Washington Information Directory
2009–2010

CQ PRESS

A Division of SAGE
Washington, D.C.

CQ Press
2300 N Street, N.W., Suite 800
Washington, DC 20037

Phone: 202-729-1900; toll-free, 1-866-4CQ-PRESS
   (1-866-427-7737)

Web: www.cqpress.com

Cover photo (top, middle) courtesy of Corbis. ©Frank
Polich/Pool/Corbis.

Washington Information Directory 2009–2010
   Project Editor: Linda A. Dziobek
   Research Editor: Catherine Farley
   Editorial Assistant: William Marsh
   Researchers: Liza Baron, Lisa Bhattacharji,
      Rick Docksai, Diane Goldenberg-Hart,
      Carol Horn, Sarah McGunnigle,
      Christopher Holmes Stern, Kate Stern,
      Ronald Stouffer, Patrice Thomas, Greg Valentine
   Proofreader: Inge Lockwood
   Indexers: Joan Stout Knight, Enid Zafran
   Electronic Composition: C&M Digitals (P) Ltd.
   Cover: Jeffrey Hall

   Manager, Electronic Production: Paul P. Pressau

Printed and bound in the United States of America

13   12   11   10   09   1   2   3   4   5

Library of Congress Cataloging-in-Publication Data

The Library of Congress cataloged the first edition of this
title as follows:

Washington information directory. 1975/76—
   Washington. Congressional Quarterly Inc.
   1. Washington, D.C.—Directories. 2. Washington metro-
      politan area—Directories. 3. United States—Executive
      departments—Directories. I. Congressional Quarterly Inc.
F192.3.W33   975.3'0025   75-646321

ISBN: 978-1-60426-531-6
ISSN: 0887-8064

Contents

Reference Boxes and Organization Charts

Each chapter also features a box listing the relevant committee resources in Congress.

Preface

Since 1975, the *Washington Information Directory* has been an essential resource for locating information on governmental and nongovernmental organizations in the national capital region. This trusted and user-friendly directory helps researchers find the right contact at the right organization, whether their interest is consumer product and food safety, equal employment opportunities, finance and investments, housing, nuclear energy, or a wealth of other timely topics. The directory allows the user to locate accurate, current information quickly and easily in a way that free Internet searches or a single phone call to a switchboard cannot.

In updating the *Washington Information Directory* every year, we research each existing entry to provide current addresses; phone, fax, TTY, and toll-free numbers; e-mail and Web addresses; and key officers and descriptions. Obtaining this information requires calling each organization and speaking with a member of its Washington office. In directory listings, we include contacts' direct lines whenever possible (many organizations do not publish these numbers on their Web sites in an attempt to channel all calls through an operator or answering service). When a federal department reorganizes, we assess the new divisions and directorates and reorganize the book accordingly. New government offices and nongovernmental organizations are added each year. Entries are arranged by topic, subtopic, and organization type. The result is an indispensable reference engine that makes finding up-to-date information easy, whether you are using the print or the online edition.

Some of the most notable changes made to this edition of the *Washington Information Directory* include updated and complete coverage of the new Obama administration and fully updated contact information for the 111th Congress, based on the results of the 2008 elections. Users will continue to find a handy "Resources in Congress" box at the beginning of each chapter, listing new and relevant committees and subcommittees for that chapter's topic, along with their Web site and phone number. Users may also turn to the first appendix, which offers a complete listing of each Congress committee, including its full contact information, leadership, membership, and jurisdictions.

Among reorganizations documented in this edition are realignments for the Defense Department, the Housing and Urban Development Department, the Labor Department, the National Transportation Safety Board,

the Nuclear Regulatory Commission, the Securities and Exchange Commission, and the Treasury Department. There are also new and expanded entries in the Education, Government Operations, and Housing and Development chapters, including updates on Fannie Mae and Freddie Mac.

In addition to adding new entries and updating and expanding coverage of existing entries, we enhance each edition of the *Washington Information Directory* by focusing on topics of new or renewed importance. We continue to emphasize Web-based government resources and to research new developments affecting the Freedom of Information Act and privacy legislation. In Chapter 1, Agriculture, Food, and Nutrition, we now include a reference box that not only has agency and organizational resources for food safety but also lists FDA and USDA hotlines for concerned consumers. In the "Chief Information Officers at Federal Departments and Agencies" reference box in Chapter 3, Communications and the Media, we include the key point people in the new administration. In Chapter 11, Housing and Development, we provide the new entry for the Real Estate Assessment Center within the Housing and Urban Development Department and the new MakingHomeAffordable Web site, both of which were created in response to the financial crisis.

The fully updated chapters of the *Washington Information Directory* are supplemented by two appendixes that include a guide to the members and committees of Congress; a directory of government Web sites; a list of governors and other state officials; a section on foreign diplomats and embassies, U.S. ambassadors, and State Department country offices; and current information on legislation pertaining to the Freedom of Information Act and USA PATRIOT Act. Users can search the edition in three ways: through the name index, the organization index, or the subject index.

CQ Press seeks to maintain the *Washington Information Directory*'s reputation as the most valuable, comprehensive, and authoritative reference of its kind. We welcome feedback, as it will help us to continue to improve the book's quality and functionality and to meet your needs as users. If you have general comments or suggestions for future editions, please share them by sending an e-mail to wideditor@cqpress.com.

Linda A. Dziobek
Project Editor

How to Use This Directory

The *Washington Information Directory* is designed to make your search for information quick and easy.

Each chapter covers a broad topic, and within the chapters information is divided into more specific subject areas. This arrangement allows you to find in one place the departments and agencies of the federal government, congressional committees, and nongovernmental organizations that have the information you need.

The directory divides information sources into three main categories: (1) agencies, (2) Congress, and (3) nongovernmental organizations. Each entry includes the name, address, and telephone and fax numbers of the organization; the name and title of the director or the best person to contact for information; press, hotline, and TTY numbers and Internet addresses whenever available; and a description of the work performed by the organization. Congressional committees and subcommittees appear in a box at the beginning of each chapter; a full entry for each committee appears in the first appendix.

HOW INFORMATION IS PRESENTED

The following examples represent the three main categories of entries and the other resources provided in the directory. The examples are drawn from the History and Preservation section in Chapter 4, Culture and Religion.

Agencies

In the first category, government agencies are listed. For example, the National Park Service and its acronym appear in bold type. Next, in parentheses, is the name of its parent organization, the Interior Department. Entries may also include the name of an office within the agency, in this case the Office of Cultural Resources.

National Park Service (NPS), *(Interior Dept.),* Cultural Resources, *1849 C St. N.W., #3128 20240-0001; (202) 208-7625. Fax, (202) 273-3237. Janet Matthews, Associate Director. Web, www.cr.nps.gov*

Oversees preservation of federal historic sites and administration of buildings programs. Programs include the National Register of Historic Places, National Historic and National Landmark Programs, Historic American Building Survey, Historic American Engineering Record, Archeology and Antiquities Act Program, and Technical Preservation Services. Gives grant and aid assistance and tax benefit information to properties listed in the National Register of Historic Places.

Congress

Congressional committees and subcommittees relevant to each chapter are listed in a box in the beginning of each chapter. Each committee's phone number and Web site are listed here. For a complete listing of congressional committees, including their full contact information, leadership, membership, and jurisdictions, please refer to the first appendix. Entries that appear under the "Congress" heading within each chapter are agencies under congressional authority, such as the Government Accountability Office or the Library of Congress. Each entry includes a description of the agency's activities relating to the section in which it appears.

Senate Office of Conservation and Preservation, *S416 CAP 20510; (202) 224-4550. Carl Fritter, Director.*

Develops and coordinates programs related to the conservation and preservation of Senate records and materials for the secretary of the Senate.

Nongovernmental

Thousands of nongovernmental groups have headquarters or legislative offices in or near Washington. Their staffs are often excellent information sources, and these organizations frequently maintain special libraries or information centers. Here is an example of a group with an interest in the preservation of historic sites:

Civil War Preservation Trust, *1331 H St. N.W., #1001 20005; (202) 367-1861. Fax, (202) 367-1865. O. James Lighthizer, President. General e-mail, info@civilwar.org Web, www.civilwar.org*

Membership: preservation professionals, historians, conservation activists, and citizens. Preserves endangered Civil War battlefields throughout the United States. Conducts preservation conferences and workshops. Advises local preservation groups. Monitors legislation and regulations at the federal, state, and local levels.

How the *Washington Information Directory* Works

The *Washington Information Directory* (WID) directs your search more efficiently and effectively than any other print or online search. This resource does the hard work of pinpointing the information you need. Here is an example of how to use it to find information on the preservation of historic sites and materials:

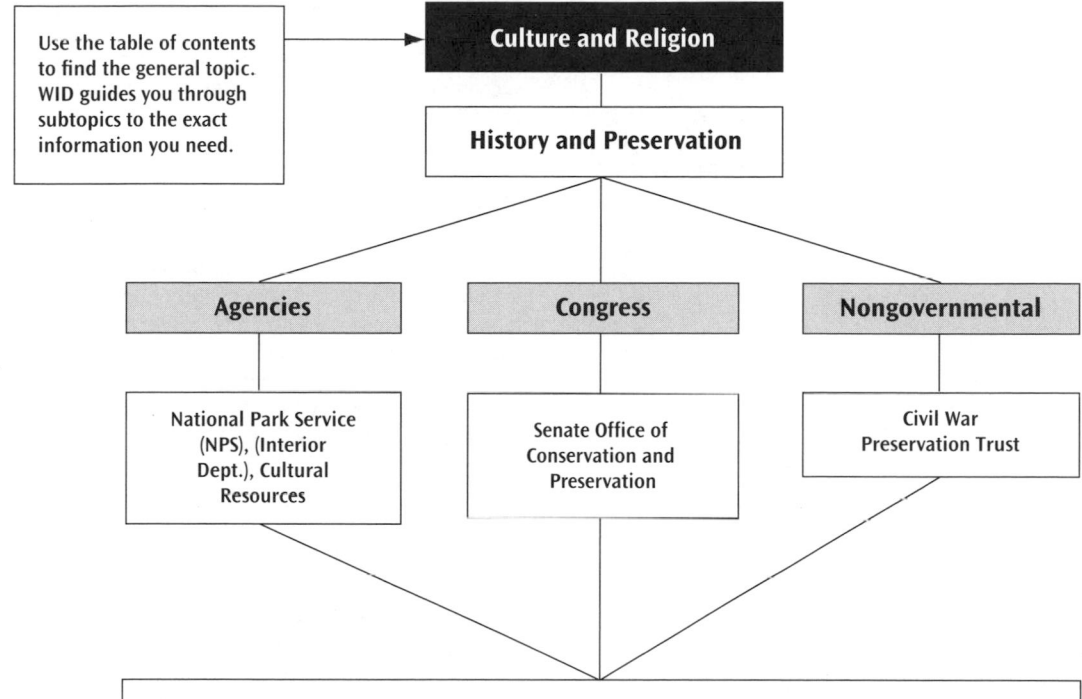

Use the table of contents to find the general topic. WID guides you through subtopics to the exact information you need.

Culture and Religion

History and Preservation

Agencies — National Park Service (NPS), (Interior Dept.), Cultural Resources

Congress — Senate Office of Conservation and Preservation

Nongovernmental — Civil War Preservation Trust

Each listing includes the name of the director or the best person to contact for information, current address, phone and fax numbers, and, whenever available, e-mail and Internet addresses, plus a brief description of the organization's purpose.

Charts and Boxes

This directory includes organization charts to make the hierarchy of federal departments and agencies easy to grasp, as well as reference boxes that provide essential agency contacts and other information. On the topic of historic sites, you can locate the National Park Service within the Interior Department (see chart on p. 277) or consult a list of sites administered by the National Park Service (see box on p. 136). A general organization chart for the federal government appears on page 843.

REFERENCE RESOURCES

Tables of Contents

The table of contents (p. iii) lists the directory's chapters and their major subheadings. A list of reference boxes and organization charts within the chapters is provided on page v. Each chapter opens with a detailed table of contents; for convenience, here again we list the boxes and charts that appear in the chapter.

Congressional Information

A section on the 111th Congress, beginning on page 724, provides extensive information about members and committees:

State Delegations. Here (p. 725) you can locate senators, representatives, and delegates by state (or territory) and congressional district.

Committees. These sections list the jurisdictions and memberships of committees and subcommittees of the House (p. 730) and Senate (p. 804), as well as the joint committees of Congress (p. 802). Also included are party leaderships and partisan committees of the House (p. 750) and Senate (p. 818).

Map of Capitol Hill

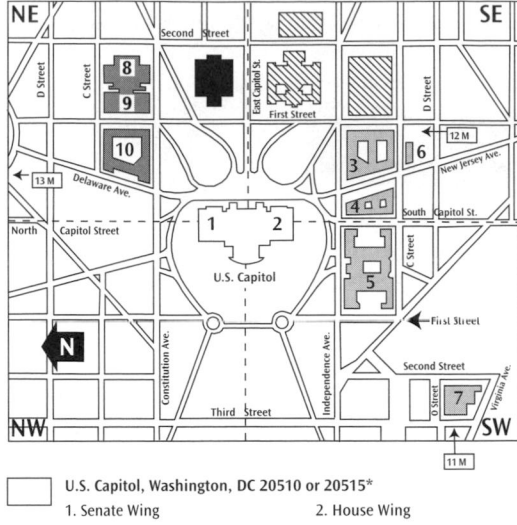

U.S. Capitol, Washington, DC 20510 or 20515*
1. Senate Wing   2. House Wing

House Office Buildings, Washington, DC 20515
3. Cannon   4. Longworth
5. Rayburn   6. O'Neill
7. Ford

Senate Office Buildings, Washington, DC 20510
8. Hart   9. Dirksen
10. Russell

Supreme Court, Washington, DC 20543

Library of Congress, Washington, DC 20540

M Subway System
11. Federal Center SW   12. Capitol South
13. Union Station

* Mail sent to the U.S. Capitol should bear the zip code of the chamber to which it is addressed.

Note: Dashed lines indicate the city's quadrants, which are noted in the corners of the map.

Members' Offices. For the House (p. 751) and Senate (p. 819), we provide each member's Capitol Hill office address, telephone and fax numbers, Internet address, key professional aide, committee assignments, and district office contact information.

Ready Reference

A section of reference lists, beginning on page 838, provides information on the following subjects:

Government Information on the Internet. Organized by branch of government, this section (p. 840) lists Web addresses for locating information on the White House, cabinet departments, Congress, and the judiciary.

State Government. The list of state officials (p. 844) provides the name, address, and telephone number for each governor, lieutenant governor, secretary of state, attorney general, and state treasurer.

Diplomats. The foreign embassies section (p. 853) gives the names, official addresses, and telephone numbers of foreign diplomats in Washington; the names of ranking U.S. diplomatic officials abroad; and the phone numbers for State Department country desk offices.

Federal Laws on Information. This section presents current information on the Freedom of Information Act (p. 866) and privacy legislation (p. 869).

Indexes

Use the name index (p. 871) to look up any person listed in the directory. Use the organization index (p. 909) to find a specific organization or agency. Use the subject index (p. 965) to locate a particular area of interest. If you need information on a specific topic but do not know a particular source, the index has entries for chapter subsections to help you find where that topic is covered. For example, on the subject of equal employment for women, you can find index entries under Equal Employment Opportunity as well as under Women.

REACHING YOUR INFORMATION SOURCE

Phoning and Faxing

Call information or toll-free numbers first. Often you can get the answer you need without searching any further. If not, an explanation of your query should put you in touch with the person who can answer your question. Rarely will you need to talk to the top administrator.

Offer to fax your query if it is difficult to explain over the phone, but make sure that the person helping you knows to expect your fax. Faxing promptly and limiting your transmission to a single page should bring the best results.

Remember that publications and documents are often available from a special office (for federal agencies, see p. 92) and, increasingly, on Web sites. Ask whether there is a faster way than by mail to receive the information you need.

Keep in mind the agency or organization, not the name of the director. Personnel changes are common, but for most inquiries you will want to stay within the organization you call, rather than track down a person who may have moved on to a new job.

Concerning congressional questions, first contact one of your members of Congress; representatives have staff assigned to answer questions from constituents. Contact a committee only if you have a technical question that cannot be answered elsewhere.

Writing

Address letters to the director of an office or organization—the contact person listed here. Your letter will be directed to the person who can answer your question. Be prepared to follow up by phone.

Using the Internet

Most agencies and governmental organizations have sites on the Internet (for federal departments and agencies, see pp. 99, 840–842) and an e-mail address for general inquiries. Information available from these sources is expanding and is usually free once you are online. If you have Internet access, try the Web site, but bear in mind that this approach is not always faster or better than a phone call: connections can be slow, menus can be complex or confusing, and information can be incomplete or out of date.

As with faxing, reserve e-mail for inquiries that may be too complex for a phone call, but phone first to establish that someone is ready to help.

ADDRESSES AND AREA CODES

Listings in the directory include full contact information, including telephone area code and, when available, room or suite number and nine-digit zip code. If an office prefers a mailing address that is different from the physical location, we provide both. Note that a call to a few listings—for example, the Social Security Administration headquarters in Baltimore and a small number of nonprofits in outlying suburbs—will incur a long distance charge.

Washington, D.C., Addresses

For brevity, entries for agencies, organizations, and congressional offices in the District of Columbia (area code 202) do not include the city as part of the address. Here is the beginning of a typical Washington entry:

Equal Employment Opportunity Commission (EEOC), *131 M St., N.E. 20002; (202) 663-4001.*

To complete the mailing address, add "Washington, DC" before the zip code.

Building Addresses

Departments and agencies generally have their own zip codes. Updates to our directory reflect the increasing use of street addresses by the federal government. Federal offices at the following locations are listed by building name or abbreviation:

The White House. Located at 1600 Pennsylvania Ave. N.W. 20500.

Dwight D. Eisenhower Executive Office Building. Located at 17th St. and Pennsylvania Ave. N.W. 20500.

New Executive Office Building. Located at 725 17th St. N.W. 20505.

Main State Building. Located at 2201 C St. N.W. 20520.

The Pentagon. Located in Arlington, Virginia, but has a Washington mailing address and different zip codes for each branch of the military.

Navy Annex. Located at Columbia Pike and Southgate Rd., Arlington, VA 20370, but most offices use a Washington mailing address.

U.S. Capitol. Abbreviated as CAP; the letters *H* and *S* before the room number indicate the House or Senate side of the building. Zip codes are 20510 for the Senate, 20515 for the House.

Senate Office Buildings. Mail for delivery to Senate office buildings does not require a street address. The zip code is 20510. Abbreviations, building names, and street locations are as follows:

SD — Dirksen Senate Office Bldg., Constitution Ave. between 1st and 2nd Sts. N.E.

SH — Hart Senate Office Bldg., 2nd St. and Constitution Ave. N.E.

SR — Russell Senate Office Bldg., Constitution Ave. between Delaware Ave. and 1st St. N.E.

House Office Buildings. Mail for delivery to House office buildings does not require a street address. The zip code is 20515. Abbreviations, building names, and street locations are as follows:

CHOB — Cannon House Office Bldg., Independence Ave. between New Jersey Ave. and 1st St. S.E.

FHOB — Ford House Office Bldg., 2nd and D Sts. S.W.

LHOB — Longworth House Office Bldg., Independence Ave. between S. Capitol St. and New Jersey Ave. S.E.

OHOB — O'Neill House Office Bldg., 300 New Jersey Ave. S.E.

RHOB — Rayburn House Office Bldg., Independence Ave. between S. Capitol and 1st Sts. S.W.

John Adams Building. Abbreviated as Adams Bldg.; located at 110 2nd St. S.E.

1 Agriculture, Food, and Nutrition

GENERAL POLICY AND ANALYSIS

Basic Resources

►AGENCIES

Agricultural Marketing Service (AMS), *(Agriculture Dept.),* *1400 Independence Ave. S.W., #3071S, MS 0201 20250-0201; (202) 720-5115. Fax, (202) 720-8477. David R. Shipman, Associate Administrator. Public Affairs, (202) 720-8998.*
Web, www.ams.usda.gov

Provides domestic and international marketing services to the agricultural industry. Administers marketing, standardization, grading, inspection, and regulatory programs; maintains a market news service to inform producers of price changes; conducts agricultural marketing research and development programs; studies agricultural transportation issues.

Agriculture Dept. (USDA), *1400 Independence Ave. S.W., #200A 20250-0002; (202) 720-3631. Fax, (202) 720-2166. Thomas J. Vilsack, Secretary; Charles Conner, Deputy Secretary. Press, (202) 720-4623. Locator, (202) 720-8732.*
Web, www.usda.gov

Serves as principal adviser to the president on agricultural policy; works to increase and maintain farm income and to develop markets abroad for U.S. agricultural products.

Agriculture Dept. (USDA), *Chief Economist, 1400 Independence Ave. S.W., #112A, Whitten Bldg. 20250-3810; (202) 720-5955. Fax, (202) 690-4915. Joseph W. Glauber, Chief Economist. Alternate phone, (202) 720-4164.*
Web, www.usda.gov/oce

Prepares economic and statistical analyses used to plan and evaluate short- and intermediate-range agricultural policy. Evaluates Agriculture Dept. policy, proposals, and legislation for their impact on the agricultural economy. Administers Agriculture Dept. economic agencies, including the Office of Risk Assessment and Cost-Benefit Analysis, the Office of Energy Policy and New Uses, the Global Change Program Office, and the World Agricultural Outlook Board.

Agriculture Dept. (USDA), *Food, Nutrition, and Consumer Services, 1400 Independence Ave. S.W., #240E 20250-0106; (202) 720-7711. Fax, (202) 690-3100. Vacant, Under Secretary; Tim O'Connor, Deputy Under Secretary (Acting).*
Web, www.fns.usda.gov

Oversees the Food and Nutrition Service and the Center for Nutrition Policy and Promotion.

Agriculture Dept. (USDA), *Outreach and Diversity, 1400 Independence Ave. S.W., MS 9473 20250; (202) 720-6350. Fax, (202) 720-7489. Carl Martin Ruiz, Director. Toll-free, (800) 880-4183.*
General e-mail, USDAoutreach@usda.gov
Web, www.usda.gov/agency/outreach

Develops, manages, and supports programs that provide information, training, and technical assistance to underserved USDA constituents. Administers the Small Farmer Outreach, Training, and Technical Assistance Program and the USDA Farm Worker Initiative. Provides policy guidance and feedback to the Agriculture Dept. on all outreach-related activities and functions.

Farm Service Agency (FSA), *(Agriculture Dept.), 1400 Independence Ave. S.W., #3086 South Bldg., MS 0501 20250-0501; (202) 720-3467. Fax, (202) 720-9105. Theresa C. Lasseter, Administrator.*
Web, www.fsa.usda.gov

Oversees farm commodity programs that provide crop loans and purchases. Administers price support programs that provide crop payments when market prices fall below specified levels; conducts programs to help obtain adequate farm and commercial storage and drying equipment for farm products; directs conservation and environmental cost sharing projects and programs to assist farmers during natural disasters and other emergencies.

►CONGRESS

For a listing of relevant congressional committees and subcommittees, please see page 3 or the Appendix.

Government Accountability Office (GAO), *Natural Resources and Environment, 441 G St. N.W., #2063 20548; (202) 512-9894. Robert A. Robinson, Managing Director.*
Web, www.gao.gov

Independent, nonpartisan agency in the legislative branch that audits the Agriculture Dept. and analyzes and reports on its handling of agriculture issues and food safety. (Formerly the General Accounting Office.)

►NONGOVERNMENTAL

Academy for Educational Development (AED), *1825 Connecticut Ave. N.W., #800 20009-5721; (202) 884-8845. Fax, (202) 884-8400. Jean Baker, Director, Center for Nutrition.*
Web, www.aed.org

Develops and manages integrated food security and nutrition programming for women and children and people living with HIV/AIDS. Offers programs that help stakeholders improve agricultural productivity and efficiency, provide training in marketing of agricultural products, enhance agricultural extension services, use agricultural water resources more efficiently, and improve the livelihoods of farmers and their families.

American Farm Bureau Federation (AFBF), *Washington Office, 600 Maryland Ave. S.W., #1000W 20024-2520; (202) 406-3600. Fax, (202) 406-3606. Bob Stallman, President.*
General e-mail, reception@fb.org
Web, www.fb.org

AGRICULTURE RESOURCES IN CONGRESS

For a complete listing of Congress committees, including their full contact information, leadership, membership, and jurisdictions, please refer to the Appendix on pages 724–837.

HOUSE:

House Agriculture Committee, (202) 225-2171.
Web, agriculture.house.gov

Subcommittee on Conservation, Credit, Energy, and Research, (202) 225-0420.

Subcommittee on Department Operations, Oversight, Nutrition, and Forestry, (202) 225-6395.

Subcommittee on General Farm Commodities and Risk Management, (202) 225-0720.

Subcommittee on Horticulture and Organic Agriculture, (202) 225-6238.

Subcommittee on Livestock, Dairy, and Poultry, (202) 225-8407.

Subcommittee on Specialty Crops, Rural Development, and Foreign Agriculture, (202) 225-2638.

House Appropriations Committee, Subcommittee on Agriculture, Rural Development, FDA, and Related Agencies, (202) 225-2638.
Web, appropriations.house.gov

House Education and Labor Committee, Subcommittee on Healthy Families and Communities, (202) 225-3725.
Web, edlabor.house.gov

House Energy and Commerce Committee, Subcommittee on Health, (202) 225-2927.
Web, energycommerce.house.gov

House Foreign Affairs Committee, (202) 225-5021.
Web, forcignaffairs.house.gov

House Science and Technology Committee, Subcommittee on Research and Science Education, (202) 225-6375.
Web, science.house.gov

House Small Business Committee, (202) 225-4038.
Web, house.gov/smbiz

Subcommittee on Finance and Tax, (202) 225-4038.

Subcommittee on Rural and Urban Entrepreneurship, (202) 225-4038.

House Ways and Means Committee, Subcommittee on Oversight, (202) 225-5522.
Web, waysandmeans.house.gov

SENATE:

Senate Agriculture, Nutrition, and Forestry Committee, (202) 224-2035.
Web, agriculture.senate.gov

Subcommittee on Domestic and Foreign Marketing, Inspection, and Plant and Animal Health, (202) 224-2035.

Subcommittee on Energy, Science, and Technology, (202) 224-2035.

Subcommittee on Nutrition and Food Assistance, Sustainable and Organic Agriculture, and General Legislation, (202) 224-2035.

Subcommittee on Production, Income Protection, and Price Support, (202) 224-2035.

Subcommittee on Rural Revitalization, Conservation, Forestry, and Credit, (202) 224-2035.

Senate Appropriations Committee, Subcommittee on Agriculture, Rural Development, FDA, and Related Agencies, (202) 224-8090.
Web, appropriations.senate.gov

Senate Banking, Housing, and Urban Affairs Committee, (202) 224-7391.
Web, banking.senate.gov

Senate Commerce, Science, and Transportation Committee, Subcommittee on Consumer Affairs, Insurance, and Automotive Safety, (202) 224-1270.
Web, commerce.senate.gov

Senate Environment and Public Works Committee, Subcommittee on Superfund and Environmental Health, (202) 224-8832.
Web, epw.senate.gov/public

Senate Finance Committee, (202) 224-4515.
Web, finance.senate.gov

Senate Health, Education, Labor, and Pensions Committee, (202) 224-5375.
Web, help.senate.gov

Senate Small Business and Entrepreneurship Committee, (202) 224-5175.
Web, sbc.senate.gov

Federation of state farm bureaus in fifty states and Puerto Rico. Promotes agricultural research. Interests include commodity programs, domestic production, marketing, education, research, financial assistance to the farmer, foreign assistance programs, rural development, the world food shortage, and inspection and certification of food.

National Assn. of State Departments of Agriculture, *1156 15th St. N.W., #1020 20005-1711; (202) 296-9680. Fax, (202) 296-9686. Stephen Hatenius, Executive Director.*
General e-mail, nasda@nasda.org
Web, www.nasda.org

Membership: commissioners, secretaries, and directors of agriculture from the fifty states, Puerto Rico, Guam, American Samoa, and the Virgin Islands. Serves as liaison between federal agencies and state governments to coordinate agricultural policies and laws. Seeks to protect consumers and the environment. Monitors legislation and regulations.

National Council of Agricultural Employers (NCAE), *1112 16th St. N.W., #920 20036-4825; (202) 728-0300. Fax, (202) 728-0303. Frank Gasperini, Executive Vice President.*

General e-mail, info@ncaeonline.org

Web, www.ncaeonline.org

Membership: employers of agricultural labor. Encourages establishment and maintenance of conditions conducive to an adequate supply of domestic and foreign farm labor.

National Farmers Union (Farmers Educational and Cooperative Union of America), *Washington Office, 400 N. Capitol St. N.W., #790 20001-1560; (202) 554-1600. Fax, (202) 554-1654. Thomas P. Buis, President.*

General e-mail, nfu.dc@nfu.org

Web, www.nfu.org

Membership: family farmers belonging to state affiliates. Interests include commodity programs, domestic production, marketing, education, research, energy and natural resources, financial assistance to farmers, Social Security for farmers, foreign programs, rural development, world food issues, and inspection and certification of food. (Headquarters in Greenwood Village, Colo.)

National Grange, *1616 H St. N.W., 10th Floor 20006-4999; (202) 628-3507. Fax, (202) 347-1091. Edward L. Luttrell, President.*

General e-mail, info@nationalgrange.org

Web, www.nationalgrange.org

Membership: farmers and others involved in agricultural production and rural community service activities. Coordinates community service programs with state grange organizations.

National Sustainable Agriculture Coalition, *110 Maryland Ave. N.E., #209 20002-5622; (202) 547-5754. Fax, (202) 547-1837. Ferd Hoefner, Policy Director.*

Web, www.sustainableagriculturecoalition.org

National alliance of farm, rural, and conservation organizations. Advocates federal policies that promote environmentally sustainable agriculture, natural resources management, and rural community development. Monitors legislation and regulations.

Rural Coalition, *1012 14th St. N.W., #1100 20005-3403; (202) 628-7160. Fax, (202) 628-7165. Lorette Picciano, Executive Director.*

General e-mail, ruralco@ruralco.org

Web, www.ruralco.org

Alliance of organizations that develop public policies benefiting rural communities. Collaborates with community-based groups on agriculture and rural development issues, including health and the environment, minority farmers, farm workers, Native Americans' rights, and rural community development. Provides rural groups with technical assistance.

Union of Concerned Scientists, *Food and Environment Program, Washington Office, 1825 K St., N.W., #800 20006-1232; (202) 223-6133. Fax, (202) 223-6162. Brise Tencer, Washington Representative.*

General e-mail, ucs@ucsusa.org

Web, www.ucsusa.org

Seeks to create a food system that encourages innovative and environmentally sustainable ways of producing high-quality, safe, and affordable food while ensuring citizens' input on how their food is grown. Focuses on reducing the unnecessary use of antibiotics and strengthening federal oversight of genetically engineered products for food and agriculture. (Headquarters in Cambridge, Mass.)

Agricultural Research, Education

▶**AGENCIES**

Agricultural Research Service *(Agriculture Dept.), 1400 Independence Ave. S.W., #302A, MS 0300 20250-0300; (202) 720-3656. Fax, (202) 720-5427. Edward B. Knipling, Administrator.*
Web, www.ars.usda.gov

Conducts research on crops, livestock, poultry, soil and water conservation, agricultural engineering, and control of insects and other pests; develops new uses for farm commodities.

Agriculture Dept. (USDA), *National Agricultural Statistics Service: Census and Survey, 1400 Independence Ave. S.W., #6306, MS 2020 20250-2020; (202) 720-4557. Fax, (202) 720-8738. Robert Bass, Director.*
General e-mail, nass@nass.usda.gov

Web, www.nass.usda.gov

Conducts a quinquennial agricultural census that provides data on crops, livestock, operator characteristics, land use, farm production expenditures, machinery and equipment, and irrigation for counties, states, regions, and the nation.

Agriculture Dept. (USDA), *Research, Education, and Economics, 1400 Independence Ave. S.W., #216W, MS 0110 20250-0110; (202) 720-5923. Fax, (202) 690-2842. Vacant, Under Secretary; Katherine Smith, Deputy Under Secretary (Acting).*
Web, www.csrees.usda.gov/ree

Coordinates agricultural research, extension, and teaching programs in the food and agricultural sciences, including human nutrition, home economics, consumer

Agriculture Department

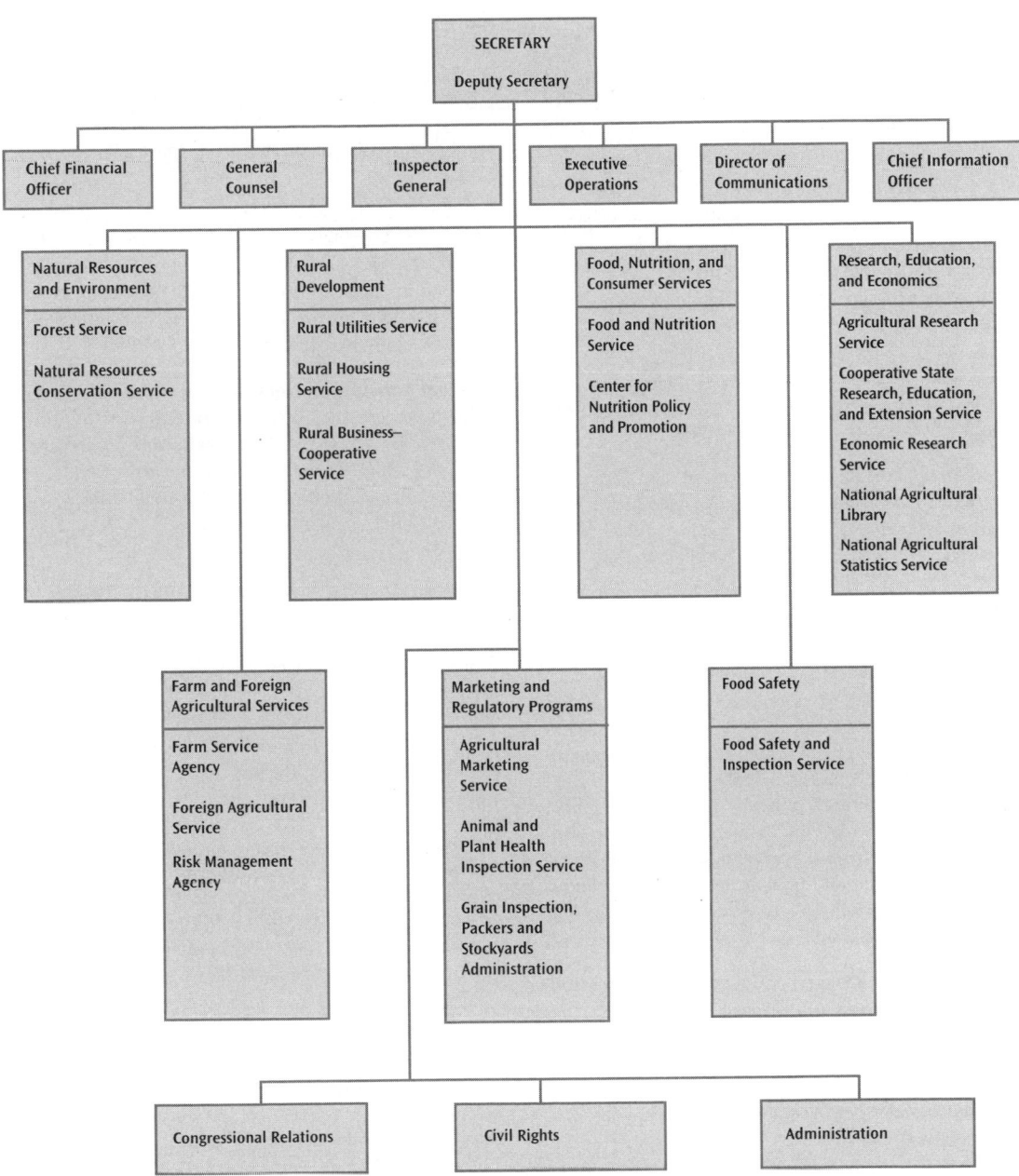

services, agricultural economics, environmental quality, natural and renewable resources, forestry and range management, animal and plant production and protection, aquaculture, and the processing, distribution, marketing, and utilization of food and agricultural products. Oversees the Agricultural Research Service; the Cooperative State Research, Education, and Extension Service; the Economic Research Service; and the National Agricultural Statistics Service.

Agriculture Dept. (USDA), *Small and Disadvantaged Business Utilization (OSDBU),* *1400 Independence Ave. S.W., #1085-S, Ag Stop 9501 20250-9501; (202) 720-7117. Fax, (202) 720-3001. Richard Ashworth, Director (Acting). Web, www.usda.gov/da/smallbus*

Provides guidance and technical assistance to small businesses seeking to do business with the USDA; monitors the development and implementation of contracting policies to prevent barriers to small business participation;

works with other federal agencies and public/private partners to increase the number of small businesses participating in the contracting arena.

Cooperative State Research, Education, and Extension Service (CSREES), *(Agriculture Dept.), 1400 Independence Ave. S.W., #305A, MS 2201 20250-2201; (202) 720-4423. Fax, (202) 720-8987. Colien Hefferan, Administrator. Information, (202) 720-4651. TTY, (202) 690-1899. Web, www.csrees.usda.gov*

Supports research, education, and extension programs in the Land-Grant University System and other partner organizations in the areas of agriculture, the environment, human health and well-being, and communities. Programs assist farmers, processors, consumers, and others in efficient, healthful production and consumption of agricultural products. Houses the National 4-H Headquarters, which coordinates the 4-H Youth Development Programs at the state and local club levels.

Cooperative State Research, Education, and Extension Service (CSREES), *(Agriculture Dept.), Competitive Programs, 800 9th St. S.W. 20024 (mailing address: 1400 Independence Ave. S.W., MS 2241, Washington, DC 20250-2241); (202) 401-1761. Fax, (202) 401-1782. Deborah L. Sheely, Deputy Administrator. General e-mail, psmith@csrees.usda.gov Web, www.csrees.usda.gov*

Administers funds to support research, education, and extension for agriculture, the environment, human health and well-being, and communities. Maintains administrative responsibility for programs in agricultural and food biosecurity; agricultural systems; animals and animal products; biotechnology and genomics; economics and commerce; families, youth, and communities; food, nutrition, and health; natural resources and environment; pest management; plants and plant products; technology and engineering; and across the spectrum of agriculture.

Cooperative State Research, Education, and Extension Service (CSREES), *(Agriculture Dept.), Science and Education Resources Development, 800 9th St. S.W. 20024 (mailing address: 1400 Independence Ave. S.W., MS 2251, Washington, DC 20250-2201); (202) 401-2855. Fax, (202) 720-3945. Franklin E. Bateler, Deputy Administrator. Web, www.csrees.usda.gov*

Provides national leadership and coordination on issues relating to food and agricultural research, higher education, and extension; assists colleges and universities in developing and maintaining education programs in the food and agricultural sciences. Seeks to ensure that colleges and universities produce the requisite number of graduates to satisfy the nation's need for individuals trained in the field. Maintains research information systems covering all publicly supported agriculture, food, human nutrition, and forestry research.

Economic Research Service *(Agriculture Dept.), 1800 M St. N.W., #4145N 20036-5831; (202) 694-5000. Fax,*

(202) 694-5757. Kitty Smith, Administrator; John Kort, Associate Administrator. General e-mail, service@ers.usda.gov Web, www.ers.usda.gov

Conducts research on economic and policy issues involving food, natural resources, and rural development.

Foreign Agricultural Service (FAS), *(Agriculture Dept.), Global Analysis, 1400 Independence Ave. S.W., #4083S 20250; (202) 720-6301. Fax, (202) 690-0727. Maurice House, Deputy Administrator. Web, www.fas.usda.gov/oga.asp*

Conducts research relevant to USDA's trade initiatives. Develops and maintains USDA's data on agricultural production, supply, and demand.

National Agricultural Library *(Agriculture Dept.), 10301 Baltimore Ave., Beltsville, MD 20705-2351; (301) 504-5248. Fax, (301) 504-7042. Eleanor Fireson, Library Director. TTY, (301) 504-6856. Reference desk, (301) 504-5755, 8:30 a.m.– 4:30 p.m. General e-mail, circinfo@nal.usda.gov Web, www.nal.usda.gov*

Principal source of agricultural information in the United States. Makes significant information available to researchers, educators, policymakers, and the public; coordinates with state land-grant and Agriculture Dept. field libraries; promotes international cooperation and exchange of information. Deeper interests include food production, food safety, human nutrition, animal welfare, plant health, water quality, rural development, technology transfer, and agricultural trade.

National Agricultural Library *(Agriculture Dept.), Alternative Farming Systems Information Center (AFSIC), 10301 Baltimore Ave., #132, Beltsville, MD 20705-2351; (301) 504-6559. Fax, (301) 504-6927. Bill Thomas, Coordinator. Web, http://afsic.nal.usda.gov*

Serves individuals and agencies seeking information on sustainability in agriculture, alternative plants and crops, farm energy options, grazing systems and alternative livestock breeds, alternative marketing and business practices, organic production, ecological pest management, and soil and water management.

National Agricultural Library *(Agriculture Dept.), Water Quality Information Center, 10301 Baltimore Ave, 1st Floor, Beltsville, MD 20705-2351; (301) 504-6077. Fax, (301) 504-6409. Joe Makuch, Coordinator. Web, www.nal.usda.gov/wqic*

Serves individuals and agencies seeking information on water quality and agriculture. Special subject areas include agricultural environmental management, irrigation, social and legal issues, water availability, and water quality.

National Agricultural Statistics Service *(Agriculture Dept.), 1400 Independence Ave. S.W., #5041, MS 2001 20250-2001; (202) 720-2707. Fax, (202) 720-9013.*

Cynthia Clark, Administrator. Information, (800) 727-9540. Print reports, (800) 999-6779.

General e-mail, nass@usda.gov

Web, www.nass.usda.gov

Prepares estimates and reports on production, supply, prices, and other items relating to the U.S. agricultural economy. Reports include statistics on field crops, fruits and vegetables, cattle, hogs, poultry, and related products. Prepares quinquennial national census of agriculture.

Office of Science and Technology Policy (OSTP), *(Executive Office of the President),* *New Executive Office Bldg., 725 17th St. N.W., #5208 20502; (202) 456-7116. Fax, (202) 456-6021. John P. Holdren, Director, Science. Science Division, (202) 456-6130; Fax, (202) 456-6027. Technology Division, (202) 456-6046; Fax, (202) 456-6040.*

General e-mail, info@ostp.gov

Web, www.ostp.gov

Provides the president with policy analysis on scientific and technological matters, including energy policy and technology issues; coordinates executive office and federal agency responses to these issues; evaluates the effectiveness of scientific and technological programs.

Rural Development *(Agriculture Dept.), Business and Cooperative Programs: Business Programs, 1400 Independence Ave. S.W., #5813-S 20250-3220; (202) 720-7287. Fax, (202) 690-0097. William F. Hagy III, Deputy Administrator.*

Web, www.rurdev.usda.gov/rbs

Conducts economic research and provides financial assistance and business planning to help farmers market their products and purchase supplies.

Rural Development *(Agriculture Dept.), Business and Cooperative Programs: Cooperative Programs, 1400 Independence Ave. S.W., #4016-S 20250-3250; (202) 720-7558. Fax, (202) 720-4641. LeAnn M. Oliver, Deputy Administrator.*

Web, www.rurdev.usda.gov/rbs

Conducts economic research and helps people living in rural areas obtain business services through cooperatives.

▶**INTERNATIONAL ORGANIZATIONS**

Consultative Group on International Agricultural Research (CGIAR), *1818 H St. N.W., MS G6-601 20433; (202) 473-8951. Fax, (202) 473-8110. Ren Wang, Director. Press, (202) 473-2396.*

General e-mail, cgiar@cgiar.org

Web, www.cgiar.org

Alliance of countries, international and regional organizations, and private foundations supporting 15 international agricultural research centers. Works with national agricultural research systems and civil society organizations, including the private sector. Interests include use of agricultural science to reduce poverty, promote agricultural growth, and protect the environment.

▶**NONGOVERNMENTAL**

National Council of Farmer Cooperatives (NCFC), *50 F St. N.W., #900 20001-1530; (202) 626 8700. Fax, (202) 626-8722. Charles F. Connor, President.*

General e-mail, info@ncfc.org

Web, www.ncfc.org

Membership: cooperative businesses owned and operated by farmers. Conducts educational programs and encourages research on agricultural cooperatives; provides statistics and analyzes trends; presents awards for research papers.

National FFA Organization, *1410 King St., #400, Alexandria, VA 22314-2749; (703) 838-5889. Fax, (703) 838-5888. Larry D. Case, Chief Executive Officer. Toll-free, (800) 772-0939.*

Web, www.ffa.org

Membership: local chapters of high school students enrolled in agricultural education and agribusiness programs. Coordinates leadership training and other activities with local chapters across the United States. Formerly known as the Future Farmers of America. (Business Center in Indianapolis, Ind.)

National 4-H Council, *7100 Connecticut Ave., Chevy Chase, MD 20815-4999; (301) 961-2800. Fax, (301) 961-2894. Donald T. Floyd Jr., President. Press, (301) 961-2972.*

Web, www.fourhcouncil.edu

4-H membership: young people across the United States learning leadership, citizenship, and life skills. National 4-H Council is a national, private-sector partner of the 4-H Youth Development Program and its parent, the Cooperative Extension System of the United States Department of Agriculture.

Fertilizer and Pesticides

▶**AGENCIES**

Agriculture Dept. (USDA), *Natural Resources Conservation Service: Pest Management, 1400 Independence Ave. S.W., #6155-S 20250; (202) 720-7838. Fax, (202) 720-2646. Benjamin F. Smallwood, Specialist.*

General e-mail, benjamin.smallwood@usda.gov

Web, www.nrcs.usda.gov/technical/ECS/pest

Formulates and recommends agency policy in coordination with the Environmental Protection Agency and other USDA agencies for the establishment of standards, procedures, and management of agronomic, forest, and horticultural use of pesticides.

Environmental Protection Agency (EPA), *Pesticide Programs, 1 Potomac Yard, 2777 Crystal Dr., Arlington, VA 22202 (mailing address: Ariel Rios Building, 1200 Pennsylvania Ave. N.W., MS 7501-P, Washington, DC 20460-7101); (703) 305-7090. Fax, (703) 308-4776.*

Debbie Edwards, Director. National Pesticide Information Center, (800) 858-7378.

Web, www.epa.gov/pesticides

Evaluates data to determine the risks and benefits of pesticides; sets standards for safe use of pesticides, including those for use on foods. Develops rules that govern labeling and literature accompanying pesticide products.

Environmental Protection Agency (EPA), *Prevention, Pesticides, and Toxic Substances (OPPTS)*, 1200 Pennsylvania Ave. N.W., #3130 EPA-E, MS 7101M 20460-7101; (202) 564-2902. Fax, (202) 564-0801. James J. Jones, Assistant Administrator (Acting). Pollution prevention and toxic substances, (202) 564-3810.

Web, www.epa.gov/oppts

Studies and makes recommendations for regulating chemical substances under the Toxic Substances Control Act; compiles list of chemical substances subject to the act; registers, controls, and regulates use of pesticides and toxic substances.

▶**NONGOVERNMENTAL**

Beyond Pesticides/National Coalition Against the Misuse of Pesticides, 701 E St. S.E., #200 20003; (202) 543-5450. Fax, (202) 543-4791. Jay Feldman, Executive Director.

General e-mail, info@beyondpesticides.org

Web, www.beyondpesticides.org

Coalition of family farmers, farm workers, consumers, home gardeners, physicians, lawyers, and others concerned about pesticide hazards and safety. Issues information to increase public awareness of environmental, public health, and economic problems caused by pesticide abuse; promotes alternatives to pesticide use, such as the integrated pest management program.

Croplife America, 1156 15th St. N.W., #400 20005-1752; (202) 296-1585. Fax, (202) 463-0474. Jay J. Vroom, President.

General e-mail, webmaster@croplifeamerica.org

Web, www.croplifeamerica.org

Membership: pesticide manufacturers. Provides information on pesticide safety, development, and use. Monitors legislation and regulations. (Formerly the American Crop Protection Assn.)

Entomological Society of America, 10001 Derekwood Lane, #100, Lanham, MD 20706-4876; (301) 731-4535. Fax, (301) 731-4538. Robin Kriegel, Executive Director.

General e-mail, esa@entsoc.org

Web, www.entsoc.org

Scientific association that promotes the science of entomology and the interests of professionals in the field. Advises on crop protection, food chain, and individual and urban health matters dealing with insect pests.

Fertilizer Institute, Union Center Plaza, 820 1st St. N.E., #430 20002-8037; (202) 962-0490. Fax, (202) 962-0577. Ford B. West, President.

General e-mail, info@tfi.org

Web, www.tfi.org

Membership: manufacturers, dealers, and distributors of fertilizer. Provides statistical data and other information concerning the effects of fertilizer and its relationship to world food production, food supply, and the environment.

Migrant Legal Action Program, 1001 Connecticut Ave. N.W., #915 20036-5524; (202) 775-7780. Fax, (202) 775-7784. Roger C. Rosenthal, Executive Director.

General e-mail, mlap@mlap.org

Web, www.mlap.org

Assists local legal services groups and private attorneys representing farm workers. Monitors legislation, regulations, and enforcement activities of the Environmental Protection Agency and the Occupational Safety and Health Administration in the area of pesticide use as it affects the health of migrant farm workers. Litigates cases concerning living and working conditions experienced by migrant farm workers. Works with local groups on implementation of Medicaid block grants.

National Agricultural Aviation Assn., 1005 E St. S.E. 20003; (202) 546-5722. Fax, (202) 546-5726. Andrew Moore, Executive Director.

General e-mail, information@agaviation.org

Web, www.agaviation.org

Membership: qualified agricultural pilots; operating companies that seed, fertilize, and spray land by air; and allied industries. Monitors legislation and regulations.

National Pest Management Assn., *Government Affairs,* 10460 North St., Fairfax, VA 22030; (703) 352-6762. Fax, (703) 352-3031. Robert M. Rosenberg, Senior Vice President.

Web, www.npmapestworld.org

Membership: pest control operators. Monitors federal regulations that affect pesticide use; provides members with technical information.

Horticulture and Gardening

▶**AGENCIES**

National Arboretum (*Agriculture Dept.*), 3501 New York Ave. N.E. 20002-1958; (202) 245-2726. Fax, (202) 245-4575. Thomas S. Elias, Director. Library, (202) 245-4538.

Web, www.usna.usda.gov

Maintains public display of plants on 446 acres; provides information and makes referrals concerning cultivated plants (exclusive of field crops and fruits); conducts plant breeding and research; maintains herbarium. Library open to the public by appointment.

Smithsonian Institution, *Botany and Horticulture Library,* 10th St. and Constitution Ave. N.W., #W422

20560-0166 (mailing address: PO Box 37012, MRC 154, Washington, DC 20017-7012); (202) 633-1685. Fax, (202) 357-1896. Robin Everly, Branch Librarian.

General e-mail, libmail.si.edu

Web, www.sil.si.edu/libraries/bothort

Collection includes books, periodicals, and videotapes on horticulture, garden history, and landscape design. Specializes in American gardens and gardening of the late nineteenth and early twentieth centuries. Open to the public by appointment. (Housed at the National Museum of Natural History.)

U.S. Botanic Garden, 100 Maryland Ave. S.W. 20001 (mailing address: 245 1st St. S.W., Washington, DC 20024); (202) 225-8333. Fax, (202) 225-1561. Holly H. Shimizu, Executive Director. Horticulture hotline, (202) 226-4785. Program and tour reservations, (202) 225-1116. Special events, (202) 226-7674.

General e-mail, usbg@aoc.gov

Web, www.usbg.gov

Collects, cultivates, and grows various plants for public display and study; identifies botanic specimens and furnishes information on proper growing methods. Conducts horticultural classes and tours.

▶**NONGOVERNMENTAL**

American Horticultural Society, 7931 E. Boulevard Dr., Alexandria, VA 22308-1300; (703) 768-5700. Fax, (703) 768-8700. Tom Underwood, Executive Director.

Web, www.ahs.org

Promotes the expansion of horticulture in the United States through educational programs for amateur and professional horticulturists. Publishes gardening magazine. Oversees historic house and farm once owned by George Washington, with gardens maintained by plant societies; house and grounds are rented for special occasions.

American Nursery and Landscape Assn., 1000 Vermont Ave. N.W., #300 20005-4914; (202) 789-2900. Fax, (202) 789-1893. Robert J. Dolibois, Executive Vice President.

Web, www.anla.org

Membership: wholesale growers, garden center retailers, landscape firms, and suppliers to the horticultural community. Monitors legislation and regulations on agricultural, environmental, and small business issues; conducts educational seminars on business management for members.

American Society for Horticultural Science (ASHS), 113 S. West St., #200, Alexandria, VA 22314-2851; (703) 836-4606. Fax, (703) 836-2024. Michael W. Neff, Executive Director.

General e-mail, ashs@ashs.org

Web, www.ashs.org

Membership: educators, government workers, firms, associations, and individuals interested in horticultural science. Promotes scientific research and education in horticulture, including international exchange of information.

Society of American Florists, 1601 Duke St., Alexandria, VA 22314-3406; (703) 836-8700. Fax, (703) 836-8705. Drew Gruenburg, Senior Vice President.

Web, www.safnow.org

Membership: growers, wholesalers, and retailers in the floriculture and ornamental horticulture industries. Interests include labor, pesticides, the environment, international trade, and toxicity of plants. Mediates industry problems.

Soil and Watershed Conservation

▶**AGENCIES**

Farm Service Agency (FSA), (Agriculture Dept.), Conservation and Environmental Programs, 1400 Independence Ave. S.W., MS 0513 20250-0513; (202) 720-6221. Fax, (202) 720-4619. Robert K. Stephenson, Director.

Web, www.fsa.usda.gov

Directs conservation and environmental projects and programs to help farmers and ranchers prevent soil erosion and contamination of natural resources.

Interior Dept. (DOI), Bird Habitat Conservation, 4501 N. Fairfax Dr., Arlington, VA 22203 (mailing address: 4401 N. Fairfax Dr., MBSP 4075, Arlington, VA 22203-1610); (703) 358-1784. Fax, (703) 358-2282. Michael J. Johnson, Chief.

General e-mail, dbhc@fws.gov

Web, http://birdhabitat.fws.gov

Membership: government and private-sector conservation experts. Works to protect, restore, and manage wetlands and other habitats for migratory birds and other animals and to maintain migratory bird and waterfowl populations.

Natural Resources Conservation Service (Agriculture Dept.), 1400 Independence Ave. S.W., #5105 20250 (mailing address: P.O. Box 2890, Washington, DC 20013-2890); (202) 720-4525. Fax, (202) 720-7690. Arlen Lancaster, Chief. Chief's Office, (202) 720-7246. Public Affairs, (202) 720-3210.

Web, www.nrcs.usda.gov

Responsible for soil and water conservation programs, including watershed protection, flood prevention, river basin surveys, and resource conservation and development. Provides landowners, operators, state and local units of government, and community groups with technical assistance in carrying out local programs. Inventories and monitors soil, water, and related resource data and resource use trends. Provides information about soil surveys, farmlands, and other natural resources.

▶**NONGOVERNMENTAL**

American Farmland Trust (AFT), 1200 18th St. N.W., #800 20036-2524; (202) 331-7300. Fax, (202) 659-8339. Jon Scholl, President.

General e-mail, jmorrill@farmland.org

Web, www.farmland.org

Works to stop the loss of farmland, enhance local food systems, and promote environmentally responsible farming practices through local, regional, and national efforts. Works with communities to keep agriculture economically viable by connecting local markets and helping farmers implement practices that protect waterways and reduce greenhouse gas emissions.

Irrigation Assn., *6540 Arlington Blvd., Falls Church, VA 22042-6638; (703) 536-7080. Fax, (703) 536-7019. Deborah Hamlin, Executive Director.*

General e-mail, webmaster@irrigation.org

Web, www.irrigation.org

Membership: companies and individuals involved in irrigation, drainage, and erosion control worldwide. Promotes efficient and effective water management through training, education, and certification programs. Interests include economic development and environmental enhancement.

National Assn. of Conservation Districts (NACD), *509 Capitol Court N.E. 20002-4937; (202) 547-6223. Fax, (202) 547-6450. Krysta Harden, Chief Executive Director.*

General e-mail, washington@nacdnet.org

Web, www.nacdnet.org

Membership: conservation districts (local subdivisions of state government). Works to promote the conservation of land, forests, and other natural resources. Interests include erosion and sediment control; water quality; forestry, water, flood plain, and range management; rural development; and urban and community conservation.

Winrock International, *1621 N. Kent St., #1200, Arlington, VA 22209-2134; (703) 525-9430. Fax, (703) 525-1744. Frank Tugwell, President.*

General e-mail, information@winrock.org

Web, www.winrock.org

Works globally to increase economic opportunity, sustain natural resources, and protect the environment. Matches local individuals and communities with new ideas and technologies.

COMMODITIES, FARM PRODUCE

▶AGENCIES

Agricultural Marketing Service (AMS), *(Agriculture Dept.), Transportation and Marketing Programs, 1400 Independence Ave. S.W., #1098, MS 0264 20250-0264; (202) 690-1300. Fax, (202) 690-0338. Barbara C. Robinson, Deputy Administrator; Bruce Blanton, Director, Transportation Services Division; Errol R. Bragg, Director, Marketing Services Division, (202) 720-8317.*

Web, www.ams.usda.gov

Promotes efficient, cost-effective marketing and transportation for U.S. agricultural products; sets standards for domestic and international marketing of organic products. Provides exporters with market information, educational services, and regulatory representation.

Agricultural Research Service *(Agriculture Dept.), National Plant Germplasm System, 5601 Sunnyside Ave., #4-2212, Beltsville, MD 20705-5139; (301) 504-5541. Fax, (301) 504-6191. Peter Bretting, National Program Leader.*

Web, www.ars-grin.gov

Network of federal and state gene banks that preserve samples of all major field crops and horticultural crops. Collects, preserves, evaluates, and catalogs germplasm and distributes it for specific purposes.

Agriculture Dept. (USDA), *Marketing and Regulatory Programs, 1400 Independence Ave. S.W., #228W, MS 0109 20250-0109; (202) 720-4256. Fax, (202) 720-5775. Vacant, Under Secretary.*

Web, www.usda.gov/mrp

Administers inspection and grading services and regulatory programs for agricultural commodities through the Agricultural Marketing Service; Animal and Plant Health Inspection Service; and Grain Inspection, Packers and Stockyards Administration.

Animal and Plant Health Inspection Service (APHIS), *(Agriculture Dept.), 1400 Independence Ave. S.W., #312E, MS 3401 20250-3401; (202) 720-3668. Fax, (202) 720-3054. Cindy Smith, Administrator.*

Web, www.aphis.usda.gov

Administers programs in cooperation with the states to prevent the spread of pests and plant diseases; certifies that U.S. exports are free of pests and disease.

Commodity Credit Corp. *(Agriculture Dept.), 1400 Independence Ave. S.W., #3702A-S, MS 0599 20250-0599; (202) 720-1068. Fax, (202) 690-1692. Steven N. Mikkelsen, Secretary of CCC (Acting).*

Web, www.fsa.usda.gov/ccc

Finances commodity stabilization programs, domestic and export surplus commodity disposal, foreign assistance, storage activities, and related programs.

Commodity Futures Trading Commission, *3 Lafayette Center, 1155 21st St. N.W. 20581-0001; (202) 418-5000. Fax, (202) 418-5533. Michael Dunn, Chair (Acting); Madge A. Bolinger, Executive Director. Information, (202) 418-5000. Library, (202) 418-5255.*

Web, www.cftc.gov

Oversees the Commodity Exchange Act, which regulates all commodity futures and options to prevent fraudulent trade practices.

Cooperative State Research, *Education, and Extension Service (CSREES), (Agriculture Dept.), 1400 Independence Ave. S.W., #305A, MS 2201 20250-2201; (202) 720-4423. Fax, (202) 720-8987. Colien Hefferan, Administrator. Information, (202) 720-4651. TTY, (202) 690-1899.*

Web, www.csrees.usda.gov

Conducts workshops on management of farmer cooperatives and educational programs on sustainable agriculture. Provides small farmers with management and marketing programs; offers training and assistance to rural communities and local officials.

Farm Service Agency (FSA), *(Agriculture Dept.),* *1400 Independence Ave. S.W., #3086 South Bldg., MS 0501 20250-0501; (202) 720-3467. Fax, (202) 720-9105. Theresa C. Lasseter, Administrator.*

Web, www.fsa.usda.gov

Administers farm commodity programs providing crop loans and purchases; provides crop payments when market prices fall below specified levels; sets acreage allotments and marketing quotas; assists farmers in areas affected by natural disasters.

Foreign Agricultural Service (FAS), *(Agriculture Dept.),* *1400 Independence Ave. S.W., #5071S, MS 1001 20250-1001; (202) 720-3935. Fax, (202) 690-2159. Michael Michener, Administrator; Vacant, General Sales Manager. TTY, (202) 720-1786. Public Affairs, (202) 720-3448.*

Web, www.fas.usda.gov

Promotes exports of U.S. commodities and assists with trade negotiations; coordinates activities of U.S. representatives in foreign countries who report on crop and market conditions; sponsors trade fairs in foreign countries to promote export of U.S. agricultural products; analyzes world demand and production of various commodities; administers food aid programs; monitors sales by private exporters; provides technical assistance and trade capacity building programs.

Foreign Agricultural Service (FAS), *(Agriculture Dept.),* *Trade Programs, 1250 Maryland Ave., Portal Bldg., 4th Floor, MS 1020 20250 (mailing address: 1400 Independence Ave. S.W., MS 1020, Washington, DC 20250-1020); (202) 720-9516. Fax, (202) 690-1171. Christian Foster, Deputy Administrator.*

Web, www.fas.usda.gov/OTP.asp

Administers market development, export credit guarantee, dairy export incentive programs, and import programs for sugar, dairy, and trade adjustment assistance.

Rural Development *(Agriculture Dept.), Business and Cooperative Programs: Business Programs, 1400 Independence Ave. S.W., #5813-S 20250-3220; (202) 720-7287. Fax, (202) 690-0097. William F. Hagy III, Deputy Administrator.*

Web, www.rurdev.usda.gov/rbs

Conducts economic research and provides financial assistance and business planning to help farmers market their products and purchase supplies.

State Dept., *Agricultural, Biotechnology, and Textile Trade Affairs, 2201 C St. N.W., #4470 20520-0002; (202) 647-3090. Fax, (202) 647-1894. Gary Clements, Director.*

Web, www.state.gov/e/eeb/tpp/c22860.htm

Develops agricultural trade policy; handles questions pertaining to international negotiations on all agricultural products covered by the World Trade Organization (WTO) and bilateral trade agreements. Negotiates bilateral textile trade agreements with foreign governments concerning cotton, wool, and synthetic textile and apparel products.

►CONGRESS

For a listing of relevant congressional committees and subcommittees, please see page 3 or the Appendix.

►NONGOVERNMENTAL

American Seed Trade Assn., *225 Reinekers Lane, #650, Alexandria, VA 22314-2878; (703) 837-8140. Fax, (703) 837-9365. Andrew W. LaVigne, President.*

Web, www.amseed.org

Membership: producers and merchandisers of seeds. Conducts seminars on research developments in corn, sorghum, soybean, garden seeds, and other farm seeds; promotes overseas seed market development.

Commodity Markets Council (CMC), *1300 L St. N.W., #1020 20005-4166; (202) 842-0400. Fax, (202) 789-7223. Christine Cochran, Vice President, Government Relations.*

Web, www.cmcmarkets.org

Federation of commodity futures exchanges, boards of trade, and industry stakeholders including commodity merchandisers, processors, and refiners; futures commission merchants; food and beverage manufacturers; transportation companies; and financial institutions. Combines members' expertise to formulate positions on market, policy, and contracting issues involving commodities, with an overall goal of facilitating growth in liquidity and transparency in cash and derivative markets. Monitors legislation and regulations. (Formerly the National Grain Trade Council.)

International Assn. of Refrigerated Warehouses, *1500 King St., #201, Alexandria, VA 22314-2730; (703) 373-4300. Fax, (703) 373-4301. J. William Hudson, President.*

General e-mail, email@iarw.org

Web, www.iarw.org

Membership: owners and operators of public refrigerated warehouses. Interests include labor, transportation, taxes, environment, safety, regulatory compliance, and food distribution. Monitors legislation and regulations. (Affiliated with the International Refrigerated Transportation Assn., the International Assn. for Cold Storage Construction, and the World Food Logistics Assn.)

National Cooperative Business Assn., *1401 New York Ave. N.W., #1100 20005-2160; (202) 638-6222. Fax, (202) 638-1374. Paul Hazen, President.*

General e-mail, ncba@ncba.coop

Web, www.ncba.coop

Alliance of cooperatives, businesses, and state cooperative associations. Provides information about starting and managing agricultural cooperatives in the United States and in developing nations. Monitors legislation and regulations.

National Council of Farmer Cooperatives (NCFC),
*50 F St. N.W., #900 20001-1530; (202) 626-8700. Fax,
(202) 626-8722. Charles F. Connor, President.*
General e-mail, info@ncfc.org

Web, www.ncfc.org

Membership: cooperative businesses owned and operated by farmers. Encourages research on agricultural cooperatives; provides statistics and analyzes trends. Monitors legislation and regulations on agricultural trade, transportation, energy, and tax issues.

U.S. Agricultural Export Development Council, *8233
Old Courthouse Rd., #200, Vienna, VA 22182-3816; (703)
556-9290. Fax, (703) 790-0845. Annie Durbin, Executive
Director.*
General e-mail, adurbin@usaedc.org

Web, www.usaedc.org

Membership: producer and agribusiness organizations. Works with the Foreign Agricultural Service on projects to create, expand, and maintain agricultural markets abroad. Sponsors seminars and workshops.

Cotton

▶**AGENCIES**

Agricultural Marketing Service (AMS), *(Agriculture
Dept.), Cotton and Tobacco Programs, 1400
Independence Ave. S.W., #2639S, MS 0224 20250-0224;
(202) 720-3193. Fax, (202) 690-1718. Darryl W. Earnest,
Deputy Administrator.*
Web, www.ams.usda.gov/cotton/index.htm

Administers cotton marketing programs; sets cotton and tobacco grading standards and conducts quality inspections based on those standards. Maintains market news service to inform producers of daily price changes.

Farm Service Agency (FSA), *(Agriculture Dept.), Fibers,
Peanuts, and Tobacco Analysis, 1400 Independence Ave.
S.W., #37605, MS 0515 20250-0515; (202) 720-3392. Fax,
(202) 690-2186. Scott Sanford, Director.*
Web, www.fsa.usda.gov

Develops production adjustment and price support programs to balance supply and demand for cotton, peanuts, and tobacco.

▶**INTERNATIONAL ORGANIZATIONS**

International Cotton Advisory Committee, *1629 K St.
N.W., #702 20006-1636; (202) 463-6660. Fax, (202) 463-
6950. Terry P. Townsend, Executive Director.*
General e-mail, secretariat@icac.org

Web, www.icac.org

Membership: cotton producing and consuming countries. Provides information on cotton production, trade, consumption, stocks, and prices.

▶**NONGOVERNMENTAL**

American Cotton Shippers Assn., *Washington Office,
1701 K St. N.W., #200 20006; (202) 296-7116. Fax, (202)
659-5322. Neal P. Gillen, Executive Vice President.*
Web, www.acsa-cotton.org

Federation of four regional cotton merchandising and shippers associations. Monitors legislation and regulations concerning international cotton trade. (Administrative offices in Memphis, Tenn.)

Cotton Council International, *Washington Office, 1521
New Hampshire Ave. N.W. 20036-1203; (202) 745-7805.
Fax, (202) 483-4040. Allen Terhaar, Executive Director.*
General e-mail, cottonusa@cotton.org

Web, www.cottonusa.org

Division of National Cotton Council of America. Promotes U.S. raw cotton exports. (Headquarters in Memphis, Tenn.)

Cotton Warehouse Assn. of America, *499 S. Capitol St.
S.W., #408 20003-4004; (202) 479-4371. Fax, (202) 479-
4375. Larry Combest, Executive Vice President.*
General e-mail, cwaa@cottonwarehouse.org

Web, www.cottonwarehouse.org

Membership: cotton compress and warehouse workers. Serves as a liaison between members and government agencies; monitors legislation and regulations.

National Cotton Council of America, *Washington
Office, 1521 New Hampshire Ave. N.W. 20036-1203;
(202) 745-7805. Fax, (202) 483-4040. A. John Maguire,
Senior Vice President.*
Web, www.cotton.org

Membership: all segments of the U.S. cotton industry. Provides statistics and information on such topics as cotton history and processing. (Headquarters in Memphis, Tenn.)

Dairy Products and Eggs

▶**AGENCIES**

Agricultural Marketing Service (AMS), *(Agriculture
Dept.), Dairy Programs, 1400 Independence Ave. S.W.,
#2968 20250-0225; (202) 720-4392. Fax, (202) 690-3410.
Dana H. Coale, Deputy Administrator.*
Web, www.ams.usda.gov/dairy/index.htm

Administers dairy product marketing and promotion programs; grades dairy products; maintains market news service on daily price changes; sets minimum price that farmers receive for milk.

Agricultural Marketing Service (AMS), *(Agriculture
Dept.), Poultry Programs, 1400 Independence Ave. S.W.,
#3932S 20250-0262; (202) 720-4476. Fax, (202) 720-5631.
Rex Barnes, Deputy Administrator.*
Web, www.ams.usda.gov/poultry/index.htm

Sets poultry and egg grading standards. Provides promotion and market news services for domestic and international markets.

Farm Service Agency (FSA), *(Agriculture Dept.), Dairy and Sweeteners Analysis, 1400 Independence Ave. S.W., #3752, MS 0516 20250-0516; (202) 720-3451. Fax, (202) 690-2186. Daniel Colacicco, Group Director.*
Web, www.fsa.usda.gov

Develops production adjustment and price support programs to balance supply and demand for certain commodities, including dairy products, sugar, and honey.

▶ **NONGOVERNMENTAL**

American Butter Institute (ABI), *2101 Wilson Blvd., #400, Arlington, VA 22201-3062; (703) 243-5630. Fax, (703) 841-9328. Jerome J. Kozak, Executive Director.*
General e-mail, AMiner@nmpf.org
Web, www.butterinstitute.org

Membership: butter manufacturers, packagers, and distributors. Interests include dairy price supports and programs, packaging and labeling, and imports. Monitors legislation and regulations.

Egg Nutrition Center, *1900 L St., #725 20036-5053; (202) 833-8850. Fax, (202) 463-0102. Vacant, Director.*
General e-mail, enc@enc-online.org
Web, www.enc-online.org

Provides information on egg nutrition and related health issues. Disseminates information on cholesterol and heart disease.

Humane Farm Animal Care, *P.O. Box 727, Herndon, VA 20172-0727; (703) 435-3883. Fax, (703) 435-3981. Adele Douglass, Chief Executive Officer.*
General e-mail, info@certifiedhumane.org
Web, www.certifiedhumane.org

Seeks to improve the welfare of farm animals by providing viable, duly monitored standards for humane food production. Sponsors the Certified Humane Raised and Handled program for meat, poultry, eggs, and products.

International Dairy Foods Assn., *1250 H St. N.W., #900 20005-3952; (202) 737-4332. Fax, (202) 331-7820. Constance E. Tipton, President.*
Web, www.idfa.org

Membership: processors, manufacturers, marketers, and distributors of dairy foods in the United States and abroad. Provides members with marketing, public relations, training, and management services. Monitors legislation and regulations. (Affiliated with the Milk Industry Foundation, the National Cheese Institute, and the International Ice Cream Assn.)

International Ice Cream Assn., *1250 H St. N.W., #900 20005-3952; (202) 737-4332. Fax, (202) 331-7820. Constance E. Tipton, President.*
Web, www.idfa.org

Membership: manufacturers and distributors of ice cream and other frozen desserts. Conducts market research. Monitors legislation and regulations.

Milk Industry Foundation, *1250 H St. N.W., #900 20005-3952; (202) 737-4332. Fax, (202) 331-7820. Constance E. Tipton, President.*
Web, www.idfa.org

Membership: processors of fluid milk and fluid-milk products. Conducts market research. Monitors legislation and regulations.

National Cheese Institute, *1250 H St. N.W., #900 20005-3952; (202) 737-4332. Fax, (202) 331-7820. Constance E. Tipton, President.*
Web, www.idfa.org

Membership: cheese manufacturers, packagers, processors, and distributors. Interests include dairy price supports and programs, packaging and labeling, and imports. Monitors legislation and regulations.

National Milk Producers Federation, *2101 Wilson Blvd., #400, Arlington, VA 22201-3062; (703) 243-6111. Fax, (703) 841-9328. Jerome J. Kozak, Chief Executive Officer.*
General e-mail, info@nmpf.org
Web, www.nmpf.org

Membership: dairy farmer cooperatives. Provides information on development and modification of sanitary regulations, product standards, and marketing procedures for dairy products.

United Egg Producers, *Government Relations, Washington Office, 1 Massachusetts Ave. N.W., #800 20001-1401; (202) 842-2345. Fax, (202) 408-7763. Howard Magwire, Vice President of Government Relations.*
General e-mail, hmagwire@mwmlaw.com
Web, www.unitedegg.org

Membership: egg marketing cooperatives and egg producers. Monitors legislation and regulations. (Headquarters in Atlanta, Ga.)

Fruits and Vegetables

▶ **AGENCIES**

Agricultural Marketing Service (AMS), *(Agriculture Dept.), Fruit and Vegetable Program, 1400 Independence Ave. S.W., #2077-S, MS 0235 20250-0235; (202) 720-4722. Fax, (202) 720-0016. Robert C. Keeney, Deputy Administrator.*
Web, www.ams.usda.gov/fv/index.htm

Administers research, marketing, promotional, and regulatory programs for fruits, vegetables, nuts, ornamental plants, and other specialty crops; focus includes international markets. Sets grading standards for fresh and processed fruits and vegetables; conducts quality inspections;

maintains market news service to inform producers of price changes.

Economic Research Service *(Agriculture Dept.), 1800 M St. N.W., #4145N 20036-5831; (202) 694-5000. Fax, (202) 694-5757. Kitty Smith, Administrator; John Kort, Associate Administrator.*

General e-mail, service@ers.usda.gov

Web, www.ers.usda.gov

Conducts market research; studies and forecasts domestic supply-and-demand trends for fruits and vegetables.

▶**NONGOVERNMENTAL**

International Banana Assn. (IBA), *1901 Pennsylvania Ave. N.W., #1100 20006-3412; (202) 303-3400. Fax, (202) 303-3433. Tom Stenzel, President.*

General e-mail, info@eatmorebananas.com

Web, www.eatmorebananas.com

Works to improve global distribution and increased consumption of bananas; collects and disseminates information about the banana industry; serves as a liaison between the U.S. government and banana-producing countries on issues of concern to the industry.

United Fresh Produce Assn., *1901 Pennsylvania Ave. N.W., #1100 20006; (202) 303-3400. Fax, (202) 303-3433. Tom Stenzel, President.*

General e-mail, info@unitedfresh.org

Web, www.unitedfresh.org

Membership: growers, shippers, wholesalers, retailers, food service operators, importers, and exporters involved in producing and marketing fresh fruits and vegetables. Represents the industry before the government and the public sector. (Formerly the United Fresh Fruit and Vegetable Assn.; name changed upon merging with the International Fresh-Cut Assn.)

U.S. Apple Assn., *8233 Old Courthouse Rd., #200, Vienna, VA 22182-3816; (703) 442-8850. Fax, (703) 790-0845. Nancy Foster, President.*

General e-mail, info@usapple.org

Web, www.usapple.org

Membership: U.S. commercial apple growers and processors, distributors, exporters, importers, and retailers of apples. Compiles statistics, including imports and exports; promotes research and marketing; provides information about apples and nutrition to educators. Monitors legislation and regulations.

Wine Institute, *Washington Office, 601 13th St. N.W., #330 South 20005-3866; (202) 408-0870. Fax, (202) 371-0061. Robert P. Koch, President; Sally Murphy, Federal Relations. Web, www.wineinstitute.org*

Membership: California wineries and affiliated businesses. Seeks international recognition for California wines; conducts promotional campaigns in other countries. Monitors legislation and regulations. (Headquarters in San Francisco, Calif.)

Grains and Oilseeds

▶**AGENCIES**

Agricultural Marketing Service (AMS), *(Agriculture Dept.), Livestock and Seed, 1400 Independence Ave. S.W., #2092S, MS 0249 20250-0249; (202) 720-5705. Fax, (202) 720-3499. Craig Morris, Deputy Administrator.*

Web, www.ams.usda.gov/lsprogram

Administers programs for marketing grain, including rice; maintains market news service to inform producers of grain market situation and daily price changes.

Farm Service Agency (FSA), *(Agriculture Dept.), Feed Grains and Oilseeds Analysis, 1400 Independence Ave. S.W., #3740S, MS 0532 20250-0532; (202) 720-2711. Fax, (202) 690-2186. Phil Sronce, Group Director.*

Web, www.fsa.usda.gov

Develops, analyzes, and implements domestic farm policy focusing on corn, soybeans, and other feed grains and oilseeds. Develops production adjustment and price support programs to balance supply and demand for these commodities.

Farm Service Agency (FSA), *(Agriculture Dept.), Food Grains, 1400 Independence Ave. S.W., MS 0518 20250-0532; (202) 720-2891. Fax, (202) 690-2186. Thomas F. Tice, Director.*

Web, www.fsa.usda.gov

Develops marketing loan and contract crop programs in support of food grain commodities, including wheat, rice, and pulse crops.

Grain Inspection, Packers and Stockyards Administration *(Agriculture Dept.), 1400 Independence Ave. S.W., #2055, MS 3601 20250-3601; (202) 720-0219. Fax, (202) 205-9237. Alan R. Christian, Administrator (Acting). Information, (202) 720-3553.*

Web, www.gipsa.usda.gov

Administers inspection and weighing program for grain, soybeans, rice, sunflower seeds, and other processed commodities; conducts quality inspections based on established standards.

▶**NONGOVERNMENTAL**

American Feed Industry Assn. (AFIA), *2101 Wilson Blvd., #916, Arlington, VA 22201; (703) 524-0810. Fax, (703) 524-1921. Joel Newman, President.*

General e-mail, afia@afia.org

Web, www.afia.org

Membership: feed manufacturers and ingredient suppliers and integrators. Conducts seminars on feed grain production, marketing, advertising, and quality control; interests include international trade.

American Soybean Assn., *Washington Office, 600 Pennsylvania Ave. S.E., #320, 20003-6300; (202) 969-7040. Fax, (202) 969-7036. John Gordley, Washington Representative. Web, www.soygrowers.com*

Membership: soybean farmers. Promotes expanded world markets and research for the benefit of soybean growers; maintains a network of state and international offices. (Headquarters in St. Louis, Mo.)

Corn Refiners Assn., *1701 Pennsylvania Ave. N.W., #950 20006-5805; (202) 331-1634. Fax, (202) 331-2054. Audrae Erickson, President.*

General e-mail, info@corn.org

Web, www.corn.org

Promotes research on technical aspects of corn refining and product development; acts as a clearinghouse for members who award research grants to colleges and universities. Monitors legislation and regulations.

National Assn. of Wheat Growers, *415 2nd St. N.E., #300 20002-4993; (202) 547-7800. Fax, (202) 546-2638. Daren Coppock, Chief Executive Officer.*

General e-mail, wheatworld@wheatworld.org

Web, www.wheatworld.org

Federation of state wheat grower associations. Sponsors annual wheat industry conference. Monitors legislation and regulations.

National Corn Growers Assn., *Public Policy, Washington Office, 122 C St. N.W., #510 20001-2109; (202) 628-7001. Fax, (202) 628-1933. Jon Doggett, Vice President.*

General e-mail, corninfo@ncga.com

Web, www.ncga.com

Represents the interests of U.S. corn farmers, including in international trade; promotes the use, marketing, and efficient production of corn; conducts research and educational activities; monitors legislation and regulations. (Headquarters in St. Louis, Mo.)

National Grain and Feed Assn., *1250 Eye St. N.W., #1003 20005-3939; (202) 289-0873. Fax, (202) 289-5388. Kendell Keith, President.*

General e-mail, info@ngfa.org

Web, www.ngfa.org

Membership: firms that process U.S. grains and oilseeds for domestic and export markets. Arbitration panel resolves disputes over trade and commercial regulations.

National Institute of Oilseed Products, *1156 15th St. N.W., #900 20005-1717; (202) 785-8450. Fax, (202) 223-9741. Richard E. Cristol, Washington Representative.*

General e-mail, niop@kellencompany.com

Web, www.niop.org

Membership: companies and individuals involved in manufacturing and trading oilseed products. Provides statistics on oilseed product imports and exports.

National Oilseed Processors Assn., *1300 L St. N.W., #1020 20005-4168; (202) 842-0463. Fax, (202) 842-9126. Thomas A. Hammer, President.*

Web, www.nopa.org

Provides information on oilseed crops, products, processing, and commodity programs; interests include international trade.

North American Export Grain Assn. (NAEGA), *1250 Eye St. N.W., #1003 20005-3939; (202) 682-4030. Fax, (202) 682-4033. Gary C. Martin, President.*

General e-mail, info@naega.org

Web, www.naega.org

Membership: grain exporting firms and others interested in the grain export industry. Provides information on grain export allowances, distribution, and current market trends; sponsors foreign seminars. Monitors legislation and regulations.

North American Millers' Assn., *600 Maryland Ave. S.W., #825W 20024-2573; (202) 484-2200. Fax, (202) 488-7416. Betsy Faga, President.*

General e-mail, info@namamillers.org

Web, www.namamillers.org

Trade association representing the dry corn, wheat, oats, and rye milling industry. Seeks to inform the public, the industry, and government about issues affecting the domestic milling industry. Monitors legislation and regulations.

USA Rice Federation, *4301 N. Fairfax Dr., #425, Arlington, VA 22203-1616; (703) 236-2300. Fax, (703) 236-2301. Betsy Ward, Chief Executive Officer.*

Web, www.usarice.com

Membership: rice producers, millers, merchants, and related firms. Provides U.S. and foreign rice trade and industry information; assists in establishing quality standards for rice production and milling. Monitors legislation and regulations.

U.S. Grains Council, *1400 K St. N.W., #1200 20005-2403; (202) 789-0789. Fax, (202) 898-0522. Kenneth Hobbie, President.*

General e-mail, grains@grains.org

Web, www.grains.org

Membership: barley, corn, and sorghum producers through checkoff support; agribusinesses including exporters; and chemical, machinery, malting, and seed companies interested in feed grain exports. Promotes development of U.S. feed grain markets overseas.

U.S. Wheat Associates, *3103 10th St. North, #300, Arlington, VA 22201; (202) 463-0999. Fax, (703) 524-4399. Alan Tracy, President.*

General e-mail, info@uswheat.org

Web, www.uswheat.org

Membership: wheat farmers. Develops export markets for the U.S. wheat industry; provides information on wheat production and marketing.

Sugar

►AGENCIES

Economic Research Service *(Agriculture Dept.)*, *1800 M St. N.W., #4145N 20036-5831; (202) 694-5000. Fax, (202) 694-5757. Kitty Smith, Administrator; John Kort, Associate Administrator.*
General e-mail, service@ers.usda.gov
Web, www.ers.usda.gov

Conducts market research; studies and forecasts domestic supply-and-demand trends for sugar and other sweeteners.

Farm Service Agency (FSA), *(Agriculture Dept.)*, **Dairy and Sweeteners Analysis,** *1400 Independence Ave. S.W., #3752, MS 0516 20250-0516; (202) 690-0734. Fax, (202) 690-2186. Daniel Colacicco, Group Director.*
Web, www.fsa.usda.gov

Develops production adjustment and price support programs to balance supply and demand for certain commodities, including dairy products, sugar, and honey.

►NONGOVERNMENTAL

American Sugar Alliance, *2111 Wilson Blvd., #600, Arlington, VA 22201-3051; (703) 351-5055. Fax, (703) 351-6698. Vickie R. Myers, Executive Director.*
General e-mail, info@sugaralliance.org
Web, www.sugaralliance.org

National coalition of sugarcane and sugarbeet farmers, processors, refiners, suppliers, workers, and others dedicated to preserving a strong domestic sweetener industry. Monitors legislation and regulations.

American Sugarbeet Growers Assn., *1156 15th St. N.W., #1101 20005-1756; (202) 833-2398. Fax, (240) 235-4291. Luther Markwart, Executive Vice President.*
General e-mail, info@americansugarbeet.org
Web, www.americansugarbeet.org

Membership: sugarbeet growers associations. Serves as liaison to U.S. government agencies, including the Agriculture Dept. and the U.S. Trade Representative; interests include international trade. Monitors legislation and regulations.

National Confectioners Assn., *8320 Old Courthouse Rd., #300, Vienna, VA 22182-3811; (703) 790-5750. Fax, (703) 790-5752. Lawrence T. Graham, President.*
General e-mail, info@candyusa.com
Web, www.candyusa.com

Membership: confectionery manufacturers and suppliers. Provides information on confectionery consumption and nutrition; sponsors educational programs and research on candy technology. Monitors legislation and regulations.

Sugar Assn., *1300 L St. N.W., #1001 20005-4263; (202) 785-1122. Fax, (202) 785-5019. Andrew Briscoe, President.*
General e-mail, sugar@sugar.org
Web, www.sugar.org

Membership: sugar processors, growers, refiners, and planters. Provides nutritional information, public education, and research on sugar. Library open to the public by appointment.

U.S. Beet Sugar Assn., *1156 15th St. N.W., #1019 20005-1704; (202) 296-4820. Fax, (202) 331-2065. James W. Johnson, President.*
General e-mail, beetsugar@aol.com
Web, www.beetsugar.org

Membership: beet sugar processors. Library open to the public by appointment.

Tobacco and Peanuts

►AGENCIES

Agricultural Marketing Service (AMS), *(Agriculture Dept.)*, **Cotton and Tobacco Programs,** *1400 Independence Ave. S.W., #2639S, MS 0224 20250-0224; (202) 720-3193. Fax, (202) 690-1718. Darryl W. Earnest, Deputy Administrator.*
Web, www.ams.usda.gov/cotton/index.htm

Administers cotton marketing programs; sets cotton and tobacco grading standards and conducts quality inspections based on those standards. Maintains market news service to inform producers of daily price changes.

Economic Research Service *(Agriculture Dept.)*, *1800 M St. N.W., #4145N 20036-5831; (202) 694-5000. Fax, (202) 694-5757. Kitty Smith, Administrator; John Kort, Associate Administrator.*
General e-mail, service@ers.usda.gov
Web, www.ers.usda.gov

Conducts market research; studies and forecasts domestic supply-and-demand trends for tobacco.

Farm Service Agency (FSA), *(Agriculture Dept.)*, **Farm Programs,** *1400 Independence Ave. S.W., MS 0510 20250-0510; (202) 720-3175. Fax, (202) 720-4726. Candace Thompson, Deputy Administrator (Acting). Press, (202) 720-7807.*
Web, www.fsa.usda.gov

Administers and manages aid programs for farmers, including conservation efforts, disaster relief, loans, subsidies, and the Tobacco Transition Payment program. Operates through county offices spread throughout the continental United States, Hawaii, and several American territories.

Farm Service Agency (FSA), *(Agriculture Dept.)*, **Fibers, Peanuts, and Tobacco Analysis,** *1400 Independence Ave. S.W., #37605, MS 0515 20250-0515; (202) 720-3392. Fax, (202) 690-2186. Scott Sanford, Director.*
Web, www.fsa.usda.gov

Develops production adjustment and price support programs to balance supply and demand for cotton, peanuts, and tobacco.

►NONGOVERNMENTAL

American Peanut Council, *1500 King St., #301, Alexandria, VA 22314-2737; (703) 838-9500. Fax, (703) 838-9508. Patrick Archer, President.*

General e-mail, info@peanutsusa.com

Web, www.peanutsusa.com

Membership: peanut growers, shellers, brokers, and manufacturers, as well as allied companies. Provides information on economic and nutritional value of peanuts; coordinates research; promotes U.S. peanut exports, domestic production, and market development.

Cigar Assn. of America, *818 Connecticut Ave. N.W., #200 20006-3919; (202) 223-8204. Fax, (202) 833-0379. Norman F. Sharp, President.*

General e-mail, nsharp@cigarassociation.org

Membership: growers and suppliers of cigar leaf tobacco; manufacturers, packagers, importers, distributors of cigars; and suppliers to the cigar industry. Monitors legislation and regulations.

Tobacco Associates, Inc., *8452 Holly Leaf Dr., McLean, VA 22102-2225; (703) 821-1255. Fax, (202) 821-1511. Clyde N. "Kirk" Wayne, President.*

General e-mail, taw@tobaccoassociatesinc.org

Web, www.tobaccoassociatesinc.org

Membership: U.S. producers of flue-cured tobacco. Promotes exports; provides information to encourage overseas market development.

FARM LOANS, INSURANCE, AND SUBSIDIES

►AGENCIES

Commodity Credit Corp. *(Agriculture Dept.), 1400 Independence Ave. S.W., #3702A-S, MS 0599 20250-0599; (202) 720-1068. Fax, (202) 690-1692. Steven N. Mikkelsen, Secretary of CCC (Acting).*

Web, www.fsa.usda.gov/ccc

Administers and finances the commodity stabilization program through loans, purchases, and supplemental payments; sells through domestic and export markets commodities acquired by the government under this program; administers some aspects of foreign food aid through the Food for Peace program; provides storage facilities.

Farm Credit Administration, *1501 Farm Credit Dr., McLean, VA 22102-5090; (703) 883-4056. Fax, (703) 790-3260. Lee Strom, Chair. TTY, (703) 883-4056.*

General e-mail, info-line@fca.gov

Web, www.fca.gov

Examines and regulates the cooperative Farm Credit System, which comprises farm credit banks, one agricultural credit bank, agricultural credit associations, and federal land credit associations. Oversees credit programs and related services for farmers, ranchers, producers and harvesters of aquatic products, farm-related service businesses, rural homeowners, agricultural and aquatic cooperatives, and rural utilities.

Farm Credit Administration, Examination, *1501 Farm Credit Dr., McLean, VA 22102-5090; (703) 883-4160. Fax, (703) 893-2978. Thomas G. McKenzie, Chief Examiner.*

General e-mail, info-line@fca.gov

Web, www.fca.gov

Enforces and oversees compliance with the Farm Credit Act. Monitors cooperatively owned member banks' and associations' compliance with laws prohibiting discrimination in credit transactions.

Farm Service Agency (FSA), (Agriculture Dept.), *1400 Independence Ave. S.W., #3086 South Bldg., MS 0501 20250-0501; (202) 720-3467. Fax, (202) 720-9105. Theresa C. Lasseter, Administrator.*

Web, www.fsa.usda.gov

Administers farm commodity programs providing crop loans and purchases; provides crop payments when market prices fall below specified levels; sets acreage allotments and marketing quotas; assists farmers in areas affected by natural disasters.

Farm Service Agency (FSA), (Agriculture Dept.), Farm Loan Programs, *1400 Independence Ave. S.W., #3605S, MS 0520 20250-0520; (202) 720-4671. Fax, (202) 690-3573. Carolyn Cooksie, Deputy Administrator.*

Web, www.fsa.usda.gov

Provides services and loans to beginning farmers and administers emergency farm loan programs.

Farm Service Agency (FSA), (Agriculture Dept.), Minority and Socially Disadvantaged Farmers Assistance, *1400 Independence Ave. S.W., MS 0503 20250-0503; (202) 720-1584. Fax, (202) 720-5398. Gypsy Banks, Director. TTY, (202) 720-5132. Toll-free, (866) 538-2610 (phone); (866) 302-1760 (fax); (866) 480-2824 (TTY).*

General e-mail, msda@wdc.usda.gov

Web, www.fsa.usda.gov

Works with minority and socially disadvantaged farmers who have concerns and questions about loan applications filed with local offices or other Farm Service Agency programs.

Farmer Mac, *1133 21st St. N.W., #600 20036-3332; (202) 872-7700. Fax, (202) 872-7713. Michael Gerber, President.*

Web, www.farmermac.com

Private corporation chartered by Congress to provide a secondary mortgage market for farm and rural housing loans. Guarantees principal and interest repayment on securities backed by farm and rural housing loans. (Farmer Mac stands for Federal Agricultural Mortgage Corp.)

Risk Management Agency *(Agriculture Dept.), 1400 Independence Ave. S.W., #6092S, MS 0801 20250-0801; (202) 690-2803. Fax, (202) 690-2818. Eldon Gould, Administrator. Information, (202) 690-0437.*

General e-mail, rma.mail@rma.usda.gov

Web, www.rma.usda.gov

Provides farmers with insurance against crops lost because of bad weather, insects, disease, and other natural causes.

Rural Development *(Agriculture Dept.), Civil Rights,* *1400 Independence Ave. S.W., #1341, MS 0703 20250; (202) 692-0090. Fax, (202) 692-0279. Thelma Floyd, Director.*

Web, www.rurdev.usda.gov/rhs/Admin/civilrights.htm

Processes Equal Employment Opportunity complaints for Rural Development employees, former employees, and applicants. Enforces compliance with the Equal Credit Opportunity Act, which prohibits discrimination on the basis of sex, marital status, race, color, religion, disability, or age in rural housing, utilities, and business programs. Provides civil rights training to Rural Development's national, state, and field staffs.

►CONGRESS

For a listing of relevant congressional committees and subcommittees, please see page 3 or the Appendix.

►NONGOVERNMENTAL

Environmental Working Group, *1436 U St. N.W., #100 20009-3987; (202) 667-6982. Fax, (202) 232-2592. Kenneth A. Cook, President.*

General e-mail, generalinfo@ewg.org

Web, www.ewg.org

Research and advocacy group that studies and publishes reports on a wide range of agricultural and environmental issues, including farm subsidies. Monitors legislation and regulations.

Farm Credit Council, *50 F St. N.W., #900 20001-1530; (202) 626-8710. Fax, (202) 626-8718. Ken Auer, President. Toll-free, (800) 525-2345.*

Web, www.fccouncil.com

Represents the Farm Credit System, a national financial cooperative that makes loans to agricultural producers, rural homebuyers, farmer cooperatives, and rural utilities. Finances the export of U.S. agricultural commodities.

FOOD AND NUTRITION

►AGENCIES

Agricultural Marketing Service (AMS), *(Agriculture Dept.), Science and Technology, 1400 Independence Ave. S.W., #3507-S 20250-0003; (202) 720-5231. Fax, (202) 720-6496. Robert L. Epstein, Deputy Administrator.*

Web, www.ams.usda.gov/science/index.htm

Provides analytical testing to AMS community programs, federal and state agencies, and the private sector food industry; participates in international food safety organizations. Tests commodities traded with specific countries and regions, including butter, honey, eggs, nuts, poultry, and meat; analyzes nutritional value of U.S. military rations.

Agricultural Research Service *(Agriculture Dept.), 1400 Independence Ave. S.W., #302A, MS 0300 20250-0300; (202) 720-3656. Fax, (202) 720-5427. Edward B. Knipling, Administrator.*

Web, www.ars.usda.gov

Conducts studies on agricultural problems of domestic and international concern through nationwide network of research centers. Studies include research on human nutrition; livestock production and protection; crop production, protection, and processing; postharvest technology; and food distribution and market value.

Agriculture Dept. (USDA), *Food, Nutrition, and Consumer Services, 1400 Independence Ave. S.W., #240E 20250-0106; (202) 720-7711. Fax, (202) 690-3100. Vacant, Under Secretary; Tim O'Connor, Deputy Under Secretary (Acting).*

Web, www.fns.usda.gov

Oversees the Food and Nutrition Service and the Center for Nutrition Policy and Promotion.

Animal and Plant Health Inspection Service (APHIS), *(Agriculture Dept.), 1400 Independence Ave. S.W., #312E, MS 3401 20250-3401; (202) 720-3668. Fax, (202) 720-3054. Cindy Smith, Administrator.*

Web, www.aphis.usda.gov

Administers animal disease control programs in cooperation with states; inspects imported animals, flowers, and plants; licenses the manufacture and marketing of veterinary biologics to ensure purity and effectiveness.

Cooperative State Research, Education, and Extension Service (CSREES), *(Agriculture Dept.), 1400 Independence Ave. S.W., #305A, MS 2201 20250-2201; (202) 720-4423. Fax, (202) 720-8987. Colien Heffernan, Administrator. Information, (202) 720-4651. TTY, (202) 690-1899.*

Web, www.csrees.usda.gov

Oversees county agents and operation of state offices that provide information on nutrition, diet, food purchase budgeting, food safety, home gardening, and other consumer concerns.

Food and Drug Administration (FDA), *(Health and Human Services Dept.), Center for Food Safety and Applied Nutrition, 5100 Paint Branch Pkwy., College Park, MD 20740-3835; (301) 436-1600. Fax, (301) 436-2668. Dr. Stephen F. Sundlof, Director.*

General e-mail, consumer@fda.gov

Web, www.cfsan.fda.gov

Develops standards of composition and quality of foods (except meat and poultry but including fish); develops safety regulations for food and color additives for foods, cosmetics, and drugs; monitors pesticide residues in foods; conducts food safety and nutrition research;

develops analytical methods for measuring food additives, nutrients, pesticides, and chemical and microbiological contaminants; recommends action to Justice Dept.

Food and Drug Administration (FDA), *(Health and Human Services Dept.), Nutritional Products Labeling and Dietary Supplements*, 5100 Paint Branch Pkwy., MS HFS800, College Park, MD 20740-3835; (301) 436 2373. Fax, (301) 436-2639. Dr. Barbara Schneeman, Director. Web, www.cfsan.fda.gov

Scientific and technical component of the Center for Food Safety and Applied Nutrition. Conducts research on nutrients; develops regulations and labeling requirements on infant formulas, medical foods, and dietary supplements, including herbs.

Food and Nutrition Service *(Agriculture Dept.)*, 3101 Park Center Dr., #906, Alexandria, VA 22302-1500; (703) 305-2060. Fax, (703) 305-2908. Enrique Gomez, Administrator (Acting). Information, (703) 305-2286. Web, www.fns.usda.gov/fns

Administers all Agriculture Dept. domestic food assistance, including the distribution of funds and food for school breakfast and lunch programs (preschool through secondary) to public and nonprofit private schools; the food stamp program; and a supplemental nutrition program for women, infants, and children (WIC).

Food and Nutrition Service *(Agriculture Dept.), Child Nutrition*, 3101 Park Center Dr., #640, Alexandria, VA 22302-1500; (703) 305-2590. Fax, (703) 305-2879. Cindy Long, Director. Press, (703) 305-2286. Web, www.fns.usda.gov/cnd

Administers the transfer of funds to state agencies for the National School Lunch Program; the School Breakfast Program; the Special Milk Program, which helps schools and institutions provide children who do not have access to full meals under other child nutrition programs with fluid milk; the Child and Adult Care Food Program, which provides children in nonresidential child-care centers and family day-care homes with year-round meal service; and the Summer Food Service Program, which provides children from low-income areas with meals during the summer months. Administers the Child Nutrition Labeling Program, which certifies that foods served in school lunch and breakfast programs meet nutritional requirements.

Food and Nutrition Service *(Agriculture Dept.), Food Distribution*, 3101 Park Center Dr., #504, Alexandria, VA 22302-1500; (703) 305-2680. Fax, (703) 305-1410. Cathie McCullough, Director. Web, www.fns.usda.gov/fdd

Provides food for the National School Lunch Program, Summer Food Service Program, and the Child and Adult Care Food Program. Administers the Commodity Supplemental Food Program for low-income pregnant and breastfeeding women, new mothers, infants, children, and the elderly. Supplies food to relief organizations for distribution following disasters. Makes commodity food and cash available through the Nutrition Services Incentive Program (formerly the Nutrition Program for the Elderly). Administers the Emergency Food Assistance Program through soup kitchens and food banks and the Food Distribution Program on Indian reservations and to Indian households elsewhere.

Food and Nutrition Service *(Agriculture Dept.), Research, Nutrition, and Analysis*, 3101 Park Center Dr., #1014, Alexandria, VA 22302-1500; (703) 305-2017. Fax, (703) 305-2576. Steve Carlson, Director. General e-mail, oaneweb@fns.usda.gov Web, www.fns.usda.gov/oane

Administers the Nutrition Education and Training Program, which provides states with grants for disseminating nutrition information to children and for in-service training of food service and teaching personnel; provides information and technical assistance in nutrition and food service management.

Food and Nutrition Service *(Agriculture Dept.), Supplemental Food Programs*, 3101 Park Center Dr., #520, Alexandria, VA 22302-1500; (703) 305-2746. Fax, (703) 305-2196. Patricia N. Daniels, Director. Web, www.fns.usda.gov

Provides health departments and agencies with federal funding for food supplements and administrative expenses to make food, nutrition education, and health services available to infants, young children, and pregnant, nursing, and postpartum women.

Food and Nutrition Service *(Agriculture Dept.), Supplemental Nutrition Assistance Program (SNAP)*, 3101 Park Center Dr., #808, Alexandria, VA 22302-1500; (703) 305-2026. Fax, (703) 305-2454. Jessica Shahin, Associate Administrator. Web, www.fns.usda.gov

Administers SNAP through state welfare agencies to provide needy persons with Electronic Benefit Transfer cards to increase food purchasing power. Provides matching funds to cover half the cost of EBT card issuance.

Food Safety and Inspection Service *(Agriculture Dept.)*, 1400 Independence Ave. S.W., #331E 20250-0003; (202) 720-7025. Fax, (202) 205-0158. Al Almonzo, Administrator. Press, (202) 720-9113. Consumer inquiries, (800) 535-4555. Web, www.usda.gov/fsis

Inspects meat, poultry, and egg products moving in interstate commerce for use as human food to ensure that they are safe, wholesome, and accurately labeled. Provides safe handling and labeling guidelines.

National Agricultural Library *(Agriculture Dept.), Food and Nutrition Information Center*, 10301 Baltimore Ave., #105, Beltsville, MD 20705-2351; (301) 504-5719. Fax, (301) 504-6409. Vacant, Coordinator. TTY, (301) 504-6369.

General e-mail, fnic@nal.usda.gov

Web, www.nal.usda.gov/fnic

Serves individuals and agencies seeking information or educational materials on food and human nutrition; lends books and audiovisual materials for educational purposes; maintains a database of food and nutrition software and multimedia programs; provides reference services; develops resource lists of health and nutrition publications. Center open to the public.

National Agricultural Library *(Agriculture Dept.),*
Food Safety Information Center, 10301 Baltimore Ave., #304, Beltsville, MD 20705-2351; (301) 504-7374. Fax, (301) 504-7680. Yvette Alonso, Coordinator. Reference, (301) 504-5515.

General e-mail, fsic@ars.usda.gov

Web, http://foodsafety.nal.usda.gov

Provides food safety information to educators, industry, researchers, and the general public. Special subject areas include pathogens and contaminants, sanitation and quality standards, food preparation and handling, and food processing and technology. The center includes the Food Safety Research Information Office, which focuses on providing information and reference services to the research community and the general public.

National Institute of Diabetes and Digestive and Kidney Diseases (National Institutes of Health),
Nutritional Sciences, 6707 Democracy Blvd., #631, MSC-5450, Bethesda, MD 20892-5450; (301) 594-8883. Fax, (301) 480-8300. Dr. Van S. Hubbard, Chief.

General e-mail, hubbardv@mail.nih.gov

Web, www.niddk.nih.gov

Supports research on nutritional requirements, dietary fiber, obesity, eating disorders, energy regulation, clinical nutrition, trace minerals, and basic nutrient functions.

National Oceanic and Atmospheric Administration (NOAA), *(Commerce Dept.),* **Seafood Inspection Program,** 1315 East-West Hwy., #10837, Silver Spring, MD 20910; (301) 713-2355. Fax, (301) 713-1081. Timothy Hansen, Director.

Web, http://seafood.nmfs.noaa.gov

Administers voluntary inspection program for fish products and fish processing plants; certifies fish for wholesomeness, safety, and condition; grades for quality. Conducts training and workshops to help U.S. importers and foreign suppliers comply with food regulations.

►CONGRESS

For a listing of relevant congressional committees and subcommittees, please see page 3 or the Appendix.

►INTERNATIONAL ORGANIZATIONS

Codex Alimentarius Commission, *U.S. Codex Office,* 1400 Independence Ave. S.W., South Bldg., #4861 20250-3700; (202) 205-7760. Fax, (202) 720-3157. Karen S. Tuck,

U.S. Codex Manager (Acting); Paulo Almeida, U.S. Associate Manager.

General e-mail, uscodex@fsis.usda.gov

Web, www.fsis.usda.gov/regulations_&_policies/codex_Alimentarius/index.asp

U.S. contact point for the principal U.N. agency concerned with food standards, food safety, and related regulation of international trade. Convenes committees in member countries to address specific commodities and issues including labeling, additives in food and veterinary drugs, pesticide residues and other contaminants, and systems for food inspection. (Located in the USDA Food Safety and Inspection Service; international headquarters in Rome.)

►NONGOVERNMENTAL

American Dietetic Assn. (ADA), *Washington Office,* 1120 Connecticut Ave. N.W., #480 20036-3989; (202) 775-8277. Fax, (202) 775-8284. Stephanie Patrick, Vice President. Press, (800) 877-1600, ext. 4802.

General e-mail, govaffairs@eatright.org or media@eatright.org

Web, www.eatright.org

Membership: dietitians and other nutrition professionals. Promotes public health and nutrition; accredits academic programs in clinical nutrition and food service management; sets standards of professional practice. Sponsors the National Center for Nutrition and Dietetics. (Headquarters in Chicago, Ill.)

American Herbal Products Assn., 8630 Fenton St., #918, Silver Spring, MD 20910; (301) 588-1171. Fax, (301) 588-1174. Michael McGuffin, President. Press, (301) 588-1171, ext. 104.

General e-mail, ahpa@ahpa.org

Web, www.ahpa.org

Membership: U.S. companies and individuals that grow, manufacture, and distribute therapeutic herbs and herbal products; associates in education, law, media, and medicine. Supports research; promotes quality standards, consumer protection, competition, and self-regulation in the industry. Monitors legislation and regulations.

American Society for Nutrition, 9650 Rockville Pike, #L5500, Bethesda, MD 20814-3990; (301) 634-7050. Fax, (301) 634-7892. John Courtney, Executive Officer.

General e-mail, sec@nutrition.org

Web, www.nutrition.org

Membership: nutritional research scientists including clinical nutritionists. Supports research on the role of human nutrition in health and disease; encourages undergraduate and graduate nutrition education; offers awards for research. (Merger of the American Society for Clinical Nutrition and the American Society for Nutritional Sciences.)

American Society for Parenteral and Enteral Nutrition (ASPEN), 8630 Fenton St., #412, Silver Spring, MD 20910-3805; (301) 587-6315. Fax, (301) 587-2365. Debra Ben Avram, Executive Director.

General e-mail, aspen@nutr.org

Web, www.nutritioncare.org

Membership: health care professionals who provide patients with intravenous nutritional support during hospitalization and rehabilitation at home. Develops nutrition guidelines; provides educational materials; conducts annual meetings.

Center for Science in the Public Interest, *1875 Connecticut Ave. N.W., #300 20009-5728; (202) 332-9110. Fax, (202) 265-4954. Michael F. Jacobson, Executive Director.*

General e-mail, cspi@cspinet.org

Web, www.cspinet.org

Conducts research on food and nutrition. Interests include eating habits, food safety regulations, food additives, organically produced foods, alcohol beverages, and links between diet and disease. Monitors U.S. and international policy.

Congressional Hunger Center, *Hall of the States Bldg., 400 N. Capitol St. N.W., #G100 20001-1592; (202) 547-7022. Fax, (202) 547-7575. Edward M. Cooney, Executive Director.*

Web, www.hungercenter.org

Works to increase public awareness of hunger in the United States and abroad. Develops strategies and trains leaders to combat hunger and facilitates collaborative efforts between organizations.

Council for Responsible Nutrition (CRN), *1828 L St. N.W., #510 20036-5104; (202) 776-7929. Fax, (202) 204-7701. Steven Mister, President.*

Web, www.crnusa.org

Membership: manufacturers, distributors, and ingredient suppliers of dietary supplements. Provides information to members; monitors Food and Drug Administration, Federal Trade Commission, and Consumer Product Safety Commission regulations.

Food & Water Watch, *1616 P St. N.W., #300 20036; (202) 683-2500. Fax, (202) 683-2501. Wenonah Hauter, Executive Director.*

General e-mail, foodandwater@fwwatch.org

Web, www.foodandwaterwatch.org

Consumer organization that advocates for stricter water and food safety regulations. Organizes public awareness campaigns and lobbies Congress. Publishes studies of agricultural, food preparation, and drinking water sanitation practices.

Food Allergy and Anaphylaxis Network (FAAN), *11781 Lee Jackson Hwy., #160, Fairfax, VA 22033-3309; (703) 691-3179. Fax, (703) 691-2713. Anne Muñoz-Furlong, Chief Executive Officer. Toll-free, (800) 929-4040.*

General e-mail, faan@foodallergy.org

Web, www.foodallergy.org

Membership: dieticians, nurses, physicians, school staff, government representatives, and members of the food and pharmaceutical industries. Seeks to educate the public about and advance research on food allergies and allergic reactions.

Food Research and Action Center (FRAC), *1875 Connecticut Ave. N.W., #540 20009-5728; (202) 986-2200. Fax, (202) 986-2525. James D. Weill, President.*

General e-mail, comments@frac.org

Web, www.frac.org

Public interest advocacy, research, and legal center that works to end hunger and poverty in the United States; offers legal assistance, organizational aid, training, and information to groups seeking to improve or expand federal food programs, including food stamp, child nutrition, and WIC (women, infants, and children) programs; conducts studies relating to hunger and poverty; coordinates network of anti-hunger organizations. Monitors legislation and regulations.

International Food Information Council, *1100 Connecticut Ave. N.W., #430 20036-4120; (202) 296-6540. Fax, (202) 296-6547. David B. Schmidt, President.*

General e-mail, foodinfo@ific.org

Web, www.ific.org

Membership: food and beverage companies and manufacturers of food ingredients. Provides the media, health professionals, and consumers with scientific information about food safety, health, and nutrition. Interests include harmonization of international food safety standards.

International Life Sciences Institute (ILSI), *North America,* *1156 15th St. N.W., #200 20005-5802; (202) 659-0074. Fax, (202) 659-3859. Sharon Weiss, Deputy Executive Director.*

General e-mail, ilsi@ilsi.org

Web, www.ilsi.org

Acts as liaison among scientists from international government agencies, concerned industries, research institutes, and universities regarding the safety of foods and chemical ingredients. Conducts research on caffeine, food coloring, oral health, human nutrition, and other food issues. Promotes international cooperation among scientists.

Physicians Committee for Responsible Medicine (PCRM), *5100 Wisconsin Ave. N.W., #400 20016; (202) 686-2210. Fax, (202) 686-2216. Dr. Neal D. Barnard, President.*

General e-mail, pcrm@pcrm.org

Web, www.pcrm.org

Membership: health care professionals, medical students, and laypersons interested in preventive medicine, nutrition, and higher standards in research. Conducts clinical research, educational programs, and public information campaigns; advocates for more effective and compassionate health-related policies in government and in public and private institutions.

Public Citizen, *Health Research Group,* *1600 20th St. N.W. 20009-1001; (202) 588-1000. Fax, (202) 588-7796. Dr. Sidney M. Wolfe, Director.*

Food Safety Resources and Contacts

The following agencies and organizations offer consumer information pertaining to food safety issues.

AGENCIES

Center for Food Safety and Applied Nutrition, Food and Drug Administration (FDA), (Health and Human Services Department)
Dr. Stephen F. Sundlof, Director, (301) 436-1600
    Office of Food Defense, Communication and Emergency Response, Faye Feldstein, Director, (301) 436-2428
    Office of Food Safety, Dr. Nega Behru, Director, (301) 436-1700
    Office of Nutrition, Labeling and Dietary Supplements, Dr. Barbara O. Schneeman, Director, (301) 436-2373
Food Safety and Inspection Service (FSIS), (Agriculture Department)
Alfred V. Almanza, Administrator, (202) 720-7025
    Office of Data Integration and Food Protection, Dr. Carol Maczka, Assistant Administrator, (202) 720-5643
Food Safety Information Center (FSIC), National Agricultural Library, (Agriculture Department)
Yvette Alonso-Haire, (301) 504-5515
Office of Food Protection, Food and Drug Administration (FDA), (Health and Human Services Department)
Dr. David Acheson, Associate Commissioner of Foods, (301) 827-4000
Office of Ground Water and Drinking Water, Environmental Protection Agency
Cynthia Dougherty, Director, (202) 564-3750
Seafood Inspection Program, National Oceanic and Atmospheric Administration (NOAA), (Commerce Department)

Timothy Hansen, Director, (301) 713-2355; (800) 422-2750

ORGANIZATIONS

Center for Food Safety
Andrew Kimbrell, Executive Director
    (202) 547-9359
Center for Science in the Public Interest
Michael F. Jacobson, Executive Director
    (202) 332-9110
Food and Water Watch
Wenonah Hauter, Executive Director
    (202) 683-2500
International Food Information Council
David B. Schmidt, President
    (202) 296-6540

HOTLINES

FDA Center for Food Safety and Applied Nutrition
    (888) SAFEFOOD; (888) 723-3366
    www.cfsan.fda.gov
Office of Data Integration and Food Protection, Food Safety and Inspection Service
24-Hour Emergency Number: (866) 395-9701
    www.fsis.usda.gov
Safe Drinking Water Hotline
    (800) 426-4791
    www.epa.gov/safewater
USDA Meat and Poultry Hotline
    (888) MPHOTLINE; (888) 674-6854
    mphotline.fsis@usda.gov
Gateway to Government Food Safety Information
    www.foodsafety.gov

General e-mail, *pcmail@citizen.org*

Web, *www.citizen.org*

Citizens' interest group that studies and reports on unsafe foods; monitors and petitions the Food and Drug Administration.

United Food and Commercial Workers International Union (UFCW), *1775 K St. N.W. 20006-1598; (202) 223-3111. Fax, (202) 466-1562. Joseph T. Hansen, President.*

Web, *www.ufcw.org*

Membership: approximately 1.3 million workers in food-related industries, including supermarkets, department stores, and packing houses and processing plants. Helps members negotiate pay, benefits, and better working conditions; conducts training programs and workshops. Monitors legislation and regulations. (Affiliated with the Canadian Labour Congress.)

Vegetarian Resource Group, *P.O. Box 1463, Baltimore, MD 21203-1463; (410) 366-8343. Fax, (410) 366-8804. Charles Stahler, Co-Director; Debra Wasserman, Co-Director.*

General e-mail, *vrg@vrg.org*

Web, *www.vrg.org*

Works to educate the public on vegetarianism and issues of health, nutrition, ecology, ethics, and world hunger.

Vegetarian Union of North America, *P.O. Box 9710 20016-9710; (202) 362-8349, option 3. Saurabh Dalal, President.*

General e-mail, *vuna@ivu.org*

Web, *www.ivu.org/vuna/english.html*

Promotes a cooperative and effective vegetarian movement throughout North America. Builds a network of vegetarian groups throughout the United States and Canada. Serves as a liaison with the worldwide vegetarian movement.

Beverages

►AGENCIES

Alcohol and Tobacco Tax and Trade Bureau (TTB), *(Treasury Dept.), 1310 G St. N.W., #300E 20220; (202) 927-5000. Fax, (202) 927-5611. John J. Manfreda, Administrator. Press, (202) 927-8062.*
Web, www.ttb.gov

Regulates the advertising and labeling of alcohol beverages, including the size of containers; enforces federal taxation of alcohol and tobacco. Authorized to refer violations to Justice Dept. for criminal prosecution.

National Clearinghouse for Alcohol and Drug Information *(Health and Human Services Dept.), Center for Substance Abuse Prevention, 11420 Rockville Pike, Rockville, MD 20852 (mailing address: P.O. Box 2345, Rockville, MD 20847-2345); (240) 221-4017. Fax, (240) 221-4292. Lisa Swanberg, Director. Information, (800) 729-6686. Press, (240) 221-4261. TTY, (800) 487-4889.*
Web, http://ncadi.samhsa.gov

Provides information, publications, mental health services, and grant applications for programs to prevent alcohol and drug abuse. Non-circulating library open to the public.

►NONGOVERNMENTAL

American Beverage Assn., *1101 16th St. N.W. 20036-6396; (202) 463-6732. Fax, (202) 659-5349. Susan Neely, President. Press, (202) 463-6770.*
General e-mail, info@ameribev.org
Web, www.ameribev.org

Membership: companies engaged in producing or distributing carbonated and non-carbonated soft drinks and bottled water. Acts as industry liaison with government and the public. (Formerly the National Soft Drink Assn.)

American Beverage Institute, *1090 Vermont Ave. N.W., #800 20005; (202) 463-7110. Fax, (202) 463-7107. Rick Berman, Executive Director.*
Web, www.abionline.org

Promotes responsible alcohol consumption in restaurants and bars. Opposes restrictions on alcohol use. Monitors legislation and regulations.

American Beverage Licensees (ABL), *5101 River Rd., #108, Bethesda, MD 20816-1560; (301) 656-1494. Fax, (301) 656-7539. Harry G. Wiles, Executive Director.*
General e-mail, info@ablusa.org
Web, www.ablusa.org

Membership: state associations of on- and off-premise beverage alcohol licensees. Monitors legislation and regulations affecting the alcohol beverage industry. (Formerly National Assn. of Beverage Retailers and National Licensed Beverage Assn.)

Beer Institute, *122 C St. N.W., #350 20001-2150; (202) 737-2337. Fax, (202) 737-7004. Jeffrey G. Becker, President. Press, (202) 289-5900.*

General e-mail, info@beerinstitute.org
Web, www.beerinstitute.org

Membership: domestic and international brewers and suppliers to the domestic brewing industry. Monitors legislation and regulations.

Center for Science in the Public Interest, *1875 Connecticut Ave. N.W., #300 20009-5728; (202) 332-9110. Fax, (202) 265-4954. Michael F. Jacobson, Executive Director.*
General e-mail, cspi@cspinet.org
Web, www.cspinet.org

Concerned with U.S. and international policy on food and alcohol, including marketing, labeling, and taxation. Opposes U.S. government promotion of alcohol products overseas.

Distilled Spirits Council of the United States, *1250 Eye St. N.W., #400 20005-3998; (202) 628-3544. Fax, (202) 682-8888. Peter H. Cressy, President.*
Web, www.discus.org

Membership: manufacturers and marketers of distilled spirits sold in the United States. Provides consumer information on alcohol-related issues and topics. Monitors legislation and regulations.

International Bottled Water Assn. (IBWA), *1700 Diagonal Rd., #650, Alexandria, VA 22314-2864; (703) 683-5213. Fax, (703) 683-4074. Joseph K. Doss, President. Information, (800) WATER-11. Press, (877) 597-7122.*
General e-mail, ibwainfo@bottledwater.org
Web, www.bottledwater.org

Serves as a clearinghouse for industry-related consumer, regulatory, and technical information; interests include international trade. Monitors state and federal legislation and regulations.

Mothers Against Drunk Driving (MADD), *Public Policy Office, 1025 Connecticut Ave. N.W., #1200 20036-5415; (202) 974-2487. Fax, (202) 293-0106. J. T. Griffin, Public Policy Director; Julie Clements, State Policy Specialist.*
General e-mail, madd@madd.org
Web, www.madd.org

Advocacy group that seeks to stop drunk driving and prevent underage drinking. Monitors legislation and regulations. (Headquarters in Irving, Texas.)

National Alcohol Beverage Control Assn. (NABCA), *4401 Ford Ave., #700, Alexandria, VA 22302-1433; (703) 578-4200. Fax, (703) 820-3551. James M. Sgueo, President.*
General e-mail, info@nabca.org
Web, www.nabca.org

Membership: distilleries, trade associations, and state agencies that control the purchase, distribution, and sale of alcohol beverages. Promotes responsible sale and consumption of these beverages. Serves as an information clearinghouse. Monitors legislation and regulations.

National Assn. of State Alcohol and Drug Abuse Directors (NASADAD), *1025 Connecticut Ave. N.W., #605 20036-5430; (202) 293-0090. Fax, (202) 293-1250. Rob Morrison, Executive Director.*
General e-mail, dcoffice@nasadad.org
Web, www.nasadad.org

Provides information on drug abuse treatment and prevention; contracts with federal and state agencies for design of programs to fight drug abuse.

National Beer Wholesalers Assn., *1101 King St., #600, Alexandria, VA 22314-2965; (703) 683-4300. Fax, (703) 683-8965. Craig Purser, President.*
General e-mail, info@nbwa.org
Web, www.nbwa.org

Works to enhance the independent beer wholesale industry. Advocates before government and the public; encourages responsible consumption of beer; sponsors programs and services to benefit members; monitors legislation and regulations.

Wine and Spirits Wholesalers of America (WSWA), *805 15th St. N.W., #430 20005-2273; (202) 371-9792. Fax, (202) 789-2405. Craig Wolf, President.*
Web, www.wswa.org

Trade association of wholesale distributors of domestic and imported wine and distilled spirits. Provides information on drinking awareness. Represents members' interests before Congress and federal agencies.

Wine Institute, *Washington Office, 601 13th St. N.W., #330 South 20005-3866; (202) 408-0870. Fax, (202) 371-0061. Robert P. Koch, President; Sally Murphy, Federal Relations.*
Web, www.wineinstitute.org

Membership: California wineries and affiliated businesses. Seeks international recognition for California wines; conducts promotional campaigns in other countries. Monitors legislation and regulations. (Headquarters in San Francisco, Calif.)

Food Industries

▶**NONGOVERNMENTAL**

American Bakers Assn. (ABA), *1300 Eye St. N.W., #700W 20005-7203; (202) 789-0300. Fax, (202) 898-1164. Robb Mackie, President.*
General e-mail, info@americanbakers.org
Web, www.americanbakers.org

Membership: wholesale baking companies and their suppliers. Promotes increased consumption of baked goods; provides consumers with nutritional information; conducts conventions. Monitors legislation and regulations.

American Frozen Food Institute, *2000 Corporate Ridge, #1000, McLean, VA 22102-7862; (703) 821-0770. Fax, (703) 821-1350. Kraig Naasz, President.*

General e-mail, info@affi.com
Web, www.affi.com

Membership: frozen food packers, distributors, and suppliers. Testifies before Congress and federal agencies.

American Meat Institute, *1150 Connecticut Ave. N.W., 12th Floor 20036; (202) 587-4200. Fax, (202) 587-4300. J. Patrick Boyle, President.*
Web, www.meatami.com

Membership: national and international meat and poultry packers, suppliers, and processors. Provides statistics on meat and poultry production and exports. Funds research projects and consumer education programs. Monitors legislation and regulations.

Bakery, Confectionery, Tobacco Workers, and Grain Millers International Union, *10401 Connecticut Ave., Kensington, MD 20895-3940; (301) 933-8600. Fax, (301) 946-8452. Frank Hurt, President.*
Web, www.bctgm.org

Membership: approximately 120,000 workers from the bakery, confectionery, grain miller, and tobacco industries. Helps members negotiate pay, benefits, and better working conditions; conducts training programs and workshops. Monitors legislation and regulations. (Affiliated with the AFL-CIO.)

Biscuit and Cracker Manufacturers' Assn., *6325 Woodside Court, #125, Columbia, MD 21046-3215; (443) 545-1645. Fax, (410) 290-8585. Stacey Sharpless, President.*
Web, www.thebcma.org

Membership: companies in the cookie and cracker industry. Provides multimedia educational materials to members.

Food Marketing Institute (FMI), *2345 Crystal Dr., #800, Arlington, VA 22202-4813; (202) 452-8444. Fax, (202) 429-4519. Leslie G. Sarasin, President. Library, (202) 452-8444.*
General e-mail, feedback@fmi.org
Web, www.fmi.org

Trade association of food retailers and wholesalers. Conducts programs in research, education, industry relations, and public affairs; participates in international conferences. Library open to the public by appointment.

Food Processing Suppliers Assn. (FPSA), *1451 Dolley Madison Blvd., #101, McLean, VA 22101-3850; (703) 761-2600. Fax, (703) 761-4334. George Melnykovich, President.*
Web, www.fpsa.org

Membership: equipment and ingredient manufacturers, suppliers, and servicers for the food, dairy, and beverage processing industry. Sponsors food engineering scholarships and the annual Process Expo. (Merger of the International Assn. of Food Industry Suppliers and the Food Processing Machinery Assn.)

Grocery Manufacturers Assn. (GMA), *1350 Eye St. N.W., #300 20005-3377; (202) 639-5900. Fax, (202) 639-5932. Pamela Bailey, President. Press, (202) 295-3938.*

General e-mail, info@gmaonline.org

Web, www.gmaonline.org

Membership: manufacturers of food, beverage, and consumer packaged goods sold through the retail grocery trade. Interests include increased productivity and growth and the safety and security of the food supply. Supplies industry information to members. Monitors legislation and regulations. (Merger of the Grocery Manufacturers Assn. and the Food Products Assn.)

International Foodservice Distributors Assn., *1410 Spring Hills Rd., #210, McLean, VA 22102; (703) 532-9400. Fax, (703) 538-4673. Mark S. Allen, President.*

Web, www.ifdaonline.org

Trade association of foodservice distribution companies that advocates the interests of members in government and industry affairs through research, education, and communication.

National Assn. of Convenience Stores (NACS), *1600 Duke St., #700, Alexandria, VA 22314-3421; (703) 684-3600. Fax, (703) 836-4564. Hank Armour, President.*

General e-mail, nacs@nacsonline.com

Web, www.nacsonline.com

Membership: convenience store retailers and industry suppliers. Advocates industry position on labor, tax, environment, alcohol, and food-related issues; conducts research and training programs. Monitors legislation and regulations.

National Automatic Merchandising Assn. (NAMA), *449 Carlisle Dr., #3, Herndon, VA 20170-5610; (703) 435-1210. Fax, (703) 435-6389. Richard M. Geerdes, President; Tom McMahon, Chief Counsel. Press, (301) 287-7113.*

Web, www.vending.org

Membership: service companies, equipment manufacturers, and product suppliers for the food and refreshment vending, coffee service, and foodservice management industries. Seeks to advance and promote the automatic merchandising and coffee service industries, provide administrative, logistical, and financial assistance to its members. (Headquarters in Chicago, Ill.)

National Council of Chain Restaurants (NCCR), *325 7th St. N.W., #1100 20004; (202) 626-8183. Fax, (202) 626-8185. Jack Whipple, President. Press, (202) 626-8127.*

General e-mail, purviss@nrf.com

Web, www.nccr.net

National trade association affiliated with the National Retail Federation. Monitors legislation and regulations.

National Grocers Assn., *1005 N. Glebe Rd., #250, Arlington, VA 22201-5758; (703) 516-0700. Fax, (703) 516-0115. Thomas K. Zaucha, President.*

General e-mail, info@nationalgrocers.org

Web, www.nationalgrocers.org

Trade association that represents independent retail and wholesale grocers. Membership also includes affiliated associations, manufacturers, and service suppliers. Provides members with educational materials through a Web site, publications, and conferences. Monitors legislation and regulations.

National Pasta Assn. (NPA), *1156 15th St. N.W., #900 20005-1717; (202) 637-5888. Fax, (202) 223-9741. Mark Vermylen, Chair.*

General e-mail, info@ilovepasta.org

Web, www.ilovepasta.org

Membership: U.S. pasta manufacturers, related suppliers, and allied industry representatives. Represents the industry on public policy issues; monitors and addresses technical issues; and organizes events and seminars for the industry.

National Restaurant Assn., *1200 17th St. N.W. 20036; (202) 331-5900. Fax, (202) 331-2429. Dawn Sweeney, Chief Executive Officer.*

General e-mail, info@dineout.org

Web, www.restaurant.org

Membership: restaurants, cafeterias, clubs, contract feeders, caterers, institutional food services, and other members of the food industry. Supports food service education and research. Monitors legislation and regulations.

Retail Bakers of America, *8400 W. Park Dr., 2nd Floor, McLean, VA 22102-3814; (703) 610-9035. Fax, (703) 610-0239. Susan Nicolais, Executive Vice President. Toll-free, (800) 638-0924.*

General e-mail, info@rbanet.com

Web, www.rbanet.com

Membership: single- and multi-unit retail bakeries and bakery-delis; donut and other specialty shops; supermarket in-store bakeries and bakery-delis; allied companies that offer equipment, ingredients, supplies, or services to these retailers; and students and teachers of secondary or postsecondary school baking programs. Provides business and training aids. Monitors legislation and regulations.

Snack Food Assn. (SFA), *1600 Wilson Blvd., #650, Rosslyn, VA 22209-2510; (703) 836-4500. Fax, (703) 836-8262. James A. McCarthy, President. Toll-free, (800) 628-1334.*

General e-mail, sfa@sfa.org

Web, www.sfa.org

Membership: snack food manufacturers and suppliers. Promotes industry sales; compiles statistics; conducts research and surveys; assists members with training and education; provides consumers with industry information. Monitors legislation and regulations.

Soyfoods Assn. of North America, *1050 17th St. N.W., #600 20036-5570; (202) 659-3520. Fax, (202) 659-3522. Nancy Chapman, Executive Director.*

General e-mail, members@soyfoods.org

Web, www.soyfoods.org

Membership: large and small soyfood companies, growers and suppliers of soybeans, nutritionists, equipment representatives, food scientists, and retailers. Promotes soybean consumption. Helps establish standards for soyfoods. Monitors legislation and regulations.

Tortilla Industry Assn., *8400 W. Park Dr., 2nd Floor, McLean, VA 22102; (703) 610-9036. Fax, (703) 610-9005. Jim Kabbani, Executive Director.*
General e-mail, info@tortilla-info.com
Web, www.tortilla-info.com

Membership: tortilla manufacturers, industry suppliers, and distributors. Promotes tortilla consumption. Provides market research and other industry-related information to its members.

UNITE HERE, *1775 K St. N.W., #620 20006-1530; (202) 393-4373. Fax, (202) 223-6213. John W. Wilhelm, President, Hospitality Industry.*
Web, www.unitehere.org

Membership: approximately 241,000 hotel and restaurant employees. Helps members negotiate pay, benefits, and better working conditions; conducts training programs and workshops. Monitors legislation and regulations. (Formerly Hotel Employees and Restaurant Employees International. Headquarters in New York.)

World Cocoa Foundation, *1411 K St. N.W., #1300 20005; (202) 737-7870. Fax, (202) 737-7832. William Guyton, President.*
General e-mail, wcf@worldcocoa.org
Web, www.worldcocoafoundation.org

Promotes a sustainable cocoa economy through economic and social development and environmental conservation in cocoa-growing communities. Helps raise funds for cocoa farmers and increases their access to modern farming practices.

Vegetarianism

▶NONGOVERNMENTAL

Farm Animal Rights Movement (FARM), *10101 Ashburton Lane, Bethesda, MD 20817-1729; (301) 530-1737. Fax, (301) 530-5683. Alex Hershaft, President.*
General e-mail, info@farmusa.org
Web, www.farmusa.org

Works to end use of animals for food. Interests include animal protection, consumer health, agricultural resources, and environmental quality. Conducts national educational campaigns, including World Farm Animals Day and the Great American Meatout. Monitors legislation and regulations.

Great American Meatout, *10101 Ashburton Lane, Bethesda, MD 20817-1729; (800) 632-8688. Fax, (301) 530-5683. Jen Riley, Media Coordinator.*

General e-mail, info@meatout.org
Web, www.meatout.org

Promotes the dietary elimination of meat. Facilitates information tables, exhibits, cooking demonstrations, and festivals nationwide. (Affiliated with Farm Animal Rights Movement.)

Vegetarian Resource Group, *P.O. Box 1463, Baltimore, MD 21203-1463; (410) 366-8343. Fax, (410) 366-8804. Charles Stahler, Co-Director; Debra Wasserman, Co-Director.*
General e-mail, vrg@vrg.org
Web, www.vrg.org

Works to educate the public on vegetarianism and issues of health, nutrition, ecology, ethics, and world hunger.

Vegetarian Union of North America, *P.O. Box 9710 20016-9710; (202) 362-8349, option 3. Saurabh Dalal, President.*
General e-mail, vuna@ivu.org
Web, www.ivu.org/vuna/english.html

Promotes a cooperative and effective vegetarian movement throughout North America. Builds a network of vegetarian groups throughout the United States and Canada. Serves as a liaison with the worldwide vegetarian movement.

World Food Assistance

▶AGENCIES

Foreign Agricultural Service (FAS), *(Agriculture Dept.),* **Capacity Building and Development,** *1400 Independence Ave. S.W., #3008S, MS 1081 20250-1030; (202) 720-6887. Fax, (202) 720-0069. Gary Groves, Deputy Administrator (Acting).*
Web, www.fas.usda.gov

Operates food aid programs, trade, science, and regulatory capacity-building projects, including training and technical assistance programs, and supports USDA's post-conflict and post-disaster reconstruction efforts.

State Dept., *Agricultural and Biotech Trade Affairs, 2201 C St. N.W., #4470 20520-5820; (202) 647-0133. Fax, (202) 647-1894. Gary Clements, Division Chief.*
Web, www.state.gov

Makes recommendations on international food policy issues such as the effects of U.S. food aid on foreign policy; studies and drafts proposals on the U.S. role in Food for Peace and World Food programs.

World Agricultural Outlook Board *(Agriculture Dept.), 1400 Independence Ave. S.W., #4419S 20250-3812; (202) 720-6030. Fax, (202) 720-4043. Gerald A. Bange, Chair.*
Web, www.usda.gov/oce

Reports to the USDA chief economist. Coordinates the department's commodity forecasting program, which develops the official prognosis of supply, utilization, and prices for commodities worldwide. Works with the National Weather Service to monitor the impact of global weather on agriculture.

▶INTERNATIONAL ORGANIZATIONS

Food and Agriculture Organization of the United Nations (FAO), *Liaison Office for North America,* 2175 K St. N.W., #500 20037-0001; (202) 653-2400. Fax, (202) 653-5760. *Daniel Gustafson, Director. Press,* (202) 653-0011.
Web, www.fao.org

Offers development assistance; collects, analyzes, and disseminates information; provides policy and planning advice to governments; acts as an international forum for debate on food and agricultural issues, including animal health and production, fisheries, and forestry; encourages sustainable agricultural development and a long-term strategy for the conservation and management of natural resources. (International headquarters in Rome.)

International Fund for Agricultural Development (IFAD), *North American Liaison Office,* 1775 K St. N.W., #410 20006; (202) 331-9099. Fax, (202) 331-9366. *Cheryl Morden, Director.*
General e-mail, nalo@ifad.org
Web, www.ifad.org

Specialized agency of the United Nations that provides the rural poor of developing nations with cost-effective ways of overcoming hunger, poverty, and malnutrition. Advocates a community-based approach to reducing rural poverty. (International headquarters in Rome.)

▶NONGOVERNMENTAL

ACDI/VOCA, 50 F St. N.W., #1075 20001-1530; (202) 683-4661. Fax, (202) 783-7204. *Carl Leonard, President.*
Alternate phone: (202) 383-4961.
General e-mail, webmaster@acdivoca.org
Web, www.acdivoca.org

Membership: farm supply, processing, and marketing cooperatives; farm credit banks; national farmer organizations; and insurance cooperatives. Provides cooperatives with training and technical, management, and marketing assistance; supports farm credit systems, agribusiness, and government agencies in developing countries. Contracts with the Agency for International Development to start farm cooperatives in other countries. (Merger of Agricultural Cooperative Development International and Volunteers in Overseas Cooperative Assistance. Affiliated with the National Council of Farmer Cooperatives.)

American Red Cross, *National Headquarters,* 2025 E St. N.W. 20006-5009; (202) 737-8300. *Gail J. McGovern, Chief Executive Officer. Press,* (202) 303-5551.
Web, www.redcross.org

Humanitarian relief and health education organization chartered by Congress. Provides food and supplies to assist in major disaster and refugee situations worldwide. Part of the international Red Cross and Red Crescent movement.

Bread for the World/Bread for the World Institute, 50 F St. N.W., #500 20001-1567; (202) 639-9400. Fax, (202) 639-9401. *David Beckmann, President.*
General e-mail, bread@bread.org
Web, www.bread.org

Christian citizens' movement that works to eradicate world hunger. Organizes and coordinates political action on issues and public policy affecting the causes of hunger.

CARE, *Washington Office,* 1625 K St. N.W., #500 20006-1611; (202) 595-2800. Fax, (202) 296-8695. *Helene Gayle, President; JoDee Winterhoff, Vice President, Policy and Advocacy.*
General e-mail, info@care.org
Web, www.care.org

Assists the developing world's poor through emergency assistance and community self-help programs that focus on sustainable development, agriculture, agroforestry, water and sanitation, health, family planning, and income generation. Community-based efforts are centered on providing resources to poor women. (U.S. headquarters in Atlanta, Ga.; international headquarters in Geneva.)

International Food Policy Research Institute (IFPRI), 2033 K St. N.W., #400 20006-1018; (202) 862-5600. Fax, (202) 467-4439. *Joachim von Braun, Director. Library,* (202) 862-5607.
General e-mail, ifpri@cgiar.org
Web, www.ifpri.org

Research organization that analyzes the world food situation and suggests ways of making food more available in developing countries. Provides various governments with information on national and international food policy. Sponsors conferences and seminars; publishes research reports. Library open to the public by appointment.

National Center for Food and Agricultural Policy, 1616 P St. N.W., #100 20036; (202) 328-5048. Fax, (202) 328-5133. *Stanley Johnson, Chief Executive Officer. Press,* (202) 328-5183.
General e-mail, ncfap@ncfap.org
Web, www.ncfap.org

Research and educational organization concerned with international food and agricultural issues. Examines public policy concerning agriculture, food safety and quality, natural resources, and the environment.

Oxfam America, *Policy, Washington Office,* 1100 15th St. N.W. #600 20005-1759; (202) 496-1180. Fax, (202) 496-1190. *Raymond C. Offenheiser, President; Jim Lyons, Vice President for Advocacy and Communications. Information,* (800) 776-9326.
Web, www.oxfamamerica.org

Funds disaster relief and self-help development projects, primarily at the international level, including food and agriculture programs; supports grassroots and community efforts to combat hunger; conducts an educational campaign and debt relief for foreign countries. (Headquarters in Boston, Mass.)

RESULTS, *750 1st St. N.E., #1040 20002-4241; (202) 783-7100. Fax, (202) 783-2818. Joanne Carter, Executive Director. General e-mail, results@results.org*

Web, www.results.org

Works to end hunger and the worst aspects of poverty nationally and worldwide; encourages grassroots and legislative support of programs and proposals dealing with hunger and hunger-related issues. Monitors legislation and regulations.

U.S. National Committee for World Food Day, *2175 K St. N.W.20437-0001; (202) 653-2404. Fax, (202) 653-5760. Patricia Young, National Coordinator.*

Web, www.worldfooddayusa.org

Consortium of 450 farm, religious, nutrition, education, consumer, relief, and development organizations. Coordinates widespread community participation in World Food Day. Distributes materials about food and hunger issues and encourages long-term action.

Winrock International, *Washington Office, 1621 N. Kent St., #1200, Arlington, VA 22209-2131; (703) 525-9430. Fax, (703) 525-1744. Frank Tugwell, President. General e-mail, information@winrock.org*

Web, www.winrock.org

Works to increase economic opportunity; sustain natural resources; protect the environment; and increase long-term productivity, equity, and responsible resource management to benefit the world's poor and disadvantaged communities. Matches innovative approaches in agriculture, natural resources management, clean energy, and leadership development with the unique needs of its partners. Links local individuals and communities with new ideas and technology. (Headquarters in Little Rock, Ark.)

Worldwatch Institute, *1776 Massachusetts Ave. N.W., 8th Floor 20036; (202) 452-1999. Fax, (202) 296-7365. Christopher Flavin, President. General e-mail, worldwatch@worldwatch.org*

Web, www.worldwatch.org

Research organization that studies the environmental, political, and economic links to world population growth and health trends. Interests include the food supply, human and environmental health, biotechnology, energy, and climate change.

LIVESTOCK AND POULTRY

►AGENCIES

Agricultural Marketing Service (AMS), *(Agriculture Dept.), Livestock and Seed, 1400 Independence Ave. S.W., #2092S, MS 0249 20250-0249; (202) 720-5705. Fax, (202) 720-3499. Craig Morris, Deputy Administrator.*

Web, www.ams.usda.gov/lsprogram

Administers meat marketing program; maintains market news service to inform producers of meat market situation

and daily price changes; develops, establishes, and revises U.S. standards for classes and grades of livestock and meat; grades, examines, and certifies meat and meat products.

Agricultural Marketing Service (AMS), *(Agriculture Dept.), Poultry Programs, 1400 Independence Ave. S.W., #3932S 20250-0262; (202) 720-4476. Fax, (202) 720-5631. Rex Barnes, Deputy Administrator.*

Web, www.ams.usda.gov/poultry/index.htm

Sets poultry and egg grading standards. Provides promotion and market news services for domestic and international markets.

Food Safety and Inspection Service *(Agriculture Dept.), 1400 Independence Ave. S.W., #331E 20250-0003; (202) 720-7025. Fax, (202) 205-0158. Al Almonzo, Administrator. Press, (202) 720-9113. Consumer inquiries, (800) 535-4555.*

Web, www.usda.gov/fsis

Inspects meat and poultry products and provides safe handling and labeling guidelines.

Grain Inspection, Packers and Stockyards Administration *(Agriculture Dept.), 1400 Independence Ave. S.W., #2055, MS 3601 20250-3601; (202) 720-0219. Fax, (202) 205-9237. Alan R. Christian, Administrator (Acting). Information, (202) 720-3553.*

Web, www.gipsa.usda.gov

Maintains competition in the marketing of livestock, poultry, grain, and meat by prohibiting deceptive and monopolistic marketing practices; tests market scales and conducts check weighings for accuracy.

►CONGRESS

For a listing of relevant congressional committees and subcommittees, please see page 3 or the Appendix.

►NONGOVERNMENTAL

American Meat Institute, *1150 Connecticut Ave. N.W., 12th Floor 20036; (202) 587-4200. Fax, (202) 587-4300. J. Patrick Boyle, President.*

Web, www.meatami.com

Membership: national and international meat and poultry packers and processors. Provides statistics on meat and poultry production and consumption, livestock, and feed grains. Funds meat research projects and consumer education programs; sponsors conferences and correspondence courses on meat production and processing. Monitors legislation and regulations.

American Sheep Industry Assn., *Washington Office, 412 1st St. S.E., #1 Lobby Level 20003; (202) 484-7134. Fax, (202) 484-0770. Fran Boyd, Washington Representative. General e-mail, info@sheepusa.org*

Web, www.sheepusa.org

Membership: sheep, wool, and mohair producers. Interests include sheep breeds, lamb and wool marketing, and wool research. Monitors legislation and regulations. (Headquarters in Denver, Colo.)

Animal Health Institute, *1325 G St. N.W., #700 20005-3104; (202) 637-2440. Fax, (202) 393-1667. Alexander S. Mathews, President.*

Web, www.ahi.org

Membership: manufacturers of drugs and other products (including vaccines, pesticides, and vitamins) for pets and food-producing animals. Monitors legislation and regulations.

Farm Animal Rights Movement (FARM), *10101 Ashburton Lane, Bethesda, MD 20817-1729; (301) 530-1737. Fax, (301) 530-5683. Alex Hershaft, President.*

General e-mail, info@farmusa.org

Web, www.farmusa.org

Works to end use of animals for food. Interests include animal protection, consumer health, agricultural resources, and environmental quality. Conducts national educational campaigns, including World Farm Animals Day and the Great American Meatout. Monitors legislation and regulations.

Humane Farm Animal Care, *P.O. Box 727, Herndon, VA 20172-0727; (703) 435-3883. Fax, (703) 435-3981. Adele Douglass, Chief Executive Officer.*

General e-mail, info@certifiedhumane.org

Web, www.certifiedhumane.org

Seeks to improve the welfare of farm animals by providing viable, duly monitored standards for humane food production. Sponsors the Certified Humane Raised and Handled program for meat, poultry, eggs, and products.

National Cattlemen's Beef Assn., *Government Affairs, Washington Office, 1301 Pennsylvania Ave. N.W., #300 20004-1701; (202) 347-0228. Fax, (202) 638-0607. Burton Elles, Vice President.*

Web, www.beefusa.org

Membership: individual cattlemen, state cattlemen's groups, and breed associations. Provides information on beef research, agricultural labor, beef grading, foreign trade, taxes, marketing, cattle economics, branding, animal health, and environmental management. (Headquarters in Denver, Colo.)

National Chicken Council, *1015 15th St. N.W., #930 20005-2622; (202) 296-2622. Fax, (202) 293-4005. George B. Watts, President.*

General e-mail, ncc@chickenusa.org

Web, www.nationalchickencouncil.com

Trade association that represents the producers and processors of 95 percent of the chickens raised in the United States. Provides information on production, marketing, and consumption of chickens. Lobbies Congress and federal agencies on legislative and regulatory developments that concern the chicken industry. Co-sponsors, with the U.S. Poultry and Egg Association, public promotion activities and educational seminars on food trends across the country.

National Pork Producers Council, *Washington Office, 122 C St. N.W., #875 20001; (202) 347-3600. Fax, (202) 347-5265. Kirk Ferrell, Vice President.*

General e-mail, pork@nppc.org

Web, www.nppc.org

Membership: pork producers and independent pork producer organizations. Interests include pork production, nutrition, the environment, trade, and federal regulations. Monitors legislation and regulations. (Headquarters in Des Moines, Iowa.)

National Renderers Assn., *801 N. Fairfax St., #205, Alexandria, VA 22314-1776; (703) 683-0155. Fax, (703) 683-2626. Thomas M. Cook, President.*

General e-mail, renderers@nationalrenderers.com

Web, http://nationalrenderers.org

Membership: manufacturers of meat meal and tallow. Compiles industry statistics; sponsors research; conducts seminars and workshops. Monitors legislation and regulations.

National Turkey Federation, *1225 New York Ave. N.W., #400 20005-6404; (202) 898-0100. Fax, (202) 898-0203. Joel Brandenberger, President.*

General e-mail, info@turkeyfed.org

Web, www.eatturkey.com

Membership: turkey growers, hatcheries, breeders, and processors. Promotes turkey consumption. Monitors legislation and regulations.

North American Meat Processors Assn. (NAMP), *1910 Association Dr., Reston, VA 20191-1501; (703) 758-1900, ext. 102. Fax, (703) 758-8001. Philip H. Kimball, Executive Director. Member services, (800) 368-3043.*

General e-mail, smoore@namp.com

Web, www.namp.com

Membership: meat and poultry companies specializing in the food service industry. Conducts seminars; interests include quality standards and procedures for handling meat and poultry. Publishes the Meat Buyers Guide.

Shelf-Stable Food Processors Assn. (SFPA), *1150 Connecticut Ave. N.W., 12th Floor 20036; (202) 587-4273. Fax, (202) 587-4303. James Hodges, Executive Secretary.*

General e-mail, sfpa@meatami.com

Web, www.meatami.com

Membership: shelf-stable food manufacturers and their suppliers. Provides information on the shelf-stable industry, particularly as it pertains to meat products. (Formerly National Meat Canners Assn.)

U.S. Hide, Skin, and Leather Assn. *(USHSLA), 1150 Connecticut Ave. N.W., 12th Floor 20036; (202) 587-4250. Fax, (202) 587-4300. John Reddington, President.*

Web, www.ushsla.org

Membership: meatpackers, brokers, dealers, processors, and exporters of hides and skins. Maintains liaison with allied trade associations and participates in programs on export statistics, hide price reporting, and freight rates; conducts seminars and consumer information programs. (Division of American Meat Institute.)

2

Business and Economics

GENERAL POLICY AND ANALYSIS

Basic Resources

►AGENCIES

Census Bureau *(Commerce Dept.)*, *Economic Programs*, *4600 Silver Hill Rd., #8H132, Suitland, MD 20746 (mailing address: MS 6000, #8H132, Washington, DC 20233-6000); (301) 763-4636. Fax, (301) 763-3842. Thomas L. Mesenbourg, Deputy Director. Toll-free, (800) 923-8282.*
Web, www.census.gov

Compiles comprehensive statistics on the level and structure of U.S. economic activity and the characteristics of industrial and business establishments at the national, state, and local levels; collects and publishes foreign trade statistics.

Commerce Dept., *1401 Constitution Ave. N.W. 20230; (202) 482-4883. Fax, (202) 482-5168. Gary Locke, Secretary; Vacant, Deputy Secretary. Information, (202) 482-2000. Library, (202) 482-5511.*
Web, www.commerce.gov

Acts as principal adviser to the president on federal policy affecting industry and commerce; promotes national economic growth and development, competitiveness, international trade, and technological development; provides business and government with economic statistics, research, and analysis; encourages minority business; promotes tourism.

Commerce Dept., *Business Liaison*, *1401 Constitution Ave. N.W., #5062 20230; (202) 482-1360. Fax, (202) 482-4054. Mary Tinsley Raul, Director.*
Web, www.doc.gov/obl

Serves as the central office for business assistance. Handles requests for information and services as well as complaints and suggestions from businesses; provides a forum for businesses to comment on federal regulations; initiates meetings on policy issues with industry groups, business organizations, trade and small business associations, and the corporate community.

Commerce Dept., *STAT-USA*, *1401 Constitution Ave. N.W., #4876, MS 4885 20230; (202) 482-3429. Fax, (202) 482-3417. Francine Krasowka, Director. Toll-free, (800) STAT-USA.*
General e-mail, stat-mail@doc.gov
Web, www.stat-usa.gov

Maintains and makes available for public use the National Trade Data Bank (NTDB) and Stat-USA-Internet.

Consumer Product Safety Commission (CPSC),
Economic Analysis, 4330 East-West Hwy., Bethesda, MD 20814; (301) 504-7705. Fax, (301) 504-0109. Gregory Rodgers, Associate Executive Director.
Web, www.cpsc.gov

Conducts studies to determine the impact of CPSC's regulations on consumers, the economy, industry, and production. Studies the potential environmental effects of commission actions.

Council of Economic Advisers *(Executive Office of the President)*, *1800 G St. N.W., 8th Floor 20006 (mailing address: 725 17th St. N.W., Washington, DC 20502); (202) 395-5042. Fax, (202) 395-6958. Christina D. Romer, Chair; Pierce E. Scranton, Chief of Staff.*
Web, www.whitehouse.gov/cea

Advisory body consisting of three members and supporting staff of economists. Monitors and analyzes the economy and advises the president on economic developments, trends, and policies and on the economic implications of other policy initiatives. Prepares the annual *Economic Report of the President* for Congress. Assesses economic implications of international policy.

Economics and Statistics Administration *(Commerce Dept.)*, *1401 Constitution Ave. N.W., #4848 20230; (202) 482-3727. Fax, (202) 482-0432. Cynthia A. Glassman, Under Secretary.*
General e-mail, esa@doc.gov
Web, www.esa.doc.gov

Advises the secretary on economic policy matters, including consumer and capital spending, inventory status, and the short- and long-term outlook in output and unemployment. Seeks to improve economic productivity and growth. Serves as departmental liaison with the Council of Economic Advisers and other government agencies concerned with economic policy. Supervises and sets policy for the Census Bureau and the Bureau of Economic Analysis.

Federal Reserve System, *Board of Governors*, *20th and C Sts. N.W., #B2046 20551 (mailing address: 20th St. and Constitution Ave. N.W., Washington, DC 20551); (202) 452-3201. Fax, (202) 452-3819. Ben S. Bernanke, Chair; Donald L. Kohn, Vice Chair. Information, (202) 452-3204. Public Affairs, (202) 452-2955. Congressional Liaison, (202) 452-3003. Locator, (202) 452-3204. Publications, (202) 452-3245.*
Web, www.federalreserve.gov

Sets U.S. monetary policy. Supervises the Federal Reserve System and influences credit conditions through the buying and selling of treasury securities in the open market, by fixing the amount of reserves depository institutions must maintain, and by determining discount rates.

Federal Trade Commission (FTC), *600 Pennsylvania Ave. N.W., #440 20580; (202) 326-2100. William Kovacic, Chair; Charles Schneider, Executive Director. Press, (202) 326-2180. Library, (202) 326-2395. Congressional Relations, (202) 326-2195.*
Web, www.ftc.gov

Promotes policies designed to maintain strong competitive enterprise and consumer protection within the U.S. economic system. Monitors trade practices and investigates cases involving monopoly, unfair restraints, or deceptive practices. Enforces Truth in Lending and Fair Credit Reporting acts. Library open to the public.

BUSINESS AND ECONOMICS RESOURCES IN CONGRESS

For a complete listing of Congress committees, including their full contact information, leadership, membership, and jurisdictions, please refer to the Appendix on pages 724–837.

JOINT COMMITTEES:

Joint Committee on Taxation, (202) 225-7377 or (202) 225-3621.
Web, www.house.gov/jct

Joint Economic Committee, (202) 224-0372.
Web, jec.senate.gov or www.house.gov/jec

HOUSE:

House Appropriations Committee, (202) 225-2771.
Web, appropriations.house.gov
    Subcommittee on Commerce, Justice, Science, and Related Agencies, (202) 225-3351.
    Subcommittee on Financial Services and General Government, (202) 225-7245.
    Subcommittee on Transportation, HUD, and Related Agencies, (202) 225-2141.

House Budget Committee, (202) 226-7200.
Web, budget.house.gov

House Energy and Commerce Committee, (202) 225-2927.
Web, energycommerce.house.gov
    Subcommittee on Commerce, Trade, and Consumer Protection, (202) 225-2927.
    Subcommittee on Health, (202) 225-2927.

House Financial Services Committee, (202) 225-7502.
Web, financialservices.house.gov
    Subcommittee on Capital Markets, Insurance, and Government Sponsored Enterprises, (202) 225-4247.

    Subcommittee on Domestic and International Monetary Policy, Trade, and Technology, (202) 225-4247.
    Subcommittee on Financial Institutions and Consumer Credit, (202) 225-4247.
    Subcommittee on Housing and Community Opportunity, (202) 225-4247.
    Subcommittee on Oversight and Investigations, (202) 225-4247.

House Judiciary Committee, (202) 225-3951.
Web, judiciary.house.gov
    Subcommittee on Commercial and Administrative Law, (202) 226-7680.
    Subcommittee on Courts, the Internet, and Intellectual Property, (202) 225-5741.

House Oversight and Government Reform Committee, (202) 225-5051.
Web, oversight.house.gov
    Subcommittee on Domestic Policy, (202) 225-5051.

House Science and Technology Committee, (202) 225-6375.
Web, science.house.gov
    Subcommittee on Technology and Innovation, (202) 225-9662.

House Small Business Committee, (202) 225-4038.
Web, www.house.gov/smbiz
    Subcommittee on Contracting and Technology, (202) 225-4038.
    Subcommittee on Finance and Tax, (202) 225-4038.

Federal Trade Commission (FTC), *Economics, 600 Pennsylvania Ave. N.W. 20580; (202) 326-3429. Fax, (202) 326-2380. Pauline M. Ippolito, Director (Acting).*
Web, www.ftc.gov/ftc/economic.htm

Provides economic analyses for consumer protection and antitrust investigations, cases, and rulemakings; advises the commission on the effect of government regulations on competition and consumers in various industries; develops special reports on competition, consumer protection, and regulatory issues.

National Economic Council *(Executive Office of the President), The White House 20502; (202) 456-2800. Fax, (202) 456-2223. Keith Hennessey, Assistant to the President for Economic Policy; Charles Blahous, Deputy Assistant to the President for Economic Policy.*
Web, www.whitehouse.gov/nec

Comprised of cabinet members and other high-ranking executive branch officials. Coordinates domestic and international economic policy-making process to facilitate the implementation of the president's economic agenda.

National Institute of Standards and Technology (NIST), *(Commerce Dept.), Global Standards and Information, 100 Bureau Dr., MS 2100, Gaithersburg, MD 20899; (301) 975-4040. Fax, (301) 926-1559. Carmiña Londoño, Group Leader. NIST Public Inquiries Unit, (301) 975-6478.*
General e-mail, gsig@nist.gov

Web, http://ts.nist.gov/standards/global

Serves as the national repository for information on voluntary industry standards and regulations for domestic and international products. Provides information on specifications, conformity assessment, test methods, domestic and international technical regulations, codes, and recommended practices.

National Women's Business Council, *409 3rd St. S.W., #210 20024; (202) 205-3850. Fax, (202) 205-6825. Carole Jean Jordan, Chair; Margaret Mankin Barton, Executive Director.*
General e-mail, info@nwbc.gov

Web, www.nwbc.gov

Independent, congressionally mandated council established by the Women's Business Ownership Act of 1988.

BUSINESS AND ECONOMICS RESOURCES IN CONGRESS

Subcommittee on Investigations and Oversight, (202) 225-4038.

Subcommittee on Regulations, Health Care and Trade, (202) 225-4038.

Subcommittee on Rural and Urban Entrepreneurship, (202) 225-4038.

House Ways and Means Committee, (202) 225-3625.

Web, waysandmeans.house.gov

Subcommittee on Trade, (202) 225-6649.

SENATE:

Senate Appropriations Committee, (202) 224-7363.

Web, appropriations.senate.gov

Subcommittee on Commerce, Justice, Science, and Related Agencies, (202) 224-5202.

Subcommittee on Financial Services and General Government, (202) 224-1133.

Subcommittee on Transportation, HUD and Related Agencies, (202) 224-7281.

Senate Banking, Housing and Urban Affairs Committee, (202) 224-7391.

Web, banking.senate.gov

Subcommittee on Economic Policy, (202) 224-2441.

Subcommittee on Financial Institutions, (202) 224-5842.

Subcommittee on Securities, Insurance, and Investment, (202) 224-4642.

Subcommittee on Security and International Trade and Finance, (202) 224-5623.

Senate Budget Committee, (202) 224-0862.

Web, budget.senate.gov

Senate Commerce, Science, and Transportation Committee, (202) 224-0411.

Web, commerce.senate.gov

Subcommittee on Consumer Affairs, Insurance and Automotive Safety, (202) 224-1270.

Subcommittee on Interstate Commerce, Trade and Tourism, (202) 224-1270.

Senate Finance Committee, (202) 224-4515.

Web, finance.senate.gov

Subcommittee on International Trade and Global Competitiveness, (202) 224-4515.

Subcommittee on Taxation, IRS Oversight, and Long-Term Growth, (202) 224-4515.

Senate Health, Education, Labor and Pension Committee, (202) 224-5375.

Web, help.senate.gov

Senate Homeland Security and Governmental Affairs Committee, (202) 224-2627.

Web, hsgac.senate.gov

Permanent Subcommittee on Investigations, (202) 224-9505.

Senate Judiciary Committee, (202) 224-7703.

Web, judiciary.senate.gov

Subcommittee on Antitrust, Competition Policy and Consumer Rights (202) 224-3406.

Senate Small Business and Entrepreneurship Committee, (202) 224-5175.

Web, sbc.senate.gov

Reviews the status of women-owned businesses nationwide and makes policy recommendations to the president, Congress, and the Small Business Administration. Assesses the role of the federal government in aiding and promoting women-owned businesses.

Small Business Administration (SBA), *409 3rd St. S.W., #7600 20416-7600; (202) 205-6605. Fax, (202) 205-6802. Sandy Baruah, Administrator; Jovita Carranza, Deputy Administrator. Press, (202) 205-6740. Toll-free information (Answer Desk), (800) 827-5722. Locator, (202) 205-6600.*
Web, www.sba.gov

Maintains and strengthens the nation's economy by aiding, counseling, assisting, and protecting the interests of small businesses and by helping families and businesses recover from natural disasters.

Treasury Dept., *1500 Pennsylvania Ave. N.W., #3330 20220; (202) 622-2000. Fax, (202) 622-0073. Timothy Geithner, Secretary, (202) 622-1100; Robert M. Kimmitt,*

Deputy Secretary. Information, (202) 622-5500. Library, (202) 622-0990.
Web, www.ustreas.gov

Serves as chief financial officer of the government and adviser to the president on economic policy. Formulates and recommends domestic and international financial, economic, tax, and broad fiscal policies; manages the public debt. Library open to the public by appointment.

Treasury Dept., *Economic Policy, 1500 Pennsylvania Ave. N.W., #3454 20220; (202) 622-2200. Fax, (202) 622-2633. Phillip Swagel, Assistant Secretary.*
Web, www.ustreas.gov

Assists and advises the Treasury secretary in the formulation and execution of domestic and international economic policies and programs; helps prepare economic forecasts for the federal budget.

Treasury Dept., *Financial Management Service, 401 14th St. S.W., #548 20227; (202) 874-7000. Fax, (202)*

Commerce Department

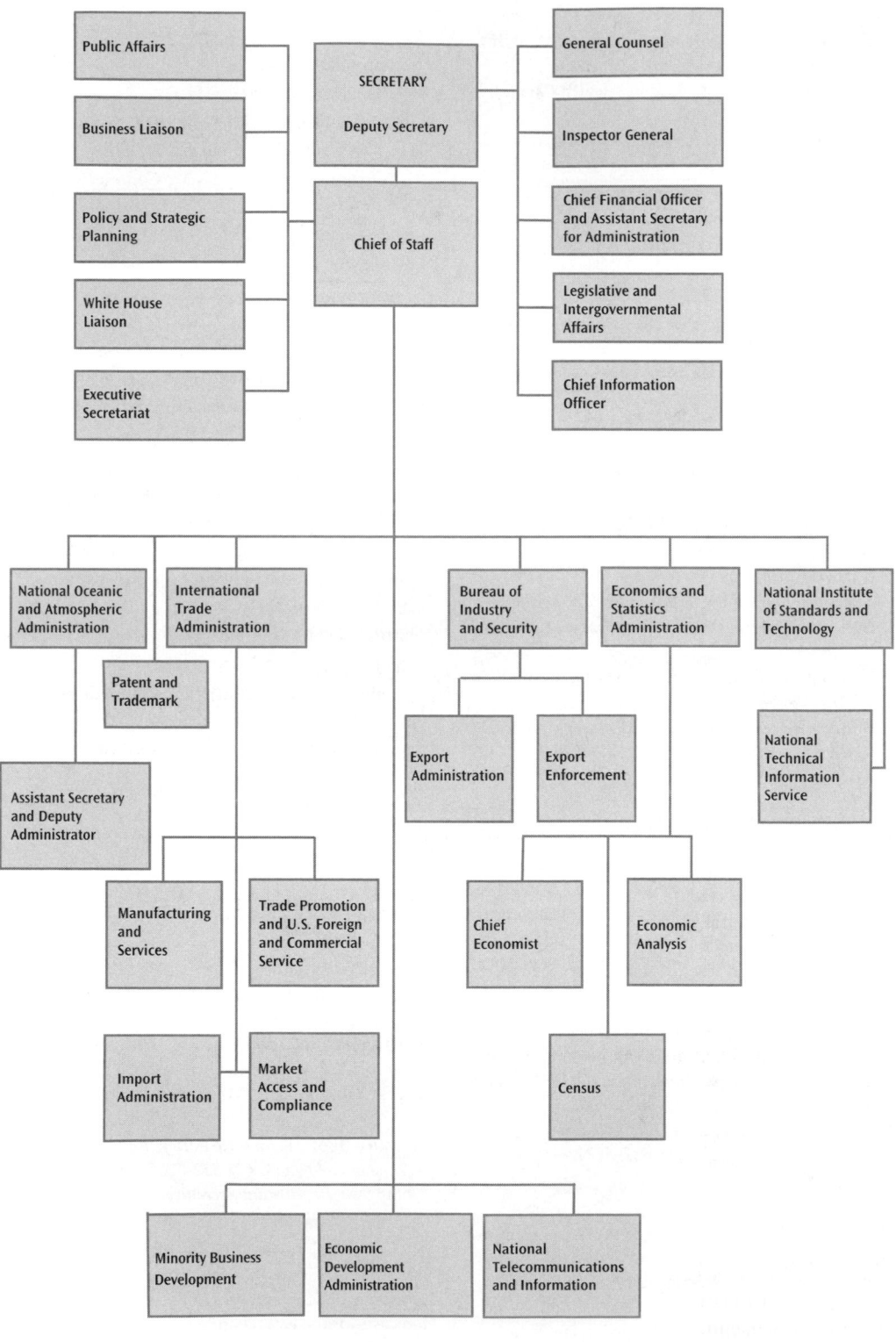

Federal Trade Commission

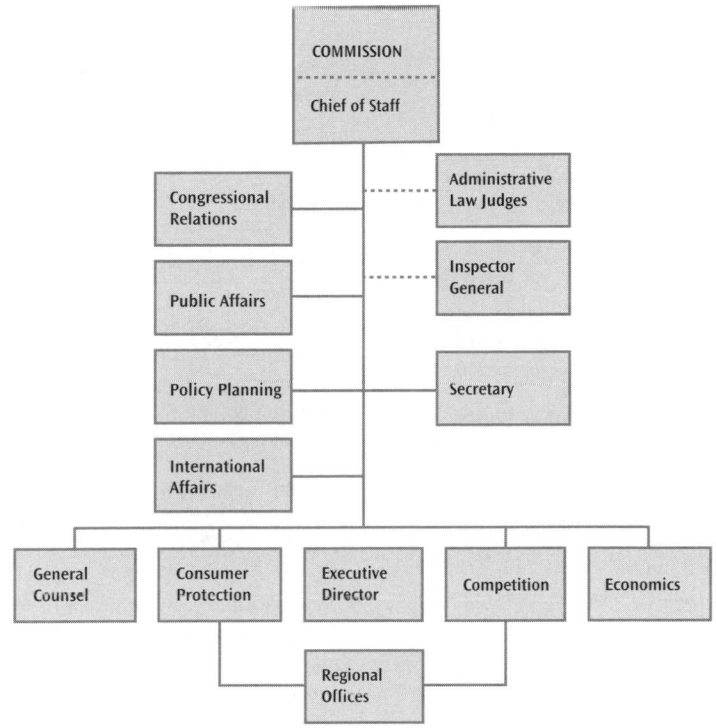

COMMISSION

Chief of Staff

Congressional Relations

Administrative Law Judges

Public Affairs

Inspector General

Policy Planning

Secretary

International Affairs

General Counsel

Consumer Protection

Executive Director

Competition

Economics

Regional Offices

---- Denotes independent operation within the agency

874-6743. Judith R. Tillman, Commissioner. Public Affairs, (202) 874-6750.

Web, www.fms.treas.gov

Serves as the government's central financial manager, responsible for cash management and investment of government trust funds, credit administration, and debt collection. Handles central accounting for government fiscal activities; promotes sound financial management practices and increased use of automated payments, collections, accounting, and reporting systems.

Treasury Dept., *Fiscal Operations and Policy,* 1500 Pennsylvania Ave. N.W., #2112 20220; (202) 622-0550. Fax, (202) 622-0962. Gary Grippo, Deputy Assistant Secretary.

Web, www.ustreas.gov

Administers Treasury Dept. financial operations. Supervises the Financial Management Service and the Bureau of the Public Debt.

►CONGRESS

For a listing of relevant congressional committees and subcommittees, please see page 32 or the Appendix.

Government Accountability Office (GAO), 441 G St. N.W., #7100 20548; (202) 512-5500. Fax, (202) 512-5507. Gene L. Dodaro, Comptroller General. Information, (202) 512-3000. Library, (202) 512-2585. Publications, (202)

512-6000. Congressional Relations, (202) 512-4400.

Web, www.gao.gov

Independent, nonpartisan agency in the legislative branch. Serves as the investigating agency for Congress; carries out legal, accounting, auditing, and claims settlement functions; makes recommendations for more effective government operations; publishes monthly lists of reports available to the public. (Formerly the General Accounting Office.)

►NONGOVERNMENTAL

American Business Conference, 1828 L St. N.W., #908 20036; (202) 822-9300. Fax, (202) 467-4070. John Endean, President.

General e-mail, abc@americanbusinessconference.org

Web, www.americanbusinessconference.org

Membership: chief executive officers of midsize, high-growth companies. Seeks a public policy role for growth companies. Studies capital formation, tax policy, regulatory reform, and international trade.

American Chamber of Commerce Executives, 4875 Eisenhower Ave., #250, Alexandria, VA 22304; (703) 998-0072. Fax, (703) 212-9512. Michael Fleming, President.

Web, www.acce.org

Membership: executives of local, state, and international chambers of commerce. Conducts for members educational programs and conferences on topics of interest, including economic development, management symposiums, and membership drives. Sponsors special interest groups for members.

American Council for Capital Formation (ACCF), *1750 K St. N.W., #400 20006; (202) 293-5811. Fax, (202) 785-8165. Mark Bloomfield, President.*
General e-mail, info@accf.org
Web, www.accf.org

Advocates tax, trade, and environmental policies conducive to saving, investment, and economic growth. Affiliated with the ACCF Center for Policy Research, which conducts and funds research on capital formation topics.

American Enterprise Institute for Public Policy Research (AEI), *Economic Policy Studies, 1150 17th St. N.W. 20036; (202) 862-5800. Fax, (202) 862-7177. Arthur Brooks, President.*
Web, www.aei.org

Conducts research. Sponsors events. Interests include monetary, tax, trade, financial services, telecommunications, regulatory policy, labor, and social security issues.

American Management Assn. International, *2345 Crystal Dr., #200, Arlington, VA 22202; (571) 481-2200. Fax, (571) 481-2211. Richard Nusbaum, Center Manager.*
Web, www.amanet.org

Membership: managers and other corporate professionals. Offers training and education programs to members. (Headquarters in New York.)

Americans for Prosperity Foundation, *1726 M St. N.W., 10th Floor 20036; (202) 349-5880. Fax, (202) 587-4599. Tim Phillips, President. Toll-free, (866) 730-0150.*
General e-mail, info@AFPhq.org
Web, www.americansforprosperity.org

Grassroots organization that seeks to educate citizens about economic policy and encourage their participation in the public policy process. Supports limited government and free markets on the local, state, and federal levels. Specific interests include Social Security, trade, and taxes.

American Society of Assn. Executives (ASAE), *1575 Eye St. N.W., #1100 20005-1103; (202) 626-2723. Fax, (202) 371-8825. John H. Graham IV, President. Library, (202) 326-9559. Press, (202) 626-2703.*
General e-mail, pr@asaecenter.org
Web, www.asaecenter.org

Conducts research and provides educational programs on association management, trends, and developments. Library open to the public. (Merged with the Center for Assn. Leadership.)

Aspen Institute, *1 Dupont Circle N.W., #700 20036; (202) 736-5800. Fax, (202) 467-0790. Walter Isaacson, President. Press, (202) 736-3849.*

General e-mail, info@aspeninstitute.org
Web, www.aspeninstitute.org

Promotes consideration of the public good in a wide variety of areas, including business management and economic development policies. Conducts educational programs; publishes reports.

The Brookings Institution, *Economic Studies Program, 1775 Massachusetts Ave. N.W. 20036-2188; (202) 797-6000. Fax, (202) 797-6181. William G. Gale, Director. Information, (202) 797-6105.*
General e-mail, escomment@brookings.edu
Web, www.brookings.edu

Sponsors economic research and publishes studies on domestic and international economics, worldwide economic growth and stability, public finance, industrial organization and regulation, labor economics, social policy, and the economics of human resources.

The Business Council, *45575 Shepard Dr., Sterling, VA 20164 (mailing address: P.O. Box 20147, Washington, DC 20041); (202) 298-7650. Fax, (202) 785-0296. Philip E. Cassidy, Executive Director.*
Web, www.businesscouncil.com

Membership: current and former chief executive officers of major corporations. Serves as a forum for business and government to exchange views and explore public policy as it affects U.S. business interests.

Business–Higher Education Forum, *2025 M St. N.W., #800 20036; (202) 367-1189. Fax, (202) 367-2269. Brian K. Fitzgerald, Executive Director.*
General e-mail, info@bhef.com
Web, www.bhef.com

Membership: chief executive officers of major corporations, foundations, colleges, and universities. Develops and promotes policy positions to enhance U.S. competitiveness. Interests include improving student achievement and readiness for college and work; and strengthening higher education, particularly in the fields of science, technology, engineering, and math.

The Business Roundtable, *1717 Rhode Island Ave. N.W., #800 20036-3026; (202) 872-1260. Fax, (202) 466-3509. John J. Castellani, President.*
General e-mail, info@businessroundtable.org
Web, www.businessroundtable.org

Membership: chief executives of the nation's largest corporations. Examines issues of concern to business, including taxation, antitrust law, international trade, employment policy, and the federal budget.

Center for Economic and Policy Research (CEPR), *1611 Connecticut Ave. N.W., #400 20009; (202) 293-5380, ext. 115. Fax, (202) 588-1356. Dean Baker, Co-Director; Mark Weisbrot, Co-Director.*
General e-mail, cepr@cepr.net
Web, www.cepr.net

Researches economic and social issues and the impact of related public policies. Presents findings to the public with the goal of better preparing citizens to choose among various policy options. Promotes democratic debate and voter education. Areas of interest include health care, trade, Social Security, taxes, housing, and the labor market.

Center for Study of Public Choice (*George Mason University*), *Carow Hall, MS 1D3, 4400 University Dr., Fairfax, VA 22030-4444; (703) 993-2330. Fax, (703) 993-2323. Don Boudreaux, Director.*
Web, www.gmu.edu/centers/publicchoice

Promotes research in public choice, an interdisciplinary approach to the study of the relationship between economic and political institutions. Interests include constitutional economics, public finance, federalism and local government, econometrics, and trade protection and regulation. Sponsors conferences and seminars. Library open to the public.

Committee for Economic Development, *2000 L St. N.W., #700 20036; (202) 296-5860. Fax, (202) 223-0776. Charles E. M. Kolb, President; Joseph J. Minarik, Senior Vice President of Research and Policy. Toll-free, (800) 676-7353.*
General e-mail, info@ced.org
Web, www.ced.org

Research organization that makes recommendations on domestic and international economic policy.

Competitive Enterprise Institute, *1899 L St. N.W., 12th Floor 20036; (202) 331-1010. Fax, (202) 331-0640. Fred L. Smith, President.*
General e-mail, info@cei.org
Web, www.cei.org

Advocates free enterprise and limited government. Produces policy analyses on tax, budget, financial services, antitrust, biotechnological, and environmental issues. Monitors legislation and litigates against restrictive regulations through its Free Market Legal Program.

Council for Social and Economic Studies, *1133 13th St. N.W., #C2 20005-4297; (202) 371-2700. Fax, (202) 371-1523. Roger Pearson, Executive Director.*
Web, www.jspes.org

Conducts research on domestic and international economic, social, and political issues. Publishes the *Journal of Social, Political, and Economic Studies.*

Council on Competitiveness, *1500 K St. N.W., #850 20005; (202) 682-4292. Fax, (202) 682-5150. Deborah Wince-Smith, President.*
General e-mail, council@compete.org
Web, www.compete.org

Membership: chief executives from business, education, and labor. Seeks increased public awareness of issues related to economic competitiveness. Works to set a national action agenda for U.S. competitiveness in global markets.

Economic Policy Institute, *1333 H St. N.W., #300 East Tower 20005-4707; (202) 775-8810. Fax, (202) 775-0819. Lawrence Mishel, President.*
General e-mail, epi@epi.org
Web, www.epinet.org

Research and educational organization that publishes analyses on economics, economic development, competitiveness, income distribution, industrial competitiveness, and investment. Conducts public conferences and seminars.

Ethics Resource Center, *2345 Crystal Dr., #201, Arlington, VA 22202; (703) 647-2185. Fax, (703) 647-2180. Patricia J. Harned, President. Information, (800) 777-1285.*
General e-mail, ethics@ethics.org
Web, www.ethics.org

Nonpartisan educational organization that fosters ethical practices among individuals and institutions. Interests include research, knowledge building, education, and advocacy.

Financial Executives International, *Washington Office, 1825 K St. N.W., #510 20006; (202) 626-7808. Fax, (202) 626-6555. Grace Hinchman, Senior Vice President.*
Web, www.financialexecutives.org

Membership: chief financial officers, treasurers, controllers, and other corporate financial managers involved in policy making. Offers professional development opportunities through peer networking, career management services, conferences, teleconferences, and publications. (Headquarters in Florham Park, N.J.)

FreedomWorks, *601 Pennsylvania Ave. N.W., North Bldg., #700 20004-2601; (202) 783-3870. Fax, (202) 942-7649. Matt Kibbe, President. Toll-free, (888) 564-6273.*
Web, www.freedomworks.org

Citizens' advocacy group that promotes reduced taxes, free trade, and deregulation. Advocates deficit reduction through spending restraint, competitiveness in financial markets, and increased private involvement in providing public services. Encourages citizens to petition members of Congress. (Formerly Citizens for a Sound Economy and Empower America.)

Good Jobs First, *1616 P St. N.W., #210 20036; (202) 232-1616. Fax, (202) 232-6680. Greg LeRoy, Executive Director.*
General e-mail, info@goodjobsfirst.org
Web, www.goodjobsfirst.org

Promotes corporate and government accountability in economic development and job growth. Provides information on state and local job subsidies. Monitors legislation and regulations.

Greater Washington Board of Trade, *1725 Eye St. N.W., #200 20006; (202) 857-5900. Fax, (202) 223-2648. James C. Dinegar, President.*
General e-mail, info@bot.org
Web, www.bot.org

Promotes and plans economic growth for the capital region. Supports business-government partnerships, technological training, and transportation planning; promotes international trade; works to increase economic viability of the city of Washington. Monitors legislation and regulations at local, state, and federal levels.

Inclusion, *1611 Connecticut Ave. N.W., #400 20009; (202) 293-5380. Fax, (202) 588-1356. Shawn Fremstad, Director.*

Web, www.inclusionist.org

Think tank that develops and promotes policies that foster social and economic inclusion, with a current focus on low-wage work in the United States. Provides information through policy reports, charts and graphs, and interactive blog entries. (Affiliated with the Center for Economic and Policy Research.)

International Business Ethics Institute, *1776 Eye St. N.W., 9th Floor 20006; (202) 296-6938. Fax, (202) 296-5897. Lori Tansey Martens, President.*

General e-mail, info@business-ethics.org

Web, www.business-ethics.org

Nonpartisan educational organization that promotes business ethics and corporate responsibility. Works to increase public awareness and dialogue about international business ethics issues through various educational resources and activities. Works with companies to assist them in establishing effective international ethics programs.

Mercatus Center *(George Mason University),* *3301 N. Fairfax Dr., #450, Arlington, VA 22201; (703) 993-4930. Fax, (703) 993-4935. Tyler Cowen, Director. Information, (800) 815-5711.*

General e-mail, mercatus@gmu.edu

Web, www.mercatus.org

Research center that studies sustained prosperity in societies and the conditions that contribute to economic success. Interests include the drivers of social, political, and economic change; international and domestic economic development; entrepreneurship and the institutions that enable it; the benefits and costs of regulatory policy; government performance and transparency; and good governance practices. Also studies the benefits of market-oriented systems using market process analysis.

National Assn. of Corporate Directors, *1133 21st St. N.W., #700 20036; (202) 775-0509. Fax, (202) 775-4857. Kenneth Daly, President.*

General e-mail, info@nacdonline.org

Web, www.nacdonline.org

Membership: executives of closely held and public companies, outside and inside directors, and stewards of corporate governance. Serves as a clearinghouse on corporate governance and current board practices. Conducts seminars; runs executive search service; sponsors insurance program for directors and officers.

National Assn. of Manufacturers (NAM), *1331 Pennsylvania Ave. N.W., #600 20004-1790; (202) 637-3000. Fax, (202) 637-3182. John Engler, President. Press, (202) 637-3134.*

General e-mail, manufacturing@nam.org

Web, www.nam.org

Represents industry views (mainly of manufacturers) to government on national and international issues. Reviews legislation, administrative rulings, and judicial decisions affecting industry. Operates a Web site for members and the public that provides information on legislative and other news; conducts programs on labor relations, occupational safety and health, regulatory and consumer affairs, environmental trade and technology, and other business issues.

National Assn. of State Auditors, Comptrollers, and Treasurers, *444 N. Capitol St. N.W., #234 20001; (202) 624-5451. Fax, (202) 624-5473. Cornelia Chebinou, Washington Director.*

Web, www.nasact.org

Membership: state officials who deal with the financial management of state government. Provides information on financial best practices and research. Monitors legislation and regulations.

National Assn. of State Budget Officers, *444 N. Capitol St. N.W., #642 20001-1501; (202) 624-5382. Fax, (202) 624-7745. Scott Pattison, Executive Director.*

General e-mail, nasbo-direct@nasbo.org

Web, www.nasbo.org

Membership: state budget and financial officers. Publishes research reports on budget-related issues. (Affiliate of the National Governors Assn.)

National Chamber Litigation Center, *1615 H St. N.W., #230 20062-2000; (202) 463-5337. Fax, (202) 463-5346. Robin S. Conrad, Executive Vice President.*

General e-mail, nclc@uschamber.org

Web, www.uschamber.com/nclc

Public policy law firm of the U.S. Chamber of Commerce. Advocates businesses' positions in court on such issues as employment, environmental, and constitutional law. Provides businesses with legal assistance and representation in legal proceedings before federal courts and agencies.

National Cooperative Business Assn., *1401 New York Ave. N.W., #1100 20005-2160; (202) 638-6222. Fax, (202) 638-1374. Paul Hazen, President.*

General e-mail, ncba@ncba.coop

Web, www.ncba.coop

Alliance of cooperatives, businesses, and state cooperative associations. Supports development of cooperative businesses; promotes and develops trade among domestic and international cooperatives. Monitors legislation and regulations.

National Economists Club, *P.O. Box 19281 20036; (703) 493-8824. Kris Bledowski, President.*

General e-mail, info@national-economists.org

Web, www.national-economists.org

Provides venues for scholars, policymakers, business leaders, and public figures to present and defend their views on timely economic topics. Offers members employment and networking opportunities.

National Retail Federation, *325 7th St. N.W., #1100 20004-2802; (202) 783-7971. Fax, (202) 737-2849. Tracy Mullin, President.*

Web, www.nrf.com

Membership: international, national, and state associations of retailers and major retail corporations. Concerned with federal regulatory activities and legislation that affect retailers, including tax, employment, trade, and credit issues. Provides information on retailing through seminars, conferences, and publications.

National Venture Capital Assn., *1655 N. Fort Myer Dr., #850, Arlington, VA 22209; (703) 524-2549. Fax, (703) 524-3940. Mark Heesen, President.*

General e-mail, info@nvca.org

Web, www.nvca.org

Membership: venture capital organizations and individuals and corporate financiers. Promotes understanding of venture capital investment. Facilitates networking opportunities and provides research data on equity investment in emerging growth companies. Monitors legislation.

Partnership for Public Service, *1100 New York Ave., #1090E 20005; (202) 775-9111. Fax, (202) 775-8885. Max Stier, President.*

General e-mail, mail@ourpublicservice.org

Web, www.ourpublicservice.org

Membership: large corporations and private businesses, including financial and information technology organizations. Seeks to improve government efficiency, productivity, and management through a cooperative effort of the public and private sectors. (Merged with the Private Sector Council.)

Private Equity Council (PEC), *950 F St. N.W., #550 20004; (202) 465-7700. Fax, (202) 639-0209. Robert W. Stewart, Vice President of Public Affairs.*

General e-mail, info@privateequitycouncil.org

Web, www.privateequitycouncil.org

Advocacy, communications, and research organization and resource center that develops, analyzes, and distributes information about the private equity industry and its contributions to the national and global economy.

Society of Competitive Intelligence Professionals (SCIP), *1700 Diagonal Rd., #600, Alexandria, VA 22314;* *(703) 739-0696. Fax, (703) 739-2524. Ken Garrison, Executive Director.*

General e-mail, mbrsrv@scip.org

Web, www.scip.org

Promotes businesses' competitiveness through a greater understanding of competitive behaviors and future strategies as well as the market dynamics in which they conduct business. Conducts seminars and conferences. Publishes the *Competitive Intelligence Magazine.*

U.S. Business and Industry Council (USBIC), *910 16th St. N.W., #300 20006; (202) 728-1980. Fax, (202) 728-1981. Kevin L. Kearns, President.*

General e-mail, council@usbusiness.org

Web, www.usbusiness.org

Advocates energy independence, reindustrialization, and effective use of natural resources and manufacturing capacity. Interests include business tax reduction, the liability crisis, defense and other federal spending, and the trade deficit. Media network distributes op-ed pieces to newspapers and radio stations.

U.S. Chamber of Commerce, *1615 H St. N.W. 20062-2000; (202) 659-6000. Fax, (202) 463-5327. Thomas J. Donohue, President. Press, (202) 463-5682. Publications, (800) 638-6582.*

Web, www.uschamber.com

Federation of businesses; trade and professional associations; state and local chambers of commerce; and American chambers of commerce abroad. Develops policy on legislative and regulatory issues important to American business; sponsors programs on management, business confidence, small business, consumer affairs, economic policy, minority business, and tax policy. Monitors legislation and regulations.

U.S. Chamber of Commerce, *Congressional and Public Affairs, 1615 H St. N.W. 20062-2000; (202) 463-5600. Fax, (202) 887-3430. Rolf T. Lundberg, Senior Vice President.*

Web, www.uschamber.com

Advocates businesses' position on government and regulatory affairs. Monitors legislation and regulations on antitrust and corporate policy, product liability, and business-consumer relations.

U.S. Chamber of Commerce, *Economic Policy, 1615 H St. N.W. 20062-2000; (202) 463-5620. Fax, (202) 463-3174. Martin A. Regalia, Chief Economist. Press, (202) 463-5682.*

Web, www.uschamber.com

Represents the business community's views on economic policy, including government spending, the federal budget, and tax issues. Forecasts the economy of the United States and other industrialized nations and projects the impact of major policy changes. Studies economic trends and analyzes their effect on the business community.

Coins and Currency

Bureau of Engraving and Printing (BEP), *(Treasury Dept.), 14th and C Sts. S.W., #119M 20228; (202) 874-2002. Fax, (202) 874-3879. Larry Felix, Director. Information, (202) 874-2000. Tours, (202) 874-2330. Web, www.moneyfactory.gov*

Designs, engraves, and prints Federal Reserve notes, military certificates, White House invitations, presidential portraits, and special security documents for the federal government. Provides information on history, design, and engraving of currency; offers public tours; maintains reading room where materials are brought for special research (for appointment, write to the BEP's Historical Resource Center).

Bureau of Engraving and Printing (BEP), *(Treasury Dept.), Mutilated Currency Division, 14th and C Sts. S.W. 20228 (mailing address: P.O. Box 37048, Washington, DC 20013); (202) 874-2141. Fax, (202) 874-5362. Allan Wibbenmeyer, Chief. Information, (866) 575-2361. Mutilation redemption, (202) 874-2131. Unfit currency and destruction of currency, (202) 874-2771. Claims, (202) 874-2397. Web, www.moneyfactory.gov*

Redeems U.S. currency that has been mutilated; develops regulations and procedures for the destruction of mutilated U.S. currency.

Federal Reserve System, *Board of Governors, 20th and C Sts. N.W., #B2046 20551 (mailing address: 20th St. and Constitution Ave. N.W., Washington, DC 20551); (202) 452-3201. Fax, (202) 452-3819. Ben S. Bernanke, Chair; Donald L. Kohn, Vice Chair. Information, (202) 452-3204. Public Affairs, (202) 452-2955. Congressional Liaison, (202) 452-3003. Locator, (202) 452-3204. Publications, (202) 452-3245. Web, www.federalreserve.gov*

Influences the availability of money as part of its responsibility for monetary policy; maintains reading room for inspection of records that are available to the public.

National Museum of American History *(Smithsonian Institution), National Numismatic Collection, 14th St. and Constitution Ave. N.W. 20013; (202) 633-3854. Fax, (202) 633-4370. Richard G. Doty, Senior Curator. Web, http://americanhistory.si.edu/collections/numismatics*

Develops and maintains collections of ancient, medieval, modern, U.S., and world coins; U.S. and world currencies; tokens; medals; orders and decorations; and traditional exchange media. Conducts research and responds to public inquiries.

Treasury Dept., *1500 Pennsylvania Ave. N.W., #3330 20220; (202) 622-2000. Fax, (202) 622-0073. Timothy Geithner, Secretary, (202) 622-1100; Robert M. Kimmitt, Deputy Secretary. Information, (202) 622-5500. Library,*

(202) 622-0990. Web, www.ustreas.gov

Oversees the manufacture of U.S. coins and currency; submits to Congress final reports on the minting of coins or any changes in currency. Library open to the public by appointment.

Treasury Dept., *Financial Management Service, 401 14th St. S.W., #548 20227; (202) 874-7000. Fax, (202) 874-6743. Judith R. Tillman, Commissioner. Public Affairs, (202) 874-6750. Web, www.fms.treas.gov*

Prepares and publishes for the president, Congress, and the public monthly, quarterly, and annual statements of government financial transactions, including reports on U.S. currency and coins in circulation.

Treasury Dept., *Treasurer of the United States, 1500 Pennsylvania Ave. N.W., #2134 20220; (202) 622-0100. Fax, (202) 622-6464. Anna Escobedo Cabral, Treasurer. Web, www.ustreas.gov*

Advises the secretary of the Treasury on matters relating to coinage, currency, and the production of other instruments issued by the United States. Serves as the national honorary director of the Savings Bond Program.

U.S. Mint *(Treasury Dept.), 801 9th St. N.W., 8th Floor 20220; (202) 354-7200. Fax, (202) 756-6200. Edmund C. Moy, Director. Information, (202) 354-7227. TTY, (202) 354-7600. Web, www.usmint.gov*

Manufactures and distributes all domestic coins; safeguards the government's holdings of precious metals; manufactures and sells commemorative coins and medals of historic interest. Maintains a sales area at Union Station in Washington, D.C., and a kiosk at its main building.

Federal Budget

Federal Financing Bank *(Treasury Dept.), 1500 Pennsylvania Ave. N.W. 20220; (202) 622-2470. Fax, (202) 622-0707. Gary H. Burner, Chief Financial Officer. General e-mail, ffb@do.treas.gov*

Web, www.ustreas.gov/ffb

Coordinates federal agency borrowing by purchasing securities issued or guaranteed by federal agencies; funds its operations by borrowing from the Treasury.

Office of Management and Budget (OMB), *(Executive Office of the President), Eisenhower Executive Office Bldg., #252 20503; (202) 395-4840. Fax, (202) 395-3888. Peter Orzag, Director. Press, (202) 395-7254. Web, www.whitehouse.gov/omb*

Prepares president's annual budget; works with the Council of Economic Advisers and the Treasury Dept. to develop the federal government's fiscal program; oversees administration of the budget; reviews government regulations; coordinates administration procurement and management policy.

Treasury Dept., *Bureau of the Public Debt,* 799 9th St. N.W., 9th Floor 20239; (202) 504-3500. Fax, (202) 504-3630. Van Zeck, Commissioner. Press, (202) 504-3502. Savings bonds, (866) 388-1776.
Web, www.publicdebt.treas.gov

Handles public debt securities, Treasury notes, and bonds; maintains all records on series EE and HH savings bonds.

Treasury Dept., *Debt Management,* 1500 Pennsylvania Ave. N.W., #2414 20220; (202) 622-2630. Fax, (202) 622-0244. Karthik Ramanathan, Director.
General e-mail, Debt.Management@do.treas.gov
Web, www.treas.gov/offices/domestic-finance/debt-management

Provides financial and economic analysis on government financing and Treasury debt management. Coordinates, analyzes, and reviews government borrowing, lending, and investment activities. Determines interest rates for government loan programs.

Treasury Dept., *Financial Market Policy,* 1500 Pennsylvania Ave. N.W., #5011 20220; (202) 622-2692. Fax, (202) 622-0974. Heidilynne Schultheiss, Director.
Web, www.ustreas.gov/offices/domestic-finance/financial-markets/fin-market-policy

Analyzes and evaluates economic and financial development, problems and proposals, and related economic matters. Provides analysis and technical assistance on regulatory issues involving financial markets.

Treasury Dept., *Policy and Legislative Review,* 1120 Vermont Ave. N.W., #916B 20005; (202) 622-2450. Fax, (202) 622-0427. Paula Farrell, Director.
Web, www.treas.gov/offices/domestic-finance/financial-markets/legislative-review

Analyzes federal credit program principles and standards, legislation, and proposals related to government borrowing, lending, and investment. Furnishes actuarial and mathematical analysis required for Treasury market financing, the Federal Financing Bank, and other government agencies.

►CONGRESS

For a listing of relevant congressional committees and subcommittees, please see page 32 or the Appendix.

Congressional Budget Office, 402 FHOB 20515; (202) 226-2700. Fax, (202) 225-7509. Douglas W. Elmendorf, Director. Information, (202) 226-2600. Publications, (202) 226-2809.
Web, www.cbo.gov

Nonpartisan office that provides the House and Senate with analyses needed for economic and budget decisions, and with the information and estimates required for the congressional budget process.

►NONGOVERNMENTAL

Concord Coalition, 1011 Arlington Blvd., #300, Arlington, VA 22209; (703) 894-6222. Fax, (703) 894-6231. Robert L. Bixby, Executive Director.
General e-mail, concordcoalition@concordcoalition.org
Web, www.concordcoalition.org

Nonpartisan grassroots organization advocating fiscal responsibility and ensuring Social Security, Medicare, and Medicaid are secure for all generations.

Institute for Policy Studies, *Foreign Policy in Focus,* 1112 16th St., #600 20036; (202) 234-9382. Fax, (202) 387-7915. Emira Woods, Director.
Web, www.fpif.org

Think tank that provides analysis of U.S. foreign policy and international affairs and recommends progressive policy alternatives. Publishes reports; organizes briefings for the public, media, and policymakers. Interests include climate change, global poverty, nuclear weapons, terrorism, and military conflict.

OMB Watch, 1742 Connecticut Ave. N.W. 20009; (202) 234-8494. Fax, (202) 234-8584. Gary Bass, Executive Director.
General e-mail, ombwatch@ombwatch.org
Web, www.ombwatch.org

Research and advocacy organization that promotes improved access to governmental decision makers, including those in the Office of Management and Budget. Promotes a just, equitable, and accountable government as well as a politically active electorate. Specific interests include the federal budget, taxes, information access, and regulatory policy.

Statistics, Economic Projections

►AGENCIES

Bureau of Economic Analysis *(Commerce Dept.),* 1441 L St. N.W., #6006 20230; (202) 606-9600. Fax, (202) 606-5311. J. Steven Landefeld, Director. Information, (202) 606-9900.
Web, www.bea.gov

Compiles, analyzes, and publishes data on measures of aggregate U.S. economic activity, including gross domestic product; prices by type of expenditure; personal income and outlays; personal savings; corporate profits; capital stock; U.S. international transactions; and foreign investment. Provides statistics of personal income and employment by industry for regions, states, metropolitan areas, and counties. Refers specific inquiries to economic specialists in the field.

Treasury Department

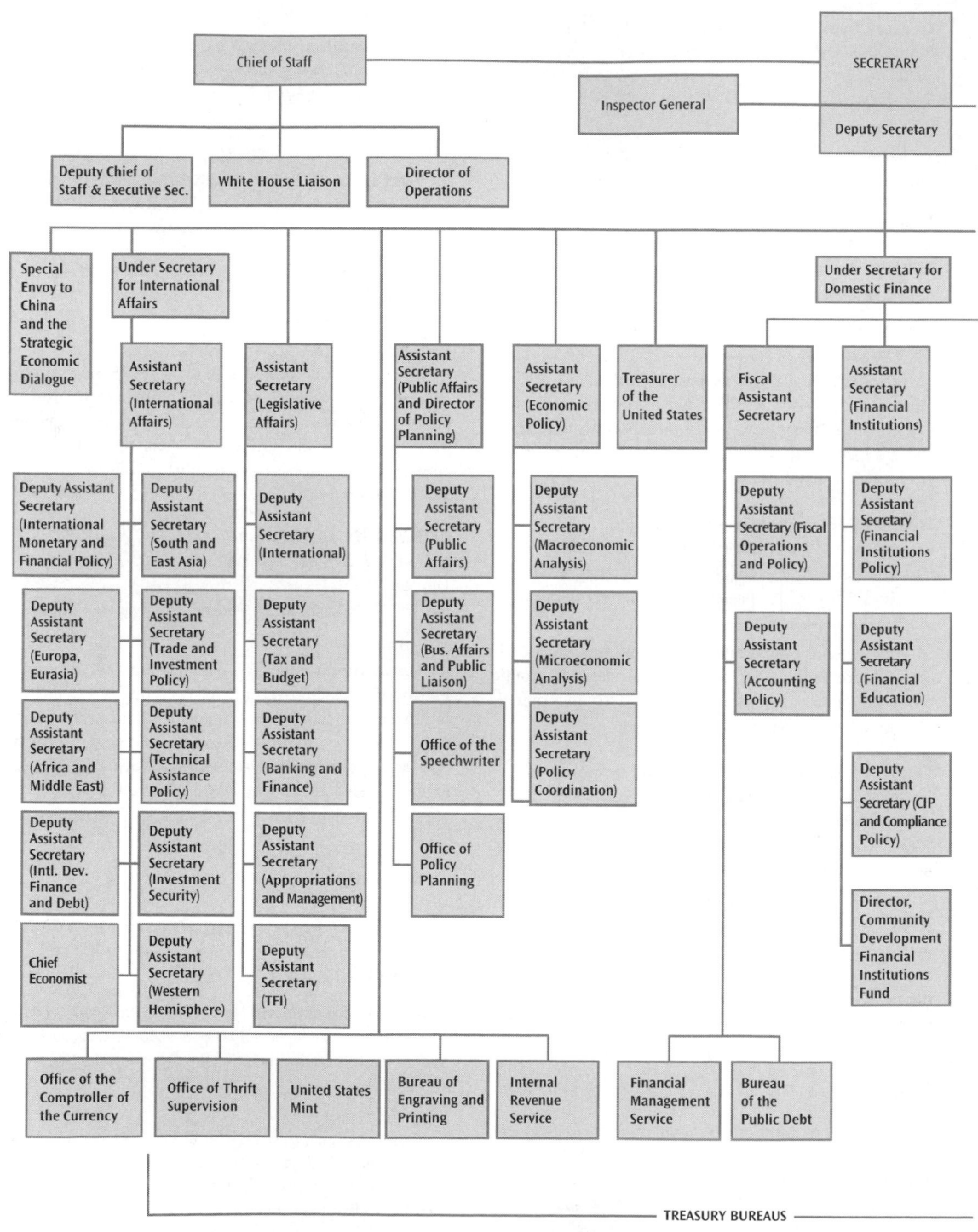

*Unless otherwise indicated, all bureaus report through the deputy secretary to the secretary.

Treasury Department

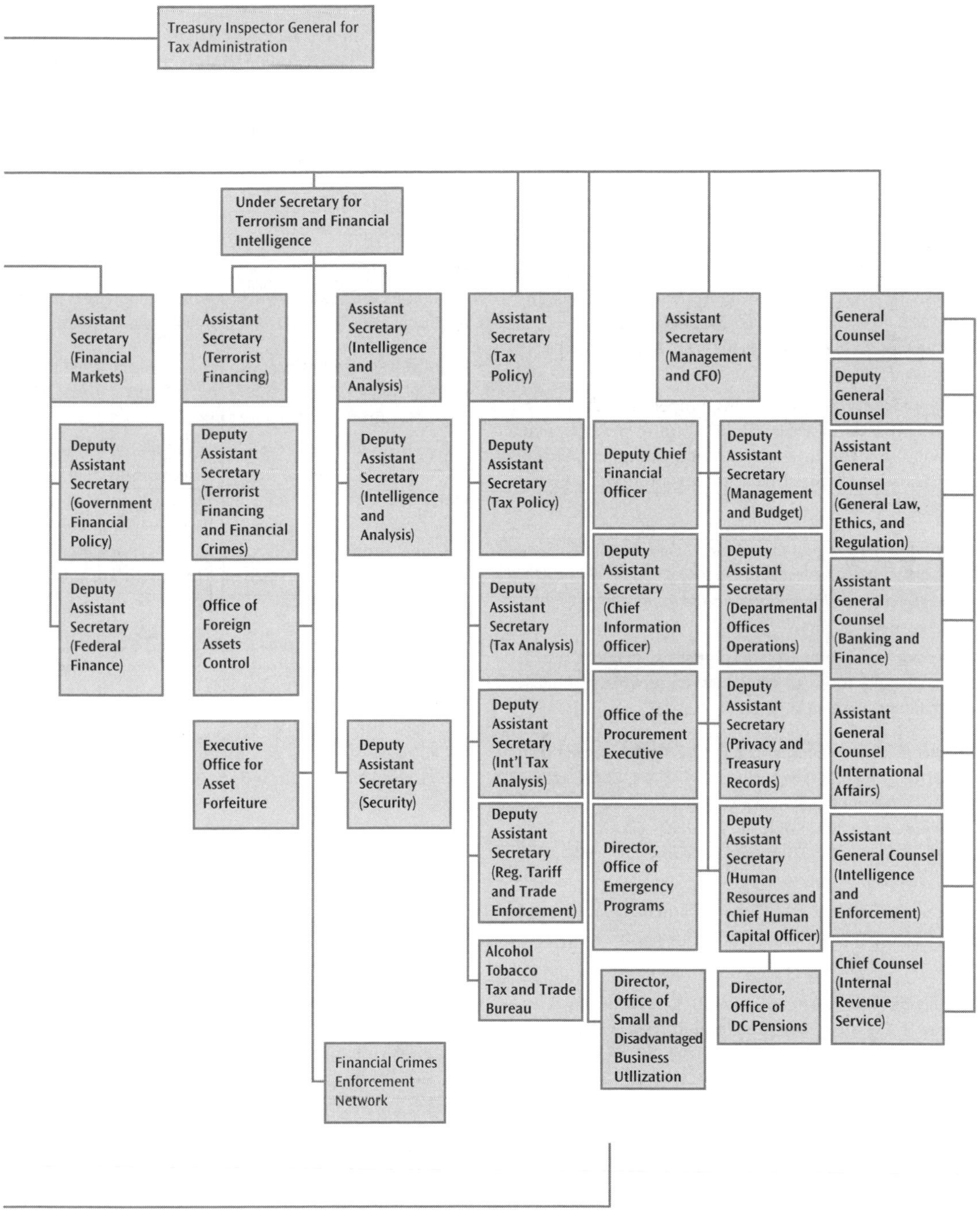

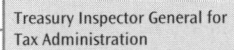

Treasury Inspector General for Tax Administration

Under Secretary for Terrorism and Financial Intelligence

Assistant Secretary (Financial Markets)

Assistant Secretary (Terrorist Financing)

Assistant Secretary (Intelligence and Analysis)

Assistant Secretary (Tax Policy)

Assistant Secretary (Management and CFO)

General Counsel

Deputy Assistant Secretary (Government Financial Policy)

Deputy Assistant Secretary (Terrorist Financing and Financial Crimes)

Deputy Assistant Secretary (Intelligence and Analysis)

Deputy Assistant Secretary (Tax Policy)

Deputy Chief Financial Officer

Deputy Assistant Secretary (Management and Budget)

Deputy General Counsel

Assistant General Counsel (General Law, Ethics, and Regulation)

Deputy Assistant Secretary (Federal Finance)

Office of Foreign Assets Control

Deputy Assistant Secretary (Tax Analysis)

Deputy Assistant Secretary (Chief Information Officer)

Deputy Assistant Secretary (Departmental Offices Operations)

Assistant General Counsel (Banking and Finance)

Executive Office for Asset Forfeiture

Deputy Assistant Secretary (Security)

Deputy Assistant Secretary (Int'l Tax Analysis)

Office of the Procurement Executive

Deputy Assistant Secretary (Privacy and Treasury Records)

Assistant General Counsel (International Affairs)

Deputy Assistant Secretary (Reg. Tariff and Trade Enforcement)

Director, Office of Emergency Programs

Deputy Assistant Secretary (Human Resources and Chief Human Capital Officer)

Assistant General Counsel (Intelligence and Enforcement)

Alcohol Tobacco Tax and Trade Bureau

Director, Office of Small and Disadvantaged Business Utilization

Director, Office of DC Pensions

Chief Counsel (Internal Revenue Service)

Financial Crimes Enforcement Network

Bureau of Labor Statistics (BLS), *(Labor Dept.),*
2 Massachusetts Ave. N.E., #4040 20212-0001; (202)
691-7800. Fax, (202) 691-7797. Keith Hall, Commissioner.
Press, (202) 691-5902.
General e-mail, blsdata-staff@bls.gov
Web, www.bls.gov

Provides statistical data on labor economics, including
labor force, employment and unemployment, hours of
work, wages, employee compensation, prices, living conditions, labor-management relations, productivity, technological developments, occupational safety and health, and
structure and growth of the economy. Publishes reports on
these statistical trends including the Consumer Price Index,
Producer Price Index, and Employment and Earnings.

Census Bureau *(Commerce Dept.), Economic Programs,*
4600 Silver Hill Rd., #8H132, Suitland, MD 20746 (mailing
address: MS 6000, #8H132, Washington, DC 20233-6000);
(301) 763-4636. Fax, (301) 763-3842. Thomas L.
Mesenbourg, Deputy Director. Toll-free, (800) 923-8282.
Web, www.census.gov

Provides data and explains proper use of data on
county business patterns, classification of industries and
commodities, and business statistics. Compiles quarterly
reports listing financial data for corporations in certain
industrial sectors.

Census Bureau *(Commerce Dept.), Governments*
Division, 4600 Silver Hill Rd., #HQ-5K156 20233; (301)
763-1489. Fax, (301) 457-3057. Stephanie Brown, Chief.
Web, www.census.gov

Provides data and explains proper use of data concerning state and local governments, employment, finance,
governmental organization, and taxation.

Census Bureau *(Commerce Dept.), Manufacturing and*
Construction, 4600 Silver Hill Rd., #7K154, Suitland, MD
20746-4600 (mailing address: change city and zip code to,
Washington, DC 20233); (301) 763-4593. Fax, (301) 768-
7783. Thomas E. Zabelsky, Division Chief.
Web, www.census.gov

Collects and distributes manufacturing, construction,
and mineral industry data. Reports are organized by commodity, industry, and geographic area.

Census Bureau *(Commerce Dept.), Service Sector*
Statistics Division, 4700 Silver Hill Rd., #8K154, Suitland,
MD 20746-2401; (301) 763-5170. Fax, (301) 457-1343.
Mark E. Wallace, Chief.
Web, www.census.gov

Provides data of five-year census programs on retail,
wholesale, and service industries. Conducts periodic monthly
or annual surveys for specific items within these industries.

Council of Economic Advisers *(Executive Office of the*
President), Statistical Office, 1800 G St. N.W., 8th Floor
20502; (202) 395-5062. Fax, (202) 395-5630. Adrianne
Pilot, Director.
Web, www.whitehouse.gov/cea

Compiles and reports aggregate economic data, including national income and expenditures, employment,
wages, productivity, production and business activity,
prices, money stock, credit, finance, government finance,
corporate profits and finance, agriculture, and international statistics, including balance of payments and
import-export levels by commodity and area. Data published in the *Annual Economic Report of the President* and
the monthly *Economic Indicators,* prepared for the congressional Joint Economic Committee.

Economic Research Service *(Agriculture Dept.), 1800*
M St. N.W., #4145N 20036-5831; (202) 694-5000. Fax,
(202) 694-5757. Kitty Smith, Administrator; John Kort,
Associate Administrator.
General e-mail, service@ers.usda.gov
Web, www.ers.usda.gov

Conducts market research; studies and forecasts domestic supply-and-demand trends for fruits and vegetables.

Federal Reserve System, *Monetary Affairs, 20th and*
C Sts. N.W., #B3022B 20551; (202) 452-2007. Fax, (202)
452-2301. Brian F. Madigan, Director.
Web, www.federalreserve.gov/research/mastaff.htm

Assists the Federal Reserve Board and the Federal
Open Market Committee in the conduct of monetary
policy, especially in the areas of finance, money and banking, and monetary policy design and implementation.
Provides expertise on open market operations, discount
window policy, and reserve markets.

Federal Reserve System, *Research and Statistics, 20th*
and C Sts. N.W., #B3048 20551; (202) 452-3301. Fax,
(202) 452-5296. David J. Stockton, Director.
Web, www.federalreserve.gov

Publishes statistical data on business finance, real estate
credit, consumer credit, industrial production, construction, and flow of funds.

Internal Revenue Service (IRS), *(Treasury Dept.),*
Statistics of Income, 500 N. Capitol St. N.W. 20001
(mailing address: P.O. Box 2608, Washington, DC 20013-
2608); (202) 874-0700. Fax, (202) 874-0983. Thomas B.
Petska, Director. Publications, (202) 874-0410.
Web, www.irs.ustreas.gov/prod/tax_stats

Provides the public and the Treasury Dept. with statistical information on tax laws. Prepares statistical information for the Commerce Dept. to use in formulating the
gross national product (GNP). Publishes *Statistics of
Income,* a series available at cost to the public.

International Trade Administration (ITA), *(Commerce*
Dept.), Manufacturing and Services: Industry Analysis,
14th St. and Constitution Ave. N.W., #2126 20230; (202)
482-6232. Fax, (202) 482-4614. Praveen Dixit, Deputy
Assistant Secretary.
Web, www.ita.doc.gov/tradestats

Analyzes international and domestic competitiveness
of U.S. industry and component sectors. Assesses impact of

regulations on competitive positions. Produces and disseminates U.S. foreign trade and related economic data. Supports U.S. international trade negotiations initiative.

National Agricultural Statistics Service *(Agriculture Dept.)*, *1400 Independence Ave. S.W., #5041, MS 2001 20250-2001; (202) 720-2707. Fax, (202) 720-9013. Cynthia Clark, Administrator. Information, (800) 727-9540. Print reports, (800) 999-6779.*
General e-mail, nass@usda.gov
Web, www.nass.usda.gov

Prepares estimates and reports on production, supply, prices, and other items relating to the U.S. agricultural economy. Reports include statistics on field crops, fruits and vegetables, cattle, hogs, poultry, and related products. Prepares quinquennial national census of agriculture.

Office of Management and Budget (OMB), *(Executive Office of the President),* **Statistical Policy,** *New Executive Office Bldg., #10201 20503; (202) 395-3093. Fax, (202) 395-7245. Katherine K. Wallman, Chief.*
Web, www.whitehouse.gov/omb

Carries out the statistical policy and coordination functions under the Paperwork Reduction Act of 1995; develops long-range plans for improving federal statistical programs; develops policy standards and guidelines for statistical data collection, classification, and publication; evaluates statistical programs and agency performance.

Securities and Exchange Commission, *Economic Analysis, 100 F St. N.E., #9461 20549; (202) 551-6600. Fax, (202) 772-9290. James A. Overdahl, Chief Economist. Information, (202) 942-8088.*
Web, www.sec.gov

Advises the SEC and its staff on economic issues as they pertain to the commission's regulatory activities. Publishes data on trading volume of the stock exchanges; compiles statistics on financial reports of brokerage firms.

U.S. International Trade Commission, *Industries, 500 E St. S.W., #504-A 20436; (202) 205-3296. Fax, (202) 205-3161. Karen Laney-Cummings, Director. Press, (202) 205-1819.*
Web, www.usitc.gov

Identifies, analyzes, and develops data on economic and technical matters related to the competitive position of the United States in domestic and world markets in agriculture and forest production, chemicals, textiles, energy, electronics, transportation, services and investments, minerals, metals, and machinery.

►**NONGOVERNMENTAL**

American Statistical Assn., *732 N. Washington St., Alexandria, VA 22314-1943; (703) 684-1221. Fax, (703) 684-2037. Toll-free, (888) 231-3473. Ronald Wasserstein, Executive Director.*
General e-mail, asainfo@amstat.org
Web, www.amstat.org

Membership: individuals interested in statistics and related quantitative fields. Advises government agencies on statistics and methodology in agency research; promotes development of statistical techniques for use in business, industry, finance, government, agriculture, and science. Promotes knowledge of statistics at all levels of education. Publishes statistical journals.

Taxes and Tax Reform

►**AGENCIES**

Alcohol and Tobacco Tax and Trade Bureau (TTB), *(Treasury Dept.), 1310 G St. N.W., #300E 20220; (202) 927-5000. Fax, (202) 927-5611. John J. Manfreda, Chief Counsel, (202) 927-8209. Press, (202) 927-8062.*
Web, www.ttb.gov

Enforces and administers revenue laws relating to firearms, explosives, alcohol, and tobacco.

Internal Revenue Service (IRS), *(Treasury Dept.), 1111 Constitution Ave. N.W. 20224; (202) 622-5000. Douglas Shulman, Commissioner. Information, (800) 829-1040. Press, (202) 622-4000. TTY, (800) 829-4059. National Taxpayer Advocate Helpline, (877) 777-4778.*
Web, www.irs.gov

Administers and enforces internal revenue laws and related statutes (except those relating to firearms, explosives, alcohol, and tobacco).

Internal Revenue Service (IRS), *(Treasury Dept.),* **Art Advisory Panel,** *1099 14th St. N.W., #4200E 20005; (202) 435-5609. Fax, (202) 435-5624. Karen Carolan, Chair.*

Panel of twenty art professionals that assists the IRS by reviewing and evaluating taxpayers' appraisals on works of art valued at $20,000 or more involved in Federal Income, Estate, and Gift taxes.

Internal Revenue Service (IRS), *(Treasury Dept.),* **Taxpayer Advocate,** *1111 Constitution Ave. N.W., #3031 20224; (202) 622-6100. Fax, (202) 622-7854. Nina E. Olson, National Taxpayer Advocate.*
Web, www.irs.gov/advocate/index.html

Helps taxpayers resolve problems with the IRS and recommends changes to prevent the problems. Represents taxpayers' interests in the formulation of policies and procedures.

Justice Dept. (DOJ), *Tax Division, 950 Pennsylvania Ave. N.W., #4141 20530; (202) 514-2901. Fax, (202) 514-5479. Nathan J. Hochman, Assistant Attorney General.*
Web, www.usdoj.gov/tax/tax.html

Acts as counsel for the Internal Revenue Service (IRS) in court litigation between the government and taxpayers (other than those handled by the IRS in the U.S. Tax Court).

Multistate Tax Commission, *444 N. Capitol St. N.W., #425 20001-1538; (202) 624-8699. Fax, (202) 624-8819. Joe Huddleston, Executive Director.*

General e-mail, mtc@mtc.gov

Web, www.mtc.gov

Membership: state governments that have enacted the Multistate Tax Compact. Promotes fair, effective, and efficient state tax systems for interstate and international commerce; works to preserve state tax sovereignty. Encourages uniform state tax laws and regulations for multistate and multinational enterprises. Maintains three regional audit offices that monitor compliance with state tax laws and encourage uniformity in taxpayer treatment. Administers program to identify businesses that do not file tax returns with states.

Treasury Dept., *Tax Policy,* 1500 Pennsylvania Ave. N.W., #3120 20220; (202) 622-0050. Fax, (202) 622-0605. Eric Solomon, Assistant Secretary.

Web, www.ustreas.gov/offices/tax-policy

Formulates and implements domestic and international tax policies and programs; conducts analyses of proposed tax legislation and programs; participates in international tax treaty negotiations; responsible for receipts estimates for the annual budget of the United States.

►JUDICIARY

U.S. Tax Court, 400 2nd St. N.W., #134 20217; (202) 521-0700. John O. Colvin, Chief Judge.

Web, www.ustaxcourt.gov

Tries and adjudicates disputes involving income, estate, and gift taxes and personal holding company surtaxes in cases in which deficiencies have been determined by the Internal Revenue Service.

►NONGOVERNMENTAL

American Enterprise Institute for Public Policy Research (AEI), *Fiscal Policy Studies,* 1150 17th St. N.W., #1100 20036; (202) 862-5800. Fax, (202) 862-7177. Kevin Hassett, Resident Scholar. Press, (202) 862-4871.

Web, www.aei.org

Conducts research on fiscal policy, taxes, and budget issues. Sponsors events.

Americans for Tax Reform, 1920 L St. N.W., #200 20036; (202) 785-0266. Fax, (202) 785-0261. Grover G. Norquist, President.

General e-mail, info@atr.org

Web, www.atr.org

Advocates reduction of federal and state taxes; encourages candidates for public office to pledge their opposition to income tax increases through a national pledge campaign.

Center on Budget and Policy Priorities, 820 1st St. N.E., #510 20002; (202) 408-1080. Fax, (202) 408-1056. Robert Greenstein, Executive Director.

General e-mail, center@cbpp.org

Web, www.cbpp.org

Research group that analyzes changes in federal and state programs, such as tax credits, Medicaid coverage and food stamps, and their effect on low- and moderate-income households.

Citizens Against Government Waste, 1301 Connecticut Ave. N.W., #400 20036; (202) 467-5300. Fax, (202) 467-4253. Thomas A. Schatz, President.

General e-mail, membership@cagw.org

Web, www.cagw.org

Taxpayer watchdog group that monitors government spending to identify how waste, mismanagement, and inefficiency in government can be eliminated. Has created criteria to identify pork-barrel spending. Publishes the annual *Congressional Pig Book,* which lists the names of politicians and their pet pork-barrel projects. Monitors legislation and regulations.

Citizens for Tax Justice, *Institute on Taxation and Economic Policy,* 1616 P St. N.W., #200 20036; (202) 299-1066. Fax, (202) 299-1065. Robert S. McIntyre, Director.

General e-mail, ctj@ctj.org

Web, www.ctj.org

Research and advocacy organization that works for progressive taxes at the federal, state, and local levels.

Federation of Tax Administrators, 444 N. Capitol St. N.W., #348 20001; (202) 624-5890. Fax, (202) 624-7888. Harley T. Duncan, Executive Director.

Web, www.taxadmin.org

Membership: state tax agencies. Provides information upon written request on tax-related issues, including court decisions and legislation. Conducts research and sponsors workshops.

FreedomWorks, 601 Pennsylvania Ave. N.W., North Bldg., #700 20004-2601; (202) 783-3870. Fax, (202) 942-7649. Matt Kibbe, President. Toll-free, (888) 564-6273.

Web, www.freedomworks.org

Citizens' advocacy group that promotes reduced taxes, free trade, and deregulation. (Formerly Citizens for a Sound Economy and Empower America.)

Institute for Research on the Economics of Taxation, 1710 Rhode Island Ave. N.W., 11th Floor 20036; (202) 463-1400. Fax, (202) 463-6199. Stephen Entin, President.

General e-mail, iret@iret.org

Web, www.iret.org

Education and research organization that analyzes all aspects of taxation. Conducts research on the economic effects of federal tax policies; publishes studies on domestic and international economic policy issues.

National Assn. of Manufacturers (NAM), *Tax and Domestic Economic Policy,* 1331 Pennsylvania Ave. N.W., #600 20004-1790; (202) 637-3076. Fax, (202) 637-3182. Dorothy Coleman, Vice President.

Web, www.nam.org

Represents industry views (mainly of manufacturers) on federal tax and budget policies; conducts conferences. Monitors legislation and regulations.

National Tax Assn., *725 15th St. N.W., #600 20005-2109; (202) 737-3325. Fax, (202) 737-7308. J. Fred Giertz, Executive Director.*

General e-mail, natltax@aol.com

Web, www.ntanet.org

Membership: tax lawyers and accountants, academics, legislators, and students. Seeks to advance understanding of tax theory, practice, and policy, as well as other aspects of public finance. Holds conferences and symposiums, including the Annual Conference on Taxation. Publishes the *National Tax Journal.*

National Taxpayers Union, *Communications, 108 N. Alfred St., 3rd Floor, Alexandria, VA 22314; (703) 683-5700. Fax, (703) 683-5722. Peter Sepp, Vice President for Policy and Communications.*

General e-mail, ntu@ntu.org

Web, www.ntu.org

Citizens' interest group that promotes tax and spending reduction at all levels of government. Supports constitutional amendments to balance the federal budget and limit taxes.

Tax Analysts, *400 S. Maple Ave., #400, Falls Church, VA 22046; (703) 533-4400. Fax, (703) 533-4444. Christopher Bergin, President. Customer Service, (800) 955-3444.*

General e-mail, cservice@tax.org

Web, www.taxanalysts.com

Nonpartisan organization that seeks to develop tax systems that are fair, simple, and efficient. Provides publications to educate tax professionals and the public about tax reform.

The Tax Council, *1301 K St. N.W., #800W 20005; (202) 822-8062. Fax, (202) 315-3413. Roger J. LeMaster, Executive Director.*

General e-mail, general@thetaxcouncil.org

Web, www.thetaxcouncil.org

Organization of corporations concerned with tax policy and legislation. Interests include tax rate, capital formation, capital gains, foreign source income, and capital cost recovery.

Tax Executives Institute, *1200 G St. N.W., #300 20005-3814; (202) 638-5601. Fax, (202) 638-5607. Timothy J. McCormally, Executive Director.*

Web, www.tei.org

Membership: accountants, lawyers, and other corporate and business employees dealing with tax issues. Sponsors seminars and conferences on federal, state, local, and international tax issues. Develops and monitors tax legislation, regulations, and administrative procedures.

Tax Foundation, *2001 L St. N.W., #1050 20036; (202) 464-6200. Fax, (202) 464-6201. Scott A. Hodge, President.*

General e-mail, tf@taxfoundation.org

Web, www.taxfoundation.org

Membership: individuals and businesses interested in federal, state, and local fiscal matters. Conducts research and prepares reports on taxes and government expenditures.

Tax Policy Center, *2100 M St. N.W. 20037; (202) 833-7200. Fax, (202) 728-0232. Leonard Burman, Director.*

Web, www.taxpolicycenter.org

Provides independent analysis of tax issues. Communicates findings to policymakers and the public. (Affiliated with the Brookings Institution and the Urban Institute.)

U.S. Conference of Mayors, *1620 Eye St. N.W., #400 20006; (202) 293-7330. Fax, (202) 293-2352. J. Thomas Cochran, Executive Director.*

General e-mail, info@usmayors.org

Web, www.usmayors.org/uscm

Membership: mayors of cities with populations of 30,000 or more. Monitors tax policy and legislation.

CONSUMER PROTECTION

►AGENCIES

Consumer Product Safety Commission (CPSC), *4330 East-West Hwy., #519, Bethesda, MD 20814; (301) 504-7908. Fax, (301) 504-0399. Nancy Nord, Chair (Acting); Patricia Semple, Executive Director. TTY, (800) 638-8270. Public Affairs, (301) 504-7908. Congressional Relations, (301) 504-7903. Product safety hotline, (800) 638-2772.*

General e-mail, info@cpsc.gov

Web, www.cpsc.gov

Establishes and enforces product safety standards; collects data; studies the causes and prevention of product-related injuries; identifies hazardous products, including imports, and recalls them from the marketplace.

Consumer Product Safety Commission (CPSC), *Hazard Identification and Reduction, 4330 East-West Hwy., #723, Bethesda, MD 20814; (301) 504-7949. Fax, (301) 504-0407. Robert J. Howell, Deputy Assistant Executive Director.*

Web, www.cpsc.gov

Establishes labeling and packaging regulations. Develops standards in accordance with the Poison Prevention Packaging Act, the Federal Hazardous Substances Act, the Consumer Products Safety Act, and the Consumer Products Safety Improvement Act.

Consumer Product Safety Commission (CPSC), *International Programs and Intergovernmental Affairs, 4330 East-West Hwy., Bethesda, MD 20814; (301) 504-7907. Fax, (301) 504-0137. Richard O'Brien, Director.*

Web, www.cpsc.gov

Coordinates international and intergovernmental efforts with respect to consumer product safety standards

Consumer Product Safety Commission

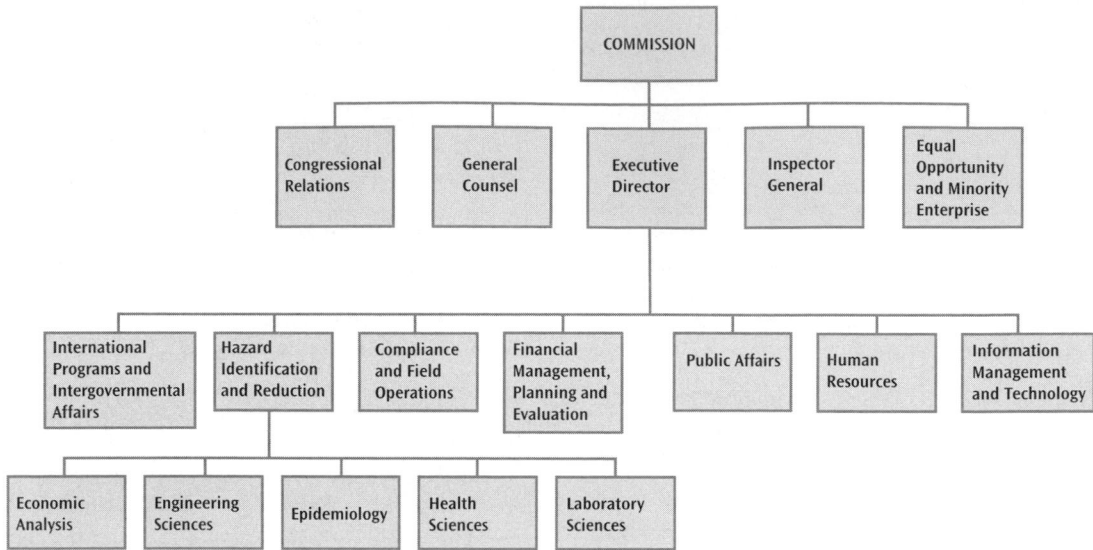

development, harmonization efforts, inspection and enforcement coordination, consumer education, and information dissemination.

Federal Trade Commission (FTC), *Consumer Response Center, 600 Pennsylvania Ave. N.W., #130 20580; (202) 326-2830. Fax, (202) 326-2012. David Torok, Director. Identity Fraud report line, (877) ID-THEFT. Toll-free, (877) FTC-HELP.*
Web, www.ftc.gov

Enforces regulations dealing with unfair or deceptive business practices in advertising, credit, marketing, and service industries; educates consumers and businesses about these regulations; conducts investigations and litigation.

General Services Administration (GSA), *Federal Citizen Information Center, 1800 F St. N.W., #G142 20405; (202) 501-1794. Fax, (202) 501-4281. Teresa N. Nasif, Director.*
Web, www.pueblo.gsa.gov

Publishes quarterly consumer information catalog that lists free and low-cost federal publications. Copies may be obtained from the Consumer Information Centers, Pueblo, CO 81009. Copies also available at Federal Information Centers.

►AGENCY AND DEPARTMENT CONSUMER CONTACTS

Commission on Civil Rights, *Public Affairs, 624 9th St. N.W., #700 20425; (202) 376-8312. Fax, (202) 376-7672. Martin Dennenfelser, Staff Director. TTY, (202) 376-8116.*
Web, www.usccr.gov

Consumer Product Safety Commission (CPSC), *Public Affairs, 4330 East-West Hwy., #519, Bethesda, MD 20814; (301) 504-7908. Fax, (301) 504-0862. Joseph Martyak, Director (Acting). TTY, (800) 638-8270. Product safety hotline, (800) 638-2772.*
General e-mail, info@cpsc.gov
Web, www.cpsc.gov

Education Dept., *Legislation and Congressional Affairs, 400 Maryland Ave. S.W., #6W300 20202-3500; (202) 401-0020. Fax, (202) 401-1438. Terrell Halaska, Assistant Secretary.*
Web, www.ed.gov

Energy Dept. (DOE), *Intergovernmental and External Affairs, 1000 Independence Ave. S.W., CI-10, #8G070 20585; (202) 586-2764. Fax, (202) 586-7314. Steven Morello, Deputy Assistant Secretary.*
Web, www.energy.gov

Federal Communications Commission (FCC), *Consumer and Governmental Affairs Bureau, 445 12th St. S.W., #5C758 20554; (202) 418-1400. Fax, (202) 418-2839. Cathy Seidel, Chief. TTY, (888) 835-5322.*
General e-mail, fccinfo@fcc.gov
Web, www.fcc.gov/cg/consumers

Federal Deposit Insurance Corp. (FDIC), *Compliance and Consumer Affairs, 550 17th St. N.W. 20429-9990; (202) 898-3911. Fax, (202) 898-3638. Robert Mooney, Deputy Director. Information, (877) ASK-FDIC. TTY, (800) 925-4618.*
General e-mail, consumer@fdic.gov
Web, www.fdic.gov

Coordinates and monitors complaints filed by consumers against federally insured state banks that are not members of the Federal Reserve System; handles complaints concerning truth-in-lending and other fair credit provisions, including charges of discrimination on the basis of sex or marital status; responds to general banking inquiries; answers questions on deposit insurance coverage.

Federal Maritime Commission, *Consumer Affairs and Dispute Resolution Services,* *800 N. Capitol St. N.W., #1082 20573; (202) 523-5807. Fax, (202) 275-0059. Ronald D. Murphy, Director.*
Web, www.fmc.gov

Federal Reserve System, *Consumer and Community Affairs,* *1709 New York Ave. N.W. 20006; (202) 452-2631. Fax, (202) 872-4995. Sandra F. Braunstein, Director. Complaints, (888) 851-1920.*
Web, www.federalreserve.gov

Food and Drug Administration (FDA), *(Health and Human Services Dept.),* **External Relations,** *5600 Fishers Lane, Parklawn, #1505, Rockville, MD 20857-0001; (301) 827-4414. Fax, (301) 827-1070. Patricia Kuntze, Senior Advisor for Consumer Affairs. Consumer inquiries, (888) 463-6332.*
Web, www.fda.gov

Food and Nutrition Service *(Agriculture Dept.),* **Communications and Governmental Affairs,** *3101 Park Center Dr., #926, Alexandria, VA 22302; (703) 305-2281. Fax, (703) 305-2312. Vacant, Director.*
Web, www.fns.usda.gov/cga

General Services Administration (GSA), *Federal Citizen Information Center,* *1800 F St. N.W., #G142 20405; (202) 501-1794. Fax, (202) 501-4281. Teresa N. Nasif, Director.*
Web, www.pueblo.gsa.gov

Interior Dept. (DOI), *Communications,* *1849 C St. N.W., #6013 20240; (202) 208-6416. Fax, (202) 208-3231. Tina Kreisher, Director. TTY, (202) 208-4817.*
Web, www.doi.gov

Justice Dept. (DOJ), *Civil Division: Consumer Litigation,* *450 5th St. N.W., #6400 20001; (202) 307-0066. Fax, (202) 514-8742. Eugene M. Thirolf, Director.*
Web, www.usdoj.gov

Merit Systems Protection Board, *1615 M St. N.W., 5th Floor 20419; (202) 653-7200. Fax, (202) 653-7130. Neil McPhie, Chair; William Spencer, Clerk of the Board. TTY, (800) 877-8339. Toll-free, (800) 209-8960; MSPB Inspector General hotline, (800) 424-9121.*
General e-mail, mspb@mspb.gov
Web, www.mspb.gov

Independent quasi-judicial agency that handles hearings and appeals involving federal employees; protects the integrity of federal merit systems and ensures adequate protection for employees against abuses by agency management. Library open to the public.

National Institute of Standards and Technology (NIST), *(Commerce Dept.),* **Inquiries,** *100 Bureau Dr., Stop 1070, Gaithersburg, MD 20899-1070; (301) 975-6478. Fax, (301) 926-1630. Sharon Seide, Head.*
General e-mail, inquiries@nist.gov
Web, www.nist.gov

Nuclear Regulatory Commission, *Public Affairs,* *11555 Rockville Pike, Rockville, MD 20852-2738; (301) 415-8200. Fax, (301) 415-3716. Eliot B. Brenner, Director; Elizabeth A. Hayden, Senior Adviser.*
General e-mail, opa@nrc.gov
Web, www.nrc.gov/what-we-do/public-affairs.html

Postal Regulatory Commission, *Public Affairs and Government Relations,* *901 New York Ave. N.W., #200 20268; (202) 789-6800. Fax, (202) 789-6886. Nanci E. Langley, Commissioner; Dan G. Blair, Chair.*
Web, www.prc.gov

Small Business Administration (SBA), *Capital Access,* *409 3rd St. S.W., #8200 20416; (202) 205-6657. Fax, (202) 205-7230. Eric R. Zarnikow, Associate Deputy Administrator.*
Web, www.sba.gov

State Dept., *Commercial and Business Affairs,* *2201 C St. N.W., #2318 20520-5820; (202) 647-1625. Fax, (202) 647-3953. J. Frank Mermoud, Special Representative for Commercial and Business Affairs.*
General e-mail, cbaweb@state.gov
Web, www.state.gov/e/eb/cba

Transportation Dept. (DOT), *Aviation Consumer Protection,* *1200 New Jersey Ave. S.E., #W96-432 20590 (mailing address: 1200 New Jersey S.E., Transportation Dept., C-75, #4107, Washington, DC 20590); (202) 366-2220. Norman Strickman, Director. Fax, (202) 366-5944. Disability-Related Problems, (800) 778-4838. TTY, (800) 455-9880.*
Web, http://airconsumer.ost.dot.gov

Transportation Security Administration (TSA), *(Homeland Security Dept.),* **Contact Center,** *601 S. 12th St., 7th Floor, Arlington, VA 22202; (866) 289-9673. James C. Murphy, Executive Director.*
General e-mail, tsa-contactcenter@dhs.gov
Web, www.tsa.gov

Treasury Dept., *Public Affairs,* *1500 Pennsylvania Ave. N.W., #3442 20220; (202) 622-2960. Fax, (202) 622-1999. Michele Davis, Assistant Secretary.*
Web, www.ustreas.gov/offices/public-affairs

U.S. Postal Service (USPS), *Office of the Consumer Advocate, 475 L'Enfant Plaza S.W. 20260-0004; (202) 268-2284. Fax, (202) 268-2304. Delores J. Killette, Vice President and Consumer Advocate. TTY, (877) 889-2457. Inquiries, (800) ASK-USPS or (800) 275-8777.*
Web, www.usps.com

Handles consumer complaints; oversees investigations into consumer problems; intercedes in local areas when problems are not adequately resolved; provides information on specific products and services; represents consumers' viewpoint before postal management bodies; initiates projects to improve the U.S. Postal Service.

Veterans Affairs Dept. (VA), *Consumer Affairs, 810 Vermont Ave. N.W., #915 20420; (202) 461-7402. Fax, (202) 273-5716. Shirley Mathis, Program Analyst.*
Web, www.va.gov

►CONGRESS

For a listing of congressional committees and subcommittees, please see page 32 or the Appendix.

►NONGOVERNMENTAL

Call for Action, *5272 River Road, #300, Bethesda, MD 20816; (301) 657-8260. Shirley Rooker, President.*
Web, www.callforaction.org

International network of consumer hotlines affiliated with local broadcast partners. Helps consumers resolve problems with businesses, government agencies, and other organizations through mediation. Provides information on privacy concerns.

Center for Auto Safety, *1825 Connecticut Ave. N.W., #330 20009-5708; (202) 328-7700. Fax, (202) 387-0140.*
General e-mail, accounts@autosafety.org
Web, www.autosafety.org

Public interest organization that receives written consumer complaints against auto manufacturers; monitors federal agencies responsible for regulating and enforcing auto and highway safety rules.

Center for Consumer Freedom, *P.O. Box 34557 20043; (202) 463-7112. Richard Berman, Executive Director.*
Web, www.consumerfreedom.com

Membership: restaurants, food companies, and consumers. Seeks to promote personal freedom and protect consumer choices in lifestyle- and health-related areas such as diet and exercise. Monitors legislation and regulations.

Consumer Federation of America, *1620 Eye St. N.W., #200 20006; (202) 387-6121. Fax, (202) 265-7989. Stephen Brobeck, Executive Director.*
General e-mail, cfa@consumerfed.org
Web, www.consumerfed.org

Federation of national, regional, state, and local pro-consumer organizations. Promotes consumer interests in banking, credit, and insurance; telecommunications; housing; food, drugs, and medical care; safety; and energy and natural resources development.

Consumers Union of the United States, *Washington Office, 1101 17th St. N.W., #500 20036; (202) 462-6262. Fax, (202) 265-9548. Ellen Bloom, Director.*
Web, www.consumersunion.org

Consumer advocacy group that represents consumer interests before Congress and regulatory agencies and litigates consumer affairs cases involving the government. Interests include consumer impact of world trade. Publishes *Consumer Reports* magazine. (Headquarters in Yonkers, N.Y.)

Council of Better Business Bureaus, *4200 Wilson Blvd., #800, Arlington, VA 22203-1838; (703) 276-0100. Fax, (703) 525-8277. Steven J. Cole, President.*
Web, www.bbb.org

Membership: businesses and Better Business Bureaus in the United States and Canada. Promotes ethical business practices and truth in national advertising; mediates disputes between consumers and businesses.

National Consumers League, *1701 K St. N.W., #1200 20006; (202) 835-3323. Fax, (202) 835-0747. Sally Greenberg, Executive Director.*
General e-mail, info@nclnet.org
Web, www.nclnet.org

Advocacy group that engages in research and educational activities related to consumer and worker issues. Interests include fraud, privacy, child labor, and food and drug safety. Web resources include fieldsofhope.org, fraud.org, lifesmarts.org, sosrx.org, stopchildlabor.org, and phishinginfo.org.

Public Citizen, *1600 20th St. N.W. 20009; (202) 588-1000. Fax, (202) 588-7798. Joan Claybrook, President.*
General e-mail, pcmail@citizen.org
Web, www.citizen.org

Public interest consumer advocacy organization comprising the following programs: Congress Watch, Auto Safety Program, Health Research Group, Litigation Group, and Global Trade Watch.

Public Justice Foundation, *1825 K St. N.W., #200 20006; (202) 797-8600. Fax, (202) 232-7203. Arthur H. Bryant, Executive Director.*
General e-mail, publicjustice@publicjustice.net
Web, www.publicjustice.net

Membership: consumer activists, trial lawyers, and public interest lawyers. Litigates to influence corporate and government decisions about products or activities adversely affecting health or safety. Interests include toxic torts, environmental protection, civil rights and civil liberties, workers' safety, consumer protection, and the preservation of the civil justice system. (Formerly Trial Lawyers for Public Justice.)

SAFE KIDS Worldwide, *1301 Pennsylvania Ave. N.W., #1000 20004; (202) 662-0600. Fax, (202) 393-2072. Martin Eichelberger, Chair; Mitch Stoler, President. General e mail, communications@safekids.org*

Web, www.safekids.org

Promotes awareness among adults that unintentional injury is the leading cause of death among children ages fourteen and under. Conducts educational programs on childhood injury prevention; sponsors National SAFE KIDS Week. (Formerly the National SAFE KIDS Campaign.)

U.S. Chamber of Commerce, *Congressional and Public Affairs, 1615 H St. N.W. 20062-2000; (202) 463-5600. Fax, (202) 887-3430. Rolf T. Lundberg, Senior Vice President. Web, www.uschamber.com*

Monitors legislation and regulations regarding business and consumer issues, including legislation and policies affecting the Federal Trade Commission, the Consumer Product Safety Commission, and other agencies.

U.S. Public Interest Research Group, *Federal Advocacy, 218 D St. S.E. 20003; (202) 546-9707. Fax, (202) 546-2461. Gary Kolman, Director. General e-mail, uspirg@pirg.org*

Web, www.uspirg.org

Conducts research and advocacy on consumer and environmental issues, including telephone rates, banking practices, insurance, campaign finance reform, product safety, toxic and solid waste; monitors private and governmental actions affecting consumers; supports efforts to challenge consumer fraud and illegal business practices. Serves as national office for state groups.

Credit Practices

►AGENCIES

Comptroller of the Currency *(Treasury Dept.), Compliance Operations and Policy, 250 E St. S.W. 20219-0001; (202) 874-4428. Fax, (202) 874-5221. Ann Jaedicke, Deputy Comptroller. Web, www.occ.treas.gov*

Develops policy for enforcing consumer laws and regulations that affect national banks, including the Bank Secrecy (BSA/AML), Truth-in-Lending, Community Reinvestment, and Equal Credit Opportunity acts.

Comptroller of the Currency *(Treasury Dept.), Law Dept., 250 E St. S.W., 8th Floor 20219; (202) 874-5200. Fax, (202) 874-5374. Julie L. Williams, First Senior Deputy Comptroller and Chief Counsel. Library, (202) 874-4720. Web, www.occ.treas.gov*

Enforces and oversees compliance by nationally chartered banks with laws prohibiting discrimination in credit transactions on the basis of sex or marital status. Enforces regulations concerning bank advertising; may issue cease-and-desist orders.

Comptroller of the Currency *(Treasury Dept.), Public Affairs, 250 E St. S.W. 20219; (202) 874-4880. Fax, (202) 874-4950. John Walsh, Chief of Staff and Public Affairs. Web, www.occ.treas.gov or helpwithmybank.gov*

Advises the comptroller on relations with the media and the banking industry.

Federal Deposit Insurance Corp. (FDIC), *Compliance and Consumer Affairs, 550 17th St. N.W. 20429-9990; (202) 898-3911. Fax, (202) 898-3638. Robert Mooney, Deputy Director. Information, (877) ASK-FDIC. TTY, (800) 925-4618. General e-mail, consumer@fdic.gov*

Web, www.fdic.gov

Coordinates and monitors complaints filed by consumers against federally insured state banks that are not members of the Federal Reserve System; handles complaints concerning truth-in-lending and other fair credit provisions, including charges of discrimination on the basis of sex or marital status; responds to general banking inquiries; answers questions on deposit insurance coverage.

Federal Deposit Insurance Corp. (FDIC), *Division of Supervision and Consumer Protection, 550 17th St. N.W. 20429; (202) 898-6880. Fax, (202) 898-3638. Sandra L. Thompson, Director. Web, www.fdic.gov*

Examines and supervises federally insured state banks that are not members of the Federal Reserve System to ascertain their safety and soundness.

Federal Reserve System, *Consumer and Community Affairs, 1709 New York Ave. N.W. 20006; (202) 452-2631. Fax, (202) 872-4995. Sandra F. Braunstein, Director. Complaints, (888) 851-1920. Web, www.federalreserve.gov*

Receives consumer complaints concerning truth-in-lending, fair credit billing, equal credit opportunity, electronic fund transfer, home mortgage disclosure, consumer leasing, and advertising; receives complaints about unregulated practices; refers complaints to district banks. The Federal Reserve monitors enforcement of fair lending laws with regard to state-chartered banks that are members of the Federal Reserve System.

Federal Trade Commission (FTC), *Financial Practices, 601 New Jersey Ave. N.W. 20580; (202) 326-3224. Fax, (202) 326-3768. Peggy Twohig, Associate Director. Web, www.ftc.gov*

Challenges unfair or deceptive financial practices, including those involving lending, loan servicing, debt negotiation, and debt collection. Enforces specific consumer credit statutes, including the Fair Debt Collection Practices Act, Equal Credit Opportunity Act, Truth-in-Lending Act, Credit Repair Organization Act, Home Ownership and Equity Protection Act, Electronic Fund Transfer Act, Consumer Leasing Act, Holder-In-Due-Course Rule, and Credit Practices Rule.

Justice Dept. (DOJ), *Civil Division: Consumer Litigation,* 450 5th St. N.W., #6400 20001; (202) 307-0066. Fax, (202) 514-8742. Eugene M. Thirolf, Director.
Web, www.usdoj.gov

Files suits to enforce the Truth-in-Lending Act and other federal statutes protecting consumers, generally upon referral by client agencies.

National Credit Union Administration, *Examination and Insurance,* 1775 Duke St., Alexandria, VA 22314-3428; (703) 518-6300. Fax, (703) 518-6499. David M. Marquis, Director. Toll-free investment hotline, (800) 755-5999.
Web, www.ncua.gov

Oversees and enforces compliance by federally chartered credit unions with the Truth-in-Lending Act, the Equal Credit Opportunity Act, and other federal statutes protecting consumers.

Office of Thrift Supervision (OTS), *(Treasury Dept.), Examinations, Supervision, and Consumer Protection,* 1700 G St. N.W., 5th Floor 20552; (202) 906-5666. Fax, (202) 898-0230. Timothy T. Ward, Deputy Director. Consumer complaints, (800) 842-6929.
Web, www.ots.treas.gov

Prepares consumer protection regulations and compliance examination procedures. Coordinates a consumer complaint process that covers federal savings associations.

Small Business Administration (SBA), *Equal Employment Opportunity and Civil Rights Compliance,* 409 3rd St. S.W., #6800 20416; (202) 205-6751. Fax, (202) 205-7580. Margareth J. Bennett, Assistant Administrator. TTY, (202) 205-7150.
Web, www.sba.gov

Reviews complaints based on disability against the Small Business Administration by recipients of its assistance in cases of alleged discrimination in credit transactions; monitors recipients for civil rights compliance.

American Bankers Assn. (ABA), *Communications,* 1120 Connecticut Ave. N.W., 8th Floor 20036; (202) 663-5315. Fax, (202) 663-7578. Virginia Dean, Executive Director.
Web, www.aba.com

Provides information on a wide range of banking issues and financial management.

American Financial Services Assn. (AFSA), 919 18th St. N.W., #300 20006-5517; (202) 296-5544. Fax, (202) 223-0321. Christopher S. Stinebert, President.
General e-mail, afsa@afsamail.org
Web, www.afsaonline.org

Trade association for the consumer credit industry. Focus includes government relations and consumer education. Monitors legislation and regulations.

National Retail Federation, 325 7th St. N.W., #1100 20004-2802; (202) 783-7971. Fax, (202) 737-2849. Tracy Mullin, President.
Web, www.nrf.com

Membership: national and state associations of retailers and major retail corporations. Provides information on credit, truth-in-lending laws, and other fair credit practices.

Product Safety, Testing

Consumer Product Safety Commission (CPSC), 4330 East-West Hwy., #519, Bethesda, MD 20814; (301) 504-7908. Fax, (301) 504-0399. Nancy Nord, Chair (Acting); Patricia Semple, Executive Director. TTY, (800) 638-8270. Public Affairs, (301) 504-7908. Congressional Relations, (301) 504-7903. Product safety hotline, (800) 638-2772.
General e-mail, info@cpsc.gov
Web, www.cpsc.gov

Establishes and enforces product safety standards; collects data; studies the causes and prevention of product-related injuries; identifies hazardous products, including imports, and recalls them from the marketplace.

Consumer Product Safety Commission (CPSC), *Compliance and Field Operations,* 4330 East-West Hwy., #610, Bethesda, MD 20814; (301) 504-7520. Fax, (301) 504-0359. John Mullan, Assistant Executive Director; Marc Schoem, Deputy Director.
Web, www.cpsc.gov

Identifies and acts on any defective consumer product already in distribution; conducts surveillance and enforcement programs to ensure industry compliance with existing safety standards; works to ensure that products imported to the United States comply with existing safety standards; conducts enforcement litigation. Participates in developing standards to ensure that the final result is enforceable; monitors recall of defective products and issues warnings to consumers when appropriate.

Consumer Product Safety Commission (CPSC), *Engineering Sciences,* 4330 East-West Hwy., #611, Bethesda, MD 20814-4408; (301) 504-7918. Fax, (301) 504-0533. Hugh M. McLaurin, Associate Executive Director.
Web, www.cpsc.gov

Develops and evaluates consumer product safety standards, test methods, performance criteria, design specifications, and quality standards; conducts and evaluates engineering tests. Collects scientific and technical data to determine potential hazards of consumer products.

Consumer Product Safety Commission (CPSC), *Epidemiology,* 4330 East-West Hwy., Bethesda, MD 20814; (301) 504-7309. Fax, (301) 504-0038. Russell H. Roegner, Assistant Executive Director.
Web, www.cpsc.gov

Collects data on consumer product-related hazards and potential hazards; determines the frequency, severity, and distribution of the various types of injuries and investigates their causes; and assesses the effects of product safety standards and programs on consumer injuries. Conducts epidemiological studies and research in the fields of consumer-related injuries.

Consumer Product Safety Commission (CPSC), *Health Sciences,* 4330 East-West Hwy., #600, Bethesda, MD 20814-4408; (301) 504-7919. Fax, (301) 504-0079. Mary Ann Danello, Associate Executive Director.
Web, www.cpsc.gov

Evaluates potential health effects and hazards of consumer products and their foreseeable uses, and performs exposure and risk assessments for product-related hazards.

Consumer Product Safety Commission (CPSC), *Laboratory Sciences,* 10901 Darnestown Rd., Gaithersburg, MD 20878; (301) 424-6421. Fax, (301) 413-7107. Andrew Stadnik, Associate Executive Director.
Web, www.cpsc.gov

Conducts engineering analyses and testing of consumer products, supports the development of voluntary and mandatory standards, and supports the agency's compliance activities through product safety assessments.

National Injury Information Clearinghouse *(Consumer Product Safety Commission),* 4330 East-West Hwy., Bethesda, MD 20814-4408; (301) 504-7921. Fax, (301) 504-0025. Pamela McDonald, Senior Technical Information Specialist. TTY, (800) 638-8270. Alternate fax, (301) 504-0127. To report consumer product-related accidents or injuries, (800) 638-2772.
General e-mail, clearinghouse@cpsc.gov
Web, www.cpsc.gov

Analyzes types and frequency of injuries resulting from consumer and recreational products. Collects injury information from consumer complaints, investigations, coroners' reports, death certificates, newspaper clippings, and statistically selected hospital emergency rooms nationwide.

▶**NONGOVERNMENTAL**

American Academy of Pediatrics, *Washington Office,* 601 13th St. N.W., #400N 20005; (202) 347-8600. Fax, (202) 393-6137. Jackie Noyes, Director. Information, (800) 336-5475.
General e-mail, kidsdocs@aap.org
Web, www.aap.org

Promotes legislation and regulations concerning child health and safety. Committee on Injury and Poison Prevention drafts policy statements and publishes information on toy safety, poisons, and other issues that affect children and adolescents. (Headquarters in Elk Grove Village, Ill.)

Cosmetic Ingredient Review, 1101 17th St. N.W., #412 20036-4702; (202) 331-0651. Fax, (202) 331-0088. F. Alan Andersen, Director.

General e-mail, cirinfo@cir-safety.org
Web, www.cir-safety.org

Voluntary self-regulatory program funded by the Cosmetic, Toiletry, and Fragrance Assn. Reviews and evaluates published and unpublished data to assess the safety of cosmetic ingredients.

Tobacco

▶**AGENCIES**

Alcohol and Tobacco Tax and Trade Bureau (TTB), *(Treasury Dept.),* 1310 G St. N.W., #300E 20220; (202) 927-5000. Fax, (202) 927-5611. John J. Manfreda, Administrator. Press, (202) 927-8062.
Web, www.ttb.gov

Enforces and administers existing federal laws and tax code provisions relating to the production and taxation of alcohol and tobacco.

Centers for Disease Control and Prevention *(Health and Human Services Dept.),* **Smoking and Health Liaison,** 395 E St. S.W., #9100 20201; (202) 245-0600. Fax, (202) 245-0602. Simon McNabb, Team Leader.
Web, www.cdc.gov/tobacco

Produces and issues the surgeon general's annual report on smoking and health; conducts public information and education programs on smoking and health. Conducts epidemiological studies, surveys, and analyses on tobacco use. Serves as liaison between governmental and nongovernmental organizations that work on tobacco initiatives.

Federal Trade Commission (FTC), *Advertising Practices,* 601 New Jersey Ave. N.W., #3223 20001 (mailing address: 600 Pennsylvania Ave. N.W., Washington, DC 20580); (202) 326-3090. Fax, (202) 326-3259. Mary Engle, Associate Director.
Web, www.ftc.gov

Monitors advertising of tobacco products under the Federal Cigarette Labeling and Advertising Act and the Comprehensive Smokeless Tobacco Health Education Act. Regulates labeling and advertising of tobacco products; administers health warnings on packages; monitors and tests claims on tobacco products for validity. Works with the Justice Dept. in enforcing the ban on tobacco advertising in the broadcast media; monitors deceptive claims and violations of laws and may refer violations to the Justice Dept. for criminal prosecution.

▶**NONGOVERNMENTAL**

Action on Smoking and Health (ASH), 2013 H St. N.W. 20006; (202) 659-4310. Fax, (202) 833-3921. John F. Banzhaf III, Executive Director.
General e-mail, vd@ash.org
Web, www.ash.org

Educational and legal organization that works to protect nonsmokers from cigarette smoking; provides information about smoking hazards and nonsmokers' rights.

Bakery, Confectionery, Tobacco Workers, and Grain Millers International Union, *10401 Connecticut Ave., Kensington, MD 20895-3940; (301) 933-8600. Fax, (301) 946-8452. Frank Hurt, President.*
Web, www.bctgm.org

Membership: approximately 120,000 workers from the bakery, confectionery, grain miller, and tobacco industries. Helps members negotiate pay, benefits, and better working conditions; conducts training programs and workshops. Monitors legislation and regulations. (Affiliated with the AFL-CIO.)

National Center for Tobacco-Free Kids, *1400 Eye St. N.W., #1200 20005; (202) 296-5469. Fax, (202) 296-5427. Matthew Myers, President. Information, (800) 803-7178.*
Web, www.tobaccofreekids.org

Seeks to reduce tobacco use by children through public policy change and educational programs. Provides technical assistance to state and local programs.

FINANCE AND INVESTMENTS

Banking

▶**AGENCIES**

Antitrust Division *(Justice Dept.), Networks and Technology Enforcement, 600 E St. N.W., #9500 20530; (202) 307-6200. Fax, (202) 616-8544. James J. Tierney, Chief.*
Web, www.usdoj.gov/atr

Investigates and litigates certain antitrust cases involving financial institutions, including securities, commodity futures, computer software, and insurance; participates in agency proceedings and rulemaking in these areas; monitors and analyzes legislation.

Comptroller of the Currency *(Treasury Dept.), 250 E St. S.W. 20219; (202) 874-5000. Fax, (202) 874-4950. John C. Dugan, Comptroller. Library, (202) 874-4720. Press, (202) 874-5770.*
Web, www.occ.treas.gov

Regulates and examines operations of national banks; establishes guidelines for bank examinations; handles mergers of national banks with regard to antitrust law. Library open to the public.

Comptroller of the Currency *(Treasury Dept.), Licensing, 250 E St. S.W. 20219; (202) 874-5060. Fax, (202) 874-5293. Lawrence E. Beard, Deputy Comptroller. Library, (202) 874-4720.*
Web, www.occ.treas.gov

Advises the comptroller on policy matters and programs related to bank corporate activities and is the primary decision maker on national bank corporate applications, including charters, mergers and acquisitions, conversions, and operating subsidiaries.

Federal Deposit Insurance Corp. (FDIC), *550 17th St. N.W. 20429; (202) 898-6974. Fax, (202) 898-3500. Sheila C. Bair, Chair; Martin J. Gruenberg, Vice Chair. Information, (877) 275-3342. Library, (202) 898-3631. Press, (202) 898-6993.*
Web, www.fdic.gov

Insures deposits in national banks and state banks. Conducts examinations of insured state banks that are not members of the Federal Reserve System.

Federal Deposit Insurance Corp. (FDIC), *Division of Supervision and Consumer Protection, 550 17th St. N.W. 20429; (202) 898-6880. Fax, (202) 898-3638. Sandra L. Thompson, Director.*
Web, www.fdic.gov

Serves as the federal regulator and supervisor of insured state banks that are not members of the Federal Reserve System. Conducts regular examinations and investigations of banks under the jurisdiction of FDIC; advises bank managers on improving policies and practices. Administers the Bank Insurance Fund, which insures deposits in commercial and savings banks, and the Savings Assn. Insurance Fund, which insures deposits in savings and loan institutions.

Federal Deposit Insurance Corp. (FDIC), *Ombudsman, 550 17th St. N.W. 20429; (703) 562-6040. Fax, (703) 562-6057. Cottrell L. Webster, Director. TTY, (800) 925-4618.*
Web, www.fdic.gov

An independent, neutral, and confidential source of assistance for the public. Provides answers to the public in the areas of depositor concerns, loan questions, asset information, bank closing issues, and any FDIC regulation or policy.

Federal Deposit Insurance Corp. (FDIC), *Resolutions and Receiverships, 1776 F St. N.W. 20429 (mailing address: 550 17th St. N.W., Washington, DC 20429); (202) 898-6525. Fax, (202) 898-6528. Mitchell Glassman, Director.*
Web, www.fdic.gov

Plans, executes, and monitors the orderly and least cost resolution of failing FDIC-insured institutions. Manages remaining liability of the federal savings and deposit insurance funds.

Federal Reserve System, *Banking Supervision and Regulation, 20th St. and Constitution Ave. N.W. 20551; (202) 452-2773. Fax, (202) 452-2770. Roger T. Cole, Director, (202) 452-2618.*
Web, www.federalreserve.gov

Supervises and regulates state banks that are members of the Federal Reserve System; supervises and inspects all bank holding companies; monitors banking practices;

Federal Deposit Insurance Corporation

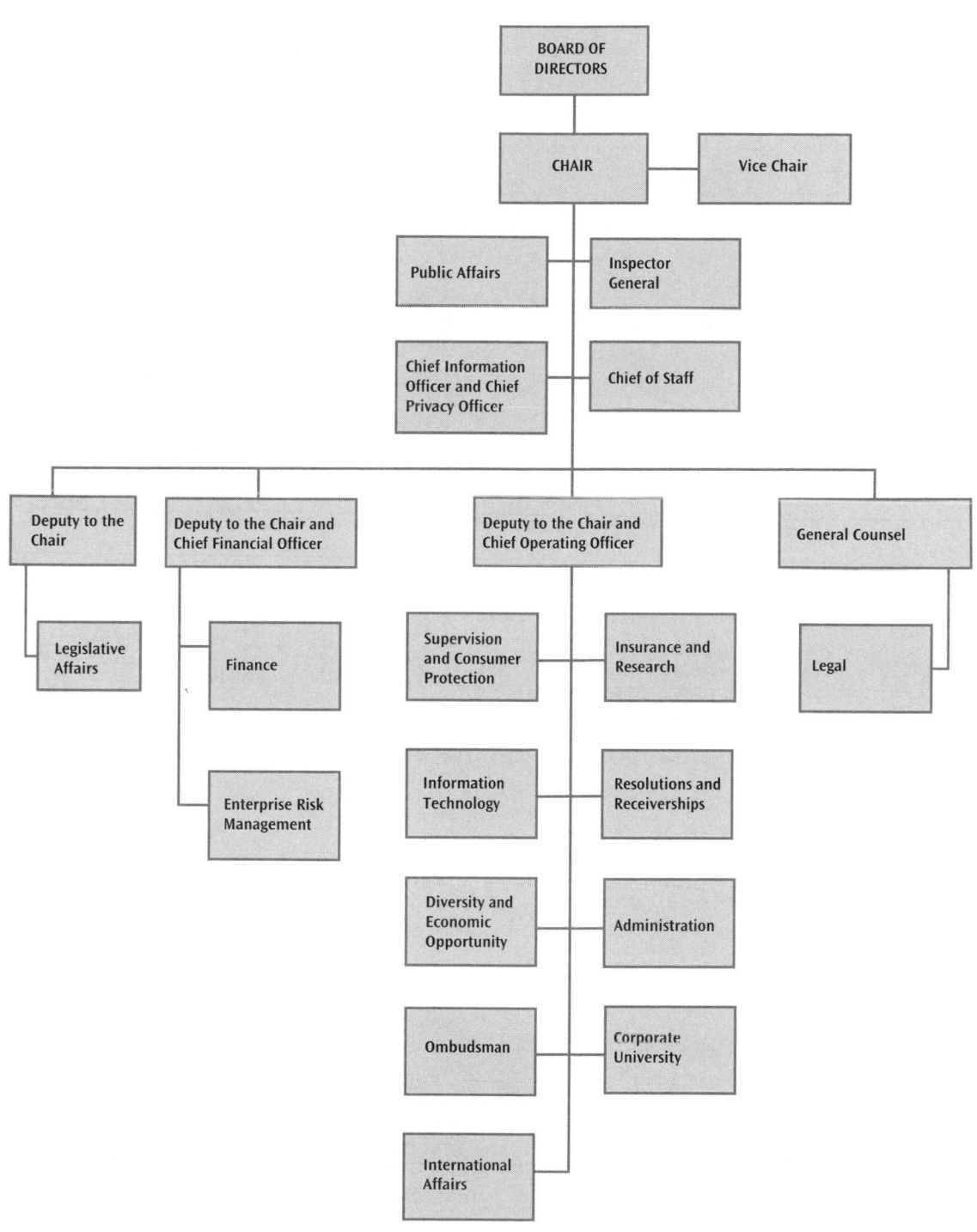

Federal Reserve System

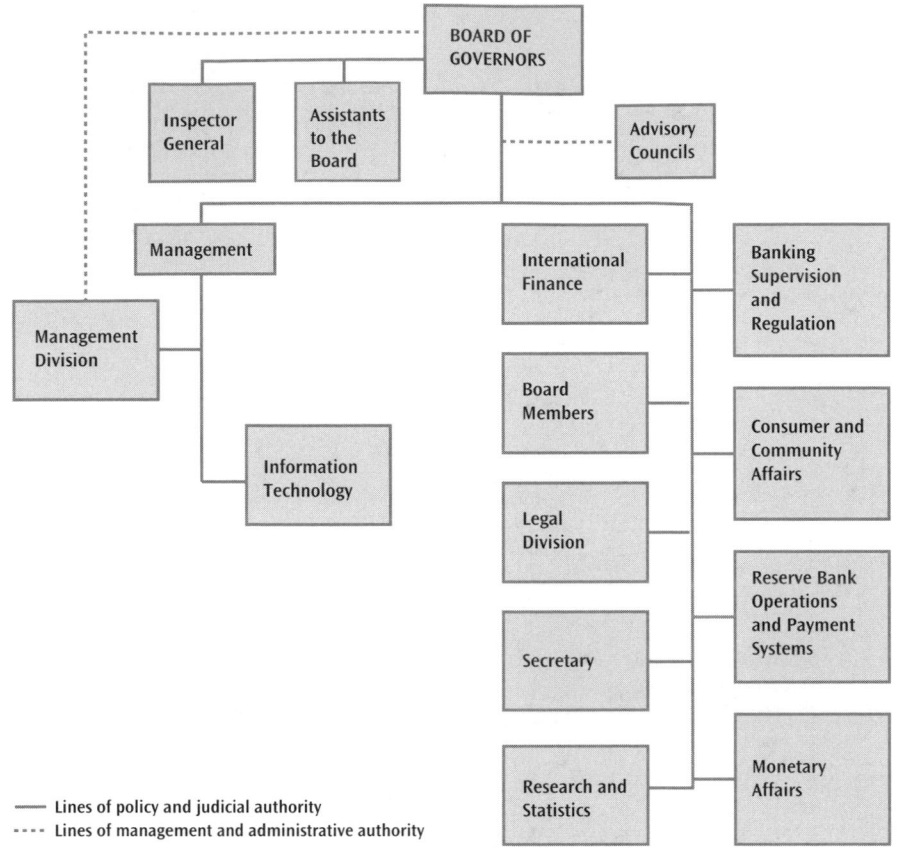

— Lines of policy and judicial authority
---- Lines of management and administrative authority

approves bank mergers, consolidations, and other changes in bank structure.

Federal Reserve System, *Board of Governors,* 20th and C Sts. N.W., #B2046 20551 (mailing address: 20th St. and Constitution Ave. N.W., Washington, DC 20551); (202) 452-3201. Fax, (202) 452-3819. Ben S. Bernanke, Chair; Donald L. Kohn, Vice Chair. Information, (202) 452-3204. Public Affairs, (202) 452-2955. Congressional Liaison, (202) 452-3003. Locator, (202) 452-3204. Publications, (202) 452-3245.
Web, www.federalreserve.gov

Serves as the central bank and fiscal agent for the government. Examines Federal Reserve banks and state member banks; supervises bank holding companies. Controls wire system transfer operations and supplies currency for depository institutions.

Federal Reserve System, *Reserve Bank Operations and Payment Systems,* 20th and C Sts. N.W., MS 195 20551; (202) 452-3963. Fax, (202) 452-2509. Dorothy LaChapelle, Associate Director.
Web, www.federalreserve.gov

Monitors budgets of Federal Reserve banks.

National Credit Union Administration, *1775 Duke St., Alexandria, VA 22314-3428; (703) 518-6300. Fax, (703) 518-6319. JoAnn Johnson, Chair. Information, (703) 518-6330. Electronic bulletin board, (703) 518-6480.*
Web, www.ncua.gov

Regulates all federally chartered credit unions; charters new credit unions; supervises and examines federal credit unions and insures their member accounts up to $100,000. Insures state-chartered credit unions that apply and are eligible. Manages the Central Liquidity Facility, which supplies emergency short-term loans to members. Conducts research on economic trends and their effect on credit unions and advises the administration's board on economic and financial policy and regulations.

Office of Management and Budget (OMB), *(Executive Office of the President), Housing, Treasury, and Commerce,* New Executive Office Bldg., #9201 20503; (202) 395-4516. Fax, (202) 395-6889. Mark Weatherly, Chief. Press, (202) 395-7254.
Web, www.whitehouse.gov/omb

Monitors the financial condition of deposit insurance funds including the Bank Insurance Fund, the Savings Assn. Insurance Fund, and the Federal Savings and Loan

Insurance Corp. (FSLIC) Resolution Fund. Monitors the Securities and Exchange Commission. Has limited oversight over the Federal Housing Finance Board and the Federal Home Loan Bank System.

Office of Thrift Supervision (OTS), *(Treasury Dept.),* *1700 G St. N.W. 20552; (202) 906-6590. Fax, (202) 898-0230. John M. Reich, Director. Information, (202) 906-6000. Library, (202) 906-6470. Press, (202) 906-6288.*
Web, www.ots.treas.gov

Charters, regulates, and examines the operations of savings and loan institutions. Library open to the public.

Securities and Exchange Commission, *Corporation Finance, 100 F St. N.E. 20549; (202) 551-3100. Fax, (202) 772-9215. John White, Director. Information, (202) 551-3000.*
Web, www.sec.gov

Receives and examines disclosure statements and other information from publicly held companies, including bank holding companies.

Securities and Exchange Commission, *Economic Analysis, 100 F St. N.E., #9461 20549; (202) 551-6600. Fax, (202) 772-9290. James A. Overdahl, Chief Economist. Information, (202) 942-8088.*
Web, www.sec.gov

Provides the commission with economic analyses of proposed rule and policy changes and other information to guide the SEC in influencing capital markets. Evaluates the effect of policy and other factors on competition within the securities industry and among competing securities markets; compiles financial statistics on capital formation and the securities industry.

Treasury Dept., *Financial Institutions, 1500 Pennsylvania Ave. N.W., #2326 20220; (202) 622-2610. Fax, (202) 622-2027. David G. Nason, Assistant Secretary.*
Web, www.ustreas.gov

Advises the under secretary for domestic finance and the Treasury secretary on financial institutions, banks, and thrifts.

►**CONGRESS**

For a listing of relevant congressional committees and subcommittees, please see page 32 or the Appendix.

►**NONGOVERNMENTAL**

American Bankers Assn. (ABA), *1120 Connecticut Ave. N.W. 20036; (202) 663-5000. Fax, (202) 663-7533. Edward Yingling, President. Information, (800) BANKERS.*
General e-mail, custserv@aba.com
Web, www.aba.com

Membership: commercial banks. Operates schools to train banking personnel; conducts conferences; formulates government relations policies for the banking community.

American Council of State Savings Supervisors, *P.O. Box 1904, Leesburg, VA 20177-1904; (703) 669-5440. Fax, (703) 669-5441. Andrea M. Falzarano, Executive Director.*
Web, www.acsss.org

Membership: supervisors and regulators of state-chartered savings associations; associate members include state-chartered savings associations and state savings banks. Monitors legislation and regulations affecting the state-chartered thrift industry.

American Institute of Certified Public Accountants, *Washington Office, 1455 Pennsylvania Ave. N.W., 10th Floor 20004-1081; (202) 737-6600. Fax, (202) 638-4512. Mark Peterson, Vice President of Congressional and Public Affairs. Press, (202) 434-9213.*
Web, www.aicpa.org

Establishes voluntary professional and ethical regulations for the profession; sponsors conferences and training workshops. Answers technical auditing and accounting questions. (Headquarters in New York.)

Assn. for Financial Professionals, *4520 East-West Hwy., #750, Bethesda, MD 20814; (301) 907-2862. Fax, (301) 907-2864. James A. Kaitz, President.*
Web, www.afponline.org

Membership: more than 16,000 members from a wide range of industries throughout all stages of their careers in various aspects of treasury and financial management. Acts as a resource for continuing education, financial tools and publications, career development, certifications, research, representation to legislators and regulators, and the development of industry standards.

Bankers' Assn. for Finance and Trade, *1120 Connecticut Ave. N.W., 3rd Floor 20036-3902; (202) 663-7575. Fax, (202) 663-5538. Rebecca Morter, Executive Director.*
General e-mail, baft@aba.com
Web, www.baft.org

Membership: U.S. commercial banks with major international operations; foreign banks with U.S. operations are affiliated as nonvoting members. Monitors activities that affect the operation of U.S. commercial and international banks and nonfinancial companies.

Center on Federal Financial Institutions, *1717 K St. N.W., #600 20036; (202) 347-5770. Fax, (202) 347-5771. Douglas J. Elliott, President.*
General e-mail, info@coffi.org
Web, www.coffi.org

Nonpartisan think tank that promotes effectiveness and efficiency in the federal government's lending and insurance activities.

Conference of State Bank Supervisors, *1155 Connecticut Ave. N.W., #500 20036-4306; (202) 296-2840. Fax, (202) 296-1928. Neil Milner, President.*
Web, www.csbs.org

Membership: state officials responsible for supervision of state-chartered banking institutions. Conducts educational programs. Monitors legislation.

Consumer Bankers Assn., *1000 Wilson Blvd., #2500, Arlington, VA 22209-3912; (703) 276-1750. Fax, (703) 528-1290. Jim Ead, President.*
Web, www.cbanet.org

Membership: federally insured financial institutions. Provides information on retail banking, including industry trends. Operates the Graduate School of Retail Bank Management to train banking personnel; conducts research and analysis on retail banking trends; sponsors conferences.

Consumer Data Industry Assn., *1090 Vermont Ave. N.W., #200 20005-4905; (202) 371-0910. Fax, (202) 371-0134. Stuart Pratt, President. Press, (202) 408-7406.*
Web, www.cdiaonline.org

Membership: credit reporting, mortgage reporting, and collection service companies. Provides information about credit rights to consumers. Monitors legislation and regulations. (Formerly Associated Credit Bureaus.)

Credit Union National Assn., *Washington Office, 601 Pennsylvania Ave. N.W., South Bldg., #600 20004-2601; (202) 638-5777. Fax, (202) 638-7734. Daniel A. Mica, President.*
Web, www.cuna.org

Confederation of credit unions from every state, the District of Columbia, and Puerto Rico. Represents federal and state chartered credit unions. Monitors legislation and regulations. (Headquarters in Madison, Wis.)

Electronic Funds Transfer Assn., *11350 Random Hills Rd., #800, Fairfax, VA 22030; (703) 934-6052. Fax, (703) 934-6058. Kurt Helwig, President.*
Web, www.efta.org

Membership: financial institutions, electronic funds transfer hardware and software providers, automatic teller machine networks, and others engaged in electronic commerce. Promotes electronic payments and commerce technologies; sponsors industry analysis. Monitors legislation and regulations.

Employment Benefits Research Institute, *American Savings Education Council, 1100 13th St. N.W., #878 20005; (202) 659-0670. Fax, (202) 775-6312. Ken McDonnell, Program Associate.*
Web, www.asec.org

Seeks to raise public awareness about long-term personal financial independence and encourage retirement savings.

Financial Services Roundtable, *1001 Pennsylvania Ave., N.W., #500 South 20004; (202) 289-4322. Fax, (202) 628-2507. Richard Whiting, Executive Director.*
General e-mail, info@fsround.org
Web, www.fsround.org

Membership: one hundred integrated financial services companies. Provides banking, insurance, investment products, and services to American consumers.

Independent Community Bankers of America, *1615 L St. N.W., #900 20036; (202) 659-8111. Fax, (202) 659-9216. Camden Fine, President. Information, (800) 422-8439.*
General e-mail, info@icba.org
Web, www.icba.org

Membership: medium-sized and smaller community banks. Interests include farm credit, deregulation, interstate banking, deposit insurance, and financial industry standards.

Mortgage Bankers Assn., *1331 L St. N.W. 20005; (202) 557-2700. Fax, (202) 721-0249. John Courson, President. Alternate fax, (202) 721-0167.*
Web, www.mbaa.org

Membership: institutions involved in real estate finance. Maintains School of Mortgage Banking and sponsors educational seminars; collects statistics on the industry.

NACHA–The Electronic Payments Assn., *13450 Sunrise Valley Dr., #100, Herndon, VA 20171; (703) 561-1100. Fax, (703) 787-0996. Jan Estep, President.*
General e-mail, info@nacha.org
Web, www.nacha.org

Membership: financial institutions involved in the ACH payment system. Promotes the use of electronic solutions for payment systems. Develops operating rules and business practices in the areas of Internet commerce, electronic bill and invoice presentment and payment, e-checks, financial electronic data interchange, international payments, and electronic benefits services. Sponsors workshops and seminars. (Formerly the National Automated Clearing House Assn.)

National Assn. of Federal Credit Unions (NAFCU), *3138 10th St. North, Arlington, VA 22201-2149; (703) 522-4770. Fax, (703) 524-1082. Fred Becker, President.*
Web, www.nafcu.org

Membership: federally chartered credit unions. Represents interests of federal credit unions before Congress and regulatory agencies and provides legislative alerts for its members. Sponsors educational meetings focusing on current financial trends, changes in legislation and regulations, and management techniques.

National Assn. of State Credit Union Supervisors, *1655 N. Fort Myer Dr., #300, Arlington, VA 22209; (703) 528-8351. Fax, (703) 528-3248. Mary Martha Fortney, President.*
General e-mail, offices@nascus.org
Web, www.nascus.org

Membership: state credit union supervisors, state-chartered credit unions, and credit union leagues. Interests include state regulatory systems; conducts educational programs for examiners.

National Bankers Assn., *1513 P St. N.W. 20005; (202) 588-5432. Fax, (202) 588-5443. Michael Grant, President. Web, www.nationalbankers.org*

Membership: minority- and women-owned financial institutions. Monitors legislation and regulations.

National Society of Accountants, *1010 N. Fairfax St., Alexandria, VA 22314-1574; (703) 549-6400. Fax, (703) 549-2984. John G. Ams, Executive Vice President. Toll-free, (800) 966-6679.*

General e-mail, members@nsacct.org

Web, www.nsacct.org

Seeks to improve the accounting profession and to enhance the status of individual practitioners. Sponsors seminars and correspondence courses on accounting, auditing, business law, and estate planning; monitors legislation and regulations affecting accountants and their small-business clients.

Transparency International USA, *1023 15th St. N.W., #300 20005; (202) 589-1616. Fax, (202) 589-1512. Nancy Boswell, President.*

General e-mail, administration@transparency-usa.org

Web, www.transparency-usa.org

Seeks to prevent corruption in international transactions. Promotes reform through effective anti-corruption laws and policies. (Headquarters in Berlin.)

Stocks, Bonds, and Securities

►AGENCIES

Bureau of the Public Debt *(Treasury Dept.),* **Public and Legislative Affairs,** *799 9th St. N.W., 9th Floor 20239; (202) 504-3535. Fax, (202) 504-3634. Kim Treat, Director.*

Web, www.treasurydirect.gov

Plans, develops, and implements communication regarding treasury securities.

Federal Reserve System, *Board of Governors, 20th and C Sts. N.W., #B2046 20551 (mailing address: 20th St. and Constitution Ave. N.W., Washington, DC 20551); (202) 452-3201. Fax, (202) 452-3819. Ben S. Bernanke, Chair; Donald L. Kohn, Vice Chair. Information, (202) 452-3204. Public Affairs, (202) 452-2955. Congressional Liaison, (202) 452-3003. Locator, (202) 452-3204. Publications, (202) 452-3245. Web, www.federalreserve.gov*

Regulates amount of credit that may be extended and maintained on certain securities in order to prevent excessive use of credit for purchase or carrying of securities.

Securities and Exchange Commission, *100 F St. N.E. 20549; (202) 551-2100. Fax, (202) 772-9200. Mary Schapiro, Chair; Diego Ruiz, Executive Director, (202) 551-4300. Press, (202) 551-4120. Investor Education and Advocacy, (202) 551-6500. Locator, (202) 551-7500. Legislative and Intergovernmental Affairs, (202) 551-2010. Web, www.sec.gov*

Requires public disclosure of financial and other information about companies whose securities are offered for public sale, traded on exchanges, or traded over the counter; issues and enforces regulations to prevent fraud in securities markets and investigates securities frauds and violations; supervises operations of stock exchanges and activities of securities dealers, investment advisers, and investment companies; regulates purchase and sale of securities, properties, and other assets of public utility holding companies and their subsidiaries; participates in bankruptcy proceedings involving publicly held companies; has some jurisdiction over municipal securities trading. Public Reference Section makes available corporation reports and statements filed with the SEC. The information is available via the Web (www.sec.gov/edgar.shtml).

Securities and Exchange Commission, *Economic Analysis, 100 F St. N.E., #9461 20549; (202) 551-6600. Fax, (202) 772-9290. James A. Overdahl, Chief Economist. Information, (202) 942-8088.*

Web, www.sec.gov

Provides the commission with economic analyses of proposed rule and policy changes and other information to guide the SEC in influencing capital markets. Evaluates the effect of policy and other factors on competition within the securities industry and among competing securities markets; compiles financial statistics on capital formation and the securities industry.

Securities and Exchange Commission, *Trading and Markets, 100 F St. N.E. 20549; (202) 551-5500. Fax, (202) 772-9273. Erik R. Sirri, Director; Daniel M. Gallagher Jr., Deputy Director. Library, (202) 551-5450.*

Web, www.sec.gov

Oversees and regulates the operations of securities markets, brokers, dealers, and transfer agents. Promotes the establishment of a national system for clearing and settling securities transactions. Works for standards among and oversees self-regulatory organizations, such as national securities exchanges, registered clearing agencies, and the National Assn. of Securities Dealers. Facilitates the development of a national market system.

Treasury Dept., *Financial Institutions Policy, 1500 Pennsylvania Ave. N.W., 1418 Main Treasury 20220; (202) 622-2730. Fax, (202) 622-0256. Mario Ugoletti, Director.*

Web, www.ustreas.gov

Coordinates department efforts on all legislation affecting financial institutions and the government agencies that regulate them. Develops department policy on all matters relating to agencies responsible for supervising financial institutions and financial markets.

Securities and Exchange Commission

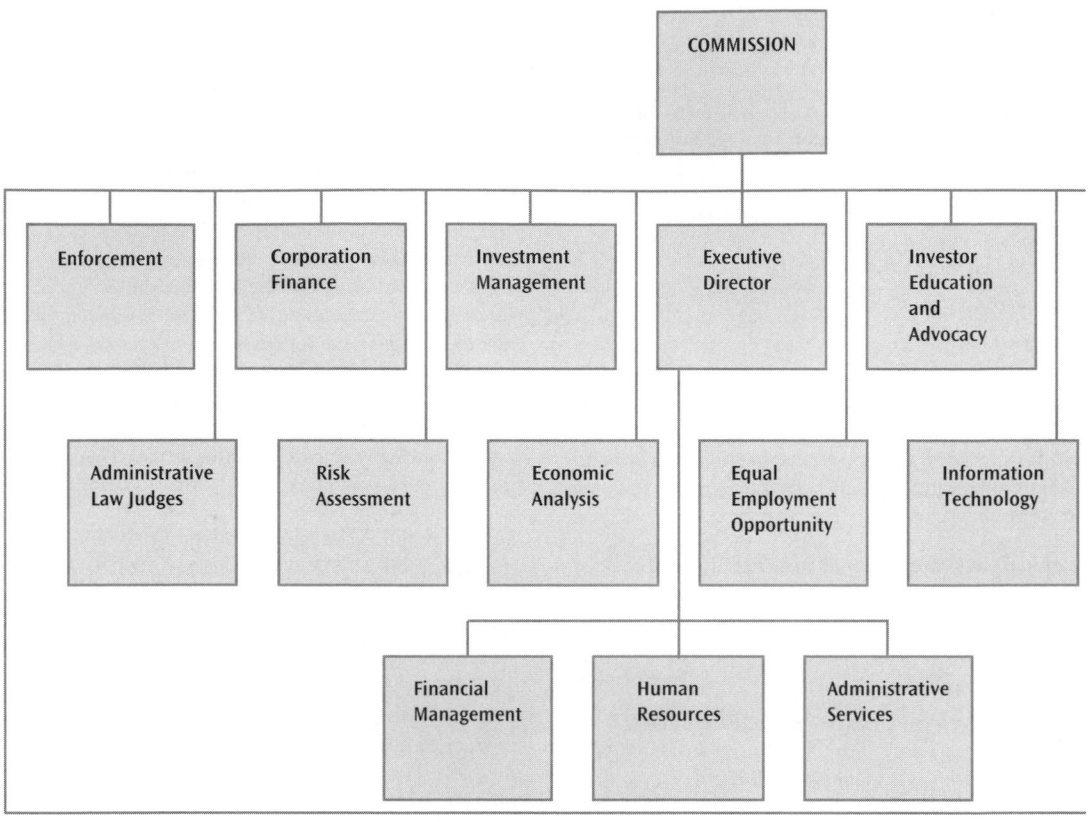

Council of Institutional Investors, *888 17th St. N.W., #500 20006; (202) 822-0800. Fax, (202) 822-0801. Ann Yerger, Executive Director.*

Web, www.cii.org

Membership: public, union, and corporate pension funds. Studies investment issues that affect pension plan assets. Focuses on corporate governance. Monitors legislation and regulations.

Financial Industry Regulation Authority (FINRA),

1735 K St. N.W. 20006-1506; (202) 728-8000. Fax, (202) 728-8075. Mary Shapiro, Chair. Member services, (301) 590-6500. Public disclosure, (800) 289-9999.

Web, www.finra.org

Membership: investment brokers and dealers authorized to conduct transactions of the investment banking and securities business under federal and state laws. Serves as the self-regulatory mechanism in the over-the-counter securities market. Operates speakers bureau. (Formerly the National Assn. of Securities Dealers.)

Futures Industry Assn., *2001 Pennsylvania Ave. N.W., #600 20006; (202) 466-5460. Fax, (202) 296-3184. John M. Damgard, President.*

General e-mail, info@futuresindustry.org

Web, www.futuresindustry.org

Membership: commodity futures brokerage firms and others interested in commodity futures. Serves as a forum for discussion of futures industry; provides market information and statistical data; offers educational programs; works to establish professional and ethical standards for members.

Investment Company Institute, *1401 H St. N.W., 12th Floor 20005-2148; (202) 326-5800. Fax, (202) 326-5899. Paul Schott Stevens, President.*

Web, www.ici.org

Membership: mutual funds and closed-end funds registered under the Investment Company Act of 1940 (including investment advisers to and underwriters of such companies) and the unit investment trust industry. Conducts research and disseminates information on issues affecting mutual funds.

Securities and Exchange Commission

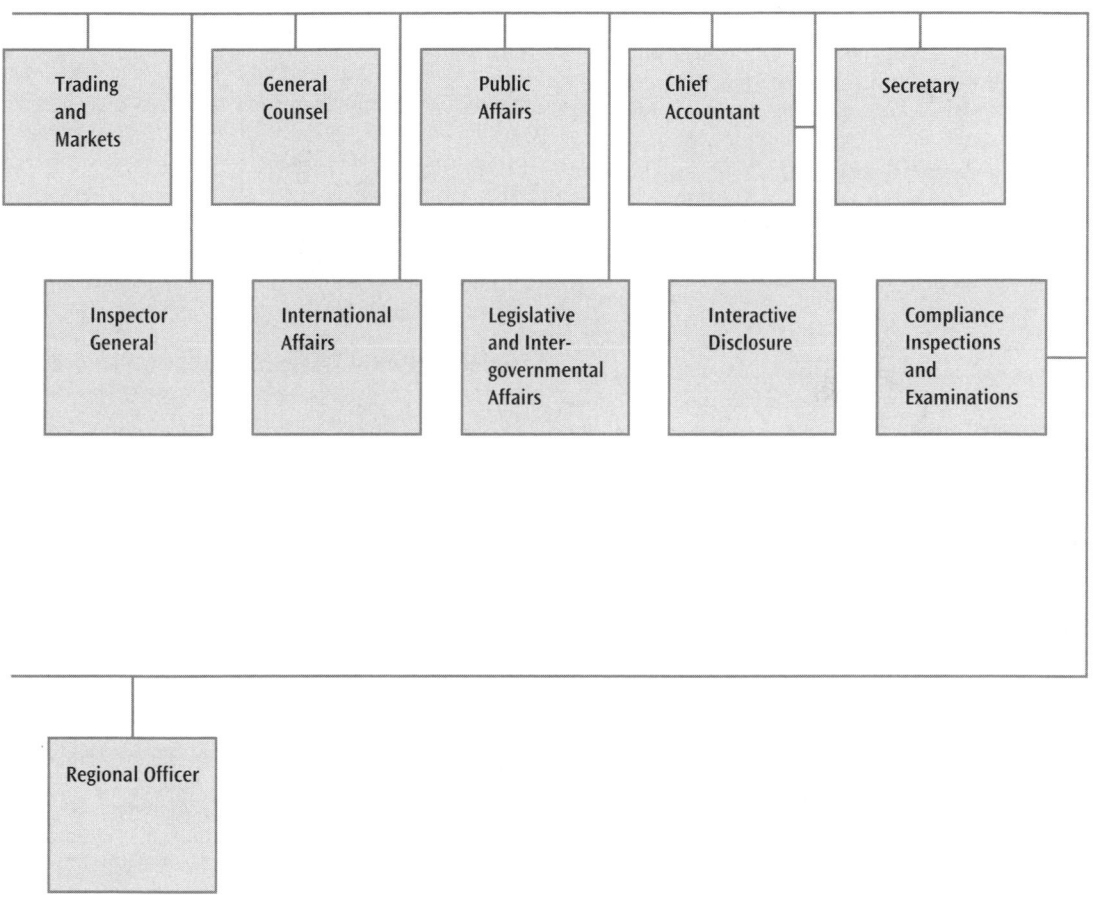

Investor Protection Trust, *919 18th St. N.W., #300 20006-5517; (202) 775-2111. Don M. Blandin, President. General e-mail, info@investorprotection.org*

Web, www.investorprotection.org

Provides noncommercial investment information to consumers to help them make informed investment decisions. Serves as an independent source of noncommercial investor education materials. Operates programs under its own auspices and uses grants to underwrite important initiatives carried out by other organizations.

Municipal Securities Rulemaking Board, *1900 Duke St., #600, Alexandria, VA 22314; (703) 797-6600. Fax, (703) 797-6700. Lynnette Kelly Hotchkiss, Executive Director.*

Web, www.msrb.org

Writes rules, subject to approval by the Securities and Exchange Commission, applicable to municipal securities brokers and dealers, in such areas as conduct, industry practices, and professional qualifications. Serves as a self-regulatory agency for the municipal securities industry.

National Assn. of Bond Lawyers, *Governmental Affairs, Washington Office,* *601 13th St., #800-S 20005-3875; (202) 682-1498. Fax, (202) 637-0217. Victoria Rostow, Director.*

General e-mail, governmentalaffairs@nabl.org

Web, www.nabl.org

Membership: municipal finance lawyers. Provides members with information on laws relating to the borrowing of money by states and municipalities and to the issuance of state and local government bonds. Monitors legislation and regulations. (Headquarters in Chicago, Ill.)

National Assn. of Real Estate Investment Trusts, *1875 Eye St. N.W., #600 20006-5413; (202) 739-9400. Fax, (202) 739-9401. Steven Wechsler, President.*
Web, www.reit.com

Membership: real estate investment trusts and corporations, partnerships, and individuals interested in real estate securities and the industry. Monitors federal and state legislation, federal taxation, securities regulation, standards and ethics, and housing and education; compiles industry statistics.

National Investor Relations Institute, *8020 Towers Crescent Dr., #250, Vienna, VA 22182; (703) 506-3570. Fax, (703) 506-3571. Jeffrey D. Morgan, President.*
Web, www.niri.org

Membership: executives engaged in investor relations and financial communications. Provides publications, educational training sessions, and research on investor relations for members; offers conferences and workshops; maintains job placement and referral services for members.

New York Stock Exchange, *Washington Office,* *801 Pennsylvania Ave. N.W., #630 20004-2685; (202) 347-4300. Fax, (202) 347-4370. Linda Dallas Rich, Senior Vice President.*
Web, www.nyse.com

Provides limited information on operations of the New York Stock Exchange; Washington office monitors legislation and regulations. (Headquarters in New York.)

North American Securities Administrators Assn., *750 1st St. N.E., #1140 20002; (202) 737-0900. Fax, (202) 783-3571. Russel Iuculano, Deputy Executive Director.*
Web, www.nasaa.org

Membership: state, provincial, and territorial securities administrators of the United States, Canada, and Mexico. Serves as the national representative of the state agencies responsible for investor protection. Works to prevent fraud in securities markets and provides a national forum to increase the efficiency and uniformity of state regulation of capital markets. Operates the Central Registration Depository, a nationwide computer link for agent registration and transfers, in conjunction with the National Assn. of Securities Dealers. Monitors legislation and regulations.

Public Company Accounting Oversight Board, *1666 K St. N.W. 20006-2803; (202) 207-9100. Fax, (202) 862-8430. Mark Olson, Chair.*
General e-mail, info@pcaobus.org
Web, www.pcaobus.org

Oversees the auditors of public companies in order to protect the interests of investors and the public.

Securities Industry and Financial Markets Assn. (SIFMA), *Washington Office, 1101 New York Ave. N.W., 8th Floor 20005; (202) 962-7300. Fax, (202) 962-7305. Timothy Ryan Jr., Chief Executive Officer.*
Web, www.sifma.org

Represents a variety of firms in all financial markets globally. Focuses on enhancing the public's trust in markets. Provides educational resources for professionals and investors in the industry. (Headquarters in New York. Merger of the Securities Industry Assn. and the Bond Market Assn.)

Securities Investor Protection Corp., *805 15th St. N.W., #800 20005-2215; (202) 371-8300. Fax, (202) 371-6728. Armando J. Bucelo Jr., Chair.*
Web, www.sipc.org

Private corporation established by Congress to administer the Securities Investor Protection Act. Provides financial protection for customers of member broker-dealers that fail financially.

Social Investment Forum, *910 17th St. N.W., #1000 20006; (202) 872-5361. Fax, (202) 775-8686. Lisa Woll, Chief Executive Officer.*
Web, www.socialinvest.org

Membership association promoting the concept, practice, and growth of socially responsible investing. Provides education and networking opportunities for members; conducts research into the outcomes of socially and environmentally conscious investments.

Tangible Assets

▶**AGENCIES**

Census Bureau *(Commerce Dept.), Manufacturing and Construction: Construction and Minerals, 4700 Silver Hill Rd., #7K044D 20233; (301) 763-4680. Fax, (301) 763-8398. Mary Susan Bucci, Chief.*
Web, www.census.gov/mcd

Collects, tabulates, and publishes statistics for the mining and construction sectors of the Economic Census; collects and tabulates data for the Manufacturing Energy Consumption Survey for the Energy Dept. concerning combustible and non-combustible energy sources for the U.S. manufacturing sector.

Commodity Futures Trading Commission, *3 Lafayette Center, 1155 21st St. N.W., 20581-0001; (202) 418-5000. Fax, (202) 418-5533. Michael Dunn, Chair (Acting); Madge A. Bolinger, Executive Director. Information, (202) 418-5000. Library, (202) 418-5255.*
Web, www.cftc.gov

Enforces federal statutes relating to commodity futures and options, including gold and silver futures and options. Monitors and regulates gold and silver leverage contracts, which provide for deferred delivery of the commodity and the payment of an agreed portion of the purchase price on margin.

Defense Logistics Agency *(Defense Dept.), Defense National Stockpile Center, 8725 John Jay Kingman Rd., #3229, Fort Belvoir, VA 22060-6223; (703) 767-5500. Fax, (703) 767-3316. Cornel A. Holder, Administrator.*
Web, www.dnsc.dla.mil

Manages the national defense stockpile of strategic and critical materials. Purchases strategic materials, including beryllium and newly developed high-tech alloys. Disposes of excess materials, including tin, silver, industrial diamond stones, tungsten, and vegetable tannin.

U.S. Geological Survey (USGS), *(Interior Dept.), Metals, 12201 Sunrise Valley Dr., MS 989, Reston, VA 20192-0002; (703) 648-4976. Fax, (703) 648-7757. Scott F. Sibley, Chief.*
Web, http://minerals.usgs.gov/minerals

Collects, analyzes, and disseminates information on ferrous and non-ferrous metals, including gold, silver, platinum group metals, iron, iron ore, steel, chromium, and nickel.

U.S. Mint *(Treasury Dept.), 801 9th St. N.W., 8th Floor 20220; (202) 354-7200. Fax, (202) 756-6200. Edmund C. Moy, Director. Information, (202) 354-7227. TTY, (202) 354-7600.*
Web, www.usmint.gov

Produces and distributes the national coinage so that the nation can conduct trade and commerce. Produces gold, silver, and platinum coins for sale to investors.

▶**NONGOVERNMENTAL**

Silver Institute, *888 18th St. N.W., #303 20006; (202) 835-0185. Fax, (202) 835-0155. Michael DiRienzo, Executive Director.*
General e-mail, info@silverinstitute.org
Web, www.silverinstitute.org

Membership: companies that mine, refine, fabricate, or manufacture silver or silver-containing products. Conducts research on new technological and industrial uses for silver. Compiles statistics by country on mine production of silver; coinage use; the production, distribution, and use of refined silver; and the conversion of refined silver into other forms, such as silverware and jewelry.

Silver Users Assn., *11240 Waples Mill Rd., #200, Fairfax, VA 22030; (703) 930-7790. Fax, (703) 359-7562. Jon Potts, President.*
General e-mail, info@mwcapitol.com
Web, www.silverusersassociation.org

Membership: users of silver, including the photographic industry, silversmiths, and other manufacturers. Conducts research on the silver market; monitors government activities in silver; analyzes government statistics on silver consumption and production.

INDUSTRIAL PRODUCTION, MANUFACTURING

▶**AGENCIES**

Bureau of Industry and Security *(Commerce Dept.), 14th St. and Constitution Ave. N.W., #3898 20230; (202) 482-1455. Fax, (202) 482-2421. Mario Mancuso, Under Secretary. Press, (202) 482-2721. Export licensing information, (202) 482-4811.*
Web, www.bis.doc.gov

Assists in providing for an adequate supply of strategic and critical materials for defense activities and civilian needs, including military requirements, and other domestic energy supplies; develops plans for industry to meet national emergencies. Studies the effect of imports on national security and recommends actions. Manages the nation's dual-use export control laws and regulations.

Census Bureau *(Commerce Dept.), Manufacturing and Construction, 4600 Silver Hill Rd., #7K154, Suitland, MD 20746-4600 (mailing address: change city and zip code to, Washington, DC 20233); (301) 763-4593. Fax, (301) 768-7783. Thomas E. Zabelsky, Division Chief.*
Web, www.census.gov

Collects and distributes manufacturing, construction, and mineral industry data. Reports are organized by commodity, industry, and geographic area.

Economic Development Administration *(Commerce Dept.), 1401 Constitution Ave. N.W., #7800 20230; (202) 482-5081. Fax, (202) 273-4781. Sandy Baruah, Assistant Secretary.*
Web, www.eda.gov

Assists U.S. firms in increasing their competitiveness against foreign imports. Certifies eligibility and provides domestic firms and industries adversely affected by increased imports with technical assistance under provisions of the Trade Act of 1974. Administers eleven regional Trade Adjustment Assistance Centers that offer services to eligible U.S. firms.

Economics and Statistics Administration *(Commerce Dept.), 1401 Constitution Ave. N.W., #4848 20230; (202) 482-3727. Fax, (202) 482-0432. Cynthia A. Glassman, Under Secretary.*
General e-mail, esa@doc.gov
Web, www.esa.doc.gov

Advises the secretary on economic policy matters, including consumer and capital spending, inventory status, and the short- and long-term outlook in output and unemployment. Seeks to improve economic productivity and growth. Serves as departmental liaison with the Council of Economic Advisers and other government agencies concerned with economic policy. Supervises and sets policy for the Census Bureau and the Bureau of Economic Analysis.

International Trade Administration (ITA), *(Commerce Dept.), Manufacturing and Services, 1401 Constitution*

Ave. N.W., #3832 20230; (202) 482-1461. Fax, (202) 482-5697. William Sutton, Assistant Secretary.

General e-mail, tdwebmaster@ita.doc.gov

Web, www.ita.doc.gov/td

Conducts industry trade analysis. Shapes U.S. trade policy. Participates in trade negotiations. Organizes trade capacity building programs. Evaluates the impact of domestic and international economic and regulatory policies on U.S. manufacturers and service industries.

Manufacturing Extension Partnership, *managed by National Institute of Standards and Technology (Commerce Dept.),* 100 Bureau Dr., MS 4800, Gaithersburg, MD 20899; (301) 975-5020. Fax, (301) 963-6556. Roger Kilmer, Director.

Web, www.mep.nist.gov

Network of nonprofit centers that assists manufacturers with such issues as process improvements, worker training, sound business practices, and technology transfer.

National Institute of Standards and Technology (NIST), *(Commerce Dept.), Weights and Measures,* 100 Bureau Dr., MS 2600, Gaithersburg, MD 20899; (301) 975-4004. Fax, (301) 975-8091. Carol Hockert, Chief.

General e-mail, owm@nist.gov

Web, www.nist.gov/owm

Promotes uniform standards among the states for packaging and labeling products and for measuring devices, including scales and commercial measurement instruments; advises manufacturers on labeling and packaging laws and on measuring device standards.

▶ **NONGOVERNMENTAL**

American National Standards Institute, *Accreditation Services, Washington Office,* 1819 L St. N.W., 6th Floor 20036; (202) 293-8020. Fax, (202) 293-9287. Joe Bhatia, President.

Web, www.ansi.org

Administers and coordinates the voluntary standardization system and conformity assessment programs for the U.S. private sector; maintains staff contacts for specific industries. Serves as U.S. member of the International Organization for Standardization (ISO) and hosts the U.S. National Committee of the International Electrotechnical Commission (IEC).

Assn. for Manufacturing Technology, 7901 Westpark Dr., McLean, VA 22102-4206; (703) 893-2900. Fax, (703) 893-1151. Bob Simpson, President.

General e-mail, amt@amtonline.org

Web, www.amtonline.org

Supports the U.S. manufacturing industry; sponsors workshops and seminars; fosters safety and technical standards. Monitors legislation and regulations.

Can Manufacturers Institute, 1730 Rhode Island Ave. N.W., #1000 20036; (202) 232-4677. Fax, (202) 232-5756. Robert Budway, President.

Web, www.cancentral.com

Represents can manufacturers and suppliers; promotes the use of the can as a form of food packaging. Conducts market research. Monitors legislation and regulations.

Envelope Manufacturers Assn., 500 Montgomery St., #550, Alexandria, VA 22314-1565; (703) 739-2200. Fax, (703) 739-2209. Maynard H. Benjamin, President.

Web, www.envelope.org

Membership: envelope manufacturers and suppliers. Monitors legislation and regulations.

Flexible Packaging Assn., 971 Corporate Blvd., #403, Linthicum, MD 21090-2211; (410) 694-0800. Fax, (410) 694-0900. Marla Donahue, President.

General e-mail, fpa@flexpack.org

Web, www.flexpack.org

Membership: companies that supply or manufacture flexible packaging. Researches packaging trends and technical developments. Compiles industry statistics. Monitors legislation and regulations.

Glass Packaging Institute, 700 N. Fairfax St., #510, Alexandria, VA 22314; (703) 684-6359. Fax, (703) 684-6048. Joseph J. Cattaneo, President.

General e-mail, info@gpi.org

Web, www.gpi.org

Membership: manufacturers of glass containers and their suppliers. Promotes industry policies to protect the environment, conserve natural resources, and reduce energy consumption; conducts research; monitors legislation affecting the industry. Interests include glass recycling.

Independent Lubricant Manufacturers Assn., 400 North Columbus St., #201, Alexandria, VA 22314; (703) 684-5574. Fax, (703) 836-8503. Celeste Powers, Executive Director.

General e-mail, ilma@ilma.org

Web, www.ilma.org

Membership: U.S. and international companies that manufacture automotive, industrial, and metalworking lubricants; associates include suppliers and related businesses. Conducts two workshops and conferences annually; compiles statistics. Monitors legislation and regulations.

Independent Office Products and Furniture Dealers Assn., 301 N. Fairfax St., #200, Alexandria, VA 22314; (703) 549-9040. Fax, (703) 683-7552. Christopher H. Bates, President. Information, (800) 542-6672.

General e-mail, info@iopfda.org

Web, www.iopfda.org

Membership: independent dealers of office products and office furniture. Serves independent dealers and works with their trading partners to develop programs and opportunities that help strengthen the dealer position in the marketplace.

Industrial Designers Society of America, *45195 Business Ct., #250, Dulles, VA 20166-6717; (703) 707-6000. Fax, (703) 787-8501. Frank Tyneski, Executive Director.*

General e-mail, idsa@idsa.org

Web, www.idsa.org

Membership: designers of products, equipment, instruments, furniture, transportation, packages, exhibits, information services, and related services. Provides the Bureau of Labor Statistics with industry information. Monitors legislation and regulations.

Industrial Energy Consumers of America, *1155 15th St. N.W., #500 20005; (202) 223-1661. Fax, (202) 530-0659. Paul N. Cicio, President.*

General e-mail, pcicio@carbonleaf.net

Web, www.ieca-us.org

National trade association that represents the manufacturing industry on energy and environmental issues. Advocates for greater diversity of and lower costs for energy. Monitors legislation and regulations.

Industrial Research Institute Inc., *2200 Clarendon Blvd., #1102, Arlington, VA 22201; (703) 647-2580. Fax, (703) 647-2581. Edward Bernstein, President.*

Web, www.iriinc.org

Membership: companies that maintain laboratories for industrial research. Seeks to improve the process of industrial research by promoting cooperative efforts among companies, between the academic and research communities, and between industry and the government. Monitors legislation and regulations concerning technology, industry, and national competitiveness.

International Sleep Products Assn., *501 Wythe St., Alexandria, VA 22314-1917; (703) 683-8371. Fax, (703) 683-4503. Richard Doyle, President.*

General e-mail, info@sleepproducts.org

Web, www.sleepproducts.org

Membership: manufacturers of bedding and mattresses. Compiles statistics on the industry. (Affiliated with Sleep Products Safety Council and the Better Sleep Council.)

Clothing and Textiles

▶AGENCIES

Federal Trade Commission (FTC), *Enforcement, 601 New Jersey Ave. N.W., 2nd Floor 20580; (202) 326-2996. Fax, (202) 326-2558. James A. Kohm, Associate Director.*

Web, www.ftc.gov

Enforces legislation concerning labels for textile fibers, wool products, fur products, and product care.

International Trade Administration (ITA), *(Commerce Dept.), Textiles and Apparel Industries, 1401 Constitution Ave. N.W., #3001A 20230; (202) 482-3737. Fax, (202) +482-2331. Matthew Priest, Deputy Assistant Secretary.*

Web, http://otexa.ita.doc.gov

Participates in negotiating bilateral textile and apparel import restraint agreements; responsible for export expansion programs and reduction of nontariff barriers for textile and apparel goods; provides data on economic conditions in the domestic textile and apparel markets, including impact of imports.

▶NONGOVERNMENTAL

American Apparel and Footwear Assn. (AAFA), *1601 N. Kent St., #1200, Arlington, VA 22209; (703) 524-1864. Fax, (703) 522-6741. Kevin M. Burke, President. Toll-free, (800) 520-2262.*

Web, www.apparelandfootwear.org

Membership: manufacturers of apparel, sewn products, footwear and their suppliers, importers, and distributors. Provides members with information on the industry, including import and export data. Interests include product flammability and trade promotion. Monitors legislation and regulations.

American Fiber Manufacturers Assn., *1530 Wilson Blvd., #690, Arlington, VA 22209; (703) 875-0432. Fax, (703) 875-0907. Paul T. O'Day, President.*

General e-mail, fcb@afma.org

Web, www.fibersource.com

Membership: U.S. producers of manufactured (man-made) fibers, filaments, and yarns. Interests include international trade, education, and environmental and technical services. Monitors legislation and regulations.

American Textile Machinery Assn., *201 Park Washington Court, Falls Church, VA 22046-4527; (703) 538-1789. Fax, (703) 241-5603. Susan A. Denston, Executive Vice President.*

General e-mail, info@atmanet.org

Web, www.atmanet.org

Membership: U.S.-based manufacturers of textile machinery and related parts and accessories. Interests include competitiveness and expansion of foreign markets. Monitors legislation and regulations.

Dry Cleaning and Laundry Institute, *14700 Sweitzer Lane, Laurel, MD 20707; (301) 622-1900. Fax, (240) 295-0685. William E. Fisher, Chief Executive Officer.*

General e-mail, administrator@ifi.org

Web, www.ifi.org

Membership: dry cleaners and launderers. Conducts research and provides information on products and services. Monitors legislation and regulations.

Footwear Distributors and Retailers of America, *1319 F St. N.W., #700 20004; (202) 737-5660. Fax, (202) 638-2615. Peter T. Mangione, President.*

General e-mail, info@fdra.org

Web, www.fdra.org

Membership: companies that operate shoe retail outlets and wholesale footwear companies with U.S. and global brands. Provides business support and government relations to members. Interests include intellectual property rights, ocean shipping rates, trade with China, and labeling regulations.

National Cotton Council of America, *Washington Office, 1521 New Hampshire Ave. N.W. 20036-1203; (202) 745-7805. Fax, (202) 483-4040. A. John Maguire, Senior Vice President.*

Web, www.cotton.org

Membership: all segments of the U.S. cotton industry. Formulates positions on trade policy and negotiations; seeks to improve competitiveness of U.S. exports; sponsors programs to educate the public about flammable fabrics. (Headquarters in Memphis, Tenn.)

National Council of Textile Organizations, *910 17th St. N.W., #1020 20006; (202) 822-8028. Fax, (202) 822-8029. Cass Johnson, President.*

Web, www.ncto.org

Membership: U.S. companies that spin, weave, knit, or finish textiles from natural fibers, and associate members from affiliated industries. Interests include domestic and world markets. Monitors legislation and regulations.

UNITE HERE, *Washington Office, 1775 K St. N.W., #620 20006; (202) 393-4373. Fax, (202) 342-2929. Tom Snyder, Political Director.*

Web, www.unitehere.org

Membership: approximately 250,000 workers in basic apparel and textiles, millinery, shoe, laundry, retail, and related industries, and in auto parts and auto supply. Assists members with contract negotiation and grievances; conducts training programs and workshops. Monitors legislation and regulations. (Headquarters in New York. Formerly the Union of Needletrades, Industrial and Textile Employers.)

Electronics and Appliances

▶**NONGOVERNMENTAL**

AHRI (Air-Conditioning, Heating, and Refrigeration Institute), *2107 Wilson Blvd., #600, Arlington, VA 22201; (703) 524-8800. Fax, (703) 562-1942. Stephen Yurek, President.*

General e-mail, information@ahrinet.org

Web, www.ahrinct.org

Membership: manufacturers of gas appliances and equipment for residential and commercial use and related industries. Advocates product improvement; provides market statistics. Monitors legislation and regulations. (Merger of the Air-Conditioning and Refrigeration Institute [ARI] and the Gas Appliance Manufacturers Assn. [GAMA].)

Consumer Electronics Assn., *1919 S. Eads St., Arlington, VA 22202; (703) 907-7600. Fax, (703) 907-7601. Gary Shapiro, President. Toll-free, (866) 858-1555.*

Web, www.ce.org

Membership: U.S. consumer electronics manufacturers. Promotes the industry; sponsors seminars and conferences; conducts research; consults with member companies. Monitors legislation and regulations. (Affiliated with Electronic Industries Alliance.)

Electronic Industries Alliance, *2500 Wilson Blvd., Arlington, VA 22201-3834; (703) 907-7500. Fax, (703) 907-7501. Dave McCurdy, Interim President.*

Web, www.eia.org

Membership: manufacturers, dealers, installers, and distributors of consumer electronics products. Provides consumer information and data on industry trends; advocates an open market. Monitors legislation and regulations.

National Electrical Contractors Assn., *3 Bethesda Metro Center, #1100, Bethesda, MD 20814; (301) 657-3110. Fax, (301) 215-4500. John Grau, Chief Executive Officer.*

Web, www.necanet.org

Membership: electrical contractors who build and service electrical wiring, equipment, and appliances. Represents members in collective bargaining with union workers; sponsors research and educational programs.

Optoelectronics Industry Development Assn., *1220 Connecticut Ave. N.W. 20036; (202) 785-4426. Fax, (202) 785-4428. Michael Lebby, President.*

Web, www.oida.org

Membership: users and suppliers of optoelectronics in North America. Promotes the global competitiveness of members; provides a forum for exchange of information; conducts workshops and conferences; sponsors research. Monitors legislation and regulations.

Steel, Metalworking, Machinery

▶**NONGOVERNMENTAL**

American Boiler Manufacturers Assn., *8221 Old Courthouse Rd., #207, Vienna, VA 22182; (703) 356-7172. Fax, (703) 356-4543. Randall Rawson, President.*

Web, www.abma.com

Membership: manufacturers of boiler systems and boiler-related products, including fuel-burning systems. Interests include energy and environmental issues.

American Gear Manufacturers Assn., *500 Montgomery St., #350, Alexandria, VA 22314-1581; (703) 684-0211. Fax, (703) 684-0242. Joe T. Franklin Jr., President.*

General e-mail, agma@agma.org

Web, www.agma.org

Membership: gear manufacturers, suppliers, and industry consultants. Conducts workshops, seminars, and conferences; develops industry standards; sponsors research. Monitors legislation and regulations.

American Institute for International Steel, *8201 Greensboro Dr., McLean, VA 22102; (703) 245-8075. Fax, (703) 610-9005. David Phelps, President.*

General e-mail, aiis@aiis.org

Web, www.aiis.org

Membership: importers and exporters of steel. Conducts research and provides analysis on manufacturing processes. Holds annual conferences.

American Machine Tool Distributors Assn., *7361 Calhoun Pl., #450, Rockville, MD 20855; (301) 738-1200. Fax, (301) 738-9499. Peter Borden, President. Information, (800) 878-2683.*

Web, www.amtda.org

Membership: distributors of machine tools. Supports advances in manufacturing and expansion of international trade. Monitors legislation and regulations.

American Wire Producers Assn., *801 N. Fairfax St., #211, Alexandria, VA 22314-1757; (703) 299-4434. Fax, (703) 299-9233. Kimberly A. Korbel, Executive Director.*

General e-mail, info@awpa.org

Web, www.awpa.org

Membership: companies that produce carbon, alloy, and stainless steel wire and wire products in the United States, Canada, and Mexico. Interests include imports of rod, wire, and wire products. Publishes survey of the domestic wire industry. Monitors legislation and regulations.

International Assn. of Bridge, Structural, Ornamental, and Reinforcing Iron Workers, *1750 New York Ave. N.W., #400 20006; (202) 383-4800. Fax, (202) 638-4856. Joseph J. Hunt, President.*

Web, www.ironworkers.org

Membership: approximately 140,000 iron workers. Helps members negotiate pay, benefits, and better working conditions; conducts training programs and workshops. Monitors legislation and regulations. (Affiliated with the AFL-CIO.)

International Assn. of Machinists and Aerospace Workers, *9000 Machinists Pl., Upper Marlboro, MD 20772-2687; (301) 967-4500. Fax, (301) 967-4588. Thomas Buffenbarger, International President. Information, (301) 967-4520. TTY, (800) 201-7165.*

Web, www.goiam.org

Membership: machinists in more than 200 industries. Helps members negotiate pay, benefits, and better working conditions; conducts training programs and workshops. Monitors legislation and regulations. (Affiliated with the AFL-CIO, the Canadian Labour Congress, the International Metalworkers Federation, the International Transport Workers' Federation, and the Railway Labor Executives Assn.)

Machinery Dealers National Assn., *315 S. Patrick St., Alexandria, VA 22314; (703) 836-9300. Fax, (703) 836-9303. Mark Robinson, Executive Vice President.*

General e-mail, office@mdna.org

Web, www.mdna.org

Membership: companies that buy and sell used capital equipment. Establishes a code of ethics for members; publishes a buyer's guide that lists members by types of machinery they sell.

National Tooling and Machining Assn., *9300 Livingston Rd., Ft. Washington, MD 20744-4998; (301) 248-6200. Fax, (301) 248-7104. Robert Akers, Chief Operating Officer.*

General e-mail, info@ntma.org

Web, www.ntma.org

Membership: members of the contract precision metalworking industry, including tool, die, mold, diecasting die, and special machining companies. Assists members in developing and expanding their domestic and foreign markets. Offers training program, insurance, and legal advice; compiles statistical information. Monitors legislation and regulations.

Outdoor Power Equipment Institute, *341 S. Patrick St., Alexandria, VA 22314; (703) 549-7600. Fax, (703) 549-7604. William G. Harley, President.*

Web, www.opei.org

Membership: manufacturers of powered lawn and garden maintenance products, components and attachments, and their suppliers. Promotes safe use of outdoor power equipment; keeps statistics on the industry; fosters exchange of information. Monitors legislation and regulations.

Sheet Metal Workers International Assn., *1750 New York Ave. N.W. 20006; (202) 783-5880. Fax, (202) 662-0880. Michael J. Sullivan, General President.*

Web, www.smwia.org

Membership: more than 150,000 U.S., Puerto Rican, and Canadian workers in the building and construction trades, manufacturing, and the railroad and shipyard industries. Assists members with contract negotiation and grievances; conducts training programs and workshops. Monitors legislation and regulations. (Affiliated with the Sheet Metal and Air Conditioning Contractors' Assn., the AFL-CIO, and the Canadian Labour Congress.)

Specialty Steel Industry of North America, *3050 K St. N.W., #400 20007; (202) 342-8450. Fax, (202) 342-8451. David A. Hartquist, Counsel.*

Web, www.ssina.com

Membership: manufacturers of products in stainless and other specialty steels. Establishes quality standards and manufacturing techniques; operates a hotline for technical questions.

Steel Manufacturers Assn., *1150 Connecticut Ave. N.W., #715 20036-3101; (202) 296-1515. Fax, (202) 296-2506. Thomas A. Danjczek, President.*

General e-mail, webmail@steelnet.org

Web, www.steelnet.org

Membership: steel producers in North America. Helps members exchange information on technical matters;

provides information on the steel industry to the public and government. Monitors legislation and regulations.

United Steel, Paper & Forestry, Rubber, Manufact., Allied Indust. & Service Workers Internat'l Union, *1150 17th St. N.W., #300 20036; (202) 778-4384. Fax, (202) 293-5308. Holly Hart, Legislative Director.*

Web, www.usw.org

Membership: More than 850,000 workers in the steel, paper, rubber, energy, chemical, pharmaceutical, and allied industries. Helps members negotiate pay, benefits, and better working conditions; conducts training programs and workshops. Monitors legislation and regulations. (Headquarters in Pittsburgh, Pa; affiliated with the AFL-CIO.)

INSURANCE

▶AGENCIES

Federal Emergency Management Agency (FEMA), *(Homeland Security Dept.), Mitigation Division, 500 C St. S.W., #406 20472; (202) 646-2781. Fax, (202) 646-7970. David I. Maurstad, Assistant Administrator.*

Web, www.fema.gov/nfip

Administers federal flood insurance programs, including the National Flood Insurance Program. Makes low-cost flood insurance available to eligible homeowners.

Small Business Administration (SBA), *Disaster Assistance, 409 3rd St. S.W., #6050 20416; (202) 205-6734. Fax, (202) 205-7728. Herbert L. Mitchell, Associate Administrator. Call center, (800) 659-2955.*

General e-mail, disastercustomerservice@sba.gov

Web, www.sba.gov

Provides victims of physical disasters with disaster and economic injury loans for homes, businesses, and personal property. Lends funds for uncompensated losses incurred from any disaster declared by the president of the United States or the administrator of the SBA. Lends funds to individual homeowners, business concerns of all sizes, and nonprofit institutions to repair or replace damaged structures and furnishings, business machinery, equipment, and inventory. Provides economic injury loans to small businesses for losses to meet necessary operating expenses, provided the business could have paid these expenses prior to the disaster.

▶CONGRESS

For a listing of relevant congressional committees and subcommittees, please see page 32 or the Appendix.

▶NONGOVERNMENTAL

American Academy of Actuaries, *1850 M St. N.W., #300 20036; (202) 223-8196. Fax, (202) 872-1948. Kevin Cronin, Executive Director.*

Web, www.actuary.org

Membership: professional actuaries practicing in the areas of life, health, liability, property, and casualty insurance; pensions; government insurance plans; and general consulting. Provides information on actuarial matters, including insurance and pensions; develops professional standards; advises public policymakers.

American Assn. for Justice, *777 6th St. N.W. 20001; (202) 965-3500. Fax, (202) 342-5484. Jon Haber, Chief Executive Officer.*

General e-mail, aaj@justice.org

Web, www.justice.org

Membership: attorneys, judges, law professors, and students. Interests include aspects of legal and legislative activity relating to the adversary system and trial by jury, including property and casualty insurance. (Formerly the Assn. of Trial Lawyers of America.)

American Council of Life Insurers, *101 Constitution Ave. N.W., #700 20001; (202) 624-2000. Fax, (202) 624-2319. Frank Keating, President.*

Web, www.acli.com

Membership: life insurance companies authorized to do business in the United States. Conducts research and compiles statistics at state and federal levels. Monitors legislation and regulations.

American Insurance Assn., *2101 L St. N.W., #400 20037; (202) 828-7100. Fax, (202) 293-1219. Leigh Ann Pusey, President. Library, (202) 828-7183. Federal Affairs, (202) 828-7496.*

Web, www.aiadc.org

Membership: companies providing property and casualty insurance. Conducts public relations and educational activities; provides information on issues related to property and casualty insurance. Library open to the public by appointment.

American Society of Pension Professionals and Actuaries, *4245 N. Fairfax Dr., #750, Arlington, VA 22203-1648; (703) 516-9300. Fax, (703) 516-9308. Brian Graff, Executive Director.*

General e-mail, asppa@asppa.org

Web, www.asppa.org

Membership: professional pension plan actuaries, administrators, consultants, and other benefits professionals. Sponsors educational programs to prepare actuaries and consultants for professional exams. Monitors legislation.

Assn. for Advanced Life Underwriting, *2901 Telestar Court, 4th Floor, Falls Church, VA 22042; (703) 641-9400. Fax, (703) 641-9885. David J. Stertzer, Chief Executive Officer.*

General e-mail, info@aalu.org

Web, www.aalu.org

Membership: specialized underwriters in the fields of estate analysis, charitable planning, business insurance, pension planning, and employee benefit plans. Monitors legislation and regulations on small-business taxes and capital formation. (Maintains an additional office in Washington, D.C.)

Consumer Federation of America, *1620 Eye St. N.W., #200 20006; (202) 387-6121. Fax, (202) 265-7989. Stephen Brobeck, Executive Director.*

General e-mail, cfa@consumerfed.org

Web, www.consumerfed.org

Federation of national, regional, state, and local pro-consumer organizations. Promotes consumer interests in banking, credit, and insurance; telecommunications; housing; food, drugs, and medical care; safety; and energy and natural resources development.

Council of Insurance Agents and Brokers, *701 Pennsylvania Ave. N.W., #750 20004; (202) 783-4400. Fax, (202) 783-4410. Ken A. Crerar, President.*

General e-mail, ciab@ciab.com

Web, www.ciab.com

Represents commercial property and casualty insurance agencies and brokerage firms. Members offer insurance products and risk management services to business, government, and the public.

ERISA Industry Committee, *1400 L St. N.W., #350 20005; (202) 789-1400. Fax, (202) 789-1120. Mark J. Ugoretz, President.*

General e-mail, eric@eric.org

Web, www.eric.org

Membership: major U.S. employers. Advocates members' positions on employee retirement, health care coverage, and welfare benefit plans. Monitors legislation and regulations.

GAMA International, *2901 Telestar Court, #140, Falls Church, VA 22042-1205; (703) 770-8184. Fax, (703) 770-8182. Jeff Hughes, Chief Executive Officer. Information, (800) 345-2687.*

Web, www.gamaweb.com

Membership: general agents and managers who provide life insurance and related financial products and services. Provides information, education, and training for members.

Independent Insurance Agents and Brokers of America, *127 S. Peyton St., Alexandria, VA 22314; (703) 683-4422. Fax, (703) 683-7556. Bob Rusbuldt, Chief Executive Officer.*

General e-mail, info@iiab.org

Web, www.independentagent.net

Provides educational and advisory services; researches issues pertaining to auto, home, business, life, and health insurance; offers cooperative advertising program to members. Political action committee monitors legislation and regulations.

Insurance Information Institute, *Washington Office, 1819 L St. N.W. 20036; (202) 833-1580. Fax, (202) 785-4676. Carolyn Gorman, Vice President.*

General e-mail, media@iii.org

Web, www.iii.org

Membership: property and casualty insurance companies. Monitors state and federal issues concerning insurance. Serves as a primary source for information, analysis, and referral concerning property and casualty insurance. (Headquarters in New York.)

Mortgage Insurance Companies of America, *1425 K St. N.W., #210 20005; (202) 682-2683. Fax, (202) 842-9252. Suzanne C. Hutchinson, Executive Vice President.*

General e-mail, info@privatemi.com

Web, www.privatemi.com

Membership: companies that provide private mortgage guarantee insurance on residential mortgage loans. Promotes the interests of the mortgage insurance industry.

National Assn. of Independent Life Brokerage Agencies, *11325 Random Hills Rd., #110, Fairfax, VA 22033; (703) 383-3081. Fax, (703) 383-6942. Jack Chiasson, Executive Director.*

Web, www.nailba.org

Membership: owners of independent life insurance agencies. Fosters the responsible and effective distribution of life and health insurance and related financial services; provides a forum for exchange of information among members. Monitors legislation and regulations.

National Assn. of Insurance and Financial Advisors, *2901 Telestar Court, Falls Church, VA 22042-1205; (703) 770-8100. Fax, (703) 770-8107. John J. Healy, Chief Executive Officer.*

General e-mail, membersupport@naifa.org

Web, www.naifa.org

Federation of affiliated state and local life underwriters. Provides information on life and health insurance and other financial services; sponsors education and training programs. (Formerly the National Assn. of Life Underwriters.)

National Assn. of Insurance Commissioners, *Washington Office, 444 N. Capitol St. N.W., #701 20001-1512; (202) 471-3990. Fax, (202) 471-3972. Therese M. Vaughan, Chief Executive Officer.*

Web, www.naic.org

Membership: state insurance commissioners, directors, and supervisors. Provides members with information on computer information services, legal and market conduct, and financial services; publishes research and statistics on the insurance industry. Monitors legislation and regulations. (Headquarters in Kansas City, Mo.)

National Assn. of Professional Insurance Agents, *400 N. Washington St., Alexandria, VA 22314-2353; (703) 836-9340. Fax, (703) 836-1279. Len Brevik, Executive Vice President; Mike Becku, Assistant Vice President, Federal Affairs, (703) 518-1365. Information, (800) 742-6900. Press, (703) 518-1352.*

General e-mail, piaweb@pianet.org

Web, www.pianet.com

Membership: independent insurance agents and brokers. Operates schools to provide agents with basic training; offers seminars and provides educational materials. Monitors legislation and regulations.

Nonprofit Risk Management Center, *15 N. King St., #203, Leesburg, VA 20176; (202) 785-3891. Fax, (703) 443-1990. Melanie Herman, Executive Director.*
General e-mail, info@nonprofitrisk.org

Web, www.nonprofitrisk.org

Provides information on insurance and risk management issues through conferences, consulting, online tools, and publications for nonprofit organizations.

National Assn. of Wholesaler-Distributors, *Government Relations, 1325 G St. N.W., #1000 20005; (202) 872-0885. Fax, (202) 785-0586. Dirk Van Dongen, President.*
General e-mail, naw@nawd.org

Web, www.naw.org

Membership: manufacturers, product sellers and their insurers, and trade associations. Promotes enactment of federal product liability tort reform legislation.

Property Casualty Insurers Assn. of America, *Washington Office, 444 N. Capitol St., #801 20001; (202) 639-0490. Fax, (202) 639-0494. Ben McKay, Senior Vice President.*
General e-mail, justinpierce@pciaa.net

Web, www.pciaa.net

Membership: companies providing property and casualty insurance. Monitors legislation and compiles statistics; interests include personal and commercial property and casualty insurance. (Headquarters in Des Plaines, Ill.)

Reinsurance Assn. of America, *1301 Pennsylvania Ave. N.W., #900 20004; (202) 638-3690. Fax, (202) 638-0936. Franklin W. Nutter, President.*
Web, www.reinsurance.org

Membership: companies writing property and casualty reinsurance. Monitors legislation and regulations.

PATENTS, COPYRIGHTS, AND TRADEMARKS

►AGENCIES

Justice Dept. (DOJ), *Civil Division: Intellectual Property, 1100 L St. N.W., #11116 20005; (202) 514-7223. Fax, (202) 307-0345. John Fargo, Director.*
General e-mail, john.fargo@usdoj.gov

Web, www.usdoj.gov

Represents the United States in patent, copyright, and trademark cases. Includes the defense of patent infringement suits; legal proceedings to establish government priority of invention; defense of administrative acts of the Register of Copyrights; and actions on behalf of the government involving the use of trademarks.

Patent and Trademark Office *(Commerce Dept.), 600 Dulany St., Madison West Bldg., #10-D44, Alexandria, VA 22314; (571) 272-8600. Fax, (571) 273-0464. Jon W. Dudas, Under Secretary. Press, (571) 272-8400. TTY, (571) 272-9950. Patent search library, (571) 272-4223.*
Web, www.uspto.gov

Grants patents, registers trademarks, and provides patent and trademark information. Library and search file of U.S. and foreign patents available for public use.

State Dept., *Intellectual Property Enforcement, 2201 C St. N.W., #4931 20520-4931; (202) 647-3251. Fax, (202) 647-1537. Dan Jacobs, Director.*
Web, www.state.gov

Handles multilateral and bilateral policy formulation involving patents, copyrights, and trademarks, and international industrial property of U.S. nationals.

U.S. Customs and Border Protection *(Homeland Security Dept.), Intellectual Property Rights and Restrictions, 1300 Pennsylvania Ave. N.W., Mint Annex 20229; (202) 325-0020. Fax, (202) 572-8744. George Frederick McCray, Chief.*
General e-mail, hqiprbranch@dhs.gov

Web, www.cbp.gov

Responsible for customs recordation of registered trademarks and copyrights. Enforces rules and regulations pertaining to intellectual property rights. Coordinates enforcement of International Trade Commission exclusion orders against unfairly competing goods. Determines admissibility of restricted merchandise and cultural properties. Provides support to and coordinates with international organizations and the Office of the U.S. Trade Representative.

►CONGRESS

For a listing of relevant congressional committees and subcommittees, please see page 32 or the Appendix.

Library of Congress, *Copyright Office, 101 Independence Ave. S.E., #403 20540; (202) 707-8350. Marybeth Peters, Register of Copyrights. Information, (202) 707-3000. TTY, (202) 707-6737. Forms and publications hotline, (202) 707-9100.*
Web, www.copyright.gov

Provides information on copyright registration procedures and requirements, copyright law, and international copyrights; registers copyright claims and maintains public records of copyright registrations. Copyright record searches conducted on an hourly fee basis. Files open to public for research during weekday business hours. Does not give legal advice on copyright matters.

►JUDICIARY

U.S. Court of Appeals for the Federal Circuit, *717 Madison Pl. N.W. 20439; (202) 633-6550. Fax, (202) 633-9623. Paul R. Michel, Chief Judge; Jan Horbaly, Clerk, (202) 312-5520.*
Web, www.cafe.uscourts.gov

Reviews decisions of U.S. Patent and Trademark Office on applications and interferences regarding patents and trademarks; hears appeals on patent infringement cases from district courts.

►NONGOVERNMENTAL

American Intellectual Property Law Assn., *241 18th St. South, #700, Arlington, VA 22202; (703) 415-0780. Fax, (703) 415-0786. Q. Todd Dickinson, Executive Director.*

General e-mail, aipla@aipla.org

Web, www.aipla.org

Membership: lawyers practicing in the field of patents, trademarks, and copyrights (intellectual property law). Holds continuing legal education conferences.

Assn. of American Publishers, *Government Affairs, 50 F St. N.W., #400 20001; (202) 347-3375. Fax, (202) 347-3690. Allan R. Adler, Vice President, Legal and Government Affairs.*

Web, www.publishers.org

Monitors copyright activity in government, Congress, and international forums and institutions. Sponsors seminars open to the public for a fee.

Intellectual Property Owners Assn., *1501 M St. N.W., #1150 20005; (202) 466-2396. Fax, (202) 507-4501. Herbert C. Wamsley, Executive Director; Dana R. Colarulli, Director of Government Relations.*

General e-mail, info@ipo.org

Web, www.ipo.org

Monitors and advocates for intellectual property legislation. Conducts educational programs to protect intellectual property through patents, trademarks, copyrights, and trade secret laws.

International Anticounterfeiting Coalition, *1730 M St. N.W., #1020 20036; (202) 223-6667. Fax, (202) 223-6668. Robert Barchiesi, President.*

General e-mail, meghan@iacc.org

Web, www.iacc.org

Works to combat counterfeiting and piracy by promoting laws, regulations, and directives to render theft of intellectual property unprofitable. Oversees anticounterfeiting programs that increase patent, trademark, copyright, service mark, trade dress, and trade secret protection. Provides information and training to law enforcement officials to help identify counterfeit and pirate products.

International Intellectual Property Alliance, *2101 L St. N.W., #1000 20037; (202) 833-4198. Fax, (202) 261-0151. Eric H. Smith, Counsel.*

General e-mail, info@iipa.com

Web, www.iipa.com

Represents U.S. copyright-based industries in efforts to improve international protection of copyrighted materials. Monitors legislation domestically and abroad; promotes enforcement reform abroad.

National Assn. of Manufacturers (NAM), *Technology Policy, 1331 Pennsylvania Ave. N.W., #600 20004-1790; (202) 637-3000. Fax, (202) 637-3182. Franklin J. Vargo, Vice President.*

General e-mail, manufacturing@nam.org

Web, www.nam.org

Develops policy and legislation on patents, copyrights, trademarks, and trade secrets.

National Music Publishers' Assn., *101 Constitution Ave. N.W., #705 East 20001; (202) 742-4375. Fax, (202) 742-4377. David M. Israelite, President.*

General e-mail, pr@nmpa.org

Web, www.nmpa.org

Works to enforce music copyrights. Sponsors litigation against copyright violators. Monitors and interprets legislation and regulations.

National School Boards Assn., *1680 Duke St., Alexandria, VA 22314; (703) 838-6722. Fax, (703) 683-7590. Anne L. Bryant, Executive Director; Francisco Negron, General Counsel.*

General e-mail, info@nsba.org

Web, www.nsba.org

Promotes a broad interpretation of copyright law to permit legitimate scholarly use of published and musical works, videotaped programs, and materials for computer-assisted instruction.

Progress and Freedom Foundation, *Center for the Study of Digital Property, 1444 Eye St. N.W., #500 20005; (202) 289-8928. Fax, (202) 289-6079. Tom Sydnor, Director.*

General e-mail, mail@pff.org

Web, www.pff.org

Conducts program on research and education on intellectual property issues related to the Internet and other digital technologies.

U.S. Chamber of Commerce, *Congressional and Public Affairs, 1615 H St. N.W. 20062-2000; (202) 463-5600. Fax, (202) 887-3430. Rolf T. Lundberg, Senior Vice President.*

Web, www.uschamber.com

Monitors legislation and regulations on patents, copyrights, and trademarks.

SALES AND SERVICES

►AGENCIES

Bureau of Labor Statistics (BLS), *(Labor Dept.), Prices and Living Conditions, 2 Massachusetts Ave. N.E., #3120 20212-0001; (202) 691-6960. Fax, (202) 691-7080. Michael W. Horrigan, Associate Commissioner.*

Web, www.bls.gov

Collects, processes, analyzes, and disseminates data relating to prices and consumer expenditures; maintains the Consumer Price Index.

Census Bureau *(Commerce Dept.), Service Sector Statistics Division,* 4700 Silver Hill Rd., #8K154, Suitland, MD 20746-2401; (301) 763-5170. Fax, (301) 457-1343. Mark E. Wallace, Chief.
Web, www.census.gov

Provides data of five-year census programs on retail, wholesale, and service industries. Conducts periodic monthly or annual surveys for specific items within these industries.

▶NONGOVERNMENTAL

American Wholesale Marketers Assn., 2750 Prosperity Ave., #530, Fairfax, VA 22031; (703) 208-3358. Fax, (703) 573-5738. Scott Ramminger, President.
General e-mail, info@awmanet.org
Web, www.awmanet.org

Membership: wholesalers, manufacturers, retailers, and brokers who sell or distribute convenience products. Conducts educational programs. Monitors legislation and regulations.

Cosmetic, Toiletry, and Fragrance Assn., 1101 17th St. N.W., #300 20036-4702; (202) 331-1770. Fax, (202) 331-1969. Mark Pollack, President (Acting).
Web, www.ctfa.org

Membership: manufacturers and distributors of finished personal care products. Represents the industry at the local, state, and national levels. Interests include scientific research, legal issues, international trade, legislation, and regulatory policy.

Council of Better Business Bureaus, 4200 Wilson Blvd., #800, Arlington, VA 22203-1838; (703) 276-0100. Fax, (703) 525-8277. Steven J. Cole, President.
Web, www.bbb.org

Membership: businesses and Better Business Bureaus in the United States and Canada. Promotes ethical business practices and truth in national advertising; mediates disputes between consumers and businesses.

Equipment Leasing and Finance Assn., 1825 K St. N.W., #900 20006; (202) 238-3400. Fax, (202) 238-3401. Kenneth Bentsen Jr., President.
General e-mail, dfenig@elfaonline.org
Web, www.elfaonline.org

Membership: independent leasing companies, banks, financial service companies, and independent brokers and suppliers to the leasing industry. Promotes the interests of the equipment leasing and finance industry; assists in the resolution of industry problems; encourages standards. Monitors legislation and regulations. (Formerly the Equipment Leasing Assn. of America.)

Grocery Manufacturers Assn. (GMA), 1350 Eye St. N.W., #300 20005-3377; (202) 639-5900. Fax, (202) 639-5932. Pamela Bailey, President. Press, (202) 295-3938.
General e-mail, info@gmaonline.org
Web, www.gmaonline.org

Membership: sales and marketing agents and retail merchandisers of food and consumer products worldwide. Sponsors research, training, and educational programs for members and their trading partners. Monitors legislation and regulations. (Merger of the Grocery Manufacturers Assn. and the Food Products Assn.)

International Cemetery, Cremation, and Funeral Assn., 107 Carpenter Dr., #100, Sterling, VA 20164; (703) 391-8400. Fax, (703) 391-8416. Robert Fells, External Chief Operating Officer. Information, (800) 645-7700.
General e-mail, rfells@iccfa.com
Web, www.iccfa.com

Membership: owners and operators of cemeteries, crematories, funeral homes, mausoleums, and columbariums. Promotes the building and proper maintenance of modern interment places; promotes high ethical standards in the industry; encourages pre-arrangement of funerals.

International Council of Shopping Centers, *Government Relations, Washington Office,* 1399 New York Ave. N.W., #720 20005; (202) 626-1400. Fax, (202) 626-1418. Betsy Laird, Senior Vice President.
General e-mail, govrel@icsc.org
Web, www.icsc.org

Membership: shopping center owners, developers, managers, retailers, contractors, and others in the industry worldwide. Provides information, including research data. Monitors legislation and regulations. (Headquarters in New York.)

International Franchise Assn., 1501 K St. N.W., #350 20005; (202) 628-8000. Fax, (202) 628-0812. Matthew R. Shay, President.
General e-mail, ifa@franchise.org
Web, www.franchise.org

Membership: national and international franchisers. Sponsors seminars, workshops, trade shows, and conferences. Monitors legislation and regulations.

National Assn. of Convenience Stores (NACS), 1600 Duke St., #700, Alexandria, VA 22314-3421; (703) 684-3600. Fax, (703) 836-4564. Hank Armour, President.
General e-mail, nacs@nacsonline.com
Web, www.nacsonline.com

Membership: convenience store retailers and industry suppliers. Advocates industry position on labor, tax, environment, alcohol, and food-related issues; conducts research and training programs. Monitors legislation and regulations.

National Assn. of Wholesaler-Distributors, 1325 G St. N.W., #1000 20005-3100; (202) 872-0885. Fax, (202) 785-0586. Dirk Van Dongen, President.

General e-mail, naw@nawd.org

Web, www.naw.org

Membership: wholesale distributors and trade associations. Provides members and government policymakers with research, education, and government relations information. Monitors legislation and regulations.

National Retail Federation, *325 7th St. N.W., #1100 20004-2802; (202) 783-7971. Fax, (202) 737-2849. Tracy Mullin, President.*

Web, www.nrf.com

Membership: international, national, and state associations of retailers and major retail corporations. Concerned with federal regulatory activities and legislation that affect retailers, including tax, employment, trade, and credit issues. Provides information on retailing through seminars, conferences, and publications.

Retail Industry Leaders Assn., *1700 N. Moore St., #2250, Arlington, VA 22209-1998; (703) 841-2300. Fax, (703) 841-1184. Sandra Kennedy, President.*

Web, www.rila.org

Membership: retailers and consumer product manufacturers in the United States and abroad. Interests include supply chain, trade, radio frequency identification (RFID), smart growth, taxes, health care, legal reform, labor issues, and energy. Monitors legislation and regulations. (Formerly International Mass Retail Assn.)

Security Industry Assn., *635 Slaters Lane, #110, Alexandria, VA 22314; (703) 683-2075. Fax, (703) 683-2469. Richard Chace, Executive Director.*

General e-mail, info@siaonline.org

Web, www.siaonline.org

Promotes expansion and professionalism in the security industry. Sponsors trade shows, develops industry standards, supports educational programs and job training, and publishes statistical research. Serves as an information source for the media and the industry.

Service Station Dealers of America/National Coalition of Petroleum Retailers and Allied Trades, *1532 Pointer Ridge Pl., Suite E, Bowie, MD 20716; (301) 390-4405. Fax, (301) 390-3161. Paul Fiore, Executive Vice President.*

General e-mail, pfiore@wmda.net

Web, www.ssda-at.org

Membership: state associations of gasoline retailers, repair facilities, car washes, and convenience stores. Interests include environmental issues, retail marketing, oil allocation, imports and exports, prices, and taxation.

Society of Consumer Affairs Professionals in Business, *675 N. Washington St., #200, Alexandria, VA 22314-1939; (703) 519-3700. Fax, (703) 549-4886. Matthew D'Uva, President.*

General e-mail, socap@socap.org

Web, www.socap.org

Membership: managers and supervisors who are responsible for consumer affairs, customer service, market research, and sales and marketing operations. Provides information on customer service techniques, market trends, and industry statistics; sponsors seminars and conferences. Monitors legislation and regulations.

Advertising

▶AGENCIES

Federal Highway Administration (FHWA), *(Transportation Dept.), Real Estate Services, 1200 New Jersey Ave. S.E., #E76-304 20590; (202) 366-0142. Fax, (202) 366-3713. Gerald Solomon, Director.*

Web, www.fhwa.dot.gov/realestate

Administers laws concerning outdoor advertising along interstate and federally aided primary highways.

Federal Trade Commission (FTC), *Advertising Practices, 601 New Jersey Ave. N.W., #3223 20001 (mailing address: 600 Pennsylvania Ave. N.W., Washington, DC 20580); (202) 326-3090. Fax, (202) 326-3259. Mary Engle, Associate Director.*

Web, www.ftc.gov

Protects consumers from deceptive and unsubstantiated advertising through law enforcement, public reports, and industry outreach. Focuses on national advertising campaigns for food, dietary supplements, and over-the-counter drugs, particularly advertising that makes claims difficult for consumers to evaluate. Monitors tobacco and alcohol advertising for unfair practices; issues reports on alcohol and cigarette labeling, advertising, and promotion. Issues reports on the marketing to children of violent movies, video games, and music recordings.

Food and Drug Administration (FDA), *(Health and Human Services Dept.), Drug Marketing, Advertising, and Communications, 10903 New Hampshire Ave., Bldg. 51, #3271, Silver Spring, MD 20903-0002; (301) 796-1200. Fax, (301) 796-2877. Thomas Abrams, Director.*

Web, www.fda.gov/cder

Monitors prescription drug advertising and labeling; investigates complaints; conducts market research on health care communications and drug issues.

▶NONGOVERNMENTAL

American Advertising Federation, *1101 Vermont Ave. N.W., #500 20005; (202) 898-0089. Fax, (202) 898-0159. James Edmund Datri, President.*

General e-mail, aaf@aaf.org

Web, www.aaf.org

Membership: advertising companies (ad agencies, advertisers, media, and services), clubs, associations, and college chapters. A founder of the National Advertising

Review Board, a self-regulatory body. Sponsors annual awards for outstanding advertising.

American Assn. of Advertising Agencies, *Washington Office, 1203 19th St. N.W., 4th Floor 20036; (202) 331-7345. Fax, (202) 857-3675. Richard O'Brien, Executive Vice President.*
General e-mail, wash@aaaadc.org

Web, www.aaaa.org

Co-sponsors the National Advertising Review Board (a self-regulatory body), the Advertising Council, and the Media/Advertising Partnership for a Drug Free America. Monitors legislation and regulations. (Headquarters in New York.)

Color Marketing Group, *5845 Richmond Hwy., #410, Alexandria, VA 22303-1865; (703) 329-8500. Fax, (703) 329-0155. James Martin, President.*
General e-mail, cmg@colormarketing.org

Web, www.colormarketing.org

Provides a forum for the exchange of noncompetitive information on color marketing. Holds meetings; sponsors special events in the United States as well as abroad.

Direct Marketing Assn., *Washington Office, 1615 L St. N.W., #1100 20036-5624; (202) 955-5030. Fax, (202) 955-0085. Linda A. Woolley, Executive Vice President of Government Affairs.*
General e-mail, privacy@the-dma.org

Web, www.the-dma.org

Membership: businesses and nonprofit organizations using and supporting direct marketing tools. Advocates standards for marketing, focusing on relevance to consumers. Provides research, education, and networking opportunities to members. Operates a service that removes consumer names from unwanted mailing lists. Monitors legislation and regulations. (Headquarters in New York.)

International Sign Assn., *1001 N. Fairfax St., #301, Alexandria, VA 22314; (703) 836-4012. Fax, (703) 836-8353. Lori Anderson, President.*
General e-mail, info@signs.org

Web, www.signs.org

Membership: manufacturers and distributors of signs. Promotes the sign industry; conducts workshops and seminars; sponsors annual competition.

Outdoor Advertising Assn. of America, *1850 M St. N.W., #1040 20036; (202) 833-5566. Fax, (202) 833-1522. Nancy Fletcher, President.*
Web, www.oaaa.org

Membership: outdoor advertising companies, operators, suppliers, and affiliates. Serves as a clearinghouse for public service advertising campaigns. Monitors legislation and regulations.

SMALL AND DISADVANTAGED BUSINESS

►AGENCIES

Agency for International Development (USAID), *Small and Disadvantaged Business Utilization/Minority Resource Center, 1300 Pennsylvania Ave. N.W., #5.8-C 20523-5800; (202) 712-1500. Fax, (202) 216-3056. Mauricio Vera, Director.*
Web, www.usaid.gov

Counsels small and minority-owned businesses on how to do business with USAID. Identifies opportunities for small businesses in subcontracting with the agency.

Commerce Dept., *Business Liaison, 1401 Constitution Ave. N.W., #5062 20230; (202) 482-1360. Fax, (202) 482-4054. Mary Tinsley Raul, Director.*
Web, www.doc.gov/obl

Serves as the central office for business assistance. Handles requests for information and services as well as complaints and suggestions from businesses; provides a forum for businesses to comment on federal regulations; initiates meetings on policy issues with industry groups, business organizations, trade and small business associations, and the corporate community.

Consumer Product Safety Commission (CPSC), *Small Business Ombudsman, 4330 East-West Hwy., Bethesda, MD 20814; (888) 531-9070. Fax, (301) 504-0121. Kevin Robinson, Ombudsman.*
General e-mail, sbo@cpsc.gov

Web, www.cpsc.gov

Provides guidance and advice about compliance with CPSC laws and regulations as well as technical assistance in resolving problems.

Farm Service Agency (FSA), *(Agriculture Dept.), Minority and Socially Disadvantaged Farmers Assistance, 1400 Independence Ave. S.W., MS 0503 20250-0503; (202) 720-1584. Fax, (202) 720-5398. Gypsy Banks, Director. TTY, (202) 720-5132. Toll-free, (866) 538-2610 (phone); (866) 302-1760 (fax); (866) 480-2824 (TTY).*
General e-mail, msda@wdc.usda.gov

Web, www.fsa.usda.gov

Works with minority and socially disadvantaged farmers who have concerns and questions about loan applications filed with local offices or other Farm Service Agency programs.

Federal Emergency Management Agency (FEMA), *(Homeland Security Dept.), Mitigation Division, 500 C St. S.W., #406 20472; (202) 646-2781. Fax, (202) 646-7970. David I. Maurstad, Assistant Administrator.*
Web, www.fema.gov/nfip

Administers federal crime and flood insurance programs. Makes low-cost flood and crime insurance available to eligible small businesses.

General Services Administration (GSA), *Small Business Utilization, 1800 F St. N.W., #6029 20405; (202) 501-1021. Fax, (202) 501-2590. Mary Parks, Associate Administrator (Acting).*

Web, www.gsa.gov

Works to increase small business procurement of government contracts. Provides policy guidance and direction for GSA Business Service Centers, which offer advice and assistance to businesses interested in government procurement.

Minority Business Development Agency *(Commerce Dept.), 14th St. and Constitution Ave. N.W., #5053 20230; (202) 482-5061. Fax, (202) 501-4698. Ronald N. Langston, Director. Information, (888) 324-1551.*

Web, www.mbda.gov

Assists minority business owners in obtaining federal loans and contract awards; produces an annual report on federal agencies' performance in procuring from minority-owned businesses. Assists minority entrepreneurs one-on-one with financial planning, marketing, management, and technical assistance. Focuses on promoting wealth in minority communities.

National Science Foundation (NSF), *Industrial Innovation and Partnerships: Small Business Innovation Research/Small Business Technology Transfer, 4201 Wilson Blvd., #590, Arlington, VA 22230; (703) 292-8050. Fax, (703) 292-9057. Kesh Narayanan, Director; Joseph Hennessey, Senior Adviser.*

General e-mail, sbir@nsf.gov

Web, www.nsf.gov/eng/iip/sbir

Serves as liaison between the small-business community and NSF offices; awards grants and contracts. Administers the Small Business Innovation Research Program, which funds research proposals from small science/high technology firms; offers incentives for commercial development, including NSF-funded research.

National Women's Business Council, *409 3rd St. S.W., #210 20024; (202) 205-3850. Fax, (202) 205-6825. Carole Jean Jordan, Chair; Margaret Mankin Barton, Executive Director.*

General e-mail, info@nwbc.gov

Web, www.nwbc.gov

Independent, congressionally mandated council established by the Women's Business Ownership Act of 1988. Reviews the status of women-owned businesses nationwide and makes policy recommendations to the president, Congress, and the Small Business Administration. Assesses the role of the federal government in aiding and promoting women-owned businesses.

Securities and Exchange Commission, *Economic Analysis, 100 F St. N.E., #9461 20549; (202) 551-6600. Fax, (202) 772-9290. James A. Overdahl, Chief Economist. Information, (202) 942-8088.*

Web, www.sec.gov

Provides the commission with economic analyses of proposed rule and policy changes and other information to guide the SEC in influencing capital markets. Evaluates the effect of policy and other factors on competition within the securities industry and among competing securities markets; compiles financial statistics on capital formation and the securities industry.

Small Business Administration (SBA), *409 3rd St. S.W., #7600 20416-7600; (202) 205-6605. Fax, (202) 205-6802. Sandy Baruah, Administrator; Jovita Carranza, Deputy Administrator. Press, (202) 205-6740. Toll-free information (Answer Desk), (800) 827-5722. Locator, (202) 205-6600.*

Web, www.sba.gov

Provides small businesses with financial and management assistance; offers loans to victims of floods, natural disasters, and other catastrophes; licenses, regulates, and guarantees some financing of small-business investment companies; conducts economic and statistical research on small businesses. SBA Answer Desk is an information and referral service. District or regional offices can be contacted for specific loan information.

Small Business Administration (SBA), *Advocacy, 409 3rd St. S.W., #7800 20416; (202) 205-6533. Fax, (202) 205-6928. Shawne Carter McGibbon, Chief Counsel (Acting).*

General e-mail, agh@adv.sba.gov

Web, www.sba.gov/advo

Acts as an advocate for small business viewpoints in regulatory and legislative proceedings. Economic Research Office analyzes the effects of government policies on small businesses and documents the contributions of small business to the economy.

Small Business Administration (SBA), *Business and Community Initiatives, 409 3rd St. S.W., #6100 20416; (202) 205-6665. Fax, (202) 205-7416. Ellen M. Thrasher, Director.*

Web, www.sba.gov/BI

Provides small businesses with instruction and counseling in marketing, accounting, product analysis, production methods, research and development, and management problems.

Small Business Administration (SBA), *Business Development, 409 3rd St. S.W., #8000 20416; (202) 205-6613. Fax, (202) 205-7267. Luz A. Hopewell, Associate Administrator, (202) 205-6460.*

General e-mail, 8abd@sba.gov

Web, www.sba.gov/8abd

Coordinates the services provided by private industry, banks, the SBA, and other government agencies—such as business development and management and technical assistance—to increase the number of small

Small Business Administration

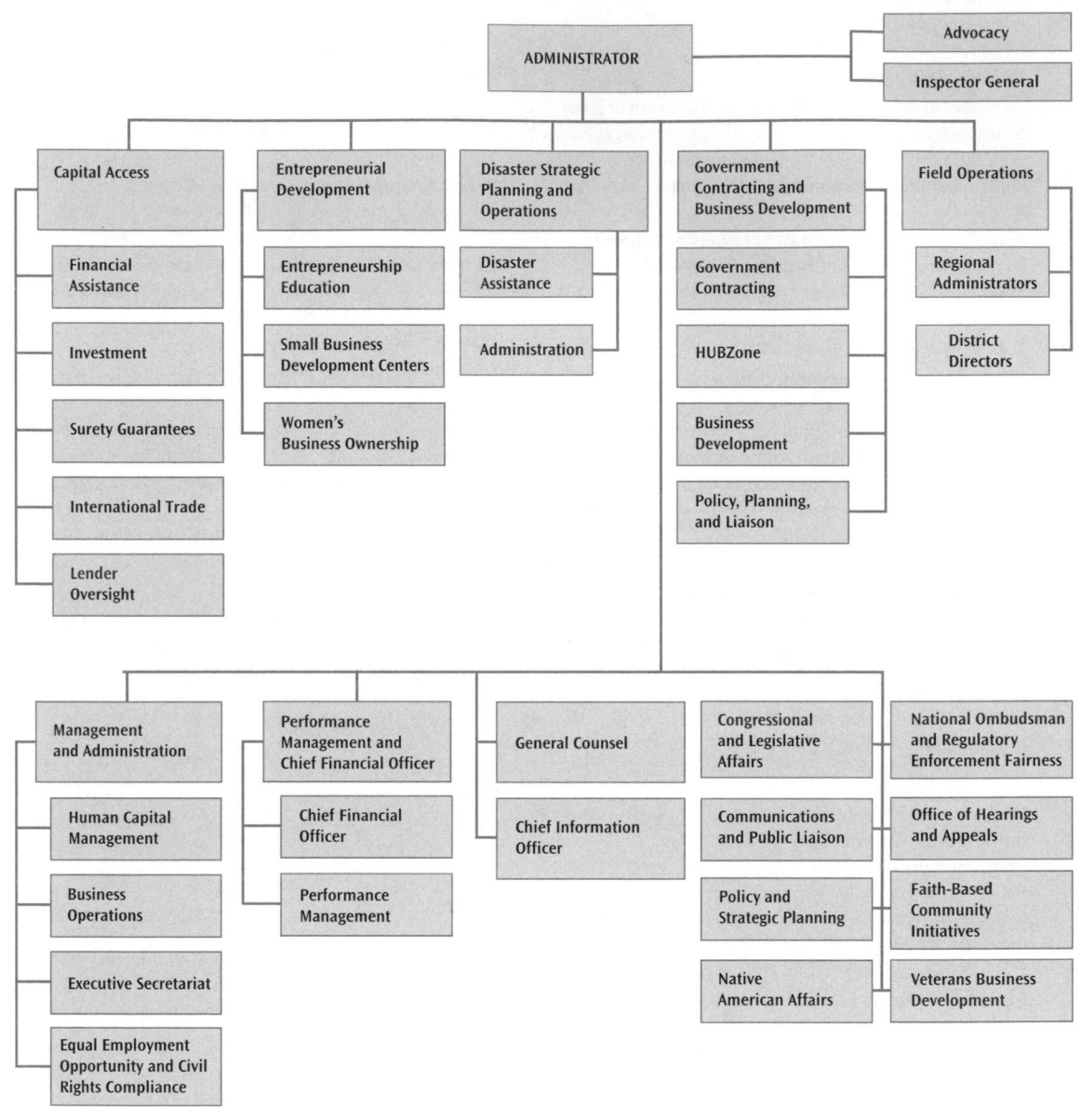

businesses owned by socially and economically disadvantaged Americans.

Small Business Administration (SBA), *Capital Access,* 409 3rd St. S.W., #8200 20416; (202) 205-6657. Fax, (202) 205-7230. Eric R. Zarnikow, Associate Deputy Administrator.
Web, www.sba.gov

Provides financial assistance to small business; focus includes surety guarantees, investment, and international trade. Makes microloans to start-up businesses and loans to established businesses for purchase of new equipment or facilities.

Small Business Administration (SBA), *Entrepreneurial Development,* 409 3rd St. S.W., 6th Floor 20416; (202) 205-6239. Anoop Prakash, Associate Administrator.
Web, www.sba.gov/ed

Responsible for business development programs of the offices of the Small Business Development Centers and the offices of Business Initiatives and Women's Business Ownership.

Small Business Administration (SBA), *Financial Assistance,* 409 3rd St. S.W., #8300 20416; (202) 205-6490. Fax, (202) 205-7722. Grady Hedgespeth, Director.
Web, www.sba.gov/services/financialassistance/index.html

Makes available guaranteed loans to aid in developing small businesses.

Small Business Administration (SBA), *Women's Business Ownership,* 409 3rd St. S.W., 6th Floor 20416; (202) 205-6673. Fax, (202) 205-7287. Wilma Goldstein, Director; Ann Bradberry, Deputy Administrator.
Web, www.sba.gov/women

Advocates for current and potential women business owners throughout the federal government and in the private sector. Provides training and counseling; offers information on national and local resources.

White House Initiative on Asian Americans and Pacific Islanders, 1401 Constitution Ave. N.W., #5612, MS 5063 20230; (202) 482-3949. Fax, (202) 501-6239. Jimmy D. Lee, Executive Director; Cianna Ferrer, Special Assistant to the Director.
General e-mail, info@aapi.gov

Web, www.aapi.gov

Develops, monitors, and coordinates federal efforts to improve the economic and community development of Asian American and Pacific Islander businesses through increased participation in federal programs and private-sector partnerships. Improves and increases the collection of data related to Asian American and Pacific Islander businesses. Suggests ways to increase the business diversification of Asian Americans and Pacific Islanders.

▶**CONGRESS**

For a listing of relevant congressional committees and subcommittees, please see page 32 or the Appendix.

▶**NONGOVERNMENTAL**

Assn. of Hispanic Advertising Agencies, 8400 Westpark Dr., 2nd Floor, McLean, VA 22102; (703) 610-9014. Fax, (7048

3) 610-9005. Horacio Gavilan, *Executive Director.*
General e-mail, info@ahaa.org

Web, www.ahaa.org

Works to grow, strengthen, and protect the Hispanic marketing and advertising industry. Strives to increase Hispanics' awareness of market opportunities and enhance professionalism of the industry.

Center for Women's Business Research, 1760 Old Meadow Rd., #500, McLean, VA 22102; (703) 556-7162. Fax, (703) 506-3266. Sharon G. Hadary, Executive Director.

Small and Disadvantaged Business Contacts at Federal Departments and Agencies

DEPARTMENTS
Agriculture, Richard Ashworth (Acting), (202) 720-7117
Commerce, Vacant, (202) 482-1472
Defense, Linda Oliver, (703) 604-0017
  Air Force, Ronald Poussard, (703) 696-1103
  Army, Tracey L. Pinson, (703) 695-9800
  Navy, Vacant, (202) 685-6485
Education, Kristi Wilson, (202) 245-6300
Energy, Brenda DeGraffemreid, (202) 586-7377
Health and Human Services, Deborah Ridgely, (202) 690-7300
Homeland Security, Kevin Boshears, (202) 447-5279 or (202) 447-5284
  Coast Guard, Gregory A. Cate, (202) 475-3757
Housing and Urban Development, Valerie Hayes (Acting), (202) 708-1428
Interior, Mark Oliver, (202) 208-3493
Justice, David Sutton, (202) 616-0521
Labor, Jose A. "Joe" Lira, (202) 693-6460
State, Gregory Mayberry, (703) 875-6822
Transportation, Brenda Neal, (202) 366-1930
Treasury, Virginia Bellamy Graham (202) 622-2826
Veterans Affairs, Gail Wegner (Acting), (202) 303-3260

AGENCIES
Agency for International Development, Mauricio Vera, (202) 712-1500
Consumer Product Safety Commission, Patricia Bittner, (301) 504-7263
Environmental Protection Agency, Jeanette L. Brown, (202) 566-2075
General Services Administration, Mary Parks (Acting), (202) 501-1021
National Aeronautics and Space Administration, David Grove, (202) 358-0795
Nuclear Regulatory Commission, Corenthis "Ren" Kelley, (301) 415-7380
Social Security Administration, Wayne McDonald, (410) 965-7467

General e-mail, info@womensbusinessresearch.org
Web, www.cfwbr.org

Conducts research on women-owned businesses.

Enterprise Development Group (EDG), 901 S. Highland St., Arlington, VA 22204; (703) 685-0510. Fax, (703) 685-4200. Haddish Welday, Finance Manager.
General e-mail, edgloan@entdevgroup.org

Web, www.entdevgroup.org

Provides micro-loans to clients in the Washington metropolitan area with low-to-moderate income in order to promote new business enterprises and individual self-sufficiency. Offers business training and pre- and post-loan technical assistance to entrepreneurs. Operates a matched savings program for low-income refugees and a car loan program for those with inadequate transportation. An independent subsidiary of the Ethiopian Community Development Council.

Maryland/District of Columbia Minority Supplier Development Council, *10770 Columbia Pike, Lower Level, #L100, Silver Spring, MD 20901; (301) 592-6700. Fax, (301) 592-6704. Kenneth E. Clark, President.*
General e-mail, info@mddccouncil.org

Web, www.mddccouncil.org

Certifies minority (Asian, African American, Hispanic, and Native American) business enterprises. Refers corporate buyers to minority suppliers and supports the development, expansion, and promotion of corporate minority supplier development programs. Offers networking opportunities and gives awards. Disseminates statistics and information. Provides consultation services, educational seminars, financial assistance, technical assistance, and training opportunities. (Regional council of the National Minority Supplier Development Council.)

National Assn. of Investment Companies, *1300 Pennsylvania Ave. N.W., #700 20004; (202) 204-3001. Fax, (202) 204-3022. Samuel J. Boyd Jr., President.*
Web, www.naicvc.com

Membership: investment companies that provide minority-owned businesses with venture capital and management guidance. Provides technical assistance; monitors legislation and regulations.

National Assn. of Negro Business and Professional Women's Clubs Inc., *1806 New Hampshire Ave. N.W. 20009; (202) 483-4206. Fax, (202) 462-7253. Sandra A. Coleman, President.*
General e-mail, nanbpwc@aol.com

Web, www.nanbpwc.org

Promotes opportunities for African American women in business; sponsors workshops and scholarships; maintains a job bank. Monitors legislation and regulations.

National Assn. of Small Business Investment Companies, *666 11th St. N.W., #750 20005; (202) 628-5055. Fax, (202) 628-5080. Brett Palmer, President.*
Web, www.nasbic.org

Membership: companies licensed by the Small Business Administration to provide small businesses with advisory services, equity financing, and long-term loans.

National Assn. of Women Business Owners, *8405 Greensboro Dr., #800, McLean, VA 22102; (800) 556-2926. Fax, (703) 506-3266. Erin M. Fuller, Executive Director.*
General e-mail, national@nawbo.org

Web, www.nawbo.org

Promotes the economic, social, and political interests of women business owners through networking, leadership and business development training, and advocacy.

National Black Chamber of Commerce, *1350 Connecticut Ave. N.W., #405 20036; (202) 466-6888. Fax, (202) 466-4918. Harry C. Alford, President.*
General e-mail, info@nationalbcc.org

Web, www.nationalbcc.org

Membership: African American–owned businesses. Educates and trains the African American community in entrepreneurship and other economic areas.

National Federation of Independent Business (NFIB), *1201 F St. N.W., #200 20004-1221; (202) 554-9000. Fax, (202) 554-0496. Dan Danner, President.*
General e-mail, media@nfib.com

Web, www.nfib.com

Membership: independent businesses. Monitors public policy issues and legislation affecting small and independent businesses, including taxation, government regulation, labor-management relations, and liability insurance.

National Gay and Lesbian Chamber of Commerce, *1612 U St. N.W., #408 20009; (202) 234-9181. Fax, (202) 234-9185. Kate Karasmeighan, Chief of Staff.*
General e-mail, info@nglcc.org

Web, www.nglcc.org

Communicates ideas and information for and between businesses and organizations. Works with state and local chambers of commerce and business groups on various issues. Advocates on behalf of lesbian, gay, bisexual, and transgender owned businesses; professionals; students of business; and corporations.

National Indian Business Assn., *1730 Rhode Island Ave. N.W., #501 20036 (mailing address: 4004 David Lane, Alexandria, VA 22311); (202) 223-3766. Fax, (202) 955-5605. Pete Homer, President.*
General e-mail, phomerje@hotmail.com

Web, www.nibanetwork.org

Channels information on programs, policies, and legislation to the Native American business community. Monitors legislation and regulations.

National Small Business Assn., *1156 15th St. N.W., #1100 20005; (202) 293-8830. Fax, (202) 872-8543. Todd McCracken, President.*
General e-mail, nsba@nsba.biz

Web, www.nsba.biz

Membership: manufacturing, wholesale, retail, service, and other small business firms and regional small-business organizations. Represents the interests of small business before Congress, the administration, and federal agencies. Services to members include a toll-free legislative hotline and group insurance.

SCORE, *1175 Herndon Pkwy., #900, Herndon, VA 20170; (202) 205-6762. Fax, (202) 205-7636. W. Kenneth Yancey Jr., Chief Executive Officer. Information, (800) 634-0245. General e-mail, media@score.org*

Web, www.score.org

Independent volunteer organization funded by the Small Business Administration through which retired, semiretired, and active business executives use their knowledge and experience to counsel small businesses. (Formerly Service Corps of Retired Executives Assn.)

Small Business and Entrepreneurship Council (SBE Council), *2944 Hunter Mill Rd., #204, Oakton, VA 22124; (703) 242-5840. Fax, (703) 242-5841. Karen Kerrigan, President.*

General e-mail, info@sbecouncil.org

Web, www.sbecouncil.org

Membership: U.S. entrepreneurs and business owners. Promotes small business growth through policy modernization and limited government. Provides networking opportunities, educational resources, and market intelligence for its members. Monitors legislation and regulations.

Small Business Legislative Council, *1100 H St. N.W., #540 20005-5476; (202) 639-8500. Fax, (202) 296-5333. John S. Satagaj, President.*

General e-mail, email@sblc.org

Web, www.sblc.org

Membership: trade associations that represent small businesses in the manufacturing, wholesale, retail, service, and other sectors. Monitors and proposes legislation and regulations to benefit small businesses.

U.S. Chamber of Commerce, *Council on Small Business, 1615 H St. N.W.20062-2000; (202) 463-5498. Fax, (202) 463-3174. Giovanni Coratolo, Executive Director.*

Web, www.uschamber.com

Seeks to enhance visibility of small businesses within the national Chamber and the U.S. business community. Provides members with information on national small business programs and legislative issues.

U.S. Hispanic Chamber of Commerce, *2175 K St. N.W., #100 20037; (202) 842-1212. Fax, (202) 842-3221. Augustine Martinez, President.*

General e-mail, ushcc@ushcc.com

Web, www.ushcc.com

Membership: Hispanic Chambers of Commerce and business organizations. Monitors legislation that affects the Hispanic business community. Provides technical assistance to Hispanic business associations and owners. Promotes public policies that enhance the economic development of its members, trade between Hispanic businesses in the United States and Latin America, and partnerships between its members and the rest of the business community.

U.S. Pan Asian American Chamber of Commerce, *1329 18th St. N.W. 20036; (202) 296-5221. Fax, (202) 296-5225. Susan Allen, President.*

General e-mail, info@uspaacc.com

Web, www.uspaacc.com

Helps Asian American–owned businesses gain access to government and corporate contracts.

U.S. Women's Chamber of Commerce, *1200 G St. N.W., #800 20005; (202) 661-4701. Fax, (202) 661-4699. Margot Dorfman, Chief Executive Officer. Toll-free, (888) 41USWCC.*

General e-mail, 360advisors@uswcc360.org

Web, www.uswcc.org

Provides services and career opportunities to women in business, including networking, leadership training, political advocacy, access to government procurement markets, and technical expertise.

3

Communications
and the Media

GENERAL POLICY AND ANALYSIS

Basic Resources

▶AGENCIES

Federal Communications Commission (FCC), *445 12th St. S.W. 20554; (202) 418-1000. Fax, (202) 418-2801. Kevin J. Martin, Chair. TTY, (888) 835-5322. National Call Center, (888) 225-5322. Reference Information Center, (202) 418-0270. Media Relations, (202) 418-0500. Consumer and Government Affairs, (202) 418-1400. Legislative Affairs, (202) 418-1900.*
General e-mail, fccinfo@fcc.gov

Web, www.fcc.gov

Regulates interstate and foreign communications by radio, television, wire, cable, microwave, and satellite; consults with other government agencies and departments on national and international matters involving wire and radio telecommunications and with state regulatory commissions on telegraph and telephone matters; reviews applications for construction permits and licenses for such services. Reference Information Center open to the public (except under high alert status orange and higher).

Federal Communications Commission (FCC), *Media Bureau: Policy Division, 445 12th St. S.W. 20554; (202) 418-2120. Fax, (202) 418-1069. Mary Beth Murphy, Division Chief.*
Web, www.fcc.gov/mb/policy

Conducts proceedings concerning broadcast, cable, and post-licensing Direct Broadcast Satellite issues. Facilitates competition in the multichannel video programming marketplace by resolving carriage and other complaints involving access to facilities. Administers FCC's programs for political broadcasting and Equal Opportunity matters.

National Telecommunications and Information Administration (NTIA), *(Commerce Dept.), 1401 Constitution Ave. N.W., #4898 20230; (202) 482-1840. Fax, (202) 501-0536. Vacant, Assistant Secretary. Press, (202) 482-7002.*
Web, www.ntia.doc.gov

Develops domestic and international telecommunications policy for the executive branch; manages federal use of radio spectrum; conducts research on radiowave transmissions and other aspects of telecommunications; serves as information source for federal and state agencies on the efficient use of telecommunications resources.

▶CONGRESS

For a listing of relevant congressional committees and subcommittees, please see page 83 or the Appendix.

Legislative Resource Center, *B106 CHOB 20515; (202) 226-5200. Fax, (202) 226-5208. Deborah Turner, Chief.*
Web, http://clerk.house.gov

Records, stores, and provides legislative status information on all bills and resolutions pending in Congress. Print publications include a biographical directory, a guide to research collection of former House members, and books on African Americans and women who have served in Congress.

Library of Congress, *Copyright Office: Licensing, 101 Independence Ave. S.E., #454 20559; (202) 707-6800. Fax, (202) 707-0905. Jim Enzinna, Chief. Information, (202) 707-3000.*

Web, www.copyright.gov/licensing

Licenses cable television companies and satellite carriers; collects and distributes royalty payments under the copyright law. Distributes licenses for making and distributing digital audio recording products and for use of certain noncommercial broadcasting. Administers Section 115 licensing for making and distributing phonorecords.

▶INTERNATIONAL ORGANIZATIONS

Inter-American Telecommunication Commission (CITEL), *(Organization of American States), 1889 F St. N.W., #348 20006; (202) 458-3004. Fax, (202) 458-6854. Clovis Baptista, Executive Secretary.*
General e-mail, citel@oas.org

Web, www.citel.oas.org

Works with the public and private sectors to facilitate the development of universal telecommunications in the Americas.

▶NONGOVERNMENTAL

Accuracy in Media (AIM), *4455 Connecticut Ave. N.W., #330 20008; (202) 364-4401. Fax, (202) 364-4098. Donald K. Irvine, Board Chair.*
General e-mail, info@aim.org

Web, www.aim.org

Analyzes print and electronic news media for bias, omissions, and errors in news; approaches media with complaints. Maintains a speakers bureau and a library on political and media topics.

Alliance for Public Technology, *919 18th St. N.W., 10th Floor 20006; (202) 263-2970. Fax, (202) 263-2960. Sylvia Rosenthal, Executive Director, (202) 263-2971. Main phone is voice and TTY accessible.*
General e-mail, apt@apt.org

Web, www.apt.org

Membership: public groups, unions, and individuals concerned with developing affordable access to information services and telecommunications technology through broadband and advanced telecommunications technologies, and promoting improved and more affordable health care, expanded educational opportunities for lifelong learning, and simplified access to technology, particularly for the elderly, residential consumers, low-income groups, and people with disabilities.

Alliance for Telecommunications Industry Solutions (ATIS), *1200 G St. N.W., #500 20005; (202) 628-6380. Fax, (202) 393-5453. Susan M. Miller, President.*

General e-mail, atispr@atis.org

Web, www.atis.org

Develops and promotes the worldwide technical and operations standards for information, entertainment, and communications technologies. Sponsors industry forums; serves as an information clearinghouse. Member of the Inter-American Telecommunication Commission (CITEL). Monitors legislation and regulations.

Center for Media and Public Affairs (CMPA), *2100 L St. N.W., #300 20037-1561; (202) 223-2942. Fax, (202) 872-4014. S. Robert Lichter, President.*

General e-mail, mail@cmpa.com

Web, www.cmpa.com

Nonpartisan research and educational organization that studies media coverage of social and political issues and campaigns, specifically information about health risks and scientific matters. Conducts surveys; publishes materials and reports.

Computer and Communications Industry Assn. (CCIA), *900 17th St. N.W., #1100 20006; (202) 783-0070. Fax, (202) 783-0534. Edward J. Black, President; Heather Greenfield, Director of Media Relations.*

General e-mail, ccia@ccianet.org

Web, www.ccianet.org

Membership: Internet service providers, software providers, and manufacturers and suppliers of computer data processing and communications-related products and services. Interests include Internet freedom, privacy and neutrality, government electronic surveillance, telecommunications policy, tax policy, federal procurement policy, communications and computer industry standards, intellectual property policies, encryption, international trade, and antitrust reform.

Free Press, Washington Office, *501 3rd St. N.W., #875 20001; (202) 265-1490. Fax, (202) 265-1489. Josh Silver, Executive Director.*

General e-mail, info@freepress.net

Web, www.freepress.net

Seeks to engage the public in media policy making. Advocates policies for more competitive and public interest–oriented media. (Headquarters in Northhampton, Mass.)

Institute for Public Representation, *600 New Jersey Ave. N.W. 20001; (202) 662-9535. Fax, (202) 662-9634. Hope Babcock, Co-Director; Angela Campbell, Co-Director; David Vladeck, Co-Director. TTY, (202) 662-9538.*

General e-mail, gulcipr@law.georgetown.edu

Web, www.law.georgetown.edu/clinics/ipr

Public interest law firm and clinical education program founded by Georgetown University Law Center. Attorneys act as counsel for groups and individuals unable to obtain effective legal representation in the areas of First Amendment and media law, environmental law, civil rights, and general public interest matters. Gives graduate fellows an opportunity to work on unique, large-scale projects.

Info Comm International, *11242 Waples Mill Rd., #200, Fairfax, VA 22030; (703) 273-7200. Fax, (703) 278-8082. Randal A. Lemke, Executive Director. Information, (800) 659-7469.*

General e-mail, customerservice@infocomm.org

Web, www.infocomm.org

Membership: video and audiovisual dealers; manufacturers and producers; and individuals. Promotes the professional AV communications industry and seeks to enhance members' ability to conduct business successfully through tradeshows, education, certification, market research, and government relations. Interests include small business issues, intellectual property, sustainable buildings, and e-Waste. Monitors legislation and regulations. (Formerly the International Communications Industries Assn.)

Media Access Project (MAP), *1625 K St. N.W., #1000 20006; (202) 232-4300. Fax, (202) 466-7656. Andrew Jay Schwartzman, President.*

General e-mail, info@mediaaccess.org

Web, www.mediaaccess.org

Public interest telecommunications law firm that promotes the public's First Amendment right to access diverse information in the electronic mass media. Represents listeners' and speakers' interests in electronic media and telecommunications issues before the FCC, other policy-making bodies, and in the courts. Monitors legislation and regulations.

Media Institute, *2300 Clarendon Blvd., #503, Arlington, VA 22201; (703) 243-5700. Fax, (703) 243-8808. Patrick D. Maines, President.*

General e-mail, info@mediainstitute.org

Web, www.mediainstitute.org

Research foundation that conducts conferences, files court briefs and regulatory comments, and sponsors programs on communications topics. Advocates a competitive media and communications industry and free-speech rights for individuals, media, and corporate speakers.

Media Matters for America, *1625 Massachusetts Ave. N.W., #300 20036; (202) 756-4100. Fax, (202) 756-4101. David Brock, Chief Executive Officer.*

Web, http://mediamatters.org

COMMUNICATIONS AND THE MEDIA RESOURCES IN CONGRESS

For a complete listing of Congress committees, including their full contact information, leadership, membership, and jurisdictions, please refer to the Appendix on pages 724–837.

JOINT COMMITTEES:

Joint Committee on the Library, (202) 224-6352.
Joint Committee on Printing, (202) 224-6352.

HOUSE:

House Administration Committee, (202) 225-2061.
Web, cha.house.gov

House Appropriations Committee, Subcommittee on Labor, Health and Human Services, Education, and Related Agencies, (202) 225-3508.
Web, appropriations.house.gov

House Energy and Commerce Committee, Subcommittee on Telecommunications and the Internet, (202) 225-2927.
Web, energycommerce.house.gov

House Judiciary Committee, (202) 225-3951.
Web, judiciary.house.gov

Subcommittee on Commercial and Administrative Law, (202) 226-7680.

Subcommittee on the Constitution, Civil Rights, and Civil Liberties, (202) 225-2825.

Subcommittee on Courts, the Internet, and Intellectual Property, (202) 225-5741.

House Oversight and Government Reform Committee, Subcommittee on Information Policy, Census, and National Archives, (202) 225-6751.
Web, oversight.house.gov

SENATE:

Senate Appropriations Committee, Subcommittee on Labor, Health and Human Services, Education, and Related Agencies, (202) 224-9145.
Web, appropriations.senate.gov

Senate Commerce, Science, and Transportation Committee, Subcommittee on Science, Technology, and Innovation, (202) 224-0415.
Web, commerce.senate.gov

Senate Foreign Relations Committee, Subcommittee on International Operations and Organizations, Democracy, and Human Rights, (202) 224-4651.
Web, foreign.senate.gov

Senate Judiciary Committee, (202) 224-7703.
Web, judiciary.senate.gov

Subcommittee on Antitrust, Competition Policy, and Consumer Rights, (202) 224-3406.

Subcommittee on the Constitution, (202) 224-5573.

Subcommittee on Terrorism, Technology, and Homeland Security, (202) 224-4933.

Senate Rules and Administration Committee, (202) 224-6352.
Web, rules.senate.gov

Web-based research and information center concerned with monitoring and analyzing print, broadcast, cable, radio, and Internet media for unreliable news and commentary. Seeks to inform journalists and the general public about specific instances of misinformation and provide resources for taking action against false claims.

Media Research Center, *325 S. Patrick St., Alexandria, VA 22314; (703) 683-9733. Fax, (703) 683-9736. L. Brent Bozell III, President. Toll-free (800) 672-1423.*
General e-mail, mrc@mediaresearch.org

Web, www.mediaresearch.org

Media-watch organization working for balanced and responsible news coverage of political issues. Records and analyzes network news programs; analyzes print media; maintains profiles of media executives and library of recordings.

National Assn. of Broadcasters (NAB), *1771 N St. N.W. 20036-2891; (202) 429-5300. Fax, (202) 429-5406. David K. Rehr, President. Press, (202) 429-5350.*
General e-mail, nab@nab.org

Web, www.nab.org

Membership: radio and television broadcast stations and broadcast networks holding an FCC license or construction permit; associate members include producers of equipment and programs. Assists members in areas of management, engineering, and research. Interests include privatization abroad and related business opportunities. Monitors legislation and regulations.

National Assn. of Regulatory Utility Commissioners, *1101 Vermont Ave. N.W., #200 20005-3521; (202) 898-2200. Fax, (202) 898-2213. Charles D. Gray, Executive Director. Press, (202) 898-9382.*
General e-mail, admin@naruc.org

Web, www.naruc.org

Membership: members of federal, state, municipal, and international regulatory commissions that have jurisdiction over utilities and carriers. Interests include telecommunications, energy, and water regulation.

National Captioning Institute, *1900 Gallows Rd. #3000, Vienna, VA 22182; (703) 917-7600. Fax, (703) 917-9878. Gene Chao, President. Main phone is voice and TTY accessible.*

Federal Communications Commission

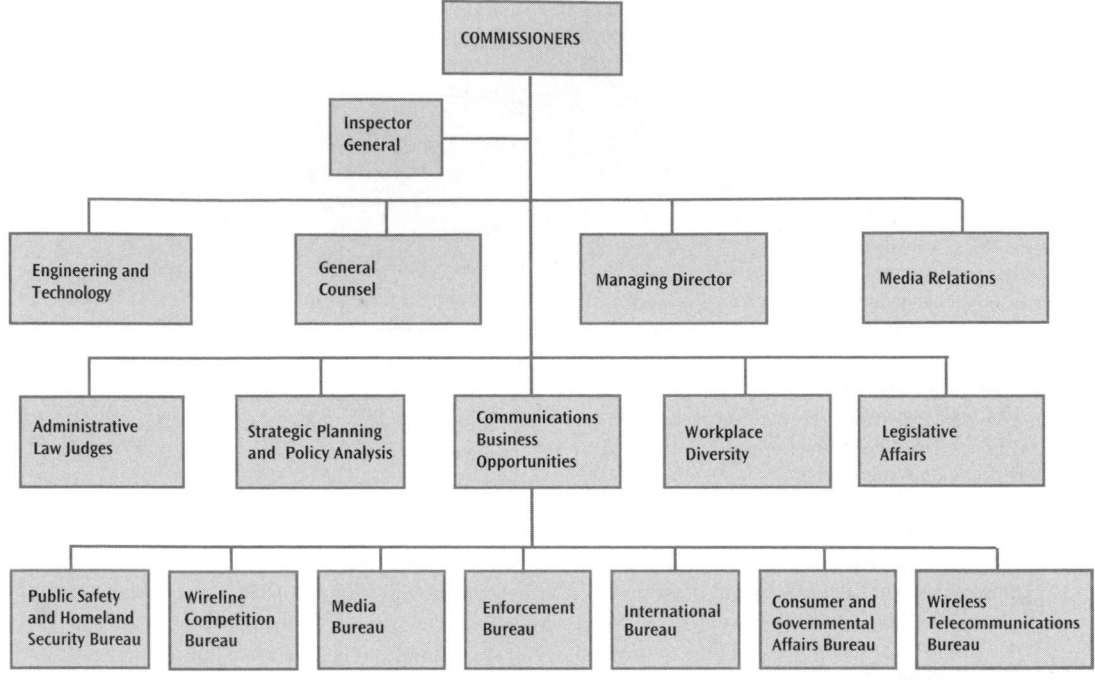

General e-mail, mail@ncicap.org

Web, www.ncicap.org

Captions television programs for the deaf and hard-of-hearing and produces audio descriptions for the blind on behalf of public and commercial broadcast television networks, cable networks, syndicators, program producers, government agencies, advertisers, and home video distributors. Produces and disseminates information about the national closed-captioning service and audio description services.

Pew Research Center for the People and the Press,
1615 L St. N.W., #700 20036; (202) 419-4350. Fax, (202) 419-4399. Andrew Kohut, President.
General e-mail, info@people-press.org

Web, http://people-press.org

Studies attitudes toward media, politics, and public policy issues through public opinion research. Conducts national surveys measuring public attentiveness to major news stories; charts trends in values and political and social attitudes. Makes survey results available free of charge to political leaders, scholars, journalists, and public interest groups.

Telecommunications for the Deaf and Hard of Hearing Inc., *8630 Fenton St., #604, Silver Spring, MD 20910-3803; (301) 589-3786. Fax, (301) 589-3797. Claude L. Stout, Executive Director. TTY, (301) 589-3006.*

General e-mail, info@tdi-online.org

Web, www.tdi-online.org

Membership: individuals, organizations, and businesses using text telephone (TTY) and video phone equipment. Promotes equal access in telecommunications, media, and information technology for people who are deaf, hard of hearing, late deafened, or deaf blind. Provides information on TTY equipment. Interests include closed captioning for television, emergency access (911), TTY and Internet relay services, and visual alerting systems. Publishes an annual TDI National Directory & Resource Guide and a quarterly news magazine, and hosts Biennial TDI Conference. Administers the Community Emergency Preparedness Information Network (CEPIN) project.

Telecommunications Industry Assn. (TIA), *2500 Wilson Blvd., #300, Arlington, VA 22201-3834; (703) 907-7700. Fax, (703) 907-7727. Grant Seiffert, President. TTY, (703) 907-7776. Press, (703) 907-7721 or (703) 907-7723.*
General e-mail, tia@tiaonline.org

Web, www.tiaonline.org

Trade association for the information and communications industry. Helps develop product standards. Advocates on behalf of domestic and international policy. Facilitates business opportunities for its members through trade shows and a job-matching service. (Represents the communications sector of the Electronic Industries Alliance.)

Cable Services

▶AGENCIES

Federal Communications Commission (FCC), *Media Bureau,* 445 12th St. S.W., 3rd Floor 20554; (202) 418-7200. Fax, (202) 418-2376. Monica Desai, Chief. General e-mail, mbinfo@fcc.gov

Web, www.fcc.gov/mb

Makes, recommends, and enforces rules governing cable television and other video distribution services; promotes industry growth, competition, and availability to the public; ensures reasonable rates for consumers in areas that do not have competition in cable service.

Federal Communications Commission (FCC), *Media Bureau: Engineering,* 445 12th St. S.W., #4-C838 20554; (202) 418-7012. Fax, (202) 418-1189. John Wong, Chief. *Web, www.fcc.gov/mb/engineering*

Provides technical advice for digital television (DTV) transition, latest cable technologies, and spectrum and broadband policies. Oversees the processing of routine cable applications.

▶NONGOVERNMENTAL

Alliance for Community Media (ACM), *666 11th St. N.W., #740 20001-4542; (202) 393-2650. Fax, (202) 393-2653. Helen Soule, Director of Information and Organizing Services.* General e-mail, acm@alliancecm.org

Web, www.alliancecm.org

Promotes local programming and participation in cable television. Interests include freedom of expression, diversity of information, and developing technologies. Monitors legislation and regulations.

CTAM, *201 N. Union St., #440, Alexandria, VA 22314; (703) 549-4200. Fax, (703) 684-1167. Char Beales, President.* General e-mail, info@ctam.com

Web, www.ctam.com

Promotes innovation in the cable and related industries in areas of marketing, research, management, and new product development. Sponsors annual marketing and research conferences; interests include international markets. CTAM stands for Cable and Telecommunications Assn. for Marketing.

National Cable Telecommunications Assn., *25 Massachusetts Ave. N.W., #100 20001-1413; (202) 222-2300. Fax, (202) 222-2411. Kyle McSlarrow, President. Press, (202) 222-2350. Government Relations, (202) 222-2410. Alternate fax, (202) 222-2351.* General e-mail, webmaster@ncta.com

Web, www.ncta.com

Membership: companies that operate cable television systems, cable television programmers, and manufacturers and suppliers of hardware and software for the industry. Represents the industry before federal regulatory agencies and Congress and in the courts; provides management and promotional aids and information on legal, legislative, and regulatory matters.

Enforcement, Judicial, and Legal Actions

▶AGENCIES

Antitrust Division *(Justice Dept.), Networks and Technology Enforcement, 600 E St. N.W., #9500 20530; (202) 307-6200. Fax, (202) 616-8544. James J. Tierney, Chief. Web, www.usdoj.gov/atr*

Reviews mergers in the areas of information technology, Internet-related businesses, financial services, and the securities industry.

Antitrust Division *(Justice Dept.), Telecommunications, 1401 H St. N.W., #8000 20530; (202) 514-5621. Fax, (202) 514-6381. Nancy M. Goodman, Chief. Press, (202) 514-2007. Web, www.usdoj.gov/atr*

Investigates and litigates antitrust cases dealing with communications and media; participates in agency proceedings and rulemaking concerning communications and media; monitors and analyzes legislation.

Federal Bureau of Investigation (FBI), *(Justice Dept.), CALEA Implementation Unit, FBI Quantico Engineering Research Facility (ERF) Building, #27958A, Quantico, VA 22135; (703) 632-4697. Fax, (703) 632-6855. Charles Barry Smith, Chief. Toll-free, (800) 551-0336. Web, www.askcalea.net*

Administers enforcement of the Communications Assistance for Law Enforcement Act (CALEA). Sets standards for telecommunications carriers concerning the development and deployment of electronic surveillance technologies. Promotes cooperation between the telecommunications industry, government entities, and law enforcement officials to develop intercept capabilities required by law enforcement.

Federal Communications Commission (FCC), *Administrative Law Judges, 445 12th St. S.W., #1C768 20554; (202) 418-2280. Fax, (202) 418-0195. Richard L. Sippel, Chief Judge. Web, www.fcc.gov/oalj*

Presides over hearings and issues initial decisions in disputes concerning FCC regulations and applications for licensing.

Federal Communications Commission (FCC), *Enforcement Bureau, 445 12th St. S.W., 3rd Floor, #7C723 20554; (202) 418-7450. Fax, (202) 418-2810. Kris*

Monteith, Chief, Enforcement Bureau. Media Relations,
(202) 418-8165.

Web, www.fcc.gov/eb

Commission's primary enforcement organization responsible for compliance with the Communications Act of 1934, the FCC's rules, Commission orders, and the terms of licenses and other authorizations. Promotes competition under the Telecommunications Act of 1996 and related regulations and ensures access to communications by the disabled. Houses the FCC's Office of Homeland Security.

►NONGOVERNMENTAL

Federal Communications Bar Assn., *1020 19th St. N.W.,*
#325 20036-6106; (202) 293-4000. Fax, (202) 293-4317.
Stanley Zenor, Executive Director.

General e-mail, fcba@fcba.org

Web, www.fcba.org

Membership: attorneys, nonattorneys, and law students in communications law who practice before the Federal Communications Commission, the courts, and state and local regulatory agencies. Cooperates with the FCC and other members of the bar on legal aspects of communications issues.

International and Satellite Communications

►AGENCIES

Federal Communications Commission (FCC),
International Bureau, 445 12th St. S.W., 6th Floor 20554;
(202) 418-0437. Fax, (202) 418-2818. Helen Domenici,
Chief.

Web, www.fcc.gov/ib

Coordinates the FCC's international policy activities; represents the FCC in international forums. Licenses international telecommunications carriers, undersea cables, international short-wave broadcasters, and satellite facilities. Coordinates the FCC's collection and dissemination of information on communications and telecommunications policy, regulation, and market developments in other countries and the policies and regulations of international organizations.

Federal Communications Commission (FCC), *Media*
Bureau: Policy Division, 445 12th St. S.W. 20554; (202)
418-2120. Fax, (202) 418-1069. Mary Beth Murphy,
Division Chief.

Web, www.fcc.gov/mb/policy

Conducts proceedings and drafts policy on post-licensing Direct Broadcast Satellite issues. Enforces the Satellite Home Viewer Enforcement Act.

Federal Communications Commission (FCC), *Wireline*
Competition Bureau, 445 12th St. S.W., 5th Floor 20554;
(202) 418-1500. Fax, (202) 418-2825. Dana Shaffer, Chief.
TTY, (202) 418-0484.

Web, www.fcc.gov/wcb

Develops and recommends FCC policies involving common carriers (wireline facilities that furnish interstate communications services for hire). Interests include deregulation, pricing policy, economic and technical aspects, numbering resources, and competition in telecommunications markets.

National Telecommunications and Information
Administration (NTIA), *(Commerce Dept.), 1401*
Constitution Ave. N.W., #4898 20230; (202) 482-1840.
Fax, (202) 501-0536. Meredith A. Baker, Assistant
Secretary (Acting). Press, (202) 482-7002.

Web, www.ntia.doc.gov

Represents the U.S. telecommunications sector (along with the State Department) in negotiating international agreements, including conferences with the International Telecommunication Union.

State Dept., *International Communications and*
Information Policy, 2201 C St. N.W., #6333, MC EEB/
CIP 20520-5820; (202) 647-5212. Fax, (202) 647-5957.
David A. Gross, U.S. Coordinator.

Web, www.state.gov/e/eeb/cip

Coordinates U.S. government international communication and information policy. Acts as a liaison for other federal agencies and the private sector in international communications issues. Promotes advancement of information and communication technology with expanded access and improved efficiency and security; the creation of business opportunities at home and abroad in this sector; resolution of telecommunications trade issues in conjunction with the Office of the U.S. Trade Representative; and the expansion of access to this technology globally.

►INTERNATIONAL ORGANIZATIONS

Intelsat, *3400 International Dr. N.W. 20008-3006; (202)*
944-6800. Fax, (202) 944-7898. David McGlade, Chief
Executive Officer.

Web, www.intelsat.com

Owns and operates a global satellite communications system and complementary terrestrial network. Helps service providers, broadcasters, corporations, and governments transmit information and content internationally.

►NONGOVERNMENTAL

Satellite Broadcasting and Communications Assn.
(SBCA), *1730 M St. N.W., #600 20036; (202) 349-3620.*
Fax, (202) 349-3621. Joseph Widoff, Executive Director.
General e-mail, info@sbca.org

Web, www.sbca.com

Membership: owners, operators, manufacturers, dealers, and distributors of satellite receiving stations; software and program suppliers; and others in the satellite services industry. Promotes use of satellite technology for broadcast delivery of video, audio, voice, broadband, and interactive services and as part of the national and global information infrastructure. Monitors legislation and regulations.

Satellite Industry Association (SIA), *1730 M St. N.W., #600 20036; (202) 349-3650. Fax, (202) 349-3622. Patricia Cooper, President.*
General e-mail, info@sia.org
Web, www.sia.org

Trade association representing global satellite operators, service providers, manufacturers, launch services providers, and ground equipment suppliers. Promotes the benefits and uses of commercial satellite technology. Monitors legislation and regulations, domestically and abroad.

Radio and Television

▶AGENCIES

Corporation for Public Broadcasting, *401 9th St. N.W. 20004-2129; (202) 879-9600. Fax, (202) 879-9700. Louise Filkins, Press Contact. Press, (202) 879-9758. Comments, (800) 272-2190.*
General e-mail, press@cpb.org
Web, www.cpb.org

Private corporation chartered by Congress under the Public Broadcasting Act of 1967 and funded by the federal government. Supports public broadcasting through grants for public radio and television stations; provides general support for national program production and operation; helps fund projects on U.S. and international news, culture, history, and natural history; studies emerging technologies, such as cable and satellite transmission, the Internet and broadband communication networks, for possible use by public telecommunications; supports training activities.

Federal Communications Commission (FCC), *Enforcement Bureau, 445 12th St. S.W., 3rd Floor, #7C723 20554; (202) 418-7450. Fax, (202) 418-2810. Kris Monteith, Chief, Enforcement Bureau. Media Relations, (202) 418-8165.*
Web, www.fcc.gov/eb

Monitors the radio spectrum and inspects broadcast stations; ensures that U.S. radio laws and FCC rules are observed. Develops activities to inform, assist, and educate licensees; provides presentations and information. Manages the Emergency Alert System. Operates the National Call Center in Gettysburg, Pa.

Federal Communications Commission (FCC), *Engineering and Technology, 445 12th St. S.W., 7th Floor 20554; (202) 418-2470. Fax, (202) 418-1944. Julius Knapp, Chief.*
General e-mail, oetinfo@fcc.gov
Web, www.fcc.gov/oet

Advises the FCC on technical and spectrum matters and assists in developing U.S. telecommunications policy.

Identifies and reviews developments in telecommunications and related technologies. Studies characteristics of radio frequency spectrum. Certifies radios and other electronic equipment to meet FCC standards.

Federal Communications Commission (FCC), *Media Bureau: Broadcast License Policy, 445 12th St. S.W., #2C337 20554; (202) 418-2600. Fax, (202) 418-2376. Monica Desai, Chief.*
Web, www.fcc.gov/mb

Responsible for the regulation of analog and digital broadcast services. Licenses, regulates, and develops audio and video services in traditional broadcasting and emerging television delivery systems, including digital television (DTV). Processes applications for licensing commercial and noncommercial radio and television broadcast equipment and facilities; handles renewals and changes of ownership; investigates public complaints.

National Endowment for the Arts (NEA), *Dance, Design, Media Arts, Museums, and Visual Arts, 1100 Pennsylvania Ave. N.W., #729 20506; (202) 682-5452. Fax, (202) 682-5721. Jeff Watson, Visual Arts Division Coordinator; Douglas Sonntag, Director, Dance; Maurice Cox, Director, Design; Ted Libbey, Director, Media Arts; Robert Frankel, Director, Museums and Visual Arts. TTY, (202) 682-5496.*
Web, www.arts.gov

Awards grants to nonprofit organizations for film, video, and radio productions; supports arts programming broadcast nationally on public television and radio.

▶NONGOVERNMENTAL

Assn. for Maximum Service Television (MSTV), *P.O. Box 9897, 4100 Wisconsin Ave. N.W. 20016; (202) 966-1956. Fax, (202) 966-9617. David L. Donovan, President.*
General e-mail, mstv@mstv.org
Web, www.mstv.org

Membership: commercial and educational television stations. Participates in FCC rulemaking proceedings; specializes in television engineering and other matters concerning the transmission structure of the nation's television system.

Center for SCREEN-TIME Awareness, *1200 29th St. N.W., Lower Level #1 20007-3363; (202) 333-9220. Fax, (202) 333-9221. Robert Kesten, Executive Director.*
General e-mail, cfstaemail@screentime.org
Web, www.screentime.org

Promotes a voluntary and dramatic reduction in the amount of screen-media watched by Americans. Sponsors National TV Turn-off Week.

Electronic Industries Alliance, *2500 Wilson Blvd., Arlington, VA 22201-3834; (703) 907-7500. Fax, (703) 907-7501. Dave McCurdy, Interim President.*
Web, www.eia.org

Membership: U.S. electronics manufacturers. Interests include common distribution, government procurement, high-definition television, and home recording rights; promotes trade, competitiveness, and export expansion through the International Business Council. Monitors legislation and regulations.

National Assn. of Broadcasters (NAB), *1771 N St. N.W. 20036-2891; (202) 429-5300. Fax, (202) 429-5406. David K. Rehr, President. Press, (202) 429-5350.*

General e-mail, nab@nab.org

Web, www.nab.org

Membership: radio and television broadcast stations and broadcast networks holding an FCC license or construction permit; associate members include producers of equipment and programs. Assists members in areas of management, engineering, and research. Interests include privatization abroad and related business opportunities. Monitors legislation and regulations.

National Public Radio, *635 Massachusetts Ave. N.W. 20001-3753; (202) 513-2000. Fax, (202) 513-3329. Vivian Schiller, President. Press, (202) 513-2300. Audience services (tapes, transcripts, and listener inquiries), (202) 513-3232.*

General e-mail, ombudsman@npr.org

Web, www.npr.org

Privately supported membership organization composed of public radio stations nationwide. Produces and distributes news and public affairs programming, congressional hearings, speeches, cultural and dramatic presentations, and programs for specialized audiences. Provides program distribution service via satellite. Represents member stations before Congress, the FCC, and other regulatory agencies.

Public Broadcasting Service, *2100 Crystal Dr., Arlington, VA 22202; (703) 739-5000. Fax, (703) 739-0775. Paula Kerger, President; Michael Getler, Ombudsman, (703) 739-5290.*

General e-mail, pbs@pbs.org

Web, www.pbs.org

Membership: public television stations nationwide. Selects, schedules, promotes, and distributes national programs; provides public television stations with educational, instructional, and cultural programming; also provides news and public affairs, science and nature, and children's programming. Assists members with technology development and fundraising.

Telephone and Telegraph

For cellular telephones, see Wireless Telecommunications

▶AGENCIES

Federal Communications Commission (FCC), *Wireline Competition Bureau, 445 12th St. S.W., 5th Floor 20554;*

(202) 418-1500. Fax, (202) 418-2825. Dana Shaffer, Chief. TTY, (202) 418-0484.

Web, www.fcc.gov/wcb

Develops and recommends FCC policies involving common carriers (wireline facilities that furnish interstate communications services for hire). Interests include deregulation, pricing policy, economic and technical aspects, numbering resources, and competition in telecommunications markets.

General Services Administration (GSA), *Federal Relay Service (FedRelay), 10304 Eaton Pl., Fairfax, VA 22030; (703) 306-6308. Patricia Stevens, Program Manager. Customer service, (800) 877-0996 (Voice/TTY, ASCII, Spanish). Toll-free, (800) 877-8339 (TTY/ASCII). VCO (Voice Carry Over), (877) 877-6280. Speech-to-Speech, (877) 877-8982. Voice, (866) 377-8642. TeleBraille, (866) 893-8340.*

General e-mail, patricia.stevens@gsa.gov

Web, www.gsa.gov/fedrelay

Provides equal telecommunications access for active and retired federal employees (civilian or military), veterans, and U.S. tribal members who are deaf, hard of hearing, or deaf-blind, or who have speech disabilities. Federal Relay Service features are: Voice, TTY, VCO, HCO, Speech-to-Speech, Spanish, Telebraille, CapTel, Video Relay Service (VRS), Internet Relay (FRSO), and Relay Conference Captioning (RCC). Publishes the U.S. Government TTY Directory, available at www.fts.gsa.gov/frs/ttydir.htm. Service is managed by the GSA.

▶NONGOVERNMENTAL

COMPTEL, *900 17th St. N.W., #400 20006; (202) 296-6650. Fax, (202) 296-7585. Jerry James, Chief Executive Officer.*

Web, www.comptel.org

Membership: providers of voice, video, and data offerings and the developers and providers of IP-based networks and services. Advocates for the competitive telecommunications industry before Congress, the FCC, and state regulatory agencies; sponsors trade shows and conferences. Monitors legislation and regulations.

National Telecommunications Cooperative Assn. (NTCA), *4121 Wilson Blvd., 10th Floor, Arlington, VA 22203-1801; (703) 351-2000. Fax, (703) 351-2001. Michael E. Brunner, Chief Executive Officer.*

General e-mail, pubrelations@ntca.org

Web, www.ntca.org

Membership: locally owned and controlled telecommunications cooperatives and companies serving rural and small-town areas. Offers educational seminars, workshops, technical assistance, and a benefits program to members. Monitors legislation and regulations.

Organization for the Promotion and Advancement of Small Telecommunications Companies (OPASTCO),

21 Dupont Circle N.W., #700 20036-1544; (202) 659-5990. Fax, (202) 659-4619. John N. Rose, President.

General e-mail, opastco@opastco.org

Web, www.opastco.org

Membership: local exchange carriers with 100,000 or fewer access lines, generally in rural areas. Provides members with educational materials and information on regulatory, legislative, and judicial issues in the telecommunications industry. Operates Foundation for Rural Education and Development.

U.S. Telecom Assn. (USTA), *607 14th St. N.W., #400 20005; (202) 326-7300. Fax, (202) 326-7333. Walter B. McCormick Jr., President.*

General e-mail, policy@ustelecom.org

Web, www.ustelecom.org

Membership: telecommunication companies and manufacturers and suppliers for these companies. Provides members with information on the industry; conducts seminars; participates in FCC regulatory proceedings.

Wireless Telecommunications

▶AGENCIES

Federal Communications Commission (FCC), *Wireless Telecommunications Bureau, 445 12th St. S.W. 20554; (202) 418-0600. Fax, (202) 418-0787. Jim Schlichting, Chief (Acting).*

Web, http://wireless.fcc.gov

Regulates domestic wireless communications, including cellular telephone, paging, personal communications services, public safety, air and maritime navigation, and other commercial and private radio services. Responsible for implementing the competitive bidding authority for spectrum auctions. Assesses new uses of wireless technologies, including electronic commerce. (Gettysburg office handles all licensing: FCC Wireless Telecommunications Bureau, Spectrum Management Resources and Technologies Division, 1270 Fairfield Rd., Gettysburg, PA 17325; (717) 338-2510.)

Homeland Security Dept. (DHS), *Science and Technology Directorate: SAFECOM Program, P.O. Box 57243 20037; (866) 969-7233. David Boyd, Director. Press, (202) 254-2385.*

General e-mail, SAFECOM@dhs.gov

Web, www.safecomprogram.gov

Serves as the umbrella program to help state, local, tribal, and federal public safety agencies build more effective and interoperable wireless communications. Develops processes to advance communications standards. Researches emerging technology. Provides training, grants, and technical assistance for radio, voice, and data communications systems. Web site provides information on topics relevant to emergency response communications and features best practices.

U.S. Secret Service *(Homeland Security Dept.),* **Financial Crimes Division,** *950 H St. N.W., #5300 20223; (202) 406-9330. Fax, (202) 406-5016. John Large, Special Agent in Charge.*

Web, www.secretservice.gov/financial_crimes.shtml

Plans, reviews, and coordinates criminal investigations involving reports of bank fraud, credit fraud, telecommunications and computer crimes, fraudulent securities, and electronic funds transfer fraud.

▶NONGOVERNMENTAL

CTIA—The Wireless Assn., *1400 16th St. N.W., #600 20036; (202) 785-0081. Fax, (202) 785-0721. Steve Largent, President.*

General e-mail, info@ctia.org

Web, www.ctia.org

Membership: system operators, equipment manufacturers, engineering firms, and others engaged in the cellular telephone and mobile communications industry in domestic and world markets. Monitors legislation and regulations.

Enterprise Wireless Alliance, *8484 Westpark Dr., #630, McLean, VA 22102; (703) 528-5115. Fax, (703) 524-1074. Mark E. Crosby, Chief Executive Officer. Toll-free, (800) 886-4222.*

General e-mail, customerservice@enterprisewireless.org

Web, www.ita-relay.com

Membership: enterprise wireless companies, dealers, and trade associations. Serves as an information source on radio frequencies, licensing, new products and technology, and market conditions. Monitors legislation and regulations. (Merger of the American Mobile Telecommunications Assn., the Licensing Assistance Office, the Council of Independent Communication Suppliers, and the Industrial Telecommunications Assn.)

PCIA—The Wireless Infrastructure Assn., *901 N. Washington St., #600, Alexandria, VA 22314; (703) 739-0300. Fax, (703) 836-1608. Michael T. N. Fitch, President. Information, (800) 759-0300. Press, (703) 535-7409*

Web, www.pcia.com

Represents companies that make up the wireless telecommunications infrastructure industry. Supports wireless communications and information infrastructure, and manages AWS Clearinghouse (www.awsclearinghouse.com), which facilitates the process of cost sharing in spectrum relocation.

Utilities Telecom Council (UTC), *1901 Pennsylvania Ave. N.W., 5th Floor 20006; (202) 872-0030. Fax, (202) 872-1331. William Moroney, President.*

Web, www.utc.org

Membership: companies that own, manage, or provide critical telecommunications systems in support of their core business, including energy, gas, and water utility companies, pipeline companies, and radio and international critical infrastructure organizations. Participates in FCC rulemaking proceedings. Interests include radio spectrum for fixed and mobile wireless communication and technological, legislative, and regulatory developments affecting telecommunications operations of energy utilities.

Wireless Communications Assn. International, *1333 H St. N.W., #700 West 20005-4754; (202) 452-7823. Fax, (202) 452-0041. Fred Campbell, President.*
Web, www.wcai.com

Membership: system operators, program suppliers, equipment manufacturers and service providers, application developers, and others involved in the wireless broadband industry (including stationary, nomadic, and portable access to broadband). Develops standards; promotes technological advancement, spectrum harmonization, and worldwide growth of the industry. Monitors legislation and regulations.

GOVERNMENT INFORMATION

▶AGENCIES

General Services Administration (GSA), *National Contact Center* (800) 333-4636. Stuart Willoughby, *Program Manager, (202) 501-9121. TTY, (800) 326-2996.*
Web, www.info.gov

Operates a toll-free hotline that provides information in English and Spanish on all federal government agencies, programs, and services. Operated under contract by the ICT Group in Lakeland, Florida.

National Archives and Records Administration (NARA), *8601 Adelphi Rd., #4200, College Park, MD 20740-6001; (866) 272-6272. Fax, (301) 837-0483. Adrienne C. Thomas, Archivist of the United States (Acting). Press, (202) 357-5300. Fax directory, www.archives.gov/about/ organization/fax-lst.html.*
Web, www.archives.gov

Identifies, preserves, and makes available federal government documents of historic value; administers a network of regional storage centers and archives and operates the presidential library system. Collections include photographs, graphic materials, films, and maps; holdings include records generated by foreign governments (especially in wartime) and by international conferences, commissions, and exhibitions.

National Archives and Records Administration (NARA), *Center for Legislative Archives, 700 Pennsylvania Ave. N.W., #8E 20408; (202) 357-5350. Fax, (202) 357-5911. Richard H. Hunt, Director, (202) 357-5376.*
Web, www.archives.gov/legislative/index.html

Collects and maintains records of congressional committees and legislative files from 1789 to the present. Publishes inventories and guides to these records.

National Archives and Records Administration (NARA), *Electronic and Special Media Records Services, 8601 Adelphi Rd., #5320, College Park, MD 20740-6001; (301) 837-0470. Fax, (301) 837-3681. Michael R. Carlson, Director, (301) 837-1578.*
General e-mail, cer@nara.gov
Web, www.archives.gov/research/electronic-records

Preserves, maintains, and makes available electronic records of the U.S. government in all subject areas. Provides researchers with magnetic tape, CD, DVD, and other copies of electronic records on a cost-recovery basis. Distributes lists of holdings.

National Archives and Records Administration (NARA), *Federal Register, 800 N. Capitol St. N.W., #700 20001 (mailing address: 8601 Adelphi Rd., College Park, MD 20740-6001); (202) 741-6000. Fax, (202) 741-6012. Raymond Mosley, Director. TTY, (202) 741-6086. Public Laws Update Service (PLUS), (202) 741-6040.*
General e-mail, fedreg.info@nara.gov
Web, www.archives.gov/federal_register

Informs citizens of their rights and obligations by providing access to the official texts of federal laws, presidential documents, administrative regulations and notices, and descriptions of federal organizations, programs, and activities. Administers the Electoral College and the constitutional amendment process. Publications available from the U.S. Government Printing Office, (301) 317-3953, http://bookstore.gpo.gov.

National Archives and Records Administration (NARA), *Modern Records Program, 8601 Adelphi Rd., College Park, MD 20740; (301) 837-3570. Fax, (301) 837-3697. Paul M. Wester Jr., Director, (301) 837-3120.*
General e-mail, rmcommunications@nara.gov
Web, www.archives.gov

Administers programs that establish standards, guidelines, and procedures for agency records administration. Manages training programs; inspects records management practices; monitors certain records not contained in National Archives depositories.

National Archives and Records Administration (NARA), *Presidential Libraries, 8601 Adelphi Rd., #2200, College Park, MD 20740-6001; (301) 837-3250. Fax, (301) 837-3199. Sharon Fawcett, Assistant Archivist, (301) 837-1693.*
Web, www.archives.gov/presidential_libraries

Administers thirteen presidential libraries. Directs all programs relating to acquisition, preservation, publication, and research use of materials in presidential libraries; conducts oral history projects; publishes finding aids for research sources; provides reference service, including information from and about documentary holdings.

National Archives and Records Administration (NARA), *Reference Services, 8601 Adelphi Rd., #2600, College*

Chief Information Officers at Federal Departments and Agencies

DEPARTMENTS

Agriculture, Christopher Smith, (202) 720-8833

Commerce, Susanne Hilding, (202) 482-4797

Defense, John G. Grimes, (703) 695-0348

  Air Force, Lt. Gen. William Shelton,
(703) 695-6829

  Army, Lt. Gen. Jeffrey Sorenson,
(703) 697-7494

  Navy, Robert Carey, (703) 602-1800

Education, Bill Vajda, (202) 245-6640

Energy, Thomas N. Pyke Jr., (202) 586-0166

Health and Human Services, Vacant,
(202) 690-6162

Homeland Security, Richard Mangogna, (202) 447-3735

Housing and Urban Development, Lynn Allen (Acting),
(202) 708-0306

Interior, Sanjeev Bhagowlia, (202) 208-6194

Justice, Vance Hitch, (202) 514-0507

Labor, Vacant, (202) 693-4040

State, Susan H. Swart, (202) 647-2889

Transportation, Jackie Patillo (Acting), (202) 366-9201

Treasury, Michael Duffy, (202) 622-1200

Veterans Affairs, Stephanie Warren, (202) 273-8842

AGENCIES

Central Intelligence Agency, Adolfo Tarasiuk,
(703) 482-0901

Environmental Protection Agency, Linda Travers (Acting),
(202) 564-6665

Federal Emergency Management Agency, Jean Etzel
(Acting), (202) 646-3006

Federal Trade Commission, Stanley Lowe,
(202) 326-3052

General Services Administration, Casey Coleman,
(202) 501-1000

Government Accountability Office, Joseph M. Kraus,
(202) 512-6623

National Aeronautics and Space Administration,
Bobby German (Acting), (202) 358-1824

National Science Foundation, George Strawn,
(703) 292-8100

Nuclear Regulatory Commission, Darren Ash,
(301) 415-7443

Office of Personnel Management, Janet L. Barnes,
(202) 606-2150

Securities and Exchange Commission, Charles Boucher,
(202) 551-8800

Small Business Administration, Christine Rider,
(202) 205-6708

Social Security Administration, Greg Pace (Acting)
(410) 966-5739

Park, MD 20740-6001; (301) 837-3480. Fax, (301) 837-1919. Steven Tilley, Director, (301) 837-3059.

Web, www.archives.gov/research/order/textual-records-dc.html

Provides reference service for unpublished civil and military federal government records. Maintains central catalog of all library materials. Compiles comprehensive bibliographies of materials related to archival administration and records management. Permits research in American history, archival science, and records management. Maintains collections of the papers of the Continental Congress (1774–1789), U.S. State Dept. diplomatic correspondence (1789–1963), and general records of the U.S. government.

National Archives and Records Administration (NARA), *Regional Records Services,*
8601 Adelphi Rd., #3600, College Park, MD 20740-6001; (301) 837-2950. Fax, (301) 837-1617. Tom Mills, Assistant Archivist, (301) 837-1982.

Web, www.archives.gov/locations/archival-research.html

Preserves and makes available federal records at regional archives and records center facilities outside the Washington metropolitan area, serving both the public and federal agencies.

National Technical Information Service (NTIS),
(Commerce Dept.), 5285 Port Royal Rd., Springfield, VA 22161; (703) 605-6000. Fax, (703) 605-6900. Ellen Herbst, Director, (703) 605-6400. Sales department, (703) 605-6000. Toll-free, (800) 553-6847. Bookstore, (703) 605-6040.

General e-mail, info@ntis.gov

Web, www.ntis.gov

Collects and organizes technical, scientific, engineering, and business-related information generated by U.S. and foreign governments and makes it available for commercial use in the private sector. Makes available approximately 3 million works covering research and development, current events, business and management studies, translations of foreign open source reports, foreign and domestic trade, general statistics, environment and energy, health and social sciences, and hundreds of other areas. Provides computer software and computerized data files in a variety of formats, including Internet downloads. Houses the Homeland Security Information Center, a centralized source on major security concerns for health and medicine, food and agriculture, and biochemical war.

Publications Contacts at Federal Departments and Agencies

DEPARTMENTS

Agriculture, Orders, (202) 694-5050

Commerce, Orders (via NTIS), (703) 605-6000; Toll-free, (800) 553-6847

Defense

  Army, Orders (via NTIS), (703) 605-6000; Toll-free, (800) 553-6847

Education, (877) 433-7827; TTY, (877) 576-7734; Fax orders, (301) 470-1244

Energy, Orders, (202) 586-5575

Health and Human Services, Orders, (202) 619-0257

Housing and Urban Development, Orders, (800) 767-7468; Fax orders, (202) 708-2313

Justice, Orders, (800) 851-3420

Labor, Statistic orders, (202) 691-5200

State, Orders from GPO, (202) 512-1800; Toll-free, (866) 512-1800

Transportation, Orders, (301) 322-4961; Fax orders, (301) 386-5394

Treasury, Orders, (202) 622-2970; Library, (202) 622-0990

Veterans Affairs, Information, (800) 827-1000

AGENCIES

Census Bureau, Orders, (301) 763-4636

Commission on Civil Rights, Orders, (202) 376-8128

Consumer Product Safety Commission, Orders, (301) 504-7923; Fax (301) 504-0127

Corporation for National and Community Service (AmeriCorps), Orders, (800) 942-2677

Energy Information Administration, Orders, (202) 586-8800

Environmental Protection Agency, Orders, (800) 490-9198

Equal Employment Opportunity Commission, Orders, (800) 669-3362

Federal Communications Commission, Fax-on-demand, (202) 418-2830

Federal Election Commission, Orders, (800) 424-9530

Federal Emergency Management Agency, Toll-free, (800) 480-2520

Federal Reserve System, Orders, (202) 452-3244

Federal Trade Commission, Orders, (202) 326-2222

General Services Administration, Orders, (800) 488-3111

Government Accountability Office, Orders, (202) 512-6000

Government Printing Office, Orders, (202) 512-1800

International Bank for Reconstruction and Development (World Bank), Orders, (202) 473-1155

International Trade Administration, Orders from NTIS and GPO, (202) 482-5487

National Aeronautics and Space Administration, Orders, (301) 621-0390

National Archives and Records Administration, Orders, (800) 234-8861

National Endowment for the Humanities, Orders, (202) 606-8400

National Institute of Standards and Technology, Information (orders from NTIS and GPO), (301) 975-6478

National Labor Relations Board, Pamphlets, (202) 273-1991; Orders from GPO, (202) 512-1800; Toll-free, (866) 512-1800

National Park Service, Information (orders by mail only), (202) 208-4747

National Science Foundation, Orders, (703) 292-7827

National Technical Information Service, Orders, (703) 605-6000; Toll-free, (800) 553-6847

National Transportation Safety Board, Orders, (202) 314-6551

Nuclear Regulatory Commission, Orders from NRC, (301) 415-4737 or (800) 397-4209; Orders from GPO, (202) 512-1800; Toll-free, (866) 512-1800

Occupational Safety and Health Administration, Orders, (202) 693-1888; Fax (202) 693-1660

Office of Personnel Management, Information (orders from GPO), (202) 512-1800; Toll-free, (866) 512-1800; Retirement and insurance information, (202) 606-0623

Peace Corps, Orders from NTIS, (703) 605-6000 or ERIC, (800) 538-3742; Information, (800) 424-8580

Securities and Exchange Commission, Orders, (202) 551-4040

Social Security Administration, Toll-free, (800) 772-1213

U.S. Fish and Wildlife Service, Orders, (304) 876-7203; from NTIS, (800) 553-6847

U.S. Geological Survey, Orders, (888) ASK-USGS

U.S. Institute of Peace, Book orders, (800) 868-8064; Other orders, (202) 457-1700

National Security Council *(Executive Office of the President), Office of Strategic Communications and Global Outreach,* Dwight D. Eisenhower Executive Office Bldg., #302 20500; (202) 456-9271. Fax, (202) 456-9270. Dennis McDonough, Deputy Assistant. Administrative office, (202) 456-9301.

Web, www.whitehouse.gov/administration/eop/nsc

Advises U.S. government agencies on the direction and theme of the president's message. Assists in the development and coordination of communications programs that disseminate consistent and accurate messages about the U.S. government and policies to the global audience.

State Dept., *International Information Programs,* 301 4th St. S.W. 20547; (202) 453-8358. Fax, (202) 453-8356. Jeremy Curtin, Coordinator.

Web, www.state.gov/r/iip

Implements strategic communications programs— including Internet and print publications, traveling and electronically transmitted speaker programs, and information resource services—that reach key international audiences and support department initiatives. Explains U.S. foreign policy. Develops governmentwide technology policies that help disseminate this information.

►CONGRESS

For a listing of relevant congressional committees and subcommittees, please see page 83 or the Appendix.

Government Accountability Office (GAO), *Publications and Dissemination,* 441 G St. N.W., #1127E 20548; (202) 512-3598. Patrick Seeley, Director (Acting).

General e-mail, info@gao.gov

Web, www.gao.gov

Provides information to the public on federal programs, reports, and testimonies. GAO publications and information about GAO publications are available upon request in print or online. (Formerly the General Accounting Office.)

Government Printing Office (GPO), 732 N. Capitol St N.W. 20401; (202) 512-0000. Fax, (202) 512-2104. William H. Turri, Public Printer of the United States (Acting). Public Affairs, (202) 512-1957. Congressional documents, (202) 512-1808. To order government publications, (202) 512-1800 or (866) 512-1800.

General e-mail, contactcenter@gpo.gov

Web, www.gpo.gov

Prints, distributes, and sells selected publications of the U.S. Congress, government agencies, and executive departments. Provides personal assistance in locating and using government information. Makes available, for a fee, the *Monthly Catalog of U.S. Government Publications,* a comprehensive listing of all publications issued by the various departments and agencies each month. Publications are distributed to GPO Regional Depository Libraries; some titles also may be purchased in larger cities at GPO bookstores. GPO Access provides free electronic access to government publications at www.gpoaccess.gov.

Legislative Resource Center, *Clerk of the House,* B106 CHOB 20515-6612; (202) 226-5200. Deborah Turner, Chief. Web, www.clerk.house.gov/about/offices_lrc.html

Provides legislative information, records and registration, historical information, and library services to the House and the public. Reading room contains computer terminals where collections may be viewed or printed out. Collections include House and Senate journals (1st Congress to present); *Congressional Record* and its predecessors (1st Congress to present); House reports, documents, bills, resolutions, and hearings; Senate reports and documents; U.S. statutes, treaties, the *Federal Register,* U.S. codes, and numerous other documents. (See Web site or call for a complete list of collections.)

Library of Congress, *Federal Library and Information Center Committee,* 101 Independence Ave. S.E., #LA217 20540; (202) 707-4800. Fax, (202) 707-4818. Deanna Marcum, Chair.

General e-mail, flicc@loc.gov

Web, www.loc.gov/flicc

Membership: one representative from each major federal agency, one representative each from the Library of Congress and the national libraries of medicine, education, and agriculture, and one representative from each of the major Federal Information Centers. Coordinates planning, development, operations, and activities among federal libraries.

Library of Congress, *Serial and Government Publications,* 101 Independence Ave. S.E., #LM133 20540; (202) 707-5647. Mark Sweeney, Chief.

Web, www.loc.gov

Operates Newspaper and Periodical Reading Room; maintains library's collection of current domestic and foreign newspapers, current periodicals, and serially issued publications of federal, state, and foreign governments; has maintained a full government publication depository since 1979. Responds to written or telephone requests for information on government publications.

Office of History and Preservation, *Clerk of the House of Representatives,* B53 CHOB 20515-6612; (202) 226-1300. Farar P. Elliott, Chief.

Web, http://clerk.house.gov

Provides access to published documents and historical records of the House. Conducts historical research. Advises members on the disposition of their records and papers; maintains information on manuscript collections of former members; maintains biographical files on former members. Produces publications on Congress and its members.

Senate Historical Office, SH-201 20510; (202) 224-6900. Richard A. Baker, Historian.

General e-mail, historian@sec.senate.gov

Web, www.senate.gov

Public Affairs Contacts at Federal Departments and Agencies

DEPARTMENTS

Agriculture, Chris Mather, (202) 720-4623

Commerce, Kevin Griffis, (202) 482-4883

Defense, Bryant Whitman (Acting), (703) 697-9312

  Air Force, Colonel Les Kodlick,
  (703) 697-6061

  Army, Maj. Gen. Kevin J. Bergner,
  (703) 695-5135

  Marine Corps, Col. David A. Leapan,
  (703) 614-1492

  Navy, Frank Thorp, (703) 697-7391

Education, John White, (202) 401-1576

Energy, Van Leistikow, (202) 586-4940

Health and Human Services, Jenny Backus (Acting),
(202) 690-6343

Homeland Security, Sean Bob Smith (Acting), (202) 282-8010

Housing and Urban Development, Neill Coleman, (202)
708-0980

Interior, Matt Lee-Ashley, (202) 208-6416

Justice, Matthew Miller, (202) 616-2777

Labor, Paul Craven (Acting), (202) 693-4676

State, Sean McCormack, (202) 647-9606

Transportation, Jill Zuckman, (202) 366-4570

Treasury, Vacant, (202) 622-2910

Veterans Affairs, Vacant, (202) 273-5710

AGENCIES

Agency for International Development,
Joseph Fredricks, (202) 712-4300

Commission on Civil Rights, Lenore Ostrowsky, (202)
376-8582

Commodity Futures Trading Commission, Robert
Hollingfield (Acting), (202) 418-5080

Consumer Product Safety Commission, Scott Wolfson,
(301) 504-7051

Corporation for National and Community Service,
Sandy Scott, (202) 606-6724

Environmental Protection Agency, Allyn Brooks-Lasure
(Acting), (202) 564-8368

Equal Employment Opportunity Commission,
Charles Robbins, (202) 663-4191

Export–Import Bank, Phil Cogan,
(202) 565-3200

Farm Credit Administration, Michael A. Stobbe
(703) 883-4056

Federal Communications Commission, David Fiske,
(202) 418-0500

Federal Deposit Insurance Corporation, David Barr,
(202) 898-6992

Federal Election Commission, Judy Ingram,
(202) 694-1220

Federal Emergency Management Agency,
Dan Stoneking, (202) 646-4600

Serves as an information clearinghouse on Senate history, traditions, and members. Collects, organizes, and distributes to the public unpublished Senate documents; collects and preserves photographs and pictures related to Senate history; conducts an oral history program; advises senators and Senate committees on the disposition of their noncurrent papers and records. Produces publications on the history of the Senate.

Freedom of Information

▶**AGENCIES**

Justice Dept. (DOJ), *Information and Privacy,* 1425 New York Ave. N.W., #11050 20530; (202) 514-3642. Fax, (202) 514-1009. Melanie Ann Pustay, Director. Information, (202) 514-2000. TTY, (202) 514-1888.
Web, www.usdoj.gov/oip/oip.html; FOIA requests, www. usdoj.gov/oip/04_04.html

Provides federal agencies with advice and policy guidance on matters related to implementing and interpreting the Freedom of Information Act (FOIA). Litigates selected FOIA and Privacy Act cases; adjudicates administrative appeals from Justice Dept. denials of public requests for access to documents; conducts FOIA training for government agencies.

National Archives and Records Administration (NARA), *Information Security Oversight,* 700 Pennsylvania Ave. N.W., #503 20408-0001; (202) 357-5250. Fax, (202) 357-5907. William J. Bosanko, Director, (202) 357-5205.
General e-mail, isoo@nara.gov
Web, www.archives.gov/isoo/index.html

Oversees government policy on security classification of documents for federal agencies and industry; reviews procedures; monitors declassification programs of federal agencies.

National Archives and Records Administration (NARA), *Initial Processing/Declassification,* 8601 Adelphi Rd., #2600, College Park, MD 20740; (301) 837-0584. Fax, (301) 837-0346. Jeanne Schauble, Director.
Web, www.archives.gov

Public Affairs Contacts at Federal Departments and Agencies

Federal Labor Relations Authority, Catherine Emerson, (202) 218-7945

Federal Mediation and Conciliation Services, John Arnold, (202) 606-5442

Federal Reserve System, Michelle Smith, (202) 452-2955

Federal Trade Commission, Vacant, (202) 326-2180

General Services Administration, Eleni Martin, (202) 501-1231

Government Accountability Office, Chuck Young, (202) 512-4800

Government Printing Office, Gary Somerset, (202) 512-1957

Institute of Museum and Library Services, Mamie Bittner, (202) 653-4757

National Aeronautics and Space Administration, David Mould, (202) 358-1898

National Archives and Records Administration, Susan Cooper, (202) 357-5300

National Capital Planning Commission, Lisa N. MacSpadden, (202) 482-7263

National Credit Union Administration, John J. McKechnie III, (703) 518-6330

National Endowment for the Arts, Victoria Hutter (Acting), (202) 682-5570

National Endowment for the Humanities, Brian Lee, (202) 606-8446

National Labor Relations Board, Patricia Gilbert, (202) 273-1991

National Science Foundation, Jeff Nesbit, (703) 292-8070

National Transportation Safety Board, Ted Lopatkiewicz, (202) 314-6100

Nuclear Regulatory Commission, Eliot B. Brenner, (301) 415-8200

Occupational Safety and Health Review Commission, Richard C. Loeb, (202) 606-5730

Office of Personnel Management, Sedelta Verble (Acting), (202) 606-2402

Office of Special Counsel, Leslie Williamson, (202) 254-3600

Pension Benefit Guaranty Corporation, Jeffrey Speicher (Acting), (202) 326-4343

Securities and Exchange Commission, John Nester, (202) 551-4120

Selective Service System, Richard S. Flahavan, (703) 605-4100

Small Business Administration, Sean Ruston, (202) 205-6882

Social Security Administration, Mark Lassiter, (410) 965-8904

U.S. International Trade Commission, Peg O'Laughlin, (202) 205-1819

U.S. Postal Service, Gerald McKiernan, (202) 268-2599

Directs the review and declassification of records and security-classified materials in the National Archives in accordance with Executive Order 12958 and the Freedom of Information Act; assists other federal archival agencies in declassifying security-classified documents in their holdings.

►NONGOVERNMENTAL

American Civil Liberties Union (ACLU), *Washington Legislative Office, 915 15th St. N.W. 20005; (202) 544-1681. Fax, (202) 546-0738. Caroline Fredrickson, Director. Press, (202) 675-2312. Alternate fax, (202) 546-1440.*

General e-mail, media@dcaclu.org

Web, www.aclu.org/legislative

Advocates for legislation to guarantee constitutional rights and civil liberties. Monitors agency compliance with the Privacy Act and other access statutes. Produces publications. (Headquarters in New York maintains docket of cases.)

American Society of Access Professionals, *1444 Eye St. N.W., #700 20005; (202) 712-9054. Fax, (202) 216-9646. Claire Shanley, Executive Director.*

General e-mail, asap@bostrom.com

Web, www.accesspro.org

Membership: federal employees, attorneys, journalists, and others working with or interested in access-to-information laws. Seeks to improve the administration of the Freedom of Information Act, the Privacy Act, and other access statutes.

Center for National Security Studies, *1120 19th St. N.W., #800 20036; (202) 721-5650. Fax, (202) 530-0128. Kate A. Martin, Director. Press, (202) 721-5660.*

General e-mail, cnss@cnss.org

Web, www.cnss.org

Human rights and civil liberties organization specializing in national security, access to government information, government secrecy, government surveillance, intelligence oversight, and detentions.

Freedom of Information Contacts at Federal Departments and Agencies

DEPARTMENTS

Agriculture, Rita Morgan, (202) 720-8164

Commerce, Brenda Dolan, (202) 482-3707

Defense, William T. Kramer, (703) 696-4689

  Air Force, John Espinal, (703) 696-7268

  Army, Vicky Short, (703) 428-6508

  Marine Corps, Teresa D. Ross, (703) 614-4008

  Navy, Doris M. Lama, (202) 685-6545

Education, Lee Eiden, (202) 401-5848

Energy, Alexander Morris, (202) 586-5955

Health and Human Services, Robert Eckert, (202) 690-7453

Homeland Security, Vania Lockett, (703) 235-0790

Housing and Urban Development, Vicky Lewis, (202) 708-3866

Interior, Alexandra Mallus, (202) 208-5342

Justice, Carmen L. Mallon, (202) 514-FOIA

Labor, Joseph Plick, (202) 693-5527 or (202) 693-5500

State, Margaret P. Grafeld, (202) 261-8484

Transportation, Kathy Ray, (202) 366-5546

Treasury, Hugh Gilmore, (202) 622-0876 or (202) 622-0930

Veterans Affairs, Sally Wallace, (202) 461-7450

AGENCIES

Agency for International Development, Joanne Paskar, (202) 712-0960 or (202) 712-1217

Central Intelligence Agency, Scott A. Koch, (703) 613-1287

Commission on Civil Rights, Emma Monroig, (202) 376-7796

Commodity Futures Trading Commission, Stacy J. Easter, (202) 418-5011

Consumer Product Safety Commission, Alberta Mills, (301) 504-7479

Environmental Protection Agency, Larry F. Gottesman, (202) 566-1667

Equal Employment Opportunity Commission, Stephanie Garner, (202) 663-4640

Export-Import Bank, Joseph Sorbera, (202) 565-3241

Farm Credit Administration, Jane Virga, (703) 883-4020

Federal Communications Commission, Shoko B. Hair, (202) 418-1379

Federal Deposit Insurance Corp., Fred Fisch, (202) 898-6901

Federal Election Commission, Candace Salley, (202) 694-1650

Federal Emergency Management Agency, Vacant, (202) 646-3323

Federal Labor Relations Authority, William Tobey, (202) 218-7908

Federal Maritime Commission, Karen V. Gregory, (202) 523-5725

Federal Reserve, Jeanne McLaughlin, (202) 452-3684

Federal Trade Commission, Joan Fina, (202) 326-2013

General Services Administration, Sharon Lighton, (202) 501-2262

Legal Services Corp., Patricia Batie, (202) 295-1625 or (202) 295-1500

Merit Systems Protection Board, Arlin Winefordner, (202) 653-7200, ext. 1162

National Aeronautics and Space Administration, Stephen McConnell, (202) 358-0068

National Archives and Records Administration, Ramona Oliver, (301) 837-2024

National Credit Union Administration, Linda Dent, (703) 518-6540

National Endowment for the Humanities, Mary Jeffcoat, (202) 682-5505

National Labor Relations Board, Diane Bridge, (202) 273-3851

National Mediation Board, Judy Femi, (202) 692-5040

National Science Foundation, Leslie Jensen, (703) 292-8060, ext. 5065

National Transportation Safety Board, Melba D. Moye, (202) 314-6540

Nuclear Regulatory Commission, Donna Sealing, (301) 415-7169

Office of Government Ethics, William E. Gressman, (202) 482-9245

Office of Management and Budget, Dionne Hardy, (202) 395-3642

Office of Personnel Management, Ryan Witt, (202) 606-3642

Office of the U.S. Trade Representative, Sybia Harrison, (202) 395-3419

Peace Corps, Allison Tanaka (Acting), (202) 692-1186

Pension Benefit Guaranty Corp., Bill Fitzgerald, (202) 326-4040

Securities and Exchange Commission, Celia Winter, (202) 551-8300

Selective Service, Richard S. Flahaven, (703) 605-4100

Small Business Administration, Lisa J. Babcock, (202) 401-8203

Social Security Administration, Dawn S. Wiggins, (410) 966-6645

U.S. International Trade Commission, Marilyn Abbott, (202) 205-2000

U.S. Postal Service, Jane Eyre, (202) 268-2608

Radio-Television News Directors Assn. (RTNDA/ RTNDF), *1025 F St. N.W., 7th Floor 20004 (mailing address: 4121 Plank Rd., #512, Fredericksburg, VA 22407); (202) 659-6510. Fax, (202) 223-4007. Barbara Cochran, President.*

General e-mail, rtnda@rtnda.org

Web, www.rtnda.org

Membership: electronic journalists in radio, television, and all digital media. Sponsors and promotes education and advocacy concerning First Amendment issues, freedom of information, and government secrecy issues; ethics in reporting; improving coverage; implementing technology; and other news industry issues. Radio and Television News Directors Foundation (RTNDF) is the educational arm of the association.

INTERNET AND RELATED TECHNOLOGIES

►AGENCIES

Criminal Division *(Justice Dept.), Computer Crime and Intellectual Property, 1301 New York Ave. N.W., #600 20530; (202) 514-1026. Fax, (202) 514-6113. Michael DuBose, Chief.*

Web, www.usdoj.gov/criminal/cybercrime

Investigates and litigates criminal cases involving computers, intellectual property, and the Internet. Administers the Computer Crime Initiative, a program designed to combat electronic penetrations, data theft, and cyberattacks on critical information systems. Provides specialized technical and legal assistance to other Justice Dept. divisions; coordinates international efforts; formulates policies and proposes legislation on computer crime and intellectual property issues.

Cyber Crimes Center *(Homeland Security Dept.), 11320 Random Hills Rd., #400, Fairfax, VA 22030; (703) 293-8005. Fax, (703) 293-9127. Shawn Bray, Unit Chief.*

Web, www.ice.gov/about/investigations/services/ cyberbranch.htm

Focuses U.S. immigration and customs resources on the investigation of international Internet crimes, such as money laundering, financing of terrorist activities, child exploitation, intellectual property rights violations, illegal arms trafficking, drug trafficking, and stolen antiquities and art.

Defense Advanced Research Projects Agency *(Defense Dept.), 3701 N. Fairfax Dr., Arlington, VA 22203-1714; (703) 526-6629. Fax, (571) 218-4356. Anthony J. Tether, Director; John Jennings, External Relations, (703) 526-4725. Press, (703) 696-2404.*

Web, www.darpa.mil

Develops technologically advanced research ideas, assesses technical feasibility, and develops prototypes.

Federal Bureau of Investigation (FBI), *(Justice Dept.), Asset Forfeiture/Money Laundering Unit, 935 Pennsylvania Ave. N.W., #3901 20535; (202) 324-8628. Fax, (202) 324-8061. Jacqueline "Jackie" Felton, Chief, (202) 324-8635.*

Web, www.fbi.gov

Investigates crimes of fraud, theft, or embezzlement within or against financial institutions. Priorities include identity theft, mortgage and credit card fraud, asset forfeiture, and money laundering.

Federal Communications Commission (FCC), *Strategic Planning and Policy Analysis, 445 12th St. S.W., #7-C347 20554; (202) 418-2030. Fax, (202) 418-2807. Elizabeth Andrion, Chief (Acting).*

Web, www.fcc.gov/osp

Monitors developments in expansion of the global Internet and the communications industry. Reviews legal trends in intellectual property law and e-commerce issues.

General Services Administration (GSA), *Governmentwide Policy, Technology Strategy, 1800 F St. N.W., #2239 20405; (202) 501-0202. Fax, (202) 219-1533. Peter Alterman, Deputy Associate Administrator.*

General e-mail, estrategy.gov@gsa.gov

Web, www.estrategy.gov

Develops, coordinates, and defines ways that electronic and information technology business strategies can assist the Office of Management and Budget and other federal agencies to enhance access to and delivery of information and services.

National Science Foundation (NSF), *Computer and Information Sciences and Engineering (CISE), 4201 Wilson Blvd., #1105N, Arlington, VA 22230; (703) 292-8900. Fax, (703) 292-9074. Janette M. Ming, Assistant Director.*

Web, www.nsf.gov/dir/index.jsp?org=CISE

Supports investigator-initiated research in computer science and engineering. Promotes the use of advanced computing, communications, and information systems. Provides grants for research and education.

National Telecommunications and Information Administration (NTIA), *(Commerce Dept.), 1401 Constitution Ave. N.W., #4898 20230; (202) 482-1840. Fax, (202) 501-0536. Meredith A. Baker, Assistant Secretary (Acting). Press, (202) 482-7002.*

Web, www.ntia.doc.gov

Responsible for oversight of the technical management of the Internet domain name system (DNS).

Office of Management and Budget (OMB), *(Executive Office of the President), Information and Regulatory Affairs, New Executive Office Bldg., #10236 20503; (202) 395-3785. Fax, (202) 395-5167. Jasmeet Seehra, Co-Chief; Kim Nelson, Co-Chief.*

Web, www.whitehouse.gov/omb/inforeg_infopoltech

Oversees implementation and policy development under the Information Technology Reform Act of 1996 and the Paperwork Reduction Act of 1995; focuses on information technology management and substantive information policy, including records management, privacy, and computer security, and the Freedom of Information Act.

►CONGRESS

For a listing of relevant congressional committees and subcommittees, please see page 83 or the Appendix.

Government Accountability Office (GAO), *Applied Research and Methods,* 441 G St. N.W., #6133 20548; (202) 512-2700. Nancy Kingsbury, Managing Director.
Web, www.gao.gov

Assesses the quality of the nation's major statistical databases and helps adapt the government's dissemination of information to a new technological environment. Conducts congressional studies that entail specialized analysis. (Formerly the General Accounting Office.)

Government Accountability Office (GAO), *Information Technology,* 441 G St. N.W., #4480 20548; (202) 512-6253. Joel C. Willemssen, Managing Director.
Web, www.gao.gov

Seeks to make the federal government more effective in its information management by improving performance and reducing costs. Assesses best practices in the public and private sectors; makes recommendations to government agencies. Interests include information security. (Formerly the General Accounting Office.)

►NONGOVERNMENTAL

American Library Assn., *Office for Information Technology Policy,* 1615 New Hampshire Ave. N.W., 1st Floor 20009-2520; (202) 628-8410. Fax, (202) 628-8419. Emily Sheketoff, Associate Executive Director. Information, (800) 941-8476.
General e-mail, oitp@alawash.org
Web, www.ala.org/oitp

Provides policy research and analysis of developments in technology and telecommunications as they affect libraries and library users. Interests include information policy, law, and regulations; free expression on the Internet; equitable access to electronic information resources; and treaty negotiations of the United Nations World Intellectual Property Organization.

American Society for Information Science and Technology (ASIS), 1320 Fenwick Lane, #510, Silver Spring, MD 20910-3560; (301) 495-0900. Fax, (301) 495-0810. Richard Hill, Executive Director.
General e-mail, asis@asis.org
Web, www.asis.org

Membership: information specialists from such fields as computer science, linguistics, management, librarianship, engineering, law, medicine, chemistry, and education. Advocates research and development in basic and applied information science. Offers continuing education programs.

Assn. for Competitive Technology (ACT), 1401 K St. N.W., #502 20005; (202) 331-2130. Fax, (202) 331-2139. Jonathan Zuck, President.
General e-mail, info@actonline.org
Web, www.actonline.org

Membership: businesses that engage in or support the information technology industry. International education and advocacy organization for information technology companies worldwide. Interests include intellectual property, international trade, e-commerce, privacy, tax policy, and antitrust issues. Focuses predominately on the interests of small and midsized entrepreneurial technology companies. Monitors legislation and regulations.

Assn. of Research Libraries (ARL), 21 Dupont Circle N.W., #800 20036; (202) 296-2296. Fax, (202) 872-0884. Charley B. Lowry, Executive Director.
General e-mail, webmgr@arl.org
Web, www.arl.org

Federation of 123 principal libraries serving major research institutions in the United States and Canada. Interests include public access to federally funded research; federal, state, and international copyright and intellectual property laws; information technology and telecommunications policies; appropriations for selected federal and congressional agencies, national libraries, and agency programs and initiatives; scholarly communication, including publication and dissemination systems; the library's role in the transformation of research, teaching, and learning; and library performance assessment.

Business Software Alliance (BSA), 1150 18th St. N.W., #700 20036; (202) 872-5500. Fax, (202) 872-5501. Robert W. Holleyman II, President. Toll-free, (888) 667-4722.
General e-mail, software@bsa.org
Web, www.bsa.org

Membership: personal computer software publishing companies. Promotes growth of the software industry worldwide; helps develop electronic commerce. Investigates claims of software theft within corporations, financial institutions, academia, state and local governments, and nonprofit organizations. Provides legal counsel and initiates litigation on behalf of members.

Center for Democracy and Technology, 1634 Eye St. N.W., #1100 20006; (202) 637-9800. Fax, (202) 637-0968. Leslie Harris, President.
General e-mail, info@cdt.org
Web, www.cdt.org

Promotes and defends privacy and civil liberties on the Internet. Interests include social networking and access to the Internet, consumer protection and combating spyware, health information privacy and technology, government surveillance, and access to information and use of interactivity by government.

Federal Government Web Sites

CONGRESS
Government Accountability Office, www.gao.gov
House of Representatives, www.house.gov
Library of Congress, www.loc.gov
Senate, www.senate.gov

WHITE HOUSE
General Information, www.whitehouse.gov

DEPARTMENTS
Agriculture, www.usda.gov
Commerce, www.commerce.gov
Defense, www.defenselink.mil
  Air Force, www.af.mil
  Army, www.army.mil
  Marine Corps, www.usmc.mil
  Navy, www.navy.mil
Education, www.ed.gov
Energy, www.energy.gov
Health and Human Services, www.dhhs.gov
Homeland Security, www.dhs.gov
  Coast Guard, www.uscg.mil
Housing and Urban Development, www.hud.gov
Interior, www.doi.gov
Justice, www.usdoj.gov
Labor, www.dol.gov
State, www.state.gov
Transportation, www.dot.gov
Treasury, www.ustreas.gov
Veterans Affairs, www.va.gov

AGENCIES
Consumer Product Safety Commission, www.cpsc.gov
Corporation for Public Broadcasting, www.cpb.org
Drug Enforcement Administration, www.usdoj.gov/dea
Environmental Protection Agency, www.epa.gov
Export-Import Bank, www.exim.gov
Federal Aviation Administration, www.faa.gov
Federal Bureau of Investigation, www.fbi.gov
Federal Communications Commission, www.fcc.gov
Federal Deposit Insurance Corporation, www.fdic.gov
Federal Election Commission, www.fec.gov
Federal Emergency Management Agency, www.fema.gov

Federal Energy Regulatory Commission, www.ferc.gov
Federal Reserve System, www.federalreserve.gov
Federal Trade Commission, www.ftc.gov
Food and Drug Administration, www.fda.gov
General Services Administration, www.gsa.gov
Government Printing Office, www.gpo.gov
Internal Revenue Service, www.irs.gov
National Aeronautics and Space Administration, www.nasa.gov
National Archives and Records Administration, www.archives.gov
National Institute of Standards and Technology, www.nist.gov
National Institutes of Health, www.nih.gov
National Oceanic and Atmospheric Administration, www.noaa.gov
National Park Service, www.nps.gov
National Railroad Passenger Corporation (Amtrak), www.amtrak.com
National Science Foundation, www.nsf.gov
National Technical Information Service, www.ntis.gov
National Transportation Safety Board, www.ntsb.gov
Nuclear Regulatory Commission, www.nrc.gov
Occupational Safety and Health Administration, www.osha.gov
Patent and Trademark Office, www.uspto.gov
Peace Corps, www.peacecorps.gov
Pension Benefit Guaranty Corporation, www.pbgc.gov
Securities and Exchange Commisssion, www.sec.gov
Small Business Administration, www.sba.gov
Smithsonian Institution, www.si.edu
Social Security Administration, www.ssa.gov
U.S. Fish and Wildlife Service, www.fws.gov
U.S. Geological Survey, www.usgs.gov
U.S. International Trade Commission, www.usitc.gov
U.S. Postal Service, www.usps.com

Center for Digital Democracy, *1718 Connecticut Ave. N.W., #200 20009; (202) 986-2220. Fax, (301) 270-2376. Jeffrey Chester, Executive Director, (202) 494-7100.*

General e-mail, jeff@democraticmedia.org

Web, www.democraticmedia.org

Promotes understanding of the changing U.S. digital media system by disseminating information about communications options and public-interest resources. Specializes in interactive advertising in the electronic media. Interests include the public-interest potential of broadband, protecting the privacy of U.S. consumers online, and diverse ownership of new media outlets.

Coalition for Networked Information, *21 Dupont Circle N.W., #800 20036; (202) 296-5098. Fax, (202) 872-0884. Clifford A. Lynch, Executive Director.*

General e-mail, info@cni.org

Web, www.cni.org

Membership: higher education, publishing, network and telecommunications, information technology, and libraries and library organizations, as well as government agencies and foundations. Promotes networked information technology, scholarly communication, intellectual productivity, and education.

Computer and Communications Industry Assn. (CCIA), *900 17th St. N.W., #1100 20006; (202) 783-0070. Fax, (202) 783-0534. Edward J. Black, President; Heather Greenfield, Director of Media Relations.*

General e-mail, ccia@ccianet.org

Web, www.ccianet.org

Membership: Internet service providers, software providers, and manufacturers and suppliers of computer data processing and communications-related products and services. Interests include Internet freedom, privacy and neutrality, government electronic surveillance, telecommunications policy, tax policy, federal procurement policy, communications and computer industry standards, intellectual property policies, encryption, international trade, and antitrust reform.

Cyber Security Policy and Research Institute, *George Washington University, 707 22nd St. N.W., #304 20006; (202) 994-8675. Fax, (202) 994-1651. C. Dianne Martin, Director.*

General e-mail, dmartin@gwu.edu

Web, www.cpi.seas.gwu.edu

Promotes education, research, and policy analysis in the areas of computer security and privacy, computer networks, electronic commerce, e-government, and the cultural aspects of cyberspace.

Data Interchange Standards Assn. (DISA), *7600 Leesburg Pike, #430, Falls Church, VA 22043; (703) 970-4480. Fax, (703) 970-4488. Jerry C. Connors, President.*

General e-mail, info@disa.org

Web, www.disa.org

Supports the development and the use of electronic data interchange standards in electronic commerce. Sponsors workshops and seminars. Helps develop international standards.

Electronic Privacy Information Center (EPIC), *1718 Connecticut Ave. N.W., #200 20009; (202) 483-1140. Fax, (202) 483-1248. Marc Rotenberg, Executive Director.*

General e-mail, epic-info@epic.org

Web, www.epic.org

Public interest research center. Conducts research and conferences on domestic and international civil liberties issues, including privacy, free speech, information access, computer security, and encryption; litigates cases. Monitors legislation and regulations.

Entertainment Software Assn. (ESA), *575 7th St. N.W., #300 20004; (202) 223-2400. Fax, (202) 223-2401. Mike Gallagher, President.*

General e-mail, esa@theesa.com

Web, www.theesa.com

Membership: publishers of interactive entertainment software. Distributes marketing statistics and information. Administers a worldwide anti-piracy program. Established an independent rating system for entertainment software. Monitors legislation and regulations. Interests include First Amendment and intellectual property protection efforts. (Formerly the Interactive Digital Software Assn.)

Family Online Safety Institute, *815 Connecticut Ave. N.W., #220 20006; (202) 775-0130. Steven Balkam, Chief Executive Officer. Press, (202) 572-6252.*

General e-mail, fosi@fosi.org

Web, www.fosi.org

Membership: Internet industry leaders and smaller companies, web-design professionals, and individuals. Promotes safe and effective use of the Internet by children through education and information, while protecting the rights of content providers. Provides the public with information about the level of sex, nudity, violence, language used, user-generated, and harmful content in software and on the Internet. Assists parents through programs that label the content of software and the Internet.

IDEAlliance, *1421 Prince St., Alexandria, VA 22314-2805; (703) 837-1070. Fax, (703) 837-1072. David J. Steinhardt, President.*

General e-mail, info@idealliance.org

Web, www.idealliance.org

Membership: firms and customers in printing, publishing, and information technology. Helps set industry standards for electronic and web commerce and conducts studies on new information technologies.

Info Comm International, *11242 Waples Mill Rd., #200, Fairfax, VA 22030; (703) 273-7200. Fax, (703) 278-8082.*

Randal A. Lemke, Executive Director. Information, (800) 659-7469.

General e-mail, customerservice@infocomm.org

Web, www.infocomm.org

Membership: video and audiovisual dealers; manufacturers and producers; and individuals. Promotes the professional AV communications industry and seeks to enhance members' ability to conduct business successfully through tradeshows, education, certification, market research, and government relations. Interests include small business issues, intellectual property, sustainable buildings, and e-Waste. Monitors legislation and regulations. (Formerly the International Communications Industries Assn.)

Information Sciences Institute - East, *Washington Office,* 3811 N. Fairfax Dr, #200, Arlington, VA 22203; (703) 243-9422. Fax, (703) 812-3712. Forrest Houston, Manager, (703) 812-3726.

Web, www.east.isi.edu

Conducts research in advanced computer, communications, and information processing technologies. Projects include advanced communications and network research; distributed databases and pattern recognition with applications in law enforcement, inspection systems, and threat detection; and computing architectures and devices. (Headquarters in Marina del Rey, Calif.; part of the University of Southern California.)

Information Technology Industry Council (ITI), 1250 Eye St. N.W., #200 20005; (202) 737-8888. Fax, (202) 638-4922. Dean Garfield, President. Press, (202) 626-5725.

Web, www.itic.org

Membership: providers of information technology products and services. Promotes the global competitiveness of its members and advocates free trade. Seeks to protect intellectual property and encourages the use of voluntary standards. Interests include environmental conservation and energy efficiency, health information technology, increased access to high-speed broadband, protection of personal information, and U.S. export policy.

Internet Alliance, 1615 L St. N.W., #1100 20036; (202) 329-0017. Emily T. Hackett, Executive Director.

General e-mail, emilyh@internetalliance.org

Web, www.internetalliance.org

Membership: companies involved in the online industry, including marketing agencies, consulting and research organizations, entrepreneurs, financial institutions, interactive service providers, software vendors, telecommunications companies, and service bureaus. Promotes consumer confidence and trust in the Internet and monitors the effect of public policy on the Internet and its users with a focus on privacy, taxation, intellectual property, online security, unsolicited e-mail, and content regulation.

Internet Education Foundation, 1634 Eye St. N.W., #1100 20006; (202) 638-4370. Fax, (202) 637-0968. Tim Lordan, Executive Director.

General e-mail, info@neted.org

Web, www.neted.org

Sponsors educational initiatives promoting the Internet as a valuable medium for democratic participation, communications, and commerce. Funds the Congressional Internet Caucus Advisory Committee, which works to inform Congress of important Internet-related policy issues. Monitors legislation and regulations.

Internet Engineering Task Force (IETF), c/o Internet Security (ISOC), 1775 Wiehle Ave., #201, Reston, VA 20190-5108; (571) 326-9880. Fax, (703) 326-9881. Ray Pelletier, Executive Director. Alternate phone, (703) 439-2120.

General e-mail, ietf-info@ietf.org

Web, www.ietf.org

Membership: network designers, operators, vendors, and researchers from around the world who are concerned with the evolution, smooth operation, and continuing development of the Internet. Establishes working groups to address technical concerns. IETF is an organized activity of the Internet Society.

Internet Society (ISOC), 1775 Wiehle Ave., #201, Reston, VA 20190-5108; (703) 326-9880. Fax, (703) 326-9881. Lynn St. Amour, President. Alternate phone, (703) 439-2120.

General e-mail, isoc@isoc.org; Press, media@isoc.org

Web, www.isoc.org

Membership: individuals, corporations, nonprofit organizations, and government agencies. Promotes development and availability of the Internet and its associated technologies and applications; publishes international standards. Conducts research and educational programs; assists technologically developing countries in achieving Internet usage; provides information about the Internet.

Pew Internet and American Life Project, 1615 L St. N.W., #700 20036; (202) 419-4500. Fax, (202) 419-4505. Lee Rainie, Director.

General e-mail, data@pewinternet.org

Web, www.pewinternet.org

Conducts research, surveys, and analysis to explore the impact of the Internet on families, communities, education, health care, the workplace, and civic and political life. Makes its reports available online for public and academic use.

Progress and Freedom Foundation, 1444 Eye St. N.W., #500 20005; (202) 289-8928. Fax, (202) 289-6079. Ken Ferree, President.

General e-mail, mail@pff.org

Web, www.pff.org

Studies the impact of the digital revolution and its implications for public policy; sponsors seminars, conferences, and broadcasts.

Progress and Freedom Foundation, *Center for the Study of Digital Property,* 1444 Eye St. N.W., #500 20005; (202) 289-8928. Fax, (202) 289-6079. Tom Sydnor, Director.

General e-mail, mail@pff.org

Web, www.pff.org

Conducts program on research and education on intellectual property issues related to the Internet and other digital technologies.

Public Knowledge, *1875 Connecticut Ave. N.W., #650 20009; (202) 518-0020. Fax, (202) 986-2539. Gigi B. Sohn, President.*

General e-mail, pk@publicknowledge.org

Web, www.publicknowledge.org

Coalition of libraries, educators, scientists, artists, musicians, journalists, lawyers, and consumers interested in intellectual property law and technology policy as it pertains to the Internet and electronic information. Encourages openness, access, and competition in the digital age. Supports U.S. laws and policies that provide incentives to innovators as well as ensure a free flow of information and ideas to the public.

Software and Information Industry Assn. (SIIA), *1090 Vermont Ave. N.W., 6th Floor 20005-4095; (202) 289-7442. Fax, (202) 289-7097. Ken Wasch, President.*

Web, www.siia.net

Membership: softwarw and digital content companies, Promotes the industry worldwide; conducts anti-piracy program and other initiatives that protect members intellectual property; supports initiatives developed through member requests; sponsors conferences, seminars, and other events that focus on industrywide and specific interests. monitors legislation and regulations.

TechAmerica, *601 Pennsylvania Ave. N.W., North Bldg., #600, Washington, DC 20004; (202) 682-9110. Fax, (202) 682-9111. Christopher W. Hansen, Chief Executive Officer; Phillip J. Bond, President. Toll-free, (800) 284-4232. Press (703) 284-5305. General e-mail, csc@techamerica.org*

Web, www.techamerica.org

Trade association for companies offering hardware, software, electronics, telecommunications, and information technology products and services in the public and commercial sectors. Conducts market research and standards development; offers business services and networking programs to members. Lobbies governments at the local, state, federal, and international levels to facilitate growth in the technology industry. (Merger of AeA [formerly the American Electronics Assn.], the Information Technology Assn. of America [ITAA], the Government Electronics and Information and Technology Assn. [GEIA], and the Cyber Security Industry Alliance.)

Technology CEO Council, *1341 G St. N.W., #1100 20005; (202) 585-0261. Fax, (202) 393-3031. Bruce Mehlman, Executive Director.*

General e-mail, info@techceocouncil.org

Web, www.cspp.org

Membership: chief executive officers from U.S. information technology companies. Works to develop and advocate the information technology industry's public policy positions on technology and trade issues. Focuses on health care information technology, telecommunications, international trade, innovation, digital rights management, export and knowledge controls, and privacy. (Formerly the Computer Systems Policy Project.)

Telework Coalition (TelCoa), *204 E. St. N.E. 20002; (202) 266-0046. Chuck Wilsker, President. Phone and fax are same number.*

General e-mail, info@telcoa.org

Web, www.telcoa.org

Promotes telework and telecommuting, particularly in the government sector, and access to broadband services as a viable way to increase employee productivity and motivation to provide new employment opportunities for the disabled, rural, and older workers, while reducing vehicular pollution, traffic, and dependency on imported oil. Encourages adoption of telework applications such as telemedicine and distance learning. Monitors legislation and regulations.

United States Holocaust Memorial Museum, *Genocide Prevention Mapping Initiative, 100 Raoul Wallenberg Pl. S.W. 20024-2126; (202) 488-6133. Press fax, (202) 488-2695.*

General e-mail, jhefferman@ushmm.org

Web, www.ushmm.org/maps

Seeks to collect and visually present critical information on emerging crises that may lead to genocide or related crimes against humanity. Projects include "Crisis in Darfur" in Google Earth, field-based research in at-risk countries presented through the "World Is Witness" Web site, and development of an interactive "global crisis map" to help citizens, aid workers, and foreign policy professionals to determine effective prevention and response strategies.

U.S. Internet Industry Assn. (USIIA), *1800 Diagonal Rd., #600, Alexandria, VA 22314; (703) 647-7440. Fax, (703) 647-6009. David P. McClure, President.*

General e-mail, info.3@usiia.org

Web, www.usiia.org

Membership: U.S. Internet access, content, and connectivity companies. Fosters the growth and development of online commerce and communications. Monitors legislation and regulations.

MEDIA PROFESSIONS AND RESOURCES

▶AGENCIES

Federal Communications Commission (FCC), *Communications Business Opportunities, 445 12th St. S.W., #4A624 20554; (202) 418-0990. Fax, (202) 418-0235. Carolyn Fleming Williams, Director.*

General e-mail, ocboinfo@fcc.gov

Web, www.fcc.gov/ocbo

Provides technical and legal guidance and assistance to the small, minority, and female business communities in the telecommunications industry. Advises the FCC chair on small, minority, and female business issues.

Serves as liaison between federal agencies, state and local governments, and trade associations representing small, minority, and female enterprises concerning FCC policies, procedures, rulemaking activities, and increased ownership and employment opportunities.

Federal Communications Commission (FCC), *Media Bureau: Equal Employment Opportunity,* 445 12th St. S.W., #3A633 20554; (202) 418-1450. Fax, (202) 418-1797. Lewis Pulley, Assistant Chief, Policy Division, (202) 418-2120.
Web, www.fcc.gov

Responsible for the annual certification of cable television equal employment opportunity compliance. Oversees broadcast employment practices.

▶NONGOVERNMENTAL

American News Women's Club, 1607 22nd St. N.W. 20008; (202) 332-6770. Fax, (202) 265-6092. Pam Ginsbach, President.
General e-mail, anwclub@covad.net
Web, www.anwc.org

Membership: women in communications. Promotes the advancement of women in all media. Sponsors professional receptions and lectures.

Communications Workers of America (CWA), 501 3rd St. N.W. 20001; (202) 434-1100. Fax, (202) 434-1279. Larry Cohen, President.
General e-mail, cwaweb@cwa-union.org
Web, www.cwa-union.org

Membership: approximately 700,000 workers in telecommunications, journalism, publishing, cable television, electronics, and other fields. Interests include workplace democracy and restoring bargaining rights. Represents members in contract negotiation and grievances; conducts training programs and workshops. Monitors legislation and regulations. (Affiliated with the AFL-CIO.)

Freedom Forum, 555 Pennsylvania Ave. N.W. 20001; (202) 292-6100. Fax, (703) 284-3770. Charles L. Overby, Chief Executive Officer. Toll-Free Inquiries, (888) 639-7386.
General e-mail, news@freedomforum.org
Web, www.freedomforum.org

Sponsors conferences, educational activities, training, and research that promote free press, free speech, and freedom of information and that enhance the teaching and practice of journalism, both in the United States and abroad. Primary funder for the Newseum, an interactive museum of news.

Fund for Investigative Journalism, 910 17th St. N.W., 7th Floor 20006; (202) 481-1218. Fax, (703) 534-3763. Cheryl Arvidson, Executive Director.
General e-mail, fundfij@gmail.com
Web, www.fij.org

Provides investigative reporters working outside the protection and backing of major news organizations with grants for pre-publication help for investigative pieces involving corruption, malfeasance, incompetence, and societal ills in general, as well as for investigative media criticism.

International Center for Journalists (ICFJ), 1616 H St. N.W., 3rd Floor 20006; (202) 737-3700. Fax, (202) 737-0530. Joyce Barnathan, President. Press, (202) 349-7624.
General e-mail, editor@icfj.org
Web, www.icfj.org

Fosters international freedom of the press through hands-on training, workshops, seminars, online courses, fellowships, and international exchanges. Offers online mentoring and consulting; publishes media training manuals in various languages.

International Women's Media Foundation (IWMF), 1625 K St. N.W., #1275 20006; (202) 496-1992. Fax, (202) 496-1977. Jane B. Ransom, Executive Director.
General e-mail, info@iwmf.org
Web, www.iwmf.org

Researches the role of women journalists. Conducts training on career development and leadership, free press, and the media business. Publishes media training guide. Facilitates networking among women journalists.

J-Lab: The Institute for Interactive Journalism, 3201 New Mexico Ave. N.W., #330 20016; (202) 885-8100. Fax, (202) 885-8110. Jan Schaffer, Executive Director.
General e-mail, news@j-lab.org
Web, www.j-lab.org

Journalism center that facilitates innovative news experiments that use new technologies to help people engage in public policy issues. Affiliated with the American University School of Communication.

Minority Media and Telecommunications Council (MMTC), 3636 16th St. N.W., #B-366 20010; (202) 332-0500. Fax, (202) 332-0503. David Honig, Executive Director; David Lowenstein, Managing Director.
General e-mail, info@mmtconline.org
Web, www.mmtconline.org

Membership: lawyers, engineers, broadcasters, cablecasters, telecommunicators, and scholars. Provides pro bono services to the civil rights community on communication policy matters. Represents civil rights groups before the FCC on issues concerning equal opportunity and diversity. Promotes equal opportunity and civil rights in the mass media and telecommunications industries. Operates nonprofit media brokerage and offers fellowships for lawyers and law students interested in FCC practice.

National Assn. of Black Journalists (NABJ), *University of Maryland,* 8701-A Adelphi Rd., Adelphi, MD 20783-1716; (301) 445-7100. Fax, (301) 445-7101. Karen Wynn Freeman, Executive Director. Toll-free (866) 479-6225.

Media Contacts in Washington, D.C.

MAGAZINES

CQ Weekly, 1255 22nd St. N.W. 20037; (202) 419-8500

National Journal, 600 New Hampshire Ave. N.W., #400 20037; (202) 739-8400

Newsweek, 1750 Pennsylvania Ave. N.W., #1220 20006; (202) 626-2000

Time, 555 12th St. N.W., #600 North 20004; (202) 861-4000

U.S. News & World Report, 1050 Thomas Jefferson St. N.W. 20007; (202) 955-2000

NEWSPAPERS

Baltimore Sun, 1025 F St. N.W., #700 20004; (202) 452-8250 or (202) 824-8300

Christian Science Monitor, 910 16th St. N.W., #200 20006; (202) 785-4400

Los Angeles Times, 1025 F St. N.W., #700 20004; (202) 824-8300

New York Times, 1627 Eye St. N.W., #700 20006; (202) 862-0300

USA Today, 7950 Jones Branch Dr., McLean, VA 22108; (703) 854-3400

Wall Street Journal, 1025 Connecticut Ave. N.W., #800 20036; (202) 862-9200

Washington Post, 1150 15th St. N.W., 20071; (202) 334-6000

Washington Times, 3600 New York Ave. N.E. 20002; (202) 636-3000

NEWS SERVICES

Agence France-Presse, 1500 K St. N.W., #600 20005; (202) 289-0700

Associated Press, 2021 K St. N.W., 6th Floor 20006; (202) 776-9400

Gannett News Service, 7950 Jones Branch Dr., McLean, VA 22108; (703) 854-5800

McClatchy, 700 12th St. N.W., #1000; 20005; (202) 383-6000

Newhouse News Service, 1101 Connecticut Ave. N.W., #300 20036; (202) 383-7800

Reuters, 1333 H St. N.W., #500 20005; (202) 898-8300

Scripps-Howard Newspapers, 1090 Vermont Ave. N.W., #1000 20005; (202) 408-1484

United Press International, 1510 H St. N.W. 20005; (202) 898-8000

TELEVISION/RADIO NETWORKS

ABC News, 1717 DeSales St. N.W. 20036; (202) 222-7777

Cable News Network (CNN), 820 1st St. N.E. 20002; (202) 898-7900

CBS News, 2020 M St. N.W. 20036; (202) 457-4321

C-SPAN, 400 N. Capitol St. N.W., #650 20001; (202) 737-3220

Fox News, 400 N. Capitol St. N.W., #550 20001; (202) 824-6300

National Public Radio, 635 Massachusetts Ave. N.W. 20001; (202) 513-2000

NBC News, 4001 Nebraska Ave. N.W. 20016; (202) 885-4200

Public Broadcasting Service, 2100 Crystal Dr., Arlington, VA 22202; (703) 739-5000

General e-mail, nabj@nabj.org

Web, www.nabj.org

Membership: African American students and media-related professionals. Works to increase recognition of the achievements of minority journalists, to expand opportunities for minority students entering the field, and to promote balanced coverage of the African American community by the media. Seeks to expand the number of black journalists in management and to encourage black journalists to become entrepreneurs. Sponsors scholarships, internship program, and annual convention.

National Assn. of Government Communicators (NAGC), 201 Park Washington Ct., Falls Church, VA 22046-4527; (703) 538-1787. Fax, (703) 241-5603. George Selby, President. General e-mail, info@nagconline.org

Web, www.nagconline.org

National network of federal, state, and local government communications employees. Provides professional development through public meetings, exhibitions, workshops, and formal courses of instruction. Promotes high standards for the government communications profession and recognizes noteworthy service.

National Assn. of Hispanic Journalists (NAHJ), 529 14th St. N.W., #1000 20045-2001; (202) 662-7145. Fax, (202) 662-7144. Ivan Román, Executive Director. Toll-free, (888) 346-6245.

General e-mail, nahj@nahj.org

Web, www.nahj.org

Membership: professional journalists, educators, students, and others interested in encouraging and supporting the study and practice of journalism and communications by Hispanics. Promotes fair representation and treatment of Hispanics by the media. Provides professional development and computerized job referral service; compiles and updates national directory of Hispanics in the media; sponsors national high school essay contest, journalism awards, and scholarships.

Congressional News Media Galleries

The congressional news media galleries serve as liaisons between members of Congress and their staffs and accredited newspaper, magazine, and broadcasting correspondents. The galleries provide accredited correspondents with facilities to cover activities of Congress, and gallery staff members ensure that congressional press releases reach appropriate correspondents. Independent committees of correspondents working through the press galleries are responsible for accreditation of correspondents. See Accreditation in Washington, pp. 106–107.

House Periodical Press Gallery, H304 CAP 20515; (202) 225-2941. Robert M. Zatkowski, Director.

House Press Gallery, H315 CAP 20515; (202) 225-3945. Jerry Gallegos, Superintendent.

House Radio and Television Gallery, H321 CAP 20515; (202) 225-5214. Olga Ramirez Kornacki, Director.

Press Photographers Gallery, S317 CAP 20510; (202) 224-6548. Jeffrey S. Kent, Director.

Senate Periodical Press Gallery, S320 CAP 20510; (202) 224-0265. Edward V. Pesce, Director.

Senate Press Gallery, S316 CAP 20510; (202) 224-0241. Joe Keenan, Director.

Senate Radio and Television Gallery, S325 CAP 20510; (202) 224-6421. Michael Mastrian, Director.

National Assn. of Multicultural Media Executives (NAMME), *7950 Jones Branch Dr., McLean, VA 22107; (703) 854-7178. Fax, (703) 854-7181. Toni F. Laws, Executive Director. Toll-free, (888) 968-7658.*

General e-mail, info@namme.org

Web, www.namme.org

Membership: minority media managers and executives from newspapers, magazines, radio, television, cable, and electronic media. Interests include increasing diversity in the senior ranks of the media industry. Provides executive development training and mentoring for new managers. Sponsors forums and alliances for discussions on multicultural issues in the media.

National Federation of Press Women (NFPW), *P.O. Box 5556, Arlington, VA 22205; (703) 812-9487. Fax, (703) 812-4555. Carol Pierce, Executive Director. Toll-free, (800) 780-2715.*

General e-mail, presswomen@aol.com

Web, www.nfpw.org

Membership: communications professionals, both men and women. Provides professional development opportunities for members, including an annual conference. Advocates freedom of the press. Provides cost-effective libel insurance. Monitors legislation and regulations.

National Lesbian and Gay Journalists Assn. (NLGJA), *1420 K St. N.W., #910 20005; (202) 588-9888. Fax, (202) 588-1818. David Barre, Executive Director.*

General e-mail, info@nlgja.org

Web, www.nlgja.org

Works within the journalism industry to foster fair and accurate coverage of lesbian, gay, bisexual, and transgender issues. Opposes workplace bias against all minorities and provides professional development for its members.

National Press Club, *529 14th St. N.W., 13th Floor 20045; (202) 662-7500. Fax, (202) 662-7569. Donna Leinwand, President. Library, (202) 662-7523.*

General e-mail, info@press.org

Web, www.press.org

Membership: reporters, editors, writers, publishers, cartoonists, producers, librarians, and teachers of journalism at all levels. Interests include advancement of professional standards and skills, and the promotion of free expression. Provides networking opportunities and manages an online job listing site for members. Library available to members for research.

National Press Foundation (NPF), *1211 Connecticut Ave. N.W., #310 20036; (202) 663-7280. Fax, (202) 530-2855. Bob Meyers, President.*

General e-mail, npf@nationalpress.org

Web, www.nationalpress.org

Works to enhance the professional competence of journalists through in-career education projects. Sponsors conferences, seminars, fellowships, and awards; conducts public forums and international exchanges. Supports the National Press Club library.

The Newspaper Guild-CWA, *501 3rd St. N.W., 6th Floor 20001-2797; (202) 434-7177. Fax, (202) 434-1472. Bernard J. Lunzer, President.*

General e-mail, guild@cwa-union.org

Web, www.newsguild.org

Membership: journalists, sales and media professionals. Advocates for higher standards in journalism, equal employment opportunity in the newspaper industry, and advancement of members' economic interests. (Affiliated with Communications Workers of America and the AFL-CIO.)

Project for Excellence in Journalism, *1615 L St. N.W., #700 20036; (202) 419-3650. Fax, (202) 419-3699. Tom Rosenstiel, Director.*

General e-mail, mail@journalism.org

Web, www.journalism.org

Evaluates and studies the performance of the press, particularly content analysis using empirical research to quantify what is occurring in the press. Tracks key industry trends. Publishes a daily digest of media news and an annual report on American journalism. (Part of the Pew Research Center.)

Society for Technical Communication (STC), *901 N. Stuart St., #904, Arlington, VA 22203-1822; (703) 522-4114. Fax, (703) 522-2075. Susan Burton, Executive Director.*

General e-mail, stc@stc.org

Web, www.stc.org

Membership: writers, publishers, educators, editors, illustrators, and others involved in technical communication. Encourages research and develops training programs; aids educational institutions in devising curricula; awards scholarships.

Statistical Assessment Service (STATS), *2100 L St. N.W., #300 20037; (202) 223-3193. Fax, (202) 872-4014. S. Robert Lichter, President.*

Web, www.stats.org

Research and resource organization. Interests include improving the quality of scientific and statistical information in public discourse. Acts as a resource for journalists and policymakers on scientific issues and controversies. (Affiliated with the Center for Media and Public Affairs at George Mason University.)

UNITY: Journalists of Color Inc., *7950 Jones Branch Dr., McLean, VA 22107; (703) 854-3585. Fax, (703) 854-3586. Onica Makwakwa, Executive Director.*

General e-mail, info@unityjournalists.org

Web, www.unityjournalists.org

Alliance of Asian American Journalists Assn., National Assn. of Black Journalists, National Assn. of Hispanic Journalists, and the Native American Journalists Association. Fosters representative media leadership and fair promotion practices for minority journalists. Educates the industry about the accurate representation of diverse populations in coverage. Encourages diversity in newsrooms.

Washington Press Club Foundation, *529 14th St. N.W., #1115 20045; (202) 393-0613. Fax, (202) 662-7040. Suzanne Pierron, Executive Director.*

General e-mail, wpcf@wpcf.org

Web, www.wpcf.org

Seeks to advance professionalism in journalism. Sponsors programs and events to educate students and the public on the role of a free press. Awards minority grants and scholarships. Administers an oral history of women in journalism. Sponsors annual Congressional Dinner in February to welcome Congress back into session.

White House Correspondents' Assn., *600 New Hampshire Ave., #800 20037; (202) 266-7453. Fax, (202) 266-7454. Julia Whiston, Executive Director.*

General e-mail, whca@starpower.net

Web, www.whca.net

Membership: reporters with permanent White House press credentials. Acts as a liaison between reporters and White House staff. Sponsors annual WHCA Journalism Awards and Scholarships fundraising dinner.

Women's Institute for Freedom of the Press, *1940 Calvert St. N.W. 20009-1502; (202) 265-6707. Martha Allen, President.*

General e-mail, mediademocracy@wifp.org

Web, www.wifp.org

Conducts research and publishes in areas of communications and the media that are of particular interest to women. Promotes freedom of the press. Publishes a free online directory of media produced by and for women.

Accreditation in Washington

►AGENCIES

Defense Dept. (DoD), *Public Affairs, The Pentagon, #2E964 20301-1400; (703) 697-5131. Fax, (703) 695-4299. Vacant, Assistant Secretary for Public Affairs, (703) 697-9312. Press, (703) 697-5131.*

Web, www.defenselink.mil/news

Grants accreditation to Washington-based media organizations to form the National Media Pool. Selected staff of accredited groups are assigned to the media pool on a rotating basis and put on alert for short-notice deployment to the site of military operations. Issues Pentagon press passes to members of the press regularly covering the Pentagon.

Foreign Press Center *(State Dept.), 529 14th St. N.W., #800 20045; (202) 504-6300. Fax, (202) 504-6334. James Dickmeyer, Director; Gordon Duguid, Director, Washington Center.*

Web, http://fpc.state.gov/7431.htm

Provides foreign journalists with access to news sources, including wire services and daily briefings from the White House, State Dept., and Pentagon. Holds live news conferences. Foreign journalists wishing to use the center must present a letter from their news organization, letter from the embassy of the country in which their paper is published, copy of photo page of passport, copy of visa or residency (green) card, and one recent passport-size photograph.

Metropolitan Police Dept., *Police Public Information, 300 Indiana Ave. N.W., #4048 20001; (202) 727-4383. Fax, (202) 715-7760. Traci Hughes, Director.*

General e-mail, mpd@dc.gov

Web, www.mpdc.dc.gov

Serves as connection between the media and the police department. Provides application forms and issues press passes required for crossing police lines within the city of Washington. Passes are issued on a yearly basis; applicants should allow four to six weeks for processing of passes.

National Park Service (NPS), *(Interior Dept.), National Capital Region, 1100 Ohio Dr. S.W., #107 20242; (202) 619-7000. Fax, (202) 619-7220. Margaret O'Dell, Regional Director. Recorded information, (202) 619-7275. Permits, (202) 619-7225.*

Web, www.nps.gov/ncro

Regional office that administers national parks, monuments, historic sites, and recreation areas in the

Washington metropolitan area. Issues special permits required for commercial filming on public park lands. News media representatives covering public events that take place on park lands must notify the Office of Public Affairs and Tourism in advance. A White House, Capitol Hill, metropolitan police, or other policy-agency-issued press pass is required in some circumstances. Commercial filming on park lands requires a special-use permit.

State Dept., *Public Affairs Press Office,* *2201 C St. N.W., #2109 20520-6180; (202) 647-2492. Fax, (202) 647-0244. Richard Aker, Director (Acting).*

Web, www.state.gov/press

Each U.S. journalist seeking a building pass must apply in person with a letter from his or her editor or publisher, two application forms (available from the press office), and a passport-size photograph. In addition, foreign correspondents need a letter from the embassy of the country in which their organization is based. Proof of citizenship is required of all applicants. All journalists must cover the State Dept.'s daily briefing on a regular basis, and thus reside in the Washington, D.C., area. Applicants should allow three months for security clearance. Members of the press wishing to attend an individual briefing should request clearance from the press office.

White House, *Press Office,* *1600 Pennsylvania Ave. N.W. 20500; (202) 456-2580. Fax, (202) 456-6210. Robert Gibbs, Press Secretary. Comments and information, (202) 456-1111. Alternate phone, (202) 647-2492.*

Web, www.whitehouse.gov

Journalists seeking permanent accreditation must meet four criteria. The journalist must be a designated White House correspondent and expected to cover the White House daily; must be accredited by the House and Senate press galleries; must be a resident of the Washington, D.C., area, and must be willing to undergo the required Secret Service background investigation. A journalist's editor, publisher, or employer must write to the press office requesting accreditation. Freelance journalists, cameramen, or technicians wishing temporary accreditation must send letters from at least two news organizations indicating the above criteria.

► **CONGRESS**

For a listing of relevant congressional committees and subcommittees, please see page 83 or the Appendix.

► **JUDICIARY**

Supreme Court of the United States, *1 1st St. N.E. 20543; (202) 479-3000. John G. Roberts Jr., Chief Justice; Kathleen Arberg, Public Information Officer, (202) 479-3211.*

Web, www.supremecourtus.gov/publicinfo

Journalists seeking to cover the Court should be accredited by either the White House or the House or Senate press galleries, but others may apply by submitting a letter from their editors. Contact the public information office to make arrangements.

Broadcasting

► **AGENCIES**

Federal Communications Commission (FCC), *Media Bureau: Policy Division,* *445 12th St. S.W. 20554; (202) 418-2120. Fax, (202) 418-1069. Mary Beth Murphy, Division Chief.*

Web, www.fcc.gov/mb/policy

Handles complaints and inquiries concerning the equal time rule, which requires equal broadcast opportunities for all legally qualified candidates for the same office, and other political broadcast, cable, and satellite rules. Interprets and enforces related Communications Act provisions, including the requirement for sponsorship identification of all paid political broadcast, cable, and satellite announcements and the requirement for broadcasters to furnish federal candidates with reasonable access to broadcast time for political advertising.

► **NONGOVERNMENTAL**

American Women in Radio and Television (AWRT), *1760 Old Meadow Rd., #500, McLean, VA 22102; (703) 506-3290. Fax, (703) 506-3266. Maria E. Brennan, President.*

General e-mail, info@awrt.org

Web, www.awrt.org

Membership: professionals in the electronic media and full-time students in accredited colleges and universities. Promotes industry cooperation and advancement of women. Maintains foundation supporting educational programs, charitable activities, public service campaigns, and scholarships.

Broadcast Education Assn. (BEA), *1771 N St. N.W. 20036-2891; (202) 429-3935. Fax, (202) 775-2981. Heather Birks, Executive Director. Information, (888) 380-7222.*

General e-mail, beainfo@beaweb.org

Web, www.beaweb.org

Membership: universities, colleges, and faculty members offering specialized training in the radio, television, and electronic media industries. Promotes improvement of curriculum and teaching methods. Fosters working relationships among academics, students, and professionals in the industry. Interests include documentaries, international business and regulatory practices, gender issues, interactive media and emerging technologies, and electronic media law and policy. Administers scholarships in the field.

National Academy of Television Arts and Sciences (NATAS), *National Capital/Chesapeake Bay Chapter Office,* *9405 Russell Rd., Silver Spring, MD 20910-1445; (301) 587-3993. Fax, (301) 587-3993. Dianne E. Bruno, Administrator.*

General e-mail, capitalemmys@aol.com

Web, www.capitalemmys.tv

Membership: professionals in television and related fields and students in communications. Serves the Virginia, Maryland, and Washington, D.C., television community. Works to upgrade television programming; awards scholarships to junior, senior, or graduate students in communications. Sponsors annual Emmy Awards. (Headquarters in New York.)

National Assn. of Black Owned Broadcasters (NABOB), *1155 Connecticut Ave. N.W., 6th Floor 20036; (202) 463-8970. Fax, (202) 429-0657. James L. Winston, Executive Director.*

General e-mail, nabob@nabob.org

Web, www.nabob.org

Membership: minority owners and employees of radio and television stations and telecommunications properties. Provides members and the public with information on the broadcast industry and the FCC. Provides members with legal and advertising research facilities. Monitors legislation and regulations.

National Assn. of Broadcast Employees and Technicians (NABET-CWA), *501 3rd St. N.W., 6th Floor 20001; (202) 434-1254. Fax, (202) 434-1426. John S. Clark, President.*

Web, www.nabetcwa.org

Membership: approximately 10,000 commercial broadcast and cable television and radio personnel. Helps members negotiate pay, benefits, and better working conditions; conducts training programs and workshops. Monitors legislation and regulations. (Broadcast and Cable Television Workers Sector of the Communications Workers of America.)

National Assn. of Broadcasters (NAB), *1771 N St. N.W. 20036-2891; (202) 429-5300. Fax, (202) 429-5406. David K. Rehr, President. Press, (202) 429-5350.*

General e-mail, nab@nab.org

Web, www.nab.org

Membership: radio and television broadcast stations and broadcast networks holding an FCC license or construction permit; associate members include producers of equipment and programs. Assists members in areas of management, engineering, and research. Interests include privatization abroad and related business opportunities. Monitors legislation and regulations.

Radio and Television Correspondents Assn., *S-325 CAP 20510; (202) 224-6421. Fax, (202) 224-4882. Michael Mastrian, Director.*

Web, www.senate.gov/galleries/radiotv

Membership: broadcast correspondents who cover Congress. Sponsors annual dinner. Officers also serve on the executive committee of the Congressional Radio-Television Galleries and determine eligibility for broadcast media credentials in Congress. Acts as a liaison between congressional offices and members of the media, and facilitates broadcast coverage of Senate activities.

Radio-Television News Directors Assn. (RTNDA/RTNDF), *1025 F St. N.W., 7th Floor 20004 (mailing address: 4121 Plank Rd., #512, Fredericksburg, VA 22407); (202) 659-6510. Fax, (202) 223-4007. Barbara Cochran, President.*

General e-mail, rtnda@rtnda.org

Web, www.rtnda.org

Membership: local and network news executives in broadcasting, cable, and other electronic media in more than thirty countries. Serves as information source for members; provides advice on legislative, political, and judicial problems of electronic journalism; conducts international exchanges.

Press Freedom

▶**NONGOVERNMENTAL**

Fund for Independence in Journalism, *910 17th St. N.W., #700 20006; (202) 481-1244. Charles Lewis, President; Jeanne Brooks, Managing Director.*

Web, www.tfij.org

Seeks to protect, defend, and foster independent, high-quality investigative journalism. Provides legal defense and endowment support to the Center for Public Integrity and other nonprofit journalism organizations. Conducts public education.

Reporters Committee for Freedom of the Press, *1101 Wilson Blvd., #1100, Arlington, VA 22209; (703) 807-2100. Fax, (703) 807-2109. Lucy A. Dalglish, Executive Director. Legal defense hotline, (800) 336-4243.*

General e-mail, rcfp@rcfp.org

Web, www.rcfp.org

Committee of reporters and editors that provides journalists and media lawyers with a 24-hour hotline for media law and freedom of information questions. Provides assistance to journalists and media lawyers in media law court cases. Produces publications on newsgathering legal issues. Interests include freedom of speech abroad, primarily as it affects U.S. citizens in the press.

Reporters Without Borders (Reporters Sans Frontières), *Washington Office, 1500 K St. N.W., #600 20005; (202) 256-5613. Lucie Morillon, Director.*

General e-mail, lucie.morillon@rsf.org

Web, www.rsf.org

Defends journalists who have been imprisoned or persecuted while conducting their work. Works to improve the safety of journalists. Advocates for freedom of the press internationally. Sponsors annual events and awards. (Headquarters in Paris, France.)

Student Press Law Center, *1101 Wilson Blvd., #1100, Arlington, VA 22209-2275; (703) 807-1904. Fax, (703) 807-2109. Frank LoMonte, Executive Director.*

Web, www.splc.org

Collects, analyzes, and distributes information on free expression and freedom of information rights of student journalists (print and broadcast) and on violations of those rights in high schools and colleges. Provides free legal advice and referrals to students and faculty advisers experiencing censorship.

World Press Freedom Committee, *11690-C Sunrise Valley Dr., Reston, VA 20191; (703) 715-9811. Fax, (703) 620-6790. Mark Bench, Executive Director.*
General e-mail, freepress@wpfc.org
Web, www.wpfc.org

Worldwide organization of print and broadcast groups. Promotes freedom of the press and opposes government censorship, licensing of journalists, and news controls. Assists journalists in central and eastern Europe and the developing world. Participates in international conferences.

Print Media

▶NONGOVERNMENTAL

American Press Institute (API), *11690 Sunrise Valley Dr., Reston, VA 20191-1498; (703) 620-3611. Fax, (703) 620-5814. Drew Davis, President.*
General e-mail, info@americanpressinstitute.org
Web, www.americanpressinstitute.org

Promotes the continuing education and career development of newspaper men and women. Conducts seminars, workshops, and conferences. Programs include an intensive computerized newspaper management simulation and a seminar on how to build revenue and audiences in the newspaper industry.

American Society of Newspaper Editors, *11690-B Sunrise Valley Dr., Reston, VA 20191-1409; (703) 453-1122. Fax, (703) 453-1133. Scott Bosley, Executive Director.*
General e-mail, asne@asne.org
Web, www.asne.org

Membership: directing editors of daily newspapers. Conducts training on good journalistic writing. Campaigns against government secrecy. Works to improve the racial diversity of newsroom staff. Serves as information clearinghouse for newsrooms of daily newspapers. Conducts initiative for high school students and journalism advisers at www.highschooljournalism.org. Monitors legislation and regulations.

Assn. of American Publishers, *Government Affairs, 50 F St. N.W., #400 20001; (202) 347-3375. Fax, (202) 347-3690. Allan R. Adler, Vice President, Legal and Government Affairs.*
Web, www.publishers.org

Membership: U.S. publishers of books, journals, tests, and software. Provides members with information on domestic and international trade and market conditions; interests include library and educational funding,

educational reform, postal rates, new technology, taxes, copyright, censorship, and libel matters. Monitors legislation and regulations.

Essential Information, *P.O. Box 19405 20036; (202) 387-8030. Fax, (202) 234-5176. John Richard, Director.*
General e-mail, info@essential.org
Web, www.essential.org

Provides writers and the public with information on public policy matters; awards grants to investigative reporters; sponsors conference on investigative journalism. Interests include activities of multinational corporations in developing countries.

Graphic Communications Conference of the International Brotherhood of Teamsters (GCC/IBT), *1900 L St. N.W. 20036; (202) 462-1400. Fax, (202) 721-0641. George Tedeschi, President.*
Web, www.gciu.org

Membership: approximately 60,000 members of the print and publishing industries, including lithographers, photoengravers, and bookbinders. Assists members with contract negotiation and grievances; conducts training programs and workshops. Monitors legislation and regulations.

Greeting Card Assn., *1156 15th St. N.W., #900 20005; (202) 393-1778. Fax, (202) 223-9741. Valerie Cooper, Executive Vice President.*
General e-mail, info@greetingcard.org
Web, www.greetingcard.org

Membership: publishers, printers, and others involved in the greeting card industry. Monitors legislation and regulations.

IDEAlliance, *1421 Prince St., Alexandria, VA 22314-2805; (703) 837-1070. Fax, (703) 837-1072. David J. Steinhardt, President.*
General e-mail, info@idealliance.org
Web, www.idealliance.org

Membership: firms and customers in printing, publishing, and related industries. Assists members in production of color graphics and conducts studies on print media management methods.

International Newspaper Financial Executives (INFE), *14237 Bookcliff Court, #200, Purcellville, VA 20132; (703) 421-4060. Fax, (703) 421-4068. Bob Kasabian, Executive Director.*
General e-mail, membership@infe.org
Web, www.infe.org

Membership: controllers and chief financial officers of newspapers and new media. Provides members with information on business office technology, including accounting software and spreadsheet applications. Produces publications, conducts seminars, and sponsors an annual conference.

Magazine Publishers of America (MPA), *Government Affairs, Washington Office,* *1211 Connecticut Ave. N.W., #610 20036; (202) 296-7277. Fax, (202) 296-0343. Nina Link, Chief Executive Officer.*

Web, www.magazine.org/government

Membership: publishers of consumer magazines. Washington office represents members in all aspects of government relations in Washington and state capitals. Interests include intellectual property and the First Amendment, consumer protection, and marketing and advertising. (Headquarters in New York.)

National Newspaper Assn. (NNA), *Washington Office,* *2020 N. 14th St., #300, Arlington, VA 22201-2515 (mailing address: P.O. Box 50301, Arlington, VA 22205); (703) 465-8808. Fax, (703) 812-4555. Tonda Rush, Director, Public Policy.*

Web, www.nna.org

Membership: community, weekly, and daily newspapers. Provides members with advisory services; informs members of legislation and regulations that affect their business. Educational arm, the National Newspaper Foundation, conducts management seminars and conferences. (Headquarters in Columbia, Mo.)

National Newspaper Publishers Assn. (NNPA), *3200 13th St. N.W. 20010; (202) 588-8764. Fax, (202) 588-8960. John Smith, Executive Director (Acting).*

General e-mail, nnpadc@nnpa.org

Web, www.nnpa.org

Membership: newspapers owned by African Americans serving an African American audience. Assists in improving management and quality of the African American press through workshops and merit awards. Sponsors NNPA Media Services, a print and Web advertising-placement and press release distribution service.

Newspaper Assn. of America, *4401 Wilson Blvd., #900, Arlington, VA 22203-1867; (571) 366-1000. Fax, (571) 366-1195. John Sturm, President. Library, (571) 366-1193.*

Web, www.naa.org

Membership: daily and weekly newspapers, other papers, and online products published in the United States, Canada, other parts of the Western Hemisphere, and Europe. Conducts research and disseminates information on newspaper publishing, including labor relations, legal matters, government relations, technical problems and innovations, telecommunications, economic and statistical data, marketing, and training programs. Library open to the public by appointment.

NPES: The Assn. for Suppliers of Printing, Publishing, and Converting Technologies, *1899 Preston White Dr., Reston, VA 20191-4367; (703) 264-7200. Fax, (703) 620-0994. Ralph J. Nappi, President.*

General e-mail, npes@npes.org

Web, www.npes.org

Trade association representing companies that manufacture and distribute equipment, supplies, systems, software, and services for printing, publishing, and converting.

Print Communications Professionals International Inc. (PCPI), *2100 N. Potomac St., Arlington, VA 22205; (703) 534-9379. Fax, (703) 534-1858. Suzanne Morgan, President.*

General e-mail, membersolutions@pcpi.org

Web, www.pcpi.org

Membership: print buyers, communications professionals, and other purchasers of printing services. Educates members about best practices in the industry.

Printing Industries of America/Graphic Arts Technical Foundation (PIA/GATF), *Washington Office,* *601 13th St., #360N 20005-3807; (202) 730-7970. Fax, (202) 730-7987. Julie Riccio, Director of Government Affairs. TTY, (866) 742-4283.*

General e-mail, govtaffairs@piagatf.org

Web, www.piagatf.org

Membership: printing firms and businesses that service printing industries. Represents members before Congress and regulatory agencies. Assists members with labor relations, human resources management, and other business management issues. Sponsors graphic arts competition. Monitors legislation and regulations. (Headquarters in Sewickley, Pa.)

Print Services and Distribution Assn., *433 E. Monroe Ave., Alexandria, VA 22301-1693; (703) 836-6232. Fax, (703) 836-2241. Peter L. Colaianni, Executive Vice President. Toll-free, (800) 336-4641.*

General e-mail, psda@psda.org

Web, www.psda.org

Membership: companies in the business printing supply chain, including manufacturers, suppliers, and distributors of business forms, labels, commercial printing, and advertising specialties. Conducts workshops, seminars, and conferences; sponsors industry research. Monitors legislation and regulations.

Screen Printing Technical Foundation (SPTF), *10015 Main St., Fairfax, VA 22031-3489; (703) 385-1335. Fax, (703) 273-0456. Michael E. Robertson, President.*

General e-mail, sgia@sgia.org

Web, www.sgia.org/sptf

Provides screen printers, suppliers, manufacturers, and schools with technical support and training; conducts research on production practices and standards. Offers scholarships for college students, grants to schools and teachers, and workshops. (Affiliated with Specialty Graphic Imaging Assn.)

Society of National Assn. Publications (SNAP), *1760 Old Meadow Rd., #500, McLean, VA 22102; (703) 506-3285. Fax, (703) 506-3266. Amy E. Lestition, Executive Director.*

General e-mail, snapinfo@snaponline.org

Web, www.snaponline.org

Membership: association publishers and communications professionals. Works to develop high publishing standards, including high-quality editorial and advertising content in members' publications. Compiles statistics; bestows editorial and graphics awards; monitors postal regulations.

Specialized Information Publishers Assn. (SIPA), *8229 Boone Blvd., #260, McLean, VA 22102; (703) 992-9339. Fax, (703) 992-7512. Henry Greene, Executive Director. Toll-free, (800) 356-9302.*

General e-mail, sipa@sipaonline.com

Web, www.sipaonline.com

Membership: newsletter publishers, specialized information services, and vendors to that market. Serves as an information clearinghouse and provides educational resources in the field. Monitors legislation and regulations. Library open to the public. (Formerly the Newsletter and Electronic Publishers Assn.)

Specialty Graphic Imaging Assn., *10015 Main St., Fairfax, VA 22031-3489; (703) 385-1335. Fax, (703) 273-0456. Michael E. Robertson, President.*

General e-mail, sgia@sgia.org

Web, www.sgia.org

Provides screen printers, graphic imagers, digital imagers, suppliers, manufacturers, and educators with technical guidebooks, training videos, managerial support, and guidelines for safety programs. Monitors legislation and regulations. (Affiliated with Screen Printing Technical Foundation.)

4

Culture and Religion

ARTS AND HUMANITIES

▶AGENCIES

Commission of Fine Arts, *National Building Museum,*
401 F St. N.W., #312 20001-2728; (202) 504-2200.
Fax, (202) 504-2195. Earl A. Powell, Chair; Thomas
Luebke, Secretary.
General e-mail, staff@cfa.gov
Web, www.cfa.gov

Advises the federal and D.C. governments on matters of art and architecture that affect the appearance of the nation's capital.

General Services Administration (GSA), *Design*
Excellence and the Arts Division: Office of the Chief
Architect, 1800 F St. N.W. 20405; (202) 501-1888. Fax,
(202) 501-3393. Leslie Shepherd, Director.
Web, www.gsa.gov

Administers the Art in Architecture Program, which commissions publicly scaled works of art for government buildings and landscapes, and the Fine Arts Program, which manages the GSA's collection of fine artwork that has been commissioned for use in government buildings.

John F. Kennedy Center for the Performing Arts, *2700*
F St. N.W. 20566-0001; (202) 416-8000. Fax, (202) 416-
8205. Michael Kaiser, President; Stephen A. Schwarzman,
Chair. Press, (202) 416-8000. Performance and ticket
information, (202) 467-4600; Toll-free, (800) 444-1324;
TTY, (202) 416-8524.
Web, www.kennedy-center.org

National cultural center created by Congress that operates independently; funded in part by federal dollars but primarily through private gifts and sales. Sponsors educational programs; presents American and international performances in theater, music, dance, and film; sponsors the John F. Kennedy Center Education Program, which produces the annual American College Theater Festival; and presents and subsidizes events for young people. The Kennedy Center stages free daily performances open to the public and free of charge 365 days a year on its Millennium Stage in the Grand Foyer.

National Endowment for the Arts (NEA), *1100*
Pennsylvania Ave. N.W. 20506-0001; (202) 682-5400. Fax,
(202) 682-5611. Dana Gioia, Chair. Press, (202) 682-5570.
TTY, (202) 682-5496.
General e-mail, webmgr@arts.endow.gov
Web, www.arts.gov

Independent federal grant-making agency. Awards grants to nonprofit, tax-exempt arts organizations, art service organizations, federally recognized tribal communities, state and local government offices, and others, in three categories: Access to Artistic Excellence, Learning in the Arts for Children and Youth, and Challenge America: Reaching Every Community Fast-Track Review Grants.

National Endowment for the Humanities (NEH), *1100*
Pennsylvania Ave. N.W., #503 20506; (202) 606-8310.
Fax, (202) 606-8588. Carole Watson, Chair.
Information, (202) 606-8400. Library, (202) 606-8244.
Press, (202) 606-8446. TTY, (202) 606-8282.
General e-mail, info@neh.gov
Web, www.neh.gov

Independent federal grant-making agency. Awards grants to individuals and institutions for research, scholarship, and educational and public programs (including broadcasts, museum exhibitions, lectures, and symposia) in the humanities (defined as study of archaeology; history; jurisprudence; language; linguistics; literature; philosophy; comparative religion; ethics; history, criticism, and theory of the arts; and humanistic aspects of the social sciences). Funds preservation of books, newspapers, historical documents, and photographs.

President's Committee on the Arts and the
Humanities, *1100 Pennsylvania Ave. N.W., #526 20506;*
(202) 682-5409. Fax, (202) 682-5668. Henry Moran,
Executive Director.
General e-mail, pcah@pcah.gov
Web, www.pcah.gov

Helps to incorporate the arts and humanities into White House objectives. Bridges federal agencies and the private sector. Recognizes cultural excellence, engages in research, initiates special projects, and stimulates private funding.

▶CONGRESS

For a listing of relevant congressional committees and subcommittees, please see page 114 or the Appendix.

▶NONGOVERNMENTAL

Americans for the Arts, *1000 Vermont Ave. N.W., 6th*
Floor 20005; (202) 371-2830. Fax, (202) 371-0424.
Robert L. Lynch, President.
General e-mail, info@artsusa.org
Web, www.americansforthearts.org

Membership: groups and individuals promoting advancement of the arts and culture in U.S. communities. Provides information on programs, activities, and administration of local arts agencies; on funding sources and guidelines; and on government policies and programs. Monitors legislation and regulations.

America the Beautiful Fund, *725 15th St. N.W., #605*
20005-6093; (202) 638-1649. Fax, (202) 638-2175. Nanine
Bilski, President.
General e-mail, info@america-the-beautiful.org
Web, www.america-the-beautiful.org

National service organization that promotes community self-help. Offers advisory services; grants; free seeds for civic and charitable volunteer programs; and national recognition awards to local community groups for activities that promote America's heritage, culture, environment, public parks, and human services.

CULTURE AND RELIGION RESOURCES IN CONGRESS

For a complete listing of Congress committees, including their full contact information, leadership, membership, and jurisdictions, please refer to the Appendix on pages 724–837.

HOUSE:

House Administration Committee, (202) 225-2061. Web, cha.house.gov

House Appropriations Committee, Subcommittee on Interior, Environment, and Related Agencies, (202) 225-3081. Web, appropriations.house.gov

> **Subcommittee on Labor, Health and Human Services, Education, and Related Agencies,** (202) 225-3508.

House Education and Labor Committee, Subcommittee on Healthy Families and Communities, (202) 225-3725. Web, edworkforce.house.gov

House Energy and Commerce Committee, Subcommittee on Commerce, Trade, and Consumer Protection, (202) 225-2927. Web, energycommerce.house.gov

> **Subcommittee on Telecommunications and the Internet,** (202) 225-2927.

House Judiciary Committee, Subcommittee on the Constitution, Civil Rights and Civil Liberties, (202) 225-2825. Web, judiciary.house.gov

House Natural Resources Committee, Subcommittee on National Parks, Forests, and Public Lands, (202) 226-7736. Web, resourcescommittee.house.gov

House Oversight and Government Reform Committee, Subcommittee on Domestic Policy, (202) 225-6427.

Web, oversight.house.gov

> **Subcommittee on Federal Workforce, Postal Service, and the District of Columbia,** (202) 225-5147.

House Ways and Means Committee, (202) 225-3625. Web, waysandmeans.house.gov\p

SENATE:

Senate Appropriations Committee, Subcommittee on Interior, Environment, and Related Agencies, (202) 228-0774. Web, appropriations.senate.gov

> **Subcommittee on Labor, Health and Human Services, Education and Related Agencies,** (202) 224-9145.

Senate Commerce, Science, and Transportation Committee, Subcommittee on Interstate Commerce, Trade, and Tourism, (202) 224-1270. Web, commerce.senate.gov

Senate Energy and Natural Resources Committee, Subcommittee on National Parks, (202) 224-4971. Web, energy.senate.gov

Senate Finance Committee, (202) 224-4515. Web, finance.senate.gov

Senate Health, Education, Labor and Pensions Committee, (202) 224-5375. Web, help.senate.gov

Senate Judiciary Committee, (202) 224-7703. Web, judiciary.senate.gov

Senate Rules and Administration Committee, (202) 224-6352. Web, rules.senate.gov

---

Assn. of Performing Arts Presenters, *1211 Connecticut Ave. N.W., #200 20036; (202) 833-2787. Fax, (202) 833-1543. Sandra Gibson, President.*
General e-mail, info@artspresenters.org
Web, www.artspresenters.org

Connects performing artists to audiences and communities around the world. Facilitates the work of presenters, artist managers, and consultants through continuing education, regranting programs, and legislative advocacy.

Federation of State Humanities Councils, *1600 Wilson Blvd., #902, Arlington, VA 22209-2511; (703) 908-9700. Fax, (703) 908-9706. Esther Mackintosh, President.*
General e-mail, info@statehumanities.org
Web, www.statehumanities.org

Membership: humanities councils from U.S. states and territories. Provides members with information; forms partnerships with other organizations and with the private

sector to promote the humanities. Monitors legislation and regulations.

National Assembly of State Arts Agencies, *1029 Vermont Ave. N.W., 2nd Floor 20005; (202) 347-6352. Fax, (202) 737-0526. Jonathan Katz, Chief Executive Officer. TTY, (202) 347-5948.*
General e-mail, nasaa@nasaa-arts.org
Web, www.nasaa-arts.org

Membership: state and jurisdictional arts agencies. Provides members with information, resources, and representation. Interests include arts programs for rural and underserved populations and the arts as a catalyst for economic development. Monitors legislation and regulations.

National Humanities Alliance, *21 Dupont Circle N.W., #800 20036; (202) 296-4994. Fax, (202) 872-0884. Jessica Jones-Irons, Executive Director, (202) 296-4994, ext. 149.*
Web, www.nhalliance.org

Represents scholarly and professional humanities associations; associations of museums, libraries, and historical societies; higher education institutions; state humanities councils; and independent and university-based research centers. Promotes the interests of individuals engaged in research, writing, and teaching.

National League of American Pen Women, *1300 17th St. N.W. 20036-1973; (202) 785-1997. Fax, (202) 452-6868. Taylor Collins, National President.*
General e-mail, nlapw1@verizon.net

Web, www.nlapw.org

Promotes the development of the creative talents of professional women in the fields of art, letters, and music composition. Conducts and promotes literary, educational, and charitable activities. Offers scholarships, workshops, and discussion groups.

Performing Arts Alliance, *1211 Connecticut Ave. N.W., #200 20036; (202) 207-3850. Fax, (202) 833-1543. Townley Clardy, Director (Acting).*
General e-mail, info@theperformingartsalliance.org

Web, www.theperformingartsalliance.org

Membership: organizations of the professional, nonprofit performing arts and presenting fields. Through legislative and grassroots activities, advocates policies favorable to the performing arts and presenting fields.

Provisions Library Resource Center for Activism and Arts, *1875 Connecticut Ave. N.W., #1100 20009; (202) 299-0460. Fax, (202) 232-1651. Donald H. Russell, Executive Director.*
General e-mail, pl@provisionslibrary.org

Web, www.provisionslibrary.org

Library collection on politics and culture open to the public by appointment. Offers educational and arts programs concerning social change and social justice.

Wolf Trap Foundation for the Performing Arts, *1645 Trap Rd., Vienna, VA 22182-2064; (703) 255-1900. Fax, (703) 255-1905. Terrence D. Jones, President. TTY, (703) 255-9432. Media and communications fax, (703) 255-4077.*
General e-mail, wolftrap@wolftrap.org

Web, www.wolftrap.org

Established by Congress; operates as a public-private partnership between the National Park Service, which maintains the grounds, and the Wolf Trap Foundation, which sponsors performances in theater, music, and dance. Conducts educational programs for children, internships for college students, career-entry programs for young singers, and professional training for teachers and performers.

Education

▶ **AGENCIES**

Education Dept., *Arts in Education Model Development and Dissemination, 400 Maryland Ave.*
S.W. 20202-5950; (202) 260-1280. Fax, (202) 205-5630. Diane Austin, Program Specialist.
General e-mail, artsdemo@ed.gov

Web, www.ed.gov

Supports the development of innovative model programs that integrate the arts into core elementary and middle school curricula and that strengthen arts instruction in those grades. Provides grants to local education agencies and nonprofit organizations.

Education Dept., *Professional Development for Arts Educators, 400 Maryland Ave. S.W., #4W223 20202-5950; (202) 260-3778. Fax, (202) 205-5630. Isadora Bender, Program Manager.*
General e-mail, artspd@ed.gov

Web, www.ed.gov

Supports the implementation of high-quality professional development model programs in elementary and secondary education for music, dance, drama, and visual arts educators. Funds support innovative instructional methods, especially those linked to scientifically based research.

John F. Kennedy Center for the Performing Arts, *Education, 2700 F St. N.W. 20566-0001; (202) 416-8800. Fax, (202) 416-8802. Darrell Ayers, Vice President of Education. Press, (202) 416-8441. TTY, (202) 416-8728.*
Web, www.kennedy-center.org/education

Establishes and supports state committees to encourage arts education in schools; promotes community partnerships between performing arts centers and school systems (Partners in Education); provides teachers, artists, and school and arts administrators with professional development classes; offers in-house and touring performances for students, teachers, families, and the general public; arranges artist and company residencies in schools; sponsors the National Symphony Orchestra education program; presents lectures, demonstrations, and classes in the performing arts for the general public; offers internships in arts management and fellowships for visiting artists; and produces annually the Kennedy Center American College Theater Festival.

John F. Kennedy Center for the Performing Arts, *National Partnerships, 2700 F St. N.W. 20566-0001; (202) 416-8816. Fax, (202) 416-8802. Barbara Shepherd, Director. Press, (202) 416-8441. TTY, (202) 416-8410.*
General e-mail, bbshepherd@kennedy-center.org

Web, www.kennedy-center.org/education/partners

Supports community-based educational partnerships and state alliances by providing professional development, technical support, resource development, and project grants through the Kennedy Center Alliance for Arts Education Network (KCAAEN) and the Partners in Education program. These two national networks provide communities with such services as teacher professional development, policy and research formation, and arts education programming.

National Endowment for the Arts (NEA), *Arts Education, Music, Opera, and Presenting, 1100 Pennsylvania Ave. N.W. 20506-0001; (202) 682-5400. Fax, (202) 682-5611. Jan Stunkard, Division Coordinator.*

General e-mail, lowd@arts.endow.gov

Web, www.arts.gov

Provides nonprofit, tax-exempt organizations with grants to produce arts-related projects. Organizations must have been in existence for at least three years to be eligible. Also offers fellowships for published authors of creative fiction, nonfiction, poetry, and translation.

National Endowment for the Humanities (NEH), *Education, 1100 Pennsylvania Ave. N.W., #302 20506; (202) 606-8500. Fax, (202) 606-8394. William Craig Rice, Director.*

General e-mail, education@neh.gov

Web, www.neh.gov

Supports the improvement of education in the humanities. Supports projects such as curriculum and materials development, classroom resources, and faculty training and development.

National Endowment for the Humanities (NEH), *Research Programs, 1100 Pennsylvania Ave. N.W., #318 20506; (202) 606-8200. Fax, (202) 606-8204. Ann Meyer, Director; Donna McClish, Librarian, (202) 606-8244.*

Web, www.neh.gov

Sponsors fellowship programs for humanities scholars. Provides support to libraries, museums, and independent centers for advanced study.

National Gallery of Art, *Education, 6th St. and Constitution Ave. N.W. 20565 (mailing address: 2000B S. Club Dr., Landover, MD 20785); (202) 842-6273. Fax, (202) 842-6935. TTY, (202) 842-6176. Order desk, (202) 842-6263.*

General e-mail, EdResources@nga.gov

Web, www.nga.gov/education

Serves as an educational arm of the gallery by providing free programs for schools, families, and adults. Lends audiovisual educational materials free of charge to schools, colleges, community groups, libraries, and individuals. Provides answers to written and telephone inquiries about European and American art.

Smithsonian Center for Education and Museum Studies, *600 Maryland Ave. S.W., #1005 20024 (mailing address: P.O. Box 37012, MRC 508, Washington, DC 20013-7012); (202) 633-5330. Fax, (202) 633-5489. Stephanie Norby, Director.*

General e-mail, learning@si.edu

Web, www.smithsonianeducation.org

Serves as the Smithsonian's central education office. Provides elementary and secondary teachers with programs, publications, audiovisual materials, regional workshops, and summer courses on using museums and primary source materials as teaching tools. Publishes books and other educational materials for teachers.

Smithsonian Institution, *Smithsonian Resident Associates, 1100 Jefferson Dr. S.W., #3077 20560 (mailing address: P.O. Box 23293, Washington, DC 20026-3293); (202) 633-3030. Fax, (202) 786-2034. Barbara Tuceling, Director.*

General e-mail, rap@tsa.si.edu

Web, www.residentassociates.org

National cultural and educational membership organization that offers courses and lectures for adults and young people. Presents films and offers study tours on arts-, humanities-, and science-related subjects; sponsors performances, studio arts workshops, and research.

▶**NONGOVERNMENTAL**

National Art Education Assn., *1916 Association Dr., Reston, VA 20191-1590; (703) 860-8000. Fax, (703) 860-2960. Deborah Reeve, Executive Director. Toll-free, (800) 299-8321.*

General e-mail, info@arteducators.org

Web, www.arteducators.org

Membership: art teachers (elementary through university), museum staff, and manufacturers and suppliers of art materials. Issues publications on art education theory and practice, research, and current trends; provides technical assistance to art educators. Sponsors awards.

National Assn. of Schools of Art and Design, *11250 Roger Bacon Dr., #21, Reston, VA 20190-5248; (703) 437-0700. Fax, (703) 437-6312. Samuel Hope, Executive Director.*

General e-mail, info@arts-accredit.org

Web, http://nasad.arts-accredit.org

Accrediting agency for educational programs in art and design. Provides information on art and design programs at the postsecondary level; offers professional development for executives of art and design programs.

Film, Photography, and Broadcasting

▶**AGENCIES**

American Film Institute (AFI), *Silver Theatre and Cultural Center, 8633 Colesville Rd., Silver Spring, MD 20910-3916; (301) 495-6720. Fax, (301) 495-6777. Murray Horwitz, Director. Press, (301) 495-6747. Recorded information, (301) 495-6700.*

General e-mail, silverinfo@afi.com

Web, www.afi.com/silver

Shows films of historical and artistic importance. AFI theater open to the public.

National Archives and Records Administration (NARA), *Motion Picture, Sound, and Video Branch, 8601 Adelphi Rd., #3360, College Park, MD 20740-6001; (866) 272-6272. Fax, (301) 837-3620. Leslie Waffen, Chief. TTY, (301) 837-0482.*

General e-mail, mopix@nara.gov

Web, www.archives.gov

Selects and preserves audiovisual records produced or acquired by federal agencies; maintains collections from the private sector, including newsreels. Research room open to the public.

National Archives and Records Administration (NARA), *Still Picture Branch,* *NWCS #5360, 8601 Adelphi Rd., College Park, MD 20740-6001; (301) 837-3530. Fax, (301) 837-3621. Robert E. Richardson, Director. Reference desk, (301) 837-0561.*
General e-mail, stillpix@nara.gov
Web, www.archives.gov

Provides the public with copies of still pictures from the federal government; supplies guides to these materials. Collection includes still pictures from more than 150 federal agencies.

National Endowment for the Arts (NEA), *Dance, Design, Media Arts, Museums, and Visual Arts,* *1100 Pennsylvania Ave. N.W., #729 20506; (202) 682-5452. Fax, (202) 682-5721. Jeff Watson, Visual Arts Division Coordinator; Douglas Sonntag, Director, Dance; Maurice Cox, Director, Design; Ted Libbey, Director, Media Arts; Robert Frankel, Director, Museums and Visual Arts. TTY, (202) 682-5496.*
Web, www.arts.gov

Awards grants to nonprofit organizations for film, video, and radio productions; supports film and video exhibitions and workshops.

National Endowment for the Humanities (NEH), *Public Programs,* *1100 Pennsylvania Ave. N.W., #426 20506; (202) 606-8269. Fax, (202) 606-8557. Thomas C. Phelps, Director.*
General e-mail, publicpgms@neh.gov
Web, www.neh.gov

Promotes public appreciation of the humanities through support of quality public programs of broad significance, reach, and impact. Awards grants for projects that meet NEH goals and standards, including excellence in content and format, broad public appeal, and wide access to diverse audiences.

►CONGRESS

For a listing of relevant congressional committees and subcommittees, please see page 114 or the Appendix.

Library of Congress, *Motion Picture, Broadcasting, and Recorded Sound Division,* *101 Independence Ave. S.E., #LM 338 20540; (202) 707-5840. Fax, (202) 707-2371. Gregory Lukow, Chief. Recorded sound reference center, (202) 707-7833. Motion picture and television reading room, (202) 707-8572.*
Web, www.loc.gov/rr/mopic

Collections include archives of representative motion pictures (1942–present); historic films (1894–1915); early American films (1898–1926); German, Italian, and Japanese features, newsreels, and documentary films (1930–1945); and a selected collection of stills, newspaper reviews, and

U.S. government productions. Collection also includes television programs of all types (1948–present), radio broadcasts (1924–present), and sound recordings (1890–present). Tapes the library's concert series and other musical events for radio broadcast; produces recordings of music and poetry for sale to the public. American Film Institute film archives are interfiled with the division's collections. Use of collections restricted to scholars and researchers; reading room open to the public.

Library of Congress, *National Film Preservation Board,* *101 Independence Ave. S.E. 20540; (202) 707-6240. Fax, (202) 707-2371. Steve Leggett, Staff Coordinator. TTY, (202) 707-6362.*
Web, www.loc.gov/film

Administers the National Film Preservation Plan. Establishes guidelines and receives nominations for the annual selection of twenty-five films of cultural, historical, or aesthetic significance; selections are entered in the National Film Registry to ensure archival preservation in their original form.

Library of Congress, *Prints and Photographs Division,* *101 Independence Ave. S.E., #LM 339 20540; (202) 707-5836. Fax, (202) 707-6647. Helena Zinkham, Chief (Acting). TTY, (202) 707-9051. Reading room, (202) 707-6394.*
Web, www.loc.gov/rr/print

Maintains Library of Congress's collection of pictorial material not in book format, totaling more than 13.5 million items. U.S. and international collections include artists' prints; historical prints, posters, and drawings; photographs (chiefly); political and social cartoons; and architectural plans, drawings, prints, and photographs. Reference service provided in the Prints and Photographs Reading Room. Reproductions of nonrestricted material available through the Library of Congress's Photoduplication Service; prints and photographs may be borrowed through the Exhibits Office for exhibits by qualified institutions. A portion of the collections and an overview of reference services are available on the World Wide Web.

►NONGOVERNMENTAL

CINE (Council on International Nontheatrical Events), *1112 16th St. N.W., #510 20036; (202) 785-1136. Fax, (202) 785-4114. Wendy Revel, Executive Director.*
General e-mail, info@cine.org
Web, www.cine.org

Serves as peer group for emerging and established film, video, and new media professionals. Sponsors semiannual competition for film and new media; holds semiannual screening competitions and annual showcase and awards ceremonies.

Library of American Broadcasting, *Hornbake Library, University of Maryland, College Park, MD 20742; (301) 405-9160. Fax, (301) 314-2634. Chuck Howell, Curator.*
General e-mail, labcast@umd.edu
Web, www.lib.umd.edu/LAB

Maintains library and archives on the history of radio and television. Open to the public.

Motion Picture Assn. of America, *1600 Eye St. N.W. 20006; (202) 293-1966. Fax, (202) 296-7410. Dan Glickman, President. Anti-piracy hotline, (800) 662-6797. Web, www.mpaa.org*

Membership: motion picture producers and distributors. Advises state and federal governments on copyrights, censorship, cable broadcasting, and other topics; administers volunteer rating system for motion pictures; works to prevent video piracy.

Language and Literature

►AGENCIES

National Endowment for the Arts (NEA), *Literature, 1100 Pennsylvania Ave. N.W. 20506-0001; (202) 682-5757. Fax, (202) 682-5481. Garrick Davis, Division Specialist. Web, www.arts.gov*

Awards grants to published writers, poets, and translators of prose and poetry; awards grants to small nonprofit presses, literary magazines, and literature organizations that publish poetry and fiction.

►CONGRESS

For a listing of relevant congressional committees and subcommittees, please see page 114 or the Appendix.

Library of Congress, *Center for the Book, 101 Independence Ave. S.E., #LM 650 20540; (202) 707-5221. Fax, (202) 707-0269. John Y. Cole, Director. General e-mail, cfbook@loc.gov*

Web, www.loc.gov/cfbook

Seeks to broaden public appreciation of books, reading, literacy, and libraries; sponsors lectures and conferences on the educational and cultural role of the book worldwide, including the history of books and printing, television and the printed word, and the publishing and production of books; cooperates with state centers and with other organizations. Projects and programs are privately funded except for basic administrative support from the Library of Congress.

Library of Congress, *Children's Literature Center, 101 Independence Ave. S.E., #LJ100 20540; (202) 707-5535. Fax, (202) 707-4632. Sybille A. Jagusch, Chief. General e-mail, childref@loc.gov*

Web, www.loc.gov/rr/child

Provides reference and information services by telephone, by correspondence, and in person; maintains reference materials on all aspects of the study of children's literature. Sponsors lectures, symposia, and exhibits. Consultation by appointment only. Serves children indirectly through assistance given to teachers, librarians, and others who work with youth.

Library of Congress, *Poetry and Literature Center, 101 Independence Ave. S.E., #LJ120 20540; (202) 707-3302. Fax, (202) 707-9946. Carolyn T. Brown, Director; Donald Hall, Poet Laureate. Poetry Readings (recording), (202) 707-5394.*

Web, www.loc.gov/poetry

Advises the library on public literary programs and on the acquisition of literary materials. Sponsors public poetry and fiction readings, lectures, symposia, occasional dramatic performances, and other literary events. Arranges for poets to record readings of their work for the library's tape archive. The poet laureate is appointed annually by the Librarian of Congress on the basis of literary distinction.

►NONGOVERNMENTAL

Alliance Française de Washington, *2142 Wyoming Ave. N.W. 20008-3906; (202) 234-7911. Fax, (202) 234-0125. Laurent Mellier, Executive Director. General e-mail, alliance@francedc.org*

Web, www.francedc.org

Offers courses in French language and literature; presents lectures and cultural events; maintains library of French-language publications for members; offers language programs, including on-site corporate language programs.

American Councils for International Education: ACTR/ ACCELS, *1776 Massachusetts Ave. N.W., #700 20036; (202) 833-7522. Fax, (202) 833-7523. Dan E. Davidson, President. General e-mail, general@americancouncils.org*

Web, www.americancouncils.org

Advances education and research worldwide through international programs focused on academic exchange, professional training, distance learning, curriculum and test development, delivery of technical assistance, research, evaluation, and institution building. Conducts educational exchanges for high school, university, and graduate school students as well as scholars with the countries of eastern Europe, Eurasia, southeast Europe, and the Middle East.

Center for Applied Linguistics, *4646 40th St. N.W., #200 20016-1859; (202) 362-0700. Fax, (202) 362-3740. Donna Christian, President. General e-mail, info@cal.org*

Web, www.cal.org

Research and technical assistance organization that serves as a clearinghouse on application of linguistics to practical language problems. Interests include English as a second language (ESL), teacher training and material development, language education, language proficiency test development, bilingual education, and sociolinguistics.

English First, *8001 Forbes Pl., #102, Springfield, VA 22151-2205; (703) 321-8818. Fax, (703) 321-7261. Jim Boulet Jr., Executive Director. Web, www.englishfirst.org*

Seeks to make English the official language of the United States. Advocates policies that make English education available to all children. Monitors legislation and regulations. Opposes bilingual education and ballots and Clinton Executive Order 13166.

Folger Shakespeare Library, *201 E. Capitol St. S.E. 20003-1004; (202) 544-4600. Fax, (202) 544-4623. Gail Kern Paster, Director. Press, (202) 675-0342. Box Office, (202) 544-7077.*

General e-mail, webmaster@folger.edu

Web, www.folger.edu

Maintains major Shakespearean and Renaissance materials; awards fellowships for postdoctoral research; presents concerts, theater performances, poetry and fiction readings, exhibits, and other public events. Offers educational programs for elementary, secondary, high school, college, and graduate school students and teachers. Publishes the New Folger Library Shakespeare editions and, in association with the George Washington University, *Shakespeare Quarterly.*

Hurston/Wright Foundation, *6525 Belcrest Rd., #531, Hyattsville, MD 20782-2037; (301) 683-2134. Fax, (301) 277-1262. Marita Golden, President; Clyde McElvene, Executive Director.*

General e-mail, info@hurstonwright.org

Web, www.hurstonwright.org

Resource center for writers, readers, and supporters of black literature. Presents monetary awards to writers and sponsors writers' workshops.

Japan-America Society of Washington, *1819 L St. N.W., 1B Level 20036-3807; (202) 833-2210. Fax, (202) 833-2456. Amb. John R. Malott, President.*

General e-mail, jaswdc@us-japan.org

Web, www.us-japan.org/dc

Partner of the National Cherry Blossom Festival; offers lectures and films on Japan; operates a Japanese-language school and an annual nationwide language competition for high school students. Maintains library for members.

Joint National Committee for Languages, *4646 40th St. N.W., #310 20016; (202) 966-8477. Fax, (202) 966-8310. J. David Edwards, Executive Director.*

General e-mail, info@languagepolicy.org

Web, www.languagepolicy.org

Membership: translators, interpreters, and associations of language teachers (primary through postsecondary level). Supports a national policy on language study and international education. Provides forum and clearinghouse for professional language and international education associations. National Council for Languages and International Studies is the political arm.

Linguistic Society of America, *1325 18th St. N.W., #211 20036; (202) 835-1714. Fax, (202) 835-1717. Alyson Reed, Director.*

General e-mail, lsa@lsadc.org

Web, www.lsadc.org

Membership: individuals and institutions interested in the scientific analysis of language. Holds linguistic institutes every other year.

Malice Domestic Ltd., *P.O. Box 8007, Gaithersburg, MD 20898-8007. Louise Leftwich, Chair; Sky Benson, Public Relations.*

General e-mail, publicrelations@malicedomestic.org

Web, www.malicedomestic.org

Membership: authors and readers of traditional mysteries. Sponsors annual Agatha Awards and an annual convention. Awards grants to unpublished writers in the genre.

National Foreign Language Center *(University of Maryland), 5201 Paint Branch Pkwy., #2132, College Park, MD 20742; (301) 405-9828. Fax, (301) 405-9829. Catherine Ingold, Director.*

General e-mail, inquiries@nflc.org

Web, www.nflc.org

Research and policy organization that develops new strategies to strengthen foreign language competence in the United States. Conducts research on national language needs and assists policymakers in identifying priorities, allocating resources, and designing programs. Interests include the role of foreign language in higher education, national competence in critical languages, ethnic language maintenance, and K–12 and postsecondary language programs.

PEN/Faulkner Foundation, *201 E. Capitol St. S.E. 20003-1094; (202) 675-0345. Fax, (202) 675-0360. Jessica Neely, Executive Director. Alternate phone, (202) 898-9063.*

Web, www.penfaulkner.org

Sponsors an annual juried award for American fiction. Brings authors to visit public schools to discuss their work. Holds readings by noted authors of American fiction.

U.S. English, *1747 Pennsylvania Ave. N.W., #1050 20006-4682; (202) 833-0100. Fax, (202) 833-0108. Mauro E. Mujica, Chair.*

General e-mail, info@usenglish.org

Web, www.usenglish.org

Advocates English as the official language of federal and state government. Affiliate U.S. English Foundation promotes English language education for immigrants.

The Writer's Center, *4508 Walsh St., Bethesda, MD 20815; (301) 654-8664. Fax, (801) 730-6233. Charlotte Moser, Chair.*

General e-mail, postmaster@writer.org

Web, www.writer.org

Membership: writers, editors, graphic artists, and interested individuals. Supports the creation and marketing of literary texts. Sponsors workshops in writing and graphic arts, and a reading series of poetry, fiction, and plays. Maintains a book gallery.

Museums

►AGENCIES

Anacostia Community Museum *(Smithsonian Institution),* *1901 Fort Place S.E. 20020 (mailing address: P.O. Box 37012, MRC 0777, Washington, DC 20013-7012); (202) 633-4820. Fax, (202) 287-3183. Camille Akeju, Director. Press, (202) 633-4869. TTY, (202) 357-1729.*

General e-mail, info@anacostia.si.edu

Web, http://anacostia.si.edu

Explores American history, society, and creative expression from an African American perspective and encourages the collection and preservation of materials that reflect that history and tradition.

Arthur M. Sackler Gallery *(Smithsonian Institution),* *1050 Independence Ave. S.W. 20560-0707 (mailing address: P.O. Box 37012, MRC 707, Washington, DC 20013-7012); (202) 633-4880. Fax, (202) 357-4911. Julian Raby, Director. Press, (202) 633-0520. TTY, (202) 633-5285. Public programs, (202) 633-1000 (recording).*

General e-mail, publicaffairsasia@si.edu

Web, www.asia.si.edu

Exhibits Asian and Near Eastern art drawn from collections in the United States and abroad; features international exhibitions and public programs. Presents films, lectures, and concerts. Library open to the public.

Federal Council on the Arts and the Humanities, *1100 Pennsylvania Ave. N.W. 20506-0001; (202) 682-5574. Fax, (202) 682-5603. Alice M. Whelihan, Indemnity Administrator.*

Membership: leaders of federal agencies sponsoring arts-related activities. Administers the Arts and Artifacts Indemnity Act, which helps museums reduce the costs of commercial insurance for international exhibits.

Ford's Theatre National Historic Site, *511 10th St. N.W. 20004; (202) 426-6924. Fax, (202) 426-1845. Rae Emerson, Site Manager. Recorded ticket information, (202) 638-2941.*

General e-mail, NACC_FOTH_Interpretation@nps.gov

Web, www.nps.gov/foth

Administered by the National Park Service, which manages Ford's Theatre, Ford's Theatre Museum, and the Peterson House (house where Lincoln died). Presents interpretive talks, exhibits, and tours. Research library open by appointment. Functions as working stage for theatrical productions.

Frederick Douglass National Historic Site, *1411 W St. S.E. 20020; (202) 426-5961. Fax, (202) 426-0880. Eola Dance, Site Manager (Acting). TTY, (301) 864-1152. Reservations, (877) 444-6777.*

General e-mail, frdo@nps.gov

Web, www.nps.gov/frdo

Administered by the National Park Service. Museum of the life and work of abolitionist Frederick Douglass and his family. Offers tours of the home and special programs, such as documentary films, videos, and slide presentations; maintains visitors center and bookstore. Reservations are required for parties of more than ten. Online reservations can be made at www.recreation.gov.

Freer Gallery of Art *(Smithsonian Institution),* *12th St. and Independence Ave. S.W. 20560 (mailing address: P.O. Box 37012, MRC 707, Washington, DC 20013-7012); (202) 633-4880. Fax, (202) 357-4911. Julian Raby, Director. Press, (202) 633-0519. TTY, (202) 357-1729. Public programs, (202) 633-1000 (recording).*

General e-mail, publicaffairsasia@asia.si.edu

Web, www.asia.si.edu

Exhibits Asian art from the Mediterranean to Japan and late nineteenth- and early twentieth-century American art from its permanent collection, including works by James McNeill Whistler. Presents films, lectures, and concerts. Library open to the public.

Hirshhorn Museum and Sculpture Garden *(Smithsonian Institution),* *7th St. and Independence Ave. S.W. 20560 (mailing address: P.O. Box 37012, HMSG, MRC 350, Washington, DC 20013-7012); (202) 633-4674. Fax, (202) 633-8835. Richard Koshalek, Director. Information, (202) 357-2700. Press, (202) 633-4765. TTY, (202) 633-8043.*

General e-mail, hmsginquiries@hmsg.si.edu

Web, www.hirshhorn.si.edu

Preserves and exhibits contemporary American and European paintings and sculpture. Offers films, lectures, concerts, and tours of the collection.

Institute of Museum and Library Services, *1800 M St. N.W., 9th Floor 20036-5802; (202) 653-4657. Fax, (202) 653-4600. Anne-Imelda M. Radice, Director. Press, (202) 653-4632. TTY, (202) 653-4699. Public and legislative affairs, (202) 653-4757.*

General e-mail, imlsinfo@imls.gov

Web, www.imls.gov

Independent federal agency established by Congress to assist museums and libraries in increasing and improving their services. Awards grants for general operating support, conservation projects, and museum assessment to museums of all disciplines and budget sizes; helps fund museum associations.

National Archives and Records Administration (NARA), Center for the National Archives Experience, *700 Pennsylvania Ave. N.W., #G9 20408; (202) 357-5210. Fax, (202) 357-5926. Marvin Pinkert, Director. Information, (202) 357-5000. Press, (202) 357-5300.*

General e-mail, inquire@nara.gov

Web, www.archives.gov

Plans and directs activities to acquaint the public with the mission and holdings of the National Archives;

Museum Education Programs

Alexandria Archaeology, (703) 838-4399

American Assn. of Museums, Museum Assessment Program, (202) 289-1818

Arlington Arts Center, (703) 248-6800

Assn. of Science-Technology Centers, (202) 783-7200

B'nai B'rith Klutznick Museum, (202) 857-6583

C & O Canal, (301) 739-4200

Corcoran Gallery of Art, (202) 639-1700

Daughters of the American Revolution (DAR) Museum, (202) 879-3241 or (202) 628-1776

Decatur House, (202) 842-0920

Dumbarton Oaks, (202) 339-6401

Federal Reserve Board Fine Arts Program, (202) 452-3302

Folger Shakespeare Library, (202) 675-0395

Gadsby's Tavern Museum, (703) 838-4242

Institute of Museum and Library Services, (202) 653-4657

J.F.K. Center for the Performing Arts, (202) 416-8800

Lyceum, (703) 838-4994

Mount Vernon, (703) 780-2000

National Arboretum, (202) 245-2726

National Archives, (202) 357-5210

National Building Museum, (202) 272-2448

National Gallery of Art, (202) 842-6246

National Museum of Women in the Arts, (202) 783-7370

Navy Museum, (202) 433-4882

Octagon Museum, (202) 638-3221

Phillips Collection, (202) 387-2151

Smithsonian Institution

  Anacostia Community Museum, (202) 633-4821

  Arthur M. Sackler Gallery, (202) 633-0266

  Center for Education and Museum Studies, (202) 633-5330

  Freer Gallery of Art, (202) 633-0457

  Hirshhorn Museum and Sculpture Garden, (202) 633-2829

  National Air and Space Museum, (202) 633-2540

  National Museum of African Art, (202) 633-4640

  National Museum of American Art, (202) 633-7970

  National Museum of American History, (202) 633-3717

  National Museum of the American Indian, (202) 633-6900

  National Museum of Natural History, (202) 633-1077

  National Portrait Gallery, (202) 633-8500

  Renwick Gallery, (202) 633-8528 or (202) 633-2850

Textile Museum, (202) 667-0441, ext. 35

Woodrow Wilson House, (202) 387-4062

---

conducts behind-the-scenes tours; presents hands-on workshops; develops both traditional and interactive exhibits; produces publications, including teaching packets that feature historic documents.

National Cryptologic Museum *(National Security Agency), 9800 Savage Rd., Fort George Meade, MD 20755; (301) 688-5849. Fax, (301) 688-5847. Patrick Weadon, Curator. NSA Public and Media Affairs, (301) 688-6524*
General e-mail, museum@nsa.gov

Web, www.nsa.gov/museum

Documents the history of the cryptologic profession.

National Endowment for the Arts (NEA), *Dance, Design, Media Arts, Museums, and Visual Arts, 1100 Pennsylvania Ave. N.W., #729 20506; (202) 682-5452. Fax, (202) 682-5721. Jeff Watson, Visual Arts Division Coordinator; Douglas Sonntag, Director, Dance; Maurice Cox, Director, Design; Ted Libbey, Director, Media Arts; Robert Frankel, Director, Museums and Visual Arts. TTY, (202) 682-5496.*
Web, www.arts.gov

Awards grants to museums for installing and cataloging permanent and special collections; conducts traveling exhibits; trains museum professionals; conserves and preserves museum collections; and develops arts-related educational programs.

National Gallery of Art, *6th St. and Constitution Ave. N.W. 20565 (mailing address: 2000B S. Club Dr., Landover, MD 20785); (202) 737-4215. Fax, (202) 789-3044. Earl A. Powell III, Director. Information, (202) 737-4215. Press, (202) 842-6353. TTY, (202) 842-6176.*
General e-mail, pressinfo@nga.gov

Web, www.nga.gov

Created by a joint resolution of Congress, the museum is a public-private partnership that preserves and exhibits European and American paintings, sculpture, and decorative and graphic arts. Offers concerts, demonstrations, lectures, symposia, films, tours, and teacher workshops to enhance exhibitions, the permanent collection, and related topics. Lends art to museums in all fifty states and abroad through the National Lending Service. Publishes a bimonthly calendar of events.

National Museum of African Art *(Smithsonian Institution), 950 Independence Ave. S.W. 20560-0708 (mailing address: P.O. Box 37012, MRC 708, Washington, DC 20013-7012); (202) 633-4600. Fax, (202) 357-4879. Sharon Patton, Director. Press, (202) 633-4649. TTY, (202) 357-4814.*
General e-mail, nmafaweb@nmafa.si.edu

Web, http://africa.si.edu

Collects, studies, and exhibits traditional and contemporary arts of Africa. Exhibits feature objects from the permanent collection and from private and public collections worldwide. Library and photo archive open to the public by appointment.

National Museum of American History *(Smithsonian Institution)*, *14th St. and Constitution Ave. N.W., #4260, MRC 622 20560-0630; (202) 633-3435. Fax, (202) 786-2624. Brent D. Glass, Director. Library, (202) 633-3865. Press, (202) 633-3129. TTY, (202) 633-5285.*

General e-mail, glassb@si.edu

Web, http://americanhistory.si.edu

Collects and exhibits objects representative of American cultural history, applied arts, industry, national and military history, and science and technology. Library open to the public by appointment.

National Museum of Health and Medicine *(Defense Dept.)*, *6900 Georgia Ave. N.W., Bldg. 54 20307 (mailing address: AFIP P.O. Box 59685, Washington, DC 20012-0685); (202) 782-2200. Fax, (202) 782-3573. Dr. Adrianne Noe, Director.*

General e-mail, nmhminfo@afip.osd.mil

Web, http://nmhm.washingtondc.museum

Collects and exhibits medical models, tools, and teaching aids. Maintains permanent exhibits on the human body, STDs, Civil War medicine, and military contributions to medicine; collects specimens illustrating a broad range of pathological conditions. Open to the public. Study collection available for scholars by appointment.

National Museum of the American Indian *(Smithsonian Institution)*, *4th St. and Independence Ave. S.W. 20560; (202) 633-1000. Fax, (202) 633-6920. Kevin Gover, Director. Group reservations, (202) 633-6644.*

Web, www.americanindian.si.edu

Established by Congress in 1989, the museum collects, exhibits, preserves, and studies American Indian languages, literature, history, art, and culture.

National Portrait Gallery *(Smithsonian Institution)*, *800 G St. N.W. 20560 (mailing address: P.O. Box 37012, Victor Bldg., MRC 973, Washington, DC 20013-7012); (202) 633-8300. Fax, (202) 633-8243. Martin E. Sullivan, Director; Carolyn K. Carr, Deputy Director. Library, (202) 633-8230. Press, (202) 633-8293. TTY, (202) 633-5285. Library TTY, (202) 633-8229.*

General e-mail, npg@si.edu

Web, www.npg.si.edu

Exhibits paintings, photographs, sculpture, drawings, and prints of individuals who have made significant contributions to the history, development, and culture of the United States. Library open to the public.

Naval Historical Center, *Navy Art Collection, 822 Sicard St. S.E. 20374 (mailing address: 805 Kidder Breese St. S.E., Washington Navy Yard, DC 20374); (202) 433-3815. Fax, (202) 433-5635. Gale Munro, Director.*

Web, www.history.navy.mil

Holdings include more than 18,000 paintings, prints, drawings, and sculptures. Artworks depict naval ships, personnel, and action from all eras of U.S. naval history, especially the eras of World War II, the Korean War, and Desert Shield/Storm. Open to the public. Visitors without Defense Dept. or military identification must call in advance. Photo identification required.

Renwick Gallery of the Smithsonian American Art Museum *(Smithsonian Institution)*, *17th St. and Pennsylvania Ave. N.W. 20006 (mailing address: P.O. Box 37012, Renwick Gallery, MRC 510, Washington, DC 20013-7012); (202) 633-2850. Fax, (202) 275-1715. Robyn Kennedy, Chief. Press, (202) 633-8530. TTY, (202) 633-5285.*

General e-mail, info@saam.si.edu

Web, www.americanart.si.edu

Curatorial department of the Smithsonian American Art Museum. Exhibits nineteenth- to twenty-first-century American crafts.

Smithsonian American Art Museum *(Smithsonian Institution)*, *8th and F Sts. N.W. 20560 (mailing address: P.O. Box 37012, MRC 970, Washington, DC 20013-7012); (202) 633-7970. Fax, (202) 633-8535. Elizabeth Broun, Director. Library, (202) 633-8230. Press, (202) 633-8530. TTY, (202) 633-5285.*

General e-mail, saaminfo@si.edu

Web, www.americanart.si.edu

Exhibits and interprets American painting, sculpture, photographs, folk art, and graphic art in the permanent collection and temporary exhibition galleries. Library open to the public.

Smithsonian Center for Education and Museum Studies, *600 Maryland Ave. S.W., #1005 20024 (mailing address: P.O. Box 37012, MRC 508, Washington, DC 20013-7012); (202) 633-5330. Fax, (202) 633-5489. Stephanie Norby, Director.*

General e-mail, learning@si.edu

Web, www.smithsonianeducation.org

Serves as the Smithsonian's central education office. Provides elementary and secondary teachers with programs, publications, audiovisual materials, regional workshops, and summer courses on using museums and primary source materials as teaching tools. Publishes books and other educational materials for teachers.

Smithsonian Institution, *1000 Jefferson Dr. S.W., #205 20560 (mailing address: P.O. Box 37012, SIB 354, MRC 033, Washington, DC 20013-7012); (202) 633-1846. Fax, (202) 786-2377. G. Wayne Clough, Secretary; Charles Alcock, Under Secretary for Science (Acting); Richard Kurin, Under Secretary for Art, History, and Culture; Alison McNally, Under Secretary for Finance and Administration. Information, (202) 633-1000. Library, (202) 633-1700. Press, (202) 633-2400. TTY, (202) 633-5285. Locator, (202) 633-1000.*

General e-mail, info@si.edu

Web, www.si.edu

Conducts research; publishes results of studies, explorations, and investigations; presents study and reference collections on science, culture, and history; presents exhibitions in the arts, American history, technology, aeronautics and space exploration, and natural history. Smithsonian Institution sites in Washington, D.C., include the Anacostia Community Museum, Archives of American Art, Arthur M. Sackler Gallery, Arts and Industries Building, Freer Gallery of Art, Hirshhorn Museum and Sculpture Garden, National Air and Space Museum, National Museum of African Art, Renwick Gallery, Smithsonian American Art Museum, National Museum of American History, National Museum of the American Indian, National Museum of Natural History, National Portrait Gallery, National Postal Museum, National Zoological Park, S. Dillon Ripley Center, and Smithsonian Institution Building. Supports affiliates in Arizona, Florida, Maryland, Massachusetts, New York, and Panama. Autonomous organizations affiliated with the Smithsonian Institution include John F. Kennedy Center for the Performing Arts, National Gallery of Art, and Woodrow Wilson International Center for Scholars. Libraries open to the public by appointment; library catalogs are available on the Web.

Smithsonian Institution, *International Relations, 1100 Jefferson Dr. S.W., #3123 20705 (mailing address: P.O. Box 37012, Quad MRC 705, Washington, DC 20013-7012); (202) 633-4773. Fax, (202) 786-2557. Francine C. Berkowitz, Director.*
Web, www.si.edu/intrel

Fosters the development and coordinates the international aspects of Smithsonian cultural activities; facilitates basic research in history and art and encourages international collaboration among individuals and institutions.

Smithsonian Institution, *Office of Fellowships, 470 L'Enfant Plaza S.W., #7102 20013 (mailing address: P.O. Box 37012, MRC 902, Washington, DC 20013-7012); (202) 633-7070. Fax, (202) 633-7069. Catherine F. Harris, Director.*
General e-mail, siofg@si.edu
Web, www.si.edu/research+study

Provides fellowships to students and scholars for independent research projects in association with members of the Smithsonian professional research staff. Provides central management for all Smithsonian research fellowship programs. Facilitates the Smithsonian's scholarly interactions with universities, museums, and research institutions around the world.

Smithsonian Institution, *Smithsonian Museum Support Center, 4210 Silver Hill Rd., MSC Room C-2000, Suitland, MD 20746-2863; (301) 238-1030. Fax, (301) 238-3661. Gil Taylor, Librarian.*
General e-mail, libmail@si.edu
Web, www.sil.si.edu/libraries/msc

Museum collections management facility dedicated to collections, storage, research, and conservation. Library serves Smithsonian staff, other government agencies, and researchers. Open to the public by appointment.

Steven F. Udvar-Hazy Center *(Smithsonian Institution),* ***National Air and Space Museum,*** *14390 Air and Space Museum Pkwy., Chantilly, VA 20151; (202) 633-1000. Gen. John Dailey, Director; Joseph T. Anderson, Deputy Director. TTY, (202) 633-5285. Public Affairs, (703) 572-4040.*
Web, www.nasm.si.edu/udvarhazy

Displays and preserves a collection of historical aviation and space artifacts, including the B-29 Superfortress, Enola Gay, the Lockheed SR-71 Blackbird, the prototype of the Boeing 707, the space shuttle *Enterprise,* and the Concorde. Provides a center for research into the history, science, and technology of aviation and space flight.

U.S. Navy Museum (Naval Historical Center), *Bldg. 76, 805 Kidder Breese St. S.E., Washington Navy Yard 20374-5060; (202) 433-4882. Fax, (202) 433-8200. Karen Hill, Director, Education and Public Programs; Kim Nielsen, Director,*
Web, www.history.navy.mil

Collects, preserves, displays, and interprets historic naval artifacts and artwork. Presents a complete overview of U.S. naval history. Visitors without Defense Dept. or military identification must call in advance. Photo identification required.

▶**CONGRESS**

For a listing of relevant congressional committees and subcommittees, please see page 114 or the Appendix.

Library of Congress, *Interpretive Programs, 101 Independence Ave. S.E., #LA G25 20540; (202) 707-5223. Fax, (202) 707-9063. Irene Ursula Chambers, Interpretive Programs Officer. Information, (202) 707-4604.*
Web, www.loc.gov/exhibits

Handles exhibits within the Library of Congress; establishes and coordinates traveling exhibits; handles loans of library material.

▶**NONGOVERNMENTAL**

American Assn. of Museums, *1575 Eye St. N.W., #400 20005-1105; (202) 289-1818. Fax, (202) 289-6578. Ford W. Bell, President. Press, (202) 289-9125. TTY, (202) 289-8439.*
General e-mail, aaminfo@aam-us.org
Web, www.aam-us.org

Membership: individuals, institutions, museums, and museum professionals. Accredits museums; conducts educational programs; promotes international professional exchanges.

Art Services International, *1319 Powhatan St., Alexandria, VA 22314; (703) 548-4554. Fax, (703) 548-3305. Lynn K. Rogerson, Director.*
General e-mail, asi@asiexhibitions.org
Web, www.asiexhibitions.org

Organizes and circulates fine arts exhibitions to museums worldwide.

Corcoran Gallery of Art, *500 17th St. N.W. 20006-4804; (202) 639-1700. Fax, (202) 639-1768. Paul Greenhalgh, President. Press, (202) 639-1703.*

General e-mail, museum@corcoran.org

Web, www.corcoran.org

Exhibits paintings, sculpture, and drawings, primarily American. Collections include European art and works of local Washington artists. The affiliated Corcoran College of Art and Design offers BFA, MFA, and MA degrees and a continuing education program. Library open to the public by appointment.

Dumbarton Oaks, *1703 32nd St. N.W. 20007-2961; (202) 339-6410. Fax, (202) 339-6419. Jan M. Ziolkowski, Director. Information, (202) 339-6400. Recorded information, (202) 339-6401.*

General e-mail, DumbartonOaks2009@doaks.org

Web, www.doaks.org

Exhibits Byzantine and pre-Columbian art and artifacts; conducts advanced research and maintains publication programs and library collections in Byzantine and pre-Columbian studies and garden and landscape studies. Gardens open to the public Tuesday through Sunday 2:00–6:00 p.m. in summer, and 2:00–5:00 p.m. in winter (except during inclement weather and on federal holidays; fee charged March 15 through October 31); library open to qualified scholars by advance application. Administered by the trustees for Harvard University.

Hillwood Estate, Museum, and Gardens, *4155 Linnean Ave. N.W. 20008-3806; (202) 686-8500. Fax, (202) 966-7846. Frederick J. Fisher, Director. Reservations, (202) 686-8500.*

General e-mail, info@hillwoodmuseum.org

Web, www.hillwoodmuseum.org

Former residence of Marjorie Merriweather Post. Maintains and exhibits collection of Russian imperial art, including Fabergé eggs, and eighteenth-century French decorative arts; twelve acres of formal gardens. Gardens and museum open to the public by reservation; reservations required for large groups.

International Spy Museum, *800 F St. N.W. 20004; (202) 393-7798. Fax, (202) 393-7797. Peter Earnest, Executive Director; Amanda Abrell, Media Relations Manager, (202) 654-2843. TTY, (202) 654-2840. Toll-free, (866) 779-6873.*

General e-mail, other@spymuseum.org

Web, www.spymuseum.org

Educates the public about espionage, particularly human intelligence, by examining its role in and effect on current and historical events. (Affiliated with the Malrite Company.)

Marian Koshland Science Museum *(National Academy of Sciences), 500 5th St. N.W., entrance at corner of 6th and E St. N.W. 20001; (202) 334-1201. Fax, (202) 334-1548. Patrice Legro, Director. TTY, (202) 334-1306. Toll-free, (888) 567-4526.*

General e-mail, ksm@nas.edu

Web, www.koshland-science-museum.org

Strives to make studies conducted by the National Academy of Sciences more accessible to the public and to increase public understanding of the nature and value of science.

National Building Museum, *401 F St. N.W. 20001-2637; (202) 272-2448. Fax, (202) 272-2564. Chase Rynd, President. Press, (202) 272-2448, ext. 3402.*

Web, www.nbm.org

Celebrates achievements in building, architecture, urban planning, engineering, and historic preservation through educational programs, exhibitions, tours, lectures, workshops, and publications.

National Children's Museum, *955 L'Enfant Plaza North S.W., #5100 20024; (202) 675-4120. Fax, (202) 675-4140. Kathy Dwyer Southern, President. Press, (202) 675-4160.*

General e-mail, info@ncm.museum

Web, www.ncm.museum

Museum under development; scheduled to open in 2013 at National Harbor, Prince George's County, Md. (Formerly the Capital Children's Museum.)

National Geographic Museum at Explorers Hall, *17th St. and M St. N.W. 20036. Susan Norton, Director. Information, (202) 857-7588.*

Web, www.nationalgeographic.com/museum

Maintains self-guided exhibits about past and current expeditions, scientific research, and other themes in history and culture. Admission is free.

National Guard Memorial Museum, *1 Massachusetts Ave. N.W. 20001; (202) 789-0031. Fax, (202) 682-9358. Jonathan Bernstein, Director. Toll-free, (888) 226-4287.*

General e-mail, ngef@ngaus.org

Web, www.ngef.org

Features six core exhibit areas that explore the National Guard from colonial times through the world wars and the cold war to the modern era through timelines, photographs, artifacts, light, and sound.

National Museum of Women in the Arts, *1250 New York Ave. N.W. 20005-3970; (202) 783-5000. Fax, (202) 393-3234. Susan Fisher Sterling, Deputy Director. Information, (800) 222-7270. Library, (202) 783-7365.*

Web, www.nmwa.org

Acquires, researches, and presents the works of women artists from the Renaissance to the present. Promotes greater representation and awareness of women in the arts. Library open for research to the public by appointment.

Newseum, *555 Pennsylvania Ave. N.W. 20001; (202) 292-6100. Joe Urschel, Executive Director; Ken Paulson, President. Press, (202) 292-6320. Toll-free, (888) 639-7386.*

General e-mail, info@newseum.org

Web, www.newseum.org

World's only interactive museum of news. Collects items related to the history of news coverage; offers multimedia presentations and exhibits on the past, present, and future of news coverage; emphasizes the importance of the First Amendment to news coverage. (Affiliated with Freedom Forum.)

Octagon Museum, *1799 New York Ave. N.W. 20006-5291; (202) 638-3221. Fax, (202) 626-7420. Press, (202) 626-7571. Recorded Information, (202) 638-3105*
General e-mail, info@theoctagon.org

Web, www.archfoundation.org/octagon

Federal period historic residence open to the public for tours; served as the executive mansion during the War of 1812. Sponsors lectures, scholarly research, publications, and educational programs. (Owned by the American Architectural Foundation.) Group tours of 10–25 people available by appointment.

Phillips Collection, *1600 21st St. N.W. 20009; (202) 387-2151. Fax, (202) 387-2436. Dorothy Kosinski, Director. Press, (202) 387-2151, ext. 220. Membership, (202) 387-2151, ext. 268. Shop, (202) 387-2151, ext. 239.*
Web, www.phillipscollection.org

Maintains permanent collection of European and American paintings, primarily of the nineteenth through twenty-first centuries, and holds special exhibitions from the same periods. Sponsors lectures, gallery talks, and special events, including Sunday concerts (October–May). Library open to researchers and members by appointment.

Textile Museum, *2320 S St. N.W. 20008-4088; (202) 667-0441. Fax, (202) 483-0994. Daniel Walker, Director. Press, (202) 667-0441, ext. 78.*
General e-mail, info@textilemuseum.org

Web, www.textilemuseum.org

Exhibits historic and handmade textiles and carpets. Sponsors symposia, conferences, workshops, lectures, and an annual Textile Museum Fall Symposium. Library open to the public during restricted hours.

Trust for Museum Exhibitions, *1250 Connecticut Ave. N.W., #200 20036; (202) 261-6567. Fax, (202) 261-6570. Anne Townsend, Chair. Alternate phone, (202) 745-2566.*
General e-mail, thetrust@tme.org

Web, www.tme.org

Provides lending and exhibiting institutions with traveling exhibition services, which include negotiating loans, engaging guest curators, scheduling tours, fundraising, and managing registration details and catalog production.

U.S. Holocaust Memorial Museum, *100 Raoul Wallenberg Pl. S.W. 20024-2126; (202) 488-0400. Fax, (202) 488-2690. Sara Bloomfield, Director. Library, (202) 479-9717. Press, (202) 488-6133. TTY, (202) 488-0406.*
General e-mail, visitorsmail@ushmm.org

Web, www.ushmm.org

Extensive collection of photos, artifacts, and personal narratives about the Holocaust. Works to preserve documentation about the Holocaust; encourages research; provides educational resources, including conferences, publications, and public programming. Responsible for the annual Days of Remembrance of the Victims of the Holocaust. Works to prevent contemporary genocide through exhibits, public programs, and educational initiatives. Library and archives are open to the public.

Woodrow Wilson House *(National Trust for Historic Preservation), 2340 S St. N.W. 20008-4016; (202) 387-4062. Fax, (202) 483-1466. Frank Aucella, Director. Press, (202) 387-4062, ext. 18.*
Web, www.woodrowwilsonhouse.org

Georgian Revival home that exhibits furnishings and memorabilia from President Woodrow Wilson's political and postpresidential years.

Music

►AGENCIES

National Endowment for the Arts (NEA), *Arts Education, Music, Opera, and Presenting, 1100 Pennsylvania Ave. N.W. 20506-0001; (202) 682-5400. Fax, (202) 682-5611. Jan Stunkard, Division Coordinator.*
General e-mail, lowd@arts.endow.gov

Web, www.arts.gov

Awards grants to professional music training and career development institutions and to music performing, presenting, recording, and service organizations; awards fellowship grants to professional jazz musicians. Awards grants to professional opera and musical theater companies for regional touring and to organizations that provide services for opera and musical theater professionals.

National Museum of American History *(Smithsonian Institution), Music, Sports, and Entertainment, 12th St. and Constitution Ave. N.W. 20560-0616 (mailing address: P.O. Box 37012, MRC 616, Washington, DC 20013-7012); (202) 633-1707. Fax, (202) 786-2883. Gary Sturm, Chair. Press, (202) 633-3129.*
General e-mail, info@info.si.edu

Web, www.americanhistory.si.edu

Preserves American culture and heritage through collections, research, exhibitions, publications, teaching and lectures, broadcasts, and other presentations. Sponsors Jazz Appreciation Month and a chamber music program. Research areas are open by appointment.

National Symphony Orchestra *(John F. Kennedy Center for the Performing Arts), 2700 F St. N.W. 20566-0004; (202) 416-8100. Fax, (202) 416-8105. Iván Fisher, Principal Conductor. Information and reservations, (202) 467-4600; toll-free, (800) 444-1324; TTY, (202) 416-8524. Administrative Assistant, (202) 416-8100.*
Web, www.nationalsymphony.org

Year-round orchestra that presents a full range of symphonic activities: classical, pops, and educational events; national and international tours; recordings; and special events.

National Symphony Orchestra Education Program
(John F. Kennedy Center for the Performing Arts), 2700
F St. N.W. 20566-0004 (mailing address: P.O. Box 101510,
Arlington, VA 22210); (202) 416-8820. Fax, (202) 416-
8853. Carole J. Wysocki, Director. TTY, (202) 416-8728.
Web, www.kennedy-center.org/nso/nsoed

Presents wide range of activities: concerts for students
and families; fellowship program for talented high school
musicians and a young associates program for high school
students interested in arts management and professional
music careers; annual soloist competition open to high
school and college pianists, and orchestral instrumental-
ists; and Youth Orchestra Day for area youth orchestra
members selected by their conductors.

▶CONGRESS

For a listing of relevant congressional committees and
subcommittees, please see page 114 or the Appendix.

Library of Congress, *Motion Picture, Broadcasting, and*
Recorded Sound Division, 101 Independence Ave. S.E.,
#LM 338 20540; (202) 707-5840. Fax, (202) 707-2371.
Gregory Lukow, Chief. Recorded sound reference center,
(202) 707-7833. Motion picture and television reading
room, (202) 707-8572.
Web, www.loc.gov/rr/mopic

Maintains library's collection of musical and vocal
recordings; tapes the library's concert series and other
musical events for radio broadcast; produces recordings
of music and poetry for sale to the public. Collection also
includes sound recordings (1890–present). Reading room
open to the public; listening and viewing by appointment.

Library of Congress, *Music Division,* 101 Independence
Ave. S.E., #LM 113 20540; (202) 707-5503. Fax, (202)
707-0621. Susan H. Vita, Chief. Concert information,
(202) 707-5502. Reading room, (202) 707-5507.
Web, www.loc.gov/rr/perform

Maintains and services, through the Performing Arts
Reading Room, the library's collection of music manuscripts, sheet music, books, and instruments. Coordinates
the library's chamber music concert series; produces radio
broadcasts and, for sale to the public, recordings of concerts sponsored by the division; issues publications relating to the field of music and to division collections.

▶NONGOVERNMENTAL

American Music Therapy Assn., *8455 Colesville Rd., #1000,*
Silver Spring, MD 20910; (301) 589-3300. Fax, (301)
589-5175. Andrea Farbman, Executive Director.
General e-mail, info@musictherapy.org
Web, www.musictherapy.org

Promotes the therapeutic use of music by approving
degree programs and clinical training sites for therapists,
setting standards for certification of music therapists, and
conducting research in the music therapy field.

Future of Music Coalition, *1615 L St. N.W., #520 20036;*
(202) 822-2051. Fax, (202) 429-8857. Ann Chaitovitz,
Executive Director.
Web, www.futureofmusic.org

Seeks to educate the media, policymakers, and the
public on music technology issues. Identifies and promotes innovative business models that will help musicians and citizens benefit from new technologies.

League of American Orchestras, *Washington Office,* 910
17th St. N.W., #800 20006; (202) 776-0215. Fax, (202) 776-
0224. Heather Noonan, Vice President for Advocacy.
General e-mail, league@americanorchestras.org
Web, www.americanorchestras.org

Service and educational organization dedicated to
strengthening orchestras. Provides information and analysis on subjects of interest to orchestras through reports,
seminars, and other educational forums. Monitors legislation and regulations. (Headquarters in New York.)

Music Educators National Conference, *1806 Robert*
Fulton Dr., Reston, VA 20191-4348; (703) 860-4000. Fax,
(703) 860-1531. John J. Mahlmann, Executive Director.
Information, (800) 336-3768.
General e-mail, info@menc.org
Web, www.menc.org

Membership: music educators (preschool through
university). Holds biennial conference. Publishes books
and teaching aids for music educators.

National Assn. of Schools of Music, *11250 Roger Bacon*
Dr., #21, Reston, VA 20190-5248; (703) 437-0700. Fax,
(703) 437-6312. Samuel Hope, Executive Director.
General e-mail, info@arts-accredit.org
Web, http://nasm.arts-accredit.org

Accrediting agency for educational programs in music.
Provides information on music education programs;
offers professional development for executives of music
programs.

Recording Industry Assn. of America, *1025 F St. N.W.,*
10th Floor 20004; (202) 775-0101. Fax, (202) 775-7253.
Mitch Bainwol, Chief Executive Officer.
Web, www.riaa.com

Membership: creators, manufacturers, and marketers of
sound recordings. Educates members about new technology in the music industry. Advocates copyright protection
and opposes censorship. Works to prevent recording piracy,
counterfeiting, bootlegging, and unauthorized record rental
and imports. Certifies gold, platinum, and multiplatinum
recordings. Publishes statistics on the recording industry.

Washington Area Music Assn., *6263 Occoquan Forest*
Dr., Manassas, VA 20112-3011; (202) 338-1134. Fax,
(703) 393-1028. Mike Schreibman, Executive Director.
Information, (703) 368-3300.
General e-mail, dcmusic@wamadc.com
Web, www.wamadc.com

Membership: musicians, concert promoters, lawyers, recording engineers, managers, contractors, and other music industry professionals. Sponsors workshops on industry-related topics. Represents professionals from all musical genres. Serves as a liaison between the Washington-area music community and music communities nationwide.

Theater and Dance

▶AGENCIES

Ford's Theatre National Historic Site, *511 10th St. N.W. 20004; (202) 426-6924. Fax, (202) 426-1845. Rae Emerson, Site Manager. Recorded ticket information, (202) 638-2941.*
General e-mail, NACC_FOTH_Interpretation@nps.gov
Web, www.nps.gov/foth

Administered by the National Park Service, which manages Ford's Theatre, Ford's Theatre Museum, and the Peterson House (house where Lincoln died). Presents interpretive talks, exhibits, and tours. Research library open by appointment. Functions as working stage for theatrical productions.

National Endowment for the Arts (NEA), *Dance, Design, Media Arts, Museums, and Visual Arts, 1100 Pennsylvania Ave. N.W., #729 20506; (202) 682-5452. Fax, (202) 682-5721. Jeff Watson, Visual Arts Division Coordinator; Douglas Sonntag, Director, Dance; Maurice Cox, Director, Design; Ted Libbey, Director, Media Arts; Robert Frankel, Director, Museums and Visual Arts. TTY, (202) 682-5496.*
Web, www.arts.gov

Awards grants to dance services organizations and companies.

National Endowment for the Arts (NEA), *Folk and Traditional Arts, Theater, and Musical Theater, 1100 Pennsylvania Ave. N.W. 20506-0001, (202) 682-5428. Fax, (202) 682-5669. Cathy Vass, Division Coordinator, (202) 682-5523.*
Web, www.arts.gov

Awards grants to professional theater companies and theater service organizations.

Smithsonian Institution, *Discovery Theater, 1100 Jefferson Dr. S.W. 20024 (mailing address: Discovery Theater, P.O. Box 23293, Washington, DC 20026-3293); (202) 633-8700. Fax, (202) 343-1073. Roberta Gasbarre, Director. Reservations, (202) 633-8700.*
General e-mail, info@discoverytheater.org
Web, www.discoverytheater.org

Presents live theatrical performances, including storytelling, dance, music, puppetry, and plays, for young people and their families.

▶NONGOVERNMENTAL

Dance/USA, *1111 16th St. N.W., #300 20036; (202) 833-1717. Fax, (202) 833-2686. Andrea Snyder, Executive Director.*
General e-mail, danceusa@danceusa.org
Web, www.danceusa.org

Membership: professional dance companies, artists, artist managers, presenters, service organizations, educators, libraries, businesses, and individuals. Advances the art form by addressing the needs, concerns, and interests of the professional dance community through public communications, research and information services, professional development, advocacy, re-granting initiatives, and other projects.

National Assn. of Schools of Dance, *11250 Roger Bacon Dr., #21, Reston, VA 20190-5248; (703) 437-0700. Fax, (703) 437-6312. Samuel Hope, Executive Director.*
General e-mail, info@arts-accredit.org
Web, http://nasd.arts-accredit.org

Accrediting agency for educational programs in dance. Provides information on dance education programs; offers professional development for executives of dance programs.

National Assn. of Schools of Theatre, *11250 Roger Bacon Dr., #21, Reston, VA 20190-5248; (703) 437-0700. Fax, (703) 437-6312. Samuel Hope, Executive Director.*
General e-mail, info@arts-accredit.org
Web, http://nast.arts-accredit.org

Accrediting agency for educational programs in theater. Provides information on theater education programs; offers professional development for executives of theater programs.

National Conservatory of Dramatic Arts, *1556 Wisconsin Ave. N.W. 20007; (202) 333-2202. Fax, (202) 333-1753. Ray Ficca, President.*
General e-mail, ncdadrama@aol.com
Web, www.theconservatory.org

Offers an accredited two-year program in postsecondary professional actor training and a one-year program in advanced professional training. Emphasizes both physical and mental preparedness for acting in the professional entertainment industry.

Shakespeare Theatre Company, *Lansburgh Theatre, 450 7th St. N.W., and Sidney Harmon Hall, 610 F St., N.W. 20004 (mailing address: 516 8th St. S.E., Washington, DC 20003-2834); (202) 547-3230. Fax, (202) 547-0226. Chris Jennings, Managing Director. TTY, (202) 638-3863. Box office, (202) 547-1122.*
Web, www.shakespearetheatre.org

Professional resident theater that presents Shakespearean and other classical plays. Offers actor training program for youths, adults, and professional actors. Produces free outdoor summer Shakespeare plays and free Shakespeare plays for schools.

Visual Arts

►AGENCIES

National Endowment for the Arts (NEA), *Dance, Design, Media Arts, Museums, and Visual Arts,* 1100 Pennsylvania Ave. N.W., #729 20506; (202) 682-5452. Fax, (202) 682-5721. Jeff Watson, Visual Arts Division Coordinator; Douglas Sonntag, Director, Dance; Maurice Cox, Director, Design; Ted Libbey, Director, Media Arts; Robert Frankel, Director, Museums and Visual Arts. TTY, (202) 682-5496.
Web, www.arts.gov

Awards grants to nonprofit organizations for creative works and programs in the visual arts, including painting, sculpture, crafts, video, photography, printmaking, drawing, artists' books, and performance art.

National Endowment for the Arts (NEA), *Folk and Traditional Arts, Theater, and Musical Theater,* 1100 Pennsylvania Ave. N.W. 20506-0001; (202) 682-5428. Fax, (202) 682-5669. Cathy Vass, Division Coordinator, (202) 682-5523.
Web, www.arts.gov

Awards grants for design arts projects in architecture; landscape architecture; urban design and planning; historic preservation; and interior, graphic, industrial, product, and costume and fashion design.

State Dept., *Art in Embassies,* M-OBO-OM-ART, Dept. of State 20552; (703) 875-4202. Fax, (703) 875-4182. Virginia Shore, Director (Acting).
Web, http://aiep.state.gov

Exhibits American art in U.S. ambassadorial residences. Borrows artworks from artists, collectors, galleries, and museums.

►CONGRESS

For a listing of relevant congressional committees and subcommittees, please see page 114 or the Appendix.

Library of Congress, *Prints and Photographs Division,* 101 Independence Ave. S.E., #LM 339 20540; (202) 707-5836. Fax, (202) 707-6647. Helena Zinkham, Chief (Acting). TTY, (202) 707-9051. Reading room, (202) 707-6394.
Web, www.loc.gov/rr/print

Maintains Library of Congress's collection of pictorial material not in book format, totaling more than 13.5 million items. U.S. and international collections include artists' prints; historical prints, posters, and drawings; photographs (chiefly documentary); political and social cartoons; and architectural plans, drawings, prints, and photographs. Reference service provided in the Prints and Photographs Reading Room. Reproductions of nonrestricted material available through the Library of Congress's Photoduplication Service; prints and photographs may be borrowed through the Exhibits Office for exhibits by qualified institutions. A portion of the collections and an overview of reference services are available on the World Wide Web.

►NONGOVERNMENTAL

American Institute of Architects, 1735 New York Ave. N.W. 20006-5292; (202) 626-7300. Fax, (202) 626-7498. Christine McEntee, Chief Executive Officer. Library, (202) 626-7496. Press, (202) 626-7467. Toll-free, (800) 242-3837. Government Advocacy, (202) 626-7507.
General e-mail, infocentral@aia.org

Web, www.aia.org

Membership: licensed American architects, interns, architecture faculty, engineers, planners, and those in government, manufacturing, or other fields in a capacity related to architecture. Works to advance the standards of architectural education, training, and practice. Promotes the aesthetic, scientific, and practical efficiency of architecture, urban design, and planning; monitors international developments. Offers continuing and professional education programs; sponsors scholarships, internships, and awards. Houses archival collection, including documents and drawings of American architects and architecture. Library open to the public by appointment. Monitors legislation and regulations.

Foundation for Art and Preservation in Embassies, 1725 Eye St. N.W., #300 20006-2423; (202) 349-3724. Fax, (202) 349-3727. Jennifer A. Duncan, Director.
General e-mail, fapeindc@aol.com

Web, www.fapeglobal.org

Foundation established to assist the State Dept.'s Office of Foreign Buildings and Art in Embassies programs. Acquires, preserves, and exhibits American art, decorative art, and furnishings in U.S. embassies and other diplomatic facilities.

National Assn. of Schools of Art and Design, 11250 Roger Bacon Dr., #21, Reston, VA 20190-5248; (703) 437-0700. Fax, (703) 437-6312. Samuel Hope, Executive Director.
General e-mail, info@arts-accredit.org

Web, http://nasad.arts-accredit.org

Accrediting agency for educational programs in art and design. Provides information on art and design programs at the postsecondary level; offers professional development for executives of art and design programs.

HISTORY AND PRESERVATION

►AGENCIES

Advisory Council on Historic Preservation, 1100 Pennsylvania Ave. N.W., #803 20004; (202) 606-8503. Fax, (202) 606-8647. John M. Fowler, Executive Director; John Nau, Chair.
General e-mail, achp@achp.gov

Web, www.achp.gov

Advises the president and Congress on historic preservation; reviews and comments on federal projects and programs affecting historic, architectural, archaeological, and cultural resources.

Bureau of Land Management (BLM), *(Interior Dept.),* *Culture, Paleontological Resources, and Tribal Consultation,* *1620 L St. N.W., #204 20036 (mailing address: 1849 C St. N.W., #204-LS, Washington, DC 20240); (202) 452-0330. Fax, (202) 452-7701. Richard Hanes, Division Chief. Press, (202) 452-5125.*
Web, www.blm.gov/heritage

Develops bureau policy on historic preservation, archaeological resource protection, consultation with Native Americans, curation of artifacts and records, heritage education, and paleontological resource management.

General Services Administration, *Urban Development/ Good Neighbor Program, 1800 F St. N.W., #3341 20405-0001; (202) 501-1856. Fax, (202) 501-3393. Frank Giblin, Director.*
Web, www.gsa.gov/goodneighbor

Advises on locations, designs, and renovations of federal facilities in central business areas, historic districts, and local redevelopment areas where they can anchor or promote community development. Collaborates with local and national civic and other organizations. Serves as clearinghouse for good practices.

International Cultural Property Protection *(State Dept.), Bureau of Education and Cultural Affairs, 301 4th St. S.W., #334 20547-0009; (202) 453-8800. Fax, (202) 453-8803. Maria Kouroupas, Executive Director.*
General e-mail, culprop@state.gov
Web, http://exchanges.state.gov/culprop

Reviews country requests for import restrictions on archaeological or ethnological artifacts and makes recommendations on them to the State Department.

National Archives and Records Administration (NARA), *Advisory Committee on Preservation, 8601 Adelphi Rd., #2800, College Park, MD 20740-6001; (301) 837-1785. Fax, (301) 837-3701. Doris A. Hamburg, Director of Preservation Programs.*

Advises the archivist of the United States on preservation technology and research and on matters related to the continued preservation of records of the National Archives of the United States.

National Archives and Records Administration (NARA), *Cartographic and Architectural Unit, 8601 Adelphi Rd., #3320, College Park, MD 20740-6001; (301) 837-3200. Fax, (301) 837-3622. Deborah Lelansky, Cartographic Supervisor.*
General e-mail, carto@nara.gov
Web, www.archives.gov

Preserves and makes available historical records of federal agencies, including maps, charts, aerial photographs, architectural engineering drawings, patents, lighthouse plans, and ships' plans. Research room open to the public. Records are available for reproduction.

National Archives and Records Administration (NARA), *Preservation Programs, 8601 Adelphi Rd., #2800, College*

Park, MD 20740-6001; (301) 837-1785. Fax, (301) 837-3701. Doris A. Hamburg, Director. Public Affairs, (301) 357-5300. Toll-free, (866) 272-6272.
General e-mail, preserve@nara.gov
Web, www.archives.gov/preservation

Manages the preservation program for the 39 National Archives facilities across the country. Develops preservation policy, regulations, and planning. Responsible for conserving textual and nontextual (videos, sound recordings, motion pictures, and still photos) records and for reformatting and duplicating nontextual and textual records. Ensures that the storage environments are designed and maintained to prolong the life of records. Conducts research and testing for materials purchased by and used in the archives. Monitors and maintains the condition of the Charters of Freedom.

National Capital Planning Commission, *401 9th St. N.W., North Lobby, #500 20004; (202) 482-7200. Fax, (202) 482-7272. Marcel Acosta, Executive Director.*
General e-mail, info@ncpc.gov
Web, www.ncpc.gov

Central planning agency for the federal government in the national capital region, which includes the District of Columbia and suburban Maryland and Virginia. Reviews and approves plans for the preservation of certain historic and environmental features in the national capital region, including the annual federal capital improvement plan.

National Endowment for the Arts (NEA), *Folk and Traditional Arts, Theater, and Musical Theater, 1100 Pennsylvania Ave. N.W. 20506-0001; (202) 682-5428. Fax, (202) 682-5669. Cathy Vass, Division Coordinator, (202) 682-5523.*
Web, www.arts.gov

Awards grants to exceptional projects in the arts and arts education to arts organizations, art service organizations, federally recognized tribal communities, state and local government offices, and others.

National Endowment for the Humanities (NEH), *Preservation and Access, 1100 Pennsylvania Ave. N.W., #411 20005; (202) 606-8570. Fax, (202) 606-8639. Nadina Gardner, Director; Ralph Canevali, Deputy Director.*
General e-mail, preservation@neh.gov
Web, www.neh.gov

Sponsors preservation and access projects, the stabilization and documentation of material culture collections, and the U.S. newspaper program.

National Museum of American History *(Smithsonian Institution), Music, Sports, and Entertainment, 12th St. and Constitution Ave. N.W. 20560-0616 (mailing address: P.O. Box 37012, MRC 616, Washington, DC 20013-7012); (202) 633-1707. Fax, (202) 786-2883. Gary Sturm, Chair. Press, (202) 633-3129.*
General e-mail, info@info.si.edu
Web, www.americanhistory.si.edu

Collects and preserves artifacts related to U.S. cultural heritage; supports research, exhibits, performances, and educational programs. Areas of focus include ethnic and religious communities; sports, recreation, and leisure; popular entertainment and mass media; business and commercial culture; musical instruments; hand tools; and educational, civic, and voluntary organizations.

National Park Service (NPS), *(Interior Dept.),*
Cultural Resources, 1849 C St. N.W., #3128 20240-0001; (202) 208-7625. Fax, (202) 273-3237. Janet Matthews, Associate Director.
Web, www.cr.nps.gov

Oversees preservation of federal historic sites and administration of buildings programs. Programs include the National Register of Historic Places, National Historic and National Landmark Programs, Historic American Building Survey, Historic American Engineering Record, Archeology and Antiquities Act Program, and Technical Preservation Services. Gives grant and aid assistance and tax benefit information to properties listed in the National Register of Historic Places.

▶**CONGRESS**

For a listing of relevant congressional committees and subcommittees, please see page 114 or the Appendix.

Senate Office of Conservation and Preservation, *S416 CAP 20510; (202) 224-4550. Carl Fritter, Director.*

Develops and coordinates programs related to the conservation and preservation of Senate records and materials for the secretary of the Senate.

▶**NONGOVERNMENTAL**

American Historical Assn., *400 A St. S.E. 20003-3807; (202) 544-2422. Fax, (202) 544-8307. Arnita Jones, Executive Director.*
General e-mail, aha@historians.org
Web, www.historians.org

Supports public access to government information; publishes original historical research, journals, bibliographies, historical directories, and a job placement bulletin.

American Institute for Conservation of Historic and Artistic Works, *1156 15th St. N.W., #320 20005; (202) 452-9545. Fax, (202) 452-9328. Eryl P. Wentworth, Executive Director.*
General e-mail, info@aic-faic.org
Web, www.aic-faic.org

Membership: professional conservators, scientists, students, administrators, cultural institutions, and others. Promotes the knowledge and practice of the conservation of cultural property; supports research; and disseminates information on conservation.

American Studies Assn., *1120 19th St. N.W., #301 20036-3614; (202) 467-4783. Fax, (202) 467-4786. John F. Stephens, Executive Director.*

General e-mail, asastaff@theasa.net
Web, www.theasa.net

Fosters exchange of ideas about American life; supports and assists programs for teaching American studies abroad and encourages teacher and student exchanges; awards annual prizes for contributions to American studies; provides curriculum resources.

Civil War Preservation Trust, *1331 H St. N.W., #1001 20005; (202) 367-1861. Fax, (202) 367-1865. O. James Lighthizer, President.*
General e-mail, info@civilwar.org
Web, www.civilwar.org

Membership: preservation professionals, historians, conservation activists, and citizens. Preserves endangered Civil War battlefields throughout the United States. Conducts preservation conferences and workshops. Advises local preservation groups. Monitors legislation and regulations at the federal, state, and local levels.

Council on America's Military Past—U.S.A., *11125 Stonebrook Pl., Manassas, VA 20112; (703) 912-6124. Mark Magnussen, Editor. Information, (800) 398-4693.*
General e-mail, mark_magnussen@hotmail.com
Web, www.campjamp.org

Membership: historians, archaeologists, curators, writers, and others interested in military history and preservation of historic military sites, establishments, ships, and aircraft.

David S. Wyman Institute for Holocaust Studies, *1200 G St. N.W., #800 20005; (202) 434-8994. Rafael Medoff, Director.*
General e-mail, rafaelmedoff@aol.com
Web, www.wymaninstitute.org

Educates the public about U.S. response to Nazism and the Holocaust through scholarly research, public events and exhibits, publications, conferences, and educational programs.

Heritage Preservation, *1012 14th St. N.W., #1200 20005-3408; (202) 233-0800. Fax, (202) 233-0807. Larry Reger, President. Information, (888) 388-6789.*
General e-mail, info@heritagepreservation.org
Web, www.heritagepreservation.org

Membership: museums, libraries, archives, historic preservation organizations, historical societies, and conservation groups. Advocates the conservation and preservation of works of art, anthropological artifacts, documents, historic objects, architecture, and natural science specimens. Programs include Save Outdoor Sculpture, which works to inventory all U.S. outdoor sculpture; the Conservation Assessment Program, which administers grants to museums for conservation surveys of their collections; the Heritage Health Index, which documents the condition of U.S. collections; the Heritage Emergency Task Force, which helps institutions protect their collections from disasters and emergencies; and Rescue Public

Murals, which aids in the conservation of public murals throughout the United States.

National Conference of State Historic Preservation Officers, *444 N. Capitol St. N.W., #342 20001-1512; (202) 624-5465. Fax, (202) 624-5419. Nancy Schamu, Executive Director.*

Web, www.ncshpo.org

Membership: state and territorial historic preservation officers and deputy officers. Compiles statistics on programs; monitors legislation and regulations.

National Park Trust, *401 E. Jefferson St., #102, Rockville, MD 20850; (301) 279-7275. Fax, (301) 279-7211. Grace K. Lee, Executive Director.*

General e-mail, npt@parktrust.org

Web, www.parktrust.org

Protects national parks, wildlife refuges, and historic monuments. Uses funds to purchase private land within or adjacent to existing parks and land suitable for new parks; works with preservation organizations to manage acquired resources.

National Preservation Institute, *P.O. Box 1702, Alexandria, VA 22313-1702; (703) 765-0100. Fax, (703) 768-9350. Jere Gibber, Executive Director.*

General e-mail, info@npi.org

Web, www.npi.org

Conducts seminars in historic preservation and cultural resource management for those involved in the management, preservation, and stewardship of historic and cultural resources.

National Society, Colonial Dames XVII Century, *1300 New Hampshire Ave. N.W. 20036-1595; (202) 293-1700. Fax, (202) 466-6099. Sandra Quimby, Office Manager.*

Web, www.colonialdames17c.net

Membership: American women who are lineal descendants of persons who rendered civil or military service and lived in America or one of the British colonies before 1701. Preserves records and shrines; encourages historical research; awards scholarships to undergraduate and graduate students and scholarships in medicine to persons of Native American descent.

National Society, Daughters of the American Revolution, *1776 D St. N.W. 20006-5303; (202) 628-1776. Fax, (202) 879-3252. Linda G. Calvin, President. Press, (202) 879-3238.*

Web, www.dar.org

Membership: women descended from American Revolutionary War patriots. Conducts historical, educational, and patriotic activities; maintains a genealogical library, fine arts museum, and documentary collection antedating 1830. Library open to the public (nonmembers charged fee for use).

National Society of the Children of the American Revolution, *1776 D St. N.W., #224 20006-5303; (202) 638-3153. Fax, (202) 737-3162. Suzanne Reynolds, Senior National President; Rajanee Sirivanakarn, Office Manager.*

General e-mail, hq@nscar.org

Web, www.nscar.org

Membership: descendants, age twenty-two years and under, of American soldiers or patriots of the American Revolution. Conducts historical, educational, and patriotic activities; preserves places of historical interest.

National Society of the Colonial Dames of America, *2715 Que St. N.W. 20007-3071; (202) 337-2288. Fax, (202) 337-0348. Karen L. Daly, Executive Director.*

General e-mail, info@nscda.org

Web, www.nscda.org

Membership: descendants of colonists in America before 1750. Conducts historical and educational activities; maintains Dumbarton House, a museum open to the public Tuesday–Saturday; and offers lectures and concerts.

National Trust for Historic Preservation, *1785 Massachusetts Ave. N.W. 20036-2117; (202) 588-6000. Fax, (202) 588-6038. Richard Moe, President. Information, (800) 944-6847. Press, (202) 588-6141.*

General e-mail, feedback@nthp.org

Web, www.preservationnation.org

Conducts seminars, workshops, and conferences on topics related to preservation, including neighborhood conservation, main street revitalization, rural conservation, and preservation law; offers financial assistance through loan and grant programs; provides advisory services; and operates historic house sites, which are open to the public.

Preservation Action, *401 F St. N.W., #324 20001; (202) 637-7873. Fax, (202) 637-7874. Heather MacIntosh, President.*

General e-mail, mail@preservationaction.org

Web, www.preservationaction.org

Monitors legislation affecting historic preservation and neighborhood conservation. Maintains a nationwide database of activists. Promotes adequate funding for historic preservation programs and policies that support historic resource protection.

Society for American Archaeology, *900 2nd St. N.E., #12 20002-3560; (202) 789-8200. Fax, (202) 789-0284. Tobi Brimsek, Executive Director.*

General e-mail, info@saa.org

Web, www.saa.org

Promotes greater awareness, understanding, and research of archaeology on the American continents; works to preserve and publish results of scientific data and research; serves as information clearinghouse for members.

Archives and Manuscripts

▶**AGENCIES**

National Archives and Records Administration (NARA), *8601 Adelphi Rd., #4200, College Park, MD 20740-6001;*

(866) 272-6272. Fax, (301) 837-0483. Adrienne C. Thomas, Archivist of the United States (Acting). Press, (202) 357-5300. Fax directory, www.archives. gov/about/organization/fax-lst.html.

Web, www.archives.gov

Identifies, preserves, and makes available federal government documents of historic value; administers a network of regional storage centers and archives and operates the presidential library system. Collections include photographs, graphic materials, films, and maps; holdings include records generated by foreign governments (especially in wartime) and by international conferences, commissions, and exhibitions.

National Archives and Records Administration (NARA), Center for Legislative Archives, *700 Pennsylvania Ave. N.W., #8E 20408; (202) 357-5350. Fax, (202) 357-5911. Richard H. Hunt, Director, (202) 357-5376.*

Web, www.archives.gov/legislative/index.html

Collects and maintains records of congressional committees and legislative files from 1789 to the present. Publishes inventories and guides to these records.

National Archives and Records Administration (NARA), Presidential Libraries, *8601 Adelphi Rd., #2200, College Park, MD 20740-6001; (301) 837-3250. Fax, (301) 837-3199. Sharon Fawcett, Assistant Archivist, (301) 837-1693.*

Web, www.archives.gov/presidential_libraries

Administers thirteen presidential libraries. Directs all programs relating to acquisition, preservation, publication, and research use of materials in presidential libraries; conducts oral history projects; publishes finding aids for research sources; provides reference service, including information from and about documentary holdings.

National Historical Publications and Records Commission *(National Archives and Records Administration), 700 Pennsylvania Ave. N.W., #106 20408-0001; (202) 357-5010. Fax, (202) 357-5914. Kathleen Williams, Executive Director (Acting).*

General e-mail, nhprc@nara.gov

Web, www.archives.gov/nhprc

Awards grants to state and local government archives and nonprofit cultural institutions that preserve, arrange, edit, and publish documents of historical importance, including the papers of outstanding Americans. Works in partnership with state archives to provide access to records for all Americans.

National Museum of American History *(Smithsonian Institution), Archives Center, 12th St. and Constitution Ave. N.W., #1100 20560-0601 (mailing address: P.O. Box 37012, NMAH MRC 601, Washington, DC 20013-7012); (202) 633-3270. Fax, (202) 786-2453. Deborah A. Richardson, Chair. Press, (202) 633-3129. TTY, (202) 633-3270.*

General e-mail, archivescenter@si.edu

Web, www.americanhistory.si.edu/archives

Acquires, organizes, preserves, and makes available for research the museum's archival and documentary materials relating to American history and culture. Three-dimensional objects and closely related documents are in the care of curatorial divisions. Research areas are open by appointment.

Smithsonian Institution, *Archives of American Art, 750 9th St. N.W., #2200 20001 (mailing address: P.O. Box 37012, Victor Bldg., MRC 937, Washington, DC 20013-7012); (202) 633-7940. Fax, (202) 633-7994. John W. Smith, Director. Reference desk, (202) 633-7950.*

Web, www.archivesofamericanart.si.edu

Collects and preserves manuscript items, such as notebooks, sketchbooks, letters, and journals; photos of artists and works of art; tape-recorded interviews with artists, dealers, and collectors; exhibition catalogs; directories; and biographies on the history of visual arts in the United States. Library open to scholars and researchers. Reference centers that maintain microfilm copies of a selection of the Archives' collection include New York; Boston; San Francisco; and San Marino, Calif.

►CONGRESS

For a listing of relevant congressional committees and subcommittees, please see page 114 or the Appendix.

Legislative Resource Center, *Office of History and Preservation, B53 CHOB 20515; (202) 226-1300. Fax, (202) 226-5204. Farar P. Elliott, Chief.*

Web, http://clerk.house.gov

Provides access to published documents and historical records of the House. Conducts historical research. Advises members on the disposition of their records and papers; maintains information on manuscript collections of former members; maintains biographical files on former members. Produces publications on Congress and its members.

Library of Congress, *Manuscript Division, 101 Independence Ave. S.E., #LM 102 20540; (202) 707-5383. Fax, (202) 707-6336. James H. Hutson, Chief. Reading room, (202) 707-5387.*

Web, www.loc.gov/rr/mss

Maintains, describes, and provides reference service on the library's manuscript collections, including the papers of U.S. presidents and other eminent Americans. Manuscript Reading Room primarily serves serious scholars and researchers; historians and reference librarians are available for consultation.

Library of Congress, *Rare Book and Special Collections Division, 101 Independence Ave. S.E., #LJ 239 20540; (202) 707-5434. Fax, (202) 707-4142. Mark G. Dimunation, Chief. Reading room, (202) 707-3448.*

Web, www.loc.gov/rr/rarebook

Maintains collections of incunabula (books printed before 1501) and other early printed books; early imprints of American history and literature; illustrated books; early

Spanish American, Russian, and Bulgarian imprints; Confederate states imprints; libraries of famous personalities (including Thomas Jefferson, Woodrow Wilson, and Oliver Wendell Holmes); special format collections (miniature books, broadsides, almanacs, and pre-1870 copyright records); special interest collections; and special provenance collections. Reference assistance is provided in the Rare Book and Special Collections Reading Room.

Senate Historical Office, *SH-201 20510; (202) 224-6900. Richard A. Baker, Historian.*

General e-mail, historian@sec.senate.gov

Web, www.senate.gov

Serves as an information clearinghouse on Senate history, traditions, and members. Collects, organizes, and distributes to the public unpublished Senate documents; collects and preserves photographs and pictures related to Senate history; conducts an oral history program; advises senators and Senate committees on the disposition of their noncurrent papers and records. Produces publications on the history of the Senate.

▶NONGOVERNMENTAL

Assassination Archives and Research Center, *1003 K St. N.W., #640 20001-4423; (202) 393-1921. Fax, (301) 657-3699. James Lesar, President.*

General e-mail, jlesar@mindspring.com

Web, www.aarclibrary.org

Acquires, preserves, and disseminates information on political assassinations. Materials and information available on Web site and by request through mail. On-site access available to the public by appointment only.

Moorland-Spingarn Research Center *(Howard University), 500 Howard Pl. N.W., #120 20059; (202) 806-7239. Fax, (202) 806-6405. Thomas C. Battle, Director.*

Web, www.howard.edu/library/moorland-spingarn

Collects, preserves, and makes available for study numerous artifacts, books, manuscripts, newspapers, photographs, prints, recordings, and other materials documenting black history and culture in the United States, Africa, Europe, Latin America, and the Caribbean. Maintains extensive collections of black newspapers and magazines; contains the works of African American and African scholars, poets, and novelists; maintains collections on the history of Howard University.

Genealogy

▶AGENCIES

National Archives and Records Administration (NARA), *Archives 1, Research Support Branch, 700 Pennsylvania Ave. N.W. 20408; (202) 357-5400. Fax, (202) 357-5934. Vacant, Branch Chief.*

General e-mail, inquire@nara.gov

Web, www.archives.gov

Assists individuals interested in researching record holdings of the National Archives, including genealogical records; issues research cards to researchers who present photo identification. Users must be at least fourteen years of age.

National Archives and Records Administration (NARA), *Center for the National Archives Experience, 700 Pennsylvania Ave. N.W., #G9 20408; (202) 357-5210. Fax, (202) 357-5926. Marvin Pinkert, Director. Information, (202) 357-5000. Press, (202) 357-5300.*

General e-mail, inquire@nara.gov

Web, www.archives.gov

Plans and directs activities to acquaint the public with the mission and holdings of the National Archives; conducts behind-the-scenes tours; presents hands-on workshops; develops both traditional and interactive exhibits; produces publications, including teaching packets that feature historic documents.

▶CONGRESS

For a listing of relevant congressional committees and subcommittees, please see page 114 or the Appendix.

Library of Congress, *Local History and Genealogy Reading Room, 101 Independence Ave. S.E., #LJ-G42 20540; (202) 707-5537. Fax, (202) 707-1957. Stephen E. James, Chief.*

Web, www.loc.gov/rr/genealogy

Provides reference and referral service on topics related to local history, genealogy, and heraldry throughout the United States.

▶NONGOVERNMENTAL

Family History Center, *Church of Jesus Christ of Latter-Day Saints, 10000 Stoneybrook Dr., Kensington, MD 20895 (mailing address: P.O. Box 49, Kensington, MD 20895); (301) 587-0042. Jeannette Clawson, Director.*

Maintains genealogical library for research. Collection includes international genealogical index, family group record archives, microfiche registers, and the Family Search Computer Program (www.familysearch.org). Library open to the public. (Sponsored by the Church of Jesus Christ of Latter-Day Saints.)

National Genealogical Society, *3108 Columbia Pike, #300, Arlington, VA 22204-4304; (703) 525-0050. Fax, (703) 525-0052. Janet A. Alpert, President. Toll-free, (800) 473-0060.*

General e-mail, ngs@ngsgenealogy.org

Web, www.ngsgenealogy.org

Encourages study of genealogy and publication of all records that are of genealogical interest. Provides online courses and an in-depth home study program; holds an annual conference.

National Society, Daughters of the American Colonists, *2205 Massachusetts Ave. N.W. 20008-2819; (202) 667-3076. Fax, (202) 667-0571. Georgia Holder, President.*

General e-mail, nsdac@excite.com

Web, www.nsdac.org

Membership: women descended from men and women who were resident in or gave civil or military service to the colonies prior to the Revolutionary War. Maintains library of colonial and genealogical records, open to the public by appointment.

National Society, Daughters of the American Revolution, *1776 D St. N.W. 20006-5303; (202) 628-1776. Fax, (202) 879-3252. Linda G. Calvin, President. Press, (202) 879-3238.*

Web, www.dar.org

Membership: women descended from American Revolutionary War patriots. Maintains a genealogical library, which is open to the public (nonmembers charged fee for use).

Specific Cultures

▶AGENCIES

Interior Dept. (DOI), *Indian Arts and Crafts Board, 1849 C St. N.W., #2528 20240-0001; (202) 208-3773. Fax, (202) 208-5196. Meridith Stanton, Director.*

General e-mail, iacb@ios.doi.gov

Web, www.iacb.doi.gov

Advises Native American artisans and craft guilds; produces a source directory on arts and crafts of Native Americans (including Alaska Natives); maintains museums of native crafts in Montana, South Dakota, and Oklahoma; provides information on the Indian Arts and Crafts Act.

National Endowment for the Arts (NEA), *Folk and Traditional Arts, Theater, and Musical Theater, 1100 Pennsylvania Ave. N.W. 20506-0001; (202) 682-5428. Fax, (202) 682-5669. Cathy Vass, Division Coordinator, (202) 682-5523.*

Web, www.arts.gov

Seeks to preserve and enhance multicultural artistic heritage through grants for folk arts projects.

National Museum of American History *(Smithsonian Institution), Curatorial Affairs, 12th St. and Constitution Ave. N.W. 20560 (mailing address: P.O. Box 37012, MRC 664, Washington, DC 20013-7012); (202) 633-3376. Fax, (202) 633-8192. James B. Gardner, Associate Director.*

General e-mail, info@si.edu

Web, www.americanhistory.si.edu

Conducts research, develops collections, and creates exhibits on American social and public history, based on collections of folk and popular arts, ethnic and craft objects, textiles, coins, costumes and jewelry, ceramics and glass, graphic arts, musical instruments, photographs, technological innovations, appliances, and machines. Research areas are open by appointment.

Smithsonian Institution, *Center for Folklife and Cultural Heritage, 600 Maryland Ave. S.W., #2001 20024 (mailing address: P.O. Box 37012, MRC 520, Washington, DC 20013-7012); (202) 633-6440. Fax, (202) 633-6474. Richard Kennedy, Director (Acting). Press, (202) 633-5183.*

General e-mail, folklife-info@si.edu

Web, www.folklife.si.edu

Promotes and conducts research into traditional U.S. cultures and foreign folklife traditions; produces folkways recordings, films, videos, and educational programs; presents annual Smithsonian Folklife Festival in Washington, D.C.

▶CONGRESS

For a listing of relevant congressional committees and subcommittees, please see page 114 or the Appendix.

Library of Congress, *American Folklife Center, 101 Independence Ave. S.E., #LJ G49 20540; (202) 707-5510. Fax, (202) 707-2076. Margaret "Peggy" Bulger, Director.*

General e-mail, folklife@loc.gov

Web, www.loc.gov/folklife

Coordinates national, regional, state and local government, and private folklife activities; contracts with individuals and groups for research and field studies in American folklife and for exhibits and workshops; maintains the National Archive of Folk Culture (an ethnographic collection of American and international folklore, grassroots oral histories, and ethnomusicology) and the Veterans History Project (a collection of oral histories and documentary materials from veterans of World Wars I and II and the Korean, Vietnam, and Persian Gulf wars). Conducts internships at the archive; sponsors year-round concerts of traditional and ethnic music.

▶NONGOVERNMENTAL

National Council for the Traditional Arts, *1320 Fenwick Lane, #200, Silver Spring, MD 20910; (301) 565-0654. Fax, (301) 565-0472. Julia Olin, Executive Director.*

General e-mail, info@ncta.net

Web, www.ncta.net

Seeks to celebrate and honor arts of cultural and ethnic significance, including music, crafts, stories, and dance. Promotes artistic authenticity in festivals, national and international tours, concerts, radio and television programs, CD recordings, and films. Works with national parks and other institutions to create, plan, and present cultural events, exhibits, and other programs. Sponsors the annual National Folk Festival.

National Hispanic Foundation for the Arts (NHFA), *Waterfront Center, 1010 Wisconsin Ave. N.W., #650 20007; (202) 293-8330. Fax, (202) 965-5252. Richard Rodriguez, Executive Director.*

General e-mail, info@hispanicarts.org

Web, www.hispanicarts.org

Strives to increase the presence of Hispanics in the media, telecommunications, entertainment industries, and performing arts.

National Italian American Foundation, *1860 19th St. N.W. 20009; (202) 387-0600. Fax, (202) 387-0800. James R. De Santis, National Executive Director.*

General e-mail, info@niaf.org

Web, www.niaf.org

Membership: U.S. citizens of Italian ancestry. Promotes recognition of Italian American contributions to American society. Funds cultural events, educational symposia, anti-defamation programs, and grants and scholarships. Represents the interests of Italian Americans before Congress. Serves as an umbrella organization for local Italian American clubs throughout the United States.

Washington Area

►AGENCIES

National Park Service (NPS), *(Interior Dept.),* **National Capital Region,** *1100 Ohio Dr. S.W., #107 20242; (202) 619-7000. Fax, (202) 619-7220. Margaret O'Dell, Regional Director. Recorded information, (202) 619-7275. Permits, (202) 619-7225.*

Web, www.nps.gov/ncro

Provides visitors with information on Washington-area parks, monuments, and Civil War battlefields; offers press services for the media and processes special event applications and permits.

White House Visitor Center (President's Park), *1450 Pennsylvania Ave. N.W. 20230; (202) 208-1631. Fax, (202) 208-1643. Scott Tucker, Manager. Information, (202) 456-7041. TTY, (202) 456-2121.*

General e-mail, whho_presidents_park@nps.gov

Web, www.nps.gov/whho

Administered by the National Park Service. Educates visitors about the White House through videos, exhibits, and historical artifacts. Public tours are available for groups of ten or more, Tuesday through Saturday; requests must be submitted through one's member of Congress and are accepted up to six months in advance.

►CONGRESS

For a listing of relevant congressional committees and sub-committees, please see page 114 or the Appendix.

Architect of the Capitol, *Office of the Curator, S411 CAP 20515; (202) 224-2955. Diane K. Skvarla, Curator.*

Web, www.aoc.gov

Preserves artwork; maintains collection of drawings, photographs, and manuscripts on and about the Capitol and the House and Senate office buildings. Maintains records of the Architect of the Capitol. Library open to the public.

Senate Commission on Art, *S230 CAP 20510; (202) 224-2955. Sen. Harry M. Reid, D–Nev., Chair; Diane K. Skvarla, Curator of the Senate.*

General e-mail, curator@sec.senate.gov

Web, www.senate.gov/artandhistory/art/common/generic/senate_art.htm

Accepts artwork and historical objects for display in Senate office buildings and the Senate wing of the Capitol. Maintains and exhibits Senate collections (paintings, sculptures, furniture, and manuscripts); oversees and maintains old Senate and Supreme Court chambers.

►NONGOVERNMENTAL

Assn. for Preservation of Historic Congressional Cemetery, *1801 E St. S.E. 20003-2499; (202) 543-0539. Fax, (202) 543-5966. Patrick Crowley, Chair.*

General e-mail, staff@congressionalcemetery.org

Web, www.congressionalcemetery.org

Administers and maintains the Washington Parish Burial Ground (commonly known as the Congressional Cemetery). Tours available Saturdays at 11:00 a.m. in warm weather. See Web site for tour information.

Historical Society of Washington, D.C., *801 K St. N.W. 20001-3746; (202) 383-1800. Fax, (202) 383-1870. Sandy Bellamy, Executive Director, (202) 383-1810; Merrick T. Malone Esq., Chair; Yvonne Carignan, Library Director. Library, (202) 383-1850.*

General e-mail, info@historydc.org

Web, www.historydc.org

Maintains research collections on the District of Columbia. Publishes *Washington History* magazine. Library open to the public for researchers involved in projects about Washington, D.C., Tuesday through Saturday, 10:00 a.m.–5:00 p.m.; museum open Tuesday–Sunday, 10:00 a.m.–5:00 p.m.

Martin Luther King Jr. Memorial Library, **Washingtoniana Division,** *901 G St. N.W., #307 20001-4599; (202) 727-1213. Fax, (202) 727-1129. Karen Blackman-Mills, Chief (Interim).*

General e-mail, wash.dcpl@dc.gov

Web, http://dclibrary.org/washingtoniana

Maintains reference collections of District of Columbia current laws and regulations, history, and culture. Collections include biographies; travel books; memoirs and diaries; family, church, government, and institutional histories; maps (1612–present); plat books; city, telephone, and real estate directories (1822–present); census schedules; newspapers (1800–present), including the *Washington Star* microfilm (1852–1981) and microfilm of several other historic newspapers dating back to 1800, and a collection of clippings and photographs (1940–1981); periodicals; photographs; and oral history materials on local neighborhoods, ethnic groups, and businesses.

National Assn. to Restore Pride in America's Capital, *4401 Boxwood Rd., #400, Bethesda, MD 20816-1817; (301) 229-6076. Fax, (301) 229-6077. Leonard Sullivan, President.*

General e-mail, lsnarpac@bellatlantic.net

Web, www.narpac.org

National Park Service Sites in the Capital Region

The National Park Service administers most parks, circles, and monuments in the District of Columbia, as well as sites in nearby Maryland, Virginia, and West Virginia. For information on facilities not listed here, call (202) 619-7000. Web, www.nps.gov/parks.html.

Go to www.recreation.gov for information on visiting and making reservations at federal recreation sites nationwide.

Antietam National Battlefield, (301) 432-7648

Arlington House, Robert E. Lee Memorial, (703) 235-1530

C & O Canal National Historic Park, (301) 739-4200
   Great Falls Area, Maryland, (301) 767-3714

Catoctin Mountain Park, (301) 663-9330

Clara Barton National Historic Site, (301) 320-1410

Ford's Theatre National Historic Site, (202) 426-6924

Fort Washington Park, (301) 763-4600 (includes Piscataway Park)

Frederick Douglass National Historic Site, (202) 426-5961

George Washington Parkway, (703) 289-2500 (includes memorials to Theodore Roosevelt, Lyndon Johnson, and U.S. Marine Corps)

Glen Echo Park, (301) 492-6229

Great Falls Park, Virginia, (703) 757-3104

Greenbelt Park, (301) 344-3948

Harpers Ferry National Historic Park, (304) 535-6029

Manassas National Battlefield Park, (703) 754-1861

Mary McLeod Bethune National Historic Site, (202) 673-2402

Monocacy National Battlefield, (301) 662-3515

National Mall, (202) 233-3520 (includes presidential and war memorials and Pennsylvania Avenue National Historic Site)

Prince William Forest Park, (703) 221-4706

Rock Creek Park, (202) 895-6070

Thomas Stone National Historic Site, (301) 392-1776

White House, (202) 456-7041

Wolf Trap National Park, (703) 255-1800 or (703) 255-1868

Operates as an information clearinghouse and educational source on the city's history and its major current issues.

National Coalition to Save Our Mall, *9507 Overlea Dr., Rockville, MD 20850 (mailing address: P.O. Box 4709, Rockville, MD 20849); (301) 340-3938. Fax, (301) 340-3947. Judy Scott Feldman, President.*

General e-mail, jfeldman@savethemall.org

Web, www.savethemall.org

Coalition of professional and civic organizations and concerned artists, historians, and citizens promoting the protection and enhancement of the National Mall in Washington, D.C.

Supreme Court Historical Society, *224 E. Capitol St. N.E. 20003; (202) 543-0400. Fax, (202) 547-7730. David T. Pride, Executive Director.*

Web, www.supremecourthistory.org

Acquires, preserves, and displays historic items associated with the Court; conducts and publishes scholarly research. Conducts lecture programs; promotes and supports educational activities about the Court.

U.S. Capitol Historical Society, *200 Maryland Ave. N.E. 20002-5724; (202) 543-8919. Fax, (202) 544-8244. Ronald A. Sarasin, President; Donald R. Kennon, Vice President for Scholarship and Education (historian). Information, (800) 887-9318. Press, (202) 543-8919, ext. 31. Library, (202) 543-8919, ext. 27.*

General e-mail, uschs@uschs.org

Web, www.uschs.org

Membership: members of Congress, individuals, and organizations interested in the preservation of the history and traditions of the U.S. Capitol. Conducts historical research; offers tours, lectures, and films; publishes an annual historical calendar.

White House Historical Assn., *740 Jackson Pl. N.W. 20006; (202) 737-8292. Fax, (202) 789-0440. Neil W. Horstman, President.*

Web, www.whitehousehistory.org

Seeks to enhance the understanding and appreciation of the White House. Publishes books on the White House, its inhabitants, and its artworks. Net proceeds from book sales go toward the purchase of historic items for the White House permanent collection.

PHILANTHROPY, PUBLIC SERVICE, AND VOLUNTARISM

►AGENCIES

AmeriCorps *(Corporation for National and Community Service), 1201 New York Ave. N.W. 20525; (202) 606-5000. Fax, (202) 606-3475. Kristin McSwain, Director, (202) 606-6926. Volunteer recruiting information, (800) 942-2677. TTY, (800) 833-3722; local TTY, (202) 606-3472.*

General e-mail, questions@americorps.gov or info@cns.gov

Web, www.americorps.gov

Provides Americans age seventeen and older with opportunities to serve their communities on a full- or part-time basis. Participants work in the areas of education, public safety, human needs, and the environment and earn education awards for college or vocational training.

AmeriCorps *(Corporation for National and Community Service), National Civilian Community Corps,* 1201 *New York Ave. N.W. 20525; (202) 606-5000. Fax, (202) 606-3462. Merlene Mazyck, Director, (202) 606-6705. Volunteer recruiting information, (800) 942-2677. TTY, (800) 833-3722; local TTY, (202) 565-2799.*

General e-mail, webmaster@cns.gov

Web, www.americorps.gov/nccc

Provides a 10-month residential service and leadership program for men and women ages eighteen to twenty-four of all social, economic, and educational backgrounds. Works to restore and preserve the environment. Members provide disaster relief, fight forest fires, and restore homes and habitats after natural disasters.

AmeriCorps *(Corporation for National and Community Service), State and National Program,* 1201 *New York Ave. N.W. 20525; (202) 606-5000. Kristin McSwain, Director, (202) 606-6926. Information, (800) 942-2677. TTY, (800) 833-3722; local TTY, (202) 565-2799.*

General e-mail, webmaster@cns.gov

Web, www.americorps.gov

AmeriCorps State administers and oversees AmeriCorps funding distributed to governor-appointed state commissions, which distribute grants to local organizations and to such national organizations as Habitat for Humanity. AmeriCorps National provides grants directly to national public and nonprofit organizations that sponsor service programs, Indian tribes, and consortia formed across two or more states, including faith-based and community organizations, higher education institutions, and public agencies.

AmeriCorps *(Corporation for National and Community Service), Volunteers in Service to America (VISTA),* 1201 *New York Ave. N.W. 20525; (202) 606-5000. Fax, (202) 565-2789. Jean Whaley, Director, (202) 606-6943. Volunteer recruiting information, (800) 942-2677. TTY, (800) 833-3722; local TTY, (202) 565-2799.*

General e-mail, questions@americorps.gov

Web, www.americorps.gov/vista

Assigns full-time volunteers to public and private nonprofit organizations for one year to alleviate poverty in local communities. Volunteers receive a living allowance and their choice of a stipend or education award.

Corporation for National and Community Service, 1201 *New York Ave. N.W. 20525; (202) 606-5000. Fax, (202) 565-2799. Nicola Goren, Chief Executive Officer (Acting). Press, (202) 456-7381. Volunteer recruiting information, (800) 942-2677. TTY, (800) 833-3722; local TTY, (202) 565-2799.*

General e-mail, webmaster@cns.gov

Web, www.nationalservice.gov

Partners people of all ages with national and community-based organizations, schools, faith-based groups, and local agencies to assist with community needs in education, the environment, public safety, homeland security, and other areas. Programs include AmeriCorps-VISTA

(Volunteers in Service to America), AmeriCorps-NCCC (National Civilian Community Corps), Learn and Serve America, and the Senior Corps.

Learn and Serve America *(Corporation for National and Community Service),* 1201 *New York Ave. N.W. 20525; (202) 606-5000. Fax, (202) 565-2781. Amy B. Cohen, Director, (202) 606-6927. Volunteer recruiting information, (800) 942-2677. TTY, (800) 833-3722; local TTY, (202) 565-2799.*

General e-mail, lsaabout@cns.gov

Web, www.learnandserve.gov

Coordinates school-based community service programs, including the K–12 Program, for school-age children; the Higher Education Program, for undergraduate and graduate students; and School and Community-based Programs and Programs for Tribes and U.S. Territories, which support schools and nonprofit organizations that provide school-age children with community service opportunities.

Office of Faith-Based and Community Initiatives *(Executive Office of the President),* The White House 20502; *(202) 456-6708. Fax, (202) 456-7019. Jay Hein, Director.*

Web, www.whitehouse.gov/government/fbci

Strengthens and expands the role of faith-based and community organizations in addressing social needs. Centers in twelve cabinet departments and agencies work with the office in the White House to help organizations gain access to federal funding. Targeted populations include at-risk youth, ex-offenders, homeless, hungry, substance abusers, HIV/AIDS sufferers, and welfare-to-work families.

Peace Corps, 1111 *20th St. N.W. 20526; (202) 692-2100. Fax, (202) 692-2101. Jody Olsen, Director (Acting). Information, (800) 424-8580.*

Web, www.peacecorps.gov

Promotes world peace and mutual understanding between the United States and developing nations. Administers volunteer programs to assist developing countries in education, the environment, health (particularly HIV awareness and prevention), small business development, agriculture, and urban development.

Senior Corps *(Corporation for National and Community Service), Retired and Senior Volunteer Program, Foster Grandparent Program, and Senior Companion Program,* 1201 *New York Ave. N.W. 20525; (202) 606-5000. Fax, (202) 565-2789. Tess Scannell, Director, (202) 606-6925. Volunteer recruiting information, (800) 424-8867. TTY, (800) 833-3722; local TTY, (202) 565-2799.*

General e-mail, webmaster@cns.gov

Web, www.seniorcorps.gov

Network of programs that help older Americans find service opportunities in their communities, including the Retired and Senior Volunteer Program, which encourages older citizens to use their talents and experience in community service; the Foster Grandparent Program, which gives older citizens opportunities to work with exceptional children and children with special needs; and the Senior Companion Program, which recruits older citizens to help homebound adults, especially seniors, with special needs.

►CONGRESS

For a listing of relevant congressional committees and subcommittees, please see page 114 or the Appendix.

Government Accountability Office (GAO), *Education, Workforce, and Income Security,* 441 G St. N.W., #5928 20548; (202) 512-7215. Cynthia M. Fagnoni, Managing Director.
Web, www.gao.gov

Independent, nonpartisan agency in the legislative branch. Audits, analyzes, and evaluates programs of the Corporation for National and Community Service; makes reports available to the public. (Formerly the General Accounting Office.)

►NONGOVERNMENTAL

Arca Foundation, 1308 19th St. N.W. 20036; (202) 822-9193. Fax, (202) 785-1446. Anna Kuhn, Executive Director.
General e-mail, grants@arcafoundation.org
Web, www.arcafoundation.org

Awards grants to nonprofit organizations seeking to shape public policy, particularly in the areas of social equity and justice. Interests include campaign finance reform, civic participation domestically and internationally, labor and education, and diverse and competitive media.

Assn. of Fundraising Professionals (AFP), 4300 Wilson Blvd., #300, Arlington, VA 22203; (703) 684-0410. Fax, (703) 684-0540. Paulette V. Maehara, President. Information, (800) 666-3863.
General e-mail, afp@afpnet.org
Web, http://afpnet.org

Membership: individuals who serve as fundraising executives for nonprofit institutions or as members of counseling firms engaged in fundraising management. Promotes ethical standards; offers workshops; certifies members; monitors legislation and regulations. AFP Foundation promotes philanthropy and volunteerism. Library open to the public by appointment.

BoardSource, 1828 L St. N.W., #900 20036-5114; (202) 452-6262. Fax, (202) 452-6299. Linda C. Crompton, President. Toll-free, (800) 883-6262.
Web, www.boardsource.org

Works to improve the effectiveness of nonprofit organizations by strengthening their boards of directors. Operates an information clearinghouse; publishes materials on governing nonprofit organizations; assists organizations in conducting training programs, workshops, and conferences for board members and chief executives.

Capital Research Center, 1513 16th St. N.W. 20036-1480; (202) 483-6900. Fax, (202) 483-6902. Terrence M. Scanlon, President.

General e-mail, crc@capitalresearch.org
Web, www.capitalresearch.org

Conservative think tank that researches funding sources of public interest and advocacy groups. Analyzes the impact these groups have on public policy. Publishes findings in newsletters and reports.

Caring Institute, 228 7th St. S.E. 20003; (202) 547-4273. Fax, (202) 547-4510. Val J. Halamandaris, President.
General e-mail, info@caringinstitute.org
Web, www.caring-institute.org

Promotes selflessness and public service. Recognizes the achievements of individuals who have demonstrated a commitment to serving others. Operates the Frederick Douglass Museum and Hall of Fame for Caring Americans. Sponsors the National Caring Award and offers internships to high school and college students.

Center for a New American Dream, 6930 Carroll Ave., #900, Takoma Park, MD 20912; (301) 891-3683. Fax, (301) 891-3684. Jane Reese-Coulbourne, Executive Director. Information, (877) 683-7326.
General e-mail, newdream@newdream.org
Web, www.newdream.org

Promotes conservation of natural resources, recycling, and responsible consumer behavior. Distributes educational materials.

The Congressional Award, 379 FHOB 20515 (mailing address: P.O. Box 77440, Washington, DC 20013-7440); (202) 226-0130. Fax, (202) 226-0131. Erica Heyse, National Director. Toll-free, (888) 802-9273.
General e-mail, information@congressionalaward.org
Web, www.congressionalaward.org

Noncompetitive program established by Congress that recognizes the achievements of young people ages fourteen to twenty-three. Participants are awarded certificates or medals for setting and achieving goals in four areas: volunteer public service, personal development, physical fitness, and expeditions and exploration.

Council of Better Business Bureaus, *Wise Giving Alliance,* 4200 Wilson Blvd., #800, Arlington, VA 22203-1838; (703) 276-0100. Fax, (703) 525-8277. H. Art Taylor, President.
General e-mail, charities@cbbb.bbb.org
Web, www.give.org

Serves as a donor information service on national charities. Evaluates charities in relation to Better Business Bureau standards for charitable solicitation, which address charity finances, solicitations, fundraising practices, and governance. Produces quarterly guide that summarizes these findings.

Council on Foundations, 2121 Crystal Drive, Ste. 700, Arlington, VA 22202; (800) 673-9036. Steve Gunderson, President.
General e-mail, info@cof.org
Web, www.cof.org

Membership: independent community, family, and public- and company-sponsored foundations; corporate giving programs; and foundations in other countries. Promotes responsible and effective philanthropy through educational programs, publications, government relations, and promulgation of a set of principles and practices for effective grant making.

D.C. Preservation League, *401 F St. N.W., #324 20001; (202) 783-5144. Fax, (202) 783-5596. Rebecca A. Miller, Executive Director.*
General e-mail, info@dcpreservation.org
Web, www.dcpreservation.org

Participates in planning and preserving buildings and sites in Washington, D.C. Programs include protection and enhancement of the city's landmarks; educational lectures, tours, and seminars; and technical assistance to neighborhood groups. Monitors legislation and regulations.

Earth Share, *7735 Old Georgetown Rd., #900, Bethesda, MD 20814; (240) 333-0300. Fax, (240) 333-0301. Kalman Stein, President. Information, (800) 875-3863.*
General e-mail, info@earthshare.org
Web, www.earthshare.org

Federation of environmental and conservation organizations. Works with government and private payroll contribution programs to solicit contributions to member organizations for environmental research, education, and community programs. Provides information on establishing environmental giving options in the workplace.

Eugene and Agnes E. Meyer Foundation, *1400 16th St. N.W., #360 20036; (202) 483-8294. Fax, (202) 328-6850. Julie L. Rogers, President.*
General e-mail, meyer@meyerfdn.org
Web, www.meyerfoundation.org

Seeks to improve the quality of life in Washington, D.C. Awards grants to nonprofit organizations in eight program areas: arts and humanities, education, health, mental health, law and justice, neighborhood development and housing, community service, and nonprofit-sector strengthening.

Eugene B. Casey Foundation, *800 S. Frederick Ave., #100, Gaithersburg, MD 20877-4150; (301) 948-4595. Betty Brown Casey, Chair.*

Philanthropic organization that supports the arts, education, and social services in the metropolitan Washington area.

Evangelical Council for Financial Accountability, *440 W. Jubal Early Dr., #130, Winchester, VA 22601-6319; (540) 535-0103. Fax, (540) 535-0533. Dan Busby, President (Acting). Information, (800) 323-9473.*
General e-mail, info@ecfa.org
Web, www.ecfa.org

Membership: charitable, religious, international relief, and educational nonprofit U.S.-based organizations committed to evangelical Christianity. Assists members in making appropriate public disclosure of their financial practices and accomplishments. Certifies organizations that conform to standards of financial integrity and Christian ethics.

Foundation Center, *Washington Office, 1627 K St. N.W., 3rd Floor 20006-1708; (202) 331-1400. Fax, (202) 331-1739. Patricia Pasqual, Director.*
General e-mail, feedback@fdncenter.org
Web, www.foundationcenter.org/washington

Publishes foundation guides. Serves as a clearinghouse on foundations and corporate giving, nonprofit management, fundraising, and grants for individuals. Provides training and seminars on fundraising and grant writing. Operates libraries in Atlanta, Cleveland, New York, San Francisco, and Washington, D.C. Libraries open to the public. (Headquarters in New York.)

General Federation of Women's Clubs, *1734 N St. N.W. 20036-2990; (202) 347-3168. Fax, (202) 835-0246. Natasha Kalteis, Executive Director.*
General e-mail, gfwc@gfwc.org
Web, www.gfwc.org

Nondenominational, nonpartisan international organization of women volunteers. Interests include conservation, education, international and public affairs, and the arts.

Gifts In Kind International, *333 N. Fairfax St., #100, Alexandria, VA 22314; (703) 836-2121. Fax, (703) 798-3192. Barry R. Anderson, President (Interim).*
General e-mail, productdonations@giftsinkind.org
Web, www.giftsinkind.org

Encourages corporations to donate newly manufactured products to domestic and international charities. Works with companies to develop in-kind programs, coordinates the distribution of gifts to nonprofit agencies, collects tax documentation from recipients, and conducts communitywide public relations activities to encourage product giving. Serves schools and health, recreational, housing, arts, and environmental groups.

Grantmakers in Health, *1100 Connecticut Ave. N.W., #1200 20036; (202) 452-8331. Fax, (202) 452-8340. Lauren LeRoy, President.*
General e-mail, gih@gih.org
Web, www.gih.org

Seeks to increase the capacity of private sector grantmakers to enhance public health. Fosters information exchange among grantmakers. Publications include a bulletin on current news in health and human services and the *Directory of Health Philanthropy.*

Habitat for Humanity International, *Government Relations and Advocacy, 1000 Vermont Ave. N.W., #1100 20005; (202) 628-9171. Fax, (202) 628-9169. Jenny Russell, Managing Director.*
General e-mail, washingtonoffice@hfhi.org
Web, www.habitat.org

Christian ministry that seeks to eliminate poverty housing. Builds and sells homes to low-income families. Monitors legislation and regulations.

Independent Sector, *1602 L St. N.W., #900 20036; (202) 467-6100. Fax, (202) 467-6101. Diana Aviv, President.*
Web, www.independentsector.org

Membership: corporations, foundations, and national voluntary, charitable, and philanthropic organizations. Encourages volunteering, giving, and not-for-profit non-partisan initiatives by the private sector for public causes.

Institute for Justice, *901 N. Glebe Rd., #900, Arlington, VA 22203; (703) 682-9320. Fax, (703) 682-9321. Chip Mellor, President.*
General e-mail, general@ij.org
Web, www.ij.org

Sponsors seminars to train law students, grassroots activists, and practicing lawyers in applying advocacy strategies in public interest litigation. Seeks to protect individuals from arbitrary government interference in free speech, private property rights, parental school choice, and economic liberty. Litigates cases.

Institute for Sustainable Communities, *888 17th St. N.W., #610 20006; (202) 777-7575. Fax, (202) 777-7577. George Hamilton, President.*
General e-mail, isc@iscvt.org
Web, www.iscvt.org

Public interest organization that offers counseling and training in advocacy skills and strategies to nonprofit and international groups interested in such issues as civil and human rights, public health, arms control, and environmental and consumer affairs. Aids groups in making better use of resources, such as access to the media and coalition building. (Formerly the Advocacy Institute. Headquarters in Montpelier, Vt.)

Junior League of Washington, *3039 M St. N.W. 20007; (202) 337-2001. Fax, (202) 342-3148. Diana Marousek, President.*
General e-mail, office@jlw.org
Web, www.jlw.org

Educational and charitable women's organization that promotes volunteerism and works for community improvement through leadership of trained volunteers. Includes leagues in Canada, Mexico, and Great Britain. Interests include promoting volunteerism and developing the potential of women. Current emphasis is on literacy. (Assn. of Junior Leagues International headquarters in New York.)

Lutheran Volunteer Corps, *1226 Vermont Ave. N.W. 20005; (202) 387-3222. Fax, (202) 667-0037. Michael Wilker, Executive Director.*
General e-mail, staff@lutheranvolunteercorps.org
Web, www.lutheranvolunteercorps.org

Administers volunteer program in selected U.S. cities; coordinates activities with health and social service agencies, educational institutions, and environmental groups. Places volunteers in full-time positions in direct service, community organizing, advocacy, and public policy.

Mars Foundation, *6885 Elm St., McLean, VA 22101; (703) 821-4900. Fax, (703) 448-9678. Sue Martin, Assistant Secretary; O. O. Otih, Secretary-Treasurer.*

Awards grants in education, arts, health care concerns, animal wildlife environment, and history.

Morris and Gwendolyn Cafritz Foundation, *1825 K St. N.W., #1400 20006; (202) 223-3100. Fax, (202) 296-7567. Calvin Cafritz, Chair.*
Web, www.cafritzfoundation.org

Awards grants to educational, arts, and social services institutions in the metropolitan Washington area.

National Committee for Responsive Philanthropy, *2001 S St. N.W., #620 20009; (202) 387-9177. Fax, (202) 332-5084. Aaron Dorfman, Executive Director.*
General e-mail, info@ncrp.org
Web, www.ncrp.org

Directs philanthropic giving to benefit the socially, economically, and politically disenfranchised; advocates for groups that represent the poor, minorities, and women. Conducts research; organizes local coalitions. Monitors legislation and regulations.

National Human Services Assembly, *1319 F St. N.W., #402 20004; (202) 347-2080. Fax, (202) 393-4517. Irv Katz, President.*
General e-mail, nassembly@nassembly.org
Web, www.nassembly.org

Membership: national voluntary health and human service organizations. Provides collective leadership in the areas of health and human service. Provides members' professional staff and volunteers with a forum to share information. Supports public policies, programs, and resources that advance the effectiveness of health and human service organizations and their service delivery. (Formerly the National Assembly of Health and Human Services Organizations.)

Partnership for Public Service, *1100 New York Ave. N.W., #1090E 20005; (202) 775-9111. Fax, (202) 775-8885. Max Stier, President.*
General e-mail, mail@ourpublicservice.org
Web, www.ourpublicservice.org

Nonpartisan organization that seeks to revitalize public service through a campaign of educational efforts, policy research, public-private partnerships, and legislative advocacy.

Philanthropy Roundtable, *1150 17th St. N.W., #503 20036; (202) 822-8333. Fax, (202) 822-8325. Adam Meyerson, President.*
General e-mail, main@philanthropyroundtable.org
Web, www.philanthropyroundtable.org

Membership: individual donors, foundation trustees and staff, and corporate giving officers. Helps donors achieve their charitable objectives by offering counsel and peer-to-peer exchange opportunities.

Points of Light Institute, *1875 KSt. N.W., 5th Floor 20006; (202) 729-8000. Fax, (202) 729-8100. Michelle Nunn, President. Press, (202) 729-8177. Toll-free, (800) 750-7653.*

General e-mail, info@pointsoflight.org

Web, www.pointsoflight.org

Promotes mobilization of people for volunteer community service aimed at solving social problems. Offers technical assistance, training, and information services to nonprofit organizations, public agencies, corporations, and others interested in volunteering.

United Way of America, *701 N. Fairfax St., Alexandria, VA 22314; (703) 836-7100. Fax, (703) 683-7840. Brian Gallagher, President.*

Web, http://national.unitedway.org

Service association for independent local United Way organizations in the United States. Services include staff training; fundraising, planning, and communications assistance; resource management; and national public service advertising.

Volunteers of America, *1660 Duke St., Alexandria, VA 22314; (703) 341-5000. Fax, (703) 341-7000. Charles Gould, President.*

General e-mail, info@voa.org

Web, www.voa.org

Faith-based organization that promotes local human services and outreach programs. Facilitates individual and community involvement. Focuses on children at risk, abused and neglected children, older adults, homeless individuals, people with disabilities, and others.

Washington Grantmakers, *1400 16th St. N.W., #740 20036; (202) 939-3440. Fax, (202) 939-3442. Tamara Lucas Copeland, President.*

General e-mail, info@washingtongrantmakers.org

Web, www.washingtongrantmakers.org

Network of funders that partners with agencies and nongovernmental organizations in the Washington, D.C., region. Identifies and implements new and innovative forms of philanthropy. Shares best practices. Advocates for collective philanthropic community in the region.

W. O'Neil Foundation, *5454 Wisconsin Ave., #730, Chevy Chase, MD 20815; (301) 656-5848. Helene O'Neil Cobb, President.*

Awards grants to Roman Catholic interests providing for basic needs of the poor both nationally and internationally.

Youth Service America, *1101 15th St. N.W., #200 20005; (202) 296-2992. Fax, (202) 296-4030. Steven A. Culbertson, President; Christina Batcheler, Director of Communications, (202) 296-2992, ext. 128.*

General e-mail, info@ysa.org

Web, www.ysa.org

Advocates youth service at national, state, and local levels. Promotes opportunities for young people to be engaged in community service. Sponsors Global Youth Service Day. Hosts database of U.S. volunteer opportunities (www.servenet.org).

RECREATION AND SPORTS

►AGENCIES

Armed Forces Sports Council (AFSC), *4700 King St., 4th Floor, Alexandria, VA 22302-4418; (703) 681-7230. Fax, (703) 681-1616. Suba Saty, Secretariat. Toll-free, (888) 875-7529.*

General e-mail, suba.satyanarayan@us.army.mil

Web, www.armedforcessports.com

Administers and coordinates participation of U.S. military personnel within armed forces, national, and international sports activities. Includes one representative from each of the five armed services. Member of the International Military Sports Council (CISM).

Health and Human Services Dept. (HHS), *President's Council on Physical Fitness and Sports, Humphrey Bldg. #738H, 200 Independence Ave. S.W. 20201-0004; (202) 690-5187. Fax, (202) 690-5211. Melissa Johnson, Executive Director.*

Web, www.fitness.gov and www.presidentschallenge.org

Provides schools, state and local governments, recreation agencies, and employers with information on designing and implementing physical fitness programs; conducts award programs for children and adults and for schools, clubs, and other institutions.

►NONGOVERNMENTAL

American Alliance for Health, Physical Education, Recreation, and Dance, *1900 Association Dr., Reston, VA 20191-1598; (703) 476-3400. Fax, (703) 476-9527. Michael G. Davis, Chief Executive Officer.*

General e-mail, info@aahperd.org

Web, www.aahperd.org

Membership: teachers and others who work with school health, physical education, athletics, recreation, dance, and safety education programs (kindergarten through postsecondary levels). Member associations are National Assn. for Girls and Women in Sport, American Assn. for Health Education, National Dance Assn., National Assn. for Sport and Physical Education, and American Assn. for Physical Activity and Recreation.

American Canoe Assn., *1340 Central Park Blvd., #210, Fredericksburg, VA 22401; (540) 907-4460. Fax, (888) 229-3792. Martin Bartels, Executive Director.*

General e-mail, aca@americancanoe.org

Web, www.americancanoe.org

Membership: individuals and organizations interested in the promotion of canoeing, kayaking, and other paddle sports. Works to preserve the nation's recreational waterways. Sponsors programs in safety education, competition, recreation, public awareness, conservation, and public policy. Monitors legislation and regulations.

American Gaming Assn., *1299 Pennsylvania Ave. N.W., #1175 20004; (202) 552-2675. Fax, (202) 552-2676. Frank J. Fahrenkopf Jr., President.*
General e-mail, info@americangaming.org

Web, www.americangaming.org

Membership: casinos, casino and gaming equipment manufacturers, and financial services companies. Compiles statistics and serves as an information clearinghouse on the gaming industry. Administers a task force to study gambling addiction, raise public awareness of the condition, and develop assistance programs for it. Monitors legislation and regulations.

American Hiking Society, *1422 Fenwick Lane, Silver Spring, MD 20910-3328; (301) 565-6704. Fax, (301) 565-6714. Gregory Miller, President.*
General e-mail, info@americanhiking.org

Web, www.americanhiking.org

Membership: individuals and clubs interested in preserving America's trail system and protecting the interests of hikers and other trail users. Sponsors research on trail construction and a trail maintenance summer program. Provides information on outdoor volunteer opportunities on public lands.

American Medical Athletic Assn., *4405 East-West Hwy., #405, Bethesda, MD 20814-4535; (301) 913-9517. Fax, (301) 913-9520. David Watt, Executive Director. Information, (800) 776-2732.*
General e-mail, amaa@americanrunning.org

Web, www.amaasportsmed.org

Membership: sports medicine and allied health professionals. Assists members in promoting running and physical fitness to their patients and in developing their own physical fitness programs. Promotes and reports on sports medicine research and discussion. (Sister organization to American Running Assn.)

American Recreation Coalition, *1225 New York Ave. N.W., #450 20005-6405; (202) 682-9530. Fax, (202) 682-9529. Derrick A. Crandall, President.*
General e-mail, arc@funoutdoors.com

Web, www.funoutdoors.com

Membership: recreation industry associations, recreation enthusiast groups, and leading corporations in the recreation products and services sectors. Promotes health and well-being through recreation.

American Resort Development Assn., *1201 15th St. N.W., #400 20005; (202) 371-6700. Fax, (202) 289-8544. Howard Nusbaum, President.*
Web, www.arda.org

Membership: U.S. and international developers, builders, financiers, marketing companies, and others involved in resort, recreational, and community development. Serves as an information clearinghouse; monitors federal and state legislation affecting land, time share, and community development industries.

American Running Assn., *4405 East-West Hwy., #405, Bethesda, MD 20814-4535; (301) 913-9517. Fax, (301) 913-9520. David Watt, Executive Director. Information, (800) 776-2732.*
General e-mail, run@americanrunning.org

Web, www.americanrunning.org

Membership: athletes, health clubs, businesses, and individuals. Promotes proper nutrition and regular exercise. Provides members with medical advice and referrals, fitness information, and assistance in developing fitness programs. (Sister organization to American Medical Athletic Assn.)

American Sportfishing Assn., *225 Reinekers Lane, #420, Alexandria, VA 22314; (703) 519-9691. Fax, (703) 519-1872. Michael Nussman, President.*
General e-mail, info@asafishing.org

Web, www.asafishing.org

Works to ensure healthy and sustainable fish resources, to increase participation in sport fishing to expand market growth for its members. (Affiliated with the Future Fisherman Foundation and the Fish America Foundation.)

Assn. of Pool and Spa Professionals, *2111 Eisenhower Ave., #500, Alexandria, VA 22314-4698; (703) 838-0083. Fax, (703) 549-0493. Bill Weber, President.*
General e-mail, MemberServices@apsp.org

Web, www.apsp.org

Membership: manufacturers, dealers, service companies, builders, and distributors of pools, spas, and hot tubs. Promotes the industry; compiles statistics. Monitors legislation and regulations.

Bicycle Federation of America, *1612 K St. N.W., #802 20006; (202) 223-3621. Sharon Roerty, Executive Director.*
General e-mail, info@bikewalk.org

Web, www.bikewalk.org

Promotes bicycle use; conducts research, planning, and training projects; develops safety education and public information materials; offers consulting services for long-range planning and policy analysis. Works to increase public awareness of the benefits and opportunities of bicycling and walking. Manages the Campaign to Make America Walkable.

Boat Owners Assn. of the United States, *Government and Public Affairs, 880 S. Pickett St., Alexandria, VA 22304-4695; (703) 461-2864. Fax, (703) 461-2845. Margaret Podlich, Director of Government Affairs.*
General e-mail, govtaffairs@boatus.com

Web, www.boatus.com

Membership: owners of recreational boats. Represents boat-owner interests before the federal government; offers consumer protection and other services to members.

Club Managers Assn. of America, *1733 King St., Alexandria, VA 22314; (703) 739-9500. Fax, (703) 739-0124. James Singerling, Chief Executive Officer.*

General e-mail, cmaa@cmaa.org

Web, www.cmaa.org

Membership: managers of membership clubs. Promotes the profession of club management through education and other assistance.

Disabled Sports USA, *451 Hungerford Dr., #100, Rockville, MD 20850; (301) 217-0960. Fax, (301) 217-0968. Kirk M. Bauer, Executive Director, (301) 217-9838.*

General e-mail, information@dsusa.org

Web, www.dsusa.org

Offers nationwide sports rehabilitation programs; conducts sports and recreation activities and physical fitness programs for people with permanent disabilities and their families and friends; conducts workshops and competitions; participates in world championships.

FishAmerica Foundation, *225 Reinekers Lane, #420, Alexandria, VA 22314; (703) 519-9691. Fax, (703) 519-1872. Johanna Laderman, Executive Director.*

General e-mail, fishamerica@asafishing.org

Web, www.fishamerica.org

Promotes investment in grassroots fisheries, habitat conservation, restoration projects, and research. (Affiliated with the American Sportfishing Assn.)

Future Fisherman Foundation, *225 Reinekers Lane, #420, Alexandria, VA 22314; (703) 519-9691. Fax, (703) 519-1872. Anne Danielski, Executive Director.*

General e-mail, info@futurefisherman.org

Web, www.futurefisherman.org

Promotes sportfishing to youth by offering a variety of fishing and boating programs, equipment, and services to community groups and schools across the country. (Affiliated with the American Sportfishing Assn.)

National Aeronautic Assn., *Reagan National Washington Airport, Hangar 7, #202 20001; (703) 416-4888. Fax, (703) 416-4877. Jonathan Gaffney, President.*

General e-mail, naa@naa.aero

Web, www.naa.aero

Membership: persons interested in development of general and sporting aviation. Supervises sporting aviation competitions; oversees and approves official U.S. aircraft, aeronautics, and space records. Serves as U.S. representative to the International Aeronautical Federation in Lausanne, Switzerland.

National Assn. for Girls and Women in Sport, *1900 Association Dr., Reston, VA 20191-1599; (703) 476-3400. Fax, (703) 476-4566. Pamela Noakes, Executive Director.*

General e-mail, nagws@aahperd.org

Web, www.nagws.org

Membership: students, coaches, physical education teachers, athletes, athletic directors, and trainers for girls' and women's sports programs. Seeks to increase sports opportunities for women and girls; provides information on laws relating to equality of sports funds and facilities for women; hosts training sites.

National Club Assn., *1201 15th St. N.W., #450 20005; (202) 822-9822. Fax, (202) 822-9808. Susanne Wegrzyn, President.*

General e-mail, info@nationalclub.org

Web, www.nationalclub.org

Promotes the interests of private, social, and recreational clubs. Monitors legislation and regulations.

National Coalition Against Legalized Gambling, *100 Maryland Ave. N.E., #311 20002. Guy Clark, Chair. Toll-free and fax, (800) 664-2680.*

General e-mail, ncalg@ncalg.org

Web, www.ncalg.org

Compiles information on the personal, social, economic, and public health impacts of gambling and disseminates it to citizens and policymakers at the local, state, and national levels. Monitors legislation and regulations.

National Collegiate Athletic Assn. (NCAA), *Government Relations, Washington Office, 1 Dupont Circle N.W., #310 20036-1139; (202) 293-3050. Fax, (202) 293-3075. Abe L. Frank, Director.*

Web, www.ncaa.org

Membership: colleges and universities, conferences, and organizations interested in the administration of intercollegiate athletics. Certifies institutions' athletic programs; compiles records and statistics; produces publications and television programs; administers youth development programs; awards student athletes with postgraduate scholarships and degree-completion grants. (Headquarters in Indianapolis, Ind.)

National Football League Players Assn., *1133 20th St. N.W. 20036; (202) 463-2200. Fax, (202) 857-0380. Demaurice Smith, Executive Director. Toll-free, (800) 372-2000.*

Web, www.nflplayers.org

Membership: professional football players. Represents members in matters concerning wages, hours, and working conditions. Provides assistance to charitable and community organizations. Sponsors programs and events to promote the image of professional football and its players.

National Indian Gaming Assn. (NIGA), *224 2nd St. S.E. 20003; (202) 546-7711. Fax, (202) 546-1755. Mark Van Norman, Executive Director.*

General e-mail, info@indiangaming.org

Web, www.indiangaming.org

Membership: 184 Indian nations as well as other organizations, tribes, and businesses engaged in gaming enterprises. Operates as a clearinghouse for tribes, policymakers, and the public on Indian gaming issues and tribal community development.

National Recreation and Park Assn., *22377 Belmont Ridge Rd., Ashburn, VA 20148-4501; (703) 858-0784. Fax, (703) 858-0794. Barbara Tulipane, Executive Director.*
General e-mail, info@nrpa.org

Web, www.nrpa.org

Membership: park and recreation professionals and interested citizens. Promotes support and awareness of park, recreation, and leisure services; facilitates development, expansion, and management of resources; provides technical assistance for park and recreational programs; and provides professional development to members. Monitors legislation and regulations.

Poker Players Alliance, *1325 G St. N.W., #500 20005; (202) 552-7431. Fax, (202) 552-7423. John A. Pappas, Executive Director. Toll-free, (888) 448-4772. Toll-free fax, (888) 486-3138.*
General e-mail, email@pokerplayersalliance.org

Web, www.pokerplayersalliance.org

Membership: poker players and enthusiasts. Seeks to promote the game and protect players' rights. Monitors legislation and regulations.

Road Runners Club of America, *1501 Lee Hwy., #140, Arlington, VA 22209; (703) 525-3890. Fax, (703) 525-3891. Jean Knaack, Executive Director.*
General e-mail, office@rrca.org

Web, www.rrca.org

Develops and promotes road races and fitness programs, including the Children's Running Development Program and the Women's Distance Festival. Issues guidelines on road races concerning safety, legal issues, and runners with disabilities. Facilitates communication between clubs. Supports running for people with disabilities.

SnowSports Industries America, *8377-B Greensboro Dr., McLean, VA 22102-3587; (703) 556-9020. Fax, (703) 821-8276. David Ingemie, President.*
General e-mail, siamail@snowsports.org

Web, www.snowsports.org

Membership: manufacturers and distributors of ski and other outdoor sports equipment, apparel, accessories, and footwear. Interests include international markets.

Society of State Directors of Health, Physical Education, and Recreation, *1900 Association Dr., #100, Reston, VA 20191-1599; (703) 390-4599. Fax, (703) 476-0988. Grace Stevens, Executive Director (Interim).*
Web, www.thesociety.org

Membership: state directors, supervisors, and coordinators for physical and health education and recreation activities in state education departments, and other interested individuals. Seeks to improve school programs on comprehensive health, physical education, athletics, outdoor education, recreation, and safety.

Special Olympics International Inc., *1133 19th St. N.W. 20036-3604; (202) 628-3630. Fax, (202) 824-0200. Timothy P. Shriver, President (Acting).*

General e-mail, info@specialolympics.org

Web, www.specialolympics.org

Offers individuals with intellectual disabilities opportunities for year-round sports training; sponsors athletic competition worldwide in twenty-two individual and team sports.

U.S. Eventing Assn. (USEA), *525 Old Waterford Rd. N.W., Leesburg, VA 20176-2050; (703) 779-0440. Fax, (703) 779-0550. Jo Whitehouse, Chief Executive Officer.*
General e-mail, info@useventing.com

Web, www.useventing.com

Membership: individuals interested in eventing, an Olympic-recognized equestrian sport. Registers all national events to ensure that they meet the standards set by the U.S.A. Equestrian Federation. Sponsors three-day events for members from novice to Olympic levels. Provides educational materials on competition, riding, and care of horses.

U.S. Olympic Committee, *Government Relations, 1101 17th St. N.W., #601 20036; (202) 466-3399. Fax, (202) 466-5068. Vacant, Director; Karen Irish, Manager.*
Web, www.usoc.org

Responsible for training, entering, and underwriting the full expenses for U.S. teams in the Olympic, Paralympic, and Pan American Games. Supports the bid of U.S. cities to host the Olympic, Paralympic, and Pan American Games; recognizes the national governing body of each sport in these games. Promotes international athletic competition. (Headquarters in Colorado Springs, Colo.)

U.S. Parachute Assn., *5401 Southpoint Centre Blvd., Fredericksburg, VA 22407-2612; (540) 604-9740. Fax, (540) 604-9741. Edward Scott, Executive Director. Information, (800) 371-8772.*
General e-mail, uspa@uspa.org

Web, www.uspa.org

Membership: individuals and organizations interested in skydiving. Develops safety procedures; maintains training programs; issues skydiving licenses and ratings; certifies skydiving instructors; sanctions national competitions; and documents record attempts. Offers liability insurance to members. Monitors legislation and regulations.

RELIGION

▶AGENCIES

Office of Faith-Based and Community Initiatives *(Executive Office of the President), The White House 20502; (202) 456-6708. Fax, (202) 456-7019. Jay Hein, Director.*
Web, www.whitehouse.gov/government/fbci

Strengthens and expands the role of faith-based and community organizations in addressing social needs. Centers in twelve cabinet departments and agencies work with the office in the White House to help organizations gain access to federal funding. Targeted populations include at-risk youth, ex-offenders, homeless, hungry, substance abusers, HIV/AIDS sufferers, and welfare-to-work families.

▶NONGOVERNMENTAL

Alban Institute, *2121 Cooperative Way, #100, Herndon, VA 20171; (703) 964-2700. Fax, (703) 964-0370. James P. Wind, President. Information, (800) 486-1318.*

Web, www.alban.org

Nondenominational research, consulting, and educational membership organization that provides church and synagogue congregations with support and services. Interests include planning and growth, conflict resolution, leadership and staff training, spiritual development, and mission and stewardship. Conducts continuing education programs.

American Assn. of Pastoral Counselors, *9504A Lee Hwy., Fairfax, VA 22031-2303; (703) 385-6967. Fax, (703) 352-7725. Douglas M. Ronsheim, Executive Director.*

General e-mail, info@aapc.org

Web, www.aapc.org

Membership: mental health professionals with training in both religion and the behavioral sciences. Nonsectarian organization that accredits pastoral counseling centers, certifies pastoral counselors, and approves training programs.

Alliance of Baptists, *1328 16th St. N.W., #1415 20036-2206; (202) 745-7609. Fax, (202) 745-0023. Stan Hastey, Minister for Mission and Ecumenism. Toll-free, (866) 745-7609.*

General e-mail, info@allianceofbaptists.org

Web, www.allianceofbaptists.org

Membership: Baptist congregations and individuals. Interests include worship, refuge and renewal, the poor and social justice, peace, Baptist freedoms, servant leadership, biblical authority, open inquiry, and evangelism.

American Baptist Churches U.S.A., *Government Relations, Washington Office, 200 Maryland Ave. N.E. 20002; (202) 544-3400. Fax, (202) 544-0277. Curtis Ramsey-Lucas, Director. Information, (800) 222-3872.*

Web, www.nationalministries.org

Serves as liaison between American Baptist churches and government organizations. Interests include immigration, foreign and military policy, human services, employment, the environment, and civil rights. (Headquarters in Valley Forge, Pa.)

American Friends Service Committee (AFSC), *Washington Office, 1822 R St. N.W. 20009-1604; (202) 483-3341. Fax, (202) 232-3197. R. Aura Kanegis, Director.*

General e-mail, WashOfficeInfo@afsc.org

Web, www.afsc.org/locations/dc

Education, outreach, and advocacy office for the AFSC, an independent organization affiliated with the Religious Society of Friends (Quakers) in America. Sponsors domestic and international service, development, justice, and peace programs. Priorities include

---

Faith-Based and Community Initiatives Contacts at Federal Departments and Agencies

White House Office of Faith-Based and Community Initiatives, Jay Hein, (202) 456-6708, www.fbci.gov

DEPARTMENTS

Commerce, Vacant, (202) 482-4355, www.commerce.gov/fbci

Education, Vacant, (202) 219-1741, www.ed.gov/faithandcommunity

Health and Human Services, Mike Costigan, (202) 358-3595, www.hhs.gov/fbci

Compassion Capital Fund/National Resource Center, Tom Campbell, (866) CCF-5129, www.acf.hhs.gov/programs/ccf/index.html

Housing and Urban Development, Anne Marie Farias, (202) 708-2404, www.hud.gov/offices/fbci

Justice, Steven McFarland, (202) 514-2987, www.usdoj.gov/fbci

Labor, Jedd Medefind, (202) 693-6450, www.dol.gov/cfbci

Veterans Affairs, Stephen Gillard (Acting), (202) 273-7499, www.va.gov/fbci

AGENCIES

Agency for International Development, Mauricio Vera (Acting), (202) 712-4080, www.usaid.gov

Corporation for National and Community Service, John Kelly, (202) 606-6743, www.nationalservice.gov/home/site_map/index.asp

Small Business Administration, Joseph Shattan, (202) 205-9037, www.sba.gov/fbci

---

Iraq, Israel/Palestine, Colombia, civil rights and liberties, and economic justice in the United States. Interests include peace education; arms control and disarmament; social and economic justice; gay and lesbian rights, racism, sexism, and civil rights; refugees and immigration policy; crisis response and relief efforts; and international development efforts, especially in Central America, the Middle East, and southern Africa. (Headquarters in Philadelphia, Pa.)

American Humanist Assn., *1777 T St. N.W. 20009-7125; (202) 238-9088. Fax, (202) 238-9003. David Niose, President. Toll-free, (800) 837-3792.*

General e-mail, aha@americanhumanist.org

Web, www.americanhumanist.org

Seeks to educate the public about Humanism and bring Humanists together for mutual support and action. Defends the civil liberties and constitutional freedoms of Humanists and leads both local and national Humanist organizations toward progressive societal change.

American Islamic Congress, *1718 M St. N.W., #243 20036; (202) 595-3160. Fax, (202) 315-5838. Zainab Al-Suwaij, Executive Director.*

General e-mail, info@aicongress.org

Web, www.aicongress.org

Non-religious civic initiative of American Muslims challenging negative perceptions of Muslims by advocating responsible leadership and "two-way" interfaith understanding. Promotes open multicultural society and civil liberties; advocates for women's equality, free expression, and nonviolence. Encourages the denouncement of terrorism, extremism, and hate speech within the Muslim community. Interests include rebuilding schools and empowering women in Iraq. Maintains a speakers bureau.

American Jewish Committee, *Government and International Affairs, Washington Office, 1156 15th St. N.W., #1201 20005; (202) 785-4200. Fax, (202) 785-4115. Jason Isaacson, Director.*

Web, www.ajc.org

Human relations agency devoted to protecting civil and religious rights for all people. Interests include church-state issues, research on human behavior, Israel and the Middle East, Jews in the former Soviet Union, immigration, social discrimination, civil and women's rights, employment, education, housing, and international cooperation for peace and human rights. (Headquarters in New York.)

American Jewish Congress, *Washington Office, 1001 Connecticut Ave. N.W., #407 20036-5553; (202) 466-9661. Fax, (202) 466-9665. Matthew Horn, National Policy Director.*

General e-mail, washrep@ajcongress.org

Web, www.ajcongress.org

Jewish community relations and civil liberties organization. Seeks to combat anti-Semitism and other forms of bigotry in employment, education, housing, and voting. Areas of activity include church-state relations; government involvement in education; public school prayer; gun control policy; constitutional, minority, women's, and human rights; world Jewry; U.S. foreign policy in the Middle East; Arab investment in the United States; and the Arab boycott of Israel. Monitors legislation. (Headquarters in New York.)

Americans United for Separation of Church and State, *518 C St. N.E. 20002; (202) 466-3234. Fax, (202) 466-2587. Barry W. Lynn, Executive Director.*

General e-mail, americansunited@au.org

Web, www.au.org

Citizens' interest group. Opposes federal and state aid to parochial schools; works to ensure religious neutrality in public schools; supports free religious exercise; initiates litigation; maintains speakers bureau. Monitors legislation and regulations.

Baptist Joint Committee for Religious Liberty, *200 Maryland Ave. N.E., 3rd Floor 20002; (202) 544-4226. Fax, (202) 544-2094. J. Brent Walker, Executive Director.*

General e-mail, bjc@bjconline.org

Web, www.bjconline.org

Membership: Baptist conventions and conferences. Conducts research and operates an information service. Interests include religious liberty, separation of church and state, First Amendment religious issues, and government regulation of religious institutions. (Formerly the Baptist Joint Committee on Public Affairs.)

Baptist World Alliance, *405 N. Washington St., Falls Church, VA 22046; (703) 790-8980. Fax, (703) 893-5160. Neville Callam, General Secretary.*

General e-mail, bwa@bwanet.org

Web, www.bwanet.org

International Baptist organization. Conducts religious teaching and works to create a better understanding among nations. Organizes development efforts and disaster relief in less developed nations. Interests include human rights and religious liberty.

Becket Fund for Religious Liberty, *1350 Connecticut Ave. N.W., #605 20036; (202) 955-0095. Fax, (202) 955-0090. Kevin J. Hasson Esq., Chair; Scott Walter, Executive Director. Press, (202) 349-7205.*

Web, www.becketfund.org

Public interest law firm that promotes freedom of expression for people of all faiths. Works to ensure that people and institutions of all faiths, domestically and abroad, are entitled to a voice in public affairs.

B'nai B'rith International, *2020 K St. N.W., 7th Floor 20006; (202) 857-6600. Fax, (202) 857-2700. Daniel S. Mariaschin, Executive Vice President.*

General e-mail, info@bnaibrith.org

Web, www.bnaibrith.org

International Jewish organization that promotes the security and continuity of the Jewish people and the State of Israel; defends human rights; combats anti-Semitism; and promotes Jewish identity through cultural activities. Interests include strengthening family life and the education and training of youth, providing broad-based services for the benefit of senior citizens, and advocacy on behalf of Jews throughout the world.

Brethren Witness (Church of the Brethren), *Washington Office, 337 North Carolina Ave. S.E. 20003; (202) 546-3202. Fax, (202) 546-5852. Phil Jones, Director.*

General e-mail, washington_office_gb@brethren.org

Web, www.brethren.org/genbd/washofc

Organizes and coordinates political activities on social policy issues of concern to the church. Interests include military spending; civil rights and liberties; health care; conditions for the poor; refugees and immigrants; world hunger; conditions in the Middle East, Sudan, and Central America; and religious freedom. Sponsors seminars. (Headquarters in Elgin, Ill.)

Catholic Charities USA, *66 Canal Center Plaza, #600, Alexandria, VA 22314; (703) 549-1390. Fax, (703) 549-1656. Rev. Larry Snyder, President.*

General e-mail, info@catholiccharitiesusa.org

Web, www.catholiccharitiesusa.org

Member agencies and institutions provide assistance to persons of all backgrounds; community-based services include day care, counseling, food, and housing. National office provides members with advocacy and professional support, including networking, training and consulting, program development, and financial benefits. Represents the Catholic community in times of domestic disaster.

Catholic Information Center, *1501 K St. N.W., #175 20005; (202) 783-2062. Fax, (202) 783-6667. Rev. Arne Panula, Director.*

General e-mail, contract@cicdc.org

Web, www.cicdc.org

Provides information on Roman Catholicism and the Catholic church. Offers free counseling services. Includes Catholic bookstore and chapel.

Center for Islamic Pluralism, *1718 M St. N.W., #260 20036; (202) 232-1750. Fax, (866) 792-9439. Stephen Schwartz, Executive Director.*

General e-mail, schwartz@islamicpluralism.org

Web, www.islamicpluralism.org

Think tank that opposes the radicalization of Islam in America and promotes integration of moderate Muslims into the American interfaith environment. Seeks to educate the public about moderate Islam. Activities include media releases, conferences, and publications.

Center for Law and Religious Freedom, *8001 Braddock Rd., #300, Springfield, VA 22151; (703) 642-1070, ext. 2. Fax, (703) 642-1075. Gregory S. Baylor, Director.*

Web, www.clsnet.org

Provides legal assistance and advocacy on anti-abortion and religious-freedom issues. Monitors legislation and regulations. (Affiliated with the Christian Legal Society.)

Center for the Study of Islam and Democracy, *1625 Massachusetts Ave. N.W., #601 20036; (202) 265-1200. Fax, (202) 265-1222. Radwan Masmoudi, President.*

General e-mail, feedback@islam-democracy.org

Web, www.csidonline.org

Strives to merge Islamic and democratic political thought into a modern Islamic democratic discourse and improve understanding of Islam's approach to civil rights and political pluralism.

Christian Science Committee on Publication, *1660 L St. N.W., #216 20036; (202) 296-2190. Fax, (202) 296-2426. Kim Robert Walker, Federal Representative.*

Public service organization that provides information on the religious convictions and practices of Christian Scientists; maintains a speakers bureau. Monitors legislation and regulations.

Churches' Center for Theology and Public Policy, *4500 Massachusetts Ave. N.W. 20016-5632; (202) 885-8648. Fax, (202) 885-8559. Barbara G. Green, Director, (202) 885-8609.*

Web, www.cctpp.org

Studies the effect of Christian faith on political life and public policy. Interests include arms control and disarmament, health care, minority rights, and world political economy. Sponsors the Faithful Security Project and Greater Washington Interfaith Power and Light.

Conference of Major Superiors of Men (CMSM), *8808 Cameron St., Silver Spring, MD 20910; (301) 588-4030. Fax, (301) 587-4575. Rev. Paul Lininger, Executive Director.*

General e-mail, postmaster@cmsm.org

Web, www.cmsm.org

National representative body for men in religious and apostolic communities in the United States, as well as foreign missionaries. Collaborates with U.S. bishops and other key groups and organizations that serve church and society.

Council on American-Islamic Relations, *453 New Jersey Ave. S.E. 20003-4034; (202) 488-8787. Fax, (202) 488-0833. Nihad Awad, National Executive Director.*

General e-mail, info@cair.com

Web, www.cair.com

Promotes the understanding of Islam to the American public. Seeks to empower the Muslim community in the United States and protect civil liberties through political and social activism.

Episcopal Church, *Government Relations, 110 Maryland Ave. N.E., #309 20002; (202) 547-7300. Fax, (202) 547-4457. Maureen T. Shea, Director. Toll-free, (800) 228-0515.*

Web, www.episcopalchurch.org/eppn

Informs Congress, the executive branch, and governmental agencies about the actions and resolutions of the Episcopal church. Monitors legislation and regulations. (Headquarters in New York.)

Ethics and Public Policy Center, *Religion and Society Program, 1015 15th St. N.W., #900 20005; (202) 682-1200. Fax, (202) 408-0632. M. Edward Whelan III, President.*

General e-mail, ethics@eppc.org

Web, www.eppc.org

Considers implications of Judeo-Christian moral tradition for domestic and foreign policy making.

Evangelical Lutheran Church in America, *Washington Office, 122 C St. N.W., #125 20001; (202) 783-7507. Fax, (202) 783-7502. Andrew Genszler, Director.*

General e-mail, washingtonoffice@elca.org

Web, www.elca.org/advocacy

Represents the church's positions, particularly on social justice in domestic and foreign policy, and policies regarding poor and oppressed peoples. Monitors and responds to legislation and regulations. (Headquarters in Chicago, Ill.)

Faith in Public Life, *1101 Vermont Ave. N.W., 9th Floor 20005; (202) 435-0260. Fax, (202) 435-0261. Rev. Jennifer Butler, Executive Director. Press, (202) 459-8625.*

General e-mail, admin@faithinpubliclife.org

Web, www.faithinpubliclife.org

Promotes collaboration among diverse faith movements to further justice and the common good in public policy. Provides organizing and communications resources to diverse faith leaders and organizations.

Friends Committee on National Legislation (FCNL), *245 2nd St. N.E. 20002-5795; (202) 547-6000. Fax, (202) 547-6019. Joe Volk, Executive Secretary. Toll-free, (800) 630-1330. Recorded information, (202) 547-4343.*

General e-mail, fcnl@fcnl.org

Web, www.fcnl.org

Advocates for economic justice, world disarmament, international cooperation, and religious rights. Advocates on behalf of Native Americans in such areas as treaty rights, self-determination, and U.S. trust responsibilities. Conducts research and educational activities through the FCNL Education Fund. Opposes the death penalty. Monitors national legislation and policy. (Affiliated with the Religious Society of Friends [Quakers].)

General Board of Church and Society of The United Methodist Church, *100 Maryland Ave. N.E. 20002; (202) 488-5600. Fax, (202) 488-5619. James E. Winkler, General Secretary. Press, (202) 488-5630.*

General e-mail, gbcs@umc-gbcs.org

Web, www.umc-gbcs.org

One of four international general program boards of The United Methodist Church. Provides training and educational resources to member churches. Monitors legislation and regulations. Current legislative priorities are HIV and AIDS, global poverty and hunger, criminal and restorative justice, children's concerns, Iraq, and global warming and energy policy. (Has offices at the Church Center at the United Nations.)

General Conference of Seventh-day Adventists, *12501 Old Columbia Pike, Silver Spring, MD 20904-6600; (301) 680-6000. Fax, (301) 680-6090. Jan Paulsen, President.*

General e-mail, info@adventist.org

Web, www.adventist.org

World headquarters of the Seventh-day Adventist church. Interests include education, health care, humanitarian relief, and development. Supplies educational tools for the blind and the hard of hearing. Operates schools worldwide. Organizes community service–oriented youth groups.

Institute on Religion and Democracy, *1023 15th St. N.W., #601 20005-2601; (202) 682-4131. Fax, (202) 682-4136. James Tonkowich, President.*

General e-mail, mail@theird.org

Web, www.theird.org

Interdenominational bipartisan organization that supports democratic and constitutional forms of government consistent with the values of Christianity. Serves as a resource center to promote Christian perspectives on U.S. foreign policy questions. Interests include international conflicts, religious liberties, and the promotion of democratic forms of government in the United States and worldwide.

Interfaith Alliance, *1212 New York Ave. N.W., #1250 20005; (202) 238-3300. Fax, (202) 238-3301. Rev. C. Welton Gaddy, President.*

General e-mail, info@interfaithalliance.org

Web, www.interfaithalliance.org

Membership: Protestant, Catholic, Jewish, and Muslim clergy, laity, and others who favor a positive, nonpartisan role for religious faith in public life. Advocates mainstream religious values; promotes tolerance and social opportunity; opposes the use of religion to promote political extremism at national, state, and local levels. Monitors legislation and regulations.

International Religious Liberty Assn., *12501 Old Columbia Pike, Silver Spring, MD 20904-6600; (301) 680-6680. Fax, (301) 680-6695. John Graz, Secretary General.*

Web, www.irla.org

Seeks to preserve and expand religious liberty and freedom of conscience; advocates separation of church and state; sponsors international and domestic meetings and congresses.

Islamic Society of North America (ISNA), *Office of Interfaith and Community Alliances,* *110 Maryland Ave. N.E., #304 20002; (202) 544-5656. Fax, (202) 544-6636. Sayyid M. Syeed, National Director.*

General e-mail, ssyeed@isna.net

Web, www.isna.net

Conducts outreach to grassroots organizations and engages in joint programs with other religious organizations, including the National Council of Churches, the United States Conference of Catholic Bishops, the National Jewish Center for Learning and Leadership, and the Religious Action Center for Reform Judaism. Seeks to promote a positive image of Islam and Muslims to national political leaders. (Headquarters in Plainfield, Ind.)

Jesuit Conference, *Social and International Ministries,* *1016 16th St. N.W., 4th Floor 20036; (202) 462-0400. Fax, (202) 328-9212. Rev. James Stormes, Director.*

General e-mail, usjc@jesuit.org

Web, www.jesuit.org/JCOSIM

Information and advocacy organization of Jesuits and laypersons concerned with peace and social justice issues in the United States. Interests include peace and disarmament, economic justice, and issues affecting minorities, especially Native Americans, Hispanics, and African Americans.

Leadership Conference of Women Religious, *8808 Cameron St., Silver Spring, MD 20910; (301) 588-4955. Fax, (301) 587-4575. Jane Burke, Executive Director.*

Web, www.lcwr.org

Membership: Roman Catholic women who are the principal administrators of their congregations in the

United States and around the world. Offers programs and support to members; conducts research; serves as an information clearinghouse.

Loyola Foundation, *308 C St. N.E. 20002; (202) 546-9400. Fax, (202) 546-0320. A. Gregory McCarthy IV, Executive Director.*

Web, www.loyolafoundation.org

Assists overseas Catholic mission activities. Awards grants to international missionaries and Catholic dioceses for construction and capital projects.

Maryknoll Fathers and Brothers (Catholic Foreign Mission Society of America), *Washington Office, 415 Michigan Ave. N.E. 20017; (202) 832-1780. Fax, (202) 832-5195. Rev. William Boteler, Regional Director.*

Web, www.maryknollogc.org

Conducts religious teaching and other mission work for the poor in Africa, Asia, Latin America, China, Russia, and other countries. (Headquarters in Maryknoll, N.Y.)

Mennonite Central Committee, *Washington Office, 110 Maryland Ave. N.E., #502 20003; (202) 544-6564. Fax, (202) 544-2820. Rachelle Lyndaker Schlabach, Director.*

General e-mail, mccwash@mcc.org

Web, www.mcc.org/us/washington

Christian organization engaged in service and development projects. Monitors legislation and regulations affecting issues of interest to Mennonite and Brethren in Christ churches. Interests include human rights in developing countries, military spending, the environment, world hunger, poverty, and civil and religious liberties. (Headquarters in Akron, Pa.)

Muslim American Society, *6408 Edsall Rd., Alexandria, VA 22312; (703) 642-6165. Fax, (757) 299-9961. Imam Mahdi Bray, Executive Director.*

General e-mail, info@masfreedom.org

Web, www.masnet.org

Works to promote understanding between Muslims and non-Muslims. Encourages Muslims to follow Islamic principles and ways of life. Offers Islam-based solutions to societal problems. Operates the Freedom Foundation, which seeks to empower the American Muslim community through civic education, political participation, community outreach, and coalition building.

Muslim Public Affairs Council, *110 Maryland Ave. N.E., #210 20002; (202) 547-7701. Fax, (202) 547-7704. Salam Al-Marayati, Executive Director.*

General e-mail, mpac-contact@mpac.org

Web, www.mpac.org

Promotes the civil rights of American Muslims and the integration of Islam into American pluralism. Seeks an accurate portrayal of Islam and Muslims in the media and popular culture.

National Assn. of Evangelicals, *701 G St. S.W. 20024 (mailing address: P.O. Box 23269, Washington, DC 20026); (202) 789-1011. Fax, (202) 842-0392. Leith Anderson, President.*

General e-mail, nae@nae.net

Web, www.nae.net

Represents sixty Christian evangelical denominations. Interests include religious liberty; economic policy; church-state relations; public health issues, including HIV and AIDS; and immigration and refugee policy. Monitors legislation and regulations.

National Clergy Council, *109 2nd St. N.E. 20002; (202) 546-8329. Fax, (202) 546-6864. Paul C.B. Schenck, Chair; Rob Schenck, President.*

General e-mail, info@faithandaction.org

Web, www.nationalclergycouncil.org

Informal network of conservative and traditional Christian clergy and heads of religious organizations and societies. Advocates interjecting religious morality into public policy debates. Monitors legislation and regulations.

National Council of Catholic Women, *200 N. Glebe Rd., #703, Arlington, VA 22203; (703) 224-0990. Fax, (703) 224-0991. Sheila McCarron, Executive Director.*

General e-mail, nccw01@nccw.org

Web, www.nccw.org

Federation of Roman Catholic women's organizations. Provides a forum for Catholic women to research and discuss issues affecting the church and society. Interests include employment, family life, abortion, care for older adults, day care, world hunger, global water supplies, genetic engineering research, pornography legislation, and substance abuse. Special programs include volunteer respite care, leadership training for women, mentoring of mothers, and drug and alcohol abuse education. Monitors legislation and regulations.

National Council of Churches, *Washington Office, 110 Maryland Ave. N.E. 20002; (202) 544-2350. Fax, (202) 543-1297. Wesley M. Pattillo, Senior Program Director for Justice, Advocacy, and Communication, (212) 870-2227; Kevin Williams, Office Manager.*

Web, www.ncccusa.org

Membership: thirty-five Protestant, Anglican, and Orthodox denominations. Interests include racial and social equality; social welfare, economic justice, peace, and international issues; church-state relations; prayer in public schools; and federal aid to private schools. (Headquarters in New York.)

National Council of Jewish Women, *Washington Office, 1707 L St. N.W., #950 20036-4206; (202) 296-2588. Fax, (202) 331-7792. Sammie Moshenberg, Director.*

General e-mail, action@ncjwdc.org

Web, www.ncjw.org

Jewish women's membership organization. Activities include education, community service, and advocacy. Interests include women's issues; reproductive, civil, and constitutional rights; child care; judicial nominations; religion-state separation; and human needs funding issues. (Headquarters in New York.)

NCSJ: Advocates on Behalf of Jews in Russia, Ukraine, the Baltic States and Eurasia, *2020 K St. N.W., #7800 20006; (202) 898-2500. Fax, (202) 898-0822. Mark B. Levin, Executive Director.*

General e-mail, ncsj@ncsj.org

Web, www.ncsj.org

Advocacy group for the organized American Jewish community on issues concerning the former Soviet Union. Works with community and government leadership in the United States and in the former Soviet Union addressing issues of anti-Semitism, community relations, and promotion of democracy, tolerance, and U.S. engagement in the region.

NETWORK, *25 E St. N.W., #200 20001; (202) 347-9797. Fax, (202) 347-9864. Simone Campbell SSS, Executive Director.*

General e-mail, network@networklobby.org

Web, www.networklobby.org

Catholic social justice lobby that coordinates political activity and promotes economic and social justice. Monitors legislation and regulations.

Orthodox Union, *OU Institute for Public Affairs, 800 8th St. N.W., #318 20001; (202) 513-6484. Fax, (202) 289-8936. Nathan Diament, Director.*

General e-mail, ipadc@ou.org

Web, www.ou.org/public_affairs

Works to protect Jewish interests and freedoms through dissemination of policy briefings to government officials. Encourages Jewish law and a traditional perspective on public policy issues. Coordinates grassroots activities; sponsors a summer internship program for Jewish college students. (Headquarters in New York.)

Pew Forum on Religion and Public Life, *1615 L St. N.W., #700 20036; (202) 419-4550. Fax, (202) 419-4559. Luis Lugo, Director.*

General e-mail, info@pewforum.org

Web, www.pewforum.org

Nonpartisan organization that seeks to explore the impact of religion on public affairs, political behavior, the law, domestic policy, and international affairs. Conducts polling and independent research; serves as a clearinghouse and forum on these issues. Delivers findings to journalists, government officials, and other interested groups.

Presbyterian Church (U.S.A.), *Washington Office, 100 Maryland Ave. N.E., #410 20002; (202) 543-1126. Fax, (202) 543-7755. Catherine Gordon, Director (Acting).*

General e-mail, ga_washington_office@pcusa.org

Web, www.pcusa.org/washington

Provides information on the views of the general assembly of the Presbyterian church on public policy issues; monitors legislation affecting issues of concern. Interests include arms control, budget priorities, foreign policy, civil rights, religious liberty, church-state relations, economic justice, environmental justice, and public policy issues affecting women. (Headquarters in Louisville, Ky.)

Progressive National Baptist Convention Inc., *601 50th St. N.E. 20019; (202) 396-0558. Fax, (202) 398-4998. Tyrone S. Pitts, General Secretary.*

General e-mail, info@pnbc.org

Web, www.pnbc.org

Baptist denomination that supports missionaries, implements education programs, and advocates for civil and human rights.

Sojourners, *3333 14th St. N.W., #200 20010; (202) 328-8842. Fax, (202) 328-8757. Jim Wallis, Executive Director; Adam Taylor, Senior Political Director. Toll-free, (800) 714-7474.*

General e-mail, sojourners@sojo.net

Web, www.sojo.net

Membership: Catholics, Protestants, Evangelicals, and other interested Christians. Grassroots network that focuses on the intersection of faith, politics, and culture. (Merger of Sojourners and Call to Renewal.)

Union for Reform Judaism, *Religious Action Center of Reform Judaism, 2027 Massachusetts Ave. N.W. 20036; (202) 387-2800. Fax, (202) 667-9070. Rabbi David Saperstein, Director.*

General e-mail, rac@urj.org

Web, www.rac.org

Religious and educational organization concerned with social justice and religious liberty. Mobilizes the American Jewish community and serves as its advocate on issues concerning Jews around the world, including economic justice, civil rights, and international peace.

Unitarian Universalist Assn. of Congregations, *Washington Office, 1100 G St. N.W., #800 20005; (202) 393-2255. Fax, (202) 393-5494. Robert C. Keithan, Director.*

Web, www.uua.org/aboutus/professionalstaff/ advocacywitness/washingtonoffice

Monitors public policy and legislation. Interests include civil and religious liberties; the federal budget; international and interfaith affairs; human rights; and public policy affecting women, including reproductive rights policy. (Headquarters in Boston, Mass.)

United Church of Christ, *Washington Office, 100 Maryland Ave. N.E., #330 20002; (202) 543-1517. Fax, (202) 543-5994. Sandy Sorenson, Director.*

General e-mail, sorenses@ucc.org

Web, www.ucc.org

Studies public policy issues and promotes church policy on these issues; organizes legislative advocacy to address church views. Interests include health care, international peace, economic justice, the environment, climate change, and civil rights. (Headquarters in Cleveland, Ohio.)

United Jewish Communities (UJC), *Washington Office, 1720 Eye St. N.W., #800 20006; (202) 785-5900. Fax, (202) 785-4937. William Daroff, Director.*

General e-mail, dc@ujc.org

Web, www.ujc.org

Fundraising organization. Sustains and enhances the quality of Jewish life domestically and internationally. Advocates the needs of the Jewish community. Offers marketing, communications, and public relations support; coordinates a speakers bureau and Israeli emissaries. (Headquarters in New York.)

U.S. Conference of Catholic Bishops (USCCB), *3211 4th St. N.E. 20017; (202) 541-3000. Fax, (202) 541-3322. Msgr. David Malloy, General Secretary. Communications, (202) 541-3200.*

Web, www.usccb.org

Serves as a forum for bishops to exchange ideas, debate concerns of the church, and draft responses to religious and social issues. Provides information on doctrine and policies of the Roman Catholic church; develops religious education and training programs; formulates policy positions on social issues, including the economy, employment, federal budget priorities, voting rights, energy, health, housing, rural affairs, international military and political matters, human rights, the arms race, global economics, and immigration and refugee policy.

Washington Ethical Society, *7750 16th St. N.W. 20012; (202) 882-6650. Fax, (202) 829-1354. Richard Nugent, Senior Leader (Interim).*

General e-mail, wes@ethicalsociety.org

Web, www.ethicalsociety.org

A humanistic religious community that sets standards, distributes ethical culture materials, trains leaders, awards grants, publishes statements on moral issues and public policy, and coordinates national projects such as youth programs. (Affiliated with and formerly the Washington office of New York–based American Ethical Union.)

Women's Alliance for Theology, Ethics, and Ritual, *8121 Georgia Ave., #310, Silver Spring, MD 20910; (301) 589-2509. Fax, (301) 589-3150. Dianne L. Neu, Co-Director; Mary E. Hunt, Co-Director.*

General e-mail, water@hers.com

Web, www.hers.com/water

Feminist theological organization that focuses on issues concerning women and religion. Interests include social issues; work skills for women with disabilities; human rights in Latin America; and liturgies, rituals, counseling, and research.

TRAVEL AND TOURISM

▶AGENCIES

International Trade Administration (ITA), *(Commerce Dept.), Travel and Tourism Industries, 1401 Constitution Ave. N.W., #1003 20230-0001; (202) 482-0140. Fax, (202) 482-2887. Helen Marano, Director. TTY, (202) 482-4670.*

General e-mail, info@tinet.ita.doc.gov

Web, http://tinet.ita.doc.gov

Fosters international tourism trade development, including public-private partnerships; represents the United States in tourism-related meetings with foreign government officials. Assembles, analyzes, and disseminates data and statistics on travel and tourism to and from the United States.

National Park Service *(Interior Dept.), Tourism, 1201 Eye St. 20005; (202) 354-6986. Fax, (202) 571-5530. Dean T. Reeder, Director.*

General e-mail, dean_reeder@nps.gov

Web, www.nps.gov/tourism

Directs and supports the National Park Service's tourism program. Acts as liaison to government departments and agencies on tourism issues. Serves as the primary contact for national and international travel and tourism industry officials and professionals.

State Dept., *Consular Affairs: Special Issuance Agency, 1111 19th St. N.W., #200 20036; (202) 955-0198. Fax, (202) 955-0182. Gary Roach, Director. TTY, (888) 874-7793. National passport information, (877) 487-2778.*

Web, http://travel.state.gov

Administers passport laws and issues passports. (Most branches of the U.S. Postal Service and most U.S. district and state courts are authorized to accept applications and payment for passports and to administer the required oath to U.S. citizens. Completed applications are sent from the post office or court to the nearest State Dept. regional passport office for processing.) Maintains a variety of records received from the Overseas Citizens Services, including consular certificates of witness to marriage and reports of birth and death. (Individuals wishing to apply for a U.S. passport may seek additional information via the phone number or Web address listed above.)

▶CONGRESS

For a listing of relevant congressional committees and subcommittees, please see page 114 or the Appendix.

▶INTERNATIONAL ORGANIZATIONS

Organization of American States (OAS), *Tourism and Trade Section, 1889 F St. N.W., #300A 20006; (202) 458-3181. Fax, (202) 458-3190. Pamela Hamilton, Chief.*

General e-mail, tourism@oas.org

Web, www.oas.org/tourism

Responsible for matters related to tourism and its development in the hemisphere. Provides support to the Inter-American Travel Congress; works for sustainable tourism development and safety and security; promotes cooperation among international, regional, and subregional tourism offices.

▶NONGOVERNMENTAL

American Hotel and Lodging Assn., *1201 New York Ave. N.W., #600 20005-3931; (202) 289-3100. Fax, (202) 289-3199. Joseph A. McInerney, President; Thomas Corcoran, Chair. Press, (202) 289-3131.*

General e-mail, info@ahla.com

Web, www.ahla.com

Membership: state and city partner lodging associations. Provides operations, technical, educational, marketing, and communications services to members. Monitors legislation and regulations.

American Society of Travel Agents, *1101 King St., #200, Alexandria, VA 22314-2963; (703) 739-2782. Fax, (703) 684-8319. Chris Russo, President.*

General e-mail, askasta@astahq.com

Web, www.astanet.com

Membership: representatives of the travel industry. Works to safeguard the traveling public against fraud, misrepresentation, and other unethical practices. Offers training programs for travel agents. Consumer affairs department offers help for anyone with a travel complaint against a member of the association.

Center for Responsible Travel, *1333 H St. N.W., #300 East Tower 20005; (202) 347-9203. Fax, (202) 775-0819. Martha Honey, Executive Director.*

General e-mail, staff@responsibletravel.org

Web, www.responsibletravel.org

Designs, monitors, evaluates, and seeks to improve ecotourism and sustainable tourism principles and practices. (Affiliated with the Institute for Policy Studies and Stanford University and the International Ecotourism Society.)

Cruise Lines International Assn., *2111 Wilson Blvd., 8th Floor, Arlington, VA 22201; (703) 522-8463. Fax, (703) 522-3811. J. Michael Crye, President. Toll-free, (800) 595-9338.*

General e-mail, info@cruising.org

Web, www.cruising.org

Membership: chief executives of twenty-four cruise lines and other cruise industry professionals. Advises domestic and international regulatory organizations on shipping policy. Works with U.S. and international agencies to promote safety, public health, security, medical facilities, environmental awareness, and passenger protection. Monitors legislation and regulations. (Formerly the International Council of Cruise Lines.)

Destination Marketing Assn. International, *2025 M St. N.W., #500 20036-3309; (202) 296-7888. Fax, (202) 296-7889. Michael Gehrisch, President. Toll-free, (888) 275-3140.*

General e-mail, info@destinationmarketing.org

Web, www.destinationmarketing.org

Membership: travel- and tourism-related businesses, convention and meeting professionals, and tour operators. Encourages business travelers and tourists to visit local historic, cultural, and recreational areas; assists in meeting preparations. Monitors legislation and regulations. (Formerly the International Assn. of Convention and Visitor Bureaus.)

Hostelling International USA—American Youth Hostels, *8401 Colesville Rd., #600, Silver Spring, MD*

20910-9663; (301) 495-1240. Fax, (301) 495-6697. Russell Hedge, Executive Director.

General e-mail, members@hiusa.org

Web, www.hiusa.org

Provides opportunities for outdoor recreation and inexpensive educational travel and accommodations through hostelling. Member of the International Youth Hostel Federation.

International Assn. of Amusement Parks and Attractions, *1448 Duke St., Alexandria, VA 22314; (703) 836-4800. Fax, (703) 836-2824. Charles Bray, President. Press, (703) 299-5127.*

General e-mail, iaapa@iaapa.org

Web, www.iaapa.org

Membership: companies from around the world in the amusement parks and attractions industry. Conducts an international exchange program for members. Monitors legislation and regulations.

International Ecotourism Society, *1301 Clifton St. N.W. 20009; (202) 506-5033. Fax, (202) 789-7279. Kelly Bricker, Executive Director.*

General e-mail, info@ecotourism.org

Web, www.ecotourism.org

Promotes travel to natural areas in ways that conserve the environment and improve the situation of local peoples. (Affiliated with the Center for Responsible Travel.)

National Assn. of RV Parks and Campgrounds, *113 Park Ave., Falls Church, VA 22046; (703) 241-8801. Fax, (703) 241-1004. Linda Profaizer, President.*

General e-mail, info@arvc.org

Web, www.arvc.org

Represents the interests of commercial RV parks and campgrounds, park developers, membership resorts and campgrounds, and cabin and lodge resorts. Offers management services and group purchasing power. Monitors legislation and regulations.

National Business Travel Assn., *110 N. Royal St., 4th Floor, Alexandria, VA 22314-3274; (703) 684-0836. Fax, (703) 684-0263. Bill Connors, Executive Director.*

General e-mail, info@nbta.org

Web, www.nbta.org

Membership: corporate travel managers and travel suppliers. Promotes educational advancement of members and provides a forum for exchange of information on U.S. and international travel. Monitors legislation and regulations.

Passenger Vessel Assn., *901 N. Pitt St., #100, Alexandria, VA 22314; (703) 518-5005. Fax, (703) 518-5151. John R. Groundwater, Executive Director. Toll-free, (800) 807-8360.*

General e-mail, pvainfo@passengervessel.com

Web, www.passengervessel.com

Membership: owners, operators, and suppliers for U.S. and Canadian passenger vessels and international vessel companies. Interests include insurance, safety and security, and U.S. congressional impact upon dinner and excursion boats, car and passenger ferries, overnight cruise ships, and riverboat casinos. Monitors legislation and regulations.

Travel Industry Assn. of America, *1100 New York Ave. N.W., #450W 20005-3934; (202) 408-8422. Fax, (202) 408-1255. Roger J. Dow, President.*
Web, www.tia.org

Membership: business, professional, and trade associations and corporations of the travel industry and state and local associations (including official state government tourism offices) promoting tourism to a specific region or site. Encourages travel to and within the United States.

UNITE HERE, *1775 K St. N.W., #620 20006-1530; (202) 393-4373. Fax, (202) 223-6213. John W. Wilhelm, President, Hospitality Industry*
Web, www.unitehere.org

Membership: approximately 241,000 hotel and restaurant employees. Helps members negotiate pay, benefits, and better working conditions; conducts training programs and workshops. Monitors legislation and regulations. (Formerly Hotel Employees and Restaurant Employees International. Headquarters in New York.)

5 Education

GENERAL POLICY AND ANALYSIS

Basic Resources

►AGENCIES

Educational Resources Information Center (ERIC), *(Education Dept.),* 655 15th St. N.W., #500 20005; (202) 741-4298. Fax, (202) 628-3205. Lawrence Henry, Project Director. Technical Assistance and Information, (800) 538-3742.
General e-mail, ericacq@csc.com

Web, www.eric.ed.gov

Coordinates an online national information system of education literature and resources. Provides a centralized bibliographic and full-text database of journal articles and other published and unpublished materials. Available at no charge to educators worldwide. Managed by the Computer Sciences Corporation.

Education Dept., 400 Maryland Ave. S.W., #7W301 20202-0001; (202) 401-3000. Fax, (202) 401-0596. Arne Duncan, Secretary; Vacant, Deputy Secretary; Vacant, General Counsel. Information, (202) 401-2000. Press, (202) 401-1576. TTY, (800) 437-0833. Toll-free, (800) 872-5327.
Web, www.ed.gov

Establishes education policy and acts as principal adviser to the president on education matters; administers and coordinates most federal assistance programs on education.

Education Dept., *International Affairs,* 400 Maryland Ave. S.W., #7W104 20202; (202) 401-0430. Fax, (202) 401-2508. Vacant, Deputy Director.
General e-mail, international.affairs@ed.gov

Web, www.ed.gov/international

Responsible for the overall coordination of the Education Dept.'s international presence. Works with department program offices, support units, and senior leadership as well as with external partners, including other federal agencies, state and local agencies, foreign governments, international organizations, and the private sector.

Education Dept., *Legislation and Congressional Affairs,* 400 Maryland Ave. S.W., #6W300 20202-3500; (202) 401-0020. Fax, (202) 401-1438. Terrell Halaska, Assistant Secretary.
Web, www.ed.gov

Disseminates information on government programs that encourage public understanding and support for improving American education. Engages government, business, religious, and community organizations, as well as families, students, and the general public. Oversees recognition programs (Presidential Scholars, President's Education Awards, No Child Left Behind Blue Ribbon Schools).

Education Dept., *Office of Innovation and Improvement,* 400 Maryland Ave. S.W., #4W300 20202-0001; (202) 205-4500. Fax, (202) 205-4123. James Shelton, Assistant Deputy Secretary.
Web, www.ed.gov/about/offices/list/oii/index.html

Provides grants to states, schools, and community and nonprofit organizations for innovative and entrepreneurial education initiatives. Coordinates some provisions of the Elementary and Secondary Education Act as amended by the No Child Left Behind Act. Serves as the department's liaison and resource to the nonpublic education community; oversees the Family Policy Compliance Office.

Education Dept., *School Support and Technology Programs,* 400 Maryland Ave. S.W., #3E115 20202-6400; (202) 401-0039. Fax, (202) 205-5870. Jenelle Leonard, Director. Information, (800) 872-5327.
Web, www.ed.gov

Provides a coordinated strategy to focus federal resources on supporting improvements in schools; promotes development and implementation of comprehensive improvement plans that direct resources toward improved achievement for all students.

►CONGRESS

For a listing of relevant congressional committees and subcommittees, please see page 156 or the Appendix.

Government Accountability Office (GAO), *Education, Workforce, and Income Security,* 441 G St. N.W., #5928 20548; (202) 512-7215. Cynthia M. Fagnoni, Managing Director.
Web, www.gao.gov

Independent, nonpartisan agency in the legislative branch. Audits, analyzes, and evaluates Education Dept. programs; makes reports available to the public. (Formerly the General Accounting Office.)

►NONGOVERNMENTAL

Academy for Educational Development (AED), 1825 Connecticut Ave. N.W., #800 20009-5721; (202) 884-8000. Fax, (202) 884-8400. Stephen F. Moseley, President.
General e-mail, communicationsmail@aed.org

Web, www.aed.org

Works to improve access to completion of primary and secondary education in the United States and countries in Africa, Asia, Latin America, and the Middle East. Works to improve the quality of decision making in educational reform and workforce development; emphasis on teacher preparation and student achievement. Programs support children with disabilities, Migrant Head Start, high school and middle school reform, youth in transition from school to career, education for out-of-school use, and access to higher education. Prioritizes use of technology to improve learning.

EDUCATION RESOURCES IN CONGRESS

For a complete listing of Congress committees, including their full contact information, leadership, membership, and jurisdictions, please refer to the Appendix on pages 724–837.

JOINT COMMITTEES:

Joint Committee on the Library of Congress, (202) 224-6352.

HOUSE:

House Administration Committee, (202) 225-2061.
Web, cha.house.gov

House Agriculture Committee, Subcommittee on Department Operations, Oversight, Nutrition, and Forestry, (202) 225-6395.
Web, agriculture.house.gov

House Appropriations Committee, Subcommittee on Interior, Environment, and Related Agencies, (202) 225-3081.
Web, appropriations.house.gov

  Subcommittee on Labor, Health and Human Services, Education, and Related Agencies, (202) 225-3508.

  Subcommittee on Legislative Branch, (202) 226-7252.

House Education and Labor Committee, (202) 225-3725.
Web, edworkforce.house.gov

  Subcommittee on Early Childhood, Elementary, and Secondary Education, (202) 225-3725.

  Subcommittee on Healthy Families and Communities, (202) 225-3725.

  Subcommittee on Higher Education, Lifelong Learning, and Competitiveness, (202) 225-3725.

House Natural Resources Committee, (202) 225-6065.
Web, resourcescommittee.house.gov

House Oversight and Government Reform Committee, Subcommittee on Domestic Policy, (202) 225-6427.
Web, oversight.house.gov

House Science and Technology Committee, Subcommittee on Research and Science Education, (202) 225-9662.
Web, science.house.gov

SENATE:

Senate Agriculture, Nutrition, and Forestry Committee, Subcommittee on Nutrition and Food Assistance, Sustainable and Organic Agriculture, and General Legislation, (202) 224-2035.
Web, agriculture.senate.gov

Senate Appropriations Committee, Subcommittee on Interior, Environment and Related Agencies, (202) 224-7363.
Web, appropriations.senate.gov

  Subcommittee on Labor, Health and Human Services, Education and Related Agencies, (202) 224-9145.

  Subcommittee on Legislative Branch, (202) 224-3477.

Senate Banking, Housing and Urban Affairs Committee, (202) 224-7391.
Web, banking.senate.gov

Senate Commerce, Science, and Transportation Committee, Subcommittee on Science, Technology and Innovation, (202) 224-0415.
Web, commerce.senate.gov

Senate Health, Education, Labor and Pensions Committee, (202) 224-5375.
Web, help.senate.gov

  Subcommittee on Children and Families, (202) 224-5630 or (202) 224-5800.

Senate Indian Affairs Committee, (202) 224-2251.
Web, indian.senate.gov

Senate Rules and Administration Committee, (202) 224-6352.
Web, rules.senate.gov

American Institutes for Research, *1000 Thomas Jefferson St. N.W. 20007; (202) 403-5000. Fax, (202) 403-5001. Sol Pelavin, President.*
Web, www.air.org

Conducts behavioral and social science research and provides technical assistance both domestically and internationally in the areas of education, health, and workforce productivity.

America's Choice, *555 13th St. N.W., #500W 20004; (202) 783-3668. Fax, (202) 783-3672. Judy Codding, President.*
General e-mail, info@americaschoice.org
Web, www.americaschoice.org

Provides comprehensive school and instructional design services, technical assistance, and teacher professional development. Established set of internally bench-marked

Education Department

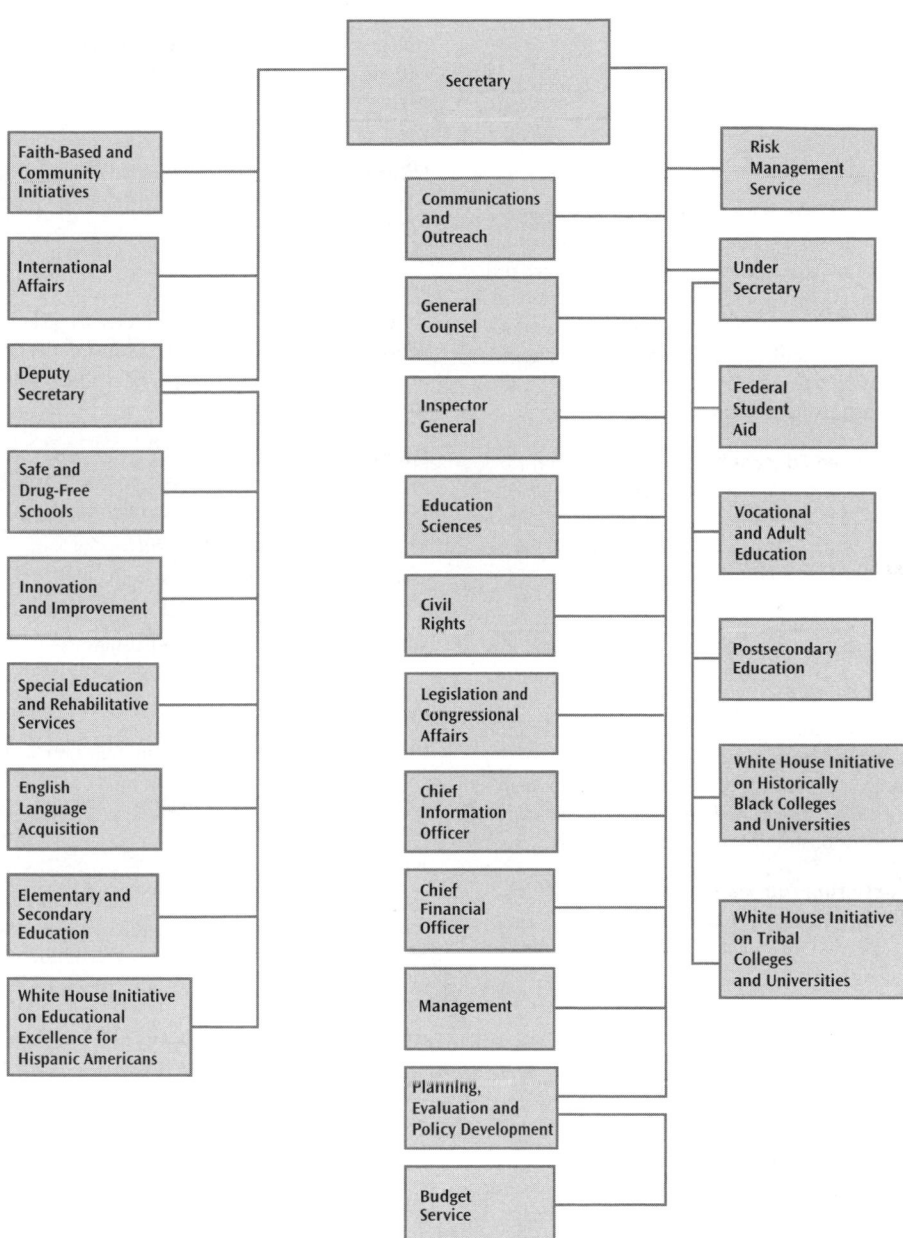

Secretary		

- Faith-Based and Community Initiatives
- International Affairs
- Deputy Secretary
- Safe and Drug-Free Schools
- Innovation and Improvement
- Special Education and Rehabilitative Services
- English Language Acquisition
- Elementary and Secondary Education
- White House Initiative on Educational Excellence for Hispanic Americans

- Communications and Outreach
- General Counsel
- Inspector General
- Education Sciences
- Civil Rights
- Legislation and Congressional Affairs
- Chief Information Officer
- Chief Financial Officer
- Management
- Planning, Evaluation and Policy Development
- Budget Service

- Risk Management Service
- Under Secretary
- Federal Student Aid
- Vocational and Adult Education
- Postsecondary Education
- White House Initiative on Historically Black Colleges and Universities
- White House Initiative on Tribal Colleges and Universities

solutions to improve American schools. (For-profit subsidiary of National Center on Education and the Economy [NCEE].)

Annenberg Public Policy Center, *529 14th St. N.W., #320 20045; (202) 879-6700. Fax, (202) 879-6707. Kathleen Hall Jamieson, Director.*
General e-mail, appcdc@appcpenn.org

Web, www.annenbergpublicpolicycenter.org

Supports research on public policy issues at the federal level. Sponsors lectures and conferences. (Headquarters in Philadelphia, Pa.; part of the University of Pennsylvania.)

Aspen Institute, *1 Dupont Circle N.W., #700 20036; (202) 736-5800. Fax, (202) 467-0790. Walter Isaacson, President. Press, (202) 736-3849.*
General e-mail, info@aspeninstitute.org

Web, www.aspeninstitute.org

Promotes consideration of the public good in a wide variety of areas, including education policy. Conducts educational programs; publishes reports.

Center for Education Reform, *910 17th St. N.W., #1120 20006; (301) 986-8088. Fax, (301) 986-1826. Jeanne Allen, President. Toll-free, (800) 521-2118.*
General e-mail, cer@edreform.com

Web, www.edreform.com

Research and informational organization that promotes education reform through grassroots advocacy. Interests include charter school laws, school choice programs, teacher qualifications, and educational standards. Web site serves as a networking forum for parents, educators, policymakers, and others interested in education reform, providing news reports and information on education seminars throughout the country.

Center for Law and Education, *Washington Office, 1875 Connecticut Ave. N.W., #510 20009-5728; (202) 986-3000. Fax, (202) 986-6648. Paul Weckstein, Co-Director; Kathleen Boundy, Co-Director. Publications, (202) 462-7688.*
General e-mail, cle@cleweb.org

Web, www.cleweb.org

Works to advance the right of all students, and low-income students in particular, to a high-quality education. Interests include testing and tracking; bilingual education; discriminatory discipline; special education; special needs for Native Americans, migrants, and Hispanics; parent, community, and student participation in education; and vocational and compensatory education. (Headquarters in Boston, Mass.)

Charles F. Kettering Foundation, *Washington Office, 444 N. Capitol St. N.W., #434 20001-1512; (202) 393-4478. Fax, (202) 393-7644. David Matthews, President (located in Ohio).*
General e-mail, hsaunders@kettering.org

Web, www.kettering.org

Works to improve the domestic policy-making process through citizen deliberation. Supports international programs focusing on unofficial, citizen-to-citizen diplomacy. Encourages greater citizen involvement in formation of public policy. Interests include public education and at-risk youths. (Headquarters in Dayton, Ohio.)

Council for Advancement and Support of Education, *1307 New York Ave. N.W., #1000 20005-4701; (202) 328-5900. Fax, (202) 387-4973. John Lippincott, President.*
General e-mail, memberservicecenter@case.org

Membership: two- and four-year colleges, universities, and independent schools. Offers professional education and training programs to members; advises members on institutional advancement issues, including fundraising, public relations programs, government relations, and management. Library open to professional members by appointment.

DECA Inc., *1908 Association Dr., Reston, VA 20191-1594; (703) 860-5000. Fax, (703) 860-4013. Edward L. Davis,* Executive Director.
Web, www.deca.org

Educational organization that helps high school and college students develop skills in marketing, management, and entrepreneurship. Promotes business and education partnerships.

Education Sector, *1201 Connecticut Ave. N.W., #850 20036; (202) 552-2840. Fax, (202) 775-5877. Kevin Carey, Research and Policy Manager.*
General e-mail, info@educationsector.org

Web, www.educationsector.org

Independent think tank dedicated to promoting sound educational policies and guiding educational debates. Produces original research and policy analysis. Monitors legislation and regulations.

Ethics Resource Center, *2345 Crystal Dr., #201, Arlington, VA 22202; (703) 647-2185. Fax, (703) 647-2180. Patricia J. Harned, President. Information, (800) 777-1285.*
General e-mail, ethics@ethics.org

Web, www.ethics.org

Nonpartisan educational organization that fosters ethical practices among individuals and institutions. Interests include research, knowledge building, education, and advocacy.

Institute for Educational Leadership, *4455 Connecticut Ave. N.W., #310 20008; (202) 822-8405. Fax, (202) 872-4050. Elizabeth L. Hale, President.*
General e-mail, iel@iel.org

Web, www.iel.org

Works with educators, human services personnel, government officials, and association executives to improve educational opportunities for youths; conducts research on education issues.

National Assn. of State Boards of Education, *277 S. Washington St., #100, Alexandria, VA 22314-3678; (703) 684-4000. Fax, (703) 836-2313. Brenda L. Welburn, Executive Director.*
General e-mail, boards@nasbe.org

Web, www.nasbe.org

Membership: members of state boards of education, state board attorneys, and executives to state boards. Works to strengthen state boards as the preeminent educational policy-making bodies for students and citizens.

National Center for Education Information, *4401A Connecticut Ave. N.W., #212 20008; (202) 362-3444. C. Emily Feistritzer, President. Phone and fax are same number.*
General e-mail, emilyf@ncei.com

Web, www.ncei.com

Specializes in survey research and data analysis of alternative teacher preparation and certification. Conducts national and state surveys of teachers, school administrators, school board presidents, state departments of education, local school districts, and individuals interested in becoming teachers.

National Center on Education and the Economy (NCEE), *555 13th St. N.W., #500 20004; (202) 783-3668. Fax, (202) 783-3672. Marc Tucker, President. General e-mail, info@ncee.org*

Web, www.ncee.org

Provides research, analysis, advocacy, tools, and technical assistance to improve the nation's school systems and student performances. (Affiliated with America's Choice and the National Institute for School Leadership.)

National Children's Museum, *955 L'Enfant Plaza North S.W., #5100 20024; (202) 675-4120. Fax, (202) 675-4140. Kathy Dwyer Southern, President. Press, (202) 675-4160. General e-mail, info@ncm.museum*

Web, www.ncm.museum

Designs, implements, and conducts studies in education. Interests include the creation and development of new educational methods, materials, and structures.

National Community Education Assn., *3929 Old Lee Hwy., #91-A, Fairfax, VA 22030-2401; (703) 359-8973. Fax, (703) 359-0972. Beth Robertson, Executive Director. General e-mail, ncea@ncea.com*

Web, www.ncea.com

Works for greater recognition of community education programs, services, and personnel. Interests include business-education partnerships to improve schools; lifelong learning; school-site child care and latchkey programs; extended learning opportunities and after-school programs; and parental involvement in public education.

National Humanities Institute (NHI), *P.O. Box 1387, Bowie, MD 20718-1387; (301) 464-4277. Fax, (301) 464-4277. Joseph Baldacchino, President. Phone and fax are the same number. General e-mail, mail@nhinet.org*

Web, www.nhinet.org

Promotes research, publishing, and teaching in the humanities. Interests include the effect of the humanities on society.

National Institute for School Leadership (NISL), *555 13th St. N.W., #500W 20004; (202) 783-3668. Robert Hughes, President. General e-mail, nislinfo@ncee.org*

Web, www.nisl.net

Offers research-based professional development programs designed to give principals the knowledge and skills they need to be instructional leaders and improve student achievement in their schools. (For-profit subsidiary of National Center on Education and the Economy [NCEE].)

National School Public Relations Assn., *15948 Derwood Rd., Rockville, MD 20855; (301) 519-0496. Fax, (301) 519-0494. Richard D. Bagin, Executive Director.*

General e-mail, nspra@nspra.org

Web, www.nspra.org

Membership: educators and individuals interested in improving communications in education. Works to improve communication between educators and the public on the needs of schools. Provides educators with information on public relations and policy developments.

Internships, Fellowships, Grants

▶**AGENCIES**

Harry S. Truman Scholarship Foundation, *712 Jackson Pl. N.W., 3rd Floor 20006-4901; (202) 395-4831. Fax, (202) 395-6995. Frederick G. Slabach, Executive Secretary. General e-mail, office@truman.gov*

Web, www.truman.gov

Memorial to Harry S. Truman established by Congress. Provides students preparing for careers in public service with scholarships. (Candidates are nominated by their respective colleges or universities while in their third year of undergraduate study.)

National Endowment for the Arts (NEA), *1100 Pennsylvania Ave. N.W. 20506-0001; (202) 682-5400. Fax, (202) 682-5611. Dana Gioia, Chair. Press, (202) 682-5570. TTY, (202) 682-5496. General e-mail, webmgr@arts.endow.gov*

Web, www.arts.gov

Independent federal grant-making agency. Awards grants to nonprofit, tax-exempt arts organizations, art service organizations, federally recognized tribal communities, state and local government offices, and others, in three categories: Access to Artistic Excellence, Learning in the Arts for Children and Youth, and Challenge America: Reaching Every Community Fast-Track Review Grants.

National Endowment for the Humanities (NEH), *1100 Pennsylvania Ave. N.W., #503 20506; (202) 606-8310. Fax, (202) 606-8588. Carole Watson, Chair. Information, (202) 606-8400. Library, (202) 606-8244. Press, (202) 606-8446. TTY, (202) 606-8282. General e-mail, info@neh.gov*

Web, www.neh.gov

Independent federal grant-making agency. Awards grants to individuals and institutions for research, scholarship, and educational and public programs (including broadcasts, museum exhibitions, lectures, and symposia) in the humanities (defined as study of archaeology; history; jurisprudence; language; linguistics; literature; philosophy; comparative religion; ethics; history, criticism, and theory of the arts; and humanistic aspects of the social sciences). Funds preservation of books, newspapers, historical documents, and photographs.

National Endowment for the Humanities (NEH), *Education, 1100 Pennsylvania Ave. N.W., #302*

20506; (202) 606-8500. Fax, (202) 606-8394. William
Craig Rice, Director.
General e-mail, education@neh.gov

Web, www.neh.gov

Offers fellowships, stipends, seminars, and institutes
for higher education faculty, school teachers, and independent scholars. Conducts research.

National Science Foundation (NSF), *Graduate*
Education, 4201 Wilson Blvd., #875, Arlington, VA 22230;
(703) 292-8630. Fax, (703) 292-9048. Carol Stoel, Director
(Acting). TTY, (800) 281-8749.
Web, www.nsf.gov

Supports activities to strengthen the education of
research scientists and engineers; promotes career development; offers pre-doctoral fellowships and traineeships for
study and research.

President's Commission on White House Fellowships,
1900 E St. N.W., #B431 20415; (202) 395-4522. Fax, (202)
395-6179. Janet Slaughter Eissenstat, Director.
Web, www.whitehouse.gov/fellows

Nonpartisan commission that provides professionals
from all sectors of national life with the opportunity to
observe firsthand the processes of the federal government.
Fellows work for one year as special assistants to cabinet
members or to principal members of the White House
staff. Qualified applicants have demonstrated superior
accomplishments early in their careers and have a commitment to leadership and public service.

Smithsonian Institution, *Office of Fellowships,* 470
L'Enfant Plaza S.W., #7102 20013 (mailing address: P.O.
Box 37012, MRC 902, Washington, DC 20013-7012);
(202) 633-7070. Fax, (202) 633-7069. Catherine F. Harris,
Director.
General e-mail, siofg@si.edu

Web, www.si.edu/research+study

Administers internships and fellowships in residence
for study and research at the Smithsonian Institution in
history of science and technology, American and cultural
history, history of art, anthropology, evolutionary and
systematic biology, environmental sciences, astrophysics
and astronomy, earth sciences, and tropical biology.

Woodrow Wilson International Center for Scholars,
1300 Pennsylvania Ave. N.W. 20004-3027; (202) 691-
4000. Fax, (202) 691-4001. Lee Hamilton, Director.
General e-mail, fellowships@wilsoncenter.org

Web, www.wilsoncenter.org

Supports research in the social studies and humanities. Awards fellowships to individuals from a wide variety
of backgrounds, including academia, government, the
nonprofit sector, the corporate world, and the professions.
Hosts public policy and senior scholars who conduct
research and write in a variety of disciplines. Offers grant
competitions through regional programs: the Asia Program, the Kennan Institute, East European Studies, and
the Canada Institute.

▶**NONGOVERNMENTAL**

American Architectural Foundation, 1799 New York
Ave. N.W. 20006; (202) 626-7318. Fax, (202) 626-7420.
Ronald E. Bogle, President.
General e-mail, info@archfoundation.org

Web, www.archfoundation.org

Seeks to advance the quality of American architecture.
Works to increase public awareness and understanding
and to apply new technology to create more humane
environments. Acts as liaison between the profession and
the public. Awards grants for architecture-oriented projects. Operates the historic Octagon Museum.

**American Assn. of University Women Educational
Foundation,** 1111 16th St. N.W. 20036; (202) 728-7602.
Fax, (202) 463-7169. Linda D. Hallman, Executive Director.
General e-mail, foundation@aauw.org

Web, www.aauw.org

Awards fellowships and grants to women for various
areas of study and educational pursuit. Offers fellowships
to foreign women coming to the United States for one
year of graduate study. Awards grants to women returning to school for postbaccalaureate education or professional development.

American Political Science Assn. (APSA), *Congressional*
Fellowship Program, 1527 New Hampshire Ave. N.W.
20036-1206; (202) 483-2512. Fax, (202) 483-2657. Jeffrey
R. Biggs, Program Director.
General e-mail, cfp@apsanet.org

Web, www.apsanet.org/about/cfp

Places mid-career political scientists, journalists, faculty
of medical schools (Robert Wood Johnson Fellowships),
and federal executives in congressional offices and committees for nine-month fellowships. Individual government
agencies nominate federal executive participants.

Business and Professional Women's Foundation,
1620 Eye St. N.W., #210 20006; (202) 293-1100.
Fax, (202) 861-0298. Diane M. Polangin, President.
General e-mail, foundation@bpw.org

Web, www.bpwfoundation.org

Works to improve women's economic status by promoting their employment at all levels in all occupations. Provides mature women seeking training and education with
scholarships and loans to increase their job skills. Awards
grants for doctoral research on women's economic issues.
(Affiliate of Business and Professional Women U.S.A.)

Center for the Study of the Presidency, 1020 19th St.
N.W., #250 20036; (202) 872-9800. Fax, (202) 872-9811.
David M. Abshire, President.
General e-mail, center@thepresidency.org

Web, www.thepresidency.org

Membership: college students, government officials,
and business leaders interested in the presidency, government, and politics. Conducts conferences, lectures, and
symposiums on domestic, economic, and foreign policy

issues. Publishes papers, essays, books, and reports on various aspects of the presidency and Congress.

Congressional Black Caucus Foundation, *1720 Massachusetts Ave. N.W. 20036-1903; (202) 263-2800. Fax, (202) 775-0773. Elsie Scott, President.*
General e-mail, info@cbcfinc.org

Web, www.cbcfinc.org

Conducts public policy research on issues of concern to African Americans. Sponsors fellowship programs in which professionals and academic candidates work on congressional committees and subcommittees. Sponsors internship, scholarship, and fellowship programs.

Council for International Exchange of Scholars, *3007 Tilden St. N.W., #5L 20008-3009; (202) 686-4000. Fax, (202) 362-3442. Sabine O'Hara, Executive Director.*
General e-mail, apprequest@cies.iie.org

Web, www.cies.org

Cooperates with the U.S. government in administering Fulbright grants for university teaching and advanced research abroad. (Affiliated with the American Council of Learned Societies.)

Council on Foundations, *2121 Crystal Drive, Ste. 700, Arlington, VA 22202; (800) 673-9036. Steve Gunderson, President.*
General e-mail, info@cof.org

Web, www.cof.org

Membership: independent community, family, and public- and company-sponsored foundations; corporate giving programs; and foundations in other countries. Promotes responsible and effective philanthropy through educational programs, publications, government relations, and promulgation of a set of principles and practices for effective grant making.

Education Trust, *1250 H St. N.W., #700 20005; (202) 293-1217. Fax, (202) 293-2605. Kati Haycock, President.*
General e-mail, lsingleton@edtrust.org

Web, www.edtrust.org

Researches and disseminates data on student achievement. Provides assistance to school districts, colleges, and other organizations to raise student achievement, especially among poor and minority students. Monitors legislation and regulations.

Foundation Center, *Washington Office, 1627 K St. N.W., 3rd Floor 20006-1708; (202) 331-1400. Fax, (202) 331-1739. Patricia Pasqual, Director.*
General e-mail, feedback@fdncenter.org

Web, www.foundationcenter.org/washington

Publishes foundation guides. Serves as a clearinghouse on foundations and corporate giving, nonprofit management, fundraising, and grants for individuals. Provides training and seminars on fundraising and grant writing. Operates libraries in Atlanta, Cleveland, New York, San Francisco, and Washington, D.C. Libraries open to the public. (Headquarters in New York.)

The Fund for American Studies (TFAS), *1706 New Hampshire Ave. N.W. 20009; (202) 986-0384. Fax, (202) 986-0390. Roger R. Ream, President. Toll-free, (800) 741-6964 (outside D.C. area).*
General e-mail, info@tfas.org

Web, www.tfas.org

Sponsors summer and semester internships for college undergraduate students on comparative political and economic systems, business and government affairs, political journalism, philanthropy, and voluntary service; grants scholarships to qualified students for study-internship programs.

Institute of International Education, *National Security Education Program, 1400 K St. N.W., #650 20005-2403; (202) 326-7697. Fax, (202) 326-7672. Chris Powers, Director. Information, (800) 618-6737.*
General e-mail, boren@iie.org

Web, www.borenawards.org

Administers Boren Awards and Language Flagship programs; provides scholarships, fellowships, and institutional grants to academics with an interest in foreign affairs and national security.

National Journalism Center, *529 14th St. N.W., #937 20045; (202) 628-1490. Fax, (202) 628-1491. Alex X. Mooney, Executive Director.*
Web, www.nationaljournalismcenter.org

Sponsors a comprehensive internship program in journalism. Operates a job bank to help place alumni in permanent media positions. Sponsors a series of training seminars that enhance students' knowledge of policy reporting in the areas of economics, education, and business.

The Washington Center for Internships and Academic Seminars, *1333 16th St. N.W. 20036-2205; (202) 238-7900. Fax, (202) 238-7700. Michael B. Smith, President. Information, (800) 486-8921.*
General e-mail, info@twc.edu

Web, http;//ies.ed.gov/nesser/

Arranges congressional, agency, and public service internships for college undergraduate students for credit. Sponsors classes and lectures as part of the internship program. Scholarships and stipends available. Fee for internship and housing assistance.

Washington Center for Politics and Journalism, *The Watergate, 600 New Hampshire Ave. N.W., 4th Floor 20037 (mailing address: P.O. Box 15239, Washington, DC 20003-0239); (202) 296-8455. Fax, (800) 858-8365. Terry Michael, Executive Director.*
General e-mail, terrymichael@wcpj.org

Web, www.wcpj.org

Offers internships in political journalism to undergraduate and graduate students and recent graduates; provides a $3,000 stipend for living expenses. The Politics & Journalism Semester provides for sixteen-week fall and winter/spring sessions, which include full-time work in

Washington news bureaus and twice weekly seminars in campaign, governance, and interest group politics for future political reporters.

Women's Research and Education Institute (WREI), *1828 L St. N.W. 20036; (202) 280-2720. Fax, (202) 332-2949. Susan Scanlan, President.*
General e-mail, wrei@wrei.org

Web, www.wrei.org

Provides data and analysis of issues affecting women and their families to policymakers, the press, and the public. Sponsors Congressional Fellowships on Women and Public Policy for graduate students who are placed in congressional offices for one academic year to work on policy issues affecting women. Its Women in the Military project advocates on policy issues affecting women in uniform through publications and conferences.

Professional Interests and Benefits

▶**NONGOVERNMENTAL**

American Assn. of Colleges for Teacher Education, *1307 New York Ave. N.W., #300 20005-4701; (202) 293-2450. Fax, (202) 457-8095. Sharon P. Robinson, President.*
General e-mail, aacte@aacte.org

Web, www.aacte.org

Membership: colleges and universities with teacher education programs. Informs members about state and federal policies affecting teacher education and about professional issues such as accreditation, certification, and assessment. Collects and analyzes information on education.

American Assn. of School Administrators, *801 N. Quincy St., #700, Arlington, VA 22203-1730; (703) 528-0700. Fax, (703) 841-1543. Daniel Domenech, Executive Director.*
General e-mail, info@aasa.org

Web, www.aasa.org

Membership: more than 13,000 educational leaders, including chief executive officers, superintendents, senior-level school administrators, cabinet members, and professors, as well as aspiring school system leaders. Seeks to support and develop effective school system leaders through publications and professional development workshops.

American Federation of School Administrators, *1101 17th St. N.W., #408 20036-4704; (202) 986-4209. Fax, (202) 986-4211. Jill Levy, President.*
General e-mail, afsa@admin.org

Web, www.admin.org

Membership: approximately 20,000 school administrators, including principals, vice principals, directors, and superintendents in the United States, Puerto Rico, and U.S. Virgin Islands. Helps members negotiate pay, benefits, and better working conditions; conducts training

programs and workshops. Monitors legislation and regulations. (Affiliated with the AFL-CIO.)

American Federation of Teachers (AFT), *555 New Jersey Ave. N.W. 20001-2079; (202) 879-4400. Fax, (202) 879-4545. Randi Weingarten, President.*
General e-mail, online@aft.org

Web, www.aft.org

Membership: 1.4 million public and private school teachers, higher education faculty, school support staff, state and local government employees, and nurses and health care professionals. Assists members with contract negotiation and grievances; conducts training programs and workshops. Monitors legislation and regulations. (Affiliated with the AFL-CIO.)

American Political Science Assn. (APSA), *1527 New Hampshire Ave. N.W. 20036-1206; (202) 483-2512. Fax, (202) 483-2657. Michael A. Brintnall, Executive Director.*
General e-mail, apsa@apsanet.org

Web, www.apsanet.org

Membership: political scientists, primarily college and university professors. Promotes scholarly inquiry into all aspects of political science, including international affairs and comparative government. Works to increase public understanding of politics; provides services to facilitate and enhance research, teaching, and professional development of its members. Acts as liaison with federal agencies, Congress, and the public. Seeks to improve the status of women and minorities in the profession. Offers congressional fellowships, workshops, and awards. Provides information on political science issues.

Assn. of School Business Officials International, *11401 N. Shore Dr., Reston, VA 20190-4232; (703) 478-0405. Fax, (703) 478-0205. John Musso, Executive Director.*
General e-mail, asboreg@asbointl.org

Web, www.asbointl.org

Membership: administrators, directors, and others involved in school business management. Works to educate members on tools, techniques, and procedures of school business management. Researches, analyzes, and disseminates information; conducts workshops.

Assn. of Teacher Educators, *8503 Euclid Ave., #4, Manassas Park, VA 20111-2400 (mailing address: P.O. Box 793, Manassas, VA 20113); (703) 331-0911. Fax, (703) 331-3666. David A. Ritchey, Executive Director.*
General e-mail, info@ate1.org

Web, www.ate1.org

Membership: individuals and public and private agencies involved with teacher education. Seeks to improve teacher education at all levels; conducts workshops and conferences; produces and disseminates publications.

Council of Chief State School Officers, *1 Massachusetts Ave. N.W., #700 20001-1431; (202) 336-7000. Fax, (202) 408-8072. Gene Wilhoit, Executive Director. Press, (202) 336-7034.*

General e-mail, info@ccsso.org

Web, www.ccsso.org

Membership: the public officials who head departments of elementary and secondary education in the states, the District of Columbia, the Department of Defense Education Activity, and five U.S. extra-state jurisdictions. Provides leadership, advocacy, and technical assistance on major educational issues. Seeks member consensus on major educational issues and advocates issue positions to civic and professional organizations, federal agencies, Congress, and the public.

Federal Education Assn., *1201 16th St. N.W., #117 20036; (202) 822-7850. Fax, (202) 822-7867. Michael Priser, President.*
General e-mail, fea@feaonline.org

Web, www.feaonline.org

Membership: teachers and personnel of Defense Dept. schools for military dependents in the United States and abroad. Helps members negotiate pay, benefits, and better working conditions. Provides professional development through workshops and publications. Monitors legislation and regulations.

International Test and Evaluation Assn., *4400 Fair Lakes Court, #104, Fairfax, VA 22033-3899; (703) 631-6220. Fax, (703) 631-6221. Lori Tremmel Freeman, Executive Director.*
General e-mail, itea@itea.org

Web, www.itea.org

Membership: engineers, scientists, managers, and other industry, government, and academic professionals interested in testing and evaluating products and complex systems. Provides a forum for information exchange; monitors international research.

National Assn. of Biology Teachers, *12030 Sunrise Valley Dr., #110, Reston, VA 20191-3409; (703) 264-9696. Fax, (703) 264-7778. Jacki Reeves-Pepin, Director of Development. Information, (800) 406-0775.*
General e-mail, office@nabt.org

Web, www.nabt.org

Membership: biology teachers and others interested in biology and life sciences education at the elementary, secondary, and collegiate levels. Provides professional development opportunities through its publication program, summer workshops, conventions, and national award programs. Interests include teaching standards, science curriculum, and issues affecting biology and life sciences education.

National Business Education Assn., *1914 Association Dr., Reston, VA 20191-1596; (703) 860-8300. Fax, (703) 620-4483. Janet M. Treichel, Executive Director.*
General e-mail, nbea@nbea.org

Web, www.nbea.org

Membership: business education teachers and others interested in the field. Provides information on business education; offers teaching materials; sponsors conferences.

Monitors legislation and regulations affecting business education.

National Council for Accreditation of Teacher Education, *2010 Massachusetts Ave. N.W., #500 20036-1023; (202) 466-7496. Fax, (202) 296-6620. James Cibulka, President.*
General e-mail, ncate@ncate.org

Web, www.ncate.org

Evaluates and accredits schools and departments of education at colleges and universities. Publishes list of accredited institutions and standards for accreditation.

National Council for the Social Studies (NCSS), *8555 16th St., #500, Silver Spring, MD 20910; (301) 588-1800. Fax, (301) 588-2049. Susan Griffin, Executive Director. Publications, (800) 683-0812.*
General e-mail, information@ncss.org

Web, www.socialstudies.org

Membership: curriculum developers, educational administrators, state supervisors, and social studies educators, including teachers of history, political science, geography, economics, civics, psychology, sociology, and anthropology. Promotes the teaching of social studies; encourages research; sponsors publications; works with other organizations to advance social studies education.

National Council of Teachers of Mathematics, *1906 Association Dr., Reston, VA 20191-1502; (703) 620-9840. Fax, (703) 476-2970. James M. Rubillo, Executive Director.*
General e-mail, nctm@nctm.org

Web, www.nctm.org

Membership: teachers of mathematics in elementary and secondary schools and two-year colleges; university teacher education faculty; students; and other interested persons. Works for the improvement of classroom instruction at all levels. Serves as forum and information clearinghouse on issues related to mathematics education. Offers educational materials and conferences. Monitors legislation and regulations.

National Education Assn. (NEA), *1201 16th St. N.W. 20036-3290; (202) 833-4000. Fax, (202) 822-7974. Dennis Van Roekel, President.*
Web, www.nea.org

Membership: more than 3.2 million educators from preschool to university graduate programs. Promotes the interest of the profession of teaching and the cause of education in the United States. Monitors legislation and regulations at state and national levels.

National Science Resources Center, *901 D St. S.W., #704-B 20024; (202) 633-2972. Fax, (202) 287-7309. Sally Goetz Shuler, Executive Director.*
General e-mail, shulers@si.edu

Web, www.nsrconline.org

Sponsored by the Smithsonian Institution and the National Academy of Sciences. Works to establish effective science programs for all students. Disseminates research information; develops curriculum materials; seeks to increase public support for change of science education through the development of strategic partnerships.

National Science Teachers Assn., *1840 Wilson Blvd., Arlington, VA 22201-3000; (703) 243-7100. Fax, (703) 243-7177. Francis Eberle, Executive Director.*
General e-mail, publicinfo@nsta.org

Web, www.nsta.org

Membership: science teachers from elementary through college levels. Seeks to improve science education; provides forum for exchange of information. Monitors legislation and regulations.

NEA Foundation for the Improvement of Education, *1201 16th St. N.W., #416 20036-3207; (202) 822-7840. Fax, (202) 822-7779. Harriet Sanford, President.*
General e-mail, foundation_info@nea.org

Web, www.neafoundation.org

Offers grants and programs to public educators to improve teaching techniques, increase classroom innovations, and otherwise further professional development. Grant areas include science, technology, engineering, and mathematics teaching and learning, with a current special emphasis on "green" grants. Program specialties include strategies for improving achievement rates for poor and minority students.

NRTA: AARP's Educator Community, *601 E St. N.W. 20049; (202) 434-2380. Fax, (202) 434-3439. Megan Stevens Hookey, Vice President (Interim). Information, (888) 687-2277.*
General e-mail, gruiz@aarp.org

Web, www.aarp.org/nrta

Membership: active and retired teachers and other school personnel (elementary through postsecondary) over age fifty. Provides members with information on relevant national issues. Provides state associations of retired school personnel with technical assistance. (Formerly the National Retired Teachers Assn.)

Teachers of English to Speakers of Other Languages Inc. (TESOL), *700 S. Washington St., #200, Alexandria, VA 22314-4287; (703) 836-0774. Fax, (703) 836-7864. Charles Amorosino, Executive Director. Information, (888) 547-3369.*
General e-mail, info@tesol.org

Web, www.tesol.org

Develops and provides information on instruction and research in the teaching of English to speakers of other languages. Sponsors professional development programs and provides career management services.

Research

▶**AGENCIES**

Education Dept., *Institute of Education Sciences, 555 New Jersey Ave. N.W., #600 20208-5500; (202) 219-1385.*

Fax, (202) 219-1402. Sue Betka, Deputy Director (Acting). Library, (202) 205-4945.
Web, www.ed.gov/about/offices/list/ies

Provides evidence on which to ground education practice and policy through the work of four centers dealing with education research, education statistics, education evaluation and regional assistance, and special education research. Funds studies on ways to improve academic achievement, conducts large-scale evaluations of federal education programs, and reports a wide array of statistics on the condition of education.

Education Dept., *National Center for Education Evaluation and Regional Assistance (NCEE), 555 New Jersey Ave. N.W. 20208-5500; (202) 219-2484. Phoebe Cottingham, Commissioner.*
Web, www.ed.gov

Conducts large-scale evaluations of education programs and practices supported by federal funds; provides research-based technical assistance to educators and policymakers; and supports the synthesis and dissemination of the results of research and evaluation.

Education Dept., *National Center for Education Research, 555 New Jersey Ave. N.W. 20208; (202) 219-1385. Lynn Okagaki, Commissioner.*
Web, http://ncer.ed.gov

Supports research that addresses the nation's education needs, from early childhood to adult education.

Education Dept., *National Center for Education Statistics, 1990 K St. N.W., #9000 20006; (202) 502-7300. Fax, (202) 502-7466. Stuart Kerechsky, Commissioner (Acting).*
Web, www.ed.gov

Primary federal entity for collecting and analyzing data related to education. Administers the National Assessment of Educational Progress (NAEP), the "Nation's Report Card."

Education Dept., *National Center for Special Education Research (NCSER), 555 New Jersey Ave. N.W. 20208-5500; (202) 219-1385. Lynn Okagaki, Commissioner (Acting).*
Web, http://ies.ed.gov/ncser/

Sponsors a comprehensive program of special education research designed to expand the knowledge and understanding of infants, toddlers, and children with disabilities.

Education Dept., *National Library of Education, 400 Maryland Ave. S.W. 20202-5721; (202) 205-5015. Fax, (202) 401-0547. Christina Dunn, Director. Information, (800) 424-1616.*
General e-mail, library@ed.gov

Web, http://ies.ed.gov/ncee/projects/nat_ed_library.asp

Federal government's main resource center for education information. Provides access to its collections to the public, the education community, and other government agencies.

Houses publications produced or funded by the Education Dept., including Educational Resources Information Center (ERIC) materials, such as current and historical programs, policies, and legislation. Provides information and answers questions on education statistics and research.

▶**NONGOVERNMENTAL**

American Educational Research Assn., *1430 K St. N.W., #1200 20005; (202) 238-3200. Fax, (202) 238-3250. Felice Levine, Executive Director.*
General e-mail, flevine@aera.net

Web, www.aera.net

Membership: educational researchers affiliated with universities and colleges, school systems, and federal and state agencies. Publishes original research in education; sponsors publication of reference works in educational research; conducts continuing education programs; studies status of women and minorities in the education field.

Council on Government Relations, *1200 New York Ave. N.W., #750 20005; (202) 289-6655. Fax, (202) 289-6698. Anthony DeCrappeo, President.*
Web, www.cogr.edu

Membership: research universities, institutes, and medical colleges maintaining federally supported programs. Advises members and makes recommendations to government agencies regarding policies and regulations affecting federally funded university research.

Ethics and Public Policy Center, *1015 15th St. N.W., #900 20005-2605; (202) 682-1200. Fax, (202) 408-0632. M. Edward Whelan III, President.*
General e-mail, ethics@eppc.org

Web, www.eppc.org

Conducts research and holds conferences on the role of formal education and morality in teaching facts, ideas, attitudes, and values.

Knowledge Alliance, *1718 Connecticut Ave. N.W., #700 20009 1162; (202) 510-0047. Fax, (202) 783-3849. Jim Kohlmoos, President.*
General e-mail, jim@knowledgeall.net

Web, www.nekia.org

Membership: regional educational laboratories, university-based educational research and development organizations, educational entrepreneurs, and technical assistance providers. Promotes use of scientifically based solutions for improving teaching and learning. (Formerly the National Education Knowledge Industry Assn.)

National Assn. of Independent Colleges and Universities, *1025 Connecticut Ave. N.W., #700 20036-5405; (202) 785-8866. Fax, (202) 835-0003. David L. Warren, Co-Chair.*
General e-mail, webmaster@naicu.edu

Web, www.naicu.edu

Membership: liberal arts colleges, research universities, church- and faith-related institutions, historically black colleges and universities, women's colleges, performing and visual arts institutions, two-year colleges; graduate schools of law, medicine, engineering, business, and other professions. Tracks campus trends; conducts research; analyzes higher education issues; and helps coordinate state-level activities. Interests include federal policies that affect student aid, taxation, and government regulation. Monitors legislation and regulations.

Pew Research Center, *1615 L St. N.W., #700 20036; (202) 419-4300. Fax, (202) 419-4349. Andrew Kohut, President.*
General e-mail, info@pewresearch.org

Web, www.pewresearch.org

Nonpartisan research organization that studies issues of public interest in America and around the world. Conducts public opinion polling and social science research; reports news; analyzes news coverage; and holds forums and briefings.

RAND Corporation, *Washington Office, 1200 S. Hayes St., Arlington, VA 22202-5050; (703) 413-1100. Fax, (703) 413-8111. Lynn Davis, Director.*
Web, www.rand.org

Research organization partially funded by federal agencies. Conducts research on education policy. (Headquarters in Santa Monica, Calif.)

LIBRARIES AND EDUCATIONAL MEDIA

▶**AGENCIES**

Institute of Museum and Library Services, *Discretionary Grant Programs, 1800 M St. N.W., 9th Floor 20036-5802; (202) 653-4700. Fax, (202) 653-4601. Anne-Imelda M. Radice, Director. Main IMLS office, (202) 653-4657.*
General e-mail, imlsinfo@imls.gov

Web, www.imls.gov

Awards federal grants to support public, academic, research, school, and special libraries. Promotes access to information through electronic networks, links between libraries, and services to individuals having difficulty using a library. Provides funding for improved library services to Native American tribal communities, Alaska Native villages, and Native Hawaiian library users. Provides federal grants for improved care of museum collections and increased professional development opportunities.

National Archives and Records Administration (NARA), *Presidential Libraries, 8601 Adelphi Rd., #2200, College Park, MD 20740-6001; (301) 837-3250. Fax, (301) 837-3199. Sharon Fawcett, Assistant Archivist, (301) 837-1693.*
Web, www.archives.gov/presidential_libraries

Administers thirteen presidential libraries. Directs all programs relating to acquisition, preservation, publication,

Libraries at Federal Departments and Agencies

DEPARTMENTS

Agriculture, (301) 504-6778

Commerce, (202) 482-5511

Defense, (703) 695-1997

Education, (202) 205-5019

Energy, (202) 586-9534

Health and Human Services Law, (202) 619-0190

Housing and Urban Development, (202) 708-2370

Interior, (202) 208-5815

Justice, (202) 514-3775

Labor, (202) 693-6600

State, (202) 647-1099

Transportation, (202) 366-0746

Treasury, (202) 622-0990

Veterans Affairs, (202) 273-8523

  Law, (202) 273-6558

AGENCIES

Agency for International Development, (202) 712-0579

Commission on Civil Rights, (202) 376-8110

Commodity Futures Trading Commission, (202) 418-5255

Consumer Product Safety Commission, (301) 504-7622

Drug Enforcement Administration, (202) 307-8932

Environmental Protection Agency, (202) 566-0556

Equal Employment Opportunity Commission, (202) 663-4630

Export-Import Bank, (202) 565-3980

Federal Communications Commission, (202) 418-0450 or (202) 418-0270

Federal Deposit Insurance Corporation, (202) 898-3631

Federal Election Commission, (202) 694-1600

Federal Labor Relations Authority, (202) 218-7975

Federal Maritime Commission, (202) 523-5762

Federal Reserve Board, (202) 452-3332

Federal Trade Commission, (202) 326-2395

Government Accountability Office

  Law, (202) 512-2585

  Technical, (202) 512-5180

International Bank for Reconstruction and Development (World Bank)/International Monetary Fund, (202) 623-7054

Merit Systems Protection Board, (202) 653-7132

National Aeronautics and Space Administration, (202) 358-0168

National Credit Union Administration Law Library, (703) 518-6540

National Endowment for the Humanities, (202) 606-8244

National Institutes of Health, (301) 496-1080 or (301) 496-5611
  Health Services Research Library, (301) 496-1080 or (301) 496-5611

National Labor Relations Board, (202) 273-3720

National Library of Medicine, (301) 496-6308

National Science Foundation, (703) 292-7830

Nuclear Regulatory Commission, (301) 415-5610

Occupational Safety and Health Review Commission, (202) 606-5100, ext. 254

Office of Thrift Supervision, (202) 906-6470

Overseas Private Investment Corporation, (202) 336-8566

Peace Corps, (202) 692-2640

Postal Regulatory Commission, (202) 789-6800

Securities and Exchange Commission, (202) 551-5450

Small Business Administration Law Library, (202) 205-6849

Smithsonian Institution, (202) 633-2240

Social Security Administration, (410) 965-6113

U.S. International Trade Commission

  Main Library, (202) 205-2630

  Law, (202) 205-3287

U.S. Postal Service, (202) 268-2904

Library of Congress Divisions and Programs

African and Middle Eastern Division, (202) 707-7937

American Folklife Center, (202) 707-5510

Asian Division, (202) 707-5420

Cataloging Distribution Service, (202) 707-6100

Center for the Book, (202) 707-5221

Children's Literature Center, (202) 707-5535

Computer Catalog Center, (202) 707-3370

Copyright Office, (202) 707-3000 or (202) 707-5959

European Division, (202) 707-5414

Federal Library and Information Center Committee, (202) 707-4800

Geography and Map Division, (202) 707-6277

Hispanic Division, (202) 707-5400

Humanities and Social Science Division, (202) 707-5530

Interpretive Programs, (202) 707-5223

Law Library, (202) 707-5065

Law Library Reading Room, (202) 707-5080

Loan Division, (202) 707-5445

Local History and Genealogy Reading Room, (202) 707-5537

Manuscript Division, (202) 707 5383

Mary Pickford Theater, (202) 707-5677 or (202) 707-8572

Microform Reading Room, (202) 707-5471

Motion Picture, Broadcasting, and Recorded Sound Division, (202) 707-5840

Music Division, (202) 707-5503

National Library Service for the Blind and Physically Handicapped, (202) 707-5100

Photoduplication Service, (202) 707-5640

Poetry and Literature Center, (202) 707-5394

Preservation Directorate, (202) 707-5213

Prints and Photographs Division, (202) 707-6394

Rare Book and Special Collections Division, (202) 707-5434 or (202) 707-4144

Science, Technology and Business Division, (202) 707-5664

Serial and Government Publications Division, (202) 707-5690

and research use of materials in presidential libraries; conducts oral history projects; publishes finding aids for research sources; provides reference service, including information from and about documentary holdings.

National Endowment for the Humanities (NEH), *Public Programs, 1100 Pennsylvania Ave. N.W., #426 20506; (202) 606-8269. Fax, (202) 606-8557. Thomas C. Phelps, Director. General e-mail, publicpgms@neh.gov*

Web, www.neh.gov

Awards grants to libraries, museums, special projects, and media for projects that enhance public appreciation and understanding of the humanities through books and other resources in American library collections. Projects include conferences, exhibitions, essays, documentaries, radio programs, and lecture series.

Smithsonian Institution, *Office of the Director: Libraries, 10th St. and Constitution Ave. N.W., #22 National Museum of Natural History 20560 (mailing address: P.O. Box 37012, MRC 154, Washington, DC 20013-7012); (202) 633-2240. Fax, (202) 786-2866. Nancy E. Gwinn, Director. TTY, (202) 357-2139. Web, www.sil.si.edu*

Unites twenty libraries into one system supported by an online catalog of the combined collections. Maintains collection of general reference, biographical, and interdisciplinary materials; serves as an information resource on institution libraries and museum studies.

▶**CONGRESS**

For a listing of relevant congressional committees and subcommittees, please see page 156 or the Appendix.

Library of Congress, *101 Independence Ave. S.E. 20540; (202) 707-5205. Fax, (202) 707-1714. James H. Billington, Librarian of Congress. Information, (202) 707-5000. Public Affairs, (202) 707-2905. Web, www.loc.gov*

Main book repository of the United States.

Library of Congress, *Center for the Book, 101 Independence Ave. S.E., #LM 650 20540; (202) 707-5221. Fax, (202) 707-0269. John Y. Cole, Director. General e-mail, cfbook@loc.gov*

Web, www.loc.gov/cfbook

Seeks to broaden public appreciation of books, reading, literacy, and libraries; sponsors lectures and conferences on the educational and cultural role of the book worldwide, including the history of books and printing, television and the printed word, and the publishing and production of books; cooperates with state centers and with other organizations. Projects and programs are privately funded except for basic administrative support from the Library of Congress.

Library of Congress, *Federal Library and Information Center Committee, 101 Independence Ave. S.E., #LA217 20540; (202) 707-4800. Fax, (202) 707-4818. Deanna Marcum, Chair. General e-mail, flicc@loc.gov*

Web, www.loc.gov/flicc

Membership: one representative from each major federal agency, one representative each from the Library of Congress and the national libraries of medicine, education, and agriculture, and one representative from each of the major Federal Information Centers. Coordinates planning, development, operations, and activities among federal libraries.

Library of Congress, Preservation, *101 Independence Ave. S.E., #LM642 20540; (202) 707-7423. Fax, (202) 707-3434. Dianne L. Van der Reyden, Director.*
General e-mail, preserve@loc.gov

Web, www.loc.gov/preserv

Responsible for preserving book and paper materials in the library's collections.

▶**NONGOVERNMENTAL**

American Library Assn., Washington Office, *1615 New Hampshire Ave. N.W., 1st Floor 20009-2520; (202) 628-8410. Fax, (202) 628-8419. Emily Sheketoff, Associate Executive Director. Toll-free, (800) 941-8478.*
General e-mail, alawash@alawash.org

Web, www.ala.org/washoff

Educational organization of librarians, trustees, and educators. Washington office monitors legislation and regulations on libraries and information science. (Headquarters in Chicago, Ill.)

American Society for Information Science and Technology (ASIS), *1320 Fenwick Lane, #510, Silver Spring, MD 20910-3560; (301) 495-0900. Fax, (301) 495-0810. Richard Hill, Executive Director.*
General e-mail, asis@asis.org

Web, www.asis.org

Membership: information specialists from such fields as computer science, linguistics, management, librarianship, engineering, law, medicine, chemistry, and education. Advocates research and development in basic and applied information science. Offers continuing education programs.

Assn. for Information and Image Management, *1100 Wayne Ave., #1100, Silver Spring, MD 20910; (301) 587-8202. Fax, (301) 587-2711. John F. Mancini, President. Information, (800) 477-2446.*
General e-mail, aiim@aiim.org

Web, www.aiim.org

Membership: manufacturers and users of image-based information systems. Works to advance the profession of information management; develops standards on such technologies as microfilm and electronic imaging.

Assn. of Research Libraries (ARL), *21 Dupont Circle N.W., #800 20036; (202) 296-2296. Fax, (202) 872-0884. Charley B. Lowry, Executive Director.*
General e-mail, webmgr@arl.org

Web, www.arl.org

Membership: major research libraries, mainly at universities, in the United States and Canada. Interests include development of library resources in all formats, subjects, and languages; computer information systems and other bibliographic tools; management of research libraries; preservation of library materials; worldwide information policy; and publishing and scholarly communication.

Council on Library and Information Resources, *1755 Massachusetts Ave. N.W., #500 20036-2124; (202) 939-4750. Fax, (202) 939-4765. Charles Henry, President.*
Web, www.clir.org

Acts on behalf of the nation's libraries, archives, and universities to develop and encourage collaborative strategies for preserving the nation's intellectual heritage and strengthening its information systems.

Gallaudet University, Library, *800 Florida Ave. N.E. 20002-3695; (202) 651-5217. Fax, (202) 651-5213. Sarah Hamrick, Director, Libary Public Services; Ulf Hedberg, Director, Deaf Library Collection Archives. TTY, (202) 651-5209. Some numbers require state relay service for voice transmission.*
General e-mail, library.help@gallaudet.edu

Web, http://library.gallaudet.edu

Maintains extensive special collection on deafness, including archival materials relating to deaf cultural history and Gallaudet University.

Info Comm International, *11242 Waples Mill Rd., #200, Fairfax, VA 22030; (703) 273-7200. Fax, (703) 278-8082. Randal A. Lemke, Executive Director. Information, (800) 659-7469.*
General e-mail, customerservice@infocomm.org

Web, www.infocomm.org

Membership: manufacturers, dealers, and specialists in educational communications products. Provides educators with information on federal funding for audiovisual, video, and computer equipment and materials; monitors trends in educational technology; conducts educational software conference on microcomputers and miniaturization. (Formerly the International Communications Industries Assn.)

Society for Imaging Science and Technology, *7003 Kilworth Lane, Springfield, VA 22151; (703) 642-9090. Fax, (703) 642-9094. Suzanne E. Grinnan, Executive Director.*
General e-mail, info@imaging.org

Web, www.imaging.org

Membership: individuals and companies worldwide in fields of imaging science and technology, including photofinishing, nonimpact printing, electronic imaging, silver halide, image preservation, and hybrid imaging systems. Gathers and disseminates technical information; fosters professional development.

Special Libraries Assn., *331 S. Patrick St., Alexandria, VA 22314-3501; (703) 647-4900. Fax, (703) 647-4901. Janice R. Lachance, Executive Director. Fax-on-demand, (888) 411-2856.*
General e-mail, sla@sla.org

Web, www.sla.org

Membership: librarians and information managers serving institutions that use or produce information in specialized areas, including business, engineering, law, the arts and sciences, government, museums, and universities. Conducts professional development programs, research projects, and an annual conference; provides a consultation service; sponsors International Special Libraries Day. Monitors legislation and regulations.

POSTSECONDARY EDUCATION

►AGENCIES

Education Dept., *Fund for the Improvement of Postsecondary Education, 1990 K St. N.W., 6th Floor 20006-8544; (202) 502-7500. Fax, (202) 502-7877. Ralph Hines, Director (Acting).*
Web, www.ed.gov/FIPSE

Works to improve postsecondary education by administering grant competitions, including the Comprehensive Program for Improvement in Postsecondary Education; the European Union–United States Atlantis Program; the Program for North American Mobility in Higher Education; the U.S.-Brazil Higher Education Consortia Program; the United States–Russia Program; and the Underground Railroad Education and Cultural Program.

Education Dept., *Office of Postsecondary Education (OPE), 1990 K St. N.W., 7th Floor 20006; (202) 502-7750. Fax, (202) 502-7677. Daniel T. Madzelan Assistant Secretary. TTY, (800) 437-0833.*
Web, www.ed.gov/about/offices/list/ope/index.html

Administers federal assistance programs for public and private postsecondary institutions; provides financial support for faculty development, construction of facilities, and improvement of graduate, continuing, cooperative, and international education; awards grants and loans for financial assistance to eligible students.

►CONGRESS

For a listing of relevant congressional committees and subcommittees, please see page 156 or the Appendix.

►NONGOVERNMENTAL

Accuracy in Academia, *4455 Connecticut Ave. N.W., #330 20008-2372; (202) 364-3085. Fax, (202) 364-4098. Malcolm A. Kline, Executive Director.*
General e-mail, info@academia.org
Web, www.academia.org

Seeks to eliminate political bias in university education, particularly discrimination against students, faculty, or administrators on the basis of political beliefs. Publishes a monthly newsletter.

ACT Inc. (American College Testing), *Washington Office, 1 Dupont Circle N.W., #340 20036-1170; (202) 223-2318. Fax, (202) 293-2223. Tom Lindsley, Director.*
Web, www.act.org

Administers ACT assessment planning and examination for colleges and universities. Provides more than one hundred assessment, research, information, and program management services in the areas of education and workforce development to elementary and secondary schools, colleges, professional associations, businesses, and government agencies. (Headquarters in Iowa City, Iowa.)

American Assn. of Colleges of Pharmacy, *1727 King St., Alexandria, VA 22314-2700; (703) 739-2330. Fax, (703) 836-8982. Lucinda L. Maine, Executive Vice President.*
General e-mail, mail@aacp.org
Web, www.aacp.org

Represents and advocates for pharmacists in the academic community. Conducts programs and activities in cooperation with other national health and higher education associations.

American Assn. of Collegiate Registrars and Admissions Officers, *1 Dupont Circle N.W., #520 20036-1135; (202) 293-9161. Fax, (202) 872-8857. Jerome Sullivan, Executive Director.*
General e-mail, info@aacrao.org
Web, www.aacrao.org

Membership: degree-granting postsecondary institutions, government agencies, higher education coordinating boards, private education organizations, and education-oriented businesses. Promotes higher education and contributes to the professional development of members working in admissions, enrollment management, financial aid, institutional research, records, and registration.

American Assn. of Community Colleges, *1 Dupont Circle N.W., #410 20036-1176; (202) 728-0200. Fax, (202) 223-9390. George R. Boggs, President.*
Web, www.aacc.nche.edu

Membership: accredited two-year community technical and junior colleges, corporate foundations, international associates, and institutional affiliates. Studies include policies for lifelong education, workforce training programs and partnerships, international curricula, enrollment trends, and cooperative programs with public schools and communities. (Affiliated with the Council for Resource Development.)

American Assn. of State Colleges and Universities, *1307 New York Ave. N.W., 5th Floor 20005; (202) 293-7070. Fax, (202) 296-5819. Constantine W. Curris, President.*
Web, www.aascu.org

Membership: presidents and chancellors of state colleges and universities. Promotes equity in education and fosters information exchange among members. Interests include student financial aid, international education programs, academic affairs, teacher education, and higher education access and affordability. Monitors legislation and regulations.

American Assn. of University Professors (AAUP), *1133 19th St. N.W., #200 20036; (202) 737-5900. Fax, (202) 737-5526. Gary Rhoades, General Secretary.*
General e-mail, aaup@aaup.org
Web, www.aaup.org

Membership: college and university faculty members. Defends faculties' academic freedom and tenure; advocates collegial governance; assists in the development of policies ensuring due process. Conducts workshops and education programs. Monitors legislation and regulations.

American Conference of Academic Deans, *1818 R St. N.W. 20009; (202) 884-7419. Fax, (202) 265-9532. Linda Cabe Halpern, Chair.*
General e-mail, information@acad-edu.org

Web, www.acad-edu.org

Membership: academic administrators of two- and four-year accredited colleges, universities, and community colleges (private and public). Fosters information exchange among members on college curricular and administrative issues.

American Council of Trustees and Alumni, *1726 M St. N.W., #802 20036-4525; (202) 467-6787. Fax, (202) 467-6784. Jerry L. Martin, Chair; Anne D. Neal, President.*
General e-mail, info@goacta.org

Web, www.goacta.org

Membership: college and university alumni and trustees interested in promoting academic freedom and excellence. Seeks to help alumni and trustees direct their financial contributions to programs that will raise educational standards at their alma maters. Promotes the role of alumni and trustees in shaping higher education policies.

American Council on Education (ACE), *1 Dupont Circle N.W., #800 20036-1193; (202) 939-9300. Fax, (202) 833-4762. Molly Corbett Broad, Co-Chair. Library, (202) 939-9405. Press, (202) 939-9365.*
Web, www.acenet.edu

Membership: colleges, universities, education associations, students with disabilities, and businesses. Conducts and publishes research; maintains offices dealing with government relations, women and minorities in higher education, management of higher education institutions, adult learning and educational credentials (academic credit for nontraditional learning, especially in the armed forces), leadership development, and international education. Library open to the public by appointment.

Assn. for Supervision and Curriculum Development, *1703 N. Beauregard St., Alexandria, VA 22311-1714; (703) 578-9600. Fax, (703) 575-5400. Gene R. Carter, Executive Director. Information, (800) 933-2723.*
General e-mail, member@ascd.org

Web, www.ascd.org

Membership: approximately 175,000 professional educators internationally, including superintendents, supervisors, principals, teachers, professors of education, and school board members. Develops programs, products, and services for educators.

Assn. of American Colleges and Universities (AACU), *1818 R St. N.W. 20009; (202) 387-3760. Fax, (202) 265-9532. Carol Geary Schneider, President.*
Web, www.aacu.org

Membership: public and private colleges, universities, and postsecondary consortia. Works to develop effective academic programs and improve undergraduate curricula and services. Seeks to encourage, enhance, and support student achievement through liberal education for all students, regardless of academic specialization or intended career.

Assn. of American Law Schools, *1201 Connecticut Ave. N.W., #800 20036-2717; (202) 296-8851. Fax, (202) 296-8869. Susan Westerberg Prager, Executive Director.*
General e-mail, aals@aals.org

Web, www.aals.org

Membership: law schools, subject to approval. Membership criteria include high-quality academic programs, faculty, scholarship, and students; academic freedom; diversity of people and viewpoints; and emphasis on public service. Hosts meetings and workshops; publishes a directory of law teachers. Advocates on behalf of legal education; monitors legislation and judicial decisions.

Assn. of American Universities, *1200 New York Ave. N.W., #550 20005; (202) 408-7500. Fax, (202) 408-8184. Robert Berdahl, President.*
Web, www.aau.edu

Membership: public and private universities with emphasis on graduate and professional education and research. Fosters information exchange among presidents of member institutions.

Assn. of Catholic Colleges and Universities, *1 Dupont Circle N.W., #650 20036; (202) 457-0650. Fax, (202) 728-0977. Richard Yanikoski, President.*
General e-mail, accu@accunet.org

Web, www.accunet.org

Membership: regionally accredited American Catholic colleges and universities. Offers affiliated status for selected international Catholic universities. Acts as a clearinghouse for information on Catholic institutions of higher education.

Assn. of Community College Trustees, *1233 20th St. N.W., #301 20036; (202) 775-4667. Fax, (202) 223-1297. J. Noah Brown, President.*
Web, www.acct.org

Provides members of community college governing boards with training in educational programs and services. Monitors federal education programs and advocates on behalf of community colleges and their trustees.

Assn. of Governing Boards of Universities and Colleges, *1133 20th St. N.W., #300 20036; (202) 296-8400. Fax, (202) 223-7053. Richard D. Lagon, President. Toll-free, (800) 356-6317.*
Web, www.agb.org

Membership: presidents, boards of trustees, regents, commissions, and other groups governing colleges, universities, and institutionally related foundations. Interests include the relationship between the president and board of trustees and other subjects relating to governance.

Colleges and Universities in the Washington Metropolitan Area

Agriculture Dept. Graduate School,
600 Maryland Ave. S.W. 20024
Switchboard: (888) 744-GRAD
Executive Director: Jerry Ice, (202) 314-3686

American University, 4400 Massachusetts Ave. N.W. 20016
Switchboard: (202) 885-1000
President: Cornelius Kerwin, (202) 885-2121

Catholic University, 620 Michigan Ave. N.E. 20064
Switchboard: (202) 319-5000
President: Rev. David M. O'Connell C.M., (202) 319-5100

Columbia Union College, 7600 Flower Ave., Takoma Park, MD 20912
Switchboard: (301) 891-4000; toll-free, (800) 835-4212
President: Weymouth Spence, (301) 891-4128

Corcoran College of Art and Design, 500 17th St. N.W. 20006
Switchboard: (202) 639-1801
Dean: Christina DePaul, (202) 639-1804

Gallaudet University, 800 Florida Ave. N.E. 20002
Switchboard: (202) 651-5000 (voice and TTY)
President: Robert R. Davila, (202) 651-5005 (voice and TTY)

George Mason University, 4400 University Dr., Fairfax, VA 22030
Switchboard: (703) 993-1000
President: Alan G. Merten, (703) 993-8700

George Washington University,
2121 Eye St. N.W. 20052
Switchboard: (202) 994-1000
President: Steven Knapp, (202) 994-6500

George Washington University at Mount Vernon Campus, 2100 Foxhall Rd. N.W. 20007
Switchboard: (202) 242-6600
Associate Vice President: Frederic A. Siegel, (202) 242-6609

Georgetown University, 37th and O Sts. N.W. 20057
Switchboard: (202) 687-0100
President: John J. DeGioia, (202) 687-4134

Howard University, 2400 6th St. N.W. 20059
Switchboard: (202) 806-6100
President: Sidney A. Ribeau, (202) 806-2500

Marymount University, 2807 N. Glebe Rd., Arlington, VA 22207
Switchboard: (703) 522-5600
President: James Bundschuh, (703) 284-1598

Paul H. Nitze School of Advanced International Studies (SAIS), Johns Hopkins University,
1740 Massachusetts Ave. N.W. 20036
Switchboard: (202) 663-5600
Dean: Jessica P. Einhorn, (202) 663-5624

Southeastern University, 501 Eye St. S.W. 20024
Switchboard: (202) 488-8162
President: Charlene Drew Jarvis, (202) 478-8200, ext. 211

Trinity University, 125 Michigan Ave. N.E. 20017
Switchboard: (202) 884-9000
President: Patricia McGuire, (202) 884-9050

University of Maryland, Rt. 1, College Park Campus, College Park, MD 20742
Switchboard: (301) 405-1000
President: C.D. Mote Jr., (301) 405-5803

University of the District of Columbia,
4200 Connecticut Ave. N.W. 20008
Switchboard: (202) 274-5000
President: Alan C. Sessions, (202) 274-5100

University of Virginia (Northern Virginia Center),
7054 Haycock Rd., Falls Church, VA 22043
UVA Switchboard: (703) 536-1100
UVA Director: Patrick Valentine, (703) 536-1118

Virginia Tech (Northern Virginia Center), 7054 Haycock Rd., Falls Church, VA 22043
VT Switchboard: (703) 538-8324
VT Director: Karen E. Akers, (703) 538-8312

Virginia Theological Seminary, 3737 Seminary Rd., Alexandria, VA 22304
Switchboard: (703) 370-6600
Dean: Ian Markham, (703) 461-1701

Assn. of Higher Education Facilities Officers, *1643 Prince St., Alexandria, VA 22314-2818; (703) 684-1446. Fax, (703) 549-2772. E. Lander Medlin, Executive Vice President.*
General e-mail, info@appa.org

Web, www.appa.org

Membership: professionals involved in the administration, maintenance, planning, and development of buildings and facilities used by colleges and universities. Interests include maintenance and upkeep of housing facilities. Provides information on campus energy management programs and campus accessibility for people with disabilities.

Assn. of Jesuit Colleges and Universities, *1 Dupont Circle N.W., #405 20036-1140; (202) 862-9893. Fax, (202)* *862-8523. Rev. Charles L. Currie, S.J., President.*
General e-mail, office@ajcunet.edu

Web, www.ajcunet.edu

Membership: American Jesuit colleges and universities. Monitors government regulatory and policy-making activities affecting higher education. Publishes the AJCU Directory and a monthly newsletter. Promotes international cooperation among Jesuit higher education institutions.

Business–Higher Education Forum, *2025 M St. N.W., #800 20036; (202) 367-1189. Fax, (202) 367-2269. Brian K. Fitzgerald, Executive Director.*
General e-mail, info@bhef.com

Web, www.bhef.com

Membership: chief executive officers of major corporations, foundations, colleges, and universities. Develops and promotes policy positions to enhance U.S. competitiveness. Interests include improving student achievement and readiness for college and work; and strengthening higher education, particularly in the fields of science, technology, engineering, and math.

Career College Assn., *1101 Connecticut Ave. N.W., #900 20036; (202) 336-6700. Fax, (202) 336-6828. Harris N. Miller, President.*
General e-mail, cca@career.org

Web, www.career.org

Membership: private postsecondary colleges and career schools in the United States. Works to expand the accessibility of postsecondary career education and to improve the quality of education offered by member schools.

College Board, *Advocacy, Government Relations, and Development, Washington Office, 1233 20th St. N.W., #600 20036-2304; (202) 741-4700. Fax, (202) 741-4743. Tom Rudin, Senior Vice President.*
Web, www.collegeboard.com

Membership: colleges and universities, secondary schools, school systems, and education associations. Provides direct student support programs and professional development for educators; conducts policy analysis and research; and advocates public policy positions that support educational excellence and promote student access to higher education. Library open to the public. (Headquarters in New York.)

Council for Christian Colleges and Universities, *321 8th St. N.E. 20002; (202) 546-8713. Fax, (202) 546-8913. Paul Corts, President.*
General e-mail, council@cccu.org

Web, www.cccu.org

Membership: accredited four-year Christian liberal arts colleges. Offers faculty development conferences on faith and the academic disciplines. Coordinates annual gathering of college administrators. Sponsors internship/seminar programs for students at member colleges. Interests include religious and educational freedom.

Council for Resource Development, *1 Dupont Circle N.W., #365 20036-1176; (202) 822-0750. Fax, (202) 822-5014. Judy Everett, President.*
General e-mail, crd@crdnet.org

Web, www.crdnet.org

Membership: college presidents, administrators, fundraisers, grant writers, and development officers at two-year colleges. Educates members on how to secure resources for their institution; conducts workshops and training programs. Monitors legislation and regulations. (Affiliated with the American Assn. of Community Colleges.)

Council of Graduate Schools, *1 Dupont Circle N.W., #230 20036-1173; (202) 223-3791. Fax, (202) 331-7157. Debra W. Stewart, President.*

General e-mail, pmcallister@cgs.nche.edu
Web, www.cgsnet.org

Membership: private and public colleges and universities with significant involvement in graduate education, research, and scholarship. Produces publications and information about graduate education; provides a forum for member schools to exchange information and ideas.

Council of Independent Colleges, *1 Dupont Circle N.W., #320 20036-1142; (202) 466-7230. Fax, (202) 466-7238. Richard Ekman, President.*
General e-mail, cic@cic.nche.edu

Web, www.cic.edu

Membership: independent liberal arts colleges and universities, and higher education affiliates and organizations. Sponsors development programs for college presidents, deans, and faculty members on topics such as leadership, financial management, academic quality, visibility, and other issues crucial to high-quality education. Holds workshops and produces publications.

Council on Social Work Education, *1725 Duke St., #500, Alexandria, VA 22314-3457; (703) 683-8080. Fax, (703) 683-8099. Julia Watkins, Executive Director.*
General e-mail, info@cswe.org

Web, www.cswe.org

Membership: educational and professional institutions, social welfare agencies, and private citizens. Promotes high-quality education in social work. Accredits social work programs.

Educational Testing Service (ETS), *Communications and Public Affairs, Washington Office, 1800 K St. N.W., #900 20006-2202; (202) 659-0616. Fax, (202) 659-8075. Kurt Landgraf, President; Charles Cascio, Vice President. TTY, (202) 659-8067.*
General e-mail, etsinfo@ets.org

Web, www.ets.org

Administers examinations for admission to educational programs and for graduate and licensing purposes; conducts instructional programs in testing, evaluation, and research in education fields. Washington office handles government and professional relations. Fee for services. (Headquarters in Princeton, N.J.)

NASPA–Student Affairs Administration in Higher Education, *1875 Connecticut Ave. N.W., #418 20009-5728; (202) 265-7500. Fax, (202) 797-1157. Gwendolyn Dungy, Executive Director.*
General e-mail, office@naspa.org

Web, www.naspa.org

Membership: student affairs administrators, deans, faculty, and graduate students at 1,400 campuses, representing 29 countries. Seeks to develop leadership and improve practices in student affairs administration. Initiates and supports programs and legislation to improve student affairs administration.

National Assn. for College Admission Counseling, *1050 N. Highland St., #400, Arlington, VA 22201; (703) 836-2222. Fax, (703) 836-8015. Joyce Smith, Chief Executive Officer. Information, (800) 822-6285.*
General e-mail, info@nacac.com

Web, wwww.nacacnet.org

Membership: high school guidance counselors, independent counselors, college and university admissions officers, and financial aid officers. Assists counselors who serve students in the college admission process. Promotes and funds research on admission counseling and on the transition from high school to college. Advocates for the rights of students in the college admission process. Sponsors national college fairs and continuing education for members.

National Assn. of College and University Attorneys, *1 Dupont Circle N.W., #620 20036-1134; (202) 833-8390. Fax, (202) 296-8379. Kathleen Curry Santora, Chief Executive Officer.*
General e-mail, nacua@nacua.org

Web, www.nacua.org

Provides information on legal developments affecting postsecondary education. Operates a clearinghouse through which attorneys on campuses are able to network with their counterparts on current legal problems.

National Assn. of College and University Business Officers, *1110 Vermont Ave. N.W., #800 20005; (202) 861-2500. Fax, (202) 861-2583. John D. Walda, President. Toll-free, (800) 462-4916.*
General e-mail, webmaster@nacubo.org

Web, www.nacubo.org

Membership: chief business officers at higher education institutions. Provides members with information on financial management, federal regulations, and other subjects related to the business administration of universities and colleges; conducts workshops on issues such as student aid, institutional budgeting, and accounting.

National Assn. of Independent Colleges and Universities, *1025 Connecticut Ave. N.W., #700 20036-5405; (202) 785-8866. Fax, (202) 835-0003. David L. Warren, Co-Chair.*
General e-mail, webmaster@naicu.edu

Web, www.naicu.edu

Membership: liberal arts colleges, research universities, church- and faith-related institutions, historically black colleges and universities, women's colleges, performing and visual arts institutions, two-year colleges; graduate schools of law, medicine, engineering, business, and other professions. Tracks campus trends; conducts research; analyzes higher education issues; and helps coordinate state-level activities. Interests include federal policies that affect student aid, taxation, and government regulation. Monitors legislation and regulations.

National Assn. of State Universities and Land Grant Colleges, *1307 New York Ave. N.W., #400 20005-4722;* *(202) 478-6040. Fax, (202) 478-6046. M. Peter McPherson, President.*
Web, www.nasulgc.org

Membership: land grant colleges; state and public research universities. Serves as clearinghouse on issues of public higher education.

National Council of University Research Administrators, *1225 19th St. N.W., #850 20036; (202) 466-3894. Fax, (202) 223-5573. Kathleen Larmett, Executive Director.*
General e-mail, info@ncura.edu

Web, www.ncura.edu

Membership: individuals engaged in administering research, training, and educational programs, primarily at colleges and universities. Encourages development of effective policies and procedures in the administration of these programs.

U.S. Student Assn., *1211 Connecticut Ave. N.W., #406 20036; (202) 640-6570. Fax, (202) 223-4005. Carmen Berkley, President.*
General e-mail, ussa@usstudents.org

Web, www.usstudents.org

Represents postsecondary students, student government associations, and state student lobby associations. Monitors legislation and regulations. Organizes students to participate in the political process through testifying in official congressional hearings, letter-writing campaigns, and face-to-face lobbying visits. Represents students in various coalitions, including the Committee for Education Funding, the Student Aid Alliance, and the Leadership Conference on Civil Rights.

Washington Higher Education Secretariat, *1 Dupont Circle N.W., #800 20036; (202) 939-9410. Fax, (202) 833-4760. Ellen R. Babby, Executive Secretary.*
General e-mail, whes@ace.nche.edu

Web, www.whes.org

Membership: national higher education associations representing the different sectors and functions in postsecondary institutions. Provides forum for discussion on national and local education issues.

College Accreditation

Many college- or university-based independent postsecondary education programs are accredited by member associations. See specific subject headings and associations within the chapter.

▶**AGENCIES**

Education Dept., *Accreditation State Liaison, 1990 K St. N.W., #7126 20006-8509; (202) 219-7011. Fax, (202) 219-7005. Nancy Regan, Director.*
Web, www.ed.gov

Reviews accrediting agencies and state approval agencies that seek initial or renewed recognition by the secretary; provides the National Advisory Committee on Institutional Quality and Integrity with staff support.

▶NONGOVERNMENTAL

Accrediting Council for Independent Colleges and Schools (ACICS), *750 1st St. N.E., #980 20002-4241; (202) 336-6780. Fax, (202) 842-2593. Al Gray, Executive Director. Toll-free, (800) 510-0746.*
General e-mail, info@acics.org

Web, www.acics.org

Accredits postsecondary institutions offering programs of study through the master's degree level that are designed to train and educate persons for careers or professions where business applications and concepts constitute or support the career or professional activity. Promotes educational excellence and ethical business practices in its member schools.

American Academy for Liberal Education (AALE), *1050 17th St. N.W., #400 20036; (202) 452-8611. Fax, (202) 452-8620. Jeffrey D. Wallin, President.*
General e-mail, info@aale.org

Web, www.aale.org

Accredits colleges, universities, and charter schools whose general education program in the liberal arts meets the academy's accreditation requirements. Provides support for institutions that maintain substantial liberal arts programs and desire to raise requirements to meet AALE standards.

Council for Higher Education Accreditation, *1 Dupont Circle N.W., #510; (202) 955-6126. Fax, (202) 955-6129. Judith S. Eaton, President.*
General e-mail, chea@chea.org

Web, www.chea.org

Advocates voluntary self-regulation of colleges and universities through accreditation; conducts recognition processes for accrediting organizations; coordinates research, debate, and processes that improve accreditation; mediates disputes and fosters communications among accrediting bodies and the higher education community.

Financial Aid to Students

▶AGENCIES

Education Dept., Federal Student Aid, *830 1st St. N.E. 20202; (202) 377-3000. Fax, (202) 275-5000. James Manning, Chief Operating Officer (Acting). Student Aid Information Center, (800) 433-3243.*
Web, www.ed.gov

Administers federal loan, grant, and work-study programs for postsecondary education to eligible individuals. Administers the Pell Grant Program, the Perkins Loan Program, the Stafford Student Loan Program (Guaranteed Student Loan)/PLUS Program, the College Work-Study Program, the Supplemental Loans for Students (SLS), and the Supplemental Educational Opportunity Grant Program.

▶NONGOVERNMENTAL

College Board, Advocacy, Government Relations, and Development, Washington Office, *1233 20th St. N.W., #600 20036-2304; (202) 741-4700. Fax, (202) 741-4743. Tom Rudin, Senior Vice President.*
Web, www.collegeboard.com

Membership: colleges and universities, secondary schools, school systems, and education associations. Provides direct student support programs and professional development for educators; conducts policy analysis and research; and advocates public policy positions that support educational excellence and promote student access to higher education. Library open to the public. (Headquarters in New York.)

College Parents of America, *2000 N. 14th St., #800, Arlington, VA 22201-2540; (703) 797-7103. Fax, (703) 875-2199. James Boyle, President. Information, (888) 761-6702.*
General e-mail, info@collegeparents.org

Web, www.collegeparents.org

Provides information and resources on savings strategies and financial aid; offers advice on the evaluation, selection, and application process; provides information on meeting the opportunities and challenges of a child's college years; offers savings and access to discounts on products and services associated with college prep and campus living. Monitors legislation and regulations on the national and state (financial, academic, and emotional) levels.

Education Finance Council, *1850 M St. N.W., #920 20036; (202) 955-5510. Fax, (202) 955-5530. Peter Warren, President.*
General e-mail, info@efc.org

Web, www.efc.org

Membership: state-based student loan secondary market organizations. Participates in the Federal Family Education Loan Program (FFELP). Works to maintain and expand student access to higher education through tax-exempt funding for loans.

National Assn. of Student Financial Aid Administrators, *1101 Connecticut Ave. N.W., #1100 20036-4303; (202) 785-0453. Fax, (202) 785-1487. Philip D. Day, President.*
General e-mail, ask@nasfaa.org

Web, www.nasfaa.org

Membership: more than 3,500 educational institutions, organizations, and individuals at postsecondary institutions who administer student financial aid. Works to ensure adequate funding for individuals seeking postsecondary education and to ensure proper management and administration of public and private financial aid funds.

National Council of Higher Education Loan Programs, *1100 Connecticut Ave. N.W., 12th Floor 20036-4110; (202) 822-2106. Fax, (202) 822-2142. Brett E. Lief, President.*

General e-mail, info@nchelp@org

Web, www.nchelp.org

Membership: agencies and organizations involved in making, servicing, and collecting Guaranteed Student Loans. Works with the Education Dept. to develop forms and procedures for administering the Federal Family Education Loan Program (FFELP). Fosters information exchange among members.

Sallie Mae, 12061 Bluemont Way, Reston, VA 20190-5684; (703) 810-3000. Fax, (703) 984-5042. Albert L. Lord, Chief Executive Officer.

Web, www.salliemae.com

Provides educational funding, debt-management services, and business and technical products to a range of business clients, including colleges, universities, and loan guarantors. Provides federal and private education loans, including Federal Stafford, PLUS, and consolidation loans.

Student Aid Alliance, 1 Dupont Circle N.W., #800 20036-1193; (202) 939-9355. Fax, (202) 833-4762. Molly Corbett Broad, Co-Chair; David L. Warren, Co-Chair.

Web, www.studentaidalliance.org

Membership: more than sixty organizations representing students, administrators, and faculty members from all sectors of higher education. Seeks to ensure adequate funding of federal aid programs. Monitors legislation and regulations. (Formerly the Alliance to Save Student Aid.)

PRESCHOOL, ELEMENTARY, SECONDARY EDUCATION

▶AGENCIES

Education Dept., *Academic Improvement and Teacher Quality Programs (AITQ),* 400 Maryland Ave. S.W. 20202; (202) 260-8228. Fax, (202) 260-8969. Joseph C. Conaty, Director.

www.ed.gov/about/offices/list/oese/aitq/index.html

Provides financial assistance to state and local educational agencies, community and faith-based organizations, and other entities to support activities to recruit and retain high-quality teaching staff and to strengthen the quality of elementary and secondary education. Divided into four program groups: the Academic Improvement Program, the High School Programs, the Teacher Quality Program, and the Early Childhood Reading Group Program; implements programs providing support for reopening and rebuilding schools in areas impacted by Hurricane Katrina; implements the 21st Century Community Learning Centers, which provide academic enrichment opportunities during nonschool hours for students attending high-poverty and low-performing schools.

Education Dept., *Elementary and Secondary Education,* 400 Maryland Ave. S.W., #3W300 20202; (202) 401-0113. Fax, (202) 205-0310. Joseph C. Conaty, Assistant Secretary (Acting).

Web, www.ed.gov/about/offices/list/oese/index.html

Administers federal assistance programs for elementary and secondary education (both public and private). Program divisions include Compensatory Education (including Title I aid for disadvantaged children); School Improvement; Migrant Education; Impact Aid; School Support and Technology Programs; and Academic Improvement and Teacher Quality Programs.

Education Dept., *Elementary and Secondary Education, Academic Improvement and Teacher Quality (AITQ): Early Childhood Reading Group,* 9400 Maryland Ave. S.W. 20202-6132; (202) 260-3793. Fax, (202) 260-8969. Deborah Spitz, Group Leader (Acting).

Administers formula and discretionary grants that support family literacy programs that provide early childhood, adult literacy, and parenting education to low-income families (Even Start); enhance early childhood literacy instruction for children in the two years before kindergarten (Early Reading First); and supports partnerships between institutions of higher education and other entities to improve the professional development of early childhood instructors (Early Childhood Educator Professional Development).

Education Dept., *Impact Aid,* 400 Maryland Ave. S.W., #3E105 20202-6244; (202) 260-3858. Fax, (202) 205-0088. Catherine Schagh, Director.

General e-mail, impact.aid@ed.gov

Web, www.ed.gov/about/offices/list/oese/impactaid

Provides funds for elementary and secondary educational activities to school districts in federally impacted areas (where federal activities such as military bases enlarge staff and reduce taxable property).

Education Dept., *Office of English Language Acquisition (OELA),* 400 Maryland Ave. S.W. 20202-6510; (202) 401-1402. Fax, (202) 205-1229. Margarita Pinkos, Director.

Web, www.ed.gov/about/offices/list/oela/index.html

Administers bilingual education programs in elementary and secondary schools to help students of limited English proficiency learn the English language. The program is designed to give students of limited English proficiency better opportunities to achieve academic success and meet grade promotion and graduation requirements. (Formerly the Office of Bilingual Education and Minority Languages Affairs.)

Education Dept., *Safe and Drug-Free Schools,* 550 12th St. S.W., #10001 20202-6450; (202) 245-7896. Fax, (202) 485-0013. William Modzeleski, Associate Assistant Deputy Secretary.

Web, www.ed.gov/offices/oese/sdfs

Develops policy for the department's drug and violence prevention initiatives for students in elementary and secondary schools and institutions of higher education. Provides financial assistance for drug and violence prevention activities. Coordinates education efforts in drug and violence prevention with those of other federal departments and agencies.

Environmental Protection Agency (EPA), *Pollution Prevention and Toxics, 1201 Constitution Ave. N.W., #3166 EPA East, MC 7401M 20460; (202) 564-3810. Fax, (202) 564-0575. Wendy Cleland-Hamnett, Director (Acting). Information, (202) 554-1404.*
Web, www.epa.gov/oppts

Manages programs on pollution prevention and new and existing chemicals in the marketplace such as asbestos, lead, and PCBs. Administers the Asbestos Loan and Grant Program to needy public and private elementary and secondary schools to eliminate health threats caused by asbestos-containing materials. Other programs include the High Production Volume Challenge Program, Sustainable Futures, the Green Chemistry Program, Green Suppliers Network, the High Production Volume Challenge Program, Design for the Environment, and the Chemical Right-to-Know Initiative.

Health and Human Services Dept. (HHS), *Head Start, 1250 Maryland Ave. S.W., 8th Floor 20024; (202) 205-8573. Fax, (202) 260-9663. Patricia Brown, Director (Acting).*
Web, www.hhs.gov/headstart

Awards grants to nonprofit and for-profit organizations and local governments for operating community Head Start programs (comprehensive development programs for children, ages three to five, of low-income families); manages a limited number of parent and child centers for families with children up to age three. Conducts research and manages demonstration programs, including those under the Comprehensive Child Care Development Act of 1988; administers the Child Development Associate scholarship program, which trains individuals for careers in child development, often as Head Start teachers.

National Agricultural Library *(Agriculture Dept.),* *Food and Nutrition Information Center, 10301 Baltimore Ave., #105, Beltsville, MD 20705-2351; (301) 504-5719. Fax, (301) 504-6409. Vacant, Coordinator. TTY, (301) 504-6369.*
General e-mail, fnic@nal.usda.gov
Web, www.nal.usda.gov/fnic

Serves as a resource center for school and child nutrition program personnel who need information on food service management and nutrition education. Center open to the public.

National Assessment Governing Board, *800 N. Capitol St. N.W., #825 20002-4233; (202) 357-6938. Fax, (202) 357-6945. Mary Crovo, Executive Director (Acting). Toll-free, (877) 977-6938.*
General e-mail, nagb@ed.gov
Web, www.nagb.org

Independent board of local, state, and federal officials, educators, and others appointed by the secretary of education and funded under the National Assessment of Educational

Progress (NAEP) program. Sets policy for NAEP, a series of tests measuring achievements of U.S. students since 1969.

White House Commission on Presidential Scholars *(Education Dept.), 400 Maryland Ave. S.W., #5E119 20202-8173; (202) 401-0961. Fax, (202) 260-7464. Melissa Apostolides, Executive Director.*
General e-mail, Presidential.Scholars@ed.gov
Web, www.ed.gov/programs/psp/about.html

Honorary recognition program that selects high school seniors of outstanding achievement in academics, community service, artistic ability, and leadership to receive the Presidential Scholars Award. Scholars travel to Washington during national recognition week to receive the award.

▶**CONGRESS**

For a listing of relevant congressional committees and subcommittees, please see page 156 or the Appendix.

▶**NONGOVERNMENTAL**

Achieve, Inc., *1775 Eye St. N.W., #410 20006; (202) 419-1540. Fax, (202) 828-0911. Michael Cohen, President.*
Web, www.achieve.org

Bipartisan organization that seeks to raise academic standards, improve performance assessments, and strengthen personal accountability among young people. Encourages high school graduates to pursue postsecondary education and rewarding careers. Monitors legislation and regulations.

Alliance for Excellent Education, *1201 Connecticut Ave. N.W., #901 20036; (202) 828-0828. Fax, (202) 828-0821. Bob Wise, President.*
Web, www.all4ed.org

Policy and advocacy organization that promotes secondary education reform, with a focus on the most at-risk students. Works to increase public awareness through conferences, reports, and press releases. Monitors legislation and regulations.

American Coal Foundation, *101 Constitution Ave. N.W., #525 East 20001-2133; (202) 463-9785. Fax, (202) 463-9786. Alma Patty, Executive Director.*
General e-mail, info@teachcoal.org
Web, www.teachcoal.org

Develops, produces, and disseminates, via the Web, coal-related educational materials and programs designed for teachers and students. Works with other coal- and energy-related groups to co-sponsor workshops for science and social studies teachers. Supported by coal producers and manufacturers of mining equipment and supplies.

American Institutes for Research, *1000 Thomas Jefferson St. N.W. 20007; (202) 403-5000. Fax, (202) 403-5001. Sol Pelavin, President. Press, (202) 403-5119.*
General e-mail, inquiry@air.org
Web, www.air.org

Conducts research on educational evaluation and improvement. Develops and implements assessment and testing services that improve student education as well as meet the requirements set forth by state and federally mandated programs. (Formerly New American Schools.)

Assn. for Childhood Education International, *17904 Georgia Ave., #215, Olney, MD 20832; (301) 570-2111. Fax, (301) 570-2212. Diane Whitehead, Executive Director (Acting). Information, (800) 423-3563.*
General e-mail, headquarters@acei.org

Web, www.acei.org

Membership: educators, parents, and professionals who work with children (infancy to adolescence). Works to promote the rights, education, and well-being of children worldwide. Holds annual conference.

Assn. for Supervision and Curriculum Development, *1703 N. Beauregard St., Alexandria, VA 22311-1714; (703) 578-9600. Fax, (703) 575-5400. Gene R. Carter, Executive Director. Information, (800) 933-2723.*
General e-mail, member@ascd.org

Web, www.ascd.org

Membership: approximately 175,000 professional educators internationally, including superintendents, supervisors, principals, teachers, professors of education, and school board members. Develops programs, products, and services for educators.

Center for Inspired Teaching, *1436 U St. N.W., #400 20009; (202) 462-1956. Fax, (202) 462-1905. Aleta Margolis, Executive Director.*
General e-mail, info@inspiredteaching.org

Web, www.inspiredteaching.org

Seeks to decrease time teachers spend maintaining discipline, increase teaching time, and improve students' ability to think critically and solve problems. Promotes education reform through the use of innovative teaching methods to motivate and challenge students. Offers professional development courses, in-classroom mentoring, and school partnerships.

Center on Education Policy, *1001 Connecticut Ave. N.W., #522 20036; (202) 822-8065. Fax, (202) 822-6008. John F. Jennings, President.*
General e-mail, cep-dc@cep-dc.org

Web, www.cep-dc.org

Advocates for public education. Interests include the federal role in education and the status and effects of state high school exit examinations. Provides expert advice upon request. Works with many other education, business, state, and civic organizations. Monitors local, state, and federal legislation and regulations.

Council of the Great City Schools, *1301 Pennsylvania Ave. N.W., #702 20004-1758; (202) 393-2427. Fax, (202) 393-2400. Mike Casserly, Executive Director.*
Web, www.cgcs.org

Membership: superintendents and school board members of large urban school districts. Provides research, legislative, and support services for members; interests include elementary and secondary education and school finance.

Editorial Projects in Education, Inc., *6935 Arlington Rd., #100, Bethesda, MD 20814-5233; (301) 280-3100. Fax, (301) 280-3200. Virginia Edwards, President. Toll-free, (800) 346 1834.*
Web, www.edweek.org

Promotes awareness of important issues in K through 12 education among professionals and the public. Publishes books and special reports on topics of interest to educators.

Home and School Institute, *MegaSkills Education Center, 1500 Massachusetts Ave. N.W. 20005; (202) 362-7889. Fax, (202) 362-9066. Dorothy Rich, President.*
Web, www.megaskillshsi.org

Works to improve the quality of education for children and parents by integrating the resources of the home, the school, and the community. Develops family training curricula and materials for home use and training programs and conferences for professionals. Programs and materials address such topics as special, bilingual, and career education; character development; and working parents.

National Assn. for College Admission Counseling, *1050 N. Highland St., #400, Arlington, VA 22201; (703) 836-2222. Fax, (703) 836-8015. Joyce Smith, Chief Executive Officer. Information, (800) 822-6285.*
General e-mail, info@nacac.com

Web, wwww.nacacnet.org

Membership: high school guidance counselors, independent counselors, college and university admissions officers, and financial aid officers. Assists counselors who serve students in the college admission process. Promotes and funds research on admission counseling and on the transition from high school to college. Advocates for the rights of students in the college admission process. Sponsors national college fairs and continuing education for members.

National Assn. for the Education of Young Children, *1313 L St. N.W., #500 20005; (202) 232-8777. Fax, (202) 328-1846. Mark R. Ginsberg, Executive Director. Information, (800) 424-2460.*
General e-mail, naeyc@naeyc.org

Web, www.naeyc.org

Membership: teachers, parents, and directors of early childhood programs. Works to improve the education of and the quality of services to children from birth through age eight. Sponsors professional development opportunities for early childhood educators. Offers an accreditation program and conducts an annual conference; issues publications.

National Assn. of Elementary School Principals, *1615 Duke St., Alexandria, VA 22314-3483; (703) 684-3345. Fax, (703) 549-5568. Gail Connelly, Executive Director. Toll-free, (800) 386-2377.*

General e-mail, naesp@naesp.org

Web, www.naesp.org

Membership: elementary school and middle school principals. Conducts workshops for members on federal and state policies and programs and on professional development. Offers assistance in contract negotiations.

National Assn. of Secondary School Principals, *1904 Association Dr., Reston, VA 20191-1537; (703) 860-0200. Fax, (703) 476-5432. Gerald Tirozzi, Executive Director. Web, www.principals.org*

Membership: principals and assistant principals of middle schools and senior high schools, both public and private, and college-level teachers of secondary education. Conducts training programs for members; serves as clearinghouse for information on secondary school administration. Student activities office provides student councils, student activity advisers, and national and junior honor societies with information on national associations.

National Congress of Parents and Teachers, *Programs, Washington Office,* *1400 L St. N.W., #300 20005-9998; (202) 289-6790. Fax, (202) 289-6791. Sheri Johnson, Director. General e-mail, info@pta.org*

Web, www.pta.org

Membership: parent-teacher associations at the preschool, elementary, and secondary levels. Washington office represents members' interests on education, funding for education, parent involvement, child protection and safety, comprehensive health care for children, AIDS, the environment, children's television and educational technology, child care, and nutrition. (Headquarters in Chicago, Ill.)

National Head Start Assn., *1651 Prince St., Alexandria, VA 22314; (703) 739-0875. Fax, (703) 739-0878. Michael McGrady, President (Acting). Web, www.nhsa.org*

Membership: organizations that represent Head Start children, families, and staff. Recommends strategies on issues affecting Head Start programs; provides training and professional development opportunities. Monitors legislation and regulations.

National School Boards Assn., *1680 Duke St., Alexandria, VA 22314; (703) 838-6722. Fax, (703) 683-7590. Anne L. Bryant, Executive Director; Francisco Negron, General Counsel. General e-mail, info@nsba.org*

Web, www.nsba.org

Federation of state school board associations. Interests include funding of public education, local governance, and quality of education programs. Sponsors seminars, an annual conference, and an information center. Monitors legislation and regulations. Library open to the public by appointment.

Reading Is Fundamental, *1825 Connecticut Ave. N.W., #400 20009-5726; (202) 536-3400. Fax, (202) 536-3518. Carol H. Rasco, President. Information, (877) RIF-READ.*

General e-mail, contactus@rif.org

Web, www.rif.org

Conducts programs and workshops to motivate young people to read. Provides young people with books and parents with services to encourage reading at home.

School Nutrition Assn., *700 S. Washington St., #300, Alexandria, VA 22314-4287; (703) 739-3900. Fax, (703) 739-3915. Barbara Belmont, Executive Director. Information, (800) 877-8822. General e-mail, servicecenter@schoolnutrition.org*

Web, www.schoolnutrition.org

Membership: state and local food service workers and supervisors, school cafeteria managers, nutrition educators, industry members, and others interested in school food programs and child nutrition. Sponsors National School Lunch Week and National School Breakfast Week. (Formerly the American School Food Service Assn.)

Teach for America, *Washington Office,* *1413 K St. N.W., 7th Floor 20005; (202) 552-2400. Fax, (202) 371-9272. Wendy Kopp, Chief Executive Officer. Information, (800) 832-1230. General e-mail, admissions@teachforamerica.org*

Web, www.teachforamerica.org

A national teacher corps of recent college graduates from all academic majors and cultural backgrounds. Participants teach for a minimum of two years in underfunded urban and rural public schools. Promotes outstanding teaching and educational equity. Monitors legislation and regulations. (Headquarters in New York.)

Private, Parochial, and Home Schooling

►AGENCIES

Education Dept., *Non-Public Education,* *400 Maryland Ave. S.W., #4W339 20202-5940; (202) 401-1365. Fax, (202) 401-1368. Jack Klenk, Director. General e-mail, oiinon-publiceducation@ed.gov*

Web, www.ed.gov/about/offices/list/oii/nonpublic/index. html

Acts as ombudsman for interests of teachers and students in non-public schools (elementary and secondary levels); reports to the secretary of education on matters relating to non-public education.

►NONGOVERNMENTAL

Americans United for Separation of Church and State, *518 C St. N.E. 20002; (202) 466-3234. Fax, (202) 466-2587. Barry W. Lynn, Executive Director. General e-mail, americansunited@au.org*

Web, www.au.org

Citizens' interest group. Opposes federal and state aid to parochial schools; works to ensure religious neutrality in public schools; supports free religious exercise; initiates litigation; maintains speakers bureau. Monitors legislation and regulations.

Council for American Private Education, *13017 Wisteria Dr., #457, Germantown, MD 20874; (301) 916-8460. Fax, (301) 916-8485. Joe McTighe, Executive Director.*
General e-mail, cape@capenet.org

Web, www.capenet.org

Coalition of national private school associations serving private elementary and secondary schools. Acts as a liaison between private education and government, other educational organizations, the media, and the public. Seeks greater access to private schools for all families. Monitors legislation and regulations.

Home School Legal Defense Assn., *1 Patrick Henry Circle, Purcellville, VA 20132 (mailing address: P.O. Box 3000, Purcellville, VA 20134-9000); (540) 338-5600. Fax, (540) 338-2733. J. Michael Smith, President.*
General e-mail, info@hslda.org

Web, www.hslda.org

Membership: families who practice home schooling. Provides members with legal consultation and defense. Initiates civil rights litigation on behalf of members. Monitors legislation and regulations.

National Assn. of Independent Schools, *Government Relations, 1620 L St. N.W., #1100 20036-5695; (202) 973-9700. Fax, (202) 973-9790. Jefferson G. Burnett, Vice President. Press, (202) 973-9717.*
General e-mail, ic@nais.org

Web, www.nais.org

Membership: independent elementary and secondary schools in the United States and abroad. Provides statistical and educational information to members. Monitors legislation and regulations.

National Catholic Educational Assn., *1077 30th St. N W, #100 20007-3852; (202) 337 6232. Fax, (202) 333-6706. Karen Ristau, President.*
General e-mail, admin@ncea.org

Web, www.ncea.org

Membership: Catholic schools (preschool through college and seminary) and school administrators. Provides consultation services to members for administration, curriculum, continuing education, religious education, campus ministry, boards of education, and union and personnel negotiations; conducts workshops and conferences; supports federal aid for private education. (Affiliated with the Assn. of Catholic Colleges and Universities.)

National Congress of Parents and Teachers, *Programs, Washington Office, 1400 L St. N.W., #300 20005-9998; (202) 289-6790. Fax, (202) 289-6791. Sheri Johnson, Director.*
General e-mail, info@pta.org

Web, www.pta.org

Membership: parent-teacher associations at the preschool, elementary, and secondary levels. Coordinates the National Coalition for Public Education, which opposes tuition tax credits and vouchers for private education. (Headquarters in Chicago, Ill.)

National Council of Churches, *Washington Office, 110 Maryland Ave. N.E. 20002; (202) 544-2350. Fax, (202) 543-1297. Wesley M. Pattillo, Senior Program Director for Justice, Advocacy, and Communication, (212) 870-2227; Kevin Williams, Office Manager.*
Web, www.ncccusa.org

Membership: Protestant, Anglican, and Eastern Orthodox churches. Opposes federal aid to private schools. (Headquarters in New York.)

U.S. Conference of Catholic Bishops (USCCB), *Secretariat of Catholic Education, 3211 4th St. N.E. 20017-1194; (202) 541-3132. Fax, (202) 541-3390. Marie A. Powell, Executive Director.*
Web, www.usccb.org

Represents Catholic bishops in the United States in public policy educational issues.

SPECIAL GROUPS IN EDUCATION

Gifted and Talented

▶**AGENCIES**

Education Dept., *Jacob K. Javits Gifted and Talented Students Education, 400 Maryland Ave. S.W., #3E124 20202-6200; (202) 260-7813. Fax, (202) 205-8969. Pat O'Connell Johnson, Program Officer.*
Web, www.ed.gov/programs/javits/index.html

Awards grants for developing programs for gifted and talented students, including the limited-English-speaking, economically disadvantaged, and disabled. Oversees the National Research Center, which administers grants for research and analysis of gifted and talented programs.

▶**NONGOVERNMENTAL**

Council for Exceptional Children (CEC), *110 N. Glebe Rd., #300, Arlington, VA 22201-5704; (703) 620-3660. Fax, (703) 264-9494. Bruce A. Ramirez, Director.*
General e-mail, service@cec.sped.org

Web, www.cec.sped.org

Membership association that advocates on behalf of children with disabilities and gifts and talents as well as special educators. Sets professional standards for the field; publishes books, journals, newsletters, and other resources; and offers professional development for teachers and administrators, including an annual convention. Sponsors the Yes I Can! Awards for children with disabilities who excel. Monitors legislation and regulations.

National Assn. for Gifted Children, *1707 L St. N.W.,*
#550 20036; (202) 785-4268. Fax, (202) 785-4248. Nancy
Green, Executive Director.
General e-mail, nagc@nagc.org
Web, www.nagc.org

Membership: teachers, administrators, state coordinators, and parents. Works for programs for intellectually and creatively gifted children in public and private schools.

Learning and Physically Disabled

►AGENCIES

Education Dept., *National Center for Special*
Education Research (NCSER), 555 New Jersey Ave. N.W.
20208-5500; (202) 219-1385. Lynn Okagaki,
Commissioner (Acting).
Web, www.ed.gov

Sponsors a comprehensive program of special education research designed to expand the knowledge and understanding of infants, toddlers, and children with disabilities.

Education Dept., *Special Education and Rehabilitative*
Services, 550 12th St. S.W., 5th Floor 20202; (202) 245-
7468. Fax, (202) 245-7638. Vacant, Assistant Secretary.
Main phone is voice and TTY accessible.
Web, www.nochildleftbehind.gov

Administers federal assistance programs for the education and rehabilitation of people with disabilities through the National Institute of Disability and Rehabilitation Research, the Office of Special Education Programs, and the Rehabilitation Services Administration; maintains a national information clearinghouse for people with disabilities.

Education Dept., *Special Education Programs, 550 12th*
St. S.W., 4th Floor 20202-3600; (202) 245-7459. Fax,
(202) 245-7614. Patty Guard, Director (Acting).
Web, www.ed.gov/about/offices/list/osers/osep/about.html

Responsible for special education programs and services designed to meet the needs and develop the full potential of children with disabilities. Programs include support for training of teachers and other professional personnel; grants for research; financial aid to help states initiate and improve their resources; and media services and captioned films for hearing impaired persons.

Office of Personnel Management (OPM), *Outreach*
Group, 1900 E St. N.W., #7412 20415; (202) 606-2773.
Anita R. Hanson, Outreach Group Manager.
Web, www.opm.gov

Provides veterans, military personnel, and federal hiring officials with information on veterans' rights and employment opportunities with the federal government. Provides outreach to colleges and universities on Schedule A hiring authorities for people with disabilities.

Smithsonian Institution, *Accessibility Program,*
14th St. and Constitution Ave. N.W., NMAH, MRC 607
20013-7012; (202) 633-2921. Fax, (202) 633-4352.
Elizabeth Ziebarth, Director. Information, (888) 783-0001.
TTY, (202) 633-4353.
General e-mail, ziebarth@si.edu
Web, www.si.edu

Coordinates the Smithsonian's efforts to improve accessibility of its programs and facilities to visitors and staff with disabilities. Serves as a resource for museums and individuals nationwide.

►CONGRESS

For a listing of relevant congressional committees and
subcommittees, please see page 156 or the Appendix.

Library of Congress, *National Library Service for the*
Blind and Physically Handicapped, 1291 Taylor St. N.W.
20542; (202) 707-5100. Fax, (202) 707-0712. Frank Kurt
Cylke, Director. Toll-free, (800) 424-8567. TDD, (202)
707-0744.
General e-mail, nls@loc.gov
Web, www.loc.gov/nls

Administers a national program of free library services for persons with physical disabilities in cooperation with regional and subregional libraries. Produces and distributes full-length books and magazines in recorded form and in Braille. Reference section answers questions relating to blindness and physical disabilities and on library services available to persons with disabilities.

►NONGOVERNMENTAL

Assn. for Education and Rehabilitation of the Blind
and Visually Impaired, *1703 N. Beauregard St., #440,*
Alexandria, VA 22311; (703) 671-4500. Fax, (703) 671-
6391. Jim Gandorf, Executive Director. Toll-free, (877)
492-2708.
General e-mail, aer@aerbvi.org
Web, www.aerbvi.org

Membership: professionals who work in all phases of education and rehabilitation of blind and visually impaired children and adults. Provides support and professional development opportunities through the sponsorship of international and regional conferences, continuing education, job exchange, professional recognition through annual awards, and several publications. Interests include an interdisciplinary approach to research in the field of visual impairment. Monitors legislation and regulations.

Assn. of University Centers on Disabilities (AUCD),
1010 Wayne Ave., #920, Silver Spring, MD 20910; (301)
588-8252. Fax, (301) 588-2842. George Jesien, Executive
Director.
General e-mail, info@aucd.org
Web, www.aucd.org

Network of facilities that diagnose and treat the developmentally disabled. Trains graduate students and professionals in the field; helps state and local agencies develop services. Interests include interdisciplinary training and services, early screening to prevent developmental disabilities, and development of equipment and programs to serve persons with disabilities.

Council for Exceptional Children (CEC), *110 N. Glebe Rd., #300, Arlington, VA 22201-5704; (703) 620-3660. Fax, (703) 264-9494. Bruce A. Ramirez, Director. General e-mail, service@cec.sped.org*

Web, www.cec.sped.org

Membership association that advocates on behalf of children with disabilities and gifts and talents as well as special educators. Sets professional standards for the field; publishes books, journals, newsletters, and other resources; and offers professional development for teachers and administrators, including an annual convention. Sponsors the Yes I Can! Awards for children with disabilities who excel. Monitors legislation and regulations.

Gallaudet University, *800 Florida Ave. N.E. 20002-3695; (202) 651-5000. Fax, (202) 651-5508. Robert R. Davila, President. Phone numbers are voice and TTY accessible. Video phone, (202) 651-5866 (or IP address, 134.231.18.170). Web, www.gallaudet.edu*

Offers undergraduate, graduate, and doctoral degree programs for deaf, hard of hearing, and hearing students. Conducts research; maintains the Laurent Clerc National Deaf Education Center and demonstration preschool, elementary (Kendall Demonstration Elementary School), and secondary programs (Model Secondary School for the Deaf). Sponsors the Center for Global Education, National Deaf Education Network and Clearinghouse, and the Cochlear Implant Education Center.

National Assn. of Private Special Education Centers, *1522 K St. N.W., #1032 20005-1202; (202) 408-3338. Fax, (202) 408-3340. Sherry L. Kolbe, Executive Director. General e-mail, napsec@aol.com*

Web, www.napsec.org

Promotes greater education opportunities for children with disabilities; provides legislators and agencies with information and testimony; formulates and disseminates positions and statements on special education issues.

National Assn. of State Directors of Special Education, *1800 Diagonal Rd., #320, Alexandria, VA 22314; (703) 519-3800. Fax, (703) 519-3808. Bill East, Executive Director, (703) 519-3800, ext. 322. TTY, (703) 519-7008. General e-mail, nasdse@nasdse.org*

Web, www.nasdse.org

Membership: state directors of special education and others interested in special education policy. Monitors legislation, policy, and research affecting special education.

VSA Arts, *818 Connecticut Ave. N.W., #600 20006; (202) 628-2800. Fax, (202) 429-0868. Soula Antoniou, President. Information, (800) 933-8721. TTY, (202) 737-0645. General e-mail, info@vsarts.org*

Web, www.vsarts.org

Initiates and supports research and program development providing arts training and programming for persons with disabilities to make classrooms and communities more inclusive. Provides technical assistance and training to VSA Arts state organizations; acts as an information clearinghouse for arts and persons with disabilities. (Affiliated with the John F. Kennedy Center for the Performing Arts.)

Minorities and Women

▶**AGENCIES**

Bureau of Indian Education (BIE), *(Interior Dept.), 1849 C St. N.W., MS 3609, MIB 20240; (202) 208-6123. Fax, (202) 208-3312. Kevin Skenandore, Director (Acting). Web, www.oiep.bia.edu*

Operates schools and promotes school improvement for Native Americans, including people with disabilities. Provides assistance to Native American pupils in public schools. Aids Native American college students. Sponsors adult education programs designed specifically for Native Americans.

Commission on Civil Rights, *Civil Rights Evaluation, 624 9th St. N.W., #740 20425; (202) 376-8582. Fax, (202) 376-7754. Martin Dannenfelser, Staff Director. Library, (202) 376-8110. Web, www.usccr.gov*

Researches federal policy on education, including desegregation. Library open to the public.

Education Dept., *Civil Rights, 550 12th St. S.W. 20202-1100; (202) 245-6700. Fax, (202) 485-0126. Stephanie Monroe, Assistant Secretary. Information, (800) 421-3481. TTY, (877) 521-2172. General e-mail, ocr@ed.gov*

Web, www.ed.gov/ocr

Enforces laws prohibiting use of federal funds for education programs or activities that discriminate on the basis of race, color, sex, national origin, age, or disability; authorized to discontinue funding.

Education Dept., *Federal TRIO Programs, 1990 K St. N.W., #7000 20006-8510; (202) 502-7600. Fax, (202) 502-7857. Linda Byrd-Johnson, Director. TTY, (202) 502-7600. Web, www.ed.gov/about/offices/list/ope/trio/index.html*

Administers programs for disadvantaged students, including Educational Opportunity Centers, Upward Bound, Upward Bound Math and Science, Talent Search, Student Support Services, the McNair Post-Baccalaureate Achievement Program, TRIO training program, TRIO Dissemination Partnership, and Child Care Access Means Parents in School program.

Education Dept., *Indian Education Programs, 400 Maryland Ave. S.W. 20202-6335; (202) 260-3774. Fax, (202) 260-7779. Cathie Carothers, Director. General e-mail, indian.education@ed.gov*

Web, www.ed.gov/about/offices/list/oese/oie/index.html

Aids local school districts with programs for Native American and Alaska Native students.

Education Dept., *Migrant Education,* *400 Maryland Ave. S.W., #3E317, LBJ 20202-6135; (202) 260-1164. Fax, (202) 205-0089. Lisa Ramirez, Director.*
Web, www.ed.gov/programs/mep/index.html

Administers programs that fund education (preschool through postsecondary) for children of migrant workers.

Education Dept., *Student Achievement and School Accountability,* *400 Maryland Ave. S.W. 20202-6132; (202) 260-0826. Fax, (202) 260-7764. Zollie Stevenson, Director.*
Web, www.ed.gov

Administers the Title I federal assistance program for education of educationally deprived children (preschool through secondary), including Native American children, homeless children, delinquents, and residents in state institutions.

Education Dept., *White House Initiative on Historically Black Colleges and Universities,* *1990 K St. N.W., 6th Floor 20006; (202) 502-7900. Fax, (202) 502-7879. Leonard L. Haynes III, Executive Director.*
General e-mail, oswhi_hbcu@ed.gov
Web, www.ed.gov/about/inits/list/whhbcu/edlite-index.html

Seeks to expand the participation of the black college community in the programs of the federal government and to engage the private sector to help achieve this objective. Hosts annual conference. Provides information about federal contracts, grants, scholarships, fellowships, and other resources available to historically black colleges and universities.

Education Dept., *Women's Educational Equity,* *400 Maryland Ave. S.W., #4W242, LBJ 20202-5950; (202) 205-3145. Fax, (202) 205-5630. Beverley A. Farrar, Program Manager.*
General e-mail, oii.weea@ed.gov
Web, www.ed.gov/programs/equity/index.html

Promotes education equity for women and girls through competitive grants to public agencies, private nonprofit organizations, and individuals. Designates most of its funding for local implementation of gender-equity policies and practice. Projects may be funded for up to four years.

Justice Dept. (DOJ), *Educational Opportunity,* *601 D St. N.W., #4300 20530; (202) 514-4092. Fax, (202) 514-8337. Jeremiah Glassman, Chief. Toll-free, (877) 292-3804.*
Web, www.usdoj.gov/crt

Initiates litigation to ensure equal opportunities in public education; enforces laws dealing with civil rights in public education.

Office of Personnel Management (OPM), *Outreach Group,* *1900 E St. N.W., #7412 20415; (202) 606-2773. Anita R. Hanson, Outreach Group Manager.*
Web, www.opm.gov

Provides veterans, military personnel, and federal hiring officials with information on veterans' rights and employment opportunities with the federal government. Provides outreach to colleges and universities on Schedule A hiring authorities for people with disabilities.

White House Initiative on Educational Excellence for Hispanic Americans *(Education Dept.),* *400 Maryland Ave. S.W., #5E110 20202-3601; (202) 401-1411. Fax, (202) 401-8377. Glorimar Nosal, Market Communications Manager.*
General e-mail, WhiteHouse.HispanicEducation@ed.gov
Web, www.yesican.gov

Promotes high quality education for Hispanic Americans and the participation of Hispanic Americans in federal education programs. Disseminates information on educational resources. Promotes parental involvement, engagement of the business community, and enrollment in college.

White House Initiative on Tribal Colleges and Universities *(Education Dept.),* *1990 K St. N.W., #7010 20006; (202) 219-7040. Fax, (202) 219-7086. Alan Schiff, Chief of Staff.*
Web, www.ed.gov/about/inits/list/whtc/edlite-index.html

Supports tribal colleges and universities (TCUs) through long-term planning, improved financial management and security, the use of new technology, enhanced physical infrastructure, and achievement of learning standards. Improves access by TCUs to federal programs. Encourages the preservation of tribal languages and traditions.

▶**CONGRESS**

For a listing of relevant congressional committees and subcommittees, please see page 156 or the Appendix.

▶**NONGOVERNMENTAL**

American Assn. of University Women (AAUW), *1111 16th St. N.W. 20036-4873; (202) 785-7700. Fax, (202) 872-1425. Linda D. Hallman, Executive Director. Library, (202) 728-7622. TTY, (202) 785-7777.*
General e-mail, info@aauw.org
Web, www.aauw.org

Membership: graduates of accredited colleges, universities, and recognized foreign institutions. Interests include equity for women and girls in education, the workplace, health care, and the family. Library open to the public by appointment.

American Indian Higher Education Consortium, *121 Oronoco St., Alexandria, VA 22314; (703) 838-0400. Fax, (703) 838-0388. Carrie L. Billy, President.*
General e-mail, info@aihec.org
Web, www.aihec.org

Membership: Tribal colleges and universities (TCUs). Objectives include increased financial support for TCUs, equitable participation in the land grant system, expanded technology programs in Indian Country, and development of an accrediting body for postsecondary institutions that serve American Indians.

Aspira Assn., *1444 Eye St. N.W., #800 20005; (202) 835-3600. Fax, (202) 835-3613. Ronald Blackburn-Moreno, President.*
General e-mail, info@aspira.org
Web, www.aspira.org

Provides Latino youth with resources necessary for them to remain in school and contribute to their community. Interests include math, science, leadership development, parental involvement, and research. Monitors legislation and regulations.

Assn. of American Colleges and Universities (AACU), *1818 R St. N.W. 20009; (202) 387-3760. Fax, (202) 265-9532. Carol Geary Schneider, President.*
Web, www.aacu.org

Serves as clearinghouse for information on women professionals in higher education. Interests include women's studies, women's centers, and women's leadership and professional development.

Assn. of American Colleges and Universities, *Office of Diversity, Equity, and Global Initiatives, 1818 R St. N.W. 20009; (202) 387-3760. Fax, (202) 265-9532. Carol Geary-Schneider, President.*
Web, www.aacu.org

Conducts a multi-project initiative over a network of colleges and universities that offers diversity leadership institutes, curriculum development, conferences on diversity in education, literature, and research grants.

Clare Booth Luce Policy Institute, *112 Elden St., Suite P, Herndon, VA 20170; (703) 318-0730. Fax, (703) 318-8867. Michelle Easton, President. Toll-free, (888) 891-4288.*
General e-mail, info@cblpi.org
Web, www.cblpi.org

Seeks to engage young women through student programs promoting conservative values and leadership. Offers mentoring, internship, and networking opportunities for young women.

Council for Opportunity in Education, *1025 Vermont Ave. N.W., #900 20005-3516; (202) 347-7430. Fax, (202) 347-0786. Arnold L. Mitchem, President.*
General e-mail, arnold.mitchem@coenet.us
Web, www.coenet.us

Represents institutions of higher learning, administrators, counselors, teachers, and others committed to advancing equal educational opportunity in colleges and universities. Works to sustain and improve educational opportunity programs such as the federally funded TRIO programs, designed to help low-income, first-generation immigrants, physically disabled students, and veterans enroll in and graduate from college.

Hispanic Assn. of Colleges and Universities, *Washington Office, 1 Dupont Circle N.W., #430 20036; (202) 833-8361. Fax, (202) 261-5082. Antonio R. Flores, President.*
General e-mail, govrel@hacu.net
Web, www.hacu.net

Membership: Hispanic-serving institutions (HSIs) and other higher education institutions committed to improving the quality of schools for Hispanics in the United States, Puerto Rico, Latin America, and Spain. Focuses on increased federal funding for HSIs; partnerships with government agencies and industry; faculty development and research; technological assistance; and financial aid and internships for Hispanic students. (Headquarters in San Antonio, Texas.)

League of United Latin American Citizens, *2000 L St. N.W., #610 20036; (202) 833-6130. Fax, (202) 833-6135. Brent Wilkes, Executive Director. Toll-free, (877) LULAC-01.*
General e-mail, info@lulac.org
Web, www.lulac.org

Seeks to increase the number of minorities, especially Hispanics, attending postsecondary schools; supports legislation to increase educational opportunities for Hispanics and other minorities; provides scholarship funds and educational and career counseling.

The Links Inc., *1200 Massachusetts Ave. N.W. 20005-4501; (202) 842-8686. Fax, (202) 842-4020. Gwendolyn B. Lee, President.*
Web, www.linksinc.org

Predominantly African American women's service organization that works with the educationally disadvantaged and culturally deprived; focuses on arts, services for youth, and national and international trends and services.

NAACP Legal Defense and Educational Fund, *Washington Office, 1444 Eye St. N.W., 10th Floor 20005; (202) 682-1300. Fax, (202) 682-1312. Leslie M. Proll, Director.*
Web, www.naacpldf.org

Civil rights litigation group that provides legal information about civil rights and advice on educational discrimination against women and minorities; monitors federal enforcement of civil rights laws. Not affiliated with the National Assn. for the Advancement of Colored People (NAACP). (Headquarters in New York.)

National Alliance of Black School Educators, *310 Pennsylvania Ave. S.E. 20003; (202) 608-6310. Fax, (202) 608-6319. Quentin R. Lawson, Executive Director. Toll-free, (800) 221-2654.*
Web, www.nabse.org

Develops and recommends policy for and promotes the education of African American youth and adults; seeks to raise the academic achievement level of all African American students. Sponsors workshops and conferences on major issues in education affecting African American students and educators.

National Assn. for Equal Opportunity in Higher Education (NAFEO), *209 3rd St. S.E. 20003; (202) 552-3300. Fax, (202) 552-3330. Lezli Baskerville, President.*
Web, www.nafeo.org

Membership: historically and predominantly black colleges and universities, including public, private, land-grant, two-year, four-year, graduate, and professional schools. Represents and advocates on behalf of its member institutions and the students, faculty, and alumni they serve. Operates a national research and resource center on blacks in higher education.

National Assn. for the Advancement of Colored People (NAACP), *Washington Bureau, 1156 15th St. N.W., #915 20005-1750; (202) 463-2940. Fax, (202) 463-2953. Hilary O. Shelton, Director.*
General e-mail, washingtonbureau@naacpnet.org
Web, www.naacp.org

Membership: persons interested in civil rights for all minorities. Works for equal opportunity for minorities in all areas, including education; seeks to ensure a high-quality desegregated education for all through litigation and legislation. (Headquarters in Baltimore, Md.)

National Assn. of Colored Women's Clubs Inc. (NACWC), *1601 R St. N.W. 20009-6420; (202) 667-4080. Fax, (202) 667-2574. Marie Wright-Tolliver, President.*
Web, www.nacwc.org

Seeks to promote education; protect and enforce civil rights; raise the standard of family living; promote interracial understanding; and enhance leadership development. Awards scholarships; conducts programs in education, social service, and philanthropy.

National Assn. of State Universities and Land Grant Colleges, *Advancement of Public Black Colleges, 1307 New York Ave. N.W., #400 20005-4722; (202) 478-6040. Fax, (202) 478-6046. Vacant, Vice President.*
Web, www.nasulgc.org

Seeks to heighten awareness and visibility of public African American colleges; promotes institutional advancement. Conducts research and provides information on issues of concern; acts as a liaison with African American public colleges and universities, the federal government, and private associations. Monitors legislation and regulations.

National Clearinghouse for English Language Acquisition (NCELA), *Language Instruction Educational Programs, 2011 Eye St. N.W., #300 20006; (202) 467-0867. Fax, (202) 467-4283. Jack Levy, Director.*
General e-mail, askncela@ncela.gwu.edu
Web, www.ncela.gwu.edu

Collects, analyzes, and disseminates information relating to the effective education of linguistically and culturally diverse learners in the United States. Interests include foreign language programs, ESL programs, Head Start, Title I, migrant education, and adult education programs.

National Council of La Raza, *1126 16th St. N.W. 20036; (202) 785-1670. Fax, (202) 776-1792. Janet Murguia, President.*
General e-mail, comments@nclr.org
Web, www.nclr.org

Provides research, policy analysis, and advocacy on educational status and needs of Hispanics; promotes education reform benefiting Hispanics; develops and tests community-based models for helping Hispanic students succeed in school. Interests include counseling, testing, and bilingual, vocational, preschool through postsecondary, and migrant education.

National Council of Women's Organizations, *714 G St. N.W., #200 20003; (202) 293-4505. Fax, (202) 293-4507. Susan Scanlan, Chair.*
General e-mail, ncwo@ncwo-online.org
Web, www.womensorganizations.org

Membership: local and national women's organizations. Engages in policy work and grassroots activism to address issues of concern to women, including workplace and economic equity, education and job training, affirmative action, Social Security, child care, reproductive freedom, health, and global women's equality. Monitors legislation and regulations.

National Indian Education Assn. (NIEA), *110 Maryland Ave. N.E., #104 20002; (202) 544-7290. Fax, (202) 544-7293. Lillian A. Sparks, Executive Director.*
General e-mail, niea@niea.org
Web, www.niea.org

Represents American Indian, Alaska Native, and Native Hawaiian educators and students. Seeks to improve educational opportunities and resources for those groups nationwide while preserving their traditional cultures and values. Monitors legislation and regulations.

National Society of Black Engineers, *205 Daingerfield Rd., Alexandria, VA 22314; (703) 549-2207. Fax, (703) 683-5312. Carl Mack, Executive Director.*
General e-mail, headquarters@nsbe.org
Web, www.nsbe.org

Membership: college students studying engineering. Offers academic excellence programs, scholarships, leadership training, and professional and career development opportunities. Activities include tutorial programs, group study sessions, high school/junior high outreach programs, technical seminars and workshops, career fairs, and an annual convention.

National Women's Law Center, *11 Dupont Circle N.W., #800 20036; (202) 588-5180. Fax, (202) 588-5185. Nancy Duff Campbell, Co-President; Marcia D. Greenberger, Co-President.*
General e-mail, info@nwlc.org
Web, www.nwlc.org

Works to protect and advance the rights of women and girls at work, in school, and beyond. Maintains programs that focus on enforcing Title IX's provisions for equal treatment in education and narrowing the gender gap in athletics and the technology-oriented workplace. Other interests include equal pay and benefits, sexual harassment laws, the right to family leave, and the preservation of diversity in the workplace.

United Negro College Fund, *8260 Willow Oaks Corporate Dr., Fairfax, VA 22031-4511 (mailing address: P.O. Box 10444, Fairfax, VA 22031-0444); (703) 205-3400. Fax, (703) 205-3575. Michael Lomax, President.*
Web, www.uncf.org

Membership: private colleges and universities with historically black enrollment. Raises money for member institutions; monitors legislation and regulations.

Younger Women's Task Force, *714 G St. N.W., #200 20003; (202) 293-4505. Fax, (202) 293-4507. Shannon Lynberg, National Director.*
General e-mail, ShannonL@ywtf.org
Web, www.ywtf.org

Grassroots organization that encourages young women to engage in political activism on issues directly affecting them. Provides leadership training and a local and national network for peer mentoring; runs financial literacy programs. A project of the National Council of Women's Organizations.

SPECIAL TOPICS IN EDUCATION

Bilingual and Multicultural

▶**AGENCIES**

Education Dept., *Office of English Language Acquisition (OELA), 400 Maryland Ave. S.W. 20202-6510; (202) 401-1402. Fax, (202) 205-1229. Margarita Pinkos, Director.*
Web, www.ed.gov/about/offices/list/oela/index.html

Provides state education agencies with grants to help ensure that children with limited English proficiency, including immigrant children and youth, attain English proficiency and meet the same student academic achievement standards as other children. Provides grants for the professional development of teachers of English learners, manages the Foreign Language Assistance Program, and administers the Native American/Alaska Native Children in School Program. (Formerly the Office of Bilingual Education and Minority Language Affairs.)

▶**NONGOVERNMENTAL**

National Assn. for Bilingual Education, *1313 L St. N.W., #210 20005; (202) 898-1829. Fax, (202) 789-2866. Mary Jew, President.*
General e-mail, nabe@nabe.org
Web, www.nabe.org

Membership: educators, policymakers, paraprofessionals, publications personnel, students, researchers, and interested individuals. Works to improve educational programs for non-English-speaking students and to promote bilingualism among American students. Conducts annual conference and workshops.

National MultiCultural Institute, *3000 Connecticut Ave. N.W., #438 20008-2556; (202) 483-0700. Fax, (202) 483-5233. Elizabeth P. Salett, President.*
General e-mail, nmci@nmci.org
Web, www.nmci.org

Encourages understanding and communication among people of various ethnic backgrounds; seeks to increase awareness of different perspectives and experiences; provides multicultural training, education, and counseling programs for organizations and institutions working with diverse cultural groups; conducts two conferences annually.

Teachers of English to Speakers of Other Languages Inc. (TESOL), *700 S. Washington St., #200, Alexandria, VA 22314-4287; (703) 836-0774. Fax, (703) 836-7864. Charles Amorosino, Executive Director. Information, (888) 547-3369.*
General e-mail, info@tesol.org
Web, www.tesol.org

Develops and provides information on instruction and research in the teaching of English to speakers of other languages. Sponsors professional development programs and provides career management services.

Citizenship Education

▶**NONGOVERNMENTAL**

Close Up Foundation, *44 Canal Center Plaza, #600, Alexandria, VA 22314-1952; (703) 706-3300. Fax, (703) 706-0000. Timothy Davis, President. Toll-free, (800) 256-7387.*
General e-mail, info@closeup.org
Web, www.closeup.org

Sponsors week-long programs on American government in Washington, D.C., for middle and high school students. Produces television series featuring high school students' experiences in the program.

Horatio Alger Assn. of Distinguished Americans, *99 Canal Center Plaza, #320, Alexandria, VA 22314; (703) 684-9444. Fax, (703) 548-3822. Terrence J. Giroux, Executive Director.*
General e-mail, association@horatioalger.org
Web, www.horatioalger.org

Educates young people about the economic and personal opportunities available in the American free enterprise system. Conducts seminars on careers in public and community service; operates speakers bureau and internship program. Presents the Horatio Alger Youth Award to outstanding high school students and the Horatio Alger Award to professionals who have achieved success in their respective fields. Awards college scholarships.

League of Women Voters Education Fund (LWV), *1730 M St. N.W., #1000 20036; (202) 429-1965. Fax, (202) 429-4343. Nancy Tate, Executive Director.*
General e-mail, lwv@lwv.org

Web, www.lwv.org/lwvef

Public foundation established by the League of Women Voters of the United States. Promotes citizen knowledge of and involvement in representative government; conducts citizen education on current public policy issues; seeks to increase voter registration and turnout; sponsors candidate forums and debates.

National 4-H Council, *7100 Connecticut Ave., Chevy Chase, MD 20815-4999; (301) 961-2800. Fax, (301) 961-2894. Donald T. Floyd Jr., President. Press, (301) 961-2972.*
Web, www.fourhcouncil.edu

4-H membership: young people across America learning leadership, citizenship, and life skills. National 4-H Council strengthens and complements the 4-H youth development program of the U.S. Dept. of Agriculture's cooperative extension system of state land-grant universities. Interests include 4-H afterschool, healthy lifestyle, science engineering and technology, and youth in governance.

Presidential Classroom for Young Americans, *119 Oronoco St., Alexandria, VA 22314-2015; (703) 683-5400. Fax, (703) 548-5728. Maria Darie, Executive Director. Information, (800) 441-6533.*
General e-mail, info@presidentialclassroom.org

Web, www.presidentialclassroom.org

Offers civic education programs for high school students and volunteer opportunities for college students and adults. Provides week-long series of seminars featuring representatives of each branch of government, the diplomatic community, the military, the media, private interest groups, and both major political parties.

Washington Workshops Foundation, *3222 N St. N.W., #340 20007; (202) 965-3434. Fax, (202) 965-1018. Tom Crossan, Executive Director. Information, (800) 368-5688.*
General e-mail, info@workshops.org

Web, www.workshops.org

Educational foundation that provides introductory seminars on American government and politics to junior and senior high school students, including the congressional seminars for high school students.

Consumer Education

►AGENCIES

Agriculture Dept. (USDA), *Research, Education, and Economics,* *1400 Independence Ave. S.W., #216W, MS 0110 20250-0110; (202) 720-5923. Fax, (202) 690-2842. Vacant, Under Secretary; Katherine Smith, Deputy Under Secretary (Acting).*
Web, www.csrees.usda.gov/ree

Coordinates agricultural research, extension, and teaching programs in the food and agricultural sciences, including human nutrition, home economics, consumer services, agricultural economics, environmental quality, natural and renewable resources, forestry and range management, animal and plant production and protection, aquaculture, and the production, distribution, and utilization of food and agricultural products. Oversees the Cooperative State Research, Education, and Extension Service.

Consumer Product Safety Commission (CPSC), *Public Affairs,* *4330 East-West Hwy., #519, Bethesda, MD 20814; (301) 504-7908. Fax, (301) 504-0862. Joseph Martyak, Director (Acting). TTY, (800) 638-8270. Product safety hotline, (800) 638-2772.*
General e-mail, info@cpsc.gov

Web, www.cpsc.gov

Provides information concerning consumer product safety; works with local and state governments, school systems, and private groups to develop product safety information and education programs. Toll-free hotline accepts consumer complaints on hazardous products and injuries associated with a product and offers recorded information on product recalls and CPSC safety recommendations.

Cooperative State Research, Education, and Extension Service (CSREES), *(Agriculture Dept.),* *1400 Independence Ave. S.W., #305A, MS 2201 20250-2201; (202) 720-4423. Fax, (202) 720-8987. Colien Hefferan, Administrator. Information, (202) 720-4651. TTY, (202) 690-1899.*
Web, www.csrees.usda.gov

Oversees county agents and operation of state offices that provide information on home economics, including diet and nutrition, food budgeting, food safety, home gardening, clothing care, and other consumer concerns.

Federal Trade Commission (FTC), *Consumer and Business Education,* *600 Pennsylvania Ave. N.W. 20580; (202) 326-3268. Fax, (202) 326-3574. Carolyn Shanoff, Director. TTY, (202) 326-2502. Consumer Response Center, (877) FTC-HELP.*
Web, www.ftc.gov

Develops educational material about FTC activities in order to inform consumers about their rights and alert businesses about their compliance responsibilities.

Food and Drug Administration (FDA), *(Health and Human Services Dept.), External Relations,* *5600 Fishers Lane, Parklawn, #1505, Rockville, MD 20857-0001; (301) 827-4414. Fax, (301) 827-1070. Patricia Kuntze, Senior Advisor for Consumer Affairs. Consumer inquiries, (888) 463-6332.*
Web, www.fda.gov

Responds to inquiries on issues related to the FDA. Conducts consumer health education programs for specific groups, including women, older adults, and the educationally and economically disadvantaged. Serves as liaison with national health and consumer organizations.

Food Safety and Inspection Service *(Agriculture Dept.)*, *1400 Independence Ave. S.W., #331E 20250-0003; (202) 720-7025. Fax, (202) 205-0158. Al Almonzo, Administrator. Press, (202) 720-9113. Consumer inquiries, (800) 535-4555.*
Web, www.usda.gov/fsis

Sponsors food safety educational programs to inform the public about measures to prevent foodborne illnesses; sponsors lectures, publications, public service advertising campaigns, exhibits, and audiovisual presentations. Toll-free hotline answers food safety questions.

►**NONGOVERNMENTAL**

American Assn. of Family and Consumer Sciences, *400 N. Columbus St., #202, Alexandria, VA 22314; (703) 706-4600. Fax, (703) 706-4663. Carolyn Jackson, Executive Director (Interim). Toll-free, (800) 424-8080.*
General e-mail, staff@aafcs.org
Web, www.aafcs.org

Membership: professional home economists. Supports family and consumer sciences education; develops accrediting standards for undergraduate family and consumer science programs; trains and certifies family and consumer science professionals. Monitors legislation and regulations concerning family and consumer issues.

Family, Career, and Community Leaders of America, *1910 Association Dr., Reston, VA 20191-1584; (703) 476-4900. Fax, (703) 860-2713. Michael L. Benjamin, Executive Director.*
General e-mail, natlhdqtrs@fcclainc.org
Web, www.fcclainc.org

National vocational student organization that helps young men and women address personal, family, work, and social issues through family and consumer sciences education.

Literacy, Basic Skills

►**AGENCIES**

AmeriCorps *(Corporation for National and Community Service), Volunteers in Service to America (VISTA), 1201 New York Ave. N.W. 20525; (202) 606-5000. Fax, (202) 565-2789. Jean Whaley, Director, (202) 606-6943. Volunteer recruiting information, (800) 942-2677. TTY, (800) 833-3722; local TTY, (202) 565-2799.*
General e-mail, questions@americorps.gov
Web, www.americorps.gov/vista

Assigns volunteers to local and state education departments, to public agencies, and to private nonprofit organizations that have literacy programs. Other activities include tutor recruitment and training and the organization and

expansion of local literacy councils, workplace literacy programs, and intergenerational literacy programs.

Education Dept., *Adult Education and Literacy, 550 12th St. S.W., 11th Floor 20202-7100; (202) 245-7700. Fax, (202) 245-7838. Cheryl L. Keenan, Director.*
Web, www.ed.gov/about/offices/list/ovae/pi/AdultEd/index.html

Provides state and local education agencies and the general public with information on establishing, expanding, improving, and operating adult education and literacy programs. Emphasizes basic and life skills attainment, English literacy, and high school completion. Awards grants to state education agencies for adult education and literacy programs, including workplace and family literacy.

Education Dept., *National Institute for Literacy, 1775 Eye St. N.W., #730 20006-2401; (202) 233-2025. Fax, (202) 233-2050. Vacant, Director.*
Web, www.nifl.gov

Operates a literacy clearinghouse and an electronic national literacy and communications system; provides private literacy groups, educational institutions, and federal, state, and local agencies working on literacy with assistance; awards grants to literacy programs and individuals pursuing careers in the literacy field.

►**CONGRESS**

For a listing of relevant congressional committees and subcommittees, please see page 156 or the Appendix.

Library of Congress, *Center for the Book, 101 Independence Ave. S.E., #LM 650 20540; (202) 707-5221. Fax, (202) 707-0269. John Y. Cole, Director.*
General e-mail, cfbook@loc.gov
Web, www.loc.gov/cfbook

Promotes family and adult literacy; encourages the study of books and stimulates public interest in books, reading, and libraries; sponsors publication of a directory describing national organizations that administer literacy programs. Affiliated state centers sponsor projects and hold events that call attention to the importance of literacy.

►**NONGOVERNMENTAL**

AFL-CIO Working for America Institute, *815 16th St. N.W. 20006; (202) 508-3717. Fax, (202) 508-3719. Nancy Mills, Executive Director.*
General e-mail, info@workingforamerica.org
Web, www.workingforamerica.org

Provides labor unions, employers, education agencies, and community groups with technical assistance for workplace education programs focusing on adult literacy, basic skills, and job training. Interests include new technologies and workplace innovations.

American Society for Training and Development (ASTD), *1640 King St., Box 1443, Alexandria, VA 22313-2043; (703) 683-8100. Fax, (703) 683-1523. Tony Bingham, Chief Executive Officer.*

General e-mail, astdresearch@astd.org

Web, www.astd.org

Membership: trainers and human resource development specialists. Publishes information on workplace literacy.

Center for Applied Linguistics, *4646 40th St. N.W., #200 20016-1859; (202) 362-0700. Fax, (202) 362-3740. Donna Christian, President.*

General e-mail, info@cal.org

Web, www.cal.org

Research and technical assistance organization that serves as a clearinghouse on application of linguistics to practical language problems. Interests include English as a second language (ESL), teacher training and material development, language education, language proficiency test development, bilingual education, and sociolinguistics.

First Book, *1319 F St. N.W., #1000 20004-1155; (202) 393-1222. Fax, (202) 628-1258. Kyle Zimmer, President.*

General e-mail, staff@firstbook.org

Web, www.firstbook.org

Donates and sells books to programs serving children of low-income families. Organizes fundraisers to support and promote local literacy programs.

General Federation of Women's Clubs, *1734 N St. N.W. 20036-2990; (202) 347-3168. Fax, (202) 835-0246. Natasha Kalteis, Executive Director.*

General e-mail, gfwc@gfwc.org

Web, www.gfwc.org

Nondenominational, nonpartisan international organization of women volunteers. Develops literacy projects in response to community needs; sponsors tutoring.

National Coalition for Literacy, *P.O. Box 11592 20008; (301) 602-6358. Fax, (866) 738-3757. Jennifer Maloney, Director.*

Web, www.national-coalition-literacy.org

Members: organizations concerned with education. Promotes adult education, literacy, and English language development through public awareness campaigns and research application. Seeks to improve literacy policy nationwide.

Newspaper Assn. of America Foundation, *4401 Wilson Blvd., #900, Arlington, VA 22203; (571) 366-1007. Fax, (571) 366-1207. Jeanne Fox-Alston, Vice President.*

Web, www.naafoundation.org

Supports student programs that focus on newspaper readership and an appreciation of the First Amendment as ways of developing engaged and literate citizens. Emphasizes the use of newspapers and other media as educational tools for young people. Interests include student newspapers and the development of youth-appropriate content in community newspapers.

Reading Is Fundamental, *1825 Connecticut Ave. N.W., #400 20009-5726; (202) 536-3400. Fax, (202) 536-3518.*

Carol H. Rasco, President. Information, (877) RIF-READ. General e-mail, contactus@rif.org

Web, www.rif.org

Conducts programs and workshops to motivate young people to read. Provides young people with books and parents with services to encourage reading at home.

Science and Mathematics Education

▶AGENCIES

Education Dept., *Office of Postsecondary Education (OPE): Institutional Development and Undergraduate Education Service: Minority Science and Engineering Improvement,* *1990 K St. N.W., 6th Floor 20006-8512; (202) 502-7777. Fax, (202) 502-7861. James Laws Jr., Director.*

General e-mail, OPEMSEIP@ed.gov

Web, www.ed.gov/programs/iduesmsi/index.html

Provides grants to effect long-range improvement in science and engineering education at predominantly minority institutions and to increase the flow of underrepresented ethnic minorities, particularly minority women, into science and engineering careers.

National Aeronautics and Space Administration (NASA), *Education,* *300 E St. S.W., #9N70 20546; (202) 358-0103. Fax, (202) 358-7097. Joyce Winterton, Assistant Administrator.*

General e-mail, education@nasa.gov

Web, http://education.nasa.gov

Coordinates NASA's education programs and activities to meet national educational needs and ensure a sufficient talent pool to preserve U.S. leadership in aeronautical technology and space science.

National Museum of Natural History *(Smithsonian Institution), Naturalist Center,* *741 Miller Dr. S.E., #G2, Leesburg, VA 20175; (703) 779-9712. Fax, (703) 779-9715. Richard H. Efthim, Manager. Information, (800) 729-7725.*

General e-mail, NatCenter@si.edu

Web, www.mnh.si.edu/education/fieldtrip/planned_ programs/naturalist_center

Main study gallery contains natural history research and reference library with books and more than 36,000 objects, including minerals, rocks, plants, animals, shells and corals, insects, invertebrates, micro- and macrofossil materials, and microbiological and anthropological materials. Facilities include study equipment, such as microscopes, dissecting instruments, and plant presses. Family learning center offers hands-on activities for younger families. Operates a teachers reference center. Library open to the public. Reservations required for groups of six or more, but entry is free of charge.

National Oceanic and Atmospheric Administration (NOAA), *(Commerce Dept.), National Sea Grant College Program,* *1315 East-West Hwy., 11th Floor, Silver Spring, MD 20910; (301) 734-1088. Fax, (301) 713-0799. Leon M. Cammen, Director.*
Web, www.nsgo.seagrant.org

Provides grants, primarily to colleges and universities, for marine resource development; sponsors undergraduate and graduate education and the training of technicians at the college level.

National Science Foundation (NSF), *Education and Human Resources,* *4201 Wilson Blvd., #805, Arlington, VA 22230; (703) 292-8600. Fax, (703) 292-9179. Joan E. Ferrini-Mundy, Director (Acting).*
Web, www.nsf.gov

Develops and supports programs to strengthen science and mathematics education. Provides fellowships and grants for graduate research and teacher education, instructional materials, and studies on the quality of existing science and mathematics programs. Participates in international studies.

National Science Foundation (NSF), *Science Resources Statistics,* *4201 Wilson Blvd., #965, Arlington, VA 22230; (703) 292-8780. Fax, (703) 292-9092. Lynda T. Carlson, Director.*
Web, www.nsf.gov/statistics

Develops and analyzes U.S. and international statistics on training, use, and characteristics of scientists, engineers, and technicians.

Office of Science and Technology Policy (OSTP), *(Executive Office of the President), Science,* *New Executive Office Bldg., 725 17th St. N.W. 20502; (202) 456-6130. Fax, (202) 456-6027. Ted Wackler, Deputy Associate Director.*
General e-mail, info@ostp.gov
Web, www.ostp.gov

Advises the president and others within the EOP on the impact of science and technology on domestic and international affairs; coordinates executive office and federal agency actions related to these issues. Evaluates the effectiveness of science education programs, which include environment, life sciences, physical sciences and engineering, and social, behavioral, and educational sciences. Provides technical support to Homeland Security Dept.

▶**NONGOVERNMENTAL**

American Assn. for the Advancement of Science (AAAS), *Education and Human Resources Programs,* *1200 New York Ave. N.W., 6th Floor 20005; (202) 326-6670. Fax, (202) 371-9849. Shirley M. Malcom, Head. Main phone is voice and TTY accessible.*
General e-mail, ehr@aaas.org
Web, www.aaas.org

Membership: scientists, scientific organizations, and others interested in science and technology education. Works to increase and provide information on the status of women, minorities, and people with disabilities in the sciences and in engineering; focuses on expanding science education opportunities for women, minorities, and people with disabilities.

American Assn. of Physics Teachers, *1 Physics Ellipse, College Park, MD 20740-3845; (301) 209-3311. Fax, (301) 209-0845. Warren Hein, Executive Officer.*
General e-mail, aapt-web@aapt.org
Web, www.aapt.org

Membership: physics teachers and others interested in physics education. Seeks to advance the institutional and cultural role of physics education. Sponsors seminars and conferences; provides educational information and materials. (Affiliated with the American Institute of Physics.)

American Society for Engineering Education, *1818 N St. N.W., #600 20036-2479; (202) 331-3500. Fax, (202) 265-8504. Frank L. Huband, Executive Director. Press, (202) 331-3537.*
Web, www.asee.org

Membership: engineering faculty and administrators, professional engineers, government agencies, and engineering colleges, corporations, and professional societies. Conducts research, conferences, and workshops on engineering education. Monitors legislation and regulations.

Assn. of Science-Technology Centers, *1025 Vermont Ave. N.W., #500 20005-6310; (202) 783-7200. Fax, (202) 783-7207. Bonnie Van Dorn, Executive Director.*
General e-mail, info@astc.org
Web, www.astc.org

Membership: more than 585 science centers, science museums, and similar operations in forty-three countries. Strives to enhance the ability of its members to engage visitors in science activities and explorations of scientific phenomena. Sponsors conferences and informational exchanges on interactive exhibits, hands-on science experiences, and educational programs for children, families, and teachers; publishes journal; compiles statistics; provides technical assistance for museums; speaks for science centers before Congress and federal agencies.

Challenger Center for Space Science Education, *300 N. Lee St., #301, Alexandria, VA 22314; (703) 683-9740. Fax, (703) 683-7546. Daniel Barstaw, President.*
General e-mail, info@challenger.org
Web, www.challenger.org

Educational organization designed to stimulate interest in science, math, and technology among middle school and elementary school students. Students participate in interactive mission simulations that require training and classroom preparation. Sponsors Challenger Learning Centers across the United States, Canada, England, and Korea.

Commission on Professionals in Science and Technology, *1200 New York Ave. N.W., #113 20005; (202) 326-7080. Fax, (202) 842-1603. Lisa Frehill, Executive Director.*
General e-mail, info@cpst.org

Web, www.cpst.org

Membership: scientific societies, corporations, academic institutions, and individuals. Analyzes and publishes data on scientific and engineering human resources in the United States. Interests include employment of minorities and women, salary ranges, and supply and demand of scientists and engineers.

Mathematical Assn. of America, *1529 18th St. N.W. 20036-1358; (202) 387-5201. Fax, (202) 265-2384. Tina H. Straley, Executive Director. Information, (800) 741-9415.*
General e-mail, maahq@maa.org

Web, www.maa.org

Membership: mathematics professors and individuals worldwide with a professional interest in mathematics. Seeks to improve the teaching of collegiate mathematics. Conducts professional development programs.

National Assn. of Biology Teachers, *12030 Sunrise Valley Dr., #110, Reston, VA 20191-3409; (703) 264-9696. Fax, (703) 264-7778. Jacki Reeves-Pepin, Director of Development. Information, (800) 406-0775.*
General e-mail, office@nabt.org

Web, www.nabt.org

Membership: biology teachers and others interested in biology and life sciences education at the elementary, secondary, and collegiate levels. Provides professional development opportunities through its publication program, summer workshops, conventions, and national award programs. Interests include teaching standards, science curriculum, and issues affecting biology and life sciences education.

National Council of Teachers of Mathematics, *1906 Association Dr., Reston, VA 20191-1502; (703) 620-9840. Fax, (703) 476-2970. James M. Rubillo, Executive Director. General e-mail, nctm@nctm.org*

Web, www.nctm.org

Membership: teachers of mathematics in elementary and secondary schools and two-year colleges; university teacher education faculty; students; and other interested persons. Works for the improvement of classroom instruction at all levels. Serves as forum and information clearinghouse on issues related to mathematics education. Offers educational materials and conferences. Monitors legislation and regulations.

National Geographic Society, *1145 17th St. N.W. 20036-4688; (202) 857-7000. Fax, (202) 775-6141. John M. Fahey, President. Information, (800) 647-5463. Library, (202) 857-7783. Press, (202) 857-7027. TTY, (202) 548-9797.*
Web, www.nationalgeographic.com

Educational and scientific organization. Publishes *National Geographic, National Geographic Adventure, National Geographic Traveler, National Geographic Kids,* and *National Geographic Little Kids* magazines; produces maps, books, and films; maintains a museum; offers film-lecture series; produces television specials and the National Geographic Channel. Library open to the public.

National Science Resources Center, *901 D St. S.W., #704-B 20024; (202) 633-2972. Fax, (202) 287-7309. Sally Goetz Shuler, Executive Director.*
General e-mail, shulers@si.edu

Web, www.nsrconline.org

Sponsored by the Smithsonian Institution and the National Academy of Sciences. Works to establish effective science programs for all students. Disseminates research information; develops curriculum materials; seeks to increase public support for change of science education through the development of strategic partnerships.

National Science Teachers Assn., *1840 Wilson Blvd., Arlington, VA 22201-3000; (703) 243-7100. Fax, (703) 243-7177. Francis Eberle, Executive Director.*
General e-mail, publicinfo@nsta.org

Web, www.nsta.org

Membership: science teachers from elementary through college levels. Seeks to improve science education; provides forum for exchange of information. Monitors legislation and regulations.

World Future Society, *7910 Woodmont Ave., #450, Bethesda, MD 20814; (301) 656-8274. Fax, (301) 951-0394. Timothy Mack, President.*
General e-mail, info@wfs.org

Web, www.wfs.org

Scientific and educational organization interested in future social and technological developments on a global scale. Publishes magazines and journals.

Vocational and Adult

▶AGENCIES

Agriculture Dept. (USDA), *Graduate School, 1400 Independence Ave. S.W., #1112-S 20250; (202) 314-3686. Fax, (202) 690-3277. Jerry Ice, Chief Executive Officer; Albert Tyree, Marketing and Communications Director. Information, (888) 744-GRAD.*
General e-mail, pubaffairs@grad.usda.gov

Web, www.grad.usda.gov

Self-supporting educational institution that is open to the public. Offers continuing education courses for career advancement and personal fulfillment; offers training at agency locations.

Education Dept., *Office of Vocational and Adult Education (OVAE),* *550 12th St. S.W., #11139 20202-7100;*

(202) 245-7700. Fax, (202) 245-7838. Vacant, Assistant Secretary.

Web, www.ed.gov

Provides state and local education agencies with information on establishment, expansion, improvement, and operation of vocational technical education programs. Awards grants to state education agencies for vocational technical education programs.

► NONGOVERNMENTAL

Accrediting Commission of Career Schools and Colleges of Technology, *2101 Wilson Blvd., #302, Arlington, VA 22201; (703) 247-4212. Fax, (703) 247-4533. Michale S. McCornis, Executive Director.*

General e-mail, info@accsct.org

Web, www.accsct.org

Serves as the national accrediting agency for private postsecondary institutions offering occupational and vocational programs. Sponsors workshops and meetings on academic excellence and ethical practices in career education.

American Assn. for Adult and Continuing Education (AAACE), *10111 Martin Luther King Jr. Hwy., #200C, Bowie, MD 20720; (301) 459-6261. Fax, (301) 459-6241. Cle Anderson, Association Manager.*

General e-mail, aaace10@aol.com

Web, www.aaace.org

Membership: adult and continuing education professionals. Acts as an information clearinghouse; evaluates adult and continuing education programs; sponsors conferences, seminars, and workshops.

Assn. for Career and Technical Education (ACTE), *1410 King St., Alexandria, VA 22314; (703) 683-3111. Fax, (703) 683-7424. Janet Bray, Executive Director. Information, (800) 826-9972.*

General e-mail, acte@acteonline.org

Web, www.acteonline.org

Membership: teachers, students, supervisors, administrators, and others working or interested in career and technical education (middle school through postgraduate). Interests include the impact of high school graduation requirements on career and technical education; private sector initiatives; and the improvement of the quality and image of career and technical education. Offers an annual convention and other professional development opportunities. Monitors legislation and regulations.

Career College Assn., *1101 Connecticut Ave. N.W., #900 20036; (202) 336-6700. Fax, (202) 336-6828. Harris N. Miller, President.*

General e-mail, cca@career.org

Web, www.career.org

Acts as an information clearinghouse on trade and technical schools.

Distance Education and Training Council (DETC), *1601 18th St. N.W., #2 20009; (202) 234-5100. Fax, (202) 332-1386. Michael P. Lambert, Executive Director.*

General e-mail, detc@detc.org

Web, www.detc.org

Membership: accredited correspondence schools. Accredits distance education institutions, many of which offer vocational training.

International Assn. for Continuing Education and Training (IACET), *1760 Old Meadow Rd., #500, McLean, VA 22102; (703) 506-3275. Fax, (703) 506-3266. Sara Meier, Executive Director.*

General e-mail, iacet@iacet.org

Web, www.iacet.org

Membership: education and training organizations and individuals who use the Continuing Education Unit. (The C.E.U. is defined as ten contact hours of participation in an organized continuing education program that is noncredit.) Authorizes organizations that issue the C.E.U.; develops criteria and guidelines for use of the C.E.U.

International Technology Education Assn. (ITEA), *1914 Association Dr., #201, Reston, VA 20191-1539; (703) 860-2100. Fax, (703) 860-0353. Kendall N. Starkweather, Executive Director.*

General e-mail, itea@iteaconnect.org

Web, www.iteaconnect.org

Membership: technology education teachers, supervisors, teacher educators, and individuals studying to be technology education teachers (elementary school through university level). Technology education includes the curriculum areas of manufacturing, construction, communications, transportation, robotics, energy, design, and engineering.

National Assn. of State Directors of Career Technical Education Consortium, *8484 Georgia Ave., #320, Silver Spring, MD 20910; (301) 588-9630. Fax, (301) 588-9631. Kimberly A. Green, Executive Director.*

Web, www.careertech.org

Membership: state career education agency heads, senior staff, and business, labor, and other education officials. Advocates state and national policy to strengthen career technical education to create a foundation of skills for American workers and provide them with opportunities to acquire new and advanced skills.

National Institute for Work and Learning (AED), *1825 Connecticut Ave. N.W., 10th Floor 20009; (202) 884-8173. Fax, (202) 884-8422. Ivan Charner, Vice President.*

General e-mail, NIWL@aed.org

Web, www.aed.niwl.org

Promotes the integration of the education and employment systems to ensure lifelong learning and productivity for all Americans. Combines research, program development and evaluation, capacity building, training, and information sharing in three broad areas: learning at school, learning at work, and learning beyond school and work. (Affiliated with the Academy for Educational Development.)

SkillsUSA, *14001 SkillsUSA Way, Leesburg, VA 20176 (mailing address: P.O. Box 3000, Leesburg, VA 20177-0300); (703) 777-8810. Fax, (703) 777-8999. Timothy W. Lawrence, Executive Director.*
Web, www.skillsusa.org

Membership: students, teachers, and administrators of trade, industrial, technical, and health occupations programs at public high schools, vocational schools, and two-year colleges. Promotes strong work skills, workplace ethics, understanding of free enterprise, and lifelong education. (Formerly Vocational Industrial Clubs of America.)

University Continuing Education Assn. (UCEA), *1 Dupont Circle N.W., #615 20036; (202) 659-3130. Fax, (202) 785-0374. Kay J. Kohl, Executive Director.*
Web, www.ucea.edu

Membership: higher education institutions and non-profit organizations involved in postsecondary continuing education. Prepares statistical analyses and produces data reports for members; recognizes accomplishments in the field. Monitors legislation and regulations.

6 🕐

Employment and Labor

GENERAL POLICY AND ANALYSIS

Basic Resources

►AGENCIES

Labor Dept. (DOL), *200 Constitution Ave. N.W. 20210; (202) 693-6000. Fax, (202) 693-6111. Hilda L. Solis, Secretary; Vacant, Deputy Secretary. Library, (202) 693-6600. TTY, (877) 889-5627. Locator, (202) 693-5000. Toll-free, (866) 487-2365.*
Web, www.dol.gov

Promotes and develops the welfare of U.S. wage earners; administers federal labor laws; acts as principal adviser to the president on policies relating to wage earners, working conditions, and employment opportunities. Library open to the public, 8:15 a.m.–4:15 p.m.

Labor Dept. (DOL), *Administrative Law Judges, 800 K St. N.W., #400N 20001-8002; (202) 693-7300. Fax, (202) 693-7365. John Vittone, Chief Administrative Law Judge, (202) 693-7542; Yvonne Washington, Chief Docket Clerk. Web, www.oalj.dol.gov*

Presides over formal hearings to determine violations of minimum wage requirements, overtime payments, compensation benefits, employee discrimination, grant performance, alien certification, employee protection, the Sarbanes-Oxley Act, and health and safety regulations set forth under numerous statutes, executive orders, and regulations. With few exceptions, hearings are required to be conducted in accordance with the Administrative Procedure Act.

Labor Dept. (DOL), *Administrative Review Board, 200 Constitution Ave. N.W., #N5404 20210; (202) 693-6200. Fax, (202) 693-6220. M. Cynthia Douglass, Chair. General e-mail, Contact-OAS@dol.gov*

Web, www.dol.gov/arb/welcome.html

Issues final decisions for the secretary of labor on appeals from decisions of the administrator of the Wage and Hour Division of the Employment Standards Administration and the Office of Administrative Law Judges under a broad range of federal labor laws, including nuclear, environmental, safety and security, financial, and transportation whistle-blower protection provisions; contract compliance laws; child labor laws; immigration laws; migrant and seasonal agricultural worker protection laws; the McNamara O'Hara Service Contract Act; and the Davis-Bacon Act.

►CONGRESS

For a listing of relevant congressional committees and subcommittees, please see page 195 or the Appendix.

Government Accountability Office (GAO), *Education, Workforce, and Income Security, 441 G St. N.W., #5928 20548; (202) 512-7215. Cynthia M. Fagnoni, Managing Director.*
Web, www.gao.gov

Independent, nonpartisan agency in the legislative branch. Audits, analyzes, and evaluates Labor Dept. programs; makes reports available to the public. (Formerly the General Accounting Office.)

►NONGOVERNMENTAL

AFL-CIO (American Federation of Labor-Congress of Industrial Organizations), *815 16th St. N.W. 20006; (202) 637-5000. Fax, (202) 637-5058. John J. Sweeney, President. Library, (301) 431-6400.*
Web, www.aflcio.org

Voluntary federation of national and international labor unions in the United States. Represents members before Congress and other branches of government. Each member union conducts its own contract negotiations. Library (located in Silver Spring, Md.) open to the public.

American Civil Liberties Union (ACLU), *National Capital Area, 1400 20th St. N.W., #119 20036-5920; (202) 457-0800. Fax, (202) 452-1868. Johnny Barnes, Executive Director.*
Web, www.aclu-nca.org

Protects the civil liberties of the citizens, including federal employees, of the Washington metropolitan area. Interests include First Amendment rights, privacy, and due process.

American Enterprise Institute for Public Policy Research (AEI), *Economic Policy Studies, 1150 17th St. N.W. 20036; (202) 862-5800. Fax, (202) 862-7177. Arthur Brooks, President.*
Web, www.aei.org

Research and educational organization that studies trends in employment, earnings, the environment, health care, and income in the United States.

American Staffing Assn., *277 S. Washington St., #200, Alexandria, VA 22314-3675; (703) 253-2020. Fax, (703) 253-2053. Richard A. Wahlquist, President. General e-mail, asa@americanstaffing.net*

Web, www.americanstaffing.net

Membership: companies supplying other companies with workers on a temporary or permanent basis, with outsourcing, with human resources, and with professional employer organizations (PEOs) arrangements. Monitors legislation and regulations. Encourages the maintenance of high ethical standards and provides public relations and educational support to members.

Campaign for America's Future, *1825 K St. N.W., #400 20006; (202) 955-5665. Fax, (202) 955-5606. Robert L. Borosage, Co-Director; Roger Hickey, Co-Director. Web, www.ourfuture.org*

Operates the Campaign for America's Future and the Institute for America's Future. Advocates policies to help working people. Supports improved employee benefits, including health care, child care, and paid family leave; promotes lifelong education and training of workers.

EMPLOYMENT AND LABOR RESOURCES IN CONGRESS

For a complete listing of Congress committees, including their full contact information, leadership, membership, and jurisdictions, please refer to the Appendix on pages 724–837.

JOINT COMMITTEES:

Joint Economic Committee, (202) 224-0372.
Web, jec.senate.gov or www.house.gov/jec

HOUSE:

House Appropriations Committee, Subcommittee on Labor, Health and Human Services, Education, and Related Agencies, (202) 225-3508.
Web, appropriations.house.gov
House Education and Labor Committee, (202) 225-3725.
Web, edworkforce.house.gov
  Subcommittee on Health, Employment, Labor, and Pensions, (202) 225-3725.
  Subcommittee on Healthy Families and Communities, (202) 225-3725.
  Subcommittee on Higher Education, Lifelong Learning, and Competitiveness, (202) 225-3725.
  Subcommittee on Workforce Protections, (202) 226-3725.
House Judiciary Committee, Subcommittee on Immigration, Citizenship, Refugees, Border Security, and International Law, (202) 225-3926.
Web, judiciary.house.gov
House Oversight and Government Reform Committee, (202) 225-5051.
Web, oversight.house.gov
  Subcommittee on Domestic Policy, (202) 225-6427.
  Subcommittee on Federal Workforce, Postal Service, and the District of Columbia, (202) 225-5147.
House Small Business Committee, (202) 225-4038.
Web, www.house.gov/smbiz
  Subcommittee on Regulations, Health Care and Trade, (202) 225-4038.
House Ways and Means Committee, (202) 225-3625.
Web, waysandmeans.house.gov
  Subcommittee on Income Security and Family Support, (202) 225-1025.

  Subcommittee on Oversight, (202) 225-5522.
  Subcommittee on Trade, (202) 225-6649.

SENATE:

Senate Appropriations Committee, Subcommittee on Labor, Health and Human Services, Education and Related Agencies, (202) 224-9145.
Web, appropriations.senate.gov
Senate Finance Committee, (202) 224-4515.
Web, finance.senate.gov
  Subcommittee on International Trade and Global Competitiveness, (202) 224-4515.
  Subcommittee on Social Security, Pensions and Family Policy, (202) 225-4515.
  Subcommittee on Taxation, IRS Oversight, and Long-Term Growth, (202) 224-4515.
Senate Health, Education, Labor and Pensions Committee, (202) 224-5375.
Web, help.senate.gov
  Subcommittee on Employment and Workplace Safety, (202) 224-2621.
  Subcommittee on Retirement and Aging, (202) 224-9243.
Senate Homeland Security and Governmental Affairs Committee, (202) 224-2627.
Web, hsgac.senate.gov
  Permanent Subcommittee on Investigations, (202) 224-9505.
  Subcommittee on Oversight of Government Management, the Federal Workforce, and the District of Columbia, (202) 224-5538.
Senate Judiciary Committee, Subcommittee on Immigration, Refugees, and Border Security, (202) 224-7878.
Web, judiciary.senate.gov
Senate Small Business and Entrepreneurship Committee, (202) 224-5175.
Web, sbc.senate.gov
Senate Special Committee on Aging, (202) 224-5364.
Web, aging.senate.gov

Seeks full employment, higher wages, and increased productivity. Monitors legislation and regulations.

Center for Economic and Policy Research (CEPR), *1611 Connecticut Ave. N.W., #400 20009; (202) 293-5380, ext. 115. Fax, (202) 588-1356. Dean Baker, Co-Director; Mark Weisbrot, Co-Director.*

General e-mail, cepr@cepr.net
Web, www.cepr.net

Researches economic and social issues and the impact of related public policies. Presents findings to the public with the goal of better preparing citizens to choose among various policy options. Promotes democratic debate and voter education. Areas of interest include health care, trade, Social Security, taxes, housing, and the labor market.

Corporate Voices for Working Families, *2600 Virginia Ave. N.W., #205 20037; (202) 333-8924. Fax, (202) 333-8920. Donna Klein, President. Press, (330) 631-9298.*
Web, www.cvworkingfamilies.org

Coalition of more than fifty companies that supports flexible work policies as a way of increasing workforce retention, productivity, and loyalty while also reducing business costs.

Employment Policies Institute, *1090 Vermont Ave. N.W., #800 20005-4605; (202) 463-7650. Fax, (202) 463-7107. Richard Berman, Executive Director.*
General e-mail, epi@epionline.org
Web, www.epionline.org

Sponsors and conducts research on public policy and employment. Opposes raising the minimum wage. Monitors legislation and regulations.

Good Jobs First, *1616 P St. N.W., #210 20036; (202) 232-1616. Fax, (202) 232-6680. Greg LeRoy, Executive Director.*
General e-mail, info@goodjobsfirst.org
Web, www.goodjobsfirst.org

Promotes corporate and government accountability in economic development and job growth. Provides information on state and local job subsidies. Monitors legislation and regulations.

HR Policy Assn., *1100 13th St. N.W., #850 20005-4090 (mailing address: P.O. Box 34108, Washington, DC 20043-9998); (202) 789-8670. Fax, (202) 789-0064. Jeffrey C. McGuiness, President.*
General e-mail, webmaster@hrpolicy.org
Web, www.hrpolicy.org

Membership: corporate vice presidents in charge of employee relations. Promotes research in employee relations, particularly in federal employment policy and implementation. Interests include international labor issues, including immigration and child labor.

Inclusion, *1611 Connecticut Ave. N.W., #400 20009; (202) 293-5380. Fax, (202) 588-1356. Shawn Fremstad, Director.*
Web, www.inclusionist.org

Think tank that develops and promotes policies that foster social and economic inclusion, with a current focus on low-wage work in the United States. Provides information through policy reports, charts and graphs, and interactive blog entries. (Affiliated with the Center for Economic and Policy Research.)

National Assn. of Professional Employer Organizations, *707 N. Saint Asaph St., Alexandria, VA 22314; (703) 836-0466. Fax, (703) 836-0976. Milan P. Yager, Executive Vice President.*
General e-mail, info@napeo.org
Web, www.napeo.org

Membership: professional employer organizations. Conducts research; sponsors seminars and conferences for members. Monitors legislation and regulations.

Society for Human Resource Management, *1800 Duke St., Alexandria, VA 22314-3499; (703) 548-3440. Fax, (703) 535-6492. Laurence G. O'Neil, Chief Executive Officer; China Miner Gorman, Chief Operating Officer. Information, (800) 283-7476. Press, (703) 535-6273. TTY, (703) 548-6999. General e-mail, shrm@shrm.org*
Web, www.shrm.org

Membership: human resource management professionals. Monitors legislation and regulations concerning recruitment, training, and employment practices; occupational safety and health; compensation and benefits; employee and labor relations; and equal employment opportunity. Sponsors seminars and conferences.

U.S. Chamber of Commerce, *Economic Policy, 1615 H St. N.W. 20062-2000; (202) 463-5620. Fax, (202) 463-3174. Martin A. Regalia, Chief Economist. Press, (202) 463-5682.*
Web, www.uschamber.com

Monitors legislation and regulations affecting the business community, including employee benefits, health care, legal and regulatory affairs, transportation and telecommunications infrastructure, defense conversion, and equal employment opportunity.

International Issues

▶AGENCIES

Bureau of Labor Statistics (BLS), *(Labor Dept.), International Labor Comparison, 2 Massachusetts Ave. N.E., #2120 20212-0001; (202) 691-5654. Fax, (202) 691-5679. Constance Sorrentino, Division Chief. General e-mail, flshelp@bls.gov*
Web, www.bls.gov/fls

Issues statistical reports on labor force, productivity, employment, prices, and labor costs in foreign countries adjusted to U.S. concepts.

Employment and Training Administration *(Labor Dept.), Trade Adjustment Assistance, 200 Constitution Ave. N.W., #N5428 20210; (202) 693-3098. Fax, (202) 693-3584. Erin FitzGerald, Program Manager.*
Web, www.doleta.gov/tradeact

Assists American workers who are totally or partially unemployed because of increased imports or a shift in production; offers training, job search and relocation assistance, weekly benefits at state unemployment insurance levels, and other reemployment services.

Labor Dept. (DOL), *International Labor Affairs, 200 Constitution Ave. N.W., #C4325 20210; (202) 693-4770. Fax, (202) 693-4780. Vacant, Deputy Under Secretary. General e-mail, Contact-ILAB@dol.gov*
Web, www.dol.gov/ilab

Labor Department

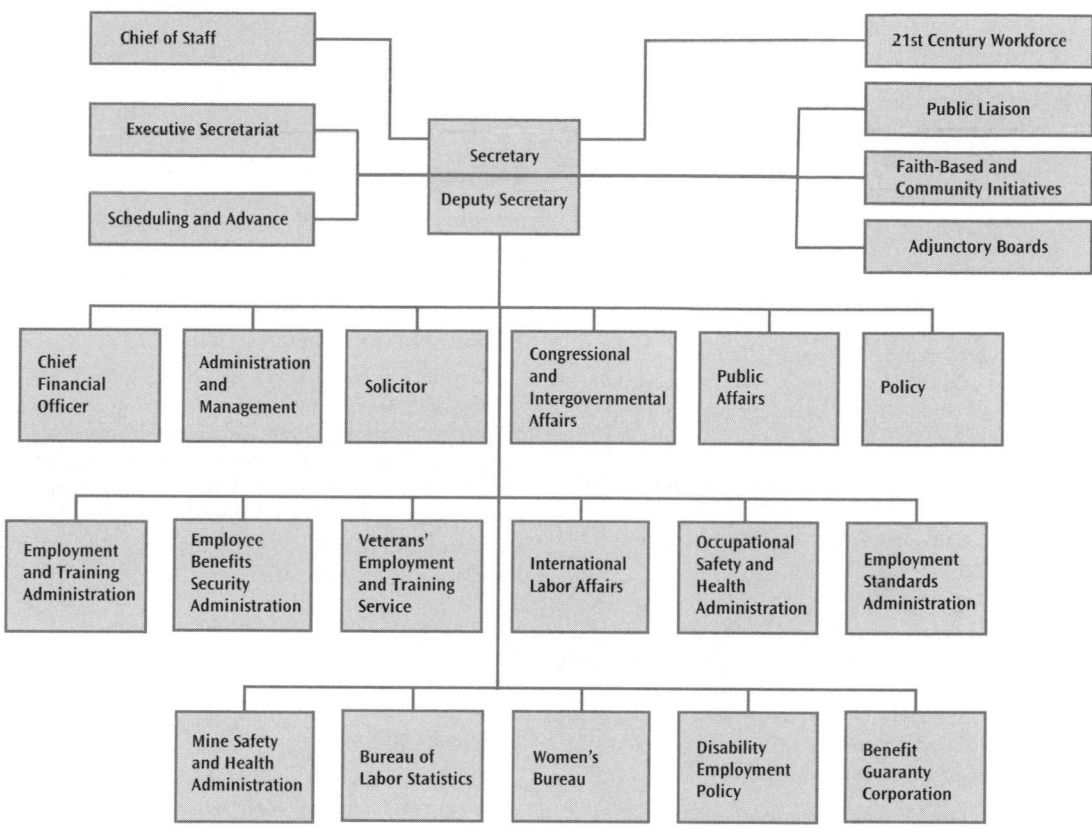

Assists in formulating international economic and trade policies affecting American workers. Represents the United States in trade negotiations. Helps administer the United States labor attaché program. Carries out overseas technical assistance projects. Represents the United States in various international organizations. Houses the Office of Trade Agreement Implementation, which is responsible for overseeing the implementation of the labor provisions of free trade agreements.

Labor Dept. *(Labor Dept.), International Labor Affairs: Trade Agreement Administration and Technical Cooperation,* 200 Constitution Ave. N.W., #S5303 20210; (202) 693-4775. Fax, (202) 693-4784. Cathryn Celeste Helm, Division Chief.
General e-mail, helm.cathryn@dol.gov

Web, www.dol.gov/ilab/programs/nao

Coordinates international technical cooperation in support of the labor provisions in free trade agreements. Provides services, information, expertise, and technical cooperation programs that support the Labor Dept.'s foreign policy objectives. Administers the U.S. government's responsibilities under the North American Free Trade Agreement on Labor Cooperation and labor chapters of U.S. regional and bilateral free trade agreements. Provides

technical assistance for post-conflict reconstruction and reintegration activities in countries key to U.S. security. Provides technical assistance globally to help countries observe international labor standards. Supports HIV/AIDS workplace preventive education in countries around the world.

Labor Dept. (DOL), *International Relations,* 200 Constitution Ave. N.W., #S5004 20210; (202) 693-4855. Fax, (202) 693-4860. Robert B. Shepard, Director.
General e-mail, Contact-OIR@dol.gov

Web, www.dol.gov/ilab/programs/oir

Provides administrative support for U.S. participation in the International Labor Organization (ILO) and Asian Pacific Economic Cooperation (APEC) and at the Paris-based Organization for Economic Cooperation and Development (OECD). Provides research on labor and employment in other countries. Facilitates information-sharing between Labor Dept. and other countries.

Labor Dept. (DOL), *U.S. Foreign Visitors Program,* 200 Constitution Ave. N.W., #S5303 20210; (202) 693-4793. Fax, (202) 693-4784. Patricia Butler, International Program Specialist.
Web, www.dol.gov/ilab/programs/oir/fvp.htm

Works with the State Dept., the Agency for International Development, and other agencies in arranging visits and training programs for foreign officials interested in U.S. labor and trade unions.

President's Committee on the International Labor Organization *(Labor Dept.), 200 Constitution Ave. N.W., #S5303 20210; (202) 693-4855. Fax, (202) 693-4860. Elaine L. Chao, Chair; Charlotte M. Ponticelli, Deputy Under Secretary.*

Advisory committee of government, employer, and worker representatives, including secretaries of state, commerce, and labor, the president's national security adviser, the president's national economic adviser, and duly appointed representatives of business and labor. Formulates and coordinates policy on the International Labor Organization (ILO); advises the president and the secretary of labor.

State Dept., *International Labor and Corporate Social Responsibility, 2201 C St. N.W., #12B61 20520; (202) 647-3663. Fax, (202) 647-3779. Mark Mittelhauser, Director, (202) 647-4327. Web, www.state.gov/g/drl/lbr*

Works with organized labor, nongovernmental organizations, international organizations, and corporations to monitor and promote worker rights and corporate social responsibility throughout the world. Contributes to U.S. foreign policy goals related to democracy promotion, trade, development, and human rights.

State Dept., *International Organization Affairs, 2201 C St. N.W., #6323 20520-6319; (202) 647-9600. Fax, (202) 736-4116. Brian Hook, Assistant Secretary. Press, (202) 647-7938. Web, www.state.gov/p/io*

Shares responsibility with the Labor Dept. and the Commerce Dept. for U.S. policy in the United Nations, the UN's specialized agencies, and other international organizations, including government relations with the International Labor Organization (ILO).

▶ CONGRESS

For a listing of relevant congressional committees and subcommittees, please see page 195 or the Appendix.

▶ INTERNATIONAL ORGANIZATIONS

International Labor Organization (ILO), *Washington Office, 1828 L St. N.W., #600 20036; (202) 653-7652. Fax, (202) 653-7687. Armand F. Pereira, Director. General e-mail, washington@ilo.org Web, www.ilo.org*

Works toward advancing social justice through the promotion of international labor standards, employment, social protection, and social dialogue. Carries out research and technical cooperation and advisory services under these four major themes and related subthemes, including labor statistics, wages, occupational safety and health and other working conditions, social security, eradication

of child labor and forced labor, equality of treatment in employment and occupation, freedom of association, and bargaining rights. Liaison office for the United States and multilateral organizations in Washington, D.C. (Headquarters in Geneva.)

▶ NONGOVERNMENTAL

American Center for International Labor Solidarity, *888 16th St. N.W., #400 20006; (202) 974-8383. Fax, (202) 974-8384. Ellie Larson, Executive Director. General e-mail, info@solidaritycenter.org*

Web, www.solidaritycenter.org

Provides assistance to free and democratic trade unions worldwide. Provides trade union leadership courses in collective bargaining, union organization, trade integration, labor-management cooperation, union administration, and political theories. Sponsors social and community development projects; focus includes child labor, human and worker rights, and the role of women in labor unions. (Affiliated with the AFL-CIO.)

International Labor Rights Forum, *2001 S St. N.W., #420 20009; (202) 347-4100. Fax, (202) 347-4885. Bama Athreya, Executive Director. General e-mail, laborrights@ilrf.org*

Web, www.laborrights.org

Promotes the enforcement of international labor rights through policy advocacy; advocates for better protection of workers. Concerns include child labor, sweatshops, and exploited workers. Monitors legislation and regulations on national and international levels.

Labor, Immigration, and Employee Benefits, *U.S. Chamber of Commerce, 1615 H St. N.W. 20062-2000; (202) 463-5522. Fax, (202) 463-5901. Angelo I. Amador, Director of Immigration. Web, www.uschamber.com*

Unites regional business organizations and companies and national trade associations to facilitate the flow of goods and people across borders while addressing national security concerns.

NumbersUSA, *1601 N. Kent St., #1100, Arlington, VA 22209; (202) 543-1341. Fax, (202) 543-3147. Roy Beck, Executive Director. General e-mail, info@numbersusa.com*

Web, www.numbersusa.com

Public policy organization that favors immigration reduction as a way of promoting economic justice for American workers. Monitors legislation and regulations.

Society for Human Resource Management, *International Programs, 1800 Duke St., Alexandria, VA 22314-3499; (703) 535-6033. Fax, (703) 258-6034. Brian Glade, Vice President. TTY, (703) 548-6999. Toll-free, (800) 283-7476. Web, www.shrm.org*

Provides human resources professionals with specialized, timely information on the worldwide business environment and its implications for the human resources profession.

Labor Standards and Practices

►AGENCIES

Bureau of Labor Statistics (BLS), *(Labor Dept.),* *Compensation and Working Conditions,* 2 Massachusetts Ave. N.E., #4130 20212; (202) 691-6300. Fax, (202) 691-6310. William Wiatrowski, Associate Commissioner.
Web, www.bls.gov/bls/proghome.htm#ocwc

Conducts annual area wage surveys to determine occupational pay information in individual labor markets. Conducts industry wage surveys, which provide wage and employee benefit information; collects data on labor costs, job injuries and illnesses, and work stoppages.

Employment Standards Administration *(Labor Dept.),* 200 Constitution Ave. N.W., #S2321 20210; (202) 693-0200. Fax, (202) 693-0218. Victoria A. Lipnic, Assistant Secretary.
Web, www.dol.gov/esa

Administers and enforces employment laws and regulations. Responsibilities include ensuring compliance among federal contractors, administering benefits claims for federal employees and other workers, and protecting workers' wages and working conditions.

Employment Standards Administration *(Labor Dept.),* *Child Labor and Special Employment,* 200 Constitution Ave. N.W., #S3510 20210; (202) 693-0072. Fax, (202) 693-1387. Arthur M. Kerschner Jr., Team Leader. Press, (202) 693-0069.
Web, www.dol.gov/esa/whd

Authorizes subminimum wages under the Fair Labor Standards Act for certain categories of workers, including full-time students, student learners, and workers with disabilities. Administers the Fair Labor Standards Act restrictions on working at home in certain industries and enforces child labor laws.

Employment Standards Administration *(Labor Dept.),* *Fair Labor Standards Act Enforcement,* 200 Constitution Ave. N.W., #S3516 20210; (202) 693-0067. Fax, (202) 693-1387. Monty Navarro, Team Leader (Acting), (202) 693-0051. Information, (866) 487-9243. TTY, (877) 889-5627.
Web, www.dol.gov/esa

Issues interpretations and rulings of the Fair Labor Standards Act of 1938, as amended (Federal Minimum Wage and Overtime Pay and Record Keeping Law).

Employment Standards Administration *(Labor Dept.),* *Federal Contract Compliance Programs,* 200 Constitution Ave. N.W., #C3325 20210; (202) 693-0101. Fax, (202) 693-1304. Vacant, Deputy Assistant Secretary.
General e-mail, ofccp-public@dol.gov
Web, www.dol.gov/esa/ofccp/index.htm

Monitors and enforces government contractors' compliance with federal laws and regulations on equal employment opportunities and affirmative action, including employment rights of minorities, women, persons with disabilities, and disabled and Vietnam-era veterans.

Employment Standards Administration *(Labor Dept.),* *Government Contracts Enforcement,* 200 Constitution Ave. N.W., #S3006 20210; (202) 693-0064. Fax, (202) 693-1087. Timothy Helm, Team Leader.
General e-mail, helm.timothy@dol.gov
Web, www.dol.gov/esa

Enforces the Davis-Bacon Act, the Walsh-Healey Public Contracts Act, the Contract Work Hours and Safety Standards Act, the Service Contract Act, and other related government contract labor standards statutes.

Employment Standards Administration *(Labor Dept.),* *Wage and Hour Division,* 200 Constitution Ave. N.W., #S3502 20210; (202) 693-0051. Fax, (202) 693-1406. Vacant, Administrator.
Web, www.dol.gov/esa/whd

Enforces the minimum-wage, overtime, record keeping, and child labor provisions of the Fair Labor Standards Act. Also enforces certain labor standards of the Immigration and Nationality Act and other laws regarding employment standards with respect to polygraphs, leave from work, agricultural workers, and the construction industry.

Employment Standards Administration *(Labor Dept.),* *Wage Determination, Service Contracts,* 200 Constitution Ave. N.W., #S3028 20210; (202) 693-0073. Fax, (202) 693-1425. Sandra Hamlett, Director.
Web, www.dol.gov/esa/whd

Issues prevailing wage determinations under the Service Contract Act of 1965 and other regulations pertaining to wage determination.

Justice Dept., *Civil Rights Division: Trafficking in Persons and Worker Exploitation Task Force,* P.O. Box 66018 20035-6018. Complaint Line, (888) 428-7581.
Web, www.usdoj.gov/crt/crim/tpwetf.htm

Seeks to prevent trafficking in persons and worker exploitation throughout the United States and to investigate and prosecute cases when such violations occur. Provides information to advocacy organizations and service providers to invite their participation to combat trafficking in persons and worker exploitation. The Complaint Line is toll-free and offers foreign language translation services in most languages as well as TTY. After business hours, the Complaint Line has a message service in English, Spanish, and Mandarin only.

►CONGRESS

For a listing of relevant congressional committees and subcommittees, please see page 195 or the Appendix.

Fair Labor Assn. (FLA), *1707 L St. N.W., #200 20036; (202) 898-1000. Fax, (202) 898-9050. Jorge Perez-Lopez, Executive Director.*
General e-mail, info@fairlabor.org

Web, www.fairlabor.org

Membership: consumer, human, and labor rights groups; apparel and footwear manufacturers and retailers; and colleges and universities. Seeks to protect the rights of workers in the United States and worldwide. Concerns include sweatshop practices, forced labor, child labor, and worker health and benefits. Monitors workplace conditions and reports findings to the public. Develops capacity for sustainable labor compliance.

Statistics and Information

►AGENCIES

Bureau of Labor Statistics (BLS), *(Labor Dept.),* *2 Massachusetts Ave. N.E., #4040 20212-0001; (202) 691-7800. Fax, (202) 691-7797. Keith Hall, Commissioner. Press, (202) 691-5902.*
General e-mail, blsdata-staff@bls.gov

Web, www.bls.gov

Collects, analyzes, and publishes data on labor economics, including employment, unemployment, hours of work, wages, employee compensation, prices, consumer expenditures, labor-management relations, productivity, technological developments, occupational safety and health, and structure and growth of the economy. Publishes reports on these statistical trends, including the Consumer Price Index, the Producer Price Index, and Employment and Earnings.

Bureau of Labor Statistics (BLS), *(Labor Dept.),* *Current Employment Statistics, 2 Massachusetts Ave. N.E., #4860 20212; (202) 691-6555. Fax, (202) 691-6641. Kenneth W. Robertson, Chief.*
General e-mail, cesinfo@bls.gov

Web, www.bls.gov/ces/home.htm

Analyzes and publishes national-level employment, hour, and earnings statistics based on data submitted by the states; develops statistical information on employment, hours, and earnings by industry for the nation, states, and metropolitan statistical areas.

Bureau of Labor Statistics (BLS), *(Labor Dept.),* *Employment and Unemployment Statistics,* *2 Massachusetts Ave. N.E., #4945 20212-0022; (202) 691-6400. Fax, (202) 691-6425. John M. Galvin, Associate Commissioner. Press, (202) 691-5902.*
General e-mail, labstathelpdesk@bls.gov

Web, www.bls.gov/bls/employment.htm

Monitors employment and unemployment trends on national and local levels; compiles data on worker and industry employment and earnings.

Bureau of Labor Statistics (BLS), *(Labor Dept.),* *International Labor Comparison, 2 Massachusetts Ave. N.E., #2120 20212-0001; (202) 691-5654. Fax, (202) 691-5679. Constance Sorrentino, Division Chief.*
General e-mail, flshelp@bls.gov

Web, www.bls.gov/fls

Issues statistical reports on labor force, productivity, employment, prices, and labor costs in foreign countries adjusted to U.S. concepts.

Bureau of Labor Statistics (BLS), *(Labor Dept.), Local Area Unemployment Statistics, 2 Massachusetts Ave. N.E., #4675 20212; (202) 691-6392. Fax, (202) 691-6459. Sharon P. Brown, Chief. Press, (202) 691-5902.*
General e-mail, lausinfo@bls.gov

Web, www.bls.gov/lau

Issues labor force and unemployment statistics for states, metropolitan statistical areas, and cities with populations of 25,000 or more.

Bureau of Labor Statistics (BLS), *(Labor Dept.), Occupational Statistics and Employment Projections, 2 Massachusetts Ave. N.E., #2135 20212; (202) 691-5700. Fax, (202) 691-5745. Dixie Sommers, Assistant Commissioner.*
General e-mail, ep-info@bls.gov

Web, www.bls.gov/emp

Develops economic, industrial, and demographic employment projections according to industry and occupation. Provides career guidance material.

Bureau of Labor Statistics (BLS), *(Labor Dept.), Productivity and Technology, 2 Massachusetts Ave. N.E., #2150 20212-0001; (202) 691-5600. Fax, (202) 691-5664. Michael Harper, Associate Commissioner. TTY, (202) 691-5618.*
General e-mail, dipsweb@bls.gov

Web, www.bls.gov/bls/productivity.htm

Develops and analyzes productivity measures for the U.S. business economy and industries, conducts research on factors affecting productivity, and provides international comparisons of productivity measures and other statistical data.

Employment and Training Administration *(Labor Dept.), Workforce Security, 200 Constitution Ave. N.W., #S4231 20210; (202) 693-3029. Fax, (202) 693-3229. Cheryl Atkinson, Administrator.*
Web, http://workforcesecurity.doleta.gov

Provides guidance and oversight with respect to federal and state unemployment compensation. Compiles statistics on state unemployment insurance programs. Studies unemployment issues related to benefits.

Occupational Safety and Health Administration (OSHA), *(Labor Dept.), Statistiscal Analysis, 200 Constitution Ave. N.W., #N3507 20210; (202) 693-1886. Fax, (202) 693-1631. Dave Schmidt, Director (Acting).*

Compiles and provides all statistical data for OSHA, such as occupational injury and illness records, which are used in setting standards and making policy.

►CONGRESS

For a listing of relevant congressional committees and subcommittees, please see page195 or the Appendix.

Unemployment Benefits

►AGENCIES

Employment and Training Administration *(Labor Dept.), Trade Adjustment Assistance, 200 Constitution Ave. N.W., #N5428 20210; (202) 693-3098. Fax, (202) 693-3584. Erin FitzGerald, Program Manager.*
Web, www.doleta.gov/tradeact

Assists American workers who are totally or partially unemployed because of increased imports or a shift in production; offers training, job search and relocation assistance, weekly benefits at state unemployment insurance levels, and other reemployment services.

Employment and Training Administration *(Labor Dept.), Workforce Security, 200 Constitution Ave. N.W., #S4231 20210; (202) 693-3029. Fax, (202) 693-3229. Cheryl Atkinson, Administrator.*
Web, http://workforcesecurity.doleta.gov

Directs and reviews the state-administered system that provides income support for unemployed workers nationwide; advises state and federal employment security agencies on wage-loss, worker dislocation, and adjustment assistance compensation programs.

►CONGRESS

For a listing of relevant congressional committees and subcommittees, please see page 195 or the Appendix.

►NONGOVERNMENTAL

National Assn. of State Workforce Agencies, *444 N. Capitol St. N.W., #142 20001; (202) 434-8020. Fax, (202) 434-8033. Richard A. Hobbie, Executive Director.*
Web, www.workforceatm.org

Membership: state workforce agency administrators. Informs members of employment training programs, unemployment insurance programs, employment services, labor market information, and legislation. Provides unemployment insurance and workforce development professionals with opportunities for networking and information exchange.

EMPLOYMENT AND TRAINING PROGRAMS

►AGENCIES

Employment and Training Administration *(Labor Dept.), 200 Constitution Ave. N.W., #S2307 20210; (202) 693-2700.*

Fax, (202) 693-2725. Douglas F. Small, Deputy Assistant Secretary. Press, (202) 693-4696. TTY, (877) 889-5627. Toll-free employment and training hotline, (877) US2-JOBS. Web, www.doleta.gov

Responsible for providing job training, employment, labor market information, and income maintenance services primarily through state and local workforce development programs.

Employment and Training Administration *(Labor Dept.), Adult Services, 200 Constitution Ave. N.W., #C4512 20210; (202) 693-3046. Fax, (202) 693-3587. Christine Ollis, Chief.*
Web, www.doleta.gov/etainfo/wrksys/wiadultservices.cfm

Responsible for adult training and services for dislocated workers funded under the Workforce Investment Act; examines training initiatives and technology. Provides targeted job training services for migrant and seasonal farm workers, Native Americans, older workers, and the disabled. Provides foreign labor certification.

Employment and Training Administration *(Labor Dept.), Business Relations Group, 200 Constitution Ave. N.W., #N4643 20210; (202) 693-3949. Fax, (202) 693-3890. Amanda Ahlstrand, Director.*
General e-mail, businessrelations@dol.gov
Web, www.doleta.gov/brg

Serves as liaison between business and industry and the workforce investment system, a network of state and local resources that connects workers to job opportunities and helps businesses recruit, train, and maintain a skilled workforce. Manages the president's High Growth Job Training Initiative with the goal of preparing workers for high growth and high demand jobs. Targeted industries include advanced manufacturing, aerospace, biotechnology, health care, and information technology.

Employment and Training Administration *(Labor Dept.), Workforce Investment, 200 Constitution Ave. N.W., #S4231 20210; (202) 693-3980. Fax, (202) 693-3981. Gay M. Gilbert, Administrator.*
Web, www.doleta.gov/etainfo/wrksys/wioffice.cfm

Oversees federal employment and training programs under the Workforce Investment Act for adults, dislocated workers, and youths and Wagner-Peyser employment services as delivered through the one-stop delivery system nationwide.

Employment and Training Administration *(Labor Dept.), Workforce Systems Support, 200 Constitution Ave. N.W., #S4231 20210; (202) 693-2793. Fax, (202) 693-3015. Janet Sten, Chief.*
Web, www.doleta.gov/usworkforce/onestop

Oversees the operation of the one-stop system, which supports the employment needs of job seekers and the human resources needs of business by assisting with recruitment, training, and retention of skilled workers. Coordinates all employment and training services offered by federal agencies. Helps develop and operate the CareerOneStop E-tools, a

Personnel Offices at Federal Departments and Agencies

Job seekers interested in additional information can explore federal government career opportunities through the government's official employment information system: (703) 724-1850. Web site, www.usajobs.opm.gov.

DEPARTMENTS

Agriculture, (202) 720-3585

Commerce, (202) 482-0433

Defense (civilian), (703) 696-4638

  Air Force (civilian), (703) 696-7895

  Defense Logistics Agency, (703) 767-6445

  Navy (civilian), (703) 695-2633

Education, (202) 401-0553

Energy, (202) 586-1234

Health and Human Services, (202) 690-6191

  Food and Drug Administration, (888) 478-4340

  Health Resources and Services Administration, (301) 827-4076

  National Institutes of Health, (301) 496-3592

Homeland Security, (202) 357-8151

  Coast Guard, (202) 475-5220 or (202) 475-5000

  Federal Emergency Management Agency, (202) 646-3962; recording, (202) 646-4040

  Transportation Security Administration, (866) 274-6438

Housing and Urban Development, (202) 708-2000

Interior, (202) 208-6761; recording, (800) 336-4562

Justice, (202) 616-3100

Labor, (202) 693-7600

State, (202) 647-9898; civil service, (202) 663-2176; foreign service, (202) 261-8849

Transportation, (202) 366-4088

Treasury, (304) 480-8000

Veterans Affairs, (202) 273-4950

AGENCIES

Administrative Office of the U. S. Courts, (202) 502-3100 and (202) 502-3800; recording, (202) 502-1271

Commodity Futures Trading Commission, (202) 418-5003; recording (202) 418-5009

Consumer Product Safety Commission, (301) 504-7925

Corporation for National and Community Service, (202) 606-5000

Environmental Protection Agency, (202) 564-4606

Equal Employment Opportunity Commission, (202) 663-4306

Export-Import Bank, (202) 565-3300

Farm Credit Administration, (703) 883-4135; recording, (703) 883-4139

Federal Communications Commission, (202) 418-0100

Federal Deposit Insurance Corporation, (703) 562-2180

Federal Election Commission, (202) 694-1080

Federal Labor Relations Authority, (202) 218-7979

Federal Mediation and Conciliation Service, (202) 606-5460

Federal Reserve Board, (202) 452-3880; recording, (202) 452-3038; toll-free, (800) 448-4894

Federal Trade Commission, (202) 326-2021

General Services Administration, (202) 501-0370

Government Accountability Office, (202) 512-5811; recording, (202) 512-6092

Government Printing Office, (202) 512-1200

National Aeronautics and Space Administration, (202) 358-1998 and (202) 358-2336

National Archives and Records Administration, (301) 837-3710

National Credit Union Administration, (703) 518-6510

National Endowment for the Arts, (202) 682-5405

National Endowment for the Humanities, (202) 606-8415

National Labor Relations Board, (202) 273-3900

National Mediation Board, (202) 692-5010

National Science Foundation, (703) 292-8180

National Transportation Safety Board, (202) 314-6239; recording, (800) 573-0937

Nuclear Regulatory Commission, (301) 415-7516

Office of Personnel Management, employment information, (202) 606-2525; recording, (202) 606-1800

Securities and Exchange Commission, (202) 551-7500

Small Business Administration, (202) 205-6780

Smithsonian Institution, (202) 633-6370

Social Security Administration, (410) 965-4506

U.S. International Trade Commission, (202) 205-2651

U.S. Postal Service, (202) 268-3646

group of Web sites that provide job, career, and workforce services information to workers, job seekers, and employers.

Housing and Urban Development Dept. (HUD), *Office of Labor Relations, 451 7th St. S.W., #2102 20410; (202) 708-0370. Fax, (202) 619-8022. Waite Madison, Executive Director.*
Web, www.hud.gov/offices/olr

Partnership between HUD and the Labor Dept. that assists low-income housing residents in obtaining job training and employment.

►CONGRESS

For a listing of relevant congressional committees and subcommittees, please see page 195 or the Appendix.

►NONGOVERNMENTAL

AFL-CIO Working America, *815 16th St. N.W. 20006; (202) 637-5137. Fax, (202) 508-6900. Karen Nussbaum, Executive Director.*
General e-mail, info@workingamerica.org
Web, www.workingamerica.org

Advocates on behalf of nonunion workers at the community, state, and national levels. Seeks to secure better jobs, health care, education, and retirement benefits for these workers. Monitors legislation and regulations. (A community affiliate of the AFL-CIO.)

AFL-CIO Working for America Institute, *815 16th St. N.W. 20006; (202) 508-3717. Fax, (202) 508-3719. Nancy Mills, Executive Director.*
General e-mail, info@workingforamerica.org
Web, www.workingforamerica.org

Provides technical assistance to labor unions, employers, education agencies, and community groups for workplace programs focusing on dislocated workers, economically disadvantaged workers, and skill upgrading. Interests include new technologies and workplace innovations.

American Society for Training and Development (ASTD), *1640 King St., Box 1443, Alexandria, VA 22313-2043; (703) 683-8100. Fax, (703) 683-1523. Tony Bingham, Chief Executive Officer.*
General e-mail, astdresearch@astd.org
Web, www.astd.org

Membership: trainers and human resource developers. Promotes workplace training programs and human resource development. Interests include productivity, job training and retraining, participative management, and unemployment. Holds conferences and provides information on technical and skills training.

National Assn. of State Workforce Agencies, *444 N. Capitol St. N.W., #142 20001; (202) 434-8020. Fax, (202) 434-8033. Richard A. Hobbie, Executive Director.*
Web, www.workforceatm.org

Membership: state employment security administrators. Informs members of federal legislation on job placement, veterans' affairs, and employment and training programs. Distributes labor market information; trains new state administrators and executive staff. Provides employment and training professionals with opportunities for networking and information exchange.

National Assn. of Workforce Boards, *1133 19th St. N.W., #400 20036; (202) 857-7900. Fax, (202) 857-7955. Ross Jackson, Executive Director.*
General e-mail, nawb@nawb.org
Web, www.nawb.org

Membership: private industry councils and state job training coordinating councils established under the Job Training Partnership Act of 1982 (renamed Workforce Boards under the Workforce Investment Act). Interests include job training opportunities for youth and unemployed, economically disadvantaged, and dislocated workers; and private sector involvement in federal employment and training policy. Provides members with technical assistance; holds conferences and seminars.

National Assn. of Workforce Development Professionals, *1133 19th St. N.W., 4th Floor 20036; (202) 589-1790. Fax, (202) 589-1799. Bridget Brown, Executive Director.*
General e-mail, info@nawdp.org
Web, www.nawdp.org

Membership: professionals and policymakers in the employment and training field. Promotes professionalism, information exchange, networking, and professional growth in the workforce development field.

National Center on Education and the Economy (NCEE), *555 13th St. N.W., #500 20004; (202) 783-3668. Fax, (202) 783-3672. Marc Tucker, President.*
General e-mail, info@ncee.org
Web, www.ncee.org

Partnership of states, school districts, corporations, foundations, and nonprofit organizations that provides tools and technical assistance for school districts to improve education and training for the workplace.

National Governors Assn. (NGA), *Center for Best Practices: Workforce Development Programs, 444 N. Capitol St. N.W., #267 20001-1512; (202) 624-5345. Fax, (202) 624-7829. Martin Simon, Director.*
Web, www.nga.org

Provides information and technical assistance to members participating in federal job training programs, including programs authorized under the federal workforce development programs; informs members of related legislation. Provides technical assistance to members in areas of work and welfare programs, youth programs, employment services, dislocated workers, and dropout prevention.

Selected Internships and Other Opportunities in the Washington Metropolitan Area

For congressional internships, contact the members' offices, listed in the appendix. For opportunities at federal agencies, visit www.studentjobs.gov and www.studentjobs.gov/d_internship.asp.

American Assn. for the Advancement of Science, Joan Abdallah, (202) 326-6670, www.aaas.org

American Civil Liberties Union, Bernice Bolden, (202) 544-1681, www.aclu.org

American Farm Bureau Federation, Dave Conover, (202) 406-3600, www.fb.org

American Federation of Teachers, Jodie Fingland, (202) 879-4400, www.aft.org

American Red Cross, Patrick Riley, (202) 303-5321, www.redcross.org

Americans for the Arts, Mahogany Payne, (202) 371-2830, www.americansforthearts.org

Amnesty International, Alison Collins, (202) 544-0200, www.amnestyusa.org

B'nai B'rith International, Eric Fusfield, (202) 857-6613, www.bnaibrith.org

The Brookings Institution, Megha Pokharel, (202) 797-6254, www.brookings.edu/admin/employment.htm

Carnegie Institution of Washington, Cady Canapp (202) 387-6400, ext. 113, www.carnegieinstitution.org

Center for Defense Information, Susanne Ostrofsky, (202) 797-5273, www.cdi.org

Center for Responsive Politics, Michael Beckel, (202) 354-0101, www.opensecrets.org

Center for Science in the Public Interest, Janet Caputo, (202) 332-9110, www.cspinet.org

Children's Defense Fund, Kanika Magee, (202) 628-8787, www.childrensdefense.org

Common Cause, Darren Cambridge, (202) 736-5726 or (202) 833-1200, www.commoncause.org

Council for Excellence in Government, Michael Huang, (202) 728-0418, www.excelgov.org

C-SPAN, Angie Seldon, (202) 626-4868, www.cspan.org

Democratic National Committee, Nicole Varma, (202) 479-5146, www.democrats.org

Friends of the Earth, Lisa Matthis, (202) 783-7400, www.foe.org

International Assn. of Chiefs of Police, Eleni Trahilis, (703) 836-6767, ext. 392, www.theiacp.org

Middle East Institute, Peter White, (202) 785-1141, ext. 206, www.mideasti.org

Motion Picture Assn. of America, Todd DeLorenzo, (202) 293-1966, ext. 106, www.mpaa.org

National Academy of Sciences, Katina Wilson, (202) 334-3400, www.nas.edu

---

National Institute for Work and Learning (AED), *1825 Connecticut Ave. N.W., 10th Floor 20009; (202) 884-8173. Fax, (202) 884-8422. Ivan Charner, Vice President. General e-mail, NIWL@aed.org*

Web, www.aed.niwl.org

Promotes the integration of the education and employment systems to ensure lifelong learning and productivity for all Americans. Combines research, program development and evaluation, capacity building, training, and information sharing in three broad areas: learning at school, learning at work, and learning beyond school and work. (Affiliated with the Academy for Educational Development.)

Telework Coalition (TelCoa), *204 E. St. N.E. 20002; (202) 266-0046. Chuck Wilsker, President. Phone and fax are same number. General e-mail, info@telcoa.org*

Web, www.telcoa.org

Promotes telework and telecommuting, particularly in the government sector, and access to broadband services as a viable way to increase employee productivity and motivation to provide new employment opportunities for disabled, rural, and older workers, while reducing vehicular pollution, traffic, and dependency on imported oil. Encourages adoption of telework applications such as telemedicine and distance learning. Monitors legislation and regulations.

U.S. Chamber of Commerce, *Institute for a Competitive Workforce, 1615 H St. N.W. 20062-2000; (202) 463-5525. Fax, (202) 887-3424. Karen Elzey, Vice President. General e-mail, icw@uschamber.com*

Web, www.uschamber.com/icw

Works with U.S. Chamber of Commerce members on workforce development issues, including educational reform, human resources, and job training.

U.S. Conference of Mayors, *Workforce Development, 1620 Eye St. N.W., #400 20006; (202) 293-7330. Fax, (202) 293-2352. Kathleen Amoroso, Assistant Executive Director. Web, www.usmayors.org*

Offers technical assistance to members participating in federal job training programs; monitors related legislation; acts as an information clearinghouse on employment and training programs.

Worldwide ERC (Employee Relocation Council), *4401 Wilson Blvd., #510, Arlington, VA 22203; (703) 842-3400.*

Selected Internships and Other Opportunities in the Washington Metropolitan Area

National Assn. for the Advancement of Colored People, Adam Lee, (202) 463-2940, www.naacp.org

National Assn. for Equal Opportunity in Higher Education, Lanitra Berger, (202) 552-3300 or (301) 650-2440, ext. 7, www.nafeo.org

National Assn. of Broadcasters, Scott Goodwin, (202) 429-5430, www.nab.org

National Center for Missing & Exploited Children, Tyrone Sharpe, (703) 274-3900, www.missingkids.com, interns@ncmec.org

National Geographic Society, Intern information recording, (202) 857-5899, www.nationalgeographic.com

National Governors Assn., Debbie Lately, (202) 624-5300, www.nga.org

National Head Start Assn., Dario Crenshaw, (703) 739-7555, www.nhsa.org

National Law Center on Homelessness and Poverty, Vibha Bhatia, (202) 638-2535, www.nlchp.org

National Organization for Women, (202) 628-8669, www.now.org

National Public Radio, Claudine Robinson, (202) 513-2000, www.npr.org

National Trust for Historic Preservation, David Field, (202) 588-6124, www.nationaltrust.org

National Wildlife Federation, Courtney Cochran, (703) 438-6265, www.nwf.org

Nature Conservancy, (703) 841-5300, www.nature.org

Points of Light Institute, (202) 729-8000, www.pointsoflight.org

Public Broadcasting Service, Brittany Thackston, (703) 739-5088, www.pbs.org

Radio Free Europe/Radio Liberty, Donna Black, (202) 457-6936, www.rferl.org

Republican National Committee, Julie Fleming, (202) 863-8743, www.rnc.org

Sierra Club, Lala Shamirvaian, (202) 547-1141, www.sierraclub.org

Special Olympics International, Andrea Cahn, (703) 836-6382, www.specialolympics.org

U.S. Chamber of Commerce, Jonathan Williams, (202) 463-5731, www.uschamber.com

United Negro College Fund, Sylvia Walker, (703) 205-3400, www.uncf.org

Urban Institute, Dawn Dangel, (202) 833-7200, www.urban.org

Veterans of Foreign Wars of the United States, Eric Hilleman, (202) 608-8352, www.vfw.org

---

Fax, (703) 527-1552. Lynn Bragg, Chief Executive Officer. General e-mail, info@erc.org

Web, www.erc.org

Membership: corporations that relocate employees and moving, real estate, and relocation management companies. Researches and recommends policies that provide a smooth transition for relocated employees and their families. Holds conferences and issues publications on employee relocation issues.

Aliens

▶**AGENCIES**

Administration for Children and Families (ACF), *(Health and Human Services Dept.), Refugee Resettlement, 901 D St. S.W., 8th Floor 20447; (202) 401-9246. Fax, (202) 401-0981. David Siegel, Director. Web, www.acf.hhs.gov/programs/orr*

Directs a domestic resettlement program for refugees; reimburses states for costs incurred in giving refugees monetary and medical assistance; awards funds to voluntary resettlement agencies for providing refugees with monetary assistance and case management; provides states and nonprofit agencies with grants for social services such as English and employment training.

Employment and Training Administration *(Labor Dept.), Foreign Labor Certification, 200 Constitution Ave. N.W., #C4312 20210; (202) 693-3010. William Carlson, Program Director. Web, www.foreignlaborcert.doleta.gov*

Sets national policies and guidelines to carry out the responsibilities of the secretary of labor pursuant to the Immigration and Nationality Act regarding the admission of foreign workers to the United States for both temporary and permanent employment; certifies whether U.S. citizens are available for positions for which admission of foreign workers is sought and whether employment of foreign nationals will adversely affect similarly employed U.S. citizens.

Apprenticeship Programs

▶**AGENCIES**

Employment and Training Administration *(Labor Dept.), National Office of Apprenticeship, 200*

Constitution Ave. N.W., #N5306 20210-0001; (202) 693-3812. Fax, (202) 693-3799. John V. Ladd, Administrator, (202). Library, (202) 693-6600.
Web, www.doleta.gov/oa

Advises the secretary of labor on the role of apprenticeship programs in employment training and on safety standards for those programs; encourages sponsors to include these standards in planning apprenticeship programs. Promotes establishment of apprenticeship programs in private industry and the public sector.

Employment and Training Administration *(Labor Dept.), Youth Services,* 200 Constitution Ave. N.W., #N4508 20210; (202) 693-3030. Fax, (202) 693-3861. Gregg Weltz, Director.
General e-mail, youthservices@dol.gov

Web, www.doleta.gov/youth_services

Administers youth grant programs designed to enhance youth education, encourage school completion, and provide career and apprenticeship opportunities. Oversees the Going Home: Serious and Violent Offender Reentry Initiative.

Dislocated Workers

▶**AGENCIES**

Employment and Training Administration *(Labor Dept.), Adult Services,* 200 Constitution Ave. N.W., #C4512 20210; (202) 693-3046. Fax, (202) 693-3587. Christine Ollis, Chief.
Web, www.doleta.gov/etainfo/wrksys/wiadultservices.cfm

Responsible for adult training and services for dislocated workers funded under the Workforce Investment Act; examines training initiatives and technology. Provides targeted job training services for migrant and seasonal farm workers, Native Americans, older workers, and the disabled. Provides foreign labor certification.

▶**NONGOVERNMENTAL**

National Assn. of Workforce Boards, *1133 19th St. N.W., #400 20036; (202) 857-7900. Fax, (202) 857-7955. Ross Jackson, Executive Director.*
General e-mail, nawb@nawb.org

Web, www.nawb.org

Membership: private industry councils and state job training coordinating councils established under the Job Training Partnership Act of 1982 (renamed Workforce Boards under the Workforce Investment Act). Interests include job training opportunities for youth and unemployed, economically disadvantaged, and dislocated workers; and private sector involvement in federal employment and training policy. Provides members with technical assistance; holds conferences and seminars.

National Governors Assn. (NGA), *Center for Best Practices: Workforce Development Programs,* 444 N. Capitol St. N.W., #267 20001-1512; (202) 624-5345. Fax, (202) 624-7829. Martin Simon, Director.
Web, www.nga.org

Provides technical assistance to members participating in employment and training activities for dislocated workers.

Migrant and Seasonal Farm Workers

▶**AGENCIES**

Employment and Training Administration *(Labor Dept.), National Farmworker Jobs Program,* 200 Constitution Ave. N.W., #C4311 20210-3945; (202) 693-2706. Fax, (202) 693-3945. Alina Walker, Program Manager.
General e-mail, walker.alina@dol.gov

Web, www.doleta.gov/msfw

Provides funds for programs that help seasonal farm workers and their families find better jobs in agriculture and other areas. Services include occupational training, education, and job development and placement.

Employment Standards Administration *(Labor Dept.), Farm and Labor Team,* 200 Constitution Ave. N.W., #S3510 20210; (202) 693-0070. Fax, (202) 693-1387. James Kessler, Team Leader. Toll-free, (866) 487-9243.

Administers and enforces the Migrant and Seasonal Agricultural Worker Protection Act, which protects migrant and seasonal agricultural workers from substandard labor practices by farm labor contractors, agricultural employers, and agricultural associations.

▶**NONGOVERNMENTAL**

Assn. of Farmworker Opportunity Programs, *1726 M St. N.W., #800 20036; (202) 828-6006. Fax, (202) 828-6005. David Strauss, Executive Director.*
General e-mail, afop@afop.org

Web, www.afop.org

Represents state-level organizations that provide job training and other services and support to migrant and seasonal farm workers. Monitors legislation and conducts research.

Migrant Legal Action Program, *1001 Connecticut Ave. N.W., #915 20036-5524; (202) 775-7780. Fax, (202) 775-7784. Roger C. Rosenthal, Executive Director.*
General e-mail, mlap@mlap.org

Web, www.mlap.org

Supports and assists local legal services, migrant education, migrant health issues, and other organizations and private attorneys with respect to issues involving the living and working conditions of migrant farm workers. Monitors legislation and regulations.

Older Workers

▶**AGENCIES**

Employment and Training Administration *(Labor Dept.), Older Worker Programs,* 200 Constitution Ave.

N.W., #S4209 20210; (202) 693-3046. Fax, (202) 693-3817. Alexandra Kielty, Program Manager.
Web, www.doleta.gov/seniors

Administers the Senior Community Service Employment Program, which provides funds for part-time, community service work-training programs; the programs pay minimum wage and are operated by national sponsoring organizations and state and territorial governments. The program is aimed at economically disadvantaged persons age fifty-five and over.

▶**NONGOVERNMENTAL**

AARP, *Senior Community Service Employment Program, 601 E St. N.W. 20049; (202) 434-2020. Fax, (202) 434-6446. Jim Seith, Director.*
Web, www.aarp.org

Conducts a federally funded work-experience program for economically disadvantaged older persons; places trainees in community service jobs and helps them reenter the labor force.

Experience Works, Inc., *4401 Wilson Blvd., #1100, Arlington, VA 22203; (703) 522-7272. Fax, (703) 522-0141. Cynthia A. Metzler, Chief Executive Officer. Toll-free, (866) 397-9757.*
Web, www.experienceworks.org

Trains and places older adults in the workforce. Seeks to increase awareness of issues affecting older workers and build support for policies and legislation benefiting older adults.

National Council on the Aging, *Senior Community Service Employment Program, 1901 L St. N.W., 4th Floor 20036; (202) 479-6631. Fax, (202) 479-0735. Sandra Nathan, Vice President, Workforce Development. Information, (202) 479-1200. TTY, (202) 479-6674.*
General e-mail, info@ncoa.org

Web, www.ncoa.org

Operates a grant through funding from the U.S. Labor Dept. under the authority of the Older Americans Act to provide workers age fifty-five and over with community service employment and training opportunities in their resident communities.

Workers with Disabilities

▶**AGENCIES**

Committee for Purchase from People Who Are Blind or Severely Disabled, *1421 Jefferson Davis Hwy., #10800, Arlington, VA 22202-3259; (703) 603-7740. Fax, (703) 603-0655. Tina Ballard, Executive Director.*
Web, www.abilityone.gov

Presidentially appointed committee. Determines which products and services are suitable for federal procurement from qualified nonprofit agencies that employ people who are blind or have other severe disabilities; seeks to increase employment opportunities for these individuals.

Employment Standards Administration *(Labor Dept.),* **Child Labor and Special Employment,** *200 Constitution Ave. N.W., #S3510 20210; (202) 693-0072. Fax, (202) 693-1387. Arthur M. Kerschner Jr., Team Leader. Press, (202) 693-0069.*
Web, www.dol.gov/esa/whd

Administers certification of special lower minimum wage rates for workers with disabilities and impaired earning capacity; wage applies in industry, sheltered workshops, hospitals, institutions, and group homes.

Equal Employment Opportunity Commission (EEOC), *131 M St. N.E. 20507; (202) 663-4001. Fax, (202) 663-4110. Naomi C. Earp, Chair. Information, (202) 663-4900. Library, (202) 663-4630. TTY, (202) 663-4191.*
Web, www.eeoc.gov

Works for increased employment of persons with disabilities, affirmative action by the federal government, and an equitable work environment for employees with mental and physical disabilities.

Office of Disability Employment Policy *(Labor Dept.),* *200 Constitution Ave. N.W., #S1303 20210; (202) 693-7880. Fax, (202) 693-7888. Vacant, Assistant Secretary. TTY, (202) 693-7881.*
Web, www.dol.gov/odep

Influences disability employment policy by developing and promoting the use of evidence-based disability employment policies and practices, building collaborative partnerships, and delivering data on employment of people with disabilities.

Office of Personnel Management (OPM), *Outreach Group, 1900 E St. N.W., #7412 20415; (202) 606-2773. Anita R. Hanson, Outreach Group Manager.*
Web, www.opm.gov

Develops policies, programs, and procedures to promote opportunities for qualified workers with disabilities, including veterans, to obtain and advance in federal employment. Administers the Disabled Veterans Affirmative Action Program.

Rehabilitation Services Administration *(Education Dept.), 400 Maryland Ave. S.W. 20202-2800; (202) 245-7488. Fax, (202) 245-7591. P. Edward Anthony, Commissioner (Acting). TTY, (800) 437-0833.*
Web, www.ed.gov/about/offices/list/osers/rsa/index.html

Coordinates and directs federal services for eligible persons with physical or mental disabilities, with emphasis on programs that promote employment opportunities. Provides vocational training and job placement; supports projects with private industry; administers grants for the establishment of supported-employment programs.

▶**NONGOVERNMENTAL**

Inter-National Assn. of Business, Industry, and Rehabilitation, *P.O. Box 15242 20003; (202) 543-6353. Fax, (202) 546-2854. Charles Harles, Executive Director.*
General e-mail, harles@inabir.org

Web, www.inabir.org

Membership: rehabilitation service organizations, state government agencies, corporations, and other groups that work to provide competitive employment for persons with disabilities.

NISH, *8401 Old Courthouse Rd., Vienna, VA 22182; (571) 226-4660. Fax, (703) 849-8916. E. Robert Chamberlin, President.*
General e-mail, info@nish.org
Web, www.nish.org

Assists work centers that employ people with severe disabilities in obtaining federal contracts under the Javits-Wagner-O'Day Act; supports community rehabilitation programs employing persons with severe disabilities.

Youth

►AGENCIES

Employment and Training Administration *(Labor Dept.), Youth Services, 200 Constitution Ave. N.W., #N4508 20210; (202) 693-3030. Fax, (202) 693-3861. Gregg Weltz, Director.*
General e-mail, youthservices@dol.gov
Web, www.doleta.gov/youth_services

Administers youth grant programs designed to enhance youth education, encourage school completion, and provide career and apprenticeship opportunities. Oversees the Going Home: Serious and Violent Offender Reentry Initiative.

Employment Standards Administration *(Labor Dept.), Child Labor and Special Employment, 200 Constitution Ave. N.W., #S3510 20210; (202) 693-0072. Fax, (202) 693-1387. Arthur M. Kerschner Jr., Team Leader. Press, (202) 693-0023.*
Web, www.dol.gov

Administers and enforces child labor, special minimum wage, and other provisions of Section 14 of the Fair Labor Standards Act. Administers the Work Experience and Career Exploration Program aimed at reducing the number of high school dropouts.

Forest Service *(Agriculture Dept.), Youth Conservation Corps, 1621 N. Kent St., Arlington, VA 22209 (mailing address: P.O. Box 96090, Washington, DC 20090-6090); (703) 605-4854. Fax, (703) 605-5115. Ransom Hughes, Program Manager.*
Web, www.fs.fed.us/people/programs/ycc.htm

Administers with the National Park Service and the Fish and Wildlife Service the Youth Conservation Corps, a summer employment and training public works program for youths ages fifteen to eighteen. The program is conducted in national parks, in national forests, and on national wildlife refuges.

Labor Dept. (DOL), *Job Corps, 200 Constitution Ave. N.W., #N4463 20210; (202) 693-3000. Fax, (202)*

693-2767. Esther R. Johnson, National Director. Information, (800) 733-5627.
Web, http://jobcorps.doleta.gov

Provides job training for disadvantaged youth at residential centers. Most of the centers are managed and operated by corporations and nonprofit organizations.

►NONGOVERNMENTAL

The Corps Network, *1100 G St. N.W. 20001; (202) 737-6272. Fax, (202) 737-6277. Sally T. Prouty, President.*
Web, www.corpsnetwork.org

Membership: youth corps programs. Produces publications on starting and operating youth corps. Offers technical assistance to those interested in launching programs and sponsors professional development workshops. Holds annual conference. Monitors legislation and regulations.

Work, Achievement, Values, and Education (WAVE), *525 School St. S.W., #500 20024; (202) 484-0103. Fax, (202) 488-7595. Larry Brown, President. Information, (800) 274-2005.*
General e-mail, mail@waveinc.org
Web, www.waveinc.org

Provides teachers and community youth development professionals with training and adaptable teaching strategies to help them motivate youths to succeed. Engages youths in hands-on lessons and activities to build confidence, strengthen communication skills, improve academic performance, and develop work skills. Involves youths in community service. Focuses on school dropouts and youths at risk of dropping out.

EQUAL EMPLOYMENT OPPORTUNITY

►AGENCIES

Commission on Civil Rights, *Civil Rights Evaluation, 624 9th St. N.W., #740 20425; (202) 376-8582. Fax, (202) 376-7754. Martin Dannenfelser, Staff Director. Library, (202) 376-8110.*
Web, www.usccr.gov

Researches federal policy in areas of equal employment and job discrimination; monitors the economic status of minorities and women, including their employment and earnings. Library open to the public.

Employment Standards Administration *(Labor Dept.), Federal Contract Compliance Programs, 200 Constitution Ave. N.W., #C3325 20210; (202) 693-0101. Fax, (202) 693-1304. Vacant, Deputy Assistant Secretary.*
General e-mail, ofccp-public@dol.gov
Web, www.dol.gov/esa/ofccp/index.htm

Monitors and enforces government contractors' compliance with federal laws and regulations on equal employment opportunities and affirmative action, including employment rights of minorities, women, persons with disabilities, and disabled and Vietnam-era veterans.

Equal Employment Opportunity Commission (EEOC),

131 M St. N.E. 20507; (202) 663-4001. Fax, (202) 663-4110. Naomi C. Earp, Chair. Information, (202) 663-4900. Library, (202) 663-4630. TTY, (202) 663-4191. Web, www.eeoc.gov

Works to end job discrimination by private and government employers based on race, color, religion, sex, national origin, disability, or age. Works to protect employees against reprisal for protest of employment practices alleged to be unlawful in hiring, promotion, firing, wages, and other terms and conditions of employment. Works for increased employment of persons with disabilities, affirmative action by the federal government, and an equitable work environment for employees with mental and physical disabilities. Enforces Title VII of the Civil Rights Act of 1964, as amended, which includes the Pregnancy Discrimination Act; Americans with Disabilities Act; Age Discrimination in Employment Act; Equal Pay Act; and, in the federal sector, rehabilitation laws. Receives charges of discrimination; attempts conciliation or settlement; can bring court action to force compliance; has review and appeals responsibility in the federal sector. Library open to the public by appointment only.

Equal Employment Opportunity Commission (EEOC),

Field Programs, 131 M St. N.E. 20507; (202) 663-4801. Fax, (202) 663-7190. Nicholas Inzeo, Director.

Provides guidance and technical assistance to employees who suspect discrimination and to employers who are working to comply with equal employment laws.

Justice Dept. (DOJ),

Civil Rights Division: Employment Litigation, 601 D St. N.W., #4040 20004 (mailing address: 950 Pennsylvania Ave. N.W., PHB 4040, Washington, DC 20530); (202) 514-3831. Fax, (202) 514-1005. John Gadzichowski, Chief. Library, (202) 514-3775. Web, www.usdoj.gov/crt/emp

Investigates, negotiates, and litigates allegations of employment discrimination by public schools, universities, state and local governments, and federally funded employers; has enforcement power. Enforces the Uniform Services Employment and Reemployment Rights Act. Members of the public are asked to contact the library with questions about access.

Office of Personnel Management (OPM),

Outreach Group, 1900 E St. N.W., #7412 20415; (202) 606-2773. Anita R. Hanson, Outreach Group Manager. Web, www.opm.gov

Provides veterans, military personnel, and federal hiring officials with information on veterans' rights and employment opportunities with the federal government. Provides outreach to colleges and universities on Schedule A hiring authorities for people with disabilities.

▶**CONGRESS**

For a listing of relevant congressional committees and subcommittees, please see page 195 or the Appendix.

▶**NONGOVERNMENTAL**

Center for Equal Opportunity,

7700 Leesburg Pike, #231, Falls Church, VA 22043; (703) 442-0066. Fax, (703) 442-0449. Roger Clegg, President; Linda Chavez, Chair. General e-mail, comment@ceousa.org

Web, www.ceousa.org

Research organization concerned with issues of race, ethnicity, and assimilation; opposes racial preferences in employment and education. Monitors legislation and regulations.

Council of Federal EEO and Civil Rights Executives,

P.O. Box 5911, Largo, MD 20792-6973; (202) 619-5151. Fax, (202) 260-0406. Delia Johnson, Co-Chair; Jorge Ponce, Co-Chair. General e-mail, EEO@fedcivilrights.org

Web, www.fedcivilrights.org

Membership: EEO/civil rights directors and professionals in the federal government. Interests include EEO, civil rights, affirmative action, and diversity. Communicates concerns to the EEO community, Congress, and federal agencies and organizations.

Equal Employment Advisory Council,

1501 M St. N.W., #400 20005; (202) 629-5650. Fax, (202) 629-5651. Jeffrey A. Norris, President. General e-mail, info@eeac.org

Web, www.eeac.org

Membership: principal equal employment officers and lawyers. Files amicus curiae (friend of the court) briefs; conducts research and provides information on equal employment law and policy. Monitors legislation and regulations.

NAACP Legal Defense and Educational Fund,

Washington Office, 1444 Eye St. N.W., 10th Floor 20005; (202) 682-1300. Fax, (202) 682-1312. Leslie M. Proll, Director. Web, www.naacpldf.org

Civil rights litigation group that provides legal information about civil rights legislation and advice on employment discrimination against women and minorities; monitors federal enforcement of equal opportunity rights laws. Not affiliated with the National Assn. for the Advancement of Colored People (NAACP). (Headquarters in New York.)

Minorities

▶**AGENCIES**

Bureau of Indian Affairs (BIA),

(Interior Dept.), Policy and Economic Development, 1849 C St. N.W., #3657

Equal Employment Contacts at Federal Departments and Agencies

DEPARTMENTS

Agriculture, Michael Watts, (202) 720-3808

Commerce, Suzan Aramaki, (202) 482-0625

Defense, Clarence A. Johnson, (703) 695-0105

  Air Force, Kimberly Litherland, (703) 695-8283

  Army, Ramón Surís-Fernández, (703) 607-1976

  Marine Corps, Janet Crickenberger, (703) 784-9385

  Navy, Judy Scott, (202) 685-6466

Education, Larry Rose, (202) 401-3560

Energy, Bill Lewis, (202) 586-6530

Health and Human Services, Robinsue Frohboese, (202) 619-0403

Homeland Security, Daniel W. Sutherland, (202) 282-8000

  Coast Guard, Capt. Jack R. Smith, (202) 372-4036

Housing and Urban Development, Linda Bradford Washington, (202) 402-6853

Interior, Sharon Eller, (202) 208-5693

Justice, Vontel Frost-Tucker, (202) 616-4800

Labor, Julia Mankata, (202) 693-6503

State, Gregory B. Smith (Acting), (202) 647-9887

Transportation, Beatrice Pacheco, (202) 366-1732 or (202) 366-4648

Treasury, Gloria Booze, (202) 622-4134

Veterans Affairs, Georgia Coffey, (202) 461-4131

AGENCIES

Commission on Civil Rights, Margaret Butler, (202) 376-7700

Commodity Futures Trading Commission, Sandra Canery, (202) 418-5116

Consumer Product Safety Commission, Kathy Buttrey, (301) 504-0107

Corporation for National and Community Service, Elizabeth Honnoll, (202) 606-6913

Environmental Protection Agency, Karen Higginbotham, (202) 564-7272

Equal Employment Opportunity Commission, Carlton Hadden, (202) 663-4599

Export-Import Bank, Patrease Jones-Brown, (202) 565-3591

Farm Credit Administration, Eric Howard, (703) 883-4481

Federal Communications Commission, Lawrence Schaffner (Acting), (202) 418-1799

Federal Deposit Insurance Corporation, Anthony Pagano, (703) 562-6062

Federal Election Commission, Carolyn Mackey-Bryant, (202) 694-1229

Federal Emergency Management Agency, Pauline Campbell, (202) 646-4122

Federal Labor Relations Authority, Bridget Sisson, (202) 218-7919

Federal Maritime Commission, Keith Gilmore, (202) 523-5806

Federal Mediation and Conciliation Service, Jerry Allen, (202) 606-5460 or (510) 273-6237

Federal Reserve Board, Sheila Clark, (202) 452-2883

Federal Trade Commission, Barbara B. Wiggs, (202) 326-2196

General Services Administration, Shirley Dade, (202) 501-0767

Merit Systems Protection Board, Charlene Proctor (Acting), (202) 653-6772, ext. 1194

National Aeronautics and Space Administration, Brenda Manuel, (202) 358-2167

National Credit Union Administration, Chrisanthy J. Loizos, (703) 518-6325

National Endowment for the Humanities, Willie V. McGhee, (202) 606-8233

National Labor Relations Board, Robert J. Poindexter, (202) 273-3891 or (202) 273-3894

National Science Foundation, Ronald Branch, (703) 292-8020

National Transportation Safety Board, Fara Guest, (202) 314-6190

Nuclear Regulatory Commission, Sandra Talley or Lori Suto-Goldsby, (301) 415-7380

Occupational Safety and Health Review Commission, Angela Roach, (202) 606-5391

Office of Personnel Management, Lorna Louis, (202) 606-2460

Peace Corps, Shirley Everest, (202) 692-2137

Securities and Exchange Commission, Alta Rodriguez, (202) 551-6040

Small Business Administration, Margareth J. Bennett, (202) 205-6750

Smithsonian Institution, Era Marshall, (202) 633-6430

Social Security Administration, A. Tracy Thurmond, Jr., (410) 965-4949

U.S. International Trade Commission, Jacqueline Waters, (202) 205-2240

U.S. Postal Service, Thais Mootz, (202) 268-6847

20240; (202) 219-4066. Fax, (202) 273-3153. Vacant, Deputy Assistant Secretary.

Web, www.doi.gov/bureau-indian-affairs.html

Develops policies and programs to promote the achievement of economic goals for members of federally recognized tribes who live on or near reservations. Provides job training; assists those who have completed job training programs in finding employment; provides loan guarantees; enhances contracting opportunities for individuals and tribes.

Employment and Training Administration (Labor Dept.), Indian and Native American Programs, 200 Constitution Ave. N.W., #S4209 20210; (202) 693-3841. Fax, (202) 693-3818. Evangeline Campbell, Program Manager.

Web, www.doleta.gov/dinap

Administers grants for training and employment-related programs to promote employment opportunity; provides unemployed, underemployed, and economically disadvantaged Native Americans and Alaska and Hawaiian Natives with funds for training, job placement, and support services.

▶NONGOVERNMENTAL

American Assn. for Affirmative Action, 888 16th St. N.W., #800 20006; (202) 349-9855, ext. 1857. Fax, (202) 355-1399. Shirley J. Wilcher, Executive Director. Information, (800) 252-8952.

General e-mail, execdir@affirmativeaction.org

Web, www.affirmativeaction.org

Membership: professional managers in the areas of affirmative action, equal opportunity, diversity, and human resources. Sponsors education, research, and training programs. Acts as a liaison with government agencies involved in equal opportunity compliance. Maintains ethical standards for the profession.

Coalition of Black Trade Unionists, 1625 L St. N.W. 20036 (mailing address: P.O. Box 66268, Washington, DC 20035-6268); (202) 429-1203. Fax, (202) 429-1114. William Lucy, President.

Web, www.cbtu.org

Monitors legislation affecting African American and other minority trade unionists. Focuses on equal employment opportunity, unemployment, and voter education and registration.

Labor Council for Latin American Advancement, 815 16th St. N.W., 4th Floor 20006; (202) 508-6919. Fax, (202) 508-6922. Gabriela D. Lemus, Executive Director General e-mail, headquarters@lclaa.org

Web, www.lclaa.org

Membership: Hispanic trade unionists. Encourages equal employment opportunity, voter registration, and participation in the political process. (Affiliated with the AFL-CIO and the Change to Win Federation.)

Mexican American Legal Defense and Educational Fund, Washington Office, 1016 16th St. N.W., #100 20036; (202) 293 2828. Fax, (202) 293-2849. Peter Zamora, Regional Counsel.

Web, www.maldef.org

Provides Mexican Americans and other Hispanics involved in class-action employment discrimination suits or complaints with legal assistance. Monitors legislation and regulations. (Headquarters in Los Angeles, Calif.)

National Assn. for the Advancement of Colored People (NAACP), Washington Bureau, 1156 15th St. N.W., #915 20005-1750; (202) 463-2940. Fax, (202) 463-2953. Hilary O. Shelton, Director.

General e-mail, washingtonbureau@naacpnet.org

Web, www.naacp.org

Membership: persons interested in civil rights for all minorities. Advises individuals with employment discrimination complaints. Seeks to eliminate job discrimination and to bring about full employment for all Americans through legislation and litigation. (Headquarters in Baltimore, Md.)

National Assn. of Hispanic Federal Executives, Inc., P.O. Box 23270 20026; (202) 239-0879. Al Gallegos, President (Acting).

General e-mail, washington@hatfe.org

Web, www.nahfe.org

Works to ensure that the needs of the Hispanic American community are addressed in the policy-making levels of the federal government by promoting career opportunities for qualified Hispanics in the federal GS/GM-13/15 grade levels and the Senior Executive Service policy-making positions.

National Assn. of Negro Business and Professional Women's Clubs Inc., 1806 New Hampshire Ave. N.W. 20009; (202) 483-4206. Fax, (202) 462-7253. Sandra A. Coleman, President.

General e-mail, nanbpwc@aol.com

Web, www.nanbpwc.org

Promotes opportunities for African American women in business; sponsors workshops and scholarships; maintains a job bank. Monitors legislation and regulations.

National Council of La Raza, 1126 16th St. N.W. 20036; (202) 785-1670. Fax, (202) 776-1792. Janet Murguia, President.

General e-mail, comments@nclr.org

Web, www.nclr.org

Provides research, policy analysis, and advocacy on Hispanic employment status and programs; provides Hispanic community-based groups with technical assistance to help develop effective employment programs with strong educational components. Works to promote understanding of Hispanic employment needs in the private sector. Interests include women in the workplace, affirmative action, equal opportunity employment, and youth employment. Monitors federal employment legislation and regulations.

National Urban League, *Washington Office,* 2901 14th Street N.W. 20009; (202) 265-8200. Fax, (202) 265-6122. *Maudine R. Cooper, President.*
Web, www.gwul.org

Social service organization concerned with the social welfare of African Americans and other minorities. Testifies before congressional committees and federal agencies on equal employment; studies and evaluates federal enforcement of equal employment laws and regulations. (Headquarters in New York.)

Society of American Indian Government Employees, *P.O. Box 7715 20044; (202) 564-0375. Fax, (208) 564-7899. Danny Garceau, Chair; Lori Windle, Vice Chair.*
General e-mail, lwindle@osmre.gov
Web, www.saige.org

Fosters the recruitment, development, and advancement of American Indians and Alaska Natives in the government workforce. Promotes communication among its members. Serves as an information clearinghouse. Coordinates training and conferences for federal employees on issues concerning American Indians and Alaska Natives. Monitors legislation and policies.

Women

►**AGENCIES**

Agriculture Dept. (USDA), *Center for Leadership Management,* 600 Maryland Ave. S.W., #330 20024-2520; (202) 314-3580. Fax, (202) 479-6813. *Kimberly Robinson, Director.*
General e-mail, lda@grad.usda.gov
Web, www.grad.usda.gov

Trains federally employed men and women with managerial potential for executive positions in the government.

Labor Dept. (DOL), *Women's Bureau,* 200 Constitution Ave. N.W., #S3002 20210; (202) 693-6710. Fax, (202) 693-6725. *Vacant, Director. Information, (800) 827-5335.*
General e-mail, Women'sBureauNetwork@dol.gov
Web, www.dol.gov/wb

Monitors women's employment issues. Promotes employment opportunities for women; sponsors workshops, job fairs, symposia, demonstrations, and pilot projects. Offers technical assistance; conducts research and provides publications on issues that affect working women; represents working women in international forums.

Office of Personnel Management (OPM), *Outreach Group,* 1900 E St. N.W., #7412 20415; (202) 606-2773. *Anita R. Hanson, Outreach Group Manager.*
Web, www.opm.gov

Promotes opportunities for women to obtain and advance in federal employment; assists federal agencies in the recruitment and employment of women. Collects and maintains statistics on women's employment.

►**NONGOVERNMENTAL**

Business and Professional Women U.S.A., 1600 Eye St. N.W., #210 20006; (202) 293-1100. Fax, (202) 861-0298. *Diane M. Polangin, President.*
General e-mail, memberservices@bpwusa.org
Web, www.bpwusa.org

Seeks to improve the status of working women through education, legislative action, and local projects. Sponsors Business and Professional Women's Foundation, which awards grants and loans, based on need, to mature women reentering the workforce or entering nontraditional fields.

Federally Employed Women, 700 N. Fairfax St., #510, Alexandria, VA 22306; (202) 898-0994. Fax, (202) 898-1535. *Sue Webster, President.*
General e-mail, few@few.org
Web, www.few.org

Membership: women and men who work for the federal government. Works to eliminate sex discrimination in government employment and to increase job opportunities for women; offers training programs. Monitors legislation and regulations.

Institute for Women's Policy Research (IWPR), 1707 L St. N.W., #750 20036; (202) 785-5100. Fax, (202) 833-4362. *Heidi Hartmann, President.*
General e-mail, iwpr@iwpr.org
Web, www.iwpr.org

Public policy research organization that focuses on women's issues, including welfare reform, family and work policies, employment and wages, and discrimination based on gender, race, or ethnicity.

National Assn. of Women Business Owners, 8405 Greensboro Dr., #800, McLean, VA 22102; (800) 556-2926. Fax, (703) 506-3266. *Erin M. Fuller, Executive Director.*
General e-mail, national@nawbo.org
Web, www.nawbo.org

Promotes the economic, social, and political interests of women business owners through networking, leadership and business development training, and advocacy.

National Council of Women's Organizations, 714 G St. N.W., #200 20003; (202) 293-4505. Fax, (202) 293-4507. *Susan Scanlan, Chair.*
General e-mail, ncwo@ncwo-online.org
Web, www.womensorganizations.org

Membership: local and national women's organizations. Engages in policy work and grassroots activism to address issues of concern to women, including workplace and economic equity, education and job training, affirmative action, Social Security, child care, reproductive freedom, health, and global women's equality. Monitors legislation and regulations.

National Women's Law Center, *11 Dupont Circle N.W., #800 20036; (202) 588-5180. Fax, (202) 588-5185. Nancy Duff Campbell, Co-President; Marcia D. Greenberger, Co-President.*

General e-mail, info@nwlc.org

Web, www.nwlc.org

Works to protect and advance the rights of women and girls at work, in school, and beyond. Maintains programs that focus on enforcing Title IX's provisions for equal treatment in education and narrowing the gender gap in athletics and the technology-oriented workplace. Other interests include equal pay and benefits, sexual harassment laws, the right to family leave, and the preservation of diversity in the workplace.

Wider Opportunities for Women, *1001 Connecticut Ave. N.W., #930 20036-5504; (202) 464-1596. Fax, (202) 464-1660. Joan Kuriansky, Executive Director.*

General e-mail, info@wowonline.org

Web, www.wowonline.org

Promotes equal employment opportunities for women through equal access to jobs and training, equal incomes, and an equitable workplace. Monitors public policy relating to jobs, affirmative action, vocational education, training opportunities, and welfare reform.

Women Work!, *1625 K St. N.W., #300 20006; (202) 467-6346. Fax, (202) 467-5366. Jill Miller, Chief Executive Officer. Information, (800) 235-2732.*

General e-mail, info@womenwork.org

Web, www.womenwork.org

Promotes economic equality for women through education, advocacy, and organizing. Monitors legislation and regulations.

LABOR-MANAGEMENT RELATIONS

►AGENCIES

Bureau of Labor Statistics (BLS), *(Labor Dept.),* **Compensation and Working Conditions,** *2 Massachusetts Ave. N.E., #4130 20212; (202) 691-6300. Fax, (202) 691-6310. William Wiatrowski, Associate Commissioner.*

Web, www.bls.gov/bls/proghome.htm#ocwc

Compiles data on wages and benefits, work stoppages, and workplace injuries, illnesses, and fatalities. Compiles data for *Employment Cost Index,* published quarterly.

Criminal Division *(Justice Dept.),* **Organized Crime and Racketeering: Labor-Management Racketeering,** *1301 New York Ave. N.W., #510 20530; (202) 514-3954. Fax, (202) 514-9837. Gerald A. Toner, Assistant Chief. Press, (202) 514-2007.*

General e-mail, criminaldivision@usdoj.gov

Reviews and advises on prosecutions of criminal violations involving labor-management relations, the operation of employee pension and health care plans, and internal affairs of labor unions.

Defense Dept. (DoD), *National Committee for Employer Support of the Guard and Reserve (ESGR), 1555 Wilson Blvd., #200, Arlington, VA 22209-2405; (703) 696-1386. Fax, (703) 896-6517. Vacant, Executive Director. Press, (703) 696-1386, ext. 537. Toll-free, (800) 336-4590.*

General e-mail, USERRA@osd.mil

Web, www.esgr.mil

Works to gain and maintain employer support for National Guard and Reserve service by recognizing outstanding support and providing information on applicable law. Volunteers provide free education, consultation, and, if necessary, mediation for employers of National Guard and Reserve members.

Employment Standards Administration *(Labor Dept.),* **Labor-Management Standards,** *200 Constitution Ave. N.W., #N5603 20210; (202) 693-0122. Fax, (202) 693-1206. Vacant, Deputy Assistant Secretary. Press, (202) 693-4676.*

General e-mail, olms-public@dol.gov

Web, www.dol.gov/esa/olms_org.htm

Administers and enforces the Labor-Management Reporting and Disclosure Act of 1959 (Landrum-Griffin Act), which guarantees union members certain rights; sets rules for electing union officers, handling union funds, and using trusteeships; requires unions to file annual financial reports with the Labor Dept. regulatory authority over relevant sections of the Civil Service Reform Act of 1980 and the Foreign Service Act of 1980.

Federal Mediation and Conciliation Service, *2100 K St. N.W. 20427; (202) 606-8100. Fax, (202) 606-4251. Arthur F. Rosenfeld, Director. Information, (202) 606-8080.*

Web, www.fmcs.gov

Assists labor and management representatives in resolving disputes in collective bargaining contract negotiation through voluntary mediation and arbitration services; awards competitive grants to joint labor-management initiatives; trains other federal agencies in mediating administrative disputes and formulating rules and regulations under the Administrative Dispute Resolution Act of 1996 and the Negotiated Rulemaking Act of 1996; provides training to unions and management in cooperative processes.

National Labor Relations Board (NLRB), *1099 14th St. N.W. 20570-0001; (202) 273-1000. Fax, (202) 273-0814. Peter C. Schaumber, Chair; Lester A. Heltzer, Executive Secretary. Library, (202) 273-3720. Press and public information, (202) 273-1991. Toll-free, (800) 667-6572. TTY (866) 315-6572.*

Web, www.nlrb.gov

Administers the National Labor Relations Act. Works to prevent and remedy unfair labor practices by employers and labor unions; conducts elections among employees to determine whether they wish to be represented by a labor union for collective bargaining purposes. Library open to the public.

National Mediation Board, *1301 K St. N.W., #250E 20005; (202) 692-5000. Fax, (202) 692-5080. Read Van de Water, Chair. Information, (202) 692-5050. Public Affairs, (202) 692-5050. TTY, (202) 692-5001.*
General e-mail, infoline@nmb.gov

Web, www.nmb.gov

Mediates labor disputes in the railroad and airline industries; determines and certifies labor representatives for those industries. Library open to the public; call for an appointment.

►CONGRESS

For a listing of relevant congressional committees and subcommittees, please see page 195 or the Appendix.

►NONGOVERNMENTAL

AFL-CIO (American Federation of Labor-Congress of Industrial Organizations), *815 16th St. N.W. 20006; (202) 637-5000. Fax, (202) 637-5058. John J. Sweeney, President. Library, (301) 431-6400.*
Web, www.aflcio.org

Voluntary federation of national and international labor unions in the United States. Represents members before Congress and other branches of government. Each member union conducts its own contract negotiations. Library (located in Silver Spring, Md.) open to the public.

American Arbitration Assn., *Government Relations, 1776 Eye St. N.W., #850 20006; (202) 739-8280,ext. 109. Fax, (202) 222-7095. Jean Baker, Vice President.*
General e-mail, BakerJ@adr.org

Web, www.adr.org

Provides alternative dispute resolution services to governments and the private sector. (Headquarters in New York.)

American Federation of Musicians, *Washington Office, 910 17th St. N.W., #1070 20006; (202) 463-0772. Fax, (202) 463-0758. Hal Ponder, Director of Government Relations.*
Web, www.afm.org

Seeks to improve the working conditions and salary of musicians. Monitors legislation and regulations affecting musicians and the arts. (Headquarters in New York.)

American Foreign Service Assn. (AFSA), *2101 E St. N.W. 20037; (202) 338-4045. Fax, (202) 338-6820. Ian Houston, Executive Director.*
General e-mail, member@afsa.org

Web, www.afsa.org

Membership: active and retired foreign service employees of federal agencies. Represents active duty foreign service personnel in labor-management negotiations; seeks to ensure adequate resources for foreign service operations and personnel. Monitors legislation and regulations related to foreign service personnel and retirees.

The Center for Union Facts, *1090 Vermont Ave. N.W., #800 20005 (mailing address: P.O. Box 34507, Washington,*

AFL-CIO

DEPARTMENTS

Civil, Human, and Women's Rights, Rosalyn Pelles, Director; (202) 637-5270

International, Barbara Shailor, Director; (202) 637-5050

Legal Dept., Jonathan Hiatt, General Counsel; (202) 637-5053

Legislation, William Samuel, Director; (202) 637-5320

Occupational Safety and Health, Peg Seminario, Director; (202) 637-5366

Office of the President, John J. Sweeney, President; (202) 637-5231

Organizing, Stewart Acuff, Director; (202) 639-6200

Politics and Field, Karen Ackerman, Director; (202) 637-5101

Public Affairs, Denise Mitchell, Special Assistant to the President; (202) 637-5340

TRADE AND INDUSTRIAL SECTORS

Building and Construction Trades, Mark Ayers, President; (202) 347-1461

Maritime Trades, Michael Sacco, President; (202) 628-6300

Metal Trades, Ronald Ault, President; (202) 508-3705

Professional Employees, Paul E. Almeida, President; (202) 638-0320

Transportation Trades, Edward Wytkind, President; (202) 628-9262

Union Label and Service Trades, Charles E. Mercer, President; (202) 508-3700

DC 20043); (202) 463-7106. Fax, (202) 463-7107. Richard Berman, Executive Director.
General e-mail, info@unionfacts.com

Web, www.unionfacts.com

Seeks to educate businesses, union members, and the public about the labor movement's political activities, specifically those of union officials. Interests include management of union dues. Monitors legislation and regulations.

Coalition of Black Trade Unionists, *1625 L St. N.W. 20036 (mailing address: P.O. Box 66268, Washington, DC 20035-6268); (202) 429-1203. Fax, (202) 429-1114. William Lucy, President.*
Web, www.cbtu.org

Monitors legislation affecting African American and other minority trade unionists. Focuses on equal employment opportunity, unemployment, and voter education and registration.

Coalition of Labor Union Women, *815 16th St. N.W., 2nd Floor 20006-1119; (202) 508-6969. Fax, (202) 508-6968. Carol S. Rosenblatt, Executive Director.*

General e-mail, getinfo@cluw.org

Web, www.cluw.org

Seeks to make unions more responsive to the needs of women in the workplace; advocates affirmative action and the active participation of women in unions. Monitors legislation and regulations.

International Brotherhood of Teamsters, *25 Louisiana Ave. N.W. 20001-2198; (202) 624-6800. Fax, (202) 624-6918. James P. Hoffa, President. Press, (202) 624-6911. General e-mail, feedback@teamster.org*

Web, www.teamster.org

Membership: more than 1.4 million workers in the transportation and construction industries, factories, offices, hospitals, warehouses, and other workplaces. Helps members negotiate pay, benefits, and better working conditions; conducts training programs and workshops. Monitors legislation and regulations.

Labor Council for Latin American Advancement, *815 16th St. N.W., 4th Floor 20006; (202) 508-6919. Fax, (202) 508-6922. Gabriela D. Lemus, Executive Director. General e-mail, headquarters@lclaa.org*

Web, www.lclaa.org

Membership: Hispanic trade unionists. Encourages equal employment opportunity, voter registration, and participation in the political process. (Affiliated with the AFL-CIO and the Change to Win Federation.)

Laborers' International Union of North America, *905 16th St. N.W. 20006-1765; (202) 737-8320. Fax, (202) 942-2307. Terence O'Sullivan, President. Web, www.liuna.org*

Membership: over 800,000 construction workers; federal, state, and local government employees; health care professionals; mail handlers; custodial service personnel; shipbuilders; and hazardous waste handlers. Helps members negotiate pay, benefits, and better working conditions; conducts training programs and workshops. Monitors legislation and regulations. (Affiliated with the AFL-CIO.)

National Assn. of Manufacturers (NAM), *Human Resources Policy, 1331 Pennsylvania Ave. N.W., #600 20004-1790; (202) 637-3127. Fax, (202) 637-3182. Jeri Kubicki, Vice President. Alternate phone, (202) 637-3000. Web, www.nam.org*

Provides information on corporate industrial relations, including collective bargaining, labor standards, international labor relations, productivity, employee benefits, health care, and other current labor issues; monitors legislation and regulations.

National Labor College, *10000 New Hampshire Ave., Silver Spring, MD 20903-1706; (301) 431-6400. Fax, (301) 628-0162. William E. Scheuerman, President. Toll-free, (800) 462-4237. Web, www.nlc.edu*

Accredited college that offers a bachelor of arts degree in labor studies disciplines and union skills. Offers graduate opportunities through programs with George Mason University and the University of Baltimore.

National Right to Work Committee, *8001 Braddock Rd., #500, Springfield, VA 22160; (703) 321-9820. Fax, (703) 321-7342. Mark Mix, President. Information, (800) 325-7892. General e-mail, info@nrtwc.org*

Web, www.nrtwc.org

Citizens' organization opposed to compulsory union membership. Supports right-to-work legislation.

National Right to Work Legal Defense Foundation, *8001 Braddock Rd., #600, Springfield, VA 22160; (703) 321-8510. Fax, (703) 321-9613. Mark Mix, President. Toll-free, (800) 336-3600. General e-mail, info@nrtw.org*

Web, www.nrtw.org

Provides free legal aid for employees in cases of compulsory union membership abuses.

Office and Professional Employees International Union, *Washington Office, 1660 L St. N.W., #801 20036; (202) 393-4464. Fax, (202) 347-0649. Michael Goodwin, International President; Nancy Wohlforth, Secretary-Treasurer. Web, www.opeiu.org*

Membership: approximately 125,000 workers, including computer analysts, programmers, and data entry operators; copywriters; nurses and other health care personnel; attorneys; law enforcement officers and security guards; accountants; secretaries; bank employees; and insurance workers and agents. Helps members negotiate pay, benefits, and better working conditions; conducts training programs and workshops. Monitors legislation and regulations. (Headquarters in New York; affiliated with the AFL-CIO.)

Public Service Research Foundation, *320D Maple Ave. East, Vienna, VA 22180-4747; (703) 242-3575. Fax, (703) 242-3579. David Y. Denholm, President. General e-mail, info@psrf.org*

Web, www.psrf.org

Independent, nonpartisan research and educational organization. Studies labor unions and labor issues with emphasis on employment in the public sector. Sponsors conferences and seminars. Library open to the public by appointment.

Service Employees International Union, *1800 Massachusetts Ave. N.W. 20036; (202) 730-7000. Fax, (202) 429-5563. Andrew L. Stern, President. Press, (202) 730-7162. TTY, (202) 730-7481. Web, www.seiu.org*

Membership: approximately two million members in Canada, the United States, and Puerto Rico among health care, public services, and property services employees. Promotes better wages, health care, and job security for workers. Monitors legislation and regulations.

United Auto Workers, *Washington Office, 1757 N St. N.W. 20036; (202) 828-8500. Fax, (202) 293-3457. Alan Reuther, Legislative Director.*
Web, www.uaw.org

Membership: approximately 750,000 active and 600,000 retired North American workers in aerospace, automotive, defense, manufacturing, steel, technical, and other industries. Assists members with contract negotiations and grievances; conducts training programs and workshops. Monitors legislation and regulations. (Headquarters in Detroit, Mich.)

United Electrical, Radio and Machine Workers of America, *815 King St., #307, Alexandria, VA 22314-5020; (703) 299-5120. Fax, (703) 299-5121. Chris Townsend, Political Action Director. Information, (412) 471-8919.*
Web, www.ueunion.org

Represents over 35,000 workers in electrical, metal working, and plastic manufacturing public sector and private nonprofit sector jobs. Membership: manufacturing assembly workers, plastic injection molders, tool and die makers, sheet metal workers, truck drivers, warehouse workers, custodians, clerical workers, graduate instructors, graduate researchers, scientists, librarians, social workers, and day care workers. (National headquarters in Pittsburgh, Pa.)

UNITE HERE, *Washington Office, 1775 K St. N.W., #620 20006; (202) 393-4373. Fax, (202) 342-2929. Tom Snyder, Political Director.*
Web, www.unitehere.org

Membership: more than 440,000 active and 400,000 retired North American workers in the apparel and textile manufacturing, distribution, and retail; industrial laundry; hotel; casino; foodservice; airport concession; and restaurant industries. Helps members negotiate pay, benefits, and better working conditions; conducts training programs and workshops. Monitors legislation and regulations. (Headquarters in New York. Formed by the merger of the former Union of Needletrades, Textiles and Industrial Employees and the Hotel Employees and Restaurant Employees International Union.)

U.S. Chamber of Commerce, *Labor, Immigration, and Employee Benefits, 1615 H St. N.W. 20062-2000; (202) 463-5522. Fax, (202) 463-3194. Randel K. Johnson, Vice President.*
Web, www.uschamber.com

Monitors legislation and regulations affecting labor-management relations, employee benefits, and immigration issues.

PENSIONS AND BENEFITS

►AGENCIES

Advisory Council on Employee Welfare and Pension Benefit Plans (ERISA Advisory Council) *(Labor Dept.),*
200 Constitution Ave. N.W., #N5623 20210; (202) 693-8668. Fax, (202) 219-8141. Larry Good, Executive Secretary.
Web, www.dol.gov/ebsa

Advises and makes recommendations to the secretary of labor under the Employee Retirement Income Security Act of 1974 (ERISA).

Bureau of Labor Statistics (BLS), *(Labor Dept.), Compensation and Working Conditions, 2 Massachusetts Ave. N.E., #4130 20212; (202) 691-6300. Fax, (202) 691-6310. William Wiatrowski, Associate Commissioner.*
Web, www.bls.gov/bls/proghome.htm#ocwc

Provides data on pensions and related work benefits.

Criminal Division *(Justice Dept.), Organized Crime and Racketeering: Labor-Management Racketeering, 1301 New York Ave. N.W., #510 20530; (202) 514-3954. Fax, (202) 514-9837. Gerald A. Toner, Assistant Chief. Press, (202) 514-2007.*
General e-mail, criminaldivision@usdoj.gov

Reviews and advises on prosecutions of criminal violations concerning the operation of employee benefit plans in the private sector.

Employee Benefits Security Administration *(Labor Dept.), 200 Constitution Ave. N.W., #S2524 20210; (202) 693-8300. Fax, (202) 219-5526. Vacant, Assistant Secretary.*
Web, www.dol.gov/ebsa

Administers, regulates, and enforces private employee benefit plan standards established by the Employee Retirement Income Security Act of 1974 (ERISA), with particular emphasis on fiduciary obligations; receives and maintains required reports from employee benefit plan administrators pursuant to ERISA.

Federal Retirement Thrift Investment Board, *1250 H St. N.W., #200 20005; (202) 942-1600. Fax, (202) 639-4428. Gregory T. Long, Executive Director.*
Web, www.frtib.gov

Administers the Thrift Savings Plan, a tax-deferred, defined contribution plan that permits federal employees and members of the uniformed services to save for additional retirement security under a program similar to private 401(k) plans.

Joint Board for the Enrollment of Actuaries, *1111 Constitution Ave. N.W., SE: OPR, Internal Revenue Service 20224; (202) 622-8229. Fax, (202) 622-8300. Patrick McDonough, Executive Director.*
Web, www.irs.gov/taxpros/actuaries/index.html

Joint board, with members from the departments of Labor and Treasury and the Pension Benefit Guaranty Corp., established under the Employee Retirement Income Security Act of 1974 (ERISA). Promulgates regulations for the enrollment of pension actuaries; examines applicants and grants certificates of enrollment; disciplines enrolled actuaries who have engaged in misconduct in the discharge of duties under ERISA.

Office of Personnel Management (OPM), *Retirement Information,* 1900 E St. N.W. 20415-1000; (202) 606-0300. Fax, (202) 606-0145. Joseph Donald, Jr., Chief. TTY, (800) 878-5707.
General e-mail, retire@opm.gov

Web, www.opm.gov/retire

Provides civil servants with information and assistance on federal retirement payments.

Pension Benefit Guaranty Corp., 1200 K St. N.W., #12000 20005-4026; (202) 326-4000. Fax, (202) 326-4016. Vincent K. Snowbarger, Director (Acting). General legal inquiries, (202) 326-4020. Locator, (202) 326-4110.
Web, www.pbgc.gov

Self-financed U.S. government corporation. Insures private-sector defined benefit pension plans; guarantees payment of retirement benefits subject to certain limitations established in the Employee Retirement Income Security Act of 1974 (ERISA). Provides insolvent multiemployer pension plans with financial assistance to enable them to pay guaranteed retirement benefits.

►CONGRESS

For a listing of relevant congressional committees and subcommittees, please see page 195 or the Appendix.

Government Accountability Office (GAO), *Education, Workforce, and Income Security,* 441 G St. N.W., #5928 20548; (202) 512-7215. Cynthia M. Fagnoni, Managing Director.
Web, www.gao.gov

Independent, nonpartisan agency in the legislative branch. Audits, analyzes, and evaluates federal agency and private sector pension programs; makes reports available to the public. (Formerly the General Accounting Office.)

►NONGOVERNMENTAL

AARP, 601 E St. N.W. 20049; (202) 434-2277. Fax, (202) 434-2320. William D. Novelli, Chief Executive Officer. Press, (202) 434-2560. TTY, (877) 434-7595. Research Info Center, (202) 434-6233.
Web, www.aarp.org

Researches and testifies on private, federal, and other government employee pension legislation and regulations; conducts seminars; provides information on preretirement preparation. Library open to the public.

American Academy of Actuaries, 1850 M St. N.W., #300 20036; (202) 223-8196. Fax, (202) 872-1948. Kevin Cronin, Executive Director.
Web, www.actuary.org

Membership: professional actuaries practicing in the areas of life, health, liability, property, and casualty insurance; pensions; government insurance plans; and general consulting. Provides information on actuarial matters, including insurance and pensions; develops professional standards; advises public policymakers.

American Benefits Council, 1501 M St. N.W., #600 20005; (202) 289-6700. Fax, (202) 289-4582. James A. Klein, President.
General e-mail, info@abcstaff.org

Web, www.americanbenefitscouncil.org

Membership: employers, consultants, banks, and service organizations. Informs members of employee benefits, including private pension benefits, health benefits, and compensation.

Americans for Secure Retirement, 1850 M St. N.W., #800 20036; (202) 289-5900. Shannon Hunt, Director.
General e-mail, info@paycheckforlife.org

Web, www.paycheckforlife.org

Works with policymakers to reform retirement policies. Monitors legislation and regulations.

American Society of Pension Professionals and Actuaries, 4245 N. Fairfax Dr., #750, Arlington, VA 22203-1648; (703) 516-9300. Fax, (703) 516-9308. Brian Graff, Executive Director.
General e-mail, asppa@asppa.org

Web, www.asppa.org

Membership: professional pension plan actuaries, administrators, consultants, and other benefits professionals. Sponsors educational programs to prepare actuaries and consultants for professional exams. Monitors legislation.

Coalition to Preserve Retirement Security, 12 S. Pitt St., Alexandria, VA 22314; (703) 684-3601. Fax, (703) 684-3417. Thomas Lussier, Administrator.
Web, www.retirementsecurity.org

Coalition of current public employees and retirees. Supports the voluntary participation of state and local employees in the Social Security system. Opposes all legislation that would compel public employees into participation in the system.

Employee Benefit Research Institute, 1100 13th St. N.W., #878 20005; (202) 659-0670. Fax, (202) 775-6312. Dallas L. Salisbury, President. Media Relations, (202) 775-6349.
General e-mail, info@ebri.org

Web, www.ebri.org

Research institute that focuses on health, savings, retirement, and economic security issues. Does not lobby and does not take policy positions.

Employers Council on Flexible Compensation, 927 15th St. N.W., #1000 20005; (202) 659-4300. David Carver, Executive Director. Information, (877) 747-3539.
General e-mail, info@ecfc.org

Web, www.ecfc.org

Represents employers who have or are considering flexible compensation plans. Supports the preservation and expansion of employee choice in savings and pension plans. Monitors legislation and regulations. Interests include cafeteria plans and 401(k) plans.

ERISA Industry Committee, *1400 L St. N.W., #350 20005; (202) 789-1400. Fax, (202) 789-1120. Mark J. Ugoretz, President.*
General e-mail, eric@eric.org

Web, www.eric.org

Membership: major U.S. employers. Advocates members' positions on employee retirement, health care coverage, and welfare benefit plans. Monitors legislation and regulations.

National Assn. of Manufacturers (NAM), *Human Resources Policy, 1331 Pennsylvania Ave. N.W., #600 20004-1790; (202) 637-3127. Fax, (202) 637-3182. Jeri Kubicki, Vice President. Alternate phone, (202) 637-3000. Web, www.nam.org*

Studies the Social Security system to ensure that its long-term status remains compatible with private sector retirement plans. Other interests include health care, pensions, cost containment, mandated benefits, and Medicare and other federal programs that affect employers. Opposed to government involvement in health care and proposed expansion of health care liability.

Pension Rights Center, *1350 Connecticut Ave. N.W., #206 20036; (202) 296-3776. Fax, (202) 833-2472. Karen W. Ferguson, Director.*
General e-mail, pensionhelp@pensionrights.org

Web, www.pensionrights.org

Works to preserve and expand pension rights; provides information and technical assistance on pension law.

Profit Sharing 401K Council of America, *Washington Office, 500 8th St. N.W., #200 20004; (202) 863-7272. Fax, (202) 863-7872. Edward Ferrigno, Vice President of Washington Affairs.*
General e-mail, ferrigno@401k.org

Web, www.psca.org

Encourages the use of profit sharing, 401(k) accounts, and related savings and incentive programs to strengthen free-enterprise systems. Provides assistance and information to member companies about the design, administration, compliance, investment, communication, and motivation practices associated with such programs.

Society of Professional Benefit Administrators, *2 Wisconsin Circle, #670, Chevy Chase, MD 20815; (301) 718-7722. Fax, (301) 718-9440. Frederick D. Hunt Jr., President. Web, http://users.erols.com/spba*

Membership: third-party administration firms that manage outside claims and benefit plans for client employers. Monitors government compliance requirements. Interests include pensions and retirement policy and funding, health funding, and the Employee Retirement Income Security Act of 1974 (ERISA).

United Mine Workers of America Health and Retirement Funds, *2121 K St. N.W., #350 20037-1801; (202) 521-2200. Fax, (202) 521-2394. Lorraine Lewis, Executive Director.*
Web, www.umwafunds.org

Labor/management trust fund that provides health and retirement benefits to coal miners. Health benefits are provided to pensioners, their dependents, and, in some cases, their survivors.

Women's Institute for a Secure Retirement (WISER), *1146 19th St. N.W., #700 20036; (202) 393-5452. Fax, (202) 393-5890. Cindy Hounsell, President.*
General e-mail, info@wiserwomen.org

Web, www.wiserwomen.org

Provides information on women's retirement issues. Monitors legislation and regulations.

WORKPLACE SAFETY AND HEALTH

▶ **AGENCIES**

Bureau of Labor Statistics (BLS), *(Labor Dept.), Compensation and Working Conditions, 2 Massachusetts Ave. N.E., #4130 20212; (202) 691-6300. Fax, (202) 691-6310. William Wiatrowski, Associate Commissioner.*

Web, www.bls.gov/bls/proghome.htm#ocwc

Compiles data on occupational safety and health.

Federal Mine Safety and Health Review Commission, *601 New Jersey Ave. N.W., #9500 20001-2021; (202) 434-9900. Fax, (202) 434-9906. Lisa Boyd, Executive Director.*
General e-mail, info@fmshrc.gov
Web, www.fmshrc.gov

Independent agency established by the Federal Mine Safety and Health Act of 1977. Holds fact-finding hearings and issues orders affirming, modifying, or vacating the labor secretary's enforcement actions regarding mine safety and health. Reading room open to the public by appointment.

Health, Safety, and Security *(Energy Dept.), 1000 Independence Ave. S.W., #7G040 20585; (301) 903-3777. Fax, (301) 903-5492. Glenn S. Podonsky, Chief Officer.*
General e-mail, HSS.Infocenter@hq.doe.gov
Web, www.hss.energy.gov

Develops policy and establishes standards to ensure safety and health protection in all department activities.

Mine Safety and Health Administration *(Labor Dept.), 1100 Wilson Blvd., #2322, Arlington, VA 22209-3939; (202) 693-9899. Fax, (202) 693-9801. Vacant, Assistant Secretary.*
General e-mail, ASMSHA@msha.gov
Web, www.msha.gov

Administers and enforces the health and safety provisions of the Federal Mine Safety and Health Act of 1977.

National Institute for Occupational Safety and Health (NIOSH), *(Centers for Disease Control and Prevention), 395 E St. S.W., Patriots Plaza, #9200 20201; (202)*

245-0625. *Christine Blanche, Director (Acting).*
Information, (800) 356-4674.
Web, www.cdc.gov/niosh

Entity within the Centers for Disease Control and Prevention in Atlanta. Supports and conducts research on occupational safety and health issues; provides technical assistance and training; develops recommendations for the Labor Dept. Operates an occupational safety and health bibliographic database (mailing address: NIOSH Clearinghouse for Occupational Safety and Health Information, 4676 Columbia Pkwy., Cincinnati, OH 45226).

Occupational Safety and Health Administration (OSHA), *(Labor Dept.),* *200 Constitution Ave. N.W., #S2315 20210; (202) 693-2000. Fax, (202) 693-1659. Jordan Barab, Assistant Secretary.*
Web, www.osha.gov

Sets and enforces rules and regulations for workplace safety and health. Implements the Occupational Safety and Health Act of 1970. Provides federal agencies and private industries with compliance guidance and assistance.

Occupational Safety and Health Administration (OSHA), *(Labor Dept.), Communications, 200 Constitution Ave. N.W., #N3647 20210; (202) 693-1999. Fax, (202) 693-1635. Jennifer Ashley, Director. Emergency hotline, (800) 321-OSHA.*
Web, www.osha.gov

Develops strategies, products, and materials to promote public understanding of OSHA standards, regulations, guidelines, policies, and activities to improve the safety and health of employees.

Occupational Safety and Health Administration (OSHA), *(Labor Dept.), Construction, 200 Constitution Ave. N.W., #N3468 20210; (202) 693-2020. Fax, (202) 693-1689. Richard Fairfax, Director (Acting).*
Web, www.osha.gov

Provides technical expertise to OSHA's enforcement personnel; initiates studies to determine causes of construction accidents; works with the private sector to promote construction safety and training.

Occupational Safety and Health Administration (OSHA), *(Labor Dept.), Cooperative and State Programs, 200 Constitution Ave. N.W., #N3700 20210; (202) 693-2200. Fax, (202) 693-1671. Steven Witt, Director.*
Web, www.osha.gov/fso/DFSO.html

Makes grants to nonprofit organizations under the New Directions Grant Program to assist in providing education, training, and technical assistance to meet the workplace safety and health needs of employers and employees; administers state enforcement and consultation programs; trains federal and private employees, OSHA and state inspectors, and state consultants.

Occupational Safety and Health Administration (OSHA), *(Labor Dept.), Enforcement Programs, 200 Constitution Ave. N.W., #N3119 20210; (202) 693-2100.*

Fax, (202) 693-1681. Richard Fairfax, Director.
Web, www.osha.gov

Interprets compliance safety standards for agency field personnel and private employees and employers.

Occupational Safety and Health Administration (OSHA), *(Labor Dept.), Standards and Guidance, 200 Constitution Ave. N.W., #N3718 20210; (202) 693-1950. Fax, (202) 693-1678. Dorothy Dougherty, Director. Press, (202) 693-1999.*
Web, www.osha.gov

Develops new or revised occupational health standards for toxic, hazardous, and carcinogenic substances; biological and safety hazards; or other harmful physical agents, such as vibration, noise, and radiation.

Occupational Safety and Health Review Commission, *1120 20th St. N.W., 9th Floor 20036-3457; (202) 606-5398. Fax, (202) 606-5050. Horace Thompson, Chair. TTY, (202) 606-5390.*
Web, www.oshrc.gov

Independent executive branch agency that adjudicates disputes between private employers and the Occupational Safety and Health Administration arising under the Occupational Safety and Health Act of 1970.

Office of Personnel Management (OPM), *Work/Life Group, 1900 E St. N.W., #7315 20415-2000; (202) 606-1858. Fax, (202) 418-9939. Marie L'Etoile, Manager. TTY, (202) 606-2532.*
General e-mail, worklife@opm.gov
Web, www.opm.gov/employment_and_benefits/worklife/index.asp

Sets policy and guides federal agencies in establishing and maintaining programs on alcohol and drug abuse, drug-free workplaces, workplace violence, work and family issues, telework, and fitness.

▶**CONGRESS**

For a listing of relevant congressional committees and subcommittees, please see page 195 or the Appendix.

▶**NONGOVERNMENTAL**

American Industrial Hygiene Assn., *2700 Prosperity Ave., #250, Fairfax, VA 22031-4321; (703) 849-8888. Fax, (703) 207-3561. Peter J. O'Neill, Executive Director.*
General e-mail, infonet@aiha.org
Web, www.aiha.org

Membership: scientists and engineers who practice industrial hygiene in government, labor, academic institutions, and independent organizations. Promotes health and safety standards in the workplace and the community; conducts research to identify potential dangers; educates workers about job-related risks; monitors safety regulations. Interests include international standards and information exchange.

Fair Labor Assn. (FLA), *1707 L St. N.W., #200 20036; (202) 898-1000. Fax, (202) 898-9050. Jorge Perez-Lopez, Executive Director.*

Occupational Safety and Health Administration

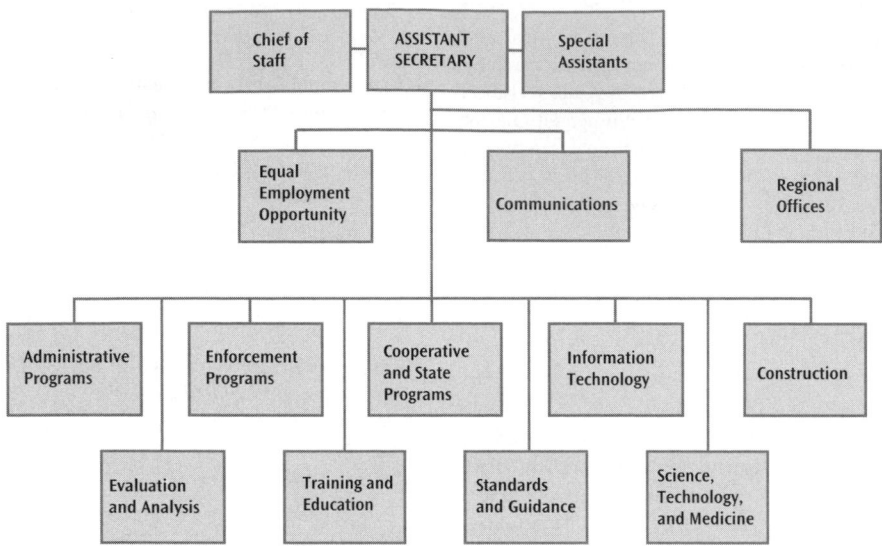

General e-mail, info@fairlabor.org

Web, www.fairlabor.org

Membership: consumer, human, and labor rights groups; apparel and footwear manufacturers and retailers; and colleges and universities. Seeks to protect the rights of workers in the United States and worldwide. Concerns include sweatshop practices, forced labor, child labor, and worker health and benefits. Monitors workplace conditions and reports findings to the public. Develops capacity for sustainable labor compliance.

Institute for a Drug-Free Workplace, *10701 Parkridge Blvd., #300, Reston, VA 20191; (703) 391-7222. Fax, (703) 391-7223. Mark A. de Bernardo, Executive Director.*
General e-mail, institute@drugfreeworkplace.org

Web, www.drugfreeworkplace.org

Coalition of businesses, business organizations, and individuals. Seeks to increase productivity, improve safety, and control insurance costs through detection and treatment of drug and alcohol abuse. Promotes fair and consistent implementation of drug abuse prevention programs; supports the right of employers to test for drugs. Monitors legislation and regulations.

ISEA—The International Safety Equipment Assn., *1901 N. Moore St., #808, Arlington, VA 22209; (703) 525-1695. Fax, (703) 528-2148. Daniel K. Shipp, President.*
General e-mail, isea@safetyequipment.org

Web, www.safetyequipment.org

Trade organization that drafts industry standards for employees' and emergency responders' personal safety and protective equipment; encourages development and use of proper equipment to deal with industrial hazards;

works to influence international standards, especially in North America. Monitors legislation and regulations.

National Assn. of Manufacturers (NAM), *Human Resources Policy, 1331 Pennsylvania Ave. N.W., #600 20004-1790; (202) 637-3127. Fax, (202) 637-3182. Jeri Kubicki, Vice President. Alternate phone, (202) 637-3000.*
Web, www.nam.org

Conducts research, develops policy, and informs members of toxic injury compensation systems, and occupational safety and health legislation, regulations, and standards internationally. Offers mediation service to business members.

National Safety Council, *Government Services, Washington Office, 1025 Connecticut Ave. N.W., #1200 20036; (202) 293-2270. Fax, (202) 293-0032. Bobby Jackson, Senior Vice President of National Programs.*
Web, www.nsc.org

Works toward the prevention of injuries and accidental deaths at work and at home, in communities, and on the road through research, education, and advocacy. Monitors legislation and regulations. (Headquarters in Itasca, Ill.)

Public Citizen, *Health Research Group, 1600 20th St. N.W. 20009-1001; (202) 588-1000. Fax, (202) 588-7796. Dr. Sidney M. Wolfe, Director.*
General e-mail, pcmail@citizen.org

Web, www.citizen.org

Citizens' interest group that studies and reports on occupational diseases; monitors the Occupational Safety and Health Administration and participates in OSHA enforcement proceedings.

Workers' Compensation

Bureau of Labor Statistics (BLS), *(Labor Dept.), Safety, Health, and Working Conditions: Occupational Safety and Health,* 2 Massachusetts Ave. N.E., #3180 20212-0001; (202) 691-6170. Fax, (202) 691-6196. William Wiatrowski, Associate Commissioner.
General e-mail, iif-staff@bls.gov

Web, www.bls.gov/iif

Compiles and publishes statistics on occupational injuries, illnesses, and fatalities.

Employment Standards Administration *(Labor Dept.), Coal Mine Workers' Compensation,* 200 Constitution Ave. N.W., #C3520 20210; (202) 693-0046. Fax, (202) 693-1395. James L. DeMarce, Director.
Web, www.dol.gov/dol/esa

Provides direction for administration of the black lung benefits program. Adjudicates all black lung claims; certifies benefit payments and maintains black lung beneficiary rolls.

Employment Standards Administration *(Labor Dept.), Workers' Compensation Programs,* 200 Constitution Ave. N.W., #S3524 20210; (202) 693-0031. Fax, (202) 693-1378. Shelby Hallmark, Director.
Web, www.dol.gov/esa/owcp_org.htm

Administers three federal workers' compensation laws: the Federal Employees' Compensation Act, the Longshore and Harbor Workers' Compensation Act and extensions, and Title IV (Black Lung Benefits Act) of the Federal Coal Mine Health and Safety Act. Also administers the Division of Energy Employees Occupational Illness Compensation Program.

Labor Dept. (DOL), *Benefits Review Board,* 200 Constitution Ave. N.W., #N5101 20210 (mailing address: P.O. Box 37601, Washington, DC 20013-7601); (202) 693-6300. Fax, (202) 693-6260. Nancy S. Dolder, Chief Public Administrative Appeals Judge.
Web, www.dol.gov/brb

Reviews appeals of workers seeking benefits under the Longshore and Harbor Workers' Compensation Act and its extensions, including the District of Columbia Workers' Compensation Act, and Title IV (Black Lung Benefits Act) of the Federal Coal Mine Health and Safety Act.

Labor Dept. (DOL), *Employees' Compensation Appeals Board,* 200 Constitution Ave. N.W., #S5220 20210; (202) 693-6360. Fax, (202) 693-6367. Alec J. Koromilas, Chair.
Web, www.dol.gov/ecab

Reviews and determines appeals of final determinations of benefit claims made by the Office of Workers' Compensation Programs under the Federal Employees' Compensation Act.

American Insurance Assn., 2101 L St. N.W., #400 20037; (202) 828-7100. Fax, (202) 293-1219. Leigh Ann Pusey, President. Library, (202) 828-7183. Federal Affairs, (202) 828-7496.
Web, www.aiadc.org

Membership: companies providing property and casualty insurance. Offers information on workers' compensation legislation and regulations; conducts educational activities. Library open to the public by appointment.

National Assn. of Manufacturers (NAM), *Human Resources Policy,* 1331 Pennsylvania Ave. N.W., #600 20004-1790; (202) 637-3127. Fax, (202) 637-3182. Jeri Kubicki, Vice President. Alternate phone, (202) 637-3000.
Web, www.nam.org

Conducts research, develops policy, and informs members of workers' compensation law; provides feedback to government agencies.

7 Energy

GENERAL POLICY AND ANALYSIS

Basic Resources

▶**AGENCIES**

Bureau of Land Management (BLM), *(Interior Dept.),*
*Minerals, Realty, and Resource Protection, 1849 C St.
N.W., #5625 20240; (202) 208-4201. Fax, (202) 208-4800.
Michael P. Nedd, Assistant Director.
Web, www.blm.gov*

Evaluates and classifies onshore oil, natural gas, geothermal resources, and all solid energy and mineral
resources, including coal and uranium, on federal lands.
Develops and administers regulations for fluid and solid
mineral leasing on national lands and on the subsurface
of land where fluid and solid mineral rights have been
reserved for the federal government.

Defense Energy Support Center (DESC), *(Defense
Dept.), 8725 John Jay Kingman Rd., #4950, Fort Belvoir,
VA 22060-6222; (703) 767-9706. Fax, (703) 767-9672.
Kim Huntley, Director. Toll-free, (800) 286-7633. Public
Affairs, (703) 767-5121.
Web, www.desc.dla.mil*

Provides the Defense Dept. and other federal agencies
with products and services to meet energy-related needs;
facilitates the cycle of storage and deployment of fuels
and other energy sources, including petroleum, electricity, and natural gas.

Energy Dept. (DOE), *1000 Independence Ave. S.W.,
#7A257 20585; (202) 586-6210. Fax, (202) 586-4403.
Steven Chu, Secretary. Information, (202) 586-5575. Press,
(202) 586-4940. Locator, (202) 586-5000.
Web, www.energy.gov*

Decides major energy policy issues and acts as principal adviser to the president on energy matters, including
strategic reserves and nuclear power; acts as principal
spokesperson for the department.

Energy Dept. (DOE), *1000 Independence Ave. S.W.,
#7B252 20585; (202) 586-5500. Fax, (202) 586-7210.
Vacant, Deputy Secretary. Information, (202) 586-5575.
Press, (202) 586-4940. Locator, (202) 586-5000.
Web, www.energy.gov*

Manages departmental programs in conservation and
renewable energy, fossil energy, energy research, the Energy
Information Administration, nuclear energy, civilian
radioactive waste management, and the power marketing
administrations.

Energy Dept. (DOE), *1000 Independence Ave. S.W.,
#7A219 20585; (202) 586-7700. Fax, (202) 586-0148.
Vacant, Under Secretary. Information, (202) 586-5575.
Press, (202) 586-4940. Locator, (202) 586-5000.
Web, www.energy.gov*

Manages departmental programs in defense, environmental safety and health, and waste management (including

radioactive and nuclear waste); responsible for all administration and management matters and for regulatory and
information programs.

Energy Dept. (DOE), *Defense Nuclear Nonproliferation:
National Nuclear Security Administration, 1000
Independence Ave. S.W., #7A049 20585; (202) 586-0645.
Fax, (202) 586-0862. Kenneth Baker, Principal Assistant
Deputy Administrator (Acting).
Web, www.nnsa.doe.gov*

Provides U.S. government agencies and departments
with technical and operational expertise on foreign
nuclear and energy issues. Oversees programs to prevent
the spread of nuclear, chemical, and biological weapons
and missiles for their delivery. Partners with Russia and
other former Soviet states to secure weapons of mass
destruction materials and expertise; works to strengthen
legal and institutional nonproliferation norms; builds
technologies to detect proliferation activities; and promotes the safe use of nuclear power.

Energy Dept. (DOE), *Economic Impact and Diversity,
1000 Independence Ave. S.W., #5B110 20585; (202) 586-
8383. Fax, (202) 586-3075. Annie Whatley, Director
(Acting).
Web, www.hr.doe.gov/ed*

Advises the secretary on the impacts of energy policies, programs, regulations, and other departmental
actions on underrepresented communities; minority educational institutions; and minority, small, and women-
owned business enterprises.

Energy Dept. (DOE), *Emergency Operations, 1000
Independence Ave. S.W., #GH060 20585; (202) 586-9892.
Fax, (202) 586-3904. Joseph J. Krol Jr., Associate
Administrator.
Web, www.energy.gov*

Works to ensure coordinated Energy Dept. responses
to energy-related emergencies. Recommends policies to
mitigate the effects of energy supply crises on the United
States; recommends government responses to energy
emergencies.

Energy Dept. (DOE), *Industrial Technologies: Inventions
and Innovation, 1000 Independence Ave. S.W., #5F039
20585-0121; (202) 586-4981. Fax, (202) 586-9234. Isaac
Chan, Supervisor.
Web, www.eere.energy.gov/inventions*

Offers financial and technical support to small businesses and individual inventors for establishing technical
performance and conducting early development of innovative ideas and inventions that have a significant energy
saving impact and future commercial market potential.

Energy Dept. (DOE), *Policy and International Affairs:
Policy Analysis, 1000 Independence Ave. S.W., #7C034,
PI-40 20585; (202) 586-8436. Fax, (202) 586-3047.
Carmen Difiglio, Deputy Assistant Secretary.
Web, www.pi.energy.gov*

ENERGY RESOURCES IN CONGRESS

For a complete listing of Congress committees, including their full contact information, leadership, membership, and jurisdictions, please refer to the Appendix on pages 724–837.

JOINT COMMITTEES:

Joint Committee on Taxation, (202) 225-7377 or (202) 225-3621.
Web, www.house.gov/jct

Joint Economic Committee, (202) 224-0372.
Web, jec.senate.gov or www.house.gov/jec

HOUSE:

House Agriculture Committee, Subcommittee on Conservation, Credit, Energy, and Research, (202) 225-0420.
Web, agriculture.house.gov

House Appropriations Committee, Subcommittee on Energy and Water Development, (202) 225-3421.
Web, appropriations.house.gov

    Subcommittee on Interior, Environment and Related Agencies, (202) 225-3081.

House Education and Labor Committee, Subcommittee on Workforce Protections, (202) 226-3725.
Web, edlabor.house.gov

House Energy and Commerce Committee, (202) 225-2927.
Web, energycommerce.house.gov

    Subcommittee on Commerce, Trade and Consumer Protection, (202) 225-2927.

    Subcommittee on Energy and Environment, (202) 225-2927.

House Foreign Affairs Committee, (202) 225-5021.
Web, foreignaffairs.house.gov

House Natural Resources Committee, (202) 225-6065.
Web, resourcescommittee.house.gov

    Subcommittee on Energy and Mineral Resources, (202) 225-9297.

    Subcommittee on National Parks, Forests and Public Lands, (202) 226-7736.

    Subcommittee on Water and Power, (202) 225-8331.

House Oversight and Government Reform Committee, Subcommittee on Domestic Policy, (202) 225-6427.
Web, oversight.house.gov

House Science and Technology Committee, (202) 225-6375.
Web, science.house.gov

    Subcommittee on Energy and Environment, (202) 225-8844.

House Select Committee on Energy Independence and Global Warming, (202) 225-4012.
Web, globalwarming.house.gov

House Small Business Committee, (202) 225-4038.
Web, www.house.gov/smbiz

Serves as principal adviser to the secretary, deputy secretary, and under secretary in formulating and evaluating departmental policy. Reviews programs, budgets, regulations, and legislative proposals to ensure consistency with departmental policy.

Energy Information Administration (EIA), *(Energy Dept.), 1000 Independence Ave. S.W., #2H027 20585; (202) 586-4361. Fax, (202) 586-0329. Howard Gruenspecht, Administrator (Acting).*
Web, www.eia.doe.gov

Collects and publishes data on national and international energy reserves, financial status of energy-producing companies, production, demand, consumption, and other areas; provides long- and short-term analyses of energy trends and data.

Energy Information Administration (EIA), *(Energy Dept.), Energy Markets and End Use, 1000 Independence Ave. S.W., #2G-090 20585; (202) 586-2589. Fax, (202) 586-9753. Margot Anderson, Director.*
Web, www.eia.doe.gov

Publishes short-term energy forecasts, collects and publishes comprehensive domestic and international energy statistics, analyzes international energy markets, conducts national energy consumption surveys, and publishes energy consumption data and analysis.

Energy Information Administration (EIA), *(Energy Dept.), Integrated Analysis and Forecasting, 1000 Independence Ave. S.W., EI-80, #2F081 20585; (202) 586-2188. Fax, (202) 586-3045. John J. Conti, Director.*
Web, www.eia.doe.gov

Analyzes and forecasts alternative energy futures. Develops, applies, and maintains modeling systems for analyzing the interactions of demand, conversion, and supply for all energy sources and their economic and environmental impacts. Concerned with emerging energy markets and U.S. dependence on petroleum imports.

Federal Energy Regulatory Commission (FERC), *(Energy Dept.), 888 1st St. N.E., #11A 20426; (202) 502-8000. Fax, (202) 502-8612. Joseph T. Kelliher, Chair. Information, (202) 502-8200. Press, (202) 502-8680.*

ENERGY RESOURCES IN CONGRESS

House Transportation and Infrastructure Committee, Subcommittee on Railroads, Pipelines, and Hazardous Materials, (202) 225-3274.
Web, transportation.house.gov
> **Subcommittee on Water Resources and Environment,** (202) 225-0060.

House Ways and Means Committee, (202) 225-3625.
Web, waysandmeans.house.gov
> **Subcommittee on Trade,** (202) 225-6649.

SENATE:

Senate Agriculture, Nutrition, and Forestry Committee, Subcommittee on Energy, Science, and Technology, (202) 224-2035.
Web, agriculture.house.gov

Senate Appropriations Committee, Subcommittee on Energy and Water Development, (202) 224-8119.
Web, appropriations.senate.gov
> **Subcommittee on Interior, Environment and Related Agencies,** (202) 224-0774.

Senate Commerce, Science, and Transportation Committee, Subcommittee on Oceans, Atmosphere, Fisheries and Coast Guard, (202) 224-4912.
Web, commerce.senate.gov
> **Subcommittee on Science, Technology, and Innovation,** (202) 224-0415.

Senate Energy and Natural Resources Committee, (202) 224-4971.
Web, energy.senate.gov

> **Subcommittee on Energy,** (202) 224-4971.
> **Subcommittee on Water and Power,** (202) 224-4971.

Senate Environment and Public Works Committee, Subcommittee on Clean Air and Nuclear Safety, (202) 224-8832.
Web, epw.senate.gov/public
> **Subcommittee on Private Sector and Consumer Solutions to Global Warming and Wildlife Protection,** (202) 224-8832.
> **Subcommittee on Public Sector Solutions to Global Warming, Oversight and Children's Health Protection,** (202) 224-8832.

Senate Finance Committee, Subcommittee on Energy, Natural Resources and Infrastructure, (202) 224-4515.
Web, finance.senate.gov

Senate Foreign Relations Committee, (202) 224-4651.
Web, foreign.senate.gov

Senate Health, Education, Labor and Pensions Committee, Subcommittee on Employment and Workplace Safety, (202) 224-2621.
Web, help.senate.gov

Senate Homeland Security and Governmental Affairs Committee, (202) 224-2627.
Web, hsgac.senate.gov

Dockets, (202) 502-8715. Public reference room, (202) 502-8371. Public inquiries, (202) 502-6088.
Web, www.ferc.gov

Independent agency that regulates the interstate transmission of electricity, natural gas, and oil, including approving rates and charges. Reviews proposals to build liquefied natural gas terminals and interstate natural gas pipelines and approves siting. Licenses and inspects nonfederal hydroelectric projects. Regulates the sale of natural gas for resale in interstate commerce and wholesale interstate sales of electricity. Ensures the reliability of high voltage interstate transmission systems. Establishes accounting and financial reporting requirements for regulated utilities.

Health, Safety, and Security *(Energy Dept.), 1000 Independence Ave. S.W., #7G040 20585; (301) 903-3777. Fax, (301) 903-5492. Glenn S. Podonsky, Chief Officer. General e-mail, HSS.Infocenter@hq.doe.gov*

Web, www.hss.energy.gov

Coordinates and integrates health, safety, environment, and security enforcement and independent oversight programs at the Energy Dept. Responsible for policy development, technical assistance, safety analysis, education, and training.

Interior Dept. (DOI), *Land and Minerals Management, 1849 C St. N.W., #6628 20240; (202) 208-6734. Fax, (202) 208-3619. C. Stephen Allred, Assistant Secretary.*
Web, www.doi.gov

Directs and supervises the Bureau of Land Management, the Minerals Management Service, and the Office of Surface Mining and Reclamation Enforcement. Supervises programs associated with land use planning, onshore and offshore minerals, surface mining reclamation and enforcement, and outer continental shelf minerals management.

Office of Management and Budget (OMB), *(Executive Office of the President), Energy, Science, and Water, New Executive Office Bldg., #8002 20503; (202) 395-3404. Fax, (202) 395-3049. Richard A. Mertens, Deputy Associate Director. Press, (202) 395-7524.*
Web, www.whitehouse.gov/omb

Energy Department

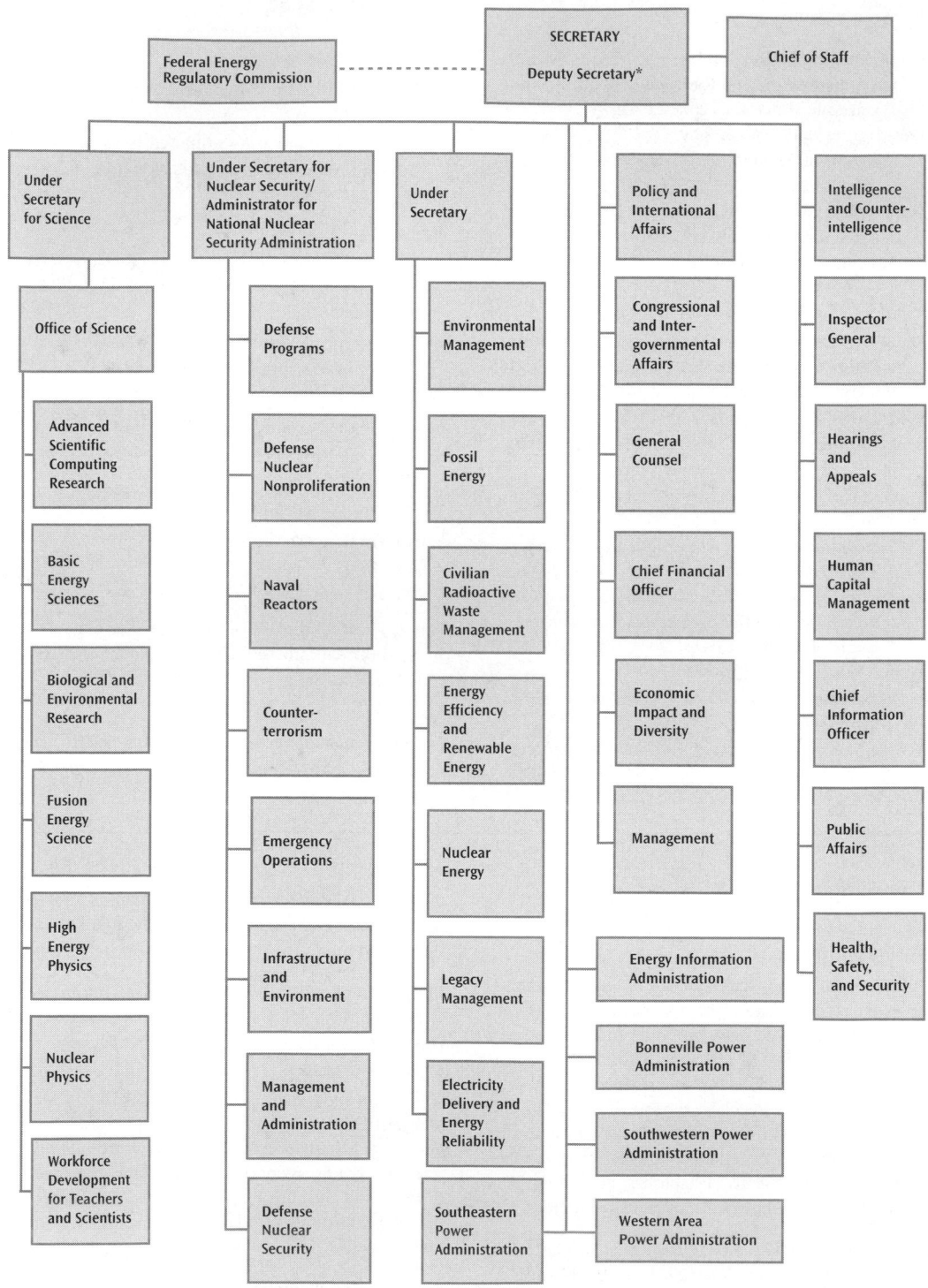

*The deputy secretary serves as the chief operating officer.

- - - - - - - - - - The FERC is an independent regulatory agency within the Dept. of Energy.

Advises and assists the president in preparing the budget for energy programs; coordinates OMB energy policy and programs.

Office of Science *(Energy Dept.),* *1000 Independence Ave. S.W., #7B058 20585; (202) 586-5430. Fax, (202) 586-4120. Patricia Dehmer, Deputy Director of Science Programs.*
Web, www.science.doe.gov

Advises the secretary on the department's physical science research and energy research and development programs; the use of multipurpose laboratories (except weapons laboratories); and education and training for basic and applied research activities. Manages the department's high energy and nuclear physics programs and the fusion energy program. Conducts environmental and health-related research and development programs, including studies of energy-related pollutants and hazardous materials.

Office of Science and Technology Policy (OSTP), *(Executive Office of the President),* *New Executive Office Bldg., 725 17th St. N.W., #5208 20502; (202) 456-7116. Fax, (202) 456-6021. John P. Holdren, Director. Science Division, (202) 456-6130; Fax, (202) 456-6027. Technology Division, (202) 456-6046; Fax, (202) 456-6040.*
General e-mail, info@ostp.gov
Web, www.ostp.gov

Provides the president with policy analysis on scientific and technological matters, including energy policy and technology issues; coordinates executive office and federal agency responses to these issues; evaluates the effectiveness of scientific and technological programs.

Treasury Dept., *Tax Analysis: Business and International Taxation,* *1500 Pennsylvania Ave. N.W., #4221 20220; (202) 622-1782. Fax, (202) 622-2969. Geraldine Gerardi, Director.*
Web, www.ustreas.gov

Negotiates tax treaties with foreign governments and participates in meetings of international organizations. Develops legislative proposals and regulations.

►**CONGRESS**

For a listing of relevant congressional committees and subcommittees, please see page 224 or the Appendix.

Government Accountability Office (GAO), *Natural Resources and Environment,* *441 G St. N.W., #2063 20548; (202) 512-9894. Robert A. Robinson, Managing Director.*
Web, www.gao.gov

Independent, nonpartisan agency in the legislative branch. Audits, analyzes, and reports on efficiency and effectiveness of the Defense, Energy, and Interior Depts. Addresses governmentwide science issues and the production, regulation, and consumption of energy. (Formerly the General Accounting Office.)

►**NONGOVERNMENTAL**

American Assn. of Blacks in Energy (AABE), *1625 K St. N.W., #405 20006; (202) 371-9530. Fax, (202) 371-9218. Frank Stewart, President.*
General e-mail, aabe@aabe.org
Web, www.aabe.org

Encourages participation of African Americans and other minorities in energy research and in formulating energy policy. Provides financial aid and scholarships to African American students who pursue careers in energy-related fields. Promotes greater awareness in private and public sectors of the impacts of energy policy on minority communities.

American Boiler Manufacturers Assn., *8221 Old Courthouse Rd., #207, Vienna, VA 22182; (703) 356-7172. Fax, (703) 356-4543. Randall Rawson, President.*
Web, www.abma.com

Membership: manufacturers of boiler systems and boiler-related products, including fuel-burning systems. Interests include energy and environmental issues.

Apollo Alliance, *1825 K St. N.W., #400 20009; (202) 587-1615. Fax, (202) 955-5606. Jerome Ringo, President; Dan Seligman, Washington Director.*
General e-mail, feedback@apolloalliance.org
Web, www.apolloalliance.org

Coalition of labor, environmental, business, and community leaders. Promotes clean energy and energy efficiency policies and initiatives as a way to reform the U.S. economy and create new industrial jobs. Monitors legislation and regulations. (Headquarters in San Francisco, Calif.)

Aspen Institute, *1 Dupont Circle N.W., #700 20036; (202) 736-5800. Fax, (202) 467-0790. Walter Isaacson, President. Press, (202) 736-3849.*
General e-mail, info@aspeninstitute.org
Web, www.aspeninstitute.org

Promotes consideration of the public good in a wide variety of areas, including energy policy. Conducts educational programs; publishes reports.

Consumer Energy Council of America, *2737 Devonshire Pl., #102 20008; (202) 468-8440. Fax, (703) 690-5920. Ellen Berman, Chief Executive Officer.*
General e-mail, outreach@cecarf.org
Web, www.cecarf.org

Analyzes economic and social effects of energy policies and advances interests of residential and small business consumers. Builds consensus on energy policy issues among public- and private-sector organizations, state and local groups, businesses, utilities, consumers, environmentalists, government agencies, and others. Interests include clean and sustainable fuels, distributed generation of electricity, and reliable electric systems. Conducts consumer education campaigns concerning fuel choices, energy conservation, and legislative and regulatory developments.

Diesel Technology Forum, *5291 Corporate Drive, #102, Frederick, MD 21703-2875; (301) 668-7230. Fax, (301) 668-7234. Allen Schaeffer, Executive Director.*
General e-mail, dtf@dieselforum.org

Web, www.dieselforum.org

Represents diesel interests, with a focus on environmental protection. Supports energy research and advises policymakers. Monitors legislation and regulations.

Energy Bar Assn., *1990 M St. N.W., #350 20036-3404; (202) 223-5625. Fax, (202) 833-5596. Lorna Wilson, Executive Director.*
General e-mail, admin@eba-net.org

Web, www.eba-net.org

Membership: lawyers interested in all areas of energy law. Interests include administration of laws covering production, development, conservation, transmission, and economic regulation of energy.

Energy Future Coalition, *1800 Massachusetts Ave. N.W., 4th Floor 20036; (202) 463-1947. Fax, (202) 887-9021. Reid Detchon, Executive Director.*
General e-mail, info@energyfuturecoalition.org

Web, www.energyfuturecoalition.org

Works to unite business, labor, and environmental groups in support of changes to U.S. energy policy. Interests include the economic, security, and environmental challenges associated with the use of fossil fuels.

Industrial Energy Consumers of America, *1155 15th St. N.W., #500 20005; (202) 223-1661. Fax, (202) 530-0659. Paul N. Cicio, President.*
General e-mail, pcicio@carbonleaf.net

Web, www.ieca-us.org

National trade association that represents the manufacturing industry on energy and environmental issues. Advocates for greater diversity of and lower costs for energy. Monitors legislation and regulations.

National Assn. of Energy Service Companies, *1615 M St. N.W., #800 20036-3213; (202) 822-0950. Fax, (202) 822-0955. Terry E. Singer, Executive Director.*
General e-mail, info@naesco.org

Web, www.naesco.org

Trade organization representing energy service companies, equipment manufacturers, affiliates of utilities, financial institutions, and governmental and other organizations involved in energy conservation and alternative energy projects. Acts as an energy information clearinghouse; sponsors conferences and seminars. Monitors legislation and regulations affecting the industry.

National Assn. of Regulatory Utility Commissioners, *1101 Vermont Ave. N.W., #200 20005-3521; (202) 898-2200. Fax, (202) 898-2213. Charles D. Gray, Executive Director. Press, (202) 898-9382.*
General e-mail, admin@naruc.org

Web, www.naruc.org

Membership: members of federal, state, municipal, and international regulatory commissions that have jurisdiction over utilities and carriers. Interests include electricity, natural gas, and nuclear power.

National Assn. of State Energy Officials (NASEO), *1414 Prince St., #200, Alexandria, VA 22314-2853; (703) 299-8800. Fax, (703) 299-6208. David Terry, Executive Director.*
General e-mail, sspencer@naseo.org

Web, www.naseo.org

Represents governor-designated energy officials from each state. Seeks to improve energy programs, provide policy analysis, and act as an information clearinghouse.

National Governors Assn. (NGA), *Center for Best Practices: Environment, Energy, and Natural Resources, 444 N. Capitol St. N.W., #267 20001-1512; (202) 624-5300. Fax, (202) 624-5825. Sue Gander, Director.*
General e-mail, webmaster@nga.org

Web, www.nga.org

Identifies best practices for energy, land-use, environment, and transportation issues and shares these with the states.

National Governors Assn. (NGA), *Natural Resources Committee, 444 N. Capitol St. N.W., #267 20001-1512; (202) 624-5300. Fax, (202) 624-7829. Michelle Cady Nellenbach, Director.*
General e-mail, webmaster@nga.org

Web, www.nga.org

Monitors legislation and regulations and makes recommendations on agriculture, energy, environment, and natural resource issues to ensure governors' views and priorities are represented in federal policies and regulations.

U.S. Chamber of Commerce, *Environment, Technology, and Regulatory Affairs, 1615 H St. N.W. 20062-2000; (202) 463-5533. Fax, (202) 887-3445. William L. Kovacs, Vice President.*
General e-mail, environment@uschamber.com

Web, www.uschamber.com

Develops policy on all issues affecting energy, including alternative energy, emerging technologies, regulatory affairs, energy taxes, telecommunications, and on- and off-shore mining of energy resources.

U.S. Conference of Mayors, *Municipal Waste Management Assn., 1620 Eye St. N.W., #400 20006; (202) 293-7330. Fax, (202) 429-0422. J. Thomas Cochran, Executive Director.*
General e-mail, info@usmayors.org

Web, www.usmayors.org/mwma

Membership: mayors of cities with populations of 30,000 or more. Brings together local government and other organizations with a common interest in the management of solid waste and broader environment issues related to environmental protection in the urban setting.

Utility Workers Union of America, *815 16th St. N.W. 20006; (202) 974-8200. Fax, (202) 974-8201. D. Michael Langford, President.*
General e-mail, webmaster@uwua.net
Web, www.uwua.net

Labor union representing approximately 50,000 workers in utilities and related industries. Helps members negotiate pay, benefits, and better working conditions; conducts training programs and workshops. Monitors legislation and regulations. (Affiliated with the AFL-CIO.)

Energy Conservation

►AGENCIES

Energy Efficiency and Renewable Energy *(Energy Dept.), 1000 Independence Ave. S.W., #6A013 20585; (202) 586-9220. Fax, (202) 586-9260. Steven Chalk, Assistant Secretary (Acting). Information, (877) 337-3463. Press, (202) 586-0462.*
General e-mail, eereic@ee.doe.gov
Web, www.eere.energy.gov

Develops and manages programs to improve foreign and domestic markets for renewable energy sources including solar, biomass, wind, geothermal, and hydropower and to increase efficiency of energy use among residential, commercial, transportation, utility, and industrial users. Administers financial and technical assistance for state energy programs, weatherization for low-income households, and implementation of energy conservation measures by schools, hospitals, local governments, and public care institutions.

Energy Efficiency and Renewable Energy *(Energy Dept.), Industrial Technologies, 1000 Independence Ave. S.W., #5F065, EE2F 20585; (202) 586-9488. Fax, (202) 586-9234. Douglas Kaempf, Program Manager.*
Web, www.eere.energy.gov/industry

Conducts research and disseminates information to increase energy end-use efficiency, promote renewable energy use and industrial applications, and reduce the volume of industrial and municipal waste.

Energy Efficiency and Renewable Energy *(Energy Dept.), Weatherization and Intergovernmental Programs, 1000 Independence Ave. S.W., #EE2K 20585; (202) 586-8038. Fax, (202) 586-1233. Gilbert P. Sperling, Director.*
Web, www.eere.energy.gov/wip

Supports private and government efforts to improve the energy efficiency of buildings and transportation. Promotes accelerated market penetration of energy efficiency and renewable energy technologies. Conducts research to make

information and energy technologies available. Administers weatherization assistance program that assists elderly and low-income persons to make their homes energy efficient. Reviews and implements building codes that promote energy efficiency in buildings.

Energy Information Administration (EIA), *(Energy Dept.), Energy Markets and End Use: Energy Consumption, 1000 Independence Ave. S.W., #2G060, EI-63 20585; (202) 586-7237. Fax, (202) 586-0018. Stephanie Battles, Director.*
Web, www.eia.doe.gov/emeu/consumption/index.html

Collects and provides data on energy consumption in the residential, commercial, and industrial sectors. Prepares analyses on energy consumption by sector and fuel type, including the impact of conservation measures.

Housing and Urban Development Dept. (HUD), *Environment and Energy, 451 7th St. S.W., #7244 20410; (202) 708-2894, ext. 4439. Fax, (202) 708-3363. Richard H. Broun, Director.*
Web, www.hud.gov/offices/cpd/environment

Develops policies promoting energy efficiency, conservation, and renewable sources of supply in housing and community development programs, including district heating and cooling systems and waste-to-energy cogeneration projects.

National Institute of Standards and Technology (NIST), *(Commerce Dept.), Building and Fire Research Laboratory, 100 Bureau Dr., MS 8600, Gaithersburg, MD 20899-8600; (301) 975-5900. Fax, (301) 975-4032. S. Shyam Sunder, Director; Hunter Fanney, Chief, Building Environment Division, (301) 975-5864.*
Web, www.bfrl.nist.gov

Develops measurement techniques, test methods, and mathematical models to encourage energy conservation in large buildings. Interests include refrigeration, lighting, infiltration and ventilation, heating and air conditioning, indoor air quality, and heat transfer in the building envelope.

►CONGRESS

For a listing of relevant congressional committees and subcommittees, please see page 224 or the Appendix.

►NONGOVERNMENTAL

Alliance to Save Energy, *1850 M St. N.W., #600 20036; (202) 857-0666. Fax, (202) 331-9588. Kateri Callahan, President.*
General e-mail, info@ase.org
Web, www.ase.org

Coalition of government, business, consumer, and labor leaders concerned with increasing the efficiency of energy use. Advocates efficient use of energy; conducts research, demonstration projects, and public education programs.

American Council for an Energy-Efficient Economy (ACEEE), *529 14th St. N.W., #600 20045-1000; (202) 507-4000. Fax, (202) 429-2248. Steve Nadel, Executive Director.*
General e-mail, info@aceee.org

Web, www.aceee.org

Independent research organization concerned with energy policy, technologies, and conservation. Interests include consumer information, energy efficiency in buildings and appliances, improved transportation efficiency, industrial efficiency, utility issues, and conservation in developing countries.

Environmental Defense, *Washington Office, 1875 Connecticut Ave. N.W., #600 20009-5728; (202) 387-3500. Fax, (202) 234-6049. Michael Roach, Office Manager. Information, (800) 684-3322. Press, (202) 572-3235.*
Web, www.edf.org

Citizens' interest group staffed by lawyers, economists, and scientists. Provides information on energy issues and advocates energy conservation measures. Interests include Antarctica and the Amazon rain forest. Provides utilities and environmental organizations with energy conservation computer models. (Headquarters in New York.)

Friends of the Earth (FOE), *1717 Massachusetts Ave. N.W., #600 20036-2008; (202) 783-7400. Fax, (202) 783-0444. Brent Blackwelder, President.*
General e-mail, foe@foe.org

Web, www.foe.org

Environmental advocacy group. Interests include global warming, conservation and renewable energy resources and air and water pollution. Specializes in federal budget and tax issues related to the environment, and World Bank and International Monetary Fund reform.

International Institute for Energy Conservation (IIEC), *10005 Leamoore Lane, #100, Vienna, VA 22181-5909; (703) 281-7263. Fax, (703) 938-5153. Nitin Pandit, President.*
Web, www.iiec.org

Works with developing nations to establish sustainable growth through efficient uses of energy. Seeks to counteract air and water pollution and the threat of global warming.

National Conference of States on Building Codes and Standards, *505 Huntmar Park Dr., #210, Herndon, VA 20170-5139; (703) 437-0100. Fax, (703) 481-3596. Vacant, Executive Director; Cynthia Wilk, Deputy Director.*
Web, www.ncsbcs.org

Membership: delegates appointed by the governors of the states and territories; local and county individuals and organizations concerned with building standards participate as associate members. Provides technical services, education, and training to members. Prepares code reports under contract. Works with national and state organizations and governmental agencies to promote the updating and adoption of model energy conservation codes for new and existing buildings.

National Insulation Assn., *12100 Sunset Hills Rd., #330, Reston, VA 20190-3233; (703) 464-6422. Fax, (703) 464-6896. Michele M. Jones, Executive Vice President.*
General e-mail, niainfo@insulation.org

Web, www.insulation.org

Membership: companies in the commercial and industrial insulation industries, including contractors, manufacturers, distributors, and fabricators. Monitors legislation and regulations.

North American Insulation Manufacturers Assn., *44 Canal Center Plaza, #310, Alexandria, VA 22314-1548; (703) 684-0084. Fax, (703) 684-0427. Kenneth D. Mentzer, President.*
General e-mail, insulation@naima.org

Web, www.naima.org

Membership: manufacturers of insulation products for use in homes, commercial buildings, and industrial facilities. Provides information on the use of insulation for thermal efficiency, sound control, and fire safety; monitors research in the industry. Interests include energy efficiency and sustainability. Monitors legislation and regulations.

Resources for the Future, *1616 P St. N.W. 20036-1400; (202) 328-5000. Fax, (202) 939-3460. Philip R. Sharp, President. Library, (202) 328-5089. Press, (202) 328-5026.*
General e-mail, info@rff.org

Web, www.rff.org

Research organization that conducts independent studies on economic and policy aspects of energy, environment, conservation, and natural resource management issues worldwide. Interests include climate change, energy, natural resource issues in developing countries, and public health.

Set America Free, *7811 Montrose Rd., #505, Potomac, MD 20854; (866) 713-7527. Fax, (301) 340-8008. Anne Korin, Chair.*
General e-mail, info@setamericafree.org

Web, www.setamericafree.org

Advocates reduction of U.S. dependence on foreign oil. Promotes plans to reduce oil consumption in the United States, specifically transitioning the transportation sector to new fuels and vehicles that can utilize them. (Affiliated with the Institute for the Analysis of Global Security.)

Sierra Club, *Washington Office, 408 C St. N.E. 20002-5818; (202) 547-1141. Fax, (202) 547-6009. Debbie Sease, Legislative Director. Press, (202) 675-6698.*
General e-mail, information@sierraclub.org

Web, www.sierraclub.org

Citizens' interest group that promotes protection and responsible use of the Earth's ecosystems and its natural resources. Focuses on combating global warming/greenhouse effect through energy conservation, efficient use of renewable energy resources, auto efficiency, and constraints on deforestation. Monitors federal, state, and local legislation relating to the environment and natural resources. (Headquarters in San Francisco, Calif.)

Union of Concerned Scientists, *Strategy and Policy, Washington Office,* *1825 K St. N.W., #800 20006-3962; (202) 223-6133. Fax, (202) 223-6162. Alden Meyer, Director. General e-mail, ucs@ucsusa.org*

Web, www.ucsusa.org

Independent group of scientists and citizens that advocate safe and sustainable international, national, and state energy policies. Conducts research, advocacy, and educational outreach focusing on market-based strategies for the development of renewable energy and alternative fuels, transportation policy, climate change policy, and energy efficiency. (Headquarters in Cambridge, Mass.)

Worldwatch Institute, *1776 Massachusetts Ave. N.W., 8th Floor 20036; (202) 452-1999. Fax, (202) 296-7365. Christopher Flavin, President. General e-mail, worldwatch@worldwatch.org*

Web, www.worldwatch.org

Focuses on an interdisciplinary approach to solving global environmental problems. Interests include energy conservation, renewable resources, solar power, and energy use in developing countries.

International Trade and Cooperation

▶**AGENCIES**

Agency for International Development (USAID), *Bureau for Economic Growth, Agriculture, and Trade, 1300 Pennsylvania Ave. N.W., #3.9B 20523-3900; (202) 712-0670. Fax, (202) 216-3235. Mark Silverman, Deputy Assistant Administrator. Press, (202) 712-4320. Web, www.usaid.gov*

Assists with the economic growth of developing countries by providing policy, technical, and financial assistance for cost-effective, reliable energy programs and other infrastructure. Focuses on the Clean Energy Initiative, energy efficiency and conservation, public-private partnerships, increased access to energy, technology innovation, and training of officials in developing countries.

Census Bureau *(Commerce Dept.), Foreign Trade, 4600 Silver Hill Rd., #6K032, Suitland, MD 20746 (mailing address: change city to Washington, DC 20233-6700); (301) 763-2255. Fax, (301) 763-6638. William G. Bostic Jr., Chief. General e-mail, william.g.bostic.jr@census.gov*

Web, www.census.gov/trade

Provides detailed statistics on all U.S. imports and exports, including petroleum, advanced technology products, and agricultural products; organizes this information by commodity, country, state, district, and port. Compiles information for 240 trading partners, including China, Japan, and Mexico through all U.S. states and ports. Publishes the monthly economic indicator, *U.S. International Trade in Goods and Services,* in conjunction with the U.S. Bureau of Economic Analysis.

Commerce Dept., *Balance of Payments, 1441 L St. N.W., #BE-58 20230; (202) 606-9545. Fax, (202) 606-5314. Christopher L. Bach, Chief. Press, (202) 606-2649. Web, www.bea.gov*

Provides statistics on U.S. balance of trade, including figures on energy commodities.

Energy Dept. (DOE), *Emergency Operations, 1000 Independence Ave. S.W., #GH060 20585; (202) 586-9892. Fax, (202) 586-3904. Joseph J. Krol Jr., Associate Administrator.*
Web, www.energy.gov

Monitors international energy situations as they affect domestic market conditions; recommends policies on and government responses to energy emergencies; represents the United States in the International Energy Agency's emergency programs and NATO civil emergency preparedness activities.

Energy Dept. (DOE), *Nuclear Risk Reduction, 955 L'Enfant Plaza S.W., #W710 20585; (202) 586-6641. Fax, (202) 586-8272. Trisha Dedik, Assistant Deputy Administrator.*
Web, www.nnsa.doe.gov

Coordinates other departmental offices and government agencies in the implementation of U.S. nonproliferation activities. Promotes nuclear safety in the former Soviet Union and eastern Europe and assists in the shutdown of plutonium production reactors. Works with other agencies to open new markets for U.S. nuclear technology.

Energy Dept. (DOE), *Policy and International Affairs, 1000 Independence Ave. S.W., #7C016, PI-1 20585; (202) 586-8660. Fax, (202) 586-4403. Jonathan Shrier, Assistant Secretary (Acting).*
Web, www.pi.energy.gov

Advises the Energy Dept. leadership in the development of a national policy concerning domestic and international energy matters. Coordinates the varied interests of the department's divisions and other government organizations. Negotiates and manages international energy agreements.

Energy Dept. (DOE), *Policy and International Affairs; Policy Analysis, 1000 Independence Ave. S.W., #7C034, PI-40 20585; (202) 586-8436. Fax, (202) 586-3047. Carmen Difiglio, Deputy Assistant Secretary.*
Web, www.pi.energy.gov

Advises the assistant secretary and Energy Dept. leadership on energy demand and supply, energy efficiency, energy research and development, and the environment, including air quality and climate. Provides analysis for the development of domestic and international energy policy.

Responds to energy market disruptions and emergencies. Recommends science and technology policies.

Energy Information Administration (EIA), *(Energy Dept.), Integrated Analysis and Forecasting: International, Economic, and Greenhouse Gases, 1000 Independence Ave. S.W., #2H073, EI81 20585; (202) 586-2188. Fax, (202) 586-3045. Glen Sweetnam, Director. Web, www.eia.doe.gov*

Compiles, interprets, and reports international energy statistics and U.S. energy data for international energy organizations. Analyzes international energy markets; makes projections concerning world prices and trade for energy sources, including oil, natural gas, coal, and electricity; monitors world petroleum market to determine U.S. vulnerability.

Fossil Energy *(Energy Dept.), Clean Energy Collaboration, FE-27/Germantown Bldg., 1000 Independence Ave. S.W. 20585-1290; (301) 903-3820. Fax, (301) 903-1591. Barbara N. McKee, Director. Web, www.fossil.energy.gov*

Coordinates all international clean coal activities within the Office of Fossil Energy. Fosters international opportunities for U.S. energy firms. Develops and promotes international partnerships for deployment of greenhouse gas abatement technologies.

International Trade Administration (ITA), *(Commerce Dept.), Energy and Environmental Industries, 14th St. and Constitution Ave. N.W., #4053 20230; (202) 482-5225. Fax, (202) 482-5361. Patricia Sefcik, Director (Acting). Alternate fax, (202) 482-0170. Web, www.environment.ita.doc.gov*

Conducts research on the effect of federal energy policy on the business community; monitors overseas trade and investment opportunities; promotes improved market competitiveness and participation in international trade by the basic energy and environmental industries. Develops strategies to remove foreign trade barriers; conducts conferences and workshops.

Nuclear Regulatory Commission, *International Programs, #04E21 20555; (301) 415-2344. Fax, (301) 415-2400. Margaret M. Doane, Director. Web, www.nrc.gov*

Coordinates application review process for exports and imports of nuclear materials, facilities, and components. Makes recommendations on export-import licensing upon completion of review process. Conducts related policy reviews.

Office of Science *(Energy Dept.), 1000 Independence Ave. S.W., #7B058 20585; (202) 586-5430. Fax, (202) 586-4120. Patricia Dehmer, Deputy Director of Science Programs. Web, www.science.doe.gov*

Coordinates energy research, science, and technology programs among producing and consuming nations; analyzes existing international research and development activities; pursues international collaboration in research and in the design, development, construction, and operation of new facilities and major scientific experiments; participates in negotiations for international cooperation activities.

State Dept., *International Energy and Commodities Policy, 2201 C St. N.W., #4843 20520; (202) 647-3036. Fax, (202) 647-4037. Stephen J. Gallogly, Director. Web, www.state.gov*

Coordinates U.S. international energy policy related to commodities, including energy supply, and U.S. participation in the International Energy Agency; monitors cooperative multilateral and bilateral agreements related to energy; coordinates energy-related aspects of U.S. relations with other countries.

State Dept., *Nuclear Energy, Safety, and Security Affairs, 2201 C St. N.W., #3320A 20520; (202) 647-4413. Fax, (202) 647-0775. Richard J.K. Stratford, Director. Web, www.state.gov*

Coordinates and supervises international nuclear energy policy for the State Dept. Advises the secretary on policy matters relating to nonproliferation and export controls, nuclear technology and safeguards, and nuclear safety. Promotes adherence to the Nuclear Nonproliferation Treaty and other international agreements.

Treasury Dept., *International Affairs: Middle East and North Africa (MENA), 1500 Pennsylvania Ave. N.W., #5012 20220; (202) 622-1263. Fax, (202) 622-0431. Karen Mathiasen, Director. Alternate phone, (202) 622-8236. Web, www.ustreas.gov/offices/international-affairs/africa_middle-east_asia*

Represents the department in the World Bank, International Monetary Fund, and other international institutions that address energy matters. Provides economic analyses of the Middle East (including Turkey) and North Africa.

U.S. International Trade Commission, *Natural Resources and Metals, 500 E St. S.W., #511A 20436; (202) 205-3348. Fax, (202) 205-2217. Cynthia B. Foreso, Energy Analyst. General e-mail, cynthia.foreso@usitc.gov Web, www.usitc.gov*

Advisory fact-finding agency on tariffs, commercial policy, and foreign trade matters. Analyzes data on oil, crude petroleum, petroleum products, natural gas and its products, and coal and its products (including all forms of coke) traded internationally; investigates effects of tariffs on certain chemical and energy imports.

U.S. Trade Representative *(Executive Office of the President), 600 17th St. N.W., #205 20508; (202) 395-7360. Fax, (202) 395-4549. Jonathan Weinberger, Executive Secretary; Ronald Kirk, Ambassador (Acting). Press, (202) 395-3230. Web, www.ustr.gov*

Serves as principal adviser to the president and primary trade negotiator on international trade policy. Develops and coordinates energy trade matters among government agencies.

►CONGRESS

For a listing of relevant congressional committees and subcommittees, please see page 224 or the Appendix.

►INTERNATIONAL ORGANIZATIONS

European Commission, *Press and Public Diplomacy,* **Washington Office,** *2300 M St. N.W. 20037-1400; (202) 862-9500. Fax, (202) 429-1766. Anthony Smallwood, Head; John Bruton, Ambassador.*
General e-mail, relex-delusw-help@ec.europa.eu
Web, www.eurunion.org

Provides information on European Union energy policy, initiatives, research activities, and selected statistics. (Headquarters in Brussels.)

International Energy Agency *(Organization for Economic Cooperation and Development),* **Washington Office,** *2001 L St. N.W., #650 20036-4922; (202) 785-6323. Fax, (202) 785-0350. Kathleen Deboer, Director (Acting).*
General e-mail, washington.contact@oecd.org
Web, www.iea.org

Promotes cooperation in energy research among developed nations; assists developing countries in negotiations with energy-producing nations; prepares plans for international emergency energy allocation. Publishes statistics and analyses on most aspects of energy. Washington Center maintains reference library open to the public. (Headquarters in Paris.)

United Nations Information Centre, *1775 K St. N.W., #400 20006-1500; (202) 331-8670. Fax, (202) 331-9191. William Davis, Director, (202) 454-2104.*
General e-mail, unicdc@unicwash.org
Web, www.unicwash.org

Articulates U.N. priorities and activities to raise awareness of and generate support for the United Nations. Center for reference publications of the United Nations; publications include *World Energy Statistics, Energy Balances and Electricity Profiles,* and other statistical material on energy. Library open to the public by appointment.

►NONGOVERNMENTAL

Atlantic Council of the United States, *Energy and Environment Program, 1101 15th St. N.W., 11th Floor 20005-5003; (202) 778-4983, Fax, (202) 463-7241. John Lyman, Director. Information, (202) 463-7226. Press, (202) 778-4967.*
General e-mail, info@acus.org
Web, www.acus.org/tags/energy-environment

Studies and makes policy recommendations on the economic, political, and security aspects of energy supply and international environment issues. Promotes open access, clean air, and development of national energy and water-supply infrastructures.

U.S. Energy Assn., *1300 Pennsylvania Ave. N.W., #550, Mailbox 142 20004-3022; (202) 312-1230. Fax, (202) 682-1682. Barry K. Worthington, Executive Director.*
Web, www.usea.org

Membership: energy-related organizations, including professional, trade, and government groups. Participates in the World Energy Council (headquartered in London). Sponsors seminars and conferences on energy resources, policy management, technology, utilization, and conservation.

Statistics

►AGENCIES

Bureau of Labor Statistics (BLS), *(Labor Dept.),* **Producer Price Index,** *2 Massachusetts Ave. N.E., #3840 20212-0001; (202) 691-5085. Fax, (202) 691-7754. Jayson Pollock, Manager, Chemical and Energy Team; David Friedman, Associate Commissioner. Information, (202) 691-7705.*
General e-mail, ppi-info@bls.gov
Web, www.bls.gov/ppi/home.htm

Compiles statistics on energy for the Producer Price Index; analyzes movement of prices for natural gas, petroleum, coal, and electric power in the primary commercial and industrial markets. Records changes over time in the prices domestic producers receive.

Energy Information Administration (EIA), *(Energy Dept.),* **National Energy Information Center,** *1000 Independence Ave. S.W., #1E210, EI-30 20585; (202) 586-8800. Fax, (202) 586-0727. Gina Pearson, Director.*
General e-mail, infoctr@eia.doe.gov
Web, www.eia.doe.gov

Serves as the information point of contact for federal, state, and local governments; academia, businesses and industry; foreign governments and international organizations; the news media; and the public. Manages and oversees the Energy Information Administration's public Web site, printed publications, and a customer contact center.

►NONGOVERNMENTAL

American Gas Assn., *Statistics, 400 N. Capitol St. N.W., 4th Floor 20001-1598; (202) 824-7000. Fax, (202) 824-7115. Paul Pierson, Manager.*
Web, www.aga.org

Issues statistics on the gas utility industry, including supply and reserves.

American Petroleum Institute, *Statistics, 1220 L St. N.W. 20005-4070; (202) 682-8520. Fax, (202) 962-4730. Hazem Arafa, Director. Information, (202) 682-8046.*

General e-mail, statistics@api.org

Web, www.api.org

Provides basic statistical information on petroleum industry operations, market conditions, and environmental, health, and safety performance. Includes data on supply and demand of crude oil and petroleum products, exports and imports, refinery operations, drilling activities and costs, environmental expenditures, injuries, illnesses and fatalities, oil spills, and emissions.

Edison Electric Institute, *Business Information, 701 Pennsylvania Ave. N.W. 20004-2696; (202) 508-5000. Fax, (202) 508-5599. Christopher Eisenbrey, Manager. Press, (202) 508-5659.*

General e-mail, ceisenbrey@eei.org

Web, www.eei.org

Provides statistics on electric utility operations, including the *Statistical Yearbook of the Electric Utility Industry,* which contains data on the capacity, generation, sales, customers, revenue, and finances of the electric utility industry.

National Mining Assn., *Communications, 101 Constitution Ave. N.W., #500E 20001-2133; (202) 463-2600. Fax, (202) 463-2666. Carol Raulston, Senior Vice President.*

Web, www.nma.org

Collects, analyzes, and distributes statistics on the mining industry, including statistics on the production, transportation, and consumption of coal and hard rock minerals.

ELECTRICITY

▶AGENCIES

Energy Dept. (DOE), *Power Marketing Liaison Office, 1000 Independence Ave. S.W., #8G027 20585; (202) 586-5581. Fax, (202) 586-6261. R. Jack Dodd, Assistant Administrator.*

Web, www.energy.gov

Serves as a liaison among the Southeastern, Southwestern, and Western area power administrations; other federal agencies; and Congress. Coordinates marketing of electric power from federally owned hydropower projects.

Energy Information Administration (EIA), *(Energy Dept.), Coal, Nuclear, Electric, and Alternate Fuels, 1000 Independence Ave. S.W., #2H073, EI-50 20585; (202) 586-2800. Fax, (202) 287-1933. Scott Sitzer, Director.*

Web, www.eia.doe.gov

Prepares analyses and forecasts on electric power supplies, including the effects of government policies and regulatory actions on capacity, consumption, finances, and rates. Publishes statistics on electric power industry.

Tennessee Valley Authority, *Government Affairs, Washington Office, 1 Massachusetts Ave. N.W., #300 20444; (202) 898-2999. Fax, (202) 898-2998. Justin Maierhofer, Director.*

General e-mail, latootle@tva.gov

Web, www.tva.gov

Coordinates resource conservation, development, and land-use programs in the Tennessee River Valley. Produces and supplies wholesale power to municipal and cooperative electric systems, federal installations, and some industries. (Headquarters in Knoxville, Tenn.)

▶CONGRESS

For a listing of relevant congressional committees and subcommittees, please see page 224 or the Appendix.

▶NONGOVERNMENTAL

American Coalition for Clean Coal Electricity, *333 John Carlyle St., #530, Alexandria, VA 22314-5745; (703) 684-6292. Fax, (703) 684-6297. Stephen L. Miller, President.*

Web, www.cleancoalusa.org

Membership: coal, railroad, and electric utility companies and suppliers. Educates the public and policymakers about economic, technological, and scientific research on energy resources employed in generating electricity. Promotes the use of coal in generating electricity.

Electric Power Supply Assn., *1401 New York Ave., 11th Floor 20005; (202) 628-8200. Fax, (202) 628-8260. John Shelk, President.*

Web, www.epsa.org

Membership: power generators active in U.S. and global markets, power marketers, and suppliers of goods and services to the industry. Promotes competition in the delivery of electricity to consumers.

Electricity Consumers Resource Council (ELCON), *1333 H St. N.W., West Tower, 8th Floor 20005; (202) 682-1390. Fax, (202) 289-6370.*

General e-mail, elcon@elcon.org

Web, www.elcon.org

Membership: large industrial users of electricity. Promotes development of coordinated federal, state, and local policies concerning electrical supply for industrial users; studies rate structures and their impact on consumers.

National Electrical Contractors Assn., *3 Bethesda Metro Center, #1100, Bethesda, MD 20814; (301) 657-3110. Fax, (301) 215-4500.*

Web, www.necanet.org

Membership: electrical contractors who build and service electrical wiring, equipment, and appliances. Represents members in collective bargaining with union workers; sponsors research and educational programs.

National Electrical Manufacturers Assn., *1300 N. 17th St., #1752, Arlington, VA 22209-3801; (703) 841-3200. Fax, (703) 841-5900. Evan Gaddis, President. Press, (703) 841-3256. Web, www.nema.org*

Membership: manufacturers of electrical products. Develops and promotes use of electrical standards; compiles and analyzes industry statistics. Interests include efficient energy management, emerging technologies, product safety and liability, occupational safety, counterfeiting, and the environment. Monitors international trade activities, legislation, and regulations.

National Hydropower Assn., *1 Massachusetts Ave. N.W., #850 20001-1410; (202) 682-1700. Fax, (202) 682-9478. Linda Church Ciocci, Executive Director.*

General e-mail, help@hydro.org

Web, www.hydro.org

Membership: investor-owned utilities and municipal and independent companies that generate hydroelectric power and power from new water technologies; consulting, engineering, and law firms; and equipment suppliers and manufacturers. Focus includes regulatory relief, public affairs, and coalition building. Monitors legislation and regulations.

Public Utilities

►AGENCIES

Federal Energy Regulatory Commission (FERC), (Energy Dept.), Electric Reliability, *888 1st St. N.E., #81-03 20426; (202) 502-8600. Fax, (202) 219-2856. Joseph McClelland, Office Director. Web, www.ferc.gov*

Oversees the reliability and security of the nation's bulk power system. Establishes and ensures compliance with reliability and security standards for users, owners, and operators of the bulk power system.

Federal Energy Regulatory Commission (FERC), (Energy Dept.), Energy Market Regulation, *888 1st St. N.E., #8A-01 20426; (202) 502-6700. Fax, (202) 219-2836. Shelton M. Cannon, Director. Web, www.ferc.gov*

Establishes rates and power charges for electric energy transmission, sale, and interconnections. Regulates wholesale electric rates in interstate commerce. Regulates tariffs and rates related to natural gas and oil pipeline facilities and services. Ensures the reliability of the electric grid.

Federal Energy Regulatory Commission (FERC), (Energy Dept.), Energy Projects, *888 1st St. N.E., #6A01 20426; (202) 502-8700. Fax, (202) 219-0205. J. Mark Robinson, Director. Web, www.ferc.gov*

Issues licenses, permits, and exemptions for hydroelectric power and natural gas pipeline projects. Ensures safety of licensed dams and safeguards the environment.

Rural Development Utilities (Agriculture Dept.), *1400 Independence Ave. S.W., #5135-S, MS 1510 20250-1510; (202) 720-9540. Fax, (202) 720-1725. James Newby, Administrator (Acting). Information, (202) 720-1255. Web, www.usda.gov/rus*

Makes loans and loan guarantees to provide electricity, telecommunication systems, and water and waste disposal services to rural areas.

►NONGOVERNMENTAL

American Public Power Assn., *1875 Connecticut Ave. N.W., #1200 20009; (202) 467-2900. Fax, (202) 467-2910. Mark Crisson, President. Library, (202) 467-2957. Web, www.appanet.org*

Membership: local, municipally owned electric utilities nationwide. Represents industry interests before Congress, federal agencies, and the courts; provides educational programs; collects and disseminates information; funds energy research and development projects. Library open to the public by appointment.

Edison Electric Institute, *701 Pennsylvania Ave. N.W. 20004-2696; (202) 508-5000. Fax, (202) 508-5015. Thomas R. Kuhn, President. Library, (202) 508-5623. Web, www.eei.org*

Membership: investor-owned electric power companies and electric utility holding companies. Interests include electric utility operation and concerns, including conservation and energy management, energy analysis, resources and environment, cogeneration and renewable energy resources, nuclear power, and research. Provides information and statistics relating to electric energy; aids member companies in generating and selling electric energy; and conducts information forums. Library open to the public by appointment.

National Assn. of Regulatory Utility Commissioners, *1101 Vermont Ave. N.W., #200 20005-3521; (202) 898-2200. Fax, (202) 898-2213. Charles D. Gray, Executive Director. Press, (202) 898-9382.*

General e-mail, admin@naruc.org

Web, www.naruc.org

Membership: members of federal, state, municipal, and international regulatory commissions that have jurisdiction over utilities. Interests include electric utilities.

National Assn. of State Utility Consumer Advocates (NASUCA), *8380 Colesville Rd., #101, Silver Spring, MD 20910-6267; (301) 589-6313. Fax, (301) 589-6380. Charles A. Acquard, Executive Director.*

General e-mail, nasuca@nasuca.org

Web, www.nasuca.org

Membership: public advocate offices authorized by states to represent ratepayer interests before state and federal utility regulatory commissions. Monitors legislation and regulatory agencies with jurisdiction over electric utilities, telecommunications, natural gas, and water; conducts conferences.

National Rural Electric Cooperative Assn. (NRECA), *4301 Wilson Blvd., Arlington, VA 22203-1860; (703) 907-5500. Fax, (703) 907-5511. Glenn English, Chief Executive Officer.*
Web, www.nreca.org

Membership: rural electric cooperative systems and public power and utility districts. Provides members with legislative, legal, and regulatory services. Supports energy and environmental research and offers technical advice and assistance to developing countries.

Research and Development

▶**AGENCIES**

Energy Dept. (DOE), *Office of Science: Fusion Energy Sciences, SC-24/Germantown Bldg., 1000 Independence Ave. S.W. 20585; (301) 903-4941. Fax, (301) 903-8584. Steve Eckstrand, Associate Director (Acting).*
Web, www.science.doe.gov/ofes

Conducts research and development on fusion energy for electric power generation.

National Institute of Standards and Technology (NIST), *(Commerce Dept.), Electronics and Electrical Engineering Laboratory, 100 Bureau Dr., Bldg. 220, #B358, MS 8100, Gaithersburg, MD 20899-8100; (301) 975-2220. Fax, (301) 975-4091. Kent Rochford, Director (Acting).*
General e-mail, eeel@nist.gov
Web, www.eeel.nist.gov

Provides focus for research, development, and applications in the fields of electrical, electronic, quantum electric, and electromagnetic materials engineering. Interests include fundamental physical constants, practical data, measurement methods, theory, standards, technology, technical services, and international trade.

National Institute of Standards and Technology (NIST), *(Commerce Dept.), Quantum Electrical Metrology Division, 100 Bureau Dr., MS 8170, Gaithersburg, MD 20899-8170; (301) 975-2400. Fax, (301) 926-3972. Michael Kelley, Chief (Acting).*
Web, www.eeel.nist.gov/817

Conducts research to characterize and define performance parameters of electrical/electronic systems, components, and materials; applies research to advance measurement instrumentation and the efficiency of electric power transmission and distribution; develops and maintains national electrical reference standards, primarily for power, energy, and related measurements, to assist in the development of new products and promote international competitiveness.

▶**NONGOVERNMENTAL**

Electric Power Research Institute (EPRI), *Washington Office, 2000 L St. N.W., #805 20036-4913; (202)* 872-9222. *Fax, (202) 296-5436. Barbara Bauman Tyran, Director.*
Web, www.epri.com

Membership: investor- and municipally owned electric utilities and rural cooperatives. Conducts research and development in power generation and delivery technologies, including fossil fuel, nuclear, and renewable energy sources used by electric utilities. Studies energy management and utilization, including conservation and environmental issues. (Headquarters in Palo Alto, Calif.)

FOSSIL FUELS

▶**AGENCIES**

Fossil Energy *(Energy Dept.), 1000 Independence Ave. S.W., #4G084 20585-1290; (202) 586-6660. Fax, (202) 586-7847. Vacant, Assistant Secretary.*
Web, www.fe.doe.gov

Responsible for policy and management of high-risk, long-term research and development in recovering, converting, and using fossil energy, including coal, petroleum, oil shale, and unconventional sources of natural gas. Handles the petroleum reserve and the naval petroleum and oil shale reserve programs; oversees the Clean Coal Program to design and construct environmentally clean coal-burning facilities.

U.S. Geological Survey (USGS), *(Interior Dept.), Energy Resources Program, 12201 Sunrise Valley Dr., Reston, VA 20192 (mailing address: 915A National Center, Reston, VA 20192); (703) 648-6421. Fax, (703) 648-5464. Brenda S. Pierce, Program Coordinator.*
General e-mail, gd-energyprogram@usgs.gov
Web, http://energy.usgs.gov

Conducts research on geologically based energy resources of the United States and the world, including assessments of the quality, quantity, and geographic locations of natural gas, oil, gas hydrates, geothermal, and coal resources. Estimates energy resource availability and recoverability; conducts research on the deleterious environmental impacts of energy resource occurence and use.

▶**CONGRESS**

For a listing of relevant congressional committees and subcommittees, please see page 224 or the Appendix.

Coal

▶**AGENCIES**

Bureau of Land Management (BLM), *(Interior Dept.), Solid Minerals Group, 1620 L St. N.W., #501 20036 (mailing address: 1849 C St. N.W., #LS501, Washington, DC 20240); (202) 452-0350. Fax, (202) 653-7397. Mitchell Leverette, Group Manager (Acting).*

General e-mail, mitchell_leverette@blm.gov

Web, www.blm.gov/nhp/300/wo320

Evaluates and classifies coal resources on federal lands; develops and administers leasing programs. Supervises coal mining operations on federal lands; oversees pre- and postlease operations, including production phases of coal development. Oversees implementation of the Mining Law of 1872 and the Mineral Materials Act of 1955.

Energy Information Administration (EIA), *(Energy Dept.), Coal, Nuclear, Electric, and Alternate Fuels,* *1000 Independence Ave. S.W., #2H073, EI-50 20585; (202) 586-2800. Fax, (202) 287-1933. Scott Sitzer, Director.* Web, www.eia.doe.gov

Collects data, compiles statistics, and prepares analyses and forecasts on domestic coal supply, including availability, production, costs, processing, transportation, and distribution. Publishes data on the export and import of coal; makes forecasts and provides analyses on coal imports and exports.

Federal Mine Safety and Health Review Commission, *601 New Jersey Ave. N.W., #9500 20001-2021; (202) 434-9900. Fax, (202) 434-9906. Lisa Boyd, Executive Director.* General e-mail, info@fmshrc.gov

Web, www.fmshrc.gov

Independent agency established by the Federal Mine Safety and Health Act of 1977. Holds fact-finding hearings and issues orders affirming, modifying, or vacating the labor secretary's enforcement actions regarding mine safety and health. Reading room open to the public by appointment.

Fossil Energy *(Energy Dept.), Sequestration, Hydrogen, and Clean Coal Fuels,* *19901 Germantown Rd., Germantown, MD 20874 (mailing address: 1000 Independence Ave. S.W., FE 24, GTN, Washington, DC 20585-1290); (301) 903-9453. Fax, (301) 903-2238. C. Lowell Miller, Director.* Web, www.fossil.energy.gov

Fosters the development and implementation of clean coal technologies in the private sector, including carbon capture and storage and hydrogen from coal. Monitors economic and commercial efficiency program and disseminates results. Sponsors demonstrations in cooperation with the private sector.

Interior Dept. (DOI), *Surface Mining Reclamation and Enforcement,* *1951 Constitution Ave. N.W., #233 20240; (202) 208-4006. Fax, (202) 219-3106. Glenda Owens, Director (Acting). Press, (202) 208-2539.* General e-mail, gowens@osmre.gov

Web, www.osmre.gov

Administers the Surface Mining Control and Reclamation Act of 1977. Establishes and enforces national standards for the regulation and reclamation of surface coal mining and the surface effects of underground coal mining; oversees state implementation of these standards.

Mine Safety and Health Administration *(Labor Dept.),* *1100 Wilson Blvd., #2322, Arlington, VA 22209-3939; (202) 693-9899. Fax, (202) 693-9801. Vacant, Assistant Secretary.* General e-mail, ASMSHA@msha.gov

Web, www.msha.gov

Administers and enforces the health and safety provisions of the Federal Mine Safety and Health Act of 1977. Monitors underground mining and processing operations of minerals, including minerals used in construction materials; produces educational materials in engineering; and assists with rescue operations following mining accidents.

▶**CONGRESS**

For a listing of relevant congressional committees and subcommittees, please see page 224 or the Appendix.

▶**NONGOVERNMENTAL**

American Coal Foundation, *101 Constitution Ave. N.W., #525 East 20001-2133; (202) 463-9785. Fax, (202) 463-9786. Alma Patty, Executive Director.* General e-mail, info@teachcoal.org

Web, www.teachcoal.org

Develops, produces, and disseminates, via the Web, coal-related educational materials and programs designed for teachers and students. Works with other coal- and energy-related groups to co-sponsor workshops for science and social studies teachers. Supported by coal producers and manufacturers of mining equipment and supplies.

American Coke and Coal Chemicals Institute, *1140 Connecticut Ave. N.W., #705 20036-4011; (202) 452-7198. Fax, (202) 463-6573. Bruce A. Steiner, President.* General e-mail, information@accci.org

Web, www.accci.org

Membership: producers of metallurgical coke and coal; tar distillers and coal chemical producers; coke and coal brokers; equipment, materials, and service suppliers to the coke industry; builders of coke ovens and coke byproduct plants. Maintains committees on coke, coal chemicals, manufacturing, environment, safety and health, human resources, quality, governmental relations, and international affairs.

Assn. of Bituminous Contractors, *815 Connecticut Ave. N.W., #620 20006-4053; (202) 785-4440. Fax, (202) 331-8049. William H. Howe, General Counsel.* Membership: independent and general contractors that build coal mines. Represents members before the Federal Mine Safety and Health Review Commission and in collective bargaining with the United Mine Workers of America.

Bituminous Coal Operators' Assn., *1776 Eye St. N.W., #255 20006-3750; (202) 783-3195. Fax, (202) 783-4862. David M. Young, President.*

Membership: firms that mine bituminous coal. Represents members in collective bargaining with the United Mine Workers of America.

Coal Technology Assn., 601 Suffield Dr., Gaithersburg, MD 20878-2656; (301) 294-6080. Barbara A. Sakkestad, Vice President.
General e-mail, barbarasak@aol.com

Web, www.coaltechnologies.com

Membership: business professionals interested in energy (coal technology), economic, and environmental policies and regulations. Seeks to improve coal utilization technologies and to develop coal cleaning technologies. Facilitates the exchange of technical information on coal technologies through annual international conference.

National Coal Council, 1730 M St. N.W., #907 20036-4512; (202) 223-1191. Fax, (202) 223-9031. Robert A. Beck, Executive Director.
Web, www.nationalcoalcouncil.org

Membership: individuals appointed by the secretary of energy. Represents coal producers, transporters, women and minorities in mining, and manufacturers of coal-producing equipment. Makes recommendations to the secretary on issues involving coal. Monitors federal policies. Library open to the public.

National Mining Assn., 101 Constitution Ave. N.W., #500 East 20001-2133; (202) 463-2600. Fax, (202) 463-2666. Harold P. Quinn Jr., President. Press, (202) 463-2651.
General e-mail, webmaster@nma.org

Web, www.nma.org

Membership: coal producers, coal sales and transportation companies, equipment manufacturers, consulting firms, coal resource developers and exporters, coal-burning electric utility companies, and other energy companies. Collects, analyzes, and distributes industry statistics; conducts special studies of competitive fuels, coal markets, production and consumption forecasts, and industry planning. Interests include exports, coal leasing programs, coal transportation, environmental issues, health and safety, national energy policy, slurry pipelines, and research and development, including synthetic fuels. Monitors legislation and regulation. (Merged with Coal Exporters Assn. of the United States.)

United Mine Workers of America, 8315 Lee Hwy., 5th Floor, Fairfax, VA 22031-2215; (703) 208-7200. Fax, (703) 208-7132. Cecil E. Roberts, President.
Web, www.umwa.org

Membership: coal miners and other mining workers. Represents members in collective bargaining with industry. Conducts educational, housing, and health and safety training programs; monitors federal coal mining safety programs.

Oil and Natural Gas

▶**AGENCIES**

Energy Information Administration (EIA), *(Energy Dept.), Collection and Dissemination,* 1000 Independence Ave. S.W., #2E068, EI 45 20585; (202) 586-4804. Fax, (202) 586-1073. Audrey Corley, Director.
General e-mail, infoctr@eia.doe.gov

Web, www.eia.doe.gov

Collects natural gas and petroleum data for publication; disseminates publications in print and via the Web; collects and disseminates EIA oil and gas forms.

Energy Information Administration (EIA), *(Energy Dept.), Natural Gas,* 1000 Independence Ave. S.W., #BE072 20585; (202) 586-9646. Fax, (202) 586-4420. James M. Kendell, Director.
General e-mail, infoctr@eia.doe.gov

Web, www.eia.doe.gov

Collects and publishes weekly, monthly, and annual estimates of domestic natural gas. Performs analyses of the natural gas industry, including consumption, prices, and storage levels.

Energy Information Administration (EIA), *(Energy Dept.), Oil and Gas,* 1000 Independence Ave. S.W., #2G024 20585; (202) 586-6012. Fax, (202) 586-9739. Stephen Harvey, Director.
General e-mail, infoctr@eia.doe.gov

Web, www.eia.doe.gov

Collects, interprets, and publishes data on domestic production, use, and distribution of oil and natural gas; analyzes and projects oil and gas reserves, resources, production, capacity, and supply; surveys and monitors alternative fuel needs during emergencies; publishes statistics.

Energy Information Administration (EIA), *(Energy Dept.), Petroleum,* 1000 Independence Ave. S.W., #2G048 20585; (202) 586-5986. Fax, (202) 586-3873. John S. Cook, Director.
General e-mail, john.cook@eia.doe.gov

Web, www.eia.doe.gov

Collects, compiles, interprets, and publishes data on domestic production, distribution, and prices of crude oil and refined petroleum products; analyzes and projects availability of petroleum supplies. Conducts short-term forecasts and analyses of regulatory or economic impacts on oil supplies and prices.

Fossil Energy *(Energy Dept.), Naval Petroleum and Oil Shale Reserves,* 1000 Independence Ave. S.W., #3H076 20585; (202) 586-4685. Fax, (202) 586-4446. Francis Gangle, Director.
Web, www.fe.doe.gov

Develops, conserves, operates, and maintains oil fields for producing oil, natural gas, and other petroleum products.

Fossil Energy *(Energy Dept.), Oil and Natural Gas,* 1000 Independence Ave. S.W., #3E028 20585; (202) 586-5600. Fax, (202) 586-6221. Guido Dehoratiis, Deputy Assistant Secretary (Acting).
Web, www.fe.doe.gov

Responsible for research and development programs in oil and gas exploration, production, processing, and storage; studies ways to improve efficiency of oil recovery in depleted reservoirs; coordinates and evaluates research and development among government, universities, and industrial research organizations.

Internal Revenue Service (IRS), *(Treasury Dept.), Passthroughs and Special Industries: Excise Tax Branch,* 1111 Constitution Ave. N.W., #5314 20224; (202) 622-3130. Fax, (202) 622-4537. Frank Boland, Chief.
Web, www.irs.ustreas.gov

Administers excise tax programs, including taxes on diesel, gasoline, and special fuels. Advises district offices, internal IRS offices, and general inquirers on tax policy, rules, and regulations.

Minerals Management Service *(Interior Dept.), Offshore Regulatory Programs,* 381 Elden St., MS 4020, Herndon, VA 20170-4817; (703) 787-1598. Fax, (703) 787-1093. E.P. Danenberger, Chief.
Web, www.mms.gov/offshore

Administers the Outer Continental Shelf Land Act. Supervises oil and gas operations on outer continental shelf lands; oversees lease operations including exploration, drilling, and production phases of offshore oil and gas development; administers lease provisions for offshore oil and gas.

National Oceanic and Atmospheric Administration (NOAA), *(Commerce Dept.), Program, Planning, and Integration,* #15628, SS-MC3, 1315 East-West Hwy., Silver Spring, MD 20910; (301) 713-1632. Fax, (301) 713-0585. Laura Furgione, Assistant Administrator.
Web, www.noaa.gov

Develops NOAA's strategic plan. Manages designated programs using matrix principles and promotes the development of effective agency programs.

▶NONGOVERNMENTAL

AHRI (Air-Conditioning, Heating, and Refrigeration Institute), 2107 Wilson Blvd., #600, Arlington, VA 22201; (703) 524-8800. Fax, (703) 562-1942. Stephen Yurek, President.
General e-mail, information@ahrinet.org
Web, www.ahrinct.org

Membership: manufacturers of gas appliances and equipment for residential and commercial use and related industries. Advocates product improvement; provides market statistics. Monitors legislation and regulations. (Merger of the Air-Conditioning and Refrigeration Institute [ARI] and the Gas Appliance Manufacturers Assn. [GAMA].)

American Gas Assn., 400 N. Capitol St. N.W., 4th Floor 20001-1535; (202) 824-7000. Fax, (202) 824-7115. David N. Parker, President. Press, (202) 824-7204. Alternate press, (202) 824-7205.
Web, www.aga.org

Membership: natural gas utilities and pipeline companies. Interests include all technical and operational aspects of the gas industry. Publishes comprehensive statistical record of gas industry; conducts national standard testing for gas appliances. Advocates for policies that are favorable to increased supplies and lower prices. Monitors legislation and regulations.

American Petroleum Institute, 1220 L St. N.W., 12th Floor 20005; (202) 682-8000. Fax, (202) 682-8110. Jack Gerard, President. Press, (202) 682-8114.
Web, www.api.org

Membership: producers, refiners, marketers, pipeline operators, and transporters of oil, natural gas, and related products such as gasoline. Provides information on the industry, including data on exports and imports, taxation, transportation, weekly refinery operations and inventories, and drilling activity and costs; conducts research on petroleum and publishes statistical and drilling reports. Develops equipment and operating standards. Certifies compliance of equipment manufacturing and of environmental and occupational safety and health management systems.

American Petroleum Institute, *Taxation,* 1220 L St. N.W., 11th Floor 20005; (202) 682-8000. Fax, (202) 682-8049. Michael Platner, Director.
Web, www.api.org

Provides information on petroleum taxation.

American Public Gas Assn. (APGA), 201 Massachusetts Ave. N.E., #C4 20002-4988; (202) 464-2742. Fax, (202) 464-0246. Bert Kalisch, President.
General e-mail, apga@apga.org
Web, www.apga.org

Membership: municipally owned gas distribution systems. Provides information on federal developments affecting natural gas. Promotes efficiency and works to protect the interests of public gas systems. Sponsors workshops and conferences.

Compressed Gas Assn., 4221 Walney Rd., 5th Floor, Chantilly, VA 20151-2923; (703) 788-2700. Fax, (703) 961-1831. Marc Meteyer, President.
General e-mail, cga@cganet.com
Web, www.cganet.com

Membership: all segments of the compressed gas industry, including producers and distributors of compressed and liquefied gases. Promotes and coordinates technical development and standardization of the industry. Monitors legislation and regulations.

Gas Technology Institute (GTI), *Policy and Regulatory Affairs, Washington Office, 1350 Eye St. N.W., #510 20005-3355; (202) 747-0518. Fax, (202) 747-0519. Melanie Kenderdine, Vice President.*
Web, www.gastechnology.org

Membership: all segments of the natural gas industry, including producers, pipelines, and distributors. Conducts research and develops new technology for gas customers and the industry. (Headquarters in Des Plaines, Ill.)

Independent Liquid Terminals Assn. (ILTA), *1444 Eye St. N.W., #400 20005-6538; (202) 842-9200. Fax, (202) 326-8660. E. David Doane, President.*
General e-mail, info@ilta.org
Web, www.ilta.org

Membership: commercial operators of for-hire bulk liquid terminals and tank storage facilities, including those for crude oil and petroleum. Promotes the safe and efficient handling of various types of bulk liquid commodities. Sponsors workshops and seminars and publishes directories. Monitors legislation and regulations.

Independent Petroleum Assn. of America, *1201 15th St. N.W., #300 20005-2842; (202) 857-4722. Fax, (202) 857-4799. Barry Russell, President.*
Web, www.ipaa.org

Membership: independent oil and gas producers; land and royalty owners; and others with interests in domestic exploration, development, and production of oil and natural gas. Interests include leasing, prices and taxation, foreign trade, environmental restrictions, and improved recovery methods.

International Assn. of Drilling Contractors (IADC), *Government Affairs, Washington Office, 1901 L St. N.W., #702 20036-3506; (202) 293-0670. Fax, (202) 872-0047. Brian T. Petty, Senior Vice President.*
General e-mail, info@iadc.org
Web, www.iadc.org

Membership: drilling contractors, oil and gas producers, and others in the industry worldwide. Promotes safe exploration and production of hydrocarbons, advances in drilling technology, and preservation of the environment. Monitors legislation and regulations. (Headquarters in Houston, Texas.)

National Ocean Industries Assn., *1120 G St. N.W., #900 20005; (202) 347-6900. Fax, (202) 347-8650. Tom A. Fry, President.*
General e-mail, noia@noia.org
Web, www.noia.org

Membership: manufacturers, producers, suppliers, and support and service companies involved in marine, offshore, and ocean work. Interests include offshore oil and gas supply and production, pursuit of offshore renewable-energy opportunities, environmental safeguards, equipment supply, gas transmission, navigation, research and technology, and shipyards.

National Petrochemical & Refiners Assn. (NPRA), *1667 K St. N.W., #700 20006-1605; (202) 457-0480. Fax, (202) 457-0486. Charlie Drevna, President.*
General e-mail, info@npra.org
Web, www.npra.org

Membership: petroleum, petrochemical, and refining companies. Interests include allocation, imports, refining technology, petrochemicals, and environmental regulations.

National Petroleum Council, *1625 K St. N.W., #600 20006-1656; (202) 393-6100. Fax, (202) 331-8539. Marshall W. Nichols, Executive Director.*
General e-mail, info@npc.org
Web, www.npc.org

Advisory committee to the secretary of energy on matters relating to the petroleum industry, including oil and natural gas. Publishes reports concerning technical aspects of the oil and gas industries.

National Propane Gas Assn., *1150 17th St. N.W., #310 20036-4623; (202) 466-7200. Fax, (202) 466-7205. Richard R. Roldan, President.*
General e-mail, info@npga.org
Web, www.npga.org

Membership: retail marketers, producers, wholesale distributors, appliance and equipment manufacturers, equipment fabricators, and distributors and transporters of liquefied petroleum gas. Conducts research, safety, and educational programs; provides statistics on the industry.

Natural Gas Supply Assn., *805 15th St. N.W., #510 20005-2276; (202) 326-9300. Fax, (202) 326-9330. R. "Skip" Horvath, President.*
Web, www.ngsa.org

Membership: major and independent producers of domestic natural gas. Interests include the production, consumption, marketing, and regulation of natural gas. Monitors legislation and regulations.

NGVAmerica, *400 N. Capitol St. N.W. 20001; (202) 824-7366. Fax, (202) 824-7087. Richard R. Kolodziej, President. Press, (202) 824-7366.*
General e-mail, rkolodziej@ngvamerica.org
Web, www.ngvamerica.org

Membership: natural gas distributors; automobile and engine manufacturers; natural gas and hydrogen vehicle product and service suppliers; environmental groups; research and development organizations; and state and local government agencies. Advocates installation of natural gas, biomethane, and hydrogen fuel stations and development of industry standards. Helps market new products and equipment related to natural gas, biomethane, and hydrogen-powered vehicles. (Formerly known as the Natural Gas Vehicle Coalition.)

Petroleum Marketers Assn. of America (PMAA), *1901 N. Fort Myer Dr., #500, Arlington, VA 22209-1604; (703) 351-8000. Fax, (703) 351-9160. Daniel F. Gilligan, President.*

General e-mail, info@pmaa.org

Web, www.pmaa.org

Membership: state and regional associations representing independent branded and nonbranded marketers of petroleum products. Provides information on all aspects of petroleum marketing. Monitors legislation and regulations.

Service Station Dealers of America/National Coalition of Petroleum Retailers and Allied Trades, *1532 Pointer Ridge Pl., Suite E, Bowie, MD 20716; (301) 390-4405. Fax, (301) 390-3161. Paul Fiore, Executive Vice President.*

General e-mail, pfiore@wmda.net

Web, www.ssda-at.org

Membership: state associations of gasoline retailers, repair facilities, car washes, and convenience stores. Interests include environmental issues, retail marketing, oil allocation, imports and exports, prices, and taxation.

Society of Independent Gasoline Marketers of America (SIGMA), *3930 Pender Dr., #340, Fairfax, VA 22030-0985; (703) 709-7000. Fax, (703) 709-7007. Kenneth A. Doyle, Executive Vice President.*

General e-mail, sigma@sigma.org

Web, www.sigma.org

Membership: marketers and wholesalers of brand and nonbrand gasoline. Seeks to ensure adequate supplies of gasoline at competitive prices. Monitors legislation and regulations affecting gasoline supply and price.

U.S. Oil and Gas Assn., *901 F St. N.W., #601 20004-1400; (202) 638-4400. Fax, (202) 638-5967. Albert Modiano, President.*

Membership: major and independent petroleum and natural gas companies, refineries, and natural gas and petroleum product transporters and distributors. Monitors legislation and regulations affecting the petroleum industry.

Pipelines

▶AGENCIES

Federal Energy Regulatory Commission (FERC), *(Energy Dept.), Energy Market Regulation, 888 1st St. N.E., #8A-01 20426; (202) 502-6700. Fax, (202) 219-2836. Shelton M. Cannon, Director.*

Web, www.ferc.gov

Establishes and enforces maximum rates and charges for oil and natural gas pipelines; establishes oil pipeline operating rules; issues certificates for and regulates construction, sale, and acquisition of natural gas pipeline facilities. Ensures compliance with the Natural Gas Policy Act, the Natural Gas Act, and other statutes.

National Transportation Safety Board, *Railroad, Pipeline, and Hazardous Materials, 490 L'Enfant Plaza East S.W., #RPH1 20594; (202) 314-6460. Fax, (202) 314-6482. Bob Chipkevich, Director.*

Web, www.ntsb.gov

Investigates hazardous materials and petroleum pipeline accidents.

Pipeline and Hazardous Materials Safety Administration *(Transportation Dept.), Hazardous Materials Safety, 1200 New Jersey Ave. S.E., E21-317 20590; (202) 366-0656. Fax, (202) 366-5713. Theodore Willke, Associate Administrator. Information, (202) 366-4488.*

General e-mail, phmsa.hmhazmatsafety@dot.gov

Web, http://phmsa.dot.gov

Designates fuels, chemicals, and other substances as hazardous materials and regulates their transportation in interstate commerce. Provides technical assistance on hazardous waste materials transportation safety and security to state and local governments. Gathers and analyzes incident data from carriers transporting hazardous materials.

Pipeline and Hazardous Materials Safety Administration *(Transportation Dept.), Pipeline Safety, 1200 New Jersey Ave. S.E., E24-455 20590; (202) 366-4595. Fax, (202) 366-4566. Jeffrey D. Wiese, Associate Administrator (Acting).*

General e-mail, phmsa.pipelinesafety@dot.gov

Web, http://phmsa.dot.gov

Issues and enforces federal regulations for oil, natural gas, and petroleum products pipeline safety. Inspects pipelines and oversees risk management by pipeline operators.

▶NONGOVERNMENTAL

Assn. of Oil Pipe Lines (AOPL), *1808 Eye St., N.W., #300 20006; (202) 408-7970. Fax, (202) 280-1949. Shirley J. Neff, President.*

General e-mail, aopl@aopl.org

Web, www.aopl.org

Membership: oil pipeline companies. Analyzes industry statistics. Monitors legislation and regulations.

Interstate Natural Gas Assn. of America, *10 G St. N.E., #700 20002-4248; (202) 216-5900. Fax, (202) 216-0875. Donald F. Santa Jr., President. Press, (202) 216-5910.*

Web, www.ingaa.org

Membership: U.S. interstate and Canadian interprovincial natural gas pipeline companies. Commissions studies and provides information on the natural gas pipeline industry.

NUCLEAR ENERGY

▶AGENCIES

Energy Information Administration (EIA), *(Energy Dept.), Coal, Nuclear, Electric, and Alternate Fuels, 1000 Independence Ave. S.W., #2H073, EI-50 20585; (202) 586-2800. Fax, (202) 287-1933. Scott Sitzer, Director.*

Web, www.eia.doe.gov

Prepares analyses and forecasts on the availability, production, prices, processing, transportation, and distribution of nuclear energy, both domestically and internationally. Collects and publishes data concerning the uranium supply and market.

Nuclear Energy *(Energy Dept.), Laboratory Facilities Management,* 19901 Germantown Rd., #D-428, NE-32, Germantown, MD 20874-1290; (301) 903-5161. Fax, (301) 903-5434. Michael Worley, Associate Director.
Web, www.nuclear.energy.gov

Manages the design, construction, and operation of nuclear energy test facilities and Office of Energy Research reactor and supporting facilities, ensuring their safe, reliable, and environmentally sound operation and cost-effective use. Interests include international nuclear safety.

Nuclear Energy *(Energy Dept.), Radioisotope Power Systems,* NE-34/Germantown Bldg., 1000 Independence Ave. S.W., 20585-1290; (301) 903-3456. Fax, (301) 903-1510. Owen W. Lowe, Director.
Web, www.nuclear.energy.gov

Develops and produces radioisotope power systems for space applications in support of NASA. Directs all isotope production and distribution activities within the Energy Dept.; ensures a reliable supply of medical, research, and industrial isotopes consistent with customer needs. (Program will move to Office of Science in 2009.)

Nuclear Regulatory Commission, 11555 Rockville Pike, MS 016G4, Rockville, MD 20852; (301) 415-1750. Fax, (301) 415-1757. Dale E. Klein, Chair; R. William Borchardt, Executive Director. Press, (301) 415-8200.
General e-mail, opa@nrc.gov
Web, www.nrc.gov

Regulates commercial uses of nuclear energy; responsibilities include licensing, inspection, and enforcement; monitors and regulates the imports and exports of nuclear material and equipment.

Tennessee Valley Authority, *Government Affairs, Washington Office,* 1 Massachusetts Ave. N.W., #300 20444; (202) 898-2999. Fax, (202) 898-2998. Justin Maierhofer, Director.
General e-mail, latootle@tva.gov
Web, www.tva.gov

Coordinates resource conservation, development, and land-use programs in the Tennessee River Valley. Produces and supplies wholesale power to municipal and cooperative electric systems, federal installations, and some industries; interests include nuclear power generation.

►**CONGRESS**

For a listing of relevant congressional committees and subcommittees, please see page 224 or the Appendix.

►**NONGOVERNMENTAL**

American Physical Society, *Washington Office,* 529 14th St. N.W., #1050 20045-2001; (202) 662-8700. Fax, (202) 662-8711. Judy Franz, Director.

General e-mail, opa@aps.org
Web, www.aps.org

Scientific and educational society of educators, students, citizens, and scientists, including industrial scientists. Sponsors studies on issues of public concern related to physics, such as reactor safety and energy use. Informs members of national and international developments. (Headquarters in College Park, Md.)

Nuclear Energy Institute, 1776 Eye St. N.W., #400 20006-3708; (202) 739-8000. Fax, (202) 785-4019. Frank Bowman, President.
General e-mail, media@nei.org
Web, www.nei.org

Membership: utilities; industries; labor, service, and research organizations; law firms; universities; and government agencies interested in peaceful uses of nuclear energy, including the generation of electricity. Acts as a spokesperson for the nuclear power industry; provides information on licensing and plant siting, research and development, safety and security, waste disposal, and legislative and policy issues.

Nuclear Information and Resource Service, 6930 Carroll Ave., #340, Takoma Park, MD 20912-4446; (301) 270-6477. Fax, (301) 270-4291. Michael Mariotte, Executive Director.
General e-mail, nirsnet@nirs.org
Web, www.nirs.org

Information and networking clearinghouse for environmental activists and other individuals concerned about nuclear power plants, radioactive waste, and radiation and sustainable energy issues. Initiates large-scale organizing and public education campaigns and provides technical and strategic expertise to environmental groups. Library open to the public by appointment.

Public Citizen, *Energy Program,* 215 Pennsylvania Ave. S.E. 20003-1155; (202) 546-4996. Fax, (202) 546-5562. Tyson Slocum, Director.
General e-mail, cmep@citizen.org
Web, www.citizen.org/cmep

Public interest group that promotes energy efficiency and renewable energy technologies; opposes nuclear energy. Interests include nuclear plant safety and energy policy issues.

Union of Concerned Scientists, *Global Security, Washington Office,* 1707 H St. N.W., #600 20006-3962; (202) 223-6133. Fax, (202) 223-6162. Lisbeth Gronlund, Co-Director; David Wright, Co-Director.
General e-mail, ucs@ucsusa.org
Web, www.ucsusa.org

An independent public interest group of scientists and citizens concerned with U.S. energy policy, including nuclear policy and nuclear power plant safety. Monitors the performance of nuclear power plants and their regulators. (Headquarters in Cambridge, Mass.)

Nuclear Regulatory Commission

—— Direct Reporting Relationships
– – – General Supervision

Licensing and Plant Siting

▶AGENCIES

Federal Emergency Management Agency (FEMA), *(Homeland Security Dept.), Technological Hazards,* *1800 S. Bell St., Arlington, VA 22202 (mailing address: 500 C St. S.W., Mail Code 0104, Washington, DC 20472); (703) 305-0837. Fax, (703) 305-0837. Vanessa Quinn, Director (Acting), (703) 605-1535. Web, www.fema.gov*

Reviews off-site preparedness for commercial nuclear power facilities; evaluates emergency plans before plant licensing and submits findings to the Nuclear Regulatory Commission.

Nuclear Regulatory Commission, *New Reactors,* *11555 Rockville Pike, MS T6F15, Rockville, MD 20852; (301) 415-1897. Fax, (301) 415-6323. R. William Borchardt, Director. Web, www.nrc.gov*

Licenses and regulates nuclear power plants that use new designs; approves siting of new plants.

Nuclear Regulatory Commission, *Nuclear Material Safety and Safeguards, 6003 Executive Blvd., #E1-C2, Rockville, MD 20852 (mailing address: MS E1D2M, Washington, DC 20555-0001); (301) 492-3239. Fax, (301) 492-3360. Michael F. Weber, Director. Web, www.nrc.gov*

Licenses all nuclear facilities and materials except power reactors; directs principal licensing and regulation activities for the management of nuclear waste.

Nuclear Regulatory Commission, *Nuclear Reactor Regulation,* 11555 Rockville Pike, MS O13D13, Rockville, MD 20852; (301) 415-1270. Fax, (301) 415-8333. Eric J. Leeds, Director.
Web, www.nrc.gov

Licenses nuclear power plants and operators.

Research and Development

►AGENCIES

Energy Dept. (DOE), *Office of Science: Fusion Energy Sciences,* SC-24/Germantown Bldg., 1000 Independence Ave. S.W. 20585; (301) 903-4941. Fax, (301) 903-8584. Steve Eckstrand, Associate Director (Acting).
Web, www.science.doe.gov/ofes

Conducts research and development on fusion energy for electric power generation.

National Institute of Standards and Technology (NIST), *(Commerce Dept.),* ***Physics Laboratory,*** 100 Bureau Dr., Bldg. 221, #B160, Gaithersburg, MD 20899-8400; (301) 975-4200. Fax, (301) 975-3038. Katharine B. Gebbie, Director.
Web, www.physics.nist.gov

Provides national standards for radiation measurement methods and technology. Conducts research in measurement science in the fields of electron physics; ionizing radiation dosimetry; neutron physics; and optical, ultraviolet, x-ray, gamma-ray, and infrared radiometry.

Nuclear Energy *(Energy Dept.),* 1000 Independence Ave. S.W., #5A143, NE-1 20585; (202) 586-6630. Fax, (202) 586-0544. Vacant, Assistant Secretary.
Web, www.nuclear.energy.gov

Responsible for nuclear technology research and development, management of the Energy Dept.'s nuclear technology infrastructure, uranium activities, and fuel cycle issues. Supports nuclear education, including university reactor instrumentation and equipment upgrades and general support to nuclear engineering programs at U.S. universities. Leads U.S. participation in the Global Nuclear Energy Partnership, which seeks to demonstrate a more proliferation-resistant closed fuel cycle and increase the safety and security of nuclear energy.

Nuclear Energy *(Energy Dept.),* ***Radioisotope Power Systems,*** NE-34/Germantown Bldg., 1000 Independence Ave. S.W., 20585-1290; (301) 903-3456. Fax, (301) 903-1510. Owen W. Lowe, Director.
Web, www.nuclear.energy.gov

Develops and produces radioisotope power systems for space applications in support of NASA. Directs all isotope production and distribution activities within the Energy Dept.; ensures a reliable supply of medical, research, and industrial isotopes consistent with customer needs. (Program will move to Office of Science in 2009.)

Nuclear Regulatory Commission, *Nuclear Regulatory Research,* 21 Church St., MS C6D20M, Rockville, MD 20852-2746; (301) 415-6641. Fax, (301) 251-7426. Brian W. Sheron, Director.
Web, www.nrc.gov

Plans, recommends, and implements nuclear regulatory research, standards development, and resolution of safety issues for nuclear power plants and other facilities regulated by the Nuclear Regulatory Commission; develops and promulgates all technical regulations.

Safety, Security, and Waste Disposal

►AGENCIES

Defense Nuclear Facilities Safety Board, 625 Indiana Ave. N.W., #700 20004-2901; (202) 694-7080. Fax, (202) 208-6518. A.J. Eggenberger, Chair. Information, (202) 694-7000.
General e-mail, mailbox@dnfsb.gov
Web, www.dnfsb.gov

Independent board created by Congress and appointed by the president to provide external oversight of Energy Dept. defense nuclear weapons production facilities and make recommendations to the secretary of energy regarding public health and safety.

Energy Dept. (DOE), *Civilian Radioactive Waste Management,* 1000 Independence Ave. S.W., #5A085 20585; (202) 586-6842. Fax, (202) 586-6638. Christopher A. Kouts, Director (Acting).
Web, www.ocrwm.doe.gov

Responsible for obtaining a license from the Nuclear Regulatory Commission to construct and operate a geologic repository at Yucca Mountain for the permanent disposal of spent nuclear fuel from commercial nuclear reactors and high-level radioactive waste from national defense activities.

Energy Information Administration (EIA), *(Energy Dept.),* ***Coal, Nuclear, Electric, and Alternate Fuels,*** 1000 Independence Ave. S.W., #2H073, EI-50 20585; (202) 586-2800. Fax, (202) 287-1933. Scott Sitzer, Director.
Web, www.eia.doe.gov

Directs collection of spent fuel data and validation of spent nuclear fuel discharge data for the Civilian Radioactive Waste Management Office.

Environmental Management *(Energy Dept.),* ***Disposal Operations,*** Cloverleaf Bldg., 1000 Independence Ave. S.W., #2126 20585; (301) 903-1669. Fax, (301) 903-4303. Christine Gelles, Director.
Web, www.em.doe.gov

Manages Energy Dept. programs that treat, stabilize, and dispose of radioactive waste, including that generated from the decontamination and decommissioning of Energy Dept. facilities and sites. Works to develop a reliable national system for low-level waste management and techniques for treatment and immobilization of waste from former nuclear weapons complex sites. Provides technical assistance to states and Regional Disposal Compacts on the safe and effective management of commercially generated wastes.

Environmental Protection Agency (EPA), *Radiation and Indoor Air, 1310 L St. N.W., 4th Floor, MC 6601J 20005; (202) 343-9320. Fax, (202) 343-2395. Elizabeth Cotsworth, Director.*
Web, www.epa.gov/oar/oria.html

Establishes standards to regulate the amount of radiation discharged into the environment from uranium mining and milling projects, and other activities that result in radioactive emissions; and to ensure the safe disposal of radioactive waste. Fields a Radiological Emergency Response Team to respond to radiological incidents.

Federal Emergency Management Agency (FEMA), *(Homeland Security Dept.), 500 C St. S.W. 20472; (202) 646-3923. Fax, (202) 646-3875. Nancy L. Ward, Administrator (Acting). Press, (202) 646-4600. TTY, (800) 462-7585. Locator, (202) 646-2500. Disaster assistance, (800) 621-3362.*
General e-mail, femaopa@dhs.gov
Web, www.fema.gov

Assists state and local governments responding to and recovering from natural, technological, and attack-related emergencies, including in communities where accidents at nuclear power facilities have occurred and communities surrounding accidents involving transportation of radioactive materials; operates the National Emergency Training Center. Coordinates emergency preparedness, mitigation, response, and recovery activities, and planning for all federal agencies and departments.

Health, Safety, and Security *(Energy Dept.), 1000 Independence Ave. S.W., #7G040 20585; (301) 903-3777. Fax, (301) 903-5492. Glenn S. Podonsky, Chief Officer.*
General e-mail, HSS.Infocenter@hq.doe.gov
Web, www.hss.energy.gov

Develops policy and establishes standards to ensure safety and health protection in all department activities.

Health, Safety, and Security *(Energy Dept.), Health and Safety, 1000 Independence Ave. S.W., HS-10/270CC 20585-0270; (301) 903-5926. Fax, (301) 903-3445. Patricia R. Worthington, Director.*
Web, www.hss.energy.gov/healthsafety

Establishes hazardous material worker safety and health requirements and expectations for the Energy Dept. and assists in their implementation. Conducts and supports domestic and international hazardous material

health studies and programs. Supports the Labor Dept. in the implementation of the Energy Employees Occupational Illness Compensation Program Act (EEOICPA).

Health, Safety, and Security *(Energy Dept.), Nuclear Safety and Environment, 1000 Independence Ave. S.W., #6B-128 20585; (202) 586-5680. Fax, (202) 586-7330. Andrew C. Lawrence, Director.*
Web, www.hss.energy.gov

Establishes policies and guidance for environmental protection and compliance; provides technical assistance to departmental program and field offices in complying with environmental requirements.

National Transportation Safety Board, *Railroad, Pipeline, and Hazardous Materials, 490 L'Enfant Plaza East S.W., #RPH1 20594; (202) 314-6460. Fax, (202) 314-6482. Bob Chipkevich, Director.*
Web, www.ntsb.gov

Investigates accidents involving the transportation of hazardous materials.

Nuclear Regulatory Commission, *Advisory Committee on Reactor Safeguards, 11545 Rockville Pike, Rockville, MD 20852 (mailing address: Nuclear Regulatory Commission, MS T2E26, Washington, DC 20555-0001); (301) 415-7360. Fax, (301) 415-5589. Frank P. Gillespie, Executive Director.*
Web, www.nrc.gov/about-nrc/organization/acrsfuncdesc. html

Advises the commission on the licensing and operation of production and utilization facilities and related safety issues, the adequacy of proposed reactor safety standards, and technical and policy issues related to the licensing of evolutionary and passive plant designs. Submits annual report on the NRC Safety Research Program. Reviews Energy Dept. nuclear activities and facilities and provides technical advice to the Energy Dept.'s Nuclear Safety Board upon request.

Nuclear Regulatory Commission, *Enforcement, 11555 Rockville Pike, MS O4A 15A, Rockville, MD 20555; (301) 415-2741. Fax, (301) 415-3431. Cynthia A. Carpenter, Director.*
Web, www.nrc.gov

Oversees the development and implementation of policies and programs that enforce the commission's procedures concerning public health and safety. Identifies and takes action against violators.

Nuclear Regulatory Commission, *Federal and State Materials and Environmental Management Programs, 11545 Rockville Pike, MS T8D22 20852-2746; (301) 415-7197. Fax, (301) 415-6680. Charles Miller, Director.*
Web, www.nrc.gov

Implements rules and guidance in providing for the safe, environmentally sound, and secure uses and disposal of nuclear materials, and the decommissioning of regulated facilities.

Nuclear Regulatory Commission, *Investigations,* 11555 Rockville Pike, MS O3F1, Rockville, MD 20555; (301) 415-2373. Fax, (301) 415-2370. Guy P. Caputo, Director. Web, www.nrc.gov

Develops policy, procedures, and standards for investigations of licensees, applicants, and their contractors or vendors concerning wrongdoing. Refers substantiated criminal cases to the Justice Dept. Informs the commission's leadership about investigations concerning public health and safety.

Nuclear Regulatory Commission, *Nuclear Material Safety and Safeguards,* 6003 Executive Blvd., #E1-C2, Rockville, MD 20852 (mailing address: MS E1D2M, Washington, DC 20555-0001); (301) 492-3239. Fax, (301) 492-3360. Michael F. Weber, Director. Web, www.nrc.gov

Develops and implements safeguards programs; directs licensing and regulation activities for the management and disposal of nuclear waste.

Nuclear Regulatory Commission, *Nuclear Reactor Regulation,* 11555 Rockville Pike, MS O13D13, Rockville, MD 20852; (301) 415-1270. Fax, (301) 415-8333. Eric J. Leeds, Director. Web, www.nrc.gov

Conducts safety inspections of nuclear reactors. Regulates nuclear materials used or produced at nuclear power plants.

Nuclear Regulatory Commission, *Nuclear Regulatory Research,* 21 Church St., MS C6D20M, Rockville, MD 20852-2746; (301) 415-6641. Fax, (301) 251-7426. Brian W. Sheron, Director. Web, www.nrc.gov

Plans, recommends, and implements resolution of safety issues for nuclear power plants and other facilities regulated by the Nuclear Regulatory Commission.

Nuclear Regulatory Commission, *Nuclear Security and Incident Response,* 11545 Rockville Pike, MS T4D22A, Rockville, MD 20555; (301) 415-8003. Fax, (301) 415-6382. Roy P. Zimmerman, Director. Emergency, (301) 816-5100. Non-emergency, (800) 695-7403. Web, www.nrc.gov

Evaluates technical issues concerning security at nuclear facilities. Develops and directs the commission's response to incidents. Serves as point of contact with Homeland Security Dept., Energy Dept., Federal Emergency Management Agency, and intelligence and law enforcement offices and other agencies.

Nuclear Waste Technical Review Board, 2300 Clarendon Blvd., #1300, Arlington, VA 22201-3367; (703) 235-4473. Fax, (703) 235-4495. William D. Barnard, Executive Director. General e-mail, info@nwtrb.gov Web, www.nwtrb.gov

Independent board of scientists and engineers appointed by the president to review, evaluate, and report on Energy Dept. development of waste disposal systems and repositories for spent fuel and high-level radioactive waste. Oversees siting, packaging, and transportation of waste, in accordance with the Nuclear Waste Policy Act of 1987.

Pipeline and Hazardous Materials Safety Administration *(Transportation Dept.), Hazardous Materials Safety,* 1200 New Jersey Ave. S.E., E21-317 20590; (202) 366-0656. Fax, (202) 366-5713. Theodore Willke, Associate Administrator. Information, (202) 366-4488. General e-mail, phmsa.hmhazmatsafety@dot.gov Web, http://phmsa.dot.gov

Issues safety regulations and exemptions for the transportation of hazardous materials; works with the International Atomic Energy Agency on standards for international shipments of radioactive materials.

RENEWABLE ENERGIES, ALTERNATIVE FUELS

►AGENCIES

Energy Efficiency and Renewable Energy *(Energy Dept.),* 1000 Independence Ave. S.W., #6A013 20585; (202) 586-9220. Fax, (202) 586-9260. Steven Chalk, Assistant Secretary (Acting). Information, (877) 337-3463. Press, (202) 586-0462. General e-mail, eereic@ee.doe.gov Web, www.eere.energy.gov

Develops and manages programs to improve foreign and domestic markets for renewable energy sources including solar, biomass, wind, geothermal, and hydropower and to increase efficiency of energy use among residential, commercial, transportation, utility, and industrial users. Administers financial and technical assistance for state energy programs, weatherization for low-income households, and implementation of energy conservation measures by schools, hospitals, local governments, and public care institutions.

Energy Information Administration (EIA), *(Energy Dept.), Coal, Nuclear, Electric, and Alternate Fuels,* 1000 Independence Ave. S.W., #2H073, EI-50 20585; (202) 586-2800. Fax, (202) 287-1933. Scott Sitzer, Director. Web, www.eia.doe.gov

Prepares analyses on the availability, production, costs, processing, transportation, and distribution of uranium and alternative energy supplies, including biomass, solar, wind, waste, wood, and alcohol.

►CONGRESS

For a listing of relevant congressional committees and subcommittees, please see page 224 or the Appendix.

►NONGOVERNMENTAL

Electric Power Supply Assn., 1401 New York Ave., 11th Floor 20005; (202) 628-8200. Fax, (202) 628-8260. John Shelk, President

President.
Web, www.epsa.org

Membership: companies that generate electricity, steam, and other forms of energy using a broad spectrum of fossil fuel–fired and renewable technologies.

Hearth, Patio, and Barbecue Assn. (HPBA), *1901 N. Moore St., #600, Arlington, VA 22209-1708; (703) 522-0086. Fax, (703) 522-0548. Jack Goldman, President.*
General e-mail, hpba@hpba.org

Web, www.hpba.org

Membership: all sectors of the hearth products industry. Provides industry training programs to its members on the safe and efficient use of alternative fuels and appliances. Works with the Hearth Education Foundation, which certifies gas hearth, fireplace, pellet stove, and wood stove appliances and venting design specialists.

Institute for the Analysis of Global Security, *7811 Montrose Rd., #505, Potomac, MD 20854-3363 (mailing address: P.O. Box 2837, Washington, DC 20013-2837); (202) 271-0531. Gal Luft, Co-Director; Anne Korin, Co-Director. Toll-free, (866) 713-7527.*
General e-mail, info@iags.org

Web, www.iags.org

Seeks to promote public awareness about the impact of energy on the U.S. economy and national security. Advocates harnessing domestic resources and the use of new technologies in order to displace foreign oil. Monitors legislation and regulations.

National Commission on Energy Policy, *1225 Eye St. N.W., #1000 20005-5977; (202) 637-0400. Fax, (202) 637-9220. Jason S. Grumet, Executive Director.*
General e-mail, info@energycommission.org

Web, www.energycommission.org

Researches and advocates for a reduction of oil consumption in the United States. Evaluates policy options and makes recommendations to lawmakers. Monitors legislation and regulations.

National Hydrogen Assn., *1211 Connecticut Ave. N.W., #600 20036; (202) 223-5547. Fax, (202) 223-5537. Jeffrey Serfass, President.*
General e-mail, info@hydrogenassociation.org

Web, www.hydrogenassociation.org

Membership: industry, small businesses, universities, government agencies, and nonprofit organizations. Promotes use of hydrogen as an energy carrier; fosters the development and application of hydrogen technologies.

Set America Free, *7811 Montrose Rd., #505, Potomac, MD 20854; (866) 713-7527. Fax, (301) 340-8008. Anne Korin, Chair.*
General e-mail, info@setamericafree.org

Web, www.setamericafree.org

Advocates reduction of U.S. dependence on foreign oil. Promotes plans to reduce oil consumption in the United

States, specifically transitioning the transportation sector to new fuels and vehicles that can utilize them. (Affiliated with the Institute for the Analysis of Global Security.)

SRI International, *Washington Office, 1100 Wilson Blvd., #2800, Arlington, VA 22209; (703) 524-2053. Fax, (703) 247-8569. Toni Linz, Director.*
Web, www.sri.com

Conducts energy-related research and development. Interests include power generation, fuel and solar cells, clean energy storage, and advanced batteries. (Headquarters in Menlo Park, Calif.)

Alcohol Fuels

►AGENCIES

Alcohol and Tobacco Tax and Trade Bureau (TTB), *(Treasury Dept.), Regulations and Rulings, 1310 G St. N.W., #200 East 20220; (202) 927-8210. Fax, (202) 927-8602. Francis Foote, Director.*
Web, www.ttb.gov

Develops guidelines for regional offices responsible for issuing permits for producing gasohol and other ethyl alcohol fuels, whose uses include heating and operating machinery. Writes and interprets regulations for distilleries that produce ethyl alcohol fuels.

Rural Development *(Agriculture Dept.), Business and Cooperative Programs: Business Programs, 1400 Independence Ave. S.W., #5813-S 20250-3220; (202) 720-7287. Fax, (202) 690-0097. William F. Hagy III, Deputy Administrator.*
Web, www.rurdev.usda.gov/rbs

Makes loan guarantees to rural businesses, including those seeking to develop alcohol fuels production facilities.

►NONGOVERNMENTAL

Methanol Institute, *4100 N. Fairfax Dr., #740, Arlington, VA 22203; (703) 248-3636. Fax, (703) 248-3997. John E. Lynn, President.*
General e-mail, mi@methanol.org

Web, www.methanol.org

Membership: methanol producers and related industries. Encourages use of methanol fuels and development of chemical-derivative markets. Monitors legislation and regulations.

Renewable Fuels Assn., *1 Massachusetts Ave. N.W., #820 20001-1431; (202) 289-3835. Fax, (202) 289-7519.*
General e-mail, info@ethanolrfa.org

Web, www.ethanolrfa.org

Membership: companies and state governments involved in developing the domestic ethanol industry. Distributes publications on ethanol performance.

Geothermal Energy

►AGENCIES

Energy Efficiency and Renewable Energy *(Energy Dept.)*, **Geothermal Technologies**, *1000 Independence Ave. S.W., #5G067, EE-2C 20585-0121; (202) 586-2860. Fax, (202) 586-7114. Edward Wall, Program Manager. Web, www1.eere.energy.gov/geothermal*

Responsible for research and technology development of geothermal energy resources. Conducts outreach to state energy offices and consumers.

U.S. Geological Survey (USGS), *(Interior Dept.)*, **Volcano Hazards**, *12201 Sunrise Valley Dr., Reston, VA 20192 (mailing address: 904 National Center, Reston, VA 20192); (703) 648-6711. Fax, (703) 648-5483. John C. Eichelberger, Program Coordinator. Web, www.volcanoes.usgs.gov*

Provides staff support to the U.S. Geological Survey through programs in volcano hazards.

Solar, Ocean, and Wind Energy

►AGENCIES

Energy Efficiency and Renewable Energy *(Energy Dept.)*, **Solar Energy Technologies**, *1000 Independence Ave. S.W., #5H095 20585; (202) 586-1720. Fax, (202) 586-8148. Thomas Kimbis, Program Manager (Acting). Web, www1.eere.energy.gov/solar*

Supports research and development of solar technologies of all types through national laboratories and partnerships with industries and universities.

Energy Efficiency and Renewable Energy *(Energy Dept.)*, **Wind and Hydropower Technologies**, *1000 Independence Ave. S.W., #5H072, EE-2B 20585; (202) 586-5348. Fax, (202) 586-5124. Drew Ronneberg, Program Manager (Acting). Web, www1.eere.energy.gov/windandhydro*

Conducts research on wind technologies. Works with U.S. industries to develop hydropower and wind technologies.

National Oceanic and Atmospheric Administration (NOAA), *(Commerce Dept.)*, **Ocean and Coastal Resource Management**, *1305 East-West Hwy., #10411, SSMC4, Silver Spring, MD 20910; (301) 713-3155. Fax, (301) 713-4012. David Kennedy, Director. Information, (301) 713-3074. Web, http://coastalmanagement.noaa.gov*

Administers the Coastal Zone Management Act, the National Estuarine Research Reserve System, the National Marine Protected Areas Center, and the Marine Managed Areas Program to carry out NOAA's goals for preservation, conservation, and restoration management of the ocean and coastal environment.

►CONGRESS

For a listing of relevant congressional committees and subcommittees, please see page 224 or the Appendix.

►NONGOVERNMENTAL

American Wind Energy Assn., *1501 M St. N.W., #1000 20005-1700; (202) 383-2500. Fax, (202) 383-2505. Dennis Bode, Chief Executive Officer. General e-mail, windmail@awea.org Web, www.awea.org*

Membership: manufacturers, developers, operators, and distributors of wind machines; utility companies; and others interested in wind energy. Advocates wind energy as an alternative energy source; makes industry data available to the public and to federal and state legislators. Promotes export of wind energy technology.

National Ocean Industries Assn., *1120 G St. N.W., #900 20005; (202) 347-6900. Fax, (202) 347-8650. Tom A. Fry, President. General e-mail, noia@noia.org Web, www.noia.org*

Membership: manufacturers, producers, suppliers, and support and service companies involved in marine, offshore, and ocean work. Interests include ocean thermal energy and new energy sources.

Solar Electric Light Fund, *1612 K St. N.W., #402 20006-2823; (202) 234-7265. Fax, (202) 328-9512. Robert A. Freling, Executive Director. General e-mail, info@self.org Web, www.self.org*

Promotes and develops solar rural electrification and energy self-sufficiency in developing countries. Assists developing world communities and governments in acquiring, financing, and installing decentralized household and community solar electric systems.

Solar Energy Industries Assn., *805 15th St. N.W., #510 20005-2276; (202) 682-0556. Fax, (202) 682-0559. Rhone Resch, President. General e-mail, info@seia.org Web, www.seia.org*

Membership: industries with interests in the production and use of solar energy. Promotes growth of U.S. and international markets. Interests include photovoltaic, solar thermal power, and concentrating solar power. Monitors legislation and regulations.

Sustainable Buildings Industry Council, *1112 16th St. N.W., #240 20036-4818; (202) 628-7400. Fax, (202) 393-5043. Sophia Greenbaum, Executive Director. General e-mail, sbic@sbicouncil.org Web, www.sbicouncil.org*

Membership: building industry associations, corporations, small businesses, and independent professionals. Provides information on sustainable design and construction. Interests include passive solar industry and related legislation, regulations, and programs.

8 Environment and Natural Resources

GENERAL POLICY AND ANALYSIS

Basic Resources

▶**AGENCIES**

Agriculture Dept. (USDA), *Natural Resources and Environment,* 1400 Independence Ave. S.W., #217E 20250-0108; (202) 720-7173. Fax, (202) 720-0632. Vacant, Under Secretary.
Web, www.usda.gov

Formulates and promulgates policy relating to environmental activities and management of natural resources. Oversees the Forest Service and the Natural Resources Conservation Service.

Council on Environmental Quality *(Executive Office of the President),* 730 Jackson Pl. N.W. 20503; (202) 395-5750. Fax, (202) 456-6546. Nancy Sutley, Chair.
Web, www.whitehouse.og/ceq

Advises the president on environmental issues and prepares annual report on environmental quality for Congress; develops regulations for implementation of environmental impact statement law; provides information on environmental affairs.

Environmental Protection Agency (EPA), *1200 Pennsylvania Ave. N.W., #3000, MC 1101A 20460; (202) 564-4700. Fax, (202) 501-1450. Lisa P. Jackson, Administrator; Vacant, Deputy Administrator. Information, (202) 272-0167. Press, (202) 564-4355.*
Web, www.epa.gov

Administers federal environmental policies, research, and regulations; provides information on environmental subjects, including water pollution, pollution prevention, hazardous and solid waste disposal, air and noise pollution, pesticides and toxic substances, and radiation.

Environmental Protection Agency (EPA), *Children's Health Protection,* 1200 Pennsylvania Ave. N.W., #2512, MC 1107A 20460; (202) 564-2188. Fax, (202) 564-2733. Ruth McCully, Director.
Web, www.epa.gov

Supports and facilitates the EPA's efforts to protect children's and older adults' health from environmental risks, both domestically and internationally.

Environmental Protection Agency (EPA), *National Center for Environmental Assessment,* 808 17th St. N.W., #400, MC 8601D 20460; (202) 564-3322. Fax, (202) 565-0090. Peter Preuss, Director.
General e-mail, ncea.webmaster@epa.gov

Web, www.epa.gov/ncea

Evaluates animal and human health data to define environmental health hazards and estimate risk to humans.

Environmental Protection Agency (EPA), *Policy, Economics, and Innovation,* 1200 Pennsylvania Ave.

N.W., #3513, MC 1803A 20460; (202) 564-4332. Fax, (202) 501-1688. Vacant, Associate Administrator.
Web, www.epa.gov

Coordinates agency policy development and standard-setting activities.

Environmental Protection Agency (EPA), *Research and Development,* 1200 Pennsylvania Ave. N.W., #41223, MC 8101R 20460; (202) 564-6620. Fax, (202) 565-2430. Lek G. Kadeli, Assistant Administrator (Acting).
Web, www.epa.gov/ord

Develops scientific data and methods to support EPA standards and regulations; conducts exposure and risk assessments; researches applied and long-term technologies to reduce risks from pollution.

Environmental Protection Agency (EPA), *Science Advisory Board,* 1025 F St. N.W., #3600 20004 (mailing address: 1200 Pennsylvania Ave. N.W., MC 1400F, Washington, DC 20460); (202) 343-9999. Fax, (202) 233-0643. Vanessa Vu, Staff Director.
Web, www.epa.gov/sab

Coordinates nongovernment scientists and engineers who advise the administrator on scientific and technical aspects of environmental problems and issues. Evaluates EPA research projects, the technical basis of regulations and standards, and policy statements.

Health, Safety, and Security *(Energy Dept.),* 1000 Independence Ave. S.W., #7G040 20585; (301) 903-3777. Fax, (301) 903-5492. Glenn S. Podonsky, Chief Officer.
General e-mail, HSS.Infocenter@hq.doe.gov

Web, www.hss.energy.gov

Coordinates and integrates health, safety, environment, and security enforcement and independent oversight programs at the Energy Dept. Responsible for policy development, technical assistance, safety analysis, education, and training.

Housing and Urban Development Dept. (HUD), *Environment and Energy,* 451 7th St. S.W., #7244 20410; (202) 708-2894, ext. 4439. Fax, (202) 708-3363. Richard H. Broun, Director.
Web, www.hud.gov/offices/cpd/environment

Issues policies and sets standards for environmental and land-use planning and environmental management practices. Oversees HUD implementation of requirements on environment, historic preservation, archaeology, flood plain management, coastal zone management, sole source aquifers, farmland protection, endangered species, airport clear zones, explosive hazards, radon, and noise.

Interior Dept. (DOI), *1849 C St. N.W., #6151 20240; (202) 208-7351. Fax, (202) 208-6956. Kenneth L. Salazar, Secretary; David Hayes, Deputy Secretary. Information, (202) 208-3100. Library, (202) 208-5815. Press, (202) 208-6416. Locator, (202) 208-3100.*
Web, www.doi.gov

Principal U.S. conservation agency. Manages most federal land; responsible for conservation and development of mineral and water resources; responsible for conservation, development, and use of fish and wildlife resources; operates recreation programs for federal parks, refuges, and public lands; preserves and administers the nation's scenic and historic areas; reclaims arid lands in the West through irrigation; administers Native American lands and develops relationships with tribal governments.

Interior Dept. (DOI), *Policy Analysis,* *1849 C St. N.W., #3530, MS 3530 20240; (202) 208-5978. Fax, (202) 208-4867. Vacant, Director.*
Web, www.doi.gov/ppa

Analyzes how policies affect the department; makes recommendations and develops policy options for resolving natural resource problems.

Justice Dept. (DOJ), *Environment and Natural Resources,* *950 Pennsylvania Ave. N.W., #2143 20530-0001; (202) 514-2701. Fax, (202) 514-0557. Vacant, Assistant Attorney General. Press, (202) 514-2008.*
Web, www.usdoj.gov/enrd

Handles civil suits involving the federal government in all areas of the environment and natural resources; handles some criminal suits involving pollution control.

National Institute of Environmental Health Sciences *(National Institutes of Health),* *31 Center Dr., #B1C02, MSC 2256, Bethesda, MD 20892-2256; (301) 496-7719. Fax, (301) 496-0563. Dr. Linda S. Birnbaum, Director.*
General e-mail, webcenter@niehs.nih.gov

Web, www.niehs.nih.gov

Conducts and supports research on the human effects of various environmental exposures, expanding the scientific basis for making public health decisions based on the potential toxicity of environmental agents. (Most operations located in Research Triangle, N.C.)

National Oceanic and Atmospheric Administration *(NOAA),* *(Commerce Dept.),* *14th St. and Constitution Ave. N.W., #5128 20230; (202) 482-3436. Fax, (202) 408-9674. Dr. Jane Lubehenco, Under Secretary. Information, (301) 713-4000. Library, (301) 713-2600. Press, (202) 482-6090.*
Web, www.noaa.gov

Conducts research in marine and atmospheric sciences; issues weather forecasts and warnings vital to public safety and the national economy; surveys resources of the sea; analyzes economic aspects of fisheries operations; develops and implements policies on international fisheries; provides states with grants to conserve coastal zone areas; protects marine mammals; maintains a national environmental center with data from satellite observations and other sources, including meteorological, oceanic, geodetic, and seismological data centers; provides colleges and universities with grants for research, education, and marine advisory services; prepares and provides nautical and aeronautical charts and maps.

National Oceanic and Atmospheric Administration *(NOAA),* *(Commerce Dept.),* *National Environmental Satellite, Data, and Information Service,* *1335 East-West Hwy., Silver Spring, MD 20910; (301) 713-3578. Fax, (301) 713-1249. Mary Kicza, Assistant Administrator.*
Web, www.nesdis.noaa.gov

Provides satellite observations of the environment by operating polar orbiting and geostationary satellites; develops satellite techniques; increases the utilization of satellite data in environmental services.

Office of Science and Technology Policy (OSTP), *(Executive Office of the President),* *New Executive Office Bldg., 725 17th St., #5228 20502; (202) 456-7116. Fax, (202) 456-6027. John P. Holdren, Director. Press, (202) 456-6124.*
General e-mail, info@ostp.gov
Web, www.ostp.gov

Advises the president on the effects of science and technology on domestic and international affairs. Serves as a source of scientific and technological analysis for the president with respect to major policies, plans, and programs of the federal government. Leads an interagency effort to develop and implement sound science and technology policies and budgets. Works with the private sector to ensure federal investments in science and technology contribute to economic prosperity, environmental quality, and national security.

Office of Science and Technology Policy (OSTP), *(Executive Office of the President),* *National Science and Technology Council,* *New Executive Office Bldg., #725, 17th St. N.W., 5th Floor 20502-5230; (202) 456-0721. Fax, (202) 456-6021. Vacant, Director.*
General e-mail, info@ostp.gov
Web, www.ostp.gov

Coordinates research and development activities and programs that involve more than one federal agency. Activities concern earth sciences, materials, forestry research, and radiation policy.

Transportation Dept. (DOT), *Environmental Policies Team,* *1200 New Jersey Ave. S.E., #W86306 20590-0001; (202) 366-4861. Fax, (202) 366-7638. Camille H. Mittelholtz, Environmental Policies Team Leader.*
Web, www.dot.gov

Develops environmental policy and makes recommendations to the secretary; monitors Transportation Dept. implementation of environmental legislation; serves as liaison with other federal agencies and state and local governments on environmental matters related to transportation.

U.S. Geological Survey (USGS), *(Interior Dept.),* *12201 Sunrise Valley Dr., MS 100, Reston, VA 20192-0002; (703) 648-4000. Fax, (703) 648-4454. Information, (888) ASK-USGS. Library, (703) 648-4302. Press, (703) 648-4460.*
Web, www.usgs.gov

ENVIRONMENTAL RESOURCES IN CONGRESS

For a complete listing of Congress committees, including their full contact information, leadership, membership, and jurisdictions, please refer to the Appendix on pages 724–837.

HOUSE:

House Agriculture Committee, (202) 225-2171.
Web, agriculture.house.gov

  Subcommittee on Conservation, Credit, Energy, and Research, (202) 225-0420.

  Subcommittee on Department Operations, Oversight, Nutrition, and Forestry, (202) 225-6395.

  Subcommittee on Livestock, Dairy, and Poultry, (202) 225-8407.

House Appropriations Committee, Subcommittee on Agriculture, Rural Development, FDA, and Related Agencies, (202) 225-2638.
Web, appropriations.house.gov

  Subcommittee on Commerce, Justice, Science, and Related Agencies, (202) 225-3351.

  Subcommittee on Energy and Water Development, (202) 225-3421.

  Subcommittee on Interior, Environment and Related Agencies, (202) 225-3081.

House Energy and Commerce Committee, (202) 225-2927.
Web, energycommerce.house.gov

  Subcommittee on Energy and Environment (202) 225-2927.

House Natural Resources Committee, (202) 225-6065.
Web, resourcescommittee.house.gov

  Subcommittee on Energy and Mineral Resources, (202) 225-9297.

  Subcommittee on Insular Affairs, Oceans, and Wildlife (202) 226-0200.

  Subcommittee on National Parks, Forests and Public Lands, (202) 226-7736.

  Subcommittee on Water and Power, (202) 225-8331.

House Science and Technology Committee, Subcommittee on Energy and Environment, (202) 225-8844.
Web, science.house.gov

  Subcommittee on Technology and Innovation, (202) 225-9662.

House Select Committee on Energy Independence and Global Warming, (202) 225-4012.
Web, globalwarming.house.gov

House Small Business Committee, (202) 225-4038.
Web, www.house.gov/smbiz

House Transportation and Infrastructure Committee, Subcommittee on Coast Guard and Maritime Transportation, (202) 226-3587.
Web, transportation.house.gov

  Subcommittee on Railroads, Pipelines, and Hazardous Materials, (202) 225-3274.

  Subcommittee on Water Resources and Environment, (202) 225-0060.

SENATE:

Senate Agriculture, Nutrition, and Forestry Committee, (202) 224-2035.
Web, agriculture.senate.gov

  Subcommittee on Domestic and Foreign Marketing, Inspection, and Plant and Animal Health, (202) 224-2035.

Provides reports, maps, and databases that describe and analyze water, energy, biological, and mineral resources; the land surface; and the underlying geological structure and dynamic processes of the earth.

►CONGRESS

For a listing of relevant congressional committees and subcommittees, please see page 252 or the Appendix.

Government Accountability Office (GAO), *Natural Resources and Environment,* 441 G St. N.W., #2063 20548; (202) 512-9894. Robert A. Robinson, Managing Director.
Web, www.gao.gov

Independent, nonpartisan agency in the legislative branch that audits, analyzes, and reports on efficiency and effectiveness of Interior Dept. programs concerned with managing natural resources. (Formerly the General Accounting Office.)

►NONGOVERNMENTAL

American Bar Assn. (ABA), *Standing Committee on Environmental Law,* 740 15th St. N.W. 20005-1019; (202) 662-1694. Fax, (202) 638-3844. Elissa Lichtenstein, Director.
General e-mail, scel@staff.abanet.org

Web, www.abanet.org/publicserv/environmental/home.html

Conducts domestic and international projects in environmental law and policy; coordinates environmental law activities throughout the ABA.

Aspen Institute, *1 Dupont Circle N.W., #700 20036;* (202) 736-5800. Fax, (202) 467-0790. Walter Isaacson, President. Press, (202) 736-3849.
General e-mail, info@aspeninstitute.org

Web, www.aspeninstitute.org

Promotes consideration of the public good in a wide variety of areas, including environmental policy. Conducts educational programs; publishes reports.

ENVIRONMENTAL RESOURCES IN CONGRESS

Subcommittee on Energy, Science, and Technology, (202) 224-2035.

Subcommittee on Rural Revitalization, Conservation, Forestry, and Credit, (202) 224-2035.

Senate Appropriations Committee, Subcommittee on Agriculture, Rural Development, FDA, and Related Agencies, (202) 224-8090.

Web, appropriations.senate.gov

Subcommittee on Commerce, Justice, Science, and Related Agencies, (202) 224-5202.

Subcommittee on Energy and Water Development, (202) 224-8119.

Subcommittee on Interior, Environment and Related Agencies, (202) 228-0774.

Senate Commerce, Science, and Transportation Committee, (202) 224-0411.

Web, commerce.senate.gov

Subcommittee on Oceans, Atmosphere, Fisheries and the Coast Guard, (202) 224-4912.

Senate Energy and Natural Resources Committee, (202) 224-4971.

Web, energy.senate.gov

Subcommittee on Energy, (202) 224-4971.

Subcommittee on National Parks, (202) 224-4971.

Subcommittee on Public Lands and Forests, (202) 224-4971.

Subcommittee on Water and Power, (202) 224-4971.

Senate Environment and Public Works Committee, (202) 224-8832.

Web, epw.senate.gov/public

Subcommittee on Clean Air and Nuclear Safety, (202) 224-8832.

Subcommittee on Private Sector and Consumer Solutions to Global Warming and Wildlife Protection, (202) 224-8832.

Subcommittee on Public Sector Solutions to Global Warming, Oversight and Children's Health, (202) 224-8832.

Subcommittee on Superfund and Environmental Health, (202) 224-8832.

Subcommittee on Transportation Safety, Infrastructure Security and Water Quality, (202) 224-8832.

Senate Finance Committee, Subcommittee on Energy, Natural Resources and Infrastructure, (202) 224-4515.

Web, finance.senate.gov

Senate Foreign Relations Committee, Subcommittee on International Development and Foreign Assistance, Economic Affairs, and International Environmental Protection, (202) 224-4651.

Web, foreign.senate.gov

Senate Indian Affairs Committee, (202) 224-2251.

Web, indian.senate.gov

Senate Small Business and Entrepreneurship Committee, (202) 224-5175.

Web, sbc.senate.gov

Concern, *1794 Columbia Rd. N.W., #6 20009; (202) 328-8160. Fax, (202) 387-3378. Susan F. Boyd, Executive Director.*
General e-mail, concern@concern.org

Web, www.sustainable.org

Environmental education organization interested in such issues as sustainable communities and smart growth.

The Conservation Fund, *1655 N. Fort Myer Dr., #1300, Arlington, VA 22209-2156; (703) 525-6300. Fax, (703) 525-4610. Lawrence A. Selzer, President.*
General e-mail, postmaster@conservationfund.org

Web, www.conservationfund.org

Creates partnerships with the private sector, nonprofit organizations, and public agencies to promote land and water conservation.

Earth Share, *7735 Old Georgetown Rd., #900, Bethesda, MD 20814; (240) 333-0300. Fax, (240) 333-0301. Kalman Stein, President. Information, (800) 875-3863.*
General e-mail, info@earthshare.org

Web, www.earthshare.org

Federation of environmental and conservation organizations. Works with government and private payroll contribution programs to solicit contributions to member organizations for environmental research, education, and community programs. Provides information on establishing environmental giving options in the workplace.

Edison Electric Institute, *701 Pennsylvania Ave. N.W. 20004-2696; (202) 508-5000. Fax, (202) 508-5015. Thomas R. Kuhn, President. Library, (202) 508-5623.*
Web, www.eei.org

Membership: investor-owned electric power companies and electric utility holding companies. Interests include

Environmental Protection Agency

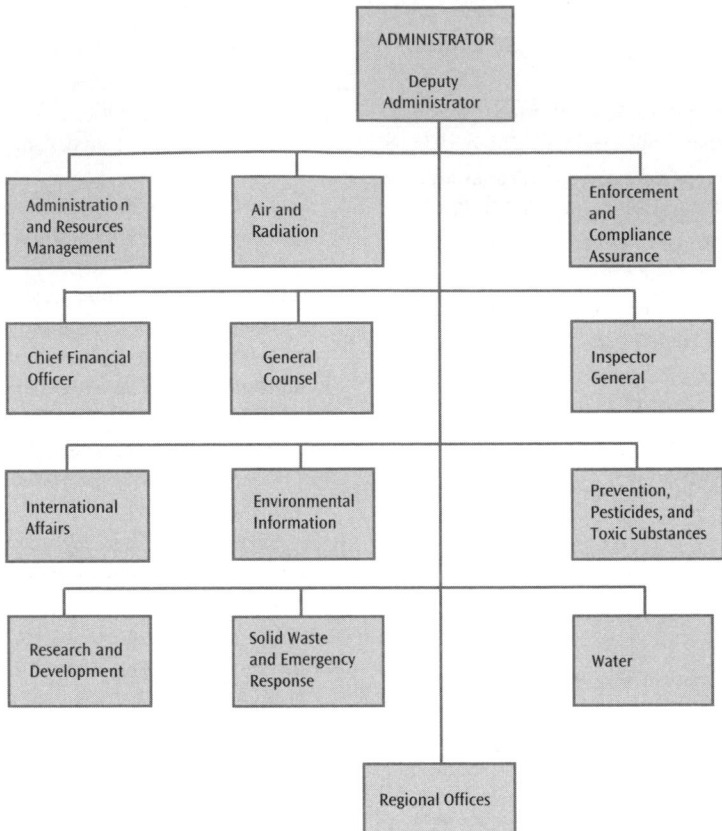

electric utility operation and concerns, including conservation and energy management, energy analysis, resources and environment, cogeneration and renewable energy resources, nuclear power, and research. Library open to the public by appointment.

Environmental and Energy Study Institute (EESI), *1112 16th St. N.W., #300 20036; (202) 628-1400. Fax, (202) 204-5244. Carol Werner, Executive Director.*
General e-mail, eesi@eesi.org

Web, www.eesi.org

Nonpartisan policy education and analysis group established by members of Congress to foster informed debate on environmental and energy issues. Interests include policies for sustainable development, energy, climate change, agriculture, transportation, and fiscal policy reform.

Environmental Council of the States, *444 N. Capitol St. N.W., #445 20001; (202) 624-3660. Fax, (202) 624-3666. R. Steven Brown, Executive Director.*
General e-mail, ecos@sso.org

Web, www.ecos.org

Works to improve the environment by providing for the exchange of ideas and experiences among states and territories; fosters cooperation and coordination among environmental management professionals.

Environmental Defense, *Washington Office, 1875 Connecticut Ave. N.W., #600 20009-5728; (202) 387-3500. Fax, (202) 234-6049. Michael Roach, Office Manager. Information, (800) 684-3322. Press, (202) 572-3235.*
Web, www.edf.org

Citizens' interest group staffed by lawyers, economists, and scientists. Takes legal action on environmental issues; provides information on pollution prevention, environmental health, wetlands, toxic substances, acid rain, tropical rain forests, and litigation of water pollution standards. (Headquarters in New York.)

Environmental Law Institute, *2000 L St. N.W., #620 20036; (202) 939-3800. Fax, (202) 939-3868. Leslie Carothers, President.*
General e-mail, law@eli.org

Web, www.eli.org

Conducts policy studies on the environment and sustainability. Publishes materials on environmental issues, sponsors education and training courses, issues policy recommendations, cosponsors conferences on environmental law, and provides technical assistance in the United States and abroad.

Environmental Working Group, *1436 U St. N.W., #100 20009-3987; (202) 667-6982. Fax, (202) 232-2592. Kenneth A. Cook, President.*

General e-mail, generalinfo@ewg.org

Web, www.ewg.org

Research and advocacy organization that studies and reports on the presence of herbicides and pesticides in food and drinking water. Monitors legislation and regulations.

Environment America, *218 D St. S.E., 2nd Floor 20003; (202) 683-1250. Fax, (202) 546-2461. Margie Alt, Executive Director.*

Web, www.environmentamerica.org

Coordinates grassroots efforts to advance environmental and consumer protection laws; conducts research on environmental issues, including toxic and solid waste, air and water pollution, pesticides, endangered species, forest and wildlife preservation, alternative energy sources, and energy conservation; compiles reports and disseminates information on such issues; drafts and monitors environmental laws; testifies on behalf of proposed environmental legislation. (Affiliated with the U.S. Public Interest Research Group.)

FreedomWorks, *601 Pennsylvania Ave. N.W., North Bldg., #700 20004-2601; (202) 783-3870. Fax, (202) 942-7649. Matt Kibbe, President. Toll-free, (888) 564-6273.*

Web, www.freedomworks.org

Education and research organization that seeks market-oriented solutions to environmental problems. Develops initiatives to balance environmental and economic considerations; supports private efforts to manage wildlife habitats.

Friends of the Earth (FOE), *1717 Massachusetts Ave. N.W., #600 20036-2008; (202) 783-7400. Fax, (202) 783-0444. Brent Blackwelder, President.*

General e-mail, foe@foe.org

Web, www.foe.org

Environmental advocacy group concerned with environmental, public health, and energy-related issues, including clean air, water, and groundwater; energy conservation; international water projects; transportation of hazardous wastes; global warming; and toxic substances and pesticides. Specializes in federal budget and tax issues related to the environment, ozone layer and groundwater protection, and World Bank and International Monetary Fund reform.

Green America, *1612 K St. N.W., #600 20006; (202) 872-5307. Fax, (202) 331-8166. Alisa Gravitz, Executive Director. Information, (800) 584-7336. Press, (202) 872-5314. TTY, (202) 822-5038.*

General e-mail, members@greenamericatoday.org

Web, www.greenamericatoday.org

Educates consumers and businesses about social and environmental responsibility. Publishes a directory of environmentally and socially responsible businesses and a financial planning guide for investment.

Izaak Walton League of America, *707 Conservation Lane, Gaithersburg, MD 20878-2983; (301) 548-0150. Fax, (301) 548-0146. David Hoskins, Executive Director. Toll-free, (800) 453-5463.*

General e-mail, general@iwla.org

Web, www.iwla.org

Grassroots organization that promotes conservation of natural resources and the environment. Interests include air and water pollution and wildlife habitat protection. Provides information on acid rain and stream cleanup efforts at the local level.

League of Conservation Voters (LCV), *1920 L St. N.W., #800 20036; (202) 785-8683. Fax, (202) 835-0491. Gene Karpinski, President.*

Web, www.lcv.org

Supports the environmental movement by advocating for sound environmental policies and helping elect environmentally concerned candidates to public office. Publishes the National Environmental Scorecard and Presidential Report Card.

National Assn. of Conservation Districts (NACD), *509 Capitol Court N.E. 20002-4937; (202) 547-6223. Fax, (202) 547-6450. Krysta Harden, Chief Executive Director.*

General e-mail, washington@nacdnet.org

Web, www.nacdnet.org

Membership: conservation districts (local subdivisions of state government). Works to promote the conservation of land, forests, and other natural resources. Interests include erosion and sediment control; water quality; forestry, water, flood plain, and range management; rural development; and urban and community conservation.

National Audubon Society, *Public Policy, Washington Office, 1150 Connecticut Ave. N.W., #600 20036-3029; (202) 861-2242. Fax, (202) 861-4290. Betsy Loyless, Senior Vice President.*

General e-mail, audubonaction@audubon.org

Web, www.audubon.org

Citizens' interest group that promotes environmental preservation. Provides information on water resources, public lands, rangelands, forests, parks, wildlife conservation, and the National Wildlife Refuge System. (Headquarters in New York.)

National Governors Assn. (NGA), *Center for Best Practices: Environment, Energy, and Natural Resources, 444 N. Capitol St. N.W., #267 20001-1512; (202) 624-5300. Fax, (202) 624-5825. Sue Gander, Director.*

General e-mail, webmaster@nga.org

Web, www.nga.org

Identifies best practices for energy, land-use, environment, and transportation issues and shares these with the states.

National Governors Assn. (NGA), *Natural Resources Committee,* 444 N. Capitol St. N.W., #267 20001-1512; (202) 624-5300. Fax, (202) 624-7829. Michelle Cady Nellenbach, Director.
General e-mail, webmaster@nga.org

Web, www.nga.org

Monitors legislation and regulations and makes recommendations on agriculture, energy, environment, and natural resource issues to ensure governors' views and priorities are represented in federal policies and regulations.

National Sustainable Agriculture Coalition, *110 Maryland Ave. N.E., #209 20002-5622; (202) 547-5754. Fax, (202) 547-1837. Ferd Hoefner, Policy Director.*
Web, www.sustainableagriculturecoalition.org

National alliance of farm, rural, and conservation organizations. Advocates federal policies that promote environmentally sustainable agriculture, natural resources management, and rural community development. Monitors legislation and regulations.

National Wildlife Federation, *11100 Wildlife Center Dr., Reston, VA 20190-5362; (703) 438-6000. Fax, (703) 438-3570. Larry J. Schweiger, President. Information, (800) 822-9919.*
General e-mail, info@nwf.org

Web, www.nwf.org

Promotes conservation of natural resources; provides information on the environment and resource management; takes legal action on environmental issues.

Natural Resources Defense Council, *Washington Office,* 1200 New York Ave. N.W., #400 20005-4709; (202) 289-6868. Fax, (202) 289-1060. Leslie Edmond, Office Manager.
General e-mail, nrdcinfo@nrdc.org

Web, www.nrdc.org

Environmental organization staffed by lawyers and scientists who conduct litigation and research. Interests include air, water, land use, forests, toxic materials, natural resources management and conservation, preservation of endangered plant species, and ozone pollution. (Headquarters in New York.)

Nature Conservancy, *4245 N. Fairfax Dr., #100, Arlington, VA 22203-1606; (703) 841-5300. Fax, (703) 841-1283. Mark Tercek, President. Information, (800) 628-6860.*
General e-mail, comment@tnc.org

Web, www.nature.org

Maintains an international system of natural sanctuaries; acquires land to protect endangered species and habitats. Collaborates with other conservation organizations, country and local governments, corporations, indigenous peoples and communities, and individuals such as fishermen, ranchers, and farmers to create management plans for natural areas.

Pew Environment Group, *1200 18th St. N.W., #500 20036; (202) 887-8800. Fax, (202) 887-8877. Josh Reichert, Managing Director.*
General e-mail, envimail@pewtrusts.org

Web, www.pewtrusts.org

Identifies and publicizes environmental issues at the national and local levels. Interests include climate change, clean air, endangered species, global warming, hazardous chemicals, national park pollution, and campaign finance reform. Opposes efforts to weaken environmental laws. Monitors legislation and regulations.

Population-Environment Balance, *2000 P St. N.W., #600 20036; (202) 955-5700. Fax, (202) 955-6161. Aaron Beckwith, Vice President.*
General e-mail, uspop@us.net

Web, www.balance.org

Grassroots organization that advocates U.S. population stabilization to safeguard the environment.

Public Employees for Environmental Responsibility (PEER), *2000 P St. N.W., #240 20036; (202) 265-7337. Fax, (202) 265-4192. Jeff Ruch, Executive Director.*
General e-mail, info@peer.org

Web, www.peer.org

Service organization for public citizens and employees of federal, state, and local resource management agencies. Defends legal rights of public employees who speak out concerning natural resource management and environmental protection issues. Monitors enforcement of environmental protection laws.

Resources for the Future, *1616 P St. N.W. 20036-1400; (202) 328-5000. Fax, (202) 939-3460. Philip R. Sharp, President. Library, (202) 328-5089. Press, (202) 328-5026.*
General e-mail, info@rff.org

Web, www.rff.org

Engages in research and education on environmental and natural resource issues, including forestry, multiple use of public lands, costs and benefits of pollution control, endangered species, environmental risk management, energy and national security, and climate resources. Interests include hazardous waste, the Superfund, and biodiversity. Library open to the public.

Science Communication Network, *2000 P St., #740 20036; (202) 463-6670. Fax, (202) 463-6671. Amy Kostant, Executive Director.*
Web, www.sciencecommunicationnetwork.org

Advocates expanded and improved coverage of environmental health reporting in the nation's media. Conducts educational workshops. Focuses on environmental health science, green chemistry, and science integrity issues.

Sierra Club, *Washington Office, 408 C St. N.E. 20002-5818; (202) 547-1141. Fax, (202) 547-6009. Debbie Sease, Legislative Director. Press, (202) 675-6698.*
General e-mail, information@sierraclub.org
Web, www.sierraclub.org

Citizens' interest group that promotes protection of natural resources. Interests include the Clean Air Act; the Arctic National Wildlife Refuge; protection of national forests, parks, and wilderness; toxins; global warming; promotion of responsible international trade; and international development lending reform. Monitors legislation and regulations. (Headquarters in San Francisco, Calif.)

Union of Concerned Scientists, *Strategy and Policy, Washington Office, 1825 K St. N.W., #800 20006-3962; (202) 223-6133. Fax, (202) 223-6162. Alden Meyer, Director.*
General e-mail, ucs@ucsusa.org
Web, www.ucsusa.org

Membership: scientists and citizens who advocate a comprehensive approach to resolving global environmental and resource concerns. Educates and mobilizes citizens on the linkages between resource depletion, environmental degradation, climate changes, consumption patterns, and population growth. (Headquarters in Cambridge, Mass.)

U.S. Chamber of Commerce, *Environment, Technology, and Regulatory Affairs, 1615 H St. N.W. 20062-2000; (202) 463-5533. Fax, (202) 887-3445. William L. Kovacs, Vice President.*
General e-mail, environment@uschamber.com
Web, www.uschamber.com

Monitors operations of federal departments and agencies responsible for environmental programs, policies, regulatory issues, and food safety. Analyzes and evaluates legislation and regulations that affect the environment.

The Wilderness Society, *1615 M St. N.W., #100 20036; (202) 833-2300. Fax, (202) 429-3958. William H. Meadows III, President.*
General e-mail, tws@tws.org
Web, www.wilderness.org

Promotes preservation of wilderness and the responsible management of federal lands, including national parks and forests, wilderness areas, wildlife refuges, and land administered by the Interior Dept.'s Bureau of Land Management.

Global Warming and Climate Change

►AGENCIES

Economic Research Service *(Agriculture Dept.), 1800 M St. N.W., #4145N 20036 5831; (202) 694-5000. Fax,* *(202) 694-5757. Kitty Smith, Administrator; John Kort, Associate Administrator.*
General e-mail, service@ers.usda.gov
Web, www.ers.usda.gov

Provides research and economic information to the USDA. Interests include economic and policy issues involving food, farming, natural resources, and rural development. Web site offers a briefing room on global climate change.

Environmental Protection Agency (EPA), *Atmospheric Programs, Climate Change Division, 1200 Pennsylvania Ave. N.W., MC 6207J 20460; (202) 343-9416. Fax, (202) 343-2202. Dina Kruger, Director.*
General e-mail, webmasters.cpd@epa.gov
Web, www.epa.gov/climatechange/ccd.html

Works to address global climate change and the associated risks to human health and the environment. Implements voluntary programs to reduce non-carbon dioxide emissions; analyzes greenhouse gas emissions and reduction options; educates the public on climate change and provides climate analysis and strategies to policymakers, experts, and U.S. climate negotiators.

U.S. Geological Survey (USGS), *(Interior Dept.), Global Change Programs, 12201 Sunrise Valley Dr., MS 104, Reston, VA 20192; (703) 648-4000. Fax, (703) 648-4454. Thomas R. Armstrong, Program Coordinator.*
Web, www.usgs.gov/global_change

Conducts research to understand the interactions among climate, earth surface processes, and ecosystems. Provides information that can be used to assess the effects of climate change and variability on landscapes, ecosystems, resources, and regions.

►CONGRESS

For a listing of relevant congressional committees and subcommittees, please see page 252 or the Appendix.

►NONGOVERNMENTAL

Climate Institute, *900 17th St. N.W., #700 20006; (202) 547-0104. Fax, (202) 547-0111. John C. Topping Jr., President.*
General e-mail, info@climate.org
Web, www.climate.org

Educates the public and policymakers on climate change (greenhouse effect, or global warming) and on the depletion of the ozone layer. Develops strategies on mitigating climate change in developing countries and in North America.

Competitive Enterprise Institute, *1899 L St. N.W., 12th Floor 20036; (202) 331-1010. Fax, (202) 331-0640. Fred L. Smith, President.*
General e-mail, info@cei.org
Web, www.cei.org

Advocates free enterprise, limited government, and free market solutions to international environmental issues, such as global warming and hazardous wastes. Produces policy analyses on tax, budget, financial services, antitrust, biotechnological, and environmental issues. Monitors legislation and litigates against restrictive regulations through its Free Market Legal Program.

George C. Marshall Institute, *1625 K St. N.W., #1050 20006; (202) 296-9655. Fax, (202) 296-9714. Jeffrey Kueter, President.*
General e-mail, info@marshall.org
Web, www.marshall.org

Analyzes the technical and scientific aspects of public policy and defense issues; produces publications on environmental science, space, national security, energy issues, and technology policy. Interests include global warming and defense policy.

Global Green USA, *Washington Office,* *1717 Massachusetts Ave. N.W., #600 20036-2002; (202) 222-0700. Fax, (202) 222-0703. Matt Petersen, President.*
General e-mail, cion@globalgreen.org
Web, www.globalgreen.org

Offers research and community-based projects to educate people about the environment and encourage improved environmental policy. Interests include climate change, elimination of weapons of mass destruction, access to clean water, green technology, and green building. Hosts the Millenium Awards and the Designing a Sustainable and Secure World Awards. (Headquarters in Santa Monica, Calif.)

International Institute for Energy Conservation (IIEC), *10005 Leamoore Lane, #100, Vienna, VA 22181-5909; (703) 281-7263. Fax, (703) 938-5153. Nitin Pandit, President.*
Web, www.iiec.org

Works with developing nations to establish sustainable growth through efficient uses of energy. Seeks to counteract air and water pollution and the threat of global warming.

National Council for Science and the Environment, *1101 17th St. N.W., #250 20036; (202) 530-5810. Fax, (202) 628-4311. Peter Saundry, Executive Director.*
General e-mail, info@ncseonline.org
Web, http://ncseonline.org

Coordinates programs that bring together individuals, institutions, and communities to discuss environmental education, research, and public policy decisions affecting the environment.

Resources for the Future, *1616 P St. N.W. 20036-1400; (202) 328-5000. Fax, (202) 939-3460. Philip R. Sharp, President. Library, (202) 328-5089. Press, (202) 328-5026.*
General e-mail, info@rff.org
Web, www.rff.org

Research organization that conducts independent studies on economic and policy aspects of energy, environment, conservation, and natural resource management issues worldwide. Interests include climate change, energy, natural resource issues in developing countries, and public health.

Science and Environmental Policy Project (SEPP), *1600 S. Eads St., #712-S, Arlington, VA 22202-2907; (703) 920-2744. S. Fred Singer, President.*
General e-mail, comments@sepp.org
Web, www.sepp.org

Works to clarify environmental problems and provide effective, economical solutions. Encourages use of scientific knowledge when making health or environmental public policy decisions.

Union of Concerned Scientists, *Strategy and Policy, Washington Office,* *1825 K St. N.W., #800 20006-3962; (202) 223-6133. Fax, (202) 223-6162. Alden Meyer, Director.*
General e-mail, ucs@ucsusa.org
Web, www.ucsusa.org

Membership: scientists and citizens who advocate a comprehensive approach to resolving global environmental and resource concerns. Educates and mobilizes citizens on the linkages between resource depletion, environmental degradation, climate changes, consumption patterns, and population growth. (Headquarters in Cambridge, Mass.)

International Issues

▶AGENCIES

Environmental Protection Agency (EPA), *International Affairs, 1200 Pennsylvania Ave. N.W., #31207, MC 2610R 20460; (202) 564-6600. Fax, (202) 565-2407. Scott Fulton, Assistant Administrator (Acting).*
Web, www.epa.gov

Coordinates the agency's work on international environmental issues and programs, including management of bilateral agreements and participation in multilateral organizations and negotiations.

International Trade Administration (ITA), *(Commerce Dept.), Energy and Environmental Industries, 14th St. and Constitution Ave. N.W., #4053 20230; (202) 482-5225. Cheryl McQueen, Director (Acting).*
General e-mail, public_affairs@ita.doc.gov
Web, www.environment.ita.doc.gov

Works to facilitate and increase export of U.S. environmental technologies, including goods and services. Conducts market analysis, business counseling, and trade promotion.

State Dept., *Ecology and Natural Resource Conservation, 2201 C St. N.W., #4333 20520; (202) 647-3367. Fax, (202) 736-7351. Vacant, Director; Harvey Lee, Deputy Director.*
Web, www.state.gov

Represents the United States in international affairs relating to natural resources. Interests include wildlife, tropical forests, and biological diversity.

State Dept., *Environmental Policy,* 2201 C St. N.W., #2657 20520; (202) 647-9266. Fax, (202) 647-5947. *Daniel Fantozzi, Director.*
Web, www.state.gov

Advances U.S. interests internationally regarding multilateral environmental organizations, chemical waste and other pollutants, and bilateral and regional environmental policies.

State Dept., *Oceans, Environment, and Science,* 2201 C St. N.W., #3880 20520-7818; (202) 647-1554. Fax, (202) 647-0217. *Reno Harnish, Assistant Secretary (Acting).* Press, (202) 647-3486.
Web, www.state.gov/g/oes/index.htm

Concerned with foreign policy as it affects natural resources and the environment, human health, the global climate, energy production, and oceans and fisheries.

►**CONGRESS**

For a listing of relevant congressional committees and subcommittees, please see page 252 or the Appendix.

►**INTERNATIONAL ORGANIZATIONS**

International Joint Commission, United States and Canada, *U.S. Section,* 2401 Pennsylvania Ave. N.W., #400 20037; (202) 736-9000. Fax, (202) 254-4562. *Irene Brooks, Chair.*
Web, www.ijc.org

Prevents and resolves disputes between the United States and Canada on transboundary water and air resources. Investigates issues upon request of the governments of the United States and Canada. Reviews applications for water resource projects. (Canadian section in Ottawa.)

International Union for the Conservation of Nature, *U.S. Office, Washington Office,* 1630 Connecticut Ave. N.W., 3rd Floor 20009; (202) 387-4826. Fax, (202) 387-4823. *Scott A. Hajost, Executive Director.*
General e-mail, postmaster@iucnus.org/usa

Web, www.iucn.org

Membership: world governments, their environmental agencies, and nongovernmental organizations. Studies conservation issues from local to global levels. Interests include protected areas, forests, oceans, polar regions, biodiversity, species survival, environmental law, sustainable use of resources, and the impact of trade on the environment. (Headquarters in Gland, Switzerland.)

Organization of American States (OAS), *Sustainable Development,* 1889 F St. N.W., #710 20006; (202) 458-3567. Fax, (202) 458-3560. *Cletus Springer, Director.*
Web, www.oas.org/dsd

Provides support to OAS technical cooperation projects. Promotes integrated and sustainable development of natural resources. Interests include international river basins, border areas, coastal zones, and emerging trade corridors.

►**NONGOVERNMENTAL**

Antarctic and Southern Ocean Coalition, 1630 Connecticut Ave. N.W., 3rd Floor 20009; (202) 234-2480. Fax, (202) 387-4823. *James N. Barnes, Executive Director.* General e-mail, secretariat@asoc.org

Web, www.asoc.org

Promotes effective implementation of the Antarctic Treaty System; works to protect the environment of the Antarctic continent and promote responsible sustainable fisheries in the Southern Ocean.

Conservation International, 2011 Crystal Dr., #500, Arlington, VA 22202; (703) 341-2400. Fax, (703) 553-0654. *Russell Mittermeier, President.* Toll-free, (800) 429-5660. Web, www.conservation.org

Works to conserve tropical rain forests through economic development; promotes exchange of debt relief for conservation programs that involve local people and organizations. Provides private groups and governments with information and technical advice on conservation efforts; supports conservation data gathering in Latin America, Africa, Asia, and the Caribbean.

Environmental Investigation Agency (EIA), P.O. Box 53343 20009; (202) 483-6621. Fax, (202) 986-8626. *Alexander von Bismarck, Director.* General e-mail, usinfo@eia-international.org

Web, www.eia-global.org

Works to expose international environmental crime, including illegal trade of wildlife, illegal logging, and sale of ozone-depleting substances. Monitors legislation and regulations. Also maintains an office in London.

Greenpeace USA, *Washington Office,* 702 H St. N.W., #300 20001; (202) 462-1177. Fax, (202) 462-4507. *Phil Radford, Executive Director.* General e-mail, info@wdc.greenpeace.org

Web, www.greenpeaceusa.org

Seeks to expose global environmental problems and to promote solutions through nonviolent direct action, lobbying, and creative communication. Interests include forests, oceans, toxins, global warming, nuclear energy, disarmament, and genetic engineering. (International office in Amsterdam, Netherlands.)

Pinchot Institute for Conservation, 1616 P St. N.W., #100 20036; (202) 797-6580. Fax, (202) 797-6583. *V. Alaric Sample, President.* General e-mail, pinchot@pinchot.org

Web, www.pinchot.org

Seeks to advance the conservation of natural resources nationally through policy research and analysis, convening and facilitation, and development of conservation leaders. Programs include Community-based Forest Stewardship, Conservation Policy and Organizational Change, Conservation Leadership and Executive Development, Conservation and the Arts, International Forest Policy and Planning, and the Milford Experimental Forest in Pennsylvania.

Winrock International, *Washington Office, 1621 N. Kent St., #1200, Arlington, VA 22209-2131; (703) 525-9430. Fax, (703) 525-1744. Frank Tugwell, President. General e-mail, information@winrock.org*

Web, www.winrock.org

Works to sustain natural resources and protect the environment. Matches innovative approaches in agriculture, natural resource management, clean energy, and leadership development with the unique needs of its partners.

World Resources Institute, *10 G St. N.E., #800 20002; (202) 729-7600. Fax, (202) 729-7610. Jonathan Lash, President. Press, (202) 729-7736. General e-mail, front@wri.org*

Web, www.wri.org

Conducts research on environmental problems and studies the interrelationships of natural resources, economic growth, and human needs. Interests include forestry and land use, renewable energy, fisheries, and sustainable agriculture. Assesses environmental policies of aid agencies.

Worldwatch Institute, *1776 Massachusetts Ave. N.W., 8th Floor 20036; (202) 452-1999. Fax, (202) 296-7365. Christopher Flavin, President. General e-mail, worldwatch@worldwatch.org*

Web, www.worldwatch.org

Focuses on an interdisciplinary approach to solving global environmental problems. Interests include energy conservation, renewable resources, solar power, and energy use in developing countries.

World Wildlife Fund (WWF), *1250 24th St. N.W. 20037-1193 (mailing address: P.O. Box 97180, Washington, DC 20090-7180); (202) 293-4800. Fax, (202) 293-9211. Carter S. Roberts, President.*

Web, www.worldwildlife.org

Conducts scientific research and analyzes policy on environmental and conservation issues, including pollution reduction, land use, forestry and wetlands management, parks, soil conservation, and sustainable development. Supports projects to promote biological diversity and to save endangered species and their habitats, including tropical forests in Latin America, Asia, and Africa. Awards grants and provides technical assistance to local conservation groups.

ANIMALS AND PLANTS

▶**AGENCIES**

Animal and Plant Health Inspection Service (APHIS), *(Agriculture Dept.), Investigative and Enforcement Services, 4700 River Rd., Unit 85, Riverdale,*

MD 20737-1234; (301) 734-8684. Fax, (301) 734-4328. Gregory Parham, Administrator. Web, www.aphis.usda.gov/ies

Provides investigative and enforcement services and leadership, direction, and support for compliance activities within the service.

Animal and Plant Health Inspection Service (APHIS), *(Agriculture Dept.), Plant Protection and Quarantine, 14th Independence Ave. S.W., #302E 20250; (202) 720-5601. Fax, (202) 690-0472. Rebecca Bech, Deputy Administrator. Antismuggling hotline, (800) 877-3835. General e-mail, aphis.web@aphis.usda.gov*

Web, www.aphis.usda.gov/plant_health

Encourages compliance with regulations that safeguard agriculture and natural resources from the risks associated with the entry, establishment, or spread of animal and plant pests and noxious weeds. Methods include requirements for the import and export of plants and plant products; partnership agreements with industry groups, community organizations, and government entities; and public education and outreach.

Food and Drug Administration (FDA), *(Health and Human Services Dept.), Center for Veterinary Medicine, 7519 Standish Pl., Rockville, MD 20855-0001; (240) 276-9000. Fax, (240) 276-9001. Dr. Bernadette Dunham, Director. General e-mail, CVMHomeP@cvm.fda.gov*

Web, www.fda.gov/cvm

Regulates the manufacture and distribution of drugs, food additives, feed, and devices for livestock and pets. Conducts research; works to ensure animal health and the safety of food derived from animals.

National Zoological Park *(Smithsonian Institution), 3001 Connecticut Ave. N.W. 20008; (202) 633-4800. Fax, (202) 673-4607. Vacant, Director. Library, (202) 633-1031. Press, (202) 633-3055. TTY, (202) 673-7800. Friends of the Zoo, (202) 633-4240.*

Web, www.nationalzoo.si.edu

Maintains a public zoo. Conducts research on animal behavior, ecology, nutrition, reproductive physiology, pathology, and veterinary medicine; operates an annex near Front Royal, Va., for the propagation and study of endangered species. Houses a unit of the Smithsonian Institution library open to qualified researchers by appointment. Interlibrary loans available.

U.S. Customs and Border Protection *(Homeland Security Dept.), Agricultural Program and Trade Liaison Office, 1300 Pennsylvania Ave. N.W., #2.5B 20229; (202) 344-3298. Fax, (202) 344-1442. Vernon Foret, Executive Director.*

Web, www.cbp.gov

Responsible for safeguarding the nation's animal and natural resources from pests and disease through inspections at ports of entry and beyond.

►CONGRESS

For a listing of relevant congressional committees and subcommittees, please see page 252 or the Appendix.

►NONGOVERNMENTAL

American Herbal Products Assn., *8630 Fenton St., #918, Silver Spring, MD 20910; (301) 588-1171. Fax, (301) 588-1174. Michael McGuffin, President. Press, (301) 588-1171, ext. 104.*
General e-mail, ahpa@ahpa.org
Web, www.ahpa.org

Membership: U.S. companies and individuals that grow, manufacture, and distribute therapeutic herbs and herbal products; associates in education, law, media, and medicine. Supports research; promotes quality standards, consumer protection, competition, and self-regulation in the industry. Monitors legislation and regulations.

American Veterinary Medical Assn., *Governmental Relations, Washington Office, 1910 Sunderland Pl. N.W. 20036-1642; (202) 789-0007. Fax, (202) 842-4360. Dr. Mark Lutschaunig, Director. Toll-free, (800) 321-1473.*
General e-mail, avmagrd@avma.org
Web, www.avma.org

Monitors legislation and regulations that influence animal and human health and advance the veterinary medical profession. (Headquarters in Schaumburg, Ill.)

Animal Health Institute, *1325 G St. N.W., #700 20005-3104; (202) 637-2440. Fax, (202) 393-1667. Alexander S. Mathews, President.*
Web, www.ahi.org

Membership: manufacturers of drugs and other products (including vaccines, pesticides, and vitamins) for pets and food-producing animals. Monitors legislation and regulations.

Assn. of American Veterinary Medical Colleges (AAVMC), *1101 Vermont Ave. N.W., #301 20005-3536; (202) 371-9195. Fax, (202) 842-0773. Dr. Marguerite Pappaionou, Executive Director.*
Web, www.aavmc.org

Membership: U.S., Canadian, and international schools and colleges of veterinary medicine, departments of comparative medicine, and departments of veterinary science in agricultural colleges. Produces veterinary reports; sponsors continuing education programs and conferences on veterinary medical issues.

Animal Rights and Welfare

►AGENCIES

Animal and Plant Health Inspection Service (APHIS), *(Agriculture Dept.), Animal Care, 4700 River Rd., Unit 84, Riverdale, MD 20737-1234; (301) 734-7833. Fax, (301) 734-4978. Chester Gipson, Deputy Administrator.*

General e-mail, ace@aphis.usda.gov
Web, www.aphis.usda.gov/animal_welfare/index.shtml

Administers laws for the breeding, exhibition, and care of animals raised for sale and research and transported commercially.

National Agricultural Library *(Agriculture Dept.), Animal Welfare Information Center, 10301 Baltimore Ave., #410, Beltsville, MD 20705; (301) 504-6212. Fax, (301) 504-7125. Jean Larson, Coordinator.*
General e-mail, awic@ars.usda.gov
Web, http://awic.nal.usda.gov

Provides information for improved animal care and use in research, testing, teaching, and exhibition.

National Institutes of Health (NIH), *(Health and Human Services Dept.), Animal Care and Use, 31 Center Drive, Bldg. 31, #B1C37, MSC 2252, Bethesda, MD 20892-2252; (301) 496-5424. Fax, (301) 480-8298. Terri Clark, Director (Acting).*
General e-mail, secoacu@od.nih.gov
Web, http://oacu.od.nih.gov

Provides guidance for the humane care and use of animals in the intramural research program at NIH.

National Institutes of Health (NIH), *(Health and Human Services Dept.), Laboratory Animal Welfare, 6705 Rockledge Dr., RLK1, #360, MSC 7982, Bethesda, MD 20892-7982; (301) 496-7163. Fax, (301) 402-7065. Patricia Brown, Director.*
General e-mail, olaw@od.nih.gov
Web, http://grants.nih.gov/grants/olaw/olaw.htm

Develops and monitors policy on the humane care and use of animals in research conducted by any public health service entity.

►CONGRESS

For a listing of relevant congressional committees and subcommittees, please see page 252 or the Appendix.

►NONGOVERNMENTAL

Alley Cat Allies, *7920 Norfolk Avenue, #600, Bethesda, MD 20814-2525; (240) 482-1980. Fax, (240) 482-1990. Donna Wilcox, Director.*
General e-mail, webmaster@alleycat.org
Web, www.alleycat.org

Clearinghouse for information on feral and stray cats. Advocates the trap-neuter-return method to reduce feral cat populations.

American Horse Protection Assn., *1000 29th St. N.W., #T100 20007; (202) 965-0500. Fax, (202) 965-9621. Robin C. Lohnes, Executive Director.*
General e-mail, info@ahpa.us

Membership: individuals, corporations, and foundations interested in protecting wild and domestic horses.

American Humane Assn., *Public Policy, Washington Office,* 206 N. Washington St., #300, Alexandria, VA 22314; (703) 836-7387. Fax, (703) 549-5437. Allie Phillips, Director of Government Affairs.
General e-mail, publicpolicy@americanhumane.org

Web, www.americanhumane.org

Membership: humane societies, government agencies, and individuals. Monitors legislation and regulations to ensure the proper treatment of all animals; assists local societies in establishing shelters and investigating cruelty cases; maintains training programs for humane society personnel. (Headquarters in Denver, Colo.)

Americans for Medical Progress Educational Foundation, 526 King St., #201, Alexandria, VA 22314; (703) 836-9595. Fax, (703) 836-9594. Jacqueline Calnan, President.
General e-mail, info@amprogress.org

Web, www.amprogress.org

Promotes and protects animal-based medical research. Serves as a media resource by fact-checking claims of animal rights groups. Conducts public education campaigns on the link between animal research and medical advances.

Animal Welfare Institute, 900 Pennsylvania Ave. S.E. 20003 (mailing address: P.O. Box 3650, Washington, DC 20027); (202) 337-2332. Fax, (202) 446-2131. Cathy Liss, President.
Web, www.awionline.org

Works to improve conditions for animals used for experimentation, to preserve species threatened with extinction, and to protect wildlife from cruel means of capture. Supports legislation to ensure the proper treatment of animals. (Merged with the Society for Animal Protective Legislation.)

Compassion Over Killing, P.O. Box 9773 20016; (301) 891-2458. Fax, (301) 891-6815. Erica Meier, Executive Director.
General e-mail, info@cok.net

Web, www.cok.net

Animal rights organization that focuses primarily on factory farming.

Council on Humane Giving, 5100 Wisconsin Ave. N.W., #400 20016; (202) 686-2210,ext. 397. Fax, (202) 686-2216. Rebecca Frye, Coordinator.
General e-mail, info@humaneseal.org

Web, www.humaneseal.org

Supports charities that conduct health-related research using nonanimal methods; sponsors the Humane Charity Seal of Approval program. Administered by the Physicians Committee for Responsible Medicine.

Doris Day Animal League, 2100 L St. N.W. 20037; (202) 452-1100. Fax, (202) 546-2193. Holly Hazard, Executive Director.

General e-mail, info@ddal.org

Web, www.ddal.org

Seeks to reduce the inhumane treatment of animals through legislative initiatives, education, and programs. Works with all levels of government to pass new protection laws and strengthen existing ones.

Farm Animal Rights Movement (FARM), 10101 Ashburton Lane, Bethesda, MD 20817-1729; (301) 530-1737. Fax, (301) 530-5683. Alex Hershaft, President.
General e-mail, info@farmusa.org

Web, www.farmusa.org

Works to end use of animals for food. Interests include animal protection, consumer health, agricultural resources, and environmental quality. Conducts national educational campaigns, including World Farm Animals Day and the Great American Meatout. Monitors legislation and regulations.

Humane Farm Animal Care, P.O. Box 727, Herndon, VA 20172-0727; (703) 435-3883. Fax, (703) 435-3981. Adele Douglass, Chief Executive Officer.
General e-mail, info@certifiedhumane.org

Web, www.certifiedhumane.org

Seeks to improve the welfare of farm animals by providing viable, duly monitored standards for humane food production. Sponsors the Certified Humane Raised and Handled program for meat, poultry, eggs, and products.

Humane Society Legislative Fund, 519 C St. N.E. 20002; (202) 676-2314. Fax, (202) 676-2300. Michael Markarian, President. Press, (301) 548-7778.
General e-mail, info@hslf.org

Web, www.hslf.org

Works to pass state and federal laws protecting animals from cruelty and suffering. (Lobbying arm of the Humane Society of the United States.)

Humane Society of the United States, 2100 L St. N.W. 20037; (202) 452-1100. Fax, (202) 778-6132. Wayne Pacelle, President.
Web, www.hsus.org

Citizens' interest group that sponsors programs in pet and equine protection, disaster preparedness and response, wildlife and habitat protection, animals in research, and farm animal welfare. Interests include legislation to protect pets, provide more humane treatment for farm animals, strengthen penalties for illegal animal fighting, and curb abusive sport hunting practices such as trophy hunting, baiting, and hounding.

National Assn. for Biomedical Research, 818 Connecticut Ave. N.W., #900 20006; (202) 857-0540. Fax, (202) 659-1902. Frankie L. Trull, President.
General e-mail, info@nabr.org

Web, www.nabr.org

Membership: scientific and medical professional societies, academic institutions, and research-oriented corporations. Supports the humane use of animals in medical research, education, and product-safety assessment.

National Horse Protection League, *Washington Office,* *1000 Vermont Ave. N.W., #200 20005; (202) 293-0570. Fax, (202) 822-4787. Bryan Buchanan, Coordinator.* General e-mail, info@horse-protection.org

Web, www.horse-protection.org

Seeks to reduce the inhumane treatment of horses through legislative initiatives and education. Interests include bringing an end to slaughter and the export of horses for human consumption, and making racing safer and healthier for horses and riders. Provides information on responsible horse care and placement. (Headquarters in Chappaqua, N.Y.)

National Research Council (NRC), *Institute for Laboratory Animal Research, 500 5th St. N.W., #KECK 687 20001; (202) 334-2590. Fax, (202) 334-1687. Joanne Zurlo, Director.* General e-mail, ilar@nas.edu

Web, www.national-academies.org/ilar

Prepares reports on subjects of importance to the animal care and use community. Develops and makes available scientific and technical information on laboratory animals and other biological research resources for the scientific community, institutional animal care and use committees, the federal government, science educators and students, and the public.

Physicians Committee for Responsible Medicine (PCRM), *5100 Wisconsin Ave. N.W., #400 20016; (202) 686-2210. Fax, (202) 686-2216. Dr. Neal D. Barnard, President.* General e-mail, pcrm@pcrm.org

Web, www.pcrm.org

Membership: health care professionals, medical students, and laypersons interested in preventive medicine, nutrition, and higher standards in research. Investigates alternatives to animal use in medical research experimentation, product testing, and education.

Scientists Center for Animal Welfare, *7833 Walker Dr., #410, Greenbelt, MD 20770; (301) 345-3500. Fax, (301) 345-3503. Joseph Bielitzki, President.* General e-mail, info@scaw.com

Web, www.scaw.com

Promotes best practices in the humane care, use, and management of animals involved in research, testing, or education in laboratory, agricultural, wildlife, or other settings.

Fish

▶**AGENCIES**

Atlantic States Marine Fisheries Commission, *1444 Eye St. N.W., 6th Floor 20005; (202) 289-6400. Fax, (202) 289-6051. John V. O'Shea, Executive Director.*

General e-mail, info@asmfc.org

Web, www.asmfc.org

Interstate compact commission of marine fisheries representatives from fifteen states along the Atlantic seaboard. Assists states in developing joint fisheries programs; works with other fisheries organizations and the federal government on environmental, natural resource, and conservation issues.

Interior Dept. (DOI), *Fish and Wildlife and Parks, 1849 C St. N.W., #3156 20240; (202) 208-4416. Fax, (202) 208-4684. Vacant, Assistant Secretary.* Web, www.doi.gov

Responsible for programs associated with the development, conservation, and use of fish, wildlife, recreational, historical, and national park system resources. Coordinates marine environmental quality and biological resources programs with other federal agencies.

Justice Dept. (DOJ), *Environmental Crimes, 601 D St. N.W., 2nd Floor 20004 (mailing address: P.O. Box 23985, Washington, DC 20026-3985); (202) 305-0321. Fax, (202) 305-0396. Stacey H. Mitchell, Chief.* Web, www.usdoj.gov

Supervises criminal cases under federal maritime law and other laws protecting marine fish and mammals. Focuses on smugglers and black market dealers of protected wildlife.

Justice Dept. (DOJ), *Wildlife and Marine Resources, 601 D St. N.W., 3rd Floor 20004 (mailing address: P.O. Box 7369, Ben Franklin Station, Washington, DC 20044-7369); (202) 305-0210. Fax, (202) 305-0275. Jean E. Williams, Chief.* Web, www.usdoj.gov

Supervises civil cases under federal maritime law and other laws protecting marine fish and mammals.

National Oceanic and Atmospheric Administration (NOAA), *(Commerce Dept.), National Marine Fisheries Service, 1315 East-West Hwy., Silver Spring, MD 20910; (301) 713-2239. Fax, (301) 713-1940. James W. Balsiger, Assistant Administrator (Acting). Press, (301) 713-2370.* Web, www.nmfs.noaa.gov

Administers marine fishing regulations, including offshore fishing rights and international agreements; conducts marine resources research; studies use and management of these resources; administers the Magnuson-Stevens Fishery Conservation and Management Act; manages and protects marine resources, especially endangered species and marine mammals, within the exclusive economic zone.

U.S. Fish and Wildlife Service *(Interior Dept.), 1849 C St. N.W., #3256 20240; (202) 208-4717. Fax, (202) 208-6817. Rowan Gould, Director (Acting). Press, (202) 208-5634. Toll-free, (800) 344-9453.* Web, www.fws.gov

Works with federal and state agencies and nonprofits to conserve, protect, and enhance fish and wildlife and their habitats for the continuing benefit of the American people.

U.S. Fish and Wildlife Service *(Interior Dept.),* *Endangered Species, 1849 C St. N.W., #3242 20240; (202) 208-4646. Fax, (202) 208-5618. Bryan Arroyo, Assistant Director.*
Web, www.endangered.fws.gov

Monitors federal policy on fish and wildlife. Reviews all federal and federally licensed projects to determine environmental effect on fish and wildlife. Responsible for maintaining the endangered species list and for protecting and restoring species to healthy numbers.

U.S. Fish and Wildlife Service *(Interior Dept.),* *Fisheries and Habitat Conservation, 1849 C St. N.W., #3240 20240; (202) 208-6394. Fax, (202) 208-5618. Gary Frazer, Assistant Director.*
Web, www.fws.gov

Develops, manages, and protects interstate and international fisheries, including fisheries of the Great Lakes, fisheries on federal lands, aquatic ecosystems, endangered species of fish, and anadromous species. Administers the National Fish Hatchery System and the National Fish and Wildlife Resource Management Offices, as well as the Habitat and Conservation and Environmental Quality Divisions.

U.S. Geological Survey (USGS), *(Interior Dept.),* *Biological Resources, 12201 Sunrise Valley Dr., Reston, VA 20192; (703) 648-4050. Fax, (703) 648-7031. Susan D. Haseltine, Associate Director for Biology.*
Web, http://biology.usgs.gov

Performs research in support of biological resource management. Monitors and reports on the status of the nation's biotic resources, including fish resources. Conducts research on fish diseases, nutrition, and culture techniques. Studies ecology of the Great Lakes and the effects of pesticides and herbicides on fish.

▶**CONGRESS**

For a listing of relevant congressional committees and subcommittees, please see page 252 or the Appendix.

▶**NONGOVERNMENTAL**

American Fisheries Society (AFS), *5410 Grosvenor Lane, #110, Bethesda, MD 20814-2199; (301) 897-8616. Fax, (301) 897-8096. Gussam Rassam, Executive Director.*
General e-mail, main@fisheries.org
Web, www.fisheries.org

Membership: biologists and other scientists interested in fisheries. Promotes the fisheries profession, the advancement of fisheries science, and conservation of renewable aquatic resources. Monitors legislation and regulations.

Grocery Manufacturers Assn. (GMA), *1350 Eye St. N.W., #300 20005-3377; (202) 639-5900. Fax, (202) 639-5932. Pamela Bailey, President. Press, (202) 295-3938.*
General e-mail, info@gmaonline.org
Web, www.gmaonline.org

Membership: manufacturers and suppliers of processed and packaged food, drinks, and juice. Serves as industry liaison between seafood processors and the federal government. (Merger of the Grocery Manufacturers Assn. and the Food Products Assn.)

International Assn. of Fish and Wildlife Agencies, *444 N. Capitol St. N.W., #725 20001; (202) 624-7890. Fax, (202) 624-7891. Matt Hogan, Executive Director.*
General e-mail, info@iafwa.org
Web, www.fishwildlife.org

Membership: federal, state, and provincial fish and wildlife management agencies in the United States, Canada, and Mexico. Encourages balanced fish and wildlife resource management.

Marine Fish Conservation Network, *600 Pennsylvania Ave. S.E., #210 20003; (202) 543-5509. Fax, (202) 543-5774. Bruce Stedman, Executive Director.*
General e-mail, network@conservefish.org
Web, www.conservefish.org

Membership: environmental organizations, commercial and recreational fishing groups, aquariums, and marine science groups. Advocates for stronger protection of marine fish and promotes their long-term sustainability.

National Fisheries Institute, *7918 Jones Branch Dr., #700, McLean, VA 22102; (703) 752-8880. Fax, (703) 752-7583. John Connelly, President. Press, (703) 752-8891.*
General e-mail, contact@nfi.org
Web, www.aboutseafood.com

Membership: vessel owners and distributors, processors, wholesalers, importers, traders, and brokers of fish and shellfish. Monitors legislation and regulations on fisheries. Advocates eating seafood for health benefits.

Ocean Conservancy, *1300 19th St. N.W., 8th Floor 20036; (202) 429-5609. Fax, (202) 872-0619. Vikki N. Spruill, President.*
General e-mail, ocean@oceanconservancy.org
Web, www.oceanconservancy.org

Works to prevent the overexploitation of living marine resources, including fisheries, and to restore depleted marine wildlife populations through research, education, and science-based advocacy.

Trout Unlimited, *1300 N. 17th St., #500, Arlington, VA 22209-2404; (703) 522-0200. Fax, (703) 284-9400. Charles F. Gauvin, President.*
General e-mail, trout@tu.org
Web, www.tu.org

Membership: individuals interested in the protection and enhancement of cold-water fish and their habitat. Sponsors research projects with federal and state fisheries agencies; maintains programs for water-quality surveillance and cleanup of streams and lakes.

Wildlife and Marine Mammals

►AGENCIES

Animal and Plant Health Inspection Service (APHIS), (Agriculture Dept.), Wildlife Services, 1400
Independence Ave. S.W., #1624S 20250-3402; (202) 720-2054. Fax, (202) 690-0053. William H. Clay, Deputy Administrator.
Web, www.aphis.usda.gov/wildlife-damage

Works to minimize damage caused by wildlife to crops and livestock, natural resources, and human health and safety. Removes or eliminates predators and nuisance birds. Interests include aviation safety and coexistence of people and wildlife in suburban areas. Oversees the National Wildlife Research Center in Ft. Collins, Colo.

Forest Service (Agriculture Dept.), Watershed, Fish, Wildlife, Air, and Rare Plants, 201 14th St. S.W. 20024; (202) 205-1205. Fax, (202) 205-1599. Anne J. Zimmermann, Director.
Web, www.fs.fed.us

Provides national policy direction and management for watershed, fish, wildlife, air, and rare plants programs on lands managed by the Forest Service.

Interior Dept. (DOI), Bird Habitat Conservation, 4501 N. Fairfax Dr., Arlington, VA 22203 (mailing address: 4401 N. Fairfax Dr., MBSP 4075, Arlington, VA 22203-1610); (703) 358-1784. Fax, (703) 358-2282. Michael J. Johnson, Chief.
General e-mail, dbhc@fws.gov
Web, http://birdhabitat.fws.gov

Membership: government and private-sector conservation experts. Works to protect, restore, and manage wetlands and other habitats for migratory birds and other animals and to maintain migratory bird and waterfowl populations.

Interior Dept. (DOI), Fish and Wildlife and Parks, 1849 C St. N.W., #3156 20240; (202) 208-4416. Fax, (202) 208-4684. Vacant, Assistant Secretary.
Web, www.doi.gov

Responsible for programs associated with the development, conservation, and use of fish, wildlife, recreational, historical, and national park system resources. Coordinates marine environmental quality and biological resources programs with other federal agencies.

Justice Dept. (DOJ), Wildlife and Marine Resources, 601 D St. N.W., 3rd Floor 20004 (mailing address: P.O. Box 7369, Ben Franklin Station, Washington, DC 20044-7369); (202) 305-0210. Fax, (202) 305-0275. Jean E. Williams, Chief.
Web, www.usdoj.gov

Responsible for criminal enforcement and civil litigation under federal fish and wildlife conservation statutes, including protection of wildlife, fish, and plant resources within U.S. jurisdiction. Monitors interstate and foreign commerce of these resources.

Marine Mammal Commission, 4340 East-West Hwy., #700, Bethesda, MD 20814; (301) 504-0087. Fax, (301) 504-0099. Timothy J. Ragen, Executive Director.
General e-mail, mmc@mmc.gov
Web, www.mmc.gov

Established by Congress to ensure protection and conservation of marine mammals. Conducts research and makes recommendations on federal programs that affect marine mammals.

Migratory Bird Conservation Commission, 4401 N. Fairfax Dr., #622, MS ARLQ622, Arlington, VA 22203; (703) 358-1716. Fax, (703) 358-2223. Eric Alvarez, Secretary.
Web, http://realty.fws.gov/mbcc.html

Established by the Migratory Bird Conservation Act of 1929. Decides which areas to purchase for use as migratory bird refuges and the price at which they are acquired.

National Oceanic and Atmospheric Administration (NOAA), (Commerce Dept.), Protected Resources, 1315 East-West Hwy., 13th Floor, Silver Spring, MD 20910; (301) 713-2332. Fax, (301) 427-2520. Jim Lecky, Director.
Web, www.nmfs.noaa.gov/prot_res

Provides guidance on the conservation and protection of marine mammals and endangered species and on the conservation and restoration of their habitats. Develops national guidelines and policies for relevant research programs; prepares and reviews management and recovery plans and environmental impact analyses.

U.S. Fish and Wildlife Service (Interior Dept.), 1849 C St. N.W., #3256 20240; (202) 208-4717. Fax, (202) 208-6817. Rowan Gould, Director (Acting). Press, (202) 208-5634. Toll-free, (800) 344-9453.
Web, www.fws.gov

Works with federal and state agencies and nonprofits to conserve, protect, and enhance fish and wildlife and their habitats for the continuing benefit of the American people.

U.S. Fish and Wildlife Service (Interior Dept.), Bird Habitat Conservation, 4501 N. Fairfax Dr., #4000, MS 4075, Arlington, VA 22203; (703) 358-1784. Fax, (703) 358-2282. Michael Johnson, Chief.
Web, www.fws.gov/birdhabitat

Coordinates U.S. activities with Canada and Mexico to protect waterfowl habitats, restore waterfowl populations, and set research priorities under the North American Waterfowl Management Plan.

U.S. Fish and Wildlife Service (Interior Dept.), Endangered Species, 1849 C St. N.W., #3242 20240; (202) 208-4646. Fax, (202) 208-5618. Bryan Arroyo, Assistant Director.
Web, www.endangered.fws.gov

Monitors federal policy on fish and wildlife. Reviews all federal and federally licensed projects to determine environmental effect on fish and wildlife. Responsible for maintaining the endangered species list and for protecting and restoring species to healthy numbers.

U.S. Fish and Wildlife Service *(Interior Dept.)*, *National Wildlife Refuge System,* 1849 C St. N.W., #3251 20240; (202) 208-5333. Fax, (202) 208-3082. Gregory Siekaniec, Chief.
Web, www.fws.gov

Determines policy for the management of wildlife. Manages the National Wildlife Refuge System and land acquisition for wildlife refuges.

U.S. Geological Survey (USGS), *(Interior Dept.)*, *Biological Resources,* 12201 Sunrise Valley Dr., Reston, VA 20192; (703) 648-4050. Fax, (703) 648-7031. Susan D. Haseltine, Associate Director for Biology.
Web, http://biology.usgs.gov

Performs research in support of biological resource management. Monitors and reports on the status of the nation's biotic resources. Conducts research on fish and wildlife, including the effects of disease and environmental contaminants on wildlife populations. Studies endangered and other species.

►CONGRESS

For a listing of relevant congressional committees and subcommittees, please see page 252 or the Appendix.

►NONGOVERNMENTAL

Animal Welfare Institute, 900 Pennsylvania Ave. S.E. 20003 (mailing address: P.O. Box 3650, Washington, DC 20027); (202) 337-2332. Fax, (202) 446-2131. Cathy Liss, President.
Web, www.awionline.org

Educational group that opposes steel jaw leghold animal traps and supports the protection of marine mammals. Interests include preservation of endangered species, reform of cruel methods of raising food animals, and humane treatment of laboratory animals. (Merged with the Society for Animal Protective Legislation.)

Defenders of Wildlife, 1130 17th St. N.W. 20036; (202) 682-9400. Fax, (202) 682-1331. Rodger Schlickeisen, President. Toll-free, (800) 385-9712.
General e-mail, defenders@defenders.org

Web, www.defenders.org

Advocacy group that works to protect wild animals and plants in their natural communities. Interests include endangered species and biodiversity. Monitors legislation and regulations.

Ducks Unlimited, *Governmental Affairs, Washington Office,* 1301 Pennsylvania Ave. N.W., #402 20004; (202) 347-1530. Fax, (202) 347-1533. Scott Sutherland, Director.
Web, www.ducks.org

Promotes waterfowl and other wildlife conservation through activities aimed at developing and restoring natural nesting and migration habitats. (Headquarters in Memphis, Tenn.)

Humane Society of the United States, 2100 L St. N.W. 20037; (202) 452-1100. Fax, (202) 778-6132. Wayne Pacelle, President.
Web, www.hsus.org

Works for the humane treatment and protection of animals. Interests include protecting endangered wildlife and marine mammals and their habitats and ending inhumane or cruel conditions in zoos.

International Assn. of Fish and Wildlife Agencies, 444 N. Capitol St. N.W., #725 20001; (202) 624-7890. Fax, (202) 624-7891. Matt Hogan, Executive Director.
General e-mail, info@iafwa.org

Web, www.fishwildlife.org

Membership: federal, state, and provincial fish and wildlife management agencies in the United States, Canada, and Mexico. Encourages balanced fish and wildlife resource management.

Jane Goodall Institute, 4245 N. Fairfax Dr., #600, Arlington, VA 22203; (703) 682-9220. Fax, (703) 682-9312. Bill Johnston, President.
Web, www.janegoodall.org

Seeks to increase primate habitat conservation, expand noninvasive primate research, and promote activities that ensure the well-being of primates. (Affiliated with Jane Goodall Institutes in Canada, Europe, Asia, and Africa.)

National Fish and Wildlife Foundation, 1133 15th St. N.W., #1100 20005; (202) 857-0166. Fax, (202) 857-0162. Jeff Trandahl, Director.
General e-mail, info@nfwf.org

Web, www.nfwf.org

Forges partnerships between the public and private sectors in support of national and international conservation activities that identify and root out causes of environmental problems that affect fish, wildlife, and plants.

National Wildlife Federation, 11100 Wildlife Center Dr., Reston, VA 20190-5362; (703) 438-6000. Fax, (703) 438-3570. Larry J. Schweiger, President. Information, (800) 822-9919.
General e-mail, info@nwf.org

Web, www.nwf.org

Educational organization that promotes preservation of natural resources; provides information on wildlife.

National Wildlife Refuge Assn., 1901 Pennsylvania Ave. N.W., #407 20006; (202) 333-9075. Fax, (202) 333-9077. Evan Hirsche, President. Toll-free, (877) 396-6972.
General e-mail, nwra@refugeassociation.org

Web, www.refugeassociation.org

Works to improve management and protection of the National Wildlife Refuge System by providing information to administrators, Congress, and the public. Advocates adequate funding and improved policy guidance for the Refuge System; assists individual refuges with particular needs.

Nature Conservancy, *4245 N. Fairfax Dr., #100, Arlington, VA 22203-1606; (703) 841-5300. Fax, (703) 841-1283. Mark Tercek, President. Information, (800) 628-6860. General e-mail, comment@tnc.org*

Web, www.nature.org

Maintains an international system of natural sanctuaries; acquires land to protect endangered species and habitats. Collaborates with other conservation organizations, country and local governments, corporations, indigenous peoples and communities, and individuals such as fishermen, ranchers, and farmers to create management plans for natural areas.

Ocean Conservancy, *1300 19th St. N.W., 8th Floor 20036; (202) 429-5609. Fax, (202) 872-0619. Vikki N. Spruill, President.*

General e-mail, ocean@oceanconservancy.org

Web, www.oceanconservancy.org

Works to conserve the diversity and abundance of life in the oceans and coastal areas, to prevent the overexploitation of living marine resources and the degradation of marine ecosystems, and to restore depleted marine wildlife populations and their ecosystems.

Wildlife Habitat Council, *8737 Colesville Rd., #800, Silver Spring, MD 20910; (301) 588-8994. Fax, (301) 588-4629. Robert J. Johnson, President.*

General e-mail, whc@wildlifehc.org

Web, www.wildlifehc.org

Membership: corporations, conservation groups, and individuals. Supports use of underdeveloped private lands for the benefit of wildlife, fish, and plant life. Provides technical assistance and educational programs; fosters information sharing among members.

The Wildlife Society, *5410 Grosvenor Lane, #200, Bethesda, MD 20814-2144; (301) 897-9770. Fax, (301) 530-2471. Michael Hutchins, Executive Director.*

General e-mail, tws@wildlife.org

Web, www.wildlife.org

Membership: wildlife biologists and resource management specialists. Provides information on management techniques, sponsors conferences, maintains list of job opportunities for members.

World Wildlife Fund (WWF), *1250 24th St. N.W. 20037-1193 (mailing address: P.O. Box 97180, Washington, DC 20090-7180); (202) 293-4800. Fax, (202) 293-9211. Carter S. Roberts, President.*

Web, www.worldwildlife.org

International conservation organization that supports and conducts scientific research and conservation projects to promote biological diversity and to save endangered species and their habitats. Awards grants for habitat protection.

POLLUTION AND TOXINS

▶**AGENCIES**

Environmental Protection Agency (EPA), *Enforcement and Compliance Assurance, 1200 Pennsylvania Ave. N.W., #3204, MC 2201A 20460; (202) 564-2440. Fax, (202) 501-3842. Catherine McCabe, Assistant Administrator (Acting).*

Web, www.epa.gov

Principal adviser to the administrator on enforcement of standards for air, water, toxic substances and pesticides; hazardous and solid waste management; and emergency preparedness programs. Investigates criminal and civil violations of environmental standards. Oversees federal facilities' environmental compliance and site cleanup. Serves as the EPA's liaison office for federal agency compliance with the National Environmental Policy Act. Manages environmental review of other agencies' projects and activities. Coordinates the EPA's environmental justice programs.

Justice Dept. (DOJ), *Environmental Crimes, 601 D St. N.W., 2nd Floor 20004 (mailing address: P.O. Box 23985, Washington, DC 20026-3985); (202) 305-0321. Fax, (202) 305-0396. Stacey H. Mitchell, Chief.*

Web, www.usdoj.gov

Conducts criminal enforcement actions on behalf of the United States for all environmental protection statutes, including air, water, pesticides, hazardous waste, wetland matters investigated by the Environmental Protection Agency, and other criminal environmental enforcement.

Justice Dept. (DOJ), *Environmental Defense, 601 D St. N.W., #8000 20004 (mailing address: P.O. Box 23986, Washington, DC 20026-3986); (202) 514-2219. Fax, (202) 514-8865. Letitia J. Grishaw, Chief.*

Web, www.usdoj.gov

Conducts litigation on air, water, noise, pesticides, solid waste, toxic substances, Superfund, and wetlands in cooperation with the Environmental Protection Agency; represents the EPA in suits involving judicial review of EPA actions; represents the U.S. Army Corps of Engineers in cases involving dredge-and-fill activity in navigable waters and adjacent wetlands; represents the Coast Guard in oil and hazardous spill cases; defends all federal agencies in environmental litigation.

Justice Dept. (DOJ), *Environmental Enforcement, 601 D St. N.W., #2121 20004 (mailing address: P.O. Box 7611, Ben Franklin Station, Washington, DC 20044-7611); (202) 514-4624. Fax, (202) 514-0097. Bruce S. Gelber, Chief.*

Web, www.usdoj.gov

Conducts civil enforcement actions on behalf of the United States for all environmental protection statutes, including air, water, pesticides, hazardous waste, wetland matters investigated by the Environmental Protection Agency, and other civil environmental enforcement.

▶**NONGOVERNMENTAL**

American Academy of Environmental Engineers,
130 Holiday Court, #100, Annapolis, MD 21401; (410)
266-3311. Fax, (410) 266-7653. Joseph S. Cavarretta,
Executive Director.
General e-mail, info@aaee.net

Web, www.aaee.net

Membership: state-licensed environmental engineers who have passed examinations in environmental engineering specialties, including general environment, air pollution control, solid waste management, hazardous waste management, industrial hygiene, radiation protection, water supply, and wastewater.

Environmental Industry Assns. (EIA), *4301 Connecticut*
Ave. N.W., #300 20008-2304; (202) 244-4700. Fax, (202)
966-4818. Bruce J. Parker, President.
General e-mail, membership@envasns.org

Web, www.envasns.org

Membership: trade associations from the waste services and environmental technology industries. Represents the National Solid Waste Management Assn. and the Waste Equipment Technology Assn.

Air Pollution

▶**AGENCIES**

Environmental Protection Agency (EPA), *Air and*
Radiation, *1200 Pennsylvania Ave. N.W., #5426, MC*
6101A 20004; (202) 564-7400. Fax, (202) 501-0986. Beth
Craig, Principal Deputy (Acting).
Web, www.epa.gov/air/index.html

Administers air quality standards and planning programs of the Clean Air Act Amendment of 1990; operates the Air and Radiation Docket and Information Center. Supervises the Office of Air Quality Planning and Standards in Durham, N.C., which develops air quality standards and provides information on air pollution control issues, including industrial air pollution. Administers the Air Pollution Technical Information Center in Research Triangle Park, N.C., which collects and provides technical literature on air pollution.

Environmental Protection Agency (EPA), *Atmospheric*
Programs, *1310 L St. N.W., 10th Floor, MC 6201J 20005;*
(202) 343-9140. Fax, (202) 343-2210. Brian J. McLean,
Director.
Web, www.epa.gov/airprogm/oar/oap.html

Responsible for acid rain and global protection programs; examines strategies for preventing atmospheric pollution and mitigating climate change.

Environmental Protection Agency (EPA), *Compliance*
Assessment and Media Programs, *1200 Pennsylvania*
Ave. N.W., #7138, MC 2223A 20460; (202) 564-2300.
Fax, (202) 564-0050. Richard F. Duffy, Director (Acting).
Web, www.epa.gov

Responsible for development and implementation of a national program of compliance concerning lead regulations and matters related to the Clean Air Act, Clean Water Act, Resource Conservation and Recovery Act, and Oil Pollution Act.

Environmental Protection Agency (EPA), *Radiation*
and Indoor Air, *1310 L St. N.W., 4th Floor, MC 6601J*
20005; (202) 343-9320. Fax, (202) 343-2395. Elizabeth
Cotsworth, Director.
Web, www.epa.gov/oar/oria.html

Administers indoor air quality control programs, including those regulating radon and environmental tobacco smoke; trains building managers in sound operation practices to promote indoor air quality.

Federal Aviation Administration (FAA), *(Transportation*
Dept.), Environment and Energy, *800 Independence Ave.*
S.W., #900W 20591; (202) 267-3576. Fax, (202) 267-5594.
Carl E. Burleson, Director.
Web, www.faa.gov/about/office_org/headquarters_offices/aep

Develops government standards for aircraft noise and emissions.

U.S. Geological Survey (USGS), *(Interior Dept.), Energy*
Resources Program, *12201 Sunrise Valley Dr., Reston, VA*
20192 (mailing address: 915A National Center, Reston, VA
20192); (703) 648-6421. Fax, (703) 648-5464. Brenda S.
Pierce, Program Coordinator.
General e-mail, gd-energyprogram@usgs.gov

Web, http://energy.usgs.gov

Conducts research on geologically based energy resources of the United States and the world; estimates energy resource availability and recoverability; anticipates and mitigates deleterious environmental impacts of energy resource extraction and use.

▶**CONGRESS**

For a listing of relevant congressional committees and subcommittees, please see page 252 or the Appendix.

▶**NONGOVERNMENTAL**

Alliance for Responsible Atmospheric Policy, *2111*
Wilson Blvd., 8th Floor, Arlington, VA 22201; (703) 243-
0344. Fax, (703) 243-2874. David Stirpe, Executive
Director.
General e-mail, info@arap.org

Web, www.arap.org

Coalition of users and producers of chlorofluorocarbons (CFCs). Seeks further study of the ozone depletion theory.

Asbestos Information Assn./North America, *Arlington,*
VA 22202-9227; (703) 560-2980. Fax, (703) 560-2981. B.J.
Pigg, President.
General e-mail, aiabjpigg@aol.com

Membership: firms that manufacture, sell, and use products containing asbestos fiber and those that mine, mill, and sell asbestos. Provides information on asbestos and health and on industry efforts to eliminate problems associated with asbestos dust; serves as liaison between the industry and federal and state governments.

American Lung Assn., *1301 Pennsylvania Ave. N.W., #800 20004-1725; (202) 785-3355. Fax, (202) 452-1805. Charles D. Connor, President; Paul Billings, Vice President of National Policy and Advocacy.*
Web, www.lungusa.org

Promotes improved lung health and the prevention of lung disease through research, education, and advocacy. Interests include antismoking campaigns; lung-related biomedical research; air pollution; and all lung diseases, including asthma, COPD, and lung cancer.

Center for Auto Safety, *1825 Connecticut Ave. N.W., #330 20009-5708; (202) 328-7700. Fax, (202) 387-0140. General e-mail, accounts@autosafety.org*
Web, www.autosafety.org

Public interest organization that conducts research on air pollution caused by auto emissions; monitors fuel economy regulations.

Center for Clean Air Policy, *750 1st. St. N.E., #940 20002; (202) 408-9260. Fax, (202) 408-8896. Ned Helme, President.*
General e-mail, general@ccap.org or tassistant@ccap.org
Web, www.ccap.org

Membership: governors, corporations, environmentalists, and academicians. Analyzes economic and environmental effects of air pollution and related environmental problems. Serves as a liaison among government, corporate, community, and environmental groups.

Climate Institute, *900 17th St. N.W., #700 20006; (202) 547-0104. Fax, (202) 547-0111. John C. Topping Jr., President.*
General e-mail, info@climate.org
Web, www.climate.org

Educates the public and policymakers on climate change (greenhouse effect, or global warming) and on the depletion of the ozone layer. Develops strategies on mitigating climate change in developing countries and in North America.

Environmental Defense, *Washington Office, 1875 Connecticut Ave. N.W., #600 20009-5728; (202) 387-3500. Fax, (202) 234-6049. Michael Roach, Office Manager. Information, (800) 684-3322. Press, (202) 572-3235.*
Web, www.edf.org

Citizens' interest group staffed by lawyers, economists, and scientists. Conducts research and provides information on pollution prevention, environmental health, and protection of the Amazon rainforest and the ozone layer. (Headquarters in New York.)

Manufacturers of Emission Controls Assn., *1730 M St. N.W., #206 20036; (202) 296-4797. Fax, (202) 331-1388. Joseph Kubsh, Executive Director.*

General e-mail, info@meca.org
Web, www.meca.org

Membership: manufacturers of motor vehicle emission control equipment. Provides information on emission technology and industry capabilities.

Pew Center on Global Climate Change, *2101 Wilson Blvd., #550, Arlington, VA 22201; (703) 516-4146. Fax, (703) 841-1422. Eileen Claussen, President.*
Web, www.pewclimate.org

Independent organization that issues information and promotes discussion by policymakers on the science, economics, and policy of climate change.

Hazardous Materials

► **AGENCIES**

Agency for Toxic Substances and Disease Registry (Health and Human Services Dept.), Washington Office, *395 E St. S.W., #9100 20201; (202) 245-0600. Fax, (202) 245-0602. Barbara A. Rogers, Associate Administrator. Press, (770) 488-0700.*
Web, www.atsdr.cdc.gov/legislation

Works with federal, state, and local agencies to minimize or eliminate adverse effects of exposure to toxic substances at spill and waste disposal sites. Maintains a registry of persons exposed to hazardous substances and of diseases and illnesses resulting from exposure to hazardous or toxic substances. Maintains inventory of hazardous substances and registry of sites closed or restricted because of contamination by hazardous material. (Headquarters in Atlanta, Ga.)

Defense Dept. (DoD), *Installations and Environment, 3400 Defense Pentagon, #3B856A 20301-3400; (703) 695-2880. Fax, (703) 693-7011. Wayne Arny, Deputy Under Secretary.*
Web, www.acq.osd.mil/ie

Oversees and offers policy guidance for all Defense Dept. installations and environmental programs.

Environmental Protection Agency (EPA), *Chemical Control, 1200 Pennsylvania Ave. N.W., #4146, MC 7405M 20460; (202) 564-4760. Fax, (202) 564-4745. Jim Willis, Director.*
Web, www.epa.gov

Selects and implements control measures for new and existing chemicals that present a risk to human health and the environment. Oversees and manages regulatory evaluation and decision-making processes. Evaluates alternative remedial control measures under the Toxic Substances Control Act and makes recommendations concerning the existence of unreasonable risk from exposure to chemicals. Develops generic and chemical-specific rules for new chemicals.

Environmental Protection Agency (EPA), *Emergency Management, 1200 Pennsylvania Ave. N.W., #1448, MC*

5104A 20460; (202) 564-8600. Fax, (202) 564-8222. Deborah Y. Dietrich, Director. Toll-free hotline, (800) 535-0202.
Web, www.epa.gov/oem

Develops and administers chemical emergency preparedness and prevention programs; reviews effectiveness of programs; prepares community right-to-know regulations. Provides guidance materials, technical assistance, and training. Implements the preparedness and community right-to-know provisions of the Superfund Amendments and Reauthorization Act of 1986.

Environmental Protection Agency (EPA), *Enforcement and Compliance Assurance, 1200 Pennsylvania Ave. N.W., #3204, MC 2201A 20460; (202) 564-2440. Fax, (202) 501-3842. Catherine McCabe, Assistant Administrator (Acting).*
Web, www.epa.gov

Enforces laws that protect public health and the environment from hazardous materials, pesticides, and toxic substances.

Environmental Protection Agency (EPA), *Pollution Prevention and Toxics, 1201 Constitution Ave. N.W., #3166 EPA East, MC 7401M 20460; (202) 564-3810. Fax, (202) 564-0575. Wendy Cleland-Hamnett, Director (Acting). Information, (202) 554-1404.*
Web, www.epa.gov/oppts

Assesses the health and environmental hazards of existing chemical substances and mixtures; collects information on chemical use, exposure, and effects; maintains inventory of existing chemical substances; reviews new chemicals and regulates the manufacture, distribution, use, and disposal of harmful chemicals.

Environmental Protection Agency (EPA), *Prevention, Pesticides, and Toxic Substances (OPPTS), 1200 Pennsylvania Ave. N.W., #3130 EPA-E, MS 7101M 20460-7101; (202) 564-2902. Fax, (202) 564-0801. James J. Jones, Assistant Administrator (Acting). Pollution prevention and toxic substances, (202) 564-3810.*
Web, www.epa.gov/oppts

Studies and makes recommendations for regulating chemical substances under the Toxic Substances Control Act; compiles list of chemical substances subject to the act; registers, controls, and regulates use of pesticides and toxic substances.

Environmental Protection Agency (EPA), *Solid Waste and Emergency Response, 1200 Pennsylvania Ave. N.W., MC 5101T 20460; (202) 566-0200. Fax, (202) 566-0207. Barry N. Breen, Assistant Administrator (Acting). Superfund/Resource conservation and recovery hotline, (800) 424-9346; local, (703) 412-9810. TTY, (800) 553-7672; local, (703) 412-3323.*
Web, www.epa.gov/swerrims

Administers and enforces the Superfund act; manages the handling, cleanup, and disposal of hazardous wastes.

Housing and Urban Development Dept. (HUD),
Healthy Homes and Lead Hazard Control, 451 7th St.

S.W., #8236 20410; (202) 708-0310. Fax, (202) 755-1000. Jon L. Gant, Director.
Web, www.hud.gov/lea

Advises HUD offices, other agencies, health authorities, and the housing industry on lead poisoning prevention. Develops regulations for lead-based paint; conducts research; makes grants to state and local governments for lead hazard reduction and inspection of housing.

Justice Dept. (DOJ), *Environmental Enforcement, 601 D St. N.W., #2121 20004 (mailing address: P.O. Box 7611, Ben Franklin Station, Washington, DC 20044-7611); (202) 514-4624. Fax, (202) 514-0097. Bruce S. Gelber, Chief.*
Web, www.usdoj.gov

Represents the United States in civil cases under environmental laws that involve the handling, storage, treatment, transportation, and disposal of hazardous waste. Recovers federal money spent to clean up hazardous waste sites or sues defendants to clean up sites under Superfund.

National Response Center *(Homeland Security Dept.), 2100 2nd St. S.W., #2111B 20593-0001; (202) 267-2428. Fax, (202) 267-1322. Syed Qadir, Chief. TTY, (202) 267-4477. Hotline, (800) 424-8802; local, (202) 267-2675. General e-mail, lst-nrcinfo@comdt.uscg.mil*
Web, www.nrc.uscg.mil

Maintains twenty-four-hour hotline for reporting oil spills, hazardous materials accidents, chemical releases, or known or suspected terrorist threats. Notifies appropriate federal officials to reduce the effects of accidents.

National Transportation Safety Board, *Railroad, Pipeline, and Hazardous Materials, 490 L'Enfant Plaza East S.W., #RPH1 20594; (202) 314-6460. Fax, (202) 314-6482. Bob Chipkevich, Director.*
Web, www.ntsb.gov

Investigates railroad, pipeline hazardous materials, natural gas, and liquid pipeline accidents and other accidents involving the transportation of hazardous materials.

Pipeline and Hazardous Materials Safety Administration *(Transportation Dept.), 1200 New Jersey Ave. S.E., #E27-300 20590; (202) 366-4433. Fax, (202) 366-3666. Vacant, Administrator. Hazardous Materials Information Center, (800) 467-4922. To report an incident, (800) 424-8802.*
Web, www.phmsa.dot.gov

Oversees the safe and secure movement of hazardous materials to industry and consumers by all modes of transportation, including pipelines. Works to eliminate transportation-related deaths and injuries. Promotes transportation solutions to protect communities and the environment.

Pipeline and Hazardous Materials Safety Administration *(Transportation Dept.), Hazardous Materials Safety, 1200 New Jersey Ave. S.E., E21-317 20590; (202) 366-0656. Fax, (202) 366-5713. Theodore Willke, Associate Administrator.*

General e-mail, phmsa.hmhazmatsafety@dot.gov

Web, http://phmsa.dot.gov

Designates substances as hazardous materials and regulates their transportation in interstate commerce; coordinates international standards regulations.

Pipeline and Hazardous Materials Safety Administration (Transportation Dept.), Pipeline Safety, 1200 New Jersey Ave. S.E., E24-455 20590; (202) 366-4595. Fax, (202) 366-4566. Jeffrey D. Wiese, Associate Administrator (Acting).

General e-mail, phmsa.pipelinesafety@dot.gov

Web, http://phmsa.dot.gov

Issues and enforces federal regulations for hazardous liquids pipeline safety.

State Dept., Environmental Policy, 2201 C St. N.W., #2657 20520; (202) 647-9266. Fax, (202) 647-5947. Daniel Fantozzi, Director.

Web, www.state.gov

Advances U.S. interests internationally regarding multilateral environmental organizations, chemical waste and other pollutants, and bilateral and regional environmental policies.

►CONGRESS

For a listing of relevant congressional committees and subcommittees, please see page 252 or the Appendix.

►NONGOVERNMENTAL

Alliance of Hazardous Materials Professionals, 9650 Rockville Pike, Bethesda, MD 20814; (301) 634-7430. Fax, (301) 634-7431. A. Cedric Calhoun, Executive Director. Toll-free, (800) 437-0137.

General e-mail, academy@achmm.org

Web, www.achmm.org

Membership: professionals who work with hazardous materials and environmental, health, and safety issues. Offers professional development and networking opportunities to members. Members must be certified by the Institute of Hazardous Materials Management (IHMM).

Center for Health, Environment, and Justice, 150 S. Washington St., #300, Falls Church, VA 22046-2921 (mailing address: P.O. Box 6806, Falls Church, VA 22040-6806); (703) 237-2249. Fax, (703) 237-8389. Lois Marie Gibbs, Executive Director.

General e-mail, chej@chej.org

Web, www.chej.org

Provides citizens' groups, individuals, and municipalities with support and information on solid and hazardous waste. Sponsors workshops, a speakers bureau, leadership development conference, and convention. Operates a toxicity data bank on the environmental and health effects of common chemical compounds; maintains a registry of technical experts to assist in solid and

hazardous waste problems; gathers information on polluting corporations.

Chlorine Institute Inc., 1300 Wilson Blvd., Arlington, VA 22209; (703) 741-5760. Fax, (703) 741-6068. Arthur Dungan, President.

General e-mail, aonna@cl2.com

Web, www.chlorineinstitute.org

Safety, health, and environmental protection center of the chlor-alkali (chlorine, caustic soda, caustic potash, and hydrogen chloride) industry. Interests include employee health and safety, resource conservation and pollution abatement, control of chlorine emergencies, product specifications, and public and community relations. Publishes technical pamphlets and drawings.

Consumer Specialty Products Assn., 900 17th St. N.W., #300 20006; (202) 872-8110. Fax, (202) 872-8114. Christopher Cathcart, President.

General e-mail, info@cspa.org

Web, www.cspa.org

Membership: manufacturers, marketers, packagers, and suppliers in the chemical specialties industry. Focus includes cleaning products and detergents, nonagricultural pesticides, disinfectants, automotive and industrial products, polishes and floor finishes, antimicrobials, air care products and candles, and aerosol products. Monitors scientific developments; conducts surveys and research; provides chemical safety information and consumer education programs; sponsors National Inhalants and Poisons Awareness and Aerosol Education Bureau. Monitors legislation and regulations.

Dangerous Goods Advisory Council, 1100 H St. N.W., #740 20005; (202) 289-4550. Fax, (202) 289-4074. Michael Morrissette, President.

General e-mail, info@dgac.org

Web, www.dgac.org

Membership: shippers, carriers, container manufacturers and conditioners, emergency response and spill cleanup companies, and trade associations. Promotes safety in the domestic and international transportation of hazardous materials. Provides information and educational services; sponsors conferences, workshops, and seminars. Advocates uniform hazardous materials regulations. (Formerly Hazardous Materials Advisory Council.)

Environmental Technology Council, 1112 16th St. N.W. 20036; (202) 783-0870. Fax, (202) 737-2038. David R. Case, Executive Director. Press, (202) 783-0870, ext. 202.

General e-mail, mail@etc.org

Web, www.etc.org

Membership: environmental service firms. Interests include the recycling, detoxification, and disposal of hazardous and industrial waste and cleanup of contaminated industrial sites; works to encourage permanent and technology-based solutions to environmental problems. Provides the public with information.

Institute of Hazardous Materials Management (IHMM), *11900 Parklawn Dr., #450, Rockville, MD 20852-2624; (301) 984-8969. Fax, (301) 984-1516. James Gaidry, Executive Director.*

General e-mail, ihmminfo@ihmm.org

Web, www.ihmm.org

Seeks to educate professionals and the general public about proper handling of hazardous materials. Administers the Certified Hazardous Materials Manager program.

International Assn. of Heat and Frost Insulators and Allied Workers, *9602 Martin Luther King Hwy., Lanham, MD 20706-1839; (301) 731-9101. Fax, (301) 731-5058. James A. Grogan, President.*

General e-mail, iiiatf@insulators.org

Web, www.insulators.org

Membership: approximately 18,000 workers in insulation industries. Helps members negotiate pay, benefits, and better working conditions; conducts training programs and workshops. Monitors legislation and regulations. (Affiliated with the AFL-CIO.)

National Insulation Assn., *12100 Sunset Hills Rd., #330, Reston, VA 20109-3233; (703) 464-6422. Fax, (703) 464-6896. Michele M. Jones, Executive Vice President.*

General e-mail, niainfo@insulation.org

Web, www.insulation.org

Membership: companies in the commercial and industrial insulation industries, including contractors, manufacturers, distributors, and fabricators. Monitors legislation and regulations.

Rachel Carson Council Inc., *P.O. Box 10779, Silver Spring, MD 20914; (301) 593-7507. Fax, (301) 593-7508. Diana Post, President.*

General e-mail, rccouncil@aol.com

Web, www.rachelcarsoncouncil.org

Acts as a clearinghouse for information on pesticides and alternatives to their use; maintains extensive data on toxicity and the effects of pesticides on humans, domestic animals, and wildlife. Library open to the public by appointment.

Radiation Protection

▶AGENCIES

Armed Forces Radiobiological Research Institute *(Defense Dept.), 8901 Wisconsin Ave., Bethesda, MD 20889-5603; (301) 295-1210. Fax, (301) 295-4967. Col. Patricia K. Lillis-Hearne (MC, USA), Director. Public Affairs, (301) 295-1953.*

Web, www.afrri.usuhs.mil

Serves as the principal ionizing radiation radiobiology research laboratory under the jurisdiction of the Uniformed Services of the Health Sciences. Participates in international conferences and projects.

Environmental Protection Agency (EPA), *Radiation and Indoor Air, 1310 L St. N.W., 4th Floor, MC 6601J 20005; (202) 343-9320. Fax, (202) 343-2395. Elizabeth Cotsworth, Director.*

Web, www.epa.gov/oar/oria.html

Establishes standards to regulate the amount of radiation discharged into the environment from uranium mining and milling projects and other activities that result in radioactive emissions; and to ensure safe disposal of radioactive waste. Fields a Radiological Emergency Response Team. Administers the nationwide Environmental Radiation Ambient Monitoring System (ERAMS), which analyzes environmental radioactive contamination.

Food and Drug Administration (FDA), *(Health and Human Services Dept.), Center for Devices and Radiological Health, 9200 Corporate Blvd., #100E, Rockville, MD 20850; (240) 276-3939. Fax, (240) 276-3943. Daniel G. Schultz, Director.*

Web, www.fda.gov/cdrh

Administers national programs to control exposure to radiation; establishes standards for emissions from consumer and medical products; conducts factory inspections. Accredits and certifies mammography facilities and personnel; provides physicians and consumers with guidelines on radiation-emitting products. Conducts research, training, and educational programs.

▶NONGOVERNMENTAL

Institute for Science and International Security, *236 Massachusetts Ave. N.E., #500 20002; (202) 547-3633. Fax, (202) 547-3634. David Albright, President.*

General e-mail, isis@isis-online.org

Web, www.isis-online.org

Analyzes scientific and policy issues affecting national and international security, including the problems of war, regional and global arms races, the spread of nuclear weapons, and the environmental, health, and safety hazards of nuclear weapons production.

National Council on Radiation Protection and Measurements (NCRP), *7910 Woodmont Ave., #400, Bethesda, MD 20814-3095; (301) 657-2652. Fax, (301) 907-8768. David A. Schauer, Executive Director. Information, (800) 229-2652.*

General e-mail, ncrp@ncrponline.org; for publications, www.ncrppublications.org

Web, www.ncrponline.org

Nonprofit organization chartered by Congress that collects and analyzes information and provides recommendations on radiation protection and measurement. Studies radiation emissions from household items and from office and medical equipment. Holds annual conference; publishes reports on radiation protection and measurement.

Recycling and Solid Waste

▶AGENCIES

Environmental Protection Agency (EPA), *Solid Waste and Emergency Response,* 1200 Pennsylvania Ave. N.W., MC 5101T 20460; (202) 566-0200. Fax, (202) 566-0207. Barry N. Breen, Assistant Administrator (Acting). Superfund/Resource conservation and recovery hotline, (800) 424-9346; local, (703) 412-9810. TTY, (800) 553-7672; local, (703) 412-3323.
Web, www.epa.gov/swerrims

Administers and enforces the Resource Conservation and Recovery Act.

▶CONGRESS

For a listing of relevant congressional committees and subcommittees, please see page 252 or the Appendix.

▶NONGOVERNMENTAL

Alliance of Foam Packaging Recyclers (AFPR), *1298 Cronson Blvd., #201, Crofton, MD 21114; (410) 451-8340. Fax, (410) 451-8343. Betsy Steiner, Executive Director. Information, (800) 944-8448.*
General e-mail, info@epspackaging.org

Web, www.epspackaging.org

Membership: companies that recycle foam packaging material. Coordinates national network of collection centers for postconsumer foam packaging products; helps to establish new collection centers.

American Chemistry Council, *1300 Wilson Blvd., Arlington, VA 22209; (703) 741-5000. Fax, (703) 741-6000. Cal Dooley, President.*
Web, www.americanchemistry.com

Seeks to increase plastics recycling; conducts research on disposal of plastic products; sponsors research on waste-handling methods, incineration, and degradation; supports programs that test alternative waste management technologies. Monitors legislation and regulations. (Merged with Plastic Foodservice Packaging Group.)

Assn. of State and Territorial Solid Waste Management Officials, *444 N. Capitol St. N.W., #315 20001; (202) 624-5828. Fax, (202) 624-7875. Mary Zdanowicz, Executive Director.*
Web, www.astswmo.org

Membership: state and territorial solid waste management officials. Works with the Environmental Protection Agency to develop policy on solid and hazardous waste.

Container Recycling Institute, *1776 Massachusetts Ave. N.W., #800 20036-1904; (202) 263-0999. Fax, (202) 263-0949. Pat Franklin, Executive Director.*
General e-mail, info@container-recycling.org

Web, www.container-recycling.org

Studies alternatives for reducing container and packaging waste; researches container and packaging reuse and recycling options; serves as an information clearinghouse on container deposit legislation.

Environmental Industry Assns. (EIA), *4301 Connecticut Ave. N.W., #300 20008-2304; (202) 244-4700. Fax, (202) 966-4818. Bruce J. Parker, President.*
General e-mail, membership@envasns.org

Web, www.envasns.org

Membership: organizations engaged in refuse collection, processing, and disposal. Provides information on solid and hazardous waste management and waste equipment; sponsors workshops.

Foodservice Packaging Institute (FPI), *150 S. Washington St., #204, Falls Church, VA 22046; (703) 538-2800. Fax, (703) 538-2187. John Burke, President.*
General e-mail, fpi@fpi.org

Web, www.fpi.org

Membership: manufacturers, suppliers, and distributors of disposable products used in food service, packaging, and consumer products. Promotes the use of disposables for commercial and home use.

Glass Packaging Institute, *700 N. Fairfax St., #510, Alexandria, VA 22314; (703) 684-6359. Fax, (703) 684-6048. Joseph J. Cattaneo, President.*
General e-mail, info@gpi.org

Web, www.gpi.org

Membership: manufacturers of glass containers and their suppliers. Promotes industry policies to protect the environment, conserve natural resources, and reduce energy consumption; conducts research; monitors legislation affecting the industry. Interests include glass recycling.

Institute for Local Self-Reliance, *927 15th St. N.W., 4th Floor 20005; (202) 898-1610. Fax, (202) 898-1612. Neil N. Seldman, President.*
General e-mail, info@ilsr.org

Web, www.ilsr.org

Conducts research and provides technical assistance on environmentally sound economic development for government, small businesses, and community organizations. Advocates the development of a materials policy at local, state, and regional levels to reduce per capita consumption of raw materials and to shift from dependence on fossil fuels to reliance on renewable resources.

Institute of Scrap Recycling Industries, Inc., *1615 L St. N.W., #600 20036-5610; (202) 662-8500. Fax, (202) 626-0900. Robin K. Wiener, President.*
General e-mail, isri@isri.org

Web, www.isri.org

Represents processors, brokers, and consumers of scrap and recyclable paper, glass, plastic, textiles, rubber, and ferrous and nonferrous metals.

Integrated Waste Services Assn., *1730 Rhode Island Ave. N.W., #700 20036; (202) 467-6240. Fax, (202) 289-3588. Edward Michaels, President.*

General e-mail, imcneil@wte.org

Web, www.wte.org

Membership: companies that design, build, and operate resource recovery facilities. Promotes integrated solutions to municipal solid waste management issues. Encourages the use of waste-to-energy technology.

National Recycling Coalition, *805 15th St. N.W., #425 20005; (202) 789-1430. Fax, (202) 789-1431. Ed Skernolis, Executive Director.*

General e-mail, info@nrc-recycle.org

Web, www.nrc-recycle.org

Membership: public officials; community recycling groups; local, state, and national agencies; environmentalists; waste haulers; solid waste disposal consultants; and private recycling companies. Encourages recycling to reduce waste, preserve resources, and promote economic development.

Secondary Materials and Recycled Textiles Assn. (SMART), *131 E. Broad St., #206, Falls Church, VA 22046; (703) 538-1000. Fax, (703) 538-6305. Peter Mayberry, Executive Director.*

General e-mail, maryann@smartasn.org

Web, www.smartasn.org

Membership: organizations and individuals involved in producing, shipping, and distributing recycled textiles and other textile products. Sponsors educational programs; publishes newsletters.

Solid Waste Assn. of North America (SWANA), *1100 Wayne Ave., #700, Silver Spring, MD 20910-7219 (mailing address: P.O. Box 7219, Silver Spring, MD 20907-7219); (301) 585-2898. Fax, (301) 589-7068. John Skinner, Executive Director.*

Web, www.swana.org

Membership: government and private industry officials who manage municipal solid waste programs. Interests include waste reduction, collection, recycling, combustion, and disposal. Conducts training and certification programs. Operates solid waste information clearinghouse. Monitors legislation and regulations.

U.S. Conference of Mayors, *Municipal Waste Management Assn., 1620 Eye St. N.W., #400 20006; (202) 293-7330. Fax, (202) 429-0422. J. Thomas Cochran, Executive Director.*

General e-mail, info@usmayors.org

Web, www.usmayors.org/mwma

Organization of local governments and private companies involved in planning and developing solid waste management programs, including pollution prevention, waste-to-energy, and recycling. Assists communities with financing, environmental assessments, and associated policy implementation.

Water Pollution

▶AGENCIES

Environmental Protection Agency (EPA), *Ground Water and Drinking Water, 1200 Pennsylvania Ave. N.W., EPA East, MC 4601M 20460; (202) 564-3750. Fax, (202) 564-3753. Cynthia Dougherty, Director. Toll-free hotline, (800) 426-4791.*

Web, www.epa.gov/ogwdw

Develops standards for the quality of drinking water supply systems; regulates underground injection of waste and protection of groundwater wellhead areas under the Safe Drinking Water Act; provides information on public water supply systems.

Environmental Protection Agency (EPA), *Municipal Support, 1200 Pennsylvania Ave. N.W., #7119A EPA East, MC 4204M 20460; (202) 564-0749. Fax, (202) 501-2346. Sheila E. Frace, Director.*

Web, www.epa.gov

Directs programs to assist in the design and construction of municipal sewage systems; develops programs to ensure efficient operation and maintenance of municipal wastewater treatment facilities; implements programs for prevention of water pollution.

Environmental Protection Agency (EPA), *Science and Technology, 1200 Pennsylvania Ave. N.W., #5231 EPA West, MC 4301T 20460; (202) 566-0430. Fax, (202) 566-0441. Ephraim S. King, Director.*

General e-mail, ost.comments@epa.gov

Web, www.epa.gov/ost

Develops and coordinates water pollution control programs for the Environmental Protection Agency; assists state and regional agencies in establishing water quality standards and planning local water resources management; develops guidelines for industrial and municipal wastewater discharge; provides grants for water quality monitoring and swimming advisories at recreational coastal and Great Lakes beaches.

Environmental Protection Agency (EPA), *Wastewater Management, 1200 Pennsylvania Ave. N.W., #7116A EPA East, MC 4201M 20460; (202) 564-0748. Fax, (202) 501-2338. James A. Hanlon, Director.*

Web, www.epa.gov

Oversees the issuance of water permits. Responsible for the Pretreatment Program regulating industrial discharges to local sewage treatment. Oversees the State Revolving Funds Program, which provides assistance for the construction of wastewater treatment plants.

National Drinking Water Advisory Council, *1200 Pennsylvania Ave. N.W., #2104 20460; (202) 564-4094. Fax, (202) 564-3753. Veronica Blette, Designated Federal Officer.*

Web, www.epa.gov/safewater/ndwac/council.html

Advises the EPA administrator on activities, functions, and policies relating to implementation of the Safe Drinking Water Act.

National Oceanic and Atmospheric Administration (NOAA), *(Commerce Dept.), Office of Response and Restoration, 1305 East-West Hwy., 10th Floor, Bldg. 4, Silver Spring, MD 20910; (301) 713-2989. Fax, (301) 713-4389. David Westerholm, Director.*
Web, www.nos.noaa.gov/programs/orr.html

Provides information on damage to marine ecosystems caused by pollution. Offers information on spill trajectory projections and chemical hazard analyses. Researches trends of toxic contamination on U.S. coastal regions.

U.S. Coast Guard (USCG), *(Homeland Security Dept.), Incident Management and Preparedness, 2100 2nd St. S.W., #2100, CG-533 20593-0001; (202) 372-2230. Fax, (202) 372-2905. Cmdr. Anthony Lloyd, Chief. Locator, (202) 372-8724. Public Affairs, (202) 372-4600.*
Web, http://homeport.uscg.mil

Oversees cleanup operations after spills of oil and other hazardous substances in U.S. waters, on the outer continental shelf, and in international waters. Reviews coastal zone management and enforces international standards for pollution prevention and response.

U.S. Coast Guard (USCG), *(Homeland Security Dept.), National Pollution Funds Center, 4200 Wilson Blvd., #1000, Arlington, VA 22203; (202) 493-6700. Fax, (202) 493-6900. William Grawe, Director (Acting). Locator, (202) 372-8724. Public Affairs, (202) 372-4600.*
Web, www.uscg.mil/npfc

Certifies the financial responsibility of vessels and companies involved in oil exploration and transportation in U.S. waters and on the outer continental shelf; manages the Oil Spill Liability Trust Fund under the Oil Pollution Act of 1990.

►CONGRESS

For a listing of relevant congressional committees and subcommittees, please see page 252 or the Appendix.

►NONGOVERNMENTAL

Assn. of State and Interstate Water Pollution Control Administrators, *1221 Connecticut Ave. N.W., 2nd Floor 20036; (202) 756-0600. Fax, (202) 756-0605. Linda Eichmiller, Executive Director.*
General e-mail, admin1@asiwpca.org
Web, www.asiwpca.org

Membership: administrators of state water pollution agencies and related associations. Represents the states' concerns on implementation, funding, and reauthorization of the Clean Water Act. Monitors legislation and regulations.

Clean Water Action, *1010 Vermont Ave. N.W., #1100 20005; (202) 895-0420. Fax, (202) 895-0438. John DeCock, Chief Executive Officer.*
General e-mail, cwa@cleanwater.org
Web, www.cleanwateraction.org

Citizens' organization interested in clean, safe, and affordable water. Works to influence public policy through education, technical assistance, and grassroots organizing. Interests include toxins and pollution, drinking water, water conservation, sewage treatment, pesticides, mass burn incineration, bay and estuary protection, and consumer water issues. Monitors legislation and regulations.

Ocean Conservancy, *1300 19th St. N.W., 8th Floor 20036; (202) 429-5609. Fax, (202) 872-0619. Vikki N. Spruill, President.*
General e-mail, ocean@oceanconservancy.org
Web, www.oceanconservancy.org

Protects the health of oceans and seas. Advocates policies that restrict discharge of pollutants harmful to marine ecosystems.

Water Environment Federation, *601 Wythe St., Alexandria, VA 22314-1994; (703) 684-2400. Fax, (703) 684-2492. William Bertera, Executive Director.*
Web, www.wef.org

Membership: civil and environmental engineers, wastewater treatment plant operators, scientists, government officials, and others concerned with water quality. Works to preserve and improve water quality worldwide. Provides the public with technical information and educational materials. Monitors legislation and regulations.

RESOURCES MANAGEMENT

►AGENCIES

Bureau of Land Management (BLM), *(Interior Dept.), Renewable Resources and Planning, 1849 C St. N.W., MIB 5644 20240; (202) 208-4896. Fax, (202) 208-5010. Edwin Robertson, Assistant Director.*
General e-mail, woinfo@blm.gov
Web, www.blm.gov

Develops and implements natural resource programs for renewable resources use and protection, including management of forested land, rangeland, wild horses and burros, wildlife habitats, endangered species, soil and water quality, recreation, and cultural programs.

Interior Dept. (DOI), *1849 C St. N.W., #6151 20240; (202) 208-7351. Fax, (202) 208-6956. Kenneth L. Salazar, Secretary; David Hayes, Deputy Secretary. Information, (202) 208-3100. Library, (202) 208-5815. Press, (202) 208-6416. Locator, (202) 208-3100.*
Web, www.doi.gov

Manages most federal land through its component agencies. Responsible for conservation and development of mineral, water, and fish and wildlife resources. Operates recreation programs for federal parks, refuges, and public lands. Preserves and administers scenic and historic areas. Administers Native American lands and develops relationships with tribal governments.

Tennessee Valley Authority, *Government Affairs, Washington Office,* 1 Massachusetts Ave. N.W., #300 20444; (202) 898-2999. Fax, (202) 898-2998. Justin Maierhofer, Director.
General e-mail, latootle@tva.gov

Web, www.tva.gov

Coordinates resource conservation, development, and land-use programs in the Tennessee River Valley. Activities include forestry and wildlife development.

▶**NONGOVERNMENTAL**

National Assn. of Conservation Districts (NACD), 509 Capitol Court N.E. 20002-4937; (202) 547-6223. Fax, (202) 547-6450. Krysta Harden, Chief Executive Director.
General e-mail, washington@nacdnet.org

Web, www.nacdnet.org

Membership: conservation districts (local subdivisions of state government). Works to promote the conservation of land, forests, and other natural resources. Interests include erosion and sediment control; water quality; forestry, water, flood plain, and range management; rural development; and urban and community conservation.

Renewable Natural Resources Foundation, 5430 Grosvenor Lane, #220, Bethesda, MD 20814-2193; (301) 493-9101. Fax, (301) 493-6148. Robert D. Day, Executive Director.
General e-mail, info@rnrf.org

Web, www.rnrf.org

Consortium of professional, scientific, and education organizations working to advance scientific and public education in renewable natural resources. Encourages the application of sound scientific practices to resource management and conservation. Fosters interdisciplinary cooperation among its member organizations.

U.S. Chamber of Commerce, *Environment, Technology, and Regulatory Affairs,* 1615 H St. N.W. 20062-2000; (202) 463-5533. Fax, (202) 887-3445. William L. Kovacs, Vice President.
General e-mail, environment@uschamber.com

Web, www.uschamber.com

Develops policy on all issues affecting the production, use, and conservation of natural resources, including fuel and nonfuel minerals, timber, water, public lands, on- and offshore energy, wetlands, and endangered species.

Forests and Rangelands

▶**AGENCIES**

Forest Service *(Agriculture Dept.),* 201 14th St. S.W., #4NW 20250 (mailing address: 1400 Independence Ave. S.W., MS 1144, Washington, DC 20250-1144); (202) 205-1661. Fax, (202) 205-1765. Abigail Kimbell, Chief. Press, (202) 205-8333.
Web, www.fs.fed.us

Manages national forests and grasslands for outdoor recreation and sustained yield of renewable natural resources, including timber, water, forage, fish, and wildlife. Cooperates with state and private foresters; conducts forestry research.

Forest Service *(Agriculture Dept.),* **International Programs,** 1099 14th St. N.W., #5500W 20005; (202) 273-4695. Fax, (202) 273-4750. Valdis E. Mezainis, Director.
Web, www.fs.fed.us/global

Responsible for the Forest Service's involvement in international forest conservation efforts. Analyzes international resource issues; promotes information exchange; provides planning and technical assistance. Interests include tropical forests and sustainable forest management.

Forest Service *(Agriculture Dept.),* **National Forest System,** 201 14th St. S.W., #3NW 20250 (mailing address: 1400 Independence Ave. S.W., MS 1106, Washington, DC 20250-1106); (202) 205-1523. Fax, (202) 205-1758. Joel Holtrop, Deputy Chief.
Web, www.fs.fed.us

Manages 191 million acres of forests and rangelands. Products and services from these lands include timber, water, forage, wildlife, minerals, and recreation.

Forest Service *(Agriculture Dept.),* **Research and Development,** 201 14th St. S.W., #1NW 20250 (mailing address: 1400 Independence Ave. S.W., MS 1120, Washington, DC 20250-1120); (202) 205-1665. Fax, (202) 205-1530. Ann M. Bartuska, Deputy Chief for Research.
Web, www.fs.fed.us

Conducts biological, physical, and economic research related to forestry, including studies on harvesting methods, acid deposition, international forestry, the effects of global climate changes on forests, and forest products. Provides information on the establishment, improvement, and growth of trees, grasses, and other forest vegetation. Works to protect forest resources from fire, insects, diseases, and animal pests. Examines the effect of forest use activities on water quality, soil erosion, and sediment production. Conducts continuous forest survey and analyzes outlook for future supply and demand.

Forest Service *(Agriculture Dept.),* **State and Private Forestry,** 201 14th St. S.W., # 2NW 20024-1109 (mailing address: 1400 Independence Ave. S.W., MS 1109, Washington, DC 20250-1109); (202) 205-1657. Fax, (202) 205-1174. James E. Hubbard, Deputy Chief.
Web, www.fs.fed.us

Interior Department

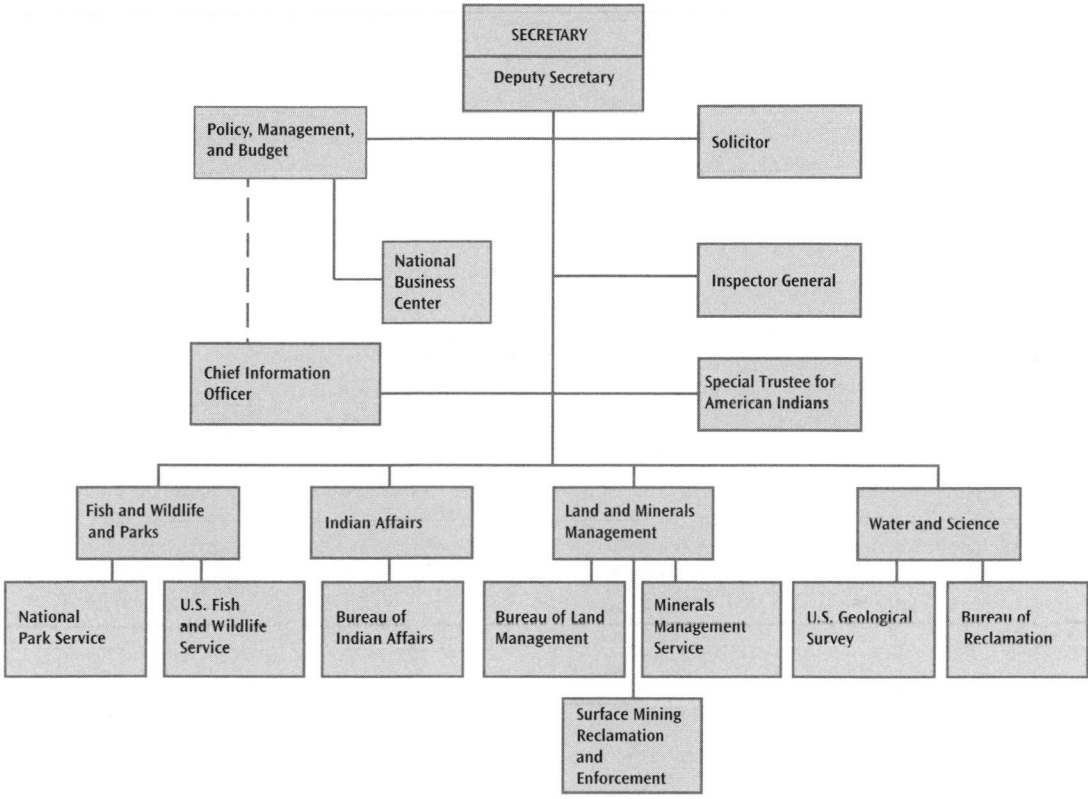

— — — Indicates a support or advisory relationship with the unit rather than a direct reporting relationship

Assists state and private forest owners with the protection and management of 574 million acres of forest and associated watershed lands. Assistance includes fire control, protecting forests from insects and diseases, land-use planning, developing multiple-use management, and improving practices in harvesting, processing, and marketing of forest products.

Forest Service *(Agriculture Dept.), Youth Conservation Corps, 1621 N. Kent St., Arlington, VA 22209 (mailing address: P.O. Box 96090, Washington, DC 20090-6090); (703) 605-4854. Fax, (703) 605-5115. Ransom Hughes, Program Manager.*
Web, www.fs.fed.us/people/programs/ycc.htm

Administers with the National Park Service and the Fish and Wildlife Service the Youth Conservation Corps, a summer employment and training public works program for youths ages fifteen to eighteen. The program is conducted in national parks, in national forests, and on national wildlife refuges.

▶**CONGRESS**

For a listing of relevant congressional committees and subcommittees, please see page 252 or the Appendix.

▶**NONGOVERNMENTAL**

American Forest and Paper Assn., *Government Affairs, 1111 19th St. N.W., #800 20036; (202) 463-2700. Fax, (202) 463-2471. Elizabeth VanDersarl, Vice President. General e-mail, info@afandpa.org*

Web, www.afandpa.org

Membership: wood and specialty products manufacturers and those in related associations. Interests include tax, housing, environmental, international trade, natural resources, and land-use issues that affect the wood products industry.

American Forests, *734 15th St. N.W., #800 20005 (mailing address: P.O. Box 2000, Washington, DC 20013-2000); (202) 737-1944. Fax, (202) 737-2457. Deborah Gangloff, Executive Director. General e-mail, info@amfor.org*

Web, www.americanforests.org

Citizens' interest group that promotes protection and responsible management of forests and natural resources. Provides information on conservation, public land policy, urban forestry, and timber management. Promotes an international tree-planting campaign to help mitigate global warming.

Forest Resources Assn., *600 Jefferson Plaza, #350, Rockville, MD 20852; (301) 838-9385. Fax, (301) 838-9481. Richard Lewis, President.*
General e-mail, fra@forestresources.org

Web, www.forestresources.org

Membership: logging contractors, pulpwood dealers, suppliers, and consumers. Administers programs to improve the productivity, safety, and efficiency of pulpwood harvesting and transport; provides information on new equipment, tools, and methods; works to ensure continued access to the timberland base. Monitors legislation and regulations.

International Wood Products Assn., *4214 King St. West, Alexandria, VA 22302; (703) 820-6696. Fax, (703) 820-8550. Brent McClendon, Executive Vice President.*
General e-mail, info@iwpawood.org

Web, www.iwpawood.org

Membership: companies that handle imported wood products. Encourages environmentally responsible forest management and international trade in wood products. Sponsors research and environmental education on tropical forestry. (Affiliated with the Tropical Forest Foundation.)

National Assn. of State Foresters, *444 N. Capitol St. N.W., #540 20001; (202) 624-5415. Fax, (202) 624-5407. James Farrell, Executive Director.*
General e-mail, nasf@stateforesters.org

Web, www.stateforesters.org

Membership: directors of state forestry agencies from all states, the District of Columbia, and U.S. territories. Members manage and protect more than two-thirds of the nation's forests, as well as assist private landowners in managing their forests. Monitors legislation and regulations.

National Forest Foundation, *2715 M St. N.W., #100 20007; (202) 298-6740. Fax, (202) 298-6758. William Possiel, President.*
General e-mail, info@natlforests.org

Web, www.natlforests.org

Established by Congress to support the U.S. Forest Service in its management of public lands. Promotes research and multiple-use, cooperative forestry. Interests include conservation, preservation, recreation, wildlife, and environmental education.

National Lumber and Building Material Dealers Assn., *2025 M St. N.W., #800 20036-3309; (202) 367-1169. Fax, (202) 367-2169. Michael O'Brian, President. Toll-free, (800) 634-8645.*
General e-mail, nlbmda@dealer.org

Web, www.dealer.org

Membership: federated associations of retailers in the lumber and building material industries. Provides statistics training and networking opportunities to members. Monitors legislation and regulations.

Save America's Forests, *4 Library Court S.E. 20003; (202) 544-9219. Fax, (202) 544-7462. Carl Ross, Executive Director.*
General e-mail, forests@saveamericasforests.org

Web, www.saveamericasforests.org

Coalition of environmental and public interest groups, businesses, and individuals. Advocates comprehensive nationwide laws to prevent deforestation and to protect forest ecosystems.

Society of American Foresters, *5400 Grosvenor Lane, Bethesda, MD 20814-2198; (301) 897-8720. Fax, (301) 897-3690. Michael Goergen, Executive Vice President. Toll-free, (866) 897-8720.*
General e-mail, safweb@safnet.org

Web, www.safnet.org

Association of forestry professionals. Provides technical information on forestry, accredits forestry programs in universities and colleges, and publishes scientific forestry journals.

Sustainable Forestry Initiative, *1600 Wilson Blvd., #810, Arlington, VA 22209; (703) 875-9500. Fax, (703) 875-9510. Kathy Abusow, President.*
Web, www.sfiprogram.org

Works to ensure protection of forests while continuing to produce wood and paper products as needed by the economy. Encourages perpetual growing and harvesting of trees and protection of wildlife, plants, soil, water, and air quality. Seeks to mitigate illegal logging. Interests include the economic, environmental, cultural, and legal issues related to forestry.

Land Resources and Rights

▶**AGENCIES**

Bureau of Land Management (BLM), *(Interior Dept.), 1849 C St. N.W., #5662, MS 5628 20240; (202) 208-3801. Fax, (202) 208-5242. Vacant, Director. Press, (202) 452-5125.*
General e-mail, woinfo@blm.gov

Web, www.blm.gov

Manages public lands and federally owned mineral resources, including oil, gas, and coal. Resources managed and leased include wildlife habitats, timber, minerals, open space, wilderness areas, forage, and recreational resources. Surveys federal lands and maintains public land records.

Bureau of Land Management (BLM), *(Interior Dept.), Lands, Realty, and Cadastral Survey, 1620 L St. N.W. 20036 (mailing address: 1849 C St. N.W., MS 1000LS, Washington, DC 20240); (202) 452-7779. Fax, (202) 452-7708. Jeff Holdren, Manager.*
Web, www.blm.gov

Oversees use, acquisition, and disposal of public lands. Conducts the Public Lands Survey; authorizes rights-of-way on public lands, including roads and power lines.

Bureau of Reclamation *(Interior Dept.)*, 1849 C St. N.W., #7554, 7069 MIB 20240; (202) 513-0501. Fax, (202) 513-0309. John McDonald, Commissioner (Acting). Press, (202) 513-0684.

Web, www.usbr.gov

Responsible for acquisition, administration, management, and disposal of water in seventeen western states. Water resource development projects include dams, power plants, and canals.

Interior Dept. (DOI), *Bird Habitat Conservation,* 4501 N. Fairfax Dr., Arlington, VA 22203 (mailing address: 4401 N. Fairfax Dr., MBSP 4075, Arlington, VA 22203-1610); (703) 358-1784. Fax, (703) 358-2282. Michael J. Johnson, Chief.

General e-mail, dbhc@fws.gov

Web, http://birdhabitat.fws.gov

Membership: government and private-sector conservation experts. Works to protect, restore, and manage wetlands and other habitats for migratory birds and other animals and to maintain migratory bird and waterfowl populations.

Interior Dept. (DOI), *Board of Land Appeals,* 801 N. Quincy St., #300, Arlington, VA 22203; (703) 235-3750. Fax, (703) 235-8349. H. Barry Holt, Chief Administrative Judge.

Web, www.doi.gov

Adjunct office of the interior secretary that decides appeals from decisions rendered by the Bureau of Land Management, the Minerals Management Service, the Office of Surface Mining and Reclamation Enforcement, and the Bureau of Indian Affairs concerning the use and disposition of public lands and minerals. Issues final decisions concerning the Surface Mining Control and Reclamation Act of 1977.

Interior Dept. (DOI), *Land and Minerals Management,* 1849 C St. N.W., #6628 20240; (202) 208-6734. Fax, (202) 208-3619. C. Stephen Allred, Assistant Secretary.

Web, www.doi.gov

Directs and supervises the Bureau of Land Management, the Minerals Management Service, and the Office of Surface Mining and Reclamation Enforcement. Supervises programs associated with land use planning, onshore and offshore minerals, surface mining reclamation and enforcement, and outer continental shelf minerals management.

Interior Dept. (DOI), *Surface Mining Reclamation and Enforcement,* 1951 Constitution Ave. N.W., #233 20240; (202) 208-4006. Fax, (202) 219-3106. Glenda Owens, Director (Acting). Press, (202) 208-2539.

General e-mail, gowens@osmre.gov

Web, www.osmre.gov

Regulates surface mining of coal and surface effects of underground coal mining. Responsible for reclamation of abandoned coal mine lands.

Natural Resources Conservation Service *(Agriculture Dept.)*, 1400 Independence Ave. S.W., #5105 20250

(mailing address: P.O. Box 2890, Washington, DC 20013-2890); (202) 720-4525. Fax, (202) 720-7690. Arlen Lancaster, Chief. Chief's Office, (202) 720-7246. Public Affairs, (202) 720-3210.

Web, www.nrcs.usda.gov

Responsible for soil and water conservation programs, including watershed protection, flood prevention, river basin surveys, and resource conservation and development. Provides landowners, operators, state and local units of government, and community groups with technical assistance in carrying out local programs.

Tennessee Valley Authority, *Government Affairs, Washington Office,* 1 Massachusetts Ave. N.W., #300 20444; (202) 898-2999. Fax, (202) 898-2998. Justin Maierhofer, Director.

General e-mail, latootle@tva.gov

Web, www.tva.gov

Coordinates resource conservation, development, and land-use programs in the Tennessee River Valley. Provides information on land usage in the region.

▶CONGRESS

For a listing of relevant congressional committees and subcommittees, please see page 252 or the Appendix.

▶NONGOVERNMENTAL

American Geological Institute, 4220 King St., Alexandria, VA 22302-1502; (703) 379-2480. Fax, (703) 379-7563. P. Patrick Leahy, Executive Director.

General e-mail, agi@agiweb.org

Web, www.agiweb.org

Membership: earth science societies and associations. Maintains computerized database of the world's geoscience literature (available to the public for a fee).

American Resort Development Assn., 1201 15th St. N.W., #400 20005; (202) 371-6700. Fax, (202) 289-8544. Howard Nusbaum, President.

Web, www.arda.org

Membership: U.S. and international developers, builders, financiers, marketing companies, and others involved in resort, recreational, and community development. Serves as an information clearinghouse; monitors federal and state legislation affecting land, time share, and community development industries.

Land Trust Alliance, 1660 L St. N.W., #1100 20036; (202) 638-4725. Fax, (202) 638-4730. Rand Wentworth, President.

General e-mail, info@lta.org

Web, www.landtrustalliance.org

Membership: organizations and individuals who work to conserve land resources. Serves as a forum for the exchange of information; conducts research and public education programs. Monitors legislation and regulations.

National Assn. of Conservation Districts (NACD), 509 Capitol Court N.E. 20002-4937; (202) 547-6223. Fax,

(202) 547-6450. Krysta Harden, Chief Executive Director.

General e-mail, washington@nacdnet.org

Web, www.nacdnet.org

Membership: conservation districts (local subdivisions of state government). Works to promote the conservation of land, forests, and other natural resources. Interests include erosion and sediment control; water quality; forestry, water, flood plain, and range management; rural development; and urban and community conservation.

Public Lands Council, *1301 Pennsylvania Ave. N.W., #300 20004-1701; (202) 347-5355. Fax, (202) 638-0607. Jeff Eisenberg, Executive Director.*

Web, www.beefusa.org

Membership: cattle and sheep ranchers who hold permits and leases to graze livestock on public lands. (Affiliated with the National Cattlemen's Beef Association.)

Scenic America, *1250 Eye St. N.W., #750A 20005; (202) 638-4630. Fax, (202) 638-3171. Kevin E. Fry, President.*

General e-mail, fry@scenic.org

Web, www.scenic.org

Membership: national, state, and local groups concerned with land-use control, growth management, and landscape protection. Works to enhance the scenic quality of America's communities and countryside. Provides information and technical assistance on scenic byways, tree preservation, economics of aesthetic regulation, billboard and sign control, scenic areas preservation, and growth management.

Wallace Genetic Foundation, *4910 Massachusetts Ave. N.W., #221 20016; (202) 966-2932. Fax, (202) 966-3370. Patricia M. Lee, Co-Executive Director; Carolyn H. Sand, Co-Executive Director.*

General e-mail, president@wallacegenetic.org

Web, www.wallacegenetic.org

Supports national and international nonprofits in the areas of agricultural research, preservation of farmland, ecology, conservation, and sustainable development.

Metals and Minerals

▶**AGENCIES**

Bureau of Land Management (BLM), *(Interior Dept.), Minerals, Realty, and Resource Protection, 1849 C St. N.W., #5625 20240; (202) 208-4201. Fax, (202) 208-4800. Michael P. Nedd, Assistant Director.*

Web, www.blm.gov

Evaluates and classifies onshore oil, natural gas, geothermal resources, and all solid energy and mineral resources, including coal and uranium, on federal lands. Develops and administers regulations for fluid and solid mineral leasing on national lands and on the subsurface

of land where fluid and solid mineral rights have been reserved for the federal government.

Interior Dept. (DOI), *Board of Land Appeals, 801 N. Quincy St., #300, Arlington, VA 22203; (703) 235-3750. Fax, (703) 235-8349. H. Barry Holt, Chief Administrative Judge.*

Web, www.doi.gov

Adjunct office of the interior secretary that decides appeals from decisions rendered by the Bureau of Land Management, the Minerals Management Service, the Office of Surface Mining and Reclamation Enforcement, and the Bureau of Indian Affairs concerning the use and disposition of public lands and minerals. Issues final decisions concerning the Surface Mining Control and Reclamation Act of 1977.

Interior Dept. (DOI), *Land and Minerals Management, 1849 C St. N.W., #6628 20240; (202) 208-6734. Fax, (202) 208-3619. C. Stephen Allred, Assistant Secretary.*

Web, www.doi.gov

Directs and supervises the Bureau of Land Management, the Minerals Management Service, and the Office of Surface Mining and Reclamation Enforcement. Supervises programs associated with land use planning, onshore and offshore minerals, surface mining reclamation and enforcement, and outer continental shelf minerals management.

Interior Dept. (DOI), *Water and Science, 1849 C St. N.W., #6657, MS 6640 20240; (202) 208-3186. Fax, (202) 208-3324. Vacant, Assistant Secretary.*

Web, www.doi.gov

Administers departmental water, scientific, and research activities. Directs and supervises the Bureau of Reclamation and the U.S. Geological Survey.

Minerals Management Service *(Interior Dept.), 1849 C St. N.W., MS 4230 20240; (202) 208-3500. Fax, (202) 208-7242. Walter Cruickshank, Director (Acting). Press, (202) 208-3985.*

Web, www.mms.gov

Collects and accounts for revenues from onshore and offshore minerals production; disburses royalties to the federal government and Native American groups; oversees development of offshore resources, especially oil and natural gas.

Minerals Management Service *(Interior Dept.), Minerals Revenue Management, Washington Office, 1849 C St. N.W., #4226, MS 4230 20240; (202) 208-3512. Fax, (202) 501-0247. Greg Gould, Associate Director.*

Web, www.mrm.mms.gov

Collects and manages royalties on minerals produced on federal and Native American lands. (Headquarters and accounting center in Denver, Colo.)

Minerals Management Service *(Interior Dept.), Offshore Regulatory Programs, 381 Elden St., MS 4020,*

Herndon, VA 20170-4817; (703) 787-1598. Fax, (703) 787-1093. E.P. Danenberger, Chief.
Web, www.mms.gov/offshore

Oversees postlease operations, including exploration, drilling, and production phases of oil and gas development. Ensures compliance with environmental statutes and regulations.

State Dept., *International Energy and Commodities Policy,* 2201 C St. N.W., #4843 20520; (202) 647-3036. Fax, (202) 647-4037. Stephen J. Gallogly, Director.
Web, www.state.gov

Coordinates U.S. international energy policy related to commodities, including energy supply, and U.S. participation in the International Energy Agency; monitors cooperative multilateral and bilateral agreements related to energy; coordinates energy-related aspects of U.S. relations with other countries.

U.S. Geological Survey (USGS), *(Interior Dept.),* *Mineral Resources Program,* 12201 Sunrise Valley Dr., #3A204, MS 913, Reston, VA 20192; (703) 648-6110. Fax, (703) 648-6057. Kathleen M. Johnson, Program Coordinator.
Web, www.minerals.usgs.gov

Coordinates mineral resource activities for the Geological Survey, including research and information on U.S. and international mineral resources, baseline information on earth materials, and geochemical and geophysical instrumentation and applications.

▶CONGRESS

For a listing of relevant congressional committees and subcommittees, please see page 252 or the Appendix.

▶NONGOVERNMENTAL

Aluminum Assn., 1525 Wilson Blvd., #600, Arlington, VA 22209; (703) 358-2960. Fax, (703) 358-2961. J. Stephen Larkin, President.
Web, www.aluminum.org

Represents the aluminum industry. Develops voluntary standards and technical data; compiles statistics concerning the industry. Monitors legislation and regulations.

American Iron and Steel Institute, 1140 Connecticut Ave. N.W., #705 20036; (202) 452-7100. Fax, (202) 463-6573. Thomas Gibson, President. Press, (202) 452-7116.
General e-mail, steelnews@steel.org
Web, www.steel.org

Represents the iron and steel industry. Publishes statistics on iron and steel production; promotes the use of steel; conducts research. Monitors legislation and regulations. (Maintains offices in Detroit, Mich., and Pittsburgh, Pa.)

American Zinc Assn., 2025 M St. N.W., #800 20036; (202) 367-1151. Fax, (202) 367-2232. George Vary, Executive Director.

General e-mail, zincinfo@zinc.org
Web, www.zinc.org

Membership: primary and secondary producers of zinc metal, zinc oxide, and zinc dust. Provides information on zinc. Monitors legislation and regulations. (Affiliated with the International Zinc Assn.)

Mineralogical Society of America, 3635 Concorde Pkwy., #500, Chantilly, VA 20151-1125; (703) 652-9950. Fax, (703) 652-9951. Nancy Ross, President.
General e-mail, business@minsocam.org
Web, www.minsocam.org

Membership: mineralogists, petrologists, crystallographers, geochemists, educators, students, and others interested in mineralogy. Conducts research; sponsors educational programs; promotes industrial application of mineral studies.

National Mining Assn., 101 Constitution Ave. N.W., #500 East 20001-2133; (202) 463-2600. Fax, (202) 463-2666. Harold P. Quinn Jr., President. Press, (202) 463-2651.
General e-mail, webmaster@nma.org
Web, www.nma.org

Membership: domestic producers of coal and industrial-agricultural minerals and metals; manufacturers of mining equipment; engineering and consulting firms; and financial institutions. Interests include mine-leasing programs, mine health and safety, research and development, public lands, and minerals availability. Monitors legislation and regulations.

Salt Institute, 700 N. Fairfax St., #600, Alexandria, VA 22314; (703) 549-4648. Fax, (703) 548-2194. Richard L. Hanneman, President.
General e-mail, info@saltinstitute.org
Web, www.saltinstitute.org

Membership: North American salt companies and overseas companies that produce dry salt for use in food, animal feed, highway de-icing, water softening, and chemicals. Sponsors education and training projects with the Bureau of Mines and the Food and Drug Administration. Monitors legislation and regulations.

Native American Trust Resources

▶AGENCIES

Bureau of Indian Affairs (BIA), *(Interior Dept.),* Trust Services, 1849 C St. N.W., MS 4620 20240; (202) 208-5831. Fax, (202) 219-1255. Vicki Forrest, Deputy Bureau Director.
Web, www.doi.gov/bureau-indian-affairs-html

Assists in developing and managing bureau programs involving Native American trust resources (agriculture, forestry, wildlife, water, irrigation, real property management probate, and title records.)

Interior Dept. (DOI), *Office of the Solicitor: Indian Affairs,* *1849 C St. N.W., MS 6513 20240; (202) 208-3401. Fax, (202) 219-1791. Edith Blackwell, Associate Solicitor. Web, www.doi.gov*

Advises the Bureau of Indian Affairs and the secretary of the interior on all legal matters, including its trust responsibilities toward Native Americans and their natural resources.

Justice Dept. (DOJ), *Indian Resources,* *601 D St. N.W., #3507 20004 (mailing address: P.O. Box 44378, L'Enfant Plaza, Washington, DC 20026-4378); (202) 305-0269. Fax, (202) 305-0271. S. Craig Alexander, Chief. Web, www.usdoj.gov*

Represents the United States in suits, including trust violations, brought on behalf of individual Native Americans and Native American tribes against the government. Also represents the United States as trustee for Native Americans in court actions involving protection of Native American land and resources.

Minerals Management Service *(Interior Dept.),* *Minerals Revenue Management, Washington Office, 1849 C St. N.W., #4226, MS 4230 20240; (202) 208-3512. Fax, (202) 501-0247. Greg Gould, Associate Director. Web, www.mrm.mms.gov*

Collects and manages royalties on minerals produced on federal and Native American lands. (Headquarters and accounting center in Denver, Colo.)

►CONGRESS

For a listing of relevant congressional committees and subcommittees, please see page 252 or the Appendix.

►NONGOVERNMENTAL

Native American Rights Fund, *Washington Office, 1712 N St. N.W. 20036-2907; (202) 785-4166. Fax, (202) 822-0068. Richard Guest, Staff Attorney; Dawn Baum, Staff Attorney. Web, www.narf.org*

Provides Native Americans and Alaska Natives with legal assistance in land claims, water rights, hunting, and other areas. Practices federal Indian law. (Headquarters in Boulder, Colo.)

Ocean Resources

►AGENCIES

Council on Environmental Quality *(Executive Office of the President), Committee on Ocean Policy, 722 Jackson Pl. N.W. 20503; (202) 456-3892. Fax, (202) 456-2710. Nancy Sutley, Chair. Web, http://ocean.ceq.gov*

Cabinet-level committee that coordinates the ocean-related activities of executive branch departments and agencies.

National Oceanic and Atmospheric Administration (NOAA), *(Commerce Dept.), Marine and Aviation Operations, 8403 Colesville Rd., 5th Floor, Silver Spring, MD 20910; (301) 713-1045. Fax, (301) 713-1541. Jonathan Bailey, Director. Web, www.omao.noaa.gov*

Uniformed service of the Commerce Dept. that operates and manages NOAA's fleet of hydrographic, oceanographic, and fisheries research ships and aircraft. Supports NOAA's scientific programs.

National Oceanic and Atmospheric Administration (NOAA), *(Commerce Dept.), National Environmental Satellite, Data, and Information Service, 1335 East-West Hwy., Silver Spring, MD 20910; (301) 713-3578. Fax, (301) 713-1249. Mary Kicza, Assistant Administrator. Web, www.nesdis.noaa.gov*

Disseminates worldwide environmental data through a system of meteorological, oceanographic, geophysical, and solar-terrestrial data centers.

National Oceanic and Atmospheric Administration (NOAA), *(Commerce Dept.), National Marine Sanctuaries, 1305 East-West Hwy., 11th Floor, Silver Spring, MD 20910; (301) 713-3125. Fax, (301) 713-0404. Daniel J. Basta, Director. General e-mail, sanctuaries@noaa.gov*

Web, www.sanctuaries.noaa.gov

Administers the National Marine Sanctuary Program, which seeks to protect the ecology and the recreational and cultural resources of marine and Great Lakes waters.

National Oceanic and Atmospheric Administration (NOAA), *(Commerce Dept.), National Sea Grant College Program, 1315 East-West Hwy., 11th Floor, Silver Spring, MD 20910; (301) 734-1088. Fax, (301) 713-0799. Leon M. Cammen, Director. Web, www.nsgo.seagrant.org*

Provides institutions with grants for marine research, education, and advisory services; provides marine environmental information.

National Oceanic and Atmospheric Administration (NOAA), *(Commerce Dept.), Ocean and Coastal Resource Management, 1305 East-West Hwy., #10411, SSMC4, Silver Spring, MD 20910; (301) 713-3155. Fax, (301) 713-4012. David Kennedy, Director. Information, (301) 713-3074. Web, http://coastalmanagement.noaa.gov*

Administers the Coastal Zone Management Act, the National Estuarine Research Reserve System, the National Marine Protected Areas Center, and the Marine Managed Areas Program to carry out NOAA's goals for preservation, conservation, and restoration management of the ocean and coastal environment.

National Oceanic and Atmospheric Administration (NOAA), *(Commerce Dept.), Special Projects, 1305 East-West Hwy., Silver Spring, MD 20910; (301) 713-3000. Fax, (301) 713-4384. Brent Ache, Chief.*

Web, www.nos.noaa.gov

Conducts national studies and develops policies on ocean management and use along the U.S. coastline and the exclusive economic zone.

▶**CONGRESS**

For a listing of relevant congressional committees and subcommittees, please see page 252 or the Appendix.

▶**NONGOVERNMENTAL**

Blue Frontier Campaign, *P.O. Box 19367 20036; (202) 387-8030. Fax, (202) 234-5176. David Helvarg, President. General e-mail, info@bluefront.org*

Web, www.bluefront.org

Promotes ocean conservation. Seeks to strengthen unity among ocean conservationists and encourage public awareness at the local, regional, and national levels.

Coastal States Organization, *444 N. Capitol St. N.W., #322 20001; (202) 508-3860. Fax, (202) 508-3843. Kristen Fletcher, Executive Director. General e-mail, kzultner@coastalstates.org*

Web, www.coastalstates.org

Nonpartisan organization that represents governors of U.S. coastal states, territories, and commonwealths on management of coastal, Great Lakes, and marine resources. Interests include ocean dumping, coastal pollution, wetlands preservation and restoration, national oceans policy, and the outer continental shelf. Gathers and analyzes data to assess state coastal needs; sponsors and participates in conferences and workshops.

Joint Ocean Commission Initiative, *c/o Meridian Institute, 1920 L St. N.W., #500 20036; (202) 354-6440. Fax, (202) 354-6441. Laura Cantral, Senior Staff Member. General e-mail, lcantral@merid.org*

Web, www.jointoceancommission.org

Provides policy information on ocean conservation and releases Ocean Policy Report Cards that analyze the effectiveness of policy initiatives on ocean and coast protection. (Formed by the U.S. Commission on Ocean Policy and the Pew Oceans Commission.)

Marine Technology Society, *5565 Sterrett Pl., #108, Columbia, MD 21044; (410) 884-5330. Fax, (410) 884-9060. Richard Lawson, Executive Director. General e-mail, membership@mtsociety.org*

Web, www.mtsociety.org

Membership: scientists, engineers, technologists, and others interested in marine science and technology. Provides information on marine science, technology, and education.

National Ocean Industries Assn., *1120 G St. N.W., #900 20005; (202) 347-6900. Fax, (202) 347-8650. Tom A. Fry, President. General e-mail, noia@noia.org*

Web, www.noia.org

Membership: manufacturers, producers, suppliers, and support and service companies involved in marine, offshore, and ocean work. Interests include offshore oil and gas supply and production, deep-sea mining, ocean thermal energy, and new energy sources.

Oceana, *1350 Connecticut Ave. N.W., #500 20036; (202) 833-3900. Fax, (202) 833-2070. Andrew F. Sharpless, Chief Executive Officer. Toll-free, (877) 7-OCEANA. General e-mail, info@oceana.org*

Web, www.oceana.org

Promotes ocean conservation both nationally and internationally; pursues policy changes to reduce pollution and protect fish, marine mammals, and other forms of sea life. Conducts specific two- to five-year scientific, legal, policy, and advocacy campaigns. Monitors legislation and regulations.

Outer Continental Shelf

▶**AGENCIES**

Minerals Management Service *(Interior Dept.),* **Offshore Energy and Minerals Management,** *1849 C St. N.W., MS 5438 20240-0001; (202) 208-3530. Fax, (202) 208-6048. Chris Oynes, Associate Director; Robert P. LaBelle, Deputy Associate Director. Web, www.mms.gov/offshore*

Administers the Outer Continental Shelf Lands Act. Evaluates, classifies, and supervises oil, gas, and other mineral reserves and operations on outer continental shelf lands; manages the submerged lands of the outer continental shelf. Oversees prelease operations; administers offshore oil and gas leasing.

U.S. Geological Survey (USGS), *(Interior Dept.),* **Coastal and Marine Geology Program,** *12201 Sunrise Valley Dr., Reston, VA 20192 (mailing address: 915B National Center, Reston, VA 20192); (703) 648-6422. Fax, (703) 648-5464. John W. Haines, Program Coordinator. Web, http://marine.usgs.gov*

Handles resource assessment, exploration research, and marine geologic and environmental studies on U.S. coastal regions and the outer continental shelf.

▶**CONGRESS**

For a listing of relevant congressional committees and subcommittees, please see page 252 or the Appendix.

Parks and Recreation Areas

▶**AGENCIES**

Bureau of Land Management (BLM), *(Interior Dept.),* **Culture, Paleontological Resources, and Tribal Consultation,** *1620 L St. N.W., #204 20036 (mailing address: 1849 C St. N.W., #204-LS, Washington, DC*

20240); (202) 452-0330. Fax, (202) 452-7701. Richard Hanes, Division Chief. Press, (202) 452-5125.
Web, www.blm.gov/heritage

Identifies and manages cultural heritage and recreation programs on public lands.

Bureau of Land Management (BLM), *(Interior Dept.),* ***Recreation and Visitor Services,*** *1620 L St. N.W., #302 20036 (mailing address: 1849 C St. N.W., #302-LS, Washington, DC 20240); (202) 452-5040. Fax, (202) 452-7709. Bob Ratcliffe, Director.*
Web, www.blm.gov

Develops recreation opportunities on public lands.

Bureau of Reclamation *(Interior Dept.), 1849 C St. N.W., #7554, 7069 MIB 20240; (202) 513-0501. Fax, (202) 513-0309. John McDonald, Commissioner (Acting). Press, (202) 513-0684.*
Web, www.usbr.gov

Responsible for acquisition, administration, management, and disposal of lands in seventeen western states associated with bureau water resource development projects. Provides overall policy guidance for land use, including agreements with public agencies for outdoor recreation, fish and wildlife enhancement, and land use authorizations such as leases, licenses, permits, and rights of way.

Forest Service *(Agriculture Dept.), **Recreation and Heritage Resources,** 201 14th St. S.W., 4th Floor Central 20250-1125 (mailing address: 1400 Independence Ave. S.W., Washington, DC 20250); (202) 205-1706. Fax, (202) 205-1145. James S. Bedwell, Director.*
Web, www.fs.fed.us/recreation

Develops policy and sets guidelines on administering national forests and grasslands for recreational purposes. (The Forest Service administers some of the lands designated as national recreation areas.)

Interior Dept. (DOI), *Fish and Wildlife and Parks, 1849 C St. N.W., #3156 20240; (202) 208-4416. Fax, (202) 208-4684. Vacant, Assistant Secretary.*
Web, www.doi.gov

Responsible for programs associated with the development, conservation, and use of fish, wildlife, recreational, historical, and national park system resources. Coordinates marine environmental quality and biological resources programs with other federal agencies.

National Park Service (NPS), *(Interior Dept.), 1849 C St. N.W., #3115 20240; (202) 208-4621. Fax, (202) 208-7889. Dan Wenk, Director (Acting). Press, (202) 208-6843. Washington area activities, (202) 619-7275 (recording). General e-mail, asknps@nps.gov*
Web, www.nps.gov

Administers national parks, monuments, historic sites, and recreation areas. Oversees coordination, planning, and financing of public outdoor recreation programs at all levels of government. Conducts recreation research

surveys; administers financial assistance program to states for planning and development of outdoor recreation programs. (Some lands designated as national recreation areas are not under NPS jurisdiction.)

National Park Service (NPS), *(Interior Dept.), **Policy,** 1849 C St. N.W., #7252 20240; (202) 208-7456. Fax, (202) 219-8835. Bernard Fagan, Chief.*
Web, www.nps.gov/policy

Researches and develops management policy on matters relating to the National Park Service; makes recommendations on the historical significance of national trails and landmarks.

Tennessee Valley Authority, *Government Affairs, **Washington Office,** 1 Massachusetts Ave. N.W., #300 20444; (202) 898-2999. Fax, (202) 898-2998. Justin Maierhofer, Director.*
General e-mail, latootle@tva.gov
Web, www.tva.gov

Operates Land Between the Lakes, a national recreation and environmental education area located in western Kentucky and Tennessee.

U.S. Fish and Wildlife Service *(Interior Dept.), **National Wildlife Refuge System,** 1849 C St. N.W., #3251 20240; (202) 208-5333. Fax, (202) 208-3082. Gregory Siekaniec, Chief.*
Web, www.fws.gov

Manages the National Wildlife Refuge System. Most refuges are open to public use; activities include bird and wildlife watching, fishing, hunting, and environmental education.

▶**CONGRESS**

For a listing of relevant congressional committees and subcommittees, please see page 252 or the Appendix.

▶**NONGOVERNMENTAL**

American Hiking Society, *1422 Fenwick Lane, Silver Spring, MD 20910-3328; (301) 565-6704. Fax, (301) 565-6714. Gregory Miller, President.*
General e-mail, info@americanhiking.org
Web, www.americanhiking.org

Membership: individuals and clubs interested in preserving America's trail system and protecting the interests of trail users. Provides information on outdoor volunteer opportunities on public lands.

American Recreation Coalition, *1225 New York Ave. N.W., #450 20005-6405; (202) 682-9530. Fax, (202) 682-9529. Derrick A. Crandall, President.*
General e-mail, arc@funoutdoors.com
Web, www.funoutdoors.com

Membership: recreation industry associations, recreation enthusiast groups, and leading corporations in the recreation products and services sectors. Promotes health and well-being through recreation.

National Park Foundation, *1201 Eye St. N.W., #550B 20005; (202) 354-6460. Fax, (202) 371-2066. Vacant, President.*

General e-mail, ask-npf@nationalparks.org

Web, www.nationalparks.org

Encourages private sector support of the national park system; provides grants and sponsors educational and cultural activities. Chartered by Congress and chaired by the interior secretary.

National Parks Conservation Assn., *1300 19th St. N.W., #300 20036-6404; (202) 223-6722. Fax, (202) 659-0650. Tom Kiernan, President. Information, (800) 628-7275.*

General e-mail, npca@npca.org

Web, www.npca.org

Citizens' interest group that seeks to protect national parks and other park system areas.

National Park Trust, *401 E. Jefferson St., #102, Rockville, MD 20850; (301) 279-7275. Fax, (301) 279-7211. Grace K. Lee, Executive Director.*

General e-mail, npt@parktrust.org

Web, www.parktrust.org

Protects national parks, wildlife refuges, and historic monuments. Uses funds to purchase private land within or adjacent to existing parks and land suitable for new parks; works with preservation organizations to manage acquired resources.

National Recreation and Park Assn., *22377 Belmont Ridge Rd., Ashburn, VA 20148-4501; (703) 858-0784. Fax, (703) 858-0794. Barbara Tulipane, Executive Director.*

General e-mail, info@nrpa.org

Web, www.nrpa.org

Membership: park and recreation professionals and interested citizens. Promotes support and awareness of park, recreation, and leisure services; facilitates development, expansion, and management of resources; provides technical assistance for park and recreational programs; and provides professional development to members. Monitors legislation and regulations.

Rails-to-Trails Conservancy, *2121 Ward Court N.W. 20037; (202) 331-9696. Fax, (202) 223-9257. Keith Laughlin, President.*

Web, www.railtrails.org

Promotes the conversion of abandoned railroad corridors into hiking and biking trails for public use. Provides public education programs and technical and legal assistance. Publishes trail guides. Monitors legislation and regulations.

Scenic America, *1250 Eye St. N.W., #750A 20005; (202) 638-4630. Fax, (202) 638-3171. Kevin E. Fry, President.*

General e-mail, fry@scenic.org

Web, www.scenic.org

Membership: national, state, and local groups concerned with land-use control, growth management, and landscape protection. Works to enhance the scenic quality of America's communities and countryside. Provides information and technical assistance on scenic byways, tree preservation, economics of aesthetic regulation, billboard and sign control, scenic areas preservation, and growth management.

Student Conservation Assn., *Washington Office, 1800 N. Kent St., #102, Arlington, VA 22209; (703) 524-2441. Fax, (703) 524-2451. Flip Hagood, Senior Vice President, Strategic Initiatives.*

Web, www.thesca.org

Service organization that provides youth and adults with opportunities for training and work experience in natural resource management and conservation. Volunteers serve in national parks, forests, wildlife refuges, and other public lands. (Headquarters in Charlestown, N.H.)

World Wildlife Fund (WWF), *1250 24th St. N.W. 20037-1193 (mailing address: P.O. Box 97180, Washington, DC 20090-7180); (202) 293-4800. Fax, (202) 293-9211. Carter S. Roberts, President.*

Web, www.worldwildlife.org

International conservation organization that provides funds and technical assistance for establishing and maintaining parks.

Water Resources

▶**AGENCIES**

Army Corps of Engineers *(Defense Dept.), 441 G St. N.W., #3K05 20314-1000; (202) 761-0001. Fax, (202) 761-4463. Lt. Gen. Robert L. Van Antwerp (USACE), Chief of Engineers.*

Web, www.usace.army.mil

Provides local governments with disaster relief, flood control, navigation, and hydroelectric power services.

Bureau of Reclamation *(Interior Dept.), 1849 C St. N.W., #7554, 7069 MIB 20240; (202) 513-0501. Fax, (202) 513-0309. John McDonald, Commissioner (Acting). Press, (202) 513-0684.*

Web, www.usbr.gov

Administers federal programs for water and power resource development and management in seventeen western states; oversees municipal and industrial water supplies, hydroelectric power generation, irrigation, flood control, water quality improvement, river regulation, fish and wildlife enhancement, and outdoor recreation.

Environmental Protection Agency (EPA), *Wetlands Division, 1200 Pennsylvania Ave. N.W., #7231A, MC 4502T 20460; (202) 566-0535. Fax, (202) 566-1349. David Evans, Director.*

General e-mail, wetlands.hotline@epa.gov

Web, www.epa.gov/owow/wetlands

Manages dredge-and-fill program under section 404 of the Clean Water Act. Coordinates federal policies affecting wetlands. Promotes public awareness of wetland preservation and management. Encourages the development of stronger wetland programs at the state level. Awards and manages Wetlands Program Development Grants.

Interstate Commission on the Potomac River Basin, *51 Monroe St., #PE-8, Rockville, MD 20850; (301) 984-1908. Fax, (301) 984-5841. Joseph K. Hoffman, Executive Director.*
General e-mail, info@icprb.org
Web, www.potomacriver.org

Nonregulatory interstate compact commission established by Congress to control and reduce water pollution and to restore and protect living resources in the Potomac River and its tributaries. Monitors water quality; assists metropolitan water utilities; seeks innovative methods to solve water supply and land resource problems. Provides information and educational materials on the Potomac River basin.

Office of Management and Budget (OMB), *(Executive Office of the President), Water and Power, New Executive Office Bldg., #8002 20503; (202) 395-3404. Fax, (202) 395-4817. Eugene Ebner, Chief.*
Web, www.whitehouse.gov/omb

Reviews all plans and budgets related to federal or federally assisted water power and related land resource projects.

Rural Development Utilities *(Agriculture Dept.), 1400 Independence Ave. S.W., #5135-S, MS 1510 20250-1510; (202) 720-9540. Fax, (202) 720-1725. James Newby, Administrator (Acting). Information, (202) 720-1255.*
Web, www.usda.gov/rus

Makes loans and provides technical assistance for development, repair, and replacement of water and waste disposal systems in rural areas.

Smithsonian Environmental Research Center *(Smithsonian Institution), 647 Contees Wharf Rd., Edgewater, MD 21037 (mailing address: P.O. Box 28, Edgewater, MD 21037-0028); (443) 482-2200. Fax, (443) 482-2380. Anson H. Hines, Director. Press, (443) 482-2400.*
Web, www.serc.si.edu

Serves as a research center on water ecosystems in the coastal zone.

Tennessee Valley Authority, *Government Affairs, Washington Office, 1 Massachusetts Ave. N.W., #300 20444; (202) 898-2999. Fax, (202) 898-2998. Justin Maierhofer, Director.*
General e-mail, latootle@tva.gov
Web, www.tva.gov

Coordinates resource conservation, development, and land-use programs in the Tennessee River Valley. Operates the river control system; projects include flood control, navigation development, and multiple-use reservoirs.

U.S. Geological Survey (USGS), *(Interior Dept.), Water Resources, 12201 Sunrise Valley Dr., MS 409, Reston, VA 20192; (703) 648-5215. Fax, (703) 648-7031. Matthew C. Larsen, Associate Director for Water.*
Web, http://water.usgs.gov

Administers the Water Resources Research Act of 1990. Assesses the quantity and quality of surface and groundwater resources; collects, analyzes, and disseminates data on water use and the effect of human activity and natural phenomena on hydrologic systems. Provides federal agencies, state and local governments, international organizations, and foreign governments with scientific and technical assistance.

►CONGRESS

For a listing of relevant congressional committees and subcommittees, please see page 252 or the Appendix.

►NONGOVERNMENTAL

American Rivers, *1101 14th St. N.W., #1400 20005; (202) 347-7550. Fax, (202) 347-9240. Rebecca Wodder, President.*
General e-mail, amrivers@amrivers.org
Web, www.americanrivers.org

Works to preserve and protect the nation's river systems through public information and advocacy. Collaborates with grassroots river and watershed groups, other conservation groups, sporting and recreation groups, businesses, local citizens, and various federal, state, and tribal agencies. Monitors legislation and regulations.

American Water Works Assn., *Washington Office, 1300 Eye St. N.W., #701W 20005; (202) 628-8303. Fax, (202) 628-2846. Tom Curtis, Deputy Executive Director.*
Web, www.awwa.org

Membership: municipal water utilities, manufacturers of equipment for water industries, water treatment companies, and individuals. Provides information on drinking water treatment; publishes voluntary standards for the water industry. (Headquarters in Denver, Colo.)

Assn. of State Drinking Water Administrators (ASDWA), *1401 Wilson Blvd., #1225, Arlington, VA 22209; (703) 812-9505. Fax, (703) 812-9506. James D. Taft, Executive Director.*
General e-mail, info@asdwa.org
Web, www.asdwa.org

Membership: state officials responsible for the drinking water supply and enforcement of safety standards. Monitors legislation and regulations.

Environmental Defense, *Washington Office, 1875 Connecticut Ave. N.W., #600 20009-5728; (202) 387-3500. Fax, (202) 234-6049. Michael Roach, Office Manager. Information, (800) 684-3322. Press, (202) 572-3235.*
Web, www.edf.org

Citizens' interest group staffed by lawyers, economists, and scientists. Takes legal action on environmental issues;

provides information on pollution prevention, environmental health, water resources, and water marketing. (Headquarters in New York.)

Irrigation Assn., *6540 Arlington Blvd., Falls Church, VA 22042-6638; (703) 536-7080. Fax, (703) 536-7019. Deborah Hamlin, Executive Director.*
General e-mail, webmaster@irrigation.org

Web, www.irrigation.org

Membership: companies and individuals involved in irrigation, drainage, and erosion control worldwide. Promotes efficient and effective water management through training, education, and certification programs. Interests include economic development and environmental enhancement.

Izaak Walton League of America, *707 Conservation Lane, Gaithersburg, MD 20878-2983; (301) 548-0150. Fax, (301) 548-0146. David Hoskins, Executive Director. Toll-free, (800) 453-5463.*
General e-mail, general@iwla.org

Web, www.iwla.org

Grassroots organization that promotes conservation of natural resources and the environment. Coordinates a citizen action program to monitor and improve the condition of local streams.

National Assn. of Conservation Districts (NACD), *509 Capitol Court N.E. 20002-4937; (202) 547-6223. Fax, (202) 547-6450. Krysta Harden, Chief Executive Director.*
General e-mail, washington@nacdnet.org

Web, www.nacdnet.org

Membership: conservation districts (local subdivisions of state government). Develops national policies and works to promote the conservation of water resources. Interests include erosion and sediment control and control of nonpoint source pollution.

National Assn. of Flood and Stormwater Management Agencies (NAFSMA), *1333 H St. N.W., West Tower, 10th Floor 20005; (202) 218-4133. Fax, (202) 478-1734. Susan Gilson, Executive Director.*
Web, www.nafsma.org

Membership: state, county, and local governments, and special flood management districts concerned with management of water resources. Monitors legislation and regulations.

National Assn. of Regulatory Utility Commissioners, *1101 Vermont Ave. N.W., #200 20005-3521; (202)*
898-2200. Fax, (202) 898-2213. Charles D. Gray, Executive Director. Press, (202) 898-9382.*
General e-mail, admin@naruc.org

Web, www.naruc.org

Membership: members of federal, state, municipal, and international regulatory commissions that have jurisdiction over utilities. Interests include water.

National Assn. of Water Companies (NAWC), *2001 L St. N.W., #850 20036; (202) 833-8383. Fax, (202) 331-7442. Peter L. Cook, Executive Director.*
Web, www.nawc.org

Membership: privately owned, regulated water companies. Provides members with information on legislative and regulatory issues and other subjects.

National Utility Contractors Assn. (NUCA), *4301 N. Fairfax Dr., #360, Arlington, VA 22203-1627; (703) 358-9300. Fax, (703) 358-9307. Bill Hillman, Chief Executive Officer.*
Web, www.nuca.com

Membership: contractors who perform water, sewer, and other underground utility construction. Sponsors conferences; conducts surveys. Monitors public works legislation and regulations.

National Water Resources Assn. (NWRA), *3800 N. Fairfax Dr., #4, Arlington, VA 22203; (703) 524-1544. Fax, (703) 524-1548. Larry Libeu, President.*
General e-mail, nwra@nwra.org

Web, www.nwra.org

Membership: conservation and irrigation districts, municipalities, and others interested in water resources. Works for the development and maintenance of water resource projects in the western reclamation states. Represents interests of members before Congress and regulatory agencies.

Rural Community Assistance Partnership (RCAP), *1522 K St. N.W., #400 20005; (202) 408-1273. Fax, (202) 408-8165. Robert Stewart, Executive Director. Toll-free, (800) 321-7227.*
General e-mail, info@rcap.org

Web, www.rcap.org

Provides expertise to rural communities on wastewater disposal, protection of groundwater supply, and access to safe drinking water. Targets communities with predominately low-income or minority populations. Offers outreach policy analysis, training, and technical assistance to elected officials and other community leaders, utility owners and operators, and residents.

9 Government Operations

GENERAL POLICY AND ANALYSIS

Basic Resources

▶**AGENCIES**

Domestic Policy Council *(Executive Office of the President),* *The White House 20502; (202) 456-5594. Fax, (202) 456-5557. Melody Barnes, Director. Web, www.whitehouse.gov/dpc*

Comprised of cabinet officials and staff members. Coordinates the domestic policy-making process to facilitate the implementation of the president's domestic agenda throughout federal agencies in such major domestic policy areas as agriculture, education, energy, environment, health, housing, labor, and veterans affairs.

Executive Office of the President, *Public Liaison, Dwight D. Eisenhower Executive Office Bldg., #144 20502; (202) 456-2380. Fax, (202) 456-6218. Tina Tchen, Director. Web, www.whitehouse.gov/administration/eop/opl*

Promotes presidential priorities through outreach to concerned constituencies and public interest groups.

Federal Bureau of Investigation (FBI), *(Justice Dept.), Human Resources, 935 Pennsylvania Ave. N.W., #10903 20535; (202) 324-3514. Fax, (202) 324-1091. John G. Raucci, Assistant Director.*

Performs background investigations of presidential appointees. Oversees recruitment and hiring for the FBI.

General Services Administration (GSA), *1800 F St. N.W., #6137 20405; (202) 501-0800. Paul F. Troughy, Administrator (Acting); Barney Brasseux, Deputy Administrator; Brian D. Miller, Inspector General. Press, (202) 501-1231. Web, www.gsa.gov*

Establishes policies for managing federal government property, including construction and operation of buildings and procurement and distribution of supplies and equipment; manages transportation and telecommunications. Manages disposal of surplus federal property. Responsible for www.USA.gov.

General Services Administration (GSA), *Citizen Services and Communications, 1800 F St. N.W., #6121 20405-0001; (202) 501-0705. Fax, (202) 208-1709. Vacant, Associate Administrator; Lindsey Willis, Press. Web, www.gsa.gov*

Seeks to improve the way the federal government provides the public with access to information and services. Coordinates responses to inquiries from both the general public and news media. Maintains an information network for agency employees with regard to items of interest to federal workers. Administers the Web site www.USA.gov, a comprehensive search engine of government information; call (800) FED-INFO for information by phone.

General Services Administration (GSA), *Governmentwide Policy, 1800 F St. N.W., #5240 20405; (202) 501-8880. Fax, (202) 501-8898. Stan Kaczmarczyk, Associate Administrator (Acting). Web, www.gsa.gov/ogp*

Coordinates GSA policy-making activities, including areas of personal and real property, travel and transportation, information technology, regulatory information, and use of federal advisory committees; promotes collaboration between government and the private sector in developing policy and management techniques; works to integrate acquisition, management, and disposal of government property.

General Services Administration (GSA), *National Contact Center, G-132, 1800 F St. N.W., 20405–0001; (800) 333-4636. Stuart Willoughby, Program Manager, (202) 501-9121. TTY, (800) 326-2996. Web, www.info.gov*

Responds to inquiries about federal programs and services. Gives information or locates particular agencies or persons best suited to help with specific concerns.

General Services Administration (GSA), *Office of the Chief Acquisition Officer, 1800 F St. N.W., #4040 20405; (202) 501-1043. Fax, (202) 501-1986. Rodney Lantier, Senior Procurement Executive (Acting). Web, www.gsa.gov/chiefacquisitionofficer*

Develops and implements federal government acquisition policies and procedures; administers Federal Acquisition Regulation (FAR) for civilian agencies. Manages several GSA-specific and governmentwide acquisition database systems. Conducts pre-award and post-award contract reviews; suspends and debars contractors for unsatisfactory performance; coordinates and promotes governmentwide career management and training programs for contracting personnel.

National Archives and Records Administration (NARA), *Federal Register, 800 N. Capitol St. N.W., #700 20001 (mailing address: 8601 Adelphi Rd., College Park, MD 20740-6001); (202) 741-6000. Fax, (202) 741-6012. Raymond Mosley, Director. TTY, (202) 741-6086. Public Laws Update Service (PLUS), (202) 741-6040. General e-mail, fedreg.info@nara.gov*

Web, www.archives.gov/federal_register

Informs citizens of their rights and obligations by providing access to the official texts of federal laws, presidential documents, administrative regulations and notices, and descriptions of federal organizations, programs, and activities. Administers the Electoral College and the constitutional amendment process. Publications available from the U.S. Government Printing Office, (301) 317-3953, http://bookstore.gpo.gov.

Office of Administration *(Executive Office of the President), 725 17th St. N.W., #532 20503; (202) 456-2861. Fax, (202) 456-6512. Cameron Moody, Director. Web, www.whitehouse.gov/oa*

GOVERNMENT OPERATIONS RESOURCES IN CONGRESS

For a complete listing of Congress committees, including their full contact information, leadership, membership, and jurisdictions, please refer to the Appendix on pages 724–837.

HOUSE:

House Administration Committee, (202) 225-2061.
Web, cha.house.gov

House Appropriations Committee, (202) 225-2771.
Web, appropriations.house.gov

    Subcommittee on Commerce, Justice, Science, and Related Agencies, (202) 225-3351.

    Subcommittee on Financial Services and General Government, (202) 225-7245.

    Subcommittee on Legislative Branch, (202) 226-7252.

House Budget Committee, (202) 226-7200.
Web, budget.house.gov

House Education and Labor Committee, Subcommittee on Workforce Protections, (202) 225-3725.
Web, edworkforce.house.gov

House Financial Services Committee, (202) 225-4247.
Web, financialservices.house.gov

House Judiciary Committee, (202) 225-3951.
Web, judiciary.house.gov

    Subcommittee on Courts, the Internet, and Intellectual Property, (202) 225-5741.

House Oversight and Government Reform Committee, (202) 225-5051.
Web, oversight.house.gov

    Subcommittee on Domestic Policy, (202) 225-6427.

    Subcommittee on Federal Workforce, Postal Service, and the District of Columbia, (202) 225-5147.

    Subcommittee on Government Management, Organization, and Procurement, (202) 225-3741.

    Subcommittee on Information Policy, Census, and National Archives, (202) 225-6751.

House Rules Committee, (202) 225-9091.
Web, rules.house.gov

House Small Business Committee, (202) 225-4038.
Web, www.house.gov/smbiz

House Standards of Official Conduct Committee, (202) 225-7103.
Web, www.house.gov/ethics

House Ways and Means Committee, (202) 225-3625.
Web, waysandmeans.house.gov

    Subcommittee on Oversight, (202) 225-5522.

SENATE:

Senate Appropriations Committee, (202) 224-7363.
Web, appropriations.senate.gov

    Subcommittee on Commerce, Justice, Science, and Related Agencies, (202) 224-5202.

    Subcommittee on Financial Services and General Government, (202) 224-1133.

    Subcommittee on Legislative Branch, (202) 224-3477.

Senate Budget Committee, (202) 224-0642.
Web, budget.senate.gov

Senate Environment and Public Works Committee, (202) 224-8832.
Web, epw.senate.gov/public

    Subcommittee on Transportation and Infrastructure, (202) 224-8832

Senate Finance Committee, (202) 224-4515.
Web, finance.senate.gov

Senate Homeland Security and Governmental Affairs Committee, (202) 224-2627.
Web, hsgac.senate.gov

    Permanent Subcommittee on Investigations, (202) 224-9505.

    Subcommittee on Federal Financial Management, Government Information, and International Security, (202) 224-4551.

    Subcommittee on Oversight of Government Management, the Federal Workforce, and the District of Columbia, (202) 224-5538.

Senate Judiciary Committee, (202) 224-7703.
Web, judiciary.senate.gov

    Subcommittee on Administrative Oversight and the Courts, (202) 224-8352.

Senate Rules and Administration Committee, (202) 224-6352.
Web, rules.senate.gov

Senate Select Committee on Ethics, (202) 224-2981.
Web, ethics.senate.gov

Senate Small Business and Entrepreneurship Committee, (202) 224-5175.
Web, sbc.senate.gov

Provides administrative support services to the Executive Office of the President, including financial management and information technology support, human resources management, library and research assistance, facilities management, procurement, printing and graphics support, security, and mail and messenger operations.

White House Offices

OFFICE OF THE PRESIDENT

President, Barack Obama

1600 Pennsylvania Ave. N.W. 20500; (202) 456-1414; fax, (202) 456-2461

Web, www.whitehouse.gov

E-mail, president@whitehouse.gov

Chief of Staff, Rahm Emanuel, Chief of Staff, (202) 456-6798

Jim Messina, Mona Sutphen, Deputy Chiefs of Staff, (202) 456-6798

Advance, Vacant, Director, (202) 456-5309 or (202) 456-5309

Cabinet Liaison, Vacant, Director, (202) 456-2572

Communications, Anita Dunn (Acting), Director, (202) 456-7910

Media Affairs, Christina Reynolds, Director, (202) 456-2131

Speechwriting, Jonathan Fevreay, Director, (202) 456-2170

Counsel, Gregory B. Craig, White House Counsel, (202) 456-2632

Faith-Based and Community Initiatives, Vacant, Director, (202) 456-6708

Intergovernmental Affairs, Vacant, Director, (202) 456-2896

Legislative Affairs, Phil Schiliro, Assistant to the President, (202) 456-2230

  House Liaison, Daniel A. Turton, Deputy Assistant to the President, (202) 456-6620

  Senate Liaison, Shawn Maher, Deputy Assistant to the President, (202) 456-6620

Management and Administration, Bradley J. Kiley, Assistant to the President, (202) 456-5400

  White House Intern Program, Vacant, Coordinator, (202) 456-2500

  White House Military Office, Louis Caldera, Director, (202) 757-2151 or (202) 757-1374

National AIDS Policy, Jeffrey S. Crowley, Director, (202) 456-7320

National Intelligence, Vacant, Director, (202) 201-1001

National Security Adviser, General James Jones (202) 456-9491

Political Affairs, Patrick Gaspard, Deputy Assistant to the President, (202) 456-6257

Presidential Personnel, Donald H. Gips, Assistant to the President, (202) 456-9713

Press Secretary, Robert Gibbs, Press Secretary, (202) 456-2673

Public Liaison, Christina M. Tchen, Director, (202) 456-2380

Scheduling and Advance, Alyssa Mastromonaco, Director, (202) 456-2514

Staff Secretary, Lisa Brown, (202) 456-2702

  Correspondence, Vacant, Director, Recording and voice mail, (202) 456-5465

Strategic Initiatives, Barry Jackson, Director, (202) 456-2108

USA Freedom Corps, Henry C. Lozano, Director, (202) 456-7381

OFFICE OF THE FIRST LADY

First Lady, Michelle Obama

1600 Pennsylvania Ave. N.W. 20500; (202) 456-7064

Web, www.whitehouse.gov/firstlady

E-mail, first.lady@whitehouse.gov

Chief of Staff, Jackie Norris, Chief of Staff, (202) 456-7064

Communications, Camille Johnston, Director. Katie McCormick-Lelyveld, Press Secretary, (202) 456-6313

OFFICE OF THE VICE PRESIDENT

Vice President, Joseph R. Biden Jr.

1600 Pennsylvania Ave. N.W. 20500

Web, www.whitehouse.gov/vicepresident

E-mail, vice.president@whitehouse.gov

Chief of Staff, Ronald A. Klain, Chief of Staff, (202) 456-9000

Communications, Jay Carney, Press Secretary, (202) 456-9042

Dr. Jill Biden, Wife of the Vice President, (202) 456-7458

Office of Management and Budget (OMB), *(Executive Office of the President),* Eisenhower Executive Office Bldg., #252 20503; (202) 395-4840. Fax, (202) 395-3888. Peter Orszag, Director. Press, (202) 395-7254. *Web, www.whitehouse.gov/omb*

Works with other federal agencies to develop and maintain the Web site ExpectMore.gov, which uses the Program Assessment Rating Tool (PART) to gauge the effectiveness of federal programs. Holds programs accountable for improving their performance and management.

Office of Management and Budget (OMB), *(Executive Office of the President), Federal Procurement Policy, New Executive Office Bldg., #9013 20503; (202) 395-3501. Fax, (202) 395-5105. Lesley A. Field, Deputy Administrator. Web, www.whitehouse.gov/omb/procurement*

Oversees and coordinates government procurement policies, regulations, and procedures. Responsible for cost accounting rules governing federal contractors and subcontractors. Interests include effective use of competition, cost effective contracting for vehicles, and managing a useful information technology system for federal procurement managers.

Office of Management and Budget (OMB), *(Executive Office of the President), Housing, Treasury, and Commerce, New Executive Office Bldg., #9201 20503; (202) 395-4696. Fax, (202) 395-6825. Mark Weatherly, Deputy Associate Director. Web, www.whitehouse.gov/omb*

Examines, evaluates, and suggests improvements for agencies and programs within the Housing, Treasury, and Commerce Depts.

The Cabinet of Barack Obama

The president's cabinet includes the vice president and the heads of the fifteen executive departments. In addition, every president has discretion to elevate any number of other government officials to cabinet-rank status. The cabinet is primarily an advisory group.

Joseph R. Biden Jr., Vice President, (202) 456-7549
Web, www.whitehouse.gov/vicepresident
E-mail, vice.president@whitehouse.gov

EXECUTIVE DEPARTMENT CABINET MEMBERS
Agriculture Dept., Thomas J. Vilsack, Secretary, (202) 720-3631
Web, www.usda.gov
E-mail, agsec@usda.gov

Commerce Dept., Gary Locke, Secretary, (202) 482-2112
Web, www.commerce.gov

Defense Dept., Robert M. Gates, Secretary, (703) 692-7100
Web, www.defenselink.mil

Education Dept., Arne Duncan, Secretary, (202) 401-3000
Web, www.ed.gov

Energy Dept., Steven Chu, Secretary, (202) 586-6210
Web, www.energy.gov
E-mail, The.Secretary@hq.doe.gov

Health and Human Services Dept., Kathleen Sebelius, Secretary, (202) 690-7000
Web, www.hhs.gov

Homeland Security Dept., Janet Napolitano, Secretary, (202) 282-8000
Web, www.dhs.gov

Housing and Urban Development Dept., Shaun L. S. Donovan, Secretary, (202) 708-0417
Web, www.hud.gov

Interior Dept., Kenneth L. Salazar, Secretary, (202) 208-7351
Web, www.doi.gov

Justice Dept., Eric H. Holder Jr., Attorney General, (202) 514-2001

Web, www.usdoj.gov
E-mail, AskDOJ@usdoj.gov

Labor Dept., Hilda Solis, Secretary, (202) 693-6001
Web, www.dol.gov

State Dept., Hillary Rodham Clinton, Secretary, (202) 647-9572
Web, www.state.gov

Transportation Dept., Raymond L. LaHood, Secretary, (202) 366-1111
Web, www.dot.gov
E-mail, dot.comments@dot.gov

Treasury Dept., Timothy F. Geithner, Secretary (202) 622-1100
Web, www.ustreas.gov

Veterans Affairs Dept., Eric K. Shinseki, Secretary, (202) 273-4800
Web, www.va.gov

OTHER CABINET-RANK OFFICIALS
Environmental Protection Agency, Lisa P. Jackson, Administrator, (202) 564-4700
Web, www.epa.gov

Office of Management and Budget, Peter Orzag, Director, (202) 395-4840
Web, www.whitehouse.gov/omb

Office of National Drug Control Policy, Edward H. Jurith, Director, (202) 395-6700
Web, www.whitehousedrugpolicy.gov

Office of the U.S. Trade Representative, Ronald Kirk (Acting), U.S. Trade Representative (202) 395-6890
Web, www.ustr.gov
E-mail, contactustr@ustr.eop.gov

Office of the White House Chief of Staff, Rahm Emanuel, Chief of Staff, (202) 456-6798
Web, www.whitehouse.gov

Office of Management and Budget (OMB), *(Executive Office of the President), Information and Regulatory Affairs,* Old Executive Office Bldg., #262 20503; (202) 395-4852. Fax, (202) 395-6102. Kevin Neyland, Administrator (Acting).
Web, www.whitehouse.gov/omb

Oversees development of federal regulatory programs. Supervises agency information management activities in accordance with the Paperwork Reduction Act of 1995, as amended; reviews agency analyses of the effect of government regulatory activities on the U.S. economy.

Office of Management and Budget (OMB), *(Executive Office of the President), Performance and Personnel Management,* New Executive Office Bldg., #7236 20503; (202) 395-5017. Fax, (202) 395-5738. Vacant, Deputy Assistant Director.
Web, www.whitehouse.gov/omb

Examines, evaluates, and suggests improvements for agencies and programs within the Office of Personnel Management and the Executive Office of the President.

Regulatory Information Service Center *(General Services Administration),* 1800 F St. N.W., #3039 20405; (202) 482-7340. Fax, (202) 482-7360. David Pritzker, Senior Attorney. Information, (202) 482-7340.
General e-mail, risc@gsa.gov
Web, www.gsa.gov/risc

Provides the president, Congress, and the public with information on federal regulatory policies and their effects on society; recommends ways to make regulatory information more accessible to government officials and the public. Publishes the *Unified Agenda of Federal Regulatory and Deregulatory Actions.* See www.reginfo.gov for information about government regulations.

Government Accountability Office

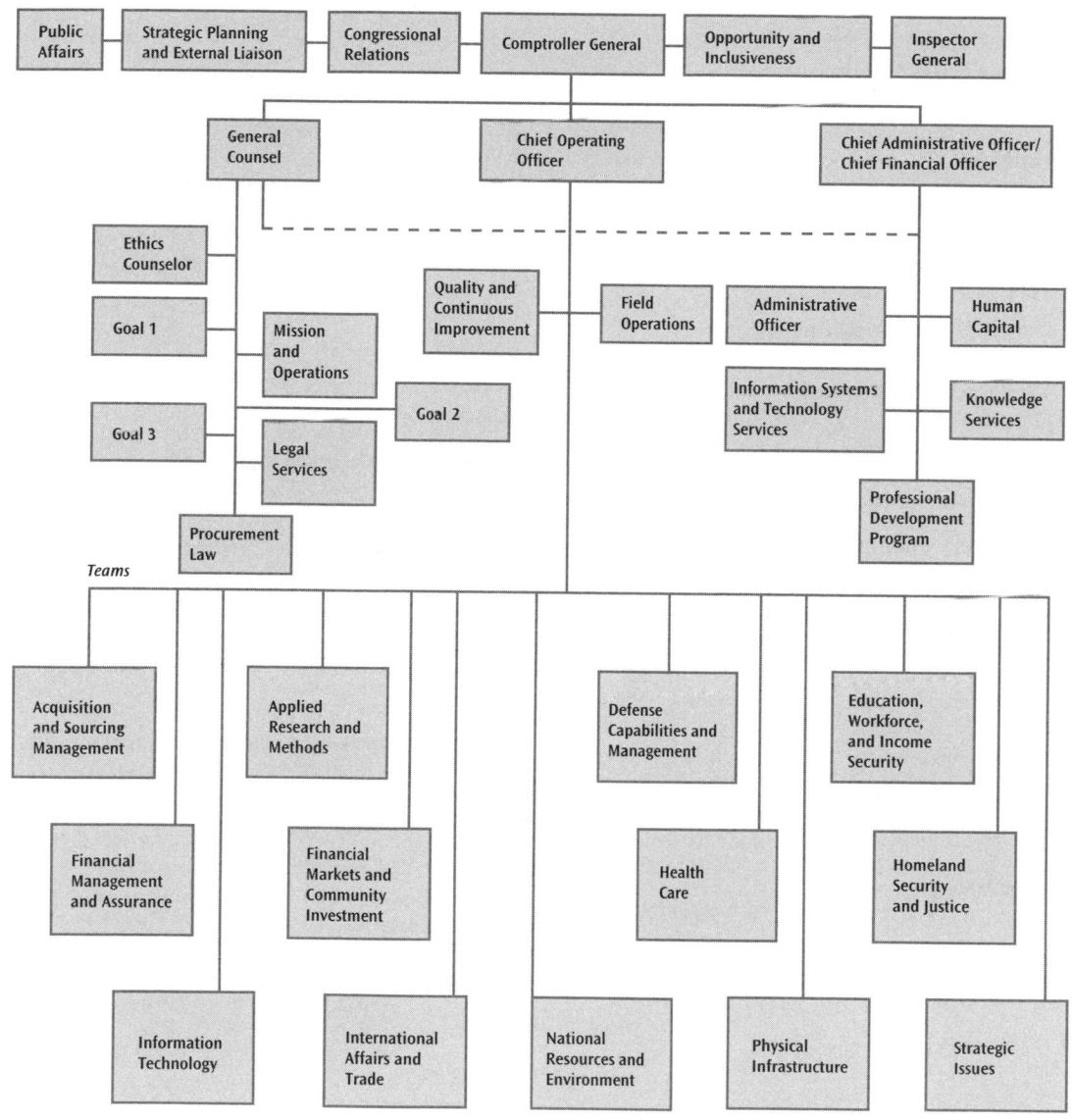

- - - - Indicates a support or advisory relationship with the teams/units rather than a direct reporting relationship

▶CONGRESS

For a listing of relevant congressional committees and subcommittees, please see page 290 or the Appendix.

Government Accountability Office (GAO), *441 G St. N.W., #7100 20548; (202) 512-5500. Fax, (202) 512-5507. Gene L. Dodaro, Comptroller General. Information, (202) 512-3000. Library, (202) 512-2585. Publications, (202) 512-6000. Congressional Relations, (202) 512-4400. Web, www.gao.gov*

Independent, nonpartisan agency in the legislative branch. Serves as the investigating agency for Congress; carries out legal, accounting, auditing, and claims settlement functions; makes recommendations for more effective government operations; publishes monthly lists of reports available to the public. (Formerly the General Accounting Office.)

▶NONGOVERNMENTAL

The Brookings Institution, *Governance Studies, 1755 Massachusetts Ave. N.W. 20036; (202) 797-6090. Fax, (202) 797-6144. Darrell West, Director, (202) 797-6481. Information, (202) 797-6000. Press, (202) 797-6105. Web, www.brookings.edu/governance.aspx*

Explores the formal and informal political institutions of democratic governments to assess how they govern, how their practices compare, and how citizens and government servants can advance sound government.

Center for Plain Language, *3936 Rickover Rd., Silver Spring, MD 20902; (301) 523-8563. Don Byrne, Executive Director.*
General e-mail, center@centerforplainlanguage.org

Web, www.centerforplainlanguage.org

Advocates plain-language/reader-focused writing through education and training within government, the private sector, and academia.

Center for Regulatory Effectiveness (CRE), *1601 Connecticut Ave. N.W., #500 20009; (202) 265-2383. James J. Tozzi, Executive Director.*
General e-mail, comments@thecre.com

Web, www.thecre.com

Clearinghouse for methods to improve the federal regulatory process and public access to data and information used to develop federal regulations. Conducts analyses of the activities of the OMB Office of Information and Regulatory Affairs and serves as a regulatory watchdog over executive branch agencies. Advocates on regulatory issues.

Center for the Study of the Presidency, *1020 19th St. N.W., #250 20036; (202) 872-9800. Fax, (202) 872-9811. David M. Abshire, President.*
General e-mail, center@thepresidency.org

Web, www.thepresidency.org

Membership: college students, government officials, and business leaders interested in the presidency, government, and politics. Conducts conferences, lectures, and symposiums on domestic, economic, and foreign policy issues. Publishes papers, essays, books, and reports on various aspects of the presidency and Congress.

Federal Managers Assn., *1641 Prince St., Alexandria, VA 22314-2818; (703) 683-8700. Fax, (703) 683-8707. Darryl Perkinson, National President; Vacant, Executive Director.*
General e-mail, info@fedmanagers.org

Web, www.fedmanagers.org

Seeks to improve the effectiveness of federal supervisors and managers and the operations of the federal government. Interests include cost-effective government restructuring, competitive civil service pay and benefits, and maintaining the core values of the civil service.

Partnership for Public Service, *1100 New York Ave. N.W., #1090E 20005; (202) 775-9111. Fax, (202) 775-8885. Max Stier, President.*
General e-mail, mail@ourpublicservice.org

Web, www.ourpublicservice.org

Membership: large corporations and private businesses, including financial and information technology organizations. Seeks to improve government efficiency, productivity, and management through a cooperative effort of the public and private sectors. (Merged with the Private Sector Council.)

Project on Government Secrecy, *Federation of American Scientists (FAS), 1725 DeSales St. N.W., 6th Floor 20036; (202) 546-3300. Fax, (202) 675-1010. Steven Aftergood, Project Director. Press, (202) 454-4680.*
General e-mail, fas@fas.org

Web, www.fas.org/programs/ssp/govsec/index.html

Promotes public access to government information and fosters development of rational information security policies. Works to reduce the scope of government secrecy, including national security classification and declassification policies. Publishes hard-to-find government documents online.

The Reg-Markets Center at AEI, *1150 17th St. N.W., #1100 20036; (202) 862-5847. Fax, (202) 862-7169. Robert W. Hahn, Executive Director.*
General e-mail, center@Reg-Markets.org

Web, www.reg-markets.org

Evaluates the impact of laws and government regulations on the economy and offers suggestions for reform.

Understanding Government, *1312 18th St. N.W., #510 20036; (202) 775-8080. Charles Peters, President; Ned Hodgman, Executive Director.*
General e-mail, info@understandinggov.org

Web, www.understandinggov.org

Seeks to stimulate more informed reporting and analyses of government activities. Funds studies of government programs to improve implementation of policy and expenditures.

Washington Center for Complexity and Public Policy, *1233 20th St. N.W., #610 20036-7322; (202) 429-3733. T. Irene Sanders, Executive Director.*
General e-mail, info@complexsys.org

Web, www.complexsys.org

Promotes new approaches to public policy making based on chaos theory and complexity theory. Conducts research and educational programs, using strategic thinking and planning, futures research, and intelligence analysis and public policy making.

Buildings and Services

►AGENCIES

Federal Protective Service (FPS), *(Homeland Security Dept.), 800 N. Capitol St., 5th Floor 20002; (202) 732-8000. Fax, (202) 732-8109. Gary Schenkel, Director. National Hotline, (866) 347-2423.*
Web, www.ice.gov

Law enforcement agency. Oversees security and law enforcement for all buildings under charge and control of the General Services Administration, and properties held by DHS components not under GSA jurisdiction.

General Services Administration (GSA), *Federal Acquisition Institute, 9820 Belvoir Rd., Ft. Belvoir, VA 22060; (703) 805-2300. Fax, (703) 805-2111. Karen Tica, Director, (703) 805-2333.*

General e-mail, Karen.Tica@fai.gov

Web, www.fai.gov

Fosters development of a professional acquisition workforce governmentwide; collects and analyzes acquisition workforce data; helps agencies identify and recruit candidates for the acquisitions field; develops instructional materials; evaluates training and career development programs.

General Services Administration (GSA), *Federal Acquisition Service, 2200 Crystal Dr., 11th Floor, Arlington, VA 22202; (703) 605-5400. Fax, (703) 605-9955. Jim Williams, Commissioner. National Customer Service Center (NCSC), (800) 488-3111 and NCSCcustomer.service@gsa.gov.*

General e-mail, contactfas@gsa.gov

Web, www.gsa.gov/fas

Responsible for providing federal agencies with common-use goods and nonpersonal services and for procurement and supply, transportation and travel management, and disposal of surplus personal property.

General Services Administration (GSA), *National Capital Region, 301 7th St. S.W., #7022 20407; (202) 708-9100. Fax, (202) 708-9966. Sharon Banks, Regional Administrator (Acting).*

Web, www.gsa.gov/ncr

Provides federal agencies with office space and property management services, supplies, telecommunications, transportation, construction services, energy conservation and recycling services, and information technology support; has equal status with regional offices.

General Services Administration (GSA), *Public Buildings Service, 1800 F St. N.W., #6340 20405; (202) 501-1100. Fax, (202) 219-2310. Tony Costa, Commissioner (Acting).*

Web, www.gsa.gov/pbs

Administers the acquisition, construction, maintenance, and operation of buildings owned or leased by the federal government. Manages and disposes of federal real estate.

General Services Administration (GSA), *Public Buildings Service, Organizational Resources, 1800 F St. N.W., #4340 20405; (202) 501-0971. Fax, (202) 501-3296. Sean Mildrew, Assistant Commissioner.*

Web, www.gsa.gov/pbs

Oversees operations of federal buildings, including facility management, safety programs, personnel hiring and training, purchasing and divesting of equipment, and contracting of services and vendors.

General Services Administration (GSA), *Real Property Asset Management, 1800 F St. N.W., #7300 20405; (202) 208-6918. Fax, (202) 208-1480. John Smith, Assistant Commissioner (Acting); Cathy Kronopolus, Chief of Staff (Acting).*

General e-mail, real.property@gsa.gov

Web, www.gsa.gov

Develops, promotes, and assesses compliance with management policies and regulations for the effective and efficient stewardship of federal real property assets and alternative workplaces. Provides oversight and guidance for governmentwide real property asset management plans and related activities, including the use and disposal of excess real property.

General Services Administration (GSA), *Transportation Management Policy, 1800 F St. N.W., #1221 20405; (202) 208-7629. Fax, (202) 501-6742. Henry L. Maury, Director, (202) 208-7928.*

Web, www.gsa.gov/transportationpolicy

Seeks to improve the management and control of procured transportation services governmentwide, promoting regulatory flexibility and business incentives and tools.

Ethics in Government

►AGENCIES

Office of Government Ethics, *1201 New York Ave. N.W., #500 20005-3917; (202) 482-9300. Fax, (202) 482-9237. Robert Cusick, Director.*

General e-mail, contactusoge@oge.gov

Web, www.usoge.gov

Administers executive branch policies relating to financial disclosure, employee conduct, and conflict-of-interest laws. Works to prevent conflicts of interest on the part of federal employees, and to resolve those that do occur. Provides educational materials and training; hosts annual conference; manages e-mail list service to notify federal ethics officials of changes in law and regulations, http://listserv.access.gpo.gov.

U.S. Office of Special Counsel, *1730 M St. N.W., #218 20036-4505; (202) 254-3600. Fax, (202) 653-5161. William E. Reukauf, Special Counsel (Acting); Vacant, Director of Communications. TTY, (800) 877-8339. Issues relating to the Hatch Act, (800) 854-2824.*

Web, www.osc.gov

Investigates allegations of prohibited personnel practices and prosecutes individuals who violate federal statutes and regulations governing federal employees, military veterans, and reservists. Receives and refers federal employee disclosures of waste, fraud, inefficiency, mismanagement, and other violations in the federal government. Enforces the Hatch Act, which limits political activity by most federal and District of Columbia employees.

►CONGRESS

For a listing of relevant congressional committees and subcommittees, please see page 290 or the Appendix.

►NONGOVERNMENTAL

Center for Public Integrity, *910 17th St. N.W., #700 20006; (202) 466-1300. Fax, (202) 466-1102.*

Bill Buzenberg, Executive Director. Press, (202) 481-1225.

Web, www.publicintegrity.org

Conducts investigative research and publishes reports on public policy issues in the United States and around the world. Organizes and supports investigative journalists committed to transparent and comprehensive reporting. Interests include the environment, public health, public accountability, federal and state lobbying, war profiteering, and financial disclosure.

Citizens Against Government Waste, 1301 Connecticut Ave. N.W., #400 20036; (202) 467-5300. Fax, (202) 467-4253. Thomas A. Schatz, President. Information, (800) 232-6479.

Web, www.cagw.org

Nonpartisan organization that seeks to eliminate waste, mismanagement, and inefficiency in the federal government. Monitors legislation, regulations, and the budget process.

Citizens for Responsibility and Ethics in Washington, 1400 Eye St. N.W., #450 20005; (202) 408-5565. Fax, (202) 588-5020. Melanie Sloan, Executive Director.

General e-mail, info@citizensforethics.org

Web, www.citizensforethics.org

Promotes ethics and accountability in government and public life. Investigates, reports, and litigates government misconduct. Seeks to enforce government disclosure of information.

Fund for Constitutional Government (FCG), 122 Maryland Ave. N.E. 20002; (202) 546-3799. Fax, (202) 543-3156. Anne B. Zill, President; Conrad Martin, Executive Director.

General e-mail, info@fcgonline.org

Web, www.fcgonline.org

Promotes an open and accountable government. Seeks to expose and correct corruption in the federal government and private sector through research and public education. Sponsors the Electronic Privacy Information Center, the Government Accountability Project, the Project on Government Oversight, and OpenThe Government.org

Government Accountability Project, 1612 K St. N.W., #1100 20006; (202) 408-0034. Fax, (202) 408-9855. Mark Cohen, Executive Director.

Web, www.whistleblower.org

Membership: federal employees, union members, professionals, and interested citizens. Provides legal and strategic counsel to employees in the public and private sectors who seek to expose corporate and government actions that are illegal, wasteful, or repressive; aids such employees in personnel action taken against them; assists grassroots organizations investigating corporate wrongdoing, government inaction, or corruption. Promotes policy and legal reforms of whistle-blower laws.

Project on Government Oversight, 1100 G St. N.W., #900 20001-4542; (202) 347-1122. Fax, (202) 347-1116. Danielle Brian, Executive Director.

General e-mail, pogo@pogo.org

Web, www.pogo.org

Public interest organization that works to expose waste, fraud, abuse, and conflicts of interest in all aspects of federal spending.

Sunlight Foundation, 1818 N St. N.W., #410 20036; (202) 742-1520. Fax, (202) 742-1524. Ellen S. Miller, Executive Director.

General e-mail, info@sunlightfoundation.com

Web, www.sunlightfoundation.com

Utilizes new information technology to enable citizens to research federal government actions. Seeks to reduce corruption and ensure greater transparency and accountability by the government. Produces OpenCongress.org and other tools; offers "transparency grants" for development of databases and Web sites. Offers online tutorials on the role of money in politics.

Executive Reorganization

▶AGENCIES

Office of Management and Budget (OMB), *(Executive Office of the President), President's Management Council,* Dwight D. Eisenhower Executive Office Bldg., #260 20503; (202) 456-7070. Fax, (202) 456-5938. Vacant, Chair.

Web, www.whitehouse.gov/omb

Membership: chief operating officers of federal government departments and agencies. Responsible for implementing the management improvement initiatives of the administration. Develops and oversees improved governmentwide management and administrative systems; formulates long-range plans to promote these systems; works to resolve interagency management problems and to implement reforms.

▶CONGRESS

For a listing of relevant congressional committees and subcommittees, please see page 290 or the Appendix.

Government Accountability Office (GAO), *Information Technology,* 441 G St. N.W., #4480 20548; (202) 512-6253. Joel C. Willemssen, Managing Director.

Web, www.gao.gov

Seeks to make the federal government more effective in its information management by improving performance and reducing costs. Assesses best practices in the public and private sectors; makes recommendations to government agencies. Interests include information security. (Formerly the General Accounting Office.)

CENSUS, POPULATION DATA

►AGENCIES

Census Bureau *(Commerce Dept.)*, *4600 Silver Hill Rd., #8H-010, North Bldg., Suitland, MD 20746 (for mailing address, change city and zip code to: Washington, DC 20233-0100); (301) 763-2135. Fax, (301) 763-3761. Thomas L. Mesenbourg Jr., Director (Acting). Information, (301) 763-3961. Library, (301) 763-2135. Press, (301) 763-3030 (pio@census.gov).*
General e-mail, pio@census.gov

Web, www.census.gov

Conducts surveys and censuses (including the decennial census of population and the American Community Survey, as well as the economic census and census of governments every five years); collects and analyzes demographic, social, economic, housing, agricultural, and foreign trade data and data on governments; publishes statistics for use by federal, state, and local governments, Congress, businesses, planners, and the public. Library open to the public.

Census Bureau *(Commerce Dept.)*, **Decennial Census,** *4600 Silver Hill Rd., #8H-122, Suitland, MD 20746 (for mailing address, change city and zip code to: Washington, DC 20233-7000); (301) 763-1764. Fax, (301) 763-8867. Arnold A. Jackson, Associate Director.*
Web, www.census.gov/2010census

Provides data from the 2000 decennial census (including general plans and procedures); economic, demographic, and population statistics; and information on trends. Conducts preparation for the next census.

Census Bureau *(Commerce Dept.)*, **Housing and Household Economic Statistics,** *4600 Silver Hill Rd., #7H-174, Suitland, MD 20746 (for mailing address, change city and zip code to: Washington, DC 20233-8500); (301) 763-3234. Fax, (301) 763-3232. David S. Johnson, Chief.*
General e-mail, hhes-info@census.gov

Web, www.census.gov

Develops statistical programs for the decennial census, the American Community Survey, and for other surveys on housing, income, poverty, and the labor force. Collects and explains the proper use of economic, social, and demographic data. Responsible for the technical planning, analysis, and publication of data from current surveys, including the decennial census, the American Community Survey, the American Housing Survey, the Current Population Survey, and the Survey of Income and Program Participation.

Census Bureau *(Commerce Dept.)*, **Population Division,** *4600 Silver Hill Rd., #5H-174, Suitland, MD 20746 (for mailing address, change city and zip code to: Washington, DC 20233-8800); (301) 763-2071. Fax, (301) 763-2516. Enrique J. Lamas, Chief. Information, (301) 763-3030. Toll-free, (866) 758-1060.*

General e-mail, pop@census.gov

Web, www.census.gov/population/www

Prepares population estimates and projections for national, state, and local areas and congressional districts. Provides data on demographic and social statistics in the following areas: families and households, marital status and living arrangements, farm population, migration and mobility, population distribution, ancestry, fertility, child care, race and ethnicity, language patterns, school enrollment, educational attainment, and voting.

►CONGRESS

For a listing of relevant congressional committees and subcommittees, please see page 290 or the Appendix.

►NONGOVERNMENTAL

Population Assn. of America, *8630 Fenton St., #722, Silver Spring, MD 20910; (301) 565-6710. Fax, (301) 565-7850. Stephanie Dudley, Executive Director.*
General e-mail, info@popassoc.org

Web, www.popassoc.org

Membership: university, government, and industry researchers in demography. Publishes newsletters, monitors legislation and related government activities, and supports collaboration of demographers. Holds annual technical sessions to present papers on domestic and international population issues and statistics.

Population Reference Bureau, *1875 Connecticut Ave. N.W., #520 20009-5728; (202) 483-1100. Fax, (202) 328-3937. William P. Butz, President. Toll-free, (800) 877-9881.*
General e-mail, popref@prb.org

Web, www.prb.org

Educational organization engaged in information dissemination, training, and policy analysis on domestic and international population trends and issues. Interests include international development and family planning programs, the environment, and U.S. social and economic policy. Library open to the public.

CIVIL SERVICE

►AGENCIES

National Archives and Records Administration (NARA), *Information Security Oversight, 700 Pennsylvania Ave. N.W., #503 20408-0001; (202) 357-5250. Fax, (202) 357-5907. William J. Bosanko, Director, (202) 357-5205.*
General e-mail, isoo@nara.gov

Web, www.archives.gov/isoo/index.html

Oversees the security classification system throughout the executive branch; reports to the president on implementation of the security classification system. Develops and disseminates security education materials. Oversees the Classified Information Nondisclosure Agreement, which

Financial Officers for Federal Departments and Agencies

DEPARTMENTS

Agriculture, Jon Holladay (Acting), (202) 720-5539

Commerce, Lisa Casias (Acting), (202) 482-4951

Defense, Robert Hale, (703) 695-3237

   Air Force, Vacant, (703) 697-1974

   Army, Peter Kunkel, (703) 614-4356

   Navy, John McNair (Acting), (703) 697-2325

Education, Thomas Skelly (Acting), (202) 401-0085

Energy, Steve Isakowitz, (202) 586-4171

Health and Human Services, Sheila Conley, (202) 690-7084

Homeland Security, Peggy Sherry (Acting), (202) 447-5751

   Coast Guard, Robert Branham, (202) 372-3407

Housing and Urban Development, Vacant, (202) 708-1946

Interior, James E. Cason, (202) 208-6149

Justice, Lee J. Lofthus, (202) 514-3101

Labor, Lisa Doherty Fiely (Acting), (202) 693-6800

State, James L. Millett, (202) 647-7490

Transportation, Lana Hurdle (Acting), (202) 366-9191

Treasury

   Chief Financial Officer, Vacant, (202) 622-0410

   Comptroller of the Currency, John C. Dugan, (202) 874-4900

Veterans Affairs, Rita Reed (Acting), (202) 273-5583

AGENCIES

Advisory Council on Historic Preservation, Danielle Pannell, (202) 606-8503

Agency for International Development, David Ostermeyer, (202) 712-0988 or (202) 712-1980

Central Intelligence Agency, Brian Shortley, (703) 482-6044

Commission on Civil Rights, Tina Louise Martin, (202) 376-8356

Commodity Futures Trading Commission, Mark Carney, (202) 418-5477

Consumer Product Safety Commission, Edward E. Quist, (301) 504-7655; Deborah Hodge, (301) 504-7130

Corporation for National and Community Service, Jerry Bridges, (202) 606-6683

Corporation for Public Broadcasting, Bill Tayman, (202) 879-9600

Environmental Protection Agency, Maryann Froehlich (Acting), (202) 564-1151

Equal Employment Opportunity Commission, Jeffrey A. Smith, (202) 663-4200

Export-Import Bank, John F. Simonson, (202) 565-3952

Farm Credit Administration, Stephen Smith, (703) 883-4275

Federal Bureau of Investigation, Richard Haley, (202) 324-1345

Federal Communications Commission, Mark Stephens, (202) 418-1925

Federal Deposit Insurance Corporation, Steven O. App, (202) 898-8732

Federal Election Commission, Brian Duffy, (202) 694-1007

Federal Emergency Management Agency, Norman Dong, (202) 646-3545

Federal Energy Regulatory Commission, Thomas R. Herlihy, (202) 502-8300

Federal Home Loan Mortgage Corporation (Freddie Mac), Anthony Piszel, (703) 903-3946

---

bars federal employees from disclosing classified and sensitive government information.

Office of Personnel Management (OPM), *1900 E St. N.W., #5H09 20415-0001; (202) 606-1800. Fax, (202) 606-2573. John Berry, Director. Press, (202) 606-2402. TTY, (202) 606-2532.*
Web, www.opm.gov

Administers civil service rules and regulations; sets policy for personnel management, labor-management relations, workforce effectiveness, and employment within the executive branch; manages federal personnel activities, including recruitment, pay comparability, and benefit programs.

Office of Personnel Management (OPM), *Human Capital, Leadership, and Merit System Accountability, 1900 E St. N.W., #7470 20415-0001; (202) 606-1575. Fax,*

(202) 606-1798. Kevin E. Mahoney, Associate Director. General e-mail, oversight@opm.gov

Web, www.opm.gov

Monitors federal agencies' personnel practices and ensures that they abide by the Merit Systems Principles. Develops policies and programs in human capital management.

Office of Personnel Management (OPM), *Human Capital Planning and Measurement Group, 1900 E St. N.W., #7675 20405; (202) 606-5181. Fax, (202) 606-2663. Judith Rutkin, Manager.*
General e-mail, joseph.kennedy@opm.gov

Web, www.opm.gov

Responsible for formulating strategies, standards, and metrics to support the successful implementation of human capital management governmentwide.

Financial Officers for Federal Departments and Agencies

Federal Labor Relations Authority, Thomas Beck (202) 218-7945

Federal Maritime Commission, Anthony Haywood (Acting), (202) 523-5800

Federal Mediation and Conciliation Service, Fran Leonard, (202) 606-3661

Federal National Mortgage Association (Fannie Mae), David Johnson, (202) 752-7000

Federal Reserve System, Vacant, (202) 452-2767

Federal Trade Commission, James D. Baker, (202) 326-3168

General Services Administration, Kathleen M. Turco, (202) 501-1721

Government Accountability Office, Sallyann Harper, (202) 512-5800

International Bank for Reconstruction and Development (World Bank), Vincenzo La Via, (202) 473-1988

John F. Kennedy Center for the Performing Arts, Lynne Pratt, (202) 416-8653

Merit Systems Protection Board, Stephen Smith, (202) 653-6772

National Academy of Sciences, Van An, (202) 334-2446

National Aeronautics and Space Administration, Ronald Spoehel, (202) 358-0978

National Archives and Records Administration, Valerie Spargo, (301) 837-3015

National Credit Union Administration, Mary Ann Woodson, (703) 518-6570

National Endowment for the Arts, Sandra Stueckler, (202) 682-5491

National Endowment for the Humanities, John Gleason, (202) 606-8336

National Labor Relations Board, Vacant, (202) 273-4230

National Mediation Board, June D. W. King, (202) 692-5010

National Railroad Passenger Corporation (Amtrak), William H. Campbell, (202) 906-3301

National Science Foundation, Thomas Cooley, (703) 292-8200

National Transportation Safety Board, Steven Goldberg, (202) 314-6210

Nuclear Regulatory Commission, Jim Dyer, (301) 415-7322

Occupational Safety and Health Review Commission, Richard Loeb, (202) 606-5390

Office of Management and Budget, Robert O'Neil, (202) 395-6190

Office of Personnel Management, Mark Reger, (202) 606-1918

Overseas Private Investment Corporation, Howard L. Burris, (202) 336-8510

Peace Corps, George Schutter, (202) 692-1600

Pension Benefit Guaranty Corporation, Patricia Kelly, (202) 326-4060, ext. 6296

Postal Regulatory Commission, Steven W. Williams, (202) 789-6840

Securities and Exchange Commission, Kristine Chadwick, (202) 551-7860

Small Business Administration, Jonathan Carver (Acting), (202) 205-6449

Smithsonian Institution, Alice C. Maroni, (202) 633-7120

Social Security Administration, Mary Glenn-Croft, (410) 965-2910

U.S. International Trade Commission, Patricia Katsourous, (202) 205-2678

U.S. Postal Service, Glen Walker, (202) 268-5272

Office of Personnel Management (OPM), *Workforce Information and Planning Group, 1900 E St. N.W., #7439 20415-0001; (202) 606-1449. Fax, (202) 606-1719. Gary A. Lukowski, Group Manager.*
General e-mail, fedstats@opm.gov
Web, www.opm.gov/feddata

Official government source of statistics on the government workforce. Produces information and analyses for the Office of Personnel Management, Congress, and the public on statistical aspects of the federal civilian workforce, including trends in composition, grade levels, minority employment, sizes of agencies, and salaries.

U.S. Office of Special Counsel, *1730 M St. N.W., #218 20036-4505; (202) 254-3600. Fax, (202) 653-5161. William E. Reukauf, Special Counsel (Acting); Vacant, Director of Communications. TTY, (800) 877-8339. Issues relating to the Hatch Act, (800) 854-2824.*
Web, www.osc.gov

Interprets federal laws, including the Hatch Act, concerning political activities allowed by certain federal employees; investigates allegations of Hatch Act violations and conducts prosecutions. Investigates and prosecutes complaints under the Whistleblower Protection Act.

►**CONGRESS**

For a listing of relevant congressional committees and subcommittees, please see page 290 or the Appendix.

►**NONGOVERNMENTAL**

American Federation of Government Employees (AFGE), *80 F St. N.W. 20001; (202) 737-8700. Fax, (202) 639-6490. John Gage, President. Press, (202) 639-6419. Membership, (202) 639-6410.*
General e-mail, comments@afge.org
Web, www.afge.org

Inspectors General for Federal Departments and Agencies

Departmental and agency inspectors general are responsible for identifying and reporting program fraud and abuse, criminal activity, and unethical conduct in the federal government. In the legislative branch, the Government Accountability Office also has a fraud and abuse hotline: (202) 512-7470. Check www.ignet.gov for additional listings.

DEPARTMENTS

Agriculture, Phyllis K. Fong, (202) 720-8001

Hotline, (800) 424-9121; (202) 690-1622, Washington area

Commerce, Todd Zinser, (202) 482-4661

Hotline, (800) 424-5197; (202) 482-2495, Washington area

Defense, Gordon S. Heddell (Acting), (703) 604-8300

Hotline, (800) 424-9098

Education, Mary Mitchelson (Acting), (202) 245-6900

Hotline, (800) 647-8733

Energy, Gregory H. Friedman, (202) 586-4393

Hotline, (800) 541-1625; (202) 586-4073, Washington area

Health and Human Services, Daniel Levinson, (202) 619-3148

Hotline, (800) 447-8477

Homeland Security and FEMA, Richard L. Skinner, (202) 254-4100

Hotline, (800) 323-8603

Housing and Urban Development, Kenneth M. Donohue, (202) 708-0430

Hotline, (800) 347-3735

Interior, Earl E. Devaney, (202) 208-5745

Hotline, (800) 424-5081; (202) 208-5300 in Washington

Justice, Glenn A. Fine, (202) 514-3435

Hotline, (800) 869-4499

Labor, Gordon S. Heddell, (202) 693-5100

Hotline, (800) 347-3756; (202) 693-6999 Washington area

State, Harold W. Geisel, (202) 663-3061

Hotline, (800) 409-9926; (202) 647-3320, Washington area

Transportation, Calvin L. Scovel III, (202) 366-1959

Hotline, (800) 424-9071

Treasury, Eric Thorson, (202) 622-1090

Hotline, (800) 359-3898

Veterans Affairs, George J. Opfer, (202) 565-8620

Hotline, (800) 488-8244

AGENCIES

Agency for International Development, Donald A. Gambatesa, (202) 712-1150

Hotline, (800) 230-6539

Central Intelligence Agency, John Helgerson, (703) 874-2553

Hotline, (703) 482-0623

Environmental Protection Agency, Bill A. Roderick (Acting), (202) 566-0847

Hotline, (888) 546-8740

Federal Deposit Insurance Corporation, Jon T. Rymer, (703) 562-6386

Hotline, (800) 964-3342

Federal Labor Relations Authority, Francine Eichler, (202) 218-7744

Hotline, (800) 331-3572

General Services Administration, Brian D. Miller, (202) 501-0450

Hotline, (800) 424-5210; (202) 501-1780 Washington area

National Aeronautics and Space Administration, Robert W. Cobb, (202) 358-1220

Hotline, (800) 424-9183

National Science Foundation, Allison Lerner, (703) 292-7100

Hotline, (800) 428-2189

Nuclear Regulatory Commission, Hubert T. Bell, (301) 415-5930

Hotline, (800) 233-3497

Office of Personnel Management, Patrick E. McFarland, (202) 606-1200

Hotline, (202) 606-1800

Small Business Administration, Vacant, (202) 205-6586

Hotline, (800) 767-0385

Social Security Administration, Patrick P. O'Carroll Jr., (410) 966-8385

Hotline, (800) 269-0271

U.S. Postal Service, David C. Williams, (703) 248-2100

Hotline, (888) 877-7644

Membership: approximately 600,000 federal and District of Columbia government employees. Provides legal services to members; assists members with contract negotiations and grievances. Monitors legislation and regulations. (Affiliated with the AFL-CIO.)

Blacks in Government, *3005 Georgia Ave. N.W. 20001-3807; (202) 667-3280. Fax, (202) 667-3705. J. David Reeves, President.*
General e-mail, big@bignet.org
Web, www.bignet.org

Advocacy organization for public employees. Promotes equal opportunity and career advancement for African American government employees; provides career development information; seeks to eliminate racism in the federal workforce; sponsors programs, business meetings, and social gatherings; represents interests of African American government workers to Congress and the executive branch; promotes voter education and registration.

Council for Excellence in Government, *Public Employees Roundtable, 1301 K St. N.W., #450 West 20005; (202) 728-0418. Fax, (202) 728-0422. Lynn Jennings, Chief Executive Officer.*

General e-mail, ceg@excelgov.org

Web, www.excelgov.org

Membership: professional and managerial associations and unions representing a wide range of public employees at all levels. Sponsors conferences, celebrations, and publicity events to educate the public about the contributions of public employees.

Federally Employed Women, *700 N. Fairfax St., #510, Alexandria, VA 22306; (202) 898-0994. Fax, (202) 898-1535. Sue Webster, President.*

General e-mail, few@few.org

Web, www.few.org

Membership: women and men who work for the federal government. Works to eliminate sex discrimination in government employment and to increase job opportunities for women; offers training programs. Monitors legislation and regulations.

Federal Managers Assn., *1641 Prince St., Alexandria, VA 22314-2818; (703) 683-8700. Fax, (703) 683-8707. Darryl Perkinson, National President; Vacant, Executive Director.*

General e-mail, info@fedmanagers.org

Web, www.fedmanagers.org

Seeks to improve the effectiveness of federal supervisors and managers and the operations of the federal government. Interests include cost-effective government restructuring, competitive civil service pay and benefits, and maintaining the core values of the civil service.

Senior Executives Assn., *820 1st St. N.E., #700 20002; (202) 927-7000. Fax, (202) 927-5192. Carol A. Bonosaro, President.*

General e-mail, action@seniorexecs.org

Web, www.seniorexecs.org

Professional association representing Senior Executive Service members and other federal career executives. Sponsors professional education. Interests include management improvement. Monitors legislation and regulations.

Dismissals and Disputes

▶**AGENCIES**

Merit Systems Protection Board, *1615 M St. N.W., 5th Floor 20419; (202) 653-7200. Fax, (202) 653-7130. Neil*

McPhie, Chair; William Spencer, Clerk of the Board. TTY, (800) 877-8339. Toll-free, (800) 209-8960; MSPB Inspector General hotline, (800) 424-9121.

General e-mail, mspb@mspb.gov

Web, www.mspb.gov

Independent quasi-judicial agency that handles hearings and appeals involving federal employees; protects the integrity of federal merit systems and ensures adequate protection for employees against abuses by agency management. Library open to the public.

Merit Systems Protection Board, *Appeals Counsel, 1615 M St. N.W. 20419; (202) 653-6772, ext. 1243. Fax, (202) 653-7130. Neil Agmcphie, Chair.*

General e-mail, settlement@mspb.gov

Web, www.mspb.gov/sites/mspb/pages/The Appeal Process. aspx

Analyzes and processes petitions for review of appeals decisions from the regional offices; prepares opinions and orders for board consideration; analyzes and processes cases that are reopened and prepares proposed depositions.

Merit Systems Protection Board, *Policy and Evaluations, 1615 M St. N.W. 20419; (202) 653-6180. Fax, (202) 653-7211. John Crum, Director. Information, (800) 209-8960 (option 2). TTY, (800) 877-8339.*

General e-mail, studies@mspb.gov

Web, www.mspb.gov/sites/mspb/pages/MSPB Studies.aspx

Conducts studies on the civil service and other executive branch merit systems; reports to the president and Congress on whether federal employees are adequately protected against political abuses and prohibited personnel practices. Conducts annual oversight review of the Office of Personnel Management.

Merit Systems Protection Board, *Washington Regional Office, 1800 Diagonal Rd., #205, Alexandria, VA 22314-2840; (703) 756-6250. Fax, (703) 756-7112. Jeremiah Cassidy, Regional Director.*

General e-mail, washingtonregion@mspb.gov

Web, www.mspb.gov

Hears and decides appeals of adverse personnel actions (such as removals, suspensions for more than fourteen days, and reductions in grade or pay), retirement, and performance-related actions for federal civilian employees who work in the Washington area, Virginia, North Carolina, or in overseas areas not covered by other regional board offices. Federal civilian employees who work outside Washington should contact the Merit Systems Protection Board regional office in their area.

Office of Personnel Management (OPM), *General Counsel, 1900 E St. N.W., #7353 20415-0001; (202) 606-1700. Fax, (202) 606-2609. Elaine Kaplan, General Counsel.*

Web, www.opm.gov

Represents the federal government before the Merit Systems Protection Board, other administrative tribunals, and the courts.

Office of Personnel Management

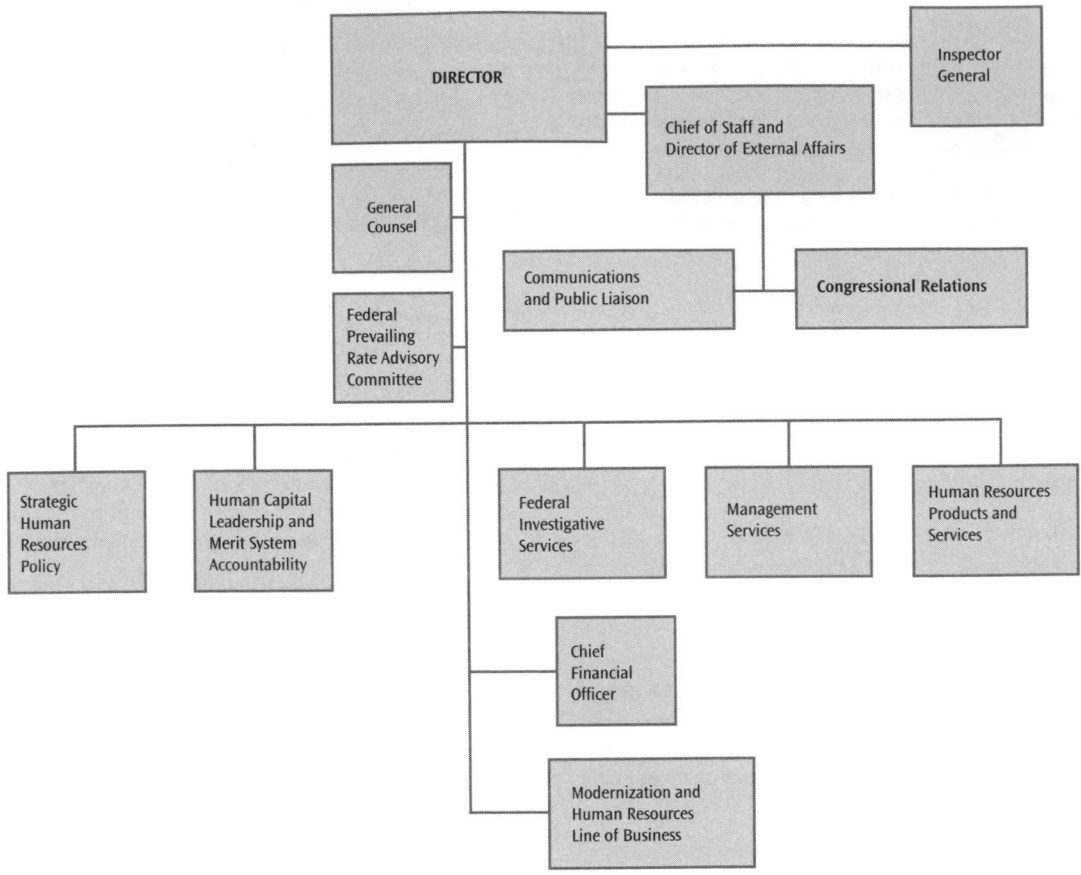

Office of Personnel Management (OPM), *Strategic Human Resources Policy, Employee Accountability Group, 1900 E St. N.W., #7H28 20415-0001; (202) 606-1972. Fax, (202) 606-2613. Dennis McPeters, Chief. General e-mail, er@opm.gov*

Web, www.opm.gov/er

Develops, implements, and interprets policy on governmentwide employee relations. Intervenes in or seeks reconsideration of erroneous third-party decisions.

U.S. Office of Special Counsel, *1730 M St. N.W., #218 20036-4505; (202) 254-3600. Fax, (202) 653-5161. William E. Reukauf, Special Counsel (Acting); Vacant, Director of Communications. TTY, (800) 877-8339. Issues relating to the Hatch Act, (800) 854-2824. Web, www.osc.gov*

Investigates allegations of prohibited personnel practices, including reprisals against whistleblowers (federal employees who disclose waste, fraud, inefficiency, and wrongdoing by supervisors of federal departments and agencies). Initiates necessary corrective or disciplinary action. Enforces the Hatch Act, which limits political activity by most federal and District of Columbia employees.

▶**JUDICIARY**

U.S. Court of Appeals for the Federal Circuit, *717 Madison Pl. N.W. 20439; (202) 633-6550. Fax, (202) 633-9623. Paul R. Michel, Chief Judge; Jan Horbaly, Clerk, (202) 312-5520. Web, www.cafe.uscourts.gov*

Reviews decisions of the Merit Systems Protection Board.

Hiring, Recruitment, and Training

▶**AGENCIES**

Office of Personnel Management (OPM), *Center for Merit System Accountability, 1900 E St. N.W., #6484 20415-5100; (202) 606-2786. Fax, (202) 606-0557. Jeffrey E. Sumberg, Deputy Associate Director. Web, www.opm.gov*

Responsible for training and curriculum development programs for government executives and supervisors. Administers executive personnel systems, including those for the Senior Executive Service (SES) and personnel in executive positions not in SES.

Office of Personnel Management (OPM), *Federal Investigative Services, 1900 E St. N.W., #2H31 20415-0001; (202) 606-1042. Fax, (202) 606-2390. Kathy Dillaman, Associate Director.*
Web, www.opm.gov/extra/investigate

Initiates and conducts investigations of new federal employees; determines whether applicants and appointees are suitable for positions.

Office of Personnel Management (OPM), *Human Resources Products and Services, 1900 E St. N.W., #4310 20415-1000; (202) 606-0600. Fax, (202) 606-2711. Kay T. Ely, Associate Director.*
Web, www.opm.gov/products_and_services

Manages federal human resources policy, including staffing, compensation, benefits, labor relations, and position classification.

Office of Personnel Management (OPM), *Intergovernmental Personnel Act Mobility Program, 1900 E St. N.W., #7463 20415-0001; (202) 606-2430. Fax, (202) 606 1798. Angela Graham Humes, Program Head.*
General e-mail, ipa@opm.gov
Web, www.opm.gov/programs/ipa

Implements temporary personnel exchanges between federal agencies and nonfederal entities, including state and local governments, institutions of higher education, and other organizations.

Office of Personnel Management (OPM), *Outreach Group, 1900 E St. N.W., #7412 20415; (202) 606-2773. Anita R. Hanson, Outreach Group Manager.*
Web, www.opm.gov

Provides veterans, military personnel, and federal hiring officials with information on veterans' rights and employment opportunities with the federal government. Provides outreach to colleges and universities on Schedule A hiring authorities for people with disabilities.

Office of Personnel Management (OPM), *Standards, Competencies, and Assessments Development, 1900 E St. N.W., #6H31 20415-0001; (202) 606-3600. Fax, (202) 606-4841. Andrea Bright, Chief, (202) 606-3590.*
General e-mail, fedclass@opm.gov
Web, www.opm.gov/fedclass

Develops job classification standards for occupations in the general schedule and federal wage system.

Office of Personnel Management (OPM), *Strategic Human Resources Policy, 1900 E St. N.W., #6566 20415-0001; (202) 606-6500. Fax, (202) 606-1637. Nancy H. Kichak, Associate Director.*

Responsible for development of policy concerning human resources throughout the federal government covering the areas of pay and performance, employee and family support, workforce relations, and training and development. Also responsible for research and development of workforce information needed for policy making.

Labor-Management Relations

►AGENCIES

Federal Labor Relations Authority, *1400 K St. N.W., 2nd Floor 20424-0001; (202) 218-7770. Fax, (202) 482-6659. Carol W. Pope, Chair; Catherine Emerson, Executive Director (Acting).*
Web, www.flra.gov

Oversees the federal labor-management relations program; administers the law that protects the right of nonpostal federal employees to organize, bargain collectively, and participate through labor organizations of their own choosing.

Federal Service Impasses Panel *(Federal Labor Relations Authority), 1400 K St. N.W., 2nd Floor 20424-0001; (202) 218-7790. Fax, (202) 482-6674. H. Joseph Schimansky, Executive Director; Vacant, Chair.*
Web, www.flra.gov/fsip/panel.html

Assists in resolving contract negotiation impasses over conditions of employment between federal agencies and labor organizations representing federal employees.

Office of Personnel Management (OPM), *General Counsel, 1900 E St. N.W., #7353 20415-0001; (202) 606-1700. Fax, (202) 606-2609. R. Alan Miller, General Counsel (Acting).*
Web, www.opm.gov

Advises the government on law and legal policy relating to federal labor-management relations; represents the government before the Merit Systems Protection Board.

Office of Personnel Management (OPM), *Workforce Relations and Accountability Policy, 1900 E St. N.W., #7H28 20415-0001; (202) 606-2930. Fax, (202) 606-2613. Anna A. Mazzi, Deputy Associate Director.*
Web, www.opm.gov

Develops policy for government agencies and unions regarding employee- and labor-management relations.

►NONGOVERNMENTAL

National Alliance of Postal and Federal Employees (NAPFE), *1620 11th St. N.W. 20001; (202) 939-6325. Fax, (202) 939-6389. James M. McGee, President.*
General e-mail, headquarters@napfe.org
Web, www.napfe.com

Membership: approximately 70,000 postal and federal employees. Helps members negotiate pay, benefits, and better working conditions; conducts training programs and workshops. Monitors legislation and regulations.

National Assn. of Government Employees (NAGE), *Washington Office,* 601 N. Fairfax St., #125, Alexandria, VA 22314; (703) 519-0300. Fax, (703) 519-0311. David J. Holway, National President. Toll-free, (866) 412-7790. General e-mail, nage@erols.com

Web, www.nage.org

Membership: approximately 200,000 federal government employees. Helps members negotiate pay, benefits, and better working conditions; conducts training programs and workshops. Monitors legislation and regulations. (Headquarters in Quincy, Mass.)

National Federation of Federal Employees, 805 15th St. N.W., #500 20005; (202) 216-4420. Fax, (202) 898-1861. Richard Brown, National President. General e-mail, cbythrow@nffe.org

Web, www.nffe.org

Membership: approximately 100,000 employees throughout various agencies within the federal government. Helps members negotiate pay, benefits, and better working conditions; conducts training programs and workshops. Monitors legislation and regulations.

National Treasury Employees Union (NTEU), 1750 H St. N.W. 20006; (202) 572-5500. Fax, (202) 572-5644. Colleen Kelly, President. General e-mail, nteu-pr@nteu.org

Web, www.nteu.org

Membership: approximately 150,000 employees from the Treasury Dept. and thirty-two other federal agencies and departments. Helps members negotiate pay, benefits, and better working conditions; conducts training programs and workshops. Monitors legislation and regulations.

Public Service Research Foundation, 320D Maple Ave. East, Vienna, VA 22180-4747; (703) 242-3575. Fax, (703) 242-3579. David Y. Denholm, President. General e-mail, info@psrf.org

Web, www.psrf.org

Independent, nonpartisan research and educational organization. Studies labor unions and labor issues with emphasis on employment in the public sector. Sponsors conferences and seminars. Library open to the public by appointment.

Pay and Employee Benefits

▶**AGENCIES**

Bureau of Labor Statistics (BLS), *(Labor Dept.),* *Compensation and Working Conditions,* 2 Massachusetts Ave. N.E., #4130 20212; (202) 691-6300. Fax, (202) 691-6310. William Wiatrowski, Associate Commissioner. Web, www.bls.gov/bls/proghome.htm#ocwc

Develops the National Compensation Survey. Analyzes, distributes, and disseminates information on occupational earnings, benefits, and compensation cost trends.

Labor Dept. (DOL), *Federal Employees' Compensation,* 200 Constitution Ave. N.W., #S3229 20210; (202) 693-0040. Fax, (202) 693-1497. Douglas Fitzgerald, Director. TTY, (877) 889-5627. General inquiries: toll-free, (866) 999-3322. Specific claims: toll-free, (866) 692-7487 (customers should contact their district office first, www. dol.gov/esa/owcp/contacts/fecacont.htm).

Web, www.dol.gov/esa/owcp/dfec

Administers the Federal Employees Compensation Act, which provides disability compensation for federal employees, including wage replacement benefits, medical treatment, vocational rehabilitation, and other benefits.

Office of Personnel Management (OPM), *Federal Prevailing Rate Advisory Committee,* 1900 E St. N.W., #5526 20415; (202) 606-1000. Fax, (202) 606-2573. Charles E. Brooks, Chair.

Advises OPM on pay systems for blue-collar and other federal workers.

Office of Personnel Management (OPM), *Insurance Services,* 1900 E St. N.W., #3415 20415; (202) 606-0745. Fax, (202) 606-0633. Lorraine E. Dettman, Assistant Director.

Web, www.opm.gov/insure

Administers group life insurance for federal employees and retirees; negotiates rates and benefits with health insurance carriers; settles disputed claims. Administers the Federal Employees' Health Benefits (FEHB), the Federal Employees' Group Life Insurance (FEGLI), the Federal Long Term Care Insurance (FLTCIP), and the Flexible Spending Accounts (FSA) programs.

Office of Personnel Management (OPM), *Pay Administration Group,* 1900 E St. N.W., #7H31 20415; (202) 606-2838. Fax, (202) 606-4264. Jeanne Jacobson, Manager.

Web, www.opm.gov/oca/payrates/index.htm

Responsible for the General Schedule and locality pay adjustment process for white-collar federal workers. Supports the Federal Salary Council and the president's "pay agent" (composed of the directors of OPM and the Office of Management and Budget and the secretary of labor). Annual report of the pay agent and General Schedule pay rates are available on OPM's Web site. Supports the Federal Prevailing Rate Advisory Committee and provides regulations and policies for the administration of the federal wage system for blue-collar federal employees. Administers the nonforeign area cost of living allowance program for federal employees outside the forty-eight contiguous states.

Office of Personnel Management (OPM), *Performance and Pay Systems,* 1900 E St. N.W., #7H31 20415; (202) 418-3163. Fax, (202) 606-0824. Chuck Grimes, Deputy Associate Director; Barbara W. Colchao, Group Manager, (202) 606-2720. General e-mail, pay-performance-policy@opm.gov

Web, www.opm.gov/perform

Sets policy and implements the performance appraisal and pay-for-performance system for federal employees.

Office of Personnel Management (OPM), *Retirement and Insurance Services,* 1900 E St. N.W., #4312 20415; (202) 606-0462. Fax, (202) 606-1163. Kathleen McGettigan, Deputy Associate Director. TTY, (800) 878-5707. Toll-free, (888) 767-6738.
General e-mail, retire@opm.gov

Web, www.opm.gov/retire; Forms, www.opm.gov/forms/html/ri.asp

Implements federal policy and regulations on retirement and insurance benefits.

Office of Personnel Management (OPM), *Retirement Information,* 1900 E St. N.W. 20415-1000; (202) 606-0300. Fax, (202) 606-0145. Joseph Donald Jr., Chief. TTY, (800) 878-5707.
General e-mail, retire@opm.gov

Web, www.opm.gov/retire

Responds to telephone inquiries on retirement law and health and life insurance; handles reports of annuitants' deaths; conducts interviews on individual cases; makes appropriate referrals.

Office of Personnel Management (OPM), *Retirement Services,* 1900 E St. N.W., #3305 20415; (202) 606-0300. Fax, (202) 606-0066. Joseph Donald Jr., Assistant Director. TTY, (800) 878-5707. Toll-free, (888) 767-6738.
General e-mail, retire@opm.gov

Web, www.opm.gov/retire

Administers the civil service and federal employees' retirement systems; responsible for monthly annuity payments and other benefits; organizes and maintains retirement records; distributes information on retirement and on insurance programs for annuitants.

▶NONGOVERNMENTAL

National Active and Retired Federal Employees Assn. (NARFE), 606 N. Washington St., Alexandria, VA 22314; (703) 838-7760. Fax, (703) 838-7785. Margaret L. Baptiste, President. Member relations, (800) 456-8410.
General e-mail, hq@narfe.org

Web, www.narfe.org

Works to preserve the integrity of the civil service retirement system. Provides members with information about benefits for retired federal employees and for survivors of deceased federal employees. Monitors legislation and regulations.

FEDERAL CONTRACTS AND PROCUREMENT

▶AGENCIES

Committee for Purchase from People Who Are Blind or Severely Disabled, 1421 Jefferson Davis Hwy., #10800, Arlington, VA 22202-3259; (703) 603-7740. Fax, (703) 603-0655. Tina Ballard, Executive Director.
Web, www.abilityone.gov

Presidentially appointed committee. Determines which products and services are suitable for federal procurement from qualified nonprofit agencies that employ people who are blind or have other severe disabilities; seeks to increase employment opportunities for these individuals.

Comptroller of the Currency *(Treasury Dept.),* *Acquisition Management,* 250 E St. S.W. 20219; (202) 874-5040. Fax, (202) 874-5625. Wes McKee, Director.
Web, www.occ.treas.gov

Responsible for procuring all of the goods and services required by the Office of the Comptroller of the Currency through federal contracting, interagency agreements, and cooperative agreements. Ensures that small businesses owned and controlled by minorities, women, and individuals with disabilities are given the opportunity to participate in contracts with the Comptroller of the Currency.

General Services Administration (GSA), *Civilian Board of Contract Appeals,* 1800 M St. N.W., 6th Floor 20036; (202) 606-8820. Fax, (202) 606-0019. Stephen M. Daniels, Chair. For filings, (202) 501-0116.
Web, www.cbca.gsa.gov

Hears and decides contract disputes between government contractors and agencies, excluding the departments of Defense, Army, Navy, and Air Force; the National Aeronautics and Space Administration; the U.S. Postal Service; the Postal Regulatory Commission; and the Tennessee Valley Authority. Provides alternative dispute resolution services on contract-related matters to excluded agencies when jointly requested by the agency and its contractor.

General Services Administration (GSA), *Federal Procurement Data System–Next Generation (FPDS-NG),* 2011 Crystal City Dr., Crystal Park 1, #911, Arlington, VA 22202. Help Desk, (703) 390-5360.
Web, www.fpds-ng.gov

Service contracted out by GSA to Global Computer Enterprise that collects procurement data from all federal government contracts and disseminates these data via the Internet. Reports include agency identification, products or services purchased, dollar obligation, principal place of performance, and contractor identification; also provides socioeconomic indicators such as business size and business ownership type.

General Services Administration (GSA), *Governmentwide Policy,* 1800 F St. N.W., #5240 20405; (202) 501-8880. Fax, (202) 501-8898. Stan Kaczmarczyk, Associate Administrator (Acting).
Web, www.gsa.gov/ogp

Coordinates GSA policy-making activities, including areas of personal and real property, travel and transportation, information technology, regulatory information, and use of federal advisory committees; promotes collaboration between government and the private sector in developing policy and management techniques; works to integrate acquisition, management, and disposal of government property.

General Services Administration (GSA), *Office of the Chief Acquisition Officer,* 1800 F St. N.W., #4040 20405; (202) 501-1043. Fax, (202) 501-1986. Rodney Lantier, Senior Procurement Executive (Acting).
Web, www.gsa.gov/chiefacquisitionofficer

Develops and implements federal government acquisition policies and procedures; administers Federal Acquisition Regulation (FAR) for civilian agencies. Manages several GSA-specific and governmentwide acquisition database systems. Conducts pre-award and post-award contract reviews; suspends and debars contractors for unsatisfactory performance; coordinates and promotes governmentwide career management and training programs for contracting personnel.

General Services Administration (GSA), *Small Business Utilization,* 1800 F St. N.W., #6029 20405; (202) 501-1021. Fax, (202) 501-2590. Vacant, Associate Administrator.
Web, www.gsa.gov

Works to increase small business procurement of government contracts. Provides policy guidance and direction for GSA Business Service Centers, which offer advice and assistance to businesses interested in government procurement.

Minority Business Development Agency *(Commerce Dept.),* 14th St. and Constitution Ave. N.W., #5053 20230; (202) 482-5061. Fax, (202) 501-4698. Ronald N. Langston, Director. Information, (888) 324-1551.
Web, www.mbda.gov

Assists minority business owners in obtaining federal loans and contract awards; produces an annual report on federal agencies' performance in procuring from minority-owned businesses. Assists minority entrepreneurs one-on-one with financial planning, marketing, management, and technical assistance. Focuses on promoting wealth in minority communities.

Office of Management and Budget (OMB), *(Executive Office of the President), Federal Procurement Policy,* New Executive Office Bldg., #9013 20503; (202) 395-3501. Fax, (202) 395-5105. Lesley A. Field, Deputy Administrator.
Web, www.whitehouse.gov/omb/procurement

Oversees and coordinates government procurement policies, regulations, and procedures. Responsible for cost accounting rules governing federal contractors and subcontractors. Interests include effective use of competition, cost effective contracting for vehicles, and managing a useful information technology system for federal procurement managers.

▶**CONGRESS**

For a listing of relevant congressional committees and subcommittees, please see page 290 or the Appendix.

Government Accountability Office (GAO), *Procurement Law Division,* 441 G St. N.W., #7494 20548; (202)

512-6071. Fax, (202) 512-8316. Vacant, Managing Associate General Counsel.
Web, www.gao.gov

Considers and rules on the proposed or actual award of a government contract upon receipt of a written protest. (Formerly the General Accounting Office.)

▶**NONGOVERNMENTAL**

Coalition for Government Procurement, 1990 M St. N.W., #450 20036; (202) 331-0975. Fax, (202) 822-9788. Larry Allen, Executive Vice President.
General e-mail, info@thecgp.org
Web, www.thecgp.org

Alliance of business firms that sell to the federal government. Seeks equal opportunities for businesses to sell to the government; monitors practices of the General Services Administration and government procurement legislation and regulations.

National Contract Management Assn. (NCMA), 21740 Beaumeade Circle, #125, Ashburn, VA 20147; (571) 382-0082. Fax, (703) 448-0939. Neal J. Couture, Executive Director. Information, (800) 344-8096.
Web, www.ncmahq.org

Membership: individuals concerned with administering, procuring, negotiating, and managing government and commercial contracts and subcontracts. Sponsors Certified Professional Contracts Manager Program and various educational and professional programs.

National Institute of Governmental Purchasing (NIGP), 151 Spring St., #300, Herndon, VA 20170-5223; (703) 736-8900. Fax, (703) 736-2818. Rick Grimm, Chief Executive Officer. Information, (800) 367-6447.
Web, www.nigp.org

Membership: governmental purchasing departments, agencies, and organizations at the federal, state, and local levels in the United States and Canada. Provides public procurement officers with technical assistance and information, training seminars, and professional certification.

Professional Services Council (PSC), 4401 Wilson Blvd., Arlington, VA 22203; (703) 875-8059. Fax, (703) 875-8922. Stan Z. Soloway, President.
Web, www.pscouncil.org

Membership: associations and firms that provide local, state, federal, and international governments with professional, engineering, and technical services. Analyzes the process by which the government awards contracts to private firms. Monitors legislation and regulations. (Merged with Contract Services Assn. of America.)

POSTAL SERVICE

▶**AGENCIES**

U.S. Postal Service (USPS), 475 L'Enfant Plaza S.W. 20260-0001; (202) 268-2000. Fax, (202) 268-5211. John E.

Procurement Officers for Federal Departments and Agencies

DEPARTMENTS

Agriculture, Pearlie Reed, (202) 720-3291

Commerce, Helen Hurcombe, (202) 482-4248

Defense, Shay Assad, (703) 695-7145

Education, Hugh Hurwitz, (202) 245-6289

Energy, Ed Simpson, (202) 287-1310

Health and Human Services, Marty Brown, (202) 690-8554 or (202) 690-7195

Homeland Security, Richard Gunderson, (202) 282-8000

Housing and Urban Development, Vacant, (202) 708-0600

Interior, Debra Sonderman, (202) 208-6352

Justice, James W. Johnston, (202) 307-2000

Labor, Sandra Foster, (202) 693-4570

State, Cathy Read, (703) 875-6639

Transportation, Mark Welch, (202) 366-4971

Treasury, Thomas Sharpe, (202) 622-1039

Veterans Affairs, Glenn D. Haggstrom, (202) 461-6858

AGENCIES

Consumer Product Safety Commission, Donna Hutton, (301) 504-7009

Corporation for National and Community Service, Ritchie T. Vinson, (202) 606-6988

Environmental Protection Agency, John Gherardini (Acting), (202) 564-4310

Export-Import Bank, Mark Pitra, (202) 565-3338

Farm Credit Administration, Philip J. Shebest, (703) 883-4135

Federal Communications Commission, Wilma Mooney, (202) 418-1865

Federal Deposit Insurance Corporation, Michael J. Rubino, (703) 562-2224

Federal Emergency Management Agency, Jacob Hansen, (202) 646-3757

Federal Maritime Commission, Michael Kilby, (202) 523-5900

Federal Mediation and Conciliation Service, Sam Baumgardner, (202) 606-8111

Federal Reserve System, Michael E. Kelly, (202) 728-5862

Federal Trade Commission, Tim Smith (Acting) (202) 326-2733

General Services Administration, David Drabkin, (202) 501-1043

National Aeronautics and Space Administration, Thomas Luedtke, (202) 358-2090

National Labor Relations Board, Angela Crawford, (202) 273-4040

National Mediation Board, Denise Murdock, (202) 692-5010

National Science Foundation, Diane Harris, (703) 292-4587

Nuclear Regulatory Commission, Mary Lynn Scott, (301) 415-7305

Office of Personnel Management, Ronald Flom, (202) 606-3207

Securities and Exchange Commission, Sharon Sheehan, (202) 551-7005

Small Business Administration, Lance Petteway, (202) 205-6622

Social Security Administration, Diane L. Rose, (410) 965-9455

U.S. International Trade Commission, Jerome Williams, (202) 205-2736

U.S. Postal Service, Susan M. Brownell, (202) 268-4040

Potter, *Postmaster General. Library, (202) 268-2904. Press, (202) 268-2155. Locator, (202) 268-2020.*
Web, www.usps.com

Offers postal service throughout the country as an independent establishment of the executive branch. Library open to the public by appointment.

U.S. Postal Service (USPS), *Inspection Service, 475 L'Enfant Plaza S.W., #3100 20260-2100; (202) 268-4264. Fax, (202) 268-7316. William Gilligan, Chief Postal Inspector. Fraud and abuse hotline, (877) 876-2455. Web, http://postalinspectors.uspis.gov*

Investigates criminal violations of postal laws, such as theft of mail or posted valuables, assaults on postal employees, organized crime in postal-related matters, and prohibited mailings. Conducts internal audits; investigates postal activities to determine effectiveness of procedures;

monitors compliance of individual post offices with postal regulations.

►CONGRESS

For a listing of relevant congressional committees and subcommittees, please see page 290 or the Appendix.

Consumer Services

►AGENCIES

U.S. Postal Service (USPS), *Customer Service Development, 475 L'Enfant Plaza S.W. 20260; (202) 268-5301. Fax, (202) 268-3301. Stephen Karney, Senior Vice President, Customer Relations. Web, www.usps.com*

Develops policies, plans, and programs for commercial mailers to improve customer satisfaction. Directs the Business Partners program. Activities include local postal customer councils, the National Postal Forum, and the Mailers' Technical Advisory Committee.

U.S. Postal Service (USPS), *Office of the Consumer Advocate,* *475 L'Enfant Plaza S.W. 20260-0004; (202) 268-2284. Fax, (202) 268-2304. Delores J. Killette, Vice President and Consumer Advocate. TTY, (877) 889-2457. Inquiries, (800) ASK-USPS or (800) 275-8777.* Web, www.usps.com

Provides information to consumers on USPS services and products. Receives and attempts to settle consumer grievances.

U.S Postal Service (USPS), *Policies and Procedures Information,* *1735 N. Lynn St., 3rd Floor, Rosslyn, VA 22209; (703) 292-3962. Kevin Coleman, Manager.* Web, www.usps.gov

Produces and provides information on many USPS publications.

U.S. Postal Service (USPS), *Stamp Acquisition and Distribution,* *1735 N. Lynn St., #5008, Arlington, VA 22209-6432; (703) 292-3808. Fax, (703) 292-4095. Andre Boykins, Acquisitions Manager; Charles Delaney, Distribution Manager.* Web, www.usps.com

Manufactures and distributes postage stamps and postal stationery; develops inventory controls.

Employee and Labor Relations

U.S. Postal Service (USPS), *Employee Development and Diversity,* *475 L'Enfant Plaza S.W., #9301 20260-5600; (202) 268-6567. Fax, (202) 268-4263. Susan M. La Chance, Vice President.* Web, www.usps.com

Responsible for policy and planning with regard to employee development and diversity.

U.S. Postal Service (USPS), *Employee Resource Management,* *475 L'Enfant Plaza S.W., #9840 20260-4200; (202) 268-3783. Fax, (202) 268-3803. Deborah Giannoni-Jackson, Vice President.* Web, www.usps.com

Drafts and implements employment policies and practices and safety and health guidelines.

U.S. Postal Service (USPS), *Labor Relations,* *475 L'Enfant Plaza S.W., #9014 20260-4100; (202) 268-7447. Fax, (202) 268-3074. Douglas A. Tulino, Vice President.* Web, www.usps.com

Handles collective bargaining and contract administration for the U.S. Postal Service.

American Postal Workers Union (APWU), *AFL-CIO,* *1300 L St. N.W. 20005; (202) 842-4200. Fax, (202) 842-4297. William Burrus, President.* Web, www.apwu.org

Membership: approximately 330,000 postal employees, including clerks, motor vehicle operators, maintenance operators, and retirees. Assists members with contract negotiation and grievances; conducts training programs and workshops. Monitors legislation and regulations. (Affiliated with the Postal, Telegraph, and Telephone International and the AFL-CIO.)

National Alliance of Postal and Federal Employees (NAPFE), *1628 11th St. N.W. 20001; (202) 939-6325. Fax, (202) 939-6389. James M. McGee, President.* General e-mail, headquarters@napfe.org

Web, www.napfe.com

Membership: approximately 70,000 postal and federal employees. Helps members negotiate pay, benefits, and better working conditions; conducts training programs and workshops. Monitors legislation and regulations.

National Assn. of Letter Carriers, *AFL-CIO,* *100 Indiana Ave. N.W. 20001-2144; (202) 393-4695. Fax, (202) 737-1540. William H. Young, President.* General e-mail, nalcinf@nalc.org

Web, www.nalc.org

Membership: approximately 300,000 city letter carriers working for, or retired from, the U.S. Postal Service. Assists members with contract negotiation and grievances; conducts training programs and workshops. Monitors legislation and regulations. (Affiliated with the AFL-CIO and the Union Network International.)

National Assn. of Postal Supervisors, *1727 King St., #400, Alexandria, VA 22314-2753; (703) 836-9660. Fax, (703) 836-9665. Ted Keating, President.* General e-mail, napshq@naps.org

Web, www.naps.org

Membership: more than 35,000 present and former postal supervisors. Management association that cooperates with other postal management associations, unions, and the U.S. Postal Service to improve the efficiency of the postal service; promotes favorable working conditions and broader career opportunities for all postal employees; provides members with information on current functions and legislative issues of the postal service.

National Assn. of Postmasters of the United States, *8 Herbert St., Alexandria, VA 22305-2600; (703) 683-9027. Fax, (703) 683-6820. Ken Engstrom, Executive Director.* General e-mail, napusinfo@napus.org

Web, www.napus.org

Membership: present and former postmasters of the United States. Professional organization that promotes high-quality mail service and favorable relations between the postal service and the public; works with other postal groups and levels of management in the interest of postal matters and the welfare of its members. Assists postmasters facing discipline or other adverse actions.

National League of Postmasters, *1 Beltway Center, 5904 Richmond Hwy., #500, Alexandria, VA 22303-1864; (703) 329-4550. Fax, (703) 329-0466. Charley W. Mapa, President.*

General e-mail, information@postmasters.org

Web, www.postmasters.org

Represents postmasters in labor negotiations with the U.S. Postal Service and in legislative matters of concern. Works to improve the salaries, working hours, and working conditions of postmasters.

National Rural Letter Carriers' Assn., *1630 Duke St., 4th Floor, Alexandria, VA 22314-3465; (703) 684-5545. Fax, (703) 548-8735. Don Cantriel, President.*

Web, www.nrlca.org

Membership: approximately 104,000 rural letter carriers working for, or retired from, the U.S. Postal Service. Seeks to improve rural mail delivery. Negotiates labor agreements affecting members; conducts training programs and workshops. Monitors legislation and regulations.

National Star Route Mail Contractors Assn., *324 E. Capitol St. N.E. 20003-3897; (202) 543-1661. Fax, (202) 543-8863. John V. Maraney, Executive Director.*

General e-mail, info@starroutecontractors.org

Web, www.starroutecontractors.org

Membership: contractors for highway mail transport and selected rural route deliverers. Acts as liaison between contractors and the U.S. Postal Service, the Transportation Dept., the Labor Dept., and Congress concerning contracts, wages, and other issues. Monitors legislation and regulations.

Mail Rates and Classification

▶AGENCIES

Postal Regulatory Commission, *901 New York Ave. N.W., #200 20268-0001; (202) 789-6800. Fax, (202) 789-6886. Dan G. Blair, Chair.*

General e-mail, ann.fisher@prc.gov

Web, www.prc.gov

Independent agency with regulatory oversight over the U.S. Postal Service. Develops and maintains regulations concerning postal rates; consults with the Postal Service on delivery service standards and performance measures; consults with the State Dept. on international postal policies; prevents anticompetitive postal practices; and adjudicates complaints.

U.S. Postal Service (USPS), *Business Mail Acceptance, 475 L'Enfant Plaza S.W., #2P836 20260; (202) 268-8086. Fax, (202) 268-8273. Angela Burns, Manager.*

Web, www.usps.com

Implements policies governing the acceptance and verification of business mail by the U.S. Postal Service.

U.S. Postal Service (USPS), *Mailing Standards, 475 L'Enfant Plaza S.W., #3436 20260-3436; (202) 268-7261. Fax, (202) 268-4955. Sharon Daniel, Manager.*

Web, www.usps.com

Issues policy statements on domestic mail classification matters. Ensures the accuracy of policies developed by the Postal Regulatory Commission with respect to domestic mail classification schedules.

U.S. Postal Service (USPS), *Pricing and Classification, 475 L'Enfant Plaza S.W., #5014 20260-5014; (202) 268-2244. Fax, (202) 268-5773. Maura Robinson, Vice President.*

Web, www.usps.com

Sets prices for U.S. Postal Service product lines using competitive pricing methods.

▶NONGOVERNMENTAL

Alliance of Nonprofit Mailers, *1211 Connecticut Ave. N.W., #610 20036-2705; (202) 462-5132. Fax, (202) 462-0423. Anthony W. Conway, Executive Director.*

General e-mail, alliance@nonprofitmailers.org

Web, www.nonprofitmailers.org

Works to maintain reasonable mail rates for nonprofit organizations. Represents member organizations before Congress, the U.S. Postal Service, the Postal Regulatory Commission, and the courts on nonprofit postal rate and mail classification issues.

Assn. for Postal Commerce, *1901 N. Fort Myer Dr., #401, Arlington, VA 22209-1609; (703) 524-0096. Fax, (703) 524-1871. Gene A. Del Polito, President.*

Web, www.postcom.org

Membership: companies and organizations interested in advertising (Standard Mail A) mail. Provides members with information about postal policy, postal rates, and legislation regarding postal regulations. Monitors legislation and regulations.

DMA Nonprofit Federation, *1111 19th St. N.W., #1180 20036; (202) 628-4380. Fax, (202) 628-4383. Xenia Boone, Executive Director. Alternate phone, (202) 861-2447.*

General e-mail, nonprofitfederation@the-dma.org

Web, www.nonprofitfederation.org

Membership: educational, cultural, fraternal, religious, and scientific organizations that mail nonprofit second-, third-, or fourth-class mail. Serves as liaison between members and the U.S. Postal Service; represents nonprofit members' interests on the Mailers' Technical Advisory Committee. Monitors legislation and regulations impacting nonprofits' advocacy and fundraising. Sponsors education programs on direct-response fundraising.

Mailing and Fulfillment Service Assn. (MFSA), *1421 Prince St., #410, Alexandria, VA 22314-2806; (703) 836-9200. Fax, (703) 548-8204. Ken Garner, President.*

General e-mail, mfsa@mfsanet.org

Web, www.mfsanet.org

Membership: Direct mail advertising services, order-fulfillment businesses, and their suppliers. Serves as a clearinghouse for members on improving methods of using the mail for advertising. Sponsors workshops and conferences; accredits fulfillment companies.

Parcel Shippers Assn. (PSA), *1420 King St., #620, Alexandria, VA 22314; (571) 257-7617. Fax, (571) 257-7613. J. Pierce Myers, Executive Vice President. General e-mail, psa@parcelshippers.org*

Web, www.parcelshippers.org

Voluntary organization of business firms concerned with the shipment of parcels. Works to improve parcel post rates and service; represents members before the Postal Regulatory Commission in matters regarding parcel post rates. Monitors legislation and regulations.

Stamps, Postal History

Smithsonian Institution, *National Postal Museum, 2 Massachusetts Ave. N.E. 20013 (mailing address: P.O. Box 37012, Washington, DC 20013); (202) 633-5555. Fax, (202) 633-9393. Allen Kane, Director. TTY, (202) 633-9849. Tours, (202) 633-5534. Web, http://postalmuseum.si.edu*

Exhibits postal history and stamp collections; provides information on world postal and stamp history.

U.S. Postal Service (USPS), *Citizens' Stamp Advisory Committee, 1735 N. Lynn St., #5013, Arlington, VA 22209-6432; (703) 292-3727. Fax, (703) 292-3634. Terry McCaffrey, Stamp Development Manager. Web, www.usps.com*

Reviews stamp subject nominations. Develops the annual Stamp Program and makes subject and design recommendations to the Postmaster General.

U.S. Postal Service (USPS), *Stamp Acquisition and Distribution, 1735 N. Lynn St., #5008, Arlington, VA 22209-6432; (703) 292-3808. Fax, (703) 292-4095. Andre Boykins, Acquisitions Manager; Charles Delaney, Distribution Manager. Web, www.usps.com*

Manufactures and distributes postage stamps and postal stationery.

U.S. Postal Service (USPS), *Stamp Development, 1735 N. Lynn St., #5013, Arlington, VA 22209-6432; (703) 292-3727. Fax, (703) 292-3634. Terry McCaffrey, Manager. Web, www.usps.com*

Manages the stamp selection function; develops the basic stamp pre-production design; manages relationship with stamp collecting community.

PUBLIC ADMINISTRATION

Office of Management and Budget (OMB), *(Executive Office of the President), President's Management Council, Dwight D. Eisenhower Executive Office Bldg., #260 20503; (202) 456-7070. Fax, (202) 456-5938. Clay Johnson III, Chair. Web, www.whitehouse.gov/omb*

Membership: chief operating officers of federal government departments and agencies. Responsible for implementing the management improvement initiatives of the administration. Develops and oversees improved governmentwide management and administrative systems; formulates long-range plans to promote these systems; works to resolve interagency management problems and to implement reforms.

President's Commission on White House Fellowships, *1900 E St. N.W., #B431 20415; (202) 395-4522. Fax, (202) 395-6179. Janet Slaughter Eissenstat, Director. Web, www.whitehouse.gov/fellows*

Nonpartisan commission that provides professionals from all sectors of national life with the opportunity to observe firsthand the processes of the federal government. Fellows work for one year as special assistants to cabinet members or to principal members of the White House staff. Qualified applicants have demonstrated superior accomplishments early in their careers and have a commitment to leadership and public service.

For a listing of relevant congressional committees and subcommittees, please see page 290 or the Appendix.

American Society for Public Administration, *1301 Pennsylvania Ave., #840 20004; (202) 393-7878. Fax, (202) 638-4952. Antoinette Samuel, Executive Director. General e-mail, info@aspanet.org*

Web, www.aspanet.org

Membership: government administrators, public officials, educators, researchers, and others interested in public administration. Presents awards to distinguished professionals in the field; sponsors workshops and conferences; disseminates information about public administration. Promotes high ethical standards for public service.

Assn. of Government Accountants, *2208 Mount Vernon Ave., Alexandria, VA 22301; (703) 684-6931. Fax, (703) 548-9367. Relmond Van Daniker, Executive Director. Toll-free, (800) 242-7211. General e-mail, agmembers@agacgfm.org*

Web, www.agacgfm.org

Membership: professionals engaged in government accounting, auditing, budgeting, and information systems. Sponsors education, research, and conferences; administers certification program.

Federally Employed Women, *700 N. Fairfax St., #510, Alexandria, VA 22306; (202) 898-0994. Fax, (202) 898-1535. Sue Webster, President.*
General e-mail, few@few.org

Web, www.few.org

Membership: women and men who work for the federal government. Works to eliminate sex discrimination in government employment and to increase job opportunities for women; offers training programs. Monitors legislation and regulations.

International City/County Management Assn., *777 N. Capitol St. N.E., #500 20002-4201; (202) 289-4262. Fax, (202) 962-3500. Robert J. O'Neill Jr., Executive Director. Member services, (202) 962-3680.*
General e-mail, customerservices@icma.org

Web, www.icma.org

Membership: appointed managers and administrators of cities, towns, counties, and other local governments around the world; local government employees; academics; and citizens. Provides technical assistance to local governments in the United States and abroad to develop professional practices and ethical, transparent government. Services include research and development, performance measurement, and consulting. Sponsors workshops and conferences. Publishes resources for local government management professionals.

International Public Management Assn. for Human Resources (IPMA-HR), *1617 Duke St., Alexandria, VA 22314; (703) 549-7100. Fax, (703) 684-0948. Neil Reichenberg, Executive Director.*
General e-mail, ipma@ipma-hr.org

Web, www.ipma-hr.org

Membership: personnel professionals from federal, state, and local governments. Provides information on training procedures, management techniques, and legislative developments on the federal, state, and local levels.

National Academy of Public Administration, *900 7th St. N.W., #600 20005; (202) 347-3190. Fax, (202) 393-0993. Jennifer L. Dorn, President.*
General e-mail, academy@napawash.org

Web, www.napawash.org

Membership: scholars and administrators in public management. Offers assistance to federal, state, and local government agencies, public officials, foreign governments, foundations, and corporations on problems related to public administration.

National Assn. of Schools of Public Affairs and Administration (NASPAA), *1029 Vermont Ave. N.W., #1100 20005; (202) 628-8965. Fax, (202) 626-4978. Laurel McFarland, Executive Director.*
General e-mail, naspaa@naspaa.org

Web, www.naspaa.org

Membership: universities, government agencies, corporations, and professional associations interested in the advancement of education, research, and training in public management. Serves as a clearinghouse for information on public administration and public affairs programs in colleges and universities. Accredits master's degree programs in public affairs, public policy, and public administration.

National Foundation for Women Legislators, *910 16th St. N.W., #100 20006; (202) 293-3040. Fax, (202) 293-5430. Robin Read, President.*
General e-mail, nfwl@womenlegislators.org

Web, www.womenlegislators.org

Provides leadership development and networking resources to women leaders at both the state and federal levels of government.

National Women's Political Caucus, *1003 K St. N.W., #637 20001 (mailing address: P.O. Box 50476, Washington, DC 20091); (202) 785-1100. Fax, (202) 370-6306. Lulu Flores, President; Clare C. Giesen, Executive Director.*
General e-mail, info@nwpc.org

Web, www.nwpc.org

Seeks to increase the number of women in policy-making positions in federal, state, and local government. Identifies, recruits, trains, and supports pro-choice women candidates for public office. Monitors agencies and provides names of qualified women for high- and mid-level appointments.

Women in Government Relations, *801 N. Fairfax St., #211, Alexandria, VA 22314-1757; (703) 299-8546. Fax, (703) 299-9233. Emily Bardach, Executive Director.*
General e-mail, info@wgr.org

Web, www.wgr.org

Membership: professionals in business, trade associations, and government whose jobs involve governmental relations at the federal, state, or local level. Serves as a forum for exchange of information among its members.

STATE AND LOCAL GOVERNMENT

▶AGENCIES

Census Bureau *(Commerce Dept.), Governments Division, 4600 Silver Hill Rd., #HQ-5K156 20233; (301) 763-1489. Fax, (301) 457-3057. Stephanie Brown, Chief.*
Web, www.census.gov

Compiles annual *Federal Expenditures by State* (available to the public), which provides information on overall federal grants-in-aid expenditures to state and local governments; collects data on finances, employment, and structure of the public sector; and serves as national clearinghouse on state and local audit reports. Computer data obtainable from Data User Services, (301) 457-4100.

Executive Office of the President, *Public Liaison and Intergovernmental Affairs, White House 20502; (202) 456-2896. Fax, (202) 456-7015. Valerie Jarrett, Senior Adviser; Christina M. Tchen, Director of Public Liaison.*
Web, www.whitehouse.gov/administration/eop/opl

Seeks to build relationships with constituents and to connect citizens with their elected officials.

General Services Administration (GSA), *Subacquisition Systems, Federal Domestic Assistance Catalog Staff, 211 Crystal Dr., #911, Arlington, VA 22202; (202) 605-3404. Fax, (202) 501-4067. Earl Warrington, Director.*
Web, www.cfda.gov

Disseminates information on federal domestic assistance programs through the CFDA Web site. Information includes all types of federal aid and explains types of assistance, eligibility requirements, application process, and suggestions for writing proposals. Printed version and CD-ROM may be ordered from the Superintendent of Documents, U.S. Government Printing Office 20402; (202) 512-1800, or toll-free, (866) 512-1800, or online at bookstore.gpo.gov or www.cfda.gov.

Housing and Urban Development Dept. (HUD), *Policy Development and Research, 451 7th St. S.W., #8100 20410-6000; (202) 708-1600. Fax, (202) 619-8000. Vacant, Assistant Secretary.*
Web, www.huduser.org

Assesses and maintains information on housing needs, market conditions, and programs; conducts research on housing and community development issues such as building technology, economic development, and urban planning.

Multistate Tax Commission, *444 N. Capitol St. N.W., #425 20001-1538; (202) 624-8699. Fax, (202) 624-8819. Joe Huddleston, Executive Director.*
General e-mail, mtc@mtc.gov
Web, www.mtc.gov

Membership: state governments that have enacted the Multistate Tax Compact. Promotes fair, effective, and efficient state tax systems for interstate and international commerce; works to preserve state tax sovereignty. Encourages uniform state tax laws and regulations for multistate and multinational enterprises. Maintains three regional audit offices that monitor compliance with state tax laws and encourage uniformity in taxpayer treatment. Administers program to identify businesses that do not file tax returns with states.

Office of Management and Budget (OMB), *(Executive Office of the President), Federal Financial Management, New Executive Office Bldg., #6025 20503; (202) 395-3993. Fax, (202) 395-3952. Vacant, Controller.*
Web, www.whitehouse.gov/omb/financial

Facilitates exchange of information on financial management standards, techniques, and processes among officers of state and local governments.

▶**CONGRESS**

For a listing of relevant congressional committees and subcommittees, please see page 290 or the Appendix.

Government Accountability Office (GAO), *Education, Workforce, and Income Security, 441 G St. N.W., #5928 20548; (202) 512-7215. Cynthia M. Fagnoni, Managing Director.*
Web, www.gao.gov

Independent, nonpartisan agency in the legislative branch. Responsible for intergovernmental relations activities. Reviews the effects of federal grants and regulations on state and local governments. Works to reduce intergovernmental conflicts and costs. Seeks to improve the allocation and targeting of federal funds to state and local governments through changes in federal funding formulas. (Formerly the General Accounting Office.)

▶**NONGOVERNMENTAL**

American Legislative Exchange Council (ALEC), *1101 Vermont Ave. N.W., 11th Floor 20005; (202) 466-3800. Fax, (202) 466-3801. Alan B. Smith, Executive Director.*
General e-mail, jamselle@alec.org
Web, www.alec.org

Nonpartisan educational and research organization for state legislators. Conducts research and provides information and model state legislation on public policy issues. Supports the development of state policies to limit government, expand free markets, promote economic growth, and preserve individual liberty.

Assn. of Public Treasurers of the United States and Canada, *962 Wayne Ave., #910, Silver Spring, MD 20910; (301) 495-5560. Fax, (301) 495-5561. Lindsay Dively, Executive Director.*
General e-mail, info@aptusc.org
Web, www.aptusc.org

Provides continuing education and certification programs for public treasury and financial officials. Monitors legislation and regulations.

Coalition of Northeastern Governors (CONEG), *Policy Research Center, Inc., 400 N. Capitol St. N.W., #382 20001; (202) 624-8450. Fax, (202) 624-8463. Anne D. Stubbs, Executive Director.*
General e-mail, coneg@sso.org
Web, www.coneg.org

Membership: governors of eight northeastern states (Connecticut, Maine, Massachusetts, New Hampshire, New Jersey, New York, Rhode Island, and Vermont). Addresses common issues of concern such as energy, economic development, transportation, and the environment; serves as an information clearinghouse and liaison among member states and with the federal government.

Council of State Governments (CSG), *Washington Office, 444 N. Capitol St. N.W., #401 20001; (202) 624-5460. Fax, (202) 624-5452. Chris Whatley, Director.*
General e-mail, csgdc@csg.org
Web, www.csg.org

Membership: governing bodies of states, commonwealths, and territories, and various affiliated national organizations of state officials. Promotes interstate, federal-state, and state-local cooperation; interests include education, transportation, human services, housing, natural resources, and economic development. Provides services to affiliates and associated organizations, including the National Assn. of State Treasurers, National Assn. of Government Labor Officials, and other state administrative organizations in specific fields. Monitors legislation and executive policy. (Headquarters in Lexington, Ky.)

Government Finance Officers Assn. (GFOA), *Federal Liaison Center, Washington Office,* *1301 Pennsylvania Ave., #309 20004-1714; (202) 393-8020. Fax, (202) 393-0780. Susan Gaffney, Director.* *General e-mail, federalliaison@gfoa.org* *Web, www.gfoa.org*

Membership: state and local government finance managers. Offers training and publications in public financial management. Conducts research in public fiscal management, design and financing of government programs, and formulation and analysis of government fiscal policy. (Headquarters in Chicago, Ill.)

International Municipal Lawyers Assn. (IMLA), *7910 Woodmont Ave., #1440, Bethesda, MD 20814; (202) 466-5424. Fax, (202) 785 0152. Chuck Thompson, General Counsel.* *General e-mail, info@imla.org* *Web, www.imla.org*

Membership: local government attorneys and public law practitioners. Acts as a research service for members in all areas of municipal law; participates in litigation of municipal and constitutional law issues.

National Assn. of Bond Lawyers, *Governmental Affairs, Washington Office, 601 13th St., #800-S 20005-3875; (202) 682-1498. Fax, (202) 637-0217. Victoria Rostow, Director.* *General e-mail, governmentalaffairs@nabl.org* *Web, www.nabl.org*

Membership: municipal finance lawyers. Provides members with information on laws relating to the borrowing of money by states and municipalities and to the issuance of state and local government bonds. Monitors legislation and regulations. (Headquarters in Chicago, Ill.)

National Assn. of Clean Water Agencies, *1816 Jefferson Pl. N.W. 20036; (202) 833-2672. Fax, (202) 833-4657. Ken Kirk, Executive Director.* *General e-mail, info@nacwa.org* *Web, www.nacwa.org*

Represents the interests of the country's publicly owned wastewater treatment works and various affiliates, including public affiliate members that convey wastewater, public and private organizations, law firms representing public clean water agencies, and nonprofit or academic organizations. Interests include water quality and ecosystem protection issues such as watershed management. Sponsors conferences. Monitors legislation and regulations.

National Assn. of Counties (NACo), *25 Massachusetts Ave. N.W., #500 20001; (202) 393-6226. Fax, (202) 942-4281. Larry Naake, Executive Director. Press, (202) 942-4220.* *General e-mail, pbeddoe@naco.org* *Web, www.naco.org*

Membership: county governments and county officials and their staffs through NACo's affiliates. Conducts research, supplies information, and provides technical and public affairs assistance on issues affecting counties. Interests include homeland security, drug abuse, access to health care, and public-private partnerships. Monitors legislation and regulations.

National Assn. of Regional Councils, *1666 Connecticut Ave. N.W., #300 20009; (202) 986-1032. Fax, (202) 986-1038. Fred Abousleman, Executive Director.* *Web, www.narc.org*

Membership: regional councils of local governments, councils of government, and metropolitan planning organizations. Works to improve local governments' ability to deal with common public needs, address regional issues, and reduce public expense. Interests include housing, urban and rural planning, transportation, the environment, homeland security and emergency preparedness, workforce development, economic and community development, and aging.

National Assn. of Secretaries of State, *444 N. Capitol St. N.W., #401 20001; (202) 624-3525. Fax, (202) 624-3527. Leslie Reynolds, Executive Director.* *General e-mail, nass@nass.org* *Web, www.nass.org*

Organization of secretaries of state and lieutenant governors or other comparable state officials from the fifty states, the District of Columbia, Guam, Puerto Rico, and the U.S. Virgin Islands. Interests include budget and finance, elections and voting, business services and licensing, and e-government.

National Assn. of State Budget Officers, *444 N. Capitol St. N.W., #642 20001-1501; (202) 624-5382. Fax, (202) 624-7745. Scott Pattison, Executive Director.* *General e-mail, nasbo-direct@nasbo.org* *Web, www.nasbo.org*

Membership: state budget and financial officers. Publishes research reports on budget-related issues. (Affiliate of the National Governors Assn.)

National Assn. of Towns and Townships (NATaT), *1130 Connecticut Ave. N.W., #300 20036; (202) 454-3954. Fax, (202) 331-1598. Jennifer Imo, Federal Director Toll-free, (866) 830-0008.* *General e-mail, info@natat.org* *Web, www.natat.org*

Membership: towns, townships, small communities, and others interested in supporting small town government. Provides local government officials from small jurisdictions with technical assistance, educational services, and public policy support; conducts research and coordinates training for local government officials nationwide. Interests include tax benefits for local public service volunteers, local economic development, water and wastewater infrastructure, transportation improvements, and allocation of federal resources. Holds an annual conference. (Affiliated with National Center for Small Communities.)

National Black Caucus of Local Elected Officials (NBC/LEO), *c/o National League of Cities, 1301 Pennsylvania Ave. N.W. 20004-1763; (202) 626-3168. Fax, (202) 626-3043. Daisy W. Lynum, President. Press, (202) 626-3003. Web, www.nbc-leo.org*

Membership: African American elected officials at the local level and other interested individuals. Seeks to increase African American participation on the National League of City's steering and policy committees. Informs members on issues, and plans strategies to achieve objectives through legislation and direct action. Interests include cultural diversity, local government and community participation, housing, economics, the family, and human rights.

National Black Caucus of State Legislators, *444 N. Capitol St. N.W., #622 20001; (202) 624-5457. Fax, (202) 508-3826. LaKimba DeSadier Walker, Executive Director. Web, www.nbcsl.com*

Membership: African American state legislators. Promotes effective leadership among African American state legislators through education, research, and training; serves as an information network and clearinghouse for members.

National Conference of State Legislatures, *Washington Office, 444 N. Capitol St. N.W., #515 20001; (202) 624-5400. Fax, (202) 737-1069. Carl Tubbesing, Deputy Executive Director. General e-mail, info@ncsl.org*

Web, www.ncsl.org

Coordinates and represents state legislatures at the federal level; conducts research, produces videos, and publishes reports in areas of interest to state legislatures; conducts an information exchange program on intergovernmental relations; sponsors seminars for state legislators and their staffs. Interests include unfunded federal mandates, state-federal law conflict, and fiscal integrity. Monitors legislation and regulations. (Headquarters in Denver, Colo.)

National Foundation for Women Legislators, *910 16th St. N.W., #100 20006; (202) 293-3040. Fax, (202) 293-5430. Robin Read, President. General e-mail, nfwl@womenlegislators.org*

Web, www.womenlegislators.org

Provides leadership development and networking resources to women leaders at both the state and federal levels of government.

National Governors Assn. (NGA), *444 N. Capitol St. N.W., #267 20001-1512; (202) 624-5300. Fax, (202) 624-5313. Raymond C. Scheppach, Executive Director. Press, (202) 624-5334. Web, www.nga.org*

Membership: governors of states, commonwealths, and territories. Provides members with policy and technical assistance. Makes policy recommendations to Congress and the president on community and economic development; education; international trade and foreign relations; energy and the environment; health care and welfare reform; agriculture; transportation, commerce, and technology; communications; criminal justice; public safety; and workforce development.

National League of Cities, *1301 Pennsylvania Ave. N.W., #550 20004; (202) 626-3000. Fax, (202) 626-3043. Donald J. Borut, Executive Director. General e-mail, info@nlc.org*

Web, www.nlc.org

Membership: cities and state municipal leagues. Provides city leaders with training, technical assistance, and publications; investigates needs of local governments in implementing federal programs that affect cities. Holds two annual conferences; conducts research; sponsors awards. Monitors legislation and regulations. (Affiliates include National Black Caucus of Local Elected Officials.)

Public Risk Management Assn. (PRIMA), *500 Montgomery St., #750, Alexandria, VA 22314; (703) 528-7701. Fax, (703) 739-0200. Lisa Lopinsky, Executive Director. Information, (703) 528-7701. General e-mail, info@primacentral.org*

Web, www.primacentral.org

Membership: state and local governments and their risk management practitioners, including benefits and insurance managers, and private sector organizations. Develops and teaches cost-effective management techniques for handling public liability issues; promotes professional development of its members. Gathers and disseminates information about risk management to public and private sectors.

Public Technology Institute (PTI), *1301 Pennsylvania Ave. N.W., #830 20004-1725; (202) 626-2400. Fax, (202) 626-2498. Alan R. Shark, Executive Director. Press, (202) 626-2467. Toll-free, (866) 664-6368. General e-mail, info@pti.org*

Web, www.pti.org

Cooperative research, development, and technology-transfer organization of cities and counties in North America. Assists local governments in increasing efficiency, reducing costs, improving services, and developing public enterprise programs to help local officials create revenues and serve citizens. Participates in international conferences.

Southern Governors' Assn., *444 N. Capitol St. N.W., #200 20001-1512; (202) 624-5897. Fax, (202) 624-7797. Diane Duff, Executive Director. General e-mail, sga@sso.org*

Web, www.southerngovernors.org

Membership: governors of fifteen southern states, plus the territories of Puerto Rico and the U.S. Virgin Islands, and corporate affiliates. Provides a regional, bipartisan forum for governors to help formulate and implement national policy; works to enhance the region's competitiveness nationally and internationally, to explore common problems, and to coordinate regional initiatives.

Stateline.org, *901 E St. N.W., #700 20004; (202) 419-4450. Fax, (202) 419-4453. Gene Gibbons, Executive Editor.*
General e-mail, editor@stateline.org

Web, www.stateline.org

Independent online news site and forum for journalists who cover state government and legislation, as well as state officials, students, and citizens. Encourages debate on state-level issues such as health care, tax and budget policy, the environment, immigration, and welfare reform. Sponsors professional development conferences and workshops for the news media.

U.S. Conference of Mayors, *1620 Eye St. N.W., #400 20006; (202) 293-7330. Fax, (202) 293-2352. J. Thomas Cochran, Executive Director.*
General e-mail, info@usmayors.org

Web, www.usmayors.org/uscm

Membership: mayors of cities with populations of 30,000 or more. Promotes city-federal cooperation; publishes reports and conducts meetings on federal programs, policies, and initiatives that affect urban and suburban interests. Serves as a clearinghouse for information on urban and suburban problems.

Western Governors' Assn., *Washington Office, 400 N. Capitol St. N.W., #388 20001; (202) 624-5402. Fax, (202) 624-7707. Shanna Brown, Director (Acting).*
Web, www.westgov.org

Independent, nonpartisan organization of governors from eighteen western states, two Pacific territories, and one commonwealth. Identifies and addresses key policy and governance issues in natural resources, clean energy and alternative transportation fuels, the environment, radioactive waste transportation, human services, economic development, international relations, and public management. (Headquarters in Denver, Colo.)

Women In Government, *1319 F St. N.W., #710 20004; (202) 333-0825. Fax, (202) 333-0875. Mary Brooks Beatty, President. Policy Resource Center, (888) 333-0164.*
General e-mail, wig@womeningovernment.org

Web, www.womeningovernment.org

Membership: women state legislators. Seeks to enhance the leadership role of women policymakers by providing issue education and leadership training. Sponsors seminars and conducts educational research.

Washington Area

▶CONGRESS

For a listing of relevant congressional committees and subcommittees, please see page 290 or the Appendix.

Local Government in the Washington Metropolitan Area

DISTRICT OF COLUMBIA

Executive Office of the Mayor
Adrian M. Fenty, Mayor
John A. Wilson Building
1350 Pennsylvania Ave. N.W., Suite 310, 20004; (202) 727-6300; fax, (202) 727-0505
E-mail, mayor@dc.gov
Web, www.dc.gov

MARYLAND

Montgomery County
Isiah Leggett, County Executive
101 Monroe St., 2nd Floor, Rockville, MD 20850; (240) 777-2500; fax, (240) 777-2517
E-mail, ocemail@montgomerycountymd.gov
Web, www.montgomerycountymd.gov

Prince George's County
Jack B. Johnson, County Executive
14741 Gov. Oden Bowie Dr., #5032, Upper Marlboro, MD 20772; (301) 952-4131; fax, (301) 952-3784
E-mail, countyexecutive@co.pg.md.us
Web, www.co.pg.md.us

VIRGINIA
City of Alexandria
William D. Euille, Mayor
301 King St., #2300, Alexandria, VA 22314; (703) 838-4500; fax, (703) 838-6433
E-mail, alexvamayor@aol.com
Web, www.alexandriava.gov

Arlington County
Ron Carlee, County Manager
2100 Clarendon Blvd., #302, Arlington, VA 22201; (703) 228-3120; fax, (703) 228-3218
E-mail, countymanager@arlingtonva.us
Web, www.arlingtonva.us

Fairfax County
Anthony H. Griffin, County Executive
12000 Government Center Pkwy., #552, Fairfax, VA 22035; (703) 324-2531; fax, (703) 324-3956
E-mail, coexec@fairfaxcounty.gov
Web, www.fairfaxcounty.gov

City of Falls Church
F. Wyatt Shields, City Manager
300 Park Ave., #303E, Falls Church, VA 22046; (703) 248-5004; fax, (703) 248-5146
E-mail, city-manager@fallschurchva.gov
Web, www.fallschurchva.gov

►NONGOVERNMENTAL

Metropolitan Washington Council of Governments,
777 N. Capitol St. N.E., #300 20002-4239; (202) 962-3200.
Fax, (202) 962-3201. David Robertson, Executive Director.
Press, (202) 962-3250. TTY, (202) 962-3213.
General e-mail, ccogdtp@mwcog.org

Web, www.mwcog.org

Membership: local governments in the Washington area, plus members of the Maryland and Virginia legislatures and the U.S. Congress. Analyzes and develops regional responses to issues such as the environment, affordable housing, economic development, health, population growth, human and social services, public safety, and transportation.

Walter E. Washington Convention Center Authority,
801 Mt. Vernon Pl. N.W. 20001; (202) 249-3000. Fax,
(202) 249-3533. Greg O'Dell, Chief Executive Officer.
Information, (800) 368-9000. Press, (202) 249-3217.
Web, www.dcconvention.com

Promotes national and international conventions and trade shows; hosts local events; fosters redevelopment of downtown Washington.

10 ✚ Health

GENERAL POLICY AND ANALYSIS

Basic Resources

▶**AGENCIES**

Agency for Health Care Research and Quality *(Health and Human Services Dept.)*, *540 Gaither Rd., Rockville, MD 20850; (301) 427-1364. Fax, (301) 427-1873. Dr. Carolyn M. Clancy, Director.*
General e-mail, info@ahrq.gov

Web, www.ahrq.gov/about

Works to improve the quality, safety, effectiveness, and efficiency of health care in the United States. Promotes improvements in clinical practices and in organizing, financing, and delivering health care services. Conducts and supports comparative effectiveness research, demonstration projects, evaluations, and training; disseminates information on a wide range of activities.

Centers for Disease Control and Prevention (CDC), *(Health and Human Services Dept.)*, **Washington Office,** *395 E St. S.W. 20201; (202) 245-0600. Fax, (202) 245-0602. Donald Shriber, Associate Director. Public inquiries, (800) 232-4636.*

Web, www.cdc.gov/washington

Collaborates with state and local health departments to further health promotion; prevention of disease, injury, and disability; and preparedness for new health threats. Strategies include monitoring the health of individuals, detecting and investigating health problems, conducting research to enhance prevention, developing and advocating public health policies, implementing prevention strategies, promoting healthy behaviors, fostering safe and healthful environments, and providing leadership and training. (Headquarters in Atlanta, Ga.: 1600 Clifton Rd. N.E. 30333.)

Federal Trade Commission (FTC), *Advertising Practices, 601 New Jersey Ave. N.W., #3223 20001 (mailing address: 600 Pennsylvania Ave. N.W., Washington, DC 20580); (202) 326-3090. Fax, (202) 326-3259. Mary Engle, Associate Director.*
Web, www.ftc.gov

Protects consumers from deceptive and unsubstantiated advertising through law enforcement, public reports, and industry outreach. Evaluates the nutritional and health benefits of foods and the safety and effectiveness of dietary supplements, drugs, and medical devices, particularly as they relate to weight loss.

Food and Drug Administration (FDA), *(Health and Human Services Dept.)*, *10903 New Hampshire Ave., Bldg. 1, #3300, Silver Spring, MD 20993; (301) 796-4540. Fax, (301) 847-3536. Dr. Margaret A. Hamburg, Commissioner. Press, (301) 827-6242. Public Affairs, (301) 827-6250. Library (Rockville), (301) 827-5703. Main Library (White Oak in Silver Spring), (301) 796-2039. Toll-free, (888) 463-6332.*
Web, www.fda.gov

Conducts research and develops standards on the composition, quality, and safety of drugs, cosmetics, medical devices, radiation-emitting products, foods, food additives, and infant formulas, including imports. Develops labeling and packaging standards; conducts inspections of manufacturers; issues orders to companies to recall and/or cease selling or producing hazardous products; enforces rulings and recommends action to Justice Dept. when necessary. Libraries open to the public; 24-hour advance appointment required.

Food and Drug Administration (FDA), *(Health and Human Services Dept.)*, **International and Special Programs,** *5600 Fishers Lane, #15A55, Rockville, MD 20857; (301) 827-4480. Fax, (301) 827-1451. Lou Valdez, Associate Commissioner.*
Web, www.fda.gov/oia/homepage.htm

Serves as the principal FDA liaison with foreign counterpart agencies, international organizations, and U.S. government agencies on international issues. Coordinates agency involvement in international trade, harmonization, and technical assistance; administers programs for foreign scientists and other international visitors.

Food and Drug Administration (FDA), *(Health and Human Services Dept.)*, **Regulatory Affairs,** *5600 Fishers Lane, #14101, #HFC01, Rockville, MD 20857; (301) 827-3101. Fax, (301) 443-6591. Michael Chappell, Associate Commissioner (Acting).*
Web, www.fda.gov/ora

Directs and coordinates the FDA's compliance activities; manages field offices; advises FDA commissioner on domestic and international regulatory policies.

Health and Human Services Dept. (HHS), *200 Independence Ave. S.W., #615F 20201; (202) 690-7000. Fax, (202) 690-7203. Kathleen Sebelius, Secretary; Tevi David Troy, Deputy Secretary. Press, (202) 690-6343. TTY, (800) 877-8339. Internship Contact, (202) 690-6139. Locator, (202) 619-0257. Toll-free, (877) 696-6775.*
Web, www.hhs.gov

Acts as principal adviser to the president on health and welfare plans, policies, and programs of the federal government. Encompasses the Centers for Medicare and Medicaid Services, the Administration for Children and Families, the Public Health Service, and the Centers for Disease Control and Prevention.

Health and Human Services Dept. (HHS), *National Committee on Vital and Health Statistics, 3311 Toledo Rd., #2402, Hyattsville, MD 20782; (301) 458-4200. Fax, (301) 458-4022. Marjorie S. Greenberg, Executive Secretary, (301) 458-4245.*
Web, www.ncvhs.hhs.gov

Statutory public advisory body on health data statistics and national health information policy. Serves as a national forum on health data. Aims to accelerate the evolution of public and private health information systems toward more uniform, shared data standards within the context of privacy and security concerns.

Health and Human Services Dept. (HHS), *Planning and Evaluation,* *200 Independence Ave. S.W., #415F 20201; (202) 690-7858. Fax, (202) 690-7383. Vacant, Assistant Secretary.*
Web, http://aspe.hhs.gov

Provides policy advice and makes recommendations to the secretary on the full range of department planning, including Medicare, Medicaid, health care services, human resources, health care facilities development and financing, biomedical research, and health care planning.

Health and Human Services Dept. (HHS), *Preparedness and Response (ASPR),* *200 Independence Ave. S.W., #638-G 20201; (202) 205-2882. Fax, (202) 690-6512. Craig Vanderwagen, Assistant Secretary.*
General e-mail, craig.vanderwagen@hhs.gov
Web, www.hhs.gov/aspr

Directs activities of HHS relating to the protection of the civilian population from acts of bioterrorism and other public health emergencies. Serves as the secretary's principal adviser on matters relating to bioterrorism and public health emergencies.

Health and Human Services Dept. (HHS), *President's Council on Bioethics,* *1425 New York Ave. N.W., #C100 20005; (202) 296-4669. Fax, (202) 296-3528. Edmund D. Pellegrino, Chair; F. Daniel Davis, Executive Director.*
General e-mail, info@bioethics.gov
Web, www.bioethics.gov

Advises the president on ethical issues related to advances in biomedical science and technology, including stem cell research, assisted reproduction, cloning, end of life care, and the protection of human subjects in research.

Health Resources and Services Administration *(Health and Human Services Dept.),* *5600 Fishers Lane, #1405, Rockville, MD 20857; (301) 443-2216. Fax, (301) 443-1246. Mary Wakefield, Administrator. Information, (301) 443-3376. Press, (301) 443-3376.*
Web, www.hrsa.gov

Administers federal health service programs related to access, quality, equity, and cost of health care. Supports state and community efforts to deliver care to underserved areas and groups with special health needs.

Health Resources and Services Administration *(Health and Human Services Dept.), Rural Health Policy,* *5600 Fishers Lane, #9A42, Rockville, MD 20857; (301) 443-0835. Fax, (301) 443-2803. Tom Morris, Associate Administrator (Acting).*
General e-mail, tmorris@hrsa.gov
Web, www.ruralhealth.hrsa.gov

Works with federal agencies, states, and the private sector to develop solutions to health care problems in rural communities. Administers grants to rural communities and supports rural health services research. Studies the effects of Medicare and Medicaid programs on rural access to health care.

National Center for Health Statistics *(Centers for Disease Control and Prevention),* *3311 Toledo Rd., #7204, Hyattsville, MD 20782; (301) 458-4500. Fax, (301) 458-4020. Dr. Edward J. Sondik, Director. Information, (301) 458-4636.*
Web, www.cdc.gov/nchs

Compiles, analyzes, and disseminates national statistics on population health characteristics, health facilities and human resources, health costs and expenditures, and health hazards. Interests include international health statistics.

National Institute for Occupational Safety and Health (NIOSH), *(Centers for Disease Control and Prevention),* *395 E St. S.W., Patriots Plaza, #9200 20201; (202) 245-0625. Christine Blanche, Director (Acting). Information, (800) 356-4674.*
Web, www.cdc.gov/niosh

Supports and conducts research on occupational safety and health issues; provides technical assistance and training; organizes international conferences and symposia; develops recommendations for the Labor Dept. Operates occupational safety and health bibliographic databases; publishes documents on occupational safety and health.

National Institutes of Health (NIH), *(Health and Human Services Dept.),* *1 Center Dr., Bldg. 1, #126, MSC-0148, Bethesda, MD 20892-0148; (301) 496-2433. Fax, (301) 402-2700. Raynard Kington, Director (Acting). Press, (301) 496-4461.*
Web, www.nih.gov

Supports and conducts biomedical research into the causes and prevention of diseases and furnishes information to health professionals and the public. Comprises research institutes *(see Health Topics: Research and Advocacy, this chapter),* and other components (the National Library of Medicine, the Warren Grant Magnuson Clinical Center, the National Center for Research Resources, the John E. Fogarty International Center, the Division of Research Grants, and the Division of Computer Research and Technology). All institutes are located in Bethesda, except the National Institute of Environmental Health Sciences, P.O. Box 12233, Research Triangle Park, N.C. 27709.

National Library of Medicine *(National Institutes of Health), National Center for Biotechnology Information: PubMed Central,* *8600 Rockville Pike, Bldg. 38A, 8th Floor, Bethesda, MD 20894; (301) 496-2475. Fax, (301) 480-4559. Dr. David J. Lipman, Director.*
General e-mail, info@ncbi.nlm.nih.gov
Web, www.ncbi.nlm.nih.gov or www.pubmedcentral.nih.gov

Publicly accessible digital archive of life sciences journal literature.

Public Health and Science *(Health and Human Services Dept.),* *5600 Fishers Lane, #18-66, Rockville, MD 20857; (301) 443-4000. Fax, (301) 443-3574. Rear Adm. Steven K. Galson, Surgeon General (Acting), (301) 594-5400.*
Web, www.surgeongeneral.gov

Directs activities of the Public Health Service. Serves as the secretary's principal adviser on health concerns;

HEALTH RESOURCES IN CONGRESS

For a complete listing of Congress committees, including their full contact information, leadership, membership, and jurisdictions, please refer to the Appendix on pages 724–837.

HOUSE:

House Agriculture Committee, Subcommittee on Department Operations, Oversight, Nutrition, and Forestry, (202) 225-6395.
Web, agriculture.house.gov

House Appropriations Committee, Subcommittee on Agriculture, Rural Development, FDA, and Related Agencies, (202) 225-2638.
Web, appropriations.house.gov

    Subcommittee on Labor, Health and Human Services, Education, and Related Agencies, (202) 225-3508.

House Budget Committee, (202) 226-7200.
Web, budget.house.gov

House Education and Labor Committee, Subcommittee on Health, Employment, Labor, and Pensions, (202) 225-3725.
Web, edworkforce.house.gov

    Subcommittee on Healthy Families and Communities, (202) 225-3725.

    Subcommittee on Workforce Protections, (202) 225-3725.

House Energy and Commerce Committee, Subcommittee on Energy and Environment (202) 225-2927.
Web, energycommerce.house.gov

    Subcommittee on Health, (202) 225-2927.

House Foreign Affairs Committee, Subcommittee on Africa and Global Health, (202) 226-7812.
Web, foreignaffairs.house.gov

House Natural Resources Committee, (202) 225-6065.
Web, resourcescommittee.house.gov

House Oversight and Government Reform Committee, (202) 225-5051.
Web, oversight.house.gov

    Subcommittee on Domestic Policy, (202) 225-6427.

House Science and Technology Committee, Subcommittee on Research and Science Education, (202) 225-9662.
Web, science.house.gov

House Small Business Committee, (202) 225-4038.
Web, www.house.gov/smbiz

    Subcommittee on Regulations and Health Care, (202) 225-4038.

House Veterans' Affairs Committee, (202) 225-9756.
Web, veterans.house.gov

    Subcommittee on Health, (202) 225-9154.

---

exercises specialized responsibilities in various health areas, including domestic and global health. Advises the public on smoking, AIDS, immunization, diet, nutrition, disease prevention, and other general health issues, including responses to bioterrorism. Oversees activities of all members of the Public Health Service Commissioned Corps. For information on avian and pandemic flu, go to PandemicFlu.gov.

Public Health and Science *(Health and Human Services Dept.), Disease Prevention and Health Promotion,* 1101 Wootton Parkway, #LL100, Rockville, MD 20852; (240) 453-8280. Fax, (240) 453-8282. Penelope Slade-Sawyer, Director. Alternate phone, (202) 453-8250.
Web, www.odphp.osophs.dhhs.gov

Develops national policies for disease prevention, clinical preventive services, and health promotion; assists the private sector and agencies with disease prevention, clinical preventive services, and health promotion activities.

Public Health and Science *(Health and Human Services Dept.), National Health Information Center,* P.O. Box 1133 20013-1133; (301) 565-4167. Fax, (301) 984-4256. Eric Davis, Project Manager. Information, (800) 336-4797.

General e-mail, healthfinder@nhic.org

Web, www.health.gov/nhic or www.healthfinder.org

A project of the office of Disease Prevention and Health Promotion; provides referrals on health topics and resources.

▶CONGRESS

For a listing of relevant congressional committees and subcommittees, please see page 320 or the Appendix.

Government Accountability Office (GAO), *Health Care,* 441 G St. N.W., #5A14 20548; (202) 512-7114. Marjorie E. Kanof, Managing Director.
Web, www.gao.gov

Independent, nonpartisan agency in the legislative branch. Audits all federal government health programs, including those administered by the departments of Defense, Health and Human Services, and Veterans Affairs. (Formerly the General Accounting Office.)

▶INTERNATIONAL ORGANIZATIONS

International Bank for Reconstruction and Development (World Bank), *Human Development*

HEALTH RESOURCES IN CONGRESS

House Ways and Means Committee, (202) 225-3625.
Web, waysandmeans.house.gov
>**Subcommittee on Health,** (202) 225-3943.

SENATE:

Senate Agriculture, Nutrition, and Forestry Committee, Subcommittee on Nutrition and Food Assistance, Sustainable and Organic Agriculture, and General Legislation, (202) 224-2035.
Web, agriculture.senate.gov

Senate Appropriations Committee, Subcommittee on Agriculture, Rural Development, FDA, and Related Agencies, (202) 224-7363.
Web, appropriations.senate.gov
>**Subcommittee on Labor, Health and Human Services, Education, and Related Agencies,** (202) 224-7363.

Senate Banking, Housing and Urban Affairs Committee, (202) 224-7391.
Web, banking.senate.gov

Senate Budget Committee, (202) 224 0642.
Web, budget.senate.gov

Senate Commerce, Science, and Transportation Committee, Subcommittee on Science, Technology, and Innovation, (202) 224-0415.
Web, commerce.senate.gov

Senate Environment and Public Works Committee, Subcommittee on Clean Air and Nuclear Safety, (202) 224-8832.

Web, epw.senate.gov/public
>**Subcommittee on Superfund and Environmental Health,** (202) 224-8832.
>**Subcommittee on Transportation Safety, Infrastructure Security and Water Quality,** (202) 224-8832.

Senate Finance Committee, (202) 224-4515.
Web, finance.senate.gov
>**Subcommittee on Health Care,** (202) 224-4515.

Senate Health, Education, Labor, and Pensions Committee, (202) 224-5375.
Web, help.senate.gov
>**Subcommittee on Children and Families,** (202) 224-5630 or (202) 224-5800.
>**Subcommittee on Employment and Workplace Safety,** (202) 224-2621.
>**Subcommittee on Retirement and Aging,** (202) 224-9243.

Senate Indian Affairs Committee, (202) 224-2251.
Web, indian.senate.gov

Senate Judiciary Committee, Subcommittee on Crime and Drugs, (202) 224-0558.
Web, judiciary.senate.gov

Senate Small Business and Entrepreneurship Committee, (202) 224-5175.
Web, sbc.senate.gov

Senate Special Committee on Aging, (202) 224-5364.
Web, aging.senate.gov

Network, 1818 H St. N.W., #G7-702, MSC-G8-801 20433; (202) 473-4946. Fax, (202) 522-3235. Joy Phumaphi, Vice President. Alternate phone, (202) 473-1000.
Web, www.worldbank.org

Provides member countries with support for initiatives concerning family planning and population. Promotes a reproductive health approach that integrates family planning, maternal and adolescent health, and prevention of sexually transmitted diseases, especially HIV/AIDS.

Pan American Health Organization, *525 23rd St. N.W. 20037; (202) 974-3000. Fax, (202) 974-3663. Dr. Mirta Roses Periago, Director. Library, (202) 974-3305.*
Web, www.paho.org

Works to extend health services to underserved populations of its member countries and to control or eradicate communicable diseases; promotes cooperation among governments to solve public health problems. Library open to the public by appointment. (Regional Office for the Americas of the World Health Organization, which is headquartered in Geneva.)

World Federation of Public Health Assns., *800 Eye St. N.W. 20001-3710; (202) 777-2742. Fax, (202) 777-2533. Dr. Barbara Hatcher, Washington Secretariat.*

General e-mail, info@wfpha.org
Web, www.wfpha.org

International, multiprofessional, and civil society organization that seeks to promote and protect global public health. Sponsors triennial international congress.

▶**NONGOVERNMENTAL**

Academy for Educational Development (AED), *1825 Connecticut Ave. N.W., #800 20009-5721; (202) 884-8000. Fax, (202) 884-8400. Stephen F. Moseley, President. General e-mail, communicationsmail@aed.org*
Web, www.aed.org

Implements global health programs that address malnutrition and food security, HIV/AIDS, malaria, and other infectious diseases. Working with public health organizations and U.S. government agencies, uses innovative social marketing and behavior change communication programs, research and evaluation, and sound public health practice to help people adopt healthier lifestyles. Areas of emphasis include prevention of HIV/AIDS and sexually transmitted diseases, obesity, teen pregnancy, nutrition and exercise, tobacco prevention, and media and health literacy.

American Clinical Laboratory Assn., *1100 New York Ave. N.W., #725 West 20005; (202) 637-9466. Fax, (202) 637-2050. Alan Mertz, President.*
Web, www.clinical-labs.org

Membership: laboratories and laboratory service companies. Advocates laws and regulations that recognize the role of laboratory services in cost-effective health care. Works to ensure the confidentiality of patient test results. Provides education, information, and research materials to members.

American Public Health Assn., *800 Eye St. N.W. 20001; (202) 777-2430. Fax, (202) 777-2534. Dr. Georges Benjamin, Executive Director.*
General e-mail, comments@apha.org
Web, www.apha.org

Membership: health providers, educators, environmentalists, policymakers, and health officials at all levels working both within and outside of governmental organizations and educational institutions. Works to protect communities from serious, preventable health threats. Strives to ensure that community-based health promotion and disease prevention activities and preventive health services are universally accessible in the United States. Develops standards for scientific procedures in public health.

Assn. of State and Territorial Health Officials, *2231 Crystal Dr., #450, Arlington, VA 22202; (202) 371-9090. Fax, (571) 527-3189. Dr. Paul Jarris, Executive Director.*
Web, www.astho.org

Membership: executive officers of state and territorial health departments. Serves as legislative review agency and information source for members. Alternate Web site: www.statepublichealth.org.

The Brookings Institution, *Economic Studies Program, 1775 Massachusetts Ave. N.W. 20036-2188; (202) 797-6000. Fax, (202) 797-6181. William G. Gale, Director. Information, (202) 797-6105.*
General e-mail, escomment@brookings.edu
Web, www.brookings.edu

Studies federal health care issues and health programs, including Medicare, Medicaid, and long-term care.

Center for Economic and Policy Research (CEPR), *1611 Connecticut Ave. N.W., #400 20009; (202) 293-5380,ext. 115. Fax, (202) 588-1356. Dean Baker, Co-Director; Mark Weisbrot, Co-Director.*
General e-mail, cepr@cepr.net
Web, www.cepr.net

Researches economic and social issues and the impact of related public policies. Presents findings to the public with the goal of better preparing citizens to choose among various policy options. Promotes democratic debate and voter education. Areas of interest include health care, trade, Social Security, taxes, housing, and the labor market.

Center for Studying Health System Change, *600 Maryland Ave. S.W., #550 20024; (202) 484-5261. Fax, (202) 484-9258. Paul B. Ginsburg, President.*
General e-mail, hscinfo@hschange.org
Web, www.hschange.org

Designs and conducts studies focused on the U.S. health care system, documenting changes in the financing, delivery, and quality of health care and the effects of those changes on people. Policy research areas include health insurance coverage and costs, access to care, quality and care delivery, and health care markets. Funded in part by the Robert Wood Johnson Foundation. (Affiliated with Mathematica Policy Research Inc.)

Forum for State Health Policy Leadership, *444 N. Capitol St. N.W., #515 20001; (202) 624-8171. Fax, (202) 737-1069. Donna C. Folkemer, Director.*
Web, www.ncsl.org/programs/health/forum

Researches state health laws and programs. Provides health policymakers, administrators, and others with information on state health programs and policies. (Affiliated with the National Conference of State Legislatures.)

Global Health Council, *1111 19th St. N.W., #1120 20036; (202) 833-5900. Fax, (202) 833-0075. Vacant, President.*
General e-mail, ghc@globalhealth.org
Web, www.globalhealth.org

Membership: health care professionals, NGOs, foundations, corporations, government agencies, and academic institutions. Works to promote better health around the world by assisting those who work for improvement and equity in global health to secure the information and resources they need to work effectively.

Grantmakers in Health, *1100 Connecticut Ave. N.W., #1200 20036; (202) 452-8331. Fax, (202) 452-8340. Lauren LeRoy, President.*
General e-mail, gih@gih.org
Web, www.gih.org

Seeks to increase the capacity of private sector grantmakers to enhance public health. Fosters information exchange among grantmakers. Publications include a bulletin on current news in health and human services and the *Directory of Health Philanthropy*.

Healthcare Leadership Council, *1001 Pennsylvania Ave. N.W., #550 South 20004; (202) 452-8700. Fax, (202) 296-9561. Mary R. Grealy, President; Michael Freeman, Executive Vice President for Communications.*
General e-mail, mfreeman@hlc.org
Web, www.hlc.org

Membership: health care leaders who examine major health issues, including access and affordability. Works to implement new public policies.

Health Policy Institute, *3300 Whitehaven St. N.W., #5000, Box 571444 20057-1485; (202) 687-0880. Fax, (202) 687-3110. Karen Pollitz, Research Professor.*
Web, http://ihcrp.georgetown.edu

Health and Human Services Department

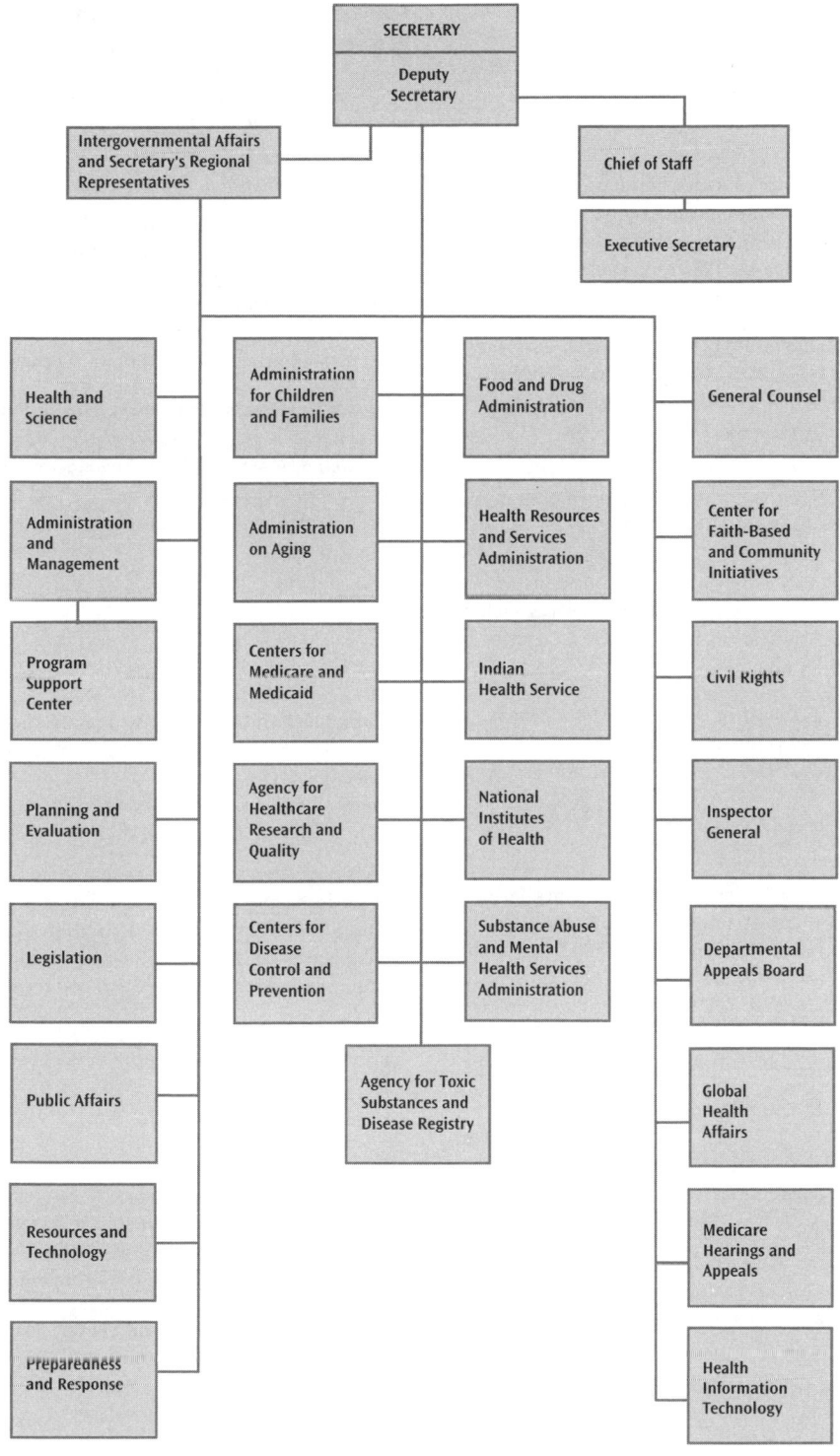

Research branch of Georgetown University. Interests include quality of care, cost effectiveness, outcomes research, structure and impact of managed care, health privacy, and access to care.

Henry J. Kaiser Family Foundation, *1330 G St. N.W. 20005; (202) 347-5270. Fax, (202) 347-5274. Drew Altman, President.*
Web, www.kff.org

Offers information on major health care issues. Conducts research and communications programs. Monitors legislation and regulations. (Headquarters in Menlo Park, Calif. Not affiliated with Kaiser Permanente or Kaiser Industries.)

International Epidemiology Institute, *1455 Research Blvd., #550, Rockville, MD 20850; (301) 424-1054. Fax, (301) 424-1053. William J. Blot, Chief Executive Officer.*
General e-mail, info@iei.ws

Web, www.ieiltd.com

Investigates biomedical problems and environmental health issues for the public and private sectors, universities, and other institutions. Conducts studies and clinical trials. Helps identify potential risks and benefits associated with new medicines and new medical devices, including implants. (Affiliated with Vanderbilt University in Nashville, Tenn.)

National Assn. of Counties (NACo), *25 Massachusetts Ave. N.W., 5th Floor 20001-2028; (202) 942-4234. Fax, (202) 942-4281. Paul Beddoe, Associate Legislative Director.*
General e-mail, pbeddoe@naco.org

Web, http://capwiz.com/naco

Promotes federal understanding of county governments' role in providing, funding, and overseeing health services at the local level. Interests include indigent health care, Medicaid and Medicare, prevention of and services for HIV infection and AIDS, long-term care, mental health, maternal and child health, and traditional public health programs conducted by local health departments.

National Assn. of County and City Health Officials, *1100 17th St. N.W., 2nd Floor 20036; (202) 783-5550. Fax, (202) 783-1583. Robert M. Pestronk, Executive Director.*
General e-mail, info@naccho.org

Web, www.naccho.org

Represents the nation's 2,850 local health departments. Develops resources and programs to support local public health practices and systems. Submits health policy proposals to the federal government.

National Committee for Quality Assurance, *1100 13th St. N.W., #1000 20005; (202) 955-3500. Fax, (202) 955-3599. Margaret E. O'Kane, President.*
Web, www.ncqa.org

Provides information on the quality of health care provided by health care institutions and individual providers. Assesses and reports on managed care plans

through accreditation and performance measurement programs.

National Forum for Health Care Quality Measurement and Reporting (National Quality Forum), *601 13th St. N.W., #500 North 20005; (202) 783-1300. Fax, (202) 783-3434. Dr. Janet Corrigan, President. Press, (202) 783-1300, ext. 179.*
General e-mail, info@qualityforum.org

Web, www.qualityforum.org

Works to improve the quality of health care in the United States by setting national priorities and goals for performance improvement, endorsing national consensus standards for measuring and publicly reporting on performances, and promoting the attainment of national goals through education and outreach programs.

National Governors Assn. (NGA), *Health Division,* *444 N. Capitol St. N.W., #267 20001-1512; (202) 624-5343. Fax, (202) 624-7818. Kathleen Nolan, Director. Information, (202) 624-5300.*
General e-mail, knolan@nga.org

Web, www.nga.org

Provides technical assistance regarding the Title 21 Program, state oversight of managed care, public/private efforts to improve health care quality, and long-term care services.

National Health Council, *1730 M St. N.W., #500 20036-4505; (202) 785-3910. Fax, (202) 785-5923. Myrl Weinberg, President.*
General e-mail, info@nhcouncil.org

Web, www.nationalhealthcouncil.org

Membership: voluntary health agencies, associations, and business, insurance, and government groups interested in health. Conducts research on health and health-related issues; serves as an information clearinghouse on health careers. Monitors legislation and regulations.

National Health Policy Forum, *2131 K St. N.W., #500 20037; (202) 872-1390. Fax, (202) 862-9837. Judith Miller Jones, Director.*
General e-mail, nhpf@gwu.edu

Web, www.nhpf.org

Nonpartisan policy analysis and research organization that provides executive branch and congressional staff with information on financing and delivery of health care services. Affiliated with George Washington University.

National Vaccine Information Center, *407 Church St., Suite H, Vienna, VA 22180; (703) 938-3783. Fax, (703) 938-5768. Barbara Loe Fisher, President.*
General e-mail, contactnvic@gmail.com

Web, www.nvic.org

Educational organization that supports informed vaccination decisions, including the option to forego vaccination. Provides assistance to parents of children who have experienced vaccine reactions and publishes information on diseases and vaccines. Monitors vaccine research, legislation, and regulations.

Partnership for Prevention, *1015 18th St. N.W., #300 20036; (202) 833-0009. Fax, (202) 833-0113. Dr. Corinne G. Husten, President (Interim).*
General e-mail, info@prevent.org
Web, www.prevent.org

Seeks to make prevention a priority in national health policy and practice. Coordinates the prevention-oriented efforts of federal health agencies, corporations, states, and nonprofit organizations in order to achieve the Healthy People 2010 national prevention goals.

Physicians for Human Rights, *Washington Office, 1156 15th St. N.W., #1001 20005; (202) 728-5335. Fax, (202) 728-3053. John Bradshaw, Director, ext. 304.*
General e-mail, phrusa@phrusa.org
Web, www.physiciansforhumanrights.org

Mobilizes health professionals to promote health and human rights globally. Investigates and seeks to end and prevent human rights abuses. Interests include the AIDS epidemic and prison health care. (Headquarters in Cambridge, Mass.)

Public Citizen, *Health Research Group, 1600 20th St. N.W. 20009-1001; (202) 588-1000. Fax, (202) 588-7796. Dr. Sidney M. Wolfe, Director.*
General e-mail, pcmail@citizen.org
Web, www.citizen.org

Citizens' interest group that conducts policy-oriented research on health care issues. Interests include hospital quality and costs, doctors' fees, physician discipline and malpractice, state administration of Medicare programs, workplace safety and health, unnecessary surgery, comprehensive health planning, dangerous drugs, carcinogens, and medical devices. Favors a single-payer (Canadian-style), comprehensive health program.

RAND Corporation, *Health Unit, Washington Office, 1200 S. Hayes St., Arlington, VA 22202-5050; (703) 413-1100. Fax, (703) 413-8111. Dr. Ross Anthony, Director of Global Health, ext. 5265. Media Relations, ext. 5117.*
Web, www.rand.org/health

Research organization that assesses health issues, including alternative reimbursement schemes for health care. Monitors national and international trends. (Headquarters in Santa Monica, Calif.)

Regulatory Affairs Professionals Society, *5635 Fishers Lane, #550, Rockville, MD 20852; (301) 770-2920. Fax, (301) 770-2924. Sherry Keramidas, Executive Director.*
General e-mail, raps@raps.org
Web, www.raps.org

Membership: regulatory professionals in the health care product sector worldwide. Promotes the safety and effectiveness of health care products. Supports the regulatory profession with resources, including education and certification. Monitors legislation and regulations.

Health Insurance, Managed Care

►AGENCIES

Centers for Medicare and Medicaid Services (CMS), *(Health and Human Services Dept.), Center for Medicare Management, 7500 Security Blvd., C5-01-14, Baltimore, MD 21244; (410) 786-4164. Fax, (410) 786-0192. Elizabeth Richter, Director (Acting).*
Web, www.cms.hhs.gov

Manages the traditional fee-for-service Medicare program, which includes the development of payment policy and management of Medicare fee-for-service contractors. (Formerly the Health Care Financing Administration.)

►CONGRESS

For a listing of relevant congressional committees and subcommittees, please see page 320 or the Appendix.

Congressional Budget Office, *Health and Human Resources, 419 FHOB 20515; (202) 226-2666. Fax, (202) 225-3149. Bruce Vavrichek, Assistant Director.*
Web, www.cbo.gov

Analyzes program and budget issues in the areas of health, education, employment and training, and social services. Examines the potential effects on the private sector of proposed federal mandates in those areas. Prepares reports to Congress.

►NONGOVERNMENTAL

Alliance for Health Reform, *1444 Eye St. N.W., #910 20005; (202) 789-2300. Fax, (202) 789-2233. Edward F. Howard, Executive Vice President.*
General e-mail, info@allhealth.org
Web, www.allhealth.org

Nonpartisan organization that advocates health care reform, including cost containment and coverage for all. Sponsors conferences and seminars for journalists, business leaders, policymakers, and the public.

American Medical Assn. (AMA), *Government Relations, Washington Office, 25 Massachusetts Ave. N.W., #600 20001; (202) 789-7400. Fax, (202) 789-7485. Richard Deem, Senior Vice President.*
Web, www.ama-assn.org

Membership: physicians, residents, and medical students. Provides information on health care. Monitors legislation and regulations. (Headquarters in Chicago, Ill.)

America's Health Insurance Plans, *601 Pennsylvania Ave., South Bldg. N.W., #500 20004; (202) 778-3200. Fax, (202) 770-0500. Karen Ignagni, President. Press, (202) 778-8494.*
General e-mail, ahip@ahip.org
Web, www.ahip.org

Membership: companies providing medical expense, long-term care, disability income, dental, supplemental, and stop-loss insurance and reinsurance to consumers, employers, and public purchasers. Advocates evidence-based medicine, targeted strategies to give all Americans access to health care, and health care cost savings through regulatory, legal, and other reforms. Provides educational programs and legal counsel. Monitors legislation and regulations. (Merger of the American Assn. of Health Plans and Health Insurance Assn. of America.)

Blue Cross and Blue Shield Assn., *Washington Office,* *1310 G St. N.W. 20005; (202) 626-4780. Fax, (202) 626-4833. Scott Serota, President. Press, (202) 662-4825.* *Web, www.bluecares.com*

Membership: Blue Cross and Blue Shield insurance plans, which operate autonomously at the local level. Certifies member plans; acts as consultant to plans in evaluating new medical technologies and contracting with doctors and hospitals. Operates a national network to collect, analyze, and disseminate data. (Headquarters in Chicago, Ill.)

Center for Health Transformation, *1425 K St. N.W., #450 20005; (202) 375-2001. Fax, (202) 375-2036. Nancy Desmond, Chief Executive Officer.* *General e-mail, info@healthtransformation.net* *Web, www.healthtransformation.net*

Promotes transformational change of health and the health care system by identifying better solutions and raising public awareness. Activities include building coalitions, creating communications initiatives, and coordinating educational events and projects. Monitors legislation and regulations.

Center for Studying Health System Change, *600 Maryland Ave. S.W., #550 20024; (202) 484-5261. Fax, (202) 484-9258. Paul B. Ginsburg, President.* *General e-mail, hscinfo@hschange.org* *Web, www.hschange.org*

Analyzes private and public insurance coverage, the uninsured, and the cost of health care. Interests include managed care, Medicare+Choice and Medicaid managed care, changes in health care costs, the rising number of uninsured Americans, and changes in employer-sponsored coverage. Funded primarily by the Robert Wood Johnson Foundation.

Council for Affordable Health Insurance, *127 S. Peyton St., #210, Alexandria, VA 22314; (703) 836-6200. Fax, (703) 836-6550. Merrill Matthews Jr., Director.* *General e-mail, mail@cahi.org* *Web, www.cahi.org*

Membership: insurance carriers in the small group, individual, and senior markets, business groups, doctors, actuaries, and insurance brokers. Research and advocacy organization devoted to free market solutions to America's health care problems. Promotes reform measures, including health savings accounts, tax equity, universal access, medical price disclosure prior to treatment, and caps on malpractice awards. Serves as a liaison with businesses, provider organizations, and public interest groups. Monitors legislation and regulations at state and federal levels.

Employee Benefit Research Institute, *1100 13th St. N.W., #878 20005; (202) 659-0670. Fax, (202) 775-6312.*

Dallas L. Salisbury, President. Media Relations, (202) 775-6349. *General e-mail, info@ebri.org* *Web, www.ebri.org*

Research institute that focuses on health, savings, retirement, and economic security issues. Does not lobby and does not take policy positions.

Employers Council on Flexible Compensation, *927 15th St. N.W., #1000 20005; (202) 659-4300. David Carver, Executive Director. Information, (877) 747-3539.* *General e-mail, info@ecfc.org* *Web, www.ecfc.org*

Represents employers who have or are considering flexible compensation plans. Supports the preservation and expansion of employee choice in health insurance coverage. Monitors legislation and regulations.

Galen Institute, *P.O. Box 320010, Alexandria, VA 22320; (703) 299-8900. Fax, (703) 299-0721. Grace-Marie Turner, President.* *General e-mail, galen@galen.org* *Web, www.galen.org*

Provides ideas and information on health care financing, focusing on initiatives that advance consumer choice. Advocates savings accounts, competition among private plans in Medicare, and other free-market health reform ideas.

National Academy of Social Insurance, *1776 Massachusetts Ave. N.W., #615 20036-1904; (202) 452-8097. Fax, (202) 452-8111. Pamela J. Larson, Executive Vice President.* *General e-mail, nasi@nasi.org* *Web, www.nasi.org*

Promotes research and education on Social Security, Medicare, health care financing, and related public and private programs; assesses social insurance programs and their relationship to other programs; supports research and leadership development. Acts as a clearinghouse for social insurance information.

National Assn. of Health Underwriters, *2000 N. 14th St., #450, Arlington, VA 22201; (703) 276-0220. Fax, (703) 841-7797. Janet Trautwein, Executive Vice President. Public Relations, (703) 276-3835.* *General e-mail, nahu@nahu.org* *Web, www.nahu.org*

Membership: more than 20,000 licensed health insurance agents, brokers, consultants, and benefit professionals nationwide. Offers continuing education programs as well as business-development tools. Promotes private health insurance market solutions. Monitors legislation and regulations.

National Assn. of Manufacturers (NAM), *Human Resources Policy, 1331 Pennsylvania Ave. N.W., #600 20004-1790; (202) 637-3127. Fax, (202) 637-3182. Jeri Kubicki, Vice President. Alternate phone, (202) 637-3000.* *Web, www.nam.org*

Interests include health care, Social Security, pensions, employee benefits, cost containment, mandated benefits, Medicare, and other federal programs that affect employers. Opposed to government involvement in health care.

National Business Group on Health, *50 F St. N.W., #600 20001; (202) 628-9320. Fax, (202) 628-9244. Helen Darling, President.*
General e-mail, info@businessgrouphealth.org
Web, www.businessgrouphealth.org

Membership: large corporations with an interest in health care benefits. Interests include reimbursement policies, disease prevention and health promotion, hospital cost containment, health care planning, corporate education, Medicare, and retiree medical costs. Monitors legislation and regulations. (Formerly the Washington Business Group on Health.)

National Coalition on Health Care, *1120 G St. N.W., #810 20005; (202) 638-7151. Fax, (202) 638-7166. Vacant, Executive Director.*
General e-mail, info@nchc.org
Web, www.nchc.org

Membership: insurers, labor organizations, large and small businesses, consumer groups, and healthcare providers. Advocates for improved access to affordable health care coverage and improved quality of care. Monitors legislation and regulations.

National Health Care Anti-Fraud Assn., *1201 New York Ave. N.W., #1120 20005; (202) 659-5955. Fax, (202) 785-6764. Louis Saccoccio, Executive Director.*
General e-mail, nhcaa@nhcaa.org
Web, www.nhcaa.org

Membership: health insurance companies and regulatory and law enforcement agencies. Members work to identify, investigate, and prosecute individuals defrauding health care reimbursement systems.

Society of Professional Benefit Administrators, *2 Wisconsin Circle, #670, Chevy Chase, MD 20815; (301) 718-7722. Fax, (301) 718-9440. Frederick D. Hunt Jr., President.*
Web, http://users.erols.com/spba

Membership: third-party administration firms that manage employee benefit plans for client employers. Interests include health care and insurance legislation and regulations, revision of Medicare programs, and health care cost containment. Monitors industry trends, government compliance requirements, and developments in health care financing.

Hospitals

▶AGENCIES

Centers for Medicare and Medicaid Services (CMS), *(Health and Human Services Dept.), Survey and Certification Group, 7500 Security Blvd., S2-12-25,* Baltimore, MD 21244; (410) 786-3160. Fax, (410) 786-0194. Thomas E. Hamilton, Director.
Web, www.cms.hhs.gov

Enforces health care and safety standards for hospitals, nursing homes, and other health care facilities. (Formerly the Health Care Financing Administration.)

Mark O. Hatfield Clinical Research Center *(National Institutes of Health), 10 Center Dr., Bethesda, MD 20892; (301) 496-3315 (Admissions). Dr. John I. Gallin, Director. Patient Recruitment, (800) 411-1222; Public Information, (301) 496-4000.*
Web, http://clinicalcenter.nih.gov

Provides in-patient care and conducts clinical research. Promotes the application of scientific laboratory research to benefit patient health and medical care. With the Warren Grant Magnuson Clinical Center, forms the NIH Clinical Center.

NIH Clinical Center *(National Institutes of Health), 10 Center Dr., Bldg. 10 CRC, #6-2551, MSC-1504, Bethesda, MD 20892-1504; (301) 496-4114. Fax, (301) 402-0244. Dr. John I. Gallin, Director. Communications, (301) 496-2563.*
Web, http://clinicalcenter.nih.gov

Serves as a clinical research center for the NIH; patients are referred by physicians and self-referred throughout the United States and overseas.

▶CONGRESS

For a listing of relevant congressional committees and subcommittees, please see page 320 or the Appendix.

▶NONGOVERNMENTAL

American Hospital Assn., Washington Office, *325 7th St. N.W., #700 20004-2802; (202) 638-1100. Fax, (202) 626-2345. Richard Umbdenstock, President.*
Web, www.aha.org

Membership: hospitals, other inpatient care facilities, outpatient centers, Blue Cross plans, areawide planning agencies, regional medical programs, hospital schools of nursing, and individuals. Conducts research and education projects in such areas as provision of comprehensive care, hospital economics, hospital facilities and design, and community relations; participates with other health care associations in establishing hospital care standards. Monitors legislation and regulations. (Headquarters in Chicago, Ill.)

Assn. of Academic Health Centers, *1400 16th St. N.W., #720 20036; (202) 265-9600. Fax, (202) 265-7514. Dr. Steven Wartman, President.*
Web, www.aahcdc.org

Membership: academic health centers (composed of a medical school, a teaching hospital, and at least one other health professional school or program). Participates in studies and public debates on health professionals' training and education, patient care, and biomedical research.

Federation of American Hospitals, *801 Pennsylvania Ave. N.W., #245 20004-2604; (202) 624-1500. Fax, (202) 737-6462. Charles N. Kahn III, President.*
Web, www.fah.org

Membership: privately owned or managed community hospitals and health systems. Interests include national health care issues, such as cost containment, Medicare and Medicaid, the tax code, and the hospital workforce. Monitors legislation and regulations.

National Assn. of Children's Hospitals, *401 Wythe St., Alexandria, VA 22314; (703) 684-1355. Fax, (703) 684-1589. Lawrence A. McAndrews, President.*
Web, www.childrenshospitals.net

Membership: more than 140 children's hospitals nationwide. Assists member hospitals in addressing public policy issues that affect their ability to provide clinical care, education, research, and advocacy. (Affiliated with the National Assn. of Children's Hospitals and Related Institutions.)

National Assn. of Children's Hospitals and Related Institutions, *401 Wythe St., Alexandria, VA 22314; (703) 684-1355. Fax, (703) 684-1589. Lawrence A. McAndrews, President.*
Web, www.childrenshospitals.net

Advocates and promotes education and research on child health care related to children's hospitals; compiles statistics and provides information on pediatric hospitalizations. (Affiliated with the National Assn. of Children's Hospitals.)

National Assn. of Public Hospitals and Health Systems, *1301 Pennsylvania Ave. N.W., #950 20004; (202) 585-0100. Fax, (202) 585-0101. Larry S. Gage, President. General e-mail, naph@naph.org*
Web, www.naph.org

Membership: city and county public hospitals, state universities, and hospital districts and authorities. Works to improve and expand health care in hospitals; interests include Medicaid patients and vulnerable populations, including AIDS patients, the homeless, the mentally ill, and non-English-speaking patients. Holds annual regional meetings. Monitors legislation and regulations.

Medicaid and Medicare

▶**AGENCIES**

Centers for Medicare and Medicaid Services (CMS), *(Health and Human Services Dept.), 200 Independence Ave. S.W., #314G 20201; (202) 690-6726. Fax, (202) 690-6262. Vacant, Administrator.*
Web, www.cms.hhs.gov

Administers Medicare (a health insurance program for persons with disabilities or age sixty-five or older who are eligible to participate) and Medicaid (a health insurance program for persons judged unable to pay for

health services). (Formerly the Health Care Financing Administration.)

Centers for Medicare and Medicaid Services (CMS), *(Health and Human Services Dept.), Center for Medicare Management, 7500 Security Blvd., C5-01-14, Baltimore, MD 21244; (410) 786-4164. Fax, (410) 786-0192. Elizabeth Richter, Director (Acting).*
Web, www.cms.hhs.gov

Manages the contractual framework for the Medicare program; establishes and enforces performance standards for contractors who process and pay Medicare claims. Issues regulations and guidelines for administration of the Medicare program. (Formerly the Health Care Financing Administration.)

Centers for Medicare and Medicaid Services (CMS), *(Health and Human Services Dept.), Chronic Care Improvement Program, 7500 Security Blvd., C5-05-27, Baltimore, MD 21244-1850; (410) 786-3000. Fax, (410) 786-0765. Vacant, Administrator. TTY, (866) 226-1819. Local TTY, (410) 786-0727. Public Affairs, (202) 690-6145.*
Web, www.cms.hhs.gov

Administers coverage policy for Medicare persons with renal disease, chronic kidney failure, and the Program for All-Inclusive Care for the Elderly (PACE). Coordinates coverage under new treatment methods. (Formerly the Health Care Financing Administration.)

Centers for Medicare and Medicaid Services *(Health and Human Services Dept.), Clinical Standards and Quality, 7500 Security Blvd., S3-02-01, Baltimore, MD 21244; (410) 786-6841. Fax, (410) 786-6857. Barry Straube, Director.*
Web, www.cms.hhs.gov

Develops, establishes, and enforces standards that regulate the quality of care of hospitals and other health care facilities under Medicare and Medicaid programs. Administers operations of survey and peer review organizations that enforce health care standards, primarily for institutional care. Oversees clinical laboratory improvement programs and end stage renal disease networks. Monitors providers' and suppliers' compliance with standards. (Formerly the Health Care Financing Administration.)

Centers for Medicare and Medicaid Services (CMS), *(Health and Human Services Dept.), Disabled and Elderly Health Group, 7500 Security Blvd., S2-14-27, Baltimore, MD 21244; (410) 786-8624. Fax, (410) 786-9004. Melissa Halbert, Director (Acting).*
Web, www.cms.hhs.gov

Approves state Medicaid plan amendments and waivers to serve the disabled and elderly population. Organizes and administers grant programs that assist persons with disabilities to participate fully in communities. (Formerly the Health Care Financing Administration.)

Centers for Medicare and Medicaid Services (CMS), *(Health and Human Services Dept.), Information*

Services, 7500 Security Blvd., N3-15-25, Baltimore, MD 21244-1850; (410) 786-1800. Fax, (410) 786-1810. Julie Boughn, Director.
Web, www.cms.hhs.gov

Serves as primary federal statistical office for disseminating economic data on Medicare and Medicaid. (Formerly the Health Care Financing Administration.)

Centers for Medicare and Medicaid Services (CMS), *(Health and Human Services Dept.), Medicaid,* 7500 Security Blvd., #C5-22-23, Baltimore, MD 21244; (410) 786-3870. Fax, (410) 786-0025. Jackie Garner, Director (Acting); William Lasowski, Deputy Director. Alternate phone, (202) 690-7428.
Web, www.cms.hhs.gov

Administers and monitors Medicaid programs to ensure program quality and financial integrity; promotes beneficiary awareness and access to services. (Formerly the Health Care Financing Administration.)

Health Resources and Services Administration *(Health and Human Services Dept.), Rural Health Policy,* 5600 Fishers Lane, #9A42, Rockville, MD 20857; (301) 443-0835. Fax, (301) 443-2803. Tom Morris, Associate Administrator (Acting).
General e-mail, tmorris@hrsa.gov
Web, www.ruralhealth.hrsa.gov

Studies the effects of Medicare and Medicaid programs on rural access to health care.

►NONGOVERNMENTAL

Blue Cross and Blue Shield Assn., *Washington Office,* 1310 G St. N.W. 20005; (202) 626-4780. Fax, (202) 626-4833. Scott Serota, President. Press, (202) 662-4825.
Web, www.bluecares.com

Acts as the primary contractor for the federal government in administration of Medicare Part A, which covers hospitalization and institutional care for persons with disabilities and persons age sixty-five or older. (Headquarters in Chicago, Ill.)

Federation of American Hospitals, 801 Pennsylvania Ave. N.W., #245 20004-2604; (202) 624-1500. Fax, (202) 737-6462. Charles N. Kahn III, President.
Web, www.fah.org

Membership: investor-owned, for-profit hospitals and health care systems. Studies Medicaid and Medicare reforms. Maintains speakers bureau; compiles statistics on investor-owned hospitals. Monitors legislation and regulations.

National Committee to Preserve Social Security and Medicare, 10 G St. N.E., #600 20002-4215; (202) 216-0420. Fax, (202) 216-0446. Barbara Kennelly, President. Press, (202) 216-8378.
Web, www.ncpssm.org

Educational and advocacy organization that focuses on Social Security and Medicare programs and on related income security and health issues. Interests include retirement income protection, health care reform, and the quality of life of seniors. Monitors legislation and regulations.

Medical Devices and Technology

►AGENCIES

Food and Drug Administration (FDA), *(Health and Human Services Dept.), Center for Devices and Radiological Health,* 9200 Corporate Blvd., #100E, Rockville, MD 20850; (240) 276-3939. Fax, (240) 276-3943. Daniel G. Schultz, Director.
Web, www.fda.gov/cdrh

Evaluates safety, efficacy, and labeling of medical devices; classifies devices; establishes performance standards; assists in legal actions concerning medical devices; coordinates research and testing; conducts training and educational programs. Maintains an international reference system to facilitate trade in devices. Library open to the public.

Food and Drug Administration (FDA), *(Health and Human Services Dept.), Combination Products,* 15800 Crabbs Branch Way, #200, HFG-3, Rockville, MD 20855; (301) 427-1934. Fax, (301) 427-1935. Thinh Nguyen, Director.
General e-mail, combination@fda.gov
Web, www.fda.gov/oc/combination

Created to streamline the processing of complex drug-device, drug-biologic, and device-biologic combination products. Responsibilities cover the entire regulatory life cycle of combination products, including jurisdiction decisions as well as the timeliness and effectiveness of pre-market review, and the consistency and appropriateness of post-market regulation.

Food and Drug Administration (FDA), *(Health and Human Services Dept.), Small Manufacturers International and Consumer Assistance,* 1350 Piccard Dr., HFZ-220, Rockville, MD 20850; (240) 276-3150. Fax, (240) 276-3151. John F. Stigi, Director, (240) 276-3150, ext. 124. Manufacture Assistance, (800) 638-2041. Consumer Assistance, (240) 276-3103. Fax-on-demand, (800) 899-0381.
General e-mail, dsmica@cdrh.fda.gov
Web, www.fda.gov/cdrh/devadvice

Serves as liaison between small-business manufacturers of medical devices and the FDA. Assists manufacturers in complying with FDA regulatory requirements; sponsors seminars.

Lister Hill National Center for Biomedical Communications, *(National Library of Medicine),* 8600 Rockville Pike, Bethesda, MD 20894; (301) 496-4441. Fax, (301) 402-0118. Dr. Clement McDonald, Director. Visitor's Center, (301) 496-7771.
Web, http://lhncbc.nlm.nih.gov

A research and development division of the National Library of Medicine. Conducts and supports research and development in the dissemination of high-quality imagery, medical language processing, high-speed access to biomedical information, intelligent database systems development, multimedia visualization, knowledge management, data mining, and machine-assisted indexing.

National Institute of Biomedical Imaging and Bioengineering *(National Institutes of Health), 31 Center Dr., Bldg. 31, #1C14, MSC-2281, Bethesda, MD 20892-2281; (301) 496-8859. Fax, (301) 480-0679. Dr. Roderic I. Pettigrew, Director. Public Liaison, (301) 451-6768.*
General e-mail, info@nibib.nih.gov

Web, www.nibib.nih.gov

Conducts and supports research and development of biomedical imaging and bioengineering techniques and devices to improve the prevention, detection, and treatment of disease.

National Institutes of Health (NIH), *(Health and Human Services Dept.), Technology Transfer, 6011 Executive Blvd., #325, MSC 7660, Rockville, MD 20852-3804; (301) 496-7057. Fax, (301) 402-0220. Mark L. Rohrbaugh, Director.*
General e-mail, NIHOTT@mail.nih.gov

Web, http://ott.od.nih.gov

Evaluates, protects, monitors, and manages the NIH invention portfolio. Oversees patent prosecution, negotiates and monitors licensing agreements, and provides oversight and central policy review of cooperative research and development agreements. Also manages the patent and licensing activities for the Food and Drug Administration (FDA). Responsible for the central development and implementation of technology transfer policies for three research components of the Public Health Service—the NIH, the FDA, and the Centers for Disease Control and Prevention.

▶NONGOVERNMENTAL

Advanced Medical Technology Assn., *701 Pennsylvania Ave. N.W., #800 20004; (202) 783-8700. Fax, (202) 783-8750. Stephen J. Ubl, President.*
General e-mail, info@advamed.org

Web, www.advamed.org

Membership: manufacturers of medical devices, diagnostic products, and health care information systems. Interests include safe and effective medical devices; conducts educational seminars. Monitors legislation, regulations, and international issues. (Formerly Health Industry Manufacturers Assn.)

American Assn. for Homecare, *2011 Crystal Dr., #725, Arlington, VA 22202; (703) 836-6263. Fax, (703) 836-6730. Tyler J. Wilson, President.*
General e-mail, info@aahomecare.org

Web, www.aahomecare.org

Membership: home medical equipment and services providers; respiratory and infusion therapy organizations; hospice organizations; rehabilitation and assistive technology organizations; state homecare associations; and equipment manufacturers. Interests include preserving access to high-quality equipment and services. Provides education, training, and information about industry trends and legislative and regulatory developments. Supports legislative and regulatory policies that promote clinical and technological advances in the homecare setting.

American Institute of Ultrasound in Medicine, *14750 Sweitzer Lane, #100, Laurel, MD 20707-5906; (301) 498-4100. Fax, (301) 498-4450. Carmine Valente, Executive Director.*
General e-mail, admin@aium.org

Web, www.aium.org

Membership: medical professionals who use ultrasound technology in their practices. Promotes multidisciplinary research and education in the field of diagnostic ultrasound through conventions and educational programs. Monitors international research.

American Medical Informatics Assn., *4915 St. Elmo Ave., #401, Bethesda, MD 20814; (301) 657-1291. Fax, (301) 657-1296. Don E. Detmer, President and CEO.*
General e-mail, mail@amia.org

Web, www.amia.org

Membership: doctors and other medical professionals in the applied informatics field. Provides members information on medical systems and the use of computers in the health care field. Promotes use of computers and information systems in patient care; conducts and promotes research on medical technology; encourages development of universal standards, terminology, and coding systems.

American Orthotic and Prosthetic Assn., *330 John Carlyle St., #200, Alexandria, VA 22314; (571) 431-0876. Fax, (571) 431-0899. Brian L. Gustin, President.*
Web, www.aopanet.org

Membership: companies that manufacture or supply artificial limbs and braces. Provides information on the profession.

American Roentgen Ray Society, *44211 Slatestone Court, Leesburg, VA 20176-5109; (703) 729-3353. Fax, (703) 729-4839. Susan B. Cappitelli, Executive Director. Toll-free, (800) 438-2777.*
General e-mail, info@arrs.org

Web, www.arrs.org

Membership: physicians and researchers in radiology and allied sciences. Publishes research; conducts conferences; presents scholarships and awards; monitors international research.

Health Industry Distributors Assn., *310 Montgomery St., Alexandria, VA 22314-1516; (703) 549-4432. Fax, (703) 549-6495. Matthew Rowan, President.*
General e-mail, mail@hida.org

Web, www.hida.org

Membership: medical products distributors. Sponsors and conducts educational programs and training seminars. Monitors legislation and regulations.

Optical Society of America, *2010 Massachusetts Ave. N.W. 20036; (202) 223-8130. Fax, (202) 223-1096. Elizabeth Rogan, Executive Director.*
General e-mail, info@osa.org
Web, www.osa.org

Membership: researchers, educators, manufacturers, students, and others interested in optics and photonics worldwide. Promotes research and information exchange; conducts conferences.

Program for Appropriate Technology in Health, *Washington Office, 1800 K St. N.W., #800 20006; (202) 822-0033. Fax, (202) 457-1466. Patricia Daunas, Administrator.*
General e-mail, info@path.org
Web, www.path.org

Seeks to improve the safety and availability of health products and technologies worldwide, particularly in developing countries. Interests include reproductive health, immunization, maternal-child health, AIDS, and nutrition.

Nursing Homes and Hospices

►AGENCIES

Centers for Medicare and Medicaid Services (CMS), *(Health and Human Services Dept.), Nursing Homes and Continuing Care Services, 7500 Security Blvd., S2-12-25-07, Baltimore, MD 21244-1850; (410) 786-3870. Fax, (410) 786-6730. Cynthia Graunke, Director.*
Web, www.cms.hhs.gov

Monitors compliance of nursing homes, psychiatric hospitals, and long-term and intermediate care facilities with government standards. Focus includes quality of care, environmental conditions, and participation in Medicaid and Medicare programs. Coordinates health care programs for the mentally challenged. (Formerly the Health Care Financing Administration.)

Centers for Medicare and Medicaid Services (CMS), *(Health and Human Services Dept.), Survey and Certification Group, 7500 Security Blvd., S2-12-25, Baltimore, MD 21244; (410) 786-3160. Fax, (410) 786-0194. Thomas E. Hamilton, Director.*
Web, www.cms.hhs.gov

Enforces health care and safety standards for nursing homes and other long-term care facilities. (Formerly the Health Care Financing Administration.)

►NONGOVERNMENTAL

AARP, *Federal Affairs Health and Long-Term Care Team, 601 E St. N.W. 20049; (202) 434-3770. Fax, (202)* 434-3745. David Certner, Director of Federal Affairs. Main switchboard, (202) 434-2277.*
Web, www.aarp.org

Maintains the Legal Counsel for the Elderly, which advocates on behalf of older residents of the District of Columbia who reside in nursing homes and board and care homes. Monitors legislation and regulations.

American College of Health Care Administrators, *12100 Sunset Hills Rd., #130, Reston, VA 20190; (703) 739-7900. Fax, (703) 435-4390. Marianna Grachek, President.*
General e-mail, abell@achca.org
Web, www.achca.org

Membership: administrators of long-term health care organizations and facilities, including home health care programs, hospices, day care centers for the elderly, nursing and hospital facilities, retirement communities, and mental health care centers. Conducts research on statistical characteristics of nursing home and other medical administrators; conducts seminars and workshops; offers education courses; provides certification for administrators.

American Health Care Assn., *1201 L St. N.W. 20005; (202) 842-4444. Fax, (202) 842-3860. Bruce Yarwood, President. Library, (202) 898-2842. Publication orders, (800) 321-0343.*
Web, www.ahcancal.org

Association of facility-based long-term care providers and affiliates of state health organizations. Advocates for high-quality care and services for frail, elderly, and disabled Americans to government, business leaders, and the general public. Provides information, education, and administrative tools. Monitors legislation and regulations. Library open to the public by appointment only.

Assisted Living Federation of America, *1650 King St., #602, Alexandria, VA 22314; (703) 894-1805. Fax, (703) 894-1831. Richard Grimes, President.*
General e-mail, info@alfa.org
Web, www.alfa.org

Represents owner-operators of senior living and continuing care residences and others involved in the industry. Promotes the development of standards and increased awareness for the senior living industry. Provides members with information on policy, funding access, and quality of care. Interests include informed choice, safe environments, caring and competent staff, and funding alternatives to increase accessibility to senior communities. Monitors legislation and regulations.

Consumer Consortium on Assisted Living, *2342 Oak St., Falls Church, VA 22046; (703) 533-8121. Kathleen Cameron, Chair.*
General e-mail, info@ccal.org
Web, www.ccal.org

Educates consumers, trains professionals, and advocates for assisted living issues.

Hospice Foundation of America, *1621 Connecticut Ave. N.W., #300 20009; (202) 638-5419. Fax, (202) 638-5312. Amy Tucci, President. Toll-free, (800) 854-3402.*
General e-mail, info@hospicefoundation.org

Web, www.hospicefoundation.org

Acts as an advocate for the hospice style of health care through ongoing programs of public education and training, information dissemination, and research.

National Assn. for Home Care and Hospice, *228 7th St. S.E. 20003; (202) 547-7424. Fax, (202) 547-3540. Val J. Halamandaris, President.*
General e-mail, webmaster@nahc.org

Web, www.nahc.org

Promotes high-quality hospice, home care, and other community services for those with chronic health problems or life-threatening illness. Conducts research and provides information on related issues. Works to educate the public concerning health and social policy matters. Monitors legislation and regulations.

National Center for Assisted Living, *1201 L St. N.W. 20005; (202) 842-4444. Fax, (202) 842-3860. Karl Polzer, Senior Director for Assisted Living Policy.*
General e-mail, kpolzer@ncal.org

Web, www.ncal.org

Membership: assisted living professionals. Provides networking opportunities and professional development. Publishes a consumer's guide to assist in the selection of an assisted living facility. With affiliate American Health Care Association (AHCA), maintains the Mark A. Jerstad Information Resource Center and hosts educational seminars and an annual convention. Monitors legislation and regulations.

National Consumer Voice for Quality Long-term Care (NCCNHR), *1828 L St. N.W., #801 20036; (202) 332-2275. Fax, (202) 332-2949. Sarah F. Wells, Executive Director.*
General e-mail, nccnhr@nccnhr.org

Web, www.nccnhr.org

Seeks to improve the long-term care system and quality of life for residents in nursing homes and other facilities for the elderly; coordinates the Campaign for Quality Care. Promotes citizen participation in all aspects of nursing homes; acts as clearinghouse for nursing home advocacy.

National Hospice and Palliative Care Organization, *1731 King St., Alexandria, VA 22314; (703) 837-1500. Fax, (703) 837-1233. Don Schumacher, President. Press, (703) 837-3139. Toll-free consumer information and referral helpline, (800) 658-8898.*
General e-mail, nhpco_info@nhpco.org

Web, www.nhpco.org

Membership: institutions and individuals providing hospice and palliative care and other interested organizations and individuals. Promotes supportive care for the terminally ill and their families; sets hospice program standards; provides information on hospices. Monitors legislation and regulations. Consumer Web site can be found at www.caringinfo.org.

National Long-Term Care Ombudsman Resource Center, *1828 L St. N.W., #801 20036; (202) 332-2275. Fax, (202) 332-2949. Lori Smetanka, Director.*
General e-mail, ombudcenter@nccnhr.org

Web, www.ltcombudsman.org

Provides technical assistance, management guidance, policy analysis, and program development information on behalf of state and substate ombudsman programs. (Affiliate of the National Citizens' Coalition for Nursing Home Reform.)

Pharmaceuticals

►AGENCIES

Federal Trade Commission (FTC), *Advertising Practices, 601 New Jersey Ave. N.W., #3223 20001 (mailing address: 600 Pennsylvania Ave. N.W., Washington, DC 20580); (202) 326-3090. Fax, (202) 326-3259. Mary Engle, Associate Director.*
Web, www.ftc.gov

Protects consumers from deceptive and unsubstantiated advertising through law enforcement, public reports, and industry outreach. Evaluates the nutritional and health benefits of foods and the safety and effectiveness of dietary supplements, drugs, and medical devices, particularly as they relate to weight loss.

Food and Drug Administration (FDA), *(Health and Human Services Dept.), Center for Drug Evaluation and Research,* *10903 New Hampshire Ave., Silver Spring, MD 20993; (301) 796-5400. Fax, (301) 847-8752. Dr. Janet Woodcock, Director. Press, (301) 796-4540.*
Web, www.fda.gov/cder

Reviews and approves applications to investigate and market new drugs; monitors prescription drug advertising; works to harmonize drug approval internationally.

Food and Drug Administration (FDA), *(Health and Human Services Dept.), Center for Drug Evaluation and Research: Generic Drugs,* *7519 Standish Pl., Rockville, MD 20855; (240) 276-9310. Fax, (240) 276-9327. Gary Buehler, Director.*
Web, www.fda.gov/cder/ogd

Oversees generic drug review process to ensure the safety and effectiveness of approved drugs.

Food and Drug Administration (FDA), *(Health and Human Services Dept.), Center for Drug Evaluation and Research: Pharmaceutical Science and New Drug Quality Assessment,* *10903 New Hampshire Ave., Silver Spring, MD 20993; (301) 796-1900. Fax, (301) 796-9748. Moheb Nasr, Director.*
Web, www.fda.gov/cder/ondc

Reviews the critical quality attributes and manufacturing processes of new drugs, establishes quality standards to ensure safety and efficacy, and facilitates new drug development.

Food and Drug Administration (FDA), *(Health and Human Services Dept.), Drug Marketing, Advertising, and Communications,* 10903 New Hampshire Ave., Bldg. 51, #3271, Silver Spring, MD 20903-0002; (301) 796-1200. Fax, (301) 796-2877. Thomas Abrams, Director.
Web, www.fda.gov/cder

Monitors prescription drug advertising and labeling; investigates complaints; conducts market research on health care communications and drug issues.

National Institutes of Health (NIH), *(Health and Human Services Dept.), Dietary Supplements,* 6100 Executive Blvd., #3B01, MSC-7517, Bethesda, MD 20892-7517; (301) 435-2920. Fax, (301) 480-1845. Paul M. Coates, Director.
General e-mail, ods@nih.gov

Web, http://ods.od.nih.gov

Provides accurate, up-to-date information on dietary supplements. Reviews the current scientific evidence on the safety and efficacy of dietary supplements on the market to evaluate the need for further research. Conducts and coordinates scientific research within the NIH relating to dietary supplements. Plans, organizes, and supports conferences, workshops, and symposia on scientific topics related to dietary supplements.

Public Health Service *(Health and Human Services Dept.), Orphan Products Development,* 5600 Fishers Lane, #6A55, Rockville, MD 20857; (301) 827-3666. Fax, (301) 827-0017. Timothy Coté, Director.
Web, www.fda.gov/orphan

Promotes the development of drugs, devices, and alternative medical food therapies for rare diseases or conditions. Coordinates activities on the development of orphan drugs among federal agencies, manufacturers, and organizations representing patients.

▶**NONGOVERNMENTAL**

American Assn. of Colleges of Pharmacy, 1727 King St., Alexandria, VA 22314-2700; (703) 739-2330. Fax, (703) 836-8982. Lucinda L. Maine, Executive Vice President.
General e-mail, mail@aacp.org

Web, www.aacp.org

Represents and advocates for pharmacists in the academic community. Conducts programs and activities in cooperation with other national health and higher education associations.

American Assn. of Pharmaceutical Scientists, 2107 Wilson Blvd., #700, Arlington, VA 22201-3042; (703) 243-2800. Fax, (703) 243-9650. John Lisack Jr., Executive Director. Public Relations, (703) 248-4744.
General e-mail, aaps@aaps.org

Web, www.aapspharmaceutica.com

Membership: pharmaceutical scientists from biomedical, biotechnological, and health care fields. Promotes pharmaceutical sciences as an industry. Represents scientific interests within academia and public and private institutions. Monitors legislation and regulations.

American Pharmacists Assn., 2215 Constitution Ave., N.W., 20037-2985; (202) 628-4410. Fax, (202) 783-2351. Vacant, Chief Executive Officer. Information, (800) 237-2742. Library, (202) 429-7524.
Web, www.pharmacist.com

Membership: practicing pharmacists, pharmaceutical scientists, and pharmacy students. Promotes professional education and training; publishes scientific journals and handbooks on nonprescription drugs; monitors international research. Library open to the public by appointment.

American Society for Pharmacology and Experimental Therapeutics, 9650 Rockville Pike, Bethesda, MD 20814-3995; (301) 634-7060. Fax, (301) 634-7061. Dr. Christine K. Carrico, Executive Officer.
General e-mail, info@aspet.org

Web, www.aspet.org

Membership: researchers and teachers involved in basic and clinical pharmacology primarily in the United States and Canada.

American Society of Health-System Pharmacists, 7272 Wisconsin Ave., Bethesda, MD 20814; (301) 657-3000. Fax, (301) 664-8862. Henri Manasse, Chief Executive Officer.
Web, www.ashp.org

Membership: pharmacists who practice in organized health care settings such as hospitals, health maintenance organizations, and long-term care facilities. Provides publishing and educational programs designed to help members improve pharmaceutical services; accredits pharmacy residency and pharmacy technician training programs. Monitors legislation and regulations.

Consumer Healthcare Products Assn., 900 19th St. N.W., #700 20006; (202) 429-9260. Fax, (202) 223-6835. Linda Suydam, President.
Web, www.chpa-info.org

Membership: manufacturers and distributors of nonprescription medicines; associate members include suppliers, advertising agencies, research and testing laboratories, and others. Promotes the role of self medication in health care. Monitors legislation and regulations.

Drug Policy Alliance, Washington Office, 925 15th St. N.W., 2nd Floor 20005; (202) 683-2030. Fax, (202) 216-0803. Bill Piper, Director.
General e-mail, dc@drugpolicy.org

Web, www.drugpolicy.org

Seeks to broaden debate on drug policy to include considering alternatives to incarceration, expanding maintenance therapies, and restoring constitutional protections.

Studies drug policy in other countries. Monitors legislation and regulations. (Headquarters in New York.)

Generic Pharmaceutical Assn., *2300 Clarendon Blvd., #400, Arlington, VA 22201; (703) 647-2480. Fax, (703) 647-2481. Kathleen D. Jeager, Chief Executive Officer. General e-mail, info@gphaonline.org*

Web, www.gphaonline.org

Membership: manufacturers and distributors of generic pharmaceuticals and pharmaceutical chemicals and suppliers of goods and services to the generic pharmaceutical industry. Monitors legislation and regulations. Attempts to increase availability and public awareness of generic medicines.

Healthcare Distribution Management Assn., *901 N. Glebe Rd., #1000, Arlington, VA 22203; (703) 787-0000. Fax, (703) 812-5282. John Gray, President. Web, www.healthcaredistribution.org*

Membership: distributors of pharmaceutical and health-related products and information. Serves as a forum on major industry issues. Researches and disseminates information on distribution issues and management practices. Monitors legislation and regulations. (Formerly the National Wholesale Druggists' Assn.)

Long Term Care Pharmacy Alliance, *1776 Massachusetts Ave. N.W., #410 20036; (202) 386-7559. Fax, (202) 386-7560. Darrell McKigney, Executive Director. General e-mail, info@ltcpa.org*

Web, www.ltcpa.org

Membership: Long-term pharmacies and group purchasing organizations that serve most of the long-term care pharmacy industry nationwide. Monitors legislation and regulations.

National Assn. of Chain Drug Stores, *413 N. Lee St., Alexandria, VA 22314 (mailing address: P.O. Box 1417-D49, Alexandria, VA 22314); (703) 549-3001. Fax, (703) 836-4869. Steven Anderson, President. Web, www.nacds.org*

Membership: chain drug retailers; associate members include manufacturers, suppliers, publishers, and advertising agencies. Provides information on the pharmacy profession, community pharmacy practice, and retail prescription drug economics.

National Community Pharmacists Assn., *100 Daingerfield Rd., Alexandria, VA 22314; (703) 683-8200. Fax, (703) 683-3619. Bruce Roberts, Executive Vice President. General e-mail, info@ncpanet.org*

Web, www.ncpanet.org

Membership: independent pharmacy owners, including independent pharmacies, independent pharmacy franchises, and independent chains. Promotes the interests of independent community pharmacists to compete in the health care market. Monitors legislation and regulations.

National Council on Patient Information and Education, *4915 St. Elmo Ave., #505, Bethesda, MD 20814-6082; (301) 656-8565. Fax, (301) 656-4464. W. Ray Bullman, Executive Vice President. General e-mail, ncpie@ncpie.info*

Web, www.talkaboutrx.org

Membership: organizations of health care professionals, pharmaceutical manufacturers, federal agencies, voluntary health organizations, and consumer groups. Works to improve communication between health care professionals and patients about the appropriate use of medicines; produces educational resources; conducts public affairs programs; sponsors awards program. Additional information can be found at www.bemedwise.org and www.mustforseniors.org (medication use safety training for seniors).

National Pharmaceutical Council, *1894 Preston White Dr., Reston, VA 20191-5433; (703) 620-6390. Fax, (703) 476-0904. Dan Leonard, President. General e-mail, info@npcnow.org*

Web, www.npcnow.org

Membership: pharmaceutical manufacturers that research and produce trade-name prescription medication and other pharmaceutical products. Sponsors and conducts scientific analyses of the use of pharmaceuticals and the clinical and economic value of innovation.

Parenteral Drug Assn. (PDA), *4350 East-West Hwy., #150, Bethesda, MD 20814; (301) 656-5900. Fax, (301) 986-0296. Robert Myers, President. General e-mail, info@pda.org*

Web, www.pda.org

Membership: scientists involved in the development, manufacture, quality control, and regulation of pharmaceuticals/biopharmaceuticals and related products. Provides science, technology, and regulatory information and education to the pharmaceutical and biopharmaceutical community. Influences FDA regulatory process.

Pharmaceutical Care Management Assn., *601 Pennsylvania Ave. N.W., 7th Floor 20004; (202) 207-3610. Fax, (202) 207-3623. Mark Merritt, President. General e-mail, info@pcmanet.org*

Web, www.pcmanet.org

Membership: companies providing managed care pharmacy and pharmacy benefits management. Promotes legislation, research, education, and practice standards that foster high-quality, affordable pharmaceutical care.

Pharmaceutical Research and Manufacturers of America, *950 F St. N.W., #300 20004; (202) 835-3400. Fax, (202) 835-3414. Billy Tauzin, President. Web, www.phrma.org*

Membership: research-based pharmaceutical and biotechnology companies that orginate, develop, and manufacture prescription drugs. Advocates public policies that encourage discovery of new medicines. Provides

Food and Drug Administration

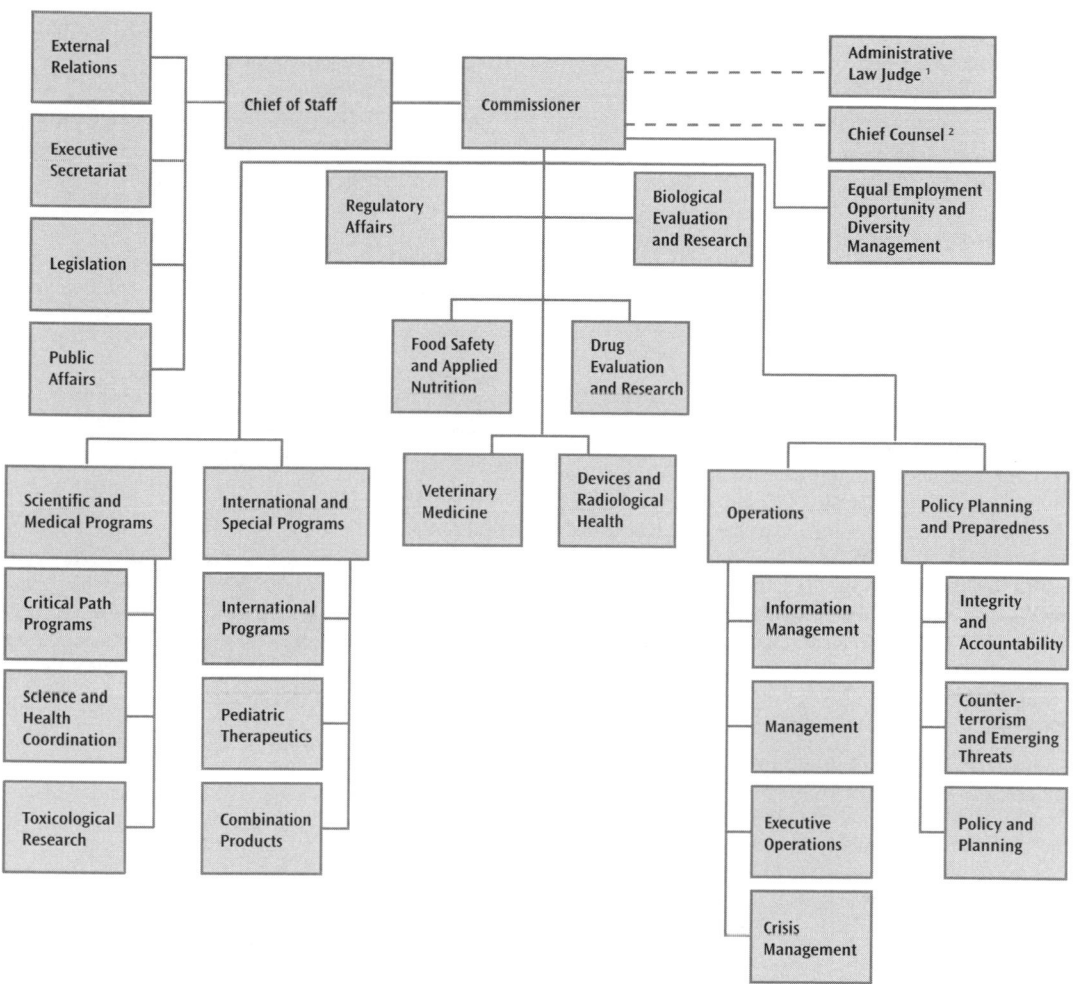

- - - [1]Reports directly to the Secretary of Health and Human Services (HHS)
- - - [2]The Office of the Chief Counsel is part of the Office of the General Counsel
of the Department of Health and Human Services

consumer information on drug abuse, the safe and effective use of prescription medicines, and developments in important areas, including the treatment of HIV/AIDS.

U.S. Pharmacopeia Convention, *12601 Twinbrook Pkwy., Rockville, MD 20852; (301) 881-0666. Fax, (301) 816-8299. Roger L. Williams, Chief Executive Officer. General e-mail, usp@usp.org*

Web, www.usp.org

Establishes and revises standards for drug strength, quality, purity, packaging, labeling, and storage. Publishes drug use information, official drug quality standards, patient education materials, and consumer drug references. Interests include international standards.

HEALTH PROFESSIONS

►AGENCIES

Centers for Medicare and Medicaid Services *(Health and Human Services Dept.), Clinical Standards and Quality, 7500 Security Blvd., S3-02-01, Baltimore, MD 21244; (410) 786-6841. Fax, (410) 786-6857. Barry Straube, Director.*
Web, www.cms.hhs.gov

Oversees professional review and other medical review programs; establishes guidelines; prepares issue papers relating to legal aspects of professional review and quality assurance. (Formerly the Health Care Financing Administration.)

Clinician Recruitment and Services *(Health and Human Services Dept.), National Health Service Corps,* 5600 Fishers Lane, #8-37, Rockville, MD 20857; (301) 594-4400. Fax, (301) 594-4981. Tamara Overby, Director. Toll-free, (800) 221-9393.
Web, www.nhsc.bhpr.hrsa.gov

Supplies communities experiencing a shortage of health care personnel with doctors and other medical professionals.

Health Resources and Services Administration *(Health and Human Services Dept.), Health Education Assistance Loan Branch,* 5600 Fishers Lane, #9-105, Parklawn Bldg., Rockville, MD 20857; (301) 443-1540. Fax, (301) 443-0795. Judy Rodgers, Branch Chief. To speak with a HEAL representative, (877) 411-4325.
Web, www.bhpr.hrsa.gov/dsa/healsite

Insures loans provided by private lenders to students attending eligible health professions schools under the Public Health Service Act. New loans to student borrowers have been discontinued. Refinancing has been terminated.

Health Resources and Services Administration *(Health and Human Services Dept.), Health Professions,* 5600 Fishers Lane, #905, Rockville, MD 20857; (301) 443-5794. Fax, (301) 443-2111. Diane Espinosa, Associate Administrator (Acting).
Web, www.healthworkforceinfo.org

Supports primary care and public health education and practice. Supports recruitment of health care professionals, including nursing and allied health professionals, for underserved populations. Administers categorical training programs, scholarship and loan programs, and minority and disadvantaged assistance programs. Oversees National Practitioner Data Bank.

Health Resources and Services Administration *(Health and Human Services Dept.), National Health Services Corps,* 5600 Fishers Lane, #8A55, Rockville, MD 20857; (301) 594-4130. Fax, (301) 594-4076. Richard J. Smith III, Director. Hotline, (800) 221-9393.
Web, www.bhpr.hrsa.gov/nhsc

Supplies communities experiencing a shortage of health care personnel with doctors and other medical professionals.

Health Resources and Services Administration *(Health and Human Services Dept.), National Practitioner Data Bank,* 5600 Fishers Lane, #8-103, Rockville, MD 20857; (301) 443-2300. Fax, (301) 443-6725. Darryl Gray, Division Director. Information, (800) 767-6732.
Web, www.npdb-hipdb.hrsa.gov

Provides information on reports of malpractice payments, adverse state licensure, clinical privileges, and society membership actions (only to eligible state licensing boards, hospitals, and other health care entities) about physicians, dentists, and other licensed health care practitioners.

National Institutes of Health (NIH), *(Health and Human Services Dept.), Minority Opportunities in Research,* 45 Center Dr., Bldg. 45, #2AS37, MSC 6200, Bethesda, MD 20892-6200; (301) 594-3900. Fax, (301) 480-2753. Dr. Clifton A. Poodry, Director.
Web, www.nigms.nih.gov

Administers research and research training programs aimed at increasing the number of minority biomedical scientists. Funds grants, fellowships, faculty development awards, and development of research facilities.

Public Health and Science *(Health and Human Services Dept.), Public Health Service Commissioned Corps: Force Management (OCCFM),* 1101 Wootton Pkwy., Plaza Level, Rockville, MD 20852; (240) 453-6161. Fax, (240) 453-6109. Rear Adm. Denise S. Canton, Director. General information, (877) 463-6327. Application information, (800) 279-1605.
General e-mail, OCCFMHelpdesk@hhs.gov
Web, www.usphs.gov

Responsible for the overall force management of the U.S. Public Health Service Commissioned Corps, health professionals with a wide range of specialties who respond to emergencies, conduct research, and care for patients in underserved communities through federal agencies such as the National Institutes of Health and the Centers for Disease Control and Prevention.

▶CONGRESS

For a listing of relevant congressional committees and subcommittees, please see page 320 or the Appendix.

▶NONGOVERNMENTAL

AFT Healthcare, 555 New Jersey Ave. N.W. 20001; (202) 879-4491. Fax, (202) 879-4597. Mary Lehman MacDonald, Director.
General e-mail, afthealthcare@aft.org
Web, www.aft.org/healthcare

Membership: nurses and other health care workers. Assists members with contract negotiation and grievances; conducts training programs and workshops. Monitors legislation and regulations. (Division of the American Federation of Teachers.)

American Assn. for Health Education, 1900 Association Dr., Reston, VA 20191-1599; (703) 476-3437. Fax, (703) 476-6638. Becky J. Smith, Executive Director.
General e-mail, aahe@aahperd.org
Web, www.aahperd.org/aahe

Membership: health educators and allied health professionals in community and volunteer health agencies, educational institutions, and businesses. Develops health education programs; monitors legislation.

American Assn. of Colleges of Pharmacy, 1727 King St., Alexandria, VA 22314-2700; (703) 739-2330. Fax, (703) 836-8982. Lucinda L. Maine, Executive Vice President.

General e-mail, mail@aacp.org

Web, www.aacp.org

Membership: teachers and administrators representing colleges of pharmacy accredited by the American Council on Pharmaceutical Education. Sponsors educational programs; conducts research; provides career information; helps administer the Pharmacy College Admissions Test.

American College of Health Care Administrators, *12100 Sunset Hills Rd., #130, Reston, VA 20190; (703) 739-7900. Fax, (703) 435-4390. Marianna Grachek, President.*

General e-mail, abell@achca.org

Web, www.achca.org

Membership: administrators of long-term health care organizations and facilities, including home health care programs, hospices, day care centers for the elderly, nursing and hospital facilities, retirement communities, and mental health care centers. Conducts research on statistical characteristics of nursing home and other medical administrators; conducts seminars and workshops; offers education courses; provides certification for administrators.

American Health Lawyers Assn., *1025 Connecticut Ave. N.W., #600 20036; (202) 833-1100. Fax, (202) 833-1105. Peter Leibold, Executive Vice President.*

General e-mail, info@healthlawyers.org

Web, www.healthlawyers.org

Membership: corporate, institutional, and government lawyers interested in the health field; law students; and health professionals. Serves as an information clearinghouse on health law; sponsors health law educational programs and seminars.

American Medical Group Assn., *1422 Duke St., Alexandria, VA 22314-3403; (703) 838-0033. Fax, (703) 548-1890. Donald W. Fisher, President.*

Web, www.amga.org

Membership: medical group practices. Compiles statistics on group practice. Sponsors a foundation for research and education programs. Advocates the multispecialty group practice model of health care delivery. Provides educational and networking programs and publications, benchmarking data services, and financial and operations assistance. Monitors legislation and regulations.

American Society of Consultant Pharmacists, *1321 Duke St., 4th Floor, Alexandria, VA 22314-3563; (703) 739-1300. Fax, (703) 739-1321. John Feather, Executive Director. Toll-free phone, (800) 355-2727. Toll-free fax, (800) 220-1321.*

General e-mail, info@ascp.com

Web, www.ascp.com

Membership: dispensing and clinical pharmacists who provide services to long-term care facilities. Monitors legislation and regulations.

American Speech-Language-Hearing Assn. (ASHA), *2200 Research Blvd., Rockville, MD 20850-3289; (301) 296-5700. Fax, (301) 296-8580. Arlene Pietranton, Executive Director. Press, (301) 296-8732. Toll-free hotline (except Alaska, Hawaii, and Maryland), (800) 638-8255 (voice and TTY accessible).*

General e-mail, actioncenter@asha.org

Web, www.asha.org

Membership: specialists in speech-language pathology and audiology. Sponsors professional education programs; acts as accrediting agent for graduate programs; certifies audiologists and speech language pathologists. Advocates the rights of the communicatively disabled; provides information on speech, hearing, and language problems. Provides referrals to speech-language pathologists and audiologists. Interests include national and international standards for bioacoustics and noise.

Assn. for Healthcare Philanthropy, *313 Park Ave., #400, Falls Church, VA 22046; (703) 532-6243. Fax, (703) 532-7170. William C. McGinly, President.*

General e-mail, ahp@ahp.org

Web, www.ahp.org

Membership: hospital and health care executives who manage fundraising activities and organizations and individuals who provide consulting services for such activities. Acts as a clearinghouse on philanthropy and offers programs, services, and publications to members.

Assn. for Prevention Teaching and Research, *1001 Connecticut Ave. N.W., #610 20036; (202) 463-0550. Fax, (202) 463-0555. Allison L. Lewis, Executive Director. Toll-free, (866) 520-2787.*

General e-mail, info@aptrweb.org

Web, www.aptrweb.org

Membership: faculty, researchers, residents, and students within schools of medicine, schools of public health, schools of nursing, schools of pharmacy, physician assistant programs, graduate programs for public health, and health agencies. Works to advance population-based and public health education, research, and service. (Formerly the Assn. of Teachers of Preventive Medicine.)

Assn. of Reproductive Health Professionals, *1901 L St. N.W., #300 20036; (202) 466-3825. Fax, (202) 466-3826. Wayne C. Shields, President.*

General e-mail, arhp@arhp.org

Web, www.arhp.org

Membership: obstetricians, gynecologists, other physicians, researchers, clinicians, and educators. Educates health professionals and the public on reproductive health issues, including family planning, contraception, HIV/AIDS and other sexually transmitted diseases, abortion, menopause, infertility, and cancer prevention and detection.

Assn. of Schools of Allied Health Professions, *4400 Jenifer St. N.W., #333 20015; (202) 237-6481. Fax, (202) 237-6485. Thomas W. Elwood, Executive Director.*

General e-mail, thomas@asahp.org

Web, www.asahp.org

Membership: two- and four-year colleges and academic health science centers with allied health professional training programs; administrators, educators, and practitioners; and professional societies. Serves as information resource; works with the Health and Human Services Dept. to conduct surveys of allied health education programs. Interests include health promotion and disease prevention, ethics in health care, and the participation of women and persons with disabilities in allied health. Monitors legislation and regulations.

Assn. of Schools of Public Health, *1101 15th St. N.W., #910 20005; (202) 296-1099. Fax, (202) 296-1252. Harrison C. Spencer, President.*
General e-mail, info@asph.org

Web, www.asph.org

Membership: deans, faculty, and students of accredited graduate schools of public health. Promotes improved education and training of professional public health personnel; interests include disease prevention, health promotion, and international health.

Assn. of State and Territorial Health Officials, *2231 Crystal Dr., #450, Arlington, VA 22202; (202) 371-9090. Fax, (571) 527-3189. Dr. Paul Jarris, Executive Director. Web, www.astho.org*

Membership: executive officers of state and territorial health departments. Serves as legislative review agency and information source for members. Alternate Web site: www.statepublichealth.org.

Assn. of University Programs in Health Administration, *2000 14th St. North, #780, Arlington, VA 22201; (703) 894-0940. Fax, (703) 894-0941. Kristi Donovan, CAE, Senior Director of Professional Affairs. General e-mail, aupha@aupha.org*

Web, www.aupha.org

Membership: university-based educational programs, faculty, practitioners, and provider organizations. Works to improve the field of health care management and practice by educating entry-level professional managers.

Council on Education for Public Health, *800 Eye St. N.W., #202 20001-3710; (202) 789-1050. Fax, (202) 789-1895. Laura Rasar King, Executive Director. Web, www.ceph.org*

Accredits schools of public health and graduate programs in public health. Works to strengthen public health programs through research and other means.

Healthcare Financial Management Assn., *Washington Office, 1133 Connecticut Ave. N.W., 11th Floor 20036; (202) 296-2920. Fax, (202) 223-9771. Richard Gundling, Vice President. Information, (800) 252-4362. Web, www.hfma.org*

Membership: health care financial management specialists. Offers educational programs; provides information on financial management of health care. (Headquarters in Westchester, Ill.)

Hispanic-Serving Health Professions Schools Inc., *1120 Connecticut Ave. N.W., #261 20036; (202) 293-2701. Fax, (202) 293-2704. Maria Soto-Greene, President. General e-mail, hshps@hshps.org*

Web, www.hshps.org

Seeks to increase representation of Hispanics in all health care professions. Monitors legislation and regulations.

National Assn. of County and City Health Officials, *1100 17th St. N.W., 2nd Floor 20036; (202) 783-5550. Fax, (202) 783-1583. Robert M. Pestronk, Executive Director. General e-mail, info@naccho.org*

Web, www.naccho.org

Membership: city, county, and district health officers. Provides members with information on national, state, and local health developments. Works to develop the technical competence, managerial capacity, and leadership potential of local public health officials.

National Assn. of Healthcare Access Management, *2025 M St. N.W., #800 20036-3309; (202) 367-1125. Fax, (202) 367-2125. Steven Kemp, Executive Director. General e-mail, info@naham.org*

Web, www.naham.org

Promotes professional growth and recognition of health care patient access managers; provides instructional videotapes; sponsors educational programs.

National Center for Homeopathy, *801 N. Fairfax St., #306, Alexandria, VA 22314; (703) 548-7790. Fax, (703) 548-7792. Sharon Stevenson, Executive Director. General e-mail, info@nationalcenterforhomeopathy.org*

Web, www.nationalcenterforhomeopathy.org

Educational organization for professionals, groups, associations, and individuals interested in homeopathy and homeotherapeutics. Promotes health through homeopathy; conducts education programs; holds annual conference; publishes magazine.

National Organization for Competency Assurance, *2025 M St. N.W., #800 20036-3309; (202) 367-1165. Fax, (202) 367-2165. Jim Kendzel, Executive Director. General e-mail, info@noca.org*

Web, www.noca.org

Membership: certifying agencies and other groups that issue credentials to health professionals. Promotes public understanding of competency assurance certification programs for health professions and occupations. Oversees commission that establishes certification program standards. Monitors regulations.

Chiropractors

▶**NONGOVERNMENTAL**

American Chiropractic Assn., *1701 Clarendon Blvd., 2nd Floor, Arlington, VA 22209; (703) 276-8800. Fax, (703)*

243-2593. *Kevin P. Corcoran, Executive Vice President.*
Toll-free, (800) 986-4636.
General e-mail, memberinfo@amerchiro.org

Web, www.acatoday.org

Promotes professional growth and recognition for chiropractors. Interests include health care coverage, sports injuries, physical fitness, internal disorders, and orthopedics. Supports foundation for chiropractic education and research. Monitors legislation and regulations.

Foundation for the Advancement of Chiropractic Tenets and Science, *1110 N. Glebe Rd., #650, Arlington, VA 22201-5722; (703) 528-5000. Fax, (703) 528-5023. Robert N. Pohtos, Executive Director.*
General e-mail, chiro@chiropractic.org

Web, www.chiropractic.org

Offers financial aid for education and research programs in colleges and independent institutions; studies chiropractic services in the United States; provides international relief and development programs. (Affiliate of the International Chiropractors Assn.)

International Chiropractors Assn., *1110 N. Glebe Rd., #650, Arlington, VA 22201-5722; (703) 528-5000. Fax, (703) 528-5023. Robert N. Pohtos, Executive Director.*
General e-mail, chiro@chiropractic.org

Web, www.chiropractic.org

Membership: chiropractors, students, educators, and laypersons. Seeks to increase public awareness of chiropractic care. Supports research on health issues; administers scholarship program; monitors legislation and regulations.

Dental Care

▶AGENCIES

National Institute of Dental and Craniofacial Research *(National Institutes of Health), 31 Center Dr., MSC-2290, Bldg. 31, #2C39, Bethesda, MD 20892-2290; (301) 496-3571. Fax, (301) 402-2185. Lawrence A. Tabak, Director. Information, (301) 496-4261.*
Web, www.nidcr.nih.gov

Conducts and funds research on the causes, prevention, and treatment of oral diseases and conditions. Monitors international research.

▶NONGOVERNMENTAL

American College of Dentists, *839 Quince Orchard Blvd., Suite J, Gaithersburg, MD 20878; (301) 977-3223. Fax, (301) 977-3330. Stephen Ralls, Executive Director.*
General e-mail, office@acd.org

Web, www.acd.org

Honorary society of dentists. Fellows are elected based on their contributions to education, research, dentistry, and community and civic organizations. Interests include ethics, professionalism, and dentistry in health care.

American Dental Assn. (ADA), *Government Relations, Washington Office, 1111 14th St. N.W., #1100 20005; (202) 898-2400. Fax, (202) 898-2437. Bill Prentice, Director.*
Web, www.ada.org

Conducts research, provides dental education materials, compiles statistics on dentistry and dental care. Monitors legislation and regulations. (Headquarters in Chicago, Ill.)

American Dental Education Assn., *1400 K St., #1100 20005; (202) 289-7201. Fax, (202) 289-7204. Dr. Richard W. Valachovic, Executive Director.*
General e-mail, adea@adea.org

Web, www.adea.org

Membership: U.S. and Canadian dental schools; advanced, hospital, and allied dental education programs; corporations; and faculty and students. Works to influence education, research, and the delivery of oral health care for the improvement of public health. Provides information on dental teaching and research and on admission requirements of U.S. dental schools; publishes a monthly journal and newsletter.

Dental Trade Alliance, *2300 Clarendon Blvd., #1003, Arlington, VA 22201; (703) 379-7755. Fax, (703) 931-9429. Gary W. Price, Chief Executive Officer.*
General e-mail, info@dentaltradealliance.org

Web, www.dentaltradealliance.org

Membership: dental laboratories and distributors and manufacturers of dental equipment and supplies. Collects and disseminates statistical and management information; conducts studies, programs, and projects of interest to the industry; acts as liaison with government agencies. (Formerly the American Dental Trade Assn.)

International and American Assns. for Dental Research, *1619 Duke St., Alexandria, VA 22314-3406; (703) 548-0066. Fax, (703) 548-1883. Dr. Christopher H. Fox, Executive Director.*
General e-mail, research@iadr.org

Web, www.dentalresearch.org

Membership: professionals engaged in dental research worldwide. Conducts annual convention, conferences, and symposia.

National Dental Assn., *3517 16th St. N.W. 20010; (202) 588-1697. Fax, (202) 588-1244. Robert S. Johns, Executive Director.*
Web, www.ndaonline.org

Promotes the interests of ethnic minority dentists through recruitment, educational and financial services, and federal legislation and programs.

Medical Researchers

▶AGENCIES

National Institutes of Health (NIH), *(Health and Human Services Dept.), Office of Intramural Training*

and Education, *2 Center Dr., Bldg. 2, #2E04, MSC 0240, Bethesda, MD 20892-0240; (301) 496-2427. Fax, (301) 594-9606. Sharon Milgram, Director.*

General e-mail, trainingwww@mail.nih.gov

Web, www.training.nih.gov

Administers programs and initiatives to recruit and develop individuals who participate in research training activities on the NIH's main campus as well as other facilities across the country. Maintains an interactive Web site for the various research training programs and handbooks for postdoctoral fellows, graduate students, post-baccalaureate trainees, and summer interns. Supports the training mission of the intramural program through placement, retention, support, and tracking of trainees at all levels, as well as program delivery and evaluation. Administers the NIH Academy and the Summer Internship Program.

▶NONGOVERNMENTAL

American Assn. for Clinical Chemistry, *1850 K St. N.W., #625 20006; (202) 857-0717. Fax, (202) 833-4576. Richard G. Flaherty, Executive Vice President.*

General e-mail, info@aacc.org

Web, www.aacc.org

International society of chemists, physicians, and other scientists specializing in clinical chemistry. Provides educational and professional development services; presents awards for outstanding achievement. Monitors legislation and regulations.

American Assn. of Immunologists, *9650 Rockville Pike, Bethesda, MD 20814-3994; (301) 634-7178. Fax, (301) 634-7887. M. Michele Hogan, Executive Director.*

General e-mail, infoaai@aai.org

Web, www.aai.org

Membership: scientists working in virology, bacteriology, biochemistry, genetics, immunology, and related disciplines. Conducts training courses and workshops; compiles statistics; participates in international conferences. Monitors legislation and regulations.

American Medical Writers Assn., *30 W. Gude Dr., #525, Rockville, MD 20850-1161; (301) 294-5303. Fax, (301) 294-9006. Donna Munari, Executive Director.*

General e-mail, amwa@amwa.org

Web, www.amwa.org

Provides professional education and additional services to writers, editors, and others in the field of biomedical communication.

American Society for Clinical Laboratory Science, *6701 Democracy Blvd., #300, Bethesda, MD 20817; (301) 657-2768. Fax, (301) 657-2909. Elissa Passiment, Executive Vice President.*

General e-mail, ascls@ascls.org

Web, www.ascls.org

Membership: clinical laboratory scientists. Conducts continuing education programs for clinical laboratory scientists and laboratory practitioners. Monitors legislation and regulations.

American Society for Clinical Pathology, *Washington Office, 1225 New York Ave. N.W., #250 20005-6156; (202) 347-4450. Fax, (202) 347-4453. Jeff Jacobs, Vice President, Public Policy. Information, (800) 267-2727.*

General e-mail, info@ascp.org

Web, www.ascp.org

Membership: pathologists, residents, and other physicians; clinical scientists; registered certified medical technologists; and technicians. Promotes continuing education, educational standards, and research in pathology. Monitors legislation, regulations, and international research. (Headquarters in Chicago, Ill.)

Assn. of Public Health Laboratories, *8515 Georgia Ave., #700, Silver Spring, MD 20910; (240) 485-2745. Fax, (240) 485-2700. Scott Becker, Executive Director.*

Web, www.aphl.org

Membership: state and local public health, environmental, and agricultural laboratories. Acts as a liaison to the Centers for Disease Control and Prevention. Administers the National Laboratory Training Network, which assesses, develops, and delivers continuing education for laboratory practitioners. Implements international training and assistance programs for developing nations. Acts as a liaison between public health laboratories and other laboratory systems during crises.

Coalition for the Advancement of Medical Research (CAMR), *2021 K St. N.W., #305 20006; (202) 725-0339. Amy Comstock Rick, President.*

General e-mail, CAMResearch@yahoo.com

Web, www.CAMRAdvocacy.org

Membership: nationally recognized patient organizations, universities, scientific societies, foundations, and individuals with life-threatening illnesses and disorders. Advocates for research and technologies in regenerative medicine, including stem cell research and somatic cell nuclear transfer.

Society of Toxicology, *1821 Michael Faraday Dr., #300, Reston, VA 20190; (703) 438-3115. Fax, (703) 438-3113. Shawn Lamb, Executive Director.*

General e-mail, sothq@toxicology.org

Web, www.toxicology.org

Membership: scientists from academic institutions, government, and industry worldwide who work in toxicology. Promotes professional development, exchange of information, and research to improve the health of humans, animals, and the environment.

Nurses and Physician Assistants

▶AGENCIES

National Institute of Nursing Research *(National Institutes of Health), 31 Center Dr., Bldg. 31, #5B05, MSC-2178, Bethesda, MD 20892-2178; (301) 496-8230. Fax, (301) 594-3405. Dr. Patricia A. Grady, Director, (301) 496-8237.*

Web, http://ninr.nih.gov

Provides grants and awards for nursing research and research training. Research focus includes health promotion and disease prevention, quality of life, health disparities, and end-of-life issues.

▶NONGOVERNMENTAL

AFT Healthcare, *555 New Jersey Ave. N.W. 20001; (202) 879-4491. Fax, (202) 879-4597. Mary Lehman MacDonald, Director.*
General e-mail, afthealthcare@aft.org
Web, www.aft.org/healthcare

Membership: nurses and other health care workers. Assists members with contract negotiation and grievances; conducts training programs and workshops. Monitors legislation and regulations. (Division of the American Federation of Teachers.)

American Academy of Physician Assistants (AAPA), *950 N. Washington St., Alexandria, VA 22314-1552; (703) 836-2272. Fax, (703) 684-1924. Bill Leinweber, Chief Executive Officer.*
General e-mail, aapa@aapa.org
Web, www.aapa.org

Membership: physician assistants and physician assistant students. Sponsors continuing medical education programs for recertification of physician assistants; offers malpractice insurance. Interests include health care reform, quality of care, research, and laws and regulations affecting physician assistant practice and patients. Monitors legislation and regulations.

American Assn. of Colleges of Nursing, *1 Dupont Circle N.W., #530 20036-1120; (202) 463-6930. Fax, (202) 785-8320. Geraldine P. Bednash, Executive Director.*
Web, www.aacn.nche.edu

Promotes high-quality baccalaureate and graduate nursing education; works to secure federal support of nursing education, nursing research, and student financial assistance; operates databank providing information on enrollments, graduations, salaries, and other conditions in nursing higher education. Interests include international practices.

American College of Nurse-Midwives, *8403 Colesville Rd., #1550, Silver Spring, MD 20910; (240) 485-1800. Fax, (240) 485-1818. Lorrie Kline Kaplan, Executive Director. Press, (240) 485-1822.*
General e-mail, info@acnm.org
Web, www.midwife.org

Membership: certified midwives and nurse-midwives who preside at deliveries. Accredits midwifery education programs; establishes clinical practice studies. Interests include preventive health care for women.

American Nurses Assn., *8515 Georgia Ave., #400, Silver Spring, MD 20910; (301) 628-5000. Fax, (301) 628-5001. Linda Stierle, Chief Executive Officer. Toll-free, (800) 274-4262.*

General e-mail, info@ana.org
Web, www.nursingworld.org

Membership: registered nurses. Promotes high standards of nursing practice, economic and general welfare of nurses in the workplace, and a positive and realistic view of nursing. Affiliated organizations include the American Nurses Foundation, the American Academy of Nursing, the American Nurses Credentialing Center, and the Center for American Nurses. Monitors legislation and regulations.

National Assn. of Nurse Practitioners in Women's Health, *505 C St. N.E. 20002; (202) 543-9693. Fax, (202) 543-9858. Susan Wysocki, President.*
General e-mail, info@npwh.org
Web, www.npwh.org

Develops standards for nurse practitioner training and practices. Sponsors continuing education. Provides accreditation of women's health nurse practitioner programs. Provides the public and government with information on nurse practitioner education, practice, and women's health issues.

National Black Nurses Assn., *8630 Fenton St., #330, Silver Spring, MD 20910-3803; (301) 589-3200. Fax, (301) 589-3223. Millicent Gorham, Executive Director.*
General e-mail, nbna@erols.com
Web, www.nbna.org

Membership: African American nurses from the United States, the eastern Caribbean, and Africa. Fosters improvement in the level of care available to minorities, conducts continuing education programs, and builds relationships with public and private agencies and organizations to exert influence on laws and programs. Conducts and publishes research.

Physical and Occupational Therapy

▶NONGOVERNMENTAL

American Occupational Therapy Assn., *4720 Montgomery Lane, Bethesda, MD 20824 (mailing address: P.O. Box 31220, Bethesda, MD 20824-1220); (301) 652-2682. Fax, (301) 652-7711. Fred Somers, Executive Director. TTY, (800) 377-8555.*
General e-mail, info@aota.org
Web, www.aota.org

Membership: registered occupational therapists, certified occupational therapy assistants, and students. Associate members include businesses and organizations supportive of occupational therapy. Accredits educational programs and credentials occupational therapists. Supports research and sponsors scholarships, grants, and fellowships. Library is open to the public by appointment.

American Physical Therapy Assn., *1111 N. Fairfax St., Alexandria, VA 22314-1488; (703) 684-2782. Fax, (703) 684-7343. John Barnes, Chief Executive Officer.*

Information, (800) 999-2782. TTY, (703) 683-6748.

General e-mail, svcctr@apta.org

Web, www.apta.org

Membership: physical therapists, assistants, and students. Establishes professional standards and accredits physical therapy programs; seeks to improve physical therapy education, practice, and research.

Physicians

▶**NONGOVERNMENTAL**

American Academy of Dermatology, *1350 Eye St. N.W., #870 20005-4355; (202) 842-3555. Fax, (202) 842-4355. David M. Pariser, President.*

Web, www.aad.org

Membership: practicing dermatologists. Promotes the science and art of medicine and surgery related to the skin, hair, and nails. Advocates for high-quality dermatologic care and for higher standards of care. Monitors legislation and regulations.

American Academy of Family Physicians, *Washington Office, 2021 Massachusetts Ave. N.W. 20036; (202) 232-9033. Fax, (202) 232-9044. Rosemarie Sweeney, Vice President.*

General e-mail, fp@aafp.org

Web, www.aafp.org

Membership: family physicians, family practice residents, and medical students. Sponsors continuing medical education programs; promotes family practice residency programs. Monitors legislation and regulations. (Headquarters in Leawood, Kan.)

American Academy of Otolaryngology—Head and Neck Surgery, *1650 Diagonal Rd., Alexandria, VA 22314; (703) 836-4444. Fax, (703) 683-5100. Dr. David R. Nielsen, Chief Executive Officer. Press, (703) 535-3754. General e-mail, newsroom@entnet.org*

Web, www.entnet.org

Membership: otolaryngologists—head and neck surgeons. Supports the advancement of scientific medical research. Provides continuing medical education for members. Monitors legislation, regulations, and international research.

American Assn. of Colleges of Osteopathic Medicine, *5550 Friendship Blvd., #310, Chevy Chase, MD 20815-7231; (301) 968-4100. Fax, (301) 968-4101. Dr. Stephen C. Shannon, President.*

General e-mail, webmaster@aacom.org

Web, www.aacom.org

Administers a centralized application service for osteopathic medical colleges; supports an increase in the number of minority and economically disadvantaged students in osteopathic colleges; maintains an information database; sponsors recruitment programs. Monitors legislation and regulations.

American Assn. of Naturopathic Physicians, *4435 Wisconsin Ave. N.W., #403 20016; (202) 237-8150. Fax, (202) 237-8152. Karen Howard, Executive Director. Toll-free, (866) 538-2267.*

General e-mail, member.services@naturopathic.org

Web, www.naturopathic.org

Promotes naturopathic physician education and acceptance of naturopathic medicine in the nation's health care system.

American College of Cardiology, *2400 N St. N.W. 20037; (202) 375-6000. Fax, (202) 375-7000. Dr. Jack Lewin, Chief Executive Officer. Press, (202) 375-6476.*

General e-mail, resource@acc.org

Web, www.acc.org

Membership: physicians, surgeons, and scientists specializing in cardiovascular health care. Sponsors programs in continuing medical education; collaborates with national and international cardiovascular organizations.

American College of Emergency Physicians, Government Affairs, Washington Office, *2121 K St. N.W., #325 20037-1801; (202) 728-0610. Fax, (202) 728-0617. Dean Wilkerson, Executive Director.*

General e-mail, pr@acep.org

Web, www.acep.org

Membership: physicians, residents, and interns. Interests include Medicare and Medicaid legislation and regulations, medical liability, overcrowding in emergency departments, access to emergency care, bioterrorism and terrorism preparedness, managed care, and adult and pediatric emergencies. Disseminates public education materials. (Headquarters in Dallas, Texas.)

American College of Obstetricians and Gynecologists, *409 12th St. S.W. 20024-2188 (mailing address: P.O. Box 96920, Washington, DC 20090-6920); (202) 638-5577. Fax, (202) 479-6826. Dr. Ralph Hale, Executive Vice President. Press, (202) 484-3321.*

Web, www.acog.org

Membership: medical specialists in obstetrics and gynecology. Monitors legislation, regulations, and international research on maternal and child health care.

American College of Osteopathic Surgeons, *123 N. Henry St., Alexandria, VA 22314-2903; (703) 684-0416. Fax, (703) 684-3280. Guy D. Beaumont Jr., Executive Director.*

General e-mail, info@facos.org

Web, www.facos.org

Membership: osteopathic surgeons in disciplines of neurosurgery, thoracic surgery, cardiovascular surgery, urology, plastic surgery, and general surgery. Offers members continuing surgical education programs and use of the ACOS-sponsored coding and reimbursement online database. Monitors legislation and regulations.

American College of Preventive Medicine, *1307 New York Ave. N.W., #200 20005; (202) 466-2044. Fax, (202) 466-2662. Michael Barry, Executive Director.*
General e-mail, info@acpm.org

Web, www.acpm.org

Membership: physicians in general preventive medicine, public health, international health, occupational medicine, and aerospace medicine. Provides educational opportunities; advocates public policies consistent with scientific principles of the discipline; supports the investigation and analysis of issues relevant to the field.

American College of Radiology, *1891 Preston White Dr., Reston, VA 20191; (703) 648-8900. Fax, (703) 295-6773. Dr. Harvey L. Neiman, Executive Director.*
General e-mail, info@acr.org

Web, www.acr.org

Membership: certified radiologists and medical physicists in the United States and Canada. Develops programs in radiation protection, technologist training, practice standards, and health care insurance; maintains a placement service for radiologists; participates in international conferences.

American College of Surgeons, *Washington Office, 1640 Wisconsin Ave. N.W. 20007; (202) 337-2701. Fax, (202) 337-4271. Christian Shalgian, Associate Director.*
General e-mail, cshalgian@facs.org

Web, www.facs.org

Monitors legislation and regulations concerning surgery; conducts continuing education programs and sponsors scholarships for graduate medical education. Interests include hospital cancer programs, trauma care, hospital accreditation, and international research. (Headquarters in Chicago, Ill.)

American Health Quality Assn., *1155 21st St. N.W., #202 20036; (202) 331-5790. Fax, (202) 331-9334. David G. Schulke, Executive Vice President.*
General e-mail, info@ahqa.org

Web, www.ahqa.org

National network of private Quality Improvement Organizations (QIOs) that seek to improve health care provider performance through provider performance measurement feedback, teaching self-assessment techniques, responding to consumer complaints and appeals, and initiating community-based quality improvement programs. Monitors legislation and regulations.

American Medical Assn. (AMA), *Government Relations, Washington Office, 25 Massachusetts Ave. N.W., #600 20001; (202) 789-7400. Fax, (202) 789-7485. Richard Deem, Senior Vice President.*
Web, www.ama-assn.org

Membership: physicians, residents, and medical students. Provides information on the medical profession and health care; cooperates in setting standards for medical schools and hospital intern and residency training programs; offers physician placement service and counseling

on management practices; provides continuing medical education. Interests include international research and peer review. Monitors legislation and regulations. (Headquarters in Chicago, Ill.)

American Osteopathic Assn., *Washington Office, 1090 Vermont Ave. N.W., #510 20005; (202) 414-0140. Fax, (202) 544-3525. Sydney Olson, Director. Information, (800) 962-9008.*
General e-mail, ktaylor@osteopathic.org

Web, www.osteopathic.org

Membership: osteopathic physicians. Promotes public health, education, and research; accredits osteopathic educational institutions. Monitors legislation and regulations. (Headquarters in Chicago, Ill.)

American Podiatric Medical Assn., *9312 Old Georgetown Rd., Bethesda, MD 20814-1698; (301) 581-9200. Fax, (301) 530-2752. Dr. Glenn Gastwirth, Executive Director.*
Web, www.apma.org

Membership: podiatrists in affiliated and related societies. Interests include advocacy in legislative affairs, health policy and practice, scientific meetings, and public education.

American Psychiatric Assn., *1000 Wilson Blvd., #1825, Arlington, VA 22209-3901; (703) 907-7300. Fax, (703) 907-1085. Dr. James Scully, Medical Director. Library, (703) 907-8648. Press, (703) 907-8640.*
General e-mail, apa@psych.org

Web, www.psych.org

Membership: psychiatrists. Promotes availability of high-quality psychiatric care; provides the public with information; assists state and local agencies; conducts educational programs for professionals and students in the field; participates in international meetings and research. Library open to members.

American Society of Addiction Medicine, *4601 N. Park Ave., Upper Arcade, #101, Chevy Chase, MD 20815-4520; (301) 656-3920. Fax, (301) 656-3815. Eileen McGrath, Executive Vice President.*
General e-mail, email@asam.org

Web, www.asam.org

Membership: physicians and medical students. Supports the study and provision of effective treatment and care for people with alcohol and drug dependencies; educates physicians. Monitors legislation and regulations.

American Society of Nuclear Cardiology, *4550 Montgomery Ave., #780 North, Bethesda, MD 20814; (301) 215-7575. Fax, (301) 215-7113. Steve Carter, Executive Director.*
General e-mail, info@asnc.org

Web, www.asnc.org

Membership: physicians, scientists, technologists, and other professionals engaged in nuclear cardiology practice or research. Provides professional education programs; establishes standards and guidelines for training and practice; promotes research worldwide. Works with agreement states to monitor user-licensing requirements of the Nuclear Regulatory Commission.

American Society of Transplant Surgeons, *2461 S. Clark St., #640, Arlington, VA 22202; (703) 414-7870. Fax, (703) 414-7874. John Roberts, President. General e-mail, asts@asts.org*

Web, www.asts.org

Promotes education and research of organ and tissue transplantation for patients with end stage organ failure. Provides information for policy decisions affecting the practice of transplantation. Offers professional development for transplant colleagues.

Assn. of American Medical Colleges (AAMC), *2450 N St. N.W. 20037; (202) 828-0400. Fax, (202) 828-1125. Dr. Darrell G. Kirch, President.*

Web, www.aamc.org

Membership: U.S. schools of medicine, councils of deans, teaching hospitals, academic societies, medical students, and residents. Administers Medical College Admission Test.

Assn. of Professors of Medicine, *2501 M St. N.W., #550 20037-1325; (202) 861-9351. Fax, (202) 861-9731. Bergitta E. Smith, Executive Vice President. General e-mail, apm@im.org*

Web, www.im.org/apm

Membership: chairs of internal medicine departments at all U.S. medical schools and several affiliated teaching hospitals. Provides services, training, and educational opportunities for leaders in internal medicine departments. Monitors legislation and regulations. (Affiliated with Alliance for Academic Internal Medicine.)

Clerkship Directors in Internal Medicine, *2501 M St. N.W., #550 20037-1325; (202) 861-9351. Fax, (202) 861-9731. Bergitta E. Smith, Executive Vice President. General e-mail, cdim@im.org*

Web, www.im.org/cdim

Membership: directors of third- and fourth-year internal medicine clerkships at U.S. and Canadian medical schools. (Affiliated with Alliance for Academic Internal Medicine.)

College of American Pathologists, *Washington Office, 1350 Eye St. N.W., #590 20005-3305; (202) 354-7100. Fax, (202) 354-7155. John Scott, Vice President. Information, (800) 392-9994.*

Web, www.cap.org

Membership: physicians who are board certified in clinical or anatomic pathology. Accredits laboratories and provides them with proficiency testing programs; promotes the practice of pathology and laboratory medicine worldwide. Monitors legislation and regulations. (Headquarters in Northfield, Ill.)

National Medical Assn., *1012 10th St. N.W. 20001; (202) 347-1895. Fax, (202) 371-1162. Dr. Mohammad N. Akhter, Executive Director.*

Web, www.nmanet.org

Membership: minority physicians. Supports increased participation of minorities in the health professions, especially medicine.

Vision Care

▶AGENCIES

National Eye Institute *(National Institutes of Health), 31 Center Dr., Bldg. 31, #6A03, MSC-2510, Bethesda, MD 20892; (301) 496-2234. Fax, (301) 496-9970. Dr. Paul A. Sieving, Director. Information, (301) 496-5248.*

Web, www.nei.nih.gov

Conducts and supports research, training, health information dissemination, and other programs with respect to blinding eye diseases, visual disorders, mechanisms of visual function, preservation of sight, and the special health problems and requirements of the blind.

▶NONGOVERNMENTAL

American Academy of Ophthalmology, *Governmental Affairs, Washington Office, 1101 Vermont Ave. N.W., #700 20005-3570; (202) 737-6662. Fax, (202) 737-7061. Cathy G. Cohen, Vice President.*

Web, www.aao.org

Membership: eye physicians and surgeons. Provides information on eye diseases. Monitors legislation, regulations, and international research. (Headquarters in San Francisco, Calif.)

American Academy of Optometry, *6110 Executive Blvd., #506, Rockville, MD 20852; (301) 984-1441. Fax, (301) 984-4737. Lois Schoenbrun, Executive Director. General e-mail, AAOptom@AAOptom.org*

Web, www.aaopt.org

Membership: optometrists and students of optometry. Conducts research and continuing education. Interests include primary care optometry, contact lenses, low vision, and diseases of the eye.

American Board of Opticianry and National Contact Lens Examiners Board, *6506 Loisdale Rd., #209, Springfield, VA 22150; (703) 719-5800. Fax, (703) 719-9144. Michael Robey, Executive Manager. General e-mail, mail@abo-ncle.org*

Web, www.abo-ncle.org

Establishes standards for opticians who dispense eyeglasses and contact lenses. Administers professional exams and awards certification; maintains registry of certified eyeglass and contact lens dispensers. Adopts and enforces continuing education requirements; assists state licensing boards; approves educational offerings for recertification requirements.

American Optometric Assn., *Washington Office, 1505 Prince St., #300, Alexandria, VA 22314; (703) 739-9200. Fax, (703) 739-9497. Jon Hymes, Director, ext. 1371. General e-mail, jfhymes@aoa.org*

Web, www.aoa.org

Membership: optometrists, optometry students, and paraoptometric assistants and technicians in a federation of state, student, and armed forces optometric associations. Sets professional standards and provides research and information on eye care to the public. Monitors legislation and regulations and acts as liaison with international optometric groups and government optometrists; conducts continuing education programs for optometrists and provides information on eye care. (Headquarters in St. Louis, Mo.)

American Society of Cataract and Refractive Surgery, *4000 Legato Rd., #700, Fairfax, VA 22033; (703) 591-2220. Fax, (703) 591-0614. David Karcher, Executive Director. Web, www.ascrs.org*

Membership: more than 9,000 ophthalmologists who specialize in cataract and refractive surgery. Offers educational programs and services to its members. Monitors regulations affecting ophthalmic practices. Sponsors independent research. Maintains a foundation dedicated to improving public understanding of ophthalmology and providing eye care to underserved parts of the world.

Assn. for Research in Vision and Ophthalmology, *12300 Twinbrook Pkwy., #250, Rockville, MD 20852; (240) 221-2900. Fax, (240) 221-0370. Joanne Angle, Executive Director.*
General e-mail, arvo@arvo.org
Web, www.arvo.org

Promotes eye and vision research; issues awards for significant research and administers research grant program.

Assn. of Schools and Colleges of Optometry, *6110 Executive Blvd., #420, Rockville, MD 20852; (301) 231-5944. Fax, (301) 770-1828. Martin A. Wall, Executive Director.*
General e-mail, admini@opted.org
Web, www.opted.org

Membership: U.S. and Puerto Rican optometry schools and colleges and foreign affiliates. Provides information about the Optometry College Admission Test to students. Supports the international development of optometric education. Monitors legislation and regulations.

Contact Lens Society of America, *441 Carlisle Dr., Herndon, VA 20170; (703) 437-5100. Fax, (703) 437-0727. Tina M. Schott, Executive Director.*
General e-mail, tinaschott@clsa.info
Web, www.clsa.info

Membership: contact lens professionals. Conducts courses and continuing education seminars for contact lens fitters and technicians.

Eye Bank Assn. of America, *1015 18th St. N.W., #1010 20036-5504; (202) 775-4999. Fax, (202) 429-6036. Patricia Aiken-O'Neill, President.*
General e-mail, info@restoresight.org
Web, www.restoresight.org

Membership: eye banks in Brazil, Canada, England, Italy, Japan, Saudi Arabia, Taiwan, and the United States.

Sets and enforces medical standards for eye banking; seeks to increase donations to eye, tissue, and organ banks; conducts training and certification programs for eye bank technicians; compiles statistics; accredits eye banks.

International Eye Foundation, *10801 Connecticut Ave., Kensington, MD 20895; (240) 290-0263. Fax, (240) 290-0269. Victoria M. Sheffield, President.*
General e-mail, ief@iefusa.org
Web, www.iefusa.org

Operates blindness prevention programs focusing on cataracts, trachoma, "river blindness," and childhood blindness, including vitamin A deficiency. Provides affordable ophthalmic instruments, equipment, and supplies to eye hospitals in developing countries to help lower surgical costs. Works to strengthen management and financial sustainability of eye hospitals and clinics in developing countries. Works with the World Health Organization, ministries of health, and international and indigenous organizations in Africa, Asia, Latin America, and eastern Europe to promote eye care.

Optical Laboratories Assn., *11096 Lee Hwy., #A101, Fairfax, VA 22030; (703) 359-2830. Fax, (703) 359-2834. Robert L. Dziuban, Executive Director. Toll-free, (800) 477-5652.*
General e-mail, ola@ola-labs.org
Web, www.ola-labs.org

Membership: optical laboratories. Promotes the eyewear industry; sponsors conferences. Monitors legislation and regulations.

Vision Council, *1700 Diagonal Rd., #500, Alexandria, VA 22314; (703) 548-4560. Fax, (703) 548-4580. Ed Greene, Chief Executive Officer. Toll-free, (866) 826-0290.*
General e-mail, info@thevisioncouncil.org
Web, www.thevisioncouncil.org

Sponsors trade shows and public relations programs for the ophthalmic industry. Educates the public on developments in the optical industry. Represents manufacturers and distributors of optical products and equipment.

HEALTH SERVICES FOR SPECIAL GROUPS

►**AGENCIES**

Administration for Children and Families (ACF), *(Health and Human Services Dept.), 901 D St. S.W., #600 20447 (mailing address: 370 L'Enfant Promenade S.W., Washington, DC 20201); (202) 401-2337. Fax, (202) 401-4678. Public Affairs, (202) 401-9215.*
Web, www.acf.hhs.gov

Administers and funds programs for Native Americans, children, youth, families, and those with developmental disabilities. Responsible for Social Services Block Grants to the states. Provides agencies with technical assistance; administers Head Start program; funds the National

Runaway Switchboard, (800) RUNAWAY (786-2929), the Domestic Violence Hotline, (800) 799-7233, the National Teen Dating Abuse Help Line, (866) 331-9474, and programs for abused children.

Centers for Medicare and Medicaid Services (CMS), *(Health and Human Services Dept.), Nursing Homes and Continuing Care Services,* 7500 Security Blvd., S2-12-25-07, Baltimore, MD 21244-1850; (410) 786-3870. Fax, (410) 786-6730. Cynthia Graunke, Director. *Web, www.cms.hhs.gov*

Monitors compliance of nursing homes, psychiatric hospitals, and long-term and intermediate care facilities with government standards. Focus includes quality of care, environmental conditions, and participation in Medicaid and Medicare programs. Coordinates health care programs for the mentally challenged. (Formerly the Health Care Financing Administration.)

Health Resources and Services Administration *(Health and Human Services Dept.), Policy and Development,* 5600 Fishers Lane, #C26, Rockville, MD 20857; (301) 594-4300. Fax, (301) 594-4997. Elisabeth Handley, Director. *Web, www.bphc.hrsa.gov*

Awards grants to public and nonprofit migrant, community, and health care centers to provide direct health care services in areas that are medically underserved. Provides staff support for National Advisory Council on Migrant Health. Administers Consolidated Health Centers Program and other bureau-funded programs.

Health Resources and Services Administration *(Health and Human Services Dept.), Primary Health Care,* 5600 Fishers Lane, #17-105, Rockville, MD 20857; (301) 594-4110. Fax, (301) 594-4072. James Macrae, Associate Administrator. *Web, www.bphc.hrsa.gov*

Advocates accessible primary health care for underserved communities and individuals. Promotes partnerships in public and private health care delivery communities. Researches and analyzes effectiveness of community-based systems of care.

Health Resources and Services Administration *(Health and Human Services Dept.), Primary Health Care: Minority and Special Populations,* 5600 Fishers Lane, #16-105, Rockville, MD 20857; (301) 594-4303. Fax, (301) 443-0248. Capt. Henry Lopez Jr., Director. *Web, www.bphc.hrsa.gov*

Advocates to improve the health of racial and ethnic minority populations and others who experience difficulty in accessing health care, through the development of health policies and programs that will increase access and eliminate health disparities. Advises the associate administrator for primary care on public health activities affecting ethnic, racial, and other minority groups, including migrant and seasonal farmworkers, homeless persons, persons living in public housing, older adults, and women.

Immigration and Customs Enforcement (ICE), *(Homeland Security Dept.), Immigration Health*

Services, 1220 L St. N.W., #500 20005; (202) 732-0100. Fax, (202) 732-0095. Capt. (Dr.) José H. Rodriguez, Director. *Web, www.icehealth.org*

Works to improve the health of new immigrants and detained aliens in the United States; promotes increased access to comprehensive primary and preventive health care.

Indian Health Service *(Health and Human Services Dept.),* 801 Thompson Ave., #440, Rockville, MD 20852; (301) 443-1083. Fax, (301) 443-4794. Robert G. McSwain, Director. Information, (301) 443-3593. *Web, www.ihs.gov*

Acts as the health advocate for and operates hospitals and health centers that provide preventive, curative, and community health care for Native Americans and Alaska Natives. Provides and improves sanitation and water supply systems in Native American and Alaska Native communities.

National Institute of Child Health and Human Development *(National Institutes of Health), National Center for Medical Rehabilitation Research,* 6100 Executive Blvd., Bldg. 6100, #2A-03, MSC 7510, Bethesda, MD 20892; (301) 402-2242. Fax, (301) 402-0832. Dr. Michael Weinrich, Director, (301) 402-4201. *Web, www.nichd.nih.gov/about/ncmrr*

Fosters the development of scientific knowledge needed to enhance the health, productivity, independence, and quality of life of persons with disabilities. Supports a program of basic and applied research promoting tissue plasticity, assistive technology and devices, improved outcomes, and increased patient participation.

National Institute on Deafness and Other Communication Disorders *(National Institutes of Health),* 31 Center Dr., #3C02, MSC-2320, Bethesda, MD 20892-2320; (301) 402-0900. Fax, (301) 402-1590. Dr. James F. Battey Jr., Director. Information, (301) 496-7243. TTY, (301) 402-0252. *General e-mail, nidcdinfo@nidcd.nih.gov*

Web, www.nidcd.nih.gov

Conducts and supports research and research training and disseminates information on hearing disorders and other communication processes, including diseases that affect hearing, balance, smell, taste, voice, speech, and language. Monitors international research.

Public Health and Science *(Health and Human Services Dept.), Minority Health,* 1101 Wootton Pkwy., #600, Rockville, MD 20852; (240) 453-2882. Fax, (240) 453-2883. Dr. Garth Graham, Deputy Assistant Secretary. Information, (800) 444-6472. *General e-mail, info@omhrc.gov*

Web, www.omhrc.gov

Oversees the implementation of the secretary's Task Force on Black and Minority Health and legislative mandates; develops programs to meet the health care needs of minorities; awards grants to coalitions of minority community organizations and to minority AIDS education and prevention projects.

Rehabilitation Services Administration *(Education Dept.)*, *400 Maryland Ave. S.W. 20202-2800; (202) 245-7488. Fax, (202) 245-7591. P. Edward Anthony, Commissioner (Acting). TTY, (800) 437-0833. Web, www.ed.gov/about/offices/list/osers/rsa/index.html*

Allocates funds to state agencies and nonprofit organizations for programs serving eligible physically and mentally disabled persons; services provided by these funds include medical and psychological treatment as well as establishment of supported-employment and independent-living programs.

▶**CONGRESS**

For a listing of relevant congressional committees and subcommittees, please see page 320 or the Appendix.

▶**NONGOVERNMENTAL**

Assn. of Clinicians for the Underserved, *1420 Spring Hill Rd., #600, Tysons Corner, VA 22102; (703) 442-5318. Fax, (703) 562-8801. Kathie Westpheling, Executive Director. General e-mail, acu@clinicians.org*

Web, www.clinicians.org

Membership: clinicians, advocates, and health care organizations. Works to improve the health of underserved populations and eliminate health disparities in the United States. Educates and supports health care clinicians serving these populations. Interests include health care access, transdisciplinary approaches to health care, workforce development and diversity, pharmaceutical access, and health information technology.

Catholic Health Assn. of the United States, *1875 Eye St. N.W., #1000 20006; (202) 296-3993. Fax, (202) 296-3997. Sister Carol Keehan, President. Web, www.chausa.org*

Concerned with the health care needs of the poor and disadvantaged. Promotes health care reform, including universal insurance coverage, and more cost-effective, affordable health care.

Easter Seals, *Washington Office, 1425 K St. N.W., #200 20005; (202) 347-3066. Fax, (202) 737-7914. Randall Rutta, Executive Vice President. TTY, (202) 347-7385. Web, www.easterseals.com*

Federation of state and local groups with programs that help people with disabilities achieve independence. Washington office monitors legislation and regulations. Affiliates assist individuals with a broad range of disabilities, including muscular dystrophy, cerebral palsy, stroke, speech and hearing loss, blindness, amputation, and learning disabilities. Services include physical, occupational, vocational, and speech therapy; speech, hearing, physical, and vocational evaluation; psychological testing and counseling; personal and family counseling; and special education programs. (Headquarters in Chicago, Ill.)

Farm Worker Health Services, *1221 Massachusetts Ave. N.W., #5 20005-4526; (202) 347-7377. Fax, (202) 347-6385. Oscar C. Gomez, Chief Executive Officer. General e-mail, mail@farmworkerhealth.org*

Web, www.farmworkerhealth.org

Provides technical assistance to community-based organizations that provide health and social services to farmworkers and their families.

National Assn. of Community Health Centers, *7200 Wisconsin Ave., #210, Bethesda, MD 20814; (301) 347-0400. Fax, (301) 347-0459. Tom Van Coverden, President. General e-mail, contact@nachc.com*

Web, www.nachc.com

Membership: community, migrant, public housing, and homeless health centers. Provides the medically underserved with health services; seeks to ensure the continued development of community health care programs through policy analysis, research, technical assistance, publications, education, and training.

National Health Law Program, *Washington Office, 1444 Eye St. N.W., #1105 20005; (202) 289-7661. Fax, (202) 289-7724. Emily Spitzer, Director. General e-mail, nhelpdc@healthlaw.org*

Web, www.healthlaw.org

Organization of lawyers representing the economically disadvantaged, minorities, and older adults on issues concerning federal, state, and local health care programs. Offers technical assistance, workshops, seminars, and training for health law specialists. (Headquarters in Los Angeles, Calif.)

Older Adults

▶**AGENCIES**

National Institute on Aging *(National Institutes of Health), 31 Center Dr., Bldg. 31, #5C35, MSC-2292, Bethesda, MD 20892-2292; (301) 496-9265. Fax, (301) 496-2525. Dr. Richard J. Hodes, Director. Communications and Public Liaison, (301) 496-1752. Information Center, (800) 222-2225. Alzheimer's Disease Education and Referral Center, (800) 438-4380. Web, www.nia.nih.gov*

Conducts and supports biomedical, social, and behavioral research and training related to the aging process and the diseases and special problems of the aged. Manages the Alzheimer's Disease Education and Referral Center (www.alzheimer.org).

▶**NONGOVERNMENTAL**

AARP, *601 E St. N.W. 20049; (202) 434-2277. Fax, (202) 434-2320. William D. Novelli, Chief Executive Officer. Press, (202) 434-2560. TTY, (877) 434-7595. Research Info Center, (202) 434-6233. Web, www.aarp.org*

Membership: people fifty years of age and older. Conducts educational and counseling programs in areas concerning older adults, such as widowed persons services, health promotion, housing, and consumer protection. Library open to the public.

AARP, *Federal Affairs Health and Long-Term Care Team,* 601 E St. N.W. 20049; (202) 434-3770. Fax, (202) 434-3745. David Certner, Director of Federal Affairs. Main switchboard, (202) 434-2277.
Web, www.aarp.org

Maintains the Legal Counsel for the Elderly, which advocates on behalf of older residents of the District of Columbia who reside in nursing homes and board and care homes. Monitors legislation and regulations.

AARP Foundation, 601 E St. N.W. 20049; (202) 434-6200. Fax, (202) 434-6593. Robin Talbert, Director. Press, (202) 434-2560.
Web, www.aarp.org/foundation

Seeks to educate the public on aging issues; sponsors conferences and produces publications on age-related concerns. Interests include aging and living environments for older persons. Funds age-related research, educational grants, legal hotlines, senior employment programs, and reverse mortgage projects. (Affiliated with AARP.)

Alliance for Aging Research, 2021 K St. N.W., #305 20006; (202) 293-2856. Fax, (202) 785-8574. Daniel P. Perry, Executive Director.
General e-mail, info@agingresearch.org
Web, www.agingresearch.org

Membership: senior corporate and foundation executives, science leaders, and congressional representatives. Citizen advocacy organization that seeks to improve the health and independence of older Americans through public and private research.

Alliance for Retired Americans, 815 16th St. N.W., 4th Floor North 20006-4104; (202) 637-5399. Fax, (202) 637-5398. Barbara Esterling, President. Information, (888) 373-6497.
Web, www.retiredamericans.org

Supports expansion of Medicare, improved health programs, national health care, and reduced cost of drugs. Nursing Home Information Service provides information on nursing home standards and regulations. Monitors legislation and regulations. (Affiliate of the AFL-CIO.)

Alzheimer's Assn., *Public Policy, Washington Office,* 1319 F St. N.W., #500 20004-1106; (202) 393-7737. Fax, (866) 865-0270. Robert Egge, Senior Vice President. Information, (800) 272-3900.
Web, www.alz.org

Offers family support services and educates the public about Alzheimer's disease, a neurological disorder mainly affecting the brain tissue in older adults. Promotes research and long-term care protection; maintains liaison with Alzheimer's associations abroad. Monitors legislation and regulations. (Headquarters in Chicago, Ill.)

American Assn. for Geriatric Psychiatry, 7910 Woodmont Ave., #1050, Bethesda, MD 20814-3004; (301) 654-7850. Fax, (301) 654-4137. Christine de Vries, Vice President.
General e-mail, main@aagponline.org
Web, www.aagponline.org

Works to improve the practice of geriatric psychiatry and knowledge about it through education, research, and advocacy. Monitors legislation and regulations.

American Assn. of Homes and Services for the Aging, *Advocacy,* 2519 Connecticut Ave. N.W. 20008-1520; (202) 783-2242. Fax, (202) 783-2255. Susan M. Weiss, Senior Vice President.
General e-mail, info@aahsa.org
Web, www.aahsa.org

Membership: nonprofit homes, housing, and health-related facilities for the elderly sponsored by religious, fraternal, labor, private, and governmental organizations. Conducts research on long-term care for the elderly; sponsors institutes and workshops on accreditation, financing, and institutional life. Monitors legislation and regulations.

Gerontological Society of America, 1220 L St. N.W., #901 20005-4018; (202) 842-1275. Fax, (202) 842-1150. James Appleby, Executive Director.
General e-mail, geron@geron.org
Web, www.geron.org

Scientific organization of researchers, educators, and professionals in the field of aging. Promotes the study of aging and the application of research to public policy. Interests include health and civic engagement.

National Assn. for Home Care and Hospice, 228 7th St. S.E. 20003; (202) 547-7424. Fax, (202) 547-3540. Val J. Halamandaris, President.
General e-mail, webmaster@nahc.org
Web, www.nahc.org

Membership: home care professionals and paraprofessionals. Advocates the rights of the elderly, infirm, and terminally ill to remain independent in their own homes as long as possible. Monitors legislation and regulations.

National Consumer Voice for Quality Long-term Care (NCCNHR), 1828 L St. N.W., #801 20036; (202) 332-2275. Fax, (202) 332-2949. Sarah F. Wells, Executive Director.
General e-mail, nccnhr@nccnhr.org
Web, www.nccnhr.org

Seeks to improve the long-term care system and quality of life for residents in nursing homes and other facilities for the elderly; coordinates the Campaign for Quality Care. Promotes citizen participation in all aspects of nursing homes; acts as clearinghouse for nursing home advocacy.

National Council on the Aging, 1901 L St. N.W., 4th Floor 20036; (202) 479-1200. Fax, (202) 479-0735. James P. Firman, President. Press, (202) 479-6975. TTY, (202) 479-6674.

General e-mail, info@ncoa.org

Web, www.ncoa.org

Promotes the physical, mental, and emotional health of older persons and studies adult day care and community-based long-term care. Monitors legislation and regulations.

National Hispanic Council on Aging, *734 15th St. N.W., #1050 20005; (202) 347-9733. Fax, (202) 347-9735. Yanira Cruz, President.*

General e-mail, nhcoa@nhcoa.org

Web, www.nhcoa.org

Membership: senior citizens, health care workers, professionals in the field of aging, and others in the United States and Puerto Rico who are interested in topics related to Hispanics and aging.

National Long-Term Care Ombudsman Resource Center, *1828 L St. N.W., #801 20036; (202) 332-2275. Fax, (202) 332-2949. Lori Smetanka, Director.*

General e-mail, ombudcenter@nccnhr.org

Web, www.ltcombudsman.org

Provides technical assistance, management guidance, policy analysis, and program development information on behalf of state and substate ombudsman programs. (Affiliate of the National Citizens' Coalition for Nursing Home Reform.)

National Osteoporosis Foundation, *1232 22nd St. N.W. 20037-1292; (202) 223-2226. Fax, (202) 223-2237. Leo Schargorodski, Executive Director. Toll-free, (800) 231-4222.*

General e-mail, nofmail@nof.org

Web, www.nof.org

Volunteer health organization that seeks to prevent osteoporosis and related bone fractures, to promote lifelong bone health, to improve the lives of those affected by osteoporosis, and to find a cure through programs of awareness, advocacy, and public health education and research. Monitors international research.

Prenatal, Maternal, and Child Health Care

▶AGENCIES

Centers for Medicare and Medicaid Services (CMS), *(Health and Human Services Dept.), Medicaid, 7500 Security Blvd., #C5-22-23, Baltimore, MD 21244; (410) 786-3870. Fax, (410) 786-0025. Dennis G. Smith, Director; William Lasowski, Deputy Director. Alternate phone, (202) 690-7428.*

Web, www.cms.hhs.gov

Develops health care policies and programs for needy children under Medicaid; works with the Public Health Service and other related agencies to coordinate the department's child health resources. (Formerly the Health Care Financing Administration.)

Environmental Protection Agency (EPA), *Children's Health Protection, 1200 Pennsylvania Ave. N.W., #2512, MC 1107A 20460; (202) 564-2188. Fax, (202) 564-2733. Ruth McCully, Director.*

Web, www.epa.gov

Supports and facilitates the EPA's efforts to protect children's and older adults' health from environmental risks, both domestically and internationally.

Health Resources and Services Administration *(Health and Human Services Dept.), Maternal and Child Health, 5600 Fishers Lane, #18-05, Rockville, MD 20857; (301) 443-2170. Fax, (301) 443-1797. Dr. Peter C. van Dyck, Associate Administrator.*

Web, www.mchb.hrsa.gov

Administers block grants to states for mothers and children and for children with special health needs; awards funding for research training, genetic disease testing, counseling and information dissemination, hemophilia diagnostic and treatment centers, and demonstration projects to improve the health of mothers and children. Interests also include emergency medical services for children, universal newborn hearing screening, and traumatic brain injury.

Health Resources and Services Administration *(Health and Human Services Dept.), National Vaccine Injury Compensation Program, 5600 Fishers Lane, Parklawn Bldg., #11C-26, Rockville, MD 20857; (301) 443-6593. Fax, (301) 443-8196. Dr. Geoffrey Evans, Director. Toll-free hotline, (800) 338-2382.*

Web, www.hrsa.gov/vaccinecompensation

Provides no-fault compensation to individuals injured by certain childhood vaccines (rotavirus vaccine; diphtheria and tetanus toxoids and pertussis vaccine; measles, mumps, and rubella vaccine; varicella, hepatitis A and B, HiB vaccine; polio and inactivated polio vaccine; and influenza, pneumococcal, meningococcal, and human papillomavirus vaccines).

National Institute of Child Health and Human Development *(National Institutes of Health), 31 Center Dr., Bldg. 31, #2A03, MSC-2425, Bethesda, MD 20892-2425; (301) 496-3454. Fax, (301) 402-1104. Dr. Duane F. Alexander, Director. Information, (301) 496-5133.*

Web, www.nichd.nih.gov

Conducts research and research training on biological and behavioral human development. Studies reproduction and population statistics, perinatal biology and infant mortality, congenital defects, nutrition, human learning and behavior, medical rehabilitation, and mental retardation. Interests include UNICEF and other international organizations.

National Institute of Child Health and Human Development *(National Institutes of Health), Center for Research for Mothers and Children, 6100 Executive Blvd., #4B05, Bethesda, MD 20892-7510; (301) 496-5098. Fax, (301) 480-7773. Dorothy Tucker, Director.*

Web, www.nichd.nih.gov/about/org/crmc

Supports biomedical and behavioral science research and training for maternal and child health care. Areas of study include fetal development, maternal-infant health problems, HIV-related diseases in childbearing women, roles of nutrients and hormones in child growth, developmental disabilities, and behavioral development. Also supports research into the effects and effectiveness of pharmaceuticals on maternal and child health.

Public Health and Science *(Health and Human Services Dept.), Adolescent Pregnancy Programs,* 1101 *Wootton Pkwy., 7th Floor, Rockville, MD 20852; (240) 453-2828. Fax, (240) 453-2829. Alicia Richmond-Scott, Director (Acting). Alternate phone, (240) 453-2800.*
General e-mail, oapp@hhs.gov

Web, http://hhs.gov/opa

Awards, administers, and evaluates research and demonstration grants through the Adolescent Family Life Program, which funds community health care and pregnancy prevention programs. Administers a program that provides pregnant adolescents and children of teenage parents with comprehensive health education and social services, and a program that focuses on sexual abstinence. Interests include adolescent sexual behavior, adoption, and early childbearing.

▶**NONGOVERNMENTAL**

Advocates for Youth, *2000 M St. N.W., #750 20036; (202) 419-3420. Fax, (202) 419-1448. James Wagoner, President.*
General e-mail, information@advocatesforyouth.org

Web, www.advocatesforyouth.org

Seeks to reduce the incidence of unintended teenage pregnancy and AIDS through public education, training and technical assistance, research, and media programs.

Alliance for Healthy Homes, *50 F St. N.W., #300 20001; (202) 347-7610. Fax, (202) 347-0058. Patrick MacRoy, Executive Director.*
General e-mail, afhh@afhh.org

Web, www.afhh.org

Seeks to protect children from lead and other environmental health hazards. Develops and promotes prevention programs; promotes effective federal programs and standards. Helps community-based organizations identify health hazards in homes and document substandard conditions to achieve changes in policies and practices in high-risk communities.

American Academy of Child and Adolescent Psychiatry, *3615 Wisconsin Ave. N.W. 20016-3007; (202) 966-7300. Fax, (202) 966-2891. Virginia Q. Anthony, Executive Director.*
Web, www.aacap.org

Membership: child and adolescent psychiatrists trained to promote healthy development and to evaluate, diagnose, and treat children, adolescents, and families affected by mental illness. Sponsors annual meeting and review for medical board examinations. Provides information on child and adolescent development and mental illnesses. Monitors international research and U.S. legislation concerning children with mental illness.

American Academy of Pediatrics, *Washington Office, 601 13th St. N.W., #400N 20005; (202) 347-8600. Fax, (202) 393-6137. Jackie Noyes, Director. Information, (800) 336-5475.*
General e-mail, kidsdocs@aap.org

Web, www.aap.org

Advocates for maternal and child health legislation and regulations. Interests include increased access and coverage for persons under age twenty-one, immunizations, injury prevention, environmental hazards, child abuse, emergency medical services, biomedical research, Medicaid, disabilities, pediatric AIDS, substance abuse, and nutrition. (Headquarters in Elk Grove Village, Ill.)

American College of Nurse-Midwives, *8403 Colesville Rd., #1550, Silver Spring, MD 20910; (240) 485-1800. Fax, (240) 485-1818. Lorrie Kline Kaplan, Executive Director. Press, (240) 485-1822.*
General e-mail, info@acnm.org

Web, www.midwife.org

Membership: certified midwives and nurse-midwives who preside at deliveries. Accredits midwifery education programs; establishes clinical practice studies. Interests include preventive health care for women.

American College of Obstetricians and Gynecologists, *409 12th St. S.W. 20024-2188 (mailing address: P.O. Box 96920, Washington, DC 20090-6920); (202) 638-5577. Fax, (202) 479-6826. Dr. Ralph Hale, Executive Vice President. Press, (202) 484-3321.*
Web, www.acog.org

Membership: medical specialists in obstetrics and gynecology. Monitors legislation, regulations, and international research on maternal and child health care.

Assn. of Maternal and Child Health Programs (AMCHP), *2030 M St. N.W., #350 20036; (202) 775-0436. Fax, (202) 775-0061. Michael Fraser, Chief Executive Officer.*
General e-mail, info@amchp.org

Web, www.amchp.org

Membership: state public health leaders and others. Works to improve the health and well-being of women, children, and youth, including those with special health care needs and their families.

Assn. of Women's Health, Obstetric, and Neonatal Nurses, *2000 L St. N.W., #740 20036; (202) 261-2400. Fax, (202) 728-0575. Kim L. Armour, President. Press, (202) 371-1997. Toll-free, (800) 673-8499.*
Web, www.awhonn.org

Promotes the health of women and newborns. Provides nurses with information and support. Produces educational materials and legislative programs.

Children's Defense Fund, *25 E St. N.W. 20001; (202)* 628-8787. Fax, (202) 662-3510. Marian Wright Edelman, President.
General e-mail, cdfinfo@childrensdefense.org
Web, www.childrensdefense.org

Advocacy group concerned with programs for children and youth. Assesses adequacy of the Early and Periodic Screening, Diagnosis, and Treatment Program for Medicaid-eligible children. Promotes adequate prenatal care for adolescent and lower-income women; works to prevent adolescent pregnancy.

Guttmacher Institute, *Public Policy, Washington Office,* 1301 Connecticut Ave. N.W., #700 20036-3902; (202) 296-4012. Fax, (202) 223-5756. Cory L. Richards, Executive Vice President.
General e-mail, policyinfo@guttmacher.org
Web, www.guttmacher.org

Conducts research, policy analysis, and public education in reproductive health issues, including maternal and child health. (Headquarters in New York.)

Healthy Teen Network, *1501 St. Paul St., #124,* Baltimore, MD 21202; (410) 685-0410. Fax, (410) 685-0481. Pat Paluzzi, Executive Director.
General e-mail, healthyteens@healthyteennetwork.org
Web, www.healthyteennetwork.org

Membership: health and social work professionals, community and state leaders, and individuals. Promotes services to prevent and resolve problems associated with adolescent sexuality, pregnancy, and parenting. Helps to develop stable and supportive family relationships through program support and evaluation. Monitors legislation and regulations. (Formerly the National Organization on Adolescent Pregnancy, Parenting and Prevention Inc.)

Lamaze International, *2025 M St. N.W., #800* 20036-3309; (202) 367-1128. Fax, (202) 367-2128. Linda Harmon, Executive Director. Information, (800) 368-4404.
General e-mail, info@lamaze.org
Web, www.lamaze.org

Membership: supporters of the Lamaze philosophy of childbirth, including parents, physicians, childbirth educators, and other health professionals. Trains and certifies Lamaze educators. Provides referral service for parents seeking Lamaze classes.

March of Dimes, *Government Affairs, Washington Office,* 1146 19th St. N.W., #600 20036; (202) 659-1800. Fax, (202) 296-2964. Marina L. Weiss, Senior Vice President.
Web, www.marchofdimes.com

Works to prevent birth defects, low birth weight, and infant mortality. Awards grants for research and provides funds for treatment of birth defects. Medical services grantees provide prenatal counseling. Monitors legislation and regulations. (Headquarters in White Plains, N.Y.)

National Assn. of Children's Hospitals and Related Institutions, *401 Wythe St., Alexandria, VA 22314; (703)* 684-1355. Fax, (703) 684-1589. Lawrence A. McAndrews, President.
Web, www.childrenshospitals.net

Advocates and promotes education and research on child health care related to children's hospitals; compiles statistics and provides information on pediatric hospitalizations. (Affiliated with the National Assn. of Children's Hospitals.)

National Assn. of School Psychologists, *4340 East-West Hwy., Bethesda, MD 20814; (301) 657-0270. Fax, (301)* 657-0275. Susan Gorin, Executive Director.
Web, www.nasponline.org

Membership: organizations interested in developing mental health services for children. Fosters information exchange; advises local, state, and federal agencies that develop children's mental health services.

National Center for Education in Maternal and Child Health, *2115 Wisconsin Ave. N.W., #601 20007 (mailing address: Georgetown University, Box 571272, Washington, DC 20057-1272); (202) 784-9770. Fax, (202) 784-9777.* Dr. Rochelle Mayer, Director.
General e-mail, mchgroups@georgetown.edu
Web, www.ncemch.org

Collects and disseminates information about maternal and child health to health professionals and the general public. Carries out special projects for the U.S. Maternal and Child Health Bureau. Library open to the public by appointment. (Affiliated with Georgetown University.)

National Organization on Fetal Alcohol Syndrome, *1200 Eton Court N.W., 3rd Floor 20007; (202) 785-4585.* Fax, (202) 466-6456. Tom Donaldson, President. Information, (800) 666-6327.
General e-mail, information@nofas.org
Web, www.nofas.org

Works to eradicate fetal alcohol syndrome and alcohol-related birth defects through public education, conferences, medical school curricula, and partnerships with federal programs interested in fetal alcohol syndrome.

Pediatric/Adolescent Gastroesophageal Reflux Assn. (PAGER), *P.O. Box 486, Buckeystown, MD 21717. Beth Anderson, Director. Message Center, (301) 601-9541.*
General e-mail, gergroup@aol.com
Web, www.reflux.org, or in Spanish, www.ReflujoEnNinos.org

Promotes public awareness of pediatric gastroesophageal reflux (GER) and provides support for those who suffer from it. Researches GER and acts as a clearinghouse for information on the disorder.

Zero to Three: National Center for Infants, Toddlers, and Families, *2000 M St. N.W., #200 20036; (202)* 638-1144. Fax, (202) 638-0851. Matthew Melmed, Executive Director. Publications, (800) 899-4301.

General e-mail, 0to3@zerotothree.org

Web, www.zerotothree.org

Works to improve infant health, mental health, and development. Sponsors training programs for professionals; offers fellowships. Provides private and government organizations with information on infant development issues.

HEALTH TOPICS: RESEARCH AND ADVOCACY

►AGENCIES

Armed Forces Institute of Pathology *(Defense Dept.),* *6825 16th St. N.W., Bldg. 54 20306-6000; (202) 782-2100. Fax, (202) 782-9376. Dr. Florabel G. Mullick, Director. General e-mail, telepath@afip.osd.mil*

Web, www.afip.org

Maintains a central laboratory of pathology for consultation and diagnosis of pathologic tissue for the Defense Dept., other federal agencies, and civilian pathologists. Conducts research and provides instruction in advanced pathology and related subjects; monitors international research.

Armed Forces Radiobiological Research Institute *(Defense Dept.),* *8901 Wisconsin Ave., Bethesda, MD 20889-5603; (301) 295-1210. Fax, (301) 295-4967. Col. Patricia K. Lillis-Hearne (MC, USA), Director. Public Affairs, (301) 295-1953.*

Web, www.afrri.usuhs.mil

Serves as the principal ionizing radiation radiobiology research laboratory under the jurisdiction of the Uniformed Services of the Health Sciences. Participates in international conferences and projects.

Fogarty International Center *(National Institutes of Health),* *31 Center Dr., MSC 2220, Bethesda, MD 20892-2220 (mailing address: 9000 Rockville Pike, Bldg. 31, #B2C02, Bethesda, MD 20892-2220); (301) 496-1415. Fax, (301) 402-2173. Roger I. Glass, Director. General e-mail, ficinfo@nih.gov*

Web, www.fic.nih.gov

Promotes and supports international scientific research and training to reduce disparities in global health. Leads formulation and implementation of international biomedical research and policy. Supports the conduct of research in high-priority global health areas and helps build research capacity in the developing world.

Health and Human Services Dept. (HHS), *Human Research Protections, 1101 Wootton Pkwy., The Tower Bldg., #200, Rockville, MD 20852; (240) 453-6900. Fax, (240) 453-6909. Dr. Jerry Menikoff, Director. General e-mail, ohrp@hhs.gov*

Web, www.hhs.gov/ohrp

Promotes the rights, welfare, and well-being of subjects involved in research conducted or supported by the Health and Human Services Dept.; helps to ensure that research is carried out in accordance with federal regulations by providing clarification and guidance, developing educational programs and materials, and maintaining regulatory oversight.

Health Resources and Services Administration *(Health and Human Services Dept.), Health Care Systems Bureau: Transplantation, 5600 Fishers Lane, #12C-06, Rockville, MD 20857; (301) 443-7577. Fax, (301) 594-6095. Richard Durbin, Director (Acting).*

Web, www.organdonor.gov

Implements provisions of the National Organ Transplant Act. Provides information on federal, state, and private programs involved in transplantation; supports a national computerized network for organ procurement and matching; maintains information on transplant recipients; awards grants to organ procurement organizations. Administers the C.W. Bill Young Cell Transplantation Program and the National Cord Blood Inventory.

Health, Safety, and Security *(Energy Dept.), Health and Safety, 1000 Independence Ave. S.W., HS-10/270CC 20585-0270; (301) 903-5926. Fax, (301) 903-3445. Patricia R. Worthington, Director.*

Web, www.hss.energy.gov/healthsafety

Evaluates and establishes standards related to radiation, industrial hygiene, worker safety, and occupational medicine at Energy Dept. facilities and surrounding communities. Oversees epidemiologic studies.

Mark O. Hatfield Clinical Research Center *(National Institutes of Health), 10 Center Dr., Bethesda, MD 20892; (301) 496-3315 (Admissions). Dr. John I. Gallin, Director. Patient Recruitment, (800) 411-1222; Public Information, (301) 496-4000.*

Web, http://clinicalcenter.nih.gov

Provides in-patient care and conducts clinical research. Promotes the application of scientific laboratory research to benefit patient health and medical care. With the Warren Grant Magnuson Clinical Center, forms the NIH Clinical Center.

National Heart, Lung, and Blood Institute *(National Institutes of Health), 31 Center Dr., Bldg. 31, #5A48, MSC-2486, Bethesda, MD 20892-2486; (301) 496-5166. Fax, (301) 402-0818. Dr. Elizabeth G. Nabel, Director. Press, (301) 496-4236.*

Web, www.nhlbi.nih.gov

Collects and disseminates information on diseases of the heart, lungs, and blood, on sleep disorders, and on transfusion medicine, with an emphasis on disease prevention. Conducts educational programs for scientists and clinicians; participates in international research.

National Institute of Diabetes and Digestive and Kidney Diseases *(National Institutes of Health), 31 Center Dr., Bldg. 31, #9A52, MSC-2560, Bethesda, MD*

20892-2560 (mailing address: 9000 Rockville Pike, Bldg. 31, #9A52, Bethesda, MD 20892-2220); (301) 496-5877. Fax, (301) 402-2125. Dr. Griffin Rodgers, Director. Press, (301) 496-3583.
Web, www.niddk.nih.gov

Conducts and supports basic and clinical research and research training on diabetes and other endocrine and metabolic diseases, digestive diseases, nutrition, obesity, and kidney, urologic, and hematologic diseases. Web site provides evidence-based health information.

National Institute of General Medical Sciences

(National Institutes of Health), 45 Center Dr., #2AN12B, MSC-6200, Bethesda, MD 20892-6200; (301) 594-2172. Fax, (301) 402-0156. Dr. Jeremy M. Berg, Director.
Web, www.nigms.nih.gov

Primarily supports basic biomedical research and training that lays the foundation for advances in disease diagnosis, treatment, and prevention. Areas of special interest include bioinformatics, cell biology, genetics, infectious diseases, and trauma, burn, and perioperative injury and wound healing. Major initiatives include the Pharmacogenetics Research Network and the Protein Structure Initiative.

National Institutes of Health (NIH), *(Health and Human Services Dept.)*, 1 Center Dr., Bldg. 1, #126, MSC-0148, Bethesda, MD 20892-0148; (301) 496-2433. Fax, (301) 402-2700. Raynard Kington, Director (Acting). Press, (301) 496-4461.
Web, www.nih.gov

Supports and conducts biomedical research on the causes and prevention of diseases; furnishes health professionals and the public with information.

National Institutes of Health (NIH), *(Health and Human Services Dept.)*, Center for Information Technology, 10401 Fernwood Rd., Bethesda, MD 20817; (301) 496-5703. Fax, (301) 402-1754. John F. Jones Jr., Director (Acting).
Web, http://cit.nih.gov

Responsible for incorporating computers into biomedical research information, technology, security, and administrative procedures of the NIH. Serves as the primary scientific and technological resource for the NIH in the areas of high performance computing, database applications, mathematics, statistics, laboratory automation, engineering, computer science and technology, telecommunications, and information resources management.

National Institutes of Health (NIH), *(Health and Human Services Dept.)*, Center for Scientific Review, 6701 Rockledge Dr., #3030, MSC-7776, Bethesda, MD 20892-7776; (301) 435-1114. Fax, (301) 480-3965. Antonio Scarpa, Director.
Web, www.csr.nih.gov

Conducts scientific merit review of research grant and fellowship applications submitted to the NIH. Participates in formulating grant and award policies.

National Institutes of Health (NIH), *(Health and Human Services Dept.)*, Minority Opportunities in Research, 45 Center Dr., Bldg. 45, #2AS37, MSC 6200, Bethesda, MD 20892-6200; (301) 594-3900. Fax, (301) 480-2753. Dr. Clifton A. Poodry, Director.
Web, www.nigms.nih.gov

Administers research and research training programs aimed at increasing the number of minority biomedical scientists. Funds grants, fellowships, faculty development awards, and development of research facilities.

National Institutes of Health (NIH), *(Health and Human Services Dept.)*, National Center for Complementary and Alternative Medicine, 31 Center Dr., Bldg. 31, #2B11, MSC-2182, Bethesda, MD 20892-2182; (301) 435-6826. Fax, (301) 435-6549. Dr. Josephine Briggs, Director. Information, (888) 644-6226. TTY, (866) 464-3615. Clearinghouse International, (301) 519-3153. General e-mail, nccam-info@nccam.nih.gov
Web, www.nccam.nih.gov

Conducts and supports research on complementary and alternative medicine; trains researchers and disseminates information to practitioners and the public.

National Institutes of Health (NIH), *(Health and Human Services Dept.)*, National Center for Research Resources, 9000 Rockville Pike, Bldg. 31, #3B11, MSC-2128, Bethesda, MD 20892-2128; (301) 496-5793. Fax, (301) 402-0006. Barbara Alving, Director. General e-mail, info@ncrr.nih.gov
Web, www.ncrr.nih.gov

Supports primary research to create and develop critical resources, models, and technologies. Provides biomedical researchers with access to diverse instrumentation, technologies, basic and clinical research facilities, animal models, genetic stocks, materials, and other resources.

National Institutes of Health (NIH), *(Health and Human Services Dept.)*, National Center on Minority Health and Health Disparities (NCMHD), 2 Democracy Plaza, 6707 Democracy Blvd., #800, MSC-5465, Bethesda, MD 20892-5465; (301) 402-1366. Fax, (301) 480-4049. Dr. John Ruffin, Director.
Web, www.ncmhd.nih.gov

Promotes minority health and leads, coordinates, supports, and assesses the NIH's effort to eliminate health disparities. Conducts and supports basic clinical, social, and behavioral research; promotes research infrastructure and training; fosters emerging programs; disseminates information; and reaches out to minority and other communities suffering from health disparities.

National Institutes of Health (NIH), *(Health and Human Services Dept.)*, Science Policy, 9000 Rockville Pike, Bldg. 1, #103, Bethesda, MD 20892; (301) 496-2122. Fax, (301) 402-1759. Dr. Amy Patterson, Director (Acting).
Web, www1.od.nih.gov/osp

Advises the NIH director on science policy issues affecting the medical research community. Participates in

National Institutes of Health

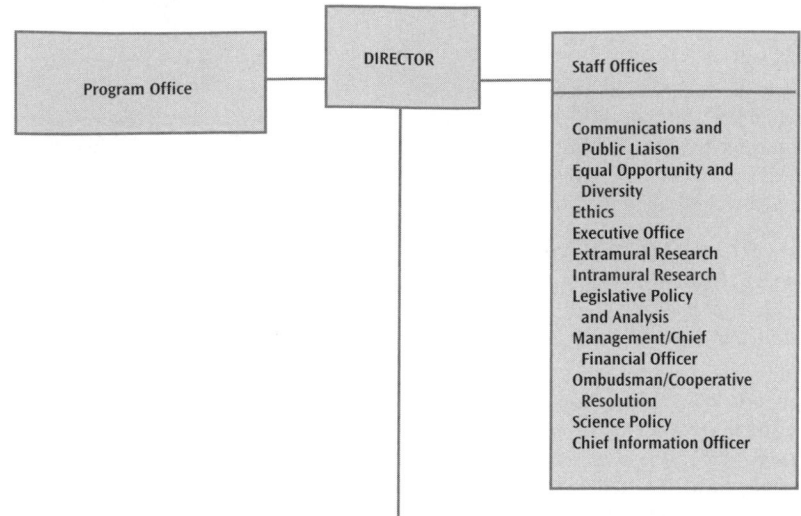

Program Office	DIRECTOR	Staff Offices

Staff Offices:
- Communications and Public Liaison
- Equal Opportunity and Diversity
- Ethics
- Executive Office
- Extramural Research
- Intramural Research
- Legislative Policy and Analysis
- Management/Chief Financial Officer
- Ombudsman/Cooperative Resolution
- Science Policy
- Chief Information Officer

Center for Information Technology
Center for Scientific Review
Clinical Center
John E. Fogarty International Center for Advanced Study in the Health Sciences
National Cancer Institute
National Center for Complementary and Alternative Medicine
National Center for Research Resources
National Center on Minority Health and Health Disparities
National Eye Institute
National Heart, Lung, and Blood Institute

National Human Genome Research Institute
National Institute of Allergy and Infectious Diseases
National Institute of Arthritis and Musculoskeletal and Skin Diseases
National Institute of Biomedical Imaging and Bioengineering
National Institute of Child Health and Human Development
National Institute of Dental and Craniofacial Research
National Institute of Diabetes and Digestive and Kidney Diseases

National Institute of Environmental Health Sciences
National Institute of General Medical Sciences
National Institute of Mental Health
National Institute of Neurological Disorders and Stroke
National Institute of Nursing Research
National Institute on Aging
National Institute on Alcohol Abuse and Alcoholism
National Institute on Deafness and Other Communication Disorders
National Institute on Drug Abuse
National Library of Medicine

the development of new policy and program initiatives. Monitors and coordinates agency planning and evaluation activities. Plans and implements a comprehensive science education program. Develops and implements NIH policies and procedures for the safe conduct of recombinant DNA and other biotechnology activities.

National Institutes of Health (NIH), *(Health and Human Services Dept.),* **Stem Cell Task Force,** *9000 Rockville Pike, Bethesda, MD 20892; (301) 496-9746. Fax, (301) 402-2265. Dr. Story Landis, Chair. Press, (301) 496-5787. General e-mail, stemcell@mail.nih.gov*

Web, http://stemcells.nih.gov

The federal government's primary source for stem cell research, policy, and funding. Enables and speeds the pace of stem cell research by identifying resources and developing measures to enhance such resources. Seeks the advice of scientific leaders in stem cell research about the challenges to advancing the stem cell research agenda and strategies to overcome them.

National Library of Medicine *(National Institutes of Health),* *8600 Rockville Pike, Bldg. 38, #2E17, MSC-3808, Bethesda, MD 20894-6075; (301) 496-6221. Fax, (301) 496-4450. Dr. Donald A.B. Lindberg, Director. Reference, (888) 346-3656. Communications, (301) 496-6308. General e-mail, custserv@nlm.nih.gov*

Web, www.nlm.nih.gov

Offers medical library services and computer-based reference service to the public, health professionals, libraries in medical schools and hospitals, and research institutions. Operates a toxicology information service for the scientific community, industry, and federal agencies. Assists medical libraries through the National Network of Libraries of Medicines. Assists in the improvement of basic library resources.

National Library of Medicine *(National Institutes of Health),* **Health Information Programs Development,** *8600 Rockville Pike, Bldg. 38, #2S20, MSC-12, Bethesda, MD 20894; (301) 496-2311. Fax, (301) 496-4450. Elliot Siegel, Associate Director.*

General e-mail, custserv@nlm.nih.gov

Web, www.nlm.nih.gov

Facilitates worldwide use of the library's medical databases through agreements with individual nations, international organizations, and commercial vendors. Helps the library acquire and share international biomedical literature; promotes international collaboration in creating new databases. Conducts programs for international visitors.

National Library of Medicine *(National Institutes of Health), National Center for Biotechnology Information: PubMed Central,* 8600 Rockville Pike, Bldg. 38A, 8th Floor, Bethesda, MD 20894; (301) 496-2475. Fax, (301) 480-4559. Dr. David J. Lipman, Director.
General e-mail, info@ncbi.nlm.nih.gov

Web, www.ncbi.nlm.nih.gov or www.pubmedcentral.nih.gov

Publicly accessible digital archive of life sciences journal literature.

Naval Medical Research Center *(Defense Dept.),* 503 Robert Grant Ave., #1W28, Silver Spring, MD 20910-7500; (301) 319-7400. Fax, (301) 319-7410. Capt. Christopher Daniel, Commanding Officer.
Web, www.nmrc.navy.mil

Performs basic and applied biomedical research in areas of military importance, including infectious diseases, hyperbaric medicine, wound repair enhancement, environmental stress, and immunobiology. Provides support to field laboratories and naval hospitals; monitors research internationally.

NIH Clinical Center *(National Institutes of Health),* 10 Center Dr., Bldg. 10 CRC, #6-2551, MSC-1504, Bethesda, MD 20892-1504; (301) 496-4114. Fax, (301) 402-0244. Dr. John I. Gallin, Director. Communications, (301) 496-2563.
Web, http://clinicalcenter.nih.gov

Serves as a clinical research center for the NIH; patients are referred by physicians and self-referred throughout the United States and overseas.

Walter Reed Army Institute of Research *(Defense Dept.),* 503 Robert Grant Ave., Silver Spring, MD 20910-7500; (301) 319-9100. Fax, (301) 319-9227. Col. Kent Kester, Commander. Public Affairs Officer, (301) 319-9471. General e-mail, wrair.publicaffairs@amedd.army.mil

Web, www.wrair.army.mil

Provides research, education, and training in support of the Defense Dept.'s health care system. Develops vaccines and drugs to prevent and treat infectious diseases. Other research efforts include surveillance of naturally occurring infectious diseases of military importance and study of combat casualty care (blood loss, resuscitation, and brain and other organ system trauma), battle casualties, operational stress, sleep deprivation, and medical countermeasures against biological and chemical agents.

▶CONGRESS

For a listing of relevant congressional committees and subcommittees, please see page 320 or the Appendix.

▶NONGOVERNMENTAL

AcademyHealth, 1150 17th St. N.W., #600 20036; (202) 292-6700. Fax, (202) 292-6800. W. David Helms, Chief Executive Officer.
Web, www.academyhealth.org

Membership: individuals and organizations with an interest in health services research, including health policymakers, universities, private research organizations, professional associations, consulting firms, advocacy organizations, insurers, managed care companies, health care systems, and pharmaceutical companies. Serves as an information clearinghouse on health services research and policy; communicates with policymakers concerning state and federal health policies; works to increase public and private funding for health services research, including comparative effectiveness and public health systems and services research. Offers professional development and training programs for health services researchers and policymakers. Monitors legislation and regulations. (Formerly Academy for Health Services Research and Health Policy.)

American Physiological Society, 9650 Rockville Pike, #330, Bethesda, MD 20814-3991; (301) 634-7118. Fax, (301) 634-7241. Dr. Martin Frank, Executive Director.
Web, www.the-aps.org

Researches how the body and its organ systems function. Promotes scientific research, education, and dissemination of information through publication of peer-reviewed journals; monitors international research. Offers travel fellowships for scientific meetings; encourages minority participation in physiological research. Works to establish standards for the humane care and use of laboratory animals. Publishes fourteen scientific journals and a newsletter.

American Public Health Assn., 800 Eye St. N.W. 20001; (202) 777-2430. Fax, (202) 777-2534. Dr. Georges Benjamin, Executive Director.
General e-mail, comments@apha.org

Web, www.apha.org

Membership: health providers, educators, environmentalists, policymakers, and health officials at all levels working both within and outside of governmental organizations and educational institutions. Works to protect communities from serious, preventable health threats. Strives to ensure that community-based health promotion and disease prevention activities and preventive health services are universally accessible in the United States. Develops standards for scientific procedures in public health.

American Trauma Society, 7611 S. Osborne Rd., #202, Upper Marlboro, MD 20772-2656; (301) 574-4300. Fax, (301) 574-4301. Harry Teter, Executive Director.

General e-mail, info@amtrauma.org

Web, www.amtrauma.org

Seeks to prevent trauma and improve its treatment. Coordinates programs aimed at reducing the incidence and severity of trauma; sponsors research; provides training to nurses and others involved in the trauma field. Monitors legislation and regulations.

Center for Applied Proteomics and Molecular Medicine (*George Mason University*), *MSN 4E3, 10900 University Blvd., Manassas, VA 20110; (703) 993-9526. Fax, (703) 993-4288. Lance Liotta, Co-Director; Emanuel Petricoin III, Co-Director.*

General e-mail, proteomics@gmu.edu

Web, www.gmu.edu/departments/lifesciences/proteomics

Researches blood-based protein biomarker discovery and molecular analysis of tissue in order to tailor treatment to individual patients. Participates in clinical trials.

Foundation for the National Institutes of Health, *9650 Rockville Pike, Bethesda, MD 20814-3999; (301) 402-5311. Fax, (301) 480-2752. Amy Porter, Executive Director.*

General e-mail, foundation@fnih.org

Web, www.fnih.org

Established by Congress to support the NIH's mission of developing new knowledge through biomedical research. Works to foster collaborative relationships in education, research, and related activities between the NIH, industry, academia, and nonprofit organizations; supports basic and clinical research to advance medical knowledge; supports training and advanced education programs for future researchers; and invests in educational programs related to medical research.

Howard Hughes Medical Institute, *4000 Jones Bridge Rd., Chevy Chase, MD 20815-6789; (301) 215-8500. Fax, (301) 215-8863. Thomas R. Cech, President.*

Web, www.hhmi.org

Conducts biomedical research programs in major academic medical centers, hospitals, and universities. Areas of research include cell biology, computational biology, genetics, immunology, neuroscience, and structural biology. Maintains a grants program in science education, including precollege, undergraduate, graduate, and postgraduate levels. Supports selected biomedical researchers in foreign countries.

Institute for Alternative Futures (IAF), *100 N. Pitt St., #235, Alexandria, VA 22314-3134; (703) 684-5880. Fax, (703) 684-0640. Jonathan Peck, President.*

General e-mail, futurist@altfutures.com

Web, www.altfutures.com

Research and educational organization that explores the implications of scientific developments and facilitates planning efforts. Works with state and local governments, Congress, international organizations, federal government, and regional associations; conducts seminars. Interests include pharmaceutical research, health care, telecommunications, artificial intelligence, energy, the environment, and sustainability.

Institute of Medicine, *500 5th St. N.W. 20001; (202) 334-3300. Fax, (202) 334-3851. Harvey V. Fineberg, President. Library, (202) 334-2125. Press, (202) 334-2138.*

General e-mail, iomwww@nas.edu

Web, www.iom.edu

Seeks to improve health nationally; provides evidence-based advice to policymakers, health professionals, the private sector, and the public. National Academy of Sciences George E. Brown Jr. Library open to the public by appointment.

Johns Hopkins University Applied Physics Laboratory, *Biomedicine Facilities, 11100 Johns Hopkins Rd., Laurel, MD 20723-6099; (240) 228-5000. Fax, (240) 228-1093. Dr. Dexter G. Smith, Biomedicine Business Area Executive, ext. 5879. Information, (240) 228-5021.*

Web, www.jhuapl.edu/areas/biomed/index.asp

Research and development organization that seeks to improve warfighter survivability, sustainment, and performance through battlefield trauma prevention and mitigation, along with medical device evaluation and development. Programs include improvement of soldier protection equipment, the development of a neurally integrated upper extremity prosthetic, and blast-related traumatic brain injury research.

National Institute of Environmental Health Sciences (*National Institutes of Health*), *31 Center Dr., #B1C02, MSC 2256, Bethesda, MD 20892-2256; (301) 496-7719. Fax, (301) 496-0563. Dr. Linda S. Birnbaum, Director.*

General e-mail, webcenter@niehs.nih.gov

Web, www.niehs.nih.gov

Conducts and supports research on the human effects of various environmental exposures, expanding the scientific basis for making public health decisions based on the potential toxicity of environmental agents. (Most operations located in Research Triangle, N.C.)

National Sleep Foundation, *1522 K St. N.W., #500 20005-1253; (202) 347-3471. Fax, (202) 347-3472. David Cloud, Chief Executive Director.*

General e-mail, nsf@sleepfoundation.org

Web, www.sleepfoundation.org

Supports sleep-related public education and research to understand sleep problems and sleep disorders, including insomnia, sleep apnea, and narcolepsy. Works to prevent sleep-related accidents, especially those that involve driving. Monitors legislation and regulations related to sleep, alertness, and safety, such as hours-of-service rules for commercial drivers.

Obesity Society, *8630 Fenton St., #814, Silver Spring, MD 20910; (301) 563-6526. Fax, (301) 563-6595. Ann Kenworthy, Executive Vice President (Interim).*

Web, www.naaso.org

Promotes research, education, and advocacy to better understand, prevent, and treat obesity. Informs the medical community and the public of new advances.

Research!America, *1101 King St., #520, Alexandria, VA 22314-2960; (703) 739-2577. Fax, (703) 739-2372. Mary Woolley, President. Information, (800) 366-2873.*
General e-mail, info@researchamerica.org

Web, www.researchamerica.org

Membership: academic institutions, professional societies, voluntary health organizations, corporations, and individuals interested in promoting medical research. Provides information on the benefits of medical and health research and seeks to increase funding for research.

SRI International, *Washington Office, 1100 Wilson Blvd., #2800, Arlington, VA 22209; (703) 524-2053. Fax, (703) 247-8569. Toni Linz, Director.*
Web, www.sri.com

Research and consulting organization. Conducts studies on biotechnology, genetic engineering, drug metabolism, cancer, toxicology, disease control systems, and other areas of basic and applied research; monitors international research. (Headquarters in Menlo Park, Calif.)

Alternative Medicine

►AGENCIES

Food and Drug Administration (FDA), *(Health and Human Services Dept.), Center for Food Safety and Applied Nutrition, 5100 Paint Branch Pkwy., College Park, MD 20740-3835; (301) 436-1600. Fax, (301) 436-2668. Dr. Stephen F. Sundlof, Director.*
General e-mail, consumer@fda.gov

Web, www.cfsan.fda.gov

Develops standards for dietary supplements taken as part of alternative medicine treatments. Conducts research about dietary supplements and nutrition in general.

National Institutes of Health (NIH), *(Health and Human Services Dept.), National Center for Complementary and Alternative Medicine, 31 Center Dr., Bldg. 31, #2B11, MSC-2182, Bethesda, MD 20892-2182; (301) 435-6826. Fax, (301) 435-6549. Dr. Josephine Briggs, Director. Information, (888) 644-6226. TTY, (866) 464-3615. Clearinghouse International, (301) 519-3153.*
General e-mail, nccam-info@nccam.nih.gov

Web, www.nccam.nih.gov

Conducts research for the government on complementary and alternative medicine. Works with the Food and Drug Administration (FDA) to develop regulations for the research and use of alternative medicine.

►NONGOVERNMENTAL

American Assn. for Health Freedom, *1350 Constitution Ave. N.W., 5th Floor 20036; (202) 467-1985. Gretchen Dubeau, Executive Director. Toll-free, (800) 230-2762.*

General e-mail, office@healthfreedom.net

Web, www.healthfreedom.net

Advocates on behalf of health care practitioners who use alternative therapies in patient care. Promotes a comprehensive approach to health and medical freedom for both physicians and patients. Monitors legislation and regulations. (Formerly the American Preventive Medical Assn.)

American Assn. of Naturopathic Physicians, *4435 Wisconsin Ave. N.W., #403 20016; (202) 237-8150. Fax, (202) 237-8152. Karen Howard, Executive Director. Toll-free, (866) 538-2267.*
General e-mail, member.services@naturopathic.org

Web, www.naturopathic.org

Membership: naturopathic physicians who are licensed as primary health care providers. Promotes the combination of modern medicine and natural and traditional therapies, including therapeutic nutrition, botanical medicine, homeopathy, and natural childbirth.

American Music Therapy Assn., *8455 Colesville Rd., #1000, Silver Spring, MD 20910; (301) 589-3300. Fax, (301) 589-5175. Andrea Farbman, Executive Director.*
General e-mail, info@musictherapy.org

Web, www.musictherapy.org

Promotes the therapeutic use of music by approving degree programs and clinical training sites for therapists, setting standards for certification of music therapists, and conducting research in the music therapy field.

National Center for Homeopathy, *801 N. Fairfax St., #306, Alexandria, VA 22314; (703) 548-7790. Fax, (703) 548-7792. Sharon Stevenson, Executive Director.*
General e-mail, info@nationalcenterforhomeopathy.org

Web, www.nationalcenterforhomeopathy.org

Promotes health through homeopathy. Seeks to educate the public about homeopathic medicine and increase its availability in the United States.

Arthritis

►AGENCIES

National Institute of Arthritis and Musculoskeletal and Skin Diseases *(National Institutes of Health), 31 Center Dr., Bldg. 31, #4C32, MSC-2350, Bethesda, MD 20892-2350; (301) 496-4353. Fax, (301) 402-3607. Dr. Stephen I. Katz, Director. Information, (301) 496-8190.*
Web, www.niams.nih.gov

Conducts and funds research on arthritis, rheumatic, skin, muscle, and bone diseases and musculoskeletal disorders. Funds national arthritis centers.

National Institute of Arthritis and Musculoskeletal and Skin Diseases *(National Institutes of Health), Information Clearinghouse, 1 AMS Circle, Bethesda, MD 20892-3675; (301) 495-4484. Fax, (301) 718-6366. Vacant, Project Manager. TTY, (301) 565-2966. Toll-free, (877) 226-4267.*

General e-mail, niamsinfo@mail.nih.gov

Web, www.niams.nih.gov

Supports medical research into the causes, treatment, and prevention of diseases of the bones, muscles, joints, and skin. Provides general information on health conditions and referrals to organizations.

Blood and Bone Marrow

►AGENCIES

Health Resources and Services Administration *(Health and Human Services Dept.), Health Care Systems Bureau: Transplantation, 5600 Fishers Lane, #12C-06, Rockville, MD 20857; (301) 443-7577. Fax, (301) 594-6095. Richard Durbin, Director (Acting).*
Web, www.organdonor.gov

Administers the National Marrow Donor Program, which maintains a registry of potential unrelated bone marrow donors.

National Heart, Lung, and Blood Institute *(National Institutes of Health), Blood Diseases and Resources, 6701 Rockledge Dr., #9030, MSC-7950, Bethesda, MD 20892-7950; (301) 435-0080. Fax, (301) 480-0867. Dr. Keith Hoots, Director.*
Web, www.nhlbi.nih.gov/about/dbdr

Administers and conducts research and training programs to improve the diagnosis, prevention, and treatment of blood diseases and related disorders. Works to ensure the efficient and safe use and adequate supply of high-quality blood and blood products.

National Heart, Lung, and Blood Institute *(National Institutes of Health), Health Information Center, P.O. Box 30105, Bethesda, MD 20824-0105; (301) 592-8573. Fax, (301) 592-8563. Press, (301) 496-4236. TTY, (240) 629-3255. General e-mail, nhlbinfo@nhlbi.nih.gov*
Web, www.nhlbi.nih.gov/health/infoctr

Provides public and patient education materials on the prevention and treatment of heart, lung, and blood diseases. Issues clinical practice guidelines for health professionals.

National Heart, Lung, and Blood Institute *(National Institutes of Health), Transfusion Medicine and Cellular Therapeutic Branch, 6701 Rockledge Dr., #9030, MSC-7950, Bethesda, MD 20892-7950; (301) 435-0065. Fax, (301) 480-1067. Dr. Simone Glynn, Director.*
Web, www.nhlbi.nih.gov/about/dbdr

Supports research and research training in transfusion medicine, stem cell biology and disease, clinical cellular medicine, and blood supply adequacy and safety.

National Institute of Diabetes and Digestive and Kidney Diseases *(National Institutes of Health), Hematology, 6707 Democracy Blvd., MSC-5458, Bethesda, MD 20892-5458; (301) 594-7717. Fax, (301) 480-3510. Dr. Daniel Wright, Director. Press, (301) 496-3585.*
Web, www.niddk.nih.gov

Supports basic research on and clinical studies of the states of blood cell formation, mobilization, and release. Interests include anemia associated with chronic diseases, iron and white blood cell metabolism, and genetic control of hemoglobin.

Warren Grant Magnuson Clinical Center *(National Institutes of Health), Transfusion Medicine, 10 Center Dr., Bldg. 10, #1C711, MSC-1184, Bethesda, MD 20892-1184; (301) 496-9702. Fax, (301) 402-1360. Dr. Harvey G. Klein, Chief. Information, (301) 496-4506. Press, (301) 496-2563.*
Web, www.cc.nih.gov/dtm/index.html

Supplies blood and blood components for research and patient care. Provides training programs and conducts research in the preparation and transfusion of blood and blood products. Research topics include hepatitis, automated cell separation, immunohematology, and AIDS transmittal through transfusions.

►NONGOVERNMENTAL

AABB, *8101 Glenbrook Rd., Bethesda, MD 20814-2749; (301) 907-6977. Fax, (301) 907-6895. Karen Shoos Lipton, Executive Officer. Press, (301) 215-6496.*
General e-mail, aabb@aabb.org

Web, www.aabb.org

Membership: hospital and community blood centers, transfusion and transplantation services, and individuals involved in transfusion and transplantation medicine and related biological therapies. Develops and implements standards, accreditation and educational programs, and services that optimize patient and donor care and safety. Encourages the voluntary donation of blood and other tissues and organs through education and public information. (Formerly the American Assn. of Blood Banks.)

American Red Cross, *National Headquarters, 2025 E St. N.W. 20006-5009; (202) 737-8300. Gail J. McGovern, Chief Executive Officer. Press, (202) 303-5551.*
Web, www.redcross.org

Humanitarian relief and health education organization chartered by Congress; provides services in the United States and internationally. Collects blood and maintains blood centers; conducts research; operates the national bone marrow registry and a rare-donor registry; operates transfusion alternative program. Conducts training programs in nursing and first aid; trains volunteers. Serves as U.S. member of the International Federation of Red Cross and Red Crescent Societies.

Cancer

►AGENCIES

National Cancer Institute *(National Institutes of Health), 31 Center Dr., Bldg. 31, #11A48, MSC-2590, Bethesda, MD 20892-2590; (301) 496-5615. Fax, (301) 402-0338. Dr. John Niederhuber, Director. Press, (301) 496-6641. Toll-free, (800) 422-6237.*
Web, www.cancer.gov

Conducts and funds research on the causes, diagnosis, treatment, prevention, control, and biology of cancer and the rehabilitation of cancer patients; administers the National Cancer Program; coordinates international research activities. Sponsors regional and national cancer information services.

National Cancer Institute *(National Institutes of Health), Cancer Content Management,* 6116 Executive Blvd., #300A, Rockville, MD 20852; (301) 496-9096. Fax, (301) 480-8105. Richard Manrow, Associate Director. Web, www.cancer.gov

Collects and disseminates scientific information on cancer biology, etiology, screening, prevention, treatment, and supportive care. Evaluates and develops new media formats for cancer information.

National Cancer Institute *(National Institutes of Health), Cancer Prevention,* 6130 Executive Blvd., #2040, Bethesda, MD 20892; (301) 496-6616. Fax, (301) 496-9931. Dr. Peter Greenwald, Director. Web, http://prevention.cancer.gov

Seeks to plan, direct, implement, and monitor cancer research focused on early detection, cancer risk, chemo-prevention, and supportive care. Focuses on intervention in the process of carcinogenesis to prevent development into invasive cancer. Supports various approaches, from pre-clinical discovery and development of biomarkers and chemoprevention agents, including pharmaceuticals and micronutrients, to Phase III clinical testing. Programs are carried out with other National Cancer Institute divisions, NIH institutes, and federal and state agencies.

National Cancer Institute *(National Institutes of Health), Translational Research Program,* 6116 Executive Blvd., #7013, MSC-8347, Bethesda, MD 20892-8347; (301) 496-8528. Fax, (301) 408-5046. Dr. Toby T. Hecht, Associate Director (Acting). Web, http://trp.cancer.gov

Encourages the study of organ-specific cancers and leukemia. Promotes and funds interdisciplinary research and information exchange between basic and clinical science to move basic research findings from the laboratory to applied settings involving patients and populations. Encourages laboratory and clinical scientists to work collaboratively to plan, design, and implement research programs on cancer prevention, detection, diagnosis, treatment, and control.

President's Cancer Panel, *c/o National Cancer Institute,* 6116 Executive Blvd., #220, MSC-8349, Bethesda, MD 20892-8349; (301) 451-9399. Fax, (301) 435-1832. Dr. Abby Sandler, Executive Secretary. General e-mail, pcp-r@mail.nih.gov

Web, http://pcp.cancer.gov

Presidentially appointed committee that monitors and evaluates the National Cancer Program; reports to the president and Congress.

▶**NONGOVERNMENTAL**

American Cancer Society, *Cancer Action Network, Washington Office,* 901 E St. N.W., #500 20004; (202)

661-5700. Fax, (202) 661-5750. Daniel E. Smith, President. Web, www.acscan.org

Supports evidence-based policy and legislation designed to eliminate cancer as a major health problem; works to encourage elected officials and candidates to make cancer a top national priority. Monitor legislation and regulations. (Headquarters in Atlanta, Ga.)

American Institute for Cancer Research, 1759 R St. N.W. 20009-2583; (202) 328-7744. Fax, (202) 328-7226. Marilyn Gentry, Executive Director. Information, (800) 843-8114. General e-mail, aicrweb@aicr.org

Web, www.aicr.org

Funds cancer research in areas of diet and nutrition; sponsors education programs. Library open to the public by appointment.

American Society for Radiation and Oncology (ASTRO), 8280 Willow Oaks Corporate Dr., #500, Fairfax, VA 22031; (703) 502-1550. Fax, (703) 502-7852. Laura Thevenot, Chief Executive Officer. Toll-free, (800) 962-7876. Web, www.astro.org

Radiation oncology, biology, and physics organization that seeks to improve patient care through education, clinical practice, the advancement of science, and advocacy.

American Society of Clinical Oncology, 2318 Mill Rd., #800, Alexandria, VA 22314; (571) 483-1300. Fax, (571) 366-9530. Richard C. Schilsky, President. General e-mail, asco@asco.org

Web, www.asco.org

Membership: physicians and scientists specializing in cancer prevention, treatment, education, and research. Promotes exchange of information in clinical research and patient care relating to all stages of cancer; monitors international research.

Assn. of Community Cancer Centers, 11600 Nebel St., #201, Rockville, MD 20852-2557; (301) 984-9496. Fax, (301) 770-1949. Christian Downs, Executive Director. Web, www.accc-cancer.org

Membership: individuals from community hospitals involved in multidisciplinary cancer programs, including physicians, administrators, nurses, medical directors, pharmacists, and other members of the cancer care team.

Breast Cancer Network of Strength, *Mid-Atlantic Affiliate,* 441 Carlisle Dr., Suite C, Herndon, VA 20170; (703) 437-9595. Fax, (703) 437-8387. Traci Richards, Executive Director. General e-mail, mid-atlantic@networkofstrength.org

Web, www.networkofstrength.org/mid-atlantic

Supports people touched by breast cancer through peer support, educational programs, local resources, and advocacy to improve the quality of health care. (Headquarters in Chicago, Ill.)

Candlelighters Childhood Cancer Foundation, *10400 Connecticut Ave., #205, Kensington, MD 20895 (mailing address: P.O. Box 498, Kensington, MD 20895-0498); (301) 962-3520. Fax, (301) 962-3521. Ruth Hoffman, Executive Director. Information, (800) 366-2223. General e-mail, staff@candlelighters.org*

Web, www.candlelighters.org

Membership: families of children with cancer, survivors of childhood cancer, and health and education professionals. Serves as an information and educational network; sponsors self-help groups for parents of children and adolescents with cancer. Monitors legislation and regulations.

Leukemia and Lymphoma Society of America, *National Area Chapter, 5845 Richmond Hwy., #800, Alexandria, VA 22303; (703) 399-2900. Fax, (703) 399-2901. Donna McKelvey, Executive Director. Information, (800) 955-4572.*

Web, www.lls.org

Voluntary health organization that funds blood cancer research, education, and patient services. Seeks to find cures for leukemia, lymphoma, Hodgkin's disease, and myeloma, and to improve the quality of life of patients and their families. Local chapters provide leukemia and lymphoma patients with disease and treatment information, financial assistance, counseling, and referrals. (Headquarters in White Plains, New York.)

National Breast Cancer Coalition, *1101 17th St., N.W., #1300 20036; (202) 296-7477. Fax, (202) 265-6854. Frances M. Visco, President. Toll-free, (800) 622-2838.*

Web, www.stopbreastcancer.org

Membership: organizations, local coalitions, and individuals. Advocates increased funding for research to prevent and treat breast cancer; promotes better access to screening and care; conducts training for breast cancer activists.

National Coalition for Cancer Survivorship, *1010 Wayne Ave., #770, Silver Spring, MD 20910-5600; (301) 650-9127. Fax, (301) 565-9670. Ellen L. Stovall, President. Toll-free information and publications, (877) 622-7937. General e-mail, info@canceradvocacy.org*

Web, www.canceradvocacy.org

Membership: survivors of cancer (newly diagnosed to long-term), their families and friends, health care providers, and support organizations. Disseminates information, including the Cancer Survival Toolbox, about living with cancer diagnosis and treatment; works to reduce cancer-based discrimination in employment and insurance.

Ovarian Cancer National Alliance, *910 17th St. N.W., #1190 20006; (202) 331-1332. Fax, (202) 331-2292. Karen Orloff Kaplan, Chief Executive Officer. Toll-free, (866) 399-6262.*

General e-mail, ocna@ovariancancer.org

Web, www.ovariancancer.org

Advocates at the federal and state levels for adequate and sustained funding for ovarian cancer research and awareness programs. Promotes legislation that would improve the quality of life and access to care for all cancer patients.

Diabetes, Digestive Diseases

▶AGENCIES

National Diabetes Information Clearinghouse *(National Institutes of Health), 1 Information Way, Bethesda, MD 20892-3560; (800) 860-8747. Fax, (703) 738-4929. April Borchevsky, Senior Information Specialist. TTY, (866) 549-1162.*

General e-mail, ndic@info.niddk.nih.gov

Web, www.diabetes.niddk.nih.gov

Provides health professionals and the public with information on the symptoms, causes, treatments, and general nature of diabetes.

National Digestive Diseases Information Clearinghouse *(National Institutes of Health), 2 Information Way, Bethesda, MD 20892-3570; (800) 891-5389. Fax, (703) 738-4929. Michael Walker, Senior Information Specialist.*

General e-mail, nddic@info.niddk.nih.gov

Web, www.digestive.niddk.nih.gov

Provides health professionals and the public with information on the symptoms, causes, treatments, and general nature of digestive diseases and ailments.

National Institute of Diabetes and Digestive and Kidney Diseases *(National Institutes of Health), Diabetes, Endocrinology, and Metabolic Diseases, 31 Center Dr., #9A27, MSC-2560, Bethesda, MD 20892-2560; (301) 496-7348. Fax, (301) 480-6792. Judith E. Fradkin, Director. Press, (301) 496-3585.*

Web, www.niddk.nih.gov

Provides research funding and support for basic and clinical research in the areas of type 1 and type 2 diabetes and other metabolic disorders, including cystic fibrosis; endocrinology and endocrine disorders; obesity, neuroendocrinology, and energy balance; and development, metabolism, and basic biology of liver, fat, and endocrine tissues.

National Institute of Diabetes and Digestive and Kidney Diseases *(National Institutes of Health), Digestive Diseases and Nutrition, 31 Center Dr., #9A27, MSC-2560, Bethesda, MD 20892-2560; (301) 496-1333. Fax, (301) 480-7926. Stephen James, Director. Press, (301) 496-3585.*

Web, www.niddk.nih.gov

Awards grants and contracts to support basic nutritional and clinical research on digestive diseases. Conducts and supports research concerning liver and biliary diseases; pancreatic diseases; gastrointestinal disease, including neuroendocrinology, motility, immunology, absorption, and transport in the gastrointestinal tract; nutrient metabolism; obesity; and eating disorders.

▶NONGOVERNMENTAL

American Diabetes Assn. (ADA), *1701 N. Beauregard St., Alexandria, VA 22311; (703) 549-1500. Fax, (703) 836-7439. Larry Hausner, Chief Executive Officer. Information, (800) 232-3472.*

Web, www.diabetes.org

Works to improve access to quality care and to eliminate discrimination against people because of their diabetes. Provides local affiliates with education, information, and referral services. Conducts and funds research on diabetes. Monitors international research. Monitors legislation and regulations.

American Gastroenterological Assn., *4930 Del Ray Ave., Bethesda, MD 20814; (301) 654-2055. Fax, (301) 654-5920. Robert B. Greenberg, Executive Vice President. General e-mail, member@gastro.org*

Web, www.gastro.org

Membership: gastroenterology clinicians, scientists, health care professionals, and educators. Sponsors scientific research on digestive diseases; disseminates information on new methods of prevention and treatment. Monitors legislation and regulations. (Affiliated with the Foundation of Digestive Health and Nutrition.)

Endocrine Society, *8401 Connecticut Ave., #900, Chevy Chase, MD 20815-5817; (301) 941-0200. Fax, (301) 941-0259. Scott Hunt, Executive Director.*

Web, www.endo-society.org

Membership: scientists, doctors, health care educators, clinicians, nurses, and others interested in endocrine glands and their disorders. Promotes endocrinology research and clinical practice; sponsors seminars and conferences; gives awards and travel grants.

Juvenile Diabetes Research Foundation, *Governmental Relations, Washington Office, 1400 K St. N.W., #1212 20005; (202) 371-9746. Fax, (202) 371-2760. Cynthia Rice, Vice President. Information, (800) 533-1868. General e-mail, advocacy@jdrf.org*

Web, www.jdrf.org

Conducts research, education, and public awareness programs aimed at improving the lives of people with type 1 (juvenile) diabetes and finding a cure for diabetes and its related complications. Monitors legislation and regulations. (Headquarters in New York.)

Pediatric/Adolescent Gastroesophageal Reflux Assn. (PAGER), *P.O. Box 486, Buckeystown, MD 21717. Beth Anderson, Director. Message Center, (301) 601-9541. General e-mail, gergroup@aol.com*

Web, www.reflux.org, or in Spanish, www.ReflujoEnNinos.org

Promotes public awareness of pediatric gastroesophageal reflux (GER) and provides support for those who suffer from it. Researches GER and acts as a clearinghouse for information on the disorder.

Family Planning and Population

▶AGENCIES

Agency for International Development (USAID), *Global Health: Population and Reproductive Health, 1300 Pennsylvania Ave. N.W., 3rd Floor 20523-3600; (202) 712-1261. Fax, (202) 216-3485. Scott Radloff, Director. Web, www.usaid.gov/our_work/global_health/pop*

Provides programs in family planning and reproductive health. Conducts related research.

Census Bureau *(Commerce Dept.), Fertility and Family Statistics, 4600 Silver Hill Rd., #7H484C, Suitland, MD 20746-8800; (301) 763-2416. Fax, (301) 457-3500. Martin O'Connell, Branch Chief. Press, (301) 763-3030. Web, www.census.gov*

Provides data and statistics on fertility and family composition. Conducts census and survey research on the number of children, households and living arrangements, and current child spacing patterns of women in the United States, especially working mothers. Conducts studies on child care.

National Institute of Child Health and Human Development *(National Institutes of Health), Center for Population Research, 6100 Executive Blvd., #8B-07, Bethesda, MD 20892-7510; (301) 496-1101. Fax, (301) 496-0962. Dr. Florence P. Haseltine, Director. Press, (301) 496-5133.*

Web, www.nichd.nih.gov

Supports biomedical and behavioral research on reproductive processes influencing human fertility and infertility; develops methods for regulating fertility; evaluates the safety and effectiveness of contraceptive methods; conducts research on the reproductive motivation of individuals and the causes and consequences of population change.

Public Health and Science *(Health and Human Services Dept.), Population Affairs, 1101 Wootton Pkwy., #700, Rockville, MD 20852; (240) 453-2800. Fax, (240) 453-2801. Dr. Susan Orr, Deputy Assistant Secretary. General e-mail, opa@hhs.gov*

Web, www.hhs.gov/opa

Responsible for Title X Family Planning Program, which provides family planning services, health screening services, and screening for STDs (including HIV) to all who want and need them, with priority given to low-income persons; the Title XX Adolescent Family Life Program, including demonstration projects to develop, implement, and evaluate program interventions to promote abstinence from sexual activity among adolescents and to provide comprehensive health care, education, and social services to pregnant and parenting adolescents; and for planning, monitoring, and evaluating population research.

Public Health and Science (*Health and Human Services Dept.*), *Population Affairs: Clearinghouse,* P.O. Box 30686, Bethesda, MD 20824-0686; (866) 640-7827. Fax, (866) 592-3299. Nina Corin, Project Director. General e-mail, info@opaclearinghouse.org

Web, www.opaclearinghouse.org

Federally contracted program that collects and disseminates information on family planning, general reproductive health care, and related topics, including adoption, adolescent pregnancy prevention, contraception, HIV/AIDS, sexually transmitted diseases, and abstinence. (Formerly Family Life Information Exchange.)

►**INTERNATIONAL ORGANIZATIONS**

International Bank for Reconstruction and Development (World Bank), *Human Development Network,* 1818 H St. N.W., #G7-702, MSC-G8-801 20433; (202) 473-4946. Fax, (202) 522-3235. Joy Phumaphi, Vice President. Alternate phone, (202) 473-1000. Web, www.worldbank.org

Provides member countries with support for initiatives concerning family planning and population. Promotes a reproductive health approach that integrates family planning, maternal and adolescent health, and prevention of sexually transmitted diseases, especially HIV/AIDS.

►**NONGOVERNMENTAL**

Advocates for Youth, 2000 M St. N.W., #750 20036; (202) 419-3420. Fax, (202) 419-1448. James Wagoner, President. General e-mail, information@advocatesforyouth.org

Web, www.advocatesforyouth.org

Seeks to reduce the incidence of unintended teenage pregnancy and AIDS through public education, training and technical assistance, research, and media programs.

American Society for Reproductive Medicine, *J. Benjamin Younger Office of Public Affairs,* 409 12th St. S.W., #203 20024-2188; (202) 863-2494. Fax, (202) 484-4039. Sean B. Tipton, Public Affairs Director. Web, www.asrm.org/washington/maingov.html

Works to advance knowledge in infertility, reproductive medicine, and biology. Supports education activities for medical professionals and the public. Monitors legislation and regulations in reproductive medicine. (Headquarters in Birmingham, Ala.).

Guttmacher Institute, *Public Policy, Washington Office,* 1301 Connecticut Ave. N.W., #700 20036-3902; (202) 296-4012. Fax, (202) 223-5756. Cory L. Richards, Executive Vice President. General e-mail, policyinfo@guttmacher.org

Web, www.guttmacher.org

Conducts research, policy analysis, and public education in reproductive health, fertility regulation, population, and related areas of U.S. and international health. (Headquarters in New York.)

National Abortion Federation (NAF), 1660 L St. N.W., #450 20036; (202) 667-5881. Fax, (202) 667-5890. Vicki Saporta, President. Toll-free, (800) 772-9100. General e-mail, naf@prochoice.org

Web, www.prochoice.org

Federation of facilities providing abortion services in the United States and Canada. Offers information on medical, legal, and social aspects of abortion; sets quality standards for abortion care. Conducts training workshops and seminars. Monitors legislation and regulations.

National Family Planning and Reproductive Health Assn., 1627 K St. N.W., 12th Floor 20006-1702; (202) 293-3114. Fax, (202) 293-1990. Mary Jane Gallagher, President. General e-mail, info@nfprha.org

Web, www.nfprha.org

Represents family planning providers, including nurses, nurse practitioners, administrators, and other health care professionals nationwide. Provides advocacy, education, and training for those in the family planning and reproductive health care field. Interests include family planning for the low-income and uninsured, and reducing rates of unintended pregnancy.

Planned Parenthood Federation of America, *Public Policy, Washington Office,* 1110 Vermont Ave. N.W., #300 20005; (202) 973-4800. Fax, (202) 296-3242. Laurie Rubiner, Vice President. Press, (202) 973-4882. Web, www.plannedparenthood.org

Educational, research, and medical services organization. Washington office conducts research and monitors legislation on fertility-related health topics, including reproductive health, contraception, family planning, international population control, and abortion. (Headquarters in New York accredits affiliated local centers, which offer medical services, birth control, and family planning information.)

Population Action International, 1300 19th St. N.W., #200 20036; (202) 557-3400. Fax, (202) 728-4177. Amy Coen, President. General e-mail, pai@popact.org

Web, www.populationaction.org

Promotes population stabilization through public education and universal access to voluntary family planning. Library open to the public by appointment.

Population Connection, 2120 L St. N.W., #500 20037; (202) 332-2200. Fax, (202) 332-2302. John Seager, President. General e-mail, info@populationconnection.org

Web, www.populationconnection.org

Membership: persons interested in sustainable world populations. Promotes the expansion of domestic and international family planning programs; supports a voluntary population stabilization policy and women's access to abortion and family planning services; works to protect the earth's resources and environment. (Formerly Zero Population Growth.)

Population-Environment Balance, *2000 P St. N.W., #600 20036; (202) 955-5700. Fax, (202) 955-6161. Aaron Beckwith, Vice President.*
General e-mail, uspop@us.net
Web, www.balance.org

Grassroots organization that advocates U.S. population stabilization to safeguard the environment.

Population Institute, *107 2nd St. N.E. 20002; (202) 544-3300. Fax, (202) 544-0068. Robert Walker, Executive Vice President.*
General e-mail, info@populationinstitute.org
Web, www.populationinstitute.org

Encourages leaders of developing nations to balance population growth through resource management; works with leaders of industrial nations to help achieve a balance between population and natural resources. Seeks to slow excessive population growth. Works with leaders in developing and industrialized nations to help achieve a balance among the world population, the global environment, and natural resources.

Population Reference Bureau, *1875 Connecticut Ave. N.W., #520 20009-5728; (202) 483-1100. Fax, (202) 328-3937. William P. Butz, President. Toll-free, (800) 877-9881.*
General e-mail, popref@prb.org
Web, www.prb.org

Educational organization engaged in information dissemination, training, and policy analysis on domestic and international population trends and issues. Interests include international development and family planning programs, the environment, and U.S. social and economic policy. Library open to the public.

Genetic Disorders

▶**AGENCIES**

Health Resources and Services Administration *(Health and Human Services Dept.), Genetic Services: Maternal and Child Health, 5600 Fishers Lane, #18A-19, Rockville, MD 20857; (301) 443-1080. Fax, (301) 480-1312. Dr. Michele A. Lloyd-Puryear, Chief. Alternate fax, (301) 594-0878.*
Web, www.mchb.hrsa.gov

Awards funds, including demonstration grants, to develop or enhance regional, local, and state genetic screening, diagnostic, counseling, and follow-up programs; assists states in their newborn screening programs; provides funding for regional hemophilia treatment centers. Supports comprehensive care for individuals and families with Cooley's anemia, and those with sickle cell anemia identified through newborn screening. Supports educational programs.

National Heart, Lung, and Blood Institute *(National Institutes of Health), Blood Diseases Program, 6701 Rockledge Dr., #90930, Bethesda, MD 20892-7950; (301) 435-0050. Fax, (301) 480-0867. Dr. Charles Peterson, Director.*
Web, www.nhlbi.nih.gov

Supports research into the diagnosis and treatment of genetic blood disorders and continuing education programs for professionals and the public.

National Human Genome Research Institute *(National Institutes of Health), 31 Center Dr., Bldg. 31, #4B09, MSC-2152, Bethesda, MD 20892-2152; (301) 496-0844. Fax, (301) 402-0837. Dr. Alan Guttmacher, Director (Acting). Information, (301) 402-0911.*
Web, www.genome.gov

Conducts and funds a broad range of studies aimed at understanding the structure and function of the human genome and its role in health and disease. Supports the development of resources and technology that will accelerate genome research and its application to human health. Studies the ethical, legal, and social implications of genome research, and supports the training of investigators, as well as the dissemination of genome information to the public and to health professionals.

National Institute of Allergy and Infectious Diseases *(National Institutes of Health), Allergy, Immunology, and Transplantation, 6610 Rockledge Dr., #3111, Bethesda, MD 20892-7640; (301) 496-1886. Fax, (301) 402-0175. Dr. Daniel Rotrosen, Director. Information, (301) 496-5717.*
Web, www3.niaid.nih.gov/about/organization/dait

Focuses on the immune system as it functions to maintain health and as it malfunctions to produce disease; interests include allergies, asthma, immune deficiencies, transplantation of organs and tissue, and genetics. Monitors international research.

National Institute of Diabetes and Digestive and Kidney Diseases *(National Institutes of Health), Hematology, 6707 Democracy Blvd., MSC-5458, Bethesda, MD 20892-5458; (301) 594-7717. Fax, (301) 480-3510. Dr. Daniel Wright, Director. Press, (301) 496-3585.*
Web, www.niddk.nih.gov

Supports basic research on and clinical studies of the states of blood cell formation, mobilization, and release. Interests include anemia associated with chronic diseases, iron and white blood cell metabolism, and genetic control of hemoglobin.

National Institute of General Medical Sciences *(National Institutes of Health), Genetics and Developmental Biology, 45 Center Dr., #2AS25N, MSC-6200, Bethesda, MD 20892-6200; (301) 594-0943. Fax, (301) 480-2228. Judith H. Greenberg, Director.*
Web, www.nigms.nih.gov/about/overview/gdb.htm

Supports research and research training in genetics.

National Institutes of Health (NIH), *(Health and Human Services Dept.), Biotechnology Activities, 6705*

Rockledge Dr., #750, MSC-7985, Bethesda, MD 20892-7985; (301) 496-9838. Fax, (301) 496-9839. Dr. Amy P. Patterson, Director.

Web, http://oba.od.nih.gov/oba/index.html

Reviews requests submitted to the NIH involving genetic testing, recombinant DNA technology, and xenotransplantation, and implements research guidelines.

▶NONGOVERNMENTAL

Center for Sickle Cell Disease *(Howard University), 1840 7th St. N.W. 20001; (202) 865-8284. Fax, (202) 232-6719. Dr. Victor Gordeuk, Director.*

Web, www.sicklecell.howard.edu

Screens and tests for sickle cell disease; conducts research; promotes public education and community involvement; provides counseling and patient care.

Cystic Fibrosis Foundation, *6931 Arlington Rd., #200, Bethesda, MD 20814; (301) 951-4422. Fax, (301) 951-6378. Robert J. Beall, President. Information, (800) 344-4823.*

General e-mail, info@cff.org

Web, www.cff.org

Conducts research on cystic fibrosis, a genetic disease affecting the respiratory and digestive systems. Focuses on medical research to identify a cure and to improve quality of life for those living with cystic fibrosis.

Genetic Alliance, *4301 Connecticut Ave. N.W., #404 20008-2369; (202) 966-5557. Fax, (202) 966-8553. Sharon Terry, President.*

General e-mail, info@geneticalliance.org

Web, www.geneticalliance.org

Coalition of government, industry, advocacy organizations, and private groups that seeks to advance genetic research and its applications. Promotes increased funding for research, improved access to services, and greater support for emerging technologies, tests, and treatments. Advocates on behalf of individuals and families living with genetic conditions.

Genetics Society of America, *9650 Rockville Pike, Bethesda, MD 20814; (301) 634-7300. Fax, (301) 634-7079. Sherry Marts, Executive Director. Toll-free, (866) 486-4363.*

General e-mail, smarts@genetics-gsa.org

Web, www.genetics-gsa.org

Facilitates professional cooperation among persons working in genetics and related sciences. Advocates for research funding; sponsors meetings.

Kennedy Institute of Ethics *(Georgetown University), Healy Hall, 37th and O Sts. N.W., 4th Floor 20057; (202) 687-8099. Fax, (202) 687-8089. G. Madison Powers, Director. Library, (202) 687-3885. Toll-free, United States and Canada, (888) 246-3849 and (888) 436-3849.*

General e-mail, kicourse@georgetown.edu

Web, http://kennedyinstitute.georgetown.edu

Carries out teaching and research on medical ethics, including legal and ethical definitions of death, allocation of health resources, and recombinant DNA and human gene therapy. Sponsors the annual Intensive Bioethics Course. Conducts international programs. Serves as the home of the National Reference Center for Bioethics Literature (http://bioethics.georgetown.edu) and the National Information Resource on Ethics and Human Genetics (http://genthx.georgetown.edu), both supported by the NIH. Provides free reference assistance and bibliographic databases covering all ethical issues in health care, genetics, and biomedical research. Library open to the public.

March of Dimes, *Government Affairs, Washington Office, 1146 19th St. N.W., #600 20036; (202) 659-1800. Fax, (202) 296-2964. Marina L. Weiss, Senior Vice President.*

Web, www.marchofdimes.com

Works to prevent and treat birth defects. Awards grants for research and provides funds for treatment of birth defects. Monitors legislation and regulations. (Headquarters in White Plains, N.Y.)

Heart Disease, Strokes

▶AGENCIES

National Heart, Lung, and Blood Institute *(National Institutes of Health), Cardiovascular Diseases, 6701 Rockledge Dr., #8030, Bethesda, MD 20892-7940; (301) 435-0466. Fax, (301) 480-7971. Sonia Skarlatos, Director (Acting).*

Web, www.nhlbi.nih.gov/about/dcvd/index.htm

Conducts and funds research on the prevention, causes, and treatment of heart and vascular diseases.

National Heart, Lung, and Blood Institute *(National Institutes of Health), Health Information Center, P.O. Box 30105, Bethesda, MD 20824-0105; (301) 592-8573. Fax, (301) 592-8563. Press, (301) 496-4236. TTY, (240) 629-3255.*

General e-mail, nhlbinfo@nhlbi.nih.gov

Web, www.nhlbi.nih.gov/health/infoctr

Acquires, maintains, and disseminates information on cholesterol, high blood pressure, heart attack awareness, and asthma to the public and health professionals. Provides reference and referral services. Library open to the public.

National Institute of Neurological Disorders and Stroke *(National Institutes of Health), 31 Center Dr., Bldg. 31, #8A52, MSC-2540, Bethesda, MD 20892-2540; (301) 496-9746. Fax, (301) 496-0296. Dr. Story Landis, Director. Information, (301) 496-5751. Toll-free, (800) 352-9424.*

Web, www.ninds.nih.gov

Conducts research and disseminates information on the causes, prevention, diagnosis, and treatment of neurological disorders and stroke; supports basic research in related scientific areas. Provides research grants to public and private institutions and individuals. Operates a program of contracts for the funding of research and research-support efforts.

▶NONGOVERNMENTAL

American Heart Assn., Washington Office, 1150 Connecticut Ave. N.W., #300 20036; (202) 785-7900. Fax, (202) 785-7950. Sue A. Nelson, Vice President for Federal Advocacy. Toll-free, (800) 242-8721.
Web, www.americanheart.org

Membership: physicians, scientists, and other interested individuals. Supports research, treatment, and community service programs that provide information about heart disease and stroke; participates in international conferences and research. Monitors legislation and regulations. (Headquarters in Dallas, Texas.)

WomenHeart, 818 18th St. N.W., #930 20006; (202) 728-7199. Fax, (202) 728-7238. Lisa M. Tate, Chief Executive Officer.
General e-mail, mail@womenheart.org

Web, www.womenheart.org

Patient-centered organization that seeks to advance women's heart health through advocacy, community education, and patient support. Comprised of patients and their families, health care providers, advocates, and interested consumers.

HIV and AIDS

▶AGENCIES

Centers for Disease Control and Prevention (CDC), *(Health and Human Services Dept.), Washington Office,* 395 E St. S.W. 20201; (202) 245-0600. Fax, (202) 245-0602. Donald Shriber, Associate Director. Public inquiries, (800) 232-4636.
Web, www.cdc.gov/washington

Conducts research to prevent and control acquired immune deficiency syndrome (AIDS); promotes public awareness through guidelines for health care workers, educational packets for schools, and monthly reports on incidences of AIDS. (Headquarters in Atlanta, Ga.: 1600 Clifton Rd. N.E. 30333.)

Food and Drug Administration (FDA), *(Health and Human Services Dept.), Center for Biologics Evaluation and Research,* 1401 Rockville Pike, #200 North, Rockville, MD 20852-1448 (mailing address: 5515 Security Lane, #7100, Rockville, MD 20852), (301) 827-0372. Fax, (301) 827-0440. Dr. Jesse L. Goodman, Director. Press and publications, (301) 827-2000.
Web, www.fda.gov/cber

Develops testing standards for vaccines, blood supply, and blood products and derivatives to prevent transmission of the human immunodeficiency virus (HIV); regulates biological therapeutics; helps formulate international standards. Serves as the focus for AIDS activities within the FDA.

Food and Drug Administration (FDA), *(Health and Human Services Dept.), Center for Drug Evaluation and Research,* 10903 New Hampshire Ave., Silver Spring, MD 20993; (301) 796-5400. Fax, (301) 847-8752. Dr. Janet Woodcock, Director. Press, (301) 796-4540.
Web, www.fda.gov/cder

Approves new drugs for AIDS and AIDS-related diseases. Reviews and approves applications to investigate and market new drugs; works to harmonize drug approval internationally.

Health Resources and Services Administration *(Health and Human Services Dept.), HIV/AIDS Bureau,* 5600 Fishers Lane, #705, Rockville, MD 20857; (301) 443-1993. Fax, (301) 443-9645. Deborah Parham Hopson, Associate Administrator.
Web, www.hab.hrsa.gov

Administers grants to support health care programs for AIDS patients, including those that reimburse low-income patients for drug expenses. Provides patients with AIDS and HIV-related disorders with ambulatory and community-based care. Conducts AIDS/HIV education and training activities for health professionals.

National Institute of Allergy and Infectious Diseases *(National Institutes of Health), AIDS,* 6700-B Rockledge Dr., #4142, Bethesda, MD 20892-7620; (301) 496-0545. Fax, (301) 402-1505. Dr. Carl Dieffenbach, Director. Toll-free hotline, (800) 342-2437.
Web, www3.niaid.nih.gov/about/organization/daids

Primary institute at the NIH for HIV/AIDS research. Plans, implements, manages, and evaluates programs in fundamental research, discovery, and development of therapies for HIV infection and its complications, and discovery and development of vaccines and other prevention strategies. Conducts a network of AIDS clinical trials and preclinical drug development research. Supports epidemiological studies and research into AIDS vaccines. Studies the pathogenesis of HIV infection.

National Institutes of Health (NIH), *(Health and Human Services Dept.), Office of AIDS Research,* 5635 Fishers Lane, #4000, Rockville, MD 20892 (mailing address: 5635 Fishers Lane, #4000, Rockville, MD 20852); (301) 496-0357. Fax, (301) 496-2119. Jack E. Whitescarver, Director.
Web, www.oar.nih.gov

Responsible for the scientific, budgetary, legislative, and policy elements of the NIH AIDS research program. Plans, coordinates, evaluates, and funds all NIH AIDS research.

Public Health and Science *(Health and Human Services Dept.), HIV/AIDS Policy,* 200 Independence Ave. S.W., #736E 20201; (202) 690-5560. Fax, (202) 690-7560. Christopher H. Bates, Director (Interim). HIV/AIDS Information, http://aids.gov.
Web, www.hhs.gov/ophs/ohap

Coordinates national AIDS policy, sets priorities, recommends funding, and helps implement all Public Health Service HIV programs. Monitors progress of prevention and control programs; serves as a liaison with governmental and private organizations.

Public Health and Science *(Health and Human Services Dept.), Minority Health, 1101 Wootton Pkwy., #600, Rockville, MD 20852; (240) 453-2882. Fax, (240) 453-2883. Dr. Garth Graham, Deputy Assistant Secretary. Information, (800) 444-6472.*
General e-mail, info@omhrc.gov
Web, www.omhrc.gov

Oversees the implementation of the secretary's Task Force on Black and Minority Health and legislative mandates; develops programs to meet the health care needs of minorities; awards grants to coalitions of minority community organizations and to minority AIDS education and prevention projects.

State Dept., *U.S. Global AIDS Coordinator, 2100 Pennsylvania Ave. N.W., Bldg. SA-29, #200 20037 (mailing address: 2201 C St. N.W., Washington, DC 20520); (202) 663-2304. Fax, (202) 663-2979. Vacant, Ambassador. Information, (202) 663-2440. Press, (202) 663-2708.*
General e-mail, SGAC_Public_Affairs@state.gov
Web, www.pepfar.gov

Oversees and coordinates all U.S. international HIV/AIDS activities, including implementation of the President's Emergency Plan for AIDS Relief.

Walter Reed Army Institute of Research *(Defense Dept.), U.S. Military HIV Research Program, 1600 East Gude Dr., Rockville, MD 20850-5318; (301) 251-5083. Fax, (301) 251-5020. Col. Nelson L. Michael, Director. Public affairs, (301) 251-5070.*
General e-mail, info@hivresearch.org
Web, www.hivresearch.org

Conducts HIV research, encompassing vaccine development, prevention, disease surveillance, and care and treatment options.

Warren Grant Magnuson Clinical Center *(National Institutes of Health), Transfusion Medicine, 10 Center Dr., Bldg. 10, #1C711, MSC-1184, Bethesda, MD 20892-1184; (301) 496-9702. Fax, (301) 402-1360. Dr. Harvey G. Klein, Chief. Information, (301) 496-4506. Press, (301) 496-2563.*
Web, www.cc.nih.gov/dtm/index.html

Supplies blood and blood components for patient care and research. Conducts research on diseases transmissible by blood, primarily AIDS and hepatitis.

▶**NONGOVERNMENTAL**

AIDS Action, *1730 M St. N.W., #611 20036; (202) 530-8030. Fax, (202) 530-8031. Rebecca Haag, Executive Director.*
General e-mail, aidsaction@aidsaction.org
Web, www.aidsaction.org

Promotes and monitors legislation on AIDS research and education and on related public policy issues.

AIDS Alliance for Children, Youth, and Families, *1600 K St. N.W., #200 20006; (202) 785-3564. Fax, (202) 785-3579. Carole Preston, Executive Director. Toll-free, (888) 917-2437.*
General e-mail, info@aids-alliance.org
Web, www.aids-alliance.org

Conducts research and disseminates information on health care and HIV issues. Develops and promotes policy aimed at improving the health and welfare of children, youth, and families affected by HIV. Provides training and technical assistance to health care providers and consumers.

American Red Cross, *National Headquarters, 2025 E St. N.W. 20006-5009; (202) 737-8300. Gail J. McGovern, Chief Executive Officer. Press, (202) 303-5551.*
Web, www.redcross.org

Humanitarian relief and health education organization chartered by Congress. Conducts public education campaigns on AIDS. Part of the international Red Cross and Red Crescent movement.

Children's AIDS Fund, *P.O. Box 16433 20041; (703) 433-1560. Fax, (800) 557-8529. Anita M. Smith, President. Toll-free, (866) 829-1560.*
General e-mail, info@childrensaidsfund.org
Web, www.childrensaidsfund.org

Provides care, services, resources, referrals, and education to children and their families affected by HIV disease. Focuses on children from birth through age 24 who are infected with, are orphaned by, or will potentially be orphaned by HIV.

The Foundation for AIDS Research (amfAR), *Public Policy, Washington Office, 1150 17th St. N.W., #406 20036; (202) 331-8600. Fax, (202) 331-8606. Chris Collins, Vice President. Information, (800) 392-6327.*
Web, www.amfar.org

Supports funding for basic biomedical and clinical AIDS research; promotes AIDS prevention education worldwide; advocates effective AIDS-related public policy. Monitors legislation, regulations, and international research. (Headquarters in New York.)

Human Rights Campaign (HRC), *1640 Rhode Island Ave. N.W. 20036; (202) 628-4160. Fax, (202) 347-5323. Joe Solmonese, Executive Director. TTY, (202) 216-1572. Toll-free, (800) 777-4723.*
General e-mail, hrc@hrc.org
Web, www.hrc.org

Promotes legislation to fund AIDS research.

National AIDS Fund, *729 15th St. N.W., 9th Floor 20005-1511; (202) 408-4848. Fax, (202) 408-1818. Kandy Ferree, President.*
Web, www.aidsfund.org

Channels resources to community-based organizations to fight HIV/AIDS at the local level. Provides grants and other support to nearly 400 organizations, principally for prevention efforts.

National Assn. of People with AIDS, *8401 Colesville Rd., #508, Silver Spring, MD 20910; (240) 247-0880. Fax, (240) 247-0574. Frank Oldham Jr., President.*
General e-mail, info@napwa.org

Web, www.napwa.org

Membership: people with AIDS or HIV disease. Provides capacity-building assistance to health departments and to organizations that work with people living with HIV/AIDS; contributes to educational campaigns about AIDS. Programs include AIDSWATCH and National HIV Testing Day.

National Minority AIDS Council, *1931 13th St. N.W. 20009-4432; (202) 483-6622. Fax, (202) 483-1135. Paul A. Kawata, Executive Director.*
General e-mail, info@nmac.org

Web, www.nmac.org

Works to build the capacity of small faith- and community-based organizations delivering HIV/AIDS services in communities of color. Holds national conferences; administers treatment and research programs and training; disseminates electronic and printed resource materials; conducts public policy advocacy.

Infectious Diseases, Allergies

▶**AGENCIES**

National Institute of Allergy and Infectious Diseases *(National Institutes of Health), 31 Center Dr., Bldg. 31, #7A03, MSC-2520, Bethesda, MD 20892-2520; (301) 496-2263. Fax, (301) 496-4409. Dr. Anthony S. Fauci, Director.*
Web, www.niaid.nih.gov

Conducts and funds research on infectious diseases, allergies, and other immunological disorders; biodefense and development of bioterrorism countermeasures; and vaccine development. Sponsors and participates in educational programs and conferences. Participates in international research, especially on AIDS and HIV.

▶**NONGOVERNMENTAL**

Allergy and Asthma Network Mothers of Asthmatics, *2751 Prosperity Ave., #150, Fairfax, VA 22031-4397; (703) 641-9595. Fax, (703) 573-7794. Nancy Sander, President. Information, (800) 878-4403.*
General e-mail, info@aanma.org

Web, www.aanma.org

Membership: families dealing with asthma and allergies. Works to eliminate suffering and death due to asthma, allergies, and related conditions through education, advocacy, and community outreach.

Asthma and Allergy Foundation of America, *1233 20th St. N.W., #402 20036; (202) 466-7643. Fax, (202) 466-8940. Bill McLin, President. Information, (800) 727-8462.*
General e-mail, info@aafa.org

Web, www.aafa.org

Provides information on asthma and allergies; awards research grants to asthma and allergic disease professionals; offers in-service training to allied health professionals, child care providers, and others.

Food Allergy and Anaphylaxis Network (FAAN), *11781 Lee Jackson Hwy., #160, Fairfax, VA 22033-3309; (703) 691-3179. Fax, (703) 691-2713. Anne Munoz-Furlong, Chief Executive Officer. Toll-free, (800) 929-4040.*
General e-mail, faan@foodallergy.org

Web, www.foodallergy.org

Membership: dieticians, nurses, physicians, school staff, government representatives, and members of the food and pharmaceutical industries. Seeks to educate the public about and advance research on food allergies and allergic reactions.

National Center for Biodefense and Infectious Diseases *(George Mason University), MSN 1H8, 10900 University Blvd., Manassas, VA 20110; (703) 993-4271. Fax, (703) 993-4280. Charles Bailey, Director. Alternate phone, (703) 993-8545.*
General e-mail, biodefense@gmu.edu

Web, http://ncbid.gmu.edu

Studies infectious diseases that are emerging worldwide due to an increasingly mobile society. Studies infections caused by biological agents. (Associated with the Department of Molecular and Microbiology at George Mason University.)

National Foundation for Infectious Diseases, *4733 Bethesda Ave., #750, Bethesda, MD 20814-5228; (301) 656-0003. Fax, (301) 907-0878. Leonard Novick, Executive Director.*
General e-mail, info@nfid.org

Web, www.nfid.org

Works to educate the public and health care professionals about the causes, treatment, and prevention of infectious diseases.

Kidney Disease

▶**AGENCIES**

Centers for Medicare and Medicaid Services (CMS), *(Health and Human Services Dept.), Chronic Care Improvement Program, 7500 Security Blvd., C5-05-27, Baltimore, MD 21244-1850; (410) 786-3000. Fax, (410) 786-0765. Vacant, Administrator. TTY, (866) 226-1819. Local TTY, (410) 786-0727. Public Affairs, (202) 690-6145.*
Web, www.cms.hhs.gov

Administers coverage policy for Medicare persons with renal disease, chronic kidney failure, and the Program for All-Inclusive Care for the Elderly (PACE). Coordinates coverage under new treatment methods. (Formerly the Health Care Financing Administration.)

National Institute of Allergy and Infectious Diseases *(National Institutes of Health), Allergy, Immunology, and Transplantation,* 6610 Rockledge Dr., #3111, Bethesda, MD 20892-7640; (301) 496-1886. Fax, (301) 402-0175. Dr. Daniel Rotrosen, Director. Information, (301) 496-5717.
Web, www3.niaid.nih.gov/about/organization/dait

Focuses on the immune system as it functions to maintain health and as it malfunctions to produce disease; interests include allergies, asthma, immune deficiencies, transplantation of organs and tissue, and genetics. Monitors international research.

National Institute of Diabetes and Digestive and Kidney Diseases *(National Institutes of Health), Kidney, Urologic, and Hematologic Diseases,* 6707 Democracy Blvd., #625, Bethesda, MD 20892; (301) 496-6325. Fax, (301) 480-3510. Dr. Robert Star, Director. Information, (301) 594-7717. Press, (301) 496-3585.
Web, www.niddk.nih.gov

Funds research on the prevention, diagnosis, and treatment of renal disorders. Conducts research and reviews grant proposals concerning maintenance therapy for persons with chronic kidney, urologic, and renal diseases.

National Institute of Diabetes and Digestive and Kidney Diseases *(National Institutes of Health), National Kidney and Urologic Diseases Information Clearinghouse,* 3 Information Way, Bethesda, MD 20892-3580; (301) 654-4415. Fax, (703) 738-4929. Darlene Kerr, Project Manager. Information, (800) 891-5390. Press, (301) 496-3585.
Web, http://kidney.niddk.nih.gov

Supplies health care providers and the public with information on the symptoms, causes, treatments, and general nature of kidney and urologic diseases.

▶ **NONGOVERNMENTAL**

American Kidney Fund, 6110 Executive Blvd., #1010, Rockville, MD 20852; (301) 881-3052. Fax, (301) 881-0898. LaVarne A. Burton, Executive Director. Information, (800) 638-8299.
General e-mail, helpline@kidneyfund.org
Web, www.kidneyfund.org

Voluntary health organization that gives financial assistance to kidney disease victims. Disseminates public service announcements and public education materials; sponsors research grants and conferences for professionals; promotes organ donation for transplantation.

National Kidney Foundation, *Government Relations, Washington Office,* 1401 K St. N.W., #702 20005; (202) 216-9257. Fax, (202) 216-9258. Troy Zimmerman, Director. Information, (800) 889-9559.
General e-mail, info@kidney.org
Web, www.kidney.org

Supports funding for kidney dialysis and other forms of treatment for kidney disease; provides information on detection and screening of kidney diseases; supports organ

transplantation programs. Monitors legislation, regulations, and international research. (Headquarters in New York.)

Lung Diseases

▶ **AGENCIES**

National Heart, Lung, and Blood Institute *(National Institutes of Health), Health Information Center,* P.O. Box 30105, Bethesda, MD 20824-0105; (301) 592-8573. Fax, (301) 592-8563. Press, (301) 496-4236. TTY, (240) 629-3255.
General e-mail, nhlbinfo@nhlbi.nih.gov
Web, www.nhlbi.nih.gov/health/infoctr

Acquires, maintains, and disseminates information on asthma and other lung ailments. Provides reference and referral services.

National Heart, Lung, and Blood Institute *(National Institutes of Health), Lung Diseases,* 6701 Rockledge Dr., #10042, Bethesda, MD 20892; (301) 435-0233. Fax, (301) 480-3557. James P. Kiley, Director.
Web, www.nhlbi.nih.gov

Plans and directs research and training programs in lung diseases, including research on causes, treatments, prevention, and health education.

▶ **NONGOVERNMENTAL**

American Lung Assn., 1301 Pennsylvania Ave. N.W., #800 20004-1725; (202) 785-3355. Fax, (202) 452-1805. Charles D. Connor, President; Paul Billings, Vice President of National Policy and Advocacy.
Web, www.lungusa.org

Promotes improved lung health and the prevention of lung disease through research, education, and advocacy. Interests include antismoking campaigns; lung-related biomedical research; air pollution; and all lung diseases, including asthma, COPD, and lung cancer.

Cystic Fibrosis Foundation, 6931 Arlington Rd., #200, Bethesda, MD 20814; (301) 951-4422. Fax, (301) 951-6378. Robert J. Beall, President. Information, (800) 344-4823.
General e-mail, info@cff.org
Web, www.cff.org

Conducts research on cystic fibrosis, a genetic disease affecting the respiratory and digestive systems. Focuses on medical research to identify a cure and to improve quality of life for those living with cystic fibrosis.

Minority Health

▶ **AGENCIES**

Agency for Health Care Research and Quality *(Health and Human Services Dept.),* 540 Gaither Rd., Rockville, MD 20850; (301) 427-1364. Fax, (301) 427-1873. Dr. Carolyn M. Clancy, Director.

General e-mail, info@ahrq.gov

Web, www.ahrq.gov/about

Researches health care quality among minorities. Identifies and devises solutions for disparities in access to care, diagnosis, and treatment of illness. Provides health care professionals with research on minority health.

Health and Human Services Dept. (HHS), *Civil Rights,* *200 Independence Ave. S.W., #515F 20201; (202) 619-0403. Fax, (202) 619-3437. Robinsue Frohboese, Director (Acting). TTY, (800) 537-7697. Toll-free hotline, (800) 368-1019.*

Web, www.hhs.gov/ocr

Administers and enforces laws prohibiting discrimination on the basis of race, color, sex, national origin, religion, age, or disability in programs receiving federal funds from the department; authorized to discontinue funding. Responsible for health information privacy under the Health Insurance Portability and Accountability Act.

Health and Human Services Dept. (HHS), *Minority* *Health, 1101 Wootton Pkwy., #600, Rockville, MD 20852; (240) 453-2882. Fax, (240) 453-2883. Dr. Garth Graham, Deputy Assistant Secretary. Information, (800) 444-6472. General e-mail, info@omhrc.gov*

Web, www.omhrc.gov

Promotes improved health among racial and ethnic minority populations. Advises the secretary and the Office of Public Health and Science on public health program activities affecting American Indian and Alaska Native, African American, Asian American and Pacific Islander, and Hispanic populations. Awards grants to minority AIDS education and prevention projects to administer health promotion, education, and disease prevention programs.

Health and Human Services Dept. (HHS), *Minority* *Health Resource Center, 1101 Wootton Pkwy., #650, Rockville, MD 20852 (mailing address: P.O. Box 37337, Washington, DC 20013-7337); (301) 251-1797. Fax, (301) 251-2160. Jose Tarcisio M. Carneiro, Director. Information, (800) 444-6472. TTY, (301) 251-1432. General e-mail, info@omhrc.gov*

Web, www.omhrc.gov

Serves as a national resource and referral service on minority health issues. Distributes information on health topics such as substance abuse, cancer, heart disease, violence, diabetes, HIV/AIDS, and infant mortality. Provides free services, including customized database searches, publications, mailing lists, and referrals regarding American Indian and Alaska Native, African American, Asian American and Pacific Islander, and Hispanic populations.

Health Resources and Services Administration *(Health and Human Services Dept.), Minority Health and Health Disparities, 5600 Fishers Lane, #6C26, Rockville, MD 20857; (301) 443-2964. Fax, (301) 443-7853. Dr. Tanya Pagán Raggio-Ashley, Director. General e-mail, ask@hrsa.gov*

Web, www.hrsa.gov/omh

Sponsors programs and activities that address the special health needs of racial and ethnic minorities. Advises the administrator on minority health issues affecting the Health Resources and Services Administration (HRSA) and policy development; collects data on minority health activities within HRSA; represents HRSA programs affecting the health of racial and ethnic minorities to the health community and organizations in the public, private, and international sectors.

Indian Health Service *(Health and Human Services Dept.), 801 Thompson Ave., #440, Rockville, MD 20852; (301) 443-1083. Fax, (301) 443-4794. Robert G. McSwain, Director. Information, (301) 443-3593.*

Web, www.ihs.gov

Acts as the health advocate for and operates hospitals and health centers that provide preventive, curative, and community health care for Native Americans and Alaska Natives. Provides and improves sanitation and water supply systems in Native American and Alaska Native communities.

National Institutes of Health (NIH), *(Health and Human Services Dept.), National Center on Minority Health and Health Disparities (NCMHD), 2 Democracy Plaza, 6707 Democracy Blvd., #800, MSC-5465, Bethesda, MD 20892-5465; (301) 402-1366. Fax, (301) 480-4049. Dr. John Ruffin, Director.*

Web, www.ncmhd.nih.gov

Promotes minority health and leads, coordinates, supports, and assesses the NIH's effort to eliminate health disparities. Conducts and supports basic clinical, social, and behavioral research; promotes research infrastructure and training; fosters emerging programs; disseminates information; and reaches out to minority and other communities suffering from health disparities.

Public Health and Science *(Health and Human Services Dept.), Minority Health, 1101 Wootton Pkwy., #600, Rockville, MD 20852; (240) 453-2882. Fax, (240) 453-2883. Dr. Garth Graham, Deputy Assistant Secretary. Information, (800) 444-6472. General e-mail, info@omhrc.gov*

Web, www.omhrc.gov

Oversees the implementation of the secretary's Task Force on Black and Minority Health and legislative mandates; develops programs to meet the health care needs of minorities; awards grants to coalitions of minority community organizations and to minority AIDS education and prevention projects.

▶NONGOVERNMENTAL

Asian and Pacific Islander American Health Forum, *Washington Office, 1828 L St. N.W., #802 20036; (202) 466-7772. Fax, (202) 466-6444. Dr. Ho Luong Tran, Chief Executive Officer. General e-mail, healthinfo@apiahf.org*

Web, www.apiahf.org

Works to improve the health status of and access to care by Asian Americans and Pacific Islanders and to address health disparities, including disability and mental health, HIV/AIDS, domestic violence, smoking, and cancer. Monitors legislation in the areas of health, politics, and social and economic issues that affect Asian Americans and Pacific Islanders.

National Alliance for Hispanic Health, *1501 16th St. N.W. 20036; (202) 387-5000. Fax, (202) 265-8027. Dr. Jane L. Delgado, President.*
General e-mail, alliance@hispanichealth.org
Web, www.hispanichealth.org

Assists agencies and groups serving the Hispanic community in general health care and in targeting health and psychosocial problems; provides information, technical assistance, health care provider training, and policy analysis; coordinates and supports research. Interests include mental health, chronic diseases, substance abuse, maternal and child health, youth issues, juvenile delinquency, and access to care.

National Council of Urban Indian Health, *924 Pennsylvania Ave. S.E. 20003; (202) 544-0344. Fax, (202) 544-9394. Geoffrey Roth, Executive Director.*
General e-mail, gfine@ncuih.org
Web, www.ncuih.org

Membership: Indian health care providers. Supports accessible, high-quality health care programs for American Indians and Alaska Natives living in urban communities. Provides education and training. Monitors legislation and funding.

National Hispanic Medical Assn., *1411 K St. N.W., #1100 20005; (202) 628-5895. Fax, (202) 628-5898. Elena V. Rios, President.*
General e-mail, nhma@nhmamd.org
Web, www.nhmamd.org

Provides policymakers and health care providers with information and support to strengthen the delivery of health care to Hispanic communities in the United States. Areas of interest include high-quality care and increased opportunities in medical education for Latinos. Works with federal officials, other Hispanic advocacy groups, and Congress to eliminate disparities in health care for minorities.

National Minority AIDS Council, *1931 13th St. N.W. 20009-4432; (202) 483-6622. Fax, (202) 483-1135. Paul A. Kawata, Executive Director.*
General e-mail, info@nmac.org
Web, www.nmac.org

Works to build the capacity of small faith- and community-based organizations delivering HIV/AIDS services in communities of color. Holds national conferences; administers treatment and research programs and training; disseminates electronic and printed resource materials; conducts public policy advocacy.

Neurological and Muscular Disorders

▶AGENCIES

National Institute of Neurological Disorders and Stroke *(National Institutes of Health), 31 Center Dr., Bldg. 31, #8A52, MSC-2540, Bethesda, MD 20892-2540; (301) 496-9746. Fax, (301) 496-0296. Dr. Story Landis, Director. Information, (301) 496-5751. Toll-free, (800) 352-9424. Web, www.ninds.nih.gov*

Conducts and funds research on neurological diseases. Monitors international research.

▶NONGOVERNMENTAL

Alzheimer's Assn., *Public Policy, Washington Office, 1319 F St. N.W., #500 20004-1106; (202) 393-7737. Fax, (866) 865-0270. Vacant, Senior Vice President. Information, (800) 272-3900.*
Web, www.alz.org

Offers family support services and educates the public about Alzheimer's disease, a neurological disorder mainly affecting the brain tissue in older adults. Promotes research and long-term care protection; maintains liaison with Alzheimer's associations abroad. Monitors legislation and regulations. (Headquarters in Chicago, Ill.)

Brain Injury Assn. of America, *1608 Spring Hill Rd., #110, Vienna, VA 22182; (703) 761-0750. Fax, (703) 761-0755. Susan H. Connors, President. Information, (800) 444-6443.*
General e-mail, info@biausa.org
Web, www.biausa.org

Works to improve the quality of life for persons with traumatic brain injuries and for their families. Promotes the prevention of head injuries through public awareness and education programs. Offers state-level support services for individuals and their families. Monitors legislation and regulations.

Epilepsy Foundation, *8301 Professional Pl. East, #200, Landover, MD 20785; (301) 459-3700. Fax, (301) 577-2684. Eric Hargis, Chief Executive Officer. Information, (800) 332-1000. Library, (800) 332-4050.*
General e-mail, postmaster@efa.org
Web, www.epilepsyfoundation.org

Promotes research and treatment of epilepsy; makes research grants; disseminates information and educational materials. Affiliates provide direct services for people with epilepsy and make referrals when necessary. Library open to the public by appointment.

Foundation for the Advancement of Chiropractic Tenets and Science, *1110 N. Glebe Rd., #650, Arlington, VA 22201-5722; (703) 528-5000. Fax, (703) 528-5023. Robert N. Pohtos, Executive Director.*
General e-mail, chiro@chiropractic.org
Web, www.chiropractic.org

Offers financial aid for education and research programs in colleges and independent institutions; studies chiropractic services in the United States; provides international relief and development programs. (Affiliate of the International Chiropractors Assn.)

National Multiple Sclerosis Society, *Washington Office,* *1800 M St. N.W., #750 South 20036; (202) 296-5363. Fax, (202) 296-3425. Christopher Broullire, Chapter President.* *General e-mail, information@msandyou.org*

Web, www.msandyou.org

Seeks to advance medical knowledge of multiple sclerosis, a disease of the central nervous system; disseminates information worldwide. Patient services include individual and family counseling, exercise programs, equipment loans, medical and social service referrals, transportation assistance, back-to-work training programs, and in-service training seminars for nurses, homemakers, and physical and occupational therapists. (Headquarters in New York.)

Society for Neuroscience, *1121 14th St. N.W., #1010 20005; (202) 962-4000. Fax, (202) 962-4941. Marty Saggese, Executive Director.* *General e-mail, info@sfn.org*

Web, www.sfn.org

Membership: scientists and physicians worldwide who research the brain, spinal cord, and nervous system. Interests include the molecular and cellular levels of the nervous system; systems within the brain, such as vision and hearing; and behavior produced by the brain. Promotes education in the neurosciences and the application of research to treat nervous system disorders.

Spina Bifida Assn., *4590 MacArthur Blvd. N.W., #250 20007-4226; (202) 944-3285. Fax, (202) 944-3295. Cindy Brownstein, Chief Executive Officer. Information, (800) 621-3141.* *General e-mail, sbaa@sbaa.org*

Web, www.spinabifida.org

Membership: individuals with spina bifida, their supporters, and concerned professionals. Offers educational programs, scholarships, and support services; acts as a clearinghouse; provides referrals and information about treatment and prevention. Serves as U.S. member of the International Federation for Hydrocephalus and Spina Bifida, which is headquartered in Geneva. Monitors legislation and regulations.

United Cerebral Palsy Assns., *1660 L St. N.W., #700 20036-5602; (202) 776-0406. Fax, (202) 776-0414. Stephen Bennett, President. Information, (800) 872-5827. Main phone is voice and TTY accessible.* *General e-mail, info@ucp.org*

Web, www.ucp.org

National network of state and local affiliates that assists individuals with cerebral palsy and other developmental disabilities and their families. Provides parent education, early intervention, employment services, family support and respite programs, therapy, assistive technology, and vocational training. Promotes research on cerebral palsy; supports the use of assistive technology and community-based living arrangements for persons with cerebral palsy and other developmental disabilities.

Skin Disorders

►AGENCIES

National Institute of Arthritis and Musculoskeletal and Skin Diseases *(National Institutes of Health), 31 Center Dr., Bldg. 31, #4C32, MSC-2350, Bethesda, MD 20892-2350; (301) 496-4353. Fax, (301) 402-3607. Dr. Stephen I. Katz, Director. Information, (301) 496-8190.* *Web, www.niams.nih.gov*

Supports research on the causes and treatment of skin diseases, including psoriasis, eczema, and acne.

►NONGOVERNMENTAL

American Academy of Facial Plastic and Reconstructive Surgery, *310 S. Henry St., Alexandria, VA 22314; (703) 299-9291. Fax, (703) 299-8898. Stephen C. Duffy, Executive Vice President.* *General e-mail, info@aafprs.org*

Web, www.aafprs.org

Membership: facial plastic and reconstructive surgeons and other board-certified surgeons whose focus is surgery of the face, head, and neck. Promotes research and study in the field. Helps train residents in facial plastic and reconstructive surgery; offers continuing medical education. Sponsors scientific and medical meetings, international symposia, fellowship training program, seminars, and workshops. Provides videotapes on facial plastic and reconstructive surgery.

Substance Abuse

►AGENCIES

Education Dept., *Safe and Drug-Free Schools, 550 12th St. S.W., #10001 20202-6450; (202) 245-7896. Fax, (202) 485-0013. William Modzeleski, Associate Assistant Deputy Secretary.* *Web, www.ed.gov/offices/oese/sdfs*

Develops policy for the department's drug and violence prevention initiatives for students in elementary and secondary schools and institutions of higher education. Provides financial assistance for drug and violence prevention activities. Coordinates education efforts in drug and violence prevention with those of other federal departments and agencies.

Health Resources and Services Administration *(Health and Human Services Dept.), Policy and Development,*

5600 Fishers Lane, #C26, Rockville, MD 20857; (301) 594-4300. Fax, (301) 594-4997. Elisabeth Handley, Director. Web, www.bphc.hrsa.gov

Provides grants to health centers to expand services to include behavioral health and substance abuse services.

National Institute on Alcohol Abuse and Alcoholism *(National Institutes of Health)*, 5635 Fishers Lane, MSC-9304, Bethesda, MD 20892-9304; (301) 443-3885. Fax, (301) 443-7043. Dr. Kenneth Warren, Director (Acting). Information, (301) 443-3860. Web, www.niaaa.nih.gov

Supports basic and applied research on preventing and treating alcoholism and alcohol-related problems; conducts research and disseminates findings on alcohol abuse and alcoholism. Participates in international research.

National Institute on Drug Abuse *(National Institutes of Health)*, 6001 Executive Blvd., #5274, MSC-9581, Bethesda, MD 20892-9581; (301) 443-6480. Fax, (301) 443-9127. Dr. Nora Volkow, Director. Information, (301) 443-1124. Press, (301) 443-6245. TTY, (888) 889-6432. Web, www.nida.nih.gov

Conducts and sponsors research on the prevention, effects, and treatment of drug abuse. Monitors international policy and research.

Office of National Drug Control Policy (ONDCP), *(Executive Office of the President)*, 750 17th St. N.W. 20503; (202) 395-6700. Fax, (202) 395-6680. Edward H. Jurith, Director (Acting). Drug Policy Information Clearinghouse, (800) 666-3332. Web, www.whitehousedrugpolicy.gov

Establishes policies and oversees the implementation of a national drug control strategy with the goal of reducing illicit drug use, manufacturing, trafficking, and drug-related crimes, violence, and health consequences. Coordinates the international and domestic anti-drug efforts of executive branch agencies and ensures that such efforts sustain and complement state and local anti-drug activities. Advises the president and the National Security Council on drug control policy. (Clearinghouse address: P.O. Box 6000, Rockville, MD 20849-6000.)

Substance Abuse and Mental Health Services Administration *(Health and Human Services Dept.)*, 1 Choke Cherry Rd., #8-1065, Rockville, MD 20857; (240) 276-2000. Fax, (240) 276-2010. Eric Broderick, Administrator (Acting). Communications, (240) 276-2130. General e-mail, info@samhsa.hhs.gov

Web, www.samhsa.gov

Facilitates recovery for people with or at risk for substance abuse and mental illness through formula grants to states and communities.

Substance Abuse and Mental Health Services Administration *(Health and Human Services Dept.)*, **Center for Substance Abuse Prevention,** 1 Choke Cherry Rd., #4-1056, Rockville, MD 20857; (240) 276-2420. Fax, (240) 276-2430. Frances Harding, Director. TTY, (800) 487-4889. Workplace Helpline, (800) WORKPLACE. Web, http://prevention.samhsa.gov

Promotes strategies to prevent alcohol and drug abuse. Operates the National Clearinghouse for Alcohol and Drug Information, which provides information, publications, and grant applications for programs to prevent substance abuse. (Clearinghouse address: http://ncadi. samhsa.gov or P.O. Box 2345, Rockville, MD 20847.)

Substance Abuse and Mental Health Services Administration *(Health and Human Services Dept.)*, **Center for Substance Abuse Treatment,** 1 Choke Cherry Rd., #5-1015, Rockville, MD 20857; (240) 276-1660. Fax, (240) 276-1670. Dr. H. Westley Clark, Director. TTY, (800) 487-4889. Treatment referral, literature, and reports, (800) 662-4357. Web, www.csat.samhsa.gov

Develops and supports policies and programs that improve and expand treatment services for alcoholism, substance abuse, and addiction. Administers grants that support private and public addiction prevention and treatment services. Evaluates alcohol treatment programs and other drug treatment programs and delivery systems.

▶**INTERNATIONAL ORGANIZATIONS**

International Commission for the Prevention of Alcoholism and Drug Dependency, 12501 Old Columbia Pike, Silver Spring, MD 20904; (301) 680-6719. Fax, (301) 680-6707. Dr. Peter N. Landless, Executive Director. General e-mail, the_icpa@hotmail.com

Web, www.health20-20.org/icpa.htm

Membership: health officials, physicians, educators, clergy, and judges worldwide. Promotes scientific research on prevention of alcohol and drug dependencies; provides information about medical effects of alcohol and drugs; conducts world congresses.

▶**NONGOVERNMENTAL**

American Legacy Foundation, 1724 Massachusetts Ave. N.W. 20036; (202) 454-5555. Fax, (202) 454-5599. Cheryl Healton, President. General e-mail, info@americanlegacy.org

Web, www.americanlegacy.org

Develops programs to disseminate information on the health effects of tobacco. Provides prevention and cessation services through grants, technical training and assistance, youth activism, partnerships, and community outreach.

American Society of Addiction Medicine, 4601 N. Park Ave., Upper Arcade, #101, Chevy Chase, MD 20815-4520; (301) 656-3920. Fax, (301) 656-3815. Eileen McGrath, Executive Vice President. General e-mail, email@asam.org

Web, www.asam.org

Membership: physicians and medical students. Supports the study and provision of effective treatment and care for people with alcohol and drug dependencies; educates physicians. Monitors legislation and regulations.

Assn. for Addiction Professionals (NAADAC), *1001 N. Fairfax St., #201, Alexandria, VA 22314; (703) 741-7686. Fax, (703) 741-7698. Cynthia Moreno Tuohy, Executive Director. Information, (800) 548-0497.*
General e-mail, naadac@naadac.org

Web, www.naadac.org

Provides information on drug dependency treatment, research, and resources. Works with private groups and federal agencies concerned with treating and preventing alcoholism and drug abuse; certifies addiction counselors; holds workshops and conferences for treatment professionals. (Formerly National Assn. of Alcoholism and Drug Abuse Counselors.)

Employee Assistance Professionals Assn., *4350 N. Fairfax Dr., #410, Arlington, VA 22203; (703) 387-1000. Fax, (703) 522-4585. John Maynard, Chief Executive Officer.*
General e-mail, info@eapassn.org

Web, www.eapassn.org

Membership: professionals in the workplace who assist employees and their family members with personal and behavioral problems, including health, marital, family, financial, alcohol, drug, legal, emotional, stress, or other personal problems that adversely affect employee job performance and productivity.

National Assn. of State Alcohol and Drug Abuse Directors (NASADAD), *1025 Connecticut Ave. N.W., #605 20036-5430; (202) 293-0090. Fax, (202) 293-1250. Rob Morrison, Executive Director.*
General e-mail, dcoffice@nasadad.org

Web, www.nasadad.org

Provides information on drug abuse treatment and prevention; contracts with federal and state agencies for design of programs to fight drug abuse.

Therapeutic Communities of America, *1601 Connecticut Ave. N.W., #803 20009; (202) 296-3503. Fax, (202) 518-5475. Patricia Beauchemin, Executive Director.*
General e-mail, tca.office@verizon.net

Web, www.therapeuticcommunitiesofamerica.org

Membership: nonprofit organizations that provide substance abuse and mental health treatment and rehabilitation. Provides policy analysis and educates the public on substance abuse and treatment issues. Promotes the interests of therapeutic communities, their clients, and staffs. Monitors legislation and regulations.

Women's Health

▶ AGENCIES

National Heart, Lung, and Blood Institute *(National Institutes of Health), Women's Health Initiative,* *2 Rockledge Center, #10018, MS 7936, 6701 Rockledge Dr., Bethesda, MD 20892-7935; (301) 402-2900. Fax, (301) 480-5158. Jacques Rossouw, Project Officer. Information, (301) 592-8573. Press, (301) 496-4236.*
General e-mail, nm9o@nih.gov

Web, www.nhlbi.nih.gov/whi

During post-clinical trial, seeks to explain the postmenopausal hormone therapy findings and other clinical trial findings of the fifteen-year research project and to investigate the impact of genetic and biological markers on common diseases affecting postmenopausal women.

National Institutes of Health (NIH), *(Health and Human Services Dept.), Office of Research on Women's Health, 6707 Democracy Blvd., #400, MSC-5484, Bethesda, MD 20892-5484; (301) 402-1770. Fax, (301) 402-1798. Dr. Vivian W. Pinn, Director.*
Web, http://orwh.od.nih.gov

Collaborates with NIH institutes and centers to establish NIH goals and policies for research related to women's health and sex- or gender-based studies of the differences between women and men. Supports expansion of research on diseases, conditions, and disorders that affect women; monitors inclusion of women and minorities in clinical research; develops opportunities and support for recruitment and advancement of women in biomedical careers.

Public Health and Science *(Health and Human Services Dept.), Women's Health, 200 Independence Ave. S.W., #712E 20201; (202) 690-7650. Fax, (202) 401-4005. Dr. Wanda K. Jones, Deputy Assistant Secretary. Information, (800) 994-9662. TTY, (888) 220-5446.*
Web, www.womenshealth.gov/owh or www.womenshealth. gov and www.girlshealth.gov

Promotes better health for girls and women as well as health equity through sex/gender-specific approaches. Methods include educating health professionals and motivating behavior change in consumers through the dissemination of health information.

▶ NONGOVERNMENTAL

Black Women's Health Imperative, *1726 M St. N.W., #300 20036; (202) 548-4000. Fax, (202) 543-9743. Eleanor Hinton-Hoytt, President.*
General e-mail, info@blackwomenshealth.org

Web, www.blackwomenshealth.org

Provides the tools and information for African American women to prevent health problems, to recognize symptoms and early warning signs, and to understand all of the options available for their specific health situations. Achieves these ends through community outreach, advocacy, resources and research, and education. (Formerly the National Black Women's Health Project.)

Eating Disorders Coalition for Research, Policy, and Action, *720 7th St. N.W., #300 20001; (202) 543-9570. David Jaffe, Executive Director.*
Web, www.eatingdisorderscoalition.org

Seeks greater national and federal recognition of eating disorders. Promotes recognition of eating disorders as a public health priority and the implementation of more accessible treatment and more effective prevention programs. Monitors legislation and regulations.

Institute for Women's Policy Research (IWPR), *1707 L St. N.W., #750 20036; (202) 785-5100. Fax, (202) 833-4362. Heidi Hartmann, President.*
General e-mail, iwpr@iwpr.org

Web, www.iwpr.org

Public policy research organization that focuses on women's issues, including health care and comprehensive family and medical leave programs.

National Research Center for Women and Families, *1701 K St. N.W., #700 20006; (202) 223-4000. Fax, (202) 223-4242. Diana Zuckerman, Executive Director.*
General e-mail, info@center4research.org

Web, www.center4research.org

Utilizes scientific and medical research to improve the quality of women's lives and the lives of family members. Seeks to educate policymakers about medical and scientific research through hearings, meetings, and publications.

National Women's Health Network, *1413 K St. N.W., 4th Floor 20005; (202) 682-2640. Fax, (202) 682-2648. Cynthia Pearson, Executive Director.*
General e-mail, nwhn@nwhn.org

Web, www.nwhn.org

Acts as an information clearinghouse on women's health issues; monitors federal health policies and legislation. Interests include older women's health issues, sexual and reproductive health, contraception, menopause, abortion, unsafe drugs, AIDS, breast cancer, and universal health.

Society for Women's Health Research, *1025 Connecticut Ave. N.W., #701 20036; (202) 223-8224. Fax, (202) 833-3472. Phyllis Greenberger, President.*
General e-mail, info@womenshealthresearch.org

Web, www.womenshealthresearch.org

Promotes public and private funding for women's health research and changes in public policies affecting women's health. Seeks to advance women as leaders in the health professions and to inform policymakers, educators, and the public of research outcomes. Sponsors meetings; produces reports and educational videotapes.

WomenHeart, *818 18th St. N.W., #930 20006; (202) 728-7199. Fax, (202) 728-7238. Lisa M. Tate, Chief Executive Officer.*
General e-mail, mail@womenheart.org

Web, www.womenheart.org

Patient-centered organization that seeks to advance women's heart health through advocacy, community education, and patient support. Comprised of patients and their families, health care providers, advocates, and interested consumers.

MENTAL HEALTH

►AGENCIES

National Institute of Mental Health *(National Institutes of Health), 6001 Executive Blvd., #8235, Rockville, MD 20892; (301) 443-3673. Fax, (301) 443-2578. Dr. Thomas R. Insel, Director. Information, (301) 443-4513. Press, (301) 443-4536. TTY, (301) 443-8431.*
General e-mail, nimhinfo@nih.gov

Web, www.nimh.nih.gov

Conducts research on the cause, diagnosis, treatment, and prevention of mental disorders; provides information on mental health problems and programs. Participates in international research.

National Institute of Mental Health *(National Institutes of Health), Developmental Translational Research, 6001 Executive Blvd., #6200, Bethesda, MD 20892; (301) 443-5944. Fax, (301) 480-4415. Mary Ellen Oliveri, Director.*
Web, www.nimh.nih.gov/about/organization/ddtr/index. shtml

Promotes research programs concerning the prevention of mental disorders and the promotion of mental health.

National Institute of Mental Health *(National Institutes of Health), Neuroscience and Basic Behavioral Science, 6001 Executive Blvd., #7204, Rockville, MD 20892; (301) 443-3563. Fax, (301) 443-1731. Linda S. Brady, Director.*
Web, www.nimh.nih.gov

Supports research programs in the areas of basic neuroscience, genetics, basic behavioral science, research training, resource development, technology development, drug discovery, and research dissemination. Responsible for ensuring that relevant basic science knowledge is generated to create improved diagnosis, treatment, and prevention of mental and behavioral disorders.

National Institute of Mental Health *(National Institutes of Health), Special Populations, 6001 Executive Blvd., #8125, MSC-9659, Bethesda, MD 20892; (301) 443-2847. Fax, (301) 443-8552. Robert A. Mays, Director (Acting).*
Web, www.nimh.nih.gov

Sets research policy on women and underrepresented racial and ethnic minorities. Administers the minority institutions programs, which support research on and research training for minorities in the mental health field.

National Institutes of Health *(Health and Human Services Dept.), Behavioral and Social Sciences Research, 31 Center Dr., Bldg. 31, #B1C19, Bethesda, MD 20892-0183; (301) 402-1146. Fax, (301) 402-1150. Dr. Christine Bachrach, Director (Acting).*
Web, http://obssr.od.nih.gov

Information Sources on Women's Health

AIDSinfo (NIH), (800) 448-0440; TTY, (888) 480-3739, http://aidsinfo.nih.gov

American College of Nurse-Midwives, (240) 485-1800, www.midwife.org

American College of Obstetricians and Gynecologists, Public Information, (202) 484-3321, www.acog.org

American Society for Reproductive Medicine, (202) 863-2494, www.asrm.org

Assn. of Maternal and Child Health Programs, (202) 775-0436, www.amchp.org

Assn. of Reproductive Health Professionals, (202) 466-3825, www.arhp.org

Assn. of Women's Health, Obstetric, and Neonatal Nurses, (800) 673-8499, www.awhonn.org

Guttmacher Institute, (202) 296-4012; toll-free, (800) 772-9100, www.guttmacher.org

Healthfinder (HHS), www.healthfinder.gov

Lamaze International, (202) 367-1128; toll-free, (800) 368-4404, www.lamaze.org

Maternal and Child Health Bureau (HHS), (301) 443-2170, www.mchb.hrsa.gov

Medem Network, www.medem.com

Medline (NIH), www.nlm.nih.gov/medlineplus/womenshealth.html

National Abortion Federation, (202) 667-5881; Hotline, (800) 231-4222, www.prochoice.org

National Breast Cancer Coalition, (202) 296-7477; toll-free (800) 622-2838, www.stopbreastcancer.org

National Cancer Institute (NIH), (800) 422-6237; TTY, (800) 332-8615, www.cancer.gov

National Center for Education in Maternal and Child Health (Georgetown Univ.), (202) 784-9770, www.ncemch.org

National Coalition for Women With Heart Disease, (202) 728-7199, www.womenheart.org

National Family Planning and Reproductive Health Assn., (202) 293-3114, www.nfprha.org

National Institute of Allergy and Infectious Diseases (NIH), AIDS, toll-free hotline, (800) 342-2437, www.niaid.nih.gov/factsheets/womenhiv.htm

National Institute of Child Health and Human Development (NIH), Program and Public Liaison, (301) 496-0536, www.nichd.nih.gov/womenshealth

National Institute on Aging (NIH), Information Center, (800) 222-2225; TTY, (800) 222-4225, www.nia.nih.gov

National Maternal and Child Health Clearinghouse (HHS), (888) 275-4772, www.ask.hrsa.gov/mch.cfm

National Osteoporosis Foundation, (202) 223-2226; toll-free, (800) 231-4222, www.nof.org

National Research Center for Women and Families, (202) 223-4000, www.center4research.org

National Women's Health Information Center (HHS), (800) 994-9662, TDD (888) 220-5446, www.womenshealth.gov, www.girlshealth.gov

National Women's Health Network, (202) 347-1140, www.nwhn.org

Office of Research on Women's Health (NIH), (301) 402-1770, http://orwh.od.nih.gov

Planned Parenthood Federation of America, (202) 785-3351, www.plannedparenthood.org

Society for Women's Health Research, (202) 223-8224, www.womenshealthresearch.org

United States National Library of Medicine (NIH), Communications, (301) 496-6308, www.nlm.nih.gov

Women's Mental Health Consortium, National Institute of Mental Health (NIH), www.nimh.nih.gov/healthinformation/depwomen.cfm

Y-Me National Breast Cancer Organization, (703) 437-9595; toll-free hotline, (800) 221-2141, www.y-me.org

---

Works to advance behavioral and social sciences training, to integrate a biobehavioral perspective across the NIH, and to improve communication among scientists and with the public. Develops funding initiatives for research and training. Sets priorities for research. Provides training and career development opportunities for behavioral and social scientists. Links minority students with mentors. Organizes cultural workshops and lectures.

Substance Abuse and Mental Health Services Administration *(Health and Human Services Dept.),* *1 Choke Cherry Rd., #8-1065, Rockville, MD 20857; (240)*

276-2000. Fax, (240) 276-2010. Eric Broderick, Administrator (Acting). Communications, (240) 276-2130. General e-mail, info@samhsa.hhs.gov

Web, www.samhsa.gov

Facilitates recovery for people with or at risk for substance abuse and mental illness through formula grants to states and communities.

Substance Abuse and Mental Health Services Administration *(Health and Human Services Dept.), Center for Mental Health Services, 1 Choke Cherry Rd., #6-1057, Rockville, MD 20857; (240) 276-1310. Fax,*

(240) 276-1320. A. Kathryn Power, Director. Information, (800) 789-2647. TTY, (866) 889-2647.

Web, http://mentalhealth.samhsa.gov

Works with federal agencies and state and local governments to demonstrate, evaluate, and disseminate service delivery models to treat mental illness, promote mental health, and prevent the developing or worsening of mental illness. Operates the National Mental Health Information Center.

▶CONGRESS

For a listing of relevant congressional committees and subcommittees, please see page 320 or the Appendix.

▶NONGOVERNMENTAL

American Academy of Child and Adolescent Psychiatry, *3615 Wisconsin Ave. N.W. 20016-3007; (202) 966-7300. Fax, (202) 966-2891. Virginia Q. Anthony, Executive Director.*

Web, www.aacap.org

Membership: child and adolescent psychiatrists trained to promote healthy development and to evaluate, diagnose, and treat children, adolescents, and families affected by mental illness. Sponsors annual meeting and review for medical board examinations. Provides information on child and adolescent development and mental illnesses. Monitors international research and U.S. legislation concerning children with mental illness.

American Assn. of Pastoral Counselors, *9504A Lee Hwy., Fairfax, VA 22031-2303; (703) 385-6967. Fax, (703) 352-7725. Douglas M. Ronsheim, Executive Director.*

General e-mail, info@aapc.org

Web, www.aapc.org

Membership: mental health professionals with training in both religion and the behavioral sciences. Nonsectarian organization that accredits pastoral counseling centers, certifies pastoral counselors, and approves training programs.

American Assn. of Suicidology, *5221 Wisconsin Ave. N.W. 20015; (202) 237-2280. Fax, (202) 237-2282.*

General e-mail, info@suicidology.org

Web, www.suicidology.org

Membership: educators, researchers, suicide prevention centers, school districts, volunteers, and survivors affected by suicide. Works to understand and prevent suicide; serves as an information clearinghouse.

American Bar Assn. (ABA), *Commission on Mental and Physical Disability Law, 740 15th St. N.W., 9th Floor 20005-1022; (202) 662-1570. Fax, (202) 442-3439. John Parry, Director.*

General e-mail, cmpdl@abanet.org

Web, www.abanet.org/disability

Serves as a clearinghouse for information on mental and physical disability law. Publishes a report on mental and physical disability law, law digest, and handbooks. Provides a directory of lawyers who practice disability law, a directory on law school disability curricula, and a directory on law students with disabilities.

American Mental Health Counselors Assn., *801 N. Fairfax St., #304, Alexandria, VA 22314; (703) 548-6002. Fax, (703) 548-4775. Dr. W. Mark Hamilton, Executive Director. Toll-free, (800) 326-2642.*

Web, www.amhca.org

Membership: professional counselors and graduate students in the mental health field. Sponsors leadership training and continuing education programs for members; holds annual conference. Monitors legislation and regulations. (Affiliated with the American Counseling Assn.)

American Psychiatric Assn., *1000 Wilson Blvd., #1825, Arlington, VA 22209-3901; (703) 907-7300. Fax, (703) 907-1085. Dr. James Scully, Medical Director. Library, (703) 907-8648. Press, (703) 907-8640.*

General e-mail, apa@psych.org

Web, www.psych.org

Membership: psychiatrists. Promotes availability of high-quality psychiatric care; provides the public with information; assists state and local agencies; conducts educational programs for professionals and students in the field; participates in international meetings and research. Library open to members.

American Psychological Assn., *750 1st St. N.E. 20002-4242; (202) 336-5500. Fax, (202) 336-6069. Norman B. Anderson, Chief Executive Officer. Library, (202) 336-5640. TTY, (202) 336-6123. Toll-free, (800) 374-2721.*

Web, www.apa.org

Membership: professional psychologists, educators, and behavioral research scientists. Supports research, training, and professional services; works toward improving the qualifications, competence, and training programs of psychologists. Monitors international research and U.S. legislation on mental health.

American Psychosomatic Society, *6728 Old McLean Village Dr., McLean, VA 22101; (703) 556-9222. Fax, (703) 556-8729. George K. Degnon, Executive Director.*

General e-mail, info@psychosomatic.org

Web, www.psychosomatic.org

Promotes and advances scientific understanding of relationships among biological, psychological, social, and behavioral factors in health and disease.

Anxiety Disorders Assn. of America, *8730 Georgia Ave., #600, Silver Spring, MD 20910; (240) 485-1001. Fax, (240) 485-1035. Alies Muskin, Chief Operating Officer.*

Web, www.adaa.org

Membership: clinicians and researchers who treat and study anxiety disorders; individuals with anxiety disorders and their families; and other interested individuals. Promotes prevention, treatment, and cure of anxiety disorders by disseminating information, linking individuals with treatment facilities, and encouraging research and advancement of scientific knowledge.

Assn. of Black Psychologists, *P.O. Box 55999 20040-5999; (202) 722-0808. Fax, (202) 722-5941. Dorothy A. Holmes, President.*
General e-mail, abpsi_office@abpsi.org

Web, www.abpsi.org

Membership: psychologists, psychology students, and others in the mental health field. Develops policies to foster mental health in the African American community; holds annual convention.

Bazelon Center for Mental Health Law, *1101 15th St. N.W., #1212 20005; (202) 467-5730. Fax, (202) 223-0409. Robert Bernstein, Executive Director. TTY, (202) 467-4232.*
General e-mail, info@bazelon.org

Web, www.bazelon.org

Public interest law firm. Works to establish and advance the legal rights of children and adults with mental disabilities and ensure their equal access to services and resources needed for full participation in community life. Provides technical support to lawyers and other advocates. Conducts test case litigation to defend rights of persons with mental disabilities. Conducts policy analysis, builds coalitions, issues advocacy alerts, publishes handbooks, and maintains advocacy resources online. Monitors legislation and regulations.

Mental Health America, *2000 N. Beauregard St., 12th Floor, Alexandria, VA 22311; (703) 684-7722. Fax, (703) 684-5968. David L. Shern, President. Information, (800) 969-6642.*
General e-mail, infoctr@nmha.org

Web, www.nmha.org

Works to increase accessible and appropriate care for adults and children with mental disorders. Informs and educates the public about mental illnesses and available treatment. Supports research on illnesses and services.

National Alliance on Mental Illness, *2107 Wilson Blvd., Colonial Pl. III, #300, Arlington, VA 22201-3042; (703) 524-7600. Fax, (703) 524-9094. Michael Fitzpatrick, Executive Director. Helpline, (800) 950-6264.*
General e-mail, info@nami.org

Web, www.nami.org

Membership: mentally ill individuals and their families and friends. Works to eradicate mental illness and improve the lives of those affected by brain disorders; sponsors public education and research. Monitors legislation and regulations. (Formerly the National Alliance for the Mentally Ill.)

National Assn. of Psychiatric Health Systems, *701 13th St. N.W., #950 20005; (202) 393-6700. Fax, (202) 783-6041. Mark Covall, President.*
General e-mail, naphs@naphs.org

Web, www.naphs.org

Membership: behavioral health care systems that are committed to the delivery of responsive, accountable, and clinically effective treatment and prevention and care programs for children, adolescents, adults, and older adults with mental and substance use disorders.

National Assn. of School Psychologists, *4340 East-West Hwy., Bethesda, MD 20814; (301) 657-0270. Fax, (301) 657-0275. Susan Gorin, Executive Director.*
Web, www.naspweb.org

Membership: organizations interested in developing mental health services for children. Fosters information exchange; advises local, state, and federal agencies that develop children's mental health services.

National Assn. of State Mental Health Program Directors, *66 Canal Center Plaza, #302, Alexandria, VA 22314-1591; (703) 739-9333. Fax, (703) 548-9517. Robert W. Glover, Executive Director.*
Web, www.nasmhpd.org

Membership: officials in charge of state mental health agencies. Compiles data on state mental health programs. Fosters collaboration among members; provides technical assistance and consultation. Maintains research institute. Operates under a cooperative agreement with the National Governors Association.

National Council for Community Behavioral Healthcare, *1701 K St. N.W., #400 20006; (202) 684-7457. Fax, (202) 684-7472. Linda Rosenberg, President.*
General e-mail, communications@thenationalcouncil.org

Web, www.TheNationalCouncil.org

Membership: community mental health agencies and state community mental health associations. Conducts research on community mental health activities; provides information, technical assistance, and referrals. Operates a job bank; publishes newsletters and a membership directory. Monitors legislation and regulations affecting community mental health facilities.

Suicide Prevention Action Network (SPAN USA), *1025 Vermont Ave. N.W., #1066 20005; (202) 449-3600. Fax, (202) 449-3601. Vacant, Executive Director.*
General e-mail, info@spanusa.org

Web, www.spanusa.org

Supports development, funding, and evaluation of suicide prevention programs; access to care and support programs; a national research agenda; and training and assistance for families, activists, and professionals involved in suicide prevention. Advocates development and implementation of a national strategy for suicide prevention. Monitors legislation and regulations.

The Treatment Advocacy Center, *200 N. Glebe Rd., #730, Arlington, VA 22203; (703) 294-6001. Fax, (703) 294-6010. Rosanna Esposito, Executive Director (Interim). Information, (703) 294-6008.*
General e-mail, info@treatmentadvocacycenter.org

Web, www.treatmentadvocacycenter.org

Works to eliminate legal and other barriers to treatment of severe mental illness.

U.S. Psychiatric Rehabilitation Assn., *601 Global Way, #106, Linthicum, MD 21090; (410) 789-7054. Fax, (410) 789-7675. Marcie Granahan, Chief Executive Officer.*

General e-mail, info@uspra.org

Web, www.uspra.org

Membership: agencies, mental health practitioners, policymakers, family groups, and consumer organizations. Supports the community adjustment of persons with psychiatric disabilities. Promotes the role of rehabilitation in mental health systems; opposes discrimination based on mental disability. Certifies psychosocial rehabilitation practitioners. (Formerly the International Assn. of Psychosocial Rehabilitation Services.)

11 Housing and Development

GENERAL POLICY AND ANALYSIS

Basic Resources

►**AGENCIES**

Economic Development Administration *(Commerce Dept.)*, *1401 Constitution Ave. N.W., #7800 20230; (202) 482-5081. Fax, (202) 273-4781. Sandy Baruah, Assistant Secretary.*
Web, www.eda.gov

Advises the commerce secretary on domestic economic development. Administers development assistance programs that provide financial and technical aid to economically distressed areas to stimulate economic growth and create jobs. Awards public works and technical assistance grants to public institutions, nonprofit organizations, and Native American tribes; assists state and local governments with economic adjustment problems caused by long-term or sudden economic dislocation.

General Services Administration (GSA), *Subacquisition Systems, Federal Domestic Assistance Catalog Staff, 211 Crystal Dr., #911, Arlington, VA 22202; (202) 605-3404. Fax, (202) 501-4067. Earl Warrington, Director.*
Web, www.cfda.gov

Disseminates information on federal domestic assistance programs through the CFDA Web site. Information includes all types of federal aid and explains types of assistance, eligibility requirements, application process, and suggestions for writing proposals. Printed version and CD-ROM may be ordered from the Superintendent of Documents, U.S. Government Printing Office 20402; (202) 512-1800, or toll-free, (866) 512-1800, or online at bookstore.gpo.gov or www.cfda.gov.

Housing and Urban Development Dept. (HUD), *451 7th St. S.W., #10000 20410; (202) 708-0417. Fax, (202) 708-2476. Shaun Donovan, Secretary. Information, (202) 708-1112. Library, (202) 708-2370. TTY, (202) 708-1455. Congressional and Intergovernmental Relations, (202) 708-0005. Locator, (202) 401-0388.*
Web, www.hud.gov

Responsible for federal programs concerned with housing needs, fair housing opportunities, and improving and developing the nation's urban and rural communities. Administers mortgage insurance, rent subsidy, preservation, rehabilitation, and antidiscrimination in housing programs. Advises the president on federal policy and makes legislative recommendations on housing and community development issues.

Housing and Urban Development Dept. (HUD), *HUD USER, P.O. Box 23268 20026-3268; (800) 245-2691. Fax, (202) 708-9981. Ryan Callahan, Project Manager. TTY, (800) 927-7589.*
General e-mail, helpdesk@huduser.org
Web, www.huduser.org

Research information service and clearinghouse for HUD research reports. Provides information on past and current HUD research; maintains HUD USER, an in-house database. Extensive collection of publications and documents available online.

Housing and Urban Development Dept. (HUD), *Policy Development and Research, 451 7th St. S.W., #8100 20410-6000; (202) 708-1600. Fax, (202) 619-8000. Vacant, Assistant Secretary.*
Web, www.huduser.org

Studies ways to improve the effectiveness and equity of HUD programs; analyzes housing and urban issues, including national housing goals, the operation of housing financial markets, the management of housing assistance programs, and statistics on federal and housing insurance programs; conducts the American Housing Survey; develops policy recommendations to improve federal housing programs. Works to increase the affordability of rehabilitated and newly constructed housing through technological and regulatory improvements.

Housing and Urban Development Dept. (HUD), *Program Evaluation, 451 7th St. S.W., #8146 20410; (202) 708-0574. Fax, (202) 708-3141. Kevin J. Neary, Director. General e-mail, Kevin.J.Neary@hud.gov*
Web, www.hud.gov

Conducts research, program evaluations, and demonstrations for all HUD housing, community development, and fair housing and equal opportunity programs.

Office of Management and Budget (OMB), *(Executive Office of the President), Housing, New Executive Office Bldg., #9226 20503; (202) 395-4516. Fax, (202) 395-1307. Michelle Enger, Chief.*
Web, www.whitehouse.gov/omb

Assists and advises the OMB director in budget preparation, reorganizations, and evaluations of Housing and Urban Development Dept. programs.

►**CONGRESS**

For a listing of relevant congressional committees and subcommittees, please see page 381 or the Appendix.

►**NONGOVERNMENTAL**

Center for Economic and Policy Research (CEPR), *1611 Connecticut Ave. N.W., #400 20009; (202) 293-5380,ext. 115. Fax, (202) 588-1356. Dean Baker, Co-Director; Mark Weisbrot, Co-Director.*
General e-mail, cepr@cepr.net
Web, www.cepr.net

Researches economic and social issues and the impact of related public policies. Presents findings to the public with the goal of better preparing citizens to choose among various policy options. Promotes democratic debate and voter education. Areas of interest include health care, trade, Social Security, taxes, housing, and the labor market.

HOUSING AND DEVELOPMENT RESOURCES IN CONGRESS

For a complete listing of Congress committees, including their full contact information, leadership, membership, and jurisdictions, please refer to the Appendix on pages 724–837.

HOUSE:

House Agriculture Committee, Subcommittee on Conservation, Credit, Energy, and Research, (202) 225-0420.
Web, agriculture.house.gov
Subcommittee on Rural Development, Biotechnology, Specialty Crops, and Foreign Agriculture, (202) 225-8248.
House Appropriations Committee, (202) 225-2771.
Web, appropriations.house.gov
Subcommittee on Agriculture, Rural Development, FDA, and Related Agencies, (202) 225-2638.
Subcommittee on Financial Services and General Government, (202) 225-7245.
Subcommittee on Transportation, HUD, and Related Agencies, (202) 225-2141.
House Budget Committee, (202) 226-7200.
Web, budget.house.gov
House Education and Labor Committee, Subcommittee on Healthy Families and Communities, (202) 225-3725.
Web, edlabor.house.gov
House Financial Services Committee, (202) 225-7502.
Web, financialservices.house.gov
Subcommittee on Capital Markets, Insurance and Government Sponsored Enterprises, (202) 225-4247.
Subcommittee on Domestic Monetary Policy and Technology, (202) 225-4247.
Subcommittee on Financial Institutions and Consumer Credit, (202) 225-4247.
Subcommittee on International Monetary Policy and Trade, (202) 225-4247.
Subcommittee on Housing and Community Opportunity, (202) 225-4247.
Subcommittee on Oversight and Investigations, (202) 225-4247.
House Judiciary Committee, Subcommittee on the Constitution, Civil Rights, and Civil Liberties, (202) 225-2825.
Web, judiciary.house.gov
House Small Business Committee, Subcommittee on Rural Development, Entrepreneurship, and Trade, (202) 225-4038.
Web, www.house.gov/smbiz
House Transportation and Infrastructure Committee, Subcommittee on Economic Development, Public Buildings, and Emergency Management, (202) 225-9961.
Web, transportation.house.gov

House Ways and Means Committee, (202) 225-3625.
Web, waysandmeans.house.gov
Subcommittee on Oversight, (202) 225-5522.

SENATE:

Senate Agriculture, Nutrition, and Forestry Committee, Subcommittee on Rural Revitalization, Conservation, Forestry, and Credit, (202) 224-2035.
Web, agriculture.senate.gov
Senate Appropriations Committee, (202) 224-7363.
Web, appropriations.senate.gov
Subcommittee on Agriculture, Rural Development, FDA, and Related Agencies, (202) 224-8090.
Web, appropriations.senate.gov
Subcommittee on Financial Services and General Government, (202) 224-1133.
Subcommittee on Transportation, HUD and Related Agencies, (202) 224-7281.
Senate Banking, Housing and Urban Affairs Committee, (202) 224-7391.
Web, banking.senate.gov
Subcommittee on Economic Policy, (202) 224-2441.
Subcommittee on Financial Institutions, (202) 224-5842.
Subcommittee on Housing, Transportation and Community Development, (202) 224-7391.
Subcommittee on Securities, Insurance, and Investment, (202) 224-7391.
Senate Budget Committee, (202) 224-0642.
Web, budget.senate.gov
Senate Environment and Public Works Committee, (202) 224-8832.
Web, epw.senate.gov/public
Senate Finance Committee, (202) 224-4515.
Web, finance.senate.gov
Senate Homeland Security and Governmental Affairs Committee, (202) 224-2627.
Web, hsgac.senate.gov
Senate Indian Affairs Committee, (202) 224-2251.
Web, indian.senate.gov
Senate Judiciary Committee, Subcommittee on the Constitution, (202) 224-5573.
Web, judiciary.senate.gov
Senate Small Business and Entrepreneurship Committee, (202) 224-5175.
Web, sbc.senate.gov
Senate Special Committee on Aging, (202) 224-5364.
Web, aging.senate.gov

Housing and Urban Development Department

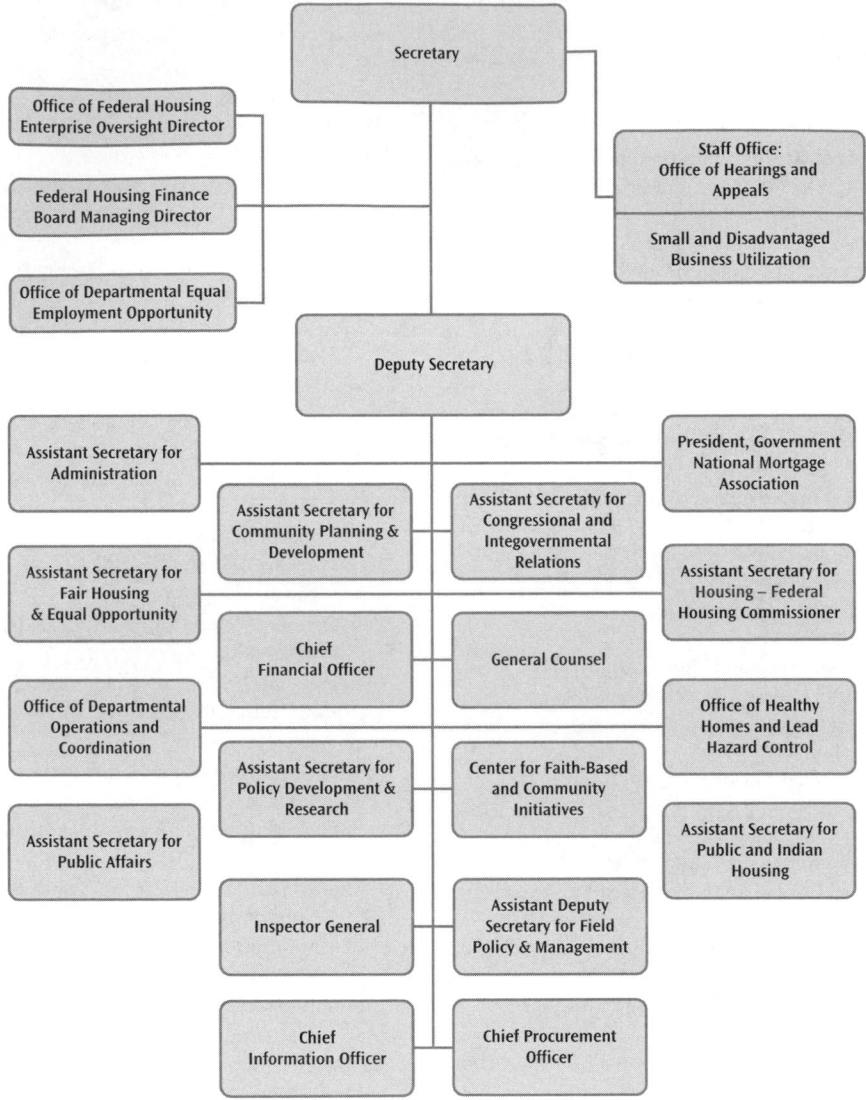

Secretary

Office of Federal Housing Enterprise Oversight Director

Federal Housing Finance Board Managing Director

Office of Departmental Equal Employment Opportunity

Staff Office: Office of Hearings and Appeals

Small and Disadvantaged Business Utilization

Deputy Secretary

Assistant Secretary for Administration

Assistant Secretary for Community Planning & Development

Assistant Secretaty for Congressional and Integovernmental Relations

President, Government National Mortgage Association

Assistant Secretary for Fair Housing & Equal Opportunity

Assistant Secretary for Housing – Federal Housing Commissioner

Chief Financial Officer

General Counsel

Office of Departmental Operations and Coordination

Office of Healthy Homes and Lead Hazard Control

Assistant Secretary for Policy Development & Research

Center for Faith-Based and Community Initiatives

Assistant Secretary for Public Affairs

Assistant Secretary for Public and Indian Housing

Inspector General

Assistant Deputy Secretary for Field Policy & Management

Chief Information Officer

Chief Procurement Officer

Center for Housing Policy, *1801 K St. N.W., #M100 20006-1301; (202) 466-2121. Fax, (202) 466-2122. Jeffrey Lubell, Executive Director.*
General e-mail, nhc@nhc.org

Web, www.nhc.org

Researches and develops fundamentals of housing policy. Seeks to create new policies that integrate housing into overall social and economic goals. Sponsors educational forums and publishes reports (available online). (Research affiliate of the National Housing Conference.)

Housing and Development Law Institute, *630 Eye St. N.W. 20001-3736; (202) 289-3400. Fax, (202) 289-3401. Lisa L. Walker, Executive Director.*
General e-mail, hdli@hdli.org

Web, www.hdli.org

Assists agencies and developers that administer public housing and community redevelopment programs in addressing common legal concerns and problems; publishes a quarterly compilation of nationwide case law affecting housing agencies; conducts seminars on legal issues and practices in the housing and community development field.

Institute for Local Self-Reliance, *927 15th St. N.W., 4th Floor 20005; (202) 898-1610. Fax, (202) 898-1612. Neil N. Seldman, President.*
General e-mail, info@ilsr.org
Web, www.ilsr.org

Conducts research and provides technical assistance on environmentally sound economic development for government, small businesses, and community organizations.

National Assn. of Housing and Redevelopment Officials, *630 Eye St. N.W. 20001-3736; (202) 289-3500. Fax, (202) 289-8181. Saul Ramirez, Executive Director. Toll-free, (877) 866-2476.*
Web, www.nahro.org

Membership: housing, community, and urban development practitioners and organizations, and state and local government agencies and personnel. Works with federal government agencies to improve community development and housing programs; conducts training programs.

Statistics

▶**AGENCIES**

Census Bureau *(Commerce Dept.), Governments Division, 4600 Silver Hill Rd., #HQ-5K156 20233; (301) 763-1489. Fax, (301) 457-3057. Stephanie Brown, Chief.*
Web, www.census.gov

Compiles the annual *Federal Expenditures by State,* which provides information on federal domestic spending, federal grants programs, and federal aid to states.

Census Bureau *(Commerce Dept.), Housing and Household Economic Statistics, 4600 Silver Hill Rd., #7H-174, Suitland, MD 20746 (for mailing address, change city and zip code to: Washington, DC 20233-8500); (301) 763-3234. Fax, (301) 763-3232. David S. Johnson, Chief.*
General e-mail, hhes-info@census.gov
Web, www.census.gov

Publishes decennial census of housing and the American Housing Survey, which describe housing inventory characteristics. Also publishes a quarterly survey of market absorption. Survey on housing vacancy is available on the Web site.

Census Bureau *(Commerce Dept.), Manufacturing and Construction, 4600 Silver Hill Rd., #7K154, Suitland, MD 20746-4600 (for mailing address, change city and zip code to: Washington, DC 20233); (301) 763-4593. Fax, (301) 768-7783. Thomas E. Zabelsky, Division Chief.*
Web, www.census.gov

Publishes statistics on the value of construction put in place; housing starts, sales, and completions; building permits; price index of single-family homes sold; characteristics of new housing; and expenditures for residential improvements. Conducts a census of construction industries every five years.

Housing and Urban Development Dept. (HUD), Economic Affairs, *451 7th St. S.W., #8204 20410-6000; (202) 708-3080. Fax, (202) 708-1159. Kurt Usowski, Deputy Assistant Secretary.*
Web, www.hud.gov

Directs research in public finance and urban economic development; assembles data on housing markets; conducts annual housing surveys; analyzes financial instruments used in housing.

International Trade Administration (ITA), *(Commerce Dept.), Manufacturing and Services: Manufacturing, 14th St. and Constitution Ave. N.W., #2800 20230; (202) 482-1872. Fax, (202) 482-0856. Vacant, Assistant Secretary.*
Web, www.trade.gov

Analyzes and maintains data on international construction and engineering. Monitors production costs, prices, financial and labor conditions, technological changes, distribution, markets, trade patterns, and other aspects of these industries. Promotes international trade, develops competitive assessments, and assists engineering and construction companies in obtaining overseas construction projects.

Office of Thrift Supervision (OTS), *(Treasury Dept.), Financial Monitoring and Analysis, 1700 G St. N.W., 6th Floor 20552; (202) 906-5680. Fax, (202) 906-6527. James Caton, Director.*
General e-mail, public.info@ots.treas.gov
Web, www.ots.treas.gov

Provides housing and mortgage statistics, including terms and rates of conventional home mortgages, and asset and liability information for thrift institutions insured by the Savings Assn. Insurance Fund.

COMMUNITY AND REGIONAL DEVELOPMENT

▶**AGENCIES**

Administration for Children and Families (ACF), *(Health and Human Services Dept.), Office of Community Services, 370 L'Enfant Promenade S.W., 5th Floor 20447; (202) 401-9333. Fax, (202) 401-4694. Yolanda J. Butler, Director (Acting).*
Web, www.acf.hhs.gov

Administers the Community Services Block Grant and Discretionary Program Grants.

Administration for Native Americans *(Health and Human Services Dept.), 370 L'Enfant Promenade S.W., 8th Floor West Aerospace Center 20447-0002; (202) 690-7776. Fax, (202) 690-7441. Vacant, Commissioner. Toll-free, (877) 922-9262.*
General e-mail, ana@acf.hhs.gov
Web, www.acf.hhs.gov/programs/ana

Awards grants for locally determined social and economic development strategies; promotes Native American economic and social self-sufficiency; funds tribes and Native American and Native Hawaiian organizations. Commissioner chairs the Intradepartmental Council on Indian Affairs, which coordinates Native American–related programs.

Army Corps of Engineers *(Defense Dept.),* *441 G St. N.W., #3K05 20314-1000; (202) 761-0001. Fax, (202) 761-4463. Lt. Gen. Robert L. Van Antwerp (USACE), Chief of Engineers.*
Web, www.usace.army.mil

Provides local governments with disaster relief, flood control, navigation, and hydroelectric power services.

Community Development Financial Institutions Fund *(Treasury Dept.),* *601 13th St. N.W., #200 South 20005; (202) 622-8662. Fax, (202) 622-9102. Donna J. Gambrell, Director.*
General e-mail, cdfihelp@cdfi.treas.gov
Web, www.cdfifund.gov

Works to build private markets, create healthy local tax revenues, and expand the availability of credit, investment capital, and financial services in low-income urban, rural, and Native communities.

Defense Dept. (DoD), *Office of Economic Adjustment,* *400 Army-Navy Dr., #200, Arlington, VA 22202-4704; (703) 604-6020. Fax, (703) 604-5843. Patrick J. O'Brien, Director.*
General e-mail, patrick.obrien@wso.whs.mil
Web, www.oea.gov

Civilian office that helps community officials develop strategies and coordinate plans to alleviate the economic effect of major defense program changes, including base closings (BRAC) and contract cutbacks. Assists communities where defense activities are being expanded. Serves as the staff for the Economic Adjustment Committee, an interagency group that coordinates federal defense economic adjustment activities.

Empowerment Programs *(Agriculture Dept.),* *Cooperative Development, 1400 Independence Ave. S.W., MS 3254 20250; (202) 720-3350. Fax, (202) 690-2750. John H. Wells, Director. Information, (800) 645-4712.*
General e-mail, cdpwebmaster@wdc.usda.gov
Web, www.ezec.gov and www.rurdev.usda.gov

Provides information about federal empowerment zones and enterprise communities in economically distressed rural areas.

Housing and Urban Development Dept. (HUD), *Block Grant Assistance, 451 7th St. S.W., #7286 20410; (202) 708-3587. Fax, (202) 401-2044. Stan Gimont, Director. Press, (202) 708-0685.*
Web, www.hud.gov/offices/cpd

Provides grants on a formula basis to states, cities, and urban counties to be used for a wide range of eligible activities selected by the grantee.

Housing and Urban Development Dept. (HUD), *Community Planning and Development, 451 7th St. S.W., #7100 20410; (202) 708-2690. Fax, (202) 708-3336. Nelson Bregón, General Deputy Assistant Secretary.*
Web, www.hud.gov/offices/cpd

Provides cities and states with community and economic development and housing assistance, including community development block grants. Encourages public-private partnerships in urban development and private sector initiatives. Oversees enterprise zone development program.

Housing and Urban Development Dept. (HUD), *Environment and Energy, 451 7th St. S.W., #7244 20410; (202) 708-2894, ext. 4439. Fax, (202) 708-3363. Richard H. Broun, Director.*
Web, www.hud.gov/offices/cpd/environment

Issues policies and sets standards for environmental and land-use planning and for environmental management practices. Develops policies promoting energy efficiency, conservation, and renewable sources of supply in housing and community development programs, including district heating and cooling systems and wastes-to-energy cogeneration projects.

Housing and Urban Development Dept. (HUD), *Field Management, 451 7th St. S.W., #7154 20410; (202) 708-2565. Fax, (202) 401-9681. Ronald J. Herbert, Director.*
Web, www.hud.gov

Acts as liaison and coordinates all activities between the Office of Community Planning and Development and regional and field offices; evaluates the performance of regional and field offices. Conducts policy analyses and evaluations of community planning and development programs, including the Community Development Block Grant Program, the Empowerment Zones/Enterprise Communities Program, and the McKinney Act programs.

Housing and Urban Development Dept. (HUD), *States Division, 451 7th St. S.W., #7184 20410; (202) 708-1322. Fax, (202) 401-2044. Diane Lobasso, Director.*
Web, www.hud.gov/offices/cpd/communitydevelopment/programs/index.cfm

Provides states with grants for distribution to small cities (fewer than 50,000 persons) and counties (fewer than 200,000 persons) that do not receive funding through the Entitlement Community Development Block Grant Program. Funds benefit low- and moderate-income persons, eliminate slums and blighted conditions, or meet other urgent community development needs. All states (except Hawaii), plus Puerto Rico, receive State Community Development Block Grant (CDBG) program funding. In Hawaii, HUD provides funding directly to the local governments. A separate program also provides funding to the U.S. territories.

Housing and Urban Development Dept. (HUD), *Technical Assistance, 451 7th St. S.W., #7216 20410; (202) 708-3176. Fax, (202) 619-5979. Mark A. "Marty" Horwarth, Director.*
Web, www.hud.gov/offices.cpd

Develops program policies and designs and implements technical assistance plans for state and local governments for use in community planning and development programs.

►CONGRESS

For a listing of relevant congressional committees and subcommittees, please see page 381 or the Appendix.

►NONGOVERNMENTAL

American Planning Assn., *1776 Massachusetts Ave. N.W., #400 20036-1904; (202) 872-0611. Fax, (202) 872-0643. Paul W. Farmer, Executive Director (Chicago); Jeffrey Soule, Director of Policy and Outreach. Web, www.planning.org*

Membership: professional planners and others interested in urban, suburban, and rural planning. Serves as a clearinghouse for planners. Sponsors professional development workshops conducted by the American Institute of Certified Planners. Prepares studies and technical reports; conducts seminars and conferences.

American Resort Development Assn., *1201 15th St. N.W., #400 20005; (202) 371-6700. Fax, (202) 289-8544. Howard Nusbaum, President. Web, www.arda.org*

Membership: U.S. and international developers, builders, financiers, marketing companies, and others involved in resort, recreational, and community development. Serves as an information clearinghouse; monitors federal and state legislation affecting land, time share, and community development industries.

Center for Community Change, *1536 U St. N.W. 20009; (202) 339-9300. Fax, (202) 387-4896. Deepak Bhargava, Executive Director. Toll-free, (877) 777-1536. General e-mail, info@communitychange.org Web, www.communitychange.org*

Works to strengthen grassroots organizations that help low-income people, working-class people, and minorities develop skills and resources to improve their communities and change the policies and institutions that affect their lives. Monitors legislation and regulations.

CFED, *1200 G St. N.W., #400 20005; (202) 408-9788. Fax, (202) 408-9793. Andrea Levere, President. General e-mail, info@cfed.org Web, www.cfed.org*

Works to expand economic opportunity and participation by bringing together community practice, public policy, and private markets in new and effective ways. (Formerly the Corporation for Enterprise Development.)

Council of State Community Development Agencies, *1825 K St. N.W., #515 20006; (202) 293-5820. Fax, (202) 293-2820. Dianne E. Taylor, Executive Director. General e-mail, coscda@coscda.org Web, www.coscda.org*

Membership: directors and staff of state community development agencies. Promotes common interests among the states, including community and economic development, housing, homelessness, infrastructure, and state and local planning.

Institute for Sustainable Communities, *888 17th St. N.W., #610 20006; (202) 777-7575. Fax, (202) 777-7577. Betty Weiss, Director of Community Initiatives. General e-mail, isc@iscvt.org Web, www.iscvt.org*

Provides training and technical assistance to communities to engage citizens in developing and implementing plans for a sustainable future.

International Institute of Site Planning, *715 G St. S.E. 20003; (202) 546-2322. Fax, (202) 546-2722. Beatriz de Winthuysen Coffin, Director. General e-mail, iisitep@aol.com Web, www.gis.net/~iisp*

Directs research and provides information on site planning development and design of sites and buildings; conducts study and travel programs.

Land Trust Alliance, *1660 L St. N.W., #1100 20036; (202) 638-4725. Fax, (202) 638-4730. Rand Wentworth, President. General e-mail, info@lta.org Web, www.landtrustalliance.org*

Membership: organizations and individuals who work to conserve land resources. Serves as a forum for the exchange of information; conducts research and public education programs. Monitors legislation and regulations.

Local Initiatives Support Corp., *Washington Office, 1825 K St. N.W., #1100 20006; (202) 785-2908. Fax, (202) 835-8931. Michael Tierney, Executive Vice President. Web, www.lisc.org*

Provides community development corporations with financial and technical assistance to build affordable housing and revitalize distressed neighborhoods. (Headquarters in New York.)

National Assn. of Conservation Districts (NACD), *509 Capitol Court N.E. 20002-4937; (202) 547-6223. Fax, (202) 547-6450. Krysta Harden, Chief Executive Director. General e-mail, washington@nacdnet.org Web, www.nacdnet.org*

Membership: conservation districts (local subdivisions of state government). Works to promote the conservation of land, forests, and other natural resources. Interests include erosion and sediment control; water quality, forestry, water, flood plain, and range management; rural development; and urban and community conservation.

National Assn. of Counties (NACo), *Community and Economic Development, 25 Massachusetts Ave. N.W., 5th Floor 20001; (202) 393-6226. Fax, (202) 942-4281. Daria Daniel, Associate Legislative Director. Web, www.naco.org*

Membership: county governments. Conducts research and provides information on community development block grants, assisted low-income housing, and other housing and economic development programs. Monitors legislation and regulations.

National Assn. of Development Organizations, *400 N. Capitol St. N.W., #390 20001; (202) 624-7806. Fax, (202) 624-8813. Matthew D. Chase, Executive Director.*
General e-mail, info@nado.org

Web, www.nado.org

Membership: organizations interested in regional, local, and rural economic development. Provides information on federal, state, and local development programs and revolving loan funds; sponsors conferences and seminars.

National Assn. of Regional Councils, *1666 Connecticut Ave. N.W., #300 20009; (202) 986-1032. Fax, (202) 986-1038. Fred Abousleman, Executive Director.*
Web, www.narc.org

Membership: regional councils of local governments and metropolitan planning organizations. Works with member local governments to encourage areawide economic growth and cooperation between public and private sectors, with emphasis on community development.

National Community Development Assn., *522 21st St. N.W., #120 20006; (202) 293-7587. Fax, (202) 887-5546. Cardell Cooper, Executive Director.*
Web, www.ncdaonline.org

Membership: local governments that administer federally supported community and economic development, housing, and human service programs.

National Trust for Historic Preservation, *1785 Massachusetts Ave. N.W. 20036-2117; (202) 588-6000. Fax, (202) 588-6038. Richard Moe, President. Information, (800) 944-6847. Press, (202) 588-6141.*
General e-mail, feedback@nthp.org

Web, www.preservationnation.org

Conducts seminars, workshops, and conferences on topics related to preservation, including neighborhood conservation, main street revitalization, rural conservation, and preservation law; offers financial assistance through loan and grant programs; provides advisory services; and operates historic house sites, which are open to the public.

Partners for Livable Communities, *1429 21st St. N.W., 2nd Floor 20036; (202) 887-5990. Fax, (202) 466-4845. Robert H. McNulty, President.*
Web, www.livable.com

Promotes working partnerships among public, private, and governmental sectors to improve the quality of life and economic development at local and regional levels. Conducts conferences and workshops; maintains referral clearinghouse; provides technical assistance.

Scenic America, *1250 Eye St. N.W., #750A 20005; (202) 638-4630. Fax, (202) 638-3171. Kevin E. Fry, President.*

General e-mail, fry@scenic.org

Web, www.scenic.org

Membership: national, state, and local groups concerned with land-use control, growth management, and landscape protection. Works to enhance the scenic quality of America's communities and countryside. Provides information and technical assistance on scenic byways, tree preservation, economics of aesthetic regulation, billboard and sign control, scenic areas preservation, and growth management.

Smart Growth America, *1707 L St. N.W., #1050 20036; (202) 207-3355. Fax, (202) 207-3349. Geoff Anderson, President. Press, (202) 412-7930.*
General e-mail, sga@smartgrowthamerica.org

Web, www.smartgrowthamerica.org

Coalition of advocacy groups that supports citizen-driven planning that coordinates development, transportation, revitalization of older areas, and preservation of open space and the environment.

Smart Growth Leadership Institute (Smart Growth America), *1707 L St. N.W., #1050 20036; (202) 207-3355. Fax, (202) 207-3349. Tamar Shapiro, Executive Director.*
General e-mail, info@sgli.org

Web, www.sgli.org

Provides technical and strategic assistance to communities working to achieve smart growth, including presentations and workshops, reviews and evaluations of the regulatory frameworks that shape community development patterns, training in coalition building, and direct consultations.

Rural Areas

▶**AGENCIES**

Agriculture Dept. (USDA), *Rural Development, 1400 Independence Ave. S.W., #205W 20250-0107; (202) 720-4581. Fax, (202) 720-2080. Sheryl L. Cook, Under Secretary (Acting).*
Web, www.rurdev.usda.gov

Acts as chief adviser to the secretary on agricultural credit and related matters; coordinates rural development policies and programs throughout the federal government; supervises the Rural Utilities Service, Rural Housing Service, and Rural Business-Cooperative Service.

Farm Service Agency (FSA), *(Agriculture Dept.), Farm Loan Programs, 1400 Independence Ave. S.W., #3605S, MS 0520 20250-0520; (202) 720-4671. Fax, (202) 690-3573. Carolyn Cooksie, Deputy Administrator.*
Web, www.fsa.usda.gov

Supports rural development through farm program loans, including real estate, farm production, and emergency loans.

National Agricultural Library *(Agriculture Dept.),* *Rural Information Center,* 10301 Baltimore Ave., #132, Beltsville, MD 20705-2351; (800) 633-7701. Fax, (301) 504-5181. William Thomas, Coordinator, (301) 504-6559. General e-mail, ric@nal.usda.gov

Web, http://ric.nal.usda.gov

Provides services for rural communities, local officials, organizations, businesses, and rural citizens in the interest of maintaining rural areas. Interests include community development, tourism promotion, water quality, recycling, and technology transfer.

Rural Development *(Agriculture Dept.),* **Business and Cooperative Programs: Business Programs,** 1400 Independence Ave. S.W., #5813-S 20250-3220; (202) 720-7287. Fax, (202) 690-0097. William F. Hagy III, Deputy Administrator. Web, www.rurdev.usda.gov/rbs

Promotes rural economic development by providing financial assistance and business planning to community businesses.

Rural Development Utilities *(Agriculture Dept.),* 1400 Independence Ave. S.W., #5135-S, MS 1510 20250-1510; (202) 720-9540. Fax, (202) 720-1725. James Newby, Administrator (Acting). Information, (202) 720-1255. Web, www.usda.gov/rus

Makes loans and loan guarantees to rural electric and telephone companies providing service in rural areas. Administers the Rural Telephone Bank, which provides supplemental financing from federal sources. Makes loans for economic development and creation of jobs in rural areas, for water and waste disposal, and for distance learning and telemedicine.

Rural Housing Service *(Agriculture Dept.),* 1400 Independence Ave. S.W., #5014, MS 0701 20250-0701; (202) 690-1533. Fax, (202) 690-0500. James C. Alsop, Administrator (Acting). Web, www.rurdev.usda.gov/rhs

Offers financial assistance to apartment dwellers and homeowners in rural areas; provides funds to construct or improve community facilities.

▶**CONGRESS**

For a listing of relevant congressional committees and subcommittees, please see page 381 or the Appendix.

▶**NONGOVERNMENTAL**

Farm Credit Council, 50 F St. N.W., #900 20001-1530; (202) 626-8710. Fax, (202) 626-8718. Ken Auer, President. Toll-free, (800) 525-2345. Web, www.fccouncil.com

Represents the Farm Credit System, a national financial cooperative that makes loans to agricultural producers, rural homebuyers, farmer cooperatives, and rural utilities. Finances the export of U.S. agricultural commodities.

Housing Assistance Council, 1025 Vermont Ave. N.W., #606 20005-3516; (202) 842-8600. Fax, (202) 347-3441. Moises Loza, Executive Director. General e-mail, hac@ruralhome.org

Web, www.ruralhome.org

Operates in rural areas and in cities of fewer than 25,000 citizens. Advises low-income and minority groups seeking federal assistance for improving rural housing and community facilities; studies and makes recommendations for state and local housing policies; makes low-interest loans for housing programs for low-income and minority groups living in rural areas, including Native Americans and farm workers.

Irrigation Assn., 6540 Arlington Blvd., Falls Church, VA 22042-6638; (703) 536-7080. Fax, (703) 536-7019. Deborah Hamlin, Executive Director. General e-mail, webmaster@irrigation.org

Web, www.irrigation.org

Membership: companies and individuals involved in irrigation, drainage, and erosion control worldwide. Promotes efficient and effective water management through training, education, and certification programs. Interests include economic development and environmental enhancement.

National Cooperative Business Assn., 1401 New York Ave. N.W., #1100 20005-2160; (202) 638-6222. Fax, (202) 638-1374. Paul Hazen, President. General e-mail, ncba@ncba.coop

Web, www.ncba.coop

Alliance of cooperatives, businesses, and state cooperative associations. Provides information about starting and managing agricultural cooperatives in the United States and in developing nations. Monitors legislation and regulations.

National Council of Farmer Cooperatives (NCFC), 50 F St. N.W., #900 20001-1530; (202) 626-8700. Fax, (202) 626-8722. Charles F. Connor, President. General e-mail, info@ncfc.org

Web, www.ncfc.org

Membership: cooperative businesses owned and operated by farmers. Encourages research on agricultural cooperatives; provides statistics and analyzes trends. Monitors legislation and regulations on agricultural trade, transportation, energy, and tax issues.

National Rural Electric Cooperative Assn. (NRECA), 4301 Wilson Blvd., Arlington, VA 22203-1860; (703) 907-5500. Fax, (703) 907-5511. Glenn English, Chief Executive Officer. Web, www.nreca.org

Membership: rural electric cooperative systems and public power and utility districts. Provides members with legislative, legal, and regulatory services.

National Telecommunications Cooperative Assn. (NTCA), 4121 Wilson Blvd., 10th Floor, Arlington, VA

22203-1801; (703) 351-2000. Fax, (703) 351-2001.
Michael E. Brunner, Chief Executive Officer.
General e-mail, pubrelations@ntca.org

Web, www.ntca.org

Membership: locally owned and controlled telecommunications cooperatives and companies serving rural and small-town areas. Offers educational seminars, workshops, technical assistance, and a benefits program to members. Monitors legislation and regulations.

Rural Coalition, 1012 14th St. N.W., #1100 20005-3403; (202) 628-7160. Fax, (202) 628-7165. Lorette Picciano, Executive Director.
General e-mail, ruralco@ruralco.org

Web, www.ruralco.org

Alliance of organizations that develop public policies benefiting rural communities. Collaborates with community-based groups on agriculture and rural development issues, including health and the environment, minority farmers, farm workers, Native Americans' rights, and rural community development. Provides rural groups with technical assistance.

Rural Community Assistance Partnership (RCAP), 1522 K St. N.W., #400 20005; (202) 408-1273. Fax, (202) 408-8165. Robert Stewart, Executive Director. Toll-free, (800) 321-7227.
General e-mail, info@rcap.org

Web, www.rcap.org

Provides expertise to rural communities on wastewater disposal, protection of groundwater supply, and access to safe drinking water. Targets communities with predominately low-income or minority populations. Offers outreach policy analysis, training, and technical assistance to elected officials and other community leaders, utility owners and operators, and residents.

Specific Regions

►AGENCIES

Appalachian Regional Commission, 1666 Connecticut Ave. N.W., #700 20009-1068; (202) 884-7660. Fax, (202) 884-7693. Thomas M. Hunter, Executive Director, (202) 884-7700; Anne B. Pope, Federal Co-Chair. Press, (202) 884-7771.
General e-mail, info@arc.gov

Web, www.arc.gov

Federal-state-local partnership for economic development of the region including West Virginia and parts of Alabama, Georgia, Kentucky, Maryland, Mississippi, New York, North Carolina, Ohio, Pennsylvania, South Carolina, Tennessee, and Virginia. Plans and provides technical and financial assistance and coordinates federal and state efforts for economic development of Appalachia.

Bureau of Reclamation *(Interior Dept.),* 1849 C St. N.W., #7554, 7069 MIB 20240; (202) 513-0501. Fax, (202) 513-0309. John McDonald, Commissioner (Acting). Press, (202) 513-0684.
Web, www.usbr.gov

Administers federal programs for water and power resource development and management in seventeen western states; oversees municipal and industrial water supplies, hydroelectric power generation, irrigation, flood control, water quality improvement, river regulation, fish and wildlife enhancement, and outdoor recreation.

Interstate Commission on the Potomac River Basin, 51 Monroe St., #PE-8, Rockville, MD 20850; (301) 984-1908. Fax, (301) 984-5841. Joseph K. Hoffman, Executive Director.
General e-mail, info@icprb.org

Web, www.potomacriver.org

Nonregulatory interstate compact commission established by Congress to control and reduce water pollution and to restore and protect living resources in the Potomac River and its tributaries. Monitors water quality; assists metropolitan water utilities; seeks innovative methods to solve water supply and land resource problems. Provides information and educational materials on the Potomac River basin.

National Capital Planning Commission, 401 9th St. N.W., North Lobby, #500 20004; (202) 482-7200. Fax, (202) 482-7272. Marcel Acosta, Executive Director.
General e-mail, info@ncpc.gov

Web, www.ncpc.gov

Central planning agency for the federal government in the national capital region, which includes the District of Columbia and suburban Maryland and Virginia. Reviews and approves plans for the physical growth and development of the national capital area, using environmental, historic, and land-use criteria.

Tennessee Valley Authority, *Government Affairs,* *Washington Office,* 1 Massachusetts Ave. N.W., #300 20444; (202) 898-2999. Fax, (202) 898-2998. Justin Maierhofer, Director.
General e-mail, latootle@tva.gov

Web, www.tva.gov

Coordinates resource conservation, development, and land-use programs in the Tennessee River Valley. Produces and supplies wholesale power to municipal and cooperative electric systems, federal installations, and some industries. (Headquarters in Knoxville, Tenn.)

►NONGOVERNMENTAL

Greater Washington Board of Trade, 1725 Eye St. N.W., #200 20006; (202) 857-5900. Fax, (202) 223-2648. James C. Dinegar, President.
General e-mail, info@bot.org

Web, www.bot.org

Promotes and plans economic growth for the capital region. Supports business-government partnerships, technological training, and transportation planning; promotes international trade; works to increase economic viability of the city of Washington. Monitors legislation and regulations at local, state, and federal levels.

New England Council, *Washington Office,* 331 *Constitution Ave. N.E. 20002; (202) 547-0048. Fax, (202) 547-9149. Jeff Turcotte, Director of Federal Affairs. General e-mail, dcoffice@newenglandcouncil.com*

Web, www.newenglandcouncil.com

Provides information on business and economic issues concerning New England; serves as liaison between the New England congressional delegations and business community. (Headquarters in Boston, Mass.)

Northeast–Midwest Institute, *50 F St. N.W., #950 20001; (202) 544-5200. Fax, (202) 544-0043. Tom Wolfe, Executive Director.*

General e-mail, info@nemw.org

Web, www.nemw.org

Public policy research organization that promotes the economic vitality of the northeast and midwest regions. Interests include distribution of federal funding to regions, economic development, human resources, energy, and natural resources.

Urban Areas

►AGENCIES

General Services Administration (GSA), *Urban Development/Good Neighbor Program, 1800 F St. N.W., #3341 20405-0001; (202) 501-1856. Fax, (202) 501-3393. Frank Giblin, Director. Web, www.gsa.gov/goodneighbor*

Advises on locations, designs, and renovations of federal facilities in central business areas, historic districts, and local redevelopment areas where they can anchor or promote community development. Collaborates with local and national civic and other organizations. Serves as clearinghouse for good practices.

Housing and Urban Development Dept. (HUD), *Affordable Housing Programs, 451 7th St. S.W., #7164 20410; (202) 708-2684. Fax, (202) 708-1744. Clifford Taffet, Director. Web, www.hud.gov*

Coordinates with cities to convey publicly owned, abandoned property to low-income families in exchange for their commitment to repair, occupy, and maintain the property.

Housing and Urban Development Dept. (HUD), *Economic Development, 451 7th St. S.W., #7136 20410; (202) 708-4091. Fax, (202) 401-2231. Vacant, Deputy Assistant Secretary. Web, www.hud.gov*

Manages economic development programs, including Empowerment Zones/Renewal Communities, Rural Housing and Economic Development, Brownfields Economic Development Initiatives, and YOUTHBUILD. Encourages private-public partnerships for development through neighborhood development corporations. Formulates policies and legislative proposals on economic development.

NeighborWorks America, *1325 G St. N.W., #800 20005-3100; (202) 220-2300. Fax, (202) 376-2600. Kenneth D. Wade, Chief Executive Officer.*

Web, www.nw.org

Chartered by Congress to assist localities in developing and operating local neighborhood-based programs designed to reverse decline in urban residential neighborhoods and rural communities. Oversees the National NeighborWorks Network, an association of local nonprofit organizations concerned with urban and rural development. (Formerly the Neighborhood Reinvestment Corp.)

►NONGOVERNMENTAL

The Brookings Institution, *Metropolitan Policy Program, 1717 Massachusetts Ave. N.W., 3rd Floor 20036-2001; (202) 797-6139. Fax, (202) 797-2965. Bruce Katz, Director.*

General e-mail, metro@brookings.edu

Web, www.brookings.edu/metro

Helps U.S. cities and metropolitan areas identify, advance, and implement the policies needed to achieve their full economic, fiscal, and social potential. Conducts research at the national, state, and local levels to develop and augment public policy ideas toward this end. Monitors legislation and regulations.

Center for Neighborhood Enterprise, *1625 K St. N.W., #1200 20006; (202) 518-6500. Fax, (202) 588-0314. Robert L. Woodson Sr., President. Information, (866) 518-1263.*

General e-mail, info@ncne.com

Web, www.ncne.com

Provides community and faith-based organizations with training, technical assistance, and additional sources of support. Addresses homelessness and deteriorating neighborhoods. (Formerly known as the National Center for Neighborhood Enterprise.)

International Downtown Assn., *734 15th St. N.W., #610 20005; (202) 393-6801. Fax, (202) 393-6869. David M. Feehan, President.*

General e-mail, question@ida-downtown.org

Web, www.ida-downtown.org

Membership: organizations, corporations, public agencies, and individuals interested in the development and management of city downtown areas. Supports cooperative efforts between the public and private sectors to revitalize downtowns and adjacent neighborhoods; provides members with information, technical assistance, and advice.

International Economic Development Council, *734 15th St. N.W., #900 20005; (202) 223-7800. Fax, (202) 223-4745. Jeffrey Finkle, President.*
General e-mail, mail@iedconline.org

Web, www.iedconline.org

Membership: public economic development directors, chamber of commerce staff, utility executives, academicians, and others who design and implement development programs. Provides information to members on job creation, attraction, and retention.

Milton S. Eisenhower Foundation, *1875 Connecticut Ave. N.W., #410 20009-5728; (202) 234-8104. Fax, (202) 234-8484. Alan Curtis, President.*
General e-mail, info@eisenhowerfoundation.org

Web, www.eisenhowerfoundation.org

Strives to help inner-city communities combat violence by supporting programs with proven records of success. Provides funding, technical assistance, evaluation, and supervision to communities wishing to replicate successful programs.

National Assn. for the Advancement of Colored People (NAACP), *Washington Bureau, 1156 15th St. N.W., #915 20005-1750; (202) 463-2940. Fax, (202) 463-2953. Hilary O. Shelton, Director.*
General e-mail, washingtonbureau@naacpnet.org

Web, www.naacp.org

Membership: persons interested in civil rights for all minorities. Works to eliminate discrimination in housing and urban affairs. Interests include programs for urban redevelopment, urban homesteading, and low-income housing. Supports programs that make affordable rental housing available to minorities and that maintain African American ownership of urban and rural land. (Headquarters in Baltimore, Md.)

National Assn. of Neighborhoods, *1300 Pennsylvania Ave. N.W., #700 20004; (202) 332-7766. Fax, (202) 529-2976. Ricardo C. Byrd, Executive Director.*
General e-mail, staff@nanworld.org

Web, www.nanworld.org

Federation of neighborhood groups that provides technical assistance to local governments, neighborhood groups, and businesses. Seeks to increase influence of grassroots groups on decisions affecting neighborhoods; sponsors training workshops promoting neighborhood awareness.

National League of Cities, *1301 Pennsylvania Ave. N.W., #550 20004; (202) 626-3000. Fax, (202) 626-3043. Donald J. Borut, Executive Director; Sherry Appel, Director of Media Relations, (202) 626-3003.*
General e-mail, info@nlc.org

Web, www.nlc.org

Membership: cities and state municipal leagues. Aids city leaders in developing programs; investigates needs of local governments in implementing federal community development programs.

National Urban League, *Washington Office, 2901 14th Street N.W. 20009; (202) 265-8200. Fax, (202) 265-6122. Maudine R. Cooper, President.*
Web, www.gwul.org

Social service organization concerned with the social welfare of African Americans and other minorities. Conducts legislative and policy analysis on housing and urban affairs. Operates a job bank. (Headquarters in New York.)

Urban Institute, *Metropolitan Housing and Communities Policy Center, 2100 M St. N.W., #500 20037; (202) 833-7200. Fax, (202) 872-9322. Robert D. Reischauer, President; Vacant, Director. Public Affairs, (202) 261-5709.*
General e-mail, paffairs@ui.urban.org

Web, www.urban.org/center/met

Research organization that deals with urban problems. Researches federal, state, and local policies; focus includes community development block grants, neighborhood rehabilitation programs, and housing issues.

Urban Land Institute, *1025 Thomas Jefferson St. N.W., #500W 20007-5201; (202) 624-7000. Fax, (202) 624-7140. Richard Rosan, President. Information, (800) 321-5011. Library, (202) 624-7137.*
Web, www.uli.org

Membership: land developers, planners, state and federal agencies, financial institutions, home builders, consultants, and realtors. Provides responsible leadership in the use of land to enhance the total environment; monitors trends in new community development. Library open to the public by appointment for a fee.

U.S. Conference of Mayors, *1620 Eye St. N.W., #400 20006; (202) 293-7330. Fax, (202) 293-2352. J. Thomas Cochran, Executive Director.*
General e-mail, info@usmayors.org

Web, www.usmayors.org/uscm

Membership: mayors of cities with populations of 30,000 or more. Promotes city-federal cooperation; publishes reports and conducts meetings on federal programs, policies, and initiatives that affect urban and suburban interests. Serves as a clearinghouse for information on urban and suburban problems.

CONSTRUCTION

▶AGENCIES

Census Bureau *(Commerce Dept.), Manufacturing and Construction, 4600 Silver Hill Rd., #7K154, Suitland, MD 20746-4600 (for mailing address, change city and zip code to: Washington, DC 20233); (301) 763-4593. Fax, (301) 768-7783. Thomas E. Zabelsky, Division Chief.*
Web, www.census.gov

Publishes statistics on the value of construction put in place; housing starts, sales, and completions; building permits; price index of single-family homes sold; characteristics of new housing; and expenditures for residential improvements. Conducts a census of construction industries every five years.

General Services Administration (GSA), *Public Buildings Service, 1800 F St. N.W., #6340 20405; (202) 501-1100. Fax, (202) 219-2310. Tony Costa, Commissioner (Acting).*
Web, www.gsa.gov/pbs

Administers the acquisition, construction, maintenance, and operation of buildings owned or leased by the federal government. Manages and disposes of federal real estate.

International Trade Administration (ITA), *(Commerce Dept.), Manufacturing and Services: Manufacturing, 14th St. and Constitution Ave. N.W., #2800 20230; (202) 482-1872. Fax, (202) 482-0856. Vacant, Assistant Secretary.*
Web, www.trade.gov

Analyzes and maintains data on international construction and engineering. Monitors production costs, prices, financial and labor conditions, technological changes, distribution, markets, trade patterns, and other aspects of these industries. Promotes international trade, develops competitive assessments, and assists engineering and construction companies in obtaining overseas construction projects.

▶**NONGOVERNMENTAL**

American Public Works Assn., *Washington Office, 1401 K St. N.W., 11th Floor 20005; (202) 408-9541. Fax, (202) 408-9542. Peter B. King, Executive Director.*
General e-mail, apwa.dc@apwa.net
Web, www.apwa.net

Membership: engineers, architects, and others who maintain and manage public works facilities and services. Conducts research and education and promotes exchange of information on transportation and infrastructure-related issues. (Headquarters in Kansas City, Mo.)

American Subcontractors Assn., *1004 Duke St., Alexandria, VA 22314-3588; (703) 684-3450. Fax, (703) 836-3482. Colette Nelson, Executive Vice President.*
General e-mail, asaoffice@asa-hq.com
Web, www.asaonline.com

Membership: construction subcontractors, specialty contractors, and their suppliers. Addresses business, contract, and payment issues affecting all subcontractors. Interests include procurement laws, payment practices, and lien laws. Monitors legislation and regulations.

Associated Builders and Contractors, *4250 N. Fairfax Dr., 9th Floor, Arlington, VA 22203-1607; (703) 812-2000. Fax, (703) 812-8202. M. Kirk Pickerel, President.*
General e-mail, info@abc.org
Web, www.abc.org

Membership: construction contractors engaged primarily in nonresidential construction, subcontractors, and suppliers. Sponsors apprenticeship, safety, and training programs. Provides labor relations information; compiles statistics. Monitors legislation and regulations.

Associated General Contractors of America, *2300 Wilson Blvd., #400, Arlington, VA 22201; (703) 548-3118. Fax, (703) 548-3119. Stephen E. Sandherr, Chief Executive Officer.*
General e-mail, info@agc.org
Web, www.agc.org

Membership: general contractors engaged primarily in nonresidential construction; subcontractors; suppliers; accounting, insurance and bonding, and law firms. Conducts training programs, conferences, seminars, and market development activities for members. Produces position papers on construction issues. Monitors legislation and regulations.

Construction Management Assn. of America, *7926 Jones Branch Dr., #800, McLean, VA 22102-3303; (703) 356-2622. Fax, (703) 356-6388. Bruce D'Agostino, President.*
General e-mail, info@cmaanet.org
Web, www.cmaanet.org

Promotes the development of construction management as a profession through publications, education, a certification program, and an information network. Serves as an advocate for construction management in the legislative, executive, and judicial branches of government.

Construction Specifications Institute, *99 Canal Center Plaza, #300, Alexandria, VA 22314-1588; (703) 684-0300. Fax, (703) 684-0465. Walter T. Marlowe, Executive Director. Information, (800) 689-2900.*
General e-mail, csi@csinet.org
Web, http://csinet.org

Membership: architects, engineers, contractors, and others in the construction industry. Promotes construction technology; publishes reference materials to help individuals prepare construction documents; sponsors certification programs for construction specifiers and manufacturing representatives.

Mechanical Contractors Assn. of America, *1385 Piccard Dr., Rockville, MD 20850; (301) 869-5800. Fax, (301) 990-9690. John R. Gentille, Executive Vice President.*
Web, www.mcaa.org

Membership: mechanical contractors and members of related professions. Seeks to improve building standards and codes. Provides information, publications, and training programs; conducts seminars and annual convention. Monitors legislation and regulations.

National Assn. of Home Builders (NAHB), *1201 15th St. N.W. 20005-2800; (202) 266-8200. Fax, (202) 266-8400. Jerry M. Howard, Chief Executive Officer. Press, (202) 266-8254. Toll-free, (800) 368-5242.*

General e-mail, info@nahb.org

Web, www.nahb.org

Membership: contractors, builders, architects, engineers, mortgage lenders, and others interested in home building and residential real estate construction. Participates in updating and developing building codes and standards; offers technical information.

National Assn. of Minority Contractors, *1300 Pennsylvania Ave. N.W., #700 20001; (202) 204-3093. Fax, (202) 789-7349. Richard Copeland, President. Toll-free, (866) 688-6262.*

Web, www.namcdc.org

Membership: minority businesses and related firms, associations, and individuals serving those businesses in the construction industry. Advises members on commercial and government business; develops resources for technical assistance and training; provides bid information on government contracts.

National Assn. of Plumbing-Heating-Cooling Contractors, *180 S. Washington St., Falls Church, VA 22046 (mailing address: P.O. Box 6808, Falls Church, VA 22040-6808); (703) 237-8100. Fax, (703) 237-7442. Dwight L. "Ike" Casey, Executive Vice President. Information, (800) 533-7694.*

Web, www.phccweb.org

Provides education and training for plumbing, heating, and cooling contractors and their employees. Offers career information, internships, and scholarship programs for business and engineering students to encourage careers in the plumbing and mechanical contracting field.

National Electrical Contractors Assn., *3 Bethesda Metro Center, #1100, Bethesda, MD 20814; (301) 657-3110. Fax, (301) 215-4500. John Grau, Chief Executive Officer.*

Web, www.necanet.org

Membership: electrical contractors who build and service electrical wiring, equipment, and appliances. Represents members in collective bargaining with union workers; sponsors research and educational programs.

National Utility Contractors Assn. (NUCA), *4301 N. Fairfax Dr., #360, Arlington, VA 22203-1627; (703) 358-9300. Fax, (703) 358-9307. Bill Hillman, Chief Executive Officer.*

Web, www.nuca.com

Membership: contractors who perform water, sewer, and other underground utility construction. Sponsors conferences; conducts surveys. Monitors public works legislation and regulations.

Sheet Metal and Air Conditioning Contractors National Assn., *4201 Lafayette Center Dr., Chantilly, VA 20151-1209; (703) 803-2980. Fax, (703) 803-3732. Vincent R. Sandusky, Chief Executive Officer.*

General e-mail, info@smacna.org

Web, www.smacna.org

Membership: unionized sheet metal and air conditioning contractors. Provides information on standards and installation and fabrication methods.

Society for Marketing Professional Services, *44 Canal Center Plaza, #444, Alexandria, VA 22314; (703) 549-6117. Fax, (703) 549-2498. Ronald D. Worth, Chief Executive Officer. Information, (800) 292-7677.*

General e-mail, info@smps.org

Web, www.smps.org

Membership: individuals who provide professional services to the building industry. Assists individuals who market design services in the areas of architecture, engineering, planning, interior design, landscape architecture, and construction management. Provides seminars, workshops, and publications for members. Maintains job banks.

Sustainable Buildings Industry Council, *1112 16th St. N.W., #240 20036-4818; (202) 628-7400. Fax, (202) 393-5043. Sophia Greenbaum, Executive Director.*

General e-mail, sbic@sbicouncil.org

Web, www.sbicouncil.org

Provides information on all aspects of sustainable design and construction: energy efficiency, renewable technologies, daylighting, healthy indoor environments, sustainable building materials and products, and resource conservation.

U.S. Green Building Council, *1800 Massachusetts Ave. N.W., #300 20036; (202) 828-7422. Fax, (202) 828-5110. S. Richard Fedrizzi, President. Information, (800) 795-1747. Customer care, (202) 742-3792.*

General e-mail, info@usgbc.org

Web, www.usgbc.org

Promotes buildings that are environmentally responsible, profitable, and healthy. Rates green buildings in order to accelerate implementation of environmentally friendly design practices.

Architecture and Design

▶**AGENCIES**

General Services Administration (GSA), *Design Excellence and the Arts Division: Office of the Chief Architect, 1800 F St. N.W. 20405; (202) 501-1888. Fax, (202) 501-3393. Leslie Shepherd, Director.*

Web, www.gsa.gov

Administers the Art in Architecture Program, which commissions publicly scaled works of art for government buildings and landscapes, and the Fine Arts Program, which manages the GSA's collection of fine artwork that has been commissioned for use in government buildings.

National Endowment for the Arts (NEA), *Folk and Traditional Arts, Theater, and Musical Theater, 1100 Pennsylvania Ave. N.W. 20506-0001; (202) 682-5428.*

Fax, (202) 682-5669. Cathy Vass, Division Coordinator, (202) 682-5523.

Web, www.arts.gov

Awards grants for design arts projects in architecture; landscape architecture; urban design and planning; historic preservation; and interior, graphic, industrial, product, and costume and fashion design.

▶ NONGOVERNMENTAL

American Institute of Architects, *1735 New York Ave. N.W. 20006-5292; (202) 626-7300. Fax, (202) 626-7498. Christine McEntee, Chief Executive Officer. Library, (202) 626-7496. Press, (202) 626-7467. Toll-free, (800) 242-3837. Government Advocacy, (202) 626-7507. General e-mail, infocentral@aia.org*

Web, www.aia.org

Membership: licensed American architects, interns, architecture faculty, engineers, planners, and those in government, manufacturing, or other fields in a capacity related to architecture. Works to advance the standards of architectural education, training, and practice. Promotes the aesthetic, scientific, and practical efficiency of architecture, urban design, and planning; monitors international developments. Offers continuing and professional education programs; sponsors scholarships, internships, and awards. Houses archival collection, including documents and drawings of American architects and architecture. Library open to the public by appointment. Monitors legislation and regulations.

American Nursery and Landscape Assn., *1000 Vermont Ave. N.W., #300 20005-4914; (202) 789-2900. Fax, (202) 789-1893. Robert J. Dolibois, Executive Vice President; Warren Quinn, Director.*

Web, www.anla.org

Serves as an information clearinghouse on the technical aspects of nursery and landscape business and design.

American Society of Interior Designers, *608 Massachusetts Ave. N.E. 20002-6006; (202) 546-3480. Fax, (202) 546-3240. Michael Alin, Executive Director. General e-mail, asid@asid.org*

Web, www.asid.org

Offers certified professional development courses addressing the technical, professional, and business needs of designers; bestows annual scholarships, fellowships, and awards; supports licensing efforts at the state level.

American Society of Landscape Architects, *636 Eye St. N.W. 20001-3736; (202) 898-2444. Fax, (202) 898-1185. Nancy Somerville, Executive Vice President. Toll-free, (888) 999-2752. General e-mail, info@asla.org*

Web, www.asla.org

Membership: professional landscape architects. Advises government agencies on land-use policy and environmental matters. Accredits university-level programs in landscape architecture; conducts professional education seminars for members.

Assn. of Collegiate Schools of Architecture, *1735 New York Ave. N.W. 20006; (202) 785-2324. Fax, (202) 628-0448. Michael J. Monti, Executive Director. General e-mail, info@acsa-arch.org*

Web, www.acsa-arch.org

Membership: U.S. and Canadian institutions that offer at least one accredited architecture degree program. Conducts workshops and seminars for architecture school faculty; presents awards for student and faculty excellence in architecture; publishes a guide to architecture schools in North America.

Industrial Designers Society of America, *45195 Business Ct., #250, Dulles, VA 20166-6717; (703) 707-6000. Fax, (703) 787-8501. Frank Tyneski, Executive Director. General e-mail, idsa@idsa.org*

Web, www.idsa.org

Membership: designers of products, equipment, instruments, furniture, transportation, packages, exhibits, information services, and related services. Provides the Bureau of Labor Statistics with industry information. Monitors legislation and regulations.

Landscape Architecture Foundation, *818 18th St. N.W., #810 20006; (202) 331-7070. Fax, (202) 331-7079. Barbara Deutsch, Executive Director. General e-mail, laf@lafoundation.org*

Web, www.lafoundation.org

Conducts research and provides educational and scientific information on sustainable land design and development and related fields. Awards scholarships and fellowships.

National Architectural Accrediting Board Inc., *1735 New York Ave. N.W. 20006; (202) 783-2007. Fax, (202) 783-2822. Andrea S. Rutledge, Executive Director. General e-mail, info@naab.org*

Web, www.naab.org

Accredits Bachelor, Master, and Doctor of Architecture degree programs.

National Assn. of Schools of Art and Design, *11250 Roger Bacon Dr., #21, Reston, VA 20190-5248; (703) 437-0700. Fax, (703) 437-6312. Samuel Hope, Executive Director. General e-mail, info@arts-accredit.org*

Web, http://nasad.arts-accredit.org

Accrediting agency for educational programs in art and design. Provides information on art and design programs at the postsecondary level; offers professional development for executives of art and design programs.

National Council of Architectural Registration Boards, *1801 K St. N.W., #700-K 20006-1310; (202) 783-6500.*

Fax, (202) 783-0290. Lenore M. Lucey, Executive Vice President.
Web, www.ncarb.org

Membership: state architectural licensing boards. Develops examinations used in U.S. states and territories for licensing architects; certifies architects.

PLANET (Professional Landcare Network), *950 Herndon Pkwy., #450, Herndon, VA 20170; (703) 736-9666. Fax, (703) 736-9668. Sabeena Hickman, Chief Operating Officer. Toll-free, (800) 395-2522.*
General e-mail, info@landcarenetwork.org

Web, www.landcarenetwork.org

Membership: lawn care professionals, exterior maintenance contractors, installation/design/building professionals, and interiorscapers. Provides members with education, business management and marketing tools, and networking opportunities. Offers certification program. Focus is the green industry. Monitors legislation. (Merger of the Associated Landscape Contractors of America and the Professional Lawn Care Assn. of America.)

Codes, Standards, and Research

▶**AGENCIES**

Architectural and Transportation Barriers Compliance Board (Access Board), *1331 F St. N.W., #1000 20004-1111; (202) 272-0080. Fax, (202) 272-0081. David M. Capozzi, Executive Director. TTY, (202) 272-0082. TTY toll-free, (800) 993-2822. Toll-free technical assistance, (800) 872-2253.*
General e-mail, info@access-board.gov

Web, www.access-board.gov

Develops and maintains accessibility requirements for buildings, transit vehicles, telecommunications equipment, and electronic and information technology. Provides technical assistance and training on these guidelines and standards. Enforces access standards for federally funded facilities through the Architectural Barriers Act.

Environmental Protection Agency (EPA), *Radiation and Indoor Air, 1310 L St. N.W., 4th Floor, MC 6601J 20005; (202) 343-9320. Fax, (202) 343-2395. Elizabeth Cotsworth, Director.*
Web, www.epa.gov/oar/oria.html

Establishes standards for measuring radon; develops model building codes for state and local governments; provides states and building contractors with technical assistance and training on radon detection and mitigation.

Federal Housing Administration (FHA), *(Housing and Urban Development Dept.), Manufactured Housing Programs, 451 7th St. S.W., #9164 20410; (202) 708-6423. Fax, (202) 708-4213. Elizabeth Cocke, Deputy Administrator. TTY, (202) 708-1455. Consumer complaints, (800) 927-2891.*
Web, www.hud.gov/offices/hsg/sfh/mhs/mhshome.cfm

Establishes and maintains standards for selection of new materials and methods of construction; evaluates technical suitability of products and materials; develops uniform, preemptive, and mandatory national standards for manufactured housing; enforces standards through design review and quality control inspection of factories; administers a national consumer protection program.

Housing and Urban Development Dept. (HUD), *Affordable Housing Research and Technology, 451 7th St. S.W., #8134 20410; (202) 708-4370. Fax, (202) 708-5873. Kevin J. Neary, Director (Acting).*
Web, www.hud.gov

Studies regulatory barriers to housing, such as land development and building codes and zoning. Conducts building technology research on housing affordability, environmental hazards, and energy efficiency. Reviews and assesses changes in building codes and standards. Conducts demonstrations on innovative building construction techniques.

Housing and Urban Development Dept. (HUD), *Healthy Homes and Lead Hazard Control, 451 7th St. S.W., #8236 20410; (202) 708-0310. Fax, (202) 755-1000. Jon L. Gant, Director.*
Web, www.hud.gov/lea

Advises HUD offices, other agencies, health authorities, and the housing industry on lead poisoning prevention. Develops regulations for lead-based paint; conducts research; makes grants to state and local governments for lead hazard reduction and inspection of housing.

National Institute of Building Sciences, *1090 Vermont Ave. N.W., #700 20005-4905; (202) 289-7800. Fax, (202) 289-1092. Henry L. Green, President.*
General e-mail, nibs@nibs.org

Web, www.nibs.org

Public-private partnership authorized by Congress to improve the regulation of building construction, facilitate the safe introduction of innovative building technology, and disseminate performance criteria and other technical information.

National Institute of Standards and Technology (NIST), *(Commerce Dept.), Building and Fire Research Laboratory, 100 Bureau Dr., MS 8600, Gaithersburg, MD 20899-8600; (301) 975-5900. Fax, (301) 975-4032. S. Shyam Sunder, Director; Hunter Fanney, Chief, Building Environment Division, (301) 975-5864.*
Web, www.bfrl.nist.gov

Performs analytical, laboratory, and field research in the area of building technology and its applications for building usefulness, safety, and economy; produces performance criteria and evaluation, test, and measurement methods for building owners, occupants, designers, manufacturers, builders, and federal, state, and local regulatory authorities.

Occupational Safety and Health Administration (OSHA), *(Labor Dept.), Standards and Guidance,* 200 *Constitution Ave. N.W., #N3718 20210; (202) 693-1950. Fax, (202) 693-1678. Dorothy Dougherty, Director.*

Administers regulations for fire safety standards; sponsors programs for maritime, fire protection, mechanical, and electrical industries.

U.S. Fire Administration *(Homeland Security Dept.),* 16825 S. Seton Ave., Emmitsburg, MD 21727; (301) 447-1000. Fax, (301) 447-1346. Gregory B. Cade, Assistant Administrator.
Web, www.usfa.dhs.gov

Conducts research and collects, analyzes, and disseminates data on combustion, fire prevention, firefighter safety, and the management of fire prevention organizations; studies and develops arson prevention programs and fire prevention codes; maintains the National Fire Data System.

▶**NONGOVERNMENTAL**

Air Conditioning, Heating, and Refrigeration Institute, *Legislative and Regulatory Affairs,* 2111 *Wilson Blvd., #500, Arlington, VA 22201; (703) 524-8800. Fax, (703) 528-3816. Don Davis, Chief Executive Officer. General e-mail, ahri@ahrinet.org*
Web, www.ahrinet.org

Represents manufacturers of central air conditioning and commercial refrigeration equipment. Develops product performance rating standards and administers programs to verify manufacturers' certified ratings.

American Society of Civil Engineers, *1801 Alexander Bell Dr., Reston, VA 20191-4400; (703) 295-6300. Fax, (703) 295-6333. Patrick Natale, Executive Director. Toll-free, (800) 548-2723. Government Relations, (202) 789-7850.*
Web, www.asce.org

Membership: professionals and students in civil engineering. Develops and produces consensus standards for construction documents and building codes. Maintains the Civil Engineering Research Foundation, which focuses national attention and resources on the research needs of the civil engineering profession. Participates in international conferences.

American Society of Heating, Refrigerating, and Air Conditioning Engineers, *Government Affairs,* 1828 L St. *N.W., #906 20036-5104; (202) 833-1830. Fax, (202) 833 0118. Douglas E. "Doug" Read, Director.*
Web, www.ashrae.org

Membership: engineers for the heating and cooling industry in the United States and abroad, including students. Sponsors research, meetings, and educational activities. Develops industry standards; publishes technical data. Monitors legislation and regulations.

Assn. of Pool and Spa Professionals, *2111 Eisenhower Ave., #500, Alexandria, VA 22314-4698; (703) 838-0083. Fax, (703) 549-0493. Bill Weber, President.*

General e-mail, MemberServices@apsp.org
Web, www.apsp.org

Membership: manufacturers, dealers, service companies, builders, and distributors of pools, spas, and hot tubs. Promotes the industry; compiles statistics. Monitors legislation and regulations.

Center for Auto Safety, *1825 Connecticut Ave. N.W., #330 20009-5708; (202) 328-7700. Fax, (202) 387-0140. General e-mail, accounts@autosafety.org*
Web, www.autosafety.org

Monitors Federal Trade Commission warranty regulations and HUD implementation of federal safety and construction standards for manufactured mobile homes.

International Code Council, *500 New Jersey Ave. N.W., 6th Floor 20001-2070; (202) 370-1800. Fax, (202) 783-2348. Richard P. "Rick" Weiland, Chief Executive Officer. Toll-free, (888) 422-7233.*
Web, www.iccsafe.org

Membership association dedicated to building safety and fire prevention. Develops codes used to construct residential and commercial buildings, including homes and schools.

NAHB Research Center, *400 Prince George's Blvd., Upper Marlboro, MD 20774; (301) 249-4000. Fax, (301) 430-6180. Michael Luzier, President. Toll-free, (800) 638-8556.*
Web, www.nahbrc.org

Conducts contract research and product labeling and certification for U.S. industry, government, and trade associations related to home building and light commercial industrial building. Interests include energy conservation, new technologies, international research, public health issues, affordable housing, special needs housing for the elderly and persons with disabilities, building codes and standards, land development, and environmental issues. (Affiliated with the National Assn. of Home Builders [NAHB].)

National Conference of States on Building Codes and Standards, *505 Huntmar Park Dr., #210, Herndon, VA 20170-5139; (703) 437-0100. Fax, (703) 481-3596. Vacant, Executive Director; Cynthia Wilk, Deputy Director.*
Web, www.ncsbcs.org

Membership: individuals and organizations concerned with building standards. Works with HUD to ensure that manufactured housing conforms to HUD standards and codes; assists states in improving their building codes, standards, and regulations; promotes local, state, and interstate cooperation.

National Fire Protection Assn., *Government Affairs, Washington Office,* 1401 K St. N.W., #500 20005; (202) 898-0222. Fax, (202) 898-0044. Nancy McNabb, Director.
General e-mail, wdc@nfpa.org
Web, www.nfpa.org

Membership: individuals and organizations interested in fire protection. Develops and updates fire protection codes and standards; sponsors technical assistance programs; collects fire data statistics. Monitors legislation and regulations. (Headquarters in Quincy, Mass.)

Materials and Labor

▶NONGOVERNMENTAL

American Forest and Paper Assn., *Government Affairs, 1111 19th St. N.W., #800 20036; (202) 463-2700. Fax, (202) 463-2471. Elizabeth VanDersarl, Vice President. General e-mail, info@afandpa.org*

Web, www.afandpa.org

Membership: wood and specialty products manufacturers and those in related associations. Interests include tax, housing, environmental, international trade, natural resources, and land-use issues that affect the wood and paper products industry.

Architectural Woodwork Institute, *46179 Westlake Dr., #120, Potomac Falls, VA 20165; (571) 323-3636. Fax, (571) 323-3630. Philip Duvic, Executive Vice President. General e-mail, info@awinet.org*

Web, www.awinet.org

Promotes the use of architectural woodworking; establishes industry standards; conducts seminars and workshops; certifies professionals in the industry. Monitors legislation and regulations.

Asbestos Information Assn./North America, *1745 Jefferson Davis Highway, Arlington, VA 22202-9227; (703) 560-2980. Fax, (703) 560-2981. B.J. Pigg, President. General e-mail, aiabjpigg@aol.com*

Membership: firms that manufacture, sell, and use products containing asbestos fiber and those that mine, mill, and sell asbestos. Provides information on asbestos and health and on industry efforts to eliminate problems associated with asbestos dust; serves as liaison between the industry and federal and state governments.

Asphalt Roofing Manufacturers Assn., *1156 15th St. N.W., #900 20005; (202) 207-0917. Fax, (202) 223-9741. Reed Hitchcock, Director. General e-mail, arma@kellencompany.com*

Web, www.asphaltroofing.org

Membership: manufacturers of bitumen-based roofing products. Assists in developing local building codes and standards for asphalt roofing products. Provides technical information; supports research. Monitors legislation and regulations.

Assn. of the Wall and Ceiling Industries, *513 W. Broad St., #210, Falls Church, VA 22046-3257; (703) 538-1600. Fax, (703) 534-8307. Steven A. Etkin, Executive Vice President. Web, www.awci.org*

Membership: contractors and suppliers working in the wall and ceiling industries. Sponsors conferences and seminars. Monitors legislation and regulations.

Brick Industry Assn., *1850 Centennial Park Dr., #301, Reston, VA 20191-1542; (703) 620-0010. Fax, (703) 620-3928. Richard A. Jennison, President. General e-mail, birnkinfo@bia.org*

Web, www.gobrick.com

Membership: manufacturers and distributors of clay brick. Provides technical expertise and assistance; promotes bricklaying vocational education programs; maintains collection of technical publications on brick masonry construction. Monitors legislation and regulations.

Building Systems Councils of the National Assn. of Home Builders, *1201 15th St. N.W., 7th Floor 20005-2800; (202) 266-8576. Fax, (202) 266-8141. Jeremy Bertrand, Executive Director. Toll-free, (800) 368-5242. Web, www.nahb.org/buildingsystems*

Membership: manufacturers and suppliers of home building products and services. Represents all segments of the industry. Assists in developing National Assn. of Home Builders policies regarding building codes, legislation, and government regulations affecting manufacturers of model-code-complying, factory-built housing (includes concrete, log, modular, and panelized); sponsors educational programs; conducts plant tours of member operations.

Composite Panel Assn., *19465 Deerfield Ave., #306, Leesburg, VA 20176; (703) 724-1128. Fax, (703) 724-1588. Thomas A. Julia, President. General e-mail, info@pbmdf.com*

Web, www.pbmdf.com

Membership: manufacturers of particleboard, medium-density fiberboard, and hardboard. Promotes use of these materials; conducts industry education; offers a certification program for recycled and low emitting products (Environmentally Preferable Products). Monitors legislation and regulations.

Door and Hardware Institute, *14150 Newbrook Dr., #200, Chantilly, VA 20151-2232; (703) 222-2010. Fax, (703) 222-2410. Jerry S. Heppes, Chief Executive Officer. General e-mail, info@dhi.org*

Web, www.dhi.org

Membership: companies and individuals that manufacture or distribute doors and related fittings. Promotes the industry. Interests include building security, life safety and exit devices, and compliance with the Americans with Disabilities Act. Monitors legislation and regulations.

Gypsum Assn., *6525 Belcrest Rd., #400, Hyattsville, MD 20782; (301) 277-8686. Fax, (301) 277-8747. Michael A. Gardner, Executive Director. General e-mail, info@gypsum.org*

Web, www.gypsum.org

Membership: manufacturers of gypsum wallboard and plaster. Assists members, code officials, builders, designers, and others with technical problems and building code questions; publishes *Fire Resistance Design Manual* referenced by major building codes; conducts safety programs for member companies. Monitors legislation and regulations.

Hardwood, Plywood, and Veneer Assn., *1825 Michael Faraday Dr., Reston, VA 20190-5350; (703) 435-2900. Fax, (703) 435-2537. Clifford "Kip" Howlett, President.*
General e-mail, hpva@hpva.org

Web, www.hpva.org

Membership: manufacturers, distributors, wholesalers, suppliers, and sales agents of hardwood, plywood, veneer, and laminated wood floor. Disseminates business information; sponsors workshops and seminars; conducts research.

International Assn. of Bridge, Structural, Ornamental, and Reinforcing Iron Workers, *1750 New York Ave. N.W., #400 20006; (202) 383-4800. Fax, (202) 638-4856. Joseph J. Hunt, President.*
Web, www.ironworkers.org

Membership: approximately 140,000 iron workers. Helps members negotiate pay, benefits, and better working conditions; conducts training programs and workshops. Monitors legislation and regulations. (Affiliated with the AFL-CIO.)

International Assn. of Heat and Frost Insulators and Allied Workers, *9602 Martin Luther King Hwy., Lanham, MD 20706-1839; (301) 731-9101. Fax, (301) 731-5058. James A. Grogan, President.*
General e-mail, iiiatf@insulators.org

Web, www.insulators.org

Membership: approximately 18,000 workers in insulation industries. Helps members negotiate pay, benefits, and better working conditions; conducts training programs and workshops. Monitors legislation and regulations. (Affiliated with the AFL-CIO.)

International Brotherhood of Boilermakers, Iron Ship Builders, Blacksmiths, Forgers, and Helpers, *Government Affairs, Washington Office, 2722 Merrilee Dr., #360, Fairfax, VA 22031; (703) 560-1493. Fax, (703) 560-2584. Bridget P. Martin, Director.*
Web, www.boilermakers.org

Membership: approximately 80,000 workers in construction, repair, maintenance, manufacturing, and related industries in the United States and Canada. Helps members negotiate pay, benefits, and better working conditions; conducts training programs and workshops. Monitors legislation and regulations. (Headquarters in Kansas City, Kan.; affiliated with the AFL-CIO.)

International Brotherhood of Electrical Workers (IBEW), *900 7th St. N.W. 20001; (202) 833-7000. Fax, (202) 728-7676. Edwin D. Hill, President.*
General e-mail, web@ibew.org

Web, www.ibew.org

Helps members negotiate pay, benefits, and better working conditions; conducts training programs and workshops. Monitors legislation and regulations. (Affiliated with the AFL-CIO.)

International Brotherhood of Teamsters, *25 Louisiana Ave. N.W. 20001-2198; (202) 624-6800. Fax, (202) 624-6918. James P. Hoffa, President. Press, (202) 624-6911.*

General e-mail, feedback@teamster.org

Web, www.teamster.org

Membership: more than 1.4 million workers in the transportation and construction industries, factories, offices, hospitals, warehouses, and other workplaces. Helps members negotiate pay, benefits, and better working conditions; conducts training programs and workshops. Monitors legislation and regulations.

International Union of Bricklayers and Allied Craftworkers, *620 F St. N.W. 20004; (202) 783-3788. Fax, (202) 393-0219. John J. Flynn, President. Toll-free, (888) 880-8222.*
General e-mail, askbac@bacweb.org

Web, www.bacweb.org

Membership: bricklayers, stonemasons, and other skilled craftworkers in the building industry. Helps members negotiate pay, benefits, and better working conditions; conducts training programs and workshops. Monitors legislation and regulations. (Affiliated with the AFL-CIO and the International Masonry Institute.)

International Union of Operating Engineers, *1125 17th St. N.W. 20036; (202) 429-9100. Fax, (202) 778-2616. Vincent J. Giblin, President.*
Web, www.iuoe.org

Membership: approximately 400,000 operating engineers, including heavy equipment operators, mechanics, and surveyors in the construction industry, and stationary engineers, including operations and building maintenance staff. Helps members negotiate pay, benefits, and better working conditions; conducts training programs and workshops. Monitors legislation and regulations. (Affiliated with the AFL-CIO.)

International Union of Painters and Allied Trades, *1750 New York Ave. N.W., 8th Floor 20006; (202) 637-0700. Fax, (202) 637-0771. James A. Williams, President.*
General e-mail, mail@iupat.org and askthegeneral president@iupat.org

Web, www.iupat.org

Membership: more than 140,000 painters, glaziers, floor covering installers, signmakers, show decorators, and workers in allied trades in the United States and Canada. Helps members negotiate pay, benefits, and better working conditions; conducts training programs and workshops. Monitors legislation and regulations. (Affiliated with the AFL-CIO.)

Kitchen Cabinet Manufacturers Assn., *1899 Preston White Dr., Reston, VA 20191-5435; (703) 264-1690. Fax, (703) 620-6530. C. Richard Titus, Executive Vice President.*
General e-mail, info@kcma.org

Web, www.kcma.org

Represents cabinet manufacturers and suppliers to the industry. Provides government relations, management statistics, marketing information, and plant tours. Administers cabinet testing and certification programs.

National Concrete Masonry Assn., *13750 Sunrise Valley Dr., Herndon, VA 20171-4662; (703) 713-1900. Fax, (703) 713-1910. Robert D. Thomas, President.*
General e-mail, ncma@ncma.org

Web, www.ncma.org

Membership: producers of concrete masonry and suppliers of related goods and services. Conducts research; provides members with technical, marketing, government relations, and communications assistance.

National Glass Assn., *8200 Greensboro Dr., #302, McLean, VA 22102-3881; (703) 442-4890. Fax, (703) 442-0630. Philip J. James, President. Toll-free, (866) 342-5642.*
Web, www.glass.org

Membership: companies in flat (architectural and automotive) glass industry. Provides education and training programs to promote quality workmanship, ethics, and safety standards in the architectural, automotive, and window and door glass industries. Acts as a clearinghouse for information and links professionals with job listings, suppliers, and technical support. Monitors legislation and regulations.

National Insulation Assn., *12100 Sunset Hills Rd., #330, Reston, VA 20190-3233; (703) 464-6422. Fax, (703) 464-6896. Michele M. Jones, Executive Vice President.*
General e-mail, niainfo@insulation.org

Web, www.insulation.org

Membership: companies in the commercial and industrial insulation industries, including contractors, manufacturers, distributors, and fabricators. Monitors legislation and regulations.

National Lumber and Building Material Dealers Assn., *2025 M St. N.W., #800 20036-3309; (202) 367-1169. Fax, (202) 367-2169. Michael O'Brian, President. Toll-free, (800) 634-8645.*
General e-mail, nlbmda@dealer.org

Web, www.dealer.org

Membership: federated associations of retailers in the lumber and building material industries. Provides statistics training and networking opportunities to members. Monitors legislation and regulations.

National Paint and Coatings Assn., *1500 Rhode Island Ave. N.W. 20005; (202) 462-6272. Fax, (202) 462-8549. J. Andrew Doyle, President.*
Web, www.paint.org

Membership: paint and coatings manufacturers, raw materials suppliers, and distributors. Provides educational and public outreach programs for the industry; interests include health, safety, and the environment. Monitors legislation and regulations.

North American Insulation Manufacturers Assn., *44 Canal Center Plaza, #310, Alexandria, VA 22314-1548; (703) 684-0084. Fax, (703) 684-0427. Kenneth D. Mentzer, President.*
General e-mail, insulation@naima.org

Web, www.naima.org

Membership: manufacturers of insulation products for use in homes, commercial buildings, and industrial facilities. Provides information on the use of insulation for thermal efficiency, sound control, and fire safety; monitors research in the industry. Interests include energy efficiency and sustainability. Monitors legislation and regulations.

Operative Plasterers' and Cement Masons' International Assn. of the United States and Canada, *11720 Beltsville Dr., #700, Beltsville, MD 20705; (301) 623-1000. Fax, (301) 623-1032. Patrick D. Finley, President.*
General e-mail, opcmiaintel@opcmia.org

Web, www.opcmia.org

Membership: approximately 58,000 cement masons and plasterers. Helps members negotiate pay, benefits, and better working conditions; conducts training programs and workshops. Monitors legislation and regulations. (Affiliated with the AFL-CIO.)

Portland Cement Assn., *500 New Jersey Ave. N.W., 7th Floor 20001-1005; (202) 408-9494. Fax, (202) 408-0877. John S. Shaw, Senior Vice President of Government Affairs.*
Web, www.cement.org

Membership: producers of portland cement. Monitors legislation and regulations.

Roof Coatings Manufacturers Assn., *1156 15th St. N.W. #900 20005; (202) 207-0919. Fax, (202) 223-9741. Reed B. Hitchcock, Vice President.*
General e-mail, questions@roofcoatings.org

Web, www.roofcoatings.org

Represents the manufacturers of cold-applied protective roof coatings, cements, and systems, and the suppliers of products, equipment, and services to and for the roof coating manufacturing industry.

Sheet Metal Workers International Assn., *1750 New York Ave. N.W. 20006; (202) 783-5880. Fax, (202) 662-0880. Michael J. Sullivan, General President.*
Web, www.smwia.org

Membership: more than 150,000 U.S., Puerto Rican, and Canadian workers in the building and construction trades, manufacturing, and the railroad and shipyard industries. Assists members with contract negotiation and grievances; conducts training programs and workshops. Monitors legislation and regulations. (Affiliated with the Sheet Metal and Air Conditioning Contractors' Assn., the AFL-CIO, and the Canadian Labour Congress.)

FIRE PREVENTION AND CONTROL

▶**AGENCIES**

Consumer Product Safety Commission (CPSC), *Hazard Identification and Reduction, 4330 East-West Hwy., #723, Bethesda, MD 20814; (301) 504-7949. Fax, (301)*

504-0407. *Robert J. Howell, Deputy Assistant Executive Director.*
Web, www.cpsc.gov

Proposes, evaluates, and develops standards and test procedures for safety of consumer products. Reports injuries resulting from use of products.

Forest Service *(Agriculture Dept.), Fire and Aviation Management,* 201 14th St. S.W. 20250 *(mailing address: 1400 Independence Ave. S.W., MS 1107, Washington, DC 20250-0003); (202) 205-1483. Fax, (202) 205-1401. Tom Harbour, Director.*
Web, www.fs.fed.us/fire

Responsible for aviation and fire management programs, including fire control planning and prevention, suppression of fires, and the use of prescribed fires. Provides state foresters with financial and technical assistance for fire protection in forests and on rural lands.

National Institute of Standards and Technology (NIST), *(Commerce Dept.), Building and Fire Research Laboratory,* 100 Bureau Dr., MS 8600, Gaithersburg, MD 20899-8600; (301) 975-5900. Fax, (301) 975-4032. S. Shyam Sunder, Director; Hunter Fanney, Chief, Building Environment Division, (301) 975-5864.*
Web, www.bfrl.nist.gov

Conducts basic and applied research on fire and fire resistance of construction materials; develops testing methods, standards, design concepts, and technologies for fire protection and prevention.

National Institute of Standards and Technology (NIST), *(Commerce Dept.), Fire Research,* 100 Bureau Dr., MS 8660, Gaithersburg, MD 20899-8600; (301) 975-6598. Fax, (301) 975-4052. Anthony Hamins, Chief. TTY, (301) 975-8295.*
Web, www.bfrl.nist.gov/fris

Conducts research on fire safety and metrology. Develops models to measure the behavior and mitigate the impact of large-scale fires. Operates the Fire Research Information Service, Fire Dynamics Group, and a large-scale fire test facility. Studies smoke components of flames, the burning of polymeric materials, and fire detection and suppression systems.

Occupational Safety and Health Administration (OSHA), *(Labor Dept.), Standards and Guidance,* 200 Constitution Ave. N.W., #N3718 20210; (202) 693-1950. Fax, (202) 693-1678. Dorothy Dougherty, Director.*

Administers regulations for fire safety standards; sponsors programs for maritime, fire protection, mechanical, and electrical industries.

U.S. Fire Administration *(Homeland Security Dept.),* 16825 S. Seton Ave., Emmitsburg, MD 21727; (301) 447-1000. Fax, (301) 447-1346. Gregory B. Cade, Assistant Administrator.*
Web, www.usfa.dhs.gov

Conducts research and collects, analyzes, and disseminates data on combustion, fire prevention, firefighter safety, and the management of fire prevention organizations;

studies and develops arson prevention programs and fire prevention codes; maintains the National Fire Data System.

U.S. Fire Administration *(Homeland Security Dept.), National Fire Academy,* 16825 S. Seton Ave., Emmitsburg, MD 21727-8998; (301) 447-1117. Fax, (301) 447-1173. Denis Onieal, Superintendent.*
Web, www.usfa.dhs.gov/nfa

Trains fire officials and related professionals in fire prevention and management, current firefighting technologies, and the administration of fire prevention organizations.

► **NONGOVERNMENTAL**

International Assn. of Fire Chiefs, 4025 Fair Ridge Dr., #300, Fairfax, VA 22033-2868; (703) 273-0911. Fax, (703) 273-9363. Mark Light, Executive Director.*
Web, www.iafc.org

Membership: fire service chiefs and chief officers. Conducts research on fire control; testifies before congressional committees. Monitors legislation and regulations affecting fire safety codes.

International Assn. of Fire Fighters, 1750 New York Ave. N.W., #300 20006-5395; (202) 737-8484. Fax, (202) 737-8418. Harold A. Schaitberger, General President.*
General e-mail, pr@iaff.org
Web, www.iaff.org

Membership: more than 288,000 professional firefighters and emergency medical personnel. Assists members with contract negotiation and grievances; conducts training programs and workshops. Monitors legislation and regulations. (Affiliated with the AFL-CIO and the Canadian Labour Congress.)

**National Fire Protection Assn., *Government Affairs, Washington Office,* 1401 K St. N.W., #500 20005; (202) 898-0222. Fax, (202) 898-0044. Nancy McNabb, Director.*
General e-mail, wdc@nfpa.org
Web, www.nfpa.org

Membership: individuals and organizations interested in fire protection. Develops and updates fire protection codes and standards; sponsors technical assistance programs; collects fire data statistics. Monitors legislation and regulations. (Headquarters in Quincy, Mass.)

HOUSING

► **AGENCIES**

Federal Housing Administration (FHA), *(Housing and Urban Development Dept.), Housing Assistance and Grant Administration,* 451 7th St. S.W., #6134 20410-8000; (202) 708-3000. Fax, (202) 708-3104. Willie Spearmon, Director.*
Web, www.hud.gov/offices/hsg/mfh/hsgmfbus.cfm

Directs and oversees the housing assistance and grant programs, including project-based Section 8 housing assistance, Section 202/811 capital advance and project rental assistance programs, the assisted-living conversion program (ALCP), rent supplements, service coordinator, and congregate housing services grant programs.

Federal Housing Administration (FHA), *(Housing and Urban Development Dept.), Housing Assistance Contract Administration Oversight,* 451 7th St. S.W., #6138 20410-8000; (202) 402-2677. Fax, (202) 708-1010. *Deborah Lear, Director.*
Web, www.hud.gov/offices/hsg/mfh/mfbroch/mfbroc2.cfm

Administers Section 8 contracts and other rental subsidy programs. Ensures that Section 8 subsidized properties meet the department's goal of providing decent, safe, and sanitary housing to low-income families.

Federal Housing Administration (FHA), *(Housing and Urban Development Dept.), Multifamily Housing,* 451 7th St. S.W., #6106 20410; (202) 708-2495. Fax, (202) 708-2583. *Carol J. Galante, Deputy Assistant Secretary.*
Web, www.hud.gov/offices/hsg/hsgmulti.cfm

Determines risk and administers programs associated with government-insured mortgage programs, architectural procedures, and land development programs for multifamily housing. Administers the Rural Rental Housing Program and the development of congregate housing facilities that provide affordable housing, adequate space for meals, and supportive services.

Federal Housing Administration (FHA), *(Housing and Urban Development Dept.), Single Family Housing,* 451 7th St. S.W., #9282 20410; (202) 708-3175. Fax, (202) 708-2582. *Phillip Murray, Deputy Assistant Secretary,* (202) 708-1515.
Web, www.hud.gov/offices/hsg/sfh/hsgsingle.cfm

Determines risk and administers programs associated with government-insured mortgage programs for single family housing. Administers requirements to obtain and maintain federal government approval of mortgages.

Housing and Urban Development Dept. (HUD), *Entitlement Communities,* 451 7th St. S.W., #7282 20410; (202) 708-1577. Fax, (202) 401-2044. *Steve Johnson, Director.*
Web, www.hud.gov/offices/cpd/communitydevelopment/ programs/entitlement/index.cfm#MORE

Provides entitled cities and counties with block grants to provide housing, community, revitalization, and economic opportunity for low- and moderate-income people.

Housing and Urban Development Dept. (HUD), *Housing,* 451 7th St. S.W., #9100 20410; (202) 708-2601. Fax, (202) 708-2580. *Brian D. Montgomery, Assistant Secretary.* TTY, (202) 708-1455.
Web, www.hud.gov/offices/hsg/index.cfm

Administers housing programs, including the production, financing, and management of housing; directs preservation and rehabilitation of the housing stock; manages regulatory programs.

Rural Housing Service *(Agriculture Dept.),* 1400 *Independence Ave. S.W., #5014, MS 0701 20250-0701; (202) 690-1533. Fax, (202) 690-0500. James C. Alsop, Administrator (Acting).*
Web, www.rurdev.usda.gov/rhs

Offers financial assistance to apartment dwellers and homeowners in rural areas.

Rural Housing Service *(Agriculture Dept.), Housing Programs,* 1400 Independence Ave. S.W., #5014 20250-0780; (202) 690-1533. Fax, (202) 690-0500. James C. Alsop, Administrator (Acting). Press, (202) 720-6903.
Web, www.rurdev.usda.gov/rhs

Makes loans and grants in rural communities (population under 20,000) to low-income borrowers, including the elderly and persons with disabilities, for buying, building, or improving single-family houses. Makes grants to communities for rehabilitating single-family homes.

▶CONGRESS

For a listing of relevant congressional committees and subcommittees, please see page 381 or the Appendix.

▶NONGOVERNMENTAL

Center for Housing Policy, 1801 K St. N.W., #M100 20006-1301; (202) 466-2121. Fax, (202) 466-2122. *Jeffrey Lubell, Executive Director.*
General e-mail, nhc@nhc.org

Web, www.nhc.org

Researches and develops fundamentals of housing policy. Seeks to create new policies that integrate housing into overall social and economic goals. Sponsors educational forums and publishes reports (available online). (Research affiliate of the National Housing Conference.)

Enterprise Community Partners, 10227 Wincopin Circle, #500, Columbia, MD 21044; (410) 964-1230. Fax, (410) 964-1918. *Norman B. Rice, Chair. Toll-free, (800) 624-4298.*
Web, www.enterprisecommunity.org

Works with local groups to help provide decent, affordable housing for low-income individuals and families.

Habitat for Humanity International, *Government Relations and Advocacy,* 1000 Vermont Ave. N.W., #1100 20005; (202) 628-9171. Fax, (202) 628-9169. *Jenny Russell, Managing Director.*
General e-mail, washingtonoffice@hfhi.org

Web, www.habitat.org

Christian ministry that seeks to eliminate poverty housing. Builds and sells homes to low-income families. Monitors legislation and regulations.

Housing Assistance Council, 1025 Vermont Ave. N.W., #606 20005-3516; (202) 842-8600. Fax, (202) 347-3441. *Moises Loza, Executive Director.*
General e-mail, hac@ruralhome.org

Web, www.ruralhome.org

Operates in rural areas and in cities of fewer than 25,000 citizens. Advises low-income and minority groups seeking federal assistance for improving rural housing and community facilities; studies and makes recommendations for state and local housing policies; makes low-interest loans for housing programs for low-income and minority groups living in rural areas, including Native Americans and farm workers.

National Housing and Rehabilitation Assn., *HousingOnline.com, 1400 16th St. N.W., #420 20036; (202) 939-1750. Fax, (202) 265-4435. Peter H. Bell, Executive Director.* Web, www.housingonline.com

Membership: historic rehabilitation businesses, development firms and organizations and city, state, and local agencies concerned with affordable multifamily housing. Monitors government policies affecting multifamily development and rehabilitation.

National Housing Conference, *1801 K St. N.W., #M100 20006-1301; (202) 466-2121. Fax, (202) 466-2122. Conrad Egan, President.* General e-mail, nhc@nhc.org

Web, www.nhc.org

Membership: state and local housing officials, community development specialists, builders, bankers, lawyers, civic leaders, tenants, architects and planners, labor and religious groups, and national housing and housing-related organizations. Mobilizes public support for community development and affordable housing programs; conducts educational sessions.

National Leased Housing Assn., *1900 L St. N.W., #300 20036; (202) 785-8888. Fax, (202) 785-2008. Denise B. Muha, Executive Director.* General e-mail, info@hudnlha.com

Web, www.hudnlha.com

Membership: public and private organizations and individuals concerned with multifamily, government-assisted housing programs. Conducts training seminars. Monitors legislation and regulations.

National Low Income Housing Coalition, *727 15th St. N.W., 6th Floor 20005; (202) 662-1530. Fax, (202) 393-1973. Sheila Crowley, President.* General e-mail, info@nlihc.org

Web, www.nlihc.org

Membership: organizations and individuals that support low-income housing. Works to end the affordable housing crisis in America. Interests include the needs of the lowest-income people and those who are homeless. Monitors legislation.

National Rural Housing Coalition, *1250 Eye St. N.W., #902 20005; (202) 393-5229. Fax, (202) 393-3034. Robert A. Rapoza, Legislative Director.* Web, www.nrhcweb.org

Advocates improved housing for low-income rural families; works to increase public awareness of rural housing problems. Monitors legislation.

Fair Housing, Special Groups

▶**AGENCIES**

Federal Housing Administration (FHA), *(Housing and Urban Development Dept.), Multifamily Asset Management, 451 7th St. S.W., #6160 20410; (202) 708-3730. Fax, (202) 401-5978. Beverly J. Miller, Director.* Web, www.hud.gov

Responsible for the management of multifamily property and the physical and financial management of the HUD portfolio.

Housing and Urban Development Dept. (HUD), *Fair Housing and Equal Opportunity, 451 7th St. S.W., #5100 20410-2000; (202) 708-4252. Fax, (202) 708-4483. Bryan Greene, Assistant Secretary (Acting). Housing discrimination hotline, (800) 669-9777.* Web, www.hud.gov/offices/fheo/index.cfm

Monitors compliance with legislation requiring equal opportunities in housing for minorities, persons with disabilities, and families with children. Monitors compliance with construction codes to accommodate people with disabilities in multifamily dwellings. Hotline answers inquiries about housing discrimination.

Housing and Urban Development Dept. (HUD), *Native American Programs, 451 7th St. S.W., #4126 20410-5000; (202) 401-7914. Fax, (202) 401-7909. Rodger J. Boyd, Deputy Assistant Secretary.* Web, www.hud.gov/groups/nativeamericans.cfm

Administers federal assistance for Native American tribes. Assistance programs focus on housing and community and economic development through competitive and formula grants. Funds for approved activities are provided directly to tribes or Alaska Native villages or to a tribally designated housing authority.

Housing and Urban Development Dept. (HUD), *Program Standards: FHIP/FHAP Support, 451 7th St. S.W., #5222 20410; (202) 402-6949. Fax, (202) 708-6211. Aztec Jacobs, Director.* Web, www.hud.gov

Awards grants to public and private organizations and to state and local agencies. Funds projects that educate the public about fair housing rights; programs are designed to prevent or eliminate discriminatory housing practices; investigates housing discrimination complaints. Administers the Fair Housing Initiative and the Fair Housing Assistance Programs (FHIP/FHAP).

Justice Dept. (DOJ), *Civil Rights Division, 950 Pennsylvania Ave. N.W. 20530; (202) 514-2151. Fax, (202)*

514-0293. *Loretta King, Assistant Attorney General (Acting). Press, (202) 514-2007. TTY, (202) 514-0716. Web, www.usdoj.gov/crt*

Enforces federal civil rights laws prohibiting discrimination on the basis of race, color, religion, sex, disability, age, or national origin in housing, public accommodations and facilities, and credit and federally assisted programs.

Office of Thrift Supervision (OTS), *(Treasury Dept.), Examinations, Supervision, and Consumer Protection, 1700 G St. N.W., 5th Floor 20552; (202) 906-5666. Fax, (202) 898-0230. Timothy T. Ward, Deputy Director. Consumer complaints, (800) 842-6929. Web, www.ots.treas.gov*

Handles complaints of discrimination against minorities and women by savings and loan associations; assists minority-owned or minority-controlled savings and loan institutions.

Rural Development *(Agriculture Dept.), Civil Rights, 1400 Independence Ave. S.W., #1341, MS 0703 20250; (202) 692-0090. Fax, (202) 692-0279. Thelma Floyd, Director. Web, www.rurdev.usda.gov/rhs/Admin/civilrights.htm*

Enforces compliance with laws prohibiting discrimination in credit transactions on the basis of sex, marital status, race, color, religion, age, or disability. Ensures equal opportunity in granting Rural Economic and Community Development housing, farm ownership, and operating loans and a variety of community and business program loans.

▶**NONGOVERNMENTAL**

AARP Foundation, *Consumer Fraud Prevention Project, 601 E St. N.W. 20049; (202) 434-6055. Fax, (202) 434-6470. Bridget Small, General Program Manager. General e-mail, bsmall@aarp.org and litigation@aarp.org Web, www.aarp.org*

Supports affordable and appropriate housing for older Americans, including shared housing, continuing care, retirement and assisted living communities, and home equity conversion. Provides education and outreach to older consumers to help them protect against financial fraud and abuse that endanger savings and assets and damage creditworthiness. Offers resources on reverse mortgages and other alternatives (online at www.aarp .org/money).

ACORN (Assn. of Community Organizations for Reform Now), *Washington Office, 739 8th St. S.E. 20003; (202) 547-2500. Fax, (202) 546-2483. Steve Kest, Executive Director. General e-mail, dcacorn@acorn.org Web, www.acorn.org*

Works to advance the interests of minority and low-income families through community organizing and action. Interests include jobs, living wages, housing, welfare reform, and community reinvestment.

American Assn. of Homes and Services for the Aging, *Advocacy, 2519 Connecticut Ave. N.W. 20008-1520; (202) 783-2242. Fax, (202) 783-2255. Susan M. Weiss, Senior Vice President. General e-mail, info@aahsa.org Web, www.aahsa.org*

Membership: nonprofit nursing homes, housing, and health-related facilities for the elderly. Provides research and technical assistance on housing and long-term care for the elderly; conducts certification program for retirement housing professionals. Operates a capital formation program to procure financing for new housing facilities for the elderly. Monitors legislation and regulations.

B'nai B'rith International, *Center for Senior Services, 2020 K St. N.W., 7th Floor 20006; (202) 857-2785. Fax, (202) 857-2782. Mark D. Olshan, Director. Toll-free, (888) 388-4224. General e-mail, seniors@bnaibrith.org Web, www.bnaibrith.org*

Advocates on behalf of the aging population in America. Works with local groups to sponsor federally assisted housing for independent low-income senior citizens and persons with disabilities, regardless of race or religion.

Center for Community Change, *1536 U St. N.W. 20009; (202) 339-9300. Fax, (202) 387-4896. Deepak Bhargava, Executive Director. Toll-free, (877) 777-1536. General e-mail, info@communitychange.org Web, www.communitychange.org*

Works to strengthen grassroots organizations that help low-income people, working-class people, and minorities develop skills and resources to improve their communities and change the policies and institutions that affect their lives. Monitors legislation and regulations.

National American Indian Housing Council, *50 F St. N.W., #3300 20001-1565; (202) 789-1754. Fax, (202) 789-1758. Paul Lumley, Executive Director. Toll-free, (800) 284-9165. Web, www.naihc.net*

Membership: Native American housing authorities. Clearinghouse for information on Native American housing issues; works for safe and sanitary dwellings for Native American and Alaska Native communities; monitors policies of the Housing and Urban Development Dept. and housing legislation; provides members with training and technical assistance in managing housing assistance programs.

National Assn. for the Advancement of Colored People (NAACP), *Washington Bureau, 1156 15th St. N.W., #915 20005-1750; (202) 463-2940. Fax, (202) 463-2953. Hilary O. Shelton, Director. General e-mail, washingtonbureau@naacpnet.org Web, www.naacp.org*

Membership: persons interested in civil rights for all minorities. Works to eliminate discrimination in housing and urban affairs. Supports programs that make affordable rental housing available to minorities and that maintain African American ownership of land. (Headquarters in Baltimore, Md.)

National Assn. of Real Estate Brokers, *9831 Greenbelt Rd., #309, Lanham, MD 20706; (301) 552-9340. Fax, (301) 552-9216. Maria Kong, President; Tawanda Barnett, Office Manager.*
General e-mail, nareb3@aol.com
Web, www.nareb.com

Membership: minority real estate brokers, appraisers, contractors, property managers, and salespersons. Works to prevent discrimination in housing policies and practices; conducts regional seminars on federal policy, legislation, and regulations; advises members on procedures for procuring federal contracts.

National Council of La Raza, *1126 16th St. N.W. 20036; (202) 785-1670. Fax, (202) 776-1792. Janet Murguia, President.*
General e-mail, comments@nclr.org
Web, www.nclr.org

Helps Hispanic community-based groups obtain funds, develop and build low-income housing and community facilities, and develop and finance community economic development projects; conducts research and provides policy analysis on the housing status and needs of Hispanics; monitors legislation on fair housing and government funding for low-income housing.

National Council on the Aging, *1901 L St. N.W., 4th Floor 20036; (202) 479-1200. Fax, (202) 479-0735. James P. Firman, President. Press, (202) 479-6975. TTY, (202) 479-6674.*
General e-mail, info@ncoa.org
Web, www.ncoa.org

Serves as an information clearinghouse on aging. Works to ensure quality housing for older persons. Monitors legislation and regulations.

Public and Subsidized Housing

▶**AGENCIES**

Housing and Urban Development Dept. (HUD), *Public Housing and Voucher Programs, 451 7th St. S.W., #4204 20410-5000; (202) 708-1380. Fax, (202) 708-0690. David Vargas, Deputy Assistant Secretary.*
Web, www.hud.gov

Establishes policies and procedures for low-income public housing and rental assistance programs, including special needs for the elderly and disabled, standards for rental and occupancy, utilities and maintenance engineering, and financial management.

Public and Indian Housing *(Housing and Urban Development Dept.), Housing Voucher Management and Operations, 451 7th St. S.W., #4210 20410; (202)*

708-0477. Fax, (202) 401-7974. Milan Ozdinec, Deputy Assistant Secretary.*
Web, www.hud.gov/offices/pih/about/offices.cfm

Administers certificate and housing voucher programs and moderate rehabilitation authorized by Section 8 of the Housing Act of 1937, as amended. Provides rental subsidies to lower-income families.

Public and Indian Housing *(Housing and Urban Development Dept.), Public Housing Investments, 451 7th St. S.W., #4130 20410-0050; (202) 401-8812. Fax, (202) 401-7910. Dominique Blom, Deputy Assistant Secretary.*
Web, www.hud.gov/offices/pih

Establishes development policies and procedures for low-income housing programs, including criteria for site approval and construction standards; oversees administration of the Comprehensive Improvement Assistance Program for modernizing existing public housing. Administers the HOPE VI Program.

▶**NONGOVERNMENTAL**

Council of Large Public Housing Authorities, *1250 Eye St. N.W., #901 20005-3922; (202) 638-1300. Fax, (202) 638-2364. Sunia Zaterman, Executive Director.*
General e-mail, info@clpha.org
Web, www.clpha.org

Works to preserve and improve public housing through advocacy, research, policy analysis, and public education.

Public Housing Authorities Directors Assn., *511 Capitol Court N.E., #200 20002-4937; (202) 546-5445. Fax, (202) 546-2280. Timothy G. Kaiser, Executive Director.*
Web, www.phada.org

Membership: executive directors of public housing authorities. Serves as liaison between members and the Housing and Urban Development Dept. and Congress; conducts educational seminars and conferences. Monitors legislation and regulations.

Urban Institute, *Metropolitan Housing and Communities Policy Center, 2100 M St. N.W., #500 20037; (202) 833-7200. Fax, (202) 872-9322. Robert D. Reischauer, President; Vacant, Director. Public Affairs, (202) 261-5709.*
General e-mail, paffairs@ui.urban.org
Web, www.urban.org/center/met

Research organization that deals with urban problems. Researches housing policy problems, including housing management, public housing programs, finance, and rent control.

REAL ESTATE

▶**AGENCIES**

Federal Emergency Management Agency (FEMA), *(Homeland Security Dept.), Mitigation Division,*

500 C St. S.W., #406 20472; (202) 646-2781. Fax, (202) 646-7970. David I. Maurstad, Assistant Administrator. Web, www.fema.gov/nfip

Administers federal flood insurance programs, including the National Flood Insurance Program. Makes low-cost flood insurance available to eligible homeowners.

Federal Highway Administration (FHWA), *(Transportation Dept.), Real Estate Services, 1200 New Jersey Ave. S.E., #E76-304 20590; (202) 366-0142. Fax, (202) 366-3713. Gerald Solomon, Director. Web, www.fhwa.dot.gov/realestate*

Funds and oversees acquisition of land by states for federally assisted highways; provides financial assistance to relocate people and businesses forced to move by highway construction; cooperates in administering program for the use of air rights in connection with federally aided highways; administers the Highway Beautification Act to control billboards and junkyards along interstate and federally aided primary highways.

General Services Administration (GSA), *Public Buildings Service, 1800 F St. N.W., #6340 20405; (202) 501-1100. Fax, (202) 219-2310. Tony Costa, Commissioner (Acting). Web, www.gsa.gov/pbs*

Administers the acquisition, construction, maintenance, and operation of buildings owned or leased by the federal government. Manages and disposes of federal real estate.

Housing and Urban Development Dept. (HUD), *Affordable Housing Programs, 451 7th St. S.W., #7164 20410; (202) 708-2684. Fax, (202) 708-1744. Clifford Taffet, Director. Web, www.hud.gov*

Administers the Uniform Relocation Assistance and Real Property Acquisition Policies Act of 1970, as amended, and other laws requiring that relocation assistance be given to persons displaced by federally assisted housing and community development programs.

Housing and Urban Development Dept. (HUD), *Real Estate Settlement Procedures Act (RESPA) and Interstate Land Sales, 451 7th St. S.W., #9154 20410; (202) 708-0502. Fax, (202) 708-4559. Ivy Jackson, Director. General e-mail, hsg-respa@hud.gov Web, www.hud.gov/offices/hsg/sfh/ils/ilshome.cfm*

Responsible for helping home buyers become better shoppers for settlement services and eliminating kickbacks and referral fees that unnecessarily increase the costs of certain settlement services. Administers the Interstate Land Sales Full Disclosure Act, which requires land developers who sell undeveloped land through interstate commerce or the mail to disclose required information about the land to the purchaser prior to signing a sales contract and to file information with the federal government.

Small Business Administration (SBA), *Disaster Assistance, 409 3rd St. S.W., #6050 20416; (202) 205-6734. Fax, (202) 205-7728. Herbert L. Mitchell, Associate Administrator. Call center, (800) 659-2955. General e-mail, disastercustomerservice@sba.gov Web, www.sba.gov*

Provides victims of physical disasters with disaster and economic injury loans for homes, businesses, and personal property. Lends funds for uncompensated losses incurred from any disaster declared by the president of the United States or the administrator of the SBA. Lends funds to individual homeowners, business concerns of all sizes, and nonprofit institutions to repair or replace damaged structures and furnishings, business machinery, equipment, and inventory. Provides economic injury loans to small businesses for losses to meet necessary operating expenses, provided the business could have paid these expenses prior to the disaster.

►CONGRESS

For a listing of relevant congressional committees and subcommittees, please see page 381 or the Appendix.

►NONGOVERNMENTAL

American Homeowners Foundation, *6776 Little Falls Rd., Arlington, VA 22213-1213; (703) 536-7776. Fax, (703) 536-7079. Bruce N. Hahn, President. Toll-free, (800) 489-7776. General e-mail, amerhome@americanhomeowners.org Web, www.americanhomeowners.org*

Publishes books, model contracts, and special studies to help homeowners buy, sell, finance, or build homes.

American Homeowners Grassroots Alliance, *6776 Little Falls Rd., Arlington, VA 22213-1213; (703) 536-7776. Fax, (703) 536-7079. Bruce N. Hahn, President. General e-mail, AHGA@americanhomeowners.org Web, www.americanhomeowners.org*

Consumer advocacy group that focuses on issues with significant economic impact on home owners and home ownership. Monitors legislation and regulations.

American Land Title Assn., *1828 L St. N.W., #705 20036; (202) 296-3671. Fax, (202) 223-5843. Kurt Pfotenhauer, Chief Executive Officer. General e-mail, service@alta.org Web, www.alta.org*

Membership: land title insurance underwriting companies, abstracters, and title insurance agents. Searches, reviews, and insures land titles to protect real estate investors, including home buyers and mortgage lenders; provides industry information. Monitors legislation and regulations.

American Resort Development Assn., *1201 15th St. N.W., #400 20005; (202) 371-6700. Fax, (202) 289-8544. Howard Nusbaum, President. Web, www.arda.org*

Membership: U.S. and international developers, builders, financiers, marketing companies, and others involved in resort, recreational, and community development. Serves as an information clearinghouse; monitors federal and state legislation.

American Society of Appraisers, *555 Herndon Pkwy., #125, Herndon, VA 20170; (703) 478-2228. Fax, (703) 742-8471. Laurie M. Saunders, Executive Vice President. Toll-free, (800) 272-8258.*
General e-mail, asainfo@appraisers.org

Web, www.appraisers.org

Membership: accredited appraisers of real property, including land, houses, and commercial buildings; business valuation; machinery and technical specialties; yachts; aircraft; public utilities; personal property, including antiques, fine art, residential contents; gems and jewelry. Affiliate members include students and professionals interested in appraising. Provides technical information; accredits appraisers; provides consumer information programs.

Appraisal Foundation, *1155 15th St. N.W., #1111 20005; (202) 347-7722. Fax, (202) 347-7727. David S. Bunton, President.*
General e-mail, info@appraisalfoundation.org

Web, www.appraisalfoundation.org

Ensures that appraisers are qualified to offer their services by promoting uniform appraisal standards and establishing education, experience, and examination requirements.

Appraisal Institute, *Public Affairs, Washington Office, 122 C St. N.W., #360 20001; (202) 298-6449. Fax, (202) 298-5547. William "Bill" Garber, Director of Government and External Relations.*
Web, www.appraisalinstitute.org

Provides Congress, regulatory agencies, and the executive branch with information on appraisal matters. (Headquarters in Chicago, Ill.)

Assn. of Foreign Investors in Real Estate, *1300 Pennsylvania Ave. N.W. 20004-3020; (202) 312-1400. Fax, (202) 312-1401. James A. Fetgatter, Chief Executive.*
General e-mail, afireinfo@afire.org

Web, www.afire.org

Represents foreign institutions that are interested in the laws, regulations, and economic trends affecting the U.S. real estate market. Informs the public and the government of the contributions foreign investment makes to the U.S. economy. Examines current issues and organizes seminars for members.

International Real Estate Federation, *U.S. Chapter, 1916 Wilson Blvd., #306, Arlington, VA 22201; (703) 524-4279. Fax, (703) 991-6256. Tyler Clay, President.*
General e-mail, info@fiabci-usa.com

Web, www.fiabci-usa.com

Membership: real estate professionals in the fields of appraisal, brokerage, counseling, development, financing, and property management. Sponsors seminars, workshops, and conferences. (International headquarters in Paris.)

Manufactured Housing Institute, *2101 Wilson Blvd., #610, Arlington, VA 22201-3040; (703) 558-0400. Fax, (703) 558-0401. Gail Cardwell, President.*
General e-mail, info@manufacturedhousing.org

Web, www.manufacturedhousing.org

Represents community owners and developers, financial lenders, and builders, suppliers, and retailers of manufactured and modular homes. Provides information on manufactured and modular home construction standards, finance, site development, property management, and marketing.

National Assn. of Home Builders (NAHB), *1201 15th St. N.W. 20005-2800; (202) 266-8200. Fax, (202) 266-8400. Jerry M. Howard, Chief Executive Officer. Press, (202) 266-8254. Toll-free, (800) 368-5242.*
General e-mail, info@nahb.org

Web, www.nahb.org

Membership: contractors, builders, architects, engineers, mortgage lenders, and others interested in home building and residential real estate construction. Offers educational programs and information on housing policy and mortgage finance in the United States. Library open to the public by appointment.

National Assn. of Real Estate Brokers, *9831 Greenbelt Rd., #309, Lanham, MD 20706; (301) 552-9340. Fax, (301) 552-9216. Maria Kong, President; Tawanda Barnett, Office Manager.*
General e-mail, nareb3@aol.com

Web, www.nareb.com

Membership: minority real estate brokers, appraisers, contractors, property managers, and salespersons. Works to prevent discrimination in housing policies and practices; conducts regional seminars on federal policy, legislation, and regulations; advises members on procedures for procuring federal contracts.

National Assn. of Real Estate Investment Trusts, *1875 Eye St. N.W., #600 20006-5413; (202) 739-9400. Fax, (202) 739-9401. Steven Wechsler, President.*
Web, www.reit.com

Membership: real estate investment trusts and corporations, partnerships, and individuals interested in real estate securities and the industry. Monitors federal and state legislation, federal taxation, securities regulation, standards and ethics, and housing and education; compiles industry statistics.

National Assn. of Realtors, *Government Affairs, Washington Office, 500 New Jersey Ave. N.W. 20001-2020; (202) 383-1000. Fax, (202) 383-7580. Jerry Giovaniello, Senior Vice President.*
Web, www.realtor.org

Sets standards of ethics for the real estate business; promotes education, research, and exchange of information. Monitors legislation and regulations. (Headquarters in Chicago, Ill.)

The Real Estate Roundtable, *801 Pennsylvania Ave. N.W., #720 20004; (202) 639-8400. Fax, (202) 639-8442. Jeffrey D. DeBoer, President.*
General e-mail, info@rer.org

Web, www.rer.org

Membership: real estate owners, advisers, builders, investors, lenders, and managers. Serves as forum for public policy issues, including taxes, the environment, capital, credit, and investments.

Society of Industrial and Office Realtors, *1201 New York Ave., #350 20005-6126; (202) 449-8200. Fax, (202) 216-9325. Richard Hollander, Executive Vice President.*
General e-mail, admin@sior.com

Web, www.sior.com

Membership: commercial and industrial real estate brokers worldwide. Certifies brokers; sponsors seminars and conferences; mediates and arbitrates business disputes for members; sponsors a speakers bureau. (Affiliated with the National Assn. of Realtors.)

Mortgages and Finance

▶AGENCIES

Fannie Mae (Federal Housing Finance Agency), *3900 Wisconsin Ave. N.W. 20016-2892; (202) 752-7000. Fax, (202) 752-3616. Herbert M. Allison Jr., Chief Executive Officer. Information, (800) 732-6643. Press, (202) 752-7111. Web, www.fanniemae.com and www.fhfa.gov*

Congressionally chartered, shareholder-owned corporation under conservatorship of the Federal Housing Finance Agency. Makes mortgage funds available by buying conventional and government-insured mortgages in the secondary mortgage market; raises capital through sale of short- and long-term obligations, mortgages, and stock; issues and guarantees mortgage-backed securities. (Fannie Mae stands for Federal National Mortgage Assn.)

Farmer Mac, *1133 21st St. N.W., #600 20036-3332; (202) 872-7700. Fax, (202) 872-7713. Michael Gerber, President. Web, www.farmermac.com*

Private corporation chartered by Congress to provide a secondary mortgage market for farm and rural housing loans. Guarantees principal and interest repayment on securities backed by farm and rural housing loans. (Farmer Mac stands for Federal Agricultural Mortgage Corp.)

Federal Housing Administration (FHA), *(Housing and Urban Development Dept.), Multifamily Housing Development, 451 7th St. S.W., #6136 20410-8000; (202) 708-1142. Fax, (202) 708-3104. Joyce Allen, Director. TTY, (202) 708-1455.*
Web, www.hud.gov/offices/hsg/mfh/mfbroch/mfbroc3.cfm

Establishes procedures for the origination of FHA-insured mortgages for multifamily housing. Administers the mortgage insurance programs for rental, cooperative, and condominium housing, nursing homes, and assisted living systems.

Federal Housing Administration (FHA), *(Housing and Urban Development Dept.), Single Family Program Development, 451 7th St. S.W., #9278 20410-8000; (202) 708-2121. Fax, (202) 708-4308. Margaret E. Burns, Director.*
Web, www.hud.gov/offices/hsg/sfh/hsgsingle.cfm

Establishes procedures for mortgage insurance programs related to the purchase or rehabilitation of single family homes.

Federal Housing Administration (FHA), *(Housing and Urban Development Dept.), Title I Insurance, 451 7th St. S.W., #9266 20410; (202) 708-2121. Fax, (202) 708-4308. Joanne Kuczma, Director.*
Web, www.hud.gov

Sets policy for Title I loans on manufactured home and property improvement loans. Provides information to lenders on policy issues.

Federal Housing Finance Agency (FHFA), *1700 G St. N.W. 20552-0100; (866) 796-5595. Fax, (202) 414-3823. James B. Lockhart III, Director.*
General e-mail, fhfainfo@fhfa.gov

Web, www.fhfa.gov

Regulates and works to ensure the financial soundness of Fannie Mae (Federal National Mortgage Assn.), Freddie Mac (Federal Home Loan Mortgage Corp.), and the twelve Federal Home Loan banks. FHFA was formed by a legislative merger of the Office of Federal Housing Enterprise Oversight (OFHEO), the Federal Housing Finance Board, and HUD's Government-sponsored Enterprise (GSE) mission team.

Freddie Mac (Federal Housing Finance Agency), *8200 Jones Branch Dr., McLean, VA 22102-3100; (703) 903-3001. Fax, (703) 903-3495. Robert R. Glauber, Chair (Interim); John A. Koskinen, Chief Executive Officer (Interim). Information, (703) 903-2000. Press, (703) 903-2438. Web, www.freddiemac.com and www.fhfa.gov*

Chartered by Congress to support homeownership and rental housing by increasing the flow of funds for residential mortgages and mortgage-related securities. Issues mortgage passthrough securities and debt instruments in capital markets toward this end. (Freddie Mac stands for Federal Home Loan Mortgage Corp.)

Ginnie Mae *(Housing and Urban Development Dept.), 550 12th St. S.W., 3rd Floor 20024 (mailing address: 451 7th St. S.W., #B-133, Washington, DC 20410); (202) 708-0926. Fax, (202) 485-0206. Joseph J. Murin, President; Thomas Weakland, Executive Vice President (Acting). Web, www.ginniemae.gov*

Supports government housing objectives by establishing secondary markets for residential mortgages. Serves as a vehicle for channeling funds from the securities markets into the mortgage market through mortgage-backed securities programs and helps to increase the supply of credit available for housing. Guarantees privately issued securities backed by Federal Housing Administration, Veterans Affairs Dept., and Farmers Home Administration mortgages. (Ginnie Mae stands for Government National Mortgage Assn.)

Housing and Urban Development Dept. (HUD),
Housing, *451 7th St. S.W., #9100 20410; (202) 708-2601. Fax, (202) 708-2580. Brian D. Montgomery, Assistant Secretary. TTY, (202) 708-1455.*
Web, www.hud.gov/offices/hsg/index.cfm

Administers all Federal Housing Administration (FHA) mortgage insurance programs; approves and monitors all lending institutions that conduct business with HUD.

Office of Thrift Supervision (OTS), *(Treasury Dept.),*
1700 G St. N.W. 20552; (202) 906-6590. Fax, (202) 898-0230. John M. Reich, Director. Information, (202) 906-6000. Library, (202) 906-6470. Press, (202) 906-6288.
Web, www.ots.treas.gov

Charters, regulates, and examines the operations of savings and loan institutions; focus includes mortgage rates. Library open to the public by appointment.

►CONGRESS

For a listing of relevant congressional committees and subcommittees, please see page 381 or the Appendix.

►NONGOVERNMENTAL

American Bankers Assn. (ABA), *1120 Connecticut Ave. N.W. 20036; (202) 663-5000. Fax, (202) 663-7533. Edward Yingling, President. Information, (800) BANKERS.*
General e-mail, custserv@aba.com

Web, www.aba.com

Membership: insured depository institutions involved in finance, including community banking. Provides information on issues that affect the industry. Monitors economic issues affecting savings institutions; publishes real estate lending survey. Monitors legislation and regulations. (America's Community Bankers merged with the American Banking Assn.)

Center for Responsible Lending, *Washington Office, 910 17th St. N.W., #500 20006; (202) 349-1850. Fax, (202) 289-9009. Eric Halperin, Director.*
Web, www.responsiblelending.org

Protects homeownership and family wealth by working to eliminate abusive financial practices. Encourages policy decisions to eliminate such practices. Provides legal knowledge to advocates and policymakers; researches predatory lending practices; provides a Web-based archive of information for public use.

Mortgage Bankers Assn., *1331 L St. N.W. 20005; (202) 557-2700. Fax, (202) 721-0249. John Courson, President. Alternate fax, (202) 721-0167.*
Web, www.mbaa.org

Membership: institutions involved in real estate finance. Maintains School of Mortgage Banking; collects statistics on the industry. Conducts seminars and workshops in specialized areas of mortgage finance. Monitors legislation and regulations.

Mortgage Insurance Companies of America, *1425 K St. N.W., #210 20005; (202) 682-2683. Fax, (202) 842-9252. Suzanne C. Hutchinson, Executive Vice President.*
General e-mail, info@privatemi.com

Web, www.privatemi.com

Membership: companies that provide guaranteed insurance on residential, high-ratio mortgage loans. Insures members against loss from default on low down payment home mortgages and provides coverage that acts as a credit enhancement on mortgage securities.

National Assn. of Affordable Housing Lenders, *1600 K St. N.W., #210 20006; (202) 293-9850. Fax, (202) 293-9852. Judith A. Kennedy, President.*
General e-mail, naahl@naahl.org

Web, www.naahl.org

Membership: lenders who specialize in providing private capital for affordable housing and community development in low- and moderate-income areas. Serves as an information clearinghouse; provides education, training, and direct technical assistance. Monitors legislation and regulations.

National Assn. of Local Housing Finance Agencies, *2025 M St. N.W., #800 20036-3309; (202) 367-1197. Fax, (202) 367-2197. John C. Murphy, Executive Director.*
General e-mail, info@nalhfa.org

Web, www.nalhfa.org

Membership: professionals of city and county governments that finance affordable housing. Provides professional development programs in new housing finance and other areas. Monitors legislation and regulations.

National Assn. of Mortgage Brokers, *7900 Westpark Dr., #T309, McLean, VA 22102; (703) 342-5900. Fax, (703) 342-5905. Roy DeLoach, Chief Executive Officer.*
Web, www.namb.org

Membership: mortgage brokers. Seeks to improve the mortgage broker industry. Offers educational programs to members. Provides referrals. Monitors legislation and regulations.

National Council of State Housing Agencies, *444 N. Capitol St. N.W., #438 20001; (202) 624-7710. Fax, (202) 624-5899. Barbara J. Thompson, Executive Director.*
General e-mail, info@ncsha.org

Web, www.ncsha.org

Membership: state housing finance agencies. Promotes greater opportunities for lower-income people to rent or buy affordable housing.

Resources for Mortgage Financing and Other Housing Assistance

The following agencies and organizations offer consumer information pertaining to mortgages and other housing issues.

Center for Responsible Lending, Washington, DC, office, (202) 349-1850, www.responsiblelending.org

Center on Budget and Policy Priorities, (202) 408-1080, www.cbpp.org

Consumer Federation of America, (202) 387-6121, www.consumerfed.org

Council for Affordable and Rural Housing, (703) 837-9001, www.carh.org

Fannie Mae, (202) 752-7000, www.fanniemae.com

The Finance Project, Economic Success Clearinghouse, (202) 628.4200, www.financeproject.org

Freddie Mac, (703) 903-3001, www.freddiemac.com

Housing and Urban Development Dept., (202) 708-1112, www.hud.gov

Housing Assistance Council, (202) 842-8600, www.ruralhome.org

Mortgage Bankers Assn., (202) 557-2700, www.mortgagebankers.org

National Assn. of Development Companies, (703) 748-2575, www.nadco.org

National Assn. of Home Builders, (202) 266-8200; toll-free, (800) 368-5254, www.nahb.org

National Assn. Of Local Housing Finance Agencies, (202) 367-1197, www.nalhfa.org

National Assn. of Mortgage Brokers, (703) 342-5900, www.namb.org

National Assn. of Realtors, (800) 874-6500, www.realtor.org

National Council of State Housing Agencies, (202) 624-7710, www.ncsha.org

National Housing Conference, (202) 466-2121, www.nhc.org

National Housing Law Project, Headquarters, (510) 251-9400; Washington, DC, office, (202) 347-8775 www.nhlp.org

National Housing Trust, (202) 333-8931, www.nhtinc.org

National Leased Housing Assn., (202) 785-8888, www.hudnlha.com

National Low Income Housing Coalition, (202) 662-1530, www.nlihc.org

National Reverse Mortgage Lenders Assn., (202) 939-1760, www.reversemortgage.org or www.nrmla.org

NeighborhoodWorks America, (202) 220-2300, www.nw.org

Smart Growth America, (202) 207-3355, www.smartgrowthamerica.org

Urban Institute, (202) 833-7200, www.urban.org

National Reverse Mortgage Lenders Assn., *1400 16th St. N.W., #420 20036; (202) 939-1760. Fax, (202) 265-4435. Peter H. Bell, President. Web, www.nrmlaonline.org*

National trade association for firms that originate, service, and invest in reverse mortgages. Monitors legislation and regulations.

Property Management

▶AGENCIES

Bureau of Land Management (BLM), *(Interior Dept.), Lands, Realty, and Cadastral Survey, 1620 L St. N.W. 20036 (mailing address: 1849 C St. N.W., MS 1000LS, Washington, DC 20240); (202) 452-7779. Fax, (202) 452-7708. Jeff Holdren, Manager. Web, www.blm.gov*

Oversees use, acquisition, and disposal of public lands. Conducts the Public Lands Survey; authorizes rights-of-way on public lands, including roads and power lines.

Federal Housing Administration (FHA), *(Housing and Urban Development Dept.), Multifamily Asset Management, 451 7th St. S.W., #6160 20410; (202) 708-3730. Fax, (202) 401-5978. Beverly J. Miller, Director. Web, www.hud.gov*

Services mortgages developed under HUD's multifamily mortgage insurance programs, including the Community Disposal Program; reviews management of multifamily housing projects and administers project-based subsidy programs; advises state housing agencies that administer multifamily projects.

Federal Housing Administration (FHA), *(Housing and Urban Development Dept.), Procurement Management, 451 7th St. S.W., #2222 20410; (202) 402-7166. Fax, (202) 708-3698. Thomas Dussault, Director. Web, www.hud.gov*

Develops and implements policies and procedures and conducts contract administration for the Office of Housing and the Federal Housing Administration headquarters' procurement actions.

Real Estate Assessment Center *(Housing and Urban Development Dept.), 550 12th St. S.W., #100 20410; (202) 475-7949. Fax, (202) 485-0286. James David Reeves, Deputy Assistant Secretary. Toll-free, (888) 245-4860. General e-mail, REAC_TAC@hud.gov Web, www.hud.gov/reac*

Conducts physical inspections and surveys of resident satisfaction in publicly owned, insured, or subsidized housing. Assesses financial condition and management operations of public housing agencies.

▶NONGOVERNMENTAL

Building Owners and Managers Assn. International, *1101 15th St. N.W., #800 20005; (202) 408-2662. Fax, (202) 326-6377. Henry Chamberlain, President. Web, www.boma.org*

Membership: office building owners and managers. Reviews changes in model codes and building standards; conducts seminars and workshops on building operation and maintenance issues; sponsors educational and training programs. Monitors legislation and regulations.

Community Associations Institute, *225 Reinekers Lane, #300, Alexandria, VA 22314; (703) 548-8600. Fax, (703) 684-1581. Edward D. Thomas, Chief Executive Officer. Toll-free, (888) 224-4321. Web, www.caionline.org*

Membership: homeowner associations, builders, lenders, owners, managers, realtors, insurance companies, and public officials. Provides members with information on creating, financing, and maintaining common facilities and services in condominiums and other planned developments.

National Apartment Assn., *4300 Wilson Blvd., #400, Arlington, VA 22203; (703) 518-6141. Fax, (703) 248-9440. Doug Culkin, Executive Vice President. Web, www.naahq.org*

Membership: state and local associations of owners, managers, investors, developers, and builders of apartment houses or other rental properties. Conducts educational and professional certification programs. Monitors legislation and regulations.

National Assn. of Home Builders (NAHB), *1201 15th St. N.W. 20005-2800; (202) 266-8200. Fax, (202) 266-8400. Jerry M. Howard, Chief Executive Officer. Press, (202) 266-8254. Toll-free, (800) 368-5242. General e-mail, info@nahb.org*

Web, www.nahb.org

Membership: contractors, builders, architects, engineers, mortgage lenders, and others interested in home building and residential real estate construction. Offers a Registered Apartment Managers certification program; provides educational programs and information on apartment construction and management, condominiums and cooperatives, multifamily rehabilitation, and low-income and federally assisted housing. Library open to the public by appointment.

National Assn. of Housing and Redevelopment Officials, *630 Eye St. N.W. 20001-3736; (202) 289-3500. Fax, (202) 289-8181. Saul Ramirez, Executive Director. Toll-free, (877) 866-2476. Web, www.nahro.org*

Membership: housing, community, and urban development practitioners and organizations, and state and local government agencies and personnel. Conducts studies and provides training and certification in the operation and management of rental housing; develops performance standards for low-income rental housing operations.

National Assn. of Housing Cooperatives, *1444 Eye St. N.W., #700 20005-6542; (202) 737-0797. Fax, (202) 216-9646. Dee Ann Walker, Executive Director. General e-mail, info@coophousing.org*

Web, www.coophousing.org

Membership: housing cooperative professionals, developers, and individuals. Promotes housing cooperatives; sets standards; provides technical assistance in all phases of cooperative housing; sponsors educational programs and on-site training; monitors legislation; maintains an information clearinghouse on housing cooperatives.

National Assn. of Industrial and Office Properties (NAIOP), *2201 Cooperative Way, #300, Herndon, VA 20171-3034; (703) 904-7100. Fax, (703) 904-7942. Thomas J. Bisacquino, President. General e-mail, naiop@naiop.org*

Web, www.naiop.org

Membership: developers, planners, designers, builders, financiers, and managers of industrial and office properties. Provides research and continuing education programs. Monitors legislation and regulations on capital gains, real estate taxes, impact fees, growth management, environmental issues, and hazardous waste liability.

National Center for Housing Management, *12021 Sunset Hills Rd., #210, Reston, VA 20190; (703) 435-9393. Fax, (703) 435-9775. W. Glenn Stevens, President. Toll-free, (800) 368-5625. General e-mail, service@nchm.org*

Web, www.nchm.org

Private corporation created by executive order to meet housing management and training needs. Conducts research, demonstrations, and educational and training programs in all types of multifamily housing management. Develops and implements certification systems for housing management programs.

National Cooperative Business Assn., *1401 New York Ave. N.W., #1100 20005-3160; (202) 638-6222. Fax, (202) 638-1374. Paul Hazen, President. General e-mail, ncba@ncba.coop*

Web, www.ncba.coop

Alliance of cooperatives, businesses, and state cooperative associations. Provides information about starting and managing housing cooperatives. Monitors legislation and regulations.

National Multi Housing Council, *1850 M St. N.W., #540 20036-5803; (202) 974-2300. Fax, (202) 775-0112. Doug Bibby, President.*
General e-mail, info@nmhc.org

Web, www.nmhc.org

Membership: owners, financiers, managers, and developers of multifamily housing. Advocates policies and programs at the federal, state, and local levels to increase the supply and quality of multifamily units in the United States; serves as a clearinghouse on rent control, condominium conversion, taxes, fair housing, and environmental issues.

Property Management Assn., *7900 Wisconsin Ave., #305, Bethesda, MD 20814; (301) 657-9200. Fax, (301) 907-9326. Thomas B. Cohn, Executive Director.*
General e-mail, info@pma-dc.org

Web, www.pma-dc.org

Membership: property managers and firms that offer products and services needed in the property management field. Promotes information exchange on property management practices.

12 International Affairs

INTERNATIONAL AFFAIRS RESOURCES IN CONGRESS

For a complete listing of Congress committees, including their full contact information, leadership, membership, and jurisdictions, please refer to the Appendix on pages 724–837.

HOUSE:

House Agriculture Committee, Subcommittee on Rural Development, Biotechnology, Specialty Crops, and Foreign Agriculture, (202) 225-8248.
Web, agriculture.house.gov

House Appropriations Committee, Subcommittee on Commerce, Justice, Science, and Related Agencies, (202) 225-3351.
Web, appropriations.house.gov

    Subcommittee on Interior, Environment and Related Agencies, (202) 225-3081.

    Subcommittee on State, Foreign Operations, and Related Programs, (202) 225-2041.

House Energy and Commerce Committee, Subcommittee on Commerce, Trade and Consumer Protections, (202) 225-2927.
Web, energycommerce.house.gov

House Financial Services Committee, Subcommittee on International Monetary Policy and Trade, (202) 225-4247.
Web, financialservices.house.gov

House Foreign Affairs Committee, (202) 225-5021.
Web, foreignaffairs.house.gov

    Subcommittee on Africa and Global Health, (202) 226-7812.

    Subcommittee on Asia, the Pacific, and the Global Environment, (202) 226-7825.

    Subcommittee on Europe, (202) 226-7820.

    Subcommittee on International Organizations, Human Rights and Oversight, (202) 226-6434.

    Subcommittee on the Middle East and South Asia, (202) 225-3345.

    Subcommittee on Terrorism, Nonproliferation and Trade, (202) 226-1500.

    Subcommittee on the Western Hemisphere, (202) 226-9980.

House Homeland Security Committee, (202) 226-2616.
Web, homeland.house.gov

    Subcommittee on Border, Maritime and Global Counterterrorism, (202) 226-2616.

House Judiciary Committee, Subcommittee on Crime, Terrorism and Homeland Security, (202) 225-5727.
Web, judiciary.house.gov

    Subcommittee on Immigration, Citizenship, Refugees, Border Security, and International Law, (202) 225-3926.

House Natural Resources Committee, (202) 225-6065.
Web, resourcescommittee.house.gov

    Subcommittee on Insular Affairs, Oceans, and Wildlife, (202) 226-0200.

House Oversight and Government Reform Committee, Subcommittee on National Security and Foreign Affairs, (202) 225-2548.
Web, oversight.house.gov

House Small Business Committee, Subcommittee on Finance and Tax, (202) 225-4038.
Web, www.house.gov/smbiz

    Subcommittee on Regulations, Health Care and Trade, (202) 225-4038.

House Transportation and Infrastructure Committee, Subcommittee on Coast Guard and Marine Transportation, (202) 226-3587.
Web, transportation.house.gov

House Ways and Means Committee, Subcommittee on Trade, (202) 225-6649.
Web, waysandmeans.house.gov

GENERAL POLICY AND ANALYSIS

Basic Resources

▶**AGENCIES**

Agency for International Development (USAID), *Conflict Management and Mitigation,* 1300 *Pennsylvania Ave. N.W., #2.9 20523; (202) 712-0197. Neil Levine, Director.*
General e-mail, conflict@usaid.gov

Web, www.usaid.gov/our_work/cross-cutting_programs/ conflict

Supports USAID's work as it relates to conflict management, fragility, political instability, and extremism. Applies best practices of conflict management to areas such as democracy and governance, economic growth, natural resource management, and peace-building efforts.

Defense Dept. (DoD), *International Security Affairs, The Pentagon, #3-C852A 20301-2400; (703) 695-4351. Fax, (703) 697-7230. Vacant, Assistant Secretary.*
Web, www.defenselink.mil

Advises the secretary of defense and recommends policies on regional security issues (except those involving countries of the former Soviet Union or NATO members).

National Security Council (NSC), *(Executive Office of the President), International Economic Affairs, The White House 20504; (202) 456-9281. Fax, (202) 456-9280. John Herrmann, Special Assistant to the President.*
Web, www.whitehouse.gov/nsc

INTERNATIONAL AFFAIRS RESOURCES IN CONGRESS

JOINT:

Joint Economic Committee, (202) 224-0372.

Web, jec.senate.gov or www.house.gov/jec

SENATE:

Senate Agriculture, Nutrition, and Forestry Committee, Subcommittee on Domestic and Foreign Marketing, Inspection, and Plant and Animal Health, (202) 224-2035.

Web, agriculture.senate.gov

Senate Appropriations Committee, Subcommittee on Commerce, Justice, Science, and Related Agencies, (202) 224-5202.

Web, appropriations.senate.gov

> **Subcommittee on Interior, Environment and Related Agencies,** (202) 228-0774.

> **Subcommittee on State, Foreign Operations, and Related Programs,** (202) 224-7284.

Senate Banking, Housing, and Urban Affairs Committee, Subcommittee on Security and International Trade and Finance, (202) 224-5623.

Web, banking.senate.gov

Senate Commerce, Science, and Transportation Committee, Subcommittee on Oceans, Atmosphere, Fisheries and the Coast Guard, (202) 224-4912.

Web, commerce.senate.gov

Senate Energy and Natural Resources Committee, (202) 224-4971.

Web, energy.senate.gov

Senate Finance Committee, Subcommittee on International Trade and Global Competitiveness, (202) 224-4515.

Web, finance.senate.gov

Senate Foreign Relations Committee, (202) 224-4651.

Web, foreign.senate.gov

> **Subcommittee on African Affairs,** (202) 224-4651.

> **Subcommittee on East Asian and Pacific Affairs,** (202) 224-4651.

> **Subcommittee on European Affairs,** (202) 224-4651.

> **Subcommittee on International Development and Foreign Assistance, Economic Affairs, and International Environmental Protection,** (202) 224-4651.

> **Subcommittee on International Operations and Organizations, Democracy, and Human Rights,** (202) 224-4651.

> **Subcommittee on Near Eastern and South and Central Asian Affairs,** (202) 224-4651.

> **Subcommittee on Western Hemisphere, Peace Corps, and Narcotics Affairs,** (202) 224-4651.

Senate Homeland Security and Governmental Affairs Committee, (202) 224-2627.

Web, hsgac.senate.gov

> **Permanent Subcommittee on Investigations,** (202) 224-9505.

Senate Judiciary Committee, Subcommittee on Crime and Drugs, (202) 224-0558.

Web, judiciary.senate.gov

> **Subcommittee on Human Rights and the Law,** (202) 224-1158.

> **Subcommittee on Immigration, Refugees, and Border Security,** (202) 224-7878.

> **Subcommittee on Terrorism, Technology, and Homeland Security,** (202) 224-4933.

Senate Small Business and Entrepreneurship Committee, (202) 224-5175.

Web, sbc.senate.gov

Advises the president, the National Security Council, and the National Economic Council on all aspects of U.S. foreign policy dealing with U.S. international economic policies.

National Security Council *(Executive Office of the President), Office of Strategic Communications and Global Outreach,* Dwight D. Eisenhower Executive Office Bldg., #302 20500, (202) 456-9271. Fax, (202) 456-9270. Dennis McDonough, Deputy Assistant. Administrative office, (202) 456-9301.
Web, www.whitehouse.gov/administration/eop/nsc

Advises U.S. government agencies on the direction and theme of the president's message. Assists in the development and coordination of communications programs that disseminate consistent and accurate messages

about the U.S. government and policies to the global audience.

Office of Science and Technology Policy (OSTP), *(Executive Office of the President),* New Executive Office Bldg., #5236 20502; (202) 456-7116. Fax, (202) 456-6021. John Halder, Director, Science.
General e-mail, info@ostp.gov
Web, www.ostp.gov

Advises the president on science and technology matters as they affect national security; coordinates science and technology initiatives at the interagency level. Interests include nuclear materials, security, nuclear arms reduction, and counterterrorism.

President's Foreign Intelligence Advisory Board *(Executive Office of the President),* New Executive Office

Bldg., #5020 20502; (202) 456-2352. Fax, (202) 395-3403. Vacant, Chair; Vacant, Executive Director.
Web, www.whitehouse.gov/pfiab

Members appointed by the president. Assesses the quality, quantity, and adequacy of foreign intelligence collection and of counterintelligence activities by all government agencies; advises the president on matters concerning intelligence and national security.

State Dept., *2201 C St. N.W. 20520; (202) 647-5291. Fax, (202) 647-6424. Hillary Clinton, Secretary; James Steinburg, Deputy Secretary. Information, (202) 647-4000. Press, (202) 647-2492.*
Web, www.state.gov

Directs and coordinates U.S. foreign relations and interdepartmental activities of the U.S. government overseas.

State Dept., *Consular Affairs, 2201 C St. N.W., #6811 20520-4818; (202) 647-9576. Fax, (202) 647-9622. Janice L. Jacobs, Assistant Secretary. TTY, (888) 874-7793. National Passport Information Center (fees are charged for calls to this number), (877) 487-2778 with credit card. Assistance to U.S. citizens overseas, (888) 407-4747; (317) 472-2328 from overseas.*
Web, http://travel.state.gov

Issues passports to U.S. citizens and visas to immigrants and nonimmigrants seeking to enter the United States. Provides protection, assistance, and documentation for U.S. citizens abroad.

State Dept., *Democracy and Global Affairs, 2201 C St. N.W., #7250 20520; (202) 647-6240. Fax, (202) 647-0753. Vacant, Under Secretary.*
Web, www.state.gov

Advises the secretary on international issues. Divisions include Democracy, Human Rights, and Labor; Oceans and International Environmental and Scientific Affairs; Population, Refugees, and Migration; Women's Issues; and Monitor and Combat Trafficking in Persons.

State Dept., *Intelligence and Research, 2201 C St. N.W., #6468 20520-6531; (202) 647-9177. Fax, (202) 736-4688. John Dinger, Assistant Secretary (Acting).*
Web, www.state.gov

Coordinates foreign policy–related research, analysis, and intelligence programs for the State Dept. and other federal agencies.

State Dept., *International Conferences, 2201 C St. N.W., #4334A 20520-6319; (202) 647-6875. Fax, (202) 647-5996. Edward P. Malcik, Managing Director.*
Web, www.state.gov

Coordinates U.S. participation in international conferences and accredits delegations.

State Dept., *International Organization Affairs, 2201 C St. N.W., #6323 20520-6319; (202) 647-9600. Fax, (202) 736-4116. Brian Hook, Assistant Secretary. Press, (202) 647-7938.*
Web, www.state.gov/p/io

Coordinates and develops policy guidelines for U.S. participation in the United Nations and in other international organizations and conferences.

State Dept., *Management, 2201 C St. N.W., #7207 20520; (202) 647-1500. Fax, (202) 647-0168. Patrick F. Kennedy, Under Secretary.*
Web, www.state.gov

Serves as principal adviser to the secretary on management matters, including budgetary, administrative, and personnel policies of the department and the Foreign Service.

State Dept., *Policy Planning Staff, 2201 C St. N.W., #7311 20520; (202) 647-2372. Fax, (202) 647-0844. Anne-Marie Slaughter, Director.*
Web, www.state.gov

Advises the secretary and other State Dept. officials on foreign policy matters.

State Dept., *Political Affairs, 2201 C St. N.W., #7240 20520; (202) 647-2471. Fax, (202) 647-4780. William J. Burns Jr., Under Secretary.*
Web, www.state.gov

Assists in the formulation and conduct of foreign policy and in the overall direction of the department; coordinates interdepartmental activities of the U.S. government abroad.

State Dept., *Public Diplomacy and Public Affairs, 2201 C St. N.W., #7261 20520; (202) 647-9199. Fax, (202) 647-9140. Vacant, Under Secretary.*
Web, www.state.gov

Seeks to broaden public affairs discussion on foreign policy with U.S. citizens, media, and institutions. Provides cultural and educational exchange opportunities and international information programs to people in the United States and abroad.

State Dept., *Public Diplomacy and Public Affairs: Bureau of Educational and Cultural Affairs, 301 4th St. S.W., #534 20547; (202) 203-7470. Fax, (202) 203-7469. Sheldon Yuspeh, Executive Director.*
Web, www.state.gov

Seeks to promote mutual understanding between the people of the United States and other countries through international educational and training programs. Promotes personal, professional, and institutional ties between private citizens and organizations in the United States and abroad; presents U.S. history, society, art, and culture to overseas audiences.

U.S. Institute of Peace, *1200 17th St. N.W., #200 20036; (202) 457-1700. Fax, (202) 429-6063. J. Robinson West, Chair; Richard H. Solomon, President. TTY, (202) 457-1719. General e-mail, info@usip.org*
Web, www.usip.org

Independent, nonpartisan institution established by Congress. Aims to prevent and resolve violent international conflicts, promote post-conflict stability, and increase peace-building capacity, tools, and intellectual capital worldwide.

►CONGRESS

For a listing of relevant congressional committees and subcommittees, please see page 412 or the Appendix.

Government Accountability Office (GAO), *International Affairs and Trade,* 441 G St. N.W., #4962 20548; (202) 512-3101. Jacquelyn L. Williams-Bridgers, Managing Director.
Web, www.gao.gov

Independent, nonpartisan agency in the legislative branch. Audits, analyzes, and evaluates international programs; makes unclassified reports available to the public. (Formerly the General Accounting Office.)

House Democracy Assistance Commission, *341 FHOB 20515; (202) 226-1641. Fax, (202) 226-6062. Rep. David E. Price, D–N.C., Chair; John Lis, Staff Director.*
General e-mail, hdac@mail.house.gov

Web, http://hdac.house.gov

Provides advice to members and staff of parliaments of select countries that have established or are developing democratic governments. Makes recommendations to the U.S. Agency for International Development (USAID) regarding material assistance to foreign countries.

Library of Congress, *Serial and Government Publications,* 101 Independence Ave. S.E., #LM133 20540; (202) 707-5647. Mark Sweeney, Chief.
Web, www.loc.gov

Collects and maintains information on governmental and nongovernmental organizations that are internationally based, financed, and sponsored. Responds to written or telephone requests to provide information on the history, structure, operation, and activities of these organizations. Some book material available for interlibrary loan through the Library of Congress Loan Division.

►INTERNATIONAL ORGANIZATIONS

European Commission, *Press and Public Diplomacy, Washington Office,* 2300 M St. N.W. 20037-1400; (202) 862-9500. Fax, (202) 429-1766. Anthony Smallwood, Head; John Bruton, Ambassador.
General e-mail, relex-delusw-help@ec.europa.eu

Web, www.eurunion.org

Provides information on European Union energy policy, initiatives, research activities, and selected statistics. (Headquarters in Brussels.)

International Bank for Reconstruction and Development (World Bank), *1818 H St. N.W. 20433; (202) 473-1000. Fax, (202) 477-6391. Robert B. Zoellick, President; Eli Whitney Debevoise II, U.S. Executive Director. Press, (202) 473-7660. Bookstore, (202) 458-4500.*
General e-mail, gchopra@worldbank.org

Web, www.worldbank.org

International development institution funded by government membership subscriptions and borrowings on private capital markets. Encourages the flow of public and private foreign investments into developing countries through loans, grants, and technical assistance. Finances foreign economic development projects in agriculture, environmental protection, education, public utilities, telecommunications, water supply, sewerage, public health, and other areas.

International Crisis Group, *Washington Office,* 1629 K St. N.W., #450 20006; (202) 785-1601. Fax, (202) 785-1630. Mark L. Schneider, Senior Vice President.
General e-mail, washington@crisisgroup.org

Web, www.crisisgroup.org

Private, multinational organization that seeks to prevent international conflict. Writes and distributes reports and raises funds. (Headquarters in Brussels.)

International Monetary Fund (IMF), *700 19th St. N.W. 20431; (202) 623-7000. Fax, (202) 623-4661. Meg Lundsager, U.S. Executive Director. Press, (202) 623-7100. Public Affairs, (202) 623-7300.*
Web, www.imf.org

International organization of 185 member countries that promotes policies for financial stability and economic growth, works to prevent financial crises, and helps members solve balance-of-payments problems through loans funded by member contributions.

Organisation for Economic Co-operation and Development (OECD), *Washington Center,* 2001 L St. N.W., #650 20036-4922; (202) 785-6323. Fax, (202) 785-0350. Kathleen Deboer, Director (Acting).
General e-mail, washington.contact@oecd.org

Web, www.oecdwash.org

Membership: thirty nations, including Australia, Canada, Japan, Mexico, New Zealand, the United States, and western European nations. Serves as a forum for government officials to exchange information on their countries' policies. The Washington Center maintains a reference library open to the public. (Headquarters in Paris.)

Organization of American States (OAS), *17th St. and Constitution Ave. N.W. 20006 (mailing address: 1889 F St. N.W., Washington, DC 20006); (202) 458-3000. Fax, (202) 458-3967. José Miguel Insulza, Secretary General. Library, (202) 458-6041.*
Web, www.oas.org

Membership: the United States, Canada, and all independent Latin American and Caribbean countries. Funded by quotas paid by member states and by contributions to special multilateral funds. Works to promote democracy, eliminate poverty, and resolve disputes among member nations. Provides member states with technical and advisory services in cultural, educational, scientific, social, and economic areas. Library open to the public.

United Nations Information Centre, *1775 K St. N.W., #400 20006-1500; (202) 331-8670. Fax, (202) 331-9191. William Davis, Director, (202) 454-2104.*

State Department

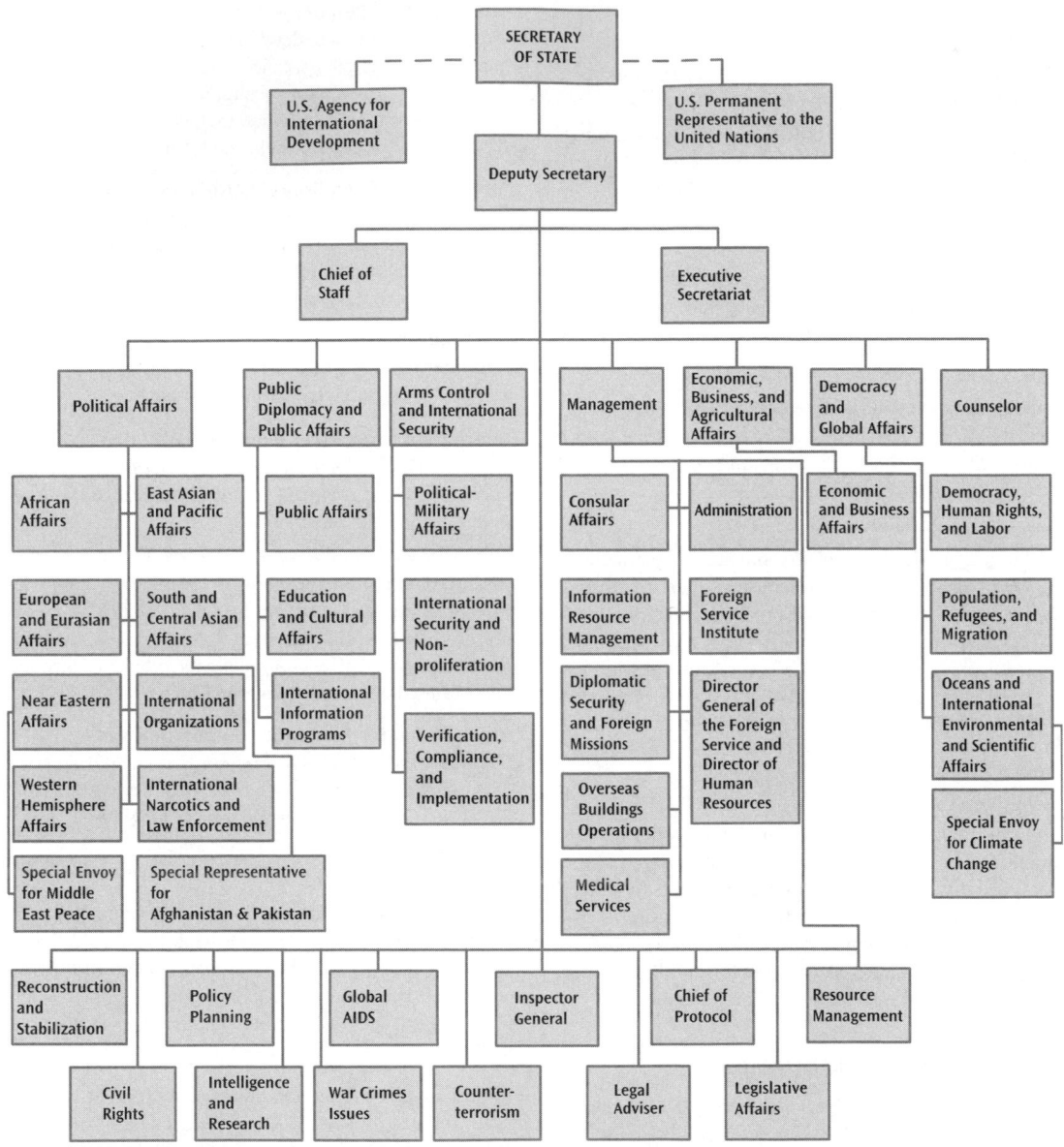

— — — Denotes independent agencies that receive guidance from the Secretary of State.

General e-mail, unicdc@unicwash.org

Web, www.unicwash.org

Lead United Nations (U.N.) office in Washington. Center for reference publications of the U.N. Library, open to the public; includes all official U.N. records and publications.

▶NONGOVERNMENTAL

American Enterprise Institute for Public Policy Research (AEI), *Foreign and Defense Policy Studies,* 1150 17th St. N.W., #1100 20036; (202) 862-5872. Fax, (202) 862-4877. Danielle Pletka, Vice President. Information, (202) 862-5800. Press, (202) 862-4871. Web, www.aei.org

Research and educational organization that conducts conferences, seminars, and debates and sponsors research on international affairs.

Aspen Institute, *1 Dupont Circle N.W., #700 20036; (202) 736-5800. Fax, (202) 467-0790. Walter Isaacson, President. Press, (202) 736-3849.* General e-mail, info@aspeninstitute.org

Web, www.aspeninstitute.org

Promotes consideration of the public good in a wide variety of areas, including international policy. Conducts educational programs; publishes reports.

Assn. on Third World Affairs, Inc., *1717 K St. N.W., #600 20036; (202) 973-0157. Fax, (202) 775-7465. Lorna Hahn, Executive Director.*
General e-mail, info@atwa.org
Web, www.atwa.org

Membership: individuals and groups interested in developing nations and nations in transition. Promotes research projects; arranges lectures and conferences; holds Capitol Hill conference series featuring ambassadors, members of Congress, and other distinguished persons.

Atlantic Council of the United States, *1101 15th St. N.W., 11th Floor 20005; (202) 463-7226. Fax, (202) 463-7241. Frederick Kempe, President.*
General e-mail, info@acus.org
Web, www.acus.org

Conducts studies and makes policy recommendations on U.S. foreign security and international economic policies in the Atlantic and Pacific communities; sponsors conferences and educational exchanges.

The Brookings Institution, *Foreign Policy Studies, 1775 Massachusetts Ave. N.W. 20036; (202) 797-6000. Fax, (202) 797-6004. Carlos Pascual, Director. Publications, (202) 797-6105.*
Web, www.brookings.edu

Conducts studies on foreign policy, national security, regional and global affairs, and economic policies. Includes four policy centers: Saban Center for Middle East Policy, the Center for Northeast Asian Policy Studies, the Center on the United States and Europe, and the John L. Thornton China Center.

Carnegie Endowment for International Peace, *1779 Massachusetts Ave. N.W. 20036; (202) 483-7600. Fax, (202) 483-1840. Jessica T. Mathews, President.*
General e-mail, info@carnegieendowment.org
Web, www.carnegieendowment.org

Conducts research on international affairs and U.S. foreign policy. Program activities cover a broad range of military, political, and economic issues; sponsors panel discussions. (Affiliate office in Moscow.)

Center for Strategic and International Studies, *1800 K St. N.W., #400 20006; (202) 887-0200. Fax, (202) 775-3199. John J. Hamre, President. Publications, (202) 775-3160.*
Web, www.csis.org

A bipartisan organization that seeks to advance global security and prosperity by providing strategic insights and practical policy solutions to decision makers. Expertise includes defense and international security, emerging global issues, and regional transformation.

Center for the Advanced Study of Language, *(University of Maryland), 7005 52nd Ave., College Park, MD 20742 (mailing address: University of Maryland, Box*

25, College Park, MD 20742-0025); (301) 226-8800. Fax, (301) 226-8811. Richard Brecht, Executive Director.
General e-mail, info@casl.umd.edu
Web, www.casl.umd.edu

Works to improve the performance of foreign language professionals in the federal government. Joint venture with the National Security Agency; collaborates with government agencies. Conducts research, conferences, and workshops on topics such as Arabic media and detecting deception in language and cultural context.

Center of Concern, *1225 Otis St. N.E. 20017; (202) 635-2757. Fax, (202) 832-9494. Fr. James Hug S.J., President.*
General e-mail, coc@coc.org
Web, www.coc.org

Independent, interdisciplinary organization that conducts social analysis, theological reflection, policy advocacy, and public education on issues of international justice and peace.

Charles F. Kettering Foundation, *Washington Office, 444 N. Capitol St. N.W., #434 20001-1512; (202) 393-4478. Fax, (202) 393-7644. David Matthews, President (located in Ohio).*
General e-mail, hsaunders@kettering.org
Web, www.kettering.org

Works to improve the domestic policy-making process through citizen deliberation. Supports international programs focusing on unofficial, citizen-to-citizen diplomacy. Encourages greater citizen involvement in formation of public policy. Interests include public education and at-risk youths. (Headquarters in Dayton, Ohio.)

Citizens for Global Solutions, *420 7th St. S.E. 20003; (202) 546-3950. Fax, (202) 546-3749. Don Kraus, Chief Executive Officer.*
General e-mail, info@globalsolutions.org
Web, www.globalsolutions.org

Encourages U.S. global engagement on a broad range of foreign policy issues, including U.N. reform, international law and justice, health and the environment, international institutions, and peace and security.

Citizens Network for Foreign Affairs (CNFA), *1828 L St. N.W., #710 20036; (202) 296-3920. Fax, (202) 296-3948. John H. Costello, President.*
General e-mail, info@cnfa.org
Web, www.cnfa.org

Public policy and education organization that works to involve Americans in the foreign policy process. Advocates a more collaborative partnership between the public and private sectors to promote global economic growth.

Coalition for American Leadership Abroad (COLEAD), *2101 E St. N.W. 20037; (202) 944-5519. Fax, (202) 338-6820. Harry C. Blaney III, President.*
General e-mail, colead@afsa.org
Web, www.colead.org

Works to improve U.S. foreign policies and assistance programs. Supports communication with international organizations to address threats to world peace. Interests include sustainable development and the environment, human rights and humanitarian assistance, arms control, and international trade. Supports the involvement of nongovernmental organizations, academic communities, churches, state and local governments, and citizens in international affairs. Interested in strengthening foreign affairs education and career development in public and private sectors.

Council on Foreign Relations, *Washington Office, 1777 F St. N.W. 20006; (202) 509-8400. Fax, (202) 509-8490. Kay King, Director.*
General e-mail, dcmeetings@cfr.org
Web, www.cfr.org

Promotes understanding of U.S. foreign policy and international affairs. Awards research grants through its International Affairs Fellowship Program. (Headquarters in New York.)

David S. Wyman Institute for Holocaust Studies, *1200 G St. N.W., #800 20005; (202) 434-8994. Rafael Medoff, Director.*
General e-mail, rafaelmedoff@aol.com
Web, www.wymaninstitute.org

Educates the public about U.S. response to Nazism and the Holocaust through scholarly research, public events and exhibits, publications, conferences, and educational programs.

Democracy Coalition Project, *1120 19th St. N.W. 20036; (202) 721-5630. Fax, (202) 721-5658.*
General e-mail, info@demcoalition.org
Web, www.demcoalition.org

Research and advocacy organization that promotes establishing and strengthening open democratic societies and respect for human rights worldwide. Policy agenda includes improving international responses to democratic crises, encouraging the donor community to support emerging democracies, and promoting reform of the United Nations through greater collaboration among democratic governments. Hosts panel discussions, makes presentations, and publishes reports.

Eisenhower Institute, *915 15th St. N.W., 8th Floor 20005; (202) 628-4444. Fax, (202) 628-4445. Jeffrey M. Blavatt, Chief Executive Officer; Susan Eisenhower, Senior Fellow.*
General e-mail, info@eisenhowerinstitute.org
Web, www.eisenhowerinstitute.org

Nonpartisan research and educational organization modeled on President Eisenhower's legacy of public policy formation and leadership, stressing pursuit of facts, respectful dialogue, and a focus on the future. Provides scholarships, fellowships, internships, and other sponsored opportunities for students to participate in dialogue with prominent figures and to pursue study of public policy and related fields. (Affiliated with Gettysburg College in Gettysburg, Pa.)

Freedom House, *1301 Connecticut Ave. N.W., 6th Floor 20036; (202) 296-5101. Fax, (202) 293-2840. Jennifer L. Windsor, Executive Director.*

General e-mail, info@freedomhouse.org
Web, www.freedomhouse.org

Promotes human rights, democracy, free markets, the rule of law, independent media, and U.S. engagement in international affairs through education, advocacy, and training initiatives. Collects and analyzes data on political rights and civil liberties worldwide; publishes comparative surveys and reports; sponsors conferences and training programs.

Friends Committee on National Legislation (FCNL), *245 2nd St. N.E. 20002-5795; (202) 547-6000. Fax, (202) 547-6019. Joe Volk, Executive Secretary. Toll-free, (800) 630-1330. Recorded information, (202) 547-4343.*
General e-mail, fcnl@fcnl.org
Web, www.fcnl.org

Seeks to broaden public interest and affect legislation and policy concerning regional and global institutions, peace processes, international development, and the work of the United Nations. (Affiliated with the Religious Society of Friends [Quakers].)

IFES, *1101 15th St. N.W., 3rd Floor 20005; (202) 828-8507. Fax, (202) 452-0804. Jean-Pierre Kingsley, President.*
Web, www.ifes.org

Supports electoral and other democratic institutions in emerging democracies. Holds conferences; observes election activities in more than 120 countries. Provides technical assistance. Conducts education and training programs and conferences. (Formerly the International Foundation for Election Systems.)

Institute for Foreign Policy Analysis, *1725 DeSales St. N.W., #402 20036; (202) 463-7942. Fax, (202) 785-2785. Robert L. Pfaltzgraff Jr., President.*
Web, www.ifpa.org

Trains policy analysts in the fields of foreign policy and national security. Sponsors research and workshops.

Institute for Policy Studies, *1112 16th St. N.W., #600 20036; (202) 234-9382. Fax, (202) 387-7915. John Cavanagh, Director.*
General e-mail, info@ips-dc.org
Web, www.ips-dc.org

Research and educational organization. Interests include foreign policy, inequality in the common good, international development, human rights, and national security.

Institute of International Education, *National Security Education Program, 1400 K St. N.W., #650 20005-2403; (202) 326-7697. Fax, (202) 326-7672. Chris Powers, Director. Information, (800) 618-6737.*
General e-mail, boren@iie.org
Web, www.borenawards.org

Administers Boren Awards and Language Flagship programs; provides scholarships, fellowships, and institutional grants to academics with an interest in foreign affairs and national security.

Institute of World Politics, *1521 16th St. N.W. 20036; (202) 462-2101. Fax, (202) 462-1527. John Lenczowski, President.*

General e-mail, info@iwp.edu

Web, www.iwp.edu

Offers master's degree in international affairs, foreign policy, methods of statecraft, and political philosophy.

International Center, *1025 Vermont Ave. N.W., #300 20005; (202) 263-5630. Fax, (202) 637-2007. Virginia Foote, President.*

Web, www.theintlcenter.org

Research organization concerned with U.S. foreign policy. Has sponsored U.S. delegations to more than twenty countries. Current activities include the New Forests Project and the U.S.-Vietnam Trade Council Education Forum.

International Republican Institute (IRI), *1225 Eye St. N.W., #700 20005-3987; (202) 408-9450. Fax, (202) 408-9462. Lorne Craner, President.*

Web, www.iri.org

Created under the National Endowment for Democracy Act. Fosters democratic self-rule through closer ties and cooperative programs with political parties and other nongovernmental institutions overseas.

National Defense Council Foundation, *1600 Wilson Blvd., #960, Arlington, VA 22209; (571) 216-1928. Fax, (703) 807-2073. James L. Martin, Chair.*

General e-mail, ndfhq@yahoo.com

Web, www.ndcf.org

Studies defense and foreign affairs issues faced by the United States. Informs Congress and the media on socioeconomic, political, and military issues that affect the United States. Interests include low-intensity conflict, drug control, and energy security concerns.

National Democratic Institute for International Affairs (NDI), *2030 M St. N.W., 5th Floor 20036; (202) 728-5500. Fax, (202) 728-5520. Kenneth Wollack, President.*

General e-mail, contactndi@ndi.org

Web, www.ndi.org

Conducts nonpartisan international programs to help maintain and strengthen democratic institutions worldwide. Focuses on party building, governance, and electoral systems.

National Endowment for Democracy, *1025 F St. N.W., #800 20004; (202) 378-9700. Fax, (202) 378-9407. Carl Gershman, President; Barbara Haig, Vice President for Program Planning and Evaluation.*

General e-mail, info@ned.org

Web, www.ned.org

Grant-making organization that receives funding from Congress. Awards grants to private organizations involved in democratic development abroad, including

the areas of democratic political processes; pluralism; and education, culture, and communications.

National Peace Foundation, *666 11th St. N.W., #202 20001; (202) 783-7030. Fax, (202) 783-7040. Sarah Harder, President.*

General e-mail, npf@nationalpeace.org

Web, www.nationalpeace.org

Seeks to prevent conflict and build peace in the United States and around the world by developing citizen networks, advancing peace education and conflict prevention and resolution skills, and promoting democratic values through international travel/exchange programs.

National Security Archive, *Gelman Library, George Washington University, 2130 H St. N.W., #701 20037; (202) 994-7000. Fax, (202) 994-7005. Thomas Blanton, Executive Director.*

General e-mail, nsarchiv@gwu.edu

Web, www.nsarchive.org

Research institute and library that provides information on U.S. foreign and economic policy and national security affairs. Maintains and publishes collection of declassified and unclassified documents obtained through the Freedom of Information Act. Archive open to the public by appointment.

Nixon Center, *1615 L St. N.W., #1250 20036-5651; (202) 887-1000. Fax, (202) 887-5222. Dimitri K. Simes, President.*

General e-mail, mail@nixoncenter.org

Web, www.nixoncenter.org

Works to develop new principles for U.S. global engagement and security. (Affiliated with the Richard Nixon Library and Birthplace Foundation.)

Paul H. Nitze School of Advanced International Studies, *1740 Massachusetts Ave. N.W. 20036; (202) 663-5624. Fax, (202) 663-5621. Jessica P. Einhorn, Dean. Information, (202) 663-5600. Press, (202) 663-5626.*

Web, www.sais-jhu.edu

Offers graduate and non-degree programs in international relations, economics, public policy, regional and functional studies, and foreign languages. Sponsors the Johns Hopkins Foreign Policy Institute and several other research centers.

Pew Global Attitudes Project, *1615 L St. N.W., #700 20036; (202) 419-4400. Fax, (202) 419-4399. Andrew Kohut, President.*

General e-mail, info@pewglobal.org

Web, www.pewglobal.org

Conducts public opinion surveys about world affairs and makes results available to journalists, academics, policymakers, and the public. Attempts to gauge attitudes in every region of the world toward globalization, democracy, trade, and other key issues. (A Pew Research Center project.)

United Nations Assn. of the USA, *Washington Office,*
1779 Massachusetts Ave. N.W., #610 20036; (202)
462-3446. Fax, (202) 462-3448. Steven A. Dimoff, Vice
President.
General e-mail, unadc@unausa.org

Web, www.unausa.org

Research and educational organization focusing on
international institutions, multilateral diplomacy, U.S.
foreign policy, and international economics. Coordinates
Model United Nations program for high school and university students. Monitors legislation and regulations.
(Headquarters in New York.)

U.S. Conference of Catholic Bishops (USCCB),
International Justice and Peace, 3211 4th St. N.E.
20017-1194; (202) 541-3160. Fax, (202) 541-3339.
Stephen Colecchi, Director.
General e-mail, jphdmail@usccb.org

Web, www.usccb.org

Works with the U.S. State Dept., foreign government
offices, and international organizations on issues of peace,
justice, and human rights.

U.S. Travel Assn., *1100 New York Ave. N.W., #450 20005;*
(202) 408-2120. Fax, (202) 408-1255. Kristy Chandler,
Director of Communications for the Travel Industry Assn..
General e-mail, kchandler@ustravel.org

Web, www.USTravel.org

Encourages travel as a way to improve the United
States' image abroad. Mobilizes businesses and government leaders to interact with international visitors. (Affiliated with the Travel Industry Assn.)

Washington Institute of Foreign Affairs, *2121*
Massachusetts Ave. N.W. 20008; (202) 332-1616. Fax,
(202) 332-0108. Sheila C. Schmidt, Executive Director.
General e-mail, WIFADC@aol.com

Web, http://WIFADC.org

Membership: former government officials, retired
military professionals, educators, and others concerned
with foreign affairs. Seeks to promote greater understanding of foreign policy issues.

Women in International Security, *CPASS, School of*
Foreign Service, Georgetown University, 3600 N St. N.W.
20007; (202) 687-3366. Fax, (202) 687-3233. Jolynn
Shoemaker, Executive Director.
General e-mail, wiisinfo@georgetown.edu

Web, http://wiis.georgetown.edu

Seeks to advance the role of women in international
relations. Maintains a database of women foreign and
defense policy specialists worldwide; organizes conferences
in the United States, Europe, the former Soviet Union, and
Asia; disseminates information on jobs, internships, and
fellowships for women in international affairs.

Women's Foreign Policy Group, *1875 Connecticut Ave.*
N.W., #720 20009-5728; (202) 884-8597. Fax, (202)
884-8487. Patricia Ellis, President.

General e-mail, wfpg@wfpg.org

Web, www.wfpg.org

Promotes women's leadership and women's interests
in international affairs professions. Conducts policy
programs, mentoring, and research.

Diplomats and Foreign Agents

▶**AGENCIES**

Foreign Service Institute *(State Dept.), 4000 Arlington*
Blvd., Arlington, VA 22204-1500 (mailing address: U.S.
Department of State, Washington, DC 20522-4201); (703)
302-6729. Fax, (703) 302-7227. Ruth Whiteside, Director.
Student messages and course information, (703) 302-7144.
Web, www.state.gov/m/fsi

Provides training for U.S. government personnel
involved in foreign affairs agencies, including employees
of the State Dept., the Agency for International Development, and the Defense Dept. Includes the Schools of
Applied Information Technology, Language Studies, Leadership and Management, and Professional and Area Studies as well as the Transition Center and the Assn. for
Diplomatic Studies and Training.

Justice Dept. (DOJ), *Foreign Agents Registration Unit,*
1400 New York Ave. N.W., #100 20005; (202) 514-1216.
Fax, (202) 514-2836. Heather H. Hunt, Chief.
Web, www.fara.gov

Receives and maintains the registration of agents
representing foreign countries, companies, organizations,
and individuals. Compiles semi-annual report on foreign
agent registrations. Foreign agent registration files are
open for public inspection.

State Dept., *Career Development and Assignments,*
2201 C St. N.W., #2328 20520-6258 (mailing address: HR/
CDA, Washington, DC 20520-6258); (202) 647-1692. Fax,
(202) 647-0277. Scott DeLisi, Director.
Web, www.state.gov

Coordinates programs related to the professional
development of American members of the Foreign
Service, including career development and assignment
counseling programs, training, and presidential appointments and resignations.

State Dept., *Diplomatic Security Bureau, 2201 C St.*
N.W., #6316 20520; (202) 647-6290. Fax, (202) 647-0953.
Gregg Starr, Director.
General e-mail, DSPublicAffairs@state.gov

Web, www.state.gov

Provides a secure environment for conducting U.S.
diplomacy and promoting American interests abroad and
in the United States.

State Dept., *Family Liaison, 2201 C St. N.W., #1239*
20520-0108; (202) 647-1076. Fax, (202) 647-1670. Leslie
Teixeira, Director.

General e-mail, flo@state.gov

Web, www.state.gov/m/dghr/flo

Works to improve the quality of life of U.S. government employees and their family members assigned to, or returning from, a U.S. embassy abroad. Areas of interest are education and youth, family member employment, and support services for those in crisis. Manages the worldwide Community Liaison Office program.

State Dept., *Foreign Missions,* 2201 C St. N.W., #2238 20520; (202) 647-3417. Fax, (202) 736-4145. Justine Sincavage, Deputy Assistant Secretary.
Web, www.state.gov

Regulates the benefits, privileges, and immunities granted to foreign missions and their personnel in the United States on the basis of the treatment accorded U.S. missions abroad and considerations of national security and public safety.

State Dept., *Human Resources,* 2201 C St. N.W., #6218 20520; (202) 647-9898. Fax, (202) 647-5080. Vacant, Director General of the Foreign Service and Director of Human Resources.
Web, http://careers.state.gov

Directs human resource policies of the State Dept. and Foreign Service.

State Dept., *Medical Services,* 2401 E St. N.W., #L218 20522-0102; (202) 663-1611. Fax, (202) 663-1613. Dr. Thomas W. Yun, Medical Director.
Web, www.state.gov

Operates a worldwide primary health care system for U.S. citizen employees, and eligible family members, of participating U.S. government agencies. Conducts physical examinations of Foreign Service officers and candidates; provides clinical services; assists with medical evacuation of patients overseas.

State Dept., *Overseas Schools,* 2401 E St. N.W., #H328 20037; (202) 261-8200. Fax, (202) 261-8224. Keith D. Miller, Director.
General e-mail, OverseasSchools@state.gov

Web, www.state.gov/m/a/os

Promotes high-quality educational opportunities at the elementary and secondary school levels for dependents of American citizens carrying out the programs and interests of the U.S. government abroad.

State Dept., *Protocol,* 2201 C St. N.W., #1232 20520; (202) 647-4543. Fax, (202) 647-3980. Vacant, Chief. Press, (202) 647-2299.
Web, www.state.gov

Serves as principal adviser to the president, vice president, the secretary, and other high-ranking government officials on matters of diplomatic procedure governed by law or international customs and practice.

▶**CONGRESS**

For a listing of relevant congressional committees and subcommittees, please see page 412 or the Appendix.

▶**NONGOVERNMENTAL**

American Foreign Service Assn. (AFSA), 2101 E St. N.W. 20037; (202) 338-4045. Fax, (202) 338-6820. Ian Houston, Executive Director (Acting).
General e-mail, member@afsa.org

Web, www.afsa.org

Membership: active and retired foreign service employees of the State Dept., Agency for International Development, Foreign Commercial Service, and the Foreign Agricultural Service. Offers scholarship program; maintains club for members; represents active duty foreign service personnel in labor-management negotiations. Seeks to ensure adequate resources for foreign service operations and personnel. Interests include business-government collaboration and international trade. Monitors legislation and regulations related to foreign service personnel and retirees.

Council of American Ambassadors, 888 17th St. N.W., #306 20006-3312; (202) 296-3757. Fax, (202) 296-0926. Bruce S. Gelb, President; Carolyn M. Gretzinger, Executive Director.
General e-mail, council@americanambassadors.org

Web, www.americanambassadors.org

Membership: U.S. ambassadors. Seeks to educate the public on foreign policy issues affecting the national interest.

Executive Council on Diplomacy, 818 Connecticut Ave. N.W., #1200 20006-2702; (202) 466-5199. Fax, (202) 872-8696. Solveig Spielmann, Executive Director.
Web, www.ibgc.com

Brings foreign diplomats from international organizations such as the United Nations and World Bank into contact with their U.S. counterparts. Provides a forum for discussion on issues such as agriculture, international trade, education, and the arts.

Institute for the Study of Diplomacy *(Georgetown University),* 1316 36th St. N.W. 20007; (202) 965-5735. Fax, (202) 965-5652. Paula Newberg, Director.
Web, http://isd.georgetown.edu

Part of the Edmund A. Walsh School of Foreign Service. Focuses on the practical implementation of foreign policy objectives; draws on academic research and the concrete experience of diplomats and other members of the policy community.

Humanitarian Aid

▶**AGENCIES**

Administration for Children and Families (ACF), *(Health and Human Services Dept.), Refugee Resettlement,* 901 D St. S.W., 8th Floor 20447; (202) 401-9246. Fax, (202) 401-0981. David Siegel, Director.
Web, www.acf.hhs.gov/programs/orr

Directs a domestic resettlement program for refugees; reimburses states for costs incurred in giving refugees monetary and medical assistance; awards funds to voluntary resettlement agencies for providing refugees with monetary assistance and case management; provides states and nonprofit agencies with grants for social services such as English and employment training.

Agency for International Development (USAID),
Democracy, Conflict, and Humanitarian Assistance, 1300 Pennsylvania Ave. N.W., #8.06-084 20523-8601; (202) 712-0100. Fax, (202) 216-3397. Dirk Dijkerman, Assistant Administrator (Acting).
Web, www.usaid.gov

Manages U.S. foreign disaster assistance, emergency and developmental food aid, democracy programs, conflict management programs, and programs to assist countries transitioning out of crises. Assists U.S. voluntary organizations, schools, and hospitals abroad. Serves as USAID's liaison to the U.S. military.

Agency for International Development (USAID),
Global Health, 1300 Pennsylvania Ave. N.W., #3.64 20523-3100; (202) 712-0540. Fax, (202) 216-3485. Gloria Steele, Assistant Administrator (Acting).
Web, www.usaid.gov/our_work/global_health

Participates in global efforts to stabilize world population growth and support women's reproductive rights. Focus includes family planning; reproductive health care; infant, child, and maternal health; and prevention of sexually transmitted diseases, especially AIDS. Conducts demographic and health surveys; educates girls and women.

Agency for International Development (USAID),
Transition Initiatives, 1300 Pennsylvania Ave. N.W., #B3.06-124 20523-8602; (202) 712-0730. Fax, (202) 216-3406. Robert Jenkins, Director (Acting).
General e-mail, rjenkins@usaid.gov
Web, www.usaid.gov/our_work/cross-cutting_programs/transition_initiatives

Provides efficient short-term assistance to countries in crisis in order to stabilize their governments.

Agency for International Development (USAID), U.S.
Foreign Disaster Assistance, 1300 Pennsylvania Ave. N.W., #8.6 20523-8602; (202) 712-0400. Fax, (202) 216-3106. Peter Morris, Deputy Administrator (Acting).
Web, www.usaid.gov/hum_response/ofda

Office within the Democracy, Conflict, and Humanitarian Assistance Bureau. Administers disaster relief and preparedness assistance to foreign countries to save lives and alleviate human suffering. Aids displaced persons in disaster situations and helps other countries manage natural disasters and complex emergencies.

Defense Dept. (DoD), *Stability Operations,* 2500 Defense
Pentagon, OASD #5E384 20301-2500; (703) 697-5022. Fax, (703) 697-5353. Vacant, Deputy Assistant Secretary.
Web, www.defenselink.mil

Develops policy and plans for department provision of humanitarian assistance, refugee affairs, U.S. international information programs, and international peacekeeping and peace enforcement activities. Develops policy related to creating, identifying, training, exercising, and committing military forces for peacekeeping and peace enforcement activities.

Public Health Service *(Health and Human Services
Dept.), Global Health Affairs,* 200 Independence Ave. S.W. 20201; (202) 260-0399. Fax, (202) 260-0396. Jim Kulckowski, Director (Acting).
Web, www.globalhealth.gov

Represents the Health and Human Services Dept. before other governments, U.S. government agencies, international organizations, and the private sector on international and refugee health issues. Promotes international cooperation; provides health-related humanitarian and developmental assistance.

State Dept., *Coordinator for Reconstruction and
Stabilization,* 2121 Virginia Ave. N.W., 7th Floor 20037; (202) 663-0323. Fax, (202) 663-0327. John Herbst, Coordinator.
General e-mail, scrs_info@state.gov
Web, www.crs.state.gov

Coordinates the U.S. government's civilian capacity to prepare for post-conflict situations abroad. Reconstructs societies recovering from conflict in order to help them reach a sustainable path toward peace and democracy.

State Dept., *Population, Refugees, and Migration,* 2201
C St. N.W., #5805 20520-5824; (202) 647-7360. Fax, (202) 647-8162. Vacant, Assistant Secretary. Information, (202) 663-1071.
Web, www.state.gov/g/prm

Develops and implements policies and programs on matters relating to international refugees, internally displaced persons, and victims of conflict, including repatriation and resettlement programs; funds and monitors overseas relief, assistance, and repatriation programs; manages refugee admission to the United States.

▶CONGRESS

For a listing of relevant congressional committees and subcommittees, please see page 412 or the Appendix.

▶INTERNATIONAL ORGANIZATIONS

International Committee of the Red Cross (ICRC),
Washington Office, 1100 Connecticut Ave. N.W., #500 20036; (202) 587-4600. Fax, (202) 587-4696. Geoff Loane, Head of Delegation.
General e-mail, washington.was@icrc.org
Web, www.icrc.org

Serves as the ICRC's main point of contact with U.S. authorities on issues concerning operations and international humanitarian law. Visits people held by the U.S. government in Guantanamo Bay, Cuba. (Headquarters in Geneva.)

International Disaster Relief Organizations

Action Against Hunger, (212) 967-7800; toll-free (877) 777-1420, www.actionagainsthunger.org

American Jewish Joint Distribution Committee, (212) 687-6200, www.jdc.org

American Red Cross, (800) 435-7669 or (202) 303-4498, www.redcross.org

AmeriCares, (800) 486-4357 or (203) 658-9557, www.americares.org

CARE, (800) 521-2273 or (202) 595-2800, www.care.org

Catholic Relief Services, (888) 277-7575, www.catholicrelief.org

Christian Children's Fund, (800) 776-6767, www.christianchildrensfund.org

Church World Service, (800) 297-1516 or (888) 279-2767 CROP Program, or (202) 544-2350, www.churchworldservice.org

Direct Relief International, (805) 964-4767, www.directrelief.org

Doctors of the World, USA, (212) 226-9890, www.doctorsoftheworld.org

Episcopal Relief and Development, (800) 334-7626, ext. 5129, www.er-d.org

InterAction, (202) 667-8227, www.interaction.org

International Federation of Red Cross/Red Crescent, (212) 338 0161, www.ifrc.org

International Medical Corps, (800) 481-4462 or (202) 828-5155, www.imcworldwide.org

International Rescue Committee, (877) 733-8433 or (202) 822-0043, www.theirc.org

Islamic Relief USA, (888) 479-4968 or (202) 347-0774, www.irw.org

Lutheran World Relief, (800) 597-5972, www.lwr.org

Mercy Corps, (800) 292-3355 or (503) 796-6800, www.mercycorps.org

Operation USA, (800) 678-7255, www.opusa.org

Oxfam America, (800) 776-9326, www.oxfamamerica.org

Save the Children, (800) 728-3843 or (202) 640-6600, www.savethechildren.org

UNICEF, (800) 486-4233, www.unicefusa.org

World Food Programme, (202) 653-0010, www.wfp.org

World Health Organization, (202) 974-3459, www.who.int

World Vision, (888) 511-6593 or (800) 777-5777, www.worldvision.org

---

International Organization for Migration (IOM), *Washington Office, 1752 N St. N.W., #700 20036; (202) 862-1826. Fax, (202) 862-1879. Richard E. Scott, Regional Representative.*
General e-mail, mrfwashington@iom.int

Web, www.iom.int

Nonpartisan organization that plans and operates refugee resettlement, national migration, and humanitarian assistance programs at the request of its member governments. Recruits skilled professionals for developing countries. (Headquarters in Geneva.)

Pan American Health Organization, *525 23rd St. N.W. 20037; (202) 974-3000. Fax, (202) 974-3663. Dr. Mirta Roses Periago, Director. Library, (202) 974-3305.*
Web, www.paho.org

Works to extend health services to underserved populations of its member countries and to control or eradicate communicable diseases; promotes cooperation among governments to solve public health problems. Library open to the public by appointment. (Regional Office for the Americas of the World Health Organization, which is headquartered in Geneva.)

United Nations High Commissioner for Refugees, *Washington Office, 1775 K St. N.W., #300 20006-1502; (202) 296-5191. Fax, (202) 296-5660. Michel Gabaudan, Regional Representative.*

General e-mail, usawa@unhcr.org

Web, www.unhcr.org

Works with governments and voluntary organizations to protect and assist refugees worldwide. Promotes long-term alternatives to refugee camps, including voluntary repatriation, local integration, and resettlement overseas. (Headquarters in Geneva.)

U.S. Fund for the United Nations Children's Fund, *Public Policy and Advocacy, Washington Office, 1775 K St. N.W., #360 20006; (202) 296-4242. Fax, (202) 296-4060. Martin S. Rendón, Vice President.*
General e-mail, OPPA@unicefusa.org

Web, www.unicefusa.org

Serves as information reference service on UNICEF; advocates policies to advance the well-being of the world's children. Interests include international humanitarian assistance, U.S. volunteerism, child survival, and international health. (Headquarters in New York.)

▶ NONGOVERNMENTAL

American Red Cross, *National Headquarters, 2025 E St. N.W. 20006-5009; (202) 737-8300. Gail J. McGovern, Chief Executive Officer. Press, (202) 303-5551.*
Web, www.redcross.org

Service organization chartered by Congress to provide domestic and international disaster relief and to act as a medium of communication between the U.S. armed forces and their families in time of war and for armed forces personnel stationed overseas in case of emergencies. Coordinates the distribution of supplies, funds, and technical assistance for relief in major foreign disasters through the International Federation of Red Cross and Red Crescent Societies and the International Committee of the Red Cross, both headquartered in Geneva.

Bikes for the World, *3108 17th St. North, Arlington, VA 22201; (703) 525-0931. Keith Oberg, Director. General e-mail, info@bikesfortheworld.org*

Web, http://bikesfortheworld.org

Collects unwanted bicycles and related paraphernalia in the United States and delivers them to low-cost community development programs assisting the poor in developing countries. (Sponsored by the Washington Area Bicyclist Assn.)

The Campaign for Innocent Victims in Conflict (CIVIC), *1605 Connecticut Ave. N.W., 3rd Floor 20009; (202) 558-6958. Fax, (623) 321-7076. Sarah Holewinski, Executive Director.*

General e-mail, info@civicworldwide.org

Web, www.civicworldwide.org

Advocates for aid to civilians injured and families of those killed by the warring parties involved. Seeks to set international standards for warring parties to make amends to war victims.

Central American Resource Center, *1460 Columbia Rd. N.W. 20009; (202) 328-9799. Fax, (202) 328-7894. Saul Solorzano, Executive Director.*

General e-mail, info@carecendc.org

Web, http://carecendc.org

Helps Central American and Latino immigrants obtain and maintain legal status. Seeks to address the legal and social service needs of Latinos in the Washington area; to facilitate Latinos' transition to life in the United States; and to provide Latinos with the resources and leadership skills necessary to promote the community's development. Works closely with other community-based agencies.

Christian Children's Fund (CCF), *Washington Office, 1717 N St. N.W. 20036; (202) 955-7951. Fax, (202) 955-6166. Laura N. Henderson, Director.*

General e-mail, washington@ccfusa.org

Web, www.christianchildrensfund.org

Nonsectarian humanitarian organization that promotes improved child welfare standards and services worldwide by supporting long-term sustainable development. Provides children in emergency situations brought on by war, natural disaster, and other circumstances with education, medical care, food, clothing, and shelter. Provides aid and promotes the development potential of children of all backgrounds. (Headquarters in Richmond, Va.)

Health Volunteers Overseas, *1900 L St. N.W., #310 20036; (202) 296-0928. Fax, (202) 296-8018. Nancy A. Kelly, Executive Director.*

General e-mail, info@hvousa.org

Web, www.hvousa.org

Operates training programs in developing countries for health professionals who wish to teach low-cost health care delivery practices.

International Rescue Committee, *Washington Office, 1730 M St. N.W., #505 20036; (202) 822-0166. Fax, (202) 822-0089. Anne C. Richard, Vice President. General e-mail, advocacy@theirc.org*

Web, www.theirc.org

Provides worldwide emergency aid, protection, resettlement services, educational support, and advocacy for refugees, displaced persons, and victims of oppression and violent conflict; recruits volunteers. (Headquarters in New York.)

Jesuit Refugee Service/USA, *1016 16th St. N.W., #400 20036; (202) 462-0400. Fax, (202) 328-9212. Mitzi Schroeder, Director of Policy; Kenneth Gavin S.J., National Director. General e-mail, jrsusa@jesuit.org*

Web, www.jrsusa.org

U.S. Jesuit organization that aids refugees worldwide. Provides information on refugee problems; places individual Jesuits and lay people in refugee work abroad. Monitors refugee- and immigration-related legislation. (International headquarters in Rome.)

Mental Disability Rights International, *1156 15th St. N.W., #1001 20005; (202) 296-0800. Fax, (202) 728-3053. Eric Rosenthal, Executive Director.*

General e-mail, mdri@mdri.org

Web, www.mdri.org

Challenges discrimination of and abuse faced by people with mental disabilities worldwide. Documents conditions, publishes reports, and trains grassroots advocates.

National Council of Churches, *Washington Office, 110 Maryland Ave. N.E. 20002; (202) 544-2350. Fax, (202) 543-1297. Wesley M. Pattillo, Senior Program Director for Justice, Advocacy, and Communication, (212) 870-2227; Kevin Williams, Office Manager.*

Web, www.ncccusa.org

Works to foster cooperation among Christian congregations across the nation in programs concerning poverty, racism, family, environment, and international humanitarian objectives. (Headquarters in New York.)

Program for Appropriate Technology in Health, *Washington Office, 1800 K St. N.W., #800 20006; (202) 822-0033. Fax, (202) 457-1466. Patricia Daunas, Administrator.*

General e-mail, info@path.org

Web, www.path.org

Seeks to improve the safety and availability of health products and technologies worldwide, particularly in developing countries. Interests include reproductive health, immunization, maternal-child health, AIDS, and nutrition.

Refugees International, *2001 S St. N.W., #700 20009; (202) 828-0110. Fax, (202) 828-0819. Ken Bacon, President.*
General e-mail, ri@refintl.org
Web, www.refugeesinternational.org

Advocates for assistance and protection for displaced people worldwide. Conducts field studies to identify basic needs and makes recommendations to policymakers and aid agencies.

Southeast Asia Resource Action Center (SEARAC), *1628 16th St. N.W., 3rd Floor 20009; (202) 667-4690. Fax, (202) 667-6449. Doua Thor, Executive Director.*
General e-mail, searac@searac.org
Web, www.searac.org

Assists Southeast Asians (from Cambodia, Laos, and Vietnam) in the United States with resettlement. Advocates for refugee rights. Interests include education, immigration, health and aging, citizenship development, Indochinese self-help organizations, and economic development.

Unitarian Universalist Service Committee, *1100 G St. N.W., #800 20001; (202) 393-2255. Fax, (202) 393-5494. Shelly Maskowitz, Manager of Public Policy.*
General e-mail, info@uusc.org
Web, www.uusc.org

Secular human rights organization fighting race, gender, environmental, and economic injustice worldwide. Partners with civil liberty organizations defending right to water, workers' rights, and the democratic process. Responds to disasters. Provides education through travel and workcamps.

U.S. Committee for Refugees and Immigrants, *2231 Crystal Dr., #350, Arlington, VA 22202; (202) 347-3507. Fax, (703) 769-4241. Lavinia Limon, President.*
General e-mail, uscri@uscri.org
Web, www.refugees.org

Defends rights of refugees in the United States and abroad. Helps immigrants and refugees adjust to American society; assists in resettling recently arrived immigrants and refugees; offers information, counseling services, and temporary living accommodations through its member agencies nationwide; issues publications on refugees and refugee resettlement; collects and disseminates information on refugee issues. Monitors legislation and regulations.

U.S. Conference of Catholic Bishops (USCCB), *Migration and Refugee Services, 3211 4th St. N.E. 20017; (202) 541 3352. Fax, (202) 722-0755. Johnny Young, Executive Director.*
General e-mail, mrs@usccb.org
Web, www.usccb.org/mrs

Advocates for immigrants, refugees, migrants, and victims of human trafficking. Works with legislative and executive branches of the U.S. government and with national and international organizations such as the U.N.

High Commissioner for Refugees to promote fair and responsive immigration and refugee policy.

Women for Women International, *4455 Connecticut Ave. N.W., #200 20008; (202) 737-7705. Fax, (202) 737-7709. Zainab Salbi, President.*
General e-mail, general@womenforwomen.org
Web, www.womenforwomen.org

Helps women in war-torn regions rebuild their lives through financial and emotional support, job skills training, rights education, access to capital, and assistance for small business development.

World Vision, *Washington Office, 300 Eye St. N.E. 20002; (202) 572-6300. Fax, (202) 572-6480. George Ward, Senior Vice President.*
Web, www.worldvision.org

Christian humanitarian and development organization with focus on poverty worldwide. Provides emergency disaster relief and long-term development programs domestically and abroad. (Headquarters in Seattle, Wash.)

Information and Exchange Programs

▶**AGENCIES**

Broadcasting Board of Governors, *330 Independence Ave. S.W., #3360 20237; (202) 203-4545. Fax, (202) 203-4568. Jeffrey Trimble, Executive Director.*
Web, www.bbg.gov

Established by Congress to supervise all U.S. government nonmilitary international broadcasting, including Voice of America, Radio and TV Marti, Radio Free Europe/Radio Liberty, Radio Free Asia, and the Middle East Broadcasting Networks (MBN). Assesses the quality and effectiveness of broadcasts with regard to U.S. foreign policy objectives; reports annually to the president and to Congress.

Graduate School USDA (Agriculture Dept.), *International Institute, 600 Maryland Ave. S.W., #320 20024-2520; (202) 314-3500. Fax, (202) 479-6803. David Simpson, Director (Acting).*
General e-mail, intlinst@grad.usda.gov
Web, www.grad.usda.gov

Offers professional training and educational services to employees of foreign governments, international organizations, nongovernmental agencies, and employees of U.S. agencies engaged in international activities. Areas of concentration include governance and democratization, international conflict resolution, privatization, environmental management, and management skills and systems development. Conducts courses in Washington, D.C., San Francisco, and other locations worldwide.

Voice of America *(International Broadcasting Bureau),* *330 Independence Ave. S.W., #3300 20237; (202) 203-4500. Fax, (202) 203-4513. Danforth Austin, Director. Information, (202) 203-4959.* *Web, www.voa.gov*

A multimedia international broadcasting service funded by the U.S. government through the Broadcasting Board of Governors. Broadcasts news, information, educational, and cultural programming to an estimated worldwide audience of more than 134 million people. Programs are produced in forty-five languages.

▶NONGOVERNMENTAL

Alliance for International Educational and Cultural Exchange, *1776 Massachusetts Ave. N.W., #620 20036; (202) 293-6141. Fax, (202) 293-6144. Michael McCarry, Executive Director.* *General e-mail, info@alliance-exchange.org*

Web, www.alliance-exchange.org

Promotes public policies that support the growth of international exchange between the United States and other countries. Provides professional representation, resource materials, publications, and public policy research for those involved in international exchanges.

American Bar Assn. (ABA), *International Legal Exchange Program (ILEX), 740 15th St. N.W. 20005-1022; (202) 662-1660. Fax, (202) 662-1669. Christina Heid, Director.* *Web, www.abanet.org/intlaw/nglproj/ilex/home.html*

Facilitates entry into the United States for foreign lawyers offered training in U.S. law firms. Serves as designated U.S. government sponsor for the J-1 visa and accepts applications from foreign lawyers.

American Council of Young Political Leaders, *2131 K St. N.W., #400 20037; (202) 857-0999. Fax, (202) 857-0027. Linda Rotunno, Chief Executive Officer.* *Web, www.acypl.org*

Bipartisan political education organization that promotes understanding of foreign policy between state and local leaders and their counterparts abroad. Sponsors conferences and political study tours for American and foreign political leaders between the ages of twenty-five and forty.

Business–Higher Education Forum, *2025 M St. N.W., #800 20036; (202) 367-1189. Fax, (202) 367-2269. Brian K. Fitzgerald, Executive Director.* *General e-mail, info@bhef.com*

Web, www.bhef.com

Membership: chief executive officers of major corporations, museums, colleges, and universities. Promotes the development of industry-university alliances around the world. Provides countries in central and eastern Europe with technical assistance in enterprise development, management training, market economics, education, and infrastructure development.

Center for Intercultural Education and Development, *330 Whitehaven St. N.W., #1000 20007 (mailing address: P.O. Box 579400, Georgetown University, Washington, DC 20057-9400); (202) 687-1400. Fax, (202) 687-2555. Chantal Santelices, Director.* *Web, www.georgetown.edu/CIED*

Designs and administers programs aimed at improving the quality of life of economically disadvantaged people; provides technical education, job training, leadership skills development, and business management training; runs programs in Central America, the Caribbean, Central Europe, and Southeast Asia.

Council for International Exchange of Scholars, *3007 Tilden St. N.W., #5L 20008-3009; (202) 686-4000. Fax, (202) 362-3442. Sabine O'Hara, Executive Director.* *General e-mail, apprequest@cies.iie.org*

Web, www.cies.org

Cooperates with the U.S. government in administering Fulbright grants for university teaching and advanced research abroad. (Affiliated with the American Council of Learned Societies.)

English-Speaking Union, *Washington Office, P.O. Box 58068 20037; (202) 234-4602. Fax, (202) 234-4639. Mark Olshaker, Executive Director.* *General e-mail, esuwdc@verizon.net*

Web, www.esuwdc.org

International educational and cultural organization that promotes exchange programs with countries in which English is a major language; sponsors scholarships for studies in English-speaking countries; sponsors annual Shakespeare competition among Washington metropolitan area schools. (Headquarters in New York.)

Institute of International Education, *Washington Office, 1400 K St. N.W., #650 20005-2403; (202) 898-0600. Fax, (202) 326-7754. Allan Goodman, President.* *Web, www.iie.org*

Educational exchange, technical assistance, and training organization that arranges professional programs for international visitors; conducts training courses in energy, environment, journalism, human resource development, educational policy and administration, and business-related fields; provides developing countries with short- and long-term technical assistance in human resource development; arranges professional training and support for staff of human rights organizations; sponsors fellowships and applied internships for midcareer professionals from developing countries; manages programs sending U.S. teachers, undergraduate and graduate students, and professionals abroad; implements contracts and cooperative agreements for the State Dept., the U.S. Agency for International Development, foreign governments, philanthropic foundations, multilateral banks, and other organizations. (Headquarters in New York.)

International Research and Exchanges Board (IREX), *2121 K St. N.W., #700 20037; (202) 628-8188. Fax, (202) 628-8189. W. Robert Pearson, President.*

General e-mail, newsroom@irex.org

Web, www.irex.org

Provides programs, grants, and consulting expertise in more than 100 countries to improve the quality of education, strengthen independent media, and foster pluralistic civil society development.

Meridian International Center, *1630 Crescent Pl. N.W. 20009; (202) 667-6800. Fax, (202) 667-1475. Stuart Holliday, President. Information, (202) 667-6670.*

General e-mail, info@meridian.org

Web, www.meridian.org

Conducts international educational and cultural programs; provides foreign visitors and diplomats in the United States with services, including cultural orientation, seminars, and language assistance. Offers world affairs programs and international exhibitions for Americans.

NAFSA: Assn. of International Educators, *1307 New York Ave. N.W., 8th Floor 20005-4701; (202) 737-3699. Fax, (202) 737-3657. Marlene M. Johnson, Executive Director. Publications, (866) 538-1927.*

General e-mail, inbox@nafsa.org

Web, www.nafsa.org

Membership: individuals engaged in the field of international education and exchange at the post-secondary level. Promotes educational opportunities across national boundaries. Sets and upholds standards of good practice and provides professional education and training.

National Council for International Visitors, *1420 K St. N.W., #800 20005-2401; (202) 842-1414. Fax, (202) 289-4625. Sherry L. Mueller, President. Information, (800) 523-8101.*

General e-mail, info@nciv.org

Web, www.nciv.org

National network of nonprofit and community organizations that provides hospitality to international visitors. Seeks to improve international relations through professional and personal communications and exchanges. Provides training, networking, and information services.

Radio Free Europe/Radio Liberty, *Washington Office, 1201 Connecticut Ave. N.W., 4th Floor 20036; (202) 457-6900. Fax, (202) 457-6992. Jeffrey Gedmin, President. Press, (202) 457-6947.*

General e-mail, info@rferl.org

Web, www.rferl.org

Independent radio broadcast service funded by federal grants to promote and support democracy. Broadcasts programs to Afghanistan, the former Yugoslavia, Iraq, Romania, and the states of the former Soviet Union; programming includes news, analysis, and specials on political developments. Research materials available to the public by appointment.

Sister Cities International, *1301 Pennsylvania Ave. N.W., #850 20004; (202) 347-8630. Fax, (202) 393-6524. Patrick Madden, President.*

General e-mail, info@sister-cities.org

Web, www.sister-cities.org

A network of more than 2,400 partnerships between U.S. and foreign cities. Promotes global cooperation at the municipal level, cultural understanding, and economic stimulation through exchanges of citizens, ideas, and materials. Serves as information clearinghouse for economic and sustainability issues and as program coordinator for trade missions. Sponsors youth programs.

World Learning, *Visitor Exchange Program, 1015 18th St. N.W., #1000 20036-5272; (202) 898-0950. Fax, (202) 842-0885. Peter C. Simpson, Director.*

General e-mail, pidt@worldlearning.org

Web, www.worldlearning.org

Assists public and private organizations engaged in international cooperation and business. Works with governments and private counterparts to support foreign professional exchanges. Develops technical training programs and educational curricula for foreign visitors. Provides technical expertise, management support, travel, and business development services. Administered by World Learning's Project in International Development division. (Formerly Delphi International.)

Youth for Understanding USA, *6400 Goldsboro Rd., #100, Bethesda, MD 20817; (240) 235-2100. Fax, (240) 235-2104. Michael Finnell, President. TTY, (800) 787-8000. Teen Information, (800) TEENAGE.*

Web, www.yfu-usa.org

Educational organization that administers cross-cultural exchange programs for secondary school students. Administers scholarship programs that sponsor student exchanges.

War, Conflict, and Peacekeeping

► **AGENCIES**

State Dept., *Coordinator for Reconstruction and Stabilization, 2121 Virginia Ave. N.W., 7th Floor 20037; (202) 663-0323. Fax, (202) 663-0327. John Herbst, Coordinator.*

General e-mail, scrs_info@state.gov

Web, www.crs.state.gov

Coordinates the U.S. government's civilian capacity to prepare for post-conflict situations abroad. Reconstructs societies recovering from conflict in order to help them reach a sustainable path toward peace and democracy.

State Dept., *Policy Planning Staff, 2201 C St. N.W., #7311 20520; (202) 647-2372. Fax, (202) 647-0844. Anne-Marie Slaughter, Director.*

Web, www.state.gov

Advises the secretary and other State Dept. officials on foreign policy matters, including international peacekeeping and peace enforcement operations.

U.S. Institute of Peace, *1200 17th St. N.W., #200 20036; (202) 457-1700. Fax, (202) 429-6063. J. Robinson West, Chair; Richard H. Solomon, President. TTY, (202) 457-1719.*
General e-mail, info@usip.org

Web, www.usip.org

Independent, nonpartisan institution established by Congress. Aims to prevent and resolve violent international conflicts, promote post-conflict stability, and increase peace-building capacity, tools, and intellectual capital worldwide.

▶CONGRESS

For a listing of relevant congressional committees and subcommittees, please see page 412 or the Appendix.

▶NONGOVERNMENTAL

Act Now to Stop War and End Racism (ANSWER) Coalition, *1247 E St. S.E. 20003; (202) 544-3389,ext. 14. Fax, (202) 280-1022. Sarah Sloan, National Staff Coordinator.*
General e-mail, info@answercoalition.org

Web, www.answercoalition.org

Works to end war and conflict, with current emphasis on ending the occupation in Iraq, Afghanistan, and Pakistan. Conducts demonstrations with other peace and anti-war groups, especially ethnic and cultural identity groups concerned with ending racism.

Fourth Freedom Forum, *1111 19th St. N.W., 12th Floor 20036; (202) 464-6007. Fax, (202) 238-9604. Alistair Millar, Vice President.*
General e-mail, amillar@fourthfreedom.org

Web, www.fourthfreedom.org

Researches nonviolent resolution options for international conflict and sponsors media communications and public education campaigns to encourage citizen awareness. Encourages economic power over military power; supports economic incentives and sanctions to end conflict and secure peace. (Headquarters in Goshen, Ind.)

Genocide Intervention Network, *1333 H St. N.W., 1st Floor 20005; (202) 481-8220. Fax, (202) 682-1867. Mark Hanis, Executive Director.*
General e-mail, info@genocideintervention.net

Web, www.genocideintervention.net

Works to protect all civilians from genocide and other crises and empower individuals and communities with tools to prevent and stop genocide. Promotes international intervention as an effective method of ending widespread violence.

International Peace Operations Assn. (IPOA), *1900 L St. N.W., #320 20036-5027; (202) 464-0721. Fax, (202) 464-0726. Doug Brooks, President.*
General e-mail, ipoa@ipoaonline.org

Web, www.ipoaonline.org

Membership: private-sector service companies involved in all sectors of peace and stability operations around the world, including mine clearance, logistics, security, training, and emergency humanitarian aid. Works to institute standards and codes of conduct. Monitors legislation.

Just Foreign Policy, *4410 Massachusetts Ave. N.W., #290 20016; (202) 448-2898. Chelsea Mozen, Director.*
General e-mail, info@justforeignpolicy.org

Web, www.justforeignpolicy.org

Nonpartisan membership organization that seeks to influence U.S. foreign policy through education, organization, and mobilization of citizens. Advocates cooperation, international law, and diplomacy as means to achieve a just foreign policy.

National Peace Foundation, *666 11th St. N.W., #202 20001; (202) 783-7030. Fax, (202) 783-7040. Sarah Harder, President.*
General e-mail, npf@nationalpeace.org

Web, www.nationalpeace.org

Seeks to prevent conflict and build peace in the United States and around the world by developing citizen networks, advancing peace education and conflict prevention and resolution skills, and promoting democratic values through international travel/exchange programs.

Psychologists for Social Responsibility (PsySR), *208 Eye St. N.E. 20002; (202) 543-5347. Fax, (202) 543-5348. Colleen Cordes, Executive Director.*
General e-mail, psysr@psysr.org

Web, www.psysr.org

Applies psychological knowledge and skills to promote peace and social justice at the community, national, and international levels. Facilitates support for victims and survivors of violence, advocates for basic human needs, and encourages the use of psychology in public policy decision making.

Refugees International, *2001 S St. N.W., #700 20009; (202) 828-0110. Fax, (202) 828-0819. Ken Bacon, President.*
General e-mail, ri@refintl.org

Web, www.refugeesinternational.org

Advocates for assistance and protection for displaced people worldwide. Conducts field studies to identify basic needs and makes recommendations to policymakers and aid agencies.

Save Darfur Coalition, *2120 L St. N.W., #335 20037; (800) 917-2034. Fax, (202) 478-6312. Jerry Fowler, President. Media office, (202) 478-6174.*
General e-mail, info@savedarfur.org

Web, www.savedarfur.org

Alliance of more than 180 faith-based, advocacy, and human rights organizations concerned with genocide in the Darfur region of Sudan. Seeks to raise public awareness about conditions in Darfur. Utilizes media outreach, public education, coalition building, and grassroots mobilization to compel policymakers in the United States and abroad to aid the people of Darfur.

Veterans for America (VFA), *1025 Vermont Ave. N.W., 3rd Floor 20005; (202) 483-9222. Bobby Muller, President. General e-mail, vet@gmail.com*

Web, www.veteransforamerica.org

Works to engage the American public in support of policies addressing the needs of veterans, those currently in the military, and victims of wars overseas. Encourages policy and public discourse around the causes, conduct, and consequences of war.

Voters for Peace, *2842 N. Calvert St., Baltimore, MD 21218; (443) 708-8360. Kevin Zeese, Executive Director. Web, www.votersforpeace.us*

Educates, organizes, and mobilizes voters to end the occupation in Iraq and prevent future wars of aggression.

Win Without War, *1000 Vermont Ave. N.W., #200 20005; (202) 822-2075. Fax, (202) 822-4787. Tom Andrews, National Director. General e-mail, info@winwithoutwarus.org*

Web, www.winwithoutwarus.org

Coalition of national organizations promoting international cooperation and agreements as the best means for securing peace. Encourages U.S. foreign policies of counterterrorism and weapons proliferation, but opposes unilateral military preemption.

IMMIGRATION AND NATURALIZATION

►AGENCIES

Administration for Children and Families (ACF), *(Health and Human Services Dept.), Refugee Resettlement, 901 D St. S.W., 8th Floor 20447; (202) 401-9246. Fax, (202) 401-0981. David Siegel, Director. Web, www.acf.hhs.gov/programs/orr*

Directs a domestic resettlement program for refugees; reimburses states for costs incurred in giving refugees monetary and medical assistance; awards funds to voluntary resettlement agencies for providing refugees with monetary assistance and case management; provides states and nonprofit agencies with grants for social services such as English and employment training.

Justice Dept. (DOJ), Civil Division: Immigration Litigation, *450 5th St. N.W. 20539 (mailing address: P.O. Box 878, Ben Franklin Station, Washington, DC 20044); (202) 616-4900. Fax, (202) 307-8837. Thomas W. Hussey, Director. Information, (202) 616-4900. Web, www.usdoj.gov*

Handles most civil litigation arising under immigration and nationality laws.

Justice Dept. (DOJ), *Executive Office for Immigration Review, 5107 Leesburg Pike, #2600, Falls Church, VA 22041; (703) 305-0169. Fax, (703) 305-0985. Kevin Ohlson, Director. TTY, (800) 828-1120. Web, www.usdoj.gov/eoir*

Quasi-judicial body that includes the Board of Immigration Appeals and offices of the chief immigration judge and the chief administration hearing officer. Interprets immigration laws; conducts hearings and hears appeals on immigration issues.

Justice Dept. (DOJ), *Special Investigations, 1301 New York Ave. N.W., John C. Keeney Bldg., #200 20530; (202) 616-2492. Fax, (202) 616-2491. Eli M. Rosenbaum, Director. Web, www.usdoj.gov*

Identifies Nazi war criminals who illegally entered the United States after World War II. Tracks war criminals within the United States with connections to other world genocidal conflicts. Handles legal action to ensure denaturalization and/or deportation.

State Dept., *Visa Services, 2401 E St. N.W., #6811 20522-0106; (202) 663-1225. Fax, (202) 663-6811. Stephen Edson, Deputy Assistant Secretary. Web, http://travel.state.gov/visa/visa_1750.html*

Supervises visa issuance system, which is administered by U.S. consular offices abroad.

U.S. Citizenship and Immigration Services (USCIS), *(Homeland Security Dept.), 20 Massachusetts Ave. N.W. 20529; (202) 282-8000 (switchboard). Fax, (202) 272-1322. Vacant, Director. Press, (202) 272-1200. Information, (800) 375-5283 or TTY, (800) 767-1833. Web, www.uscis.gov*

Responsible for the administration of immigration and naturalization adjudication functions and establishing immigration services policies and priorities.

►CONGRESS

For a listing of relevant congressional committees and subcommittees, please see page 412 or the Appendix.

►INTERNATIONAL ORGANIZATIONS

International Catholic Migration Commission (ICMC), *Washington Office, 3211 4th St. N.E., #453-A 20017-1194; (202) 541-3389. Johan Ketelers, Secretary General; Jane Bloom, U.S. Liaison Officer. General e-mail, bloom@icmc.net*

Web, www.icmc.net

Supports ICMC's worldwide programs by liaising with the U.S. government, nongovernmental organizations, and the American public. Works with refugees, internally displaced persons, and forced migrants. Responds to refugees' immediate needs while working for return to and reintegration in their home country, local integration, or resettlement in a third country. (Headquarters in Geneva.)

International Organization for Migration (IOM),
*Washington Office, 1752 N St. N.W., #700 20036; (202)
862-1826. Fax, (202) 862-1879. Richard E. Scott, Regional
Representative.*
General e-mail, mrfwashington@iom.int

Web, www.iom.int

Nonpartisan organization that plans and operates
refugee resettlement, national migration, and humanitarian assistance programs at the request of its member governments. Recruits skilled professionals for developing
countries. (Headquarters in Geneva.)

▶**NONGOVERNMENTAL**

Alexis de Tocqueville Institution, *611 Pennsylvania Ave.
S.E., #298 20003; (202) 437-7435. Fax, (866) 433-3480.
Kenneth P. Brown Jr., President.*
General e-mail, kenbrown@adti.net

Web, www.adti.net

Public policy research organization that studies the
spread of democracy around the world. Works to increase
public understanding of the cultural and economic benefits associated with democracy. Supports pro-immigration policy reform, technology policy reform, and trade
policy reform.

American Immigration Lawyers Assn., *1331 G St. N.W.,
#300 20005; (202) 507-7600. Fax, (202) 783-7853. Jeanne
Butterfield, Executive Director.*
Web, www.aila.org

Bar association for attorneys interested in immigration
law. Provides information and continuing education programs on immigration law and policy; offers workshops
and conferences. Monitors legislation and regulations.

Center for Immigration Studies, *1522 K St. N.W., #820
20005-1202; (202) 466-8185. Fax, (202) 466-8076. Mark
Krikorian, Executive Director.*
General e-mail, center@cis.org

Web, www.cis.org

Nonpartisan organization that conducts research and
policy analysis of the economic, social, demographic, and
environmental impact of immigration on the United States.
Sponsors symposiums.

Ethiopian Community Development Council, Inc., *901
S. Highland St., Arlington, VA 22204; (703) 685-0510. Fax,
(703) 685-0529. Tsehaye Teferra, President.*
General e-mail, info@ecdcinternational.org

Web, www.ecdcinternational.org

Seeks to improve quality of life for African immigrants
and refugees in the United States through local and
national programs. Interests include the resettlement and
acculturation of refugees, health education, and cultural
outreach for communities. Also provides business loans
and management training for minority- and women-
owned businesses in the Washington metropolitan area.

Federation for American Immigration Reform (FAIR),
*25 Massachusetts Ave. N.W., #330 20001; (202) 328-7004.
Fax, (202) 387-3447. Daniel A. Stein, President.*

General e-mail, fair@fairus.org

Web, www.fairus.org

Organization of individuals interested in immigration
reform. Monitors immigration laws and policies.

Lutheran Immigration and Refugee Service, *Washington
Office, 122 C St. N.W., #125 20001-2172; (202) 626-7833.
Fax, (202) 783-7502. Gregory Chen, Director.*
General e-mail, lirsdc@lirs.org

Web, www.lirs.org

Provides refugees in the United States with resettlement assistance, follow-up services, and immigration
counseling. Funds local projects that provide social and
legal services to all refugees, including undocumented
persons. (Headquarters in Baltimore, Md.)

Migration Policy Institute, *1400 16th St. N.W., #300
20036; (202) 266-1940. Fax, (202) 266-1900. Demetrios
G. Papademetriou, President.*
General e-mail, info@migrationpolicy.org

Web, www.migrationpolicy.org

Nonpartisan think tank that studies the movement of
people worldwide. Provides analysis, development, and
evaluation of migration, integration, and refugee policies
at local, national, and international levels.

National Council of La Raza, *1126 16th St. N.W. 20036;
(202) 785-1670. Fax, (202) 776-1792. Janet Murguia,
President.*
General e-mail, comments@nclr.org

Web, www.nclr.org

Provides research, policy analysis, and advocacy relating to immigration policy and programs. Monitors federal legislation on immigration, legalization, employer
sanctions, employment discrimination, and eligibility of
immigrants for federal benefit programs. Assists community-based groups involved in immigration and education
services and educates employers about immigration laws.

National Immigration Forum, *50 F St. N.W., #300
20001; (202) 347-0040. Fax, (202) 347-0058. Ali Noorani,
Executive Director. Press, (202) 383-5987.*
General e-mail, info@immigrationforum.org

Web, www.immigrationforum.org

Pro-immigration advocacy organization that provides
policy analysis, research, and updates on immigration
policy developments to members and allies across the
country. Monitors legislation and regulations related to
immigrants and immigration. Works in coalition with
broad cross-section of immigrant advocacy, immigrant-
serving, religious, business, and labor organizations to
advance policies welcoming to immigrants.

NumbersUSA, *1601 N. Kent St., #1100, Arlington, VA
22209; (202) 543-1341. Fax, (202) 543-3147. Roy Beck,
Executive Director.*
General e-mail, info@numbersusa.com

Web, www.numbersusa.com

Public policy organization that favors immigration reduction as a way of promoting economic justice for American workers. Monitors legislation and regulations.

Pew Hispanic Center, *1615 L St. N.W., #700 20036; (202) 419-3600. Fax, (202) 419-3608. Paul Taylor, Director. Information, (202) 419-3606.*
General e-mail, info@pewhispanic.org

Web, www.pewhispanic.org

Seeks to improve understanding of the U.S. Hispanic population and its impact on the nation, as well as explore Latino views on a range of social matters and public policy issues. Conducts public opinion surveys and other studies that are made available to the public.

U.S. Border Control, *8180 Greensboro Dr., #1070, McLean, VA 22102; (703) 740-8668. Fax, (202) 740-9755. Edward I. Nelson, Director.*
General e-mail, info@usbc.org

Web, www.usbc.org

Seeks to curb illegal immigration by securing borders and reforming immigration policies. Monitors legislation and regulations.

U.S. Committee for Refugees and Immigrants, *2231 Crystal Dr., #350, Arlington, VA 22202; (202) 347-3507. Fax, (703) 769-4241. Lavinia Limon, President.*
General e-mail, uscri@uscri.org

Web, www.refugees.org

Defends rights of refugees in the United States and abroad. Helps immigrants and refugees adjust to American society; assists in resettling recently arrived immigrants and refugees; offers information, counseling services, and temporary living accommodations through its member agencies nationwide; issues publications on refugees and refugee resettlement; collects and disseminates information on refugee issues. Monitors legislation and regulations.

U.S. Conference of Catholic Bishops (USCCB), *Migration and Refugee Services, 3211 4th St. N.E. 20017; (202) 541-3352. Fax, (202) 722-8755. Johnny Young, Executive Director.*
General e-mail, mrs@usccb.org

Web, www.usccb.org/mrs

Advocates for immigrants, refugees, migrants, and victims of human trafficking. Works with legislative and executive branches of the U.S. government and with national and international organizations such as the U.N. High Commissioner for Refugees to promote fair and responsive immigration and refugee policy.

INTERNATIONAL LAW AND AGREEMENTS

▶AGENCIES

Commission on Security and Cooperation in Europe *(Helsinki Commission), 234 FHOB 20515; (202)*
225-1901. Fax, (202) 226-4199. Sen. Benjamin L. Cardin, D–Md., Chair; Rep. Alcee L. Hastings, D–Fla., Co-Chair; Fred L. Turner, Chief of Staff.
General e-mail, info@csce.gov

Web, www.csce.gov

Independent agency created by Congress. Membership includes individuals from the executive and legislative branches. Monitors and encourages compliance with the Helsinki Accords, a series of agreements with provisions on security, economic, environmental, human rights, and humanitarian issues; conducts hearings; serves as an information clearinghouse for issues in eastern and western Europe, Canada, and the United States relating to the Helsinki Accords.

Federal Bureau of Investigation (FBI), *(Justice Dept.), International Operations, 935 Pennsylvania Ave. N.W., #7825 20535; (202) 324-3000. Fax, (202) 324-5292. Carol K. O. Lee, Assistant Director (Acting).*

Supports FBI involvement in international investigations; oversees liaison offices in U.S. embassies abroad. Maintains contacts with other federal agencies; Interpol; foreign police and security officers based in Washington, D.C.; and national law enforcement associations.

Securities and Exchange Commission, *International Affairs, 100 F St. N.E., MS 1004 20549; (202) 551-6690. Fax, (202) 772-9281. Ethiopis Tafara, Director.*
Web, www.sec.gov

Acts as liaison with enforcement and diplomatic officials abroad; coordinates international enforcement activities for the securities markets; obtains evidence from abroad relating to investigations and litigation. Develops agreements with foreign countries to assist commission enforcement and regulatory efforts.

State Dept., *International Claims and Investment Disputes, 2430 E St. N.W., #203 20037-2800; (202) 776-8360. Fax, (202) 776-8389. Jeffrey Kovar, Assistant Legal Adviser.*
Web, www.state.gov

Handles claims by foreign governments and their nationals against the U.S. government, as well as claims against the State Dept. for negligence under the Federal Tort Claims Act. Administers the Iranian claims program and negotiates agreements with other foreign governments on claims settlements.

State Dept., *Law Enforcement and Intelligence, 2201 C St. N.W., #5419 20520; (202) 647-7324. Fax, (202) 647-4802. Clifton Johnson, Assistant Legal Adviser.*
Web, www.state.gov

Negotiates extradition treaties, legal assistance treaties in criminal matters, and other agreements relating to international criminal matters.

State Dept., *Legal Adviser, 2201 C St. N.W., #6421 20520-6310; (202) 647-9598. Fax, (202) 647-7096. Joan Donoghue, Legal Adviser (Acting).*
Web, www.state.gov/s/l

Provides the secretary and the department with legal advice on domestic and international problems; participates in international negotiations; represents the U.S. government in international litigation and in international conferences related to legal issues.

State Dept., *Political-Military Affairs,* 2201 C St. N.W., #6212 20520; (202) 647-9022. Fax, (202) 736-4779. Frank Ruggiero, Assistant Secretary (Acting).
Web, www.state.gov

Principal link between State Dept. and Defense Dept. Provides policy direction in the areas of international security, security assistance, military operations, defense strategy and policy, military use of space, and defense trade.

State Dept., *Treaty Affairs,* 2201 C St. N.W., #5420 20520; (202) 647-1345. Fax, (202) 647-9844. Aviril Haines, Assistant Legal Adviser for Treaty Affairs.
Web, www.state.gov/s/l/treaty

Provides legal advice on treaties and other international agreements, including constitutional questions, drafting, negotiation, and interpretation of treaties; maintains records of treaties and executive agreements.

State Dept., *War Crimes Issues,* 2201 C St. N.W., #7419A 20520; (202) 647-5072. Fax, (202) 736-4495. Clint Williamson, Director; Vacant, Deputy Director.
Web, www.state.gov/s/wci

Oversees U.S. stance on the creation of courts and other judicial mechanisms to bring perpetrators of crimes under international law to justice. Engages in diplomacy with foreign governments whose nationals have been captured in the war on terrorism. Has primary responsibility for policy on Iraqi war crimes.

Transportation Dept. (DOT), *International Aviation,* 1200 New Jersey Ave. S.E., #W86-316 20590; (202) 366-2423. Fax, (202) 366-3694. Paul L. Gretch, Director.
Web, www.dot.gov

Responsible for international aviation regulation and negotiations, including fares, tariffs, and foreign licenses; represents the United States at international aviation meetings.

▶**CONGRESS**

For a listing of relevant congressional committees and subcommittees, please see page 412 or the Appendix.

▶**INTERNATIONAL ORGANIZATIONS**

INTERPOL, *Washington Office,* INTERPOL-USNCB, U.S. Justice Dept. 20530; (202) 616-9000. Fax, (202) 616-8400. Martin Renkiewicz, Director.
Web, www.usdoj.gov/usncb

U.S. national central bureau for INTERPOL; participates in international investigations on behalf of U.S. police; coordinates the exchange of investigative information on crimes, including drug trafficking, counterfeiting, missing persons, and terrorism. Coordinates law enforcement requests for investigative assistance in the United States and abroad. Assists with extradition processes. Serves as liaison between foreign and U.S. law enforcement agencies at federal, state, and local levels. (Headquarters in Lyons, France.)

▶**NONGOVERNMENTAL**

American Arbitration Assn., *Government Relations,* 1776 Eye St. N.W., #850 20006; (202) 739-8280, ext. 109. Fax, (202) 222-7095. Jean Baker, Vice President.
General e-mail, BakerJ@adr.org
Web, www.adr.org

Provides dispute resolution services and information. Administers international arbitration and mediation systems. (Headquarters in New York.)

American Bar Assn. (ABA), *International Law,* 740 15th St. N.W. 20005; (202) 662-1660. Fax, (202) 662-1669. Leanne Pfautz, Director.
General e-mail, intlaw@abanet.org
Web, www.abanet.org/intlaw

Monitors and makes recommendations concerning developments in the practice of international law that affect ABA members and the public. Conducts programs, including International Legal Exchange, and produces publications covering the practice of international law.

American Society of International Law, 2223 Massachusetts Ave. N.W. 20008-2864; (202) 939-6000. Fax, (202) 797-7133. Elizabeth Andersen, Executive Director.
Web, www.asil.org

Membership: lawyers, political scientists, economists, government officials, and students. Conducts research and study programs on international law. Holds an annual meeting on current issues in international law. Library open to the public, 9:00 a.m.–5:00 p.m.

Antarctic and Southern Ocean Coalition, 1630 Connecticut Ave. N.W., 3rd Floor 20009; (202) 234-2480. Fax, (202) 387-4823. James N. Barnes, Executive Director.
General e-mail, secretariat@asoc.org
Web, www.asoc.org

Promotes effective implementation of the Antarctic Treaty System; works to protect the environment of the Antarctic continent and promote responsible sustainable fisheries in the Southern Ocean.

Inter-American Bar Assn., 1211 Connecticut Ave. N.W., #202 20036; (202) 466-5944. Fax, (202) 466-5946. Maryanne Cordier, Secretary General.
General e-mail, iaba@iaba.org
Web, www.iaba.org

Membership: lawyers and bar associations in the Western Hemisphere with associate members in Europe and Asia. Works to promote uniformity of national and international laws; holds conferences; makes recommendations to national governments and organizations. Library open to the public.

World Jurist Assn., *7910 Woodmont Ave., #1440, Bethesda, MD 20814; (202) 466-5428. Fax, (202) 452-8540. Margaret M. Henneberry, Executive Vice President. General e-mail, wja@worldjurist.org*

Web, www.worldjurist.org

Membership: lawyers, law professors, judges, law students, and nonlegal professionals worldwide. Conducts research; promotes world peace through adherence to international law; holds biennial world conferences. (Affiliates, at same address, include World Assn. of Judges, World Assn. of Law Professors, World Assn. of Lawyers, and World Business Assn.)

Americans Abroad

►**AGENCIES**

Administration for Children and Families (ACF), *(Health and Human Services Dept.), Refugee Resettlement, 901 D St. S.W., 8th Floor 20447; (202) 401-9246. Fax, (202) 401-0981. David Siegel, Director. Web, www.acf.hhs.gov/programs/orr*

Provides benefits and services to refugees, Cuban and Haitian entrants, asylees, trafficking and torture victims, repatriated U.S. citizens, and unaccompanied alien children. Seeks to help individuals achieve economic self-sufficiency and social adjustment within the shortest time possible following arrival to the United States.

Foreign Claims Settlement Commission of the United States *(Justice Dept.), 600 E St. N.W., #6002 20579; (202) 616-6975. Fax, (202) 616-6993. Mauricio Tamargo, Chair; Judith H. Lock, Administrative Officer. Web, www.usdoj.gov/FCSC*

Processes claims by U.S. nationals against foreign governments for property losses sustained.

State Dept., *American Citizens Services and Crisis Management, 2201 C St. N.W., SA-29, 4th Floor 20520-2818; (202) 647-9019. Fax, (202) 647-3732. Michelle Bernier Toth, Director. Toll-free, (888) 407-4747. Web, http://travel.state.gov*

Handles matters involving protective services for Americans abroad, including arrests, assistance in death cases, loans, medical emergencies, welfare and whereabouts inquiries, travel warnings and consular information, nationality and citizenship determination, document issuance, judicial and notarial services, estates, property claims, third-country representation, and disaster assistance.

State Dept., *Children's Issues, 2201 C St. N.W., SA-29, 4th Floor 20520-2818; (202) 736-9130. Fax, (202) 736-9133. Julie Furuta-Toy, Director; Kathleen Ruckman,*

Deputy Director. Recorded consular information, (202) 736-7000. Toll-free, (888) 407-4747. Web, http://travel.state.gov/family/family_1732.html

Assists with consular aspects of children's services and fulfills U.S. treaty obligations relating to the abduction of children. Advises foreign service posts on international parental child abduction and transnational adoption.

State Dept., *Consular Affairs: Special Issuance Agency, 1111 19th St. N.W., #200 20036; (202) 955-0198. Fax, (202) 955-0182. Gary Roach, Director. TTY, (888) 874-7793. National passport information, (877) 487-2778. Web, http://travel.state.gov*

Administers passport laws and issues passports. (Most branches of the U.S. Postal Service and most U.S. district and state courts are authorized to accept applications and payment for passports and to administer the required oath to U.S. citizens. Completed applications are sent from the post office or court to the nearest State Dept. regional passport office for processing.) Maintains a variety of records received from the Overseas Citizens Services, including consular certificates of witness to marriage and reports of birth and death. (Individuals wishing to apply for a U.S. passport may seek additional information via the phone number or Web address listed above.)

State Dept., *International Claims and Investment Disputes, 2430 E St. N.W., #203 20037-2800; (202) 776-8360. Fax, (202) 776-8389. Jeffrey Kovar, Assistant Legal Adviser. Web, www.state.gov*

Handles claims by U.S. government and citizens against foreign governments; handles claims by owners of U.S. flag vessels for reimbursements of fines, fees, licenses, and other direct payments for illegal seizures by foreign governments in international waters under the Fishermen's Protective Act.

State Dept., *Policy Review and Interagency Liaison, 2100 Pennsylvania Ave. N.W., 4th Floor 20037; (202) 736-9110. Fax, (202) 736-9111. Edward A. Betancourt, Director. Recorded consular information, (202) 647-5225. Toll-free, (888) 407-4747. Web, www.state.gov*

Offers guidance concerning the administration and enforcement of laws on citizenship and on the appropriate documentation of Americans traveling and residing abroad; gives advice on legislative matters, including implementation of new laws, and on treaties and agreements; reconsiders the acquisition and loss of U.S. citizenship in complex cases; and administers the overseas federal benefits program.

Boundaries

►**AGENCIES**

Saint Lawrence Seaway Development Corp. *(Transportation Dept.), 1200 New Jersey Ave. S.E., #W32-300 20590; (202) 366-0091. Fax, (202) 366-7147.*

Collister "Terry" Johnson, Administrator. Toll-free, (800) 785-2779.

Web, www.greatlakes-seaway.com

Operates and maintains the Saint Lawrence Seaway within U.S. territorial limits; conducts development programs and coordinates activities with its Canadian counterpart.

State Dept., *Mexican Affairs,* 2201 C St. N.W., #3909 20520-6258; (202) 647-9894. Fax, (202) 647-5752. Daniel Darrach, Border Coordinator.

Web, www.state.gov

Acts as liaison between the United States and Mexico in international boundary and water matters as defined by binational treaties and agreements. Also involved with border health and environmental issues, new border crossings, and significant modifications to existing crossings.

►INTERNATIONAL ORGANIZATIONS

International Boundary Commission, *United States and Canada,* U.S. Section, 2401 Pennsylvania Ave. N.W., #475 20037; (202) 736-9100. Fax, (202) 254-4562. Paul Hipsley, Commissioner (Acting).

Web, www.internationalboundarycommission.org

Defines and maintains the international boundary line between the United States and Canada. Rules on applications for approval of projects affecting boundary or transboundary waters. Assists the United States and Canada in protecting the transboundary environment. Alerts the governments to emerging issues that may give rise to bilateral disputes. Commissioners represent only the commission, not the government that appointed them. (Canadian section in Ottawa.)

International Joint Commission, United States and Canada, *U.S. Section,* 2401 Pennsylvania Ave. N.W., #400 20037; (202) 736-9000. Fax, (202) 254-4562. Irene Brooks, Chair.

Web, www.ijc.org

Handles disputes concerning the use of boundary waters; negotiates questions dealing with the rights, obligations, and interests of the United States and Canada along the border; establishes procedures for the adjustment and settlement of questions. (Canadian section in Ottawa.)

Extradition

►AGENCIES

Justice Dept. (DOJ), *International Affairs,* 1301 New York Ave. N.W., #800 20005 (mailing address: P.O. Box 27330, Washington, DC 20038-7330); (202) 514-0000. Fax, (202) 514-0080. Mary Ellen Warlow, Director.

Web, www.usdoj.gov

Performs investigations necessary for extradition of fugitives from the United States and other nations. Handles

U.S. and foreign government requests for mutual legal assistance, including documentary evidence.

State Dept., *Law Enforcement and Intelligence,* 2201 C St. N.W., #5419 20520; (202) 647-7324. Fax, (202) 647-4802. Clifton Johnson, Assistant Legal Adviser.

Web, www.state.gov

Negotiates and approves extradition of fugitives between the United States and other nations.

►NONGOVERNMENTAL

Center for National Security Studies, 1120 19th St. N.W., #800 20036; (202) 721-5650. Fax, (202) 530-0128. Kate A. Martin, Director. Press, (202) 721-5660.

General e-mail, cnss@cnss.org

Web, www.cnss.org

Monitors and conducts research on extradition, intelligence, national security, and civil liberties.

Fishing, Law of the Sea

►AGENCIES

National Oceanic and Atmospheric Administration (NOAA), *(Commerce Dept.), National Marine Fisheries Service,* 1315 East-West Hwy., Silver Spring, MD 20910; (301) 713-2239. Fax, (301) 713-1940. James W. Balsiger, Assistant Administrator (Acting). Press, (301) 713-2370.

Web, www.nmfs.noaa.gov

Administers marine fishing regulations, including offshore fishing rights and international agreements.

State Dept., *Oceans and Fisheries,* 2201 C St. N.W., #3880 20520; (202) 647-2396. Fax, (202) 647-0217. David A. Balton, Deputy Assistant Secretary.

Web, www.state.gov

Coordinates U.S. negotiations concerning international fishing and oceans issues. Handles foreign fleets fishing in U.S. waters and U.S. fleets fishing in foreign waters or the open seas.

►CONGRESS

For a listing of relevant congressional committees and subcommittees, please see page 412 or the Appendix.

Human Rights

►AGENCIES

Commission on Security and Cooperation in Europe (Helsinki Commission), 234 FHOB 20515; (202) 225-1901. Fax, (202) 226-4199. Sen. Benjamin L. Cardin, D–Md., Chair; Rep. Alcee L. Hastings, D–Fla., Co-Chair; Fred L. Turner, Chief of Staff.

General e-mail, info@csce.gov

Web, www.csce.gov

Independent agency created by Congress. Membership includes individuals from the executive and legislative branches. Monitors and encourages compliance with the human rights provisions of the Helsinki Accords; conducts hearings; serves as an information clearinghouse for human rights issues in eastern and western Europe, Canada, and the United States relating to the Helsinki Accords.

Congressional–Executive Commission on China, 243
FHOB 20515; (202) 226-3766. Fax, (202) 226-3804. Sen. Byron L. Dorgan, D-N. Dak., Chair; Rep. Sander M. Levin, D-Mich., Co-Chair; Charlotte Oldham-Moore, Staff Director.

General e-mail, infocecc@mail.house.gov

Web, www.cecc.gov

Independent agency created by Congress. Membership includes individuals from the executive and legislative branches. Monitors human rights and the development of the rule of law in the People's Republic of China. Submits an annual report to the president and Congress.

State Dept., *Democracy, Human Rights, and Labor,*
2201 C St. N.W., #7802 20520-7812; (202) 647-2126. Fax, (202) 647-5283. Karen Stewart, Assistant Secretary (Acting).
Web, www.state.gov/g/drl

Implements U.S. policies relating to human rights, labor, and religious freedom; prepares annual review of human rights worldwide; provides the U.S. Citizenship and Immigration Services with advisory opinions regarding asylum petitions.

State Dept., *Global Affairs: International Women's*
Issues, 2201 C St. N.W., #6805 20520; (202) 647-7285. Fax, (202) 647-7288. Melanne Verveer, Ambassador at Large for Global Women's Issues.
Web, www.state.gov/g/wi

Works to promote the human rights of women within U.S. foreign policy. Participates in international organizations and conferences; advises other U.S. agencies; disseminates information. Reports to under secretary for democracy and global affairs.

State Dept., *Monitor and Combat Trafficking in*
Persons, 1800 G St. N.W., #2201 20520; (202) 312-9639. Fax, (202) 312-9637. Nan Kemmerely, Director (Acting).
General e-mail, tipoutreach@state.gov

Web, www.state.gov/g/tip

Combats trafficking in persons domestically and internationally. Publishes annual *Trafficking in Persons Report,* which assesses the progress of other governments, analyzes best practices and new data, and summarizes U.S. efforts to combat human trafficking at home.

U.S. Commission on International Religious Freedom,
800 N. Capitol St. N.W., #790 20002; (202) 523-3240. Fax, (202) 523-5020. Jane Standish, Executive Director.
General e-mail, communications@uscirf.gov

Web, www.uscirf.gov

Agency created by the International Religious Freedom Act of 1998 to monitor religious freedom worldwide and to advise the president, the secretary of state, and Congress on how best to promote it.

▶CONGRESS

For a listing of relevant congressional committees and subcommittees, please see page 412 or the Appendix.

▶NONGOVERNMENTAL

Amnesty International USA, *Washington Office,* 600
Pennsylvania Ave. S.E., 5th Floor 20003; (202) 544-0200. Fax, (202) 546-7142. Betsy Hawkings, Managing Director of Government Relations.
Web, www.amnestyusa.org

International organization that works for the release of men and women imprisoned anywhere in the world for their beliefs, political affiliation, color, ethnic origin, sex, language, or religion, provided they have neither used nor advocated violence. Opposes torture and the death penalty; urges fair and prompt trials for all political prisoners. (U.S. headquarters in New York.)

Center for Human Rights and Humanitarian Law, 4801
Massachusetts Ave. N.W. 20016-8084; (202) 274-4180. Fax, (202) 274-0783. Hadar Harris, Executive Director.
General e-mail, humlaw@wcl.american.edu

Web, www.wcl.american.edu/humright/center

Seeks to promote human rights and humanitarian law. Establishes training programs for judges, lawyers, and law schools; assists emerging democracies and other nations in developing laws and institutions that protect human rights; organizes conferences with public and private institutions. (Affiliated with the Washington College of Law at American University.)

Free the Slaves, 514 10th St. N.W., 7th Floor 20004;
(202) 638-1865. Fax, (202) 638-0599. Jolene Smith, Executive Director. Toll-free, (866) 324-3733.
General e-mail, info@freetheslaves.net

Web, http://freetheslaves.net

Researches modern slavery and funds the work of grassroots antislavery organizations. Partners with concerned businesses and nongovernmental organizations to remove slavery from product supply chains and build a consumer movement that chooses slave-free goods. Maintains a video library, holds public presentations, and distributes educational materials. Monitors legislation and regulations.

Genocide Watch, P.O. Box 809 20044; (703) 448-0222.
Gregory Stanton, President.
General e-mail, genocidewatch@aol.com

Web, www.genocidewatch.org

Educates the public and policymakers about the causes, processes, and warning signs of genocide; seeks to create the institutions and the political will to prevent and stop genocide and to bring perpetrators of genocide to justice. (Chair of the International Campaign to End Genocide.)

Global Rights, *1200 18th St. N.W., #602 20036; (202) 822-4600. Fax, (202) 822-4606. Mary McClymont, Executive Director.*
Web, www.globalrights.org

Public interest law center concerned with promoting and protecting international human rights. Conducts educational programs and conferences; provides information regarding human rights violations; monitors the electoral and judicial process in several countries.

Human Rights First, *Washington Office, 100 Maryland Ave. N.E., #500 20002-5625; (202) 547-5692. Fax, (202) 543-5999. Elisa Massimino, Executive Director.*
General e-mail, dibelloS@humanrightsfirst.org

Web, www.humanrightsfirst.org

Promotes human rights as guaranteed by the International Bill of Human Rights. Mobilizes the legal community to protect the rule of law. (Headquarters in New York; formerly the Lawyers Committee for Human Rights.)

Human Rights Watch, *Washington Office, 1630 Connecticut Ave. N.W., #500 20009; (202) 612-4321. Fax, (202) 612-4372. Tom Malinowski, Advocacy Director.*
General e-mail, hrwdc@hrw.org

Web, www.hrw.org

International, nonpartisan human rights organization that monitors human rights violations worldwide. Subdivided into six regional concentrations—Africa, Americas, Asia, Europe and Central Asia, Middle East and North Africa, and South Asia. Coordinates thematic projects on women's rights, arms sales, and prisons. Sponsors fact-finding missions to various countries; publicizes violations and encourages international protests; maintains file on human rights violations. (Headquarters in New York.)

International Assn. of Official Human Rights Agencies (IAOHRA), *444 N. Capitol St. N.W., #536 20001; (202) 624-5410. Fax, (202) 624-8185. Leon W. Russell, President; Shannon Bennett, Director.*
General e-mail, iaohra@sso.org

Web, www.iaohra.org

Works with government and human rights agencies worldwide to identify needs common to civil rights enforcement. Offers management training for human rights executives and civil rights workshops for criminal justice agencies; develops training programs in investigative techniques, settlement and conciliation, and legal theory. Serves as an information clearinghouse on human rights laws and enforcement.

International Justice Mission, *P.O. Box 58147 20037-8147; (703) 465-5495. Fax, (703) 465-5499. Gary A. Haugen, President.*
General e-mail, contact@ijm.org

Web, www.ijm.org

Seeks to help people suffering injustice and oppression who cannot rely on local authorities for relief. Documents and monitors conditions of abuse and oppression, educates churches and the public about abuses, and mobilizes intervention on behalf of victims.

Jubilee Campaign USA, *9689-C Main St., Fairfax, VA 22031; (703) 503-0791. Danny Smith, President.*
General e-mail, jubilee@jubileecampaign.org

Web, www.jubileecampaign.org

Promotes human rights and religious liberty for ethnic and religious minorities in countries that oppress them. Advocates the release of prisoners of conscience and revising laws to achieve this. Especially interested in ending the exploitation of children.

Polaris Project, *P.O. Box 77892 20013; (202) 745-1001. Fax, (202) 745-1119. Katherine Chon, President; Amb. Mark Lagon, Executive Director.*
General e-mail, info@polarisproject.org

Web, www.polarisproject.org

Grassroots organization that fights human trafficking at the local, national, and international levels with an emphasis on policy advocacy and survivor support.

Robert F. Kennedy Center for Justice and Human Rights, *1367 Connecticut Ave. N.W., #200 20036-1859; (202) 463-7575. Fax, (202) 463-6606. Lynn Delaney, Executive Director.*
General e-mail, info@rfkcenter.org

Web, www.rfkcenter.org

Presents annual book, journalism, and human rights awards and carries out programs that support the work of the human rights award laureates in their countries. Investigates and reports on human rights; campaigns to heighten awareness of these issues, stop abuses, and encourage governments, international organizations, and corporations to adopt policies that ensure respect for human rights.

Rugmark Foundation, *2001 S St. N.W., #430 20009; (202) 234-9050. Fax, (202) 347-4885. Nina Smith, Executive Director.*
General e-mail, info@rugmark.org

Web, www.rugmark.org

International human rights organization working to end child labor in Indian, Nepalese, and Pakistani handmade carpet industries. Runs schools and rehabilitation centers for former child workers.

Torture Abolition and Survivors Support Coalition International (TASSC), *4121 Harewood Rd. N.E., Suite B 20017-1597; (202) 529-2991. Fax, (202) 529-8334. Demissie Abebe, Director.*
General e-mail, info@tassc.org

Web, www.tassc.org

Coalition of torture survivors seeking to end torture through public education and political advocacy. Provides resources and information to survivors of torture.

Unitarian Universalist Service Committee, *1100 G St. N.W., #800 20001; (202) 393-2255. Fax, (202) 393-5494. Shelly Maskowitz, Manager of Public Policy. General e-mail, info@uusc.org*

Web, www.uusc.org

Secular human rights organization fighting race, gender, environmental, and economic injustice worldwide. Partners with civil liberty organizations defending right to water, workers' rights, and the democratic process. Responds to disasters. Provides education through travel and workcamps.

World Organization for Human Rights USA, *2029 P St. N.W., #301 20036; (202) 296-5702. Fax, (202) 296-5704. Therese Harris, Executive Director. General e-mail, info@humanrightsusa.org*

Web, www.humanrightsusa.org

Seeks to prevent torture and other major human rights abuses through litigation in U.S. courts, focusing on U.S. compliance with international human rights norms.

Narcotics Trafficking

▶**AGENCIES**

Defense Dept. (DoD), *Counternarcotics, 1510 Defense Pentagon, #4A275 20301-1510; (703) 614-8847. Fax, (703) 697-4682. Ed Frathingham, Deputy Assistant Secretary (Acting). Web, www.defenselink.mil/policy/solic/cn*

Coordinates and monitors Defense Dept. support of civilian drug law enforcement agencies and interagency efforts to detect and monitor the maritime and aerial transit of illegal drugs into the United States. Represents the secretary on drug control matters outside the department.

Drug Enforcement Administration (DEA), *(Justice Dept.), 700 Army-Navy Dr., Arlington, VA 22202 (mailing address: 8701 Morrissette Dr., Springfield, VA 22152); (202) 307-8000. Fax, (202) 307-4540. Michelle Leonhart, Administrator (Acting). Press, (202) 307-7977. Locator, (202) 307-4132. Web, www.dea.gov*

Assists foreign narcotics agents; cooperates with the State Dept., embassies, the Agency for International Development, and international organizations to strengthen narcotics law enforcement and to reduce supply and demand in developing countries; trains and advises narcotics enforcement officers in developing nations.

State Dept., International Narcotics and Law Enforcement Affairs, *2201 C St. N.W., #7333 20520-7512; (202) 647-8464. Fax, (202) 736-4885. David T. Johnson, Assistant Secretary. General e-mail, samuelcm@state.gov*

Web, www.state.gov/p/inl

Coordinates efforts to establish and facilitate stable criminal justice systems in order to strengthen international law enforcement and judicial effectiveness, bolster cooperation in legal affairs, and support the rule of law, while respecting human rights. Seeks to disrupt the overseas production and trafficking of illicit drugs by means of counter-drug and anti-crime assistance and coordination with foreign nations and international organizations.

U.S. Coast Guard (USCG), *(Homeland Security Dept.), Law Enforcement Command (CG-531), 2100 2nd St. S.W., #3110 20593-0001; (202) 372-2160. Fax, (202) 372-2913. Michael Giglio, Chief. Web, www.uscg.mil/hq/g-o/g-opl*

Oversees enforcement of federal laws and treaties and other international agreements to which the United States is party on, over, and under the high seas and waters subject to the jurisdiction of the United States; jurisdiction includes narcotics, migration interdiction, and fisheries.

U.S. Customs and Border Protection *(Homeland Security Dept.), Border Patrol, 1300 Pennsylvania Ave. N.W., #6.5E 20229; (202) 344-2050. Fax, (202) 344-3140. David V. Aguilar, Chief. Web, www.cbp.gov*

Mobile uniformed law enforcement arm of the Homeland Security Dept. Primary mission is to detect and prevent the illegal trafficking of people and contraband across U.S. borders.

U.S. Customs and Border Protection *(Homeland Security Dept.), Field Operations, 1300 Pennsylvania Ave. N.W., #2.4A 20229; (202) 344-1620. Fax, (202) 344-2777. Thomas Winkowski, Assistant Commissioner. Hotline to report suspicious activity, (800) 232-5378. Web, www.cbp.gov*

Interdicts and seizes contraband, including narcotics and other drugs, at the U.S. border.

INTERNATIONAL TRADE AND DEVELOPMENT

▶**AGENCIES**

Antitrust Division *(Justice Dept.), Foreign Commerce, 450 5th St. N.W., #1100 20530; (202) 514-2464. Fax, (202) 514-4508. Edward T. Hand, Chief. Web, www.usdoj.gov/atr*

Acts as the division's liaison with foreign governments and international organizations including the European Union. Works with the State Dept. to exchange information with foreign governments concerning investigations involving foreign corporations and nationals.

Bureau of Economic Analysis *(Commerce Dept.), International Economics, 1441 L St. N.W., #6063 20005; (202) 606-9900. Fax, (202) 606-5311. Obie G. Whichard, Associate Director. Web, www.bea.gov*

U.S. Customs and Border Protection

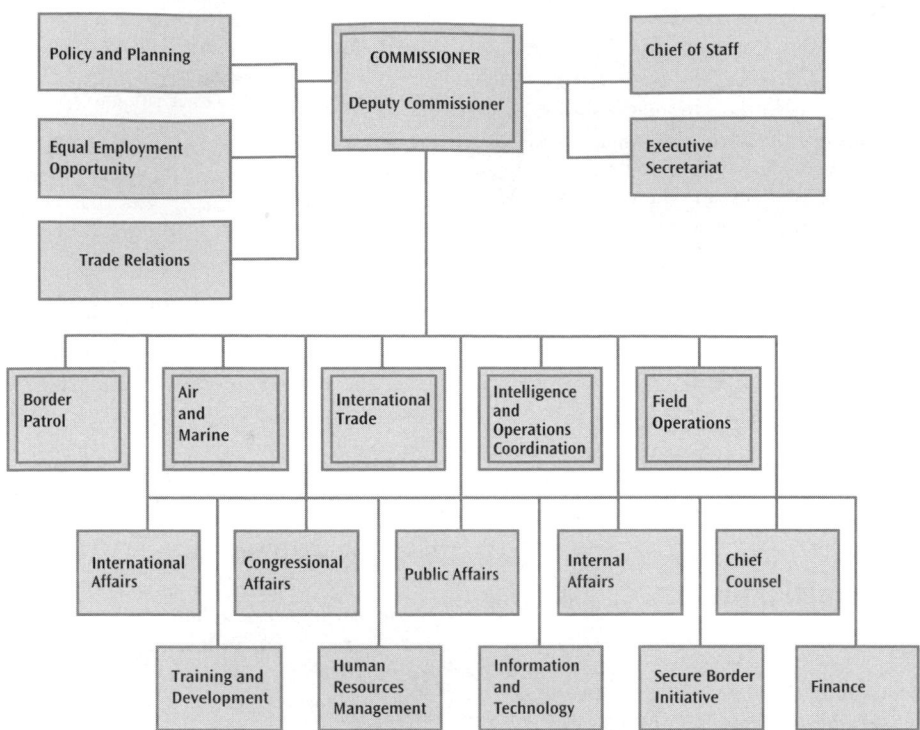

Compiles statistics under the International Investment and Trade in Services Survey Act for an ongoing study of foreign direct investment in the United States and direct investment abroad by the United States. (Visit www.bea.gov/bea/surveys/iussurv.htm for information on the surveys.)

Bureau of Industry and Security *(Commerce Dept.),*
14th St. and Constitution Ave. N.W., #3898 20230; (202) 482-1455. Fax, (202) 482-2421. Mario Mancuso, Under Secretary. Press, (202) 482-2721. Export licensing information, (202) 482-4811.
Web, www.bis.doc.gov

Administers Export Administration Act; coordinates export administration programs of federal departments and agencies; maintains control lists and performs export licensing for the purposes of national security, foreign policy, and short supply. Monitors impact of foreign boycotts on the United States; ensures availability of goods and services essential to industrial performance on contracts for national defense. Assesses availability of foreign products and technology to maintain control lists and licensing.

Census Bureau *(Commerce Dept.), Foreign Trade, 4600 Silver Hill Rd., #6K032, Suitland, MD 20746 (for mailing address, change city to: Washington, DC 20233-6700); (301) 763-2255. Fax, (301) 763-6638. William G. Bostic Jr., Chief.*

General e-mail, william.g.bostic.jr@census.gov
Web, www.census.gov/trade

Provides data on all aspects of foreign trade in commodities.

Committee on Foreign Investment in the United States *(Treasury Dept.),* 1500 Pennsylvania Ave. N.W., #5221 20220; (202) 622-1860. Fax, (202) 622-0391. Mark Jaskowiak, Staff Chair.

Reviews foreign acquisition of U.S. companies and determines whether they pose national security threats. Conducts investigations into such acquisitions.

Consumer Product Safety Commission (CPSC),
International Programs and Intergovernmental Affairs, 4330 East-West Hwy., Bethesda, MD 20814; (301) 504-7907. Fax, (301) 504-0137. Richard O'Brien, Director.
Web, www.cpsc.gov

Coordinates international and intergovernmental efforts with respect to consumer product safety standards development, harmonization efforts, inspection and enforcement coordination, consumer education, and information dissemination.

Export-Import Bank of the United States, *811 Vermont Ave. N.W., #1215 20571; (202) 565-3545. Fax, (202) 565-3513. Vacant, Chair; Vacant, Vice Chair. Press,*

(202) 565-3200. TTY, (202) 565-3377. Toll-free hotline, (800) 565-3946; in Washington, (202) 565-3946.
Web, www.exim.gov

Independent agency of the U.S. government. Aids in financing exports of U.S. goods and services; offers direct credit to borrowers outside the United States; guarantees export loans made by commercial lenders, working capital guarantees, and export credit insurance; conducts an intermediary loan program. Hotline advises businesses in using U.S. government export programs.

Federal Trade Commission (FTC), *International Affairs,* *600 Pennsylvania Ave. N.W., #H382 20580; (202) 326-3051. Fax, (202) 326-2884. Randolph W. Tritell, Director.*
Web, www.ftc.gov

Assists in the enforcement of antitrust laws by arranging appropriate cooperation and coordination with foreign governments in international cases and with the antitrust division of the Justice Dept. Negotiates bilateral and multilateral antitrust agreements and represents the United States in international antitrust policy forums.

Foreign Trade Zones Board *(Commerce Dept.), 1401 Constitution Ave. N.W., #2111 20230; (202) 482-2862. Fax, (202) 482-0002. Andrew McGilvray, Executive Secretary.*
Web, www.trade.gov/ftz

Authorizes public and private corporations to establish foreign trade zones to which foreign and domestic goods can be brought without being subject to customs duties.

International Trade Administration (ITA), *(Commerce Dept.), 14th St. and Constitution Ave. N.W., #3850 20230; (202) 482-2867. Fax, (202) 482-2925. Michelle O'Neill, Under Secretary (Acting). Press, (202) 482-3809. Publications, (202) 482-5487. Trade information, (800) 872-8723.*
Web, www.trade.gov

Seeks to strengthen the competitiveness of U.S. industry, promote trade and investment, and ensure fair trade and compliance with trade law and agreements.

International Trade Administration (ITA), *(Commerce Dept.), Global Trade Programs, Ronald Reagan Bldg., 14th St. and Constitution Ave. N.W., #2500-RRB 20230; (202) 482-4207. Fax, (202) 482-7800. Blanche Ziv, Program Manager.*
Web, www.export.gov

Promotes and directs programs to expand exports abroad; manages overseas trade missions; conducts trade fair certification programs. Participates in trade fairs and technology seminars to introduce American products abroad. Provides the business community with sales and trade information through an automated system, which allows a direct connection between U.S. and overseas offices.

International Trade Administration (ITA), *(Commerce Dept.), Import Administration, 14th St. and Constitution*

Ave. N.W., #3099B 20230; (202) 482-1780. Fax, (202) 482-0947. Ronald Lorentzen, Assistant Secretary (Acting).
Web, http://ia.ita.doc.gov

Enforces antidumping and countervailing duty statutes if foreign goods are subsidized or sold at less than fair market value. Evaluates and processes applications by U.S. international air- and seaport communities seeking to establish limited duty-free zones. Administers the Statutory Import Program, which governs specific tariff schedules and imports and determines whether property left abroad by U.S. agencies may be imported back into the United States.

International Trade Administration (ITA), *(Commerce Dept.), Manufacturing and Services, 14th St. and Constitution Ave. N.W., #3832 20230; (202) 482-1461. Fax, (202) 482-5697. Mary Saunders, Assistant Secretary (Acting).*
Web, www.trade.gov

Seeks to strengthen the international competitiveness of U.S. businesses; coordinates export promotion programs and trade missions; compiles and analyzes trade data. Divisions focus on basic industries, service industries and finance, technology and aerospace, consumer goods, tourism, and environmental technologies exports.

International Trade Administration (ITA), *(Commerce Dept.), Manufacturing and Services: Industry Analysis, 14th St. and Constitution Ave. N.W., #2126 20230; (202) 482-6232. Fax, (202) 482-4614. Praveen Dixit, Deputy Assistant Secretary.*
Web, www.ita.doc.gov/tradestats

Monitors and analyzes U.S. international trade and competitive performance, foreign direct investment in the United States, and international economic factors affecting U.S. trade; identifies future trends and problems. Annual reports include *U.S. Industrial Trade Outlook* and *Foreign Direct Investment in the United States: Transactions.* Foreign Trade Reference Room open to the public.

International Trade Administration (ITA), *(Commerce Dept.), Market Access and Compliance, 14th St. and Constitution Ave. N.W., #3868A 20230; (202) 482-3022. Fax, (202) 482-5444. Stephen Jacobs, Assistant Secretary (Acting).*
Web, www.mac.doc.gov

Develops and implements trade and investment policies affecting countries, regions, or international organizations to improve U.S. market access abroad. Provides information and analyses of foreign market barriers and economic conditions to the U.S. private sector; monitors foreign compliance with trade agreements signed with the United States.

International Trade Administration (ITA), *(Commerce Dept.), NAFTA and North and Central America and the Caribbean (ONCAC), 14th St. and Constitution Ave. N.W., #3024 20230; (202) 482-0393. Fax, (202) 482-5865. Geri Word, Director.*
Web, www.ita.doc.gov

International Trade Administration

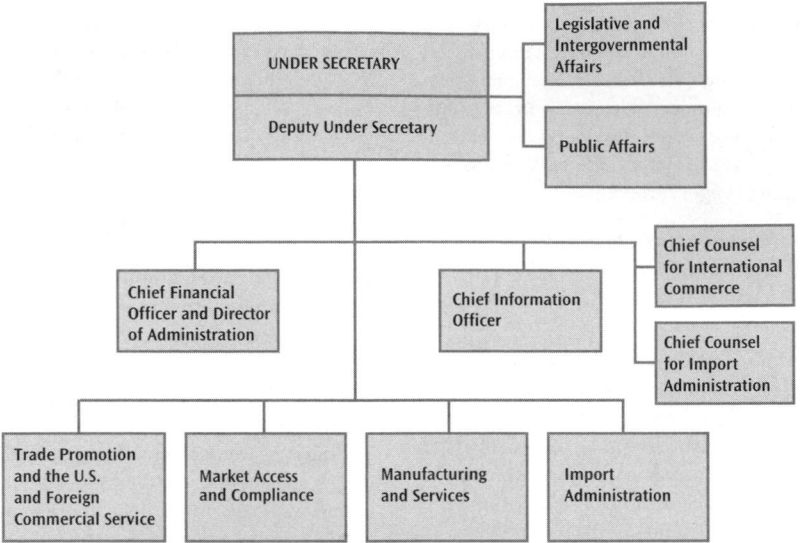

Coordinates Commerce Dept. activities regarding NAFTA (North American Free Trade Agreement), FTAA (Free Trade Areas of the Americas), and other Western Hemisphere free trade agreements.

International Trade Administration (ITA), *(Commerce Dept.), Trade Information Center, RRB-TIC, 14th St. and Constitution Ave. N.W. 20230; (202) 482-0543. Fax, (202) 482-4473. Susan Lusi, Director. Information, (800) 872-8723.*
General e-mail, tic@mail.doc.gov

Web, www.export.gov

Counsels U.S. businesses on export matters and on programs and services provided by the agencies that are members of the Trade Promotion Coordinating Committee to facilitate exports. Agencies include, but are not limited to, the Agriculture and Commerce departments, Export-Import Bank, Overseas Private Investment Corp., and the Agency for International Development.

International Trade Administration (ITA), *(Commerce Dept.), Trade Promotion and U.S. and Foreign Commercial Service, 14th St. and Constitution Ave. N.W., #3802 20230; (202) 482-5777. Fax, (202) 482-5013. Rochell Lepsitz, Assistant Secretary (Acting).*
Web, www.ita.doc.gov

Promotes the export of U.S. goods and services; protects and advocates U.S. business interests abroad; provides counseling and information on overseas markets, international contacts, and trade promotion.

National Institute of Standards and Technology (NIST), *(Commerce Dept.), National Center for Standards and Certification Information, 100 Bureau Dr., MS 2100, Gaithersburg, MD 20899-2160; (301)* 975-4040. Fax, (301) 926-1559. Carmina Londono, Chief; Anne Weininger, Group Leader.*
General e-mail, ncsci@nist.gov

Web, www.nist.gov

Provides research services on standards, technical regulations, and conformity assessment procedures for nonagricultural products. Serves as central repository for standards-related information in the United States. Has access to U.S., foreign, and international documents and contact points through its role as the U.S. national inquiry point under the World Trade Organization Agreement on Technical Barriers to Trade. Global Standards and Information group receives submissions from selected countries of proposed standards for review by U.S. technical experts.

Overseas Private Investment Corp., *1100 New York Ave. N.W. 20527; (202) 336-8400. Fax, (202) 408-9859. Lawrence Spinelli, President (Acting). Press, (202) 336-8744.*
General e-mail, info@opic.gov

Web, www.opic.gov

Provides assistance through political risk insurance, direct loans, and loan guarantees to qualified U.S. private investors to support their investments in less developed countries. Offers preinvestment information and counseling. Provides insurance against the risks of expropriation, political violence, and inconvertibility of local currency.

President's Export Council *(Commerce Dept.), 14th St. and Constitution Ave. N.W., #4043 20230; (202) 482-1124. Fax, (202) 482-4452. J. Marc Chittum, Director.*
Web, www.ita.doc.gov/pec

Advises the president on all aspects of export trade, including export controls, promotion, and expansion.

Small Business Administration (SBA), *International Trade,* 409 3rd St. S.W., 8th Floor 20416; (202) 205-6720. Fax, (202) 205-7272. Luz A. Hopewell, Director. Web, www.sba.gov/international

Offers instruction, assistance, and information on exporting through counseling and conferences. Helps businesses gain access to export financing through loan guarantee programs. Ensures interests of small businesses are considered and reflected in trade negotiations.

State Dept., *Commercial and Business Affairs,* 2201 C St. N.W., #2318 20520-5820; (202) 647-1625. Fax, (202) 647-3953. J. Frank Mermoud, Special Representative for Commercial and Business Affairs. General e-mail, cbaweb@state.gov

Web, www.state.gov/e/eb/cba

Serves as primary contact in the State Dept. for U.S. businesses. Coordinates efforts to facilitate U.S. business interests abroad, ensures that U.S. business interests are given sufficient consideration in foreign policy, and provides assistance to firms with problems overseas (such as claims and trade complaints). Works with agencies in the Trade Promotion Coordinating Committee to support U.S. business interests overseas.

State Dept., *Economic, Energy, and Agricultural Affairs,* 2201 C St. N.W., #7256 20520-7512; (202) 647-7575. Fax, (202) 647-9763. Vacant, Under Secretary. Web, www.state.gov/e

Advises the secretary on formulation and conduct of foreign economic policies and programs, including international monetary and financial affairs, trade, telecommunications, energy, agriculture, commodities, investments, and international transportation issues. Coordinates economic summit meetings.

State Dept., *Economic, Energy, and Business Affairs,* 2201 C St. N.W., #4932 20520-5820; (202) 647-7971. Fax, (202) 647-5713. David B. Nelson, Assistant Secretary (Acting). Web, www.state.gov/e/eb

Formulates and implements policies related to U.S. economic relations with foreign countries, including international business practices, communications and information, trade, finance, investment, development, natural resources, energy, and transportation.

State Dept., *Investment Affairs,* 2201 C St. N.W., #4669 20520-5820; (202) 736-4762. Fax, (202) 647-0320. Wesley S. Scholz, Director. Web, www.state.gov

Develops U.S. investment policy. Makes policy recommendations regarding multinational enterprises and the expropriation of and compensation for U.S. property overseas. Negotiates bilateral and multilateral investment agreements. Coordinates the State Dept.'s position with respect to the Committee on Foreign Investments in the United States.

State Dept., *Terrorism, Finance, and Economic Sanctions Policy,* 2201 C St. N.W., #4657 20520; (202) 647-7489. Fax, (202) 647-4064. Steven Bondy, Director. Web, www.state.gov

Develops and implements U.S. sanctions of embargoed countries and countries known to house terrorists. Coordinates U.S. participation in multilateral strategic trade control and revisions related to the export of strategically critical high-technology goods. Cooperates with the Commerce, Defense, and Treasury Depts. regarding export controls.

State Dept., *Trade Policy and Programs,* 2201 C St. N.W., #4652, EEB/TPP 20520-5820; (202) 647-5991. Fax, (202) 647-1894. Bill Craft, Administrator. General e-mail, ebtpp@state.gov

Web, www.state.gov/e/eb/tpp

Develops and administers policies and programs on international trade, including trade negotiations and agreements, import relief, unfair trade practices, trade relations with developing countries, export development, and export controls (including controls imposed for national security or foreign policy purposes).

Trade Promotion Coordinating Committee, 14th St. and Constitution Ave. N.W., #2112 20230; (202) 482-5455. Fax, (202) 482-4137. Gary Locke, Chair; Patrick Kirwan, Director. Web, www.export.gov

Coordinates all export promotion and export financing activities of the U.S. government. Composed of representatives from the departments of Commerce, State, Treasury, Defense, Homeland Security, Interior, Agriculture, Labor, Transportation, and Energy, OMB, U.S. Trade Representative, Council of Economic Advisers, EPA, Small Business Administration, AID, Export-Import Bank, Overseas Private Investment Corporation, and the U.S. Trade and Development Agency.

Treasury Dept., *Foreign Assets Control,* 1500 Pennsylvania Ave. N.W., Annex Bldg., #2233 20220; (202) 622-2500. Fax, (202) 622-1657. Adam Szubin, Director. Fax-on-demand, (202) 622-0077. Web, www.ustreas.gov/ofac

Administers and enforces economic and trade sanctions against targeted foreign countries, terrorists, international narcotics traffickers, and those engaged in activities related to the proliferation of weapons of mass destruction. Acts under presidential wartime and national emergency powers, as well as under authority granted by specific legislation, to impose controls on transactions and freeze foreign assets under U.S. jurisdiction.

Treasury Dept., *International Trade,* 1500 Pennsylvania Ave. N.W., #5204 20220; (202) 622-1733. Fax, (202) 622-1731. T. Whittier Warthin, Director. Web, www.ustreas.gov

Formulates Treasury Dept. foreign trade policies and coordinates them with other agencies through the U.S. Trade Representative.

Treasury Dept., *Investment Security*, *1500 Pennsylvania Ave. N.W., #3205 20220; (202) 622-1860. Fax, (202) 622-9212. Mark Jaskowiak, Deputy Assistant Secretary (Acting).*
General e-mail, cifius@do.treas.gov

Web, www.ustreas.gov

Oversees foreign investment and U.S. open investment policy.

U.S. Customs and Border Protection *(Homeland Security Dept.), 1300 Pennsylvania Ave. N.W., #4.4A 20229; (202) 344-2001. Fax, (202) 344-1380. W. Ralph Basham, Commissioner. Information, (202) 344-2130. Library, (202) 344-1350. Press, (202) 344-1780.*
Web, www.cbp.gov

Assesses and collects duties and taxes on imported merchandise; processes persons and baggage entering the United States; collects import and export data for international trade statistics; controls export carriers and goods to prevent fraud and smuggling. Library open to the public by appointment.

U.S. Customs and Border Protection *(Homeland Security Dept.), Commercial Targeting and Enforcement, 1300 Pennsylvania Ave. N.W., #L.11 20229; (202) 863-6550. Fax, (202) 863-6060. Don Yando, Executive Director.*
Web, www.cbp.gov

Enforces compliance with all commercial import requirements; collects import statistics; assesses and collects countervailing and antidumping duties after determinations have been made by the Commerce Dept. in conjunction with the U.S. International Trade Commission.

U.S. International Trade Commission, *500 E St. S.W. 20436; (202) 205-2000. Fax, (202) 205-2798. Shara L. Aranoff, Chair. Reference Library, (202) 205-2630.*
Web, www.usitc.gov

Provides Congress, the president, and the U.S. trade representative with technical information and advice on trade and tariff matters. Determines the impact of imports on U.S. industries in antidumping and countervailing duty investigations. Directs actions against certain unfair trade practices, such as intellectual property infringement. Investigates and reports on U.S. industries and the global trends that affect them. Publishes the *Harmonized Tariff Schedule of the United States.* Library open to the public.

U.S. Trade and Development Agency, *1000 Wilson Blvd., #1600, Arlington, VA 22209-3901; (703) 875-4357. Fax, (703) 875-4009. Leo Caolia Zork, Director (Acting).*
General e-mail, info@ustda.gov

Web, www.ustda.gov

Assists U.S. companies exporting to developing and middle-income countries. Provides grants for feasibility studies. Offers technical assistance and identifies commercial opportunities in these countries.

U.S. Trade Representative *(Executive Office of the President), 600 17th St. N.W., #205 20508; (202) 395-7360. Fax, (202) 395-4549. Devorah Adler, Executive Secretary; Ambassador Ron Kirk, U.S. Trade Representative. Press, (202) 395-3230.*
Web, www.ustr.gov

Serves as principal adviser to the president and primary trade negotiator on international trade policy. Develops and coordinates U.S. trade policy, including commodity and direct investment matters, import remedies, East-West trade policy, U.S. export expansion policy, and the implementation of MTN (Multilateral Trade Negotiations) agreements. Conducts international trade negotiations and represents the United States in World Trade Organization (WTO) matters.

U.S. Trade Representative *(Executive Office of the President), Intergovernmental Affairs and Public Liaison, 600 17th St. N.W., #100 20508; (202) 395-6120. Fax, (202) 395-3692. Lisa A. Garcia, Assistant U.S. Trade Representative for Intergovernmental Affairs, and Public Liaison.*
Web, www.ustr.gov

Serves as chief private sector advisory committee for the president, U.S. trade representative, and Congress on all matters concerning U.S. trade policy. Interests include the North American Free Trade Agreement (NAFTA) and the World Trade Organization (WTO).

▶**CONGRESS**

For a listing of relevant congressional committees and subcommittees, please see page 412 or the Appendix.

▶**INTERNATIONAL ORGANIZATIONS**

European Commission, *Press and Public Diplomacy, Washington Office, 2300 M St. N.W. 20037-1400; (202) 862-9500. Fax, (202) 429-1766. Anthony Smallwood, Head; John Bruton, Ambassador.*
General e-mail, relex-delusw-help@ec.europa.eu

Web, www.eurunion.org

Provides information on European Union energy policy, initiatives, research activities, and selected statistics. (Headquarters in Brussels.)

Food and Agriculture Organization of the United Nations (FAO), *Liaison Office for North America, 2175 K St. N.W., #500 20037-0001; (202) 653-2400. Fax, (202) 653-5760. Daniel Gustafson, Director. Press, (202) 653-0011.*
Web, www.fao.org

Offers development assistance; collects, analyzes, and disseminates information; provides policy and planning advice to governments; acts as an international forum for debate on food and agricultural issues, including animal health and production, fisheries, and forestry; encourages sustainable agricultural development and a long-term strategy for the conservation and management of natural resources. (International headquarters in Rome.)

Inter-American Development Bank, *1300 New York Ave. N.W. 20577; (202) 623-1000. Fax, (202) 623-3096. Luis Alberto Morena, President; Miguel San Juan, U.S. Executive Director. Information, (202) 623-1000. Library, (202) 623-3211. Press, (202) 623-1371.*
Web, www.iadb.org

Promotes, through loans and technical assistance, the investment of public and private capital in member countries of Latin America and the Caribbean for social and economic development purposes. Facilitates economic integration of the Latin American region. Library open to the public by appointment.

International Bank for Reconstruction and Development (World Bank), *1818 H St. N.W. 20433; (202) 473-1000. Fax, (202) 477-6391. Robert B. Zoellick, President; Eli Whitney Debevoise II, U.S. Executive Director. Press, (202) 473-7660. Bookstore, (202) 458-4500.*
General e-mail, gchopra@worldbank.org
Web, www.worldbank.org

International development institution funded by government membership subscriptions and borrowings on private capital markets. Encourages the flow of public and private foreign investment into developing countries through loans, grants, and technical assistance; collects data on selected economic indicators, world trade, and external public debt. Finances economic development projects in agriculture, environmental protection, education, public utilities, telecommunications, water supply, sewerage, public health, and other areas.

International Centre for Settlement of Investment Disputes, *1818 H St. N.W. 20433; (202) 458-1534. Fax, (202) 522-2615. Nassib Ciade, Secretary General.*
Web, www.worldbank.org/icsid

World Bank affiliate that handles the conciliation and arbitration of investment disputes between contracting states and foreign investors.

International Development Assn., *1818 H St. N.W. 20433; (202) 458-2552. Fax, (202) 522-2515. Akihiko Nishio, Director.*
Web, www.worldbank.org/ida

Affiliate of the World Bank funded by membership contributions and transfers of funds from the World Bank. Provides long-term interest-free loans and grants to the poorest countries.

International Monetary Fund (IMF), *Statistics, 700 19th St. N.W. 20431; (202) 623-4714. Fax, (202) 623-6460. Adelheid Burgi-Schmelz, Director. Publications, (202) 623-7430.*
Web, www.imfstatistics.org

Publishes monthly *International Financial Statistics (IFS),* which includes comprehensive financial data for most countries, and *Direction of Trade Statistics,* a quarterly publication, which includes the distribution of exports and imports for 152 countries. Annual statistical

publications include the *Balance of Payments Statistics Yearbook, Direction of Trade Statistics Yearbook, Government Finance Statistics Yearbook,* and *International Financial Statistics Yearbook.* Subscriptions available to the public. All four publications are available on CD-ROM and on the Web site.

Organisation for Economic Co-operation and Development (OECD), *Washington Center, 2001 L St. N.W., #650 20036-4922; (202) 785-6323. Fax, (202) 785-0350. Kathleen Deboer, Director (Acting).*
General e-mail, washington.contact@oecd.org
Web, www.oecdwash.org

Membership: thirty nations, including Australia, Canada, Japan, Mexico, New Zealand, the United States, and western European nations. Funded by membership contributions. Serves as a forum for members to exchange information and coordinate their economic policies; compiles statistics. Washington Center sells OECD publications and software; maintains a reference library that is open to the public. (Headquarters in Paris.)

United Nations Information Centre, *1775 K St. N.W., #400 20006-1500; (202) 331-8670. Fax, (202) 331-9191. William Davis, Director, (202) 454-2104.*
General e-mail, unicdc@unicwash.org
Web, www.unicwash.org

Lead United Nations (U.N.) office in Washington. Center for reference publications of the United Nations; publications include statistical compilations on international trade and development, national accounts, growth of world industry, and demographic statistics. Library open to the public.

▶JUDICIARY

U.S. Court of Appeals for the Federal Circuit, *717 Madison Pl. N.W. 20439; (202) 633-6550. Fax, (202) 633-9623. Paul R. Michel, Chief Judge; Jan Horbaly, Clerk, (202) 312-5520.*
Web, www.cafe.uscourts.gov

▶NONGOVERNMENTAL

Assn. of Foreign Investors in Real Estate, *1300 Pennsylvania Ave. N.W. 20004-3020; (202) 312-1400. Fax, (202) 312-1401. James A. Fetgatter, Chief Executive.*
General e-mail, afireinfo@afire.org
Web, www.afire.org

Represents foreign institutions that are interested in the laws, regulations, and economic trends affecting the U.S. real estate market. Informs the public and the government of the contributions foreign investment makes to the U.S. economy. Examines current issues and organizes seminars for members.

Assn. of Women in International Trade, *1707 L St. N.W., #570 20036; (202) 293-2948. Fax, (202) 293-0495. Tanya Kemp, President.*

General e-mail, wiidc@wiit.org

Web, www.wiit.org

Membership: women and men from all sectors concerned with international trade, including import-export firms, government, corporations, and nonprofit organizations. Provides members with opportunities for professional development. Maintains job bank and sponsors mentoring program.

Center for Global Development, *1776 Massachusetts Ave. N.W., #301 20036; (202) 416-0700. Fax, (202) 416-0750. Nancy Birdsall, President.*

General e-mail, info@cgdev.org

Web, www.cgdev.org

Works to reduce global poverty and inequality through policy-oriented research and active engagement on development issues with policymakers and the public. Conducts independent research to develop practical ideas for global prosperity.

Center for International Private Enterprise, *1155 15th St. N.W., #700 20005-2706; (202) 721-9200. Fax, (202) 721-9250. Thomas J. Donohue, President; John D. Sullivan, Executive Director.*

General e-mail, cipe@cipe.org

Web, www.cipe.org

Works to strengthen private voluntary business organizations worldwide and to promote participation in the formation of public policy. Cooperates with local, national, regional, and multilateral institutions promoting private enterprise. (Affiliated with the U.S. Chamber of Commerce.)

Coalition for Employment Through Exports, *1100 Connecticut Ave. N.W., #810 20036-4101; (202) 296-6107. Fax, (202) 296-9709. Edmund B. Rice, President.*

General e-mail, info@usaexport.org

Web, www.usaexport.org

Membership: major U.S. exporters and banks. Works to ensure adequate lending authority for the Export-Import Bank and other trade finance facilities as well as aggressive export financing policies for the United States.

Economic Strategy Institute, *3050 K St. N.W., #220 20007; (202) 965-9484. Fax, (202) 965-1104. Clyde V. Prestowitz Jr., President.*

General e-mail, kheidinger@econstrat.org

Web, www.econstrat.org

Works to increase U.S. economic competitiveness through research on domestic and international economic policies, industrial and technological developments, and global security issues. Testifies before Congress and government agencies.

Emergency Committee for American Trade, *900 17th St. N.W., #1150 20006; (202) 659-5147. Fax, (202) 659-1347. Calman J. Cohen, President.*

General e-mail, ecattrade@ecattrade.com

Web, www.ecattrade.com

Membership: U.S. corporations interested in international trade and investment. Supports liberalized trade and investment and opposes restrictions on U.S. exports and imports.

Federation of International Trade Assns., *11654 Plaza America Dr., #120, Reston, VA 20191; (703) 621-1900. Fax, (703) 620-4922. Kimberly Park, Executive Director. Toll-free, (800) 969-FITA.*

General e-mail, info@fita.org

Web, www.fita.org

Membership: local, regional, and national trade associations throughout North America that have an international mission. Works to increase North American exports.

G-7 Council, *888 16th St. N.W., #740 20006; (202) 223-0774. Fax, (202) 861-0790. David Smick, Co-Chair; Manuel Johnson, Co-Chair.*

Membership: international economic policy experts and business leaders, including former G-7 officials. Advocates promoting the international economy over national economies. Promotes cooperation and coordination among the G-7 countries and other industrial nations.

Global Business Dialogue, *1140 Connecticut Ave. N.W., #950 20036; (202) 463-5074. Fax, (202) 463-7075. R.K. Morris, President.*

General e-mail, comments@gbdinc.org

Web, www.gbdinc.org and www.ttalk.biz

Promotes discussion of trade and investment within the global business community.

Institute for Sustainable Communities, *888 17th St. N.W., #610 20006; (202) 777-7575. Fax, (202) 777-7577. Betty Weiss, Director of Community Initiatives.*

General e-mail, isc@iscvt.org

Web, www.iscvt.org

Provides training and technical assistance to communities to engage citizens in developing and implementing plans for a sustainable future.

International Business Ethics Institute, *1776 Eye St. N.W., 9th Floor 20006; (202) 296-6938. Fax, (202) 296-5897. Lori Tansey Martens, President.*

General e-mail, info@business-ethics.org

Web, www.business-ethics.org

Nonpartisan educational organization that promotes business ethics and corporate responsibility. Works to increase public awareness and dialogue about international business ethics issues through various educational resources and activities. Works with companies to assist them in establishing effective international ethics programs.

International Management and Development Institute, *700 12th St. N.W., #800 20005; (202) 879-3371. Fax, (202) 879-3375. Don L. Bonker, President.*

General e-mail, imdimail@aol.com

Web, www.imdi-usa.com

Educational organization that works to improve government-business understanding and international economic and trade cooperation worldwide through policy seminars and research on international economic and trade issues.

National Assn. of Manufacturers (NAM), *International Economic Affairs, 1331 Pennsylvania Ave. N.W., #600 20004; (202) 637-3000. Fax, (202) 637-3182. Franklin J. Vargo, Vice President.*
Web, www.nam.org

Represents manufacturing business interests on international economic issues, including trade, international investment and financial affairs, and multinational corporations.

National Customs Brokers and Forwarders Assn. of America, *1200 18th St. N.W., #901 20036; (202) 466-0222. Fax, (202) 466-0226. Barbara Reilly, Executive Vice President. General e-mail, staff@ncbfaa.org*
Web, www.ncbfaa.org

Membership: customs brokers and freight forwarders in the United States. Fosters information exchange within the industry. Monitors legislation and regulations.

National Foreign Trade Council, *1625 K St. N.W., #200 20006-1604; (202) 887-0278. Fax, (202) 452-8160. William A. Reinsch, President. General e-mail, nftcinformation@nftc.org*
Web, www.nftc.org

Membership: U.S. companies engaged in international trade and investment. Advocates open international trading, export expansion, and policies to assist U.S. companies competing in international markets. Provides members with information on international trade topics. Sponsors seminars and conferences.

Organization for International Investment, *1225 19th St. N.W., #501 20036; (202) 659-1903. Fax, (202) 659-2293. Nancy McLernon, President.*
Web, www.ofii.org

Membership: U.S. subsidiaries of international companies. Provides data on international investment in the United States, including reports on exports, tax revenue, and job creation. Monitors legislation and regulations concerning the business operations of U.S. subsidiaries.

Peterson Institute for International Economics (IIE), *1750 Massachusetts Ave. N.W. 20036; (202) 328-9000. Fax, (202) 328-5432. C. Fred Bergsten, Director.*
Web, www.petersoninstitute.org

Conducts studies and makes policy recommendations on international monetary affairs, trade, investment, energy, exchange rates, commodities, and North-South and East-West economic relations.

United States Council for International Business, *Washington Office, 1400 K St. N.W., #905 20005; (202)*

371-1316. Fax, (202) 371-8249. Timothy Deal, Senior Vice President. General e-mail, info@uscib.org
Web, www.uscib.org

Membership: multinational corporations, service companies, law firms, and business associations. Represents U.S. business positions before intergovernmental bodies, foreign governments, and business communities. Promotes an open system of world trade, finance, and investment. (Headquarters in New York.)

U.S. Chamber of Commerce, *International Division, 1615 H St. N.W. 20062-2000; (202) 463-5460. Fax, (202) 463-3114. Myron Brilliant, Senior Vice President. Alternate fax, (202) 463-3173.*
Web, www.uschamber.com

Provides liaison with network of U.S. chambers of commerce abroad; administers bilateral business councils; responsible for international economic policy development; informs members of developments in international affairs, business economics, and trade; sponsors seminars and conferences.

Washington International Trade Assn., *1300 Pennsylvania Ave. N.W., #350 20004-3014; (202) 312-1600. Fax, (202) 312-1601. James Wilkinson, Executive Director. General e-mail, events@wita.org*
Web, www.wita.org

Membership: trade professionals. Conducts programs and provides neutral forums to discuss international trade issues. Monitors legislation and regulations.

Women Thrive Worldwide, *1825 Connecticut Ave. N.W., #600 20009; (202) 884-8396. Fax, (202) 884 8366. Ritu Sharma, President. General e-mail, thrive@womenthrive.org*
Web, www.womenthrive.org

Advocates international economic policies and human rights that support women worldwide in ending poverty. Researches and develops economic trade policies that reduce poverty, illiteracy, illness, and violence in developing countries.

World Cocoa Foundation, *1411 K St. N.W., #1300 20005; (202) 737-7870. Fax, (202) 737-7832. William Guyton, President. General e-mail, wcf@worldcocoa.org*
Web, www.worldcocoafoundation.org

Promotes a sustainable cocoa economy through economic and social development and environmental conservation in cocoa-growing communities. Helps raise funds for cocoa farmers and increases their access to modern farming practices.

World Shipping Council, *1156 15th St. N.W., #300 20005; (202) 589-1230. Fax, (202) 589-1231. Christopher L. Koch, President.*

General e-mail, info@worldshipping.org

Web, www.worldshipping.org

Membership association representing the liner shipping industry. Works with policymakers and other industry groups interested in international transportation issues, including maritime security, regulatory policy, tax issues, safety, the environment, harbor dredging, and trade infrastructure. Monitors legislation and regulations.

Development Assistance

►AGENCIES

Agency for International Development (USAID), *Economic Growth, Agriculture, and Trade,* 1300 Pennsylvania Ave. N.W., #3.09 20523-3900; (202) 712-0670. Fax, (202) 216-3235. Vacant, Assistant Administrator.

Web, www.usaid.gov

Works to foster increased capability of foreign missions to collaborate with governments, entrepreneurs, and other local institutions and individuals to encourage country-based assistance programs. Divisions focus on economic growth (including business, agriculture, microenterprise development, and institutional reform); the environment and energy use; human capacity development (including education and training); and women in development.

Agency for International Development (USAID), *Education,* 1300 Pennsylvania Ave. N.W., #3.9-37 20523-3901; (202) 712-4273. Fax, (202) 216-3229. Joseph P. Carney, Director.

Web, www.usaid.gov

Provides field support, technical leadership, and research to help foreign missions and countries manage and develop their human resources. Improves the means of basic and higher education as well as training. Administers the AID Participant Training Program, which provides students and midcareer professionals from developing countries with academic and technical training, and the Entrepreneur International Initiative, a short-term training/trade program that matches developing country entrepreneurs with American counterparts to familiarize them with American goods, services, and technology.

Foreign Agricultural Service (FAS), *(Agriculture Dept.),* 1400 Independence Ave. S.W., #5071S, MS 1001 20250-1001; (202) 720-3935. Fax, (202) 690-2159. Vacant, Administrator; Vacant, General Sales Manager. TTY, (202) 720-1786. Public Affairs, (202) 720-3448.

Web, www.fas.usda.gov

Administers the U.S. foreign food aid program with the Agency for International Development. Responsible for Title I of the Food for Peace program, the Food for Progress program, and the Section 416(b) program, which provides developing countries with surplus commodities.

Millennium Challenge Corp., 875 15th St. N.W. 20005; (202) 521-3600. Fax, (202) 521-3700. Rodney Bent, Chief Executive Officer (Acting).

General e-mail, web@mcc.gov

Web, www.mcc.gov

Government corporation that provides financial assistance to developing nations that encourage economic freedom. Funds are used for agricultural development, education, enterprise and private-sector development, governance, health, and building trade capacity. Monitors legislation and regulations.

Peace Corps, 1111 20th St. N.W. 20526; (202) 692-2100. Fax, (202) 692-2101. Jody Olsen, Director (Acting). Information, (800) 424-8580.

Web, www.peacecorps.gov

Promotes world peace and mutual understanding between the United States and developing nations. Administers volunteer programs to assist developing countries in education, the environment, health (particularly HIV awareness and prevention), small business development, agriculture, and urban development.

Treasury Dept., *Development Policy,* 1500 Pennsylvania Ave. N.W., #5417 20220; (202) 622-9124. Fax, (202) 622-0664. John Hurley, Director.

Web, www.treasury.gov

Responsible for multilateral development banks and broader development policy issues.

►INTERNATIONAL ORGANIZATIONS

United Nations Development Programme (UNDP), *Washington Office,* 1775 K St. N.W., #420 20006; (202) 331-9130. Fax, (202) 331-9363. Frederick Tipson, Director.

Web, www.undp.org

Funded by voluntary contributions from national governments. Administers United Nations' support for economic and social development in developing countries, democratic governance, poverty reduction, crisis prevention and recovery, energy and the environment, and HIV/AIDS.

►NONGOVERNMENTAL

Academy for Educational Development (AED), 1825 Connecticut Ave. N.W., #800 20009-5721; (202) 884-8000. Fax, (202) 884-8400. Stephen F. Moseley, President.

General e-mail, communicationsmail@aed.org

Web, www.aed.org

Works in all the major areas of human development to solve critical social problems and improve education, health, and economic opportunities for the least advantaged in 150 developing countries throughout the world.

ACDI/VOCA, 50 F St. N.W., #1075 20001-1530; (202) 683-4661. Fax, (202) 783-7204. Carl Leonard, President. Alternate phone: (202) 383-4961.

General e-mail, webmaster@acdivoca.org

Web, www.acdivoca.org

Recruits professionals for voluntary, short-term technical assistance to cooperatives, environmental groups, and agricultural enterprises, upon request, in developing countries and emerging democracies. (ACDI/VOCA resulted from the 1997 merger of Agricultural Cooperative Development International and Volunteers in Overseas Cooperative Assistance.)

Adventist Development and Relief Agency International, *12501 Old Columbia Pike, Silver Spring, MD 20904; (301) 680-6380. Fax, (301) 680-6370. Charles Sandefur, President. Toll-free, (800) 424-2372.*

Web, www.adra.org

Worldwide humanitarian agency of the Seventh-day Adventist Church. Works to alleviate poverty in developing countries and responds to disasters. Sponsors activities that improve health, foster economic and social well-being, and build self-reliance.

American Jewish World Service, Washington Office, *1001 Connecticut Ave. N.W., #1200 20036-3405; (202) 408-1380. Fax, (202) 379-4310. Vacant, Director.*

Web, www.ajws.org

International development organization that works to alleviate poverty, hunger, and disease. Provides grants to grassroots organizations; offers volunteer services, advocacy, and education for society building, sustainable development, and protection of human rights. Promotes global citizenship within the Jewish community. (Headquarters in New York.)

Ashoka: Innovators for the Public, *1700 N. Moore St., #2000, Arlington, VA 22209; (703) 527-8300. Fax, (703) 527-8383. Diana Wells, President.*

General e-mail, servicecenter@ashoka.org

Web, www.ashoka.org

Supports fellowships for individuals with ideas for social change in sixty developing nations. Provides fellows with research support, organizational networking, legal counseling, economic support, and business consulting. Seeks to educate the public about the developing world and the work of its fellows.

CARE, Washington Office, *1625 K St. N.W., #500 20006-1611; (202) 595-2800. Fax, (202) 296-8695. Helene Gayle, President; JoDee Winterhoff, Vice President, Policy and Advocacy.*

General e-mail, info@care.org

Web, www.care.org

Assists the developing world's poor through emergency assistance and community self-help programs that focus on sustainable development, agriculture, agroforestry, water and sanitation, health, family planning, and income generation. Community-based efforts are centered on providing resources to poor women. (U.S. headquarters in Atlanta, Ga.; international headquarters in Geneva.)

Center for Intercultural Education and Development, *330 Whitehaven St. N.W., #1000 20007 (mailing address: P.O. Box 579400, Georgetown University, Washington, DC 20057-9400); (202) 687-1400. Fax, (202) 687-2555. Chantal Santelices, Director.*

Web, www.georgetown.edu/CIED

Designs and administers programs aimed at improving the quality of life of economically disadvantaged people; provides technical education, job training, leadership skills development, and business management training; runs programs in Central America, the Caribbean, Central Europe, and Southeast Asia.

CHF International, *8601 Georgia Ave., #800, Silver Spring, MD 20910-3440; (301) 587-4700. Fax, (301) 587-7315. Michael E. Doyle, President. Communications, (301) 563-1823.*

General e-mail, mailbox@chfinternational.org

Web, www.chfinternational.org

Works under contract with the Agency for International Development, United Nations, and World Bank to strengthen local government housing departments abroad.

Citizens Development Corps, *1420 K St. N.W., 7th Floor 20005; (202) 872-0933. Fax, (202) 872-0923. Michael Levett, President. Toll-free, (800) 394-1945.*

General e-mail, info@cdc.org

Web, www.cdc.org

Delivers programs and services that foster economic growth and democratic stability in emerging markets and transitional economies worldwide. Develops new jobs and competitive private sectors; promotes regional and global trade and international investments; builds public-private business partnerships. Mobilizes volunteers who provide training, technical assistance, and mentoring to entrepreneurs, organizations and institutions, and local and regional governments.

Development Group for Alternative Policies, *927 15th St. N.W., 4th Floor 20005; (202) 898-1566. Fax, (202) 898-1612. Douglas Hellinger, Executive Director.*

General e-mail, dgap@developmentgap.org

Web, www.developmentgap.org

Works with grassroots organizations in developing countries to promote changes in international economic policies to benefit the poor.

InterAction, *1400 16th St. N.W., #210 20036; (202) 667-8227. Fax, (202) 667-8236. Samuel Worthington, President.*

General e-mail, ia@interaction.org

Web, www.interaction.org

Alliance of U.S.-based international development and humanitarian nongovernmental organizations. Provides a forum for exchange of information on development assistance issues, including food aid and other relief services, migration, and refugee affairs. Monitors legislation and regulations.

International Center for Research on Women, *1120 20th St. N.W., #500N 20036; (202) 797-0007. Fax, (202) 797-0020. Geeta Rao Gupta, President.*
General e-mail, info@icrw.org
Web, www.icrw.org

Advances gender equality and human rights, fights poverty, and promotes sustainable economic and social development through research, publications, and media outreach. Conducts empirical research and promotes practical, evidence-based solutions that enable women to control their own lives and fully participate in their societies.

National Peace Corps Assn., *1900 L St. N.W., #404 20036-5002; (202) 293-7728. Fax, (202) 293-7554. Kevin Quigley, President.*
General e-mail, news@rpcv.org
Web, www.peacecorpsconnect.org

Membership: returned Peace Corps volunteers, staff, and interested individuals. Promotes a global perspective in the United States; seeks to educate the public about the developing world; supports Peace Corps programs; maintains network of returned volunteers.

Partners for Livable Communities, *1429 21st St. N.W., 2nd Floor 20036; (202) 887-5990. Fax, (202) 466-4845. Robert H. McNulty, President.*
Web, www.livable.com

Provides technical assistance, support services, and information to assist communities in creating better living environments. Works in the Caribbean, South America, and Europe on public-private partnerships and resource development to improve living environments. Conducts conferences and workshops; maintains referral clearinghouse.

Salvation Army World Service Office, *615 Slaters Lane, Alexandria, VA 22313; (703) 684-5528. Fax, (703) 684-5536. Lt. Col. Daniel Starrett, Executive Director.*
General e-mail, sawso@usn.salvationarmy.org
Web, www.sawso.org

Works in Russia and the other states of the former Soviet Union, Latin America, the Caribbean, Africa, Asia, and the South Pacific to provide technical assistance in support of local Salvation Army programs of health services (including HIV/AIDS), community development, education, institutional development, microenterprise, and relief and reconstruction assistance. (International headquarters in London.)

United Way International, *701 N. Fairfax St., Alexandria, VA 22314-2045; (703) 519-0092. Fax, (703) 519-0097. Teresa Hall Bartels, President.*
General e-mail, uwi@unitedway.org
Web, www.uwint.org

Membership: independent United Way organizations in countries outside the United States. Provides United Way fundraising campaigns with technical assistance; trains volunteers and professionals; operates an information exchange for affiliated organizations.

Vital Voices Global Partnership, *1625 Massachusetts Ave. N.W., #850 20036; (202) 861-2625. Fax, (202) 296-4142. Susan Davis, Co-Chair; Bobbie Greene McCarthy, Co-Chair; Alyse Nelson Bloom, President.*
General e-mail, info@vitalvoices.org
Web, www.vitalvoices.org

Worldwide organization of volunteers with governmental, corporate, or other leadership expertise that trains and mentors emerging women leaders in Asia, Africa, Eurasia, Latin America, and the Middle East. Seeks to expand women's political participation and representation, increase women's entrepreneurship and business leadership, and combat human rights violations affecting women.

Finance, Monetary Affairs

▶**AGENCIES**

Commerce Dept., *Balance of Payments, 1441 L St. N.W., #BE-58 20230; (202) 606-9545. Fax, (202) 606-5314. Christopher L. Bach, Chief. Press, (202) 606-2649.*
Web, www.bea.gov

Compiles, analyzes, and publishes quarterly U.S. balance-of-payments figures.

Federal Reserve System, *International Finance, 20th and C Sts. N.W., #B1242C 20551-0001; (202) 452-3770. Fax, (202) 452-6424. Nathan Sheets, Director. Press, (202) 452-3799.*
Web, www.federalreserve.gov

Provides the Federal Reserve's board of governors with economic analyses of international developments. Compiles data on exchange rates.

State Dept., *International Finance and Development, 2201 C St. N.W., #4950 20520; (202) 647-9496. Fax, (202) 647-5713. David B. Nelson, Principal Deputy Assistant Secretary.*
Web, www.state.gov

Formulates and implements policies related to multinational investment and insurance; activities of the World Bank and regional banks in the financial development of various countries; bilateral aid; international monetary reform; international antitrust cases; and international debt, banking, and taxation.

State Dept., *Monetary Affairs, 2201 C St. N.W., #4880 20520; (202) 647-9792. Fax, (202) 647-7453. Marlene Sakaue, Director.*
Web, www.state.gov

Monitors global macroeconomic developments and identifies financial trends and potential crises in countries affecting U.S. interests. Formulates debt relief policies and negotiates debt relief agreements.

Treasury Dept., *International Affairs, 1500 Pennsylvania Ave. N.W., #3432 20220; (202) 622-0656.*

Fax, (202) 622-0417. Vacant, Under Secretary. Press, (202) 622-2920.

Web, www.ustreas.gov

Coordinates and implements U.S. international economic and financial policy in cooperation with other government agencies. Works to improve the structure and stabilizing operations of the international monetary and investment system; monitors developments in international gold and foreign exchange operations; coordinates policies and programs of development lending institutions; coordinates Treasury Dept. participation in direct and portfolio investment by foreigners in the United States; studies international monetary, economic, and financial issues; analyzes data on international transactions.

Treasury Dept., *Trade Finance and Investment Negotiations,* 1500 Pennsylvania Ave. N.W., #5419 20220; (202) 622-2120. Fax, (202) 622-0967. Steven F. Tvardek, Director.

Web, www.ustreas.gov

Heads the U.S. delegation to the Participants and Working Party on Export Credits and Credit Guarantees of the Organisation for Economic Cooperation and Development, negotiating agreements to reduce subsidies in export credit support. Negotiates bilateral investment treaties (BITs) and the investment portion of free trade agreements (FTAs) with foreign governments.

►CONGRESS

For a listing of relevant congressional committees and subcommittees, please see page 412 or the Appendix.

►INTERNATIONAL ORGANIZATIONS

International Finance Corp., 2121 Pennsylvania Ave. N.W. 20433 (mailing address: 1818 H St. N.W., HIIK-1111, Washington, DC 20433); (202) 473-1000. Fax, (202) 477-6391. Lars Thunell, Executive Vice President. Press, (202) 473-7660.

Web, www.ifc.org

World Bank affiliate that promotes private enterprise in developing countries through direct investments in projects that establish new businesses or expand, modify, or diversify existing businesses; provides its own financing or recruits financing from other sources. Gives developing countries technical assistance in capital market development, privatization, corporate restructuring, and foreign investment.

International Monetary Fund (IMF), 700 19th St. N.W. 20431; (202) 623-7000. Fax, (202) 623-4661. Meg Lundsager, U.S. Executive Director. Press, (202) 623-7100. Public Affairs, (202) 623-7300.

Web, www.imf.org

International organization of 185 member countries that promotes policies for financial stability and economic growth, works to prevent financial crises, and helps members solve balance-of-payments problems through loans funded by member contributions.

Multilateral Investment Guarantee Agency, 1800 G St. N.W., #U-1200 20433 (mailing address: 1818 H St. N.W., Washington, DC 20433); (202) 473-9809. Fax, (202) 522-2620. Izumi Kobayashi, Executive Vice President. Press, (202) 473-0844.

General e-mail, migaenquiry@worldbank.org

Web, www.miga.org

World Bank affiliate that encourages foreign investment in developing countries. Provides guarantees against losses due to currency transfer, expropriation, war, civil disturbance, and breach of contract. Advises member developing countries on means of improving their attractiveness to foreign investors. Membership open to World Bank member countries.

►NONGOVERNMENTAL

Bankers' Assn. for Finance and Trade, 1120 Connecticut Ave. N.W., 3rd Floor 20036-3902; (202) 663-7575. Fax, (202) 663-5538. Rebecca Morter, Executive Director.

General e-mail, baft@aba.com

Web, www.baft.org

Membership: U.S. commercial banks with major international operations; foreign banks with U.S. operations are affiliated as nonvoting members. Monitors activities that affect the operation of U.S. commercial and international banks and nonfinancial companies.

Bretton Woods Committee, 1726 M St. N.W., #200 20036; (202) 331-1616. Fax, (202) 785-9423. James C. Orr, Executive Director.

General e-mail, info@brettonwoods.org

Web, www.brettonwoods.org

Works to increase public understanding of the World Bank, the regional development institutions, the International Monetary Fund, and the World Trade Organization.

Institute of International Finance, 1333 H St. N.W., #800 20005; (202) 857-3600. Fax, (202) 775-1430. Charles H. Dallara, Managing Director. Press, (202) 331-8183.

General e-mail, info@iif.com

Web, www.iif.com

Membership: financial services companies from over sixty countries. Provides analysis and research on emerging markets. Identifies and analyzes regulatory, financial, and economic policy issues. Promotes the development of sound financial systems with particular emphasis on emerging markets.

Transparency International USA, 1023 15th St. N.W., #300 20005; (202) 589-1616. Fax, (202) 589-1512. Nancy Boswell, President.

General e-mail, administration@transparency-usa.org

Web, www.transparency-usa.org

Seeks to prevent corruption in international transactions. Promotes reform through effective anti-corruption laws and policies. (Headquarters in Berlin.)

REGIONAL AFFAIRS

See also Foreign Embassies, U.S. Ambassadors, and Country Desk Offices (appendix)

Africa

For North Africa, see Near East and South Asia

►AGENCIES

African Development Foundation (ADF), *1400 Eye St. N.W., #1000 20005-2248; (202) 673-3916. Fax, (202) 673-3810. Lloyd Pierson, President. Press, (202) 673-3916, ext. 111.*
General e-mail, info@usadf.gov
Web, www.usadf.gov

Established by Congress to work with and fund organizations and individuals involved in community-based development projects in Africa. Gives preference to projects involving extensive participation by local Africans.

Agency for International Development (USAID), *Africa Bureau, 1300 Pennsylvania Ave. N.W., #4.08C 20523-4801; (202) 712-0500. Fax, (202) 216-3008. Earl Gost, Senior Deputy Assistant Administrator. Press, (202) 712-4300.*
Web, www.usaid.gov/regions/afr

Advises the AID administrator on U.S. policy toward developing countries in Africa.

State Dept., *Bureau of African Affairs, 2201 C St. N.W., #6234A 20520-3430; (202) 647-4440. Fax, (202) 647-6301. Phillip Carter, Assistant Secretary (Acting).*
Web, www.state.gov

Advises the secretary on U.S. policy toward sub-Saharan Africa. Directors, assigned to different regions in Africa, aid the assistant secretary.

State Dept., *Central African Affairs, 2201 C St. N.W., #4244 20520-2902; (202) 647-2080. Fax, (202) 647-1726. Karl Wycoff, Director.*
Web, www.state.gov

Includes Burundi, Cameroon, Central African Republic, Chad, the Democratic Republic of Congo, the Republic of Congo, Equatorial Guinea, Gabon, Rwanda, and Sao Tomé and Principe.

State Dept., *East African Affairs, 2201 C St. N.W., #5238 20520; (202) 647-8852. Fax, (202) 647-0810. James Knight, Director.*
Web, www.state.gov

Includes Comoros, Djibouti, Eritrea, Ethiopia, Kenya, Madagascar, Mauritius, Seychelles, Somalia, Tanzania, and Uganda.

State Dept., *Southern African Affairs, 2201 C St. N.W., #4236 20520; (202) 647-9836. Fax, (202) 647-5007. Maryjo Wills, Director.*
Web, www.state.gov

Includes Angola, Botswana, Lesotho, Malawi, Mozambique, Namibia, South Africa, Swaziland, Zambia, and Zimbabwe.

State Dept., *Sudan Programs Group, 2201 C St. N.W., #5819 20520; (202) 647-4531. Fax, (202) 647-4553. Timothy Shortley, Senior Representative.*
Web, www.state.gov

Represents the U.S. government's interests in Sudan and Darfur/South Sudan.

State Dept., *West African Affairs, 2201 C St. N.W., #4246 20520-3430; (202) 647-3395. Fax, (202) 647-4855. Don Heflin, Director (Acting).*
Web, www.state.gov

Includes Benin, Burkina Faso, Cape Verde, Côte d'Ivoire, the Gambia, Ghana, Guinea, Guinea-Bissau, Liberia, Mali, Mauritania, Niger, Nigeria, Senegal, Sierra Leone, and Togo.

►CONGRESS

For a listing of relevant congressional committees and subcommittees, please see page 412 or the Appendix.

Library of Congress, *African and Middle Eastern Division, 101 Independence Ave. S.E., #LJ220 20540; (202) 707-7937. Fax, (202) 252-3180. Mary Jane Deeb, Chief. Reading room, (202) 707-4188.*
Web, www.loc.gov/rr/amed

Maintains collections of African, Near Eastern, and Hebraic material. Prepares bibliographies and special studies relating to Africa and the Middle East. Reference service and reading rooms available to the public.

►INTERNATIONAL ORGANIZATIONS

International Bank for Reconstruction and Development (World Bank), *Africa, 1818 H St. N.W., #J5093 20433; (202) 458-2858. Fax, (202) 477-0380. Obiageli Ezekwesili, Vice President. Information, (202) 473-9156. Press, (202) 473-3548.*
Web, www.worldbank.org

Works to fight poverty and improve the living standards of low- and middle-income people in the countries of sub-Saharan Africa by providing loans, grants, policy advice, technical assistance, and knowledge-sharing services. Areas of interest include finance, economic development, education, water supply, agriculture, public health, and environmental protection.

►NONGOVERNMENTAL

Africa Faith and Justice Network (AFJN), *125 Michigan Ave. N.E., #481 20017; (202) 884-9780. Fax, (202) 884-9774. Rev. Rocco Puopolo SX, Executive Director. General e-mail, afjn@afjn.org*

Web, www.afjn.org

Advocates with Catholic missionary congregations and Africa-focused coalitions for U.S. economic and political policies that benefit Africa. Promotes the Catholic view of peace building, human rights, and social justice. Interests include ending armed conflict, equitable trade with and investment in Africa, and sustainable development.

Africare, *440 R St. N.W. 20001-1935; (202) 462-3614. Fax, (202) 464-0867. Julius E. Coles, President. Web, www.africare.org*

Seeks to improve the quality of life in rural Africa through development of water resources, increased food production, and delivery of health services.

TransAfrica/TransAfrica Forum, *1629 K St. N.W., #1100 20006; (202) 223-1960. Fax, (202) 223-1966. Nicole Lee, Executive Director. Library, (202) 223-1960, ext. 137. General e-mail, info@transafricaforum.org*

Web, www.transafricaforum.org

Focuses on U.S. foreign policy toward African nations, the Caribbean, Latin America, and peoples of African descent. Provides members with information on foreign policy issues. The Arthur R. Ashe Foreign Policy Library is open to the public by appointment.

United States Holocaust Memorial Museum, *Genocide Prevention Mapping Initiative, 100 Raoul Wallenberg Pl. S.W. 20024-2126; (202) 488-6133. Press fax, (202) 488-2695. General e-mail, jhefferman@ushmm.org*

Web, www.ushmm.org/maps

Seeks to collect and visually present critical information on emerging crises that may lead to genocide or related crimes against humanity. Projects include "Crisis in Darfur" in Google Earth, field-based research in at-risk countries presented through the "World Is Witness" Web site, and development of an interactive "global crisis map" to help citizens, aid workers, and foreign policy professionals to determine effective prevention and response strategies.

East Asia and the Pacific

►AGENCIES

Agency for International Development (USAID), *Asia and Near East Bureau, 1300 Pennsylvania Ave. N.W., #4.09-034 20523-4900; (202) 712-0200. Fax, (202) 216-3386. Vacant, Assistant Administrator. Web, www.usaid.gov/regions/ane*

Advises the AID administrator on U.S. economic development policy in Asia and the Near East.

Defense Dept. (DoD), *Asian and Pacific Security Affairs, The Pentagon, #5D688 20301-2400; (703) 695-4175. Fax, (703) 614-7626. Derek J. Mitchell, Deputy Under Secretary. Press, (703) 695-3895. Web, www.defenselink.mil*

Advises the assistant secretary for international security affairs on matters dealing with Asia and the Pacific.

Japan–United States Friendship Commission, *1201 15th St. N.W., #330 20005-2842; (202) 653-9800. Fax, (202) 653-9802. Eric J. Gangloff, Executive Director. General e-mail, jusfc@jusfc.gov*

Web, www.jusfc.gov

Independent agency established by Congress that makes grants and administers funds and programs promoting educational and cultural exchanges between Japan and the United States.

State Dept., *Bureau of East Asian and Pacific Affairs, 2201 C St. N.W., #6205 20520-6205; (202) 647-6600. Fax, (202) 647-7350. Vacant, Assistant Secretary. Press, (202) 647-2538. Web, www.state.gov/p/eap*

Advises the secretary on U.S. policy toward East Asian and Pacific countries. Directors assigned to specific countries within the bureau aid the assistant secretary.

State Dept., *Australia, New Zealand, and Pacific Island Affairs, 2201 C St. N.W., #4312 20520; (202) 736-4741. Fax, (202) 647-0118. Alcy Frelick, Director. Web, www.state.gov*

State Dept., *Chinese and Mongolian Affairs, 2201 C St. N.W., #4318 20520; (202) 647-6803. Fax, (202) 647-6820. David Shear, Director. Press, (202) 647-2538. Web, www.state.gov*

State Dept., *Japanese Affairs, 2201 C St. N.W., #4206 20520; (202) 647-2913. Fax, (202) 647-4402. Karen Kelley, Director (Acting). Web, www.state.gov*

State Dept., *Korean Affairs, 2201 C St. N.W., #4206 20520; (202) 647-7700. Fax, (202) 647-7388. Kurt Tong, Director. Web, www.state.gov*

State Dept., *Mainland Southeast Asia Affairs, 2201 C St. N.W., #5206 20520-6310; (202) 647-3132. Fax, (202) 647-3069. Stephen Blake, Director. Web, www.state.gov*

Handles issues related to Americans missing in action in Indochina; serves as liaison with Congress, international organizations, and foreign governments on developments in these countries. Includes Thailand, Cambodia, Laos, Vietnam, and Burma.

State Dept., *Maritime Southeast Asia Affairs,* *2201 C St. N.W., #5210 20520; (202) 647-3276. Fax, (202) 736-4559. Karmala Lakhdir, Director.*
Web, www.state.gov

Includes the Philippines, Malaysia, Brunei, Indonesia, East Timor, and Singapore.

State Dept., *Taiwan Coordination,* *2201 C St. N.W., #4312 20520; (202) 647-7711. Fax, (202) 647-0076. Ted Mann, Director.*
Web, www.state.gov

U.S.-China Economic and Security Review Commission, *444 N. Capitol St. N.W., #602, Hall of the States 20001; (202) 624-1407. Fax, (202) 624-1406. T. Scott Bunton, Executive Director.*
General e-mail, contact@uscc.gov
Web, www.uscc.gov

Investigates the national security implications of the bilateral trade and economic relationship between China and the United States. Makes recommendations to Congress based on its findings.

▶CONGRESS

For a listing of relevant congressional committees and subcommittees, please see page 412 or the Appendix.

Library of Congress, *Asian Division,* *101 Independence Ave. S.E., #LJ149 20540; (202) 707-5240. Fax, (202) 252-3336. Hwa-Wei Lee, Chief. Reading Room, (202) 707-5426.*
Web, www.loc.gov/rr/asian

Maintains collections of Chinese, Korean, Japanese, Southeast Asian, and South Asian material. Reference service is provided in the Asian Reading Room.

▶INTERNATIONAL ORGANIZATIONS

International Bank for Reconstruction and Development (World Bank), *East Asia and Pacific, 1818 H St. N.W., MC 9-910 20433; (202) 458-0127. Fax, (202) 477-0169. James W. Adams, Vice President. Press, (202) 458-5964.*
Web, www.worldbank.org

Works to fight poverty and improve the living standards of low- and middle-income people in the countries of East Asia and the Pacific by providing loans, policy advice, technical assistance, and knowledge-sharing services. Areas of interest include finance, economic development, education, water supply, agriculture, public health, and environmental protection.

▶NONGOVERNMENTAL

American Institute in Taiwan, *1700 N. Moore St., #1700, Arlington, VA 22209-1385; (703) 525-8474. Fax,*
(703) 841-1385. Barbara Schrage, Managing Director; Raymond Burghardt, Chair.
Web, www.ait.org.tw

Chartered by Congress to coordinate commercial, cultural, and other activities between the people of the United States and Taiwan. Represents U.S. interests and maintains offices in Taiwan.

Asia Foundation, *Washington Office,* *1779 Massachusetts Ave. N.W., #815 20036; (202) 588-9420. Fax, (202) 588-9409. Nancy Yuan, Vice President.*
General e-mail, info@asiafound-dc.org
Web, www.asiafoundation.org

Provides grants and technical assistance in Asia and the Pacific islands (excluding the Middle East). Seeks to strengthen legislatures, legal and judicial systems, market economies, the media, and nongovernmental organizations. (Headquarters in San Francisco, Calif.)

Asia Policy Point (APP), *1730 Rhode Island Ave. N.W., #414 20036; (202) 822-6040. Fax, (202) 822-6044. Mindy Kotler, Director.*
General e-mail, access@jiaponline.org
Web, www.jiaponline.org

Studies Japanese and Northeast Asian security and public policies as they relate to the United States. Researches and analyzes issues affecting Japan's relationship with the West. (Formerly the Japan Information Access Project.)

Asia Society Washington Center, *1575 Eye St. N.W., #325 20005; (202) 833-2742. Fax, (202) 833-0189. Jack Garrity, Director.*
General e-mail, dcinfo@asiasoc.org
Web, www.asiasociety.org/dc

Membership: individuals, organizations, and corporations interested in Asia and the Pacific (excluding the Middle East). Sponsors seminars and lectures on political, economic, and cultural issues. (Headquarters in New York.)

East-West Center Washington, *1819 L St. N.W., #200 20036; (202) 327-9752. Fax, (202) 293-1402. Satu Limaye, Director.*
General e-mail, washington@eastwestcenter.org
Web, www.eastwestcenter.org

Promotes strengthening of relations and understanding among countries and peoples of Asia, the Pacific, and the United States. Plans to undertake substantive programming activities, including collaborative research, training, seminars, and outreach; publications; and congressional study groups. (Headquarters in Honolulu.)

Heritage Foundation, *Asian Studies Center,* *214 Massachusetts Ave. N.E. 20002-4999; (202) 608-6140. Fax, (202) 675-1779. Walter Lohman, Director. Press, (202) 608-6153.*
Web, www.heritage.org

Conducts research and provides information on U.S. policies in Asia and the Pacific. Interests include economic and security issues in the Asia Pacific region. Hosts speakers and visiting foreign policy delegations; sponsors conferences.

Japan-America Society of Washington, *1819 L St. N.W., 1B Level 20036-3807; (202) 833-2210. Fax, (202) 833-2456. Amb. John R. Malott, President.*
General e-mail, jaswdc@us-japan.org

Web, www.us-japan.org/dc

Conducts programs on U.S.-Japan trade, politics, and economic issues. Cultural programs include lectures, films, a Japanese-language school, and assistance to Japanese performing artists. Maintains library for members. Sponsors National Cherry Blossom Festival.

Japan Productivity Center for Socio-Economic Development, *Washington Office, 910 17th St. N.W., #1025 20006-4926; (202) 833-1404. Fax, (202) 833-1406. Kazuteru Kuroda, Director.*
General e-mail, kuroda@jpc-sed.org

Web, www.jpc-sed.org

Promotes education and exchange of information between Japanese and American businesspeople by coordinating overseas meetings and visits for participating countries. (Headquarters in Tokyo.)

National Congress of Vietnamese Americans, *6433 Northarena Dr., Springfield, VA 22150; (703) 971-9178. Fax, (703) 719-5764. Nguyen Nguc Bich, President. Toll-free, (877) 592-4140.*
General e-mail, info@ncvaonline.org

Web, www.ncvaonline.org

Advances the cause of Vietnamese Americans by encouraging them to actively participate in their communities as civic-minded citizens engaged in education, culture, and civic liberties.

Taipei Economic and Cultural Representative Office (TECRO), *4201 Wisconsin Ave. N.W. 20016; (202) 895-1800. Fax, (202) 966-0825. Amb. Jason Yuan, Representative. Press, (202) 895-1850.*
General e-mail, tecroinfodc@tecro-inf.org

Web, www.taiwanembassy.org/US/mp.asp?mp=12

Represents political, economic, and cultural interests of the government of the Republic of China (Taiwan) in the United States.

United States Asia Pacific Council, *1819 L St. N.W., #200 20036; (202) 327-9752. Fax, (202) 293-1402. Mark Borthwick, Executive Director.*
General e-mail, info@usapc.org

Web, www.eastwestcenter.org

Membership: U.S. corporations and representatives from business, government, education, research, and journalism interested in the advancement of the U.S. relationship with Asian and Pacific nations. Works on practical government and business policy issues to increase trade, investment, and economic development in the region. (Formerly the Pacific Economic Cooperation Council. Affiliated with East-West Center.)

U.S.-Asia Institute, *232 E. Capitol St. N.E. 20003; (202) 747-5889. Fax, (202) 543-1748. Ben Wu, President.*
General e-mail, usasiainstitute@verizon.net

Web, www.usasiainstitute.org

Organization of individuals interested in Asia. Encourages communication among political and business leaders in the United States and Asia. Interests include foreign policy, international trade, Asian and American cultures, education, and employment. Conducts research and sponsors conferences and workshops in cooperation with the State Dept. to promote greater understanding between the United States and Asian nations. Conducts programs that take congressional staff members to Japan, China, and other Asian nations.

U.S.-China Business Council, *1818 N St. N.W., #200 20036-2470; (202) 429-0340. Fax, (202) 775-2476. John Frisbie, President.*
General e-mail, info@uschina.org

Web, www.uschina.org

Member-supported organization that represents U.S. companies engaged in business relations with the People's Republic of China. Participates in U.S. policy issues relating to China and other international trade. Publishes research reports. (Maintains offices in Beijing and Shanghai.)

Europe

(Includes the Baltic states)

►**AGENCIES**

Agency for International Development (USAID), Europe and Eurasia Bureau, *1300 Pennsylvania Ave. N.W., #5.06 20523-5600; (202) 712-0290. Fax, (202) 216-3057. Ken Yamashita, Assistant Administrator (Acting).*
Web, www.usaid.gov/regions/europe_eurasia

Advises the AID administrator on U.S. economic development policy in Europe and Eurasia.

Defense Dept. (DOD), European and NATO Policy, *The Pentagon, #5B652 20301-2900; (703) 695-5553. Fax, (703) 571-9637. Mary Warlick, Deputy Assistant Secretary (Acting).*
Web, www.defenselink.mil

Advises the assistant secretary for international security affairs on matters dealing with Europe and NATO.

International Trade Administration (ITA), *(Commerce Dept.), Trade Information Center, RRB-TIC, 14th St. and Constitution Ave. N.W. 20230; (202) 482-0543. Fax, (202) 482-4473. Susan Lusi, Director. Information, (800) 872-8723.*
General e-mail, tic@mail.doc.gov

Web, www.export.gov

Provides information on trade and investment in central and eastern Europe. Disseminates information on potential trade partners, regulations and incentives, and trade promotion; encourages private enterprise in the region.

State Dept., *Bureau of European and Eurasian Affairs, 2201 C St. N.W., #6228 20520; (202) 647-9626. Fax, (202) 647-5575. Daniel Fata, Assistant Secretary. Information, (202) 647-6925.*
Web, www.state.gov

Advises the secretary on U.S. policy toward European and Eurasian countries. Directors assigned to specific countries within the bureau aid the assistant secretary.

State Dept., *Central European Affairs, 2201 C St. N.W., #4228 20520; (202) 647-1484. Fax, (202) 647-5117. Claire Pierangelo, Director.*
Web, www.state.gov

Includes Austria, Bulgaria, Czech Republic, Germany, Hungary, Liechtenstein, Poland, Romania, Slovak Republic, Slovenia, and Switzerland.

State Dept., *European Security and Political Affairs, 2201 C St. N.W., #6511 20520; (202) 647-1626. Fax, (202) 647-1369. Bruce Turner, Director.*
Web, www.state.gov

Coordinates and advises, with the Defense Dept. and other agencies, the U.S. mission to NATO and the U.S. delegation to the Organization for Security and Co-operation in Europe regarding political, military, and arms control matters.

State Dept., *European Union and Regional Affairs, 2201 C St. N.W., #5424 20520; (202) 647-3932. Fax, (202) 647-9959. William Lucas, Director.*
Web, www.state.gov

Handles all matters concerning the European Union, the Council of Europe, and the Organisation for Economic Co-operation and Development, with emphasis on trade issues. Monitors export controls and economic activities for the North Atlantic Treaty Organization and the Organization for Security and Co-operation in Europe.

State Dept., *Nordic and Baltic Affairs, 2201 C St. N.W., #5428 20520; (202) 647-5669. Fax, (202) 736-4170. Robert Gilchrist, Director.*
Web, www.state.gov

Includes Denmark, Estonia, Finland, Iceland, Latvia, Lithuania, Norway, and Sweden.

State Dept., *South Central European Affairs, 2201 C St. N.W., #5227 20520; (202) 647-0608. Fax, (202) 647-1838. Jason Hyland, Director.*
Web, www.state.gov

Includes Albania, Bosnia-Herzegovina, Croatia, Kosovo, Macedonia, and Serbia and Montenegro.

State Dept., *Southern European Affairs, 2201 C St. N.W., #5511 20520; (202) 647-6112. Fax, (202) 647-5087. Kathleen Fitzpatrick, Director.*
Web, www.state.gov

Includes Cyprus, Greece, and Turkey.

State Dept., *Western European Affairs, 2201 C St. N.W., #5218 20520; (202) 647-3072. Fax, (202) 647-3459. Pamela Spratlen, Director.*
Web, www.state.gov

Includes Andorra, Belgium, Bermuda, France, Ireland, Italy, Luxembourg, Malta, Monaco, the Netherlands, Portugal, Réunion, San Marino, Spain, the United Kingdom, and the Vatican.

►CONGRESS

For a listing of relevant congressional committees and subcommittees, please see page 412 or the Appendix.

Library of Congress, *European Division, 101 Independence Ave. S.E., #LJ-250 20540; (202) 707-5414. Fax, (202) 707-8482. Georgette M. Dorn, Chief (Acting). Reference desk, (202) 707-4515.*
Web, www.loc.gov/rr/european

Provides reference service on the library's European collections (except collections on Spain, Portugal, and the British Isles). Prepares bibliographies and special studies relating to European countries, including Russia and the other states of the former Soviet Union and eastern bloc. Maintains current unbound Slavic language periodicals and newspapers, which are available at the European Reference Desk.

►INTERNATIONAL ORGANIZATIONS

European Commission, *Press and Public Diplomacy, Washington Office, 2300 M St. N.W. 20037-1400; (202) 862-9500. Fax, (202) 429-1766. Anthony Smallwood, Head; John Bruton, Ambassador.*
General e-mail, relex-delusw-help@ec.europa.eu

Web, www.eurunion.org

Information and public affairs office in the United States for the European Union, which includes the European Economic Community, the European Coal and Steel Community, and the European Atomic Energy Community. Provides social policy data on the European Union and provides statistics and documents on member countries, including those related to energy, economics, development and cooperation, commerce, agriculture, industry, and technology. Library open to the public by appointment. (Headquarters in Brussels.)

International Bank for Reconstruction and Development (World Bank), *Europe and Central Asia,* 600 19th St. N.W. 20431 (mailing address: 1818 H St. N.W., MS H121202, Washington, DC 20433); (202) 458-8154. Fax, (202) 522-2758. Shigeo Katsu, Vice President.
General e-mail, ecainformation@worldbank.org

Web, www.worldbank.org

Works to fight poverty and improve the living standards of low- and middle-income people in the countries of eastern Europe by providing loans, policy advice, technical assistance, and knowledge-sharing services. Areas of interest include finance, economic development, education, water supply, agriculture, public health, and environmental protection.

▶**NONGOVERNMENTAL**

American Bar Assn. (ABA), *Rule of Law Initiative,* 740 15th St. N.W., 8th Floor 20005-1022; (202) 662-1950. Fax, (202) 662-1597. Rob Boone, Program Director.
General e-mail, ROFL@staff.abanet.org

Web, www.abanet.org/rol

Promotes the rule of law and specific legal reforms in the emerging democracies of central and eastern Europe, Russia, and the other states of the former Soviet Union; recruits volunteer legal professionals from the United States and western Europe. Interests include civil, criminal, commercial, and environmental law; judicial restructuring; bar development; and legal education and research.

American Hellenic Institute, 1220 16th St. N.W. 20036-3202; (202) 785-8430. Fax, (202) 785-5178. Nick Larigakis, Executive Director.
General e-mail, info@ahiworld.org

Web, www.ahiworld.org

Works to strengthen relations between Greece and Cyprus and the United States and within the American Hellenic community.

British-American Business Assn., P.O. Box 16482 20041; (202) 293-0010. Fax, (202) 296-3332. Michael Ferguson, President.
General e-mail, info@babawashington.org

Web, www.babawashington.org

Organization dedicated to the development of business relations between the United Kingdom and the United States.

British American Security Information Council (BASIC), 110 Maryland Ave. N.E., #205 20002-5620; (202) 546-8055. Fax, (202) 546-8056. Paul Ingram, Executive Director.
General e-mail, basicus@basicint.org

Web, www.basicint.org

Independent analysis and advocacy organization that researches global security issues, including nuclear policies, military strategies, armaments, and disarmament. Assists in the development of global security policies, promotes public awareness, and facilitates exchange of information on both sides of the Atlantic.

European-American Business Council, 919 18th St. N.W., #220 20006; (202) 828-9104. Fax, (202) 828-9106. Michael Maibach, President.
General e-mail, eabc@eabc.org

Web, www.eabc.org

Membership: American companies with operations in Europe and European companies with operations in the United States. Works for free and fair trade and investment between the United States and the European Union.

European Institute, 1001 Connecticut Ave. N.W., #220 20036; (202) 895-1670. Fax, (202) 362-1088. Joelle Attinger, President.
General e-mail, info@europeaninstitute.org

Web, www.europeaninstitute.org

Membership: governments and multinational corporations. Provides an independent forum for business leaders, government officials, journalists, academics, and policy experts. Organizes seminars and conferences. Interests include international finance, economics, energy, telecommunications, defense and procurement policies, the integration of central Europe into the European Union and NATO, and relations with Asia and Latin America.

German American Business Council, 2000 M St. N.W., #335 20036; (202) 955-5595. Fax, (202) 955-5597. Ulrich Gamerdinger, Executive Director.
General e-mail, info@gabcwashington.com

Web, http://gabcwashington.com

Promotes closer ties between Germany and the United States through improved communication between embassies, industry, governments, and academia.

German Marshall Fund of the United States, 1744 R St. N.W. 20009; (202) 745-3950. Fax, (202) 265-1662. Craig Kennedy, President.
General e-mail, info@gmfus.org

Web, www.gmfus.org

American institution created by a gift from Germany as a permanent memorial to Marshall Plan aid. Seeks to stimulate exchange of ideas and promote cooperation between the United States and Europe. Awards grants to promote the study of international and domestic policies; supports comparative research and debate on key issues.

Irish National Caucus, P.O. Box 15128 20003-0849; (202) 544-0568. Fax, (202) 488-7537. Sean McManus, President.
General e-mail, sean@irishnationalcaucus.org

Web, www.irishnationalcaucus.org

Educational organization concerned with protecting human rights in Northern Ireland. Seeks to end anti-Catholic discrimination in Northern Ireland through implementation of the McBride Principles, initiated in 1984. Advocates nonviolence and supports the peace process in Northern Ireland. Monitors legislation and regulations.

Joint Baltic American National Committee, *400 Hurley Ave., Rockville, MD 20850; (301) 340-1954. Fax, (301) 309-1406. Karl Altau, Managing Director.*
General e-mail, jbanc@jbanc.org

Web, www.jbanc.org

Washington representative of the Estonian, Latvian, and Lithuanian American communities in the United States; acts as a representative on issues affecting the Baltic states.

National Federation of Croatian Americans, *2401 Research Blvd., #115, Rockville, MD 20850; (301) 208-6650. Fax, (301) 208-6659. Edward Andrus, President.*
General e-mail, nfcahdq@verizon.net

Web, www.nfcaonline.com

Membership: Croatian American organizations. Promotes independence, democracy, business and economic development, human rights, and a free-market economy in Croatia and Bosnia-Herzegovina. Supports equal rights in these countries regardless of ethnicity or religious beliefs.

Latin America, Canada, and the Caribbean

▶AGENCIES

Agency for International Development (USAID), *Latin America and the Caribbean Bureau, 1300 Pennsylvania Ave. N.W., #5.09 20523-5900; (202) 712-4800. Fax, (202) 216-3012. Deborah Kennedy, Assistant Administrator (Acting). Press, (202) 712-4793.*
Web, www.usaid.gov/regions/lac

Advises the AID administrator on U.S. policy toward developing Latin American and Caribbean countries. Designs and implements assistance programs for developing nations.

Defense Dept. (DoD), *Western Hemisphere Policy, 2400 Defense Pentagon, #5D435 20301-2400; (703) 614-0446. Fax, (703) 697-4945. Frank Mora, Deputy Assistant Secretary.*
Web, www.defenselink.mil

Advises the assistant secretary for international security affairs on inter-American matters; aids in the development of U.S. policy toward Latin America.

Inter-American Foundation, *901 N. Stuart St., 10th Floor, Arlington, VA 22203; (703) 306-4301. Fax, (703) 306-4365. Larry Palmer, President.*

General e-mail, info@iaf.gov

Web, www.iaf.gov

Supports small-scale Latin American and Caribbean social and economic development efforts through grass-roots development programs, grants, and fellowships.

International Trade Administration (ITA), *(Commerce Dept.), NAFTA and North and Central America and the Caribbean (ONCAC), 14th St. and Constitution Ave. N.W., #3024 20230; (202) 482-0393. Fax, (202) 482-5865. Geri Word, Director.*
Web, www.ita.doc.gov

Coordinates Commerce Dept. activities regarding NAFTA (North American Free Trade Agreement), FTAA (Free Trade Areas of the Americas), and other Western Hemisphere free trade agreements.

State Dept., *Andean Affairs, 2201 C St. N.W., #4915 20520; (202) 647-1715. Fax, (202) 647-2628. Kevin Whitaker, Director.*
Web, www.state.gov

Includes Bolivia, Colombia, Ecuador, Peru, and Venezuela.

State Dept., *Brazilian, Southern Cone Affairs, 2201 C St. N.W., #4258 20520; (202) 647-2407. Fax, (202) 736-7825. Milton Drucker, Director.*
Web, www.state.gov

Includes Argentina, Brazil, Chile, Paraguay, and Uruguay.

State Dept., *Bureau of Western Hemisphere Affairs, 2201 C St. N.W., #6262 20520; (202) 647-5780. Fax, (202) 647-0834. Thomas A. Shannon, Assistant Secretary. Press, (202) 647-4252.*
Web, www.state.gov

Advises the secretary on U.S. policy toward Canada, Latin America, and the Caribbean. Directors assigned to specific regions within the bureau aid the assistant secretary.

State Dept., *Canadian Affairs, 2201 C St. N.W., #3030 20520; (202) 647-2170. Fax, (202) 647-4088. Edwin Nolan, Director.*
Web, www.state.gov

State Dept., *Caribbean Affairs, 2201 C St. N.W., #4262 20520-6258; (202) 647-5088. Fax, (202) 647-2901. Velia de Pirro, Director.*
Web, www.state.gov

Includes Anguilla, Antigua and Barbuda, Aruba, Bahamas, Barbados, British Virgin Islands, Cayman Islands, Dominica, Dominican Republic, Grenada, Guyana, Haiti, Jamaica, Martinique, Montserrat, Netherlands Antilles, St. Kitts and Nevis, St. Lucia, St. Vincent and the Grenadines, Suriname, Trinidad and Tobago, and Turks and Caicos Islands.

State Dept., *Central American Affairs,* *2201 C St. N.W.,*
#5906 20520; (202) 647-4087. Fax, (202) 647-2597.
Christopher Webster, Director.
Web, www.state.gov

Includes Belize, Costa Rica, El Salvador, Guatemala,
Honduras, Nicaragua, and Panama.

State Dept., *Cuban Affairs,* *2201 C St. N.W., #3234*
20520; (202) 647-9272. Fax, (202) 647-7095. Bisa
Williams, Coordinator.
Web, www.state.gov

State Dept., *Mexican Affairs,* *2201 C St. N.W., #3909*
20520-6258; (202) 647-9894. Fax, (202) 647-5752. Daniel
Darrach, Border Coordinator.
Web, www.state.gov

Acts as liaison between the United States and Mexico
in international boundary and water matters as defined by
binational treaties and agreements. Also involved with
border health and environmental issues, new border crossings, and significant modifications to existing crossings.

State Dept., *U.S. Mission to the Organization of*
American States, *2201 C St. N.W., #5914 20520-6258;*
(202) 647-9376. Fax, (202) 647-0911. Hector E. Morales
Jr., U.S. Permanent Representative.
Web, www.state.gov

Formulates U.S. policy and represents U.S. interests at
the Organization of American States (OAS).

►CONGRESS

For a listing of relevant congressional committees and
subcommittees, please see page 412 or the Appendix.

Library of Congress, *Hispanic Division,* *101*
Independence Ave. S.E., #LJ-205 20540; (202) 707-5400.
Fax, (202) 707-2005. Georgette M. Dorn, Chief. Reference
staff and reading room, (202) 707-5397.
Web, www.loc.gov/rr/hispanic

Orients researchers and scholars in the area of
Iberian, Latin American, Caribbean, and U.S. Latino
studies. Primary and secondary source materials are
available in the library's general collections for the study
of all periods, from pre-Columbian to the present,
including recordings of 640 authors reading their own
material. All major subject areas are represented with
emphasis on history, literature, and the social sciences;
the "Archive of Hispanic Literature on Tape" is available
in the reading room.

►INTERNATIONAL ORGANIZATIONS

Inter-American Development Bank, *1300 New York*
Ave. N.W. 20577; (202) 623-1000. Fax, (202) 623-3096.
Luis Alberto Morena, President; Miguel San Juan, U.S.
Executive Director. Information, (202) 623-1000. Library,
(202) 623-3211. Press, (202) 623-1371.
Web, www.iadb.org

Promotes, through loans and technical assistance, the
investment of public and private capital in member countries of Latin America and the Caribbean for social and
economic development purposes. Facilitates economic
integration of the Latin American region. Library open to
the public by appointment.

International Bank for Reconstruction and
Development (World Bank), *Latin America and the*
Caribbean, *1850 Eye St. N.W. 20433 (mailing address:*
1818 H St. N.W., MS I8-800, Washington, DC 20433);
(202) 473-0897. Fax, (202) 676-9271. Pamela Cox, Vice
President.
Web, www.worldbank.org

Works to fight poverty and improve the living standards of poor and middle-income people in the countries
of Latin America and the Caribbean by providing loans,
policy advice, technical assistance, and knowledge-sharing
services. Areas of interest include finance, economic
development, education, water supply, agriculture, public
health, and environmental protection.

Organization of American States (OAS), *17th St. and*
Constitution Ave. N.W. 20006 (mailing address: 1889 F St.
N.W., Washington, DC 20006); (202) 458-3000. Fax,
(202) 458-3967. José Miguel Insulza, Secretary General.
Library, (202) 458-6041.
Web, www.oas.org

Membership: the United States, Canada, and all
independent Latin American and Caribbean countries.
Funded by quotas paid by member states and by contributions to special multilateral funds. Works to promote
democracy, eliminate poverty, and resolve disputes among
member nations. Provides member states with technical
and advisory services in cultural, educational, scientific,
social, and economic areas. Library open to the public.

United Nations Economic Commission for Latin
America and the Caribbean, *Washington Office,* *1825*
K St. N.W., #1120 20006-1210; (202) 955-5613. Fax, (202)
296-0826. Inés Bustillo, Director.
General e-mail, info@eclac.org
Web, www.eclac.org

Membership: Latin American, Caribbean, and some
industrially developed Western nations. Seeks to
strengthen economic relations between countries both
within and outside Latin America through research and
analysis of socioeconomic problems, training programs,
and advisory services to member governments. (Headquarters in Santiago, Chile.)

► NONGOVERNMENTAL

Caribbean-Central American Action, *1818 N St. N.W.,*
#310 20036-2473; (202) 466-7464. Fax, (202) 822-0075.
Anton Edmunds, Executive Director. Press, (202)
466-7464, ext. 24.
General e-mail, info@c-caa.org
Web, www.c-caa.org

Promotes trade and investment in Caribbean Basin countries; encourages democratic public policy in member countries and works to strengthen private initiatives.

Center for International Policy, *1717 Massachusetts Ave. N.W., #801 20036-2001; (202) 232-3317. Fax, (202) 232-3440. William Goodfellow, Executive Director. General e-mail, cip@ciponline.org*

Web, www.ciponline.org

Research and educational organization concerned with peace and security worldwide. Special interests include military spending, U.S. intelligence policy, and U.S. policy toward Asia, Colombia, and Cuba. Publishes the *International Policy Report.*

Council of the Americas, Americas Society, *Washington Office, 1615 L St. N.W., #250 20036; (202) 659-8989. Fax, (202) 659-7755. Eric Farnsworth, Vice President. Web, www.counciloftheamericas.org*

Membership: businesses with interests and investments in Latin America. Seeks to expand the role of private enterprise in development of the region. (Headquarters in New York.)

Guatemala Human Rights Commission/USA, *3321 12th St. N.E. 20017-4008; (202) 529-6599. Fax, (202) 526-4611. Amanda Martin, Director. General e-mail, ghrc-usa@ghrc-usa.org*

Web, www.ghrc-usa.org

Provides information and collects and makes available reports on human rights violations in Guatemala; publishes a quarterly report of documented cases of specific abuses. Takes on special projects and leads delegations to further sensitize the public and the international community to human rights abuses in Guatemala.

Council on Hemispheric Affairs, *1250 Connecticut Ave. N.W., #1C 20036; (202) 223-4975. Fax, (202) 223-4979. Larry R. Birns, Director. General e-mail, coha@coha.org*

Web, www.coha.org

Seeks to expand interest in inter-American relations and increase press coverage of Latin America and Canada. Monitors U.S., Latin American, and Canadian relations, with emphasis on human rights, trade, growth of democratic institutions, freedom of the press, and hemispheric economic and political developments; provides educational materials and analyzes issues. Issues annual survey on human rights and freedom of the press.

Inter-American Dialogue, *1211 Connecticut Ave. N.W., #510 20036-2701; (202) 822-9002. Fax, (202) 822-9553. Peter Hakim, President. General e-mail, meetings@thedialogue.org*

Web, www.thedialogue.org

Serves as a forum for communication and exchange among leaders of the Americas. Provides analyses and policy recommendations on issues of hemispheric concern. Interests include economic integration, trade, and the strengthening of democracy in Latin America. Hosts private and public exchanges; sponsors conferences and seminars; publishes daily newsletter, *Latin America Advisor.*

Latin America Working Group, *424 C St. N.E. 20002; (202) 546-7010. Fax, (202) 543-7647. Lisa Haugaard, Executive Director. General e-mail, lawg@lawg.org*

Web, www.lawg.org

Represents more than sixty organizations concerned with Latin America. Encourages U.S. policies toward Latin America that promote human rights, justice, peace, and sustainable development.

Pan American Development Foundation, *1889 F St. N.W., 2nd Floor 20006; (202) 458-3969. Fax, (202) 458-6316. John Sanbrailo, Executive Director. General e-mail, padf-dc@padf.org*

Web, www.padf.org

Works with the public and private sectors to improve the quality of life throughout the Caribbean and Latin America. Associated with the Organization of American States (OAS).

Partners of the Americas, *1424 K St. N.W., #700 20005-2410; (202) 628-3300. Fax, (202) 628-3306. Stephen Vetter, President. Press, (202) 637-6222. General e-mail, info@partners.net*

Web, www.partners.net

Membership: individuals in the United States, Latin America, and the Caribbean. Sponsors technical assistance projects and cultural exchanges between the United States, Latin America, and the Caribbean; supports self-help projects in agriculture, public health, education, and democratic participation.

U.S.-Mexico Chamber of Commerce, *5510 Cherokee Ave., #120, Alexandria, VA 22312; (703) 752-4752. Fax, (703) 642-1088. Albert C. Zapanta, President. General e-mail, news-hq@usmcoc.org*

Web, www.usmcoc.org

Promotes trade and investment between the United States and Mexico. Provides members with information and expertise on conducting business between the two countries as pertains to NAFTA. Serves as a clearinghouse for information.

Washington Office on Latin America, *1666 Connecticut Ave. N.W., #400 20009; (202) 797-2171. Fax, (202) 797-2172. Joy Olson, Executive Director. General e-mail, wola@wola.org*

Web, www.wola.org

Acts as a liaison between government policymakers and groups and individuals concerned with human rights and U.S. policy in Latin America and the Caribbean. Serves as an information resource center; monitors legislation.

Near East and South Asia

(Includes North Africa)

►AGENCIES

Agency for International Development (USAID), *Asia and Near East Bureau,* 1300 Pennsylvania Ave. N.W., #4.09-034 20523-4900; (202) 712-0200. Fax, (202) 216-3386. Vacant, Assistant Administrator.
Web, www.usaid.gov/regions/ane

Advises the AID administrator on U.S. economic development policy in Asia and the Near East.

Defense Dept. (DoD), *International Security Affairs: Middle East,* The Pentagon, #5B712 20301-2400; (703) 697-1335. Fax, (703) 693-6795. Colin Kahl, Deputy Under Secretary. Press, (703) 697-5333.
Web, www.defenselink.mil

Advises the assistant secretary for international security affairs on matters dealing with the Near East and South Asia.

State Dept., *Afghanistan Affairs,* 2201 C St. N.W., #5310 20520-6258; (202) 647-5175. Fax, (202) 647-5505. Henry Ensher, Director.
Web, www.state.gov

State Dept., *Arabian Peninsula Affairs,* 2201 C St. N.W., #4224 20520-6243; (202) 647-6184. Fax, (202) 736-4459. Andrew Steinfeld, Director.
General e-mail, nea-arp-dl@state.gov
Web, www.state.gov

Includes Bahrain, Kuwait, Oman, Qatar, Saudi Arabia, United Arab Emirates, and Yemen.

State Dept., *Bureau of Near Eastern Affairs,* 2201 C St. N.W., #6242 20520-6243; (202) 647-7209. Fax, (202) 736-4462. Vacant, Assistant Secretary.
Web, www.state.gov

Advises the secretary on U.S. policy toward countries of the Near East and North Africa. Directors assigned to specific countries within the bureau aid the assistant secretary.

State Dept., *Bureau of South and Central Asian Affairs,* 2201 C St. N.W., #6254 20520-6258; (202) 736-4325. Fax, (202) 736-4333. Richard A. Boucher, Assistant Secretary.
Web, www.state.gov

Advises the secretary on U.S. policy toward South Asian countries. Directors assigned to specific countries within the bureau aid the assistant secretary.

State Dept., *Egypt and Levant Affairs,* 2201 C St. N.W., #5250 20520-6243; (202) 647-2670. Fax, (202) 647-0989. Nicole Shampaine, Director. Press, (202) 647-5919.
Web, www.state.gov

Includes Egypt, Jordan, Lebanon, and Syria.

State Dept., *Iran Affairs,* 2201 C St. N.W., #1058 20520; (202) 647-2520. Fax, (202) 647-2526. Todd Schwartz, Director.
Web, www.state.gov

Advises the secretary on Iranian affairs.

State Dept., *Iraq Affairs,* 2201 C St. N.W., #2808 20520; (202) 647-5692. Fax, (202) 736-4464. George N. Sibley, Director. Press, (202) 647-5150.
Web, www.state.gov

State Dept., *Israeli-Palestinian Affairs,* 2201 C St. N.W., #6251 20520; (202) 647-3672. Fax, (202) 736-4461. Thomas Goldberger, Director.
Web, www.state.gov

State Dept., *Middle East Partnership Initiative,* 5-A4 Central 20520; (202) 776-8500. Fax, (202) 776-8445. Timothy Andrews, Director.
General e-mail, nea-grants@state.gov
Web, http://mepi.state.gov/mepi

Funds programs that seek to advance democracy in the Middle East. Encourages reform in the areas of politics, economics, education, and women's rights.

State Dept., *Near Eastern Affairs,* 2201 C St. N.W., #6250 20520; (202) 647-2300. Fax, (202) 736-4460. Stephanie P. Williams, Director.
Web, www.state.gov

Includes Algeria, Libya, Morocco, and Tunisia.

State Dept., *Pakistan and Bangladesh Affairs,* 2201 C St. N.W., #5247 20520-6258; (202) 647-6711. Fax, (202) 647-3001. Brent Hartley, Deputy Director.
Web, www.state.gov

State Dept., *South Central Asian Affairs,* 2201 C St. N.W., #5251 20520-6243; (202) 647-2141. Fax, (202) 736-4463. Michael Owen, Director. Press, (202) 736-4255.
Web, www.state.gov

Includes Bhutan, India, Maldives, Nepal, and Sri Lanka.

►CONGRESS

For a listing of relevant congressional committees and subcommittees, please see page 412 or the Appendix.

Library of Congress, *African and Middle Eastern Division,* 101 Independence Ave. S.E., #LJ220 20540; (202) 707-7937. Fax, (202) 252-3180. Mary Jane Deeb, Chief. Reading room, (202) 707-4188.
Web, www.loc.gov/rr/amed

Maintains collections of African, Near Eastern, and Hebraic material. Prepares bibliographies and special studies relating to Africa and the Middle East. Reference service and reading rooms available to the public.

Library of Congress, *Asian Division,* 101 Independence Ave. S.E., #LJ149 20540; (202) 707-5240. Fax, (202)

252-3336. Hwa-Wei Lee, Chief. Reading Room, (202) 707-5426.
Web, www.loc.gov/rr/asian

Maintains collections of Chinese, Korean, Japanese, Southeast Asian, and South Asian material. Reference service is provided in the Asian Reading Room.

►INTERNATIONAL ORGANIZATIONS

International Bank for Reconstruction and Development (World Bank), *Middle East and North Africa,* 600 19th St. N.W. 20433 (mailing address: 1818 H St. N.W., #H10-163, Washington, DC 20433); (202) 473-7305. Fax, (202) 477-0810. Daniela Gressani, Vice President.
Web, www.worldbank.org

Works to fight poverty and improve the living standards of low- and middle-income people in the countries of the Middle East and North Africa by providing loans, policy advice, technical assistance, and knowledge-sharing services. Areas of interest include finance, economic development, education, water supply, agriculture, public health, and environmental protection.

International Bank for Reconstruction and Development (World Bank), *South Asia,* 1818 H St. N.W., MSN 10-1003 20433; (202) 458-4735. Fax, (202) 522-3707. Isabel Guerrero, Vice President.
Web, www.worldbank.org

Works to fight poverty and improve the living standards of low- and middle-income people in the countries of South Asia by providing loans, policy advice, technical assistance, and knowledge-sharing services. Areas of interest include finance, economic development, education, water supply, agriculture, public health, and environmental protection.

League of Arab States, *Washington Office,* 1100 17th St. N.W., #602 20036; (202) 265-3210. Fax, (202) 331-1525. Amb. Hussein Hassouna, Director.
General e-mail, arableague@aol.com
Web, www.arableague-us.org

Membership: Arab countries in the Near East, North Africa, and the Indian Ocean. Coordinates members' policies in political, cultural, economic, and social affairs; mediates disputes among members and between members and third parties. Washington office maintains the Arab Information Center. (Headquarters in Cairo.)

►NONGOVERNMENTAL

American Israel Public Affairs Committee, 251 H St. N.W. 20001-2017; (202) 639-5200. Fax, (202) 347-4889. Howard Kohr, Executive Director.
General e-mail, help@aipac.org
Web, www.aipac.org

Works to maintain and improve relations between the United States and Israel.

American Jewish Congress, *Washington Office,* 1001 Connecticut Ave. N.W., #407 20036-5553; (202) 466-9661. Fax, (202) 466-9665. Matthew Horn, National Policy Director.
General e-mail, washrep@ajcongress.org
Web, www.ajcongress.org

National Jewish organization that advocates the maintenance and improvement of U.S.-Israeli relations through legislation, public education, and joint economic ventures. Interests include the Arab boycott of Israel and foreign investment in the United States. (Headquarters in New York.)

American Kurdish Information Network (AKIN), 2722 Connecticut Ave. N.W., #42 20008-5366; (202) 483-6444. Kani Xulam, Director.
General e-mail, akin@kurdistan.org
Web, www.kurdistan.org

Membership: Americans of Kurdish origin, recent Kurdish immigrants and refugees, and others. Collects and disseminates information about the Kurds, an ethnic group living in parts of Turkey, Iran, Iraq, and Syria. Monitors human rights abuses against Kurds; promotes self-determination in Kurdish homelands; fosters Kurdish American friendship and understanding.

American Near East Refugee Aid (ANERA), 1522 K St. N.W., #600 20005-1251; (202) 842-2766. Fax, (202) 682-1637. William Corcoran, President.
General e-mail, anera@anera.org
Web, www.anera.org

Works with local institutions to provide development, health, education, and employment programs to Palestinian communities and impoverished families throughout the Middle East. (Field offices in the West Bank, Gaza, Lebanon, and Jordan.)

AMIDEAST, 1730 M St. N.W., #1100 20036-4500; (202) 776-9600. Fax, (202) 776-7000. Theodore H. Kattouf, President.
General e-mail, inquiries@amideast.org
Web, www.amideast.org

Promotes understanding and cooperation between Americans and the people of the Middle East and North Africa through education, information, and development programs. Produces educational material to help improve teaching about the Arab world in American schools and colleges.

Asia Society Washington Center, 1575 Eye St. N.W., #325 20005; (202) 833-2742. Fax, (202) 833-0189. Jack Garrity, Director.
General e-mail, dcinfo@asiasoc.org
Web, www.asiasociety.org/dc

Membership: individuals, organizations, and corporations interested in Asia and the Pacific (excluding the Middle East). Sponsors seminars and lectures on political, economic, and cultural issues. (Headquarters in New York.)

Center for Contemporary Arab Studies (*Georgetown University*), 241 Intercultural Center, 37th and O St. N.W. 20057-1020; (202) 687-5793. Fax, (202) 687-7001. Michael Hudson, Director.
General e-mail, ccasinfo@georgetown.edu

Web, http://ccas.georgetown.edu

Sponsors lecture series, seminars, and conferences. Conducts a community outreach program that assists secondary school teachers in the development of instructional materials on the Middle East; promotes the study of the Arabic language in area schools. Offers master's degree program in Arab studies.

Foundation for Democracy in Iran, 7831 Woodmont Ave., #395, Bethesda, MD 20814; (301) 946-2918. Fax, (301) 942-5341. Kenneth Timmerman, Executive Director.
General e-mail, exec@iran.org

Web, www.iran.org

Seeks to foster democracy in Iran. Acts as a clearinghouse for information pertaining to opposition efforts in Iran.

Foundation for Middle East Peace, 1761 N St. N.W. 20036-2801; (202) 835-3650. Fax, (202) 835-3651. Amb. Philip C. Wilcox Jr., President.
General e-mail, info@fmep.org

Web, www.fmep.org

Educational organization that seeks to promote understanding and resolution of the Israeli-Palestinian conflict. Publishes bimonthly *Report on Israeli Settlement in the Occupied Territories;* provides media with information; and awards grants to organizations and activities that contribute to the solution of the conflict.

Institute for Palestine Studies, *Washington Office*, 3501 M St. N.W. 20007-2624; (202) 342-3990. Fax, (202) 342-3927. Linda Butler, Director. Press, (202) 342-3990, ext. 19.
General e-mail, jps@palestine-studies.org

Web, www.palestine-studies.org

Scholarly research institute that specializes in the history and development of the Palestine problem, the Arab-Israeli conflict, and their peaceful resolution. (Headquarters in Beirut, Lebanon.)

Institute of Turkish Studies (*Georgetown University*), Intercultural Center, Box 571033 20057-1033; (202) 687-0295. Fax, (202) 687-3780. David C. Cuthell, Executive Director.
General e-mail, director@turkishstudies.org

Web, www.turkishstudies.org

Independent grant-making organization that supports and encourages the development of Turkish studies in American colleges and universities. Awards grants to individual scholars and educational institutions in the United States.

MEMRI (Middle East Media Research Institute), P.O. Box 27837 20038-7837; (202) 955-9070. Fax, (202) 955-9077. Steven Stalinsky, Executive Director.
General e-mail, memri@memri.org

Web, www.memri.org

Explores the Middle East through the region's media. Seeks to inform the debate over U.S. policy in the Middle East.

Middle East Institute, 1761 N St. N.W. 20036-2882; (202) 785-1141. Fax, (202) 331-8861. Amb. Wendy Chamberlin, President. Library, (202) 785-1141, ext. 222. Press, (202) 785-1141, ext. 236. Language Dept., (202) 785-1141, ext. 237.
General e-mail, nmoqueet@mei.edu

Web, www.mideasti.org

Membership: individuals interested in the Middle East. Seeks to broaden knowledge of the Middle East through research, conferences and seminars, language classes, lectures, and exhibits. Library open to members and the press Monday through Thursday 12:00–8:00 p.m.

Middle East Policy Council, 1730 M St. N.W., #512 20036-4505; (202) 296-6767. Fax, (202) 296-5791. Chas W. Freeman Jr., President.
General e-mail, info@mepc.org

Web, www.mepc.org

Encourages public discussion and understanding of issues affecting U.S. policy in the Middle East. Sponsors conferences for the policy community; conducts workshops for high school teachers nationwide.

Middle East Research and Information Project, 1500 Massachusetts Ave. N.W., #119 20005; (202) 223-3677. Fax, (202) 223-3604. Christopher J. Toensing, Executive Director.
General e-mail, ctoensing@merip.org

Web, www.merip.org

Works to educate the public about the contemporary Middle East. Focuses on U.S. policy in the region and issues of human rights and social justice.

National Council on U.S.-Arab Relations, 1730 M St. N.W., #503 20036; (202) 293-6466. Fax, (202) 293-7770. John Duke Anthony, President.
General e-mail, info@ncusar.org

Web, www.ncusar.org

Educational organization that works to improve mutual understanding between the United States and the Arab world. Serves as a clearinghouse on Arab issues and maintains speakers bureau. Coordinates trips for U.S. professionals and congressional delegations to the Arab world.

National U.S.-Arab Chamber of Commerce, 1023 15th St. N.W., 4th Floor 20005; (202) 289-5920. Fax, (202) 289-5938. David Hamod, President.

General e-mail, info@nusacc.org

Web, www.nusacc.org

Promotes trade between the United States and the Arab world. Offers members informational publications, research and certification services, and opportunities to meet with international delegations.

New Israel Fund, *1101 14th St. N.W., 6th Floor 20005-5639; (202) 842-0900. Fax, (202) 842-0991. Naomi Chazan, Chair. Press, (202) 513-7824. General e-mail, info@nif.org*

Web, www.nif.org

International philanthropic partnership of North Americans, Israelis, and Europeans. Supports activities that defend civil and human rights, promote Jewish-Arab equality and coexistence, advance the status of women, nurture tolerance, bridge social and economic gaps, encourage government accountability, and assist citizen efforts to protect the environment. Makes grants and provides capacity-building assistance to Israeli public interest groups; trains civil rights lawyers.

United Palestinian Appeal (UPA), *1330 New Hampshire Ave. N.W., #104 20036-6350; (202) 659-5007. Fax, (202) 296-0224. Samer Badawi, Executive Director. General e-mail, contact@helpupa.com*

Web, www.helpupa.com

Charitable organization dedicated to improving the quality of life for Palestinians in the Middle East, particularly those in the West Bank, the Gaza Strip, and refugee camps. Provides funding for community development projects, health care, education, children's services, and emergency relief. Funded by private donations from individuals and foundations in the United States and Arab world.

Washington Institute for Near East Policy, *1828 L St. N.W., #1050 20036; (202) 452-0650. Fax, (202) 223-5364. Robert Satloff, Executive Director. Web, www.washingtoninstitute.org*

Research and educational organization that seeks to improve the effectiveness of U.S. policy in the Near East by promoting debate among policymakers, journalists, and scholars.

Washington Kurdish Institute, *611 4th St. S.W. 20024; (202) 484-0140. Shwan Ziad, Executive Director. General e-mail, wki@kurd.org*

Web, www.kurd.org

Membership: scholars, human rights practitioners, Middle East and foreign policy experts, and Kurds from around the world.

Women's Alliance for Peace and Human Rights in Afghanistan, *P.O. Box 77057 20013-7057; (202) 882-1432. Zieba Shorish-Shamley, Executive Director. General e-mail, nisasahar@comcast.net*

Web, www.wapha.org

U.S.-based organization that advocates for Afghan women's sociopolitical and economic rights. Seeks to achieve full restoration of Afghan women's and girls' rights and Afghan women's full participation in the restoration of their country.

Russia and New Independent States

For the Baltic states, see Europe

▶**AGENCIES**

Agency for International Development (USAID), Europe and Eurasia Bureau, *1300 Pennsylvania Ave. N.W., #5.06 20523-5600; (202) 712-0290. Fax, (202) 216-3057. Ken Yamashita, Assistant Administrator (Acting). Web, www.usaid.gov/regions/europe_eurasia*

Advises the AID administrator on U.S. economic development policy in Europe and Eurasia.

State Dept., *Caucasus Affairs and Regional Conflicts, 2201 C St. N.W., #4220 20520-7512; (202) 647-8741. Fax, (202) 736-7915. Baxter Hunt, Director. Web, www.state.gov*

Includes Armenia, Azerbaijan, and Georgia.

State Dept., *Central Asian Affairs, 2201 C St. N.W., #4212 20520; (202) 647-9370. Fax, (202) 736-4710. Tom Hushek, Director. Web, www.state.gov*

Covers affairs of Kazakhstan, Kyrgyzstan, Tajikistan, Turkmenistan, and Uzbekistan.

State Dept., *Russian Affairs, 2201 C St. N.W., #4417 20520-7512; (202) 647-9806. Fax, (202) 647-8980. Ian Kelly, Director. Web, www.state.gov*

State Dept., *Ukraine, Moldova, and Belarus Affairs, 2201 C St. N.W., #4427 20520-7512; (202) 647-8671. Fax, (202) 647-3506. Robert Boehme, Director. Web, www.state.gov*

▶**CONGRESS**

For a listing of relevant congressional committees and subcommittees, please see page 412 or the Appendix.

Library of Congress, *European Division, 101 Independence Ave. S.E., #LJ-250 20540; (202) 707-5414. Fax, (202) 707-8482. Georgette M. Dorn, Chief (Acting). Reference desk, (202) 707-4515. Web, www.loc.gov/rr/european*

Provides reference service on the library's European collections (except collections on Spain, Portugal, and the British Isles). Prepares bibliographies and special studies relating to European countries, including Russia and the other states of the former Soviet Union and eastern bloc. Maintains current unbound Slavic language periodicals and newspapers, which are available at the European Reference Desk.

►INTERNATIONAL ORGANIZATIONS

International Bank for Reconstruction and Development (World Bank), *Europe and Central Asia,* *600 19th St. N.W. 20431 (mailing address: 1818 H St. N.W., MS H121202, Washington, DC 20433); (202) 458-8154. Fax, (202) 522-2758. Shigeo Katsu, Vice President. General e-mail, ecainformation@worldbank.org*

Web, www.worldbank.org

Works to fight poverty and improve the living standards of low- and middle-income people in the countries of eastern Europe and central Asia, including states of the former Soviet Union, by providing loans, policy advice, technical assistance, and knowledge-sharing services. Interests include finance, economic development, education, water supply, agriculture, public health, and environmental protection.

►NONGOVERNMENTAL

American Bar Assn. (ABA), *Rule of Law Initiative, 740 15th St. N.W., 8th Floor 20005-1022; (202) 662-1950. Fax, (202) 662-1597. Rob Boone, Program Director. General e-mail, ROFL@staff.abanet.org*

Web, www.abanet.org/rol

Promotes the rule of law and specific legal reforms in the emerging democracies of central and eastern Europe, Russia, and the other states of the former Soviet Union; recruits volunteer legal professionals from the United States and western Europe. Interests include civil, criminal, commercial, and environmental law; judicial restructuring; bar development; and legal education and research.

American Councils for International Education: ACTR/ ACCELS, *1776 Massachusetts Ave. N.W., #700 20036; (202) 833-7522. Fax, (202) 833-7523. Dan E. Davidson, President. General e-mail, general@americancouncils.org*

Web, www.americancouncils.org

Advances education and research worldwide through international programs focused on academic exchange, professional training, distance learning, curriculum and test development, delivery of technical assistance, research, evaluation, and institution building. Conducts educational exchanges for high school, university, and graduate school students as well as scholars with the countries of eastern Europe, Eurasia, southeast Europe, and the Middle East.

Armenian Assembly of America, *1140 19th St. N.W., #600 20036; (202) 393-3434. Fax, (202) 638-4904. Bryan Ardouny, Executive Director. General e-mail, info@aaainc.org*

Web, www.aaainc.org

Promotes public understanding and awareness of Armenian issues; advances research and data collection and disseminates information on the Armenian people; advocates greater Armenian American participation in the American democratic process; works to alleviate human suffering of Armenians.

Armenian National Committee of America (ANCA), *1711 N St. N.W. 20036; (202) 775-1918. Fax, (202) 775-5648. Kenneth V. Hachikian, Chair. General e-mail, anca@anca.org*

Web, www.anca.org

Armenian American grassroots political organization. Works to advance concerns of the Armenian American community. Interests include strengthening U.S.-Armenian relations.

Eurasia Foundation, *1350 Connecticut Ave. N.W., #1000 20036-1730; (202) 234-7370. Fax, (202) 234-7377. William Horton Beebe-Center, President. General e-mail, eurasia@eurasia.org*

Web, www.eurasia.org

Grant-making organization that funds programs that build democratic and free market institutions in Russia, Central Asia, the Caucasus, and western Eurasia. Interests include economic and governmental reform, development of the nonprofit sector, and projects in media and communications.

Free Congress Research and Education Foundation (FCF), *1423 Powhatan St., #2, Alexandria, VA 22314; (703) 837-0030. Fax, (703) 837-0031. Paul M. Weyrich, Chair. Web, www.freecongress.org*

Public policy research and education foundation. Pioneers coalition-building efforts; seeks to improve conservatives' effectiveness in the political process. Hosts an annual Russian Forum.

Institute for European, Russian, and Eurasian Studies *(George Washington University), 1957 E St. N.W., #412 20052-0001; (202) 994-6340. Fax, (202) 994-5436. Hope M. Harrison, Director. General e-mail, ieresgwu@gwu.edu*

Web, www.ieres.org

Studies and researches European, Russian, and Eurasian affairs. (Affiliated with the George Washington University Elliott School of International Affairs.)

Jamestown Foundation, *1111 16th St. N.W., #320 20036; (202) 483-8888. Fax, (202) 483-8337. Glen E. Howard, President. General e-mail, pubs@jamestown.org*

Web, www.jamestown.org

Provides policymakers with information about events and trends in societies that are strategically or tactically important to the United States and that frequently restrict access to such information. Serves as an alternative source to official or intelligence channels, especially with regard to Eurasia and terrorism.

Kennan Institute for Advanced Russian Studies, *One Woodrow Wilson Plaza, 1300 Pennsylvania Ave. N.W. 20004-3027; (202) 691-4100. Fax, (202) 691-4247. Blair A. Ruble, Director.*
General e-mail, kennan@wilsoncenter.org
Web, www.wilsoncenter.org/kennan

Offers residential research scholarships to academic scholars and to specialists from government, media, and the private sector for studies to improve American knowledge about Russia and the former Soviet Union. Sponsors lectures; publishes reports; promotes dialogue between academic specialists and policymakers. (Affiliated with the Woodrow Wilson International Center for Scholars.)

NCSJ: Advocates on Behalf of Jews in Russia, Ukraine, the Baltic States and Eurasia, *2020 K St. N.W., #7800 20006; (202) 898-2500. Fax, (202) 898-0822. Mark B. Levin, Executive Director.*
General e-mail, ncsj@ncsj.org
Web, www.ncsj.org

Membership: national Jewish organizations and local federations. Coordinates efforts by members to aid Jews in the former Soviet Union.

Open Society Institute, *Eastern Europe/Former Soviet Union Project, 1120 19th St. N.W., 8th Floor 20036; (202) 721-5600. Fax, (202) 530-0128. Stephen Rickard, Director, Washington Office.*
General e-mail, info@osi-dc.org
Web, www.soros.org/initiatives/washington

Serves as a resource for government agencies, multilateral institutions, and nongovernmental organizations interested in the region. Promotes open societies in the region. Provides policy briefings and political analysis. Oversees OSI foundations established in the region. (Affiliated with the Soros Foundation Network.)

Ukrainian National Information Service, *Washington Office, 311 Massachusetts Ave. N.E., Lower Level 20002; (202) 547-0018. Fax, (202) 543-5502. Michael Sawkiw Jr., Director.*
General e-mail, unis@ucca.org
Web, www.ucca.org

Information bureau of the Ukrainian Congress Committee of America in New York. Provides information and monitors U.S. policy on Ukraine and the Ukrainian community in the United States and abroad. (Headquarters in New York.)

U.S.-Russia Business Council, *1110 Vermont Ave. N.W., #350 20005; (202) 739-9180. Fax, (202) 659-5920. Edward Verona, President. Press, (202) 739-9187.*
General e-mail, info@usrbc.org
Web, www.usrbc.org

Membership: U.S. companies involved in trade and investment in Russia. Promotes commercial ties between the United States and Russia.

U.S.-Ukraine Foundation, *1701 K St. N.W., #903 20006; (202) 223-2228. Fax, (202) 223-1224. Nadia K. McConnell, President.*
General e-mail, info@usukraine.org
Web, www.usukraine.org

Encourages and facilitates democratic and human rights development and free market reform in the Ukraine. Creates and sustains communications channels between the United States and Ukraine. Manages the U.S.-Ukraine Community Partnerships Program.

U.S. Territories and Associated States

► **AGENCIES**

Interior Dept. (DOI), *Insular Affairs, 1849 C St. N.W., MS 2428 20240; (202) 208-4736. Fax, (202) 219-1989. Nik Pula, Director.*
Web, www.doi.gov/oia

Promotes economic, social, and political development of U.S. territories (Guam, American Samoa, the Virgin Islands, and the Commonwealth of the Northern Mariana Islands). Supervises federal programs for the Freely Associated States (Federated States of Micronesia, Republic of the Marshall Islands, and Republic of Palau).

► **CONGRESS**

For a listing of relevant congressional committees and subcommittees, please see page 412 or the Appendix.

American Samoa's Delegate to Congress, *2422 RHOB 20515; (202) 225-8577. Fax, (202) 225-8757. Del. Eni F.H. Faleomavaega, D–Am. Samoa.*
General e-mail, Faleomavaega@mail.house.gov
Web, www.house.gov/faleomavaega

Represents American Samoa in Congress.

Guam's Delegate to Congress, *427 CHOB 20515; (202) 225-1188. Fax, (202) 226-0341. Del. Madeleine Z. Bordallo, D–Guam.*
Web, www.house.gov/bordallo

Represents Guam in Congress.

Puerto Rican Resident Commissioner, *126 CHOB 20515; (202) 225-2615. Fax, (202) 225-2154. Luis G. Fortuno, R–P.R., Resident Commissioner.*
Web, www.house.gov/fortuno

Represents the Commonwealth of Puerto Rico in Congress.

Virgin Islands' Delegate to Congress, *1510 LHOB 20515; (202) 225-1790. Fax, (202) 225-5517. Del. Donna M. Christensen, D–Virgin Is..*
Web, www.house.gov/christian-christensen

Represents the Virgin Islands in Congress.

► **NONGOVERNMENTAL**

Puerto Rico Federal Affairs Administration, *1100 17th St. N.W., #800 20036; (202) 778-0710. Fax, (202) 778-0721. Richard Figueroa, Executive Director. Press, (202) 778-0710.*
General e-mail, info@prfaa.com

Web, www.prfaa.com

Represents the governor and the government of the Commonwealth of Puerto Rico before Congress and the executive branch; conducts research; serves as official press information center for the Commonwealth of Puerto Rico. Monitors legislation and regulations.

U.S. Virgin Islands Department of Tourism,
Washington Office, 444 N. Capitol St. N.W., #305 20001; (202) 624-3590. Fax, (202) 624-3594. Loan Sewer, Manager. Toll-free, (800) 372-8784.
Web, www.usvitourism.vi

Provides information about the U.S. Virgin Islands; promotes tourism. (Headquarters in St. Thomas.)

Private Equity Council (PEC), *950 F St. N.W., #550 20004; (202) 465-7700. Fax, (202) 639-0209. Robert W. Stewart, Vice President of Public Affairs.*
General e-mail, info@privatequitycouncil.org

Web, www.privateequitycouncil.org

Advocacy, communications, and research organization and resource center that develops, analyzes, and distributes information about the private equity industry and its contributions to the national and global economy.

13 ⚖ Law and Justice

GENERAL POLICY AND ANALYSIS

Basic Resources

►AGENCIES

Executive Office for U.S. Attorneys *(Justice Dept.)*, *950 Pennsylvania Ave. N.W., #2242 20530-0001; (202) 514-2121. Fax, (202) 616-2278. Kenneth E. Melson, Director. Linda Jones, Public Affairs, Information, (202) 514-2121.*
Web, www.usdoj.gov/usao/eousa

Provides the offices of U.S. attorneys with technical assistance and supervision in areas of legal counsel, personnel, and training. Publishes the *U.S. Attorneys' Manual* and *United States Attorneys' Bulletin.* Administers the Attorney General's Office of Legal Education, which conducts workshops and seminars to develop the litigation skills of the department's attorneys in criminal and civil trials. Develops and implements Justice Dept. procedures for collecting criminal fines.

Justice Dept. (DOJ), *950 Pennsylvania Ave. N.W. 20530-0001; (202) 514-2001. Fax, (202) 307-6777. Eric Holder, Attorney General; David Ogden, Deputy Attorney General; Thomas Perrelli, Associate Attorney General. Information, (202) 514-2000. Meaghan McDavid, Public Affairs, (202) 514-2007.*
General e-mail, askdoj@usdoj.gov
Web, www.usdoj.gov

Serves as counsel for the U.S. government. Represents the government in enforcing the law in the public interest. Plays key role in protecting against criminals and subversion, in ensuring healthy competition of business in the U.S. free enterprise system, in safeguarding the consumer, and in enforcing drug, immigration, and naturalization laws. Plays a significant role in protecting citizens through effective law enforcement, crime prevention, crime detection, and prosecution and rehabilitation of offenders. Conducts all suits in the Supreme Court in which the United States is concerned. Represents the government in legal matters generally, furnishing legal advice and opinions to the president, the cabinet, and to the heads of executive departments, as provided by law. Justice Dept. organization includes divisions on antitrust, civil law, civil rights, criminal law, environment and natural resources, and taxes, as well as the Bureau of Alcohol, Tobacco, Firearms, and Explosives; Drug Enforcement Administration; Executive Office for Immigration Review; Federal Bureau of Investigation; Federal Bureau of Prisons; Foreign Claims Settlement Commission; Office of Justice Programs; U.S. Attorneys, U.S. Marshals Service, U.S. Parole Commission; and U.S. Trustees.

Justice Dept. (DOJ), *Legal Policy, 950 Pennsylvania Ave. N.W., #4234 20530-0001; (202) 514-4601. Fax, (202) 514-2424. Kevin Jones, Assistant Attorney General (Acting).*
Web, www.usdoj.gov/olp

Develops and implements the Justice Dept.'s major policy initiatives, often with the cooperation of other offices within the department and among other agencies. Works with Office of Legislative Affairs to promote the department's policies in Congress.

Justice Dept. (DOJ), *Professional Responsibility, 950 Pennsylvania Ave. N.W., #3266 20530-0001; (202) 514-3365. Fax, (202) 514-5050. H. Marshall Jarrett, Counsel.*
Web, www.usdoj.gov/opr

Receives and reviews allegations of misconduct by Justice Dept. attorneys; refers cases that warrant further review to appropriate investigative agency or unit; makes recommendations to the attorney general for action on certain misconduct cases.

Justice Dept. (DOJ), *Solicitor General, 950 Pennsylvania Ave. N.W., #5143 20530-0001; (202) 514-2203. Fax, (202) 514-9769. Elena Kagan, Solicitor General. Information on pending cases, (202) 514-2218.*
Web, www.usdoj.gov/osg

Represents the federal government before the Supreme Court of the United States.

Legal Services Corp., *3333 K St. N.W., 3rd Floor 20007-3522; (202) 295-1500. Fax, (202) 337-6797. Helaine M. Barnett, President. Information, (202) 295-1500. Public Reading Room, (202) 295-1502.*
Web, www.lsc.gov

Independent federal corporation established by Congress. Awards grants to local agencies that provide the poor with legal services. Library open to the public.

Office of Justice Programs (OJP), *(Justice Dept.), 810 7th St. N.W. 20531; (202) 307-5933. Fax, (202) 514-7805. Laurie Robinson, Assistant Attorney General. TTY, (202) 616-3867.*
Web, www.ojp.usdoj.gov

Provides federal leadership, coordination, and assistance in developing the nation's capacity to prevent and control crime, administer justice, and assist crime victims. Includes the Bureau of Justice Assistance, which supports state and local criminal justice strategies; the Bureau of Justice Statistics, which collects, analyzes, and disseminates criminal justice data; the National Institute of Justice, which is the primary research and development agency of the Justice Dept.; the Office of Juvenile Justice and Delinquency Prevention, which supports state and local efforts to combat juvenile crime and victimization; the Office of Victims of Crime, which provides support for crime victims and leadership to promote justice and healing for all crime victims; and the Community Capacity Development Office, which provides resources to support community-based anti-crime efforts.

►CONGRESS

For a listing of relevant congressional committees and subcommittees, please see page 468 or the Appendix.

LAW AND JUSTICE RESOURCES IN CONGRESS

For a complete listing of Congress committees, including their full contact information, leadership, membership, and jurisdictions, please refer to the Appendix on pages 724–837.

HOUSE:

House Administration Committee, (202) 225-2061.
Web, cha.house.gov
  Subcommittee on Capitol Security, (202) 225-2061.

House Appropriations Committee, Subcommittee on Commerce, Justice, Science, and Related Agencies, (202) 225-3351.
Web, appropriations.house.gov
  Subcommittee on Homeland Security, (202) 225-5834.

House Education and Labor Committee, Subcommittee on Healthy Families and Communities, (202) 225-3725.
Web, edlabor.house.gov
  Subcommittee on Workforce Protections, (202) 225-3725.

House Energy and Commerce Committee, Subcommittee on Commerce, Trade and Consumer Protections, (202) 225-2927.
Web, energycommerce.house.gov
  Subcommittee on Health, (202) 225-2927.

House Financial Services Committee, Subcommittee on Financial Institutions and Consumer Credit, (202) 225-4247.
Web, financialservices.house.gov

House Homeland Security Committee, (202) 226-2616.
Web, homeland.house.gov
  Subcommittee on Border, Maritime and Global Counterterrorism, (202) 226-2616.

House Judiciary Committee, (202) 225-3951.

Web, judiciary.house.gov
  Subcommittee on Commercial and Administrative Law, (202) 226-7680.
  Subcommittee on the Constitution, Civil Rights, and Civil Liberties, (202) 225-2825.
  Subcommittee on Courts, the Internet, and Intellectual Property, (202) 225-5741.
  Subcommittee on Crime, Terrorism and Homeland Security, (202) 225-5727.
  Subcommittee on Immigration, Citizenship, Refugees, Border Security, and International Law, (202) 225-3926.

House Natural Resources Committee, (202) 225-6065.
Web, resourcescommittee.house.gov

House Oversight and Government Reform Committee, (202) 225-5051.
Web, oversight.house.gov
  Subcommittee on Domestic Policy, (202) 225-6427.
  Subcommittee on Government Management, Organization, and Procurement, (202) 225-3741.

House Small Business Committee, Subcommittee on Regulations and Health Care, (202) 225-4038.
Web, www.house.gov/smbiz

House Standards of Official Conduct Committee, (202) 225-7103.
Web, www.house.gov/ethics

House Ways and Means Committee, (202) 225-3625.
Web, waysandmeans.house.gov
  Subcommittee on Oversight, (202) 225-5522.

Government Accountability Office (GAO), *Homeland Security and Justice, 441 G St. N.W., #6169 20548; (202) 512-3610. Norm J. Rabkin, Managing Director. Documents, (202) 512-6000.*
Web, www.gao.gov

Independent, nonpartisan agency in the legislative branch. Audits, analyzes, and evaluates federal administration of homeland security programs and activities; makes some reports available to the public. (Formerly the General Accounting Office.)

▶JUDICIARY

Administrative Office of the U.S. Courts, *1 Columbus Circle N.E. 20544-0001; (202) 502-2600. James C. Duff, Director.*
Web, www.uscourts.gov/adminoff.html

Provides administrative support to the federal courts, including the procurement of supplies and equipment; the administration of personnel, budget, and financial control services; and the compilation and publication of statistical data and reports on court business. Implements

the policies of the Judicial Conference of the United States and supports its committees. Recommends plans and strategies to manage court business. Procures needed resources, legislation, and other assistance for the judiciary from Congress and the executive branch.

Federal Judicial Center, *1 Columbus Circle N.E. 20002-8003; (202) 502-4160. Fax, (202) 502-4099. Barbara J. Rothstein, Director. Library, (202) 502-4153. Public Affairs, (202) 502-4250.*
Web, www.fjc.gov

Conducts research on the operations of the federal court system; develops and conducts continuing education and training programs for judges and judicial personnel; and makes recommendations to improve the administration of the courts.

Judicial Conference of the United States, *1 Columbus Circle N.E., #7-425 20544; (202) 502-2400. Fax, (202) 502-1144. John G. Roberts Jr., Chief Justice of the United States, Chair; James C. Duff, Secretary.*
Web, www.uscourts.gov

LAW AND JUSTICE RESOURCES IN CONGRESS

SENATE:

Senate Appropriations Committee, Subcommittee on Commerce, Justice, Science, and Related Agencies, (202) 224-5202.
Web, appropriations.senate.gov

Subcommittee on Homeland Security, (202) 224-8244.

Senate Commerce, Science, and Transportation Committee, Subcommittee on Consumer Affairs, Insurance, and Automotive Safety, (202) 224-1270.
Web, commerce.senate.gov

Subcommittee on Oceans, Atmosphere, Fisheries and the Coast Guard, (202) 224-4912.

Senate Finance Committee, Subcommittee on Taxation, IRS Oversight, and Long-Term Growth, (202) 224-4515.
Web, finance.senate.gov

Senate Foreign Relations Committee, Subcommittee on Western Hemisphere, Peace Corps, and Narcotics Affairs, (202) 224-4651
Web, foreign.senate.gov

Senate Health, Education, Labor, and Pension Committee, (202) 224-5375.
Web, help.senate.gov

Subcommittee on Children and Families, (202) 224-5630 or (202) 224-5800.

Subcommittee on Employment and Workplace Safety, (202) 224-2621.

Senate Homeland Security and Governmental Affairs Committee, (202) 224-2627.
Web, hsgac.senate.gov

Permanent Subcommittee on Investigations, (202) 224-9505.

Senate Indian Affairs Committee, (202) 224-2251.
Web, indian.senate.gov

Senate Judiciary Committee, (202) 224-7703.
Web, judiciary.senate.gov

Subcommittee on Administrative Oversight and the Courts, (202) 224-8352.

Subcommittee on Antitrust, Competition Policy and Consumer Rights (202) 224-3406.

Subcommittee on the Constitution, (202) 224-5573.

Subcommittee on Crime and Drugs, (202) 224-0558.

Subcommittee on Human Rights and the Law, (202) 224-1158.

Subcommittee on Immigration, Refugees, and Border Security, (202) 224-7878.

Subcommittee on Terrorism, Technology, and Homeland Security, (202) 224-4933.

Senate Rules and Administration Committee, (202) 224-6352.
Web, rules.senate.gov

Senate Select Committee on Ethics, (202) 224-2981.
Web, ethics.senate.gov

Senate Small Business and Entrepreneurship Committee, (202) 224-5175.
Web, sbc.senate.gov

Senate Special Committee on Aging, (202) 224-5364.
Web, aging.senate.gov

Serves as the policy-making and governing body for the administration of the federal judicial system; advises Congress on the creation of new federal judgeships. Interests include international judicial relations.

Supreme Court of the United States, *1 1st St. N.E. 20543; (202) 479-3000. John G. Roberts Jr., Chief Justice.*
Web, *www.supremecourtus.gov/publicinfo*

Highest appellate court in the federal judicial system. Interprets the U.S. Constitution, federal legislation, and treaties. Provides information on new cases filed, the status of pending cases, and admissions to the Supreme Court Bar. Library open to Supreme Court bar members only.

►NONGOVERNMENTAL

AEI Legal Center for the Public Interest, *1150 17th St. N.W. 20036; (202) 862-580. Fax, (202) 862-7171. Arthur C. Brooks, President.*
General e-mail, sara.wexler@aei.org
Web, *www.AEILegalCenter.org*

Public interest law center and information clearinghouse. Studies judicial issues and the impact of the legal system on the private sector; sponsors seminars; does not litigate cases. (Merger of the National Legal Center for the Public Interest and the American Enterprise Institute.)

Alliance for Justice, *11 Dupont Circle N.W., 2nd Floor 20036-1213; (202) 822-6070. Fax, (202) 822-6068. Nan Aron, President.*
General e-mail, alliance@afj.org
Web, *www.afj.org*

Membership: public interest lawyers and advocacy, environmental, civil rights, and consumer organizations. Promotes reform of the legal system to ensure access to the courts; monitors selection of federal judges; works to preserve the rights of nonprofit organizations to advocate on behalf of their constituents.

American Assn. for Justice, *777 6th St. N.W. 20001; (202) 965-3500. Fax, (202) 342-5484. Jon Haber, Chief Executive Officer.*

Justice Department

General e-mail, aaj@justice.org

Web, www.justice.org

Membership: attorneys, judges, law professors, and students. Works to strengthen the civil justice system and the right to trial by jury. Interests include victims' rights, property and casualty insurance, revisions of federal rules of evidence, criminal code, jurisdictions of courts, juries, and consumer law. (Formerly the Assn. of Trial Lawyers of America.)

American Bar Assn. (ABA), *Washington Office,*
740 15th St. N.W. 20005-1019; (202) 662-1000. Fax, (202) 662-1099. Henry F. White Jr., Executive Director. Information, (202) 662-1010. Library, (202) 662-1011.

Web, www.abanet.org

Composed of the Governmental Affairs Office, Public Services Division, Government and Public Sector Lawyers Division, International Law and Practice Section, Criminal Justice Section, Taxation Section, Individual Rights and Responsibilities Section, Dispute Resolution Section, Administrative Law and Regulatory Practice Section, and others. Acts as a clearinghouse for the association's legislative activities and communicates the status of important bills and regulations to state and local bar associations and to all sections concerned with major governmental activities that affect the legal profession. Publishes the *ABA Washington Letter,* a monthly online legislative analysis, and *ABA Washington Summary,* a daily online publication. (Headquarters in Chicago, Ill.)

American Constitution Society for Law and Policy,
1333 H St. N.W., 11th Floor 20005; (202) 393-6181. Fax, (202) 393-6189. David Lyle, Executive Director (Acting). General e-mail, info@acslaw.org

Web, www.acslaw.org

National association of lawyers, law students, judges, legal scholars, and policymakers that promotes a progressive vision of constitutional law and public policy. Produces issue briefs and publications. Organizes lectures, conferences, seminars, and two annual student competitions.

American Tort Reform Assn., 1101 Connecticut Ave. N.W., #400 20036-4351; (202) 682-1163. Fax, (202) 682-1022. Sherman Joyce, President.
Web, www.atra.org

Membership: businesses, associations, trade groups, professional societies, and individuals interested in reforming the civil justice system in the United States. Develops model state legislation and position papers on tort reform. Works with state coalitions in support of tort reform legislation.

Center for Study of Responsive Law, 1530 P St. N.W. 20005 (mailing address: P.O. Box 19367, Washington, DC 20036); (202) 387-8030. Fax, (202) 234-5176. John Richard, Administrator.
General e-mail, csrl@csrl.org
Web, www.csrl.org

Consumer interest clearinghouse that conducts research and holds conferences on public interest law. Interests include white-collar crime, the environment, occupational health and safety, the postal system, banking deregulation, insurance, freedom of information policy, and broadcasting.

Death Penalty Information Center, 1101 Vermont Ave. N.W., #701 20005; (202) 289-2275. Fax, (202) 289-7336. Richard Dieter, Executive Director.
General e-mail, dpic@deathpenaltyinfo.org
Web, www.deathpenaltyinfo.org

Provides the media and public with analysis and information on issues concerning capital punishment. Conducts briefings for journalists; prepares reports; issues press releases.

Federal Bar Assn., 1220 N. Fillmore St., #444, Arlington, VA 22201; (571) 481-9100. Fax, (571) 481-9090. Jack D. Lockridge, Executive Director.
General e-mail, fba@fedbar.org
Web, www.fedbar.org

Membership: attorneys employed by the federal government or practicing before federal courts or agencies. Conducts research and programs in fields that include tax, environment, veterans health, intellectual property, Social Security, transportation, Native American, antitrust, immigration, and international law; concerns include professional ethics, legal education (primarily continuing education), and legal services.

The Federalist Society, 1015 18th St. N.W., #425 20036; (202) 822-8138. Fax, (202) 296-8061. Eugene B. Meyer, President.
General e-mail, info@fed-soc.org
Web, www.fed-soc.org

Promotes awareness of federalist principles among lawyers, judges, law professors, law students, and the general public. Sponsors lectures, debates, and seminars.

HALT—An Organization of Americans for Legal Reform, 1612 K St. N.W., #510 20006-2802; (202) 887-8255. Fax, (202) 887-9699. James C. Turner, Executive Director. Toll-free, (888) 367-4258.
General e-mail, halt@halt.org
Web, www.halt.org

Public interest organization concerned with legal reform. Interests include freedom of information, small claims reform, lawyer accountability, and judicial integrity. Conducts research on alternative dispute resolution programs for delivery of legal services, including arbitration, legal clinics, and mediation services; provides educational and self-help manuals for consumers on the legal process.

Lawyers for Civil Justice, 1140 Connecticut Ave. N.W., #503 20036-4013; (202) 429-0045. Fax, (202) 429-6982. Gregory Lederer, President.
Web, www.lfcj.com

Membership: defense lawyers and corporate counsel. Interests include tort reform, litigation cost containment, and tort and product liability. Monitors legislation and regulations affecting civil justice reform.

National Assn. for the Advancement of Colored People (NAACP), Washington Bureau, 1156 15th St. N.W., #915 20005-1750; (202) 463-2940. Fax, (202) 463-2953. Hilary O. Shelton, Director.
General e-mail, washingtonbureau@naacpnet.org
Web, www.naacp.org

Membership: persons interested in civil rights for all minorities. Seeks, through litigation, to end discrimination in all areas, including discriminatory practices in the administration of justice. Studies and recommends policy on court administration and jury selection. Maintains branch offices in many state and federal prisons. (Headquarters in Baltimore, Md.)

National Bar Assn., 1225 11th St. N.W. 20001-4217; (202) 842-3900. Fax, (202) 289-6170. John Crump, Executive Director.
General e-mail, info@nationalbar.org
Web, www.nationalbar.org

Membership: primarily minority attorneys, legal professionals, judges, and law students. Interests include legal education and improvement of the judicial process. Sponsors legal education seminars in all states that require continuing legal education for lawyers.

National Center for State Courts, Government Relations, 2425 Wilson Blvd., #350, Arlington, VA 22201; (703) 841-5601. Fax, (703) 841-5645. Kay Farley, Executive Director. Toll-free, (800) 532-0204, ext. 5601.
General e-mail, govrel@ncsc.dni.us
Web, www.ncsconline.org/d_gov/govindex.html

Works to improve state court systems through research, technical assistance, and training programs. Monitors legislation affecting court systems; interests include state-federal jurisdiction, family law, criminal justice, court administration, international agreements, and

General Counsels for Federal Departments and Agencies

DEPARTMENTS

Agriculture, James Michael Kelly, (202) 720-3351

Commerce, Barbara Fredericks (Acting), (202) 482-4772

Defense, Daniel Dell'orto (Acting), (703) 695-3341

  Air Force, Robert Maguire (Acting), (703) 697-0941

  Army, Levator Norsworth Jr. (Acting), (703) 697-9235

  Navy, Frank Jimenez, (703) 614-1994

Education, Charles Rose , (202) 401-6000

Energy, Eric J. Fygi (Acting), (202) 586-5281

Health and Human Services, Vacant, (202) 690-7741

Homeland Security, Ivan Fong, (202) 282-9673

Housing and Urban Development, Helen R. Karovsky, (202) 708-2244

Interior, Arthur Gary (Acting), (202) 208-4423

Justice, David Barron (Acting), (202) 514-2051

Labor, Vacant, (202) 693-5260

State, Erich Hart, (202) 647-9598

Transportation, Rosalind A. Knapp (Acting), (202) 366-4702

Treasury, Robert Hoyt, (202) 622-0283

Veterans Affairs, John Thompson (Acting), (202) 273-6660

AGENCIES

Advisory Council on Historic Preservation, Javier Marques, (202) 606-8503

Agency for International Development, Alan Swendiman, (202) 712-0900

Central Intelligence Agency, John Rizzo (Acting), (703) 482-1951

Commission on Civil Rights, David T. Blackwood, (202) 376-7622

Commodity Futures Trading Commission, Terry Arbit, (202) 418-5120

Consumer Product Safety Commission, Cheryl A. Falvey, (301) 504-7642

Corporation for National Service, Frank Trinity, (202) 606-5000, ext. 6677

Environmental Protection Agency, Patricia Hirsch, (202) 564-8040

Equal Employment Opportunity Commission, Ronald Cooper, (202) 663-4702

Export-Import Bank, Kamil Cook (Acting), (202) 565-3229

Farm Credit Administration, Charles R. Rawls, (703) 883-4020

Federal Communications Commission, Matthew Berry, (202) 418-1700

Federal Deposit Insurance Corporation, Michael Bradfield, (202) 898-3645

Federal Election Commission, Thomasenia Duncan, (202) 694-1650

Federal Emergency Management Agency, David Trissell, (202) 646-4105

Federal Energy Regulatory Commission, Cynthia Marlette, (202) 502-6000

Federal Labor Relations Authority, Vacant, (202) 218-7910

---

automated information systems. Serves as secretariat for eleven state court organizations, including the Conference of Chief Justices, Conference of State Court Administrators, American Judges Assn., and National Assn. for Court Management. (Headquarters in Williamsburg, Va.)

National Institute of Military Justice, *4801 Massachusetts Ave. N.W. 20016; (202) 274-4322. Fax, (202) 274-4226. Eugene R. Fidell, President. General e-mail, nimj@wcl.american.edu*

Web, www.nimj.org

Seeks to advance fair administration of military justice and improve public understanding of the military justice system. Offers assistance in court cases related to military justice law and policy. Monitors legislation and regulations. Does not represent individuals. (Affiliated with the Washington College of Law at American University.)

National Whistleblower Center, *3238 P St. N.W. 20007-2756 (mailing address: P.O. Box 3768, Washington, DC 20027); (202) 342-1903. Fax, (202) 342-1904. Stephen M. Kohn, Executive Director (Acting). General e-mail, contact@whistleblowers.org*

Web, www.whistleblowers.org

Supports and represents employee whistleblowers. Works to ensure that whistleblower disclosures about improper government and industry actions that are harmful to the environment and the public health are defended and heard. Operates attorney referral service through National Whistleblower Legal Defense and Education Fund.

RAND Corporation, *Washington Office, 1200 S. Hayes St., Arlington, VA 22202-5050; (703) 413-1100. Fax, (703) 413-8111. Lynn Davis, Director. Web, www.rand.org*

Analyzes current problems of the American civil and criminal justice systems and evaluates recent and pending changes and reforms. (Headquarters in Santa Monica, Calif.)

State Justice Institute, *1650 King St., #600, Alexandria, VA 22314; (703) 684-6100. Fax, (703) 684-7618. Janice Munsterman, Executive Director. Web, www.statejustice.org*

Awards grants to state courts and to state agencies for development and training programs that improve state courts' judicial administration and raise their performance standards. Interests include judicial education, court-media relations, federal-state relations, victim assistance, immigration issues, and senior citizen issues.

General Counsels for Federal Departments and Agencies

Federal Maritime Commission, Peter King (Acting), (202) 523-5740

Federal Mediation and Conciliation Service, Dawn Starr, (202) 606-5444

Federal Reserve System, Scott Alvarez, (202) 452-3583

Federal Trade Commission, David Shonka (Acting), (202) 326-2424

General Services Administration, Lennard Loewentritt, (202) 501-2200

International Bank for Reconstruction and Development (World Bank), Scott White (Acting), (202) 458-2600

Merit Systems Protection Board, B. Chad Bungard, (202) 653-7171

National Aeronautics and Space Administration, Michael C. Wholley, (202) 358-2450

National Credit Union Administration, Robert M. Fenner, (703) 518-6540

National Endowment for Humanities, Heather Gottry (Acting), (202) 606-8322

National Endowment for the Arts, Karen Elias (Acting), (202) 682-5418

National Labor Relations Board, Ronald Meisburg, (202) 273-3700

National Mediation Board, Mary L. Johnson, (202) 692-5040

National Railroad Passenger Corporation (Amtrak), Eleanor Acheson, (202) 906-2198

National Science Foundation, Lawrence Rudolph, (703) 292-8060

National Transportation Safety Board, Gary L. Halbert, (202) 314-6080

Nuclear Regulatory Commission, Karen D. Cyr, (301) 415-1743

Occupational Safety and Health Review Commission, Vacant, (202) 606-5410

Office of Personnel Management, Vacant, (202) 606-1700

Overseas Private Investment Corporation, Mark Garfinkel, (202) 336-8410

Peace Corps, Carl Sossebbe (Acting), (202) 692-2150

Pension Benefit Guaranty Corporation, Judith Starr, (202) 326-4020, ext. 4400

Postal Regulatory Commission, Stephen Sharfman, (202) 789-6820

Securities and Exchange Commission, Andrew Vollmer, (202) 551-5100

Small Business Administration, Nina Levine, (202) 205-6642

Smithsonian Institution, Marsha Shane (Acting), (202) 633-5099

Social Security Administration, David Black, (410) 965-0600

U.S. International Trade Commission, James M. Lyons, (202) 205-3061

U.S. Postal Service, Mary Anne Gibbons, (202) 268-2950

U.S. Chamber of Commerce, *Congressional and Public Affairs, 1615 H St. N.W. 20062-2000; (202) 463-5600. Fax, (202) 887-3430. Rolf T. Lundberg, Senior Vice President.*
Web, www.uschamber.com

Federation of individuals; firms; corporations; trade and professional associations; and local, state, and regional chambers of commerce. Monitors legislation and regulations in administrative law, antitrust policy, civil justice reform, and product liability reform.

U.S. Chamber of Commerce, *Institute for Legal Reform, 1615 H St. N.W. 20062-2000; (202) 463-5724. Fax, (202) 463-5302. Lisa A. Rickard, President.*
General e-mail, ilr@uschamber.com
Web, www.instituteforlegalreform.org

Works to make the civil justice system simpler, fairer, and faster. Strives to reduce excessive litigation. Hosts public forums on legal and tort reform.

Washington Legal Foundation, *2009 Massachusetts Ave. N.W. 20036; (202) 588-0302. Fax, (202) 588-0386. Daniel J. Popeo, General Counsel.*
General e-mail, administration@wlf.org
Web, www.wlf.org

Public interest law and policy center. Interests include constitutional law, government regulation, media law, and criminal justice; litigates on behalf of small businesses, members of Congress, and victims of violent crimes who bring civil suits against their attackers.

Women's Bar Assn., *2020 Pennsylvania Ave. N.W., #446 20006; (202) 639-8880. Fax, (202) 639-8889. Carol Montoya, Executive Director.*
General e-mail, admin@wbadc.org
Web, www.wbadc.org

Membership: women and men who are judges, attorneys in the public and private sectors, law students, and lawyers at home who remain professionally active. Promotes appointment of members to positions in the judiciary and legislative policies that foster the advancement of women.

World Jurist Assn., *7910 Woodmont Ave., #1440, Bethesda, MD 20814; (202) 466-5428. Fax, (202) 452-8540. Margaret M. Henneberry, Executive Vice President.*
General e-mail, wja@worldjurist.org
Web, www.worldjurist.org

Membership: lawyers, law professors, judges, law students, and nonlegal professionals worldwide. Conducts research; promotes world peace through adherence to international law; holds biennial world conferences. (Affiliates, at same address, include World Assn. of Judges, World Assn. of Law Professors, World Assn. of Lawyers, and World Business Assn.)

Dispute Resolution

►AGENCIES

Justice Dept. (DOJ), *Dispute Resolution, 950 Pennsylvania Ave. N.W., #5738 20530-0001; (202) 305-4439. Fax, (202) 616-9570. Joanna Jacobs, Director (Acting).*
Web, www.usdoj.gov/odr

Division of the office of the associate attorney general. Coordinates Justice Dept. activities related to dispute resolution. Responsible for alternative dispute resolution (ADR), policy, and training. Manages the Interagency ADR Working Group.

►NONGOVERNMENTAL

American Arbitration Assn., *Government Relations, 1776 Eye St. N.W., #850 20006; (202) 739-8280,ext. 109. Fax, (202) 222-7095. Jean Baker, Vice President.*
General e-mail, BakerJ@adr.org

Web, www.adr.org

Provides alternative dispute resolution services to governments and the private sector. (Headquarters in New York.)

American Bar Assn. (ABA), *Dispute Resolution, 740 15th St. N.W., 7th Floor 20005-1009; (202) 662-1680. Fax, (202) 662-1683. Kimberly Knight, Executive Director. Press, (202) 662-1698.*
General e-mail, dispute@abanet.org

Web, www.abanet.org/dispute

Acts as a clearinghouse on dispute resolution; supports alternative methods to litigation for resolving disputes; provides technical assistance.

Assn. for Conflict Resolution, *5151 Wisconsin Ave. N.W., #500 20016; (202) 464-9700. Fax, (202) 464-9720. Douglas M. Kleine, Executive Director.*
General e-mail, membership@acrnet.org

Web, www.acrnet.org

Membership: mediators, arbitrators, facilitators, and others involved in conflict resolution and collaborative decision making. Provides professional development and educational opportunities for members and the public through its conferences, publications, and Web site. Offers referrals for mediation. (The Assn. for Conflict Resolution is a merger of the Academy of Family Mediators, the Conflict Resolution Education Network, and the Society of Professionals in Dispute Resolution.)

Center for Dispute Settlement, *1666 Connecticut Ave. N.W., #500 20009-1039; (202) 265-9572. Fax, (202) 332-3951. Linda R. Singer, President.*

General e-mail, cds@cdsusa.org

Web, www.cdsusa.org

Designs, implements, and evaluates alternative and nonjudicial methods of dispute resolution. Mediates disputes. Provides training in dispute resolution for public and private institutions, individuals, and communities.

Council of Better Business Bureaus, *Dispute Resolution, 4200 Wilson Blvd., #800, Arlington, VA 22203-1838. Steven J. Cole, President.*
General e-mail, bbb@bbb.org

Web, www.dr.bbb.org

Administers mediation and arbitration programs through Better Business Bureaus nationwide to assist in resolving disputes between businesses and consumers. Assists with unresolved disputes between car owners and automobile manufacturers. Maintains pools of certified arbitrators nationwide. Provides mediation training.

HALT—An Organization of Americans for Legal Reform, *1612 K St. N.W., #510 20006-2802; (202) 887-8255. Fax, (202) 887-9699. James C. Turner, Executive Director. Toll-free, (888) 367-4258.*
General e-mail, halt@halt.org

Web, www.halt.org

Public interest organization concerned with legal reform. Interests include freedom of information, small claims reform, lawyer accountability, and judicial integrity. Conducts research on alternative dispute resolution programs for delivery of legal services, including arbitration, legal clinics, and mediation services; provides educational and self-help manuals for consumers on the legal process.

National Assn. for Community Mediation (NAFCM), *1514 Upshur St. N.W. 20011; (202) 545-8866. Fax, (202) 545-8873. Irvin Foster, Executive Director.*
General e-mail, nafcm@nafcm.org

Web, www.nafcm.org

Supports the maintenance and growth of community-based mediation programs and processes. Provides information on the development and practice of community mediation; encourages regional and national collaborative projects among community mediation programs.

Judicial Appointments

►AGENCIES

Justice Dept. (DOJ), *Legal Policy, 950 Pennsylvania Ave. N.W., #4234 20530-0001; (202) 514-4601. Fax, (202) 514-2424. Kevin Jones, Assistant Attorney General (Acting).*
Web, www.usdoj.gov/olp

Investigates and processes prospective candidates for presidential appointment (subject to Senate confirmation) to the federal judiciary.

►CONGRESS

For a listing of relevant congressional committees and subcommittees, please see page 468 or the Appendix.

►JUDICIARY

Administrative Office of the U.S. Courts, *1 Columbus Circle N.E. 20544-0001; (202) 502-2600. James C. Duff, Director.*
Web, www.uscourts.gov/adminoff.html

Supervises all administrative matters of the federal court system, except the Supreme Court. Transmits to Congress the recommendations of the Judicial Conference of the United States concerning creation of federal judgeships and other legislative proposals.

Judicial Conference of the United States, *1 Columbus Circle N.E., #7-425 20544; (202) 502-2400. Fax, (202) 502-1144. John G. Roberts Jr., Chief Justice of the United States, Chair; James C. Duff, Secretary.*
Web, www.uscourts.gov

Serves as the policy-making and governing body for the administration of the federal judicial system; advises Congress on the creation of new federal judgeships. Interests include international judicial relations.

►NONGOVERNMENTAL

Alliance for Justice, *Judicial Selection Project, 11 Dupont Circle N.W., 2nd Floor 20036-6919; (202) 822-6070. Fax, (202) 822-6068. Nan Aron, President; Caroline Lerner, Lead Attorney.*
General e-mail, alliance@afj.org

Web, www.afj.org

Monitors candidates for vacancies in the federal judiciary; independently reviews nominees' records; maintains statistics on the judiciary.

Committee for Justice, *722 12th St. N.W., 4th Floor 20005; (202) 270-7748. Fax, (202) 204-4861. Curt Levey, Executive Director.*
General e-mail, contact@committeeforjustice.org

Web, www.committeeforjustice.org

Defends and promotes constitutionalist judicial nominees and the rule of law.

BUSINESS AND TAX LAW

Antitrust

►AGENCIES

Antitrust Division *(Justice Dept.), 950 Pennsylvania Ave. N.W., #1220 20530-0001; (202) 514-2481. Fax, (202) 616-2645. Christine A. Varney, Assistant Attorney General. Press, (202) 514-2007.*
General e-mail, antitrust.atr@usdoj.gov

Web, www.usdoj.gov/atr

Enforces antitrust laws to prevent monopolies and unlawful restraint of trade; has civil and criminal jurisdiction; coordinates activities with the Bureau of Competition of the Federal Trade Commission.

Antitrust Division *(Justice Dept.), Antitrust Documents Group, 450 6th St. N.W., #1024 20530; (202) 514-2481. Fax, (202) 514-3763. Janie M. Ingalls, Chief.*
General e-mail, atrdocsgrp@usdoj.gov

Web, www.usdoj.gov/atr

Maintains files and handles requests for information on federal civil and criminal antitrust cases; provides the president and Congress with copies of statutory reports prepared by the division on a variety of competition-related issues; issues opinion letters on whether certain business activity violates antitrust laws.

Antitrust Division *(Justice Dept.), Litigation I, 1401 H St. N.W., #4000 20530; (202) 307-0001. Fax, (202) 307-5802. Joshua H. Soven, Chief.*
General e-mail, atr.personnel@usdoj.gov

Web, www.usdoj.gov/atr/sections.htm

Investigates and litigates cases involving dairy, health care, paper, and insurance.

Antitrust Division *(Justice Dept.), Litigation II, 1401 H St. N.W., #3000 20530; (202) 307-0924. Fax, (202) 514-9033. Maribeth Petrizzi, Chief.*
Web, www.usdoj.gov/atr/sections.htm

Investigates and litigates cases involving defense, waste, and banking.

Antitrust Division *(Justice Dept.), Litigation III, 325 7th St. N.W., #300 20530-0001; (202) 616-5935. Fax, (202) 514-7308. John R. Read, Chief.*
Web, www.usdoj.gov/atr

Investigates and litigates certain antitrust cases involving such commodities as movies, radio, TV, newspapers, performing arts, sports, toys, and credit and debit cards. Handles certain violations of antitrust laws that involve patents, copyrights, and trademarks. Deals with mergers and acquisitions.

Antitrust Division *(Justice Dept.), Networks and Technology Enforcement, 600 E St. N.W., #9500 20530; (202) 307-6200. Fax, (202) 616-8544. James J. Tierney, Chief.*
Web, www.usdoj.gov/atr

Investigates and litigates certain antitrust cases involving either communications industries or financial institutions, including securities, commodity futures, and insurance firms; participates in agency proceedings and rulemaking in these areas.

Antitrust Division *(Justice Dept.), Transportation, Energy, and Agriculture, 325 7th St. N.W., #500 20530; (202) 307-6349. Fax, (202) 307-2784. Donna N. Kooperstein, Chief.*
Web, www.usdoj.gov/atr

Enforces antitrust laws in the airline, railroad, motor carrier, barge line, ocean carrier, and energy industries. Litigates antitrust cases pertaining to agriculture and related commodities. Participates in proceedings before the Federal Energy Regulatory Commission, Environmental Protection Agency, and Agriculture Dept.

Comptroller of the Currency *(Treasury Dept.)*, *250 E St. S.W. 20219; (202) 874-5000. Fax, (202) 874-4950. John C. Dugan, Comptroller. Library, (202) 874-4720. Press, (202) 874-5770.*
Web, www.occ.treas.gov

Regulates and examines operations of national banks; establishes guidelines for bank examinations; handles mergers of national banks with regard to antitrust law. Library open to the public.

Federal Communications Commission (FCC), *Wireline Competition Bureau, 445 12th St. S.W. 20554; (202) 418-1500. Fax, (202) 418-2825. Julie Veach, Chief (Acting).*
Web, www.fcc.gov/wcb

Regulates mergers involving common carriers (wireline facilities that furnish interstate communications services).

Federal Deposit Insurance Corp. (FDIC), *Division of Supervision and Consumer Protection, 550 17th St. N.W. 20429; (202) 898-6880. Fax, (202) 898-3638. Sandra L. Thompson, Director.*
Web, www.fdic.gov

Studies and analyzes applications for mergers, consolidations, acquisitions, and assumption transactions between insured banks.

Federal Energy Regulatory Commission (FERC), *(Energy Dept.), 888 1st St. N.E., #11A 20426; (202) 502-8000. Fax, (202) 502-8612. Joseph T. Kelliher, Chair. Information, (202) 502-8200. Press, (202) 502-8680. Dockets, (202) 502-8715. Public reference room, (202) 502-8371. Public inquiries, (202) 502-6088.*
Web, www.ferc.gov

Regulates mergers, consolidations, and acquisitions of electric utilities; regulates the acquisition of interstate natural gas pipeline facilities.

Federal Maritime Commission, *800 N. Capitol St. N.W., #1046 20573-0001; (202) 523-5725. Fax, (202) 523-0014. Vacant, Chair; Austin L. Schmitt, Director of Operations. TTY, (800) 877-8339. Locator, (202) 523-5773. General e-mail, secretary@fmc.gov*
Web, www.fmc.gov

Regulates the foreign ocean shipping of the United States; reviews agreements (on rates, schedules, and other matters) filed by ocean common carriers for compliance with shipping statutes and grants limited antitrust immunity. Library open to the public.

Federal Reserve System, *Banking Supervision and Regulation, 20th St. and Constitution Ave. N.W. 20551; (202) 452-2773. Fax, (202) 452-2770. Roger T. Cole, Director, (202) 452-2618.*
Web, www.federalreserve.gov

Approves bank mergers, consolidations, and other alterations in bank structure.

Federal Trade Commission (FTC), *Competition, 600 Pennsylvania Ave. N.W., #394 20580; (202) 326-3300. Fax,*

(202) 326-2884. David Wales Jr., Director (Acting). Press, (202) 326-2180. Toll-free, (877) 382-4357.
General e-mail, antitrust@ftc.gov
Web, www.ftc.gov

Enforces antitrust laws and investigates possible violations, mergers and acquisitions, and anticompetitive practices; seeks voluntary compliance and pursues civil judicial remedies; reviews premerger filings; coordinates activities with the Antitrust Division of the Justice Dept.

Federal Trade Commission (FTC), *Competition: Anticompetitive Practices, 601 New Jersey Ave. N.W., #6264 20001 (mailing address: 600 Pennsylvania Ave. N.W., Washington, DC 20580); (202) 326-2584. Fax, (202) 326-3496. Melanie Sabo, Assistant Director. Toll-free, (877) 382-4357.*
General e-mail, antitrust@ftc.gov
Web, www.ftc.gov

Investigates nonmerger anticompetitive practices in a variety of industries.

Federal Trade Commission (FTC), *Competition: Compliance, 601 New Jersey Ave. N.W., #5222 20001 (mailing address: 600 Pennsylvania Ave. N.W., Washington, DC 20580); (202) 326-2152. Fax, (202) 326-3396. Daniel P. Ducore, Assistant Director, (202) 326-2526. General e-mail, bcompliance@ftc.gov*
Web, www.ftc.gov/bc/mission

Monitors and enforces competition orders. Investigates possible violations of the Hart-Scott-Rodino Act.

Federal Trade Commission (FTC), *Competition: Healthcare Services and Products, 601 New Jersey Ave. N.W., #7223 20001 (mailing address: 600 Pennsylvania Ave. N.W., Washington, DC 20580); (202) 326-3759. Fax, (202) 326-3384. Markus H. Meier, Assistant Director. General e-mail, antitrust@ftc.gov*
Web, www.ftc.gov

Investigates and litigates nonmerger anticompetitive practices in the health care industry, including the pharmaceutical industry.

Federal Trade Commission (FTC), *Competition: Honors Paralegal Program, 601 New Jersey Ave. N.W., #6137 20580; (202) 326-3619. Fax, (202) 326-3496. Sara Dillon, Coordinator.*
General e-mail, honorsparalegals@ftc.gov
Web, www.ftc.gov/ftc/oed/hrmo/hpp/index.5htm

Administers paralegal program for individuals considering a career in law, economics, business, or public service. Honors paralegals are given significant responsibility and hands-on experience while assisting attorneys and economists in the investigation and litigation of antitrust matters. Applicants are appointed for 14-month terms.

Federal Trade Commission (FTC), *Competition: Mergers I, 601 New Jersey Ave. N.W., #5108 20001 (mailing address: 600 Pennsylvania Ave. N.W., Washington, DC 20580); (202) 326-3106. Fax, (202) 326-2655. Michael Moiseyev, Assistant Director.*

General e-mail, antitrust@ftc.gov

Web, www.ftc.gov/bc/mission

Investigates and litigates antitrust violations in mergers and acquisitions in the pharmaceutical, defense, and medical product industries.

Federal Trade Commission (FTC), *Competition: Mergers II, 601 New Jersey Ave. N.W., #6120 20001 (mailing address: 600 Pennsylvania Ave. N.W., Washington, DC 20580); (202) 326-2749. Fax, (202) 326-2071. Catharine M. Moscatelli, Assistant Director.* General e-mail, antitrust@ftc.gov

Web, www.ftc.gov/bc/mission

Investigates and litigates antitrust violations in mergers and acquisitions in the chemicals, technology, retail, book, music, and other industries.

Federal Trade Commission (FTC), *Competition: Mergers III, 601 New Jersey Ave. N.W., #7119 20001 (mailing address: 600 Pennsylvania Ave. N.W., Washington, DC 20580); (202) 326-2805. Fax, (202) 326-3383. Phillip Broyles, Assistant Director.* General e-mail, antitrust@ftc.gov

Web, www.ftc.gov/bc/mission

Investigates and litigates antitrust violations in mergers and acquisitions concerning the oil and energy industries.

Federal Trade Commission (FTC), *Competition: Mergers IV, 601 New Jersey Ave. N.W., #5245 20001 (mailing address: 600 Pennsylvania Ave. N.W., Washington, DC 20580); (202) 326-2350. Fax, (202) 326-2286. Matthew J. Reilly, Assistant Director (Acting).* General e-mail, antitrust@ftc.gov

Web, www.ftc.gov/bc/mission

Investigates and litigates antitrust violations in mergers and acquisitions concerning the hospital industry, the grocery food product industry, and the media.

Federal Trade Commission (FTC), *Competition: Premerger Notification, 600 Pennsylvania Ave. N.W., #H-301 20580; (202) 326-2740. Fax, (202) 326-2624. Robert L. Jones, Deputy Assistant Director.* General e-mail, antitrust@ftc.gov

Web, www.ftc.gov/bc/mission

Reviews filings under the Hart-Scott-Rodino Act.

Surface Transportation Board *(Transportation Dept.), 395 E St. S.W. 20423-0001; (202) 245-0245. Fax, (202) 245-0458. Charles D. Nottingham, Chair, (202) 245-0200. Library, (202) 245-0406. TTY, (800) 877-8339.* Web, www.stb.dot.gov

Regulates rail rate disputes, railroad consolidations, rail line construction proposals, line abandonments, and rail car service. Library open to the public.

▶**CONGRESS**

For a listing of relevant congressional committees and subcommittees, please see page 468 or the Appendix.

▶**NONGOVERNMENTAL**

American Antitrust Institute (AAI), *2919 Ellicott St. N.W., #1000 20008-1022; (202) 276-6002. Fax, (202) 966-8711. Albert A. "Bert" Foer, President.* Web, www.antitrustinstitute.org

Pro-antitrust organization that provides research and policy analysis to journalists, academic researchers, lawyers, economists, businesspeople, government officials, courts, and the general public. Seeks to educate the public on the importance of fair competition. Monitors legislation and regulations on competition-oriented policies.

Assn. of Corporate Counsel, *1025 Connecticut Ave. N.W., #200 20036-5425; (202) 293-4103. Fax, (202) 293-4701. Frederick J. Krebs, President.* General e-mail, webmistress@acc.com

Web, www.acc.com

Membership: practicing attorneys in corporate law departments and in legal departments of other private-sector organizations. Provides information on corporate law issues, including securities, health and safety, the environment, intellectual property, litigation, international legal affairs, pro bono work, and labor benefits. Monitors legislation and regulations, with primary focus on issues affecting in-house attorneys' ability to practice law. (Formerly American Corporate Counsel.)

The Business Roundtable, *1717 Rhode Island Ave. N.W., #800 20036-3026; (202) 872-1260. Fax, (202) 466-3509. John J. Castellani, President.* General e-mail, info@businessroundtable.org

Web, www.businessroundtable.org

Membership: chief executives of the nation's largest corporations. Examines issues of concern to business, including antitrust law.

Bankruptcy

▶**AGENCIES**

Executive Office for U.S. Trustees *(Justice Dept.), 20 Massachusetts Ave. N.W., #8000 20530; (202) 307-1391. Fax, (202) 307-0672. Clifford J. White III, Director.* General e-mail, ustrustee.program@usdoj.gov

Web, www.usdoj.gov/ust

Handles the administration and oversight of bankruptcy and liquidation cases filed under the Bankruptcy Reform Act, including detecting and combating bankruptcy fraud. Provides individual U.S. trustee offices with administrative and management support.

Justice Dept. (DOJ), *Legal Policy, 950 Pennsylvania Ave. N.W., #4234 20530-0001; (202) 514-4601. Fax, (202) 514-2424. Kevin Jones, Assistant Attorney General (Acting).* Web, www.usdoj.gov/olp

Studies and develops policy for improvement of the criminal and civil justice systems, including bankruptcy reform policy.

►CONGRESS

For a listing of relevant congressional committees and subcommittees, please see page 468 or the Appendix.

►JUDICIARY

Administrative Office of the U.S. Courts, *Bankruptcy Judges Division,* 1 Columbus Circle N.E., #4-250 20544-0001; (202) 502-1900. Fax, (202) 502-1988. *Francis F. Szczebak, Chief.*
Web, www.uscourts.gov

Provides administrative assistance and support in the operation of U.S. bankruptcy courts.

►NONGOVERNMENTAL

American Bankruptcy Institute, *44 Canal Center Plaza, #400, Alexandria, VA 22314-1592; (703) 739-0800. Fax, (703) 739-1060. Samuel Gerdano, Executive Director.*
General e-mail, info@abiworld.org

Web, www.abiworld.org

Membership: lawyers; federal and state legislators; and representatives of accounting and financial services firms, lending institutions, credit organizations, and consumer groups. Provides information and educational services on insolvency, reorganization, and bankruptcy issues; sponsors conferences, seminars, and workshops.

National Assn. of Consumer Bankruptcy Attorneys, *2300 M St. N.W., #800 20037; (202) 331-8005. Fax, (202) 331-8535. Maureen Thompson, Legislative Director.*
General e-mail, admin@nacba.org

Web, www.nacba.org

Advocates on behalf of consumer debtors and their attorneys. Files amicus briefs on behalf of parties in the U.S. courts of appeal and Supreme Court, and provides educational programs and workshops for attorneys. Monitors legislation and regulations.

Tax Violations

►AGENCIES

Internal Revenue Service (IRS), *(Treasury Dept.), Procedures and Administration,* 1111 Constitution Ave. N.W., #5501 20224; (202) 622-3400. Fax, (202) 622-4914. *Deborah Butler, Associate Chief Counsel. Press, (202) 622-4000.*
Web, www.irs.gov

Oversees field office litigation of civil cases that involve underpayment of taxes when the taxpayer chooses to challenge the determinations of the Internal Revenue Service (IRS) in the U.S. Tax Court, or when the taxpayer chooses to pay the amount in question and sue the IRS for a refund. Reviews briefs and defense letters prepared by field offices for tax cases; drafts legal advice memos; prepares tax litigation advice memoranda; coordinates

litigation strategy. Makes recommendations concerning appeal and certiorari. Prepares tax regulations, rulings, and other published guidance regarding the Internal Revenue Code, as enacted.

Justice Dept. (DOJ), *Tax Division,* 950 Pennsylvania Ave. N.W., #4141 20530; (202) 514-2901. Fax, (202) 514-5479. *Nathan J. Hochman, Assistant Attorney General.*
Web, www.usdoj.gov/tax/tax.html

Authorizes prosecution of all criminal cases involving tax violations investigated and developed by the Internal Revenue Service (IRS); represents the IRS in civil litigation except in U.S. Tax Court proceedings; represents other agencies, including the departments of Defense and Interior, in cases with state or local tax authorities.

►CONGRESS

For a listing of relevant congressional committees and subcommittees, please see page 468 or the Appendix.

►JUDICIARY

U.S. Tax Court, *400 2nd St. N.W., #134 20217; (202) 521-0700. John O. Colvin, Chief Judge.*
Web, www.ustaxcourt.gov

Tries and adjudicates disputes involving income, estate, and gift taxes and personal holding company surtaxes in cases in which deficiencies have been determined by the Internal Revenue Service.

►NONGOVERNMENTAL

American Bar Assn. (ABA), *Taxation Section,* 740 15th St. N.W., 10th Floor 20005-1019; (202) 662-8670. Fax, (202) 662-8682. *William J. Wilkins, Section Chair.*
General e-mail, tax@abanet.org

Web, www.abanet.org/tax

Studies and recommends policies on taxation; provides information on tax issues; sponsors continuing legal education programs; monitors tax laws and legislation.

CIVIL RIGHTS

►AGENCIES

Commission on Civil Rights, *624 9th St. N.W., #700 20425; (202) 376-7700. Fax, (202) 376-7672. Gerald A. Reynolds, Chair; Abigail Thernstrom, Vice Chair; Martin Dannenfelser, Staff Director. Library, (202) 376-8110. Press, (202) 376-8582. TTY, (202) 376-8116.*
General e-mail, referral@usccr.gov

Web, www.usccr.gov

Assesses federal laws and policies of government agencies and studies legal developments to determine the nature and extent of denial of equal protection under the law on the basis of race, color, religion, sex, national origin, age, or disability in many areas, including employment, voting rights, education, administration of justice, and housing. Reports and makes recommendations to the president and Congress; serves as national clearinghouse for civil rights information. Conducts studies relating to discrimination against certain groups, including women, African Americans, Hispanics, Asians, Native Americans, and Pacific Islanders. Issues public service announcements to discourage discrimination or denials of equal protection of the laws. Library open to the public.

Education Dept., *Civil Rights,* 550 12th St. S.W. 20202-1100; (202) 245-6700. Fax, (202) 485-0126. Stephanie Monroe, Assistant Secretary. Information, (800) 421-3481. TTY, (877) 521-2172. General e-mail, ocr@ed.gov

Web, www.ed.gov/ocr

Enforces laws prohibiting use of federal funds for education programs or activities that discriminate on the basis of race, color, sex, national origin, age, or disability; authorized to discontinue funding.

Equal Employment Opportunity Commission (EEOC), 131 M St. N.E. 20507; (202) 663-4001. Fax, (202) 663-4110. Naomi C. Earp, Chair. Information, (202) 663-4900. Library, (202) 663-4630. TTY, (202) 663-4191. Web, www.eeoc.gov

Works to end job discrimination by private and government employers based on race, color, religion, sex, national origin, disability, or age. Works to protect employees against reprisal for protest of employment practices alleged to be unlawful in hiring, promotion, firing, wages, and other terms and conditions of employment. Works for increased employment of persons with disabilities, affirmative action by the federal government, and an equitable work environment for employees with mental and physical disabilities. Enforces Title VII of the Civil Rights Act of 1964, as amended, which includes the Pregnancy Discrimination Act; Americans with Disabilities Act; Age Discrimination in Employment Act; Equal Pay Act; and, in the federal sector, rehabilitation laws. Receives charges of discrimination; attempts conciliation or settlement; can bring court action to force compliance; has review and appeals responsibility in the federal sector. Library open to the public by appointment only.

Health and Human Services Dept. (HHS), *Civil Rights,* 200 Independence Ave. S.W., #515F 20201; (202) 619-0403. Fax, (202) 619-3437. Robinsue Frohboese, Director (Acting). TTY, (800) 537-7697. Toll-free hotline, (800) 368-1019. Web, www.hhs.gov/ocr

Administers and enforces laws prohibiting discrimination on the basis of race, color, sex, national origin, religion, age, or disability in programs receiving federal funds from the department; authorized to discontinue funding. Responsible for health information privacy under the Health Insurance Portability and Accountability Act.

Justice Dept. (DOJ), *Civil Rights Division,* 950 Pennsylvania Ave. N.W. 20530; (202) 514-2151. Fax, (202) 514-0293. Loretta King, Assistant Attorney General (Acting). Press, (202) 514-2007. TTY, (202) 514-0716. Web, www.usdoj.gov/crt

Enforces federal civil rights laws prohibiting discrimination on the basis of race, color, religion, sex, disability, age, or national origin in voting, education, employment, credit, housing, public accommodations and facilities, and federally assisted programs.

Labor Dept. (DOL), *Civil Rights Center,* 200 Constitution Ave. N.W., #N4123 20210; (202) 693-6500. Fax, (202) 693-6505. Ramón Suris Fernandez, Director. Library, (202) 693-6613. TTY, (877) 889-5627. General e-mail, civilrightscenter@dol.gov

Web, www.dol.gov/oasam/programs/crc

Resolves complaints of discrimination on the basis of race, color, religion, sex, national origin, age, or disability in programs funded by the department. Library open to the public.

▶**CONGRESS**

For a listing of relevant congressional committees and subcommittees, please see page 468 or the Appendix.

▶**NONGOVERNMENTAL**

American Assn. for Affirmative Action, 888 16th St. N.W., #800 20006; (202) 349-9855, ext. 1857. Fax, (202) 355-1399. Shirley J. Wilcher, Executive Director. Information, (800) 252-8952. General e-mail, execdir@affirmativeaction.org

Web, www.affirmativeaction.org

Membership: professional managers in the areas of affirmative action, equal opportunity, diversity, and human resources. Sponsors education, research, and training programs. Acts as a liaison with government agencies involved in equal opportunity compliance. Maintains ethical standards for the profession.

Appleseed: A Network of Public Interest Justice Centers, 727 15th St. N.W., 11th Floor 20005; (202) 347-7960. Fax, (202) 289-8009. Betsy Cavendish, Director. General e-mail, info@appleseeds.net

Web, www.appleseeds.net

Network of sixteen public interest justice centers in the United States and Mexico advocating for universal access to legal help through its pro bono network.

Center for Neighborhood Enterprise, 1625 K St. N.W., #1200 20006; (202) 518-6500. Fax, (202) 588-0314. Robert L. Woodson Sr., President. Information, (866) 518-1263. General e-mail, info@ncne.com

Web, www.ncne.com

Provides community and faith-based organizations with training, technical assistance, and additional sources of support. Addresses issues such as youth violence, substance abuse, teen pregnancy, homelessness, joblessness,

Selected Minorities-Related Resources

See also Small and Disadvantaged Business Contacts at Federal Departments and Agencies on page 77 and Information Sources on Women's Health on page 375.

ADVOCACY AND ANTIDISCRIMINATION

American-Arab Anti-Discrimination Committee, www.adc.org

Anti-Defamation League, www.adl.org

Arab American Institute, www.aaiusa.org

Human Rights Campaign, www.hrc.org

Japanese American Citizens League, www.jacl.org

Mexican American Legal Defense and Educational Fund, www.maldef.org

NAACP (National Assn. for the Advancement of Colored People), www.naacp.org

National Council of La Raza, www.nclr.org

National Gay and Lesbian Task Force, www.thetaskforce.org

National Organization for Women, www.now.org

(OCA) Organization of Chinese Americans, www.ocanatl.org

Rainbow/PUSH Coalition, www.rainbowpush.org

BUSINESS AND LABOR

Business and Professional Women USA, www.bpwusa.org

Center for Women's Business Research, www.nfwbo.org

Council of Federal EEO and Civil Rights Executives, www.fedcivilrights.org

Minority Business Enterprise Legal Defense and Education Fund, Inc., www.mbeldef.org

National Assn. of Hispanic Federal Executives, Inc., www.nahfe.org

National Assn. of Minority Contractors, www.namcline.org

National Assn. of Women Business Owners, www.nawbo.org

National Black Chamber of Commerce, www.nationalbcc.org

National Indian Business Assn., www.nibanetwork.org

National U.S.-Arab Chamber of Commerce, www.nusacc.org

U.S. Hispanic Chamber of Commerce, www.ushcc.com

U.S. Pan Asian American Chamber of Commerce, www.uspaacc.com

EDUCATION

American Assn. for Affirmative Action, www.affirmativeaction.org

American Indian Higher Education Consortium, www.aihec.org

Assn. of American Colleges and Universities, www.aacu.org

Assn. of Research Libraries, www.arl.org/diversity

---

poor education, and deteriorating neighborhoods. (Formerly known as the National Center for Neighborhood Enterprise.)

Citizens' Commission on Civil Rights, *2000 M St. N.W., #400 20036-3307; (202) 659-5565. Fax, (202) 223-5302. William L. Taylor, Chair; Dianne M. Piché, Executive Director. General e-mail, citizens@cccr.org*

Web, www.cccr.org

Bipartisan commission of former federal officials. Monitors compliance of federal agencies and judicial bodies with civil rights laws and education laws; conducts social science research and provides technical and legal assistance to other civil rights and public interest groups; interests include low- and moderate-income housing, voting rights, employment, school desegregation, and education of the disadvantaged.

Leadership Conference on Civil Rights, *1629 K St. N.W., 10th Floor 20006; (202) 466-3311. Fax, (202) 319-0924. Wade Henderson, President. General e-mail, info@civilrights.org*

Web, www.civilrights.org

Coalition of national organizations representing minorities, women, labor, older Americans, people with disabilities, and religious groups. Works for enactment and enforcement of civil rights, human rights, and social welfare legislation; acts as clearinghouse for information on civil rights legislation and regulations.

NAACP Legal Defense and Educational Fund, *Washington Office, 1444 Eye St. N.W., 10th Floor 20005; (202) 682-1300. Fax, (202) 682-1312. Leslie M. Proll, Director. Web, www.naacpldf.org*

Civil rights litigation group that provides legal information on civil rights issues, including employment, housing, and educational discrimination; monitors federal enforcement of civil rights laws. Not affiliated with the National Assn. for the Advancement of Colored People (NAACP). (Headquarters in New York.)

National Black Justice Coalition, *1638 R St. N.W., #300 20006; (202) 319-1552. Fax, (202) 319-0924. H. Alexander Robinson, Chief Executive Officer. General e-mail, info@nbjcoalition.org*

Web, www.nbjcoalition.org

Selected Minorities-Related Resources

EDUCATION

National Assn. for Equal Opportunity in Higher Education, www.nafeo.org

GOVERNMENT, LAW, AND PUBLIC POLICY

Asian American Justice Center, www.advancingequality. org

Blacks in Government, www.bignet.org

Congressional Black Caucus Foundation, Inc., www.cbcfinc.org

Congressional Hispanic Caucus Institute, www.chci.org

Council on American-Islamic Relations, www.cair.com

Institute for Women's Policy Research, www.iwpr.org

Joint Center for Political and Economic Studies, www.jointcenter.org

Leadership Conference on Civil Rights, www.civilrights.org

National Congress of American Indians, www.ncai.org

National Women's Law Center, www.nwlc.org

National Women's Political Caucus, www.nwpc.org

Society of American Indian Government Employees, www.saige.org

HEALTH

Asian and Pacific Islander American Health Forum, www.apiahf.org

National Alliance for Hispanic Health, www.hispanichealth.org

National Black Nurses Assn., www.nbna.org

National Council of Urban Indian Health, www.ncuih.org

National Hispanic Medical Assn., www.nhmamd.org

National Minority AIDS Council, www.nmac.org

MEDIA

Center for Digital Democracy, www.democraticmedia.org

International Women's Media Foundation, www.iwmf.org

Media Access Project, www.mediaaccess.org

Minority Media and Telecommunications Council, www.mmtconline.org

National Assn. of Black Owned Broadcasters, www.nabob.org

National Assn. of Minority Media Executives, www.namme.org

National Lesbian and Gay Journalists Assn., www.nlgja.org

UNITY: Journalists of Color, Inc., www.unityjournalists.org

Seeks equality for black, lesbian, gay, bisexual, and transgender people by fighting racism and homophobia through education initiatives.

Poverty and Race Research Action Council, *1015 15th St. N.W., #400 20005; (202) 906-8023. Fax, (202) 842-2885. Philip Tegeler, Executive Director.*
General e-mail, info@prrac.org

Web, www.prrac.org

Facilitates cooperative links between researchers and activists who work on race and poverty issues. Publishes bimonthly *Poverty and Race* and a civil rights history curriculum guide. Policy research areas include housing, education, and health disparities.

African Americans

▶**NONGOVERNMENTAL**

Blacks in Government, *3005 Georgia Ave. N.W. 20001-3807; (202) 667-3280. Fax, (202) 667-3705. J. David Reeves, President.*

General e-mail, big@bignet.org

Web, www.bignet.org

Advocacy organization for public employees. Promotes equal opportunity and career advancement for African American government employees; provides career development information; seeks to eliminate racism in the federal workforce; sponsors programs, business meetings, and social gatherings; represents interests of African American government workers to Congress and the executive branch; promotes voter education and registration.

Congressional Black Caucus Foundation, *1720 Massachusetts Ave. N.W. 20036-1903; (202) 263-2800. Fax, (202) 775-0773. Elsie Scott, President.*
General e-mail, info@cbcfinc.org

Web, www.cbcfinc.org

Conducts research and programs on public policy issues of concern to African Americans. Sponsors fellowship programs in which professionals and academic candidates work on congressional committees and subcommittees. Holds issue forums and leadership seminars. Provides elected officials, organizations, and researchers with statistical, demographic, public policy, and political information. Sponsors internship, scholarship, and fellowship programs.

Joint Center for Political and Economic Studies, *1090 Vermont Ave. N.W., #1100 20005-4928; (202) 789-3500. Fax, (202) 789-6385. Ralph B. Everett, President. Web, www.jointcenter.org*

Documents and analyzes the political and economic status of African Americans and other minority populations, focusing on economic advancement, social policy, and political participation. Publishes an annual profile of African American elected officials in federal, state, and local government; disseminates information through forums, conferences, publications, and the Internet.

Lincoln Institute for Research and Education, *P.O. Box 254, Great Falls, VA 22066; (703) 759-4278. Fax, (703) 759-4597. Jay Parker, President. Web, www.lincolnreview.com*

Public policy research group that studies issues of interest to middle-class African Americans, including business, economics, employment, education, national defense, health, and culture. Sponsors seminars.

National Assn. for the Advancement of Colored People (NAACP), *Washington Bureau, 1156 15th St. N.W., #915 20005-1750; (202) 463-2940. Fax, (202) 463-2953. Hilary O. Shelton, Director. General e-mail, washingtonbureau@naacpnet.org*

Web, www.naacp.org

Membership: persons interested in civil rights for all minorities. Works for the political, educational, social, and economic equality and empowerment of minorities through legal, legislative, and direct action. (Headquarters in Baltimore, Md.)

National Assn. of Colored Women's Clubs Inc. (NACWC), *1601 R St. N.W. 20009-6420; (202) 667-4080. Fax, (202) 667-2574. Marie Wright-Tolliver, President. Web, www.nacwc.org*

Seeks to promote education; protect and enforce civil rights; raise the standard of family living; promote interracial understanding; and enhance leadership development. Awards scholarships; conducts programs in education, social service, and philanthropy.

National Black Caucus of Local Elected Officials (NBC/LEO), *c/o National League of Cities, 1301 Pennsylvania Ave. N.W. 20004-1763; (202) 626-3168. Fax, (202) 626-3043. Daisy W. Lynum, President. Press, (202) 626-3003. Web, www.nbc-leo.org*

Membership: African American elected officials at the local level and other interested individuals. Seeks to increase African American participation on the National League of City's steering and policy committees. Informs members on issues, and plans strategies to achieve objectives through legislation and direct action. Interests include cultural diversity, local government and community participation, housing, economics, the family, and human rights.

National Black Caucus of State Legislators, *444 N. Capitol St. N.W., #622 20001; (202) 624-5457. Fax, (202) 508-3826. LaKimba DeSadier Walker, Executive Director. Web, www.nbcsl.com*

Membership: African American state legislators. Promotes effective leadership among African American state legislators through education, research, and training; serves as an information network and clearinghouse for members.

National Council of Negro Women, *633 Pennsylvania Ave. N.W. 20004-2605; (202) 737-0120. Fax, (202) 737-0476. Alfreda V. Davis, Executive Director (Interim). Web, www.ncnw.org*

Seeks to advance opportunities for African American women, their families, and communities through research, advocacy, and national and community-based programs in the United States and Africa.

National Urban League, *Washington Office, 2901 14th Street N.W. 20009; (202) 265-8200. Fax, (202) 265-6122. Maudine R. Cooper, President. Web, www.gwul.org*

Social service organization concerned with the social welfare of African Americans and other minorities. Seeks elimination of racial segregation and discrimination; monitors legislation, policies, and regulations to determine impact on minorities; interests include employment, health, welfare, education, housing, and community development. (Headquarters in New York.)

Project 21, *National Center for Public Policy, 501 Capitol Ct. N.E., #200 20002; (202) 543-4110. Fax, (202) 543-5975. Mychal Massie, Chair; David W. Almasi, Executive Director. General e-mail, project21@nationalcenter.org*

Web, www.nationalcenter.org

Emphasizes spirit of entrepreneurship, sense of family, and traditional values among African Americans.

Washington Government Relations Group, *1001 Pennsylvania Ave. N.W., 6th Floor 20004; (202) 742-6630. Fax, (202) 742-6501. Yvonne McIntyre, President. General e-mail, info@wgrginc.org*

Web, www.wgrginc.org

Works to enrich the careers and leadership abilities of African American government relations professionals. Increases dialogue between members and senior-level policymakers to produce public policy solutions.

Hispanics

▶**NONGOVERNMENTAL**

Congressional Hispanic Caucus Institute, *911 2nd St. N.E. 20002; (202) 543-1771. Fax, (202) 546-2143. Nydia M. Velazquez, D–N.Y., Chair, (202) 225-2361; Esther Aguilera, President.*

General e-mail, chci@chci.org

Web, www.chci.org

Develops educational and leadership programs to familiarize Hispanic students with policy-related careers and to encourage their professional development. Aids in the developing of future Latino leaders. Provides scholarship, internship, and fellowship opportunities.

League of United Latin American Citizens, 2000 L St. N.W., #610 20036; (202) 833-6130. Fax, (202) 833-6135. Brent Wilkes, Executive Director. Toll-free, (877) LULAC-01.

General e-mail, info@lulac.org

Web, www.lulac.org

Seeks full social, political, economic, and educational rights for Hispanics in the United States. Programs include housing projects for the poor, employment and training for youth and women, and political advocacy on issues affecting Hispanics, including immigration. Operates National Educational Service Centers (LNESCs) and awards scholarships. Holds exposition open to the public.

Mexican American Legal Defense and Educational Fund, *Washington Office,* 1016 16th St. N.W., #100 20036; (202) 293-2828. Fax, (202) 293-2849. Peter Zamora, Regional Counsel.

Web, www.maldef.org

Works with Congress and the White House to promote legislative advocacy for minority groups. Interests include equal employment, voting rights, bilingual education, immigration, and discrimination. Monitors legislation and regulations. (Headquarters in Los Angeles, Calif.)

National Council of La Raza, 1126 16th St. N.W. 20036; (202) 785-1670. Fax, (202) 776-1792. Janet Murguia, President.

General e-mail, comments@nclr.org

Web, www.nclr.org

Seeks to reduce poverty of and discrimination against Hispanic Americans. Offers assistance to Hispanic community-based organizations. Conducts research and policy analysis. Interests include education, employment and training, asset development, immigration, language access issues, civil rights, and housing and community development. Monitors legislation and regulations.

National Puerto Rican Coalition, Inc., 1100 G St. N.W., #805 20005; (202) 223-3915. Fax, (202) 429-2223. Rafael A. Fanntauzzi, President.

General e-mail, nprc@nprcinc.org

Web, www.nprcinc.org

Membership: Puerto Rican organizations and individuals. Analyzes and advocates for public policy that benefits Puerto Ricans; offers training and technical assistance to Puerto Rican organizations and individuals; develops national communication network for Puerto Rican community-based organizations and individuals.

U.S. Conference of Catholic Bishops (USCCB), *Secretariat for Hispanic Affairs,* 3211 4th St. N.E. 20017-1194; (202) 541-3150. Fax, (202) 722-8717. Ronaldo M. Cruz, Executive Director.

General e-mail, hispanicaffairs@usccb.org

Web, www.usccb.org/hispanicaffairs

Acts as an information clearinghouse on communications and pastoral and liturgical activities; serves as liaison for other church institutions and government and private agencies concerned with Hispanics; provides information on legislation; acts as advocate for Hispanics within the National Conference of Catholic Bishops.

Lesbian, Gay, Bisexual, and Transgender People

►NONGOVERNMENTAL

Dignity USA, 721 8th St. S.E. 20003 (mailing address: P.O. Box 15279, Washington, DC 20003-0279); (202) 546-2235. Fax, (781) 521-3954. Mark Matson, President. Information, (800) 877-8797.

General e-mail, dignity@dignitywashington.org

Web, www.dignitywashington.org

Membership: gay, lesbian, bisexual, and transgender Catholics, their families, and friends. Works to promote spiritual development, social interaction, educational outreach, and acceptance within the Catholic community.

Gay and Lesbian Activists Alliance of Washington (GLAA), P.O. Box 75265 20013; (202) 667-5139. Mitch Wood, President.

General e-mail, equal@glaa.org

Web, www.glaa.org

Advances the rights of gays and lesbians within the Washington community. (Affiliated with International Lesbian and Gay Assn., Brussels, Belgium.)

Gay and Lesbian Victory Fund and Leadership Institute, 1133 15th St. N.W., #350 20005; (202) 842-8679. Fax, (202) 289-3863. Chuck Wolfe, President.

General e-mail, victory@victoryfund.org

Web, www.victoryfund.org

Supports the candidacy of openly gay and lesbian individuals in federal, state, and local elections.

Human Rights Campaign (HRC), 1640 Rhode Island Ave. N.W. 20036; (202) 628-4160. Fax, (202) 347-5323. Joe Solmonese, Executive Director. TTY, (202) 216-1572. Toll-free, (800) 777-4723.

General e-mail, hrc@hrc.org

Web, www.hrc.org

Provides campaign support and educates the public to ensure the rights of lesbians and gays at home, work, school, and in the community. Works to prohibit workplace discrimination based on sexual orientation, combat hate crimes, repeal the policy on gays and lesbians in the military, and fund AIDS research, care, and prevention.

Log Cabin Republicans, *1901 Pennsylvania Ave. N.W., #902 20006; (202) 347-5306. Fax, (202) 347-5224. Chris Scalise, President.*
General e-mail, info@logcabin.org

Web, www.logcabin.org

Membership: lesbian and gay Republicans. Educates conservative politicians and voters on gay and lesbian issues; disseminates information; conducts seminars for members. Raises campaign funds. Monitors legislation and regulations.

National Center for Transgender Equality (NCTE), *1325 Massachusetts Ave. N.W., #700 20005; (202) 903-0112. Fax, (202) 393-2241. Mara Keisling, Executive Director.*
General e-mail, ncte@nctequality.org

Web, www.nctequality.org

Works to advance the equality of transgender people through advocacy, collaboration, and empowerment, and to make them safe from discrimination and violence. Provides resources to local efforts nationwide.

National Gay and Lesbian Task Force and Policy Institute (NGLTF), *1325 Massachusetts Ave. N.W., #600 20005-4164; (202) 393-5177. Fax, (202) 393-2241. Rea Carey, Executive Director.*
General e-mail, thetaskforce@thetaskforce.org

Web, www.thetaskforce.org

Educates the media and the public on issues affecting the lesbian and gay community. Interests include grassroots organizations, civil rights, antigay violence, sodomy law reform, and gays on campus. Monitors legislation.

National Lesbian and Gay Journalists Assn. (NLGJA), *1420 K St. N.W., #910 20005; (202) 588-9888. Fax, (202) 588-1818. David Barre, Executive Director.*
General e-mail, info@nlgja.org

Web, www.nlgja.org

Works within the journalism industry to foster fair and accurate coverage of lesbian, gay, bisexual, and transgender issues. Opposes workplace bias against all minorities and provides professional development for its members.

National Organization for Women (NOW), *1100 H St. N.W., 3rd Floor 20005; (202) 628-8669. Fax, (202) 785-8576. Kim Gandy, President. TTY, (202) 331-9002.*
Web, www.now.org

Membership: women and men interested in feminist civil rights. Promotes the development and enforcement of legislation prohibiting discrimination on the basis of sexual orientation. Works toward achieving constitutional equality for women. Organizes membership and provides education. Monitors legislation and regulations.

Parents, Families, and Friends of Lesbians and Gays (PFLAG), *1726 M St. N.W., #400 20036; (202) 467-8180. Fax, (202) 467-8194. Jody M. Huckaby, Executive Director.*

General e-mail, info@pflag.org

Web, www.pflag.org

Promotes the health and well-being of gay, lesbian, transgender, and bisexual persons, their families, and their friends through support, education, and advocacy. Works to change public policies and attitudes toward gay, lesbian, transgender, and bisexual persons. Monitors legislation and regulations. Library open to the public.

Servicemembers Legal Defense Network (SLDN), *P.O. Box 65301 20035-5301; (202) 328-3244. Fax, (202) 797-1635. Aubrey Sarvis, Executive Director.*
General e-mail, sldn@sldn.org

Web, www.sldn.org

Provides legal assistance to individuals affected by the military's policy on gays and lesbians. Monitors legislation and regulations.

Sexual Minority Youth Assistance League (SMYAL), *410 7th St. S.E. 20003-2707; (202) 546-5940. Fax, (202) 544-1306. Andrew Barnett, Executive Director. TTY, (202) 464-4548.*
General e-mail, supporterinfo@smyal.org

Web, www.smyal.org

Provides support to youth who are lesbian, gay, bisexual, transgender, intersex, or who may be questioning their sexuality. Facilitates youth center and support groups; promotes HIV/AIDS awareness; coordinates public education programs about homophobia. Offers individual counseling.

Native Americans

▶**AGENCIES**

Administration for Native Americans *(Health and Human Services Dept.),* *370 L'Enfant Promenade S.W., 8th Floor West Aerospace Center 20447-0002; (202) 690-7776. Fax, (202) 690-7441. Vacant, Commissioner. Toll-free, (877) 922-9262.*
General e-mail, ana@acf.hhs.gov

Web, www.acf.hhs.gov/programs/ana

Awards grants for locally determined social and economic development strategies; promotes Native American economic and social self-sufficiency; funds tribes and Native American and Native Hawaiian organizations. Commissioner chairs the Intradepartmental Council on Indian Affairs, which coordinates Native American–related programs.

Bureau of Indian Affairs (BIA), *(Interior Dept.),* *1849 C St. N.W., #4611, MS 4141 20240; (202) 208-5116. Fax, (202) 208-6334. George Skibine, Assistant Secretary (Acting). Press, (202) 219-4150.*
General e-mail, opa@doi.gov

Web, www.doi.gov/bia

Works with federally recognized Indian tribal governments and Alaska Native communities in a government-to-government relationship. Encourages and supports tribes' efforts to govern themselves and to provide needed programs and services on the reservations. Manages land held in trust for Indian tribes and individuals. Funds educational benefits, road construction and maintenance, social services, police protection, economic development efforts, and special assistance to develop governmental and administrative skills.

►CONGRESS

For a listing of relevant congressional committees and subcommittees, please see page 468 or the Appendix.

►JUDICIARY

U.S. Court of Federal Claims, *717 Madison Pl. N.W. 20005; (202) 357-6400. Fax, (202) 357-6401. Edward J. Damich, Chief Judge; John Buckley, Clerk (Acting). Web, www.uscfc.uscourts.gov*

Deals with Native American tribal claims against the government that are founded upon the Constitution, congressional acts, government regulations, and contracts. Examples include congressional reference cases; patent cases; claims for land, water, and mineral rights; and the accounting of funds held for Native Americans under various treaties.

►NONGOVERNMENTAL

National Congress of American Indians, *1301 Connecticut Ave. N.W., #200 20036; (202) 466-7767. Fax, (202) 466-7797. Jacqueline Johnson, Executive Director. General e-mail, ncai@ncai.org*

Web, www.ncai.org

Membership: Native American and Alaska Native governments and individuals. Provides information and serves as general advocate for tribes. Monitors legislative and regulatory activities affecting Native American affairs.

Native American Rights Fund, *Washington Office, 1712 N St. N.W. 20036-2907; (202) 785-4166. Fax, (202) 822-0068. Richard Guest, Staff Attorney; Dawn Baum, Staff Attorney. Web, www.narf.org*

Provides Native Americans and Alaska Natives with legal assistance in land claims, water rights, hunting, and other areas. Practices federal Indian law. (Headquarters in Boulder, Colo.)

Navajo Nation, *Washington Office, 750 1st St. N.E., #1010 20002; (202) 682-7390. Fax, (202) 682-7391. Sharon Clahchischilliage, Executive Director. General e-mail, dpete@nnwo.org*

Web, www.nnwo.org

Monitors legislation and regulations affecting the Navajo people; serves as an information clearinghouse on the Navajo Nation. (Headquarters in Window Rock, Ariz.)

Older Adults

►AGENCIES

Administration on Aging (AoA), *(Health and Human Services Dept.), 1 Massachusetts Ave. N.W. 20201; (202) 619-0724. Fax, (202) 357-3555. Edwin Walker, Assistant Secretary (Acting). Press, (202) 401-4541. TTY, (800) 877-8339. Eldercare Locator, (800) 677-1116. General e-mail, AoAInfo@aoa.gov*

Web, www.aoa.gov

Advocacy agency for older Americans and their concerns. Collaborates with tribal organizations, community and national organizations, and state and area agencies to implement grant programs and services designed to improve the quality of life for older Americans, such as information and referral, adult day care, elder abuse prevention, home-delivered meals, in-home care, transportation, and services for caregivers.

►CONGRESS

For a listing of relevant congressional committees and subcommittees, please see page 468 or the Appendix.

►NONGOVERNMENTAL

AARP, *601 E St. N.W. 20049; (202) 434-2277. Fax, (202) 434-2320. William D. Novelli, Chief Executive Officer. Press, (202) 434-2560. TTY, (877) 434-7595. Research Info Center, (202) 434-6233. Web, www.aarp.org*

Membership organization for persons age fifty and older. Provides members with training, employment information, and volunteer programs; offers financial services, including insurance, investment programs, and consumer discounts; makes grants through AARP Andrus Foundation for research on aging. Monitors legislation and regulations and disseminates information on issues affecting older Americans, including age discrimination, Social Security, Medicaid and Medicare, pensions and retirement, and consumer protection. (Formerly the American Assn. of Retired Persons.)

Alliance for Retired Americans, *815 16th St. N.W., 4th Floor North 20006-4104; (202) 637-5399. Fax, (202) 637-5398. Barbara Esterling, President. Information, (888) 373-6497. Web, www.retiredamericans.org*

Alliance of retired members of unions affiliated with the AFL-CIO, senior citizen clubs, associations, councils, and other groups. Seeks to nationalize health care services and to strengthen benefits to older adults, including improved Social Security payments, increased employment, and education and health programs. Offers prescription drug program and vision care Medicare supplement. (Affiliate of the AFL-CIO.)

Gray Panthers, *1612 K St. N.W., #300 20006; (202) 737-6637. Fax, (202) 737-1160. Susan Murany, Executive Director. Information, (800) 280-5362.*

General e-mail, info@graypanthers.org

Web, www.graypanthers.org

Intergenerational educational and advocacy organization that promotes peace and economic and social justice for all people; seeks universal health care, the preservation of Social Security, affordable housing, access to education, and jobs for all with a living wage.

National Caucus and Center for the Black Aged, Inc., *1220 L St. N.W., #800 20005-2407; (202) 637-8400. Fax, (202) 347-0895. Karyne Jones, President.*

General e-mail, info@ncba-aged.org

Web, www.ncba-aged.org

Concerned with issues that affect older African Americans. Sponsors employment and housing programs for older adults and education and training for professionals in gerontology. Monitors legislation and regulations.

National Council on the Aging, *1901 L St. N.W., 4th Floor 20036; (202) 479-1200. Fax, (202) 479-0735. James P. Firman, President. Press, (202) 479-6975. TTY, (202) 479-6674.*

General e-mail, info@ncoa.org

Web, www.ncoa.org

Serves as an information clearinghouse on training, technical assistance, advocacy, and research on every aspect of aging. Provides information on social services for older persons. Monitors legislation and regulations.

National Hispanic Council on Aging, *734 15th St. N.W., #1050 20005; (202) 347-9733. Fax, (202) 347-9735. Yanira Cruz, President.*

General e-mail, nhcoa@nhcoa.org

Web, www.nhcoa.org

Membership: senior citizens, health care workers, professionals in the field of aging, and others in the United States and Puerto Rico who are interested in topics related to Hispanics and aging. Provides research training, policy analysis, consulting, and technical assistance; sponsors seminars, workshops, and management internships.

National Senior Citizens Law Center, *1444 Eye St. N.W., #1100 20005; (202) 289-6976. Fax, (202) 289-7224. Paul Nathanson, Executive Director (Interim).*

General e-mail, nsclc@nsclc.org

Web, www.nsclc.org

Provides training, technical assistance, and litigation for attorneys representing the elderly poor and persons with disabilities. Represents clients before Congress and federal departments and agencies. Focus includes Social Security, Medicare, Medicaid, nursing home residents' rights, home health care, pensions, and protective services. Funded by the Administration on Aging and various charitable foundations.

Seniors Coalition, *4401 Fair Lakes Ct., #210, Fairfax, VA 22033; (703) 896-7615. Fax, (866) 728-5450. Dave Herman, Executive Director. Toll-free, (800) 325-9891.*

General e-mail, tsc@senior.org

Web, www.senior.org

Seeks to protect the quality of life and economic well-being of older Americans. Interests include health care, Social Security, taxes, pharmaceutical issues, and Medicare. Conducts seminars and monitors legislation and regulations.

60 Plus, *1600 Wilson Blvd., #960, Arlington, VA 22209; (888) 560-7587. Fax, (703) 807-2073. James L. Martin, President.*

General e-mail, info@60plus.org

Web, www.60plus.org

Advocates for the rights of senior citizens. Interests include free enterprise, less government regulation, and tax reform. Works to eliminate estate taxes. Publishes rating system of members of Congress. Monitors legislation and regulations.

United Seniors Assn.—USA Next, *3900 Jermantown Rd., #450, Fairfax, VA 22030 (mailing address: P.O. Box 2038, Purcellville, VA 20132); (703) 359-6500. Fax, (703) 359-6510. Charles W. Jarvis, Chair.*

Works to educate Americans of all ages about issues concerning seniors, their children, and grandchildren.

Women

▶**NONGOVERNMENTAL**

Assn. for Women in Science, *1200 New York Ave. N.W., #650 20005; (202) 326-8940. Fax, (202) 326-8960. Janet Bandows Koster, Executive Director.*

General e-mail, awis@awis.org

Web, www.awis.org

Promotes equal opportunity for women in scientific professions; provides career and funding information. Provides educational scholarships for women in science. Interests include international development.

Center for Women Policy Studies, *1776 Massachusetts Ave. N.W., #450 20036; (202) 872-1770. Fax, (202) 296-8962. Leslie R. Wolfe, President.*

General e-mail, cwps@centerwomenpolicy.org

Web, www.centerwomenpolicy.org

Policy and advocacy organization concerned with women's issues, including educational and employment equity for women, women and AIDS, violence against women, economic opportunity for low-income women, women's health, and reproductive laws.

Church Women United, *Washington Office, 100 Maryland Ave. N.E., #100 20002; (202) 544-8747. Fax, (202) 544-9133. Patricia Burkhardt, Legislative Coordinator. Toll-free, (800) 298-5551.*

General e-mail, cwu-dc@churchwomen.org

Web, www.churchwomen.org

Ecumenical women's organization dedicated to spirituality and faith-based advocacy. Interests include defense policy, employment, family stability, health, human rights, justice, world peace, and hunger and poverty issues, especially as they affect women and children. (Headquarters in New York.)

Independent Women's Forum (IWF), *4400 Jenifer St., 7240 20015-2113; (202) 419-1820. Fax, (202) 419-1821. Michelle D. Bernard, President. Press, (202) 349-5889. Toll-free (800) 224-6000.*
General e-mail, info@iwf.org

Web, www.iwf.org

Membership: women and men interested in advancing limited government, equality under the law, property rights, free markets, strong families, and a powerful and effective national defense and foreign policy. Publishes policy papers; makes appearances on radio and television broadcasts; maintains speakers bureau. Interests include school choice, Social Security and health care reform, the war in Iraq, and democracy promotion and women's human rights in the Middle East.

Jewish Women International, *2000 M St. N.W., #720 20036; (202) 857-1300. Fax, (202) 857-1380. Loribeth Weinstein, Executive Director. Toll-free, (800) 343-2823.*
General e-mail, jwi@jwi.org

Web, www.jwi.org

Organization of Jewish women in the United States. Interests include emotional health of children and youth, family violence, women's health care, civil and constitutional rights, community service, and anti-Semitism.

National Council of Women's Organizations, *714 G St. N.W., #200 20003; (202) 293-4505. Fax, (202) 293-4507. Susan Scanlan, Chair.*
General e-mail, ncwo@ncwo-online.org

Web, www.womensorganizations.org

Membership: local and national women's organizations. Engages in policy work and grassroots activism to address issues of concern to women, including workplace and economic equity, education and job training, affirmative action, Social Security, child care, reproductive freedom, health, and global women's equality. Monitors legislation and regulations.

National Organization for Women (NOW), *1100 H St. N.W., 3rd Floor 20005; (202) 628-8669. Fax, (202) 785-8576. Kim Gandy, President. TTY, (202) 331-9002. Web, www.now.org*

Membership: women and men interested in feminist civil rights. Uses traditional and nontraditional forms of political activism, including nonviolent civil disobedience, to improve the status of all women regardless of age, income, sexual orientation, or race. Maintains liaisons with counterpart organizations worldwide.

National Partnership for Women and Families, *1875 Connecticut Ave. N.W., #650 20009-5731; (202) 986-2600. Fax, (202) 986-2539. Debra L. Ness, President.*
General e-mail, info@nationalpartnership.org

Web, www.nationalpartnership.org

Advocacy organization that promotes fairness in the workplace, access to high-quality health care, and policies that help women and men meet the demands of work and family. Publishes and disseminates information in print and on the Web to heighten awareness of work and family issues. Monitors legislative activity and pending Supreme Court cases and argues on behalf of family issues before Congress and in the courts.

National Women's Law Center, *11 Dupont Circle N.W., #800 20036; (202) 588-5180. Fax, (202) 588-5185. Nancy Duff Campbell, Co-President; Marcia D. Greenberger, Co-President.*
General e-mail, info@nwlc.org

Web, www.nwlc.org

Works to expand and protect women's legal rights through advocacy and public education. Interests include reproductive rights, health, education, employment, income security, and family support.

OWL: The Voice of Midlife and Older Women, *1828 L St. N.W., #801 20036; (202) 332-2573. Fax, (202) 332-2949. Ashley B. Carson, Executive Director. Information, (800) 825-3695.*
General e-mail, owlinfo@owl-national.org

Web, www.owl-national.org

Grassroots organization concerned with the social and economic problems of middle-aged and older women. Interests include health care, Social Security, pension rights, housing, employment, women as caregivers, effects of budget cuts, and issues relating to health insurance and long-term care.

Quota International, *1420 21st St. N.W. 20036; (202) 331-9694. Fax, (202) 331-4395. Kathleen Treiber, Executive Director.*
General e-mail, staff@quota.org

Web, www.quota.org

International service organization that links members in fourteen countries in a worldwide network of service and friendship. Interests include deaf, hard-of-hearing, and speech-impaired individuals and disadvantaged women and children. Maintains the We Share Foundation, a charitable organization.

Women's Action for New Directions, *Washington Office, 322 4th St. N.E. 20002; (202) 544-5055. Fax, (202) 544-7612. Marie Rietmann, Public Policy Director.*
General e-mail, peace@wand.org

Web, www.wand.org

Seeks to empower women to act politically to reduce violence and militarism and redirect excessive military resources toward unmet human and environmental needs. Monitors legislation on federal budget priorities. (Headquarters in Arlington, Mass.)

Women's Institute for Freedom of the Press, *1940 Calvert St. N.W. 20009-1502; (202) 265-6707.*
General e-mail, mediademocracy@wifp.org

Web, www.wifp.org

Operates as a national and international network of media and media-concerned women and men. Publishes the *Directory of Women's Media*, a series on media democracy, and *Voices for Media Democracy*, a newsletter.

Women's Research and Education Institute (WREI), *1828 L St. N.W. 20036; (202) 280-2720. Fax, (202) 332-2949. Susan Scanlan, President.*
General e-mail, wrei@wrei.org

Web, www.wrei.org

Analyzes policy-relevant information on women's issues. Sponsors fellowships in congressional offices; educates the public through reports and conferences. Interests include women's employment and economic status; women in nontraditional occupations; military women and veterans; older women; women's health issues; and women and immigration. Library open to the public.

YWCA of the USA (YWCA USA), *1015 18th St. N.W., #1100 20036; (202) 467-0801. Fax, (202) 467-0802. Lorraine Cole, Chief Executive Officer.*
General e-mail, info@ywca.org

Web, www.ywca.org

Strives to empower women and girls and to eliminate racism. Provides services and programs concerning child care and youth development, economic empowerment, global awareness, health and fitness, housing and shelter, leadership development, racial justice and human rights, and violence prevention. (YWCA stands for Young Women's Christian Association.)

Other Minority Groups

▶**NONGOVERNMENTAL**

American-Arab Anti-Discrimination Committee (ADC), *1732 Wisconsin Ave. N.W. 20007; (202) 244-2990. Fax, (202) 244-7968. Kareem W. Shora, Executive Director.*
General e-mail, adc@adc.org

Web, www.adc.org

Nonpartisan and nonsectarian organization that seeks to protect the rights and heritage of Americans of Arab descent. Works to combat discrimination against Arab Americans in employment, education, and political life and to prevent stereotyping of Arabs in the media. Monitors legislation and regulations. Library open to the public.

Anti-Defamation League, *Washington Office, 1100 Connecticut Ave. N.W., #1020 20036 (mailing address: P.O. Box 96226, Washington, DC 20090-6226); (202) 452-8310. Fax, (202) 296-2371. David Friedman, Regional Director.*
General e-mail, washington-dc@adl.org

Web, www.adl.org

Seeks to combat anti-Semitism and other forms of bigotry. Interests include discrimination in employment, housing, voting, and education; U.S. foreign policy in the Middle East; and the treatment of Jews worldwide. Monitors legislation and regulations affecting Jewish interests

and the civil rights of all Americans. (Headquarters in New York.)

Asian American Justice Center (AAJC), *1140 Connecticut Ave. N.W., #1200 20036; (202) 296-2300. Fax, (202) 296-2318. Karen K. Narasaki, President.*
General e-mail, information@advancingequality.org

Web, www.advancingequality.org

Works to advance the human and civil rights of Asian Americans through advocacy, public policy, public education, and litigation. Promotes civic engagement and works to create an inclusive society in communities on local, regional, and national levels. Interests include affirmative action, hate crimes, media diversity, census, immigrant rights, language access, and voting rights. (Formerly known as National Asian Pacific American Legal Consortium.)

Japanese American Citizens League, *Washington Office, 1828 L St. N.W., #802 20036; (202) 223-1240. Fax, (202) 296-8082. Floyd Mori, Executive Director.*
General e-mail, dc@jacl.org

Web, www.jacl.org

Monitors legislative and regulatory activities affecting the rights of Japanese Americans. Supports civil rights of all Americans, with a focus on Asian and Asian Pacific Americans. (Headquarters in San Francisco, Calif.)

National Federation of Filipino American Assns., *2607 24th St. N.W., #4 20008-2600; (202) 986-1153. Fax, (202) 478-5109. Greg Macubenta, National Chair.*
General e-mail, admin@naffaa.org

Web, www.naffaa.org

Nonpartisan affiliation of more than five hundred Filipino American institutions and umbrella organizations. Conducts conferences; monitors legislation.

OCA (Organization of Asian Pacific Americans), *National Center, 1322 18th St. N.W. 20036-1803; (202) 223-5500. Fax, (202) 296-0540. George Wu, Executive Director.*
General e-mail, oca@ocanational.org

Web, www.ocanational.org

Advocacy group seeking to advance the social, political, and economic well-being of Asian Pacific Americans in the United States. (Formerly the Organization of Chinese Americans.)

Organization of Chinese American Women, *4641 Montgomery Ave., #208, Bethesda, MD 20814; (301) 907-3898. Fax, (301) 907-3899. Janet Biermann, Executive Director.*
General e-mail, info@ocawwomen.org

Web, www.ocawwomen.org

Promotes equal rights and opportunities for Chinese and other Asian Pacific American women in professional and nonprofessional fields. Provides members with leadership and skills training and newly arrived immigrants with career development.

CONSTITUTIONAL LAW AND CIVIL LIBERTIES

►AGENCIES

Commission on Civil Rights, *624 9th St. N.W., #700 20425; (202) 376-7700. Fax, (202) 376-7672. Gerald A. Reynolds, Chair; Abigail Thernstrom, Vice Chair; Martin Dannenfelser, Staff Director. Library, (202) 376-8110. Press, (202) 376-8582. TTY, (202) 376-8116. General e-mail, referral@usccr.gov*

Web, www.usccr.gov

Assesses federal laws and policies of government agencies and studies legal developments to determine the nature and extent of denial of equal protection under the law on the basis of race, color, religion, sex, national origin, age, or disability in many areas, including employment, voting rights, education, administration of justice, and housing. Reports and makes recommendations to the president and Congress; serves as national clearinghouse for civil rights information. Conducts studies relating to discrimination against certain groups, including women, African Americans, Hispanics, Asians, Native Americans, and Pacific Islanders. Issues public service announcements to discourage discrimination or denials of equal protection of the laws. Library open to the public.

Justice Dept. (DOJ), *Legal Counsel, 950 Pennsylvania Ave. N.W., #5218 20530-0001; (202) 514-2041. Fax, (202) 514-0539. David Barron, Assistant Attorney General (Acting).*
Web, www.usdoj.gov

Advises the attorney general, the president, and executive agencies on questions regarding constitutional law.

►CONGRESS

For a listing of relevant congressional committees and subcommittees, please see page 468 or the Appendix.

►JUDICIARY

Supreme Court of the United States, *1 1st St. N.E. 20543; (202) 479-3000. John G. Roberts Jr., Chief Justice.*
Web, www.supremecourtus.gov/publicinfo

Highest appellate court in the federal judicial system. Interprets the U.S. Constitution, federal legislation, and treaties. Provides information on new cases filed, the status of pending cases, and admissions to the Supreme Court Bar. Library open to Supreme Court bar members only.

►NONGOVERNMENTAL

American Civil Liberties Union (ACLU), *Washington Legislative Office, 915 15th St. N.W. 20005; (202) 544-1681. Fax, (202) 546-0738. Caroline Fredrickson, Director. Press, (202) 675-2312. Alternate fax, (202) 546-1440. General e-mail, media@dcaclu.org*

Web, www.aclu.org/legislative

Initiates test court cases and advocates legislation to guarantee constitutional rights and civil liberties. Focuses on First Amendment rights, minority and women's rights, gay and lesbian rights, and privacy; supports legalized abortion, opposes government-sponsored school prayer and legislative restrictions on television content. Washington office monitors legislative and regulatory activities and public policy. Library open to the public by appointment. (Headquarters in New York maintains docket of cases.)

American Constitution Society for Law and Policy, *1333 H St. N.W., 11th Floor 20005; (202) 393-6181. Fax, (202) 393-6189. David Lyle, Executive Director (Acting). General e-mail, info@acslaw.org*

Web, www.acslaw.org

National association of lawyers, law students, judges, legal scholars, and policymakers that promotes a progressive vision of constitutional law and public policy. Produces issue briefs and publications. Organizes lectures, conferences, seminars, and two annual student competitions.

Center for Individual Rights, *1233 20th St. N.W., #300 20036; (202) 833-8400. Fax, (202) 833-8410. Terence J. "Terry" Pell, President. Toll-free, (877) 426-2665. General e-mail, cir@cir-usa.org*

Web, www.cir-usa.org

Public interest law firm that supports reform of the civil justice system on the basis of private rights and individual responsibility. Interests include discrimination law, freedom of speech, and civil rights law.

Ethics and Public Policy Center, *1015 15th St. N.W., #900 20005-2605; (202) 682-1200. Fax, (202) 408-0632. M. Edward Whelan III, President. General e-mail, ethics@eppc.org*

Web, www.eppc.org

Examines current issues of jurisprudence, especially those relating to constitutional interpretation.

First Amendment Center, *555 Pennsylvania Ave. N.W. 20001; (615) 727-1600. Fax, (202) 292-6295. Gene Policinski, Executive Director. General e-mail, info@fac.org*

Web, www.firstamendmentcenter.org

Works to preserve and protect First Amendment freedoms through information and education. Serves as a nonpartisan forum for the study and exploration of free-expression issues, including freedom of speech, the press, religion, and the rights to assemble and to petition the government. The center is an operating program of the Freedom Forum and is associated with the Newseum. Affiliated with Vanderbilt University through the Vanderbilt Institute for Public Policy Studies.

Institute for Justice, *901 N. Glebe Rd., #900, Arlington, VA 22203; (703) 682-9320. Fax, (703) 682-9321. Chip Mellor, President. General e-mail, general@ij.org*

Web, www.ij.org

Supreme Court Justices

CHIEF JUSTICE

John G. Roberts Jr.

Appointed chief justice by President George W. Bush, sworn in Sept. 29, 2005.

ASSOCIATE JUSTICES

John Paul Stevens

Appointed by President Ford, sworn in Dec. 19, 1975.

Antonin Scalia

Appointed by President Reagan, sworn in Sept. 26, 1986.

Anthony M. Kennedy

Appointed by President Reagan, sworn in Feb. 18, 1988.

David H. Souter

Appointed by President George Bush, sworn in Oct. 9, 1990. Retired June 2009.

Clarence Thomas

Appointed by President George Bush, sworn in Oct. 23, 1991.

Ruth Bader Ginsburg

Appointed by President Clinton, sworn in Aug. 10, 1993.

Stephen G. Breyer

Appointed by President Clinton, sworn in Aug. 3, 1994.

Samuel A. Alito Jr.

Appointed by President George W. Bush, sworn in Jan. 31, 2006.

Sponsors seminars to train law students, grassroots activists, and practicing lawyers in applying advocacy strategies in public interest litigation. Seeks to protect individuals from arbitrary government interference in free speech, private property rights, parental school choice, and economic liberty. Litigates cases.

National Organization for Women (NOW), *1100 H St. N.W., 3rd Floor 20005; (202) 628-8669. Fax, (202) 785-8576. Kim Gandy, President. TTY, (202) 331-9002.*
Web, www.now.org

Membership: women and men interested in civil rights for women. Works to end discrimination based on gender, to preserve abortion rights, and to pass an equal rights amendment to the Constitution.

OSI (Open Society Institute), *Washington Office, 1120 19th St. N.W., 8th Floor 20036; (202) 721-5600. Fax, (202) 530-0128. Stephen Rickard, Director.*
General e-mail, info@osi-dc.org
Web, www.soros.org/initiatives/washington

Addresses violations of civil liberties in the United States. Interests include criminal and civil justice reform, global economic policies, and women's rights. (Headquarters in New York. Affiliated with the Soros Foundation Network.)

Abortion and Reproductive Issues

▶NONGOVERNMENTAL

Assn. of Reproductive Health Professionals, *1901 L St. N.W., #300 20036; (202) 466-3825. Fax, (202) 466-3826. Wayne C. Shields, President.*
General e-mail, arhp@arhp.org
Web, www.arhp.org

Membership: obstetricians, gynecologists, other physicians, researchers, clinicians, and educators. Educates health professionals and the public on reproductive health issues, including family planning, contraception, HIV/AIDS and other sexually transmitted diseases, abortion, menopause, infertility, and cancer prevention and detection.

Catholics for Choice, *1436 U St. N.W., #301 20009-3997; (202) 986-6093. Fax, (202) 332-7995. Jon O'Brien, President.*
General e-mail, cffc@catholicsforchoice.org
Web, www.catholicsforchoice.org

Works to change church positions and public policies that limit individual freedom, particularly those related to sexuality and reproduction. Provides the public, policymakers, and groups working for change with information and analysis.

Feminists for Life of America, *P.O. Box 320667, Alexandria, VA 22320; (703) 836-3354. Serrin M. Foster, President.*
General e-mail, info@feministsforlife.org
Web, www.feministsforlife.org

Membership: women and men who advocate classical feminism, including its anti-abortion position. Opposes abortion, euthanasia, and capital punishment; seeks to redress economic and social conditions that cause women to choose abortion.

March for Life Fund, *P.O. Box 90300 20090; (202) 543-3377. Fax, (202) 543-8202. Nellie J. Gray, President.*
General e-mail, info@marchforlife.org
Web, www.marchforlife.org

Membership: individuals and organizations that support government action prohibiting abortion. Sponsors annual march in Washington each January 22. Monitors legislation and regulations.

NARAL Pro-Choice America, *1156 15th St. N.W., #700 20005; (202) 973-3000. Fax, (202) 973-3096. Nancy Keenan, President. Press, (202) 973-3032.*
Web, www.prochoiceamerica.org

Membership: persons who support using the political process to guarantee women a range of reproductive choices, including preventing unintended pregnancy, bearing healthy children, and choosing legal abortion. (Formerly National Abortion and Reproductive Rights Action League.)

National Abortion Federation (NAF), *1660 L St. N.W., #450 20036; (202) 667-5881. Fax, (202) 667-5890. Vicki Saporta, President. Toll-free, (800) 772-9100.*

General e-mail, naf@prochoice.org

Web, www.prochoice.org

Membership: abortion providers. Seeks to preserve and enhance the quality and accessibility of abortion care.

National Committee for a Human Life Amendment, *1500 Massachusetts Ave. N.W., #24 20005; (202) 393-0703. Fax, (202) 347-1383. Michael A. Taylor, Executive Director. General e-mail, info@nchla.org*

Web, www.nchla.org

Supports legislation and a constitutional amendment prohibiting abortion.

National Organization for Women (NOW), *1100 H St. N.W., 3rd Floor 20005; (202) 628-8669. Fax, (202) 785-8576. Kim Gandy, President. TTY, (202) 331-9002. Web, www.now.org*

Membership: women and men interested in civil rights for women. Works to preserve abortion rights.

National Right to Life Committee, *512 10th St. N.W. 20004-1401; (202) 626-8800. Fax, (202) 347-3119. David N. O'Steen, Executive Director. General e-mail, nrlc@nrlc.org*

Web, www.nrlc.org

Association of fifty state right-to-life organizations. Opposes abortion, infanticide, and euthanasia; supports legislation prohibiting abortion except when the life of the mother is endangered. Operates an information clearinghouse and speakers bureau. Monitors legislation and regulations.

National Women's Health Network, *1413 K St. N.W., 4th Floor 20005; (202) 682-2640. Fax, (202) 682-2648. Cynthia Pearson, Executive Director. General e-mail, nwhn@nwhn.org*

Web, www.nwhn.org

Advocacy organization interested in women's health. Seeks to preserve legalized abortion; monitors legislation and regulations; testifies before Congress.

National Women's Political Caucus, *1003 K St. N.W., #637 20001 (mailing address: P.O. Box 50476, Washington, DC 20091); (202) 785-1100. Fax, (202) 370-6306. Lulu Flores, President; Clare C. Giesen, Executive Director. General e-mail, info@nwpc.org*

Web, www.nwpc.org

Advocacy group that seeks greater involvement of women in politics. Supports legalized abortion.

Religious Coalition for Reproductive Choice, *1025 Vermont Ave. N.W., #1130 20005; (202) 628-7700. Fax, (202) 628-7716. Rev. Carlton W. Veazey, President. General e-mail, info@rcrc.org*

Web, www.rcrc.org

Coalition of religious groups favoring birth control, sexuality education, and access to legal abortion. Opposes constitutional amendments and federal and state legislation restricting access to abortion services in most cases.

U.S. Conference of Catholic Bishops (USCCB), *Secretariat of Pro-Life Activities, 3211 4th St. N.E. 20017-1194; (202) 541-3070. Fax, (202) 541-3054. Tom Grenchik, Executive Director. Publications, (800) 235-8722. General e-mail, prolife@usccb.org*

Web, www.usccb.org/prolife

Provides information on the position of the Roman Catholic Church on abortion. Monitors legislation on abortion, embryonic stem-cell research, human cloning, and related issues. Promotes alternatives to abortion.

Claims Against the Government

►AGENCIES

Justice Dept. (DOJ), *Civil Division: National Courts, 1100 L St. N.W., #12124 20530; (202) 514-7300. Fax, (202) 307-0972. Jeanne E. Davidson, Director. Web, www.usdoj.gov*

Represents the United States in the U.S. Court of Federal Claims, except in cases involving taxes, lands, or Native American claims.

Justice Dept. (DOJ), *Environment and Natural Resources, 950 Pennsylvania Ave. N.W., #2143 20530-0001; (202) 514-2701. Fax, (202) 514-0557. Vacant, Assistant Attorney General. Press, (202) 514-2008. Web, www.usdoj.gov/enrd*

Represents the United States in the U.S. Court of Federal Claims in cases arising from acquisition of property or related matters.

Justice Dept. (DOJ), *Tax Division, 950 Pennsylvania Ave. N.W., #4141 20530; (202) 514-2901. Fax, (202) 514-5479. Nathan J. Hochman, Assistant Attorney General. Web, www.usdoj.gov/tax/tax.html*

Represents the United States and its officers in all civil and criminal litigation arising under the internal revenue laws, other than proceedings in the United States Tax Court.

State Dept., *International Claims and Investment Disputes, 2430 E St. N.W., #203 20037-2800; (202) 776-8360. Fax, (202) 776-8389. Jeffrey Kovar, Assistant Legal Adviser. Web, www.state.gov*

Handles claims by U.S. government and citizens against foreign governments, as well as claims by foreign governments and their nationals against the U.S. government; negotiates international claims agreements. Handles claims against the State Dept. for negligence (under the Federal Tort Claims Act) and claims by owners of U.S. flag vessels due to illegal seizures by foreign governments in international waters (under the Fishermen's Protective Act).

►CONGRESS

For a listing of relevant congressional committees and subcommittees, please see page 468 or the Appendix.

►JUDICIARY

U.S. Court of Federal Claims, *717 Madison Pl. N.W. 20005; (202) 357-6400. Fax, (202) 357-6401. Edward J. Damich, Chief Judge; John Buckley, Clerk (Acting). Web, www.uscfc.uscourts.gov*

Renders judgment on any nontort claims for monetary damages against the United States founded upon the Constitution, statutes, government regulations, and government contracts. Examples include compensation for taking of property, claims arising under construction and supply contracts, certain patent cases, and cases involving the refund of federal taxes. Hears cases involving Native American claims.

Privacy

►AGENCIES

Federal Communications Commission (FCC), *Wireline Competition Bureau, 445 12th St. S.W. 20554; (202) 418-1500. Fax, (202) 418-2825. Julie Veach, Chief (Acting). Web, www.fcc.gov/wcb*

Creates and recommends policy goals, objectives, programs, and plans for the FCC on matters concerning wireline telecommunications. Objectives include promoting competition in wireline services and markets, deregulation, encouraging economically efficient investment in wireline telecommunications infrastructure, expanding the availability of wireline telecommunications services, and fostering economic growth.

Federal Trade Commission (FTC), *Financial Practices, 601 New Jersey Ave. N.W. 20580; (202) 326-3224. Fax, (202) 326-3768. Peggy Twohig, Associate Director. Web, www.ftc.gov*

Enforces the Fair Credit Reporting Act, which requires credit bureaus to furnish correct and complete information to businesses evaluating credit, insurance, or job applications.

Office of Management and Budget (OMB), *(Executive Office of the President), Information and Regulatory Affairs, New Executive Office Bldg., #10236 20503; (202) 395-3785. Fax, (202) 395-5167. Jasmeet Seehra, Co-Chief; Kim Nelson, Co-Chief. Web, www.whitehouse.gov/omb/inforeg_infopoltech*

Oversees implementation of the Privacy Act of 1974 and other privacy- and security-related statutes. Issues guidelines and regulations.

Privacy and Civil Liberties Oversight Board, *1600 Pennsylvania Ave. N.W. 20502. Fax, (202) 456-1066. Mark A. Robbins, Executive Director. General e-mail, privacyboard@who.eop.gov Web, www.whitehouse.gov/administration/eop/pclob*

The five-member board advises the president and other senior executive branch officials to ensure that privacy concerns and civil liberties are considered in the implementation of laws, regulations, and executive branch policies related to terrorism. The board is appointed by and serves at the pleasure of the president. Members are confirmed by the Senate.

►CONGRESS

For a listing of relevant congressional committees and subcommittees, please see page 468 or the Appendix.

►NONGOVERNMENTAL

ASIS International, *1625 Prince St., Alexandria, VA 22314-2818; (703) 519-6200. Fax, (703) 519-6299. Michael J. Stack, Chief Executive Officer. General e-mail, asis@asisonline.org Web, www.asisonline.org*

Membership: security professionals worldwide. Interests include all aspects of security, with emphasis on counterterrorism, computer security, privacy issues, government security, and the availability of job-related information for employers determining an employee's suitability for employment. (Formerly the American Society for Industrial Security.)

Assn. of Direct Response Fundraising Counsel, *1612 K St. N.W., #510 20006-2849; (202) 293-9640. Robert S. Tigner, General Counsel. General e-mail, adrfco@msn.com Web, www.adrfco.org*

Membership: businesses in the direct response fundraising industry. Establishes standards of ethical practice in such areas as ownership of direct mail donor lists and mandatory disclosures by fundraising counsel. Educates nonprofit organizations and the public on direct mail fundraising. Represents members' interests before the federal and state governments.

Call for Action, *5272 River Road, #300, Bethesda, MD 20816; (301) 657-8260. Shirley Rooker, President. Web, www.callforaction.org*

International network of consumer hotlines affiliated with local broadcast partners. Helps consumers resolve problems with businesses, government agencies, and other organizations through mediation. Provides information on privacy concerns.

Center for Democracy and Technology, *1634 Eye St. N.W., #1100 20006; (202) 637-9800. Fax, (202) 637-0968. Leslie Harris, President. General e-mail, info@cdt.org Web, www.cdt.org*

Promotes and defends privacy and civil liberties on the Internet. Interests include social networking and access to the Internet, consumer protection and combating spyware, health information privacy and technology, government surveillance, and access to information and use of interactivity by government.

Communications Workers of America (CWA), *501 3rd St. N.W. 20001; (202) 434-1100. Fax, (202) 434-1279. Larry Cohen, President.*

General e-mail, cwaweb@cwa-union.org

Web, www.cwa-union.org

Membership: telecommunications, broadcast, and printing and publishing workers. Opposes electronic monitoring of productivity, eavesdropping by employers, and misuse of drug and polygraph tests.

Consumers Union of the United States, *Washington Office, 1101 17th St. N.W., #500 20036; (202) 462-6262. Fax, (202) 265-9548. Ellen Bloom, Director.*

Web, www.consumersunion.org

Consumer advocacy group active in protecting the privacy of consumers. Interests include credit report accuracy. (Headquarters in Yonkers, N.Y.)

Electronic Privacy Information Center (EPIC), *1718 Connecticut Ave. N.W., #200 20009; (202) 483-1140. Fax, (202) 483-1248. Marc Rotenberg, Executive Director.*

General e-mail, epic-info@epic.org

Web, www.epic.org

Public interest research center. Conducts research and conferences on domestic and international civil liberties issues, including privacy, free speech, information access, computer security, and encryption; litigates cases. Monitors legislation and regulations.

National Assn. of State Utility Consumer Advocates (NASUCA), *8380 Colesville Rd., #101, Silver Spring, MD 20910-6267; (301) 589-6313. Fax, (301) 589-6380. Charles A. Acquard, Executive Director.*

General e-mail, nasuca@nasuca.org

Web, www.nasuca.org

Membership: public advocate offices authorized by states to represent ratepayer interests before state and federal utility regulatory commissions. Supports privacy protection for telephone customers.

National Consumers League, *1701 K St. N.W., #1200 20006; (202) 835-3323. Fax, (202) 835-0747. Sally Greenberg, Executive Director.*

General e-mail, info@nclnet.org

Web, www.nclnet.org

Advocacy group concerned with privacy rights of consumers. Interests include credit and financial records, medical records, direct marketing, telecommunications, and workplace privacy.

U.S. Public Interest Research Group (USPIRG), *218 D St. S.E. 20003; (202) 546-9707. Fax, (202) 546-2461. Gary Kalman, Director.*

General e-mail, uspirg@pirg.org

Web, www.uspirg.org

Coordinates grassroots efforts to advance consumer protection laws. Works for the protection of privacy rights, particularly in the area of fair credit reporting.

Religious Freedom

▶**NONGOVERNMENTAL**

American Jewish Congress, *Washington Office, 1001 Connecticut Ave. N.W., #407 20036-5553; (202) 466-9661. Fax, (202) 466-9665. Matthew Horn, National Policy Director.*

General e-mail, washrep@ajcongress.org

Web, www.ajcongress.org

Advocacy organization that seeks to uphold civil and constitutional rights. Litigates cases involving prayer in public schools, tuition tax credits, equal access, and religious symbols on public property. (Headquarters in New York.)

Americans for Religious Liberty, *P.O. Box 6656, Silver Spring, MD 20916; (301) 260-2988. Fax, (301) 260-2989. Edd Doerr, President.*

General e-mail, info@arlinc.org

Web, www.arlinc.org

Educational organization concerned with issues involving the separation of church and state. Opposes government-sponsored school prayer and tax support for religious institutions; supports religious neutrality in public education; defends abortion rights. Provides legal services in litigation cases. Maintains speakers bureau.

Americans United for Separation of Church and State, *518 C St. N.E. 20002; (202) 466-3234. Fax, (202) 466-2587. Barry W. Lynn, Executive Director.*

General e-mail, americansunited@au.org

Web, www.au.org

Citizens' interest group that opposes government-sponsored prayer in public schools and tax aid for parochial schools.

Christian Legal Society, *8001 Braddock Rd., #300, Springfield, VA 22151; (703) 642-1070. Fax, (703) 642-1075. Samuel B. Casey, Chief Executive Officer.*

General e-mail, clshq@clsnet.org

Web, www.clsnet.org

Membership: attorneys, judges, law professors, law students, and others. Seeks to create and mobilize a national grassroots network of Christians to advocate equal access to justice for the poor, religious freedom, the sanctity of human life, and biblical conflict resolution.

International Religious Liberty Assn., *12501 Old Columbia Pike, Silver Spring, MD 20904-6600; (301) 680-6680. Fax, (301) 680-6695. John Graz, Secretary General.*

Web, www.irla.org

Seeks to preserve and expand religious liberty and freedom of conscience; advocates separation of church and state; sponsors international and domestic meetings and congresses.

National Assn. of Evangelicals, *701 G St. S.W. 20024 (mailing address: P.O. Box 23269, Washington, DC 20026); (202) 789-1011. Fax, (202) 842-0392. Leith Anderson, President.*

Privacy Resources

See government agencies' individual Web sites for their privacy policies and freedom of information procedures.

AGENCIES AND CONGRESS

Federal Trade Commission, ID Theft, www.ftc.gov/idtheft; Privacy Initiatives, www.ftc.gov/privacy; Identity Theft Hotline, (877) 438-4338

House Judiciary Committee, Subcommittee on the Constitution, Civil Rights, and Civil Liberties, (202) 225-2825, www.judiciary.house.gov

National Do-Not-Call Registry, toll-free, (888) 382-1222, TTY, (866) 290-4236, www.fcc.gov/cgb/donotcall

Office of Management and Budget (concerning the Privacy Act), (202) 395-3647, www.whitehouse.gov/omb/privacy/index.html

Senate Judiciary Committee, Subcommittee on the Constitution, (202) 224-5573, www.judiciary.senate.gov

U.S. Postal Service, www.usps.com/privacyoffice/welcome.htm

NONGOVERNMENTAL

American Bar Association, Lawyer Referral Service, (202) 662-1000, www.findlegalhelp.org

American Civil Liberties Union, (202) 544-1681, www.aclu.org/privacy/index.html

Call for Action, (301) 657-8260, www.callforaction.org

Center for Democracy and Technology, (202) 637-9800, www.cdt.org

Center for National Security Studies, (202) 721-5650, www.cnss.org

Center for Study of Responsive Law, (202) 387-8030, www.csrl.org

Consumer Data Industry Assn., (202) 371-0910, www.cdiaonline.org

Consumer Privacy Guide, www.consumerprivacyguide.org

Consumers Union of the United States, (202) 462-6262, www.consumersunion.org

Direct Marketing Assn., Do-Not-Call Registry, (202) 955-5030, www.the-dma.org

Electronic Privacy Information Center, (202) 483-1140, www.epic.org

Health Privacy Project, www.healthprivacy.org

National Consumers League, (202) 835-3323, www.nclnet.org

Online Privacy Alliance, (202) 637-5600, www.privacyalliance.org

Privacy Site (EPIC), www.privacy.org

U.S. Postal Inspection Service, (877) 876-2455, postalinspectors.uspis.gov

U.S. Public Interest Research Group (USPIRG), (202) 546-9707, www.uspirg.org

---

General e-mail, nae@nae.net

Web, www.nae.net

Membership: evangelical churches, organizations (including schools), and individuals. Supports religious freedom. Monitors legislation and regulations.

National Council of Churches, *Washington Office, 110 Maryland Ave. N.E. 20002; (202) 544-2350. Fax, (202) 543-1297. Wesley M. Pattillo, Senior Program Director for Justice, Advocacy, and Communication, (212) 870-2227; Kevin Williams, Office Manager.*
Web, www.ncccusa.org

Membership: Protestant, Anglican, and Orthodox churches. Opposes government-sponsored prayer in public schools. Provides information on the school prayer issue. (Headquarters in New York.)

Separation of Powers

►NONGOVERNMENTAL

Public Citizen Litigation Group, *1600 20th St. N.W. 20009; (202) 588-1000. Fax, (202) 588-7795. Brian Wolfman, Director of Litigation. Press, (202) 588-7741. General e-mail, litigation@citizen.org*

Web, www.citizen.org/litigation

Conducts litigation for Public Citizen, a citizens' interest group, in cases involving separation of powers; represents individuals and groups with similar interests.

CRIMINAL LAW

►AGENCIES

Criminal Division *(Justice Dept.), 950 Pennsylvania Ave. N.W., #2107 20530-0001; (202) 514-2601. Fax, (202) 514-9412. Lanny A. Breuer, Assistant Attorney General (Acting).*
General e-mail, Criminal.Division@usdoj.gov

Web, www.usdoj.gov/criminal

Enforces all federal criminal laws except those specifically assigned to the antitrust, civil rights, environment and natural resources, and tax divisions of the Justice Dept. Supervises and directs U.S. attorneys in the field on criminal matters and litigation; supervises international extradition proceedings. Coordinates federal enforcement efforts against white-collar crime, fraud, and child pornography; handles civil actions under customs, liquor, narcotics, gambling, and firearms laws; coordinates enforcement activities against organized crime. Directs the National Asset Forfeiture Program for seizing the proceeds of criminal activity. Investigates and prosecutes criminal offenses involving public integrity and subversive activities, including treason, espionage, and sedition; Nazi war crimes; and related criminal offenses. Handles all civil cases relating to internal security and counsels federal departments and agencies regarding internal security matters. Drafts responses on proposed and pending criminal law legislation.

Criminal Division *(Justice Dept.)*, *Enforcement Operations: International Prisoner Transfer Unit*, *1301 New York Ave. N.W., John C. Keeney Bldg., 12th Floor 20005 (mailing address: 950 Pennsylvania Ave. N.W., Criminal Division, Washington, DC 20530-0001); (202) 514-3173. Fax, (202) 514-9003. Paula A. Wolff, Chief. General e-mail, international.prisoner.transfer@usdoj.gov*

Web, www.usdoj.gov/criminal/oeo

Implements prisoner transfer treaties with foreign countries.

Federal Bureau of Investigation (FBI), *(Justice Dept.)*, *935 Pennsylvania Ave. N.W., #7176 20535-0001; (202) 324-3444. Fax, (202) 323-2079. Robert S. Mueller III, Director. Information, (202) 324-3000. Press, (202) 324-3691. Web, www.fbi.gov*

Investigates all violations of federal criminal laws except those assigned specifically to other federal agencies. Exceptions include alcohol, counterfeiting, and tobacco violations (Justice Dept. and Commerce Dept.); customs violations and illegal entry of aliens (Homeland Security Dept.); and postal violations (U.S. Postal Service). Priorities include protecting the United States against terror attacks; protecting civil rights; combating public corruption at all levels, transnational/national criminal organizations and enterprises, white-collar crime, and significant violent crime; and supporting federal, state, local, and international partners. Services to other law enforcement agencies include fingerprint identifications, laboratory services, police training, and access to the National Crime Information Center (a communications network among federal, state, and local police agencies).

Federal Bureau of Investigation (FBI), *(Justice Dept.)*, *Victim Assistance*, *935 Pennsylvania Ave. N.W., #3329 20535; (202) 324-1339. Fax, (202) 324-1311. Kathryn McKay Turman, Program Director. Toll-free, (866) 828-5320. General e-mail, victim.assistance@ic.fbi.gov*

Web, www.fbi.gov/hq/cid/victimassist/home.htm

Ensures that victims of crimes investigated by the FBI are identified, offered assistance, and given information about case events. Manages the Victim Assistance Program in the fifty-six FBI field offices as well as the FBI's international offices. Trains agents and personnel to work with victims. Coordinates resources and services to victims in cases of terrorism and crimes against citizens that occur outside the United States. Coordinates with other federal agencies on behalf of victims.

Office of Justice Programs (OJP), *(Justice Dept.)*, *National Institute of Justice*, *810 7th St. N.W., 7th Floor 20531; (202) 307-2942. Fax, (202) 307-6394. David W. Hagy, Director (Acting). Press, (202) 307-0703. Web, www.ojp.usdoj.gov/nij*

Conducts research on all aspects of criminal justice, including crime prevention, enforcement, adjudication, and corrections; evaluates programs; develops model programs using new techniques. Serves as an affiliated institute of the United Nations Crime Prevention and Criminal Justice Program (UNCPCJ); studies transnational issues, especially within the Western Hemisphere. Maintains the National Criminal Justice Reference Service, which provides information on criminal justice research: (800) 851-3420; in Maryland, (301) 519-5500; Web, www.ncjrs.gov.

Office of Justice Programs (OJP), *(Justice Dept.)*, *Victims of Crime*, *810 7th St. N.W., 8th Floor 20531; (202) 307-5983. Fax, (202) 514-6383. John W. Gillis, Director. TTY, (202) 514-7908. Resource Center, (800) 851-3420 or TTY (877) 712-9279. Victim hotline, (800) 331-0075 or TTY, (800) 833-6885. Web, www.ovc.gov*

Works to advance the rights of and improve services to the nation's crime victims. Supports programs and initiatives to assist other federal agencies, state and local governments, tribal governments, private nonprofit organizations, and the international community in their efforts to aid victims of violent and nonviolent crime. Provides emergency funding and services for victims of terrorism and mass violence and victims of human trafficking. Funds the development of training and technical assistance for victim service providers and other professionals through the Training and Technical Assistance Center, (866) 682-8822 or TTY (866) 682-8880. Funds demonstration projects and coordinates annual observances of National Crime Victims' Rights Week.

▶**CONGRESS**

For a listing of relevant congressional committees and subcommittees, please see page 468 or the Appendix.

▶**INTERNATIONAL ORGANIZATIONS**

INTERPOL, *Washington Office*, *INTERPOL-USNCB, U.S. Justice Dept. 20530; (202) 616-9000. Fax, (202) 616-8400. Martin Renkiewicz, Director. Web, www.usdoj.gov/usncb*

U.S. national central bureau for INTERPOL; participates in international investigations on behalf of U.S. police; coordinates the exchange of investigative information on crimes, including drug trafficking, counterfeiting, missing persons, and terrorism. Coordinates law enforcement requests for investigative assistance in the United States and abroad. Assists with extradition processes. Serves as liaison between foreign and U.S. law enforcement agencies at federal, state, and local levels. (Headquarters in Lyons, France.)

▶**NONGOVERNMENTAL**

American Bar Assn. (ABA), *Criminal Justice, Washington Office*, *740 15th St. N.W., 10th Floor 20005-1009; (202) 662-1500. Fax, (202) 662-1501. Jack Hanna, Director. Press, (202) 662-1090. General e-mail, crimjustice@abanet.org*

Web, www.abanet.org/crimjust

Responsible for all matters pertaining to criminal law and procedure for the association. Studies and makes recommendations on all facets of the criminal and juvenile justice systems, including sentencing, juries, pre-trial procedures, grand juries, and white-collar crime. (Headquarters in Chicago, Ill.)

Justice Policy Institute, *1003 K St. N.W., #500 20001-4425; (202) 558-7974. Fax, (202) 558-7978. Tracy Velázquez, Executive Director. General e-mail, info@justicepolicy.org*

Web, www.justicepolicy.org

Research, advocacy, and policy development organization. Analyzes current and emerging adult and juvenile criminal justice problems; educates the public about criminal justice issues; provides technical assistance to communities seeking to reform incarceration policies. Interests include new prison construction, alternatives to incarceration, anti-gang legislation, and curfew laws.

National Assn. of Attorneys General, *2030 M St. N.W., 8th Floor 20036; (202) 326-6000. Fax, (202) 331-1427. James McPherson, Executive Director (Acting). Press, (202) 326-6027. General e-mail, feedback@naag.org*

Web, www.naag.org

Membership: attorneys general of the states, territories, and commonwealths. Fosters interstate cooperation on legal and law enforcement issues, conducts policy research and analysis, and facilitates communication between members and all levels of government.

(For list of attorneys general, see Governors and Other State Officials in appendix.)

National Assn. of Crime Victim Compensation Boards, *P.O. Box 7054, Alexandria, VA 22307; (703) 780-3200. Dan Eddy, Executive Director. General e-mail, nacvcb@aol.com*

Web, www.nacvcb.org

Provides state compensation agencies with training and technical assistance. Provides public information on victim compensation.

National Assn. of Criminal Defense Lawyers, *1660 L St. N.W., 12th Floor 20036; (202) 872-8600. Fax, (202) 872-8690. Norman L. Reimer, Executive Director. General e-mail, assist@nacdl.org*

Web, www.nacdl.org

Membership: criminal defense attorneys. Provides members with continuing legal education programs, a brief bank, an ethics hotline, and specialized assistance in such areas as forensic science. Offers free legal assistance to members threatened with sanctions for providing ethical but aggressive representation. Interests include eliminating mandatory minimum sentencing, forensic lab reform, death penalty reform, and minimizing the effect on civil liberties of the wars on terrorism and drugs. Monitors legislation and regulations and advocates for a rational and humane criminal justice policy.

National Center for Victims of Crime, *2000 M St. N.W., #480 20036; (202) 467-8700. Fax, (202) 467-8701. Mary Lou Leary, Executive Director. TTY, (800) 211-7996. Crime victims hotline, (800) 394-2255. General e-mail, webmaster@ncvc.org*

Web, www.ncvc.org

Works with victims' groups and criminal justice agencies to protect the rights of crime victims through state and federal statutes and policies. Promotes greater responsiveness to crime victims through training and education; provides research and technical assistance in the development of victim-related legislation.

National Crime Prevention Council, *2345 Crystal Dr., 5th Floor, Arlington, VA 22202; (202) 466-6272. Fax, (202) 296-1356. Alfonso E. "Al" Lenhardt, President. Publications office, (800) 627-2911. Web, www.ncpc.org*

Educates public on crime prevention through media campaigns, supporting materials, and training workshops; sponsors McGruff public service campaign; runs demonstration programs in schools.

National District Attorneys' Assn. (NDAA), *44 Canal Center Plaza, #110, Alexandria, VA 22314; (703) 549-9222. Fax, (703) 836-3195. Scott Burns, Executive Director (Interim). Web, www.ndaa.org*

Membership: prosecutors. Sponsors conferences and workshops on such topics as criminal justice, district attorneys, the courts, child abuse, national traffic laws, community prosecution, violence against women, gun violence, and others. Conducts research; provides information, training, and technical assistance to prosecutors; and analyzes policies related to improvements in criminal prosecution.

National Organization for Victim Assistance, *510 King St., #424, Alexandria, VA 22314; (703) 535-6682. Fax, (703) 535-5500. Will Marling, Executive Director. Toll-free and referral line, (800) 879-6682. General e-mail, nova@trynova.org*

Web, www.trynova.org

Membership: persons involved with victim and witness assistance programs, criminal justice professionals, researchers, crime victims, and others interested in victims' rights. Monitors legislation; provides victims and victim support programs with technical assistance, referrals, and program support; provides information on victims' rights.

Child Abuse, Domestic Violence, and Sexual Assault

▶**AGENCIES**

Administration for Children and Families *(Health and Human Services Dept.), Family and Youth Services,*

1250 Maryland Ave. S.W., 8th Floor 20201; (202) 205-8347. Fax, (202) 205-9721. Curtis Porter, Associate Commissioner (Acting).

Web, www.acf.hhs.gov/programs/fysb

Administers federal discretionary grant programs for projects serving runaway and homeless youth and for projects that deter youth involvement in gangs. Provides youth service agencies with training and technical assistance. Monitors federal policies, programs, and legislation. Supports research on youth development issues, including gangs, runaways, and homeless youth. Operates national clearinghouse on families and youth. Issues grants and monitors abstinence education programs.

Criminal Division *(Justice Dept.), Child Exploitation and Obscenity, 1400 New York Ave. N.W., 6th Floor 20530; (202) 514-5780. Fax, (202) 514-1793. Andrew Oosterbaan, Chief.*

Web, www.usdoj.gov/criminal/ceos

Enforces federal child exploitation, obscenity, and pornography laws; prosecutes cases involving violations of these laws, including international trafficking and kidnapping. Maintains collection of briefs, pleadings, and other material for use by federal, state, and local prosecutors. Assists the U.S. Attorney's Office with investigations, trials, and appeals pertaining to these offenses. Advises and trains law enforcement personnel, federal prosecutors, and Justice Dept. officials.

Defense Dept. (DoD), *Sexual Assault Prevention and Response, 1401 Wilson Blvd., #402, Arlington, VA 22209; (703) 696-9422. Fax, (703) 696-9437. Kaye H. Whitley, Director. Hotline, (800) 342-9647.*

General e-mail, SAPRO@wso.whs.mil

Web, www.sapr.mil

Serves as the single point of accountability for the Defense Dept.'s sexual assault policy. Responsible for improving prevention and ensuring support for victims and accountability of offenders. Publishes an online newsletter.

Justice Department (DOJ), *Violence Against Women, 800 K St. N.W., #920 20530; (202) 307-6026. Fax, (202) 305-2589. Catherine Pierce, Director (Acting). TTY, (202) 307-2277. National Domestic Violence Hotline, (800) 799-SAFE.*

Web, www.ovw.usdoj.gov

Seeks more effective policies and services to combat domestic violence, sexual assault, stalking, and other crimes against women. Helps administer grants to states to fund shelters, crisis centers, and hotlines, and to hire law enforcement officers, prosecutors, and counselors specializing in cases of sexual violence and other violent crimes against women.

Office of Justice Programs (OJP), *(Justice Dept.), National Institute of Justice, 810 7th St. N.W., 7th Floor 20531; (202) 307-2942. Fax, (202) 307-6394. David W. Hagy, Director (Acting). Press, (202) 307-0703.*

Web, www.ojp.usdoj.gov/nij

Conducts research on all aspects of criminal justice, including AIDS issues for law enforcement officials. Studies on rape and domestic violence available from the National Criminal Justice Reference Service: (800) 851-3420; in Maryland, (301) 519-5500; Web, www.ncjrs.gov.

►NONGOVERNMENTAL

American Bar Assn. (ABA), *Center on Children and the Law, 740 15th St. N.W. 20005-1022; (202) 662-1720. Fax, (202) 662-1755. Howard Davidson, Director.*

General e-mail, ctrchildlaw@abanet.org

Web, www.abanet.org/child

Provides state and private child welfare organizations with training and technical assistance. Interests include child abuse and neglect, adoption, foster care, and medical neglect.

Rape, Abuse, and Incest National Network (RAINN), *2000 L St. N.W., #406 20036; (202) 544-1034. Fax, (202) 544-3556. Scott Berkowitz, President. National Sexual Assault Hotline, (800) 656-4673.*

General e-mail, info@rainn.org

Web, www.rainn.org

Links sexual assault victims to confidential local services through national sexual assault hotline. Provides extensive public outreach and education programs nationwide on sexual assault prevention, prosecution, and recovery. Promotes national policy efforts to improve services to victims.

Drug Control

►AGENCIES

Criminal Division *(Justice Dept.), Narcotic and Dangerous Drugs, 1400 New York Ave. N.W., #1100 20530; (202) 514-0917. Fax, (202) 514-6112. Wayne Raabe, Director. Press, (202) 514-2007.*

Web, www.usdoj.gov/criminal

Investigates and prosecutes participants in criminal syndicates involved in the large-scale importation, manufacture, shipment, or distribution of illegal narcotics and other dangerous drugs. Trains agents and prosecutors in the techniques of major drug litigation.

The DEA Museum and Visitors Center *(Justice Dept.), 700 Army Navy Dr., Arlington, VA 22202; (202) 307-3463. Fax, (202) 307-8956. Sean Fearns, Director.*

Web, www.deamuseum.org

Seeks to educate the public on the role and impact of federal drug law enforcement through state-of-the-art exhibits, displays, interactive stations, and outreach programs. Admission is free; groups of fifteen or more should call ahead for reservations.

Defense Dept. (DoD), *Counternarcotics, 1510 Defense Pentagon, #4A275 20301-1510; (703) 614-8847. Fax,*

(703) 697-4682. Ed Frathingham, Deputy Assistant Secretary (Acting).
Web, www.defenselink.mil/policy/solic/cn

Advises the secretary on Defense Dept. policies and programs in support of federal counternarcotics operations and the implementation of the president's national drug control policy.

Drug Enforcement Administration (DEA), *(Justice Dept.), 700 Army-Navy Dr., Arlington, VA 22202 (mailing address: 8701 Morrissette Dr., Springfield, VA 22152); (202) 307-8000. Fax, (202) 307-4540. Michelle Leonhart, Director (Acting). Press, (202) 307-7977. Locator, (202) 307-4132.*
Web, www.dea.gov

Enforces federal laws and statutes relating to narcotics and other dangerous drugs, including addictive drugs, depressants, stimulants, and hallucinogens; manages the National Narcotics Intelligence System in cooperation with federal, state, and local officials; investigates violations and regulates legal trade in narcotics and dangerous drugs. Provides school and community officials with drug abuse policy guidelines. Provides information on drugs and drug abuse.

Federal Bureau of Investigation (FBI), *(Justice Dept.), 935 Pennsylvania Ave. N.W., #7176 20535-0001; (202) 324-3444. Fax, (202) 323-2079. Robert S. Mueller III, Director. Information, (202) 324-3000. Press, (202) 324-3691.*
Web, www.fbi.gov

Shares responsibility with the Drug Enforcement Administration for investigating violations of federal criminal drug laws; investigates organized crime involvement with illegal narcotics trafficking.

Food and Drug Administration (FDA), *(Health and Human Services Dept.), Center for Drug Evaluation and Research, 10903 New Hampshire Ave., Silver Spring, MD 20993; (301) 796-5400. Fax, (301) 847-8752. Dr. Janet Woodcock, Director. Press, (301) 796-4540.*
Web, www.fda.gov/cder

Makes recommendations to the Justice Dept.'s Drug Enforcement Administration on narcotics and dangerous drugs to be controlled.

Interior Dept. (DOI), *Law Enforcement: Border and Drug Coordination, 1849 C St. N.W., MS 7354 20240; (202) 208-6891. Fax, (202) 219-1185. Mark Harvey, Branch Chief (Acting).*
Web, http://doi.gov/law_enforcement.html

Oversees drug enforcement activities for law enforcement branches of DOI bureaus, including National Park Service, Bureau of Land Management, Fish and Wildlife Service, and Bureau of Indian Affairs. Coordinates drug enforcement on DOI lands with federal agencies, including the ONDCP and DEA. Develops and implements DOI counter-drug policy and strategy.

Office of Justice Programs (OJP), *(Justice Dept.), Justice Assistance, 810 7th St. N.W., 4th Floor 20531; (202)*

616-6500. Fax, (202) 305-1367. James H. Burch II, Director (Acting).
General e-mail, askbja@usdoj.gov
Web, www.ojp.usdoj.gov/bja

Awards grants and provides eligible state, local, and tribal governments with training and technical assistance to enforce laws relating to narcotics and other dangerous drugs.

Office of National Drug Control Policy (ONDCP), *(Executive Office of the President), 750 17th St. N.W. 20503; (202) 395-6700. Fax, (202) 395-6680. Edward H. Jurith, Director (Acting). Drug Policy Information Clearinghouse, (800) 666-3332.*
Web, www.whitehousedrugpolicy.gov

Establishes policies and oversees the implementation of a national drug control strategy with the goal of reducing illicit drug use, manufacturing, trafficking, and drug-related crimes, violence, and health consequences. Coordinates the international and domestic anti-drug efforts of executive branch agencies and ensures that such efforts sustain and complement state and local anti-drug activities. Advises the president and the National Security Council on drug control policy. (Clearinghouse address: P.O. Box 6000, Rockville, MD 20849-6000.)

U.S. Coast Guard (USCG), *(Homeland Security Dept.), Law Enforcement Command (CG-531), 2100 2nd St. S.W., #3110 20593-0001; (202) 372-2160. Fax, (202) 372-2913. Michael Giglio, Chief.*
Web, www.uscg.mil/hq/g-o/g-opl

Combats smuggling of narcotics and other drugs into the United States via the Atlantic and Pacific Oceans and the Gulf of Mexico. Works with U.S. Customs and Border Protection on drug law enforcement; interdicts illegal migrants; enforces domestic fisheries laws and international fisheries agreements.

U.S. Customs and Border Protection *(Homeland Security Dept.), Border Patrol, 1300 Pennsylvania Ave. N.W., #6.5E 20229; (202) 344-2050. Fax, (202) 344-3140. David V. Aguilar, Chief.*
Web, www.cbp.gov

Mobile uniformed law enforcement arm of the Homeland Security Dept. Primary mission is to detect and prevent the illegal trafficking of people and contraband across U.S. borders.

U.S. Customs and Border Protection *(Homeland Security Dept.), Field Operations, 1300 Pennsylvania Ave. N.W., #2.4A 20229; (202) 344-1620. Fax, (202) 344-2777. Thomas Winkowski, Assistant Commissioner. Hotline to report suspicious activity, (800) 232-5378.*
Web, www.cbp.gov

Interdicts and seizes contraband, including narcotics and other drugs, at the U.S. border.

U.S. Immigration and Customs Enforcement (ICE), *(Homeland Security Dept.), 500 12th St. S.W.*

20024-6121; (202) 514-1900. Fax, (202) 307-9911. Julie L. Myers, Assistant Secretary. Press, (202) 732-4242. Hotline to report suspicious activity, (866) 347-2423.
Web, www.ice.gov

Investigates narcotics smuggling, including money laundering, document and identity fraud, and immigration enforcement; interdicts flow of narcotics into the United States.

►**NONGOVERNMENTAL**

Drug Policy Alliance, *Washington Office, 925 15th St. N.W., 2nd Floor 20005; (202) 683-2030. Fax, (202) 216-0803. Bill Piper, Director.*
General e-mail, dc@drugpolicy.org
Web, www.drugpolicy.org

Supports reform of current drug control policy. Advocates medical treatment to control drug abuse; opposes random drug testing. Sponsors the annual International Conference on Drug Policy Reform. (Headquarters in New York.)

Marijuana Policy Project, *P.O. Box 77492 20013; (202) 462-5747. Fax, (202) 232-0442. Robert D. Kampia, Executive Director.*
General e-mail, info@mpp.org
Web, www.mpp.org

Promotes reform of marijuana policies and regulations. Opposes the prohibition of responsible growing and use of marijuana by adults. Interests include allowing doctors to prescribe marijuana to seriously ill patients and eliminating criminal penalties for marijuana use.

National Assn. of State Alcohol and Drug Abuse Directors (NASADAD), *1025 Connecticut Ave. N.W., #605 20036-5430; (202) 293-0090. Fax, (202) 293-1250. Rob Morrison, Executive Director.*
General e-mail, dcoffice@nasadad.org
Web, www.nasadad.org

Provides information on drug abuse treatment and prevention; contracts with federal and state agencies for design of programs to fight drug abuse.

National Organization for the Reform of Marijuana Laws (NORML), *1600 K St. N.W., #501 20006-2832; (202) 483-5500. Fax, (202) 483-0057. Allen St. Pierre, Executive Director.*
General e-mail, norml@norml.org
Web, www.norml.org

Works to reform federal, state, and local marijuana laws and policies. Educates the public and conducts litigation on behalf of marijuana consumers. Monitors legislation and regulations.

RAND Corporation, *Drug Policy Research Center, Washington Office, 1200 S. Hayes St., Arlington, VA 22202-5050; (703) 413-1100. Fax, (703) 413-8111. Beau Kilmer, Co-Director; Rosalie Liccardo Pacula, Co-Director.*
Web, www.rand.org/centers/dprc

Studies and analyzes the nation's drug problems and policies. Emphasis on empirical research and policy recommendations; interests include international and local policy, trafficking, interdiction, modeling and forecasting, prevention, and treatment. Provides policymakers with information. (Headquarters in Santa Monica, Calif.)

Gun Control

►**AGENCIES**

Bureau of Alcohol, Tobacco, Firearms, and Explosives (ATF), *(Justice Dept.), 650 Massachusetts Ave. N.W., #8000 20226; (202) 927-8700. Fax, (202) 927-8876. Kenneth E. Melson, Director (Acting).*
Web, www.atf.gov

Enforces and administers laws to eliminate illegal possession and use of firearms. Investigates criminal violations and regulates legal trade, including imports and exports. To report illegal firearms activity, (800) 283-4867; firearms theft hotline, (888) 930-9275.

►**NONGOVERNMENTAL**

Brady Campaign, *1225 Eye St. N.W., #1100 20005; (202) 898-0792. Fax, (202) 371-9615. Paul Helmke, President.*
Web, www.bradycampaign.org

Public interest organization that works for gun control legislation and serves as an information clearinghouse. Monitors legislation and regulations.

Brady Center to Prevent Gun Violence, *1225 Eye St. N.W., #1100 20005; (202) 289-7319. Fax, (202) 371-9615. Paul Helmke, President.*
Web, www.bradycenter.org

Educational, research, and legal action organization that seeks to allay gun violence, especially among children. Library open to the public. (Affiliated with Brady Campaign.)

Citizens Committee for the Right to Keep and Bear Arms, *Publications and Public Affairs, Washington Office, 1250 Connecticut Ave. N.W., #200 20036; (202) 326-5259. Fax, (202) 898-1939. John M. Snyder, Director. Toll-free, (800) 486-6963.*
General e-mail, gundean@aol.com
Web, www.ccrkba.org

Concerned with rights of gun owners. Maintains National Advisory Council, composed of members of Congress and distinguished Americans, to provide advice on issues concerning the right to keep and bear arms. (Headquarters in Bellevue, Wash.)

Coalition to Stop Gun Violence, *1424 L St. N.W., #2-1 20005; (202) 408-0061. Fax, (202) 408-0062. Michael K. Beard, President; Joshua Horwitz, Executive Director.*
General e-mail, csgv@csgv.org
Web, www.csgv.org

Membership: 45 national organizations and 100,000 individuals. Works to reduce gun violence by fostering effective community and national action.

Educational Fund to Stop Gun Violence, *1424 L St. N.W., #2-1 20005; (202) 408-7560. Fax, (202) 408-0062. Michael K. Beard, President; Joshua Horwitz, Executive Director.*
Web, www.csgv.org

Works to reduce handgun violence through education; assists schools and organizations in establishing antiviolence programs; maintains a firearms litigation clearinghouse; promotes legislation to close illegal gun markets; trains grassroots activists. Monitors legislation and regulations. (Affiliated with the Coalition to Stop Gun Violence.)

Gun Owners of America, *8001 Forbes Pl., #102, Springfield, VA 22151; (703) 321-8585. Fax, (703) 321-8408. Lawrence D. Pratt, Executive Director.*
General e-mail, goamail@gunowners.org

Web, www.gunowners.org

Seeks to preserve the right to bear arms and to protect the rights of law-abiding gun owners. Administers foundation that provides gun owners with legal assistance in suits against the federal government. Monitors legislation, regulations, and international agreements.

National Rifle Assn. of America (NRA), *11250 Waples Mill Rd., Fairfax, VA 22030; (703) 267-1000. Fax, (703) 267-3976. Wayne LaPierre, Executive Vice President. Press, (703) 267-3820. Toll-free, (800) 672-3888.*
Web, www.nra.org

Membership: target shooters, hunters, gun collectors, gunsmiths, police officers, and others interested in firearms. Promotes shooting sports and recreational shooting and safety; studies and makes recommendations on firearms laws. Opposes gun control legislation. (Affiliated with the Institute for Legislative Action, the NRA's lobbying arm.)

Juvenile Justice

▶AGENCIES

Education Dept., *Student Achievement and School Accountability, 400 Maryland Ave. S.W. 20202-6132; (202) 260-0826. Fax, (202) 260-7764. Zollie Stevenson, Director.*
Web, www.ed.gov

Funds state and local institutions responsible for providing neglected or delinquent children with free public education.

Office of Justice Programs (OJP), *(Justice Dept.), Juvenile Justice and Delinquency Prevention, 810 7th St. N.W. 20531; (202) 307-5911. Fax, (202) 514-6382. Jeff Slowikowski, Administrator (Acting). Clearinghouse, (800) 851-3420.*
Web, www.ojjdp.ncjrs.org

Administers federal programs related to prevention and treatment of juvenile delinquency, missing and exploited children, child victimization, and research and evaluation of the juvenile justice system; coordinates with youth programs of the departments of Agriculture, Education, Housing and Urban Development, Interior, and Labor, and of the Substance Abuse and Mental Health Services Administration, including the Center for Studies of Crime and Delinquency. Operates the Juvenile Justice Clearinghouse.

▶NONGOVERNMENTAL

Coalition for Juvenile Justice, *1710 Rhode Island Ave. N.W., 10th Floor 20036; (202) 467-0864. Fax, (202) 887-0738. Nancy Gannon Hornberger, Executive Director. General e-mail, info@juvjustice.org*

Web, www.juvjustice.org

Represents state juvenile justice advisory groups. Promotes the improvement of the juvenile justice system and the prevention of juvenile delinquency.

Organized Crime

▶AGENCIES

Criminal Division *(Justice Dept.), Narcotic and Dangerous Drugs, 1400 New York Ave. N.W., #1100 20530; (202) 514-0917. Fax, (202) 514-6112. Wayne Raabe, Director. Press, (202) 514-2007.*
Web, www.usdoj.gov/criminal

Investigates and prosecutes participants in criminal syndicates involved in the large-scale importation, manufacture, shipment, or distribution of illegal narcotics and other dangerous drugs. Trains agents and prosecutors in the techniques of major drug litigation.

Criminal Division *(Justice Dept.), Organized Crime and Racketeering, 1301 New York Ave. N.W., #700 20005; (202) 514-3594. Fax, (202) 514-3601. Bruce G. Ohr, Chief. General e-mail, criminaldivision@us.doj.gov*

Web, www.usdoj.gov/criminal

Enforces federal criminal laws when subjects under investigation are alleged racketeers or part of syndicated criminal operations; coordinates efforts of federal, state, and local law enforcement agencies against organized crime, including emerging international groups. Cases include infiltration of legitimate businesses and labor unions, public corruption, labor-management racketeering, and violence that disrupts the criminal justice process.

Federal Bureau of Investigation (FBI), *(Justice Dept.), Organized Crime, 935 Pennsylvania Ave. N.W., #3352 20535-0001; (202) 324-5625. Fax, (202) 324-0880. Matthew Heron, Section Chief.*
Web, www.fbi.gov/hq/cid/orgcrime/ocshome.htm

Coordinates all FBI organized crime investigations. Determines budget, training, and resource needs for investigations, including those related to international organized crime.

Other Violations

▶AGENCIES

Bureau of Alcohol, Tobacco, Firearms, and Explosives (ATF), *(Justice Dept.),* *650 Massachusetts Ave. N.W., #8000 20226; (202) 927-8700. Fax, (202) 927-8876. Kenneth E. Nelson, Director (Acting).*
Web, www.atf.gov

Performs law enforcement functions relating to alcohol (beer, wine, distilled spirits), tobacco, arson, explosives, and destructive devices; investigates criminal violations and regulates legal trade.

Criminal Division *(Justice Dept.),* *Asset Forfeiture and Money Laundering, 1400 New York Ave. N.W., #10100 20530; (202) 514-1263. Fax, (202) 514-5522. Richard Weber, Chief.*
Web, www.usdoj.gov/afmls

Investigates and prosecutes money laundering and criminal and civil forfeiture offenses involving illegal transfer of funds within the United States and from the United States to other countries. Oversees and coordinates legislative policy proposals. Advises U.S. attorneys' offices in multidistrict money laundering and criminal and civil forfeiture prosecutions. Represents Justice Dept. in international anti–money laundering and criminal and civil forfeiture initiatives.

Criminal Division *(Justice Dept.),* *Fraud, 1400 New York Ave. N.W., #4100 20005; (202) 514-7023. Fax, (202) 514-7021. Steven A. Tyrrell, Chief.*
Web, www.usdoj.gov/criminal/fraud

Administers federal enforcement activities related to fraud and white-collar crime. Focuses on frauds against government programs, transnational and multidistrict fraud, and cases involving the security and commodity exchanges, banking practices, and consumer victimization.

Federal Bureau of Investigation (FBI), *(Justice Dept.),* *Counterintelligence, 935 Pennsylvania Ave. N.W., #4012 20535; (202) 324-4614. Fax, (202) 324-0848. Daniel L. Cloyd, Assistant Director.*
Web, www.fbi.gov/hq/ci/cointell.htm

Provides centralized management and oversight of all foreign counterintelligence investigations. Integrates law enforcement with intelligence efforts to investigate violations of federal laws against espionage, including economic espionage. Seeks to prevent foreign acquisition of weapons of mass destruction, penetration of the U.S. intelligence community and government agencies and contractors, and compromise of U.S. critical national assets.

Federal Bureau of Investigation (FBI), *(Justice Dept.),* *Cyber Division, 935 Pennsylvania Ave. N.W., #5835 20535; (202) 324-1380. Fax, (202) 324-2840. Shawn Henry, Assistant Director.*
Web, www.fbi.gov/cyberinvest/cyberhome.htm

Coordinates the investigations of federal violations in which the Internet or computer networks are exploited for terrorist, foreign government–sponsored intelligence, or criminal activities, including copyright violations, fraud, pornography, child exploitation, and malicious computer intrusions.

Federal Bureau of Investigation (FBI), *(Justice Dept.),* *Economic Crimes, 935 Pennsylvania Ave. N.W., #3925 20535; (202) 324-6352. Fax, (202) 324-8072. Robert McMenomy, Chief. Press, (202) 324-3691.*
General e-mail, robert.mcmenomy@ic.fbi.gov
Web, www.fbi.gov

Investigates, reduces, and prevents significant financial crimes against individuals, businesses, and industries by safeguarding the integrity and credibility of corporations, securities and commodities markets, investment vehicles, and the insurance industry. Reinforces compliance in the corporate world and promotes investor confidence in the United States' financial markets. Categorizes the frauds it investigates into four separate classifications: corporate fraud, securities and commodities fraud, insurance fraud (non–health care related), and mass marketing fraud.

Justice Dept., *Civil Rights Division: Trafficking in Persons and Worker Exploitation Task Force, P.O. Box 66018 20035-6018. Complaint Line, (888) 428-7581.*
Web, www.usdoj.gov/crt/crim/tpwetf.htm

Seeks to prevent trafficking in persons and worker exploitation throughout the United States and to investigate and prosecute cases when such violations occur. Provides information to advocacy organizations and service providers to invite their participation to combat trafficking in persons and worker exploitation. The Complaint Line is toll-free and offers foreign language translation services in most languages as well as TTY. After business hours, the Complaint Line has a message service in English, Spanish, and Mandarin only.

Justice Dept. (DOJ), *National Security Division, 950 Pennsylvania Ave. N.W., #7339 20530; (202) 514-1057. Fax, (202) 353-9836. David S. Kris, Assistant Attorney General.*
General e-mail, nsd.public@usdoj.gov
Web, www.usdoj.gov/nsd

Coordinates the Justice Dept.'s intelligence, counterterrorism, counterespionage, and other national security activities. Provides legal assistance and advice, in coordination with the Office of Legal Counsel as appropriate, to all branches of government on matters of national security law and policy.

National Security Division *(Justice Dept.),* *Counterterrorism and Counterespionage, 10th St. and Constitution Ave. N.W., #2649 20530; (202) 514-0849. Fax, (202) 514-8714. David S. Kris, Assistant Attorney General.*
Web, www.usdoj.gov/nsd

Investigates and prosecutes incidents of international and domestic terrorism involving U.S. interests, domestic violent crime, firearms, and explosives violations. Provides legal advice on federal statutes relating to murder, assault, kidnapping, threats, robbery, weapons and explosives control, malicious destruction of property, and aircraft and sea piracy.

U.S. Customs and Border Protection *(Homeland Security Dept.), Field Operations,* 1300 Pennsylvania Ave. N.W., #2.4A 20229; (202) 344-1620. Fax, (202) 344-2777. *Thomas Winkowski, Assistant Commissioner. Hotline to report suspicious activity, (800) 232-5378. Web, www.cbp.gov*

Combats smuggling and the unreported transportation of funds in excess of $10,000; enforces statutes relating to the processing and regulation of people, carriers, cargo, and mail into and out of the United States. Investigates counterfeiting, child pornography, commercial fraud, and Internet crimes.

U.S. Postal Service (USPS), *Inspection Service,* 475 L'Enfant Plaza S.W., #3100 20260-2100; (202) 268-4264. Fax, (202) 268-7316. *William Gilligan, Chief Postal Inspector. Fraud and abuse hotline, (877) 876-2455. Web, http://postalinspectors.uspis.gov*

Protects mail, postal funds, and property from violations of postal laws, such as mail fraud or distribution of obscene materials.

U.S. Secret Service *(Homeland Security Dept.),* 950 H St. N.W., #8300 20223; (202) 406-5700. Fax, (202) 406-5246. *Mark Sullivan, Director. Information, (202) 406-5708. Web, www.secretservice.gov*

Protects the president and vice president of the United States and their immediate family members, foreign heads of state and their spouses, and other individuals as designated by the president. Investigates threats against these protectees; protects the White House, vice president's residence, and foreign missions; and plans and implements security designs for national special security events. Investigates violations of laws relating to counterfeiting of U.S. currency; financial crimes, including access device fraud, financial institution fraud, identity theft, and computer fraud; and computer-based attacks on the financial, banking, and telecommunications infrastructure.

▶**NONGOVERNMENTAL**

International Anticounterfeiting Coalition, 1730 M St. N.W., #1020 20036; (202) 223-6667. Fax, (202) 223-6668. *Robert Barchiesi, President. General e-mail, meghan@iacc.org Web, www.iacc.org*

Works to combat counterfeiting and piracy by promoting laws, regulations, and directives to render theft of intellectual property unprofitable. Oversees anticounterfeiting programs that increase patent, trademark, copyright, service mark, trade dress, and trade secret protection. Provides information and training to law enforcement officials to help identify counterfeit and pirate products.

Stalking Resource Center, 2000 M St. N.W., #480 20036; (202) 467-8700. Fax, (202) 467-8701. *Michelle Garcia, Director. General e-mail, src@ncvc.org Web, www.ncvc.org/src/main.aspx*

Acts as an information clearinghouse on stalking. Works to raise public awareness of the dangers of stalking.

Encourages the development of multidisciplinary responses to stalking in local communities. Offers practitioner training and peer-to-peer exchange programs. (Affiliated with the National Center for Victims of Crime.)

Sentencing and Corrections

▶**AGENCIES**

Federal Bureau of Prisons *(Justice Dept.),* 320 1st St. N.W., #654 20534; (202) 307-3198. Fax, (202) 514-6878. *Harley G. Lappin, Director, (202) 307-3250. Press, (202) 514-6551. Inmate locator service, (202) 307-3126. Web, www.bop.gov*

Supervises operations of federal correctional institutions, community treatment facilities, and commitment and management of federal inmates; oversees contracts with local institutions for confinement and support of federal prisoners. Regional offices are responsible for administration; central office in Washington coordinates operations and issues standards and policy guidelines. Central office includes Federal Prison Industries, a government corporation providing prison-manufactured goods and services for sale to federal agencies, and the National Institute of Corrections, an information and technical assistance center on state and local corrections programs.

Federal Bureau of Prisons *(Justice Dept.), Health Services,* 320 1st St. N.W., #1054 20534; (202) 307-3055. Fax, (202) 307-0826. *Rear Adm. Newton E. Kendig, Assistant Director. Web, www.bop.gov*

Administers health care and treatment programs for prisoners in federal institutions.

Federal Bureau of Prisons *(Justice Dept.), Industries, Education, and Vocational Training—UNICOR,* 400 1st St. N.W. 20534 (mailing address: 320 1st St. N.W., Washington, DC 20534); (202) 305-3500. Fax, (202) 305-7340. *Paul M. Laird, Assistant Director. Customer Service, (800) 827-3168. Web, www.unicor.gov*

Administers program whereby inmates in federal prisons produce goods and services that are sold to the federal government.

Federal Bureau of Prisons *(Justice Dept.), National Institute of Corrections,* 320 1st St. N.W., #5007 20534; (202) 307-3106. Fax, (202) 307-3361. *Morris L. Thigpen, Director. Toll-free, (800) 995-6423. Web, www.nicic.org*

Offers technical assistance and training for upgrading state and local corrections systems through staff development, research, and evaluation of correctional operations and programs. Acts as a clearinghouse on correctional information.

Justice Dept. (DOJ), *Pardon Attorney,* 1425 New York Ave. N.W., #11000 20530; (202) 616-6070. Fax, (202) 616-6069. *Ronald L. Rodgers, Pardon Attorney. Web, www.usdoj.gov/pardon*

Receives and reviews petitions to the president for all forms of executive clemency, including pardons and sentence reductions; initiates investigations and prepares the deputy attorney general's recommendations to the president on petitions.

Office of Justice Programs (OJP), *(Justice Dept.),* **Justice Assistance,** *810 7th St. N.W., 4th Floor 20531; (202) 616-6500. Fax, (202) 305-1367. James H. Burch II, Director (Acting).*
General e-mail, askbja@usdoj.gov

Web, www.ojp.usdoj.gov/bja

Provides states and communities with funds and technical assistance for corrections demonstration projects.

Office of Justice Programs (OJP), *(Justice Dept.),* **National Institute of Justice,** *810 7th St. N.W., 7th Floor 20531; (202) 307-2942. Fax, (202) 307-6394. David W. Hagy, Director (Acting). Press, (202) 307-0703.*
Web, www.ojp.usdoj.gov/nij

Conducts research on all aspects of criminal justice, including crime prevention, enforcement, adjudication, and corrections. Maintains the National Criminal Justice Reference Service, which provides information on corrections research: (800) 851-3420; in Maryland, (301) 519-5500; Web, www.ncjrs.gov.

U.S. Parole Commission *(Justice Dept.), 5550 Friendship Blvd., #420, Chevy Chase, MD 20815-7286; (301) 492-5990. Fax, (301) 492-5307. Edward F. Reilly Jr., Chair.*
Web, www.usdoj.gov/uspc

Makes release and revocation decisions for all federal prisoners serving sentences of more than one year for offenses committed before November 1, 1987, and for D.C. Code offenders serving parolable offenses or subject to a term of supervised release.

U.S. Sentencing Commission, *1 Columbus Circle N.E., #2-500 South Lobby 20002-8002; (202) 502-4500. Fax, (202) 502-4699. Ricardo H. Hinojosa, Chair.*
Web, www.ussc.gov

Establishes sentencing guidelines and policy for all federal courts, including guidelines prescribing the appropriate form and severity of punishment for those convicted of federal crimes. Provides training and research on sentencing-related issues. Serves as an information resource. Library open to the public.

▶JUDICIARY

Administrative Office of the U.S. Courts, *1 Columbus Circle N.E. 20544-0001; (202) 502-2600. James C. Duff, Director.*
Web, www.uscourts.gov/adminoff.html

Supervises all administrative matters of the federal court system, except the Supreme Court; collects statistical data on business of the courts.

Administrative Office of the U.S. Courts, *Probation and Pretrial Services, 1 Columbus Circle N.E., #4-300 20544-0001; (202) 502-1600. Fax, (202) 502-1677. John M. Hughes, Assistant Director.*

Determines the resource and program requirements of the federal and pre-trial services system. Provides policy guidance, program evaluation services, management and technical assistance, and training to probation and pre-trial services officers.

▶NONGOVERNMENTAL

American Bar Assn. (ABA), *Criminal Justice, Washington Office, 740 15th St. N.W., 10th Floor 20005-1009; (202) 662-1500. Fax, (202) 662-1501. Jack Hanna, Director. Press, (202) 662-1090.*
General e-mail, crimjustice@abanet.org

Web, www.abanet.org/crimjust

Studies and makes recommendations on all aspects of the correctional system, including overcrowding in prisons and the privatization of prisons and correctional institutions. (Headquarters in Chicago, Ill.)

American Civil Liberties Union Foundation, *National Prison Project, 915 15th St. N.W., 7th Floor 20005; (202) 393-4930. Fax, (202) 393-4931. Elizabeth Alexander, Executive Director.*
Web, www.aclu.org/prisons/prisonsmain.cfm

Litigates on behalf of prisoners through class action suits. Seeks to improve prison conditions and the penal system; serves as resource center for prisoners' rights; operates an AIDS education project.

American Correctional Assn. (ACA), *206 N. Washington St., #200, Alexandria, VA 22314; (703) 224-0000. Fax, (703) 224-0179. James A. Gondles Jr., Executive Director. Information, (800) 222-5646.*
Web, www.aca.org

Membership: corrections professionals in all aspects of corrections, including juvenile and adult facilities, community facilities, and academia; affiliates include state and regional corrections associations in the United States and Canada. Conducts and publishes research; provides state and local governments with technical assistance; certifies corrections professionals. Offers professional development courses and accreditation programs. Monitors legislation and regulation. Interests include criminal justice issues, correctional standards, and accreditation programs. Library open to the public.

Amnesty International USA, *Washington Office, 600 Pennsylvania Ave. S.E., 5th Floor 20003; (202) 544-0200. Fax, (202) 546-7142. Betsy Hawkings, Managing Director of Government Relations.*
Web, www.amnestyusa.org

International organization that opposes retention or reinstitution of the death penalty; advocates humane treatment of all prisoners. (U.S. headquarters in New York.)

Catholics Against Capital Punishment, *P.O. Box 5706, Bethesda, MD 20824-5706; (301) 652-1125. Fax, (301) 654-0925. Frank McNeirny, National Coordinator.*
General e-mail, ellen.frank@verizon.net

Web, www.cacp.org

Seeks to inform the public about the Catholic Church's position against capital punishment.

Families Against Mandatory Minimums, *1612 K St. N.W., #700 20006; (202) 822-6700. Fax, (202) 822-6704. Julie Stewart, President.*
General e-mail, famm@famm.org

Web, www.famm.org

Seeks to repeal statutory mandatory minimum prison sentences. Works to increase public awareness of inequity of mandatory minimum sentences through grassroots efforts and media outreach programs.

NAACP Legal Defense and Educational Fund,
Washington Office, *1444 Eye St. N.W., 10th Floor 20005; (202) 682-1300. Fax, (202) 682-1312. Leslie M. Proll, Director.*
Web, www.naacpldf.org

Civil rights litigation group that supports abolition of capital punishment; assists attorneys representing prisoners on death row; focuses public attention on race discrimination in the application of the death penalty. Not affiliated with the National Assn. for the Advancement of Colored People (NAACP). (Headquarters in New York.)

National Center on Institutions and Alternatives, *7222 Ambassador Rd., Baltimore, MD 21244; (410) 265-1490. Fax, (410) 597-9656. Herbert J. Hoelter, Chair.*
General e-mail, hhoelter@ncianet.org

Web, www.ncianet.org

Seeks to reduce incarceration as primary form of punishment imposed by criminal justice system; advocates use of extended community service, work-release, and halfway house programs; operates residential programs; provides defense attorneys and courts with specific recommendations for sentencing and parole. (Affiliated with the Augustus Institute. Headquarters in Baltimore, Md.)

National Coalition to Abolish the Death Penalty, *1705 DeSales St. N.W., 5th Floor 20036; (202) 331-4090. Fax, (202) 331-4099. Diann Rust-Tierney, Executive Director.*
General e-mail, info@ncadp.org

Web, www.ncadp.org

Membership: organizations and individuals opposed to the death penalty. Maintains collection of death penalty research. Provides training, resources, and conferences. Works with families of murder victims; tracks execution dates. Monitors legislation and regulations.

Prison Fellowship Ministries, *44180 Riverside Pkwy., Lansdowne, VA 20176; (703) 478-0100. Fax, (703) 456-4060. Mark L. Earley, President. Toll-free, (877) 478-0100.*
Web, www.pfm.org

Religious organization that ministers to prisoners and ex-prisoners, victims, and the families involved. Offers counseling, seminars, and support for readjustment after release; works to increase the fairness and effectiveness of the criminal justice system.

The Sentencing Project, *514 10th St. N.W., #1000 20004; (202) 628-0871. Fax, (202) 628-1091. Marc Mauer, Executive Director.*
General e-mail, staff@sentencingproject.org

Web, www.sentencingproject.org

Engages in research and advocacy on criminal justice policy issues, including sentencing, incarceration, racial disparity, alternatives to incarceration, and felony disenfranchisement. Publishes books and briefings.

LAW ENFORCEMENT

▶ AGENCIES

Criminal Division *(Justice Dept.),* **Computer Crime and Intellectual Property,** *1301 New York Ave. N.W., #600 20530; (202) 514-1026. Fax, (202) 514-6113. Michael DuBose, Chief.*
Web, www.usdoj.gov/criminal/cybercrime

Investigates and litigates criminal cases involving computers, intellectual property, and the Internet. Administers the Computer Crime Initiative, a program designed to combat electronic penetrations, data theft, and cyberattacks on critical information systems. Provides specialized technical and legal assistance to other Justice Dept. divisions; coordinates international efforts; formulates policies and proposes legislation on computer crime and intellectual property issues.

Federal Bureau of Investigation (FBI), *(Justice Dept.),* **Law Enforcement Coordination,** *935 Pennsylvania Ave. N.W. 20535; (202) 324-7126. Fax, (202) 324-0920. Louis F. Quijas, Assistant Director.*
General e-mail, olec@leo.gov

Web, www.fbi.gov/hq/olec/olec.htm

Advises FBI executives on the use of state and local law enforcement and resources in criminal, cyber, and counterterrorism investigations. Coordinates the bureau's intelligence-sharing and technological efforts with state and local law enforcement. Serves as a liaison with the Homeland Security Dept. and other federal entities.

Federal Law Enforcement Training Center *(Homeland Security Dept.),* **Washington Operations,** *555 11th St. N.W., #400 20004-1300; (202) 233-0260. Fax, (202) 233-0258. Connie Patrick, Director.*
General e-mail, FLECT-WashingtonOffice@dhs.gov

Web, www.fletc.gov

Trains federal law enforcement personnel from more than eighty agencies, excluding the Federal Bureau of Investigation and the Drug Enforcement Administration. (Headquarters in Glynco, Ga.)

Interior Dept. (OLESEM), *Law Enforcement, Security, and Emergency Management, 1849 C St. N.W., MS7354-MIB 20240; (202) 208-5773. Fax, (202) 208-1369. Larry R. Parkinson, Deputy Assistant Secretary; Kim Thorsen, Director. Watch Office, (202) 208-4108.*

General e-mail, os_olesem_ple@ios.doi.gov

Web, www.doi.gov/watch_office/about_olesem

Provides leadership, policy guidance, and oversight to the Interior Dept.'s law enforcement, homeland security, emergency management, and security programs. Works to protect critical infrastructure facilities, national icons, and monuments; develops law enforcement staffing models; establishes departmental training requirements and monitors their implementation; oversees the hiring of key law enforcement and security personnel; establishes emergency management procedures; develops and implements emergency management plans and programs; and oversees and reviews law enforcement and security budgets.

Internal Revenue Service (IRS), *(Treasury Dept.),* *Criminal Investigation,* *1111 Constitution Ave. N.W., #2501 20224; (202) 622-3200. Eileen C. Mayer, Chief. Tax fraud hotline, (800) 829-0433.*
Web, www.irs.gov

Investigates money laundering and violations of the tax law. Lends support in counterterrorism and narcotics investigations conducted in conjunction with other law enforcement agencies, both foreign and domestic.

National Institute of Standards and Technology (NIST), *(Commerce Dept.),* *Law Enforcement Standards,* *100 Bureau Dr., Bldg. 220, #B208, MS-8102, Gaithersburg, MD 20899-8102; (301) 975-2757. Fax, (301) 948-0978. Mark Stolorow, Director.*
General e-mail, oles@nist.gov

Web, www.eeel.nist.gov/oles

Answers inquiries and makes referrals concerning the application of science and technology to the criminal justice community; maintains information on standards and current research; prepares reports and formulates standards for the National Institute of Justice and the Homeland Security Dept.

Office of Justice Programs (OJP), *(Justice Dept.),* *Justice Assistance,* *810 7th St. N.W., 4th Floor 20531; (202) 616-6500. Fax, (202) 305-1367. James H. Burch II, Director (Acting).*
General e-mail, askbja@usdoj.gov

Web, www.ojp.usdoj.gov/bja

Provides funds to eligible state and local governments and to nonprofit organizations for criminal justice programs, primarily those that combat drug trafficking and other drug-related crime.

Transportation Security Administration (TSA), *(Homeland Security Dept.),* *Federal Air Marshal Service,* *TSA-18, 601 S. 12th St., Arlington, VA 22202; (703) 487-3400. Fax, (703) 487-3405. Dana A. Brown, Director.*
Web, www.tsa.gov/lawenforcement/programs/fams.shtm

Protects air security in the United States. Promotes public confidence in the U.S. civil aviation system. Deploys marshals on flights around the world to detect and deter hostile acts targeting U.S. air carriers, airports, passengers, and crews.

Treasury Dept., *Financial Crimes Enforcement Network,* *2070 Chain Bridge Rd., Vienna, VA 22183 (mailing address: P.O. Box 39, Vienna, VA 22183-0039); (703) 905-3591. Fax, (703) 905-3690. James H. Freis Jr., Director. Financial institutions hotline, (866) 556-3974.*
General e-mail, webmaster@fincen.gov

Web, www.fincen.gov

Administers an information network in support of federal, state, and local law enforcement agencies in the prevention and detection of terrorist financing, money-laundering operations, and other financial crimes. Administers the Bank Secrecy Act.

U.S. Marshals Service *(Justice Dept.),* *1750 Crystal Dr., Arlington, VA 22202 (mailing address: #1200 CS-3, Washington, DC 20530-1000); (202) 307-9001. Fax, (202) 307-5040. John F. Clark, Director. Public Affairs, (202) 307-9065.*
General e-mail, us.marshals@usdoj.gov

Web, www.usmarshals.gov

Acts as the enforcement arm of the federal courts and U.S. attorney general. Responsibilities include court and witness security, prisoner custody and transportation, prisoner support, maintenance and disposal of seized and forfeited property, and special operations. Administers the Federal Witness Security Program. Apprehends fugitives, including those wanted by foreign nations and believed to be in the United States; oversees the return of fugitives apprehended abroad and wanted by U.S. law enforcement. Carries out the provisions of the Adam Walsh Child Protection and Safety Act.

▶**CONGRESS**

For a listing of relevant congressional committees and subcommittees, please see page 468 or the Appendix.

▶**NONGOVERNMENTAL**

Feminist Majority Foundation, *National Center for Women and Policing,* *1600 Wilson Blvd., #801, Arlington, VA 22209; (703) 522-2214. Fax, (703) 522-2219. Margaret Moore, Director.*
Web, www.feminist.org/other/ncwp.asp

Seeks to increase the number of women at all ranks of policing and law enforcement. Sponsors conferences and training programs.

International Assn. of Chiefs of Police, *515 N. Washington St., Alexandria, VA 22314-2357; (703) 836-6767. Fax, (703) 836-4543. Daniel N. Rosenblatt, Executive Director. Toll-free, (800) 843-4227.*
General e-mail, information@theiacp.org

Web, www.theiacp.org

Membership: foreign and U.S. police executives and administrators at federal, state, and local levels. Consults and conducts research on all aspects of police activity; conducts training programs and develops educational aids; conducts public education programs.

Law Enforcement Alliance of America, *5538 Port Royal Rd., Springfield, VA 22151; (703) 847-2677. Fax, (703) 556-6485. James J. Fotis, Executive Director. Toll-free, (800) 766-8578.*
General e-mail, info@leaa.org

Web, www.leaa.org

Membership: law enforcement professionals, citizens, and victims of crime. Advocacy group on law and order issues.

National Black Police Assn., *30 Kennedy St. N.W., #101 20011; (202) 986-2070. Fax, (202) 986-0410. Ronald E. Hampton, Executive Director.*
General e-mail, nbpanatofc@worldnet.att.net

Web, www.blackpolice.org

Membership: local, state, and regional African American police associations. Works to improve the relationship between police departments and minorities; to evaluate the effect of criminal justice policies and programs on the minority community; to recruit minority police officers; to eliminate police corruption, brutality, and racial discrimination; and to educate and train police officers.

National Criminal Justice Assn., *720 7th St. N.W., 3rd Floor 20001-3716; (202) 628-8550. Fax, (202) 448-1723. Cabell C. Cropper, Executive Director. Press, (202) 448-1713.*
General e-mail, info@ncja.org

Web, www.ncja.org

Membership: criminal justice organizations and professionals. Provides members and interested individuals with technical assistance and information.

National Organization of Black Law Enforcement Executives, *4609F Pinecrest Office Park Dr., Alexandria, VA 22312-1442; (703) 658-1529. Fax, (703) 658-9479. Jessie Lee, Executive Director.*
General e-mail, noble@noblenational.org

Web, www.noblenational.org

Membership: African American police chiefs and senior law enforcement executives. Works to increase community involvement in the criminal justice system and to enhance the role of African Americans in law enforcement. Provides urban police departments with assistance in police operations, community relations, and devising strategies to sensitize the criminal justice system to the problems of the African American community.

National Sheriffs' Assn., *1450 Duke St., Alexandria, VA 22314-3490; (703) 836-7827. Fax, (703) 683-6541. Aaron D. Kennard, Executive Director. Toll-free, (800) 424-7827.*
General e-mail, exec@sheriffs.org

Web, www.sheriffs.org

Membership: sheriffs and other municipal, state, and federal law enforcement officers. Conducts research and training programs for members in law enforcement, court procedures, and corrections. Publishes *Sheriff* magazine and an e-newsletter.

Police Executive Research Forum, *1120 Connecticut Ave. N.W., #930 20036; (202) 466-7820. Fax, (202) 466-7826. Chuck Wexler, Executive Director.*
General e-mail, perf@policeforum.org

Web, www.policeforum.org

Membership: law enforcement executives. Conducts research on law enforcement issues and methods of disseminating criminal justice and law enforcement information.

Police Foundation, *1201 Connecticut Ave. N.W., #200 20036-2636; (202) 833-1460. Fax, (202) 659-9149. Hubert Williams, President.*
General e-mail, pfinfo@policefoundation.org

Web, www.policefoundation.org

Research and education foundation that conducts studies to improve police procedures; provides technical assistance for innovative law enforcement strategies, including community-oriented policing. Houses the National Center for the Study of Police and Civil Disorder.

LEGAL PROFESSIONS AND RESOURCES

▶NONGOVERNMENTAL

American Assn. of Visually Impaired Attorneys, *1155 15th St. N.W., #1004 20005-2706; (202) 467-5081. Fax, (202) 467-5085. Mitch Pomerantz, President. Press, (203) 877-4108. Toll-free, (800) 424-8666.*
General e-mail, austingl@bellsouth.net

Web, www.visuallyimpairedattorneys.org

Membership: visually impaired lawyers and law students. Provides members with legal information; acts as an information clearinghouse on legal materials available in Braille, in large print, on computer disc, and on tape. (Formerly the American Blind Lawyers Assn. Affiliated with American Council of the Blind.)

American Bar Assn. (ABA), *International Law, 740 15th St. N.W. 20005; (202) 662-1660. Fax, (202) 662-1669. Leanne Pfautz, Director.*
General e-mail, intlaw@abanet.org

Web, www.abanet.org/intlaw

Monitors and makes recommendations concerning developments in the practice of international law that affect ABA members and the public. Conducts programs, including International Legal Exchange, and produces publications covering the practice of international law.

American Health Lawyers Assn., *1025 Connecticut Ave. N.W., #600 20036; (202) 833-1100. Fax, (202) 833-1105. Peter Leibold, Executive Vice President.*
General e-mail, info@healthlawyers.org

Web, www.healthlawyers.org

Membership: corporate, institutional, and government lawyers interested in the health field; law students;

and health professionals. Serves as an information clearinghouse on health law; sponsors health law educational programs and seminars.

American Inns of Court Foundation, *1229 King St., 2nd Floor, Alexandria, VA 22314; (703) 684-3590. Fax, (703) 684-3607. Brig. Gen. David Carey (USA, Ret.), Executive Director.*
General e-mail, info@innsofcourt.org
Web, www.innsofcourt.org

Promotes professionalism, ethics, civility, and legal skills of judges, lawyers, academicians, and law students in order to improve the quality and efficiency of the justice system.

Asian American Justice Center (AAJC), *1140 Connecticut Ave. N.W., #1200 20036; (202) 296-2300. Fax, (202) 296-2318. Karen K. Narasaki, President.*
General e-mail, information@advancingequality.org
Web, www.advancingequality.org

Works to advance the human and civil rights of Asian Americans through advocacy, public policy, public education, and litigation. Promotes civic engagement and works to create an inclusive society in communities on local, regional, and national levels. Interests include affirmative action, hate crimes, media diversity, census, immigrant rights, language access, and voting rights. (Formerly known as National Asian Pacific American Legal Consortium.)

Assn. of American Law Schools, *1201 Connecticut Ave. N.W., #800 20036-2717; (202) 296-8851. Fax, (202) 296-8869. Susan Westerberg Prager, Executive Director.*
General e-mail, aals@aals.org
Web, www.aals.org

Membership: law schools, subject to approval. Membership criteria include high-quality academic programs, faculty, scholarship, and students; academic freedom; diversity of people and viewpoints; and emphasis on public service. Hosts meetings and workshops; publishes a directory of law teachers. Advocates on behalf of legal education; monitors legislation and judicial decisions.

Federal Circuit Bar Assn., *1620 Eye St. N.W., #900 20006; (202) 466-3923. Fax, (202) 833-1061. James E. Brookshire, Executive Director.*
Web, www.fedcirbar.org

Represents practitioners before the Court of Appeals for the Federal Circuit. Fosters discussion between different groups within the legal community; sponsors regional seminars; publishes a scholarly journal.

Hispanic National Bar Assn., *1001 Connecticut Ave. N.W., #507 20036 (mailing address: P.O. Box 14347, Ben Franklin Station, Washington, DC 20044); (202) 223-4777. Fax, (202) 223-2324. Ramona Romero, President.*
General e-mail, info@hnba.com
Web, www.hnba.com

Membership: Hispanic American attorneys, judges, professors, paralegals, and law students. Seeks to increase professional opportunities in law for Hispanic Americans and to increase Hispanic American representation in law schools. (Affiliated with National Hispanic Leadership Agenda and the American Bar Assn.)

International Law Institute, *1055 Thomas Jefferson St. N.W., #M-100 20007; (202) 247-6006. Fax, (202) 247-6010. Kim Phan, Executive Director.*
General e-mail, training@ili.org
Web, www.ili.org

Performs scholarly research, offers training programs, and provides technical assistance in the area of international law. Sponsors international conferences.

National Consumer Law Center, *Washington Office, 1001 Connecticut Ave. N.W., #510 20036-5528; (202) 452-6252. Fax, (202) 463-9462. Lauren Saunders, Managing Attorney.*
General e-mail, consumerlaw@nclc.org
Web, www.consumerlaw.org

Provides lawyers funded by the Legal Services Corp. with research and assistance; provides lawyers with training in consumer and energy law. (Headquarters in Boston, Mass.)

National Court Reporters Assn., *8224 Old Courthouse Rd., Vienna, VA 22182-3808; (703) 556-6272. Fax, (703) 556-6291. Mark J. Golden, Executive Director. TTY, (703) 556-6289. Toll-free, (800) 272-6272.*
General e-mail, msic@ncrahq.org
Web, www.ncraonline.org

Membership organization that offers certification and continuing education for court reporting and captioning. Acts as a clearinghouse on technology and information for and about court reporters; certifies legal video specialists. Monitors legislation and regulations.

Street Law, Inc., *1010 Wayne Ave., #870, Silver Spring, MD 20910; (301) 589-1130. Fax, (301) 589-1131. Edward O'Brien, Executive Director.*
Web, www.streetlaw.org

International educational organization that promotes public understanding of law, the legal system, democracy, and human rights. Provides curriculum materials, training, and technical assistance to secondary school systems, law schools, departments of corrections, juvenile justice systems, bar associations, community groups, and state, local, and foreign governments.

Data and Research

▶**AGENCIES**

Justice Dept. (DOJ), *Community Oriented Policing Services (COPS),* *1100 Vermont Ave. N.W. 20530 (mailing address: for overnight delivery, use zip code 20005); (202) 3071480. Fax, (202) 616-5899. Carl R. Peed, Director, (202) 616-2888. Press, (202) 616-9602. Congressional Relations, (202) 514-9079. Outside Washington, (800) 421-6770.*

General e-mail, askCopsRC@usdoj.gov

Web, www.cops.usdoj.gov

Awards grants to tribal, state, and local law enforcement agencies to hire and train community policing professionals, acquire and deploy crime-fighting technologies, and develop and test policing strategies. Provides publications and other educational materials on a wide range of law enforcement concerns and community policing topics. Community policing emphasizes crime prevention through partnerships between law enforcement and citizen.

Office of Justice Programs (OJP), *(Justice Dept.),* **Bureau of Justice Statistics,** *810 7th St. N.W., 2nd Floor 20531; (202) 307-0765. Fax, (202) 307-5846. Jeffrey L. Sedgwick, Director.*
General e-mail, askbjs@usdoj.gov

Web, www.ojp.usdoj.gov/bjs

Collects, evaluates, publishes, and provides statistics on criminal justice. Data available from the National Criminal Justice Reference Service: P.O. Box 6000, Rockville, MD 20849-6000; toll-free, (800) 851-3420; international callers, (301) 519-5500; TTY (877) 712-9279; and from the National Archive of Criminal Justice Data in Ann Arbor, MI, (800) 999-0960.

Office of Justice Programs (OJP), *(Justice Dept.),* **National Institute of Justice,** *810 7th St. N.W., 7th Floor 20531; (202) 307-2942. Fax, (202) 307-6394. David W. Hagy, Director (Acting). Press, (202) 307-0703.*
Web, www.ojp.usdoj.gov/nij

Conducts research on all aspects of criminal justice, including crime prevention, enforcement, adjudication, and corrections; evaluates programs; develops model programs using new techniques. Serves as an affiliated institute of the United Nations Crime Prevention and Criminal Justice Programme (UNCPCJ); studies transnational issues. Maintains the National Criminal Justice Reference Service, which provides information on criminal justice, including activities of the Office of National Drug Control Policy and law enforcement in Latin America: (800) 851-3420 or (301) 519-5500; Web, www.ncjrs.gov.

▶**CONGRESS**

For a listing of relevant congressional committees and subcommittees, please see page 468 or the Appendix.

Library of Congress, *Law Library,* *101 Independence Ave. S.E., #LM240 20540; (202) 707-5065. Rubens Medina, Law Librarian. Reading room, (202) 707-5080. Reference information, (202) 707-5079.*
Web, www.loc.gov/law

Maintains collections of foreign, international, and comparative law texts organized jurisdictionally by country; covers all legal systems—common, civil, Roman, canon, religious, and ancient and medieval law. Services include a public reading room; a microtext facility, with readers and printers for microfilm and microfiche; and foreign law/rare book reading areas. Staff of legal specialists is competent in approximately forty languages; does not provide advice on legal matters.

▶**JUDICIARY**

Administrative Office of the U.S. Courts, *1 Columbus Circle N.E. 20544-0001; (202) 502-2600. James C. Duff, Director.*
Web, www.uscourts.gov/adminoff.html

Supervises all administrative matters of the federal court system, except the Supreme Court; prepares statistical data and reports on the business of the courts, including reports on juror utilization; caseloads of federal, public, and community defenders; and types of cases adjudicated.

Administrative Office of the U.S. Courts, *Statistics,* *1 Columbus Circle N.E., #2-250 20544; (202) 502-1442. Fax, (202) 502-1411. Steven R. Schlesinger, Chief. Press, (202) 502-2600.*
Web, www.uscourts.gov

Compiles information and statistics from civil, criminal, appeals, and bankruptcy cases. Publishes statistical reports on court management; juror utilization; federal offenders; equal access to justice; the Financial Privacy Act; caseloads of federal, public, and community defenders; and types of cases adjudicated.

Supreme Court of the United States, *Library,* *1 1st St. N.E. 20543; (202) 479-3037. Fax, (202) 479-3477. Judith Gaskell, Librarian.*
Web, www.supremecourtus.gov

Maintains collection of Supreme Court documents dating from the mid-1800s. Records, briefs, and depository documents available for public use.

▶**NONGOVERNMENTAL**

Justice Research and Statistics Assn., *777 N. Capitol St. N.E., #801 20002; (202) 842-9330. Fax, (202) 842-9329. Joan C. Weiss, Executive Director.*
General e-mail, cjinfo@jrsa.org

Web, www.jrsa.org

Provides information on the collection, analysis, dissemination, and use of data concerning crime and criminal justice at the state level; serves as liaison between the Justice Dept. Bureau of Justice Statistics and the states; develops standards for states on the collection, analysis, and use of statistics. Offers courses in criminal justice software and in research and evaluation methodologies in conjunction with its annual conference.

PUBLIC INTEREST LAW

▶**AGENCIES**

Legal Services Corp., *3333 K St. N.W., 3rd Floor 20007-3522; (202) 295-1500. Fax, (202) 337-6797. Helaine M. Barnett, President. Information, (202) 295-1500. Public Reading Room, (202) 295-1502.*
Web, www.lsc.gov

Independent federal corporation established by Congress. Awards grants to local agencies that provide the poor with legal services. Library open to the public.

►CONGRESS

For a listing of relevant congressional committees and subcommittees, please see page 468 or the Appendix.

►NONGOVERNMENTAL

AEI Legal Center for the Public Interest, 1150 17th St. N.W. 20036; (202) 862-580. Fax, (202) 862-7171. Vacant, President.
General e-mail, sara.wexler@aei.org

Web, www.AEILegalCenter.org

Public interest law center and information clearinghouse. Studies judicial issues and the impact of the legal system on the private sector; sponsors seminars; does not litigate cases. (Merger of the National Legal Center for the Public Interest and the American Enterprise Institute.)

Alliance for Justice, 11 Dupont Circle N.W., 2nd Floor 20036-1213; (202) 822-6070. Fax, (202) 822-6068. Nan Aron, President.
General e-mail, alliance@afj.org

Web, www.afj.org

Membership: public interest lawyers and advocacy, environmental, civil rights, and consumer organizations. Promotes reform of the legal system to ensure access to the courts; monitors selection of federal judges; works to preserve the rights of nonprofit organizations to advocate on behalf of their constituents.

American Bar Assn. (ABA), *Commission on Mental and Physical Disability Law,* 740 15th St. N.W., 9th Floor 20005-1022; (202) 662-1570. Fax, (202) 442-3439. John Parry, Director.
General e-mail, cmpdl@abanet.org

Web, www.abanet.org/disability

Serves as a clearinghouse for information on mental and physical disability law. Publishes a report on mental and physical disability law, law digest, and handbooks. Provides a directory of lawyers who practice disability law, a directory on law school disability curricula, and a directory on law students with disabilities.

Bazelon Center for Mental Health Law, 1101 15th St. N.W., #1212 20005; (202) 467-5730. Fax, (202) 223-0409. Robert Bernstein, Executive Director. TTY, (202) 467-4232.
General e-mail, info@bazelon.org

Web, www.bazelon.org

Public interest law firm. Works to establish and advance the legal rights of children and adults with mental disabilities and ensure their equal access to services and resources needed for full participation in community life. Provides technical support to lawyers and other advocates. Conducts test case litigation to defend rights of persons with mental disabilities. Conducts policy analysis, builds coalitions, issues advocacy alerts, publishes handbooks, and maintains advocacy resources online. Monitors legislation and regulations.

Center for Law and Education, *Washington Office,* 1875 Connecticut Ave. N.W., #510 20009-5728; (202) 986-3000. Fax, (202) 986-6648. Paul Weckstein, Co-Director; Kathleen Boundy, Co-Director. Publications, (202) 462-7688.
General e-mail, cle@cleweb.org

Web, www.cleweb.org

Assists local legal services programs in matters concerning education, civil rights, and provision of legal services to low-income persons; litigates some cases for low-income individuals. (Headquarters in Boston, Mass.)

Center for Law and Social Policy, 1015 15th St. N.W., #400 20005; (202) 906-8000. Fax, (202) 842-2885. Alan W. Houseman, Director.
General e-mail, info@clasp.org

Web, www.clasp.org

Public policy organization with expertise in national, state, and local policy affecting low-income Americans. Seeks to improve the economic security and educational and workforce prospects of low-income children, youth, adults, and families.

Center for Study of Responsive Law, 1530 P St. N.W. 20005 (mailing address: P.O. Box 19367, Washington, DC 20036); (202) 387-8030. Fax, (202) 234-5176. John Richard, Administrator.
General e-mail, csrl@csrl.org

Web, www.csrl.org

Consumer interest clearinghouse that conducts research and holds conferences on public interest law. Interests include white-collar crime, the environment, occupational health and safety, the postal system, banking deregulation, insurance, freedom of information policy, and broadcasting.

Institute for Justice, 901 N. Glebe Rd., #900, Arlington, VA 22203; (703) 682-9320. Fax, (703) 682-9321. Chip Mellor, President.
General e-mail, general@ij.org

Web, www.ij.org

Sponsors seminars to train law students, grassroots activists, and practicing lawyers in applying advocacy strategies in public interest litigation. Seeks to protect individuals from arbitrary government interference in free speech, private property rights, parental school choice, and economic liberty. Litigates cases.

Institute for Public Representation, 600 New Jersey Ave. N.W. 20001; (202) 662-9535. Fax, (202) 662-9634. Hope Babcock, Co-Director; Angela Campbell, Co-Director; David Vladeck, Co-Director. TTY, (202) 662-9538.
General e-mail, gulcipr@law.georgetown.edu

Web, www.law.georgetown.edu/clinics/ipr

Public interest law firm funded by Georgetown University Law Center that studies federal administrative law and federal court litigation. Interests include communications law, environmental protection, and disability rights.

Lawyers' Committee for Civil Rights Under Law, *1401 New York Ave. N.W., #400 20005-2124; (202) 662-8600. Fax, (202) 783-0857. Barbara R. Arnwine, Executive Director. Toll-free, (888) 299-5227.*

Web, www.lawyerscommittee.org

Provides minority groups and the poor with legal assistance in such areas as voting rights, employment discrimination, education, environment, and equal access to government services and benefits.

Migrant Legal Action Program, *1001 Connecticut Ave. N.W., #915 20036-5524; (202) 775-7780. Fax, (202) 775-7784. Roger C. Rosenthal, Executive Director.*

General e-mail, mlap@mlap.org

Web, www.mlap.org

Provides both direct representation to farm workers and technical assistance and support to health, education, and legal services programs for migrants. Monitors legislation and regulations.

National Assn. of Consumer Bankruptcy Attorneys, *2300 M St. N.W., #800 20037; (202) 331-8005. Fax, (202) 331-8535. Maureen Thompson, Legislative Director.*

General e-mail, admin@nacba.org

Web, www.nacba.org

Advocates on behalf of consumer debtors and their attorneys. Files amicus briefs on behalf of parties in the U.S. courts of appeal and Supreme Court, and provides educational programs and workshops for attorneys. Monitors legislation and regulations.

National Consumer Law Center, *Washington Office, 1001 Connecticut Ave. N.W., #510 20036-5528; (202) 452-6252. Fax, (202) 463-9462. Lauren Saunders, Managing Attorney.*

General e-mail, consumerlaw@nclc.org

Web, www.consumerlaw.org

Provides lawyers funded by the Legal Services Corp. with research and assistance; researches problems of low-income consumers and develops alternative solutions. (Headquarters in Boston, Mass.)

National Health Law Program, *Washington Office, 1444 Eye St. N.W., #1105 20005; (202) 289-7661. Fax, (202) 289-7724. Emily Spitzer, Director.*

General e-mail, nhelpdc@healthlaw.org

Web, www.healthlaw.org

Organization of lawyers representing the economically disadvantaged, minorities, and older adults on issues concerning federal, state, and local health care programs. Offers technical assistance, workshops, seminars, and training for health law specialists. (Headquarters in Los Angeles, Calif.)

National Legal Aid and Defender Assn., *1140 Connecticut Ave. N.W., #900 20036; (202) 452-0620. Fax, (202) 872-1031. Jo-Ann Wallace, President.*

General e-mail, info@nlada.org

Web, www.nlada.org

Membership: local organizations and individuals providing indigent clients, including prisoners, with legal aid and defender services. Serves as a clearinghouse for member organizations; provides training and support services.

Public Citizen Litigation Group, *1600 20th St. N.W. 20009; (202) 588-1000. Fax, (202) 588-7795. Brian Wolfman, Director of Litigation. Press, (202) 588-7741.*

General e-mail, litigation@citizen.org

Web, www.citizen.org/litigation

Conducts litigation for Public Citizen, a citizens' interest group, in the areas of consumer rights, employee rights, health and safety, government and corporate accountability, and separation of powers; represents other individuals and citizens' groups with similar interests.

Public Justice Foundation, *1825 K St. N.W., #200 20006; (202) 797-8600. Fax, (202) 232-7203. Arthur H. Bryant, Executive Director.*

General e-mail, publicjustice@publicjustice.net

Web, www.publicjustice.net

Membership: consumer activists, trial lawyers, and public interest lawyers. Litigates to influence corporate and government decisions about products or activities adversely affecting health or safety. Interests include toxic torts, environmental protection, civil rights and civil liberties, workers' safety, consumer protection, and the preservation of the civil justice system. (Formerly Trial Lawyers for Public Justice.)

14

Military Personnel and Veterans

GENERAL POLICY AND ANALYSIS

Basic Resources

▶AGENCIES

Air Force Dept. *(Defense Dept.), Force Management Integration,* 1660 Air Force Pentagon, #5E818 20330-1660; (703) 614-4751. Fax, (703) 693-4244. Barbara J. Barger, Deputy Assistant Secretary. Web, www.af.mil

Civilian office that coordinates military and civilian personnel policies of the Air Force Dept. Focus includes pay; health care; education and training; commissaries, PXs, and service clubs; recruitment; retirement; and veterans affairs.

Air Force Dept. *(Defense Dept.), Manpower and Personnel,* 1040 Air Force Pentagon, #4D765 20330-1040; (703) 697-6088. Fax, (703) 697-6091. Lt. Gen. Richard Newton III, Deputy Chief of Staff. Web, www.af.mil

Military office that coordinates military and civilian personnel policies of the Air Force Dept.

Army Dept. *(Defense Dept.), G-1,* 300 Army Pentagon, #2E446 20310-0300; (703) 697-8060. Fax, (703) 695-1377. Michael D. Rochelle, Deputy Chief of Staff. Web, www.army.mil

Military office that coordinates military and civilian personnel policies of the Army Dept.

Army Dept. *(Defense Dept.), Human Resources Policy Directorate,* 300 Army Pentagon, #2C453 20310-0300; (703) 695-5418. Fax, (703) 695-6988. Maj. Gen. John R. Hawkins III, Director. Web, www.armyg1.army.mil/hr/default.asp

Military office that coordinates military personnel policies of the Army Dept. Focus includes health promotion, equal opportunity, drug and alcohol abuse, retirement, suicide prevention, housing, uniform policy, and women in the army.

Army Dept. *(Defense Dept.), Manpower and Reserve Affairs,* 111 Army Pentagon, #2E460 20310-0111; (703) 697-9253. Fax, (703) 692-9000. Thomas R. Lamont, Assistant Secretary. Web, www.asamra.army.pentagon.mil

Civilian office that reviews policies and programs for Army personnel and reserves; makes recommendations to the secretary of the Army.

Defense Dept. (DoD), *Community Relations and Public Liaison,* 1400 Defense Pentagon, 2D982 20301-1400; (703) 695-2113. Fax, (703) 697-2577. Roxie Merritt, Director. Toll-free, (800) 342-9647. Web, www.americasupportsyou.mil

Administers Pentagon tours and Defense Dept. speakers programs for the public; hosts Joint Civilian Orientation Conference (JCOC) for nominated civilians interested in military and defense careers. Handles community outreach, including America Supports You, a home front program intended to bolster morale and community support of U.S. military troops.

Defense Dept. (DoD), *Military Personnel Policy,* 4000 Defense Pentagon, #5A678 20301-4000; (703) 571-0116. Fax, (703) 571-0120. William J. Carr, Deputy Under Secretary. Web, www.defenselink.mil/prhome/mpp.html

Military office that coordinates military personnel policies of the Defense Dept. and reviews military personnel policies of the individual services.

Defense Dept. (DoD), *Personnel and Readiness,* 4000 Defense Pentagon, #3E788 20301-4000; (703) 695-5254. Fax, (703) 571-0847. Gail H. McGinn, Under Secretary (Acting). Web, www.defenselink.mil/prhome

Coordinates civilian and military personnel policies of the Defense Dept. and reviews personnel policies of the individual services. Handles equal opportunity policies; serves as focal point for all readiness issues. Administers Military OneSource, a 24/7 toll-free information and referral telephone service for matters relating to education, financial aid, relocation, housing, child care, counseling, and other employee concerns. Military OneSource is available worldwide to military personnel and their families. Toll-free, (800) 342-9647; international, (800) 3429-6477; international collect, (484) 530-5908; www.militaryonesource.com.

Defense Dept. (DoD), *Public Communications,* 2521 S. Clark St., #1700, Arlington, VA 22202 (mailing address: 1400 Defense Pentagon, Washington, DC 20301-1400); (703) 428-0711. Fax, (703) 697-3501. David McWilliams, Director. Press, (703) 697-5131. Web, www.defenselink.mil

Responds to public inquiries on Defense Dept. personnel.

Navy Dept. *(Defense Dept.), Manpower and Reserve Affairs,* 1000 Navy Pentagon, #4E590 20350-1000; (703) 695-4333. Fax, (703) 614-4103. H. C. "Barney" Barnum, Assistant Secretary (Acting). Web, www.donhq.navy.mil/mra

Civilian office that reviews policies of the U.S. Naval Academy, Navy and Marine Corps service schools, and officer candidates' training and Reserve Officer Training Corps (ROTC) programs. Advises the secretary of the Navy on education matters, including voluntary education programs.

Navy Dept. *(Defense Dept.), Manpower, Personnel, Training, Education, and Policy Division N13,* 2 Navy Annex, #3066 20370; (703) 614-5571. Fax, (703) 614-5595. Adm. Daniel Holloway, Director. Web, www.navy.mil

Military office that coordinates naval personnel policies, including promotions, professional development, and compensation, for officers and enlisted personnel.

MILITARY PERSONNEL AND VETERANS RESOURCES IN CONGRESS

For a complete listing of Congress committees, including their full contact information, leadership, membership, and jurisdictions, please refer to the Appendix on pages 724–837.

HOUSE:

House Appropriations Committee, (202) 225-2771. Web, appropriations.house.gov
 Subcommittee on Defense, (202) 225-2847.
 Subcommittee on Military Construction, Veterans Affairs, and Related Agencies, (202) 225-3047.

House Armed Services Committee, (202) 225-4151. Web, armedservices.house.gov
 Subcommittee on Air and Land Forces, (202) 225-4151.
 Subcommittee on Military Personnel, (202) 225-4151.a
 Subcommittee on Oversight and Investigations, (202) 225-4151.
 Subcommittee on Readiness, (202) 225-4151.
 Subcommittee on Seapower and Expeditionary Forces, (202) 225-4151.
 Subcommittee on Strategic Forces, (202) 225-4151.
 Subcommittee on Terrorism and Unconventional Threats and Capabilities, (202) 225-4151.

House Financial Services Committee, Subcommittee on Financial Institutions and Consumer Credit, (202) 225-4247. Web, financialservices.house.gov
 Subcommittee on Housing and Community Opportunity, (202) 225-4247.
 Subcommittee on Oversight and Investigations, (202) 225-4247.

House Foreign Affairs Committee, (202) 225-5021. Web, foreignaffairs.house.gov

House Oversight and Government Reform Committee, (202) 225-5051. Web, oversight.house.gov
 Subcommittee on National Security and Foreign Affairs, (202) 225-2548.

House Veterans' Affairs Committee, (202) 225-9756. Web, veterans.house.gov

 Subcommittee on Disability Assistance and Memorial Affairs, (202) 225-9164.
 Subcommittee on Economic Opportunity, (202) 226-5491.
 Subcommittee on Health, (202) 225-9154.
 Subcommittee on Oversight and Investigations, (202) 225-3569.

SENATE:

Senate Appropriations Committee, (202) 224-7363. Web, appropriations.senate.gov
 Subcommittee on Defense, (202) 224-6688.
 Subcommittee on Military Construction, Veterans Affairs, and Related Agencies, (202) 224-8224.

Senate Armed Services Committee, (202) 224-3871. Web, armed-services.senate.gov
 Subcommittee on Airland, (202) 224-3871.
 Subcommittee on Emerging Threats and Capabilities, (202) 224-3871.
 Subcommittee on Personnel, (202) 224-3871.
 Subcommittee on Readiness and Management Support, (202) 224-3871.
 Subcommittee on Seapower, (202) 224-3871.
 Subcommittee on Strategic Forces, (202) 224-3871.

Senate Banking, Housing and Urban Affairs Committee, Subcommittee on Financial Institutions, (202) 224-5842. Web, banking.senate.gov

Senate Foreign Relations Committee, (202) 224-4651. Web, foreign.senate.gov

Senate Homeland Security and Governmental Affairs Committee, (202) 224-2627. Web, hsgac.senate.gov

Senate Veterans' Affairs Committee, (202) 224-9126. Web, veterans.senate.gov

---

Navy Dept. *(Defense Dept.), Naval Personnel,* 2 Navy Annex, #2077 20370; (703) 614-1101. Fax, (703) 693-1746. Vice Adm. Mark E. Ferguson III, Chief. Web, www.navy.mil

Responsible for planning and programming of manpower and personnel resources, budgeting for Navy personnel, developing systems to manage total force manpower and personnel resources, and assignment of Navy personnel.

Selective Service System, 1515 Wilson Blvd., Arlington, VA 22209-2425; (703) 605-4010. Fax, (703) 605-4006.

William A. Chatfield, Director. Locator, (703) 605-4000. Web, www.sss.gov

Supplies the armed forces with manpower when authorized; registers male citizens of the United States ages eighteen to twenty-five. In an emergency, would institute a draft and would provide alternative service assignments to men classified as conscientious objectors.

U.S. Coast Guard (USCG), *(Homeland Security Dept.), Human Resources Directorate (CG-1),* 2100 2nd St. S.W., #5410 20593-0001; (202) 475-5000. Fax, (202)

475-5940. *Rear Adm. Jody Breckenridge, Assistant Commandant.*
Web, www.uscg.mil/hr

Responsible for hiring, recruiting, and training all military and nonmilitary Coast Guard personnel.

►CONGRESS

For a listing of relevant congressional committees and subcommittees, please see page 513 or the Appendix.

►NONGOVERNMENTAL

Air Force Assn., *1501 Lee Hwy., Arlington, VA 22209-1198; (703) 247-5800. Fax, (703) 247-5853. Michael M. Dunn, Executive Director. Information, (800) 727-3337. Press, (703) 247-5850.*
Web, www.afa.org

Membership: civilians and active duty, reserve, retired, and cadet personnel of the Air Force. Informs members and the public of developments in the aerospace field. Monitors legislation and Defense Dept. policies. Library on aviation history open to the public by appointment.

Air Force Sergeants Assn., *5211 Auth Rd., Suitland, MD 20746; (301) 899-3500. Fax, (301) 899-8136. Richard M. Dean, Executive Director. Toll-free, (800) 638-0594. General e-mail, staff@hqafsa.org*

Web, www.hqafsa.org

Membership: active duty, reserve, National Guard, and retired enlisted Air Force personnel. Monitors and advocates legislation and policies that promote quality of life benefits for its members.

America's Heroes of Freedom (AHOF), *P.O. Box 18984 20036-18984; (214) 789-4505. Susan Brewer, President. General e-mail, susan@americasheroes.us*

Web, www.americasheroes.us

Works to provide education, support, and recovery assistance to members of the military, law enforcement, fire and rescue services, and civil services. Provides education forums on post-traumatic stress disorder. Also works with traumatized children in a mentorship program.

Assn. of the United States Army, *2425 Wilson Blvd., Arlington, VA 22201; (703) 841-4300. Fax, (703) 525-9039. Gordon R. Sullivan, President. Information, (800) 336-4570.*
Web, www.ausa.org

Membership: civilians and active duty and retired members of the armed forces. Conducts symposia on defense issues and researches topics that affect the military.

Fleet Reserve Assn., *125 N. West St., Alexandria, VA 22314-2754; (703) 683-1400. Fax, (703) 549-6610. Joseph L. Barnes, National Executive Director. Information, (800) 372-1924.*
General e-mail, news-fra@fra.org

Web, www.fra.org

Membership: active duty, reserve, and retired Navy, Marine Corps, and Coast Guard personnel. Works to safeguard the compensation, benefits, and entitlements of sea services personnel. Recognized by the Veterans Affairs Dept. to assist veterans and widows of veterans with benefit claims.

Marine Corps League, *8626 Lee Hwy., #201, Fairfax, VA 22031-3070 (mailing address: P.O. Box 3070, Merrifield, VA 22116); (703) 207-9588. Fax, (703) 207-0047. Michael A. Blum, Executive Director. Toll-free, (800) 625-1775.*
Web, www.mcleague.org

Membership: active duty, retired, and reserve Marine Corps groups. Promotes the interests of the Marine Corps and works to preserve its traditions; assists veterans and their survivors. Monitors legislation and regulations.

Military Order of the World Wars, *435 N. Lee St., Alexandria, VA 22314; (703) 683-4911. Fax, (703) 683-4501. Brig. Gen. Roger C. Bultman, Chief of Staff. Toll-free, (877) 320-3774.*
Web, www.militaryorder.net

Membership: retired and active duty commissioned officers, warrant officers, and flight officers. Supports a strong national defense; supports patriotic education in schools; presents awards to outstanding Junior and Senior Reserve Officers Training Corps (ROTC) cadets, Boys Scouts, and Girl Scouts.

National Assn. for Uniformed Services, *5535 Hempstead Way, Springfield, VA 22151-4094; (703) 750-1342. Fax, (703) 354-4380. Maj. Gen. William M. Matz Jr. (USA Ret.), President. Information, (800) 842-3451. General e-mail, naus@naus.org*

Web, www.naus.org

Membership: active duty, reserve, and retired officers and enlisted personnel of all uniformed services and their families and survivors. Supports legislation that benefits military personnel and veterans. (Affiliated with the Society of Military Widows.)

Navy League of the United States, *2300 Wilson Blvd., #200, Arlington, VA 22201-3308; (703) 528-1775. Fax, (703) 528-2333. Stephen R. Pietropaoli, National Executive Director. Toll-free, (800) 356-5760. General e-mail, service@navyleague.org*

Web, www.navyleague.org

Membership: retired and reserve military personnel and civilians interested in the U.S. Navy, Marine Corps, Coast Guard, and Merchant Marine. Distributes literature, provides speakers, and conducts seminars to promote interests of the sea services. Monitors legislation.

Noncommissioned Officers Assn., *National Capital Office, P.O. Box 427, Alexandria, VA 22313; (703) 549-0311. Fax, (703) 549-0245. H. Gene Overstreet, President; Richard C. Schneider, Executive Director for Government Affairs.*
General e-mail, rschneider@ncoadc.org

Web, www.ncoausa.org

Congressionally chartered fraternal organization of active duty, reserve, guard, and retired enlisted military personnel. Sponsors job fairs to assist members in finding employment. (Headquarters in San Antonio, Texas.)

United Service Organizations (USO), *World Headquarters, 2111 Wilson Blvd., #1200, Arlington, VA 22201; (703) 908-6400. Fax, (202) 908-6401. Stan D. Gibson, President. Toll-free, (800) 876-7469.*
Web, www.uso.org

Voluntary civilian organization chartered by Congress. Provides military personnel and their families in the United States and overseas with social, educational, and recreational programs.

U.S. Army Warrant Officers Assn., *462 Herndon Pkwy., #207, Herndon, VA 20170-5235; (703) 742-7727. Fax, (703) 742-7728. Donald E. Hess, Executive Director (Acting). Toll-free, (800) 587-2962.*
General e-mail, usawoa@cavtel.net

Web, www.usawoa.org

Membership: active duty, guard, reserve, and retired and former warrant officers. Monitors and makes recommendations to Defense Dept., Army Dept., and Congress on policies and programs affecting Army warrant officers and their families.

DEFENSE PERSONNEL

Chaplains

▶AGENCIES

Air Force Dept. *(Defense Dept.), Chief of Chaplains, Bolling AFB, 112 Luke Ave. 20032; (202) 767-4577. Fax, (202) 404-7841. Maj. Gen. Cecil Richardson, Chief of Chaplains.*
General e-mail, afhc@pentagon.af.mil

Web, www.usafhc.af.mil

Oversees chaplains and religious services within the Air Force; maintains liaison with religious denominations.

Armed Forces Chaplains Board *(Defense Dept.), OUSD (P&R) MPP-AFCB, 4000 Defense Pentagon, #2E341 20301-4000; (703) 697-9015. Fax, (703) 693-2280. Maj. Gen. Douglas L. Carver (USA), Chair; Col. Thomas E. Preston, Executive Director.*
General e-mail, afcb@osd.mil

Web, www.defenselink.mil/prhome/mppchaplain.html

Membership: chiefs and deputy chiefs of chaplains of the armed services; works to coordinate religious policies and services among the military branches.

Army Dept. *(Defense Dept.), Chief of Chaplains, 2700 Army Pentagon, #2A514A 20310-2700; (703) 695-1133. Fax, (703) 695-9834. Douglas L. Carver, Chief of Chaplains.*
Web, www.occh.army.mil

Oversees chaplains and religious services within the Army; maintains liaison with religious denominations.

Marine Corps *(Defense Dept.), Chaplain, 2 Navy Annex, #1056 20380-1775; (703) 614-4627. Fax, (703) 693-2907. Rear Adm. Mark Tidd, Chaplain.*
Web, www.hqmc.usmc.mil

Oversees chaplains and religious services within the Marine Corps; maintains liaison with religious denominations.

National Guard Bureau *(Defense Dept.), Chaplain Services, 1411 Jefferson Davis Hwy., #9500, Arlington, VA 22202-3231; (703) 607-5229. Fax, (703) 607-5295. Col. John B. Ellington Jr., Chief Chaplain. Public Affairs, (703) 607-2584.*
General e-mail, chaplain@ngb.ang.af.mil

Web, www.ngb.army.mil/jointstaff/ss/hc/default.aspx

Represents the Chief National Guard Bureau on all aspects of the chaplains' mission. Directs and oversees the activities and policies of the National Guard Chaplain Services. Oversees chaplains and religious services within the National Guard; maintains liaison with religious denominations.

Navy Dept. *(Defense Dept.), Chief of Chaplains, N097, 2 Navy Annex, #1056 20370-0400; (703) 614-4043. Fax, (703) 614-4725. Rear Adm. Robert F. Burt, Chief.*
Web, www.navy.mil/local/crb

Oversees chaplains and religious services within the Navy; maintains liaison with religious denominations.

U.S. Coast Guard *(Homeland Security Dept.), Chaplain, 2100 2nd St. S.W., #2112 20593-0001; (202) 372-4434. Fax, (202) 372-4962. Capt. William F. Cuddy Jr., Chaplain; Cmdr. Daniel E. McKay, Deputy Chaplain.*
Web, www.uscg.mil/hq/chaplain

Oversees chaplains and religious services within the Coast Guard; maintains liaison with religious denominations.

▶NONGOVERNMENTAL

Military Chaplains Assn. of the United States of America, *P.O. Box 7056, Arlington, VA 22207-7056; (703) 533-5890. Gary R. Pollitt, Executive Director. Phone and fax are the same number.*
General e-mail, chaplains@mca-usa.org

Web, www.mca-usa.org

Membership: chaplains of all faiths in all branches of the armed services and chaplains of veterans affairs and civil air patrol. Provides training opportunities for chaplains and a referral service concerning chaplains and chaplaincy.

National Conference on Ministry to the Armed Forces, *7724 Silver Sage Ct., Springfield, VA 22153; (703) 608-2100. Jack Williamson, Executive Director.*
Web, www.ncmaf.org

Offers support to the Armed Forces Chaplains Board, the chief of chaplains of each service, and chaplains throughout the military and Veterans Affairs Dept.; disseminates information on matters affecting service personnel welfare.

Civilian Employees

►AGENCIES

Air Force Dept. *(Defense Dept.), Civilian Force Policy,* 2221 S. Clark St., #500, Arlington, VA 22202; (703) 604-8122. Fax, (703) 604-5060. Ermelinda Rodriguez-Heffner, Chief.
Web, www.af.mil

Civilian office that monitors and reviews Air Force policies, benefits and entitlements, civilian pay, career programs, and external and internal placement of staff.

Air Force Dept. *(Defense Dept.), Personnel Policy,* 1040 Air Force Pentagon, #4D950 20330-1040; (703) 695-6770. Fax, (703) 614-8523. Brig. Gen. Darrell Jones, Director.
Web, www.af.mil

Implements and evaluates Air Force civilian personnel policies; serves as the principal adviser to the Air Force personnel director on civilian personnel matters and programs.

Army Dept. *(Defense Dept.), Civilian Personnel,* 300 Army Pentagon, #2C453 20310-0300; (703) 695-5701. Fax, (703) 695-6997. Susan Duncan, Assistant G-1 for Civilian Personnel.
Web, www.cpol.army.mil

Develops and reviews Army civilian personnel policies and advises the Army leadership on civilian personnel matters.

Army Dept. *(Defense Dept.), Equal Employment Opportunity and Civil Rights,* 1225 S. Clark St., #200, Crystal Gateway 2, Arlington, VA 22202; (703) 604-0580. Fax, (703) 604-0685. Jay D. Aronowitz, Deputy Assistant Secretary (Acting).
Web, http://eeoa.army.pentagon.mil/web/index.cfm

Civilian office that administers equal employment opportunity and civil rights programs and policies for civilian employees of the Army.

Defense Dept. (DoD), *Civilian Assistance and Re-Employment (CARE),* 1400 Key Blvd., #B-200, Arlington, VA 22209-5144; (703) 696-1799. Fax, (703) 696-5416. Jeffrey L. Nelson, Chief.
Web, www.cpms.osd.mil/care

Manages transition programs for Defense Dept. civilians, including placement, separation incentives, early retirement, and transition assistance programs.

Marine Corps *(Defense Dept.), Human Resources and Organizational Management,* 1120, Code ARH, Arlington, VA 20380-1775; (703) 614-1300. Fax, (703) 693-1963. Hal P. Wright, Director; Albert Washington, Deputy Equal Employment Opportunities Officer.
Web, www.chro.usmc.mil

Develops and implements personnel and equal employment opportunity programs for civilian employees of the Marine Corps.

Navy Dept. *(Defense Dept.), Civilian Human Resources,* 1000 Navy Pentagon, #4D548 20350-1000; (703) 695-2633. Fax, (703) 693-4959. Patricia C. Adams, Deputy Assistant Secretary.
General e-mail, patricia.c.adams@navy.mil
Web, www.hq.navy.mil/shhro

Civilian office that develops and reviews Navy and Marine Corps civilian personnel and equal opportunity programs and policies.

U.S. Coast Guard (USCG), *(Homeland Security Dept.), Human Resources Directorate (CG-1),* 2100 2nd St. S.W., #5410 20593-0001; (202) 475-5000. Fax, (202) 475-5940. Rear Adm. Jody Breckenridge, Assistant Commandant.
Web, www.uscg.mil/hr

Responsible for hiring, recruiting, and training all military and nonmilitary Coast Guard personnel.

U.S. Coast Guard (USCG), *(Homeland Security Dept.), Military and Civilian Equal Opportunity,* 2100 2nd St. S.W., #B432 20593-0001; (202) 372-4000. Fax, (202) 372-4920. Johnny McAfee, Manager, (202) 372-4260.
Web, www.uscg.mil

Manages military and civilian internal equal employment opportunity programs.

Equal Opportunity

►AGENCIES

Air Force Dept. *(Defense Dept.), Military Equal Opportunity,* 1040 Air Force Pentagon, #4D950 20330-1040; (703) 692-2171. Fax, (703) 695-4083. Dwayne E. Walker, Program Manager.
Web, www.af.mil

Military office that develops and administers Air Force equal opportunity programs and policies.

Army Dept. *(Defense Dept.), Equal Employment Opportunity and Civil Rights,* 1225 S. Clark St., #200, Crystal Gateway 2, Arlington, VA 22202; (703) 604-0580. Fax, (703) 604-0685. Jay D. Aronowitz, Director (Acting).
Web, http://eeoa.army.pentagon.mil/web/index.cfm

Develops policy and conducts program reviews for the Dept. of Army Civilian Equal Employment Opportunity and Affirmative Employment Programs.

Defense Dept. (DoD), *Defense Dept. Advisory Committee on Women in the Services,* 4000 Defense Pentagon, #2C548A 20301-4000; (703) 697-2122. Fax, (703) 614-6233. Col. Denise Dailey (USA), Military Director.
General e-mail, dacowits@osd.mil
Web, www.defenselink.mil/dacowits

Provides the DoD with advice and recommendations on matters and policies relating to the recruitment and retention, treatment, employment, integration, and well-being of highly qualified professional women in the armed forces, as well as issues related to military families.

Defense Dept. (DoD), *Diversity Management and Equal Opportunity,* 4000 Defense Pentagon, #5D641 20301-4000; (703) 571-9321. Fax, (703) 571-9338. Clarence A. Johnson, Director. Web, www.defenselink.mil/prhome/eo.html

Formulates equal employment opportunity policy for the Defense Dept. Evaluates civil rights complaints from military personnel, including issues of sexual harassment and recruitment.

Marine Corps *(Defense Dept.),* *Equal Opportunity and Diversity Management,* HQUSMC, MNRA (MPE), 3280 Russell Rd., Quantico, VA 22134-5103; (703) 784-9371. Fax, (703) 784-9814. Col. Otto Rutt, Head. Web, www.marines.mil

Military office that develops, monitors, and administers Marine Corps equal opportunity programs.

Navy Dept. *(Defense Dept.),* *Diversity Directorate,* Navy Annex, #3633 20370; (703) 614-6854. Fax, (703) 614-6502. Capt. Ken J. Barrett, Director. Web, www.npc.navy.mil

Military office that develops and administers Navy diversity programs and policies.

U.S. Coast Guard (USCG), *(Homeland Security Dept.),* *Military and Civilian Equal Opportunity,* 2100 2nd St. S.W., #B432 20593-0001; (202) 372-4000. Fax, (202) 372-4920. Johnny McAfee, Manager, (202) 372-4260. Web, www.uscg.mil

Administers equal opportunity regulations for Coast Guard military personnel.

▶**NONGOVERNMENTAL**

Human Rights Campaign (HRC), 1640 Rhode Island Ave. N.W. 20036; (202) 628-4160. Fax, (202) 347-5323. Joe Solmonese, Executive Director. TTY, (202) 216-1572. Toll-free, (800) 777-4723. General e-mail, hrc@hrc.org Web, www.hrc.org

Promotes legislation affirming the rights of lesbians and gays. Focus includes discrimination in the military.

Minerva Center, 20 Granada Rd., Pasadena, MD 21122-2708; (410) 437-5379. Fax, (410) 990-9646. Linda Grant De Pauw, Director. Web, www.minervacenter.com

Encourages the study of women in war and women and the military. Focus includes current U.S. servicewomen; women veterans; women in war and the military abroad; and the preservation of artifacts, oral history, and first-hand accounts of women's experience in military service.

Servicemembers Legal Defense Network (SLDN), P.O. Box 65301 20035-5301; (202) 328-3244. Fax, (202) 797-1635. Aubrey Sarvis, Executive Director.

General e-mail, sldn@sldn.org

Web, www.sldn.org

Provides legal assistance to individuals affected by the military's policy on gays and lesbians. Monitors legislation and regulations.

Family Services

▶AGENCIES

Air Force Dept. *(Defense Dept.),* *Family Matters,* 201 12th St. South, #413, Arlington, VA 22202; (703) 604-0196. Fax, (703) 604-0323. Gretchen Shannon, Chief. Web, www.afcrossroads.com

Military policy office that monitors and reviews services provided to Air Force families and civilian employees with family concerns; oversees Airmen and Family Readiness Centers.

Air Force Dept. *(Defense Dept.),* *Manpower and Personnel,* 1040 Air Force Pentagon, #4D765 20330-1040; (703) 697-6088. Fax, (703) 697-6091. Lt. Gen. Richard Newton III, Deputy Chief of Staff. Web, www.af.mil

Military office that responds to inquiries concerning deceased Air Force personnel and their beneficiaries; refers inquiries to the Military Personnel Center at Randolph Air Force Base in San Antonio, Texas.

Army Dept. *(Defense Dept.),* *Casualty and Mortuary Affairs,* 200 Stovall St., #4S47, Alexandria, VA 22332-0481; (703) 325-7990. Fax, (703) 325-0134. Lt. Col. Michiyo Montague, Chief. Web, www.army.mil

Handles notifications concerning deceased and wounded soldiers; bedside travel and transportation orders; mortuary assistance, including military funeral honors program and return of personal effects; current and past conflict POWs and MIAs; management of cemeteries; and casualty-related FOIA requests. Verifies beneficiaries of deceased Army Dept. personnel for benefits distribution, and handles short- and long-term case management for bereaved and surviving family members. (Allied with the Casualty and Mortuary Affairs Operations Center.)

Army Dept. *(Defense Dept.),* *Casualty and Mortuary Affairs Operations Center (CMAOC),* 200 Stovall St., #4S43, Alexandria, VA 22332; (800) 626-3317. Col. Carl Johnson, Director. General e-mail, CMAOCWEB@conus.army.mil

The 24/7 operations center that handles notifications concerning deceased and wounded soldiers.

Army Dept. *(Defense Dept.),* *Family and Morale, Welfare, and Recreation Command,* 4700 King St., Alexandria, VA 22302-4401; (703) 681-7469. Fax, (703) 681-7446. Col. Brick Miller, Commander. Web, www.armymwr.com

Military office that directs operations of Army recreation, community service, child development, and youth activity centers. Handles dependent education in conjunction with the Defense Dept.

Defense Dept. (DoD), *Education Activity,* 4040 N. Fairfax Dr., Arlington, VA 22203-1635; (703) 588-3200. Fax, (703) 588-3701. Shirley A. Miles, Director. Web, www.dodea.edu

Civilian office that maintains school system for dependents of all military personnel and eligible civilians in the United States and abroad; advises the secretary of defense on overseas education matters; supervises selection of teachers in schools for military dependents.

Defense Dept. (DoD), *Management Support,* 4000 Defense Pentagon, #5A734 20301-4000; (703) 697-7191. Fax, (703) 695-1977. Carolee Van Horn, Director. Web, www.defenselink.mil

Coordinates policies related to quality of life of military personnel and their families.

Marine Corps *(Defense Dept.), Casualty Section,* HQUSMC, 3280 Russell Rd., Quantico, VA 22134-5102; (703) 784-9512. Fax, (703) 784-4134. Gerald Castle, Head. Toll-free, (800) 847-1597. General e-mail, casualtysection@manpower.usmc.mil

Web, www.manpower.usmc.mil

Confirms beneficiaries of deceased Marine Corps personnel for benefits distribution.

Marine Corps *(Defense Dept.), Personal and Family Readiness Division,* HQUSMC, M and RA (MR), 3280 Russell Rd., Quantico, VA 22134-5103; (703) 784-9501. Fax, (703) 432-9269. Timothy "T. R." Larsen, Director. Web, www.usmc-mccs.org

Sponsors family service centers located on major Marine Corps installations. Oversees the administration of policies affecting the quality of life of Marine Corps military families. Administers relocation assistance programs.

Navy Dept. *(Defense Dept.), Personal and Community Readiness,* Navy Annex, #1612 20370-5000; (703) 614-4259. Fax, (703) 693-4199. Thomas Yavorski, Liaison. Web, www.npc.navy.mil

Acts as liaison between D.C. area and Navy quality of life programs located in Tenn., which provide naval personnel and families being sent overseas with information and support; addresses problems of abuse and sexual assault within families; helps Navy spouses find employment; facilitates communication between Navy families and Navy officials; and assists in relocating Navy families during transition from military to civilian life.

U.S. Coast Guard (USCG), *(Homeland Security Dept.), Worklife Programs,* 2100 2nd St. S.W., #B419 20593-0835; (202) 372-4084. Fax, (202) 372-4906. Lt. Cmdr. Michael Albert, Chief. Alternate phone number, (202) 475-5141. Web, www.uscg.mil/worklife

Offers broad array of human services to individuals in the Coast Guard and their families, including child care, elderly care, educational services, domestic violence counseling, sexual abuse counseling, health care, transition and relocation benefits, and special needs.

▶**CONGRESS**

For a listing of relevant congressional committees and subcommittees, please see page 513 or the Appendix.

▶**NONGOVERNMENTAL**

Air Force Aid Society Inc., 241 18th St. South, #202, Arlington, VA 22202-3409; (703) 607-3034. Fax, (703) 607-3022. Lt. Gen. John D. Hopper Jr., Chief Executive Officer. Web, www.afas.org

Membership: Air Force active duty, reserve, and retired military personnel and their dependents. Provides active duty and retired Air Force military personnel with personal emergency loans for basic needs, travel, or dependents' health expenses; assists families of active duty, deceased, or retired Air Force personnel with postsecondary education grants.

Armed Forces Hostess Assn., 6604 Army Pentagon, #1E541 20310-6604; (703) 614-0350. Fax, (703) 697-5542. Rosemarie Nemeth, President. Alternate phone number, (703) 614-0485. General e-mail, afha@hqda.army.mil

Web, www.army.mil/afha

Volunteer office staffed by spouses of military personnel of all services. Serves as an information clearinghouse for military and civilian Defense Dept. families; maintains information on military bases in the United States and abroad; issues information handbook for families in the Washington area.

American Red Cross, *Service to the Armed Forces,* 2025 E St. N.W., 2nd Floor 20006; (202) 303-6156. Fax, (202) 303-0216. Sherri L. Brown, Vice President, (202) 303-6512. Call Center (24/7), (202) 303-6156. Web, www.redcross.org

Provides emergency services for active duty armed forces personnel and their families, including reporting and communications, financial assistance, information and referral, and counseling. Mandated by Congress. Contacts military personnel in family emergencies; provides military personnel with verification of family situations for emergency leave applications.

Army Distaff Foundation (Knollwood), 6200 Oregon Ave. N.W. 20015-1543; (202) 541-0149. Fax, (202) 364-2856. Maj. Gen. Donald C. Hilbert (USA, Ret.), Executive Director. Information, (800) 541-4255. Web, www.armydistaff.org

Nonprofit continuing care retirement community for career military officers and their families. Provides retirement housing and health care services.

Army Emergency Relief, *200 Stovall St., #5N13, Alexandria, VA 22332; (703) 428-0000. Fax, (703) 325-7183. Gen. Robert F. Foley (Ret.), Executive Director. Toll-free, (866) 878-6378.*
General e-mail, aer@aerhq.org

Web, www.aerhq.org

Provides emergency financial assistance to soldiers and their family members who are on extended active duty and are members of the U.S. Army or U.S. Army Reserves; provides financial assistance for family members to further their education.

EX-POSE, Ex-Partners of Servicemembers for Equality, *P.O. Box 11191, Alexandria, VA 22312-0191; (703) 941-5844. Fax, (703) 212-6951. Nancy K. Davis, Office Manager.*
General e-mail, ex-pose@juno.com

Web, www.ex-pose.org

Membership: current and former partners of military members, both officers and enlisted, and other interested parties. Educates current and former spouses about potential benefits that may be gained or lost through divorce, including retirement pay, survivors' benefits, and medical, commissary, and exchange benefits. Provides information concerning legal resources and related federal laws and regulations. Serves as an information clearinghouse.

Federal Education Assn., *1201 16th St. N.W., #117 20036; (202) 822-7850. Fax, (202) 822-7867. Michael Priser, President.*
General e-mail, fea@feaonline.org

Web, www.feaonline.org

Membership: teachers and personnel of Defense Dept. schools for military dependents in the United States and abroad. Helps members negotiate pay, benefits, and better working conditions. Provides professional development through workshops and publications. Monitors legislation and regulations.

Fisher House Foundation, *1401 Rockville Pike, #600, Rockville, MD 20852; (301) 294-8560. Fax, (301) 294-8562. David A. Coker, Executive Director. Toll-free, (888) 294-8560.*
General e-mail, info@fisherhouse.org

Web, www.fisherhouse.org

Builds new group homes on the grounds of major military and VA hospitals to enable families of hospitalized service members to stay within walking distance. Donates the Fisher Houses to the U.S. government. Administers the Hero Miles Program, which uses donated frequent flier miles to purchase airline tickets for hospitalized service members and their families. Provides scholarships for military children.

Freedom Alliance, *22570 Markey Court, #240, Dulles, VA 20166; (703) 444-7940. Fax, (703) 444-6620. Tom Kilgannon, President. Toll-free, (800) 475-6620.*
Web, www.freedomalliance.org

Promotes strong national defense and honors military service. Awards monetary grants to wounded troops; assists soldiers and their families with housing and travel expenses; provides active duty troops with meals, clothing, entertainment, and other comforts. Offers a scholarship fund for soldiers' children.

National Military Family Assn., *2500 N. Van Dorn St., #102, Alexandria, VA 22315; (703) 931-6632. Fax, (703) 931-4600. Mary Scott, Chair; Joyce Raezer, Executive Director.*
General e-mail, families@nmfa.org

Web, www.nmfa.org

Membership: active duty and retired military, National Guard, and reserve personnel of all U.S. uniformed services, civilian personnel, families, and other interested individuals. Works to improve the quality of life for military families.

Naval Services FamilyLine, *1043 Harwood St. S.E., #100, Washington Navy Yard, DC 20374-5067; (202) 433-2333. Fax, (202) 433-4622. Josi Hunt, Chair.*
General e-mail, nsfamline@aol.com

Web, www.lifelines.navy.mil/FamilyLine

Offers support services to spouses of Navy, Marine Corps, and Coast Guard personnel; disseminates information on all aspects of military life; fosters sense of community among sea service personnel and their families.

Navy–Marine Corps Relief Society, *875 N. Randolph St., #225, Arlington, VA 22203-1977; (703) 696-4904. Fax, (703) 696-0144. Steve Abbot, President.*
Web, www.nmcrs.org

Assists active duty and retired Navy and Marine Corps personnel and their families in times of need. Disburses interest-free loans and grants. Provides educational scholarships and loans, visiting nurse services, thrift shops, food lockers, budget counseling, and volunteer training.

Our Military Kids, Inc., *6861 Elm St., #2-A, McLean, VA 22101; (703) 734-6654. Fax, (703) 734-6503. Linda Davidson, Co–Executive Director.*
General e-mail, omkinquiry@ourmilitarykids.org

Web, www.ourmilitarykids.org

Provides grants for extracurricular activities for school-aged children of deployed and severely injured Reserve and National Guard military personnel.

Financial Services

▶AGENCIES

Air Force Dept. *(Defense Dept.),* **Financial Management and Comptroller,** *1130 Air Force Pentagon, #4E978 20330-1130; (703) 697-1974. Fax, (703) 693-1996. Richard Hartley, Assistant Secretary (Acting).*
Web, www.saffm.hq.af.mil

Advises the secretary of the Air Force on policies relating to financial services for military and civilian personnel.

Defense Dept. (DoD), *Accounting and Finance Policy Analysis,* 1100 Defense Pentagon, #3C653A 20301-1100; (703) 697-3200. Fax, (703) 695-4283. Robert McNamara, Director.
Web, www.defenselink.mil

Develops accounting policy for the Defense Dept. federal management regulation.

► **CONGRESS**

For a listing of relevant congressional committees and subcommittees, please see page 513 or the Appendix.

► **NONGOVERNMENTAL**

Armed Forces Benefit Assn., *909 N. Washington St., Alexandria, VA 22314; (703) 549-4455. Fax, (703) 706-5961. Gen. Ralph E. Eberhart (USAF, Ret.), President.*
General e-mail, info@afba.com

Web, www.afba.com

Membership: active duty and retired personnel of the uniformed services, federal civilian employees, government contractors, first responders, and family members. Offers low-cost health and life insurance and financial, banking, and investment services worldwide.

Army and Air Force Mutual Aid Assn., *102 Sheridan Ave., Fort Myer, VA 22211-1110; (703) 522-3060. Fax, (703) 528-2662. Maj. Walt Lincoln (USA, Ret.), President. Information, (866) 422-3622.*
General e-mail, info@aafmaa.com

Web, www.aafmaa.com

Private organization that offers member and family life insurance products and survivor assistance services to all Army and Air Force personnel under age sixty-six, active duty, Guard, Reserve, retired West Point and Air Force Academy alumni, and Army and Air Force ROTC cadets under contract.

Army Emergency Relief, *200 Stovall St., #5N13, Alexandria, VA 22332; (703) 428-0000. Fax, (703) 325-7183. Gen. Robert F. Foley (Ret.), Executive Director. Toll-free, (866) 878-6378.*
General e-mail, aer@aerhq.org

Web, www.aerhq.org

Provides emergency financial assistance to soldiers and their family members who are on extended active duty and are members of the U.S. Army or U.S. Army Reserves; provides financial assistance for family members to further their education.

Defense Credit Union Council, *601 Pennsylvania Ave. N.W., South Bldg., #600 20004-2601; (202) 638-3950. Fax, (202) 638-3410. Roland Arteaga, President.*
General e-mail, dcuc1@cuna.com

Web, www.dcuc.org

Trade association of credit unions serving the Defense Dept.'s military and civilian personnel. Works with the National Credit Union Administration to solve problems concerning the operation of credit unions for the military community; maintains liaison with the Defense Dept.

Health Care

► **AGENCIES**

Air Force Dept. *(Defense Dept.),* **Health Benefits,** *1500 Wilson Blvd., #120, Arlington, VA 22209; (202) 588-6650. Fax, (202) 767-1455. Lt. Col. James Clapsaddle, Chief.*
Web, www.af.mil

Military office that develops and administers health benefits and policies for Air Force military personnel. Oversees modernization of Air Force medical facilities.

Air Force Dept. *(Defense Dept.),* **Surgeon General,** *1780 Air Force Pentagon, #4C882 20330-1780; (703) 692-6800. Fax, (703) 692-6610. Lt. Gen. (Dr.) James G. Roudebush, Surgeon General.*
Web, www.airforcemedicine.afms.mil

Directs the provision of medical and dental services for Air Force personnel and their beneficiaries.

Army Dept. *(Defense Dept.),* **Command Policies and Programs,** *1225 S. Clark St., Crystal City, VA 22202; (703) 604-0617. Lt. Col. Thomas Languirand, Chief, (703) 604-0670.*
Web, www.armyg1.army.mil

Develops policies and initiatives to enhance soldiers' health, fitness, and morale. Interests include weight control and suicide prevention.

Army Dept. *(Defense Dept.),* **Surgeon General,** *5109 Leesburg Pike, #672, Falls Church, VA 22041-3258; (703) 681-3000. Fax, (703) 681-3167. Lt. Gen. Eric Shoomaker, Surgeon General.*
General e-mail, OTSGWebPublisher@amedd.army.mil

Web, www.armymedicine.army.mil

Directs the provision of medical and dental services for Army personnel and their dependents.

Army Dept. *(Defense Dept.),* **Warrior Transition Brigade,** *6900 Georgia Ave. N.W., Bldg. 38 20307; (202) 782-6746. Fax, (202) 782-4545. Col. Terrence J. McKenrick, Commander.*
Web, www.wramc.amedd.army.mil

Provides leadership, command, and control for wounded soldiers' health and welfare, military administrative requirements, and readiness. Collaborates with medical providers in order to facilitate quality care, disposition, and transition. Supports the needs of wounded warriors and their families; supports the professional growth of all personnel.

Army Dept. *(Defense Dept.),* **Wounded Warrior Program (AW2),** *200 Stovall St., #6N09, Alexandria, VA 22332-0400; (703) 325-1530. Fax, (703) 325-1516. Col. James S. Rice, Chief. Toll-free, (800) 237-1336. Overseas, (312) 221-8186.*

General e-mail, aw2@conus.army.mil

Web, www.aw2.army.mil

Incorporates several existing programs to provide holistic support services for severely disabled soldiers and their families. Provides each soldier with a personal AW2 advocate. Tracks and monitors severely disabled soldiers beyond their medical retirement.

Defense Dept. (DoD), *Health Affairs: Clinical Program Policy, 1200 Defense Pentagon, #3E1082 20301-1200; (703) 681-1708. Fax, (703) 697-4197. Jack W. Smith, Director. Web, www.defenselink.mil*

Administers the medical benefits programs for active duty and retired military personnel and dependents in the Defense Dept.; develops policies relating to medical programs.

Marine Corps *(Defense Dept.),* **Personal and Family Readiness Division,** *HQUSMC, M and RA (MR), 3280 Russell Rd., Quantico, VA 22134-5103; (703) 784-9501. Fax, (703) 432-9269. Timothy "T. R." Larsen, Director. Web, www.usmc-mccs.org*

Military office that directs Marine Corps health care, family violence, and drug and alcohol abuse policies and programs.

Naval Medical Research Center *(Defense Dept.), 503 Robert Grant Ave., #1W28, Silver Spring, MD 20910-7500; (301) 319-7400. Fax, (301) 319-7410. Capt. Christopher Daniel, Commanding Officer. Web, www.nmrc.navy.mil*

Performs basic and applied biomedical research in areas of military importance, including infectious diseases, hyperbaric medicine, wound repair enhancement, environmental stress, and immunobiology. Provides support to field laboratories and naval hospitals; monitors research internationally.

Navy Dept. *(Defense Dept.),* **Manpower and Reserve Affairs: Health Affairs,** *1000 Navy Pentagon, #4D548 20350-1000; (703) 693-5365. Fax, (703) 675-1211. Cmdr. Ann Swap, Director, (703) 693-0238. Web, www.navy.mil*

Reviews medical programs for Navy and Marine Corps military personnel and develops and reviews policies relating to these programs.

Navy Dept. *(Defense Dept.),* **Patient Administration/ TriCare Operations,** *23rd and E Sts. N.W., #1000 20372-5300; (202) 762-3152. Fax, (202) 762-3743. Capt. Clarence Thomas, Head. Web, www.med.navy.mil*

Military office that interprets and oversees the implementation of Navy health care policy. Assists in the development of eligibility policy for medical benefits programs for Navy and Marine Corps military personnel.

Navy Dept. *(Defense Dept.),* **Surgeon General,** *23rd and E Sts. N.W., #1215 20372-5120; (202) 762-3701. Fax, (202) 762-3750. Vice Adm. Adam M. Robinson, Surgeon General. Web, www.navy.mil*

Directs the provision of medical and dental services for Navy and Marine Corps personnel and their dependents; oversees the Navy's Bureau of Medicine and Surgery.

U.S. Coast Guard (USCG), *(Homeland Security Dept.),* **Health and Safety,** *2100 2nd St. S.W., CG-11 20593-0001; (202) 475-5130. Fax, (202) 475-5909. Rear Adm. Mark Tedesco, Director. General e-mail, darlene.byrd@uscg.mil*

Web, www.uscg.mil

Oversees all health, safety, and work-life aspects of the Coast Guard, including the operation of medical and dental clinics and sick bays on ships. Investigates Coast Guard accidents, such as the grounding of ships and downing of aircraft. Oversees all work-life–related programs, including health promotion, mess halls and galleys, and individual and family support groups.

Walter Reed Army Institute of Research *(Defense Dept.), 503 Robert Grant Ave., Silver Spring, MD 20910-7500; (301) 319-9100. Fax, (301) 319-9227. Col. Kent Kester, Commander. Public Affairs Officer, (301) 319-9471. General e-mail, wrair.publicaffairs@amedd.army.mil*

Web, www.wrair.army.mil

Provides research, education, and training in support of the Defense Dept.'s health care system. Develops vaccines and drugs to prevent and treat infectious diseases. Other research efforts include surveillance of naturally occurring infectious diseases of military importance and study of combat casualty care (blood loss, resuscitation, and brain and other organ system trauma), battle casualties, operational stress, sleep deprivation, and medical countermeasures against biological and chemical agents.

▶NONGOVERNMENTAL

Assn. of Military Osteopathic Physicians and Surgeons, *1796 Severn Hills Lane, Severn, MD 21144-1061; (410) 519-8217. Fax, (410) 519-7657. Jim Yonts, Executive Director. General e-mail, jim@amops.org*

Web, www.amops.org

Membership: osteopathic physicians who work or have worked for or with the military or federal government and osteopathic medical students in the Health Professions Scholarship Program. Promotes the advancement of osteopathic principles in military and federal practice and institutions and the recognition of the unique aspects of practice in the uniformed services. Sponsors annual continuing medical education conference.

Assn. of Military Surgeons of the United States, *9320 Old Georgetown Rd., Bethesda, MD 20814-1653; (301) 897-8800. Fax, (301) 530-5446. Maj. Gen. George K. Anderson (USAF, Ret.), Executive Director. General e-mail, amsus@amsus.org*

Web, www.amsus.org

Membership: health professionals, including nurses, dentists, pharmacists, and physicians, who work or have worked for the U.S. Public Health Service, the VA, or the Army, Navy, Air Force, Guard, and Reserves, and students. Works to improve all phases of federal health services.

Comfort for America's Uniformed Services (CAUSE), *6315 Bren Mar Dr., #175, Alexandria, VA 22312; (703) 750-6458. Barbara Lau, Executive Director.*
General e-mail, info@cause-usa.org

Web, www.cause-usa.org

Provides comfort items and organizes recreational programs for U.S. military service personnel undergoing medical treatment or recuperating in government hospitals or rehabilitation facilities.

Commissioned Officers Assn. of the U.S. Public Health Service, *8201 Corporate Dr., #200, Landover, MD 20785; (301) 731-9080. Fax, (301) 731-9084. Gerard M. Farrell, Executive Director.*
Web, www.coausphs.org

Membership: commissioned officers of the U.S. Public Health Service. Supports expansion of federal health care facilities, including military facilities.

Injured Marine Semper Fi Fund, *715 Broadway St., Quantico, VA 22134 (mailing address: Wounded Warrior Center, Box 555193, Camp Pendleton, CA 92055); (703) 640-0181. Fax, (703) 640-0192. Karen Guenther, Executive Director.*
General e-mail, info@semperfifund.org

Web, www.semperfifund.org

Provides financial assistance to marines injured in combat and training, other service members injured while in direct support of marine units, and families of marines for expenses during hospitalization, rehabilitation, and recovery.

Missing in Action, Prisoners of War

▶AGENCIES

Air Force Dept. *(Defense Dept.), Manpower and Personnel, 1040 Air Force Pentagon, #4D765 20330-1040; (703) 697-6088. Fax, (703) 697-6091. Lt. Gen. Richard Newton III, Deputy Chief of Staff.*
Web, www.af.mil

Military office that responds to inquiries about missing in action (MIA) personnel for the Air Force; refers inquiries to the Military Personnel Center at Randolph Air Force Base in San Antonio, Texas.

Army Dept. *(Defense Dept.), Past Conflict Repatriations Branch, U.S. Army Human Resources Command, 200 Stovall St., #S15, Alexandria, VA 22332-0482; (703) 325-0680. Fax, (703) 325-1808. Eric Wolf, Chief. Toll-free, (800) 892-2490.*
Web, www.army.mil

Military office responsible for past conflict policy regarding prisoner of war (POW) and missing in action (MIA) personnel for the Army. Responds to inquiries and distributes information about past conflict Army POWs and MIAs to the next of kin.

Defense Dept. (DoD), *Defense Prisoners of War/Missing Personnel, 241 18th St. South, Crystal Square 4, #800, Arlington, VA 22202; (703) 699-1102. Fax, (703) 602-1890. Amb. Charles A. Ray, Deputy Assistant Secretary.*
Web, www.dtic.mil/dpmo

Civilian office responsible for policy matters relating to prisoners of war and missing personnel issues. Represents the Defense Dept. before Congress, the media, veterans organizations, and prisoner of war and missing personnel families.

Defense Dept. (DoD), *Public Communications, 2521 S. Clark St., #1700, Arlington, VA 22202 (mailing address: 1400 Defense Pentagon, Washington, DC 20301-1400); (703) 428-0711. Fax, (703) 697-3501. David McWilliams, Director. Press, (703) 697-5131.*
Web, www.defenselink.mil

Responds to public inquiries on Defense Dept. personnel.

Marine Corps *(Defense Dept.), Casualty Section, HQUSMC, 3280 Russell Rd., Quantico, VA 22134-5102; (703) 784-9512. Fax, (703) 784-4134. Gerald Castle, Head. Toll-free, (800) 847-1597.*
General e-mail, casualtysection@manpower.usmc.mil

Web, www.manpower.usmc.mil

Military office that responds to inquiries about missing in action (MIA) personnel for the Marine Corps and distributes information about Marine Corps MIAs to the next of kin.

Navy Dept. *(Defense Dept.), Naval Personnel, 2 Navy Annex, #2077 20370; (703) 614-1101. Fax, (703) 693-1746. Vice Adm. Mark E. Ferguson III, Chief.*
Web, www.navy.mil

Military office that responds to inquiries about missing in action (MIA) personnel for the Navy and distributes information about Navy MIAs.

State Dept., *Mainland Southeast Asia Affairs, 2201 C St. N.W., #5206 20520-6310; (202) 647-3132. Fax, (202) 647-3069. Stephen Blake, Director.*
Web, www.state.gov

Handles issues related to Americans missing in action in Indochina; serves as liaison with Congress, international organizations, and foreign governments on developments in these countries. Includes Thailand, Cambodia, Laos, Vietnam, and Burma.

▶CONGRESS

For a listing of relevant congressional committees and subcommittees, please see page 513 or the Appendix.

▶NONGOVERNMENTAL

National League of Families of American Prisoners and Missing in Southeast Asia, *1005 N. Glebe Rd., #170,*

Arlington, VA 22201; (703) 465-7432. Fax, (703) 465-7433. Ann Mills Griffiths, Executive Director. General e-mail, info@pow-miafamilies.org

Web, www.pow-miafamilies.org

Membership: family members of MIAs and POWs and returned POWs of the Vietnam War are voting members; nonvoting associate members include veterans and other interested people. Works for the release of all prisoners of war, an accounting of the missing, and repatriation of the remains of those who have died serving their country in Southeast Asia. Works to raise public awareness of these issues; maintains regional and state coordinators.

Pay and Compensation

▶AGENCIES

Air Force Dept. *(Defense Dept.), Manpower and Personnel (A1P): Compensation and Travel Policy,* HQUSAF/A15, 201 12th St. South, #413, Arlington, VA 22202-4306; (703) 604-8130. Fax, (703) 604-0321. Jean Love, Chief. Web, www.af.mil

Military office that develops and administers Air Force military personnel pay and compensation policies.

Army Dept. *(Defense Dept.), Military Compensation and Entitlements,* 111 Army Pentagon, #2E469 20310-0111; (703) 697-1482. Fax, (703) 693-7072. Col. Maurenia D. Wade, Assistant Deputy, (703) 695-4394. Web, www.asamra.army.mil

Military office that provides oversight of the development and administration of and compliance with Army military personnel pay and compensation policies.

Defense Dept. (DoD), *Compensation,* 4000 Defense Pentagon, #2B279 20301-4000; (703) 695-3177. Fax, (703) 697-0202. Virginia Penrod, Director. Web, www.defenselink.mil/militarypay

Coordinates military pay and compensation policies with the individual service branches and advises the secretary of defense on compensation policy.

Marine Corps *(Defense Dept.), Military Manpower Policy,* 3280 Russell Rd., #4 West, Quantico, VA 22134-5103; (703) 784-9350. Fax, (703) 784-9812. Michael F. Applegate, Director; Maj. Paul Gulbrandsen, Compensation/Incentive Officer. Web, www.marines.mil

Military office that develops and administers Marine Corps personnel pay and compensation policies.

Navy Dept. *(Defense Dept.), Military Pay and Compensation Policy,* 2 Navy Annex, #3608 20370-5000; (703) 614-2053. Fax, (703) 695-3311. Jeri Busch, Head. TTY, (866) 297-1971. Toll-free, (866) 827-5672. General e-mail, nxaq_n130@navy.mil

Web, www.npc.navy.mil/careerinfo/PayandBenefits/N130

Military office that develops and administers Navy military pay, compensation, and personnel policies.

Recruitment

▶AGENCIES

Air Force Dept. *(Defense Dept.), Air Force Commissioning Programs,* 2221 S. Clark St., #500, Arlington, VA 22202; (703) 604-8129. Fax, (703) 604-5061. Col. Vic Sowers, Chief. Web, www.af.mil

Military office that establishes Air Force officer commissioning policies and programs.

Air Force Dept. *(Defense Dept.), Force Management,* 1235 S. Clark St., #301, Arlington, VA 22202; (703) 604-0423. Fax, (703) 604-1657. John T. Park, Chief. Web, www.af.mil

Military office that oversees Air Force accession and retention policies for officers and enlisted personnel.

Defense Dept. (DoD), *Accession Policy,* 4000 Defense Pentagon, #2B271 20301-4000; (703) 695-5525. Fax, (703) 614-9272. Curt Gilroy, Director. Web, www.defenselink.mil

Military office that develops Defense Dept. recruiting programs and policies, including advertising, market research, and enlistment standards. Coordinates with the individual services on recruitment of military personnel.

Marine Corps *(Defense Dept.), Recruiting Command,* 3280 Russell Rd., Quantico, VA 22134-5103; (703) 784-9400. Fax, (703) 784-9863. Brig. Gen. Robert E. Milstead Jr., Commanding General. Web, www.marines.mil

Military office that administers and executes policies for Marine Corps officer and enlisted recruitment programs.

Retirement, Separation

▶AGENCIES

Armed Forces Retirement Home—Washington, 3700 N. Capitol St. N.W. 20011-8400; (202) 730-3556. Fax, (202) 730-3492. David Watkins, Director. Toll-free, (800) 422-9988. General e-mail, publicaffairs@afrh.gov

Web, www.afrh.gov

Gives domiciliary and medical care to retired members of the armed services or career service personnel unable to earn a livelihood. Formerly known as U.S. Soldiers' and Airmen's Home. (Armed Forces Retirement Home in Gulfport, Miss., is being rebuilt and will reopen in 2010.)

Army Dept. *(Defense Dept.), Army Career and Alumni Program,* 200 Stovall St., #7S07, Alexandria, VA

22332-0476; (703) 325-3591. Fax, (703) 325-4072. James
T. Hoffman, Chief.
Web, www.acap.army.mil

Military office that provides Army military personnel
and Defense Dept. civilian personnel with information concerning transition benefits and job assistance for separating
service members, civilian personnel, and their families.

Army Dept. *(Defense Dept.), Retirement Services,*
DAPE-HRP-RS0, 200 Stovall St., #5N37, Alexandria, VA
22332-0470; (703) 325-9158. Fax, (703) 325-8947. John
W. Radke, Chief.
Web, www.armyg1.army.mil/rso

Military office that administers retirement programs
for Army military personnel.

Defense Dept. (DoD), *Compensation,* 4000 Defense
Pentagon, #2B279 20301-4000; (703) 695-3177. Fax, (703)
697-0202. Virginia Penrod, Director.
Web, www.defenselink.mil/militarypay

Develops retirement policies and reviews administration of retirement programs for all Defense Dept. military
personnel.

Marine Corps *(Defense Dept.), Retired Activities,* 3280
Russell Rd., Quantico, VA 22134-5103; (703) 784-9312.
Fax, (703) 784-9834. Wesley R. Combs, Head. Toll-free,
(800) 336-4649.
Web, www.marines.mil

Military office that administers retirement programs
and benefits for Marine Corps retirees and the Marine
Corps retirement community survivor benefit plan.

Marine Corps *(Defense Dept.), Separation and
Retirement,* 3280 Russell Rd., Quantico, VA 22134-5103;
(703) 784-9304. Fax, (703) 784-9834. Steven M.
Hanscom, Head.
Web, www.manpower.usmc.mil

Military office that processes Marine Corps military
personnel retirements and separations but does not
administer benefits.

▶ **NONGOVERNMENTAL**

Army Distaff Foundation (Knollwood), 6200 Oregon
Ave. N.W. 20015-1543; (202) 541-0149. Fax, (202) 364-
2856. Maj. Gen. Donald C. Hilbert (USA, Ret.), Executive
Director. Information, (800) 541-4255.
Web, www.armydistaff.org

Nonprofit continuing care retirement community for
career military officers and their families. Provides retirement housing and health care services.

MILITARY EDUCATION AND TRAINING

▶ **AGENCIES**

Air Force Dept. *(Defense Dept.), Force Management
Integration,* 1660 Air Force Pentagon, #5E818

20330-1660; (703) 614-4751. Fax, (703) 693-4244.
Barbara J. Barger, Deputy Assistant Secretary.
Web, www.af.mil

Civilian office that monitors and reviews education
policies of the U.S. Air Force Academy at Colorado
Springs and officer candidates' training and Reserve Officers Training Corps (ROTC) programs for the Air Force.
Advises the secretary of the Air Force on education matters, including graduate education, voluntary education
programs, and flight, specialized, and recruit training.

Air Force Dept. *(Defense Dept.), Personnel Policy,* 1040
Air Force Pentagon, #4D950 20330-1040; (703) 695-6770.
Fax, (703) 614-8523. Brig. Gen. Darrell Jones, Director.
Web, www.af.mil

Supervises operations and policies of all professional
military education, including continuing education programs. Oversees operations and policies of Air Force service schools, including technical training for newly enlisted
Air Force personnel.

Army Dept. *(Defense Dept.), Collective Training
Division,* 400 Army Pentagon, #1E163 20310-0400; (703)
692-8370. Fax, (703) 692-7292. Col. Eric Johnson, Chief.
Web, www.army.mil

Military office that plans and monitors program
resources for active duty and reserve unit training readiness
programs.

Army Dept. *(Defense Dept.), Education,* 200 Stovall St.,
Attn.: AHRC-PDE, #3N07, Alexandria, VA 22332-0472;
(703) 325-9800. Fax, (703) 325-7476. Ileen Rogers, Chief.
Web, www.army.mil/wellbeing/education.html

Military office that manages the operations and
policies of voluntary education programs for active
duty Army personnel. Administers the tuition assistance
program and basic army special skills program.

Army Dept. *(Defense Dept.), Military Personnel
Management,* 300 Army Pentagon, #1D429 20310-0300;
(703) 695-5871. Fax, (703) 695-6025. Maj. Gen. Gina
Farrisee, Director.
Web, www.hqda.army.mil

Military office that supervises operations and policies
of the U.S. Military Academy and officer candidates' training and Reserve Officers Training Corps (ROTC) programs. Advises the chief of staff of the Army on academy
and education matters.

Civil Air Patrol, *National Capital Wing, Washington
Office,* 200 McChord St., #111, Bolling AFB 20032-0000;
(202) 767-4405. Fax, (202) 767-5695. Col. Richard J.
Cooper, Wing Commander, (202) 767-7776.
General e-mail, cc@natcapwg.cap.gov

Web, www.natcapwg.cap.gov

Official auxiliary of the U.S. Air Force. Sponsors a cadet
training and education program for junior and senior high
school age students. Cadets who have earned the Civil Air
Patrol's Mitchell Award are eligible to enter the Air Force
at an advanced pay grade. Conducts emergency services,

homeland security missions, and an aerospace education program for adults. (Headquarters at Maxwell Air Force Base, Ala.)

Defense Acquisition University *(Defense Dept.), 9820 Belvoir Rd., Fort Belvoir, VA 22060-5565; (703) 805-3360. Fax, (703) 805-2639. Frank J. Anderson Jr., President. Toll-free, (800) 845-7606. Registrar, (703) 805-5142. Web, www.dau.mil*

Academic institution that offers courses to military and civilian personnel who specialize in acquisition and procurement. Conducts research to support and improve management of defense systems acquisition programs.

Defense Dept. (DoD), *Accession Policy, 4000 Defense Pentagon, #2B271 20301-4000; (703) 695-5525. Fax, (703) 614-9272. Curt Gilroy, Director. Web, www.defenselink.mil*

Reviews and develops education policies of the service academies, service schools, graduate and voluntary education programs, education programs for active duty personnel, tuition assistance programs, and officer candidates' training and Reserve Officers Training Corps (ROTC) programs for the Defense Dept. Advises the secretary of defense on education matters.

Defense Dept. (DoD), *Readiness and Training, 4000 Defense Pentagon, #1E537 20301-4000; (703) 695-2618. Fax, (703) 693-7382. Daniel E. Gardner, Director. Web, www.asamra.army.mil/prhome/readiness.html*

Develops, reviews, and analyzes legislation, policies, plans, programs, resource levels, and budgets for the training of military personnel and military units. Develops the substantive-based framework, working collaboratively across the defense, federal, academic, and private sectors, for the global digital knowledge environment. Manages with other government agencies the sustainability and modernization of DoD ranges.

Industrial College of the Armed Forces *(Defense Dept.), Fort Lesley J. McNair, 408 4th Ave. S.W., Bldg. #59 20319-5062; (202) 685-4278. Fax, (202) 685-4339. Rear Adm. Garry E. Hall, Commandant. Administration, (202) 685-4333. Web, www.ndu.edu/ICAF*

Division of National Defense University. Offers professional level courses for senior military officers and senior civilian government officials. Academic program focuses on management of national resources, mobilization, and industrial preparedness.

Marine Corps *(Defense Dept.), Alfred M. Gray Research Center, 2040 Broadway St., Quantico, VA 22134; (703) 784-2240. Fax, (703) 784-4665. Kurt Sanftleben, Director. Library, (703) 784-4411. Archives, (703) 784-4685. Web, www.mcu.usmc.mil/MCRCweb*

Supports the professional, military, educational, and academic needs of the students and faculty of the Marine Corps University. Acts as a central research facility for marines in operational units worldwide. Houses the library and archives of the Marine Corps.

Marine Corps *(Defense Dept.), Training and Education Command, 1019 Elliot Rd., Quantico, VA 22134-5001; (703) 784-3730. Fax, (703) 784-0012. Brig. Gen. Melvin Spiese, Commanding General. Web, www.tecom.usmc.mil*

Military office that develops and implements training and education programs for regular and reserve personnel and units.

National Defense University *(Defense Dept.), Fort Lesley J. McNair, 300 5th Ave. 20319-5066; (202) 685-3938. Fax, (202) 685-3931. Lt. Gen. Frances C. Wilson (USMC), President. Help Desk, (202) 685-3824. Web, www.ndu.edu*

Specialized university sponsored by the Joint Chiefs of Staff to prepare individuals for senior executive duties in the national security establishment. Offers master of science degrees in national resource strategy and national security strategy, as well as nondegree programs and courses.

National War College *(Defense Dept.), Fort Lesley J. McNair, 300 D St. S.W., Bldg. #61 20319-5078; (202) 685-4341. Fax, (202) 685-3993. Maj. Gen. Robert P. Steel (USAF), Commandant. Information, (202) 685-3674. Web, www.ndu.edu/nwc*

Division of National Defense University. Offers professional level courses for senior military officers, senior civilian government officials, and foreign officers. Academic program focuses on the formulation and implementation of national security policy and military strategy.

Navy Dept. *(Defense Dept.), Manpower and Reserve Affairs, 1000 Navy Pentagon, #4E590 20350-1000; (703) 695-4333. Fax, (703) 614-4103. H. C. "Barney" Barnum, Assistant Secretary (Acting). Web, www.donhq.navy.mil/mra*

Civilian office that reviews policies of the U.S. Naval Academy, Navy and Marine Corps service schools, and officer candidates' training and Reserve Officer Training Corps (ROTC) programs. Advises the secretary of the Navy on education matters, including voluntary education programs.

Uniformed Services University of the Health Sciences *(Defense Dept.), 4301 Jones Bridge Rd., Bethesda, MD 20814-4799; (301) 295-3013. Fax, (301) 295-1960. Dr. Charles L. Rice, President. Information, (301) 295-3166. Registrar, (301) 295-3101. Web, www.usuhs.mil*

An accredited four-year medical school under the auspices of the Defense Dept. Awards doctorates and master's degrees in health- and science-related fields. The Graduate School of Nursing awards a master of science and a doctoral degree in nursing.

U.S. Coast Guard (USCG), *(Homeland Security Dept.), Human Resources Directorate (CG-1), 2100 2nd St. S.W., #5410 20593-0001; (202) 475-5000. Fax, (202)*

475-5940. *Rear Adm. Jody Breckenridge, Assistant Commandant.*

Web, www.uscg.mil/hr

Responsible for hiring, recruiting, and training all military and nonmilitary Coast Guard personnel.

U.S. Naval Academy *(Defense Dept.), 121 Blake Rd., Annapolis, MD 21402-5000; (410) 293-1500. Fax, (410) 293-3133. Vice Adm. Jeffrey L. Fowler, Superintendent; Capt. Stephen B. Latta, Dean of Admissions. Visitor information, (410) 263-6933. Candidate guidance, (410) 293-4361. Public Affairs, (410) 293-2291.*

General e-mail, pao@usna.edu

Web, www.usna.edu

Provides undergraduate education for young men and women who have been nominated by members of their state's congressional delegation or, in some cases, the president or vice president of the United States. Graduates receive bachelor of science degrees and are commissioned as either an ensign in the U.S. Navy or a second lieutenant in the U.S. Marine Corps.

►CONGRESS

For a listing of relevant congressional committees and subcommittees, please see page 513 or the Appendix.

►NONGOVERNMENTAL

Assn. of Military Colleges and Schools of the U.S., *3604 Glenbrook Rd., Fairfax, VA 22031-3211; (703) 272-8406. Fax, (703) 280-1082. Rudolph H. Ehrenberg Jr., Executive Director.*

Web, www.amcsus.org

Membership: nonfederal military colleges, junior colleges, and secondary schools that emphasize character development, leadership, and knowledge. Interests include Reserve Officers Training Corps (ROTC). Publishes a newsletter; sponsors an annual meeting and outreach activities.

George and Carol Olmsted Foundation, *201 Park Washington Court, Falls Church, VA 22046; (703) 536-3500. Fax, (703) 536-5020. Larry R. Marsh, President. Toll-free, (877) 656-4527.*

Web, www.olmstedfoundation.org

Administers grants for two years of graduate study overseas, including foreign language study, for selected officers of the armed forces.

Military Order of the World Wars, *435 N. Lee St., Alexandria, VA 22314; (703) 683-4911. Fax, (703) 683-4501. Brig. Gen. Roger C. Bultman, Chief of Staff. Toll-free, (877) 320-3774.*

Web, www.militaryorder.net

Membership: retired and active duty commissioned officers, warrant officers, and flight officers. Presents awards to outstanding Reserve Officers Training Corps (ROTC) cadets; gives awards to Boy Scouts and Girl Scouts; conducts youth leadership conferences.

Navy League of the United States, *2300 Wilson Blvd., #200, Arlington, VA 22201-3308; (703) 528-1775. Fax,*

(703) 528-2333. *Stephen R. Pietropaoli, National Executive Director. Toll-free, (800) 356-5760.*

General e-mail, service@navyleague.org

Web, www.navyleague.org

Sponsors Naval Sea Cadet Corps and Navy League Sea Cadet Corps for young people ages eleven through eighteen years. Graduates are eligible to enter the Navy at advanced pay grades.

Servicemembers Opportunity Colleges, *1307 New York Ave. N.W., 5th Floor 20005-4701; (202) 667-0079. Fax, (202) 667-0622. Katherine Snead, Director. Information, (800) 368-5622.*

General e-mail, socmail@aascu.org

Web, www.soc.aascu.org

Partnership of higher education associations, educational institutions, the Defense Dept., and the military services. Offers credit courses and degree programs to military personnel and their families stationed in the United States and around the world.

MILITARY GRIEVANCES AND DISCIPLINE

►AGENCIES

Air Force Dept. *(Defense Dept.), Air Force Personnel Council, 1535 Command Dr., EE Wing, 3rd Floor, Andrews AFB, MD 20762-7002; (240) 857-5739. Fax, (240) 857-1814. Col. Venetia E. Brown, Director, (240) 857-3138.*

Web, www.af.mil

Military office that administers boards that review appeal cases. Administers the Clemency and Parole Board, Discharge Review Board, Decorations Board, and Personnel Board.

Air Force Dept. *(Defense Dept.), Air Force Review Boards Agency, 1535 Command Dr., #E302, Andrews AFB, MD 20762-7002; (240) 857-3137. Fax, (240) 857-3136. Joe G. Lineberger, Director.*

Web, www.af.mil

Civilian office that responds to complaints from Air Force military and civilian personnel and assists in seeking corrective action.

Air Force Dept. *(Defense Dept.), Complaints Resolution Directorate, 1400 Air Force Pentagon, #4E1081 22209; (703) 588-1531. Fax, (703) 696-2555. Col. John Dowless, Chief.*

Web, www.af.mil

Military office that handles complaints and requests for assistance from civilians and Air Force and other military personnel.

Army Dept. *(Defense Dept.), Army Review Boards Agency, 1901 S. Bell St., 2nd Floor, Arlington, VA 22202-4508; (703) 607-1597. Fax, (703) 607-0542.*

Catherine C. Mitrano, Deputy Assistant Secretary. Information, (703) 602-1714.
Web, http://arba.army.pentagon.mil

Civilian office that administers boards reviewing appeals cases. Administers the Ad Hoc Board, Army Grade Determination Review Board, Army Board for Correction of Military Records, Army Active Duty Board, Disability Rating Review Board, Discharge Review Board, Elimination Review Board, Army Clemency and Parole Board, Physical Disability Review Board, and Physical Disability Appeals Board.

Army Dept. *(Defense Dept.),* **Human Resources Policy Directorate,** *300 Army Pentagon, #2C453 20310-0300; (703) 695-5418. Fax, (703) 695-6988. Maj. Gen. John R. Hawkins III, Director.*
Web, www.armyg1.army.mil/hr/default.asp

Military office that receives complaints from Army military personnel and assists in seeking corrective action.

Defense Dept. (DoD), *Diversity Management and Equal Opportunity,* 4000 Defense Pentagon, #5D641 20301-4000; (703) 571-9321. Fax, (703) 571-9338. Clarence A. Johnson, Director.
Web, www.defenselink.mil/prhome/eo.html

Formulates equal employment opportunity policy for the Defense Dept. Evaluates civil rights complaints from military personnel, including issues of sexual harassment and recruitment.

Defense Dept. (DoD), *Legal Policy,* 4000 Defense Pentagon, #5E604 20301-4000; (703) 697-3387. Fax, (703) 693-6708. Col. Shawn Shumake, Director.
Web, www.defenselink.mil

Coordinates policy in a variety of personnel-related areas.

Defense Dept. (DoD), *Sexual Assault Prevention and Response,* 1401 Wilson Blvd., #402, Arlington, VA 22209; (703) 696-9422. Fax, (703) 696-9437. Kaye H. Whitley, Director. Hotline, (800) 342-9647.
General e-mail, SAPRO@wso.whs.mil
Web, www.sapr.mil

Serves as the single point of accountability for the Defense Dept.'s sexual assault policy. Responsible for improving prevention and ensuring support for victims and accountability of offenders. Publishes an online newsletter.

Marine Corps *(Defense Dept.),* **Inspector General of the Marine Corps,** 2 Navy Annex 20380-1775 (mailing address: Headquarters, U.S. Marine Corps, Code IG, Washington, DC 20380-1775); (703) 614-1533. Fax, (703) 697-6690. Brig. Gen. Kenneth J. Lee, Inspector General.
Web, www.hqmc.usmc.mil/ig/ig.nsf

Military office that investigates complaints from Marine Corps personnel and assists in seeking corrective action.

Navy Dept. *(Defense Dept.),* **Council of Review Boards,** 720 Kennon St. S.E., Bldg. 36, #309, Washington Navy Yard, DC 20374-5023; (202) 685-6408. Fax, (202) 685-6610. Col. Mark D. Franklin, Director.
Web, www.donhq.navy.mil/corb

Military office that administers boards that review appeal cases for the Navy and the Marine Corps. Composed of the Physical Evaluation Board, the Naval Discharge Review Board, the Naval Clemency and Parole Board, the Combat-Related Special Compensation (CRSC) Branch, and the Board for Decorations and Medals.

Navy Dept. *(Defense Dept.),* **Manpower and Reserve Affairs,** 1000 Navy Pentagon, #4E590 20350-1000; (703) 695-4333. Fax, (703) 614-4103. H. C. "Barney" Barnum, Assistant Secretary (Acting).
Web, www.donhq.navy.mil/mra

Civilian office that receives complaints from Navy and Marine Corps military personnel and assists in seeking corrective action.

▶**CONGRESS**

For a listing of relevant congressional committees and subcommittees, please see page 513 or the Appendix.

▶**NONGOVERNMENTAL**

National Institute of Military Justice, 4801 Massachusetts Ave. N.W. 20016; (202) 274-4322. Fax, (202) 274-4226. Eugene R. Fidell, President.
General e-mail, nimj@wcl.american.edu
Web, www.nimj.org

Seeks to advance fair administration of military justice and improve public understanding of the military justice system. Offers assistance in court cases related to military justice law and policy. Monitors legislation and regulations. Does not represent individuals. (Affiliated with the Washington College of Law at American University.)

Servicemembers Legal Defense Network (SLDN), P.O. Box 65301 20035-5301; (202) 328-3244. Fax, (202) 797-1635. Aubrey Sarvis, Executive Director.
General e-mail, sldn@sldn.org
Web, www.sldn.org

Provides legal assistance to individuals affected by the military's policy on gays and lesbians. Monitors legislation and regulations.

Correction of Military Records

▶**AGENCIES**

Air Force Dept. *(Defense Dept.),* **Board for the Correction of Military Records,** 1535 Command Dr., EE Wing, 3rd Floor, Andrews AFB, MD 20762-7002; (240) 857-3502. Fax, (240) 857-9207. Algie Walker, Executive Director.
Web, www.af.mil

Civilian board that reviews appeals for corrections to Air Force personnel records and makes recommendations to the secretary of the Air Force.

Army Dept. *(Defense Dept.)*, **Board for the Correction of Military Records,** *1901 S. Bell St., 2nd Floor, Crystal Mall 4, Arlington, VA 22202-4508; (703) 607-1621. Fax, (703) 602-0935. Conrad V. Meyer, Director.*
Web, http://arba.army.pentagon.mil

Civilian board that reviews appeals for corrections to Army personnel records and makes recommendations to the secretary of the Army.

Defense Dept. (DoD), *Legal Policy, 4000 Defense Pentagon, #5E604 20301-4000; (703) 697-3387. Fax, (703) 693-6708. Col. Shawn Shumake, Director.*
Web, www.defenselink.mil

Coordinates policy for armed services boards charged with correcting military records.

Navy Dept. *(Defense Dept.)*, **Board for Correction of Naval Records,** *2 Navy Annex, #2432 20370-5100; (703) 614-1402. Fax, (703) 614-9857. W. Dean Pfeiffer, Executive Director.*
Web, www.hq.navy.mil/bcnr/bcnr.htm

Civilian board that reviews appeals for corrections to Navy and Marine Corps personnel records and makes recommendations to the secretary of the Navy.

U.S. Coast Guard (USCG), *(Homeland Security Dept.)*, **Board for Correction of Military Records,** *245 Murray Lane, #5126, MS 900 20528; (202) 447-0497. Fax, (202) 447-5694. Rear Adm. Dorothy J. Ulmer, Chair.*
General e-mail, cgbcmr@dhs.gov
Web, www.uscg.mil/legal/BCMR.asp

Civilian board (an adjunct to the U.S. Coast Guard) that reviews appeals for corrections to Coast Guard personnel records and makes recommendations to the general counsel of the Homeland Security Dept.

Legal Proceedings

▶**AGENCIES**

Air Force Dept. *(Defense Dept.)*, **Air Force Personnel Council,** *1535 Command Dr., EE Wing, 3rd Floor, Andrews AFB, MD 20762-7002; (240) 857-5739. Fax, (240) 857-1814. Col. Venetia E. Brown, Director, (240) 857-3138.*
Web, www.af.mil

Military office that administers review boards, including the Clemency and Parole Board, which in turn reviews cases of military prisoners and makes recommendations to the secretary of the Air Force.

Air Force Dept. *(Defense Dept.)*, **Judge Advocate General,** *1420 Air Force Pentagon 20330-1420; (703) 614-5732. Fax, (703) 614-8894. Lt. Gen. Jack L. Rives, Judge Advocate General.*
Web, www.af.mil

Military office that prosecutes and defends Air Force personnel during military legal proceedings. Gives legal advice and assistance to Air Force staff.

Army Dept. *(Defense Dept.)*, **Army Clemency and Parole Board,** *Crystal Mall 4, 1901 S. Bell St., 2nd Floor, Arlington, VA 22202-4508; (703) 607-1504. Fax, (703) 607-2047. James E. Vick, Chair.*
Web, www.army.mil

Civilian and military board that reviews cases of military prisoners and makes recommendations to the secretary of the Army; reviews suspension of less-than-honorable discharges and restoration of prisoners to active duty or parole.

Army Dept. *(Defense Dept.)*, **Judge Advocate General,** *2200 Army Pentagon, #2B514 20310-2200; (703) 697-5151. Fax, (703) 693-0600. Lt. Gen. Scott C. Black, Judge Advocate General.*
Web, www.jagcnet.army.mil

Military policy office for the field offices that prosecute and defend Army personnel during military legal proceedings. Serves as an administrative office for military appeals court, which hears legal proceedings involving Army personnel.

Defense Dept. (DoD), *Court of Appeals for the Armed Forces, 450 E St. N.W. 20442-0001; (202) 761-1448. Fax, (202) 761-4672. William DeCicco, Clerk of the Court. Library, (202) 761-1466.*
Web, www.armfor.uscourts.gov

Serves as the appellate court for cases involving dishonorable or bad conduct discharges, confinement of a year or more, and the death penalty, and for cases certified to the court by the judge advocate general of an armed service. Less serious cases are reviewed by the individual armed services. Library open to the public.

Marine Corps *(Defense Dept.)*, **Judge Advocate,** *3000 Marine Corps Pentagon, #4D558 20350-3000; (703) 614-2737. Fax, (703) 614-5775. Brig. Gen. James C. Walker, Staff Judge Advocate.*
Web, www.hqmc.usmc.mil

Military office that administers legal proceedings involving Marine Corps personnel.

Navy Dept. *(Defense Dept.)*, **Council of Review Boards,** *720 Kennon St. S.E., Bldg. 36, #309, Washington Navy Yard, DC 20374-5023; (202) 685-6408. Fax, (202) 685-6610. Col. Mark D. Franklin, Director.*
Web, www.donhq.navy.mil/corb

Includes the Naval Clemency Board, which reviews cases of Navy and Marine Corps prisoners; the Naval Discharge Review Board, which considers former service members' less-than-honorable discharge for potential upgrade; the Physical Evaluation Board, which makes determinations about physical fitness for continuation of military service; and the Combat-Related Special Compensation Board, which makes determinations about combat-related conditions and appropriate compensation. All boards make recommendations to the secretary of the Navy.

Navy Dept. *(Defense Dept.)*, **Judge Advocate General,** *1322 Patterson Ave. S.E., #3000, Washington Navy Yard,*

DC 20374-5066; (703) 614-7420. Fax, (703) 697-4610. Vice Adm. Bruce E. MacDonald, Judge Advocate General. Web, www.jag.navy.mil

Military office that administers the Judge Advocate General's Corps, which conducts legal proceedings involving Navy and Marine Corps personnel.

Military Police and Corrections

►AGENCIES

Army Dept. *(Defense Dept.), Provost Marshal General: Policy Division,* 2800 Army Pentagon, DAPM-OPS, #MF748 20310-2800; (703) 693-9478. Fax, (703) 693-6580. Col. Charles Tennison, Chief. Web, www.army.mil

Develops policies and supports military police and corrections programs in all branches of the U.S. military. Operates the Military Police Management Information System (MPMIS), which automates incident reporting and tracks information on facilities, staff, and inmates, including enemy prisoners of war.

Defense Dept. (DoD), *Legal Policy,* 4000 Defense Pentagon, #5E604 20301-4000; (703) 697-3387. Fax, (703) 693-6708. Col. Shawn Shumake, Director. Web, www.defenselink.mil

Coordinates and reviews Defense Dept. policies and programs relating to deserters.

Marine Corps *(Defense Dept.), Corrections,* CMC HQUSMC PSL, 2 Navy Annex, #3316 20380-1775; (703) 614-1480. Fax, (703) 614-3499. Abel Galaviz, Chief Warrant Officer. Web, http://usmc.mil

Military office that develops Marine Corps policies and responds to inquiries relating to deserters. Oversees Marine Corps brigs (correctional facilities) for prisoners and detainees in the United States and overseas.

MILITARY HISTORY AND HONORS

►AGENCIES

Air Force Dept. *(Defense Dept.), Air Force History, Programs, and Policy,* HQ USAF/HO, 1190 Air Force Pentagon, #5E823 20330-1190; (703) 697-5600. Fax, (703) 693-3496. Clarence R. "Dick" Anderegg, Director. Reference, (202) 404-2264. Web, www.af.mil

Publishes histories, studies, monographs, and reference works; directs worldwide Air Force History and Museums Program and provides guidance to the Air Force Historical Research Agency at Maxwell Air Force Base in Alabama; supports Air Force Air Staff agencies and responds to inquiries from the public and the U.S. government.

Army Dept. *(Defense Dept.), Institute of Heraldry,* 9325 Gunston Rd., Bldg. 1466, #S112, Fort Belvoir, VA 22060-5579; (703) 806-4970. Fax, (703) 806-4964. Charles Mugno, Director. Information, (703) 806-4971. General e-mail, TIOHWebmaster@conus.army.mil Web, www.tioh.hqda.pentagon.mil

Furnishes heraldic services to the armed forces and other U.S. government agencies, including the Executive Office of the President. Responsible for research, design, development, and standardization of official symbolic items, including seals, decorations, medals, insignias, badges, flags, and other items awarded to or authorized for official wear or display by government personnel and agencies. Limited research and information services on these items are provided to the general public.

Army Dept. *(Defense Dept.), U.S. Army Center of Military History,* Fort Lesley J. McNair, 103 3rd Ave., Bldg. 35 20319-5058; (202) 685-2706. Fax, (202) 685-4570. Jeffrey C. Clarke, Director. Library, (202) 685-4042. Web, www.history.army.mil

Publishes the official history of the Army. Provides information on Army history; coordinates Army museum system and art program. Works with Army school system to ensure that history is included in curriculum. Sponsors professional appointments, fellowships, and awards. Collections and library facilities open to the public by appointment.

Defense Dept. (DoD), *Historical Office,* 1777 N. Kent St., #5000, Arlington, VA 22209; (703) 588-7890. Fax, (703) 588-7572. Stuart Rochester, Chief Historian. Web, www.odam.osd.mil/hist/index.htm

Collects, compiles, and publishes documents and data on the history of the Defense Dept. and the office of the secretary; coordinates historical activities of the Defense Dept. and prepares special studies at the request of the secretary.

Defense Dept. (DoD), *Joint History Office,* 9999 Defense Pentagon, #1A466 20318-9999; (703) 695-2114. Fax, (703) 614-6243. Brig. Gen. David A. Armstrong (USA, Ret.), Director, (703) 695-2137. General e-mail, David.Armstrong@js.pentagon.mil Web, www.defenselink.mil

Provides historical support services to the chair of the Joint Chiefs of Staff and the Joint Staff, including research; writes the official history of the Joint Chiefs. Supervises field programs encompassing nine Unified Commands and all deployed Joint Task Forces.

Marine Corps *(Defense Dept.), History Division,* Marine Corps University, 3078 Moreell Ave., Quantico, VA 22134; (703) 432-4877. Fax, (703) 432-5054. Charles P. Neimeyer, Director. Reference, (703) 432-4874. Web, www.history.usmc.mil

Writes official histories of the corps for government agencies and the public; answers inquiries about Marine Corps history.

National Archives and Records Administration (NARA), *Reference Services, 8601 Adelphi Rd., #2600, College Park, MD 20740-6001; (301) 837-3480. Fax, (301) 837-1919. Steven Tilley, Director, (301) 837-3059. Web, www.archives.gov/research/order/textual-records-dc.html*

Contains Army records from the Revolutionary War to the Vietnam War, Navy records from the Revolutionary War to the Korean War, and Air Force records from 1947 to 1954. Handles records captured from enemy powers at the end of World War II and a small collection of records captured from the Vietnamese. Conducts research in response to specific inquiries; makes records available for reproduction or examination in research room.

National Museum of American History *(Smithsonian Institution), Division of Military History and Diplomacy, 14th St. and Constitution Ave. N.W., NMAH-4032, MRC 620 20560-0620; (202) 633-3950. Jennifer Locke Jones, Chair. Web, http://americanhistory.si.edu*

Maintains collections relating to the history of the U.S. armed forces, U.S. military technology, and the American flag; includes manuscripts, documents, correspondence, uniforms, ordnance material of European and American origin, and other personal memorabilia of armed forces personnel of all ranks. Research areas are open by appointment.

National Museum of Health and Medicine *(Defense Dept.), 6900 Georgia Ave. N.W., Bldg. 54 20307 (mailing address: AFIP P.O. Box 59685, Washington, DC 20012-0685); (202) 782-2200. Fax, (202) 782-3573. Dr. Adrianne Noe, Director. General e-mail, nmhminfo@afip.osd.mil Web, http://nmhm.washingtondc.museum*

Maintains exhibits related to pathology and the history of medicine, particularly military medicine during the Civil War. Open to the public. Study collection available for scholars by appointment.

National Park Service (NPS), *(Interior Dept.), 1849 C St. N.W., #3115 20240; (202) 208-4621. Fax, (202) 208-7889. Dan Wenk, Director (Acting). Press, (202) 208-6843. Washington area activities, (202) 619-7275 (recording). General e-mail, asknps@nps.gov Web, www.nps.gov*

Administers national parks, monuments, historic sites, and recreation areas. Responsible for national battlefields, selected historic forts, and other sites associated with U.S. military history.

Naval Historical Center, *Navy Art Collection, 822 Sicard St. S.E. 20374 (mailing address: 805 Kidder Breese St. S.E., Washington Navy Yard, DC 20374); (202) 433-3815. Fax, (202) 433-5635. Gale Munro, Director. Web, www.history.navy.mil*

Holdings include more than 18,000 paintings, prints, drawings, and sculptures. Artworks depict naval ships, personnel, and action from all eras of U.S. naval history, especially the eras of World War II, the Korean War, and Desert Shield/Storm. Open to the public. Visitors without Defense Dept. or military identification must call in advance. Photo identification required.

Naval History and Heritage *(Navy Dept.), 805 Kidder Breese St. S.E., Washington Navy Yard, DC 20374-5060; (202) 433-2210. Fax, (202) 433-3593. Rear Adm. Jay DeLoach (Ret.), Director. Library, (202) 433-4132. Museum, (202) 433-4882. Art Gallery, (202) 433-3815. Archives, (202) 433-3224. Web, www.history.navy.mil*

Produces publications on naval history. Maintains historical files on Navy ships, operations, shore installations, and aviation. Collects Navy art, artifacts, and photographs. Library, archives, museum, and gallery are open to the public. (Formerly the Naval Historical Center.)

The Old Guard Museum, *Fort Myer, VA 22211-1199 (mailing address: 3rd Infantry, The Old Guard, ATTN: ANOG-OGM, 201 Jackson St., Fort Myer, VA 22211-1199); (703) 696-6670. Fax, (703) 696-4256. Kirk Heflin, Director. Web, www.army.mil/oldguard*

Preserves the artifacts and history of the 3rd U.S. Infantry Regiment (The Old Guard), the Army's official ceremonial unit and escort to the president. (Museum is moving and will reopen in 2010. Archives are available by appointment.)

U.S. Coast Guard (USCG), *(Homeland Security Dept.), Historian, 2100 2nd St. S.W., #B717 20593-0001; (202) 372-4650. Fax, (202) 372-4984. Robert M. Browning, Chief Historian. Web, www.uscg.mil/hq/g-cp/history/collect.html*

Collects and maintains Coast Guard historical materials, including service artifacts, documents, photographs, and books. Archives are available to the public by appointment only.

U.S. Navy Museum (Naval Historical Center), *Bldg. 76, 805 Kidder Breese St. S.E., Washington Navy Yard 20374-5060; (202) 433-4882. Fax, (202) 433-8200. Karen Hill, Director, Education and Public Programs; Kim Nielsen, Director of Museum. Web, www.history.navy.mil*

Collects, preserves, displays, and interprets historic naval artifacts and artwork. Presents a complete overview of U.S. naval history. Visitors without Defense Dept. or military identification must call in advance. Photo identification required.

▶**NONGOVERNMENTAL**

Aerospace Education Foundation, *1501 Lee Hwy., #400, Arlington, VA 22209; (703) 247-5800. Fax, (703) 247-5853. Gen. Michael M. Dunn, Executive Director. Information, (800) 727-3337.*

General e-mail, aefstaff@aef.org

Web, www.afa.org

Promotes knowledge and appreciation of U.S. civilian and military aerospace development and history. (Affiliated with the Air Force Assn.)

Air Force Historical Foundation, *1535 Command Dr., #A-122, Andrews AFB, MD 20762-7002 (mailing address: P.O. Box 790, Clinton, MD 20735-0790); (301) 736-1959. Fax, (301) 981-3574. Col. Charles Thomas "Tom" Bradley (USAF, Ret.), Executive Director.*

General e-mail, execdir@afhistoricalfoundation.org

Web, www.afhistoricalfoundation.org

Membership: individuals interested in the history of the U.S. Air Force and U.S. air power. Bestows awards on Air Force Academy and Air War College students and to other active duty personnel. Funds research and publishes books on aviation and Air Force history.

Council on America's Military Past—U.S.A., *11125 Stonebrook Pl., Manassas, VA 20112; (703) 912-6124. Mark Magnussen, Editor. Information, (800) 398-4693.*

General e-mail, mark_magnussen@hotmail.com

Web, www.campjamp.org

Membership: historians, archaeologists, curators, writers, and others interested in military history and preservation of historic military sites, establishments, ships, and aircraft.

Marine Corps Heritage Foundation, *3800 Fettler Park Dr., #104, Dumfries, VA 22025; (703) 640-7965. Fax, (703) 640-9546. Lt. Gen. G. Ron Christmas (USMC, Ret.), President. Toll-free, (800) 397-7585.*

General e-mail, info@marineheritage.org

Web, www.marineheritage.org

Preserves and promotes Marine Corps history through education, awards, and publications. Offers funding for the study of Marine Corps history. Funds the ongoing development of the National Museum of the Marine Corps.

National Guard Educational Foundation, *1 Massachusetts Ave. N.W. 20001; (202) 408-5887. Fax, (202) 682-9358. Lt. Jonathan Bernstein, Director. Library, (202) 408-5890. Toll-free (888) 226-4287.*

General e-mail, ngef@ngef.org

Web, www.ngef.org

Promotes public awareness of the National Guard by providing information about its history and traditions. Museum and library open to the public.

National Museum of American Jewish Military History, *1811 R St. N.W. 20009; (202) 265-6280. Fax, (202) 234-5662. Col. Herb Rosenbleeth, Executive Director.*

Web, www.nmajmh.org

Collects, preserves, and displays memorabilia of Jewish men and women in the military; conducts research; sponsors seminars; provides information on the history of Jewish participation in the U.S. armed forces.

Naval Historical Foundation, *1306 Dahlgren Ave. S.E., Washington Navy Yard, DC 20374-5055; (202) 678-4333. Fax, (202) 889-3565. Vice Adm. Robert F. Dunn (Ret.), President.*

Web, www.navyhistory.org

Collects private documents and artifacts relating to naval history; maintains collection on deposit with the Library of Congress for public reference; conducts oral history and heritage speakers programs; raises funds to support the Navy Museum and historical programs.

Cemeteries and Memorials

▶**AGENCIES**

American Battle Monuments Commission, *Courthouse Plaza 2, 2300 Clarendon Blvd., #500, Arlington, VA 22201-3367; (703) 696-6900. Fax, (703) 696-6666. Brig. Gen. John W. Nicholson (USA, Ret.), Secretary.*

General e-mail, info@abmc.gov

Web, www.abmc.gov

Maintains military cemeteries and memorials on foreign soil and certain memorials in the United States; provides next of kin with grave site and related information. Manages twenty-four overseas military cemeteries.

Army Dept. *(Defense Dept.), Arlington National Cemetery: Interment Services, Arlington, VA 22211; (703) 607-8585. Fax, (703) 607-8583. Vicki Tanner, Chief. Visitor Services, (703) 607-8000. Eligibility recorded information, (703) 607-8000.*

Web, www.arlingtoncemetery.org

Arranges interment services and provides eligibility information for burials at Arlington National Cemetery.

Veterans Affairs Dept. (VA), *National Cemetery Administration, 810 Vermont Ave. N.W., #400 20420; (202) 273-5146. Fax, (202) 273-6709. Steve Muro, Under Secretary for Memorial Affairs (Acting). Information on burial eligibility, (800) 827-1000.*

Web, www.cem.va.gov

Administers VA national cemeteries; furnishes markers and headstones for deceased veterans; administers state grants to establish, expand, and improve veterans' cemeteries. Provides presidential memorial certificates to next of kin.

▶**CONGRESS**

For a listing of relevant congressional committees and subcommittees, please see page 513 of the Appendix.

▶**NONGOVERNMENTAL**

Air Force Memorial Foundation, *1501 Lee Hwy., Arlington, VA 22209-1109; (703) 979-0674. Fax, (703) 979-0556. Lt. Gen. Michael M. Dunn (USAF Ret.), President; Col. Peter Lindquist, Managing Director.*

Web, www.airforcememorial.org

Supervises the design and construction of an Air Force memorial to honor the achievements of men and women who have served in the U.S. Air Force and its predecessors, such as the Army Air Forces.

U.S. Navy Memorial Foundation, *701 Pennsylvania Ave. N.W., #123 20004-2608; (202) 737-2300. Fax, (202) 737-2308. Rear Adm. Richard A. Buchanan (USN, Ret.), President.*
Web, www.navymemorial.org

Educational foundation authorized by Congress. Focuses on U.S. naval history; built and supports the national Navy memorial to honor those who serve or have served in the naval services.

Women in Military Service for America Memorial Foundation, *200 N. Glebe Rd., #400, Arlington, VA 22203 (mailing address: Dept. 560, Washington, DC 20042-0560); (703) 533-1155. Fax, (703) 931-4208. Brig. Gen. Wilma L. Vaught (USAF, Ret.), President. Information, (800) 222-2294.*
General e-mail, hq@womensmemorial.org
Web, www.womensmemorial.org

Authorized by Congress to create, support, and build the national memorial to honor women who serve or have served in the U.S. armed forces from the Revolutionary War to the present. Mailing address is for donations.

Ceremonies, Military Bands

▶AGENCIES

Air Force Dept. *(Defense Dept.), Air Force Bands, 1690 Air Force Pentagon, #5C279 20330; (703) 695-0019. Fax, (703) 693-9601. Col. Dennis Layendecker, Chief of Music.*
Web, www.bands.af.mil

Disseminates information to the public regarding various Air Force bands, including their schedules and performances. Oversees policy, training, and personnel assignments for Air Force bands.

Army Dept. *(Defense Dept.), Army Field Band, 4214 Field Band Dr., Fort Meade, MD 20755-5330; (301) 677-6231. Fax, (301) 677-7980. Col. Thomas H. Palmatier, Commander.*
General e-mail, field.band@usarmy.mil
Web, www.army.mil/fieldband

Supports the Army by providing musical services for official military ceremonies and community events. Sponsors vocal and instrumental clinics for high school and college students.

Army Dept. *(Defense Dept.), Ceremonies and Special Events, Fort Lesley J. McNair, 103 3rd Ave., Bldg. 42 20319-5058; (202) 685-2983. Fax, (202) 685-3379. Phil Fowler, Director, (202) 685-2980; Gary S. Davis, Ceremonies Chief; Tina Peck, Special Events Coordinator.*
Web, www.jfhqncr.northcom.mil

Coordinates and schedules public ceremonies and special events, including appearances of all armed forces bands and honor guards.

Army Dept. *(Defense Dept.), The U.S. Army Band, Attn: TUSAB, 400 McNair Rd., Fort Myer, VA 22211-1306; (703) 696-3718. Fax, (703) 696-0279. Col. Thomas Rotondi Jr., Commander.*
Web, www.usarmyband.com

Supports the Army by providing musical services for official military ceremonies and community events.

Defense Dept. (DoD), *Community Relations and Public Liaison, 1400 Defense Pentagon, 2D982 20301-1400; (703) 695-2113. Fax, (703) 697-2577. Roxie Merritt, Director. Toll-free, (800) 342-9647.*
Web, www.americasupportsyou.mil

Coordinates public outreach events of the Office of the Secretary of Defense and coordinates its activities with the Joint Staff. Coordinates military band color guard requests. Administers America Supports You, a coalition of more than 250 nonprofit groups that support troops and their families. Also administers Military OneSource, a 24/7 toll-free information and referral telephone service for matters relating to education, financial aid, relocation, housing, child care, counseling, and other employee concerns. Military OneSource is available worldwide to military personnel and their families. Toll-free, (800) 342-9647; international, (800) 3429-6477; international collect, (484) 530-5908; www.militaryonesource.com.

Marine Corps *(Defense Dept.), Marine Band, Marine Barracks Annex, 600 Virginia Ave. S.E. 20003; (202) 433-5809. Fax, (202) 433-4752. Col. Michael J. Colburn, Director. Concert information line, (202) 433-4011.*
Web, www.marineband.usmc.mil

Supports the Marine Corps by providing musical services for official military ceremonies and community events.

Navy Dept. *(Defense Dept.), Navy Band, 617 Warrington Ave. S.E., Washington Navy Yard, DC 20374-5054; (202) 433-3676. Fax, (202) 433-4108. Cmdr. George N. Thompson, Commanding Officer. Performance hotline, (202) 433-2525.*
Web, www.navyband.navy.mil

Supports the Navy by providing musical services for official military ceremonies and community events.

U.S. Naval Academy *(Defense Dept.), Band, 101 Buchanan Rd., Annapolis, MD 21402-1258; (410) 293-3282. Fax, (410) 293-2116. Lt. Cmdr. Brian Walden, Director. Concert information, (410) 293-0263.*
Web, www.usna.edu/USNABand

The Navy's oldest continuing musical organization. Supports the Navy by providing musical services for official military ceremonies and community events.

U.S. Naval Academy *(Defense Dept.), Drum and Bugle Corps, U.S. Naval Academy, Alumni Hall, 675 Decatur*

Rd., Annapolis, MD 21402-5086; (410) 293-3602. Fax, (410) 293-4508. Jeff Weir, Corps Director.

General e-mail, weir@usna.edu

Web, www.usna.edu/USNADB

The oldest drum and bugle corps in the United States. Plays for Brigade of Midshipmen at sporting events, pep rallies, parades, and daily formations. Supports the Navy by providing musical services for official military ceremonies and community events.

RESERVES AND NATIONAL GUARD

▶AGENCIES

Air Force Dept. *(Defense Dept.)*, **Air Force Reserve**, *1150 Air Force Pentagon, #4D762 20330-1150; (703) 695-9225. Fax, (703) 695-8959. Lt. Gen. Charles E. Stenner Jr., Chief.*

Military office that coordinates and directs Air Force Reserve matters (excluding the Air National Guard).

Air Force Dept. *(Defense Dept.)*, **Reserve Affairs**, *1660 Air Force Pentagon, #5D742 20330-1660; (703) 697-6375. Fax, (703) 695-2701. Ronald Winter, Deputy Assistant Secretary (Acting).*
Web, www.af.mil

Civilian office that reviews and monitors Air Force Reserve and Air National Guard.

Army Dept. *(Defense Dept.)*, **Army Reserve**, *2400 Army Pentagon, #2B548 20310-2400; (703) 601-0841. Fax, (703) 697-1891. Lt. Gen. Jack C. Stultz, Chief.*
Web, www.armyreserve.army.mil/arweb/contactinfo

Military office that coordinates and directs Army Reserve matters (excluding the Army National Guard).

Army Dept. *(Defense Dept.)*, **Reserve Affairs**, *111 Army Pentagon, #2E460 20310-0111; (703) 693-3783. Fax, (703) 693-3783. Danny Pummill, Deputy Assistant Secretary (Acting).*
Web, www.asamra.army.pentagon.mil

Oversees training, military preparedness, and mobilization for all active and reserve members of the Army.

Defense Dept. (DoD), **Reserve Affairs**, *1500 Defense Pentagon, #2E556 20301-1500; (703) 697-6631. Fax, (703) 697-1682. David McGinnis, Assistant Secretary (Acting).*
Web, www.defenselink.mil

Civilian office that addresses national guard and reserve component issues.

Marine Corps *(Defense Dept.)*, **Reserve Affairs**, *3280 Russell Rd., Quantico, VA 22134-5103; (703) 784-9102. Fax, (703) 784-9805. Brig. Gen. James M. Lariviere, Director.*
Web, www.usmc.mil

Military office that coordinates and directs Marine Corps Reserve matters.

National Guard Bureau *(Defense Dept.)*, *1411 Jefferson Davis Hwy., Arlington, VA 22202-3231; (703) 614-3087. Fax, (703) 614-0274. Gen. Craig McKinley, Chief.*
Web, www.ngb.army.mil

Military office that oversees and coordinates activities of the Air National Guard and Army National Guard.

National Guard Bureau *(Defense Dept.)*, **Air National Guard**, *NGB/CF, 1411 Jefferson Davis Hwy., Arlington, VA 22202-3231; (703) 614-8033. Fax, (703) 692-9056. Lt. Gen. Harry M. "Bud" Wyatt III, Director.*
Web, www.ang.af.mil

Military office that coordinates and directs Air National Guard matters.

National Guard Bureau *(Defense Dept.)*, **Army National Guard**, *111 S. George Mason Dr., Arlington, VA 22204; (703) 607-7000. Fax, (703) 607-7088. Lt. Gen. Clyde A. Vaughn, Director, (703) 607-7003.*
Web, http://ng.army.mil

Military office that coordinates and directs Army National Guard matters.

National Guard Bureau *(Defense Dept.)*, **Chaplain Services**, *1411 Jefferson Davis Hwy., #9500, Arlington, VA 22202-3231; (703) 607-5229. Fax, (703) 607-5295. Col. John B. Ellington Jr., Chief Chaplain. Public Affairs, (703) 607-2584.*
General e-mail, chaplain@ngb.ang.af.mil
Web, www.ngb.army.mil/jointstaff/ss/hc/default.aspx

Represents the Chief National Guard Bureau on all aspects of the chaplains' mission. Directs and oversees the activities and policies of the National Guard Chaplain Services. Oversees chaplains and religious services within the National Guard; maintains liaison with religious denominations.

Navy Dept. *(Defense Dept.)*, **Navy Reserve**, *2000 Navy Pentagon, CNO-N095, #4E426 20350-2000; (703) 693-5758. Fax, (703) 693-5760. Vice Adm. Dirk Debbink, Chief of Navy Reserve.*
Web, www.navy.mil

Military office that coordinates and directs Navy Reserve matters.

Navy Dept. *(Defense Dept.)*, **Reserve Affairs**, *1000 Navy Pentagon, #4D548 20350-1000; (703) 614-1327. Fax, (703) 693-4959. H. C. "Barney" Barnum, Assistant Secretary (Acting).*
Web, www.navy.mil

Civilian office that reviews Navy and Marine Corps Reserve policies.

U.S. Coast Guard (USCG), *(Homeland Security Dept.)*, **Reserve and Training**, *1900 Half St. S.W., #JR08-1139 20593-0001; (202) 475-5422. Fax, (202) 475-5940. Rear Adm. Daniel R. May, Director.*
Web, www.uscg.mil/hq/cg1/cg13

Oversees and is responsible for training all U.S. Coast Guard reserve and active duty forces.

►**NONGOVERNMENTAL**

Assn. of Civilian Technicians, *12620 Lake Ridge Dr.,*
Lake Ridge, VA 22192-2354; (703) 494-4845. Fax, (703)
494-0961. Terry W. Garnett, President.
Web, www.actnat.com

Membership: federal civil service employees of the
National Guard. Represents members before federal agencies
and Congress.

**Enlisted Assn. of the National Guard of the United
States,** *3133 Mt. Vernon Ave., Alexandria,*
VA 22305-2640; (703) 519-3846. Fax, (703) 519-3849.
Michael P. Cline, Executive Director. Information,
(800) 234-3264.
General e-mail, eangus@eangus.org
Web, www.memberconnections.com/eangus

Membership: active duty and retired enlisted members and veterans of the National Guard. Promotes a
strong national defense and National Guard. Sponsors
scholarships, conducts seminars, and provides information concerning members and their families.

National Guard Assn. of the United States,
1 Massachusetts Ave. N.W. 20001-1431; (202) 789-0031.
Fax, (202) 682-9358. Brig. Gen. Stephen M. Koper (Ret.),
President.
General e-mail, ngaus@ngaus.org
Web, www.ngaus.org

Membership: active duty and retired officers of the
National Guard. Works to promote a strong national
defense and to maintain a strong, ready National Guard.

Naval Reserve Assn., *1619 King St., Alexandria, VA*
22314-2793; (703) 548-5800. Fax, (703) 683-3647. Rear
Adm. Casey Coane, Executive Director. Toll-free, (866)
672-4968.
Web, www.navy-reserve.org

Membership: active duty, inactive, and retired Navy
and Navy Reserve officers and their families. Supports
and promotes U.S. military and naval policies, particularly the interests of the Navy and Navy Reserve. Offers
education programs for naval reservists and potential
naval commissioned officers and financial assistance for
education of family members. Provides the public with
information on national security issues. Assists members
with Navy Reserve careers, military retirement, and veterans' benefits.

Reserve Officers Assn. of the United States,
1 Constitution Ave. N.E. 20002-5618; (202) 479-2200.
Fax, (202) 547-1641. Dennis M. McCarthy
(USMC, Ret.), Executive Director. Information,
(800) 809-9448.
Web, www.roa.org

Membership: active duty and inactive commissioned
officers of all uniformed services. Supports continuation
of a reserve force to enhance national security.

VETERANS

►**AGENCIES**

Armed Forces Retirement Home—Washington, *3700*
N. Capitol St. N.W. 20011-8400; (202) 730-3556. Fax,
(202) 730-3492. David Watkins, Director. Toll-free, (800)
422-9988.
General e-mail, publicaffairs@afrh.gov
Web, www.afrh.gov

Gives domiciliary and medical care to retired members of the armed services or career service personnel
unable to earn a livelihood. Formerly known as U.S.
Soldiers' and Airmen's Home. (Armed Forces Retirement
Home in Gulfport, Miss., is being rebuilt and will reopen
in 2010.)

Center for Minority Veterans *(Veterans Affairs Dept.),*
810 Vermont Ave. N.W. 20420; (202) 461-6191. Fax, (202)
273-7092. Lucretia M. McClenney, Director.
Web, www1.va.gov/centerforminorityveterans

Advises the secretary on adoption and implementation of policies and programs affecting minority veterans,
specifically Pacific Islander, Asian American, African
American, Hispanic/Latino, and Native American, including American Indian, Alaska Native, and Native Hawaiian,
veterans.

Center for Women Veterans *(Veterans Affairs Dept.),*
810 Vermont Ave. N.W., #435, MC-00W 20420; (202)
461-6193. Fax, (202) 273-7092. Irene Trowell-Harris,
Director.
Web, www1.va.gov/womenvet

Advises the secretary and promotes research on matters related to women veterans; seeks to ensure that
women veterans receive benefits and services on par with
those of male veterans.

Veterans Affairs Dept. (VA), *810 Vermont Ave. N.W.,*
MC-00 20420; (202) 461-4800. Fax, (202) 495-5463. Gen.
Eric K. Shinseki, Secretary; W. Scott Gould, Deputy
Secretary. Press, (202) 461-7500. Locator, (202) 273-5400.
Web, www.va.gov

Administers programs benefiting veterans, including disability compensation, pensions, education, home
loans, insurance, vocational rehabilitation, medical care
at veterans' hospitals and outpatient facilities, and burial
benefits.

Veterans Affairs Dept. (VA), *National Cemetery*
Administration, *810 Vermont Ave. N.W., #400 20420;*
(202) 273-5146. Fax, (202) 273-6709. Steve Muro, Under
Secretary for Memorial Affairs (Acting). Information on
burial eligibility, (800) 827-1000.
Web, www.cem.va.gov

Administers VA national cemeteries; furnishes markers and headstones for deceased veterans; administers

Veterans Affairs Department

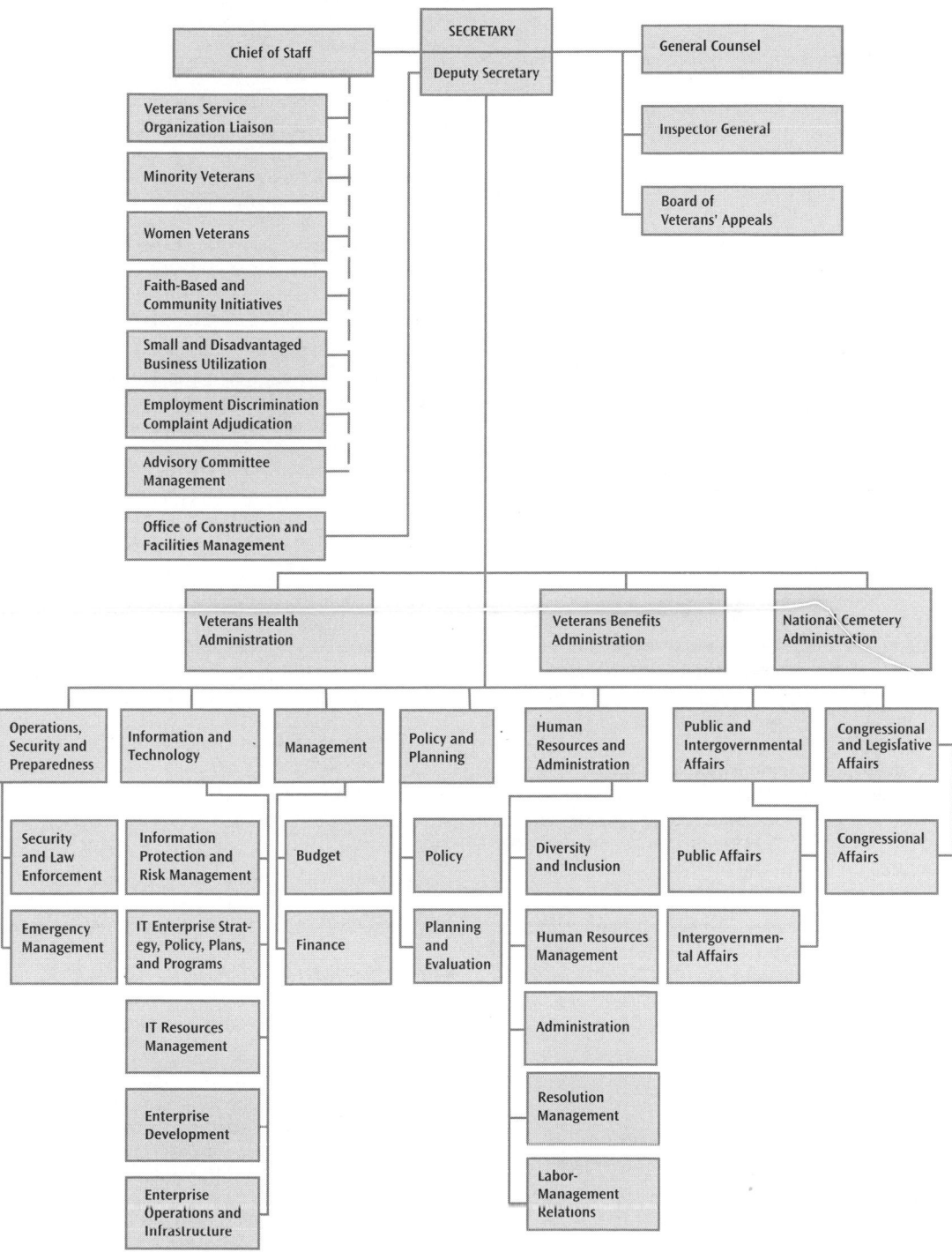

Denotes offices for which Chief of Staff coordinates staff actions.

state grants to establish, expand, and improve veterans' cemeteries. Provides presidential memorial certificates to next of kin.

Veterans Affairs Dept. (VA), *Policy and Planning,* 810 Vermont Ave. N.W., #300, MS 008 20420; (202) 461-5800. Fax, (202) 273-5993. Karen W. Pane, Assistant Secretary (Acting).
Web, www.va.gov

Serves as the single, departmentwide repository, clearinghouse, and publication source for veterans' demographic and statistical information. Manages policy and planning processes; supplies policymakers with analytical reports on improving services for veterans and their families.

Veterans Benefits Administration (VBA), *(Veterans Affairs Dept.),* 1800 G St. N.W. 20223 (mailing address: 810 Vermont Ave. N.W., #520, Washington, DC 20420); (202) 461-9301. Fax, (202) 275-3591. Patrick W. Dunne, Under Secretary. Toll-free insurance hotline, (800) 669-8477.
Web, www.vba.va.gov

Administers nonmedical benefits programs for veterans and their dependents and survivors. Benefits include veterans' compensation and pensions, survivors' benefits, education and rehabilitation assistance, home loan benefits, insurance coverage, and burials. (Directs benefits delivery nationwide through regional offices and veterans' insurance offices in Philadelphia and St. Paul.)

Veterans Benefits Administration (VBA), *(Veterans Affairs Dept.), Compensation and Pension Service,* 810 Vermont Ave. N.W., #645, MS 21 20420; (202) 461-9700. Fax, (202) 275-5661. Brad Mayes, Director. Toll-free, (800) 827-1000.
Web, www.vba.va.gov/bln/21/index.htm

Administers disability payments; handles claims for burial and plot allowances by veterans' survivors. Provides information on and assistance with benefits legislated by Congress for veterans of active military, naval, or air service.

▶CONGRESS

For a listing of relevant congressional committees and subcommittees, please see page 513 or the Appendix.

Government Accountability Office (GAO), *Education, Workforce, and Income Security,* 441 G St. N.W., #5928 20548; (202) 512-7215. Cynthia M. Fagnoni, Managing Director.
Web, www.gao.gov

Independent, nonpartisan agency in the legislative branch that audits, analyzes, and evaluates Veterans Affairs Dept. programs; makes reports available to the public. (Formerly the General Accounting Office.)

▶NONGOVERNMENTAL

American Legion, 1608 K St. N.W. 20006; (202) 861-2700. Fax, (202) 861-2786. John F. Sommer Jr., Executive Director.
Web, www.legion.org

Membership: honorably discharged veterans who served on active duty during periods of declared military conflict. Chartered by Congress to assist veterans with claims for benefits; offers a large array of programs and services for veterans and their families.

American Red Cross, *Service to the Armed Forces,* 2025 E St. N.W., 2nd Floor 20006; (202) 303-6156. Fax, (202) 303-0216. Sherri L. Brown, Vice President, (202) 303-6512. Call Center (24/7), (202) 303-6156.
Web, www.redcross.org

Assists veterans and their dependents with claims for benefits on a limited basis; provides emergency services for active duty armed forces personnel and their families.

American Veterans of World War II, Korea, and Vietnam (AMVETS), 4647 Forbes Blvd., Lanham, MD 20706-4380; (301) 459-9600. Fax, (301) 459-7924. James B. "Jim" King, Executive Director. Toll-free, (877) 726-8387.
Web, www.amvets.org

Membership: those who served honorably in the military after September 15, 1940. Helps members obtain benefits; participates in community programs; operates a volunteer service that donates time to hospitalized veterans. Monitors legislation and regulations.

Blinded Veterans Assn., 477 H St. N.W. 20001-2694; (202) 371-8880. Fax, (202) 371-8258. Thomas H. Miller, Executive Director. Toll-free, (800) 669-7079.
General e-mail, bva@bva.org
Web, www.bva.org

Chartered by Congress to assist veterans with claims for benefits. Seeks out blinded veterans to make them aware of benefits and services available to them.

Catholic War Veterans U.S.A., 441 N. Lee St., Alexandria, VA 22314-2301; (703) 549-3622. Fax, (703) 684-5196. Jose Garcia, Executive Director.
Web, www.cwv.org

Recognized by the Veterans Affairs Dept. to assist veterans with claims for benefits. Conducts community service programs; offers scholarships for children; supports benefits for Vietnam veterans commensurate with those received by World War II veterans.

Disabled American Veterans, *National Service and Legislative Headquarters,* 807 Maine Ave. S.W. 20024-2410; (202) 554-3501. Fax, (202) 554-3581. Arthur H. Wilson, National Adjutant; David Gorman, Executive Director.
Web, www.dav.org

Chartered by Congress to assist veterans with claims for benefits; represents veterans seeking to correct alleged errors in military records. Assists families of veterans with disabilities. (Headquarters in Cold Spring, Ky.)

Jewish War Veterans of the U.S.A., *1811 R St. N.W. 20009; (202) 265-6280. Fax, (202) 234-5662. Herb Rosenbleeth, National Executive Director.*
Web, www.jwv.org

Recognized by the Veterans Affairs Dept. to assist veterans with claims for benefits. Offers programs in community relations and services, foreign affairs, national defense, and veterans' affairs. Monitors legislation and regulations that affect veterans.

Marine Corps League, *8626 Lee Hwy., #201, Fairfax, VA 22031-3070 (mailing address: P.O. Box 3070, Merrifield, VA 22116); (703) 207-9588. Fax, (703) 2 07-0047. Michael A. Blum, Executive Director. Toll-free, (800) 625-1775.*
Web, www.mcleague.org

Membership: active duty, retired, and reserve Marine Corps groups. Chartered by Congress to assist veterans with claims for benefits. Operates a volunteer service program in VA hospitals.

Military Officers Assn. of America, *201 N. Washington St., Alexandria, VA 22314-2539; (703) 549-2311. Fax, (703) 838-8173. Vice Adm. Norbert R. Ryan Jr. (USN, Ret.), President. Information, (800) 234-6622.*
General e-mail, msc@moaa.org

Web, www.moaa.org

Membership: officers, former officers, and surviving spouses of officers of the uniformed services. Assists members, their dependents, and survivors with military personnel matters, including service status and retirement problems; provides employment assistance. Monitors legislation affecting active duty officers, retirees, and veterans' affairs, health, and military compensation issues.

Military Order of the Purple Heart of the U.S.A.,
5413-B Backlick Rd., Springfield, VA 22151-3960; (703) 642-5360. Fax, (703) 642-1841. John P. Leonard, National Adjutant. Toll-free, (877) 320-3774.
General e-mail, info@purpleheart.org

Web, www.purpleheart.org

Membership: veterans awarded the Purple Heart for combat wounds. Chartered by Congress to assist veterans with claims for benefits. Conducts service and welfare work on behalf of disabled and needy veterans and their families.

National Coalition for Homeless Veterans, *333 1/2 Pennsylvania Ave. S.E. 20003-1148; (202) 546-1969. Fax, (202) 546-2063. Cheryl Beversdorf, President. Toll-free, (800) VET-HELP. Toll-free fax, (888) 233-8582.*
General e-mail, nchv@nchv.org

Web, www.nchv.org

Provides technical assistance to service providers; advocates on behalf of homeless veterans.

National Veterans Legal Services Program, *1600 K St. N.W., #500 20006 (mailing address: P.O. Box 65762, Washington, DC 20035); (202) 265-8305. Fax, (202) 328-0063. Ronald B. Abrams, Co-Executive Director; Barton F. Stichman, Co-Executive Director.*
General e-mail, info@nvlsp.org

Web, www.nvlsp.org

Represents the interests of veterans through educational programs, advocacy, public policy programming, and litigation.

Noncommissioned Officers Assn., *National Capital Office,* *P.O. Box 427, Alexandria, VA 22313; (703) 549-0311. Fax, (703) 549-0245. H. Gene Overstreet, President; Richard C. Schneider, Executive Director for Government Affairs.*
General e-mail, rschneider@ncoadc.org

Web, www.ncoausa.org

Congressionally chartered and accredited by the Veterans Affairs Dept. to assist veterans and widows of veterans with claims for benefits. (Headquarters in San Antonio, Texas.)

Paralyzed Veterans of America, *801 18th St. N.W. 20006-3517; (202) 872-1300. Fax, (202) 785-4452. Homer Townsend, Executive Director. Information, (800) 424-8200. TTY, (800) 795-4327.*
General e-mail, info@pva.org

Web, www.pva.org

Congressionally chartered veterans service organization that assists veterans with claims for benefits. Distributes information on special education for paralyzed veterans; advocates for high-quality care and supports and raises funds for medical research.

Retired Enlisted Assn., *Washington Office,* *909 N. Washington St., #301, Alexandria, VA 22314-1555; (703) 684-1981. Fax, (703) 548-4876. Deirdre Holleman, Executive Director. Toll-free, (800) 554-8732.*
General e-mail, treadmin@treadc.org

Web, www.treadc.org

Membership: enlisted personnel who have retired for length of service or medical reasons from the active duty, reserve, or guard components of the armed forces. Runs scholarship, legislative, and veterans service programs. (Headquarters in Aurora, Colo.)

Veterans for America (VFA), *1025 Vermont Ave. N.W., 3rd Floor 20005; (202) 483-9222. Bobby Muller, President.*
General e-mail, vet@gmail.com

Web, www.veteransforamerica.org

Works to engage the American public in support of policies addressing the needs of veterans, those currently in the military, and victims of wars overseas. Encourages policy and public discourse around the causes, conduct, and consequences of war.

Veterans of Foreign Wars of the United States, *National Veterans Service, 200 Maryland Ave. N.E. 20002; (202) 543-2239. Fax, (202) 543-6719. Robert E. Wallace, Executive Director, Washington Office. General e-mail, vfw@vfwdc.org*

Web, www.vfw.org

Chartered by Congress to assist veterans with claims for benefits, including disability compensation, education, and pensions. Inspects VA health care facilities and cemeteries. Monitors medical updates and employment practices regarding veterans. (Headquarters in Kansas City, Mo.)

Veterans of Modern Warfare, *Washington Office, 8605 Cameron St., #400, Silver Spring, MD 20910 (mailing address: P.O. Box 96503, Washington, DC 20090); Fax, (301) 585-0519. Donald Overton, Executive Director. Toll-free, (888) 445-9891.*

Web, www.vmwusa.org

Provides information and assistance in obtaining benefits for all active duty National Guard, Reserve, and Coast Guard service members, as well as any veteran who has served in the U.S. Armed Forces since August 2, 1990. Advocates for veterans. Affiliated with the National Gulf War Resource Center. (Headquarters in Kansas City, Mo.)

Veterans of the Battle of the Bulge, *P.O. Box 101418, Arlington, VA 22210-4418; (703) 528-4058. Demetri "Dee" Parris, President; Nancy Monson, Administrative Director. Web, www.battleofthebulge.org*

Membership: veterans who served in the Battle of the Bulge and their families; historians; and other interested individuals. Maintains historical data on the Battle of the Bulge and sponsors reunions, memorial services, and educational programs.

Vietnam Veterans of America, *8605 Cameron St., #400, Silver Spring, MD 20910-3710; (301) 585-4000. Fax, (301) 585-0519. John P. Rowan, President. Information, (800) VVA-1316. General e-mail, vva@vva.org*

Web, www.vva.org

Congressionally chartered membership organization that provides information on legislation that affects Vietnam era veterans and their families. Engages in legislative and judicial advocacy in areas relevant to Vietnam era veterans. Provides information concerning benefits and initiates programs that ensure access to education and employment opportunities. Promotes full accounting of POWs and MIAs.

Appeals of VA Decisions

►**AGENCIES**

Defense Dept. (DoD), *Legal Policy, 4000 Defense Pentagon, #5E604 20301-4000; (703) 697-3387. Fax, (703) 693-6708. Col. Shawn Shumake, Director. Web, www.defenselink.mil*

Coordinates policy in a variety of personnel-related areas.

Veterans Affairs Dept. (VA), *Board of Veterans' Appeals, 811 Vermont Ave. N.W., #845 20420; (202) 565-5436. Fax, (202) 565-4720. James P. Terry, Chair. Web, www.va.gov/vbs/bva*

Final appellate body within the department; reviews claims for veterans' benefits on appeal from agencies of original jurisdiction. Decisions of the board are subject to review by the U.S. Court of Appeals for Veterans Claims.

►**JUDICIARY**

U.S. Court of Appeals for the Federal Circuit, *717 Madison Pl. N.W. 20439; (202) 633-6550. Fax, (202) 633-9623. Paul R. Michel, Chief Judge; Jan Horbaly, Clerk, (202) 312-5520. Web, www.cafe.uscourts.gov*

Reviews decisions concerning the Veterans' Judicial Review Provisions.

U.S. Court of Appeals for Veterans Claims, *625 Indiana Ave. N.W., #900 20004-2950; (202) 501-5890. Fax, (202) 501-5848. William P. Greene Jr., Chief Judge. Web, www.vetapp.gov*

Independent court that reviews decisions of the VA's Board of Veterans' Appeals concerning benefits. Focuses primarily on disability benefits claims.

►**NONGOVERNMENTAL**

American Legion, *Claims Services, Veterans Affairs, and Rehabilitation Division, 1608 K St. N.W. 20006; (202) 861-2700. Fax, (202) 861-0404. Steve Smithson, Deputy Director. Web, www.legion.org*

Membership: honorably discharged veterans who served during declared military conflicts. Assists veterans with appeals before the Veterans Affairs Dept. for compensation and benefits claims.

American Legion, *Discharge Review and Correction Boards Unit, 1608 K St. N.W. 20006-2847; (202) 861-2700. Fax, (202) 861-2728. Ray Spencer, Supervisor. Web, www.legion.org*

Membership: honorably discharged veterans who served during declared military conflicts. Represents before the Defense Dept. former military personnel seeking to upgrade less-than-honorable discharges and to correct alleged errors in military records.

Disabled American Veterans, *National Service and Legislative Headquarters, 807 Maine Ave. S.W. 20024-2410; (202) 554-3501. Fax, (202) 554-3581. David Gorman, Executive Director; Arthur H. Wilson, National Adjutant. Web, www.dav.org*

Oversees regional offices in assisting disabled veterans with claims, benefits, and appeals, including upgrading less-than-honorable discharges. Monitors legislation. (Headquarters in Cold Spring, Ky.)

National Veterans Legal Services Program, *1600 K St. N.W., #500 20006 (mailing address: P.O. Box 65762, Washington, DC 20035); (202) 265-8305. Fax, (202) 328-0063. Ronald B. Abrams, Co-Executive Director; Barton F. Stichman, Co-Executive Director.*
General e-mail, info@nvlsp.org

Web, www.nvlsp.org

Represents the interests of veterans through educational programs, advocacy, public policy programming, and litigation.

Veterans of Foreign Wars of the United States,
National Veterans' Services, 200 Maryland Ave. N.E. 20002-5724; (202) 543-2239. Fax, (202) 543-6719. Vacant, Representative to U.S. Court of Appeals for Veterans Claims; Robert E. Wallace, Executive Director.
Web, www.vfwdc.org

Assists veterans and their dependents and survivors with appeals before the Veterans Affairs Dept. for benefits claims. Assists with cases in the U.S. Court of Appeals for Veterans Claims.

Education, Economic Opportunity

▶AGENCIES

Office of Personnel Management (OPM), *Outreach Group, 1900 E St. N.W., #7412 20415; (202) 606-2773. Anita R. Hanson, Outreach Group Manager.*
Web, www.opm.gov

Provides veterans, military personnel, and federal hiring officials with information on veterans' rights and employment opportunities with the federal government. Provides outreach to colleges and universities on Schedule A hiring authorities for people with disabilities.

Small Business Administration (SBA), *Veterans Business Development, 409 3rd St. S.W., 5th Floor 20416; (202) 205-6773. Fax, (202) 205-7292. William D. Elmore, Associate Administrator.*
Web, www.sba.gov/vets

Coordinates programs to give special consideration to veterans in loan, counseling, procurement, and training programs and in transition training sessions. Oversees federal procurement programs for veteran-owned small businesses.

Veterans Benefits Administration (VBA), *(Veterans Affairs Dept.), Education Service, 1800 G St. N.W., #601 20006 (mailing address: 810 Vermont Ave. N.W.,* *Washington, DC 20420); (202) 461-9800. Fax, (202) 275-1653. Keith M. Wilson, Director. G.I. Bill information, (888) 442-4551.*
Web, www.va.gov

Administers VA's education program, including financial support for veterans' education and for spouses and dependent children of deceased and disabled veterans; provides eligible veterans and dependents with educational assistance under the G.I. Bill and Veterans Educational Assistance Program. Provides postsecondary institutions with funds, based on their enrollment of eligible veterans.

Veterans Benefits Administration (VBA), *(Veterans Affairs Dept.), Loan Guaranty Service, 810 Vermont Ave. N.W., #525 20420; (202) 461-9500. Fax, (202) 275-3523. Mark Bologna, Director.*
Web, www.homeloans.va.gov

Guarantees private institutional financing of home loans (including manufactured home loans) for veterans; provides disabled veterans with direct loans and grants for specially adapted housing; administers a direct loan program for Native American veterans living on trust land.

Veterans Benefits Administration (VBA), *(Veterans Affairs Dept.), Vocational Rehabilitation and Employment Service, MS28, 1800 G St. N.W., #501 20006 (mailing address: 810 Vermont Ave. N.W., Washington, DC 20420); (202) 461-9600. Fax, (202) 275-5122. Ruth Fanning, Director.*
Web, www.va.gov

Administers VA's vocational rehabilitation and employment program, which provides service-disabled veterans with services and assistance; helps veterans to become employable and to obtain and maintain suitable employment.

Veterans' Employment and Training Service *(Labor Dept.), 200 Constitution Ave. N.W., #S1325 20210; (202) 693-4700. Fax, (202) 693-4754. John McWilliam, Assistant Secretary.*
Web, www.dol.gov/vets

Works with and monitors state employment offices to see that preference is given to veterans seeking jobs; advises the secretary on veterans' issues.

Veterans' Employment and Training Service *(Labor Dept.), Operations, Grants, and Transition Programs, 200 Constitution Ave. N.W., #S1325 20210; (202) 693-4707. Fax, (202) 693-4755. Gordon J. Burke Jr., Director.*
Web, www.dol.gov/vets

Investigates veterans' complaints of job or benefits loss because of active or reserve duty military service. Operates in conjunction with state offices to create employment opportunities for veterans. Assists transitioning service members in gaining high-quality employment. Provides grants to organizations nationwide to prevent and eliminate homelessness among veterans.

▶NONGOVERNMENTAL

Blinded Veterans Assn., *477 H St. N.W. 20001-2694; (202) 371-8880. Fax, (202) 371-8258. Thomas H. Miller, Executive Director. Toll-free, (800) 669-7079. General e-mail, bva@bva.org*

Web, www.bva.org

Provides blind and disabled veterans with vocational rehabilitation and employment services.

National Assn. of State Workforce Agencies, *444 N. Capitol St. N.W., #142 20001; (202) 434-8020. Fax, (202) 434-8033. Richard A. Hobbie, Executive Director. Web, www.workforceatm.org*

Membership: state employment security administrators. Provides veterans' employment and training professionals with opportunities for networking and information exchange. Monitors legislation and regulations that affect veterans' employment and training programs involving state employment security agencies.

Paralyzed Veterans of America, *801 18th St. N.W. 20006-3517; (202) 872-1300. Fax, (202) 785-4452. Homer Townsend, Executive Director. Information, (800) 424-8200. TTY, (800) 795-4327. General e-mail, info@pva.org*

Web, www.pva.org

Congressionally chartered veterans service organization that assists veterans with claims for benefits. Promotes access to educational and public facilities and to public transportation for people with disabilities; seeks modification of workplaces.

Health Care, VA Hospitals

▶AGENCIES

Army Dept. *(Defense Dept.),* **Wounded Warrior Program** *(AW2), 200 Stovall St., #6N09, Alexandria, VA 22332-0400; (703) 325-1530. Fax, (703) 325-1516. Col. James S. Rice, Chief. Toll-free, (800) 237-1336. Overseas, (312) 221-8186. General e-mail, aw2@conus.army.mil*

Web, www.aw2.army.mil

Incorporates several existing programs to provide holistic support services for severely disabled soldiers and their families. Provides each soldier with a personal AW2 advocate. Tracks and monitors severely disabled soldiers beyond their medical retirement.

Defense Dept. (DoD), *Deployment Health Support, 5113 Leesburg Pike, #901, Falls Church, VA 22041-3226; (703) 578-8500. Fax, (703) 578-8501. Dr. Michael E. Kilpatrick, Deputy Director. Web, www.deploymentlink.osd.mil*

Advises the secretary of defense on measures to improve the health of deployed forces. Maintains communication between the Defense Dept., service members, veterans, and their families.

Public Health and Science *(Health and Human Services Dept.),* **Military Liaison and Veterans Affairs,** *5600 Fishers Lane, Park Lawn Bldg., #18-66, Rockville, MD 20857; (301) 443-4000. Fax, (301) 443-3574. Capt. Bryan Jones, Director. Web, www.hhs.gov*

Advises the assistant secretary on health issues that affect veterans and military personnel. Works to identify the health-related needs of veterans and their families and to facilitate the delivery of services.

Veterans Affairs Dept. (VA), *Construction and Facilities Management, 810 Vermont Ave., N.W. 20420; (202) 461-8009. Fax, (202) 565-4155. Donald H. Orndoff, Director. Web, www.va.gov/facmgt/*

Principal construction and real estate arm of the Veterans Administration.

Veterans Health Administration (VHA), *(Veterans Affairs Dept.), 810 Vermont Ave. N.W., #800 20420; (202) 461-7000. Fax, (202) 273-5787. Dr. Michael Kussman, Under Secretary. Web, www1.va.gov/health/index.asp*

Oversees all health care policies for all eligible veterans. Recommends policy and administers medical and hospital services for eligible veterans. Publishes guidelines on treatment of veterans exposed to Agent Orange.

Veterans Health Administration (VHA), *(Veterans Affairs Dept.),* **Academic Affiliations,** *1800 G St. N.W., #870 20006; (202) 461-9490. Fax, (202) 461-9855. Dr. Malcolm Cox, Chief. Web, www.va.gov/oaa*

Administers education and training programs for health professionals, students, and residents through partnerships with affiliated academic institutions.

Veterans Health Administration (VHA), *(Veterans Affairs Dept.),* **Dentistry,** *810 Vermont Ave. N.W., MS 112-D 20420; (202) 461-6951. Fax, (202) 273-9105. Dr. Timothy O. Ward, Under Secretary. Web, www.va.gov/dental*

Administers and coordinates VA oral health care programs; dental care delivered in a VA setting; administration of oral research, education, and training for VA oral health personnel; delivery of care to VA patients in private practice settings.

Veterans Health Administration (VHA), *(Veterans Affairs Dept.),* **Geriatrics and Extended Care,** *810*

Vermont Ave. N.W., MS 114 20420; (202) 461-6750. Fax, (202) 273-9131. Dr. James F. Burris, Chief Consultant. Web, www.va.gov/geriatricsshg

Administers research, educational, and clinical health care programs in geriatrics at VA and community nursing homes, personal care homes, VA domiciliaries, and state veterans' homes and in hospital-based home care.

Veterans Health Administration (VHA), *(Veterans Affairs Dept.),* ***Mental Health Services,*** *810 Vermont Ave. N.W., MS 116 20420; (202) 461-7350. Fax, (202) 273-9069. Dr. Ira R. Katz, Chief Consultant. Web, www.mentalhealth.va.gov*

Develops ambulatory and inpatient psychiatry and psychology programs for the mentally ill and for drug and alcohol abusers; programs are offered in VA facilities and twenty-one Veterans Integrated Service Networks. Incorporates special programs for veterans suffering from post-traumatic stress disorders, serious mental illness, addictive disorders, and homelessness.

Veterans Health Administration (VHA), *(Veterans Affairs Dept.),* ***Office of the Assistant Deputy Under Secretary for Health Policy and Planning,*** *810 Vermont Ave. N.W., 8th Floor 20420; (202) 461-7100. Fax, (202) 273-9030. Pat Vandenberg, Director. Web, www.va.gov*

Coordinates and develops departmental planning to distribute funds to VA field facilities.

Veterans Health Administration (VHA), *(Veterans Affairs Dept.),* ***Patient Care Services,*** *810 Vermont Ave. N.W., #975, MS 11 20420; (202) 273-8474. Fax, (202) 273-9274. Dr. Madhuika "Madhu" Agarwal, Chief Officer. Web, www.va.gov*

Manages clinical programs of the VA medical care system.

Veterans Health Administration (VHA), *(Veterans Affairs Dept.),* ***Readjustment Counseling Service,*** *810 Vermont Ave. N.W., #675, MS 15 20420; (202) 461-6525. Fax, (202) 273-9071. Alfonso R. Batres, Chief Officer. Web, www.vetcenter.va.gov and www.va.gov*

Responsible for community-based centers for veterans nationwide. Provides outreach and counseling services for war-related psychological problems and transition to civilian life. Offers bereavement counseling to surviving family members.

Veterans Health Administration (VHA), *(Veterans Affairs Dept.),* ***Research and Development,*** *810 Vermont Ave. N.W., #900, MS 12 20420; (202) 461-1700, Fax, (202) 254-0460. Dr. Joel Kupersmith, Chief. Web, www.va.gov*

Formulates and implements policy for the research and development program of the Veterans Health Administration; advises the under secretary for health on research-related matters and on management of the VA's health care system; represents the VA in interactions with external organizations in matters related to biomedical and health services research.

Veterans Health Administration (VHA), *(Veterans Affairs Dept.),* ***Voluntary Service,*** *810 Vermont Ave. N.W., #10C2 20420; (202) 461-7300. Fax, (202) 273-9040. Laura Balun, Director. Web, www.va.gov/volunteer*

Supervises volunteer programs in VA medical centers.

►CONGRESS

For a listing of relevant congressional committees and subcommittees, please see page 513 or the Appendix.

►NONGOVERNMENTAL

National Assn. of Veterans Administration Physicians and Dentists, *P.O. Box 15418, Arlington, VA 22215-0418; (202) 414-0782. Fax, (202) 408-1231. Samuel V. Spagnolo, President. Web, www.navapd.org*

Seeks to improve the quality of care and conditions at VA hospitals. Monitors legislation and regulations on veterans' health care.

National Conference on Ministry to the Armed Forces, *Endorsers Conference for Veterans Affairs Chaplaincy, 7724 Silver Sage Ct., Springfield, VA 22153; (703) 608-2100. Jack Williamson, Executive Director. General e-mail, jack@ncmaf.org*

Web, www.ncmaf.org

Encourages religious ministry to veterans in VA hospitals and centers and at the Defense Dept.

Paralyzed Veterans of America, *801 18th St. N.W. 20006-3517; (202) 872-1300. Fax, (202) 785-4452. Homer Townsend, Executive Director. Information, (800) 424-8200. TTY, (800) 795-4327. General e-mail, info@pva.org*

Web, www.pva.org

Congressionally chartered veterans service organization. Consults with the Veterans Affairs Dept. on the establishment and operation of spinal cord injury treatment centers.

Spouses, Dependents, and Survivors

►AGENCIES

Air Force Dept. *(Defense Dept.),* ***Manpower and Personnel,*** *1040 Air Force Pentagon, #4D765 20330-1040;*

(703) 697-6088. Fax, (703) 697-6091. Lt. Gen. Richard Newton III, Deputy Chief of Staff.
Web, www.af.mil

Military office that responds to inquiries concerning deceased Air Force personnel and their beneficiaries; refers inquiries to the Military Personnel Center at Randolph Air Force Base in San Antonio, Texas.

Army Dept. *(Defense Dept.), Casualty and Mortuary Affairs, 200 Stovall St., #4S47, Alexandria, VA 22332-0481; (703) 325-7990. Fax, (703) 325-0134. Lt. Col. Michiyo Montague, Chief.*
Web, www.army.mil

Handles notifications concerning deceased and wounded soldiers; bedside travel and transportation orders; mortuary assistance, including military funeral honors program and return of personal effects; current and past conflict POWs and MIAs; management of cemeteries; and casualty-related FOIA requests. Verifies beneficiaries of deceased Army Dept. personnel for benefits distribution, and handles short- and long-term case management for bereaved and surviving family members. (Allied with the Casualty and Mortuary Affairs Operations Center.)

Army Dept. *(Defense Dept.), Casualty and Mortuary Affairs Operations Center (CMAOC), 200 Stovall St., #4S43, Alexandria, VA 22332; (800) 626-3317. Col. Carl Johnson, Director.*
General e-mail, CMAOCWEB@conus.army.mil

The 24/7 operations center that handles notifications concerning deceased and wounded soldiers.

Marine Corps *(Defense Dept.), Casualty Section, HQUSMC, 3280 Russell Rd., Quantico, VA 22134-5102; (703) 784-9512. Fax, (703) 784-4134. Gerald Castle, Head. Toll-free, (800) 847-1597.*
General e-mail, casualtysection@manpower.usmc.mil
Web, www.manpower.usmc.mil

Confirms beneficiaries of deceased Marine Corps personnel for benefits distribution.

Veterans Health Administration (VHA), *(Veterans Affairs Dept.), Readjustment Counseling Service: Bereavement Counseling for Surviving Family Members, 810 Vermont Ave. N.W., #675, MS 15 20420; (202) 461-6525. Fax, (202) 461-6530. Alfonso R. Batres, Chief Officer. Bereavement services information, (202) 461-6530.*
General e-mail, vet.center@va.gov
Web, www.vetcenter.va.gov

Offers bereavement counseling to parents, spouses, siblings, and children of armed forces personnel who died in service to their country and to family members of reservists and those in the National Guard who died while federally activated. Services include outreach, counseling,

and referrals. Counseling provided without cost at community-based Vet Centers.

▶NONGOVERNMENTAL

American Gold Star Mothers Inc., *2128 Leroy Pl. N.W. 20008-1893; (202) 265-0991. Fax, (202) 265-6963. Georgianna Carter Krell, National President.*
General e-mail, goldstarmoms@yahoo.com
Web, www.goldstarmoms.com

Membership: mothers who have lost sons or daughters in military service. Members serve as volunteers in VA hospitals and around the country.

Army and Air Force Mutual Aid Assn., *102 Sheridan Ave., Fort Myer, VA 22211-1110; (703) 522-3060. Fax, (703) 528-2662. Maj. Walt Lincoln (USA, Ret.), President. Information, (866) 422-3622.*
General e-mail, info@aafmaa.com
Web, www.aafmaa.com

Private service organization that offers member and family insurance services to Army and Air Force officers. Recognized by the Veterans Affairs Dept. to assist veterans and their survivors with claims for benefits.

Army Distaff Foundation (Knollwood), *6200 Oregon Ave. N.W. 20015-1543; (202) 541-0149. Fax, (202) 364-2856. Maj. Gen. Donald C. Hilbert (USA, Ret.), Executive Director. Information, (800) 541-4255.*
Web, www.armydistaff.org

Nonprofit continuing care retirement community for career military officers and their families. Provides retirement housing and health care services.

EX-POSE, Ex-Partners of Servicemembers for Equality, *P.O. Box 11191, Alexandria, VA 22312-0191; (703) 941-5844. Fax, (703) 212-6951. Nancy K. Davis, Office Manager.*
General e-mail, ex-pose@juno.com
Web, www.ex-pose.org

Membership: current and former partners of military members, both officers and enlisted, and other interested parties. Educates current and former spouses about potential benefits that may be gained or lost through divorce, including retirement pay, survivors' benefits, and medical, commissary, and exchange benefits. Provides information concerning legal resources and related federal laws and regulations. Serves as an information clearinghouse.

Society of Military Widows, *5535 Hempstead Way, Springfield, VA 22151; (703) 750-1342,ext. 1009. Fax, (703) 354-4380. Marilyn Savage, President; Steve Hein, Marketing Director.*
Web, www.militarywidows.org

Membership: widows of active, reserve, or veteran military personnel. Serves the interests of widows of servicemen; provides support programs and information. Monitors legislation concerning military widows' benefits. (Affiliated with the National Assn. for Uniformed Services.)

Tragedy Assistance Program for Survivors (TAPS), *910 17th St. N.W., #800 20009; (202) 588-8277. Fax, (202) 588-0784. Bonnie Carroll, Executive Director. Toll-free 24-hr crisis intervention hotline, (800) 959-8277.*

General e-mail, info@taps.org

Web, www.taps.org

Offers peer-based emotional support to those who have lost a loved one in military service. Has caseworkers who act as liaisons to military and veterans agencies. Provides 24-hour crisis intervention services and grief and trauma counseling information referrals. Hosts weekly online support meeting and sponsors annual survivors seminar and youth camp.

15

National and Homeland Security

GENERAL POLICY AND ANALYSIS

Basic Resources

▶**AGENCIES**

Please note that all sections of the Homeland Security Dept. use the following mailing address: Washington, DC 20528. Their physical locations are provided below.

Air Force Dept. *(Defense Dept.), 1670 Air Force Pentagon, #4E878 20330-1670; (703) 697-7376. Fax, (703) 695-8809. Michael B. Donley, Secretary; Vacant, Under Secretary. Press, (703) 695-0640.*
Web, www.af.mil

Civilian office that develops and reviews Air Force national security policies in conjunction with the chief of staff of the Air Force and the secretary of defense.

Air Force Dept. *(Defense Dept.), Chief of Staff, 1670 Air Force Pentagon, #4E929 20330-1670; (703) 697-9225. Fax, (703) 693-9297. Gen. Norton A. Schwartz, Chief of Staff.*
Web, www.hq.af.mil

Military office that develops and directs Air Force national security policies in conjunction with the secretary of the Air Force and the secretary of defense.

Army Dept. *(Defense Dept.), 101 Army Pentagon, #3E560 20310-0101; (703) 695-1717. Fax, (703) 697-8036. Peter "Pete" Geren, Secretary.*
Web, www.army.mil

Civilian office that develops and reviews Army national security policies in conjunction with the chief of staff of the Army and the secretary of defense.

Army Dept. *(Defense Dept.), Chief of Staff, 200 Army Pentagon, #3E528 20310-0200; (703) 697-0900. Fax, (703) 614-5268. Gen. George W. Casey Jr., Chief of Staff.*
Web, www.army.mil

Military office that develops and administers Army national security policies in conjunction with the secretary of the Army and the secretary of defense.

Defense Dept. (DoD), *1000 Defense Pentagon, #3E880 20301-1000; (703) 692-7100. Fax, (703) 571-8951. Robert M. Gates, Secretary; Gordon R. England, Deputy Secretary. Information, (703) 428-0711. Pentagon operator, (703) 545-6700. Press, (703) 697-5131. Tours, (703) 614-1642.*
Web, www.defenselink.mil

Civilian office that develops national security policies and has overall responsibility for administering national defense; responds to public and congressional inquiries about national defense matters.

Defense Dept. (DoD), *Global Security Affairs, 2900 Defense Pentagon, #3C653A 20301-2900; (703) 697-7728. Fax, (703) 695-4079. Joseph A. Benkert, Assistant Secretary.*
Web, www.defenselink.mil

Develops and coordinates national security and defense strategies and advises on the resources, forces, and contingency plans necessary to implement those strategies. Ensures the integration of defense strategy into the department's resource allocation, force structure development, weapons system acquisition, and budgetary processes. Evaluates the capability of forces to accomplish defense strategy.

Defense Dept. (DoD), *Homeland Defense and America's Security Affairs, 2600 Defense Pentagon, #5D414 20301-2600; (703) 697-5664. Fax, (703) 697-5375. Vacant, Assistant Secretary.*
Web, www.defenselink.mil

Serves as primary liaison between the Defense Dept. and the Homeland Security Dept. Supervises all Defense Dept. homeland defense activities.

Defense Dept. (DoD), *Installations and Environment, 3400 Defense Pentagon, #3B856A 20301-3400; (703) 695-2880. Fax, (703) 693-7011. Wayne Arny, Deputy Under Secretary.*
Web, www.acq.osd.mil/ie

Oversees and offers policy guidance for all Defense Dept. installations and environmental programs.

Defense Dept. (DoD), *Joint Chiefs of Staff, 9999 Defense Pentagon, #2E872 20318-9999; (703) 697-9121. Fax, (703) 697-6002. Adm. Michael G. Mullen, Chair.*
Web, www.dtic.mil/jcs

Joint military staff office that assists the president, the National Security Council, and the secretary of defense in developing national security policy and in coordinating operations of the individual armed services.

Defense Dept. (DoD), *Policy, 2000 Defense Pentagon, #3E806 20301-2000; (703) 697-7200. Fax, (703) 697-6602. Porter Verga, Deputy Under Secretary for Policy.*
Web, www.defenselink.mil/policy/index.html

Civilian office responsible for policy matters relating to international security issues and political-military affairs. Oversees such areas as arms control, foreign military sales, intelligence collection and analysis, and NATO and regional security affairs.

Defense Dept. (DoD), *Special Operations and Low-Intensity Conflict, 2500 Defense Pentagon, #3C852A 20301-2500; (703) 695-9667. Fax, (703) 693-6335. Michael G. Vickers, Assistant Secretary.*
Web, www.defenselink.mil

Serves as special staff assistant and civilian adviser to the secretary of defense on matters related to special operations and low-intensity conflict. Responsible for the Army's Green Berets, the Navy Seals, and other special operations forces. Oversees counterdrug efforts and humanitarian and refugee affairs for the Defense Dept.

Defense Energy Support Center (DESC), *(Defense Dept.), 8725 John Jay Kingman Rd., #4950, Fort Belvoir,*

NATIONAL AND HOMELAND SECURITY RESOURCES IN CONGRESS

For a complete listing of Congress committees, including their full contact information, leadership, membership, and jurisdictions, please refer to the Appendix on pages 724–837.

HOUSE:

House Appropriations Committee, (202) 225-2771.
Web, appropriations.house.gov
   Subcommittee on Defense, (202) 225-2847.
   Subcommittee on Energy and Water
      Development, (202) 225-3421.
   Subcommittee on Financial Services and General
      Government, (202) 225-7245.
   Subcommittee on Homeland Security,
      (202) 225-5834.
   Subcommittee on Interior, Environment and
      Related Agencies, (202) 225-3081.
   Subcommittee on Military Construction,
      Veterans Affairs, and Related Agencies, (202)
      225-3047.
   Subcommittee on State, Foreign Operations, and
      Related Programs, (202) 225-2041.
House Armed Services Committee, (202) 225-4151.
Web, armedservices.house.gov
   Subcommittee on Air and Land Forces,
      (202) 225-4151.
   Subcommittee on Military Personnel,
      (202) 225-4151.
   Subcommittee on Readiness, (202) 225-4151.
   Subcommittee on Strategic Forces, (202) 225-4151.
   Subcommittee on Terrorism and Unconventional
      Threats and Capabilities, (202) 225-4151.
House Energy and Commerce Committee, (202)
   225-2927.
Web, energycommerce.house.gov
   Subcommittee on Health, (202) 225-2927.
House Financial Services Committee,
   Subcommittee on Housing and Community
   Opportunity, (202) 225-4247.
Web, financialservices.house.gov
House Foreign Affairs Committee, (202) 225-5021.
Web, foreignaffairs.house.gov
   Subcommittee on Terrorism, Nonproliferation
      and Trade, (202) 226-1500.
House Homeland Security Committee,
   (202) 226-2616.
Web, homeland.house.gov

   Subcommittee on Border, Maritime and Global
      Counterterrorism, (202) 226-2616.
   Subcommittee on Emergency Communications,
      Preparedness, and Response, (202) 226-2616.
   Subcommittee on Emerging Threats,
      Cyber-Security, and Science and Technology,
      (202) 226-2616.
   Subcommittee on Intelligence, Information
      Sharing and Terrorism Risk Assessment,
      (202) 226-2616.
   Subcommittee on Management, Investigations,
      and Oversight, (202) 226-2616.
House Judiciary Committee, Subcommittee on
   Crime, Terrorism and Homeland Security,
   (202) 225-5727.
Web, judiciary.house.gov
   Subcommittee on Immigration, Citizenship,
      Refugees, Border Security, and International
      Law, (202) 225-3926.
   Subcommittee on the Constitution, Civil Rights,
      and Civil Liberties, (202) 225-2825.
House Oversight and Government Reform
   Committee, (202) 225-5051.
Web, oversight.house.gov
   Subcommittee on Information Policy, Census,
      and National Archives, (202) 225-6751.
   Subcommittee on National Security and Foreign
      Affairs, (202) 225-2548.
House Permanent Select Committee on Intelligence,
   (202) 225-7690.
Web, intelligence.house.gov
   Subcommittee on Technical and Tactical
      Intelligence, (202) 225-7690.
   Subcommittee on Terrorism, Human
      Intelligence, Analysis, and
      Counterintelligence, (202) 225-7690.
   Subcommittee on Intelligence Community
      Management, (202) 225-7690.
   Subcommittee on Oversight and Investigations,
      (202) 225-7690.

VA 22060-6222; (703) 767-9706. Fax, (703) 767-9672. Kim Huntley, Director. Toll-free, (800) 286-7633. Public Affairs, (703) 767-5121.
Web, www.desc.dla.mil

   Provides the Defense Dept. and other federal agencies with products and services to meet energy-related needs; facilitates the cycle of storage and deployment of fuels and other energy sources, including petroleum, electricity, and natural gas.

Homeland Security Dept. (DHS), *Nebraska Ave. Complex, 3801 Nebraska Ave. N.W. 20528; (202) 282-8000. Fax, (202) 282-8236. Janet Napolitano, Secretary; Paul A. Schneider, Deputy Secretary. Press, (202) 282-8010. Web, www.dhs.gov*

   Responsible for the development and coordination of a comprehensive national strategy to protect the United States against terrorist attacks and other threats and hazards. Coordinates the strategy of the executive branch with

NATIONAL AND HOMELAND SECURITY RESOURCES IN CONGRESS

House Science and Technology Committee, Subcommittee on Technology and Innovation, (202) 225-9662.
Web, science.house.gov

House Transportation and Infrastructure Committee, (202) 225-4472.
Web, transportation.house.gov

Subcommittee on Economic Development, Public Buildings and Emergency Management, (202) 225-9961.

SENATE:

Senate Appropriations Committee, (202) 224-7363.
Web, appropriations.senate.gov

Subcommittee on Defense, (202) 224-6688.

Subcommittee on Energy and Water Development, (202) 224-8119.

Subcommittee on Financial Services and General Government, (202) 224-1133.

Subcommittee on Homeland Security, (202) 224-8244.

Subcommittee on Interior, Environment and Related Agencies, (202) 228-0774.

Subcommittee on Military Construction, Veterans Affairs, and Related Agencies, (202) 224-8224.

Subcommittee on State, Foreign Operations, and Related Programs, (202) 224-7284.

Senate Armed Services Committee, (202) 224-3871.
Web, armed-services.senate.gov

Subcommittee on Airland, (202) 224-3871.

Subcommittee on Emerging Threats and Capabilities, (202) 224-3871.

Subcommittee on Personnel, (202) 224-3871.

Subcommittee on Readiness and Management Support, (202) 224-3871.

Subcommittee on Seapower, (202) 224-3871.

Subcommittee on Strategic Forces, (202) 224-3871.

Senate Banking, Housing, and Urban Affairs Committee, Subcommittee on Securities, Insurance, and Investment, (202) 224-4642.
Web, banking.senate.gov

Subcommittee on Security and International Trade and Finance, (202) 224-5623.

Senate Commerce, Science, and Transportation Committee, (202) 224-0411.
Web, commerce.senate.gov

Senate Environment and Public Works Committee, Subcommittee on Clean Air and Nuclear Safety, (202) 224-8832.
Web, epw.senate.gov/public

Subcommittee on Transportation and Infrastructure, (202) 224-8832.

Subcommittee on Transportation Safety, Infrastructure Security and Water Quality, (202) 224-8832.

Senate Foreign Relations Committee, (202) 224-4651.
Web, foreign.senate.gov

Subcommittee on International Operations and Organizations, Democracy, and Human Rights, (202) 224-4651.

Senate Health, Education, Labor, and Pensions Committee, (202) 224-5375.
Web, help.senate.gov

Senate Homeland Security and Governmental Affairs Committee, (202) 224-2627.
Web, hsgac.senate.gov

Permanent Subcommittee on Investigations, (202) 224-9505.

Subcommittee on Federal Financial Management, Government Information, Federal Services, and International Security, (202) 224-4551.

Subcommittee on Oversight of Government Management, the Federal Workforce, and the District of Columbia, (202) 224-5538.

Subcommittee on State, Local and Private Sector Preparedness and Integration, (202) 224-2627.

Senate Judiciary Committee, (202) 224-7703.
Web, judiciary.senate.gov

Subcommittee on Immigration, Refugees, and Border Security, (202) 224-7878.

Subcommittee on Terrorism, Technology, and Homeland Security, (202) 224-4933.

Subcommittee on the Constitution, (202) 224-5573.

Senate Select Committee on Intelligence, (202) 224-1700.
Web, intelligence.senate.gov

those of state and local governments and private entities to detect, prepare for, protect against, respond to, and recover from terrorist attacks and other emergencies in the United States.

Homeland Security Dept. (DHS), *Science and Technology Directorate, 7th and D Sts. S.W. 20528; (202) 254-6006. Fax, (202) 254-5704. Bradley Buswell, Under Secretary. Press, (202) 282-8010.*
Web, www.dhs.gov/scienceandtechnology

Responsible for oversight and coordination of the development and augmentation of homeland security technology.

Marine Corps *(Defense Dept.), Commandant, Marine Corps Headquarters, 3000 Marine Corps Pentagon, #4E734 20350-3000; (703) 614-2500. Fax, (703) 697-7246. Gen. James T. Conway, Commandant. Information, (703) 614-8010. Press, (703) 614-1492.*
Web, www.hqmc.usmc.mil

Military office that develops and directs Marine Corps national security policies in conjunction with the secretary of defense and the secretary of the Navy.

National Security Council (NSC), *(Executive Office of the President),* The White House 20504; (202) 456-9491. Fax, (202) 456-9490. Gen. James Jones, National Security Adviser. Press, (202) 456-9271.
Web, www.whitehouse.gov/nsc

Advises the president on domestic, foreign, and military policies relating to national security.

Navy Dept. *(Defense Dept.),* 1000 Navy Pentagon, #4E686 20350-1000; (703) 695-3131. Fax, (703) 693-9545. B. J. Penn, Secretary; Under Secretary (Acting). Information, (703) 697-7491.
Web, www.navy.mil

Civilian office that develops and reviews Navy and Marine Corps national security policies in conjunction with the chief of naval operations, the commandant of the Marine Corps, and the secretary of defense.

Navy Dept. *(Defense Dept.), Naval Operations,* 2000 Navy Pentagon, #4E658 20350-2000; (703) 695-5664. Fax, (703) 693-9408. Adm. Gary Roughead, Chief.
Web, www.navy.mil

Military office that develops Navy national security policies in conjunction with the secretary of defense and the secretary of the Navy and in cooperation with the commandant of the Marine Corps.

State Dept., *Foreign Missions,* 2201 C St. N.W., #2238 20520; (202) 647-3417. Fax, (202) 736-4145. Justine Sincavage, Deputy Assistant Secretary.
Web, www.state.gov

Authorized to control the numbers, locations, and travel privileges of foreign diplomats and diplomatic staff in the United States.

State Dept., *Political-Military Affairs,* 2201 C St. N.W., #6212 20520; (202) 647-9022. Fax, (202) 736-4779. Frank Ruggiero, Assistant Secretary (Acting).
Web, www.state.gov

Responsible for security affairs policy; acts as a liaison between the Defense Dept. and the State Dept.

U.S. Coast Guard (USCG), *(Homeland Security Dept.),* 2100 2nd St. S.W. 20593-0001; (202) 372-4411. Fax, (202) 372-4960. Adm. Thad W. Allen, Commandant. Locator, (202) 372-8724. Public Affairs, (202) 372-4620.
Web, www.uscg.mil

Provides homeland security for U.S. harbors, ports, and coastlines. Implements heightened security measures for commercial, tanker, passenger, and merchant vessels. Enforces federal laws on the high seas and navigable waters of the United States and its possessions; maintains a state of military readiness to assist the Navy in time of war or when directed by the president.

►CONGRESS

For a listing of relevant congressional committees and subcommittees, please see page 546 or the Appendix.

Government Printing Office, *Security and Intelligent Documents Unit,* 732 N. Capitol St. N.W. 20401; (202) 512-2285. Benjamin Brink, Assistant Public Printer.
Web, www.gpo.gov/projects/security.htm

Works with other federal agencies to ensure the safe and secure design, production, and distribution of security and intelligence documents such as U.S. passports, social security cards, travel documents, birth certificates, driver's licenses, and immigration forms. Develops electronic and other fraud and counterfeit protection features. Helps establish domestic and international standards for security and other sensitive documents.

►NONGOVERNMENTAL

Air Force Assn., 1501 Lee Hwy., Arlington, VA 22209-1198; (703) 247-5800. Fax, (703) 247-5853. Michael M. Dunn, Executive Director. Information, (800) 727-3337. Press, (703) 247-5850.
Web, www.afa.org

Membership: civilians and active duty, reserve, retired, and cadet personnel of the Air Force. Informs members and the public of developments in the aerospace field. Monitors legislation and Defense Dept. policies. Library on aviation history open to the public by appointment.

American Assn. for the Advancement of Science (AAAS), *Center for Science, Technology, and Security Policy,* 1200 New York Ave. N.W., 11th Floor 20005; (202) 326-6440. Fax, (202) 789-0455. Ginger Pinholster, Director. Press, (202) 326-6431.
General e-mail, cstspinfo@aaas.org
Web, http://cstsp.aaas.org

Encourages the integration of science and public policy to enhance national and international security. Facilitates communication among academic centers, policy institutions, and policymakers. (Supported by the Science, Technology, and Security Initiative of the MacArthur Foundation.)

American Conservative Union (ACU), 1007 Cameron St., Alexandria, VA 22314-2426; (703) 836-8602. Fax, (703) 836-8606. Dennis E. Whitfield, Executive Vice President. Toll-free, (800) 228-7345.
General e-mail, acu@conservative.org
Web, www.conservative.org

Legislative interest organization concerned with national defense policy, legislation related to nuclear weapons, U.S. strategic position vis-à-vis the former Soviet Union, missile defense programs, U.S. troops under U.N. command, and U.S. strategic alliance commitments.

American Enterprise Institute for Public Policy Research (AEI), *Foreign and Defense Policy Studies,*

1150 17th St. N.W., #1100 20036; (202) 862-5872. Fax, (202) 862-4877. Danielle Pletka, Vice President. Information, (202) 862-5800. Press, (202) 862-4871.

Web, www.aei.org

Research and educational organization that conducts conferences, seminars, and debates and sponsors research on national security, defense policy, and arms control.

American Security Council Foundation, *1250 24th St. N.W. 20037; (202) 263-3661. Fax, (202) 263-3662. Gary James, Operations Manager.*

General e-mail, info@ascf.org

Web, www.ascfusa.org

Bipartisan organization that promotes developing and maintaining military, economic, and diplomatic strength to preserve national security. Monitors legislation and conducts educational activities.

Aspen Institute, *1 Dupont Circle N.W., #700 20036; (202) 736-5800. Fax, (202) 467-0790. Walter Isaacson, President. Press, (202) 736-3849.*

General e-mail, info@aspeninstitute.org

Web, www.aspeninstitute.org

Promotes consideration of the public good in a wide variety of areas, including homeland security policies. Conducts educational programs; publishes reports.

Assn. of the United States Army, *2425 Wilson Blvd., Arlington, VA 22201; (703) 841-4300. Fax, (703) 525-9039. Gordon R. Sullivan, President. Information, (800) 336-4570.*

Web, www.ausa.org

Membership: civilians and active duty and retired members of the armed forces. Conducts symposia on defense issues and researches topics that affect the military.

Atlantic Council of the United States, *1101 15th St. N.W., 11th Floor 20005; (202) 463-7226. Fax, (202) 463-7241. Frederick Kempe, President.*

General e-mail, info@acus.org

Web, www.acus.org

Conducts studies and makes policy recommendations on U.S. foreign security and international economic policies in the Atlantic and Pacific communities; sponsors conferences and educational exchanges.

The Brookings Institution, *Foreign Policy Studies, 1775 Massachusetts Ave. N.W. 20036; (202) 797-6000. Fax, (202) 797-6004. Carlos Pascual, Director. Publications, (202) 797-6105.*

Web, www.brookings.edu

Research and educational organization that focuses on major national security topics, including U.S. armed forces, weapons decisions, terrorism threats, employment policies, and the security aspects of U.S. foreign relations.

Business Executives for National Security (BENS), *1717 Pennsylvania Ave. N.W., #350 20006-4603;*

(202) 296-2125. Fax, (202) 296-2490. Charles G. Boyd, Chief Executive Officer.

General e-mail, bens@bens.org

Web, www.bens.org

Monitors legislation on national security issues from a business perspective; holds conferences, congressional forums, and other meetings on national security issues; works with other organizations on defense policy issues.

Center for Naval Analyses (CNA), *4825 Mark Center Dr., Alexandria, VA 22311-1850; (703) 824-2000. Fax, (703) 824-2942. Christine H. Fox, President.*

General e-mail, inquiries@cna.org

Web, www.cna.org

Conducts research on weapons acquisitions, tactical problems, and naval operations.

Center for Security Policy, *1901 Pennsylvania Ave. N.W., #201 20006-3439; (202) 835-9077. Fax, (202) 835-9066. Frank J. Gaffney Jr., President.*

General e-mail, info@centerforsecuritypolicy.org

Web, www.centerforsecuritypolicy.org

Educational institution concerned with U.S. defense and foreign policy. Interests include relations between the United States and the former Soviet Union, arms control compliance and verification policy, and technology transfer policy.

Committee on the Present Danger, *P.O. Box 33249 20033-3249; (202) 207-3696. Fax, (202) 207-0191. George P. Shultz, Co-Chair; R. James Woolsey, Co-Chair.*

General e-mail, info@defenddemocracy.org

Web, www.committeeonthepresentdanger.org

International, nonpartisan education and advocacy organization concerned with militant Islamist groups and their terrorist activities within Muslim countries and around the world. Supports policies that use various means—military, economic, political, social—to address this threat. Members include former government officials, academics, writers, and other foreign policy experts.

Conservative Caucus, *450 Maple Ave. East, Vienna, VA 22180-4724; (703) 938-9626. Fax, (703) 281-4108. Howard Phillips, Chair.*

General e-mail, info@conservativeusa.org

Web, www.conservativeusa.org

Legislative interest organization that promotes grassroots activity on national defense and foreign policy.

Defense Orientation Conference Assn. (DOCA), *9271 Old Keene Mill Rd., #200, Burke, VA 22015-4202; (703) 451-1200. Fax, (703) 451-1201. David W. Morris, Executive Vice President.*

General e-mail, info@doca.org

Web, www.doca.org

Membership: citizens interested in national defense. Under the auspices of the Defense Dept., promotes

Defense Department

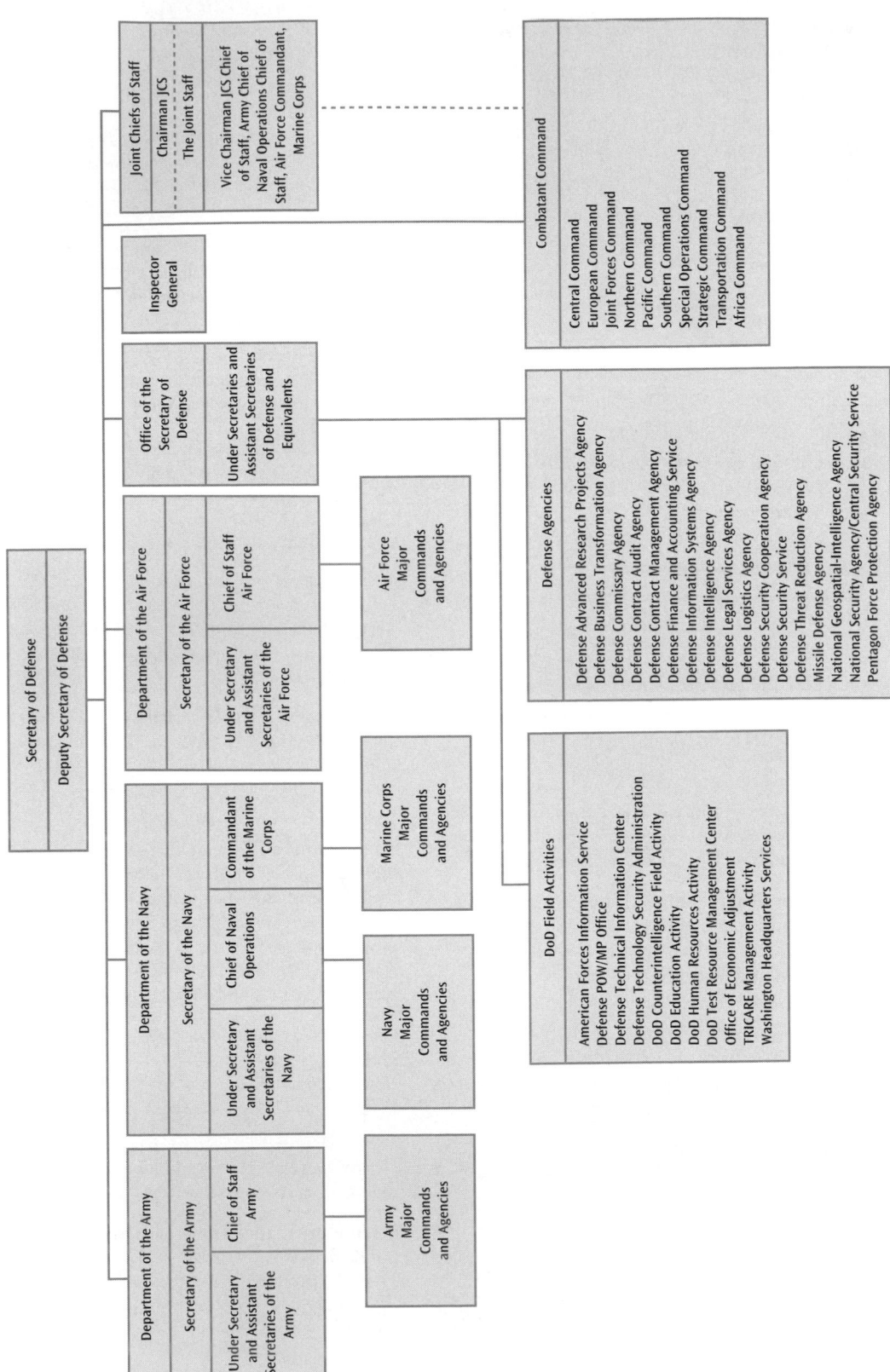

Secretary of Defense

Deputy Secretary of Defense

Department of the Army

Secretary of the Army

Under Secretary and Assistant Secretaries of the Army

Chief of Staff Army

Army Major Commands and Agencies

Department of the Navy

Secretary of the Navy

Under Secretary and Assistant Secretaries of the Navy

Chief of Naval Operations

Commandant of the Marine Corps

Navy Major Commands and Agencies

Marine Corps Major Commands and Agencies

Department of the Air Force

Secretary of the Air Force

Under Secretary and Assistant Secretaries of the Air Force

Chief of Staff Air Force

Air Force Major Commands and Agencies

Office of the Secretary of Defense

Under Secretaries and Assistant Secretaries of Defense and Equivalents

Inspector General

Joint Chiefs of Staff

Chairman JCS

The Joint Staff

Vice Chairman JCS Chief of Staff, Army Chief of Naval Operations Chief of Staff, Air Force Commandant, Marine Corps

Combatant Command

Central Command
European Command
Joint Forces Command
Northern Command
Pacific Command
Southern Command
Special Operations Command
Strategic Command
Transportation Command
Africa Command

DoD Field Activities

American Forces Information Service
Defense POW/MP Office
Defense Technical Information Center
Defense Technology Security Administration
DoD Counterintelligence Field Activity
DoD Education Activity
DoD Human Resources Activity
DoD Test Resource Management Center
Office of Economic Adjustment
TRICARE Management Activity
Washington Headquarters Services

Defense Agencies

Defense Advanced Research Projects Agency
Defense Business Transformation Agency
Defense Commissary Agency
Defense Contract Audit Agency
Defense Contract Management Agency
Defense Finance and Accounting Service
Defense Information Systems Agency
Defense Intelligence Agency
Defense Legal Services Agency
Defense Logistics Agency
Defense Security Cooperation Agency
Defense Security Service
Defense Threat Reduction Agency
Missile Defense Agency
National Geospatial-Intelligence Agency
National Security Agency/Central Security Service
Pentagon Force Protection Agency

---------- Dotted lines mean coordination but not reporting

continuing education of members on national security issues through visits to embassies and tours of defense installations in the United States and abroad.

Ethics and Public Policy Center, 1015 15th St. N.W., #900 20005-2605; (202) 682-1200. Fax, (202) 408-0632. M. Edward Whelan III, President.
General e-mail, ethics@eppc.org
Web, www.eppc.org

Considers implications of Judeo-Christian moral tradition for domestic and foreign policy making. Conducts research and holds conferences on foreign policy, including the role of the U.S. military abroad.

Henry L. Stimson Center, 1111 19th St. N.W., 12th Floor 20036; (202) 223-5956. Fax, (202) 238-9604. Ellen Laipson, President.
General e-mail, info@stimson.org
Web, www.stimson.org

Research and educational organization that studies arms control and international security, focusing on policy, technology, and politics.

Homeland Security Institute, 2900 S. Quincy St., #800, Arlington, VA 22206-2233; (703) 416-3550. Fax, (703) 416-3530. Philip Anderson, Director.
General e-mail, homelandsecurity@hsi.dhs.gov
Web, www.homelandsecurity.org

Public-service research organization that examines the homeland security challenges faced by the United States in the twenty-first century. Explores issues, conducts research, works to promote dialogue, and provides executive education through workshops, conferences, publications, and outreach programs. Funded by the Homeland Security Dept.

Hudson Institute, *National Security Studies,* 1015 15th St. N.W., 6th Floor 20005; (202) 974-2400. Fax, (202) 974-2410. Kenneth R. Weinstein, Chief Executive Officer. Press, (202) 974-2417.
General e-mail, info@hudson.org
Web, www.hudson.org

Public policy research organization that conducts studies on U.S. overseas bases, U.S.-NATO relations, and missile defense programs. Focuses on long-range implications for U.S. national security.

Institute for Foreign Policy Analysis, 1725 DeSales St. N.W., #402 20036; (202) 463-7942. Fax, (202) 785-2785. Robert L. Pfaltzgraff Jr., President.
Web, www.ifpa.org

Trains policy analysts in the fields of foreign policy and national security. Sponsors research and workshops.

Institute of International Education, *National Security Education Program,* 1400 K St. N.W., #650 20005-2403; (202) 326-7697. Fax, (202) 326-7672. Chris Powers, Director. Information, (800) 618-6737.

General e-mail, boren@iie.org
Web, www.borenawards.org

Administers Boren Awards and Language Flagship programs; provides scholarships, fellowships, and institutional grants to academics with an interest in foreign affairs and national security.

Jewish Institute for National Security Affairs (JINSA), 1779 Massachusetts Ave. N.W., #515 20036-2131; (202) 667-3900. Fax, (202) 667-0601. Tom Neumann, Executive Director.
General e-mail, info@jinsa.org
Web, www.jinsa.org

Seeks to educate the public about the importance of effective U.S. defense capability and inform the U.S. defense and foreign affairs community about Israel's role in Mediterranean and Middle Eastern affairs. Sponsors lectures and conferences; facilitates dialogue between security policymakers, military officials, diplomats, and the general public.

Marine Corps League, 8626 Lee Hwy., #201, Fairfax, VA 22031-3070 (mailing address: P.O. Box 3070, Merrifield, VA 22116); (703) 207-9588. Fax, (703) 207-0047. Michael A. Blum, Executive Director. Toll-free, (800) 625-1775.
Web, www.mcleague.org

Membership: active duty, retired, and reserve Marine Corps groups. Promotes the interests of the Marine Corps and works to preserve its traditions; assists veterans and their survivors. Monitors legislation and regulations.

National Institute for Public Policy, 9302 Lee Hwy., #750, Fairfax, VA 22031-6053; (703) 293-9181. Fax, (703) 293-9198. Keith B. Payne, President.
Web, www.nipp.org

Studies public policy and its relation to national security. Interests include arms control, strategic weapons systems and planning, and foreign policy.

National Security Whistleblowers Coalition, P.O. Box 320518, Alexandria, VA 22320; (703) 519-3640. Sibel Edmonds, President.
General e-mail, info@nswbc.org
Web, www.nswbc.org

Membership: current or former federal employees or civilians who uncover fraud, waste, and abuse in government operations pertaining to national security. Aids intelligence and military whistleblowers by promoting public education about whistleblowing and government and legal reform. Provides a community for whistleblowers experiencing retaliation and alienation.

Navy League of the United States, 2300 Wilson Blvd., #200, Arlington, VA 22201-3308; (703) 528-1775. Fax, (703) 528-2333. Stephen R. Pietropaoli, National Executive Director. Toll-free, (800) 356-5760.
General e-mail, service@navyleague.org
Web, www.navyleague.org

Homeland Security Department

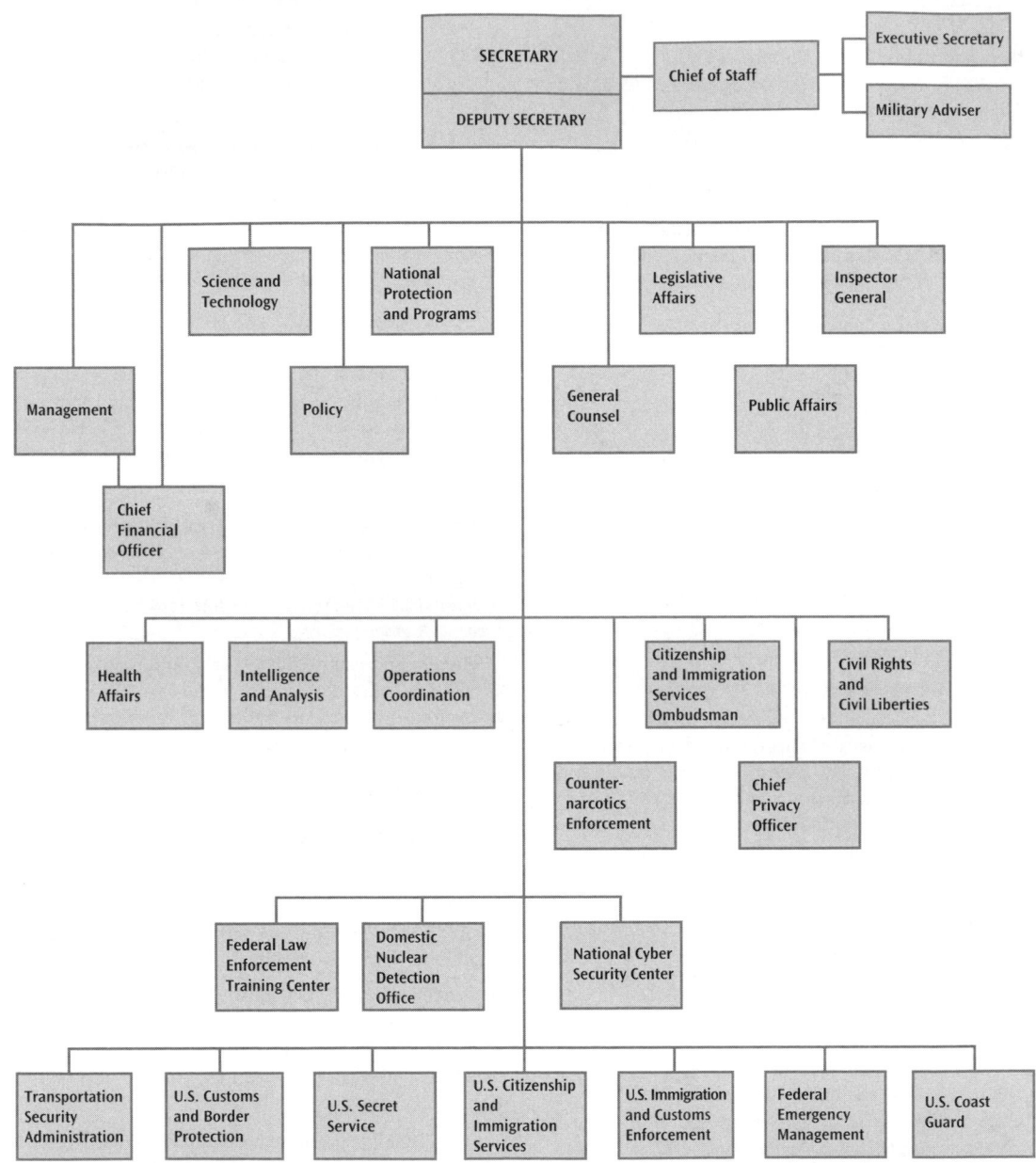

Membership: retired and reserve military personnel and civilians interested in the U.S. Navy, Marine Corps, Coast Guard, and Merchant Marine. Distributes literature, provides speakers, and conducts seminars to promote interests of the sea services. Monitors legislation.

RAND Corporation, *Washington Office,* *1200 S. Hayes St., Arlington, VA 22202-5050; (703) 413-1100. Fax, (703) 413-8111. Lynn Davis, Director.*
Web, www.rand.org

Conducts research on national security issues, including political/military affairs of the former Soviet Union and U.S. strategic policy. (Headquarters in Santa Monica, Calif.)

World Security Institute, *1779 Massachusetts Ave. N.W. 20036-2109; (202) 332-0900. Fax, (202) 462-4559. Bruce G. Blair, President. Press, (202) 797-5273.*
General e-mail, info@worldsecurityinstitute.org

Web, www.worldsecurityinstitute.org

Seeks to develop innovative approaches to communication, education, and cooperation on the social, economic, environmental, political, and military components of national security. Provides news- and research-based analysis to policymakers in the United States and abroad through publications and other services.

World Security Institute, *Center for Defense Information,* *1779 Massachusetts Ave. N.W., #615 20036-2109; (202) 332-0900. Fax, (202) 462-4559. Theresa Hitchens, Director. Press, (202) 797-5273.*
General e-mail, info@worldsecurityinstitute.org

Web, www.cdi.org

Educational organization that advocates a strong defense while opposing excessive expenditures for weapons and policies that increase the risk of war. Interests include the defense budget, weapons systems, and troop levels. Provides Congress, the Pentagon, the State Dept., the media, and the public with appraisals of military matters.

Civil Rights and Liberties

▶AGENCIES

Homeland Security Dept. (DHS), *Civil Rights and Civil Liberties,* *245 Murray Lane, Bldg. 410, MS 0800 20528-0800; (202) 401-1474. Fax, (202) 401-4708. Timothy J. Keefer, Civil Rights and Civil Liberties Officer. Toll-free, (866) 644-8360. TTY, (202) 401-0470 or toll-free, (866) 644-8361.*
General e-mail, civil.liberties@dhs.gov

Web, www.dhs.gov

Provides legal and policy advice to the secretary and senior officers of the department on civil rights and civil liberties issues; maintains dialogue with minority communities; investigates and resolves complaints filed by members of the public.

Homeland Security Dept. (DHS), *Privacy Office,* *245 Murray Lane, Bldg. 110 20528-0800; (703) 235-0780. Fax, (703) 235-0442. Mary Ellen Callahan, Chief Privacy Officer.*
General e-mail, privacy@dhs.gov

Web, www.dhs.gov/xabout/structure/editorial_0338.shtm

Responsible for ensuring that department policies and use of technology sustain individual privacy. Makes annual report to Congress and enforces the provisions of the 1974 Privacy Act and evaluates legislative and regulatory proposals involving collection, use, and disclosure of personal information by the federal government.

Justice Dept. (DOJ), *Information and Privacy,* *1425 New York Ave. N.W., #11050 20530; (202) 514-3642. Fax, (202) 514-1009. Melanie Ann Pustay, Director. Information, (202) 514-2000. TTY, (202) 514-1888.*
Web, www.usdoj.gov/oip/oip.html; FOIA requests, www .usdoj.gov/oip/04_04.html

Provides federal agencies with advice and policy guidance on matters related to implementing and interpreting the Freedom of Information Act (FOIA). Litigates selected FOIA and Privacy Act cases; adjudicates administrative appeals from Justice Dept. denials of public requests for access to documents; conducts FOIA training for government agencies.

Office of Management and Budget (OMB), *(Executive Office of the President), Information and Regulatory Affairs,* *New Executive Office Bldg., #10236 20503; (202) 395-3785. Fax, (202) 395-5167. Jasmeet Seehra, Co-Chief; Kim Nelson, Co-Chief.*
Web, www.whitehouse.gov/omb/inforeg_infopoltech

Oversees implementation of the Privacy Act of 1974 and other privacy- and security-related statutes. Issues guidelines and regulations.

Privacy and Civil Liberties Oversight Board, *1600 Pennsylvania Ave. N.W. 20502. Fax, (202) 456-1066. Mark A. Robbins, Executive Director.*
General e-mail, privacyboard@who.eop.gov

Web, www.whitehouse.gov/administration/eop/pclob

The five-member board advises the president and other senior executive branch officials to ensure that privacy concerns and civil liberties are considered in the implementation of laws, regulations, and executive branch policies related to terrorism. The board is appointed by and serves at the pleasure of the president. Members are confirmed by the Senate.

▶CONGRESS

For a listing of relevant congressional committees and subcommittees, please see page 546 or the Appendix.

▶NONGOVERNMENTAL

American Civil Liberties Union (ACLU), *Washington Legislative Office,* *915 15th St. N.W. 20005; (202) 544-1681. Fax, (202) 546-0738. Caroline Fredrickson, Director. Press, (202) 675-2312. Alternate fax, (202) 546-1440.*
General e-mail, media@dcaclu.org

Web, www.aclu.org/legislative

Advocates for legislation to guarantee constitutional rights and civil liberties. Monitors agency compliance with the Privacy Act and other access statutes. Produces publications. (Headquarters in New York maintains docket of cases.)

American Society of Access Professionals, *1444 Eye St. N.W., #700 20005; (202) 712-9054. Fax, (202) 216-9646. Claire Shanley, Executive Director.*
General e-mail, asap@bostrom.com

Web, www.accesspro.org

Membership: federal employees, attorneys, journalists, and others working with or interested in access-to-information laws. Seeks to improve the administration of the Freedom of Information Act, the Privacy Act, and other access statutes.

Center for Democracy and Technology, *1634 Eye St. N.W., #1100 20006; (202) 637-9800. Fax, (202) 637-0968. Leslie Harris, President.*

General e-mail, info@cdt.org

Web, www.cdt.org

Promotes civil liberties and democratic values in computer and communications media, both in the United States and abroad. Interests include free speech, privacy, and freedom of information. Monitors legislation and regulations.

Center for National Security Studies, *1120 19th St. N.W., #800 20036; (202) 721-5650. Fax, (202) 530-0128. Kate A. Martin, Director. Press, (202) 721-5660.* General e-mail, cnss@cnss.org

Web, www.cnss.org

Human rights and civil liberties organization specializing in national security, access to government information, government secrecy, government surveillance, intelligence oversight, and detentions.

Electronic Privacy Information Center (EPIC), *1718 Connecticut Ave. N.W., #200 20009; (202) 483-1140. Fax, (202) 483-1248. Marc Rotenberg, Executive Director.* General e-mail, epic-info@epic.org

Web, www.epic.org

Public interest research center. Conducts research and conferences on domestic and international civil liberties issues, including privacy, free speech, information access, computer security, and encryption; litigates cases. Monitors legislation and regulations.

Radio-Television News Directors Assn. (RTNDA/ RTNDF), *1025 F St. N.W., 7th Floor 20004 (mailing address: 4121 Plank Rd., #512, Fredericksburg, VA 22407); (202) 659-6510. Fax, (202) 223-4007. Barbara Cochran, President.* General e-mail, rtnda@rtnda.org

Web, www.rtnda.org

Membership: electronic journalists in radio, television, and all digital media. Sponsors and promotes education and advocacy concerning First Amendment issues, freedom of information, and government secrecy issues; ethics in reporting; improving coverage; implementing technology; and other news industry issues. Radio and Television News Directors Foundation (RTNDF) is the educational arm of the association.

Reporters Committee for Freedom of the Press, *1101 Wilson Blvd., #1100, Arlington, VA 22209; (703) 807-2100. Fax, (703) 807-2109. Lucy A. Dalglish, Executive Director. Legal defense hotline, (800) 336-4243.* General e-mail, rcfp@rcfp.org

Web, www.rcfp.org

Membership: reporters, news editors, publishers, and lawyers from the print and broadcast media. Maintains a legal defense and research fund for members of the news media involved in freedom of the press court cases; interests include access to information and privacy issues faced by journalists covering antiterrorism initiatives and military actions abroad.

Defense and Homeland Security Budgets

▶AGENCIES

Defense Contract Audit Agency (DCAA), *(Defense Dept.), 8725 John Jay Kingman Rd., #2135, Fort Belvoir, VA 22060-6219; (703) 767-3200. Fax, (703) 767-3267. April G. Stephenson, Director.* Web, www.dcaa.mil

Performs all contract audits for the Defense Dept. Provides Defense Dept. personnel responsible for procurement and contract administration with accounting and financial advisory services regarding the negotiation, administration, and settlement of contracts and subcontracts.

Defense Dept. (DoD), *Comptroller, 1100 Defense Pentagon, #3E770 20301-1100; (703) 695-3237. Fax, (703) 693-0582. Robert F. Hale, Comptroller. Press, (703) 571-9229.* Web, www.defenselink.mil/comptroller

Supervises and reviews the preparation and implementation of the defense budget. Advises the secretary of defense on fiscal matters. Collects and distributes information on the department's management of resources.

Homeland Security Dept. (DHS), *Chief Financial Officer, 7th and D Sts. S.W. 20528; (202) 447-5751. Fax, (202) 447-5172. Peggy Sherry, Chief Financial Officer (Acting).* Web, www.dhs.gov

Responsible for the Homeland Security Dept.'s budget, budget justifications, supplemental spending bill figures, and five-year financial blueprint.

Homeland Security Dept. (DHS), *Management Directorate, 3801 Nebraska Ave. N.W. 20528; (202) 447-3400. Fax, (202) 447-3713. Elaine Duke, Under Secretary.* Web, www.dhs.gov

Responsible for Homeland Security Dept. budget, appropriations, expenditure of funds, accounting and finance, procurement, human resources and personnel, information technology systems, facilities, property, equipment and all material resources, and performance measurement.

Office of Management and Budget (OMB), *(Executive Office of the President), Homeland Security, 725 17th St. N.W., New Executive Office Bldg., #9208 20503; (202) 395-5090. Fax, (202) 395-0850. Steve Mertens, Chief.* Web, www.whitehouse.gov/omb

Assists and advises the OMB director on budget preparation, proposed legislation, and evaluations of Homeland Security Dept. programs, policies, and activities.

Office of Management and Budget (OMB), *(Executive Office of the President), National Security, 725 17th St. N.W., New Executive Office Bldg., #10001 20503; (202) 395-3884. Fax, (202) 395-3307. Kathleen Peroff, Deputy Associate Director.* Web, www.whitehouse.gov/omb

Supervises preparation of the Defense Dept., intelligence community, and veterans affairs portions of the federal budget.

►CONGRESS

For a listing of relevant congressional committees and subcommittees, please see page 546 or the Appendix.

Government Accountability Office (GAO), *Defense Capabilities and Management,* 441 G St. N.W., #4030 20548; (202) 512-4300. Henry L. Hinton Jr., Managing Director.
Web, www.gao.gov

Independent, nonpartisan agency in the legislative branch. Audits, analyzes, and evaluates defense spending programs; makes unclassified reports available to the public. (Formerly the General Accounting Office.)

Government Accountability Office (GAO), *Homeland Security and Justice,* 441 G St. N.W., #6169 20548; (202) 512-3610. Norm J. Rabkin, Managing Director.
Documents, (202) 512-6000.
Web, www.gao.gov

Independent, nonpartisan agency in the legislative branch. Audits, analyzes, and evaluates federal administration of homeland security programs and initiatives related to national preparedness. Makes some reports available to the public. (Formerly the General Accounting Office.)

►NONGOVERNMENTAL

Center for Strategic and Budgetary Assessments (CSBA), 1667 K St. N.W., #900 20006-1659; (202) 331-7990. Fax, (202) 331-8019. Andrew F. Krepinevich, President.
General e-mail, info@csbaonline.org
Web, www.csbaonline.org

Conducts detailed analyses of defense spending; makes results available to members of Congress, the executive branch, the media, academics, other organizations, and the general public.

Institute for Policy Studies, *Foreign Policy in Focus,* 1112 16th St., #600 20036; (202) 234-9382. Fax, (202) 387-7915. Emira Woods, Director.
Web, www.fpif.org

Think tank that provides analysis of U.S. foreign policy and international affairs and recommends progressive policy alternatives. Publishes reports; organizes briefings for the public, media, and policymakers. Interests include climate change, global poverty, nuclear weapons, terrorism, and military conflict.

National Campaign for a Peace Tax Fund, 2121 Decatur Pl. N.W. 20008-1923; (202) 483-3751. Bethany Criss, Executive Director. Toll-free, (888) 732-2382.
General e-mail, info@peacetaxfund.org
Web, www.peacetaxfund.org

Supports legislation permitting taxpayers who are conscientiously opposed to military expenditures to have the military portion of their income tax money placed in a separate, nonmilitary fund.

Women's Action for New Directions, *Washington Office,* 322 4th St. N.E. 20002; (202) 544-5055. Fax, (202) 544-7612. Marie Rietmann, Public Policy Director.
General e-mail, peace@wand.org
Web, www.wand.org

Seeks to redirect federal spending priorities from military spending toward domestic needs; works to develop citizen expertise through education and political involvement; provides educational programs and material about nuclear and conventional weapons; monitors defense legislation, budget policy legislation, and legislation affecting women. (Headquarters in Arlington, Mass.)

Military Aid and Peacekeeping

►AGENCIES

Commission on Security and Cooperation in Europe (Helsinki Commission), 234 FHOB 20515; (202) 225-1901. Fax, (202) 226-4199. Sen. Benjamin L. Cardin, D–Md., Chair; Rep. Alcee L. Hastings, D–Fla., Co-Chair; Fred L. Turner, Chief of Staff.
General e-mail, info@csce.gov
Web, www.csce.gov

Independent agency created by Congress. Membership includes individuals from the executive and legislative branches. Studies and evaluates international peacekeeping and peace enforcement operations, particularly as they relate to the Helsinki Accords.

Defense Dept. (DoD), *Defense Security Cooperation Agency,* 201 12th St. South, #203, Arlington, VA 22202-5408; (703) 604-6604. Fax, (703) 602-5403. Vice Adm. Jeffrey A. Wieringa, Director. Public Affairs, (703) 604-6617.
Web, www.dsca.mil

Administers foreign military sales and other security assistance programs. Develops budgetary proposals for foreign military financing and training programs. Provides support for security cooperation programs, such as overseas humanitarian assistance and Warsaw Initiative programs. Serves as executive agent for five regional centers for security studies.

Defense Dept. (DoD), *European and NATO Policy,* The Pentagon, #5B652 20301-2900; (703) 695-5553. Fax, (703) 571-9637. Mary Warlick, Deputy Assistant Secretary (Acting).
Web, www.defenselink.mil

Advises the assistant secretary for international security affairs on matters dealing with Europe and NATO.

Defense Dept. (DoD), *International Security Affairs,* The Pentagon, #3-C852A 20301-2400; (703) 695-4351. Fax, (703) 697-7230. Vacant, Assistant Secretary.
Web, www.defenselink.mil

Advises the secretary of defense and recommends policies on regional security issues (except those involving countries of the former Soviet Union or NATO members).

State Dept., *Arms Control and International Security,* *2201 C St. N.W., #7208 20520-7512; (202) 647-1049. Fax, (202) 736-4397. Vacant, Under Secretary.*
Web, www.state.gov

Works with the secretary of state to develop policy on foreign security assistance programs and technology transfer.

State Dept., *European Security and Political Affairs,* *2201 C St. N.W., #6511 20520; (202) 647-1626. Fax, (202) 647-1369. Bruce Turner, Director.*
Web, www.state.gov

Coordinates and advises, with the Defense Dept. and other agencies, the U.S. mission to NATO and the U.S. delegation to the Organization for Security and Co-operation in Europe regarding political, military, and arms control matters.

State Dept., *International Organization Affairs,* *2201 C St. N.W., #6323 20520-6319; (202) 647-9600. Fax, (202) 736-4116. Brian Hook, Assistant Secretary. Press, (202) 647-7938.*
Web, www.state.gov/p/io

Coordinates and develops policy guidelines for U.S. participation in the United Nations and in other international organizations and conferences.

State Dept., *Policy Planning Staff,* *2201 C St. N.W., #7311 20520; (202) 647-2372. Fax, (202) 647-0844. Anne-Marie Slaughter, Director.*
Web, www.state.gov

Advises the secretary and other State Dept. officials on foreign policy matters, including international peacekeeping and peace enforcement operations.

State Dept., *Political-Military Affairs,* *2201 C St. N.W., #6212 20520; (202) 647-9022. Fax, (202) 736-4779. Frank Ruggiero, Assistant Secretary (Acting).*
Web, www.state.gov

Responsible for security affairs policy and operations for the non-European area.

State Dept., *United Nations Political Affairs,* *2201 C St. N.W., #6334 20520-6319; (202) 647-2392. Fax, (202) 647-0039. Jeff L. Baily, Director.*
Web, www.state.gov

Deals with United Nations political and institutional matters and international security affairs.

U.S. Institute of Peace, *1200 17th St. N.W., #200 20036; (202) 457-1700. Fax, (202) 429-6063. J. Robinson West, Chair; Richard H. Solomon, President. TTY, (202) 457-1719.*
General e-mail, info@usip.org
Web, www.usip.org

Independent, nonpartisan institution established by Congress. Aims to prevent and resolve violent international conflicts, promote post-conflict stability, and increase peace-building capacity, tools, and intellectual capital worldwide.

►CONGRESS

For a listing of relevant congressional committees and subcommittees, please see page 546 or the Appendix.

Government Accountability Office (GAO), *Defense Capabilities and Management,* *441 G St. N.W., #4030 20548; (202) 512-4300. Henry L. Hinton Jr., Managing Director.*
Web, www.gao.gov

Independent, nonpartisan agency in the legislative branch. Audits, analyzes, and evaluates international programs, including U.S. participation in international peacekeeping and peace enforcement operations; makes unclassified reports available to the public. (Formerly the General Accounting Office.)

►INTERNATIONAL ORGANIZATIONS

Inter-American Defense Board, *2600 16th St. N.W. 20441-0002; (202) 939-6600. Fax, (202) 387-2880. Rear Adm. Elis Treidler Öberg, Chair.*
Web, www.jid.org

Membership: military officers from twenty-six countries of the Western Hemisphere. Plans for the collective self-defense of the American continents. Develops procedures for standardizing military organization and operations; operates the Inter-American Defense Board and Inter-American Defense College. Advises the Organization of American States on military and defense matters.

Joint Mexican–United States Defense Commission, *U.S. Section,* *The Pentagon, #2E773, 5134 Joint Staff 20318-5134; (703) 695-8162. Fax, (703) 614-8945. Gen. Burton M. Field (USAF), Chair.*

Composed of military delegates of the two countries. Studies problems concerning the common defense of the United States and Mexico.

►NONGOVERNMENTAL

International Peace Operations Assn. (IPOA), *1900 L St. N.W., #320 20036-5027; (202) 464-0721. Fax, (202) 464-0726. Doug Brooks, President.*
General e-mail, ipoa@ipoaonline.org
Web, www.ipoaonline.org

Membership: private-sector service companies involved in all sectors of peace and stability operations around the world, including mine clearance, logistics, security, training, and emergency humanitarian aid. Works to institute standards and codes of conduct. Monitors legislation.

National Peace Foundation, *666 11th St. N.W., #202 20001; (202) 783-7030. Fax, (202) 783-7040. Sarah Harder, President.*

General e-mail, npf@nationalpeace.org

Web, www.nationalpeace.org

Seeks to prevent conflict and build peace in the United States and around the world by developing citizen networks, advancing peace education and conflict prevention and resolution skills, and promoting democratic values through international travel/exchange programs.

ARMS CONTROL, DISARMAMENT, AND THREAT REDUCTION

►AGENCIES

Defense Dept. (DoD), *Chemical and Biological Defense Program,* 3050 Defense Pentagon, #3C257 20301-3050; (703) 693-9410. Fax, (703) 695-0476. Jean Reed, Special Assistant for Chemical and Biological Defense and Chemical Demilitarization Programs.
Web, www.acq.osd.mil

Coordinates, integrates, and provides oversight for the Joint Services Chemical and Biological Defense Program. Provides oversight for the Chemical Weapons Demilitarization Program.

Defense Dept. (DoD), *Global Security Affairs,* 2900 Defense Pentagon, #3C653A 20301-2900; (703) 697-7728. Fax, (703) 695-4079. Joseph A. Benkert, Assistant Secretary.
Web, www.defenselink.mil

Advises the secretary on reducing and countering nuclear, biological, chemical, and missile threats to the United States and its forces and allies; arms control negotiations, implementation, and verification policy; nuclear weapons policy, denuclearization, threat reduction, and nuclear safety and security; and technology transfer.

Defense Dept. (DoD), *Plans,* 2000 Defense Pentagon, 20301-2000; (703) 571-9242. Fax, (703) 614-9698. Janine Davidson, Deputy Assistant Secretary; Michael McNerney, Principal Director. Press, (703) 692-3918.
Web, www.defenselink.mil

Formulates national policies to prevent and counter the proliferation of nuclear, chemical, and biological weapons; missiles; and conventional technologies. Devises arms control agreements, export controls, technology transfer policies, and military planning policies.

Defense Threat Reduction Agency *(Defense Dept.),* 8725 John Jay Kingman Rd., MS 6201, Fort Belvoir, VA 22060-6201; (703) 767-4883. Fax, (703) 767-5830. Maj. Gen. Randy E. Manner, Director. Press, (703) 767-5870.
Web, www.dtra.mil

Seeks to reduce the threat to the United States and its allies from weapons of mass destruction; conducts technology security activities, cooperative threat reduction programs, arms control treaty monitoring, and on-site inspection; provides technical support on weapons of mass destruction matters to the Defense Dept. components.

Energy Dept. (DOE), *Defense Nuclear Nonproliferation: National Nuclear Security Administration,* 1000 Independence Ave. S.W., #7A049 20585; (202) 586-0645. Fax, (202) 586-0862. Kenneth Baker, Deputy Administrator (Acting).
Web, www.nnsa.doe.gov

Provides U.S. government agencies and departments with technical and operational expertise on foreign nuclear and energy issues. Oversees programs to prevent the spread of nuclear, chemical, and biological weapons and missiles for their delivery. Partners with Russia and other former Soviet states to secure weapons of mass destruction materials and expertise; works to strengthen legal and institutional nonproliferation norms; builds technologies to detect proliferation activities; and promotes the safe use of nuclear power.

Nonproliferation *(Executive Office of the President),* Dwight D. Eisenhower Executive Office Bldg., #361 20506; (202) 456-9181. Fax, (202) 456-9180. Gary Samore, Special Adviser to the President and Senior Director.

Responsible for policies concerning arms proliferation and control in the context of homeland security.

State Dept., *Bureau of International Security and Nonproliferation (ISN),* 2201 C St. N.W., #3932 20520; (202) 647-9612. Fax, (202) 736-4863. C. S. Eliot Kang, Assistant Secretary (Acting); Philip A. Foley, Principal Deputy Assistant Secretary (Acting).
Web, www.state.gov/t/isn

Leads U.S. efforts to prevent the spread of weapons of mass destruction (WMD, including nuclear, chemical, and biological weapons) and their delivery systems; spearheads efforts to promote international consensus on WMD proliferation; supports efforts of foreign partners to prevent, protect against, and respond to the threat or use of WMD by terrorists.

State Dept., *Plans, Policy, and Analysis,* 2201 C St. N.W., #2811 20520; (202) 647-7775. Fax, (202) 647-8998. Kevin O'Keefe, Director.
Web, www.state.gov

Responsible for critical infrastructure and protection, military security assistance, counterinsurgency strategy, space policy and peacekeeping, and political military policy.

►CONGRESS

For a listing of relevant congressional committees and subcommittees, please see page 546 or the Appendix.

►NONGOVERNMENTAL

Arms Control Assn., 1313 L St. N.W., #130 20005; (202) 463-8270. Fax, (202) 463-8273. Daryl G. Kimball, Executive Director.
General e-mail, aca@armscontrol.org

Web, www.armscontrol.org

Nonpartisan organization that seeks to broaden public interest and support for arms control and disarmament in national security policy. Publishes *Arms Control Today.*

Council for a Livable World, *322 4th St. N.E.*
20002-5824; (202) 543-4100. Fax, (202) 543-6297.
John D. Isaacs, Executive Director.
General e-mail, advocacy@clw.org

Web, www.clw.org

Citizens' interest group that supports arms control treaties, reduced military spending, peacekeeping, and tight restrictions on international arms sales.

Federation of American Scientists (FAS), *1725 DeSales St. N.W., 6th Floor 20036; (202) 546-3300. Fax, (202) 675-1010. Henry Kelly, President.*
General e-mail, fas@fas.org

Web, www.fas.org

Opposes the global arms race and supports nuclear disarmament and limits on government secrecy. Promotes learning technologies and conducts studies and monitors legislation on U.S. weapons policy; provides the public with information on arms control and related issues.

Friends Committee on National Legislation (FCNL),
245 2nd St. N.E. 20002-5795; (202) 547-6000. Fax, (202) 547-6019. Joe Volk, Executive Secretary. Toll-free, (800) 630-1330. Recorded information, (202) 547-4343.
General e-mail, fcnl@fcnl.org

Web, www.fcnl.org

Supports world disarmament; international cooperation; domestic, economic, peace, and social justice issues; and improvement in relations between the United States and the former Soviet Union. Opposes conscription. Affiliated with the Religious Society of Friends (Quakers).

GlobalSecurity.org, *300 N. Washington St., #B-100, Alexandria, VA 22314-2540; (703) 548-2700. Fax, (703) 548-2424. John E. Pike, Director.*
General e-mail, info@globalsecurity.org

Web, www.globalsecurity.org

Provides background information and covers developing news stories on the military, weapons proliferation, space, homeland security, and intelligence. Offers profiles of agencies, systems, facilities, and current operations as well as a library of primary documentation.

High Frontier, *500 N. Washington St., Alexandria, VA 22314-2314; (703) 535-8774. Fax, (703) 535-8776. Henry Cooper, Director.*
General e-mail, high.frontier@verizon.net

Web, www.highfrontier.org

Educational organization that provides information on missile defense programs and proliferation. Advocates development of a single-stage-to-orbit space vehicle, a moon base program, and a layered missile defense system. Operates speakers bureau; monitors defense legislation.

Nonproliferation Policy Education Center (NPEC),
1718 M St. N.W., #244 20036-4504; (202) 466-4406. Fax, (202) 659-5429. Henry D. Sokolski, Executive Director.
General e-mail, npec@npec-web.org

Web, www.npec-web.org

Conducts and publishes research on strategic weapons proliferation issues and makes it available to the press, congressional and executive branch staff, foreign officials, and international organizations.

Nuclear Threat Initiative (NTI), *1747 Pennsylvania Ave. N.W., 7th Floor 20006; (202) 296-4810. Fax, (202) 296-4811. Charles B. Curtis, President.*
General e-mail, contact@nti.org

Web, www.nti.org

Works to reduce threats from nuclear, biological, and chemical weapons.

Peace Action, *1100 Wayne Ave., #1020, Silver Spring, MD 20910-5642; (301) 565-4050. Fax, (301) 565-0850. Kevin Martin, Executive Director.*
Web, www.peace-action.org

Grassroots organization that supports a negotiated comprehensive test ban treaty. Seeks a reduction in the military budget and a transfer of those funds to nonmilitary programs. Works for an end to international arms trade. (Merger of Sane and The Nuclear Freeze.)

Physicians for Social Responsibility (PSR), *1875 Connecticut Ave. N.W., #1012 20009-5747; (202) 667-4260. Fax, (202) 667-4201. Michael McCally, Executive Director.*
General e-mail, psrnatl@psr.org

Web, www.psr.org

Membership: doctors, nurses, health scientists, and concerned citizens. Works toward the elimination of nuclear and other weapons of mass destruction, the achievement of a sustainable environment, and the reduction of violence and its causes. Conducts public education programs, monitors policy, and serves as a liaison with other concerned groups.

Union of Concerned Scientists, *Global Security, Washington Office, 1707 H St. N.W., #600 20006-3962; (202) 223-6133. Fax, (202) 223-6162. Lisbeth Gronlund, Co-Director; David Wright, Co-Director.*
General e-mail, ucs@ucsusa.org

Web, www.ucsusa.org

Facilitates the effective participation of lay scientists in policy debates through the Global Security Program, which works to educate the public, media, and policymakers. Works to lay the groundwork for long-term policy changes internationally. Plays a unique role in increasing the number of independent scientists and technical analysts working professionally on security issues worldwide. (Headquarters in Cambridge, Mass.)

Union of Concerned Scientists, *Strategy and Policy, Washington Office, 1825 K St. N.W., #800 20006-3962; (202) 223-6133. Fax, (202) 223-6162. Alden Meyer, Director.*
General e-mail, ucs@ucsusa.org

Web, www.ucsusa.org

Works to advance international security policies and agreements that restrict the spread of weapons of mass destruction and reduce the risk of war. Promotes international nonproliferation through reductions in fissile materials and through arms control measures, including a comprehensive nuclear testing ban, restrictions on ballistic missile defenses, and dismantlement of nuclear warheads. Encourages the use of collective security forces, such as the United Nations, to alleviate conflicts. (Headquarters in Cambridge, Mass.)

World Security Institute, *Center for Defense Information,* 1779 Massachusetts Ave. N.W., #615 20036-2109; (202) 332-0900. Fax, (202) 462-4559. *Theresa Hitchens, Director. Press, (202) 797-5273. General e-mail, info@worldsecurityinstitute.org*

Web, www.cdi.org

Educational organization that advocates a strong defense while opposing excessive expenditures for weapons and policies that increase the risk of war. Interests include the defense budget, weapons systems, and troop levels. Provides Congress, the Pentagon, the State Dept., the media, and the public with appraisals of military matters.

Nuclear Weapons and Power

▶**AGENCIES**

Defense Nuclear Facilities Safety Board, 625 Indiana Ave. N.W., #700 20004-2901; (202) 694-7080. Fax, (202) 208-6518. A.J. Eggenberger, Chair. Information, (202) 694-7000. *General e-mail, mailbox@dnfsb.gov*

Web, www.dnfsb.gov

Independent board created by Congress and appointed by the president to provide external oversight of Energy Dept. defense nuclear weapons production facilities and make recommendations to the secretary of energy regarding public health and safety.

Energy Dept. (DOE), *Defense Programs,* 1000 Independence Ave. S.W., #4A019 20585; (202) 586-2179. Fax, (202) 586-5670. Brig. Gen. Garrett Harencak, Deputy Administrator (Acting). *Web, www.nnsa.doe.gov*

Responsible for nuclear weapons research, development, and engineering; performs laser fusion research and development.

Energy Dept. (DOE), *International Regimes and Agreements,* 1000 Independence Ave. S.W., NA243 20585-0001; (202) 586-0589. Fax, (202) 586-7623. Richard Goorevich, Director. *Web, www.energy.gov*

Develops and implements policies concerning nuclear materials and equipment; participates in international negotiations involving nuclear policy; supports activities of the International Atomic Energy Agency.

Homeland Security Dept. (DHS), *Domestic Nuclear Detection,* 1120 Vermont Ave. N.W. 20528; (202) 254-7000. Chuck Galloway, Director (Acting). *General e-mail, DNDOinfo@dhs.gov*

Web, www.dhs.gov/DNDO

Seeks to improve the nation's capability to detect and report unauthorized attempts to import, possess, store, develop, or transport nuclear or radiological material for use against the nation, and to further enhance this capability over time. Oversees the development of an integrated global and domestic nuclear detection program and the deployment of a nuclear detection system.

National Security Council (NSC), *(Executive Office of the President), Defense Policy and Strategy,* The White House 20504; (202) 456-9191. Fax, (202) 456-9190. Barry Pavel, Special Assistant to the President. *Web, www.whitehouse.gov/nsc*

Advises the assistant to the president for national security affairs on matters concerning defense policy.

Navy Dept. *(Defense Dept.), Naval Nuclear Propulsion,* 1240 Isaac Hull Ave. S.E., Washington Navy Yard, DC 20376-8010; (202) 781-6174. Fax, (202) 781-6403. Adm. Kirkland H. Donald, Director. *Web, www.navy.mil*

Responsible for naval nuclear propulsion.

State Dept., *Nuclear Energy, Safety, and Security Affairs,* 2201 C St. N.W., #3320A 20520; (202) 647-4413. Fax, (202) 647-0775. Richard J.K. Stratford, Director. *Web, www.state.gov*

Coordinates U.S. government activities that support safeguards against proliferation of nuclear weapons.

▶**CONGRESS**

For a listing of relevant congressional committees and subcommittees, please see page 546 or the Appendix.

▶**NONGOVERNMENTAL**

Institute for Science and International Security, 236 Massachusetts Ave. N.E., #500 20002; (202) 547-3633. Fax, (202) 547-3634. David Albright, President. *General e-mail, isis@isis-online.org*

Web, www.isis-online.org

Conducts research and analysis on nuclear weapons production and nonproliferation issues.

BORDERS, CUSTOMS, AND IMMIGRATION

▶**AGENCIES**

Federal Law Enforcement Training Center *(Homeland Security Dept.), Washington Operations,* 555 11th St. N.W., #400 20004-1300; (202) 233-0260. Fax, (202) 233-0258. Connie Patrick, Director.

General e-mail, FLECT-WashingtonOffice@dhs.gov

Web, www.fletc.gov

Trains law enforcement personnel from seventy-six federal agencies. Areas of enforcement include customs, other import and export restrictions, drug control, immigration, financial crimes, transportation, and extradition. (Headquarters in Glynco, Ga.)

Homeland Security Dept. (DHS), *Citizenship and Immigration Services Ombudsman, MS 1225 20528-1225; (202) 357-8100. Fax, (202) 357-0042. Michael Dougherty, Ombudsman.*

General e-mail, cisombudsman@dhs.gov

Web, www.dhs.gov/cisombudsman

Assists individuals and employers in resolving problems with the U.S. Citizenship and Immigration Services (USCIS); proposes changes in the administrative practices of USCIS in an effort to mitigate identified problems.

Interior Dept. (DOI), *Law Enforcement: Border and Drug Coordination, 1849 C St. N.W., MS 7354 20240; (202) 208-6891. Fax, (202) 219-1185. Bruce Marto, Branch Chief.*

Web, http://doi.gov/law_enforcement.html

Provides technical direction and assistance in the development of border practices, as well as supervision of field coordinators for the southwest, southeast, and northern borders. Coordinates with DHS's Border and Transportation Security, Customs and Border Protection, U.S. Border Patrol, and other external entities.

U.S. Citizenship and Immigration Services (USCIS), *(Homeland Security Dept.), 20 Massachusetts Ave. N.W. 20529; (202) 282-8000 (switchboard). Fax, (202) 272-1322. Vacant, Director. Press, (202) 272-1200. Information, (800) 375-5283 or TTY, (800) 767-1833. Web, www.uscis.gov*

Responsible for the delivery of immigration and citizenship services. Priorities include the promotion of national security, the elimination of immigration adjudications backlog, and the implementation of measures to improve service delivery.

U.S. Customs and Border Protection *(Homeland Security Dept.), Agricultural Program and Trade Liaison Office, 1300 Pennsylvania Ave. N.W., #2.5B 20229; (202) 344-3298. Fax, (202) 344-1442. Vernon Foret, Executive Director.*

Web, www.cbp.gov

Responsible for safeguarding the nation's animal and natural resources from pests and disease through inspections at ports of entry and beyond.

U.S. Customs and Border Protection *(Homeland Security Dept.), Border Patrol, 1300 Pennsylvania Ave. N.W., #6.5E 20229; (202) 344-2050. Fax, (202) 344-3140. David V. Aguilar, Chief.*

Web, www.cbp.gov

Mobile uniformed law enforcement arm of the Homeland Security Dept. Primary mission is to detect

---

Immigration Reform Resources

America's Voice, (202) 463-8602, www.americasvoice.org

Center for Community Change, (202) 339-9300, www.communitychange.org

Center for Immigration Studies, (202) 466-8185, www.cis.org

Federation for American Immigration Reform, (202) 328-7004, www.fairus.org

Migration Policy Institute, (202) 266-1940, www.migrationpolicy.org or www.migrationinformation.org

Minutemen Civil Defense Corps, (520) 829-3112, www.minutemenhq.com

National Council of La Raza, (202) 785-1670, www.nclr.org

National Immigration Forum, (202) 347-0040, www.immigrationforum.org

NumbersUSA, (703) 816-8820, www.numbersUSA.com

Team America PAC, (703) 255-1399, www.teamamericapac.org

U.S. Border Control, (703) 356-6567, www.usbc.org

U.S. Committee for Refugees and Immigrants, (202) 347-3507, www.refugees.org

U.S. Conference of Catholic Bishops, Migration and Refugee Services, (202) 541-3352 or (202) 541-3448, www.usccb.org/mrs

---

and prevent the illegal trafficking of people and contraband across U.S. borders.

U.S. Immigration and Customs Enforcement (ICE), *(Homeland Security Dept.), 500 12th St. S.W. 20024-6121; (202) 514-1900. Fax, (202) 307-9911. Julie L. Myers, Assistant Secretary. Press, (202) 732-4242. Hotline to report suspicious activity, (866) 347-2423. Web, www.ice.gov*

Enforces immigration and customs laws within the United States. Focuses on the protection of specified federal buildings and on air and marine enforcement. Undertakes investigations and conducts interdictions.

▶**CONGRESS**

For a listing of relevant congressional committees and subcommittees, please see page 546 or the Appendix.

DEFENSE TRADE AND TECHNOLOGY

▶**AGENCIES**

Advisory Committee on Export Policy *(Commerce Dept.), 14th St. and Constitution Ave. N.W., #3889 20230;*

(202) 482-5863. Fax, (202) 501-2815. Ralph Kessler, Chair (Acting).
Web, www.bis.doc.gov

Committee of cabinet-level secretaries and heads of other government offices. Considers export licensing policies and actions, especially those concerning national security and other major policy matters; reviews export licensing applications; advises the assistant secretary of export administration on policy matters.

Bureau of Industry and Security *(Commerce Dept.),* 14th St. and Constitution Ave. N.W., #3898 20230; (202) 482-1455. Fax, (202) 482-2421. Mario Mancuso, Under Secretary. Press, (202) 482-2721. Export licensing information, (202) 482-4811.
Web, www.bis.doc.gov

Administers Export Administration Act; maintains control lists and performs export licensing for the purposes of national security, foreign policy, and prevention of short supply.

Bureau of Industry and Security *(Commerce Dept.),* **Export Enforcement,** 14th St. and Constitution Ave. N.W., #3723 20230; (202) 482-3618. Fax, (202) 482-4173. Vacant, Assistant Secretary; Kevin Delli-Collei, Deputy Assistant Secretary.
Web, www.bis.doc.gov

Enforces dual-use export controls on exports of U.S. goods and technology for purposes of national security, nonproliferation, counterterrorism, foreign policy, and short supply. Enforces the antiboycott provisions of the Export Administration Regulations.

Defense Dept. (DoD), *Chemical, Biological, Radiation, and Nuclear Defense Information Analysis Center* **(CBIAC),** Aberdeen Proving Ground–Edgewood Area, P.O. Box 196, Gunpowder, MD 21010-0196; (410) 676-9030. Fax, (410) 676-9703. Ronald L. Evans, Director; James M. King, Deputy Director.
General e-mail, cbiac@battelle.org

Web, www.cbiac.apgea.army.mil

Defense Dept. information analysis center operated by Battelle Memorial Institute. Serves as Defense Dept.'s focal point for information related to chemical, biological, radiological, and nuclear (CBRN) defense. Collects and analyzes information pertaining to CBRN defense and homeland security. Identifies and implements high-priority research and development projects. Disseminates technical information to planners, scientists, and military field personnel. Supports Defense Dept., other federal agencies, contractors, and state and local governments.

Defense Dept. (DoD), *Defense Technology Security Administration,* 2850 Eisenhower Ave., Alexandria, VA 22314; (703) 325-3295. James Hursch, Deputy Under Secretary (Acting).
Web, www.defenselink.mil/policy

Develops and implements technology security policy for international transfers of defense-related goods, services, and technologies. Participates in interagency and international activities and regimes that monitor, control,

and prevent transfers that could threaten U.S. national security interests.

Defense Dept. (DoD), *International Cooperation,* 3070 Defense Pentagon, #3A280 20301-3070; (703) 697-4172. Fax, (703) 693-2026. Alfred G. Volkman, Director.
Web, www.acq.osd.mil/ic

Advises the under secretary of defense for Acquisitions, Technology, and Logistics on cooperative research and development, production, procurement, and follow-up support programs with foreign nations; monitors the transfer of secure technologies to foreign nations.

Energy Dept. (DOE), *International Regimes and Agreements,* 1000 Independence Ave. S.W., NA243 20585-0001; (202) 586-0589. Fax, (202) 586-7623. Richard Goorevich, Director.
Web, www.energy.gov

Develops policies concerning nuclear material and equipment exports, nuclear material transfers and retransfers, and regional nonproliferation.

National Security Council (NSC), *(Executive Office of the President), International Economic Affairs,* The White House 20504; (202) 456-9281. Fax, (202) 456-9280. John Herrmann, Special Assistant to the President.
Web, www.whitehouse.gov/nsc

Advises the president, the National Security Council, and the National Economic Council on all aspects of U.S. foreign policy dealing with U.S. international economic policies.

Nuclear Regulatory Commission, *International Programs,* #04E21 20555; (301) 415-2344. Fax, (301) 415-2400. Margaret M. Doane, Director.
Web, www.nrc.gov

Coordinates application review process for exports and imports of nuclear materials, facilities, and components. Makes recommendations on export-import licensing upon completion of review process. Conducts related policy reviews.

State Dept., *Bureau of International Security and Nonproliferation (ISN),* 2201 C St. N.W., #3932 20520; (202) 647-9612. Fax, (202) 736-4863. Vacant, Assistant Secretary; Vacant, Principal Deputy Assistant Secretary.
Web, www.state.gov/t/isn

Leads U.S. efforts to prevent the spread of weapons of mass destruction (WMD, including nuclear, chemical, and biological weapons) and their delivery systems; spearheads efforts to promote international consensus on WMD proliferation; supports efforts of foreign partners to prevent, protect against, and respond to the threat or use of WMD by terrorists.

State Dept., *Defense Trade Controls,* 2401 E St. N.W., SA-1, #H1200 20037 (mailing address: PM/DDTC, SA-1, 12th Floor, Bureau of Political Military Affairs, Washington, DC 20522-0112); (202) 663-2861. Fax, (202) 261-8199. Robert Kovac, Managing Director.
Web, www.pmddtc.state.gov

Air Force Department

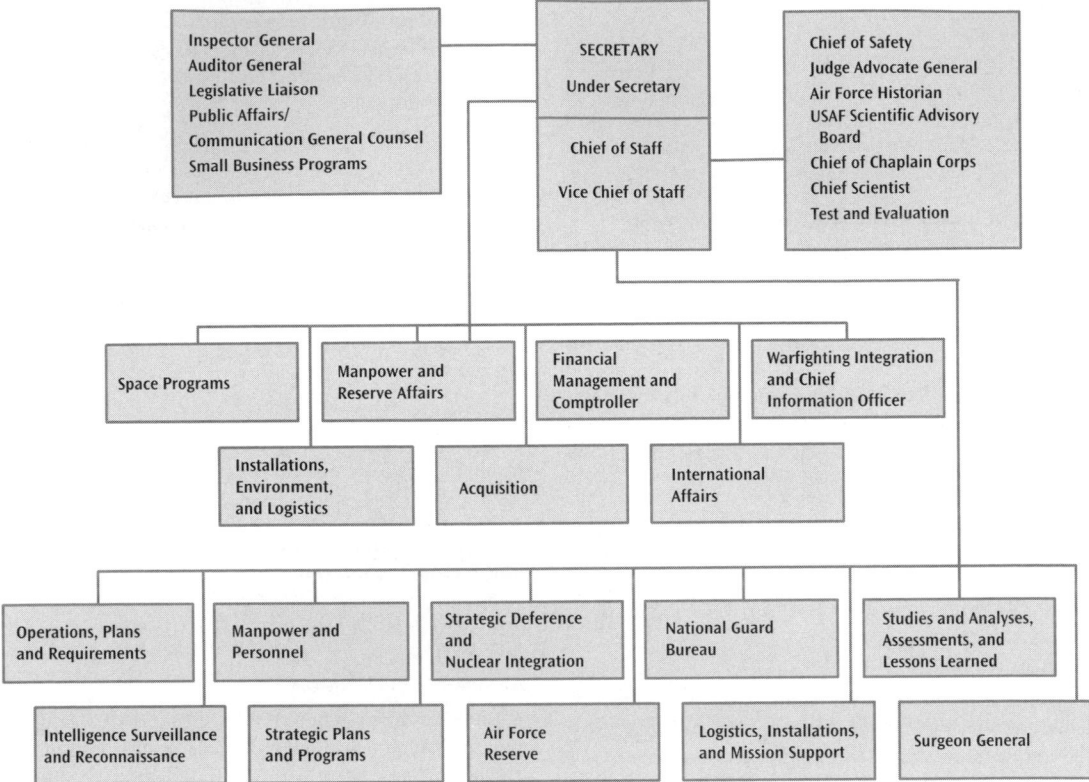

Controls the commercial export of defense articles, services, and related technical data; authorizes the permanent export and temporary import of such items.

State Dept., *Terrorism, Finance, and Economic Sanctions Policy,* 2201 C St. N.W., #4657 20520; (202) 647-7489. Fax, (202) 647-4064. Steven Bondy, Director. Web, www.state.gov

Develops and implements U.S. sanctions of embargoed countries and countries known to house terrorists. Coordinates U.S. participation in multilateral strategic trade control and revisions related to the export of strategically critical high-technology goods. Cooperates with the Commerce, Defense, and Treasury Depts. regarding export controls.

Treasury Dept., *Foreign Assets Control,* 1500 Pennsylvania Ave. N.W., Annex Bldg., #2233 20220; (202) 622-2500. Fax, (202) 622-1657. Adam Szubin, Director. Fax-on-demand, (202) 622-0077. Web, www.ustreas.gov/ofac

Authorized under the revised Trading with the Enemy Act, the International Emergency Economic Powers Act, and the United Nations Participation Act to control financial and commercial dealings with certain countries and their foreign nationals in times of war or emergencies. Regulations involving foreign assets control, narcotics,

nonproliferation, and commercial transactions currently apply in varying degrees to Angola, Cuba, Iran, Iraq, Libya, North Korea, Sierra Leone, Sudan, the Taliban, and Yugoslavia.

►CONGRESS

For a listing of relevant congressional committees and subcommittees, please see page 546 or the Appendix.

Research and Development

►AGENCIES

Air Force Dept. *(Defense Dept.), Acquisition,* 1060 Air Force Pentagon, #4E962 20330-1060; (703) 697-6361. Fax, (703) 693-6400. Sue C. Payton, Assistant Secretary. Web, www.af.mil

Air Force office that directs and reviews Air Force research, development, and acquisition of weapons systems.

Air Force Dept. *(Defense Dept.), Scientific Research,* 875 N. Randolph St., #3112, Arlington, VA 22203-1768; (703) 696-7551. Fax, (703) 696-9556. Brendan B. Godfrey, Director. Web, www.afosr.af.mil

Sponsors and sustains basic research; assists in the transfer of research results to the war fighter; supports Air Force goals of control and maximum utilization of air and space.

Army Corps of Engineers *(Defense Dept.), Research and Development,* 441 G St. N.W., #3Z10 20314-1000; (202) 761-1415. Fax, (202) 761-0907. James R. Houston, Director, (601) 634-2000.
Web, www.usace.army.mil

Supports the research and development efforts of the corps by providing strategic planning and strategic direction and oversight, developing policy and doctrine, developing national program integration, and advising the chief of engineers on science and technology issues.

Army Dept. *(Defense Dept.), Acquisition, Logistics, and Technology,* 103 Army Pentagon, #2E532 20310-0103; (703) 695-6153. Fax, (703) 697-4003. Dean G. Popps, Assistant Secretary (Acting). Press, (703) 697-7592.
Web, https://webportal.saalt.army.mil

Civilian office that directs and reviews Army acquisition research and development of weapons systems and missiles.

Army Dept. *(Defense Dept.), Research and Technology,* 103 Army Pentagon, #2E533 20310-0103; (703) 692-1830. Fax, (703) 692-1836. Thomas Killion, Deputy Assistant Secretary.
Web, www.army.mil

Sponsors and supports basic research at Army laboratories, universities, and other public and private organizations; assists in the transfer of research and technology to the field.

Defense Advanced Research Projects Agency *(Defense Dept.),* 3701 N. Fairfax Dr., Arlington, VA 22203-1714; (703) 526-6629. Fax, (571) 218-4356. Anthony J. Tether, Director; John Jennings, External Relations, (703) 526-4725. Press, (703) 696-2404.
Web, www.darpa.mil

Helps maintain U.S. technological superiority and guard against unforeseen technological advances by potential adversaries; determines which proposals for future projects related to national security deserve further research.

Defense Dept. (DoD), *Defense Research and Engineering,* 3030 Defense Pentagon, #3E1062 20301-3030; (703) 697-5776. Fax, (703) 693-7167. Vacant, Director; Alan R. Shaffer, Principal Deputy Director.
Web, www.dod.mil/ddre

Civilian office responsible for policy, guidance, and oversight for the Defense Dept.'s Science and Technology Program. Serves as focal point for in-house laboratories, university research, and other science and technology matters.

Defense Dept. (DoD), *Missile Defense Agency,* 7100 Defense Pentagon 20301-7100; (703) 695-6344. Fax, (703)

614-9777. Maj. Gen. Patrick J. O'Reilly (USA), Director; Adm. Joseph Horn, Deputy Director.
Web, www.mda.mil

Manages and directs the ballistic missile defense acquisition and research and development programs. Seeks to deploy improved theater missile defense systems and to develop options for effective national missile defenses while increasing the contribution of defensive systems to U.S. and allied security.

Defense Technical Information Center *(Defense Dept.),* 8725 John Jay Kingman Rd., #0944, Fort Belvoir, VA 22060-6218; (703) 767-9100. Fax, (703) 767-9183. Paul R. Ryan, Administrator. Registration, (703) 767-8200. Toll-free, (800) 225-3842.
Web, www.dtic.mil

Acts as a central repository for the Defense Dept.'s collection of current and completed research and development efforts in all fields of science and technology. Disseminates research and development information to contractors, grantees, and registered organizations working on government research and development projects, particularly for the Defense Dept. Users must register with the center.

Marine Corps *(Defense Dept.), Systems Command,* 2200 Lester St., Quantico, VA 22134-6050; (703) 432-1800. Fax, (703) 432-3535. Brig. Gen. Michael Brogan, Commanding General.
Web, www.marcorsyscom.usmc.mil

Military office that directs Marine Corps research, development, and acquisition.

National Communications System *(Homeland Security Dept.), President's National Security Telecommunications Advisory Committee,* NCS, 245 Murray Lane, Bldg. 410, MS 8510 20528-8510; (703) 235-5525. Fax, (703) 235-5696. Keisha Gebreyes, Program Manager. Press, (703) 235-5516.
General e-mail, nstac1@dhs.gov

Web, www.ncs.gov/nstac/nstac.html

Advises the president, the National Security Council, the Office of Science and Technology Policy, and the Office of Management and Budget on specific measures to improve national security and emergency preparedness telecommunications for the federal government.

Naval Research Laboratory *(Defense Dept.), Research,* 4555 Overlook Ave. S.W. 20375-5320; (202) 767-3301. Fax, (202) 404-2676. John A. Montgomery, Director. Press, (202) 767-2541.
Web, www.nrl.navy.mil

Conducts scientific research and develops advanced technology for the Navy. Areas of research include radar systems, radiation technology, tactical electronic warfare, and weapons guidance systems.

Navy Dept. *(Defense Dept.), Office of Naval Research,* 875 N. Randolph St., #1425, Arlington, VA 22203-1995;

Army Department

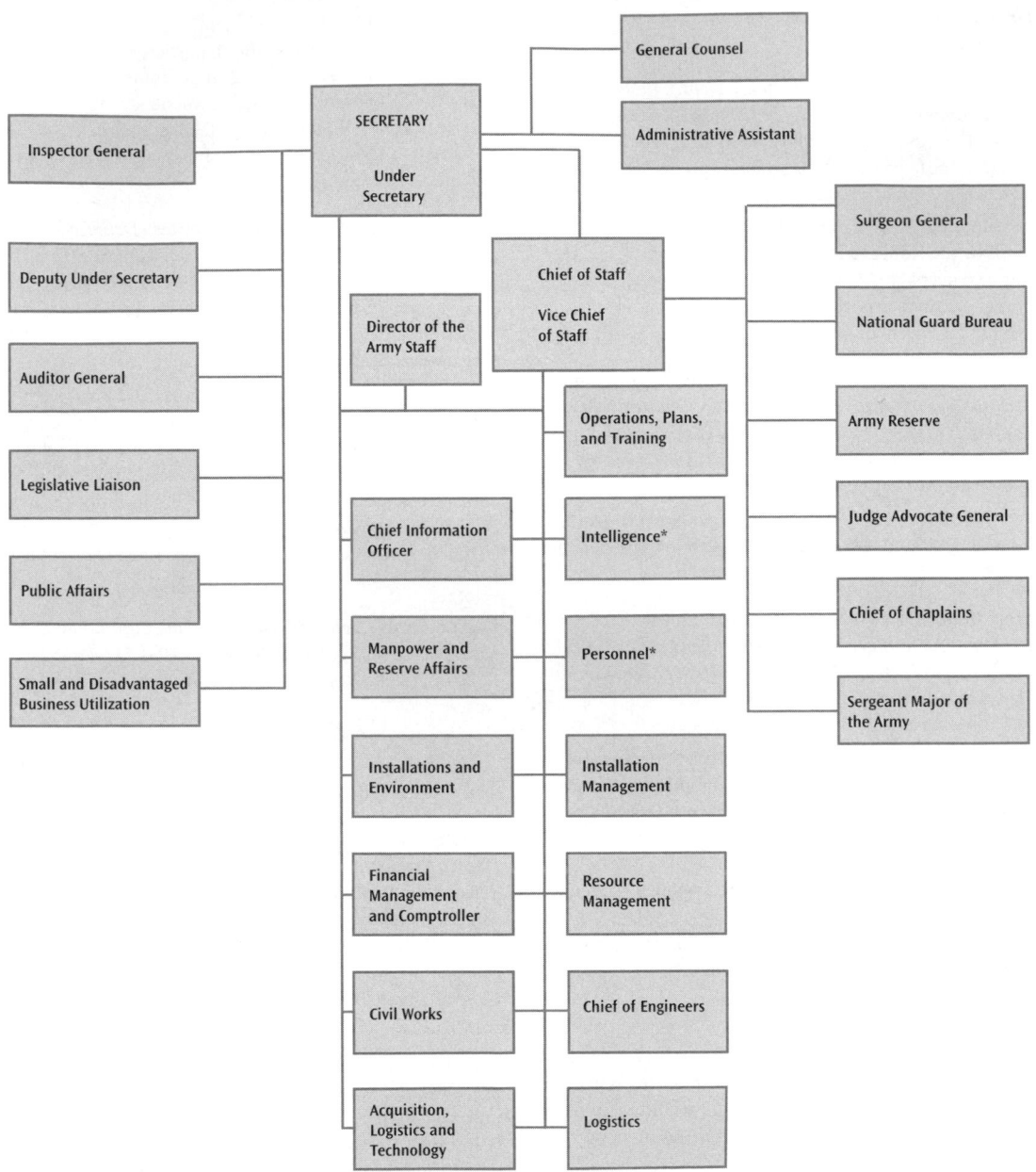

* General Counsel Oversight

(703) 696-5031. Fax, (703) 696-4065. Adm. Nevin P. Carr Jr., Chief.
Web, www.onr.navy.mil

Oversees the offices of Naval Research, Naval Technology, and Advanced Technology; works to ensure transition of research and technology to the fleet; sponsors and supports basic research at Navy laboratories, universities, and other public and private organizations.

Navy Dept. *(Defense Dept.), Research, Development, and Acquisition,* 1000 Navy Pentagon, #4E665

20350-1000; (703) 695-6315. Fax, (703) 697-0172. Sean J. Stackley, Assistant Secretary. Press, (703) 695-6950.
Web, www.navy.mil

Civilian office that directs and reviews Navy and Marine Corps research and development of weapons systems.

Office of Science and Technology Policy (OSTP),
(Executive Office of the President), New Executive Office Bldg., #5236 20502; (202) 456-7116. Fax, (202) 456-6021. John P. Holdren, Director.

Navy Department

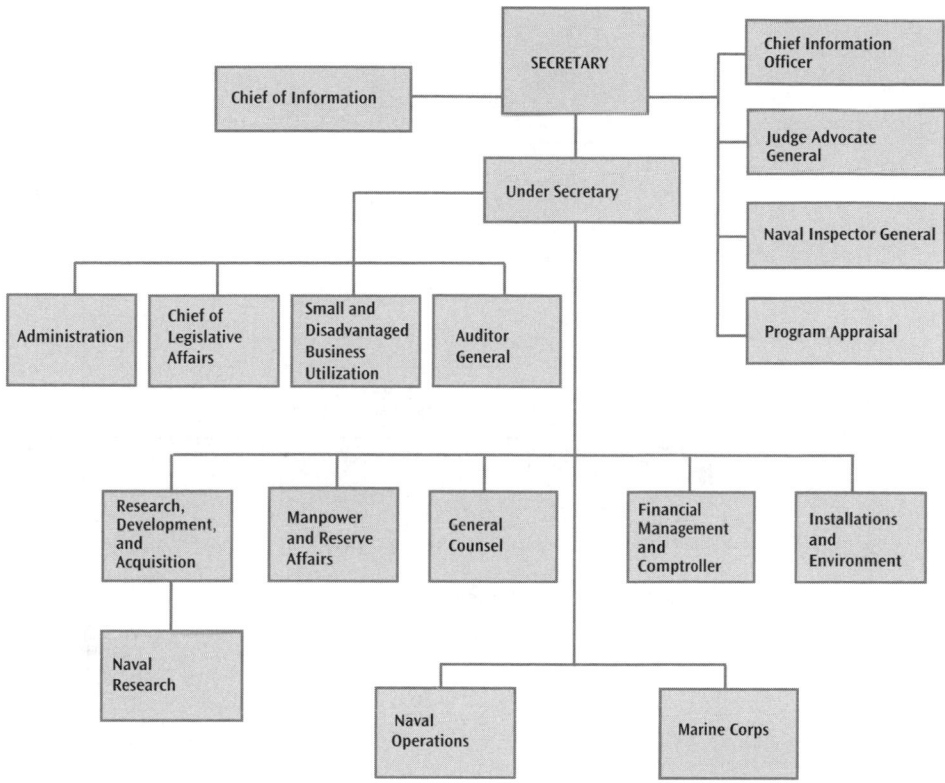

General e-mail, info@ostp.gov

Web, www.ostp.gov

Advises the president on science and technology matters as they affect national security; coordinates science and technology initiatives at the interagency level. Interests include nuclear materials, security, nuclear arms reduction, and counterterrorism.

State Dept., *Intelligence and Research,* 2201 C St. N.W., #6468 20520-6531; (202) 647-9177. Fax, (202) 736-4688. *John Dinger, Assistant Secretary (Acting).* *Web, www.state.gov*

Coordinates foreign policy–related research, analysis, and intelligence programs for the State Dept. and other federal agencies.

U.S. Coast Guard (USCG), *(Homeland Security Dept.),* *Engineering and Logistics,* 1900 Half St. S.W., #J9-1029 20593-0001; (202) 475-5554. Fax, (202) 475-5954. Adm. Thomas P. Ostebo, Assistant Commandant; Jeffrey G. Orner, Deputy Assistant Commandant. Public Affairs, (202) 372-4600. *Web, www.uscg.mil*

Develops and maintains engineering standards for the building of ships and other Coast Guard craft. Publishes *Engineering, Electronics and Logistics Quarterly,* available on the Web site.

►CONGRESS

For a listing of relevant congressional committees and subcommittees, please see page 546 or the Appendix.

►NONGOVERNMENTAL

American Society of Naval Engineers (ASNE), *1452 Duke St., Alexandria, VA 22314-3458; (703) 836-6727. Fax, (703) 836-7491. Dennis K. Kruse, Executive Director. General e-mail, asnehq@navalengineers.org*

Web, www.navalengineers.org

Membership: civilian, active duty, and retired naval engineers. Provides forum for an exchange of information between industry and government involving all phases of naval engineering.

Analytic Services (ANSER/HSI), *2900 S. Quincy St., #800, Arlington, VA 22206-2233; (703) 416-2000. Fax, (703) 416-8408. Ruth David, President. Toll-free, (800) 368-4173. Web, www.anser.org*

Systems analysis organization funded by government contracts. Conducts weapons systems analysis.

Armed Forces Communications and Electronics Assn. (AFCEA), *4400 Fair Lakes Court, Fairfax, VA 22033-3899; (703) 631-6100. Fax, (703) 631-4693. Kent Schneider, President. Toll-free, (800) 336-4583.*

U.S. Coast Guard

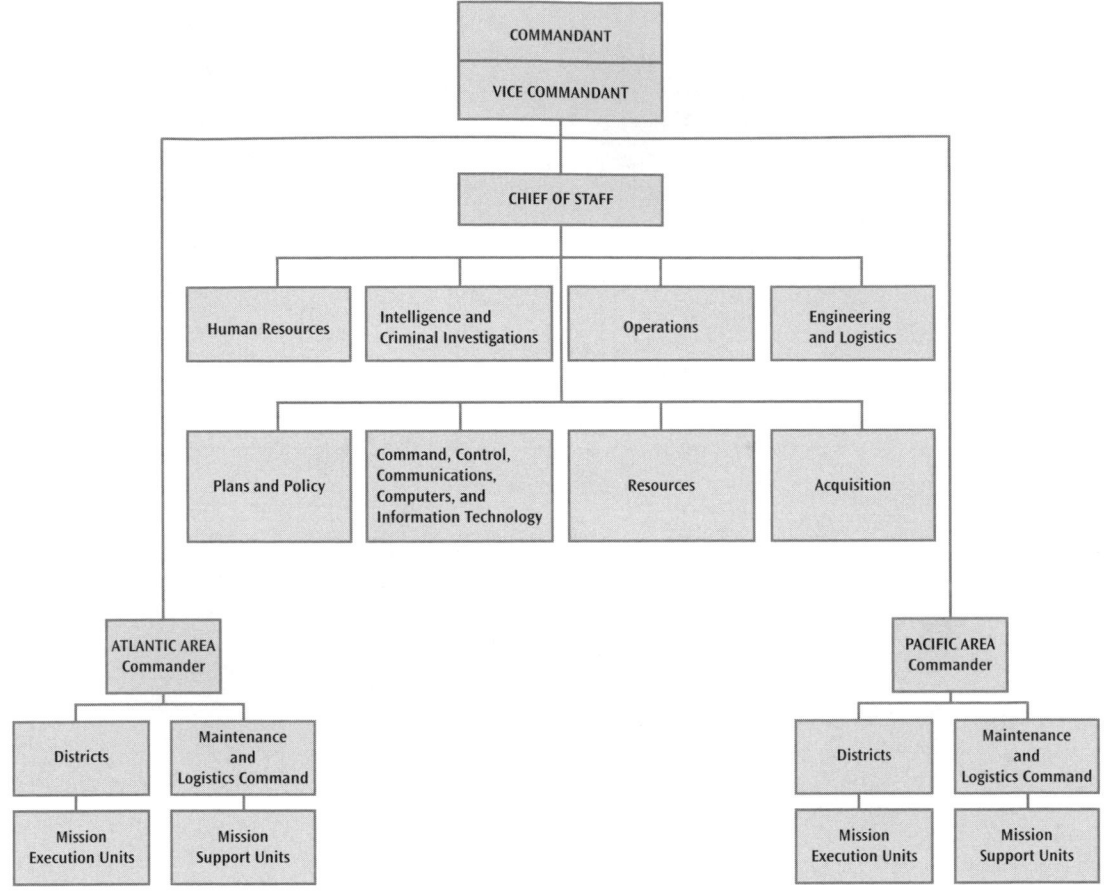

General e-mail, info@afcea.org

Web, www.afcea.org

Membership: industrial organizations, scientists, and military and government personnel in the fields of communications, electronics, computers, and electrical engineering. Consults with the Defense Dept. and other federal agencies on design and maintenance of command, control, communications, computer, and intelligence systems; holds shows displaying latest communications products.

Institute for Defense Analyses (IDA), *4850 Mark Center Dr., Alexandria, VA 22311-1882; (703) 845-2000. Fax, (703) 845-2588. Larry D. Welch (USAF, Ret.), President. Library, (703) 845-2087.*
Web, www.ida.org

Federally funded research and development center that focuses on national security and defense. Conducts research, systems evaluation, and policy analysis for Defense Dept. and other agencies.

Johns Hopkins University Applied Physics Laboratory, *11100 Johns Hopkins Rd., Laurel, MD 20723-6099; (240) 228-5000. Fax, (240) 228-1093. Richard T. Roca, Director. Public Affairs, (443) 778-5113.*
Web, www.jhuapl.edu

Research and development organization that conducts research for the Defense Dept. (primarily the Navy) and other state and federal agencies. Interests include weapons systems and satellites.

Logistics Management Institute (LMI), *2000 Corporate Ridge, McLean, VA 22102-7805; (703) 917-9800. Fax, (703) 917-7597. Nelson M. Ford, President. Toll-free, (800) 213-4817.*
Web, www.lmi.org

Conducts research on military and nonmilitary logistics, including transportation, supply and maintenance, force management, weapons support, acquisition, health systems, international programs, energy and environment, mathematical modeling, installations, operations, and information systems.

Military Operations Research Society (MORS), *1703 N. Beauregard St., #450, Alexandria, VA 22311-1745; (703) 933-9070. Fax, (703) 933-9066. Kirsta L Paternostro, Chief Executive Officer.*
General e-mail, morsoffice@mors.org

Web, www.mors.org

Membership: professional analysts of military operations. Fosters information exchange; promotes professional development and high ethical standards; educates members on emerging issues, analytical techniques, and applications of research.

The Society of American Military Engineers, *607 Prince St., Alexandria, VA 22314-3117; (703) 549-3800. Fax, (703) 684-0231. Robert D. Wolff, Executive Director. Information, (800) 336-3097. Press, (703) 549-3800, ext. 140.*
General e-mail, editor@same.org

Web, www.same.org

Membership: military and civilian engineers, architects, and construction professionals. Conducts workshops and conferences on subjects related to military engineering.

SRI International, *Washington Office, 1100 Wilson Blvd., #2800, Arlington, VA 22209; (703) 524-2053. Fax, (703) 247-8569. Toni Linz, Director.*
Web, www.sri.com

Research organization supported by government and private contracts. Conducts research on military technology, including lasers and computers. Other interests include strategic planning and armed forces interdisciplinary research. (Headquarters in Menlo Park, Calif.)

EMERGENCY PREPAREDNESS AND RESPONSE

▶AGENCIES

Army Corps of Engineers *(Defense Dept.),* **Contingency Operations and Preparedness,** *441 G St. N.W. 20314-1000; (202) 761-4601. Edward J. Hecker, Chief.*
Web, www.usace.army.mil

Assists military combatant commands, as well as federal, state, and local emergency management and emergency response organizations, with mitigation, planning, training, and exercises to build and sustain capabilities to protect from and respond to any emergency or disaster, including natural disasters and terrorist attacks involving weapons of mass destruction.

Civil Air Patrol, *National Capital Wing, Washington Office, 200 McChord St., #111, Bolling AFB 20032-0000; (202) 767-4405. Fax, (202) 767-5695. Col. Richard J. Cooper, Wing Commander, (202) 767-7776.*
General e-mail, cc@natcapwg.cap.gov

Web, www.natcapwg.cap.gov

Official auxiliary of the U.S. Air Force. Conducts search-and-rescue missions for the Air Force; participates in emergency airlift and disaster relief missions. (Headquarters at Maxwell Air Force Base, Ala.)

Energy Dept. (DOE), *Emergency Operations, 1000 Independence Ave. S.W., #GH060 20585; (202) 586-9892. Fax, (202) 586-3904. Joseph J. Krol Jr., Associate Administrator.*
Web, www.energy.gov

Works to ensure coordinated Energy Dept. responses to energy-related emergencies. Recommends policies to mitigate the effects of energy supply crises on the United States; recommends government responses to energy emergencies.

Federal Emergency Management Agency (FEMA), *(Homeland Security Dept.), 500 C St. S.W. 20472; (202) 646-3923. Fax, (202) 646-3875. Nancy L. Ward, Administrator (Acting). Press, (202) 646-4600. TTY, (800) 462-7585. Locator, (202) 646-2500. Disaster assistance, (800) 621-3362.*
General e-mail, femaopa@dhs.gov

Web, www.fema.gov

Manages federal response and recovery efforts following natural disasters, terrorist attacks, and all other kinds of national emergencies. Initiates mitigation activities; works with state and local emergency managers; manages the National Flood Insurance Program.

Federal Emergency Management Agency (FEMA), *(Homeland Security Dept.), Disaster Assistance, 500 C St. S.W. 20472; (202) 646-3642. Fax, (202) 646-2730. James Walke, Assistant Administrator (Acting).*
Web, www.fema.gov

Responsible for coordination of the president's disaster relief program.

Federal Emergency Management Agency (FEMA), *(Homeland Security Dept.), Disaster Operations, 500 C St. S.W., #238 20472; (202) 646-3692. Fax, (202) 646-4060. Robert F. "Bob" Powers, Assistant Administrator (Acting). Press, (202) 646-4600.*
Web, www.fema.gov

Responsible for coordination of federal response assets in the event of an emergency.

Federal Emergency Management Agency (FEMA), *(Homeland Security Dept.), Grant Programs, 800 K St. N.W., 9th Floor 20528; (202) 646-3272. W. Ross Ashley III, Assistant Administrator.*
Web, www.fema.gov/government/grant

Assists states, local communities, regional authorities, and tribal jurisdictions to prevent, deter, and respond to terrorists and other threats to national security through funding, training, and exercises designed to increase responsiveness.

Federal Emergency Management Agency (FEMA), *(Homeland Security Dept.), Mitigation Division, 500 C*

St. S.W., #406 20472; (202) 646-2781. Fax, (202) 646-7970. David I. Maurstad, Assistant Administrator. Web, www.fema.gov/nfip

Administers federal flood insurance programs, including the National Flood Insurance Program. Makes low-cost flood insurance available to eligible homeowners.

Federal Emergency Management Agency (FEMA), (Homeland Security Dept.), National Continuity Programs, 500 C St. S.W. 20472; (202) 646-4145. Fax, (202) 646-3921. Patricia Buckingham, Assistant Administrator (Acting).
Web, www.fema.gov

Responsible for the coordination of all Federal Emergency Management Agency national security programs.

Federal Emergency Management Agency (FEMA), (Homeland Security Dept.), National Incident Management System (NIMS) Integration, 999 E St. N.W., #313 20463; (202) 646-3850. Fax, (202) 646-3061. Donald Grant, Director. TTY, (800) 462-7585. Disaster Assistance, (800) 621-FEMA.
General e-mail, FEMA-NIMS@dhs.gov

Web, www.fema.gov/emergency/nims/index.shtm

Oversees the NIMS. Integrates federal, state, local, and tribal emergency response and preparedness practices into a national framework. Seeks to enable all responders to work together effectively through such means as standardized structures and procedures and interoperable communications systems.

Federal Emergency Management Agency (FEMA), (Homeland Security Dept.), Technological Hazards, 1800 S. Bell St., Arlington, VA 22202 (mailing address: 500 C St. S.W., Mail Code 0104, Washington, DC 20472); (703) 305-0837. Fax, (703) 305-0837. Vanessa Quinn, Director (Acting), (703) 605-1535.
Web, www.fema.gov

Helps FEMA prepare to respond to disasters and incidents of all kinds. Coordinates and develops plans, resources, assessments, and national standards for emergency response operations. Oversees standards for emergency response operations. Oversees community response plans for chemical and nuclear hazards. Develops and delivers grant opportunities and education and training programs for the emergency management and first responder communities.

Health and Human Services Dept. (HHS), National Disaster Medical System, 409 3rd St. S.W., #330 20024; (202) 205-7978. Fax, (800) 872-5945. Jack Beall, Chief.
Web, http://ndms.hhs.gov

Supports federal agencies in the management and coordination of federal medical response to major emergencies and federally declared disasters, such as natural disasters, technological disasters, major transportation accidents, and acts of terrorism, including events involving weapons of mass destruction. Maintains a national capability to provide medical and emotional care in the form of teams, supplies, and equipment at a disaster site, in transit from the impacted area, and into participating definitive care facilities.

Homeland Security Dept. (DHS), Cyber and Security Communications, 1110 N. Glebe Rd., Arlington, VA 20528; (202) 282-8000 (DHS Switchboard). Fax, (202) 447-3237. Rear Adm. Mike Brown, Assistant Secretary.
Web, www.dhs.gov

Works with other federal agencies in developing comprehensive plans to prevent and mitigate cyber-based attacks.

Homeland Security Dept. (DHS), Infrastructure Protection, 3801 Nebraska Ave. N.W., Bldg. 18 20528; (703) 235-3945. Fax, (202) 447-3250. James L. Snyder, Assistant Secretary (Acting).
Web, www.dhs.gov

Identifies and assesses threats to the nation's physical and informational structure from acts of terrorism or natural disasters. Coordinates programs to respond to and quickly recover from attacks or other emergencies.

Homeland Security Dept. (DHS), National Protection and Programs Directorate, 3801 Nebraska Ave., Bldg. 17 20528; (202) 282-8400. Fax, (202) 447-3237. Dallas Brown, Chief Operating Officer.
Web, www.dhs.gov

Identifies and assesses threats to the nation's physical and informational infrastructure; issues warnings to prevent damage.

National Response Center (Homeland Security Dept.), 2100 2nd St. S.W., #2111B 20593-0001; (202) 267-2428. Fax, (202) 267-1322. Syed Qadir, Chief. TTY, (202) 267-4477. Hotline, (800) 424-8802; local, (202) 267-2675.
General e-mail, lst-nrcinfo@comdt.uscg.mil

Web, www.nrc.uscg.mil

Maintains twenty-four-hour hotline for reporting oil spills, hazardous materials accidents, chemical releases, or known or suspected terrorist threats. Notifies appropriate federal officials to reduce the effects of accidents.

Nuclear Regulatory Commission, Nuclear Security and Incident Response, 11545 Rockville Pike, MS T4D22A, Rockville, MD 20555; (301) 415-8003. Fax, (301) 415-6382. Roy P. Zimmerman, Director. Emergency, (301) 816-5100. Non-emergency, (800) 695-7403.
Web, www.nrc.gov

Evaluates technical issues concerning security at nuclear facilities. Develops and directs the commission's response to incidents. Serves as point of contact with Homeland Security Dept., Energy Dept., Federal Emergency Management Agency, and intelligence and law enforcement offices and other agencies.

Small Business Administration (SBA), Disaster Assistance, 409 3rd St. S.W., #6050 20416; (202) 205-6734. Fax, (202) 205-7728. Herbert L. Mitchell, Associate Administrator. Call center, (800) 659-2955.

General e-mail, disastercustomerservice@sba.gov

Web, www.sba.gov

Provides victims of physical disasters with disaster and economic injury loans for homes, businesses, and personal property. Lends funds for uncompensated losses incurred from any disaster declared by the president of the United States or the administrator of the SBA. Lends funds to individual homeowners, business concerns of all sizes, and nonprofit institutions to repair or replace damaged structures and furnishings, business machinery, equipment, and inventory. Provides economic injury loans to small businesses for losses to meet necessary operating expenses, provided the business could have paid these expenses prior to the disaster.

Transportation Dept. (DOT), *Intelligence, Security, and Emergency Response,* 1200 New Jersey Ave. S.E., #56125 20590; (202) 366-6525. Fax, (202) 366-7261. Michael Lowder, Director.
Web, www.dot.gov

Advises the secretary on transportation intelligence and security policy. Acts as liaison with the intelligence community, federal agencies, corporations, and interest groups; administers counterterrorism strategic planning processes. Develops, coordinates, and reviews transportation emergency preparedness programs for use in emergencies affecting national defense and in emergencies caused by natural and man-made disasters and crisis situations.

U.S. Coast Guard (USCG), *(Homeland Security Dept.),* **Counterterrorism and Defense Operations,** 2100 2nd St. S.W., #3121 20593-0001; (202) 372-2101. Fax, (202) 372-2911. Capt. Eugene Gray, Chief.
Web, www.uscg.mil

Ensures that the Coast Guard can mobilize effectively during national emergencies, including those resulting from enemy military attack.

U.S. Fire Administration *(Homeland Security Dept.),* 16825 S. Seton Ave., Emmitsburg, MD 21727; (301) 447-1000. Fax, (301) 447-1346. Gregory B. Cade, Assistant Administrator.
Web, www.usfa.dhs.gov

Provides public education, first responder training, technology, and data initiatives in an effort to prevent losses due to fire and related emergencies. Administers the Emergency Management Institute and the National Fire Academy for firefighters and emergency management personnel.

► **CONGRESS**

For a listing of relevant congressional committees and subcommittees, please see page 546 or the Appendix.

► **NONGOVERNMENTAL**

American Red Cross, *Disaster Preparedness and Response,* 2025 E St. N.W. 20006-5009; (202) 303-5000.

Fax, (202) 303-0061. Gail J. McGovern, President. Press, (202) 303-5551. Donations, (800) RED-CROSS. Toll-free, (800) 733-2767; in Spanish, (800) 257-7575.
Web, www.redcross.org/services/disaster

Chartered by Congress to administer disaster relief. Provides disaster victims with food, shelter, first aid, medical care, and access to other available resources. Feeds emergency workers; handles inquiries from concerned family members outside the disaster area; helps promote disaster preparedness and prevention.

Community Emergency Preparedness Information Network (CEPIN), 8630 Fenton St., #604, Silver Spring, MD 20910-3822; (301) 589-3786. Fax, (301) 589-3797. Neil McDevitt, Program Director. TTY, (301) 589-3006.
General e-mail, pr@cepintdi.org
Web, www.cepintdi.org

Develops disaster preparedness training programs for deaf and hard of hearing consumers and responders. Sponsored by Telecommunications for the Deaf and Hard of Hearing (TDI) and administered by the Homeland Security Dept.

International Assn. of Chiefs of Police, *Advisory Committee for Patrol and Tactical Operations,* 515 N. Washington St., Alexandria, VA 22314-2357; (703) 836-6767. Fax, (703) 836-4543. Ed Wortman, Chair; Nancy Kollo, Staff Liaison, ext. 813. Toll-free, (800) THE-IACP.
General e-mail, kollon@theiacp.org
Web, www.theiacp.org

Membership: foreign and U.S. police executives and administrators. Maintains liaison with civil defense and emergency service agencies; prepares guidelines for police cooperation with emergency and disaster relief agencies during emergencies.

National Assn. of State EMS Officials (NASEMSO), 201 Park Washington Ct., Falls Church, VA 22046-4527; (703) 538-1799. Fax, (703) 241-5603. Elizabeth B. Armstrong, Executive Director.
General e-mail, info@nasemso.org
Web, www.nasemso.org

Works to provide leadership and support for the development of effective emergency medical services (EMS) systems throughout the United States; to formulate national EMS policy; and to foster communication and sharing among state EMS officials.

National Emergency Management Assn., *Washington Office,* 444 N. Capitol St. N.W., #401 20001-1557; (202) 624-5460. Fax, (202) 624-5875. Kristin C. Robinson, Government Relations Director.
Web, www.nemaweb.org

Professional association of state emergency managers. Promotes improvement of emergency management through strategic partnerships and innovative programs.

National Voluntary Organizations Active in Disaster (NVOAD), 1501 Lee Hwy., #206, Arlington,

VA 22209-1109; (703) 778-5088. Fax, (703) 778-5091. Diana Rothe-Smith, Executive Director. General e-mail, info@nvoad.org

Web, www.nvoad.org

Seeks to promote communication, cooperation, coordination, and collaboration among voluntary agencies that participate in disaster response, relief, and recovery nationally.

The Salvation Army Disaster Service, *2626 Pennsylvania Ave. N.W. 20037-1618; (202) 756-2600. Fax, (202) 464-7200. Bobby Lancaster, Divisional Secretary. Web, www.salvationarmyusa.org*

Provides disaster victims and rescuers with emergency support, including food, clothing, and counseling services.

Coordination and Partnerships

▶AGENCIES

Federal Bureau of Investigation (FBI), *(Justice Dept.),* **National Joint Terrorism Task Force (National JTTF),** *935 Pennsylvania Ave. N.W. 20535-0001; (571) 280-5688. Pat Sullivan, Unit Chief. Web, www.fbi.gov*

Group of more than forty agencies from the fields of intelligence, public safety, and federal, state, and local law enforcement that collects terrorism information and intelligence and funnels it to the more than one hundred JTTFs (teams of local, state, and federal agents based at FBI field offices), various terrorism units within the FBI, and partner agencies. Helps the FBI with terrorism investigations.

Federal Emergency Management Agency (FEMA), *(Homeland Security Dept.),* **Emergency Management Institute,** *16825 S. Seton Ave., Emmitsburg, MD 21727; (301) 447-1286. Fax, (301) 447-1497. Cortez Lawrence, Superintendent. General e-mail, netcwebmaster@dhs.gov*

Web, www.fema.gov

Provides federal, state, tribal, and local government personnel and some private organizations engaged in emergency management with technical, professional, and vocational training. Educational programs include hazard mitigation, emergency preparedness, and disaster response.

Federal Emergency Management Agency (FEMA), *(Homeland Security Dept.),* **Grant Programs,** *800 K St. N.W., 9th Floor 20528; (202) 646-3272. W. Ross Ashley III, Assistant Administrator. Web, www.fema.gov/government/grant*

Assists states, local communities, regional authorities, and tribal jurisdictions to prevent, deter, and respond to terrorist and other threats to national security through funding, training, and exercises designed to increase responsiveness.

Federal Emergency Management Agency (FEMA), *(Homeland Security Dept.), Office of National Capital Region Coordination (ONCRC),* *500 C St. S.W. 20472; (202) 212-1500. Ken Wall, Assistant Director. Web, www.fema.gov*

Oversees and coordinates federal programs and domestic preparedness initiatives for state, local, and regional authorities in the District of Columbia, Maryland, and Virginia.

Homeland Security Dept. (DHS), *Federal Coordinator for Gulf Coast Rebuilding,* *MS 1250 20528-1250; (202) 325-0190. Fax, (202) 325-0060. Janet Woodka, Federal Coordinator. Web, www.dhs.gov*

Responsible for developing a long-term rebuilding plan for the region in the aftermath of hurricanes Katrina, Rita, and Wilma; coordinating federal efforts; and helping state and local officials reach consensus on their vision for the region.

Homeland Security Dept. (DHS), *Office of Policy: Private Sector,* *Nebraska Ave. Complex, 3801 Nebraska Ave. N.W., Bldg. 1, 3rd Floor 20528; (202) 282-8484. Fax, (202) 282-8401. Bridger McGaw, Assistant Secretary (Acting). Press, (202) 282-8010. Web, www.dhs.gov*

Works to facilitate outreach to industry and flow of information between industry and the department on security topics ranging from protecting critical infrastructure from sabotage to securing computer networks from hackers.

Homeland Security Dept. (DHS), *Operations Coordination and Planning,* *3801 Nebraska Ave. N.W., Bldg. 3, #3126 20528; (202) 282-9580. Fax, (202) 282-8191. Roger T. Rufe Jr., Director. Web, www.dhs.gov*

Collects and fuses intelligence and enforcement activities information that may have a terrorist nexus from a variety of federal, state, territorial, tribal, local, and private sector partners to continually monitor the nation's threat environment. Coordinates incident management activities within the department and with state governors, homeland security advisors, law enforcement partners, and critical infrastructure operators in all states and major urban areas nationwide.

Homeland Security Dept. (DHS), *Science and Technology Directorate: SAFECOM Program,* *P.O. Box 57243 20037; (866) 969-7233. David Boyd, Director. Press, (202) 254-2385. General e-mail, SAFECOM@dhs.gov*

Web, www.safecomprogram.gov

Serves as the federal umbrella program to help state, local, tribal, and federal public safety agencies improve public safety response through more effective and efficient interoperable wireless communications. Works with existing federal communications initiatives and key

Federal Emergency Management Agency

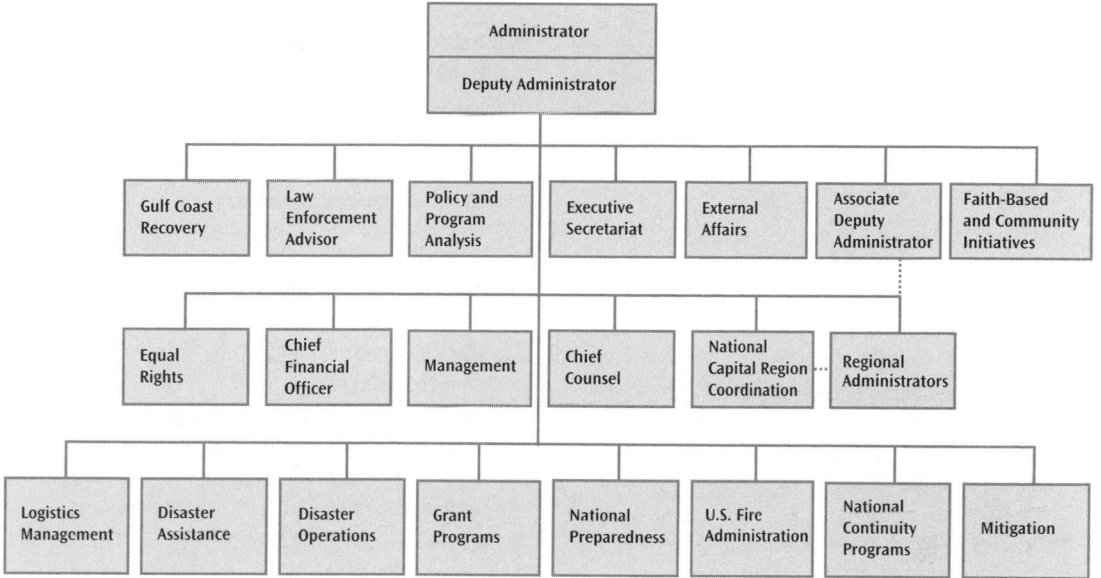

······ Dotted lines signify coordination.

public safety agencies to develop better technologies and processes to coordinate existing and future cross-jurisdictional systems and networks.

►CONGRESS

For a listing of relevant congressional committees and subcommittees, please see page 546 or the Appendix.

►INFORMATION SHARING AND ANALYSIS CENTERS

A 1998 decision directive issued by President Bill Clinton defined various infrastructure industries critical to the national economy and public well-being. The directive proposed the creation of Information Sharing and Analysis Centers (ISACs), which would be established by each critical infrastructure industry to communicate with its members, its government partners, and other ISACs about threat indications, vulnerabilities, and protection strategies. Each ISAC is led by a government agency or private entity. ISACs led by Washington-area agencies or companies are listed below.

Emergency Management and Response-ISAC, *16825 S. Seton Ave., Emmitsburg, MD 21727-8920; (301) 447-1325. Fax, (301) 447-1034. Hugh Wood, Emergency Response Support Branch Chief, USFA, (301) 447-1087. General e-mail, emr-isac@dhs.gov*

Web, www.usfa.dhs.gov/emr-isac

Collects, analyzes, and disseminates information to support the critical infrastructure protection and resilience efforts of the nation's emergency services sector. Researches current physical and cyber protection issues,

operates an information center, issues alerts and messages, and prepares instructional materials relevant to the emergency services community.

Financial Services ISAC, *21355 Ridgetop Circle, Dulles, VA 20166; (888) 732-2812. Fax, (571) 434-6009. Gary Owen, Chair; Bill Nelson, President. General e-mail, admin@fsisac.com*

Web, www.fsisac.com

Provides a confidential venue for sharing security vulnerabilities and solutions, including data obtained from such sources as other ISACs, law enforcement agencies, technology providers, and security associations. Works to facilitate trust, cooperation, and information sharing among its participants and assesses proactive means of mitigating cybersecurity risks.

Food Industry ISAC, *c/o Food Marketing Institute, 2345 Crystal Dr., #800, Arlington, VA 22202-4801; (202) 452-8544. Fax, (202) 429-4519. Leslie G. Sarasin, President, Food Marketing Institute. General e-mail, foodisac@fmi.org*

Web, www.fmi.org/isac

Assembles information and analyses that enable the food industry to report, identify, and reduce its vulnerabilities to malicious attack and to recover from attack; helps the Information Analysis and Infrastructure Protection Directorate at the Homeland Security Dept. and the Federal Bureau of Investigation's weapons of mass destruction operations unit identify credible threats and craft alerts to the industry; provides experts in threat assessment to the FBI. (The Food Industry ISAC operations have been suspended until a need arises.)

Domestic Disaster Relief Organizations

Adventist Development & Relief Agency International, (800) 424-ADRA, www.adra.org

America's Second Harvest, (800) 771-2303, www.secondharvest.org

American Red Cross, (800) RED-CROSS or (202) 303-4498, www.redcross.org

AmeriCares, (800) 486-4357, www.americares.org

Ananda Marga Universal Relief Team, Inc., (301) 984-0217, www.amurt.net

Catholic Charities USA, (703) 549-1390, www.catholiccharitiesusa.org

Catholic Relief Services, (800) 736-3467, www.catholicrelief.org

Children's Miracle Network (Osmond Foundation for the Children of the World), (801) 278-8900, www.cmn.org

Children's Network International, (877) 264-2243, www.childrensnetworkinternational.org

Church World Service, (800) 297-1516 or (888) 297-2767, www.churchworldservice.org

Direct Relief International, (805) 964-4767, www. directrelief.org

Doctors of the World, USA, (212) 226-9890, www.doctorsoftheworld.org

Episcopal Relief and Development, (800) 334-7626, www.er-d.org

Federal Employee Education and Assistance Fund (FEEA), (202) 554-0007, www.feea.org

Feed The Children, (800) 627-4556, www.feedthechildren.org

Habitat for Humanity International, (800) 422-4828, www.habitat.org

InterAction, (202) 667-8227, www.interaction.org

International Federation of Red Cross/Red Crescent, (212) 338-0161, www.ifrc.org

International Rescue Committee, (212) 551-3000, www.theirc.org

Islamic Relief USA, (888) 479-4968, www.irw.org

Medical Teams International, (800) 959-4325 or (503) 624-1000, www.nwmedicalteams.org

Mercy Corps, (800) 292-3355 or (503) 796-6800, www.mercycorps.org

Operation Blessing International Relief and Development Corporation, (800) 730-2537 or (757) 226-3401, www.ob.org

Operation USA, (800) 678-7255, www.opusa.org

Oxfam America, (800) 776-9326, www.oxfamamerica.org

Rebuilding Together, Inc., (800) 473-4229 or (202) 483-9083, www.rebuildingtogether.org

Save the Children, (800) 728-3843, www. savethechildren.org

United Methodist Committee on Relief, (800) 554-8583 or (202) 548-4002, www.umcor.org

United Way of America, (703) 836-7100, www.unitedway.org

World Health Organization, (202) 974-3458, www.who.int

World Vision, (888) 511-6548 or (202) 572-6300, www.worldvision.org

---

Surface Transportation ISAC, *c/o EWA Information and Infrastructure Technologies, Inc.,* 13873 Park Center Rd., #200, Herndon, VA 20171-5406; (866) 784-7221. Fax, (703) 478-7654. Paul G. Wolfe, Director.
General e-mail, st-isac@surfacetransportationisac.org

Web, www.surfacetransportationisac.org

Collects, analyzes, and distributes critical security and threat information from worldwide resources; shares best security practices and provides 24/7 immediate physical and cyberthreat warnings.

Telecommunications ISAC *(Homeland Security Dept.),* *c/o National Coordinating Center for Telecommunications,* 245 Murray Lane, MS8510 20520; (703) 235-5080. Fax, (703) 235-5696.
General e-mail, ncs@ncs.gov

Web, www.ncs.gov/ncc

Supports the national critical infrastructure protection goals of government and industry. Facilitates voluntary collaboration and information sharing among its

participants; gathers information on vulnerabilities, threats, intrusions, and anomalies from the telecommunications industry, government, and other sources; develops baseline statistics and analyzes the data to avert or mitigate impact upon the telecommunications infrastructure.

WaterISAC, 1620 Eye St. N.W., #500 20006-4027; (888) 426-4722. Michael Arceneaux, Managing Director.
General e-mail, tramposch@waterisac.org

Web, www.waterisac.org

Gathers, analyzes, and disseminates threat information concerning the water community from utilities' security incident reports and agencies of the federal government. Provides the water community with access to sensitive information and resources about cyber, physical, and contamination threats.

▶ **NONGOVERNMENTAL**

International Assn. of Chiefs of Police, *Advisory Committee for Patrol and Tactical Operations,*

515 N. Washington St., Alexandria, VA 22314-2357; (703) 836-6767. Fax, (703) 836-4543. Ed Wortman, Chair; Nancy Kollo, Staff Liaison, ext. 813. Toll-free, (800) THE-IACP. General e-mail, kollon@theiacp.org

Web, www.theiacp.org

Membership: foreign and U.S. police executives and administrators. Maintains liaison with civil defense and emergency service agencies; prepares guidelines for police cooperation with emergency and disaster relief agencies during emergencies.

National Governors Assn., *Center for Best Practices: Homeland Security and Technology Division,* 444 N. Capitol St. N.W. 20001-1512; (202) 624-5300. Fax, (202) 624-5313. Raymond C. Scheppach, Executive Director; Chris Logan, Program Director.
Web, www.nga.org/center

Provides support to governors in responding to the challenges of homeland security through technical assistance and policy research, and by facilitating their participation in national discussion and initiatives.

National Voluntary Organizations Active in Disaster (NVOAD), 1501 Lee Hwy., #206, Arlington, VA 22209-1109; (703) 778-5088. Fax, (703) 778-5091. Diana Rothe-Smith, Executive Director.
General e-mail, info@nvoad.org

Web, www.nvoad.org

Seeks to promote communication, cooperation, coordination, and collaboration among voluntary agencies that participate in disaster response, relief, and recovery nationally.

Emergency Communications

►AGENCIES

Air Force Dept. *(Defense Dept.),* **Warfighting Integration and Chief Information Officer,** 1800 Air Force Pentagon, #4E1050 20330-1800; (703) 695-6829. Fax, (703) 697-7512. Lt. Gen. William L. Shelton, Chief Warfighting Integration and Information Officer. Press, (703) 695-0640.
General e-mail, safxc.workflow@pentagon.af.mil

Web, www.safxc.af.mil

Responsible for policy making, planning, programming, and evaluating performance of the Air Force's command, control, communications, and computer (C-4) system.

Army Dept. *(Defense Dept.),* **Chief Information Officer IG-6,** 107 Army Pentagon, #3E604 20310-0107; (703) 695-4366. Fax, (703) 695-3091. Lt. Gen. Jeffrey Sorenson, Chief Information Officer.
Web, www.army.mil

Oversees policy and budget for the Army's information systems and programs.

Defense Dept. (DoD), *Command, Control, Communications, and Computer Systems,* 6000 Joint

Staff Pentagon, #2D864 20318-6000; (703) 695-6478. Fax, (703) 614-2945. Vice Adm. Nancy E. Brown (USN), Director; Maj. Gen. Michael Basla (USA), Vice Director. Web, www.defenselink.mil

Military office that sets policy throughout the Defense Dept. for command, control, communications, and computer (C-4) matters.

Defense Dept. (DoD), *Networks and Information Integration,* 6000 Defense Pentagon, #3E1030 20301-6000; (703) 695-0348. Fax, (703) 614-8060. John G. Grimes, Assistant Secretary. Web, www.defenselink.mil/cio.nii

Civilian office with policy oversight for all command, control, and communications matters.

Defense Dept. (DoD), *White House Communications Agency,* U.S. Naval Station—Anacostia Annex, 2743 Defense Blvd. S.W., #220 20373-5815; (202) 757-5530. Fax, (202) 757-5529. Col. James A. Lien, Commander. Web, www.defenselink.mil

Responsible for presidential communications.

Federal Communications Commission (FCC), *Emergency Alert System,* 445 12th St. S.W., #7-A807 20554; (202) 418-1199. Fax, (202) 418-2790. Bonnie Gay, EAS Coordinator.
General e-mail, eas@fcc.gov

Web, www.fcc.gov/eb/eas

Develops rules and regulations for the Emergency Alert System, which is the national warning system the president would use to communicate with the public during a national emergency in the event that access to normal media outlets becomes unavailable. It is also used by state and local officials for weather-related and man-made emergencies.

Federal Communications Commission (FCC), *Public Safety and Homeland Security,* 445 12th St. S.W., #7-C485 20554; (202) 418-1300. Fax, (202) 418-2817. David Furth, Chief (Acting). Press, (202) 418-2668.
General e-mail, PSHSBinfo@fcc.gov

Web, www.fcc.gov/pshs

Develops, recommends, and administers the FCC's policies pertaining to public safety communications issues, including 911 and E911. Responsible for the operability and interoperability of public safety communications, communications infrastructure protection and disaster response, and network security and reliability.

National Communications System *(Homeland Security Dept.),* 245 Murray Lane, Bldg. 410, MS 8510 20528-8510; (703) 235-5516. Fax, (703) 235-5696. James J. Madon, Director.
General e-mail, ncsweb1@dhs.gov

Web, www.ncs.gov

Ensures that the federal government has the necessary communications capabilities to permit its continued operation during a national emergency, including war;

provides the Federal Emergency Management Agency with communications support as it directs the nation's recovery from a major disaster.

National Communications System *(Homeland Security Dept.), President's National Security Telecommunications Advisory Committee,* NCS, 245 Murray Lane, Bldg. 410, MS 8510 20528-8510; *(703) 235-5525. Fax, (703) 235-5696. Keisha Gebreyes, Program Manager. Press, (703) 235-5516.*
General e-mail, nstac1@dhs.gov

Web, www.ncs.gov/nstac/nstac.html

Advises the president, the National Security Council, the Office of Science and Technology Policy, and the Office of Management and Budget on specific measures to improve national security and emergency preparedness telecommunications for the federal government.

National Response Center *(Homeland Security Dept.),* 2100 2nd St. S.W., #2111B 20593-0001; *(202) 267-2428. Fax, (202) 267-1322. Syed Qadir, Chief. TTY, (202) 267-4477. Hotline, (800) 424-8802; local, (202) 267-2675.*
General e-mail, lst-nrcinfo@comdt.uscg.mil

Web, www.nrc.uscg.mil

Maintains twenty-four-hour hotline for reporting oil spills, hazardous materials accidents, chemical releases, or known or suspected terrorist threats. Notifies appropriate federal officials to reduce the effects of accidents.

▶**NONGOVERNMENTAL**

Community Emergency Preparedness Information Network (CEPIN), 8630 Fenton St., #604, Silver Spring, MD 20910-3822; *(301) 589-3786. Fax, (301) 589-3797. Neil McDevitt, Program Director. TTY, (301) 589-3006.*
General e-mail, pr@cepintdi.org

Web, www.cepintdi.org

Develops disaster preparedness training programs for deaf and hard of hearing consumers and responders. Sponsored by Telecommunications for the Deaf and Hard of Hearing (TDI) and administered by the Homeland Security Dept.

Industrial and Military Planning and Mobilization

▶**AGENCIES**

Bureau of Industry and Security *(Commerce Dept.), Strategic Industries and Economic Security,* 14th St. and Constitution Ave. N.W., #3876 20230; *(202) 482-4506. Fax, (202) 482-5650. Michael Vaccaro, Director (Acting).*
General e-mail, pbean@bis.doc.gov

Web, www.bis.doc.gov

Administers the Defense Production Act and provides industry with information on the allocation of resources falling under the jurisdiction of the act; conducts studies on industrial mobilization for the federal government.

Defense Logistics Agency *(Defense Dept.), Logistics Operations and Readiness,* 8725 John Jay Kingman Rd., Fort Belvoir, VA 22060-6221; *(703) 767-1600. Fax, (703) 767-7733. Rear Adm. Mark F. Heinrich, Director. Information, (703) 767-6200.*

Oversees management, storage, and distribution of items used to support Defense Dept. logistics. Provides logistics policy, with an emphasis on modernizing business systems and maximizing readiness and combat logistics support.

Maritime Administration *(Transportation Dept.), Emergency Preparedness,* West Bldg., 1200 New Jersey Ave. S.E., #W23-304 20590; *(202) 366-5900. Fax, (202) 366-5904. Thomas M.P. Christensen, Director.*
Web, http://marad.dot.gov

Plans for the transition of merchant shipping from peacetime to wartime operations under the direction of the National Shipping Authority. Participates in interagency planning and policy development for maritime security–related directives. Coordinates port personnel and the military for deployments through the commercial strategic seaports. Represents the United States at the NATO Planning Board for Ocean Shipping. (The National Shipping Authority is a stand-by organization that is activated upon the declaration of a war or other national emergency.)

Maritime Administration *(Transportation Dept.), National Security,* West Bldg., 1200 New Jersey Ave. S.E., W25-2091212 20590; *(202) 366-5400. Fax, (202) 493-2180. James E. Caponiti, Associate Administrator and Deputy Administrator (Acting).*
Web, www.marad.gov

Ensures that merchant shipping is available in times of war or national emergency.

Maritime Administration *(Transportation Dept.), Ship Operations,* 1200 New Jersey Ave. S.E., #W25-302 20590; *(202) 366-1875. Fax, (202) 366-3954. William H. Cahill, Director.*
Web, http://marad.dot.gov/offices/ship

Maintains the National Defense Reserve Fleet, a fleet of older vessels traded in by U.S. flag operators that are called into operation during emergencies; manages and administers the Ready Reserve Force, a fleet of ships available for operation within four to twenty days, to meet the nation's sealift readiness requirements.

▶**CONGRESS**

For a listing of relevant congressional committees and subcommittees, please see page 546 or the Appendix.

▶**NONGOVERNMENTAL**

National Defense Industrial Assn. (NOIA), 2111 Wilson Blvd., #400, Arlington, VA 22201-3061; *(703) 522-1820. Fax, (703) 522-1885. Lt. Gen. Lawrence Farrell (USA, Ret.), President, (703) 247-2550.*
Web, www.ndia.org

Membership: U.S. citizens and businesses interested in national security. Also open to individuals and businesses in nations that have defense agreements with the United States. Provides information and expertise on defense preparedness issues; works to increase public awareness of national defense preparedness through education programs; serves as a forum for dialogue between the defense industry and the government.

National Defense Transportation Assn. (NDTA), *50 S. Pickett St., #220, Alexandria, VA 22304-7296; (703) 751-5011. Fax, (703) 823-8761. Lt. Gen. Kenneth Wykle (USA, Ret.), President.*
Web, www.ndtahq.com

Membership: transportation service companies. Maintains liaison with the Defense Dept., the Transportation Dept., and the Transportation Security Administration to prepare emergency transportation plans.

Shipbuilders Council of America, *1455 F St. N.W., #225 20005; (202) 347-5462. Fax, (202) 347-5464. Matt Paxton, President.*
Web, www.shipbuilders.org

Membership: commercially focused shipyards that repair and build ships, and allied industries and associations. National trade association representing the competitive shipyard industry that makes up the core shipyard industrial base in the United States. Monitors legislation and regulations.

Infrastructure Protection

▶**AGENCIES**

Energy Dept. (DOE), *Electricity Delivery and Energy Reliability, 1000 Independence Ave. S.W., #8H033 20585; (202) 586-1411. Fax, (202) 586-1472. Patricia Hoffman, Assistant Secretary (Acting).*
Web, www.doe.energy.gov

Leads the federal response to energy emergencies, guides technology research and development on the security and reliability of the nation's energy systems, provides training and support for stakeholders, and works to assess and mitigate energy system vulnerabilities. Works in conjunction with the Homeland Security Dept. and other DOE programs, federal groups, state and local governments, and private industry.

Federal Bureau of Investigation (FBI), *(Justice Dept.), Cyber Division, 935 Pennsylvania Ave. N.W., #5835 20535; (202) 324-1380. Fax, (202) 324-2840. Shawn Henry, Assistant Director.*
Web, www.fbi.gov/cyberinvest/cyberhome.htm

Coordinates the investigations of federal violations in which the Internet or computer networks are exploited for terrorist, foreign government–sponsored intelligence, or criminal activities, including copyright violations, fraud, pornography, child exploitation, and malicious computer intrusions.

Federal Protective Service (FPS), *(Homeland Security Dept.), 800 N. Capitol St., 5th Floor 20002; (202) 732-8000. Fax, (202) 732-8109. Gary Schenkel, Director. National Hotline, (866) 347-2423.*
Web, www.ice.gov

Works to ensure that appropriate levels of security are in place in General Services Administration–managed facilities throughout the United States. Conducts assessments on all GSA-controlled facilities to evaluate threats and tailor appropriate security countermeasures. Has enforcement capability to detain and arrest people, seize goods or conveyances, obtain arrest and search warrants, respond to incidents and emergency situations, provide protection during demonstrations or civil unrest, and to be deputized for law enforcement response in special situations.

Homeland Security Dept. (DHS), *Infrastructure Protection, 3801 Nebraska Ave. N.W., Bldg. 18 20528; (703) 235-3945. Fax, (202) 447-3250. James L. Snyder, Assistant Secretary (Acting).*
Web, www.dhs.gov

Assigned the lead responsibility for coordinating the collection and analysis of intelligence and information pertaining to threats against U.S. infrastructure. Handles the merging of capabilities to identify and assess current and future threats to homeland infrastructure; identifies and assesses vulnerabilities, takes preventive action, and issues timely warnings. Develops partnerships and communication lines with state and local governments and the private sector. Administers the Homeland Security Advisory System, which conveys threat information.

National Aeronautics and Space Administration (NASA), *Security and Program Protection, 300 E St. S.W., #9U70 20546; (202) 358-2010. Fax, (202) 358-3238. Jack L. Forsythe, Assistant Administrator.*
Web, www.hq.nasa.gov/office/ospp

Serves as the focal point for policy formulation, oversight, coordination, and management of NASA's security, counterintelligence, counterterrorism, emergency preparedness and response, and continuity of operations programs.

National Cyber Security Center *(Homeland Security Dept.), Cybersecurity and Communications, 245 Murray Lane S.W., Bldg. 410, MS 8570 20528-8570; (202) 282-8000 (DHS switchboard). Fax, (703) 235-5150. Rod Beckstrom, Director. Press, (202) 282-8010.*

Coordinates warning and response procedures involving threats to cyberspace. Operates (in partnership with US-CERT) the National Cyber Alert System, which provides information on computer security vulnerabilities, their potential impact, and means to counter threats. Works with state and local government, the private sector, and the international community to reduce cyberspace vulnerability.

National Institute of Standards and Technology (NIST), *(Commerce Dept.), Computer Security, 100 Bureau Dr., MS 8930, Gaithersburg, MD 20899-8930;*

(301) 975-8443. Fax, (301) 948-1233. William C. "Curt" Barker, Chief.

Web, www.csrc.nist.gov

Works to improve information systems security by raising awareness of information technology risks, vulnerabilities, and protection requirements; researches and advises government agencies of risks; devises measures for cost-effective security and privacy of sensitive federal systems.

Transportation Security Administration (TSA),
(Homeland Security Dept.), 601 S. 12th St., 7th Floor, Arlington, VA 22202-4220; (571) 227-2801. Fax, (571) 227-1398. Gale D. Rossides, Assistant Secretary (Acting). Press, (571) 227-2829. Questions and concerns regarding travel can be submitted to the TSA Contact Center, toll-free, (866) 289-9673.

General e-mail, TSA-ContactCenter@dhs.gov

Web, www.tsa.gov/public

Responsible for aviation, rail, land, and maritime transportation security. Programs and interests include the stationing of federal security directors and federal passenger screeners at airports, the Federal Air Marshal Program, improved detection of explosives, and enhanced port security.

Transportation Security Administration (TSA),
(Homeland Security Dept.), Freedom Center, 13555 EDS Dr., Herndon, VA 20171; (866) 655-7023. Donald Zimmerman, Deputy Executive Director; James "Jim" Quinlin, Chief of Staff, (703) 563-3601.

Web, www.tsa.gov

Provides continual federal, state, and local coordination, communications, and domain awareness for all of the Homeland Security Dept.'s transportation-related security activities worldwide. Transportation domains include highway, rail, shipping, and aviation.

Treasury Dept., *Domestic Finance: Critical Infrastructure Protection and Compliance Policy, 1500 Pennsylvania Ave. N.W. 20220; (202) 622-6560. Fax, (202) 622-2310. Vacant, Deputy Assistant Secretary.*

General e-mail, OCIP@do.treas.gov

Web, www.treas.gov/offices

Works with the private sector to improve the protection of the nation's financial infrastructure. Maintains protections for nonpublic personal financial information through implementation and enforcement of the Bank Secrecy Act and the Right to Financial Privacy Act. Develops regulations to protect the nation's financial system from money launderers and financiers of terrorism. Serves as the department's principal liaison with the Homeland Security Dept. on infrastructure protection issues.

U.S. Coast Guard (USCG), *(Homeland Security Dept.), Marine Safety, Security, and Stewardship, 2100 2nd St. S.W., #3200 20593; (202) 372-1001. Fax, (202) 372-2900. Rear Adm. Brian M. Salerno, Assistant Commandant.*

Web, www.uscg.mil/uscg.shtm

Establishes and enforces regulations for port safety; environmental protection; vessel safety, inspection, design, documentation, and investigation; licensing of merchant vessel personnel; and shipment of hazardous materials.

U.S. Computer Emergency Readiness Team (US-CERT),
(Homeland Security Dept.), 245 Murray Lane S.W., Bldg. 410, MS 8570 20528-8570; (202) 282-8000 (DHS switchboard). Fax, (703) 235-5150. Michael Witt, Deputy Director (Acting). Press, (202) 282-8010.

General e-mail, info@us-cert.gov

Web, www.us-cert.gov

Works with the National Cyber Security Division and the Computer Emergency Response Team at Carnegie Mellon University in a public-private partnership to prevent and mitigate cyber attacks. Seeks to enhance the ability of the Homeland Security Dept. to provide a coordinated warning and response system. (US-CERT is the operational branch of the National Cyber Security Division, Homeland Security Dept.)

U.S. Secret Service *(Homeland Security Dept.), Financial Crimes Division, 950 H St. N.W., #5300 20223; (202) 406-9330. Fax, (202) 406-5016. John Large, Special Agent in Charge.*

Web, www.secretservice.gov/financial_crimes.shtml

Investigates crimes associated with financial institutions. Jurisdiction includes bank fraud, access device fraud involving credit and debit cards, telecommunications and computer crimes, fraudulent identification, fraudulent government and commercial securities, and electronic funds transfer fraud.

►CONGRESS

For a listing of relevant congressional committees and subcommittees, please see page 546 or the Appendix.

►NONGOVERNMENTAL

National Cyber Security Alliance, *1101 Pennsylvania Ave. N.W., #600 20004; (202) 756-2278. Fax, (202) 756-0217. Michael Kaiser, Executive Director. Press, (202) 463-0013.*

General e-mail, ncsaRon@aol.com

Web, www.staysafeonline.org

Public-private partnership that promotes computer safety and responsible online behavior. Designated by the Homeland Security Dept. to provide tools and resources to help home users, small businesses, and schools stay safe online. Online resources include tips, a self-guided cyber security test and checklist, and educational materials.

SANS Institute, *8120 Woodmont Ave., #205, Bethesda, MD 20814-2784; (301) 951-0102. Fax, (301) 951-0140. Alan Paller, Director. Alternate phone, (301) 654-7267.*

General e-mail, info@sans.org

Web, www.sans.org

Develops, maintains, and makes available at no cost the largest collection of research documents about information security. Operates Internet Storm Center, the Internet's early warning system.

TechAmerica, *601 Pennsylvania Ave. N.W., North Bldg., #600 20004; (202) 682-9110. Fax, (202) 682-9111. Christopher W. Hansen, Chief Executive Officer; Phillip J. Bond, President. Press, (703) 284-5305. Toll-free, (800) 284-4232.*

General e-mail, csc@techamerica.org

Web, www.techamerica.org

Membership: cyber security software, hardware, and services companies. Advocates the improvement of cyber security through public policy, technology, education, and awareness. (Merger of AeA [formerly the American Electronics Assn.], the Information Technology Assn. of America [ITAA], the Government Electronics and Information and Technology Assn. [GEIA], and the Cyber Security Industry Alliance.)

Public Health and Environment

►AGENCIES

Centers for Disease Control and Prevention (CDC), *(Health and Human Services Dept.), Washington Office, 395 E St. S.W. 20201; (202) 245-0600. Fax, (202) 245-0602. Donald Shriber, Associate Director. Public inquiries, (800) 232-4636.*

Web, www.cdc.gov/washington

Supports the CDC's Bioterrorism and Preparedness and Response Program, which ensures the rapid development of federal, state, and local capacity to respond to bioterrorism. (Headquarters in Atlanta, Ga.: 1600 Clifton Rd. N.E. 30333.)

Environmental Protection Agency (EPA), *Emergency Management, 1200 Pennsylvania Ave. N.W., #1448, MC 5104A 20460; (202) 564-8600. Fax, (202) 564-8222. Deborah Y. Dietrich, Director. Toll-free hotline, (800) 535-0202.*

Web, www.epa.gov/oem

Responsible for planning for and responding to the harmful effects of the release or dissemination of toxic chemicals. Areas of responsibility include helping state and local responders plan for emergencies; coordinating with key federal partners; training first responders; and providing resources in the event of a terrorist incident.

Health and Human Services Dept. (HHS), *National Disaster Medical System, 409 3rd St. S.W., #330 20024; (202) 205-7978. Fax, (800) 872-5945. Jack Beall, Chief.*

Web, http://ndms.hhs.gov

Cooperative, federally coordinated program for federal, state, and local governments, private businesses, and civilian volunteers that works to ensure the availability of medical resources following a disaster.

Health and Human Services Dept. (HHS), *Preparedness and Response (ASPR), 200 Independence Ave. S.W., #638-G 20201; (202) 205-2882. Fax, (202) 690-6512. Craig Vanderwagen, Assistant Secretary.*

General e-mail, craig.vanderwagen@hhs.gov

Web, www.hhs.gov/aspr

Responsible for coordinating U.S. medical and public health preparedness and response to emergencies, including acts of biological, chemical, and nuclear terrorism. Oversees bioterrorism preparedness grant funding for state and local governments.

National Institute of Allergy and Infectious Diseases *(National Institutes of Health), 31 Center Dr., Bldg. 31, #7A03, MSC-2520, Bethesda, MD 20892-2520; (301) 496-2263. Fax, (301) 496-4409. Dr. Anthony S. Fauci, Director.*

Web, www.niaid.nih.gov

Responsible for basic research and development of new medical tools to detect and counter a bioterrorist attack. Conducts research aimed at understanding the organisms that might be used as agents of bioterrorism and the human immune system's response to them. Initiatives include the development of safer, next-generation smallpox vaccines. Shares capabilities and resources with the U.S. Army Medical Research Institute of Infectious Diseases at Fort Detrick, Md.

►CONGRESS

For a listing of relevant congressional committees and subcommittees, please see page 546 or the Appendix.

►NONGOVERNMENTAL

American Red Cross, *Disaster Preparedness and Response, 2025 E St. N.W. 20006-5009; (202) 303-5000. Fax, (202) 303-0061. Gail J. McGovern, President. Press, (202) 303-5551. Donations, (800) RED-CROSS. Toll-free, (800) 733-2767; in Spanish, (800) 257-7575.*

Web, www.redcross.org/services/disaster

Chartered by Congress to administer disaster relief. Provides disaster victims with food, shelter, first aid, medical care, and access to other available resources. Feeds emergency workers; handles inquiries from concerned family members outside the disaster area; helps promote disaster preparedness and prevention.

National Assn. of State EMS Officials (NASEMSO), *201 Park Washington Ct., Falls Church, VA 22046-4527; (703) 538-1799. Fax, (703) 241-5603. Elizabeth B. Armstrong, Executive Director.*

General e-mail, info@nasemso.org

Web, www.nasemso.org

Works to provide leadership and support for the development of effective emergency medical services (EMS) systems throughout the United States; to formulate national EMS policy; and to foster communication and sharing among state EMS officials.

National Center for Biodefense and Infectious Diseases *(George Mason University)*, *MSN 1H8, 10900 University Blvd., Manassas, VA 20110; (703) 993-4271. Fax, (703) 993-4280. Charles Bailey, Director. Alternate phone, (703) 993-8545.*
General e-mail, biodefense@gmu.edu

Web, http://ncbid.gmu.edu

Researches the prevention, diagnosis, and treatment of infectious diseases caused by biological agents. Works to develop new environmental detection methods for these agents. Manages graduate programs in biodefense. (Associated with the Department of Molecular and Microbiology at George Mason University.)

National Vaccine Information Center, *407 Church St., Suite H, Vienna, VA 22180; (703) 938-3783. Fax, (703) 938-5768. Barbara Loe Fisher, President.*
General e-mail, contactnvic@gmail.com

Web, www.nvic.org

Educates the public and provides research on vaccination safety procedures and effectiveness; supports reform of the vaccination system; publishes information on diseases and vaccines; and monitors legislation and regulations. Areas of recent interest include provisions of the Homeland Security Act relating to vaccination laws and vaccination campaigns for anthrax and smallpox.

Selective Service

►AGENCIES

Selective Service System, *1515 Wilson Blvd., Arlington, VA 22209-2425; (703) 605-4010. Fax, (703) 605-4006. William A. Chatfield, Director. Locator, (703) 605-4000.*
Web, www.sss.gov

Supplies the armed forces with manpower when authorized; registers male citizens of the United States ages eighteen to twenty-five. In an emergency, would institute a draft and would provide alternative service assignments to men classified as conscientious objectors.

►CONGRESS

For a listing of relevant congressional committees and subcommittees, please see page 546 or the Appendix.

Strategic Stockpiles

►AGENCIES

Defense Dept. (DoD), *Industrial Policy,* *3330 Defense Pentagon, #3C855A 20301-3300; (703) 697-0051. Fax, (703) 695-4277. Gary A. Powell, Deputy Under Secretary (Acting).*
Web, www.acq.osd.mil/ip

Develops and oversees strategic, industrial, and critical materials policies, including oversight of the National Defense Stockpile.

Defense Logistics Agency *(Defense Dept.),* **Defense National Stockpile Center,** *8725 John Jay Kingman Rd., #3229, Fort Belvoir, VA 22060-6223; (703) 767-5500. Fax, (703) 767-3316. Cornel A. Holder, Administrator.*
Web, www.dnsc.dla.mil

Manages the national defense stockpile of strategic and critical materials. Purchases strategic materials, including beryllium and newly developed high-tech alloys. Disposes of excess materials, including tin, silver, industrial diamond stones, tungsten, and vegetable tannin.

Fossil Energy *(Energy Dept.),* **Naval Petroleum and Oil Shale Reserves,** *1000 Independence Ave. S.W., #3H076 20585; (202) 586-4685. Fax, (202) 586-4446. Francis Gangle, Director (Acting).*
Web, www.fe.doe.gov

Develops, conserves, operates, and maintains oil fields for producing oil, natural gas, and other petroleum products.

►CONGRESS

For a listing of relevant congressional committees and subcommittees, please see page 546 or the Appendix.

INTELLIGENCE AND COUNTERTERRORISM

►AGENCIES

Air Force Dept. *(Defense Dept.),* **Intelligence, Surveillance, and Reconnaissance (ISR),** *1700 Air Force Pentagon, #5E665 20330-1700; (703) 695-5613. Fax, (703) 697-4903. Lt. Gen. David Deptula, Deputy Chief of Staff.*
General e-mail, afxoi.workflow@pentagon.af.mil

Web, www.af.mil

Responsible for policy formulation, planning, evaluation, oversight, and leadership of Air Force intelligence, surveillance, and reconnaissance capabilities.

Army Dept. *(Defense Dept.),* **Intelligence,** *1000 Army Pentagon, #2E408 20310-1000; (703) 695-3033. Fax, (703) 697-7605. Richard P. Zahner, Deputy Chief of Staff.*
Web, www.army.mil

Military office that directs Army intelligence activities and coordinates activities with other intelligence agencies.

Central Intelligence Agency (CIA), *CIA Headquarters, 930 Dolley Madison Blvd., McLean, VA 20505 (mailing address: change to CIA Headquarters, Washington, DC 20505); (703) 482-0623. Fax, (703) 482-1739. Leon E. Panetta, Director of Central Intelligence; Stephen R. Kappes, Deputy Director; Michael J. Morell, Director of Intelligence. Information, (703) 482-0623.*
Web, www.cia.gov

Coordinates the intelligence functions of government agencies as they relate to national security and advises the National Security Council on those functions; gathers and evaluates intelligence relating to national security and distributes the information to government agencies in the national security field.

Defense Dept. (DoD), *Intelligence,* *5000 Defense Pentagon, #3E834 20301-5000; (703) 695-0971. Fax, (703) 693-5706. James R. Clapper Jr., Under Secretary.*
Web, www.defenselink.mil

Responsible for ensuring the secretary of defense's access to intelligence information.

Defense Dept. (DoD), *Intelligence Oversight,* *7200 Defense Pentagon, #2E1052 20301-7200; (703) 275-6550. Fax, (703) 275-6590. William R. Dugan, Assistant to the Secretary.*
Web, www.dod.mil/atsdio

Responsible for the independent oversight of all Defense Dept. intelligence, counterintelligence, and related activities, and for the formulation of intelligence oversight policy; reviews intelligence operations and investigates and reports on possible violations of federal law or regulations.

Defense Dept. (DoD), *Networks and Information Integration,* *6000 Defense Pentagon, #3E1030 20301-6000; (703) 695-0348. Fax, (703) 614-8060. John G. Grimes, Assistant Secretary.*
Web, www.defenselink.mil/cio.nii

Civilian office that advises and makes recommendations to the secretary of defense on the management of all Defense Dept. intelligence and communications programs, resources, and activities.

Defense Dept. (DoD), *Special Operations and Low-Intensity Conflict,* *2500 Defense Pentagon, #3C852A 20301-2500; (703) 695-9667. Fax, (703) 693-6335. Michael G. Vickers, Assistant Secretary.*
Web, www.defenselink.mil

Serves as special staff assistant and civilian adviser to the secretary of defense on matters related to special operations and international terrorism.

Defense Information Systems Agency (DISA), *(Defense Dept.),* *701 S. Courthouse Rd., Arlington, VA 22204-2199; (703) 607-6001. Fax, (703) 607-4082. Lt. Gen. Caroll F. Pollett (USA), Director. Press, (703) 607-6900.*
General e-mail, cosa@disa.mil
Web, www.disa.mil

The Defense Dept. agency responsible for information technology and the central manager for major portions of the defense information infrastructure. Units include the White House Communications Agency.

Defense Intelligence Agency *(Defense Dept.),* *7400 Defense Pentagon, #3E630 20301-7400; (703) 695-7353. Fax, (703) 614-8115. Lt. Gen. Ronald L. Burgess Jr. (USA), Director.*

General e-mail, public_affairs@misc.pentagon.mil
Web, www.dia.mil

Collects and evaluates foreign military-related intelligence information to satisfy the requirements of the secretary of defense, Joint Chiefs of Staff, selected components of the Defense Dept., and other authorized agencies.

Energy Dept. (DOE), *Intelligence and Counterintelligence,* *1000 Independence Ave. S.W., #GA-293 20585; (202) 586-2610. Fax, (202) 287-5999. Rolf Mowatt-Larssen, Director; Stanley J. Borgia, Director of Counterintelligence (Acting); Douglas Nousen, Deputy Director of Counterintelligence (Acting); Alex Goodale, Deputy Director of Intelligence.*
Web, www.energy.gov

Identifies, neutralizes, and deters intelligence threats directed at Energy Dept. facilities, personnel, information, and technology.

Federal Bureau of Investigation (FBI), *(Justice Dept.),* *Counterterrorism,* *935 Pennsylvania Ave. N.W., #5012 20535; (202) 324-2770. Fax, (202) 324-7050. Michael J. Heimbach, Assistant Director. Press, (202) 324-3691.*
Web, www.fbi.gov

Collects, analyzes, and shares information and intelligence with authorities to combat international terrorism operations within the United States and in support of extraterritorial investigations, domestic terrorism operations, and counterterrorism. Maintains the Joint Terrorism Task Force, which includes representatives from the Defense Dept., Energy Dept., Federal Emergency Management Agency, CIA, U.S. Customs and Border Protection, U.S. Secret Service, and Immigration and Customs Enforcement.

Federal Bureau of Investigation (FBI), *(Justice Dept.),* *Critical Incident Response Group: Strategic Information and Operations Center,* *935 Pennsylvania Ave. N.W., #5712 20535; (202) 323-3300. Fax, (202) 323-2079. Ethel McGuire, Section Chief. Press, (202) 324-3691. General e-mail, sioc@ic.fbi.gov*
Web, www.fbi.gov

Serves as a twenty-four-hour crisis management and information processing center. Coordinates initial and crisis response investigations of violations of federal law relating to terrorism, sabotage, espionage, treason, sedition, and other matters affecting national security.

Federal Bureau of Investigation (FBI), *(Justice Dept.),* *National Joint Terrorism Task Force (National JTTF),* *935 Pennsylvania Ave. N.W. 20535-0001, (571) 280-5688. Pat Sullivan, Unit Chief.*
Web, www.fbi.gov

Group of more than forty agencies from the fields of intelligence, public safety, and federal, state, and local law enforcement that collects terrorism information and intelligence and funnels it to the more than one hundred JTTFs (teams of local, state, and federal agents based at FBI field offices), various terrorism units within

Office of the Director of National Intelligence

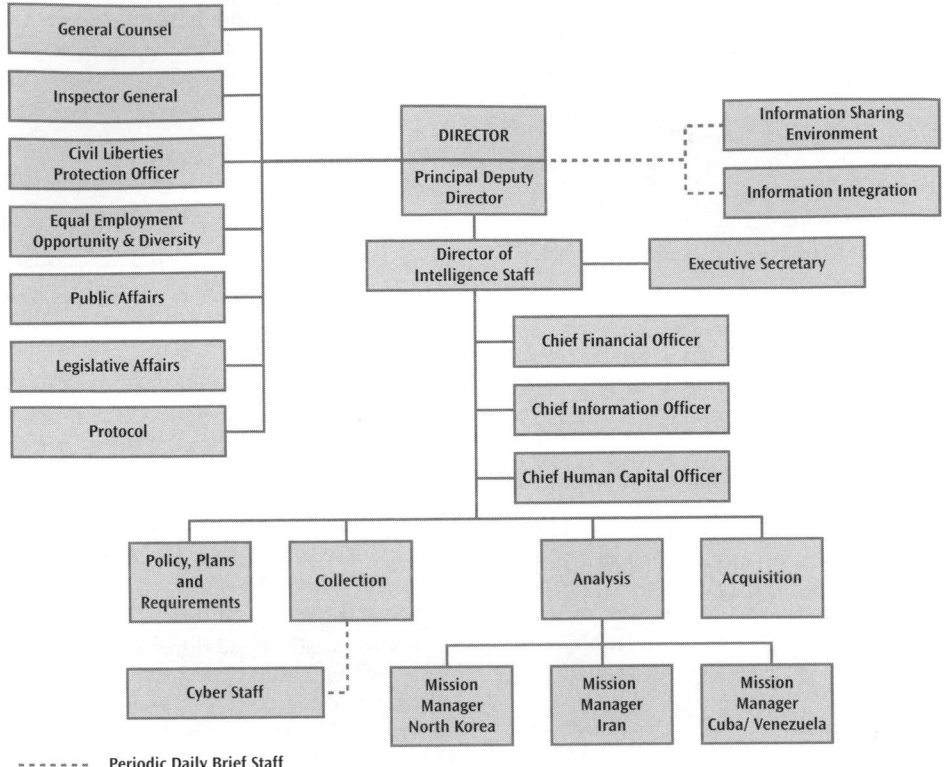

the FBI, and partner agencies. Helps the FBI with terrorism investigations.

Homeland Security Council *(Executive Office of the President),* The White House 20500; (202) 456-6317. John Brennan, Assistant to the President for Counterterrorism and Homeland Security.
Web, www.whitehouse.gov/infocus/homeland

Advises the president on combating global terrorism and homeland security policy.

Homeland Security Dept. (DHS), *Nebraska Ave. Complex, 3801 Nebraska Ave. N.W. 20528; (202) 282-8000. Fax, (202) 282-8236. Janet Napolitano, Secretary; Paul A. Schneider, Deputy Secretary. Press, (202) 282-8010.*
Web, www.dhs.gov

Responsible for the development and coordination of a comprehensive national strategy to protect the United States against terrorist attacks and other threats and hazards. Coordinates the strategy of the executive branch with those of state and local governments and private entities to detect, prepare for, protect against, respond to, and recover from terrorist attacks and other emergencies in the United States.

Homeland Security Dept. (DHS), *Intelligence and Analysis, 3801 Nebraska Ave. N.W., Bldg. 19 20528; (202)*

447-3275. Fax, (202) 282-8810. Roger Mackin, Under Secretary (Acting).
Web, www.dhs.gov

Uses intelligence from multiple sources to identify and assess current and future threats to the United States; provides guidance to the secretary on homeland security issues.

Justice Dept. (DOJ), *National Security Division, 950 Pennsylvania Ave. N.W., #7339 20530; (202) 514-1057. Fax, (202) 353-9836. David S. Kris, Assistant Attorney General.*
General e-mail, nsd.public@usdoj.gov
Web, www.usdoj.gov/nsd

Coordinates the Justice Dept.'s intelligence, counterterrorism, counterespionage, and other national security activities. Provides legal assistance and advice, in coordination with the Office of Legal Counsel as appropriate, to all branches of government on matters of national security law and policy.

Marine Corps *(Defense Dept.), Intelligence, 2 Navy Annex, #3229 20380-1775; (703) 614-2522. Fax, (703) 614-5888. Richard M. Lake, Director.*
Web, http://hqinet001.hqmc.usmc.mil/dirint/default.html

Military office that directs Marine Corps intelligence activities and coordinates activities with other intelligence agencies.

National Aeronautics and Space Administration (NASA), Security and Program Protection, 300 E St. S.W., #9U70 20546; (202) 358-2010. Fax, (202) 358-3238. Jack L. Forsythe, Assistant Administrator.
Web, www.hq.nasa.gov/office/ospp

Serves as the focal point for policy formulation, oversight, coordination, and management of NASA's security, counterintelligence, counterterrorism, emergency preparedness and response, and continuity of operations programs.

National Geospatial-Intelligence Agency (Defense Dept.), 4600 Sangamore Rd., #378, Bethesda, MD 20816-5003; (301) 227-7300. Fax, (301) 227-3696. Vice Adm. Robert B. Murrett, Director. Maps and imagery products, (800) 455-0899.
General e-mail, queries1@nga.mil

Web, www.nga.mil

Combat support agency that provides imagery and geospatial information to national policymakers and military forces in support of national defense objectives; incorporates the missions and functions of the former Defense Mapping Agency and Defense Dissemination Program Office.

National Reconnaissance Office (Defense Dept.), 14675 Lee Rd., Chantilly, VA 20151-1715; (703) 808-1198. Fax, (703) 808-1171. Scott F. Large, Director.
Web, www.nro.gov

Researches, develops, and operates intelligence satellites. Gathers intelligence for various purposes, including indications and warnings, monitoring of arms control agreements, military operations and exercises, and monitoring of natural disasters and other environmental issues.

National Security Agency (NSA), (Defense Dept.), 9800 Savage Rd., #6272, Fort Meade, MD 20755-6000; (301) 688-6524. Fax, (301) 688-6198. Lt. Gen. Keith B. Alexander (USA), Director; John C. "Chris" Inglis, Deputy Director.
General e-mail, nsapao@nsa.gov

Web, www.nsa.gov

Provides technology, products, and services to secure information and information infrastructure critical to U.S. national security interests. Organizes and controls all foreign signals collection and processing activities of the United States in accordance with requirements established by the Defense Dept., the Office of the Director of National Intelligence, and by national policies with the advice of the National Foreign Intelligence Board.

National Security Division (Justice Dept.), Counterterrorism and Counterespionage, 10th St. and Constitution Ave. N.W., #2649 20530; (202) 514-0849. Fax, (202) 514-8714. David S. Kris, Assistant Attorney General.
Web, www.usdoj.gov/nsd

Investigates and prosecutes incidents of international and domestic terrorism involving U.S. interests, domestic violent crime, firearms, and explosives violations. Provides legal advice on federal statutes relating to murder, assault, kidnapping, threats, robbery, weapons and explosives control, malicious destruction of property, and aircraft and sea piracy.

National Security Division (Justice Dept.), Intelligence, 950 Pennsylvania Ave. N.W., #7339 20530; (202) 514-5600. Fax, (202) 305-4949. Matthew G. Olsen, Deputy Assistant Attorney General.
Web, www.usdoj.gov/nsd

Prepares and files all applications for electronic surveillance and physical search under the Foreign Intelligence Act of 1978. Advises various client agencies, including the Central Intelligence Agency, the Federal Bureau of Investigation, and the Defense and State Depts., on questions of law, regulation, and guidelines, as well as the legality of domestic and overseas intelligence operations.

Navy Dept. (Defense Dept.), Naval Intelligence, 2000 Navy Pentagon, #4E360 20350-2000; (703) 614-0281. Fax, (703) 697-6800. Vice Adm. David Dorsett, Commander.
Web, www.navy.mil

Military office that directs Navy intelligence activities and coordinates activities with other intelligence agencies.

Office of the Director of National Intelligence (DNI), 20511; (703) 773-8600. Dennis C. Blair, Director of National Intelligence; Peter Lavoy, Principal Deputy Director. Press, (202) 201-1111. Switchboard, (703) 773-8600.
Web, www.dni.gov

Leads a unified intelligence community and serves as the principal adviser to the president on intelligence matters. Orders the collection of new intelligence to ensure the sharing of information among agencies and to establish common standards for the intelligence community's personnel. Responsible for determining the annual budgets for all national intelligence agencies and for directing how these funds are spent.

Office of the Director of National Intelligence (DNI), National Counterterrorism Center (NCTC), Liberty Crossing 20505; (571) 280-6202. Fax, (571) 280-5551. Michael E. Leiter, Director. Public Affairs, (571) 280-6160.
Web, www.nctc.gov

Serves as a hub for terrorism threat–related information collected domestically and abroad. Responsible for assessing, integrating, and disseminating threat information and its analysis; maintaining an all-source database on known and suspected terrorists; and identifying collection requirements related to the terrorist threat Prepares the daily terrorist threat matrix. Participates in strategic planning for counterterrorism operations.

Office of the Director of National Intelligence (DNI), National Intelligence Council, CIA Headquarters, Langley, VA 20505; (703) 482-6724. Fax, (703) 482-8632. Peter Lavoy, Chair.
Web, www.dni.gov/nic

Supports the director of national intelligence and serves as the intelligence community's center for mid- and long-term strategic thinking. Provides a focal point for policy-makers' inquiries and needs. Establishes contacts with private sector and academic experts in the intelligence field.

President's Foreign Intelligence Advisory Board

(Executive Office of the President), *New Executive Office Bldg., #5020 20502; (202) 456-2352. Fax, (202) 395-3403. Vacant, Chair; Vacant, Executive Director.*
Web, www.whitehouse.gov/pfiab

Members appointed by the president. Assesses the quality, quantity, and adequacy of foreign intelligence collection and of counterintelligence activities by all government agencies; advises the president on matters concerning intelligence and national security.

State Dept., *Counterterrorism,* 2201 C St. N.W., #2509 20520; (202) 647-9892. Fax, (202) 647-9256. Ronald Schlicher, Coordinator (Acting). Press, (202) 647-1845.
Web, www.state.gov/s/ct

Implements U.S. counterterrorism policy and coordinates activities with foreign governments; responds to terrorist acts; works to promote a stronger counterterrorism stance worldwide.

State Dept., *Diplomatic Security Bureau,* 2201 C St. N.W., #6316 20520; (202) 647-6290. Fax, (202) 647-0953. Gregg Starr, Director.
General e-mail, DSPublicAffairs@state.gov

Web, www.state.gov

Conducts the Anti-Terrorism Assistance Program, which provides training to foreign governments fighting terrorism.

State Dept., *Intelligence and Research,* 2201 C St. N.W., #6468 20520-6531; (202) 647-9177. Fax, (202) 736-4688. John Dinger, Assistant Secretary (Acting).
Web, www.state.gov

Coordinates foreign policy–related research, analysis, and intelligence programs for the State Dept. and other federal agencies.

Terrorist Screening Center, *935 Pennsylvania Ave. N.W. 20535; (703) 418-9128. Fax, (703) 418-9563. Leonard C. Boyle, Director. Toll-free, (866) 872-5678.*
General e-mail, tsc@tsc.gov

Web, www.fbi.gov/terrorinfo/counterterrorism/tsc.htm

Coordinates access to terrorist watch lists from multiple agencies. Provides operational support to federal screeners and state and local law enforcement officials.

Transportation Dept. (DOT), *Intelligence, Security, and Emergency Response,* 1200 New Jersey Ave. S.E., #56125 20590; (202) 366-6525. Fax, (202) 366-7261. Michael Lowder, Director.
Web, www.dot.gov

Advises the secretary on transportation intelligence and security policy. Acts as liaison with the intelligence community, federal agencies, corporations, and interest groups; administers counterterrorism strategic planning processes. Develops, coordinates, and reviews transportation emergency preparedness programs for use in emergencies affecting national defense and in emergencies caused by natural and man-made disasters and crisis situations.

Transportation Security Administration (TSA),
(Homeland Security Dept.), Intelligence and Analysis, TSA-10, 601 S. 12th St., 6th Floor, Arlington, VA 22202-4220; (703) 601-3100. Fax, (703) 601-3290. Stephen N. Wood, Assistant Administrator.
Web, www.tsa.gov

Oversees TSA's intelligence gathering and information sharing as they pertain to national security and the safety of the nation's transportation systems.

Treasury Dept., *Terrorism and Financial Intelligence,* 1500 Pennsylvania Ave. N.W., #4326 20220; (202) 622-8260. Fax, (202) 622-1914. Stuart A. Levey, Under Secretary. Press, (202) 622-2960.
Web, www.ustreas.gov

Manages the Treasury Dept.'s efforts against financial networks supporting global terrorism.

Treasury Dept., *Terrorism and Financial Intelligence: Terrorist Financing,* 1500 Pennsylvania Ave. N.W. 20220; (202) 622-1655. Fax, (202) 622-3915. Vacant, Assistant Secretary. Press, (202) 622-2960.
Web, www.ustreas.gov

Sets strategy and policy for combating the financing of terrorism both domestically and abroad.

U.S. Coast Guard (USCG), *(Homeland Security Dept.), Intelligence and Criminal Investigations,* 2100 2nd St. S.W., #3316 20593-0001; (202) 372-2700. Fax, (202) 372-2956. James F. Sloan, Assistant Commandant. Public Affairs, (202) 372-4600.
Web, www.uscg.mil

Manages all Coast Guard intelligence activities and programs.

U.S. Customs and Border Protection *(Homeland Security Dept.), Intelligence Operations Coordination,* 1300 Pennsylvania Ave. N.W., #4.2D 20229; (202) 344-2230. Fax, (202) 344-2231. Alvin Gamble, Executive Director.
General e-mail, cbp.anti-terrorism@dhs.gov

Web, www.cbp.gov

Coordinates the effort to prevent the introduction of weapons of mass destruction into the United States and to prevent international terrorists from obtaining weapons of mass destruction materials, technologies, arms, funds, and other support.

►CONGRESS

For a listing of relevant congressional committees and subcommittees, please see page 546 or the Appendix.

►INTERNATIONAL ORGANIZATIONS

INTERPOL, *Washington Office,* INTERPOL-USNCB, U.S. Justice Dept. 20530; (202) 616-9000. Fax, (202) 616-8400. Martin Renkiewicz, Director.
Web, www.usdoj.gov/usncb

U.S. national central bureau for INTERPOL; interacts in international investigations of terrorism on behalf of U.S. police. Serves as liaison between foreign and U.S. law enforcement agencies. Headquarters office sponsors forums enabling foreign governments to discuss counterterrorism policy. (Headquarters in Lyons, France.)

►NONGOVERNMENTAL

ASIS International, 1625 Prince St., Alexandria, VA 22314-2818; (703) 519-6200. Fax, (703) 519-6299. Michael J. Stack, Chief Executive Officer.
General e-mail, asis@asisonline.org

Web, www.asisonline.org

Membership: security administrators from around the world who protect the assets and personnel of private and public organizations. Sponsors seminars and workshops on counterterrorism. (Formerly the American Society for Industrial Security.)

Assn. for Intelligence Officers (AFIO), 6723 Whittier Ave., #3200, McLean, VA 22101-4533; (703) 790-0320. Fax, (703) 991-1278. Elizabeth A. Bancroft, Executive Director.
General e-mail, afio@afio.com

Web, www.afio.com

Membership: current and former military and civilian intelligence officers. Encourages public support for intelligence agencies; supports increased intelligence education in colleges and universities.

Center for National Security Studies, 1120 19th St. N.W., #800 20036; (202) 721-5650. Fax, (202) 530-0128. Kate A. Martin, Director. Press, (202) 721-5660.
General e-mail, cnss@cnss.org

Web, www.cnss.org

Monitors and conducts research on civil liberties and intelligence and national security, including activities of the Central Intelligence Agency and the Federal Bureau of Investigation.

Foundation for the Defense of Democracies (FDD), P.O. Box 33249 20033-0249; (202) 207-0190. Fax, (202) 207-0191. Clifford D. May, President; Mark Dubowitz, Executive Director.
General e-mail, info@defenddemocracy.org

Web, www.defenddemocracy.org

Conducts research and education related to the war on terrorism and the promotion of democracy.

National Security Archive, Gelman Library, George Washington University, 2130 H St. N.W., #701 20037; (202) 994-7000. Fax, (202) 994-7005. Thomas Blanton, Executive Director.

General e-mail, nsarchiv@gwu.edu

Web, www.nsarchive.org

Research institute and library that provides information on U.S. foreign and economic policy and national security affairs. Maintains and publishes collection of declassified and unclassified documents obtained through the Freedom of Information Act. Archive open to the public by appointment.

Potomac Institute for Policy Studies, *International Center for Terrorism Studies (ICTS),* 901 N. Stuart St., #200, Arlington, VA 22203-1821; (703) 525-0770. Fax, (703) 525-0299. Michael S. Swetnam, Chief Executive Officer.
General e-mail, webmaster@potomacinstitute.org

Web, www.potomacinstitute.org

Public policy research institute that conducts studies on key science and technology issues. Areas of focus for the ICTS include the potential for terrorism in the form of biological, chemical, or nuclear violence, as well as information warfare and cyberterrorism.

Terrorism Research Center, 901 N. Glebe Rd., #901, Arlington, VA 22203; (877) 635-0816. Fax, (703) 935-2666. Cal Temple, President.
General e-mail, TRC@terrorism.com

Web, www.terrorism.com

Independent institute dedicated to research and training in the areas of terrorism and homeland security.

Internal (Agency) Security

►AGENCIES

Air Force Dept. *(Defense Dept.), Special Investigations,* 1140 Air Force Pentagon, #5B919 20330-1140; (703) 697-1955. Fax, (703) 695-4346. Col. Kevin J. Jacobsen, Director.
Web, www.osi.andrews.af.mil

Develops and implements policy on investigations of foreign intelligence, terrorism, and other crimes as they relate to Air Force security.

Army Dept. *(Defense Dept.), Counterintelligence, Foreign Disclosure, and Security,* 1000 Army Pentagon, #2D350 20310-1000; (703) 695-1007. Fax, (703) 695-3149. Gary B. Turnbow, Director.
Web, www.army.mil

Responsible for foreign disclosure, policy formation, planning, programming, oversight, and representation for counterintelligence, human intelligence, and security countermeasures of the Army.

Defense Dept. (DoD), *Counterintelligence,* 5000 Defense Pentagon, #3C260 20301-5000; (703) 697-4768. Fax, (703) 695-8217. Toby Sullivan, Director.
Web, www.defenselink.mil

Oversees counterintelligence policy and oversight to protect against espionage and other foreign intelligence activities, sabotage, international terrorist activities, and assassination efforts of foreign powers, organizations, or persons directed against the Defense Dept.

Defense Security Service *(Defense Dept.), 1340 Braddock Pl., Alexandria, VA 22314-1651; (703) 325-5364. Fax, (703) 325-7426. Kathleen M. Watson, Director. Press, (703) 325-9546.*
Web, www.dss.mil

Administers programs to protect classified government information and resources, including the National Industrial Security Program (NISP). Serves the Defense Dept. and other executive departments and agencies. Operates DSS Academy to educate, train, and enhance awareness of security matters.

Energy Dept. (DOE), *Intelligence and Counterintelligence, 1000 Independence Ave. S.W., #GA-293 20585; (202) 586-2610. Fax, (202) 287-5999. Rolf Mowatt-Larssen, Director; Stanley J. Borgia, Director of Counterintelligence (Acting); Alex Goodale, Deputy Director of Intelligence.*
Web, www.energy.gov

Identifies, neutralizes, and deters intelligence threats directed at Energy Dept. facilities, personnel, information, and technology.

National Archives and Records Administration (NARA), *Information Security Oversight, 700 Pennsylvania Ave. N.W., #503 20408-0001; (202) 357-5250. Fax, (202) 357-5907. William J. Bosanko, Director, (202) 357-5205. General e-mail, isoo@nara.gov*

Web, www.archives.gov/isoo/index.html

Administers governmentwide national security classification program under which information is classified, declassified, and safeguarded for national security purposes.

National Security Agency (NSA), *(Defense Dept.), 9800 Savage Rd., #6272, Fort Meade, MD 20755-6000; (301) 688-6524. Fax, (301) 688-6198. Lt. Gen. Keith B. Alexander (USA), Director; John C. "Chris" Inglis, Deputy Director. General e-mail, nsapao@nsa.gov*

Web, www.nsa.gov

Maintains and operates the Defense Dept.'s Computer Security Center; ensures communications and computer security within the government.

Navy Dept. *(Defense Dept.), Naval Criminal Investigative Service, Bldg. 111, 716 Sicard St. S.E., #2000, Washington Navy Yard, DC 20388-5380; (202) 433-8800. Fax, (202) 433-9619. Thomas A. Betro, Director. Press, (202) 433-9624.*
Web, www.ncis.navy.mil

Handles felony criminal investigations, counterintelligence, counterterrorism, and security for the Navy Dept., working with federal, state, local, and foreign agencies to investigate crimes; processes security clearances for the Navy Dept.

State Dept., *Countermeasures, 1801 N. Lynn St., Rosslyn, VA 22209; (703) 312-3460. Fax, (571) 345-3844. Patrick D. Donovan, Deputy Assistant Secretary.*
Web, www.state.gov

Responsible for Physical and Technical Security Programs for State Dept. officials and for the Diplomatic Courier Program.

State Dept., *Diplomatic Security Service, 2201 C St. N.W. 20520; (202) 647-7277. Fax, (202) 647-0122. Gregg Starr, Director. Diplomatic Service Command Center, (571) 345-3146.*
Web, www.state.gov

Oversees the safety and security of all U.S. government employees at U.S. embassies and consulates abroad. Responsible for the safety of the secretary of state and all foreign dignitaries below head of state level who are visiting the United States. Conducts background investigations of potential government employees, investigates passport and visa fraud, and warns government employees of any counterintelligence dangers they might encounter.

State Dept., *Security Infrastructure, 1801 N. Lynn St., Rosslyn, VA 22209; (571) 345-3788. Fax, (571) 345-3792. Donald R. Reid, Senior Coordinator.*
Web, www.state.gov

Manages matters relating to security infrastructure in the functional areas of information security, computer security, and personnel security and suitability.

MILITARY INSTALLATIONS

▶AGENCIES

Army Dept. *(Defense Dept.), Installations and Environment, 110 Army Pentagon, #3E464 20310-0110; (703) 697-8161. Fax, (703) 614-7394. Joseph F. Calcara, Deputy Assistant Secretary.*
General e-mail, asaie.webmaster@hqda.army.mil

Web, www.asaie.army.mil

Civilian office that manages all Army installations.

Defense Dept. (DoD), *Installations and Environment, 3400 Defense Pentagon, #3B856A 20301-3400; (703) 695-2880. Fax, (703) 693-7011. Wayne Arny, Deputy Under Secretary.*
Web, www.acq.osd.mil/ie

Oversees and offers policy guidance for all Defense Dept. installations and environmental programs.

Defense Dept. (DoD), *International Security Affairs, The Pentagon, #3-C852A 20301-2400; (703) 695-4351. Fax, (703) 697-7230. Vacant, Assistant Secretary.*
Web, www.defenselink.mil

Negotiates and monitors defense cooperation agreements, including base rights, access and prepositioning, exchange programs, and status of forces agreements with foreign governments in assigned geographic areas of responsibility.

►**CONGRESS**

For a listing of relevant congressional committees and subcommittees, please see page 546 or the Appendix.

Base Closings, Economic Impact

►**AGENCIES**

Air Force Dept. *(Defense Dept.), Base Realignment and Closure,* 1665 Air Force Pentagon, #5C266 20330-1665; (703) 604-5270. Joe Morganti, Director.
Web, www.af.mil

Military office that provides management oversight for implementing base closings and base realignment under the Base Realignment Act (BRAC).

Air Force Dept. *(Defense Dept.), Installations,* 1665 Air Force Pentagon, #4B941, SAF/IEI 20330-1665; (703) 695-3592. Fax, (703) 693-7568. Kathleen Ferguson, Deputy Assistant Secretary.
General e-mail, safiei.workflow@pentagon.af.mil
Web, www.af.mil

Civilian office that plans and reviews the building, repairing, renovating, and closing of Air Force bases.

Army Dept. *(Defense Dept.), Employment Policy,* 2461 Eisenhower Ave., #148, Alexandria, VA 22322-0300; (703) 325-9989. Fax, (703) 325-3524. Sheila Dent, Chief.
Web, www.army.mil

Military office responsible for employment policies to assist civilian personnel in cases of Defense Dept. program changes, including base closings.

Defense Dept. (DoD), *Civilian Assistance and Re-Employment (CARE),* 1400 Key Blvd., #B-200, Arlington, VA 22209-5144; (703) 696-1799. Fax, (703) 696-5416. Jeffrey L. Nelson, Chief.
Web, www.cpms.osd.mil/care

Manages transition programs for Defense Dept. civilians, including placement, separation incentives, early retirement, and transition assistance programs.

Defense Dept. (DoD), *Office of Economic Adjustment,* 400 Army-Navy Dr., #200, Arlington, VA 22202-4704; (703) 604-6020. Fax, (703) 604-5843. Patrick J. O'Brien, Director.
General e-mail, patrick.obrien@wso.whs.mil
Web, www.oea.gov

Civilian office that helps community officials develop strategies and coordinate plans to alleviate the economic effect of major defense program changes, including base closings and contract cutbacks. Assists communities where defense activities are being expanded. Serves as the staff for the Economic Adjustment Committee, an interagency group that coordinates federal defense economic adjustment activities.

Marine Corps *(Defense Dept.), Land Use and Military Construction,* 2 Navy Annex 20380-1775; (703) 695-8202. Fax, (703) 695-8550. Col. David L. Spasojevich, Head.
Web, www.hqmc.usmc.mil

Military office that reviews studies on base closings under the Base Realignment Act (BRAC).

Commissaries, PXs, and Service Clubs

►**AGENCIES**

Defense Dept. (DoD), *Army and Air Force Exchange, Washington Office,* 2511 Jefferson Davis Hwy., #11600, Arlington, VA 22202-3922; (703) 604-7523. Fax, (703) 604-7510. Gregg Cox, Director.
Web, www.hqmc.usmc.mil

Coordinates Army and Air Force PX matters with other Defense Dept. offices. (Headquarters in Dallas, Texas.)

Defense Dept. (DoD), *Defense Commissary Agency, Washington Office,* Crystal Square 4, 241 S. 18th St., #302, Arlington, VA 22202-3411; (703) 602-0157. Fax, (703) 602-2584. Dan W. Sclater, Chief, Washington Office.
General e-mail, dan.sclater@osd.mil
Web, www.commissaries.com

Serves as a liaison for the Defense Commissary Agency. Monitors legislation and regulations. (Headquarters in Fort Lee, Va.)

Navy Dept. *(Defense Dept.), Manpower and Reserve Affairs,* 1000 Navy Pentagon, #4E590 20350-1000; (703) 695-4333. Fax, (703) 614-4103. H. C. "Barney" Barnum, Assistant Secretary (Acting).
Web, www.donhq.navy.mil/mra

Civilian office that develops policies for Navy and Marine Corps commissaries, exchanges, and service clubs and reviews their operations.

Navy Dept. *(Defense Dept.), Navy Exchange Service Command, Washington Office,* 200 12th St. South, #1400, Arlington, VA 22202, (703) 607-0072. Fax, (703) 607-1167. Alexander Douvres, Director. Navy Exchange, (800) 628-3924.
Web, www.navy-nex.com

Civilian office that serves as a liaison among the Navy Exchange Service Command, the Navy Supply Systems Command, Congress, and the Defense Dept. (Headquarters in Virginia Beach, Va.)

►CONGRESS

For a listing of relevant congressional committees and subcommittees, please see page 546 or the Appendix.

►NONGOVERNMENTAL

American Logistics Assn., *1133 15th St. N.W., #640 20005-2710; (202) 466-2520. Fax, (202) 296-4419. Patrick B. Nixon, President.*
Web, www.ala-national.org

Membership: suppliers of military commissaries and exchanges. Acts as liaison between the Defense Dept. and service contractors; monitors legislation and testifies on issues of interest to members.

United Service Organizations (USO), *World Headquarters, 2111 Wilson Blvd., #1200, Arlington, VA 22201; (703) 908-6400. Fax, (202) 908-6401. Stan D. Gibson, President. Toll-free, (800) 876-7469.*
Web, www.uso.org

Voluntary civilian organization chartered by Congress. Provides military personnel and their families in the United States and overseas with social, educational, and recreational programs.

Construction, Housing, and Real Estate

►AGENCIES

Air Force Dept. *(Defense Dept.), Civil Engineering, Headquarters USAF/A7C, 1235 S. Clark St., Arlington, VA 22202; (703) 693-4301. Fax, (703) 693-4893. Maj. Gen. Del Eulberg, Director.*
Web, www.af.mil

Military office that plans and directs construction of Air Force facilities in the United States and overseas.

Air Force Dept. *(Defense Dept.), Housing Operations and Management, 1235 S. Clark St., #1000, Arlington, VA 22202; (703) 604-4252. Fax, (703) 604-2484. Connie M. Lotfi, Chief.*
General e-mail, connie.lotfi@pentagon.af.mil
Web, www.af.mil

Military office that manages the operation of Air Force housing on military installations in the United States and overseas.

Air Force Dept. *(Defense Dept.), Installations, 1665 Air Force Pentagon, #4B941, SAF/IEI 20330-1665; (703) 695-3592. Fax, (703) 693-7568. Kathleen Ferguson, Deputy Assistant Secretary.*
General e-mail, safiei.workflow@pentagon.af.mil
Web, www.af.mil

Civilian office that plans and reviews construction policies and programs of Air Force military facilities (including the Military Construction Program), housing programs, and real estate buying, selling, and leasing in the United States.

Army Corps of Engineers *(Defense Dept.), 441 G St. N.W., #3K05 20314-1000; (202) 761-0001. Fax, (202) 761-4463. Lt. Gen. Robert L. Van Antwerp (USACE), Chief of Engineers.*
Web, www.usace.army.mil

Military office that establishes policy and designs, directs, and manages civil works and military construction projects of the Army Corps of Engineers; directs the Army's real estate leasing and buying for military installations and civil works projects.

Army Dept. *(Defense Dept.), Army Housing, 2511 Jefferson Davis Hwy., Arlington, VA 22202-3926; (703) 604-2476. Fax, (703) 601-0731. Deborah Reynolds, Chief.*
Web, www.hqda.army.mil

Military office that plans, directs, and administers the construction and maintenance of Army family housing. Also responsible for unaccompanied personnel.

Army Dept. *(Defense Dept.), Installations and Environment, 110 Army Pentagon, #3E464 20310-0110; (703) 697-8161. Fax, (703) 614-7394. Joseph F. Calcara, Deputy Assistant Secretary.*
General e-mail, asaie.webmaster@hqda.army.mil
Web, www.asaie.army.mil

Civilian office that reviews housing programs, the construction of Army military facilities, and the buying and leasing of real estate in the United States and overseas.

Defense Dept. (DoD), *Facility Investment and Management, 3400 Defense Pentagon, #5C646 20301-3400; (703) 695-6774. Fax, (703) 693-2659. Michael McAndrew, Director.*
Web, www.acq.osd.mil/ie/irm

Determines requirements and policies for military construction; facility sustainment, restoration, and modernization; and base operations except for housing. Prepares and defends the annual military construction bill before Congress; manages real property; oversees facilities operation and installation, hosts nation programs, energy and water resource management, and utilities acquisition and privatization; and reports on base structure.

Marine Corps *(Defense Dept.), Facilities, 3250 Catlin Ave., #235, Quantico, VA 22134-5001; (703) 784-2331. Fax, (703) 784-2332. E.C. Rushing Jr., Director.*
Web, www.quantico.usmc.mil/activities.htm

Control point for the Marine Corps divisions of public works, family housing, and natural resources and environmental affairs.

Marine Corps *(Defense Dept.), Land Use and Military Construction, 2 Navy Annex 20380-1775; (703) 695-8202. Fax, (703) 695-8550. Col. David L. Spasojevich, Head.*
Web, www.hqmc.usmc.mil

Military office responsible for military construction and the acquisition, management, and disposal of Marine Corps real property.

Navy Dept. *(Defense Dept.), Installations and Facilities,* 1000 Navy Pentagon, #4E731 20350-1000; (703) 693-4527. Fax, (703) 693-1165. Howard Snow, Deputy Assistant Secretary (Acting). Web, www.navy.mil

Civilian office that monitors and reviews construction of Navy military facilities and housing and the buying and leasing of real estate in the United States and overseas.

Navy Dept. *(Defense Dept.), Naval Facilities Engineering Command,* 1322 Patterson Ave. S.E., #1000, Washington Navy Yard, DC 20374-5065; (202) 685-9499. Fax, (202) 685-1463. Rear Adm. W. Gregory "Greg" Shear Jr., Commander. Press, (202) 685-9108. Web, www.navfac.navy.mil

Military command that plans, designs, and constructs facilities for Navy and other Defense Dept. activities around the world and manages Navy public works, utilities, environmental programs, and real estate.

Navy Dept. *(Defense Dept.), Real Estate,* 1322 Patterson Ave. S.E., #1000, Washington Navy Yard, DC 20374-5065; (202) 685-9198. Fax, (202) 685-1585. Jim Leary, Director. Web, www.navfac.navy.mil

Military office that directs the Navy's real estate leasing, buying, and disposition for military installations.

U.S. Coast Guard (USCG), *(Homeland Security Dept.), Housing Programs,* CG-1223, 2100 2nd St. S.W. 20593-0001; (202) 475-5407. Fax, (202) 475-5929. Melissa Fredrickson, Director.

Provides housing and management for uniformed Coast Guard personnel.

► **CONGRESS**

For a listing of relevant congressional committees and subcommittees, please see page 546 or the Appendix.

PROCUREMENT, ACQUISITION, AND LOGISTICS

► **AGENCIES**

Air Force Dept. *(Defense Dept.), Acquisition,* 1060 Air Force Pentagon, #4E962 20330-1060; (703) 697-6361. Fax, (703) 693-6400. Sue C. Payton, Assistant Secretary. Web, www.af.mil

Air Force office that directs and reviews Air Force procurement policies and programs.

Air Force Dept. *(Defense Dept.), Contracting,* 1060 Air Force Pentagon, #700 20330-1060; (703) 588-7004. Fax, (703) 588-1067. Roger S. Correll, Deputy Assistant Secretary. Web, www.af.mil

Develops, implements, and enforces contracting policies on Air Force acquisitions worldwide, including research and development services, weapons systems, logistics services, and operational contracts.

Air Force Dept. *(Defense Dept.), Global Power Programs,* 1500 Wilson Blvd., #1100, Arlington, VA 22209; (703) 588-7170. Fax, (703) 588-6196. Maj. Gen. Jay H. Lindell, Director. Web, www.af.mil

Military office that directs Air Force acquisition and development programs within the tactical arena.

Army Dept. *(Defense Dept.), Procurement,* 103 Army Pentagon, #2E533 20310-0103; (703) 695-4101. Fax, (703) 695-9386. Edward Harrington, Deputy Assistant Secretary. Web, www.army.mil

Directs and reviews Army procurement policies and programs.

Criminal Division *(Justice Dept.), Federal Procurement Fraud,* 10th St. and Constitution Ave. N.W., #3100 20530; (202) 616-0440. Barbara Corprew, Associate Deputy. Web, www.usdoj.gov

Interdepartmental unit that investigates fraud in federal procurement contracting.

Defense Acquisition University *(Defense Dept.),* 9820 Belvoir Rd., Fort Belvoir, VA 22060-5565; (703) 805-3360. Fax, (703) 805-2639. Frank J. Anderson Jr., President. Toll-free, (800) 845-7606. Registrar, (703) 805-5142. Web, www.dau.mil

Academic institution that offers courses to military and civilian personnel who specialize in acquisition and procurement. Conducts research to support and improve management of defense systems acquisition programs.

Defense Contract Audit Agency (DCAA), *(Defense Dept.),* 8725 John Jay Kingman Rd., #2135, Fort Belvoir, VA 22060-6219; (703) 767-3200. Fax, (703) 767-3267. April G. Stephenson, Director. Web, www.dcaa.mil

Performs all contract audits for the Defense Dept. Provides Defense Dept. personnel responsible for procurement and contract administration with accounting and financial advisory services regarding the negotiation, administration, and settlement of contracts and subcontracts.

Defense Dept. (DoD), *Acquisition, Technology, and Logistics,* 3010 Defense Pentagon, #3E1010 20301-3010; (703) 697-7021. Fax, (703) 697-5471. John J. Young Jr., Under Secretary. Web, www.acq.osd.mil

Formulates and directs policy relating to the department's purchasing system, research and development, logistics, advanced technology, international programs, environmental security, industrial base, and nuclear, biological, and chemical programs. Oversees all defense procurement and acquisition programs.

Defense Dept. (DoD), *Armed Services Board of Contract Appeals, Skyline 6, 7th Floor, 5109 Leesburg Pike, Falls Church, VA 22041-3208; (703) 681-8502. Fax, (703) 681-8535. Paul Williams, Chair.*
Web, www.law.gwu.edu/asbca

Adjudicates disputes arising under Defense Dept. contracts.

Defense Dept. (DoD), *Defense Acquisition Regulations System (DARS) Directorate and DARS Council, 3062 Defense Pentagon, #2E1004 20301-3062; (703) 602-0131. Fax, (703) 602-0350. Linda Neilson, Director.*
Web, www.acq.osd.mil/dpap

Develops procurement regulations and manages procurement cases for the Defense Dept.

Defense Dept. (DoD), *Defense Procurement and Acquisition Policy, 3060 Defense Pentagon, #3B855 20301-3060; (703) 695-7145. Fax, (703) 693-1142. Shay Assad, Director.*
Web, www.acq.osd.mil/dpap

Responsible for all acquisition and procurement policy matters for the Defense Dept. Serves as principal adviser to the under secretary of defense for acquisition, technology, and logistics on strategies relating to all major weapon systems programs, major automated information systems programs, and services acquisitions.

Defense Dept. (DoD), *Logistics and Materiel Readiness, 3500 Defense Pentagon, #1E518 20301-3500; (703) 697-1369. Fax, (703) 693-0555. Jack Bell, Deputy Under Secretary.*
Web, www.acq.osd.mil/log

Formulates and implements department policies and programs for the conduct of logistics, maintenance, materiel readiness, strategic mobility, and sustainable support.

Defense Dept. (DoD), *Operational Test and Evaluation, 1700 Defense Pentagon, #3D947 20301-1700; (703) 697-3654. Fax, (703) 693-5248. Charles E. McQueary, Director. Press, (703) 693-7780.*
Web, www.dote.osd.mil

Ensures that major acquisitions, including weapons systems, are operationally effective and suitable prior to full-scale investment. Provides the secretary of defense and Congress with independent assessment of these programs.

Defense Logistics Agency *(Defense Dept.), 8725 John Jay Kingman Rd., #2533, Fort Belvoir, VA 22060-6221; (703) 767-5200. Fax, (703) 767-5207. Vice Adm. Alan S. Thompson (USN), Director. Press, (703) 767-6200.*
Web, www.dla.mil

Administers defense contracts; acquires, stores, and distributes food, clothing, medical, and other supplies used by the military services and other federal agencies; administers programs related to logistical support for the military

services; and assists military services with developing, acquiring, and using technical information and defense materiel and disposing of materiel no longer needed.

Marine Corps *(Defense Dept.), Contracts, 2 Navy Annex 20380-1775; (703) 695-6326. Fax, (703) 695-6382. Richard Sweeney, Deputy Commandant.*
Web, www.hqmc.usmc.mil

Military office that directs Marine Corps procurement programs.

Navy Dept. *(Defense Dept.), Acquisition and Logistics Management, 1000 Navy Pentagon, #BF992A 20350-1000; (703) 614-9445. Fax, (703) 614-9394. Adm. Kathleen Dussault, Deputy Assistant Secretary.*
Web, www.acquisition.navy.mil

Directs and reviews Navy acquisition and procurement policy.

Navy Dept. *(Defense Dept.), Military Sealift Command, Bldg. 210, Washington Navy Yard, DC 20398-5540; (202) 685-5001. Fax, (202) 685-5020. Rear Adm. Robert D. Reilly, Commander. Press, (202) 685-5055.*
Web, www.msc.navy.mil

Provides sea transportation of equipment, fuel, supplies, and ammunition to sustain U.S. forces.

U.S. Coast Guard (USCG), *(Homeland Security Dept.), Acquisition, 1900 Half St. S.W., #110939 20538; (202) 475-3101. Fax, (202) 475-3900. Adm. Gary Blore, Assistant Commandant. Public Affairs, (202) 372-4600.*
Web, www.uscg.mil

Administers all procurement made through the Acquisition Contract Support Division.

U.S. Coast Guard (USCG), *(Homeland Security Dept.), Logistics Management, 2100 2nd St. S.W. 20593-0001; (202) 475-5649. Fax, (202) 475-5958. Capt. Richard T. Gromlich, Director. Public Affairs, (202) 372-4600.*
Web, www.uscg.mil

Sets policy and procedures for the procurement, distribution, maintenance, and replacement of materiel and personnel for the Coast Guard.

►CONGRESS

For a listing of relevant congressional committees and subcommittees, please see page 546 or the Appendix.

Government Accountability Office (GAO), *Defense Capabilities and Management, 441 G St. N.W., #4030 20548; (202) 512-4300. Henry L. Hinton Jr., Managing Director.*
Web, www.gao.gov

Independent, nonpartisan agency in the legislative branch. Audits, analyzes, and evaluates Defense Dept. acquisition programs; makes unclassified reports available to the public. (Formerly the General Accounting Office.)

►NONGOVERNMENTAL

National Defense Transportation Assn. (NDTA), *50 S. Pickett St., #220, Alexandria, VA 22304-7296; (703) 751-5011. Fax, (703) 823-8761. Lt. Gen. Kenneth Wykle (USA, Ret.), President.*
Web, www.ndtahq.com

Membership: transportation users, manufacturers, and mode carriers; information technology firms; and related military, government, and civil interests worldwide. Promotes a strong U.S. transportation capability through coordination of private industry, government, and the military.

TechAmerica, *Public Sector Group, 1401 Wilson Blvd., #1100, Arlington, VA 22209; (703) 522-5055. Fax, (703) 525-2279. Christopher W. Hansen, Chief Executive Officer; Phillip J. Bond, President. Press, (703) 284-5305. Toll-free, (800) 284-4232.*

General e-mail, csc@techamerica.org
Web, www.techamerica.org

Membership: companies providing information technology and electronics products and services to government organizations at the federal, state, and local levels. Provides industry trends, forecasts, and standards development. Monitors federal policy and practices in acquiring technology products and services; represents the industry's views on acquisition regulations in federal agencies; serves as the focal point through which the government communicates with the technology industry on procurement policy and other matters affecting the business-government relationship. (Merger of AeA [formerly the American Electronics Assn.], the Information Technology Assn. of America [ITAA], the Government Electronics and Information and Technology Assn. [GEIA], and the Cyber Security Alliance.)

16 Science and Technology

GENERAL POLICY AND ANALYSIS

Basic Resources

▶AGENCIES

National Digital Information Infrastructure and Preservation Program (NDIIPP), *(Library of Congress), Office of Strategic Initiatives,* 101 Independence Ave. S.E. 20540-1300; (202) 707-3300. Fax, (202) 707-0815. Jim Gallagher, Deputy Assistant Librarian (Acting).
Web, www.digitalpreservation.gov

Oversees development of a national strategy to collect, archive, and preserve digital content, and directs the activities of the Information Technology Directorate.

National Institutes of Health (NIH), *(Health and Human Services Dept.), Office of Intramural Training and Education,* 2 Center Dr., Bldg. 2, #2E04, MSC 0240, Bethesda, MD 20892-0240; (301) 496-2427. Fax, (301) 594-9606. Sharon Milgram, Director.
General e-mail, trainingwww@mail.nih.gov

Web, www.training.nih.gov

Administers programs and initiatives to recruit and develop individuals who participate in research training activities on the NIH's main campus as well as other facilities across the country. Maintains an interactive Web site for the various research training programs and handbooks for postdoctoral fellows, graduate students, post-baccalaureate trainees, and summer interns. Supports the training mission of the intramural program through placement, retention, support, and tracking of trainees at all levels, as well as program delivery and evaluation. Administers the NIH Academy and the Summer Internship Program.

National Institutes of Health (NIH), *(Health and Human Services Dept.), Science Policy,* 9000 Rockville Pike, Bldg. 1, #103, Bethesda, MD 20892; (301) 496-2122. Fax, (301) 402-1759. Dr. Amy Patterson, Director (Acting).
Web, www1.od.nih.gov/osp

Advises the NIH director on science policy issues affecting the medical research community. Participates in the development of new policy and program initiatives. Monitors and coordinates agency planning and evaluation activities. Plans and implements a comprehensive science education program. Develops and implements NIH policies and procedures for the safe conduct of recombinant DNA and other biotechnology activities.

National Museum of Natural History *(Smithsonian Institution),* 10th St. and Constitution Ave. N.W. 20560-0106 (mailing address: P.O. Box 37012, Washington, DC 20013-7012); (202) 633-2664. Fax, (202) 357-4779. Cristian Samper, Director. Library, (202) 633-1680. General Smithsonian Information, (202) 633-1000.
Web, www.nmnh.si.edu

Conducts research and maintains exhibitions and collections relating to the natural sciences. Collections are organized into seven research and curatorial departments: anthropology, botany, entomology, invertebrate zoology, mineral sciences, paleobiology, and vertebrate zoology.

National Science Board *(National Science Foundation),* 4201 Wilson Blvd., #1220, Arlington, VA 22230; (703) 292-7000. Fax, (703) 292-9008. Craig R. Robinson, Executive Officer (Acting). TTY, (800) 281-8749.
General e-mail, NSBoffice@nsf.gov

Web, www.nsf.gov/NSB

Formulates policy for the National Science Foundation; advises the president on national science policy.

National Science Foundation (NSF), 4201 Wilson Blvd., #1205, Arlington, VA 22230; (703) 292-5111. Fax, (703) 292-9232. Arden L. Bement Jr., Director. Library, (703) 292-7830. TTY, (800) 281-8749. Publications, (703) 292-7827. Government Affairs, (703) 292-8070.
General e-mail, info@nsf.gov

Web, www.nsf.gov

Sponsors scientific and engineering research; develops and helps implement science and engineering education programs; fosters dissemination of scientific information; promotes international cooperation within the scientific community; and assists with national science policy planning.

National Science Foundation (NSF), *Human Resource Development,* 4201 Wilson Blvd., #815, Arlington, VA 22230; (703) 292-8640. Fax, (703) 292-9018. James Wyche, Director.
Web, www.nsf.gov

Supports and encourages participation in scientific and engineering research by women, minorities, and people with disabilities. Awards grants and scholarships.

National Science Foundation (NSF), *Science Resources Statistics,* 4201 Wilson Blvd., #965, Arlington, VA 22230; (703) 292-8780. Fax, (703) 292-9092. Lynda T. Carlson, Director.
Web, www.nsf.gov/statistics

Compiles, analyzes, and disseminates quantitative information about domestic and international resources devoted to science, engineering, and technology. Provides information to other federal agencies for policy formulation.

SCIENCE AND TECHNOLOGY RESOURCES IN CONGRESS

For a complete listing of Congress committees, including their full contact information, leadership, membership, and jurisdictions, please refer to the Appendix on pages 724–837.

HOUSE:

House Administration Committee, (202) 225-2061.
Web, cha.house.gov

House Agriculture Committee, Subcommittee on Conservation, Credit, Energy, and Research, (202) 225-0420.
Web, agriculture.house.gov

House Appropriations Committee, Subcommittee on Commerce, Justice, Science, and Related Agencies, (202) 225-3351.
Web, appropriations.house.gov

    Subcommittee on Interior, Environment and Related Agencies, (202) 225-3081.

    Subcommittee on Labor, Health and Human Services, Education, and Related Agencies, (202) 225-3508.

House Education and Labor Committee, (202) 225-3725.
Web, edworkforce.house.gov

    Subcommittee on Early Childhood, Elementary, and Secondary Education, (202) 225-3725.

    Subcommittee on Higher Education, Lifelong Learning, and Competitiveness, (202) 225-3725.

House Energy and Commerce Committee, (202) 225-2927.
Web, energycommerce.house.gov

    Subcommittee on Communications, Technology, and the Internet, (202) 225-2927.

House Homeland Security Committee, Subcommittee on Emerging Threats, Cyber-Security, and Science and Technology, (202) 226-2616.
Web, homeland.house.gov

House Judiciary Committee, Subcommittee on Courts, the Internet, and Intellectual Property, (202) 225-5741.
Web, judiciary.house.gov

House Natural Resources Committee, (202) 225-6065.
Web, resourcescommittee.house.gov

    Subcommittee on Energy and Mineral Resources, (202) 225-9297.

    Subcommittee on Insular Affairs, Oceans, and Wildlife, (202) 226-0200.

    Subcommittee on National Parks, Forests and Public Lands, (202) 226-7736.

    Subcommittee on Water and Power, (202) 225-8331.

House Oversight and Government Reform Committee, Subcommittee on Domestic Policy, (202) 225-6427.
Web, oversight.house.gov

    Subcommittee on Information Policy, Census, and National Archives, (202) 225-6751.

House Science and Technology Committee, (202) 225-6375.
Web, science.house.gov

    Subcommittee on Energy and Environment, (202) 225-8844.

    Subcommittee on Investigations and Oversight, (202) 225-8772.

    Subcommittee on Research and Science Education, (202) 225-9662.

    Subcommittee on Space and Aeronautics, (202) 225-7858.

    Subcommittee on Technology and Innovation, (202) 225-9662.

House Select Committee on Energy Independence and Global Warming, (202) 225-4012.
Web, globalwarming.house.gov

Office of Management and Budget (OMB), *(Executive Office of the President), Energy, Science, and Water,* *New Executive Office Bldg., #8002 20503; (202) 395-3404. Fax, (202) 395-3049. Richard A. Mertens, Deputy Associate Director. Press, (202) 395-7524.*
Web, www.whitehouse.gov/omb

Assists and advises the OMB director in budget preparation; analyzes and evaluates programs in space and science, including the activities of the National Science Foundation and the National Aeronautics and Space Administration; coordinates OMB science, energy, and space policies and programs.

Office of Science *(Energy Dept.), 1000 Independence Ave. S.W., #7B058 20585; (202) 586-5430. Fax, (202) 586-4120. Patricia Dehmer, Deputy Director of Science Programs.*
Web, www.science.doe.gov

Advises the secretary on the department's physical science and energy research and development programs; the management of the nonweapons multipurpose laboratories; and education and training activities required for basic and applied research. Manages the department's high energy physics, nuclear physics, fusion energy sciences, basic energy sciences, health and environmental

SCIENCE AND TECHNOLOGY RESOURCES IN CONGRESS

House Small Business Committee, Subcommittee on Contracting and Technology, (202) 225-4038.

Web, www.house.gov/smbiz

SENATE:

Senate Agriculture, Nutrition, and Forestry Committee, Subcommittee on Energy, Science, and Technology, (202) 224-2035.

Web, agriculture.senate.gov

Senate Appropriations Committee, Subcommittee on Commerce, Justice, Science, and Related Agencies, (202) 224-5202.

Web, appropriations.senate.gov

Subcommittee on Interior, Environment and Related Agencies, (202) 228-0774.

Subcommittee on Labor, Health and Human Services, Education, and Related Agencies, (202) 224-9145.

Senate Commerce, Science, and Transportation Committee, (202) 224-0411.

Web, commerce.senate.gov

Subcommittee on Aviation Operations, Safety, and Security, (202) 224-9000

Subcommittee on Consumer Protection, Product Safety, and Insurance, (202) 224-1270.

Subcommittee on Oceans, Atmosphere, Fisheries and the Coast Guard, (202) 224-4912.

Subcommittee on Science, and Space, (202) 224-9000.

Subcommittee on Surface Transportation and Merchant Marine Infastructure, Safety, and Security, (202) 224-9000.

Senate Energy and Natural Resources Committee, (202) 224-4971.

Web, energy.senate.gov

Subcommittee on Energy, (202) 224-4971.

Subcommittee on Public Lands and Forests, (202) 224-4971.

Subcommittee on Water and Power, (202) 224-4971.

Senate Environment and Public Works Committee, Subcommittee on Clean Air and Nuclear Safety, (202) 224-8832.

Web, epw.senate.gov/public

Subcommittee on Private Sector and Consumer Solutions to Global Warming and Wildlife Protection, (202) 224-8832.

Subcommittee on Public Sector Solutions to Global Warming, Oversight and Children's Health, (202) 224-8832.

Senate Health, Education, Labor, and Pensions Committee, (202) 224-5375.

Web, help.senate.gov

Senate Judiciary Committee, Subcommittee on Terrorism, Technology, and Homeland Security, (202) 224-4933.

Web, judiciary.senate.gov

Senate Rules and Administration Committee, (202) 224-6352.

Web, rules.senate.gov

Senate Small Business and Entrepreneurship Committee, (202) 224-5175.

Web, sbc.senate.gov

Senate Special Committee on Aging, (202) 224-5364.

Web, aging.senate.gov

---

research, and computational and technology research. Provides and operates the large-scale facilities required for research in the physical and life sciences.

Office of Science and Technology Policy (OSTP), *(Executive Office of the President), New Executive Office Bldg., 725 17th St., #5228 20502; (202) 456-7116. Fax, (202) 456-6027. John P. Holdren, Director. Press, (202) 456-6124.*

General e-mail, info@ostp.gov

Web, www.ostp.gov

Advises the president on the effects of science and technology on domestic and international affairs. Serves as a source of scientific and technological analysis for the president with respect to major policies, plans, and programs of the federal government. Leads an interagency effort to develop and implement sound science and technology policies and budgets. Works with the private sector to ensure federal investments in science and technology contribute to economic prosperity, environmental quality, and national security.

Office of Science and Technology Policy (OSTP), *(Executive Office of the President), Science, New Executive Office Bldg., 725 17th St. N.W. 20502; (202) 456-6130. Fax, (202) 456-6027. Ted Wackler, Director (Acting).*

General e-mail, info@ostp.gov

Web, www.ostp.gov

Analyzes policies and advises the president and others within the EOP on biological, physical, social, and behavioral sciences and on engineering; coordinates executive office and federal agency actions related to these issues. Evaluates the effectiveness of government science programs.

Office of Science and Technology Policy (OSTP), *(Executive Office of the President), Technology,* New *Executive Office Bldg., 725 17th St. N.W., #5236 20502; Aneesh Chopra, Associate Director and Chief Technology Adviser to the President. (202) 456-6046. Fax, (202) 456-6021. General e-mail, info@ostp.gov*

Web, www.ostp.gov

►**CONGRESS**

For a listing of relevant congressional committees and subcommittees, please see page 592 or the Appendix.

►**NONGOVERNMENTAL**

American Assn. for Laboratory Accreditation (A2LA), *5301 Buckeystown Pike, #350, Frederick, MD 21704; (301) 644-3248. Fax, (301) 662-2974. Peter S. Unger, President. General e-mail, info@a2la.org*

Web, www.a2la.org

Monitors and accredits laboratories that test construction materials and perform acoustics and vibration, biological, calibration, chemical, electrical, environmental, geotechnical, mechanical, nondestructive, and thermal testing. Offers laboratory-related training and programs for accreditation of inspection bodies, proficiency testing providers, and reference material producers.

American Assn. for the Advancement of Science (AAAS), *1200 New York Ave. N.W., 12th Floor 20005; (202) 326-6640. Fax, (202) 371-9526. Alan I. Leshner, Executive Officer. Information, (202) 326-6400. General e-mail, ehr@aaas.org*

Web, www.aaas.org

Membership: scientists, affiliated scientific organizations, and individuals interested in science. Fosters scientific education; monitors and seeks to influence public policy and public understanding of science and technology; encourages scientific literacy among minorities and women. Sponsors national and international symposia, workshops, and meetings; publishes *Science* magazine.

American Assn. for the Advancement of Science (AAAS), *Scientific Freedom, Responsibility, and Law Program,* 1200 New York Ave. N.W., 8th Floor 20005; (202) 326-6600. Fax, (202) 289-4950. Mark S. Frankel, Director.

Web, www.aaas.org/spp/sfrl

Focuses on professional ethics and law in science and engineering and on the social implications of science and technology. Collaborates with other professional groups on these activities; provides technical assistance to organizations developing codes of ethics or educational programs on research integrity.

American Council of Independent Laboratories (ACIL), *1629 K St. N.W., #400 20006; (202) 887-5872. Fax, (202) 887-0021. Eddie Van Aken, Executive Director. General e-mail, info@acil.org*

Web, www.acil.org

Membership: independent commercial laboratories. Promotes professional and ethical business practices in providing analysis, testing, and research in engineering, microbiology, analytical chemistry, and environmental geosciences.

Assn. for Women in Science, *1200 New York Ave. N.W., #650 20005; (202) 326-8940. Fax, (202) 326-8960. Janet Bandows Koster, Executive Director. General e-mail, awis@awis.org*

Web, www.awis.org

Promotes equal opportunity for women in scientific professions; provides career and funding information. Provides educational scholarships for women in science. Interests include international development.

Council of Scientific Society Presidents, *1550 M St. N.W. 20005 (mailing address: 1155 16th St. N.W., #0-1015, Washington, DC 20036); (202) 872-6230. Fax, (202) 872-4079. Martin Apple, President. General e-mail, cssp@acs.org*

Web, www.cssp.us

Membership: presidents, presidents-elect, and immediate past presidents of professional scientific societies and federations. Supports professional science education. Serves as a forum for discussion of emerging scientific issues, formulates national science policy, and develops the nation's scientific leadership.

Federation of American Scientists (FAS), *1725 DeSales St. N.W., 6th Floor 20036; (202) 546-3300. Fax, (202) 675-1010. Henry Kelly, President. General e-mail, fas@fas.org*

Web, www.fas.org

Conducts studies and monitors legislation on issues and problems related to science and technology, especially U.S. nuclear arms policy, energy, arms transfer, and civil aerospace issues.

George C. Marshall Institute, *1625 K St. N.W., #1050 20006; (202) 296-9655. Fax, (202) 296-9714. Jeffrey Kueter, President. General e-mail, info@marshall.org*

Web, www.marshall.org

Analyzes the technical and scientific aspects of public policy issues; produces publications on environmental science, space, national security, bioterrorism, and technology policy.

Government-University-Industry Research Roundtable (GUIRR), *509 5th St. N.W. #509 20001; (202) 334-3486. Fax, (202) 334-1369. Susan Sauer Sloan, Director.*

General e-mail, guirr@nas.edu

Web, www.nationalacademies.org/guirr

Forum sponsored by the National Academy of Sciences, National Academy of Engineering, and Institute of Medicine. Provides scientists, engineers, and members of government, academia, and industry with an opportunity to discuss ways of improving the infrastructure for science and technology research.

Knowledge Ecology International (KEI), *Consumer Project on Technology,* 1621 Connecticut Ave. N.W., #500 20009; (202) 332-2670. Fax, (202) 332-2673. James Love, Director.
Web, www.keionline.org

Advocates consumer access to health care, electronic commerce, competition policy, and information regarding intellectual property rights.

National Academy of Sciences (NAS), 2101 Constitution Ave. N.W. 20418; (202) 334-2000. Fax, (202) 334-2419. Ralph J. Cicerone, President; E. William Colglazier, Executive Officer. Library, (202) 334-2125. Press, (202) 334-2138. Publications, (888) 624-8373; in Washington, (202) 334-3313.
General e-mail, news@nas.edu

Web, www.nationalacademies.org

Congressionally chartered independent organization that advises the federal government on questions of science, technology, and health. Library open to the public by appointment. (Affiliated with the National Academy of Engineering, the Institute of Medicine, and the National Research Council.)

National Geographic Society, *Committee for Research and Exploration,* 1145 17th St. N.W. 20036-4688; (202) 775-7844. Fax, (202) 429-5729. Peter H. Raven, Chair. TTY, (800) 548-9797.
General e-mail, cre@ngs.org

Web, www.nationalgeographic.com/research

Sponsors basic research grants in the sciences, including anthropology, archaeology, astronomy, biology, botany, ecology, physical and human geography, geology, oceanography, paleontology, and zoology. To apply for grants, see Web site.

National Research Council (NRC), 500 5th St. N.W., #1153 20001; (202) 334-2000. Fax, (202) 334-2419. Ralph J. Cicerone, President. Library, (202) 334-2125. Press, (202) 334-2138. Publications, (888) 624-8373; in Washington, (202) 334-3313.
General e-mail, news@nas.edu

Web, www.nationalacademies.org/nrc

Serves as the principal operating agency of the National Academy of Sciences, National Academy of Engineering, and Institute of Medicine. Program units focus on physical, social, and life sciences; applications of science, including medicine, transportation, and education; international affairs; and U.S. government policy. Library open to the public by appointment.

SAMA Group of Assns., 225 Reinekers Lane, #625, Alexandria, VA 22314-2875; (703) 836-1360. Fax, (703) 836-6644. Clark Mulligan, President.

Membership: manufacturers and distributors of laboratory products and optical instruments. (SAMA stands for Scientific Apparatus Makers Assn. Affiliated with the Opto-Precision Instrument Assn. and the Laboratory Products Assn.)

Society of Research Administrators International, 1901 N. Moore St., #1004, Arlington, VA 22209; (703) 741-0140. Fax, (703) 741-0142. Christopher Daniels, Executive Director.
General e-mail, info@srainternational.org

Web, www.srainternational.org

Membership: scientific and medical research administrators in the United States and other countries. Educates the public about the profession; offers professional development services; sponsors mentoring and awards programs. Monitors legislation and regulations.

Union of Concerned Scientists, *Strategy and Policy, Washington Office,* 1825 K St. N.W., #800 20006-3962; (202) 223-6133. Fax, (202) 223-6162. Alden Meyer, Director.
General e-mail, ucs@ucsusa.org

Web, www.ucsusa.org

An independent alliance of more than 100,000 concerned citizens and scientists that augments rigorous scientific analysis with innovative thinking and committed citizen advocacy to build a cleaner, healthier environment and a safer world. (Headquarters in Cambridge, Mass.)

Data, Statistics, and Reference

▶**AGENCIES**

Dibner Library of the History of Science and Technology *(Smithsonian Institution),* 14th St. and Constitution Ave. N.W., NMAH 1041/MRC 672 20013-7012; (202) 633-3872. Nancy E. Gwinn, Director.
General e-mail, Dibnerlibrary@si.edu

Web, www.sil.si.edu/libraries/Dibner

Collection includes major holdings in the history of science and technology dating from the fifteenth century to the nineteenth century. Extensive collections in engineering, transportation, chemistry, mathematics, physics, electricity, and astronomy. Open to the public by appointment.

National Aeronautics and Space Administration (NASA), *Science Proposal Support Office,* Goddard Space Flight Center, Code 605, Greenbelt, MD 20771; (301) 286-7354. Fax, (301) 286-1771. David Leisawitz, Chief.
Web, http://gsfc.nasa.gov

Supports the writing of proposals for NASA.

National Aeronautics and Space Administration (NASA), *Solar System Exploration Data Services,*

Goddard Space Flight Center, Code 690.1, Greenbelt, MD 20771; (301) 286-6695 (Access Service Office). Fax, (301) 286-1635. Edwin Grayzeck, Program Manager, Planetary Data System.
Web, http://ssedso.gsfc.nasa.gov

Coordinates data management and archiving plans within NASA's Science Mission. Operates the National Space Science Data Center (NSSDC) as a permanent archive for data associated with NASA's missions; the Crustal Dynamics Data Information System (CDDIS); and the Planetary Data System (PDS).

National Institute of Standards and Technology (NIST), (Commerce Dept.), Information Services Division: Research Library, 100 Bureau Dr., MS 2500, Gaithersburg, MD 20899-2500; (301) 975-3052. Fax, (301) 869-8071. Mary-Deirdre Coraggio, Director. TTY, (301) 975-8295.
General e-mail, library@nist.gov

Web, http://nvl.nist.gov

Creates and maintains a knowledge base that supports research and administrative needs for the institute. Includes material on engineering, chemistry, physics, mathematics, and the materials and computer sciences.

National Institute of Standards and Technology (NIST), (Commerce Dept.), Measurement Services, 100 Bureau Dr., MS 2300, Gaithersburg, MD 20899; (301) 975-8424. Fax, (301) 971-2183. Robert Watters Jr., Chief.
Web, www.nist.gov

Disseminates physical, chemical, and engineering measurement standards and provides services to ensure accurate and compatible measurements, specifications, and codes on a national and international scale.

National Institute of Standards and Technology (NIST), (Commerce Dept.), Standard Reference Data, 100 Bureau Dr., MS 2300, Gaithersburg, MD 20899-2300; (301) 975-2208. Fax, (301) 926-0416. Joan Sauerwein, Supervisory Measurement Services Product Specialist. Public Inquiries Unit, (301) 975-2208.
General e-mail, data@nist.gov

Web, www.nist.gov/srd

Collects and disseminates critically evaluated physical, chemical, and materials properties data in the physical sciences and engineering for use by industry, government, and academic laboratories. Develops databases in a variety of formats, including disk, CD-ROM, and online.

National Institute of Standards and Technology (NIST), (Commerce Dept.), Statistical Engineering, 100 Bureau Dr., Bldg. 222, A-247, MS 8980, Gaithersburg, MD 20899-8980; (301) 975-2839. Fax, (301) 975-3144. Antonio Passolo, Chief.
Web, www.nist.gov/itl/div898

Promotes the use of effective statistical techniques for planning analysis of experiments in the physical sciences within industry and government; interprets experiments and data collection programs.

National Museum of American History (Smithsonian Institution), Library, 14th St. and Constitution Ave. N.W., MRC 630 20560-0630; (202) 633-3865. Fax, (202) 357-4256. Lucien Rossignol, Chief Librarian.
Web, www.sil.si.edu

Collection includes materials on the history of science and technology, with concentrations in engineering, transportation, and applied science. Maintains collection of trade catalogs and materials about expositions and world fairs. Open to the public by appointment. Research areas are open by appointment.

National Oceanic and Atmospheric Administration (NOAA), (Commerce Dept.), Central Library, Library and Information Services, 1315 East-West Hwy., SSMC3, 2nd Floor, Silver Spring, MD 20910; (301) 713-2607. Fax, (301) 713-4599. Neal Kaske, Director. Reference service, (301) 713-2600, ext. 124.
General e-mail, library.reference@noaa.gov

Web, www.lib.noaa.gov

Collection includes electronic NOAA documents, reports, and videos; electronic and print journals; the NOAA Photo Library; bibliographic database of other NOAA libraries; and climate data. Makes interlibrary loans; library open to the public.

National Oceanic and Atmospheric Administration (NOAA), (Commerce Dept.), National Environmental Satellite, Data, and Information Service, 1335 East-West Hwy., Silver Spring, MD 20910; (301) 713-3578. Fax, (301) 713-1249. Mary Kicza, Assistant Administrator.
Web, www.nesdis.noaa.gov

Acquires and disseminates global environmental (marine, atmospheric, solid earth, and solar-terrestrial) data. Operates the following data facilities: National Climatic Data Center, Asheville, N.C.; National Geophysical Data Center, Boulder, Colo.; and National Oceanographic Data Center, Washington, D.C. Maintains comprehensive data and information referral service.

National Oceanic and Atmospheric Administration (NOAA), (Commerce Dept.), National Oceanographic Data Center, 1315 East-West Hwy., SSMC3, 4th Floor, Silver Spring, MD 20910-3282; (301) 713-3270. Fax, (301) 713-3300. Margarita Gregg, Director.
General e-mail, services@nodc.noaa.gov

Web, www.noaa.gov

Offers a wide range of oceanographic data on the Web, on disk, and on CD-ROM; provides research scientists with data processing services; prepares statistical summaries and graphical data products. (Fee charged for some services.)

National Technical Information Service (NTIS), (Commerce Dept.), 5285 Port Royal Rd., Springfield, VA 22161; (703) 605-6000. Fax, (703) 605-6900. Ellen Herbst, Director, (703) 605-6400. Sales department, (703) 605-6000. Toll-free, (800) 553-6847. Bookstore, (703) 605-6040.
General e-mail, info@ntis.gov

Web, www.ntis.gov

Collects and organizes technical, scientific, engineering, and business-related information generated by U.S. and foreign governments and makes it available for commercial use in the private sector. Makes available approximately 3 million works covering research and development, current events, business and management studies, translations of foreign open source reports, foreign and domestic trade, general statistics, environment and energy, health and social sciences, and hundreds of other areas. Provides computer software and computerized data files in a variety of formats, including Internet downloads. Houses the Homeland Security Information Center, a centralized source on major security concerns for health and medicine, food and agriculture, and bio-chemical war.

Smithsonian Institution, *Office of the Director:* *Libraries, 10th St. and Constitution Ave. N.W., #22 National Museum of Natural History 20560 (mailing address: P.O. Box 37012, MRC 154, Washington, DC 20013-7012); (202) 633-2240. Fax, (202) 786-2866. Nancy E. Gwinn, Director. TTY, (202) 357-2139.* *Web, www.sil.si.edu*

Maintains collection of general reference, biographical, and interdisciplinary materials; serves as an information resource on institution libraries, a number of which have collections in scientific subjects, including horticulture, botany, science and technology, and anthropology.

U.S. Geological Survey (USGS), *(Interior Dept.),* *Library Services, 12201 Sunrise Valley Dr., MS 950, Reston, VA 20192; (703) 648-4302. Fax, (703) 648-6373. Bob Bier, Librarian.* *General e-mail, library@usgs.gov* *Web, http://library.usgs.gov*

Maintains collection of books, periodicals, serials, maps, and technical reports on geology, mineral and water resources, mineralogy, paleontology, petrology, soil and environmental sciences, biology, and physics and chemistry as they relate to natural sciences. Open to the public; makes interlibrary loans.

U.S. Geological Survey (USGS), *(Interior Dept.), Science Information and Library Services (SILS), 12201 Sunrise Valley Dr., #1C204, Reston, VA 20192 (mailing address: 507 National Center, Reston, VA 20192-1507); (703) 648-5953. Fax, (703) 648-5548. Information and U.S. maps, (888) ASK-USGS or (888) 275-8747.* *General e-mail, ask@usgs.gov* *Web, www.usgs.gov*

Collects, organizes, and distributes cartographic, geographic, hydrologic, biologic, and other natural science information; offers maps, reports, and other publications, offers digital cartographic data, digital aerial photographic data, and space imagery and manned spacecraft photographs for sale. Acts as a clearinghouse for cartographic and geographic data.

►CONGRESS

For a listing of relevant congressional committees and subcommittees, please see page 592 or the Appendix.

Government Accountability Office (GAO), *Publications and Dissemination, 441 G St. N.W., #1127E 20548; (202) 512-512-3598. Patrick Seeley, Director (Acting).* *General e-mail, info@gao.gov*

Web, www.gao.gov

Provides information to the public on federal programs, reports, and testimonies. GAO publications and information about GAO publications are available upon request in print or online. (Formerly the General Accounting Office.)

Library of Congress, *Science, Technology, and Business, 101 Independence Ave. S.E., #LA5204 20540; (202) 707-5664. Fax, (202) 707-1925. William J. Sittig, Chief. Science reading room, (202) 707-5639. Technical reports, (202) 707-5655.* *Web, www.loc.gov/rr/scitech*

Offers reference service by telephone, by correspondence, and in person. Maintains a collection of more than 3 million reports on science, technology, business management, and economics.

►NONGOVERNMENTAL

American Statistical Assn., *732 N. Washington St., Alexandria, VA 22314-1943; (703) 684-1221. Fax, (703) 684-2037. Toll-free, (888) 231-3473. Ronald Wasserstein, Executive Director.* *General e-mail, asainfo@amstat.org*

Web, www.amstat.org

Membership: individuals interested in statistics and related quantitative fields. Advises government agencies on statistics and methodology in agency research; promotes development of statistical techniques for use in business, industry, finance, government, agriculture, and science. Promotes knowledge of statistics at all levels of education. Publishes statistical journals.

Commission on Professionals in Science and Technology, *1200 New York Ave. N.W., #113 20005; (202) 326-7080. Fax, (202) 842-1603. Lisa Frehill, Executive Director.* *General e-mail, info@cpst.org*

Web, www.cpst.org

Membership: scientific societies, corporations, academic institutions, and individuals. Analyzes and publishes data on scientific and engineering human resources in the United States. Interests include employment of minorities and women, salary ranges, and supply and demand of scientists and engineers.

International Programs

►AGENCIES

International Trade Administration (ITA), *(Commerce Dept.), Manufacturing and Services: Manufacturing, 14th St. and Constitution Ave. N.W., #2800 20230; (202)*

482-1872. Fax, (202) 482-0856. Vacant, Assistant Secretary.
Web, www.trade.gov

Conducts analyses and competitive assessments of high-tech industries, including aerospace, automotive, and industrial machinery. Develops trade policies for these industries, negotiates market access for U.S. companies, assists in promoting exports through trade missions, shows, and fairs in major overseas markets.

National Institute of Standards and Technology (NIST), *(Commerce Dept.), International and Academic Affairs, 100 Bureau Dr., Bldg. 101, #A200, Gaithersburg, MD 20899-1090; (301) 975-3069. Fax, (301) 975-3530. Claire Saundry, Director.*
General e-mail, inquiries@nist.gov
Web, www.nist.gov/oiaa/oiaa1.htm

Represents the institute in international functions; coordinates programs with foreign institutions; assists scientists from foreign countries who visit the institute for consultation. Administers a postdoctoral research associates program.

National Oceanic and Atmospheric Administration (NOAA), *(Commerce Dept.), National Environmental Satellite, Data, and Information Service, 1335 East-West Hwy., Silver Spring, MD 20910; (301) 713-3578. Fax, (301) 713-1249. Mary Kicza, Assistant Administrator.*
Web, www.nesdis.noaa.gov

Acquires and disseminates global environmental data: marine, atmospheric, solid earth, and solar-terrestrial. Participates, with the National Meteorological Center, in the United Nations World Weather Watch Programme developed by the World Meteorological Organization. Manages U.S. civil earth-observing satellite systems and atmospheric, oceanographic, geophysical, and solar data centers. Provides the public, businesses, and government agencies with environmental data and information products and services.

National Science Foundation (NSF), *International Science and Engineering, 4201 Wilson Blvd., #935, Arlington, VA 22230; (703) 292-8710. Fax, (703) 292-9067. Larry Weber, Director.*
Web, www.nsf.gov/oise

Serves as the foundation's focal point for international scientific and engineering activities; promotes new partnerships between U.S. scientists and engineers and their foreign colleagues; provides support for U.S. participation in international scientific organizations.

National Weather Service *(National Oceanic and Atmospheric Administration), National Centers for Environmental Prediction, 5200 Auth Rd., #101, Camp Springs, MD 20746; (301) 763-8016. Fax, (301) 763-8434. Louis W. Uccellini, Director.*
Web, www.ncep.noaa.gov

The National Center for Environmental Prediction and the National Environmental Satellite, Data, and Information Service are part of the World Weather Watch Programme developed by the United Nations World Meteorological Organization. Collects and exchanges data with other nations; provides other national weather service offices, private meteorologists, and government agencies with products, including forecast guidance products.

Office of Science and Technology Policy (OSTP), *(Executive Office of the President), New Executive Office Bldg., #5236 20502; (202) 456-7116. Fax, (202) 456-6021. John P. Holdren, Director.*
General e-mail, info@ostp.gov
Web, www.ostp.gov

Advises the president on science and technology matters as they affect national security; coordinates science and technology initiatives at the interagency level. Interests include nuclear materials, security, nuclear arms reduction, and counterterrorism.

Smithsonian Institution, *International Relations, 1100 Jefferson Dr. S.W., #3123 20705 (mailing address: P.O. Box 37012, Quad MRC 705, Washington, DC 20013-7012); (202) 633-4773. Fax, (202) 786-2557. Francine C. Berkowitz, Director.*
Web, www.si.edu/intrel

Fosters the development and coordinates the international aspects of Smithsonian scientific activities; facilitates basic research in the natural sciences and encourages international collaboration among individuals and institutions.

State Dept., *Oceans, Environment, and Science, 2201 C St. N.W., #3880 20520-7818; (202) 647-1554. Fax, (202) 647-0217. Reno Harnish, Assistant Secretary (Acting). Press, (202) 647-3486.*
Web, www.state.gov/g/oes/index.htm

Formulates and implements policies and proposals for U.S. international scientific, technological, environmental, oceanic and marine, Arctic and Antarctic, and space programs; coordinates international science and technology policy with other federal agencies.

State Dept., *Technological and Specialized Agencies, 2201 C St. N.W., #5333 20520; (202) 647-1044. Fax, (202) 647-8902. Michael Glover, Director.*
Web, www.state.gov

Oversees U.S. participation in international scientific and technical organizations, including the International Atomic Energy Agency; the United Nations Environment Programme; the Commission on Sustainable Development; and the United Nations Educational, Scientific, and Cultural Organization. Works to ensure that United Nations agencies follow United Nations Conference on Environment and Development recommendations on sustainable growth.

▶**INTERNATIONAL ORGANIZATIONS**

InterAcademy Panel on International Issues, *500 5th St. N.W., #528 20001 (mailing address: 500 5th St. N.W.,*

Washington, DC 20001); (202) 334-2804. Fax, (202) 334-2139. John Boright, U.S. Contact.
Web, www.interacademies.net

Membership: academies of science in countries worldwide. Promotes communication among leading authorities in the natural and social sciences; establishes regional networks of academies to identify critical issues, thereby building capacity for advice to governments and international organizations. Interests include science education and sustainable management of water, energy, and other resources. (National Academy of Sciences is U.S. member. Headquarters is in Trieste, Italy.)

►NONGOVERNMENTAL

American Assn. for the Advancement of Science (AAAS), *International Office,* 1200 New York Ave. N.W., 11th Floor 20005; (202) 326-6650. Fax, (202) 289-4958. Vaughan Turekian, Chief International Officer.
Web, www.aaas.org

Promotes international cooperation among scientists. Helps build scientific infrastructure in developing countries. Works to improve the quality of scientific input in international discourse.

Asia Policy Point (APP), *1730 Rhode Island Ave. N.W.,* #414 20036; (202) 822-6040. Fax, (202) 822-6044. Mindy Kotler, Director.
General e-mail, access@jiaponline.org
Web, www.jiaponline.org

Studies Japanese and northeast Asian science, security, and public policy and their relationship to U.S. foreign policy. (Formerly the Japan Information Access Project.)

National Research Council (NRC), *International Affairs,* 500 5th St. N.W., #528 20001; (202) 334-3817. Fax, (202) 334-2139. John Boright, Executive Director.
Web, www.nationalacademies.org/nrc

Serves the international interests of the National Research Council, National Academy of Sciences, National Academy of Engineering, and Institute of Medicine. Promotes effective application of science and technology to the economic and social problems of industrialized and developing countries, and advises U.S. government agencies.

Research Applications

►AGENCIES

Defense Technical Information Center (*Defense Dept.*), 8725 John Jay Kingman Rd., #0944, Fort Belvoir, VA 22060-6218; (703) 767-9100. Fax, (703) 767-9183. Paul R. Ryan, Administrator. Registration, (703) 767-8200. Toll-free, (800) 225-3842.
Web, www.dtic.mil

Acts as a central repository for the Defense Dept.'s collection of current and completed research and development efforts in all fields of science and technology.

Disseminates research and development information to contractors, grantees, and registered organizations working on government research and development projects, particularly for the Defense Dept. Users must register with the center.

National Aeronautics and Space Administration (NASA), *Science Mission Directorate,* 300 E St. S.W., #3C26 20546; (202) 358-3889. Fax, (202) 358-3092. Edward J. Weiler, Associate Administrator.
General e-mail, science@hq.nasa.gov
Web, http://science.hq.nasa.gov/directorate/index.html

Seeks to understand space phenomena and the origins, evolution, and structure of the universe. Sponsors scientific research that both enables and is enabled by NASA's exploration activities. Exchanges information with the science community; develops and deploys satellites and probes in collaboration with NASA's partners to answer fundamental questions requiring the view from and into space. Primary areas of study are astrophysics, earth sciences, heliophysics, and planetary science.

National Institute of Standards and Technology (NIST), *(Commerce Dept.),* 100 Bureau Dr., Bldg. 101, #A1134, Gaithersburg, MD 20899-1000 (mailing address: 100 Bureau Dr., MS 1000, Gaithersburg, MD 20899); (301) 975-2300. Fax, (301) 869-8972. Patrick Gallagher, Deputy Director.
Web, www.nist.gov

Nonregulatory agency that serves as national reference and measurement laboratory for the physical and engineering sciences. Works with industry, government agencies, and academia; promotes U.S. innovation and industrial competitiveness. Research interests include electronics, manufacturing, chemistry, materials science, nanotechnology, quantum information science, hydrogen, and homeland security.

National Institute of Standards and Technology (NIST), *(Commerce Dept.), Technology Innovation Program (TIP),* 100 Bureau Dr., MS 4700, Gaithersburg, MD 20899-4700; (888) 847-6478. Marc G. Stanley, Director.
General e-mail, tip@nist.gov
Web, www.nist.gov/tip

Provides cost-shared grants to industry (small and medium-size businesses), universities, and other research institutions for highly innovative, potentially high-return research and design projects that address critical national and societal needs in NIST's areas of technical competence.

National Institutes of Health (NIH), *(Health and Human Services Dept.), Technology Transfer,* 6011 Executive Blvd., #325, MSC 7660, Rockville, MD 20852-3804; (301) 496-7057. Fax, (301) 402-0220. Mark L. Rohrbaugh, Director.
General e-mail, NIHOTT@mail.nih.gov
Web, http://ott.od.nih.gov

Evaluates, protects, monitors, and manages the NIH invention portfolio. Oversees patent prosecution, negotiates and monitors licensing agreements, and provides oversight and central policy review of cooperative research and development agreements. Also manages the patent and licensing activities for the Food and Drug Administration (FDA). Responsible for the central development and implementation of technology transfer policies for three research components of the Public Health Service—the NIH, the FDA, and the Centers for Disease Control and Prevention.

National Science Foundation (NSF), *National Nanotechnology Initiative, 4201 Wilson Blvd., #505, Arlington, VA 22230; (703) 292-8301. Fax, (703) 292-9013. Mihail C. Roco, Chair.*
General e-mail, info@nnco.nano.gov

Web, http://nano.gov

Coordinates multiagency efforts in understanding nanoscale phenomena and furthering nanotechnology research and development.

▶**NONGOVERNMENTAL**

American National Standards Institute, *Accreditation Services, Washington Office, 1819 L St. N.W., 6th Floor 20036; (202) 293-8020. Fax, (202) 293-9287. Joe Bhatia, President.*
Web, www.ansi.org

Administers and coordinates the voluntary standardization system and conformity assessment programs for the U.S. private sector; maintains staff contacts for specific industries. Serves as U.S. member of the International Organization for Standardization (ISO) and hosts the U.S. National Committee of the International Electrotechnical Commission (IEC).

Institute for Alternative Futures (IAF), *100 N. Pitt St., #235, Alexandria, VA 22314-3134; (703) 684-5880. Fax, (703) 684-0640. Jonathan Peck, President.*
General e-mail, futurist@altfutures.com

Web, www.altfutures.com

Research and educational organization that explores the implications of scientific developments and facilitates planning efforts. Works with state and local governments, Congress, international organizations, federal government, and regional associations; conducts seminars. Interests include pharmaceutical research, health care, telecommunications, artificial intelligence, energy, the environment, and sustainability.

National Center for Advanced Technologies (NCAT), *1000 Wilson Blvd., #1700, Arlington, VA 22209-3901; (703) 358-1081. Fax, (703) 358-1181. Dan Forest, President.*
General e-mail, ncat@ncat.com

Web, www.ncat.com

Encourages U.S. competition in the world market by uniting government, industry, and university efforts to develop advanced technologies. (Affiliated with the Aerospace Industries Assn. of America.)

Public Technology Institute (PTI), *1301 Pennsylvania Ave. N.W., #830 20004-1725; (202) 626-2400. Fax, (202) 626-2498. Alan R. Shark, Executive Director. Press, (202) 626-2467. Toll-free, (866) 664-6368.*
General e-mail, info@pti.org

Web, www.pti.org

Cooperative research, development, and technology-transfer organization of cities and counties in North America. Applies available technological innovations and develops other methods to improve public services.

RAND Corporation, *Washington Office, 1200 S. Hayes St., Arlington, VA 22202-5050; (703) 413-1100. Fax, (703) 413-8111. Lynn Davis, Director.*
Web, www.rand.org

Research organization. Interests include energy, emerging technologies and critical systems, space and transportation, technology policies, international cooperative research, water resources, ocean and atmospheric sciences, and other technologies in defense and nondefense areas. (Headquarters in Santa Monica, Calif.)

SRI International, *Washington Office, 1100 Wilson Blvd., #2800, Arlington, VA 22209; (703) 524-2053. Fax, (703) 247-8569. Toni Linz, Director.*
Web, www.sri.com

Research and consulting organization that conducts basic and applied research for government, industry, and business. Interests include engineering, physical and life sciences, and international research. (Headquarters in Menlo Park, Calif.)

Scientific Research Practices

▶**AGENCIES**

Education Dept., *Office of the Chief Financial Officer, Financial Management Operations, LBJ Bldg., 400 Maryland Ave. S.W., #4C112 20202-4331; (202) 260-3353. Fax, (202) 205-0765. Gary Wood, Director.*
General e-mail, jeffrey.rodaman@ed.gov

Web, www.ed.gov/about/offices/list/ocfo/humansub.html

Advises grantees and applicants for department-supported research on regulations for protecting human subjects. Provides guidance to the Education Dept. on the requirements for complying with the regulations. Serves as the primary Education Dept. contact for matters concerning the protection of human subjects in research.

Energy Dept. (DOE), *Life and Medical Science Division: Human Subjects Research Program, 19901 Germantown Rd., #SC-23.2, Germantown, MD 20874-1290; (301) 903-3213. Fax, (301) 903-0567. Sharlene Weatherwax, Director; Elizabeth White, Program Manager.*
General e-mail, humansubjects@science.doe.gov

Web, http://humansubjects.energy.gov

Works to protect the rights and welfare of human subject research volunteers by establishing guidelines and enforcing regulations on scientific research that uses human subjects, including research that involves identifiable or high-risk data, worker populations or subgroups; humans testing devices, products, or materials; and bodily materials. Acts as an educational and technical resource to investigators, administrators, and institutional research boards.

Health and Human Services Dept. (HHS), *Human Research Protections,* 1101 Wootton Pkwy., The Tower Bldg., #200, Rockville, MD 20852; (240) 453-6900. Fax, (240) 453-6909. Dr. Jerry Menikoff, Director.
General e-mail, ohrp@hhs.gov

Web, www.hhs.gov/ohrp

Promotes the rights, welfare, and well-being of subjects involved in research conducted or supported by the Health and Human Services Dept.; helps to ensure that research is carried out in accordance with federal regulations by providing clarification and guidance, developing educational programs and materials, and maintaining regulatory oversight.

Health and Human Services Dept. (HHS), *President's Council on Bioethics,* 1425 New York Ave. N.W., #C100 20005; (202) 296-4669. Fax, (202) 296-3528. Edmund D. Pellegrino, Chair; F. Daniel Davis, Executive Director.
General e-mail, info@bioethics.gov

Web, www.bioethics.gov

Advises the president on ethical issues related to advances in biomedical science and technology, including stem cell research, assisted reproduction, cloning, end of life care, and the protection of human subjects in research.

Health and Human Services Dept. (HHS), *Research Integrity,* 1101 Wootton Pkwy., The Tower Bldg., #750, Rockville, MD 20852; (240) 453-8200. Fax, (301) 443-5351. Chris B. Pascal, Director.
Web, www.ori.dhhs.gov

Seeks to promote the quality of Public Health Service extramural and intramural research programs. (Extramural programs provide funding to research institutions that are not part of the federal government. Intramural programs provide funding for research conducted within federal government facilities.) Develops policies and regulations that protect from retaliation individuals who disclose information about scientific misconduct; administers assurance program; provides technical assistance to institutions during inquiries and investigations of scientific misconduct; reviews institutional findings and recommends administrative actions to the assistant secretary of Health and Human Services; sponsors educational programs and activities for professionals interested in research integrity.

National Aeronautics and Space Administration (NASA), *Chief Health and Medical Officer,* 300 E St. S.W., #5G39 20546; (202) 358-2390. Fax, (202) 358-3349. Dr. Richard S. Williams, Chief Health and Medical Officer.
Web, www.hq.nasa.gov/office/chmo

Monitors human and animal research and clinical practice to ensure that NASA adheres to appropriate medical and ethical standards and satisfies all regulatory and statutory requirements.

National Institutes of Health (NIH), *(Health and Human Services Dept.), Animal Care and Use,* 31 Center Drive, Bldg. 31, #B1C37, MSC 2252, Bethesda, MD 20892-2252; (301) 496-5424. Fax, (301) 480-8298. Terri Clark, Director (Acting).
General e-mail, secoacu@od.nih.gov

Web, http://oacu.od.nih.gov

Provides guidance for the humane care and use of animals in the intramural research program at NIH.

National Institutes of Health (NIH), *(Health and Human Services Dept.), Human Subjects Research,* 9000 Rockville Pike, Warren G. Magnuson Clinical Center, Bldg. 10, #2C146, MS 1154, Bethesda, MD 20892-1154; (301) 402-3444. Fax, (301) 402-3443. Charlotte Holden, Director (Acting).
Web, http://ohsr.od.nih.gov

Helps NIH investigators understand and comply with ethical principles and regulatory requirements involved in human subjects research. Assists NIH components in administering and regulating human subjects research activities.

National Institutes of Health (NIH), *(Health and Human Services Dept.), Laboratory Animal Welfare,* 6705 Rockledge Dr., RLK1, #360, MSC 7982, Bethesda, MD 20892-7982; (301) 496-7163. Fax, (301) 402-7065. Patricia Brown, Director.
General e-mail, olaw@od.nih.gov

Web, http://grants.nih.gov/grants/olaw/olaw.htm

Develops and monitors policy on the humane care and use of animals in research conducted by any public health service entity.

National Institutes of Health (NIH), *Stem Cell Task Force,* 9000 Rockville Pike, Bethesda, MD 20892; (301) 496-9746. Fax, (301) 402-2265. Dr. Story Landis, Chair. Press, (301) 496-5787.
General e-mail, stemcell@mail.nih.gov

Web, http://stemcells.nih.gov

The federal government's primary source for stem cell research, policy, and funding. Enables and speeds the pace of stem cell research by identifying resources and developing measures to enhance such resources. Seeks the advice of scientific leaders in stem cell research about the challenges to advancing the stem cell research agenda and strategies to overcome them.

▶NONGOVERNMENTAL

American Assn. for the Advancement of Science (AAAS), *Scientific Freedom, Responsibility, and Law Program,* 1200 New York Ave. N.W., 8th Floor 20005; (202) 326-6600. Fax, (202) 289-4950. Mark S. Frankel, Director.
Web, www.aaas.org/spp/sfrl

Focuses on professional ethics and law in science and engineering and on the social implications of science and technology. Collaborates with other professional groups on these activities; provides technical assistance to organizations developing codes of ethics or educational programs on research integrity.

American Society of Laboratory Animal Practitioners (ASLAP), *P.O. Box 125, Adamstown, MD 21710; (301) 874-4826. Fax, (301) 874-6195. Karl Field, President. General e-mail, ASLAP-info@aslap.org*

Web, www.aslap.org

Promotes the acquisition and dissemination of knowledge and information among veterinarians and veterinary students with an interest in laboratory animal practice.

Do No Harm: The Coalition of Americans for Research Ethics, *1100 H St. N.W., #700 20005; (202) 347-6840. Fax, (202) 347-6849. Gene Tarne, Communications Director. Web, www.stemcellresearch.org*

Membership: researchers and health care, bioethic, and legal professionals interested in scientific research conducted on human embryos. Serves as an information clearinghouse supporting adult stem cell research and other research that does not require use of embryonic stem cells or the destruction of human embryos.

Humane Society of the United States, *Animal Research Issues, 700 Professional Dr., Gaithersburg, MD 20879; (301) 258-3040. Fax, (301) 258-7760. Martin Stephens, Vice President. Web, www.hsus.org/animals_in_research*

Seeks to end the suffering of animals in research. Promotes the use of alternatives that replace, refine, or reduce the use of animals in scientific research, education, and consumer product testing. Conducts outreach programs aimed toward the public and the scientific community.

Scientists Center for Animal Welfare, *7833 Walker Dr., #410, Greenbelt, MD 20770; (301) 345-3500. Fax, (301) 345-3503. Joseph Bielitzki, President. General e-mail, info@scaw.com*

Web, www.scaw.com

Promotes best practices in the humane care, use, and management of animals involved in research, testing, or education in laboratory, agricultural, wildlife, or other settings.

BIOLOGY AND LIFE SCIENCES

▶**AGENCIES**

Armed Forces Radiobiological Research Institute *(Defense Dept.), 8901 Wisconsin Ave., Bethesda, MD 20889-5603; (301) 295-1210. Fax, (301) 295-4967. Col. Patricia K. Lillis-Hearne (MC, USA), Director. Public Affairs, (301) 295-1953. Web, www.afrri.usuhs.mil*

Serves as the principal ionizing radiation radiobiology research laboratory under the jurisdiction of the Uniformed Services of the Health Sciences. Participates in international conferences and projects.

National Aeronautics and Space Administration (NASA), *Human Research Program, 300 E St. S.W., #7V20 20546; (202) 358-2320. Fax, (202) 358-2886. Stephen Davison, Program Executive. Web, www.hq.nasa.gov*

Conducts NASA's life sciences research.

National Institute of General Medical Sciences *(National Institutes of Health), 45 Center Dr., #2AN12B, MSC-6200, Bethesda, MD 20892-6200; (301) 594-2172. Fax, (301) 402-0156. Dr. Jeremy M. Berg, Director. Web, www.nigms.nih.gov*

Primarily supports basic biomedical research and training that lays the foundation for advances in disease diagnosis, treatment, and prevention. Areas of special interest include bioinformatics, cell biology, genetics, infectious diseases, and trauma, burn, and perioperative injury and wound healing. Major initiatives include the Pharmacogenetics Research Network and the Protein Structure Initiative.

National Museum of Natural History *(Smithsonian Institution), Library, 10th St. and Constitution Ave. N.W., #51 20560-0154 (mailing address: P.O. Box 37012, Washington, DC 20013-7012); (202) 633-1680. Fax, (202) 357-1896. Ann Juneau, Head, (202) 633-4939. General e-mail, libmail@si.edu*

Web, www.sil.si.edu

Maintains reference collections covering anthropology, biodiversity, biology, botany, ecology, entomology, ethnology, mineral sciences, paleobiology, and zoology; permits on-site use of the collections. Open to the public by appointment; makes interlibrary loans.

National Museum of Natural History *(Smithsonian Institution), Naturalist Center, 741 Miller Dr. S.E., #G2, Leesburg, VA 20175; (703) 779-9712. Fax, (703) 779-9715. Richard H. Efthim, Manager. Information, (800) 729-7725. General e-mail, NatCenter@si.edu*

Web, www.mnh.si.edu/education/fieldtrip/planned_ programs/naturalist_center

Main study gallery contains natural history research and reference library with books and more than 36,000 objects, including minerals, rocks, plants, animals, shells and corals, insects, invertebrates, micro- and macrofossil materials, and microbiological and anthropological materials. Facilities include study equipment, such as microscopes, dissecting instruments, and plant presses. Family learning center offers hands-on activities for younger families. Operates a teachers reference center. Library open to the public. Reservations required for groups of six or more, but entry is free of charge.

National Oceanic and Atmospheric Administration (NOAA), *(Commerce Dept.), National Marine Fisheries*

Service, 1315 East-West Hwy., Silver Spring, MD 20910; (301) 713-2239. Fax, (301) 713-1940. James W. Balsiger, Assistant Administrator (Acting). Press, (301) 713-2370. Web, www.nmfs.noaa.gov

Conducts research and collects data on marine ecology and biology; collects, analyzes, and provides information through the Marine Resources Monitoring, Assessment, and Prediction Program. Administers the Magnuson-Stevens Fishery Conservation and Management Act and marine mammals and endangered species protection programs. Works with the Army Corps of Engineers on research into habitat restoration and conservation.

Naval Medical Research Center *(Defense Dept.),* 503 Robert Grant Ave., #1W28, Silver Spring, MD 20910-7500; (301) 319-7400. Fax, (301) 319-7410. Capt. Christopher Daniel, Commanding Officer. Web, www.nmrc.navy.mil

Performs basic and applied biomedical research in areas of military importance, including infectious diseases, hyperbaric medicine, wound repair enhancement, environmental stress, and immunobiology. Provides support to field laboratories and naval hospitals; monitors research internationally.

U.S. Geological Survey (USGS), *(Interior Dept.),* **Biological Resources,** 12201 Sunrise Valley Dr., Reston, VA 20192; (703) 648-4050. Fax, (703) 648-7031. Susan D. Haseltine, Associate Director for Biology. Web, http://biology.usgs.gov

Performs research in support of biological resource management. Monitors and reports on the status of the nation's biotic resources. Conducts research on wildlife, fish, insects, and plants, including the effects of disease and environmental contaminants on endangered and other species.

▶NONGOVERNMENTAL

American Institute of Biological Sciences, 1444 Eye St. N.W., #200 20005; (202) 628-1500. Fax, (202) 628-1509. Richard O'Grady, Executive Director. General e-mail, admin@aibs.org

Web, www.aibs.org

Membership: biologists, biology educators, and biological associations. Promotes interdisciplinary cooperation among members engaged in biological research and education; conducts educational programs for members; reviews projects supported by government grants. Monitors legislation and regulations.

American Society for Biochemistry and Molecular Biology, 9650 Rockville Pike, Bethesda, MD 20814; (301) 634-7145. Fax, (301) 634-7126. Barbara A. Gordon, Executive Director. General e-mail, asbmb@asbmb.org

Web, www.asbmb.org

Professional society of biological chemists. Participates in International Union of Biochemistry and Molecular Biology. Monitors legislation and regulations.

American Society for Cell Biology, 8120 Woodmont Ave., #750, Bethesda, MD 20814-2762; (301) 347-9300. Fax, (301) 347-9310. Joan Goldberg, Executive Director. General e-mail, ascbinfo@ascb.org

Web, www.ascb.org

Membership: scientists who have education or research experience in cell biology or an allied field. Promotes scientific exchange worldwide; organizes courses, workshops, and symposia. Monitors legislation and regulations.

American Society for Microbiology, 1752 N St. N.W. 20036; (202) 737-3600. Fax, (202) 942-9333. Michael I. Goldberg, Executive Director. Press, (202) 942-9297. General e-mail, oed@asmusa.org

Web, www.asm.org

Membership: microbiologists. Encourages education, training, scientific investigation, and application of research results in microbiology and related subjects; participates in international research.

American Type Culture Collection, 10801 University Blvd., Manassas, VA 20110-2209 (mailing address: P.O. Box 1549, Manassas, VA 20108); (703) 365-2700. Fax, (703) 365-2750. Raymond H. Cypess, President. Toll-free, (800) 638-6597. General e-mail, sales@atcc.org

Web, www.atcc.org

Provides biological products, technical services, and educational programs to government agencies, academic institutions, and private industry worldwide. Serves as a repository of living cultures and genetic material.

AOAC International, 481 N. Frederick Ave., #500, Gaithersburg, MD 20877-2417; (301) 924-7077. Fax, (301) 924-7089. E. James Bradford, Executive Director. Information, (800) 379-2622. General e-mail, aoac@aoac.org

Web, www.aoac.org

International association of analytical science professionals, companies, government agencies, nongovernmental organizations, and institutions. Promotes methods validation and quality measurements in the analytical sciences. Supports the development, testing, validation, and publication of reliable chemical and biological methods of analyzing foods, drugs, feed, fertilizers, pesticides, water, forensic materials, and other substances.

Biophysical Society, 9650 Rockville Pike, Bethesda, MD 20814-3998; (301) 634-7114. Fax, (301) 634-7133. Rosalba Kampman, Executive Director. General e-mail, society@biophysics.org

Web, www.biophysics.org

Membership: scientists, professors, and researchers engaged in biophysics or related fields. Encourages development and dissemination of knowledge in biophysics through meetings, publications, and outreach activities.

Carnegie Institution of Washington, *1530 P St. N.W. 20005-1910; (202) 387-6400. Fax, (202) 387-8092. Richard A. Meserve, President. Web, www.ciw.org*

Conducts research in plant biology, developmental biology, earth and planetary sciences, astronomy, and global ecology at the Carnegie Institution's six research departments: Dept. of Embryology (Baltimore, Md.); Geophysical Laboratory (Washington, D.C.); Dept. of Global Ecology (Stanford, Calif.); Dept. of Plant Biology (Stanford, Calif.); Dept. of Terrestrial Magnetism (Washington, D.C.); and The Observatories (Pasadena, Calif., and Las Campanas, Chile).

Ecological Society of America, *1990 M St. N.W., #700 20036; (202) 833-8773. Fax, (202) 833-8775. Katherine S. McCarter, Executive Director. General e-mail, esahq@esa.org*

Web, www.esa.org

Promotes research in ecology and the scientific study of the relationship between organisms and their past, present, and future environments. Interests include biotechnology; management of natural resources, habitats, and ecosystems to protect biological diversity; and ecologically sound public policies.

Federation of American Societies for Experimental Biology (FASEB), *9650 Rockville Pike, Bethesda, MD 20814-3998; (301) 634-7000. Fax, (301) 634-7001. Guy C. Fogleman, Executive Director. Web, www.faseb.org*

Advances biological science through collaborative advocacy for research policies that promote scientific progress and education and lead to improvements in human health. Provides educational meetings and publications to disseminate biological research results.

Biotechnology

▶AGENCIES

Cooperative State Research, Education, and Extension Service (CSREES), *(Agriculture Dept.), Competitive Programs, 800 9th St. S.W. 20024 (mailing address: 1400 Independence Ave. S.W., MS 2241, Washington, DC 20250-2241); (202) 401-1761. Fax, (202) 401-1782. Deborah L. Sheely, Deputy Administrator. General e-mail, psmith@csrees.usda.gov*

Web, www.csrees.usda.gov

Administers competitive research grants for biotechnology in the agricultural field. Oversees research in biotechnology.

Environmental Protection Agency (EPA), *Prevention, Pesticides, and Toxic Substances (OPPTS), 1200 Pennsylvania Ave. N.W., #3130 EPA-E, MS 7101M 20460-7101; (202) 564-2902. Fax, (202) 564-0801. James J. Jones, Assistant Administrator (Acting). Pollution prevention and toxic substances, (202) 564-3810. Web, www.epa.gov/oppts*

Studies and makes recommendations for regulating chemical substances under the Toxic Substances Control Act; compiles list of chemical substances subject to the act; registers, controls, and regulates use of pesticides and toxic substances.

National Institutes of Health (NIH), *(Health and Human Services Dept.), Biotechnology Activities, 6705 Rockledge Dr., #750, MSC-7985, Bethesda, MD 20892-7985; (301) 496-9838. Fax, (301) 496-9839. Dr. Amy P. Patterson, Director. Web, http://oba.od.nih.gov/oba/index.html*

Reviews requests submitted to the NIH involving genetic testing, recombinant DNA technology, and xeno-transplantation, and implements research guidelines.

National Library of Medicine *(National Institutes of Health), National Center for Biotechnology Information, 8600 Rockville Pike, Bldg. 38A, 8th Floor, Bethesda, MD 20894; (301) 496-2475. Fax, (301) 480-4559. Dr. David J. Lipman, Director. General e-mail, info@ncbi.nlm.nih.gov*

Web, www.ncbi.nlm.nih.gov or www.pubmedcentral.nih.gov

Creates automated systems for storing and analyzing knowledge of molecular biology and genetics. Develops new information technologies to aid in understanding the molecular processes that control human health and disease. Conducts basic research in computational molecular biology.

National Science Foundation (NSF), *Biological Sciences, 4201 Wilson Blvd., #605, Arlington, VA 22230; (703) 292-8400. Fax, (703) 292-9154. James P. Collins, Chair. Web, www.nsf.gov/bio.start.htm*

Serves as a forum for addressing biotechnology research issues, sharing information, identifying gaps in scientific knowledge, and developing consensus among concerned federal agencies. Facilitates continuing cooperation among federal agencies on topical issues.

▶NONGOVERNMENTAL

Biotechnology Industry Organization, *1201 Maryland Ave. S.W., #900 20024; (202) 962-9200. Fax, (202) 488-6301. James Greenwood, President. General e-mail, bio@bio.org*

Web, www.bio.org

Membership: U.S. and international companies engaged in biotechnology. Monitors government activities at all levels; promotes educational activities; conducts workshops.

Friends of the Earth (FOE), *1717 Massachusetts Ave. N.W., #600 20036-2008; (202) 783-7400. Fax, (202) 783-0444. Brent Blackwelder, President. General e-mail, foe@foe.org*

Web, www.foe.org

Monitors legislation and regulations on issues related to seed industry consolidation and patenting laws and on business developments in agricultural biotechnology and their effect on farming, food production, genetic resources, and the environment.

Genetic Alliance, *4301 Connecticut Ave. N.W., #404 20008-2369; (202) 966-5557. Fax, (202) 966-8553. Sharon Terry, President. General e-mail, info@geneticalliance.org*

Web, www.geneticalliance.org

Coalition of government, industry, advocacy organizations, and private groups that seeks to advance genetic research and its applications. Promotes increased funding for research, improved access to services, and greater support for emerging technologies, tests, and treatments. Advocates on behalf of individuals and families living with genetic conditions.

The J. Craig Venter Institute, *9704 Medical Center Drive, Rockville, MD 20850; (301) 795-7000. Fax, (301) 838-0208. J. Craig Venter, President. Web, www.jcvi.org*

Research institute that advances the science of genomics; the understanding of its ethical, legal, and economic implications for society; and the communication of those results to the scientific community, the public, and policymakers. Produces reports; offers courses, workshops, and internships.

Kennedy Institute of Ethics *(Georgetown University), Healy Hall, 37th and O Sts. N.W., 4th Floor 20057; (202) 687-8099. Fax, (202) 687-8089. G. Madison Powers, Director. Library, (202) 687-3885. Toll-free, United States and Canada, (888) 246-3849 and (888) 436-3849. General e-mail, kicourse@georgetown.edu*

Web, http://kennedyinstitute.georgetown.edu

Carries out teaching and research on medical ethics, including legal and ethical definitions of death, allocation of health resources, and recombinant DNA and human gene therapy. Sponsors the annual Intensive Bioethics Course. Conducts international programs. Serves as the home of the National Reference Center for Bioethics Literature (http://bioethics.georgetown.edu) and the National Information Resource on Ethics and Human Genetics (http://genthx.georgetown.edu), both supported by the NIH. Provides free reference assistance and bibliographic databases covering all ethical issues in health care, genetics, and biomedical research. Library open to the public.

Botany

►**AGENCIES**

National Arboretum *(Agriculture Dept.), 3501 New York Ave. N.E. 20002-1958; (202) 245-2726. Fax, (202) 245-4575. Thomas S. Elias, Director. Library, (202) 245-4538. Web, www.usna.usda.gov*

Maintains public display of plants on 446 acres; provides information and makes referrals concerning cultivated plants (exclusive of field crops and fruits);

conducts plant breeding and research; maintains herbarium. Library open to the public by appointment.

National Museum of Natural History *(Smithsonian Institution), Botany, 10th St. and Constitution Ave. N.W., MRC 166 20560 (mailing address: P.O. Box 37012, MRC 166, Washington, DC 20013-7012); (202) 633-0920. Fax, (202) 786-2563. Warren Wagner, Chair. Library, (202) 633-2146. Web, www.nmnh.si.edu*

Conducts botanical research worldwide; furnishes information on the identification, distribution, and local names of flowering plants; studies threatened and endangered plant species.

Smithsonian Institution, *Botany and Horticulture Library, 10th St. and Constitution Ave. N.W., #W422 20560-0166 (mailing address: PO Box 37012, MRC 154, Washington, DC 20017-7012); (202) 633-1685. Fax, (202) 357-1896. Robin Everly, Branch Librarian. General e-mail, libmail.si.edu*

Web, www.sil.si.edu/libraries/bothort

Collections include taxonomic botany, plant morphology, general botany, history of botany, grasses, and algae. Permits on-site use of collections (appointment necessary); makes interlibrary loans. (Housed at the National Museum of Natural History.)

►**CONGRESS**

For a listing of relevant congressional committees and subcommittees, please see page 592 or the Appendix.

U.S. Botanic Garden, *100 Maryland Ave. S.W. 20001 (mailing address: 245 1st St. S.W., Washington, DC 20024); (202) 225-8333. Fax, (202) 225-1561. Holly H. Shimizu, Executive Director. Horticulture hotline, (202) 226-4785. Program and tour reservations, (202) 225-1116. Special events, (202) 226-7674. General e-mail, usbg@aoc.gov*

Web, www.usbg.gov

Collects, cultivates, and grows various plants for public display and study; identifies botanic specimens and furnishes information on proper growing methods. Conducts horticultural classes and tours.

►**NONGOVERNMENTAL**

American Society for Horticultural Science (ASHS), *113 S. West St., #200, Alexandria, VA 22314-2851; (703) 836-4606. Fax, (703) 836-2024. Michael W. Neff, Executive Director. General e-mail, ashs@ashs.org*

Web, www.ashs.org

Membership: educators, government workers, firms, associations, and individuals interested in horticultural science. Promotes scientific research and education in horticulture, including international exchange of information.

American Society of Plant Biologists, *15501 Monona Dr., Rockville, MD 20855-2768; (301) 251-0560. Fax, (301) 279-2996. Crispin Taylor, Executive Director. Web, www.aspb.org*

Membership: plant physiologists, plant biochemists, and molecular biologists. Seeks to educate and promote public interest in the plant sciences. Publishes journals; provides placement service for members; sponsors awards, annual conference, meetings, courses, and seminars.

National Assn. of Plant Patent Owners, *1000 Vermont Ave. N.W., 3rd Floor 20005-4914; (202) 789-2900. Fax, (202) 789-1893. Craig Regelbrugge, Administrator.*
Web, www.anla.org

Membership: owners of patents on newly propagated horticultural plants. Informs members of plant patents issued, provisions of patent laws, and changes in practice. Promotes the development, protection, production, and distribution of new varieties of horticultural plants. Works with international organizations of plant breeders on matters of common interest. (Affiliated with the American Nursery and Landscape Assn.)

Zoology

▶AGENCIES

National Museum of Natural History *(Smithsonian Institution), Entomology, 10th St. and Constitution Ave. N.W., MRC 105 20560-0105 (mailing address: P.O. Box 37012, Washington, DC 20013-7012); (202) 633-1033. Fax, (202) 786-3141. Terry L. Erwin, Chair. Library, (202) 633-1680.*
Web, www.nmnh.si.edu, or for research, www.sil.si.edu/research

Conducts worldwide research in entomology. Maintains the national collection of insects; lends insect specimens to specialists for research and classification. Library open to the public by appointment.

National Museum of Natural History *(Smithsonian Institution), Invertebrate Zoology, 10th St. and Constitution Ave. N.W., MRC 163 20560 (mailing address: P.O. Box 37012, Washington, DC 20013-7012); (202) 633-1740. Fax, (202) 357-3043. Rafael Lemaitre, Chair. Library, (202) 633-1680.*
Web, www.nmnh.si.edu, or for research, www.sil.si.edu/research

Conducts research on the identity, morphology, histology, life history, distribution, classification, and ecology of marine, terrestrial, and freshwater invertebrate animals (except insects); maintains the national collection of invertebrate animals; aids exhibit and educational programs; conducts pre- and postdoctoral fellowship programs; provides facilities for visiting scientists in the profession.

National Museum of Natural History *(Smithsonian Institution), Vertebrate Zoology, 10th St. and Constitution Ave. N.W., MRC 163 20560 (mailing address: P.O. Box 37012, Washington, DC 20013-7012); (202) 633-1740. Fax, (202) 357-3043. Richard P. Vari, Chair. Library, (202) 633-1680.*
Web, www.nmnh.si.edu, or for research, www.sil.si.edu/research

Conducts research worldwide on the systematics, ecology, evolution, zoogeography, and behavior of mammals, birds, reptiles, amphibians, and fish; maintains the national collection of specimens.

▶NONGOVERNMENTAL

Assn. of Zoos and Aquariums, *8403 Colesville Rd., #710, Silver Spring, MD 20910-3314; (301) 562-0777. Fax, (301) 562-0888. Jim Maddy, Executive Director.*
General e-mail, generalinquiry@aza.org
Web, www.aza.org

Membership: interested individuals and professionally run zoos and aquariums in North America. Administers professional accreditation program; participates in worldwide conservation, education, and research activities.

Entomological Society of America, *10001 Derekwood Lane, #100, Lanham, MD 20706-4876; (301) 731-4535. Fax, (301) 731-4538. Robin Kriegel, Executive Director.*
General e-mail, esa@entsoc.org
Web, www.entsoc.org

Scientific association that promotes the science of entomology and the interests of professionals in the field. Advises on crop protection, food chain, and individual and urban health matters dealing with insect pests.

Jane Goodall Institute, *4245 N. Fairfax Dr., #600, Arlington, VA 22203; (703) 682-9220. Fax, (703) 682-9312. Bill Johnston, President.*
Web, www.janegoodall.org

Seeks to increase primate habitat conservation, expand noninvasive primate research, and promote activities that ensure the well-being of primates. (Affiliated with Jane Goodall Institutes in Canada, Europe, Asia, and Africa.)

ENGINEERING

▶AGENCIES

National Institute of Standards and Technology (NIST), *(Commerce Dept.), Electronics and Electrical Engineering Laboratory, 100 Bureau Dr., Bldg. 220, #B358, MS 8100, Gaithersburg, MD 20899-8100; (301) 975-2220. Fax, (301) 975-4091. Kent Rochford, Director (Acting).*
General e-mail, eeel@nist.gov
Web, www.eeel.nist.gov

Provides focus for research, development, and applications in the fields of electrical, electronic, quantum electric, and electromagnetic materials engineering. Interests include fundamental physical constants, practical data, measurement methods, theory, standards, technology, technical services, and international trade.

National Institute of Standards and Technology (NIST), *(Commerce Dept.), Manufacturing Engineering Laboratory, 100 Bureau Dr., Bldg. 220, #B322, MS 8200,*

Gaithersburg, MD 20899-8220; (301) 975-3400. Fax, (301) 948-5668. Howard Haray, Director (Acting).
Web, www.mel.nist.gov

Collects technical data, develops standards in production engineering, and publishes findings; produces the technical base for proposed standards and technology for industrial and mechanical engineering; provides instrument design, fabrication, and repair. Helps establish international standards.

National Science Foundation (NSF), *Engineering,* 4201 Wilson Blvd., #505N, Arlington, VA 22230; (703) 292-8300. Fax, (703) 292-9013. Thomas Peterson, Assistant Director.
Web, www.nsf.gov/dir/index.jsp?org=ENG

Directorate that supports fundamental research and education in engineering through grants and special equipment awards. Programs are designed to enhance international competitiveness and to improve the quality of engineering in the United States.

▶NONGOVERNMENTAL

American Assn. of Engineering Societies, 6522 Meadowridge Rd., #101, Elkridge, MD 21075; (202) 296-2237. Fax, (202) 296-1151. William Koffel, Executive Director.
Web, www.aaes.org

Federation of engineering societies; members work in industry, construction, government, academia, and private practice. Advances the knowledge, understanding, and practice of engineering. Serves as delegate to the World Federation of Engineering Organizations.

American Council of Engineering Companies, 1015 15th St. N.W., 8th Floor 20005-2605; (202) 347-7474. Fax, (202) 898-0068. David A. Raymond, President.
General e-mail, acec@acec.org
Web, www.acec.org

Membership: practicing consulting engineering firms and state, local, and regional consulting engineers councils. Serves as an information clearinghouse for member companies in such areas as legislation, legal cases, marketing, management, professional liability, business practices, and insurance. Monitors legislation and regulations.

American Society for Engineering Education, 1818 N St. N.W., #600 20036-2479; (202) 331-3500. Fax, (202) 265-8504. Frank L. Huband, Executive Director. Press, (202) 331-3537.
Web, www.asee.org

Membership: engineering faculty and administrators, professional engineers, government agencies, and engineering colleges, corporations, and professional societies. Conducts research, conferences, and workshops on engineering education. Monitors legislation and regulations.

American Society of Civil Engineers (ASCE), 1801 Alexander Bell Dr., Reston, VA 20191-4400; (703) 295-6300. Fax, (703) 295-6333. Patrick Natale, Executive

Director. Toll-free, (800) 548-2723. Government Relations, (202) 789-7850.
Web, www.asce.org

Membership: professionals and students in civil engineering. Develops and produces consensus standards for construction documents and building codes. Maintains the Civil Engineering Research Foundation, which focuses national attention and resources on the research needs of the civil engineering profession. Participates in international conferences.

ASFE, 8811 Colesville Rd., #G106, Silver Spring, MD 20910; (301) 565-2733. Fax, (301) 589-2017. John P. Bachner, Executive Vice President.
General e-mail, info@asfe.org
Web, www.asfe.org

Membership: consulting geotechnical and geoenvironmental engineering firms. Conducts seminars and a peer review program on quality control policies and procedures in geotechnical engineering. (Formerly the Assn. of Soil and Foundation Engineers.)

ASME, *Government Relations, Washington Office,* 1828 L St. N.W., #906 20036-5104; (202) 785-3756. Fax, (202) 429-9417. Kathryn Holmes, Director.
General e-mail, grdept@asme.org
Web, www.asme.org

Serves as a clearinghouse for sharing of information among federal, state, and local governments and the engineering profession. Monitors legislation and regulations. (Formerly the American Society of Mechanical Engineers. Headquarters in New York.)

Institute of Electrical and Electronics Engineers–USA (IEEE-USA), *Washington Office,* 2001 L St. N.W., #700 20036-5104; (202) 785-0017. Fax, (202) 785-0835. Chris Brantley, Managing Director.
General e-mail, ieeeusa@ieee.org
Web, www.ieeeusa.org

U.S. arm of an international technological and professional organization concerned with all areas of electrotechnology policy, including aerospace, computers, communications, biomedicine, electric power, and consumer electronics. (Headquarters in New York.)

International Microelectronics and Packaging Society, 611 2nd St. N.E. 20002; (202) 548-4001. Fax, (202) 548-6115. Michael O'Donoghue, Executive Director.
General e-mail, imaps@imaps.org
Web, www.imaps.org

Membership: persons and companies involved in the microelectronics industry worldwide. Integrates disciplines of science and engineering; fosters exchange of information among complementary technologies, including ceramics, thin and thick films, fuel cells, extreme cold environments, surface mounts, semiconductor packaging, discrete semiconductor devices, monolithic circuits, and multichip modules; disseminates technical knowledge.

International Test and Evaluation Assn., *4400 Fair Lakes Court, #104, Fairfax, VA 22033-3899; (703) 631-6220. Fax, (703) 631-6221. Lori Tremmel Freeman, Executive Director.*
General e-mail, itea@itea.org

Web, www.itea.org

Membership: engineers, scientists, managers, and other industry, government, and academic professionals interested in testing and evaluating products and complex systems. Provides a forum for information exchange; monitors international research.

National Academy of Engineering, *2101 Constitution Ave. N.W., #218 20418; (202) 334-3201. Fax, (202) 334-1680. Charles M. Vest, President.*
Web, www.nae.edu

Society whose members are elected in recognition of important contributions to the field of engineering and technology. Shares responsibility with the National Academy of Sciences for examining questions of science and technology at the request of the federal government; promotes international cooperation. (Affiliated with the National Academy of Sciences.)

National Society of Black Engineers, *205 Daingerfield Rd., Alexandria, VA 22314; (703) 549-2207. Fax, (703) 683-5312. Carl Mack, Executive Director.*
General e-mail, headquarters@nsbe.org

Web, www.nsbe.org

Membership: college students studying engineering. Offers academic excellence programs, scholarships, leadership training, and professional and career development opportunities. Activities include tutorial programs, group study sessions, high school/junior high outreach programs, technical seminars and workshops, career fairs, and an annual convention.

National Society of Professional Engineers (NSPE), *1420 King St., Alexandria, VA 22314-2794; (703) 684-2800. Fax, (703) 836-4875. Larry Jacobson, Executive Director.*
General e-mail, memserv@nspe.org

Web, www.nspe.org

Membership: U.S. licensed professional engineers from all disciplines. Holds engineering seminars; operates an information center.

ENVIRONMENTAL AND EARTH SCIENCES

▶AGENCIES

National Aeronautics and Space Administration (NASA), *Science Mission Directorate, 300 E St. S.W., #3C26 20546; (202) 358-3889. Fax, (202) 358-3092. Edward J. Weiler, Associate Administrator.*

General e-mail, science@hq.nasa.gov

Web, http://science.hq.nasa.gov/directorate/index.html

Engages the science community, sponsors scientific research, and collaborates with NASA's partners to answer fundamental questions in environment and earth science. Researches the origin, evolution, and structure of the universe, the solar system, and the integrated functioning of the earth and the sun.

National Oceanic and Atmospheric Administration (NOAA), *(Commerce Dept.), 14th St. and Constitution Ave. N.W., #5128 20230; (202) 482-3436. Fax, (202) 408-9674. Vacant, Under Secretary. Information, (301) 713-4000. Library, (301) 713-2600. Press, (202) 482-6090.*
Web, www.noaa.gov

Conducts research in marine and atmospheric sciences; issues weather forecasts and warnings vital to public safety and the national economy; surveys resources of the sea; analyzes economic aspects of fisheries operations; develops and implements policies on international fisheries; provides states with grants to conserve coastal zone areas; protects marine mammals; maintains a national environmental center with data from satellite observations and other sources, including meteorological, oceanic, geodetic, and seismological data centers; provides colleges and universities with grants for research, education, and marine advisory services; prepares and provides nautical and aeronautical charts and maps.

National Oceanic and Atmospheric Administration (NOAA), *(Commerce Dept.), Central Library, Library and Information Services, 1315 East-West Hwy., SSMC3, 2nd Floor, Silver Spring, MD 20910; (301) 713-2607. Fax, (301) 713-4599. Neal Kaske, Director. Reference service, (301) 713-2600, ext. 124.*
General e-mail, library.reference@noaa.gov

Web, www.lib.noaa.gov

Collection includes electronic NOAA documents, reports, and videos; electronic and print journals; the NOAA Photo Library; bibliographic database of other NOAA libraries; and climate data. Makes interlibrary loans; library open to the public.

National Science Foundation (NSF), *Geosciences, 4201 Wilson Blvd., #705N, Arlington, VA 22230; (703) 292-8500. Fax, (703) 292-9042. Timothy Killeer, Assistant Director.*
Web, www.nsf.gov

Directorate that supports research about the earth, including its atmosphere, continents, oceans, and interior. Works to improve the education and human resource base for the geosciences; participates in international and multidisciplinary activities, especially to study changes in the global climate.

National Science Foundation (NSF), *Polar Programs, 4201 Wilson Blvd., #755S, Arlington, VA 22230; (703) 292-8030. Fax, (703) 292-9081. Karl A. Erb, Director.*
Web, www.nsf.gov/dir/index.jsp?org=OPP

Funds and manages U.S. activity in Antarctica; provides grants for arctic programs in polar biology and medicine, earth sciences, atmospheric sciences, meteorology, ocean sciences, and glaciology. The Polar Information Program serves as a clearinghouse for polar data and makes referrals on specific questions.

Smithsonian Environmental Research Center
(Smithsonian Institution), 647 Contees Wharf Rd., Edgewater, MD 21037 (mailing address: P.O. Box 28, Edgewater, MD 21037-0028); (443) 482-2200. Fax, (443) 482-2380. Anson H. Hines, Director. Press, (443) 482-2400.
Web, www.serc.si.edu

Performs laboratory and field research that measures physical, chemical, and biological interactions to determine the mechanisms of environmental responses to humans' use of air, land, and water. Evaluates properties of the environment that affect the functions of living organisms. Maintains research laboratories, public education program, facilities for controlled environments, and estuarine and terrestrial lands.

United States Arctic Research Commission, *4350 N. Fairfax Dr., #510, Arlington, VA 22203; (703) 525-0111. Fax, (703) 525-0114. John Farrell, Executive Director. Web, www.arctic.gov*

Presidential advisory commission that develops policy for arctic research; assists the interagency Arctic Research Policy Committee in implementing a national plan of arctic research; recommends improvements in logistics, data management, and dissemination of arctic information.

U.S. Geological Survey (USGS), *(Interior Dept.), 12201 Sunrise Valley Dr., MS 100, Reston, VA 20192-0002; (703) 648-4000. Fax, (703) 648-4454. Information, (888) ASK-USGS. Library, (703) 648-4302. Press, (703) 648-4460. Web, www.usgs.gov*

Provides reports, maps, and databases that describe and analyze water, energy, biological, and mineral resources; the land surface; and the underlying geological structure and dynamic processes of the earth.

U.S. Geological Survey (USGS), *(Interior Dept.), Library Services, 12201 Sunrise Valley Dr., MS 950, Reston, VA 20192; (703) 648-4302. Fax, (703) 648-6373. General e-mail, library@usgs.gov*
Web, http://library.usgs.gov

Maintains collection of books, periodicals, serials, maps, and technical reports on geology, mineral and water resources, mineralogy, paleontology, petrology, soil and environmental sciences, biology, and physics and chemistry as they relate to natural sciences. Open to the public; makes interlibrary loans.

▶**CONGRESS**

For a listing of relevant congressional committees and subcommittees, please see page 592 or the Appendix.

▶**NONGOVERNMENTAL**

American Geophysical Union, *2000 Florida Ave. N.W. 20009-1277; (202) 462-6900. Fax, (202) 328-0566. Robert Van Hook, Executive Director (Interim). Information, (800) 966-2481.*
General e-mail, service@agu.org
Web, www.agu.org

Membership: scientists and technologists who study the environments and components of the earth, sun, and solar system. Promotes international cooperation; disseminates information.

Atmospheric Sciences

▶**AGENCIES**

National Science Foundation (NSF), *Atmospheric Sciences, 4201 Wilson Blvd., #775, Arlington, VA 22230; (703) 292-8520. Fax, (703) 292-9022. Jarvis Moyers, Division Director.*
Web, www.nsf.gov/div/index.jsp?div=ATM

Supports research on the earth's atmosphere and the sun's effect on it, including studies of the physics, chemistry, and dynamics of the earth's upper and lower atmospheres and its space environment; climate processes and variations; and the natural global cycles of gases and particles in the earth's atmosphere.

National Weather Service *(National Oceanic and Atmospheric Administration), 1325 East-West Hwy., #18150, Silver Spring, MD 20910; (301) 713-9095. Fax, (301) 713-0610. John L. Hayes, Administrator.*
Web, www.nws.noaa.gov

Issues warnings of hurricanes, severe storms, and floods; provides weather forecasts and services for the general public and for aviation and marine interests. National Weather Service forecast office, (703) 260-0107.

National Weather Service *(National Oceanic and Atmospheric Administration), Climate Prediction Center, 5200 Auth Rd., Camp Springs, MD 20746; (301) 763-8000 (ext. 7500 or 7535). Fax, (301) 763-8125. Wayne Higgins, Director.*
Web, www.cpc.ncep.noaa.gov

Provides climate forecasts, assesses the impact of short-term climate variability, and warns of potentially extreme climate-related events.

National Weather Service *(National Oceanic and Atmospheric Administration), National Centers for Environmental Prediction, 5200 Auth Rd., #101, Camp Springs, MD 20746; (301) 763-8016. Fax, (301) 763-8434. Louis W. Uccellini, Director.*
Web, www.ncep.noaa.gov

The National Center for Environmental Prediction and the National Environmental Satellite, Data, and Information Service are part of the World Weather Watch

Programme developed by the United Nations World Meteorological Organization. Collects and exchanges data with other nations; provides other national weather service offices, private meteorologists, and government agencies with products, including forecast guidance products.

▶**NONGOVERNMENTAL**

Alliance for Responsible Atmospheric Policy, *2111 Wilson Blvd., 8th Floor, Arlington, VA 22201; (703) 243-0344. Fax, (703) 243-2874. David Stirpe, Executive Director.*
General e-mail, info@arap.org
Web, www.arap.org

Coalition of users and producers of chlorofluorocarbons (CFCs). Seeks further study of the ozone depletion theory.

Climate Institute, *900 17th St. N.W., #700 20006; (202) 547-0104. Fax, (202) 547-0111. John C. Topping Jr., President.*
General e-mail, info@climate.org
Web, www.climate.org

Educates the public and policymakers on climate change (greenhouse effect, or global warming) and on the depletion of the ozone layer. Develops strategies on mitigating climate change in developing countries and in North America.

Pew Center on Global Climate Change, *2101 Wilson Blvd., #550, Arlington, VA 22201; (703) 516-4146. Fax, (703) 841-1422. Eileen Claussen, President.*
Web, www.pewclimate.org

Independent organization that issues information and promotes discussion by policymakers on the science, economics, and policy of climate change.

Geology and Earth Sciences

▶**AGENCIES**

National Museum of Natural History *(Smithsonian Institution), Mineral Sciences, 10th St. and Constitution Ave. N.W., MRC 119 20560 (mailing address: P.O. Box 37012, Washington, DC 20013-7012); (202) 633-1860. Fax, (202) 357-2476. Sorena Sorensen, Chair. Library, (202) 633-1692.*
Web, www.minerals.si.edu

Conducts research on gems, minerals, meteorites, rocks, and ores. Interests include mineralogy, petrology, volcanology, and geochemistry. Maintains the Global Volcanism Network, which reports worldwide volcanic and seismic activity.

National Museum of Natural History *(Smithsonian Institution), Naturalist Center, 741 Miller Dr. S.E., #G2, Leesburg, VA 20175; (703) 779-9712. Fax, (703) 779-9715. Richard H. Efthim, Manager. Information, (800) 729-7725.*

General e-mail, NatCenter@si.edu
Web, www.mnh.si.edu/education/fieldtrip/planned_programs/naturalist_center

Main study gallery contains natural history research and reference library with books and more than 36,000 objects, including minerals, rocks, plants, animals, shells and corals, insects, invertebrates, micro- and macrofossil materials, and microbiological and anthropological materials. Facilities include study equipment, such as microscopes, dissecting instruments, and plant presses. Family learning center offers hands-on activities for younger families. Operates a teachers reference center. Library open to the public. Reservations required for groups of six or more, but entry is free of charge.

National Museum of Natural History *(Smithsonian Institution), Paleobiology, 10th St. and Constitution Ave. N.W., MRC 121 20560 (mailing address: P.O. Box 37012, Washington, DC 20013-7012); (202) 633-1312. Fax, (202) 786-2832. Conrad L. Labanderia, Chair.*
Web, www.nmnh.si.edu/paleo

Conducts research worldwide on invertebrate paleontology, paleobotany, sedimentology, and vertebrate paleontology; provides information on paleontology. Maintains national collection of fossil organisms and sediment samples.

National Science Foundation (NSF), *Earth Sciences, 4201 Wilson Blvd., #785, Arlington, VA 22230; (703) 292-8550. Fax, (703) 292-9025. Robert Detrick, Division Director.*
Web, www.nsf.gov/div/index.jsp?div=EAR

Provides grants for research in geology, geophysics, geochemistry, and related fields, including tectonics, hydrologic sciences, and continental dynamics.

U.S. Geological Survey (USGS), *(Interior Dept.), Earthquake Hazards, 12201 Sunrise Valley Dr., Reston, VA 20192 (mailing address: 905 National Center, Reston, VA 20192); (703) 648-6714. Fax, (703) 648-6717. David Applegate, Senior Science Advisor.*
Web, http://earthquake.usgs.gov

Manages geologic, geophysical, and engineering investigations, including assessments of hazards from earthquakes; conducts research on the mechanisms and occurrences of earthquakes worldwide and their relationship to the behavior of the crust and upper mantle; develops methods for predicting the time, place, and magnitude of earthquakes; conducts engineering and geologic studies on ground failures.

U.S. Geological Survey (USGS), *(Interior Dept.), Geology, 12201 Sunrise Valley Dr., MS 911, Reston, VA 20192; (703) 648-6600. Fax, (703) 648-7031. Tim Miller, Associate Director (Acting).*
Web, http://geology.usgs.gov

Conducts onshore and offshore geologic research and investigation. Produces information on geologic hazards, such as earthquakes and volcanoes; geologic information for use in the management of public lands and national policy determinations; information on the chemistry and physics of the earth; and geologic, geophysical, and geochemical maps and analyses to address environmental, resource, and geologic hazards concerns. Participates in international research.

U.S. Geological Survey (USGS), *(Interior Dept.),* *National Cooperative Geologic Mapping Program,* *12201 Sunrise Valley Dr., MS 908, Reston, VA 20192; (703) 648-6943. Fax, (703) 648-6937. Peter Lyttle, Program Coordinator.* *Web, http://ncgmp.usgs.gov*

Produces geologic maps; makes maps available to public and private organizations.

U.S. Geological Survey (USGS), *(Interior Dept.),* *Volcano Hazards, 12201 Sunrise Valley Dr., Reston, VA 20192 (mailing address: 904 National Center, Reston, VA 20192); (703) 648-6711. Fax, (703) 648-5483. John C. Eichelberger, Program Coordinator.* *Web, www.volcanoes.usgs.gov*

Manages geologic, geophysical, and engineering investigations, including assessments of hazards from volcanoes; conducts research worldwide on the mechanisms of volcanoes and on igneous and geothermal systems. Issues warnings of potential volcanic hazards.

▶**NONGOVERNMENTAL**

American Geological Institute, *4220 King St., Alexandria, VA 22302-1502; (703) 379-2480. Fax, (703) 379-7563. P. Patrick Leahy, Executive Director.* *General e-mail, agi@agiweb.org*

Web, www.agiweb.org

Membership: earth science societies and associations. Maintains a computerized database with worldwide information on geology, engineering and environmental geology, oceanography, and other geological fields (available to the public for a fee).

Oceanography

▶**AGENCIES**

National Museum of Natural History *(Smithsonian Institution), Botany, 10th St. and Constitution Ave. N.W., MRC 166 20560 (mailing address: P.O. Box 37012, MRC 166, Washington, DC 20013-7012); (202) 633-0920. Fax, (202) 786-2563. Warren Wagner, Chair. Library, (202) 633-2146. Web, www.nmnh.si.edu*

Investigates the biology, evolution, and classification of tropical and subtropical marine algae and seagrasses. Acts as curator of the national collection in this field. Develops and participates in scholarly programs.

National Museum of Natural History *(Smithsonian Institution), Invertebrate Zoology, 10th St. and Constitution Ave. N.W., MRC 163 20560 (mailing address: P.O. Box 37012, Washington, DC 20013-7012); (202) 633-1740. Fax, (202) 357-3043. Rafael Lemaitre, Chair. Library, (202) 633-1680.* *Web, www.nmnh.si.edu, or for research, www.sil.si.edu/research*

Conducts research on the identity, morphology, histology, life history, distribution, classification, and ecology of marine, terrestrial, and freshwater invertebrate animals (except insects); maintains the national collection of invertebrate animals; aids exhibit and educational programs; conducts pre- and postdoctoral fellowship programs; provides facilities for visiting scientists in the profession.

National Museum of Natural History *(Smithsonian Institution), Library, 10th St. and Constitution Ave. N.W., #51 20560-0154 (mailing address: P.O. Box 37012, Washington, DC 20013-7012); (202) 633-1680. Fax, (202) 357-1896. Ann Juneau, Head, (202) 633-4939.* *General e-mail, libmail@si.edu*

Web, www.sil.si.edu

Maintains reference collections covering anthropology, biodiversity, biology, botany, ecology, entomology, ethnology, mineral sciences, paleobiology, and zoology; permits on-site use of the collections. Open to the public by appointment; makes interlibrary loans.

National Museum of Natural History *(Smithsonian Institution), Vertebrate Zoology, 10th St. and Constitution Ave. N.W., MRC 163 20560 (mailing address: P.O. Box 37012, Washington, DC 20013-7012); (202) 633-1740. Fax, (202) 357-3043. Richard P. Vari, Chair. Library, (202) 633-1680.* *Web, www.nmnh.si.edu, or for research, www.sil.si.edu/research*

Processes, sorts, and distributes to scientists specimens of marine vertebrates; engages in taxonomic sorting, community analysis, and specimen and sample data management.

National Oceanic and Atmospheric Administration (NOAA), *(Commerce Dept.), Marine and Aviation Operations, 8403 Colesville Rd., 5th Floor, Silver Spring, MD 20910; (301) 713-1045. Fax, (301) 713-1541. Jonathan Bailey, Director.* *Web, www.omao.noaa.gov*

Uniformed service of the Commerce Dept. that operates and manages NOAA's fleet of hydrographic, oceanographic, and fisheries research ships and aircraft. Supports NOAA's scientific programs.

National Oceanic and Atmospheric Administration (NOAA), *(Commerce Dept.), National Oceanographic Data Center, 1315 East-West Hwy., SSMC3, 4th Floor, Silver Spring, MD 20910-3282; (301) 713-3270. Fax, (301) 713-3300. Margarita Gregg, Director.* *General e-mail, services@nodc.noaa.gov*

Web, www.noaa.gov

Offers a wide range of oceanographic data on the Web, on disk, and on CD-ROM; provides research scientists with data processing services; prepares statistical summaries and graphical data products. (Fee charged for some services.)

National Oceanic and Atmospheric Administration (NOAA), *(Commerce Dept.), National Ocean Service, 1305 East-West Hwy., SSMC4, Silver Spring, MD 20910; (301) 713-3074. Fax, (301) 713-4269. John H. Dunnigan, Assistant Administrator.*
Web, www.nos.noaa.gov

Manages charting and geodetic services, oceanography and marine services, coastal resource coordination, and marine survey operations.

National Science Foundation (NSF), *Ocean Sciences, 4201 Wilson Blvd., #725, Arlington, VA 22230; (703) 292-8580. Fax, (703) 292-9085. Julie D. Morris, Director.*
Web, www.geo.nsf.gov/oce

Awards grants and contracts for acquiring, upgrading, and operating oceanographic research facilities that lend themselves to shared usage. Facilities supported include ships, submersibles, and shipboard and shorebased data logging and processing equipment. Supports development of new drilling techniques and systems.

U.S. Geological Survey (USGS), *(Interior Dept.), Coastal and Marine Geology Program, 12201 Sunrise Valley Dr., Reston, VA 20192 (mailing address: 915B National Center, Reston, VA 20192); (703) 648-6422. Fax, (703) 648-5464. John W. Haines, Program Coordinator.*
Web, http://marine.usgs.gov

Surveys the continental margins and the ocean floor to provide information on the mineral resources potential of submerged lands.

▶**NONGOVERNMENTAL**

Marine Technology Society, *5565 Sterrett Pl., #108, Columbia, MD 21044; (410) 884-5330. Fax, (410) 884-9060. Richard Lawson, Executive Director.*
General e-mail, membership@mtsociety.org
Web, www.mtsociety.org

Membership: scientists, engineers, technologists, and others interested in marine science and technology. Provides information on marine science, technology, and education.

National Ocean Industries Assn., *1120 G St. N.W., #900 20005; (202) 347-6900. Fax, (202) 347-8650. Tom A. Fry, President.*
General e-mail, noia@noia.org
Web, www.noia.org

Membership: manufacturers, producers, suppliers, and support and service companies involved in marine, offshore, and ocean work. Interests include offshore oil and gas supply and production, deep-sea mining, ocean thermal energy, and new energy sources.

MATHEMATICAL, COMPUTER, AND PHYSICAL SCIENCES

▶**AGENCIES**

National Institute of Standards and Technology (NIST), *(Commerce Dept.), 100 Bureau Dr., Bldg. 101, #A1134, Gaithersburg, MD 20899-1000 (mailing address: 100 Bureau Dr., MS 1000, Gaithersburg, MD 20899); (301) 975-2300. Fax, (301) 869-8972. Patrick Gallagher, Deputy Director.*
Web, www.nist.gov

Nonregulatory agency that serves as national reference and measurement laboratory for the physical and engineering sciences. Works with industry, government agencies, and academia; promotes U.S. innovation and industrial competitiveness. Research interests include electronics, manufacturing, chemistry, materials science, nanotechnology, quantum information science, hydrogen, and homeland security.

National Institute of Standards and Technology (NIST), *(Commerce Dept.), Information Technology Laboratory, 100 Bureau Dr., Bldg. 225, #B264, Gaithersburg, MD 20899-8900; (301) 975-2900. Fax, (301) 975-2378. Cita M. Furlani, Director.*
Web, www.itl.nist.gov

Offers support in mathematical and computer sciences to all institute programs and federal agencies; provides consultations, methods, and research supporting the institute's scientific and engineering projects.

National Science Foundation (NSF), *Mathematical and Physical Sciences, 4201 Wilson Blvd., #1005, Arlington, VA 22230; (703) 292-8800. Fax, (703) 292-9151. Tony F. Chan, Assistant Director.*
Web, www.nsf.gov/dir/index.jsp?org=MPS

Directorate that supports research in the mathematical and physical sciences; divisions focus on physics, chemistry, materials research, mathematical sciences, and astronomical sciences. Works to improve the education and human resource base for these fields; participates in international and multidisciplinary activities.

▶**NONGOVERNMENTAL**

Carnegie Institution of Washington, *1530 P St. N.W. 20005-1910; (202) 387-6400. Fax, (202) 387-8092. Richard A. Meserve, President.*
Web, www.ciw.org

Conducts research in plant biology, developmental biology, earth and planetary sciences, astronomy, and global ecology at the Carnegie Institution's six research departments: Dept. of Embryology (Baltimore, Md.); Geophysical Laboratory (Washington, D.C.); Dept. of Global Ecology (Stanford, Calif.); Dept. of Plant Biology (Stanford, Calif.); Dept. of Terrestrial Magnetism (Washington, D.C.); and The Observatories (Pasadena, Calif., and Las Campanas, Chile).

Chemistry

►AGENCIES

National Institute of Standards and Technology (NIST), *(Commerce Dept.), Center for Neutron Research,* 100 Bureau Dr., Bldg. 235, Gaithersburg, MD 20899-6100; (301) 975-6210. Fax, (301) 869-4770. Robert Dimeo, Director (Acting).
General e-mail, ncnr@nist.gov

Web, www.ncnr.nist.gov

Provides neutron measurement capabilities to the U.S. research community.

National Institute of Standards and Technology (NIST), *(Commerce Dept.), Chemical Science and Technology Laboratory,* 100 Bureau Dr., Bldg. 227, #A311, MS 8300, Gaithersburg, MD 20899-8300; (301) 975-8300. Fax, (301) 975-3845. Willie E. May, Director.
Web, www.cstl.nist.gov

Develops uniform chemical measurement methods; provides federal agencies and industry with advisory and research services in the areas of analytical chemistry, biotechnology, chemical engineering, and physical chemistry; conducts interdisciplinary research efforts with other NIST laboratories.

National Institute of Standards and Technology (NIST), *(Commerce Dept.), Materials Science and Engineering Laboratory,* 100 Bureau Dr., MS 8500, Gaithersburg, MD 20899-8500; (301) 975-5658. Fax, (301) 975-5012. Eric J. Amis, Director (Acting).
Web, www.msel.nist.gov

Provides measurements, data, standards, reference materials, concepts, and technical information fundamental to the processing, microstructure, properties, and performance of materials; addresses the scientific basis for new advanced materials; operates four materials divisions: ceramics, materials reliability, metallurgy, and polymers.

National Science Foundation (NSF), *Chemistry,* 4201 Wilson Blvd., #1055, Arlington, VA 22230; (703) 292-4954. Fax, (703) 292-9037. Luis Echegoyen, Director.
Web, www.nsf.gov/div/index.jsp?org=CHE

Awards grants to research programs in organic and macromolecular chemistry, experimental and theoretical physical chemistry, analytical and surface chemistry, and inorganic, bioinorganic, and organometallic chemistry; provides funds for instruments needed in chemistry research; coordinates interdisciplinary programs. Monitors international research.

National Science Foundation (NSF), *Materials Research,* 4201 Wilson Blvd., #1065, Arlington, VA 22230; (703) 292-8810. Fax, (703) 292-9035. Zakya H. Kafafi, Director.
Web, www.nsf.gov/materials

Provides grants for research in condensed matter physics; solid-state and materials, chemistry, polymers, metallic materials and nanostructures, ceramics, electronic and photonic materials, and condensed matter and materials theory. Supports multidisciplinary research in these areas through Materials Research Science and Engineering Centers (MRSEC) and national facilities such as the National High Magnetic Field Laboratory (NHMFL) and Synchrotron Radiation Center (SCR); funds major instrumentation projects as well as the acquisition and development of instrumentation for research to create new or advance current capabilities; and encourages international collaboration to positively impact the global advancement of materials research.

►NONGOVERNMENTAL

American Assn. for Clinical Chemistry, 1850 K St. N.W., #625 20006; (202) 857-0717. Fax, (202) 833-4576. Richard G. Flaherty, Executive Vice President.
General e-mail, info@aacc.org

Web, www.aacc.org

International society of chemists, physicians, and other scientists specializing in clinical chemistry. Provides educational and professional development services; presents awards for outstanding achievement. Monitors legislation and regulations.

American Chemical Society, 1155 16th St. N.W. 20036; (202) 872-4600. Fax, (202) 872-4615. Madeleine Jacobs, Executive Director. Information, (800) 227-5558. Library, (202) 872-4513.
General e-mail, help@acs.org

Web, www.chemistry.org

Membership: professional chemists and chemical engineers. Maintains educational programs, including those that evaluate college chemistry departments and high school chemistry curricula. Administers grants and fellowships for basic research; sponsors international exchanges; presents achievement awards. Library open to the public by appointment.

American Chemical Society, *Petroleum Research Fund,* 1155 16th St. N.W. 20036; (202) 872-4481. Fax, (202) 872-6319. W. Christopher Hollinsed, Director.
General e-mail, prfinfo@acs.org

Web, www.acsprf.org

Makes grants to nonprofit institutions for advanced scientific education and fundamental research related to the petroleum industry in chemistry, geology, and engineering.

American Chemistry Council, 1300 Wilson Blvd., Arlington, VA 22209; (703) 741-5000. Fax, (703) 741-6001. Cal Dooley, President.
Web, www.americanchemistry.com

Membership: manufacturers of basic industrial chemicals. Provides members with technical research, communications services, and legal affairs counseling. Interests include environmental safety and health, transportation, energy, and international trade and security. Monitors legislation and regulations.

AOAC International, *481 N. Frederick Ave., #500, Gaithersburg, MD 20877-2417; (301) 924-7077. Fax, (301) 924-7089. E. James Bradford, Executive Director. Information, (800) 379-2622.*
General e-mail, aoac@aoac.org

Web, www.aoac.org

International association of analytical science professionals, companies, government agencies, nongovernmental organizations, and institutions. Promotes methods validation and quality measurements in the analytical sciences. Supports the development, testing, validation, and publication of reliable chemical and biological methods of analyzing foods, drugs, feed, fertilizers, pesticides, water, forensic materials, and other substances.

Society of the Plastics Industry, *1667 K St. N.W., #1000 20006; (202) 974-5200. Fax, (202) 296-7005. William Carteaux, President.*
Web, www.plasticsindustry.org

Promotes the plastics industry. Monitors legislation and regulations.

Synthetic Organic Chemical Manufacturers Assn. (SOCMA), *1850 M St. N.W., #700 20036; (202) 721-4100. Fax, (202) 296-8120. Joseph Acker, President.*
Web, www.socma.org

Membership: companies that manufacture, distribute, and market organic chemicals, and providers of custom chemical services. Interests include international trade, environmental and occupational safety, chemical security, and health issues; conducts workshops and seminars. Promotes commercial opportunities for members. Monitors legislation and regulations.

Computer Sciences

►AGENCIES

National Coordination Office for Networking and Information Technology Research and Development, *4201 Wilson Blvd., Bldg. II-405, Arlington, VA 22230; (703) 292-4873. Fax, (703) 292-9097. Chris L. Greer, Director.*
General e-mail, nco@nitrd.gov

Web, www.nitrd.gov

Coordinates multi-agency research and development projects that involve computing, communications, and technology research and development. Reports to the National Science and Technology Council; provides information to Congress, U.S. and foreign organizations, and the public.

National Institute of Standards and Technology (NIST), *(Commerce Dept.), Information Technology Laboratory,* *100 Bureau Dr., Bldg. 225, #B264, Gaithersburg, MD 20899-8900; (301) 975-2900. Fax,*

(301) 975-2378. Cita M. Furlani, Director.
Web, www.itl.nist.gov

Advises federal agencies on automatic data processing management and use of information technology; helps federal agencies maintain up-to-date computer technology support systems, emphasizing computer security techniques; recommends federal information processing standards; conducts research in computer science and technology.

National Science Foundation (NSF), *Computer and Information Sciences and Engineering (CISE), 4201 Wilson Blvd., #1105N, Arlington, VA 22230; (703) 292-8900. Fax, (703) 292-9074. Janette M. Ming, Assistant Director.*
Web, www.nsf.gov/dir/index.jsp?org=CISE

Supports investigator-initiated research in computer science and engineering. Promotes the use of advanced computing, communications, and information systems. Provides grants for research and education.

National Science Foundation (NSF), *Computer and Network Systems, 4201 Wilson Blvd., #1175, Arlington, VA 22230; (703) 292-8950. Fax, (703) 292-9010. Taieb Znati, Director.*
Web, www.nsf.gov/div/index.jsp?org=CNS

Supports research and education activities that strive to create new computing and networking technologies and that explore new ways to utilize existing technologies. Seeks to foster the creation of better abstractions and tools for designing, building, analyzing, and measuring future systems. Supports the computing infrastructure that is required for experimental computer science and coordinates cross-divisional activities that foster integration of research and education and broadening of participation in the computer, information science, and engineering (CISE) workforce. Awards grants.

National Science Foundation (NSF), *Computing and Communication Foundations, 4201 Wilson Blvd., #1115, Arlington, VA 22230; (703) 292-8910. Fax, (703) 292-9059. Sampath Kannan, Division Director.*
Web, www.nsf.gov/div/index.jsp?org=CCF

Supports research and educational activities exploring the foundations of computing and communication devices and their usage. Seeks advances in computing and communication theory, algorithms for computer and computational sciences, and architecture and design of computers and software. Awards grants.

National Science Foundation (NSF), *Cyberinfrastructure, 4201 Wilson Blvd., #1145, Arlington, VA 22230; (703) 292-8970. Fax, (703) 292-9060. Ed Seidel, Director.*
Web, www.nsf.gov/dir/index.jsp?org=oci

Supports the development of computing and information infrastructure and helps advance all science and engineering domains. Infrastructure is made accessible to researchers and educators nationwide.

National Science Foundation (NSF), *Information and Intelligence Systems,* 4201 Wilson Blvd., #1125N, Arlington, VA 22230; (703) 292-8930. Fax, (703) 2 92-9073. Haym Hirsh, Director.
Web, www.nsf.gov/div/index.jsp?org—IIS

Supports research and education that develops new knowledge about the role people play in the design and use of information technology; advances the ability to represent, collect, store, organize, visualize, and communicate about data and information; and advances knowledge about how computational systems can perform tasks autonomously, robustly, and with flexibility. Awards grants.

►NONGOVERNMENTAL

American Council for Technology and Industry Advisory Council (ACT/IAC), 3040 Williams Dr., #610, Fairfax, VA 22031; (703) 208-4800. Fax, (703) 208-4805. Kenneth Allen, Executive Director.
General e-mail, act-iac@actgov.org

Web, www.actgov.org

Brings government and industry IT executives together to enhance government's ability to use information technologies. Activities include conferences, white papers, professional development programs, and other events to foster education, the exchange of information, and collaboration.

Center for Strategic and International Studies, *Technology and Public Policy Program,* 1800 K St. N.W., #400 20006; (202) 775-3175. Fax, (202) 775-3199. James A. Lewis, Director and Senior Fellow
General e-mail, techpolicy@csis.org

Web, www.csis.org/tech

Conducts and publishes research on emerging technologies, intelligence reform, and space and globalization programs.

Computer and Communications Industry Assn. (CCIA), 900 17th St. N.W., #1100 20006; (202) 783-0070. Fax, (202) 783-0534. Edward J. Black, President; Heather Greenfield, Director of Media Relations.
General e-mail, ccia@ccianet.org

Web, www.ccianet.org

Membership: Internet service providers, software providers, and manufacturers and suppliers of computer data processing and communications-related products and services. Interests include Internet freedom, privacy and neutrality, government electronic surveillance, telecommunications policy, tax policy, federal procurement policy, communications and computer industry standards, intellectual property policies, encryption, international trade, and antitrust reform.

Information Technology Industry Council (ITI), 1250 Eye St. N.W., #200 20005; (202) 737-8888. Fax, (202) 638-4922. Dean Garfield, President. Press, (202) 626-5725.
Web, www.itic.org

Membership: providers of information technology products and services. Promotes the global competitiveness of its members and advocates free trade. Seeks to protect intellectual property and encourages the use of voluntary standards. Interests include environmental conservation and energy efficiency, health information technology, increased access to high-speed broadband, protection of personal information, and U.S. export policy.

Institute of Electrical and Electronics Engineers–USA (IEEE-USA), *Washington Office,* 2001 L St. N.W., #700 20036-5104; (202) 785-0017. Fax, (202) 785-0835. Chris Brantley, Managing Director.
General e-mail, ieeeusa@ieee.org

Web, www.ieeeusa.org

U.S. arm of an international technological and professional organization. Interests include promoting career and technology policy interests of members. (Headquarters in New York.)

Software and Information Industry Assn. (SIIA), 1090 Vermont Ave. N.W., 6th Floor 20005-4095; (202) 289-7442. Fax, (202) 289-7097. Ken Wasch, President.
Web, www.siia.net

Membership: software and digital content companies. Promotes the industry worldwide; conducts anti-piracy program and other initiatives that protect members' intellectual property; supports initiatives developed through member requests; sponsors conferences, seminars, and other events that focus on industrywide and specific interests. Monitors legislation and regulations.

TechAmerica, 601 Pennsylvania Ave. N.W., North Bldg., #600 20004; (202) 682-9110. Fax, (202) 682-9111. Christopher W. Hansen, Chief Executive Officer; Phillip J. Bond, President. Press, (703) 284-5305. Toll-free, (800) 284-4232.
General e-mail, csc@techamerica.org

Web, www.techamerica.org

Trade association for companies offering hardware, software, electronics, telecommunications, and information technology products and services to the public and commercial sectors. Conducts market research and standards of development; offers business services and networking programs to members. Lobbies governments at the local, state, federal, and international levels to facilitate growth in the technology industry. (Merger of AeA [formerly the American Electronics Assn.], the Information Technology Assn. of American [ITAA], the Government Electronics and Information and Technology Assn. [GEIA], and the Cyber Security Industry Alliance.)

Mathematics

▶AGENCIES

National Institute of Standards and Technology (NIST), *(Commerce Dept.), Information Technology Laboratory,* 100 Bureau Dr., Bldg. 225, #B264, Gaithersburg, MD 20899-8900; (301) 975-2900. Fax, (301) 975-2378. Cita M. Furlani, Director.
Web, www.itl.nist.gov

Develops improved mathematical and statistical models and computational methods; consults on their use. Manages and operates NIST central computing facilities.

National Science Foundation (NSF), *Mathematical and Physical Sciences,* 4201 Wilson Blvd., #1005, Arlington, VA 22230; (703) 292-8800. Fax, (703) 292-9151. Tony F. Chan, Assistant Director.
Web, www.nsf.gov/dir/index.jsp?org=MPS

Provides grants for research in the mathematical sciences in the following areas: classical and modern analysis, geometric analysis, topology and foundations, algebra and number theory, applied and computational mathematics, and statistics and probability. Maintains special projects program, which supports scientific computing equipment for mathematics research and several research institutes. Sponsors conferences, workshops, and postdoctoral research fellowships. Monitors international research.

▶NONGOVERNMENTAL

American Statistical Assn., 732 N. Washington St., Alexandria, VA 22314-1943; (703) 684-1221. Fax, (703) 684-2037. Toll-free, (888) 231-3473. Ronald Wasserstein, Executive Director.
General e-mail, asainfo@amstat.org

Web, www.amstat.org

Membership: individuals interested in statistics and related quantitative fields. Advises government agencies on statistics and methodology in agency research; promotes development of statistical techniques for use in business, industry, finance, government, agriculture, and science. Promotes knowledge of statistics at all levels of education. Publishes statistical journals.

Conference Board of the Mathematical Sciences, 1529 18th St. N.W. 20036; (202) 293-1170. Fax, (202) 293-3412. Ronald C. Rosier, Administrative Officer.
Web, www.cbmsweb.org

Membership: presidents of sixteen mathematical sciences professional societies. Serves as a forum for discussion of issues of concern to the mathematical sciences community.

Mathematical Assn. of America, 1529 18th St. N.W. 20036-1358; (202) 387-5201. Fax, (202) 265-2384. Tina H. Straley, Executive Director. Information, (800) 741-9415.
General e-mail, maahq@maa.org

Web, www.maa.org

Membership: mathematics professors and individuals worldwide with a professional interest in mathematics. Seeks to improve the teaching of collegiate mathematics. Conducts professional development programs.

Physics

▶AGENCIES

National Institute of Standards and Technology (NIST), *(Commerce Dept.), Materials Science and Engineering Laboratory,* 100 Bureau Dr., MS 8500, Gaithersburg, MD 20899-8500; (301) 975-5658. Fax, (301) 975-5012. Eric J. Amis, Director (Acting).
Web, www.msel.nist.gov

Provides measurements, data, standards, reference materials, concepts, and technical information fundamental to the processing, microstructure, properties, and performance of materials; addresses the scientific basis for new advanced materials; operates four materials divisions: ceramics, materials reliability, metallurgy, and polymers.

National Institute of Standards and Technology (NIST), *(Commerce Dept.), Physics Laboratory,* 100 Bureau Dr., Bldg. 221, #B160, Gaithersburg, MD 20899-8400; (301) 975-4200. Fax, (301) 975-3038. Katharine B. Gebbie, Director.
Web, www.physics.nist.gov

Conducts research to improve measurement capability and quantitative understanding of basic physical processes that underlie measurement science; investigates structure and dynamics of atoms and molecules; provides national standards for time and frequency and for measurement of radiation; develops radiometric and wavelength standards; analyzes national measurement needs.

National Science Foundation (NSF), *Materials Research,* 4201 Wilson Blvd., #1065, Arlington, VA 22230; (703) 292-8810. Fax, (703) 292-9035. Zakya H. Kafafi, Director.
Web, www.nsf.gov/materials

Provides grants for research in condensed matter physics; solid-state and materials, chemistry, polymers, metallic materials and nanostructures, ceramics, electronic and photonic materials and condensed matter and materials theory. Supports multidisciplinary research in these areas through Materials Research Science and Engineering Centers (MRSEC) and national facilities such as the National High Magnetic Field Laboratory (NHMFL) and Synchrotron Radiation Center (SCR); funds major instrumentation projects as well as the acquisition and development of instrumentation for research to create new or advance current capabilities; and encourages international collaboration to positively impact the global advancement of materials research.

National Science Foundation (NSF), *Physics,* 4201 Wilson Blvd., #1015, Arlington, VA 22230; (703) 292-8890. Fax, (703) 292-9078. Joseph L. Dehmer, Director.
Web, www.nsf.gov/div/index.jsp?org=PHY

Awards grants for research and special programs in atomic, molecular, and optical physics; elementary particle physics; and nuclear, theoretical, and gravitational physics.

Science *(Energy Dept.), High Energy Physics,* 19901 Germantown Rd., Germantown, MD 20874-1290 (mailing address: SC-25/Germantown Bldg., U.S. DOE, 1000 Independence Ave. S.W., Washington, DC 20585-1290); (301) 903-3624. Fax, (301) 903-2597. Dennis Kovar, Associate Director.
Web, www.science.doe.gov/hep

Provides grants and facilities for research in high energy (or particle) physics. Constructs, operates, and maintains particle accelerators used in high energy research.

Science *(Energy Dept.), Nuclear Physics,* 19901 Germantown Rd., Germantown, MD 20874-1290 (mailing address: SC-26/Germantown Bldg., U.S. DOE, 1000 Independence Ave. S.W., Washington, DC 20585-1290); (301) 903-3613. Fax, (301) 903-3833. Eugene Henry, Associate Director (Acting).
Web, www.science.doe.gov/np

Provides grants and facilities for research in nuclear physics. Manages the nuclear data program. Develops, constructs, and operates accelerator facilities and detectors used in nuclear physics research.

▶**NONGOVERNMENTAL**

American Institute of Physics, 1 Physics Ellipse, College Park, MD 20740-3843; (301) 209-3100. Fax, (301) 209-0843. H. Frederick Dylla, Executive Director.
Web, www.aip.org

Fosters cooperation within the physics community; improves public understanding of science; disseminates information on scientific research.

American Institute of Physics, *Center for History of Physics,* 1 Physics Ellipse, College Park, MD 20740-3843; (301) 209-3165. Fax, (301) 209-0882. Gregory Wood, Director.
General e-mail, chp@aip.org
Web, www.aip.org/history

Records and preserves the history of modern physics and allied fields, including astronomy, geophysics, and optics. Maintains a documentation program containing interviews, unpublished data, and historical records. Manages the Niels Bohr Library, which is open to the public by appointment.

American Physical Society, *Washington Office,* 529 14th St. N.W., #1050 20045-2001; (202) 662-8700. Fax, (202) 662-8711. Judy Franz, Director.
General e-mail, opa@aps.org
Web, www.aps.org

Scientific and educational society of educators, students, citizens, and scientists, including industrial scientists. Sponsors studies on issues of public concern related

to physics, such as reactor safety and energy use. Informs members of national and international developments. (Headquarters in College Park, Md.)

Optical Society of America, 2010 Massachusetts Ave. N.W. 20036; (202) 223-8130. Fax, (202) 223-1096. Elizabeth Rogan, Executive Director.
General e-mail, info@osa.org
Web, www.osa.org

Membership: researchers, educators, manufacturers, students, and others interested in optics and photonics worldwide. Promotes research and information exchange; conducts conferences.

Weights and Measures, Metric System

▶**AGENCIES**

National Institute of Standards and Technology (NIST), *(Commerce Dept.), Materials Science and Engineering Laboratory,* 100 Bureau Dr., MS 8500, Gaithersburg, MD 20899-8500; (301) 975-5658. Fax, (301) 975-5012. Eric J. Amis, Director (Acting).
Web, www.msel.nist.gov

Provides technical leadership for the nation's materials measurement and standards infrastructure, using its expertise to anticipate and respond to measurement-related industry needs in many areas of technology, including microelectronics, automotive, and health care.

National Institute of Standards and Technology (NIST), *(Commerce Dept.), Measurement Services,* 100 Bureau Dr., MS 2300, Gaithersburg, MD 20899; (301) 975-8424. Fax, (301) 971-2183. Robert Watters Jr., Chief.
Web, www.nist.gov

Disseminates physical, chemical, and engineering measurement standards and provides services to ensure accurate and compatible measurements, specifications, and codes on a national and international scale.

National Institute of Standards and Technology (NIST), *(Commerce Dept.), Weights and Measures,* 100 Bureau Dr., MS 2600, Gaithersburg, MD 20899; (301) 975-4004. Fax, (301) 975-8091. Henry V. Opperman, Chief.
General e-mail, owm@nist.gov
Web, www.nist.gov/owm

Promotes uniformity in weights and measures law and enforcement. Provides weights and measures agencies with training and technical assistance; assists state and local agencies in adapting their weights and measures to meet national standards; conducts research; sets uniform standards and regulations.

National Institute of Standards and Technology (NIST), *(Commerce Dept.), Weights and Measures: Laws*

and Metric Group, *100 Bureau Dr., MS 2600, Gaithersburg, MD 20899; (301) 975-4004. Fax, (301) 975-8091. Ken Butcher, Group Leader.*
General e-mail, owm@nist.gov

Web, www.nist.gov/metric

Coordinates federal metric conversion transition to ensure consistency; provides the public with technical and general information about the metric system; assists state and local governments, businesses, and educators with metric conversion activities.

▶**CONGRESS**

For a listing of relevant congressional committees and subcommittees, please see page 592 or the Appendix.

SOCIAL SCIENCES

▶**AGENCIES**

National Institutes of Health *(Health and Human Services Dept.), Behavioral and Social Sciences Research, 31 Center Dr., Bldg. 31, #B1C19, Bethesda, MD 20892-0183; (301) 402-1146. Fax, (301) 402-1150. Dr. Christine Bachrach, Director (Acting).*
Web, http://obssr.od.nih.gov

Works to advance behavioral and social sciences training, to integrate a biobehavioral perspective across the NIH, and to improve communication among scientists and with the public. Develops funding initiatives for research and training. Sets priorities for research. Provides training and career development opportunities for behavioral and social scientists. Links minority students with mentors. Organizes cultural workshops and lectures.

National Museum of Natural History *(Smithsonian Institution), Anthropology, 10th St. and Constitution Ave. N.W., MRC 112 20560-0112 (mailing address: P.O. Box 37012, Washington, DC 20013-7012); (202) 633-1920. Fax, (202) 357-2208. J. Daniel Rogers, Chair. Library, (202) 633-1640.*
Web, http://anthropology.si.edu

Conducts research on paleo-Indian archaeology and prehistory, New World origins, and paleoecology. Maintains anthropological and human studies film archives. Museum maintains public exhibitions of human cultures.

National Museum of Natural History *(Smithsonian Institution), Library, 10th St. and Constitution Ave. N.W., #51 20560-0154 (mailing address: P.O. Box 37012, Washington, DC 20013-7012); (202) 633-1680. Fax, (202) 357-1896. Ann Juneau, Head, (202) 633-4939.*
General e-mail, libmail@si.edu

Web, www.sil.si.edu

Maintains reference collections covering anthropology, biodiversity, biology, botany, ecology, entomology, ethnology, mineral sciences, paleobiology, and zoology; permits on-site use of the collections. Open to the public by appointment; makes interlibrary loans.

National Science Foundation (NSF), *Social, Behavioral, and Economic Sciences, 4201 Wilson Blvd., #905, Arlington, VA 22230; (703) 292-8700. Fax, (703) 292-9083. David Lightfoot, Assistant Director.*
Web, www.nsf.gov/dir/index.jsp?org=SBE

Directorate that awards grants for research in behavioral and cognitive sciences, social and economic sciences, science resources studies, and international programs. Provides support for workshops, symposia, and conferences.

▶**NONGOVERNMENTAL**

American Anthropological Assn., *2200 Wilson Blvd., #600, Arlington, VA 22201; (703) 528-1902. Fax, (703) 528-3546. William E. Davis III, Executive Director.*
Web, www.aaanet.org

Membership: anthropologists, educators, students, and others interested in anthropological studies. Publishes research studies of member organizations, sponsors workshops, and disseminates to members information concerning developments in anthropology worldwide.

American Institutes for Research, *1000 Thomas Jefferson St. N.W. 20007; (202) 403-5000. Fax, (202) 403-5001. Sol Pelavin, President. TTY, (877) 334-3499.*
Web, www.air.org

Conducts behavioral and social science research and provides technical assistance both domestically and internationally in the areas of education, health, and workforce productivity.

American Psychological Assn., *750 1st St. N.E. 20002-4242; (202) 336-5500. Fax, (202) 336-6069. Norman B. Anderson, Chief Executive Officer. Library, (202) 336-5640. TTY, (202) 336-6123. Toll-free, (800) 374-2721.*
Web, www.apa.org

Membership: professional psychologists, educators, and behavioral research scientists. Supports research, training, and professional services; works toward improving the qualifications, competence, and training programs of psychologists. Monitors international research and U.S. legislation on mental health.

American Sociological Assn., *1307 New York Ave. N.W., #700 20005; (202) 383-9005. Fax, (202) 638-0882. Sally Hillsman, Executive Officer. TTY, (202) 638-0981.*
General e-mail, executive.office@asanet.org

Web, www.asanet.org

Membership: sociologists, social scientists, and others interested in research, teaching, and application of sociology in the United States and internationally. Sponsors professional development program, teaching resources center, and education programs; offers fellowships for minorities.

Consortium of Social Science Assns., *1701 K St. N.W., #1150 20006; (202) 842-3525. Fax, (202) 842-2788. Howard J. Silver, Executive Director.*
General e-mail, cossa@cossa.org

Web, www.cossa.org

Consortium of associations in the fields of criminology, economics, history, political science, psychology, sociology, statistics, geography, linguistics, law, and social science. Advocates support for research and monitors federal funding in the social and behavioral sciences; conducts seminars.

Council for Social and Economic Studies, *1133 13th St. N.W., #C2 20005-4297; (202) 371-2700. Fax, (202) 371-1523. Roger Pearson, Executive Director.*

General e-mail, socecon@aol.com

Web, www.jspes.org and www.mankindquarterly.org

Publishes peer-reviewed journals focusing on social and economic studies, anthropology, psychology, and genetics.

Human Resources Research Organization (HumRRO), *66 Canal Center Plaza, #400, Alexandria, VA 22314; (703) 549-3611. Fax, (703) 549-9025. William J. Strickland, President.*

Web, www.humrro.org

Studies, designs, develops, surveys, and evaluates personnel systems, chiefly in the workplace. Interests include personnel selection and promotion, career progression, performance appraisal, training, and program evaluation.

Institute for the Study of Man, *1133 13th St. N.W., #C2 20005-4297; (202) 371-2700. Fax, (202) 371-1523. Roger Pearson, Executive Director.*

General e-mail, iejournal@aol.com

Web, www.jies.org

Publishes academic journals, books, and monographs in areas related to Indo-European anthropology, archaeology, linguistics, cultural history, and mythology. Sponsors seminars.

Geography and Mapping

▶**AGENCIES**

Census Bureau *(Commerce Dept.), Geography, 4600 Silver Hill Rd., #HQ-4H174 20233-7400; (301) 763-2131. Fax, (301) 763-4710. Timothy Trainor, Chief.*

Web, www.census.geo.gov

Manages the MAF TIGER system, a nationwide geographic and address database; prepares maps for use in conducting censuses and surveys and for showing their results geographically; determines names and current boundaries of legal geographic units; defines names and boundaries of selected statistical areas; develops geographic code schemes; maintains computer files of area measurements, geographic boundaries, and map features with address ranges.

National Archives and Records Administration (NARA), *Cartographic and Architectural Unit, 8601 Adelphi Rd., #3320, College Park, MD 20740-6001; (301) 837-3200. Fax, (301) 837-3622. Deborah Lelansky, Cartographic Supervisor.*

General e-mail, carto@nara.gov

Web, www.archives.gov

Makes information available on federal government cartographic records, architectural drawings, and aerial mapping films; prepares descriptive guides and inventories of records. Library open to the public. Records may be reproduced for a fee.

National Geospatial-Intelligence Agency *(Defense Dept.), 4600 Sangamore Rd., #378, Bethesda, MD 20816-5003; (301) 227-7300. Fax, (301) 227-3696. Vice Adm. Robert B. Murrett, Director. Maps and imagery products, (800) 455-0899.*

General e-mail, queries1@nga.mil

Web, www.nga.mil

Combat support agency that provides imagery and geospatial information to national policymakers and military forces in support of national defense objectives; incorporates the missions and functions of the former Defense Mapping Agency and Defense Dissemination Program Office.

National Oceanic and Atmospheric Administration (NOAA), *(Commerce Dept.), National Geodetic Survey, 1315 East-West Hwy., N-NGS12, SSMC-3, #8657, Silver Spring, MD 20910-3282; (301) 713-3222. Fax, (301) 713-4175. Juliana P. Blackwell, Director.*

Web, http://geodesy.noaa.gov

Develops and maintains the National Spatial Reference System, a national geodetic reference system that serves as a common reference for latitude, longitude, height, scale, orientation, and gravity measurements. Maps the nation's coastal zone and waterways; conducts research and development programs to improve the collection, distribution, and use of spatial data; coordinates the development and application of new surveying instrumentation and procedures.

State Dept., *Office of the Geographer and Global Issues, 2201 C St. N.W., #6722 20520; (202) 647-2021. Fax, (202) 647-0504. Lee R. Schwartz, Director.*

Web, www.state.gov

Advises the State Dept. and other federal agencies on geographic and cartographic matters. Furnishes technical and analytical research and advice in the field of geography.

U.S. Board on Geographic Names, *12201 Sunrise Valley Dr., Reston, VA 20192-0523 (mailing address: 523 National Center, Reston, VA 20192); (703) 648-4552. Fax, (703) 648-4549. Louis Yost, Executive Secretary, U.S. Board on Geographic Names and Domestic Names Committee; Randall Flynn, Executive Secretary, Foreign Names Committee, (301) 227-1407.*

Web, http://geonames.usgs.gov

Interagency organization established by Congress to standardize geographic names. Board members are representatives from the departments of Agriculture,

Commerce, Defense, Homeland Security, Interior, and State; the Central Intelligence Agency; the Government Printing Office; the Library of Congress; and the U.S. Postal Service. Sets policy governing the use of both domestic and foreign geographic names as well as underseas feature names and Antarctic feature names.

U.S. Geological Survey (USGS), *(Interior Dept.),* **Geography Program,** *12201 Sunrise Valley Dr., MS 516, Reston, VA 20192; (703) 648-7413. Fax, (703) 648-5792. D. Bryant Cramer, Associate Director for Geography. Web, http://geography.usgs.gov*

Conducts research; collects, compiles, and analyzes information about features of the earth's surface; develops and maintains a digital geographic/cartographic database and assists users in applying spatial data; coordinates federal mapping activities; encourages the development of surveying and mapping techniques. Maintains federal government responsibility for the nation's land-observing satellites (Landsat 5 and Landsat 7).

U.S. Geological Survey (USGS), *(Interior Dept.),* **Geospatial Information,** *12201 Sunrise Valley Dr., Reston, VA 20192 (mailing address: 108 National Center, Reston, VA 20192); (703) 648-7145. Fax, (703) 648-6821. Mark DeMulder, Chief. Web, www.usgs.gov/ngpo*

Plans and coordinates information dissemination activities.

U.S. Geological Survey (USGS), *(Interior Dept.), Science Information and Library Services (SILS),* *12201 Sunrise Valley Dr., #1C204, Reston, VA 20192 (mailing address: 507 National Center, Reston, VA 20192-1507); (703) 648-5953. Fax, (703) 648-5548. Information and U.S. maps, (888) ASK-USGS or (888) 275-8747. General e-mail, ask@usgs.gov*

Web, www.usgs.gov

Collects, organizes, and distributes cartographic, geographic, hydrologic, biologic, and other natural science information; offers maps, reports, and other publications; offers digital cartographic data, digital aerial photographic data, and space imagery and manned spacecraft photographs for sale. Acts as a clearinghouse for cartographic and geographic data.

▶**CONGRESS**

For a listing of relevant congressional committees and subcommittees, please see page 592 or the Appendix.

Library of Congress, Geography and Map Division, *101 Independence Ave. S.E., #LM B02 20540; (202) 707-8530. John R. Hébert, Chief. Reference and reading room, (202) 707-6277. Web, www.loc.gov/rr/geogmap*

Maintains cartographic collection of maps, atlases, globes, and reference books. Reference service provided; reading room open to the public. Interlibrary loans available through the library's loan division; photocopies, when not limited by copyright or other restriction, available through the library's photoduplication service.

▶**NONGOVERNMENTAL**

American Congress on Surveying and Mapping, *6 Montgomery Village Ave., #403, Gaithersburg, MD 20879; (240) 632-9716. Fax, (240) 632-1321. Curtis W. Sumner, Executive Director. General e-mail, info@acsm.net*

Web, www.acsm.net

Membership: professionals working worldwide in surveying, cartography, geodesy, and geographic/land information systems (computerized mapping systems used in urban, regional, and environmental planning). Sponsors workshops and seminars for surveyors and mapping scientists; participates in accreditation of college and university surveying and related degree programs; grants fellowships; develops and administers certification programs for hydrographers and technician surveyors. Monitors legislation and regulations.

Assn. of American Geographers, *1710 16th St. N.W. 20009-3198; (202) 234-1450. Fax, (202) 234-2744. Douglas Richardson, Executive Director. General e-mail, gaia@aag.org*

Web, www.aag.org

Membership: educators, students, business executives, government employees, and scientists in the field of geography. Seeks to advance professional studies in geography and encourages the application of geographic research in education, government, and business.

National Geographic Maps, *1145 17th St. N.W. 20036-4688; (202) 775-7852. Fax, (202) 429-5704. Allen Carroll, Chief Cartographer. Map orders, (800) 962-1643. Web, www.nationalgeographic.com*

Produces and sells to the public political, physical, and thematic maps, atlases, and globes. (Affiliated with the National Geographic Society.)

SPACE SCIENCES

▶**AGENCIES**

Air Force Dept. *(Defense Dept.),* **Space Programs,** *1670 Air Force Pentagon, #4D859 20330-1640; (703) 693-5799. Fax, (703) 614-3998. Gary E. Payton, Under Secretary. Web, www.af.mil*

Manages the planning, programming, and acquisition of space systems for the Air Force and other military services.

Federal Aviation Administration (FAA), *(Transportation Dept.), Commercial Space Transportation,* *800 Independence Ave. S.W., #331, AST-1 20591; (202) 267-7793. Fax, (202) 267-5450. George Nield, Associate Administrator. Web, http://ast.faa.gov*

Promotes and facilitates the operation of commercial expendable space launch vehicles by the private sector; licenses and regulates these activities.

National Aeronautics and Space Administration

(**NASA**), *300 E St. S.W. 20546-0001 (mailing address: NASA Headquarters, Washington, DC 20546); (202) 358-1010. Fax, (202) 358-3251. Christopher Scolese, Administrator (Acting). Information, (202) 358-0000. TTY, (800) 877-8339.*
Web, www.nasa.gov

Develops, manages, and has oversight of the agency's programs and missions. Interacts with Congress and state officials and responds to national and international inquiries. Serves as the administrative office for the agency.

National Aeronautics and Space Administration

(**NASA**), *Aeronautics Research Mission Directorate, 300 E St. S.W., #6A70 20546 (mailing address: NASA Headquarters, Mail Code 6J39A, Washington, DC 20546); (202) 358-4600. Fax, (202) 358-2920. Jaiwon Shin, Associate Administrator.*
Web, www.aerospace.nasa.gov

Conducts research in aerodynamics, materials, structures, avionics, propulsion, high-performance computing, human factors, aviation safety, and space transportation in support of national space and aeronautical research and technology goals. Manages the following NASA research centers: Ames (Moffett Field, Calif.); Dryden (Edwards, Calif.); Langley (Hampton, Va.); and Glenn (Cleveland, Ohio).

National Aeronautics and Space Administration

(**NASA**), *Chief Engineer, 300 E St. S.W., #6V87 20546; (202) 358-1823. Fax, (202) 358-3296. Michael Ryschkewitsch, Chief Engineer.*
Web, http://oce.nasa.gov

Serves as the agency's principal adviser on matters pertaining to the technical readiness and execution of programs and projects.

National Aeronautics and Space Administration

(**NASA**), *Chief Health and Medical Officer, 300 E St. S.W., #5G39 20546; (202) 358-2390. Fax, (202) 358-3349. Dr. Richard S. Williams, Chief Health and Medical Officer.*
Web, www.hq.nasa.gov/office/chmo

Ensures the health and safety of NASA employees in space and on the ground. Develops health and medical policy, establishes guidelines for health and medical practices, oversees health care delivery, and monitors human and animal research standards within the agency.

National Aeronautics and Space Administration

(**NASA**), *Education, 300 E St. S.W., #9N70 20546; (202) 358-0103. Fax, (202) 358-7097. Joyce Winterton, Assistant Administrator.*
General e-mail, education@nasa.gov
Web, http://education.nasa.gov

Coordinates NASA's education programs and activities to meet national educational needs and ensure a sufficient talent pool to preserve U.S. leadership in aeronautical technology and space science.

National Aeronautics and Space Administration

(**NASA**), *Exploration Systems Mission Directorate, 300 E St. S.W., #7J17 20546 (mailing address: NASA headquarters, Mail ESMD, Washington, DC 20546); (202) 358-7246. Fax, (202) 358-4174. Douglas R. Cooke, Associate Administrator.*
Web, http://exploration.nasa.gov

Creates capabilities and supporting research and technologies to enable sustainable and affordable space exploration. Responsible for developing the launch systems and vehicles that will carry humans into space following the retirement of the space shuttle. Developing Lunar Reconnaissance Orbiter (LRO) mission and supports future human exploration of the moon.

National Aeronautics and Space Administration

(**NASA**), *Goddard Space Flight Center, 8800 Greenbelt Rd., Code 100, Greenbelt, MD 20771; (301) 286-2000. Fax, (301) 286-1714. Robert Strain, Director. Information, (301) 286-5121.*
Web, www.nasa.gov/centers/Goddard/home

Conducts space and earth science research; develops and operates flight missions; maintains spaceflight tracking and data acquisition networks; develops technology and instruments; develops and maintains advanced information systems for the display, analysis, archiving, and distribution of space and earth science data; and develops National Oceanic and Atmospheric Administration (NOAA) satellite systems that provide environmental data for forecasting and research.

National Aeronautics and Space Administration

(**NASA**), *Heliophysics Science Division, Goddard Space Flight Center, Code 670, Greenbelt, MD 20771; (301) 286-5839. Fax, (301) 286-5348. James A. Slavin, Director.*
Web, http://hsd.gsfc.nasa.gov

Provides scientific expertise necessary to achieve NASA's strategic science goals in solar physics, heliospheric physics, geospace physics, and space weather. Houses the Solar Physics Laboratory, the Heliospheric Physics Laboratory, the Geospace Physics Laboratory, and the Space Weather Laboratory.

National Aeronautics and Space Administration

(**NASA**), *Institutions and Management, 300 E St. S.W., #4V13 20546; (202) 358-1809. Fax, (202) 358-2834. Thomas Luedtke, Associate Administrator.*
Web, www.nasa.gov

Serves to integrate and support programs, facilities, and information at NASA in order to carry out the agency's mission more effectively

National Aeronautics and Space Administration

(**NASA**), *NASA Advisory Council, 300 E St. S.W. 20546; (202) 358-3636. Fax, (202) 358-3030. Ken Ford, Chair; Marguerite Broadwell, Executive Director. Alternate phone, (202) 358-1894.*
Web, www.hq.nasa.gov/office/oer/nac

Advises the administrator on NASA's aeronautics and space plans and programs. The council consists of six

National Aeronautics and Space Administration

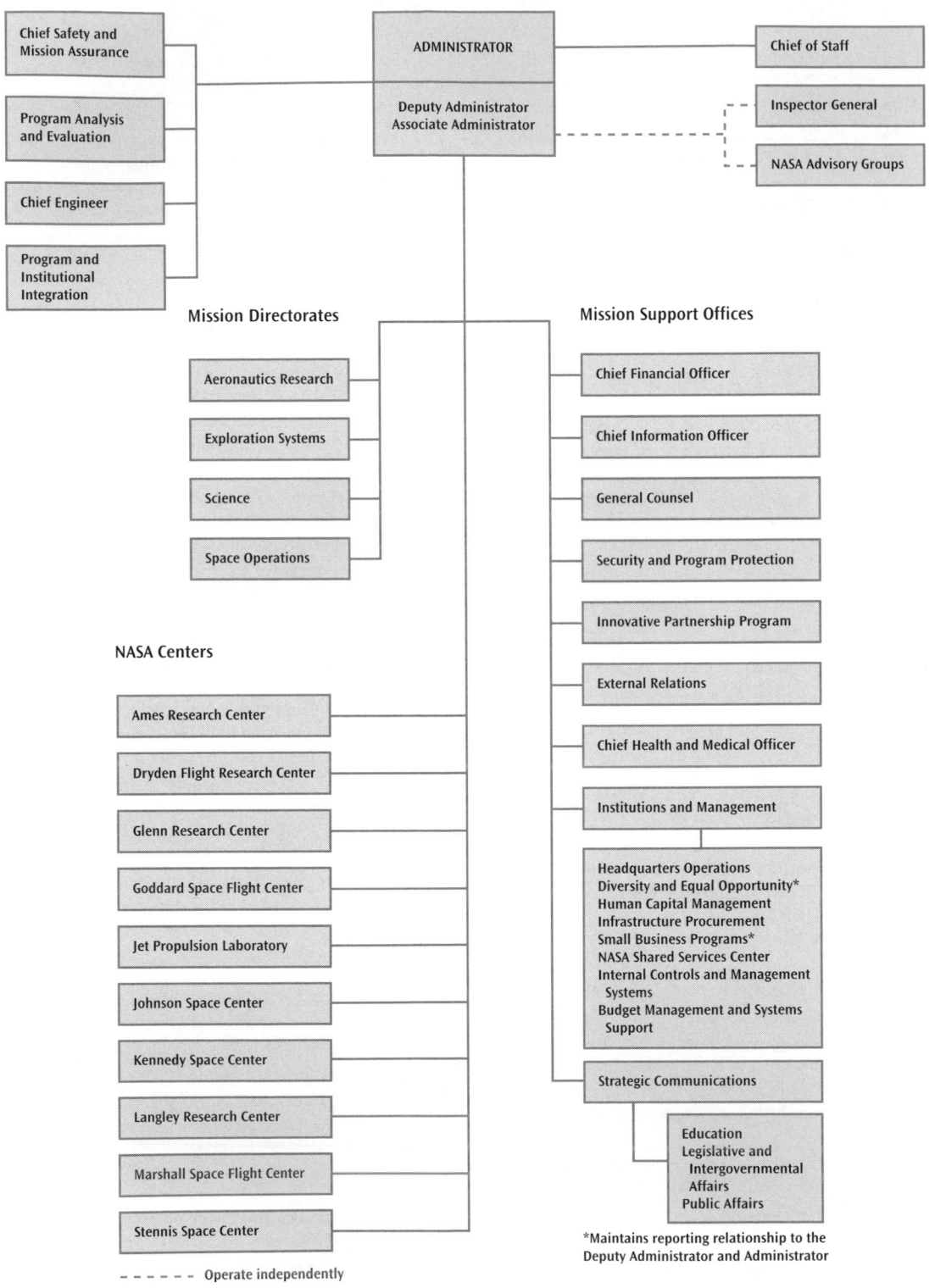

Chief Safety and Mission Assurance

Program Analysis and Evaluation

Chief Engineer

Program and Institutional Integration

ADMINISTRATOR

Deputy Administrator Associate Administrator

Chief of Staff

Inspector General

NASA Advisory Groups

Mission Directorates

Aeronautics Research

Exploration Systems

Science

Space Operations

Mission Support Offices

Chief Financial Officer

Chief Information Officer

General Counsel

Security and Program Protection

Innovative Partnership Program

External Relations

Chief Health and Medical Officer

Institutions and Management

**Headquarters Operations
Diversity and Equal Opportunity*
Human Capital Management
Infrastructure Procurement
Small Business Programs*
NASA Shared Services Center
Internal Controls and Management
  Systems
Budget Management and Systems
  Support**

Strategic Communications

**Education
Legislative and
  Intergovernmental
  Affairs
Public Affairs**

NASA Centers

Ames Research Center

Dryden Flight Research Center

Glenn Research Center

Goddard Space Flight Center

Jet Propulsion Laboratory

Johnson Space Center

Kennedy Space Center

Langley Research Center

Marshall Space Flight Center

Stennis Space Center

– – – – – Operate independently

*Maintains reporting relationship to the
Deputy Administrator and Administrator

committees: Aeronautics, Audit and Finance, Exploration, Human Capital, Science, and Space Operations.

National Aeronautics and Space Administration (NASA), *National Space Science Data Center,* Goddard Space Flight Center, Code 690.1, Greenbelt, MD 20771; (301) 286-7355. Fax, (301) 286-1771. Edwin Grayzeck, Program Manager, Planetary Data System.
Web, http://nssdc.gsfc.nasa.gov

Acquires, catalogs, and distributes NASA mission data to the international space science community, including research organizations and scientists, universities, and other interested organizations worldwide. Provides software tools and network access to promote collaborative data analysis. (Mail data requests to above address, attention: Code 690.1/ Request Coordination Office, or phone [301] 286-6695.)

National Aeronautics and Space Administration (NASA), *Safety and Mission Assurance,* 300 E St. S.W., #5V39 20546; (202) 358-2406. Fax, (202) 358-2699. Bryan D. O'Connor, Chief.
Web, www.hq.nasa.gov/office/codeq

Evaluates the safety and reliability of NASA systems and programs. Alerts officials to technical execution and physical readiness of NASA projects.

National Aeronautics and Space Administration (NASA), *Science Mission Directorate,* 300 E St. S.W., #3C26 20546, (202) 358-3889. Fax, (202) 358-3092. Edward J. Weiler, Associate Administrator.
General e-mail, science@hq.nasa.gov

Web, http://science.hq.nasa.gov/directorate/index.html

Conducts all in-orbit exploration of space. Areas of research include life sciences (people, animals, and plants), materials (crystals and minerals), and microgravity effects observed in space. Participates in international projects and conferences.

National Aeronautics and Space Administration (NASA), *Sciences and Exploration Directorate,* Goddard Space Flight Center, 8800 Greenbelt Rd., Code 600, Greenbelt, MD 20771; (301) 286-6066. Fax, (301) 286-1772. Nicholas E. White, Director.
Web, http://science.gsfc.nasa.gov

Plans, organizes, implements, and evaluates a broad system of theoretical and experimental scientific research in the study of the earth-sun system, the solar system and the origins of life, and the birth and evolution of the universe. Activities include modeling and basic research, flight experiment development, and data analysis.

National Aeronautics and Space Administration (NASA), *Security and Program Protection,* 300 E St. S.W., #9U70 20546; (202) 358-2010. Fax, (202) 358-3238. Jack L. Forsythe, Assistant Administrator.
Web, www.hq.nasa.gov/office/ospp

Serves as the focal point for policy formulation, oversight, coordination, and management of NASA's security, counterintelligence, counterterrorism, emergency preparedness and response, and continuity of operations programs.

National Aeronautics and Space Administration (NASA), *Solar System Exploration Data Services,* Goddard Space Flight Center, Code 690.1, Greenbelt, MD 20771; (301) 286-6695 (Access Service Office). Fax, (301) 286-1635. Edwin Grayzeck, Program Manager, Planetary Data System.
Web, http://ssedso.gsfc.nasa.gov

Coordinates data management and archiving plans within NASA's Science Mission. Operates the National Space Science Data Center (NSSDC) as a permanent archive for data associated with NASA's missions; the Crustal Dynamics Data Information System (CDDIS); and the Planetary Data System (PDS).

National Aeronautics and Space Administration (NASA), *Space Operations,* 300 E St. S.W., #7K39 20546 (mailing address: NASA Headquarters, #7L18, Washington, DC 20546); (202) 358-2015. Fax, (202) 358-2838. William H. Gerstenmaier, Associate Administrator.
Web, www.hq.nasa.gov/somd

Responsible for space transportation systems operations, including U.S. participation in international missions. Administers the development, testing, and production phases of the space shuttle. Manages the international space station, space shuttle program, and space and flight support.

National Aeronautics and Space Administration (NASA), *Space Physics Data Facility,* Goddard Space Flight Center, Code 612.4, Greenbelt, MD 20771; (301) 286-7794. Fax, (301) 286-1771. Robert E. McGuire, Head.
Web, http://spdf.gsfc.nasa.gov

Designs and implements multimission and multidisciplinary data services, innovative ground data system concepts, educational programs, modeling, and visualization research to strategically advance NASA's solar-terrestrial program and general understanding of the earth-sun system.

National Air and Space Museum *(Smithsonian Institution),* 6th St. and Independence Ave. S.W. 20013-7012; (202) 633-1000. Fax, (202) 357-2426. Gen. John R. Dailey, Director. Library, (202) 633-2320. TTY, (202) 357-1505. Education office, (202) 633-2540. Tours, (202) 633-2563.
Web, www.nasm.si.edu

Collects, preserves, and exhibits astronautical objects and equipment of historical interest, including aircraft, spacecraft, and communications and weather satellites. Library open to the public by appointment.

National Oceanic and Atmospheric Administration (NOAA), *(Commerce Dept.), Space Commercialization,* 14th St. and Constitution Ave. N.W., #6818 20230; (202) 482-6125. Fax, (202) 482-4429. Charles S. Baker, Director (Acting).
General e-mail, space.commerce@noaa.gov

Web, www.nesdis.noaa.gov/space

The principal unit for space commerce within NOAA and the Commerce Dept. Promotes economic growth and technological advancement of U.S. commercial space industry focusing on several commercial space industry sectors, including satellite navigation, satellite imagery, space transportation, and entrepreneurial space business. Participates in discussions of national space policy and other space-related issues.

Steven F. Udvar-Hazy Center *(Smithsonian Institution),* **National Air and Space Museum,** *14390 Air and Space Museum Pkwy., Chantilly, VA 20151; (202) 633-1000. Gen. John R. Dailey, Director; Joseph T. Anderson, Deputy Director. TTY, (202) 633-5285. Public Affairs, (703) 572-4040. Web, www.nasm.si.edu/udvarhazy*

Displays and preserves a collection of historical aviation and space artifacts, including the B-29 Superfortress, Enola Gay, the Lockheed SR-71 Blackbird, the prototype of the Boeing 707, the space shuttle *Enterprise,* and the Concorde. Provides a center for research into the history, science, and technology of aviation and space flight.

▶**CONGRESS**

For a listing of relevant congressional committees and subcommittees, please see page 592 or the Appendix.

▶**INTERNATIONAL ORGANIZATIONS**

European Space Agency (ESA), Washington Office, *955 L'Enfant Plaza S.W., #7800 20024; (202) 488-4158. Fax, (202) 488-4930. Frederic Nordlund, Head. Web, www.esa.int*

Intergovernmental agency that promotes international collaboration in space research and development and the use of space technology for peaceful purposes. Members include Austria, Belgium, Denmark, Finland, France, Germany, Greece, Ireland, Italy, Luxembourg, the Netherlands, Norway, Portugal, Spain, Sweden, Switzerland, and the United Kingdom; Canada participates in some programs. (Headquarters in Paris.)

▶**NONGOVERNMENTAL**

Aerospace Education Foundation, *1501 Lee Hwy., #400, Arlington, VA 22209; (703) 247-5800. Fax, (703) 247-5853. Gen. Michael M. Dunn, Executive Director. Information, (800) 727-3337. General e-mail, aefstaff@aef.org Web, www.afa.org*

Promotes knowledge and appreciation of U.S. civilian and military aerospace development and history. (Affiliated with the Air Force Assn.)

Aerospace Industries Assn. (AIA), *1000 Wilson Blvd., #1700, Arlington, VA 22209-3928; (703) 358-1000. Fax, (703) 358-1012. Marion Blakey, President. Press, (703) 358-1076. General e-mail, aia@aia-aerospace.org Web, www.aia-aerospace.org*

Represents manufacturers of commercial, military, and business aircraft; helicopters; aircraft engines; missiles; spacecraft; and related components and equipment. Interests include international standards and trade.

American Astronautical Society, *6352 Rolling Mill Pl., #102, Springfield, VA 22152; (703) 866-0020. Fax, (703) 866-3526. James R. Kirkpatrick, Executive Director. General e-mail, aas@astronautical.org Web, www.astronautical.org*

Scientific and technological society of researchers, scientists, astronauts, and other professionals in the field of astronautics and spaceflight engineering. Organizes national and local meetings and symposia; promotes international cooperation.

American Institute of Aeronautics and Astronautics (AIAA), *1801 Alexander Bell Dr., #500, Reston, VA 20191; (703) 264-7500. Fax, (703) 264-7551. Robert Dickman, Executive Director. Information, (800) 639-2422. General e-mail, custserv@aiaa.org Web, www.aiaa.org*

Membership: engineers, scientists, and students in the fields of aeronautics and astronautics. Holds workshops on aerospace technical issues for congressional subcommittees; sponsors international conferences. Offers computerized database through its Technical Information Service.

National Research Council (NRC), Aeronautics and Space Engineering Board, *500 5th St. N.W., Keck W932, 9th Floor 20001; (202) 334-2858. Fax, (202) 334-2482. Richard E. Rowberg, Director (Acting). General e-mail, aseb@nas.org Web, www.nationalacademies.org/aseb*

Membership: aeronautics and space experts. Advises government agencies on aeronautics and space engineering research, technology, experiments, international programs, and policy. Library open to the public by appointment.

National Research Council (NRC), Space Studies Board, *Keck Center, 500 5th St. N.W., 10th Floor 20001; (202) 334-3477. Fax, (202) 334-3701. Richard E. Rowberg, Director (Acting). General e-mail, ssb@nas.edu Web, www.nationalacademies.org/ssb*

Provides advice to the government on space policy issues and issues concerning space science activities, including space-based astrophysics, heliophysics, solar system exploration, earth science, and microgravity life and physical sciences. Produces discipline-based "Decadal Surveys," which sets priorities for government investments over ten-year time periods.

National Space Society, *1620 Eye St. N.W., #615 20006; (202) 429-1600. Fax, (202) 463-8497. George Whitesides, Executive Director. General e-mail, nsshq@nss.org Web, www.nss.org*

Membership: individuals interested in space programs and applications of space technology. Provides information on NASA, commercial space activities, and international cooperation; promotes public education on space exploration and development; conducts conferences and workshops; publishes quarterly magazine. Monitors legislation and regulations.

Resources for the Future, *1616 P St. N.W. 20036-1400; (202) 328-5000. Fax, (202) 939-3460. Philip R. Sharp, President. Library, (202) 328-5089. Press, (202) 328-5026. General e-mail, info@rff.org*

Web, www.rff.org

Examines the economic aspects of U.S. space policy, including policy on the space shuttle, unmanned rockets, communications satellites, and the space station. Focuses on the role of private business versus that of government.

Space Policy Institute *(George Washington University), 1957 E St. N.W., #403 20052; (202) 994-7292. Fax, (202) 994-1639. Scott Pace, Director. General e-mail, spi@gwu.edu*

Web, www.gwu.edu/~spi

Conducts research on space policy issues; organizes seminars, symposia, and conferences. Focuses on civilian space activities, including competitive and cooperative interactions on space between the United States and other countries.

Young Astronaut Council, *5200 27th St. N.W. 20015; (301) 617-0923. Fax, (301) 776-0858. T. Wendell Butler, President. General e-mail, youngastronauts@aol.com*

Promotes improved math and science skills through aerospace activities for children ages three to sixteen. Encourages children to pursue careers in aerospace fields.

Astronomy

▶AGENCIES

National Aeronautics and Space Administration (NASA), *Science Mission Directorate, 300 E St. S.W., #3C26 20546; (202) 358-3889. Fax, (202) 358-3092. Edward J. Weiler, Associate Administrator. General e-mail, science@hq.nasa.gov*

Web, http://science.hq.nasa.gov/directorate/index.html

Administers programs that study the composition, energy, mass, position, size, and properties of celestial bodies within the universe, as observed from Earth; participates in international research efforts. Administers NASA's rocket programs.

National Science Foundation (NSF), *Astronomical Sciences, 4201 Wilson Blvd., #1045S, Arlington, VA 22230; (703) 292-8820. Fax, (703) 292-9034. Craig Foltz, Division Director (Acting).*

Web, www.nsf.gov/div/index.jsp?org=AST

Provides grants for ground-based astronomy and astronomical research on planetary astronomy, stellar astronomy and astrophysics, galactic astronomy, extragalactic astronomy and cosmology, and advanced technologies and instrumentation. Maintains astronomical facilities; participates in international projects.

U.S. Naval Observatory *(Defense Dept.), 3450 Massachusetts Ave. N.W. 20392-5420; (202) 762-1467. Fax, (202) 762-1489. Steven Warren, Superintendent. Information, (202) 762-1438. General e-mail, webmaster@usno.navy.mil*

Web, www.usno.navy.mil

Determines the precise positions and motions of celestial bodies. Operates the U.S. master clock. Provides the U.S. Navy and Defense Dept. with astronomical and timing data for navigation, precise positioning, and command, control, and communications.

▶NONGOVERNMENTAL

American Astronomical Society, *2000 Florida Ave. N.W., #400 20009-1231; (202) 328-2010. Fax, (202) 234-2560. Kevin Marvel, Executive Officer. Press, (301) 286-2010, ext. 116. General e-mail, aas@aas.org*

Web, www.uas.org

Membership: astronomers and other professionals interested in the advancement of astronomy in North America and worldwide. Publishes technical journals; holds scientific meetings; participates in international organizations; awards research grants.

American Geophysical Union, *2000 Florida Ave. N.W. 20009-1277; (202) 462-6900. Fax, (202) 328-0566. Robert Van Hook, Executive Director (Interim). Information, (800) 966-2481. General e-mail, service@agu.org*

Web, www.agu.org

Membership: scientists and technologists who study the environments and components of the earth, sun, and solar system. Promotes international cooperation; disseminates information.

Assn. of Universities for Research in Astronomy (AURA), *1212 New York Ave. N.W., #450 20005; (202) 483-2101. Fax, (202) 483-2106. William S. Smith, President. Web, www.aura-astronomy.org*

Consortium of universities. Manages three ground-based observatories and the International Gemini Project for the National Science Foundation and manages the Space Telescope Science Institute for the National Aeronautics and Space Administration.

17 ⚖

Social Services and Disabilities

GENERAL POLICY AND ANALYSIS

Basic Resources

►AGENCIES

Administration for Children and Families (ACF),
*(Health and Human Services Dept.), 901 D St. S.W.,
#600 20447 (mailing address: 370 L'Enfant Promenade
S.W., Washington, DC 20201); (202) 401-2337. Fax, (202)
401-4678. Daniel C. Schneider, Assistant Secretary
(Acting). Public Affairs, (202) 401-9215.
Web, www.acf.hhs.gov*

Administers and funds programs for Native Americans, low-income families and individuals, and persons with disabilities. Responsible for Social Services Block Grants to the states; coordinates Health and Human Services Dept. policy and regulations on child protection, day care, foster care, adoption services, child abuse and neglect, and special services for those with disabilities. Administers the Head Start program and funds the National Runaway Switchboard, (800) 621-4000, and the Domestic Violence Hotline, (800) 799-7233; TTY, (800) 787-3224.

Administration for Children and Families (ACF),
*(Health and Human Services Dept.), Office of
Community Services, 370 L'Enfant Promenade S.W., 5th
Floor 20447; (202) 401-9333. Fax, (202) 401-4694.
Yolanda J. Butler, Director (Acting).
Web, www.acf.hhs.gov*

Administers the Community Services Block Grant and Discretionary Grant programs and the Low-Income Home Energy Assistance Block Grant Program for heating, cooling, and weatherizing low-income households.

Administration for Native Americans *(Health and
Human Services Dept.), 370 L'Enfant Promenade S.W.,
8th Floor West Aerospace Center 20447-0002; (202)
690-7776. Fax, (202) 690-7441. Vacant, Commissioner.
Toll-free, (877) 922-9262.
General e-mail, ana@acf.hhs.gov
Web, www.acf.hhs.gov/programs/ana*

Awards grants for locally determined social and economic development strategies; promotes Native American economic and social self-sufficiency; funds tribes and Native American and Native Hawaiian organizations. Commissioner chairs the Intradepartmental Council on Indian Affairs, which coordinates Native American–related programs.

AmeriCorps *(Corporation for National and Community
Service), Volunteers in Service to America (VISTA),
1201 New York Ave. N.W. 20525; (202) 606-5000. Fax,
(202) 565-2789. Jean Whaley, Director, (202) 606-6943.
Volunteer recruiting information, (800) 942-2677. TTY,
(800) 833-3722; local TTY, (202) 565-2799.
General e-mail, questions@americorps.gov
Web, www.americorps.gov/vista*

Assigns full-time volunteers to public and private nonprofit organizations for one year to alleviate poverty in local communities. Volunteers receive a living allowance and their choice of a stipend or education award.

Bureau of Indian Affairs (BIA), *(Interior Dept.),
Indian Services, Human Services, 1849 C St. N.W., MS
4513-MIB 20240-4001; (202) 513-7642. Fax, (202) 208-
2648. Carl J. Artman, Assistant Secretary. Public Affairs,
(202) 208-3710.
General e-mail, www.doi.gov/bureau-indian-affairs.html*

Gives assistance, in accordance with state payment standards, to American Indians and Alaska Natives of federally recognized tribes living on or near reservations and in tribal service areas, and provides family and individual counseling and child welfare services. Assists tribal and Indian landowners with managing natural and energy trust resources; builds and maintains housing, transportation, energy, and irrigation infrastructure; and provides law enforcement protection, corrections, and administration of justice services on federal Indian lands.

Corporation for National and Community Service,
*1201 New York Ave. N.W. 20525; (202) 606-5000. Fax,
(202) 565-2799. Nicola Goren, Chief Executive Officer
(Acting). Press, (202) 456-7381. Volunteer recruiting
information, (800) 942-2677. TTY, (800) 833-3722; local
TTY, (202) 565-2799.
General e-mail, webmaster@cns.gov*

Web, www.nationalservice.gov

Independent corporation that administers federally sponsored domestic volunteer programs that provide disadvantaged citizens with services, including AmeriCorps, AmeriCorps-VISTA (Volunteers in Service to America), AmeriCorps-NCCC (National Civilian Community Corps), Learn and Serve America, and the National Senior Service Corps.

Food and Nutrition Service *(Agriculture Dept.), 3101
Park Center Dr., #906, Alexandria, VA 22302-1500; (703)
305-2060. Fax, (703) 305-2908. Enrique Gomez,
Administrator (Acting). Information, (703) 305-2286.
Web, www.fns.usda.gov/fns*

Administers all Agriculture Dept. domestic food assistance, including the distribution of funds and food for school breakfast and lunch programs (preschool through secondary) to public and nonprofit private schools; the food stamp program; and a supplemental nutrition program for women, infants, and children (WIC).

Food and Nutrition Service *(Agriculture Dept.), Food
Distribution, 3101 Park Center Dr., #504, Alexandria, VA
22302-1500; (703) 305-2680. Fax, (703) 305-1410. Cathie
McCullough, Director.
Web, www.fns.usda.gov/fdd*

Administers the purchasing and distribution of food to state agencies for child care centers, public and private schools, public and nonprofit charitable institutions, and summer camps. Coordinates the distribution of special commodities, including surplus cheese and butter. Administers the National Commodity Processing Program, which facilitates distribution, at reduced prices, of processed foods to state agencies.

Food and Nutrition Service *(Agriculture Dept.),* *Supplemental Nutrition Assistance Program (SNAP),* *3101 Park Center Dr., #808, Alexandria, VA 22302-1500; (703) 305-2026. Fax, (703) 305-2454. Jessica Shahin, Associate Administrator (Acting).* *Web, www.fns.usda.gov*

Administers SNAP through state welfare agencies to provide needy persons with Electronic Benefit Transfer cards to increase food purchasing power. Provides matching funds to cover half the cost of EBT card issuance.

Health and Human Services Dept. (HHS), *200 Independence Ave. S.W., #615F 20201; (202) 690-7000. Fax, (202) 690-7203. Kathleen Sebelius, Secretary; Tevi David Troy, Deputy Secretary. Press, (202) 690-6343. TTY, (800) 877-8339. Internship Contact, (202) 690-6139. Locator, (202) 619-0257. Toll-free, (877) 696-6775.* *Web, www.hhs.gov*

Acts as principal adviser to the president on health and welfare plans, policies, and programs of the federal government. Encompasses the Centers for Medicare and Medicaid Services, the Administration for Children and Families, the Public Health Service, and the Centers for Disease Control and Prevention.

Health and Human Services Dept. (HHS), *Disability, Aging, and Long-Term Care Policy, 200 Independence Ave. S.W., #424E 20201; (202) 690-6443. Fax, (202) 401-7733. Vacant, Deputy Assistant Secretary.* *Web, http://aspe.hhs.gov/info/orgmission.shtm/#date*

Responsible for the development of financing and service organization/delivery policy—including planning, policy and budget analysis, review of regulations, and formulation of legislation—and for the development and coordination of research and evaluation on issues related to disability, aging, and long-term care policy.

Health and Human Services Dept. (HHS), *Planning and Evaluation, Human Services Policy: Economic Support for Families, 200 Independence Ave. S.W., #404E.5 20201; (202) 690-7148. Fax, (202) 690-6562. Canta Pian, Director.* *Web, www.aspe.hhs.gov*

Collects and disseminates information on human services programs that provide nonelderly populations, including families with children, with cash, employment, training, and related assistance.

Office of Faith-Based and Neighborhood Partnerships *(Executive Office of the President), The White House 20502; (202) 456-6708. Fax, (202) 456-7019. Joshua Dubois, Director.* *Web, www.whitehouse.gov*

▶**CONGRESS**

For a listing of relevant congressional committees and subcommittees, please see page 629 or the Appendix.

Government Accountability Office (GAO), *Education, Workforce, and Income Security, 441 G St. N.W., #5928 20548; (202) 512-7215. Cynthia M. Fagnoni, Managing Director.* *Web, www.gao.gov*

Independent, nonpartisan agency in the legislative branch. Audits, analyzes, and evaluates Health and Human Services Dept. and Corporation for National and Community Service programs; makes reports available to the public. (Formerly the General Accounting Office.)

▶**NONGOVERNMENTAL**

American Enterprise Institute for Public Policy Research (AEI), *Social and Individual Responsibility Project, 1150 17th St. N.W. 20036; (202) 862-5904. Fax, (202) 862-5802. Douglas J. Besharov, Director.* *Web, www.aei.org*

Research and education organization that conducts studies on social welfare policies, including family and welfare policies. Interests include children, child abuse and neglect, divorce, drug abuse, family breakdown, poverty, out-of-wedlock births, and welfare programs.

American Public Human Services Assn., *1133 19th St. N.W., #400 20036; (202) 682-0100. Fax, (202) 289-6555. Jerry Friedman, Executive Director.* *Web, www.aphsa.org*

Membership: state and local human services administrators. Dedicated to developing, promoting, and implementing public human services policies that improve the health and well-being of families, children, adults, and the elderly. Provides training and technical assistance; operates a job bank.

ACORN (Assn. of Community Organizations for Reform Now), *Washington Office, 739 8th St. S.E. 20003; (202) 547-2500. Fax, (202) 546-2483. Steve Kest, Executive Director.* *General e-mail, dcacorn@acorn.org* *Web, www.acorn.org*

Works to advance the interests of minority and low-income families through community organizing and action. Interests include jobs, living wages, housing, welfare reform, and community reinvestment.

Catholic Charities USA, *66 Canal Center Plaza, #600, Alexandria, VA 22314; (703) 549-1390. Fax, (703) 549-1656. Rev. Larry Snyder, President.* *General e-mail, info@catholiccharitiesusa.org* *Web, www.catholiccharitiesusa.org*

Member agencies and institutions provide assistance to persons of all backgrounds; community-based services include day care, counseling, food, and housing. National office provides members with advocacy and professional

SOCIAL SERVICES AND DISABILITIES RESOURCES IN CONGRESS

For a complete listing of Congress committees, including their full contact information, leadership, membership, and jurisdictions, please refer to the Appendix on pages 724–837.

HOUSE:

House Agriculture Committee, Subcommittee on Department Operations, Oversight, Nutrition, and Forestry, (202) 225-6395.
Web, agriculture.house.gov

House Appropriations Committee, Subcommittee on Agriculture, Rural Development, FDA, and Related Agencies, (202) 225-2638.
Web, appropriations.house.gov

Subcommittee on Financial Services and General Government, 202-225-7245.

Subcommittee on Labor, Health and Human Services, Education, and Related Agencies, (202) 225-3508.

Subcommittee on Transportation, HUD, and Related Agencies, (202) 225-2141.

House Education and Labor Committee, (202) 225-3725.
Web, edworkforce.house.gov

Subcommittee on Early Childhood, Elementary, and Secondary Education, (202) 225-3725.

Subcommittee on Health, Employment, Labor, and Pensions, (202) 225-3725.

Subcommittee on Healthy Families and Communities, (202) 225-3725.

Subcommittee on Higher Education, Lifelong Learning, and Competitiveness, (202) 225-3725.

House Energy and Commerce Committee, Subcommittee on Health, (202) 226-2424.
Web, energycommerce.house.gov

House Small Business Committee, Subcommittee on Regulations, Health Care and Trade, (202) 225-4038.
Web, www.house.gov/smbiz

House Veterans' Affairs Committee, Subcommittee on Disability Assistance and Memorial Affairs, (202) 225-9164.
Web, veterans.house.gov

House Ways and Means Committee, (202) 225-3625.
Web, waysandmeans.house.gov

Subcommittee on Health, (202) 225-3943.

Subcommittee on Income Security and Family Support, (202) 225-1025.

Subcommittee on Social Security, (202) 225-9263.

SENATE:

Senate Agriculture, Nutrition, and Forestry Committee, (202) 224-2035.
Web, agriculture.senate.gov

Subcommittee on Nutrition and Food Assistance, Sustainable and Organic Agriculture, and General Legislation, (202) 224-2035.

Senate Appropriations Committee, Subcommittee on Agriculture, Rural Development, FDA, and Related Agencies, (202) 224-8090.
Web, appropriations.senate.gov

Subcommittee on Labor, Health and Human Services, Education, and Related Agencies, (202) 224-9145.

Subcommittee on Transportation, HUD and Related Agencies, (202) 224-7281.

Senate Finance Committee, Subcommittee on Health Care, (202) 224-4515.
Web, finance.senate.gov

Subcommittee on Social Security, Pensions and Family Policy, (202) 225-4515.

Senate Health, Education, Labor, and Pensions Committee, (202) 224-5375.
Web, help.senate.gov

Subcommittee on Children and Families, (202) 224-5630.

Subcommittee on Retirement and Aging, (202) 224-9243.

Senate Special Committee on Aging, (202) 224-5364.
Web, aging.senate.gov

Senate Veterans' Affairs Committee, (202) 224-9126.
Web, veterans.senate.gov

support, including networking, training and consulting, program development, and financial benefits. Represents the Catholic community in times of domestic disaster.

Center for Community Change, *1536 U St. N.W. 20009; (202) 339-9300. Fax, (202) 387-4896. Deepak Bhargava, Executive Director. Toll-free, (877) 777-1536. General e-mail, info@communitychange.org*

Web, www.communitychange.org

Works to strengthen grassroots organizations that help low-income people, working-class people, and

minorities develop skills and resources to improve their communities and change the policies and institutions that affect their lives. Monitors legislation and regulations.

Center for Law and Social Policy, *1015 15th St. N.W., #400 20005; (202) 906-8000. Fax, (202) 842-2885. Alan W. Houseman, Director. General e-mail, info@clasp.org*

Web, www.clasp.org

Public policy organization with expertise in national, state, and local policy affecting low-income Americans.

Seeks to improve the economic security and educational and workforce prospects of low-income children, youth, adults, and families.

Center for the Study of Social Policy, *1575 Eye St. N.W., #500 20005-3922; (202) 371-1565. Fax, (202) 371-1472. Frank Farrow, Director.*
Web, www.cssp.org

Assists states and communities in organizing, financing, and delivering human services, with a focus on children and families. Helps build capacity for local decision making; helps communities use informal supports in the protection of children; promotes nonadversarial approach to class action litigation on behalf of dependent children.

Christian Relief Services, *2550 Huntington Ave., #200, Alexandria, VA 22303; (703) 317-9086. Fax, (703) 317-9690. Bryan L. Krizek, Chief Executive Officer. Information, (800) 33-RELIEF.*
General e-mail, info@christianrelief.org

Web, www.christianrelief.org

Promotes economic development and the alleviation of poverty in urban areas of the United States, Appalachia, Native American reservations, and Africa. Donates medical supplies and food; administers housing, hospital, and school construction programs; provides affordable housing for low-income individuals and families.

Coalition on Human Needs, *1120 Connecticut Ave. N.W., #910 20036; (202) 223-2532. Fax, (202) 223-2538. Deborah Weinstein, Executive Director.*
General e-mail, info@chn.org

Web, www.chn.org

Promotes public policies that address the needs of low-income Americans. Members include civil rights, religious, labor, and professional organizations and service providers concerned with the well-being of children, women, the elderly, and people with disabilities.

Community Action Partnership, *1140 Connecticut Ave. N.W., #1210 20036; (202) 265-7546. Fax, (202) 265-5048. Donald W. Mathis, President.*
General e-mail, info@communityactionpartnership.com

Web, www.communityactionpartnership.com

Provides community action agencies with information, training, and technical assistance; advocates, at all levels of government, for low-income people.

Council on Social Work Education, *1725 Duke St., #500, Alexandria, VA 22314-3457; (703) 683-8080. Fax, (703) 683-8099. Julia Watkins, Executive Director.*
General e-mail, info@cswe.org

Web, www.cswe.org

Membership: educational and professional institutions, social welfare agencies, and private citizens. Promotes high-quality education in social work. Accredits social work programs.

Food Research and Action Center (FRAC), *1875 Connecticut Ave. N.W., #540 20009-5728; (202) 986-2200. Fax, (202) 986-2525. James D. Weill, President.*
General e-mail, comments@frac.org

Web, www.frac.org

Public interest advocacy, research, and legal center that works to end hunger and poverty in the United States; offers legal assistance, organizational aid, training, and information to groups seeking to improve or expand federal food programs, including food stamp, child nutrition, and WIC (women, infants, and children) programs; conducts studies relating to hunger and poverty; coordinates network of antihunger organizations. Monitors legislation and regulations.

Foundation for International Community Assistance (FINCA), *1101 14th St. N.W., 11th Floor 20005; (202) 682-1510. Fax, (202) 682-1535. Rupert Scofield, President.*
General e-mail, info@villagebanking.org

Web, www.villagebanking.org

Provides financial services to low-income entrepreneurs outside the United States in order to create jobs, build assets, and improve standards of living. Delivers microfinance products and services through a network of wholly owned programs in Africa, Eurasia, the Middle East, and Latin America, operating on commercial principals of performance and sustainability. Focuses efforts on those living on less than $2/day.

Goodwill Industries International, *15810 Indianola Dr., Rockville, MD 20855; (301) 530-6500. Fax, (301) 530-1516. Jim Gibbons, President. Toll-free, (800) 741-0186.*
General e-mail, contactus@goodwill.org

Web, www.goodwill.org

Serves people with disabilities, low-wage workers, and others by providing education and career services, as well as job placement opportunities and post-employment support. Helps people become independent, tax-paying members of their communities.

Grameen Foundation, *50 F St. N.W., 8th Floor 20001; (202) 628-3560. Fax, (202) 628-3880. Alex Counts, President. Toll-free, (888) 764-3872.*
Web, www.grameenfoundation.org

Seeks to eliminate poverty by providing microfinance and technology products and services in sub-Saharan Africa, Asia, the Arab world, and the Americas. Focuses on assistance to women seeking to start or expand their own businesses. Identifies and promotes large-scale strategies that move people out of poverty.

Hudson Institute, *National Security Studies, 1015 15th St. N.W., 6th Floor 20005; (202) 974-2400. Fax, (202) 974-2410. Kenneth R. Weinstein, Chief Executive Officer. Press, (202) 974-2417.*
General e-mail, info@hudson.org

Web, www.hudson.org

Studies welfare policy; helps states create welfare reform programs.

Institute for Women's Policy Research (IWPR), *1707 L St. N.W., #750 20036; (202) 785-5100. Fax, (202) 833-4362. Heidi Hartmann, President.*
General e-mail, iwpr@iwpr.org

Web, www.iwpr.org

Public policy research organization that focuses on women's issues, including welfare reform, family and work policies, employment and wages, and discrimination based on gender, race, or ethnicity.

National Assn. for the Advancement of Colored People (NAACP), *Washington Bureau, 1156 15th St. N.W., #915 20005-1750; (202) 463-2940. Fax, (202) 463-2953. Hilary O. Shelton, Director.*
General e-mail, washingtonbureau@naacpnet.org

Web, www.naacp.org

Membership: persons interested in civil rights for all minorities. Interests include welfare reform and related social welfare matters. Administers programs that create employment and affordable housing opportunities and that improve health care. Monitors legislation and regulations. (Headquarters in Baltimore, Md.)

National Assn. of Social Workers, *750 1st St. N.E., #700 20002-4241; (202) 408-8600. Fax, (202) 336-8313. Elizabeth J. Clark, Executive Director; Elvira Craig de Silva, President.*
General e-mail, membership@naswdc.org

Web, www.socialworkers.org/pace

Membership: graduates of accredited social work education programs and students in accredited programs. Promotes the interests of social workers and their clients; promotes professional standards; certifies members of the Academy of Certified Social Workers; conducts research.

National Community Action Foundation (NCAF), *1 Massachusetts Ave. N.W., #310 20001; (202) 842-2092. Fax, (202) 842-2095. David A. Bradley, Executive Director.*
General e-mail, DavidBradley@ncaf.org

Web, www.ncaf.org

Organization for community action agencies concerned with issues that affect the poor. Provides information on Community Services Block Grants, low-income energy assistance, employment and training, weatherization of low-income housing, nutrition, and the Head Start program.

National Human Services Assembly, *1319 F St. N.W., #402 20004; (202) 347-2080. Fax, (202) 393-4517. Irv Katz, President.*
General e-mail, nassembly@nassembly.org

Web, www.nassembly.org

Membership: national voluntary health and human service organizations. Provides collective leadership in the areas of health and human service. Provides members' professional staff and volunteers with a forum to share information. Supports public policies, programs, and resources that advance the effectiveness of health and human service organizations and their service delivery. (Formerly the National Assembly of Health and Human Services Organizations.)

National Urban League, *Washington Office, 2901 14th Street N.W. 20009; (202) 265-8200. Fax, (202) 265-6122. Maudine R. Cooper, President.*
Web, www.gwul.org

Social service organization concerned with the social welfare of African Americans and other minorities. (Headquarters in New York.)

Poverty and Race Research Action Council, *1015 15th St. N.W., #400 20005; (202) 906-8023. Fax, (202) 842-2885. Philip Tegeler, Executive Director.*
General e-mail, info@prrac.org

Web, www.prrac.org

Facilitates cooperative links between researchers and activists who work on race and poverty issues. Publishes bimonthly *Poverty and Race* and a civil rights history curriculum guide. Policy research areas include housing, education, and health disparities.

Public Welfare Foundation, *1200 U St. N.W. 20009-4443; (202) 965-1800. Fax, (202) 265-8851. Deborah Leff, President.*
General e-mail, info@publicwelfare.org

Web, www.publicwelfare.org

Seeks to assist disadvantaged populations overcome barriers to full participation in society. Awards grants to nonprofits in the following areas: criminal and juvenile justice, health reform, and workers' rights.

Salvation Army, *P.O. Box 269, Alexandria, VA 22313-0269; (703) 684-5500. Fax, (703) 684-3478. Israel Gaither, National Commander.*
General e-mail, usn_national_commander@usn.salvation-army.org

Web, www.salvationarmy.org

International religious social welfare organization that provides social services, including counseling, youth and senior citizens services, emergency help, foster care, settlement and day care, tutoring for the mentally disabled, programs for people with physical disabilities, prison work, summer camps, community centers, employment services, rehabilitation programs for alcohol and drug abusers, missing persons bureaus, and residences for the homeless. (International headquarters in London.)

Share Our Strength, *1730 M St. N.W., #700 20036; (202) 393-2925. Fax, (202) 347-5868. Bill Shore, Executive Director. Toll-free, (800) 969-4767.*
General e-mail, info@strength.org

Web, www.strength.org

Works to alleviate and prevent hunger and poverty for families and children in the United States and around the world. Meets immediate demands for food by providing food assistance; treats malnutrition and other consequences of hunger; promotes economic independence among people in need while seeking long-term solutions to hunger and poverty. Helps mobilize industries, organizations, and individuals to contribute their talents to anti-hunger efforts.

Stalking Resource Center, *2000 M St. N.W., #480 20036; (202) 467-8700. Fax, (202) 467-8701. Michelle Garcia, Director.*

General e-mail, src@ncvc.org

Web, www.ncvc.org/src/main.aspx

Acts as an information clearinghouse on stalking. Works to raise public awareness of the dangers of stalking. Encourages the development of multidisciplinary responses to stalking in local communities. Offers practitioner training and peer-to-peer exchange programs. (Affiliated with the National Center for Victims of Crime.)

United Jewish Communities (UJC), *Washington Office, 1720 Eye St. N.W., #800 20006; (202) 785-5900. Fax, (202) 785-4937. William Daroff, Director.*

General e-mail, dc@ujc.org

Web, www.ujc.org

Fundraising organization. Sustains and enhances the quality of Jewish life domestically and internationally. Advocates the needs of the Jewish community. Offers marketing, communications, and public relations support; coordinates a speakers bureau and Israeli emissaries. (Headquarters in New York.)

Urban Institute, *2100 M St. N.W. 20037; (202) 833-7200. Fax, (202) 728-0232. Robert D. Reischauer, President. Information, (202) 261-5709. Library, (202) 261-5688. General e-mail, paffairs@urban.org*

Web, www.urban.org

Nonpartisan public policy research and education organization. Interests include states' use of federal funds; delivery of social services to specific groups, including children of mothers in welfare reform programs; retirement policy, income, and community-based services for the elderly; job placement and training programs for welfare recipients; health care cost containment and access; food stamps; child nutrition; the homeless; housing; immigration; justice policy and prisoner reentry; federal, state, and local tax policy; and education policy. Library open to the public by appointment.

U.S. Conference of City Human Services Officials, *1620 Eye St. N.W., 4th Floor 20006; (202) 293-7330. Fax, (202) 293-2352. Crystal D. Swann, Assistant Executive Director. General e-mail, info@usmayors.org*

Web, www.usmayors.org/humanservices

Promotes improved social services for specific urban populations through meetings, technical assistance, and training programs for members; fosters information exchange among federal, state, and local governments, human services experts, and other groups concerned with human services issues. (Affiliate of the U.S. Conference of Mayors.)

CHILDREN AND FAMILIES

▶AGENCIES

Administration for Children and Families (ACF), *(Health and Human Services Dept.), 901 D St. S.W., #600 20447 (mailing address: 370 L'Enfant Promenade S.W., Washington, DC 20201); (202) 401-2337. Fax, (202) 401-4678. Daniel C. Schneider, Assistant Secretary (Acting). Public Affairs, (202) 401-9215.*

Web, www.acf.hhs.gov

Plans, manages, and coordinates national assistance programs that promote stability, economic security, responsibility, and self-support for families; supervises programs and the use of funds to provide the most needy with aid and to increase alternatives to public assistance. Programs include Temporary Assistance to Needy Families, Child Welfare, Head Start, Child Support Enforcement, Low-Income Home Energy Assistance, Community Services Block Grant, and Refugee Resettlement Assistance.

Administration for Children and Families (ACF) *(Health and Human Services Dept.), Children's Bureau, 1250 Maryland Ave. S.W., 8th Floor 20029; (202) 205-8618. Fax, (202) 205-9721. Joseph Bock, Associate Commissioner (Acting).*

Web, www.acf.hhs.gov/programs/cb

Works with state and local agencies to develop programs that focus on preventing the abuse of children in troubled families, protecting children from further abuse, and finding permanent placements for those who cannot safely return to their homes. Administers grants.

Administration for Children and Families (ACF), *(Health and Human Services Dept.), Child Support Enforcement, 901 D St. S.W. 20447 (mailing address: 370 L'Enfant Promenade S.W., Washington, DC 20447); (202) 401-9370. Fax, (202) 401-5494. Donna Bonar, Deputy Commissioner (Acting). Information, (202) 401-9373.*

Web, www.acf.hhs.gov/programs/cse

Helps states develop, manage, and operate child support programs. Maintains the Federal Parent Locator Service, which provides state and local child support agencies with information for locating absent parents. State enforcement agencies locate absent parents, establish paternity, establish and enforce support orders, and collect child support payments.

Administration for Children and Families (ACF) *(Health and Human Services Dept.), Family and Youth Services, 1250 Maryland Ave. S.W., 8th Floor 20201; (202)*

205-8347. Fax, (202) 205-9721. Maiso Bryant, Associate Commissioner (Acting).
Web, www.acf.hhs.gov/programs/fysb

Administers federal discretionary grant programs for projects serving runaway and homeless youth and for projects that deter youth involvement in gangs. Provides youth service agencies with training and technical assistance. Monitors federal policies, programs, and legislation. Supports research on youth development issues, including gangs, runaways, and homeless youth. Operates national clearinghouse on families and youth. Issues grants and monitors abstinence education programs.

Administration for Children and Families (ACF),
(Health and Human Services Dept.), Family Assistance,
901 D St. S.W. 20447 (mailing address: 370 L'Enfant Promenade S.W., Washington, DC 20447); (202) 401-9275. Fax, (202) 205-5887. Ann Barbagallo, Director (Acting).
Web, www.acf.hhs.gov/programs/ofa

Provides leadership, direction, and technical guidance to the states and territories on administration of the TANF (Temporary Assistance to Needy Families) Block Grant. Focuses efforts to increase economic independence and productivity for families. Provides direction and guidance in collection and dissemination of performance and other data for these programs.

Cooperative State Research, Education, and Extension Service *(Agriculture Dept.), Families, 4-H, and Nutrition, 800 9th St. S.W. 20024 (mailing address: 1400 Independence Ave., S.W., Washington, DC 20250-2225); (202) 720-2908. Fax, (202) 720-9366. Dan Kugler, Deputy Administrator (Acting).*
Web, www.csrees.usda.gov

Administers education programs with state land-grant universities and county governments for rural and urban youth ages five to nineteen. Projects provide youth with development skills and experience in the fields of science and technological literacy, nutrition, environment, natural resources, health, leadership, citizenship, service, and personal growth and responsibility.

Food and Nutrition Service *(Agriculture Dept.), Child Nutrition, 3101 Park Center Dr., #640, Alexandria, VA 22302 1500; (703) 305-2590. Fax, (703) 305-2879. Cindy Long, Director. Press, (703) 305-2286.*
Web, www.fns.usda.gov/cnd

Administers the transfer of funds to state agencies for the National School Lunch Program; the School Breakfast Program; the Special Milk Program, which helps schools and institutions provide children who do not have access to full meals under other child nutrition programs with fluid milk; the Child and Adult Care Food Program, which provides children in nonresidential child-care centers and family day-care homes with year-round meal service; and the Summer Food Service Program, which provides children from low-income areas with meals during the summer months. Administers the Child Nutrition Labeling Program, which certifies that foods served in school lunch and breakfast programs meet nutritional requirements.

Food and Nutrition Service *(Agriculture Dept.),*
Research, Nutrition, and Analysis, 3101 Park Center Dr., #1014, Alexandria, VA 22302-1500; (703) 305-2017. Fax, (703) 305-2576. Steve Carlson, Director.
General e-mail, oaneweb@fns.usda.gov
Web, www.fns.usda.gov/oane

Administers the Nutrition Education and Training Program, which provides states with grants for disseminating nutrition information to children and for in-service training of food service and teaching personnel; provides information and technical assistance in nutrition and food service management.

Food and Nutrition Service *(Agriculture Dept.),*
Supplemental Food Programs, 3101 Park Center Dr., #520, Alexandria, VA 22302-1500; (703) 305-2746. Fax, (703) 305-2196. Patricia N. Daniels, Director.
Web, www.fns.usda.gov

Provides health departments and agencies with federal funding for food supplements and administrative expenses to make food, nutrition education, and health services available to infants, young children, and pregnant, nursing, and postpartum women.

Health and Human Services Dept. (HHS), *Head Start,*
1250 Maryland Ave. S.W., 8th Floor 20024; (202) 205-8573. Fax, (202) 260-9663. Patricia Brown, Director (Acting).
Web, www.hhs.gov/headstart

Awards grants to nonprofit and for-profit organizations and local governments for operating community Head Start programs (comprehensive development programs for children, ages three to five, of low-income families); manages a limited number of parent and child centers for families with children up to age three. Conducts research and manages demonstration programs, including those under the Comprehensive Child Care Development Act of 1988; administers the Child Development Associate scholarship program, which trains individuals for careers in child development, often as Head Start teachers.

Health and Human Services Dept. (HHS), *Planning and Evaluation, Human Services Policy: Children and Youth Policy, 200 Independence Ave. S.W., #405F 20201; (202) 690-7409. Fax, (202) 690-5514. Martha Moorehouse, Director.*
Web, www.hhs.gov

Develops policies and procedures for programs that benefit children, youth, and families. Interests include child protection, domestic violence, family support, gang violence, child care and development, and care for drug-exposed, runaway, and homeless children and their families.

Justice Department (DOJ), *Violence Against Women,* *800 K St. N.W., #920 20530; (202) 307-6026. Fax, (202) 305-2589. Catherine Pierce, Director (Acting). TTY, (202) 307-2277. National Domestic Violence Hotline, (800) 799-SAFE.*
Web, www.ovw.usdoj.gov

Seeks more effective policies and services to combat domestic violence, sexual assault, stalking, and other crimes against women. Helps administer grants to states to fund shelters, crisis centers, and hotlines, and to hire law enforcement officers, prosecutors, and counselors specializing in cases of sexual violence and other violent crimes against women.

National Institute of Child Health and Human Development *(National Institutes of Health), Center for Research for Mothers and Children, 6100 Executive Blvd., #4B05, Bethesda, MD 20892-7510; (301) 496-5098. Fax, (301) 480-7773. Dorothy Tucker, Director.*
Web, www.nichd.nih.gov/about/org/crmc

Supports biomedical and behavioral science research and training for maternal and child health care. Areas of study include fetal development, maternal-infant health problems, HIV-related diseases in childbearing women, roles of nutrients and hormones in child growth, developmental disabilities, and behavioral development. Also supports research into the effects and effectiveness of pharmaceuticals on maternal and child health.

Office of Justice Programs (OJP), *(Justice Dept.), Juvenile Justice and Delinquency Prevention, 810 7th St. N.W. 20531; (202) 307-5911. Fax, (202) 514-6382. Jeff Slowikowski, Administrator (Acting). Clearinghouse, (800) 851-3420.*
Web, www.ojjdp.ncjrs.org

Administers federal programs related to prevention and treatment of juvenile delinquency, missing and exploited children, child victimization, and research and evaluation of the juvenile justice system; coordinates with youth programs of the departments of Agriculture, Education, Housing and Urban Development, Interior, and Labor, and of the Substance Abuse and Mental Health Services Administration, including the Center for Studies of Crime and Delinquency. Operates the Juvenile Justice Clearinghouse.

▶**CONGRESS**

For a listing of relevant congressional committees and subcommittees, please see page 629 or the Appendix.

▶**NONGOVERNMENTAL**

Alliance for Children and Families, *Public Policy and Civil Engagement Office, 1001 Connecticut Ave. N.W., #601 20036; (202) 429-0400. Fax, (202) 429-0178. Patrick Lester, Senior Vice President, Public Policy.*
General e-mail, policy@alliance1.org
Web, www.alliance1.org

Provides resources and leadership to more than 300 nonprofit child- and family-serving organizations in the United States and Canada. Works to strengthen community-based programs and services to families, children, and communities. Monitors legislation. (Headquarters in Milwaukee, Wis. Affiliated with United Neighborhood Centers of America.)

American Assn. for Marriage and Family Therapy, *112 S. Alfred St., Alexandria, VA 22314; (703) 838-9808. Fax, (703) 838-9805. Michael Bowers, Executive Director.*
General e-mail, central@aamft.org
Web, www.aamft.org

Membership: professional marriage and family therapists. Promotes professional standards in marriage and family therapy through training programs; provides the public with educational material and online referral service for marriage and family therapy.

American Bar Assn. (ABA), *Center on Children and the Law, 740 15th St. N.W. 20005-1022; (202) 662-1720. Fax, (202) 662-1755. Howard Davidson, Director.*
General e-mail, ctrchildlaw@abanet.org
Web, www.abanet.org/child

Works to increase lawyer representation of children; sponsors speakers and conferences; monitors legislation. Interests include child sexual abuse and exploitation, missing and runaway children, parental kidnapping, child support, foster care, and adoption of children with special needs.

American Coalition for Fathers and Children, *Washington Office, 1718 M St. N.W., #187 20036; (800) 978-3237. Fax, (703) 442-5313. Michael McCormick, Executive Director.*
General e-mail, info@acfc.org
Web, www.acfc.us

Advocates for reform of family law and promotes equal rights for all parties affected by the breakup of a family unit. Seeks to prevent separation of children from fathers and grandparents and the emotional and psychological damage to children that might result from custody battles. Monitors legislation concerning family law. (Headquarters in Lake Forest, Calif.)

American Humane Assn., *Public Policy, Washington Office, 206 N. Washington St., #300, Alexandria, VA 22314; (703) 836-7387. Fax, (703) 549-5437. Allie Phillips, Director of Government Affairs.*
General e-mail, publicpolicy@americanhumane.org
Web, www.americanhumane.org

Membership: humane societies, individuals, and government agencies concerned with child and animal protection laws. Prepares model state legislation on child abuse and its prevention; publishes surveys on child and animal abuse and state abuse laws. (Headquarters in Denver, Colo.)

American Youth Work Center, *1331 H St. N.W., #701 20005; (202) 785-0764. Fax, (202) 728-0657. William Treanor, Executive Director.*

General e-mail, info@youthtoday.org

Web, www.youthtoday.org

Publishes *Youth Today: The Newspaper on Youth Work.* Coverage includes juvenile justice and community-based youth services, including runaway shelters, hotlines, crisis intervention centers, drug programs, alternative education, and job training and placement. Provides youth programs with information on dealing effectively with young people.

America's Promise Alliance, *1110 Vermont Ave. N.W., #900 20005; (202) 657-0600. Fax, (202) 657-0601. Alma Johnson Powell, Chair; Margueritte W. Kondracke, President.*

General e-mail, publications@americaspromise.org

Web, www.americaspromise.org

Works with national and local organizations to support America's youth. Interests include adult mentoring, safe environments, physical and psychological health, effective education, and opportunities to help others. Seeks to reduce the high school dropout rate.

Boys and Girls Clubs of America, *Washington Office, 1325 G St. N.W., #500 20005; (202) 478-6200. Roxanne Spillett, President (located in Atlanta).*

General e-mail, info@bgca.org

Web, www.bgca.org

National network of neighborhood-based facilities that provide programs for underserved children six to eighteen years old, conducted by professional staff. Programs emphasize leadership development, education and career exploration, financial literacy, health and life skills, the arts, sports, fitness and recreation, and family outreach. (Headquarters in Atlanta, Ga.)

Boy Scouts of America, *National Capitol Area Council, Marriott Scout Service Center, 9190 Rockville Pike, Bethesda, MD 20814-3897; (301) 530-9360. Fax, (301) 564-9513. Alan F. Lambert, Scout Executive.*

Web, www.boyscouts-ncac.org

Educational service organization for youth that supports more than 300 local councils that provide quality youth programs, including cub scouting, boy scouting, and venturing. (Headquarters in Irving, Texas.)

Children's Defense Fund, *25 E St. N.W. 20001; (202) 628-8787. Fax, (202) 662-3510. Marian Wright Edelman, President.*

General e-mail, cdfinfo@childrensdefense.org

Web, www.childrensdefense.org

Advocacy group concerned with programs and policies for children and youth, particularly poor and minority children. Interests include health care, child welfare and mental health, early childhood development, education and youth development, child care, job training and employment, and family support. Works to ensure educational and job opportunities for youth.

Children's Home Society and Family Services, *8555 16th St., #600, Silver Spring, MD 20910; (301) 587-7068. Fax, (301) 587-3869. Colleen McLain, Executive Director.*

General e-mail, inquire@chsfs.org

Web, www.chsfs.org

Provides information on international adoption; sponsors seminars and workshops for adoptive and prospective adoptive parents. (Headquarters in St. Paul, Minn.)

Children's Rights Council (CRC), *8181 Professional Pl., #240, Landover, MD 20785; (301) 459-1220. Fax, (301) 459-1227. Myrna B. Murdoch, Chief Executive Officer. Toll-free, (800) 787-KIDS.*

General e-mail, crdc@erols.com

Web, www.crckids.org

Membership: parents and professionals. Works to strengthen families through education and advocacy. Supports family formation and preservation. Conducts conferences and serves as an information clearinghouse. Interests include children whose parents are separated, unwed, or divorced.

Child Welfare League of America, *2345 Crystal Dr., #250, Arlington, VA 22202; (703) 412-2400. Fax, (703) 412-2401. Christine L. James-Brown, President.*

Web, www.cwla.org

Membership: public and private child welfare agencies. Develops standards for the field; provides information on adoption, day care, foster care, group home services, child protection, residential care for children and youth, services to pregnant adolescents and young parents, and other child welfare issues.

Christian Children's Fund (CCF), *Washington Office, 1717 N St. N.W. 20036; (202) 955-7951. Fax, (202) 955-6166. Laura N. Henderson, Director.*

General e-mail, washington@ccfusa.org

Web, www.christianchildrensfund.org

Works internationally to ensure the survival, protection, and development of children. Promotes the improvement in quality of life of children within the context of family, community, and culture. Helps children in unstable situations brought on by war, natural disasters, and other high-risk circumstances. (Headquarters in Richmond, Va.)

Coalition for Marriage, Family, and Couples Education (CMFCE), *5310 Belt Rd. N.W. 20015-1961; (202) 362-3332. Fax, (202) 362-0973. Diane Sollee, Director.*

General e-mail, cmfce@smartmarriages.com

Web, www.smartmarriages.com

Acts as a clearinghouse for marriage educators and couples seeking courses on marriage and relationships. Maintains a directory of marriage education courses and other outlets for marriage educator training. Hosts annual marriage education conference. Supports community initiatives, legislation, and research.

Council for Professional Recognition, *Child Development Associate National Credentialing Program,* 2460 16th St. N.W. 20009-3575; (202) 265-9090. Fax, (202) 265-9161. Deborah Jordan, Deputy Director.
General e-mail, feedback@cdacouncil.org

Web, www.cdacouncil.org

Promotes high standards for early childhood teachers. Awards credentials to family day care, preschool, home visitor, and infant-toddler caregivers.

Cradle of Hope, 8630 Fenton St., #310, Silver Spring, MD 20910; (301) 587-4400. Fax, (301) 588-3091. Linda Perilstein, Executive Director.
General e-mail, cradle@cradlehope.org

Web, www.cradlehope.org

International adoption center specializing in the placement of children from the former Soviet Union, Eastern Europe, China, and Latin America. Offers pre- and post-adoption support services. Sponsors the Bridge of Hope program, a summer camp where older Russian children meet and spend time with potential host families, in several U.S. locations, including the Washington, D.C., metro region.

Every Child Matters, 2000 M St. N.W., #203 20036; (202) 223-8177. Fax, (202) 223-8499. Michael Petit, President, (202) 223-8870.
General e-mail, info@everychildmatters.org

Web, www.everychildmatters.org

Works to make children's needs a political priority through public education activities. Interests include prevention of child abuse and neglect, improvement of the health of low-income children, solutions in child care, early childhood education, and after-school programs.

Family and Home Network, P.O. Box 545, Merrifield, VA 22116; (703) 352-1072. Fax, (703) 352-1076. Cathy Meyers, Executive Director.
General e-mail, fahn@familyandhome.org

Web, www.familyandhome.org

Provides information and support for parents who stay home, or who would like to stay home (full or part time), to raise their children, in the United States and abroad. Monitors legislation and regulations relating to family issues. (Formerly Mothers at Home.)

Generations United, 1333 H St. N.W., #900 20005; (202) 289-3979. Fax, (202) 289-3952. Donna M. Butts, Executive Director.
General e-mail, gu@gu.org

Web, www.gu.org

Membership organization that promotes intergenerational programs and public policies. Focuses on the economic, social, and personal benefits of intergenerational cooperation. Encourages collaboration between organizations that represent different age groups.

Girl Scouts of the U.S.A., *Public Policy and Advocacy,* 816 Connecticut Ave. N.W., 3rd Floor 20006; (202) 659-3780. Fax, (202) 331-8065. Laurie Westley, Senior Vice President.
Web, www.girlscouts.org

Educational service organization for girls ages five to seventeen that promotes personal development through social action, leadership, and other projects. Areas of advocacy include girls' healthy living, increasing girls' participation in STEM (science, technology, engineering, and math) fields, financial literacy, career education, and supporting girls in underserved communities. (Headquarters in New York.)

International Youth Advocate Foundation, P.O. Box 39127 20016; (202) 244-6410. Fax, (202) 244-6396. Mubarak E. Awad, Director.
General e-mail, mawad@iyaf.org

Web, www.iyaf.org

Supports the development and operation of community-based services for at-risk youth and their families. (Formerly the National Youth Advocate Program. Affiliated with Youth Advocate Program International.)

Kidsave, *Washington Office,* 5165 MacArthur Blvd. N.W. 20016; (202) 237-7283. Fax, (202) 237-7080. Terry Baugh, President.
General e-mail, info@kidsave.org

Web, www.kidsave.org

Maintains programs that provide children age eight and older in orphanages and foster care the opportunity for weekend visits and short stays with families in the community with the goal of permanent adoption or long-term mentoring. Monitors child welfare legislation and regulations worldwide.

National Assn. for the Education of Young Children, 1313 L St. N.W., #500 20005; (202) 232-8777. Fax, (202) 328-1846. Mark R. Ginsberg, Executive Director. Information, (800) 424-2460.
General e-mail, naeyc@naeyc.org

Web, www.naeyc.org

Membership: early childhood professionals and parents. Works to improve the quality of early childhood care and education. Administers national accreditation system for early childhood programs. Maintains information service.

National Black Child Development Institute, 1313 L St. N.W., #110 20005-4110; (202) 833-2220. Fax, (202) 833-8222. Carol Brunson Day, President.
General e-mail, moreinfo@nbcdi.org

Web, www.nbcdi.org

Advocacy group for African American children, youth, and families. Interests include child care, adoption, and health, and early childhood education. Provides information on government policies that affect African American children, youth, and families.

National Campaign to Prevent Teen and Unplanned Pregnancy, *1776 Massachusetts Ave. N.W., #200 20036; (202) 478-8500. Fax, (202) 478-8588. Sarah S. Brown, Chief Executive Officer.*
General e-mail, campaign@teenpregnancy.org

Web, www.teenpregnancy.org

Nonpartisan initiative that seeks to reduce the U.S. teen pregnancy rate. Provides education and information regarding contraception.

National Center for Missing and Exploited Children, *Charles B. Wang International Children's Building, 699 Prince St., Alexandria, VA 22314-3175; (703) 274-3900. Fax, (703) 274-2200. Ernest Allen, President. TTY, (800) 826-7653. Toll-free hotline, (800) 843-5678.*
Web, www.missingkids.com

Private organization funded primarily by the Justice Dept. Assists parents and citizens' groups in locating and safely returning missing children; offers technical assistance to law enforcement agencies; coordinates public and private missing children programs; maintains database that coordinates information on missing children.

National Child Support Enforcement Assn., *1109 Spring St., #700, Silver Spring, MD 20910; (240) 595-6600. Fax, (301) 587-1683. Colleen Delaney Eubanks, Executive Director.*
Web, www.ncsea.org

Promotes enforcement of child support obligations and educates social workers, attorneys, judges, and other professionals on child support issues. Fosters exchange of ideas among child support professionals. Monitors legislation and regulations.

National Coalition Against Domestic Violence, *Washington Office, 1633 Q St. N.W., #210 20009; (202) 745-1211. Fax, (202) 745-0088. Rita Smith, Executive Director. TTY, (202) 745-2042.*
General e-mail, PublicPolicy@ncadv.org

Web, www.ncadv.org

Monitors legislation and public policy initiatives concerning violence against women and family safety. Work includes empowering victims, promoting and coordinating direct services, and educating the public about domestic violence. (Headquarters in Denver, Colo.)

National Collaboration for Youth, *1319 F St. N.W., #402 20004; (202) 347-2080. Fax, (202) 393-4517. Irv Katz, President.*
Web, www.nydic.org

Membership: national youth-serving organizations. Works to improve members' youth development programs through information exchange and other support. Raises public awareness of youth issues. Monitors legislation and regulations. (Affiliate of the National Human Services Assembly.)

National Congress of Parents and Teachers, *Programs, Washington Office, 1400 L St. N.W., #300 20005-9998;*
(202) 289-6790. Fax, (202) 289-6791. Sheri Johnson, Director.
General e-mail, info@pta.org

Web, www.pta.org

Membership: parent-teacher associations at the preschool, elementary, and secondary levels. Supports school breakfast and lunch programs; works as an active member of the Child Nutrition Forum, which supports federally funded nutrition programs for children. (Headquarters in Chicago, Ill.)

National Council for Adoption, *225 N. Washington St., Alexandria, VA 22314-2561; (703) 299-6633. Fax, (703) 299-6004. Chuck Johnson, Chief Operating Officer.*
General e-mail, ncfa@adoptioncouncil.org

Web, www.adoptioncouncil.org

Organization of individuals, national and international agencies, and corporations interested in adoption. Supports adoption through legal, ethical agencies; advocates the right to confidentiality in adoption. Conducts research and holds conferences; provides information; supports pregnancy counseling, maternity services, and counseling for infertile couples. Monitors legislation and regulations.

National Family Caregivers Assn., *10400 Connecticut Ave., #500, Kensington, MD 20895-3944; (301) 942-6430. Fax, (301) 942-2302. Suzanne Mintz, President. Toll-free, (800) 896-3650.*
General e-mail, info@thefamilycaregiver.org

Web, www.thefamilycaregiver.org

Seeks to increase the quality of life of family caregivers by providing support and information; works to raise public awareness of caregiving through educational activities.

National Fatherhood Initiative, *101 Lake Forest Blvd., #360, Gaithersburg, MD 20877; (301) 948-0599. Fax, (301) 948-4325. Roland Warren, President.*
General e-mail, info@fatherhood.org

Web, www.fatherhood.org

Works to improve the well-being of children by increasing the proportion of children growing up with involved, responsible, and committed fathers. Provides curricula, training, and assistance to state and community fatherhood initiatives. Conducts public awareness campaigns and research. Monitors legislation.

National 4-H Council, *7100 Connecticut Ave., Chevy Chase, MD 20815-4999; (301) 961-2800. Fax, (301) 961-2894. Donald T. Floyd Jr., President. Press, (301) 961-2972.*
Web, www.fourhcouncil.edu

4-H membership: young people across the United States learning leadership, citizenship, and life skills. National 4-H Council is a national, private-sector partner of the 4-H Youth Development Program and its parent, the Cooperative Extension System of the U.S. Department of Agriculture.

National Head Start Assn., *1651 Prince St., Alexandria, VA 22314; (703) 739-0875. Fax, (703) 739-0878. Michael McGrady, President (Acting).*
Web, www.nhsa.org

Membership: organizations that represent Head Start children, families, and staff. Recommends strategies on issues affecting Head Start programs; provides training and professional development opportunities. Monitors legislation and regulations.

National Network for Youth, *1140 Connecticut Ave. N.W., #210 20036; (202) 783-7949. Fax, (202) 783-7955. Victoria Wagner, Executive Director.*
General e-mail, info@nn4youth.org
Web, www.nn4youth.org

Membership: providers of services related to runaway and homeless youth. Offers technical assistance to new and existing youth projects. Monitors legislation and regulations.

National Network to End Domestic Violence, *2001 S St. N.W., #400 20009; (202) 543-5566. Fax, (202) 543-5626. Sue Else, President. TTY, (800) 787-3224. National Domestic Violence Hotline, (800) 799-7233.*
Web, www.nnedv.org

Represents state domestic violence coalitions at the federal level. Advocates for stronger legislation against domestic violence.

National Urban League, *Washington Office, 2901 14th Street N.W. 20009; (202) 265-8200. Fax, (202) 265-6122. Maudine R. Cooper, President.*
Web, www.gwul.org

Social service organization concerned with the social welfare of African Americans and other minorities. Youth Development division provides local leagues with technical assistance for youth programs and seeks training opportunities for youth within Urban League programs. (Headquarters in New York.)

Orphan Foundation of America, *21351 Gentry Dr., #130, Sterling, VA 20166; (571) 203-0270. Fax, (571) 203-0273. Eileen McCaffrey, Executive Director.*
General e-mail, help@orphan.org
Web, www.orphan.org

Advocates for orphaned, abandoned, and homeless teenage youths. Provides scholarships, research, information, emergency cash grants, volunteer programs, guidance, and support. Interests include the rights of orphaned children, transition from youth foster care to young adult independence, and breaking the welfare cycle. Learning center provides training and educational materials.

Rape, Abuse, and Incest National Network (RAINN), *2000 L St. N.W., #406 20036; (202) 544-1034. Fax, (202) 544-3556. Scott Berkowitz, President. National Sexual Assault Hotline, (800) 656-4673.*
General e-mail, info@rainn.org
Web, www.rainn.org

Links sexual assault victims to confidential local services through national sexual assault hotline. Provides extensive public outreach and education programs nationwide on sexual assault prevention, prosecution, and recovery. Promotes national policy efforts to improve services to victims.

Stop Child Predators, *1919 M St. N.W., #470 20036; (202) 234-0090. Fax, (202) 234-2806. Stacie D. Rumenap, Executive Director.*
General e-mail, srumenap@stopchildpredators.org
Web, www.stopchildpredators.org

Advocacy organization that seeks to protect children from crime and hold their victimizers accountable. Works with victims' families, law enforcement, and decision makers to develop effective policies and solutions. Goals include establishing penalty enhancements for those who commit sexual offenses against children and creating an integrated nationwide sex offender registry.

Voices for America's Children, *1000 Vermont Ave. N.W., #700 20005-1202; (202) 289-0777. Fax, (202) 289-0776. William Bentley, President.*
General e-mail, voices@voices.org
Web, www.voices.org

Membership: private, nonprofit, state- and community-based child advocacy organizations. Works for safety, security, health, and education for all children by strengthening and building child advocacy organizations. (Formerly the National Assn. of Child Advocates.)

Older Adults

▶AGENCIES

Administration on Aging (AoA), *(Health and Human Services Dept.), 1 Massachusetts Ave. N.W. 20201; (202) 619-0724. Fax, (202) 357-3555. Edwin Walker, Assistant Secretary (Acting). Press, (202) 401-4541. TTY, (800) 877-8339. Eldercare Locator, (800) 677-1116.*
General e-mail, AoAInfo@aoa.gov
Web, www.aoa.gov

Advocacy agency for older Americans and their concerns. Collaborates with tribal organizations, community and national organizations, and state and area agencies to implement grant programs and services designed to improve the quality of life for older Americans, such as information and referral, adult day care, elder abuse prevention, home-delivered meals, in-home care, transportation, and services for caregivers.

Senior Corps *(Corporation for National and Community Service), Retired and Senior Volunteer Program, Foster Grandparent Program, and Senior Companion Program, 1201 New York Ave. N.W. 20525; (202) 606-5000. Fax, (202) 565-2789. Tess Scannell, Director, (202) 606-6925. Volunteer recruiting*

Resources for Older Adults

See also Information Sources on Women's Health on page 375.

AGENCIES

Administration on Aging (AoA), (202) 619-0724, www.aoa.gov

Centers for Medicare and Medicaid Services (CMS), (877) 267-2323 or (800) 633-4227, www.cms.hhs.gov

Employment and Training Administration, Older Worker Program, (202) 693-3046, www.doleta.gov/seniors

National Assn. of Area Agencies on Aging, Eldercare Locator, (800) 667-1116, www.eldercare.gov

National Institute on Aging (NIA), (301) 496-1752, www.nia.nih.gov (No phone number)

National Institutes of Health (NIH), Senior Health, nihseniorhealth.gov

Social Security Administration (SSA), (800) 772-1213, www.ssa.gov

Veterans Affairs Dept., (800) 827-1000, www.va.gov

ADVOCACY

AARP, (888) OUR-AARP or (202) 434-2277, www.aarp.org

Legal Services Network, (888) 687-2277

Alliance for Retired Americans, (888) 373-6497 or (202) 637-5399, www.retiredamericans.org

Gray Panthers, (800) 280-5362 or (202) 737-6637, www.graypanthers.org

National Caucus and Center on Black Aged, Inc., (202) 637-8400, www.ncba-aged.org

National Committee to Preserve Social Security and Medicare, (800) 966-1935 or (202) 216-0420, www.ncpssm.org

National Consumers League, (202) 835-3323, www.nclnet.org and www.sosrx.org

National Hispanic Council on Aging, (202) 347-9733, www.nhcoa.org

Seniors Coalition, (800) 325-9891, www.senior.org

60 Plus, (888) 560-7587 or (703) 807-2070, www.60plus.org

United Seniors Assn. Inc. (USA Next), (703) 359-6500

HEALTH

Alliance for Aging Research, (202) 293-2856, www.agingresearch.org

Alzheimer's Assn., (800) 272-3900, www.alz-nca.org

American Assn. for Geriatric Psychiatry, (301) 654-7850, www.aagpgpa.org or www.gmhfonline.org

Families USA, (202) 628-3030, www.familiesusa.org

National Osteoporosis Foundation, (800) 231-4222 or (202) 223-2226, www.nof.org

HOUSING, NURSING HOMES, ASSISTED LIVING

Armed Forces Retirement Home—Washington, (800) 422-9988, www.afrh.gov

Army Distaff Foundation, (800) 541-4255, or (202) 541-0149, www.armydistaff.org

B'nai B'rith International, Center for Senior Services, (202) 857-2785, www.bnaibrith.org/centers/senior_services.cfm

Consumer Consortium on Assisted Living, (703) 533-8121, www.ccal.org

National Citizens' Coalition for Nursing Home Reform, (202) 332-2275, www.nursinghomeaction.org

SERVICES, COMMUNITY SERVICE

American Veterans (AMVETS), (877) 726-8387, www.amvets.org,

Close Up Foundation, (800) 256-7387 or (703) 706-3300, www.closeup.org

Jewish Council for the Aging of Greater Washington, (301) 255-4200, www.jcagw.org

National Council on the Aging, (202) 479-1200, www.ncoa.org

National Senior Service Corps, (800) 424-8867 or (202) 606-5000, www.seniorcorps.org

Senior Community Service Employment Program, (202) 693-3842, www.doleta.gov/seniors

---

information, (800) 424-8867. TTY, (800) 833-3722; local TTY, (202) 565-2799.

General e-mail, webmaster@cns.gov

Web, www.seniorcorps.gov

Network of programs that help older Americans find service opportunities in their communities, including the Retired and Senior Volunteer Program, which encourages older citizens to use their talents and experience in community service; the Foster Grandparent Program, which gives older citizens opportunities to work with exceptional children and children with special needs, and the Senior Companion Program, which recruits older citizens to help homebound adults, especially seniors, with special needs.

▶ **CONGRESS**

For a listing of relevant congressional committees and subcommittees, please see page 629 or the Appendix.

▶**NONGOVERNMENTAL**

AARP, *601 E St. N.W. 20049; (202) 434-2277. Fax, (202) 434-2320. William D. Novelli, Chief Executive Officer. Press, (202) 434-2560. TTY, (877) 434-7595. Research Info Center, (202) 434-6233.*
Web, www.aarp.org

Membership: people fifty years of age and older. Conducts educational and counseling programs in areas concerning older adults, such as widowed persons services, health promotion, housing, and consumer protection. Library open to the public.

Alliance for Retired Americans, *815 16th St. N.W., 4th Floor North 20006-4104; (202) 637-5399. Fax, (202) 637-5398. Barbara Esterling, President. Information, (888) 373-6497.*
Web, www.retiredamericans.org

Seeks to strengthen benefits to the elderly, including improved Social Security payments, increased employment, and education and health programs. (Affiliate of the AFL-CIO.)

Experience Works, Inc., *4401 Wilson Blvd., #1100, Arlington, VA 22203; (703) 522-7272. Fax, (703) 522-0141. Cynthia A. Metzler, Chief Executive Officer. Toll-free, (866) 397-9757.*
Web, www.experienceworks.org

Trains and places older adults in the workforce. Seeks to increase awareness of issues affecting older workers and build support for policies and legislation benefiting older adults.

Families USA, *1201 New York Ave. N.W., #1100 20005; (202) 628-3030. Fax, (202) 347-2417. Ron Pollack, Executive Director.*
General e-mail, info@familiesusa.org
Web, www.familiesusa.org

Organization of American families whose interests include health care and long-term care, Social Security, Medicare, and Medicaid. Monitors legislation and regulations affecting the elderly. Focuses on communities of color.

Jewish Council for the Aging of Greater Washington, *11820 Parklawn Dr., #200, Rockville, MD 20852; (301) 255-4200. Fax, (301) 231-9360. David N. Gamse, Executive Director.*
General e-mail, seniorhelpline@accessjca.org
Web, www.accessjca.org

Nonsectarian organization that provides programs and services throughout the metropolitan D.C. area to help older people continue living independent lives. Offers employment services, computer training, adult day care, social day care, transportation, information services and referrals for transportation and in-home services, exercise classes, volunteer opportunities, and one-on-one consultation.

National Assn. of Area Agencies on Aging, *1730 Rhode Island Ave. N.W., #1200 20036; (202) 872-0888. Fax, (202) 872-0057. Sandy Markwood, Chief Executive Officer.*
Web, www.n4a.org

Works to establish an effective national policy on aging; provides local agencies with training and technical assistance; disseminates information to these agencies and the public. Monitors legislation and regulations.

National Assn. of Area Agencies on Aging, *Eldercare Locator, 1730 Rhode Island Ave. N.W., #1200 20036; (202) 872-0888. Fax, (202) 872-0057. Helen Eltzeroth, Manager. Toll-free, (800) 677-1116.*
General e-mail, eldercarelocator@n4a.org
Web, www.eldercare.gov

National toll-free directory assistance service that helps older people and caregivers locate local support resources for aging Americans. Refers people to agencies or organizations that deal with meal services, home care, transportation, housing alternatives, home repair, recreation, social activities, and legal services. (Provided by the U.S. Administration on Aging and administered by the National Assn. of Area Agencies on Aging and the National Assn. of State Units on Aging.)

National Assn. of State Units on Aging, *1201 15th St. N.W., #350 20005-2842; (202) 898-2578. Fax, (202) 898-2583. Martha Roherty, Executive Director.*
General e-mail, nyahya@nasua.org
Web, www.nasua.org

Membership: state and territorial governmental units that deal with the elderly. Provides members with information, technical assistance, and professional training. Monitors legislation and regulations.

National Caucus and Center for the Black Aged, Inc., *1220 L St. N.W., #800 20005-2407; (202) 637-8400. Fax, (202) 347-0895. Karyne Jones, President.*
General e-mail, info@ncba-aged.org
Web, www.ncba-aged.org

Concerned with issues that affect older African Americans. Sponsors employment and housing programs for older adults and education and training for professionals in gerontology. Monitors legislation and regulations.

National Council on the Aging, *1901 L St. N.W., 4th Floor 20036; (202) 479-1200. Fax, (202) 479-0735. James P. Firman, President. Press, (202) 479-6975. TTY, (202) 479-6674.*
General e-mail, info@ncoa.org
Web, www.ncoa.org

Serves as an information clearinghouse on training, technical assistance, advocacy, and research on every aspect of aging. Provides information on social services for older persons. Monitors legislation and regulations.

National Hispanic Council on Aging, *734 15th St. N.W., #1050 20005; (202) 347-9733. Fax, (202) 347-9735. Yanira Cruz, President.*

General e-mail, nhcoa@nhcoa.org

Web, www.nhcoa.org

Membership: senior citizens, health care workers, professionals in the field of aging, and others in the United States and Puerto Rico who are interested in topics related to Hispanics and aging. Provides research training, policy analysis, consulting, and technical assistance; sponsors seminars, workshops, and management internships.

DISABILITIES

▶AGENCIES

Administration for Children and Families (ACF), *(Health and Human Services Dept.), Administration on Developmental Disabilities,* 200 Independence Ave. S.W., #405D 20201; (202) 690-6590. Fax, (202) 690-6904. Faith McCormick, Commissioner (Acting). TTY, (202) 690-6415. *Web, www.acf.hhs.gov/programs/add*

Administers the Developmental Disabilities Assistance and Bill of Rights Act of 2000, providing grants for state protection and advocacy systems for people with developmental disabilities; state councils on developmental disabilities; university centers for developmental disabilities education, research, and services; and projects of national significance that must be addressed on a local level affecting people with developmental disabilities and their families. Also administers the disability provisions in the Help America Vote Act.

Architectural and Transportation Barriers Compliance Board (Access Board), 1331 F St. N.W., #1000 20004-1111; (202) 272-0080. Fax, (202) 272-0081. David M. Capozzi, Executive Director. TTY, (202) 272-0082. TTY toll-free, (800) 993-2822. Toll-free technical assistance, (800) 872-2253. *General e-mail, info@access-board.gov*

Web, www.access-board.gov

Develops and maintains accessibility requirements for buildings, transit vehicles, telecommunications equipment, and electronic and information technology. Provides technical assistance and training on these guidelines and standards. Enforces access standards for federally funded facilities through the Architectural Barriers Act.

Committee for Purchase from People Who Are Blind or Severely Disabled, 1421 Jefferson Davis Hwy., #10800, Arlington, VA 22202-3259; (703) 603-7740. Fax, (703) 603-0655. Tina Ballard, Executive Director. *Web, www.abilityone.gov*

Presidentially appointed committee. Determines which products and services are suitable for federal procurement from qualified nonprofit agencies that employ people who are blind or have other severe disabilities; seeks to increase employment opportunities for these individuals.

Education Dept., *Special Education and Rehabilitative Services,* 550 12th St. S.W., 5th Floor 20202; (202) 245-7468. Fax, (202) 245-7638. Tracy R. Justesen, Assistant Secretary. Main phone is voice and TTY accessible. *Web, www.nochildleftbehind.gov*

Provides information on federal legislation and programs and national organizations concerning individuals with disabilities.

Employment Standards Administration *(Labor Dept.), Coal Mine Workers' Compensation,* 200 Constitution Ave. N.W., #C3520 20210; (202) 693-0046. Fax, (202) 693-1395. James L. DeMarce, Director. *Web, www.dol.gov/dol/esa*

Provides direction for administration of the black lung benefits program. Adjudicates all black lung claims; certifies benefit payments and maintains black lung beneficiary rolls.

Equal Employment Opportunity Commission (EEOC), *Legal Counsel, Americans with Disabilities Act Policy Division,* 131 M St. N.E. 20507; (202) 663-4637. Fax, (202) 663-4639. Christopher J. Kuczynski, Assistant Legal Counsel. TTY, (202) 663-7026.

Provides interpretations, opinions, and technical assistance on the ADA provisions relating to employment.

Justice Dept. (DOJ), *Civil Rights Division, Disability Rights,* 1425 New York Ave. N.W., #4039 20005 (mailing address: 950 Pennsylvania Ave., 7th Floor, Washington, DC 20530); (202) 307-0663. Fax, (202) 307-1198. John L. Wodatch, Chief. Information, (800) 514-0301. TTY, (800) 514-0383. *Web, www.usdoj.gov/crt/drs/drshane.htm*

Litigates cases under Titles I, II, and III of the Americans with Disabilities Act, which prohibits discrimination on the basis of disability in places of public accommodation and in all activities of state and local government. Provides technical assistance to businesses and individuals affected by the law.

National Council on Disability, 1331 F St. N.W., #850 20004-1107; (202) 272-2004. Fax, (202) 272-2022. John R. Vaughn, Chair. TTY, (202) 272-2074. *General e-mail, ncd@ncd.gov*

Web, www.ncd.gov

Independent federal agency providing advice to the president, Congress, and executive branch agencies to promote policies and programs that ensure equal opportunity for individuals with disabilities and enable individuals with disabilities to achieve self-sufficiency and full integration into society.

National Institute of Child Health and Human Development *(National Institutes of Health), National Center for Medical Rehabilitation Research,* 6100 Executive Blvd., Bldg. 6100, #2A-03, MSC 7510, Bethesda, MD 20892; (301) 402-2242. Fax, (301) 402-0832. Dr. Michael Weinrich, Director, (301) 402-4201. *Web, www.nichd.nih.gov/about/ncmrr*

Fosters the development of scientific knowledge needed to enhance the health, productivity, independence, and quality of life of persons with disabilities. Supports a program of basic and applied research promoting tissue plasticity, assistive technology and devices, improved outcomes, and increased patient participation.

National Institute on Disability and Rehabilitation Research *(Education Dept.), 550 12th St. S.W., #6056 20024-6122 (mailing address: 400 Maryland Ave. S.W., MS 6038, Washington, DC 20202-2700); (202) 245-7640. Fax, (202) 245-7630. Ruth Brannon, Director (Acting). Web, www.ed.gov/about/offices/list/osers/nidrr/index.html*

Awards grants for research programs in rehabilitating people with disabilities from birth to adulthood; provides information on developments in the field; awards grants and contracts for scientific, technical, and methodological research; coordinates federal research programs on rehabilitation; offers fellowships to individuals conducting research in the field.

Office of Disability Employment Policy *(Labor Dept.), 200 Constitution Ave. N.W., #S1303 20210; (202) 693-7880. Fax, (202) 693-7888. Vacant, Assistant Secretary. TTY, (202) 693-7881. Web, www.dol.gov/odep*

Seeks to eliminate physical and psychological barriers to the disabled through education and information programs; promotes education, training, rehabilitation, and employment opportunities for people with disabilities.

Rehabilitation Services Administration *(Education Dept.), 400 Maryland Ave. S.W. 20202-2800; (202) 245-7488. Fax, (202) 245-7591. P. Edward Anthony, Commissioner (Acting). TTY, (800) 437-0833. Web, www.ed.gov/about/offices/list/osers/rsa/index.html*

Coordinates and directs major federal programs for eligible physically and mentally disabled persons. Administers distribution of grants for training and employment programs and for establishing supported-employment and independent-living programs. Provides vocational training and job placement.

Smithsonian Institution, *Accessibility Program, 14th St. and Constitution Ave. N.W., NMAH, MRC 607 20013-7012; (202) 633-2921. Fax, (202) 633-4352. Elizabeth Ziebarth, Director. Information, (888) 783-0001. TTY, (202) 633-4353. General e-mail, ziebarth@si.edu Web, www.si.edu*

Coordinates the Smithsonian's efforts to improve accessibility of its programs and facilities to visitors and staff with disabilities. Serves as a resource for museums and individuals nationwide.

Social Security Administration (SSA), *Disability Determinations, 3570 Annex Bldg., 6401 Security Blvd., Baltimore, MD 21235; (410) 965-1250. Fax, (410) 965-6503. Ruby Burrell, Associate Commissioner. Information, (800) 772-1213. TTY, (800) 325-0778. Web, www.ssa.gov/disability*

Administers and regulates the disability insurance program and disability provisions of the Supplemental Security Income (SSI) program.

▶CONGRESS

For a listing of relevant congressional committees and subcommittees, please see page 629 or the Appendix.

Library of Congress, *National Library Service for the Blind and Physically Handicapped, 1291 Taylor St. N.W. 20542; (202) 707-5100. Fax, (202) 707-0712. Frank Kurt Cylke, Director. Toll-free, (800) 424-8567. TDD, (202) 707-0744. General e-mail, nls@loc.gov Web, www.loc.gov/nls*

Administers a national program of free library services for persons with physical disabilities in cooperation with regional and subregional libraries. Produces and distributes full-length books and magazines in recorded form and in Braille. Reference section answers questions relating to blindness and physical disabilities and on library services available to persons with disabilities.

▶NONGOVERNMENTAL

American Assn. of People with Disabilities (AAPD), *1629 K St. N.W., #503 20006; (202) 457-0046. Fax, (202) 457-0473. Andrew J. Imparato, President. TTY, (202) 457-0046. Toll-free, (800) 840-8844. General e-mail, communications@aapd.com Web, www.aapd.com*

Works to organize the disability community to effect political, economic, and social change through programs on employment, independent living, and assistive technology. Seeks to educate the public and policymakers on issues affecting persons with disabilities. Works in coalition with other organizations toward full enforcement of disability and antidiscrimination laws.

American Bar Assn. (ABA), *Commission on Mental and Physical Disability Law, 740 15th St. N.W., 9th Floor 20005-1022; (202) 662-1570. Fax, (202) 442-3439. John Parry, Director. General e-mail, cmpdl@abanet.org Web, www.abanet.org/disability*

Serves as a clearinghouse for information on mental and physical disability law. Publishes a report on mental and physical disability law, law digest, and handbooks. Provides a directory of lawyers who practice disability law, a directory on law school disability curricula, and a directory on law students with disabilities.

American Counseling Assn., *Rehabilitation, 5999 Stevenson Ave., Alexandria, VA 22304-3300; (703) 823-9800. Fax, (703) 823-0252. Richard Yep, Executive Director. Information, (800) 347-6647. TTY, (703) 823-6862. Web, www.counseling.org*

Membership: counselors, counselor educators, and graduate students in the rehabilitation field, and other interested persons. Establishes counseling and research standards; encourages establishment of rehabilitation facilities; conducts leadership training and continuing education programs; serves as a liaison between counselors and clients. Monitors legislation and regulations.

American Medical Rehabilitation Providers Assn. (AMRPA), *1710 N St. N.W. 20036; (202) 223-1920. Fax, (202) 223-1925. Carolyn Zollar, Vice President, Government Relations. Information, (888) 346-4624. Web, www.amrpa.org*

Membership: freestanding rehabilitation hospitals and rehabilitation units of general hospitals, outpatient rehabilitation facilities, skilled nursing facilities, and others. Provides leadership, advocacy, and resources to develop medical rehabilitation services and supports for persons with disabilities and others in need of services. Acts as a clearinghouse for information to members on the nature and availability of services.

American Network of Community Options and Resources (ANCOR), *1101 King St., #380, Alexandria, VA 22314; (703) 535-7850. Fax, (703) 535-7860. Renee Pietrangelo, Chief Executive Officer. General e-mail, ancor@ancor.org*

Web, www.ancor.org

Membership: privately operated agencies and corporations that provide support and services to people with disabilities. Advises and works with regulatory and consumer agencies that serve people with disabilities; provides information and sponsors seminars and workshops. Monitors legislation and regulations.

American Occupational Therapy Assn., *4720 Montgomery Lane, Bethesda, MD 20824 (mailing address: P.O. Box 31220, Bethesda, MD 20824-1220); (301) s652-2682. Fax, (301) 652-7711. Fred Somers, Executive Director. TTY, (800) 377-8555. General e-mail, info@aota.org*

Web, www.aota.org

Membership: registered occupational therapists, certified occupational therapy assistants, and students. Associate members include businesses and organizations supportive of occupational therapy. Accredits educational programs and credentials occupational therapists. Supports research and sponsors scholarships, grants, and fellowships. Library is open to the public by appointment.

American Orthotic and Prosthetic Assn., *330 John Carlyle St., #200, Alexandria, VA 22314; (571) 431-0876. Fax, (571) 431-0899. Kimber Nation, Executive Director (Acting) Web, www.aopanet.org*

Membership: companies that manufacture or supply artificial limbs and braces.

American Physical Therapy Assn., *1111 N. Fairfax St., Alexandria, VA 22314-1488; (703) 684-2782. Fax, (703) 684-7343. John Barnes, Chief Executive Officer. Information, (800) 999-2782. TTY, (703) 683-6748.*

General e-mail, svcctr@apta.org

Web, www.apta.org

Membership: physical therapists, assistants, and students. Establishes professional standards and accredits physical therapy programs; seeks to improve physical therapy education, practice, and research.

American Speech-Language-Hearing Assn. (ASHA), *2200 Research Blvd., Rockville, MD 20850-3289; (301) 296-5700. Fax, (301) 296-8580. Arlene Pietranton, Executive Director. Press, (301) 296-8732. Toll-free hotline (except Alaska, Hawaii, and Maryland), (800) 638-8255 (voice and TTY accessible). General e-mail, actioncenter@asha.org*

Web, www.asha.org

Membership: specialists in speech-language pathology and audiology. Sponsors professional education programs; acts as accrediting agent for graduate programs; certifies audiologists and speech language pathologists. Advocates the rights of the communicatively disabled; provides information on speech, hearing, and language problems. Provides referrals to speech-language pathologists and audiologists. Interests include national and international standards for bioacoustics and noise.

Assn. of University Centers on Disabilities (AUCD), *1010 Wayne Ave., #920, Silver Spring, MD 20910; (301) 588-8252. Fax, (301) 588-2842. George Jesien, Executive Director. General e-mail, info@aucd.org*

Web, www.aucd.org

Network of facilities that diagnose and treat the developmentally disabled. Trains graduate students and professionals in the field; helps state and local agencies develop services. Interests include interdisciplinary training and services, early screening to prevent developmental disabilities, and development of equipment and programs to serve persons with disabilities.

Brain Injury Assn. of America, *1608 Spring Hill Rd., #110, Vienna, VA 22182; (703) 761-0750. Fax, (703) 761-0755. Susan H. Connors, President. Information, (800) 444-6443. General e-mail, info@biausa.org*

Web, www.biausa.org

Works to improve the quality of life for persons with traumatic brain injuries and for their families. Promotes the prevention of head injuries through public awareness and education programs. Offers state-level support services for individuals and their families. Monitors legislation and regulations.

Consortium for Citizens with Disabilities (CCD), *1660 L St. N.W., #701 20036; (202) 783-2229. Fax, (202) 783-8250. Martie Ford, Chair. General e-mail, info@c-c-d.org*

Web, www.c-c-d.org

Coalition of national disability organizations. Advocates national public policy that ensures the self-determination, independence, empowerment, and integration in all aspects of society for children and adults with disabilities.

Disabled American Veterans, *National Service and Legislative Headquarters,* *807 Maine Ave. S.W. 20024-2410; (202) 554-3501. Fax, (202) 554-3581. Arthur H. Wilson, National Adjutant; David Gorman, Executive Director.*
Web, www.dav.org

Chartered by Congress to assist veterans with claims for benefits; represents veterans seeking to correct alleged errors in military records. Assists families of veterans with disabilities. (Headquarters in Cold Spring, Ky.)

Disabled Sports USA, *451 Hungerford Dr., #100, Rockville, MD 20850; (301) 217-0960. Fax, (301) 217-0968. Kirk M. Bauer, Executive Director, (301) 217-9838. General e-mail, information@dsusa.org*
Web, www.dsusa.org

Offers nationwide sports rehabilitation programs; conducts sports and recreation activities and physical fitness programs for people with permanent disabilities and their families and friends; conducts workshops and competitions; participates in world championships.

Easter Seals, *Washington Office,* *1425 K St. N.W., #200 20005; (202) 347-3066. Fax, (202) 737-7914. Randall Rutta, Executive Vice President. TTY, (202) 347-7385. Web, www.easterseals.com*

Federation of state and local groups with programs that help people with disabilities achieve independence. Washington office monitors legislation and regulations. Affiliates assist individuals with a broad range of disabilities, including muscular dystrophy, cerebral palsy, stroke, speech and hearing loss, blindness, amputation, and learning disabilities. Services include physical, occupational, vocational, and speech therapy; speech, hearing, physical, and vocational evaluation; psychological testing and counseling; personal and family counseling; supported employment; special education programs; social clubs and day and residential camps; and transportation, referral, and follow-up programs. (Headquarters in Chicago, Ill.)

Epilepsy Foundation, *8301 Professional Pl. East, #200, Landover, MD 20785; (301) 459-3700. Fax, (301) 577-2684. Eric Hargis, Chief Executive Officer. Information, (800) 332-1000. Library, (800) 332-4050. General e-mail, postmaster@efa.org*
Web, www.epilepsyfoundation.org

Promotes research and treatment of epilepsy; makes research grants; disseminates information and educational materials. Affiliates provide direct services for people with epilepsy and make referrals when necessary. Library open to the public by appointment.

Girl Scouts of the U.S.A., *Public Policy and Advocacy,* *816 Connecticut Ave. N.W., 3rd Floor 20006; (202) 659-3780. Fax, (202) 331-8065. Laurie Westley, Senior Vice President.*
Web, www.girlscouts.org

Educational service organization for girls ages five to seventeen. Promotes personal development through social action, leadership, and such programs as Girl Scouting for Handicapped Girls. (Headquarters in New York.)

Goodwill Industries International, *15810 Indianola Dr., Rockville, MD 20855; (301) 530-6500. Fax, (301) 530-1516. Jim Gibbons, President. Toll-free, (800) 741-0186. General e-mail, contactus@goodwill.org*
Web, www.goodwill.org

Serves people with disabilities, low-wage workers, and others by providing education and career services, as well as job placement opportunities and post-employment support. Helps people become independent, tax-paying members of their communities.

Helen A. Kellar Institute for Human Disabilities, *George Mason University, 4400 University Dr., MS 1F2, Fairfax, VA 22030; (703) 993-3670. Fax, (703) 993-3681. Michael M. Behrmann, Director.*
Web, http://kihd.gmu.edu

Combines resources from local, state, national, public, and private affiliations to develop products, services, and programs for persons with disabilities.

International Code Council, *500 New Jersey Ave. N.W., 6th Floor 20001-2070; (202) 370-1800. Fax, (202) 783-2348. Richard P. "Rick" Weiland, Chief Executive Officer. Toll-free, (888) 422-7233.*
Web, www.iccsafe.org

Provides review board for the American National Standards Institute accessibility standards, which ensure that buildings are accessible to persons with physical disabilities.

National Assn. of Councils on Developmental Disabilities, *1660 L St. N.W., #700 20036; (202) 506-5813. Fax, (202) 506-5846. Michael Brogioli, Chief Executive Officer. General e-mail, info@nacdd.org*
Web, www.nacdd.org

Membership: state and territorial councils authorized by the Developmental Disabilities Act, which promotes the interests of people with developmental disabilities and their families. Monitors legislation and regulations.

National Coalition for Disability Rights, *ADA Watch,* *601 Pennsylvania Ave. N.W., #900S 20004; (202) 448-9928. Jim Ward, President. General e-mail, jimward@ncdr.org*
Web, www.adawatch.org

Alliance of disability, civil rights, and social justice organizations. Seeks to raise awareness about disabilities and civil rights.

National Council on Independent Living, *1710 Rhode Island Ave. N.W., 5th Floor 20036; (202) 207-0334. Fax, (202) 207-0341. Kelly Buckland, Executive Director. TTY, (202) 207-0340. Toll-free, (877) 525-3400.*

General e-mail, ncil@ncil.org

Web, www.ncil.org

Membership: independent living centers, their staff and volunteers, and individuals with disabilities. Seeks to strengthen independent living centers; facilitates the integration of people with disabilities into society; provides training and technical assistance; sponsors referral service and speakers bureau.

National Dissemination Center for Children with Disabilities (NICHCY), *1825 Connecticut Ave. N.W., 7th Floor 20009 (mailing address: P.O. Box 1492, Washington, DC 20013-1492); (202) 884-8200. Fax, (202) 884-8441. Stephen Luke, Director. Information, (800) 695-0285. Main phone is voice and TTY accessible. General e-mail, nichcy@aed.org*

Web, www.nichcy.org

Federally funded clearinghouse that provides information on disabilities in infants, toddlers, children, and youth. Provides research-based information on effective educational practices. Offers personal responses to specific questions, referrals to other organizations, and prepared information packets.

National Multiple Sclerosis Society, *Washington Office, 1800 M St. N.W., #750 South 20036; (202) 296-5363. Fax, (202) 296-3425. Christopher Broullire, Chapter President. General e-mail, information@msandyou.org*

Web, www.msandyou.org

Seeks to advance medical knowledge of multiple sclerosis, a disease of the central nervous system; disseminates information worldwide. Patient services include individual and family counseling, exercise programs, equipment loans, medical and social service referrals, transportation assistance, back-to-work training programs, and in-service training seminars for nurses, homemakers, and physical and occupational therapists. (Headquarters in New York.)

National Organization on Disability, *910 16th St. N.W., #410 20006-2988; (202) 293-5960. Fax, (202) 293-7999. Carol Glazer, President. General e-mail, ability@nod.org*

Web, www.nod.org

Administers the Community Partnership Program, a network of communities that works to remove barriers and address educational, employment, social, and transportation needs of people with disabilities. Provides members with information and technical assistance; sponsors annual community awards competition; makes referrals. Monitors legislation and regulations.

National Rehabilitation Assn., *633 S. Washington St., Alexandria, VA 22314; (703) 836-0850. Fax, (703) 836-0848. Beverlee Stafford, Executive Director. TTY, (703) 836-0849, or toll-free, (888) 258-4295. General e-mail, info@rehab.org*

Web, www.nationalrehab.org

Membership: administrators, counselors, therapists, disability examiners, vocational evaluators, instructors, job placement specialists, disability managers in the corporate sector, and others interested in rehabilitation of the physically and mentally disabled. Sponsors conferences and workshops. Monitors legislation and regulations.

National Rehabilitation Information Center (NARIC), *8201 Corporate Dr., #600, Landover, MD 20785; (301) 459-5900. Fax, (301) 459-4263. Mark Odum, Director. Information, (800) 346-2742. TTY, (301) 459-5984. General e-mail, naricinfo@heitechservices.com*

Web, www.naric.com

Provides information on disability and rehabilitation research. Acts as referral agency for disability and rehabilitation facilities and programs.

Paralyzed Veterans of America, *801 18th St. N.W. 20006-3517; (202) 872-1300. Fax, (202) 785-4452. Homer Townsend, Executive Director. Information, (800) 424-8200. TTY, (800) 795-4327. General e-mail, info@pva.org*

Web, www.pva.org

Congressionally chartered veterans service organization that assists veterans with claims for benefits. Distributes information on special education for paralyzed veterans; advocates for high-quality care and supports and raises funds for medical research.

RESNA, *1700 N. Moore St., #1540, Arlington, VA 22209-1903; (703) 524-6686. Fax, (703) 524-6630. Nell Bailey, Executive Director. TTY, (703) 524-6639. General e-mail, membership@resna.org*

Web, www.resna.org

Membership: engineers, health professionals, persons with disabilities, and others concerned with rehabilitation engineering and assistive technology. Promotes and supports developments in rehabilitation engineering; acts as an information clearinghouse. (RESNA stands for Rehabilitation Engineering and Assistive Technology Society of North America.)

Special Olympics International Inc., *1133 19th St. N.W. 20036-3604; (202) 628-3630. Fax, (202) 824-0200. Timothy P. Shriver, President (Acting). General e-mail, info@specialolympics.org*

Web, www.specialolympics.org

Offers individuals with intellectual disabilities opportunities for year-round sports training; sponsors athletic competition worldwide in twenty-two individual and team sports.

Spina Bifida Assn., *4590 MacArthur Blvd. N.W., #250 20007-4226; (202) 944-3285. Fax, (202) 944-3295. Cindy Brownstein, Chief Executive Officer. Information, (800) 621-3141. General e-mail, sbaa@sbaa.org*

Web, www.spinabifida.org

Membership: individuals with spina bifida, their supporters, and concerned professionals. Offers educational programs, scholarships, and support services; acts as a clearinghouse; provides referrals and information about treatment and prevention. Serves as U.S. member of the International Federation for Hydrocephalus and Spina Bifida, which is headquartered in Geneva. Monitors legislation and regulations.

United Cerebral Palsy Assns., *1660 L St. N.W., #700 20036-5602; (202) 776-0406. Fax, (202) 776-0414. Stephen Bennett, President. Information, (800) 872-5827. Main phone is voice and TTY accessible.*
General e-mail, info@ucp.org

Web, www.ucp.org

National network of state and local affiliates that assists individuals with cerebral palsy and other developmental disabilities and their families. Provides parent education, early intervention, employment services, family support and respite programs, therapy, assistive technology, and vocational training. Promotes research on cerebral palsy; supports the use of assistive technology and community-based living arrangements for persons with cerebral palsy and other developmental disabilities.

VSA Arts, *818 Connecticut Ave. N.W., #600 20006; (202) 628-2800. Fax, (202) 429-0868. Soula Antoniou, President. Information, (800) 933-8721. TTY, (202) 737-0645.*
General e-mail, info@vsarts.org

Web, www.vsarts.org

Initiates and supports research and program development providing arts training and programming for persons with disabilities to make classrooms and communities more inclusive. Provides technical assistance and training to VSA Arts state organizations; acts as an information clearinghouse for arts and persons with disabilities. (Affiliated with the John F. Kennedy Center for the Performing Arts.)

Blind and Visually Impaired

▶**AGENCIES**

Committee for Purchase from People Who Are Blind or Severely Disabled, *1421 Jefferson Davis Hwy., #10800, Arlington, VA 22202-3259; (703) 603-7740. Fax, (703) 603-0655. Tina Ballard, Executive Director.*
Web, www.abilityone.gov

Presidentially appointed committee. Determines which products and services are suitable for federal procurement from qualified nonprofit agencies that employ people who are blind or have other severe disabilities; seeks to increase employment opportunities for these individuals.

▶**CONGRESS**

For a listing of relevant congressional committees and subcommittees, please see page 629 or the Appendix.

Library of Congress, *National Library Service for the Blind and Physically Handicapped,* *1291 Taylor St. N.W. 20542; (202) 707-5100. Fax, (202) 707-0712. Frank Kurt Cylke, Director. Toll-free, (800) 424-8567. TDD, (202) 707-0744.*
General e-mail, nls@loc.gov

Web, www.loc.gov/nls

Administers a national program of free library services for persons with physical disabilities in cooperation with regional and subregional libraries. Produces and distributes full-length books and magazines in recorded form and in Braille. Reference section answers questions relating to blindness and physical disabilities and on library services available to persons with disabilities.

▶**NONGOVERNMENTAL**

American Assn. of Visually Impaired Attorneys, *1155 15th St. N.W., #1004 20005-2706; (202) 467-5081. Fax, (202) 467-5085. Mitch Pomerantz, President. Press, (203) 877-4108. Toll-free, (800) 424-8666.*
General e-mail, austingl@bellsouth.net

Web, www.visuallyimpairedattorneys.org

Membership: visually impaired lawyers and law students. Provides members with legal information; acts as an information clearinghouse on legal materials available in Braille, in large print, on computer disc, and on tape. (Formerly the American Blind Lawyers Assn. Affiliated with American Council of the Blind.)

American Council of the Blind (ACB), *2200 Wilson Blvd., #650, Arlington, VA 22201; (202) 467-5081. Fax, (703) 465-5085. Melanie Brunson, Executive Director. Toll-free, 2:00–5:00 p.m. EST, (800) 424-8666.*
General e-mail, info@acb.org

Web, www.acb.org

Membership organization serving blind and visually impaired individuals. Interests include Social Security, telecommunications, rehabilitation services, transportation, education, and architectural access. Provides blind individuals with information and referral services, including legal referrals; advises state organizations and agencies serving the blind; sponsors scholarships for the blind and visually impaired.

American Foundation for the Blind, *Public Policy Center,* *1660 L St. N.W., #513 20036; (202) 822-0830. Fax, (202) 822-0830. Paul W. Schroeder, Vice President, Policy and Programs.*
General e-mail, afbgov@afb.net

Web, www.afb.org/gov.asp

Advocates equality of access and opportunity for the blind and visually impaired. Conducts research and provides consulting; develops and implements public policy and legislation. Maintains the Helen Keller Archives and M.C. Migel Memorial Library at its headquarters in New York.

Assn. for Education and Rehabilitation of the Blind and Visually Impaired, *1703 N. Beauregard St., #440,*

Alexandria, VA 22311; (703) 671-4500. Fax, (703) 671-6391. Jim Gandorf, Executive Director. Toll-free, (877) 492-2708.

General e-mail, aer@aerbvi.org

Web, www.aerbvi.org

Membership: professionals who work in all phases of education and rehabilitation of blind and visually impaired children and adults. Provides support and professional development opportunities through the sponsorship of international and regional conferences, continuing education, job exchange, professional recognition through annual awards, and several publications. Interests include an interdisciplinary approach to research in the field of visual impairment. Monitors legislation and regulations.

Blinded Veterans Assn., 477 H St. N.W. 20001-2694; (202) 371-8880. Fax, (202) 371-8258. Thomas H. Miller, Executive Director. Toll-free, (800) 669-7079.

General e-mail, bva@bva.org

Web, www.bva.org

Chartered by Congress to assist veterans with claims for benefits. Seeks out blinded veterans to make them aware of benefits and services available to them.

National Industries for the Blind (NIB), 1310 Braddock Pl., Alexandria, VA 22314-1691; (703) 310-0500. Kevin Lynch, Chief Executive Officer.

Web, www.nib.org

Works to develop and improve opportunities for evaluating, training, employing, and advancing people who are blind and visually disabled. Develops business opportunities in the federal, state, and commercial marketplaces for organizations employing people with severe vision disabilities.

Prevention of Blindness Society of Metropolitan Washington, 1775 Church St. N.W. 20036; (202) 234-1010. Fax, (202) 234-1020. Michele Hartlove, Executive Director.

General e-mail, mail@youreyes.org

Web, www.youreyes.org

Conducts preschool and elementary school screening program and glaucoma screening; provides information and referral service on eye health care; assists low-income persons in obtaining eye care and provides eyeglasses for a nominal fee to persons experiencing financial stress; conducts macular degeneration support group.

Deaf and Hard of Hearing

▶AGENCIES

General Services Administration (GSA), *Federal Relay Service (FedRelay),* 10304 Eaton Pl., Fairfax, VA 22030; (703) 306-6308. Patricia Stevens, Program Manager. Customer service, (800) 877 0996 (Voice/TTY, ASCII, Spanish). Toll-free, (800) 877-8339 (TTY/ASCII). VCO (Voice Carry Over), (877) 877-6280. Speech-to-Speech, (877) 877-8982. Voice, (866) 377-8642. TeleBraille, (866) 893-8340.

General e-mail, patricia.stevens@gsa.gov

Web, www.gsa.gov/fedrelay

Provides equal telecommunications access for active and retired federal employees (civilian or military), veterans, and U.S. tribal members who are deaf, hard of hearing, deaf-blind, or have speech disabilities. Federal Relay Service features are: Voice, TTY, VCO, HCO, Speech-to-Speech, Spanish, Telebraille, CapTel, Video Relay Service (VRS), Internet Relay (FRSO), and Relay Conference Captioning (RCC). Publishes the U.S. Government TTY Directory, available at www.fts.gsa.gov/frs/ttydir.htm. Service is managed by the GSA.

National Institute on Deafness and Other Communication Disorders *(National Institutes of Health),* 31 Center Dr., #3C02, MSC-2320, Bethesda, MD 20892-2320; (301) 402-0900. Fax, (301) 402-1590. Dr. James F. Battey Jr., Director. Information, (301) 496-7243. TTY, (301) 402-0252.

General e-mail, nidcdinfo@nidcd.nih.gov

Web, www.nidcd.nih.gov

Conducts and supports research and research training and disseminates information on hearing disorders and other communication processes, including diseases that affect hearing, balance, smell, taste, voice, speech, and language. Monitors international research.

▶NONGOVERNMENTAL

Alexander Graham Bell Assn. for the Deaf and Hard of Hearing, 3417 Volta Pl. N.W. 20007-2778; (202) 337-5220. Fax, (202) 337-8314. Alexander T. Graham, Executive Director. TTY, (202) 337-5221.

General e-mail, info@agbell.org

Web, www.agbell.org

Provides hearing-impaired children in the United States and abroad with information and special education programs; works to improve employment opportunities for deaf persons; acts as a support group for parents of deaf persons.

American Academy of Audiology, 11730 Plaza America Dr., #300, Reston, VA 20190; (703) 790-8466. Fax, (703) 790-8631. Cheryl Kreider Carey, Executive Director. Toll-free, (800) 222-2336.

General e-mail, info@audiology.org

Web, www.audiology.org

Membership: audiologists. Provides consumer information on testing and treatment for hearing loss; sponsors research, awards, and continuing education for audiologists.

American Speech-Language-Hearing Assn. (ASHA), 2200 Research Blvd., Rockville, MD 20850-3289; (301) 296-5700. Fax, (301) 296-8580. Arlene Pietranton, Executive Director. Press, (301) 296-8732. Toll-free hotline

(except Alaska, Hawaii, and Maryland), (800) 638-8255 (voice and TTY accessible).
General e-mail, actioncenter@asha.org

Web, www.asha.org

Membership: specialists in speech-language pathology and audiology. Sponsors professional education programs; acts as accrediting agent for graduate programs; certifies audiologists and speech language pathologists. Advocates the rights of the communicatively disabled; provides information on speech, hearing, and language problems. Provides referrals to speech-language pathologists and audiologists. Interests include national and international standards for bioacoustics and noise.

Better Hearing Institute, *1444 Eye St. N.W., #700 20005; (202) 449-1100. Fax, (202) 216-9646. Sergei Kochkin, Executive Director. Hearing helpline, (800) 327-9355. Main phone is voice and TTY accessible.*
General e-mail, mail@betterhearing.org

Web, www.betterhearing.org

Educational organization that conducts national public information programs on hearing loss, hearing aids, and other treatments. (Affiliated with the Hearing Loss Assn. of America.)

Community Emergency Preparedness Information Network (CEPIN), *8630 Fenton St., #604, Silver Spring, MD 20910-3822; (301) 589-3786. Fax, (301) 589-3797. Neil McDevitt, Program Director. TTY, (301) 589-3006.*
General e-mail, pr@cepintdi.org

Web, www.cepintdi.org

Develops disaster preparedness training programs for deaf and hard of hearing consumers and responders. Sponsored by Telecommunications for the Deaf and Hard of Hearing (TDI) and administered by the Homeland Security Dept.

Gallaudet University, *800 Florida Ave. N.E. 20002-3695; (202) 651-5000. Fax, (202) 651-5508. Robert R. Davila, President. Phone numbers are voice and TTY accessible. Video phone, (202) 651-5866 (or IP address, 134.231.18.170).*
Web, www.gallaudet.edu

Offers undergraduate, graduate, and doctoral degree programs for deaf, hard of hearing, and hearing students. Conducts research; maintains the Laurent Clerc National Deaf Education Center and demonstration preschool, elementary (Kendall Demonstration Elementary School), and secondary programs (Model Secondary School for the Deaf). Sponsors the Center for Global Education, National Deaf Education Network and Clearinghouse, and the Cochlear Implant Education Center.

Hearing Industries Assn., *1444 Eye St. N.W., #700 20005; (202) 449-1090. Fax, (202) 216-9646. Carole M. Rogin, Executive Director.*
General e-mail, mspangler@bostrom.com

Web, www.hearing.org

Membership: hearing aid manufacturers and companies that supply hearing aid components.

Hearing Loss Assn. of America, *7910 Woodmont Ave., #1200, Bethesda, MD 20814; (301) 657-2248. Fax, (301) 913-9413. Brenda Battat, Executive Director. Main phone is voice and TTY accessible.*
General e-mail, info@hearingloss.org

Web, www.hearingloss.org

Promotes understanding of the nature, causes, and remedies of hearing loss. Provides hearing-impaired people with support and information. Seeks to educate the public about hearing loss and the problems of the hard of hearing. Provides travelers with information on assistive listening devices in museums, theaters, and places of worship. (Formerly Self Help for Hard of Hearing People.)

Laurent Clerc National Deaf Education Center, *Public Relations, Products, and Training, 800 Florida Ave. N.E. 20002-3695; (202) 651-5340 (Voice and TTY). Fax, (202) 651-5708. Edward Bosso, Dean. Toll-free, (800) 526-9105. Web, http://clerccenter.gallaudet.edu*

Provides information on topics dealing with hearing loss and deafness for children and young adults up to age twenty-one. (Affiliated with Gallaudet University.)

National Assn. of the Deaf, *8630 Fenton St., #820, Silver Spring, MD 20910-3819; (301) 587-1788. Fax, (301) 587-1791. Nancy J. Bloch, Chief Executive Officer. TTY, (301) 587-1789.*
Web, www.nad.org

Membership: state associations and affiliate organizations that promote, protect, and preserve the rights and quality of life of deaf and hard of hearing individuals in the United States. Provides civil rights advocacy, grassroots and youth leadership development, and legal expertise in areas of education, employment, health care, mental health, rehabilitation, technology, telecommunications, and transportation. Services include public information and dissemination, information and referral services, technical assistance, training seminars, national and regional conferences, legal and public policy analysis, guidance and research, and litigation consultation services that are provided to volunteer officers and membership of state association and organizational affiliates.

Registry of Interpreters for the Deaf, *333 Commerce St., Alexandria, VA 22314; (703) 838-0030. Fax, (703) 838-0454. Clay Nettles, Executive Director. TTY, (703) 838-0459.*
General e-mail, info@rid.org

Web, www.rid.org

Trains and certifies interpreters; maintains registry of certified interpreters; establishes certification standards. Sponsors training workshops and conferences.

Telecommunications for the Deaf and Hard of Hearing Inc., *8630 Fenton St., #604, Silver Spring, MD*

20910-3803; (301) 589-3786. Fax, (301) 589-3797. Claude L. Stout, Executive Director. TTY, (301) 589-3006.
General e-mail, info@tdi-online.org
Web, www.tdi-online.org

Membership: individuals, organizations, and businesses using text telephone (TTY) and video phone equipment. Promotes equal access in telecommunications, media, and information technology for people who are deaf, hard of hearing, late deafened, or deaf blind. Provides information on TTY equipment. Interests include closed captioning for television, emergency access (911), TTY and Internet relay services, and visual alerting systems. Publishes an annual TDI National Directory & Resource Guide and a quarterly news magazine, and hosts Biennial TDI Conference. Administers the Community Emergency Preparedness Information Network (CEPIN) project.

Intellectual and Developmental Disabilities

►AGENCIES

Administration for Children and Families (ACF),
(Health and Human Services Dept.), Administration on Developmental Disabilities, 200 Independence Ave. S.W., #405D 20201; (202) 690-6590. Fax, (202) 690-6904. Faith McCormick, Commissioner (Acting). TTY, (202) 690-6415.
Web, www.acf.hhs.gov/programs/add

Administers the Developmental Disabilities Assistance and Bill of Rights Act of 2000, providing grants for state protection and advocacy systems for people with developmental disabilities; state councils on developmental disabilities; university centers for developmental disabilities education, research, and services; and projects of national significance that must be addressed on a local level affecting people with developmental disabilities and their families. Also administers the disability provisions in the Help America Vote Act.

►NONGOVERNMENTAL

AAIDD (American Assn. on Intellectual and Developmental Disabilities), 501 3rd St. N.W., #200 20001-2760; (202) 387-1968. Fax, (202) 387-2193. M. Doreen Croser, Executive Director. Toll-free, (800) 424-3688.
Web, www.aaidd.org

Association for professionals who work in the field of intellectual and developmental disabilities. Provides information on legal rights, services, and facilities for people (including children) with intellectual and developmental disabilities.

The Arc, Governmental Affairs, Washington Office, 1660 L St. N.W., #701 20036; (202) 783-2229. Fax, (202) 783-8250. Paul Marchand, Director.

General e-mail, GAOinfo@thearc.org
Web, www.thearc.org

Membership: individuals interested in assisting people with intellectual and developmental disability. Provides information on government programs and legislation concerning intellectual and developmental disability; oversees and encourages support for local groups that provide direct services for people with intellectual and developmental disability. (Headquarters in Silver Spring, Md.)

Autism Society of America, 7910 Woodmont Ave., #300, Bethesda, MD 20814-3067; (301) 657-0881. Fax, (301) 657-0869. Lee Grossman, President. Information, (800) 328-8476.
General e-mail, info@autismsocietyofamerica.org
Web, www.autism-society.org

Monitors legislation and regulations affecting support, education, training, research, and other services for individuals with autism. Offers referral service and information to the public.

Best Buddies International, Washington Office, 300 D St. S.W., 9th Floor 20004; (202) 554-4801. Fax, (202) 554-4805. Lisa Derx, Vice President. Information, (800) 892-8339.
Web, www.bestbuddies.org

Volunteer organization that provides companionship and jobs to people with intellectual disabilities worldwide. (Headquarters in Miami, Fla.)

Joseph P. Kennedy Jr. Foundation, 1133 19th St. N.W., 12th Floor 20036-3604; (202) 393-1250. Fax, (202) 824-0351. Steve Eidelman, Executive Director (Acting).
General e-mail, eidelman@jpkf.org
Web, www.jpkf.org

Seeks to enhance the quality of life of persons with intellectual disabilities and their families.

National Assn. of State Directors of Developmental Disability Services (NASDDDS), 113 Oronoco St., Alexandria, VA 22314; (703) 683-4202. Fax, (703) 684-1395. Nancy Thaler, Executive Director.
Web, www.nasddds.org

Membership: chief administrators of state intellectual and developmental disability programs. Coordinates exchange of information on intellectual and developmental disability programs among the states; provides information on state programs.

National Children's Center, 6200 2nd St. N.W. 20011; (202) 722-2300. Fax, (202) 722-2383. Philip Campbell, Chief Executive Officer.
Web, www.nccinc.org

Provides educational, social, and clinical services to infants, children, and adults with intellectual and other developmental disabilities. Services provided through a 24-hour intensive treatment program, group homes and independent living programs, educational services, adult treatment programs, and early intervention programs for infants with disabilities or infants at high risk. Operates a child development center for children with and without disabilities.

National Disability Rights Network, *900 2nd St. N.E., #211 20002; (202) 408-9514. Fax, (202) 408-9520. Curtis L. Decker, Executive Director. TTY, (202) 408-9521. General e-mail, info@ndrn.org*

Web, www.ndrn.org

Membership: agencies working for the rights of the intellectually or developmentally disabled and clients of the vocational rehabilitation system. Provides state agencies with training and technical assistance; maintains an electronic mail network. Monitors legislation and regulations. (Formerly the National Assn. of Protection and Advocacy Systems.)

U.S. Psychiatric Rehabilitation Assn., *601 Global Way, #106, Linthicum, MD 21090; (410) 789-7054. Fax, (410) 789-7675. Marcie Granahan, Chief Executive Officer. General e-mail, info@uspra.org*

Web, www.uspra.org

Membership: agencies, mental health practitioners, policymakers, family groups, and consumer organizations. Supports the community adjustment of persons with psychiatric disabilities. Promotes the role of rehabilitation in mental health systems; opposes discrimination based on mental disability. Certifies psychosocial rehabilitation practitioners. (Formerly the International Assn. of Psychosocial Rehabilitation Services.)

HOMELESSNESS

▶AGENCIES

Education Dept., *Adult Education and Literacy,* *550 12th St. S.W., 11th Floor 20202-7100; (202) 245-7700. Fax, (202) 245-7838. Cheryl L. Keenan, Director. Web, www.ed.gov/about/offices/list/ovae/pi/AdultEd/index.html*

Provides state and local agencies and community-based organizations with assistance in establishing education programs for homeless adults.

Education Dept., *Title I Office: Education for Homeless Children and Youth Program,* *400 Maryland Ave. S.W., #3W214, FB-6 20202-6132; (202) 401-0962. Fax, (202) 260-7764. John McLaughlin, Program Specialist. Toll-free, (800) 872-5327. Web, www.ed.gov/programs/homeless*

Provides formula grants to education agencies in the states, Puerto Rico, and through the Bureau of Indian Affairs to Native Americans to educate homeless children and youth and to establish an office of coordinator of education for homeless children and youth in each jurisdiction.

Emergency Food and Shelter National Board Program, *701 N. Fairfax St., #310, Alexandria, VA 22314-2064; (703) 706-9660. Fax, (703) 706-9677. Sharon Bailey, Vice President. Web, www.efsp.unitedway.org*

Public/private partnership that administers the Emergency Food and Shelter Program under the McKinney-Vento Act. Gives supplemental assistance to programs that provide the homeless and persons in need with shelter, food, and support services.

Housing and Urban Development Dept. (HUD), *Community Planning and Development,* *451 7th St. S.W., #7100 20410; (202) 708-2690. Fax, (202) 708-3336. Nelson Bregón Genesa, Assistant Secretary. Web, www.hud.gov/offices/cpd*

Gives supplemental assistance to facilities that aid the homeless; awards grants for innovative programs that address the needs of homeless families with children.

Housing and Urban Development Dept. (HUD), *Special Needs Assistance Programs: Community Assistance,* *451 7th St. S.W., #7262 20410; (202) 708-1234. Fax, (202) 708-3617. Brian Fitzmaurice, Director. Web, www.hud.gov*

Advises and represents the secretary on homelessness matters; promotes cooperation among federal agencies on homelessness issues; coordinates assistance programs for the homeless under the McKinney Act. Trains HUD field staff in administering homelessness programs. Distributes funds to eligible nonprofit organizations, cities, counties, tribes, and territories for shelter, care, transitional housing, and permanent housing for the disabled homeless. Programs provide for acquisition and rehabilitation of buildings, prevention of homelessness, counseling, and medical care. Administers the Federal Surplus Property Program and spearheads the initiative to lease HUD-held homes to the homeless.

▶NONGOVERNMENTAL

Housing Assistance Council, *1025 Vermont Ave. N.W., #606 20005-3516; (202) 842-8600. Fax, (202) 347-3441. Moises Loza, Executive Director. General e-mail, hac@ruralhome.org*

Web, www.ruralhome.org

Provides low-income housing development groups in rural areas with seed money loans and technical assistance; assesses programs designed to respond to rural housing needs; makes recommendations for federal and state involvement; publishes technical guides and reports on rural housing issues.

National Alliance to End Homelessness, *1518 K St. N.W., #410 20005; (202) 638-1526. Fax, (202) 638-4664. Nan Roman, President. General e-mail, naeh@naeh.org*

Web, www.endhomelessness.org

Policy and educational organization that works to prevent, alleviate, and end problems of the homeless. Provides data and research to policymakers and the public; encourages public-private collaboration for stronger programs to reduce the homeless population.

National Coalition for Homeless Veterans, *333 1/2 Pennsylvania Ave. S.E. 20003-1148; (202) 546-1969. Fax, (202) 546-2063. Cheryl Beversdorf, President. Toll-free, (800) VET-HELP. Toll-free fax, (888) 233-8582. General e-mail, nchv@nchv.org*

Web, www.nchv.org

Provides technical assistance to service providers; advocates on behalf of homeless veterans.

National Coalition for the Homeless, *2201 P St. N.W. 20037; (202) 462-4822. Fax, (202) 462-4823. Michael Stoops, Executive Director. General e-mail, info@nationalhomeless.org*

Web, www.nationalhomeless.org

Advocacy network of persons who are or have been homeless, state and local coalitions, other activists, service providers, housing developers, and others. Seeks to create the systemic and attitudinal changes necessary to end homelessness. Works to meet the needs of persons who are homeless or at risk of becoming homeless.

National Law Center on Homelessness and Poverty, *1411 K St. N.W., #1400 20005; (202) 638-2535. Fax, (202) 628-2737. Maria Foscarinis, Executive Director. General e-mail, nlchp@nlchp.org*

Web, www.nlchp.org

Legal advocacy group that works to prevent and end homelessness through impact litigation, legislation, and education. Conducts research on homelessness issues. Acts as a clearinghouse for legal information and technical assistance. Monitors legislation and regulations.

National Policy and Advocacy Council on Homelessness, *1140 Connecticut Ave., #1210 20036; (202) 714-5378. Fax, (202) 386-6037. Brad Paul, President; Jeremy Rosen, Executive Director. General e-mail, info@npach.org*

Web, www.npach.org

Seeks to end homelessness through grassroots advocacy, education, and partnerships. Advocates for federal policies in collaboration with local communities.

Salvation Army, *P.O. Box 269, Alexandria, VA 22313-0269; (703) 684-5500. Fax, (703) 684-3478. Israel Gaither, National Commander. General e-mail, usn_national_commander@usn.salvationarmy.org*

Web, www.salvationarmy.org

International religious social welfare organization that provides the homeless with residences and social services, including counseling, emergency help, and employment services. (International headquarters in London.)

U.S. Conference of Mayors, *Task Force on Hunger and Homelessness, 1620 Eye St. N.W. 20006; (202) 293-7330. Fax, (202) 293-2352. Eugene T. Lowe, Assistant Executive Director. Web, www.usmayors.org*

Tracks trends in hunger, homelessness, and community programs that address homelessness and hunger in U.S. cities; issues reports. Monitors legislation and regulations.

SOCIAL SECURITY

▶AGENCIES

Employment Standards Administration *(Labor Dept.),* **Coal Mine Workers' Compensation,** *200 Constitution Ave. N.W., #C3520 20210; (202) 693-0046. Fax, (202) 693-1395. James L. DeMarce, Director. Web, www.dol.gov/dol/esa*

Provides direction for administration of the black lung benefits program. Adjudicates all black lung claims; certifies benefit payments and maintains black lung beneficiary rolls.

Social Security Administration (SSA), *6401 Security Blvd., Baltimore, MD 21235; (410) 965-3120. Fax, (410) 966-1463. Michael J. Astrue, Commissioner; Jason Fichtner, Deputy Commissioner (Acting). Information, (800) 772-1213. Press, (410) 965-1720. TTY, (800) 325-0778. Web, www.ssa.gov*

Administers national Social Security programs and the Supplemental Security Income program.

Social Security Administration (SSA), *Central Operations, 1500 Woodlawn Dr., Baltimore, MD 21241; (410) 966-7000. Fax, (410) 966-6005. Carolyn L. Simmons, Associate Commissioner. Information, (800) 772-1213.*

Reviews and authorizes claims for benefits under the disability insurance program and all claims for beneficiaries living abroad; certifies benefits payments; maintains beneficiary rolls.

Social Security Administration (SSA), *Disability Adjudication and Review, 5107 Leesburg Pike, #1600, Falls Church, VA 22041-3255; (703) 605-8200. Fax, (703) 605-8201. David Foster, Deputy Commissioner. Web, www.ssa.gov*

Administers a nationwide system of administrative law judges who conduct hearings and decide appealed cases concerning benefits provisions. Reviews decisions for appeals council action, if necessary, and renders the secretary's final decision. Reviews benefits cases on disability, retirement and survivors' benefits, and supplemental security income.

Social Security Administration (SSA), *Disability Determinations, 3570 Annex Bldg., 6401 Security Blvd., Baltimore, MD 21235; (410) 965-1250. Fax, (410)*

Social Security Administration

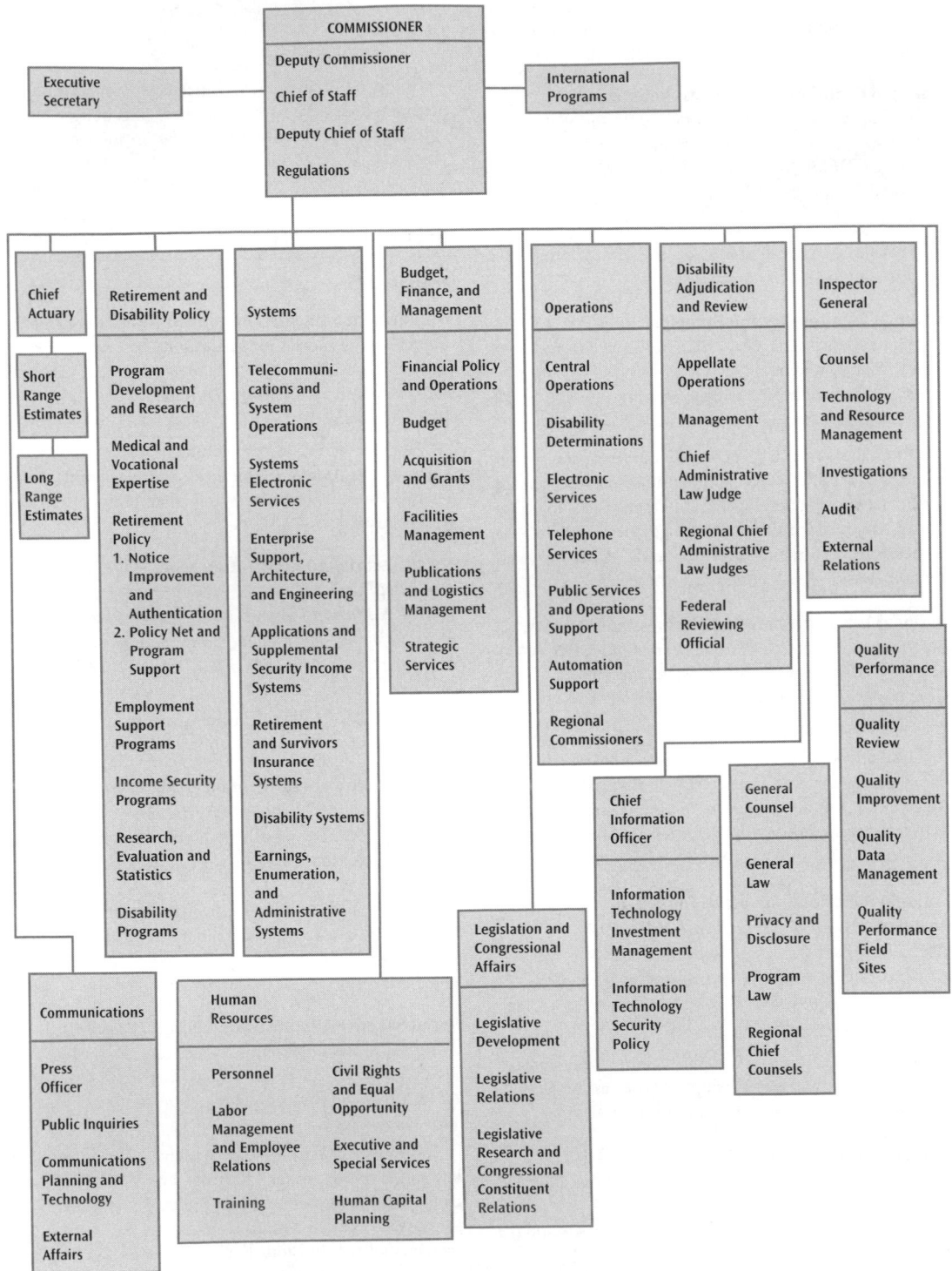

COMMISSIONER
Deputy Commissioner
Chief of Staff
Deputy Chief of Staff
Regulations

Executive Secretary

International Programs

Chief Actuary
Short Range Estimates
Long Range Estimates

Retirement and Disability Policy
Program Development and Research
Medical and Vocational Expertise
Retirement Policy
1. Notice Improvement and Authentication
2. Policy Net and Program Support
Employment Support Programs
Income Security Programs
Research, Evaluation and Statistics
Disability Programs

Systems
Telecommunications and System Operations
Systems Electronic Services
Enterprise Support, Architecture, and Engineering
Applications and Supplemental Security Income Systems
Retirement and Survivors Insurance Systems
Disability Systems
Earnings, Enumeration, and Administrative Systems

Budget, Finance, and Management
Financial Policy and Operations
Budget
Acquisition and Grants
Facilities Management
Publications and Logistics Management
Strategic Services

Operations
Central Operations
Disability Determinations
Electronic Services
Telephone Services
Public Services and Operations Support
Automation Support
Regional Commissioners

Disability Adjudication and Review
Appellate Operations
Management
Chief Administrative Law Judge
Regional Chief Administrative Law Judges
Federal Reviewing Official

Inspector General
Counsel
Technology and Resource Management
Investigations
Audit
External Relations

Quality Performance
Quality Review
Quality Improvement
Quality Data Management
Quality Performance Field Sites

Chief Information Officer
Information Technology Investment Management
Information Technology Security Policy

General Counsel
General Law
Privacy and Disclosure
Program Law
Regional Chief Counsels

Legislation and Congressional Affairs
Legislative Development
Legislative Relations
Legislative Research and Congressional Constituent Relations

Communications
Press Officer
Public Inquiries
Communications Planning and Technology
External Affairs

Human Resources
Personnel
Labor Management and Employee Relations
Training
Civil Rights and Equal Opportunity
Executive and Special Services
Human Capital Planning

965-6503. *Ruby Burrell, Associate Commissioner. Information, (800) 772-1213. TTY, (800) 325-0778. Web, www.ssa.gov/disability*

Provides direction for administration of the disability insurance program, which is paid out of the Social Security Trust Fund. Administers disability and blindness provisions of the Supplemental Security Income (SSI) program. Responsible for claims filed under black lung benefits program before July 1, 1973.

Social Security Administration (SSA), *Income Security Programs, 6401 Security Blvd., #252, Altmeyer Bldg., Baltimore, MD 21235; (410) 965-5641. Fax, (410) 965-8582. JoEllen Felice, Associate Commissioner. Web, www.ssa.gov*

Develops policies and procedures for administering the Retirement and Survivors' Insurance (RSI) programs and the Supplemental Security Income (SSI) program for the elderly, blind, and disabled. Develops agreements with the states and other agencies that govern state supplementation programs, Medicaid eligibility, food stamps, and fiscal reporting processes.

Social Security Administration (SSA), *Operations, 6401 Security Blvd., West High Rise, #1204, Baltimore, MD 21235; (410) 965-3143. Fax, (410) 966-7941. Linda S. McMahon, Deputy Commissioner. Information, (800) 772-1213. TTY, (410) 965-4404. Web, www.ssa.gov*

Issues Social Security numbers, maintains earnings and beneficiary records, authorizes claims, certifies benefits, and makes postadjudicative changes in beneficiary records for retirement, survivors', and disability insurance and black lung claims. Maintains toll-free number for workers who want information on future Social Security benefits.

Social Security Administration (SSA), *Research, Evaluation, and Statistics, 500 E St. S.W., #825 20254; (202) 358-6082. Fax, (202) 358-6079. Manuel de la Puente, Associate Commissioner. Publications, (202) 358-6263. Web, www.ssa.gov*

Compiles statistics on beneficiaries; conducts research on the economic status of beneficiaries and the relationship between Social Security, the American people, and the economy; analyzes the effects of proposed Social Security legislation, especially on lower- and middle-income individuals and families; disseminates results of research and statistical programs through publications.

►CONGRESS

For a listing of relevant congressional committees and subcommittees, please see page 629 or the Appendix.

Government Accountability Office (GAO), *Education, Workforce, and Income Security, 441 G St. N.W., #5928 20548; (202) 512-7215. Cynthia M. Fagnoni, Managing Director. Web, www.gao.gov*

Independent, nonpartisan agency in the legislative branch that audits, analyzes, and evaluates programs within the Dept. of Health and Human Services, including Social Security; makes reports available to the public. (Formerly the General Accounting Office.)

►NONGOVERNMENTAL

AARP, *601 E St. N.W. 20049; (202) 434-2277. Fax, (202) 434-2320. William D. Novelli, Chief Executive Officer. Press, (202) 434-2560. TTY, (877) 434-7595. Research Info Center, (202) 434-6233. Web, www.aarp.org*

Membership: persons fifty and older. Works to address members' needs and interests through education, advocacy, and service. Monitors legislation and regulations and disseminates information on issues affecting older Americans, including issues related to Social Security. (Formerly the American Assn. of Retired Persons.)

National Academy of Social Insurance, *1776 Massachusetts Ave. N.W., #615 20036-1904; (202) 452-8097. Fax, (202) 452-8111. Pamela J. Larson, Executive Vice President. General e-mail, nasi@nasi.org*

Web, www.nasi.org

Promotes research and education on Social Security, Medicare, health care financing, and related public and private programs; assesses social insurance programs and their relationship to other programs; supports research and leadership development. Acts as a clearinghouse for social insurance information.

National Committee to Preserve Social Security and Medicare, *10 G St. N.E., #600 20002-4215; (202) 216-0420. Fax, (202) 216-0446. Barbara Kennelly, President. Press, (202) 216-8378. Web, www.ncpssm.org*

Educational and advocacy organization that focuses on Social Security and Medicare programs and on related income security and health issues. Interests include retirement income protection, health care reform, and the quality of life of seniors. Monitors legislation and regulations.

18 Transportation

GENERAL POLICY AND ANALYSIS

Basic Resources

▶**AGENCIES**

Architectural and Transportation Barriers Compliance Board (Access Board), *1331 F St. N.W., #1000 20004-1111; (202) 272-0080. Fax, (202) 272-0081. David M. Capozzi, Executive Director. TTY, (202) 272-0082. TTY toll-free, (800) 993-2822. Toll-free technical assistance, (800) 872-2253.*
General e-mail, info@access-board.gov

Web, www.access-board.gov

Develops and maintains accessibility requirements for buildings, transit vehicles, telecommunications equipment, and electronic and information technology. Provides technical assistance and training on these guidelines and standards. Enforces access standards for federally funded facilities through the Architectural Barriers Act.

National Transportation Safety Board, *490 L'Enfant Plaza East S.W. 20594-2000; (202) 314-6035. Fax, (202) 314-6018. Mark V. Rosenker, Chair (Acting). Information, (202) 314-6000. Press, (202) 314-6100.*
Web, www.ntsb.gov

Promotes transportation safety through independent investigations of accidents and other safety problems. Makes recommendations for safety improvement.

National Transportation Safety Board, *Research and Engineering, 490 L'Enfant Plaza East S.W. 20594-2000; (202) 314-6500. Fax, (202) 314-6599. Vernon S. Ellingstad, Director.*
Web, www.ntsb.gov

Evaluates effectiveness of federal, state, and local safety programs. Identifies transportation safety issues not being addressed by government or industry. Conducts studies on specific safety problems.

National Transportation Safety Board, *Safety Recommendations and Advocacy, 490 L'Enfant Plaza East S.W. 20594-2000; (202) 314-6170. Fax, (202) 314-6178. Elaine Weinstein, Director, (202) 314-6171.*
Web, www.ntsb.gov

Makes transportation safety recommendations to federal and state agencies on all modes of transportation. Produces the annual "Most Wanted" list of critical transportation safety projects.

Office of Management and Budget (OMB), *(Executive Office of the President), Transportation, New Executive Office Bldg., #9002 20503; (202) 395-5704. Fax, (202) 395-4797. Andrew Abrams, Chief. Press, (202) 395-7254.*
Web, www.whitehouse.gov/omb

Assists and advises the OMB director on budget preparation, proposed legislation, and evaluations of Transportation Dept. programs, policies, and activities.

Pipeline and Hazardous Materials Safety Administration *(Transportation Dept.), 1200 New Jersey Ave. S.E., #E27-300 20590; (202) 366-4433. Fax, (202) 366-3666. Vacant, Administrator. Hazardous Materials Information Center, (800) 467-4922. To report an incident, (800) 424-8802.*
Web, www.phmsa.dot.gov

Oversees the safe and secure movement of hazardous materials to industry and consumers by all modes of transportation, including pipelines. Works to eliminate transportation-related deaths and injuries. Promotes transportation solutions to protect communities and the environment.

Pipeline and Hazardous Materials Safety Administration *(Transportation Dept.), Hazardous Materials Safety, 1200 New Jersey Ave. S.E. 20590; (202) 366-0656. Fax, (202) 366-5713. Theodore Willke, Associate Administrator. Information, (202) 366-4488. Hazardous Materials Information Center, (800) 467-4922.*
General e-mail, phmsa.hmhazmatsafety@dot.gov

Web, http://hazmat.dot.gov

Federal safety authority for the transportation of hazardous materials by air, rail, highway, and water. Works to reduce dangers of hazardous materials transportation. Issues regulations for classifications, communications, shipper and carrier operations, training and security requirements, and packaging and container specifications.

Pipeline and Hazardous Materials Safety Administration *(Transportation Dept.), Pipeline Safety, 1200 New Jersey Ave. S.E., E24-455 20590; (202) 366-4595. Fax, (202) 366-4566. Jeffrey D. Wiese, Associate Administrator (Acting).*
General e-mail, phmsa.pipelinesafety@dot.gov

Web, http://phmsa.dot.gov

Issues and enforces federal regulations for oil, natural gas, and petroleum products pipeline safety. Inspects pipelines and oversees risk management by pipeline operators.

Research and Innovative Technology Administration *(Transportation Dept.), 1200 New Jersey Ave. S.E. 20590; (202) 366-7582. Fax, (202) 493-2381. Vacant, Administrator; Steven K. Smith, Deputy Administrator (Acting).*
General e-mail, ritainfo@dot.gov

Web, www.rita.dot.gov

Coordinates and manages the department's research portfolio and expedites implementation of innovative technologies. Oversees the Bureau of Transportation Statistics, Volpe National Transportation Systems Center (in Cambridge, Mass.), and the Transportation Safety Institute (in Oklahoma City).

Research and Innovative Technology Administration *(Transportation Dept.), Bureau of Transportation Statistics, 1200 New Jersery Ave. S.E., #E34-314 20590; (202) 366-1270. Fax, (202) 366-3640. Steve Dillingham, Director. Information, (800) 853-1351.*

TRANSPORTATION RESOURCES IN CONGRESS

For a complete listing of Congress committees, including their full contact information, leadership, membership, and jurisdictions, please refer to the Appendix on pages 724–837.

HOUSE:

House Appropriations Committee, (202) 225-2771.
Web, appropriations.house.gov
  Subcommittee on Energy and Water
    Development, (202) 225-3421.
  Subcommittee on Financial Services and General
    Government, (202) 225-7245.
  Subcommittee on Homeland Security, (202) 225-5834.
  Subcommittee on Transportation, HUD, and
    Related Agencies, (202) 225-2141.
House Energy and Commerce Committee,
  Subcommittee on Commerce, Trade and
  Consumer Protection, (202) 225-2927.
Web, energycommerce.house.gov
House Homeland Security Committee, (202) 226-2616.
Web, homeland.house.gov
  Subcommittee on Border, Maritime and Global
    Counterterrorism, (202) 226-2616.
  Subcommittee on Transportation Security and
    Infrastructure Protection, (202) 226-2616.
House Natural Resources Committee, Subcommittee
  on Water and Power, (202) 225-8331.
Web, resourcescommittee.gov
House Science and Technology Committee,
  Subcommittee on Space and Aeronautics, (202)
  225-7858.
Web, science.house.gov
  Subcommittee on Technology and Innovation,
    (202) 225-7858.
House Select Committee on Energy Independence
  and Global Warming, (202) 225-4012.
Web, globalwarming.house.gov
House Transportation and Infrastructure
  Committee, (202) 225-4472.
Web, transportation.house.gov
  Subcommittee on Aviation, (202) 225-9161.
  Subcommittee on Coast Guard and Maritime
    Transportation, (202) 226-3587.
  Subcommittee on Economic Development, Public
    Buildings and Emergency Management, (202)
    225-9961.
  Subcommittee on Highways and Transit, (202)
    225-9989.
  Subcommittee on Railroads, Pipelines, and
    Hazardous Materials, (202) 225-3274.
  Subcommittee on Water Resources and
    Environment, (202) 225-0060.

SENATE:

Senate Appropriations Committee, (202) 224-7363.
Web, appropriations.senate.gov
  Subcommittee on Energy and Water
    Development, (202) 224-8119.

  Subcommittee on Homeland Security, (202)
    224-8244.
  Subcommittee on Transportation, HUD and
    Related Agencies, (202) 224-7281.
Senate Banking, Housing and Urban Affairs
  Committee, (202) 224-7391.
Web, banking.senate.gov
  Subcommittee on Housing, Transportation and
    Community Development, (202) 224-6542.
Senate Commerce, Science, and Transportation
  Committee, (202) 224-0411.
Web, commerce.senate.gov
  Subcommittee on Aviation Operations, Safety,
    and Security, (202) 224-9000.
  Subcommittee on Consumer Affairs, Insurance,
    and Automotive Safety, (202) 224-1270.
  Subcommittee on Interstate Commerce, Trade
    and Tourism, (202) 224-1270.
  Subcommittee on Oceans, Atmosphere, Fisheries
    and the Coast Guard, (202) 224-4912.
  Subcommittee on Science, Technology, and
    Innovation, (202) 224-0415.
  Subcommittee on Space, Aeronautics, and
    Related Sciences, (202) 224-0415.
  Subcommittee on Surface Transportation and
    Merchant Marine Infrastructure, Safety and
    Security, (202) 224-9000.
Senate Energy and Natural Resources Committee,
  Subcommittee on Water and Power, (202)
  224-4971.
Web, energy.senate.gov
Senate Environment and Public Works Committee,
  Subcommittee on Transportation and
  Infrastructure, (202) 224-8832.
Web, epw.senate.gov/public
  Subcommittee on Transportation Safety,
    Infrastructure Security and Water Quality,
    (202) 224-8832.
Senate Finance Committee, Subcommittee on
  Energy, Natural Resources and Infrastructure,
  (202) 224-4515.
Web, finance.senate.gov
Senate Health, Education, Labor, and Pensions
  Committee, (202) 224-5375.
Web, help.senate.gov
Senate Homeland Security and Governmental
  Affairs Committee, (202) 224-2627.
Web, hsgac.senate.gov
Senate Special Committee on Aging, (202) 224-5364.
Web, aging.senate.gov

Transportation Department

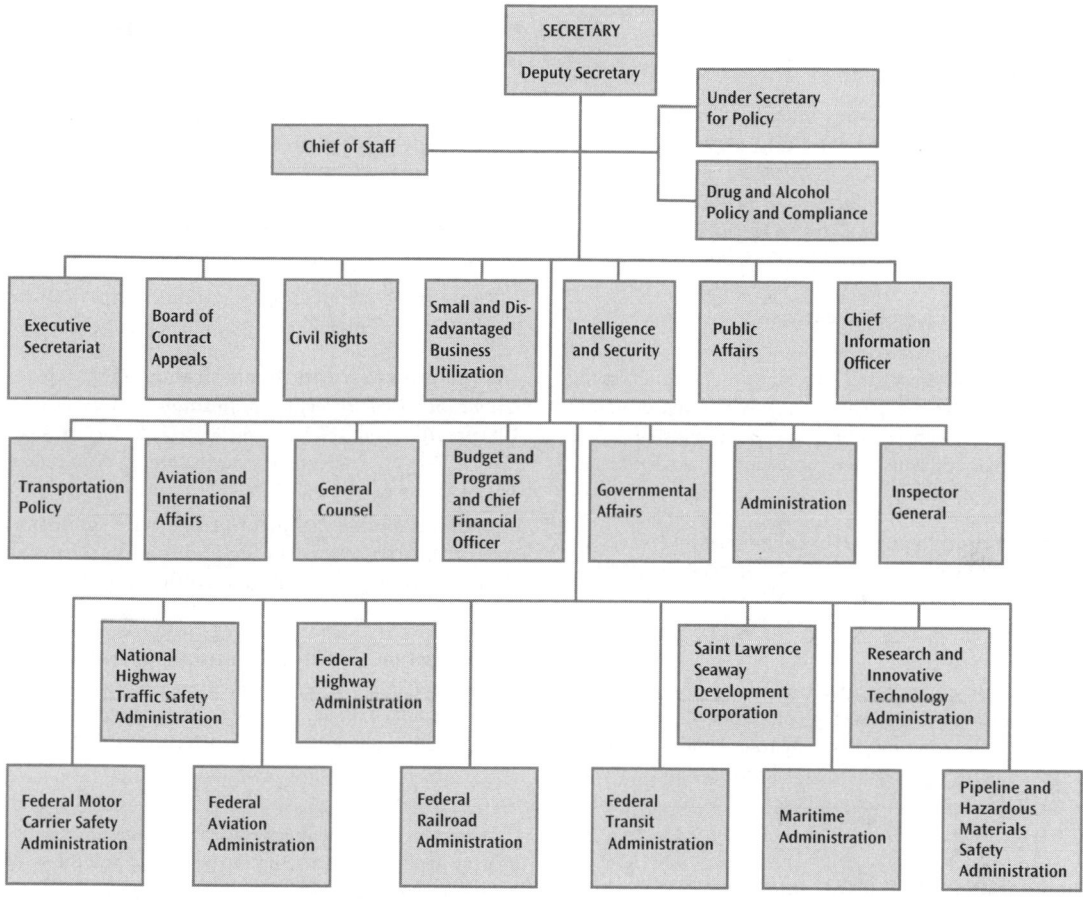

General e-mail, answers@bts.gov

Web, www.bts.gov

Works to improve public awareness of the nation's transportation systems. Collects, analyzes, and publishes a comprehensive, cross-modal set of transportation statistics.

Research and Innovative Technology Administration
(Transportation Dept.), Research, Development, and Technology, 1200 New Jersey Ave. S.E., #E33-304 20590-0001; (202) 366-5447. Fax, (202) 366-3671. Jan Brecht-Clark, Associate Administrator.
Web, www.rita.dot.gov

Supports transportation innovation research, engineering, education, and safety training. Focus includes intermodal transportation; partnerships among government, universities, and industry; and economic growth and competitiveness through use of new technologies. Monitors international research.

Transportation Dept. (DOT), *1200 New Jersey Ave. S.E. 20590; (202) 366-4000. Fax, (202) 208-7351. Raymond L. LaHood, Secretary. Press, (202) 366-4570.*

General e-mail, dot.comments@dot.gov

Web, www.dot.gov

Responsible for shaping and administering policies and programs to protect and enhance the transportation system and services. Includes the Federal Aviation Administration, Federal Highway Administration, Federal Motor Carrier Safety Administration, Federal Railroad Administration, Maritime Administration, National Highway Traffic Safety Administration, Pipeline and Hazardous Materials Safety Administration, Research and Innovative Technology Administration, Federal Transit Administration, and the Saint Lawrence Seaway Development Corp. The Surface Transportation Board is also administratively affiliated, but decisionally independent.

Transportation Dept. (DOT), *Aviation and*
International Affairs, 1200 New Jersey Ave. S.E., #W88-318 20590; (202) 366-8822. Fax, (202) 493-2005. Susan McDermott, Assistant Secretary (Acting). Press, (202) 366-5582.
Web, http://ostpxweb.dot.gov/aviation

Develops and implements public policy related to the airline industry and international civil aviation. Administers laws and regulations over a range of aviation trade issues, including U.S. and foreign carrier economic authority to engage in air transportation, small community transportation, the establishment of mail rates within Alaska and in the international market, and access at U.S. airports.

Transportation Dept. (DOT), *Aviation Consumer Protection, 1200 New Jersey Ave. S.E., #W96-432 20590 (mailing address: 1200 New Jersey S.E., Transportation Dept., C-75, #4107, Washington, DC 20590); (202) 366-2220. Norman Strickman, Director. Fax, (202) 366-5944. Disability-Related Problems, (800) 778-4838. TTY, (800) 455-9880.*
Web, www.airconsumer.ost.dot.gov

Refers consumer complaints to appropriate departmental offices; advises the secretary on consumer issues; coordinates citizen participation activities and promotes joint projects with consumer interest groups; serves as ombudsman for consumer protection affairs; publishes educational materials.

Transportation Dept. (DOT), *Environmental Policies Team, 1200 New Jersey Ave. S.E., #W86306 20590-0001; (202) 366-4861. Fax, (202) 366-7638. Camille H. Mittelholtz, Environmental Policies Team Leader.*
Web, www.dot.gov

Develops environmental policy and makes recommendations to the secretary; monitors Transportation Dept. implementation of environmental legislation; serves as liaison with other federal agencies and state and local governments on environmental matters related to transportation.

Transportation Dept. (DOT), *Intelligence, Security, and Emergency Response, 1200 New Jersey Ave. S.E., #56125 20590; (202) 366-6525. Fax, (202) 366-7261. Michael Lowder, Director.*
Web, www.dot.gov

Advises the secretary on transportation intelligence and security policy. Acts as liaison with the intelligence community, federal agencies, corporations, and interest groups; administers counterterrorism strategic planning processes. Develops, coordinates, and reviews transportation emergency preparedness programs for use in emergencies affecting national defense and in emergencies caused by natural and man-made disasters and crisis situations.

Transportation Dept. (DOT), *Safety, Energy, and Environment, 1200 New Jersey Ave. S.E., #W84-310 20590; (202) 366-4416. Fax, (202) 366-0263. Linda L. Lawson, Director.*
Web, http://ostpxweb.ost.dot.gov/policy/safetycontact.htm

Develops, coordinates, and evaluates public policy with respect to safety, environmental, energy, and accessibility issues affecting all aspects of transportation. Assesses the economic and institutional implications of domestic transportation matters. Oversees legislative and regulatory proposals affecting transportation. Provides advice on research and development requirements. Develops

policy proposals to improve the performance, safety, and efficiency of the transportation system.

Transportation Security Administration (TSA), *(Homeland Security Dept.), 601 S. 12th St., 7th Floor, Arlington, VA 22202-4220; (571) 227-2801. Fax, (571) 227-1398. Gale D. Rossides, Administrator (Acting). Press, (571) 227-2829. Questions and concerns regarding travel can be submitted to the TSA Contact Center, toll-free, (866) 289-9673.*
General e-mail, TSA-ContactCenter@dhs.gov
Web, www.tsa.gov/public

Protects the nation's transportation systems to ensure freedom of movement for people and commerce.

Transportation Security Administration (TSA), *(Homeland Security Dept.), Acquisition, TSA-25, 601 S. 12th St., Arlington, VA 20598-6028; (571) 227-1795. Fax, (571) 227-2911. Rick Gunderson, Assistant Administrator.*
Web, www.tsa.gov

Administers contract grants, cooperative agreements, and other transactions in support of TSA's mission. Develops acquisitions strategies, policies, programs, and processes.

Transportation Security Administration (TSA), *(Homeland Security Dept.), Intelligence and Analysis, TSA-10, 601 S. 12th St., 6th Floor, Arlington, VA 22202-4220; (703) 601-3100. Fax, (703) 601-3290. Stephen N. Wood, Assistant Administrator.*
Web, www.tsa.gov

Oversees TSA's intelligence gathering and information sharing as they pertain to national security and the safety of the nation's transportation systems.

Transportation Security Administration (TSA), *(Homeland Security Dept.), Legislative Affairs, TSA-5, 601 S. 12th St., Arlington, VA 20598-6028; (571) 227-2717. Claire Heffernan, Assistant Administrator (Acting).*
Web, www.tsa.gov

Serves as the TSA's primary point of contact for Congress. Coordinates responses to congressional inquiries, verifies hearings and witnesses, and delivers testimony related to the nation's transportation security.

Transportation Security Administration (TSA), *(Homeland Security Dept.), Strategic Communications and Public Affairs, TSA-4, 601 S. 12th St., Arlington, VA 20598-6028; (571) 227-2829. Fax, (571) 227-2552. Kristin Lee, Assistant Administrator.*
Web, www.tsa.gov

Responsible for TSA's communications and public information outreach, both externally and internally.

Transportation Security Administration (TSA), *(Homeland Security Dept.), Transportation Sector Network Management, TSA-28, 601 S. 12th St., Arlington, VA 20598-6028; (571) 227-4640. Fax, (571) 227-2932. John P. Sammon, Assistant Administrator.*
Web, www.tsa.gov

Transportation Security Administration

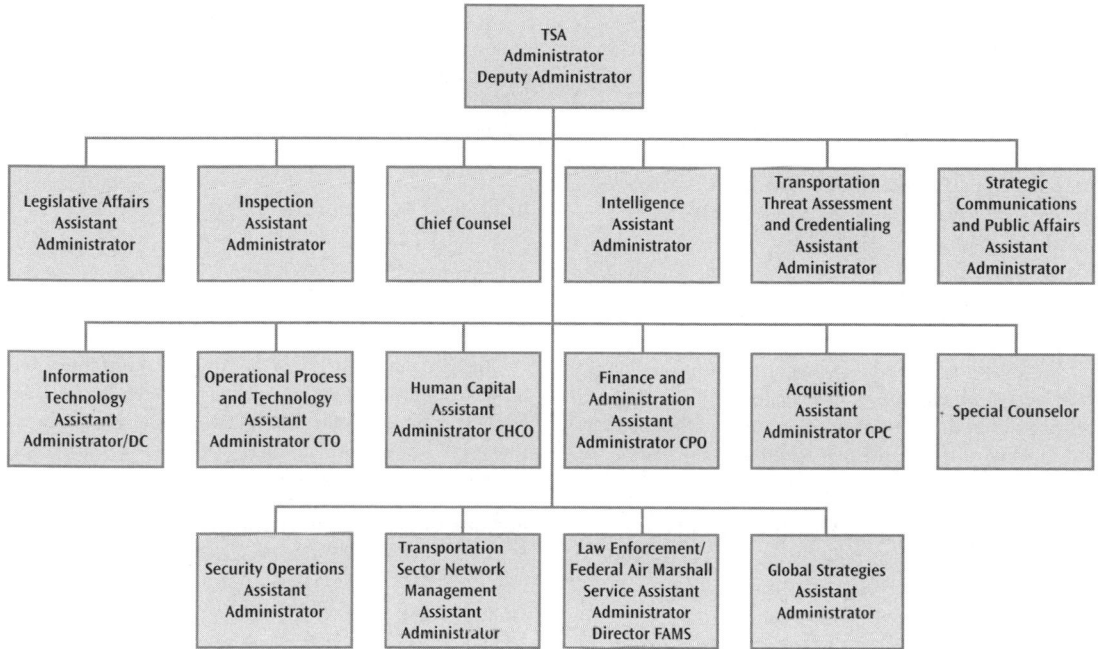

Formulates policy and shares information related to security in various segments of the transportation industry, including commercial airports, commercial airlines, general aviation, mass transit and passenger rail, freight rail, maritime, highway and motor carrier, pipeline and air cargo. Coordinates with the U.S. Coast Guard, the lead agency for maritime security.

Transportation Security Administration (TSA), *(Homeland Security Dept.), Transportation Threat Assessment and Credentialing, TSA-19, 601 S. 12th St., Arlington, VA 20598-6028; (571) 227-3603. Gregory R. Wellen, Assistant Administrator.*
Web, www.tsa.gov

Conducts a range of programs designed to ensure that known or suspected terrorists do not gain access to sensitive areas of the nation's transportation system, including the Alien Flight, Registered Traveler, Secure Flight, and Transportation Worker Identification Credential programs and Hazmat Materials Truck Drivers Background Checks.

U.S. Customs and Border Protection *(Homeland Security Dept.), Field Operations, 1300 Pennsylvania Ave. N.W., #2.4A 20229; (202) 344-1620. Fax, (202) 344-2777 Thomas Winkowski, Assistant Commissioner. Press, (202) 344-1780. Hotline to report suspicious activity, (800) 232-5378.*
Web, www.cbp.gov

Enforces statutes relating to the processing and regulation of people, baggage, cargo, and mail in and out of the United States; assesses and collects customs duties, excise taxes, fees, and penalties due on imported merchandise; administers certain navigation laws.

► CONGRESS

For a listing of relevant congressional committees and subcommittees, please see page 656 or the Appendix.

Government Accountability Office (GAO), *Physical Infrastructure, 441 G St. N.W., #2057 20548; (202) 512-6737. Patricia Dalton, Managing Director.*
Web, www.gao.gov

Independent, nonpartisan agency in the legislative branch. Audits, analyzes, and evaluates performance of the Transportation Dept. and its component agencies; makes reports available to the public. (Formerly the General Accounting Office.)

► NONGOVERNMENTAL

American Concrete Pavement Assn. (ACPA), *Washington Office, 500 New Jersey Ave. N.W., 7th Floor 20001; (202) 638-2272. Fax, (202) 638-2688. Gerald F. Voigt, President.*
Web, www.pavement.com

Provides members with project assistance, educational workshops, and training programs. Researches concrete pavement design, construction, and rehabilitation.

American Public Works Assn., *Washington Office, 1401 K St. N.W., 11th Floor 20005; (202) 408-9541. Fax, (202) 408-9542. Peter B. King, Executive Director.*

General e-mail, apwa.dc@apwa.net

Web, www.apwa.net

Membership: engineers, architects, and others who maintain and manage public works facilities and services. Conducts research and education and promotes exchange of information on transportation and infrastructure-related issues. (Headquarters in Kansas City, Mo.)

Americans for Transportation Mobility, *U.S. Chamber of Commerce, 1615 H St. N.W., 6th Floor 20062-2000; (202) 463-5600. Fax, (202) 887-3430. Janet F. Kavinoky, Executive Director.*
General e-mail, mobility@uschamber.com

Web, www.a-t-m.org

Works to make the U.S. transportation infrastructure safer and more efficient. Educates the public and elected officials about the value of transportation to the economy and quality of life. (Affiliated with the U.S. Chamber of Commerce.)

Assn. for Safe International Road Travel, *11769 Gainsborough Rd., Potomac, MD 20854-3247; (301) 983-5252. Fax, (301) 983-3663. Cathy Silberman, Executive Director.*
General e-mail, asirt@asirt.org

Web, www.asirt.org

Promotes road safety through education and advocacy with governments in the United States and abroad. Serves as information resource for governments, study abroad programs, travel organizations, nongovernmental organizations, and individual travelers.

Assn. of Metropolitan Planning Organizations, *Transportation, 1029 Vermont Ave., #710 20005; (202) 296-7051. Fax, (202) 296-7054. DeLania Hardy, Executive Director.*
Web, www.ampo.org

Membership: more than 385 metropolitan councils of elected officials and transportation professionals responsible for planning local transportation systems. Provides a forum for professional and organizational development; sponsors conferences and training programs.

Assn. of Transportation Law Professionals, *P.O. Box 5407, Annapolis, MD 21403; (410) 268-1311. Fax, (410) 268-1322. Lauren Michalski, Executive Director.*
General e-mail, Michalski@atlp.org

Web, www.atlp.org

Provides members with continuing educational development in transportation law and practice. Interests include railroad, motor, energy, pipeline, antitrust, labor, logistics, safety, environmental, air, and maritime matters. (Formerly the Assn. for Transportation Law, Logistics, and Policy.)

Diesel Technology Forum, *5291 Corporate Drive, #102, Frederick, MD 21703-2875; (301) 668-7230. Fax, (301) 668-7234. Allen Schaeffer, Executive Director.*

General e-mail, dtf@dieselforum.org

Web, www.dieselforum.org

Membership: vehicle and engine manufacturers, component suppliers, petroleum refineries, and emissions control device makers. Provides information on diesel power technology use and efforts to improve fuel efficiency and emissions control. Monitors legislation and regulations.

Institute of Navigation, *3975 University Dr., #390, Fairfax, VA 22030-2520; (703) 383-9688. Fax, (703) 383-9689. Lisa Beaty, Director of Operations.*
General e-mail, membership@ion.org

Web, www.ion.org

Membership: individuals and organizations interested in navigation. Encourages research in navigation and establishment of uniform practices in navigation operations and education; conducts symposia on air, space, marine, and land navigation.

Institute of Transportation Engineers (ITE), *1099 14th St. N.W., #300 West 20005-3438; (202) 289-0222. Fax, (202) 289-7722. Philip J. Caruso, Deputy Executive Director.*
General e-mail, ite_staff@ite.org

Web, www.ite.org

Membership: international professional transportation engineers. Conducts research, seminars, and training sessions; provides professional and scientific information on transportation standards and recommended practices.

International Brotherhood of Teamsters, *25 Louisiana Ave. N.W. 20001-2198; (202) 624-6800. Fax, (202) 624-6918. James P. Hoffa, President. Press, (202) 624-6911.*
General e-mail, feedback@teamster.org

Web, www.teamster.org

Membership: more than 1.4 million workers in the transportation and construction industries, factories, offices, hospitals, warehouses, and other workplaces. Helps members negotiate pay, benefits, and better working conditions; conducts training programs and workshops. Monitors legislation and regulations.

National Defense Transportation Assn. (NDTA), *50 S. Pickett St., #220, Alexandria, VA 22304-7296; (703) 751-5011. Fax, (703) 823-8761. Lt. Gen. Kenneth Wykle (USA, Ret.), President.*
Web, www.ndtahq.com

Membership: transportation users, manufacturers, and mode carriers; information technology firms; and related military, government, and civil interests worldwide. Promotes a strong U.S. transportation capability through coordination of private industry, government, and the military.

National Research Council (NRC), *Transportation Research Board, 500 5th St. N.W. 20001; (202) 334-2934. Fax, (202) 334-2003. Robert E. Skinner Jr., Executive Director. Library, (202) 334-2989. Press, (202) 334-2138.*
Web, www.trb.org

Promotes research in transportation systems planning and administration and in the design, construction, maintenance, and operation of transportation facilities. Provides information to state and national highway and transportation departments; operates research information services; conducts studies, conferences, and workshops; publishes technical reports. Library open to the public by appointment.

National Research Council (NRC), *Transportation Research Board Library, 500 5th St. N.W. 20001; (202) 334-2989. Fax, (202) 334-2527. Barbara Post, Information Services Manager. Press, (202) 334-3252.*
Web, www.trb.org

Primary archive for the Transportation Research Board, Highway Research Board, Strategic Highway Research Program, and Marine Board. Subject areas include transportation, aviation, engineering, rail, roads, and transit.

Sheet Metal Workers International Assn., *1750 New York Ave. N.W. 20006; (202) 783-5880. Fax, (202) 662-0880. Michael J. Sullivan, General President.*
Web, www.smwia.org

Membership: more than 150,000 U.S., Puerto Rican, and Canadian workers in the building and construction trades, manufacturing, and the railroad and shipyard industries. Assists members with contract negotiation and grievances; conducts training programs and workshops. Monitors legislation and regulations. (Affiliated with the Sheet Metal and Air Conditioning Contractors' Assn., the AFL-CIO, and the Canadian Labour Congress.)

Surface Transportation Policy Partnership, *1707 L St. N.W., #1050 20036-4602; (202) 466-2636. Fax, (202) 466-2247. Anne P. Canby, President. Press, (202) 466-2641. General e-mail, stpp@transact.org*

Web, www.transact.org

Advocates transportation policy and investments that conserve energy, protect environmental and aesthetic quality, strengthen the economy, promote social equity, and make communities more livable.

United Transportation Union, *Washington Office, 304 Pennsylvania Ave. S.E. 20003; (202) 543-7714. Fax, (202) 543-0015. James A. Stem, Legislative Director. General e-mail, jamesastem@aol.com*

Web, www.utu.org

Membership: approximately 150,000 workers in the transportation industry. Helps members negotiate pay, benefits, and better working conditions; conducts training programs and workshops. Monitors legislation and regulations. (Headquarters in Cleveland, Ohio.)

Freight and Intermodalism

▶**AGENCIES**

Federal Railroad Administration *(Transportation Dept.), Policy and Communications, West Bldg., 1200*

New Jersey Ave. S.E., MS 15 20590; (202) 493-6400. Fax, (202) 493-6401. Timothy Barkley, Director. Web, www.fra.dot.gov

Promotes intermodal movement of freight involving rail transportation; studies economics and industry practices.

Maritime Administration *(Transportation Dept.), Infrastructure Development and Congestion Mitigation, West Bldg., 1200 New Jersey Ave. S.E. 20590; (202) 366-5474. Fax, (202) 366-6988. Richard L. Walker, Director. Web, http://marad.dot.gov*

Provides coordination and management of port infrastructure projects; provides leadership in national congestion mitigation efforts that involve waterway and port issues; promotes the development and improved utilization of ports and port facilities, including intermodal connections, terminals, and distribution networks; and provides technical information and advice to other agencies and organizations concerned with intermodal development. Information and advice include the analysis of intermodal economics, the development of applicable information systems, investigation of institutional and regulatory impediments, and the application of appropriate transportation management systems.

Surface Transportation Board *(Transportation Dept.), 395 E St. S.W. 20423-0001; (202) 245-0245. Fax, (202) 245-0458. Charles D. Nottingham, Chair, (202) 245-0200. Library, (202) 245-0406. TTY, (800) 877-8339. Web, www.stb.dot.gov*

Regulates rates for water transportation and intermodal connections in noncontiguous domestic trade (between the mainland and Alaska, Hawaii, or U.S. territories). Library open to the public.

▶**NONGOVERNMENTAL**

American Moving and Storage Assn., *1611 Duke St., Alexandria, VA 22314-3406; (703) 683-7410. Fax, (703) 683-7527. Linda Bauer Darr, President. General e-mail, info@moving.org*

Web, www.moving.org

Represents members' views before the Transportation Dept. and other government agencies. Conducts certification and training programs. Provides financial support for research on the moving and storage industry.

Intermodal Assn. of North America, *11785 Beltsville Dr., #1100, Calverton, MD 20705-4048; (301) 982-3400. Fax, (301) 982-4815. Joni Casey, President. General e-mail, IANA@intermodal.org*

Web, www.intermodal.org

Membership: railroads, stacktrain operators, water carriers, motor carriers, marketing companies, and suppliers to the intermodal industry. Promotes intermodal transportation of freight. Monitors legislation and regulations.

National Assn. of Chemical Distributors (NACD), *1555 Wilson Blvd., #700, Arlington, VA 22209-2442; (703) 527-6223. Fax, (703) 527-7747. Chris Jahn, President. General e-mail, nacdpublicaffairs@nacd.com*

Web, www.nacd.com

Membership: firms involved in purchasing, processing, blending, storing, transporting, and marketing of chemical products. Provides members with information on such topics as training, safe handling and transport of chemicals, liability insurance, and environmental issues. Manages the NACD Chemical Educational Foundation. Monitors legislation and regulations.

National Customs Brokers and Forwarders Assn. of America, *1200 18th St. N.W., #901 20036; (202) 466-0222. Fax, (202) 466-0226. Barbara Reilly, Executive Vice President. General e-mail, staff@ncbfaa.org*

Web, www.ncbfaa.org

Membership: customs brokers and freight forwarders in the United States. Fosters information exchange within the industry. Monitors legislation and regulations.

National Industrial Transportation League, *1700 N. Moore St., #1900, Arlington, VA 22209-1904; (703) 524-5011. Fax, (703) 524-5017. Ruth Carlton, President. General e-mail, info@nitl.org*

Web, www.nitl.org

Membership: air, water, and surface shippers and receivers, including industries, corporations, chambers of commerce, and trade associations. Monitors legislation and regulations.

AIR TRANSPORTATION

▶AGENCIES

Civil Air Patrol, *National Capital Wing, Washington Office, 200 McChord St., #111, Bolling AFB 20032-0000; (202) 767-4405. Fax, (202) 767-5695. Col. Richard J. Cooper, Wing Commander, (202) 767-7776. General e-mail, cc@natcapwg.cap.gov*

Web, www.natcapwg.cap.gov

Official civilian auxiliary of the U.S. Air Force. Primary function is to conduct search-and-rescue missions for the Air Force. Maintains an aerospace education program for adults and a cadet program for junior and senior high school students. (Headquarters at Maxwell Air Force Base, Ala.)

Federal Aviation Administration (FAA), *(Transportation Dept.), 800 Independence Ave. S.W. 20591; (202) 267-3111. Fax, (202) 267-5047. J. Randolph Babbitt, Administrator. Press, (202) 267-3883. Toll-free, (866) 835-5322. Web, www.faa.gov*

Regulates air commerce to improve aviation safety; promotes development of a national system of airports; develops and operates a common system of air traffic control and air navigation for both civilian and military aircraft; prepares the annual National Aviation System Plan.

Federal Aviation Administration (FAA), *(Transportation Dept.), Air Traffic Organization: Acquisition and Business Services, 800 Independence Ave. S.W., #1019, AJA-O 20591; (202) 267-7222. Fax, (202) 267-5738. James H. Washington, Vice President. Web, www.faa.gov/about/office_org/headquarters_offices/ato*

Advises and assists in developing concepts for applying new technologies to meet long-range national airspace system requirements and for system acquisition, engineering, and management activities.

Federal Aviation Administration (FAA), *(Transportation Dept.), Aviation Policy, Planning, and Environment, 800 Independence Ave. S.W., #1005, APEP-1 20591-0001; (202) 267-3927. Fax, (202) 267-5800. Nancy D. LoBue, Assistant Administrator (Acting). Web, www.faa.gov/about/office_org/headquarters_offices/aep*

Leads the FAA's strategic policy and planning efforts, coordinates the agency's reauthorization before Congress, and is responsible for national aviation policies and strategies in the environment and energy arenas, including aviation activity forecasts, economic analyses, aircraft noise and emissions research and policy, environmental policy, and aviation insurance.

Federal Aviation Administration (FAA), *(Transportation Dept.), Environment and Energy, 800 Independence Ave. S.W., #900W 20591; (202) 267-3576. Fax, (202) 267-5594. Carl E. Burleson, Director. Web, www.faa.gov/about/office_org/headquarters_offices/aep*

Responsible for environmental affairs and energy conservation for aviation, including implementation and administration of various aviation-related environmental acts.

Federal Aviation Administration (FAA), *(Transportation Dept.), International Aviation, 600 Independence Ave. S.W., #10B, 6th Floor East, API-1 20591; (202) 385-8900. Fax, (202) 267-7198. Dorothy Reimold, Assistant Administrator (Acting). Web, www.faa.gov/other_visit/aviation_industry/international_aviation*

Coordinates all activities of the FAA that involve foreign relations; acts as liaison with the State Dept. and other agencies concerning international aviation; provides other countries with technical assistance on civil aviation problems; formulates international civil aviation policy for the United States.

Federal Aviation Administration (FAA), *(Transportation Dept.), Operations: Systems Engineering and Safety, 1250 Maryland Ave. S.W., 3rd Floor 20024 (mailing address: 800 Independence Ave. S.W.,*

Federal Aviation Administration

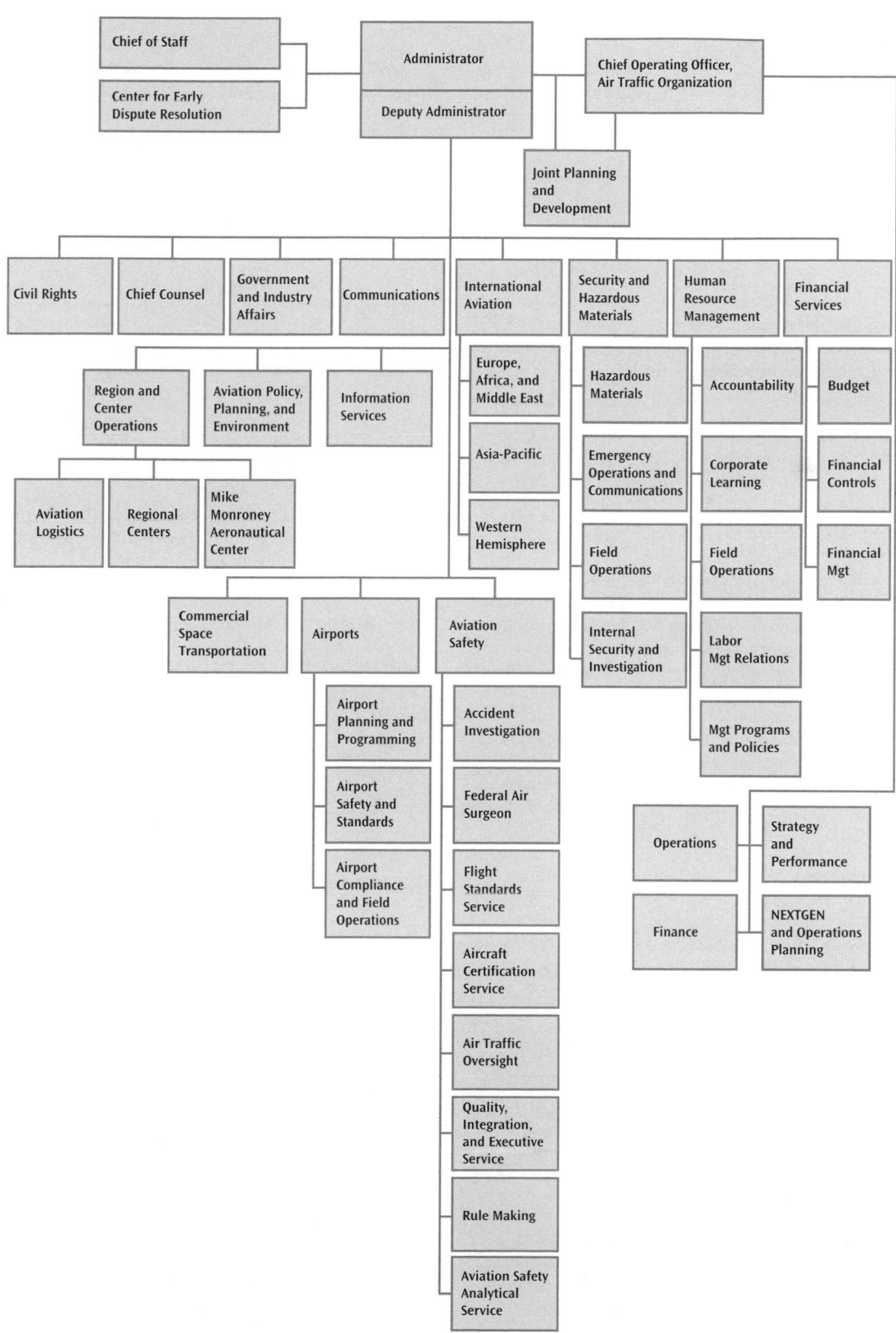

Washington*, DC 20591); (202) 385-7100. Fax, (202) 385-7105. James H. Williams, Director.
Web, www.faa.gov

Designs and maintains the National Airspace System (NAS) Enterprise Architecture and provides systems engineering and safety expertise to bridge the gap between today's NAS and the Next Generation Air Transportation System (NextGen).

International Trade Administration (ITA), (Commerce Dept.), Transportation and Machinery, 14th St. and Constitution Ave. N.W., #4036 20230-0001; (202) 482-0554. Fax, (202) 482-0674. Henry P. Misisco, Director.
Web, http://trade.gov/mas/index.asp

Promotes the export of U.S. aerospace, automotive, and machinery products; compiles and analyzes industry data; seeks to secure a favorable position for the U.S. aerospace, auto, and machinery industries in global markets through policy and trade agreements.

Justice Dept. (DOJ), Civil Division: Torts Branch, Aviation and Admiralty Litigation, 1425 New York Ave. N.W., #10100 20005 (mailing address: P.O. Box 14271, Washington*, DC 20044-4271); (202) 616-4000. Fax, (202) 616-4002. Peter F. Frost, Director.
Web, www.usdoj.gov

Represents the federal government in civil suits arising from aviation and admiralty incidents and accidents. In aviation, handles tort litigation for the government's activities in the operation of the air traffic control system, regulation of air commerce, weather services, aeronautical charting, and operation of its own civil and military aircraft. In admiralty, defends the government's placement and maintenance of maritime navigational aids, its nautical charting and dredging activities, and its operation and maintenance of U.S. and contract-operated vessels. Brings cases for government cargo damage, pollution cleanups, and damage to U.S. locks, dams, and navaids.

National Aeronautics and Space Administration (NASA), Aeronautics Research Mission Directorate, 300 E St. S.W., #6A70 20546 (mailing address: NASA Headquarters, Mail Code 6J39A, Washington, DC 20546); (202) 358-4600. Fax, (202) 358-2920. Jaiwon Shin, Associate Administrator.
Web, www.aerospace.nasa.gov

Conducts research in aerodynamics, materials, structures, avionics, propulsion, high-performance computing, human factors, aviation safety, and space transportation in support of national space and aeronautical research and technology goals. Manages the following NASA research centers: Ames (Moffett Field, Calif.); Dryden (Edwards, Calif.); Langley (Hampton, Va.); and Glenn (Cleveland, Ohio).

National Air and Space Museum (Smithsonian Institution), 6th St. and Independence Ave. S.W. 20013-7012; (202) 633-1000. Fax, (202) 357-2426. Gen. John R. Dailey, Director. Library, (202) 633-2320. TTY, (202)

357-1505. Education office, (202) 633-2540. Tours, (202) 633-2563.
Web, www.nasm.si.edu

Maintains exhibits and collections on aeronautics, pioneers of flight, and early aircraft through modern air technology. Library open to the public by appointment.

National Mediation Board, 1301 K St. N.W., #250E 20005; (202) 692-5000. Fax, (202) 692-5080. Read Van de Water, Chair. Information, (202) 692-5050. TTY, (202) 692-5001. Public Affairs, (202) 692-5050.
General e-mail, infoline@nmb.gov
Web, www.nmb.gov

Mediates labor disputes in the airline and railroad industries; determines and certifies labor representatives for the industry.

Research and Innovative Technology Administration (Transportation Dept.), Bureau of Transportation Statistics: Airline Information, 1200 New Jersey Ave. S.E., #E-34, RTS-42 20590; (202) 366-4373. Fax, (202) 366-3383. Anne Suissa, Assistant Director.
Web, www.bts.gov/oai

Develops, interprets, and enforces accounting and reporting regulations for the aviation industry; issues air carrier reporting instructions, waivers, and due-date extensions.

Steven F. Udvar-Hazy Center (Smithsonian Institution), National Air and Space Museum, 14390 Air and Space Museum Pkwy., Chantilly, VA 20151; (202) 633-1000. Gen. John R. Dailey, Director; Joseph T. Anderson, Deputy Director. TTY, (202) 633-5285. Public Affairs, (703) 572-4040.
Web, www.nasm.si.edu/udvarhazy

Displays and preserves a collection of historical aviation and space artifacts, including the B-29 Superfortress, Enola Gay, the Lockheed SR-71 Blackbird, the prototype of the Boeing 707, the space shuttle Enterprise, and the Concorde. Provides a center for research into the history, science, and technology of aviation and space flight.

Transportation Dept. (DOT), Aviation Analysis, 1200 New Jersey Ave. S.E., #W86-481 20590; (202) 366-5903. Fax, (202) 366-7638. Todd Homan, Director. Press, (202) 366-5582.
Web, www.dot.gov

Analyzes essential air service needs of communities; directs subsidy policy and programs; guarantees air service to small communities; conducts research for the department on airline mergers, international route awards, and employee protection programs; administers the air carrier fitness provisions of the Federal Aviation Act; registers domestic and foreign air carriers; enforces charter regulations for tour operators.

Transportation Dept. (DOT), Aviation and International Affairs, 1200 New Jersey Ave. S.E., #W88-318 20590; (202) 366-8822. Fax, (202) 493-2005. Susan

McDermott, Assistant Secretary (Acting). Press, (202) 366-5582.
Web, http://ostpxweb.dot.gov/aviation

Formulates domestic and international aviation policy. Assesses the performance of the U.S. aviation network in meeting public needs. Studies the social and economic conditions of the aviation industry, including airline licensing, antitrust concerns, and the effect of government policies.

Transportation Dept. (DOT), *Aviation Audits, West Bldg., 1200 New Jersey Ave. S.E., 7th Floor 20590-0001; (202) 366-8751. Fax, (202) 366-1975. Ann Calvaresi Barr, Assistant Inspector General.*
Web, www.dot.gov

Provides auditing services for airline economic programs.

Transportation Dept. (DOT), *Aviation Consumer Protection, 1200 New Jersey Ave. S.E., #W96-432 20590 (mailing address: 1200 New Jersey S.E., Transportation Dept., C-75, #4107, Washington, DC 20590); (202) 366-2220. Norman Strickman, Director. Fax, (202) 366-5944. Disability-Related Problems, (800) 778-4838. TTY, (800) 455-9880.*
Web, www.airconsumer.ost.dot.gov

Addresses complaints about airline service and consumer-protection matters. Conducts investigations, provides assistance, and reviews regulations affecting air carriers.

▶**CONGRESS**

For a listing of relevant congressional committees and subcommittees, please see page 656 or the Appendix.

▶**NONGOVERNMENTAL**

Aeronautical Repair Station Assn., *121 N. Henry St., Alexandria, VA 22314-2903; (703) 739-9543. Fax, (703) 739-9488. Sarah MacLeod, Executive Director.*
General e-mail, arsa@arsa.org
Web, www.arsa.org

Membership: repair stations that have Federal Aviation Administration certificates or comparable non-U.S. certification; associate members are suppliers and distributors of components and parts. Works to improve relations between repair stations and manufacturers. Interests include establishing uniformity in the application, interpretation, and enforcement of FAA regulations. Monitors legislation and regulations.

Aerospace Education Foundation, *1501 Lee Hwy., #400, Arlington, VA 22209; (703) 247-5800. Fax, (703) 247-5853. Gen. Michael M. Dunn, Executive Director. Information, (800) 727-3337.*
General e-mail, aefstaff@aef.org
Web, www.afa.org

Promotes knowledge and appreciation of U.S. civilian and military aerospace development and history. (Affiliated with the Air Force Assn.)

Aerospace Industries Assn. (AIA), *1000 Wilson Blvd., #1700, Arlington, VA 22209-3928; (703) 358-1000. Fax, (703) 358-1012. Marion Blakey, President. Press, (703) 358-1076.*
General e-mail, aia@aia-aerospace.org
Web, www.aia-aerospace.org

Represents manufacturers of commercial, military, and business aircraft; helicopters; aircraft engines; missiles; spacecraft; and related components and equipment. Interests include international standards and trade.

AIR Conference (Airline Industrial Relations Conference), *1300 19th St. N.W., #750 20036-1651; (202) 861-7550. Fax, (202) 861-7557. Mark Burdette, President.*
General e-mail, office@aircon.org
Web, www.aircon.org

Membership: domestic and international scheduled air carriers. Monitors developments and collects data on trends in airline labor relations.

Aircraft Owners and Pilots Assn. (AOPA), *Legislative Affairs, Washington Office, 601 Pennsylvania Ave. N.W., #875 South Bldg. 20004-2636; (202) 737-7950. Fax, (202) 737-7951. Lorraine Howerton, Vice President. Toll-free for members, (800) 872-2672.*
Web, www.aopa.org

Membership: owners and pilots of general aviation aircraft. Washington office monitors legislation and regulations. Headquarters office provides members with a variety of aviation-related services; issues airport directory and handbook for pilots; sponsors the Air Safety Foundation. (Headquarters in Frederick, Md.)

Air Line Pilots Assn. International, *1625 Massachusetts Ave. N.W. 20036; (703) 689-2270. Fax, (703) 689-4370. John Prater, President. Press, (703) 481-4440. Toll-free, (888) 359-2572.*
Web, www.alpa.org

Membership: airline pilots in the United States and Canada. Promotes air travel safety; assists investigations of aviation accidents. Monitors legislation and regulations. (Affiliated with the AFL-CIO and the Canadian Labour Conference.)

Air Transport Assn. of America, *1301 Pennsylvania Ave. N.W., #1100 20004-1707; (202) 626-4000. Fax, (202) 626-4166. James C. May, President. Press, (202) 626-4173.*
General e-mail, ata@airlines.org
Web, www.airlines.org

Membership: U.S. scheduled air carriers. Promotes aviation safety and the facilitation of air transportation for passengers and cargo. Monitors legislation and regulations.

American Helicopter Society (AHS International), *217 N. Washington St., Alexandria, VA 22314-2538; (703) 684-6777. Fax, (703) 739-9279. Morris E. "Rhett" Flater, Executive Director.*
General e-mail, staff@vtol.org
Web, www.vtol.org

Membership: individuals and organizations interested in vertical flight. Acts as an information clearinghouse for technical data on helicopter design improvement, aerodynamics, and safety. Awards the Vertical Flight Foundation Scholarship to college students interested in helicopter technology.

American Institute of Aeronautics and Astronautics (AIAA), *1801 Alexander Bell Dr., #500, Reston, VA 20191; (703) 264-7500. Fax, (703) 264-7551. Robert Dickman, Executive Director. Information, (800) 639-2422.*
General e-mail, custserv@aiaa.org

Web, www.aiaa.org

Membership: engineers, scientists, and students in the fields of aeronautics and astronautics. Holds workshops on aerospace technical issues for congressional subcommittees; sponsors international conferences. Offers computerized database through its Technical Information Service.

Assn. of Flight Attendants–CWA, *501 3rd St. N.W. 20001-2797; (202) 434-1300. Fax, (202) 434-1319. Patricia A. Friend, President. Press, (202) 434-0586.*
General e-mail, info@afacwa.org

Web, www.afanet.org

Membership: approximately 55,000 flight attendants. Helps members negotiate pay, benefits, and better working conditions; conducts training programs and workshops. Monitors legislation and regulations. (Affiliated with the AFL-CIO.)

Cargo Airline Assn., *1220 19th St. N.W., #400 20036-2438; (202) 293-1030. Fax, (202) 293-4377. Stephen A. Alterman, President.*
General e-mail, info@cargoair.org

Web, www.cargoair.org

Membership: cargo airlines and other firms interested in the development and promotion of air freight.

Coalition of Airline Pilots Assns. (CAPA), *1101 Pennsylvania Ave. N.W., #6646 20004; (202) 756-2956. Fax, (202) 756-7509. Paul Onorato, President.*
General e-mail, capapilots@capapilots.org

Web, www.capapilots.org

Trade association of more than 22,000 professional pilots. Addresses safety, security, legislative, and regulatory issues affecting flight deck crews.

General Aviation Manufacturers Assn. (GAMA), *1400 K St. N.W., #801 20005-2485; (202) 393-1500. Fax, (202) 842-4063. Peter J. Bunce, President.*
General e-mail, info@gama.aero

Web, www.gama.aero

Membership: manufacturers of business, commuter, and personal aircraft and manufacturers of engines, avionics, and related equipment. Monitors legislation and regulations; sponsors safety and public information programs.

Helicopter Assn. International, *1635 Prince St., Alexandria, VA 22314-2818; (703) 683-4646. Fax, (703) 683-4745. Matthew Zuccaro, President.*
General e-mail, questions@rotor.com

Web, www.rotor.com

Membership: owners, manufacturers, and operators of helicopters and affiliated companies in the civil helicopter industry. Provides information on use and operation of helicopters; offers business management and aviation safety courses; sponsors annual industry exposition. Monitors legislation and regulations.

International Assn. of Machinists and Aerospace Workers, *9000 Machinists Pl., Upper Marlboro, MD 20772-2687; (301) 967-4500. Fax, (301) 967-4588. Thomas Buffenbarger, International President. Information, (301) 967-4520. TTY, (800) 201-7165.*
Web, www.goiam.org

Membership: machinists in more than 200 industries. Helps members negotiate pay, benefits, and better working conditions; conducts training programs and workshops. Monitors legislation and regulations. (Affiliated with the AFL-CIO, the Canadian Labour Congress, the International Metalworkers Federation, the International Transport Workers' Federation, and the Railway Labor Executives Assn.)

National Aeronautic Assn., *Reagan Washington National Airport, Hangar 7, #202 20001; (703) 416-4888. Fax, (703) 416-4877. Jonathan Gaffney, President.*
General e-mail, naa@naa.aero

Web, www.naa.aero

Membership: persons interested in development of general and sporting aviation. Supervises sporting aviation competitions; oversees and approves official U.S. aircraft, aeronautics, and space records. Serves as U.S. representative to the International Aeronautical Federation in Lausanne, Switzerland.

National Agricultural Aviation Assn., *1005 E St. S.E. 20003; (202) 546-5722. Fax, (202) 546-5726. Andrew Moore, Executive Director.*
General e-mail, information@agaviation.org

Web, www.agaviation.org

Membership: qualified agricultural pilots; operating companies that seed, fertilize, and spray land by air; and allied industries. Monitors legislation and regulations.

National Air Carrier Assn., *1000 Wilson Blvd., #1700, Arlington, VA 22209-3901; (703) 358-8060. Fax, (703) 358-8070. Thomas Zoeller, President.*
Web, www.naca.cc

Membership: air carriers certified for charter and scheduled operations. Monitors legislation and regulations.

National Air Transportation Assn., *4226 King St., Alexandria, VA 22302-1507; (703) 845-9000. Fax, (703) 845-8176. James K. Coyne, President. Information, (800) 808-6282.*
Web, www.nata.aero

Membership: companies that provide on-demand air charter, aircraft sales, flight training, maintenance and repair, avionics, and other services. Manages education foundation; compiles statistics; provides business assistance programs. Monitors legislation and regulations.

National Assn. of State Aviation Officials, *1 Reagan Washington National Airport, Hangar 7, #218 20001; (703) 417-1880. Fax, (703) 417-1885. Henry M. Ogrodzinski, President.*
Web, www.nasao.org

Membership: state aeronautics agencies that deal with aviation issues, including regulation. Seeks uniform aviation laws; manages an aviation research and education foundation.

National Business Aviation Assn. (NBAA), *1200 18th St. N.W., #400 20036-2527; (202) 783-9000. Fax, (202) 331-8364. Ed Bolen, President.*
General e-mail, info@nbaa.org
Web, www.nbaa.org

Membership: companies owning and operating aircraft for business use, suppliers, and maintenance and air fleet service companies. Conducts seminars and workshops in business aviation management. Sponsors annual civilian aviation exposition. Monitors legislation and regulations.

Regional Airline Assn., *2025 M St. N.W., #800 20036-3309; (202) 367-1170. Fax, (202) 367-2170. Roger Cohen, President.*
General e-mail, raa@raa.org
Web, www.raa.org

Membership: regional airlines that provide passenger, scheduled cargo, and mail service. Issues annual report on the industry.

RTCA, *1828 L St. N.W., #805 20036; (202) 833-9339. Fax, (202) 833-9434. Margaret T. Jenny, President.*
General e-mail, info@rtca.org
Web, www.rtca.org

Membership: federal agencies, aviation organizations, and commercial firms interested in aeronautical systems. Develops and publishes standards for aviation, including minimum operational performance standards for equipment; conducts research, makes recommendations, and issues reports on the field of aviation electronics and telecommunications. (Formerly the Radio Technical Commission for Aeronautics.)

Airports

▶AGENCIES

Animal and Plant Health Inspection Service (APHIS), *(Agriculture Dept.), Wildlife Services, 1400 Independence Ave. S.W., #1624S 20250-3402; (202) 720-2054. Fax, (202) 690-0053. William H. Clay, Deputy Administrator.*
Web, www.aphis.usda.gov/wildlife-damage

Works to minimize damage caused by wildlife to human health and safety. Interests include aviation safety; works with airport managers to reduce the risk of bird strikes. Oversees the National Wildlife Research Center in Ft. Collins, Colo.

Bureau of Land Management (BLM), *(Interior Dept.), Lands, Realty, and Cadastral Survey, 1620 L St. N.W. 20036 (mailing address: 1849 C St. N.W., MS 1000LS, Washington, DC 20240); (202) 452-7779. Fax, (202) 452-7708. Jeff Holdren, Manager.*
Web, www.blm.gov

Operates the Airport Lease Program, which leases public lands for use as public airports.

Federal Aviation Administration (FAA), *(Transportation Dept.), Airports, 800 Independence Ave. S.W., #600E, ARP-1 20591; (202) 267-8738. Fax, (202) 267-5301. D. Kirk Shaffer, Associate Administrator.*
Web, www.faa.gov/airports_airtraffic/airports

Makes grants for development and improvement of publicly operated and owned airports and some privately owned airports; certifies safety design standards for airports; administers the congressional Airport Improvement Program; oversees construction and accessibility standards for people with disabilities. Questions about local airports are usually referred to a local FAA field office.

Maryland Aviation Administration, *P.O. Box 8766, BWI Airport, MD 21240-0766; (410) 859-7060. Fax, (410) 850-4729. Timothy L. Campbell, Executive Director. Information, (800) 435-9294. Press, (410) 859-7027. TTY, (410) 859-7227.*
Web, www.marylandaviation.com and www.bwiairport.com

Responsible for aviation operations, planning, instruction, and safety in Maryland; operates Baltimore/Washington International Thurgood Marshall Airport (BWI) and Martin State Airport.

Metropolitan Washington Airports Authority, *1 Aviation Circle 20001-6000; (703) 417-8610. Fax, (703) 417-8949. James E. Bennett, President. Information, (703) 417-8600. Press, (703) 417-8370.*
Web, www.mwaa.com

Independent interstate agency created by Virginia and the District of Columbia with the consent of Congress; operates Washington Dulles International Airport and Ronald Reagan Washington National Airport.

▶NONGOVERNMENTAL

Airports Council International (ACI), *1775 K St. N.W., #500 20006; (202) 293-8500. Fax, (202) 331-1362. Greg Principato, President.*
General e-mail, postmaster@aci-na.org
Web, www.aci-na.org

Membership: authorities, boards, commissions, and municipal departments operating public airports. Serves as liaison with government agencies and other aviation organizations; works to improve passenger and freight facilitation; acts as clearinghouse on engineering and operational aspects of airport development. Monitors legislation and regulations.

American Assn. of Airport Executives, *601 Madison St., #400, Alexandria, VA 22314; (703) 824-0500. Fax, (703) 820-1395. Charles M. Barclay, President.*
Web, www.aaae.org

Membership: airport managers, superintendents, consultants, government officials, authorities and commissioners, and others interested in the construction, management, and operation of airports. Conducts examination for and awards the professional designation of Accredited Airport Executive.

Aviation Safety and Security

▶**AGENCIES**

Federal Aviation Administration (FAA),
(Transportation Dept.), Air Traffic Organization, 800 Independence Ave. S.W., #1018A, AJA-O 20591; (202) 493-5602. Fax, (202) 267-5085. Hank Krakowski, Chief Operating Officer. Press, (202) 267-3883.
Web, www.faa.gov/about/office_org/headquarters_offices/ato

Operates the national air traffic control system; employs air traffic controllers at airport towers, en route air traffic control centers, and flight service stations; maintains the National Flight Data Center.

Federal Aviation Administration (FAA),
(Transportation Dept.), Air Traffic Organization: Technical Operations Services, 800 Independence Ave. S.W., #700E, ATO-W 20591; (202) 267-3366. Fax, (202) 267-5015. Steven B. Zaidman, Vice President.
Web, www.faa.gov/about/office_org/headquarters_offices/ato

Conducts research and development programs aimed at providing procedures, facilities, and devices needed for a safe and efficient system of air navigation and air traffic control.

Federal Aviation Administration (FAA),
(Transportation Dept.), Aviation Safety: Accident Investigation, 800 Independence Ave. S.W., #840, AAI-1 20591; (202) 267-9612. Fax, (202) 267-5043. Hooper Harris, Director (Acting).
Web, www.faa.gov/about/office_org/headquarters_offices/avs/offices/aai

Investigates aviation accidents and incidents to detect unsafe conditions and trends in the national airspace system and to coordinate corrective action.

Federal Aviation Administration (FAA),
(Transportation Dept.), Aviation Safety: Aerospace Medicine, 800 Independence Ave. S.W., #800W, AAM-1
20591; (202) 267-3535. Fax, (202) 267-5399. Dr. Frederick E. Tilton, Federal Air Surgeon; Dr. James Fraser, Deputy Federal Air Surgeon.*
Web, www.faa.gov/education_research/research/med_humanfacs/aeromedical

Responsible for the medical activities and policies of the FAA; designates, through regional offices, aviation medical examiners who conduct periodic medical examinations of all air personnel; regulates and oversees drug and alcohol testing programs for pilots, air traffic controllers, and others who hold safety-sensitive positions; maintains a Civil Aerospace Medical Institute in Oklahoma City.

Federal Aviation Administration (FAA),
(Transportation Dept.), Aviation Safety: Aircraft Certification Service, 800 Independence Ave. S.W., #800E, AIR-1 20591-0004; (202) 267-8235. Fax, (202) 267-5364. Dorenda Baker, Director.
Web, www.faa.gov/aircraft/air_cert

Certifies all aircraft for airworthiness; approves designs and specifications for new aircraft, aircraft engines, propellers, and appliances; supervises aircraft manufacturing and testing.

Federal Aviation Administration (FAA),
(Transportation Dept.), Aviation Safety: Flight Standards Service, 800 Independence Ave. S.W., #821, AFS-1 20591; (202) 267-8237. Fax, (202) 267-5230. John Allen, Director. Press, (202) 267-3883.
Web, www.faa.gov/about/office_org/headquarters_offices/avs/offices/afs

Sets certification standards for air carriers, commercial operators, air agencies, and air personnel (except air traffic control tower operators); directs and executes certification and inspection of flight procedures, operating methods, air personnel qualification and proficiency, and maintenance aspects of airworthiness programs; manages the registry of civil aircraft and all official air personnel records; supports law enforcement agencies responsible for drug interdiction.

Federal Aviation Administration (FAA),
(Transportation Dept.), En Route and Oceanic Services, 600 Independence Ave. S.W., #FOB 10-B, 3E 1500 20591; (202) 385-8501. Fax, (202) 493-4306. Richard J. Ducharme, Vice President (Acting).
Web, www.faa.gov

Provides satellite-based capability for en route navigation and a color display for en route controllers. Improves the safety of hazardous weather avoidance. Increases operations efficiency through the use of cockpit surveillance and other means. Resolves support issues.

Federal Bureau of Investigation (FBI), *(Justice Dept.), Criminal Investigative Division, 935 Pennsylvania Ave. N.W., #3012 20535; (202) 324-4260. Fax, (202) 324-0027. Kenneth W. Kaiser, Assistant Director.*
Web, www.fbi.gov

National Transportation Safety Board

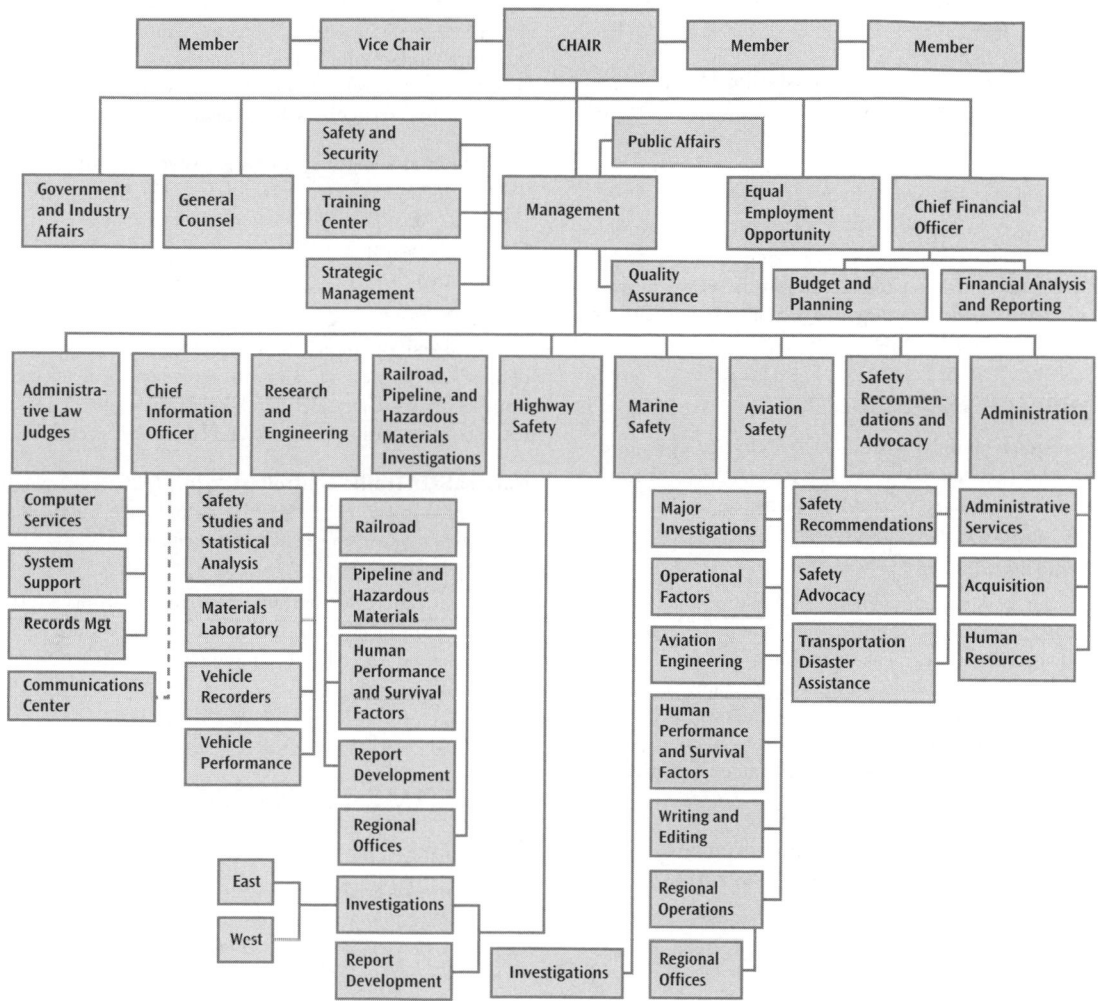

- - - - - Under the oversight of the Chief Information Officer

Investigates cases of aircraft hijacking, destruction of aircraft, and air piracy. Works with TSA and FAA to ensure security of national air carrier systems in areas of violent crime, organized crime, civil rights, corruption, and financial crimes.

Federal Communications Commission (FCC),
Enforcement Bureau, 445 12th St. S.W., 3rd Floor, #7C723 20554; (202) 418-7450. Fax, (202) 418-2810. Kris Monteith, Chief, Enforcement Bureau. Media Relations, (202) 418-8165.
Web, www.fcc.gov/eb

Provides technical services to aid the Federal Aviation Administration in locating aircraft in distress; provides interference resolution for air traffic control radio frequencies.

National Transportation Safety Board, *Aviation Safety, 490 L'Enfant Plaza East S.W., #5400 20594-0001; (202)*

314-6300. Fax, (202) 314-6309. Thomas E. Hauter, Director. Information, (202) 314-6540. Press, (202) 314-6100. Toll-free, (800) 877-6799.
Web, www.ntsb.gov

Responsible for management, policies, and programs in aviation safety and for aviation accident investigations. Manages programs on special investigations, safety issues, and safety objectives. Acts as U.S. representative in international investigations.

Transportation Security Administration (TSA), *(Homeland Security Dept.), 601 S. 12th St., 7th Floor, Arlington, VA 22202-4220; (571) 227-2801. Fax, (571) 227-1398. Gale D. Rossides, Administrator (Acting). Press, (571) 227-2829. Questions and concerns regarding travel can be submitted to the TSA Contact Center, toll-free, (866) 289-9673. General e-mail, TSA-ContactCenter@dhs.gov*
Web, www.tsa.gov/public

Protects the nation's transportation system. Performs and oversees airport security, including passenger and baggage screeners, airport federal security directors, and air marshals.

Transportation Security Administration (TSA),
(Homeland Security Dept.), Federal Air Marshal Service, TSA-18, 601 S. 12th St., Arlington, VA 22202; (703) 487-3400. Fax, (703) 487-3405. Dana A. Brown, Director.
Web, www.tsa.gov/lawenforcement/programs/fams.shtm

Protects air security in the United States. Promotes public confidence in the U.S. civil aviation system. Deploys marshals on flights around the world to detect and deter hostile acts targeting U.S. air carriers, airports, passengers, and crews.

▶**NONGOVERNMENTAL**

Aerospace Medical Assn., *320 S. Henry St., Alexandria, VA 22314-3579; (703) 739-2240. Fax, (703) 739-9652. Dr. Russell B. Rayman, Executive Director.*
General e-mail, inquiries@asma.org
Web, www.asma.org

Membership: physicians, flight surgeons, aviation medical examiners, flight nurses, scientists, technicians, and specialists in clinical, operational, and research fields of aerospace medicine. Promotes programs to improve aerospace medicine and maintain safety in aviation by examining and monitoring the health of aviation personnel; members may consult in aircraft investigation and cockpit design.

Air Traffic Control Assn., *1101 King St., #300, Alexandria, VA 22314-2963; (703) 299-2430. Fax, (703) 299-2437. Peter F. Dumont, President.*
General e-mail, info@atca.org
Web, www.atca.org

Membership: air traffic controllers, flight service station specialists, pilots, aviation engineers and manufacturers, and others interested in air traffic control systems. Compiles and publishes information and data concerning air traffic control; provides information to members, Congress, and federal agencies.

American Assn. of Airport Executives, *601 Madison St., #400, Alexandria, VA 22314; (703) 824-0500. Fax, (703) 820-1395. Charles M. Barclay, President.*
Web, www.aaae.org

Maintains the Transportation Security Clearinghouse, which matches fingerprints and other personal information from airport and airline employees against FBI databases.

Flight Safety Foundation, *601 Madison St., #300, Alexandria, VA 22314-1756; (703) 739-6700. Fax, (703) 739-6708. William R. Voss, President. Press, (703) 739-6700, ext. 126.*
General e-mail, info@flightsafety.org
Web, www.flightsafety.org

Membership: aerospace manufacturers, domestic and foreign airlines, energy and insurance companies, educational institutions, and organizations and corporations interested in flight safety. Sponsors seminars, publishes literature, and conducts studies and safety audits on air safety for governments and industries. Administers award programs that recognize achievements in air safety.

International Society of Air Safety Investigators (ISASI), *107 E. Holly Ave., #11, Sterling, VA 20164-5405; (703) 430-9668. Fax, (703) 430-4970. Frank S. Del Gandio, President.*
General e-mail, isasi@erols.com
Web, www.isasi.org

Membership: specialists who investigate and seek to define the causes of aircraft accidents. Encourages improvement of air safety and investigative procedures through information exchange and educational seminars.

National Air Traffic Controllers Assn., *1325 Massachusetts Ave. N.W. 20005; (202) 628-5451. Fax, (202) 628-5767. Patrick Forrey, President.*
Web, www.natca.org

Seeks to increase air traffic controller staffing levels, improve working conditions, and encourage procurement of more modern, reliable equipment. Concerned with airport safety worldwide.

MARITIME TRANSPORTATION

▶**AGENCIES**

Army Corps of Engineers *(Defense Dept.), 441 G St. N.W., #3K05 20314-1000; (202) 761-0001. Fax, (202) 761-4463. Lt. Gen. Robert L. Van Antwerp (USACE), Chief of Engineers.*
Web, www.usace.army.mil

Provides local governments with navigation, flood control, disaster relief, and hydroelectric power services.

Federal Maritime Commission, *800 N. Capitol St. N.W., #1046 20573-0001; (202) 523-5725. Fax, (202) 523-0014. Vacant, Chair; Austin L. Schmitt, Director of Operations. TTY, (800) 877-8339. Locator, (202) 523-5773.*
General e-mail, secretary@fmc.gov
Web, www.fmc.gov

Regulates the foreign ocean shipping of the United States; enforces maritime shipping laws and regulations regarding rates and charges, freight forwarding, passengers, and port authorities. Library open to the public.

Federal Maritime Commission, *Trade Analysis, 800 N. Capitol St. N.W., #940 20573-0001; (202) 523-5796. Fax, (202) 523-4372. Florence A. Carr, Director. Library, (202) 523-5762.*
Web, www.fmc.gov

Regulates the rates charged for shipping in foreign commerce; licenses and enforces regulations concerning ocean freight forwarders; issues certificates of financial responsibility to ensure that carriers refund fares and meet their liability in case of death, injury, or nonperformance.

Justice Dept. (DOJ), *Civil Division: Torts Branch, Aviation and Admiralty Litigation, 1425 New York Ave. N.W., #10100 20005 (mailing address: P.O. Box 14271, Washington, DC 20044-4271); (202) 616-4000. Fax, (202) 616-4002. Peter F. Frost, Director.*
Web, www.usdoj.gov

Represents the federal government in civil suits concerning the maritime industry, including ships, shipping, and merchant marine personnel. Handles civil cases arising from admiralty incidents and accidents, including oil spills.

Maritime Administration *(Transportation Dept.), West Bldg., 1200 New Jersey Ave. S.E., #W22300 20590; (202) 366-5823. Fax, (202) 366-3890. Vacant, Maritime Administrator; James E. Caponiti, Deputy Maritime Administrator (Acting). Press, (202) 366-5807.*
General e-mail, pao_marad@dot.gov

Web, http://marad.dot.gov

Conducts research on shipbuilding and operations; provides financing guarantees and a tax-deferred fund for shipbuilding; promotes the maritime industry; operates the U.S. Merchant Marine Academy in Kings Point, New York.

Maritime Administration *(Transportation Dept.), Business and Workforce Development, West Bldg., 1200 New Jersey Ave. S.E. 20590; (202) 366-5737. Fax, (202) 366-6988. Jean E. McKeever, Associate Administrator.*
Web, http://marad.dot.gov

Works with private industry to develop standardized ship designs and improved shipbuilding techniques and materials; offices dealing with cargo preference, Title XI, war risk insurance, and workforce development.

Maritime Administration *(Transportation Dept.), Cargo Preference and Domestic Trade, West Bldg., 1200 New Jersey Ave. S.E., 2nd Floor 20590; (202) 366-5515. Fax, (202) 366-7901. Thomas Harrelson, Director.*
General e-mail, cargo.marad@dot.gov

Web, http://marad.dot.gov

Enforces cargo preference laws and regulations. Promotes and monitors the use of U.S. flag vessels in the movement of cargo in domestic and international trade.

Maritime Administration *(Transportation Dept.), Environment and Compliance, West Bldg., 1200 New Jersey Ave. S.E., W21-326 20590; (202) 366-1924. Fax, (202) 366-6988. Joseph Byrne, Associate Administrator.*
General e-mail, Joseph.byrne@dot.gov

Web, www.marad.dot.gov; Public Affairs, marad-pao@dot.gov

Focuses on environmental stewardship, maritime safety, and maritime security; maritime research and development; and maritime international and domestic rules, regulations, and standards.

Maritime Administration *(Transportation Dept.), Financial Approvals and Marine Insurance, West Bldg., 1200 New Jersey Ave. S.E., 2nd Floor 20590; (202) 366-2279. Fax, (202) 366-7901. Edmond J. Fitzgerald, Director.*
Web, www.marad.dot.gov

Conducts financial analyses of commercial shipping and calculates guideline rates for carriage of preference cargoes. Administers war risk insurance program. Performs economic soundness analysis for Title XI Program.

Maritime Administration *(Transportation Dept.), International Activities, West Bldg., 1200 New Jersey Ave. S.E. 20590; (202) 366-5773. Fax, (202) 366-3746. Gregory B. Hall, Director.*
Web, http://marad.dot.gov

Formulates the agency's position on international issues affecting the U.S. maritime industry with the goal of reducing or eliminating international barriers to trade and improving market access.

Maritime Administration *(Transportation Dept.), Maritime Workforce Development, West Bldg., 1200 New Jersey Ave. S.E., 2nd Floor 20590; (202) 366-5469. Fax, (202) 366-7901. Anne Dougherty, Director.*
Web, www.marad.dot.gov

Administers programs for the U.S. Merchant Marine Academy and State Academies. Promotes maritime workforce development.

Maritime Administration *(Transportation Dept.), National Security, West Bldg., 1200 New Jersey Ave. S.E., W25-2091212 20590; (202) 366-5400. Fax, (202) 493-2180. James E. Caponiti, Deputy Administrator (Acting).*
Web, www.marad.gov

Ensures that merchant shipping is available in times of war or national emergency.

Maritime Administration *(Transportation Dept.), Policy and Plans, West Bldg., 1200 New Jersey Ave. S.E. 20590; (202) 366-4468. Fax, (202) 366-7403. Janice G. Weaver, Director.*
Web, http://marad.dot.gov

Supports the agency's policy development process with research, analysis, and documentation. Assesses the effects of legislative and regulatory proposals on maritime programs and maritime industries. Investigates the effects of national and global events on maritime policy and operations.

Maritime Administration *(Transportation Dept.), Shipyard and Marine Finance, West Bldg., 1200 New Jersey Ave. S.E., 2nd Floor 20590; (202) 366-5744. Fax, (202) 366-7901. Jean E. McKeever, Director (Acting).*
Web, http://marad.dot.gov

Provides ship financing guarantees for ship construction and shipyard modernization; administers the Capital Construction Fund Program.

National Oceanic and Atmospheric Administration (NOAA), *(Commerce Dept.), National Ocean Service,*

1305 East-West Hwy., SSMC4, Silver Spring, MD 20910; (301) 713-3074. Fax, (301) 713-4269. John H. Dunnigan, Assistant Administrator.
Web, www.nos.noaa.gov

Manages charting and geodetic services, oceanography and marine services, coastal resource coordination, and marine survey operations.

Navy Dept. *(Defense Dept.), Military Sealift Command,* Bldg. 210, Washington Navy Yard, DC 20398-5540; (202) 685-5001. Fax, (202) 685-5020. Rear Adm. Robert D. Reilly, Commander. Press, (202) 685-5055.
Web, www.msc.navy.mil

Provides sea transportation of equipment, fuel, supplies, and ammunition to sustain U.S. forces.

Surface Transportation Board *(Transportation Dept.),* 395 E St. S.W. 20423-0001; (202) 245-0245. Fax, (202) 245-0458. Charles D. Nottingham, Chair, (202) 245-0200. Library, (202) 245-0406. TTY, (800) 877-8339.
Web, www.stb.dot.gov

Regulates rates for water transportation and intermodal connections in noncontiguous domestic trade (between the mainland and Alaska, Hawaii, or U.S. territories). Library open to the public.

U.S. Coast Guard (USCG), *(Homeland Security Dept.),* 2100 2nd St. S.W. 20593-0001; (202) 372-4411. Fax, (202) 372-4960. Adm. Thad W. Allen, Commandant. Locator, (202) 372-8724. Public Affairs, (202) 372-4620.
Web, www.uscg.mil

Carries out search-and-rescue missions in and around navigable waters and on the high seas; enforces federal laws on the high seas and navigable waters of the United States and its possessions; conducts marine environmental protection programs; administers boating safety programs; inspects and regulates construction, safety, and equipment of merchant marine vessels; establishes and maintains a system of navigation aids; carries out domestic icebreaking activities; maintains a state of military readiness to assist the Navy in time of war or when directed by the president.

U.S. Coast Guard (USCG), *(Homeland Security Dept.), Investigations and Casualty Analysis,* CG-545, 2100 2nd St. S.W., #2404 20593-0001; (202) 372-1029. Fax, (202) 372-1907. Capt. Michael P. Rand, Chief.
General e-mail, michael.p.rand@uscg.mil

Web, www.uscg.mil/hq/cg5/cg545.asp

Handles disciplinary proceedings for merchant marine personnel. Compiles and analyzes records of marine casualties. Focuses on marine safety and environmental protection through marine inspection activities, including investigation of spills and the Drug and Alcohol Program Inspectors (DAPI) initiative.

U.S. Coast Guard (USCG), *(Homeland Security Dept.), Strategic Analysis,* 2100 2nd St. S.W., #2316 20593-0001; (202) 372-2695. Fax, (202) 372-4976. Capt. Samuel M. Neill, Chief.
Web, www.uscg.mil

Identifies and analyzes emerging geopolitical, economic, and environmental issues and trends; develops specific recommendations to improve the strategic and operational posture of the U.S. Coast Guard.

►CONGRESS

For a listing of relevant congressional committees and subcommittees, please see page 656 or the Appendix.

►NONGOVERNMENTAL

American Maritime Congress, *400 N. Capitol St. N.W., #G-50 20001; (202) 347-8020. Fax, (202) 347-1550. Matt Dwyer, Legislative Representative.*
General e-mail, diannelauer@americanmaritime.org

Web, www.americanmaritime.org

Organization of U.S.-flag carriers engaged in oceanborne transportation. Conducts research and provides information on the U.S.-flag merchant marine.

Boat Owners Assn. of the United States, *Government and Public Affairs, 880 S. Pickett St., Alexandria, VA 22304-4695; (703) 461-2864. Fax, (703) 461-2845. Margaret Podlich, Director of Government Affairs.*
General e-mail, govtaffairs@boatus.com

Web, www.boatus.com

Membership: owners of recreational boats. Represents boat-owner interests before the federal government; offers consumer protection and other services to members.

Chamber of Shipping of America, *1730 M St. N.W., #407 20036-4517; (202) 775-4399. Fax, (202) 659-3795. Joseph J. Cox, President.*
Web, www.knowships.org

Represents U.S.-based companies that own, operate, or charter oceangoing tankers, container ships, and other merchant vessels engaged in domestic and international trade.

Maritime Institute for Research and Industrial Development, *1025 Connecticut Ave. N.W., #507 20036; (202) 463-6505. Fax, (202) 223-9093. C. James Patti, President.*
General e-mail, jpatti@miraid.org

Membership: U.S.-flag ship operators. Promotes the development of the U.S. merchant marine. Interests include the use of private commercial merchant vessels by the Defense Dept., enforcement of cargo preference (Jones Act) laws for U.S.-flag ships, and maintenance of cabotage laws.

National Marine Manufacturers Assn., *Government Relations, Washington Office, 444 N. Capitol St. N.W., #645 20001-1559; (202) 737-9750. Fax, (202) 628-4716. John McKnight, Director of Environmental Affairs and DC Government Affairs.*
Web, www.nmma.org

Membership: recreational marine equipment manufacturers. Promotes boating safety and the development of boating facilities. Serves as liaison with Congress and regulatory agencies. Monitors legislation and regulations. (Headquarters in Chicago, Ill.)

Shipbuilders Council of America, *1455 F St. N.W., #225 20005; (202) 347-5462. Fax, (202) 347-5464. Matt Paxton, President.*
Web, www.shipbuilders.org

Membership: commercially focused shipyards that repair and build ships, and allied industries and associations. National trade association representing the competitive shipyard industry that makes up the core shipyard industrial base in the United States. Monitors legislation and regulations.

Transportation Institute, *5201 Auth Way, Camp Springs, MD 20746-4211; (301) 423-3335. Fax, (301) 423-0634. James L. Henry, President.*
General e-mail, info@trans-inst.org
Web, www.trans-inst.org

Membership: U.S.-flag maritime shipping companies. Conducts research on freight regulation and rates, government subsidies and assistance, domestic and international maritime matters, maritime safety, ports, Saint Lawrence Seaway, shipbuilding, and regulation of shipping.

World Shipping Council, *1156 15th St. N.W., #300 20005; (202) 589-1230. Fax, (202) 589-1231. Christopher L. Koch, President.*
General e-mail, info@worldshipping.org
Web, www.worldshipping.org

Membership association representing the liner shipping industry. Works with policymakers and other industry groups interested in international transportation issues, including maritime security, regulatory policy, tax issues, safety, the environment, harbor dredging, and trade infrastructure. Monitors legislation and regulations.

Maritime Safety

▶**AGENCIES**

Federal Communications Commission (FCC),
Enforcement Bureau, 445 12th St. S.W., 3rd Floor, #7C723 20554; (202) 418-7450. Fax, (202) 418-2810. Kris Monteith, Chief, Enforcement Bureau. Media Relations, (202) 418-8165.
Web, www.fcc.gov/eb

Provides technical services to the U.S. Coast Guard for locating ships in distress. Provides policy and program support for maritime radiotelegraph inspection.

National Oceanic and Atmospheric Administration (NOAA), *(Commerce Dept.), National Ocean Service: Office of Coast Survey, 1315 East-West Hwy., #6147, SSMC3, Silver Spring, MD 20910-3282; (301) 713-2770. Fax, (301) 713-4019. Capt. Steven R. Barnum, Director.*
Web, www.chartmaker.ncd.noaa.gov

Directs programs and conducts research to support fundamental scientific and engineering activities and resource development for safe navigation of the nation's waterways and territorial seas. Constructs, prints, and distributes nautical charts.

National Response Center *(Homeland Security Dept.), 2100 2nd St. S.W., #2111B 20593-0001; (202) 267-2428. Fax, (202) 267-1322. Syed Qadir, Chief. TTY, (202) 267-4477. Hotline, (800) 424-8802; local, (202) 267-2675. General e-mail, lst-nrcinfo@comdt.uscg.mil*
Web, www.nrc.uscg.mil

Maintains twenty-four-hour hotline for reporting oil spills, hazardous materials accidents, chemical releases, or known or suspected terrorist threats. Notifies appropriate federal officials to reduce the effects of accidents.

National Transportation Safety Board, *Marine Safety, 490 L'Enfant Plaza East S.W., #6313 20594-0001; (202) 314-6450. Fax, (202) 314-6454. John Spencer, Director.*
Web, www.ntsb.gov

Investigates selected marine transportation accidents, including major marine accidents that involve U.S. Coast Guard operations or functions. Determines the facts upon which the board establishes probable cause; makes recommendations on matters pertaining to marine transportation safety and accident prevention.

Occupational Safety and Health Administration (OSHA), *(Labor Dept.), Maritime, 200 Constitution Ave. N.W., #N3609 20210-0001; (202) 693-2086. Fax, (202) 693-1663. Joseph V. Daddura, Director.*
Web, www.osha.gov

Writes occupational safety and health standards and guidance products for the maritime industry.

Occupational Safety and Health Administration (OSHA), *(Labor Dept.), Maritime Enforcement, 200 Constitution Ave. N.W., #N3610 20210-0001; (202) 693-2399. Fax, (202) 693-1681. Stephen Butler, Director.*
Web, www.osha.gov

Interprets maritime safety and health regulations to ensure consistency of enforcement.

U.S. Coast Guard (USCG), *(Homeland Security Dept.), Boating Safety, 2100 2nd St. S.W., #3100 20593-0001; (202) 372-1062. Fax, (202) 372-1933. Jeffrey Hoedt, Chief.*
Web, www.uscgboating.org

Establishes and enforces safety standards for recreational boats and associated equipment; sets boater education standards; coordinates nationwide public awareness and information programs.

U.S. Coast Guard (USCG), *(Homeland Security Dept.), Design and Engineering Standards, CG-521, 2100 2nd St. S.W., #1218 20593-0001; (202) 372-1353. Fax, (202) 372-1925. Comdt. Charles Rawson, Chief.*
Web, www.uscg.mil

Develops standards; responsible for general vessel arrangements, naval architecture, vessel design and construction, and transport of bulk dangerous cargoes. Supports national advisory committees and national professional organizations to achieve industry standards.

U.S. Coast Guard (USCG), *(Homeland Security Dept.), Investigations and Casualty Analysis, CG-545, 2100 2nd St. S.W., #2404 20593-0001; (202) 372-1029. Fax, (202) 372-1907. Capt. Michael P. Rand, Chief.*
General e-mail, michael.p.rand@uscg.mil
Web, www.uscg.mil/hq/cg5/cg545.asp

Compiles and analyzes records of accidents involving commercial vessels that result in loss of life, serious injury, or substantial damage.

U.S. Coast Guard (USCG), *(Homeland Security Dept.), Marine Safety Center, 2100 2nd St. S.W. 20593; (202) 475-3400. Fax, (202) 475-3920. Capt. Patrick Little, Commanding Officer.*
General e-mail, msc@uscg.mil
Web, www.uscg.mil/hq/msc

Reviews and approves commercial vessel plans and specifications to ensure technical compliance with federal safety and pollution abatement standards.

U.S. Coast Guard (USCG), *(Homeland Security Dept.), Marine Safety, Security, and Stewardship, 2100 2nd St. S.W., #3200 20593; (202) 372-1001. Fax, (202) 372-2900. Rear Adm. Brian M. Salerno, Assistant Commandant.*
Web, www.uscg.mil/uscg.shtm

Establishes and enforces regulations for port safety; environmental protection; vessel safety, inspection, design, documentation, and investigation; licensing of merchant vessel personnel; and shipment of hazardous materials.

U.S. Coast Guard (USCG), *(Homeland Security Dept.), Response Policy, CG-53, 2100 2nd St. S.W., #3100 20593-0001; (202) 372-2010. Fax, (202) 372-2901. Adm. Joseph Castillo, Assistant Commandant.*
Web, www.uscg.mil

Conducts search-and-rescue and polar and domestic ice-breaking operations. Regulates waterways under U.S. jurisdiction. Operates the Coast Guard Command Center; participates in defense operations and homeland security; enforces boating safety; assists with law enforcement/drug interdictions.

▶NONGOVERNMENTAL

Cruise Lines International Assn., *2111 Wilson Blvd., 8th Floor, Arlington, VA 22201; (703) 522-8463. Fax, (703) 522-3811. J. Michael Crye, President. Toll-free, (800) 595-9338.*
General e-mail, info@cruising.org
Web, www.cruising.org

Membership: chief executives of twenty-four cruise lines and other cruise industry professionals. Advises domestic and international regulatory organizations on shipping policy. Works with U.S. and international agencies

to promote safety, public health, security, medical facilities, environmental awareness, and passenger protection. Monitors legislation and regulations. (Formerly the International Council of Cruise Lines.)

National Maritime Safety Assn., *919 18th St. N.W., #901 20006; (202) 587-4830. Fax, (202) 587-4888. Charles T. "Chuck" Carroll Jr., Executive Director.*
Web, www.nmsa.us

Represents the marine cargo handling industry in safety and health matters arising under various statutes, including the Occupational Safety and Health Act. Serves as a clearinghouse on information to help reduce injuries and illnesses in the marine cargo handling workplace. Monitors legislation and regulations.

U.S. Coast Guard Office of Auxiliary and Boating Safety, *2100 2nd St. S.W., #3501 20593-0001; (202) 372-1260. Fax, (202) 372-1920. Capt. Mark D. Rizzo, Chief Director.*
Web, http://nws.cgaux.org and www.uscgboating.org

Seeks to minimize the loss of life, personal injury, property damage, and environmental impact associated with the use of recreational boats in order to maximize safe use and enjoyment of U.S. waterways by the public. Offers public education programs and free vessel safety inspections. Works with the U.S. Coast Guard and others involved in waterways activities to maintain marine safety.

Ports and Waterways

▶AGENCIES

Army Corps of Engineers *(Defense Dept.), Civil Works, 441 G St. N.W. 20314-1000; (202) 761-0099. Fax, (202) 761-8992. Maj. Gen. Merdith W. B. Temple, Deputy Commanding General for Civil and Emergency Operations.*
Web, www.usace.army.mil

Coordinates field offices that oversee harbors, dams, levees, waterways, locks, reservoirs, and other construction projects designed to facilitate transportation, flood control, and environmental restoration projects. Major projects include the Mississippi, Missouri, and Ohio Rivers.

Federal Maritime Commission, *Agreements, 800 N. Capitol St. N.W., #940 20573-0001; (202) 523-5793. Fax, (202) 523-4372. Jeremiah D. Hospital, Office Director.*
Web, www.fmc.gov

Analyzes agreements between terminal operators and shipping companies for docking facilities and agreements among ocean common carriers.

Maritime Administration *(Transportation Dept.), Intermodal System Development, West Bldg., 1200 New Jersey Ave. S.E. 20590; (202) 366-4721. Fax, (202) 366-6988. H. Keith Lesnick, Associate Administrator.*
Web, http://marad.dot.gov

Responsible for direction and administration of port and intermodal transportation development and port readiness for national defense.

Saint Lawrence Seaway Development Corp.
(Transportation Dept.), 1200 New Jersey Ave. S.E., #W32-300 20590; (202) 366-0091. Fax, (202) 366-7147. Collister "Terry" Johnson, Administrator. Toll-free, (800) 785-2779. Web, www.greatlakes-seaway.com

Operates and maintains the Saint Lawrence Seaway within U.S. territorial limits; conducts development programs and coordinates activities with its Canadian counterpart.

Tennessee Valley Authority, *Government Affairs, Washington Office, 1 Massachusetts Ave. N.W., #300 20444; (202) 898-2999. Fax, (202) 898-2998. Justin Maierhofer, Director.*
General e-mail, latootle@tva.gov

Web, www.tva.gov

Coordinates resource conservation, development, and land-use programs in the Tennessee River Valley. Operates the river control system; projects include flood control, navigation development, and multiple-use reservoirs.

U.S. Coast Guard (USCG), *(Homeland Security Dept.), 2100 2nd St. S.W. 20593-0001; (202) 372-4411. Fax, (202) 372-4960. Adm. Thad W. Allen, Commandant. Locator, (202) 372-8724. Public Affairs, (202) 372-4620.*
Web, www.uscg.mil

Enforces rules and regulations governing the safety and security of ports and anchorages and the movement of vessels in U.S. waters. Supervises cargo transfer operations, storage, and stowage; conducts harbor patrols and waterfront facility inspections; establishes security zones and monitors vessel movement.

►NONGOVERNMENTAL

American Assn. of Port Authorities (AAPA), *1010 Duke St., Alexandria, VA 22314-3589; (703) 684-5700. Fax, (703) 684-6321. Kurt J. Nagle, President. Press, (703) 706-4714.*
General e-mail, info@aapa-ports.org

Web, www.aapa-ports.org

Membership: public port authorities in the Western Hemisphere. Provides technical and economic information on port finance, construction, operation, and security.

American Waterways Operators, *801 N. Quincy St., #200, Arlington, VA 22203-1708; (703) 841-9300. Fax, (703) 841-0389. Thomas A. Allegretti, President.*
Web, www.americanwaterways.com

Membership: operators of barges, tugboats, and towboats on navigable coastal and inland waterways. Acts as liaison with Congress, the U.S. Coast Guard, the Army Corps of Engineers, and the Maritime Administration. Monitors legislation and regulations.

International Longshore and Warehouse Union (ILWU), *Washington Office, 1025 Connecticut Ave. N.W., #507 20036; (202) 463-6265. Fax, (202) 467-4875. Lindsay McLaughlin, Legislative Director.*
General e-mail, washdc@ilwu.org

Web, www.ilwu.org

Membership: approximately 60,000 longshore and warehouse personnel. Helps members negotiate pay, benefits, and better working conditions; conducts training programs and workshops. Monitors legislation and regulations. (Headquarters in San Francisco, Calif.; affiliated with the AFL-CIO.)

International Longshoremen's Assn., *Washington Office, 1101 17th St. N.W., #400 20036-4704; (202) 955-6304. Fax, (202) 955-6048. John Bowers Jr., Legislative Director.*
General e-mail, iladc@aol.com

Web, www.ilaunion.org

Membership: approximately 65,000 longshore personnel. Helps members negotiate pay, benefits, and better working conditions; conducts training programs and workshops. Monitors legislation and regulations. (Headquarters in New York; affiliated with the AFL-CIO.)

National Assn. of Waterfront Employers, *919 18th St. N.W., #901 20006; (202) 587-4800. Fax, (202) 587-4888. Charles T. "Chuck" Carroll Jr., Executive Director.*
Web, www.nawe.us

Membership: private sector stevedore companies and marine terminal operators, their subsidiaries, and other waterfront-related employers. Legislative interests include trade, antitrust, insurance, port security, and user-fee issues. Monitors legislation and regulations.

National Waterways Conference, *4650 Washington Blvd., #608, Arlington, VA 22201; (703) 243-4090. Fax, (866) 371-1390. Amy W. Larson, President.*
General e-mail, info@waterways.org

Web, www.waterways.org

Membership: petroleum, coal, chemical, electric power, building materials, iron and steel, and grain companies; port authorities; water carriers; and others interested or involved in waterways. Sponsors educational programs on waterways. Monitors legislation and regulations.

Passenger Vessel Assn., *901 N. Pitt St., #100, Alexandria, VA 22314; (703) 518-5005. Fax, (703) 518-5151. John R. Groundwater, Executive Director. Toll-free, (800) 807-8360.*
General e-mail, pvainfo@passengervessel.com

Web, www.passengervessel.com

Membership: owners, operators, and suppliers for U.S. and Canadian passenger vessels and international vessel companies. Interests include insurance, safety and security, and U.S. congressional impact upon dinner and excursion boats, car and passenger ferries, overnight cruise ships, and riverboat casinos. Monitors legislation and regulations.

Waterways Council, Inc., *801 N. Quincy St., #200, Arlington, VA 22203; (703) 373-2261. Fax, (703) 373-2037. Cornel J. Martin, President. Press, (301) 565-5329 or dcolbert@vesselalliance.com.*

General e-mail, cmartin@vesselalliance.com

Web, www.waterwayscouncil.org

Membership: port authorities, waterways carriers, shippers, shipping associations, and waterways advocacy groups. Advocates for a modern and well-maintained system of inland waterways and port infrastructure. Monitors legislation and regulations.

MOTOR VEHICLES

►AGENCIES

Federal Highway Administration (FHWA),
(Transportation Dept.), East Bldg., 1200 New Jersey Ave. S.E., #300 20590-0001; (202) 366-0650. Fax, (202) 366-3244. Jeffrey F. Paniati, Deputy Administrator (Acting). Press, (202) 366-0660.
Web, www.fhwa.dot.gov

Administers federal-aid highway programs with money from the Highway Trust Fund; works to improve highway and motor vehicle safety; coordinates research and development programs on highway and traffic safety, construction costs, and the environmental impact of highway transportation; administers regional and territorial highway building programs and the highway beautification program.

Federal Motor Carrier Safety Administration
(Transportation Dept.), Bus and Truck Standards and Operations, 1200 New Jersey Ave. S.E., #N64-330 20590; (202) 366-2362. Fax, (202) 366-8842. Chuck Horan, Director.
Web, www.fmcsa.dot.gov

Regulates motor vehicle size and weight on federally aided highways; conducts studies on issues relating to motor carrier transportation; promotes uniformity in state and federal motor carrier laws and regulations.

Transportation Security Administration (TSA),
(Homeland Security Dept.), Freedom Center, 13555 EDS Dr., Herndon, VA 20171; (866) 655-7023. Donald Zimmerman, Deputy Executive Director; James "Jim" Quinlin, Chief of Staff, (703) 563-3601.
Web, www.tsa.gov

Provides continual federal, state, and local coordination, communications, and domain awareness for all of the Homeland Security Dept.'s transportation-related security activities worldwide. Transportation domains include highway, rail, shipping, and aviation.

►CONGRESS

For a listing of relevant congressional committees and subcommittees, please see page 656 or the Appendix.

►NONGOVERNMENTAL

American Assn. of Motor Vehicle Administrators (AAMVA), *4301 Wilson Blvd., #400, Arlington, VA 22203-1753; (703) 522-4200. Fax, (703) 522-1553. Neil Schuster, President (Acting). Press, (703) 908-8287.*
Web, www.aamva.org

Membership: officials responsible for administering and enforcing motor vehicle and traffic laws in the United States and Canada. Promotes uniform laws and regulations for vehicle registration, driver's licenses, and motor carrier services; provides administrative evaluation services for safety equipment.

American Automobile Assn. (AAA), *Washington Office, 607 14th St. N.W., #200 20005-2000; (202) 942-2050. Fax, (202) 783-4788. Jill Ingrassia, Managing Director of Government Relations and Traffic Safety Advocacy.*
General e-mail, jingrassia@national.AAA.org
Web, www.aaa.com

Membership: state and local automobile associations. Provides members with travel services. Interests include all aspects of highway transportation, travel and tourism, safety, drunk driving, economics, federal aid, and legislation that affects motorists. (Headquarters in Heathrow, Fla.)

American Bus Assn., *700 13th St. N.W., #575 20005-5923; (202) 842-1645. Fax, (202) 842-0850. Peter J. Pantuso, President. Toll-free, (800) 283-2877.*
General e-mail, abainfo@buses.org
Web, www.buses.org

Membership: privately owned intercity bus companies, state associations, travel/tourism businesses, bus manufacturers, and those interested in the bus industry. Monitors legislation and regulations.

American Trucking Assns., *950 N. Glebe Rd., #210, Arlington, VA 22203-4181; (703) 838-1700. Fax, (703) 838-1994. William P. Graves, President.*
General e-mail, membership@trucking.org
Web, www.truckline.com

Membership: state trucking associations, individual trucking and motor carrier organizations, and related supply companies. Maintains departments on industrial relations, law, management systems, research, safety, traffic, state laws, taxation, communications, legislation, economics, and engineering.

Electric Drive Transportation Assn. (EDTA), *1101 Vermont Ave. N.W., #401 20005-3347; (202) 408-0774. Fax, (202) 408-7610. Brian P. Wynne, President.*
General e-mail, info@electricdrive.org
Web, www.electricdrive.org

Membership: automotive and other equipment manufacturers, utilities, technology developers, component suppliers, and government agencies. Conducts public policy advocacy, education, industry networking, and international conferences in the areas of battery, hybrid, and fuel cell electric drive technologies and infrastructures.

Highway Loss Data Institute, *1005 N. Glebe Rd., #800, Arlington, VA 22201; (703) 247-1600. Fax, (703) 247-1595. Adrian Lund, President. Press, (703) 247-1530.*
Web, www.iihs.org

Research organization that gathers, processes, and publishes data on the ways in which insurance losses vary among different kinds of vehicles. (Affiliated with Insurance Institute for Highway Safety.)

International Parking Institute, *701 Kenmore Ave., #200, Fredericksburg, VA 22401 (mailing address: P.O. Box 7167, Fredericksburg, VA 22404-7167); (540) 371-7535. Fax, (540) 371-8022. Sean Conrad, Executive Director.*
General e-mail, ipi@parking.org

Web, www.parking.org

Membership: operators, designers, and builders of parking lots and structures. Provides leadership to the parking industry; supports professional development; works with transportation and related fields.

Motorcycle Industry Council, *Government Relations, Washington Office, 1235 South Clark St., #600, Arlington, VA 22202; (703) 416-0444. Fax, (703) 416-2269. Kathy Van Kleeck Sr., Vice President.*
Web, www.mic.org

Membership: manufacturers and distributors of motorcycles, mopeds, and related parts, accessories, and equipment. Monitors legislation and regulations. (Headquarters in Irvine, Calif.)

National Assn. of Regulatory Utility Commissioners, *1101 Vermont Ave. N.W., #200 20005-3521; (202) 898-2200. Fax, (202) 898-2213. Charles D. Gray, Executive Director. Press, (202) 898-9382.*
General e-mail, admin@naruc.org

Web, www.naruc.org

Membership: members of federal, state, municipal, and international regulatory commissions that have jurisdiction over motor and common carriers. Interests include motor carriers.

National Institute for Automotive Service Excellence, *101 Blue Seal Dr. S.E., #101, Leesburg, VA 20175; (703) 669-6600. Fax, (703) 669-6123. Timothy Zilke, President. Toll-free, (888) 273-8378.*
General e-mail, webmaster@ase.org

Web, www.ase.com

Administers program for testing and certifying automotive technicians; researches methods to improve technician training.

National Motor Freight Traffic Assn., *1001 N. Fairfax St., #600, Alexandria, VA 22314; (703) 838-1810. Fax, (703) 683-6296. Vacant, Executive Director.*
General e-mail, customerservice@nmfta.org

Web, www.nmfta.org

Membership: motor carriers of general goods in interstate and intrastate commerce. Publishes *National Motor Freight Classification.*

National Parking Assn., *1112 16th St. N.W., #840 20036-4880; (202) 296-4336. Fax, (202) 296-3102. Martin L. Stein, President. Toll-free, (800) 647-PARK.*
General e-mail, info@npapark.org

Web, www.npapark.org

Membership: parking garage operators, parking consultants, universities, municipalities, medical centers, and vendors. Offers information and research services; sponsors seminars and educational programs on garage design and equipment. Monitors legislation and regulations.

National Private Truck Council, *950 N. Glebe Rd., #530, Arlington, VA 22203-4183; (703) 683-1300. Fax, (703) 683-1217. Gary F. Petty, Chief Executive Officer.*
Web, www.nptc.org

Membership: manufacturers, retailers, distributors, wholesalers, and suppliers that operate their own private truck fleets in conjunction with their nontransportation businesses. Interests include standards, best practices, benchmarking, federal regulatory compliance, peer-to-peer networking, and business economics. Supports economic deregulation of the trucking industry and uniformity in state taxation of the industry. NPTC Institute supports continuing education and certification programs.

National Tank Truck Carriers (NTTC), *950 N. Glebe Rd., #520, Arlington, VA 22203-4183; (703) 838-1960. Fax, (703) 838-8860. John Conley, President.*
General e-mail, nttc@tanktruck.org

Web, www.tanktruck.org

Focuses on issues of the tank truck industry and represents the industry before Congress and federal agencies.

NATSO, Inc., *1737 King St., #200, Alexandria, VA 22314; (703) 549-2100. Fax, (703) 684-4525. Lisa J. Mullings, President. Toll-free, (888) 275-6287.*
General e-mail, headquarters@natso.com

Web, www.natso.com

Membership: travel plaza and truck stop operators and suppliers to the truck stop industry. Provides credit information and educational training programs. Monitors legislation and regulations. Operates the NATSO Foundation, which promotes highway safety.

NGVAmerica, *400 N. Capitol St. N.W. 20001; (202) 824-7366. Fax, (202) 824-7087. Richard R. Kolodziej, President. Press, (202) 824-7366.*
General e-mail, rkolodziej@ngvamerica.org

Web, www.ngvamerica.org

Membership: natural gas distributors; automobile and engine manufacturers; natural gas and hydrogen vehicle product and service suppliers; environmental groups; research and development organizations; and state and local government agencies. Advocates installation of natural gas, biomethane, and hydrogen fuel stations and development of industry standards. Helps market new products and equipment related to natural gas, biomethane, and hydrogen-powered vehicles. (Formerly known as the Natural Gas Vehicle Coalition.)

Truckload Carriers Assn., *555 E. Braddock Rd., Alexandria, VA 22314; (703) 838-1950. Fax, (703) 836-6610. Chris Burruss, President.*
General e-mail, tca@truckload.org
Web, www.truckload.org

Membership: truckload carriers and suppliers to the truckload industry. Provides information and educational programs to members. Represents intercity common and contract trucking companies before Congress, federal agencies, courts, and the media.

Union of Concerned Scientists, *Clean Vehicles Program, Washington Office, 1825 K St. N.W., #800 20006-1232; (202) 223-6133. Fax, (202) 223-6162. Michelle Robinson, Director.*
General e-mail, ucs@ucsusa.org
Web, www.ucsusa.org

Develops and promotes strategies to reduce the adverse effects of the U.S. transportation system with a focus on encouraging automakers to build and sell battery-electric, hybrid-electric, and fuel cell vehicles; cleaning up conventional automobiles; and cleaning up heavy trucks and buses. (Headquarters in Cambridge, Mass.)

Highways

▶AGENCIES

Federal Highway Administration (FHWA), *(Transportation Dept.), Infrastructure, 1200 New Jersey Ave. S.E., #E75-312 20590; (202) 366-0371. Fax, (202) 366-3988. King W. Gee, Associate Administrator.*
Web, www.fhwa.dot.gov/infrastructure

Provides guidance and oversight for planning, design, construction, and maintenance operations relating to federal aid, direct federal construction, and other highway programs; establishes design guidelines and specifications for highways built with federal funds.

Federal Highway Administration (FHWA), *(Transportation Dept.), National Highway Institute, 4600 N. Fairfax Dr., #800, Arlington, VA 22203-1555; (703) 235-0520. Fax, (703) 235-0593. Rick Barnaby, Director. Toll-free, (877) 558-6873.*
Web, www.nhi.fhwa.dot.gov

Develops and administers, in cooperation with state highway departments, technical training programs for agency, state, and local highway department employees.

Federal Highway Administration (FHWA), *(Transportation Dept.), Policy and Governmental Affairs, 1200 New Jersey Ave. S.E., #E81-123 20590-0001; (202) 366-0585. Fax, (202) 366-3590. James Cheatham, Associate Administrator (Acting).*
Web, www.fhwa.dot.gov

Develops policy and administers the Federal Highway Administration's international programs. Conducts policy studies and analyzes legislation; makes recommendations; compiles and reviews highway-related data. Represents the administration at international conferences; administers foreign assistance programs.

Federal Highway Administration (FHWA), *(Transportation Dept.), Real Estate Services, 1200 New Jersey Ave. S.E., #E76-304 20590; (202) 366-0142. Fax, (202) 366-3713. Gerald Solomon, Director.*
Web, www.fhwa.dot.gov/realestate

Funds and oversees acquisition of land by states for federally assisted highways; provides financial assistance to relocate people and businesses forced to move by highway construction; cooperates in administering program for the use of air rights in connection with federally aided highways; administers the Highway Beautification Act to control billboards and junkyards along interstate and federally aided primary highways.

Federal Highway Administration (FHWA), *(Transportation Dept.), Research, Development and Technology, 6300 Georgetown Pike, #T306, McLean, VA 22101-2296; (202) 493-3999. Fax, (202) 493-3170. Michael Trentacoste, Associate Administrator.*
Web, www.fhwa.dot.gov/orgrdat.htm

Conducts highway research and development programs; studies safety, location, design, construction, operation, and maintenance of highways; cooperates with state and local highway departments in utilizing results of research.

U.S. Coast Guard (USCG), *(Homeland Security Dept.), 2100 2nd St. S.W. 20593-0001; (202) 372-4411. Fax, (202) 372-4960. Adm. Thad W. Allen, Commandant. Locator, (202) 372-8724. Public Affairs, (202) 372-4620.*
Web, www.uscg.mil

Regulates the construction, maintenance, and operation of bridges across U.S. navigable waters.

▶NONGOVERNMENTAL

American Assn. of State Highway and Transportation Officials (AASHTO), *444 N. Capitol St. N.W., #249 20001-1512; (202) 624-5800. Fax, (202) 624-5806. John Horsley, Executive Director.*
General e-mail, info@aashto.org
Web, www.transportation.org

Membership: the transportation departments of the 50 states, the District of Columbia, and Puerto Rico, and affiliated agencies, including the U.S. Department of Transportation as a non-voting ex-officio member. Maintains committees on all modes of transportation and departmental affairs.

American Road and Transportation Builders Assn. (ARTBA), *1219 28th St. N.W. 20007-3389; (202) 289-4434. Fax, (202) 289-4435. T. Peter Ruane, President.*
Web, www.artba.org

Membership: highway and transportation contractors; federal, state, and local engineers and officials; construction equipment manufacturers and distributors; and others interested in the transportation construction industry. Serves as liaison with government; provides information on highway engineering and construction developments.

Intelligent Transportation Society of America, *1100 17th St. N.W., #1200 20036-4601; (202) 484-4847. Fax, (202) 484-3483. Scott Belcher, President. Press, (202) 721-4205. General e-mail, info@itsa.org*

Web, www.itsa.org

Advocates application of electronic, computer, and communications technology to make surface transportation more efficient and to save lives, time, and money. Coordinates research, development, and implementation of intelligent transportation systems by government, academia, and industry.

International Bridge, Tunnel and Turnpike Assn., *1146 19th St. N.W., #800 20036-3725; (202) 659-4620. Fax, (202) 659-0500. Patrick D. Jones, Executive Director. General e-mail, ibtta@ibtta.org*

Web, www.ibtta.org

Membership: public and private operators of toll facilities and associated industries. Conducts research; compiles statistics.

International Road Federation (IRF), *Madison Place, 500 Montgomery St., #525, Alexandria, VA 22314; (703) 535-1001. Fax, (703) 535-1007. C. Patrick Sankey, Director General. General e-mail, info@irfnews.org*

Web, www.irfnews.org

Membership: contractors, consultants, equipment manufacturers, researchers, and others involved in the road building industry. Administers fellowship program that allows foreign engineering students to study at U.S. graduate schools. Maintains interest in roads and highways worldwide.

Road Information Program, *1726 M St. N.W., #401 20036-4521; (202) 466-6706. Fax, (202) 785-4722. William M. Wilkins, Executive Director. General e-mail, trip@tripnet.org*

Web, www.tripnet.org

Organization of transportation specialists; conducts research on economic and technical transportation issues; promotes consumer awareness of the condition of the national road and bridge system.

Manufacturing and Sales

►AGENCIES

International Trade Administration (ITA), *(Commerce Dept.), Transportation and Machinery, 14th St. and Constitution Ave. N.W., #4036 20230-0001; (202)*

482-0554. Fax, (202) 482-0674. Henry P. Misisco, Director. Web, http://trade.gov/mas/index.asp

Promotes the export of U.S. aerospace, automotive, and machinery products; compiles and analyzes industry data; seeks to secure a favorable position for the U.S. aerospace, auto, and machinery industries in global markets through policy and trade agreements.

►NONGOVERNMENTAL

Alliance of Automobile Manufacturers, *1401 Eye St. N.W., #900 20005; (202) 326-5500. Fax, (202) 326-5598. Dave McCurdy, President. Web, www.autoalliance.org*

Trade association of ten major automakers. Provides advocacy on automotive issues focusing primarily on environment, energy, and safety. Seeks to harmonize global automotive standards.

American Automotive Leasing Assn., *675 N. Washington St., #410, Alexandria, VA 22314-1939; (703) 548-0777. Fax, (703) 548-1925. Pamela Sederholm, Executive Director. Web, www.aalafleet.com*

Membership: automotive commercial fleet leasing and management companies. Monitors legislation and regulations.

American International Automobile Dealers Assn., *211 N. Union St., #300, Alexandria, VA 22314; (703) 519-7800. Fax, (703) 519-7810. Cody Lusk, President. Toll-free, (800) 462-4232. General e-mail, goaiada@aiada.org*

Web, www.aiada.org

Promotes a favorable market for international nameplate automobiles in the United States through education of policymakers and the general public. Monitors legislation and regulations concerning tariffs, quotas, taxes, fuel economy, and clean air initiatives.

Assn. of International Automobile Manufacturers, *2111 Wilson Blvd., #1150, Arlington, VA 22201; (703) 525-7788. Fax, (703) 525-8817/3289. Michael J. Stanton, President. Web, www.aiam.org*

Membership: automobile manufacturers and parts suppliers. Monitors legislation and regulations.

Automotive Aftermarket Industry Assn. (AAIA), *7101 Wisconsin Ave., #1300, Bethesda, MD 20814; (301) 654-6664. Fax, (301) 654-3299. Kathleen Schmatz, President. General e-mail, aaia@aftermarket.org*

Web, www.aftermarket.org

Membership: domestic and international manufacturers, manufacturers' representatives, retailers, and distributors in the automotive aftermarket industry, which involves service of a vehicle after it leaves the dealership. Offers educational programs, conducts research, and provides members with technical and international trade services; acts as liaison with government; sponsors annual marketing conference and trade shows.

Automotive Parts Remanufacturers Assn., *4215 Lafayette Center Dr., #3, Chantilly, VA 20151-1243; (703) 968-2772. Fax, (703) 968-2878. William C. Gager, President.*
General e-mail, mail@apra.org

Web, www.apra.org

Membership: rebuilders and remanufacturers of automotive parts. Conducts educational programs on transmission, brake, clutch, water pump, air conditioning, electrical parts, heavy-duty brake, and carburetor rebuilding.

Automotive Recyclers Assn. (ARA), *9113 Church St., Manassas, VA 20110; (703) 385-1001. Fax, (703)385-1494. Michael E. Wilson, Chief Executive Officer. Toll-free, (888) 385-1005.*
General e-mail, staff@a-r-a.org

Web, www.a-r-a.org

Membership: retail and wholesale firms involved in the dismantling and sale of used motor vehicle parts. Works to increase the efficiency of businesses in the automotive recycling industry. Cooperates with public and private agencies to encourage further automotive recycling efforts.

Coalition for Auto Repair Equality, *119 Oronoco St., Suite 300, Alexandria, VA 22314-2015; (703) 519-7555. Fax, (703) 519-7747. Ray Pohlman, President (Acting). Toll-free, (800) 229-5380.*
General e-mail, Sandy@careauto.org

Web, www.careauto.org

Works to promote greater competition in the automotive after market repair industry in order to protect consumers. Monitors state and federal legislation that impacts motorists and the automotive after market repair industry.

Japan Automobile Manufacturers Assn. (JAMA), *Washington Office, 1050 17th St. N.W., #410 20036; (202) 296-8537. Fax, (202) 872-1212. William C. Duncan, General Director.*
General e-mail, jama@jama.org

Web, www.jama.org

Membership: Japanese motor vehicle manufacturers. Interests include energy, market, trade, and environmental issues. (Headquarters in Tokyo.)

National Automobile Dealers Assn. (NADA), *8400 Westpark Dr., McLean, VA 22102-3591; (703) 821-7000. Fax, (703) 821-7075. Phillip Brady, President. Press, (703) 821-7121. Toll-free, (800) 252-6232.*
General e-mail, nadainfo@nada.org

Web, www.nada.org

Membership: domestic and imported franchised new car and truck dealers. Publishes the *National Automobile Dealers Used Car Guide* (Blue Book).

Recreation Vehicle Dealers Assn. of North America (RVDA), *3930 University Dr., Fairfax, VA 22030-2515; (703) 591-7130. Fax, (703) 591-0734. Michael A. Molino, President.*
General e-mail, info@rvda.org

Web, www.rvda.org

Serves as liaison between the recreation vehicle industry and government; interests include government regulation of safety, trade, warranty, and franchising; provides members with educational services; works to improve service standards for consumers.

Recreation Vehicle Industry Assn. (RVIA), *1896 Preston White Dr., Reston, VA 20191-4363 (mailing address: P.O. Box 2999, Reston, VA 20195-0999); (703) 620-6003. Fax, (703) 620-5071. Richard Coon, President.*
Web, www.rvia.org

Membership: manufacturers of recreation vehicles and their suppliers. Compiles shipment statistics and other technical data; provides consumers and the media with information on the industry. Assists members' compliance with American National Standards Institute requirements for recreation vehicles. Monitors legislation and regulations.

Tire Industry Assn., *1532 Pointer Ridge Pl., Suite G, Bowie, MD 20716-1883; (301) 430-7280. Fax, (301) 430-7283. Dan Beach, President. Toll-free, (800) 876-8372.*
General e-mail, info@tireindustry.org

Web, www.tireindustry.org

Membership: all segments of the tire industry, including those that manufacture, repair, recycle, sell, service, or use new or retreaded tires and also suppliers that furnish equipment or services to the industry. Interests include environmental and small-business issues and quality control in the industry. Promotes government procurement of retreaded tires. Monitors legislation and regulations. (Created July 2002 by the merger of the International Tire and Rubber Assn. and the Tire Assn. of North America.)

Truck Renting and Leasing Assn., *675 N. Washington St., #410, Alexandria, VA 22314-1939; (703) 299-9120. Fax, (703) 299-9115. Peter J. Vroom, President.*
Web, www.trala.org

Membership: vehicle renting and leasing companies and suppliers to the industry. Acts as liaison with state and federal legislative bodies and regulatory agencies. Interests include truck security and safety, tort reform, operating taxes and registration fees, insurance, and environmental issues.

Truck Trailer Manufacturers Assn. (TTMA), *1020 Princess St., Alexandria, VA 22314; (703) 549-3010. Fax, (703) 549-3014. Richard P. Bowling, President.*
General e-mail, ttma@erols.com

Web, www.ttmanet.org

Membership: truck trailer manufacturing and supply companies. Serves as liaison between its members and government agencies.

United Auto Workers, *Washington Office, 1757 N St. N.W. 20036; (202) 828-8500. Fax, (202) 293-3457. Alan Reuther, Legislative Director.*
Web, www.uaw.org

Membership: approximately 750,000 active and 600,000 retired North American workers in aerospace, automotive, defense, manufacturing, steel, technical, and other industries. Assists members with contract negotiations and grievances; conducts training programs and workshops. Monitors legislation and regulations. (Headquarters in Detroit, Mich.)

UNITE HERE, *Washington Office, 1775 K St. N.W., #620 20006; (202) 393-4373. Fax, (202) 342-2929. Tom Snyder, Political Director.*
Web, www.unitehere.org

Membership: approximately 250,000 workers in basic apparel and textiles, millinery, shoe, laundry, retail, and related industries, and in auto parts and auto supply. Assists members with contract negotiation and grievances; conducts training programs and workshops. Monitors legislation and regulations. (Headquarters in New York. Formerly the Union of Needletrades, Industrial and Textile Employers.)

Traffic Safety

▶**AGENCIES**

Federal Highway Administration (FHWA),
(Transportation Dept.), Operations, 1200 New Jersey Ave. S.E., #E86-205 20590-0001; (202) 366-9210. Fax, (202) 366-3225. Jeffrey A. Lindley, Associate Administrator. Press, (202) 366-4650.
Web, www.fhwa.dot.gov/operations

Fosters the efficient management and operation of the highway system. Responsible for congestion management, pricing, ITS deployment, traffic operations, emergency management, and freight management. Includes offices of Transportation Management, Freight Management and Operations, and Transportation Operations.

Federal Motor Carrier Safety Administration
(Transportation Dept.), 1200 New Jersey Ave. S.E., #W60-311 20590; (202) 366-1927. Fax, (202) 366-3224. Rose McMurray, Deputy Administrator (Acting).
Web, www.fmcsa.dot.gov

Partners with federal, state, and local enforcement agencies, the motor carrier industry, safety groups, and organized labor in efforts to reduce bus- and truck-related crashes.

Federal Motor Carrier Safety Administration
(Transportation Dept.), Bus and Truck Standards and Operations, 1200 New Jersey Ave. S.E., #N64-330 20590;

(202) 366-2362. Fax, (202) 366-8842. Chuck Horan, Director.
Web, www.fmcsa.dot.gov

Interprets and disseminates national safety regulations regarding commercial drivers' qualifications, maximum hours of service, accident reporting, and transportation of hazardous materials. Sets minimum levels of financial liability for trucks and buses. Responsible for Commercial Driver's License Information Program.

National Highway Traffic Safety Administration
(Transportation Dept.), West Bldg., 1200 New Jersey Ave. S.E. 20590; (202) 366-1836. Fax, (202) 366-2106. Ron Medford, Deputy Administrator (Acting). Press, (202) 366-9550. Toll-free 24-hour hotline, (888) 327-4236.
Web, www.nhtsa.gov

Implements motor vehicle safety programs; issues federal motor vehicle safety standards; conducts testing programs to determine compliance with these standards; funds local and state motor vehicle and driver safety programs; conducts research on motor vehicle development, equipment, and auto and traffic safety. The Auto Safety Hotline provides safety information and handles consumer problems and complaints involving safety-related defects.

National Highway Traffic Safety Administration
(Transportation Dept.), National Driver Register, 1200 New Jersey Ave. S.E., #W55-123 20590-0001; (202) 366-4800. Fax, (202) 366-2746. Sean H. McLaurin, Chief.
Web, www-nrd.nhtsa.dot.gov/departments/nrd-30/ncsa/ndr.html

Maintains and operates the National Driver Register, a program in which states exchange information on motor vehicle driving records to ensure that drivers with suspended licenses in one state cannot obtain licenses in any other state.

National Transportation Safety Board, *Highway Safety, 490 L'Enfant Plaza East S.W., HS-1 20594-0001; (202) 314-6440. Fax, (202) 459-9334. Bruce A. Magladry, Director. Press, (202) 314-6100.*
Web, www.ntsb.gov

In cooperation with states, investigates selected highway transportation accidents to compile the facts upon which the board determines probable cause; works to prevent similar recurrences; makes recommendations on matters pertaining to highway safety and accident prevention.

▶**NONGOVERNMENTAL**

AAA Foundation for Traffic Safety, *607 14th St. N.W., #201 20005; (202) 638-5944. Fax, (202) 638-5943. J. Peter Kissinger, President. To order educational materials, (800) 305-7233.*
General e-mail, info@aaafoundation.org
Web, www.aaafoundation.org

Sponsors "human factor" research on traffic safety issues, including bicycle, pedestrian, and road safety; supplies traffic safety educational materials to elementary and secondary schools, commercial driving schools, law enforcement agencies, motor vehicle administrations, and programs for older drivers.

Advocates for Highway and Auto Safety, *750 1st St. N.E., #901 20002-8007; (202) 408-1711. Fax, (202) 408-1699. Judith Lee Stone, President.*
General e-mail, advocates@saferoads.org
Web, www.saferoads.org

Coalition of insurers, citizens' groups, and public health and safety organizations. Advocates public policy designed to reduce deaths, injuries, and economic costs associated with motor vehicle crashes and fraud and theft involving motor vehicles. Interests include safety belts and child safety seats, drunk driving abuse, motorcycle helmets, vehicle crashworthiness, and speed limits. Monitors legislation and regulations.

American Highway Users Alliance, *1101 14th St. N.W., #750 20005; (202) 857-1200. Fax, (202) 857-1220. Gregory M. Cohen, President.*
General e-mail, info@highways.org
Web, www.highways.org

Membership: companies and associations representing major industry and highway user groups. Develops information, analyzes public policy, and advocates legislation to improve roadway safety and efficiency and to increase the mobility of the American public. (Affiliated with the Roadway Safety Foundation.)

American Trucking Assns., *Safety, Security, and Operations Policy, 950 N. Glebe Rd., #210, Arlington, VA 22203; (703) 838-1847. Fax, (703) 836-1748. David J. Osiecki, Vice President.*
Web, www.truckline.com

Membership: state trucking associations, individual trucking and motor carrier organizations, and related supply companies. Provides information on safety for the trucking industry. Develops safety training programs for motor carriers and drivers.

Center for Auto Safety, *1825 Connecticut Ave. N.W., #330 20009-5708; (202) 328-7700. Fax, (202) 387-0140. General e-mail, accounts@autosafety.org*
Web, www.autosafety.org

Public interest organization that receives written consumer complaints against auto manufacturers; monitors federal agencies responsible for regulating and enforcing auto and highway safety rules.

Commercial Vehicle Safety Alliance (CVSA), *1101 17th St. N.W., #803 20036-4713; (202) 775-1623. Fax, (202) 775-1624. Stephen F. Campbell, Executive Director. General e-mail, cvsahq@cvsa.org*
Web, www.cvsa.org

Membership: U.S., Canadian, and Mexican officials responsible for administering and enforcing commercial motor carrier safety laws. Works to increase on-highway inspections, prevent duplication of inspections, improve the safety of equipment operated on highways, and improve compliance with hazardous materials transportation regulations.

Governors Highway Safety Assn., *444 N. Capitol St. N.W., #722 20001; (202) 789-0942. Fax, (202) 789-0946. Barbara L. Harsha, Executive Director.*
General e-mail, headquarters@ghsa.org
Web, www.ghsa.org

Membership: state officials who manage highway safety programs. Interprets technical data concerning highway safety. Represents the states in policy debates on national highway safety issues.

Institute of Transportation Engineers (ITE), *1099 14th St. N.W., #300 West 20005-3438; (202) 289-0222. Fax, (202) 289-7722. Philip J. Caruso, Deputy Executive Director.*
General e-mail, ite_staff@ite.org
Web, www.ite.org

Membership: international professional transportation engineers. Interests include safe and efficient surface transportation; provides professional and scientific information on transportation standards and recommended practices.

Insurance Institute for Highway Safety, *1005 N. Glebe Rd., #800, Arlington, VA 22201; (703) 247-1500. Fax, (703) 247-1588. Adrian Lund, President.*
Web, www.highwaysafety.org

Membership: property and casualty insurance associations and individual insurance companies. Conducts research and provides data on highway safety; seeks ways to reduce losses from vehicle crashes. (Affiliated with Highway Loss Data Institute.)

Mothers Against Drunk Driving (MADD), *Public Policy Office, 1025 Connecticut Ave. N.W., #1200 20036-5415; (202) 974-2487. Fax, (202) 293-0106. J. T. Griffin, Public Policy Director; Julie Clements, State Policy Specialist. General e-mail, madd@madd.org*
Web, www.madd.org

Advocacy group that seeks to stop drunk driving and prevent underage drinking. Monitors legislation and regulations. (Headquarters in Irving, Texas.)

National Crash Analysis Center *(George Washington University), 20101 Academic Way, Ashburn, VA 20147; (703) 726-3600. Fax, (703) 726-3530. Cing-Dao "Steve" Kan, Director. Library, (703) 726-8236. General e-mail, library@ncac.gwu.edu*
Web, www.ncac.gwu.edu

Conducts advanced crash research on transportation safety and security issues; applies research for the development and evaluation of vehicle safety systems, road features and hardware, and infrastructure systems. Interests include improving crash and pre-crash analysis methods, computer simulation, modeling, and methods in crash avoidance studies. Collaborates with the Federal Highway Administration and the National Highway Traffic Safety Administration.

National Safety Council, *Government Services, Washington Office, 1025 Connecticut Ave. N.W., #1200 20036; (202) 293-2270. Fax, (202) 293-0032. Bobby Jackson, Senior Vice President of National Programs.* Web, www.nsc.org

Chartered by Congress. Conducts research and provides educational and informational services on highway safety, child passenger safety, and motor vehicle crash prevention; promotes policies to reduce accidental deaths and injuries. Monitors legislation and regulations. (Headquarters in Itasca, Ill.)

National School Transportation Assn. (NSTA), *113 South West St., 4th Floor, Alexandria, VA 22314; (703) 684-3200. Fax, (703) 684-3212. Danielle S. Abe, Director of Marketing and Operations. Toll-free, (800) 222-NSTA. General e-mail, info@yellowbuses.org*

Web, www.yellowbuses.org

Membership: private owners who operate school buses on contract, bus manufacturers, and allied companies. Primary area of interest and research is school bus safety.

Network of Employers for Traffic Safety, *344 Maple Ave. West, #357, Vienna, VA 22180; (703) 273-6005. Fax, (703) 273-7122. Jack Hanley, Executive Director (Interim). General e-mail, nets@trafficsafety.org*

Web, www.trafficsafety.org

Dedicated to reducing the human and economic cost associated with highway crashes. Helps employers develop and implement workplace highway safety programs. Provides technical assistance.

Roadway Safety Foundation, *1101 14th St. N.W., #750 20005; (202) 857-1200. Fax, (202) 857-1220. Gregory M. Cohen, President. General e-mail, info@highways.org*

Web, www.roadwaysafety.org

Conducts highway safety programs to reduce automobile-related accidents and deaths. (Affiliated with American Highway Users Alliance.)

Rubber Manufacturers Assn., *1400 K St. N.W., #900 20005; (202) 682-4800. Fax, (202) 682-4854. Donald Shea, President. General e-mail, info@rma.org*

Web, www.rma.org

Membership: American tire manufacturers. Provides consumers with information on tire care and safety.

United Motorcoach Assn. (UMA), *113 S. West St., 4th Floor, Alexandria, VA 22314-2824; (703) 838-2929. Fax, (703) 838-2950. Victor S. Parra, Chief Executive Officer. Toll-free, (800) 424-8262. General e-mail, info@uma.org*

Web, www.uma.org

Membership: professional bus and motorcoach companies and suppliers and manufacturers in the industry. Provides information, offers technical assistance, conducts research, and monitors legislation. Interests include insurance, safety programs, and credit.

RAIL TRANSPORTATION

▶AGENCIES

Federal Railroad Administration *(Transportation Dept.), 1200 New Jersey Ave. S.E., 3rd Floor 20590; (202) 493-6014. Fax, (202) 493-6008. Karen Rae, Deputy Administrator. Press, (202) 493-6000.* Web, www.fra.dot.gov

Develops national rail policies; enforces rail safety laws; administers financial assistance programs available to states and the rail industry; conducts research and development on improved rail safety.

Federal Railroad Administration *(Transportation Dept.), Policy and Communications, West Bldg., 1200 New Jersey Ave. S.E., MS 15 20590; (202) 493-6400. Fax, (202) 493-6401. Timothy Barkley, Director.* Web, www.fra.dot.gov

Plans, coordinates, and administers activities related to railroad economics, finance, traffic and network analysis, labor management, and transportation planning, as well as intermodal, environmental, emergency response, and international programs.

Federal Railroad Administration *(Transportation Dept.), Railroad Development, 1200 New Jersey Ave. S.E., 3rd Floor 20590; (202) 493-6381. Fax, (202) 493-6330. Mark E. Yachmetz, Associate Administrator.* Web, www.fra.dot.gov

Administers federal assistance programs for national, regional, and local rail services, including freight service assistance, service continuation, and passenger service. Conducts research on and development of new rail technologies.

Federal Railroad Administration *(Transportation Dept.), Safety, 1200 New Jersey Ave. S.E., 3rd Floor 20590; (202) 493-6300. Fax, (202) 493-6309. Jo Strang, Associate Administrator.* Web, www.fra.dot.gov

Administers and enforces federal laws and regulations that promote railroad safety, including track maintenance, inspection and equipment standards, operating practices, and transportation of explosives and other hazardous materials. Conducts inspections and reports on railroad equipment facilities and accidents. All safety and/or security issues, such as bomb threats or biochemical threats, are managed by security specialists.

National Mediation Board, *1301 K St. N.W., #250E 20005; (202) 692-5000. Fax, (202) 692-5080. Read Van de Water, Chair. Information, (202) 692-5050. TTY, (202) 692-5001. Public Affairs, (202) 692-5050.*
General e-mail, infoline@nmb.gov

Web, www.nmb.gov

Mediates labor disputes in the airline and railroad industries; determines and certifies labor representatives for the industry.

National Railroad Passenger Corp. (Amtrak), *60 Massachusetts Ave. N.E. 20002; (202) 906-3000. Joseph H. Boardman, President. Press, (202) 906-3860. Travel and ticket information, consumer relations and complaints (800) 872-7245.*
Web, www.amtrak.com

Quasi-public corporation created by the Rail Passenger Service Act of 1970 to improve and develop intercity passenger rail service.

National Transportation Safety Board, *Railroad, Pipeline, and Hazardous Materials Investigations, 490 L'Enfant Plaza East S.W., #RPH1 20594; (202) 314-6460. Fax, (202) 314-6482. Bob Chipkevich, Director. Press, (202) 314-6100.*
Web, www.ntsb.gov

Investigates passenger train accidents, including rapid rail transit and rail commuter systems, freight rail accidents with substantial damage to determine probable cause, pipeline accidents, and hazardous materials accidents; makes recommendations on rail transportation, pipeline, and hazardous materials safety, and accident prevention.

Railroad Retirement Board, *Legislative Affairs, Washington Office, 1310 G St. N.W., #500 20005-3004; (202) 272-7742. Fax, (202) 272-7728. Margaret S. Lindsley, Director.*
General e-mail, ola@rrb.gov

Web, www.rrb.gov

Assists congressional offices with inquiries on retirement, spouse, survivor, unemployment, and sickness benefits for railroad employees and retirees. Assists with legislation. (Headquarters in Chicago, Ill.)

Surface Transportation Board *(Transportation Dept.), 395 E St. S.W. 20423-0001; (202) 245-0245. Fax, (202) 245-0458. Charles D. Nottingham, Chair, (202) 245-0200. Library, (202) 245-0406. TTY, (800) 877-8339.*
Web, www.stb.dot.gov

Regulates rail rate disputes, railroad consolidations, rail line construction proposals, line abandonments, and rail car service. Library open to the public.

Surface Transportation Board *(Transportation Dept.), Public Assistance, Governmental Affairs, and*

Compliance, 395 E St. S.W., #1202 20423-0001; (202) 245-0245. Fax, (202) 245-0461. Matthew Wallen, Director. Press, (202) 245-0234. TTY, (800) 877-8339. Toll-free, (866) 254-1792.
General e-mail, Congressional.Public.Services@stb.dot.gov

Web, www.stb.dot.gov

Informs members of Congress, the public, and the media of board actions. Prepares testimony for hearings; comments on proposed legislation; assists the public in matters involving transportation regulations.

U.S. Coast Guard (USCG), *(Homeland Security Dept.), 2100 2nd St. S.W. 20593-0001; (202) 372-4411. Fax, (202) 372-4960. Adm. Thad W. Allen, Commandant. Locator, (202) 372-8724. Public Affairs, (202) 372-4620.*
Web, www.uscg.mil

Regulates the construction, maintenance, and operation of bridges across U.S. navigable waters, including railway bridges.

▶**CONGRESS**

For a listing of relevant congressional committees and subcommittees, please see page 656 or the Appendix.

▶**NONGOVERNMENTAL**

American Short Line and Regional Railroad Assn. (ASLRRA), *50 F St. N.W., #7020 20001; (202) 628-4500. Fax, (202) 628-6430. Richard F. Timmons, President.*
General e-mail, aslrra@aslrra.org

Web, www.aslrra.org

Membership: independently owned short line and regional railroad systems. Assists members with technical and legal questions; compiles information on laws, regulations, and other matters affecting the industry.

Assn. of American Railroads, *50 F St. N.W., 4th Floor 20001-1564; (202) 639-2100. Fax, (202) 639-2558. Edward R. Hamberger, President. Press, (202) 639-2556.*
General e-mail, info@aar.org

Web, www.aar.org

Membership: major freight railroads in the United States, Canada, and Mexico, as well as Amtrak. Provides information on freight railroad operations, safety and maintenance, economics and finance, management, and law and legislation; conducts research; issues statistical reports.

Brotherhood of Maintenance of Way Employees, *International Brotherhood of Teamsters, Washington Office, 25 Louisiana Ave. N.W., 7th Floor 20001; (202) 508-6448. Fax, (202) 508-6150. Freddie N. Simpson, President.*
General e-mail, bmwe_dc@bmwewash.org

Web, www.bmwe.org

Membership: rail industry workers and others. Assists members with contract negotiation and grievances; conducts training programs and workshops. Monitors legislation and regulations. (Headquarters in Southfield, Mich.)

International Assn. of Machinists and Aerospace Workers, *Transportation Communications International Union,* 3 Research Pl., Rockville, MD 20850-3279; (301) 948-4910. Fax, (301) 948-1369. Robert A. Scardelletti, President.
Web, www.tcunion.org

Membership: approximately 50,000 railway workers. Assists members with contract negotiation and grievances; conducts training programs and workshops. Monitors legislation and regulations. (Affiliated with the AFL-CIO and Canadian Labour Congress.)

National Assn. of Railroad Passengers,
900 2nd St. N.E., #308 20002-3557; (202) 408-8362. Fax, (202) 408-8287. Ross B. Capon, Executive Director.
General e-mail, narp@narprail.org
Web, www.narprail.org

Consumer organization. Works to expand and improve U.S. intercity and commuter rail passenger service, increase federal funds for mass transit, ensure fair treatment for rail freight transportation, and address environmental concerns pertaining to mass transit. Opposes subsidies for intercity trucking; works with Amtrak on scheduling, new services, fares, and advertising.

National Assn. of Regulatory Utility Commissioners,
1101 Vermont Ave. N.W., #200 20005-3521; (202) 898-2200. Fax, (202) 898-2213. Charles D. Gray, Executive Director. Press, (202) 898-9382.
General e-mail, admin@naruc.org
Web, www.naruc.org

Membership: members of federal, state, municipal, and international regulatory commissions that have jurisdiction over motor and common carriers. Interests include railroads.

National Railway Labor Conference, *1901 L St. N.W., #500 20036-3506; (202) 862-7200. Fax, (202) 862-7230. Ken Gradia, Chair.*
Web, www.nrlc.ws

Assists member railroad lines with labor matters; negotiates with railroad labor representatives.

Railway Supply Institute (RSI), *50 F St. N.W., #7030 20001; (202) 347-4664. Fax, (202) 347-0047. Thomas D. Simpson, Executive Director.*
General e-mail, rsi@railwaysupply.org
Web, www.rsiweb.org

Membership: railroad and rail rapid transit suppliers. Conducts research on safety and new technology; monitors legislation.

TRANSIT SYSTEMS

▶**AGENCIES**

Federal Transit Administration *(Transportation Dept.), 1200 New Jersey Ave. S.E., #E57-310 20590; (202) 366-4040. Fax, (202) 366-9854. Vacant, Administrator;*

Matthew Welbes, Deputy Administrator (Acting). Information and Press, (202) 366-4043.
Web, www.fta.dot.gov

Responsible for developing improved mass transportation facilities, equipment, techniques, and methods; assists state and local governments in financing mass transportation systems.

Federal Transit Administration *(Transportation Dept.), Budget and Policy, 1200 New Jersey Ave. S.E., #E52-323 20590; (202) 366-4050. Fax, (202) 366-7989. Robert Tuccillo, Associate Administrator. Press, (202) 366-4043.*
Web, www.fta.dot.gov

Develops budgets, programs, legislative proposals, and policies for the federal transit program; evaluates program proposals and their potential impact on local communities; coordinates private sector initiatives of the agency.

Federal Transit Administration *(Transportation Dept.), Program Management, 1200 New Jersey Ave. S.E., 4th Floor 20590; (202) 366-4020. Fax, (202) 366-7951. Susan E. Schruth, Associate Administrator.*
Web, www.fta.dot.gov/office/program

Administers capital planning and operating assistance grants and loan activities; monitors transit projects in such areas as environmental impact, special provisions for the elderly and people with disabilities, efficiency, and investment.

Federal Transit Administration *(Transportation Dept.), Research, Demonstration, and Innovation, 1200 New Jersey Ave. S.E., #E43-431 20590; (202) 366-4052. Fax, (202) 366-3765. Vincent Valdes, Associate Administrator.*
Web, www.fta.dot.gov/office/research

Provides industry and state and local governments with contracts, cooperative agreements, and grants for testing, developing, and demonstrating methods of improved mass transportation service and technology.

Maryland Transit Administration, *6 St. Paul St., Baltimore, MD 21202; (410) 767-3943. Fax, (410) 333-3279. Paul J. Wiedefeld, Administrator; Tony Brown, Assistant Administrator, (410) 767-8769. Information, (866) RIDE-MTA. Press, (410) 767-3931. TTY, (410) 539-3497. Wheelchair accessibility, (410) MTA-LIFT.*
Web, www.mtamaryland.com

Responsible for mass transit programs in Maryland; provides MARC commuter rail service for Baltimore, Washington, and suburbs in Maryland and West Virginia.

National Transportation Safety Board, *Railroad, Pipeline, and Hazardous Materials Investigations, 490 L'Enfant Plaza East S.W., #RPH1 20594; (202) 314-6460. Fax, (202) 314-6482. Bob Chipkevich, Director. Press, (202) 314-6100.*
Web, www.ntsb.gov

Investigates passenger train accidents, including rapid rail transit and rail commuter systems, freight rail accidents with substantial damage to determine probable cause, pipeline accidents, and hazardous materials accidents;

makes recommendations on rail transportation, pipeline, and hazardous materials safety, and accident prevention.

Surface Transportation Board *(Transportation Dept.)*, *395 E St. S.W. 20423-0001; (202) 245-0245. Fax, (202) 245-0458. Charles D. Nottingham, Chair, (202) 245-0200. Library, (202) 245-0406. TTY, (800) 877-8339.*
Web, www.stb.dot.gov

Regulates mergers and through-route requirements for the intercity bus industry. Library open to the public.

Virginia Railway Express (VRE), *1500 King St., #202, Alexandria, VA 22314; (703) 684-1001. Fax, (703) 684-1313. Dale Zehner, Chief Executive Officer. Press, (703) 838-5416. TTY, (703) 684-0551. Toll-free, (800) 743-3873. General e-mail, gotrains@vre.org*

Web, www.vre.org

Regional transportation partnership that provides commuter rail service from Fredericksburg and Manassas, Va., to Washington, D.C.

Washington Metropolitan Area Transit Authority (Metro), *600 5th St. N.W. 20001; (202) 962-1234. Fax, (202) 962-1133. John B. Catoe, General Manager. Information, (202) 637-7000. TTY, (202) 638-3780. Web, www.metroopensdoors.com*

Provides bus and rail transit service to Washington, D.C., and neighboring Maryland and Virginia communities; assesses and plans for transportation needs. Provides fare, schedule, and route information; promotes accessibility for persons with disabilities and the elderly.

▶**CONGRESS**

For a listing of relevant congressional committees and subcommittees, please see page 656 or the Appendix.

▶**NONGOVERNMENTAL**

Amalgamated Transit Union (ATU), *5025 Wisconsin Ave. N.W. 20016-4139; (202) 537-1645. Fax, (202) 244-7824. Warren S. George, President. General e-mail, dispatch@atu.org*

Web, www.atu.org

Membership: transit workers in the United States and Canada, including bus, van, ambulance, subway, and light rail operators; clerks, baggage handlers, and maintenance employees in urban transit, over-the-road, and school bus industries; and municipal workers. Assists members with contract negotiations and grievances; conducts training programs and seminars. Monitors legislation and regulations. (Affiliated with the AFL-CIO.)

American Bus Assn., *700 13th St. N.W., #575 20005-5923; (202) 842-1645. Fax, (202) 842-0850. Peter J.*

Pantuso, President. Toll-free, (800) 283-2877. General e-mail, abainfo@buses.org

Web, www.buses.org

Membership: privately owned intercity bus companies, state associations, travel/tourism businesses, bus manufacturers, and those interested in the bus industry. Monitors legislation and regulations.

American Public Transportation Assn. (APTA), *1666 K St. N.W., #1100 20006-1215; (202) 496-4800. Fax, (202) 496-4324. William W. Millar, President. General e-mail, apta@apta.com*

Web, www.apta.com

Membership: rapid rail and motor bus systems and manufacturers, suppliers, and consulting firms. Compiles data on the industry; promotes research. Monitors legislation and regulations.

Community Transportation Assn. of America, *1341 G St. N.W., 10th Floor 20005; (202) 628-1480. Fax, (202) 737-9197. Dale J. Marsico, Executive Director. Press, (202) 247-1921. TTY, (800) 527-8279. Toll-free, (800) 891-0590. Web, www.ctaa.org*

Works to improve mobility for the elderly, the poor, and persons with disabilities; concerns include rural, small-city, and specialized transportation.

National Assn. of Railroad Passengers, *900 2nd St. N.E., #308 20002-3557; (202) 408-8362. Fax, (202) 408-8287. Ross B. Capon, Executive Director. General e-mail, narp@narprail.org*

Web, www.narprail.org

Consumer organization. Works to expand and improve U.S. intercity and commuter rail passenger service, increase federal funds for mass transit, ensure fair treatment for rail freight transportation, and address environmental concerns pertaining to mass transit. Opposes subsidies for intercity trucking; works with Amtrak on scheduling, new services, fares, and advertising.

United Motorcoach Assn. (UMA), *113 S. West St., 4th Floor, Alexandria, VA 22314-2824; (703) 838-2929. Fax, (703) 838-2950. Victor S. Parra, Chief Executive Officer. Toll-free, (800) 424-8262. General e-mail, info@uma.org*

Web, www.uma.org

Membership: professional bus and motorcoach companies and suppliers and manufacturers in the industry. Provides information, offers technical assistance, conducts research, and monitors legislation. Interests include insurance, safety programs, and credit.

19 🏛

U.S. Congress and Politics

ACCESS TO CONGRESSIONAL INFORMATION

Basic Resources

►AGENCIES

National Archives and Records Administration (NARA), *Federal Register, 800 N. Capitol St. N.W., #700 20001 (mailing address: 8601 Adelphi Rd., College Park, MD 20740-6001); (202) 741-6000. Fax, (202) 741-6012. Raymond Mosley, Director. TTY, (202) 741-6086. Public Laws Update Service (PLUS), (202) 741-6040. General e-mail, fedreg.info@nara.gov*

Web, www.archives.gov/federal_register

Assigns public law numbers to enacted legislation, executive orders, and proclamations. Responds to inquiries on public law numbers. Assists inquirers in finding presidential signing or veto messages in the *Weekly Compilation of Presidential Documents* and the *Public Papers of the Presidents.* Compiles slip laws and annual *United States Statutes at Large;* compiles indexes for finding statutory provisions. Operates Public Laws Update Service (PLUS) and Public Law Electronic Notification System (PENS), which provide information by telephone or e-mail on new legislation. Coordinates the functions of the Electoral College and the constitutional amendment process. Publications available from the U.S. Government Printing Office.

►CONGRESS

For a listing of relevant congressional committees and subcommittees, please see page 689 or the Appendix.

Government Printing Office (GPO), *Contact Center, 732 N. Capitol St. N.W. 20401; (202) 512-0086. Fax, (202) 512-2104. William Kurtz, Director. Toll-free, (866) 512-1800; in DC area, (202) 512-1800. Public Relations, (202) 512-1957. General e-mail, ContactCenter@gpo.gov*

Web, www.gpoaccess.gov

Prints and distributes federal and congressional documents, prints, public laws, reports, and House calendars. Documents may be obtained electronically (www.gpo access.gov), ordered (P.O. Box 979050, St. Louis, MO 63197-9000), or purchased from GPO's online bookstore (http://bookstore.gpo.gov). Information about government documents and agencies at all levels is available from government information librarians at http://govtinfo .org. Information about how to locate the *Congressional Record* and other documents in the 1,400 federal depository libraries is also available at www.gpoaccess.gov or by calling (202) 512-1530.

Legislative Resource Center, *Records and Registration, B106 CHOB 20515-6612; (202) 226-5200. Fax, (202) 226-4874. Steve Pingeton, Manager. Web, http://clerk.house.gov*

Maintains and distributes House bills, reports, public laws, and documents to members' offices, committee staffs, and the general public. (Telephone requests are accepted.)

Library of Congress, *Main Reading Room, 101 Independence Ave. S.E., #LJ 100 20540; (202) 707-3399. Fax, (202) 707-1957. James H. Billington, Librarian of Congress. Web, www.thomas.loc.gov*

Makes available bills, resolutions, laws, and other legislative documentation, such as committee hearing transcripts and prints.

Office of History and Preservation, *Clerk of the House of Representatives, B53 CHOB 20515-6612; (202) 226-1300. Farar P. Elliott, Chief. Web, http://clerk.house.gov*

Provides access to published documents and historical records of the House. Conducts historical research. Advises members on the disposition of their records and papers; maintains information on manuscript collections of former members; maintains biographical files on former members. Produces publications on Congress and its members.

Senate Executive Clerk, *S138 CAP 20510; (202) 224-4341. Michelle Haynes, Executive Clerk.*

Maintains and distributes copies of treaties submitted to the Senate for ratification; provides information on submitted treaties and nominations. (Shares distribution responsibility with Senate Printing and Document Services, [202] 224-7701.)

Senate Historical Office, *SH-201 20510; (202) 224-6900. Richard A. Baker, Historian. General e-mail, historian@sec.senate.gov*

Web, www.senate.gov

Serves as an information clearinghouse on Senate history, traditions, and members. Collects, organizes, and distributes to the public unpublished Senate documents; collects and preserves photographs and pictures related to Senate history; conducts an oral history program; advises senators and Senate committees on the disposition of their noncurrent papers and records. Produces publications on the history of the Senate.

Senate Office of Conservation and Preservation, *S416 CAP 20510; (202) 224-4550. Carl Fritter, Director.*

Develops and coordinates programs related to the conservation and preservation of Senate records and materials for the secretary of the Senate.

Senate Printing and Document Services, *SH-B04 20510-7106; (202) 224-7701. Fax, (202) 228-2815. Karen Moore, Director. General e-mail, orders@sec.senate.gov*

Web, www.senate.gov/legislative/common/generic/Doc_ Room.htm

Maintains and distributes Senate bills, reports, public laws, and documents. To obtain material send a self-addressed mailing label or fax with request. Documents and information may be accessed on the Web site.

U.S. CONGRESS AND POLITICS RESOURCES IN CONGRESS

For a complete listing of Congress committees, including their full contact information, leadership, membership, and jurisdictions, please refer to the Appendix on pages 724–837.

HOUSE:

House Administration Committee, (202) 225-2061. Web, cha.house.gov

    Subcommittee on Capitol Security, (202) 225-2061.

    Subcommittee on Elections, (202) 225-2061.

House Appropriations Committee, (202) 225-2771. Web, appropriations.house.gov

    Subcommittee on Financial Services and General Government, (202) 225-7245.

    Subcommittee on Legislative Branch, (202) 226-7252.

House Judiciary Committee, (202) 225-3951. Web, judiciary.house.gov

    Subcommittee on the Constitution, Civil Rights, and Civil Liberties, (202) 225-2825.

House Oversight and Government Reform Committee, (202) 225-5051. Web, oversight.house.gov

    Subcommittee on Domestic Policy, (202) 225-6427.

    Subcommittee on Federal Workforce, Postal Service, and the District of Columbia, (202) 225-3741.

    Subcommittee on Government Management, Organization, and Procurement, (202) 225-3741.

House Rules Committee, (202) 225-9091. Web, rules.house.gov

    Subcommittee on the Legislative and Budget Process, (202) 225-9091.

    Subcommittee on Rules and Organization of the House, (202) 225-9091.

House Standards of Official Conduct Committee, (202) 225-7103. Web, www.house.gov/ethics

House Transportation and Infrastructure Committee, Subcommittee on Economic Development, Public Buildings and Emergency Management, (202) 225 9961.

Web, transportation.house.gov

House Ways and Means Committee, (202) 225-3625. Web, waysandmeans.house.gov

JOINT:

Joint Committee on Printing, (202) 224-6352.

Joint Committee on the Library, (202) 224-6352.

SENATE:

Senate Appropriations Committee, (202) 224-7363. Web, appropriations.senate.gov

    Subcommittee on Financial Services and General Government, (202) 224-1133.

    Subcommittee on Legislative Branch, (202) 224-3477.

Senate Finance Committee, (202) 224-4515. Web, finance.senate.gov

Senate Homeland Security and Governmental Affairs Committee, (202) 224-2627. Web, hsgac.senate.gov

    Permanent Subcommittee on Investigations, (202) 224-9505.

    Subcommittee on Federal Financial Management, Government, Information, and International Security, (202) 224-4551.

    Subcommittee on Oversight of Government Management, the Federal Workforce, and the District of Columbia, (202) 224-5538.

Senate Judiciary Committee, (202) 224-7703. Web, judiciary.senate.gov

    Subcommittee on the Constitution, (202) 224-5573.

Senate Rules and Administration Committee, (202) 224-6352. Web, rules.senate.gov

Senate Select Committee on Ethics, (202) 224-2981. Web, ethics.senate.gov

---

▶ NEWS SERVICES

Congressional Quarterly Inc., *1255 22nd St. N.W. 20037; (202) 419-8500. Robert W. Merry, President. Toll-free, (800) 432-2250.*
Web, www.cq.com

Provides news, analysis, and information on government. Products include the *CQ Weekly,* online legislative tracking services, print and electronic news updates, and abstracts and full text of the *Congressional Record.* (Affiliated with the *St. Petersburg Times.*)

CQ Press, *2300 N St. N.W., #800 20037; (202) 729-1900. Fax, (800) 380-3810. John Jenkins, President and Publisher. Toll-free, (866) 427-7737.*
General e-mail, customerservice@cqpress.com

Web, www.cqpress.com

Publishes books, directories, periodicals, and Web products on U.S. government, history, and politics. Products include the *Congressional Staff Directory, CQ Weekly, CQ Press Encyclopedia of American Government,* and *CQ Researcher.* (A division of SAGE Publications.)

► **NONGOVERNMENTAL**

White House Correspondents' Assn., *600 New Hampshire Ave., #800 20037; (202) 266-7453. Fax, (202) 266-7454. Julia Whiston, Executive Director. General e-mail, whca@starpower.net*

Web, www.whca.net

Membership: reporters with permanent White House press credentials. Acts as a liaison between reporters and White House staff. Sponsors annual WHCA Journalism Awards and Scholarships fundraising dinner.

Congressional Record

The Congressional Record, *published daily when Congress is in session, is a printed account of proceedings on the floor of the House and Senate. A Daily Digest section summarizes the day's action on the floor and in committees and lists committee meetings scheduled for the following day. An index is published biweekly and at the close of sessions of Congress. Since January 1995, House members have not been allowed to edit their remarks before they appear in the* Record, *but senators retain this privilege. Material not spoken on the floor may be inserted through unanimous consent to revise or extend a speech and is published in a distinctive typeface. Grammatical, typographical, and technical corrections are also permitted.*

► **CONGRESS**

For a listing of relevant congressional committees and subcommittees, please see page 689 or the Appendix.

Government Printing Office Main Bookstore (GPO), *Congressional Order Desk, 710 N. Capitol St. N.W. 20401; (202) 512-1808. Fax, (202) 512-2104. Esther Edmonds, Manager, (202) 512-1694. Bookstore Contact Center, (866) 512-1800; in DC area, (202) 512-1800. General e-mail, ContactCenter@gpo.gov*

Web, http://bookstore.gpo.gov

Sells copies of and subscriptions to the *Congressional Record.* Expert help from government information librarians is available at http://govtinfo.org. Orders may be placed on Web site, by phone or fax, or by writing to P.O. Box 979050, St. Louis, MO 63197-9000. The *Congressional Record* from 1994 to the present is available online at www.gpoaccess.gov.

Library of Congress, *Law Library, 101 Independence Ave. S.E., #LM240 20540; (202) 707-5065. Rubens Medina, Law Librarian. Reading room, (202) 707-5080. Reference information, (202) 707-5079. Web, www.loc.gov/law*

Copies of the *Congressional Record* are available for reading. Terminals in the reading room provide access to a computer system containing bill digests from the 93rd Congress to date. The *Congressional Record* can also be accessed online at thomas.loc.gov.

► **NONGOVERNMENTAL**

Martin Luther King Jr. Memorial Library, *901 G St. N.W. 20001-4599; (202) 727-1101. Fax, (202) 727-1129. Pamela Stovall, Associate Director. Information, (202) 727-0321. TTY, (202) 727-2145. Hours of operation, (202) 727-1111 (recording). Government division, (202) 727-1261.*

Web, www.dclibrary.org

Maintains collection of *Congressional Record* from 1879 to the present, available in various formats (bound volumes, microfilm, microfiche, and electronic).

Schedules, Status of Legislation

Information can also be obtained from the Congressional Record *(Daily Digest) and from individual congressional committees (see 111th Congress, p. 724).*

► **CONGRESS**

For a listing of relevant congressional committees and subcommittees, please see page 689 or the Appendix.

Calendars of the U.S. House of Representatives and History of Legislation, *Clerk of the House of Representatives, H154 CAP 20515-6601; (202) 225-7000. Lorraine C. Miller, Clerk. General e-mail, info.clerkweb@mail.house.gov*

Web, http://clerk.house.gov

Issued daily when the House is in session and available on the Web site. Provides capsule legislative history of all measures reported by House and Senate committees; provides additional reference material in the *Congressional Record.* Subject index included in each Monday edition or in the edition published on the first day the House is in session. (Also available from the Contact Center, Government Printing Office 20402; [202] 512-1808 or in electronic format at www.gpoaccess.gov.)

House Democratic Cloakroom, *H222 CAP 20515; (202) 225-7330. Barry K. Sullivan, Manager. House floor action, (202) 225-7400. Legislative program, (202) 225-1600.*

Provides information about House floor proceedings.

House Republican Cloakroom, *H223 CAP 20515; (202) 225-7350. Tim J. Harroun, Manager, (202) 225-4060. House floor action, (202) 225-7430. Legislative program, (202) 225-2020.*

Provides information about House floor proceedings.

Legislative Resource Center, *B106 CHOB 20515; (202) 226-5200. Fax, (202) 226-5208. Deborah Turner, Chief. Web, http://clerk.house.gov*

Records, stores, and provides legislative status information on all bills and resolutions pending in Congress.

Legislative Resource Center, *Clerk of the House, B106 CHOB 20515-6612; (202) 226-5200. Deborah Turner, Chief. Web, www.clerk.house.gov/about/offices_lrc.html*

Provides legislative information, records and registration, historical information, and library services to the House and the public. Reading room contains computer terminals where collections may be viewed or printed out. Collections include House and Senate journals (1st Congress to present); *Congressional Record* and its predecessors (1st Congress to present); House reports, documents, bills, resolutions, and hearings; Senate reports and documents; U.S. statutes, treaties, the *Federal Register*, U.S. codes, and numerous other documents. (See Web site or call for a complete list of collections.)

Legislative Resource Center, *Records and Registration,* B106 CHOB 20515-6612; (202) 226-5200. Fax, (202) 226-4874. Steve Pingeton, Manager.
Web, http://clerk.house.gov

Provides videotapes of House floor proceedings.

Library of Congress, *Main Reading Room,* 101 Independence Ave. S.E., #LJ 100 20540; (202) 707-3399. Fax, (202) 707-1957. James H. Billington, Librarian of Congress.
Web, www.thomas.loc.gov

Makes available online via THOMAS (thomas.loc.gov) various legislative databases, including House Floor This Week, Bill Summary and Status (1973 to present), Public Laws (1973 to present), the *Congressional Record,* and committee reports.

Senate Democratic Cloakroom, S225 CAP 20510; (202) 224-4691. Joe Lapia Jr., Assistant. Senate floor action, (202) 224-8541.
Provides information about Senate floor proceedings.

Senate Republican Cloakroom, S226 CAP 20510; (202) 224-6191. Robert White, Senior Assistant. Senate floor action, (202) 224-8601.
Provides information about Senate floor proceedings.

►NEWS SERVICES

Associated Press, *Washington Office,* 1100 13th St. N.W., #700 20005-4076; (202) 641-9000. Fax, (202) 263-8860. Ron Fournier, Bureau Chief.
General e-mail, info@ap.org
Web, www.ap.org

Publishes daybook that lists congressional committee meetings and hearings and their location and subject matter. Fee for services. (Headquarters in New York.)

CQ Today, 1255 22nd St. N.W. 20037; (202) 419-8621. Fax, (202) 833-1635. Subscriptions, (202) 419-8599; toll-free, (800) 432-2250.
Web, www.cq.com

Provides daily news and analysis about Congress; lists daily committee meetings and hearings, complete witness lists, floor proceedings, and future scheduled committee meetings and hearings. Fee for services. (A publication of Congressional Quarterly Inc.)

CQ.com, 1255 22nd St. N.W. 20037; (202) 419-8511. Subscriptions and demonstrations, (202) 419-8279. Toll-free, (800) 432-2250.
Web, www.cq.com

Provides online congressional news and analysis, including legislative summaries, votes, testimony, and archival and reference materials. Provides hearing and markup schedules, including time and location, meeting agendas, and full witness listings. Fee for services. (Affiliated with Congressional Quarterly Inc.)

United Press International (UPI), 1433 19th St. N.W. 20005; (202) 898-8000. Fax, (202) 371-1239.
Web, www.upi.com

Wire service that lists congressional committee meetings and hearings, locations, and subject matter. Fee for services.

Washington Post, 1150 15th St. N.W. 20071; (202) 334-6000. Fax, (202) 469-3883. Katharine Weymouth, Publisher; Marcus Brauchli, Editor in Chief. Toll-free, (800) 627-1150.
General e-mail, national@washpost.com
Web, www.washingtonpost.com

Lists congressional committee meetings and hearings, locations, and subject matter.

CAMPAIGNS AND ELECTIONS

►AGENCIES

Election Assistance Commission, 1225 New York Ave. N.W. 20005; (202) 566-3100. Fax, (202) 566-3128. Gineen Beach, Chair. Toll-free, (866) 747-1471.
General e-mail, HAVAinfo@eac.gov
Web, www.eac.gov

Serves as national information clearinghouse on the administration of federal elections. Responsible for the review of voting system guidelines and the experience of states in implementing them. Tests and certifies voting system hardware and software. Studies election technology, accessibility to voting, voter statistics, voter fraud, and voter eligibility.

Federal Communications Commission (FCC), *Media Bureau: Policy Division,* 445 12th St. S.W. 20554; (202) 418-2120. Fax, (202) 418-1069. Mary Beth Murphy, Division Chief.
Web, www.fcc.gov/mb/policy

Handles complaints and inquiries concerning the equal time rule, which requires equal broadcast opportunities for all legally qualified candidates for the same office, and other political broadcast, cable, and satellite rules. Interprets and enforces related Communications Act provisions, including the requirement for sponsorship identification of all paid political broadcast, cable, and satellite announcements and the requirement for

Federal Election Commission

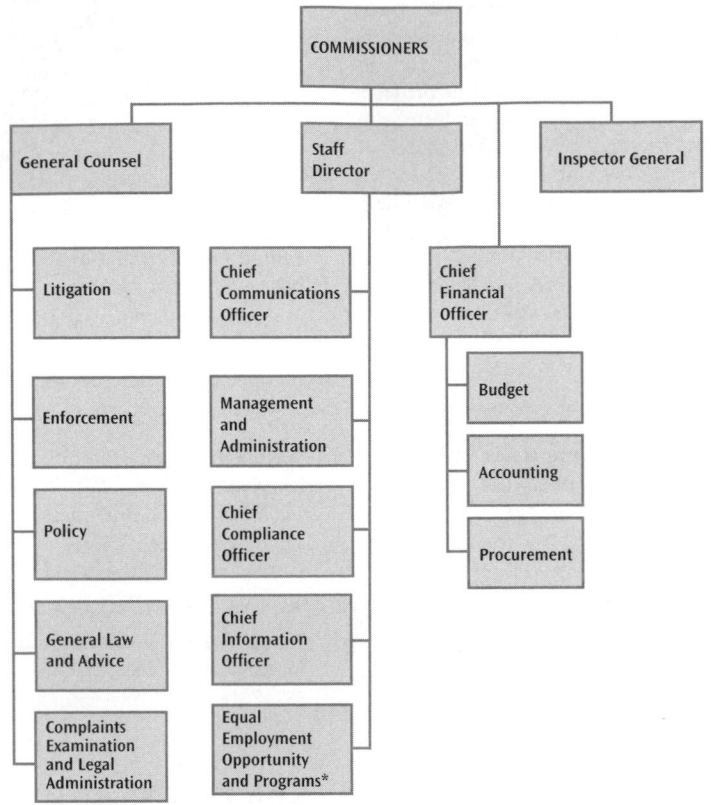

*Reports to the Staff Director for management and administrative purposes; however, has direct reporting authority to the Commission on all EEO matters.

broadcasters to furnish federal candidates with reasonable access to broadcast time for political advertising.

Federal Election Commission (FEC), *999 E St. N.W. 20463; (202) 694-1000. Steven T. Walther, Chair. Information, (202) 694-1100. Press, (202) 694-1220. Toll-free information, (800) 424-9530. Web, www.fec.gov*

Formulates, administers, and enforces policy with respect to the Federal Election Campaign Act of 1971 as amended, including campaign disclosure requirements, contribution and expenditure limitations, and public financing of presidential nominating conventions and campaigns. Receives campaign finance reports; makes rules and regulations; conducts audits and investigations. Serves as an election information clearinghouse. Makes copies of campaign finance reports available for inspection.

Federal Election Commission (FEC), *Public Disclosure, 999 E St. N.W. 20463; (202) 694-1120. Fax, (202) 501-0693. Patricia Young, Director. Information, (800) 424-9530. General e-mail, pubrec@fec.gov Web, www.fec.gov*

Makes available for public inspection and copying the detailed campaign finance reports on contributions and

expenditures filed by candidates for federal office, their supporting political committees, and individuals and committees making expenditures on behalf of a candidate. Maintains copies of all reports and statements filed since 1972.

Justice Dept. (DOJ), *Election Crimes, 1400 New York Ave. N.W. 20005; (202) 514-1421. Fax, (202) 514-3003. Craig C. Donsanto, Director. Press, (202) 514-2007. Web, www.usdoj.gov*

Supervises enforcement of federal criminal laws related to campaigns and elections. Oversees investigation of deprivation of voting rights; intimidation and coercion of voters; denial or promise of federal employment or other benefits; illegal political contributions, expenditures, and solicitations; and all other election violations referred to the division.

▶ CONGRESS

For a listing of relevant congressional committees and subcommittees, please see page 689 or the Appendix.

House Commission on Congressional Mailing Standards (Franking Commission), *2233 RHOB 20515; (202) 225-2061. Fax, (202) 226-2774. Michael Capuano, Chair; Ellen A. McCarthy, Staff Director. Web, http://cha.house.gov/services/franking.aspx*

Issues regulations governing mass mailings by members' offices. Receives complaints, conducts investigations, and issues decisions on disputes arising from the alleged abuse of franked mail by House members.

Legislative Resource Center, *Records and Registration,* *B106 CHOB 20515-6612; (202) 226-5200. Fax, (202) 226-4874. Steve Pingeton, Manager.*
Web, http://clerk.house.gov

Receives personal financial disclosure reports for members of the House, candidates for the House, and certain employees. Open for public inspection.

►**NONGOVERNMENTAL**

American Bar Assn. (ABA), *Standing Committee on Election Law, 740 15th St. N.W. 20005-1022; (202) 662-1694. Fax, (202) 638-3844. Elizabeth M. Yang, Director.*
General e-mail, election@abanet.org

Web, www.abanet.org/publicserv/election/home.html

Studies ways to improve the U.S. election and campaign process.

Assn. of Political Affairs Professionals, *600 Pennsylvania Ave. S.E., #330 20003; (202) 544-9815. Fax, (202) 544-9816. Wayne Johnson, Chair.*
General e-mail, info@theaapc.org

Web, www.theaapc.org

Membership: political consultants, media specialists, campaign managers, corporate public affairs officers, pollsters, public officials, academicians, fundraisers, lobbyists, college students, and congressional staffers. Focuses on ethics of the profession; provides members with opportunities to meet industry leaders and learn new techniques and emerging technologies.

Campaign Finance Institute, *1990 M St. N.W., #380 20036-3422; (202) 969-8890. Fax, (202) 969-5612. Michael J. Malbin, Executive Director.*
General e-mail, info@CFInst.org

Web, www.cfinst.org

Conducts objective research and educates about campaign financing. Makes recommendations for policy changes in campaign financing. (Affiliated with George Washington University.)

Campaign Legal Center, *1640 Rhode Island Ave. N.W., #650 20036; (202) 736-2200. Fax, (202) 736-2222. J. Gerald Hebert, Executive Director.*
General e-mail, info@campaignlegalcenter.org

Web, www.campaignlegalcenter.org

Dedicated to improving the elections process by promoting voluntary, realistic standards of campaign conduct.

Center for Responsive Politics, *1101 14th St. N.W., #1030 20005-5635; (202) 857-0044. Fax, (202) 857-7809. Sheila Krumholz, Executive Director.*
General e-mail, info@crp.org

Web, www.opensecrets.org

Conducts research on Congress and related issues, with particular interest in campaign finance and congressional operations.

Commission on Presidential Debates, *1200 New Hampshire Ave. N.W., #445 20036; (202) 872-1020. Fax, (202) 783-5923. Frank J. Fahrenkopf Jr., Co-Chair; Paul G. Kirk Jr., Co-Chair.*
Web, www.debates.org

Independent, nonpartisan organization established to sponsor general election presidential and vice presidential debates and to undertake educational and research activities related to the debates.

Common Cause, *1133 19th St. N.W., 9th Floor 20036; (202) 833-1200. Fax, (202) 659-3716. Bob Edgar, President, (202) 736-5740. Press, (202) 736-5770.*
Web, www.commoncause.org

Nonpartisan citizens' legislative interest group. Records and analyzes campaign contributions to congressional candidates and campaign committees, particularly those from political action committees, and soft money contributions to national political parties.

CQ MoneyLine, *1255 22nd St. N.W. 20037; (202) 419-8599. General e-mail, questions@cq.com*

Web, http://moneyline.cq.com

Monitors and reports on money as it is used in campaigns, political action committees, 527s, political parties, and by lobbyists. (Affiliated with Congressional Quarterly Inc.)

Electionline.org, *901 E St. N.W. 20007; (202) 552-2027. Doug Chapin, Director.*
General e-mail, info@electionline.org

Web, www.electionline.org

Online resource providing news and analysis on election reform. (Project of the Pew Center on the States.)

Public Campaign, *1320 19th St. N.W., #M1 20036; (202) 293-0222. Fax, (202) 293-0202. Nick Nyhart, President.*
General e-mail, info@publicampaign.org

Web, www.publicampaign.org

National grassroots organization interested in campaign finance reform. Supports the Clean Money Campaign, a voluntary program in which candidates receive a set amount of public financing for elections if they reject private money and limit spending.

Election Statistics and Apportionment

►**AGENCIES**

Census Bureau *(Commerce Dept.),* ***Census Redistricting Data,*** *4600 Silver Hill Rd., #8H019, Suitland, MD 20746 (for mailing address, change city and zip code to: Washington, DC 20233); (301) 763-6525. Fax, (301) 763-4348. Catherine C. McCully, Chief.*
Web, www.census.gov/rdo

Provides state legislatures with population figures for use in legislative redistricting.

Census Bureau *(Commerce Dept.), Customer Services Center,* *4600 Silver Hill Rd., North Bldg., 8th Floor, Suitland, MD 20746 (mailing address: Customer Service, Bureau of the Census, MS-0801, Washington, DC 20233); (301) 763-4636. Fax, (301) 763-3842. Barbara A. Harris, Chief. Press, (301) 763-3030. Orders, (800) 923-8282.*
Web, www.census.gov

Main contact for information about the Census Bureau's products and services. Census data and maps on counties, municipalities, and other small areas are available on the Web site and in libraries.

Census Bureau *(Commerce Dept.), Population Division,* *4600 Silver Hill Rd., #5H-174, Suitland, MD 20746 (for mailing address, change city and zip code to: Washington, DC 20233-8800); (301) 763-2071. Fax, (301) 763-2516. Enrique J. Lamas, Chief. Information, (301) 763-3030. Toll-free, (866) 758-1060.*
General e-mail, pop@census.gov
Web, www.census.gov/population/www

Computes every ten years the population figures that determine the number of representatives each state may have in the House of Representatives.

►CONGRESS

For a listing of relevant congressional committees and subcommittees, please see page 689 or the Appendix.

Clerk of the House of Representatives, *H154 CAP 20515-6601; (202) 225-7000. Lorraine C. Miller, Clerk; Janice Wallace, Chief. Publication Services, (202) 225-1908.*
Web, http://clerk.house.gov

Publishes biennial compilation of statistics on congressional and presidential elections.

►NONGOVERNMENTAL

Common Cause, *State Organization, 1133 19th St. N.W., 9th Floor 20036; (202) 833-1200. Fax, (202) 659-3716. Karen Hobert Flynn, Vice President for State Operations, (860) 549-1220; Tora Wang, Vice President of Research; Susannah Goodman, Director of Voting and Election Reform, (202) 736-5777. Press, (202) 736-5770.*
Web, www.commoncause.org

Nonpartisan citizens' interest group. Seeks to alter procedures governing redistricting by the establishment of independent redistricting commissions. Serves as an information clearinghouse; provides research and support for regional field offices.

Voting, Political Participation

►NONGOVERNMENTAL

America Votes, *1401 New York Ave. N.W., #720 20005; (202) 962-7240. Fax, (202) 962-7241. Greg Speed, Executive Director.*

General e-mail, info@americavotes.org
Web, www.americavotes.org

Coalition that seeks to increase voter registration, education, and participation in electoral politics.

Arab American Institute, *1600 K St. N.W., #601 20006; (202) 429-9210. Fax, (202) 429-9214. James J. Zogby, President.*
General e-mail, aai@aaiusa.org
Web, www.aaiusa.org

Advocacy group concerned with political issues affecting Arab Americans. Seeks to involve the Arab American community in party politics and the electoral process.

Center for Civic Education, *Government Relations, Washington Office, 1743 Connecticut Ave. N.W. 20009-1108; (202) 861-8800. Fax, (202) 861-8811. Mark J. Molli, Director.*
General e-mail, dc@civiced.org
Web, www.civiced.org

Fosters participation in civic life by citizens. Interests include the U.S. Constitution, American political traditions, and the rights and responsibilities of citizens. Develops curriculum and national standards for elementary and secondary school students; administers international civic education programs. (Headquarters in Los Angeles, Calif.)

Center for Progressive Leadership, *1133 19th St. N.W., 9th Floor 20036; (202) 775-2003. Fax, (202) 318-0485. Peter Murray, President.*
Web, www.progressleaders.org

Provides training and development for youths interested in progressive political leadership and activism. Seeks to increase progressive influence in key states and connect aspiring leaders with established ones through networking events, mentorship programs, online forums, and fellowship programs.

Clare Booth Luce Policy Institute, *112 Elden St., Suite P, Herndon, VA 20170; (703) 318-0730. Fax, (703) 318-8867. Michelle Easton, President. Toll-free, (888) 891-4288.*
General e-mail, info@cblpi.org
Web, www.cblpi.org

Seeks to engage young women through student programs promoting conservative values and leadership. Offers mentoring, internship, and networking opportunities for young women.

Coalition of Black Trade Unionists, *1625 L St. N.W. 20036 (mailing address: P.O. Box 66268, Washington, DC 20035-6268); (202) 429-1203. Fax, (202) 429-1114. William Lucy, President.*
Web, www.cbtu.org

Monitors legislation affecting African American and other minority trade unionists. Focuses on equal employment opportunity, unemployment, and voter education and registration.

Resources for Political Participation

NATIONWIDE CAMPAIGNS

Democratic Congressional Campaign Committee, (202) 863-1500, www.dccc.org

Democratic Governors Assn., (202) 772-5600, www.democraticgovernors.org

Democratic National Committee (DNC), (202) 863-8000, www.democrats.org

Democratic Senatorial Campaign Committee, (202) 224-2447, www.dscc.org

FairVote–The Center for Voting and Democracy, (301) 270-4616, www.fairvote.org

Fieldworks, (202) 667-4400, www.fieldworksonline.com

Generation Engage, (202) 465-4807, www.generationengage.com

Green Party of the United States, (202) 319-7191, www.gp.org

League of Women Voters (LWV), (202) 429-1965, www.lwv.org

Libertarian Party, (202) 333-0008, www.lp.org

National Republican Congressional Committee, (202) 479-7000, www.nrcc.org

National Republican Senatorial Committee, (202) 675-6000, www.nrsc.org

Republican Governors Assn., (202) 662-4140, www.rga.org

Republican National Committee (RNC), (202) 863-5000, www.rnc.org

Rock the Vote, (202) 719-9910, www.rockthevote.com

IN MARYLAND, VIRGINIA, AND WASHINGTON, D.C.

District of Columbia Board of Elections and Ethics, (202) 727-2525, www.dcboee.org

DC Vote, (202) 462-6000, www.dcvote.org

Maryland State Board of Elections, (800) 222-8683, www.elections.state.md.us

Volunteer on Election Day in Maryland, www.elections.state.md.us/get_involved

Virginia State Board of Elections, (800) 552-9745, www.sbe.virginia.gov

Volunteer on Election Day in Virginia, www.sbe.virginia.gov/cms/Voter_Information/Local_Voter_Registration_Offices/Index.asp

---

Democracy 21, *1875 Eye St. N.W., #500 20006-5415; (202) 429-2008. Fax, (202) 293-2660. Fred Wertheimer, President. Press, (202) 429-2008.*
General e-mail, info@Democracy21.org
Web, www.democracy21.org

Focuses on using the communications revolution to strengthen democracy and on eliminating the influence of big money in American politics.

Democratic National Committee (DNC), *Campaign Division, 430 S. Capitol St. S.E. 20003-4024; (202) 863-8000. Fax, (202) 863-8174. Gov. Tim Kaine, Chair. Press, (202) 863-8148.*
General e-mail, info@democrats.org
Web, www.democrats.org

Responsible for electoral activities at the federal, state, and local levels; sponsors workshops to recruit Democratic candidates and to provide instruction in campaign techniques; conducts party constituency outreach programs; coordinates voter registration; plans the party's quadrennial presidential nominating convention.

FairVote, *6930 Carroll Ave., #610, Takoma Park, MD 20912; (301) 270-4616. Fax, (301) 270-4133. Robert Richie, Executive Director.*
General e-mail, info@fairvote.org
Web, www.fairvote.org

Studies how voting systems affect participation, representation, and governance both domestically and internationally. Advocates for universal voter registration, a national popular vote for president, instant run-off voting, and a constitutionally protected right to vote. (Formerly the Center for Voting and Democracy.)

Generation Engage, *900 19th St. N.W. 20006; (202) 986-1223. Adrian Talbott, Executive Director.*
General e-mail, BuildTheFuture@generationengage.org
Web, www.generationengage.org

Bipartisan youth civic engagement initiative that recruits young, local leaders to involve young people, particularly nonstudents and first-time voters, in politics.

Internet Education Foundation, *1634 Eye St. N.W., #1100 20006; (202) 638-4370. Fax, (202) 637-0968. Tim Lordan, Executive Director.*
General e-mail, info@neted.org
Web, www.neted.org

Sponsors educational initiatives promoting the Internet as a valuable medium for democratic participation, communications, and commerce. Funds the Congressional Internet Caucus Advisory Committee, which works to inform Congress of important Internet-related policy issues. Monitors legislation and regulations.

Joint Center for Political and Economic Studies, *1090 Vermont Ave. N.W., #1100 20005-4928; (202) 789-3500. Fax, (202) 789-6385. Ralph B. Everett, President.*
Web, www.jointcenter.org

Documents and analyzes the political and economic status of African Americans and other minority populations, focusing on economic advancement, social policy, and political participation. Publishes an annual profile of African American elected officials in federal, state, and local government; disseminates information through forums, conferences, publications, and the Internet.

Labor Council for Latin American Advancement, *815 16th St. N.W., 4th Floor 20006; (202) 508-6919. Fax, (202) 508-6922. Gabriela D. Lemus, Executive Director. General e-mail, headquarters@lclaa.org*

Web, www.lclaa.org

Membership: Hispanic trade unionists. Encourages equal employment opportunity, voter registration, and participation in the political process. (Affiliated with the AFL-CIO and the Change to Win Federation.)

League of Women Voters (LWV), *1730 M St. N.W., #1000 20036-4508; (202) 429-1965. Fax, (202) 429-0854. Mary G. Wilson, President; Nancy E. Tate, Executive Director. Press, (202) 429-1965 ext. 332. General e-mail, lwv@lwv.org*

Web, www.lwv.org

Membership: women and men interested in nonpartisan political action and study. Works to increase participation in government; provides information on voter registration and balloting. Interests include social policy, natural resources, international relations, and representative government.

National Assn. of Latino Elected and Appointed Officials Educational Fund, *Washington Office, 600 Pennsylvania Ave. S.E., #230 20003; (202) 546-2536. Fax, (202) 546-4121. William Ramos, Director. General e-mail, info@naleo.org*

Web, www.naleo.org

Research and advocacy group that provides civic affairs information and assistance on legislation affecting Hispanics. Encourages Hispanic participation in local, state, and national politics. Interests include the health and social, economic, and educational welfare of Hispanics. (Headquarters in Los Angeles, Calif.)

National Black Caucus of Local Elected Officials (NBC/LEO), *c/o National League of Cities, 1301 Pennsylvania Ave. N.W. 20004-1763; (202) 626-3168. Fax, (202) 626-3043. Daisy W. Lynum, President. Press, (202) 626-3003. Web, www.nbc-leo.org*

Membership: African American elected officials at the local level and other interested individuals. Seeks to increase African American participation on the National League of City's steering and policy committees. Informs members on issues, and plans strategies to achieve objectives through legislation and direct action. Interests include cultural diversity, local government and community participation, housing, economics, the family, and human rights.

National Black Caucus of State Legislators, *444 N. Capitol St. N.W., #622 20001; (202) 624-5457. Fax,*

(202) 508-3826. LaKimba DeSadier Walker, Executive Director. Web, www.nbcsl.com

Membership: African American state legislators. Promotes effective leadership among African American state legislators through education, research, and training; serves as an information network and clearinghouse for members.

National Coalition on Black Civic Participation, *1900 L St. N.W., #700 20036; (202) 659-4929. Fax, (202) 659-5025. Melanie L. Campbell, Executive Director. General e-mail, ncbcp@ncbcp.org*

Web, www.bigvote.org

Seeks to increase black voter civic participation to eliminate barriers to political participation for African Americans. Sponsors a variety of voter education, registration, and get-out-the-vote and protect-the-vote activities, including Operation Big Vote, Black Youth Vote, Black Women's Roundtable, the Information Resource Center, Civic Engagement, Voices of the Electorate, and the Unity Black Voter Empowerment Campaign. Monitors legislation and regulations.

National Congress of Black Women, *1251 4th St. S.E., #200 20024; (202) 678-6788. E. Faye Williams, Chair. General e-mail, info@nationalcongressbw.org*

Web, www.npcbw.org

Nonpartisan political organization that encourages African American women to participate in the political process. Advocates nonpartisan voter registration and encourages African American women to engage in other political activities. Develops positions and participates in platform development and strategies that address the needs of communities at every level of government.

National Women's Political Caucus, *1003 K St. N.W., #637 20001 (mailing address: P.O. Box 50476, Washington, DC 20091); (202) 785-1100. Fax, (202) 370-6306. Lulu Flores, President; Clare C. Giesen, Executive Director. General e-mail, info@nwpc.org*

Web, www.nwpc.org

Advocacy group that seeks greater involvement of women in politics. Seeks to identify, recruit, and train women for elective and appointive political office, regardless of party affiliation; serves as an information clearinghouse on women in politics, particularly during election campaigns; publishes directory of women holding federal and state offices.

Republican National Committee (RNC), *Political, 310 1st St. S.E. 20003; (202) 863-8600. Fax, (202) 863-8820. Gentry Collins, Director. Press, (202) 863-8614. General e-mail, info@gop.org*

Web, www.rnchq.org

Responsible for electoral activities at the federal, state, and local levels; operates party constituency outreach programs; coordinates voter registration.

Women's Voices. Women Vote, *1707 L St. N.W., #750 20036; (202) 659-9570. Fax, (202) 833-4362. Page S. Gardner, President; Sharon Flynn, Executive Director. Web, www.wvwv.org*

Project targeting unmarried women to increase their voter participation. Research plan includes reviewing existing national and state data and conducting focus groups and national and state surveys.

Younger Women's Task Force, *714 G St. N.W., #200 20003; (202) 293-4505. Fax, (202) 293-4507. Shannon Lynberg, National Director.*
General e-mail, ShannonL@ywtf.org
Web, www.ywtf.org

Grassroots organization that encourages young women to engage in political activism on issues directly affecting them. Provides leadership training and a local and national network for peer mentoring; runs financial literacy programs. A project of the National Council of Women's Organizations.

CAPITOL

Capitol switchboard, (202) 224-3121; Federal Relay Service (TTY), (800) 877-8359 and, in DC area, (202) 224-3091. See also 111th Congress (p. 724) for each member's office.

▶ CONGRESS

For a listing of relevant congressional committees and subcommittees, please see page 689 or the Appendix.

Architect of the Capitol, *SB15 CAP 20515; (202) 228-1793. Fax, (202) 228-1893. Stephen T. Ayers, Architect (Acting). Flag Office, (202) 228-4239. Web, www.aoc.gov*

Maintains the Capitol and its grounds, the House and Senate office buildings, Capitol power plant, Robert A. Taft Memorial, Thurgood Marshall Federal Judiciary Building, Capitol Police headquarters, and buildings and grounds of the Supreme Court and the Library of Congress; operates the Botanic Garden and Senate restaurants. Acquires property and plans and constructs buildings for Congress, the Supreme Court, and the Library of Congress. Assists in deciding which artwork, historical objects, and exhibits are to be accepted for display in the Capitol and is responsible for their care and repair, as well as the maintenance and restoration of murals and architectural elements throughout the Capitol complex. Arranges inaugural ceremonies and other ceremonies held in the buildings or on the grass. Flag office flies American flags over the Capitol at legislators' request.

Architect of the Capitol, *Office of the Curator, S411 CAP 20515; (202) 224-2955. Diane K. Skvarla, Curator. Web, www.aoc.gov*

Preserves artwork; maintains collection of drawings, photographs, and manuscripts on and about the Capitol and the House and Senate office buildings. Maintains records of the Architect of the Capitol. Library open to the public.

Capitol Police, *119 D St. N.E. 20510; (202) 224-9806. Fax, (202) 228-2592. Phillip D. Morse Sr., Chief. TTY, (202) 225-1904. Public information, (202) 224-1677. General e-mail, ASKUSCP@cap_police.senate.gov*
Web, www.uscapitolpolice.gov

Responsible for security for the Capitol, House and Senate office buildings, and Botanic Garden; approves demonstration permits.

Senate Commission on Art, *S230 CAP 20510; (202) 224-2955. Sen. Harry M. Reid, D–Nev., Chair; Diane K. Skvarla, Curator of the Senate.*
General e-mail, curator@sec.senate.gov
Web, www.senate.gov/artandhistory/art/common/generic/senate_art.htm

Accepts artwork and historical objects for display in Senate office buildings and the Senate wing of the Capitol. Maintains and exhibits Senate collections (paintings, sculptures, furniture, and manuscripts); oversees and maintains old Senate and Supreme Court chambers.

Superintendent of the House Office Buildings, *B341 RHOB 20515; (202) 225-4141. William M. Weidemeyer, Superintendent.*

Oversees construction, maintenance, and operation of House office buildings; assigns office space to House members under rules of procedure established by the Speaker's office and the House Office Building Commission.

Superintendent of the Senate Office Buildings, *SD-G45 20510; (202) 224-5023. Robin Morey, Superintendent.*

Oversees construction, maintenance, and operation of Senate office buildings.

U.S. Botanic Garden, *100 Maryland Ave. S.W. 20001 (mailing address: 245 1st St. S.W., Washington, DC 20024); (202) 225-8333. Fax, (202) 225-1561. Holly H. Shimizu, Executive Director. Horticulture hotline, (202) 226-4785. Program and tour reservations, (202) 225-1116. Special events, (202) 226-7674.*
General e-mail, usbg@aoc.gov
Web, www.usbg.gov

Collects, cultivates, and grows various plants for public display and study.

▶ NONGOVERNMENTAL

U.S. Capitol Historical Society, *200 Maryland Ave. N.E. 20002-5724; (202) 543-8919. Fax, (202) 544-8244. Ronald A. Sarasin, President; Donald R. Kennon, Vice President for Scholarship and Education (historian). Information, (800) 887-9318. Press, (202) 543-8919, ext. 31. Library, (202) 543-8919, ext. 27.*

General e-mail, uschs@uschs.org

Web, www.uschs.org

Membership: members of Congress, individuals, and organizations interested in the preservation of the history and traditions of the U.S. Capitol. Conducts historical research; offers tours, lectures, and films; publishes an annual historical calendar.

Tours and Events

►CONGRESS

For a listing of relevant congressional committees and subcommittees, please see page 689 or the Appendix.

The House and Senate public galleries are open when Congress is in session. The House galleries are also open when the House is not in session. Free gallery passes are available from any congressional office.

Capitol Police, *Protective Services, 119 D St. N.E., #614 20510; (202) 224-9596. Donald A. Rouiller, Commander.*

Handles administrative and protective aspects of all special events held on the Capitol grounds. Accepts applications for demonstration permits and for visiting musical performances and submits them to the police board for approval. Coordinates all VIP arrivals.

Congressional Accessibility Services, *The Capitol 20510; (202) 224-4048. Fax, (202) 228-4679. David Hauck, Director. TTY, (202) 224-4049.*
Web, www.visitthecapitol.gov and www.aoc.gov

Office works to make the Capitol and its grounds and buildings accessible to members of Congress and the public.

Sergeant at Arms and Doorkeeper of the Senate, *S151 CAP 20510-7200; (202) 224-2341. Terrance W. Gainer, Sergeant at Arms and Doorkeeper.*
Web, www.senate.gov/reference/office/sergeant_at_arms.htm

Enforces rules and regulations of the Senate public gallery. Responsible for security of the Capitol and Senate buildings. Approves visiting band performances on the Senate steps. (To arrange for performances, contact your senator.)

Sergeant at Arms of the House of Representatives, *H124 CAP 20515-6611; (202) 225-2456. Fax, (202) 225-3233. Wilson L. "Bill" Livingood, Sergeant at Arms.*
Web, www.clerk.house.gov/art_history/house_history/ sergeants_at_arms.html

Enforces rules and regulations of the House public gallery. Responsible for the security of the Capitol and House buildings. Approves visiting band performances on the House steps. (To arrange for performances, contact your representative.)

U.S. Capitol Visitor Center, *The Capitol 20510; (202) 593-1746. Fax, (202) 228-3233. Terrie Rouse, Chief Executive Officer for Visitor Services; Maurice Parrish,*

Deputy Chief Executive Officer for Visitor Services. Press, (202) 593-1833. TTY, (202) 224-4049. Visitor information, (202) 225-6827.
Web, www.visitthecapitol.gov

Offers the general public free guided tours of the interior of the U.S. Capitol. Provides accommodations for visitors with special needs.

►NONGOVERNMENTAL

U.S. Capitol Historical Society, *200 Maryland Ave. N.E. 20002-5724; (202) 543-8919. Fax, (202) 544-8244. Ronald A. Sarasin, President; Donald R. Kennon, Vice President for Scholarship and Education (historian). Information, (800) 887-9318. Press, (202) 543-8919, ext. 31. Library, (202) 543-8919, ext. 27.*
General e-mail, uschs@uschs.org

Web, www.uschs.org

Offers tours, lectures, and films; maintains information centers in the Capitol.

CAUCUSES: ORGANIZATIONS OF MEMBERS

►HOUSE AND SENATE

California Democratic Congressional Delegation, *102 CHOB 20515; (202) 225-3072. Fax, (202) 225-3336. Rep. Zoe Lofgren, D–Calif., Chair; Ricky Le, Policy Adviser.*
Web, www.house.gov/lofgren/cdcd/index.aspx

Pursues a common legislative agenda. Seeks to educate Congress on California's various contributions to the United States.

Commission on Security and Cooperation in Europe (Helsinki Commission), *234 FHOB 20515; (202) 225-1901. Fax, (202) 226-4199. Sen. Benjamin L. Cardin, D–Md., Chair; Rep. Alcee L. Hastings, D–Fla., Co-Chair; Fred L. Turner, Chief of Staff.*
General e-mail, info@csce.gov

Web, www.csce.gov

Independent agency created by Congress. Membership includes individuals from the executive and legislative branches. Monitors and encourages compliance with the Helsinki Accords, a series of agreements with provisions on security, economic, environmental, human rights, and humanitarian issues; conducts hearings; serves as an information clearinghouse for issues in eastern and western Europe, Canada, and the United States relating to the Helsinki Accords.

Congressional Arts Caucus, *2469 RHOB 20515; (202) 225-3615. Rep. Louise M. Slaughter, D–N.Y., Co-Chair; Rep. Christopher Shays, R–Conn., Co-Chair.*
Web, www.artsactionfund.org/congress/default_015.asp

Works to secure adequate funding for federal initiatives concerning art, including the National Endowment for the Arts (NEA).

Congressional Asian Pacific American Caucus, *1713 LHOB 20515; (202) 225-2631. Rep. Mike Honda, D–Calif., Chair; Del. Eni F.H. Faleomavaega, D–Am. Samoa, Vice Chair; Victoria Tung, Executive Director. Toll-free, (800) 643-4715.*
Web, www.honda.house.gov/capac

Establishes policies and educates Congress about issues relating to persons of Asian and Pacific Islands ancestry who are citizens, nationals, or residents of the United States.

Congressional Black Caucus, *2444 RHOB 20515; (202) 225-2661. Rep. Barbara Lee, D–Calif., Chair; Del. Donna M. Christensen, D–Virgin Is., Co-Chair; Rep. Emanuel Cleaver II, D–Mo., Co-Chair; Rep. G. K. Butterfield, D–N.C., Co-Chair; Rep. Yvette Clark, D–N.Y., Co-Chair; Patricia Willoughby, Executive Director.*
General e-mail, congressionalblackcaucus@mail.house.gov

Web, www.thecongressionalblackcaucus.com

Promotes the legislative concerns of black and minority citizens.

Congressional Fire Services Caucus, *239 CHOB 20510; (202) 225-7896. Rep. Robert E. Andrews, D–N.J., Co-Chair; Sen. Thomas Carper, D-Del., Sen. Susan M. Collins, R–Maine, Co-Chair; Sen. Christopher J. Dodd, D–Conn., Co-Chair; Rep. Jo Ann Emerson, R–Mo., Co-Chair; Rep. Steny H. Hoyer, D–Md., Co-Chair; Rep. Peter T. King, R–N.Y., Co-Chair; Sen. John McCain, R–Ariz., Co-Chair.*

Seeks to increase awareness of fire and emergency services issues. Largest bipartisan caucus in Congress.

Congressional Fire Services Institute, *900 2nd St. N.E., #303 20002-3557; (202) 371-1277. Fax, (202) 682-3473. William M. Webb, Executive Director.*
General e-mail, update@cfsi.org
Web, www.cfsi.org

Seeks to educate Congress on fire and emergency services issues through various programs for members and their staffs.

Congressional Hispanic Caucus, *2466 RHOB 20515; (202) 225-2361. Fax, (202) 226-0327. Rep. Nydia M. Velázquez, D–N.Y., Chair; Rep. Charles A. Gonzalez, D–Tex., 1st Vice Chair; Rep. Rubén Hinojosa, D-Texas, 2nd Vice Chair; Rep. John T. Salazar, D–Colo., Whip; Miguel Ayala, Communications Director.*
Web, www.house.gov/baca/chc

Seeks to promote and advance, through the legislative process, issues facing Hispanic Americans.

Congressional Internet Caucus, *2240 RHOB 20515; (202) 225-5431. Rep. Rick Boucher, D–Va., Co-Chair; Rep. Bob Goodlatte, R–Va., Co-Chair; Sen. Patrick Leahy, D–Vt., Co-Chair; Brandon Ritchie, Staff Contact.*
Web, www.netcaucus.org

Promotes growth of the Internet, including government participation; educates members and congressional staff about the Internet.

Congressional Port Security Caucus, *1124 LHOB 20515; (202) 225-3176. Rep. Henry E. Brown Jr., R–S.C.,* *Co-Chair; Rep. C.A. "Dutch" Ruppersberger, D–Md., Co-Chair; Sen. Susan M. Collins, R–Maine, Co-Chair; Sen. Daniel K. Inouye, D–Hawaii, Co-Chair; Chris Berardini, Chief of Staff.*

Acts as a clearinghouse for information relating to port security. Seeks adequate funding for port grant programs.

Congressional Privacy Caucus, *2108 RHOB 20510; (202) 225-2836. Rep. Joe Barton, R–Texas, Co-Chair; Sen. Christopher J. Dodd, D–Conn., Co-Chair; Rep. Edward J. Markey, D–Mass., Co-Chair; Mark Bayer, Legislative Director.*

Educates Congress on matters of individual privacy and allows members to serve as advocates for personal privacy.

Congressional Task Force on International HIV/AIDS, *1035 LHOB 20515; (202) 225-3106. Rep. Barbara Lee, D–Calif., Co-Chair; Rep. Jim McDermott, D–Wash., Co-Chair; Anne Grady, Staff Contact.*
Web, www.house.gov/mcdermott/issues_hivaids.shtml

Studies the spread of HIV/AIDS in the developing world; helps plan the U.S. government's response.

Long Island Congressional Delegation, *2243 RHOB 20515; (202) 225-2601. Rep. Gary L. Ackerman, D–N.Y., Chair; Jedd I. Moskowitz, Chief of Staff.*

Promotes the interest of Long Island, New York, and pursues a common legislative agenda to this effect.

New York State Congressional Delegation, *2354 RHOB 20515; (202) 225-4365. Rep. Charles B. Rangel, D–N.Y., Chair; Wendy Featherson, Legislative Assistant.*

Promotes issues of importance to New York State.

Senate-House Steering Committee on Retirement Security, *1501-LHOB 20510; (202) 225-2611. Sen. Jeff Bingaman, D–N.M., Co-Chair; Rep. Earl Pomeroy, D–N.D., Co-Chair; Diane Oakley, Staff Contact.*

Seeks to raise awareness about pension and retirement issues and pursues policies that will improve retirement security for all Americans.

Silk Road Caucus, *420 CHOB 20515; (202) 225-2411. Rep. Gary L. Ackerman, D–N.Y., Co-Chair; Rep. Joseph R. Pitts, R–Pa., Co-Chair; Sen. Sam Brownback, R–Kan., Co-Chair; Sen. Mary L. Landrieu, D–La., Co-Chair; Betsy Christian, Legislative Director.*
Web, www.house.gov/pitts/silkroad.htm

Seeks to foster economic growth, democracy, and the rule of law in the nations of Central Asia and the Caucasus.

U.S. Assn. of Former Members of Congress, *1401 K St. N.W., #503 20005-3417; (202) 222-0972. Fax, (202) 222-0977. John Rhodes, President.*
General e-mail, admin@usafmc.org
Web, www.usafmc.org

Nonpartisan organization of former members of Congress. Acts as a congressional alumni association; sponsors educational projects, including the Congress to Campus program, which provides support for colleges and universities to host visits of former representatives and senators.

►HOUSE

Ad Hoc Congressional Committee for Irish Affairs, 339
CHOB 20515; (202) 225-7896. Rep. Joseph Crowley, D–N.Y., Co-Chair; Rep. Eliot L. Engel, D–N.Y., Co-Chair; Rep. Peter T. King, R–N.Y., Co-Chair; Adam Paulson, Legislative Assistant.

Aims to bring peace, justice, and an end to violence in Northern Ireland by sponsoring legislation and hearings in support of the Irish people.

Bi-Partisan Congressional Pro-Life Caucus, 2373 RHOB
20515; (202) 225-3765. Rep. Christopher H. Smith, R–N.J., Co-Chair; Rep. Bart Stupak, D–Mich., Co-Chair; Autumn Fredericks, Staff Coordinator.

Provides information and advances legislation related to anti-abortion concerns.

Congressional Aerospace Caucus, 2467 RHOB 20515;
(202) 225-5916. Rep. Norm Dicks, D–Wash., Co-Chair; Rep. Vernon J. Ehlers, R–Mich., Co-Chair; Andrew S. DeMott, Legislative Assistant.

Seeks to revitalize the U.S. aeronautics and space program by providing legislative support and acting as an information clearinghouse.

Congressional Automotive Caucus, 2183 RHOB 20515;
(202) 225-3761. Rep. Dale E. Kildee, D–Mich., Co-Chair; Rep. Fred Upton, R–Mich., Co-Chair; Mark Ratner, Legislative Assistant.

Seeks to solve the various problems and answer the needs of the U.S. automotive industry.

Congressional Bearing Caucus, 1401 LHOB 20515;
(202) 225-5501. Rep. John M. Spratt Jr., D–S.C., Co-Chair; Vacant, Co-Chair; Dawn Myers O'Connell, Chief of Staff.

Provides support to the U.S. bearing industry, which it views as crucial to domestic security.

Congressional Bi-Partisan Pro-Choice Caucus, 2469
RHOB 20515; (202) 225-3615. Rep. Diana L. DeGette, D–Colo., Co-Chair; Rep. Louise M. Slaughter, D–N.Y., Co-Chair; Maggie Juliand, Senior Legislative Assistant.

Promotes the right to choose and is concerned with all issues surrounding family planning and sexuality education.

Congressional Caucus for Women's Issues, 2367 RHOB
20515; (202) 225-2111. Rep. Lois Capps, D–Calif., Co-Chair; Rep. Cathy McMorris Rodgers, R–Wash., Co-Chair; Dana Thomas, Legislative Staff.

Works to set the policy agenda for women and families through introduction of various bills.

Congressional Caucus on Intellectual Property Promotion and Piracy Prevention, 2402 RHOB 20515;
(202) 225-8901. Rep. Howard Coble, R–N.C., Co-Chair; Rep. Mary Bono Mack, R–Calif., Co-Chair; Rep. Adam Smith, D–Wash., Co-Chair; Rep. Robert Wexler, D–Fla., Co-Chair; Jonathan Pawlow, Legislative Assistant.

Consults experts in order to foresee legislation needed on intellectual property protection and domestic and international piracy issues.

Congressional Caucus on Korea, 125 CHOB 20515-
0533; (202) 225-7084. Rep. Michael E. Capuano, D–Mass., Honorary Chair; Rep. Edward R. Royce, R–Calif., Co-Chair; Rep. Diane E. Watson, D–Calif., Co-Chair; Abdul Henderson, Legislative Director.

Coordinates Congress's efforts to strengthen democracy throughout the Korean Peninsula. Monitors the North Korean refugee situation.

Congressional Children's Caucus, 2435 RHOB 20515;
(202) 225-3816. Rep. Sheila Jackson Lee, D–Tex., Co-Chair; Rep. Ileana Ros-Lehtinen, R–Fla., Co-Chair; Daryle Doss, Chief of Staff.

Formulates the national agenda on all matters relating to children, including health care and adoption.

Congressional Coast Guard Caucus, 2454 RHOB 20515;
(202) 225-3111. Rep. Howard Coble, R–N.C., Co-Chair; Rep. William D. Delahunt, D–Mass., Co-Chair; Rep. Gene Taylor, D–Miss., Co-Chair; Doug Gascon, Legislative Assistant.

Works to advance the needs of the U.S. Coast Guard in Congress and seeks adequate funding for its mission.

Congressional Glaucoma Caucus, 2232 RHOB 20515;
(202) 225-5936. Rep. Charles B. Rangel, D–N.Y., Co-Chair; Rep. Edolphus Towns, D–N.Y., Co-Chair; Del. Donna M. Christensen, D–Virgin Is., Co-Chair; Shrita Sterlin, Communications Director.

Advances research regarding the treatment of glaucoma through new funding.

Congressional Hispanic Caucus Institute, 911 2nd St.
N.E. 20002; (202) 543-1771. Fax, (202) 546-2143. Nydia M. Velazquez, D–N.Y., Chair, (202) 225-2361; Esther Aguilera, President.
General e-mail, chci@chci.org

Web, www.chci.org

Develops educational and leadership programs to familiarize Hispanic students with policy-related careers and to encourage their professional development. Aids in the developing of future Latino leaders. Provides scholarship, internship, and fellowship opportunities.

Congressional Human Rights Commission, 2170 RHOB
20515; (202) 225-3599. Rep. James P. McGovern, D–Mass., Co-Chair; Rep. Frank R. Wolf, R–Va., Co-Chair; Elizabeth Hoffman, Legislative Assistant, (202) 225-3599.

Seeks to protect human rights through legislation and various forums.

Congressional Immigration Reform Caucus, 2348
RHOB 20515; (202) 225-0508. Rep. Brian P. Bilbray, R–Calif., Chair; Emily E. Sanders, Executive Director.
Web, www.house.gov/bilbray/immreformmsg.shtml

Initiates new immigration policy designed to protect America's borders, including a visa tracking system and reform of the U.S. Immigration and Naturalization Service.

Congressional Native American Caucus, *2107 RHOB 20515; (202) 225-3611. Rep. Dale E. Kildee, D–Mich., Chair; Rep. Tom Cole, R-Okla., Co-Chair; Kimberly Teehee, Senior Adviser.*

Educates Congress about issues affecting Native Americans and allows for dialogue between the caucus and Native American leaders.

Congressional Steel Caucus, *2256 RHOB 20515; (202) 225-2461. Rep. Tim Murphy, R–Pa., Co-Chair; Rep. Peter J. Visclosky, D–Ind., Co-Chair; Kevin Spicer, Legislative Director.*
Web, www.house.gov/english/steelcaucus.shtml

Works to preserve American jobs in the steel industry and to advance the interests of steel workers.

Congressional Task Force on International HIV/AIDS, *1035 LHOB 20515; (202) 225-3106. Rep. Barbara Lee, D–Calif., Co-Chair; Rep. Jim McDermott, D–Wash., Co-Chair; Anne Grady, Staff Contact.*
Web, www.house.gov/mcdermott/issues_hivaids.shtml

Studies the spread of HIV/AIDS in the developing world; helps plan the U.S. government's response.

Congressional Task Force on Tobacco and Health, *1032 LHOB 20515-3819; (202) 225-5836. Rep. Todd Russell Platts, R–Pa., Chair; Scott Miller, Chief of Staff.*

Creates public health legislation that aims to protect children and adults from the dangers of tobacco products.

Congressional Urban Caucus, *2301 RHOB 20515; (202) 225-4001. Rep. Chaka Fattah, D–Pa., Chair; Rep. Michael R. Turner, R–Ohio, Vice Chair; Brenden Chainey, Legislative Counsel.*

Sponsors legislation aimed at repairing urban problems and informs Congress of urban issues in relevant cities.

House Army Caucus, *2369 RHOB 20515; (202) 225-6105. Rep. Chet Edwards, D–Texas, Co-Chair; Rep. John M. McHugh, R–N.Y., Co-Chair; John C. Conger, Legislative Director.*

Seeks to advance the Army's needs as well as assist the Army in presenting programs to Congress.

House Biofuels Caucus, *1727 LHOB 20515; (202) 225-2865. Rep. Dennis Moore, D–Kan., Co-Chair; Rep. Stephanie Herseth Sandlin, D–S.D., Co-Chair; Rep. John M. Shimkus, R–Ill., Co-Chair; Sarah Lochner, Legislative Assistant.*

Promotes the production and use of alcohol fuels, especially ethanol.

House Rural Health Care Coalition, *1501 LHOB 20515; (202) 225-2611. Rep. Earl Pomeroy, D–N.D., Co-Chair; Rep. Greg Walden, R–Ore., Co-Chair; Melanie Rhinehart, Staff Contact.*

Promotes concerns about urban biases in federal health policy.

Iraqi Women's Caucus, *320 CHOB 20515; (202) 225-5071. Rep. Kay Granger, R–Texas, Co-Chair; Rep. Ellen O.*

Tauscher, D–Calif., Co-Chair; Rachel Carter, Communications Director.

Promotes the role of women in the Iraqi government through training programs fostering involvement in the democratic process.

Medical Technology Caucus, *103 CHOB 20515-2303; (202) 225-2871. Rep. Anna G. Eshoo, D–Calif., Co-Chair; Rep. Baron Hill, D-Ind., Co-Chair; Rep. Charles Boustany, R-La., Co-Chair; Rep. Eric Paulsen, R.-Minn., Co-Chair; Erin Katzelnick-Wise, Legislative Director.*

Provides a forum on medical technology issues but does not take a position on any matter.

Military Veterans Caucus, *2211 RHOB 20575; (202) 225-2165. Rep. Gus Bilirakis, R–Fla., Co-Chair; Rep. Collin C. Peterson, D–Minn., Co-Chair; Rep. Mike Thompson, D-Calif., Co-Chair; Chris Iacaruso, Senior Legislative Assistant.*

Seeks to advance the issues of American military personnel, active and retired.

National Parks Caucus, *2231 RHOB 20515; (202) 225-4436. Rep. Brian Baird, D–Wash., Co-Chair; Rep. Mark Souder, R–Ind., Co-Chair; Adam Howard, Legislative Director.*

Seeks to preserve the National Parks and raise awareness of the problems facing the parks.

Northeast Agricultural Caucus, *2417 RHOB 20515; (202) 225-5546. Rep. Tim Holden, D–Pa., Co-Chair; Vacant, Co-Chair; Liz Hermson, Legislative Assistant.*

Seeks to educate members on agricultural matters.

Northeast–Midwest Congressional Coalition, *2365 RHOB 20515-2308; (202) 225-6211. Rep. Steven C. LaTourette, R–Ohio, Co-Chair; Rep. James L. Oberstar, D–Minn., Co-Chair; Mary Cronin, Legislative Director.*

Develops public policies emphasizing regional equity, manufacturing efficiency, and sustainable development.

Older Americans Caucus, *2454 RHOB 20515; (202) 225-3111. Rep. William D. Delahunt, D–Mass., Co-Chair; Rep. Shelley Berkley, D–Nev., Co-Chair; Davida Walsh, Legislative Assistant.*

Acts as an information clearinghouse for aging issues and advocates in the interests of older Americans.

Prescription Drug Task Force, *2305 RHOB 20515; (202) 225-4076. Rep. Marion Berry, D–Ark., Co-Chair; Vacant, Co-Chair; Cynthia Blankenship, Legislative Assistant.*

Serves as a clearinghouse for information and works to ensure reasonable and affordable access to prescription drugs for all Americans.

Republican Study Committee, *424 CHOB 20515; (202) 226-9717. Rep. Tom Price, R–Ga., Chair; Rep. Trent Franks, R-Ariz., Co-Chair; Rep. Scott Garrett, R-N.J., Co-Chair; Rep. Jim Jordan, R-Ohio, Co-Chair; Rep. Mary Fallin, R-Okla., Co-Chair; Paul Teller, Executive Director. General e-mail, RSC@mail.house.gov*
Web, www.rsc.tomprice.house.gov/contact

Works to advance a conservative social and economic agenda.

United Nations Working Group, *2161 RHOB 20515; (202) 225-2464. Rep. Eliot L. Engel, D–N.Y., Co-Chair; Rep. Nita M. Lowey, D–N.Y., Co-Chair; Jason B. Steinbaum, Chief of Staff.*

Seeks to strengthen U.S. leadership in the United Nations, make reforms, and honor the United States' financial commitments to the international organization.

U.S.-Mexico Congressional Caucus, *233 CHOB 20515; (202) 225-2305. Rep. David Dreier, R–Calif., Chair; Rep. Howard L. Berman, D–Calif., Vice Chair; Rep. Lucille Roybal-Allard, D–Calif., Vice Chair; Vacant, Vice Chair; Rachel Leman, Legislative Assistant.*

Promotes dialogue between the United States and Mexico regarding issues arising from integration of both economies.

Western Caucus, *123 CHOB 20515; (202) 225-0453. Rep. Rob Bishop, R–Utah, Chair; Rep. Dean Heller, R–Nev., Policy Chair; Cody Stewart, Legislative Contact.*

Works to better the quality of rural life through environmental and natural resource policies.

▶SENATE

Centrist Coalition, *SH-706 20510; (202) 224-4041. Sen. Joseph I. Lieberman, I–Conn., Co-Chair; Sen. Olympia J. Snowe, R–Maine, Co-Chair; Clarine Nardi Riddle, Chief of Staff.*

Discusses concerns and the effect of the budget on Social Security and Medicare in the future.

Northeast–Midwest Senate Coalition, *SH-728 20510; (202) 224-4642. Sen. Susan M. Collins, R–Maine, Co-Chair; Sen. Jack Reed, D–R.I., Co-Chair; Chris Hickling, Legislative Director.*

Promotes the interests of the Northeast and Midwest and works to influence legislation.

Senate Auto Caucus, *SR-269 20510; (202) 224-6221. Sen. Carl Levin, D–Mich., Co-Chair; Sen. George V. Voinovich, R–Ohio, Co-Chair; Alison Pascale, Legislative Assistant.*

Discusses issues affecting the automotive industry, including transportation, safety, and the environment.

Senate Cancer Coalition, *SH-303 20510; (202) 224-6521. Sen. Sam Brownback, R–Kan., Co-Chair; Sen. Dianne Feinstein, D–Calif., Co-Chair; Melanie Benning, Legislative Director.*

Seeks to educate the Senate and the public about cancer and to promote the nation's commitment to cancer research.

Senate Hunger Caucus, *SR-404 20510; (202) 224-4843. Sen. Blanche L. Lincoln, D–Ark., Co-Chair; Sen. Richard Durbin, D–Ill., Co-Chair; Ted Serafini, Legislative Assistant.*

Advocates for legislative solutions to the problem of hunger in the United States and internationally.

Senate National Guard Caucus, *SR-274 20510; (202) 224-5721. Sen. Christopher S. Bond, R–Mo., Co-Chair; Sen. Patrick Leahy, D–Vt., Co-Chair; Bo Prosch, Legislative Assistant.*

Represents the interests of the National Guard before the Senate.

Senate Steel Caucus, *SH-711 20510; (202) 224-4254. Sen. John D. Rockefeller IV, D–W.Va., Co-Chair; Sen. Arlen Specter, R–Pa., Co-Chair; Scott Boos, Legislative Assistant.*

Advocates the interests of the steel industry and works to preserve American jobs in the industry.

Western States Coalition, *SH-511 20510; (202) 224-2651. Sen. Max S. Baucus, D–Mont., Co-Chair; Sen. Byron L. Dorgan, D–N.D., Co-Chair; Sen. Dianne Feinstein, D–Calif., Co-Chair; Sen. Orrin G. Hatch, R–Utah, Co-Chair; Vacant, Co-Chair; Paul Wilkins, Legislative Director.*

Coordinates legislation addressing the special needs of citizens in the Western states.

CONGRESS AT WORK

See 111th Congress (p. 724) for member's offices and committee assignments and for rosters of congressional committees and subcommittees.

▶CONGRESS

For a listing of relevant congressional committees and subcommittees, please see page 689 or the Appendix.

Emergency Planning, Preparedness, and Operations, *192 FHOB 20515-6462; (202) 226-0950. Fax, (202) 226-6598. J. Curtis Coughlin, Director.*

Liaises between the House and the Homeland Security Dept., the U.S. Capitol Police, and other responders in the coordination of response to emergency situations.

House Recording Studio, *B310 RHOB 20515; (202) 225-3941. Pat Hirsch, Director. TTY, (202) 225-6269.*

Assists House members in making tape recordings. Provides daily gavel-to-gavel television coverage of House floor proceedings.

Interparliamentary Affairs, *H232 CAP 20510; (202) 225-0100. Kay King, Director.*

Assists the House Speaker with international travel and the reception of foreign legislators.

Interparliamentary Services, *SH-808 20510; (202) 224-3047. Sally Walsh, Director.*

Provides support to senators participating in interparliamentary conferences and other international travel. Responsible for financial, administrative, and protocol functions.

Office of Photography, *B302 RHOB 20515; (202) 225-7122. Tina Agee, Manager (Acting).*

Provides House members with photographic assistance.

U.S. House of Representatives

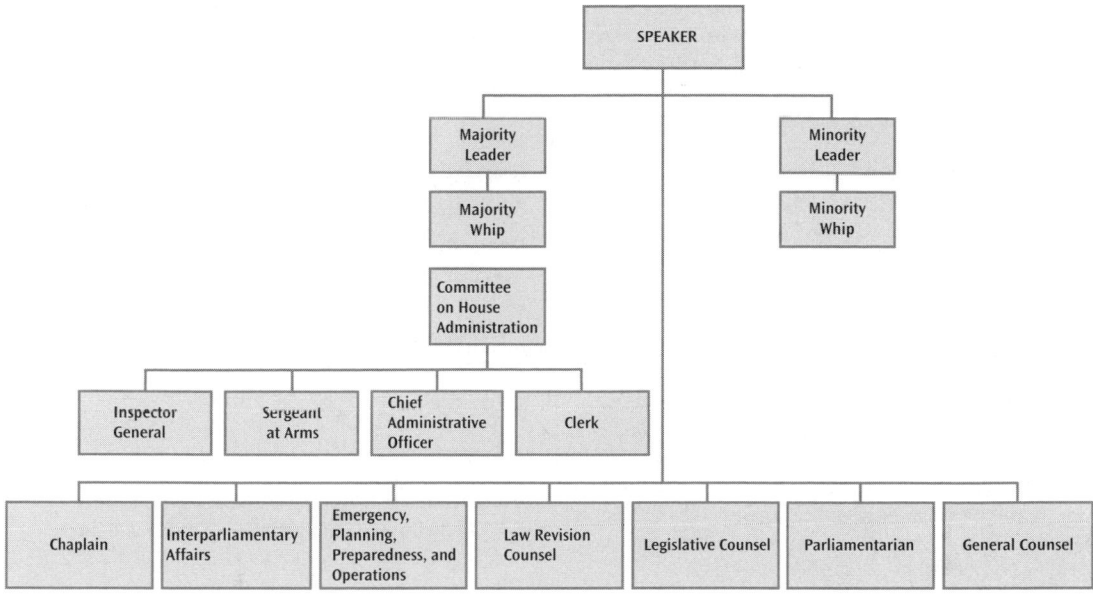

Parliamentarian of the House of Representatives,
H209 CAP 20515; (202) 225-7373. John V. Sullivan, Parliamentarian.

Advises presiding officers on parliamentary procedures and committee jurisdiction over legislation; prepares and maintains a compilation of the precedents of the House.

Parliamentarian of the Senate, *S133 CAP 20510; (202) 224-6128. Alan S. Frumin, Parliamentarian.*

Advises presiding officers on parliamentary procedures and committee jurisdiction over legislation; prepares and maintains a compilation of the precedents of the Senate.

Senate Democratic Communications Center, *S318 CAP 20510; (202) 224-1430. Fax, (202) 228-5576. Sen. Harry M. Reid, D–Nev., Chair; James Patrick Manley, Chief Spokesperson, (202) 224-2939.*
Web, http://democrats.senate.gov

Offers radio, television, and Internet services to Senate Democrats and their staffs to more effectively disseminate information to constituents at home.

Sergeant at Arms and Doorkeeper of the Senate,
Senate Photo Studio, SD-G85 20510; (202) 224-6000. Bill Allen, Manager.

Provides Senate members with photographic assistance.

Sergeant at Arms and Doorkeeper of the Senate,
Senate Recording Studio, ST-29 CAP 20510; (202) 224-4979. Dave Bass, Manager.

Assists Senate members in making radio and video tape recordings and live satellite broadcasts; televises Senate floor proceedings for broadcast by C-SPAN (Cable-Satellite Public Affairs Network).

Leadership

►HOUSE

See House Leadership and Partisan Committees (p. 750)

House Democratic Caucus, *202A CHOB 20515; (202) 225-1400. Fax, (202) 226-4412. Rep. John B. Larson, D–Conn., Chair.*
General e-mail, democratic.caucus@mail.house.gov
Web, www.dems.gov

Membership: House Democrats. Selects Democratic leadership; formulates party rules and floor strategy; considers caucus members' recommendations on major issues; votes on the Democratic Steering and Policy Committee's recommendations for Democratic committee assignments.

House Democratic Steering and Policy Committee, *H204 CAP, Washington, DC 20515; (202) 225-0100. Fax, (202) 225-4188. Rep. Nancy Pelosi, D–Calif., Chair; Rep. Rosa L. DeLauro, D–Conn., Co-Chair; Rep. George Miller, D–Calif., Co-Chair.*
Web, http://speaker.house.gov

Makes recommendations to the Democratic leadership on party policy and priorities and participates in decision making with the leadership.

House Republican Conference, *1420 LHOB 20515; (202) 225-5107. Fax, (202) 226-0154. Rep. Mike Pence, R–Ind., Chair; Rep. Cathy McMorris Rodgers, R–Wash., Vice Chair; Rep. John Carter, R–Texas, Secretary; Marc Short, Chief of Staff.*
General e-mail, GOP@mail.house.gov
Web, www.gop.gov

Membership: House Republicans. Selects Republican leadership; formulates party rules and floor strategy, and considers party positions on major legislation; votes on the Republican Committee on Committees' recommendations for House committee chairs and Republican committee assignments; publishes *Weekly Floor Briefing* and *Daily Floor Briefing*, which analyze pending legislation.

House Republican Policy Committee, *B-58 CHOB 20515; (202) 225-6168. Fax, (202) 225-0931. Rep. Thaddeus McCotter, R–Mich., Chair; Patrick Rothwell, Chief of Staff. Web, http://policy.house.gov*

Studies legislation and makes recommendations on House Republican policies and positions on proposed legislation.

House Republican Steering Committee, *1011 LHOB 20515; (202) 225-6205. Rep. John A. Boehner, R–Ohio, Minority Leader.*

Makes Republican committee assignments and nominates committee chairmen subject to approval by the House Republican Conference and entire House of Representatives.

Majority Leader of the House of Representatives, *H107 CAP 20515; (202) 225-3130. Fax, (202) 226-0663. Rep. Steny H. Hoyer, D–Md., Majority Leader; Terry Lierman, Chief of Staff. Web, www.majorityleader.gov*

Serves as chief strategist and floor spokesperson for the majority party in the House.

Majority Whip of the House of Representatives, *H329 CAP 20515-6503; (202) 226-3210. Fax, (202) 225-9253. Rep. James E. Clyburn, D–S.C., Majority Whip; Yelberton R. Watkins, Chief of Staff. Web, http://majoritywhip.house.gov*

Serves as assistant majority leader in the House; helps marshal majority forces in support of party strategy.

Minority Leader of the House of Representatives, *H204 CAP 20515-6537; (202) 225-4000. Fax, (202) 225-5117. Rep. John A. Boehner, R–Ohio, Minority Leader; Paula T. Nowakowski, Chief of Staff. Web, http://republicanleader.house.gov*

Serves as chief strategist and floor spokesperson for the minority party in the House.

Minority Whip of the House of Representatives, *H307 CAP 20515; (202) 225-0197. Fax, (202) 226-1115. Rep. Eric Cantor, R–Va., Minority Whip; Steven C. Stombres, Chief of Staff. Web, http://republicanwhip.house.gov*

Serves as assistant minority leader in the House; helps marshal minority forces in support of party strategy.

Speaker of the House of Representatives, *Speaker's Office, H232 CAP 20515; (202) 225-0100. Fax, (202) 225-4188. Rep. Nancy Pelosi, D–Calif., Speaker; John Lawrence, Chief of Staff. Web, http://speaker.house.gov*

Presides over the House while in session; preserves decorum and order; announces vote results; recognizes members for debate and introduction of bills, amendments, and motions; refers bills and resolutions to committees; decides points of order; appoints House members to conference committees; votes at own discretion.

▶SENATE

See Senate Leadership and Partisan Committees (p. 818)

Democratic Policy Committee, *SH-419 20510; (202) 224-3232. Fax, (202) 228-3432. Sen. Byron L. Dorgan, D–N.D., Chair; T. Charles Cooper, Staff Director. Web, http://democrats.senate.gov/dpc*

Studies and makes recommendations to the Democratic leadership on legislation for consideration by the Senate; prepares policy papers and develops Democratic policy initiatives.

Democratic Steering and Outreach Committee, *SH-712 20510; (202) 224-9048. Fax, (202) 224-5476. Debbie Stabenow, Chair; Kriston Alford McIntosh, Staff Director. Web, www.democrats.senate.gov/steering*

Makes Democratic committee assignments subject to approval by the Senate Democratic Conference. Develops and maintains relationships with leaders and organizations outside of Congress.

Majority Leader of the Senate, *S221 CAP 20510-7010; (202) 224-2158. Fax, (202) 224-7362. Sen. Harry M. Reid, D–Nev., Majority Leader; Gary Myrick, Chief of Staff. Web, www.reid.senate.gov*

Serves as chief strategist and floor spokesperson for the majority party in the Senate.

Majority Whip of the Senate, *S208 CAP 20510-7012; (202) 224-9447. Fax, (202) 228-0400. Sen. Richard J. Durbin, D–Ill., Majority Whip; Patrick J. Souders, Chief of Staff. Web, www.durbin.senate.gov*

Serves as assistant majority leader in the Senate; helps marshal majority forces in support of party strategy.

Minority Leader of the Senate, *S230 CAP 20510; (202) 224-3135. Fax, (202) 228-2574. Sen. Mitch McConnell, R–Ky., Minority Leader; Kyle Simmons, Chief of Staff. Web, www.mcconnell.senate.gov*

Serves as chief strategist and floor spokesperson for the minority party in the Senate.

Minority Whip of the Senate, *S208 CAP 20510-7022; (202) 224-2708. Fax, (202) 228-1507. Sen. Jon Kyl, R–Ariz., Minority Whip; Lisa Wolski, Chief of Staff.*

Serves as assistant minority leader in the Senate; helps marshal minority forces in support of party strategy.

President Pro Tempore of the Senate, *SH-311 20510; (202) 224-3954. Sen. Robert C. Byrd, D–W.Va., President Pro Tempore. Web, http://byrd.senate.gov*

U.S. Senate

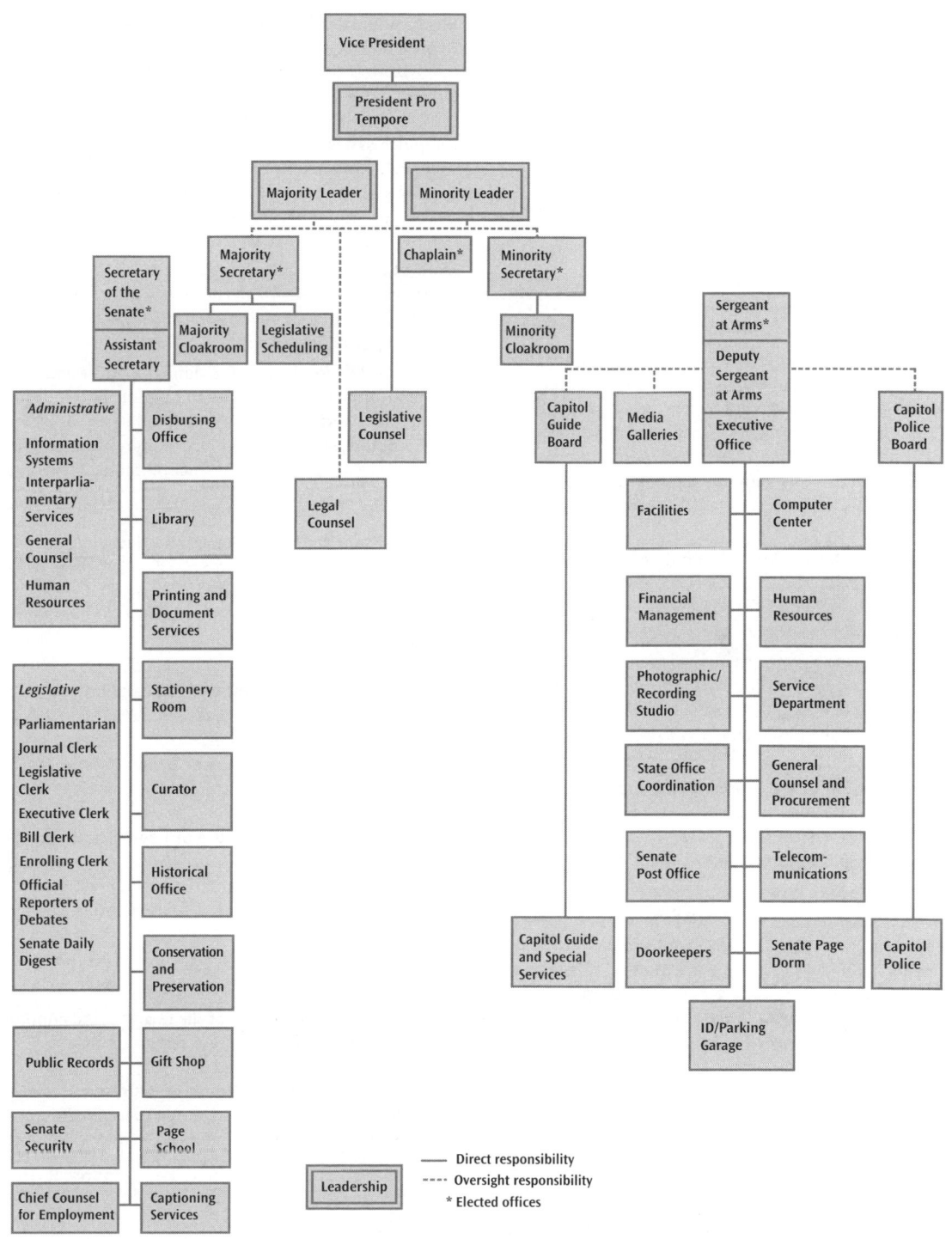

Presides over the Senate in the absence of the vice president.

Senate Democratic Conference, *S309 CAP 20510; (202) 224-3735. Sen. Harry M. Reid, D–Nev., Chair; Sen. Charles E. Schumer, D–N.Y., Vice Chair; Sen. Patty Murray, D–Wash., Secretary; Thomas J. Ingram, Chief of Staff. Web, www.democrats.senate.gov*

Membership: Democratic senators. Selects Democratic leadership; formulates party rules and floor strategy and considers party positions on major legislation; votes on the Democratic Steering Committee's recommendations for Democratic committee assignments.

Senate Republican Conference, *SH-405 20510; (202) 224-2764. Fax, (202) 224-6984. Sen. Lamar Alexander, R–Tenn., Chair. Web, http://src.senate.gov/public*

Membership: Republican senators. Serves as caucus and central coordinating body of the party. Organizes and elects Senate Republican leadership; votes on Republican Committee on Committees' recommendations for Senate committee chairs and Republican committee assignments. Staff provides various support and media services for Republican members.

Senate Republican Policy Committee, *SR-347 20510; (202) 224-2946. Fax, (202) 224-1235. Sen. John Ensign, R–Nev., Chair; Pamela Theissen, Staff Director. Web, http://rpc.senate.gov*

Studies and makes recommendations to the Republican leader on the priorities and scheduling of legislation on the Senate floor; prepares policy papers and develops Republican policy initiatives.

Vice President of the United States, *President of the Senate, The White House 20500; (202) 456-7549. Joseph R. Biden Jr., President of the Senate. General e-mail, vice.president@whitehouse.gov*

Web, www.whitehouse.gov/vicepresident

Presides over the Senate while in session; preserves decorum and order; announces vote results; recognizes members for debate and introduction of bills, amendments, and motions; decides points of order; votes only in the case of a tie. (President pro tempore of the Senate presides in the absence of the vice president.)

Officers

▶**HOUSE**

Chaplain of the House of Representatives, *HB25 CAP 20515; (202) 225-2509. Fax, (202) 226-4928. Rev. Daniel P. Coughlin, Chaplain. General e-mail, daniel.coughlin@mail.house.gov*

Web, http://chaplain.house.gov

Opens each day's House session with a prayer and offers other religious services to House members, their families, and staffs. (Prayer sometimes offered by visiting chaplain.)

Chief Administrative Officer of the House of Representatives, *HB30 CAP 20515; (202) 225-1487. Fax, (202) 226-6999. Daniel P. Beard, Chief Administrative Officer.*

Responsible for House member and staff payrolls; computer system; internal mail, office furnishings and supplies; telecommunications; tour guides; nonlegislative functions of the House printing services, recording studio, and records office; and other administrative areas.

Clerk of the House of Representatives, *H154 CAP 20515-6601; (202) 225-7000. Lorraine C. Miller, Clerk; Janice Wallace, Chief. Publication Services, (202) 225-1908. Web, http://clerk.house.gov*

Responsible for direction of duties of House employees; receives lobby registrations and reports of campaign expenditures and receipts of House candidates; disburses funds appropriated for House expenditures; responsible for other activities necessary for the continuing operation of the House.

Floor Assistant to the Speaker of the House of Representatives, *H209 CAP 20515; (202) 225-0100. Jerry L. Hartz, Senior Floor Assistant to the Speaker.*

Assists the majority leadership and members on legislative matters.

General Counsel of the House of Representatives, *219 CHOB 20515; (202) 225-9700. Fax, (202) 226-1360. Irvin B. Nathan, General Counsel.*

Advises House members and committees on legal matters.

Inspector General of the House of Representatives, *386 FHOB 20515; (202) 226-1250. Fax, (202) 225-4240. James "Jim" Cornell, Inspector General; Michael Benner, Deputy Inspector General; Theresa M. Grafenstine, Deputy Inspector General. General e-mail, HouseIG@mail.house.gov*

Web, www.house.gov/IG

Conducts periodic audits of the financial and administrative functions of the House and joint entities.

Legislative Counsel of the House of Representatives, *136 CHOB 20515-6721; (202) 225-6060. Fax, (202) 225-3437. M. Pope Barrow, Legislative Counsel. Web, www.house.gov/legcoun/index.shtml*

Assists House members and committees in drafting legislation.

Sergeant at Arms of the House of Representatives, *H124 CAP 20515-6611; (202) 225-2456. Fax, (202) 225-3233. Wilson L. "Bill" Livingood, Sergeant at Arms.*

Web, www.clerk.house.gov/art_history/house_history/ sergeants_at_arms.html

Maintains order on the House floor; executes orders from the Speaker of the House. Serves on the Capitol Police Board and Capitol Guide Board; oversees Capitol security (with Senate Sergeant at Arms) and protocol.

►SENATE

Chaplain of the Senate, *S332 CAP 20510-7002; (202) 224-2510. Fax, (202) 224-9686. Barry C. Black, Chaplain.*

Opens each day's Senate session with a prayer and offers other religious services to Senate members, their families, and staffs. (Prayer sometimes offered by visiting chaplain.)

Legal Counsel of the Senate, *SH-642 20510-7250; (202) 224-4435. Fax, (202) 224-3391. Morgan J. Frankel, Legal Counsel.*

Advises Senate members and committees on legal matters.

Legislative Counsel of the Senate, *SD-668 20510-7250; (202) 224-6461. Fax, (202) 224-0567. James W. Fransen, Legislative Counsel.*

Assists Senate members and committees in drafting legislation.

Majority Secretary of the Senate, *S118 CAP 20510-7024; (202) 224-5551. Lula J. Davis, Secretary; Tim Mitchell, Assistant Secretary.*

Assists the majority leader and majority party in the Senate.

Minority Secretary of the Senate, *S337 CAP 20510-7014; (202) 224-3835. Fax, (202) 224-2860. David J. Schiappa, Secretary; Laura Dove, Assistant Secretary.*

Assists the minority leader and the minority party in the Senate.

Secretary of the Senate, *S312 CAP 20510; (202) 224-3622. Nancy Erickson, Secretary of the Senate; Robert Paxton, Chief of Staff. Information, (202) 224-4883.*
Web, www.senate.gov/reference/office/secretary_of_senate .htm

Chief legislative, financial, and administrative officer of the Senate. Responsible for direction of duties of Senate employees and administration of oaths; receives lobby registrations and reports of campaign expenditures and receipts of Senate candidates; responsible for other day-to-day Senate activities.

Sergeant at Arms and Doorkeeper of the Senate, *S151 CAP 20510-7200; (202) 224-2341. Terrance W. Gainer, Sergeant at Arms and Doorkeeper.*
Web, www.senate.gov/reference/office/sergeant_at_arms .htm

Oversees the Senate wing of the Capitol; doormen; Senate pages; and telecommunication, photographic, supply, and janitorial services. Maintains order on the Senate floor and galleries; oversees Capitol security (with House Sergeant at Arms); sits on the Capitol Police Board and Capitol Guide Board.

Pay and Perquisites

►CONGRESS

For a listing of relevant congressional committees and subcommittees, please see page 689 or the Appendix.

Attending Physician, *H166 CAP 20515-8907; (202) 225-5421. Dr. Bryan Monahan, Attending Physician; Christopher R. Picaut, Chief of Staff.*

Provides members with primary care, first aid, emergency care, and environmental/occupational health services; provides House and Senate employees, visiting dignitaries, and tourists with first-aid and emergency care.

Clerk of the House of Representatives, *H154 CAP 20515-6601; (202) 225-7000. Lorraine C. Miller, Clerk; Janice Wallace, Chief. Publication Services, (202) 225-1908.*
Web, http://clerk.house.gov

Prepares and submits quarterly reports covering the receipts and expenditures of the House, including disbursements by each committee and each member's office and staff. Reports available from the Legislative Resource Center.

House Commission on Congressional Mailing Standards (Franking Commission), *2233 RHOB 20515; (202) 225-2061. Fax, (202) 226-2774. Michael Capuano, Chair; Ellen A. McCarthy, Staff Director.*
Web, http://cha.house.gov/services/franking.aspx

Oversight of the use of franked mail by House members.

Secretary of the Senate, *S312 CAP 20510; (202) 224-3622. Nancy Erickson, Secretary of the Senate; Robert Paxton, Chief of Staff. Information, (202) 224-4883.*
Web, www.senate.gov/reference/office/secretary_of_senate .htm

Prepares and submits semiannual reports covering the receipts and expenditures of the Senate, including data on each committee and each member's office and staff. Reports available from the Government Printing Office.

►NONGOVERNMENTAL

National Taxpayers Union, *Communications, 108 N. Alfred St., 3rd Floor, Alexandria, VA 22314; (703) 683-5700. Fax, (703) 683-5722. Peter Sepp, Vice President for Policy and Communications.*
General e-mail, ntu@ntu.org
Web, www.ntu.org

Citizens' interest group that publishes reports on congressional pay and perquisites, including pensions and the franking privilege.

Standards of Conduct

►AGENCIES

Justice Dept. (DOJ), *Public Integrity,* 1400 New York Ave. N.W., #12100 20005; (202) 514-1412. Fax, (202) 514-3003. William M. Welch II, Chief.
Web, www.usdoj.gov

Conducts investigations of wrongdoing in selected cases that involve alleged corruption of public office or violations of election law by public officials, including members of Congress.

►CONGRESS

For a listing of relevant congressional committees and subcommittees, please see page 689 or the Appendix.

Legislative Resource Center, *Records and Registration,* B106 CHOB 20515-6612; (202) 226-5200. Fax, (202) 226-4874. Steve Pingeton, Manager.
Web, http://clerk.house.gov

Receives and maintains the financial disclosure records of House members, officers, employees, candidates, and certain legislative organizations. Receives reports from committee chairs on foreign travel by members and staff. Records open for public inspection.

Secretary of the Senate, *Public Records: Ethics,* SH-232 20510; (202) 224-0322. Pamela B. Gavin, Superintendent of Public Records.
Web, www.senate.gov/lobby

Receives and maintains the financial disclosure records of Senate members, officers, employees, candidates, and legislative organizations. Receives reports from committee chairs on foreign travel by senators and staff. Records open for public inspection, 9:00 a.m.–5:30 p.m.

CONGRESSIONAL SUPPORT GROUPS

►CONGRESS

For a listing of relevant congressional committees and subcommittees, please see page 689 or the Appendix.

Congressional Budget Office, 402 FHOB 20515; (202) 226-2700. Fax, (202) 225-7509. Douglas W. Elmendorf, Director. Information, (202) 226-2600. Publications, (202) 226-2809.
Web, www.cbo.gov

Nonpartisan office that provides the House and Senate with analyses needed for economic and budget decisions, and with the information and estimates required for the congressional budget process.

Government Accountability Office (GAO), 441 G St. N.W., #7100 20548; (202) 512-5500. Fax, (202) 512-5507. Gene Dodaro, Acting Comptroller General. Information,

(202) 512-3000. Library, (202) 512-2585. Publications, (202) 512-6000. Congressional Relations, (202) 512-4400.
Web, www.gao.gov

Independent, nonpartisan agency in the legislative branch. Serves as the investigating agency for Congress; carries out legal, accounting, auditing, and claims settlement functions; makes recommendations for more effective government operations; publishes monthly lists of reports available to the public. (Formerly the General Accounting Office.)

Law Revision Counsel, H2-304 FHOB 20515-6711; (202) 226-2411. Fax, (202) 225-0010. Peter G. LeFevre, Law Revision Counsel.
Web, http://uscode.house.gov

Develops and updates an official classification of U.S. laws. Codifies, cites, and publishes the U.S. Code.

Legal Counsel of the Senate, SH-642 20510-7250; (202) 224-4435. Fax, (202) 224-3391. Morgan J. Frankel, Legal Counsel.

Advises Senate members and committees on legal matters.

Legislative Counsel of the House of Representatives, 136 CHOB 20515-6721; (202) 225-6060. Fax, (202) 225-3437. M. Pope Barrow, Legislative Counsel.
Web, www.house.gov/legcoun/index.shtml

Assists House members and committees in drafting legislation.

Legislative Counsel of the Senate, SD-668 20510-7250; (202) 224-6461. Fax, (202) 224-0567. James W. Fransen, Legislative Counsel.

Assists Senate members and committees in drafting legislation.

Library of Congress, *Congressional Research Service,* 101 Independence Ave. S.E., #LM 203 20540; (202) 707-5775. Daniel P. Mulhollan, Director. Information, (202) 707-5700. Services not available to the public.

Provides policy and legal analysis to committees and members of the House and Senate, regardless of party affiliation. Using multiple disciplines and research methodologies, assists at every stage of the legislative process, from early considerations that precede bill drafting, through committee hearings and floor debate, to the oversight of enacted laws and various agency activities.

Liaison Offices

►CONGRESS

For a listing of relevant congressional committees and subcommittees, please see page 689 or the Appendix.

National Institutes of Health (NIH), *(Health and Human Services Dept.),* **Legislative Policy and Analysis,** 1 Center Drive, MSC 0160, Bethesda, MD 20892-0160;

(301) 496-3471. Fax, (301) 496-0840. Marc Smolonsky, Associate Director for Legislative Policy and Analysis. Web, http://olpa.od.nih.gov

Briefs members of Congress and their staffs on NIH priorities and programs. Coordinates visits to NIH by members of Congress and their staffs. Serves as the NIH legislative liaison to Congress. Advises the NIH director and program offices of legislative activities. Prepares the director and other senior staff members to testify at congressional hearings. Analyzes pending legislation to assess the likely impact on NIH.

Office of Personnel Management (OPM),
Congressional Relations, 1900 E St. N.W., #5H30 20415; (202) 606-1300. Susan G. Marshall, Director.

Provides House and Senate members with information on federal civil service matters, especially those pertaining to federal employment, retirement, and health benefits programs.

►HOUSE

Air Force Liaison, *B322 RHOB 20515-0001; (202) 225-6656. Fax, (202) 685-2592. Michael Fleck, Chief. Alternate phone, (202) 685-4531. General e-mail, usaf@mail.house.gov*

Provides House members with services and information on all matters related to the U.S. Air Force.

Army Liaison, *B325 RHOB 20515; (202) 225-3853. Fax, (202) 685-2674. Christopher Hughes, Chief. Web, www.army.mil*

Provides House members with services and information on all matters related to the U.S. Army.

Navy–Marine Corps Liaison, *B324 RHOB 20515; (202) 225-7808 (Navy). Fax, (202) 685-6077. Capt. Joseph McClain, Navy Director; Col. David J. Furness, Marine Corps Director. Marine Corps, (202) 225-7124.*

Provides House members with services and information on all matters related to the U.S. Navy and the U.S. Marine Corps.

U.S. Coast Guard Liaison, *B320 RHOB 20515; (202) 225-4775. Fax, (202) 426-6081. Mark Meservey, Chief.*

Provides House members with services and information on all matters related to the U.S. Coast Guard.

Veterans Affairs Dept., *Congressional Liaison Service, B328 RHOB 20515; (202) 225-2280. Fax, (202) 453-5225. Patricia J. Covington, Director; Pamela Mugg, Assistant Director. Web, www.va.gov*

Provides House members with services and information on all matters related to veterans' benefits and services.

White House Legislative Affairs, *White House 20502; (202) 456-2230. Fax, (202) 456-3343. Phil Schiliro, Assistant to the President for Legislative Affairs; Dan Turton, Deputy Director (House); Shawn Maher, Deputy Director (Senate).*

Serves as a liaison between the president and the House of Representatives.

►SENATE

Air Force Liaison, *SR-182 20510; (202) 224-2481. Fax, (202) 685-2575. Dan Dunlop, Director. General e-mail, SAFIIS@pentagon.af.mil*

Provides senators with services and information on all matters related to the U.S. Air Force.

Army Liaison, *SR-183 20510; (202) 224-2881. Fax, (202) 685-2570. Col. Martin Schwetzer, Chief.*

Provides senators with services and information on all matters related to the U.S. Army.

Navy–Marine Corps Liaison, *SR-182 20510; (202) 224-4682 (Navy). Fax, (202) 685-6005. Capt. John Nowell, Navy Director; Col. Phil Skuta, Marine Corps Director.*

Provides senators with services and information on all matters related to the U.S. Navy and the U.S. Marine Corps.

U.S. Coast Guard Liaison, *SR-183 20510; (202) 224-2913. Fax, (202) 755-1695. Edward St. Pierre, Chief.*

Provides senators with services and information on all matters related to the U.S. Coast Guard.

Veterans Affairs Dept., *Congressional Liaison Service, SR-189 20510; (202) 224-5351. Fax, (202) 453-5218. Patricia J. Covington, Director; Pamela Mugg, Assistant Director.*

Provides senators with services and information on all matters related to veterans' benefits and services.

White House Legislative Affairs, *White House 20502; (202) 456-2230. Fax, (202) 456-3343. Phil Schiliro, Assistant to the President for Legislative Affairs; Dan Turton, Deputy Director (House); Shawn Maher, Deputy Director (Senate).*

Serves as a liaison between the Senate and the president.

Libraries

►CONGRESS

For a listing of relevant congressional committees and subcommittees, please see page 689 or the Appendix.

Legislative Resource Center, *Library Services, B106 CHOB 20515; (202) 226-5200. Fax, (202) 226-5207. Deborah Turner, Chief. Web, http://clerk.house.gov*

Serves as the statutory and official depository of House reports, hearings, prints, and documents for the clerk of the House. Includes the divisions of Library Services, Public Information, Records and Registration, and the House Document Room.

Library of Congress, *Congressional Research Service, 101 Independence Ave. S.E., #LM 203 20540; (202)*

Congressional Liaisons at Federal Departments and Agencies

DEPARTMENTS

Agriculture, Vacant, (202) 720-7095

Commerce, Frederick Siger, (202) 482-5835

Defense, Robert Wilkie, (703) 697-6210

Air Force, Maj. Gen. Hawk Carlisle, (703) 697-8153

Army, Maj. Gen. Bernard Shampouy, (703) 697-6767

Navy, Rear Adm. Mike Miller, (703) 697-7146

Education, Gabriella Gomez, (202) 401-0020

Energy, Lisa Epifani, (202) 586-5450

Health and Human Services, Vacant, (202) 690-6786

Homeland Security, Chani Wiggins, (202) 447-5890

Housing and Urban Development, Mark Studdert, (202) 708-0380

Interior, Christopher Mansour, (202) 208-7693

Justice, Ronald Weich, (202) 514-2141

Labor, Vacant, (202) 693-4600

State, Richard Verma, (202) 647-4204

Transportation, Dana Gusham, (202) 366-4573

Treasury, Kim Wallace, (202) 622-1900

Veterans Affairs, Patricia Covington, (202) 224-5351

AGENCIES

Agency for International Development, Vacant, (202) 712-4300

Commission on Civil Rights, Chris Byrnes, (202) 376-7670

Commodity Futures Trading Commission, Douglas Leslie, (202) 418-5080

Consumer Product Safety Commission, Jack Horner, (301) 504-7903, ext. 7660

Corporation for National and Community Service, Kathleen Ott, (202) 606-5000, ext. 6732

Environmental Protection Agency, Vacant, (202) 564-5200

Equal Employment Opportunity Commission, Sylvia Anderson, (202) 663-4191

Export-Import Bank, Frank Tillotson, (202) 565-3216

Farm Credit Administration, Martha Schober, (703) 883-4056

Federal Communications Commission, Kevin Washington, (202) 418-1900

Federal Deposit Insurance Corporation, Eric Spitler, (202) 898-3837

Federal Election Commission, Duane Pugh, (202) 694-1006

Federal Emergency Management Agency, Dan Shulman, (202) 646-4500

Federal Labor Relations Authority, Jill Crumpacker, (202) 218-7945

Federal Maritime Commission, Lucille Marvin, (202) 523-5740

Federal Mediation and Conciliation Service, John Arnold, (202) 606-5442

Federal Reserve System, Laricke Blanchard, (202) 452-3456

707-5775. *Daniel P. Mulhollan, Director. Information, (202) 707-5700. Services not available to the public.*

Provides members of Congress and committees with general reference assistance.

Library of Congress, *Law Library, 101 Independence Ave. S.E., #LM240 20540; (202) 707-5065. Rubens Medina, Law Librarian. Reading room, (202) 707-5080. Reference information, (202) 707-5079.*
Web, www.loc.gov/law

Maintains collections of foreign, international, and comparative law texts organized jurisdictionally by country; covers all legal systems—common, civil, Roman, canon, religious, and ancient and medieval law. Services include a public reading room; a microtext facility, with readers and printers for microfilm and microfiche; and foreign law/rare book reading areas. Staff of legal specialists is competent in approximately forty languages; does not provide advice on legal matters.

Library of the Senate, *SR-B15 20510; (202) 224-7106. Fax, (202) 229-0879. Mary Cornaby, Librarian.*

Maintains special collection for Senate private use of primary source legislative materials, including reports,

hearing transcripts, prints, documents, and debate proceedings. (Not open to the public.)

Pages

▶CONGRESS

For a listing of relevant congressional committees and subcommittees, please see page 689 or the Appendix.

House of Representatives Page Program, *H154 CAP 20515; (202) 225-7000. Rep. Dale E. Kildee, D–Mich., Chair; Ellen C. McNamara, Coordinator.*

Oversees and enforces rules and regulations concerning the House page program.

House of Representatives Page School, *101 Independence Ave. S.E., #LJ A15 20540-9996; (202) 225-9003. Fax, (202) 225-9001. Linda G. Miranda, Principal.*

Provides education for pages of the House.

Senate Page School, *U.S. Senate 20510-7248; (202) 224-3926. Kathryn S. Weeden, Principal.*

Provides education for pages of the Senate.

Congressional Liaisons at Federal Departments and Agencies

Federal Trade Commission, Jeanne Bumpus, (202) 326-2195

General Services Administration, Kevin Messner, (202) 501-0563

Legal Services Corporation, Treefa Aziz, (202) 295-1614

Merit Systems Protection Board, Rosalyn Wilcots, (202) 653-6772, ext. 1278

National Aeronautics and Space Administration, William B. Brunner III, (202) 358-1948

National Credit Union Administration, John J. McKechnie III, (703) 518-6330

National Endowment for the Arts, Ann Guthrie Hingston, (202) 682-5434

National Endowment for the Humanities, Andrew Hazlett, (202) 606-8355

National Labor Relations Board, Lester A. Heltzer, (202) 273-1067

National Mediation Board, Mary L. Johnson, (202) 692-5040

National Science Foundation, Geoffrey Nesbit, (703) 292-8070

National Transportation Safety Board, Cheryl McCullough, (202) 314-6121

Nuclear Regulatory Commission, Rebecca L. Schmidt, (301) 415-1776

Occupational Safety and Health Review Commission, Richard Loeb, (202) 606-5100, ext. 207

Office of Personnel Management, Susan G. Marshall, (202) 606-1300

Office of Special Counsel, Jim Mitchell, (202) 254-3714

Pension Benefit Guaranty Corporation, Renee Duncan, (202) 326-4010

Postal Regulatory Commission, Nanci E. Langley, (202) 789-6887

Securities and Exchange Commission, Jonathan Burks, (202) 551-2010

Selective Service System, Richard S. Flahavan, (703) 605-4100

Small Business Administration, C. Edward Rowe III, (202) 205-6703

Smithsonian Institution, Nell Payne, (202) 633-5125

Social Security Administration, Diane Garro, (410) 965-2386

Surface Transportation Board, Matt Wallen, (202) 245-0231

Tennessee Valley Authority, Justin Maierhofer, (202) 898-2995

U.S. International Trade Commission, Dominic Bianchi, (202) 205-3141

U.S. Postal Service, Marie Therese Dominguez, (202) 268-2506

Sergeant at Arms and Doorkeeper of the Senate, *Senate Page Program, Webster Hall, #11 20510; (202) 228-1291. Elizabeth Roach, Director.*

Oversees and enforces rules and regulations concerning Senate pages after they have been appointed.

Staff

▶**CONGRESS**

For a listing of relevant congressional committees and subcommittees, please see page 689 or the Appendix.

Human Resources, *House Resume Referral Service, H2-215 FHOB 20515-6201; (202) 225-2926. Fax, (202) 226-7514. Jason Hite, Director.*

Provides members, committees, and administrative offices of the House of Representatives, as well as job applicants, with placement and referral services.

Senate Placement Office, *SH-116 20510; (202) 224-9167. TTY, (202) 224-4215. Web, www.senate.gov/employment*

Provides members, committees, and administrative offices of the Senate with placement and referral services. Compiles *Senate Employment Bulletin,* a weekly listing of available jobs. (Printed version available on Tuesdays; online version available Friday evenings.)

▶**NONGOVERNMENTAL**

Congressional Legislative Staff Assn., *P.O. Box 1991 LHOB 20007; (202) 224-6441. Brian Clifford, President. General e-mail, brian_clifford@barrasso.sentae.gov or info@congressionalstaffers.org*

Web, www.congressionalstaffers.org

Nonpartisan professional organization of legislative assistants, legislative directors, legal counsels, and committee staff. Meets to discuss mutual concerns, exchange information, and hear guest speakers; holds seminars on issues pending on the House floor.

Congressional Management Foundation, *513 Capitol Court N.E., #300 20002; (202) 546-0100. Fax, (202) 547-0936. Beverly Bell, Executive Director.*

General e-mail, cmf@cmfweb.org

Web, www.cmfweb.org

Nonpartisan organization that provides members of Congress and their staffs with management information and services through seminars, consultation, research, and publications.

Federal Bar Assn., *1220 N. Fillmore St., #444, Arlington, VA 22201; (571) 481-9100. Fax, (571) 481-9090. Jack D. Lockridge, Executive Director.*

General e-mail, fba@fedbar.org

Web, www.fedbar.org

Organization of bar members who are present or former staff members of the House, Senate, Library of Congress, Supreme Court, Government Accountability Office, or Government Printing Office, or attorneys in legislative practice before federal courts or agencies.

House Chiefs of Staff Assn., *1009 LHOB 20515; (202) 225-6411. George McElwee, President.*

Professional and social organization of House administrative assistants and chiefs of staff. Meets to discuss mutual concerns and exchange information. Sponsors orientation program for new chiefs of staff. Meets with administrative, congressional, and international personnel for off-the-record briefings.

POLITICAL ADVOCACY

►AGENCIES

Justice Dept. (DOJ), *Foreign Agents Registration Unit, 1400 New York Ave. N.W., #100 20005; (202) 514-1216. Fax, (202) 514-2836. Heather H. Hunt, Chief.*

Web, www.fara.gov

Receives and maintains the registration of agents representing foreign countries, companies, organizations, and individuals. Compiles semi-annual report on foreign agent registrations. Foreign agent registration files are open for public inspection.

►CONGRESS

For a listing of relevant congressional committees and subcommittees, please see page 689 or the Appendix.

Legislative Resource Center, *Records and Registration, B106 CHOB 20515-6612; (202) 226-5200. Fax, (202) 226-4874. Steve Pingeton, Manager.*

Web, http://clerk.house.gov

Receives and maintains lobby registrations and quarterly financial reports of lobbyists. Administers the statutes of the Federal Regulation of Lobbying Act of 1995 and counsels lobbyists. Receives and maintains agency filings made under the requirements of Section 319 of the Interior Dept. and Related Agencies Appropriations Act for fiscal 1990 (known as the Byrd amendment). Open for public inspection.

►NONGOVERNMENTAL

American League of Lobbyists, *P.O. Box 30005, Alexandria, VA 22310; (703) 960-3011. Patti Jo Baber, Executive Director.*

General e-mail, info@alldc.org

Web, www.alldc.org

Membership: lobbyists and government relations and public affairs professionals. Works to improve the skills, ethics, and public image of lobbyists. Monitors lobby legislation; conducts educational programs on public issues, lobbying techniques, and other topics of interest to membership.

Citizens United, *1006 Pennsylvania Ave. S.E. 20003-2142; (202) 547-5420. Fax, (202) 547-5421. David N. Bossie, President.*

General e-mail, info@citizensunited.org

Web, www.citizensunited.org

Advocates key elements of the conservative legislative and policy agenda.

Political Action Committees and 527s

The following are some key political action committees (PACs) based in Washington. Note that many other organizations listed in this book operate their own PACs.

►LABOR

Active Ballot Club *(United Food and Commercial Workers International Union, AFL-CIO), 1775 K St. N.W. 20006; (202) 223-3111. Fax, (202) 728-1830. Joseph T. Hansen, President; Anthony M. "Marc" Perrone, Treasurer.*

Web, www.ufcw.org

Air Line Pilots Assn. PAC, *1625 Massachusetts Ave. N.W., 8th Floor 20036; (703) 689-2270. W. Randolph Helling, Treasurer.*

Web, www.alpa.org

Amalgamated Transit Union—Cope, *5025 Wisconsin Ave. N.W. 20016; (202) 537-1645. Fax, (202) 244-7824. Oscar Owens, Treasurer.*

General e-mail, dispatch@atu.org

Web, www.atu.org

American Federation of State, County, and Municipal Employees (AFSCME), *1625 L St. N.W. 20036-5687; (202) 429-1000. Fax, (202) 429-1293. William Lucy, Secretary-Treasurer. Press, (202) 429-1145. TTY, (202) 659-0446.*

Web, www.afscme.org

American Federation of Teachers Committee on Political Education, *555 New Jersey Ave. N.W. 20001; (202) 879-4436. Fax, (202) 393-6375. Elizabeth M. "Liz"*

Ratings of Members of Congress

The following organizations either publish voting records on selected issues or rate members of Congress.

AFL–CIO, 815 16th St. N.W. 20006; (202) 637-5000.
Web, www.aflcio.org

American Conservative Union, 1007 Cameron St., Alexandria, VA 22314-2426; (703) 836-8602.
Web, www.conservative.org

American Farm Bureau Federation, 600 Maryland Ave. S.W., #1000W 20024; (202) 406-3600.
Web, www.fb.org

Americans for Democratic Action, 1625 K St. N.W., #210 20006; (202) 785-5980.
Web, www.adaction.org

Citizens Against Government Waste, 1301 Connecticut Ave. N.W., #400 20036; (202) 467-5300.
Web, www.cagw.org

Human Rights Campaign, 1640 Rhode Island Ave. N.W. 20036-3278; (800) 777-4723 or (202) 628-4160; TTY, (202) 216-1572.
Web, www.hrc.org

Leadership Conference on Civil Rights, 1629 K St. N.W., 10th Floor 20006; (202) 466-3311.
Web, www.civilrights.org

League of Conservation Voters, 1920 L St. N.W., #800 20036; (202) 785-8683.
Web, www.lcv.org

NAACP (National Assn. for the Advancement of Colored People), 4805 Mt. Hope Drive, Baltimore, MD 21215; (410) 580-5777
Web, www.naacp.org

NARAL Pro-Choice America, 1156 15th St. N.W., #700 20005; (202) 973-3000.
Web, www.prochoiceamerica.org

National Assn. of Social Workers-PACE (Political Action for Candidate Election), 750 1st St. N.E., #700 20002; (202) 408-8600.
Web, www.socialworkers.org/pace

National Federation of Independent Business, 1201 F St. N.W., #200 20004-1221; (202) 554-9000.
Web, www.nfib.com

National Right to Life Committee, 512 10th St. N.W. 20004; (202) 626-8800.
Web, www.nrlc.org

National Taxpayers Union, 108 N. Alfred St., 3rd Floor, Alexandria, VA 22314; (703) 683-5700.
Web, www.ntu.org

Population Connection, 2120 L St. N.W., #500 20037; (800) 767-1956 or (202) 332-2200.
Web, www.populationconnection.org

Public Citizen, Congress Watch, 215 Pennsylvania Ave. S.E., 3rd Floor 20003; (202) 546-4996.
Web, www.citizen.org

U.S. Chamber of Commerce, Congressional Affairs, 1615 H St. N.W. 20062; (202) 659-6000.
Web, www.uschamber.com

U.S. Student Assn., Congressional Scorecard, 1211 Connecticut Ave. N.W., #406 20036; (202) 640-6570.
Web, www.usstudents.org

Smith, *Political Director; Toni Cortese, Treasurer. Press, (202) 879-4458.*
General e-mail, lsmith@aft.org

Web, www.aft.org

Committee on Letter Carriers Political Education

(National Assn. of Letter Carriers), 100 Indiana Ave. N.W. 20001-2144; (202) 393-4695. Fax, (202) 756-7400. Jane E. Broendel, Treasurer.
Web, www.nalc.org

Committee on Political Action of the American Postal Workers Union, AFL-CIO, *1300 L St. N.W. 20005; (202) 842-4215. Fax, (202) 842-8530. Terry R. Stapleton, Treasurer.*
Web, www.apwu.org

CWA-COPE Political Contributions Committee

(Communications Workers of America, AFL-CIO), 501 3rd St. N.W., #1070 20001-2797; (202) 434-1491. Fax, (202) 434-1481. Jeffrey A. Rechenbach, Treasurer.
Web, www.cwa-union.org

Engineers Political Education Committee/ International Union of Operating Engineers, *1125 17th*

St. N.W. 20036; (202) 429-9100. Fax, (202) 778-2688. Christopher Hanley, Treasurer.
Web, www.iuoe.org

International Brotherhood of Electrical Workers Committee on Political Education, *900 7th St. N.W. 20001; (202) 728-6046. Fax, (202) 728-6144. Brian Baker, Director, Political and Legislative Affairs; Lindell K. Lee, Treasurer. Press, (202) 728-6132.*
Web, www.ibew.org

The International Brotherhood of Teamsters, *Federal Legislation and Regulation, 25 Louisiana Ave. N.W. 20001-2194; (202) 624-8741. Fax, (202) 624-8973. Lisa Kinard, Director; C. Thomas "Tom" Keegel, Treasurer. Press, (202) 624-6911.*
General e-mail, drive@teamster.org
Web, www.teamster.org

Ironworkers Political Action League, *1750 New York Ave. N.W., #400 20006; (202) 383-4800. Fax, (202) 638-4856. Dave Kolbe, Political and Legislative Representative; Walter Wise, General Treasurer.*
Web, www.ironworkers.org

Laborers' Political League of Laborers' International Union of North America, *905 16th St. N.W. 20006-1765; (202) 942-2234. Fax, (202) 942-2307. Bevin Albertani, Legislative and Political Director; Armand E. Sabitoni, General Secretary–Treasurer.*
Web, www.liuna.org

Machinists Non-Partisan Political League *(International Assn. of Machinists and Aerospace Workers, AFL-CIO), 9000 Machinists Pl., Upper Marlboro, MD 20772-2687; (301) 967-4575. Fax, (301) 967-4595. Matthew McKinnon, Legislative and Political Director; Warren L. Mart, General Secretary–Treasurer.*
Web, www.iamaw.org

National Education Assn., *Government Relations, 1201 16th St. N.W. 20036-3290; (202) 822-7300. Fax, (202) 822-7741. Diane Shust, Director; Rebecca Pringle, Secretary-Treasurer. Press, (202) 822-7200.*
Web, www.nea.org

Seafarers Political Activity Donation *(Seafarers International Union of North America), 5201 Auth Way, Camp Springs, MD 20746-4275; (301) 899-0675. Fax, (301) 899-7355. Terry Turner, National Director, Political Action and Governmental Relations; David W. Heindel, Secretary-Treasurer. Press, (301) 899-0675, ext. 4303.*
Web, www.seafarers.org

Sheet Metal Workers International Assn. Political Action League, *1750 New York Ave. N.W., 6th Floor 20006-5386; (202) 662-0887. Fax, (202) 662-0880. Vince Panvini, Political Director; Joseph J. Nigro, Treasurer. Press, (202) 783-5880.*
General e-mail, info@smwia.org
Web, www.smwia.org

United Mine Workers of America, *Coal Miners PAC, 8315 Lee Hwy., Fairfax, VA 22031-2215; (703) 208-7200. Fax, (703) 208-7264. Daniel J. Kane, Secretary-Treasurer.*
Web, www.umwa.org

▶**NONCONNECTED**

American AIDS PAC, *1224 M St. N.W., #300 20005; (202) 628-7770. Fax, (202) 628-7773. Thomas F. Sheridan, Treasurer.*
General e-mail, info@aidspac.org
Web, www.aidspac.org

American Sugarbeet Growers Assn. PAC, *1156 15th St. N.W., #1101 20005; (202) 833-2398. Fax, (240) 235-4291. Pam Alther, Financial Manager.*
Web, www.americansugarbeet.org

America Votes, *1401 New York Ave. N.W., #720 20005; (202) 962-7240. Fax, (202) 962-7241. Carl Pope, President (Interim).*
General e-mail, info@americavotes.org
Web, www.americavotes.org

Seeks to mobilize Americans to register and vote around critical issues.

Automotive Free International Trade PAC, *1625 Prince St., #225, Alexandria, VA 22314-2889; (703) 684-8880. Fax, (703) 684-8920. Mary Drape Hanagan, Executive Director.*
General e-mail, information@afitpac.com
Web, www.afitpac.com

Black America's PAC, *2029 P St. N.W., #202 20036; (202) 785-9619. Fax, (202) 785-9621. Alvin Williams, President. Toll-free, (877) 722-6722.*
General e-mail, bampac@bampac.org
Web, www.bampac.org

Club for Growth, *2001 L St. N.W., #600 20036; (202) 955-5500. Fax, (202) 955-9466. Patrick J. Toomey, President; David Keating, Executive Director.*
General e-mail, www.clubforgrowth.org/contactus.php
Web, www.clubforgrowth.org

Promotes mainly Republican candidates with conservative economic policies and voting records.

Council for a Livable World, *322 4th St. N.E. 20002-5824; (202) 543-4100. Fax, (202) 543-6297. John D. Isaacs, Executive Director.*
General e-mail, advocacy@clw.org
Web, www.clw.org

Supports congressional candidates who advocate arms control and cutting the military budget.

Deloitte and Touche LLP Federal PAC, *555 12th St. N.W., #500 20004-1207; (202) 879-5600. Fax, (202) 347-4299. Cindy M. Stevens, Treasurer.*
Web, www.dtfederalpac.com

EMILY's List, *1120 Connecticut Ave. N.W., 11th Floor 20036; (202) 326-1400. Fax, (202) 326-1415. Ellen R. Malcolm, President.*
Web, www.emilyslist.org

Raises money to support pro-choice Democratic women candidates for political office.

Gay & Lesbian Victory Fund and Leadership Institute, *1133 15th St. N.W., #350 20005; (202) 842-8679. Fax, (202) 289-3863. Chuck Wolfe, President.*
General e-mail, victory@victoryfund.org
Web, www.victoryfund.org

Identifies, trains, and supports open lesbian, gay, bisexual, and transgender candidates and officials at the local, state, and federal levels of government. Raises funds for endorsed candidates.

GOPAC, *1101 16th St. N.W., #201 20036; (202) 464-5170. Fax, (202) 464-5177. Frank J. Donatelli, National Chair; David Avella, Executive Director.*
General e-mail, info@gopac.org
Web, www.gopac.org

Recruits and trains conservative Republican candidates for local and state office.

KPMG PAC, *P.O. Box 18254 20036-9998; (202) 533-5816. Fax, (202) 533-8516. Stephen E. Allis, Treasurer.*
Web, www.kpmg.com

National Committee for an Effective Congress, *122 C St. N.W., #650 20001; (202) 639-8300. Fax, (202) 638-2122. James E. Byron, Treasurer.*
General e-mail, info@ncec.org
Web, www.ncec.org

Supports liberal or progressive candidates in marginal races.

New Politics Institute, *729 15th St. N.W., 2nd Floor 20005; (202) 544-9200. Fax, (202) 547-2929. Simon Rosenberg, President.*
General e-mail, info@ndnpac.org
Web, www.ndnpac.org

Studies progressive politics as it relates to the rise in conservatism, changing voter trends, and new media strategies for campaigns.

New Republican Majority Fund, *P.O. Box 53176 20009; (202) 462-1717. Brent Boyles, Treasurer.*

PricewaterhouseCoopers PAC, *1301 K St. N.W., #800 West 20005-3333; (202) 312-7738. Fax, (202) 312-7742. Emily Gnadt, Manager; Laura Cox Kaplan, Treasurer.*
Web, http://pwc.com

Progressive Majority, *1825 K St. N.W., #450 20006; (202) 408-8603. Fax, (202) 429-0755. Gloria A. Totten, President.*
General e-mail, progressivemajority@progressivemajority .org
Web, www.progressivemajority.org

Identifies, trains, and supports progressive candidates for public office at the state and local levels. Prioritizes recruitment of candidates of color and people new to the political process.

WISH List, *333 N. Fairfax St., #302, Alexandria, VA 22314; (703) 778-5550. Fax, (703) 778-5554. Pat Carpenter, President.*
General e-mail, WISH@thewishlist.org
Web, www.thewishlist.org

Identifies, trains, and helps elect pro-choice Republican women candidates across the United States.

▶ TRADE, MEMBERSHIP, AND HEALTH

Action Committee for Rural Electrification (National Rural Electric Cooperative Assn.), *4301 Wilson Blvd., Arlington, VA 22203-1860; (703) 907-5500. Fax, (703) 907-5516. Michael Whalen, Manager.*
General e-mail, nreca@nreca.coop
Web, www.nreca.coop

American Assn. for Justice PAC, *1050 31st St. N.W. 20007; (202) 965-3500. Fax, (202) 338-8709. Heather Tureen, Director. Toll-free, (800) 424-2725.*
Web, www.justice.org

(Formerly the Assn. of Trial Lawyers of America.)

American Bankers Assn. BankPAC, *1120 Connecticut Ave. N.W., 8th Floor 20036; (202) 663-5113. Fax, (202) 663-7544. Gary W. Fields, Treasurer.*
Web, www.aba.com

American Dental PAC, *1111 14th St. N.W., 11th Floor 20005; (202) 898-2424. Fax, (202) 898-2437. Kathleen B. Ford, Director; Roger Triftshauser, Treasurer.*
Web, www.ada.org

American Health Care Assn. Political Action Committee (AHCA-PAC), *1201 L St. N.W. 20005-4015; (202) 842-4444. Fax, (202) 842-3860. Stacie Aman, Political Action Director.*
Web, www.ahca.org

American Medical Assn. PAC, *25 Massachusetts Ave. N.W., #600 20001; (202) 789-7400. Fax, (202) 789-7469. Kevin Walker, Executive Director.*
Web, www.ama-assn.org

BUILD PAC of the National Assn. of Home Builders, *1201 15th St. N.W. 20005-2800; (202) 266-8470. Fax, (202) 266-8572. Cheryl Caulfield, Assistant Staff Vice President.*
Web, www.nahb.org

Credit Union Legislative Action Council, *601 Pennsylvania Ave. N.W., #600, South Bldg. 20004-2601; (202) 638-5777. Fax, (202) 638-7734. Trey Hawkins, Political Affairs Director.*
Web, www.cuna.org

Dealers Election Action Committee of the National Automobile Dealers Assn., *8400 Westpark Dr., McLean, VA 22102; (703) 821-7110. Fax, (703) 442-3168. Scott Spurgeon, Director.*
Web, www.nada.org

Human Rights Campaign PAC (HRC), *1640 Rhode Island Ave. N.W. 20036; (202) 628-4160. Fax, (202) 347-5323. Joe Salmonese, President. TTY, (202) 216-1572.*
General e-mail, hrc@hrc.org
Web, www.hrc.org

Supports candidates for state and federal office who favor gay and lesbian rights.

Independent Insurance Agents and Brokers of America Political Action Committee (InsurPac), *412 1st St. S.E., #300 20003-1804; (202) 863-7000. Fax, (202) 863-7015. Jennifer Dlugasch, Director; Nathan Riedel, Vice President of Political Affairs.*
Web, www.independentagent.com

National Active and Retired Federal Employees PAC (NARFE), *606 N. Washington St., Alexandria, VA 22314-1914; (703) 838-7760. Fax, (703) 838-7785. Margaret L. Baptiste, President. Press, (703) 838-7760, ext. 369. Member relations, (800) 456-8410.*
General e-mail, hq@narfe.org

Web, www.narfe.org

National Assn. of Broadcasters Television and Radio Political Action Committee, *1771 N St. N.W. 20036; (202) 429-5301. Fax, (202) 775-2157. Anne Brady, Director.*
General e-mail, nab@nab.org

Web, www.nab.org

National Assn. of Insurance and Financial Advisors PAC, *2901 Telestar Ct., Falls Church, VA 22042-1205; (703) 770-8100. Fax, (703) 770-8151. Magenta Ishak, Director.*
General e-mail, mishak@naifa.org

Web, www.naifa.org

National Assn. of Social Workers Political Action for Candidate Election, *750 1st St. N.E., #700 20002-4241; (202) 408-8600. Fax, (202) 336-8311. Brian Dautch, Manager, Government Relations and Political Action.*
General e-mail, info@naswdc.org

Web, www.socialworkers.org

National Beer Wholesalers Assn. PAC, *1101 King St., #600, Alexandria, VA 22314-2944; (703) 683-4300. Fax, (703) 683-8965. Linda Auglis, Director.*
General e-mail, info@nbwa.org

Web, www.nbwa.org

National Committee to Preserve Social Security and Medicare PAC, *10 G St. N.E., #600 20002-4215; (202) 216-0420. Fax, (202) 216-0446. Phillip Rotondi, Administrator. Press, (202) 216-8378.*
Web, www.ncpssm.org

Physical Therapy Political Action Committee (PT-PAC), *1111 N. Fairfax St., Alexandria, VA 22314-1488; (703) 684-2782. Fax, (703) 684-7343. R. Scott Ward, President.*
Web, www.apta.org

Women's Campaign Forum, *734 15th St. N.W., #500 20005; (202) 393-8164. Fax, (202) 393-0649. Siobhan "Sam" Bennett, President. Toll-free, (800) 446-8170.*
Web, www.wcfonline.org

Political Interest Groups

▶**NONGOVERNMENTAL**

Alexis de Tocqueville Institution, *611 Pennsylvania Ave. S.E., #298 20003; (202) 437-7435. Fax, (866) 433-3480. Kenneth P. Brown Jr., President.*

General e-mail, kenbrown@adti.net

Web, www.adti.net

Public policy research organization that conducts, sponsors, and publishes research and analysis. Advocates individual political and economic freedom, limited government, and free markets.

American Conservative Union (ACU), *1007 Cameron St., Alexandria, VA 22314-2426; (703) 836-8602. Fax, (703) 836-8606. Dennis E. Whitfield, Executive Vice President. Toll-free, (800) 228-7345.*
General e-mail, acu@conservative.org

Web, www.conservative.org

Legislative interest organization that focuses on defense, foreign policy, economics, the national budget, taxes, and legal and social issues. Monitors legislation and regulations.

American Family Voices, *1015 18th St. N.W., #204 20036; (202) 393-4352. Fax, (202) 331-0131. Michael Lux, President.*
General e-mail, afv@americanfamilyvoices.org

Web, www.americanfamilyvoices.org

Assists and advocates on behalf of middle-class and low-income families dealing with economic, health care, and consumer issues.

Americans for Democratic Action, *1625 K St. N.W., #210 20006-1611; (202) 785-5980. Fax, (202) 785-5969. Amy F. Isaacs, National Director; Richard Parker, President.*
General e-mail, info@adaction.org

Web, www.adaction.org

Legislative interest organization that seeks to strengthen civil, constitutional, women's, family, workers', and human rights.

Americans for Prosperity Foundation, *1726 M St. N.W., 10th Floor 20036; (202) 349-5880. Fax, (202) 587-4599. Tim Phillips, President. Toll-free, (866) 730-0150.*
General e-mail, info@AFPhq.org

Web, www.americansforprosperity.org

Grassroots organization that seeks to educate citizens about economic policy and encourage their participation in the public policy process. Supports limited government and free markets on the local, state, and federal levels. Specific interests include Social Security, trade, and taxes.

Americans United For Change, *1850 K St. N.W. 20036 (mailing address: P.O. Box 65321, Washington, DC 20035); (202) 470-6954. Fax, (202) 331-0131. Brad Woodhouse, President. Press, (202) 470-5878.*
Web, http://americansunitedforchange.org

The Brookings Institution, *1775 Massachusetts Ave. N.W. 20036; (202) 797-6000. Fax, (202) 797-6004. Strobe Talbott, President. Press, (202) 797-6105.*
Web, www.brookings.edu

Public policy research organization that seeks to improve the performance of American institutions, the effectiveness of government programs, and the quality of public policy through research and analysis. Sponsors lectures, debates, and policy forums.

Campaign for America's Future, *1825 K St. N.W., #400 20006; (202) 955-5665. Fax, (202) 955-5606. Robert L. Borosage, Co-Director; Roger Hickey, Co-Director.*
Web, www.ourfuture.org

Operates the Campaign for America's Future and the Institute for America's Future. Advocates policies to help working people. Supports improved employee benefits, including health care, child care, and paid family leave; promotes lifelong education and training of workers. Seeks full employment, higher wages, and increased productivity. Monitors legislation and regulations.

Cato Institute, *1000 Massachusetts Ave. N.W. 20001-5403; (202) 842-0200. Fax, (202) 842-3413. Edward H. Crane III, President. Press, (202) 842-0200, ext. 800.*
General e-mail, cato@cato.org
Web, www.cato.org

Public policy research organization that advocates limited government and individual liberty. Interests include privatization and deregulation, low and simple taxes, and reduced government spending. Encourages voluntary solutions to social and economic problems.

Center for American Progress, *1333 H St. N.W., 10th Floor 20005; (202) 682-1611. Fax, (202) 682-1867. John D. Podesta, President.*
General e-mail, progress@americanprogress.org
Web, www.americanprogress.org

Nonpartisan research and educational institute that strives to ensure opportunity for all Americans. Advocates policies to create sustained economic growth and new opportunities. Supports fiscal discipline, shared prosperity, and investments in people through education, health care, and workforce training.

Center for National Policy, *1 Massachusetts Ave. N.W., #333 20001; (202) 682-1800. Fax, (202) 682-1818. Timothy J. Roemer, President.*
General e-mail, cmaxwell@cnponline.org
Web, www.cnponline.org

Public policy research and educational organization that serves as a forum for development of national policy alternatives. Studies issues of national and international concern, focusing on national security; sponsors conferences and symposia.

Christian Coalition of America, *P.O. Box 37030 20013-7030; (202) 479-6900. Fax, (202) 479-4260. Roberta Combs, President. Press, (202) 549-6257.*
General e-mail, coalition@cc.org
Web, www.cc.org

Membership: individuals who support traditional, conservative Christian values. Represents members' views to all levels of government and to the media.

Citizens Against Government Waste, *1301 Connecticut Ave. N.W., #400 20036; (202) 467-5300. Fax, (202) 467-4253. Thomas A. Schatz, President. Information, (800) 232-6479.*
Web, www.cagw.org

Nonpartisan organization that seeks to eliminate waste, mismanagement, and inefficiency in the federal government. Monitors legislation, regulations, and the budget process.

Committee for a Responsible Federal Budget, *1630 Connecticut Ave. N.W., 7th Floor 20009; (202) 986-6599. Fax, (202) 986-3696. Maya MacGuineas, President.*
General e-mail, crfb@newamerica.net
Web, www.crfb.org

Bipartisan, nonprofit organization that educates the public about issues that have significant fiscal policy impact. Monitors legislation and regulation. (Affiliated with the New America Foundation.)

Common Cause, *1133 19th St. N.W., 9th Floor 20036; (202) 833-1200. Fax, (202) 659-3716. Bob Edgar, President, (202) 736-5740. Press, (202) 736-5770.*
Web, www.commoncause.org

Nonpartisan citizens' legislative interest group that works for institutional reform in federal and state government. Advocates partial public financing of congressional election campaigns, ethics in government, nuclear arms control, oversight of defense spending, tax reform, and a reduction of political action committee influence in Congress.

Concerned Women for America, *1015 15th St. N.W., #1100 20005; (202) 488-7000. Fax, (202) 488-0806. Beverly LaHaye, Chair. Press, (202) 488-7000, ext. 126.*
Web, www.cwfa.org

Educational organization that seeks to protect the rights of the family and preserve Judeo-Christian values. Monitors legislation affecting family and religious issues.

Concord Coalition, *1011 Arlington Blvd., #300, Arlington, VA 22209; (703) 894-6222. Fax, (703) 894-6231. Robert L. Bixby, Executive Director.*
General e-mail, concordcoalition@concordcoalition.org
Web, www.concordcoalition.org

Nonpartisan grassroots organization advocating fiscal responsibility and ensuring Social Security, Medicare, and Medicaid are secure for all generations.

Conservative Caucus, *450 Maple Ave. East, Vienna, VA 22180-4724; (703) 938-9626. Fax, (703) 281 1100. Howard Phillips, Chair.*
General e-mail, info@conservativeusa.org
Web, www.conservativeusa.org

Legislative interest organization that promotes grassroots activity on issues such as national defense and economic and tax policy. The Conservative Caucus Research, Analysis, and Education Foundation studies public issues including Central American affairs, defense policy, and federal funding of political advocacy groups.

Eagle Forum, Washington Office, *316 Pennsylvania Ave. S.E., #203 20003; (202) 544-0353. Fax, (202) 547-6996. Colleen Holmes, Executive Director.*
General e-mail, eagle@eagleforum.org

Web, www.eagleforum.org

Legislative interest group that supports conservative, pro-family policies at all levels of government. Concerns include abortion, affirmative action, education, national defense, and taxes. (Headquarters in St. Louis, Mo.)

Family Research Council, *801 G St. N.W. 20001-3729; (202) 393-2100. Fax, (202) 393-2134. Tony Perkins, President. Toll-free, (800) 225-4008.*
Web, www.frc.org

Legislative interest organization that analyzes issues affecting the family and seeks to ensure that the interests of the family are considered in the formulation of public policy.

Feminist Majority, *1600 Wilson Blvd., #801, Arlington, VA 22209-2505; (703) 522-2214. Fax, (703) 522-2219. Eleanor Smeal, President.*
General e-mail, femmaj@feminist.org

Web, www.feministmajority.org

Legislative interest group that seeks to increase the number of feminists running for public office; promotes a national feminist agenda.

Free Congress Research and Education Foundation (FCF), *1423 Powhatan St., #2, Alexandria, VA 22314; (703) 837-0030. Fax, (703) 837-0031. Paul M. Weyrich, Chair.*
Web, www.freecongress.org

Research and education foundation that promotes traditional values, conservative governance, and institutional reform. Studies judicial/political issues, electoral process, and public policy. Trains citizens to participate in a democracy.

FreedomWorks, *601 Pennsylvania Ave. N.W., North Bldg., #700 20004-2601; (202) 783-3870. Fax, (202) 942-7649. Matt Kibbe, President; Dick Armey, Chair. Toll-free, (888) 564-6273.*
Web, www.freedomworks.org

Recruits, educates, trains, and mobilizes citizens to promote lower taxes, less government, and greater economic freedom.

Frontiers of Freedom, *11781 Lee Jackson Memorial Hwy., 3rd Floor, Fairfax, VA 22033; (703) 246-0110. Fax, (703) 246-0129. George C. Landrith, President.*
General e-mail, info@ff.org

Web, www.ff.org

Seeks to increase personal freedom through a reduction in the size of government. Interests include property rights, regulatory and tax reform, global warming, national missile defense, Internet regulation, school

vouchers, and Second Amendment rights. Monitors legislation and regulations.

The Heritage Foundation, *214 Massachusetts Ave. N.E. 20002-4999; (202) 546-4400. Fax, (202) 546-8328. Edwin J. Feulner, President. Press, (202) 675-1761.*
General e-mail, info@heritage.org

Web, www.heritage.org

Public policy research organization that conducts research and analysis and sponsors lectures, debates, and policy forums advocating individual freedom, limited government, the free market system, and a strong national defense.

Interfaith Alliance, *1212 New York Ave. N.W., #1250 20005; (202) 238-3300. Fax, (202) 238-3301. Rev. C. Welton Gaddy, President.*
General e-mail, info@interfaithalliance.org

Web, www.interfaithalliance.org

Membership: Protestant, Catholic, Jewish, and Muslim clergy, laity, and others who favor a positive, nonpartisan role for religious faith in public life. Advocates mainstream religious values; promotes tolerance and social opportunity; opposes the use of religion to promote political extremism at national, state, and local levels. Monitors legislation and regulations.

Log Cabin Republicans, *1901 Pennsylvania Ave. N.W., #902 20006; (202) 347-5306. Fax, (202) 347-5224. Chris Scalise, President.*
General e-mail, info@logcabin.org

Web, www.logcabin.org

Membership: lesbian and gay Republicans. Educates conservative politicians and voters on gay and lesbian issues; disseminates information; conducts seminars for members. Raises campaign funds. Monitors legislation and regulations.

Millennium Institute, *2111 Wilson Blvd., #700, Arlington, VA 22201-3357; (703) 351-5081. Fax, (703) 351-9292. Hans R. Herren, President.*
General e-mail, info@millennium-institute.org

Web, www.millennium-institute.org

Research and development firm that provides computer modeling services for planning and building a sustainable economic and ecological future.

National Center for Policy Analysis, Washington Office, *601 Pennsylvania Ave. N.W., #900 South Bldg. 20004-3615; (202) 220-3082. Fax, (202) 220-3096. John C. Goodman, President.*
General e-mail, ncpa@ncpa.org

Web, www.ncpa.org

Conducts research and policy analysis; disseminates others' outside research in the areas of tax reform, health care, the environment, criminal justice, education, social security, and welfare reform. (Headquarters in Dallas, Texas.)

National Jewish Democratic Council, *P.O. Box 75308 20013-5308; (202) 216-9060. Fax, (202) 216-9061. Ira N. Forman, Executive Director.*
General e-mail, njdc@njdc.org

Web, www.njdc.org

Encourages Jewish involvement in the Democratic party and its political campaigns. Monitors and analyzes domestic and foreign policy issues that concern the American Jewish community.

National Organization for Women (NOW), *1100 H St. N.W., 3rd Floor 20005; (202) 628-8669. Fax, (202) 785-8576. Kim Gandy, President. TTY, (202) 331-9002.*
Web, www.now.org

Advocacy organization that works for women's civil rights. Acts through demonstrations, court cases, and legislative efforts to improve the status of all women. Interests include increasing the number of women in elected and appointed office, improving women's economic status and health coverage, ending violence against women, preserving abortion rights, and abolishing discrimination based on gender, race, age, and sexual orientation.

National Taxpayers Union, *Communications, 108 N. Alfred St., 3rd Floor, Alexandria, VA 22314; (703) 683-5700. Fax, (703) 683-5722. Peter Sepp, Vice President for Policy and Communications.*
General e-mail, ntu@ntu.org

Web, www.ntu.org

Citizens' interest group that promotes tax and spending reduction at all levels of government. Supports constitutional amendments to balance the federal budget and limit taxes.

National Woman's Party, *144 Constitution Ave. N.E. 20002-5608; (202) 546-1210. Fax, (202) 546-3997. Audrey Sheppard, President. Press, (202) 546-1210, ext. 10.*
General e-mail, info@sewallbelmont.org

Web, www.sewallbelmont.org

Membership: women seeking equality under the law. Supports the Equal Rights Amendment and other legislation to eliminate discrimination against women.

New America Foundation, *1899 L St. N.W., #400 20036; (202) 986-2700. Fax, (202) 986-3696. Steve Coll, President.*
General e-mail, info@newamerica.net

Web, www.newamerica.net

Ideologically diverse public policy institute that seeks to nurture the next generation of public intellectuals. Sponsors research, writing, conferences, and events. Funds studies of government programs. Seeks to stimulate more informed reporting and analyses of government activities.

People for the American Way (PFAW), *2000 M St. N.W., #400 20036; (202) 467-4999. Fax, (202) 293-2672. Kathryn Kolbert, President. Toll-free, (800) 326-7329.*

General e-mail, pfaw@pfaw.org

Web, www.pfaw.org

Nonpartisan organization that promotes civil rights and liberties through legal advocacy, media and Internet outreach, and a national grassroots network of members and volunteers. Conducts public education programs on constitutional issues, including free expression and religious liberty. Advocates for election reform and encourages registration and civic participation. Conducts leadership development programs for college students, African American religious leaders, and Hispanic community leaders.

Progress and Freedom Foundation, *1444 Eye St. N.W., #500 20005; (202) 289-8928. Fax, (202) 289-6079. Ken Ferree, President.*
General e-mail, mail@pff.org

Web, www.pff.org

Studies the impact of the digital revolution and its implications for public policy; sponsors seminars, conferences, and broadcasts.

Public Advocate of the United States, *5613 Leesburg Pike, #17, Falls Church, VA 22041; (703) 845-1808. Eugene Delgaudio, President.*
Web, www.publicadvocateusa.org

Educational grassroots organization that promotes a limited role for the federal government and conservative life choices. Opposes federal gay rights laws.

Public Affairs Council, *2033 K St. N.W., #700 20006; (202) 872-1790. Fax, (202) 835-8343. Douglas G. Pinkham, President.*
General e-mail, pac@pac.org

Web, www.pac.org

Membership: public affairs professionals. Informs and counsels members on public affairs programs. Sponsors conferences on election issues, government relations, and political trends. Sponsors the Foundation for Public Affairs.

Public Citizen, *Congress Watch, 215 Pennsylvania Ave. S.E., 3rd Floor 20003; (202) 546-4996. Fax, (202) 546-5562. David Arkush, Director.*
Web, www.citizen.org/congress

Citizens' interest group engaged in public education, research, media outreach, and citizen activism. Interests include campaign finance reform, consumer protection, financial services, public health and safety, government reform, trade, and the environment.

Rainbow PUSH Coalition, *Public Policy Institute, 727 15th St. N.W., #1200 20005; (202) 393-7874. Fax, (202) 393-1495. Jesse L. Jackson Sr., President; Martin L. King, Chair; Kimberly Marcus, Executive Director. Press, (773) 373-3366.*
General e-mail, info@rainbowpush.org

Web, www.rainbowpush.org

Independent political organization concerned with U.S. domestic and foreign policy. Interests include D.C. statehood, civil rights, defense policy, agriculture, HIV/AIDS, poverty, the economy, energy, the environment, hate crimes, and social justice. (Headquarters in Chicago, Ill.)

Republican Jewish Coalition, 50 F St. N.W., #100 20001; (202) 638-6688. Fax, (202) 638-6694. Matthew Brooks, Executive Director.
General e-mail, rjc@rjchq.org

Web, www.rjchq.org

Legislative interest group that works to build support among Republican party decision makers on issues of concern to the Jewish community; studies domestic and foreign policy issues affecting the Jewish community; supports a strong relationship between the United States and Israel.

Students for Saving Social Security (S4), 1600 Wilson Blvd., #960, Arlington, VA 22209; (202) 290-6880. Fax, (703) 807-2073. Jo Jensen, Executive Director, (603) 738-6778.
General e-mail, staff@secureourfuture.org

Web, www.secureourfuture.org

Network of university students that advocates for Social Security reform to allow the option of individual investment accounts. Conducts campaigns to raise students' awareness of Social Security funding issues and encourage political engagement.

Taxpayers for Common Sense, 651 Pennsylvania Ave. S.E. 20003; (202) 546-8500. Fax, (202) 546-8511. Brian Alexander, President. Toll-free, (800) 829- 7293.
General e-mail, info@taxpayer.net

Web, www.taxpayer.net

Works with elected officials and testifies before congressional committees about reducing government waste. Brings government waste to the attention of the media. Works with grassroots citizen groups.

Third Way, 1025 Connecticut Ave. N.W., #501 20036; (202) 775-3768. Fax, (202) 775-0430. Jonathan Cowan, President.
General e-mail, contact@third-way.com

Web, www.third-way.com

Think tank that works with moderate and progressive legislators to develop modern solutions to economic, cultural, and national security issues. Conducts studies and polls; develops policy papers and strategy documents.

Traditional Values Coalition, *Washington Office,* 139 C St. S.E. 20003; (202) 547-8570. Fax, (202) 546-6403. Andrea S. Lafferty, Executive Director.
General e-mail, mail@traditionalvalues.org

Web, www.traditionalvalues.org

Legislative interest group that supports religious liberties and traditional, conservative Judeo-Christian values.

Interests include anti-abortion issues, pornography, decreased federal funding for the arts, parental rights, and the promotion of school prayer. Opposes gay rights legislation. (Headquarters in Anaheim, Calif.)

20/20 Vision, 8403 Colesville Rd., #640, Silver Spring, MD 20910; (301) 587-1782. Fax, (301) 587-1848. Tom Z. Collina, Executive Director. Toll-free, (800) 669-1782.
General e-mail, vision@2020vision.org

Web, www.2020vision.org

Pro-democracy advocacy group that encourages members to spend twenty minutes each month communicating their opinions to policymakers. Targets legislative issues in particular districts and provides information on current issues. Interests include ending the production of weapons of mass destruction, protecting the environment, and ending U.S. dependency on fossil fuel.

Urban Institute, 2100 M St. N.W. 20037; (202) 833-7200. Fax, (202) 728-0232. Robert D. Reischauer, President. Information, (202) 261-5709. Library, (202) 261-5688.
General e-mail, paffairs@urban.org

Web, www.urban.org

Nonpartisan research and education organization. Investigates U.S. social and economic problems; encourages discussion on solving society's problems, improving and implementing government decisions, and increasing citizens' awareness of public choices. Library open to the public by appointment.

U.S. Chamber of Commerce, *Grassroots Action Information Network (GAIN),* 1615 H St. N.W. 20062-2000; (202) 463-5604. Fax, (202) 463-3190. William "Bill" Miller, National Political Director. Press, (202) 463-5682.
General e-mail, vfb@uschamber.com

Web, www.voteforbusiness.com

Federation that works to enact pro-business legislation; tracks election law legislation; coordinates the chamber's candidate endorsement program and its grassroots lobbying activities.

Women Legislators' Lobby (WiLL), *Policy and Programs,* 322 4th St. N.E. 20002; (202) 544-5055. Fax, (202) 544-7612. Marie Rietmann, Public Policy Director.
General e-mail, info@wand.org

Web, www.wand.org

Bipartisan group of women state legislators. Sponsors conferences, training workshops, issue briefings, and seminars; provides information and action alerts on ways federal policies affect states. Interests include federal budget priorities, national security, and arms control. Monitors related legislation and regulations. (National office in Arlington, Mass. Affiliated with Women's Action for New Directions.)

Women's Policy Inc., 409 12th St. S.W., #310 20024; (202) 554-2323. Fax, (202) 554-2346. Cynthia A. Hall, President.

General e-mail, webmaster@womenspolicy.org

Web, www.womenspolicy.org

Nonpartisan organization that provides legislative analysis and information services on congressional actions affecting women and their families.

POLITICAL PARTY ORGANIZATIONS

Democratic

Democratic Congressional Campaign Committee, *430 S. Capitol St. S.E. 20003; (202) 863-1500. Fax, (202) 485-3436. Rep. Chris Van Hollen, D–Md., Chair. Comment line, (202) 485-3573.*
General e-mail, dccc@dccc.org

Web, www.dccc.org

Provides Democratic House candidates with financial and other campaign services.

Democratic Governors Assn., *1401 K St. N.W., #200 20005; (202) 772-5600. Fax, (202) 772-5602. Gov. Brian Schweitzer, D–Mont., Chair; Nathan Daschle, Executive Director.*
Web, www.democraticgovernors.org

Serves as a liaison between governors' offices and Democratic Party organizations; assists Democratic gubernatorial candidates.

Democratic Leadership Council, *600 Pennsylvania Ave. S.E., #400 20003; (202) 546-0007. Fax, (202) 544-5002. Harold Ford Jr., Chair; Alvin From, Chief Executive Officer.*
Web, www.ndol.org

Organization of Democratic members of Congress, governors, state and local officials, and concerned citizens. Builds consensus within the Democratic Party on public policy issues, including economic growth, national security, national service, and expansion of opportunity for all Americans.

Democratic National Committee (DNC), *430 S. Capitol St. S.E. 20003-4024; (202) 863-8000. Fax, (202) 863-8063. Gov. Tim Kaine, Chair. Press, (202) 863-8148.*
General e-mail, info@democrats.org

Web, www.democrats.org

Formulates and promotes Democratic Party policies and positions; assists Democratic candidates for state and national office; organizes national political activities; works with state and local officials and organizations.

Democratic National Committee (DNC), *Assn. of State Democratic Chairs, 430 S. Capitol St. S.E. 20003-4024; (202) 488-5120. Fax, (202) 479-5123. Ann Fishman, Executive Director. Press, (202) 863-8148.*

General e-mail, info@democrats.org

Web, www.democrats.org

Acts as a liaison between state parties and the DNC; works to strengthen state parties for national, state, and local elections; conducts fundraising activities for state parties.

Democratic National Committee (DNC), Communications, *430 S. Capitol St. S.E. 20003-4024; (202) 863-8148. Fax, (202) 863-8174. Brad Woodhouse, Director.*
General e-mail, DNCPress@dnc.org

Web, www.democrats.org

Assists federal, state, and local Democratic candidates and officials in delivering a coordinated message on current issues; works to improve and expand relations with the press and to increase the visibility of Democratic officials and the Democratic Party.

Democratic National Committee (DNC), *Finance, 430 S. Capitol St. S.E. 20003-4024; (202) 863-8000. Fax, (202) 863-8082. Rufus Gifford, Director. Press, (202) 863-8148.*
General e-mail, info@democrats.org

Web, www.democrats.org

Responsible for developing the Democratic Party's financial base. Coordinates fundraising efforts for and gives financial support to Democratic candidates in national, state, and local campaigns.

Democratic National Committee (DNC), *Research, 430 S. Capitol St. S.E. 20003-4024; (202) 479-5113. Fax, (202) 350-6015. Vacant, Director. Press, (202) 863-8148.*
General e-mail, info@democrats.org

Web, www.democrats.org

Provides Democratic elected officials, candidates, state party organizations, and the general public with information on Democratic Party policy and programs.

Democratic Senatorial Campaign Committee, *120 Maryland Ave. N.E. 20002-5610; (202) 224-2447. Fax, (202) 969-0354. Rep. Robert Menendez, D–N.J., Chair; J.B. Poersch, Executive Director.*
General e-mail, info@dscc.org

Web, www.dscc.org

Provides Democratic senatorial candidates with financial, research, and consulting services.

Woman's National Democratic Club, *Committee on Public Policy, 1526 New Hampshire Ave. N.W. 20036; (202) 232-7363. Fax, (202) 986-2791. Elizabeth "Betsy" Clark, Chair.*
General e-mail, info@democraticwoman.org

Web, www.democraticwoman.org

Studies issues and presents views to congressional committees, the Democratic Party Platform Committee, Democratic leadership groups, elected officials, and other interested groups.

Young Democrats of America, *910 17th St. N.W., #215 20006 (mailing address: P.O. Box 77496, Washington, DC 20013-8496); (202) 639-8585. Fax, (202) 318-3221. David Hardt, President. Press, (202) 256-7183.*
General e-mail, office@yda.org

Web, www.yda.org

Official youth arm of the Democratic Party with state and local chapters. Uses grassroots activist workshops, candidate schools, campaign operative training, and other activities to encourage interest in the political process. Fundraises and monitors legislation and regulations.

Republican

College Republican National Committee, *600 Pennsylvania Ave. S.E., #215 20003-4316; (202) 608-1411. Fax, (202) 608-1429. Charles Smith, National Chair; Ethan Eilon, Executive Director. Information, (888) 765-3564.*
General e-mail, info@crnc.org

Web, www.crnc.org

Membership: Republican college students. Promotes grassroots support for the Republican Party and provides campaign assistance.

National Federation of Republican Women, *124 N. Alfred St., Alexandria, VA 22314; (703) 548-9688. Fax, (703) 548-9836. Shirley Sadler, President.*
General e-mail, mail@nfrw.org

Web, www.nfrw.org

Organizes volunteers for support of Republican candidates for national, state, and local offices; encourages candidacy of Republican women; sponsors campaign management schools. Recruits Republican women candidates for office.

National Republican Congressional Committee, *320 1st St. S.E. 20003; (202) 479-7000. Fax, (202) 863-0693. Rep. Pete Sessions, R–Tex., Chair; Guy Harrison, Executive Director.*
Web, www.nrcc.org

Provides Republican House candidates with campaign assistance, including financial, public relations, media, and direct mail services.

National Republican Senatorial Committee (NRSC), *425 2nd St. N.E. 20002; (202) 675-6000. Fax, (202) 675-4730. Sen. John Cornyn, R–Texas, Chair; Rob Jesmer, Executive Director.*
General e-mail, info@nrsc.org

Web, www.nrsc.org

Provides Republican senatorial candidates with financial and public relations services.

Republican Governors Assn., *1747 Pennsylvania Ave. N.W., #250 20006; (202) 662-4140. Fax, (202) 662-4924.*

Gov. Mark Sanford, R–S.C., Chair; Nick Ayers, Executive Director. Press, (202) 662-4156.
Web, www.rga.org

Serves as a liaison between governors' offices and Republican Party organizations; assists Republican candidates for governor.

Republican Main Street Partnership, *325 7th St. N.W., #610 20004; (202) 393-4353. Fax, (202) 393-4354. Tom Davis, President; Amory Houghton, Chair.*
General e-mail, news@rmsp.org

Web, www.republicanmainstreet.org

Membership: centrist Republican Party members and public officials. Develops and promotes moderate Republican policies.

Republican National Committee (RNC), *310 1st St. S.E. 20003; (202) 863-8500. Fax, (202) 863-8820. Michael Steele, President. Press, (202) 863-8614.*
General e-mail, info@gop.com

Web, www.rnc.org

Develops and promotes Republican Party policies and positions; assists Republican candidates for state and national office; sponsors workshops to recruit Republican candidates and provide instruction in campaign techniques; organizes national political activities; works with state and local officials and organizations.

Republican National Committee (RNC), Communications, *310 1st St. S.E. 20003; (202) 863-8614. Fax, (202) 863-8773. Trevor Francis, Director; Alex Conant, Press Secretary.*
General e-mail, RNcommunications@gop.com

Web, www.rnc.org

Assists federal, state, and local Republican candidates and officials in delivering a coordinated message on current issues; works to improve and expand relations with the press and to increase the visibility of Republican officials and the Republican message.

Republican National Committee (RNC), Counsel, *310 1st St. S.E. 20003; (202) 863-8638. Fax, (202) 863-8654. Vacant, General Counsel; Heather Sidwell, Deputy Counsel. Press, (202) 863-8614.*
General e-mail, counsel@gop.com

Web, www.rnc.org

Responsible for legal affairs of the RNC, including equal time and fairness cases before the Federal Communications Commission. Advises the RNC and state parties on redistricting and campaign finance law compliance.

Republican National Committee (RNC), Finance, *310 1st St. S.E. 20003; (202) 863-8720. Fax, (202) 863-8690. Vacant, Director; Debbie Lee Hardy, Deputy Director.*
General e-mail, finance@gop.com

Web, www.rnc.org

Responsible for developing the Republican Party's financial base. Coordinates fundraising efforts for and gives financial support to Republican candidates in national, state, and local campaigns.

Republican National Hispanic Assembly, *12125 Windsor Hall Way, Herndon, VA 20170; (206) 984-9153. Raul "Danny" Vargas, Chair; Larry Meneses, Vice Chair. General e-mail, info@rnha.org*

Web, www.rnha.org

Seeks to develop a strong, effective, and informed Hispanic Republican constituency. Encourages Hispanic Americans to seek office at all levels of government; provides information and offers advisory services to Republican candidates, officeholders, and party organizations.

Ripon Society, *1300 L St. N.W., #900 20005; (202) 216-1008. George McNeill, Chief Administrative Officer. General e-mail, info@riponsoc.org*

Web, www.riponsoc.org

Membership: moderate Republicans. Works for the adoption of moderate policies within the Republican party.

Other Political Parties

Green Party of the United States, *1711 18th St. N.W. 20009 (mailing address: P.O. Box 57065, Washington, DC 20037); (202) 319-7191. Fax, (202) 319-7193. Brent McMillan, Political Director. Press, (202) 518-5624. Toll-free, (866) 414-7336. General e-mail, info@greenparty.org*

Web, www.gp.org

Committed to environmentalism, nonviolence, social justice, and grassroots organizing.

Libertarian Party, *2600 Virginia Ave. N.W., #200 20037; (202) 333-0008. Fax, (202) 333-0072. Robert Kraus, Executive Director (Acting); Vacant, Political Director. Press, (202) 333-0008, ext. 225. Toll-free, (800) 353-2887. General e-mail, info@hq.lp.org*

Web, www.lp.org

Nationally organized political party. Seeks to bring libertarian ideas into the national political debate. Believes in the primacy of the individual over government; supports property rights, free trade, and eventual elimination of taxes.

111th Congress

Delegations to the 111th Congress

Following are the senators and representatives of state delegations for the 111th Congress. This information is current as of May 1, 2009. Senators are presented first and listed according to seniority. Representatives follow, listed by district. Freshman members appear in italics and "AL" indicates at-large members.

ALABAMA

Richard C. Shelby (R)
Jeff Sessions (R)
 1. Jo Bonner (R)
 2. *Bobby Bright (D)*
 3. Mike Rogers (R)
 4. Robert B. Aderholt (R)
 5. *Parker Griffith (D)*
 6. Spencer Bachus (R)
 7. Artur Davis (D)

ALASKA

Lisa Murkowski (R)
Mark Begich (D)
 AL Don Young (R)

AMERICAN SAMOA

AL Eni F. H. Faleomavaega (D)

ARIZONA

John McCain (R)
Jon Kyl (R)
 1. *Anne Kirkpatrick (D)*
 2. Trent Franks (R)
 3. John Shadegg (R)
 4. Ed Pastor (D)
 5. Harry Mitchell (D)
 6. Jeff Flake (R)
 7. Raúl M. Grijalva (D)
 8. Gabrielle Giffords (D)

ARKANSAS

Blanche L. Lincoln (D)
Mark Pryor (D)
 1. Marion Berry (D)
 2. Vic Snyder (D)
 3. John Boozman (R)
 4. Mike Ross (D)

CALIFORNIA

Dianne Feinstein (D)
Barbara Boxer (D)
 1. Mike Thompson (D)
 2. Wally Herger (R)
 3. Dan Lungren (R)
 4. *Tom McClintock (R)*
 5. Doris Matsui (D)
 6. Lynn Woolsey (D)
 7. George Miller (D)
 8. Nancy Pelosi (D)
 9. Barbara Lee (D)
 10. Ellen O. Tauscher (D)
 11. Jerry McNerney (D)
 12. Jackie Speier (D)
 13. Pete Stark (D)
 14. Anna G. Eshoo (D)
 15. Mike Honda (D)
 16. Zoe Lofgren (D)
 17. Sam Farr (D)
 18. Dennis A. Cardoza (D)
 19. George P. Radanovich (R)
 20. Jim Costa (D)
 21. Devin Nunes (R)
 22. Kevin McCarthy (R)
 23. Lois Capps (D)
 24. Elton Gallegly (R)
 25. Howard P. "Buck" McKeon (R)
 26. David Dreier (R)
 27. Brad Sherman (D)
 28. Howard L. Berman (D)
 29. Adam Schiff (D)
 30. Henry A. Waxman (D)
 31. Xavier Becerra (D)
 32. Vacant
 33. Diane E. Watson (D)
 34. Lucille Roybal-Allard (D)
 35. Maxine Waters (D)
 36. Jane Harman (D)
 37. Laura Richardson (D)
 38. Grace F. Napolitano (D)
 39. Linda Sánchez (D)
 40. Edward R. Royce (R)
 41. Jerry Lewis (R)
 42. Gary Miller (R)
 43. Joe Baca (D)
 44. Ken Calvert (R)
 45. Mary Bono Mack (R)
 46. Dana Rohrabacher (R)
 47. Loretta Sanchez (D)
 48. John Campbell (R)
 49. Darrell Issa (R)
 50. Brian P. Bilbray (R)
 51. Bob Filner (D)
 52. Duncan Hunter (R)
 53. Susan Davis (D)

COLORADO

Mark Udall (D)
Michael F. Bennet (D)
 1. Diana L. DeGette (D)
 2. *Jared Polis (D)*
 3. John T. Salazar (D)
 4. *Betsy Markey (D)*
 5. Doug Lamborn (R)
 6. *Mike Coffman (R)*
 7. Ed Perlmutter (D)

CONNECTICUT

Christopher J. Dodd (D)
Joseph I. Lieberman (I)
 1. John B. Larson (D)
 2. Joe Courtney (D)
 3. Rosa L. DeLauro (D)
 4. *Jim Himes (D)*
 5. Christopher Murphy (D)

DELAWARE

Thomas R. Carper (D)
Edward E. "Ted" Kaufman (D)
 AL Michael N. Castle (R)

DISTRICT OF COLUMBIA

AL Eleanor Holmes Norton (D)

FLORIDA

Bill Nelson (D)
Mel Martinez (R)
1. Jeff Miller (R)
2. F. Allen Boyd Jr. (D)
3. Corrine Brown (D)
4. Ander Crenshaw (R)
5. Ginny Brown-Waite (R)
6. Clifford B. Stearns (R)
7. John L. Mica (R)
8. *Alan Grayson (D)*
9. Gus Bilirakis (R)
10. C. W. "Bill" Young (R)
11. Kathy Castor (D)
12. Adam H. Putnam (R)
13. Vern Buchanan (R)
14. Connie Mack (R)
15. *Bill Posey (R)*
16. *Tom Rooney (R)*
17. Kendrick B. Meek (D)
18. Ileana Ros-Lehtinen (R)
19. Robert Wexler (D)
20. Debbie Wasserman Schultz (D)
21. Lincoln Diaz-Balart (R)
22. Ron Klein (D)
23. Alcee L. Hastings (D)
24. *Suzanne M. Kosmas (D)*
25. Mario Diaz-Balart (R)

GEORGIA

Saxby Chambliss (R)
Johnny Isakson (R)
1. Jack Kingston (R)
2. Sanford D. Bishop Jr. (D)
3. Lynn A. Westmoreland (R)
4. Hank Johnson (D)
5. John Lewis (D)
6. Tom Price (R)
7. John Linder (R)
8. Jim Marshall (D)
9. Nathan Deal (R)
10. Paul C. Broun (R)
11. Phil Gingrey (R)
12. John Barrow (D)
13. David Scott (D)

GUAM

AL Madeleine Z. Bordallo (D)

HAWAII

Daniel K. Inouye (D)
Daniel K. Akaka (D)
1. Neil Abercrombie (D)
2. Mazie K. Hirono (D)

IDAHO

Michael D. Crapo (R)
James E. Risch (R)
1. *Walt Minnick (D)*
2. Mike Simpson (R)

ILLINOIS

Richard J. Durbin (D)
Roland W. Burris (D)
1. Bobby L. Rush (D)
2. Jesse L. Jackson Jr. (D)
3. Daniel Lipinski (D)
4. Luis V. Gutierrez (D)
5. *Mike Quigley (D)*
6. Peter Roskam (R)
7. Danny K. Davis (D)
8. Melissa Bean (D)
9. Jan Schakowsky (D)
10. Mark Steven Kirk (R)
11. *Debbie Halvorson (D)*
12. Jerry F. Costello (D)
13. Judy Biggert (R)
14. Bill Foster (D)
15. Timothy V. Johnson (R)
16. Donald A. Manzullo (R)
17. Phil Hare (D)
18. *Aaron Schock (R)*
19. John M. Shimkus (R)

INDIANA

Richard G. Lugar (R)
Evan Bayh (D)
1. Peter J. Visclosky (D)
2. Joe Donnelly (D)
3. Mark Souder (R)
4. Steve Buyer (R)
5. Dan Burton (R)
6. Mike Pence (R)
7. André Carson (D)
8. Brad Ellsworth (D)
9. Baron Hill (D)

IOWA

Charles E. Grassley (R)
Tom Harkin (D)
1. Bruce Braley (D)
2. Dave Loebsack (D)
3. Leonard L. Boswell (D)
4. Tom Latham (R)
5. Steve King (R)

KANSAS

Sam Brownback (R)
Pat Roberts (R)
1. Jerry Moran (R)
2. *Lynn Jenkins (R)*
3. Dennis Moore (D)
4. Todd Tiahrt (R)

KENTUCKY

Mitch McConnell (R)
Jim Bunning (R)
1. Ed Whitfield (R)
2. *Brett Guthrie (R)*
3. John Yarmuth (D)
4. Geoff Davis (R)
5. Hal Rogers (R)
6. Ben Chandler (D)

LOUISIANA

Mary L. Landrieu (D)
David Vitter (R)
1. Steve Scalise (R)
2. *Anh Joseph Cao (R)*
3. Charlie Melancon (D)
4. *John Fleming (R)*
5. Rodney Alexander (R)
6. *Bill Cassidy (R)*
7. Charles Boustany Jr. (R)

MAINE

Olympia J. Snowe (R)
Susan M. Collins (R)
1. *Chellie Pingree (D)*
2. Michael Michaud (D)

MARYLAND

Barbara A. Mikulski (D)
Benjamin L. Cardin (D)
1. *Frank M. Kratovil Jr. (D)*
2. C. A. "Dutch" Ruppersberger (D)
3. John P. Sarbanes (D)
4. Donna Edwards (D)
5. Steny H. Hoyer (D)
6. Roscoe G. Bartlett (R)
7. Elijah E. Cummings (D)
8. Chris Van Hollen (D)

MASSACHUSETTS

Edward M. Kennedy (D)
John F. Kerry (D)
1. John W. Olver (D)
2. Richard E. Neal (D)
3. James P. McGovern (D)
4. Barney Frank (D)
5. Niki Tsongas (D)
6. John F. Tierney (D)
7. Edward J. Markey (D)
8. Michael E. Capuano (D)
9. Stephen F. Lynch (D)
10. William D. Delahunt (D)

MICHIGAN

Carl Levin (D)
Debbie Stabenow (D)
  1. Bart Stupak (D)
  2. Peter Hoekstra (R)
  3. Vernon J. Ehlers (R)
  4. Dave Camp (R)
  5. Dale E. Kildee (D)
  6. Fred Upton (R)
  7. *Mark Schauer (D)*
  8. Mike Rogers (R)
  9. *Gary Peters (D)*
  10. Candice Miller (R)
  11. Thaddeus McCotter (R)
  12. Sander M. Levin (D)
  13. Carolyn Cheeks Kilpatrick (D)
  14. John Conyers Jr. (D)
  15. John D. Dingell (D)

MINNESOTA

Vacancy
Amy Klobuchar (D)
  1. Tim Walz (D)
  2. John Kline (R)
  3. *Erik Paulsen (R)*
  4. Betty McCollum (D)
  5. Keith Ellison (D)
  6. Michele Bachmann (R)
  7. Collin C. Peterson (D)
  8. James L. Oberstar (D)

MISSISSIPPI

Thad Cochran (R)
Roger F. Wicker (R)
  1. Travis Childers (D)
  2. Bennie G. Thompson (D)
  3. *Gregg Harper (R)*
  4. Gene Taylor (D)

MISSOURI

Christopher S. Bond (R)
Claire McCaskill (D)
  1. William Lacy Clay (D)
  2. Todd Akin (R)
  3. Russ Carnahan (D)
  4. Ike Skelton (D)
  5. Emanuel Cleaver (D)
  6. Sam Graves (R)
  7. Roy D. Blunt (R)
  8. Jo Ann Emerson (R)
  9. *Blaine Luetkemeyer (R)*

MONTANA

Max S. Baucus (D)
Jon Tester (D)
  AL Dennis Rehberg (R)

NEBRASKA

E. Benjamin Nelson (D)
Mike Johanns (R)
  1. Jeff Fortenberry (R)
  2. Lee Terry (R)
  3. Adrian Smith (R)

NEVADA

Harry M. Reid (D)
John Ensign (R)
  1. Shelley Berkley (D)
  2. Dean Heller (R)
  3. *Dina Titus (D)*

NEW HAMPSHIRE

Judd Gregg (R)
Jeanne Shaheen (D)
  1. Carol Shea-Porter (D)
  2. Paul Hodes (D)

NEW JERSEY

Frank R. Lautenberg (D)
Robert Menendez (D)
  1. Robert E. Andrews (D)
  2. Frank A. LoBiondo (R)
  3. *John Adler (D)*
  4. Christopher H. Smith (R)
  5. Scott Garrett (R)
  6. Frank Pallone Jr. (D)
  7. *Leonard Lance (R)*
  8. William J. Pascrell Jr. (D)
  9. Steve Rothman (D)
  10. Donald M. Payne (D)
  11. Rodney P. Frelinghuysen (R)
  12. Rush Holt (D)
  13. Albio Sires (D)

NEW MEXICO

Jeff Bingaman (D)
Tom Udall (D)
  1. *Martin T. Heinrich (D)*
  2. *Harry Teague (D)*
  3. *Ben R. Luján (D)*

NEW YORK

Charles E. Schumer (D)
Kirsten Gillibrand (D)
  1. Timothy H. Bishop (D)
  2. Steve Israel (D)
  3. Peter T. King (R)
  4. Carolyn McCarthy (D)
  5. Gary L. Ackerman (D)
  6. Gregory W. Meeks (D)
  7. Joseph Crowley (D)
  8. Jerrold Nadler (D)
  9. Anthony D. Weiner (D)
  10. Edolphus Towns (D)
  11. Yvette Clarke (D)
  12. Nydia M. Velázquez (D)
  13. *Michael McMahon (D)*
  14. Carolyn B. Maloney (D)
  15. Charles B. Rangel (D)
  16. José E. Serrano (D)
  17. Eliot L. Engel (D)
  18. Nita M. Lowey (D)
  19. John Hall (D)
  20. *Scott Murphy (D)*
  21. *Paul D. Tonko (D)*
  22. Maurice D. Hinchey (D)
  23. John M. McHugh (R)
  24. Michael Arcuri (D)
  25. *Dan Maffei (D)*
  26. *Christopher Lee (R)*
  27. Brian Higgins (D)
  28. Louise M. Slaughter (D)
  29. *Eric J.J. Massa (D)*

NORTH CAROLINA

Richard M. Burr (R)
Kay Hagan (D)
  1. G. K. Butterfield (D)
  2. Bob Etheridge (D)
  3. Walter B. Jones (R)
  4. David E. Price (D)
  5. Virginia Foxx (R)
  6. Howard Coble (R)
  7. Mike McIntyre (D)
  8. *Larry Kissell (D)*
  9. Sue Myrick (R)
  10. Patrick McHenry (R)
  11. Heath Shuler (D)
  12. Melvin L. Watt (D)
  13. Brad Miller (D)

NORTH DAKOTA

Kent Conrad (D)
Byron L. Dorgan (D)
  AL Earl Pomeroy (D)

OHIO

George V. Voinovich (R)
Sherrod Brown (D)
  1. *Steve Driehaus (D)*
  2. Jean Schmidt (R)
  3. Michael Turner (R)
  4. Jim Jordan (R)
  5. Robert E. Latta (R)
  6. Charlie Wilson (D)
  7. *Steve Austria (R)*
  8. John A. Boehner (R)
  9. Marcy Kaptur (D)

10. Dennis J. Kucinich (D)
11. *Marcia L. Fudge (D)*
12. Patrick J. Tiberi (R)
13. Betty Sutton (D)
14. Steven C. LaTourette (R)
15. *Mary Jo Kilroy (D)*
16. *John A. Buccieri (D)*
17. Tim Ryan (D)
18. Zack Space (D)

OKLAHOMA

James M. Inhofe (R)
Tom Coburn (R)
1. John Sullivan (R)
2. Dan Boren (D)
3. Frank D. Lucas (R)
4. Tom Cole (R)
5. Mary Fallin (R)

OREGON

Ron Wyden (D)
Jeff Merkley (D)
1. David Wu (D)
2. Greg Walden (R)
3. Earl Blumenauer (D)
4. Peter A. DeFazio (D)
5. *Kurt Schrader (D)*

PENNSYLVANIA

Arlen Specter (D)
Robert P. Casey (D)
1. Robert A. Brady (D)
2. Chaka Fattah (D)
3. Kathy Dahlkemper (D)
4. Jason Altmire (D)
5. *Glenn W. Thompson (R)*
6. Jim Gerlach (R)
7. Joe Sestak (D)
8. Patrick Murphy (D)
9. Bill Shuster (R)
10. Christopher P. Carney (D)
11. Paul E. Kanjorski (D)
12. John P. Murtha (D)
13. Allyson Y. Schwartz (D)
14. Mike Doyle (D)
15. Charlie Dent (R)
16. Joseph R. Pitts (R)
17. Tim Holden (D)
18. Tim Murphy (R)
19. Todd Russell Platts (R)

PUERTO RICO

AL *Pedro D. Pierluisi (D)*

RHODE ISLAND

Jack Reed (D)
Sheldon Whitehouse (D)
1. Patrick J. Kennedy (D)
2. James R. Langevin (D)

SOUTH CAROLINA

Lindsey O. Graham (R)
Jim DeMint (R)
1. Henry E. Brown Jr. (R)
2. Joe Wilson (R)
3. J. Gresham Barrett (R)
4. Bob Inglis (R)
5. John M. Spratt Jr. (D)
6. James E. Clyburn (D)

SOUTH DAKOTA

Tim Johnson (D)
John Thune (R)
AL Stephanie Herseth Sandlin (D)

TENNESSEE

Lamar Alexander (R)
Bob Corker (R)
1. *Phil Roe (R)*
2. John J. Duncan Jr. (R)
3. Zach Wamp (R)
4. Lincoln Davis (D)
5. Jim Cooper (D)
6. Bart Gordon (D)
7. Marsha Blackburn (R)
8. John S. Tanner (D)
9. Steve Cohen (D)

TEXAS

Kay Bailey Hutchison (R)
John Cornyn (R)
1. Louie Gohmert (R)
2. Ted Poe (R)
3. Sam Johnson (R)
4. Ralph M. Hall (R)
5. Jeb Hensarling (R)
6. Joe Barton (R)
7. John Culberson (R)
8. Kevin Brady (R)
9. Al Green (D)
10. Michael McCaul (R)
11. K. Michael Conaway (R)
12. Kay Granger (R)
13. Mac Thornberry (R)
14. Ron Paul (R)
15. Rubén Hinojosa (D)
16. Silvestre Reyes (D)
17. Chet Edwards (D)
18. Sheila Jackson Lee (D)
19. Randy Neugebauer (R)
20. Charles A. Gonzalez (D)
21. Lamar Smith (R)
22. *Pete Olson (R)*
23. Ciro D. Rodriguez (D)
24. Kenny Marchant (R)
25. Lloyd Doggett (D)
26. Michael Burgess (R)
27. Solomon P. Ortiz (D)
28. Henry Cuellar (D)
29. Gene Green (D)
30. Eddie Bernice Johnson (D)
31. John R. Carter (R)
32. Pete Sessions (R)

UTAH

Orrin G. Hatch (R)
Robert F. Bennett (R)
1. Rob Bishop (R)
2. Jim Matheson (D)
3. *Jason Chaffetz (R)*

VERMONT

Patrick Leahy (D)
Bernard Sanders (I)
AL Peter Welch (D)

VIRGIN ISLANDS

AL Donna M. Christensen (D)

VIRGINIA

James H. Webb Jr. (D)
Mark Warner (D)
1. Rob Wittman (R)
2. *Glenn C. Nye (D)*
3. Robert C. Scott (D)
4. J. Randy Forbes (R)
5. *Tom Perriello (D)*
6. Bob Goodlatte (R)
7. Eric I. Cantor (R)
8. Jim Moran (D)
9. Rick Boucher (D)
10. Frank R. Wolf (R)
11. *Gerry Connolly (D)*

WASHINGTON

Patty Murray (D)
Maria Cantwell (D)
1. Jay Inslee (D)
2. Rick Larsen (D)
3. Brian Baird (D)
4. Doc Hastings (R)

5. Cathy McMorris
   Rodgers (R)
6. Norm Dicks (D)
7. Jim McDermott (D)
8. Dave Reichert (R)
9. Adam Smith (D)

WEST VIRGINIA

Robert C. Byrd (D)
John D. Rockefeller IV (D)

1. Alan B. Mollohan (D)
2. Shelley Moore Capito (R)
3. Nick J. Rahall II (D)

WISCONSIN

Herb Kohl (D)
Russell D. Feingold (D)
1. Paul D. Ryan (R)
2. Tammy Baldwin (D)
3. Ron Kind (D)

4. Gwen Moore (D)
5. F. James Sensenbrenner Jr. (R)
6. Thomas E. Petri (R)
7. David R. Obey (D)
8. Steve Kagen (D)

WYOMING

Michael B. Enzi (R)
John Barrasso (R)
   AL Cynthia M. Lummis (R)

House Committees

The standing and select committees of the U.S. House of Representatives follow. Each listing includes the room number, office building, zip code, telephone and fax numbers, Web address, e-mail address if available, key majority and minority staff members, jurisdiction for each full committee, and party ratio. Subcommittees are listed under the full committees. Members are listed in order of seniority on the committee or subcommittee. Many committees and subcommittees may be contacted via Web-based e-mail forms found on their Web sites.

Democrats, the current majority, are shown in roman type; Republicans, in the minority, appear in italic. Vacancy indicates that a committee or subcommittee seat had not been filled as of May 1, 2009. The partisan committees of the House are listed on page 750. The area code for all phone and fax numbers is (202). A phone number and/or office number next to either the Majority or Minority Staff Director indicates a change from the full committee's office number and/or phone number. If no numbers are listed, the individual's office number and phone number are the same as for the full committee.

AGRICULTURE

Office: 1301 LHOB 20515-6001
Phone: 225-2171 **Fax:** 225-8510
Web: agriculture.house.gov
E-mail: agriculture@mail.house.gov
Majority Chief of Staff: Rob Larew
Minority Staff Director: Nicole Scott 225-0029 1305 LHOB

Jurisdiction: (1) adulteration of seeds, insect pests, and protection of birds and animals in forest reserves; (2) agriculture generally; (3) agricultural and industrial chemistry; (4) agricultural colleges and experiment stations; (5) agricultural economics and research; (6) agricultural education extension services; (7) agricultural production and marketing, and stabilization of prices of agricultural products and commodities (not including distribution outside of the United States); (8) animal industry and diseases of animals; (9) commodities exchanges; (10) crop insurance and soil conservation; (11) dairy industry; (12) entomology and plant quarantine; (13) extension of farm credit and farm security; (14) livestock inspection, poultry inspection, meat and meat products inspection, and seafood and seafood products inspection; (15) forestry in general, and forest reserves other than those created from the public domain; (16) human nutrition and home economics; (17) plant industry, soils, and agricultural engineering; (18) rural electrification; (19) rural development; (20) water conservation related to activities of the Department of Agriculture. The chair and ranking minority member are ex officio members of all subcommittees of which they are not regular members.
Party Ratio: D 28 R-18

Collin C. Peterson, Minn., Chair	*Frank D. Lucas, Okla., Ranking Minority Member*
Tim Holden, Pa.	*Bob Goodlatte, Va.*
Mike McIntyre, N.C.	*Rep. Jerry Moran, Kans.*
Leonard L. Boswell, Iowa	*Timothy V. Johnson, Ill.*
Joe Baca, Calif.	*Sam Graves, Mo.*
Dennis A. Cardoza, Calif.	*Mike Rogers, Alab.*
David Scott, Ga.	*Steve King, Iowa*
Jim Marshall, Ga.	*Randy Neugebauer, Tex.*
Stephanie Herseth Sandlin, S.D.	*K. Michael Conaway, Tex.*
Henry Cuellar, Tex.	*Jeff Fortenberry, Neb.*
	Jean Schmidt, Ohio

Jim Costa, Calif.	*Adrian Smith, Neb.*
Brad Ellsworth, Ind.	*Robert E. Latta, Ohio*
Tim Walz, Minn.	*Phil Roe, Tenn.*
Steve Kagen, Wisc.	*Blaine Luetkemeyer, Mo.*
Kurt Schrader, Oreg.	*Glenn W. Thompson, Pa.*
Debbie Halvorson, Ill.	*Bill Cassidy, La.*
Kathy Dahlkemper, Pa.	*Cynthia M. Lummis, Wyo.*
Eric J. J. Massa, N.Y.	
Bobby Bright, Ala.	
Betsy Markey, Colo.	
Frank M. Kratovil Jr., Md.	
Mark Schauer, Mich.	
Larry Kissell, N.C.	
John A. Boccieri, Ohio	
Scott Murphy, N.Y.	
Earl Pomeroy, N.D.	
Travis Childers, Miss.	
Walt Minnick, Idaho	

Subcommittees

Conservation, Credit, Energy, and Research
Office: 1336 LHOB **Phone:** 225-0420
Tim Holden (Chair), Stephanie Herseth Sandlin, Debbie Halvorson, Kathy Dahlkemper, Betsy Markey, Mark Schauer, Larry Kissell, John A. Boccieri, Mike McIntyre, Jim Costa, Brad Ellsworth, Tim Walz, Eric J.J. Massa, Bobby Bright, Frank M. Kratovil Jr., Walt Minnick, Earl Pomeroy, Vacancy
Bob Goodlatte, Jerry Moran, Sam Graves, Mike Rogers, Steve King, Randy Neugebauer, Jean Schmidt, Adrian Smith, Robert E. Latta, Blaine Luetkemeyer, Glenn W. Thompson, Bill Cassidy

Department Operations, Oversight, Nutrition, and Forestry
Office: 1407 LHOB **Phone:** 225-6395
Joe Baca (Chair), Henry Cuellar, Steve Kagen, Kurt Schrader, Kathy Dahlkemper, Travis Childers
Jeff Fortenberry, Steve King, Jean Schmidt, Cynthia Lummis

General Farm Commodities and Risk Management
Office: 1407 LHOB **Phone:** 225-0720
Leonard L. Boswell (Chair), Jim Marshall, Brad Ellsworth, Tim Walz, Kurt Schrader, Stephanie Herseth Sandlin, Betsy Markey, Larry Kissell, Debbie Halvorson, Earl Pomeroy, Travis Childers

Jerry Moran (Ranking Minority Member), Timothy V. Johnson, Sam Graves, Steve King, K. Michael Conaway, Robert E. Latta, Blaine Luetkemeyer

Horticulture and Organic Agriculture
Office: 1336 LHOB   **Phone:** 225-6238
Dennis A. Cardoza (Chair), Eric J.J. Massa, Jim Costa, Kurt Schrader, Frank M. Kratovil Jr., Vacancy
Jean Schmidt, Jerry Moran, Timothy V. Johnson, Cynthia Lummis

Livestock, Dairy, and Poultry
Office: 1336 LHOB   **Phone:** 225-8407
David Scott (Chair), Jim Costa, Steve Kagen, Frank M. Kratovil Jr., Tim Holden, Leonard L. Boswell, Joe Baca, Dennis A. Cardoza, Betsy Markey, Walt Minnick, Vacancy
Randy Neugebauer, Bob Goodlatte, Mike Rogers, Steve King, K. Michael Conaway, Adrian Smith, Phil Roe

Rural Development, Biotechnology, Specialty Crops, and Foreign Agriculture
Office: 1407 LHOB   **Phone:** 225-8248
Mike McIntyre (Chair), Bobby Bright, Jim Marshall, Henry Cuellar, Larry Kissell, Walt Minnick
K. Michael Conaway, Phil Roe, Glenn W. Thompson, Bill Cassidy

APPROPRIATIONS

Office: H-218 CAP 20515-6015
Phone: 225-2771
Web: appropriations.house.gov
Majority Staff Director: Beverly Aimaro Pheto
Minority Staff Director: Jeff S. Shockey 225-3481 1016 LHOB
Jurisdiction: (1) appropriation of the revenue for the support of the Government; (2) rescissions of appropriations contained in appropriations acts; (3) transfers of unexpected balances; (4) Bills and Joint Resolutions reported by other Committees that provide new entitlement authority as defined in Section 3(9) of the Congressional Budget Act of 1974 and referred to the Committee under Clause 4(a)(2).
Party Ratio: D 37-R 23

David R. Obey, Wisc., Chair	Jerry Lewis, Calif., Ranking
John P. Murtha, Pa.	Minority Member
Norm Dicks, Wash.	C. W. "Bill" Young, Fla.
Alan B. Mollohan, W.Va.	Hal Rogers, Ky.
Marcy Kaptur, Ohio	Frank R. Wolf, Va.
Peter J. Visclosky, Ind.	Jack Kingston, Ga.
Nita M. Lowey, N.Y.	Rodney P. Frelinghuysen, N.J.
José E. Serrano, N.Y.	Todd Tiahrt, Kan.
Rosa L. DeLauro, Conn.	Zach Wamp, Tenn.
Jim Moran, Va.	Tom Latham, Iowa
John W. Olver, Mass.	Robert B. Aderholt, Ala.
Ed Pastor, Ariz.	Jo Ann Emerson, Mo.
David E. Price, N.C.	Kay Granger, Tex.
Chet Edwards, Tex.	Mike Simpson, Idaho
Patrick J. Kennedy, R.I.	John Culberson, Tex.
Maurice D. Hinchey, N.Y.	Mark Steven Kirk, Ill.
Lucille Roybal-Allard, Calif.	Ander Crenshaw, Fla.

Sam Farr, Calif.	Dennis Rehberg, Mont.
Jesse L. Jackson Jr., Ill.	John R. Carter, Tex.
Carolyn Cheeks Kilpatrick, Mich.	Rodney Alexander, La.
	Ken Calvert, Calif.
F. Allen Boyd Jr., Fla.	Jo Bonner, Ala.
Chaka Fattah, Pa.	Steven C. LaTourette, Ohio
Steve Rothman, N.J.	Tom Cole, Okla.
Sanford D. Bishop Jr., Ga.	
Marion Berry, Ark.	
Barbara Lee, Calif.	
Adam Schiff, Calif.	
Mike Honda, Calif.	
Betty McCollum, Minn.	
Steve Israel, N.Y.	
Tim Ryan, Ohio	
C. A. "Dutch" Ruppersberger, Md.	
Ben Chandler, Ky.	
Debbie Wasserman Schultz, Fla.	
Ciro D. Rodriguez, Tex.	
Lincoln Davis, Tenn.	
John T. Salazar, Colo.	

Subcommittees

Agriculture, Rural Development, Food and Drug Administration, and Related Agencies
Office: 2362A RHOB   **Phone:** 225-2638
Rosa L. DeLauro (Chair), Sam Farr, F. Allen Boyd Jr., Sanford D. Bishop, Lincoln Davis, Marcy Kaptur, Maurice D. Hinchey, Jesse L. Jackson Jr.
Jack Kingston (Ranking Minority Member), Tom Latham, Jo Ann Emerson, Rodney Alexander

Commerce, Justice, Science, and Related Agencies
Office: H-309 CAP   **Phone:** 225-3351
Alan B. Mollohan (Chair), Patrick J. Kennedy, Chaka Fattah, Adam Schiff, Mike Honda, C. A. "Dutch" Ruppersberger, Peter J. Visclosky, José E. Serrano
Frank R. Wolf (Ranking Minority Member), John Culberson, Robert B. Aderholt, Jo Bonner

Defense
Office: H-149 CAP   **Phone:** 225-2847
John P. Murtha (Chair), Norm Dicks, Peter J. Visclosky, Jim Moran, Marcy Kaptur, F. Allen Boyd, Steve Rothman, Sanford D. Bishop, Maurice D. Hinchey, Carolyn Cheeks Kilpatrick
C. W. "Bill" Young (Ranking Minority Member), Rodney P. Frelinghuysen, Todd Tiahrt, Jack Kingston, Kay Granger, Hal Rogers

Energy and Water Development, and Related Agencies
Office: 2362B RHOB   **Phone:** 225-3421
Peter J. Visclosky (Chair), Chet Edwards, Ed Pastor, Marion Berry, Chaka Fattah, Steve Israel, Tim Ryan, John W. Olver, Lincoln Davis, John T. Salazar
Rodney Frelinghuysen (Ranking Minority Member), Zach Wamp, Mike Simpson, Dennis Rehberg, Ken Calvert, Rodney Alexander

APPROPRIATIONS (continued)

Financial Services and General Government
Office: 1040A LHOB   **Phone:** 225-7245

José E. Serrano (Chair), Debbie Wasserman Schultz, Rosa L. DeLauro, Chet Edwards, F. Allen Boyd Jr., Chaka Fattah, Barbara Lee, Adam Schiff

Jo Ann Emerson (Ranking Minority Member), John Culberson, Mark Steven Kirk, Ander Crenshaw

Homeland Security
Office: B307 RHOB   **Phone:** 225-5834

David E. Price (Chair), José E. Serrano, Ciro D. Rodriguez, C.A. Dutch Ruppersberger, Alan Mollohan, Nita M. Lowey, Lucille Roybal-Allard, Sam Farr, Steve Rothman

Hal Rogers (Ranking Minority Member), John R. Carter, John Culberson, Mark Steven Kirk, Ken Calvert

Interior, Environment, and Related Agencies
Office: B308 RHOB   **Phone:** 225-3081

Norm Dicks (Chair), Jim Moran, Alan B. Mollohan, Ben Chandler, Maurice D. Hinchey, John W. Olver, Ed Pastor, David E. Price

Mike Simpson (Ranking Minority Member), Ken Calvert, Steven C. LaTourette, Tom Cole

Labor, Health and Human Services, Education, and Related Agencies
Office: 2358 RHOB   **Phone:** 225-3508

David R. Obey (Chair), Nita M. Lowey, Rosa L. DeLauro, Jesse L. Jackson Jr., Patrick J. Kennedy, Lucille Roybal-Allard, Barbara Lee, Tom Udall, Mike Honda, Betty McCollum, Tim Ryan, Jim Moran

Todd Tiahrt (Ranking Minority Member), Dennis Rehberg, Rodney Alexander, Jo Bonner, Tom Cole

Legislative Branch
Office: H-147 CAP   **Phone:** 226-7252

Debbie Wasserman Schultz (Chair), Mike Honda, Betty McCollum, Tim Ryan, C. A. "Dutch" Ruppersberger, Ciro D. Rodriguez

Robert B. Aderhold (Ranking Minority Member), Steven C. LaTourette, Tom Cole

Military Construction, Veterans Affairs, and Related Agencies
Office: H-143 CAP   **Phone:** 225-3047

Chet Edwards (Chair), Sam Farr, John T. Salazar, Norm Dicks, Patrick J. Kennedy, Sanford D. Bishop Jr., Marion Berry, Steve Israel

Zach Wamp (Ranking Minority Member), Ander Crenshaw, C. W. "Bill" Young, John R. Carter

State, Foreign Operations, and Related Programs
Office: HB-26 CAP   **Phone:** 225-2041

Nita M. Lowey (Chair), Jesse L. Jackson Jr., Adam Schiff, Steve Israel, Ben Chandler, Steve Rothman, Barbara Lee, Betty McCollum

Kay Granger (Ranking Minority Member), Mark Steven Kirk, Ander Crenshaw, Dennis Rehberg

Transportation, Housing and Urban Development, and Related Agencies
Office: 2358 RHOB   **Phone:** 225-2141

John W. Olver (Chair), Ed Pastor, Ciro D. Rodriguez, Marcy Kaptur, David E. Price, Lucille Roybal-Allard, Marion Berry, Carolyn Cheeks Kilpatrick

Tom Lantham (Ranking Minority Member), Frank R. Wolf, John R. Carter, Steven C. LaTourette

Select Intelligence Oversight Panel
Office: H-149 CAP   **Phone:** 225-2847

Rush Holt (Chair), Dave Obey, John P. Murtha, Silvestre Reyes, Norm Dicks, Nita M. Lowey, Adam Schiff, Steve Israel

Ken Calvert (Ranking Minority Member), Jerry Lewis, C. W. Bill Young, Pete Hoekstra, Rodney P. Frelinghuysen

ARMED SERVICES

Office: 2120 RHOB 20515-6035
Phone: 225-4151 **Fax:** 225-9077
Web: armedservices.house.gov
Majority Staff Director: Erin C. Conaton
Jurisdiction: (1) ammunition depots, forts, arsenals, Army, Navy and Air Force reservations and establishments; (2) common defense generally; (3) conservation, development, and use of naval petroleum reserves and oil shale reserves; (4) the Department of Defense generally, including the Departments of the Army, Navy, and Air Force generally; (5) interoceanic canals generally, including measures relating to the maintenance, operation, and administration of interoceanic canals; (6) United States Merchant Marine Academy (Kings Point, N.Y.), and state maritime academies; (7) military applications of nuclear energy; (8) tactical intelligence and intelligence-related activities of the Department of Defense; (9) national security aspects of the merchant marine, including financial assistance for the construction and operation of vessels, the maintenance of the United States shipbuilding and ship repair industrial base, cabotage (trade or transport in coastal waters or air space, or between two points within a country), cargo preference and merchant marine personnel as these matters relate to the national security; (10) pay, promotion, retirement, and other benefits and privileges of members of the armed forces; (11) scientific research and development in support of the armed services; (12) selective service; (13) size and composition of the Army, Navy, Marine Corps, and Air Force; (14) soldiers' and sailors' homes; (15) strategic and critical materials necessary for the common defense. In addition to its legislative jurisdiction under the preceding provisions (and its general oversight functions under clause 2(b) (1), the committee has special oversight functions provided for in clause 3(a) with respect to international arms control and disarmament and military dependents education.
Party Ratio: D 37-R 25

Ike Skelton, Mo., Chair
John M. Spratt, S.C.
Solomon P. Ortiz, Tex.
Gene Taylor, Miss.
Neil Abercrombie, Hawaii
Silvestre Reyes, Tex.
Vic Snyder, Ark.
Adam Smith, Wash.
Loretta Sanchez, Calif.
Mike McIntyre, N.C.
Ellen O. Tauscher, Calif.
Robert A. Brady, Pa.
Robert E. Andrews, N.J.
Susan Davis, Calif.
James R. Langevin, R.I.
Jim Cooper, Tenn.
Jim Marshall, Ga.
Madeleine Z. Bordallo, Guam
Brad Ellsworth, Ind.
Patrick Murphy, Pa.
Hank Johnson, Ga.
Carol Shea-Porter, N.H.
Joe Courtney, Conn.
Dave Loebsack, Iowa
Joe Sestak, Pa.
Gabrielle Giffords, Ariz.
Niki Tsongas, Mass.
Glenn C. Nye, Va.
Chellie Pingree, Maine
Larry Kissell, N.C.
Martin T. Heinrich, N.M.
Frank M. Kratovil Jr., Md.
Eric J. J. Massa, N.Y.
Bobby Bright, Alab.
Dan Boren Okla.
Scott Murphy N.Y.

John M. McHugh, N.Y., Ranking Minority Member
Roscoe G. Bartlett, Md.
Howard P. "Buck" McKeon, Calif.
Mac Thornberry, Tex.
Walter B. Jones, N.C.
Todd Akin, Mo.
J. Randy Forbes, Va.
Jeff Miller, Fla.
Joe Wilson, S.C.
Frank A. LoBiondo, N.J.
Tom Cole, Okla.
Rob Bishop, Utah
Michael Turner, Ohio
John Kline, Minn.
Mike Rogers, Ala.
Trent Franks, Ariz.
Bill Shuster, Pa.
Cathy McMorris Rodgers, Wash.
K. Michael Conaway, Tex.
Geoff Davis, Ky.
Doug Lamborn, Colo.
Rob Wittman, Va.
Mary Fallin, Okla.
Duncan D. Hunter, Calif.
John Fleming, La.
Mike Coffman, Colo.
Tom Rooney, Fla.

Subcommittees

Air and Land Forces

Office: 2120 RHOB   **Phone:** 225-4151

Neil Abercrombie (Chair), John M. Spratt, Silvestre Reyes, Adam Smith, Mike McIntyre, Ellen O. Tauscher, Robert A. Brady, Jim Cooper, Jim Marshall, Joe Sestak, Gabrielle Giffords, Niki Tsongas, Larry Kissell, Frank M. Kratovil Jr., Eric J. J Massa, Bobby Bright, Vacancy

Roscoe Bartlett (Ranking Minority Member), Cathy McMorris Rodgers, Mary Fallin, Duncan D. Hunter, John Fleming, Mike Coffman, Howard P. Buck McKeon, Todd Akin, Jeff Miller, Joe Wilson, Frank A. LoBiondo, Rob Bishop, Michael Turner

Military Personnel

Office: 2120 RHOB   **Phone:** 225-4151

Susan Davis (Chair), Vic Snyder, Loretta Sanchez, Nancy Boyda, Patrick Murphy, Carol Shea-Porter, Niki Tsongas

Joe Wilson (Ranking Minority Member), Walter B. Jones, John Kline, Tom Rooney, Rob Wittman, Mary Fallin, John Fleming

Oversight and Investigations

Office: 2120 RHOB   **Phone:** 225-4151

Susan Davis (Chair), Vic Snyder, Loretta Sanchez, Madeleine Z. Bordallo, Patrick J. Murphy, Hank Johnson, Carol Shea-Porter, Dave Loebsack, Niki Tsongas

Rob Wittman (Ranking Minority Member), Walter B. Jones, Mike Rogers, Trent Franks, Cathy McMorris Rodgers, Doug Lamborn, Duncan D. Hunter

Readiness

Office: 2120 RHOB   **Phone:** 225-4151

Solomon P. Ortiz (Chair), Gene Taylor, Neil Abercrombie, Silvestre Reyes, Jim Marshall, Madeleine Z. Bordallo, Hank Johnson, Carol Shea-Porter, Joe Courtney, Dave Loebsack, Gabrielle Giffords, Glenn C. Nye, Larry Kissell, Martin T. Heinrich, Frank M. Kratovil Jr., Bobby Bright, Vacancy

J. Randy Forbes (Ranking Minority Member), Rob Bishop, Mike Rogers, Trent Franks, Bill Shuster, Cathy McMorris Rodgers, K. Michael Conaway, Doug Lamborn, Rob Wittman, Mary Fallin, John Fleming, Frank A. LoBiondo

Seapower and Expeditionary Forces

Office: 2120 RHOB   **Phone:** 225-4151

Gene Taylor (Chair), Solomon P. Ortiz, James R. Langevin, Rick Larsen, Brad Ellsworth, Joe Courtney, Joe Sestak, Glenn C. Nye, Chellie Pingree, Eric J. J. Massa

Todd Akin (Ranking Minority Member), Rob Wittman, Roscoe C. Bartlett, J. Randy Forbes, Duncan D. Hunter, Mike Coffman, Tom Rooney

Strategic Forces

Office: 2120 RHOB   **Phone:** 225-4151

Ellen O. Tauscher (Chair), John M. Spratt Jr., Loretta Sanchez, Robert E. Andrews, James R. Langevin, Rick Larsen, Martin T. Heinrich, Vacancy

Michael Turner (Ranking Minority Member), Howard P. Buck McKeon, Mac Thornberry, Trent Franks, Doug Lamborn

Terrorism and Unconventional Threats and Capabilities

Office: 2120 RHOB   **Phone:** 225-4151

Adam Smith (Chair), Mike McIntyre, Robert E. Andrews, James R. Langevin, Jim Cooper, Jim Marshall, Brad Ellsworth, Patrick J. Murphy, Bobby Bright, Vacancy

Jeff Miller (Ranking Minority Member), Frank A. LoBiondo, John Kline, Bill Shuster, K. Michael Conaway, Tom Rooney, Mac Thornberry

BUDGET

Office: 207 CHOB 20515-6065
Phone: 226-7200
Web: budget.house.gov
E-mail: Budget.Democrats@mail.house.gov
Majority Staff Director: Thomas S. Kahn
Minority Staff Director: Austin Smythe 226-7270 B-71 CHOB

BUDGET (continued)

Jurisdiction: (1) all concurrent resolutions on the budget (as defined in Section 3 of the Congressional Budget and Impoundment Control Act of 1974), other matters required to be referred to the committee under Titles III and IV of that Act, and other measures setting forth appropriate levels of budget totals for the United States Government; (2) measures relating to the budget process generally; (3) measures relating to the establishment, extension, and enforcement of special controls over the federal budget, including the budgetary treatment of off-budget federal agencies and measures providing exemption from reduction under any order issued under Part C of the Balanced Budget and Emergency Deficit Control Act of 1985; (4) the Committee shall have the duty: (A) to report the matters required to be reported by it under Titles III and IV of the Congressional Budget and Impoundment Control Act of 1974; (B) to make continuing studies of the effect on budget outlays of relevant existing and proposed legislation and to report the results of such studies to the House on a recurring basis; (C) to request and evaluate continuing studies of tax expenditures to devise methods of coordinating tax expenditures, policies, and programs with direct budget outlays, and to report the results of such studies to the House on a recurring basis; and (D) to review, on a continuing basis, the conduct by the Congressional Budget Office of its functions and duties.

Party Ratio: D 24-R 15

John M. Spratt, S.C., Chair	*Paul D. Ryan, Wisc.,*
Allyson Y. Schwartz, Pa.	*Ranking Minority*
Marcy Kaptur, Ohio	*Member*
Xavier Becerra, Calif.	*Scott Garrett, N.J.*
Lloyd Doggett, Tex.	*Mario Diaz-Balart, Fla.*
Earl Blumenauer, Ore.	*Jeb Hensarling, Tex.*
Marion Berry, Ark.	*Mike Simpson, Idaho*
F. Allen Boyd Jr., Fla.	*Patrick McHenry, N.C.*
James P. McGovern, Mass.	*Connie Mack, Fla.*
Niki Tsongas, Mass.	*John Campbell, Calif.*
Bob Etheridge, N.C.	*Jim Jordan, Ohio*
Betty McCollum, Minn.	*Devin Nunes, Calif.*
Charlie Melancon, La.	*Robert B. Aderholt, Ala.*
John Yarmuth, Ky.	*Cynthia M. Lummis, Wyo.*
Robert E. Andrews, N.J.	*Steve Austria, Ohio*
Rosa L. DeLauro, Conn.	*Gregg Harper, Miss.*
Chet Edwards, Tex.	*Robert Latta Ohio*
Robert C. Scott, Va.	
James R. Langevin, R.I.	
Rick Larsen, Wash.	
Timothy H. Bishop, N.Y.	
Gwen Moore, Wisc.	
Gerry Connolly, Va.	
Kurt Schrader, Oreg.	

EDUCATION AND LABOR

Office: 2181 RHOB 20515-6100
Phone: 225-3725
Web: edworkforce.house.gov
Majority Staff Director: Mark Zuckerman

Minority Staff Director: Sally L. Stroup 225-4527 2101 RHOB

Jurisdiction: (1) child labor; (2) Gallaudet University (Washington, D.C.), Howard University (Washington, D.C.), Howard University Hospital (Washington, D.C.); (3) convict labor and the entry of goods made by convicts into interstate commerce; (4) food programs for children in schools; (5) labor standards and labor statistics; (6) measures relating to education or labor generally; (7) mediation and arbitration of labor disputes; (8) regulation or prevention of importation of foreign laborers under contract; (9) Employees Compensation Appeals Board (Labor); (10) vocational rehabilitation; (11) wages and hours of labor; (12) welfare of miners; (13) work incentive programs. In addition to its legislative jurisdiction under the preceding provisions (and its general oversight function under clause 2 (b)(1), the Committee has the special oversight function provided for in clause 3 (c) with respect to domestic educational programs and institutions, and programs of student assistance, which are within the jurisdiction of other committees.

Party Ratio: D 29-R 19

George Miller, Calif., Chair	*Howard P. "Buck" McKeon,*
Dale E. Kildee, Mich.	*Calif., Ranking Minority*
Donald M. Payne, N.J.	*Member*
Robert E. Andrews, N.J.	*Thomas E. Petri, Wisc.*
Robert C. Scott, Va.	*Peter Hoekstra, Mich.*
Lynn Woolsey, Calif.	*Michael N. Castle, Del.*
Rubén Hinojosa, Tex.	*Mark Souder, Ind.*
Carolyn McCarthy, N.Y.	*Vernon J. Ehlers, Mich.*
John F. Tierney, Mass.	*Judy Biggert, Ill.*
Dennis J. Kucinich, Ohio	*Todd Russell Platts, Pa.*
David Wu, Ore.	*Joe Wilson, S.C.*
Rush Holt, N.J.	*John Kline, Minn.*
Susan Davis, Calif.	*Cathy McMorris Rodgers,*
Danny K. Davis, Ill.	*Wash.*
Raúl M. Grijalva, Ariz.	*Tom Price, Ga.*
Timothy H. Bishop, N.Y.	*Rob Bishop, Utah*
Joe Sestak, Pa.	*Brett Guthrie, Ky.*
Dave Loebsack, Iowa	*Bill Cassidy, La.*
Mazie K. Hirono, Hawaii	*Tom McClintock, Calif.*
Jason Altmire, Pa.	*Duncan D. Hunter, Calif.*
John Yarmuth, Ky.	*Phil Roe, Tenn.*
Phil Hare, Ill.	*Glenn W. Thompson, Pa.*
Yvette Clarke, N.Y.	
Joe Courtney, Conn.	
Carol Shea-Porter, N.H.	
Marcia L. Fudge, Ohio	
Jared Polis, Colo.	
Paul D. Tonko, N.Y.	
Pedro Pierluisi, P.R.	
Gregorio C. Sablan, Northern Mariana Islands	
Dina Titus, Nev.	
Vacancy	

Subcommittees

Early Childhood, Elementary, and Secondary Education
Office: 2181 RHOB   **Phone:** 225-3725

Dale E. Kildee (Chair), Donald M. Payne, Robert C. Scott, Rush Holt, Susan Davis, Raúl M. Grijalva, Joe Sestak, Dave Loebsack, Mazie K. Hirono, Jared Polis, Pedro Pierluisi, Gregorio C. Sablan, Lynn Woosley, Rubén Hinojosa, Dennis J. Kucinich, Jason Altmire, Dina Titus, Vacancy

Michael N. Castle (Ranking Minority Member), Thomas E. Petri, Peter Hoekstra, Mark Souder, Vernon J. Ehlers, Judy Biggert, Todd Russell Platts, Cathy McMorris Rodgers, Rob Bishop, Bill Cassidy, Tom McClintock, Duncan D. Hunter

Health, Employment, Labor, and Pensions
Office: 2181 RHOB **Phone:** 225-3725

Robert E. Andrews (Chair), David Wu, Phil Hare, John F. Tierney, Dennis J. Kucinich, Marcia L. Fudge, Dale E. Kildee, Carolyn McCarthy, Rush Holt, Joe Sestak, Dave Loebsack, Yvette D. Clarke, Joe Courtney

John Kline (Ranking Minority Member), Joe Wilson, Cathy McMorris Rodgers, Tom Price, Brett Guthrie, Tom McClintock, Duncan D. Hunter, Phil Roe

Healthy Families and Communities
Office: 2181 RHOB **Phone:** 225-3725

Carolyn McCarthy (Chair), Yvette Clarke, Robert C. Scott, Carol Shea-Porter, Paul D. Tonko, Jared Polis, George Miller, Vacancy

Todd Russell Platts (Ranking Minority Member), Howard P. "Buck" McKeon, Brett Guthrie, Phil Roe, Glenn "GT" Thompson

Higher Education, Lifelong Learning, and Competitiveness
Office: 2181 RHOB **Phone:** 225-3725

Rubén Hinojosa (Chair), Timothy H. Bishop, Jason Altmire, Joe Courtney, Paul D. Tonko, Dina Titus, Robert E. Andrews, John F. Tierney, David Wu, Susan Davis, Mazie K. Hirono, Marcia L. Fudge, Jared Polis, Pedro Pierluisi

Brett Guthrie (Ranking Minority Member), Howard P. "Buck" McKeon, Michael N. Castle, Mark Souder, Vernon J. Ehlers, Judy Biggert, Bill Cassidy, Phil Roe, Glenn "GT" Thompson

Workforce Protections
Office: 2181 RHOB **Phone:** 225-3725

Lynn Woosley (Chair), Carol Shea-Porter, Donald M. Payne, Raúl M. Grijalva, Timothy H. Bishop, Phil Hare, Gregorio C. Sablan

Tom Prince (Ranking Minority Member), Pete Hoekstra, Joe Wilson, John Kline

ENERGY AND COMMERCE

Office: 2125 RHOB 20515-6115
Phone: 225-2927
Web: energycommerce.house.gov
Majority Chief of Staff: Dennis B. Fitzgibbons
Minority Chief of Staff: David L. Cavicke 225-3641
2322A RHOB

Jurisdiction: (1) biomedical research and development; (2) consumer affairs and consumer protection; (3) health and health facilities (except health care supported by payroll deductions); (4) interstate energy compacts; (5) interstate and foreign commerce generally; (6) measures relating to the exploration, production, storage, supply, marketing, pricing, and regulation of energy resources, including all fossil fuels, solar energy, and other unconventional or renewable energy resources; (7) conservation of energy resources; (8) energy information generally; (9) the generation and marketing of power (except by federally chartered or Federal regional power marketing authorities); the reliability and interstate transmission of, and ratemaking for, all power, and siting of generation facilities, except the installation of interconnections between Government water power projects; (10) measures relating to general management of the Department of Energy, and the management and all functions of the Federal Energy Regulatory Commission; (11) national energy policy generally; (12) public health and quarantine; (13) regulation of the domestic nuclear energy industry, including regulation of research and development reactors and nuclear regulatory research; (14) regulation of interstate and foreign communications; (15) travel and tourism. The Committee has the same jurisdiction with respect to regulation of nuclear facilities and of use of nuclear energy as it has with respect to regulation of non-nuclear facilities and of use of non-nuclear energy. In addition to its legislative jurisdiction under the preceding provisions (and its general oversight functions under clause 2(b)(1)), the Committee has the special oversight function provided for in clause 3(e) with respect to all laws, programs, and government activities affecting nuclear and other energy, and non-military nuclear energy and research and development, including the disposal of nuclear waste.

Party Ratio: D 31-R 26

Henry A. Waxman, Calif., Chair	*Joe Barton, Tex., Ranking Minority Member*
John D. Dingell, Mich.	*Ralph M. Hall, Tex.*
Edward J. Markey, Mass.	*Fred Upton, Mich.*
Rick Boucher, Va.	*Clifford B. Stearns, Fla.*
Frank Pallone Jr., N.J.	*Nathan Deal, Ga.*
Bart Gordon, Tenn.	*Ed Whitfield, Ky.*
Bobby L. Rush, Ill.	*John M. Shimkus, Ill.*
Anna G. Eshoo, Calif.	*John Shadegg, Ariz.*
Bart Stupak, Mich.	*Roy D. Blunt, Mo.*
Eliot L. Engel, N.Y.	*Steve Buyer, Ind.*
Gene Green, Tex.	*George P. Radanovich, Calif.*
Diana L. DeGette, Colo., Vice Chair	*Joseph R. Pitts, Pa.*
Lois Capps, Calif.	*Mary Bono Mack, Calif.*
Mike Doyle, Pa.	*Greg Walden, Ore.*
Jane Harman, Calif.	*Lee Terry, Neb.*
Jan Schakowsky, Ill.	*Mike Rogers, Mich.*
Charles A. Gonzalez, Tex.	*Sue Myrick, N.C.*
Jay Inslee, Wash.	*John Sullivan, Okla.*
Tammy Baldwin, Wis.	*Tim Murphy, Pa.*
Mike Ross, Ark.	*Michael Burgess, Tex.*
Anthony D. Weiner, N.Y.	*Marsha Blackburn, Tenn.*

ENERGY AND COMMERCE (continued)

Jim Matheson, Utah
G. K. Butterfield, N.C.
Charlie Melancon, La.
John Barrow, Ga.
Baron Hill, Ind.
Doris Matsui, Calif.
Donna M. Christensen, V.I.
Kathy Castor, Fla.
John P. Sarbanes, Md.
Chris Murphy, Conn.
Zack Space, Ohio
Jerry McNerney, Calif.
Betty Sutton, Ohio
Bruce Braley, Iowa
Peter Welch, Vt.

Phil Gingrey, Ga.
Steve Scalise, La.

Subcommittees

Commerce, Trade, and Consumer Protection
Office: 2125 RHOB   **Phone:** 225-2927
Bobby L. Rush (Chair), Jan Schakowsky (Vice Chair), John P. Sarbanes, Betty Sutton, Frank Pallone Jr., Bart Gordon, Bart Stupak, Gene Green, Charles A. Gonzalez, Anthony D. Weiner, Jim Matheson, G.K. Butterfield, John Barrow, Doris Matsui, Kathy Castor, Zack Space, Bruce Braley, Diana L. DeGette
Ed Whitefield (Ranking Minority Member), Clifford B. Stearns, George P. Radanovich, Joseph R. Pitts, Mary Bono Mack, Lee Terry, Sue Myrick, John Sullivan, Michael Burgess, Marsha Blackburn

Communications, Technology, and the Internet
Office: 2125 RHOB   **Phone:** 225-2927
Rick Boucher (Chair), Edward J. Markey, Bart Gordon, Bobby L. Rush, Anna G. Eshoo, Bart Stupak, Diana L. DeGette, Mike Doyle, Jay Inslee, Anthony D. Weiner, G.K. Butterfield, Charlie Melancon, Baron Hill, Doris Matsui, Donna M. Christensen, Kathy Castor, Chris Murphy, Zack Space, Jerry McNerny, Peter Welch, John D. Dingell
Clifford B. Stearns (Ranking Minority Member), Fred Upton, Nathan Deal, John M. Shimkus, Steve Buyer, George P. Radanovich, Mary Bono Mack, Greg Walden, Lee Terry

Energy and Environment
Office: 2125 RHOB   **Phone:** 225-2927
Edward J. Markey (Chair), Mike Doyle, Jay Inslee, G. K. Butterfield, Charlie Melancon, Baron Hill, Doris Matsui, Jerry McNerney, Peter Welch, John D. Dingell, Rick Boucher, Frank Pallone Jr., Eliot L. Engel, Gene Green, Lois Capps, Jane Harman, Charles A. Gonzalez, Tammy Baldwin, Mike Ross, Jim Matheson, John Barrow
Fred Upton (Ranking Minority Member), Ralph M. Hall, Ed Whitfield, John M. Shimkus, John Shadegg, Roy D. Blunt, Mary Bono Mack, Greg Walden, Mike Rogers, Sue Myrick, John Sullivan, Michael Burgess, Marsha Blackburn

Health
Office: 2125 RHOB   **Phone:** 225-2927
Frank Pallone Jr. (Chair), John D. Dingell, Henry A. Waxman, Anna G. Eshoo, Eliot L. Engel, Gene Green,

Diana L. DeGette, Lois Capps, Jan Schakowsky, Tammy Baldwin, Mike Ross, Anthony D. Weiner, Jim Matheson, Jane Harman, Charles A. Gonzalez, John Barrow, Donna M. Christensen, Kathy Castor, John P. Sarbanes, Chris Murphy, Zack Space, Betty Sutton, Bruce Braley
Nathan Deal (Ranking Minority Member), Ralph M. Hall, John Shadegg, Steve Buyer, Joseph R. Pitts, Mike Rogers, Sue Myrick, John Sullivan, Tim Murphy, Michael Burgess, Marsha Blackburn

Oversight and Investigations
Office: 2125 RHOB   **Phone:** 225-2927
Bart Stupak (Chair), Bruce Braley (Vice Chair), Edward J. Markey, Diana L. DeGette, Mike Doyle, Jan Schakowsky, Mike Ross, Donna M. Christensen, Peter Welch, Gene Green, Betty Sutton, Jay Inslee
John M Shimkus (Ranking Minority Member), Ed Whitfield, Greg Walden, Tim Murphy, Michael Burgess, Marsha Blackburn

FINANCIAL SERVICES

Office: 2129 RHOB 20515-6050
Phone: 225-4247
Web: financialservices.house.gov
Majority Staff Director: Jeanne M. Roslanowick
Minority Chief of Staff: Larry C. Lavender 225-7502
  B-371A RHOB
  Jurisdiction: (1) banks and banking, including deposit insurance and federal monetary policy; (2) bank capital markets activities generally; (3) depository institution securities activities generally, including the activities of any affiliates, except for functional regulation under applicable securities laws not involving safety and soundness; (4) economic stabilization, defense production, renegotiation, and control of the price of commodities, rents, and services; (5) financial aid to commerce and industry (other than transportation); (6) international finance; (7) international financial and monetary organizations; (8) money and credit; including currency and the issuance of notes and redemption thereof; gold and silver, including the coinage thereof; valuation and revaluation of the dollar; (9) public and private housing; (10) urban development.
Party Ratio: D 42-R 29

Barney Frank, Mass., Chair
Paul E. Kanjorski, Pa.
Maxine Waters, Calif.
Carolyn B. Maloney, N.Y.
Luis V. Gutierrez, Ill.
Nydia M. Velázquez, N.Y.
Melvin L. Watt, N.C.
Gary L. Ackerman, N.Y.
Brad Sherman, Calif.
Gregory W. Meeks, N.Y.
Dennis Moore, Kan.
Michael E. Capuano, Mass.
Rubén Hinojosa, Tex.
William Lacy Clay, Mo.
Carolyn McCarthy, N.Y.

Spencer Bachus, Ala.,
*   Ranking Minority*
*   Member*
Michael N. Castle, Del.
Peter T. King, N.Y.
Edward R. Royce, Calif.
Frank D. Lucas, Okla.
Ron Paul, Tex.
Donald A. Manzullo, Ill.
Walter B. Jones, N.C.
Judy Biggert, Ill.
Gary Miller, Calif.
Shelley Moore Capito,
*   W.Va.*
Jeb Hensarling, Tex.

Joe Baca, Calif.
Stephen F. Lynch, Mass.
Brad Miller, N.C.
David Scott, Ga.
Al Green, Tex.
Emanuel Cleaver, Mo.
Melissa Bean, Ill.
Gwen Moore, Wisc.
Paul Hodes, N.H.
Keith Ellison, Minn.
Ron Klein, Fla.
Charlie Wilson, Ohio
Ed Perlmutter, Colo.
Joe Donnelly, Ind.
Bill Foster, Ill.
Andre Carson, Ind.
Jackie Speier, Calif.
Travis Childers, Miss.
Walt Minnick, Idaho
John Adler, N.J.
Mary Jo Kilroy, Ohio
Steve Driehaus, Ohio
Suzanne M. Kosmas, Fla.
Alan Grayson, Fla.
Jim Himes, Conn.
Gary Peters, Mich.
Dan Maffei, N.Y.

Scott Garrett, N.J.
J. Gresham Barrett, S.C.
Jim Gerlach, Pa.
Randy Neugebauer, Tex.
Tom Price, Ga.
Patrick McHenry, N.C.
John Campbell, Calif.
Adam H. Putnam, Fla.
Michele Bachmann, Minn.
Kenny Marchant, Tex.
Thaddeus McCotter, Mich.
Kevin McCarthy, Calif.
Bill Posey, Fla.
Lynn Jenkins, Kans.
Christopher Lee, N.Y.
Erik Paulsen, Minn.
Leonard Lance, N.J.

Subcommittees

Capital Markets, Insurance, and Government Sponsored Enterprises
Office: 2129 RHOB   **Phone:** 225-4247

Paul E. Kanjorski (Chair), Gary L. Ackerman, Brad Sherman, Michael E. Capuano, Rubén Hinojosa, Carolyn McCarthy, Joe Baca, Stephen F. Lynch, Brad Miller, David Scott, Nydia M. Velázquez, Carolyn B. Maloney, Melissa Bean, Gwen Moore, Paul Hodes, Ron Klein, Ed Perlmutter, Christopher Murphy, Joe Donnelly, André Carson, Jackie Speier, Travis Childers, Charlie Wilson, Bill Foster, Walt Minnick, John Adler, Mary Jo Kilroy, Suzanne M. Kosmas, Alan Grayson, Jim Himes, Gary Peters

Jeb Hensarling (Chair), Michael N. Castle, Peter T. King, Frank D. Lucas, Donald A. Manzullo, Edward R. Royce, Shelley Moore Capito, Adam H. Putnam, J. Gresham Barrett, Scott Garrett, Jim Gerlach, Tom Price, John Campbell, Michele Bachmann, Kenny Marchant, Thaddeus McCotter

Domestic Monetary Policy and Technology
Office: 2129 RHOB   **Phone:** 225-4247

Melvin L. Watt, Carolyn B. Maloney, Gregory W. Meeks, Wm. Lacy Clay, Brad Sherman, Al Green, Emanuel Cleaver II, Keith Ellison, John Adler, Suzanne M. Kosmas

Ron Paul (Ranking Minority Member), Michael N. Castle, Frank D. Lucas, Donald A. Manzullo, Walter B. Jones, Jeb Hensarling, Tom Price, Patrick McHenry, Michele Bachmann, Peter Roskam, Kenny Marchant, Dean Heller

Financial Institutions and Consumer Credit
Office: 2129 RHOB   **Phone:** 225-4247

Luis V. Guitierrez (Chair), Carolyn B. Maloney, Melvin L. Watt, Gary L. Ackerman, Brad Sherman, Dennis Moore, Paul E. Kanjorski, Maxine Waters, Rubén Hinojosa, Carolyn McCarthy, Joe Baca, Al Green, William Lacy Clay, Brad Miller, David Scott, Emanuel Cleaver, Melissa Bean, Paul Hodes, Keith Ellison, Ron Klein, Charlie Wilson, Gregory W. Meeks, Bill Foster, Ed Perlmutter, Jackie Speier, Travis Childers, Walt Minnick

Judy Biggert (Ranking Minority Member), Tom Price, Michael N. Castle, Peter T. King, Edward R. Royce, Walter B. Jones, Shelley Moore Capito, Jeb Hensarling, Scott Garrett, J. Gresham Barrett, Jim Gerlach, Randy Neugebauer, Patrick McHenry, John Campbell, Kevin McCarthy, Dean Heller

Housing and Community Opportunity
Office: 2129 RHOB   **Phone:** 225-4247

Maxine Waters (Chair), Nydia M. Velázquez, Stephen F. Lynch, Emanuel Cleaver, Al Green, William Lacy Clay, Keith Ellison, Joe Donnelly, Michael E. Capuano, Paul E. Kanjorski, Luis V. Guitierrez, Steve Driehaus, Mary Jo Kilroy, Jim Himes, Dan Maffei

Shelley Moore Capito (Ranking Minority Member), Peter T. King, Judy Biggert, Gary Miller, Scott Garrett, Randy Neugebauer, John Campbell, Thaddeus McCotter, Kevin McCarthy

International Monetary Policy and Trade
Office: 2129 RHOB   **Phone:** 225-4247

Gregory W. Meeks (Chair), Luis V. Guitierrez, Maxine Waters, Melvin L. Watt, Gwen Moore, André Carson, Steve Driehaus, Gary Peters, Dan Maffei

Ron Paul (Ranking Minority Member), Michael N. Castle, Frank D. Lucas, Donald A. Manzullo, Walter B. Jones, Jeb Hensarling, Tom Price, Patrick McHenry, Michele Bachmann, Peter Roskam, Kenny Marchant, Dean Heller

Oversight and Investigations
Office: 2129 RHOB   **Phone:** 225-4247

Dennis Moore, Stephen F. Lynch, Ron Klein, Jackie Speier, Gwen Moore, John Adler, Mary Jo Kilroy, Steve Driehaus, Alan Grayson

Gary Miller (Ranking Minority Member), Patrick McHenry, Edward R. Royce, Ron Paul, J. Gresham Barrett, Michele Bachmann, Kevin McCarthy

FOREIGN AFFAIRS

Office: 2170 RHOB 20515-6128
Phone: 225-5021
Web: foreignaffairs.house.gov
Majority Staff Director: Richard J. Kessler
Minority Staff Director: Yleem Poblete Ph.D. 226-8467
  B-360 RHOB
  Jurisdiction: (1) relations of the United States with foreign nations generally; (2) acquisition of land and buildings for embassies and legations in foreign countries; (3) establishment of boundary lines between the United States and foreign nations; (4) export

FOREIGN AFFAIRS (continued)

controls, including non-proliferation of nuclear technology and non-proliferation of nuclear hardware; (5) foreign loans; (6) international commodity agreements (other than those involving sugar), including all agreements for cooperation in the export of nuclear technology and nuclear hardware; (7) international conferences and congresses; (8) international education; (9) intervention abroad and declarations of war; (10) measures relating to the diplomatic service; (11) measures to foster commercial intercourse with foreign nations and to safeguard American business interests abroad; (12) measures relating to international economic policy; (13) neutrality; (14) protection of American citizens abroad and expatriation; (15) the American National Red Cross; (16) the International Committee of the Red Cross; (17) the International Federation of Red Cross and Red Crescent Societies; (18) trading with the enemy; (19) treaties, conventions, and international agreements; (20) the United Nations and its affiliated organizations. In addition to its legislative jurisdiction under the preceding provisions (and its general oversight function under clause 2 (b)(1), the Committee has the special oversight functions provided for in clause 3 (d) with respect to customs administration, intelligence activities relating to foreign policy, international financial and monetary organizations, and international fishing agreements.

Party Ratio: D 28-R 19

Howard L. Berman, Calif., Chair
Gary L. Ackerman, N.Y.
Eni F. H. Faleomavaega, Am. Samoa
Donald M. Payne, N.J.
Brad Sherman, Calif.
Robert Wexler, Fla.
Eliot L. Engel, N.Y.
William D. Delahunt, Mass.
Gregory W. Meeks, N.Y.
Diane E. Watson, Calif.
Russ Carnahan, Mo.
Albio Sires, N.J.
Gerry E. Connolly, Va.
Michael McMahon, N.Y.
John S. Tanner, Tenn.
Gene Green, Tex.
Lynn Woolsey
Sheila Jackson Lee, Tex.
Barbara Lee, Calif.
Shelley Berkley, Nev.
Joseph Crowley, N.Y.
Mike Ross, Ark.
Brad Miller, N.C.
David Scott, Ga.
Jim Costa, Calif.
Keith Ellison, Minn.
Gabrielle Giffords, Ariz.
Ron Klein, Fla.

Ileana Ros-Lehtinen, Fla., Ranking Minority Member
Christopher H. Smith, N.J.
Dan Burton, Ind.
Elton Gallegly, Calif.
Dana Rohrabacher, Calif.
Edward R. Royce, Calif.
Ron Paul, Tex.
Jeff Flake, Ariz.
Mike Pence, Ind.
Joe Wilson, S.C.
John Boozman, Ark.
J. Gresham Barrett, S.C.
Connie Mack, Fla.
Jeff Fortenberry, Neb.
Michael McCaul, Tex.
Ted Poe, Tex.
Bob Inglis, S.C.
Gus Bilirakis, Fla.

Subcommittees

Africa and Global Health
Office: 259A FHOB   **Phone:** 226-7812
Donald M. Payne (Chair), Diane E. Watson, Barbara Lee, Brad Miller, Gregory W. Meeks, Sheila Jackson Lee, Lynn Woolsey
Christopher H. Smith (Ranking Minority Member), Jeff Flake, John Boozman, Jeff Fortenberry

Asia, the Pacific, and the Global Environment
Office: 2401A RHOB   **Phone:** 226-7825
Eni F. H. Faleomavaega (Chair), Gary L. Ackerman, Diane E. Watson, Mike Ross, Brad Sherman, Eliot L. Engel, Gregory W. Meeks
Donald A. Manzullo (Ranking Minority Member), Bob Inglis, Dana Rohrabacher, Edward R. Royce, Jeff Flake

Europe
Office: 257 FHOB   **Phone:** 226-7820
Robert Wexler (Chair), John S. Tanner, William D. Delahunt, Albio Sires, Michael McMahon, Shelley Berkley, Brad Miller, David Scott, Jim Costa
Elton Gallegly (Ranking Minority Member), Gus Bilirakis, Joe Wilson, Ted Poe, John Boozman, Bob Inglis, J. Gresham Barrett

International Organizations, Human Rights, and Oversight
Office: 256 FHOB   **Phone:** 226-6434
William D. Delahunt (Chair), Russ Carnahan, Keith Ellison, Donald M. Payne, Robert Wexler
Dana Rohrabacher (Ranking Minority Member), Ron Paul, Ted Poe

Middle East and South Asia
Office: B358 RHOB   **Phone:** 225-3345
Gary L. Ackerman (Chair), Russ Carnahan, Michael McMahon, Sheila Jackson Lee, Shelley Berkley, Joseph Crowley, Mike Ross, Jim Costa, Keith Ellison, Ron Klein, Brad Sherman, Robert Wexler, Eliot L. Engel, Gerry E. Connolly, Gene Green, Vacancy
Dan Burton (Ranking Minority Member), Mike Pence, Joe Wilson, J. Gresham Barrett, Jeff Fortenberry, Michael McCaul, Bob Inglis, Gus Bilirakis, Dana Rohrabacher, Edward R. Royce

Terrorism, Non-Proliferation, and Trade
Office: 253 FHOB   **Phone:** 226-1500
Brad Sherman (Chair), Gerry E. Connolly, David Scott, Diane E. Watson, Michael McMahon, Sheila Jackson Lee, Ron Klein
Edward R. Royce, Ted Poe, Donald A. Manzullo, John Boozman, J. Gresham Barrett

Western Hemisphere
Office: 255 FHOB   **Phone:** 226-9980
Eliot L. Engel (Chair), Gregory W. Meeks, Albio Sires, Gene Green, Gabrielle Giffords, Eni F. H. Faleomavaega, Donald M. Payne, John S. Tanner, Barbara Lee, Joseph Crowley, Ron Klein
Connie Mack, Michael McCaul, Christopher H. Smith, Dan Burton, Elton Gallegly, Ron Paul, Jeff Fortenberry, Gus Bilirakis

HOMELAND SECURITY

Office: H2-176 FHOB 20515-6480
Phone: 226-2616   **Fax:** 226-4499
Web: homeland.house.gov
E-mail: homeland@mail.house.gov
Majority Staff Director: I. Lanier Avant
Minority Chief Counsel: Michael J. Russell 226-8417
   H2-117 FHOB
   Jurisdiction: (1) Overall homeland security policy;
(2) Organization and administration of the Department
of Homeland Security; (3) Functions of the Department
of Homeland Security relating to the following:
(a) Border security (except immigration policy and
non-border enforcement); (b) Customs (except customs
revenue); (c) Integration, analysis, and dissemination
of homeland security information; (d) Domestic
preparedness for and collective response to terrorism;
(e) Research and development; (f) Transportation
security, including cargo screening and port security. The
Committee shall review and study on a continuing basis
all Government activities relating to homeland security,
including the interaction of all departments and agencies
with the Department of Homeland Security.
Party Ratio: D 20-R 13

Bennie G. Thompson, Miss., Chair	Peter T. King, N.Y., Ranking Minority Member
Loretta Sanchez, Calif., Vice Chair	Lamar Smith, Tex.
Jane Harman, Calif.	Mark Souder, Ind.
Peter A. DeFazio, Ore.	Dan Lungren, Calif.
Eleanor Holmes Norton, D.C.	Mike Rogers, Ala.
Zoe Lofgren, Calif.	Michael McCaul, Tex.
Sheila Jackson Lee, Tex.	Charlie Dent, Pa.
Henry Cuellar, Tex.	Gus Bilirakis, Fla.
Christopher P. Carney, Pa.	Paul C. Broun, Ga.
Yvette Clarke, N.Y.	Candice Miller, Mich.
Laura Richardson, Calif.	Pete Olson, Tex.
Ann Kirkpatrick, Ariz.	Anh Joseph Cao, La.
Ben R. Luján, N.M.	Steve Austria, Ohio
William J. Pascrell Jr., N.J.	
Emmanuel Cleaver II, Mo.	
Al Green, Tex.	
Jim Himes, Conn.	
Mary Jo Kilroy, Ohio	
Eric J. J. Massa, N.Y.	
Dina Titus, Nev.	
Vacancy	

Subcommittees

Border, Maritime and Global Counterterrorism
Office: H2-176 FHOB   **Phone:** 226-2616
   Loretta Sanchez (Chair), Jane Harman, Zoe Lofgren,
Sheila Jackson Lee, Henry Cuellar, Ann Kirkpatrick,
William J. Pascrell Jr., Al Green, Eric J. J. Massa

   Mark Souder (Ranking Minority Member), Michael
McCaul, Gus Bilirakis, Mike Rogers, Candice Miller

Emergency Communications, Preparedness, and Response
Office: H2-176 FHOB   **Phone:** 226-2616
   Henry Cuellar (Chair), Eleanor Holmes Norton,
Laura Richardson, William J. Pascrell Jr., Emmanuel
Cleaver II, Dina Titus, Vacancy
   Mike Rogers (Ranking Minority Member), Pete Olson,
Anh Joseph Cao, Michael McCaul

Emerging Threats, Cybersecurity, and Science and Technology
Office: H2-176 FHOB   **Phone:** 226-2616
   Yvette D. Clarke (Chair), Loretta Sanchez, Laura
Richardson, Ben R. Luján, Mary Jo Kilroy
   Dan Lungren (Ranking Minority Member), Paul C.
Broun, Steve Austria

Intelligence, Information Sharing and Terrorism Risk Assessment
Office: H2-176 FHOB   **Phone:** 226-2616
   Jane Harman (Chair), Christopher P. Carney, Yvette D.
Clarke, Ann Kirkpatrick, Al Green, Jim Himes, Vacancy
   Michael McCaul (Ranking Minority Member), Charlie
Dent, Paul C. Broun, Mark Souder

Management, Investigations, and Oversight
Office: H2-176 FHOB   **Phone:** 226-2616
   Christopher P. Carney (Chair), Peter A. DeFazio,
William J. Pascrell Jr., Al Green, Mary Jo Kilroy
   Gus Bilirakis (Ranking Minority Member), Anh Joseph
Cao, Dan Lungren

Transportation Security and Infrastructure Protection
Office: H2-176 FHOB   **Phone:** 226-2616
   Sheila Jackson Lee (Chair), Peter A. DeFazio, Eleanor
Holmes Norton, Ann Kirkpatrick, Ben R. Luján, Emmanuel
Cleaver II, Jim Himes, Eric J. J. Massa, Dina Titus
   Charlie Dent (Ranking Minority Member), Dan
Lungren, Pete Olson, Candice Miller, Steve Austria

HOUSE ADMINISTRATION

Office: 1309 LHOB 20515-6157
Phone: 225-2061   **Fax:** 225-0882
Web: cha.house.gov
Majority Chief Counsel: S. Elizabeth Birnbaum
Minority Staff Director: Victor Arnold-Bik 225-8281
   1313 LHOB
   Jurisdiction: (1) appropriations from accounts for
committee salaries and expenses (except for the
Committee on Appropriations), House Information
Resources, and allowances and expenses of Members,
House Officers and administrative offices of the House;
(2) auditing and settling of all accounts described in (1),
above; (3) employment of persons by the House,
including clerks for Members and committees, and
reporters of debates; (4) except as provided in clause 1(q)
(11), matters relating to the Library of Congress and the

HOUSE ADMINISTRATION (continued)

House Library, statuary and pictures in the United States Capitol and House office buildings, acceptance or purchase of works of art for the United States Capitol and House office buildings, the United States Botanic Garden, management of the Library of Congress, purchase of books and manuscripts; (5) except as provided in clause 1(q)(11), matters relating to the Smithsonian Institution and the incorporation of similar institutions; (6) expenditure of accounts described in (1), above; (7) House Commission on Congressional Mailing Standards; (8) matters relating to printing and correction of the Congressional Record; (9) measures relating to accounts of the House generally; (10) measures relating to assignment of office space for Representatives and House committees; (11) measures relating to the disposition of useless executive papers; (12) measures relating to the election of the President, Vice President, and Members of the House of Representatives; corrupt practices, contested elections, credentials and qualifications of Members of the House, and federal elections generally; (13) Presidential Succession Act of 1947; (14) measures relating to services to the House, including the House Restaurant, parking facilities and administration of the House Office Buildings and of the House wing of the United States Capitol; (14) measures relating to the travel of Members of the House of Representatives; (15) measures relating to the raising, reporting and use of campaign contributions for candidates for office of Representative in the House of Representatives, Delegate to the House of Representatives, and of Resident Commissioner to the United States from Puerto Rico, as well as related provisions of the Bipartisan Campaign Reform Act of 2002 and the Lobbying Disclosure Act of 1995; campaign finance reform; lobbying; (16) Measures relating to the compensation, retirement and other benefits of the Members, officers, and employees of the Congress. In addition to its legislative jurisdiction under the preceding provisions (and its general oversight function under clause 2(b)(1), the committee has the function of performing the duties which are provided for in clause 4(d).

Party Ratio: D 6-R 3

Robert A. Brady, Pa., Chair
Zoe Lofgren, Calif., Vice Chair
Michael E. Capuano, Mass.
Charles A. Gonzalez, Tex.
Susan Davis, Calif.
Artur Davis, Ala.

Dan Lungren, Calif., Ranking Minority Member
Kevin McCarthy, Calif.
Gregg Harper, Miss.

Subcommittees

Capitol Security

Office: 1309 LHOB   **Phone:** 225-2061
   Michael E. Capuano (Chair), Robert A Brady
   Dan Lungren

Elections

Office: 1309 LHOB   **Phone:** 225-2061
   Zoe Lofgren (Chair), Charles A. Gonzalez, Susan Davis, Artur Davis
   Kevin McCarthy (Ranking Minority Member), Gregg Harper

JUDICIARY

Office: 2138 RHOB 20515-6216
Phone: 225-3951
Web: judiciary.house.gov
Majority Staff Director: Perry H. Apelbaum
Minority Chief of Staff: Sean McLaughlin 225-6906
   B-351 RHOB
   Jurisdiction: (1) the judiciary and judicial proceedings, civil and criminal; (2) administrative practice and procedure; (3) apportionment of Representatives; (4) bankruptcy, mutiny, espionage, and counterfeiting; (5) civil liberties; (6) constitutional amendments; (7) federal courts and judges, and local courts in United States territories and possessions; (8) immigration and naturalization; (9) interstate compacts generally; (10) measures relating to claims against the United States; (11) meetings of Congress, attendance of Members and their acceptance of incompatible offices; (12) national penitentiaries; (13) patents, the Patent Office, copyrights, and trademarks; (14) presidential succession; (15) continuity of congressional representation; (16) protection of trade and commerce against unlawful restraints and monopolies; (17) revision and codification of the Statutes of the United States; (18) state and territorial boundaries; (19) subversive activities affecting the internal security of the United States.
Party Ratio: D 23-R 16

John Conyers Jr., Mich., Chair
Howard L. Berman, Calif., Vice Chair
Rick Boucher, Va.
Jerrold Nadler, N.Y.
Robert C. Scott, Va.
Melvin L. Watt, N.C.
Zoe Lofgren, Calif.
Sheila Jackson Lee, Tex.
Maxine Waters, Calif.
William D. Delahunt, Mass.
Robert Wexler, Fla.
Steve Cohen, Tenn.
Hank Johnson, Ga.
Pedro Pierluisi, P.R.
Luis V. Gutierrez, Ill.
Brad Sherman, Calif.
Tammy Baldwin, Wisc.
Charles A. Gonzalez, Tex.
Anthony D. Weiner, N.Y.
Adam Schiff, Calif.
Linda Sánchez, Calif.
Debbie Wasserman Schultz, Fla.

Dan Maffei, N.Y.
Lamar Smith, Tex., Ranking Minority Member
F. James Sensenbrenner, Wisc.
Howard Coble, N.C.
Elton Gallegly, Calif.
Bob Goodlatte, Va.
Dan Lungren, Calif.
Darrell Issa, Calif.
J. Randy Forbes, Va.
Steve King, Iowa
Trent Franks, Ariz.
Louie Gohmert, Tex.
Jim Jordan, Ohio
Ted Poe, Tex.
Jason Chaffetz, Utah
Tom Rooney, Fla.
Gregg Harper, Miss.

Subcommittees

Commercial and Administrative Law
Office: H2-362 FHOB **Phone:** 226-7680

Steve Cohen (Chair), William D. Delahunt, Melvin L. Watt, Brad Sherman, Dan Maffei, Zoe Lofgren, Hank Johnson, Robert C. Scott, John Conyers Jr.

Trent Franks (Ranking Minority Member), Jim Jordan, Howard Coble, Darrell Issa, J. Randy Forbes, Steve King

Constitution, Civil Rights, and Civil Liberties
Office: B353 RHOB **Phone:** 225-2825

Jerrold Nadler (Chair), Melvin L. Watt, William D. Delahunt, Hank Johnson, Tammy Baldwin, John Conyers Jr., Steve Cohen, Brad Sherman, Sheila Jackson Lee

F. James Sensenbrenner Jr. (Ranking Minority Member), Tom Rooney, Steve King, Trent Franks, Louie Gohmert, Jim Jordan

Court and Competition Policy
Office: B352 RHOB **Phone:** 225-5741

Hank Johnson (Chair), John Conyers Jr., Rick Boucher, Robert Wexler, Charles A. Gonzalez, Sheila Jackson Lee, Melvin L. Watt, Brad Sherman, Vacancy

Howard Coble (Ranking Minority Member), Jason Chaffetz, F. James Sensenbrenner, Bob Goodlatte, Darrell Issa, Gregg Harper

Crime, Terrorism, and Homeland Security
Office: B370 RHOB **Phone:** 225-5727

Robert C. Scott (Chair), Pedro Pierluisi, Jerrold Nadler, Zoe Lofgren, Sheila Jackson Lee, Maxine Waters, Steve Cohen, Anthony D. Weiner, Debbie Wasserman Schultz, Vacancy

Louie Gohmert (Ranking Minority Member), Ted Poe, Bob Goodlatte, Dan Lungren, J. Randy Forbes, Tom Rooney

Immigration, Citizenship, Refugees, Border Security, and International Law
Office: 517 CHOB **Phone:** 225-3692

Zoe Lofgren (Chair), Howard L. Berman, Sheila Jackson Lee, Maxine Waters, Pedro Pierluisi, Luis V. Guitierrez, Linda Sánchez, Anthony D. Weiner, Charles A. Gonzalez, William D. Delahunt

Steve King (Ranking Minority Member), Gregg Harper, Elton Gallegly, Dan Lungren, Ted Poe, Jason Chaffetz

Task Force on Antitrust and Competition Policy

John Conyers Jr. (Chair), Rick Boucher, Zoe Lofgren, Sheila Jackson Lee, Maxine Waters, Steve Cohen, Hank Johnson, Brad Sherman, Anthony D. Weiner, Debbie Wasserman Shultz

F. James Sensenbrenner Jr., Bob Goodlatte, Dan Lungren, Darrell Issa, Steve King

NATURAL RESOURCES

Office: 1324 LHOB 20515-6201
Phone: 225-6065 **Fax:** 225-1931
Web: resourcescommittee.house.gov
Majority Staff Director: James H. Zoia
Minority Chief of Staff: Christopher Fluhr 225-2761
1329 LHOB

Jurisdiction: (1) environmental and habitat measures and matters of general applicability; (2) measures relating to the welfare of Native Americans, including management of Native American lands in general and special measures relating to claims which are paid out of Native American funds; (3) all matters regarding the relations of the United States with Native Americans and Native American tribes, including special oversight functions under Rule X of the Rules of the House of Representatives; (4) all matters regarding Native Alaskans and Native Hawaiians; (5) all matters related to the Federal trust responsibility to Native Americans and the sovereignty of Native Americans; (6) all matters related to the National Indian Gaming Regulatory Act of 1988 and the National Indian Gaming Commission; (7) all matters regarding insular areas of the United States; (8) all measures or matters regarding the Freely Associated States of the Marshall Islands, Micronesia, and Palau; (9) all measures or matters regarding Antarctica; (10) cooperative efforts to encourage, enhance and improve international programs for the protection of the environment and the conservation of natural resources otherwise within the jurisdiction of the Full Committee; (11) all measures and matters retained by the Full Committee under Committee rule 6(e); (12) general and continuing oversight and investigative authority over activities, policies and programs within the jurisdiction of the Committee under House Rule X.
Party Ratio: D 29-R 20

Nick J. Rahall, W.Va., Chair	*Doc Hastings, Wash,*
Dale E. Kildee, Mich.	*Ranking Minority*
Eni F. H. Faleomavaega,	*Member*
Am. Samoa	*Don Young, Alaska*
Neil Abercrombie, Hawaii	*Elton Gallegly, Calif.*
Frank Pallone Jr., N.J.	*John J. Duncan Jr., Tenn.*
Grace F. Napolitano, Calif.	*Jeff Flake, Ariz.*
Rush Holt, N.J.	*Henry E. Brown, S.C.*
Raúl M. Grijalva, Ariz.	*Cathy McMorris Rodgers,*
Madeleine Z. Bordallo,	*Wash.*
Guam	*Louie Gohmert, Tex.*
Jim Costa, Calif.	*Rob Bishop, Utah*
Dan Boren, Okla.	*Bill Shuster, Pa.*
Gregorio C. Sablan,	*Doug Lamborn, Colo.*
Mariana Islands	*Adrian Smith, Neb.*
Martin T. Heinrich, N.M.	*Rob Wittman, Va.*
George Miller, Calif.	*Paul C. Broun, Ga.*
Edward J. Markey, Mass.	*John Fleming, La.*
Peter A. DeFazio, Ore.	*Mike Coffman, Colo.*
Maurice D. Hinchey, N.Y.	*Jason Chaffetz, Utah*
Donna M. Christensen,	*Cynthia M. Lummis, Wyo.*
Virgin Islands	*Tom McClintock, Calif.*
Diana L. DeGette, Colo.	*Bill Cassidy, La.*
Ron Kind, Wisc.	
Lois Capps, Calif.	
Jay Inslee, Wash.	
Joe Baca, Calif.	
Stephanie Herseth	
Sandlin, S.D.	
John P. Sarbanes, Md.	
Carol Shea-Porter, N.H.	
Niki Tsongas, Mass.	
Frank M. Kratovil, Jr., Md.	
Pedro Pierluisi, P.R.	

NATURAL RESOURCES (continued)

Subcommittees

Energy and Mineral Resources
Office: 1626 LHOB   **Phone:** 225-9297
Jim Costa (Chair), Eni F. H. Faleomavaega, Rush Holt, Dan Boren, Gregorio C. Sablan, Martin T. Heinrich, Edward J. Markey, Maurice D. Hinchey, John P. Sarbanes, Niki Tsongas
Doug Lamborn (Ranking Minority Member), Don Young, Louie Gohmert, Elton Gallegly, Jeff Flake, John Fleming, Jason Chaffetz, Cynthia M. Lummis

Insular Affairs, Oceans, and Wildlife
Office: H2-187 FHOB   **Phone:** 226-0200
Madeleine Z. Bordallo (Chair), Dale E. Kildee, Eni F. H. Faleomavaega, Neil Abercrombie, Frank Pallone Jr., Gregorio C. Sablan, Donna M. Christensen, Diana L. DeGette, Ron Kind, Lois Capps, Carol Shea-Porter, Frank M. Kratovil Jr., Pedro Pierluisi
Henry E. Brown (Ranking Minority Member), Don Young, Jeff Flake, Doug Lamborn, Rob Wittman, John Fleming, Jason Chaffetz, Bill Cassidy

National Parks, Forests, and Public Lands
Office: 1333 LHOB   **Phone:** 226-7736
Raúl M. Grijalva (Chair), Dale E. Kildee, Neil Abercrombie, Grace F. Napolitano, Rush Holt, Madeleine Z. Bordallo, Dan Boren, Martin T. Heinrich, Peter A. DeFazio, Maurice D. Hinchey, Donna M. Christensen, Diana L. DeGette, Ron Kind, Lois Capps, Jay Inslee, Stephanie Herseth Sandlin, John P. Sarbanes, Carol Shea-Porter, Niki Tsongas, Pedro Pierluisi
Rob Bishop (Ranking Minority Member), Don Young, Elton Gallegly, John J. Duncan Jr., Jeff Flake, Henry E. Brown Jr., Louie Gohmert, Bill Shuster, Rob Wittman, Paul C. Broun, Mike Coffman, Jason Chaffetz, Cynthia M. Lummis, Tom McClintock

Water and Power
Office: 1522 LHOB   **Phone:** 225-8331
Grace F. Napolitano (Chair), George Miller, Raúl M. Grijalva, Jim Costa, Peter A. DeFazio, Jay Inslee, Joe Baca
Cathy McMorris Rodgers (Ranking Minority Member), Adrian Smith, Mike Coffman, Tom McClintock

OVERSIGHT AND GOVERNMENT REFORM

Office: 2157 RHOB 20515-6143
Phone: 225-5051
Web: oversight.house.gov
Majority Chief of Staff: Ronald A. Stroman
Minority Deputy Staff Director: Lawrence J. Brady
225-5074 B-350A RHOB
Jurisdiction: The Oversight and Government Reform Committee is the principal oversight committee in the U.S. House of Representatives and has broad oversight jurisdiction as set forth in House Rule X, clauses 1(m), 2, 3(i), and 4(c). The Committee's legislative jurisdiction includes the following areas, as set forth in House Rule

X, clause 1: (1) the federal civil service, including intergovernmental personnel, and the status of officers and employees of the United States, including their compensation, classification, and retirement; (2) municipal affairs of the District of Columbia in general, other than appropriations; (3) federal paperwork reduction; (4) government management and accounting measures, generally; (5) holidays and celebrations; (6) the overall economy, efficiency and management of government operations and activities, including federal procurement; (7) National Archives and Records Administration; (8) population and demography generally, including the Census; (9) postal service generally, including the transportation of the mails; (10) public information and records; (11) relationship of the federal government to the states and municipalities generally; and (12) reorganizations in the executive branch of the government.
Party Ratio: D 22-R 16

Edolphus Towns, N.Y., Chair	*Darrell Issa, Calif., Ranking Minority Member*
Paul E. Kanjorski, Pa.	
Carolyn B. Maloney, N.Y.	*Dan Burton, Ind.*
Elijah E. Cummings, Md.	*John M. McHugh, N.Y.*
Dennis J. Kucinich, Ohio	*John L. Mica, Fla.*
John F. Tierney, Mass.	*Mark Soulder, Ind.*
William Lacy Clay, Mo.	*Todd Russell Platts, Pa.*
Diane E. Watson, Calif.	*John J. Duncan Jr., Tenn.*
Stephen F. Lynch, Mass.	*Michael Turner, Ohio*
Jim Cooper, Tenn.	*Lynn A. Westmoreland, Ga.*
Gerry E. Connolly, Va.	*Patrick McHenry, N.C.*
Eleanor Holmes Norton, D.C.	*Brian P. Bilbray, Calif.*
Patrick J. Kennedy, R.I.	*Jim Jordan, Ohio*
Danny K. Davis, Ill.	*Jeff Flake, Ariz.*
Chris Van Hollen, Md.	*Jeff Fortenberry, Neb.*
Henry Cuellar, Tex.	*Jason Chaffetz, Utah*
Paul Hodes, N.H.	*Aaron Shock, Ill.*
Chris Murphy, Conn.	
Peter Welch, Vt.	
Bill Foster, Ill.	
Jackie Speier, Calif.	
Steve Driehaus, Ohio	

Subcommittees

Domestic Policy
Office: B349B RHOB   **Phone:** 225-6427
Dennis J. Kucinich (Chair), Elijah E. Cummings, John F. Tierney, Diane E. Watson, Jim Cooper, Patrick J. Kennedy, Peter Welch, Bill Foster
Jim Jordan (Ranking Minority Member), Dan Burton, John L. Mica, Mark Souder, Brian P. Bilbray

Federal Workforce, Postal Service, and the District of Columbia
Office: B349A RHOB   **Phone:** 225-5147
Stephen F. Lynch (Chair), Eleanor Holmes Norton, Danny K. Davis, Elijah E. Cummings, Dennis J. Kucinich, Wm. Lacy Clay, Gerry E. Connolly

Jason Chaffetz (Ranking Minority Member), John M. McHugh, John L. Mica, Jim Jordan

Government Management, Organization, and Procurement
Office: B349A RHOB   **Phone:** 225-3741

Diane E. Watson (Chair), Paul E. Kanjorski, Jim Cooper, Gerry E. Connolly, Henry Cuellar, Jackie Speier, Paul Hodes, Chris Murphy

Brian P. Bilbray (Ranking Minority Member), Todd Russell Platts, John J. Duncan Jr.

Information Policy, Census, and National Archives
Office: B349C RHOB   **Phone:** 225-6751

William Lacy Clay (Chair), Paul E. Kanjorski, Carolyn B. Maloney, Eleanor Holmes Norton, Danny K. Davis, Steve Driehaus, Diane E. Watson

Patrick McHenry (Ranking Minority Member), Lynn A. Westmoreland, John L. Mica, Jason Chaffetz

National Security and Foreign Affairs
Office: B371C RHOB   **Phone:** 225-2548

John F. Tierney (Chair), Carolyn B. Maloney, Patrick J. Kennedy, Chris Van Hollen, Paul Hodes, Chris Murphy, Peter Welch, Bill Foster, Steve Driehaus, Stephen F. Lynch, Henry Cuellar, Dennis J. Kucinich

Jeff Flake (Ranking Minority Member), Dan Burton, John M. McHugh, Todd Russell Platts, John J. Duncan Jr., Michael Turner, Lynn A. Westmoreland, Patrick McHenry

RULES

Office: H-312 CAP 20515-6269
Phone: 225-9091
Web: www.rules.house.gov
Majority Staff Director: Muftiah McCartin
Minority Staff Director: Hugh N. Halpern 225-9191
   H-152 CAP

Jurisdiction: (1) the rules and joint rules (other than rules or joint rules relating to the Code of Official Conduct), and order of business of the House; (2) recesses and final adjournments of Congress; (3) the Committee on Rules is authorized to sit and act whether or not the House is in session.

Party Ratio: D 9-R 4

Louise M. Slaughter, N.Y., Chair
James P. McGovern, Mass.
Alcee L. Hastings, Fla.
Doris Matsui, Calif.
Dennis A. Cardoza, Calif.
Michael Arcuri, N.Y.
Ed Perlmutter, Colo.
Chellie Pingree, Maine
Jared Polis, Colo.

David Dreier, Calif., Ranking Minority Member
Lincoln Diaz-Balart, Fla.
Pete Sessions, Tex.
Virginia Foxx, N.C.

Subcommittees

Legislative and Budget Process
Office: 2353 RHOB   **Phone:** 225-1313

Alcee L. Hastings (Chair), Dennis A. Cardoza (Vice Chair), Chellie Pingree, Jared Polis, Louise M. Slaughter

Lincoln Diaz-Balart (Ranking Minority Member), David Dreier

Rules and the Organization of the House
Office: 438 CHOB   **Phone:** 225-6465

James P. McGovern (Chair), Doris Matsui (Vice Chair), Michael Arcuri, Ed Perlmutter, Louise M. Slaughter

Pete Sessions (Ranking Minority Member)

SCIENCE AND TECHNOLOGY

Office: 2320 RHOB 20515-6301
Phone: 225-6375   **Fax:** 225-3895
Web: science.house.gov
Majority Staff Director: E. Charles Atkins
Minority Chief of Staff: Janet Perry Poppleton 225-6371
   389 FHOB

Jurisdiction: (1) all energy research, development, and demonstration, and projects therefor, and all federally owned or operated non-military energy laboratories; (2) astronautical research and development, including resources, personnel, equipment, and facilities; (3) civil aviation research and development; (4) environmental research and development; (5) marine research; (6) measures relating to the commercial application of energy technology; (7) standardization of weights and measures and the metric system; (8) the research and development programs of the Department of Energy, Environmental Protection Agency, Federal Aviation Administration, Federal Emergency Management Agency, National Aeronautics and Space Administration, National Institute of Standards and Technology, National Oceanic and Atmospheric Administration, National Science Foundation, National Space Council, National Weather Service, and United States Fire Administration; (9) outer space, including exploration and control thereof; (10) science scholarships; (11) scientific research, development, and demonstration, and projects therefor. In addition to its legislative jurisdiction under the preceding provisions (and its general oversight function under clause 2(b)(1), the Committee has the special oversight function provided for in clause 3(f) with respect to all non-military research and development.

Party Ratio: D 26-R 17

Bart Gordon, Tenn., Chair
Jerry F. Costello, Ill.
Eddie Bernice Johnson, Tex.
Lynn Woolsey, Calif.
David Wu, Ore.
Brian Baird, Wash.
Brad Miller, N.C.
Daniel Lipinski, Ill., Vice Chair
Gabrielle Giffords, Ariz.
Donna Edwards, Md.
Marcia L. Fudge, Ohio
Ben R. Luján, N.M.
Paul D. Tonko, N.Y.

Ralph M. Hall, Tex., Ranking Minority Member
F. James Sensenbrenner, Wisc.
Lamar Smith, Tex.
Dana Rohrabacher, Calif.
Roscoe G. Bartlett, Md.
Vernon J. Ehlers, Mich.
Frank D. Lucas, Okla.
Judy Biggert, Ill.
Todd Akin, Mo.
Randy Neugebauer, Tex.
Bob Inglis, S.C.

SCIENCE AND TECHNOLOGY (continued)

Parker Griffith, Ala.
Steve Rothman, N.J.
Jim Matheson, Utah
Lincoln Davis, Tenn.
Ben Chandler, Ky.
Russ Carnahan, Mo.
Baron Hill, Ind.
Harry Mitchell, Ariz.
Charlie Wilson, Ohio
Kathy Dahlkemper, Pa.
Alan Grayson, Fla.
Suzanne M. Kosmas, Fla.
Gary Peters, Mich.

Michael McCaul, Tex.
Mario Diaz-Balart, Fla.
Phil Gingrey, Ga.
Brian P. Bilbray, Calif.
Adrian Smith, Neb.
Paul C. Broun, Ga.
Pete Olson, Tex.

Subcommittees

Energy and Environment
Office: 2319 RHOB   **Phone:** 225-8844
    Brian Baird (Chair), Jerry F. Costello, Lynn Woolsey, Ben R. Luján, Paul D. Tonko, Eddie Bernice Johnson, Daniel Lipinski, Gabrielle Giffords, Jim Matheson, Lincoln Davis, Ben Chandler
    Bob Inglis (Ranking Minority Member), Roscoe G. Bartlett, Vernon J. Ehlers, Judy Biggert, Todd Akin, Randy Neugebauer, Mario Diaz-Balart

Investigations and Oversight
Office: B374 RHOB   **Phone:** 225-8772
    Brad Miller (Chair), Steve Rothman, Lincoln Davis, Charlie Wilson, Kathy Dahlkemper, Alan Grayson
    Paul C. Brown (Ranking Minority Member), Brian P. Bilbray

Research and Science Education
Office: 2320 RHOB   **Phone:** 225-9662
    Daniel Lipinski (Chair), Eddie Bernice Johnson, Brian Baird, Marcia L. Fudge, Paul D. Tonko, Parker Griffith, Russ Carnahan
    Vernon J. Ehlers (Ranking Minority Member), Randy Neugebauer, Brian P. Bilbray, Adrian Smith

Space and Aeronautics
Office: B374 RHOB   **Phone:** 225-7858
    Gabrielle Giffords (Chair), David Wu, Donna Edwards, Marcia L. Fudge, Parker Griffith, Steve Rothman, Baron Hill, Charlie Wilson, Alan Grayson, Suzanne M. Kosmas
    Pete Olson (Ranking Minority Member), F. James Sensenbrenner Jr., Dana Rohrabacher, Frank D. Lucas, Michael McCaul

Technology and Innovation
Office: 2320 RHOB   **Phone:** 225-9662
    David Wu (Chair), Daniel Lipinski, Donna Edwards, Ben R. Luján, Paul D. Tonko, Harry Mitchell, Gary Peters
    Adrian Smith (Ranking Minority Member), Judy Biggert, Todd Akin, Paul C. Broun

SELECT ENERGY INDEPENDENCE AND GLOBAL WARMING

Office: B-243 LHOB 20515
Phone: 225-4012   **Fax:** 225-4092
Majority Staff Director: Gerry Waldron
Minority Staff Director: R. Thomas Weimer 225-0110
    H2-346 FHOB
    Jurisdiction: investigate, study, make findings, and develop recommendations on policies, strategies, technologies and other innovations intended to reduce the dependence of the United States on foreign sources of energy and achieve substantial and permanent reductions in emissions and other activities that contribute to climate change and global warming. The Select Committee shall not have legislative jurisdiction and shall have no authority to take legislative action on any bill or resolution. The Select Committee may report to the House from time to time the results of its investigations and studies, together with such detailed findings and recommendations as it may deem advisable.
Party Ratio: D 9-R 6

Edward J. Markey, Mass., Chair
Earl Blumenauer, Ore.
Jay Inslee, Wash.
John B. Larson, Conn.
Stephanie Herseth Sandlin, S.D.
Emanuel Cleaver II, Mo.
John Hall, N.Y.
John T. Salazar, Colo.
Jackie Speier, Calif.

F. James Sensenbrenner, Wisc., Ranking Minority Member
John Shadegg, Ariz.
John Sullivan, Okla.
Marsha Blackburn, Tenn.
Candice Miller, Mich.
Shelley Moore Capito, W.V.

SELECT INTELLIGENCE

Office: H-405 CAP 20515-6415
Phone: 225-7690 **Fax:** 226-5068
Web: intelligence.house.gov
E-mail: intelligence.hpsci@mail.house.gov
Majority Staff Director: Mike Delaney
Minority Staff Director: James Lewis 225-4121
    H-405 CAP
    Jurisdiction: (1) the Central Intelligence Agency and the Director of Central Intelligence, and the National Foreign Intelligence Program as defined in section 3(6) of the National Security Act of 1947; (2) intelligence and intelligence-related activities of all other departments and agencies of the government, including but not limited to Air Force Intelligence, Surveillance, and Reconnaissance, Defense Intelligence Agency, Federal Bureau of Investigation, National Geospatial-Intelligence Agency (Defense), National Reconnaissance Office (Defense), National Security Agency (Defense), Office of Navy Intelligence, United States Army Intelligence and Security Command, United States Marine Corps

Intelligence Department, and related provisions of the Foreign Intelligence Surveillance Act of 1978 and the Provide Appropriate Tools Required to Intercept and Obstruct Terrorism (PATRIOT) Act of 2001; (3) the organization or reorganization of any department or agency of the government to the extent that the organization or reorganization relates to a function or activity involving intelligence or intelligence-related activities; (4) authorizations for appropriations, both direct and indirect, for the following (A) the Central Intelligence Agency, Director of Central Intelligence, and the National Foreign Intelligence Program as defined in section 3(6) of the National Security Act of 1947; (B) intelligence and intelligence-related activities of all other departments and agencies of the government, including but not limited to, the tactical intelligence and intelligence-related activities of the government, including but not limited to, the tactical intelligence and intelligence-related activities of the Department of Defense. Membership: The select committee shall be composed of not more than 21 Members, of whom not more than 12 may be from the same party. The select committee shall include at least one Member from (1) the Committee on Appropriations; (2) the Committee on Homeland Security; (3) the Committee on International Relations; and (4) the Committee on the Judiciary. The Speaker of the House and the Minority Leader of the House shall be ex officio members of the select committee, but shall have no vote in the committee and shall not be counted for purposes of determining a quorum. No Member of the House other than the Speaker and the Minority Leader may serve on the select committee during more than four Congresses in any period of six consecutive Congresses (disregarding for this purpose any service for less than a full session in any Congress), except that the incumbent chair or ranking minority member having served on the select committee for four Congresses and having served as chair or ranking minority member for not more than one Congress shall be eligible for reappointment to the select committee as chair or ranking minority member for one additional Congress.
Party Ratio: D 13-R 9

Silvestre Reyes, Tex., Chair
Alcee L. Hastings, Fla.
Anna G. Eshoo, Calif.
Rush Holt, N.J.
C. A. "Dutch" Ruppers-
 berger, Md.
John F. Tierney, Mass.
Mike Thompson, Calif.
Jan Schakowsky, Ill.
James R. Langevin, R.I.
Patrick Murphy, Pa.
Adam Schiff, Calif.
Adam Smith, Wash.
Dan Boren, Okla.

Peter Hoekstra, Mich.,
 Ranking Minority
 Member
Elton Gallegly, Calif.
Mac Thornberry, Tex.
Mike Rogers, Mich.
Sue Myrick, N.C.
Roy D. Blunt, Mo.
Jeff Miller, Fla.
John Kline, Minn.
K. Michael Conaway, Tex.

Subcommittees

Intelligence Community Management
Office: H-405 CAP   **Phone:** 225-7690
 Anna G. Eshoo (Chair), Rush Holt, Alcee L. Hastings, Jan Schakowsky, Patrick J. Murphy
 Sue Myrick (Ranking Minority Member), Roy D. Blunt, K. Michael Conaway

Oversight and Investigations
Office: H-405 CAP   **Phone:** 225-7690
 Jan Schakowsky (Chair), John F. Tierney, Patrick J. Murphy, C. A. "Dutch" Ruppersberger, Mike Thompson, Adam Schiff, Dan Boren
 Jeff Miller (Ranking Minority Member), Mac Thornberry, Mike Rogers, Roy Blunt, John Kline

Technical and Tactical Intelligence
Office: H-405 CAP   **Phone:** 225-7690
 C. A. "Dutch" Ruppersberger (Chair), Rush Holt, James R. Langevin, Patrick Murphy, Adam Smith, Adam Schiff
 Mac Thornberry (Ranking Minority Member), Mike Rogers, Jeff Miller, John Kline

Terrorism, Human Intelligence, Analysis, and Counterintelligence
Office: H-405 CAP   **Phone:** 225-7690
 Mike Thompson (Chair), Alcee L. Hastings, C. A. "Dutch" Ruppersberger, James R. Langevin, Adam Schiff, Adam Smith, Dan Boren
 Mike Rogers (Ranking Minority Member), Elton Gallegly, Sue Myrick, Jeff Miller, K.Michael Conaway

SMALL BUSINESS
Office: 2361 RHOB 20515-6315
Phone: 225-4038   **Fax:** 225-7209
Web: www.house.gov/smbiz
Majority Staff Director: Michael Day
Minority Staff Director: Karen Haas 225-5821 B-363 RHOB
 Jurisdiction: (1) assistance to and protection of small business, including financial aid, regulatory flexibility and paperwork reduction; (2) participation of small business enterprises in federal procurement and government contracts. In addition to its legislative jurisdiction under the preceding provisions (and its general oversight function under clause 2(b)(1), the committee has the special oversight function provided for in clause 3(g) with respect to the problems of small business.
Party Ratio: D 17-R 12

Nydia M. Velázquez, N.Y.,
 Chair
Dennis Moore, Kans.
Heath Shuler, N.C.
Kathy Dahlkemper, Pa.
Kurt Schrader, Ore.
Ann Kirkpatrick, Ariz.

Sam Graves, Mo., Ranking
 Minority Member
Roscoe G. Bartlett, Md.
Todd Akin, Mo.
Steve King, Iowa
Lynn A. Westmoreland, Ga.
Louie Gohmert, Tex.

SMALL BUSINESS (continued)

Glenn C. Nye, Va.
Michael Michaud, Maine
Melissa Bean, Ill.
Daniel Lipinski, Ill.
Jason Altmire, Pa.
Yvette D. Clarke, N.Y.
Brad Ellsworth, Ind.
Joe Sestak, Pa.
Bobby Bright, Ala.
Parker Griffith, Ala.
Debbie Halvorson, Ill.

Mary Fallin, Okla.
Vern Buchanan, Fla.
Blaine Luetkemeyer, Mo.
Aaron Shock, Ill.
Glenn W. Thompson, Pa.
Mike Coffman, Colo.

Subcommittees

Contracting and Technology
Office: 2361 RHOB   **Phone:** 225-4038
Glenn C. Nye (Chair), Yvette D. Clarke, Brad Ellsworth, Kurt Schrader, Debbie Halvorson, Melissa Bean, Joe Sestak, Parker Griffith
Aaron Schock (Ranking Minority Member), Roscoe G. Bartlett, Todd Akin, Mary Fallin, Glenn W. Thompson

Finance and Tax
Office: 2361 RHOB   **Phone:** 225-4038
Kurt Schrader (Chair), Dennis Moore, Ann Kirkpatrick, Melissa Bean, Joe Sestak, Debbie Halvorson, Glenn C. Nye, Michael Michaud
Vern Buchanan (Ranking Minority Member), Steve King, Todd Akin, Blaine Luetkemeyer, Mike Coffman

Investigations and Oversight
Office: 2361 RHOB   **Phone:** 225-4038
Jason Altmire (Chair), Heath Shuler, Brad Ellsworth, Parker Griffith
Mary Fallin (Ranking Minority Member), Louie Gohmert

Regulations and Healthcare
Office: 2361 RHOB   **Phone:** 225-4038
Kathy Dahlkemper (Chair), Daniel Lipinski, Parker Griffith, Melissa Bean, Jason Altmire, Joe Sestak, Bobby Bright
Lynn Westmoreland (Ranking Minority Member), Steve King, Vern Buchanan, Glenn W. Thompson, Mike Coffman

Rural Development, Entrepreneurship, and Trade
Office: 2361 RHOB   **Phone:** 225-4038
Heath Shuler (Chair), Michael Michaud, Bobby Bright, Kathy Dahlkemper, Ann Kirkpatrick, Yvette D. Clarke
Blaine Luetkemeyer (Ranking Minority Member), Steve King, Aaron Schock, Glenn W. Thompson

STANDARDS OF OFFICIAL CONDUCT

Office: HT-2 CAP 20515-6328
Phone: 225-7103
Web: www.house.gov/ethics

Majority Staff Director: Kenyen R. Brown
Minority Counsel: Todd Ungerecht 225-7103 HT-2 CAP
Jurisdiction: all bills, resolutions and other matters relating to the Code of Official Conduct adopted under House Rule XXIV (Code of Official Conduct); with respect to Members, officers and employees of the U.S. House of Representatives, the Committee is the supervising ethics office for the U.S. House of Representatives, and is authorized to: (1) recommend administrative actions to establish or enforce standards of official conduct; (2) investigate violations of the Code of Official Conduct or of any applicable rules, laws, or regulations governing the performance of official duties or the discharge of official responsibilities; (3) report to appropriate federal or state authorities substantial evidence of a violation of any law applicable to the performance of official duties that may have been disclosed in a Committee investigation (such reports must be approved by the House or by an affirmative vote of two-thirds of the Committee); (4) render advisory opinions regarding the propriety of any current or proposed conduct of a Member, officer or employee, and issue general guidance on such matters as necessary; and (5) consider requests for written waivers of the gift rule (clause 5 of House Rule XXV).
Party Ratio: D 5-R 5

Zoe Lofgren, Calif., Chair
Ben Chandler, Ky.
G.K. Butterfield, N.C.
Kathy Castor, Fla.
Peter Welch, Vt.

Jo Bonner, Ala., Ranking Minority Member
J. Gresham Barrett, S.C.
John Kline, Minn.
K. Michael Conaway, Tex.
Charlie Dent, Pa.

Subcommittees

To Conduct an Inquiry Regarding Representative Charles B. Rangel
Office: HT-2 CAP 20515-6328   **Phone:** 225-7103
Gene Green (Chair), Robert C. Scott
Jo Bonner, Doc Hastings

TRANSPORTATION AND INFRASTRUCTURE

Office: 2165 RHOB 20515-6256
Phone: 225-4472   **Fax:** 226-1270
Web: transportation.house.gov
Majority Staff Director: David A. Heymsfeld
Minority Chief of Staff: James W. Coon 225-9446 2163 RHOB
Jurisdiction: (1) Coast Guard, including lifesaving service, lighthouses, lightships, ocean derelicts, and the United States Coast Guard Academy (New London, Conn.); (2) federal management of emergencies and natural disasters; (3) flood control and improvement of rivers and harbors; (4) inland waterways; (5) inspection of merchant marine vessels, lights and signals, lifesaving equipment, and fire protection on such vessels; (6) navigation and the laws relating thereto, including

pilotage; (7) registering and licensing of vessels and small boats; (8) rules and international arrangements to prevent collisions at sea; (9) measures relating to the United States Capitol building and the Senate and House office buildings; (10) measures relating to the construction or maintenance of roads and post roads, other than appropriations therefore; but it shall not be in order for any bill providing general legislation in relation to roads to contain any provision for any specific road, nor for any bill in relation to a specific road to embrace a provision in relation to any other specific road; (11) measures relating to the construction or reconstruction, maintenance, and care of the buildings and grounds of the United States Botanic Garden, the Library of Congress, and the Smithsonian Institution; (12) measures relating to merchant marine, except for national security aspects of merchant marine; (13) measures relating to the purchase of sites and construction of post offices, customhouses, federal courthouses, and government buildings within the District of Columbia; (14) oil pollution and other pollution of navigable waters, including inland waters, coastal waters, and ocean waters; (15) marine affairs (including coastal zone management) as they relate to oil and other pollution of navigable waters; (16) public buildings and grounds of the United States generally; (17) public works for the benefit of navigation, including bridges and dams (other than international bridges and dams); (18) related transportation regulatory agencies; (19) roads and the safety thereof; (20) transportation, including civil aviation, railroads, water transportation, transportation safety (except automobile safety), transportation infrastructure, transportation labor, and railroad retirement and railroad unemployment (except revenue measures related thereto); (21) water power.

Party Ratio: D 46–R 30

James L. Oberstar, Minn., Chair	*John L. Mica, Fla., Ranking Minority Member*
Nick J. Rahall, W.Va.	*Don Young, Alaska*
Peter A. DeFazio, Ore.	*Thomas E. Petri, Wisc.*
Jerry F. Costello, Ill.	*Howard Coble, N.C.*
Eleanor Holmes Norton, D.C.	*John J. Duncan Jr., Tenn.*
Jerrold Nadler, N.Y.	*Vernon J. Ehlers, Mich.*
Corrine Brown, Fla.	*Frank A. LoBiondo, N.J.*
Bob Filner, Calif.	*Jerry Moran, Kans.*
Eddie Bernice Johnson, Tex.	*Gary Miller, Calif.*
Gene Taylor, Miss.	*Henry E. Brown Jr., S.C.*
Elijah E. Cummings, Md.	*Timothy V. Johnson, Ill.*
Ellen O. Tauscher, Calif.	*Todd Russell Platts, Pa.*
Leonard L. Boswell, Iowa	*Sam Graves, Mo.*
Tim Holden, Pa.	*Bill Shuster, Pa.*
Brian Baird, Wash.	*John Boozman, Ark.*
Rick Larsen, Wash.	*Shelley Moore Capito, W.Va.*
Michael E. Capuano, Mass.	*Jim Gerlach, Pa.*
Timothy H. Bishop, N.Y.	*Mario Diaz-Balart, Fla.*
Michael Michaud, Maine	*Charlie Dent, Pa.*
Russ Carnahan, Mo.	*Connie Mack, Fla.*
John T. Salazar, Colo.	*Lynn A. Westmoreland, Ga.*
Grace F. Napolitano, Calif.	*Jean Schmidt, Ohio*

Daniel Lipinski, Ill.	*Candice Miller, Mich.*
Mazie K. Hirono, Hawaii	*Mary Fallin, Okla.*
Jason Altmire, Pa.	*Vern Buchanan, Fla.*
Tim Walz, Minn.	*Robert E. Latta, Ohio*
Heath Shuler, N.C.	*Brett Guthrie, Ky.*
Michael Arcuri, N.Y.	*Anh Joseph Cao, La.*
Harry Mitchell, Ariz.	*Aaron Schock, Ill.*
Christopher P. Carney, Pa.	*Pete Olson, Tex.*
John Hall, N.Y.	
Steve Kagen, Wisc.	
Steve Cohen, Tenn.	
Laura Richardson, Calif.	
Albio Sires, N.J.	
Donna Edwards, Md.	
Solomon P. Ortiz, Tex.	
Phil Hare, Ill.	
John A. Boccieri, Ohio	
Mark Schauer, Mich.	
Betsy Markey, Colo.	
Parker Griffith, Ala.	
Michael McMahon, N.Y.	
Tom Perriello, Va.	
Dina Titus, Nev.	
Harry Teague, N.M.	

Subcommittees

Aviation
Office: 2251 RHOB   **Phone:** 225-9161

Jerry F. Costello (Chair), Russ Carnahan, Parker Griffith, Michael McMahon, Peter A. DeFazio, Eleanor Holmes Norton, Bob Filner, Eddie Bernice Johnson, Leonard L. Boswell, Tim Holden, Michael E. Capuano, Daniel Lipinski, Mazie K. Hirono, Harry Mitchell, John Hall, Steve Cohen, Laura Richardson, John A. Boccieri, Nick J. Rahall II, Corrine Brown, Elijah E. Cummings, Ellen O. Tauscher, Jason Altmire, Solomon P. Ortiz, Mark Schauer

Thomas E. Petri (Ranking Minority Member), Howard Coble, John J. Duncan, Vernon J. Ehlers, Frank A. LoBiondo, Jerry Moran, Sam Graves, John Boozman, Shelley Moore Capito, Jim Gerlach, Charlie Dent, Connie Mack, Lynn A. Westmoreland, Jean Schmidt, Mary Fallin, Vern Buchanan, Brett Guthrie

Coast Guard and Maritime Transportation
Office: 507 FHOB   **Phone:** 226-3587

Elijah E. Cummings (Chair), Corrine Brown, Rick Larsen, Gene Taylor, Brian Baird, Timothy H. Bishop, Steve Kagen, Michael McMahon, Laura Richardson

Frank A. LoBiondo (Ranking Minority Member), Don Young, Howard Coble, Vernon J. Ehlers, Todd Russell Platts, Pete Olson

Economic Development, Public Buildings, and Emergency Management
Office: 585 FHOB   **Phone:** 225-9961

Eleanor Holmes Norton (Chair), Betsy Markey, Michael Michaud, Heath Shuler, Parker Griffith, Russ Carnahan, Tim Walz, Michael Arcuri, Christopher P. Carney, Donna Edwards, Tom Perriello

TRANSPORTATION AND INFRASTRUCTURE (continued)

Mario Diaz-Balart (Ranking Minority Member), Timothy V. Johnson, Sam Graves, Shelley Moore Capito, Mary Fallin, Brett Guthrie, Anh Joseph Cao

Highways and Transit
Office: B370A RHOB **Phone:** 225-9989

Peter A. DeFazio (Chair), Nick J. Rahall II, Jerrold Nadler, Bob Filner, Ellen O. Tauscher, Tim Holden, Brian Baird, Michael E. Capuano, Timothy H. Bishop, Michael Michaud, Grace F. Napolitano, Daniel Lipinski, Mazie K. Hirono, Jason Altmire, Tim Walz, Heath Shuler, Michael Arcuri, Christopher P. Carney, Steve Cohen, Laura Richardson, Albio Sires, Donna Edwards, Gene Taylor, Leonard L. Boswell, Rick Larsen, John Hall, Steve Kagen, Solomon P. Ortiz, Phil Hare, John A. Boccieri, Mark Schauer

John J. Duncan Jr. (Ranking Minority Member), Don Young, Thomas E. Petri, Howard Coble, Jerry Moran, Gary Miller, Henry E. Brown Jr., Timothy V. Johnson, Todd Russell Platts, Bill Shuster, John Boozman, Jim Gerlach, Mario Diaz-Balart, Charlie Dent, Connie Mack, Jean Schmidt, Candice Miller, Mary Fallin, Vern Buchanan, Robert E. Latta, Aaron Schock

Railroads, Pipelines, and Hazardous Materials
Office: 589 FHOB **Phone:** 225-3274

Corrine Brown (Chair), Dina Titus, Harry Teague, Nick J. Rahall II, Jerrold Nadler, Elijah E. Cummings, Grace F. Napolitano, Jason Altmire, Tim Walz, Michael Arcuri, Christopher P. Carney, Albio Sires, Mark Schauer, Betsy Markey, Michael McMahon, Tom Perriello, Peter A. DeFazio, Jerry F. Costello, Bob Filner, Eddie Bernice Johnson, Leonard L. Boswell, Rick Larsen, Michael Michaud, Daniel Lipinski, Steve Cohen, Laura Richardson

Bill Shuster (Ranking Minority Member), Thomas E. Petri, Jerry Moran, Gary Miller, Henry E. Brown Jr., Timothy V. Johnson, Sam Graves, Jim Gerlach, Charlie Dent, Lynn A. Westmoreland, Jean Schmidt, Candice Miller, Vern Buchanan, Robert E. Latta, Brett Guthrie, Anh Joseph Cao, Aaron Schock, Pete Olson

Water Resources and Environment
Office: B376 RHOB **Phone:** 225-0060

Eddie Bernice Johnson (Chair), Jerry F. Costello, Gene Taylor, Ellen O. Tauscher, Brian Baird, Timothy H. Bishop, Russ Carnahan, Steve Kagen, Donna Edwards, Solomon P. Ortiz, Phil Hare, Dina Titus, Harry Teague, Eleanor Holmes Norton, Michael E. Capuano, Grace F. Napolitano, Mazie K. Hirono, Harry Mitchell, John Hall, Parker Griffith, Bob Filner, Corrine Brown

John Boozman (Ranking Minority Member), Don Young, John J. Duncan Jr., Vernon J. Ehlers, Frank A. LoBiondo, Gary Miller, Henry E. Brown Jr., Todd Russell Platts, Bill Shuster, Mario Diaz-Balart, Connie Mack, Lynn A. Westmoreland, Candice Miller, Robert E. Latta, Anh Joseph Cao, Pete Olson

VETERANS' AFFAIRS

Office: 333 CHOB 20515-6335
Phone: 225-9756
Web: veterans.house.gov
Majority Staff Director: Malcolm Shorter
Minority Staff Director: Kingston E. Smith 225-3527
333 CHOB

Jurisdiction: (1) veterans measures generally; (2) cemeteries of the United States in which veterans of any war or conflict are or may be buried, whether in the United States or abroad, except cemeteries administered by the Secretary of the Interior; (3) compensation, vocational rehabilitation, and education of veterans; (4) life insurance issued by the government on account of service in the Armed Forces; (5) pensions of all the wars of the United States; (6) readjustment of service personnel to civil life; (7) soldiers' and sailors' civil relief, including oversight of and appropriate modifications to the Soldiers' and Sailors' Civil Relief Act of 1940; (8) veterans hospitals, medical care and treatment of veterans.

Party Ratio: D 16-R 13

Bob Filner, Calif., Chair	*Steve Buyer, Ind., Ranking*
Corrine Brown, Fla.	*Minority Member*
Vic Snyder, Ark.	*Clifford B. Stearns, Fla.*
Michael Michaud, Maine	*Jerry Moran, Kan.*
Stephanie Herseth	*Henry E. Brown Jr., S.C.*
Sandlin, S.D.	*Jeff Miller, Fla.*
Harry Mitchell, Ariz.	*John Boozman, Ark.*
John Hall, N.Y.	*Brian P. Bilbray, Calif.*
Debbie Halvorson, Ill.	*Doug Lamborn, Colo.*
Tom Perriello, Va.	*Gus Bilirakis, Fla.*
Harry Teague, N.M.	*Vern Buchanan, Fla.*
Ciro D. Rodriguez, Tex.	*Phil Roe, Tenn.*
Joe Donnelly, Ind.	
Jerry McNerney, Calif.	
Zack Space, Ohio	
Tim Walz, Minn.	
John Adler, N.J.	
Ann Kirkpatrick, Ariz.	
Glenn C. Nye, Va.	

Subcommittees

Disability Assistance and Memorial Affairs
Office: 337 CHOB **Phone:** 225-9164

John Hall (Chair), Debbie Halvorson, Joe Donnelly, Ciro D. Rodriguez, Ann Kirkpatrick

Doug Lamborn (Ranking Minority Member), Jeff Miller, Brian P. Bilbray

Economic Opportunity
Office: 335 CHOB **Phone:** 226-5491

Stephanie Herseth Sandlin (Chair), Tom Perriello, John Adler, Ann Kirkpatrick, Harry Teague

John Boozman (Ranking Minority Member), Jerry Moran, Gus Bilirakis

Health
Office: 338 CHOB **Phone:** 225-9154

Michael Michaud (Chair), Corrine Brown, Vic Snyder, Harry Teague, Ciro D. Rodriguez, Joe Donnelly, Jerry McNerney, Glenn C. Nye, Debbie Halvorson, Tom Perriello

Henry E. Brown Jr. (Ranking Minority Member), Clifford B. Stearns, Jerry Moran, John Boozman, Gus Bilirakis, Vern Buchanan

Oversight and Investigations
Office: 337A CHOB   **Phone:** 225-3569
Harry Mitchell (Chair), Zack Space, Tim Walz, John Adler, John Hall

Phil Roe (Ranking Minority Member), Clifford B. Stearns, Brian P. Bilbray

WAYS AND MEANS

Office: 1102 LHOB 20515-6348
Phone: 225-3625   **Fax:** 225-2610
Web: waysandmeans.house.gov
Majority Staff Director: Janice A. Mays
Minority Staff Director: Jonathan G. Traub 225-4021
   1139E LHOB
Jurisdiction: (1) customs, collection districts, and ports of entry and delivery; (2) reciprocal trade agreements; (3) revenue measures generally; (4) revenue measures relating to the insular possessions; (5) the bonded debt of the United States (subject to the last sentence of clause 4(g) of rule X); (6) the deposit of public moneys; (7) transportation of dutiable goods; (8) tax exempt foundations and charitable trusts; (9) Social Security, except (A) health care and facilities programs that are supported from general revenues as opposed to payroll deductions and (B) work incentive programs.
Party Ratio: D 24-R 17

Charles B. Rangel, N.Y., Chair	*Dave Camp, Mich., Ranking Minority Member*
Pete Stark, Calif.	
Sander M. Levin, Mich.	*Wally Herger, Calif.*
Jim McDermott, Wash.	*Sam Johnson, Tex.*
John Lewis, Ga.	*Kevin Brady, Tex.*
Richard E. Neal, Mass.	*Paul D. Ryan, Wisc.*
John S. Tanner, Tenn.	*Eric Cantor, Va.*
Xavier Becerra, Calif.	*John Linder, Ga.*
Lloyd Doggett, Tex.	*Devin Nunes, Calif.*
Earl Pomeroy, N.D.	*Patrick J. Tiberi, Ohio*
Mike Thompson, Calif.	*Ginny Brown-Waite, Fla.*
John B. Larson, Conn.	*Geoff Davis, Ky.*
Earl Blumenauer, Ore.	*Dave Reichert, Wash.*
Ron Kind, Wisc.	*Charles Boustany Jr., La.*
William J. Pascrell Jr., N.J.	*Dean Heller, Nev.*
Shelley Berkley, Nev.	*Peter Roskam, Ill.*
Joseph Crowley, N.Y.	
Chris Van Hollen, Md.	
Kendrick B. Meek, Fla.	
Allyson Y. Schwartz, Pa.	
Artur Davis, Ala.	
Danny K. Davis, Ill.	

Bob Etheridge, N.C.
Linda Sánchez, Calif.
Brian Higgins, N.Y.
John Yarmuth, Ky.

Subcommittees

Health
Office: 1135 LHOB   **Phone:** 225-9343
Pete Stark (Chair), Lloyd Doggett, Mike Thompson, Xavier Becerra, Earl Pomeroy, Ron Kind, Earl Blumenauer, William J. Pascrell Jr., Shelley Berkley

Wally Herger (Ranking Minority Member), Sam Johnson, Paul D. Ryan, Devin Nunes, Ginny Brown-Waite

Income Security and Family Support
Office: B-317 RHOB   **Phone:** 225-1025
Jim McDermott (Chair), Pete Stark, Artur Davis, John Lewis, Shelley Berkley, Chris Van Hollen, Kendrick B. Meek, Sander M. Levin, Danny K. Davis

John Linder (Ranking Minority Member), Charles Boustany Jr., Dean Heller, Peter Roskam, Patrick J. Tiberi

Oversight
Office: 1136 LHOB   **Phone:** 225-5522
John Lewis (Chair), Xavier Becerra, Ron Kind, William J. Pascrell Jr., John B. Larson, Artur Davis, Danny K. Davis, Bob Etheridge, Brian Higgins

Charles Boustany Jr. (Ranking Minority Member), Dave Reichert, Peter Roskam, Paul D. Ryan, John Linder

Select Revenue Measures
Office: 1136 LHOB   **Phone:** 225-5522
Richard E. Neal (Chair), Mike Thompson, John B. Larson, Allyson Y. Schwartz, Earl Blumenauer, Joseph Crowley, Kendrick B. Meek, Brian Higgins, John Yarmuth

Patrick J. Tiberi (Ranking Minority Member), John Linder, Dean Heller, Peter Roskam, Geoff Davis

Social Security
Office: 1129 LHOB   **Phone:** 225-9263
John S. Tanner (Chair), Earl Pomeroy, Allyson Y. Schwartz, Xavier Becerra, Lloyd Doggett, Ron Kind, Joseph Crowley, Linda Sánchez, John Yarmuth

Sam Johnson (Ranking Minority Member), Kevin Brady, Patrick J. Tiberi, Ginny Brown-Waite, Dave Reichert

Trade
Office: 1104 LHOB   **Phone:** 225-6649
Sander M. Levin (Chair), John S. Tanner, Chris Van Hollen, Jim McDermott, Richard E. Neal, Lloyd Doggett, Earl Pomeroy, Bob Etheridge, Linda Sánchez

Kevin Brady (Ranking Minority Member), Geoff Davis, Dave Reichert, Wally Herger, Devin Nunes

HOUSE LEADERSHIP AND PARTISAN COMMITTEES

DEMOCRATIC LEADERS

Speaker of the House: Nancy Pelosi, Calif.
Majority Leader: Steny H. Hoyer, Md.
Majority Whip: James E. Clyburn, S.C.
Senior Chief Deputy Majority Whip: John Lewis, Ga.

DEMOCRATIC PARTISAN COMMITTEES

Democratic Congressional Campaign Committee
Office: 430 S. Capitol St. S.E. 20003-4024
Phone: 485-3419
Fax: 485-3512
Web: www.dccc.org
E-mail: dccc@dccc.org
Chris Van Hollen, Md., Chair

Democratic Caucus
Office: 202A CHOB 20515
Phone: 225-1400
Fax: 226-4412
Web: www.dems.gov
E-mail: democratic.caucus@mail.house.gov
John B. Larson, Conn., Chair
Xavier Becerra, Calif., Vice Chair

Democratic Steering and Policy Committee
Office: H-204 CAP 20515-6527
Phone: 225-0100
Fax: 225-4188
Web: speaker.house.gov
Nancy Pelosi, Calif., Chair
Rosa L. DeLauro, Conn., Co-Chair, Steering
George Miller, Calif., Co-Chair, Policy

REPUBLICAN LEADERS

Minority Leader: *John A. Boehner, Ohio*
Minority Whip: *Eric I. Cantor, Va..*

REPUBLICAN PARTISAN COMMITTEES

National Republican Congressional Committee
Office: 320 1st St. S.E. 20003-1838
Phone: 479-7000
Fax: 863-0693
Web: www.nrcc.org
E-mail: website@nrcc.org
Pete Sessions, Tex., Chair
Greg Walden, Ore., Vice Chair
Other Leadership
  (in alphabetical order)
Marsha Blackburn, Tenn., Communications Chair
Vacancy, Finance Chair
K. Michael Conaway, Tex., Auditing Chair
John Kline, Minn., Management Chair
Patrick McHenry, N.C., Finance Vice Chair
Candice Miller, Mich., Candidate Recruitment Chair

Republican Conference
Office: 1420 LHOB 20515
Phone: 225-5107
Fax: 226-0154
Web: www.gop.gov
E-mail: GOP@mail.house.gov
Mike Pence, Ind.., Chair
Cathy McMorris Rodgers, Wash.., Vice Chair
John R. Carter, Tex., Secretary

Republican Policy Committee
Office: B-58 CHOB 20515-6549
Phone: 225-6168
Fax: 225-0931
Web: policy.house.gov
Thaddeus McCotter, Mich., Chair
Michael Burgess, Tex., Vice Chair

Republican Steering Committee
Office: 1011 LHOB 20515-3508
Phone: 225-6205
Fax: 225-0704
John A. Boehner, Ohio, Minority Leader and Chair

House Members' Offices

Listed below are House members and their party, state, and district affiliation, followed by the address and telephone number for their Washington office. (The area code for all Washington, D.C., numbers is 202.) The top administrative aide and Web and e-mail addresses for each member are also provided, when available. (Most members may be contacted via the Web-based e-mail forms found on their Web sites.) These are followed by the address, telephone and fax numbers, and name of a key aide in the member's district office(s). Each listing concludes with the representative's committee assignments. For partisan committee assignments, see page 750.

As of May 13, 2009, there were 256 Democrats, 178 Republicans, and 1 vacancy in the House of Representatives.

Abercrombie, Neil, D-Hawaii (1)

Capitol Hill Office: 1502 LHOB 20515-1101; 225-2726; Fax: 225-4580; *Deputy Chief of Staff:* Kathleen L. Chapman
Web: www.house.gov/Abercrombie
E-mail: Neil.Abercrombie@mail.house.gov
District Office(s): Prince Kuhio Federal Bldg., 300 Ala Moana Blvd., #4104, Honolulu 96850-4972; (808) 541-2570; Fax: (808) 533-0133; *Chief of Staff:* Amy Asselbaye
Committee Assignment(s): Armed Services; Natural Resources

Ackerman, Gary L., D-N.Y. (5)

Capitol Hill Office: 2243 RHOB 20515-3205; 225-2601; Fax: 225-1589; *Chief of Staff:* Jedd I. Moskowitz
Web: www.house.gov/ackerman
District Office(s): 21814 Northern Blvd., #204, Bayside 11361-3505; (718) 423-2154; Fax: (718) 423-5053; *District Administrator:* Moya Berry
Committee Assignment(s): Financial Services; Foreign Affairs

Aderholt, Robert B., R-Ala. (4)

Capitol Hill Office: 1433 LHOB 20515-0104; 225-4876; Fax: 225-5587; *Chief of Staff:* Mark Busching
Web: aderholt.house.gov
-Morgan County Courthouse, 302 Lee St. N.E., P.O. Box 668, Decatur 35601-1926; (256) 350-4093; Fax: (256) 350-5056
Federal Bldg., 600 Broad St., #107, Gadsden 35901-3745; (256) 546-0201; Fax: (256) 546-8778; *Field Representative:* Jason Harper
Carl Elliott Federal Bldg., 1710 Alabama Ave., #247, Jasper 35501-5400; (205) 221-2310; Fax: (205) 221-9035; *District Field Director:* Paul Housel
Committee Assignment(s): Appropriations; Budget; Commission on Security and Cooperation in Europe

Adler, John, D-N.J. (3)

Capitol Hill Office: 1223 LHOB 20515-3003; 225-4765; Fax: 225-0778; *Chief of Staff:* Tim Lydon
Web: adler.house.gov
District Office(s): 28 N. Maple Ave., Marlton 08053-3021; *District Director:* Carol Gaskill
247 Main St., Toms River 08753-7468; (732) 914-2020; Fax (732) 914-8351; *Field Rep:* Ben Giovine
Committee Assignment(s): Financial Services, Veterans Affairs

Akin, Todd, R-Mo. (2)

Capitol Hill Office: 117 CHOB 20515-2502; 225-2561; Fax: 225-2563; *Chief of Staff:* Paul Protic
Web: www.house.gov/akin
District Office(s): 820 S. Main St., #206, St. Charles 63301-3306; (636) 949-6826; Fax: (636) 949-3832; *Area Director:* Debbie Cochran
301 Sovereign Court, #201, St. Louis 63141; (314) 590-0029; Fax: (314) 590-0037; *District Director:* Patrick Werner
Committee Assignment(s): Armed Services; Science and Technology; Small Business

Alexander, Rodney, R-La. (5)

Capitol Hill Office: 316 CHOB 20515-1805; 225-8490; Fax: 225-5639; *Chief of Staff:* Adam Terry
Web: www.house.gov/Alexander
District Office(s): 1412 Center Court, #402, Alexandria 71301-3449; (318) 445-0818; Fax: (318) 445-3776; *District Representative:* Tommie Seaton
1900 Stubbs Ave., Suite B, Monroe 71201-5751; (318) 322-3500; Fax: (318) 245-8218; *District Director:* Linda Blount
Committee Assignment(s): Appropriations

Altmire, Jason, D-Pa. (4)

Capitol Hill Office: 332 CHOB 20515-3804; 225-2565; Fax: 226-2274; *Chief of Staff:* Sharon Werner
Web: altmire.house.gov
District Office(s): 2110 McLean St., Aliquippa 15001-2964, (724) 378-0928, Fax. (724) 378-6171; *District Director:* Michelle Dorothy
2124 Freeport Road, Natrona Heights 15065-1527; (724) 226-1304; Fax (724) 226-1308
Committee Assignment(s): Education and Labor; Small Business; Transportation and Infrastructure

Andrews, Robert E., D-N.J. (1)

Capitol Hill Office: 2265 RHOB 20515-3001; 225-6501;
Fax: 225-6583; *Chief of Staff: Matt Walker*
Web: www.house.gov/Andrews
District Office(s): 506A White Horse Pike, Haddon
Heights 08035; (856) 546-5100; Fax: (609) 546-9529;
Director of Constituent Services; General Counsel:
Amanda Caruso
63 N. Broad. St., Woodbury 08096; (609) 848-3900;
District Representative: Leanne Hasbrouck
Committee Assignment(s): Armed Services; Budget;
Education and Labor

Arcuri, Michael, D-N.Y. (24)

Capitol Hill Office: 127 CHOB 20515-3224; 225-3665;
Fax: 225-1891; *Chief of Staff:* Sam Marchio
Web: arcuri.house.gov
District Office(s): 17 E. Genesee St., Auburn 13021; (315)
252-2777; Fax: (315) 252-2779; *Field Representative:*
Crystal Cornelius
16 Church St., Carriage House Right, Cortland
13045-2710; (607) 756-2470; (607) 756-2472;
Field Representative: Bob Messinger
Alexander Pirnie Federal Bldg., 10 Broad St., Room 200,
Utica 13501-1233; (315) 793-8146; Fax: (315)
798-4099; *District Director:* Joseph Johnson
Committee Assignment(s): Rules; Transportation and
Infrastructure

Baca, Joe, D-Calif. (43)

Capitol Hill Office: 1527 LHOB 20515-0543; 225-6161;
Fax: 225-8671; *Chief of Staff:* Linda Macias
Web: www.house.gov/baca
District Office(s): 201 North E St., #102, San Bernardino
92401; (909) 885-2222; Fax: (909) 888-5959; *District
Director:* Sam Garcia
Committee Assignment(s): Agriculture; Financial
Services; Natural Resources

Bachmann, Michele, R-Minn. (6)

Capitol Hill Office: 412 CHOB 20515-2306; 225-2331;
Fax: 225-6475; *Chief of Staff:* Michelle C. Marston
Web: bachmann.house.gov
District Office(s): 110 2nd St. South, #232, Waite Park
56387-1313; (320) 253-5931; (320) 240-6905
6043 Hudson Rd., #330, Woodbury 55125-1018; (651)
731-5400; Fax: (651) 731-6650; *District Director:* Julie
Quist
Committee Assignment(s): Financial Services

Bachus, Spencer, R-Ala. (6)

Capitol Hill Office: 2246 RHOB 20515-0106; 225-4921;
Fax: 225-2082; *Chief of Staff:* Michael Staley
Web: bachus.house.gov
District Office(s): 1900 International Park Dr., #107,
Birmingham 35243-4217; (205) 969-2296; Fax: (205)
969-3958; *Field Representative:* Caleb Goodwin

703 2nd Ave. North, P.O. Box 502, Clanton 35045; (205)
755-1522; Fax: (205) 755-1161; *Field Representative:*
Betty Bennett
Committee Assignment(s): Financial Services

Baird, Brian, D-Wash. (3)

Capitol Hill Office: 2443 RHOB 20515-4703; 225-3536;
Fax: 225-3478; *Chief of Staff:* Lisa Austin
Web: www.house.gov/baird
District Office(s): 120 Union Ave. S.E., #105, Olympia
98501-1332; (360) 352-9768; Fax: (360) 352-9241;
Field Representative: Sean Murphy
General O. O. Howard House, 750 Anderson St., Suite B,
Vancouver 98660-2962; (360) 695-6292; Fax: (360)
695-6197; *District Director:* Kelly Love
Committee Assignment(s): Budget; Science and
Technology; Transportation and Infrastructure

Baldwin, Tammy, D-Wisc. (2)

Capitol Hill Office: 2446 RHOB 20515-4902; 225-2906;
Fax: 225-6942; *Chief of Staff:* William M. Murat
Web: tammybaldwin.house.gov
District Office(s): 400 E. Grand Ave., #402, Beloit
53511-6229; (608) 362-2800; Fax: (608) 362-2838;
Field Representative: Helen Forbeck
10 E. Doty St., #405, Madison 53703-5103; (608)
258-9800; Fax: (608) 258-9808; *District Director:*
Curt Finkelmeyer
Committee Assignment(s): Energy and Commerce;
Judiciary

Barrett, J. Gresham, R-S.C. (3)

Capitol Hill Office: 439 CHOB 20515-4003; 225-5301;
Fax: 225-3216; *Chief of Staff:* Darryl Broome
Web: www.barrett.house.gov
District Office(s): 233 Pendleton St. N.W., Aiken
29801-3947; (803) 649-5571; Fax: (803) 648-9038;
Senior Caseworker: Kim Westbury
303 W. Beltline Blvd., Anderson 29625-1505; (864)
224-7401; Fax: (864) 225-7049; *Senior Caseworker:*
Pam Carpenter
115 Enterprise Court, Suite B, Greenwood 29649-1689;
(864) 223-8251; Fax: (864) 223-1679; *Caseworker:*
Tosha Hart
Committee Assignment(s): Financial Services; Foreign
Affairs; Standards of Official Conduct

Barrow, John, D-Ga. (12)

Capitol Hill Office: 213 CHOB 20515-1012; 225-2823;
Fax: 225-3377; *Chief of Staff:* Ashley Jones
Web: barrow.house.gov
District Office(s): 925 Laney Walker Boulevard, Suite 300,
Augusta 30901-2959; (706) 722-4494; Fax: (706)
722-4496; *District Director:* Lynthia Ross
400 Mall Blvd., Suite G, Savannah 31406-4820; (912)
354-7282; Fax: (912) 354-7782; *Constituent Services
Supervisor:* Yvonne Davis

107 Old Airport Rd., Suite A, Vidalia 30474; (912)
537-9301; Fax: (912) 537-9266; *Constituent Services
Representative*: Cynthia Reese

141 W. Haynes St., P.O. Box 1017, Sandersville 31082;
(478) 553-1923; Fax: (478) 553-9215; *Constituent
Services Representative*: Cynthia Reese

Committee Assignment(s): Energy and Commerce

Bartlett, Roscoe G., R-Md. (6)

Capitol Hill Office: 2412 RHOB 20515-2006; 225-2721;
Fax: 225-2193; *Chief of Staff*: Harold Bud Otis

Web: bartlett.house.gov

District Office(s): 1 Frederick St., Cumberland 21502-
2309; (301) 724-3105; Fax: (301) 724-3538; *District
Assistant*: Brenda Frantz

7360 Guilford Dr., #101, Frederick 21704-5128; (301)
694-3030; Fax: (301) 694-6674; *Policy Director*: Sallie
B. Taylor

11377 Robinwood Dr., Hagerstown 21742-6729; (301)
797-6043; Fax: (301) 797-2385; *Field Representative*:
Myra Kidd

15 E. Main St., #110, Westminster 21157-5066; (410)
857-1115; Fax: (410) 857-3648; *District Assistant*:
Deborah Burrell

Committee Assignment(s): Armed Services; Science and
Technology; Small Business

Barton, Joe, R-Tex. (6)

Capitol Hill Office: 2109 RHOB 20515-4306; 225-2002;
Fax: 225-3052; *Chief of Staff*: Heather Couri

Web: joebarton.house.gov

District Office(s): 6001 West I-20, #200, Arlington 76017;
(817) 543-1000; Fax: (817) 548-7029; *District
Director*: Ronald J. Wright

P.O. Box 958, Crockett 75835; (936) 544-8488; *District
Assistant*: Karla Carr

2106-A West Ennis Ave., Ennis 75119-3624; (972)
875-8488; *Field Representative*: Dub Maines

Committee Assignment(s): Energy and Commerce

Bean, Melissa, D-Ill. (8)

Capitol Hill Office: 432 CHOB 20515-1308; 225-3711;
Fax: 225-7830; *Chief of Staff*: Elizabeth Hart

Web: www.house.gov/bean

District Office(s): 1430 N. Meacham Rd., Schaumburg
60173-4836; (847) 519-3434; Fax: (847) 519-3436;
Executive Assistant: Dan Shrigley

Committee Assignment(s): Financial Services; Small
Business

Becerra, Xavier, D-Calif. (31)

Capitol Hill Office: 1119 LHOB 20515-0531; 225-6235;
Fax: 225-2202; *Chief of Staff*: Debra S. Dixon

Web: becerra.house.gov

District Office(s): 1910 W. Sunset Blvd., #560, Los
Angeles 90026-3445; (213) 483-1425; Fax: (213)
483-1429; *District Director*: Laura Arciniega

Committee Assignment(s): Budget; Ways and Means

Berkley, Shelley, D-Nev. (1)

Capitol Hill Office: 405 CHOB 20515-2801; 225-5965;
Fax: 225-3119; *Chief of Staff*: Richard Urey

Web: berkley.house.gov

District Office(s): 2340 Paseo Del Prado, #D-106,
Las Vegas 89102-4340; (702) 220-9823; Fax: (702)
220-9841; *District Director*: Tod J. Story

Committee Assignment(s): Foreign Affairs; Ways and
Means

Berman, Howard L., D-Calif. (28)

Capitol Hill Office: 2221 RHOB 20515-0528; 225-4695;
Chief of Staff: Julia A. Massimino

Web: www.house.gov/berman

District Office(s): 14546 Hamlin St., #202, Van Nuys
91411; (818) 994-7200; *District Director*: Robert J.
Blumenfield

Committee Assignment(s): Foreign Affairs; Judiciary

Berry, Marion, D-Ark. (1)

Capitol Hill Office: 2305 RHOB 20515-0401; 225-4076;
Fax: 225-5602; *Chief of Staff*: C. Chad Causey

Web: www.house.gov/berry

District Office(s): 112 S. 1st St., Cabot 72023-3007; (501)
843-3043; Fax: (501) 843-4955; *Caseworker*: Jennifer
Burleson

108 E. Huntington Ave., Jonesboro 72401-2967; (870)
972-4600; Fax: (870) 972-4605; *District Director*:
Erika L. Krennerich

Courthouse Sq., One E. 7th St., #200, Mountain Home
72653-4409; (870) 425-3510; Fax: (870) 425-3511;
Regional Representative: Joe Dillard

Committee Assignment(s): Appropriations; Budget

Biggert, Judy, R-Ill. (13)

Capitol Hill Office: 1034 LHOB 20515-1313; 225-3515;
Fax: 225-9420; *Chief of Staff*: Kathleen Lydon

Web: judybiggert.house.gov

District Office(s): 6262 Route 83, #305, Willowbrook
60527-2987; (630) 655-2052; Fax: (630) 655-1061;
District Office Manager: Sandy Henrichs

Committee Assignment(s): Education and Labor;
Financial Services; Science and Technology

Bilbray, Brian P., R-Calif. (50)

Capitol Hill Office: 2348 RHOB 20515-0550;
225-0508; Fax: 225-2558; *Chief of Staff*:
Steve S. Danon

Web: www.house.gov/Bilbray

District Office(s): 462 Stevens Ave., #107, Solana Beach
92075-2065; (858) 350-1150; Fax: (858) 350-0750;
District Director: Christy Guerin

Committee Assignment(s): Oversight and
Government Reform; Science and Technology;
Veterans' Affairs

Bilirakis, Gus, R-Fla. (9)

Capitol Hill Office: 1124 LHOB 20515-0909; 225-5755; Fax: 225-4085; *Chief of Staff:* Rebecca J. Hyder
Web: bilirakis.house.gov
District Office(s): 35111 U.S. Hwy. 19 North, Palm Harbor Professional Center, #301, Palm Harbor 34684-1934; (727) 773-2871; Fax: (727) 784-6471; *District Director:* Shawn Foster
10941 N. 56th St., Temple Terrace 33617-3000; (813) 985-8541; Fax: (813) 985-0714; *Special Assistant:* Diane Trimis
Committee Assignment(s): Foreign Affairs, Homeland Security; Veterans' Affairs

Bishop, Rob, R-Utah (1)

Capitol Hill Office: 124 CHOB 20515-4401; 225-0453; Fax: 225-5857; *Chief of Staff:* Scott B. Parker
Web: www.house.gov/robbishop
District Office(s): 6 N. Main St., Brigham City 84302-2116; (435) 734-2270; Fax: (435) 734-2290
324 25th St., Ogden 84401-2361; (801) 625-0107; Fax: (801) 625-0124; *District Director:* Peter Jenks
125 S. State St., #5420, Salt Lake City 84138-1125; (801) 532-3244; Fax: (801) 532-3583
Committee Assignment(s): Armed Services; Education and Labor; Natural Resources

Bishop, Sanford D. Jr., D-Ga. (2)

Capitol Hill Office: 2429 RHOB 20515-1002; 225-3631; Fax: 225-2203; *Chief of Staff; Administrative Assistant:* Phyllis Hallmon
Web: bishop.house.gov
District Office(s): Albany Towers, 235 Roosevelt Hwy., #216, Albany 31701-5132; (229) 439-8067; Fax: (229) 436-2099; *District Director:* Kenneth J. Cutts
18 9th St., #201, Columbus 31901-2778; (706) 320-9477; Fax: (706) 320-9479; *Field Representative:* Elaine Gillespie
137 E Jackson St., Thomasville 31792-5136; (229) 226-7789; Fax: (229) 226-7860; *Field Representative:* Michael Bryant
Committee Assignment(s): Appropriations

Bishop, Timothy H., D-N.Y. (1)

Capitol Hill Office: 306 CHOB 20515-3201; 225-3826; Fax: 225-3143; *Chief of Staff:* Pete Spiro
Web: timbishop.house.gov
District Office(s): 3680 Route 112, Suite C, Coram 11727-4140; (631) 696-6500; Fax: (631) 696-4520; *Director of Intergovernmental Affairs and Community Outreach:* Lisa Wieber
137 Hampton Rd., Southampton 11968-4923; (631) 259-8450; Fax (631) 259-8451; *Special Projects Director:* Jane Finalborgo
Committee Assignment(s): Budget; Education and Labor; Transportation and Infrastructure

Blackburn, Marsha, R-Tenn. (7)

Capitol Hill Office: 217 CHOB 20515-4207; 225-2811; Fax: 225-3004; *Chief of Staff:* Steve Brophy
Web: www.house.gov/Blackburn
District Office(s): 1850 Memorial Dr., Clarksville 37043-4603; (931) 503-0391; Fax: (931) 503-0393; *Caseworker:* Woody Parker
109 3rd Ave. S., #117, Franklin 37064-2518; (615) 591-5161; Fax: (615) 599-2916; *District Director:* Ryan Durst
7975 Stage Hills Blvd., #1, Memphis 38133-4036; (901) 382-5811; Fax: (901) 373-8215; *Deputy Chief of Staff:* Scott Golden
Committee Assignment(s): Energy and Commerce; Select Energy Independence and Global Warming

Blumenauer, Earl, D-Ore. (3)

Capitol Hill Office: 2267 RHOB 20515-3703; 225-4811; Fax: 225-8941; *Deputy Chief of Staff:* James E. Koski
Web: blumenauer.house.gov
District Office(s): 729 N.E. Oregon St., #115, Portland 97232-2184; (503) 231-2300; Fax: (503) 230-5413; *District Director:* Julia Pomeroy
Committee Assignment(s): Budget; Ways and Means; Select Energy Independence and Global Warming

Blunt, Roy D., R-Mo. (7)

Capitol Hill Office: 2229 RHOB 20515-2507; 225-6536; Fax: 225-5604; *Chief of Staff:* Amy Poe
Web: www.blunt.house.gov
District Office(s): Northpark Mall, 101 N. Rangeline Rd., Joplin 64801-4118; (417) 781-1041; Fax: (417) 781-2832; *Field Representative:* Steve McIntosh
2740-B East Sunshine St., Springfield 65804-2047; (417) 889-1800; Fax: (417) 889-4915; *District Director:* Sharon A. Nahon
Committee Assignment(s): Energy and Commerce, Permanent Select Intelligence

Boccieri, John A., D-Ohio (16)

Capitol Hill Office: 1516 LHOB 20515-3516; 225-3876; Fax: 225-3059; *Chief of Staff:* Anthony Trevena
Web: boccieri.house.gov
District Office(s): 4150 Belden Village Street, Suite 408, Canton 44718-2553; (330) 489-4414; Fax: (330) 489-4448, *District Rep:* Chris Cupples
Committee Assignment(s): Agriculture; Transportation and Infrastructure

Boehner, John A., R-Ohio (8)

Capitol Hill Office: 1011 LHOB 20515-3508; 225-6205; Fax: 225-0704; *Chief of Staff:* William C. Mick Krieger II
Web: johnboehner.house.gov
District Office(s): 12 S. Plum St., Troy 45373-5207; (937) 339-1524; Fax: (937) 339-1878; *Caseworker:* Angie Harrah

7969 Cincinnati-Dayton Rd., Suite B, West Chester 45069-6637; (513) 779-5400; Fax: (513) 779-5315; *District Chief of Staff:* Ryan Day

Bonner, Jo, R-Ala. (1)

Capitol Hill Office: 2236 RHOB 20515-0101; 225-4931; Fax: 225-0562; *Chief of Staff:* Alan C. Spencer
Web: bonner.house.gov
District Office(s): 1302 N. McKenzie St., Foley 36535-2232; (251) 943-2073; Fax: (251) 943-2093; *Field Representative:* Bryan Parker
11 North Water St., #15290, Mobile 36609; (251) 690-2811; Fax: (251) 342-0404; *District Director; Deputy Chief of Staff:* Eliska P. Morgan
Committee Assignment(s): Appropriations; Standards of Official Conduct

Bono Mack, Mary, R-Calif. (45)

Capitol Hill Office: 104 CHOB 20515-0545; 225-5330; Fax: 225-2961; *Chief of Staff:* Frank W. Cullen
Web: bono.house.gov
District Office(s): 1600 E. Florida Ave., #301, Hemet 92544-8639; (951) 658-2312; Fax: (951) 652-2562; *Deputy District Director:* Karen Brown
707 E. Tahquitz Canyon Way, #9, Palm Springs 92262-0101; (760) 320-1076; Fax: (760) 320-0596; *District Director:* Marc Alan Troast
Committee Assignment(s): Energy and Commerce

Boozman, John, R-Ark. (3)

Capitol Hill Office: 1519 LHOB 20515-0403; 225-4301; Fax: 225-5713; *Chief of Staff:* Christopher Matthew Sagely
Web: www.boozman.house.gov
District Office(s): 4943 Old Greenwood Rd., #1, Fort Smith 72903-6906; (479) 782-7787; Fax: (479) 783-7662; *Constituent Services Director:* Kathy J. Watson
303 N. Main St., #102, Harrison 72601-3508; (870) 741-6900; Fax: (870) 741-7741; *District Representative:* Sarah Hartley
213 W. Monroe St., Suite K, Lowell 72745-9451; (479) 725-0400; Fax: (479) 725-0408; *Deputy Chief of Staff:* Stacy McClure
Committee Assignment(s): Foreign Affairs; Transportation and Infrastructure; Veterans' Affairs

Bordallo, Madeleine Z., D-Guam (Non-Voting Delegate)

Capitol Hill Office: 427 CHOB 20515-5301; 225-1188; Fax: 226-0341; *Chief of Staff:* John Whitt
Web: www.house.gov/bordallo
District Office(s): 120 Father Duenas Ave., #107, Hagatna 96910-5058; (671) 477-4272; Fax: (671) 477-2587; *District Director:* James Sablan
Committee Assignment(s): Armed Services; Natural Resources

Boren, Dan, D-Okla. (2)

Capitol Hill Office: 216 CHOB 20515-3602; 225-2701; Fax: 225-3038; *Chief of Staff:* Jason L. Buckner
Web: www.house.gov/boren
District Office(s): 309 W. 1st St., Claremore 74017-8005; (918) 341-9336; Fax: (918) 342-4806; *Field Representative:* Peggy McGehee
118 East Carl Albert Parkway, McAlester 74501-5040; (918) 423-5951; Fax: (918) 423-1940; *Field Representative:* Betty L. Ford
431 W. Broadway St., Muskogee 74401-6614; (918) 687-2533; Fax: (918) 686-0128; *District Director:* Ben Harton Robinson
Committee Assignment(s): Natural Resources; Permanent Select Intelligence

Boswell, Leonard L., D-Iowa (3)

Capitol Hill Office: 1427 LHOB 20515-1503; 225-3806; Fax: 225-5608; *Chief of Staff:* Susan A. McAvoy
Web: boswell.house.gov
District Office(s): 300 E. Locust St., #320, Des Moines 50309-1852; (515) 282-1909; Fax: (515) 282-1785; *District Director:* Sally Barnhill Bowzer
Committee Assignment(s): Agriculture; Transportation and Infrastructure

Boucher, Rick, D-Va. (9)

Capitol Hill Office: 2187 RHOB 20515-4609; 225-3861; Fax: 225-0442; *Chief of Staff:* Laura E. Vaught
Web: www.boucher.house.gov
District Office(s): 188 E. Main St., Abingdon 24210-2841; (276) 628-1145; Fax: (276) 628-2203; *Deputy Chief of Staff:* Laura Lee
1 Cloverleaf Sq., Suite C-1, Big Stone Gap 24219-2355; (276) 523-5450; Fax: (276) 523-1412; *Casework Specialist:* Marsha Craiger
106 N. Washington Ave., P.O. Box 1268, Pulaski 24301-1268; (540) 980-4310; Fax: (540) 980-0629; *Casework Supervisor:* Becki Gunn
Committee Assignment(s): Energy and Commerce; Judiciary

Boustany, Charles Jr., R-La. (7)

Capitol Hill Office: 1117 LHOB 20515-1807; 225-2031; Fax: 225-5724; *Chief of Staff:* Jeff Dobrozsi
Web: boustany.house.gov
District Office(s): 800 Lafayette St., #1400, Lafayette 70501-6800; (337) 235-6322; Fax: (337) 235-6072; *District Director:* Joan A. Finley
700 Ryan St., Lake Charles 70601-4243; (337) 433-1747; Fax: (337) 433-0974; *Caseworker:* Theresa Martin
Committee Assignment(s): Ways and Means

Boyd, F. Allen Jr., D-Fla. (2)

Capitol Hill Office: 1227 LHOB 20515-0902; 225-5235; Fax: 225-5615; *Chief of Staff:* Melanie R. Morris
Web: www.house.gov/boyd

District Office(s): 30 W. Government St., #203, Panama City 32401-2739; (850) 785-0812; Fax: (850) 763-3764; *District Representative*: Carter Johnson
1650 Summit Lake Dr., #103, Tallahassee 32317-7937; (850) 561-3979; Fax: (850) 681-2902; *District Director*: Jerry Smithwick
Committee Assignment(s): Appropriations; Budget

Brady, Kevin, R-Tex. (8)

Capitol Hill Office: 301 CHOB 20515-4308; 225-4901; Fax: 225-5524; *Chief of Staff:* Doug Centilli
Web: www.house.gov/brady
E-mail: rep.brady@mail.house.gov
District Office(s): 1 Texas Commerce Plaza, 200 River Pointe Dr., #304, Conroe 77304-2817; (936) 441-5700; Fax: (936) 441-5757; *District Director*: Sarah E. Stephens
1202 Sam Houston Ave., #8, Huntsville 77340-4638; (936) 439-9542; Fax: (936) 439-9546; *Field Representative*: Brandon Reese
420 Green Ave., Orange 77630-5803; (409) 883-4197; Fax: (409) 883-6550; *Caseworker*: Vita Swarers
Committee Assignment(s):Ways and Means; Joint Economic

Brady, Robert A., D-Pa. (1)

Capitol Hill Office: 206 CHOB 20515-3801; 225-4731; Fax: 225-0088; *Chief of Staff:* Stanley V. White
Web: www.brady.house.gov
District Office(s): 1907 S. Broad St., Philadelphia 19148-2216; (215) 389-4627; Fax: (215) 389-4636; *District Director*: Shirley Gregory
The Colony Bldg., 511 Welsh St., 1st Floor, Chester 19013-4453; (610) 874-7094; Fax: (610) 874-7193; *Office Manager*: Carl Fitzgerald
Committee Assignment(s): Armed Services; House Administration; Printing; Library of Congress

Braley, Bruce, D-Iowa (1)

Capitol Hill Office: 1019 LHOB 20515-1501; 225-2911; Fax: 225-6666; *Chief of Staff:* Sarah Benzing
Web: braley.house.gov
District Office(s): 209 W. 4th St., #104, Davenport 52801-1307; (563) 323-5988; Fax: (563) 323-5231; *District Director*: Pete DeKock
350 W. 6th St., #222, Dubuque 52001-4648; (563) 557-7789; (563) 557-1324; *Caseworker:* John Murphy
501 Sycamore St., #623, Waterloo 50703-4651; (319) 287-3233; Fax: (319) 287-5104; *District Director*: Karen Erickson
Committee Assignment(s): Energy and Commerce

Bright, Bobby, D-Al (2)

Capitol Hill Office: 1205 LHOB 20515-0102; 225-2901; Fax: 225-8913; *Chief of Staff:* Margaret "Meg" Joseph
Web: bright.house.gov

District Office(s): 256 Honeysuckle Road, Suite 15, Dothan 36305-1168; (334) 794-9680; *Caseworker*: Teresa Jackson
22 Monroe St., Suite 1B, Montgomery 36104-3511; (334) 277-9113; Fax: (334) 277-8534; *District Director*: Al Allenback
Committee Assignment(s): Agriculture; Armed Services; Small Business

Broun, Paul C., R-Ga (10)

Capitol Hill Office: 325 CHOB 20515-1010; 225-4101; Fax: 226-0776; *Chief of Staff:* David Bowser
Web: broun.house.gov
District Office(s): 3706 Atlanta Highway, #3B, Athens 30606-7202; (706) 549-9588; Fax: (706) 549-9590; *Constituent Services Director:* Dessie Martin
P.O. Box 211661, 4246 Washington Rd., #6, Augusta 30917; (706) 447-3857; (706) 868-8756; *Press Secretary:* Jessica Morris
560 Falls Rd., Toccoa 30577-1661; (706) 886-1008; Fax: (706) 886-1009; *Constituent Services Director:* Wanda Tate
Committee Assignment(s): Homeland Security; Natural Resources; Science and Technology

Brown, Corrine, D-Fla. (3)

Capitol Hill Office: 2336 RHOB 20515-0903; 225-0123; Fax: 225-2256; *Chief of Staff:* Elias Ronnie Simmons
Web: www.house.gov/corrinebrown
District Office(s): 101 Union St. E., #202, Jacksonville 32202-6002; (904) 354-1652; Fax: (904) 354-2721; *District Director*: Glenel Bowden
219 Lime Ave., Orlando 32805-2248; (407) 872-0656; Fax: (407) 872-5763; *Community Development Specialist*: Susie Jackson
Committee Assignment(s): Transportation and Infrastructure; Veterans' Affairs

Brown, Henry E. Jr., R-S.C. (1)

Capitol Hill Office: 103 CHOB 20515-4001; 225-3176; Fax: 225-3407; *Deputy Chief of Staff:* Chris Berardini
Web: brown.house.gov
District Office(s): 1800 Oak St., Suite C, Myrtle Beach 29577-3141; (843) 445-6459; Fax: (843) 445-6418; *Constituent Services Representative*: Cam Crawford
5900 Core Ave., #401, North Charleston 29406-6069; (843) 747-4175; Fax: (843) 747-4711; *District Director*: Kathy Crawford
Committee Assignment(s): Natural Resources; Transportation and Infrastructure; Veterans' Affairs

Brown-Waite, Ginny, R-Fla. (5)

Capitol Hill Office: 414 CHOB 20515-0905; 225-1002; Fax: 226-6559; *Chief of Staff:* Pete Meachum

Web: brown-waite.house.gov
District Office(s): 16224 Spring Hill Drive, Brooksville 34604-8326; (352) 799-8354; Fax: (352) 799-8776; *District Director:* Shirley Anderson
Committee Assignment(s): Ways and Means

Buchanan, Vern, R-Fla. (13)

Capitol Hill Office: 218 CHOB 20515-0913; 225-5015; Fax: 226-0828; *Chief of Staff:* Dave Karvelas
Web: buchanan.house.gov
District Office(s): 2424 Manatee Avenue W., Suite 104, Bradenton 34205-4954; (941) 747-9081; Fax (941) 748-1564; *Constituent Services Representative:* Mark Gilliland
235 N. Orange Ave., #201, Sarasota 34236-8522; (941) 951-6643; Fax: (941) 951-2972; *District Director; Press Secretary:* Sally Dione Tibbetts
Committee Assignment(s): Small Business; Transportation and Infrastructure; Veterans' Affairs

Burgess, Michael, R-Tex. (26)

Capitol Hill Office: 229 CHOB 20515-4326; 225-7772; Fax: 225-2919; *Chief of Staff:* Barry Brown
Web: burgess.house.gov
District Office(s): 1100 Circle Dr., #200, Fort Worth 76119-8111; (817) 531-8454
1660 S. Stemmons Freeway, #230, Lewisville 75067-0600; (972) 434-9700; Fax: (972) 434-9705; *District Director:* Erik With
Committee Assignment(s): Energy and Commerce; Joint Economic

Burton, Dan, R-Ind. (5)

Capitol Hill Office: 2308 RHOB 20515-1405; 225-2276; Fax: 225-0016; *Chief of Staff:* Mark Alan Walker
Web: www.house.gov/burton
District Office(s): 8900 Keystone Crossing, #1050, Indianapolis 46240-2134; (317) 848-0201; Fax: (317) 846-7306; *Deputy Chief of Staff:* Matt Prine
209 S. Washington St., Marion 46952-3803; (765) 662-6770; Fax: (765) 662-6775; *Special Assistant:* Tresa Baker
Committee Assignment(s): Foreign Affairs; Oversight and Government Reform

Butterfield, G. K., D-N.C. (1)

Capitol Hill Office: 413 CHOB 20515-3301; 225-3101; Fax: 225-3354; *Chief of Staff:* Corliss B. Clemonts-James
Web: house.gov/butterfield
District Office(s): 311 W. 2nd St., P.O. Box 836, Weldon 27890-1409; (252) 538-4123; Fax: (252) 538-6516; *Regional Director:* Dollie B. Burwell
415 E. Blvd., #100, Williamston 27892-2731; (252) 789-4939; Fax: (252) 792-8113
216 W. Nash St., Suite B, Wilson 27893-3802; (252) 237-9816; Fax: (252) 291-0356

Committee Assignment(s): Commission on Security and Cooperation in Europe; Energy and Commerce; Standards of Official Conduct

Buyer, Steve, R-Ind. (4)

Capitol Hill Office: 2230 RHOB 20515-1404; 225-5037; Fax: 225-2067; *Chief of Staff:* Mike J. Copher
Web: stevebuyer.house.gov
District Office(s): 1801 I St., Bedford 47421-4223; (812) 277-9590; *Field Representative:* Brandi Hughes
100 S. Main St., Monticello 47960-2328; (574) 583-9819; *District Operations Director:* Brandt Hershman
148 N. Perry Rd., Plainfield 46168-9025; (317) 838-0404; *District Director:* Jim Huston
Committee Assignment(s): Energy and Commerce; Veterans' Affairs

Calvert, Ken, R-Calif. (44)

Capitol Hill Office: 2201 RHOB 20515-0544; 225-1986; Fax: 225-2004; *Chief of Staff:* Dave Ramey
Web: calvert.house.gov
District Office(s): 26111 Antonio Pkwy., #300, Rancho Santa Margarita 92688; (949) 888-8498; Fax: (949) 888-8524
3400 Central Ave., #200, Riverside 92506-2163; (951) 784-4300; Fax: (951) 784-5255; *District Director:* Jolyn D. Murphy
Committee Assignment(s): Appropriations

Camp, Dave, R-Mich. (4)

Capitol Hill Office: 341 CHOB 20515-2204; 225-3561; Fax: 225-9679; *Chief of Staff:* Jim Brandell
Web: camp.house.gov
District Office(s): 135 Ashman Dr., Midland 48640-5103; (989) 631-2552; Fax: (989) 631-6271; *District Director:* Eric Friedman
121 E. Front St., #202, Traverse City 49684-2500; (231) 929-4711; Fax: (231) 929-4776; *Constituent Representative:* Tarin Eisenga
Committee Assignment(s): Ways and Means; Joint Taxation

Campbell, John, R-Calif. (48)

Capitol Hill Office: 1507 LHOB 20515-0548; 225-5611; Fax: 225-9177; *Chief of Staff:* Muffy Lewis
Web: campbell.house.gov
District Office(s): 610 Newport Center Dr., #330, Newport Beach 92660-8034; (949) 756-2244; Fax: (949) 251-9309; *District Director:* Lou Penrose
Committee Assignment(s): Budget; Financial Services; Joint Economic

Cantor, Eric I., R-Va. (7)

Capitol Hill Office: 329 CHOB 20515-4607; 225-2815; Fax: 225-0011; *Chief of Staff:* Kristi Way
Web: cantor.house.gov

District Office(s): 763 Madison Rd., #207, Culpeper 22701; (540) 825-8960; Fax: (540) 825-8964; *Community Outreach*: Barbara Taylor

4201 Dominion Blvd., #110, Glen Allen 23060-6149; (804) 747-4073; Fax: (804) 747-5308; *District Director*: Jennifer Nolen

Committee Assignment(s): Ways and Means

Cao, Anh Joseph, R-La. (2)

Capitol Hill Office: 2113 RHOB 20515-1802; 225-6636; Fax: 225-1988; *Chief of Staff:* D. Clayton Hall

Web: josephcao.house.gov

District Office(s): 4640 S. Carrollton Avenue, Suite 120, New Orleans 70119-6074; (504) 483-2325; Fax: (504) 483-7944; *Deputy Chief of Staff:* Rosalind Peychaud

Committee Assignment(s): Homeland Security; Transportation and Infastructure

Capito, Shelley Moore, R-W.Va. (2)

Capitol Hill Office: 2443 LHOB 20515-4802; 225-2711; Fax: 225-7856; *Chief of Staff:* Joel Brubaker

Web: capito.house.gov

District Office(s): 4815 MacCorkle Ave. S.E., Charleston 25304-1948; (304) 925-5964; Fax: (304) 926-8912; *District Director*: Mary Elisabeth Eckerson

300 Foxcroft Ave., #102, Martinsburg 25401-5341; (304) 264-8810; Fax: (304) 264-8815; *District Field Representative*: Christ Strovel

Committee Assignment(s): Financial Services; Transportation and Infrastructure; Select Energy Independence and Global Warming

Capps, Lois, D-Calif. (23)

Capitol Hill Office: 1110 LHOB 20515-0523; 225-3601; Fax: 225-5632; *Chief of Staff:* Randolph Harrison

Web: www.house.gov/capps

District Office(s): 2675 N. Ventura Rd., #105, Port Hueneme 93041-2045; (805) 985-6807; Fax: (805) 985-6875; *District Representative*: Vanessa Hernandez

1411 Marsh St., #205, San Luis Obispo 93401-2923; (805) 546-8348; Fax: (805) 546-8368; *District Representative*: Greg Haas

301 E. Carrillo Street, Suite A, Santa Barbara 93101-1410; (805) 730-1710; Fax: (805) 730-9153; *District Director*: Sharon Siegel

Committee Assignment(s): Energy and Commerce; Natural Resources

Capuano, Michael E., D-Mass. (8)

Capitol Hill Office: 1414 LHOB 20515-2108; 225-5111; Fax: 225-9322; *Chief of Staff:* Robert E. Primus

Web: www.house.gov/Capuano

District Office(s): Roxbury Community College, Campus Library, #211, Boston 02120; (617) 621-6208

110 1st St., Cambridge 02141-2109; (617) 621-6208; Fax: (617) 621-8628; *District Director*: Jon Lenicheck

Committee Assignment(s): Financial Services; House Administration; Transportation and Infrastructure; Joint Printing

Cardoza, Dennis A., D-Calif. (18)

Capitol Hill Office: 1224 LHOB 20515-0518; 225-6131; Fax: 225-0819; *Chief of Staff:* Jennifer Fitzgerald Walsh

Web: www.house.gov/cardoza

District Office(s): 2222 M St., Suite 305, Merced 95340-3729; (209) 383-4455; Fax: (209) 726-1065; *Policy Advisor*: Stacie Dabbs-Vilciauskas

1010 I St., Suite 5800, Modesto 95354; (209) 527-1914; Fax: (209) 527-5748; *Senior Policy Advisor*: Dee Dee D'Adamo

137 E. Weber Ave., Stockton 95202-2704; (209) 946-0361; Fax: (209) 946-0347; *Field Representative*: Ellen Powell

Committee Assignment(s): Agriculture; Rules

Carnahan, Russ, D-Mo. (3)

Capitol Hill Office: 1710 LHOB 20515-2503; 225-2671; Fax: 225-7452; *Chief of Staff:* Caroline Pelot Battles

Web: www.house.gov/carnahan

District Office(s): 517 Bailey Rd., Crystal City 63019-1701; (636) 937-8039; Fax: (636) 937-7138; *Congressional Outreach Director*: T.C. Powers

8764 Manchester Rd., #203, St. Louis 63144-2735; (314) 962-1523; Fax: (314) 962-7169; *Communications Director*: Glenn Campbell

Committee Assignment(s): Foreign Affairs; Science and Technology; Transportation and Infrastructure

Carney, Christopher P., D-Pa. (10)

Capitol Hill Office: 416 CHOB 20515-3810; 225-3731; Fax: 225-9594; *Chief of Staff:* April Beeman Metwalli

Web: carney.house.gov

District Office(s): 233 Northern Blvd., #4, Clarks Summit 18411-8720; (570) 585-9988; Fax: (570) 585-9977; *District Director*: Paul Macknosky

521 Franklin St., P.O. Box 397, Shamokin 17872-6754; (570) 644-1682; (570) 644-1684; *Caseworker:* Roie Speller

175 Pine St., #103, Williamsport 17701-6549; (570) 327-1902; Fax: (570) 327-1904; *Regional Coordinator*: Susan Mathias

Committee Assignment(s): Homeland Security; Transportation and Infrastructure

Carson, André, D-Ind. (7)

Capitol Hill Office: 425 CHOB 20515-1407; 225-4011; Fax: 225-5633; *Chief of Staff:* Ellen White Quigley

Web: carson.house.gov

District Office(s): Julie M. Carson Government Center, 300 East Fall Creek Pkwy. N. Dr., Indianapolis 46205-4258; (317) 283-6516; Fax: (317) 283-6567; *District Rep*: Jarnell Craig

Committee Assignment(s): Financial Services

Carter, John R., R-Tex. (31)

Capitol Hill Office: 409 CHOB 20515-4331; 225-3864;
Fax: 225-5886; *Chief of Staff:* John Walker
Web: carter.house.gov
District Office(s): 1 Financial Center, Hwy. 35, #303,
Round Rock 78664; (512) 246-1600; Fax: (512)
246-1620; *Texas Chief of Staff:* Jonas Miller
6544 S. General Bruce Dr., Suite B, Temple 76502-5811;
(254) 933-1392; Fax: (254) 933-1650; *Regional
Director:* Greg Schannep
Committee Assignment(s): Appropriations

Cassidy, Bill, R-La. (6)

Capitol Hill Office: 506 CHOB 20515-1806; 225-3901;
Fax: 225-7313; *Chief of Staff:* Josh Robinson
Web: cassidy.house.gov
District Office(s): 5555 Hilton Avenue, Suite 100, Baton
Rouge 70808-2597; (225) 929-7711; Fax: (225)
929-7688; *District Director:* Brian McNabb
Committee Assignment(s): Agriculture; Education and
Labor; Natural Resources

Castle, Michael N., R-Del. (At Large)

Capitol Hill Office: 1233 LHOB 20515-0801;
225-4165; Fax: 225-2291; *Chief of Staff:* Michael
Quaranta
Web: www.castle.house.gov
District Office(s): 300 S. New St., #2005, Dover
19904-6726; (302) 736-1666; Fax: (302) 736-6580;
Field Representative: Kate Rohrer
201 N. Walnut St., #107, Wilmington 19801-3970; (302)
428-1902; Fax: (302) 428-1950; *District Director:*
Jeffrey A. Dayton
Committee Assignment(s): Education and Labor;
Financial Services

Castor, Kathy, D-Fla. (11)

Capitol Hill Office: 317 CHOB 20515-0911; 225-3376;
Fax: 225-5652; *Chief of Staff:* Clay Phillips
Web: castor.house.gov
District Office(s): 4144 N. Armenia Ave., #300, Tampa
33607-6435; (813) 871-2817; Fax: (813) 811-2864;
Press Secretary: Ellen Gedalius
Committee Assignment(s): Energy and Commerce;
Standards of Official Conduct

Chaffetz, Jason, R-Utah (3)

Capitol Hill Office: 1032 LHOB 20510-4403; 225-7751;
Fax: 225-5629; *Chief of Staff:* Justin Harding
Web: chaffetz.house.gov
District Office(s): 51 S. University Ave., Suite 319,
Provo 84601-4491; (801) 851-2500; Fax: (801)
851-2509
3895 W. 7800 South, West Jordan 84088-4314; (801)
282-5502; *District Director:* Jennifer Scott

Chandler, Ben, D-Ky. (6)

Capitol Hill Office: 1504 LHOB 20515-1706; 225-4706;
Fax: 225-2122; *Chief of Staff:* Denis Fleming
Web: chandler.house.gov
District Office(s): 1021 Majestic Dr., #180, Lexington
40513-1866; (859) 219-1366; Fax: (859) 219-3437;
District Director: Michael Noyes
Committee Assignment(s): Appropriations; Science and
Technology; Standards of Official Conduct

Childers, Travis, D-Miss. (1)

Capitol Hill Office: 1708 LHOB 20515-2401; 225-4306;
Fax: 225-3549; *Chief of Staff:* Brad Morris
Web: childers.house.gov
District Office(s): 523 Main St., Columbus 39701-5733;
(662) 294-1321; *Field Rep:* Eddie Longstreet
1360 Sunset Drive, Suite Two, Grenada 38901-2857;
(662) 294-1321; *Constituent Rep:* Jerriod Avant
2564 Highway 51 South, Hernando 38632-2128; (901)
833-7344; Fax: (662) 449-4836; *Constituent Rep:*
Brent Lewis
108B E. Main St., Tupelo 38804-4022; (662) 844-5437;
District Director: Richard Babb

Christensen, Donna M., D-Virgin Is.
(Non-Voting Delegate)

Capitol Hill Office: 1510 LHOB 20515-5501; 225-1790;
Fax: 225-5517; *Chief of Staff:* Monique Clendinen
Watson
Web: www.house.gov/christian-christensen
District Office(s): Sunshine Mall Space #204 and #205,
One Estate Cane, P.O. Box 5980, Frederiksted, St.
Croix 00840; (340) 778-5900; Fax: (340) 778-5111;
Executive Assistant: Luz Belardo-Webster
Nisky Business Center, #207, St. Thomas 00802; (340)
774-4408; Fax: (340) 774-8033; *St. Thomas Office
Manager:* Eddie de LaGarde
Committee Assignment(s): Energy and Commerce;
Natural Resources

Clarke, Yvette, D-N.Y. (11)

Capitol Hill Office: 1029 LHOB 20515-3211; 225-6231;
Fax: 226-0112; *Acting Chief of Staff:* Algene Sajery
Web: clarke.house.gov
District Office(s): 123 Linden Blvd., 4th Floor, Brooklyn
11226-3302; (718) 287-1142; Fax: (718) 287-1223;
Director of Community Development: Dale DeGale
Committee Assignment(s): Education and Labor;
Homeland Security; Small Business

Clay, William Lacy, D-Mo. (1)

Capitol Hill Office: 2418 RHOB 20515-2501; 225-2406;
Fax: 225-1725; *Senior Policy Adviser:* Frank Les Davis
Web: www.lacyclay.house.gov
District Office(s): 625 N. Euclid Ave., #326, St. Louis
63108; (314) 367-1970; Fax: (314) 367-1341; *Senior
District Assistant:* Gwendolyn Reed

8021 W Florissant Ave., Suite C, St. Louis 63136-1449; (314) 890-0349; Fax: (314) 427-6320; *Communications Director*: Steven Engelhardt

Committee Assignment(s): Financial Services; Oversight and Government Reform

Cleaver, Emanuel II, D-Mo. (5)

Capitol Hill Office: 1027 LHOB 20515-2505; 225-4535; Fax: 225-4403; *Chief of Staff:* Leslie Woolley

Web: www.house.gov/cleaver

District Office(s): 211 W. Maple Ave., Independence 64050-2815; (816) 833-4545; Fax: (816) 833-2991; *Community Affairs Liaison*: Nicki Cardwell

101 W. 31st St., Kansas City 64108-3318; (816) 842-4545; Fax: (816) 471-5215; *District Director*: Geoff Jolley

Committee Assignment(s): Financial Services; Homeland Security; Select Energy Independence and Global Warming

Clyburn, James E., D-S.C. (6)

Capitol Hill Office: 2135 RHOB 20515-4006; 225-3315; Fax: 225-2313; *Chief of Staff:* Yelberton R. Watkins

Web: clyburn.house.gov

District Office(s): 1225 Lady St., #200, Columbia 29201-3210; (803) 799-1100; Fax: (803) 799-9060; *Midlands Area Director*: Dalton Tresvant

Business and Technology Center, 181 East Evans St., #314, Florence 29506-2512; (843) 662-1212; Fax: (843) 662-8474; *Caseworker*: Kenneth Barnes

Coble, Howard, R-N.C. (6)

Capitol Hill Office: 2468 RHOB 20515-3306; 225-3065; Fax: 225-8611; *Chief of Staff:* Ed McDonald

Web: coble.house.gov

E-mail: howard.coble@mail.house.gov

District Office(s): 222 Sunset Ave., #101, Asheboro 27203-5668; (336) 626-3060; Fax: (336) 626-7819; *District Representative*: Rebecca Redding

P.O. Box 812, 124 W. Elm St., Graham 27253-2802; (336) 229-0159; Fax: (336) 228-7974; *District Representative*: Janine Osborne

P.O. Box 807, 805 S. Salisbury Ave., Granite Quarry 28072; (704) 209-0426; Fax: (704) 209-0428; *District Representative*: Terri Welch

2102 N. Elm St., Suite B, Greensboro 27408-5100; (336) 333-5005; Fax: (336) 333-5048; *Community Liaison*: Lindsay Morris

1634 North Main St., #101, High Point 27262-2644; (336) 886-5106; Fax: (336) 886-8740; *District Representative*: Nancy Mazza

Committee Assignment(s): Judiciary; Transportation and Infrastructure

Coffman, Mike, R-Colo. (6)

Capitol Hill Office: 1508 LHOB 20515-0606; 225-7882; Fax: 225-4623; *Chief of Staff:* Jacque Ponder

Web: coffman.house.gov

District Office(s): 9220 Kimmer Drive, Suite 220, Lone Tree 80124-2884; (720) 283-9772; Fax: (720) 283-9776; *District Director*: Andrew A. Merritt

Committee Assignment(s): Armed Services; Natural Resources; Small Business

Cohen, Steve, D-Tenn. (9)

Capitol Hill Office: 1005 LHOB 20515-4209; 225-3265; Fax: 225-5663; *Chief of Staff:* Marilyn Dillihay

Web: cohen.house.gov

District Office(s): 167 N. Main St., #369, Memphis 38103-1822; (901) 544-4131; Fax: (901) 544-4329; *District Director*: Randy Wade

Committee Assignment(s): Judiciary; Transportation and Infrastructure

Cole, Tom, R-Okla. (4)

Capitol Hill Office: 2438 RHOB 20515-3604; 225-6165; Fax: 225-3512; *Chief of Staff:* Sean P. Murphy

Web: www.cole.house.gov

District Office(s): 104 E. 12th St., Ada 74820-6502; (580) 436-5375; Fax: (580) 436-5451; *Field Representative*: Amber Pollard

711 S.W. D Ave., #201, Lawton 73501-4561; (580) 357-2131; Fax: (580) 357-7477; *Field Representative*: Keri Dennis

2420 Springer Dr., #120, Norman 73069-3965; (405) 329-6500; Fax: (405) 321-7369; *District Director*: Jill Daugherty

Committee Assignment(s): Appropriations

Conaway, K. Michael, R-Tex. (11)

Capitol Hill Office: 1527 LHOB 20515-4311; 225-3605; Fax: 225-1783; *Chief of Staff:* Richard L. Hudson Jr.

Web: conaway.house.gov

District Office(s): Brownwood City Hall, 501 Center Ave., Brownwood 76801-2809; (866) 882-3811; *Field Representative*: Mandy Locker

County Annex, 104 W. Sandstone St., Llano 78643-2319; (325) 247-2826; Fax: (325) 247-2676; *Field Representative*: Sarah Carkuff

Six Desta Dr., #2000, Midland 79705-5520; (432) 687-2390; Fax: (432) 687-0277; *District Director:* Ricky Wright

City Hall, 411 W. 8th St., 5th Floor, Odessa 79761-4422; (866) 882-3811

O. C. Fisher Federal Bldg., 33 E. Twohig Ave., #307, San Angelo 76903-6451; (325) 659-4010; Fax: (325) 659-4014; *Regional Director:* Joanne Powell

Committee Assignment(s): Agriculture; Armed Services; Standards of Official Conduct, Select Intelligence

Connolly, Gerry, D-Va. (11)

Capitol Hill Office: 327 CHOB 20515-4611; 225-1492; Fax: 225-3071; *Chief of Staff:* James Walkinshaw

Web: connolly.house.gov

District Office(s): 4115 Annandale Road, Annandale 22003-2500; (703) 256-3071; Fax: (703) 354-1284; *District Director*: Sharon Stark

Committee Assignment(s): Budget; Foreign Affairs; Oversight and Government Reform

Conyers, John Jr., D-Mich. (14)

Capitol Hill Office: 2426 RHOB 20515-2214; 225-5126; Fax: 225-0072; *Chief of Staff:* Cynthia Martin

Web: www.house.gov/conyers

District Office(s): Theodore Levin U.S. Courthouse, 231 W. Lafayette Blvd., #669, Detroit 48226-2766; (313) 961-5670; Fax: (313) 226-2085; *Press Secretary:* Karen Morgan

2615 Jefferson Ave., Trenton 48183-2803; (734) 675-4084; Fax: (734) 675-4218; *Congressional Aide:* Jane Mackey

Committee Assignment(s): Judiciary

Cooper, Jim, D-Tenn. (5)

Capitol Hill Office: 1536 LHOB 20515-4205; 225-4311; Fax: 226-1035; *Chief of Staff:* Lisa Quigley

Web: cooper.house.gov

District Office(s): 605 Church St., Nashville 37219-2314; (615) 736-5295; Fax: (615) 736-7479; *Office Manager:* Kathy Floyd-Buggs

Committee Assignment(s): Armed Services; Oversight and Government Reform

Costa, Jim, D-Calif. (20)

Capitol Hill Office: 1314 LHOB 20515-0520; 225-3341; Fax: 225-9308; *Chief of Staff:* Scott Nishioki

Web: www.house.gov/costa

E-mail: http://www.house.gov/formcosta/issue.htm

District Office(s): 2700 M St., #225, Bakersfield 93301-2370; (661) 869-1620; Fax: (661) 869-1027; *District Representative:* Tiara Cox

855 M St., #940, Fresno 93721-2757; (559) 495-1620; Fax: (559) 495-1027; *District Rep:* Rosa Rodriguez

Committee Assignment(s): Agriculture; Foreign Affairs; Natural Resources

Costello, Jerry F., D-Ill. (12)

Capitol Hill Office: 2408 RHOB 20515-1312; 225-5661; Fax: 225-0285; *Chief of Staff:* David C. Gillies

Web: www.house.gov/Costello

District Office(s): 144 Lincoln Place Court, #4, Belleville 62221-5878; (618) 233-8026; Fax: (618) 233-8765; *District Manager:* Mary Shalapin

250 W. Cherry St., Carbondale 62901-2856; (618) 529-3791; Fax: (618) 549-3768; *Staff Assistant:* Alice Tucker

1330 Swanwick St., Chester 62233-1314; (618) 826-3043; Fax: (618) 826-1923; *Staff Assistant:* Patsie Travelstead

8787 State St., #1022, East St. Louis 62203-2026; (618) 397-8833; *Staff Assistant:* Mel Frierson

2060 Delmar Ave., Suite B, Granite City 62040-4511; (618) 451-7065; Fax: (618) 451-2126; *Staff Assistant:* Dave Cueto

201 E. Nolen St., West Frankfort 62896-2437; (618) 937-6402; Fax: (618) 937-3307; *Staff Assistant:* Karl Maple

Committee Assignment(s): Science and Technology; Transportation and Infrastructure

Courtney, Joe, D-Conn. (2)

Capitol Hill Office: 215 CHOB 20515-0702; 225-2076; Fax: 225-4977; *Chief of Staff:* Jason J. Gross

Web: courtney.house.gov

District Office(s): 77 Hazard Ave., Unit J, Enfield 06082-3890; (860) 741-6011; Fax: (860) 741-6036

101 Water St., #301, Norwich 06360-5729; (860) 886-0139; Fax: (860) 886-2974; *District Director:* Jenny Contois

Committee Assignment(s): Armed Services; Education and Labor

Crenshaw, Ander, R-Fla. (4)

Capitol Hill Office: 440 CHOB 20515-0904; 225-2501; Fax: 225-2504; *Chief of Staff:* John M. Ariale

Web: crenshaw.house.gov/

District Office(s): 1061 Riverside Ave., #100, Jacksonville 32204-4151; (904) 598-0481; Fax: (904) 598-0486; *District Director:* Jacquelyn E. Smith

212 N. Marion Ave., #209, Lake City 32055-3917; (386) 365-3316; *District Representative:* Nathan Riska

Committee Assignment(s): Appropriations

Crowley, Joseph, D-N.Y. (7)

Capitol Hill Office: 2404 RHOB 20515-3207; 225-3965; Fax: 225-1909; *Chief of Staff:* Kate Winkler

Web: crowley.house.gov

District Office(s): 2800 Bruckner Blvd., #301, Bronx 10465-1907; (718) 931-1400; Fax: (718) 931-1340; *District Director:* Anne Marie Anzalone

177 Dreiser Loop, #3, Co-Op City 10475-2705; (718) 320-2314; *Community Liaison:* Paul Dominique

74-09 37th Ave., #306B, Jackson Heights 11372-6303; (718) 779-1400; Fax: (718) 505-0156; *Community Liaison:* Angela DenDekker

Committee Assignment(s): Foreign Affairs, Ways and Means

Cuellar, Henry, D-Tex. (28)

Capitol Hill Office: 336 CHOB 20515-4328; 225-1640; Fax: 225-1641; *Chief of Staff:* Terry Stinson

Web: www.house.gov/cuellar

District Office(s): 602 E. Calton Rd., #2, Laredo 78041-3693; (956) 725-0639; Fax: (956) 725-2647

320 N. Main St., #221, McAllen 78501-4699; (956) 631-4826; Fax: (956) 631-4251

100 N.F.M. 3167, Rio Grande City 78582; (956) 487-5603; Fax: (956) 488-0952

615 E. Houston St., #451, San Antonio 78205-2054; (210) 271-2851; Fax: (210) 277-6671; *Deputy Chief of Staff:* Cynthia Gaona

100 S. Austin St., #1, Seguin 78155-5702; (830) 401-0457; Fax: (830) 379-0984

Committee Assignment(s): Agriculture; Homeland Security; Oversight and Government Reform

Culberson, John, R-Tex. (7)

Capitol Hill Office: 1514 LHOB 20515-4307; 225-2571; Fax: 225-4381; *Deputy Chief of Staff:* Jamie Gahun

Web: culberson.house.gov

District Office(s): 10000 Memorial Dr., #620, Houston 77024; (713) 682-8828; Fax: (713) 680-8070; *Chief of Staff:* Tony Essalih

Committee Assignment(s): Appropriations

Cummings, Elijah E., D-Md. (7)

Capitol Hill Office: 2235 RHOB 20515-2007; 225-4741; Fax: 225-3178; *Chief of Staff:* Vernon Simms

Web: www.house.gov/cummings

District Office(s): 1010 Park Ave., Baltimore 21201-5600; (410) 685-9199; Fax: (410) 685-9399; *Special Assistant:* Michael Christianson

754 Frederick Rd., Catonsville 21228-4504; (410) 719-8777; Fax: (410) 455-0110; *Special Assistant:* Katie Malone

8267 Main St., #102, Ellicott City 21043-9903; (410) 465-8259; Fax: (410) 465-8740; *Special Assistant:* Amy Stratton

Committee Assignment(s): Oversight and Government Reform; Transportation and Infrastructure; Joint Economic

Dahlkemper, Kathy, D-Pa. (3)

Capitol Hill Office: 516 CHOB 20515-3803; 225-5406; Fax: 225-3103; *Chief of Staff:* Tina Mengine

Web: dahlkemper.house.gov

District Office(s): 208 E. Bayfront Parkway, Suite 102, Erie 16507-2405; *District Director:* John Hall

Committee Assignment(s): Agriculture; Science and Technology; Small Business

Davis, Artur, D-Ala. (7)

Capitol Hill Office: 208 CHOB 20515-0107; 225-2665; Fax: 226-9567; *Chief of Staff:* Chanelle Hardy

Web: www.house.gov/arturdavis

District Office(s): 2 20th St. North, Birmingham 35203-4007; (205) 254-1960; Fax: (205) 254-1974; *District Director:* Frank Adams

102 E. Washington St., Suite F, Demopolis 36732-2100; (334) 287-8060; Fax: (334) 287-0870; *Constituent Services Representative:* Audrey Haskin

UWA Station 40, 205 N. Washington St., Webb Hall, #236–237, Livingston 35470-2099; (205) 652-5834; Fax: (205) 652-5935; *Constituent Services Representative:* Kay Presley

Federal Bldg., 908 Alabama Ave., #112, Selma 36701-4660; (334) 877-4414; Fax: (334) 877-4489; *Deputy District Director:* Tammy Maul

Federal Bldg., 1118 Greensboro Ave., #336, Tuscaloosa 35401-2817; (205) 752-5380; Fax: (205) 752-5899; *Constituent Services Representative:* Kay Presley

Committee Assignment(s): House Administration; Ways and Means

Davis, Danny K., D-Ill. (7)

Capitol Hill Office: 2159 RHOB 20515-1307; 225-5006; Fax: 225-5641; *Chief of Staff:* Yul Edwards

Web: www.house.gov/davis

District Office(s): 2301 W. Roosevelt Rd., Broadview 60155-3828; (708) 345-6857; Fax: (708) 345-6715; *Suburban Coordinator:* Larry Shapiro

3333 W. Arthington St., #130, Chicago 60624-4102; (773) 533-7520; Fax: (773) 533-7530; *District Director:* F. Daniel Cantrell

Committee Assignment(s): Oversight and Government Reform; Ways and Means

Davis, Geoff, R-Ky. (4)

Capitol Hill Office: 1108 LHOB 20515-1704; 225-3465; Fax: 225-0003; *Chief of Staff:* Armstrong Robinson

Web: geoffdavis.house.gov

District Office(s): 1405 Greenup Ave., #236, Ashland 41101-7573; (606) 324-9898; Fax: (606) 325-9866; *Field Representative:* J. R. Reed

300 Buttermilk Pike, Suite 314, Fort Mitchell 41017-3924; (859) 426-0080; Fax: (859) 426-0061; *Deputy Chief of Staff:* John Stanton

108 W. Jefferson St., La Grange 40031-1108; (502) 222-2233; Fax: (502) 222-4060; *Field Representative:* Christina Poole

Kenton Commonwealth Center, 201 Government Street, Suite 102, Maysville 41056-1260; *Field Representative:* Bill Tom Cooper

City Bldg., 400 N. Main St., #145, Williamstown 41097-1026; (859) 824-3320; Fax: (859) 824-3340

Committee Assignment(s): Ways and Means

Davis, Lincoln, D-Tenn. (4)

Capitol Hill Office: 410 CHOB 20515-4204; 225-6831; Fax: 226-5172; *Chief of Staff:* Beecher W. Frasier III

Web: www.house.gov/lincolndavis

District Office(s): 1804 Carmack Blvd., Suite A, Columbia 38401-4132; (931) 490-8699; Fax: (931) 490-8675; *District Representative:* Glenn Myers

629 N. Main St., Jamestown 38556-3739; (931) 879-2361; Fax: (931) 879-2389; *District Representative:* John Robbins

477 N. Chancery St., Suite A1, McMinnville 37110-8901; (931) 473-7251; Fax: (931) 473-7259; *District Director:* Sammy Lowdermilk

1064 N. Gateway Ave., Rockwood 37854-4023; (865) 354-3323; Fax: (865) 354-3316; *District Representative*: Paul Scarbrough
Committee Assignment(s): Appropriations; Science and Technology

Davis, Susan, D-Calif. (53)

Capitol Hill Office: 1526 LHOB 20515-0553; 225-2040; Fax: 225-2948; *Chief of Staff:* Lisa A. Sherman
Web: www.house.gov/susandavis
District Office(s): 4305 University Ave., #515, San Diego 92105-1601; (619) 280-5353; Fax: (619) 280-5311; *District Director*: Jessica Poole
Committee Assignment(s): Armed Services; Education and Labor; House Administration; Joint Printing

Deal, Nathan, R-Ga. (9)

Capitol Hill Office: 2133 RHOB 20515-1009; 225-5211; Fax: 225-8272; *Deputy Chief of Staff:* Todd Smith
Web: www.house.gov/deal
District Office(s): 415 E. Walnut Ave., #108, Dalton 30721-4465; (706) 226-5320; Fax: (706) 278-0840; *Caseworker for Gordon, Murray, and Whitfield Counties*: Vivian Campbell
P.O. Box 1015, Gainesville 30501-1015; (770) 535-2592; Fax: (770) 535-2765; *Chief of Staff:* Chris Riley
108 W. Lafayette Sq., #102, Lafayette 30728-3507; (706) 638-7042; Fax: (706) 638-7049; *Caseworker for Catoosa, Dade, and Walker Counties*: Lonna Hightower
Committee Assignment(s): Energy and Commerce

DeFazio, Peter A., D-Ore. (4)

Capitol Hill Office: 2134 RHOB 20515-3704; 225-6416; Fax: 225-0032; *Chief of Staff:* Penny Dodge
Web: defazio.house.gov
District Office(s): 125 Central Ave., #250, P.O. Box 1557, Coos Bay 97420-2342; (541) 269-2609; Fax: (541) 269-5760; *Coastal Field Representative*: Ron Kresky
405 E. 8th Ave., Eugene 97401-2706; (541) 465-6732; Fax: (541) 465-6458; *District Director*: Karmen Fore
612 S.E. Jackson St., #9, P.O. Box 2460, Roseburg 97470-4956; (541) 440-3523; Fax: (541) 440-0511; *Field Representative*: Chris Conroy
Committee Assignment(s): Homeland Security; Natural Resources; Transportation and Infrastructure

DeGette, Diana L., D-Colo. (1)

Capitol Hill Office: 2335 RHOB 20515-0601; 225-4431; Fax: 225-5657; *Chief of Staff:* Lisa B. Cohen
Web: www.house.gov/degette
District Office(s): 600 Grant St., #202, Denver 80203-3525; (303) 844-4988; Fax: (303) 844-4996; *District Director*: Chris Arend
Committee Assignment(s): Energy and Commerce; Natural Resources

Delahunt, William D., D-Mass. (10)

Capitol Hill Office: 2454 RHOB 20515-2110; 225-3111; Fax: 225-5658; *Chief of Staff:* Mark R. Forest
Web: www.house.gov/Delahunt
E-mail: William.Delahunt@mail.house.gov
District Office(s): 146 Main St., Hyannis 02601; (508) 771-0666; Fax: (508) 790-1959; *Office Manager; District Scheduler*: Laurie Burnett
1250 Hancock St., #802-N, Quincy 02169-4346; (617) 770-3700; Fax: (617) 770-2984; *Deputy District Director*: Kim Arouca
Committee Assignment(s): Foreign Affairs; Judiciary

DeLauro, Rosa L., D-Conn. (3)

Capitol Hill Office: 2413 RHOB 20515-0703; 225-3661; Fax: 225-4890; *Chief of Staff:* Kevin Brennan
Web: www.house.gov/delauro
District Office(s): 59 Elm St., #205, New Haven 06510-2036; (203) 562-3718; Fax: (203) 772-2260; *District Director*: Jennifer Lamb
Committee Assignment(s): Appropriations; Budget

Dent, Charlie, R-Pa. (15)

Capitol Hill Office: 1009 LHOB 20515-3815; 225-6411; Fax: 226-0778; *Chief of Staff:* George S. McElwee
Web: dent.house.gov
District Office(s): 701 W. Broad St., #200, Bethlehem 18018-5229; (610) 861-9734; Fax: (610) 861-9308; *District Director*: Carol R. Halper
206 Main St., East Greenville 18041-1405; (215) 541-4106; Fax: (215) 541-4109; *Community Outreach Director*: Vincent W. O'Domski
Committee Assignment(s): Homeland Security; Standards of Official Conduct; Transportation and Infrastructure

Diaz-Balart, Lincoln, R-Fla. (21)

Capitol Hill Office: 2244 RHOB 20515-0921; 225-4211; Fax: 225-8576; *Legislative Director:* Cesar A. Gonzalez
Web: diaz-balart.house.gov
District Office(s): Savannah Bldg., 8525 N.W. 53rd Terrace, #102, Miami 33166-4520; (305) 470-8555; Fax: (305) 470-8575; *Chief of Staff:* Ana M. Carbonell
Committee Assignment(s): Rules

Diaz-Balart, Mario, R-Fla. (25)

Capitol Hill Office: 328 CHOB 20515-0925; 225-2778; Fax: 226-0346; *Chief of Staff:* Nilda Pedrosa
Web: www.house.gov/mariodiaz-balart
District Office(s): 12851 S.W. 42nd St., #131, Miami 33175-3436; (305) 225-6866; Fax: (305) 225-7432; *District Director:* Miguel A. Otero
4715 Golden Gate Pkwy., #1, Naples 34116-6901; (239) 348-1620; Fax: (239) 348-3569; *District Representative:* George Barton
Committee Assignment(s): Budget; Science and Technology; Transportation and Infrastructure

Dicks, Norm, D-Wash. (6)

Capitol Hill Office: 2467 RHOB 20515-4706; 225-5916; Fax: 226-1176; *Chief of Staff:* George Behan
Web: www.house.gov/dicks
District Office(s): 345 6th St., #500, Bremerton 98337; (360) 479-4011; Fax: (360) 479-2126; *Kitsap County Director:* Cheri Williams
332 E. 5th St., Port Angeles 98362-3207; (360) 452-3370; Fax: (360) 452-3502; *District Representative:* Judith Morris
1019 Pacific Ave., #806, Tacoma 98402-4486; (253) 593-6536; Fax: (253) 593-6551; *District Director:* Clark Mather
Committee Assignment(s): Appropriations

Dingell, John D., D-Mich. (15)

Capitol Hill Office: 2328 RHOB 20515-2215; 225-4071; *Chief of Staff:* Michael Robbins
Web: www.house.gov/Dingell
District Office(s): 19855 W. Outer Dr., #103-E, Dearborn 48124-2028; (313) 278-2936; Fax: (313) 278-3914; *Field Representative:* Josh Myers
23 E. Front St., #103, Monroe 48161-2256; (734) 243-1849; Fax: (734) 243-5559; *Office Manager:* Donna Hoffer
5 S. Washington St., Ypsilanti 48197-8408; (734) 481-1100; Fax: (734) 481-1112; *Field Representative:* Andrew LaBarre
Committee Assignment(s): Energy and Commerce

Doggett, Lloyd, D-Tex. (25)

Capitol Hill Office: 201 CHOB 20515-4325; 225-4865; Fax: 225-3073; *Chief of Staff:* Michael J. Mucchetti
Web: www.house.gov/Doggett
District Office(s): Federal Bldg., 300 E. 8th St., #763, Austin 78701-3224; (512) 916-5921; Fax: (512) 916-5108; *District Director:* Amanda Tyler
Committee Assignment(s): Budget; Ways and Means

Donnelly, Joe, D-Ind. (2)

Capitol Hill Office: 1530 LHOB 20515-1402; 225-3915; Fax: 225-6798; *Chief of Staff:* Joel R. Elliott
Web: donnelly.house.gov
District Office(s): 809 State St., #502B, La Porte 46350-3309; (219) 326-6808
300 E. Broadway, #102, Logansport 46947-3182; (574) 753-2671; Fax: (574) 753-7615
100 E. Michigan Blvd., Michigan City 46360-3265; (219) 873-1403
207 W. Colfax Ave., South Bend 46601-1606; (574) 288-2780; Fax: (574) 288-2825; *District Director:* Hodge Patel
Committee Assignment(s): Financial Services; Veterans' Affairs

Doyle, Mike, D-Pa. (14)

Capitol Hill Office: 401 CHOB 20515-3814; 225-2135; Fax: 225-3084; *Chief of Staff:* David G. Lucas
Web: www.house.gov/doyle
District Office(s): 627 Lysle Blvd., McKeesport 15132; (412) 664-4049; Fax: (412) 664-4053; *Caseworker:* Jamie Byrne
11 Duff Rd., Penn Hills 15235; (412) 241-6055; Fax: (412) 241-6820; *Caseworker:* John Jones
225 Ross St., #5, Pittsburgh 15219-2024; (412) 261-5091; *District Director:* Paul D'Alesandro
Committee Assignment(s): Energy and Commerce

Dreier, David, R-Calif. (26)

Capitol Hill Office: 233 CHOB 20515-0526; 225-2305; Fax: 225-7018; *Chief of Staff:* Brad Smith
Web: dreier.house.gov
District Office(s): 510 E. Foothill Blvd., #201, San Dimas 91773-1254; (909) 575-6226; *District Director:* Mark S. Harmsen
Committee Assignment(s): Rules

Driehaus, Steve, D-Ohio (1)

Capitol Hill Office: 408 CHOB 20515-3501; 225-2216; Fax: 225-3012; *Chief of Staff:* Greg Mecher
Web: driehaus.house.gov
District Office(s): 441 Vine St., Suite 3003, Cincinnati 45202-3003; *District Director:* Steve Brinker
Committee Assignment(s): Financial Services; Oversight and Government Reform

Duncan, John J., Jr., R-Tenn. (2)

Capitol Hill Office: 2207 RHOB 20515-4202; 225-5435; Fax: 225-6440; *Communications Director:* Amy Westmoreland
Web: www.house.gov/Duncan
District Office(s): McMinn County Courthouse, 6 E. Madison Ave., Athens 37303-3697; (423) 745-4671; Fax: (423) 745-6025; *Office Manager:* Linda Higdon
Howard H. Baker Jr. U.S. Courthouse, 800 Market St., #110, Knoxville 37902-2303; (423) 523-3772; Fax: (423) 544-0728; *Chief of Staff:* Bob Griffitts
200 E. Broadway Ave., #414, Maryville 37804-5754; (865) 984-5464; Fax: (865) 984-0521; *Office Manager:* Vickie Flynn
Committee Assignment(s): Natural Resources; Oversight and Government Reform; Transportation and Infrastructure

Edwards, Chet, D-Tex. (17)

Capitol Hill Office: 2369 RHOB 20515-4317; 225-6105; Fax: 225-0350; *Chief of Staff:* Chris Chwastyk
Web: edwards.house.gov
District Office(s): 115 S. Main St., #202, Cleburne 76033-5501; (817) 645-4743; Fax: (817) 645-4796; *Field Rep:* Victoria Sykes

111 University Dr., #216, College Station 77840-1261; (979) 691-8797; Fax: (979) 691-8939; *Field Rep*: Phil Shackelford

St. Charles Pl., 600 Austin Ave., #29, Waco 76710; (254) 752-9600; Fax: (254) 752-7769; *District Director*: Myrtle Johnson

Committee Assignment(s): Appropriations; Budget

Edwards, Donna, D-Md. (4)

Capitol Hill Office: 318 CHOB 20515-2004; 225-8699; Fax: 225-8714; *Chief of Staff*: Adrienne Christian

Web: donnaedwards.house.gov

District Office(s): 18401 Woodfield Road, Suite D, Gaithersburg 20879-4796; (301) 987-2054; *District Director*: Selena Mandy Singleton

9200 Basil Court, Suite 221, Largo 20774-5337; (301) 773-4094; *Deputy District Director*: Chonya Davis-Johnson

Committee Assignment(s): Science and Technology; Transportation and Infastructure

Ehlers, Vernon J., R-Mich. (3)

Capitol Hill Office: 2182 RHOB 20515-2203; 225-3831; Fax: 225-5144; *Chief of Staff*: William R. McBride

Web: www.house.gov/ehlers

District Office(s): Gerald R. Ford Federal Bldg., 110 Michigan St., #166, Grand Rapids 49503-2313; (616) 451-8383; Fax: (616) 454-5630; *Constituent Services Director*: Jennifer Long Duthler

Committee Assignment(s): Education and Labor; Science and Technology; Transportation and Infrastructure

Ellison, Keith, D-Minn. (5)

Capitol Hill Office: 1122 LHOB 20515-2305; 225-4755; Fax: 225-4886; *Chief of Staff*: Kari Moe

Web: ellison.house.gov

District Office(s): 2100 Plymouth Ave. North, Minneapolis 55411-3675; (612) 522-1212; Fax: (612) 522-9915; *District Director*: Brian Elliott

Committee Assignment(s): Financial Services; Foreign Affairs

Ellsworth, Brad, D-Ind. (8)

Capitol Hill Office: 513 CHOB 20515-1408; 225-4636; Fax: 225-3284; *Chief of Staff*: Cori Smith

Web: ellsworth.house.gov

District Office(s): 101 N.W. Martin Luther King Jr. Blvd., #124, Evansville 47708-1951; (812) 465-6484; Fax: (812) 422-4761; *District Director*: Patrick Scates

901 Wabash Ave., #140, Terre Haute 47807-3232; (812) 232-0523; Fax: (812) 232-0526; *Constituent Advocate*: Angela Bullock

Committee Assignment(s): Agriculture; Armed Services; Small Business

Emerson, Jo Ann, R-Mo. (8)

Capitol Hill Office: 2440 RHOB 20515-2508; 225-4404; Fax: 226-0326; *Chief of Staff*: Jeffrey C. Connor

Web: www.house.gov/emerson

District Office(s): 555 Independence Street, Suite 1400, Cape Girardeau 63703-6235; (573) 335-0101; Fax: (573) 335-1931; *District Director*: Kristi Nitsch

22 E. Columbia St., Farmington 63640-3101; (573) 756-9755; Fax: (573) 756-9762; *District Director*: Heather Garner

1301 Kingshighway Street, Rolla 65401-2926; (573) 364-2455; Fax: (573) 364-1053; *District Director*: Darren Lingle

35 Court Square, Suite 300, White Plains 65775-3453; (417) 255-1515; Fax: (417) 255-2009; *District Director*: Heather Peugh

Committee Assignment(s): Appropriations

Engel, Eliot L., D-N.Y. (17)

Capitol Hill Office: 2161 RHOB 20515-3217; 225-2464; *Legislative Director*: Emily Gibbons

Web: engel.house.gov

District Office(s): 3655 Johnson Ave., Bronx 10463-1671; (718) 796-9700; *Chief of Staff*: William F. Weitz

6 Gramatan Ave., #205, Mount Vernon 10550-3208; (914) 699-4100; *Staff Assistant*: Cynthia Miller

261 W. Nyack Rd., West Nyack 10994-1724; (845) 735-1000; *Staff Assistant*: Ricardo Rangel

Committee Assignment(s): Energy and Commerce; Foreign Affairs

Eshoo, Anna G., D-Calif. (14)

Capitol Hill Office: 205 CHOB 20515-0514; 225-8104; Fax: 225-8890; *Chief of Staff*: Jason M. Mahler

Web: eshoo.house.gov

District Office(s): 698 Emerson St., Palo Alto 94301-1609; (650) 323-2984; Fax: (650) 323-3498; *District Chief of Staff*: Karen Chapman

Committee Assignment(s): Energy and Commerce; Permanent Select Intelligence

Etheridge, Bob, D-N.C. (2)

Capitol Hill Office: 1533 LHOB 20515-3302; 225-4531; Fax: 225-5662; *Chief of Staff*: Vacancy

Web: www.house.gov/etheridge

District Office(s): 609 N. 1st St., Lillington 27546; (910) 814-0335; Fax: (910) 814-2264; *District Representative*: William Munn

333 Fayetteville Street, Suite 505, Raleigh 27601-1742; (919) 829-9122; Fax: (919) 829-9883; *District Director*: Russ Swindell

Committee Assignment(s): Budget; Ways and Means

Committee Assignment(s): Agriculture; Armed Services; Permanent Select Intelligence

Faleomavaega, Eni F. H., D-Am. Samoa (Non-Voting Delegate)

Capitol Hill Office: 2422 RHOB 20515-5201; 225-8577; Fax: 225-8757; *Chief of Staff:* Lisa W. Williams
Web: www.house.gov/Faleomavaega
E-mail: Faleomavaega@mail.house.gov
District Office(s): P.O. Drawer X, Pago Pago 96799; (684) 633-1372; Fax: (684) 633-2680; *Chief of Staff:* Alexander Iuli Godinet
Committee Assignment(s): Foreign Affairs; Natural Resources

Fallin, Mary, R-Okla. (5)

Capitol Hill Office: 1432 LHOB 20515-3605; 225-2132; Fax: 226-1463; *Chief of Staff:* Nate Webb
Web: fallin.house.gov
District Office(s): 120 N. Robinson Ave., #100, Oklahoma City 73102-7461; (405) 234-9900; Fax: (405) 234-9909; *District Director:* Denise Northrup
20 E. 9th St., #137, Shawnee 74801-6978; (405) 273-1733; *Field Representative:* Danielle Navas
Committee Assignment(s): Armed Services; Small Business; Transportation and Infrastructure

Farr, Sam, D-Calif. (17)

Capitol Hill Office: 1126 LHOB 20515-0517; 225-2861; Fax: 225-6791; *Chief of Staff:* Rochelle S. Dornatt
Web: www.farr.house.gov
District Office(s): 100 W. Alisal St., Salinas 93901; (831) 424-2229; Fax: (831) 424-7099; *District Director:* Alex J. Argo
701 Ocean St., #318, Santa Cruz 95060-4027; (831) 429-1976; *Congressional Aide:* Julian Chacon
Committee Assignment(s): Appropriations

Fattah, Chaka, D-Pa. (2)

Capitol Hill Office: 2301 RHOB 20515-3802; 225-4001; Fax: 225-5392; *Chief of Staff:* Michelle Anderson Lee
Web: www.house.gov/Fattah
District Office(s): 4104 Walnut St., Philadelphia 19104-3598; (215) 387-6404; **District Chief of Staff:** Bonnie Bowser
6632 Germantown Ave., Philadelphia 19119-2250; (215) 848-9386; *District Senior Policy Advisor:* Cindy Bass
Committee Assignment(s): Appropriations

Filner, Bob, D-Calif. (51)

Capitol Hill Office: 2428 RHOB 20515-0551; 225-8045; Fax: 225-9073; *Chief of Staff:* Tony J. Buckles
Web: www.house.gov/filner
District Office(s): 333 F St., Suite A, Chula Vista 91910-2624; (619) 422-5963; Fax: (619) 422-7290; *District Chief of Staff:* Humberto Peraza
1101 Airport Rd., Suite D, Imperial 92251-1800; (760) 355-8800; Fax: (760) 355-8802; *Community Representative:* Juanita Salas
Committee Assignment(s): Transportation and Infrastructure; Veterans' Affairs

Flake, Jeff, R-Ariz. (6)

Capitol Hill Office: 240 CHOB 20515-0306; 225-2635; Fax: 226-4386; *Chief of Staff:* Margaret J. Klessig
Web: flake.house.gov
District Office(s): 1640 S. Stapley Dr., #215, Mesa 85204-6666; (480) 833-0092; Fax: (480) 833-6314; *District Director:* Christine Chucri
Committee Assignment(s): Foreign Affairs; Natural Resources; Oversight and Government Reform

Fleming, John, R-La. (4)

Capitol Hill Office: 1023 LHOB 20515-1804; 225-2777; Fax: 225-8039, *Chief of Staff:* Lee Fletcher
Web: fleming.house.gov
District Office(s): 1606 S. Fifth St., Leesville 71446-5304; (337) 238-0778; Fax: (337) 238-0566; *District Director – Southern Region:* Lee Turner
6425 Youree Drive, Suite 350; Shreveport 71105-4634; (318) 798-2254; Fax: (318) 798-2063; *District Director – Northern Region:* Rebecca Turner Wilson

Forbes, J. Randy, R-Va. (4)

Capitol Hill Office: 2438 RHOB 20515-4604; 225-6365; Fax: 226-1170; *Chief of Staff:* Dee Gilmore
Web: www.house.gov/forbes
District Office(s): 505 Independence Pkwy., Lake Center II, #104, Chesapeake 23320-5178; (757) 382-0080; Fax: (757) 382-0780; *Constituent Services Representative.:* Tammie Bebout
2903 Blvd., Suite B, Colonial Heights 23834-2401; (804) 526-4969; Fax: (804) 526-7486; *Constituent Services Representative:* Joan Fallon
425 South Main St., Suite H, Emporia 23847-2300; (434) 634-5575; Fax: (434) 634-0511; *District Field Representative:* Rick Franklin
Committee Assignment(s): Armed Services; Judiciary

Fortenberry, Jeff, R-Neb. (1)

Capitol Hill Office: 1535 LHOB 20515-2701; 225-4806; Fax: 225-5686; *Chief of Staff:* Kelly Lungren McCollum
Web: fortenberry.house.gov
District Office(s): 629 N. Broad St., Fremont 68025-4932; (402) 727-0888; Fax: (402) 727-9130; *Field Representative:* Louis Pofhahl
301 S. 13th St., #100, Lincoln 68508-2532; (402) 438-1598; Fax: (402) 438-1604; *District Director:* John Moenning
125 S. 4th St., #101, Norfolk 68701-5200; (402) 379-2064; Fax: (402) 379-2101; *Field Representative:* Louis Pofhahl
Committee Assignment(s): Agriculture; Foreign Affairs; Oversight and Government Reform

Foster, Bill, D-Ill. (14)

Capitol Hill Office: 1339 LHOB 20515-1314; 225-2976; Fax: 225-0697; *Chief of Staff:* Jason Linde

Web: foster.house.gov

District Office(s): 27 N. River St., Batavia 60510-2666; (630) 406-1114; Fax: (630) 406-1808; *Director of Outreach:* Matt Rado

119 W. 1st St., Dixon 61021-3056; (815) 288-0680; Fax: (815) 288-0743; *Director of Outreach:* Amanda York

Committee Assignment(s): Financial Services; Oversight and Government Reform

Foxx, Virginia, R-N.C. (5)

Capitol Hill Office: 1230 LHOB 20515-3305; 225-2071; Fax: 225-2995; *Chief of Staff:* Todd W. Poole

Web: foxx.house.gov

District Office(s): 240 Hwy. 105 Extension, #200, Boone 28607-4291; (828) 265-0240; Fax: (828) 265-0390; *Field Representative:* Mark Hefner

6000 Meadowbrook Mall Court, #3, Clemmons 27012-8775; (336) 778-0211; Fax: (336) 778-2290; *Constituent Liaison:* Mike Garlow

Committee Assignment(s): Rules

Frank, Barney, D-Mass. (4)

Capitol Hill Office: 2252 RHOB 20515-2104; 225-5931; Fax: 225-0182; *Chief of Staff:* Peter Kovar

Web: www.house.gov/frank

District Office(s): 558 Pleasant St., #309, New Bedford 02740-6246; (508) 999-6462; Fax: (508) 999-6468; *Office Manager:* Ines Goncalves-Drolet

29 Crafts St., Newton 02458-1275; (617) 332-3920; Fax: (617) 332-2822; *Chief District Adviser:* Dorothy M. Reichard

The Jones Bldg., 29 Broadway St., #310, Taunton 02780; (508) 822-4796; Fax: (508) 822-8286; *District Director:* Garth Patterson

Committee Assignment(s): Financial Services

Franks, Trent, R-Ariz. (2)

Capitol Hill Office: 2435 RHOB 20515-0302; 225-4576; Fax: 225-6328; *Chief of Staff:* Tom Stallings

Web: www.house.gov/franks

District Office(s): 7121 W. Bell Rd., #200, Glendale 85308-8549; (623) 776-7911; Fax: (623) 776-7832; *District Director:* Daniel Hay

Committee Assignment(s): Armed Services; Judiciary

Frelinghuysen, Rodney P., R-N.J. (11)

Capitol Hill Office: 2442 RHOB 20515-3011; 225-5034; *Chief of Staff:* Nancy Fox

Web: frelinghuysen.house.gov

District Office(s): 30 Schuyler Pl., 2nd Floor, Morristown 07960-5128; (973) 984-0711; *District Outreach Coordinator:* Holly Kunzman

Committee Assignment(s): Appropriations

Fudge, Marcia L., D-Ohio (11)

Capitol Hill Office: 1513 LHOB 20515-3511; 225-7032; Fax: 225-1339; *Chief of Staff:* Dawn Kelly Mobely

Web: fudge.house.gov

District Office(s): 4834 Richmond Road, Suite 150, Cleveland 44128-5922; (216) 522-4900; Fax: (216) 522-4908; *Scheduler/Staff Assistant:* Linda R. Matthews

Committee Assignment(s): Education and Labor; Science and Technology

Gallegly, Elton, R-Calif. (24)

Capitol Hill Office: 2309 RHOB 20515-0524; 225-5811; Fax: 225-1100; *Chief of Staff:* Joel D. Kassiday

Web: www.house.gov/Gallegly

District Office(s): 485 Alisal Rd., Suite G-1A, Solvang 93463-3701; (805) 686-2525; Fax: (805) 686-2566; *Congressional Aide:* Steve Lavagnino

2829 Townsgate Rd., #315, Thousand Oaks 91361-3018; (805) 497-2224; Fax: (805) 497-0039; *District Director:* Paula Sheil

Committee Assignment(s): Foreign Affairs; Judiciary; Natural Resources; Permanent Select Intelligence

Garrett, Scott, R-N.J. (5)

Capitol Hill Office: 137 CHOB 20515-3005; 225-4465; Fax: 225-9048; *Chief of Staff:* Amy Smith

Web: garrett.house.gov

District Office(s): 266 Harristown Road, Glen Rock 07452-3302; (201) 712-0330; Fax: (201) 712-0930; *District Director:* Tatiana Glaven

93 Main St., Newton 07860-2056; (973) 300-2000; Fax: (973) 300-1051; *Constituent Services Rep:* Dana DiRisio

Committee Assignment(s): Budget; Financial Services

Gerlach, Jim, R-Pa. (6)

Capitol Hill Office: 308 CHOB 20515-3806; 225-4315; Fax: 225-8440; *Chief of Staff:* Krista Gaffney

Web: gerlach.house.gov

District Office(s): 111 E. Uwchlan Ave., Exton 19341-1206; (610) 594-1415; Fax: (610) 594-1419; *District Director:* Bryan Kendro

580 Main St., #4, Trappe 19426; (610) 409-2780; Fax: (610) 409-7988; *Director of Constituent Services:* Jason Carver

501 N. Park Rd., Wyomissing 19610-2919; (610) 376-7630; Fax: (610) 376-7633; *District Outreach Representative:* Pat Beck

Committee Assignment(s): Financial Services; Transportation and Infrastructure

Giffords, Gabrielle, D-Ariz. (8)

Capitol Hill Office: 1728 LHOB 20515-0308; 225-2542; Fax: 225-0378; *Chief of Staff:* Pia Carusone

Web: giffords.house.gov

District Office(s): 77 Calle Portal, Suite B-160, Sierra Vista 85635-2981; (520) 429-3115; Fax: (520) 459-5419; *Constituent Services Manager:* Shay Saucedo

1661 N. Swan Rd., #112, Tucson 85712-4051; (520) 881-3588; Fax: (520) 322-9490; *District Director:* Ron Barber

Committee Assignment(s): Armed Services; Foreign Affairs; Science and Technology

Gingrey, Phil, R-Ga. (11)

Capitol Hill Office: 119 CHOB 20515-1011; 225-2931; Fax: 225-2944; *Chief of Staff:* David Sours
Web: gingrey.house.gov
District Office(s): 219 Roswell St. N.E., Marietta 30060-2063; (770) 429-1776; Fax: (770) 795-9551; *Deputy District Director:* John O'Keefe
600 E. 1st St., Rome 30161-3149; (706) 290-1776; Fax: (706) 232-7864; *District Director:* Janet Byington
Committee Assignment(s): Energy and Commerce

Gohmert, Louie, Jr., R-Tex. (1)

Capitol Hill Office: 511 CHOB 20515-4301; 225-3035; Fax: 226-1230; *Chief of Staff:* Michael Tomberlin
Web: gohmert.house.gov
District Office(s): Gregg County Courthouse, 101 E. Methvin St., #302, Longview 75601-7200; (903) 236-8597
300 E. Shepherd Ave., Lufkin 75901-3252; (936) 632-3180
102 W. Houston St., Marshall 75670-4038; (903) 938-8386
202 E. Pillar St., #304, Nacogdoches 75961-5508; (936) 715-9514
1121 E. Southeast Loop 323, #206, Tyler 75701-9660; (903) 561-6349; Fax: (903) 561-7110; *District Director:* Jonna Fitzgerald
Committee Assignment(s): Judiciary; Natural Resources; Small Business

Gonzalez, Charles A., D-Tex. (20)

Capitol Hill Office: 303 CHOB 20515-4320; 225-3236; Fax: 225-1915; *Chief of Staff:* Leo Munoz
Web: gonzalez.house.gov
District Office(s): Federal Bldg., 727 E. Durango Blvd., Suite B-124, San Antonio 78206-1286; (210) 472-6195; Fax: (210) 472-4009; *District Director:* Susanna Benavidez
Committee Assignment(s): Energy and Commerce; House Administration; Judiciary

Goodlatte, Bob, R-Va. (6)

Capitol Hill Office: 2240 RHOB 20515-4606; 225-5431; Fax: 225-9681; *Chief of Staff:* Shelley H. Husband
Web: www.house.gov/goodlatte
District Office(s): 2 S. Main St., 1st Floor, Suite A, Harrisonburg 22801; (540) 432-2391; Fax: (540) 432-6593; *District Representative:* Ande Banks
916 Main St., #300, Lynchburg 24504; (434) 845-8306; Fax: (434) 845-8245; *District Representative:* Clarkie Patterson

Ten Franklin Rd. S.E., #540, Roanoke 24011; (540) 857-2672; Fax: (540) 857-2675; *District Director:* Peter S. Larkin
7 Court Sq., Staunton 24401; (540) 885-3861; Fax: (540) 885-3930; *District Representative:* Debbie Garrett
Committee Assignment(s): Agriculture; Judiciary

Gordon, Bart, D-Tenn. (6)

Capitol Hill Office: 2306 RHOB 20515-4206; 225-4231; Fax: 225-6887; *Chief of Staff:* Donna M. Pignatelli
Web: gordon.house.gov
District Office(s): 15 S. Jefferson Ave., Cookeville 38501-3307; (931) 528-5907; Fax: (931) 528-1165; *Field Representative:* Billy Smith
Sumner County Courthouse, 100 Public Sq., Suite B-100, Gallatin 37066-2867; (615) 451-5174; *Field Representative:* Caroline Diaz-Barriga
305 W. Main St., Murfreesboro 37130-3547; (615) 896-1986; Fax: (615) 896-8218; *District Chief of Staff:* Kent Syler
Committee Assignment(s): Energy and Commerce; Science and Technology

Granger, Kay, R-Tex. (12)

Capitol Hill Office: 320 CHOB 20515-4312; 225-5071; Fax: 225-5683; *Chief of Staff:* Robert Head
Web: kaygranger.house.gov
District Office(s): River Plaza, 1701 River Run Rd., #407, Fort Worth 76107-6548; (817) 338-0909; Fax: (817) 335-5852; *District Director:* Barbara Ragland
Committee Assignment(s): Appropriations

Graves, Sam, R-Mo. (6)

Capitol Hill Office: 1415 LHOB 20515-2506; 225-7041; Fax: 225-8221; *Chief of Staff:* Tom Brown
Web: www.house.gov/graves
District Office(s): 113 Blue Jay Dr., #100, Liberty 64068-1963; (816) 792-3976; Fax: (816) 792-0694; *Deputy Chief of Staff:* Melissa Roe
201 S. 8th St., #330, St. Joseph 64501-2275; (816) 233-9818; Fax: (816) 233-9848; *Field Rep:* Naomi Bass
Committee Assignment(s): Agriculture; Small Business; Transportation and Infrastructure

Grayson, Alan, D-Fl. (8)

Capitol Hill Office: 1605 LHOB 20515-0908; 225-2176; Fax: 225-0999; *Chief of Staff:* Julie Tagen
Web: grayson.house.gov
District Office(s): 445 N. Garland Avenue, Orlando 32801-1518; (407) 841-1757; Fax: (407) 841-1754; *District Director:* Debra Booth
Committee Assignment(s): Financial Services; Science and Technology

Green, Al, D-Tex. (9)

Capitol Hill Office: 236 CHOB 20515-4309; 225-7508; Fax: 225-2947; *Chief of Staff:* Jacqueline A. Ellis

Web: www.house.gov/algreen
District Office(s): 3003 S. Loop West, #460, Houston 77054-1301; (713) 383-9234; Fax: (713) 383-9202; *District Director*: Cynthia Buggage
Committee Assignment(s): Financial Services; Homeland Security

Green, Gene, D-Tex. (29)

Capitol Hill Office: 2372 RHOB 20515-4329; 225-1688; Fax: 225-9903; *Chief of Staff*: Rhonda Jackson
Web: www.house.gov/green
District Office(s): 909 Decker Dr., #124, Baytown 77520-4433; (281) 420-0502; Fax: (281) 420-0585
256 N. Sam Houston Pkwy. East, #29, Houston 77060-2028; (281) 999-5879; Fax: (281) 999-5716; *Caseworker*: Shirley Gonzalez
11811 I-10 East, #430, Houston 77029; (713) 330-0761; Fax: (713) 330-0807; *Caseworker*: Marlene Clowers
Committee Assignment(s): Energy and Commerce; Foreign Affairs

Griffith, Parker, D-Ala. (5)

Capitol Hill Office: 417 CHOB 20515-0105; 225-4801; Fax: 225-4392; *Chief of Staff*: Sharon Wheeler
Web: griffith.house.gov
District Office(s): Morgan County Courthouse, 302 Lee Street N.E., Fifth Floor, Room 86, P.O. Box 668, Decatur 35601-1926; (256) 355-9400; Fax: (256) 355-9406; *Caseworker*: Peggy Towns
2101 Clinton Avenue W., Suite 302, Huntsville 35805-3109; (256) 551-0190; Fax: (256) 551-0194; *District Director*: Jim McCamy
The Bevill Center for Advanced Technology, 1011 George Wallace Boulevard, Tuscumbia 35674-1726; (256) 381-3450; Fax: (256) 381-7659; *Field Rep*: Gene Tackett
Committee Assignment(s): Science and Technology; Small Business; Transportation and Infastructure

Grijalva, Raúl M., D-Ariz. (7)

Capitol Hill Office: 1440 LHOB 20515-0307; 225-2435; Fax: 225-1541; *Chief of Staff*: Gloria Montaño
Web: www.house.gov/grijalva
District Office(s): 810 E. 22nd St., #122, Tucson 85713-1751; (520) 622-6788; Fax: (520) 622-0198; *District Director*: Rubén H. Reyes
1455 S. 4th Ave., #4, Yuma 85364-4695; (928) 343-7933; Fax: (928) 343-7949; *Community Representative*: Araceli Rodriguez
Committee Assignment(s): Education and Labor; Natural Resources

Guthrie, Brett, R-Ky. (2)

Capitol Hill Office: 510 CHOB 20515-1702; 225-3501; Fax: 225-2019; *Chief of Staff*: Eric Bergren
Web: guthrie.house.gov

District Office(s): 1001 Center Street, Suite 300, Bowling Green 42101-2192; (270) 842-9896; *District Director*: Mark Lord
Committee Assignment(s): Education and Labor; Transportation and Infastructure

Gutierrez, Luis V., D-Ill. (4)

Capitol Hill Office: 2266 RHOB 20515-1304; 225-8203; Fax: 225-7810; *Chief of Staff*: Jennice Fuentes
Web: luisgutierrez.house.gov
District Office(s): 3455 W. North Ave., Chicago 60647-4841; (773) 384-1655; Fax: (773) 384-1685; *District Co-Director*: Veronica Ocassio
Committee Assignment(s): Financial Services; Judiciary

Hall, John, D-N.Y. (19)

Capitol Hill Office: 1217 LHOB 20515-3219; 225-5441; Fax: 225-3289; *Chief of Staff*: Susan Spear
Web: johnhall.house.gov
District Office(s): Putnam County Office Bldg., 40 Gleneida Ave., 3rd Floor, Carmel 10512-1705; (845) 225-3641, ext. 371; Fax: (845) 228-1480; *Executive Assistant*: Elizabeth Soto
Orange County Government Center, 255 Main St., #3232G, Goshen 10924-1619; (845) 291-4100; Fax: (845) 291-4164; *District Director*: Frank Giancamilli
Committee Assignment(s): Transportation and Infrastructure; Veterans' Affairs; Select Energy Independence and Global Warming

Hall, Ralph M., R-Tex. (4)

Capitol Hill Office: 2405 RHOB 20515-4304; 225-6673; Fax: 225-3332; *Chief of Staff*: Janet Perry Poppleton
Web: www.house.gov/ralphhall
District Office(s): Collin County Courts Facility, 1800 N. Graves St., #101, McKinney 75069-3422; (214) 726-9949; Fax: (214) 726-9363; *District Assistant*: Linda Schenck
Bowie County Courthouse, 710 James Bowie Dr., New Boston 75570-2328; (903) 628-8309; Fax: (903) 628-8320; *District Assistant*: Eric Cain
104 N. San Jacinto St., Rockwall 75087-2508; (972) 771-9118; Fax: (972) 722-0907; *District Assistant*: Thomas Hughes
101 E. Pecan St., #119, Sherman 75090-5917; (903) 892-1112; Fax: (903) 868-0264; *District Assistant*: Judy Rowton
U.S. Post Office, 320 Church St., #132, Sulphur Springs 75482-2606; (903) 885-8138; Fax: (903) 439-0874; *District Assistant*: Martha Glover
4303 Texas Blvd., #2, Texarkana 75503-3094; (903) 794-4445; Fax: (903) 794-5577; *District Assistant*: Marjorie Chandler
Committee Assignment(s): Energy and Commerce; Science and Technology

Halvorson, Debbie, D-Ill. (11)

Capitol Hill Office: 1541 LHOB 20515-1311; 225-3635; Fax: 225-3521; *Chief of Staff:* Gideon Blunstein
Web: halvorson.house.gov
District Office(s): 116 N. Chicago St., Suite 401, Joliet 60432-4288; (815) 726-4998; *District Director:* Marylin Turner
200 E. Court Street, Suite 700, Kankakee 60901-3856; *Regional Director, Grundee and Kankakee Counties:* Nick Allen
104 W. North Street, Normal 61761-2532; (815) 531-9466; *Regional Director, Woodford and McLean Counties:* Christina Rogers
Committee Assignment(s): Agriculture; Small Business; Veterans' Affairs

Hare, Phil, D-Ill. (17)

Capitol Hill Office: 428 CHOB 20515-1317; 225-5905; Fax: 225-5396; *Chief of Staff:* Tom O'Donnell
Web: hare.house.gov
District Office(s): 210 N. Broad St., Carlinville 62626-1302; (217) 854-2290; Fax: (217) 854-2261; *Staff Assistant:* Pamela Monetti
236 N. Water St., #765, Decatur 62523-1351; (217) 422-9150; Fax: (217) 422-9245; *Staff Assistant:* Patricia Dawson
261 N. Broad St., #5, Galesburg 61401-4612; (309) 342-4411; Fax: (309) 342-9749; *Staff Assistant:* Sue Schurke
2001 52nd Avenue, Suite 5, Moline 61265-6368; (309) 793-5760; Fax: (309) 762-9193; *District Director:* Pat C. O'Brien
Committee Assignment(s): Education and Labor; Transportation and Infrastructure

Harman, Jane, D-Calif. (36)

Capitol Hill Office: 2400 RHOB 20515-0536; 225-8220; Fax: 226-7290; *Chief of Staff:* John Hess
Web: www.house.gov/Harman
District Office(s): 2321 E. Rosecrans Ave., #3270, El Segundo 90245-4977; (310) 643-3636; Fax: (310) 643-6445; *Political Director:* Paul Arney
544 N. Avalon Blvd., #307, Wilmington 90744-5806; (310) 549-8282; Fax: (310) 549-8250; *District Director:* Vanessa Aramayo
Committee Assignment(s): Energy and Commerce; Homeland Security

Harper, Gregg, R-Miss. (3)

Capitol Hill Office: 307 CHOB 20515-2403; 225-5031; Fax: 225-5797; *Chief of Staff:* Michael J. Kravens
Web: harper.house.gov
District Office(s): 230 S. Whitworth Avenue, Brookhaven 39601-3343; (601) 823-3400; Fax: (601) 823-5512
823 22nd Avenue, Meridian 39301-5006; (601) 693-6681; Fax: (601) 693-1801; *Special Asst. for Constituent Services*

Hastings, Alcee L., D-Fla. (23)

Capitol Hill Office: 2353 RHOB 20515-0923; 225-1313; Fax: 225-1171; *Chief of Staff:* Lale M. Mamaux
Web: alceehastings.house.gov
District Office(s): 2701 W. Oakland Park Blvd., #200, Fort Lauderdale 33311-1363; (954) 733-2800; Fax: (954) 735-9444; *Florida Chief of Staff:* Art W. Kennedy
1755 East Tiffany Drive, West Palm Beach 33407-3224; (561) 684-0565; Fax: (561) 684-3613; *Congressional Aide:* Lewis Goldberg
Committee Assignment(s): Commission on Security and Cooperation in Europe; Rules; Permanent Select Intelligence

Hastings, Doc, R-Wash. (4)

Capitol Hill Office: 1203 LHOB 20515-4704; 225-5816; Fax: 225-3251; *Chief of Staff:* Jessica Gleason
Web: hastings.house.gov
District Office(s): 2715 St. Andrews Loop, Suite D, Pasco 99301-3386; (509) 543-9396; Fax: (509) 545-1972; *District Director:* Barbara S. Lisk
302 E. Chestnut St., Yakima 98901-2718; (509) 452-3243; Fax: (509) 452-3438; *Field Representative:* Ryan Rodruck
Committee Assignment(s): Natural Resources

Heinrich, Martin T., D-N.M. (1)

Capitol Hill Office: 1505 LHOB 20515-3101; 225-6316; Fax: 225-4975; *Chief of Staff:* Steve Haro
Web: heinrich.house.gov
District Office(s): 20 First Plaza, N.W., Suite 603, Albuquerque 87102-5803; (505) 346-6781; Fax: (505) 346-6723; *District Director:* Heather Brewer
Committee Assignment(s): Armed Services; Natural Resources

Heller, Dean, R-Nev. (2)

Capitol Hill Office: 125 CHOB 20515-2802; 225-6155; Fax: 225-5679; *Chief of Staff:* Edgar M. Abrams
Web: heller.house.gov
District Office(s): 405 Idaho St., #214, Elko 89801-3753; (775) 777-7920; Fax: (775) 777-7922; *Outreach Coordinator:* Terri Fairfield
600 Las Vegas Blvd., #680, Las Vegas 89101-6646; (702) 255-1651; Fax: (702) 255-1927; *Outreach Coordinator:* Andres Moses
400 S. Virginia St., #502, Reno 89501-2194; (775) 686-5760; Fax: (775) 686-5711; *District Director:* Verita Black Prothro
Committee Assignment(s): Ways and Means

Hensarling, Jeb, R-Tex. (5)

Capitol Hill Office: 129 CHOB 20515-4305; 225-3484; Fax: 226-4888; *Chief of Staff:* Dee Buchanan
Web: www.house.gov/hensarling
District Office(s): 100 E. Corsicana St., #205, Athens 75751-2528; (903) 675-8288; Fax: (903) 675-8351; *Regional Director:* Richard Sanders

6510 Abrams Rd., #243, Dallas 75231-7278; (214) 349-9996; Fax: (214) 349-0738; *Regional Director:* Brian Chase

Committee Assignment(s): Budget; Financial Services

Herger, Wally, R-Calif. (2)

Capitol Hill Office: 242 CHOB 20515-0502; 225-3076; *Chief of Staff:* Derek Harley
Web: www.house.gov/herger
District Office(s): 55 Independence Circle, #104, Chico 95973-4909; (530) 893-8363; *Field Representative:* Jenna Batti
410 Hemsted Dr., #115, Redding 96002-0164; (530) 223-5898; *Field Representative:* David Meurer
Committee Assignment(s): Ways and Means; Joint Taxation

Herseth Sandlin, Stephanie, D-S.D. (At Large)

Capitol Hill Office: 331 CHOB 20515-4101; 225-2801; Fax: 225-5823; *Chief of Staff:* Tessa A. Gould
Web: hersethsandlin.house.gov
E-mail: stephanie.herseth@mail.house.gov
District Office(s): 13 2nd Ave. S.E., #102, Aberdeen 57401-4239; (605) 626-3440; Fax: (605) 626-3441; *Northeast Area Director:* Maeve King
1823 W. Main St., Rapid City 57702-2566; (605) 394-5280; Fax: (605) 394-5282; *Outreach Director:* Kate Kelley
326 E. 8th St., #108, Sioux Falls 57103-7036; (605) 367-8371; Fax: (605) 367-8373; *Southeast Area Director:* Steven Dahlmeier
Committee Assignment(s): Agriculture; Natural Resources; Veterans' Affairs; Select Energy Independence and Global Warming

Higgins, Brian, D-N.Y. (27)

Capitol Hill Office: 431 CHOB 20515-3227; 225-3306; Fax: 226-0347; *Chief of Staff:* Chuck Eaton
Web: higgins.house.gov
District Office(s): Larkin Bldg., 726 Exchange St., #601, Buffalo 14210-1484; (716) 852-3501; Fax: (716) 852-3929; *District Director:* Megan Corbett
Fenton Bldg., Two E. 2nd St., #300, Jamestown 14701-5206; (716) 484-0729; Fax: (716) 484-1049; *Director:* Donna Coughlin
Committee Assignment(s): Ways and Means

Hill, Baron, D-Ind. (9)

Capitol Hill Office: 223 CHOB 20515-1409; 225-5315; Fax: 226-6866; *Chief of Staff:* John Zody
Web: baronhill.house.gov
District Office(s): 320 West 8th St., #114, Bloomington 47404-3700; (812) 336-3000; Fax: (812) 336-3355
279 Quartermaster Court, Jeffersonville 47130-3669; (812) 288-3999; Fax: (812) 288-3873; *District Director:* Vacancy
Committee Assignment(s): Energy and Commerce; Science and Technology; Joint Economic

Himes, Jim, D-Conn. (4)

Capitol Hill Office: 214 CHOB 20515-0704; 225-5541; Fax: 225-9629; *Chief of Staff:* Jason Cole
Web: himes.house.gov
District Office(s): Court Exchange, 211 State Street, Floor 2, Bridgeport 06604-4808; (866) 453-0028; Fax: (203) 579-0771; *District Director:* Kathleen D. Warner
888 Washington Boulevard, Floor 10, Stamford 06901-2902; *Constituent Services Rep:* Ginny Fox
Committee Assignment(s): Financial Services; Homeland Security

Hinchey, Maurice D., D-N.Y. (22)

Capitol Hill Office: 2431 RHOB 20515-3222; 225-6335; Fax: 226-0774; *Communications Director:* Jeff Lieberson
Web: www.house.gov/Hinchey
District Office(s): Federal Bldg., 15 Henry St., #100A, Binghamton 13901-2724; (607) 773-2768; *Federal Liaison:* Robin Malloy
123 S. Cayuga St., #201, Ithaca 14850-5582; (607) 273-1388; *Federal Liaison:* Lisa Newman
291 Wall St., Kingston 12401-3849; (845) 331-4466; *Federal Liaison:* Molly Eagan
City Hall, 16 James St., 3rd Floor, Middletown 10940-5787; (845) 344-3211; *Federal Liaison:* Carmel Wilson
20 Anawana Lake Rd., Monticello 12701 3200; (845) 791-7116; *Community Liaison:* Julie Allen
Committee Assignment(s): Appropriations; Natural Resources; Joint Economic

Hinojosa, Rubén, D-Tex. (15)

Capitol Hill Office: 2463 RHOB 20515-4315; 225-2531; Fax: 225-5688; *Chief of Staff:* Connie Humphrey
Web: hinojosa.house.gov
District Office(s): 107 S. Saint Mary's St., Beeville 78102-5619; (361) 358-8400; Fax: (361) 358-8407; *District Director:* Judy McAda
2864 W. Trenton Rd., Edinburg 78539-9232; (956) 682-5545; Fax: (956) 682-0141; *District Director:* Salomon Torres
Committee Assignment(s): Education and Labor; Financial Services

Hirono, Mazie K., D-Hawaii (2)

Capitol Hill Office: 1524 LHOB 20515-1102; 225-4906; Fax: 225-4987; *Chief of Staff:* John D. White
Web: hirono.house.gov
District Office(s): 5104 Prince Kuhio Federal Bldg., 300 Ala Moana Blvd., Honolulu 96850-0001; (808) 541-1986; Fax: (808) 538-0233; *District Director:* Joshua Wisch
Committee Assignment(s): Education and Labor; Transportation and Infrastructure

Hodes, Paul, D-N.H. (2)

Capitol Hill Office: 1317 LHOB 20515-2902; 225-5206; Fax: 225-2946; *Chief of Staff:* Matt Robinson

Web: hodes.house.gov
District Office(s): 80 Main St., Berlin 03570-2415; (603) 752-4680; *Community Representative:* Robert Theberge
18 N. Main St., Fourth Floor, Concord 03301-4926; (603) 223-9814; Fax: (603) 229-9819; *District Director:* Jane Berlin Pauley
29 Center St. Keene 03431-3351; (603) 358-1023; Fax: (603) 358-1025; *Constituent Services Representative:* Leigh Marthe
32 Main St., Littleton 03561-4072; (603) 444-8967; Fax: (603) 444-8968; *Community Representative:* Steve Huntington
221 Main St., Suite 201, Nashua 03060-2725; (603) 579-6913; Fax: (603) 579-6916: *Constituent Services Representative:* Laurie Goodman
Committee Assignment(s): Financial Services; Oversight and Government Reform

Hoekstra, Peter, R-Mich. (2)

Capitol Hill Office: 2234 RHOB 20515-2202; 225-4401; Fax: 226-0779; *Chief of Staff:* Justin Wormmeester
Web: hoekstra.house.gov
District Office(s): 210 1/2 N. Mitchell St., Cadillac 49601-1835; (231) 775-0050; Fax: (231) 775-0298; *Cadillac Area Represenative:* Jill Brown
184 South River Ave., Holland 49423-2848; (616) 395-0030; Fax: (616) 395-0271; *District Director:* Jon DeWitte
900 3rd St., #203, Muskegon 49440-1135; (231) 722-8386; Fax: (231) 722-0176; *District Project Manager:* Heather Sandberg
Committee Assignment(s): Education and Labor; Permanent Select Intelligence

Holden, Tim, D-Pa. (17)

Capitol Hill Office: 2417 RHOB 20515-3817; 225-5546; Fax: 226-0996; *Chief of Staff:* Trish Reilly
Web: www.holden.house.gov
District Office(s): 1721 N. Front St., #105, Harrisburg 17102-2391; (717) 234-5904; Fax: (717) 234-5918; *District Director:* Tim S. Smith
758 Cumberland St., Lebanon 17042-5247; (717) 270-1395; Fax: (717) 270-1095; *Office Manager:* Matthew Boyer
101 N. Centre St., #303, Pottsville 17901-2972; (570) 622-4212; Fax: (570) 628-2561; *Constituent Services Representative:* Frank Ratkiewicz
4918 Kutztown Rd., Temple 19560-1554; (610) 921-3502; Fax: (610) 921-3504; *Constituent Services Representative:* Marge Lawlor
Committee Assignment(s): Agriculture; Transportation and Infrastructure

Holt, Rush, D-N.J. (12)

Capitol Hill Office: 1214 LHOB 20515-3012; 225-5801; Fax: 225-6025; *Chief of Staff:* Christopher Hartmann
Web: holt.house.gov

District Office(s): 50 Washington Rd., West Windsor 08550-1012; (609) 750-9365; Fax: (609) 750-0618; *District Director:* Leslie Potter
Committee Assignment(s): Education and Labor; Natural Resources; Permanent Select Intelligence

Honda, Mike, D-Calif. (15)

Capitol Hill Office: 1713 LHOB 20515-0515; 225-2631; Fax: 225-2699; *Chief of Staff:* Jennifer Van der Heide
Web: honda.house.gov
District Office(s): 1999 S. Bascom Ave., #815, Campbell 95008-2200; (408) 558-8085; Fax: (408) 558-8086; *District Director:* Meri Maben
Committee Assignment(s): Appropriations; Congressional-Executive Commission on China

Hoyer, Steny H., D-Md. (5)

Capitol Hill Office: 1705 LHOB 20515-2005; 225-4131; Fax: 225-4300; *Administrative Assistant:* Jim Wood
Web: hoyer.house.gov
District Office(s): 6500 Cherrywood Lane, #310, Greenbelt 20770-1287; (301) 474-0119; Fax: (301) 474-4697; *Constituent Liaison:* Daryl Pennington
401 Post Office Rd., #202, Waldorf 20602-2738; (301) 843-1577; Fax: (301) 843-1331; *District Director:* Betsy W. Bossart

Hunter, Duncan D., R-Calif. (52)

Capitol Hill Office: 1429 LHOB 20515-0552; 225-5672; Fax: 225-0235; *Chief of Staff:* Victoria J. Middleton
Web: www.house.gov/hunter
District Office(s): 1870 Cordell Court, #206, El Cajon 92020-0916; (619) 448-5201; Fax: (619) 449-2251; *District Chief of Staff:* Rick Terrazas
Committee Assignment(s): Armed Services; Education and Labor

Inglis, Bob, R-S.C. (4)

Capitol Hill Office: 100 CHOB 20515-4004; 225-6030; Fax: 226-1177; *Chief of Staff:* Wayne Roper
Web: inglis.house.gov
District Office(s): 105 N. Spring St., #111, Greenville 29601-2859; (864) 232-1141; Fax: (864) 233-2160; *Constituent Liaison:* April Evans
464 E. Main St., #8, Spartanburg 29302-1973; (864) 582-6422; Fax: (864) 573-9478; *Constituent Liaison:* Dwayne Hatchett
Committee Assignment(s): Foreign Affairs; Science and Technology

Inslee, Jay, D-Wash. (1)

Capitol Hill Office: 403 CHOB 20515-4701; 225-6311; Fax: 226-1606; *Chief of Staff:* Brian Bonlender
Web: www.house.gov/Inslee
District Office(s): 17791 Fjord Dr. N.E., Door 112, Poulsbo 98370-8481; (360) 598-2342; Fax: (360) 598-3650; *Special Assistant for Kitsap County:* Mendy Droke

Shoreline Center, 18560 1st Ave. N.E., Suite E-800, Shoreline 98155-2150; (206) 361-0233; Fax: (206) 361-3959; *District Director*: Sharmila Swenson

Committee Assignment(s): Energy and Commerce; Natural Resources; Select Energy Independence and Global Warming

Israel, Steve, D-N.Y. (2)

Capitol Hill Office: 2457 RHOB 20515-3202; 225-3335; Fax: 225-4669; *Chief of Staff*: Jack Pratt
Web: www.house.gov/Israel
District Office(s): 150 Motor Pkwy., #108, Hauppauge 11788-5152; (631) 951-2210; Fax: (631) 951-3308; *Deputy Chief of Staff*: Tracie Holmberg
Committee Assignment(s): Appropriations

Issa, Darrell, R-Calif. (49)

Capitol Hill Office: 2347 RHOB 20515-0549; 225-3906; Fax: 225-3303; *Chief of Staff*: Dale Neugebauer
Web: issa.house.gov
District Office(s): 1800 Thibodo Rd., #310, Vista 92081-7515; (760) 599-5000; Fax: (760) 599-1178; *District Director*: Phil Paule
Committee Assignment(s): Judiciary; Oversight and Government Reform

Jackson, Jesse L., Jr., D-Ill. (2)

Capitol Hill Office: 2419 RHOB 20515-1302; 225-0773; Fax: 225-0899; *Chief of Staff*: Kenneth E. Edmonds
Web: www.house.gov/Jackson
District Office(s): 7121 S. Yates Boulevard, Chicago 60649; (773) 241-6500; Fax: (773) 241-6503; *Deputy District Administrator*: Brian Sleet
17926 S. Halsted St., Homewood 60430-2029; (708) 798-6000; Fax: (708) 798-6160; *District Administrator*: Richard J. Bryant
Committee Assignment(s): Appropriations

Jackson Lee, Sheila, D-Tex. (18)

Capitol Hill Office: 2160 RHOB 20515-4318; 225-3816; Fax: 225-3317; *Chief of Staff*: Leon C. Buck Jr.
Web: jacksonlee.house.gov
District Office(s): Mickey Leland Federal Bldg., 1919 Smith St., #1180, Houston 77002-8098; (713) 655-0050; Fax: (713) 655-1612; *District Director*: Steven James
6719 W. Montgomery Rd., #204, Houston 77091-3105; (713) 691-4882; Fax: (713) 699-8292; *Community Liaison*: Anita James
420 W. 19th St., Houston 77008-3914; (713) 861-4070; Fax: (713) 861-4323; *District Liaison*: Michael Halpin
Committee Assignment(s): Foreign Affairs; Homeland Security; Judiciary

Jenkins, Lynn, R-Kans. (2)

Capitol Hill Office: 130 CHOB 20515-1602; 225-6601; Fax: 225-7985; *Chief of Staff*: Pat Leopold

Web: lynnjenkins.house.gov
District Office(s): 701 N. Broadway St., Pittsburg 66762-3905; (620) 231-5966; Fax: (620) 231-5972; *Constituent Services Rep*: Sheila Lampe
3550 S.W. Fifth Street, Topeka 66606-1998; (785) 234-5966; Fax: (785) 234-5967; *District Scheduler/Constituent Services Rep*: Melissa Underwood
Committee Assignment(s): Financial Services

Johnson, Eddie Bernice, D-Tex. (30)

Capitol Hill Office: 1511 LHOB 20515-4330; 225-8885; Fax: 226-1477; *Chief of Staff*: Murat T. Gokcigdem
Web: www.house.gov/ebjohnson
District Office(s): 3102 Maple Ave., #600, Dallas 75201-1236; (214) 922-8885; Fax: (214) 922-7028; *District Director*: Ron Givens
Committee Assignment(s): Science and Technology; Transportation and Infrastructure

Johnson, Hank, D-Ga. (4)

Capitol Hill Office: 1133 LHOB 20515-1004; 225-1605; Fax: 226-0691; *Chief of Staff*: Daraka Satcher
Web: hankjohnson.house.gov
District Office(s): 5700 Hillandale Dr., #110, Lithonia 30058-4104; (770) 987-2291; Fax: (770) 987-8721; *District Director*: Kathy H. Register
3469 Lawrenceville Hwy., #205, Tucker 30084-5866; (770) 939-2016; Fax: (770) 939-3753; *Tucker Office Manager*: Katie Dailey
Committee Assignment(s): Armed Services; Judiciary

Johnson, Sam, R-Tex. (3)

Capitol Hill Office: 1211 LHOB 20515-4303; 225-4201; Fax: 225-1485; *Chief of Staff*: David J. Heil
Web: www.samjohnson.house.gov
District Office(s): 2929 N. Central Expressway, #240, Richardson 75080-2000; (972) 470-0892; Fax: (972) 470-9937; *District Director*: Ashlea Quinonez
Committee Assignment(s): Ways and Means

Johnson, Timothy V., R-Ill. (15)

Capitol Hill Office: 1207 LHOB 20515-1315; 225-2371; Fax: 226-0791; *Chief of Staff*: Jerome T. Clarke
Web: www.house.gov/timjohnson
District Office(s): 202 N. Prospect Rd., #203, Bloomington 61704-7920; (309) 663-7049; Fax: (309) 663-9880; *District Aide*: Beth Harding
2004 Fox Dr., Champaign 61820-7336; (217) 403-4690; Fax: (217) 403-4691; *District Director*: Jeremy Cirks
655 W. Lincoln Ave., #8, Charleston 61920-2461; (217) 348-6759; Fax: (217) 348-6761; *District Aide*: Matthew Jones
1001 N. Market St., #102, Mount Carmel 62863-1948; (618) 262-8719; Fax: (618) 262-8859; *Caseworker*: Larry Reynolds
Committee Assignment(s): Agriculture; Transportation and Infrastructure

Jones, Walter B., R-N.C. (3)

Capitol Hill Office: 2333 RHOB 20515-3303; 225-3415;
Fax: 225-3286; *Chief of Staff:* Glen Downs
Web: jones.house.gov
District Office(s): 1105-C Corporate Dr., Greenville
27858-5968; (252) 931-1003; Fax: (252) 931-1002;
District Director: Millie Lilley
Committee Assignment(s): Armed Services; Financial
Services

Jordan, Jim, R-Ohio (4)

Capitol Hill Office: 515 CHOB 20515-3504; 225-2676;
Fax: 226-0577; *Chief of Staff:* Ray Yonkura
Web: jordan.house.gov
E-mail: WriteJim@mail.house.gov
District Office(s): 100 E. Main Cross St., #201, Findlay
45840-4888; (419) 423-3210; Fax: (419) 423-3233;
Deputy District Director: Cameron Warner
3121 W. Elm Plaza, Lima 45805-2516; (419) 999-6455;
Fax: (419) 999-4238; *Deputy District Director:* Cory
Noonan
24 W. 3rd St., #314, Mansfield 44902-1299; (419)
522-5757; Fax: (419) 525-2805; *District Director:*
Fred Shimp
Committee Assignment(s): Budget; Judiciary; Oversight
and Government Reform

Kagen, Steve, D-Wisc. (8)

Capitol Hill Office: 1232 LHOB 20515-4908; 225-5665;
Fax: 225-5729; *Chief of Staff:* David Williams
Web: kagen.house.gov
District Office(s): Radisson Paper Valley, 330
W. College Ave., Appleton 54911-5872; (920)
380-0061; Fax: (920) 380-0051: *District Director:*
Craig Moser
700 E. Walnut St., Green Bay 54301-4052; (920)
437-1954; Fax: (920) 437-1978; *Deputy District
Director:* Bambi Yingst
Committee Assignment(s): Agriculture; Transportation
and Infrastructure

Kanjorski, Paul E., D-Pa. (11)

Capitol Hill Office: 2188 RHOB 20515-3811; 225-6511;
Fax: 225-0764; *Chief of Staff:* Karen M. Feather
Web: kanjorski.house.gov
E-mail: paul.kanjorski@mail.house.gov
District Office(s): 102 Pocono Blvd., Mount Pocono
18344-1412; (570) 895-4176 *District Director:*
Fred Ney
546 Spruce St., Scranton 18503-1808; (570) 496-1011;
Office Manager: Cathy Wechsler
The Stegmaier Bldg., 7 N. Wilkes-Barre Blvd., #400M,
Wilkes-Barre 18702-5283; (570) 825-2200; Fax: (570)
825-8685; *District Projects Director:* Thomas P.
Williams
Committee Assignment(s): Financial Services; Oversight
and Government Reform

Kaptur, Marcy, D-Ohio (9)

Capitol Hill Office: 2186 RHOB 20515-3509; 225-4146;
Fax: 225-7711; Deputy *Chief of Staff:* Nathan Facey
Web: kaptur.house.gov
District Office(s): 1 Maritime Plaza, 6th Floor, Toledo
43604-1853; (419) 259-7500; Fax: (419) 255-9623;
Chief of Staff: Steve Katich
Committee Assignment(s): Appropriations; Budget;
Congressional-Executive Commission on China

Kennedy, Patrick J., D-R.I. (1)

Capitol Hill Office: 407 CHOB 20515-3901; 225-4911;
Fax: 225-3290; *Chief of Staff:* Adam Brand
Web: patrickkennedy.house.gov
E-mail: Patrick.Kennedy@mail.house.gov
District Office(s): 249 Roosevelt Ave., #200, Pawtucket
02860-2134; (401) 729-5600; Fax: (401) 729-5608;
Rhode Island Chief of Staff: George Zainyeh
Committee Assignment(s): Appropriations; Oversight
and Government Reform

Kildee, Dale E., D-Mich. (5)

Capitol Hill Office: 2107 RHOB 20515-2205; 225-3611;
Fax: 225-6393; *Chief of Staff:* Callie Coffman
Web: www.house.gov/kildee
District Office(s): 916 Washington Ave., #205, Bay City
48708-5721; (989) 891-0990; Fax: (989) 891-0994;
Deputy District Director: Barbara Donnelly
432 N. Saginaw St., #410, Flint 48502-2018; (810) 239-1437;
Fax: (810) 239-1439; *District Director:* Tiffany Flynn
515 N. Washington Ave., #401, Saginaw 48607-1378;
(989) 755-8904; Fax: (989) 755-8908; *Deputy District
Director:* James Lewis
Committee Assignment(s): Education and Labor;
Natural Resources

Kilpatrick, Carolyn Cheeks, D-Mich. (13)

Capitol Hill Office: 2264 RHOB 20515-2213; 225-2261;
Fax: 225-5730; *Chief of Staff:* Kimberly Rudolph
Web: www.house.gov/Kilpatrick
District Office(s): 1274 Library St., #1B, Detroit
48226-2208; (313) 965-9004; Fax: (313) 965-9006;
District Director: Duron Marshall
3005 Biddle St., Suite A, Wyandotte 48192-5901; (734)
246-0780; Fax: (734) 246-1148; *District Director:*
John Harris
Committee Assignment(s): Appropriations

Kilroy, Mary Jo, D-Ohio (15)

Capitol Hill Office: 1237 LHOB 20515-3515; 225-2015;
Fax: 225-3529; *Chief of Staff:* Randy Borntrager
Web: kilroy.house.gov
District Office(s): 1299 Olentangy River Road, Suite 200,
Columbus 43212-3135; (614) 294-2196; Fax: (614)
294-2384; *District Director:* Samantha Hurd
Committee Assignment(s): Financial Services; Homeland
Security

Kind, Ron, D-Wisc. (3)

Capitol Hill Office: 1406 LHOB 20515-4903; 225-5506; Fax: 225-5739; *Chief of Staff:* Cynthia Brown
Web: www.house.gov/kind
District Office(s): 131 S. Barstow St., #301, Eau Claire 54701-2625; (715) 831-9214; Fax: (715) 831-9272; *Congressional Aide:* Mark Aumann
205 5th Ave. South, #400, La Crosse 54601-4059; (608) 782-2558; Fax: (608) 782-4588; *Chief of Staff:* Loren J. Kannenberg
Committee Assignment(s): Natural Resources; Ways and Means

King, Peter T., R-N.Y. (3)

Capitol Hill Office: 339 CHOB 20515-3203; 225-7896; Fax: 226-2279; *Chief of Staff:* Kevin C. Fogarty
Web: peteking.house.gov
E-mail: Pete.King@mail.house.gov
District Office(s): 1003 Park Blvd., #7, Massapequa Park 11762-2758; (516) 541-4225; Fax: (516) 541-6602; *District Director:* Anne Rosenfeld
Committee Assignment(s): Financial Services; Homeland Security

King, Steve, R-Iowa (5)

Capitol Hill Office: 1131 LHOB 20515-1505; 225-4426; Fax: 225-3193; *Chief of Staff:* S. Brenna Findley
Web: www.house.gov/steveking
District Office(s): 40 Pearl St., Council Bluffs 51503-0817; (712) 325-1404; Fax: (712) 325-1405; *District Representative:* Tim Moran
208 W. Taylor St., P.O. Box 601, Creston 50801-3766; (641) 782-2495; Fax: (641) 782-2497; *District Representative:* Laura Hartman
526 Nebraska St., Sioux City 51101-1313; (712) 224-4692; Fax: (712) 224-4693; *District Representative:* Sandy Hanlon
306 N. Grand Ave., P.O. Box 650, Spencer 51301-4141; (712) 580-7754; Fax: (712) 580-3354; *Policy Advisor:* Bill Anderson
800 Oneida St., Suite A, Storm Lake 50588-3209; (712) 732-4197; Fax: (712) 732-4217; *District Director:* Dave Ehler
Committee Assignment(s): Agriculture; Judiciary; Small Business

Kingston, Jack, R-Ga. (1)

Capitol Hill Office: 2368 RHOB 20515-1001; 225-5831; Fax: 226-2269; *Chief of Staff:* Jerr Rosenbaum
Web: kingston.house.gov
E-mail: Jack.Kingston@mail.house.gov
District Office(s): P.O. Box 40, Baxley 31515; (912) 367-7403; Fax: (912) 367-7404; *District Director:* Shiela Elliott
Federal Bldg., 805 Gloucester St., #304, Brunswick 31520-7073; (912) 265-9010; Fax: (912) 265-9013; *Caseworker:* Charles Wilson

1 Diamond Causeway, #7, Savannah 31406-7434; (912) 352-0101; Fax: (912) 352-0105; *Casework Manager:* Trish DePriest
Valdosta Federal Bldg., 401 N. Ashley St., #215, Valdosta 31601-4619; (229) 247-9188; Fax: (229) 247-9189; *Caseworker:* Christian Johnson
Committee Assignment(s): Appropriations

Kirk, Mark Steven, R-Ill. (10)

Capitol Hill Office: 1030 LHOB 20515-1310; 225-4835; Fax: 225-0837; *Chief of Staff:* Lester E. Munson III
Web: www.house.gov/kirk
District Office(s): 707 Skokie Blvd., #350, Northbrook 60062-2892; (847) 940-0202; Fax: (847) 940-7143; *District Chief of Staff:* Eric Elk
Committee Assignment(s): Appropriations

Kirkpatrick, Ann, D-Ariz. (1)

Capitol Hill Office: 1123 LHOB 20515-0301; 225-2315; Fax: 225-9739; *Chief of Staff:* Michael Frias
Web: kirkpatrick.house.gov
District Office(s): 240 S. Montezuma Street, Suite 101, Prescott 86303-4712; (928) 445-3434; Fax: (928) 445-4160, *District Director:* Virginia Turner
Committee Assignment(s): Homeland Security; Small Business; Veterans' Affairs

Kissell, Larry, D-N.C. (8)

Capitol Hill Office: 512 CHOB 20515-3308; 225-3715; Fax: 225-4036; *Chief of Staff:* Leanne Powell
Web: kissell.house.gov
District Office(s): 325 McGill Avenue, Suite 500, Concord 28027-6194; (704) 786-1612; Fax: (704) 782-1004; *Communications Director:* Brianna Atkins
6287 Raeford Road, Suite Two, Fayetteville 28304-2450; (910) 920-2070; Fax: (910) 920-2069; *Caseworker:* John Freudenberg
230 E. Franklin Street, Rockingham 28379; (910) 997-2070; Fax: (910) 997-7987; *District Director:* Thomas Thacker
Committee Assignment(s): Agriculture; Armed Services

Klein, Ron, D-Fla. (22)

Capitol Hill Office: 313 CHOB 20515-0922; 225-3026; Fax: 225-8398; *Chief of Staff:* Garrett Donovan
Web: klein.house.gov
District Office(s): 1900 Glades Road, Suite 260, Boca Raton 33431-7333; (561) 544-6910; Fax: (561) 544-2864; *District Director:* Felicia Goldstein
Committee Assignment(s): Financial Services; Foreign Affairs

Kline, John, R-Minn. (2)

Capitol Hill Office: 1210 LHOB 20515-2302; 225-2271; Fax: 225-2595; *Chief of Staff:* Jean Hinz
Web: kline.house.gov

District Office(s): 101 W. Burnsville Pkwy., #201, Burnsville 55337-2572; (952) 808-1213; Fax: (952) 808-1261; *District Director*: Mike Osskopp

Committee Assignment(s): Armed Services; Education and Labor; Standards of Official Conduct; Permanent Select Intelligence

Kosmas, Suzanne M., D-Fl. (24)

Capitol Hill Office: 238 CHOB 20515-0924; 225-2706; Fax: 226-6299; *Chief of Staff*: Leslie Pollner-Levy

Web: kosmas.house.gov

District Office(s): 12424 Research Parkway, Suite 135, Orlando 32826-3273; (407) 208-1106; Fax: (407) 208-1108; *District Director*: Valerie Guenther

1000 City Center Circle, Second Floor, Port Orange 32129-4144; (386) 756-9798; Fax: (386) 756-9903; *Constituent Services Rep.*: Terri Finger

Committee Assignment(s): Financial Services; Science and Technology

Kratovil Jr., Frank M., D-Md. (1)

Capitol Hill Office: 314 CHOB 20515-2001; 225-5311; Fax: 225-0253; *Chief of Staff*: Tim McCann

Web: kratovil.house.gov

District Office(s): 112 W. Pennsylvania Avenue, Suite 102, Bel Air 21014-3663; (410) 838-2517; Fax: (410) 838-7823; *Community Liason*: Justin Hayes

102 Turpins Lane, Centreville 21617-1029; (443) 262-9136; Fax: (443) 262-9713; *District Director*: Tyler Patton

One Plaza East, 103 E. Main Street, Suite 103, Salisbury 21801; *Community Liason*: Tamara Lee-Brooks

Kucinich, Dennis J., D-Ohio (10)

Capitol Hill Office: 2445 RHOB 20515-3510; 225-5871; Fax: 225-5745; *Chief of Staff*: Jaron Bourke

Web: kucinich.house.gov

District Office(s): 14400 Detroit Ave., Lakewood 44107-4408; (216) 228-8850; Fax: (216) 228-6465; *District Director:* Joseph Benny

Parmatown Mall, 7904 Day Dr., Parma 44129-5637; (440) 845-2707; Fax: (440) 845-2743; *Caseworker*: Christine Miles

Committee Assignment(s): Education and Labor; Oversight and Government Reform

Lamborn, Doug, R-Colo. (5)

Capitol Hill Office: 437 CHOB 20515-0605; 225-4422; Fax: 226-2638; *Chief of Staff*: Robert McCreary

Web: lamborn.house.gov

District Office(s): 415 Main St., Buena Vista 81211; (719) 520-0055; Fax: (719) 520-0840

3730 Sinton Rd., #150, Colorado Springs 80907-5086; (719) 520-0055; Fax: (719) 520-0840; *Deputy District Director*: Dan Norberg

Committee Assignment(s): Armed Services; Natural Resources; Veterans' Affairs

Lance, Leonard, R-N.J., (7)

Capitol Hill Office: 114 CHOB 20515-3007; 225-5361; Fax: 225-9460; *Chief of Staff:* Todd Mitchell

Web: lance.house.gov

District Office(s): 23 Royal Road, Suite 101, Flemington 08822-6001; (908) 788-6900; Fax: (908) 788-2869;

425 North Avenue East, Westfield 07090-1443; (908) 518-7733; Fax: (908) 518-7751

Committee Assignment(s): Financial Services

Langevin, James R., D-R.I. (2)

Capitol Hill Office: 109 CHOB 20515-3902; 225-2735; Fax: 225-5976; *Chief of Staff*: Kristin E. Nicholson

Web: www.house.gov/langevin

District Office(s): 300 Centerville Rd., #200 S., Warwick 02886-0200; (401) 732-9400; Fax: (401) 737-2982; *District Director*: C. Kenneth Wild Jr.

Committee Assignment(s): Armed Services; Budget; Permanent Select Intelligence

Larsen, Rick, D-Wash. (2)

Capitol Hill Office: 108 CHOB 20515-4702; 225-2605; Fax: 225-4420; *Chief of Staff:* Kimberly Johnston

Web: www.house.gov/Larsen

District Office(s): 104 W. Magnolia St., #206, Bellingham 98225-4345; (360) 733-4500; Fax: (360) 733-5144; *Constituent Services Representative*: Cherie Little

2930 Wetmore Ave., #9F, Everett 98201-4070; (425) 252-3188; Fax: (425) 252-6606; *District Director:* Jill McKinnie

Committee Assignment(s): Armed Services; Budget; Transportation and Infrastructure

Larson, John B., D-Conn. (1)

Capitol Hill Office: 106 CHOB 20515-0701; 225-2265; Fax: 225-1031; *Chief of Staff:* Amy O'Donnell

Web: www.house.gov/larson

District Office(s): 221 Main St., 2nd Floor, Hartford 06106-1890; (860) 278-8888; Fax: (860) 278-2111; *District Chief of Staff:* John Rossi

Committee Assignment(s): Ways and Means; Select Energy Independence and Global Warming

Latham, Tom, R-Iowa (4)

Capitol Hill Office: 2217 RHOB 20515-1504; 225-5476; Fax: 225-3301; *Chief of Staff:* James D. Carstensen

Web: www.tomlatham.house.gov

E-mail: tom.latham@mail.house.gov

District Office(s): 1421 South Bell Ave., #108A, Ames 50010-7710; (515) 232-2885; Fax: (515) 232-2844; *District Director:* Clarke Scanlon

812 Hwy. 18 East, Clear Lake 50428-1487; (641) 357-5225; Fax: (641) 357-5226; *Regional Representative*: Lois Clark

1426 Central Ave., Suite A, Fort Dodge 50501-4258; (515) 573-2738; Fax: (515) 576-7141; *Regional Representative*: Jim Oberhelman

Committee Assignment(s): Appropriations

LaTourette, Steven C., R-Ohio (14)

Capitol Hill Office: 2371 RHOB 20515-3514; 225-5731; Fax: 225-3307; *Chief of Staff:* John Guzzo
Web: www.house.gov/latourette
District Office(s): 1 Victoria Pl., #320, Painesville 44077; (440) 352-3939; Fax: (440) 352-3622; *Deputy Chief of Staff:* Dino DiSanto
P.O. Box 1132, Twinsburg 44087; (330) 425-9291; Fax: (330) 425-7071; *District Outreach:* Nick Ciofani
Committee Assignment(s): Appropriations

Latta Robert E., R-Ohio (5)

Capitol Hill Office: 1531 LHOB 20515-3505; 225-6405; Fax: 225-1985; *Chief of Staff:* Ryan Walker
Web: latta.house.gov

District Office(s): 1045 N. Main St., #6, Bowling Green 43402-1361; (419) 354-8700; Fax: (419) 354-8702; *Deputy District Director:* Everett Woodel
101 Clinton St., Suite 1200, Defiance 43512-2165; (419) 782-1996; Fax: (419) 784-9808; *District Director:* Barbara Barker
One East Main Street, Norwalk 44857-1558; (419) 668-0206; Fax: (419) 663-1361; *Senior District Representative:* Chris Molyet
Committee Assignment(s): Agriculture; Transportation and Infrastructure

Lee, Barbara, D-Calif. (9)

Capitol Hill Office: 2444 RHOB 20515-0509; 225-2661; Fax: 225-9817; *Chief of Staff:* Julie Nickson
Web: lee.house.gov
District Office(s): 1301 Clay St., #1000N, Oakland 94612-5233; (510) 763-0370; Fax: (510) 763-6538; *District Director:* Anne Taylor
Committee Assignment(s): Appropriations; Foreign Affairs

Lee, Christopher, R-N.Y. (26)

Capitol Hill Office: 1711 LHOB 20515-3226; 225-5265; Fax: 225-5910; *Chief of Staff:* Brian Schubert
Web: chrislee.house.gov
District Office(s): 1577 Ridge Road W., Greece 14615-2520; (585) 663-5570; Fax: (585) 663-5711; *Regional Manager:* Paul Cole
325 Essjay Road, Williamsville 14221-8243; (716) 634-2324; Fax: (716) 631-7610; *District Director:* Nick Langworthy
Committee Assignment(s): Financial Services

Levin, Sander M., D-Mich. (12)

Capitol Hill Office: 1236 LHOB 20515-2212; 225-4961; Fax: 226-1033; *Chief of Staff:* Hilarie Chambers
Web: www.house.gov/Levin
District Office(s): 27085 Gratiot Ave., Roseville 48066-2947; (586) 498-7122; Fax: (586) 498-7123; *District Director:* Judy Hartwell

Committee Assignment(s): Ways and Means; Congressional-Executive Commission on China; Joint Taxation

Lewis, Jerry, R-Calif. (41)

Capitol Hill Office: 2112 RHOB 20515-0541; 225-5861; Fax: 225-6498; *Chief of Staff:* Arlene Willis
Web: www.house.gov/jerrylewis
District Office(s): 1150 Brookside Ave., Suite J5, Redlands 92373-6314; (909) 862-6030; Fax: (909) 335-9155; *District Director:* Tara Clarke
Committee Assignment(s): Appropriations

Lewis, John, D-Ga. (5)

Capitol Hill Office: 343 CHOB 20515-1005; 225-3801; Fax: 225-0351; *Chief of Staff:* Michael D. Collins
Web: www.house.gov/johnlewis
District Office(s): Equitable Bldg., 100 Peachtree St. N.W., #1920, Atlanta 30303-1906; (404) 659-0116; Fax: (404) 331-0947; *District Director:* Tharon Johnson
Committee Assignment(s): Ways and Means

Linder, John, R-Ga. (7)

Capitol Hill Office: 1026 LHOB 20515-1007; 225-4272; Fax: 225-4696; *Chief of Staff:* Rob Woodall
Web: linder.house.gov
District Office(s): Lawrenceville District Office; (770) 232-3005; Fax: (770) 232-2909; *Deputy Chief of Staff:* Derick Corbett
Committee Assignment(s): Ways and Means

Lipinski, Daniel, D-Ill. (3)

Capitol Hill Office: 1717 LHOB 20515-1303; 225-5701; Fax: 225-1012; *Chief of Staff:* Jason Tai
Web: www.lipinski.house.gov
District Office(s): 6245 S. Archer Ave., Chicago 60638-2609; (312) 886-0481; Fax: (773) 767-9395; *District Director:* Vacancy
19 W. Hillgrove Ave., LaGrange 60525-2015; (708) 352-0524; Fax: (708) 352-0927
5309 W. 95th St., Oak Lawn 60453-2444; (708) 424-0853; Fax: (708) 424-1855
Committee Assignment(s): Science and Technology; Small Business; Transportation and Infrastructure

LoBiondo, Frank A., R-N.J. (2)

Capitol Hill Office: 2427 RHOB 20515-3002; 225-6572; Fax: 225-3318; *Chief of Staff:* Mary Annie Harper
Web: www.house.gov/lobiondo
District Office(s): 5914 Main St., Mays Landing 08330-1751; (609) 625-5008; Fax: (609) 625-5071; *Director of Constituent Services:* Joan Dermanoski
Committee Assignment(s): Armed Services; Transportation and Infrastructure

Loebsack, Dave, D-Iowa (2)

Capitol Hill Office: 1221 LHOB 20515-1502; 225-6576; Fax: 226-0757; *Chief of Staff:* Eric Witte
Web: loebsack.house.gov
District Office(s): 150 1st Ave. N.E., #375, Cedar Rapids 52401-1133; (319) 364-2288; Fax: (319) 364-2994; *District Director:* Robert Sueppel
125 S. Dubuque St., Iowa City 52240-4000; (319) 351-0789; Fax: (319) 351-5789; *District Representative:* David Leshtz
Committee Assignment(s): Armed Services; Education and Labor

Lofgren, Zoe, D-Calif. (16)

Capitol Hill Office: 102 CHOB 20515-0516; 225-3072; Fax: 225-3336; *Chief of Staff:* Stacey Leavandosky
Web: www.house.gov/Lofgren
District Office(s): 635 N. 1st St., Suite B, San Jose 95112-5110; (408) 271-8700; Fax: (408) 271-8713; *District Chief of Staff:* Sandra Soto
Committee Assignment(s): Homeland Security; House Administration; Judiciary; Standards of Official Conduct; Joint Library of Congress

Lowey, Nita M., D-N.Y. (18)

Capitol Hill Office: 2329 RHOB 20515-3218; 225-6506; Fax: 225-0546; *Chief of Staff:* Elizabeth Stanley
Web: www.house.gov/lowey
District Office(s): 222 Mamaroneck Ave., #310, White Plains 10605; (914) 428-1707; Fax: (914) 328-1505; *District Director:* Patricia Keegan
Committee Assignment(s): Appropriations

Lucas, Frank D., R-Okla. (3)

Capitol Hill Office: 2311 RHOB 20515-3603; 225-5565; Fax: 225-8698; *Communications Director:* Leslie Shedd
Web: www.house.gov/lucas
District Office(s): 720 S. Husband St., #7, Stillwater 74074-4665; (405) 624-6407; Fax: (405) 624-6467; *Field Rep:* Tyler Laughlin
2728 Williams Ave., Suite F, Woodward 73801; (580) 256-5752; Fax: (580) 254-3047; *Field Representative:* Troy White
10952 Northwest Expressway, Suite B, Yukon 73099-8214; (405) 373-1958; Fax: (405) 373-2046; *Chief of Staff:* Stacey Glasscock
Committee Assignment(s): Agriculture; Financial Services; Science and Technology

Luetkemeyer, Blaine, R-Mo. (9)

Capitol Hill Office: 1118 LHOB 20515-2509; 225-2956; Fax: 225-5712; *Chief of Staff:* Tonnie Wybensinger
Web: luetkemeyer.house.gov
District Office(s): 3610 Buttonwood Drive, Suite 200, Columbia 65201-3721; (573) 886-8629; Fax: (573) 886-8901

201 N. Third Street, Suite 120, Hannibal 63401-3550; (573) 231-1012; Fax: (573) 231-1014
516 Jefferson Street, Washington 63090-2706; (636) 239-2276; Fax: (636) 239-0478
Committee Assignment(s): Agriculture; Small Business

Luján, Ben R., D-N.M. (3)

Capitol Hill Office: 502 CHOB 20515-3103; 225-6190; Fax: 226-1331; *Chief of Staff:* Angela K. Ramirez
Web: lujan.house.gov
District Office(s): 811 St. Michael's Drive, Suite 104, Sante Fe 87505-7640; (505) 984-8950; Fax: (505) 986-5047
Committee Assignment(s): Homeland Security; Science and Technology

Lummis, Cynthia M., R-Wyo. (At Large)

Capitol Hill Office: 1004 LHOB 20515-5001; 225-2311; Fax: 225-3057; *Legislative Director:* Rick Axthelm
District Office(s): 100 East B Street, Room 4003, Casper 82602-1969; (307) 261-6596; Fax: (307) 261-6597; *Field Rep:* Jackie King
2120 Capitol Avenue, Suite 2015, Cheyenne 82001-3631; (307) 772-2595; Fax: (307) 772-2597; *Chief of Staff:* Tucker Fagan
404 N Street, Suite 204, Rock Springs 82901-5474; (307) 362-4095; Fax: (307) 362-4097; *Field Rep:* Pat Aullman
Committee Assignment(s): Agriculture; Budget; Natural Resources

Lungren, Dan, R-Calif. (3)

Capitol Hill Office: 2262 RHOB 20515-0503; 225-5716; Fax: 226-1298; *Chief of Staff:* Victor Arnold-Bik
Web: www.house.gov/lungren
District Office(s): 2339 Gold Meadow Way, #220, Gold River 95670-6307; (916) 859-9906; Fax: (916) 859-9976; *District Director:* Marilyn Erbes
Committee Assignment(s): Homeland Security; House Administration; Judiciary; Joint Printing; Joint Library of Congress

Lynch, Stephen F., D-Mass. (9)

Capitol Hill Office: 221 CHOB 20515-2109; 225-8273; Fax: 225-3984; *Chief of Staff:* Robert Kevin Ryan
Web: www.house.gov/lynch
E-mail: Stephen.Lynch@mail.house.gov
District Office(s): 88 Black Falcon Ave., #340, Boston 02210-2433; (617) 428-2000; Fax: (617) 428-2011; *Senior District Representative:* Dan Lynch
Plymouth County Registry of Deeds, 155 W. Elm St., #220, Brockton 02301-4326; (508) 586-5555; Fax: (508) 580-4692; *District Representative:* Shaynah Barnes
Committee Assignment(s): Financial Services; Oversight and Government Reform

Mack, Connie, R-Fla. (14)

Capitol Hill Office: 115 CHOB 20515-0914; 225-2536; Fax: 226-0439; *Chief of Staff:* Jeff Cohen
Web: mack.house.gov
District Office(s): 804 Nicholas Pkwy. East, #1, Cape Coral 33990; (239) 332-4677; Fax: (239) 332-8921; *Constituent Services Manager:* Tricia Molzow
Collier County Courthouse, 3301 E. Tamiami Trail, 1st Floor, Naples 34112-3969; (239) 774-8035; Fax: (239) 774-8065; *District Director:* Kara Wright
Committee Assignment(s): Budget; Foreign Affairs; Transportation and Infrastructure

Maffei, Dan, D-N.Y. (25)

Capitol Hill Office: 1630 LHOB 20515-3225; 225-3701; Fax: 225-4042; *Chief of Staff:* Daniel Krupnick
Web: maffei.house.gov
District Office(s): 1280 Titus Avenue, Rochester 14617-4125; (585) 336-7291; Fax: (585) 336-7274
1340 James H. Hanley Federal Building, 100 S. Clinton Street, P.O. Box 7306, Syracuse 13261-6100; (315) 423-5657; Fax: (315) 423-5669; *Communications Director/District Director:* Michael Whyland
Committee Assignment(s): Financial Services; Judiciary

Maloney, Carolyn B., D-N.Y. (14)

Capitol Hill Office: 2332 RHOB 20515-3214; 225-7944; Fax: 225-4709; *Chief of Staff:* Benjamin Chevat
Web: maloney.house.gov
District Office(s): 28-11 Astoria Blvd., Astoria 11102; (718) 932-1804; Fax: (718) 932-1805; *District Representative:* Mary Marangos
1651 3rd Ave., #311, New York 10128-3679; (212) 860-0606; Fax: (212) 860-0704; *New York Chief of Staff:* Minna R. Elias
Committee Assignment(s): Financial Services; Oversight and Government Reform; Joint Economic

Manzullo, Donald A., R-Ill. (16)

Capitol Hill Office: 2228 RHOB 20515-1316; 225-5676; Fax: 225-5284; *Chief of Staff:* Adam Magary
Web: manzullo.house.gov
District Office(s): 101 N. Virginia Street, Suite 170, Crystal Lake 60014-3456; (815) 356-9800; Fax: (815) 356-9803; *McHenry and Boone Counties Representative:* Kathleen Davis
415 S. Mulford Rd., Rockford 61108-3011; (815) 394-1231; Fax: (815) 394-3930; *District Director:* Pamela J. Sexton
Committee Assignment(s): Financial Services; Foreign Affairs; Congressional-Executive Commission on China

Marchant, Kenny, R-Tex. (24)

Capitol Hill Office: 227 CHOB 20515-4324; 225-6605; Fax: 225-0074; *Chief of Staff:* Brian Thomas
Web: marchant.house.gov

District Office(s): 9901 E. Valley Ranch Pkwy., #3035, Irving 75063-7186; (972) 556-0162; Fax: (972) 409-9704; *District Director:* Susie Miller
Committee Assignment(s): Financial Services

Markey, Betsy, D-Colo. (4)

Capitol Hill Office: 1229 LHOB 20515-0604; 225-4676; Fax: 225-5870; *Chief of Staff:* Anne Caprara
Web: betsymarkey.house.gov
District Office(s): 123 N. College Avenue, Suite 220, Fort Collins 80524-2489; (970) 221-7110; Fax: (970) 221-7240; *District Director:* Ken Bennett
822 Seventh Street, Suite Nine, Greeley 80631-3930; (970) 351-6007; Fax: (970) 351-6068; *District Rep:* Lori Ozzello
301 S. Fifth Street, Lamar 81052-2711; *District Rep:* Cheryl Webb
109 1/2 S. Third Street, Sterling 80751-4220
Committee Assignment(s): Agriculture; Transportation and Infastructure

Markey, Edward J., D-Mass. (7)

Capitol Hill Office: 2108 RHOB 20515-2107; 225-2836; *Chief of Staff:* Jeff Duncan
Web: markey.house.gov
District Office(s): 188 Concord St., #102, Framingham 01702-8315; (508) 875-2900; *Congressional Aide:* Patrick Lally
Five High St., #101, Medford 02155-3800; (781) 396-2900; *District Director:* Mark Gallagher
Committee Assignment(s): Energy and Commerce; Natural Resources; Select Energy Independence and Global Warming

Marshall, Jim, D-Ga. (8)

Capitol Hill Office: 504 CHOB 20515-1008; 225-6531; Fax: 225-3013; *Chief of Staff:* John Kirincich
Web: jimmarshall.house.gov
District Office(s): 503 Bellevue Ave., Suite C, Dublin 31021-5331; (478) 296-2023
682 Cherry St., #300, Macon 31201-7388; (478) 464-0255; Fax: (478) 464-0277; *District Director:* Hobby Stripling
City Hall, 130 First Street East, Tifton 31794-4831; (229) 556-7418
Committee Assignment(s): Agriculture; Armed Services

Massa, Eric J.J., D-N.Y. (29)

Capitol Hill Office: 1208 LHOB 20515-3229; 225-3161; Fax: 226-6599; *Chief of Staff:* Joe Racalto
Web: massa.house.gov
District Office(s): 87 W. Market Street, Corning 14830-2526; (607) 654-7566; Fax: (607) 654-7568; *Office Manager:* Jennifer Ruland
One Grove Street, Suite 101, Pittsford 14534-1328; (585) 218-0400; Fax: (585) 215-0053; *District Director:* Dave Marion
Committee Assignment(s): Agriculture; Armed Services; Homeland Security

Matheson, Jim, D-Utah (2)

Capitol Hill Office: 2434 RHOB 20515-4402; 225-3011; Fax: 225-5638; *Chief of Staff:* Stacey Alexander
Web: www.house.gov/matheson
District Office(s): 120 E. Main St., Price 84501-3050; (435) 636-3722; Fax: (435) 613-1834; *Field Representative:* Pamela Juliano
240 E. Morris Ave., #235, Salt Lake City 84115-3296; (801) 486-1236; Fax: (801) 486-1417; *State Director:* Mike Reberg
321 N. Mall Dr., #E101-B, St. George 84790-7305; (435) 627-0880; Fax: (435) 627-1473; *Field Representative:* Mike Empey
Committee Assignment(s): Energy and Commerce; Science and Technology

Matsui, Doris, D-Calif. (5)

Capitol Hill Office: 222 CHOB 20515-0505; 225-7163; Fax: 225-0566; *Chief of Staff:* Julie Eddy
Web: matsui.house.gov
District Office(s): 12-600 Robert T. Matsui U.S. Courthouse, 501 I St., Sacramento 95814-4778; (916) 498-5600; Fax: (916) 444-6117; *District Director:* Nathan T. Dietrich
Committee Assignment(s): Energy and Commerce; Ruless

McCarthy, Carolyn, D-N.Y. (4)

Capitol Hill Office: 2346 RHOB 20515-3204; 225-5516; Fax: 225-5758; *Chief of Staff:* Michael Spira
Web: carolynmccarthy.house.gov
District Office(s): 200 Garden City Plaza, #320, Garden City 11530-3338; (516) 739-3008; Fax: (516) 739-2973; *District Director:* Chris Chaffee
Committee Assignment(s): Education and Labor; Financial Services

McCarthy, Kevin, R-Calif. (22)

Capitol Hill Office: 1523 LHOB 20515-0522; 225-2915; Fax: 225-2908; *Chief of Staff:* James Min
Web: kevinmccarthy.house.gov
District Office(s): 5805 Capistrano Ave., Suite C, Atascadero 93422-7218; (805) 461-1034 or (805) 549-0390; Fax: (805) 461-1323; *Field Representative:* Michael Whiteford
4100 Empire Dr., #150, Bakersfield 93309-0409; (661) 327-3611; Fax: (661) 637-0867; *District Administrator:* Robin Lake Foster
Committee Assignment(s): Financial Services; House Administration; Joint Printing

McCaul, Michael, R-Tex. (10)

Capitol Hill Office: 131 CHOB 20515-4310; 225-2401; Fax: 225-5955; *Chief of Staff:* Greg Hill
Web: www.house.gov/mccaul
District Office(s):, 5929 Balcones Dr., #305, Austin 78731-4286; (512) 473-2357; Fax: (512) 473-0514; *Caseworker:* Thomas Brown

2000 S. Market St., #303, Brenham 77833-5800; (979) 830-8497; Fax: (979) 830-1984; *Caseworker:* Marita Mikeska
1550 Foxlake Dr., #120, Houston 77084-4739; (281) 398-1247; Fax: (281) 579-3401; *Caseworker:* Courtney Dennie
Rosewood Professional Bldg., 990 Village Square Dr., Suite B, Tomball 77375-4269; (281) 255-8372; Fax: (281) 255-0034; *Caseworker:* Sherrie Meicher
Committee Assignment(s): Foreign Affairs; Homeland Security; Science and Technology

McClintock, Tom, R-Calif. (4)

Capitol Hill Office: 508 CHOB 20515-0504; 225-2511; Fax: 225-5444; *Chief of Staff:* Igor Birman
Web: mcclintock.house.gov
District Office(s): 4230 Douglas Boulevard, Suite 200, Granite Bay 95746-5914; (916) 786-5560; Fax: (916) 786-6364; *District Director:* Dan Brennan
Committee Assignment(s): Education and Labor; Natural Resources

McCollum, Betty, D-Minn. (4)

Capitol Hill Office: 1714 LHOB 20515-2304; 225-6631; Fax: 225-1968; *Chief of Staff:* Bill Harper
Web: www.mccollum.house.gov
District Office(s): 165 Western Ave. N., #17, St. Paul 55102-4613; (651) 224-9191; Fax: (651) 224-3056; *District Director:* Joshua Straka
Committee Assignment(s): Appropriations; Budget

McCotter, Thaddeus, R-Mich. (11)

Capitol Hill Office: 1632 LHOB 20515-2211; 225-8171; Fax: 225-2667; *Chief of Staff:* Andrew Anuzis
Web: mccotter.house.gov/HoR/MI11/Home.htm
District Office(s): 17197 N. Laurel Park Dr., #533, Livonia 48152-7919; (734) 632-0314; Fax: (734) 632-0373; *Caseworker:* David Heintz
Committee Assignment(s): Financial Services

McDermott, Jim, D-Wash. (7)

Capitol Hill Office: 1035 LHOB 20515-4707; 225-3106; Fax: 225-6197; *Chief of Staff:* Mike DeCesare
Web: www.house.gov/mcdermott
District Office(s): 1809 7th Ave., #1212, Seattle 98101-1399; (206) 553-7170; Fax: (206) 553-7175; *District Director:* James Allen
Committee Assignment(s): Ways and Means

McGovern, James P., D-Mass. (3)

Capitol Hill Office: 438 CHOB 20515-2103; 225-6101; Fax: 225-5759; *Chief of Staff:* Christopher R. Philbin
Web: mcgovern.house.gov
District Office(s): 8 North Main St., #200, Attleboro 02703-2282; (508) 431-8025; Fax: (508) 431-8017; *District Representative:* Lisa Nelson

371 S. Main St., Suite 102, Fall River 02721-5348; (508) 677-0140; Fax: (508) 677-0992; *District Representative*: Maria DeCoste

255 Main St., #104, Marlborough 01752-5505; (508) 460-9292; Fax: (508) 460-6869; *District Representative*: Mary Pat Gibbons

34 Mechanic St., Worcester 01608-2424; (508) 831-7356; Fax: (508) 754-0982; *District Director*: Joe O'Brien

Committee Assignment(s): Budget; Rules

McHenry, Patrick, R-N.C. (10)

Capitol Hill Office: 224 CHOB 20515-3310; 225-2576; Fax: 225-0316; *Chief of Staff:* Parker Poling

Web: mchenry.house.gov

District Office(s): 87 4th St. N.W., Suite A, Hickory 28601-6142; (828) 327-6100; Fax: (828) 327-0316; *Constituent Services Director*: David McCrary

311 E. Marion St., #119, Shelby 28150-4611; (704) 481-0578; Fax: (704) 481-0757; *Regional Field Director*: Brett Keeter

Spruce Pine Town Hall, P.O. Box 715, Spruce Pine 28777; (828) 765-2701; Fax: (828) 765-2729; *Community Outreach Coordinator*: Laurie Moody

Committee Assignment(s): Budget; Financial Services; Oversight and Government Reform

McHugh, John M., R-N.Y. (23)

Capitol Hill Office: 2366 RHOB 20515-3223; 225-4611; Fax: 226-0621; *Chief of Staff:* Robert G. Taub

Web: mchugh.house.gov

District Office(s): 205 S. Peterboro St., Canastota 13032-1312; (315) 697-2063; Fax: (315) 697-2064; *Constituent Services Representative*: Karen Brayton

28 School St., P.O. Box 800, Mayfield 12117; (518) 661-6486; Fax: (518) 661-5704; *Constituent Services Representative*: Diane Henderson

14 Durkee Street, Suite 320, Plattsburgh 12901-2911; (518) 563-1406; Fax: (518) 561-9723; *Senior Caseworker:* Ruth Mary Ortloff

120 Washington St., #200, Watertown 13601; (315) 782-3150; Fax: (315) 782-1291; *Constituent Services Representative*: Kate Wehrle

Committee Assignment(s): Armed Services; Oversight and Government Reform

McIntyre, Mike, D-N.C. (7)

Capitol Hill Office: 2437 RHOB 20515-3307; 225-2731; Fax: 225-5773; *Chief of Staff:* Dean M. Mitchell

Web: www.house.gov/mcintyre

District Office(s): 310 Government Center Drive, N.E., Building S, Unit One, Bolivia 28422-9010; (910) 253-0158; Fax: (910) 253-0159; *Constituent Services Rep*: Mary Ellen Simmons

Federal Bldg., 301 Green St., #218, Fayetteville 28301-5048; (910) 323-0260; Fax: (910) 323-0069; *Field Representative*: Billy Barker

500 N. Cedar St., Lumberton 28358-5545; (910) 671-6223; Fax: (910) 735-0610; *Constituent Services Assistant*: Crystal Cummings

First Union Bank Bldg., 201 N. Front St., #410, Wilmington 28401; (910) 815-4959; Fax: (910) 815-4543; *Constituent Services Assistant*: Pam Campbell-Dereef

Committee Assignment(s): Commission on Security and Cooperation in Europe; Agriculture, Armed Services

McKeon, Howard P. Buck, R-Calif. (25)

Capitol Hill Office: 2184 RHOB 20515-0525; 225-1956; Fax: 226-0683; *Chief of Staff:* Robert A. Cochran

Web: mckeon.house.gov

District Office(s): 1008 W. Ave. M-14, Suite E-1, Palmdale 93551-1441; (661) 274-9688; *District Director*: Lew Stults

26650 The Old Rd., #203, Valencia 91381-0750; (661) 254-2111; Fax: (661) 254-2380; *Deputy Chief of Staff:* Bob Hauter

Committee Assignment(s): Armed Services; Education and Labor

McMahon, Michael, D-N.Y. (13)

Capitol Hill Office: 323 CHOB 20515-3213; 225-3371; Fax: 226-1272; *Chief of Staff:* Christopher S. McCannell

Web: mcmahon.house.gov

District Office(s): 8504 Fourth Avenue, Brooklyn 11209-4608; (718) 630-5277; Fax: (718) 630-5388; *District Director*: Patrick Hyland

4434 Amboy Road, Second Floor, Staten Island 10312-3866; (718) 356-8400; Fax: (718) 356-1928

Committee Assignment(s): Foreign Affairs; Transportation and Infastructure

McMorris Rodgers, Cathy, R-Wash. (5)

Capitol Hill Office: 1323 LHOB 20515-4705; 225-2006; Fax: 225-3392; *Chief of Staff:* Connie Partoyan

Web: mcmorris.house.gov

District Office(s): 555 S. Main St., Colville 99114-2503; (509) 684-3481; Fax: (509) 684-3482; *Regional Representative:* Karen Dodson

10 N. Post St., #625, Spokane 99201-0706; (509) 353-2374; Fax: (509) 353-2412; *Deputy Chief of Staff:* David A. Condon

29 S. Palouse St., Walla Walla 99362-1925; (509) 529-9358; Fax: (509) 529-9379; *Regional Representative*: Debra Casey

Committee Assignment(s): Armed Services; Education and Labor; Natural Resources

McNerney, Jerry, D-Calif. (11)

Capitol Hill Office: 312 CHOB 20515-0511; 225-1947; Fax: 225-4060; *Chief of Staff:* Nick Holder

Web: mcnerney.house.gov

District Office(s): 5776 Stoneridge Mall Rd., #175, Pleasanton 94588-2836; (925) 737-0727; Fax: (925) 737-0734; *District Director:* Nicole Alioto

2222 Grand Canal Blvd., #7, Stockton 95207-6671; (209) 476-8552; Fax: (209) 476-8587; *District Scheduler*: Alisa Alva

Committee Assignment(s): Energy and Commerce; Veterans' Affairs

Meek, Kendrick B., D-Fla. (17)

Capitol Hill Office: 1039 LHOB 20515-0917; 225-4506; Fax: 226-0777; *Chief of Staff:* Clarence Williams
Web: kendrickmeek.house.gov
District Office(s): 111 N.W. 183rd St., #315, Miami 33169-4538; (305) 690-5905; Fax: (305) 690-5951; *District Office Director*: Joyce M. Postell
10100 Pines Blvd., 3rd Floor, Bldg. B, Pembroke Pines 33026; (954) 450-6767; Fax: (954) 450-6768
Committee Assignment(s): Ways and Means

Meeks, Gregory W., D-N.Y. (6)

Capitol Hill Office: 2342 RHOB 20515-3206; 225-3461; Fax: 226-4169; *Washington Chief of Staff:* Sophia King
Web: www.house.gov/meeks
District Office(s): 1931 Mott Ave., #305, Far Rockaway 11691-4103; (718) 327-9791; Fax: (718) 327-4722; *Community Liaison:* Joan McCroud
153-01 Jamaica Ave., Jamaica 11432-3870; (718) 725-6000; Fax: (718) 725-9868; *District Office Administrator:* Marilyn Barnes
Committee Assignment(s): Financial Services; Foreign Affairs

Melancon, Charlie, D-La. (3)

Capitol Hill Office: 404 CHOB 20515-1803; 225-4031; Fax: 226-3944; *Chief of Staff:* Joseph Bonfiglio
Web: melancon.house.gov
District Office(s): 8201 W. Judge Perez Dr., Chalmette 70043-1611; (504) 297-5313; Fax: (504) 297-5325; *District Representative*: Amanda Beyeht
Ascension Parish Courthouse, 828 S. Irma Blvd., Gonzales 70737-3631; (225) 621-8490; Fax: (225) 621-8493; *District Representative*: Renee Pollet
423 Lafayette St., #107, Houma 70360-4802; (985) 876-3033; Fax: (985) 872-4449; *District Representative*: Jeri Theriot
124 E. Main St., #220-A, New Iberia 70560-3725; (337) 367-8231; Fax: (337) 369-7084; *District Representative*: Genee Champagne
Committee Assignment(s): Budget; Energy and Commerce

Mica, John L., R-Fla. (7)

Capitol Hill Office: 2313 RHOB 20515-0907; 225-4035; Fax: 226-0821; *Chief of Staff:* Russell L. Roberts
Web: www.house.gov/mica
District Office(s): 840 Deltona Blvd., Suite G, Deltona 32725-7162; (386) 860-1499; Fax: (386) 860-5730; *Caseworker*: Beth Ann Bryant

100 E. Sybelia Ave., #340, Maitland 32751-4700; (407) 657-8080; Fax: (407) 657-5353; *Caseworker*: Jean Carrero
770 W. Grenada Blvd., #315, Ormond Beach 32174-5180; (386) 676-7750; Fax: (386) 676-7748; *Caseworker*: Sue Bower
613 St. Johns Ave., #107, Palatka 32177-4643; (386) 328-1622
1 Florida Park Dr. S., #100, Palm Coast 32137-3801; (386) 246-6042
3000 N. Ponce de Leon Blvd., #1, St. Augustine 32084-8600; (904) 810-5048; Fax: (904) 810-5091; *Caseworker*: Elizabeth Buckles
Committee Assignment(s): Oversight and Government Reform; Transportation and Infrastructure

Michaud, Michael, D-Maine (2)

Capitol Hill Office: 1724 LHOB 20515-1902; 225-6306; Fax: 225-2943; *Deputy Chief of Staff*: Kim Glas
Web: michaud.house.gov
District Office(s): Key Plaza, 23 Water St., Bangor 04401-6364; (207) 942-6935; Fax: (207) 942-5907; *Deputy Chief of Staff*: John P. Graham Jr.
179 Lisbon St., Lewiston 04240-7248; (207) 782-3704; Fax: (207) 782-5330; *District Representative*: Andrea Quaid
445 Main St., Presque Isle 04769-2651; (207) 764-1036; Fax: (207) 764-1060; *District Representative*: Barbara Hayslett
16 Common St., Waterville 04901-6611; (207) 873-5713; Fax: (207) 873-5717; *Constituent Services Representative*: Tim Trafford
Committee Assignment(s): Small Business; Transportation and Infrastructure; Veterans' Affairs

Miller, Brad, D-N.C. (13)

Capitol Hill Office: 1127 LHOB 20515-3313; 225-3032; Fax: 225-0181; *Chief of Staff:* Ryan Hedgepeth
Web: www.house.gov/bradmiller
District Office(s): 125 South Elm St., #504, Greensboro 27401-2246; (336) 574-2909; Fax: (336) 574-2189; *District Liaison:* Ron Williams
1300 St. Marys St., #504, Raleigh 27605-1276; (919) 836-1313; Fax: (919) 836-1314; *District Liaison*: Gail Eluwa
Committee Assignment(s): Financial Services; Foreign Affairs; Science and Technology

Miller, Candice, R-Mich. (10)

Capitol Hill Office: 228 CHOB 20515-2210; 225-2106; Fax: 226-1169; *Chief of Staff:* Jamie Roe
Web: candicemiller.house.gov
District Office(s): 48701 Van Dyke Ave., Shelby Township 48317-2562; (586) 997-5010; Fax: (586) 997-5013; *District Director*: Karen Czernel
Committee Assignment(s): Homeland Security; Transportation and Infrastructure; Select Energy Independence and Global Warming

Miller, Gary, R-Calif. (42)

Capitol Hill Office: 2349 RHOB 20515-0542; 225-3201; Fax: 226-6962; *Chief of Staff:* John Rothrock
Web: www.house.gov/garymiller
E-mail: gary.miller@mail.house.gov
District Office(s): 1800 E. Lambert Rd., #150, Brea 92821-4396; (714) 257-1142; Fax: (714) 257-9242; *District Director:* Steven Thornton
200 Civic Center Dr., Mission Viejo 92691-5519; (949) 470-8484
Committee Assignment(s): Financial Services; Transportation and Infrastructure

Miller, George, D-Calif. (7)

Capitol Hill Office: 2205 RHOB 20515-0507; 225-2095; *Chief of Staff:* Daniel Weiss
Web: www.house.gov/georgemiller
E-mail: George.Miller@mail.house.gov
District Office(s): 1333 Willow Pass Rd., #203, Concord 94520-7931; (925) 602-1880; Fax, (925) 674-0983; *District Director:* Barbara Johnson
3220 Blume Dr., #281, Richmond 94806-5741; (510) 262-6500; Fax, (510) 222-1306; *Field Representative:* Latressa Alford
375 G St., #1, Vallejo 94590-5706; (707) 645-1888; Fax: (707) 645-1870; *Field Representative:* Kathy Hoffman
Committee Assignment(s): Education and Labor; Natural Resources

Miller, Jeff, R-Fla. (1)

Capitol Hill Office: 2439 RHOB 20515-0901; 225-4136; Fax: 225-3414; *Chief of Staff:* Daniel F. McFaul
Web: jeffmiller.house.gov
District Office(s): 348 Miracle Strip Pkwy. S.W., #24, Fort Walton Beach 32548-5263; (850) 664-1266; Fax: (850) 664-0851; *Field Representative:* Helen Hunt Rigdon
4300 Bayou Blvd., #13, Pensacola 32503-2671; (850) 479-1183; Fax: (850) 479-9394; *Field Representative:* Sharon Santurri
Committee Assignment(s): Armed Services; Veterans' Affairs; Permanent Select Intelligence

Minnick, Walt, D-Idaho (1)

Capitol Hill Office: 1517 LHOB 20515-1201; 225-6611; Fax: 225-3029; *Chief of Staff:* Kate Haas
Web: minnick.house.gov
District Office(s): 33 Broadway Avenue, Suite 251, Meridian 83642; (208) 888-3188; Fax: (208) 888-0894; *Acting District Director/Communications Director/Senior Advisor:* John M. Foster
Committee Assignment(s): Agriculture; Financial Services

Mitchell, Harry, D-Ariz. (5)

Capitol Hill Office: 1410 LHOB 20515-0305; 225-2190; Fax: 225-3263; *Chief of Staff:* Alexis C. Tameron

Web: mitchell.house.gov
District Office(s): 7201 E. Camelback Rd., #335, Scottsdale 85251-3318; (480) 946-2411; Fax: (480) 946-2446; *District Director:* Robbie Sherwood
Committee Assignment(s): Science and Technology; Transportation and Infrastructure; Veterans' Affairs

Mollohan, Alan B., D-W.Va. (1)

Capitol Hill Office: 2302 RHOB 20515-4801; 225-4172; Fax: 225-7564; *Chief of Staff:* Mary Colleen McCarty
Web: www.house.gov/mollohan
District Office(s): Post Office Bldg., #209, Clarksburg 26302-1400; (304) 623-4422; Fax: (304) 623-0571; *Caseworker:* Linda Woolridge
Federal Bldg., #232, Morgantown 26505-0720; (304) 292-3019; Fax: (304) 292-3027; *Area Representative:* Cate Johnson
Federal Bldg., 425 Juliana St., #2040, Parkersburg 26101-5352; (304) 428-0493; Fax: (304) 428-5980; *Caseworker:* Betsy Moore
Federal Bldg., 1125 Chapline St., #316, Wheeling 26003-2976; (304) 232-5390; Fax: (304) 232-5722; *Area Representative:* Cathy Abraham
Committee Assignment(s): Appropriations

Moore, Dennis, D-Kans. (3)

Capitol Hill Office: 1727 LHOB 20515-1603; 225-2865; Fax: 225-2807; *Chief of Staff:* Howard P. Bauleke
Web: moore.house.gov
District Office(s): 500 State Ave., #176, Kansas City 66101-2409; (913) 621-0832; Fax: (913) 621-1533; *Constituent Services Aide:* Alicia Deville
901 Kentucky St., #205, Lawrence 66044-2853; (785) 842-9313; Fax: (785) 843-3289
8417 Santa Fe Dr., #101, Overland Park 66212-2727; (913) 383-2013; Fax: (913) 383-2088; *Constituent Services Aide:* Cheyne Worley
Committee Assignment(s): Financial Services; Small Business

Moore, Gwen, D-Wisc. (4)

Capitol Hill Office: 1239 LHOB 20515-4904; 225-4572; Fax: 225-8135; *Chief of Staff:* Winfield Boerckel
Web: www.house.gov/gwenmoore
District Office(s): 219 N. Milwaukee St., #3A, Milwaukee 53202-5818; (414) 297-1140; Fax: (414) 297-1086; *Senior Adviser:* Shirley Ellis
Committee Assignment(s): Budget; Financial Services

Moran, Jerry, R-Kans. (1)

Capitol Hill Office: 2202 RHOB 20515-1601; 225-2715; Fax: 225-5124; *Chief of Staff:* Todd Novascone
Web: www.jerrymoran.house.gov
District Office(s): 1200 Main St., #402, P.O. Box 249, Hays 67601; (785) 628-6401; Fax: (785) 628-3791; *District Representative:* Mitchell Hall

1 N. Main, #525, P.O. Box 1128, Hutchinson 67504-1128; (620) 665-6138; Fax: (620) 665-6360; *District Representative*: Lisa Dethloff

119 W. Iron Ave., #603, Salina 67401-2600; (785) 309-0572; Fax: (785) 827-6957; *District Representative*: Steve Howe

Committee Assignment(s): Agriculture; Transportation and Infrastructure; Veterans' Affairs

Moran, Jim, D-Va. (8)

Capitol Hill Office: 2239 RHOB 20515-4608; 225-4376; Fax: 225-0017; *Chief of Staff:* Frank Shafroth

Web: moran.house.gov

District Office(s): 333 N. Fairfax St., #201, Alexandria 22314-2632; (703) 971-4700; Fax: (703) 922-9436; *District Director*: Susie Warner

Committee Assignment(s): Appropriations

Murphy, Christopher, D-Conn. (5)

Capitol Hill Office: 214 CHOB 20515-0705; 225-4476; Fax: 225-5933; *Chief of Staff:* Joshua Raymond

Web: chrismurphy.house.gov

District Office(s): 198 Main St., Danbury 06810-6662; (203) 798-2072

22-26 W. Main St., Meriden 06451-4109; (203) 630-0815; Fax: (203) 630-1903

1 Grove St., New Britain 06053-4144; (860) 223-8412; Fax: (860) 827-9009; *District Director:* Rob Michalik

49 Leavenworth St., Waterbury 06702-2115; (203) 759-7541

Committee Assignment(s): Energy and Commerce; Oversight and Government Reform

Murphy, Patrick, D-Pa. (8)

Capitol Hill Office: 1609 LHOB 20515-3808; 225-4276; Fax: 225-9511; *Chief of Staff:* Scott Fairchild

Web: patrickmurphy.house.gov

District Office(s): 414 Mill St., Bristol 19007-4813; (215) 826-1963; Fax: (215) 826-1997; *District Director*: Nat Binns

72 N. Main St., Doylestown 18901-3730; (215) 348-1194; Fax: (215) 348-1449; *Outreach Director*: Larry Glick

Committee Assignment(s): Armed Services; Permanent Select Intelligence

Murphy, Scott, D-N.Y. (20)

Capitol Hill Office: 120 CHOB 20515-3220; 225-5614; Fax: 225-1168; *Chief of Staff:* Todd Schulte

Web: scottmurphy.house.gov

District Office(s): 487 Broadway, Saratoga Springs 12866-2227; (518) 581-8247; Fax: (518) 581-8430

Murphy, Tim, R-Pa. (18)

Capitol Hill Office: 322 CHOB 20515-3818; 225-2301; Fax: 225-1844; *Chief of Staff:* Susan Mosychuk

Web: murphy.house.gov

District Office(s): 2040 Frederickson Pl., Greensburg 15601-9688; (724) 850-7312; Fax: (724) 850-7315; *Deputy Chief of Staff:* Lou Lazzaro

504 Washington Rd., Mt. Lebanon 15228-2817; (412) 344-5583; Fax: (412) 429-5092; *Caseworker:* Chris McLane

Committee Assignment(s): Energy and Commerce

Murtha, John P., D-Pa. (12)

Capitol Hill Office: 2423 RHOB 20515-3812; 225-2065; Fax: 225-5709; *Chief of Staff:* John A. Hugya

Web: www.house.gov/murtha

District Office(s): 647 Main St., #401, Johnstown 15901-2140; (814) 535-2642; Fax: (814) 539-6229; *District Director*: Mark Critz

Committee Assignment(s): Appropriations

Myrick, Sue, R-N.C. (9)

Capitol Hill Office: 230 CHOB 20515-3309; 225-1976; Fax: 225-3389; *Executive Assistant*: Hollie Arnold

Web: myrick.house.gov

District Office(s): 6525 Morrison Blvd., #402, Charlotte 28211-0501; (704) 362-1060; Fax: (704) 367-0852; *Chief of Staff:* Hal C. Weatherman

197 W. Main Ave., Gastonia 28052-4154; (704) 861-1976; Fax: (704) 864-2445; *Caseworker*: Linda Ferster

Committee Assignment(s): Energy and Commerce; Permanent Select Intelligence

Nadler, Jerrold, D-N.Y. (8)

Capitol Hill Office: 2334 RHOB 20515-3208; 225-5635; Fax: 225-6923; *Washington Director:* John Doty

Web: www.house.gov/nadler

District Office(s): 445 Neptune Ave., Brooklyn 11224-4561; (718) 373-3198; Fax: (718) 996-0039; *Constituent Services Representative*: Marilyn Daitsman

201 Varick St., #669, New York 10014-7069; (212) 367-7350; Fax: (212) 367-7356; *Constituent Services Representative*: Nnennaya Okezie

Committee Assignment(s): Judiciary; Transportation and Infrastructure

Napolitano, Grace F., D-Calif. (38)

Capitol Hill Office: 1610 LHOB 20515-0538; 225-5256; Fax: 225-0027; *Chief of Staff:* Daniel S. Chao

Web: napolitano.house.gov

District Office(s): 11627 E. Telegraph Rd., #100, Santa Fe Springs 90670-6810; (562) 801-2134; Fax: (562) 949-9144; *District Director*: Benjamin Cardenas

Committee Assignment(s): Natural Resources; Transportation and Infrastructure

Neal, Richard E., D-Mass. (2)

Capitol Hill Office: 2208 RHOB 20515-2102; 225-5601; Fax: 225-8112; *Chief of Staff:* Ann M. Jablon

Web: www.house.gov/neal

District Office(s): Post Office Bldg., 4 Congress St., Milford 01757; (508) 634-8198; Fax: (508) 634-8398; *Office Manager*: Virginia Purcell

Federal Bldg. and U.S. Courthouse, 1550 Main St., Springfield 01103; (413) 785-0325; Fax: (413) 747-0604; *District Director*: James B. Leydon

Committee Assignment(s): Ways and Means

Neugebauer, Randy, R-Tex. (19)

Capitol Hill Office: 1424 LHOB 20515-4319; 225-4005; Fax: 225-9615; *Chief of Staff:* Jeanette Whitener
Web: randy.house.gov
District Office(s): 500 Chestnut St., #819, Abilene 79602-1453; (325) 675-9779; Fax: (325) 675-5038; *Office Manager:* Sylvia Leal
1510 Scurry St., Suite B, Big Spring 79720-4441; (432) 264-7592; Fax: (432) 264-1838; *District Representative:* Lisa Brooks
611 University Ave., #220, Lubbock 79401-2206; (806) 763-1611; Fax: (806) 767-9168; *Office Manager:* Mary Whistler
Committee Assignment(s): Agriculture; Financial Services; Science and Technology

Norton, Eleanor Holmes, D-D.C. (Non-Voting Delegate)

Capitol Hill Office: 2136 RHOB 20515-5101; 225-8050; Fax: 225-3002; *Chief of Staff:* Sheila Bunn
Web: www.norton.house.gov
District Office(s): 2401 Martin Luther King Jr. Avenue, S.E., Suite 238, Washington 20020-7005; (202) 678-8900; Fax: (202) 678-8844
National Press Building, 529 14th Street , N.W., Suite 900, Washington 20045-1928; (202) 783-5065; Fax: (202) 783-5211; *District Director:* Aaron Ward
Committee Assignment(s): Homeland Security; Oversight and Government Reform; Transportation and Infrastructure

Nunes, Devin, R-Calif. (21)

Capitol Hill Office: 1013 LHOB 20515-0521; 225-2523; Fax: 225-3404; *Chief of Staff:* Johnny Amaral
Web: nunes.house.gov
District Office(s): 264 Clovis Ave., #206, Clovis 93612-1115; (559) 323-5235; Fax: (559) 323-5528; *Field Representative:* Anthony Ratekin
113 N. Church St., #208, Visalia 93291-6300; (559) 733-3861; Fax: (559) 733-3865; *District Director:* Tal Eslick
Committee Assignment(s): Budget; Ways and Means

Nye, Glenn C., D-Va. (2)

Capitol Hill Office: 116 CHOB 20515-4602; 225-4215; Fax: 225-4218; *Chief of Staff:* Angela Kouters
Web: nye.house.gov
District Office(s): 23386 Front Street, Accomac 23301; (757) 789-5092; Fax: (757) 789-5095; *Constituent Services Rep.:* Sylvia Parks
4772 Euclid Road, Suite E, Virginia Beach 23462-3800; (757) 326-6201; Fax: (757) 326-6209; *District Director:* Erika Walker-Cash
Committee Assignment(s): Armed Services; Small Business; Veterans' Affairs

Oberstar, James L., D-Minn. (8)

Capitol Hill Office: 2365 RHOB 20515-2308; 225-6211; Fax: 225-0699; *Administrative Assistant:* Bill Richard
Web: oberstar.house.gov
District Office(s): City Hall, 501 Laurel St., Brainerd 56401-3525; (218) 828-4400; Fax: (218) 828-1412; *Staff Assistant:* Ken Hasskamp
City Hall, 316 Lake St., Chisholm 55719-1718; (218) 254-5761; Fax: (218) 254-5132; *Staff Assistant:* Peter Makowski
Federal Bldg., 515 W. 1st St., #231, Duluth 55802-1302; (218) 727-7474; Fax: (218) 727-8270; *Staff Assistant:* David Boe
38265 14th Ave., #300B, North Branch 55056; (651) 277-1234; Fax: (651) 277-1235; *Director of Field Operations:* Alana Petersen
Committee Assignment(s): Transportation and Infrastructure

Obey, David R., D-Wisc. (7)

Capitol Hill Office: 2314 RHOB 20515-4907; 225-3365; *Chief of Staff:* Christina Hamilton
Web: obey.house.gov
District Office(s): 1401 Tower Ave., #307, Superior 54880-1553; (715) 398-4426; Fax: (715) 398-7121; *District Aide:* Matthew Rudig
401 5th St., #406-A, Wausau 54403-5473; (715) 842-5606; Fax: (715) 842-4488; *District Director:* Douglas J. Hill
Committee Assignment(s): Appropriations

Olson, Pete, R-Tex. (22)

Capitol Hill Office: 514 CHOB 20515-4322; 225-5951; Fax: 225-5241; *Chief of Staff:* John Wyatt
Web: olson.house.gov
District Office(s): 17225 El Camino Real, Suite 447, Houston 77058-2778; *Deputy District Director:* Tyler Nelson
1650 Highway Six, Suite 150, Sugar Land, 77478-4921; (281) 494-2690; Fax: (281) 494-2649; *District Director:* Jack Molho
Committee Assignment(s): Homeland Security; Science and Technology; Transportation and Infastructure

Olver, John W., D-Mass. (1)

Capitol Hill Office: 1111 LHOB 20515-2101; 225-5335; Fax: 226-1224; *Chief of Staff:* R. Hunter Ridgway
Web: www.house.gov/olver
District Office(s): 463 Main St., Fitchburg 01420-8045; (978) 342-8722; Fax: (978) 343-8156; *Caseworker:* Peggy Kane
57 Suffolk St., #310, Holyoke 01040-5055; (413) 532-7010; Fax: (413) 532-6543; *Caseworker:* Natalie Blais
Silvio O. Conte Federal Bldg., 78 Center St., Pittsfield 01201-6172; (413) 442-0946; Fax: (413) 443-2792; *Caseworker:* Cindy Clark
Committee Assignment(s): Appropriations

Ortiz, Solomon P., D-Tex. (27)

Capitol Hill Office: 2110 RHOB 20515-4327; 225-7742; Fax: 226-1134; *Chief of Staff:* Denise Blanchard
Web: ortiz.house.gov
District Office(s): Pasco Plaza Center, 1085 Ruben M. Torres Blvd., #B-27, Brownsville 78526-1539; (956) 541-1242; Fax: (956) 544-6915; *Office Manager:* Maria Jaross
3649 Leopard St., #510, Corpus Christi 78408-3251; (361) 883-5868; Fax: (361) 884-9201; *Caseworker:* Esther Oliver
Committee Assignment(s): Armed Services; Transportation and Infastructure

Pallone, Frank, Jr., D-N.J. (6)

Capitol Hill Office: 237 CHOB 20515-3006; 225-4671; Fax: 225-9665; *Chief of Staff:* Jeffrey C. Carroll
Web: www.house.gov/pallone
District Office(s): 504 Broadway, Long Branch 07740-5951; (732) 571-1140; Fax: (732) 870-3890; *District Field Representative:* Dawn Rebscher
Kilmer Sq., 67-69 Church St., New Brunswick 08901; (732) 249-8892; Fax: (732) 249-1335; *District Representative:* Scott Snyder
Committee Assignment(s): Energy and Commerce; Natural Resources

Pascrell, William J., Jr., D-N.J. (8)

Capitol Hill Office: 2464 RHOB 20515-3008; 225-5751; Fax: 225-5782; *Chief of Staff:* Ben Rich
Web: pascrell.house.gov
District Office(s): Bloomfield Town Hall, Bloomfield Municipal Bldg., 1 Municipal Plaza, #200-A, Bloomfield 07003-3470; (973) 680-1361; Fax: (973) 680-1617; *Field Representative:* Ann C. Mega
Passaic City Hall, 330 Passaic St., 1st Floor, Passaic 07055-5815; (973) 472-4510; *Field Representative:* Colia Anderson
Robert A. Roe Federal Bldg., 200 Federal Plaza, #500, Paterson 07505-1999; (973) 523-5152; Fax: (973) 523-0637; *Field Representative:* Celia Andersen
Committee Assignment(s): Homeland Security; Ways and Means

Pastor, Ed, D-Ariz. (4)

Capitol Hill Office: 2465 RHOB 20515-0304; 225-4065; Fax: 225-1655; *Executive Assistant:* Laura Campos
Web: www.house.gov/pastor
District Office(s): 411 N. Central Ave., #150, Phoenix 85004-2120; (602) 256-0551; Fax: (602) 257-9103; *District Director:* Elisa de la Vara
Committee Assignment(s): Appropriations

Paul, Ron, R-Tex. (14)

Capitol Hill Office: 203 CHOB 20515-4314; 225-2831; *Chief of Staff:* Tom Lizardo
Web: www.house.gov/paul

District Office(s): 601 25th St., #216, Galveston 77550-1738; (409) 766-7013; Fax: (409) 765-7036; *Field Rep.:* Twila Lindblade
122 West Way St., #301, Lake Jackson 77566-5245; (979) 285-0231; Fax: (979) 285-0271; *Casework Specialist:* Jon Watts
1501 E. Mockingbird Lane, #229, Victoria 77904-2194; (361) 576-1231; Fax: (361) 576-0381; *District Casework Director:* Jackie Gloor
Committee Assignment(s): Financial Services; Foreign Affairs; Joint Economic

Paulsen, Erik, R-Minn. (3)

Capitol Hill Office: 126 CHOB 20515-2303; 225-2871; Fax: 225-6351; *Admin. Assistant:* Dean P. Peterson
Web: paulsen.house.gov
District Office(s): 250 Prairie Center Drive, Suite 230, Eden Prairie 55344-7909; (952) 405-8510; Fax: (952) 405-8514; *Chief of Staff:* Laurie Esau
Committee Assignment(s): Financial Services

Payne, Donald M., D-N.J. (10)

Capitol Hill Office: 2310 RHOB 20515-3010; 225-3436; Fax: 225-4160; *Legislative Director:* Kerry B. McKenney
Web: www.house.gov/payne
District Office(s): 333 N. Broad St., Elizabeth 07208-3706; (908) 629-0222; Fax: (908) 629-0221; *Director of Casework Operations for Union County:* Maria Ramos
253 Martin Luther King Jr. Dr., Jersey City 07305-3427; (201) 369-0392; Fax: (201) 362-0395; *Director of Casework Operations:* Yvonne Hatchett
Martin Luther King Jr. Federal Bldg. and U.S. Courthouse, 50 Walnut St., #1016, Newark 07102-3596; (973) 645-3213; Fax: (973) 645-5902; *District **Chief of Staff:*** Adrienne Sneed-Byers
Committee Assignment(s): Education and Labor; Foreign Affairs

Pelosi, Nancy, D-Calif. (8)

Capitol Hill Office: 235 CHOB 20515-0508; 225-4965; Fax: 225-8259; *Chief of Staff:* Terri McCullough
Web: www.house.gov/pelosi
E-mail: sf.nancy@mail.house.gov
District Office(s): Phillip Burton Federal Bldg., 450 Golden Gate Ave., #145378, San Francisco 94102-3460; (415) 556-4862; Fax: (415) 861-1670; *District Director:* Dan Bernal

Pence, Mike, R-Ind. (6)

Capitol Hill Office: 1431 LHOB 20515-1406; 225-3021; Fax: 225-3382; *Chief of Staff:* William A. Smith
Web: mikepence.house.gov
District Office(s): Paramount Center, 1134 Meridian St., Anderson 46016-1713; (765) 640-2919; Fax: (765) 640-2922; *District Director:* Lani Czarniecki

107 W. Charles Street, Muncie 47305-2420; (765) 747-5566; Fax: (765) 747-5586; *Deputy District Director*: Kim Bennett

50 N. 5th St., Richmond 47374-4247; (765) 962-2883; Fax: (765) 962-3225; *Constituent Services Representative*: Debbie Berry

Committee Assignment(s): Commission on Security and Cooperation in Europe; Foreign Affairs

Perlmutter, Ed, D-Colo. (7)

Capitol Hill Office: 415 CHOB 20515-0607; 225-2645; Fax: 225-5278; *Chief of Operations*: Alison Inderfurth
Web: perlmutter.house.gov
District Office(s): 12600 W. Colfax Ave., Suite B400, Lakewood 80215-3779; (303) 274-7944; Fax: (303) 274-6455; *Chief of Staff:* Danielle Radovich Piper
Committee Assignment(s): Financial Services; Rules

Perriello, Tom, D-Va. (5)

Capitol Hill Office: 1520 LHOB 20515-4605; 225-4711; Fax: 225-5681; *Chief of Staff:* Lise Clavel
Web: perriello.house.gov
District Office(s): 104 S. First Street, Charlottesville 22902-5007; (434) 293-9631; Fax: (434) 293-9632; *District Director*: Ridge Schuyler
308 Craighead Street, Suite 102; Danville 24541-1468; (434) 791-2596; Fax: (434) 791-2598; *Caseworker*: Ebony Guy
Committee Assignment(s): Transportation and Infrastructure; Veterans' Affairs

Peters, Gary, D-Mich. (9)

Capitol Hill Office: 1130 LHOB 20515-2209; 225-5802; Fax: 226-2356; *Chief of Staff:* Eric Feldman
Web: peters.house.gov
District Office(s): Woodcrest Office Park, 560 Kirts Boulevard, Suite 105, Troy 48084-4141; (248) 273-4227; Fax: (248) 273-4704; *District Director*: Diana McBroom
Committee Assignment(s): Financial Services; Science and Technology

Peterson, Collin C., D-Minn. (7)

Capitol Hill Office: 2211 RHOB 20515-2307; 225-2165; Fax: 225-1593; *Chief of Staff:* Mark Brownell
Web: collinpeterson.house.gov
District Office(s): 714 Lake Ave., #107, Detroit Lakes 56501-3057; (218) 847-5056; Fax: (218) 847-5109; *Staff Assistant*: Jodi Dey
1420 E. College Dr., SW / WC, Marshall 56258-2065; (507) 537-2299; Fax: (507) 537-2298; *Staff Assistant*: Meg Louwagie
Minnesota Wheat Growers Bldg., 2603 Wheat Dr., Red Lake Falls 56750-4800; (218) 253-4356; Fax: (218) 253-4373; *Staff Assistant*: Wally Sparby
230 E. 3rd St., P.O. Box 50, Redwood Falls 56283; (507) 637-2270; *Staff Assistant*: Meg Louwagie

Center Point Mall, 320 4th St. S.W., Willmar 56201-3300; (320) 235-1061; Fax: (320) 235-2651; *Staff Assistant*: Mary Bertram
Committee Assignment(s): Agriculture

Petri, Thomas E., R-Wisc. (6)

Capitol Hill Office: 2462 RHOB 20515-4906; 225-2476; Fax: 225-2356; *Chief of Staff* : Debra Gebhardt
Web: www.house.gov/petri
District Office(s): 490 W. Rolling Meadows Dr., Suite B, Fond du Lac 54937; (920) 922-1180; Fax: (920) 922-4498; *District Director*: Dave Anderson
2390 State Rd. 44, Suite B, Oshkosh 54904-6438; (920) 231-6333; Fax: (920) 231-0464; *Staff Assistant*: Melissa Kok
Committee Assignment(s): Education and Labor; Transportation and Infrastructure

Pierluisi, Pedro, D-P.R.
(At Large, Non-Voting Delegate)

Capitol Hill Office: 1218 LHOB 20515-5401; 225-2615; Fax: 225-2154; *Chief of Staff:* Carmen M. Feliciano
Web: pierluisi.house.gov
District Office(s): 250 Calle Fortaleza, San Juan 00901-1713; (787) 723-6333; Fax: (787) 729-7738; *District Director*: Rosemarie (Maí) Vizcarrondo
Committee Assignment(s): Education and Labor; Judiciary; Natural Resources

Pingree, Chellie, D-Maine (1)

Capitol Hill Office: 1037 LHOB 20515-1901; 225-6116; Fax: 225-5590; *Chief of Staff:* Lisa Prosienski
Web: pingree.house.gov
District Office(s): 57 Exchange Street, Suite 302, Portland 04101-5000; (207) 774-5019; Fax: (207) 871-0720; *Constituent Services Manager*: Ann Goodridge
Committee Assignment(s): Armed Services; Rules

Pitts, Joseph R., R-Pa. (16)

Capitol Hill Office: 420 CHOB 20515-3816; 225-2411; Fax: 225-2013; *Chief of Staff:* Gabe Neville
Web: www.house.gov/pitts
District Office(s): Lancaster County Courthouse, 50 N. Duke St., Lancaster 17602-2805; (717) 393-0667; Fax: (717) 393-0924; *Constituent Services Director*: Joanne Horn
Berks County Services Bldg., 633 Court St., 14th Floor, Reading 19601; (610) 374-3637; Fax: (610) 444-5750
P.O. Box 837, Unionville 19375; (610) 444-4581; Fax: (610) 444-5750; *Constituent Services Assistant*: Nicholas Cammauf
Committee Assignment(s): Commission on Security and Cooperation in Europe; Energy and Commerce; Congressional-Executive Commission on China

Platts, Todd Russell, R-Pa. (19)

Capitol Hill Office: 2455 RHOB 20515-3819; 225-5836;
Fax: 226-1000; *Chief of Staff:* Scott Miller
Web: www.house.gov/platts
District Office(s): 59 W. Louther St., Carlisle 17013-2936;
(717) 249-0190; Fax: (717) 218-0190; *Field
Representative:* Jay Buck Swisher
22 Chambersburg St., Gettysburg 17325-1101; (717)
338-1919; Fax: (717) 334-6314; *Field Representative:*
Holly Sutphin
2209 E. Market St., York 17402-2853; (717) 600-1919;
Fax: (717) 757-5001; *District Director:* Lisa Flanagan
Committee Assignment(s): Education and Labor;
Oversight and Government Reform; Transportation
and Infrastructure

Poe, Ted, R-Tex. (2)

Capitol Hill Office: 430 CHOB 20515-4302; 225-6565;
Fax: 225-5547; *Chief of Staff:* Janet Diaz-Brown
Web: poe.house.gov
District Office(s): Bank of America Bldg., 505 Orleans St.,
#100, Beaumont 77701-3224; (409) 212-1997; Fax:
(409) 212-8711; *Caseworker:* Blake Hopper
Trans American Title Bldg., 20202 U.S. Hwy. 59 North,
#105, Humble 77348-2402; (281) 446-0242; Fax:
(281) 446-0252; *District Director:* Kristin Barrs
Committee Assignment(s): Foreign Affairs; Judiciary

Polis, Jared, D-Colo. (2)

Capitol Hill Office: 501 CHOB 20515-0602; 225-2161;
Fax: 226-7840; *Chief of Staff:* Brien E. Branton
Web: polis.house.gov
District Office(s): 4770 Baseline Road, Suite 200, Boulder
80303-2668; (303) 484-9596; Fax: (303) 568-9007;
District Director: Andy Schultheiss
Committee Assignment(s): Education and Labor; Rules

Pomeroy, Earl, D-N.D. (At Large)

Capitol Hill Office: 1501 LHOB 20515-3401; 225-2611;
Fax: 226-0893; *Chief of Staff:* Bob Siggins
Web: www.pomeroy.house.gov
District Office(s): Federal Bldg., 220 E. Rosser Ave., #376,
Bismarck 58501-3869; (701) 224-0355; Fax: (701)
224-0431; *Field Representative:* Greg Buhr
3003 32nd Ave. S.W., #6, Fargo 58103-6163; (701) 235-9760;
Fax: (701) 235-9767; *Field Representative:* Bill Heigaard
Committee Assignment(s): Agriculture; Ways and Means

Posey, Bill, R-Fla. (15)

Capitol Hill Office: 132 CHOB 20515-0915; 225-3671;
Fax: 225-3516; *Chief of Staff:* (Mr.) Dana G. Gartzke
Web: posey.house.gov
District Office(s): 2725 Judge Fran Jamieson Way,
Building C, Melbourne 32940-6605; (321) 632-1776;
Fax: (321) 639-8595; *District Director:* Kathryn
Rudloff
Committee Assignment(s): Financial Services

Price, David E., D-N.C. (4)

Capitol Hill Office: 2162 RHOB 20515-3304;
225-1784; Fax: 225-2014; *Chief of Staff:*
Jean-Louise Beard
Web: price.house.gov
District Office(s): 88 Vilcom Circle, #140, Chapel Hill
27514-1665; (919) 967-7924; Fax: (919) 967-8324;
District Liaison: Dave Russell
North Carolina Mutual Bldg., 411 W. Chapel Hill St., 6th
Floor, Durham 27707; (919) 688-3004; Fax: (919)
688-0940; *District Liaison:* Tracy Lovett
5400 Trinity Rd., #205, Raleigh 27607-3815; (919)
859-5999; Fax: (919) 859-5998; *District Director:*
Rose Auman
Committee Assignment(s): Appropriations

Price, Tom, R-Ga. (6)

Capitol Hill Office: 424 CHOB 20515-1006; 225-4501;
Fax: 225-0802; *Chief of Staff:* Matt McGinley
Web: tom.house.gov
District Office(s): 3730 Roswell Rd., #50, Marietta
30062-8818; (770) 565-4990; Fax: (770) 565-7570;
District Director: Jeff Hamling
Committee Assignment(s): Education and Labor;
Financial Services

Putnam, Adam H., R-Fla. (12)

Capitol Hill Office: 442 CHOB 20515-0912; 225-1252;
Fax: 226-0585; *Chief of Staff:* Charles Cooper
Web: adamputnam.house.gov
District Office(s): 650 E. Davidson St., Bartow 33830-
4051; (863) 534-3530; Fax: (863) 534-3559; *Deputy
Chief of Staff:* Cheryl Fulford
Committee Assignment(s): Financial Services

Quigley, Mike, D-Ill. (5)

Capitol Hill Office: 1319 LHOB 20515-1305; 225-4061;
Fax: 225-5603; *Chief of Staff:* Kimberly Walz
Web: Quigley.house.gov
District Office(s): 3742 W. Irving Park Road, Chicago
60618-3116; (773) 267-5926; Fax: (773) 267-6583

Radanovich, George P., R-Calif. (19)

Capitol Hill Office: 2410 RHOB 20515-0519; 225-4540;
Fax: 225-3402; *Chief of Staff:* Ted Maness
Web: radanovich.house.gov
District Office(s): 1040 E. Herndon, #201, Fresno
93720-3158; (559) 449-2490; Fax: (559) 449-2499;
District Director: Darren Rose
3509 Coffee Rd., Suite D-3, Modesto 95355-1357; (209)
579-5458; Fax: (209) 579-5028; *Field Representative:*
Kurt Vander Weide
Committee Assignment(s): Energy and Commerce

Rahall, Nick J., II, D-W.Va. (3)

Capitol Hill Office: 2307 RHOB 20515-4803; 225-3452;
Fax: 225-9061; *Chief of Staff:* Kent Keyser

Web: www.rahall.house.gov

District Office(s): 301 Prince St., Beckley 25801-4515; (304) 252-5000; Fax: (304) 252-9803; *Community Relations:* Kim McMillion

Federal Bldg., 601 Federal St., #1005, Bluefield 24701-3033; (304) 325-6222; Fax: (304) 325-0552; *Community Relations:* Deborah Stevens

Sidney L. Christie Federal Bldg. and Post Office, 845 5th Ave., #152, Huntington 25701-2031; (304) 522-6425; Fax: (304) 529-5716; *Community Relations:* Teri Booth

220 Dingess St., Logan 25601-3626; (304) 752-4934; Fax: (304) 752-8797; *Community Relations:* Debrina Workman

Committee Assignment(s): Natural Resources; Transportation and Infrastructure

Ramstad, Jim, R-Minn. (3)

Capitol Hill Office: 103 CHOB 20515-2303; 225-2871; Fax: 225-6351; *Chief of Staff:* Dean P. Peterson

Web: www.house.gov/ramstad

E-mail: mn03@mail.house.gov

District Office(s): 1809 Plymouth Rd. South, #300, Minnetonka 55305-1977; (952) 738-8200; Fax: (952) 738-9362; *District and Communications Director:* Lance N. Olson

Committee Assignment(s): Ways and Means

Rangel, Charles B., D-N.Y. (15)

Capitol Hill Office: 2354 RHOB 20515-3215; 225-4365; Fax: 225-0816; *Chief of Staff:* George A. Dalley

Web: rangel.house.gov

District Office(s): 163 W. 125th St., #737, New York 10027-4404; (212) 663-3900; Fax: (212) 663-4277; *District Administrator:* Vivian Jones

Committee Assignment(s): Ways and Means; Joint Taxation

Rehberg, Dennis, R-Mont. (At Large)

Capitol Hill Office: 2448 RHOB 20515-2601; 225-3211; Fax: 225-5687; *Deputy Chief of Staff:* Jay Martin

Web: www.house.gov/rehberg

District Office(s): 1201 Grand Ave., #1, Billings 59102-4281; (406) 256-1019; Fax: (406) 256-4934; *Constituent Services Representative:* Linda Price

105 Smelter Ave. N.E., #16, Great Falls 59404-1953; (406) 454-1066; Fax: (406) 454-1130; *Field Rep.:* Mike Waite

950 N. Montana Ave., Helena 59601-3858; (406) 443-7878; Fax: (406) 443-8890; *Constituent Services Representative:* Suzanne Studer

218 E. Main St., Suite B, Missoula 59802-4478; (406) 543-9550; Fax: (406) 543-0663; *Field Representative:* Larry Anderson

Committee Assignment(s): Appropriations

Reichert, Dave, R-Wash. (8)

Capitol Hill Office: 1730 LHOB 20515-4708; 225-7761; Fax: 225-4282; *Chief of Staff:* Chris Miller

Web: www.house.gov/reichert

District Office(s): 2737 78th Ave. S.E., #202, Mercer Island 98040-2843; (206) 275-3438; Fax: (206) 275-3437; *District Director:* Mariana Parks

Committee Assignment(s): Ways and Means

Reyes, Silvestre, D-Tex. (16)

Capitol Hill Office: 2433 RHOB 20515-4316; 225-4831; Fax: 225-2016; *Chief of Staff:* Perry Finney Brody

Web: www.house.gov/reyes

District Office(s): 301 N. Mesa St., #400, El Paso 79901-1301; (915) 534-4400; Fax: (915) 534-7426; *Deputy Chief of Staff:* Sal Payan

Committee Assignment(s): Armed Services; Permanent Select Intelligence

Richardson, Laura, D-Calif. (37)

Capitol Hill Office: 1725 LHOB 20515-0537; 225-7924; Fax: 225-7926; *Chief of Staff:* Kimberly C. Parker

Web: richardson.house.gov

District Office(s): 970 W. 190th St., East Tower, #900, Torrance 90502-1053; (310) 538-1190; Fax: (310) 538-9672; *District Director:* Rosa Hernandez

Committee Assignment(s): Homeland Security; Transportation and Infrastructure

Rodriguez, Ciro D., D-Tex. (23)

Capitol Hill Office: 2351 RHOB 20515-4323; 225-4511; Fax: 225-2237; *Chief of Staff:* Cesar Blanco

Web: rodriguez.house.gov

District Office(s): 209 E. Losoya St., Del Rio 78840-5118; (830) 774-5500; Fax: (830) 774-2200; *Caseworker:* Elvira Puente

100 S. Monroe Street, Eagle Pass 78852-4830; (830) 757-8398; Fax: (830) 752-1893; *Field Rep.:* Yecenia Martinez

Pecos County Courthouse, 103 W. Callaghan St., Fort Stockton 79735-7110; (432) 336-3975; Fax: (432) 336-3961

Northside Office, 6363 DeZavala Road, Suite 105, San Antonio 78249-2104; (210) 561-9421; Fax: (210) 561-9442; *Caseworker:* Brad Mayhar

Southside Office, 1313 S.E. Military Drive, Suite 101, San Antonio 78214-2850; (210) 922-1874; Fax: (210) 923-8447; *District Director:* Vacancy

Committee Assignment(s): Appropriations; Veterans' Affairs

Roe, Phil, R-Tenn. (1)

Capitol Hill Office: 419 CHOB 20515-4201; 225-6356; Fax: 225-5714; *Chief of Staff:* Andrew Duke

Web: roe.house.gov

District Office(s): Northeast State Technical Community College, 2425 Highway 75, Blountville 37617-6350; (423) 354-0144; Fax: (423) 354-0119; *District Director*: Bill B. Snodgrass
1609 College Park Drive, Suite Four, Morristown 37813-1659; (423) 254-1400; Fax: (423) 254-1403; *Caseworker*: Cheryl Bennett
Committee Assignment(s): Agriculture; Education and Labor; Veterans' Affairs

Rogers, Hal, R-Ky. (5)

Capitol Hill Office: 2406 RHOB 20515-1705; 225-4601; Fax: 225-0940; *Chief of Staff*: William E. Smith
Web: halrogers.house.gov
District Office(s): 601 Main St., Hazard 41701-1354; (606) 439-0794; Fax: (606) 439-4647; *Field Rep.*: Pat Wooten
110 Resource Court, Suite A, Prestonsburg 41653-7851; (606) 886-0844; Fax: (606) 889-0371; *Receptionist*: Tonya Conn
551 Clifty St., Somerset 42501-1782; (606) 679-8346; Fax: (606) 678-4856; *Caseworker*: Mariessa Flynn
Committee Assignment(s): Appropriations

Rogers, Mike, R-Ala. (3)

Capitol Hill Office: 324 CHOB 20515-0103; 225-3261; Fax: 225-5827; *Chief of Staff*: Marshall C. Macomber
Web: www.house.gov/mike-rogers
District Office(s): Federal Bldg., 1129 Noble St., #104, Anniston 36201-4674; (256) 236-5655; Fax: (256) 237-9203; *Field Representative*: Tripp Skipper
7550 Halcyon Summit Dr., Montgomery 36117-7008; (334) 277-4210; Fax: (334) 277-4257; *Field Representative*: Alvin Lewis
1819 Pepperell Pkwy., #203, Opelika 36801-5476; (334) 745-6221; Fax: (334) 742-0109; *Field Representative*: Cheryl Cunningham
Committee Assignment(s): Agriculture; Armed Services; Homeland Security

Rogers, Mike, R-Mich. (8)

Capitol Hill Office: 133 CHOB 20515-2208; 225-4872; Fax: 225-5820; *Chief of Staff*: Andy Keiser
Web: www.mikerogers.house.gov
District Office(s): 1000 St. Joseph Drive, Suite 100, Lansing 49085; (517) 702-8000; Fax: (517) 702-8642; *Deputy Chief of Staff*: Anne Belser
Committee Assignment(s): Energy and Commerce; Permanent Select Intelligence

Rohrabacher, Dana, R-Calif. (46)

Capitol Hill Office: 2300 RHOB 20515-0546; 225-2415; Fax: 225-0145; *Chief of Staff*: Richard T. Dykema
Web: rohrabacher.house.gov
E-mail: Dana@mail.house.gov

District Office(s): 101 Main St., #380, Huntington Beach 92648-8149; (714) 960-6483; Fax: (714) 960-7806; *District Director*: Kathleen M. Hollingsworth
Committee Assignment(s): Foreign Affairs; Science and Technology

Rooney, Tom, R-Fla. (16)

Capitol Hill Office: 1529 LHOB 20515-0916; 225-5792; Fax: 225-3132; *Chief of Staff*: Brian Crawford
Web: rooney.house.gov
District Office(s): 226 Taylor Street, Punta Gorda 33950-4422; (941) 575-9101; Fax: (941) 575-9103; *Deputy District Director*: Leah Valenti
325 S.E. Ocean Boulevard, Stuart 34944-2220; (772) 288-4668; Fax: (772) 288-4631; *District Director*: Steve Leighton
Committee Assignment(s): Armed Services; Judiciary

Ros-Lehtinen, Ileana, R-Fla. (18)

Capitol Hill Office: 2470 RHOB 20515-0918; 225-3931; Fax: 225-5620; *Chief of Staff*: Arturo A. Estopiñán
Web: www.house.gov/ros-lehtinen
District Office(s): 4960 S.W. 72nd Avenue, Suite 208, Miami 33155; (305) 668-2285; Fax: (305) 668-7968; *District Chief of Staff*: Debra Zimmerman
Committee Assignment(s): Foreign Affairs

Roskam, Peter, R-Ill. (6)

Capitol Hill Office: 507 CHOB 20515-1306; 225-4561; Fax: 225-1166; *Chief of Staff*: Steven Moore
Web: roskam.house.gov/
District Office(s): 150 S. Bloomingdale Rd., #200, Bloomingdale 60108-1494; (630) 893-9670; Fax: (630) 893-9735; *District Director*: Brian McCarthy
Committee Assignment(s): Ways and Means

Ross, Mike, D-Ark. (4)

Capitol Hill Office: 2436 RHOB 20515-0404; 225-3772; Fax: 225-1314; *Chief of Staff*: Drew Goesl
Web: www.house.gov/ross
District Office(s): Union County Courthouse, 101 N. Washington Ave., #406, El Dorado 71730-5669; (870) 881-0681; Fax: (870) 881-0683; *District Aide*: Patricia Herring
300 Exchange St., Suite A, Hot Springs 71901-4026; (501) 520-5892; Fax: (501) 520-5873; *District Aide*: Donna Blackwood
George Howard, Jr. Federal Building, 100 E. Eighth Avenue, Room 2521, Pine Bluff 71601-5070; (870) 536-3376; Fax: (870) 536-4058; *District Aide*: Geneva Dawson
221 W. Main St., Prescott 71857-3608; (870) 887-6787; Fax: (870) 887-6799; *District Field Representative*: John Wright
Committee Assignment(s): Energy and Commerce; Foreign Affairs

Rothman, Steve, D-N.J. (9)

Capitol Hill Office: 2303 RHOB 20515-3009; 225-5061; Fax: 225-5851; *Chief of Staff:* Bob Decheine
Web: rothman.house.gov
District Office(s): Court Plaza North, 25 Main St., #27, Hackensack 07601-7089; (201) 646-0808; Fax: (201) 646-1944; *District Director:* Kevin Donnelly
130 Central Ave., Jersey City 07306-2118; (201) 798-1366; Fax: (201) 798-1725; *Staff Assistant:* Al Zampella
Committee Assignment(s): Appropriations; Science and Technology

Roybal-Allard, Lucille, D-Calif. (34)

Capitol Hill Office: 2330 RHOB 20515-0534; 225-1766; Fax: 226-0350; *Chief of Staff:* Paul Cunningham
Web: www.house.gov/roybal-allard
District Office(s): Edward R. Roybal Center and Federal Bldg., 255 E. Temple St., #1860, Los Angeles 90012-3334; (213) 628-9230; Fax: (213) 628-8578; *District Chief of Staff:* Ana Figueroa
Committee Assignment(s): Appropriations

Royce, Edward R., R-Calif. (40)

Capitol Hill Office: 2185 RHOB 20515-0540; 225-4111; Fax: 226-0335; *Chief of Staff:* Amy Porter
Web: www.royce.house.gov
District Office(s): 305 N. Harbor Blvd., #300, Fullerton 92832-1938; (714) 992-8081; Fax: (714) 992-1668; *Deputy Chief of Staff:* Sara Carmack
Committee Assignment(s): Financial Services; Foreign Affairs; Congressional-Executive Commission on China

Ruppersberger, C. A. Dutch, D-Md. (2)

Capitol Hill Office: 2453 RHOB 20515-2002; 225-3061; Fax: 225-3094; *Chief of Staff:* Tara Linnehan Oursler
Web: dutch.house.gov
District Office(s): The Atrium, 375 W. Padonia Rd., #200, Timonium 21093-2130; (410) 628-2701; Fax: (410) 628-2708; *District Office Manager/Scheduler:* Carol Merkel
Committee Assignment(s): Appropriations; Permanent Select Intelligence

Rush, Bobby L., D-Ill. (1)

Capitol Hill Office: 2416 RHOB 20515-1301; 225-4372; Fax: 226-0333; *Chief of Staff:* Rev. Stanley Watkins
Web: www.house.gov/rush
District Office(s): 700 706 E. 79th St., Chicago 60619; (773) 224-6500; Fax: (773) 224-9624; *District Director:* Barbara Holt
3235 147th St., Midlothian 60445-3656; (708) 385-9550; Fax: (708) 385-3860; *Deputy District Director:* Younus Suleman
Committee Assignment(s): Energy and Commerce

Ryan, Paul D., R-Wisc. (1)

Capitol Hill Office: 1113 LHOB 20515-4901; 225-3031; Fax: 225-3393; *Chief of Staff:* Joyce Yamat Meyer
Web: www.house.gov/ryan
District Office(s): 20 S. Main St., #10, Janesville 53545-3959; (608) 752-4050; Fax: (608) 752-4711; *Constituent Services Representative:* Chad Herbert
5712 7th Ave., Kenosha 53140-4129; (262) 654-1901; Fax: (262) 654-2156; *Kenosha Field Representative:* David Craig
5455 Sheridan Rd., #125, Racine 53403; (262) 637-0510; Fax: (262) 637-5689; *Field Representative:* Teresa Mora
Committee Assignment(s): Budget; Ways and Means

Ryan, Tim, D-Ohio (17)

Capitol Hill Office: 1421 LHOB 20515-3517; 225-5261; Fax: 225-3719; *Chief of Staff:* Ron Grimes
Web: timryan.house.gov
District Office(s): 1030 E. Tallmadge Ave., Akron 44310-3563; (330) 630-7311; Fax: (330) 630-7314; *Constituent Liaison:* Sean Buchanan
Mahoning Bldg., 197 W. Market St., Warren 44481-1024; (330) 373 0074; Fax: (330) 373-0098; *Constituent Liaison:* Gene Crockett
241 Federal Plaza West, Youngstown 44503-1207; (330) 740-0193; Fax: (330) 740-0182; *Constituent Liaison:* Matthew Vadas
Committee Assignment(s): Appropriations

Sablan, Gregorio C., I-M.P. (Non-Voting Delegate)

Capitol Hill Office: 423 CHOB 20515-5601; 225-2646; Fax: 226-4249; *Chief of Staff:* Robert J. Schwalbach
Web: sablan.house.gov
District Office(s): P.O. Box 504879, Saipan 96950; (670) 323-2647; Fax: (670) 323-2649; *District Director:* Peter Michael P. Tenorio
Committee Assignment(s): Education and Labor; Natural Resources

Salazar, John T., D-Colo. (3)

Capitol Hill Office: 326 CHOB 20515-0603; 225-4761; Fax: 226-9669; *Chief of Staff:* Ronnie P. Carleton
Web: www.house.gov/salazar
District Office(s): 609 Main St., Apt. 6, Alamosa 81101-2557; (719) 587-5105; Fax: (719) 587-7137; *Regional Director:* Erin Minks
813 Main Ave. #300., Durango 81301 5485; (970) 259-1012; Fax: (970) 259-9467; *Regional Director:* John Whitney
225 North 5th St., #702, Grand Junction 81501-2611; (970) 245-7107; Fax: (970) 245-7194; *Regional Director:* Rich Baca
134 B St., Pueblo 81003-6401; (719) 543-8200; Fax: (719) 543-8204; *Regional Director:* Loretta Kennedy

Committee Assignment(s): Appropriations; Transportation and Infrastructure; Select Energy Independence and Global Warming

Sánchez, Linda, D-Calif. (39)

Capitol Hill Office: 1222 LHOB 20515-0539; 225-6676; Fax: 226-1012; *Chief of Staff:* Meaghan Johnson
Web: www.lindasanchez.house.gov
District Office(s): 17906 Crusader Ave., #100, Cerritos 90703-2694; (562) 860-5050; Fax: (562) 924-2914; *District Director:* Bill Grady
Committee Assignment(s): Judiciary; Ways and Means

Sanchez, Loretta, D-Calif. (47)

Capitol Hill Office: 1114 LHOB 20515-0547; 225-2965; Fax: 225-5859; *Chief of Staff:* Adrienne K. Elrod
Web: www.lorettasanchez.house.gov
District Office(s): 12397 Lewis St., #101, Garden Grove 92840-4695; (714) 621-0102; Fax: (714) 621-0401; *District Director:* Paula Negrete
Committee Assignment(s): Armed Services; Homeland Security; Joint Economic

Sarbanes, John P., D-Md. (3)

Capitol Hill Office: 426 CHOB 20515-2003; 225-4016; Fax: 225-9219; *Chief of Staff:* Jason Gleason
Web: sarbanes.house.gov
District Office(s): Arundel Center, 44 Calvert St., #349, Annapolis 21401-1930; (410) 295-1679; Fax: (410) 295-1682; *Government, Business and Community Affairs Director:* Brigid Smith
600 Baltimore Ave., #303, Towson 21204-4022; (410) 832-8890; Fax: (410) 832-8898; *Administrative Director:* Monica Henderson
Committee Assignment(s): Energy and Commerce; Natural Resources

Scalise, Steve, R-La. (1)

Capitol Hill Office: 429 CHOB 20515-1801; 225-3015; Fax: 226-0386; *Chief of Staff:* Lynnel Ruckert
Web: scalise.house.gov
District Office(s): 21454 Koop Dr., #1-E, Mandeville 70471-7513; (985) 893-9064; Fax: (985) 893-9707; *Florida Parishes Director:* Justin Crossie
110 Veterans Memorial Boulevard, Suite 500, Metairie 70002-4970; (504) 837-1259; Fax: (504) 837-4239; *Field Rep.:* Ramona Williamson

Schakowsky, Jan, D-Ill. (9)

Capitol Hill Office: 2367 RHOB 20515-1309; 225-2111; Fax: 226-6890; *Chief of Staff:* Cathy Hurwit
Web: www.house.gov/schakowsky
District Office(s): 5533 N. Broadway St., #2, Chicago 60640-1405; (773) 506-7100; Fax: (773) 506-9202; *District Director:* Leslie Combs

820 Davis St., #105, Evanston 60201-4400; (847) 328-3399; Fax: (847) 328-3425; *Constituent Advocate:* Abbey Eusebio
Committee Assignment(s): Energy and Commerce; Permanent Select Intelligence

Schauer, Mark, D-Mich. (7)

Capitol Hill Office: 1408 LHOB 20515-2207; 225-6276; Fax: 225-6281; *Washington Director:* B.J. Neidhardt
Web: schauer.house.gov
District Office(s): 800 W. Ganson Street, Jackson 49202-4203; (517) 780-9075; Fax: (517) 780-9081; *Chief of Staff:* Ken Brock
Committee Assignment(s): Agriculture; Transportation and Infrastructure

Schiff, Adam, D-Calif. (29)

Capitol Hill Office: 2447 RHOB 20515-0529; 225-4176; Fax: 225-5828; *Chief of Staff:* Timothy Bergreen
Web: schiff.house.gov
District Office(s): 87 N. Raymond Ave., #800, Pasadena 91103-3966; (626) 304-2727; Fax: (626) 304-0572; *District Director:* Ann Peifer
Committee Assignment(s): Appropriations; Judiciary; Permanent Select Intelligence

Schmidt, Jean, R-Ohio (2)

Capitol Hill Office: 418 CHOB 20515-3502; 225-3164; Fax: 225-1992; *Chief of Staff:* Barry Bennett
Web: www.house.gov/schmidt
District Office(s): 8044 Montgomery Rd., #540, Cincinnati 45236-2926; (513) 791-0381; Fax: (513) 791-1696; *District Director:* Gertrude Fleig
601 Chillicothe St., Portsmouth 45662-4023; (740) 354-1440; Fax: (740) 354-1144; *Caseworker:* Teresa Lewis
Committee Assignment(s): Agriculture; Transportation and Infrastructure

Schock, Aaron, R-Ill. (18)

Capitol Hill Office: 509 CHOB 20515-1318; 225-6201; Fax: 225-9249; *Chief of Staff:* Steven Shearer
Web: schock.house.gov
District Office(s): 209 W. State Street, Jacksonville 62650-2001; (217) 245-1431; Fax: (217) 243-6852; *Constituent Services Specialist:* Barbara Baker
100 N.E. Monroe Street, Room 100, Peoria 61602-1047; (309) 671-7027; Fax: (309) 671-7309; *District Chief of Staff:* Carol Merna
235 S. Sixth Street, Springfield 62701-1502; (217) 670-1653; Fax: (217) 670-1806; *Constituent Services Specialist:* Judy Hinds
Committee Assignment(s): Oversight and Government Reform; Small Business; Transportation and Infastructure

Schrader, Kurt, D-Ore. (5)

Capitol Hill Office: 1419 LHOB 20515-3705; 225-5711; Fax: 225-5699; *Chief of Staff:* Paul Gage
Web: schrader.house.gov
District Office(s): 494 State Street, Suite 210, Salem 97301; (503) 588-9100; Fax: (503) 588-5517; *District Director:* Suzanne Kunse
Committee Assignment(s): Agriculture; Budget; Small Business

Schwartz, Allyson Y., D-Pa. (13)

Capitol Hill Office: 330 CHOB 20515-3813; 225-6111; Fax: 226-0611; *Chief of Staff:* Daniel McElhatton
Web: schwartz.house.gov
District Office(s): 706 West Ave., Jenkintown 19046-2710; (215) 517-6572; Fax: (215) 517-6575; *District Director:* Julie Slavet
7219 Frankford Ave., Philadelphia 19135-1010; (215) 335-3355; Fax: (215) 333-4508; *District Representative:* Annamarie Feeney
Committee Assignment(s): Budget; Ways and Means

Scott, David, D-Ga. (13)

Capitol Hill Office: 225 CHOB 20515-1013; 225-2939; Fax: 225-4628; *Chief of Staff:* Michael Andel
Web: davidscott.house.gov
District Office(s): 173 N. Main St., Jonesboro 30236-3567; (770) 210-5073; Fax: (770) 210-5673; *District Director:* David Johnson
888 Concord Rd., S.E., #100, Smyrna 30080-4202; (770) 432-5405; Fax: (770) 432-5813; *District Office Manager:* Shirley Thomas
Committee Assignment(s): Agriculture; Financial Services; Foreign Affairs

Scott, Robert C., D-Va. (3)

Capitol Hill Office: 1201 LHOB 20515-4603; 225-8351; Fax: 225-8354; *Chief of Staff:* Joni L. Ivey
Web: www.house.gov/scott
District Office(s): 2600 Washington Ave., #1010, Newport News 23607-4333; (757) 380-1000; Fax: (757) 928-6694; *District Manager:* Gisele P. Russell
501 N. 2nd St., #401, Richmond 23219-1321; (804) 644-4845; Fax: (804) 644-6026; *Legislative Assistant:* Nkechi George Winkler
Committee Assignment(s): Budget; Education and Labor; Judiciary

Sensenbrenner, F. James, Jr., R-Wisc. (5)

Capitol Hill Office: 2449 RHOB 20515-4905; 225-5101; Fax: 225-3190; *Chief of Staff:* Thomas Schreibel
Web: www.house.gov/sensenbrenner
E-mail: sensenbrenner@mail.house.gov
District Office(s): 120 Bishops Way, #154, Brookfield 53005-6294; (262) 784-1111; *District Director:* Sally Cole
Committee Assignment(s): Judiciary; Science and Technology; Select Energy Independence and Global Warming

Serrano, José E., D-N.Y. (16)

Capitol Hill Office: 2227 RHOB 20515-3216; 225-4361; Fax: 225-6001; *Chief of Staff:* Paul Lipson
Web: www.house.gov/serrano
E-mail: jserrano@mail.house.gov
District Office(s): 788 Southern Blvd., Bronx 10455-2115; (718) 620-0084; Fax: (718) 620-0658; *Executive Secretary:* Clara E. Wagner-Anderson
Committee Assignment(s): Appropriations

Sessions, Pete, R-Tex. (32)

Capitol Hill Office: 2233 RHOB 20515-4332; 225-2231; Fax: 225-5878; *Chief of Staff:* Josh Saltzman
Web: sessions.house.gov
District Office(s): Park Central VII, 12750 Merit Dr., #1434, Dallas 75251-1229; (972) 392-0505; Fax: (972) 392-0615; *District Director:* Taylor Bledsoe
Committee Assignment(s): Rules

Sestak, Joe, D-Pa. (7)

Capitol Hill Office: 1022 LHOB 20515-3807; 225-2011; Fax: 226-0286; *Chief of Staff:* Bibiana Boerio
Web: sestak.house.gov
District Office(s): 600 N. Jackson St., #203, Media 19063-2561; (610) 892-8623; Fax: (610) 892-8628; *District Director:* Bill Walsh
Committee Assignment(s): Armed Services; Education and Labor; Small Business

Shadegg, John, R-Ariz. (3)

Capitol Hill Office: 436 CHOB 20515-0303; 225-3361; Fax: 225-3462; *Chief of Staff:* Kristin Thompson
Web: johnshadegg.house.gov
District Office(s): 301 E. Bethany Home Rd., Suite C-178, Phoenix 85012-1266; (602) 263-5300; Fax: (602) 248-7733; *Deputy District Director:* James Ashley
Committee Assignment(s): Energy and Commerce; Select Energy Independence and Global Warming

Shea-Porter, Carol, D-N.H. (1)

Capitol Hill Office: 1330 LHOB 20515-2901; 225-5456; Fax: 225-5822; *Chief of Staff:* Mike Brown
Web: shea-porter.house.gov
District Office(s): 104 Washington St., Dover 03820-3749; (603) 743-4813; Fax: (603) 743-5956; *District of Constituent Services:* Olga Clough
33 Lowell St., Manchester 03101-1641; (603) 641-9536; Fax: (603) 641-9561; *District Manager:* Terri Beyer
Committee Assignment(s): Armed Services; Education and Labor; Natural Resources

Sherman, Brad, D-Calif. (27)

Capitol Hill Office: 2242 RHOB 20515-0527; 225-5911; Fax: 225-5879; *Staff Director:* Don MacDonald
Web: bradsherman.house.gov

District Office(s): 5000 Van Nuys Blvd., #420, Sherman Oaks 91403-6126; (818) 501-9200; Fax: (818) 501-1554; *District Director:* Erin Prangley

Committee Assignment(s): Financial Services; Foreign Affairs; Judiciary

Shimkus, John M., R-Ill. (19)

Capitol Hill Office: 2452 RHOB 20515; 225-5271; Fax: 225-5880; *Chief of Staff:* Craig A. Roberts

Web: www.house.gov/shimkus

District Office(s): 221 E. Broadway, #102, Centralia 62801; (618) 532-9676; Fax: (618) 532-1896

240 Regency Centre, Collinsville 62234-4635; (618) 344-3065; Fax: (618) 344-4215; *District Director:* Deb Detmers

110 E. Locust St., #12, Harrisburg 62946-1557; (618) 252-8271; Fax: (618) 252-8317; *District Aide:* Holly Healy

120 S. Fair St., Olney 62450-2258; (618) 392-7737; Fax: (618) 392-8178

3130 Chatham Rd., Suite C, Springfield 62704; (217) 492-5090; Fax: (217) 492-5096; *District Aide:* Mary Ballard

Committee Assignment(s): Energy and Commerce

Shuler, Heath, D-N.C. (11)

Capitol Hill Office: 422 CHOB 20515-3311; 225-6401; Fax: 226-6422; *Chief of Staff:* Hayden Rogers

Web: shuler.house.gov

District Office(s): 356 Biltmore Ave., #400, Asheville 28801-4516; (828) 252-1651; Fax: (828) 252-8734; *Constituent Services and Operations Director:* Myrna Campbell

75 Peachtree Street, Suite 100, Murphy 28906-2947; (828) 835-4981; *Field Rep.:* Sandy Zimmerman

125 Bonnie Lane, Sylva 28779-8552; (828) 586-1962, ext. 223; Fax: (828) 286-1968; *Field Rep. (Western Counties):* Boyce Dietz

Committee Assignment(s): Small Business; Transportation and Infrastructure

Shuster, Bill, R-Pa. (9)

Capitol Hill Office: 204 CHOB 20515-3809; 225-2431; Fax: 225-2486; *Chief of Staff:* Jeffrey R. Loveng

Web: www.house.gov/shuster

District Office(s): 100 Lincoln Way East, Suite B, Chambersburg 17201-2274; (717) 264-8308; Fax: (717) 264-0269; *Constituent Services Representative:* Nancy Bull

310 Penn St., #200, Hollidaysburg 16648-2044; (814) 696-6318; Fax: (814) 696-6726; *District Director:* Jim Frank

647 Philadelphia St., #304, Indiana 15701-3923; (724) 463-0516; Fax: (724) 463-0518; *Constituent Services Representative:* Ron Nocco

118 W. Main St., #104, Somerset 15501-2047; (814) 443-3918; Fax: (814) 443-6373; *Constituent Services Representative:* Ron Nocco

Committee Assignment(s): Armed Services; Natural Resources; Transportation and Infrastructure

Simpson, Mike, R-Idaho (2)

Capitol Hill Office: 2312 RHOB 20515-1202; 225-5531; Fax: 225-8216; *Chief of Staff:* Lindsay J. Slater

Web: www.house.gov/simpson

District Office(s): 802 W. Bannock St., #600, Boise 83702-5843; (208) 334-1953; Fax: (208) 334-9533; *Deputy Chief of Staff:* John P. Revier

490 Memorial Dr., #103, Idaho Falls 83402-3600; (208) 523-6701; Fax: (208) 523-2384; *Staff Assistant:* Coleen Erickson

275 South 5th Ave., #275, Pocatello 83201-6400; (208) 233-2222; Fax: (208) 233-2095; *Regional Director:* Steve Brown

1341 Filmore St., #202, Twin Falls 83301-3392; (208) 734-7219; Fax: (208) 734-7244; *Staff Assistant:* Linda Culver

Committee Assignment(s): Appropriations; Budget

Sires, Albio, D-N.J. (13)

Capitol Hill Office: 1024 LHOB 20515-3013; 225-7919; Fax: 226-0792; *Chief of Staff:* Gene Martorony

Web: www.house.gov/sires

District Office(s): 630 Ave. C, #9, Bayonne 07002-3878; (201) 823-2900; Fax: (201) 858-7139; *Congressional Aide:* Conchita Smith

100 Cook Avenue, Second Floor, Carteret 07008-3065; (732) 969-9160; Fax: (732) 969-9167; *Congressional Aide:* Ada Morell

35 Journal Sq., #906, Jersey City 07306-4011; (201) 222-2828; Fax: (201) 222-0188; *District Director:* Richard Turner

Perth Amboy City Hall, 260 High Street, First Floor, Perth Amboy 08861-4451; (732) 442-0610; Fax: (732) 442-0671; *Field Rep.:* Gabriel Rodriquez

5500 Palisade Ave., Suite A, West New York 07093-2124; (201) 558-0800; Fax: (201) 617-2809; *Constituent Services Director:* Danita Torres

Committee Assignment(s): Foreign Affairs; Transportation and Infrastructure

Skelton, Ike, D-Mo. (4)

Capitol Hill Office: 2206 RHOB 20515-2504; 225-2876; *Deputy Chief of Staff:* Whitney D. Frost

Web: www.house.gov/skelton

District Office(s): 514-B NW Seven Hwy., Blue Springs 64014-2733; (816) 228-4242; *Chief of Staff:* Robert D. Hagedorn

1401 Southwest Blvd., #101, Jefferson City 65109-2484; (573) 635-3499; *Staff Assistant:* Carol Scott

219 N. Adams Ave., Lebanon 65536-3029; (417) 532-7964; *Staff Assistant:* Melissa Richardson

908 Thompson Blvd., Sedalia 65301-2241; (660) 826-2675; *Staff Assistant:* Arletta Garrett

Committee Assignment(s): Armed Services

Slaughter, Louise M., D-N.Y. (28)

Capitol Hill Office: 2469 RHOB 20515-3228;
225-3615; Fax: 225-7822; *Deputy Chief of Staff:* Greg
Regan
Web: www.louise.house.gov
District Office(s): 465 Main St., #105, Buffalo
14203-1717; (716) 853-5813; Fax: (716) 853-6347;
Community Liaison: Kathy Lenihan
1910 Pine Ave., Niagara Falls 14301-2310; (716)
282-1274; Fax: (716) 282-2479; *Staff Assistant:*
Suzanne Macri
Federal Bldg., 100 State St., #3120, Rochester
14614-1309; (585) 232-4850; Fax: (585) 232-1954;
District Director: Patricia Larke
Committee Assignment(s): Commission on Security and
Cooperation in Europe; Rules

Smith, Adam, D-Wash. (9)

Capitol Hill Office: 2402 RHOB 20515-4709; 225-8901;
Fax: 225-5893; *Chief of Staff:* Shana Chandler
Web: www.house.gov/adamsmith
District Office(s): 3600 Port of Tacoma Rd., #106,
Tacoma 98424-1040; (253) 896-3775; Fax: (253)
896-3789; *District Director:* Linda Danforth
Committee Assignment(s): Armed Services; Permanent
Select Intelligence

Smith, Adrian, R-Neb. (3)

Capitol Hill Office: 503 CHOB 20515-2703; 225-6435;
Fax: 225-0207; *Chief of Staff:* Jeff Shapiro
Web: adriansmith.house.gov
District Office(s): Grand Island: 1811 W. 2nd St., #105,
Grand Island 68803-5400; (308) 384-3900;
Fax: (308) 384-3902; *Constituent Services
Representative:* Barb Cooksley
Northern Heights Professional Plaza, 416 Valley View
Dr., #600, Scottsbluff 69361-1486; (308) 633-6333;
Fax: (308) 633-6335; *District Director:* Mary B.
Crawford
Committee Assignment(s): Agriculture; Natural
Resources; Science and Technology

Smith, Christopher H., R-N.J. (4)

Capitol Hill Office: 2373 RHOB 20515-3004; 225-3765;
Fax: 225-7768; *Chief of Staff:* Mary McDermott
Noonan
Web: www.house.gov/chrissmith
District Office(s): 1540 Kuser Rd., Suite A-9, Hamilton
08619-3828; (609) 585-7878; Fax: (609) 585-9155;
District Director for Casework: Pidge Carroll
Whiting Shopping Center, 108 Lacey Rd., #58-A, Whiting
08759-1331; (732) 350-2300; Fax: (732) 350-6260;
District Director for Public Policy: Jeff Sagnip
Committee Assignment(s): Commission on Security and
Cooperation in Europe; Committee on Foreign
Affairs; Congressional-Executive Commission on
China

Smith, Lamar, R-Tex. (21)

Capitol Hill Office: 2409 RHOB 20515-4321; 225-4236;
Fax: 225-8628; *Chief of Staff:* Jennifer Young Brown
Web: lamarsmith.house.gov
District Office(s): 3536 Bee Cave Rd., #212, Austin
78746-5474; (512) 306-0439; Fax: (512) 306-0427;
Constituent Services Liaison: Morgan McFall
301 Junction Hwy., #346C, Kerrville 78028-4247; (830)
896-0154; Fax: (830) 896-0168; *Constituent Services
Liaison:* Anne Overby
Guaranty Federal Bldg., 1100 N.E. Loop 410, #640, San
Antonio 78209; (210) 821-5024; Fax: (210) 821-5947;
District Director: Gerardo Interiano
Committee Assignment(s): Homeland Security;
Judiciary; Science and Technology

Snyder, Vic, D-Ark. (2)

Capitol Hill Office: 2210 RHOB 20515-0402; 225-2506;
Fax: 225-5903; *Chief of Staff:* David A. Boling
Web: www.house.gov/snyder
District Office(s): Prospect Bldg., 1501 N. University Ave.,
#150, Little Rock 72207-5230; (501) 324-5941; Fax:
(501) 324-6029; *District Director:* Amanda Nixon
White
Committee Assignment(s): Armed Services; Veterans'
Affairs; Joint Economic

Souder, Mark, R-Ind. (3)

Capitol Hill Office: 2231 RHOB 20515-1403; 225-4436;
Fax: 225-3479; *Chief of Staff:* Renee Kevelighan
Web: souder.house.gov
District Office(s): E. Ross Adair Federal Bldg., 1300
S. Harrison St., #3105, Fort Wayne 46802; (260)
424-3041; Fax: (260) 424-4042; *District Director:*
Derek Pillie
River Plaza, 320 N. Chicago Ave., #9B, Goshen 46528;
(574) 533-5802; Fax: (574) 534-2669
The Boathouse, 700 Park Ave., Suite D, Winona Lake
46590; (574) 269-1940; Fax: (574) 269-3112
Committee Assignment(s): Education and Labor;
Homeland Security; Oversight and Government
Reform

Space, Zack, D-Ohio (18)

Capitol Hill Office: 315 CHOB 20515-3518; 225-6265;
Fax: 225-3394; *Chief of Staff:* Stuart Chapman
Web: space.house.gov
District Office(s): 14 S. Paint St., #6, Chillicothe
45601-3203; (740) 779-1636; Fax: (740) 779-2352;
Field Representative: Cindy Cunningham
137 E. Iron Ave., Dover 44622-2254; (330) 364-4300;
Fax: (330) 364-4330; *District Director:* Ken Engstrom
17 N. 4th St., Suite A, Zanesville 43701-3409; (740)
452-6338; Fax: (740) 452-6354; *Field Representative:*
Mike Calevski
Committee Assignment(s): Energy and Commerce;
Veterans' Affairs

Speier, Jackie, D-Calif. (12)

Capitol Hill Office: 211 CHOB 20515-0512; 225-3531;
  Chief of Staff: Cookab Hasemi
Web: speier.house.gov
District Office(s): 400 S. El Camino Real, #410, San
  Mateo 94402-1729; (650) 342-0300; Fax: (650)
  375-8270; *District Director:* Margo Rosen
Committee Assignment(s): Financial Services; Oversight
  and Government Reform; Select Energy
  Independence and Global Warming

Spratt, John M., Jr., D-S.C. (5)

Capitol Hill Office: 1401 LHOB 20515-4005; 225-5501;
  Fax: 225-0464; *Chief of Staff:* Dawn Myers O'Connell
Web: www.house.gov/spratt
District Office(s): 88 Public Sq., Darlington 29532-3216;
  (843) 393-3998; Fax: (843) 393-8060; *District Aide:*
  Bobbi Damon
201 E. Main St., #305, Rock Hill 29730-4888; (803)
  327-1114; Fax: (803) 327-4330; *District
  Administrator:* Charlie McDow
707 Bultman Dr., Sumter 29150-2516; (803) 773-3362;
  Fax: (803) 773-7662; *District Aide:* Linda Mixon
Committee Assignment(s): Armed Services; Budget

Stark, Pete, D-Calif. (13)

Capitol Hill Office: 239 CHOB 20515-0513; 225-5065;
  Fax: 226-3805; *Chief of Staff:* Debbie Curtis
Web: www.house.gov/stark
District Office(s): 39300 Civic Center Dr., #220, Fremont
  94538-2324; (510) 494-1388; Fax: (510) 494-5852;
  District Director: Jo Cazenave
Committee Assignment(s): Ways and Means; Joint
  Taxation

Stearns, Clifford B., R-Fla. (6)

Capitol Hill Office: 2370 RHOB 20515-0906; 225-5744;
  Fax: 225-3973; *Chief of Staff:* Jack F. Seum
Web: www.house.gov/stearns
District Office(s): 5700 S.W. 34th St., #425, Gainesville
  32608-5329; (352) 337-0003; Fax: (352) 337-0034;
  Staff Assistant: Mary Johnson
115 S.E. 25th Ave., Ocala 34471-9179; (352) 351-8777;
  Fax: (352) 351-8011; *District Director:* John A. Konkus
1726 Kingsley Ave. S.E., #8, Orange Park 32073-4411;
  (904) 269-3203; Fax: (904) 269-3343; *Staff Assistant:*
  Sherrie Porter
Committee Assignment(s): Energy and Commerce;
  Veterans' Affairs

Stupak, Bart, D-Mich. (1)

Capitol Hill Office: 2268 RHOB 20515-2201; 225-4735;
  Fax: 225-4744; *Chief of Staff:* Scott P. Schloegel
Web: www.house.gov/stupak
District Office(s): 111 E. Chisholm St., Alpena 49707-
  2817; (989) 356-0690; Fax: (989) 356-0923;
  Congressional Aide: Sheila Phillips

Iron County Courthouse, Two S. 6th St., #3, Crystal Falls
  49920-1438; (906) 875-3751; Fax: (906) 875-3889;
  Congressional Aide: Jim Dellies
902 Ludington St., Escanaba 49829-3827; (906)
  786-4504; Fax: (906) 786-4534; *Congressional Aide:*
  Ann Fix
616 Shelden Ave., #213, Houghton 49931-1841; (906)
  482-1371; Fax: (906) 482-4855; *Congressional Aide:*
  Amy Wisti
1229 W. Washington St., Marquette 49855-3186; (906)
  228-3700; Fax: (906) 228-2305; *District
  Administrator:* Tom Baldini
Emmet County Bldg., 200 Division St., Petoskey 49770-
  2486; (231) 348-0657; Fax: (231) 348-0653;
  Congressional Aide: Sue Norkowski
575 Court St., West Branch 48861-9387; (989) 345-2258;
  Fax: (989) 345-2285; *Congressional Aide:* Lori
  Sheltrown
Committee Assignment(s): Energy and Commerce

Sullivan, John, R-Okla. (1)

Capitol Hill Office: 434 CHOB 20515-3601; 225-2211;
  Fax: 225-9187; *Chief of Staff:* Elizabeth L. Bartheld
Web: sullivan.house.gov
District Office(s): 401 S. Johnstone Ave., #348,
  Bartlesville 74003-6619; (918) 336-6500; Fax: (918)
  337-4196
5727 S. Lewis Ave., #520, Tulsa 74105-7146; (918)
  749-0014; Fax: (918) 749-0781; *District Director:*
  Richard H. Hedgecock
Committee Assignment(s): Energy and Commerce; Select
  Energy Independence and Global Warming

Sutton, Betty, D-Ohio (13)

Capitol Hill Office: 1721 LHOB 20515-3513; 225-3401;
  Fax: 225-2266; *Chief of Staff:* Nichole Francis
  Reynolds
Web: sutton.house.gov
District Office(s): Akron 44313-7038; (330) 865-8450;
  Fax: (330) 865-8470; *District Director:* Michael
  Dalton
St. Joseph Community Center, 205 W. 20th St., Suite
  M230, Lorain 44052-3777; (440) 245-5350; Fax:
  (440) 245-5355; *Lorain County Office Coordinator:*
  Kay Giardini
Committee Assignment(s): Energy and Commerce

Tanner, John S., D-Tenn. (8)

Capitol Hill Office: 1226 LHOB 20515-4208; 225-4714;
  Fax: 225-1765; *Chief of Staff:* Vickie L. Walling
Web: www.house.gov/tanner
District Office(s): Federal Bldg., 109 S. Highland St.,
  #B-7, Jackson 38301; (731) 423-4848; Fax: (731)
  427-1537; *Office Supervisor and Constituent Services
  Assistant:* Debbie Shires
8120 Hwy. 51 North, #3, Millington 38053-1702; (901)
  873-5690; Fax: (901) 873-5692; *Caseworker:* Margaret
  Black

203 W. Church St., Union City 38261-3811; (731) 885-7070; Fax: (731) 885-7094; *District Administrator*: Judy Counce

Committee Assignment(s): Foreign Affairs; Ways and Means

Tauscher, Ellen O., D-Calif. (10)

Capitol Hill Office: 2459 RHOB 20515-0510; 225-1880; Fax: 225-5914; *Chief of Staff:* Simon Limage

Web: www.house.gov/tauscher

District Office(s): 420 W. 3rd St., Antioch 94509-1274; (925) 757-7817; Fax: (925) 757-7056; *Field Representative*: Terrie Gillen

2000 Cadenasso Dr., Suite A, Fairfield 94533-6803; (707) 428-7792; Fax: (707) 438-0523; *Field Rep.*: Annie Winterfield

2121 N. California Blvd., #555, Walnut Creek 94596-3501; (925) 932-8899; Fax: (925) 932-8159; *District Director*: Jennifer Barton

Committee Assignment(s): Armed Services; Transportation and Infrastructure

Taylor, Gene, D-Miss. (4)

Capitol Hill Office: 2269 RHOB 20515-2404; 225-5772; Fax: 225-7074; *Chief of Staff:* Stephen Peranich

Web: www.house.gov/genetaylor

District Office(s): 412 Highway 90, Suite Eight, Bay St. Louis 39520-3534; (228) 469-9235; Fax: (228) 469-9291; *Caseworker*: Kathy Holland

2424 14th St., Gulfport 39501-2019; (228) 864-7670; Fax: (228) 864-3099; *District Director*: Beau Gex

Federal Bldg., 701 Main St., #215, Hattiesburg 39401; (601) 582-3246; Fax: (601) 582-3452; *Office Manager*: Anita Bourn

527 Central Ave., Laurel 39440-3919; (601) 425-3905; Fax: (601) 425-3906; *Caseworker*: Faye Heathcock

Jackson County West Rd. Division, 6900 N. Washington Ave., Ocean Springs 39564-2133; (228) 872-7950; Fax: (228) 872-7949; *Caseworker*: Nancy Mathieu

Committee Assignment(s): Armed Services; Transportation and Infrastructure

Teague, Harry, D-N.M. (2)

Capitol Hill Office: 1007 LHOB 20515-3102; 225-2365; Fax: 225-9599; *Chief of Staff:* Adrian Saenz

Web: teague.house.gov

District Office(s): 200 E. Broadway Street, Suite 200, Hobbs 88240-8425; (575) 392-8325; Fax: (575) 433-8325; *Field Rep.*: Monica Boyle

135 W. Griggs Avenue, Las Cruces 88001-1235; (575) 522-3908; Fax: (575) 523-8799; *District Director*: Bill Gomez

111 School of Mines Road, Socorro 87801-4533; (575) 835-8919; Fax: (575) 825-8931; *Field Rep.*: Dan Armijo

Committee Assignment(s): Transportation and Infrastructure; Veterans' Affairs

Terry, Lee, R-Neb. (2)

Capitol Hill Office: 2331 RHOB 20515-2702; 225-4155; Fax: 226-5452; *Chief of Staff:* Eric Hultman

Web: leeterry.house.gov

District Office(s): 11717 Burt St., #106, Omaha 68154-1500; (402) 397-9944; Fax: (402) 397-8787; *District Director*: Molly K. Lloyd

Committee Assignment(s): Energy and Commerce

Thompson, Bennie G., D-Miss. (2)

Capitol Hill Office: 2432 RHOB 20515-2402; 225-5876; Fax: 225-5898; *Chief of Staff:* I. Lanier Avant

Web: benniethompson.house.gov

District Office(s): 107 W. Madison St., Bolton 39041; (601) 866-9003; Fax: (601) 866-9036; *District Director*: Charlie Horhn

910 Courthouse Lane, Greenville 38701-3764; (662) 335-9003; Fax: (662) 334-1304; *Office Manager*: Juliet Thomas

509 Hwy. 82 West, Suite F, Greenwood 38930-5030; (662) 455-9300; Fax: (662) 453-0118; *Office Manager*: Trina N. George

3607 Medgar Evers Blvd., Jackson 39213-6364; (601) 946-9003; Fax: (601) 982-8583

263 E. Main St., P.O. Box 356, Marks 38646; (662) 326-9003; *Caseworker*: Samuel McCray

City Hall, 106 W. Green Ave., #134, Mound Bayou 38762-9594; (662) 741-9003; Fax: (662) 741-9002; *Caseworker*: Geri Adams

Committee Assignment(s): Homeland Security

Thompson, Glenn W., R-Pa. (5)

Capitol Hill Office: 124 CHOB 20515-3805; 225-5121; Fax: 225-5796; *Chief of Staff:* Jordan Clark

Web: thompson.house.gov

District Office(s): 3555 Benner Pike, Suite 101, Bellfonte 16823-8474; (814) 355-0215; Fax: (814) 353-0218; *Office Manager*: Susan Gurekovich

127 W. Spring Street, Suite C, Titusville 16354-1727; (814) 827-3985; Fax: (814) 827-7307

Committee Assignment(s): Agriculture; Education and Labor; Small Business

Thompson, Mike, D-Calif. (1)

Capitol Hill Office: 231 CHOB 20515-0501; 225-3311; Fax: 225-4335; *Chief of Staff:* Charles Jefferson

Web: mikethompson.house.gov

District Office(s): 317 3rd St., #1, Eureka 95501-0487; (707) 269-9595; Fax: (707) 269-9598; *District Representative*: Liz Murguia

430 N. Franklin St., Ft. Bragg 95437; (707) 962-0933; Fax: (707) 962-0934; *Field Representative:* Heidi Dickerson

1040 Main St., #101, Napa 94559-2605; (707) 226-9898; Fax: (707) 251-9800; *District Representative*: Cheryl Diehm

712 Main St., #1, Woodland 95695-3478; (530) 662-5272; Fax: (530) 662-5163; *District Representative*: Elly Fairclough

Committee Assignment(s): Ways and Means; Permanent Select Intelligence

Thornberry, Mac, R-Tex. (13)

Capitol Hill Office: 2209 RHOB 20515-4313; 225-3706; Fax: 225-3486; *Communications Director*: George Rasley Jr.

Web: www.house.gov/thornberry

District Office(s): 905 S. Fillmore St., #520, Amarillo 79101-3541; (806) 371-8844; Fax: (806) 371-7044; *Chief of Staff*: Bill Harris

4245 Kemp Blvd., #506, Wichita Falls 76308-2822; (940) 692-1700; Fax: (940) 692-0539; *Constituent Services*: Libby Hastings

Committee Assignment(s): Armed Services; Permanent Select Intelligence

Tiahrt, Todd, R-Kans. (4)

Capitol Hill Office: 2441 RHOB 20515-1604; 225-6216; Fax: 225-3489; *Administrative Assistant*: Jeff Kahrs

Web: www.house.gov/tiahrt

District Office(s): 155 N. Market St., #400, Wichita 67202-1818; (316) 262-8992; Fax: (316) 262-5309; *District Director*: Robert Noland

Committee Assignment(s): Appropriations

Tiberi, Patrick J., R-Ohio (12)

Capitol Hill Office: 113 CHOB 20515-3512; 225-5355; Fax: 226-4523; *Chief of Staff*: Chris Zeigler

Web: tiberi.house.gov

District Office(s): 3000 Corporate Exchange Dr., #310, Columbus 43231-7689; (614) 523-2555; Fax: (641) 818-0887 *District Director*: Mark Bell

Committee Assignment(s): Ways and Means

Tierney, John F., D-Mass. (6)

Capitol Hill Office: 2238 RHOB 20515-2106; 225-8020; Fax: 225-5915; *Chief of Staff*: Betsy Arnold

Web: www.house.gov/tierney

District Office(s): Lynn City Hall, Three City Hall Sq., #105, Lynn 01901-1028; (781) 595-7375; Fax: (781) 595-7492; *Constituent Representative*: Rose Mary Sargent

17 Peabody Sq., Peabody 01960-5646; (978) 531-1669; Fax: (978) 531-1996; *District Director*: Gary Barrett

Committee Assignment(s): Education and Labor; Oversight and Government Reform; Permanent Select Intelligence

Titus, Dina, D-Nev. (3)

Capitol Hill Office: 319 CHOB 20515-2803; 225-3252; Fax: 225-2185; *Chief of Staff:* Jay Getsema

Web: titus.house.gov

District Office(s): 8215 S. Eastern Avenue, Suite 205, Las Vegas 89123-2523; (702) 387-4941; Fax: (702) 837-0728; *District Director*: Dan Giraldo

Committee Assignment(s): Education and Labor; Homeland Security; Transportation and Infrastructure

Tonko, Paul D., D-N.Y. (21)

Capitol Hill Office(s): 128 CHOB 20515-3221; 225-5076; Fax: 225-5077; *Chief of Staff:* Michael Lehman

Web: tonko.house.gov

District Office(s): Leo W. O'Brien Federal Building, 445 Broadway, Room 827, Albany 12207-2908; (518) 465-0700; Fax: (518) 427-5107

Committee Assignment(s): Education and Labor; Science and Technology

Towns, Edolphus, D-N.Y. (10)

Capitol Hill Office: 2232 RHOB 20515-3210; 225-5936; Fax: 225-1018; *Chief of Staff:* Albert C. Wiltshire

Web: www.house.gov/towns

District Office(s): 104-08 Flatlands Ave., Brooklyn 11236-2806; (718) 272-1175; Fax: (718) 272-1203; *Special Assistant*: D. Bacon-Finch

186 Joralemon Street, Suite 1102, Brooklyn 11201-4326; (718) 855-8018; Fax: (718) 858-4542; *Special Assistant*: Edna Johnson

Committee Assignment(s): Oversight and Government Reform

Tsongas, Niki, D-Mass. (5)

Capitol Hill Office: 1607 LHOB 20515-2105; 225-3411; Fax: 226-0771; *Chief of Staff:* Katie Elbert

Web: www.house.gov/tsongas

District Office(s): 492 Main Street, Acton 01720-3939; (978) 263-1951; Fax: (978) 257-3297; *Regional Coordinator*: Jane Adams

305 Essex St., Fourth Floor. Lawrence 01840-1445; (978) 681-6200; Fax: (978) 682-6070; *Regional Coordinator/ Constituent Services Director:* June Black

11 Kearney Sq., Third Floor, Lowell 01852; (978) 459-0101; Fax: (978) 459-1907; *District Director*: Brian Martin

Committee Assignment(s): Armed Services; Budget; Natural Resources

Turner, Michael, R-Ohio (3)

Capitol Hill Office: 1740 LHOB 20515-3503; 225-6465; Fax: 225-6754; *Chief of Staff:* Stacy Palmer-Barton

Web: www.house.gov/miketurner

District Office(s): 120 W. 3rd St., #305, Dayton 45402-1819; (937) 225-2843; Fax: (937) 225-2752; *District Director:* Michael Wiehe

15 E. Main St., Wilmington 45177-2330; (937) 383-8931; Fax: (937) 383-8910; *Field Representative*: Margaret Horst

Committee Assignment(s): Armed Services; Oversight and Government Reform

Upton, Fred, R-Mich. (6)

Capitol Hill Office: 2183 RHOB 20515-2206; 225-3761; Fax: 225-4986; *Chief of Staff:* Joan Hillebrands
Web: www.house.gov/upton
District Office(s): 157 S. Kalamazoo Mall, #180, Kalamazoo 49007-4861; (269) 385-0039; Fax: (269) 385-2888; *District Representative:* Ed Sackley
800 Ship St., #106, St. Joseph 49085-2182; (269) 982-1986; Fax: (269) 982-0237; *District Representative:* Al Pscholka
Committee Assignment(s): Energy and Commerce

Van Hollen, Chris, D-Md. (8)

Capitol Hill Office: 1707 LHOB 20515-2008; 225-5341; Fax: 225-0375; *Chief of Staff:* David Weaver
Web: vanhollen.house.gov
District Office(s): 6475 New Hampshire Ave., Suite C-201, Hyattsville 20783-3275; (301) 891-6982; Fax: (301) 891-6985; *Prince George's County Outreach Director:* Julius West
51 Monroe St., #507, Rockville 20850-2406; (301) 424-3501; Fax: (301) 424-5992; *District Director:* Joan Kleinman
Committee Assignment(s): Oversight and Government Reform; Ways and Means

Velázquez, Nydia M., D-N.Y. (12)

Capitol Hill Office: 2466 RHOB 20515-3212; 225-2361; Fax: 226-0327; *Chief of Staff:* Michael Day
Web: www.house.gov/velazquez
District Office(s): 266 Broadway, #201, Brooklyn 11211-6215; (718) 599-3658; Fax: (718) 599-4537; *Director of Constituent Services:* James Counihan
16 Court St., #1006, Brooklyn 11241-1010; (718) 222-5819; Fax: (718) 222-5830; *Community Coordinator:* Daniel Wiley
173 Ave. B, New York 10009-4656; (212) 673-3997; Fax: (212) 473-5242; *Community Coordinator:* Iris Quiñones
Committee Assignment(s): Financial Services; Small Business

Visclosky, Peter J., D-Ind. (1)

Capitol Hill Office: 2256 RHOB 20515-1401; 225-2461; Fax: 225-2493; *Chief of Staff:* Charles Brimmer
Web: www.house.gov/visclosky
District Office(s): 701 E. 83rd Ave., #9, Merrillville 46410-6239; (219) 795-1844; Fax: (219) 795-1850; *District Director:* Mark Lopez
Committee Assignment(s): Appropriations

Walden, Greg, R-Ore. (2)

Capitol Hill Office: 2352 RHOB 20515-3702; 225-6730; Fax: 225-5774; *Chief of Staff:* Brian C. MacDonald
Web: walden.house.gov
District Office(s): 1051 N.W. Bond Street, Suite 400, Bend 97701-2061; (541) 389-4408; Fax: (541) 389-4452; *Director, Central Oregon Office:* Troy Ferguson
1211 Washington Ave., La Grande 97850-2535; (541) 624-2400; Fax: (541) 624-2402; *Director, Eastern Oregon Office:* Colby Marshall
843 E. Main St., #400, Medford 97504-7137; (541) 776-4646; Fax: (541) 779-0204; *District Director:* John Snider
Committee Assignment(s): Energy and Commerce

Walz, Tim, D-Minn. (1)

Capitol Hill Office: 1722 LHOB 20515-2301; 225-2472; Fax: 225-3433; *Legislative Director:* Chris Schmitter
Web: walz.house.gov
District Office(s): 227 E. Main St., #200, Mankato 56001-3573; (507) 388-2149; *Chief of Staff:* Josh Syrjamaki
1134 7th St. N.W., Rochester 55901-1732; (507) 206-0643; *Deputy District Director:* Francy Hall
Committee Assignment(s): Agriculture; Transportation and Infrastructure; Veterans' Affairs; Congressional-Executive Commission on China

Wamp, Zach, R-Tenn. (3)

Capitol Hill Office: 1436 LHOB 20515-4203; 225-3271; Fax: 225-3494; *Chief of Staff:* Helen Hardin
Web: www.house.gov/wamp
District Office(s): 900 Georgia Ave., #126, Chattanooga 37402-2282; (423) 756-2342; Fax: (423) 756-6613; *District Director:* Leigh McClure
Federal Bldg., 200 Administration Rd., #100, Oak Ridge 37830-8823; (865) 576-1976; Fax: (865) 576-3221; *District Director:* Regina McMahan
Committee Assignment(s): Appropriations

Wasserman Schultz, Debbie, D-Fla. (20)

Capitol Hill Office: 118 CHOB 20515-0920; 225-7931; Fax: 226-2052; *Chief of Staff:* Tracie Pough
Web: www.house.gov/schultz
District Office(s): 19200 W. Country Club Dr., 3rd Floor, Aventura 33180-2403; (305) 936-5724; Fax: (305) 932-9664; *Deputy District Director:* Laurie Flink
10100 Pines Blvd., Pembroke Pines 33026-6040; (954) 437-3936; Fax: (954) 437-4776; *District Director:* Jodi Davidson
Committee Assignment(s): Appropriations; Judiciary

Waters, Maxine, D-Calif. (35)

Capitol Hill Office: 2344 RHOB 20515-0535; 225-2201; Fax: 225-7854; *Chief of Staff:* Mikael Moore
Web: www.house.gov/waters
District Office(s): 10124 S. Broadway, #1, Los Angeles 90003-4535; (323) 757-8900; Fax: (323) 757-9506; *Field Representative:* April Lawrence

6033 W. Century Blvd., #807, Los Angeles 90045-6414; (310) 642-4610; Fax: (310) 642-9160; *Field Representative*: Edgar Saenz
Committee Assignment(s): Financial Services; Judiciary

Watson, Diane E., D-Calif. (33)

Capitol Hill Office: 2430 RHOB 20515-0533; 225-7084; Fax: 225-2422; *Chief of Staff*: Richard Butcher
Web: www.house.gov/watson
District Office(s): 4322 Wilshire Blvd., #302, Los Angeles 90010-3794; (323) 965-1422; Fax: (323) 965-1113; *District Chief of Staff*: Paulette Starks
Committee Assignment(s): Foreign Affairs; Oversight and Government Reform

Watt, Melvin L., D-N.C. (12)

Capitol Hill Office: 2304 RHOB 20515-3312; 225-1510; Fax: 225-1512; *Chief of Staff*: Danielle Owen
Web: www.house.gov/watt
District Office(s): 1230 W. Morehead St., #306, Charlotte 28208-5206; (704) 344-9950; Fax: (704) 344-9971; *District Director*: Torre Jessup
301 S. Greene St., #210, Greensboro 27401-2660; (336) 275-9950; Fax: (336) 379-9951; *District Liaison*: Sharon Fisher
Committee Assignment(s): Financial Services; Judiciary

Waxman, Henry A., D-Calif. (30)

Capitol Hill Office: 2204 RHOB 20515-0530; 225-3976; Fax: 225-4099; *Chief of Staff*: Patricia Delgado
Web: www.henrywaxman.house.gov
District Office(s): 8436 W. 3rd St., #600, Los Angeles 90048-4183; (323) 651-1040; Fax: (323) 655-0502; *District Office Director*: Lisa E. Pinto
Committee Assignment(s): Energy and Commerce

Weiner, Anthony D., D-N.Y. (9)

Capitol Hill Office: 2104 LHOB 20515-3209; 225-6616; Fax: 226-7253; *Chief of Staff*: Jeff Plague
Web: www.house.gov/weiner
E-mail: weiner@mail.house.gov
District Office(s): 80-02 Kew Gardens Rd., #5000, Kew Gardens 11415; (718) 520-9001; Fax: (718) 520-9010; *District Office Manager*: Joan Oppedisano
90-16 Rockaway Beach Blvd., Rockaway 11693; (718) 318-9255
Committee Assignment(s): Energy and Commerce; Judiciary

Welch, Peter, D-Vt. (At Large)

Capitol Hill Office: 1404 LHOB 20515-4501; 225-4115; Fax: 225-6790; *Chief of Staff*: Bob Rogan
Web: welch.house.gov
District Office(s): 30 Main St., 3rd Floor, #350, Burlington 05401-8427; (802) 652-2450; *State Director*: Patricia Coates
Committee Assignment(s): Energy and Commerce; Oversight and Government Reform; Standards of Official Conduct

Westmoreland, Lynn A., R-Ga. (3)

Capitol Hill Office: 1213 LHOB 20515-1003; 225-5901; Fax: 225-2515; *Chief of Staff*: Chip Lake
Web: westmoreland.house.gov
District Office(s): 1601 Hwy. 34 East, Suite B, Newnan 30265-1325; (770) 683-2033; Fax: (770) 683-2042; *District Director*: John Stacy
Committee Assignment(s): Oversight and Government Reform; Small Business; Transportation and Infrastructure

Wexler, Robert, D-Fla. (19)

Capitol Hill Office: 2241 RHOB 20515-0919; 225-3001; Fax: 225-5974; *Chief of Staff*: Eric Johnson
Web: wexler.house.gov
District Office(s): 2500 N. Military Trail, 490, Boca Raton 33431-6354; (561) 988-6302; Fax: (561) 988-6423; *District Administrator*: Wendi Lipsich
Margate City Hall, 5790 Margate Blvd., Margate 33063-3614; (954) 972-6454; Fax: (954) 974-3191; *Broward County Coordinator*: Theresa Brier
Committee Assignment(s): Foreign Affairs; Judiciary

Whitfield, Ed, R-Ky. (1)

Capitol Hill Office: 2411 RHOB 20515-1701; 225-3115; Fax: 225-3547; *Chief of Staff*: John Sparkman
Web: whitfield.house.gov
District Office(s): Municipal Bldg., 222 1st St., #307, Henderson 42420-3181; (270) 826-4180; Fax: (270) 826-6783; *Field Representative*: Ed West
1403 S. Main St., Hopkinsville 42240-2017; (270) 885-8079; Fax: (270) 885-8598; *District Director*: Michael Pape
Century Bldg., 100 Fountain Ave., #104, Paducah 42001-2771; (270) 442-6901; Fax: (270) 442-6805; *Field Representative*: Janece Everett
Monroe County Courthouse, P.O. Box 717, Tompkinsville 42167; (270) 487-9509; Fax: (270) 487-0019; *Field Representative*: Sandy Simpson
Committee Assignment(s): Energy and Commerce

Wilson, Charlie, D-Ohio (6)

Capitol Hill Office: 226 CHOB 20515-3506; 225-5705; Fax: 225-5907; *Chief of Staff*: Candace Bryan Abbey
Web: charliewilson.house.gov
District Office(s): 800 Main St., Bridgeport 43912-1477; (740) 633-5705; Fax: (740) 633-5727; *District Director*: Chris Gagin
4137 Boardman Canfield Rd., Canfield 44406-8087; (330) 533-7250; Fax: (330) 533-7136; *Field Representative*: Dennis Johnson
202 Park Ave., Suite C, Ironton 45638-1548; (740) 533-9423; Fax: (740) 533-9359; *Field Representative*: Phillip Roberts
258 Front St., Marietta 45750-2908; (740) 376-0868; Fax: (740) 376-0886; *Casework Manager*: Barb Danford

1200 Main St., Wellsville 43968-1233; (330) 532-3740;
Field Representative: Linda Persutti
Committee Assignment(s): Financial Services; Science
and Technology

Wilson, Joe, R-S.C. (2)

Capitol Hill Office: 212 CHOB 20515-4002; 225-2452;
Fax: 225-2455; *Chief of Staff:* Eric Dell
Web: joewilson.house.gov
District Office(s): 903 Port Republic St., P.O. Box 1538,
Beaufort 29901; (843) 521-2530; Fax: (843) 521-2535;
Field Representative: Cris Steele
1700 Sunset Blvd. (U.S. 378), #1, P.O. Box 7381, West
Columbia 29169; (803) 939-0041; Fax: (803)
939-0078; *District Director:* Butch Wallace
Committee Assignment(s): Armed Services; Education
and Labor; Foreign Affairs

Wittman, Rob, R-Va. (1)

Capitol Hill Office: 1318 LHOB 20515-4601; 225-4261;
Chief of Staff: Mary Springer
Web: wittman.house.gov
District Office(s): 3504 Plank Road, Suite 203,
Fredericksburg; (540) 548-1086; *District Rep.:*
Darlene Stein
508 Church Lane, P.O. Box 3106, Tappahannock 22560;
(804) 443-0668; *District Rep.:* Chris Jones
4904-B George Washington Memorial Hwy., Yorktown
23692; (757) 874-6687; *District Director:* Joe
Schumacher
Committee Assignment(s): Armed Services; Natural
Resources

Wolf, Frank R., R-Va. (10)

Capitol Hill Office: 241 CHOB 20515-4610;
225-5136; Fax: 225-0437; *Chief of Staff:* Daniel F.
Scandling
Web: www.house.gov/wolf
District Office(s): 13873 Park Center Rd., #130, Herndon
20171-3248; (703) 709-5800; Fax: (703) 709-5802;
Director of Constituent Services: Judy McCary
110 N. Cameron St., Winchester 22601-4730; (540)
667-0990; Fax: (540) 678-0402; *Constituent Services
Assistant:* Donna Crowley
Committee Assignment(s): Appropriations

Woolsey, Lynn, D-Calif. (6)

Capitol Hill Office: 2263 RHOB 20515-0506; 225-5161;
Fax: 225-5163; *Chief of Staff:* Nora Baumeister
Matus
Web: woolsey.house.gov
District Office(s): Northgate Bldg., 1050 Northgate Dr.,
#354, San Rafael 94903-2580; (415) 507-9554; Fax:
(415) 507-9601; *Field Representative:* Anita Franzi
1101 College Ave., #200, Santa Rosa 95404-3940; (707)
542-7182; Fax: (707) 542-2745; *District Director:*
Wendy Friefeld
Committee Assignment(s): Education and Labor; Foreign
Affairs; Science and Technology

Wu, David, D-Ore. (1)

Capitol Hill Office: 2338 RHOB 20515-3701; 225-0855;
Fax: 225-9497; *Chief of Staff:* Julie Tippens
Web: www.house.gov/wu
District Office(s): 620 S.W. Main St., #606, Portland
97205-3024; (503) 326-2901; Fax: (503) 326-5066;
District Director: Mary Elliott
Committee Assignment(s): Education and Labor; Science
and Technology

Yarmuth, John, D-Ky. (3)

Capitol Hill Office: 435 CHOB 20515-1703; 225-5401;
Fax: 225-5776; *Chief of Staff:* Juile Carr
Web: yarmuth.house.gov
District Office(s): Romano L. Mazzoli Federal Bldg., 600
Martin Luther King Jr. Pl., #216, Louisville 40202;
(502) 582-5129; Fax: (502) 582-5897; *District
Director:* Carolyn H. Whitaker-Tandy
Louisville Metro Southwest Government Center, 7219
Dixie Hwy., Louisville 40258-3756; (502) 933-5863;
Fax: (502) 935-6934; *Office Coordinator:* Shelly Spratt
Committee Assignment(s): Budget; Ways and Means

Young, C. W. Bill, R-Fla. (10)

Capitol Hill Office: 2407 RHOB 20515-0910; 225-5961;
Fax: 225-9764; *Chief of Staff:* Harry J. Glenn
Web: www.house.gov/young
E-mail: Bill.Young@mail.house.gov
District Office(s): 9210 113th St., Seminole 33772-2800;
(727) 394-6950; Fax: (727) 394-6955; *District
Assistant:* Sharon Ghezzi
360 Central Ave., #1480, St. Petersburg 33701-3838;
(727) 893-3191; *District Assistant:* Yvonne Gray
Committee Assignment(s): Appropriations

Young, Don, R-Alaska (At Large)

Capitol Hill Office: 2111 RHOB 20515-0201; 225-5765;
Fax: 225-0425; *Chief of Staff:* Michael Anderson
Web: donyoung.house.gov
District Office(s): Peterson Tower Bldg., 510 L St., #580,
Anchorage 99501-1959; (907) 271-5978; Fax: (907)
271-5950; *District Director:* Chad Padgett
Federal Bldg., 101 12th Ave., Box 10, Fairbanks 99701-
6236; (907) 456-0210; Fax: (907) 456-0279; *Special
Assistant:* Lanien Livingston
Hurff A. Saunders Federal Bldg., 709 W. 9th St., P.O. Box
21247, Juneau 99801-1807; (907) 586-7400; Fax:
(907) 586-8922; *Staff Assistant:* Connie McKenzie
110 Trading Bay Dr., Kenai 99611-7716; (907) 283-5808;
Fax: (907) 283-4363; *Staff Assistant:* Michelle
Blackwell
Currall Office Bldg., 540 Water St., #101, Ketchikan
99901-6378; (907) 225-6880; Fax: (907) 225-0390;
Staff Assistant: Sherrie Slick
851 E. Westpoint Dr., #307, Wasilla 99654-7183; (907)
376-7665; Fax: (907) 376-8526; *Staff Assistant:* Gerri
Sumpter
Committee Assignment(s): Natural Resources;
Transportation and Infrastructure

Joint Committees of Congress

The joint committees of Congress follow. Each listing includes room number, office building, zip code, telephone and fax numbers, Web address(es), key staffers, committee jurisdiction, and membership (in order of seniority) for each committee. Members are drawn from the Senate and House and from both parties. Vacancy indicates a seat that had not been filled as of May 1, 2009.

Democrats, the current majority, are shown in roman type; Republicans, in the minority, appear in italic. When a senator serves as chair, the vice chair usually is a representative, and vice versa. The location of the chair usually rotates from one chamber to the other at the beginning of each Congress. The area code for all phone and fax numbers is (202). A phone number and/or office number next to either the Majority or Minority Staff Director indicates a change from the full committee's office number and/or phone number. If no numbers are listed, the individual's office number and phone number are the same as for the full committee.

JOINT ECONOMIC

Office: SDOB-G01 20510
Phone: 224-7056
Web: jec.senate.gov and www.house.gov/jec
Executive Director: Michael Lawkawy
Minority Staff Director: Christopher Frenze 225-3923 433A CHOB
Jurisdiction: (1) make a continuing study of matters relating to the Economic Report of the President; (2) study means of coordinating programs in order to further the policy of this Act; and (3) as a guide to the several committees of the Congress dealing with legislation relating to the Economic Report, not later than March 1, of each year (beginning with the year 1947) to file a report with the Senate and the House of Representatives containing its findings and recommendations with respect to each of the main recommendations made by the President in the Economic Report, and from time to time to make other reports and recommendations to the Senate and the House of Representatives as it deems advisable.

Senate Members

Charles E. Schumer, N.Y., Chair	*Sam Brownback, Kan.*
Edward M. Kennedy, Mass.	*Jim DeMint, S.C.*
Jeff Bingaman, N.M.	*James E. Risch, Id.*
Amy Klobuchar, Minn.	*Robert F. Bennett, Utah*
Robert P. Casey, Pa.	
James H. Webb, Va.	

House Members

Carolyn B. Maloney, N.Y., Vice Chair	*Kevin Brady, Tex.*
Maurice D. Hinchey, N.Y.	*Ron Paul, Tex.*
Baron Hill, Ind.	*Michael Burgess, Tex.*
Loretta Sanchez, Calif.	*John Campbell, Calif.*
Elijah E. Cummings, Md.	
Vic Snyder, Ariz.	

JOINT LIBRARY OF CONGRESS

Office: SR-305 20515
Phone: 224-6352
Staff Director: Howard Gantman
Jurisdiction: considers proposals concerning the management and expansion of the Library of Congress, the development and maintenance of the U.S. Botanic Garden, the receipt of gifts for the benefit of the Library, and certain matters relating to placing of statues and other works of art in the U.S. Capitol.

Senate Members

Dianne Feinstein, Calif., Chair	*Charles E. Schumer, N.Y.*
Christopher J. Dodd, Conn.	*Robert F. Bennett, Utah*
	Vacancy

House Members

Robert A. Brady, Penn., Vice Chair	*Dan Lungren, Calif.*
Zoe Lofgren, Calif.	*Vernon Ehlers, Mich.*
Debbie Wasserman Schultz, Fla.	

JOINT PRINTING

Office: SR-305 20510-6650
Phone: 224-6352
Staff Director: Susan Wooten Wells
Deputy Staff Director: Bryan T. Dorsey 225-8281 1309 LHOB

Jurisdiction: oversees the functions of the Government Printing Office and general printing procedures of the federal government.

Senate Members

Dianne Feinstein, Calif., Vice Chair
Daniel K. Inouye, Hawaii
Patty Murray, Wash.

Robert F. Bennett, Utah
Saxby Chambliss, Ga.

House Members

Robert A. Brady, Pa., Chair
Michael E. Capuano, Mass.
Susan Davis, Calif.

Dan Lungren, Calif.
Kevin McCarthy, Calif.

JOINT TAXATION

Office: 1015 LHOB 20515-6453
Phone: 225-3621
Web: www.house.gov/jct
Chief of Staff: Edward D. Kleinbard
Deputy Chief of Staff: Thomas A. Barthold 225-7377 1015 LHOB

Jurisdiction: investigates the operation and effects of the federal system of taxation and the administration of such taxes by the Internal Revenue Service and other executive departments, establishments, or agencies; and studies and reports on methods for simplification of the tax laws.

Senate Members

Max S. Baucus, Mont., Chair
John D. Rockefeller, W.Va.
Kent Conrad, N.D.

Charles E. Grassley, Iowa
Orrin G. Hatch, Utah

House Members

Charles B. Rangel, N.Y., Vice Chair
Pete Stark, Calif.
Sander M. Levin, Mich.

Wally Herger, Calif.
Dave Camp, Mich.

Senate Committees

The standing and select committees of the U.S. Senate follow. This information is current as of May 2009. Each listing includes room number, office building, zip code, telephone and fax numbers, Web address, e-mail address if available, key majority and minority staff members, jurisdiction for the full committee, and party ratio. Subcommittees are listed under the full committees. Members are listed in order of seniority on the committee or subcommittee. Many committees and subcommittees may be contacted via Web-based e-mail forms found on their Web sites. A phone number and/or office number next to either the Majority or Minority Staff Director indicates a change from the full committee's office number and/or phone number. If no numbers are listed, the individual's office number and phone number are the same as for the full committee.

Democrats, the current majority, are shown in roman type; Republicans, in the minority, appear in italic. Joseph I. Lieberman, I-Conn., and Bernard Sanders, I-Vt., caucus with Democrats and accrue committee seniority with Democrats. The partisan committees of the Senate are listed on page 818. The area code for all phone and fax numbers is (202).

AGRICULTURE, NUTRITION, AND FORESTRY

Office: SR-328A 20510-6000
Phone: 224-2035
Web: agriculture.senate.gov
Staff Director: Mark B. Halverson
Minority Staff Director: Martha Scott Poindexter
Jurisdiction: (1) agricultural economics and agricultural research; (2) agricultural extension services and agricultural experiment stations; (3) agricultural production, agricultural marketing, and stabilization of prices; (4) agriculture and agricultural commodities; (5) animal industry and animal diseases; (6) crop insurance and soil conservation; (7) farm credit and farm security; (8) food from fresh waters; (9) food stamp programs; (10) forestry and forest reserves and wilderness areas other than those created from the public domain; (11) home economics; (12) human nutrition; (13) inspection of livestock, meat, and agricultural products and commodities; (14) pests and pesticides; (15) plant industry, soils, and agricultural engineering; (16) rural development, rural electrification, and watersheds; (17) school nutrition programs. The committee shall also study and review, on a comprehensive basis, matters relating to food, nutrition, and hunger, both in the United States and in foreign countries, and rural affairs.
Party Ratio: D 12-R 9

Tom Harkin, Iowa, Chair
Patrick Leahy, Vt.
Kent Conrad, N.D.
Max S. Baucus, Mont.
Blanche L. Lincoln, Ark.
Debbie Stabenow, Mich.
E. Benjamin Nelson, Neb.
Sherrod Brown, Ohio
Robert P. Casey, Pa.
Amy Klobuchar, Minn.
Kirsten Gillibrand, N.Y.
Michael F. Bennet, Colo.

Saxby Chambliss, Ga.,
  Ranking Minority
  Member
Richard G. Lugar, Ind.
Thad Cochran, Miss.
Mitch McConnell, Ky.
Pat Roberts, Kans.
Mike Johanns, Neb.
Charles E. Grassley, Iowa
John Thune, S.D.
Vacancy

Subcommittees

Domestic and Foreign Marketing, Inspection, and Plant and Animal Health
Office: SR-328A   **Phone:** 224-2035

Max S. Baucus (Chair), Kent Conrad, Debbie Stabenow, E. Benjamin Nelson, E. Benjamin Nelson, Robert P. Casey
Mitch McConnell (Ranking Minority Member), Pat Roberts, John Thune

Energy, Science, and Technology
Office: SR-328A   **Phone:** 224-2035

Kent Conrad (Chair), E. Benjamin Nelson, Sherrod Brown, Robert P. Casey, Amy Klobuchar
John Thune (Ranking Minority Member), Richard G. Lugar, Charles E. Grassley

Nutrition and Food Assistance, Sustainable and Organic Agriculture, and General Legislation
Office: SR-328A   **Phone:** 224-2035

Patrick Leahy (Chair), Blanche L. Lincoln, Debbie Stabenow, Sherrod Brown, Robert P. Casey, Amy Klobuchar
Richard G. Lugar (Ranking Minority Member), Thad Cochran, Mitch McConnell

Production, Income Protection and Price Support
Office: SR-328A   **Phone:** 224-2035

Blanche L. Lincoln (Chair), Patrick Leahy, Kent Conrad, Max S. Baucus, Sherrod Brown, Amy Klobuchar
Pat Roberts (Ranking Minority Member), Thad Cochran, John Thune, Charles E. Grassley

Rural Revitalization, Conservation, and Forestry and Credit
Office: SR-328A   **Phone:** 224-2035

Debbie Stabenow (Chair), Patrick Leahy, Max S. Baucus, Blanche L. Lincoln, E. Benjamin Nelson
Richard G. Lugar (Ranking Minority Member), Thad Cochran, Mitch McConnell

APPROPRIATIONS

Office: S-131 CAP 20510-6025
Phone: 224-7363
Web: appropriations.senate.gov
Staff Director: Charles J. Houy
Minority Staff Director: Bruce M. Evans 224-7257
S-146A CAP
Jurisdiction: (1) appropriation of the revenue for the support of the government, except as provided in subparagraph (e); (2) rescission of appropriations contained in appropriation acts (referred to in section 105 of title 1, United States Code); (3) the amount of new spending authority described in section 401 (c) (2) (A) and (B) of the Congressional Budget and Impoundment Control Act of 1974 which is to be effective for a fiscal year; (4) new spending authority described in section 401 (c) (2) (C) of the Congressional Budget and Impoundment Control Act of 1974 provided in bills and resolutions referred to the committee under section 401 (b) (2) of that Act.
Party Ratio: D 18-R 12

Daniel K. Inouye, Hawaii, Chair
Robert C. Byrd, W.Va.
Patrick Leahy, Vt.
Tom Harkin, Iowa
Barbara A. Mikulski, Md.
Herb Kohl, Wisc.
Patty Murray, Wash.
Byron L. Dorgan, N.D.
Dianne Feinstein, Calif.
Richard J. Durbin, Ill.
Tim Johnson, S.D.
Mary L. Landrieu, La.
Jack Reed, R.I.
Frank R. Lautenberg, N.J.
E. Benjamin Nelson, Neb.
Mark Pryor, Ark.
Jon Tester, Mont.
Arlen Specter, Pa.

Thad Cochran, Miss., Ranking Minority Member
Christopher S. Bond, Mo.
Mitch McConnell, Ky.
Richard C. Shelby, Ala.
Judd Gregg, N.H.
Robert F. Bennett, Utah
Kay Bailey Hutchison, Tex.
Sam Brownback, Kans.
Lamar Alexander, Tenn.
Susan M. Collins, Maine
George Voinovich, Ohio
Lisa Murkowski, Alaska

Subcommittees

Agriculture, Rural Development, Food and Drug Administration, and Related Agencies
Office: SD-129   **Phone:** 224-8090
Herb Kohl (Chair),Tom Harkin, Byron L. Dorgan, Dianne Feinstein, Richard J. Durbin, Tim Johnson, E. Benjamin Nelson, Jack Reed, Mark Pryor
Sam Brownback (Ranking Minority Member), Robert F. Bennett, Thad Cochran, Christopher S. Bond, Mitch McConnell, Susan M. Collins

Commerce, Justice, Science, and Related Agencies
Office: SD-144   **Phone:** 224-5202
Barbara A. Mikulski (Chair), Daniel K. Inouye, Patrick Leahy, Herb Kohl, Byron L. Dorgan, Dianne Feinstein, Jack Reed, Frank R. Lautenberg, E. Benjamin Nelson, Mark Pryor

Richard C. Shelby (Ranking Minority Member), Judd Gregg, Mitch McConnell, Kay Bailey Hutchison, Sam Brownback, Lamar Alexander, George V. Voinovich, Lisa Murkowski

Defense
Office: SD-119   **Phone:** 224-6688
Daniel K. Inouye (Chair), Robert C. Byrd, Patrick Leahy, Tom Harkin, Byron L. Dorgan, Richard J. Durbin, Dianne Feinstein, Barbara A. Mikulski, Herb Kohl, Patty Murray
Thad Cochran (Ranking Minority Member), Christopher S. Bond, Mitch McConnell, Richard C. Shelby, Judd Gregg, Kay Bailey Hutchison, Robert F. Bennett

Energy and Water Development
Office: SD-186   **Phone:** 224-8119
Byron L. Dorgan (Chair), Robert C. Byrd, Patty Murray, Dianne Feinstein, Tim Johnson, Mary L. Landrieu, Jack Reed, Frank R. Lautenberg, Tom Harkin, Jon Tester
Robert F. Bennett (Ranking Minority Member), Thad Cochran, Mitch McConnell, Christopher S. Bond, Kay Bailey Hutchison, Richard C. Shelby, Lamar Alexander, George V. Voinovich

Financial Services and General Government
Office: SD-184   **Phone:** 224-1133
Richard J. Durbin (Chair), Mary L. Landrieu, Frank R. Lautenberg, E. Benjamin Nelson, Jon Tester
Susan M. Collins (Ranking Minority Member), Christopher S. Bond, Lisa Murkowski

Homeland Security
Office: 131 CAP   **Phone:** 224-8244
Robert C. Byrd (Chair), Daniel K. Inouye, Patrick Leahy, Barbara A. Mikulski, Herb Kohl, Patty Murray, Mary L. Landrieu, Frank R. Lautenberg, Jon Tester
George V. Voinovich (Ranking Minority Member), Thad Cochran, Judd Gregg, Richard C. Shelby, Sam Brownback

Interior, Environment, and Related Agencies
Office: SD-131   **Phone:** 228-0774
Dianne Feinstein (Chair), Robert C. Byrd, Patrick Leahy, Byron L. Dorgan, Barbara A. Mikulski, Herb Kohl, Tim Johnson, Jack Reed, E. Benjamin Nelson, Jon Tester
Lamar Alexander (Ranking Minority Member), Thad Cochran, Robert F. Bennett, Judd Gregg, Lisa Murkowski, Susan M. Collins, George V. Voinovich

Labor, Health and Human Services, Education, and Related Agencies
Office: SD-131   **Phone:** 224-9145
Tom Harkin (Chair), Daniel K. Inouye, Herb Kohl, Patty Murray, Mary L. Landrieu, Richard J. Durbin, Jack Reed, Mark Pryor
Thad Cochran (Ranking Minority Member), Judd Gregg, Kay Bailey Hutchison, Richard C. Shelby, Lamar Alexander

APPROPRIATIONS (continued)

Legislative Branch
Office: SD-135   Phone: 224-3477

E. Benjamin Nelson (Chair), Mark Pryor, Jon Tester
Lisa Murkowski (Ranking Minority Member)

Military Construction, Veterans Affairs, and Related Agencies
Office: SD-125   Phone: 224-8224

Tim Johnson (Chair), Daniel K. Inouye, Mary L. Landrieu, Robert C. Byrd, Patty Murray, Jack Reed, E. Benjamin Nelson, Mark Pryor
Kay Bailey Hutchison (Ranking Minority Member), Sam Brownback, Mitch McConnell, Susan M. Collins, Lamar Alexander, Lisa Murkowski

State, Foreign Operations, and Related Programs
Office: SD-127   Phone: 224-7284

Patrick Leahy (Chair), Daniel K. Inouye, Tom Harkin, Barbara A. Mikulski, Richard J. Durbin, Tim Johnson, Mary L. Landrieu, Frank Lautenberg
Judd Gregg (Ranking Minority Member), Mitch McConnell, Robert F. Bennett, Christopher S. Bond, Sam Brownback

Transportation, Housing and Urban Development, and Related Agencies
Office: SD-133   Phone: 224-7281

Patty Murray (Chair), Robert C. Byrd, Barbara A. Mikulski, Herb Kohl, Richard J. Durbin, Byron L. Dorgan, Patrick Leahy, Tom Harkin, Dianne Feinstein, Tim Johnson, Frank R. Lautenberg
Christopher S. Bond (Ranking Minority Member), Richard C. Shelby, Robert F. Bennett, Kay Bailey Hutchison, Sam Brownback, Lamar Alexander, Susan M. Collins, George V. Voinovich

ARMED SERVICES
Office: SR-228 20510-6050
Phone: 224-3871
Web: armed-services.senate.gov
Staff Director: Richard D. DeBobes
Minority Staff Director: Joseph W. Bowab 224-4928

Jurisdiction: (1) aeronautical and space activities peculiar to or primarily associated with the development of weapons systems or military operations; (2) common defense; (3) Department of Defense, the Department of the Army, the Department of the Navy, and the Department of the Air Force, generally; (4) military research and development; (5) national security aspects of nuclear energy; (6) naval petroleum reserves, except those in Alaska; (7) pay, promotion, retirement, and other benefits and privileges of members of the armed forces, including overseas education of civilian and military dependents; (8) Selective Service System; (9) strategic and critical materials necessary for the common defense. The committee shall also study and review, on a comprehensive basis, matters relating to the common defense policy of the United States.
Party Ratio: D 15-R 11

Carl Levin, Mich., Chair
Edward M. Kennedy, Mass.
Robert C. Byrd, W.Va.
Joseph I. Lieberman, Conn.
Jack Reed, R.I.
Daniel K. Akaka, Hawaii
Bill Nelson, Fla.
E. Benjamin Nelson, Neb.
Evan Bayh, Ind.
James H. Webb, Va.
Claire McCaskill, Mo.
Mark Udall, Colo.
Kay Hagan, N.C.
Mark Begich, Alaska.
Roland W. Burris, Ill.

John McCain, Ariz., Ranking Minority Member
James M. Inhofe, Okla.
Jeff Sessions, Ala.
Saxby Chambliss, Ga.
Lindsey O. Graham, S.C.
John Thune, S.D.
Mel Martinez, Fla.
Roger F. Wicker, Miss.
Richard M. Burr, N.C.
David Vitter, La.
Susan M. Collins, Maine

Subcommittees

Airland
Office: SR-228   Phone: 224-3871

Joseph I. Lieberman (Chair), Evan Bayh, James H. Webb, Claire McCaskill, Kay Hagan, Mark Begich, Roland W. Burris
John Thune (Ranking Minority Member), James M. Inhofe, Jeff Sessions, Saxby Chambliss, Richard M. Burr

Emerging Threats and Capabilities
Office: SR-228   Phone: 224-3871

Jack Reed (Chair), Edward M. Kennedy, Robert C. Byrd, Bill Nelson, E. Benjamin Nelson, Evan Bayh, Mark Udall
Roger F. Wicker (Ranking Minority Member), Lindsey O. Graham, Mel Martinez, Richard M. Burr, Susan M. Collins

Personnel
Office: SR-228   Phone: 224-3871

E. Benjamin Nelson (Chair), Edward M. Kennedy, Joseph I. Lieberman, Daniel K. Akaka, James H. Webb, Claire McCaskill, Kay Hagan, Mark Begich, Roland W. Burris
Lindsey O. Graham (Ranking Minority Member), Saxby Chambliss, John Thune, Mel Martinez, Roger F. Wicker, David Vitter, Susan M. Collins

Readiness and Management Support
Office: SR-228   Phone: 224-3871

Evan Bayh (Chair), Robert C. Byrd, Daniel K. Akaka, Claire McCaskill, Mark Udall, Roland W. Burris
Richard M. Burr (Ranking Minority Member), James M. Inhofe, Saxby Chambliss, John Thune

Seapower
Office: SR-228   Phone: 224-3871

Edward M. Kennedy (Chair), Joseph I. Lieberman, Jack Reed, Daniel K. Akaka, Bill Nelson, James H. Webb, Kay Hagan
Mel Martinez (Ranking Minority Member), Jeff Sessions, Roger F. Wicker, David Vitter, Susan M. Collins

Strategic Forces

Office: SR-228   **Phone:** 224-3871

Bill Nelson (Chair), Robert C. Byrd, Jack Reed, E. Benjamin Nelson, Mark Udall, Mark Begich

Jeff Sessions (Ranking Minority Member), James M. Inhofe, Lindsey O. Graham, David Vitter

BANKING, HOUSING, AND URBAN AFFAIRS

Office: SD-534 20510-6075
Phone: 224-7391
Fax: 224-5137
Web: banking.senate.gov
Staff Director (Acting): Colin P.J. McGinnis
Minority Staff Director: William D. Duhnke

Jurisdiction: (1) banks, banking, and financial institutions; (2) financial aid to commerce and industry; (3) deposit insurance; (4) public and private housing; (5) federal monetary policy (including the Federal Reserve System); (6) money and credit, including currency and coinage; (7) issuance and redemption of notes; (8) commodity price controls; (9) rent controls; (10) urban development and urban mass transit; (11) economic stabilization and defense production; (12) export controls; (13) export and foreign trade promotion; (14) nursing home construction; (15) renegotiation of government contracts. In addition, the committee is mandated to study and review all matters relating to international economic policy as it affects U.S. monetary affairs, credit, and financial institutions, economic growth, and urban affairs.
Party Ratio: D 13-R 10

Christopher J. Dodd, Conn., Chair	*Richard C. Shelby, Ala., Ranking Minority Member*
Tim Johnson, S.D.	
Jack Reed, R.I.	*Robert F. Bennett, Utah*
Charles E. Schumer, N.Y.	*Jim Bunning, Ky.*
Evan Bayh, Ind.	*Michael D. Crapo, Idaho*
Robert Menendez, N.J.	*Mel Martinez, Fla.*
Daniel K. Akaka, Hawaii	*Bob Corker, Tenn.*
Sherrod Brown, Ohio	*Jim DeMint, S.C.*
Jon Tester, Mont.	*David Vitter, La.*
Herb Kohl, Wisc.	*Mike Johanns, Neb.*
Mark Warner, Va.	*Kay Bailey Hutchison, Tex.*
Jeff Merkley, Ore.	
Michael F. Bennet, Colo.	

Subcommittees

Economic Policy

Office: SR-455   **Phone:** 224-2315

Sherrod Brown (Chair), Jon Tester, Jeff Merkley, Christopher J. Dodd
Jim DeMint

Financial Institutions

Office: SH-136   **Phone:** 224-5842

Tim Johnson (Chair), Jack Reed, Charles E. Schumer, Evan Bayh, Robert Menendez, Daniel K. Akaka, Jon Tester, Herb Kohl, Jeff Merkley, Michael F. Bennet
Michael D. Crapo (Ranking Minority Member), Robert F. Bennett, Kay Bailey Hutchison, Jim Bunning, Mel Martinez, Bob Corker, Jim DeMint

Housing, Transportation, and Community Development

Office: SH-317   **Phone:** 224-4744

Robert Menendez (Chair), Tim Johnson, Jack Reed, Charles E. Schumer, Daniel K. Akaka, Sherrod Brown, Jon Tester, Herb Kohl, Mark Warner, Jeff Merkley
David Vitter (Ranking Minority Member), Kay Bailey Hutchison, Robert F. Bennett, Mike Johanns, Michael D. Crapo, Mel Martinez, Jim DeMint

Securities, Insurance, and Investment

Office: SH-728   **Phone:** 224-4642

Jack Reed (Chair), Tim Johnson, Charles E. Schumer, Evan Bayh, Robert Menendez, Daniel K. Akaka, Sherrod Brown, Mark Warner, Michael F. Bennet, Christopher J. Dodd
Jim Bunning (Ranking Minority Member), Mel Martinez, Robert F. Bennett, Michael D. Crapo, David Vitter, Mike Johanns, Bob Corker

Security and International Trade and Finance

Office: SR-131   **Phone:** 224-5623

Evan Bayh (Chair), Herb Kohl, Mark Warner, Michael F. Bennet, Christopher J. Dodd
Bob Corker (Ranking Minority Member), Mike Johanns

BUDGET

Office: SD-624 20510-6100
Phone: 224-0642
Fax: 228-2007
Web: budget.senate.gov
Staff Director: Mary A. Naylor 224-0862
Minority Staff Director: Cheryl J. Reidy 224-0856

Jurisdiction: *(1) all concurrent resolutions on the budget (as defined in Section 3 (a) (4) of the Congressional Budget Act of 1974) and all other matters required to be referred to that committee under Titles III and IV of that Act, and messages, petitions, memorials, and other matters relating thereto. (2) The committee shall have the duty (A) to report the matters required to be reported by it under Titles III and IV of the Congressional Budget and Impoundment Control Act of 1974; (B) to make continuing studies of the effect on budget outlays of relevant existing and proposed legislation and to report the results of such studies to the Senate on a recurring basis; (C) to request and evaluate continuing studies of tax expenditures, policies, and programs with direct budget outlays, and to report the results of such studies to the Senate on a recurring basis; and (D) to review, on a continuing basis, the conduct by the Congressional Budget Office of its functions and duties.*
Party Ratio: D 13-R 10
Kent Conrad, N.D., Chair

BUDGET (continued)

Patty Murray, Wash.	*Minority Member*
Ron Wyden, Ore.	*Charles E. Grassley, Iowa*
Russell D. Feingold, Wisc.	*Michael B. Enzi, Wyo.*
Robert C. Byrd, W.Va.	*Jeff Sessions, Ala.*
Bill Nelson, Fla.	*Jim Bunning, Ky.*
Debbie Stabenow, Mich.	*Michael D. Crapo, Idaho*
Robert Menendez, N.J.	*John Ensign, Nev.*
Benjamin L. Cardin, Md.	*John Cornyn, Tex.*
Bernard Sanders, Vt.	*Lindsey O. Graham, S.C.*
Sheldon Whitehouse, R.I.	*Lamar Alexander, Tenn.*
Mark Warner, Va.	
Jeff Merkley, Ore.	
Judd Gregg, N.H., Ranking	

COMMERCE, SCIENCE, AND TRANSPORTATION

Office: SR-254 20510-6125
Phone: 224-0411   **Fax:** 228-0303
Web: commerce.senate.gov
Staff Director: Ellen Doneski 224-0411
Minority Staff Director: Christine Kurth 224-1251
   SD-560
   Jurisdiction: (1) United States Coast Guard (Homeland Security); (2) coastal zone management; (3) communications; (4) highway safety; (5) inland waterways, except construction; (6) interstate commerce; (7) marine and ocean navigation, marine and ocean safety, and marine and ocean transportation, including navigational aspects of deepwater ports; (8) marine fisheries; (9) United States Merchant Marine and navigation; (10) non-military aeronautical and space sciences; (11) oceans, weather, and atmospheric activities; (12) Panama Canal and interoceanic canals generally, except as provided in subparagraph (c); (13) regulation of consumer products and services, including testing related to toxic substances, other than pesticides, and except for credit, financial services, and housing; (14) regulation of interstate common carriers, including railroads, buses, trucks, vessels, pipelines, and civil aviation; (15) science research, development, and policy, engineering research, development, and policy, and technology research, development, and policy; (16) sports; (17) standards and measurement; (18) transportation; (19) transportation and commerce aspects of Outer Continental Shelf land. The committee shall also study and review, on a comprehensive basis, all matters relating to science and technology, oceans policy, transportation, communications, and consumer affairs.
Party Ratio: D 14-R 11

John D. Rockefeller, W.Va., Chair	*Kay Bailey Hutchison, Tex., Vice Chair and Ranking Minority Member*
Daniel K. Inouye, Hawaii	*Olympia J. Snowe, Maine*
John F. Kerry, Mass.	*John Ensign, Nev.*
Byron L. Dorgan, N.D.	*Jim DeMint, S.C.*
Barbara Boxer, Calif.	*John Thune, S.D.*
Bill Nelson, Fla.	

Maria Cantwell, Wash.	*Roger F. Wicker, Miss.*
Frank R. Lautenberg, N.J.	*Johnny Isakson, Ga.*
Mark Pryor, Ark.	*David Vitter, La.*
Claire McCaskill, Mo.	*Sam Brownback, Kans.*
Amy Klobuchar, Minn.	*Mel Martinez, Fla.*
Tom Udall, N.M.	*Mike Johanns, Neb.*
Mark Warner, Va.	
Mark Begich, Alaska	

Subcommittees

Aviation Operations, Safety, and Security
Office: SH-427   **Phone:** 224-9000
   Byron L. Dorgan (Chair), Daniel K. Inouye, John F. Kerry, Barbara Boxer, Bill Nelson, Maria Cantwell, Frank R. Lautenberg, Mark Pryor, Claire McCaskill, Amy Klobuchar, Mark Warner, Mark Begich
   Jim DeMint (Ranking Minority Member), Olympia J. Snowe, John Ensign, John Thune, Roger F. Wicker, Johnny Isakson, David Vitter, Sam Brownback, Mel Martinez, Mike Johanns

Communications, Technology, and the Internet
Office: SH-427   **Phone:** 224-0415
   John F. Kerry (Chair), Daniel K. Inouye, Byron L. Dorgan, Bill Nelson, Maria Cantwell, Frank R. Lautenberg, Mark Pryor, Claire McCaskill, Amy Klobuchar, Tom Udall, Mark Warner, Mark Begich
   John Ensign (Ranking Minority Member), Olympia J. Snowe, Jim DeMint, John Thune, Roger F. Wicker, Johnny Isakson, David Vitter, Sam Brownback, Mel Martinez, Mike Johanns

Competitiveness, Innovation, and Export Promotion
Office: SH-428   **Phone:** 224-1270
   Amy Klobuchar (Chair), John F. Kerry, Byron L. Dorgan, Claire McCaskill, Tom Udall, Mark Warner, Mark Begich
   Mel Martinez (Ranking Minority Member), John Ensign, Jim DeMint, John Thune, Sam Brownback, Mike Johanns

Consumer Protection, Product Safety, and Insurance
Office: SH-428 **Phone:** 224-1270
   Mark Pryor (Chair), Byron L. Dorgan, Barbara Boxer, Bill Nelson, Claire McCaskill, Amy Klobuchar, Tom Udall
   Roger F. Wicker (Ranking Minority Member), Olympia J. Snowe, Jim DeMint, John Thune, Johnny Isakson, David Vitter

Oceans, Atmosphere, Fisheries, and Coast Guard
Office: SD-425   **Phone:** 224-4912
   Maria Cantwell (Chair), Daniel K. Inouye, John F. Kerry, Barbara Boxer, Frank R. Lautenberg, Mark Begich
   Olympia J. Snowe (Ranking Minority Member), Roger F. Wicker, Johnny Isakson, David Vitter, Mel Martinez

Science and Space
Office: SH-427   **Phone:** 224-0415
   Bill Nelson (Chair), Daniel K. Inouye, John F. Kerry, Barbara Boxer, Mark Pryor, Tom Udall, Mark Warner
   David Vitter (Ranking Minority Member), Olympia J. Snowe, John Ensign, John Thune, Johnny Isakson, Mike Johanns

Surface Transportation and Merchant Marine Infrastructure, Safety, and Security
Office: SH-427   **Phone:** 224-9000

Frank R. Lautenberg (Chair), Daniel K. Inouye, John F. Kerry, Byron L. Dorgan, Barbara Boxer, Maria Cantwell, Mark Pryor, Tom Udall, Mark Warner, Mark Begich

John Thune (Ranking Minority Member), Olympia J. Snowe, John Ensign, Jim DeMint, Roger F. Wicker, Johnny Isakson, David Vitter, Sam Brownback, Mike Johanns

ENERGY AND NATURAL RESOURCES

Office: SD-304 20510-6150
Phone: 224-4971
Fax: 224-6163
Web: energy.senate.gov/public/
Staff Director: Robert M. Simon
Minority Staff Director: McKie Campbell

Jurisdiction: (1) coal production, distribution, and utilization; (2) energy policy; (3) energy regulation and energy conservation; (4) energy related aspects of deepwater ports; (5) energy research and development; (6) extraction of minerals from oceans and Outer Continental Shelf lands; (7) hydroelectric power, irrigation, and reclamation; (8) mining education and research; (9) mining, mineral lands, mining claims, and mineral conservation; (10) national parks, recreation areas, wilderness areas, wild and scenic rivers, historic sites, military parks and battlefields, and on the public domain, preservation of prehistoric ruins and objects of interest; (11) naval petroleum reserves in Alaska; (12) non-military development of nuclear energy; (13) oil and gas production and distribution; (14) public lands and forests, including farming and grazing thereon, and mineral extraction therefrom; (15) solar energy systems; (16) territorial possessions of the United States, including trusteeships; international energy affairs and emergency preparedness; nuclear waste policy; privatization of federal assets; Trans-Alaska Pipeline System and other oil or gas pipeline transportation systems within Alaska; Alaska Native Claims Settlement Act of 1971; Alaska National Interest Lands Conservation Act of 1980; Antarctic research and energy development; Arctic research and energy development; Native Hawaiian matters. The Committee shall also study and review, on a comprehensive basis, matters relating to energy and resources development.
Party Ratio: D 13-R 10

Jeff Bingaman, N.M., Chair
Byron L. Dorgan, N.D.
Ron Wyden, Ore.
Tim Johnson, S.D.
Mary L. Landrieu, La.
Maria Cantwell, Wash.
Robert Menendez, N.J.
Blanche L. Lincoln, Ark.
Bernard Sanders, Vt.
Evan Bayh, Ind.
Debbie Stabenow, Mich.
Mark Udall, Colo.

John McCain, Ariz.
Robert F. Bennett, Utah
Jim Bunning, Ky.
Jeff Sessions, Ala.
Bob Corker, Tenn.

Jeanne Shaheen, N.H.
Lisa Murkowski, Alaska, Ranking Minority Member
Richard M. Burr, N.C.
John Barrasso. Wyo.
Sam Brownback, Kans.
James E. Risch, Idaho

Subcommittees

Energy
Office: SD-304   **Phone:** 224-4971

Maria Cantwell (Chair), Byron L. Dorgan, Ron Wyden, Mary L. Landrieu, Robert Menendez, Bernard Sanders, Evan Bayh, Debbie Stabenow, Mark Udall, Jeanne Shaheen

James E. Risch (Ranking Minority Member), Richard M. Burr, John Barrasso, Sam Brownback, Robert F. Bennett, Jim Bunning, Jeff Sessions, Bob Corker

National Parks
Office: SD-304   **Phone:** 224-4971

Mark Udall (Chair), Byron L. Dorgan, Mary L. Landrieu, Robert Menendez, Blanche L. Lincoln, Bernard Sanders, Evan Bayh, Debbie Stabenow

Richard M. Burr (Ranking Minority Member), John Barrasso, Sam Brownback, John McCain, Jim Bunning, Bob Corker

Public Lands and Forests
Office: SD-304   **Phone:** 224-4971

Ron Wyden (Chair), Tim Johnson, Mary L. Landrieu, Maria Cantwell, Robert Menendez, Blanche L. Lincoln, Mark Udall, Jeanne Shaheen

John Barrasso (Ranking Minority Member), James E. Risch, John McCain, Robert F. Bennett, Jeff Sessions, Bob Corker

Water and Power
Office: SD-304   **Phone:** 224-4971

Tim Johnson (Chair), Byron L. Dorgan, Ron Wyden, Maria Cantwell, Ken Salazar, Blanche L. Lincoln, Jon Tester

Debbie Stabenow (Ranking Minority Member), Byron L. Dorgan, Tim Johnson, Maria Cantwell, Blanche L. Lincoln, Bernard Sanders, Evan Bayh, Jeanne Shaheen

ENVIRONMENT AND PUBLIC WORKS

Office: SD-410 20510-6175
Phone: 224-8832
Web: epw.senate.gov/public
Staff Director: Bettina Poirier
Minority Staff Director: Ruth H. Van Mark 224-6176 SD-415

Jurisdiction: (1) air pollution; (2) construction and maintenance of highways; (3) environmental aspects of Outer Continental Shelf lands; (4) environmental effects of toxic substances, other than pesticides; (5) environmental policy; (6) environmental research and development; (7) fisheries and wildlife; (8) flood

ENVIRONMENT AND PUBLIC WORKS (continued)

control and improvements of rivers and harbors, including environmental aspects of deepwater ports; (9) noise pollution; (10) non-military environmental regulation and control of nuclear energy; (11) ocean dumping; (12) public buildings and improved grounds of the United States generally, including Federal buildings in the District of Columbia; (13) public works, bridges, and dams; (14) regional economic development; (15) solid waste disposal and recycling; (16) water pollution; (17) water resources. The committee shall also study and review, on a comprehensive basis, matters relating to environmental protection and resource utilization and conservation.

Party Ratio: D 12–R 7

Barbara Boxer, Calif., Chair
Max S. Baucus, Mont.
Thomas R. Carper, Del.
Frank R. Lautenberg, N.J.
Benjamin L. Cardin, Md.
Bernard Sanders, Vt.
Amy Klobuchar, Minn.
Sheldon Whitehouse, R.I.
Tom Udall, N.M.
Jeff Merkley, Ore.
Kirsten Gillibrand, N.Y.
Arlen Specter, Pa.

James M. Inhofe, Okla.,
  Ranking Minority
  Member
George V. Voinovich, Ohio
David Vitter, La.
John Barrasso, Wyo.
Michael D. Crapo, Idaho
Christopher S. Bond, Mo.
Lamar Alexander, Tenn.

Subcommittees

Children's Health
Office: SD-410   **Phone:** 224-8832
  Amy Klobuchar (Chair), Tom Udall, Jeff Merkley
  Lamar Alexander (Ranking Minority Member),

Clean Air and Nuclear Safety
Office: SD-410   **Phone:** 224-8832
  Thomas R. Carper (Chair), Max S. Baucus, Benjamin L. Cardin, Bernard Sanders, Jeff Merkley
  David Vitter (Ranking Minority Member), George V. Voinovich, Christopher S. Bond

Green Jobs and the New Economy
Office: SD-410   **Phone:** 224-8832
  Bernard Sanders (Chair), Thomas R. Carper, Kirsten Gillibrand
  Christopher S. Bond (Ranking Minority Member), George V. Voinovich

Oversight
Office: SD-410   **Phone:** 224-8832
  Sheldon Whitehouse (Chair), Tom Udall, Kirsten Gillibrand
  John Barrasso (Ranking Minority Member), David Vitter

Transportation and Infrastructure
Office: SD-410   **Phone:** 224-8832
  Max S. Baucus (Chair), Thomas R. Carper,

Frank Lautenberg, Benjamin L. Cardin, Bernard Sanders, Amy Klobuchar
  George V. Voinovich (Ranking Minority Member), David Vitter, John Barrasso

Water and Wildlife
Office: SD-410   **Phone:** 224-8832
  Benjamin L. Cardin (Chair), Frank Lautenberg, Sheldon Whitehouse, Tom Udall, Jeff Merkley
  Michael D. Crapo (Ranking Minority Member), John Barrasso, Lamar Alexander

FINANCE

Office: SD-219 20510-6200
Phone: 224-4515
Web: finance.senate.gov
Staff Director: Russell W. Sullivan
Minority Staff Director: Kolan L. Davis
  Jurisdiction: (1) bonded debt of the United States, except as provided in the Congressional Budget and Impoundment Control Act of 1974; (2) customs, collection districts, and ports of entry and delivery; (3) deposit of public moneys; (4) general revenue sharing; (5) health programs under the Social Security Act and health programs financed by a specific tax or trust fund; (6) Social Security; (7) reciprocal trade agreements; (8) revenue measures generally, except as provided in the Congressional Budget and Impoundment Control Act of 1974; (9) revenue measures relating to the insular possessions; (10) tariffs and import quotas, and matters related thereto; (11) transportation of dutiable goods.
Party Ratio: D 13–R 10

Max S. Baucus, Mont.,
  Chair
John D. Rockefeller, W.Va.
Kent Conrad, N.D.
Jeff Bingaman, N.M.
John F. Kerry, Mass.
Blanche L. Lincoln, Ark.
Ron Wyden, Ore.
Charles E. Schumer, N.Y.
Debbie Stabenow, Mich.
Maria Cantwell, Wash.
Bill Nelson, Fla.
Robert Menendez, N.J.
Thomas R. Carper, Del.

Charles E. Grassley, Iowa,
  Ranking Minority
  Member
Orrin G. Hatch, Utah
Olympia J. Snowe, Maine
Jon Kyl, Ariz.
Jim Bunning, Ky.
Michael D. Crapo, Idaho
Pat Roberts, Kans.
John Ensign, Nev.
Michael B. Enzi, Wyo.
John Cornyn, Tex.

Subcommittees

Energy, Natural Resources and Infrastructure
Office: SD-219   **Phone:** 224-4515
  Jeff Bingaman (Chair), Kent Conrad, John F. Kerry, Blanche Lincoln, Debbie Stabenow, Maria Cantwell, Bill Nelson, Thomas R. Carper

Jim Bunning, Michael D. Crapo, John Cornyn, Orrin G. Hatch, Michael B. Enzi

Health Care
Office: SD-219   Phone: 224-4515

John D. Rockefeller (Chair), Jeff Bingaman, John F. Kerry, Blanche L. Lincoln, Ron Wyden, Debbie Stabenow, Maria Cantwell, Bill Nelson, Robert Menendez, Thomas R. Carper
 Orrin G. Hatch (Ranking Minority Member), Olympia J. Snowe, John Ensign, Michael B. Enzi, John Cornyn, Jon Kyl, Jim Bunning, Michael D. Crapo

International Trade, Customs, and Global Competitiveness
Office: SD-219   Phone: 224-4515

Ron Wyden (Chair), John D. Rockefeller, Jeff Bingaman, John F. Kerry, Debbie Stabenow, Maria Cantwell, Robert Menendez
 Michael D. Crapo (Ranking Minority Member), Olympia J. Snowe, Jim Bunning, Pat Roberts

Social Security, Pensions, and Family Policy
Office: SD-219   Phone: 224-4515

Blanche L. Lincoln (Chair), John D. Rockefeller, Kent Conrad, Charles E. Schumer, Bill Nelson
 Pat Roberts (Ranking Minority Member), Jon Kyl, John Ensign

Taxation, IRS Oversight, and Long-Term Growth
Office: SD-219   Phone: 224-4515

Kent Conrad (Chair), Max S. Baucus, John D. Rockefeller IV, Ron Wyden, Charles E. Schumer, Debbie Stabenow, Maria Cantwell, Robert Menendez, Thomas R. Carper
 Jon Kyl (Ranking Minority Member), Orrin G. Hatch, Olympia J. Snowe, Pat Roberts, John Ensign, Michael B. Enzi, John Cornyn

FOREIGN RELATIONS

Office: SD-446 20510-6225
Phone: 224-4651
Web: foreign.senate.gov
Staff Director: David McKean
Minority Staff Director: Kenneth A. Myers Jr. 224-6797 SD-450
 Jurisdiction: (1) acquisition of land and buildings for embassies and legations in foreign countries; (2) boundaries of the United States; (3) diplomatic service; (4) foreign economic, military, technical, and humanitarian assistance; (5) foreign loans; (6) international activities of the American National Red Cross, the International Committee of the Red Cross, and the International Federation of Red Cross and Red Crescent Societies; (7) international aspects of nuclear energy, including nuclear transfer policy; (8) international conferences and congresses; (9) international law as it relates to foreign policy; (10) International Monetary Fund and other international organizations established primarily for

international monetary purposes (except that, at the request of the Committee on Banking, Housing, and Urban Affairs, any proposed legislation relating to such subjects reported by the Committee on Foreign Relations shall be referred to the Committee on Banking, Housing, and Urban Affairs); (11) intervention abroad and declarations of war; (12) measures to foster commercial intercourse with foreign nations and to safeguard United States business interests abroad; (13) national security and international aspects of trusteeships of the United States; (14) oceans and international environmental and scientific affairs as they relate to foreign policy; (15) protection of United States citizens abroad and expatriation; (16) relations of the United States with foreign nations generally; (17) treaties, conventions, and international agreements, and executive agreements, except reciprocal trade agreements; (18) the United Nations and its affiliated organizations; (19) World Bank group, the regional development banks, and other international organizations established primarily for development assistance purposes. The committee shall also study and review, on a comprehensive basis, matters relating to national security policy, foreign policy, and international economic policy as they relate to the foreign policy of the United States, and matters relating to food, hunger and nutrition in foreign countries.
Party Ratio: D 11-R 8

John F. Kerry, Mass., Chair	Richard G. Lugar, Ind., Ranking Minority Member
Christopher J. Dodd, Conn.	
Russell D. Feingold, Wisc.	Bob Corker, Tenn.
Barbara Boxer, Calif.	Johnny Isakson, Ga.
Robert Menendez, N.J.	James E. Risch, Idaho
Benjamin L. Cardin, Md.	Jim DeMint, S.C.
Robert P. Casey, Pa.	John Barrasso, Wyo.
James H. Webb, Va.	Roger F. Wicker, Miss.
Jeanne Shaheen, N.H.	Vacancy
Ted Kaufman, Del.	
Kirsten Gillibrand, N.Y.	

Subcommittees

African Affairs
Office: SD-439   Phone: 224-4651

Russell D. Feingold (Chair), Benjamin L. Cardin, James H. Webb, Ted Kaufman, Jeanne Shaheen
 Johnny Isakson (Ranking Minority Member), Jim DeMint, Bob Corker, James E. Risch

East Asian and Pacific Affairs
Office: SD-439   Phone: 224-4651

James H. Webb (Chair), Christopher J. Dodd, Russell D. Feingold, Barbara Boxer, Robert P. Casey, Kirsten Gillibrand
 Lisa Murkowski (Ranking Minority Member), John Barrasso, Roger F. Wicker, Vacancy

European Affairs
Office: SD-439   Phone: 224-4651

FOREIGN RELATIONS (continued)

Jeanne Shaheen (Chair), Christopher J. Dodd, Robert Menendez, Robert P. Casey, James H. Webb, Ted Kaufman
Jim DeMint (Ranking Minority Member), James E. Risch, Bob Corker, Roger F. Wicker

International Development and Foreign Assistance, Economic Affairs, and International Environmental Protection
Office: SD-439   **Phone:** 224-4651

Robert Menendez (Chair), Barbara Boxer, Benjamin L. Cardin, Robert P. Casey, Jeanne Shaheen, Kirsten Gillibrand
Bob Corker (Ranking Minority Member), Roger F. Wicker, Jim DeMint, Vacancy

International Operations and Organizations, Human Rights, Democracy, and Global Women's Issues
Office: SD-439   **Phone:** 224-4651

Barbara Boxer (Chair), Russell D. Feingold, Robert Menendez, Ted Kaufman, Jeanne Shaheen, Kirsten Gillibrand
Roger F. Wicker (Ranking Minority Member), Jim DeMint, John Barrasso, Vacancy

Near Eastern and South and Central Asian Affairs
Office: SD-439   **Phone:** 224-4651

Robert P. Casey (Chair), Christopher J. Dodd, Russell D. Feingold, Barbara Boxer, Benjamin L. Cardin, Ted Kaufman
James E. Risch (Ranking Minority Member), Bob Corker, John Barrasso, Johnny Isakson

Western Hemisphere, Peace Corps, and Global Narcotics Affairs
Office: SD-439   **Phone:** 224-4651

Christopher J. Dodd (Chair), Robert Menendez, James H. Webb, Benjamin L. Cardin, Kirsten Gillibrand
John Barrasso (Ranking Minority Member), Johnny Isakson, James E. Risch, Vacancy

HEALTH, EDUCATION, LABOR, AND PENSIONS

Office: SD-644 20510-6300
Phone: 224-5375
Web: help.senate.gov
E-mail: help_comments@help.senate.gov
Chief of Staff: J. Michael Myers
Minority Staff Director: Frank J. Macchiarola 224-6770
   SH-835
   Jurisdiction: (1) measures relating to education, labor, health, and public welfare; (2) aging; (3) agricultural colleges; (4) arts and humanities; (5) biomedical research and development, including cloning and stem cell research; (6) dietary supplements and non-prescription drugs; (7) Project Bioshield initiative (funding for research and production of vaccines against smallpox, anthrax and

botulism toxin); (8) managed care; (9) medical privacy regulation; (10) patients' rights; (11) child labor; (12) convict labor and the entry of goods made by convicts into interstate commerce; (13) domestic activities of the American National Red Cross; (14) equal employment opportunity; (15) Gallaudet University (Washington, D.C.), Howard University (Washington, D.C.), and St. Elizabeths Hospital (Washington, D.C.); (16) handicapped individuals; (17) labor standards and labor statistics; (18) mediation and arbitration of labor disputes; (19) occupational safety and health, including the welfare of miners; (20) private pension plans; (21) public health; (22) railway labor and railway retirement; (23) regulation of foreign laborers; (24) student loans; (25) wages and hours of labor. The committee shall also study and review, on a comprehensive basis, matters relating to health, education, and training, and public welfare.
Party Ratio: D 13-R 10

Edward M. Kennedy, Mass., Chair	*Michael B. Enzi, Wyo., Ranking Minority Member*
Christopher J. Dodd, Conn.	*Judd Gregg, N.H.*
Tom Harkin, Iowa	*Lamar Alexander, Tenn.*
Barbara A. Mikulski, Md.	*Richard M. Burr, N.C.*
Jeff Bingaman, N.M.	*Johnny Isakson, Ga.*
Patty Murray, Wash.	*John McCain, Ariz.*
Jack Reed, R.I.	*Orrin G. Hatch, Utah*
Bernard Sanders, Vt.	*Lisa Murkowski, Alaska*
Sherrod Brown, Ohio	*Tom Coburn, Okla.*
Robert P. Casey, Pa.	*Pat Roberts, Kans.*
Kay Hagan, N.C.	
Jeff Merkley, Ore.	
Vacancy	

Subcommittees

Children and Families
Office: SH-404B   **Phone:** 224-5630

Christopher J. Dodd (Chair), Jeff Bingaman, Patty Murray, Jack Reed, Bernard Sanders, Vacancy, Vacancy
Lamar Alexander (Ranking Minority Member), Judd Gregg, Lisa Murkowski, Orrin G. Hatch, Pat Roberts, Vacancy

Employment and Workplace Safety
Office: SH-113   **Phone:** 224-2621

Patty Murray (Chair), Christopher J. Dodd, Tom Harkin, Barbara A. Mikulski, Sherrod Brown, Vacancy, Vacancy
Johnny Isakson (Ranking Minority Member), Richard M. Burr, Lisa Murkowski, Pat Roberts, Tom Coburn, Vacancy

Retirement and Aging
Office: SD-424   **Phone:** 224-9243

Barbara A. Mikulski (Chair), Tom Harkin, Jeff Bingaman, Jack Reed, Bernard Sanders, Sherrod Brown
Richard M. Burr (Ranking Minority Member), Judd Gregg, Lamar Alexander, Johnny Isakson, Orrin G. Hatch

HOMELAND SECURITY AND GOVERNMENTAL AFFAIRS

Office: SD-340 20510-6300
Phone: 224-2627   **Fax:** 224-4469
Web: hsgac.senate.gov
Staff Director: Michael L. Alexander
Minority Staff Director: Brandon L. Milhorn 224-4751 SD-344

Jurisdiction: (1) Department of Homeland Security, except matters relating to: the Coast Guard, the Transportation Security Administration, the Federal Law Enforcement Training Center, or the Secret Service; and the United States Citizenship and Immigration Service; or the immigration functions of the United States Customs and Border Protection or the United States Immigration and Custom Enforcement or the Directorate of Border and Transportation Security; and the following functions performed by any employee of the Department of Homeland Security: any customs revenue function, including any function provided for in Section 415 of the Homeland Security Act of 2002; any commercial function or commercial operation of the Bureau of Customs and Border Protection or Bureau of Immigration and Customs Enforcement, including matters relating to trade facilitation and trade regulation; or any other function related to the above items that was exercised by the United States Customs Service on the day before the effective date of the Homeland Security Act of 2002; (2) archives of the United States; (3) budget and accounting measures, other than appropriations, except as provided in the Congressional Budget and Impoundment Control Act of 1974; (4) census and collection of statistics, including economic and social statistics; (5) congressional organization, except for any part of the matter that amends the rules or orders of the Senate; (6) federal civil service; (7) government information; (8) intergovernmental relations; (9) municipal affairs of the District of Columbia, except appropriations therefor; (10) organization and management of United States nuclear export policy; (11) organization and reorganization of the executive branch of the Government; (12) United States Postal Service; (13) status of officers and employees of the United States, including their classification, compensation, and benefits. The committee shall have the duty of (A) receiving and examining reports of the Comptroller General of the United States and of submitting such recommendations to the Senate as it deems necessary or desirable in connection with the subject matter of such reports; (B) studying the efficiency, economy, and effectiveness of all agencies and departments of the Government; (C) evaluating laws enacted to effect the reorganization of the legislative and executive branches of the Government; and (D) studying the intergovernmental relationships between the United States and the states and municipalities, and between the United States and international organizations of which the United States is a member.

Party Ratio: D 10-R 7

Joseph I. Lieberman, Conn., Chair
Carl Levin, Mich.
Daniel K. Akaka, Hawaii
Thomas R. Carper, Del.
Mark Pryor, Ark.
Mary L. Landrieu, La.
Claire McCaskill, Mo.
Jon Tester, Mont.
Roland W. Burris, Ill.
Michael F. Bennet, Colo.

Susan M. Collins, Maine, Ranking Minority Member
Tom Coburn, Okla.
John McCain, Ariz.
George V. Voinovich, Ohio
John Ensign, Nev.
Lindsey O. Graham, S.C.
Vacancy

Subcommittees

Permanent Investigations
Office: SR-199   **Phone:** 224-9505

Carl Levin (Chair), Thomas R. Carper, Mark Pryor, Claire McCaskill, Jon Tester, Michael F. Bennet
Tom Coburn (Ranking Minority Member), Susan M. Collins, John McCain, John Ensign

Contracting Oversight

Claire McCaskill, Carl Levin, Thomas R. Carper, Mark Pryor, Jon Tester
Susan M. Collins, Tom Coburn, John McCain

Disaster Recovery
Office: SH-605   **Phone:** 224-2627

Mary L. Landrieu (Chair), Claire McCaskill, Roland W. Burris
Lindsey O. Graham

Federal Financial Management, Government Information, and International Security
Office: SH-432   **Phone:** 224-4551

Thomas R. Carper (Chair), Carl Levin, Daniel K. Akaka, Mark Pryor, Claire McCaskill, Roland W. Burris
John McCain (Ranking Minority Member), Tom Coburn, George V. Voinovich, John Ensign

Oversight of Government Management, the Federal Workforce, and the District of Columbia
Office: SH-605   **Phone:** 224-5538

Daniel K. Akaka (Chair), Carl Levin, Mary L. Landrieu, Roland W. Burris, Michael F. Bennet
George V. Voinovich (Ranking Minority Member), Lindsey O. Graham

State, Local, and Private Sector Preparedness and Integration
Office: SH-613   **Phone:** 224-2627

Mark Pryor (Chair), Daniel K. Akaka, Mary L. Landrieu, Jon Tester, Michael F. Bennet
John Ensign (Ranking Minority Member), George V. Voinovich, Lindsey O. Graham

INDIAN AFFAIRS

Office: SH-838 20510-6450
Phone: 224-2251
Web: indian.senate.gov
Staff Director: Allison Binney
Minority Staff Director: David Mullon Jr.

Jurisdiction: (1) all proposed legislation, messages, petitions, memorials, and other matters relating to Indian affairs shall be referred to the committee; (2) study any and all matters pertaining to problems and opportunities of Indians, including but not limited to, Indian land management and trust responsibilities, Indian education, Indian health, special services, and Indian loan programs, the National Indian Gaming Regulatory Act of 1988, the National Indian Gaming Commission, and Indian claims against the United States.

Party Ratio: D 9-R 6

Byron L. Dorgan, N.D., Chair
Daniel K. Inouye, Hawaii
Kent Conrad, N.D.
Daniel K. Akaka, Hawaii
Tim Johnson, S.D.
Maria Cantwell, Wash.
Jon Tester, Mont.
Tom Udall, N.M.
Vacancy

John Barrasso, Wyo., Vice Chair and Ranking Minority Member
John McCain, Ariz.
Lisa Murkowski, Alaska
Tom Coburn, Okla.
Michael D. Crapo, Idaho
Mike Johanns, Neb.

JUDICIARY

Office: SD-224 20510-6275
Phone: 224-7703   **Fax:** 224-9516
Web: judiciary.senate.gov
Staff Director: Bruce A. Cohen
Minority Staff Director: Stephanie Middleton 224-5225 SD-152

Jurisdiction: (1) apportionment of Representatives; (2) bankruptcy, mutiny, espionage, and counterfeiting; (3) civil liberties; (4) constitutional amendments; (5) federal courts and federal judges; (6) government information; (7) presidential succession; (8) continuity of congressional representation; (9) holidays and celebrations; (10) immigration and naturalization; (11) interstate compacts generally; (12) judicial proceedings, civil and criminal, generally; (13) local courts in United States territories and possessions; (14) measures relating to claims against the United States; (15) national penitentiaries; (16) United States Patent and Trademark Office (Commerce); (17) patents, copyrights, and trademarks; (18) protection of trade and commerce against unlawful restraints and monopolies; (19) revision and codification of the statutes of the United States; (20) state and territorial boundary lines.

Party Ratio: D 12-R 7

Patrick Leahy, Vt., Chair
Herb Kohl, Wisc.
Dianne Feinstein, Calif.
Russell D. Feingold, Wisc.
Charles E. Schumer, N.Y.
Richard J. Durbin, Ill.
Benjamin L. Cardin, Md.
Sheldon Whitehouse, R.I.
Ron Wyden, Ore.
Amy Klobuchar, Minn.
Ted Kaufman, Del.
Arlen Specter, Pa.

Jeff Sessions, Ala., Ranking Minority Member
Orrin G. Hatch, Utah
Charles E. Grassley, Iowa
Jon Kyl, Ariz.
Lindsey O. Graham, S.C.
John Cornyn, Tex.
Tom Coburn, Okla.

Subcommittees

Administrative Oversight and the Courts
Office: SD-161   **Phone:** 224-8352

Sheldon Whitehouse (Chair), Dianne Feinstein, Russell D. Feingold, Charles E. Schumer, Benjamin L. Cardin, Ted Kaufman
Jeff Sessions (Ranking Minority Member), Charles E. Grassley, Jon Kyl, Lindsey O. Graham

Antitrust, Competition Policy and Consumer Rights
Office: SH-308   **Phone:** 224-3406

Herb Kohl (Chair), Charles E. Schumer, Sheldon Whitehouse, Ron Wyden, Amy Klobuchar, Ted Kaufman
Orrin G. Hatch (Ranking Minority Member), Charles E. Grassley, John Cornyn

The Constitution
Office: SH-807   **Phone:** 224-5573

Russell D. Feingold (Chair), Dianne Feinstein, Richard J. Durbin, Benjamin L. Cardin, Sheldon Whitehouse, Ted Kaufman
Tom Coburn (Ranking Minority Member), Lindsey O. Graham, John Cornyn

Crime and Drugs
Office: SH-305   **Phone:** 224-0558

Arlen Specter (Chair), Herb Kohl, Richard J. Durbin Dianne Feinstein, Russell D. Feingold, Charles E. Schumer, Benjamin L. Cardin, Amy Klobuchar, Ted Kaufman
Lindsey O. Graham (Ranking Minority Member), Orrin G. Hatch, Charles E. Grassley, Jeff Sessions, Tom Coburn

Immigration, Refugees, and Border Security
Office: SD-520   **Phone:** 224-7878

Charles E. Schumer (Chair), Patrick Leahy, Dianne Feinstein, Richard J. Durbin, Sheldon Whitehouse, Ron Wyden
John Cornyn (Ranking Minority Member), Charles E. Grassley, Jon Kyl, Jeff Sessions

Terrorism and Homeland Security
Office: SH-815   **Phone:** 224-4933

Benjamin L. Cardin (Chair), Herb Kohl, Dianne Feinstein, Charles E. Schumer, Richard J. Durbin, Ron Wyden, Ted Kaufman
Jon Kyl (Ranking Minority Member), Orrin G. Hatch, Jeff Sessions, John Cornyn, Tom Coburn

RULES AND ADMINISTRATION

Office: SR-305 20510-6325
Phone: 224-6352
Web: rules.senate.gov
Staff Director: Jean Bordewich
Minority Staff Director: Mary Suit Jones SR-479

Jurisdiction: (1) administration of the Senate office buildings and the Senate wing of the United States Capitol, including the assignment of office space for Senators and Senate Committees; (2) Senate organization relative to rules and procedures, and Senate rules and regulations, including Senate floor rules and Senate gallery rules; (3) corrupt practices; (4) related provisions of the Bipartisan Campaign Reform Act of 2002 and the Lobbying Disclosure Act of 1995; campaign finance reform; lobbying; (5) credentials and qualifications of Members of the Senate, contested elections, and acceptance of incompatible offices; (6) federal elections generally, including the election of the President, Vice President, and Members of the Senate; (7) Government Printing Office, and the printing and correction of the Congressional Record, as well as those matters provided for under Rule XI; (8) meetings of the Congress and attendance of Members; (9) payment of money out of the contingent fund of the Senate or creating a charge upon the same (except that any resolution relating to substantive matter within the jurisdiction of any other standing committee of the Senate shall be first referred to such committee); (10) Presidential Succession Act of 1947; (11) purchase of books and manuscripts and erection of monuments to the memory of individuals; (12) Senate Library and statuary, art, and pictures in the United States Capitol and Senate office buildings; (13) services to the Senate, including the Senate restaurant; (14) measures relating to the travel of Members of the Senate; (15) United States Capitol and Senate office buildings, the Library of Congress, the Smithsonian Institution (and the incorporation of similar institutions), and the United States Botanic Garden. The committee shall also (A) make a continuing study of the organization and operation of the Congress of the United States and shall recommend improvements in such organization and operation with a view toward strengthening the Congress, simplifying its operations, improving its relationships with other branches of the United States Government, and enabling it better to meet its responsibilities under the Constitution of the United States; and (B) identify any court proceeding or action which, in the opinion of the Committee, is of vital interest to the Congress as a constitutionally established institution of the Federal Government and call such proceeding or action to the attention of the Senate.
Party Ratio: D 11-R 8

Charles E. Schumer, N.Y., Chair
Robert C. Byrd, W.Va.
Daniel K. Inouye, Hawaii
Christopher J. Dodd, Conn.
Dianne Feinstein, Calif.
Richard J. Durbin, Ill.
E. Benjamin Nelson, Neb.
Patty Murray, Wash.
Mark Pryor, Ark.
Tom Udall, N.M.
Mark Warner, Va.

Robert F. Bennett, Utah, Ranking Minority Member
Mitch McConnell, Ky.
Thad Cochran, Miss.
Kay Bailey Hutchison, Tex.
Saxby Chambliss, Ga.
Lamar Alexander, Tenn.
John Ensign, Nev.
Pat Roberts, Kans.

SELECT ETHICS

Office: SH-220 20510-6425
Phone: 224-2981
Fax: 224-7416
Web: ethics.senate.gov
Acting Staff Director: John C. Sassaman Jr.

Jurisdiction: (1) receive complaints and investigate allegations of improper conduct which may reflect upon the Senate, violations of law, violations of the Senate Code of Official Conduct, and violations of rules and regulations of the Senate, relating to the conduct of individuals in the performance of their duties as Members of the Senate, or as officers or employees of the Senate, and to make appropriate findings of fact and conclusions with respect thereto; (2) recommend, when appropriate, disciplinary action against Members and staff; (3) recommend rules or regulations necessary to insure appropriate Senate standards of conduct; (4) report violations of any law to the proper Federal and State authorities; (5) regulate the use of the franking privilege in the Senate; (6) investigate unauthorized disclosures of intelligence information; (7) implement the Senate public financial disclosure requirements of the Ethics in Government Act of 1978; (8) regulate the receipt and disposition of gifts from foreign governments received by Members, officers, and employees of the Senate; and (9) render advisory opinions on the application of Senate rules and laws to Members, officers, and employees.
Party Ratio: D 3-R 3

Barbara Boxer, Calif., Chair
Mark Pryor, Ark.
Sherrod Brown, Ohio

Johnny Isakson, Ga., Vice Chair and Ranking Minority Member
Pat Roberts, Kan.
James E. Risch, Idaho

SELECT INTELLIGENCE

Office: SH-211 20510-6475
Phone: 224-1700
Web: intelligence.senate.gov
Staff Director: David Grannis
Minority Staff Director: Louis B. Tucker
    Jurisdiction: (1) oversee and make continuing studies of the intelligence activities and programs of the United States Government, including, but not limited to, the Central Intelligence Agency Act of 1949, Classified Information Procedures Act of 1980, classified national security information, foreign intelligence electronic surveillance, Foreign Intelligence Surveillance Act of 1978, National Security Act of 1947, National Security Agency Act of 1959, national security information, President's Foreign Intelligence Advisory Board (Executive Office of the President), Provide Appropriate Tools Required to Intercept and Obstruct Terrorism (PATRIOT) Act of 2001, security requirements for government employment; (2) submit to the Senate appropriate proposals for legislation; (3) report to the Senate concerning such intelligence activities and programs.
Party Ratio: D 8-R 7

Dianne Feinstein, Calif., Chair	*Christopher S. Bond, Mo., Ranking Minority Member*
John D. Rockefeller IV, W.Va.	*Orrin G. Hatch, Utah*
Ron Wyden, Ore.	*Olympia J. Snowe, Maine*
Evan Bayh, Ind.	*Saxby Chambliss, Ga.*
Barbara A. Mikulski, Md.	*Richard M. Burr, N.C.*
Russell D. Feingold, Wisc.	*Tom Coburn, Okla.*
Bill Nelson, Fla.	*James E. Risch, Idaho*
Sheldon Whitehouse, R.I.	

SMALL BUSINESS AND ENTREPRENEURSHIP

Office: SR-436 20510-6350
Phone: 224-5175   **Fax:** 224-5619
Web: sbc.senate.gov
Staff Director: Donald R. (Don) Cravins Jr.
Minority Staff Director: Wallace K. Hsueh 224-7884 SR-442
    Jurisdiction: (1) all proposed legislation, messages, petitions, memorials and other matters relating to the Small Business Administration; (2) any proposed legislation reported by such committee which relates to matters other than the functions of the Small Business Administration shall, at the request of the chair of any standing committee having jurisdiction over the subject matter extraneous to the functions of the Small Business Administration, be considered and reported by such standing committee prior to its consideration by the Senate; and likewise measures reported by other committees directly relating to the Small Business Administration shall, at the request of the chair of the Committee on Small Business and Entrepreneurship, be referred to the Committee on Small Business and

Entrepreneurship for its consideration of any portions of the measure dealing with the Small Business Administration, and be reported by this Committee prior to its consideration by the Senate; (3) study and survey by means of research and investigation all problems of small business enterprises.
Party Ratio: D 11-R 8

Mary L. Landrieu, La., Chair	*Olympia J. Snowe, Maine, Ranking Minority Member*
John F. Kerry, Mass.	
Carl Levin, Mich.	
Tom Harkin, Iowa	*Christopher S. Bond, Mo.*
Joseph I. Lieberman, Conn.	*David Vitter, La.*
Maria Cantwell, Wash.	*John Thune, S.D.*
Evan Bayh, Ind.	*Michael B. Enzi, Wyo.*
Mark Pryor, Ark.	*Johnny Isakson, Ga.*
Benjamin L. Cardin, Md.	*Roger F. Wicker, Miss.*
Kay Hagan, N.C.	*Vacancy*
Jeanne Shaheen, N.H.	

SPECIAL AGING

Office: SD-G31 20510-6400
Phone: 224-5364   **Fax:** 224-8600
Web: aging.senate.gov
Staff Director: Debra Bailey Whitman
Minority Deputy Staff Director: Michael Bassett SH-628
    Jurisdiction: (1) conduct a continuing study of any and all matters pertaining to problems and opportunities of older people, including, but not limited to, assisted living, elder abuse, health care, identity theft, long-term care, Medicare, Older Americans Act, prescription drugs, retirement income security, retirement pensions, rural health care, Social Security, telemedicine, problems and opportunities of maintaining health, of assuring adequate income, of finding employment, of engaging in productive and rewarding activity, of securing proper housing, and when necessary, of obtaining care or assistance. No proposed legislation shall be referred to such committee, and such committee shall not have power to report by bill, or otherwise have legislative jurisdiction. (2) The special committee shall, from time to time (but not less often than once each year), report to the Senate the results of the study conducted pursuant to paragraph (1), together with such recommendation as it considers appropriate.
Party Ratio: D 13-R 8

Herb Kohl, Wis., Chair	*Mel Martinez, Fla., Ranking Minority Member*
Ron Wyden, Ore.	
Blanche L. Lincoln, Ark.	
Evan Bayh, Ind.	*Richard C. Shelby, Ala.*
Bill Nelson, Fla.	*Susan M. Collins, Maine*
Robert P. Casey, Pa.	*Bob Corker, Tenn.*
Claire McCaskill, Mo.	*Orrin G. Hatch, Utah*
Sheldon Whitehouse, R.I.	*Sam Brownback, Kans.*
Mark Udall, Colo.	*Lindsey O. Graham, S.C.*
Kirsten Gillibrand, N.Y.	*Vacancy*
Michael F. Bennet, Colo.	
Arlen Specter, Pa.	
Vacancy	

VETERANS' AFFAIRS

Office: SR-412 20510-6375
Phone: 224-9126 **Fax:** 224-9575
Web: veterans.senate.gov
Staff Director: William E. Brew
Minority Staff Director: Marie Guadalupe Wissel
224-2074 SH-825A

Jurisdiction: (1) compensation of veterans; (2) life insurance issued by the government on account of service in the Armed Forces; (3) national cemeteries; (4) pensions of all the wars of the United States; (5) readjustment of service personnel to civil life; (6) soldiers' and sailors' civil relief, including oversight of and appropriate modifications to the Soldiers' and Sailors' Civil Relief Act of 1940; (7) veterans' hospitals, medical care and treatment of veterans; (8) veterans' measures generally; (9) vocational rehabilitation and education of veterans.

Party Ratio: D 10-R 5

Daniel K. Akaka, Hawaii, Chair
John D. Rockefeller IV, W.Va.
Patty Murray, Wash.
Bernard Sanders, Vt.
Sherrod Brown, Ohio
James H. Webb, Va.
Jon Tester, Mont.
Mark Begich, Alaska
Roland W. Burris, Ill.
Arlen Specter, Pa.

Richard M. Burr, N.C.
Ranking Minority Member
Johnny Isakson, Ga.
Roger F. Wicker, Miss.
Mike Johanns, Neb.
Lindsey O. Graham, S.C.

SENATE LEADERSHIP AND PARTISAN COMMITTEES

DEMOCRATIC LEADERS

President Pro Tempore: Robert C. Byrd, W.Va.
Majority Floor Leader: Harry M. Reid, Nev.
Assistant Floor Leader: Richard J. Durbin, Ill.
Chief Deputy Whip: Barbara Boxer, Calif.

DEMOCRATIC PARTISAN COMMITTEES

Democratic Communications Center
Office: S-318 CAP 20510
Phone: 224-2939
Fax: 228-5576
Web: democrats.senate.gov
Harry Reid, Nev., Chair

Democratic Policy Committee
Office: SH-419 20510
Phone: 224-3232
Fax: 228-3432
Web: democrats.senate.gov/dpc
Byron L. Dorgan, N.D., Chair

Regional Chairs (in alphabetical order)
Evan Bayh, Ind.
Mary L. Landrieu, La.
Jack Reed, R.I.

Democratic Senatorial Campaign Committee
Office: 120 Maryland Ave. N.E. 20002-5610
Phone: 224-2447
Fax: 969-0354
Web: www.dscc.org
E-mail: info@dscc.org
Robert Menendez, N.J., Chair

Democratic Steering and Outreach Committee
Office: SH-712 20510
Phone: 224-9048
Fax: 224-5476
Web: democrats.senate.gov/steering
Debbie Stabenow, Mich., Chair

REPUBLICAN LEADERS

Minority Floor Leader: *Mitch McConnell, Ky.*
Minority Whip: *Jon Kyl, Ariz.*

REPUBLICAN PARTISAN COMMITTEES

National Republican Senatorial Committee
Office: 425 2nd St. N.E. 20002-4914
Phone: 675-6000
Fax: 675-4730
Web: www.nrsc.org
John Cornyn, Tex., Chair
Orrin G. Hatch, Utah, Vice Chair
Richard C. Shelby, Ala., National Finance Chair

Republican Conference
Office: SH-405 20510-7060
Phone: 224-2764
Fax: 224-6984
Web: src.senate.gov
Lamar Alexander, Tenn., Chair
John Thune, S.D., Vice Chair

Republican Policy Committee
Office: SR-347 20510-7064
Phone: 224-2946
Fax: 224-1235
Web: rpc.senate.gov
John Ensign, Nev., Chair

Senate Members' Offices

Listed below are Senate members and their party and state affiliation, followed by the address and telephone and fax numbers for their Washington office. (The area code for all Washington, D.C., numbers is 202.) A top administrative aide, a Web address, and an e-mail address for each senator are also provided, when available. (Most members may be contacted via the Web-based e-mail forms found on their Web sites.) These are followed by the address, telephone and fax numbers, and name of a key aide for the senator's district office(s). Each listing concludes with the senator's committee assignments. For partisan committee assignments, see page 818.

As of May 2009, there were 57 Democrats, 40 Republicans, and 2 Independents in the Senate, with one seat pending.

Akaka, Daniel K., D-Hawaii

Capitol Hill Office: SH-141 20510-1103; 224-6361; Fax: 224-2126; *Chief of Staff:* Joan M. Ohashi
Web: akaka.senate.gov
District Office(s): 101 Aupuni St., #213, Hilo 96720-4221; (808) 935-1114; Fax: (808) 935-9064; *Staff Assistant:* Kim Sasaki
Prince Kuhio Federal Bldg., 300 Ala Moana Blvd., #3-106, P.O. Box 50144, Honolulu 96850-4977; (808) 522-8970; Fax: (808) 545-4683; *State Director:* Michael Kitamura
Committee Assignment(s): Armed Services; Banking, Housing, and Urban Affairs; Homeland Security and Governmental Affairs; Indian Affairs; Veterans' Affairs

Alexander, Lamar, R-Tenn.

Capitol Hill Office: SD-455 20510-4206; 224-4944; Fax: 228-3398; *Chief of Staff:* David Morgenstern
Web: alexander.senate.gov
District Office(s): Tri-Cities Regional Airport, 2525 Hwy. 75, #101, P.O. Box 1113, Blountville 37617-6366; (423) 325-6240; **Fax:** (423) 325-6236; *Field Representative:* Lana Moore
Joel E. Solomon Federal Bldg., 900 Georgia Ave., #260, Chattanooga 37402-2240; (423) 752-5337; Fax: (423) 752-5342; *Field Representative:* Lyndsay Botts
Federal Bldg., 109 S. Highland St., #B-9, Jackson 38301-6149; (731) 423-9344; Fax: (731) 423-8918; *Field Representative:* Matt Varino
Howard H. Baker Jr. U.S. Courthouse, 800 Market St., #112, Knoxville 37902-2303; (865) 545-4253; Fax: (865) 545-4252; *State Director:* Patrick Jaynes
Federal Bldg., 167 N. Main St., #1068, Memphis 38103-1858; (901) 544-4224; Fax: (901) 544 4227; *Field Representative:* Josh Thomas
3322 West End Ave., #120, Nashville 37203-6821; (615) 736-5129; Fax: (615) 269-4803; *Field Representative:* Michael Schulz
Committee Assignment(s): Appropriations; Budget; Environment and Public Works; Health, Education, Labor, and Pensions; Rules and Administration

Barrasso, John, R-Wyo.

Capitol Hill Office: SD-307 20510-5005; 224-6441; Fax: 224-1724; *Chief of Staff:* Shawn R. Whitman
Web: barrasso.senate.gov
District Office(s): Ewing T. Kerr Federal Building, 111 S. Wolcott Street, #2201, Casper 82601-2534; (307) 261-6413; *Field Representative:* Kelsey Campbell
2120 Capitol Avenue, #2013, Cheyenne 82001-3631; (307) 772-2451; *State Director:* Kristi Wallin
325 W. Main Street, Suite F, Riverton 82501-3448; (307) 856-6642; *Field Representative:* Pam Buline
2632 Foothill Boulevard, #101, Rock Springs 82901-4757; (307) 362-5012; *Field Representative:* Sandy DaRif
40 North Main Street, #206, Sheridan 82801; (307) 672-6456; *Field Representative:* Kendall Hartman
Committee Assignment(s): Energy and Natural Resources; Environment and Public Works; Foreign Relations; Indian Affairs

Baucus, Max S., D-Mont.

Capitol Hill Office: SH-511 20510-2602; 224-2651; Fax: 224-0515; *Chief of Staff:* Jonathan G. Selib
Web: baucus.senate.gov
District Office(s): 222 N. 32nd St., #100, Billings 59101-1954; (406) 657-6790; Fax: (406) 657-6793; *State Director:* Melodee Hanes
Federal Bldg., 32 E. Babcock St., #114, Bozeman 59715-4737; (406) 586-6104; Fax: (406) 587-9177; *Field Director:* David W. Cobb
Silver Bow Center, 125 W. Granite St., #100, Butte 59701-9200; (406) 782-8700; Fax: (406) 782 6553; *Field Director:* Kim S. Krueger
113 3rd St. North, Great Falls 59401-2525; (406) 761-1574; *Field Representative:* Bonnie J. Keller
The Empire Block, 30 W. 14th St., #206, Helena 59601-3390; (406) 449-5480; Fax: (406) 449-5484; *Field Representative:* Jillian Morgan
8 Third St. East, Kalispell 59901-4573; (406) 756-1150; Fax: (406) 756-1152; *Field Director:* Kirby A. Campbell-Rierson
1821 South Ave. West, #203, Missoula 59801-6518; (406) 329-3123; Fax: (406) 728-7610; *Field Director:* Matthew J. Jones

Committee Assignment(s): Agriculture, Nutrition, and Forestry; Environment and Public Works; Finance; Congressional-Executive Commission on China; Joint Taxation

Bayh, Evan, D-Ind.

Capitol Hill Office: SR-131 20510-1404; 224-5623; Fax: 228-1377; *Chief of Staff:* Thomas O. Sugar
Web: bayh.senate.gov
District Office(s): Winfield K. Denton Federal Bldg., 1010 Martin Luther King Blvd., #110, Evansville 47708; (812) 465-6500; **Fax:** (812) 465-6503; *Regional Coordinator:* Sandi Stewart
Federal Bldg. and U.S. Courthouse, 1300 S. Harrison St., #3161, Fort Wayne 46802-3435; (219) 426-3151; Fax: (219) 420-0060; *Regional Director:* Brent Wake
Hammond Federal Courthouse, 5400 Federal Plaza, #3200, Hammond 46320-1855; (219) 852-2763; Fax: (219) 852-2787; *Regional Coordinator:* Cynthia Walker
Market Tower, 10 W. Market St., #1650, Indianapolis 46204-5928; (317) 554-0750; Fax: (317) 554-0760; *Regional Director:* Doran Moreland
Jeffersonville Federal Center, 1201 E. 10th St., #106, Jeffersonville 47130-4284; (812) 218-2317; Fax: (812) 218-2370; *Regional Director:* Andrew Homan
Leighton Plaza, 130 S. Main St., #110, South Bend 46601-1817; (574) 236-8302; Fax: (574) 236-8319; *Regional Director:* Julie Vuckovich
Committee Assignment(s): Armed Services; Banking, Housing, and Urban Affairs; Energy and Natural Resources; Small Business and Entrepreneurship; Select Intelligence; Special Aging

Begich, Mark, D-Alaska

Capitol Hill Office: 825C SH 20510-0204; 224-3004; Fax: 224-2354; *Chief of Staff:* David S. Ramseur
Web: begich.senate.gov
District Office(s): Federal Building, 222 W. 7th Avenue, Suite 569, Anchorage 99513-7500; (907) 271-5915; Fax: (907) 258-9305; *State Director:* Susanne Fleek
101 12th Avenue, Room 206, Fairbanks, 99701-6237, (907) 456-0261; Fax: (907) 451-7290; *Regional Director:* Tom Moyer
Committee Assignment(s): Armed Services; Commerce, Science, and Transportation; Veterans' Affairs

Bennet, Michael F., D-Colo.

Capitol Hill Office: 702 SH 20510-0608; 224-5852; *Chief of Staff:* Jeff Lane
Web: bennet.senate.gov
District Office(s): 609 Main Street, Suite 110, Alamosa 81101-2557; (719) 587-0096; Fax: (719) 587-0098; *Regional Rep:* Charlotte Bobicki
409 N. Tejon Street, Suite 107, Colorado Springs 80903-1163; (719) 328-1100; Fax: (719) 328-1129; *Regional Director:* Annie Oatman-Gardner

2300 15th Street, Suite 450, Denver 80202-1184; (303) 455-7600; Fax: (303) 455-8851; *State Director:* Rosemary E. Rodriguez
835 E. Second Avenue, Suite 203, Durango 81301-5475; (970) 259-1710
Committee Assignment(s): Agriculture, Nutrition, and Forestry; Banking, Housing, and Urban Affairs; Homeland Security and Governmental Affairs; Special Aging

Bennett, Robert F., R-Utah

Capitol Hill Office: SD-431 20510-4403; 224-5444; Fax: 228-1168; *Chief of Staff:* Mary Jane Collipriest
Web: bennett.senate.gov
District Office(s): 77 N. Main Street, Cedar City 84720-2648; (435) 865-1335; Fax: (435) 865-1481; *Southern Utah Area Coordinator:* Bryan Thiriot
324 25th St., #1410, Ogden 84401-2340; (801) 625-5676; Fax: (801) 625-5692; *Northern Utah Liaison:* Joan Hellstrom
51 S. University Ave., #310, Provo 84601-4491; (801) 379-2525; Fax: (801) 374-2938; *Central Utah Area Coordinator:* Donna Sackett
Federal Bldg., 125 S. State St., #4225, Salt Lake City 84138-1188; (801) 524-5933; Fax: (801) 524-5730; *State Director:* Timothy Sheehan
Federal Bldg., 196 E. Tabernacle St., #42, St. George 84770-3474; (435) 628-5514; Fax: (435) 628-4160; *Southern Utah Area Coordinator:* Bryan Thiriot
Committee Assignment(s): Appropriations; Banking, Housing, and Urban Affairs; Energy and Natural Resources; Rules and Administration; Joint Printing; Joint Library of Congress; Joint Economic

Bingaman, Jeff, D-N.M.

Capitol Hill Office: SH-703 20510-3102; 224-5521; Fax: 224-2852; *Chief of Staff:* Stephen D. Ward
Web: bingaman.senate.gov
E-mail: senator_bingaman@bingaman.senate.gov
District Office(s): 625 Silver Ave. S.W., #130, Albuquerque 87102-3185; (505) 346-6601; Fax: (505) 346-6780; *State Director:* Terry Brunner
106-B West Main Street, Farmington 87401; (505) 325-5030; *Field Rep:* Jim Dumont
505 S. Main St., #148, Las Cruces 88001-1200; (505) 523-6561; Fax: (505) 523-6584; *Constituent Services Representative:* Rosalie Moralez
105 W. 3rd St., #409, Roswell 88201-4774; (505) 622-7113; Fax: (505) 622-3538; *Constituent Services Representative:* Iris Chavez
119 E. Marcy St., #101, Santa Fe 87501-2046; (505) 988-6647; Fax: (505) 992-8435; *State Scheduler/Field Rep:* Julia Maccini
Committee Assignment(s): Energy and Natural Resources; Finance; Health, Education, Labor, and Pensions; Joint Economic.

Bond, Christopher S., R-Mo.

Capitol Hill Office: SR-274 20510-2503; 224-5721;
Fax: 224-8149; *Deputy Chief of Staff:* Kara R. Vlasaty
Web: bond.senate.gov
District Office(s): Rush H. Limbaugh, Sr. U.S.
Courthouse, 555 Independence Street, Suite 1500,
Cape Girardeau 63703; (573) 334-7044; Fax: (573)
334-7352; *District Office Director:* Tom Schulte
1001 Cherry St., #204, Columbia 65201-7931; (573)
442-8151; Fax: (573) 442-8162; *Chief of Staff:* Brian
Klippenstein
308 E. High St., #202, Jefferson City 65101-3237; (573)
634-2488; Fax: (573) 634-6005; *Constituent Services
Director:* Liz Behrouz
911 Main St., #2224, Kansas City 64105-5321; (816)
471-7141; Fax: (816) 471-7338; *District Office
Director:* Michael Collins
300 S. Jefferson Ave., #401, Springfield 65806-2217; (417)
864-8258; Fax: (417) 864-7519; *District Office
Director:* Stacy Lynn Burks
7700 Bonhomme Ave., #615, St. Louis 63105-1998; (314)
725-4484; Fax: (314) 727-3548; *St. Louis Office
Manager:* Lane Koch
Committee Assignment(s): Appropriations; Environment
and Public Works; Small Business and
Entrepreneurship; Select Intelligence

Boxer, Barbara, D-Calif.

Capitol Hill Office: SH-112 20510-0505; 224-3553;
Fax: 224-0454; *Chief of Staff:* Laura Schiller
Web: boxer.senate.gov
District Office(s): 2500 Tulare St., #5290, Fresno 93721-
1318; (559) 497-5109; Fax: (559) 497-5111; *State
Director:* Thomas Bohigian
312 N. Spring St., #1748, Los Angeles 90012-4719; (213)
894-5000; Fax: (213) 894-5012; *California
Communications Director:* Leannah Bradley
501 I St., #7600, Sacramento 95814-7308; (916)
448-2787; Fax: (916) 448-2563; *Deputy State Director:*
Stacey Smith
201 North E St., #210, San Bernardino 92401; (909)
888-8525; Fax: (909) 888-8613; *Senior Adviser:* Alton
Garrett
600 B St., #2240, San Diego 92101-4508; (619) 239-3884;
Fax: (619) 239-5719; *San Diego County and Imperial
County Director:* Caridad Sanchez
1700 Montgomery St., #240, San Francisco 94111-1023;
(415) 403-0100; Fax: (415) 956-6701; *State
Operations Director:* Nicole Kaneko
Committee Assignment(s): Commerce, Science, and
Transportation; Environment and Public Works;
Foreign Relations; Select Ethics

Brown, Sherrod, D-Ohio

Capitol Hill Office: SR-455 20510-3505; 224-2315; Fax:
228-6321; *Chief of Staff:* James Heimbach
Web: brown.senate.gov

District Office(s): 425 Walnut St., #2310, Cincinnati
45202-3915; (513) 684-1021; Fax: (513) 684-1029;
Southwest Regional Director: Brooke Hill
1301 E. Ninth Street, #1710, Cleveland 44114-1869;
(216) 522-7272; Fax: (216) 522-2239; *State Director:*
John W. Ryan
John W. Bricker Federal Building, 200 N. High Street,
#614, Columbus 43215-2408; (614) 469-2083;
Fax: (614) 469-2171; *Constituent Services Liaison:*
Ayris R. Price
205 W. 20th Street, #M280, Lorraine 44052-3779; (440)
242-4100; Fax: (440) 242-4108; *Grants Coord.:* Leon
T. Mason III
Committee Assignment(s): Agriculture, Nutrition, and
Forestry; Banking, Housing, and Urban Affairs;
Health, Education, Labor, and Pensions; Veterans'
Affairs; Congressional-Executive Commission on
China; Select Ethics

Brownback, Sam, R-Kan.

Capitol Hill Office: SH-303 20510-1604; 224-6521;
Fax: 228-1265; *Chief of Staff:* Glen R. Chambers
Web: brownback.senate.gov
District Office(s): 811 N. Main St., Suite A, Garden City
67846-5487; (620) 275-1124; Fax: (620) 275-1837;
Regional Director: Dennis Mesa
11111 W. 95th St., #245, Overland Park 66214-1846;
(913) 492-6378; Fax: (913) 492-7253; *Deputy Chief of
Staff:* George Stafford
1001 N. Broadway St., Suite C, Pittsburg 66762-3944;
(620) 231-6040; Fax: (620) 231-6347; *Community
Development Director:* Anne Emerson
612 S. Kansas Ave., Topeka 66603-3818; (785) 233-2503;
Fax: (785) 233-2616; *Caseworker:* Jon Hummell
245 N. Waco St., #240, Wichita 67202-1131; (316) 264-8066;
Fax: (316) 264-9078; *State Director:* Chuck Alderson
Committee Assignment(s): Commission on Security and
Cooperation in Europe; Appropriations; Commerce,
Science, and Transportation; Energy and Natural
Resources; Congressional-Executive Commission on
China; Joint Economic; Special Aging

Bunning, Jim, R-Ky.

Capitol Hill Office: SH-316 20510-1703; 224-4343; Fax:
228-1373; *Chief of Staff:* Kim Taylor Dean
Web: bunning.senate.gov
District Office(s): 1717 Dixie Hwy., #220, Fort Wright
41011-4701; (859) 341-2602; Fax: (859) 331-7445;
State Director: Debbie McKinney
601 Main St., #2, Hazard 41701-1354; (606) 435-2390;
Fax: (606) 435-1761; *Field Representative:* Darlynn
Barber
1100 S. Main St., #12, Hopkinsville 42240-2079; (270)
885-1212; Fax: (270) 881-3975; *Field Representative:*
Anna Caryl Guffey
771 Corporate Dr., #105, Lexington 40503-5439; (859)
219-2239; Fax: (859) 219-3269; *Field Representative:*
Holly Hopkins

600 Dr. Martin Luther King Jr. Place, #1072-B, Louisville 40202-2230; (502) 582-5341; Fax: (502) 582-5344; *Field Representative:* Greg Smith

423 Frederica St., #305, Owensboro 42301-3013; (270) 689-9085; Fax: (270) 689-9158; *Field Representative:* Jim Askins

Committee Assignment(s): Banking, Housing, and Urban Affairs; Budget; Energy and Natural Resources; Finance

Burr, Richard M., R-N.C.

Capitol Hill Office: SR-217 20510-3308; 224-3154; Fax: 228-2981; *Chief of Staff:* Christopher Joyner
Web: burr.senate.gov
District Office(s): Federal Bldg., 151 Patton Ave., #204, Asheville 28801-2689; (828) 350-2437; Fax: (828) 350-2439; *Field Representative:* Steve Green

City Hall, 181 S. South St., #222, Gastonia 28052-4126; (704) 833-0854; Fax: (704) 833-1467; *Field Representative:* Ryan Combs

100 Coast Line St., #210, Rocky Mount 27804-5849; (252) 977-9522; Fax: (252) 977-7906; *Field Representative:* Betty Jo Shepheard

201 N. Front St., #809, Wilmington 28401-5089; (910) 251-1058; Fax: (910) 251-7975; *Field Representative:* Jason Soper

2000 W. 1st St., #508, Winston-Salem 27104-4225; (336) 631-5125; Fax: (336) 725-4493; *Field Representative:* Kathy Manship

Committee Assignment(s): Commission on Security and Cooperation in Europe; Armed Services; Energy and Natural Resources; Health, Education, Labor, and Pensions; Veterans' Affairs; Select Intelligence

Burris, Roland W., D-Ill.

Capitol Hill Office: 523 SDOB 20510-1307; 224-2854; Fax: 228-3333; *Deputy Chief of Staff:* Vera Baker-Merlini
Web: burris.senate.gov
District Office(s): John C. Kluczynski Federal Office Building, 230 S. Dearborn Street, Suite 3900, Chicago 60604-1480; (312) 886-3506; Fax: (312) 886-3514; *Chicago Office Director:* Jose Rivera

2001 52nd Avenue, Moline 61265-6368; (309) 736-1217; Fax: (309) 736-1233; *Field Rep.:* Kathryn Jennings

607 E. Adams Street, Room 1520, Springfield 62701-1635; (217) 492-5089; Fax: (217) 492-5099; *Acting Downstate Director:* Robert Stephan

Committee Assignment(s): Armed Services; Homeland Security and Governmental Affairs; Veterans' Affairs

Byrd, Robert C., D-W.Va.

Capitol Hill Office: SH-311 20510-4801; 224-3954; Fax: 228-0002; *Chief of Staff:* Barbara R. Videnieks
Web: byrd.senate.gov
District Office(s): 300 Virginia St. East, #2360, Charleston 25301; (304) 342-5855; Fax: (304) 343-7144; *State Director:* Mark Ferrell

217 W. King St., #238, Martinsburg 25401-3286; (304) 264-4626; *Administrative Manager:* Roseanna Cookie Davis

Committee Assignment(s): Appropriations; Armed Services; Budget; Rules and Administration

Cantwell, Maria, D-Wash.

Capitol Hill Office: SD-511 20510-4705; 224-3441; Fax: 228-0514; *Chief of Staff:* Katharine Lister
Web: cantwell.senate.gov
District Office(s): 2930 Wetmore Ave., #9B, Everett 98201-4044; (425) 303-0114; Fax: (425) 303-8351; *Northwest Washington Director:* Sally Hintz

815 Jadwin Ave., #G-58-A, Richland 99352-3562; (509) 946-8106; Fax: (509) 946-6937; *Central Washington Director:* David Reeploeg

915 2nd Ave., #3206, Seattle 98174-1011; (206) 220-6400; Fax: (206) 220-6404; *State Director:* Chris Endresen

Thomas S. Foley U.S. Courthouse, 920 Riverside Ave. W., #697, Spokane 99201-1008; (509) 353-2507; Fax: (509) 353-2547; *Eastern Washington Outreach Director:* Marcus Riccelli

950 Pacific Ave., #615, Tacoma 98402-4431; (253) 572-2281; Fax: (253) 572-5859; *Olympic Peninsula and Pierce County Director:* Mike English

Marshall House, 1313 Officers Row, Vancouver 98661-3856; (360) 696-7838; Fax: (360) 696-7844

Committee Assignment(s): Commerce, Science, and Transportation; Energy and Natural Resources; Finance; Indian Affairs; Small Business and Entrepreneurship

Cardin, Benjamin L., D-Md.

Capitol Hill Office: SH-509 20510-2004; 224-4524; Fax: 224-1651; *Chief of Staff:* Christopher W. Lynch
Web: cardin.senate.gov
District Office(s): 100 S. Charles St., Tower I, #1710, Baltimore 21201-2788; (410) 962-4436; Fax: (410) 962-4156; *State Director:* Bailey E. Fine

10201 Martin Luther King Jr. Hwy., #210, Bowie 20720-4000; (301) 860-0414; *Deputy State Office Director:* Carleton Atkinson

Western Maryland Railway Station, 13 Canal Street, #305, Cumberland 21502-3054; (301) 777-2957; Fax: (301) 777-2959; *Field Representative:* Robin Summerfield

129 E. Main Street, #115, Salisbury 21801-4920; (410) 546-4250; Fax: (410) 546-4252; *Field Representative:* Lee Whaley

Committee Assignment(s): Commission on Security and Cooperation in Europe; Budget; Environment and Public Works; Foreign Relations; Judiciary; Small Business and Entrepreneurship

Carper, Thomas R., D-Del.

Capitol Hill Office: SH-513 20510-0803; 224-2441; Fax: 228-2190; *Chief of Staff:* James D. Reilly
Web: carper.senate.gov

District Office(s): Federal Bldg., 300 S. New St., #2215, Dover 19904-6724; (302) 674-3308; *State Director:* Lawrence A. Windley

12 The Circle, Georgetown 19947-1501; (302) 856-7690; *Sussex County Regional Director:* Timothy Winstead

1 Christina Centre, 301 N. Walnut St., #102L-1, Wilmington 19801-3974; (302) 573-6291; *New Castle County Regional Director:* Bonnie J. Wu

Committee Assignment(s): Environment and Public Works; Finance; Homeland Security and Governmental Affairs

Casey, Robert P., D-Pa.

Capitol Hill Office: SR-383 20510-3805; 224-6324; Fax: 228-0604; *Chief of Staff:* James W. Brown

Web: casey.senate.gov

District Office(s): 840 Hamilton Street, Suite 301, Allentown 18101-2456; (610) 782-9470; Fax: (610) 782-9474

817 E. Bishop Street, Suite C, Bellefonte 16823-2321; (814) 357-0314; Fax: (814) 357-0318; *Field Representative:* Kim Bierly

17 S. Park Row, Suite B-150, Erie 16501-1162: (814) 874-5080; Fax: (814) 874-5084; *Field Representative:* Kyle Hannon

22 S. Third Street, #6, Harrisburg 17101-2105; (717) 231-7540; Fax: (717) 231-7542; *Director of Constituent Services:* Bonnie Seaman

2000 Market Street, #1870, Philadelphia 19103-3231; (215) 405-9660; Fax: (215) 405-9669; *Constituent Advocate:* Kurt Imhof

Regional Enterprise Tower, 425 Sixth Avenue, #2490, Pittsburgh 15219-1851; (412) 803-7370; Fax: (412) 803-7379; *Constituent Advocate:* Christopher Rosselot

409 Lackawanna Avenue, Suite 3C, Scranton 18503-2059; (570) 941-0930; Fax: (570) 941-0937; *State Director:* Charlie Lyons

Committee Assignment(s): Agriculture, Nutrition, and Forestry; Foreign Relations; Health, Education, Labor, and Pensions; Joint Economic; Special Aging

Chambliss, Saxby, R-Ga.

Capitol Hill Office: SR-416 20510-1007; 224-3521; Fax: 224-0103; *Chief of Staff:* Charlie Harman

Web: chambliss.senate.gov

District Office(s): 100 Galleria Pkwy., S.E., #1340, Atlanta 30339-3179; (770) 763-9090; Fax: (770) 226-8633; *State Director:* Steven Meeks

1054 Claussen Rd., #313, Augusta 30907-0311; (706) 738-0302; Fax: (706) 738-0901; *Regional Representative:* Jim Hussey

300 Mulberry St., #502, Macon 31201-5102; (478) 741-1417; Fax: (478) 741-1437; *Regional Representative:* Bill Stembridge

419-A S. Main St., P.O. Box 3217, Moultrie 31776-3217; (229) 985-2112; Fax: (229) 985-2123; *Regional Representative:* Debbie Cannon

2 E. Bryan St., #620, Savannah 31401-2638; (912) 232-3657; Fax: (912) 233-0115; *Regional Representative:* Kathryn Murph

Committee Assignment(s): Commission on Security and Cooperation in Europe; Agriculture, Nutrition, and Forestry; Armed Services; Rules and Administration; Joint Printing; Select Intelligence

Coburn, Tom, R-Okla.

Capitol Hill Office: SR-172 20510-3604; 224-5754; Fax: 224-6008; *Chief of Staff:* Michael Schwartz

Web: coburn.senate.gov

District Office(s): 711 S.W. D Ave., #202, Lawton 73501-4561; (580) 357-9878; Fax: (580) 355-3560

100 N. Broadway Ave., #1820, Oklahoma City 73102-8800; (405) 231-4941; Fax: (405) 231-5051; *State Government Relations Field Representative:* Greg Treat

1800 S. Baltimore Ave., #800, Tulsa 74119-5238; (918) 581-7651; Fax: (918) 581-7195; *State Director:* Jerry Morris

Committee Assignment(s): Health, Education, Labor, and Pensions; Homeland Security and Governmental Affairs; Indian Affairs; Judiciary; Select Intelligence

Cochran, Thad, R-Miss.

Capitol Hill Office: SD-113 20510-2402; 224-5054; Fax: 224-9450; *Chief of Staff:* T.A. Hawks

Web: cochran.senate.gov

District Office(s): 2012 15th St., #451, Gulfport 39501-2036; (228) 867-9710; *Office Director:* Myrtis Franke

188 E. Capitol St., #614, Jackson 39201-2137; (601) 965-4459; Fax: (601) 965-4919; *Office Director:* Brad David

Federal Bldg. and U.S. Courthouse, 911 E. Jackson Ave., #249, Oxford 38655-3652; (601) 236-1018; *Office Director:* Mindy Maxwell

Committee Assignment(s): Agriculture, Nutrition, and Forestry; Appropriations; Rules and Administration

Collins, Susan M., R-Maine

Capitol Hill Office: SD-413 20510-1904; 224-2523; Fax: 224-2693; *Chief of Staff:* Steven Abbott

Web: collins.senate.gov

District Office(s): 68 Sewall St., #507, Augusta 04330-6354; (207) 622-8414; Fax: (207) 622-5884; *State Office Representative:* William Card

Margaret Chase Smith Federal Bldg., 202 Harlow St., #204, P.O. Box 655, Bangor 04402-4919; (207) 945-0417; Fax: (207) 990-4604; *State Office Representative:* Carol Woodcock

160 Main St., Biddeford 04005-2580; (207) 283-1101; Fax: (207) 283-4054; *State Office Representative:* William Vail

25 Sweden St., Suite A, Caribou 04736-2149; (207) 493-7873; Fax: (207) 493-7810; *State Office Representative:* Phil Bosse

11 Lisbon St., Lewiston 04240-7117; (207) 784-6969; Fax: (207) 782-6475; *State Office Representative:* Peter Rogers

1 City Center, #100, Portland 04101; (207) 780-3575; Fax: (207) 828-0380; *State Office Representative:* Jennifer Duddy

Committee Assignment(s): Appropriations; Armed Services; Homeland Security and Governmental Affairs; Special Aging

Conrad, Kent, D-N.D.

Capitol Hill Office: SH-530 20510-3403; 224-2043; Fax: 224-7776; *Chief of Staff:* Sara G. Garland

Web: conrad.senate.gov

District Office(s): Federal Bldg., 220 E. Rosser Ave., #228, Bismarck 58501-3869; (701) 258-4648; Fax: (701) 258-1254; *State Director, Western Division:* Marty Boeckel

Federal Bldg., 657 2nd Ave. N., #306, Fargo 58102-4727; (701) 232-8030; Fax: (701) 232-6449; *State Director, Eastern Division:* Scott Stofferahn

Federal Bldg., 102 N. 4th St., #104, Grand Forks 58203-3738; (701) 775-9601; Fax: (701) 746-1990; *State Representative:* James S. Hand

Federal Bldg., 100 1st St., S.W., #105, Minot 58701-3846; (701) 852-0703; Fax: (701) 838-8196; *State Representative:* Gail Bergstad

Committee Assignment(s): Agriculture, Nutrition, and Forestry; Budget; Finance; Indian Affairs; Joint Taxation

Corker, Bob, R-Tenn.

Capitol Hill Office: SD-185 20510-4207; 224-3344; Fax: 228-0566; *Chief of Staff:* Todd Womack

Web: corker.senate.gov

District Office(s): 2525 Hwy. 75, #126, Blountville 37617-6366; (423) 323-1252; Fax: (423) 323-0358; *Field Director:* Bridget Baird

10 W. Martin Luther King Blvd., 6th Floor, Chattanooga 37402-1813; (423) 756-2757; Fax: (423) 756-5313; *State Director:* Chris Devaney

Ed Jones Federal Bldg., 109 S. Highland Ave., #B-8, Jackson 38301-6149; (731) 424-9655; Fax: (731) 424-8322; *Field Representative:* Jane Jolley

800 Market St., #121, Knoxville 37902-2349; (865) 637-4180; Fax: (865) 637-9886; *Field Representative:* David Leaverton

100 Peabody Place, #1335, Memphis 38103-3613; (901) 683-1910; Fax: (901) 575-3528; *Field Director:* Nick Kistenmacher

3322 W. End Ave., #610, Nashville 37203-1096; (615) 279-8125; Fax: (615) 279-9488; *Field Director:* Paul Goode

Committee Assignment(s): Banking, Housing, and Urban Affairs; Energy and Natural Resources; Foreign Relations; Special Aging

Cornyn, John, R-Tex.

Capitol Hill Office: SH-517 20510-4305; 224-2934; Fax: 228-2856; *Chief of Staff:* Beth Jafari

Web: cornyn.senate.gov

District Office(s): 221 W. 6th St., #1530, Austin 78701-3403; (512) 469-6034; Fax: (512) 469-6020; *State Field Director:* David James

Occidental Tower, 5005 LBJ Freeway, #1150, Dallas 75244-6199; (972) 239-1310; Fax: (972) 239-2110; *Regional Director:* Andrew Rittler

Bank of America Bldg., 222 E. Van Buren Ave., #404, Harlingen 78550-6804; (956) 423-0162; Fax: (956) 423-0193; *Regional Director:* Ana Garcia

5300 Memorial Dr., #980, Houston 77007; (713) 572-3337; Fax: (713) 572-3777; *Regional Director:* Jay Guerrero

3405 22nd St., #203, Lubbock 79410-1305; (806) 472-7533; Fax: (806) 472-7536; *Regional Director:* Brent Oden

600 Navarro St., #210, San Antonio 78205-2455; (210) 224-7485; Fax: (210) 224-8569; *Regional Director:* Daniel Mezza

100 E. Ferguson St., #1004, Tyler 75702-5706; (903) 593-0902; Fax: (903) 593-0920; *Regional Director:* Gail Green

Committee Assignment(s): Budget; Finance; Judiciary

Crapo, Michael D., R-Idaho

Capitol Hill Office: SD-239 20510-1205; 224-6142; Fax: 228-1375; *Chief of Staff, Washington, D.C.:* Peter C. Fischer

Web: crapo.senate.gov

District Office(s): 251 E. Front St., #205, Boise 83702-7312; (208) 334-1776; Fax: (208) 334-9044; *Chief of Staff:* John E. Hoehne

524 Cleveland Blvd., #220, Caldwell 83605-4080; (208) 455-0360; Fax: (208) 455-0358; *Regional Director:* A.J. Church

610 W. Hubbard St., #209, Coeur D'Alene 83814-2287; (208) 664-5490; Fax: (208) 664-0889; *Regional Director:* Karen Roetter

490 Memorial Dr., #102, Idaho Falls 83402-3600; (208) 522-9779; Fax: (208) 529-8367; *Regional Director:* Leslie Huddleston

313 D St., #106, Lewiston 83501-1894; (208) 743-1492; Fax: (208) 743-6484; *Regional Director:* Mitch Silvers

275 S. 5th Ave., #225, Pocatello 83201; (208) 236-6775; Fax: (208) 236-6935; *Regional Director:* Farhana Hibbert

202 Falls Ave., #2, Twin Falls 83301-3372; (208) 734-2515; Fax: (208) 733-0414

Committee Assignment(s): Banking, Housing, and Urban Affairs; Budget; Environment and Public Works; Finance; Indian Affairs

DeMint, Jim, R-S.C.

Capitol Hill Office: SR-340 20510-4004; 224-6121; Fax: 228-5143; *Chief of Staff:* W. Bret Bernhardt

Web: demint.senate.gov

District Office(s): 112 Custom House, 200 E. Bay St., Charleston 29401-2691; (843) 727-4525; Fax: (843) 722-4923; *First District Regional Director:* Ashley Holbrook

1901 Main St., #1475, Columbia 29201-2435; (803) 771-6112; Fax: (803) 771-6455; *State Director:* Luke P. Byars

105 N. Spring St., #109, Greenville 29601-2859; (864) 233-5366; Fax: (864) 271-8901; *Third District Regional Director:* Susan Aiken

Committee Assignment(s): Banking, Housing, and Urban Affairs; Commerce, Science, and Transportation; Foreign Relations; Joint Economic

Dodd, Christopher J., D-Conn.

Capitol Hill Office: SR-448 20510-0702; 224-2823; Fax: 224-1083; *Chief of Staff:* Miles Lackey

Web: dodd.senate.gov

District Office(s): 30 Lewis St., #101, Hartford 06103-2501; (860) 258-6940; Fax: (860) 258-6958; *State Director:* Edward H. Mann

Committee Assignment(s): Commission on Security and Cooperation in Europe; Banking, Housing, and Urban Affairs; Foreign Relations; Health, Education, Labor, and Pensions; Rules and Administration; Joint Library of Congress

Dorgan, Byron L., D-N.D.

Capitol Hill Office: SH-322 20510-3405; 224-2551; Fax: 224-1193; *Chief of Staff:* Elizabeth M. Gore

Web: dorgan.senate.gov

E-mail: senator@dorgan.senate.gov

District Office(s): Federal Bldg., 220 E. Rosser Ave., #312, P.O. Box 2579, Bismarck 58502-2579; (701) 250-4618; Fax: (701) 250-4484; *Deputy State Director:* Warren Larson

1802 32nd Ave. South, Suite B, P.O. Box 9060, Fargo 58106; (701) 239-5389; Fax: (701) 239-5512; *Deputy State Director:* Pam Gulleson

102 N. 4th St., #10, Grand Forks 58201; (701) 746-8972; Fax: (701) 746-9122

100 1st St., S.W., #105, Minot 58701; (701) 852-0703; Fax: (701) 838-8196; *Caseworker:* Gail Bergstad

Committee Assignment(s): Appropriations; Commerce, Science, and Transportation; Energy and Natural Resources; Indian Affairs; Congressional-Executive Commission on China

Durbin, Richard J., D-Ill.

Capitol Hill Office: SH-309 20510-1304; 224-2152; Fax: 228-0400; *Washington Chief of Staff:* Patrick J. Souders

Web: durbin.senate.gov

District Office(s): John C. Kluczynski Federal Bldg., 230 S. Dearborn St., 38th Floor, Chicago 60604-1505; (312) 353-4952; Fax: (312) 353-0150; *Chicago Director:* Clarisol Duque

701 N. Court St., Marion 62959-1709; (618) 998-8812; Fax: (618) 997-0176; *Staff Assistant:* Betsey Hall

525 S. 8th St., Springfield 62703-1606; (217) 492-4062; Fax: (217) 492-4382; *Downstate Director:* Bill Houlihan

Committee Assignment(s): Appropriations; Judiciary; Rules and Administration

Ensign, John, R-Nev.

Capitol Hill Office: SR-119 20510-2805; 224-6244; Fax: 228-2193; *Chief of Staff:* John P. Lopez

Web: ensign.senate.gov

District Office(s): 600 E. William St., #304, Carson City 89701-4052; (775) 885-9111; Fax: (775) 883-5590

Lloyd D. George Federal Bldg. and U.S. Courthouse, 333 Las Vegas Blvd. South, #8203, Las Vegas 89101-7075; (702) 388-6605; Fax: (702) 388-6501; *State Director:* Sonia Joya

Bruce R. Thompson Courthouse and Federal Bldg., 400 S. Virginia St., #738, Reno 89501-2125; (775) 686-5770; Fax: (775) 686-5729; *Reno/Sparks Director:* Sam Hudson

Committee Assignment(s): Budget; Commerce, Science, and Transportation; Finance; Homeland Security and Governmental Affairs; Rules and Administration

Enzi, Michael B., R-Wyo.

Capitol Hill Office: SR-379A 20510-5004; 224-3424; Fax: 228-0359; *Chief of Staff:* Flip McConnaughey

Web: enzi.senate.gov

District Office(s): Federal Center, 100 East B St., #3201, Casper 82601-1975; (307) 261-6572; Fax: (307) 261-6574; *Field Representative:* Sandy Tinsley

Federal Center, 2120 Capitol Ave., #2007, Cheyenne 82001-3631; (307) 772-2477; Fax: (307) 772-2480; *Field Representative:* Debbie McCann

1285 Sheridan Ave., #210, Cody 82414-3653; (307) 527-9444; Fax: (307) 527-9476; *Field Representative:* Karen McCreery

400 S. Kendrick Ave., #303, Gillette 82716-3803; (307) 682-6268; Fax: (307) 682-6501; *Field Representative:* Robin Bailey

P.O. Box 12470, Jackson 83002; (307) 739-9507; Fax: (307) 739-9520; *Field Representative:* Reagen Bebout

Committee Assignment(s): Budget; Finance; Health, Education, Labor, and Pensions; Small Business and Entrepreneurship

Feingold, Russell D., D-Wis.

Capitol Hill Office: SH-506 20510-4904; 224-5323; Fax: 224-2725; *Chief of Staff:* Mary Irvine

Web: feingold.senate.gov

District Office(s): 1640 Main St., Green Bay 54302-2639; (920) 465-7508; *Fox Valley Regional Coordinator:* Suzanne Brault Pagel

425 State St., #225, La Crosse 54601-3341; (608) 782-5585; *Western Regional Coordinator:* Matt Nikolay

1600 Aspen Commons, #100, Middleton 53562-4716; (608) 828-1200; *State Coordinator:* Jay Robiadek

517 E. Wisconsin Ave., #408, Milwaukee 53202-4504; (414) 276-7282; *South Central Regional Coordinator:* Jeri Gabrielson-Hashiguchi

Firstar Plaza, 401 5th St., #410, Wausau 54403-5468; (715) 848-5660; *Northern Regional Coordinator:* Karen Graff

Committee Assignment(s): Budget; Foreign Relations; Judiciary; Select Intelligence

Feinstein, Dianne, D-Calif.

Capitol Hill Office: SH-331 20510-0504; 224-3841; Fax: 228-3954; *Assistant to **Chief of Staff:*** Lauren Layton

Web: feinstein.senate.gov

District Office(s): 2500 Tulare St., #4290, Fresno 93721-1331; (559) 485-7430; Fax: (559) 485-9689; *District Director:* Shelly Abajian

11111 Santa Monica Blvd., #915, Los Angeles 90025-3343; (310) 914-7300; Fax: (310) 914-7318; *District Director:* Trevor Daley

750 B St., #1030, San Diego 92101-8126; (619) 231-9712; Fax: (619) 231-1108; *Deputy State Director:* James Peterson

1 Post St., #2450, San Francisco 94104-5240; (415) 393-0707; Fax: (415) 393-0710; *State Director:* Jim Molinari

Committee Assignment(s): Appropriations; Judiciary; Rules and Administration; Congressional-Executive Commission on China; Joint Printing; Joint Library of Congress; Select Intelligence

Gillibrand, Kirsten, D-N.Y.

Capitol Hill Office: SD-531 20510-3205; 224-4451; Fax: 228-0282; *Chief of Staff:* Jess C. Fassler

Web: gillibrand.senate.gov

District Office(s): Leo W. O'Brien Federal Office Building, 1 Clinton Ave., Room 821, Albany 12207-2202; (518) 431-0120; Fax: (518) 431-0128; *Regional Director:* Mike Russo

Larkin At Exchange, 726 Exchange Street, Suite 511, Buffalo 14210-1485; (716) 854-9725; Fax: (716) 854-9731; *Regional Director:* Laura Krolczyk

P.O. Box 273, Lowville 13367; (315) 376-6118; *Regional Director:* Susan Merrell

155 Pinelawn Road, Suite 250 North, Melville 11747-3247; (631) 249-2825; Fax: (631) 249-2847; *Regional Director:* Kirsten Walsh

780 Third Avenue, Suite 2601, New York 10017-2177; (212) 688-6262; *State Director:* Christine Falvo

Kenneth B. Keating Federal Office Building, 100 State Street, Room 4195, Rochester 14614-1318; (585) 263-6250; Fax: (585) 263-6247; *Regional Director:* Sarah Clark

James H. Hanley Federal Building, 100 South Clinton Street, Room 1470, P.O. Box 7378, Syracuse 13202; (315) 448-0470; Fax: (315) 448-0476

Committee Assignment(s): Agriculture, Nutrition, and Forestry; Environment and Public Works; Foreign Relations; Special Aging

Graham, Lindsey O., R-S.C.

Capitol Hill Office: SR-290 20510-4003; 224-5972; Fax: 224-3808; *Chief of Staff:* Richard S. Perry

Web: lgraham.senate.gov

District Office(s): 508 Hampton St., #202, Columbia 29201-2718; (803) 933-0112; Fax: (803) 933-0957; *Midlands Regional Director:* Rene Ann Tewkesbury

John L. McMillan Federal Bldg., 401 W. Evans St., #111, Florence 29501-3460; (843) 669-1505; Fax: (843) 669-9015; *Constituent Services Representative:* Alice Cooper

101 E. Washington St., #220, Greenville 29601-2732; (864) 250-1417; Fax: (864) 250-4322; *State Director:* Jane Goolsby

530 Johnnie Dodds Blvd., #202, Mt. Pleasant 29464-3029; (843) 849-3887; Fax: (843) 971-3669; *Low Country Regional Director:* Bill Tuten

140 E. Main St., #110, Rock Hill 29730-3600; (803) 366-2828; Fax: (803) 366-5353; *Constituent Services and Outreach Representative:* Piper Aheron

135 Eagles Nest Dr., Suite B, Seneca 29678; (864) 888-3330; Fax: (864) 888-3335; *State Outreach Manager, Medical and Business Sector:* Denise Bauld

Committee Assignment(s): Armed Services; Budget; Homeland Security and Governmental Affairs; Judiciary; Veterans' Affairs; Special Aging

Grassley, Charles E., R-Iowa

Capitol Hill Office: SH-135 20510-1501; 224-3744; Fax: 224-6020; *Chief of Staff:* David Young

Web: grassley.senate.gov

District Office(s): 150 First Avenue, N.E., Suite 235, Cedar Rapids 52401-1115; (319) 363-6832; *Regional Director:* Mary Day

Federal Bldg., Eight S. 6th St., #307, Council Bluffs 51501; (712) 322-7103; *Regional Director:* Donna Barry

131 W. 3rd St., #180, Davenport 52801-1419; (563) 322-4331; *Regional Director:* Penny Vacek

Federal Bldg., 210 Walnut St., #721, Des Moines 50309-2140; (515) 288-1145; *Regional Director:* Aaron McKay

Federal Courthouse, 320 6th St., #120, Sioux City 51101-1244; (712) 233-1860; *Regional Director:* Jacob Bossman

Waterloo Bldg., 531 Commercial St., #210, Waterloo 50701-5497; (319) 232-6657; *Regional Director:* Valerie Nehl

Committee Assignment(s): Agriculture, Nutrition, and Forestry; Budget; Finance; Judiciary; Joint Taxation

Gregg, Judd, R-N.H.

Capitol Hill Office: SR-393 20510-2904; 224-3324; Fax: 224-4952; *Communications Director:* Andrea Wuebker

Web: gregg.senate.gov

District Office(s): 60 Pleasant St., Berlin 03570-1947; (603) 752-2604; Fax: (603) 752-7351; *Staff Assistant:* Janet Woodward

John Fanaras Bldg., 125 N. Main St., Concord 03301-4921; (603) 225-7115; Fax: (603) 224-0198; *Chief of Staff:* Alyssa Shooshan

41 Hooksett Rd., Unit 2, Manchester 03104-2640; (603) 622-7979; Fax: (603) 622-0422; *Staff Assistant:* Peg Ouellette

16 Pease Blvd., Portsmouth 03801-2891; (603) 431-2171; Fax: (603) 431-1916; *Staff Assistant:* Anne Warburton

Committee Assignment(s): Appropriations; Budget; Health, Education, Labor, and Pensions

Hagan, Kay, D-N.C.

Capitol Hill Office: SD-521 20510-3309; 224-6342; Fax: 228-2563; *Chief of Staff:* Crystal King

Web: hagel.senate.gov

District Office(s): 310 New Bern Avenue, Raleigh 27601-1441; (919) 856-4630; Fax: (919) 856-4053; *State Director:* Melissa Midgett

Committee Assignment(s): Armed Services; Health, Education, Labor, and Pensions; Small Business and Entrepreneurship

Harkin, Tom, D-Iowa

Capitol Hill Office: SH-731 20510-1502; 224-3254; Fax: 224-9369; *Chief of Staff:* Brian Ahlberg

Web: harkin.senate.gov

District Office(s): 150 1st Ave. N., #370, Cedar Rapids 52401-1115; (319) 365-4504; Fax: (319) 365-4683; *Regional Director:* Beth Freeman

1606 Brady St., #323, Davenport 52803-4709; (563) 322-1338; Fax: (563) 322-0417; *Staff Assistant:* Alison Hart

Federal Bldg., 210 Walnut St., #733, Des Moines 50309-2106; (515) 284-4574; Fax: (515) 284-4937; *State Director:* Dianne Liepa

Federal Bldg., 350 W. 6th St., #315, Dubuque 52001-4648; (563) 582-2130; Fax: (563) 582-2342; *Staff Assistant:* Linda Lucy

Federal Bldg., 320 6th St., #110, Sioux City 51101-1244; (712) 252-1550; Fax: (712) 252-1638; *Regional Director:* Maureen Wilson

Committee Assignment(s): Agriculture, Nutrition, and Forestry; Appropriations; Health, Education, Labor, and Pensions; Small Business and Entrepreneurship

Hatch, Orrin G., R-Utah

Capitol Hill Office: SH-104 20510-4402; 224-5251; Fax: 224-6331; *Chief of Staff:* Jace Johnson

Web: hatch.senate.gov

District Office(s): 77 N. Main St., Suite 112, Cedar City 84720-2648; (435) 586-8435; Fax: (435) 586-2147; *Southern Utah Director:* Marreen Casper

Federal Bldg., 324 25th St., #1006, Ogden 84401-2341; (801) 625-5672; Fax: (801) 625-5590; *Northern Area Director:* Sandra Kester

51 S. University Ave., #320, Provo 84601-4491; (801) 375-7881; Fax: (801) 374-5005; *Central Utah Director:* Ronald W. Dean

Federal Bldg., 125 S. State St., #8402, Salt Lake City 84138-1191; (801) 524-4380; Fax: (801) 524-4379; *State Director:* Melanie Bowen

Washington County Administration Bldg., 197 E. Tabernacle St., #2, St. George 84770-3443; (435) 634-1795; Fax: (435) 634-1796; *Southern Utah Director:* Marreen Casper

Committee Assignment(s): Finance; Health, Education, Labor, and Pensions; Judiciary; Joint Taxation; Select Intelligence; Special Aging

Hutchison, Kay Bailey, R-Tex.

Capitol Hill Office: SR-284 20510-4303; 224-5922; Fax: 224-0776; *Deputy Chief of Staff:* James Christoferson

Web: hutchison.senate.gov

District Office(s): 500 Chestnut St., #1570, Abilene 79602-1470; (325) 676-2839; Fax: (325) 676-2937; *Regional Director:* Shea Woodard

961 Federal Bldg., 300 E. 8th St., Austin 78701-3226; (512) 916-5834; Fax: (512) 916-5839; *Regional Director:* John Etue

10440 N. Central Expressway, #1160, Dallas 75231-2223; (214) 361-3500; Fax: (214) 361-3502; *Regional Director:* Jim McGee

1906-G E. Tyler St., Harlingen 78550-7109; (956) 425-2253; Fax: (956) 412-1468; *Regional Director:* Julian Alvarez

1919 Smith St., #800, Houston 77002-8051; (713) 653-3456; Fax: (713) 209-3459; *Regional Director:* Jason Fuller

3133 General Hudnell Drive, Suite 120, San Antonio 78226; (210) 340-2885; Fax: (210) 349-6753; *Regional Director and State Outreach Director:* Jesse Hereford

Committee Assignment(s): Appropriations; Banking, Housing, and Urban Affairs; Commerce, Science, and Transportation; Rules and Administration

Inhofe, James M., R-Okla.

Capitol Hill Office: SR-453 20510-3603; 224-4721; Fax: 228-0380; *Chief of Staff:* Ryan Thompson

Web: inhofe.senate.gov

District Office(s): Continental Tower North, 302 N. Independence St., #104, Enid 73701-4025; (580) 234-5105; Fax: (580) 234-0929; *Field Representative:* Michael Lee

First National Center, 215 E. Choctaw Ave., #106, McAlester 74501-5069; (918) 426-0933; Fax: (918) 426-0935; *Field Representative:* Ronald Massey

1900 N.W. Expressway, #1210, Oklahoma City 73118; (405) 608-4381; Fax: (405) 608-4120; *State Director:* John R. H. Collison

1924 S. Utica, #530, Tulsa 74114-1620; (918) 581-7111; Fax: (918) 581-7770; *Executive Assistant:* Kathie Lopp
Committee Assignment(s): Armed Services; Environment and Public Works

Inouye, Daniel K., D-Hawaii

Capitol Hill Office: SH-722 20510-1102; 224-3934; *Chief of Staff:* Patrick H. DeLeon
Web: inouye.senate.gov
District Office(s): Hilo Lagoon Center, 101 Aupuni St., #205, Hilo 96720-4221; (808) 935-0844; Fax: (808) 961-5163; *Field Representative:* Delbert Nishimoto
Prince Kuhio Federal Bldg., 300 Ala Moana Blvd., #7-212, Honolulu 96850-4975; (808) 541-2542; Fax: (808) 541-2549; *Chief of Staff:* Jennifer Goto Sabas
P.O. Box 573, Kaunakakai 96748; (808) 560-3653; Fax: (808) 560-3385; *Field Representative:* William Akutagawa
P.O. Box 41, Kealakekua 96750; (808) 935-0844; Fax: (808) 961-5163; *Field Representative:* Wayne Tanaka
P.O. Box 311, 1840A Leleiona St., Lihue 96766; (808) 639-0100; Fax: (808) 246-9515; *Field Representative:* Ron Sakoda
94-403 Punono St., Mililani 96789-2566; (808) 864-5222; Fax: (808) 623-7701; *Field Representative:* Edmund Aczon
555 Iao Valley Rd., Wailuku 96793-3007; (808) 242-9702; Fax: (808) 242-7233; *Field Representative:* Ryther Barbin
Committee Assignment(s): Appropriations; Commerce, Science, and Transportation; Indian Affairs; Rules and Administration; Joint Printing

Isakson, Johnny, R-Ga.

Capitol Hill Office: SR-120 20510-1008; 224-3643; Fax: 228-0724; *Chief of Staff:* Christopher M. Carr
Web: isakson.senate.gov
District Office(s): 1 Overton Park, 3625 Cumberland Blvd., S.E., #970, Atlanta 30339-6406; (770) 661-0999; Fax: (770) 661-0768; *State Director:* Tricia Chastain
Committee Assignment(s): Commerce, Science, and Transportation; Foreign Relations; Health, Education, Labor, and Pensions; Small Business and Entrepreneurship; Veterans' Affairs; Select Ethics

Johanns, Mike, R-Neb.

Capitol Hill Office: SR-C1 20510-2707; 224-4224; Fax: 228-0436; *Chief of Staff:* Terri Moore
Web: johanns.senate.gov/public/index.cfm
District Office(s): 4111 Fourth Avenue, Suite 26, Kearney 68845-2884; (308) 236-7602; Fax: (308) 236-7473; *Central Nebraska Director of Constituent Services:* Julie Brooker
294 Federal Building, 100 Centennial Mall N., Lincoln 68508-3589; (402) 476-1400; Fax: (402) 476-0605; *State Director:* Nancy Montanez-Johner

9900 Nicholas Street, Suite 325, Omaha 68114-22114; (402) 758-8981; Fax: (402) 758-9165; *Omaha Director of Constituent Services:* Emily Brummund
115 W. Railway Street, Suite C102, Scottsbluff 69361-3185; (308) 632-6032; Fax: (308) 632-6295; *Constituent Services Rep.:* Brandi McCaslin

Johnson, Tim, D-S.D.

Capitol Hill Office: SH-136 20510-4104; 224-5842; Fax: 228-5765; *Chief of Staff:* Drey Samuelson
Web: johnson.senate.gov
District Office(s): 320 S. 1st St., #103, Aberdeen 57401-4168; (605) 226-3440, (605) 226-3962; Fax: (605) 226-2439; *Northeast Area Director:* Sharon Stroschein
405 E. Omaha St., Suite B, Rapid City 57701-2975; (605) 341-3990, (605) 341-3883; Fax: (605) 341-2207; *West River Area Director:* Darrell Shoemaker
715 S. Minnesota Ave., Sioux Falls 57104-6809; (605) 332-8896, (605) 332-8842; Fax: (605) 332-2824; *State Director:* Sharon Boysen
Committee Assignment(s): Appropriations; Banking, Housing, and Urban Affairs; Energy and Natural Resources; Indian Affairs

Kaufman, Ted, D-Del.

Capitol Hill Office: SD-G11 20510-0804; 224-5042; *Chief of Staff:* Jeffrey J. Connaughton
Web: kaufman.senate.gov
District Office(s): Windsor Building, 24 N.W. Front Street, Suite 101, Milford 19963-1463; (302) 424-8090; Fax: (302) 424-8098
1105 N. Market Street, Suite 2000, Wilmington 19801-1228; (302) 573-6345; Fax: (302) 573-6351; *State Director:* John M. DiEleuterio
Committee Assignment(s): Foreign Relations; Judiciary

Kennedy, Edward M., D-Mass.

Capitol Hill Office: SR-317 20510-2101; 224-4543; Fax: 224-2417; *Chief of Staff:* Eric Mogilnicki
Web: kennedy.senate.gov
District Office(s): John F. Kennedy Federal Bldg., Government Center, Corner of Cambridge St. and Sudbury, #2400, Boston 02203; (617) 565-3170; Fax: (617) 565-3183; *State Director:* Barbara Souliotis
Committee Assignment(s): Armed Services; Health, Education, Labor, and Pensions; Joint Economic

Kerry, John F., D-Mass.

Capitol Hill Office: SR-304 20510-2102; 224-2742; Fax: 224-8525; *Chief of Staff:* David Eckles Wade
Web: kerry.senate.gov
District Office(s): One Bowdoin Square, #1000, Boston 02114-2928; (617) 565-8519; Fax: (617) 248-3870; *State Director:* Drew O'Brien
222 Milken Blvd., #312, Fall River 02721-1623; (508) 677-0522; Fax: (508) 677-0275; *Local Relations:* Janet Lebel

1 Financial Plaza, 1350 Main St., #1208, Springfield
01103-1628; (413) 785-4610; Fax: (413) 736-1049;
Western Massachusetts Regional Director: Stephen
Meunier
Committee Assignment(s): Commerce, Science, and
Transportation; Finance; Foreign Relations; Small
Business and Entrepreneurship

Klobuchar, Amy, D-Minn.

Capitol Hill Office: SR-302 20510-2307; 224-3244;
Fax: 228-2186; *Chief of Staff:* Marjorie Duske
Web: klobuchar.senate.gov
District Office(s): 1200 Washington Avenue S., Suite 250,
Minneapolis 55415-1588; (612) 727-5220; Fax: (612)
727-5223; *State Director:* Zach Rodvold
121 Fourth Street S., Moorhead 56560-2613; (218)
287-2219; Fax: (218) 287-2936; *Regional Outreach
Director:* Andy Martin
1134 7th Street, N.W., Rochester 55901-1732; (507)
288-5321; Fax: (507) 288-2922; *Regional Outreach
Director:* Chuck Ackman
Olcott Plaza, 820 Ninth Street N., Suite 105; Virginia
55792-2300; (218) 741-9690; Fax: (218) 741-3692;
Regional Outreach Director: Jerry Fallos
Committee Assignment(s): Agriculture, Nutrition, and
Forestry; Commerce, Science, and Transportation;
Environment and Public Works; Judiciary; Joint
Economic

Kohl, Herb, D-Wis.

Capitol Hill Office: SH-330 20510-4903; 224-5653;
Fax: 224-9787; *Chief of Staff:* Paul S. Bock
Web: kohl.senate.gov
E-mail: kohl.senate.gov/gen_contact.html
District Office(s): 4321 W. College Ave., #235, Appleton
54914-3901; (414) 738-1640; Fax: (414) 738-1643;
Regional Representative: Marlene Mielke
402 Graham Ave., #206, Eau Claire 54701-2633; (715)
832-8424; Fax: (715) 832-8492; *Regional
Representative:* Marjorie Bunce
425 State St., #202, La Crosse 54601-3341; (608)
796-0045; Fax: (608) 796-0089; *Regional
Representative:* John Medinger
14 W. Mifflin St., #207, Madison 53703-2568; (608)
264-5338; Fax: (608) 264-5473; *Madison Director:*
Darcy Luoma
310 W. Wisconsin Ave., #950, Milwaukee 53203-2205;
(414) 297-4451; Fax: (414) 297-4455; *State Director:*
JoAnne Anton
Committee Assignment(s): Appropriations;
Banking, Housing, and Urban Affairs; Judiciary;
Special Aging

Kyl, Jon, R-Ariz.

Capitol Hill Office: SH-730 20510-0304; 224-4521;
Fax: 224-2207; *Chief of Staff:* Timothy M.
Glazewski
Web: kyl.senate.gov

District Office(s): 2200 E. Camelback Rd., #120,
Phoenix 85016-9021; (602) 840-1891; Fax: (602)
957-6838; *State Director:* Kimberly Wold
6840 N. Oracle Rd., #150, Tucson 85704-4252; (520)
575-8633; Fax: (520) 797-3232; *Regional Director:*
Hank Kenski
Committee Assignment(s): Finance; Judiciary

Landrieu, Mary L., D-La.

Capitol Hill Office: SH-328 20510-1804; 224-5824;
Fax: 224-9735; *Chief of Staff:* Jane L. Campbell
Web: landrieu.senate.gov
District Office(s): Old Federal Bldg., 707 Florida St.,
#326, Baton Rouge 70801-1713; (225) 389-0395;
Fax: (225) 389-0660; *State Director:* T. Bradley Keith
Capital One Tower, One Lakeshore Dr., #1260, Lake
Charles 70629-0104; (337) 436-6650; Fax: (337)
439-3762; *Regional Manager:* Mark Herbert
Hale Boggs Federal Bldg., 500 Poydras St., #1005, New
Orleans 70130-3309; (504) 589-2427; Fax: (504)
589-4023; *Regional Manager:* LaVerne Saulny
U.S. Courthouse, 300 Fannin St., #2240, Shreveport
71101-3123; (318) 676-3085; Fax: (318) 676-3100;
Deputy State Director: Tari Bradford
Committee Assignment(s): Appropriations; Energy and
Natural Resources; Homeland Security and
Governmental Affairs; Small Business and
Entrepreneurship

Lautenberg, Frank R., D-N.J.

Capitol Hill Office: SH-324 20510-3005; 224-3224;
Fax: 228-4054; TTY: 224-2087; *Chief of Staff:*
Daniel E. Katz
Web: lautenberg.senate.gov
District Office(s): 1 Port Center, 2 Riverside Dr., #505,
Camden 08103; (856) 338-8922; Fax: (856) 338-8936
1 Gateway Center, 23rd Floor, Newark 07102-5321; (973)
639-8700; Fax: (973) 639-8723; *State Director:* Steve
Lenox
Committee Assignment(s): Appropriations; Commerce,
Science, and Transportation; Environment and Public
Works

Leahy, Patrick, D-Vt.

Capitol Hill Office: SR-433 20510-4502; 224-4242;
Fax: 224-3479; *Chief of Staff:* Edward Pagano
Web: leahy.senate.gov
E-mail: leahy.senate.gov/contact.html
District Office(s): Courthouse Plaza, 199 Main St.,
Burlington 05401-8309; (802) 863-2525; *Vermont
Office Director:* Charles Ross
Federal Bldg., 87 State St., #338, P.O. Box 933,
Montpelier 05602-9505; (802) 229-0569; *Field Office
Director:* Robert Paquin
Committee Assignment(s): Agriculture, Nutrition, and
Forestry; Appropriations; Judiciary

Levin, Carl, D-Mich.

Capitol Hill Office: SR-269 20510-2202; 224-6221; Fax: 224-1388; *Chief of Staff:* David S. Lyles
Web: levin.senate.gov
District Office(s): Patrick V. McNamara Federal Bldg., 477 Michigan Ave., #1860, Detroit 48226-2576; (313) 226-6020; Fax: (313) 226-6948; *Michigan Director:* Cassandra Woods
623 Ludington St., #303, Escanaba 49829-3835; (906) 789-0052; Fax: (906) 789-0015; *Regional Representative:* Amy Berglund
Gerald R. Ford Federal Bldg., 110 Michigan Ave., N.W., #134, Grand Rapids 49503-2313; (616) 456-2531; Fax: (616) 456-5147; *Regional Representative:* Paul Troost
Michigan National Tower, 124 W. Allegan St., #1810, Lansing 48933-1716; (517) 377-1508; Fax: (517) 377-1506; *Regional Representative:* James J. Turner
Commerce Center, 301 E. Genesee St., #101, Saginaw 48607-1242; (989) 754-2494; Fax: (989) 754-2920; *Regional Representative:* Dusty Houser
207 W. Grandview Pkwy., #104, Traverse City 49684-2276; (231) 947-9569; Fax: (231) 947-9518; *Regional Representative:* Harold Chase
30500 Van Dyke Ave., #206, Warren 48093; (586) 573-9145; Fax: (586) 573-8260; *Regional Representative:* Vicki Selva
Committee Assignment(s): Armed Services; Homeland Security and Governmental Affairs; Small Business and Entrepreneurship; Congressional-Executive Commission on China; Select Intelligence

Lieberman, Joseph I., I-Conn.

Capitol Hill Office: SH-706 20510-0703; 224-4041; Fax: 224-9750; *Chief of Staff:* Clarine Nardi Riddle
Web: lieberman.senate.gov
District Office(s): One Constitution Plaza, 7th Floor, Hartford 06103; (860) 549-8463; Fax: (860) 549-8478; *State Director:* Sherry Brown
Committee Assignment(s): Armed Services; Homeland Security and Governmental Affairs; Small Business and Entrepreneurship

Lincoln, Blanche L., D-Ark.

Capitol Hill Office: SD-355 20510-0404; 224-4843; Fax: 228-1371; *Chief of Staff:* Elizabeth Hurley Burks
Web: lincoln.senate.gov
District Office(s): 101 E. Waterman St., Dumas 71639-2226; (870) 382-1023; Fax: (870) 382-1026; *Community Affairs Specialist:* Raymond Frazier
4 S. College Ave., #205, Fayetteville 72701-5347; (479) 251-1224; Fax: (479) 251-1410; *Community Affairs Specialist:* John Hicks
615 S. Main St., #315, Jonesboro 72401-2861; (870) 910-6896; Fax: (870) 910-6898; *Community Affairs Specialist:* Roger Fisher

912 W. 4th St., Little Rock 72201-2110; (501) 375-2993; Fax: (501) 375-7064; *State Director:* Donna Kay Yeargan
Miller County Courthouse, 400 Laurel St., #101, Texarkana 71854-5245; (870) 774-3106; Fax: (870) 774-7627; *Community Affairs Specialist:* Ed French
Committee Assignment(s): Agriculture, Nutrition, and Forestry; Energy and Natural Resources; Finance; Special Aging

Lugar, Richard G., R-Ind.

Capitol Hill Office: SH-306 20510-1401; 224-4814; *Chief of Staff:* Martin W. Morris
Web: lugar.senate.gov
E-mail: senator_lugar@lugar.senate.gov
District Office(s): Federal Bldg., 101 N.W. Martin Luther King Jr. Blvd., #122, Evansville 47708-1951; (812) 465-6313; *Southwest Regional Director:* Larry Ordner
Covington Plaza, 6384A W. Jefferson Blvd., Fort Wayne 46802-3075; (260) 422-1505; Fax: (260) 424-1342; *Northeast Regional Director:* Cathy Gallmeyer
Market Tower, 10 W. Market St., #1180, Indianapolis 46204-2964; (317) 226-5555; *State Director:* Lesley N. Reser
175 W. Lincolnway, #G-1, Valparaiso 46383-5559; (219) 548-8035; *Northwest Regional Director:* Celina Weatherwax
Committee Assignment(s): Agriculture, Nutrition, and Forestry; Foreign Relations

Martinez, Mel, R-Fla.

Capitol Hill Office: SR-356 20510-0906; 224-3041; Fax: 228-5171; *Chief of Staff:* Tom Weinberg
Web: martinez.senate.gov
District Office(s): 800 S. Douglas Rd., #148, Coral Gables 33134-3187; (305) 444-8332; Fax: (305) 444-8449; *South Florida Regional Director:* Laura Muñiz
2120 Main Street, #200, Fort Myers 33901-3010; (239) 332-3898; (239) 332-6447; *Southwest Regional Director:* Chad McLeod
1650 Prudential Dr., #220, Jacksonville 32207-8149; (904) 398-8586; Fax: (904) 398-8591; *North Florida Regional Director:* Kevin Doyle
Landmark Center One, 315 E. Robinson St., #475, Orlando 32801-4343; (407) 254-2573; Fax: (407) 423-0941; *Central Regional Director:* John Newstreet
1 N. Palafox St., #159, Pensacola 32502-5658; (850) 432-2603; Fax: (850) 433-2554; *Northwest Regional Director:* Kris Tande
3802 Spectrum Boulevard, Suite 106, Tampa 33612-9220; (813) 977-6450; Fax: (813) 977-6593; *Gulf Coast Regional Director:* Aileen Rodriguez
7711 N. Military Trail, #1014, West Palm Beach 33410-6423; (561) 842-8300; Fax: (561) 842-8949; *Southwest Florida Regional Director:* Steve Martino
Committee Assignment(s): Armed Services; Banking, Housing, and Urban Affairs; Commerce, Science, and Transportation; Congressional-Executive Commission on China; Special Aging

McCain, John, R-Ariz.

Capitol Hill Office: SR-241 20510-0303; 224-2235; Fax: 228-2862; *Administrative Assistant:* Mark Buse
Web: mccain.senate.gov
District Office(s): 5353 N. 16th St., #105, Phoenix 85016-3282; (602) 952-2410, Fax: (602) 952-8702; *State Director:* Paul T. Hickman
4703 S. Lakeshore Dr., #1, Tempe 85282-7159; (480) 897-6289; Fax: (480) 897-8389; *Office Manager:* Deb Jacobus
407 W. Congress St., #103, Tucson 85701-1349; (520) 670-6334; Fax: (520) 670-6637; *Office Manager:* Rosemary Alexander
Committee Assignment(s): Armed Services; Energy and Natural Resources; Health, Education, Labor, and Pensions; Homeland Security and Governmental Affairs; Indian Affairs; Select Intelligence

McCaskill, Claire, D-Mo.

Capitol Hill Office: SH-717 20510-2507; 224-6154; Fax: 228-6326; *Chief of Staff:* Julie Dwyer
Web: mccaskill.senate.gov
District Office(s): 339 Broadway St., #136, Cape Girardeau 63701-7348; (573) 651-0964; Fax: (573) 334-4278; *District Director:* Christy Ferrell
915 E. Ash Street, Columbia 65201-4853; (573) 442-7130; Fax: (573) 442-7140; *Regional Director:* Cindy Hall
Charles E. Whittaker Federal Bldg., 400 E. 9th St., #40, Plaza Level, Kansas City 64106-2607; (816) 421-1639; Fax: (816) 421-2562; *Regional Director:* Heather Corey Dillon
324 Park Central W., #101, Springfield 65806-1218; (417) 868-8745; Fax: (417) 831-1349; *District Director:* David Rauch
5850 Delmar Boulevard, Suite A, St. Louis 63112-2346; (314) 367-1364; Fax: (314) 361-8649; *Regional Director:* Michelle Sherod
Committee Assignment(s): Armed Services; Commerce, Science, and Transportation; Homeland Security and Governmental Affairs; Special Aging

McConnell, Mitch, R-Ky.

Capitol Hill Office: SR-361A 20510-1702; 224-2541; Fax: 224-2499; *Chief of Staff:* William H. Piper
Web: mcconnell.senate.gov
District Office(s): Federal Bldg., 241 E. Main St., #102, Bowling Green 42101-2175; (270) 781-1673; Fax: (270) 782-1884; *Field Representative:* LeAnn Crosby
1885 Dixie Hwy., #345, Fort Wright 41011-2679; (859) 578-0188; Fax: (859) 578-0488; *Field Representative:* Adam Howard
771 Corporate Dr., #108, Lexington 40503-5439; (859) 224-8286; Fax: (859) 224-9673; *Field Representative:* Kevin Atkins
300 S. Main St., #310, London 40741-2415; (606) 864-2026; Fax: (606) 864-2035; *Field Representative:* Donna McClure

Gene Snyder U.S. Courthouse, 601 W. Broadway, #630, Louisville 40202-2228; (502) 582-6304; Fax: (502) 582-5326; *State Director:* Larry E. Cox
Professional Arts Bldg., 2320 Broadway, #100, Paducah 42001-7146; (270) 442-4554; Fax: (270) 443-3102; *Field Representative:* Martie Wiles
Committee Assignment(s): Agriculture, Nutrition, and Forestry; Appropriations; Rules and Administration; Select Intelligence

Menendez, Robert, D-N.J.

Capitol Hill Office: SH-317 20510-3006; 224-4744; Fax: 228-2197; *Chief of Staff:* Danny O'Brien
Web: menendez.senate.gov
District Office(s): 208 White Horse Pike, #18-19, Barrington 08007-1322; (856) 757-5353; Fax: (854) 546-1526; *Deputy State Director, South Jersey:* Karin Elkis
1 Gateway Center, #1100, Newark 07102-5323; (973) 645-3030; Fax: (973) 645-0502; *State Director:* Mike Soliman
Committee Assignment(s): Banking, Housing, and Urban Affairs; Budget; Energy and Natural Resources; Finance; Foreign Relations

Merkley, Jeff, D-Ore.

Capitol Hill Office: SR-B40B 20510-3705; 224-3753; *Chief of Staff:* Michael S. Zamore
Web: merkley.senate.gov
District Office(s): 1 World Trade Center, 121 S.W. Salmon Street, Suite 1250, Portland 97204-2922; (503) 326-3386; Fax: (503) 326-2900; *State Director:* Jon Isaacs
Committee Assignment(s): Banking, Housing, and Urban Affairs; Budget; Environment and Public Works; Health, Education, Labor, and Pensions

Mikulski, Barbara A., D-Md.

Capitol Hill Office: SH-503 20510-2003; 224-4654; Fax: 224-8858; *Chief of Staff:* Julia Frifield
Web: mikulski.senate.gov
District Office(s): 60 West St., #202, Annapolis 21401-2448; (410) 263-1805; Fax: (410) 263-5949; *Director:* Denise G. Nooe
Brown's Wharf, 1629 Thames St., #400, Baltimore 21231; (410) 962-4510; Fax: (410) 962-4760; *Constituent Services Director:* Marianne Kreitner
6404 Ivy Lane, #406, Greenbelt 20770-1407; (301) 345-5517; Fax: (301) 345-7573; *Asst. to the Senator:* Pam College
32 W. Washington St., #203, Hagerstown 21740-4804; (301) 797-2826; Fax: (301) 797-2241; *Outreach Representative:* Juliana Albowicz
The Gallery Plaza Building, 212 W. Main Street, Suite 200, Salisbury 21801-5106; (410) 546-7711; Fax: (410) 546-9324
Committee Assignment(s): Appropriations; Health, Education, Labor, and Pensions; Select Intelligence

Murkowski, Lisa, R-Alaska

Capitol Hill Office: SH-709 20510-0203; 224-6665;
  Fax: 224-5301; *Chief of Staff:* Karen Y. Knutson
Web: murkowski.senate.gov
District Office(s): 510 L St., #550, Anchorage 99501-1956;
  (907) 271-3735; Fax: (907) 276-4081; *State Director:*
  Kevin Sweeney
P.O. Box 1030, 311 Willow St., Bldg. #3, Bethel 99559;
  (907) 543-1639; Fax: (907) 543-1637
101 12th Ave., #216, Fairbanks 99701-6278; (907)
  456-0233; Fax: (907) 451-7146; *Special Assistant:*
  Althea St. Martin
Hurff A. Saunders Federal Bldg., 709 W. 9th St.,
  P.O. Box 21647, Juneau 99802-1647; (907)
  586-7400; Fax: (907) 586-8922; *Staff Assistant:*
  Connie McKenzie
110 Trading Bay Dr., #105, Kenai 99611-9114; (907)
  283-5208; Fax: (907) 283-4363; *Staff Assistant:*
  Michelle Blackwell
4079 Tongass Avenue, Suite 204, Ketchikan 99901-5526;
  (907) 225-6880; Fax: (907) 225-0390; *Staff Assistant:*
  Sherrie Slick
851 E. Westpoint Dr., #307, Wasilla 99654-7183; (907)
  376-7665; Fax: (907) 376-8526; *Special Assistant:*
  Gerri Sumpter
Committee Assignment(s): Appropriations; Energy and
  Natural Resources; Health, Education, Labor, and
  Pensions; Indian Affairs

Murray, Patty, D-Wash.

Capitol Hill Office: SR-173 20510-4704; 224-2621;
  Fax: 224-0238; *Chief of Staff:* Jeff Bjornstad
Web: murray.senate.gov
District Office(s): Campus Office Park, 1161 116th Ave.,
  N.E., #214, Bellevue 98004-4602; (425) 462-4460;
  King County Director: Sergio Cuena-Flores
2930 Wetmore Ave., #903, Everett 98201-4067; (425)
  259-6515; Fax: (425) 259-7152; *Northwest Regional
  Director:* Shawn Bills
Henry M. Jackson Federal Bldg., 915 2nd Ave., #2988,
  Seattle 98174-1003; (206) 553-5545; Fax: (206)
  553-0891; *State Director:* Brian Kristjansson
10 North Post Street, Suite 600, Spokane 99201-0712;
  (509) 624-9515; Fax: (509) 624-9524; *Eastern
  Washington Director:* Judy Olson
950 Pacific Ave., #650, Tacoma 98402-4450; (253)
  572-3636; Fax: (253) 572-9089; *Southsound and
  Olympic Peninsula Director:* Mary McBride
Marshall House, 1323 Officers Row, Vancouver
  98661-3856; (360) 696-7797; Fax: (360) 696-7798;
  Southwest Washington Director: Theresa Wagner
402 E. Yakima Ave., #390, Yakima 98901-2760; (509)
  453-7462; Fax: (509) 453-7731; *Central Washington
  Director:* Rebecca Thorton
Committee Assignment(s): Appropriations;
  Budget; Health, Education, Labor, and Pensions;
  Rules and Administration; Veterans' Affairs; Joint
  Printing

Nelson, Bill, D-Fla.

Capitol Hill Office: SH-716 20510-0905; 224-5274;
  Fax: 228-2183; *Chief of Staff:* Peter J. Mitchell
Web: billnelson.senate.gov
District Office(s): 3416 S. University Dr., Ft. Lauderdale
  33328-2022; (954) 693-4851; Fax: (954) 693-4862;
  Regional Director: Willowstine Lawson
Justice Center Annex Bldg., 2000 Main St., #801, Ft.
  Myers 33901-5503; (239) 334-7760; Fax: (239)
  334-7710; *Regional Director:* Diana McGee
1301 Riverplace Blvd., #2218, Jacksonville 32207-9021;
  (904) 346-4500; Fax: (904) 346-4506; *Regional
  Director:* Michelle Barth
2925 Salzedo St., Miami 33134-6611; (305) 536-5999;
  Fax: (305) 536-5991; *Regional Director:* Laura Fatoric
Landmark Center Two, 225 E. Robinson St., #410,
  Orlando 32801-4326; (407) 872-7161; Fax: (407)
  872-7165; *Regional Director:* Celeste Brown
U.S. Courthouse Annex, 111 N. Adams St., Tallahassee
  32301-7736; (850) 942-8415; Fax: (850) 942-8450;
  Chief of Staff: Peter J. Mitchell
Sam M. Gibbons Federal Courthouse, 801 N. Florida
  Ave., 4th Floor, Tampa 33602-3849; (813) 225-7040;
  Fax: (813) 225-7050; *Regional Director:* Digna Alvarez
500 Clear Lake Ave., #125, West Palm Beach 33401-3002;
  (561) 514-0189; Fax: (561) 514-0844; *Regional
  Director:* Michelle McGovern
Committee Assignment(s): Armed Services; Budget;
  Commerce, Science, and Transportation; Finance;
  Select Intelligence; Special Aging

Nelson, E. Benjamin, D-Neb.

Capitol Hill Office: SH-720 20510-2706; 224-6551;
  Fax: 228-0012; *Chief of Staff:* Tim Becker
Web: bennelson.senate.gov
District Office(s): P.O. Box 791, South Sioux City 68776;
  (402) 209-3595; Fax: (866) 789-6460; *Staff Assistant:*
  Zach Nelson
P.O. Box 2105, Kearney 68848; (308) 293-5818; *Staff
  Assistant:* Phil Johansen
440 N. 8th St., #120, Lincoln 68508; (402) 441-4600;
  Fax: (402) 476-8753; *District Manager:* Tammy Ward
7602 Pacific St., #205, Omaha 68114-5451; (402)
  391-3411; Fax: (402) 391-4725; *Staff Assistant:* Louise
  Latimer
P.O. Box 1492, Scottsbluff 69361; (308) 631-7614;
  District Manager: Bob Holmstedt
Committee Assignment(s): Agriculture, Nutrition, and
  Forestry; Appropriations; Armed Services; Rules and
  Administration

Pryor, Mark, D-Ark.

Capitol Hill Office: SD-255 20510-0405; 224-2353;
  Fax: 228-0908; *Chief of Staff:* Robert A. Russell
Web: pryor.senate.gov
District Office(s): The River Market, 500 Clinton Ave.,
  #401, Little Rock 72201-1745; (501) 324-6336;
  Fax: (501) 324-5320; *State Director:* Randy Massanelli

Committee Assignment(s): Appropriations; Commerce, Science, and Transportation; Homeland Security and Governmental Affairs; Rules and Administration; Small Business and Entrepreneurship; Select Ethics

Reed, Jack, D-R.I.

Capitol Hill Office: SH-728 20510-3903; 224-4642; Fax: 224-4680; *Chief of Staff:* Neil D. Campbell
Web: reed.senate.gov
District Office(s): 1000 Chapel View Blvd., #290; Cranston 02920; (401) 943-3100; Fax: (401) 464-6837; *Chief of Staff:* Raymond D. Simone
#408, U.S. Courthouse, One Exchange Terrace, Providence 02903-1773; (401) 528-5200; Fax: (401) 528-5242; *Staff Assistant:* Nancy Melo
Committee Assignment(s): Appropriations; Armed Services; Banking, Housing, and Urban Affairs; Health, Education, Labor, and Pensions

Reid, Harry M., D-Nev.

Capitol Hill Office: SH-528 20510-2803; 224-3542; Fax: 224-7327; *Senior Advisor:* Bruce King
Web: reid.senate.gov
District Office(s): 600 E. William St., #302, Carson City 89701-4052; (775) 882-7343; Fax: (775) 883-1980; *Regional Representative:* Yolanda Garcia-Banuelos
Lloyd D. George Federal Bldg. and U.S. Courthouse, 333 Las Vegas Blvd. South, #8016, Las Vegas 89101-7075; (702) 388-5020; Fax: (702) 388-5030; *Southern Regional Director:* Shannon Raborn
Bruce R. Thompson Courthouse and Federal Bldg., 400 S. Virginia St., #902, Reno 89501-2109; (775) 686-5750; Fax: (775) 686-5757; *State Director:* Mary Conelly
Committee Assignment(s): Select Intelligence

Risch, James E., R-Idaho

Capitol Hill Office: SR-SRC-2 20510-1206; 224-2752; Fax: 224-2573; *Chief of Staff:* John Sandy
Web: risch.senate.gov
District Office(s): 350 N. Ninth Street, Suite 302, Boise 83702-5409; (208) 342-7985; *State Director:* Matt Ellsworth
Harbor Plaza, 610 W. Hubbard Street, Suite 121, Coeur D'Alene 83814-2286; (208) 667-6130; *Regional Director:* Sidney Smith
490 Memorial Drive, Suite 101, Idaho Falls 83402-3600; (208) 523-5541; *Staff Asst.:* Laci Jentzsch
313 D Street, Suite 106, Lewiston 83501-1894; (208) 743-0792; *Regional Director:* Mike Roach
275 S. Fifth Avenue, Suite 290, Pocatello 83201-6410; (208) 236-6017; *Regional Director:* Jeremy Field
560 Filer Avenue, Suite A, Twin Falls 83301-3923; (208) 734-6780; *Regional Director:* Mike Matthews
Committee Assignment(s): Energy and Natural Resources; Foreign Relations; Joint Economic; Select Ethics; Select Intelligence

Roberts, Pat, R-Kan.

Capitol Hill Office: SH-109 20510-1605; 224-4774; Fax: 224-3514; *Chief of Staff:* Jackie Cottrell
Web: roberts.senate.gov
E-mail: roberts.senate.gov/e-mail_pat.html
District Office(s): 100 Military Plaza, #203, Dodge City 67801-4990; (620) 227-2244; Fax: (620) 227-2264; *District Director:* Debbie Pugh
11900 College Blvd., #203, Overland Park 66210-3939; (913) 451-9343; Fax: (913) 451-9446; *District Director:* Ramona Corbin
Frank Carlson Federal Bldg., 444 S.E. Quincy St., #392, Topeka 66683-3599; (785) 295-2745; Fax: (785) 235-3665; *District Director:* Gilda Lintz
155 N. Market St., #120, Wichita 67202-1802; (316) 263-0416; Fax: (316) 263-0273; *District Director:* Karin Wisdom
Committee Assignment(s): Agriculture, Nutrition, and Forestry; Finance; Health, Education, Labor, and Pensions; Rules and Administration; Select Ethics

Rockefeller, John D. IV, D-W.Va.

Capitol Hill Office: SH-531 20510-4802; 224-6472; Fax: 224-7665; *Chief of Staff:* Katherine A. Ates
Web: rockefeller.senate.gov
E-mail: rockefeller.senate.gov/services/email.cfm
District Office(s): 220 N. Kanawha St., #1, Beckley 25801-4717; (304) 253-9704; Fax: (304) 253-2578; *Area Coordinator:* Phillip Lewis
405 Capitol St., #308, Charleston 25301-1786; (304) 3 47-5372; Fax: (304) 347-5371; *State Director:* Rochelle Goodwin
118 Adams St., #301, Fairmont 26554-2841; (304) 367-0122; Fax: (304) 367-0822; *Northern Area Coordinator:* Larry Lemon
225 W. King St., #307, Martinsburg 25401-3211; (304) 262-9285; Fax: (304) 262-9288; *Director, Eastern West Virginia Satellite Office:* Penny Porter
Committee Assignment(s): Commerce, Science, and Transportation; Finance; Veterans' Affairs; Joint Taxation; Select Intelligence

Sanders, Bernard, I-Vt.

Capitol Hill Office: SD-332 20510-4504; 224-5141; Fax: 228-0776; *Chief of Staff:* Huck Gutman
Web: sanders.senate.gov
District Office(s): 36 Chickering Dr., #103, Brattleboro 05301-4419; (802) 254-8732; Fax: (802) 254-9207; *Outreach Representative:* Sam Haskins
1 Church St., 2nd Floor, Burlington 05401-4451; (802) 862-0697; Fax: (802) 860-6370; *Outreach Director:* Phil Fiermonte
51 Depot Square, Suite 201, St. Johnsbury 05819-2796; (802) 748-0302; (802) 748-9269; *Health Policy Advisor/Outreach Rep.:* David Reynolds
Committee Assignment(s): Budget; Energy and Natural Resources; Environment and Public Works; Health, Education, Labor, and Pensions; Veterans' Affairs

Schumer, Charles E., D-N.Y.

Capitol Hill Office: SH-313 20510-3203; 224-6542; Fax: 228-3027; *Chief of Staff:* Michael B. Lynch
Web: schumer.senate.gov
District Office(s): Leo W. O'Brien Bldg., #420, Albany 12207; (518) 431-4070; Fax: (518) 431-4076; *Regional Representative:* Steve Mann
15 Henry St., #B-6, Binghamton 13901-2753; (607) 772-6792; Fax: (607) 772-8124; *Regional Representative:* Amanda Spellicy
130 S. Elmwood Ave., #660, Buffalo 14202-2371; (716) 846-4111; Fax: (716) 846-4113; *Regional Representative:* Laura Monte
2 Greenway Plaza, 145 Pine Lawn Rd., 3rd Floor, #300, Melville 11747; (631) 753-0978; Fax: (631) 753-0997; *Regional Representative:* Gerry Petrella
757 3rd Ave., #1702, New York 10017-2054; (212) 486-4430; Fax: (212) 486-7693; *State Director:* Martin Brennan
1 Park Place, #100, Peekskill 12566; (914) 734-1532; Fax: (914) 734-1673; *Regional Representative:* Mike Morey
100 State St., #3040, Rochester 14614-1317; (585) 263-5866; Fax: (585) 263-3173; *Regional Representative:* Joe Hamm
James M. Hanley Federal Bldg., 100 South Clinton St., #841, Syracuse 13261-6100; (315) 423-5471; Fax: (315) 423-5185; *Regional Representative:* Jill Harvey
Committee Assignment(s): Banking, Housing, and Urban Affairs; Finance; Judiciary; Rules and Administration; Joint Library of Congress

Sessions, Jeff, R-Ala.

Capitol Hill Office: SR-335 20510-0104; 224-4124; Fax: 224-3149; *Chief of Staff:* Rick A. Dearborn
Web: sessions.senate.gov
District Office(s): Robert S. Vance Federal Bldg., 1800 5th Ave., N., #341, Birmingham 35203-2171; (205) 731-1500; Fax: (205) 731-0221; *Field Representative:* Virginia Amason
AmSouth Center, 200 Clinton Ave., N.W., #802, Huntsville 35801-4932; (256) 533-0979; Fax: (256) 533-0745; *Field Representative:* Lisa Montgomery
Colonial Bank Center, 41 West I-65 Service Rd. N., #2003-A, Mobile 36608; (251) 414-3083; Fax: (251) 414-5845; *Field Representative:* Valerie Day
7550 Halcyon Summit Dr., #150, Montgomery 36117-7012; (334) 244-7017; Fax: (334) 244-7091; *Field Representative:* Cecelia Meeks
Committee Assignment(s): Armed Services; Budget; Energy and Natural Resources; Judiciary

Shaheen, Jeanne, D-N.H.

Capitol Hill Office: SR-G55 20510-2906; 224-2841; Fax: 228-3194; *Chief of Staff:* Maura Keefe
Web: shaeen.senate.gov
District Office(s): 50 Opera House Square, Claremont 03743-5407; (603) 542-4872; (603) 542-6582; *Special Assistant for Constituent Services:* Pam Slack

1589 Elm Street, Suite 3, Manchester 03743-5407; (603) 647-7500; *State Director:* Michael A. Vlacich
Committee Assignment(s): Commission on Security and Cooperation in Europe; Energy and Natural Resources; Foreign Relations; Small Business and Entrepreneurship

Shelby, Richard C., R-Ala.

Capitol Hill Office: SR-304 20510-0103; 224-5744; Fax: 224-3416; *Chief of Staff:* Alan Hanson
Web: shelby.senate.gov
E-mail: senator@shelby.senate.gov
District Office(s): Robert S. Vance Federal Bldg., 1800 5th Ave. N., #321, Birmingham 35203-2113; (205) 731-1384; Fax: (205) 731-1386; *District Representative:* Blair Agricola
Huntsville International Airport, 1000 Glenn Hearn Blvd. S.W., #20127, Huntsville 35824-2107; (256) 772-0460; Fax: (256) 772-8387; *District Representative:* LaFreeda Jordan
Federal Courthouse, 113 St. Joseph St., #445, Mobile 36602-3606; (251) 694-4164; Fax: (251) 694-4166; *District Representative:* Tera Johnson
Federal Courthouse, 15 Lee St., #B-28, Montgomery 36104-4007; (334) 223-7303; Fax: (334) 223-7317; *District Representative:* Vera Jordan
Federal Bldg., 1118 Greensboro Ave., #240, Tuscaloosa 35401-2816; (205) 759-5047; Fax: (205) 759-5067; *District Representative:* Melissia Davis
Committee Assignment(s): Appropriations; Banking, Housing, and Urban Affairs; Special Aging

Snowe, Olympia J., R-Maine

Capitol Hill Office: SR-154 20510-1903; 224-5344; Fax: 224-1946; *Chief of Staff:* John R. Richter
Web: snowe.senate.gov
District Office(s): 2 Great Falls Plaza, #5, Auburn 04210-5999; (207) 786-2451; Fax: (207) 782-1438; *Regional Representative:* Diane Jackson
Edmund S. Muskie Federal Bldg., 40 Western Ave., #408C, Augusta 04330-6350; (207) 622-8292; Fax: (207) 622-7295; *Regional Representative:* Debra McNeil
1 Cumberland Place, #306, Bangor 04401-5084; (207) 945-0432; Fax: (207) 941-9525; *State Director:* Gail M. Kelly
231 Main St., #2, Biddeford 04005-2497; (207) 282-4144; Fax: (207) 284-2358; *Regional Representative:* Peter Morin
3 Canal Plaza, #601, Portland 04101-6436; (207) 874-0883; Fax: (207) 874-7631; *Field Representative:* Cheryl Leeman
169 Academy St., Suite A, Presque Isle 04769-3166; (207) 764-5124; Fax: (207) 764-6420; *Regional Representative:* Sharon Campbell
Committee Assignment(s): Commerce, Science, and Transportation; Finance; Small Business and Entrepreneurship; Select Intelligence

Specter, Arlen, D-Pa.

Capitol Hill Office: SH-711 20510-3802; 224-4254; Fax: 228-1229; *Chief of Staff:* Scott Hoeflich
Web: specter.senate.gov
District Office(s): U.S. Courthouse and Federal Bldg., 504 W. Hamilton St., #3814, Allentown 18101-1500; (610) 434-1444; Fax: (610) 434-1844; *Executive Director:* Adrienne Baker Green
17 South Park Row, #B-120, Erie 16501-1156; (814) 453-3010; Fax: (814) 455-9925; *Executive Director:* Mary Styn
Federal Bldg., 228 Walnut St., #1104, Harrisburg 17101-1722; (717) 782-3951; Fax: (717) 782-4920; *Executive Director:* Josh Snyder
600 Arch St., #9400, Philadelphia 19106-1617; (215) 597-7200; Fax: (215) 597-0406; *Exec. Director:* Mike Oscar
Regional Enterprise Tower, 425 6th Ave., #1450, Pittsburgh 15219-1870; (412) 644-3400; Fax: (412) 644-4871; *Executive Director:* Stan Caldwell
310 Spruce St., #201, Scranton 18503-1413; (570) 346-2006; Fax: (570) 346-8499; *Executive Director:* Andrew Wallace
Stegmaier Bldg., 7 N. Wilkes-Barre Blvd., #377M, Wilkes-Barre 18702-5241; (570) 826-6265; Fax: (570) 826-6266; *Executive Director:* Andrew Wallace
Committee Assignment(s): Appropriations; Environment and Public Works; Judiciary; Veterans' Affairs; Special Aging

Stabenow, Debbie, D-Mich.

Capitol Hill Office: SH-133 20510-2204; 224-4822; Fax: 228-0325; *Chief of Staff:* Amanda A. Renteria
Web: stabenow.senate.gov
District Office(s): The Marquette Bldg., 243 W. Congress St., #550, Detroit 48226-3248; (313) 961-4330; Fax: (313) 961-7566; *Regional Manager:* Korey Hall
221 W. Lake Lansing Rd., #100, East Lansing 48823-8661; (517) 203-1760; Fax: (517) 203-1778; *State Director:* Teresa Plachetka
Linden Valley Plaza, 2503 S. Linden Rd., Flint 48532-5462; (810) 720-4172; Fax: (810) 720-4178; *Regional Manager:* Chris Hennessy
3280 Beltline Ct., #400, Grand Rapids 49525-9494; (616) 975-0052; Fax: (616) 975-5764; *Regional Manager:* Mary Judnich
1901 W. Ridge St., #7, Marquette 49855-3198; (906) 228-8756; Fax: (906) 228-9162; *Regional Manager:* Sheri Davie
3335 S. Airport Rd. West, #6B, Traverse City 49684-7928; (231) 929-1031; Fax: (231) 929-1250; *Regional Manager:* Brandon Fewins
Committee Assignment(s): Agriculture, Nutrition, and Forestry; Budget; Energy and Natural Resources; Finance

Tester, Jon, D-Mont.

Capitol Hill Office: SD-204 20510-2604; 224-2644; Fax: 224-8594; *Chief of Staff:* Stephanie Schriock
Web: tester.senate.gov
District Office(s): Granite Tower, 222 N. 32nd St., #101, Billings 59101-1954; (406) 252-0550; Fax: (406) 252-7768; *Field Director:* Rachel Stagg
211 Haggerty Lane, Bozeman 59715-9235; (406) 586-4450; Fax: (406) 586-7647; *Field Director:* Jennifer Madgic
Silver Bow Center, 125 W. Granite St., #211, Butte 59701-9215; (406) 723-3277; Fax: (406) 782-4717; *Field Director:* Pamela Haxby-Cote
122 W. Towne Street, Glendive MT 59330-1735; (406) 365-2391; Fax: (406) 365-8836; *Field Director:* Penny Zimmerman
119 1st Ave. North, #102, Great Falls 59401-2505; (406) 452-9585; Fax: (406) 452-9586; *Field Director:* Cheryl MacArthur
Capital One Center, 208 N. Montana Ave., #202, Helena 59601-3837; (406) 449-5401; Fax: (406) 257-3974; *State Director:* Bill Lombardi
19 2nd St. E, Suite E, Kalispell 59901-4508; (406) 257-3360; Fax: (406) 257-3774; *Field Director:* Virginia Sloan
130 W. Front St., Missoula 59802-4304; (406) 728-3003; Fax: (406) 728-2193; *Field Director:* Tracy Stone-Manning
Committee Assignment(s): Appropriations; Banking, Housing, and Urban Affairs; Homeland Security and Governmental Affairs; Indian Affairs; Veterans' Affairs

Thune, John, R-S.D.

Capitol Hill Office: SR-493 20510-4105; 224-2321; Fax: 228-5429; *Chief of Staff:* Matthew L. Zabel
Web: thune.senate.gov
District Office(s): 320 S. 1st St., #101, Aberdeen 57401-4168; (605) 225-8823; Fax: (605) 225-8468; *Northeast Regional Director:* Judy Vrchota
1313 W. Main St., Rapid City 57701-2540; (605) 348-7551; Fax: (605) 348-7208; *West River Regional Director:* Qusi Al-Haj
320 N. Main Ave., Suite B, Sioux Falls 57104-6056; (605) 334-9596; Fax: (605) 334-2591; *State Director:* Ryan Nelson
Committee Assignment(s): Agriculture, Nutrition, and Forestry; Armed Services; Commerce, Science, and Transportation; Small Business and Entrepreneurship

Udall, Mark, D-Colo.

Capitol Hill Office: SH-307 20510-0607; 224-5941; Fax: 224-6471; *Chief of Staff:* Michael L. Sozan
Web: markudall.senate.gov
District Office(s): Wayne Aspinall Federal Building, 400 Rood Avenue, Suite 215, Grand Junction 81501-2520; (970) 245-9553; Fax: (970) 245-9523; *Regional Rep.:* Jay Fetcher

8601 Turnpike Drive, Suite 206, Westminster 80031-7044; (303) 650-7820; Fax: (303) 650-7827; *State Director:* Jennifer Rokala

Committee Assignment(s): Armed Services; Energy and Natural Resources; Special Aging

Udall, Tom, D-N.M.

Capitol Hill Office: SH-110 20510-3103; 224-6621; Fax: 228-3261; *Chief of Staff:* Tom Nagle

Web: tomudall.senate.gov

District Office(s): 201 Third Street N.W., Suite 710, Albuquerque 87102-4380; (505) 346-6791; Fax: (505) 346-6720; *State Director:* Bianca Ortiz Wertheim

505 S. Main Street, Suite 118, Las Cruces 88001-1209; (575) 526-5475; Fax: (575) 523-6589; *Field Rep.:* Xochitl Torres

120 S. Federal Place, Suite 302, Santa Fe 87501-1966; (505) 988-6511; Fax: (505) 988-6514; *Field Rep.:* Michael Lopez

Committee Assignment(s): Commission on Security and Cooperation in Europe; Commerce, Science, and Transportation; Environment and Public Works; Indian Affairs; Rules and Administration

Vitter, David, R-La.

Capitol Hill Office: SH-516 20510-1805; 224-4623; Fax: 228-5061; *Chief of Staff:* Kyle Ruckert

Web: vitter.senate.gov

District Office(s): 2230 S. MacArthur Dr., #4, Alexandria 71301-3055; (318) 448-0169; Fax: (318) 448-0189; *Regional Representative:* Sarah Morrow

878 Convention St., Baton Rouge 70802-5626; (225) 383-0331; Fax: (225) 383-0952; *Community Liaison:* Brenda Clark

800 Lafayette St., #1200, Lafayette 70501-6800; (337) 262-6898; Fax: (337) 262-6373; *Southwest Regional Director:* Nicole Hebert

3221 Ryan St., Suite E, Lake Charles 70601-8780; (337) 436-0453; Fax: (337) 436-3163; *Regional Representative:* Courtney Hearod

2800 Veterans Blvd., #201, Metairie 70002; (504) 589-2753; Fax: (504) 589-2607; *State Director:* David B. Doss

1217 N. 19th St., Monroe 71201-5435; (318) 325-8120; Fax: (318) 325-9165; *Regional Representative:* Tiffany Clason

Pierremont Office Park, 920 Pierremont Rd., #113, Shreveport 71106-2079; (318) 861-0437; Fax: (318) 861-4865; *Regional Director:* Chip Layton

Committee Assignment(s): Commerce, Science, and Transportation; Environment and Public Works; Foreign Relations; Small Armed Services; Banking, Housing, and Urban Affairs; Commerce, Science, and Transportation; Environment and Public Works; Business and Entrepreneurship

Voinovich, George V., R-Ohio

Capitol Hill Office: SH-524 20510-3504; 224-3353; Fax: 228-1382; *Chief of Staff:* Phil Park

Web: voinovich.senate.gov

District Office(s): 36 E. 7th St., #2615, Cincinnati 45202-4453; (513) 684-3265; Fax: (513) 684-3269; *District Director:* Nancy K. Cahall

1240 E. 9th St., #2955, Cleveland 44199-2001; (216) 522-7095; Fax: (216) 522-7097; *District Director:* Diane Downing

37 W. Broad St., #300, Columbus 43215-4180; (614) 469-6697; Fax: (614) 469-7733; *State Director:* Beth Hansen

78 W. Washington St., Nelsonville 45764-1135; (740) 441-6410; Fax: (740) 441-6414; *District Representative:* Brandon Kern

420 Madison Ave., #1210, Toledo 43604-1221; (419) 259-3895; Fax: (419) 259-3899; *District Representative:* Wes Fahrbach

Committee Assignment(s): Appropriations; Environment and Public Works; Homeland Security and Governmental Affairs

Warner, Mark, D-Va.

Capitol Hill Office: SR-459A 20510-4606; 224-2023; Fax: 224-2530; *Chief of Staff:* Luke S. Albee

Web: warner.senate.gov

District Office(s): 180 W. Main St., Abingdon 24210-2844; (276) 628-8158; Fax: (276) 628-1036

5309 Commonwealth Centre Pkwy., Suite 401, Midlothian 23112-2633; (804) 739-0247; Fax: (804) 739-3478

101 W. Main Street, Suite 4900, Norfolk 23510-1690; (757) 441-3079; Fax: (757) 441-6250

Committee Assignment(s): Banking, Housing, and Urban Affairs; Budget; Commerce, Science, and Transportation; Rules and Administration

Webb, James H., Jr., D-Va.

Capitol Hill Office: SR-144 20510-4605; 224-4024; Fax: 228-6363; *Chief of Staff:* Paul Reagan

Web: webb.senate.gov

District Office(s): 1501 Lee Highway, #130, Arlington 22209-1109; (703) 807-0581; Fax: (703) 807-5198; *Field Representative:* Gwen Sigda

308 Craghead Street, Suite 102-4, Danville 24541-1468; (424) 792-0976; Fax: (424) 972-0960; *Field Rep.:* Tina Graham

756 Park Avenue, N.W., Norton 24273-1923; (276) 679-4925; Fax: (276) 679-4929; *Field Representative:* Gwyn Dutton

507 E. Franklin St., Richmond 23219-2309; (804) 771-2221; Fax: (804) 771-8313; *State Director:* Conaway B. Haskins III

3140 Chaparral Dr., Bldg. C, #101, Roanoke 24018-4370; (540) 772-4236; Fax: (540) 772-6870; *Field Representative:* Debra Lawson

222 Central Park Ave., #120, Virginia Beach 23462-3023; (757) 518-1674; Fax: (757) 518-1679; *Field Representative:* Jeanne Evans

Committee Assignment(s): Armed Services; Foreign Relations; Veterans' Affairs; Joint Economic

Whitehouse, Sheldon, D-R.I.

Capitol Hill Office: SH-502 20510-3905; 224-2921; Fax: 228-6362; *Chief of Staff:* Mindy Myers

Web: whitehouse.senate.gov

District Office(s): 170 Westminster St., #1100, Providence 02903-2109; (401) 453-5294; Fax: (401) 453-5085; *State Director:* George Carvalho

Committee Assignment(s): Commission on Security and Cooperation in Europe; Budget; Environment and Public Works; Judiciary; Select Intelligence; Special Aging

Wicker, Roger F., R-Miss.

Capitol Hill Office: SR-487 20510-2404; 224-6253; Fax: 228-0378; *Chief of Staff:* Michelle Barlow

Web: wicker.senate.gov/public

District Office(s): 452 Courthouse Road, Suite F, Gulfport 39507-1800; (228) 604-2383; Fax: (228) 896-4359; *Southern Regional Director:* Jennifer Schmidt

2601 Elm Street, Suite Six, Hernando 38632-2119; (662) 429-1002; Fax: (662) 429-6002; *Constituent Liaison:* Kim Chamberlin

245 E. Capitol Street, #226, Jackson 39201-2413; (601) 965-4644; Fax: (601) 965-4007; *Central Region Director:* Teresa Love

3118 Pascagoula Street, #179, Pascagoula 39567-4215; (228) 762-5400; Fax: (228) 762-0137; *Constituent Liaison:* Dee Phillips

2801 W. Main Street, Tupelo 38801-3001; (662) 844-5010; Fax: (662) 844-5030; *Constituent Liaison:* Jamie Ellis

Committee Assignment(s): Commission on Security and Cooperation in Europe; Armed Services; Commerce, Science, and Transportation; Foreign Relations; Small Business and Entrepreneurship; Veterans' Affairs

Wyden, Ron, D-Ore.

Capitol Hill Office: SD-220 20510-3703; 224-5244; Fax: 228-2717; *Chief of Staff:* Joshua R. Kardon

Web: wyden.senate.gov

District Office(s): The Jamison Bldg., 131 N.W. Hawthorne Ave., #107, Bend 97701-2957; (541) 330-9142; *Field Representative:* Dave Blair

405 E. 8th Ave., #2020, Eugene 97401-2733; (541) 431-0229; *Field Representative:* Juine Chada

Sac Annex Bldg., 105 Fir St., #201, La Grande 97850-2661; (541) 962-7691; *Field Representative:* Kathleen Cathey

Federal Courthouse, 310 W. 6th St., #118, Medford 97501-2700; (541) 858-5122; *Field Representative:* Molly McCarthy-Skundrick

1220 S.W. 3rd Ave., #585, Portland 97204-2805; (503) 326-7525; *State Director:* Lisa Rockower

707 13th St., S.E., #285, Salem 97301-4087; (503) 589-4555; *Field Representative:* Fritz Graham

Committee Assignment(s): Budget; Energy and Natural Resources; Finance; Judiciary; Select Intelligence; Special Aging

Ready Reference

Government Hotlines

DEPARTMENTS

Agriculture
Fraud, waste, and abuse hotline, (800) 424-9121
Meat and poultry safety inquiries, (800) 535-4555

Commerce
Export enforcement hotline, (800) 424-2980
Fraud, waste, and abuse hotline, (800) 424-5197
Trade Information Center, (800) 872-8723

Defense
Army Department's Casualty and Mortuary Affairs Operations Center, (800) 626–3317
Fraud, waste, and abuse hotline, (800) 424-9098
Military OneSource, (800) 342-9647

Education
Fraud, waste, and abuse hotline, (800) 647-8733
Student financial aid info., (800) 433-3243

Energy
Energy Efficiency and Renewable Energy Information Center, (877) 337-3463
Fraud, waste, mismanagement, and abuse hotline, (800) 541-1625

Health and Human Services
Fraud hotline, (800) 447-8477
General health info., (800) 336-4797
HIV/AIDS, STDs, and immunization info., including pandemic flu, (800) 232-4636
Medicare hotline (including prescription drug discounts), (800) 633-4227
National Adoption Center, (800) 862-3678
National Cancer Institute cancer info., (800) 422-6237
National Runaway Switchboard, (800) 786-2929
Traveler's health info., (877) 394-8747

Homeland Security
Flood insurance service, (800) 638-6620
Fraud, abuse, and mismanagement, (800) 323-8603
National Emergency Training Center, (800) 238-3358
Security breaches; hazardous material, chemical, and oil spills, (800) 424-8802

Housing and Urban Development
Housing discrimination hotline, (800) 669-9777

Justice
Americans With Disabilities Act info., (800) 514-0301; TTY, (800) 514-0383
Arson hotline, (888) 283-3473
Bomb hotline, (888) 283-2662
Fraud hotline, (800) 869-4499
Illegal firearms activity hotline, (800) 283-4867
National Criminal Justice Reference Service, (877) 712-9279
National Institute for Corrections Information Center, (800) 877-1461
Stolen firearms hotline, (888) 930-9275
Unfair employment practices hotline (immigration related), (800) 255-7688

Transportation
Auto safety hotline, (800) 424-9393
Aviation safety hotline, (800) 255-1111
Federal Aviation Administration consumer hotline, (800) 322-7873

Treasury
Comptroller of the Currency customer assistance hotline, (800) 613-6743
Fraud, waste, mismanagement, and abuse hotline (IRS programs), (800) 366-4484
Tax forms, tax refund info., and general info., (800) 829-3676
Tax refund status, (800) 829-4477
Taxpayer Advocate Service, (877) 777-4778
Taxpayer assistance, (800) 829-1040

Veterans Affairs
Benefits hotline, (800) 827-1000
Debt Management Center, (800) 827-0648
Fraud, waste, abuse, and mismanagement hotline, (800) 488-8244
Insurance policy info., (800) 669-8477
Persian Gulf hotline, (800) 749-8387

AGENCIES

Consumer Product Safety Commission
Product safety info., (800) 638-2772

Environmental Protection Agency
Asbestos and small business hotline, (800) 368-5888
Endangered species hotline, (800) 447-3813
National Lead Information Center, (800) 424-5323
National Pesticides Information Center, (800) 858-7378
National radon hotline, (800) 767-7236
Ozone information hotline, (800) 296-1996
Safe drinking water hotline, (800) 426-4791
Superfund hotline, (800) 424-9346; (703) 412-9810 in Washington
Wetlands information hotline, (800) 832-7828

Export-Import Bank
Export finance hotline, (800) 565-3946; (202) 565-3946 in Washington

Federal Deposit Insurance Corporation
Banking complaints and inquiries, (877) 275-3342

Federal Election Commission
Campaign finance law info., (800) 424-9530; (202) 694-1100 in Washington

General Services Administration
Federal Citizen Information Center, (800) 688-9889

Office of Special Counsel
Prohibited personnel practices info., (800) 872-9855

Small Business Administration
Fraud, waste, abuse, and mismanagement hotline, (800) 767-0385
Small business assistance, (800) 827-5722

Social Security Administration
Fraud and abuse hotline, (800) 269-0271
Social Security benefits (including Medicare) info., (800) 772-1213

Directory of Government Information on the Internet

Listed below are Web addresses that lead to executive, legislative, and judicial information on the Internet. These links were active as of April 2009. Government information can also be explored online through the www.usa.org, which is the U.S. government's official Internet portal to Web pages for federal and state governments, the District of Columbia, and U.S. territories.

EXECUTIVE BRANCH

The White House

Main: www.whitehouse.gov
News: www.whitehouse.gov/briefing_room/
President's Bio: www.whitehouse.gov/administration/ president_obama
Vice President's Bio: www.whitehouse.gov/ administration/vice_president_biden
First Lady's Bio: www.whitehouse.gov/administration/ michelle_obama
Contacting the White House: www.whitehouse.gov/contact/

Agriculture Dept.

Main: www.usda.gov
About the Agriculture Dept.: www.usda.gov/about_usda
News: www.usda.gov/newsroom/
Secretary's Bio: www.usda.gov/about_usda
Employee Directory: http://dc-directory.hqnet.usda.gov/ DLSNew/phone.aspx
Link to Regional Offices: http://usda.gov/about_usda
Department Budget: www.usda.gov/about_usda

Commerce Dept.

Main: www.commerce.gov
About the Commerce Dept.: www.commerce.gov/ about_us/index.htm
News: www.commerce.gov/Newsroom/index.htm
Secretary's Bio: www.commerce.gov/commercesecretary/ index.htm
Employee Directory: http://dir.commerce.gov
Links to State and Regional Offices:
 Census Bureau: www.census.gov/field/www/
 Commerce Dept.: www.commerce.gov/services/ index.htm
 Economic Development Administration: www.eda .gov/Resources/StateLinks.xml
Department Budget: www.osec.doc.gov/bmi/budget

Defense Dept.

Main: www.defenselink.mil
About the Defense Dept.: www.defenselink.mil/pubs/ dod101/index.html
News: www.defenselink.mil/news/
Secretary's Bio: www.defenselink.mil/bios/secdef_ bio.html

Directory of Senior Defense Officials: www.defenselink .mil/home/top-leaders/
Department Budget: www.dtic.mil/comptroller/ budgetindex.html

Education Dept.

Main: www.ed.gov
About the Education Dept.: www.ed.gov/about/landing .jhtml
News: www.ed.gov/news/landing.jhtml
Secretary's Bio: www.ed.gov/news/staff/bios/
Employee Directory: http://wdcrobcolp01.ed.gov/ CFAPPS/ employee_locator/index.cfm
State Contacts and Information: www.ed.gov/about/ contacts/state/index.html
Department Budget: www.ed.gov/about/overview/ budget/index.html

Energy Dept.

Main: www.energy.gov
About the Energy Dept.: www.energy.gov/about
News: www.energy.gov/news
Secretary's Bio: www.energy.gov/organization/leadership .htm
Employee Directory: http://phonebook.doe.gov/ callup.html
Link to Regional Offices: www.energy.gov/contact/ regional.htm
Department Budget: www.cfo.doe.gov/crorg/cf30.htm

Health and Human Services Dept.

Main: www.dhhs.gov
About the Health and Human Services Dept.: www.dhhs.gov/about
News: www.hhs.gov/news
Secretary's Bio: www.hhs.gov/about/
Employee Directory: http://directory.psc.gov/employee.htm
Link to Regional Offices: www.dhhs.gov/about/ regionmap.html
Department Budget: www.hhs.gov/budget/docbudget .htm

Homeland Security Dept.

Main: www.dhs.gov
About the Homeland Security Dept.: www.dhs.gov/ xabout

News: www.dhs.gov/ynews
Secretary's Bio: www.dhs.gov/xabout/structure/
biography_0116.shtm
Leadership Directory: www.dhs.gov/xabout/structure/
gc_1157655281546.shtm
Links to Regional Offices:
Federal Emergency Management Agency:
www.fema.gov/about/contact/statedr.shtm
U.S. Citizenship and Immigration Services:
www.uscis.gov
U.S. Secret Service: www.secretservice.gov/
field_offices.shtml
Department Budget: www.dhs.gov/xabout/budget

Housing and Urban Development Dept.

Main: www.hud.gov
About the Housing and Urban Development Dept.:
www.hud.gov/about
News: www.hud.gov/news
Interactive Self-Assessment Tool:
www.MakingHomeAffordable.gov
Secretary's Bio: www.hud.gov/about/keyhq.cfm
Employee Directory: www5.hud.gov:63001/po/i/netlocator
Link to Regional Offices: www.hud.gov/local/index.cfm
Department Budget: www.hud.gov/offices/cfo/reports/
cforept.cfm

Interior Dept.

Main: www.doi.gov
About the Interior Dept.: www.doi.gov/facts
News: www.doi.gov/news.html
Secretary's Bio: www.doi.gov/welcome.html
Employee Directory: www.doi.gov/hrm.people.
html#ppm
Links to Regional Offices:
Bureau of Indian Affairs: www.doi.gov/bia
Bureau of Land Management: www.blm.gov
National Park Service: www.nps.gov
Office of Surface Mining: www.osmre.gov/
offices/Offices.shtm
U.S. Fish and Wildlife Service: www.fws.gov/where
U.S. Geological Survey: www.usgs.gov/contact_us
Department Budget: www.doi.gov/budget

Justice Dept.

Main: www.usdoj.gov
About the Justice Dept.: www.usdoj.
gov/02organizations/index.html
News: www.usdoj.gov/03press/03_1_1.html
Attorney General's Bio: www.usdoj.gov/ag
Links to Regional Offices:
Drug Enforcement Administration: www.usdoj.gov/
dea/agency/domestic.htm
Federal Bureau of Investigation: www.fbi.gov/
contact/fo/fo.htm
Federal Bureau of Prisons: www.bop.gov/locations/
index.jsp
Department Budget: www.usdoj.gov/02organizations/
02_3.html

Labor Dept.

Main: www.dol.gov
About the Labor Dept.: www.dol.gov/dol/aboutdol/
main.htm
News: www.dol.gov/dol/media/main.htm
Secretary's Bio: www.dol.gov/_sec/welcome.htm
Employee Directory: www.dol.gov/dol/contact/
contact-phonekeypersonnel.htm
Links to Regional Offices:
Bureau of Labor Statistics: www.bls.gov/bls/
regnhome.htm
Employment and Training Administration:
http://wdr.doleta.gov/contacts
Occupational Safety and Health Administration:
www.osha.gov/dcsp/osp/index.html
Department Budget: www.dol.gov/dol/aboutdol/#budget

State Dept.

Main: www.state.gov
About the State Dept.: www.state.gov/aboutstate
News: www.state.gov/press
Secretary's Bio: www.state.gov/secretary
Employee Directory: www. state.gov/m/a/gps/directory/
Link to Regional Offices:
Passport Services: http://iafdb.travel.state.gov
Department Budget: www.state.gov/s/d/rm/rls

Transportation Dept.

Main: www.dot.gov
About the Transportation Dept.: www.dot.gov/about_
dot.html
News: www.dot.gov/affairs/briefing.htm
Secretary's Bio: www.dot.gov/bios/
Links to Regional Offices:
Federal Aviation Administration: www.faa.gov/
about/office_org
Federal Highway Administration: www.fhwa.dot
.gov/field.html
Federal Railroad Administration: www.fra.dot.gov/
us/content/373
Federal Transit Administration: www.fta.dot.gov/
regional_offices.html
Maritime Administration: www.marad.dot.gov/
about_us_landing_page/gateway_offices/gateway_
map/gateway_map.htm
National Highway Traffic Safety Administration:
www.nhtsa.dot.gov/nhtsa/whatis/
regions
Department Budget: www.dot.gov/about_dot.html

Treasury Dept.

Main: www.ustreas.gov
About the Treasury Dept.: www.ustreas.gov/
organization
News: www.ustreas.gov/press/index.html
Interactive Self-Assessment Tool: www.MakingHome
Affordable.gov
Secretary's Bio: www.ustreas.gov/organization/bios/
geithner-e.html

Directory of Treasury Officials: www.ustreas.gov/organization/officials.html

Links to Regional Offices:

Comptroller of the Currency: www.occ.treas.gov/district.htm

Financial Management Service: fms.treas.gov/aboutfms/locations.html

Internal Revenue Service: www.irs.treas.gov/localcontacts

Office of Thrift Supervision: www.ots.treas.gov/?P=Regions

Department Budget: www.ustreas.gov/offices/management/budget

Veterans Affairs Dept.

Main: www.va.gov

About the Veterans Affairs Dept.: www.va.gov/about_va/

News: www1.va.gov/opa/pressrel/index.cfm

Secretary's Bio: www1.va.gov/OPA/bios/index.asp

Link to Regional Offices: www2.va.gov/directory/guide/home.asp?isFlash=1

Department Budget: www.va.gov/budget/summary

LEGISLATIVE BRANCH

Congress

U.S. Constitution: www.archives.gov/exhibits/charters/constitution_transcript.html

Legislative Process: www.rules.house.gov; http://thomas.loc.gov/

How Laws Are Made: http://thomas.loc.gov/home/lawsmade.toc.html

Biographical Directory of the U.S. Congress: http://bioguide.congress.gov/biosearch/biosearch.asp

Election Statistics (1920–present): http://clerk.house.gov/member_info/electionInfo

House

Main: www.house.gov

Annual Calendar: www.house.gov/house/House_Calendar.shtml

Daily Business: http://clerk.house.gov/committee_info/commact.html

Committees: http://clerk.house.gov/committee_info/commact.html

Committee Hearing Schedules: http://clerk.house.gov/committee_info/commact.html

Pending Business: www.house.gov/house/

Link to Roll Call Votes: http://clerk.house.gov/legislative/legvotes.html

Leadership: www.house.gov/house/orgs_pub_hse_ldr_www.shtml

Media Galleries: www.house.gov/house/mediagallery.shtml

Senate

Main: www.senate.gov

Annual Calendar: www.senate.gov

Daily Calendar: www.senate.gov/pagelayout/legislative/a_three_sections_with_teasers/votes.htm

Committees: www.senate.gov/

Committee Hearing Schedules: www.senate.gov/pagelayout/legislative/a_three_sections_with_teasers/votes.htm

Link to Roll Call Votes: www.senate.gov/pagelayout/legislative/a_three_sections_with_teasers/votes.htm

Leadership: www.senate.gov/

Media Galleries: www.senate.gov/galleries

Executive Nominations: judiciary.senate.gov/nominations.executive.cfm

Government Accountability Office

Main: www.gao.gov

About the Government Accountability Office: www.gao.gov/about.htm

Comptroller General's Bio: www.gao.gov/cghome/index.html

GAO Reports: www.gao.gov/docsearch/repandtest.html

Government Printing Office

Main: www.gpo.gov; www.gpoaccess.gov

About the Government Printing Office: www.gpo.gov/factsheet/index.html; www. gpoaccess.gov/about

Library of Congress

Main: www.loc.gov/index.html

Online Catalog: http://catalog.loc.gov

Thomas (Legislative Information on the Internet): http://thomas.loc.gov

Copyright Office: www.copyright.gov

JUDICIAL BRANCH

The Supreme Court

Main: www.supremecourtus.gov

About the Supreme Court: www.supremecourtus.gov/about/about.html

News: www.supremecourtus.gov/publicinfo/press/pressreleases.html

Biographies of the Justices: www.supremecourtus.gov/about/biographiescurrent.pdf

Supreme Court Docket: www.supremecourtus.gov/docket/docket.html

Visiting the Supreme Court: www.supremecourtus.gov/visiting/visiting.html

Federal Judicial Center

Main: www.fjc.gov

U.S. Federal Courts

Main: www.uscourts.gov

About the U.S. Federal Courts: www.uscourts.gov/about.html

News: www.uscourts.gov/news.html

Publications: www.uscourts.gov/publications.html

Government of the United States

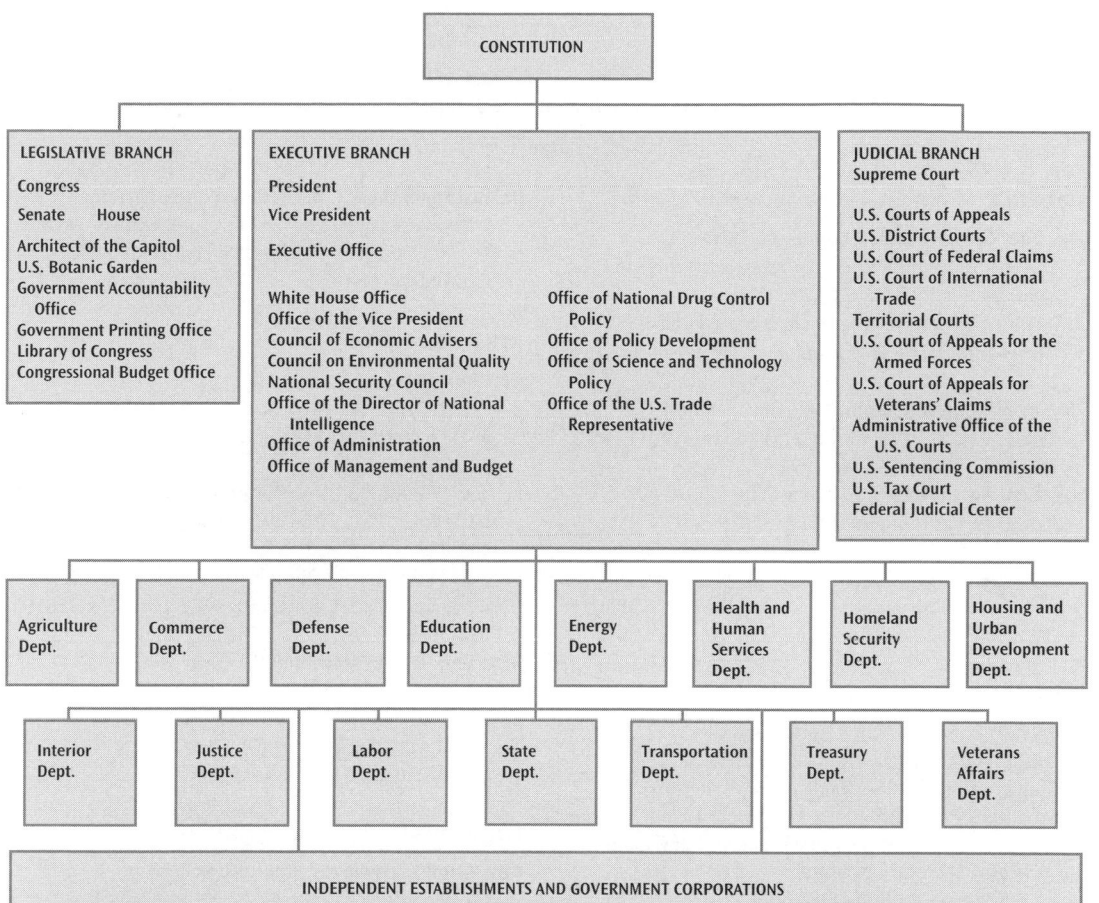

CONSTITUTION

LEGISLATIVE BRANCH

Congress

Senate   House

Architect of the Capitol
U.S. Botanic Garden
Government Accountability
  Office
Government Printing Office
Library of Congress
Congressional Budget Office

EXECUTIVE BRANCH

President

Vice President

Executive Office

White House Office
Office of the Vice President
Council of Economic Advisers
Council on Environmental Quality
National Security Council
Office of the Director of National
  Intelligence
Office of Administration
Office of Management and Budget

Office of National Drug Control
  Policy
Office of Policy Development
Office of Science and Technology
  Policy
Office of the U.S. Trade
  Representative

JUDICIAL BRANCH
Supreme Court

U.S. Courts of Appeals
U.S. District Courts
U.S. Court of Federal Claims
U.S. Court of International
  Trade
Territorial Courts
U.S. Court of Appeals for the
  Armed Forces
U.S. Court of Appeals for
  Veterans' Claims
Administrative Office of the
  U.S. Courts
U.S. Sentencing Commission
U.S. Tax Court
Federal Judicial Center

Agriculture Dept.	Commerce Dept.	Defense Dept.	Education Dept.	Energy Dept.	Health and Human Services Dept.	Homeland Security Dept.	Housing and Urban Development Dept.

Interior Dept.	Justice Dept.	Labor Dept.	State Dept.	Transportation Dept.	Treasury Dept.	Veterans Affairs Dept.

INDEPENDENT ESTABLISHMENTS AND GOVERNMENT CORPORATIONS

African Development Foundation
Broadcasting Board of Governors
Central Intelligence Agency
Commodity Futures Trading
  Commission
Consumer Product Safety Commission
Corporation for National and
  Community Service
Defense Nuclear Facilities
  Safety Board
Environmental Protection Agency
Equal Employment Opportunity
  Commission
Export-Import Bank
Farm Credit Administration
Federal Communications Commission
Federal Deposit Insurance Corp.
Federal Election Commission
Federal Housing Finance Board
Federal Labor Relations Authority
Federal Maritime Commission
Federal Mediation and Conciliation
  Service

Federal Mine Safety and Health
  Review Commission
Federal Reserve System
Federal Retirement Thrift Investment
  Board
Federal Trade Commission
General Services Administration
Inter-American Foundation
Merit Systems Protection Board
National Aeronautics and Space
  Administration
National Archives and Records
  Administration
National Capital Planning Commission
National Credit Union Administration
National Foundation on the Arts and
  the Humanities
National Labor Relations Board
National Mediation Board
National Railroad Passenger Corp. (Amtrak)
National Railroad Retirement Board
National Science Foundation
National Transportation Safety Board

Nuclear Regulatory Commission
Occupational Safety and Health Review
  Commission
Office of the Director of National
  Intelligence
Office of Government Ethics
Office of Personnel Management
Office of Special Counsel
Overseas Private Investment Corporation
Peace Corps
Pension Benefit Guaranty Corporation
Postal Regulatory Commission
Securities and Exchange Commission
Selective Service System
Small Business Administration
Social Security Administration
Tennessee Valley Authority
Trade and Development Agency
U.S. Agency for International
  Development
U.S. Commission on Civil Rights
U.S. International Trade Commission
U.S. Postal Service

Governors and Other State Officials

Political affiliations, when available, are indicated by (D) for Democrat and (R) for Republican. For key officials of the District of Columbia and other Washington-area localities, see page 315.

Alabama   Web, www.alabama.gov

Gov. Bob Riley (R), State Capitol, 600 Dexter Ave., #N-104, Montgomery 36130; Press: Jeff Emerson, (334) 242-7150; Fax, (334) 242-4495

Lt. Gov. Jim Folsom Jr. (D), Alabama State House, 11 S. Union St., #725, Montgomery 36130-6050, (334) 242-7900; Fax, (334) 242-4661

Secy. of State Beth Chapman (R), State Capitol, 600 Dexter Ave., #S-105, Montgomery 36130, (334) 242-7200; Fax, (334) 242-4993

Atty. Gen. Troy King (R), Alabama State House, 500 Dexter Ave., Montgomery 36130, (334) 242-7300; Fax, (334) 242-4891

Treasurer Kay Ivey (R), State Capitol, 600 Dexter Ave., #S-106, Montgomery 36104, (334) 242-7500; Fax, (334) 242-7592

Alaska   Web, www.alaska.gov

Gov. Sarah Palin (R), State Capitol, 3rd Floor, P.O. Box 110001, Juneau 99811-0001; Press: Meghan Stapleton (907) 465-3500; Fax, (907) 465-3532

Lt. Gov. Sean Parnell (R), State Capitol, 3rd Floor, Juneau 99811-0015, (907) 269-7460; Fax, (907) 269-0263

(No office of Secretary of State)

Atty. Gen. Wayne Anthony Ross (R), P.O. Box 110300, Juneau 99811-0300, (907) 465-2133; Fax, (907) 465-2075

In Washington, D.C.: John W. Katz, Special Counsel, Office of State-Federal Relations, State of Alaska, 444 N. Capitol St. N.W., #336 20001-1512, (202) 624-5858; Fax, (202) 624-5857

Arizona   Web, www.az.gov

Gov. Janice K. "Jan" Brewer (R), State Capitol, 1700 W. Washington St., 9th Floor, Phoenix 85007; Press: Paul Senseman, (602) 542-4331; Fax, (602) 542-1381; Toll-free, (800) 253-0883

(No office of Lieutenant Governor)

Secy. of State Ken Bennett (R), State Capitol, 1700 W. Washington St., 7th Floor, Phoenix 85007-2888, (602) 542-4285; Fax, (602) 542-1575; TTY, (602) 255-8683

Atty. Gen. Terry Goddard (D), 1275 W. Washington St., Phoenix 85007, (602) 542-5025; Fax, (602) 542-4085; Toll-free, (800) 352-8431

Treasurer Dean Martin (R), 1700 W. Washington St., 1st Floor, Phoenix 85007, (602) 604-7800; Fax, (602) 542-7176; Toll-free, (877) 365-8310

In Washington, D.C.: Brian de Vallance, Director, Washington Office of the Governor, State of Arizona, 400 N. Capitol St. N.W., #428, 20001, (202) 220-1396; Fax, (202) 624-1475.

Arkansas   Web, www.arkansas.gov

Gov. Mike Beebe (D), State Capitol, #250, Little Rock 72201; Press: Matt DeCample, (501) 683-6414; Fax, (501) 682-1382; Toll-free, (877) 727-3468; TTY, (501) 682-7515

Lt. Gov. William "Bill" A. Halter (D), State Capitol, #270, Little Rock 72201-1061, (501) 682-2144; Fax, (501) 682-2894

Secy. of State Charlie Daniels (D), State Capitol, #256, Little Rock 72201-1094, (501) 682-1010; Fax, (501) 682-3510

Atty. Gen. Dustin McDaniel (D), Tower Bldg., 323 Center St., #200, Little Rock 72201-2610, (501) 682-2007; Fax, (501) 682-8084; Toll-free, (800) 482-8982

Treasurer Martha Shoffner (D), State Capitol, #220, Little Rock 72201, (501) 682-3835; Fax, (501) 682-3842

California   Web, www.state.ca.us

Gov. Arnold Schwarzenegger (R), State Capitol, Sacramento 95814; Press: Aaron McLear, (916) 445-4571; Fax, (916) 558-3160; TTY (916) 464-1580

Lt. Gov John Garamendi (D), State Capitol, #1114, Sacramento 95814, (916) 445-8994; Fax, (916) 323-4998

Secy. of State Debra Bowen (D), 1500 11th St., #600, Sacramento 95814, (916) 653-6814; Fax, (916) 653-4795

Atty. Gen. Edmund G. Brown Jr. (D), P.O. Box 944255, Sacramento 94244-2550, (916) 322-3360; Fax, (916) 323-5341; Toll-free, (800) 952-5225; TTY, (800) 735-2929; TTY Spanish, (800) 855-3000

Treasurer Bill Lockyer (D), 915 Capitol Mall, #110, Sacramento 95814, (916) 653-2995; Fax, (916) 653-3125

In Washington, D.C.: Linda Ulrich, Director, Washington Office of the Governor, State of California, 444 N. Capitol St. N.W., #134 20001, (202) 624-5270; Fax, (202) 624-5280

Colorado   Web, www.colorado.gov

Gov. Bill Ritter Jr. (D), State Capitol, #136, Denver 80203-1792; Press: Evan Dreyer, (303) 866-6324; Fax, (303) 866-2003

Lt. Gov. Barbara O'Brien (D), State Capitol, #130, Denver 80203-1793, (303) 866-2087; Fax, (303) 866-5469

Secy. of State Bernie Buescher (R), 1700 Broadway, #250, Denver 80202, (303) 894-2200; Fax, (303) 869-4860; TTY, (303) 869-4867

Atty. Gen. John W. Suthers (R), 1525 Sherman St., 5th Floor, Denver 80203, (303) 866-4500; Fax, (303) 866-5691

Treasurer Cary Kennedy (D), State Capitol, #140, Denver 80203, (303) 866-2441; Fax, (303) 866-2123

Connecticut Web, www.ct.gov

Gov. M. Jodi Rell (R), State Capitol, 210 Capitol Ave., #202, Hartford 06106; Press: Christopher Cooper, (860) 566-4840; Toll-free, (800) 406-1527; TTY, (860) 524-7397

Lt. Gov. Michael Fedele (R), State Capitol, 210 Capitol Ave., #304, Hartford 06106, (860) 524-7384; Fax, (860) 524-7304

Secy. of State Susan Bysiewicz (D), 30 Trinity St., Hartford 06106, (860) 509-6212; Fax, (860) 509-6131

Atty. Gen. Richard Blumenthal (D), 55 Elm St., Hartford 06106, (860) 808-5318; Fax, (860) 808-5387

Treasurer Denise L. Nappier (D), 55 Elm St., Hartford 06106-1773, (860) 702- 3000; Fax, (860) 702-3043; Toll-free, (800) 618-3404

In Washington, D.C.: Julie Williams, Director, Washington Office of the Governor, State of Connecticut, 444 N. Capitol St. N.W., #317 20001, (202) 347-4535; Fax, (202) 347-7151

Delaware Web, http://delaware.gov

Gov. Jack A. Markell (D), Tatnall Bldg., 2nd Floor, William Penn St., Dover 19901; Press: Matthew Denn, (302) 744-4101; Fax, (302) 739-2775

Lt. Gov. John C. Carney Jr. (D), Tatnall Bldg., 3rd Floor, Dover 19901, (302) 744-4333; Fax, (302) 739-6965

Secy. of State Jeffrey W. Bullock (D), 401 Federal St., #3, Dover 19901, (302) 739-4111; Fax, (302) 739-3811

Atty. Gen. Joseph R. "Beau" Biden III (D), Carvel State Office Bldg., 820 N. French St., Wilmington 19801, (302) 577-8400; Fax, (302) 577-6630; TTY (302) 527-5783

Treasurer Velda Jones-Potter (D), 820 Silver Lake Blvd., # 100, Dover 19904, (302) 672-6700; Fax, (302) 739-5635

In Washington, D.C.: Emily Kuiken, Director, Washington Office of the Governor, State of Delaware, 444 N. Capitol St. N.W., #230 20001, (202) 624-7724; Fax, (202) 624-5495

Florida Web, www.myflorida.gov

Gov. Charlie Crist (R), The Capitol, 400 S. Monroe St., Tallahassee 32399-0001; Press: Erin Isaac (850) 488-5394; Fax, (850) 488-4042; TTY, (850) 922-7795

Lt. Gov. Jeff Kottkamp (R), The Capitol, 400 S. Monroe St., PL-05, Tallahassee 32399-0001, (850) 488-7146; Fax, (850) 487-0830

Secy. of State Kurt S. Browning (R), R.A. Gray Bldg., 500 S. Bronough, #15, Tallahassee 32399-0250, (850) 245-6500; Fax, (850) 245-6125

Atty. Gen. Bill McCollum (R), PL-01, The Capitol, 500 S. Bronough St., Tallahassee 32399-1050, (850) 414-6500; Fax, (850) 245-6125

Chief Financial Officer Alex Sink (D), 200 E. Gaines St., Tallahassee 32399-0300, (850) 413-2850; Fax, (850) 488-6581

In Washington, D.C.: T. Kerry Feehery, Director, Washington Office of the Governor, State of Florida, 444 N. Capitol St. N.W., #349 20001, (202) 624-5885; Fax, (202) 624-5886

Georgia Web, www.georgia.gov

Gov. Sonny Perdue (R), 203 State Capitol, Atlanta, 30334; Press: Bert Brantley, (404) 656-1776; Fax, (404) 657-7332

Lt. Gov. Casey Cagle (R), 240 State Capitol, Atlanta, 30334, (404) 656-5030; Fax, (404) 656-6739

Secy. of State Karen Handel (R), 214 State Capitol, Atlanta, 30334, (404) 656-2881; Fax, (404) 656-0513

Atty. Gen. Thurbert E. Baker (D), 40 Capitol Square S.W., Atlanta, 30334-1300, (404) 656-3300; Fax, (404) 657-8733

Treasurer W. Daniel Ebersole, 200 Piedmont Ave., W. Tower, #1204, Atlanta 30334, (404) 656-2168; Fax, (404) 656-9048

In Washington, D.C., Bradford Swann, Washington Office of the Governor, State of Georgia, 444 N. Capitol St. N.W., #376 20001, (202) 624-3681; Fax, (202) 624-3682

Hawaii Web, www.hawaii.gov

Gov. Linda Lingle (R), State Capitol, 415 S. Beretania St., Honolulu 96813; Press: Lenny Klompus, (808) 586-0034 ; Fax, (808)586-0006

Lt. Gov. James R. "Duke" Aiona Jr. (R), State Capitol, 415 S. Beretania St., Honolulu 96813, (808) 586-0255; Fax, (808) 586-0231

(No office of Secretary of State)

Atty. Gen. Mark J. Bennett (R), 425 Queen St., Honolulu 96813, (808) 586-1500; Fax, (808) 586-1239

Budget and Finance Director Georgina Kawamura, P.O. Box 150, Honolulu 96810, (808) 586-1518; Fax, (808) 586-1976

Idaho Web, www.state.id.us

Gov. C. L. "Butch" Otter (R), State Capitol, West Wing , 2nd Floor, Boise 83720-0034; Press: Jon Hanian, (208) 334-2100

Lt. Gov. Brad Little (R), State Capitol, #225, Boise 83720-0057, (208) 334-2200; Fax, (208) 334-3259

Secy. of State Ben Ysursa (R), 304 N. 8th St., #149, Boise 83720-0080, (208) 334-2300; Fax, (208) 334-2282

Atty. Gen. Lawrence G. Wasden (R), State Capitol, 2nd Floor, Boise 83720-0010, (208) 334-2400; Fax, (208) 854-8071

Treasurer Ron G. Crane (R), 304 N. 8th St., #208, Boise 83720, (208) 334-3200; Fax, (208) 332-2960

Illinois   Web, www.il.gov

Gov. Pat Quinn (D), State Capitol, #207, Springfield 62706; Press: Bob Reed (312) 814-3158; TTY, (888) 261-3336

Lt. Gov. position will be vacant until the next election. State Capitol, #214, Springfield 62706, (217) 782-7884; Fax, (217) 524-6262

Secy. of State Jesse White (D), State Capitol, #213, Springfield 62706, (217) 782-2201; Fax, (217) 785-0358

Atty. Gen. Lisa Madigan (D), 100 W. Randolph St., Chicago 60601, (312) 814-3000, Fax (312) 814-3806; TTY, (800) 964-3013

Treasurer Alexi Giannoulias (D), 100 W. Randolph St., #15-600, Chicago 60601, (312) 814-1700; Fax, (312) 814-5930; TTY, (312) 814-6592

In Washington, D.C.: Jane Mellow, Director, Washington Office of the Governor, State of Illinois, 444 N. Capitol St. N.W., #400 20001, (202) 624-7760; Fax, (202) 724-0689

Indiana   Web, www.state.in.us

Gov. Mitchell E. Daniels (R), State House, 200 W. Washington St., #206, Indianapolis 46204-2790; Press: Jane Jankowski, (317) 232-4567

Lt. Gov. Becky Skillman (R), State House, 200 W. Washington St., #333, Indianapolis 46204-2790, (317) 232-4545; Fax, (317) 232-4788

Secy. of State Todd Rokita (R), State House, 200 W. Washington St., #201, Indianapolis 46204-2790, (317) 232-6531; Fax, (317) 233-3283

Atty. Gen. Greg Zoeller (R), Indiana Government Center South, 302 W. Washington St., 5th Floor, Indianapolis 46204- 2770, (317) 232-6201; Fax, (317) 232-7979

Treasurer Richard Mourdock (R), State House, 200 W. Washington St., #242, Indianapolis 46204, (317) 232-6386; Fax, (317) 233-1780

In Washington, D.C.: Debbie Hohlt, Federal Representative, Washington Office of the Governor, State of Indiana, 1455 Pennsylvania Ave. N.W., #1140, 20004, (202) 624-1474; Fax, (202) 833-1587

Iowa   Web, www.iowa.gov

Gov. Chet Culver (D), State Capitol, 1007 E. Grand Ave., Des Moines 50319; Press: Troy Price, (515) 281-5211 ; Fax, (515) 281-0217

Lt. Gov. Patty Judge (D), State Capitol, 1007 E. Grand Ave., Des Moines 50319, (515) 281-5211; Fax, (515) 281-6611

Secy. of State Michael A. Mauro (D), State Capitol, 1007 E. Grand Ave., #105, Des Moines 50319, (515) 281-5204; Fax, (515) 242-5952

Atty. Gen. Tom Miller (D), Hoover Bldg., 2nd Floor, 1305 E. Walnut St., Des Moines 50319, (515) 281-5164; Fax, (515) 281-4209

Treasurer Michael L. Fitzgerald (D), State Capitol, 1007 E. Grand Ave., Des Moines 50319, (515) 281-5368; Fax, (515) 281-7562

In Washington, D.C.: Jon Murphy, Director (Acting), Washington Office of the Governor, State of Iowa, 400 N. Capitol St. N.W., #359 20001, (202) 624-5444; Fax, (202) 624-8189

Kansas   Web, www.accesskansas.org

Gov. Mark Parkinson (D), State Capitol, 300 S.W. 10th Ave., #212S, Topeka 66612-1590; Press: Nicole Corcoran, (785) 296-3232; Fax, (785) 368-8500

Lt. Gov. Vacant, State Capitol, 300 S.W. 10th Ave., #2231N, Topeka 66612-1590, (785) 296-2213; Fax, (785) 296-5669; TTY, (800) 766-3777

Secy. of State Ron Thornburgh (R), Memorial Hall, 120 S.W. 10th Ave., 1st Floor, Topeka 66612-1594, (785) 296-4564; Fax, (785) 296-4570

Atty. Gen. Stephen Six (D), Memorial Hall, 120 S.W. 10th Ave., 2nd Floor, Topeka 66612-1597, (785) 296-2215; Fax, (785) 296-6296; Toll-free, (888) 428-8436

Treasurer Dennis McKinney (R), Landon State Office Bldg., 900 S.W. Jackson St., #201, Topeka 66612-1235, (785) 296-3171; Fax, (785) 296-7950

In Washington, D.C.: Adam Nordstrom, Washington Representative, Washington Office of the Governor, State of Kansas, 500 New Jersey Ave. N.W., #400 20001, (202) 715-2923; Fax, (202) 638-1045

Kentucky   Web, www.kentucky.gov

Gov. Steve Beshear (D), State Capitol, 700 Capitol Ave., #100, Frankfort 40601; Press: Allison Gardner Martin (502) 564-2611; Fax, (502) 564-2517; TTY, (502) 564-9551

Lt. Gov. Daniel Mongiardo (R), State Capitol, 700 Capitol Ave., #142, Frankfort 40601, (502) 564-2611; Fax, (502) 564-2849

Secy. of State Trey Grayson (R), State Capitol, 700 Capitol Ave., #152, Frankfort 40601-3493, (502) 564-3490; Fax, (502) 564-5687

Atty. Gen. Jack Conway (D), State Capitol, 700 Capitol Ave., #118, Frankfort 40601-3449, (502) 696-5300; Fax, (502) 564-2894

Treasurer Todd Hollenbach (D), 1050 U.S. Hwy 127 S., #100, Frankfort 40601, (502) 564-4722; Fax, (502) 564-6545

In Washington, D.C.: Will Coffman, Director, Washington Office of the Governor, State of Kentucky, 444 N. Capitol St. N.W., #224 20001, (202) 220-1350; Fax, (202) 220-1359

Louisiana   Web, www.state.la.us

Gov. Bobby Jindal (R), State Capitol, 900 N. 3rd St., 4th Floor, Baton Rouge 70802-9004; Press: Melissa

Sellers, (225) 342-7015; Fax, (225) 342-7099; Toll-free, (866) 366-1121

Lt. Gov. Mitchell J. Landrieu (D), Capitol Annex, 1051 N. 3rd St., 5th Floor, Baton Rouge 70802, (225) 342-7009; Fax, (225) 342-1949

Secy. of State Jay Dardenne (R), 8585 Archives Ave., Baton Rouge 70809, (225) 922-2880; Fax, (225) 922-2003

Atty. Gen. James D. "Buddy" Caldwell (R), 300 Capitol Dr., Baton Rouge 70802, (225) 326-6705; Fax, (225) 326-6797

Treasurer John Neely Kennedy (D), State Capitol, 900 N. 3rd St., 3rd Floor, Baton Rouge 70802, (225) 342-0010; Fax, (225) 342-0046

Maine   Web, www.maine.gov

Gov. John E. Baldacci (D), 1 State House Station, Augusta 04333-0001; Press: David Farmer, (207) 287-3531; Fax, (207) 287-1034; TTY, (207) 287-6548

(No office of Lieutenant Governor)

Secy. of State Matthew Dunlap (D), 148 State House Station, Augusta 04333-0148, (207) 626-8400; Fax, (207) 287-8598

Atty. Gen. G. Steven Rowe (D), 6 State House Station, Augusta 04333-0006, (207) 626-8800; Fax, (207) 287-3145; TTY, (207) 626-8865

Treasurer David Lemoine (D), 39 State House Station, Augusta 04333-0039, (207) 624-7477; Fax, (207) 287-2367

Maryland   Web, www.maryland.gov

Gov. Martin O'Malley. (D), State House, 100 State Circle, Annapolis 21401-1925; Press: Rick Abbruzzese (410) 974-2316; Toll-free, (800) 811-8336; TTY, (800) 201-7165

Lt. Gov. Anthony G. Brown (D), State House, 100 State Circle, Annapolis 21401-1925, (410) 974-2804; Fax, (410) 974-5882

Secy. of State John P. McDonough (D), state House, 100 State Circle, Annapolis 21401, (410) 260-3848; Fax, (410) 974-5190

Atty. Gen. Douglas F. Gansler (D), 200 St. Paul Pl., Baltimore 21202, (410) 576-6300; Fax, (410) 576-6404; TTY, (410) 576-6372

Treasurer Nancy K. Kopp (D), Louis L. Goldstein Treasury Bldg., 80 Calvert St., #109, Annapolis 21401, (410) 260-7533; Fax, (410) 974-3530; Toll-free, (800) 974-0468

In Washington, D.C.: Dana Thompson, Director, Washington Office of the Governor, State of Maryland, 444 N. Capitol St. N.W., #311 20001, (202) 624-1430; Fax, (202) 783-3061

Massachusetts   Web, www.mass.gov

Gov. Deval Patrick (D), Executive Office, State House, #280, Boston 02133; Press: Kyle Sullivan, (617) 725-4005; Fax, (617) 727-9725; Toll-free, (888) 870-7770; TTY, (617) 727-3666

Lt. Gov. Timothy "Tim" P. Murray (D), State House, #360, Boston 02133, (617) 725-4005; Fax, (617) 727-9725

Secy. of the Commonwealth William Francis Galvin (D), Ashburton Pl., #1611, Boston 12108-1512, (617) 727-7030; Fax, (617) 742-4528; Toll-free, (800) 392-6090; TTY, (617) 878-3889

Atty. Gen. Martha Coakley (D), McCormack Bldg., 1 Ashburton Pl., #2010, Boston 02108-1698, (617) 727-2200; Fax, (617) 727-3251; TTY, (617) 727-4765

Treasurer Timothy P. Cahill (D), State House, #227, Boston, 02133, (617) 367-6900; Fax, (617) 248-0372

In Washington, D.C.: Caroline Powers, Director of State and Federal Relations, Washington Office of the Governor, Commonwealth of Massachusetts, 444 N. Capitol St. N.W., #208 20001, (202) 624-7713; Fax, (202) 624-7714

Michigan   Web, www.michigan.gov

Gov. Jennifer M. Granholm (D), Romney Bldg, 111 S. Capitol Ave., Lansing 48909; Press: Elizabeth Boyd, (517) 335-6397; Fax, (517) 335-6863

Lt. Gov. John D. Cherry Jr. (D), Romney Bldg., 111 S. Capitol Ave., 5th Floor, Lansing 48909, (517) 373-6800; Fax, (517) 241-3956

Secy. of State Terri Lynn Land (R), Treasury Bldg., 430 W. Allegan St., 1st Floor, Lansing 48918-9900, (517) 322-1460; Fax, (517) 373-0727; Toll-free, (888) 767-6424

Atty. Gen. Mike Cox (R), 525 W. Ottawa St., 7th Floor, Lansing 48909, (517) 373-1110; Fax, (517) 373-3042; Toll-free, (877) 765-8388

Treasurer Robert J. Kleine (D), Treasury Bldg., 430 W. Allegan St., Lansing 48922, (517) 373-3200; Fax, (517) 373-4968; TTY, (517) 636-4999

In Washington, D.C.: Genna Gent, Washington Representative, Washington Office of the Governor, State of Michigan, 444 N. Capitol St. N.W., #411 20001, (202) 624-5840; Fax, (202) 624-5841

Minnesota   Web, www.state.mn.us

Gov. Tim Pawlenty (R), 130 State Capitol, 75 Rev. Dr. Martin Luther King Jr. Blvd., #130, St. Paul 55155; Press: Brian McClung, (651) 296-3391; Fax, (651)296-2089; Toll-free, (800) 657-3717

Lt. Gov. Carol Molnau (R), 130State Capitol, 75 Rev. Dr. Martin Luther King Jr. Blvd., #130, St. Paul 55155, (651) 296-3391; Fax, (651) 296-2089

Secy. of State Mark Ritchie (D), State Capitol, 100 Rev. Dr. Martin Luther King Jr. Blvd., #180, St. Paul 55155, (651) 296-2803; Fax, (651) 297-7067; Toll-free, (877) 551-6767

Atty. Gen. Lori Swanson (D), 1400 Bremer Tower, 445 Minnesota St., St. Paul 55101, (651) 296-3353; Fax, (651) 297-4193; Toll-free, (800) 657-3787; TTY, (800) 366-4812

Commissioner of Finance Tom Hanson, 658 Cedar St., #400, St. Paul 55155, (651) 201-8000; Fax, (651) 296-8685; TTY, (800) 627-3529

In Washington, D.C.: Jason D. Rohloff, Director of Federal Affairs, Washington Office of the Governor, State of Minnesota, 400 N. Capitol St. N.W., #380 20001, (202) 624-5308; Fax, (202) 624-5425

Mississippi   Web, www.ms.gov

Gov. Haley Barbour (R), Woolfolk Bldg., 501 N. West St., 15th Floor, Jackson 39201; Press: Dan Turner, (601) 359-3150; Fax, (601) 359-3741; Toll-free, (877) 405-0733

Lt. Gov. Phil Bryant (R), New Capitol Bldg., #315, 400 High St., Jackson 39215-1018, (601) 359-3200; Fax, (601) 359-4054

Secy. of State Delbert Hosemann (R), 401 Mississippi St., Jackson 39201, (601) 359-1350; Fax, (601) 359-1499

Atty. Gen. Jim Hood (D), Walter Sillers Bldg., 550 High St., #1200, Jackson 39201, (601) 359-3680; Fax, (601) 359-3796

Treasurer Tate Reeves (R), 1101-A Woolfolk Bldg., 501 N. West St., Jackson 39201, (601) 359-3600; Fax, (601) 576-2001

Missouri   Web, www.mo.gov

Gov. Jeremiah W. "Jay" Nixon (D), State Capitol, #216, Jefferson City 65101; Press: Scott Holste, (573) 751-3222

Lt. Gov. Peter Kinder (R), State Capitol, #224 Jefferson City 65101, (573) 751-4727; Fax, (573) 751-9422

Secy. of State Robin Carnahan (D), State Capitol, #208, Jefferson City 65101, (573) 751-4936; Fax, (573) 751-2490

Atty. Gen. Chris Koster (D), Supreme Court Bldg., 207 W. High St., Jefferson City 65102, (573) 751-3321; Fax, (573) 751-0774

Treasurer Clint Zweifel (D), State Capitol, #229, Jefferson City 65101, (573) 751-2411; Fax, (573) 751-0343

Montana   Web, www.state.mt.us

Gov. Brian Schweitzer (D), State Capitol, P.O. Box 200801, Helena 59620-0801; Press: Sarah Elliot, (406) 444-3111; Fax, (406) 444-5529

Lt. Gov. John Bohlinger (R), State Capitol, P.O. Box 200801, Helena 59620-1901, (406) 444-3111; Fax, (406) 444-4648

Secy. of State Linda McCullouch (D), State Capitol, 1301 6th Ave., #260, P.O. Box 202801, Helena 59620-2801, (406) 444-2034; Fax, (406) 444-3976

Atty. Gen. Steve Bullock (D), Justice Bldg., 215 N. Sanders St., P.O. Box 201401, Helena 59620-1401, (406) 444-2026; Fax, (406) 444-3549

Director of Dept. of Administration, Janet Kelly, 125 N. Roberts St., P.O. Box 200101 Helena 59620-0101, (406) 444-3033; Fax (406) 444-6194

Nebraska   Web, www.nebraska.gov

Gov. Dave Heineman (R), State Capitol, 1445 K St., #2316, P.O. Box 96843, Lincoln 68509; Press: Jen Hein, (402) 471-2244; Fax, (402) 471-6031

Lt. Gov. Rick Sheehy (R), State Capitol, #2315, Lincoln 68509, (402) 471-2256; Fax, (402) 471-6031

Secy. of State John A. Gale (R), State Capitol, #2300, P.O.Box 94608, Lincoln 68509, (402) 471-2554; Fax, (402) 471-3237

Atty. Gen. Jon Bruning (R), State Capitol, #2115, Lincoln 68509, (402) 471-2682; Fax, (402) 471-3297

Treasurer Shane Osborn (R), State Capitol, #2005, P.O. Box 94788, Lincoln 68509, (402) 471-2455; Fax, (402) 471-4390

Nevada   Web, www.nv.gov

Gov. Jim Gibbons (R), Capitol Bldg., 101 N. Carson St., Carson City 89701; Press, Daniel Burns (775) 684-5670; Fax, (775) 684-5683

Lt. Gov. Brian Krolicki (R), Capitol Bldg., 101 N. Carson St., #2, Carson City 89701, (775) 684-7111; Fax, (775) 684-7110

Secy. of State Ross Miller (D), Capitol Bldg., 101 N. Carson St., #3, Carson City 89701-4786, (775) 684-5708

Atty. Gen. Catherine Cortez Masto (D), Capitol Complex, 100 N. Carson St., Carson City 89701-4717, (775) 684-1100

Treasurer Kate Marshall (D), Capitol Bldg., 101 N. Carson St., #4, Carson City 89701-4786, (775) 684-5600

In Washington, D.C.: Ryan McGinness, Director, Washington Office of the Governor, State of Nevada, 444 N. Capitol St. N.W., #209 20001, (202) 624-5405; Fax, (202) 624-8181

New Hampshire   Web, www.nh.gov

Gov. John Lynch (R), State House, 25 Capitol St., Concord 03301; Press: Colin Manning, (603) 271-2121; Fax, (603) 271-7680

(No office of Lieutenant Governor)

Secy. of State William M. Gardner (D), State House, 25 Capitol St., #204, Concord 03301, (603) 271-3242; Fax, (603) 271-6316

Atty. Gen. Kelly A. Ayotte (R), 33 Capitol St., Concord 03301, (603) 271-3658; Fax, (603) 271-2110; TTY, (800) 735-2964

Treasurer Catherine A. Provencher, State House Annex, 25 Capitol St., #121, Concord 03301, (603) 271-2621; Fax, (603) 271-3922

New Jersey   Web, www.newjersey.gov

Gov. Jon S. Corzine (D), State House, 125 W. State St., Trenton 08625-0001; Press: Robert Corrales, (609) 292-6000

(No office of Lieutenant Governor)

Secy. of State Nina Mitchell Wells, 125 W. State St., Trenton 08625-0300, (609) 984-1900; Fax, (609) 292-7665

Atty. Gen. Anne Milgram, 25 Market St., 8th Floor, West Wing, Trenton 08625-0080, (609) 292-4925; Fax, (609) 292-3508

Treasurer David Rousseau, State House, 125 W. State St., Trenton 08625, (609) 292-6748; Fax, (609) 984-3888

In Washington, D.C.: Clyde H. Henderson III, Director, Washington Office of the Governor, State of New Jersey, 444 N. Capitol St. N.W., #201 20001, (202) 638-0631; Fax, (202) 638-2296

New Mexico   Web, www.newmexico.gov

Gov. Bill Richardson (D), State Capitol Bldg., 490 Old Santa Fe Trail, #400, Santa Fe 87501; Press: Gilbert Gallegos, (505) 476-2200

Lt. Gov. Diane Denish (D), State Capitol Bldg., 490 Old Santa Fe Trail, #417, Santa Fe 87501, (505) 476-2250; Fax, (505) 476-2257; Toll-free, (800) 432-4406

Secy. of State Mary E. Herrera (D), State Capitol North Annex, 325 Don Gaspar Ave., #300, Santa Fe 87503, (505) 827-3600; Fax, (505) 827-3634; Toll-free, (800) 477-3632

Atty. Gen. Gary King (D), Villagra Bldg., 408 Galisteo St., Santa Fe 87501, (505) 827-6000; Fax, (505) 827-5826; Toll-free, (800) 678-1508

Treasurer James B. Lewis (D), State Treasurer's Office, 2019 Galisteo St., Bldg. K, Santa Fe 87504-0608, (505) 955-1120; Fax, (505) 955-1195

In Washington, D.C.: Tony Martinez, Director, Washington Office of the Governor, State of New Mexico, 444 N. Capitol St. N.W., #400 20001, (202) 220-1348, Fax (202) 220-1349.

New York   Web, www.state.ny.us

Gov. David A. Paterson (D), State Capitol, Albany 12224; Press: Peter Kauffmann (518) 474-7516

Lt. Gov., State Sen. Malcom Smith (D) covering, Executive Chamber, State Capitol, Albany 12224-0341, (518) 474-4623; Fax, (518) 486-4170

Secy. of State Lorraine Cortes-Vazquez (R), 1 Commerce Plaza, 99 Washington Ave., Albany 12231-0001, (518) 474-4752; Fax, (518) 474-4597

Atty. Gen. Andrew M. Cuomo (D), State Capitol, Albany 12224-0341; (518) 474-7330; Fax, (518) 402-2472; Toll-free, (800) 771-7755

Treasurer Aida Brewer, 110 State St., 2nd Floor, Albany 12207, (518) 474-4250; Fax, (518) 402-4118

In Washington, D.C.: Derek Douglas, Director, Washington Office of the Governor, State of New York, 444 N. Capitol St. N.W., #301 20001, (202) 434-7100; Fax, (202) 434-7110

North Carolina   Web, www.nc.gov

Gov. Beverly Perdue (D), State Capitol, Raleigh 27699-0301; Press: Chrissy Pearson, (919) 733-4240; Fax, (919) 715-2120

Lt. Gov. Walter Dalton (D), 310 N. Blount St., Raleigh 27601, (919) 733-7350; Fax, (919) 733-6595

Secy. of State Elaine F. Marshall (D), 2 South Salisbury St., Raleigh 27626-0622, (919) 807-2005; Fax, (919) 807-2010

Atty. Gen. Roy Cooper (D), 9001 Mail Service Ctr., Raleigh 27699-9001, (919) 716-6400; Fax, (919) 716-6750

Treasurer Janet Cowell (D), 325 N. Salisbury St., Raleigh 27603-1385, (919) 508-5176; Fax, (919) 508-5167

In Washington, D.C.: Jim McCleskey, Director, Washington Office of the Governor, State of North Carolina, 444 N. Capitol St. N.W., #332 20001, (202) 624-5830; Fax, (202) 624-5836

North Dakota   Web, www.nd.gov

Gov. John Hoeven (R), State Capitol, 600 E. Boulevard Ave., Bismarck 58505-0001; Press: Don Canton, (701) 328-2200; Fax, (701) 328-2205

Lt. Gov. Jack Dalrymple (R), State Capitol, 600 E. Boulevard Ave., Dept. 101, Bismarck 58505-0001, (701) 328-4222; Fax, (701) 328-2205

Secy. of State Al Jaeger (R), State Capitol, 600 E. Boulevard Ave., Dept. 108, Bismarck 58505-0500, (701) 328-2900; Fax, (701) 328-2992; Toll-free, (800) 352-0867; TTY, (800) 366-6888

Atty. Gen. Wayne Stenehjem (R), State Capitol, 600 E. Boulevard Ave., Dept. 125, Bismarck 58505-0040, (701) 328-2210; Fax, (701) 328-2226; TTY, (800) 366-6888

Treasurer Kelly L. Schmidt (R), State Capitol, 600 E. Boulevard Ave., Dept. 120, Bismarck 58505-0660, (701) 328-2643; Fax, (701) 328-3002

In Washington, D.C.: Krista Carman, Washington Representative, Washington Office of the Governor, State of North Dakota, 444 N. Capitol St. N.W., #837 20001-1512, (202) 624-5471; Fax, (202) 478-0811

Ohio   Web, www.ohio.gov

Gov. Ted Strickland (D), Vern Riffe Center, 77 S. High St., 30th Floor, Columbus 43215-6108; Press: Amanda Wurst, (614) 466-3555; Fax, (614) 466-9354

Lt. Gov. Lee Fisher (D), Vern Riffe Center, 77 S. High St., 30th Floor, Columbus 43215, (614) 644-3379; Fax, (614) 644-0745

Secy. of State Jennifer Brunner (D), 180 E. Broad St., 16th Floor, Columbus 43215, (614) 466-2655; Fax, (614) 644-3899

Atty. Gen. Richard Cordray (D), 30 E. Broad St., 17th Floor, Columbus 43215-3428, (614) 466-4320; Fax, (614) 466-5087

Treasurer Kevin L. Boyce (D), 30 E. Broad St., 9th Floor, Columbus 43266-0421, (614) 466-2160; Fax, (614) 644-7313; TT, (800) 228-1102

In Washington, D.C.: Drew McCracken, Director, Washington Office of the Governor, State of Ohio, 444 N. Capitol St. N.W., #546 20001, (202) 624-5844; Fax, (202) 624-5847

Oklahoma   Web, www.ok.gov

Gov. Brad Henry (D), State Capitol, 2300 N. Lincoln Blvd., #212, Oklahoma City 73105; Press: Thomas Larson (405) 521-2342; Fax, (405) 521-3353

Lt. Gov. Jari Askins (D), State Capitol, 2300 N. Lincoln Blvd., #211, Oklahoma City 73105, (405) 521-2161; Fax, (405) 522-8694

Secy. of State M. Susan Savage (D), State Capitol, 2300 N. Lincoln Blvd., #101, Oklahoma City 73105-4897, (405) 521-3912; Fax, (405) 521-3771

Atty. Gen. W. A. Drew Edmondson (D), 313 N.E. 21st St., Oklahoma City 73105, (405) 521-3921; Fax, (405) 521-6246

Treasurer Scott Meacham (D), State Capitol, 2300 N. Lincoln Blvd., #217, Oklahoma City 73105, (405) 521-3191; Fax, (405) 521-4994

Oregon   Web, www.oregon.gov

Gov. Theodore R. "Ted" Kulongoski (D), State Capitol, #160, 900 Court St., Salem 97301-4047; Press: Anna R. Taylor (503) 378-3111; Fax, (503) 378-6827

(No office of Lieutenant Governor)

Secy. of State Kate Brown (D), State Capitol, #136, Salem 97301-0722, (503) 986-1523; Fax, (503) 986-1616

Atty. Gen. John Kroger (D), Justice Bldg., 1162 Court St. N.E., Salem 97301-4096, (503) 378-4400; Fax, (503) 378-4017

Treasurer Ben Westlund (D), 350 Winter St. St., N.E., Salem 97301-3896 (503) 378-4329; Fax, (503) 373-7051

In Washington, D.C.: Dan DeSimone, Director, Washington Office of the Governor, State of Oregon, 444 N. Capitol St. N.W., #400 20001, (202) 624-7765; Fax, (202) 624-7785.

Pennsylvania   Web, www.state.pa.us

Gov. Edward G. Rendell (D), Main Capitol Bldg., #225, Harrisburg 17120; Press: Chuck Ardo, (717) 787-2500; Fax, (717) 772-8284

Lt. Gov. Catherine Baker Knoll (D), Main Capitol Bldg., #200, Harrisburg 17120-0002, (717) 787-3300; Fax, (717) 783-0150

Secy. of the Commonwealth Pedro A. Cortés (D), North Office Bldg., #302, Harrisburg 17120, (717) 787-6458; Fax, (717) 787-1734

Atty. Gen. Tom Corbett (R), Strawberry Square, 16th Floor, Harrisburg 17120, (717) 787-3391; Fax, (717) 787-8242

Treasurer Rob McCord (D), Finance Bldg., #129, Harrisburg 17120, (717) 787-2465; Fax, (717) 783-9760

In Washington, D.C.: Peter A. Peyser Jr. and Caroline Martin, Director, Washington Office of the Govenor, State of Pennsylvania, 600 New Hampshire Ave. N.W., Washington 20037, (202) 772-5806; Fax, (202) 772-1660

Rhode Island   Web, www.ri.gov

Gov. Donald L. Carcieri (R), State House, 82 Smith St., Providence 02903; Press: Jeffrey Neal, (401) 222-2080

Lt. Gov. Elizabeth Roberts (D), State House, #116, Providence 02903, (401) 222-2371; Fax, (401) 222-2012

Secy. of State A. Ralph Mollis (D), State House, #217, Providence 02903-1105, (401) 222-2357; Fax, (401) 222-1356; TTY, 711 (in state)

Atty. Gen. Patrick C. Lynch (D), 150 S. Main St., Providence 02903-2856, (401) 274-4400; Fax, (401) 222-1302

Treasurer Frank T. Caprio (D), State House, #102, Providence 02903, (401) 222-2397; Fax, (401) 222-6140

In Washington, D.C.: Tim Costa, Director, Washington Office of the Governor, State of Rhode Island, 444 N. Capitol St. N.W., #619 20001, (202) 624-3605; Fax, (202) 624-3607

South Carolina   Web, www.sc.gov

Gov. Mark Sanford (R), State House, 1st Floor, Columbia 29211; Press: Joel Sawyer, (803) 734-2100

Lt. Gov. R. André Bauer (R), State House, 1st Floor, Columbia 29201, (803) 734-2080; Fax, (803) 734-2082

Secy. of State Mark Hammond (R), 1205 Pendleton St., #525, Columbia 29201, (803) 734-2170; Fax, (803) 734-1661

Atty. Gen. Henry McMaster (R), 1000 Assembly St., #519, Columbia 29201, (803) 734-3970; Fax, (803) 734-4323

Treasurer Converse A. Chellis III (R), Wade Hampton Office Bldg., 1200 Senate St., #118, Columbia 29201, (803) 734-2016; Fax, (803) 734-2690

In Washington, D.C.: Blair Goodrich, Washington Representative, Washington Office of the Governor, State of South Carolina, 444 N. Capitol St. N.W., #203 20001, (202) 624-7784; Fax, (202) 624-7800

South Dakota   Web, www.state.sd.us

Gov. Michael Rounds (R), State Capitol, 500 E. Capitol Ave., Pierre 57501; Press: Joe Kafka, (605) 773-3212

Lt. Gov. Dennis Daugaard (R), State Capitol, 500 E. Capitol Ave., Pierre 57501-5070, (605) 773-3661; Fax, (605) 773-4711

Secy. of State Chris Nelson (R), State Capitol, 500 E. Capitol Ave., #204, Pierre 57501-5070, (605) 773-3537; Fax, (605) 773-6580

Atty. Gen. Larry Long (R), 1302 E. Hwy. 14, #1, Pierre 57501-8501, (605) 773-3215; Fax, (605) 773-4106; TTY, (605) 773-6585

Treasurer Vernon L. Larson (R), State Capitol, 500 E. Capitol Ave., #212, Pierre 57501-5070, (605) 773-3378; Fax, (605) 773-3115

Tennessee   Web, www.tn.gov

Gov. Phil Bredesen (D), State Capitol, 1st Floor, Nashville 37243-0001; Press: Lydia Lenker, (615) 741-2001

Lt. Gov. Ron Ramsey (R), 1 Legislative Plaza, Nashville 37243-0202, (615) 741-4524; Fax, (615) 741-9349

Secy. of State Tre Hargell (R), State Capitol, 1st Floor, 600 Charlotte Ave., Nashville 37243-1102, (615) 741-2819; Fax, (615) 741-5962

Atty. Gen. Robert E. Cooper Jr. (D), 425 5th Ave. North, Cordell Hull Bldg., Nashville 37243-0485, (615) 741-3491; Fax, (615) 741-2009

Treasurer David H. Lillard Jr. (R), State Capitol, 1st Floor, Nashville 37243-0225, (615) 741-2956; Fax, (615) 253-1591

Texas   Web, www.tx.gov

Gov. Rick Perry (R), State Capitol, 1100 San Jacinto, Austin 78701; Press: Allison Castle, (512) 463-2000; Fax, (512) 463-1849

Lt. Gov. David Dewhurst (R), Capitol Station, P.O. Box 12068, Austin 78711-2068, (512) 463-0001; Fax, (512) 463-0677

Secy. of State Hope Andrade, 1100 Congress Capitol Bldg., #1E.8, P.O. Box 12887, Austin 78701, (512) 463-5600; Fax, (512) 475-2761

Atty. Gen. Greg Abbott (R), 300 W. 15th St., 8th Floor, Austin 78701, (512) 463-2100; Fax, (512) 476-2653

Comptroller Susan Combs (R), Lyndon B. Johnson State Office Bldg., 111 E. 17th St., Austin 78774-0100, (512) 463-4444; Fax, (512) 475-0352

In Washington, D.C.: Ed Perez, Director, Office of State-Federal Relations, State of Texas, 10 G St. N.E., #650 20001, (202) 638-3927; Fax, (202) 628-1943

Utah   Web, www.utah.gov

Gov. Jon M. Huntsman Jr. (R), State Capitol Complex, 350 N. State St., #200, Salt Lake City 84114-2220; Press: Lisa Roskelley, (801) 538-1000; Fax, (801) 538-1528

Lt. Gov. Gary R. Herbert (R), State Capitol Complex, East Office Bldg., #220, Salt Lake City 84114-2220, (801) 538-1041; Fax, (801) 538-1133; Toll-free, (800) 705-2464

(No office of Secretary of State)

Atty. Gen. Mark Shurtleff (R), State Capitol Complex, 350 N. State St., #230, Salt Lake City 84114-2320, (801) 366-0260; Fax, (801) 538-1121

Treasurer Richard K. Ellis (R), State Capitol Complex, 350 N. State St., #180, Salt Lake City 84114-2315, (801) 538-1042; Fax, (801) 538-1465

Vermont   Web, www.vermont.gov

Gov. Jim Douglas (R), Pavilion Office Bldg., 109 State St., Montpelier 05609-0101; Press: Dennise Casey, (802) 828-3333; Fax, (802) 828-3339; TTY, (800) 649-6825

Lt. Gov. Brian Dubie (R), 115 State St., Montpelier 05633-5401, (802) 828-2226; Fax, (802) 828-3198

Secy. of State Deborah L. Markowitz (D), Redstone Bldg., 26 Terrace St., Montpelier 05609-1101, (802) 828-2363; Fax, (802) 828-2496; Toll-free, (800) 439-8683

Atty. Gen. William H. Sorrell (D), Pavilion Office Bldg., 109 State St., Montpelier 05609-1001, (802) 828-3171; Fax, (802) 828-2154; TTY, (802) 828-3665

Treasurer Jeb Spaulding (D), Pavilion Office Bldg., 109 State St., Montpelier 05609-6200, (802) 828-2301; Fax, (802) 828-2772; TTY, (800) 253-0191

Virginia   Web, www.virginia.gov

Gov. Tim Kaine (D), 1111 E. Broad St., Richmond 23219; Press: Kevin Hall, (804) 786-2211; Fax, (804) 371-6351

Lt. Gov. Bill Bolling (D), 102 Governor St., Richmond 23219, (804) 786-2078; Fax, (804) 786-7514

Secy. of the Commonwealth Katherine K. Hanley (D), 1111 E. Broad St., 4th Floor, Richmond 23219, (804) 786-2441; Fax, (804) 371-0017

Atty. Gen. Bill Mims (R), 900 E. Main St., Richmond 23219, (804) 786-2071; Fax, (804) 786-1991

Treasurer Manju Ganeriwala, 101 N. 14th St., James Monroe Bldg., 3rd Floor, Richmond 23219, (804) 225-2142; Fax, (804) 225-3187

In Washington, D.C.: Alfonso Lopez, Director, Washington Office of the Governor, Commonwealth of Virginia, 444 N. Capitol St. N.W., #214 20001, (202) 783-1769; Fax, (202) 783-7687

Washington   Web, www.access.wa.gov

Gov. Christine Gregoire (D), Legislative Bldg., 2nd Floor, Olympia 98504-0002; Press: Pearse Edwards, (360) 902-4111; Fax, (360) 753-4110

Lt. Gov. Brad Owen (D), Legislative Bldg., #220, Olympia 98504-0400, (360) 786-7700; Fax, (360) 786-7749

Secy. of State Sam Reed (R), Legislative Bldg., 2nd Floor, Olympia 98504-0220, (360) 902-4151; Fax, (360) 586-5629

Atty. Gen. Rob McKenna (R), 1125 Washington St. S.E., Olympia 98504-0100, (360) 753-6200; Fax, (360) 664-0228

Treasurer James McIntire (D), Legislative Bldg., #240, Olympia 98504-0200, (360) 902-9000; Fax, (360) 902-9044; TTY, (360) 902-8963

In Washington, D.C.: Mark Rupp, Director, Washington Office of the Governor, State of Washington, 444 N. Capitol St. N.W., #411 20001, (202) 624-3639; Fax, (202) 624-5841

West Virginia   Web, www.wv.gov

Gov. Joe Manchin III (D), Capitol Complex, 1900 Kanawha Blvd. East, Charleston 25305-0370; Press: Matthew Turner, (304) 558-2000; Toll-free, (888) 438-2731

Lt. Gov. Earl Ray Tomblin (D), Capitol Complex, Main Unit, #229, Charleston 25305, (304) 357-7801; Fax, (304) 357-7839

Secy. of State Betty Natalie E. Tennant (D), Capitol Complex, Bldg. 1, #157-K, 1900 Kanawha Blvd. East, Charleston 25305-0770, (304) 558-6000; Fax, (304) 558-0900

Atty. Gen. Darrell V. McGraw (D), Capitol Complex, Bldg. 1, #E-26, 1900 Kanawha Blvd. East, Charleston 25305-9924, (304) 558-2021; Fax, (304) 558-0140

Treasurer John D. Perdue (D), Capitol Complex, Bldg. 1, #E-145, 1900 Kanawha Blvd., Charleston 25305, (304) 558-5000; Fax, (304) 558-4097; Toll-free, (800) 422-7498; TTY, (304) 340-1598

Wisconsin   Web, www.wisconsin.gov

Gov. Jim Doyle (D), State Capitol, #115-E, Madison 53702-7863; Press: Carla Vigue, (608) 266-1212; Fax, (608) 267-8983; TTY, (608) 267-6790

Lt. Gov. Barbara Lawton (D), State Capitol, #19-E, Madison 53702, (608) 266-3516; Fax, (608) 267-3571

Secy. of State Douglas La Follette (D), 30 W. Mifflin St., 10th Floor, Madison 53703, (608) 266-8888; Fax, (608) 266-3159

Atty. Gen. J. B. Van Hollen (R), 17 W. Main St., Madison 53702, (608) 266-1221; Fax, (608) 267-2779

Treasurer Dawn Marie Sass (D), 1 S. Pinckney, #550, Madison 53707-7873, (608) 266-1714; Fax, (608) 266-2647

In Washington, D.C.: Aaron McCann, Director, Washington Office of the Governor, State of Wisconsin, 444 N. Capitol St. N.W., #613 20001, (202) 624-5870; Fax, (202) 624-5871

Wyoming   Web, www.wy.gov

Gov. David D. "Dave" Freudenthal (D), State Capitol, 200 W. 24th St., Cheyenne 82002-0010; Press: Cara Eastwood, (307) 777-7434; Fax, (307) 632-3909

(No office of Lieutenant Governor)

Secy. of State Max Maxfield (R), 106 State Capitol, 220 W. 24th St., Cheyenne 82002-0020, (307) 777-7378; Fax, (307) 777-6217

Atty. Gen. Bryce A. Salzburg, 123 State Capitol, 200 W. 24th St., Cheyenne 82002, (307) 777-7841; Fax, (307) 777-6869; TTY, (307) 777-5351

Treasurer Joseph B. Meyer (R), 200 W. 24th St., Cheyenne 82002, (307) 777-7408; Fax, (307) 777-5411

Foreign Embassies, U.S. Ambassadors, and Country Desk Offices

Following are key foreign diplomats in the United States, U.S. ambassadors or ranking diplomatic officials abroad, and country offices of the State Department that follow political, cultural, and economic developments. This information is current as of April 2009.

For information on investing or doing business abroad, contact the Commerce Department's Trade Information Center at (800) USA-TRADE (800-872-8723) or visit www.export.gov. The Office of the United States Trade Representative also offers trade information by region at www.ustr.gov/World_Regions/Section_Index.html.

Afghanistan   Web, www.embassyofafghanistan.org

Ambassador: Said Tayeb Jawad.
Chancery: 2341 Wyoming Ave. N.W. 20008; (202) 483-6410; Fax, (202) 483-6488.
U.S. Deputy Ambassador in Kabul: Francis J. Ricciardone Jr.
State Dept. Country Office: (202) 647-5175.

Albania   Web, www.albanianembassy.org

Ambassador: Aleksander Sallabanda.
Chancery: 2100 S St. N.W. 20008; (202) 223-4942; Fax, (202) 628-7342.
U.S. Ambassador in Tirana: John L. Withers, ll.
State Dept. Country Office: (202) 647-3747.

Algeria   Web, www.algeria-us.org

Ambassador: Abdallah Baali.
Chancery: 2118 Kalorama Rd. N.W. 20008; (202) 265-2800; Fax, (202) 667-2174.
U.S. Ambassador in Algiers: David Pearce.
State Dept. Country Office: (202) 647-4371.

Andorra   Web, www.andorra.be

Ambassador: Carles Font-Rossell.
U.S. Ambassador: Arnold A. Chacón (resident in Madrid, Spain).
State Dept. Country Office: (202) 647-3072.

Angola   Web, www.angola.org

Ambassador: Josefina Pitra Diakité.
Chancery: 2100-2108 16th St. N.W. 20009; (202) 785-1156; Fax, (202) 822-9049.
U.S. Ambassador in Luanda: Dan W. Mozena.
State Dept. Country Office: (202) 647-9858.

Antigua and Barbuda   Web, www.antigua-barbuda.org

Ambassador: Deborah-Mae Lovell.
Chancery: 3216 New Mexico Ave. N.W. 20016; (202) 362-5122; Fax, (202) 362-5225.
U.S. Charge d'Affaires: D. Brent Hardt (resident in Bridgetown, Barbados).
State Dept. Country Office: (202) 647-4384.

Argentina   Web, www.embassyofargentina.us

Ambassador: Hector Marcos Timerman.
Chancery: 1600 New Hampshire Ave. N.W. 20009; (202) 238-6400; Fax, (202) 332-3171.
U.S. Ambassador in Buenos Aires: Earl Anthony Wayne.
State Dept. Country Office: (202) 647-3402.

Armenia   Web, www.armeniaemb.org

Ambassador: Tatoul Markarian.
Chancery: 2225 R St. N.W. 20008; (202) 319-1976; Fax, (202) 319-2982.
U.S. Ambassador in Yerevan: Marie Yovanovitch.
State Dept. Country Office: (202) 647-6758.

Australia   Web, www.usa.embassy.gov.au

Ambassador: Dennis Richardson.
Chancery: 1601 Massachusetts Ave. N.W. 20036; (202) 797-3000; Fax, (202) 797-3168.
U.S. Chargé d'Affaires in Canberra: Daniel Klune
State Dept. Country Office: (202) 647-9690.

Austria   Web, www.austria.org

Charge d'Affaires: Andreas Riecken.
Chancery: 3524 International Court N.W. 20008; (202) 895-6700; Fax, (202) 895-6750.
U.S. Chargé d'Affaires in Vienna: Scott Kilner.
State Dept. Country Office: (202) 647-0425.

Azerbaijan   Web, www.azembassy.us

Ambassador: Yashar Aliyev.
Chancery: 2741 34th St. N.W. 20008; (202) 337-3500; Fax, (202) 337-5911.
U.S. Ambassador in Baku. Anne E. Derse.
State Dept. Country Office: (202) 647-6048.

Bahamas   Web, www.bahamas.com

Ambassador: Cornelius Smith.
Chancery: 2220 Massachusetts Ave. N.W. 20008; (202) 319-2660; Fax, (202) 319-2668.

U.S. Charge d'Affaires in Nassau: Tim Zuniga-Brown.
State Dept. Country Office: (202) 736-4322.

Bahrain   Web, www.bahrainembassy.org

Ambassador: Houda Ezra Ebrahim Nonoo.
Chancery: 3502 International Dr. N.W. 20008; (202) 342-1111; Fax, (202) 362-2192.
U.S. Ambassador in Manama: Joseph Adam Ereli.
State Dept. Country Office: (202) 647-8821.

Bangladesh   Web, www.bangladoot.org

Ambassador: M. Humayun Kabir.
Chancery: 3510 International Dr. N.W. 20008; (202) 244-0183; Fax, (202) 244-2771.
U.S. Ambassador in Dhaka: James F. Moriarty.
State Dept. Country Office: (202) 647-1450.

Barbados   Web, www.barbados.org

Ambassador: John Beale.
Chancery: 2144 Wyoming Ave. N.W. 20008; (202) 939-9200; Fax, (202) 332-7467.
U.S. Charge d'Affaires in Bridgetown: D. Brent Hardt.
State Dept. Country Office: (202) 647-4384.

Belarus   Web, www.belarusembassy.org

Charge d'Affaires: Oleg Kravchenko.
Chancery: 1619 New Hampshire Ave. N.W. 20009; (202) 986-1604; Fax, (202) 986-1805.
U.S. Charge d'Affaires in Minsk: Jonathan Moore.
State Dept. Country Office: (202) 736-4443.

Belgium   Web, www.diplobel.us

Ambassador: Jan Matthysen.
Chancery: 3330 Garfield St. N.W. 20008; (202) 333-6900; Fax, (202) 333-3079.
U.S. Charge d'Affaires in Brussels: Wayne J. Bush.
State Dept. Country Office: (202) 647-6555.

Belize   Web, www.embassyofbelize.org

Ambassador: Nestor Mendez.
Chancery: 2535 Massachusetts Ave. N.W. 20008; (202) 332-9636; Fax, (202) 332-6888.
U.S. Charge d'Affaires in Belmopan: J. A. Diffily.
State Dept. Country Office: (202) 646-7660.

Benin   Web, www.beninembassy.us

Ambassador: Cyrille S. Oguin.
Chancery: 2124 Kalorama Rd. N.W. 20008; (202) 232-6656; Fax, (202) 265-1996.
U.S. Ambassador in Cotonou: Gayleatha B. Brown.
State Dept. Country Office: (202) 647-2214.

Bhutan

The United States and Bhutan do not maintain formal diplomatic relations. Informal contact is made between the U.S. embassy and the Bhutanese embassy in New Delhi, India.
State Dept. Country Office: (202) 647-2141.

Bolivia   Web, www.bolivia-usa.org

Charge d'Affaires: Erika Dueñas.
Chancery: 3014 Massachusetts Ave. N.W. 20008; (202) 483-4410; Fax, (202) 328-3712.
U.S. Charge d'Affaires in La Paz: Krishna R. "Kris" Urs.
State Dept. Country Office: (202) 647-4193.

Bosnia and Herzegovina   Web, www.bhembassy.org

Charge d'Affaires: Svetozar Miletic.
Chancery: 2109 E St. N.W. 20037; (202) 337-1500; Fax, (202) 337-1502.
U.S. Ambassador in Sarajevo: Charles L. English.
State Dept. Country Office: (202) 647-4195.

Botswana   Web, www.botswanaembassy.org

Ambassador: Lapologang Caesar Lekoa.
Chancery: 1531-1533 New Hampshire Ave. N.W. 20036; (202) 244-4990; Fax, (202) 244-4164.
U.S. Ambassador in Gaborone: Stephen J. Nolan.
State Dept. Country Office: (202) 647-9856.

Brazil   Web, www.brasilemb.org

Ambassador: Antonio de Aguiar Patriota.
Chancery: 3006 Massachusetts Ave. N.W. 20008; (202) 238-2805; Fax, (202) 238-2827.
U.S. Ambassador in Brasilia: Clifford M. Sobel.
State Dept. Country Office: (202) 647-1926.

Brunei Darussalam   Web, www.bruneiembassy.org

Charge d'Affaires: Angela Shim.
Chancery: 3520 International Court N.W. 20008; (202) 237-1838; Fax, (202) 885-0560.
U.S. Ambassador in Bandar Seri Begawan: William E. "Bill" Todd
State Dept. Country Office: (202) 647-2769.

Bulgaria   Web, www.bulgaria-embassy.org

Ambassador: Latchezar Petkov.
Chancery: 1621 22nd St. N.W. 20008; (202) 387-0174; Fax, (202) 234-7973.
U.S. Ambassador in Sofia: Nancy McEldowney.
State Dept. Country Office: (202) 736-7152.

Burkina Faso   Web, www.burkinaembassy-usa.org

Ambassador: Paramanga Ernest Yonli.
Chancery: 2340 Massachusetts Ave. N.W. 20008; (202) 332-5577; Fax, (202) 667-1882.
U.S. Ambassador in Ouagadougou: Jeanine Jackson.
State Dept. Country Office: (202) 647-3407.

Burma (See Myanmar)

Burundi   Web, www.burundi-gov.bi

Ambassador: Celestin Niyongabo.
Chancery: 2233 Wisconsin Ave. N.W., #212 20007; (202) 342-2574; Fax, (202) 342-2578.
U.S. Ambassador in Bujumbura: Patricia Moller.
State Dept. Country Office: (202) 647-1637.

Cambodia   Web, www.embassyofcambodia.org

Ambassador: Hem Heng.
Chancery: 4530 16th St. N.W. 20011; (202) 726-7742; Fax, (202) 726-8381.
U.S. Ambassador in Phnom Penh: Carol A. Rodley.
State Dept. Country Office: (202) 647-3095.

Cameroon   Web, www.cameroonembassyusa.org

Ambassador: Joseph Bienvenu Charles Foe-Atanga.
Chancery: 2349 Massachusetts Ave. N.W. 20008; (202) 265-8790; Fax, (202) 387-3826.
U.S. Ambassador in Yaounde: Janet E. Garvey.
State Dept. Country Office: (202) 647-2973.

Canada   Web, www.canadianembassy.org

Ambassador: Michael Wilson.
Chancery: 501 Pennsylvania Ave. N.W. 20001; (202) 682-1740; Fax, (202) 682-7619.
U.S. Chargé d'Affaires in Ottawa: Terry Breese.
State Dept. Country Office: (202) 647-2170.

Cape Verde   Web, www.virtualcapeverde.net

Ambassador: Maria De Fatima Veiga.
Chancery: 3415 Massachusetts Ave. N.W. 20007; (202) 965-6820; Fax, (202) 965-1207.
U.S. Ambassador in Praia: Marianne M. Myles.
State Dept. Country Office: (202) 647-2791.

Central African Republic   Web, www.central africaine.info

Ambassador: Emmanuel Touaboy.
Chancery: 1618 22nd St. N.W. 20008; (202) 483-7800; Fax, (202) 332-9893.
U.S. Ambassador in Bangui: Frederick B. Cook.
State Dept. Country Office: (202) 647-2973.

Chad   Web, www.chadembassy-usa.org

Ambassador: Mahamoud Adam Béchir.
Chancery: 2002 R St. N.W. 20009; (202) 462-4009; Fax, (202) 265-1937.
U.S. Ambassador in N'Djamena: Louis J. Nigro.
State Dept. Country Office: (202) 647-4966.

Chile   Web, www.chile-usa.org

Ambassador: José Goñi.
Chancery: 1732 Massachusetts Ave. N.W. 20036; (202) 785-1746; Fax, (202) 887-5579.
U.S. Ambassador in Santiago: Paul E. Simons.
State Dept. Country Office: (202) 647-2575.

China   Web, www.china-embassy.org

Ambassador: Zhou Wenzhong.
Chancery: 2300 Connecticut Ave. N.W. 20008; (202) 328-2500; Fax, (202) 328-2582.
U.S. Chargé d'Affaires in Beijing: Dan Piccuta.
State Dept. Country Office: (202) 647-6803.

Colombia   Web, www.colombiaemb.org

Ambassador: Carolina Barco Isakson.
Chancery: 2118 Leroy Pl. N.W. 20008; (202) 387-8338; Fax, (202) 232-8643.
U.S. Ambassador in Bogota: William R. "Bill" Brownfield.
State Dept. Country Office: (202) 647-0464.

Comoros   Web, www.beit-salam.km

Ambassador: Mohamed Toihiri.
U.S. Ambassador: R. Niels Marquardt(resident in Antananarivo, Madagascar).
State Dept. Country Office: (202) 647-6453.

Congo, Democratic Republic of the (Zaire)   Web, www.ambardcusa.org

Ambassador: Faida M. Mitifu.
Chancery: 1726 M St. N.W., #601 20036; (202) 234-7690; Fax, (202) 234-2609.
U.S. Ambassador in Kinshasa: William John Garvelink.
State Dept. Country Office: (202) 647-2216.

Congo, Republic of the

Ambassador: Serge Mombouli.
Chancery: 4891 Colorado Ave. N.W. 20011; (202) 726-5500; Fax, (202) 726-1860.
U.S. Ambassador in Brazzaville: Alan W. Eastham.
State Dept. Country Office: (202) 647-4514.

Costa Rica   Web, www.costarica-embassy.org

Charge d'Affaires: Laura Dachner.
Chancery: 2114 S St. N.W. 20008; (202) 234-2945; Fax, (202) 265-4795.
U.S. Ambassador in San Jose: Peter Cianchette.
State Dept. Country Office: (202) 647-3559.

Côte d'Ivoire   Web, www.cotedivoirepr.ci

Ambassador: Charles Yao Koffi.
Chancery: 2424 Massachusetts Ave. N.W. 20008; (202) 797-0300; Fax, (202) 244-3088.
U.S. Ambassador in Abidjan: Wanda L. Nesbitt.
State Dept. Country Office: (202) 647-3407.

Croatia   Web, www.croatiaemb.org

Ambassador: Kolinda Grabar-Kitarovic.
Chancery: 2343 Massachusetts Ave. N.W. 20008; (202) 588-5899; Fax, (202) 588-8936.
U.S. Ambassador in Zagreb: Robert A. Bradtke.
State Dept. Country Office: (202) 647-4987.

Cuba

The United States severed diplomatic relations with Cuba in January 1961. Cuba's interests in the United States are represented by the Swiss embassy.
Cuban Interests Section: 2630 16th St. N.W. 20009; (202) 797-8518; Fax, (202) 797-8521.
U.S. interests in Cuba are represented by the U.S. Interests Section in Havana: Jonathan D. Farrar, Chief of Mission.
State Dept. Country Office: (202) 647-9272.

Cyprus   Web, www.cyprusembassy.net

Ambassador: Andreas S. Kakouris.
Chancery: 2211 R St. N.W. 20008; (202) 462-5772; Fax, (202) 483-6710.
U.S. Ambassador in Nicosia: Frank C. Urbancic Jr.
State Dept. Country Office: (202) 647-6112.

Czech Republic   Web, www.mzv.cz/washington

Ambassador: Petr Kolar.
Chancery: 3900 Spring of Freedom St. N.W. 20008; (202) 274-9100; Fax, (202) 966-8540.
U.S. Charge d'Affaires in Prague: Mary Thompson-Jones.
State Dept. Country Office: (202) 647-2005.

Denmark   Web, www.ambwashington.um.dk/en

Ambassador: Friis Arne Petersen.
Chancery: 3200 Whitehaven St. N.W. 20008; (202) 234-4300; Fax, (202) 328-1470.
U.S. Charge d'Affaires in Copenhagen: Terrence P. McCulley.
State Dept. Country Office: (202) 647-8431.

Djibouti Web, www.spp.dj

Ambassador: Roble Olhaye.
Chancery: 1156 15th St. N.W., #515 20005; (202) 331-0270; Fax, (202) 331-0302.
U.S. Ambassador in Djibouti: James C. Swan.
State Dept. Country Office: (202) 647-5082.

Dominica

Charge d'Affaires: Judith Anne Rolle.
Chancery: 3216 New Mexico Ave. N.W. 20016; (202) 364-6781; Fax, (202) 364-6791.
U.S. Charge d'Affaires: D. Brent Hardt (resident in Bridgetown, Barbados).
State Dept. Country Office: (202) 647-4384.

Dominican Republic   Web, www.domrep.org

Ambassador: Roberto Saladin.
Chancery: 1715 22nd St. N.W. 20008; (202) 332-6280; Fax, (202) 265-8057.
U.S. Charge d'Affaires in Santo Domingo: Roland W. Bullen.
State Dept. Country Office: (202) 736-4721.

East Timor   Web, www.timorlesteembassy.org

Charge d'Affaires: Jorge Camoes.
Chancery: 4201 Connecticut Ave. N.W., #504 20008; (202) 966-3202; Fax, (202) 966-3205.
U.S. Ambassador in Dili: Hans G. Klemm.
State Dept. Country Office: (202) 647-1222.

Ecuador   Web, www.ecuador.org

Ambassador: Luis Benigno Gallegos Chiriboga.
Chancery: 2535 15th St. N.W. 20009; (202) 234-7200; Fax, (202) 667-3482.
U.S. Ambassador in Quito: Heather M. Hodges.
State Dept. Country Office: (202) 647-2807.

Egypt   Web, www.egyptembassy.net

Ambassador: Sameh Shoukry.
Chancery: 3521 International Court N.W. 20008; (202) 895-5400; Fax, (202) 244-4319.
U.S. Ambassador in Cairo: Margaret Scobey.
State Dept. Country Office: (202) 647-4680.

El Salvador   Web, www.elsalvador.org

Ambassador: René Antonio León Rodríguez.
Chancery: 1400 16th St. N.W., #100 20036; (202) 265-9671; Fax, (202) 232-3763.
U.S. Charge d'Affaires in San Salvador: Robert Blau.
State Dept. Country Office: (202) 647-3505.

Equatorial Guinea   Web, guinea-equatorial.com

Ambassador: Purificación Angue Ondo.
Chancery: 2020 16th St. N.W. 20009; (202) 518-5700; Fax, (202) 518-5252.
U.S. Ambassador in Malabo: Donald C. Johnson.
State Dept. Country Office: (202) 647-2973.

Eritrea   Web, www.shabait.com/staging/index.html

Ambassador: Ghirmai Ghebremariam.
Chancery: 1708 New Hampshire Ave. N.W. 20009; (202) 319-1991; Fax, (202) 319-1304.
U.S. Ambassador in Asmara: Ronald K. McMullen.
State Dept. Country Office: (202) 647-5082.

Estonia   Web, www.estemb.org

Ambassador: Vaino Reinart.
Chancery: 2131 Massachusetts Ave. N.W. 20008; (202) 588-0101; Fax, (202) 588-0108.
U.S. Charge d'Affaires in Tallinn: Karen B. Decker.
State Dept. Country Office: (202) 647-6582.

Ethiopia   Web, www.ethiopianembassy.org

Ambassador: Samuel Assefa.
Chancery: 3506 International Dr. N.W. 20008; (202) 364-1200; Fax, (202) 587-0195.
U.S. Ambassador in Addis Ababa: Donald Y. Yamamoto.
State Dept. Country Office: (202) 647-6473.

Fiji   Web, www.fijiembassydc.com

Ambassador: Winston Thompson.
Chancery: 2000 M St., N.W. #710 20036; (202) 466-8320;
   Fax: (202) 466-8325
U.S. Ambassador in Suva: C. Steven McGann.
State Dept. Country Office: (202) 647-9690.

Finland   Web, http://finland.org

Ambassador: Pekka Lintu.
Chancery: 3301 Massachusetts Ave. N.W. 20008; (202)
   298-5800; Fax, (202) 298-6030.
U.S. Charge d'Affaires in Helsinki: Michael A. Butler.
State Dept. Country Office: (202) 647-6582.

France   Web, www.consulfrance-washington.org

Ambassador: Pierre Nicolas Vimont.
Chancery: 4101 Reservoir Rd. N.W. 20007; (202)
   944-6000; Fax, (202) 944-6166.
U.S. Ambassador in Paris: Mark Pekala.
State Dept. Country Office: (202) 647-3072.

Gabon   Web, www.legabon.org

Ambassador: Carlos Victor Boungou.
Chancery: 2034 20th St. N.W., #200 20009; (202)
   797-1000; Fax, (202) 332-0668.
U.S. Ambassador in Libreville: Eunice S. Reddick.
State Dept. Country Office: (202) 647-4514.

The Gambia   Web, www.gambiaembassy.us

Ambassador: Ajaratou Neneh Macdouall-Gaye.
Chancery: 1424 K St., N.W., #600 20005; (202) 785-1379;
   Fax, (202) 785-1430.
U.S. Ambassador in Banjul: Barry L. Wells.
State Dept. Country Office: (202) 647-0252.

Georgia   Web, www.georgiaemb.org

Ambassador: Vasil Sikharulidze.
Chancery: 2209 Massachusetts Ave. N.W. 20008; (202)
   387-2390; Fax, (202) 387-0864.
U.S. Ambassador in Tbilisi: John F. Tefft.
State Dept. Country Office: (202) 647-6795.

Germany   Web, www.germany.info

Ambassador: Klaus Scharioth.
Chancery: 4645 Reservoir Rd. N.W. 20007; (202)
   298-4000; Fax, (202) 298-4249.
U.S. Charge d'Affaires in Berlin: John M. Koenig.
State Dept. Country Office: (202) 647-2005.

Ghana   Web, www.ghanaembassy.org

Charge d'Affaires: Adolphus K. Arthur.
Chancery: 3512 International Dr. N.W. 20008; (202)
   686-4520; Fax, (202) 686-4527.
U.S. Ambassador in Accra: Donald G. Teitelbaum.
State Dept. Country Office: (202) 647-2214.

Greece   Web, www.greekembassy.org

Ambassador: Alexandros P. Mallias.
Chancery: 2217 Massachusetts Ave. N.W. 20008;
   (202) 939-1300; Fax, (202) 939-1324.
U.S. Ambassador in Athens: Daniel V. Speckhard.
State Dept. Country Office: (202) 647-6113.

Grenada   Web, www.grenadaembassyusa.org

Charge d'Affaires: Patricia Clarke.
Chancery: 1701 New Hampshire Ave. N.W. 20009;
   (202) 265-2561; Fax, (202) 265-2468.
U.S. Charge d'Affaires in Saint George's: Karen Jo
   McIsaac.
State Dept. Country Office: (202) 647-4384.

Guatemala   Web, www.guatemala.gob.gt

Ambassador: Francisco Villagrán.
Chancery: 2220 R St. N.W. 20008; (202) 745-4952; Fax,
   (202) 745-1908.
U.S. Ambassador in Guatemala City: Stephen McFarland.
State Dept. Country Office: (202) 647-3727.

Guinea   Web, www.guinee.gov.gn

Ambassador: Mory Karamoko Kaba.
Chancery: 2112 Leroy Pl. N.W. 20008; (202) 986-4300;
   Fax, (202) 986-3800.
Chargé d'Affaires in Conakry: Elizabeth Raspolic.
State Dept. Country Office: (202) 647-3469.

Guinea-Bissau   Web, www.guineabissau-government.com

   The U.S. embassy in Bissau suspended operations in
June 1998. The U.S. ambassador for Senegal, Marcia S.
Bernicat, covers matters pertaining to Guinea-Bissau.
State Dept. Country Office: (202) 647-0252.

Guyana   Web, www.guyana.org

Ambassador: Bayney Ram Karran.
Chancery: 2490 Tracy Pl. N.W. 20008; (202) 265-6900;
   Fax, (202) 232-1297.
U.S. Ambassador in Georgetown: John M. Jones.
State Dept. Country Office: (202) 647-4719.

Haiti   Web, www.haiti.org

Ambassador: Raymond A. Joseph.
Chancery: 2311 Massachusetts Ave. N.W. 20008; (202)
   332-4090; Fax, (202) 745-7215.
U.S. Ambassador in Port-au-Prince: Janet A. Sanderson.
State Dept. Country Office: (202) 736-4684.

The Holy See   Web, www.vatican.va

Ambassador: Pietro Sambi, apostolic nuncio.
Office: 3339 Massachusetts Ave. N.W. 20008; (202)
   333-7121; Fax, (202) 337-4036.
U.S. Charge d'Affaires in Vatican City: Julieta Valls Noyes.
State Dept. Country Office: (202) 647-3746.

Honduras   Web, www.hondurasemb.org

Ambassador: Roberto Flores-Bermudez.
Chancery: 3007 Tilden St. N.W. 20008; (202) 966-7702; Fax, (202) 966-9751.
U.S. Ambassador in Tegucigalpa: Hugo Llorens.
State Dept. Country Office: (202) 647-3482.

Hungary   Web, www.huembwas.org

Ambassador: Ferenc Somogyi.
Chancery: 3910 Shoemaker St. N.W. 20008; (202) 362-6730; Fax, (202) 966-8135.
U.S. Charge d'Affaires in Budapest: Jeffrey D. Levine.
State Dept. Country Office: (202) 647-3191.

Iceland   Web, www.iceland.org/us

Ambassador: Albert Jónsson.
Chancery: 1156 15th St. N.W., #1200 20005; (202) 265-6653; Fax, (202) 265-6656.
U.S. Ambassador in Reykjavik: Carol van Voorst.
State Dept. Country Office: (202) 647-8431.

India   Web, www.indianembassy.org

Ambassador: Meera Shankar.
Chancery: 2107 Massachusetts Ave. N.W. 20008; (202) 939-7000; Fax, (202) 265-4351.
U.S. Charge d'Affaires in New Delhi: A. Peter Burleigh.
State Dept. Country Office: (202) 647-2141.

Indonesia   Web, www.embassyofindonesia.org

Ambassador: Sudjadnan Parnohadiningrat.
Chancery: 2020 Massachusetts Ave. N.W. 20036; (202) 775-5200; Fax, (202) 775-5365.
U.S. Ambassador in Jakarta: Cameron R. Hume.
State Dept. Country Office: (202) 647-1221.

Iran

The United States severed diplomatic relations with Iran in April 1980. Iran's interests in the United States are represented by the Pakistani embassy.
Iranian Interests Section: 2209 Wisconsin Ave. N.W. 20007; (202) 965-4990; Fax, (202) 965-1073.
U.S. interests in Iran are represented by the Swiss embassy in Tehran.
State Dept. Country Office: (202) 647-2520.

Iraq   Web, www.iraqiembassy.us

The United States and Iraq resumed diplomatic relations in June 2004.
Ambassador: Christopher R. Hill
Chancery: 3421 Massachusetts Ave., N.W. 20007; (202) 742-1600, ext. 136
Consulate: 1801 P St. N.W. 20036; (202) 483-7500; Fax, (202) 462-5066.
Charge d'Affaires: Patricia Butenis
State Dept. Country Office: (202) 647-5692.

Ireland   Web, www.irelandemb.org

Ambassador: Michael Collins.
Chancery: 2234 Massachusetts Ave. N.W. 20008; (202) 462-3939; Fax, (202) 232-5993.
U.S. Ambassador in Dublin: Daniel Rooney.
State Dept. Country Office: (202) 647-8027.

Israel   Web, www.israelemb.org

Ambassador: Sallai Meridor.
Chancery: 3514 International Dr. N.W. 20008; (202) 364-5500; Fax, (202) 364-5607.
U.S. Ambassador in Tel Aviv: James Cunningham.
State Dept. Country Office: (202) 647-3672.

Italy   Web, www.ambwashingtondc.esteri.it/ ambasciata_ washington

Ambassador: Giovanni Castellaneta.
Chancery: 3000 Whitehaven St. N.W. 20008; (202) 612-4400; Fax, (202) 518-2154.
U.S. Charge d'Affaires in Rome: Elizabeth L. Dibble.
State Dept. Country Office: (202) 647-3746.

Jamaica   Web, www.jamaicaembassy.org

Ambassador: Anthony Johnson.
Chancery: 1520 New Hampshire Ave. N.W. 20036; (202) 452-0660; Fax, (202) 452-0081.
U.S. Charge d'Affaires in Kingston: James T. Heg.
State Dept. Country Office: (202) 736-4322.

Japan   Web, www.embjapan.org

Ambassador: Ichiro Fujisaki.
Chancery: 2520 Massachusetts Ave. N.W. 20008; (202) 238-6700; Fax, (202) 328-2187.
Charge d'Affaires: James Zumwalt.
State Dept. Country Office: (202) 647-3152.

Jordan   Web, www.jordanembassyus.org

Ambassador: Prince Zeid Ra'ad Zeid Al-Hussein.
Chancery: 3504 International Dr. N.W. 20008; (202) 966-2664; Fax, (202) 966-3110.
U.S. Ambassador in Amman: Stephen Beecroft
State Dept. Country Office: (202) 647-1022.

Kazakhstan   Web, www.kazakhembus.com

Ambassador: Erlan A. Idrissov.
Chancery: 1401 16th St. N.W. 20036; (202) 232-5488; Fax, (202) 232-5845.
U.S. Ambassador in Almaty: Richard E. Hoagland.
State Dept. Country Office: (202) 647-6859.

Kenya   Web, www.kenyaembassy.com

Ambassador: Peter N.R.O. Ogego.
Chancery: 2249 R St. N.W. 20008; (202) 387-6101; Fax, (202) 462-3829.
U.S. Ambassador in Nairobi: Michael E. Ranneberger.
State Dept. Country Office: (202) 647-8913.

Kiribati   Web, www.parliament.gov.ki

U.S. Ambassador: C. Steven McGann (resident in Suva, Fiji).
State Dept. Country Office: (202) 736-4675.

Korea, Democratic People's Republic of (North)

The United States does not have diplomatic relations with North Korea.
North Korea maintains a Permanent Mission to the United Nations: 515 E. 72nd St., #38F, New York, NY, 10021; (212) 772-0712; Fax, (212) 772-0735.
State Dept. Country Office: (202) 647-7717.

Korea, Republic of (South)   Web, www.

koreaembassyusa.org

Ambassador: Lee Tae-Sik.
Chancery: 2450 Massachusetts Ave. N.W. 20008; (202) 939-5600; Fax, (202) 387-0302.
U.S. Ambassador in Seoul: Kathleen Stephens.
State Dept. Country Office: (202) 647-7717.

Kosovo

Ambassador: Vacant
U.S. Charge d'Affaires in Pristina: Tina Kaidanow.
State Dept. Country Office: (202) 736-7729.

Kuwait Web, www.kuwaitembassy.org

Ambassador: Sheikh Salem Abdullah Al-Jaber Al-Sabah.
Chancery: 2940 Tilden St. N.W. 20008; (202) 966-0702; Fax, (202) 966-0517.
U.S. Ambassador in Kuwait City: Deborah K. Jones.
State Dept. Country Office: (202) 647-6562.

Kyrgyzstan   Web, www.kyrgyzembassy.org

Ambassador: Zamira Sydykova.
Chancery: 2360 Massachusetts Ave. N.W. 20008; (202) 449-9822; Fax, (202)386-7550.
U.S. Ambassador in Bishkek: Tatiana Gfoeller
State Dept. Country Office: (202) 647-9119.

Laos   Web, www.laoembassy.com

Ambassador: Phiane Philakone.
Chancery: 2222 S St. N.W. 20008; (202) 328 9148; Fax, (202) 232 1208.
U.S. Ambassador in Vientiane: Ravic R. Huso.
State Dept. Country Office: (202) 647-3132.

Latvia   Web, www.latvia-usa.org

Ambassador: Andrejs Pildegovics.
Chancery: 2306 Massachusetts Ave. N.W. 20008; (202) 328-2840; Fax, (202) 328-2860.
U.S. Ambassador in Riga: Charles W. Larson.
State Dept. Country Office: (202) 647-8378.

Lebanon   Web, www.lebanonembassyus.org

Ambassador: Antoine Chedid.
Chancery: 2560 28th St. N.W. 20008; (202) 939-6300; Fax, (202) 939-6324.
U.S. Ambassador in Beirut: Michele J. Sison.
State Dept. Country Office: (202) 647-1030.

Lesotho   Web, www.lesothoemb-usa.gov.ls

Ambassador: David Mohlomi Rantekoa.
Chancery: 2511 Massachusetts Ave. N.W. 20008; (202) 797-5533; Fax, (202) 234-6815.
U.S. Ambassador in Maseru: Robert Nolan.
State Dept. Country Office: (202) 647-9857

Liberia   Web, www.embassyofliberia.org

Ambassador: M. Nathaniel Barnes
Chancery: 5201 16th St. N.W. 20011; (202) 723-0437; Fax, (202) 723-0436.
U.S. Ambassador in Monrovia: Linda Thomas-Greenfield.
State Dept. Country Office: (202) 647-1540.

Libya   Web, http://libyanbureaudc.org/

Ambassador: Ali Suleiman Aujali.
Chancery: 2600 Virginia Ave. N.W., #711 20037; (202) 944-9601; Fax, (202) 944-9606.
U.S. Ambassador in Tripoli: Gene Cratz.
State Dept. Country Office: (202) 647-4674.

Liechtenstein   Web, www.liechtenstein.li/en/fl-aussenstelle-washington-home

Ambassador: Claudia Fritsche.
Chancery: 888 17th St. N.W., #1250 20006; (202) 331-0590; Fax, (202) 331-3221.
U.S. Charge d'Affaires: Leigh Carter (resident in Bern, Switzerland).
State Dept. Country Office: (202) 647-0425.

Lithuania   Web, www.ltembassyus.org

Ambassador: Audrius Bruzga.
Chancery: 2622 16th Street NW 20009; (202) 234-5860; Fax, (202) 328-0466.
U.S. Ambassador in Vilnius: John A. Cloud.
State Dept. Country Office: (202) 647-8378.

Luxembourg   Web, www.luxembourg-usa.org

Ambassador: Joseph Weyland.
Chancery: 2200 Massachusetts Ave. N.W. 20008; (202) 265-4171; Fax, (202) 328-8270.
U.S. Ambassador in Luxembourg: Ann L. Wagner.
State Dept. Country Office: (202) 647-6555.

Macedonia, Former Yugoslav Republic of

Web, www.macedonianembassy.org

Ambassador: Zoran Jolevski.
Chancery: 2129 Wyoming Ave. N.W. 20008; (202) 667-0501; Fax, (202) 667-2131.
U.S. Ambassador in Skopje: Gillian Milovanovic.
State Dept. Country Office: (202) 647-2452.

Madagascar Web: http://www.embassy.org/madagascar/

Ambassador: Jocelyn B. Radifera.
Chancery: 2374 Massachusetts Ave. N.W. 20008; (202) 265-5525; Fax, (202) 265-3034.
U.S. Ambassador in Antananarivo: R. Niels Marquardt.
State Dept. Country Office: (202) 647-6453.

Malawi Web, www.malawi.gov.mw

Ambassador: Hawa Olga Ndilowe.
Chancery: 1029 Vermont Ave., N.W. #100, 20005; (202) 721-0270; Fax, (202) 721-0288.
U.S. Ambassador in Lilongwe: Peter Bodde.
State Dept. Country Office: (202) 647-9856.

Malaysia Web, http://www.pmo.gov.my

Charge d'Affairs: Ilango Karuppannan.
Chancery: 3516 International Court N.W. 20008; (202) 572-9700; Fax, (202) 572-9882.
U.S. Ambassador in Kuala Lumpur: James R. Keith.
State Dept. Country Office: (202) 647-2931.

Maldives Web, http://www.presidencymaldives.gov.mv/pages/index.php

U.S. Ambassador: Robert O. Blake (resident in Colombo, Sri Lanka).
State Dept. Country Office: (202) 647-2351.

Mali Web, www.maliembassy.us

Ambassador: Abdoulaye Diop.
Chancery: 2130 R St. N.W. 20008; (202) 332-2249; Fax, (202) 332-6603.
U.S. Ambassador in Bamako: Gillian A. Milovanovic.
State Dept. Country Office: (202) 647-2791.

Malta Web, www.gov.mt

Ambassador: Mark Anthony Miceli.
Chancery: 2017 Connecticut Ave. N.W. 20008; (202) 462-3611; Fax, (202) 387-5470.
U.S. Charge d'Affaires in Valletta: Jason Davis.
State Dept. Country Office: (202) 647-3746.

Marshall Islands Web, www. rmiembassyus.org

Charge d'Affairs: Mr. Charles Paul
Chancery: 2433 Massachusetts Ave. N.W. 20008; (202) 234-5414; Fax, (202) 232-3236.
U.S. Ambassador: Clyde Bishop.
State Dept. Country Office: (202) 736-4683.

Mauritania Web, http://mauritaniaembassy.us/

Charge d'Affaires: Mohamed El Moctar El Alaoui Ould Youba.
Chancery: 2129 Leroy Pl. N.W. 20008; (202) 232-5700; Fax, (202) 319-2623.
U.S. Ambassador in Nouakchott: Mark Boulware.
State Dept. Country Office: (202) 647-1658.

Mauritius Web, www.maurinet.com/embgreet.html

Ambassador: Keerteecoomar Ruhee.
Chancery: 4301 Connecticut Ave. N.W., #441 20008; (202) 244-1491; Fax, (202) 966-0983.
U.S Charge d'Affaires in Port Louis: Virginia M. Blaser.
State Dept. Country Office: (202) 647-6453

Mexico Web, www.embassyofmexico.org

Ambassador: Arturo Sarukhan.
Chancery: 1911 Pennsylvania Ave. N.W. 20006; (202) 728-1600; Fax, (202) 833-4320.
Charge d'affaires: Leslie Bassett
State Dept. Country Office: (202) 647-9894.

Micronesia Web, www.fsmembassydc.org

Ambassador: Yosiwo George.
Chancery: 1725 N St. N.W. 20036; (202) 223-4383; Fax, (202) 223-4391.
U.S. Ambassador in Kolonia: Miriam K. Hughes.
State Dept. Country Office: (202) 736-4683.

Moldova Web, www.embassyrm.org

Ambassador: Nicolae Chirtoaca.
Chancery: 2101 S St. N.W. 20008; (202) 667-1130; Fax, (202) 667-1204.
U.S. Ambassador in Chisinau: Asif Chudhry
State Dept. Country Office: (202) 647-6733.

Monaco Web, http://www.monaco-usa.org/

Ambassador: Gilles Alexandre Noghes.
Chancery: 2314 Wyoming Ave., N.W. 20008; (202) 234-1530; Fax: (202) 552-5778
Charge d'Affaires: Mark Pekala (resident in Paris, France).
State Dept. Country Office: (202) 647-3072.

Mongolia Web, www.mongolianembassy.us

Ambassador: Khasbazaryn Bekhbat.
Chancery: 2833 M St. N.W. 20007; (202) 333-7117; Fax, (202) 298-9227.
U.S. Ambassador in Ulaanbaatar: Mark C. Minton.
State Dept. Country Office: (202) 647-6803.

Montenegro

Ambassador: Miodrag Vlahovic.
Chancery: 1610 New Hampshire Ave., N.W., 20009; (202) 234-6108; Fax, (202) 234-6109
U.S. Ambassador in Podgorica: Roderick W. Moore.
State Dept. Country Office: (202) 647-4330.

Morocco   Web, www.embassy.org/embassies/ma.html

Ambassador: Aziz Mekouar.
Chancery: 1601 21st St. N.W. 20009; (202) 462-7979; Fax, (202) 462-7643.
U.S. Charge d'Affaires: Robert P. Jackson.
State Dept. Country Office: (202) 647-1724.

Mozambique   Web, www.embamoc-usa.org

Ambassador: Marcos Geraldo.
Chancery: 1525 New Hampshire Ave., N.W. 20036; (202) 293-7146; Fax, (202) 835-0245.
U.S. Charge d'Affaires in Maputo: Todd Chapman.
State Dept. Country Office: (202) 647-9857.

Myanmar (Burma)   Web, www.mewashingtondc.com

Charge d'Affaires: Myint Lwin.
Chancery: 2300 S St. N.W. 20008; (202) 332-3344; Fax, (202) 332-4351.
U.S. Charge d'Affaires in Rangoon: Larry Dinger.
State Dept. Country Office: (202) 647-3132.

Namibia   Web, www.namibianembassyusa.org

Ambassador: Leonard Ilpumbu.
Chancery: 1605 New Hampshire Ave. N.W. 20009; (202) 986-0540; Fax, (202) 986-0443.
U.S. Ambassador in Windhoek: Dennise Mathieu.
State Dept. Country Office: (202) 647-9856.

Nauru   Web, www.un.int/nauru

Ambassador: Marlene Moses.
U.S. Ambassador: C. Steven McGann (resident in Suva, Fiji).
State Dept. Country Office: (202) 736-4675.

Nepal   Web, www.nepalembassyusa.org

Ambassador: Suresh Chandra Chalise.
Chancery: 2131 Leroy Pl. N.W. 20008; (202) 667-4550; Fax, (202) 667-5534.
U.S. Ambassador in Kathmandu: Nancy Powell.
State Dept. Country Office: (202) 647-1450.

The Netherlands   Web, www.netherlands-embassy.org

Ambassador: Regina Jones-Bos.
Chancery: 4200 Linnean Ave. N.W. 20008; (202) 244-5300; Fax, (202) 362-3430.
U.S. Charge d'Affaires at The Hague: Michael F. Gallagher.
State Dept. Country Office: (202) 647-6591.

New Zealand   Web, www.nzembassy.com/usa

Ambassador: Roy Ferguson.
Chancery: 37 Observatory Circle N.W. 20008; (202) 328-4800; Fax, (202) 667-5227.
U.S. Charge d'Affaires in Wellington: David Keegan.
State Dept. Country Office: (202) 736-4745.

Nicaragua

Ambassador: Arturo Jose Cruz Sequeira.
Chancery: 1627 New Hampshire Ave. N.W. 20009; (202) 939-6570; Fax, (202) 939-6542.
U.S. Ambassador in Managua: Robert J. Callahan.
State Dept. Country Office: (202) 647-1510.

Niger   Web, www.nigerembassyusa.org

Ambassador: Aminata Maiga Djibrilla Toure.
Chancery: 2204 R St. N.W. 20008; (202) 483-4224; Fax, (202) 483-3169.
U.S. Ambassador in Niamey: Bernadette M. Allen.
State Dept. Country Office: (202) 647-1658.

Nigeria   Web, www.nigeriaembassyusa.org

Charge d'Affaires: Babagana Wakil.
Chancery: 3519 International Court N.W. 20008; (202) 986-8400; Fax, (202) 362-6541.
U.S. Ambassador in Abuja: Robin Renee Sanders.
State Dept. Country Office: (202) 647-2637.

Norway   Web, http://www.norway.org/Embassy/embassy.htm

Ambassador: Wegger Christian Strommen.
Chancery: 2720 34th St. N.W. 20008; (202) 333-6000; Fax, (202) 337-0870.
U.S. Ambassador in Oslo: Benson K. Whitney.
State Dept. Country Office: (202) 647-8178.

Oman   Web, www.omanet.om

Ambassador: Hunaina Sultan Ahmed Al-Mughairy.
Chancery: 2535 Belmont Rd. N.W. 20008; (202) 387-1980; Fax, (202) 745-4933.
U.S. Ambassador in Muscat: Gary Grappo.
State Dept. Country Office: (202) 647-6558.

Pakistan   Web, http://www.pakistan-embassy.org/

Ambassador: Husain Haqqani.
Chancery: 3517 International Court N.W. 20008; (202) 243-6500; Fax, (202) 686-1534.
U.S. Ambassador in Islamabad: Anne W. Patterson.
State Dept. Country Office: (202) 647-9823.

Palau   Web, www.palauembassy.com

Ambassador: Hersey Kyota.
Chancery: 1700 Pennsylvania Ave. N.W. 20006; (202) 452-6814; Fax, (202) 452-6281.
U.S. Charge d'Affaires: Mark Bezner.
State Dept. Country Office: (202) 736-4683.

Panama   Web, www.embassyofpanama.org

Ambassador: Federico A. Humbert.
Chancery: 2862 McGill Terrace N.W. 20008; (202) 483-1407; Fax, (202) 483-8416.
U.S. Ambassador in Panama City: Barbara J. Stephenson.
State Dept. Country Office: (202) 647-3505.

Papua New Guinea   Web, www.pngembassy.org

Ambassador: Evan J. Paki.
Chancery: 1779 Massachusetts Ave. N.W., #805 20036; (202) 745-3680; Fax, (202) 745-3679.
U.S. Ambassador in Port Moresby: Leslie Rowe.
State Dept. Country Office: (202) 736-4741.

Paraguay   Web, www.embaparusa.gov.py

Ambassador: James Spalding.
Chancery: 2400 Massachusetts Ave. N.W. 20008; (202) 483-6960; Fax, (202) 234-4508.
U.S. Ambassador in Asunción: Liliana Ayalde.
State Dept. Country Office: (202) 647-1551.

Peru   Web, www.peruvianembassy.us

Ambassador: Felipe Ortiz de Zevallos.
Chancery: 1700 Massachusetts Ave. N.W. 20036; (202) 833-9860; Fax, (202) 659-8124.
U.S. Ambassador in Lima: P. Michael McKinley.
State Dept. Country Office: (202) 647-4177.

Philippines   Web, www.philippineembassy-usa.org

Ambassador: Willy Calaud Gaa.
Chancery: 1600 Massachusetts Ave. N.W. 20036; (202) 467-9300; Fax, (202) 467-9417.
U.S. Ambassador in Manila: Kristie A. Kenney.
State Dept. Country Office: (202) 647-3276.

Poland   Web, www.polandembassy.org

Ambassador: Robert Kupiecki.
Chancery: 2640 16th St. N.W. 20009; (202) 234-3800; Fax, (202) 328-6271.
U.S. Ambassador in Warsaw: Victor Ashe.
State Dept. Country Office: (202) 736-7152.

Portugal   Web, www.portugal.org

Ambassador: Joao De Vallera.
Chancery: 2012 Massachusetts Ave. N.W. 20036; (202) 328-8610; Fax, (202) 462-3726.
U.S. Ambassador in Lisbon: Thomas F. Stephenson.
State Dept. Country Office: (202) 647-3746.

Qatar   Web, www.qatarembassy.net

Ambassador: Ali Bin Fahad Al-Hajri.
Chancery: 2555 M St. N.W. 20037; (202) 274-1600; Fax, (202) 237-0061.
U.S. Ambassador in Doha: Joseph E. LeBaron
State Dept. Country Office: (202) 647-4709.

Romania   Web, www.roembus.org

Ambassador: Adrian Cosmin Vierita.
Chancery: 1607 23rd St. N.W. 20008; (202) 332-4846; Fax, (202) 232-4748.

U.S. Charge d'Affaires: Jeri Guthrie-Corn
State Dept. Country Office: (202) 647-4272.

Russia   Web, www.russianembassy.org

Ambassador: Sergei Kislyak.
Chancery: 2650 Wisconsin Ave. N.W. 20007; (202) 298-5700; Fax, (202) 298-5735.
U.S. Ambassador in Moscow: John Beyrle.
State Dept. Country Office: (202) 647-9806.

Rwanda   Web, www.rwandaembassy.org

Ambassador: Zac Nsenga.
Chancery: 1714 New Hampshire Ave. N.W. 20009; (202) 232-2882; Fax, (202) 232-4544.
U.S. Ambassador in Kigali: W. Stuart Symington.
State Dept. Country Office: (202) 647-1637.

Saint Kitts and Nevis

Web, www.stkittsnevis.org

Ambassador: Izben Cordinal Williams.
Chancery: 3216 New Mexico Ave. N.W. 20016; (202) 686-2636; Fax, (202) 686-5740.
U.S. Charge d'Affaires: D. Brent Hardt (resident in Bridgetown, Barbados).
State Dept. Country Office: (202) 647-4384.

Saint Lucia   Web, www.stlucia.gov.lc

Charge d'Affaires: Clenie Martina Jacinta Greer.
Chancery: 3216 New Mexico Ave. N.W. 20016; (202) 364-6792; Fax, (202) 364-6723.
U.S. Chargé d'Affaires: D. Brent Hardt (resident in Bridgetown, Barbados).
State Dept. Country Office: (202) 647-4384.

Saint Vincent and the Grenadines

Web, www.embsvg.com

Ambassador: Ellsworth I. A. John.
Chancery: 3216 New Mexico Ave. N.W. 20016; (202) 364-6730; Fax, (202) 364-6736.
U.S. Charge d'Affaires: D. Brent Hardt (resident in Bridgetown, Barbados).
State Dept. Country Office: (202) 647-4384.

Samoa   Web, www.govt.ws

Ambassador: Aliîoaiga Feturi Elisaia.
U.S. Charge d'Affaires: David Keegan (resident in Wellington, New Zealand).
State Dept. Country Office: (202) 736-4745.

San Marino   Web, http://www.esteri.sm/on-line/Home.html

Ambassador: Paolo Rondelli.
Chancery: 2650 Virginia Ave., N.W., 20037.
U.S. Ambassador: Mary Ellen Countryman (resident in Florence, Italy).
State Dept. Country Office: (202) 647-3072.

Sao Tomé and Principe   Web, http://www.presidencia.st

Ambassador: Ovido Manuel Barbosa Pequeno.
Chancery: 1211 Connecticut Ave. N.W., #300 20036; (202) 775-2075; Fax, (202) 775-2707.
U.S. Ambassador in Libreville: Eunice S. Reddick.
State Dept. Country Office: (202) 647-4514.

Saudi Arabia   Web, www.saudiembassy.net

Ambassador: Adel A. Al-Jubeir.
Chancery: 601 New Hampshire Ave. N.W. 20037; (202) 342-3800; Fax, (202) 944-3113.
U.S. Ambassador in Riyadh: Vacant
State Dept. Country Office: (202) 647-4709.

Senegal   Web, http://www.gouv.sn

Ambassador: Amadou Lamine Ba.
Chancery: 2112 Wyoming Ave. N.W. 20008; (202) 234-0540; Fax, (202) 332-6315.
U.S. Ambassador in Dakar: Marcia S. Bernicat.
State Dept. Country Office: (202) 647-0252.

Serbia   Web, www.serbiaembusa.org

Ambassador: Ivan Vujacic.
Chancery: 2134 Kalorama Rd. N.W. 20008; (202) 332-0333; Fax, (202) 332-3933.
U.S. Ambassador in Belgrade: Cameron Munter.
State Dept. Country Office: (202) 647-0310.

Seychelles   Web, http://www.virtualseychelles.sc

Ambassador: Ronald "Ronny" Jean Jumeau.
U.S. Charge d'Affaires: Virginia M. Blaser (resident in Port Louis, Mauritius).
State Dept. Country Office: (202) 647-6453.

Sierra Leone   Web, www.embassyofsierraleone.org

Ambassador: Bockari Kortu Stevens.
Chancery: 1701 19th St. N.W. 20009; (202) 939-9261; Fax, (202) 483-1793.
U.S. Ambassador in Freetown: June Carter Perry.
State Dept. Country Office: (202) 647-1596.

Singapore   Web, www.mfa.gov.sg/washington

Ambassador: Heng Chee Chan.
Chancery: 3501 International Pl. N.W. 20008; (202) 537-3100; Fax, (202) 537-0876.
U.S. Charge d'Affaires: Daniel Shields.
State Dept. Country Office: (202) 647-3276.

Slovak Republic   Web, www.slovakembassy-us.org

Ambassador: Peter Burian.
Chancery: 3523 International Court N.W. 20008; (202) 237-1054; Fax, (202) 237-6438.
U.S. Ambassador in Bratislava: Vincent Obsitnik.
State Dept. Country Office: (202) 647-3238.

Slovenia   Web, http://washington.embassy.si/en

Charge d'Affaires: Miriam Mozgan.
Chancery: 2410 California St., N.W., 20008; (202) 386-6610; Fax, (202) 386-6633.
U.S. Charge d'Affaires: Brad Freden.
State Dept. Country Office: (202) 736-7152.

Solomon Islands   Web, http://www.pmc.gov.sb

Ambassador: Collin David Beck.
U.S. Ambassador: Leslie V. Rowe (resident in Port Moresby, Papua New Guinea).
State Dept. Country Office: (202) 647-9690.

Somalia   Web, http://www.somali-gov.info

Washington embassy ceased operations May 1991. The U.S. embassy in Mogadishu is unstaffed. Relations are handled out of the U.S. embassy in Nairobi, Kenya.
U.S. Counselor for Somalia Affairs: Robert Patterson.
State Dept. Country Office: (202) 647-8284.

South Africa   Web, http://www.gov.za

Ambassador: Welile Augustine Witness Nhlapo.
Chancery: 3051 Massachusetts Ave. N.W. 20008; (202) 232-4400; Fax, (202) 265-1607.
U.S. Charge d'Affaires: Helen La Lime.
State Dept. Country Office: (202) 647-9862.

Spain   Web, www.spainemb.org

Ambassador: Jorge Dezcallar.
Chancery: 2375 Pennsylvania Ave. N.W. 20037; (202) 452-0100; Fax, (202) 833-5670.
U.S. Charge d'Affaires in Madrid: Arnold A. Chacón.
State Dept. Country Office: (202) 647-3746.

Sri Lanka   Web, www.slembassyusa.org

Ambassador: Jaliya Wickramasuriya.
Chancery: 2148 Wyoming Ave. N.W. 20008; (202) 483-4025; Fax, (202) 232-7181.
U.S. Ambassador in Colombo: Robert Blake.
State Dept. Country Office: (202) 647-2351.

Sudan   Web, www.sudanembassy.org

Charge d'Affaires: Akec Khoc Aciew Khoc.
Chancery: 2210 Massachusetts Ave. N.W. 20008; (202) 338-8565; Fax, (202) 667-2406.
U.S. Charge d'Affaires in Khartoum: Alberto M. Fernandez.
State Dept. Country Office: (202) 647-4531.

Suriname   Web, www.surinameembassy.org

Ambassador: Jacques Ruben Constantijn Kross.
Chancery: 4301 Connecticut Ave. N.W., #460 20008; (202) 244-7488; Fax, (202) 244-5878.
U.S. Ambassador in Paramaribo: Lisa Bobbie Schreiber Hughes.
State Dept. Country Office: (202) 647-4719.

Swaziland   Web, www.swazilandembassyus.com

Ambassador: Ephraim M. Hlophe.
Chancery: 1712 New Hampshire Ave. N.W. 20009; (202) 234-5002; Fax, (202) 234-8254.
U.S. Ambassador in Mbabane: Maurice Parker.
State Dept. Country Office: (202) 647-9858.

Sweden   Web, www.swedenabroad.se

Ambassador: Jonas Hafström.
Chancery: 2900 K St. N.W. 20007; (202) 467-2600; Fax, (202) 467-2699.
U.S. Charge d'Affaires: Robert Silverman.
State Dept. Country Office: (202) 647-8178.

Switzerland   Web, www.swissemb.org

Ambassador: Urs Ziswiler.
Chancery: 2900 Cathedral Ave. N.W. 20008; (202) 745-7900; Fax, (202) 387-2564.
U.S. Charge d'Affaires in Bern: Leigh Carter.
State Dept. Country Office: (202) 647-0425.

Syria   Web, www.syrianembassy.us

Ambassador: Imad Moustapha.
Chancery: 2215 Wyoming Ave. N.W. 20008; (202) 232-6313; Fax, (202) 234-9548.
U.S. Charge d'Affaires: Maura Connelly.
State Dept. Country Office: (202) 647-1131.

Taiwan   Web, www.tecro.org

Representation is maintained by the Taipei Economic and Cultural Representatives Office in the United States: 4201 Wisconsin Ave. N.W. 20016; (202) 895-1800; Jason Yuan, Representative.
The United States maintains unofficial relations with Taiwan through the American Institute in Taiwan: 1700 N. Moore St., Arlington, VA 22209-1996; (703) 525-8474; Steven Young, Director.
State Dept. Country Office: (202) 647-7711.

Tajikistan   Web, www.tjus.org

Ambassador: Abdujabbor Shirinov.
Chancery: 1005 New Hampshire Ave. N.W. 20037; (202) 223-6090; Fax, (202) 223-6091.
U.S. Ambassador in Dushanbe: Tracey A. Jacobson.
State Dept. Country Office: (202) 647-7644.

Tanzania   Web, www.tanzaniaembassy-us.org

Ambassador: Ombeni Y. Sefue.
Chancery: 2139 R St. N.W. 20008; (202) 939-6125; Fax, (202) 797-7408.
U.S. Charge d'Affaires: Larry Andre.
State Dept. Country Office: (202) 647-5652.

Thailand   Web, www.thaiembdc.org

Ambassador: Krit Garnjana-Goonchorn.
Chancery: 1024 Wisconsin Ave. N.W. 20007; (202) 944-3600; Fax, (202) 944-3611.

U.S. Ambassador in Bangkok: Eric G. John.
State Dept. Country Office: (202) 647-3132.

Togo   Web, http://www.republicoftogo.com

Charge d'Affaires: Lorempo Tchabre Landjergue.
Chancery: 2208 Massachusetts Ave. N.W. 20008; (202) 234-4212; Fax, (202) 232-3190.
U.S. Ambassador in Lomé: Patricia McMahon Hawkins.
State Dept. Country Office: (202) 647-2214.

Tonga

Ambassador: Fekitamoeloa 'Utoikamanu.
U.S. Ambassador: C. Steven McGann (resident in Suva, Fiji).
State Dept. Country Office: (202) 647-9690.

Trinidad and Tobago   Web, www.ttembassy.org

Ambassador: Glenda Morean-Phillip.
Chancery: 1708 Massachusetts Ave. N.W. 20036; (202) 467-6490; Fax, (202) 785-3130.
U.S. Charge d'Affaires in Port-of-Spain: Charles Shapiro.
State Dept. Country Office: (202) 647-4384.

Tunisia   Web, www.tunisiaembassy.org

Appointed ambassador: Habib Mansour.
Chancery: 1515 Massachusetts Ave. N.W. 20005; (202) 862-1850; Fax, (202) 862-1858.
U.S. Ambassador in Tunis: Robert F. Godec.
State Dept. Country Office: (202) 647-4676.

Turkey   Web, www.turkishembassy.org

Ambassador: Nabi Sensoy.
Chancery: 2525 Massachusetts Ave. N.W. 20008; (202) 612-6700; Fax, (202) 612-6744.
U.S. Ambassador in Ankara: Jim Jeffries.
State Dept. Country Office: (202) 647-6113.

Turkmenistan   Web, www.turkmenistanembassy.org

Ambassador: Meret Orazov.
Chancery: 2207 Massachusetts Ave. N.W. 20008; (202) 588-1500; Fax, (202) 588-0697.
U.S. Chargé d'Affaires: Richard E. Miles.
State Dept. Country Office: (202) 647-9031.

Tuvalu   Web, http://www.gov.tv/tiki-index.php

Ambassador: Afelee Falema Pita.
U.S. Ambassador: Larry M. Dinger (resident in Suva, Fiji).
State Dept. Country Office: (202) 647-9690.

Uganda   Web, www.ugandaembassy.com

Ambassador: Perezi Kamunanwire.
Chancery: 5911 16th St. N.W. 20011; (202) 726-7100; Fax, (202) 726-1727.
U.S. Ambassador in Kampala: Steven A. Browning.
State Dept. Country Office: (202) 647-5924.

Ukraine   Web, www.mfa.gov.ua/usa/en

Ambassador: Oleh Shamshur.
Chancery: 3350 M St. N.W. 20007; (202) 333-0606; Fax, (202) 333-0817.
U.S. Ambassador in Kiev: William B. Taylor.
State Dept. Country Office: (202) 647-8671.

United Arab Emirates   Web, www.uae-embassy.org

Ambassador: Yousef Al Otaiba.
Chancery: 3522 International Court N.W. 20008; (202) 243-2400; Fax, (202) 243-2432.
U.S. Ambassador in Abu Dhabi: Richard G. Olson, Jr.
State Dept. Country Office: (202) 647-2129.

United Kingdom   Web, www.britainusa.com

Ambassador: Nigel Sheinwald.
Chancery: 3100 Massachusetts Ave. N.W. 20008; (202) 588-6500; Fax, (202) 588-7870.
U.S. Charge d'Affaires: Richard LeBaron.
State Dept. Country Office: (202) 647-8027.

Uruguay   Web, www.uruwashi.org

Ambassador: Carlos Gianelli Derois.
Chancery: 1913 Eye St. N.W. 20006; (202) 331-1313; Fax, (202) 331-8142.
U.S. Charge d'Affairs: Robin Matthewman.
State Dept. Country Office: (202) 647-2407.

Uzbekistan   Web, www.uzbekistan.org

Ambassador: Abdulaziz Kamilov.
Chancery: 1746 Massachusetts Ave. N.W. 20036; (202) 887-5300; Fax, (202) 293-6804.
U.S. Ambassador in Tashkent: Richard B. Norland.
State Dept. Country Office: (202) 647-6765.

Vanuatu   Web, http://www.vanuatugovernment.gov.vu/index.html

U.S. Ambassador: Leslie V. Rowe (resident in Port Moresby, Papua New Guinea).
State Dept. Country Office: (202) 647-9690.

Venezuela   Web, www.embavenez-us.org

Charge d'Affaires: Angelo Rivero Santos.
Chancery: 1099 30th St. N.W. 20007; (202) 342-2214; Fax, (202) 342-6820.
U.S. Charge d'Affaires: John Caulfield.
State Dept. Country Office: (202) 647-3338.

Vietnam   Web, www.vietnamembassy-usa.org

Ambassador: Le Cong Phung.
Chancery: 1233 20th St. N.W., #400 20036; (202) 861-0737; Fax, (202) 861-0917.
U.S. Ambassador in Hanoi: Michael W. Michalak.
State Dept. Country Office: (202) 647-3132.

Western Samoa (See Samoa)

Yemen   Web, www.yemenembassy.org

Ambassador: Abdulwahab Abdulla Al-Hajjri.
Chancery: 2319 Wyoming Ave. N.W. 20008; (202) 965-4760; Fax, (202) 337-2017.
U.S. Ambassador in Sanaa: Stephen Seche.
State Dept. Country Office: (202) 647-6558.

Zaire (See Congo, Democratic Republic of the)

Zambia   Web, www.zambiaembassy.org

Ambassador: Inonge Mbikusita-Lewanika.
Chancery: 2419 Massachusetts Ave. N.W. 20008; (202) 265-9717; Fax, (202) 332-0826.
U.S. Ambassador in Lusaka: Donald E. Booth.
State Dept. Country Office: (202) 647-9857.

Zimbabwe   Web, www.zimbabwe-embassy.us

Ambassador: Machivenyika T. Mapuranga.
Chancery: 1608 New Hampshire Ave. N.W. 20009; (202) 332-7100; Fax, (202) 483-9326.
U.S. Ambassador in Harare: James D. McGee.
State Dept. Country Office: (202) 647-9852.

Freedom of Information Act

Access to government information remains a key issue in Washington. In 1966 Congress passed legislation to broaden access: the Freedom of Information Act, or FOIA (PL 89-487; codified in 1967 by PL 90-23). Amendments to expand access even further were passed into law over President Gerald Ford's veto in 1974 (PL 93-502).

Several organizations in Washington specialize in access to government information. See the "Freedom of Information" section in the Communications and the Media chapter for details (pp. 94–97). The Justice Department electronically publishes a clearinghouse of FOIA information at www.usdoj.gov/oip/index.html.

1966 Act

The 1966 act requires executive branch agencies and independent commissions of the federal government to make records, reports, policy statements, and staff manuals available to citizens who request them, unless the materials fall into one of nine exempted categories:

- secret national security or foreign policy information
- internal personnel practices
- information exempted by law (e.g., income tax returns)
- trade secrets, other confidential commercial or financial information
- inter-agency or intra-agency memos
- personal information, personnel or medical files
- law enforcement investigatory information
- information related to reports on financial institutions
- geological and geophysical information

1974 Amendments

Further clarification of the rights of citizens to gain access to government information came in late 1974, when Congress enacted legislation to remove some of the obstacles that the bureaucracy had erected since 1966. Included in the amendments are provisions that:

- Require federal agencies to publish their indexes of final opinions on settlements of internal cases, policy statements, and administrative staff manuals. If, under special circumstances, the indexes are not published, they are to be furnished to any person requesting them for the cost of duplication. The 1966 law simply required agencies to make such indexes available for public inspection and copying.
- Require agencies to release unlisted documents to someone requesting them with a reasonable description (a change designed to ensure that an agency could not refuse to provide material simply because the applicant could not give its precise title).
- Direct each agency to publish a uniform set of fees for providing documents at the cost of finding and copying them. The amendment allows waiver or reduction of those fees when in the public interest.

- Set time limits for agency responses to requests: ten working days for an initial request; twenty working days for an appeal from an initial refusal to produce documents; a possible ten-working-day extension that can be granted only once in a single case.
- Set a thirty-day time limit for an agency response to a complaint filed in court under the act; provide that the courts give such cases priority attention at the appeal, as well as the trial, level.
- Empower federal district courts to order agencies to produce withheld documents and to examine the contested materials privately (in camera) to determine if they are properly exempted.
- Require annual agency reports to Congress, including a list of all agency decisions to withhold information requested under the act; the reasons; the appeals; the results; all relevant rules; the fee schedule; and the names of officials responsible for each denial of information.
- Allow courts to order the government to pay attorneys' fees and court costs for persons winning suits against them under the act.
- Authorize a court to find that an agency employee has acted capriciously or arbitrarily in withholding information; stipulate that disciplinary action is determined by Civil Service Commission proceedings.
- Amend and clarify the wording of the national defense and national security exemption to make clear that it applies only to *properly* classified information.
- Amend the wording of the law enforcement exemption to allow withholding of information that, if disclosed, would interfere with enforcement proceedings, deprive someone of a fair trial or hearing, invade personal privacy in an unwarranted way, disclose the identity of a confidential source, disclose investigative techniques, or endanger law enforcement personnel; protect from disclosure all information from a confidential source obtained by a criminal law enforcement agency or a lawful national security investigation.
- Provide that separable non-exempt portions of requested material be released after deletion of the exempt portions.
- Require an annual report from the attorney general to Congress.

1984 Amendments

In 1984 Congress enacted legislation that clarified the requirements of the Central Intelligence Agency (CIA) to respond to citizen requests for information. Included in the amendments are provisions that:

• Authorize the CIA to close from FOIA review certain operational files that contain information on the identities of sources and methods. The measure removed the requirement that officials search the files for material that might be subject to disclosure.

• Reverse a ruling by the Justice Department and the Office of Management and Budget that invoked the Privacy Act to deny individuals FOIA access to information about themselves in CIA records. HR 5164 required the CIA to search files in response to FOIA requests by individuals for information about themselves.

• Require the CIA to respond to FOIA requests for information regarding covert actions or suspected CIA improprieties.

All agencies of the executive branch have issued regulations to implement the Freedom of Information Act. To locate a specific agency's regulations, consult the general index of the *Code of Federal Regulations* under "Information availability" or search in www.USA.gov , "FOIA Regulations."

Electronic Freedom of Information Act of 1996

In 1996 Congress enacted legislation clarifying that electronic documents are subject to the same FOIA disclosure rules as are printed documents. The 1996 law also requires federal agencies to make records available to the public in various electronic formats, such as e-mail, compact disc, and files accessible via the Internet. An additional measure seeks to improve the government's response time on FOIA requests by requiring agencies to report annually on the number of pending requests and how long it will take to respond.

Homeland Security Act of 2002

In 2002 Congress passed legislation that established the Homeland Security Department and exempted from FOIA disclosure rules certain information about national defense systems. Included in the act are provisions that:

• Grant broad exemption from FOIA requirements to information that private companies share with the government about vulnerabilities in the nation's critical infrastructure.

• Exempt from FOIA rules and other federal and state disclosure requirements any information about the critical infrastructure that is submitted voluntarily to a covered federal agency to ensure the security of this infrastructure and protected systems; require accompanying statement that such information is being submitted voluntarily in expectation of nondisclosure protection.

• Require the secretary of homeland security to establish procedures for federal agencies to follow in receiving, caring for, and storing critical infrastructure information that has been submitted voluntarily; provide criminal penalties for the unauthorized disclosure of such information.

Executive Order 13392: Improving Agency Disclosure of Information

On December 14, 2005, President George W. Bush issued Executive Order 13392: Improving Agency Disclosure of Information. The order sought to streamline the effectiveness of government agencies in responding to FOIA requests and to reduce backlogs of FOIA requests. The order did not expand the information available under FOIA. The executive order provided:

• A chief FOIA officer (at the assistant secretary or equivalent level) of each government agency to monitor FOIA compliance throughout the agency. The chief FOIA officer must inform agency heads and the attorney general of the agency's FOIA compliance performance.

• A FOIA Requester Service Center that would serve as the first point of contact for a person seeking information concerning the status of a FOIA request and appropriate information about the agency's FOIA response.

• FOIA public liaisons, supervisory officials who would facilitate further action if a requester had concerns regarding how an initial request was handled by the center staff.

• Requirement that the chief FOIA officer review and evaluate the agency's implementation and administration of FOIA pursuant to the executive order. The agency head was mandated to report the findings to the attorney general and to the director of the Office of Management and Budget. The report also must be published on the agency's Web site or in the *Federal Register.* Initial reports were submitted in June 2006, with follow-up plans included in each agency's annual FOIA reports for fiscal years 2006 and 2007 and continuing thereafter.

• The attorney general shall review the agency-specific plans and submit to the president a report on government-wide FOIA implementation. The initial report was submitted in October 2006. The Justice Department publishes annual reports of federal agency compliance on its Web site.

OPEN Government Act of 2007

On December 31, 2007, President George W. Bush signed the "Openness Promotes Effectiveness in our National (OPEN) Government Act of 2007." The OPEN Government Act amends the Freedom of Information Act (FOIA) by:

- defining "a representative of the news media";

- directing that required attorney fees be paid from an agency's appropriation rather than from the U.S. Treasury's Claims and Judgment Fund;

- prohibiting an agency from assessing search and duplication fees if it fails to comply with FOIA deadlines; and

- establishing an Office of Government Information Services within the National Archives and Records Administration to review agency compliance with FOIA.

Privacy Legislation

Privacy Act

To protect citizens from invasions of privacy by the federal government, Congress passed the Privacy Act of 1974 (PL 93-579). The act permitted individuals for the first time to inspect information about themselves contained in federal agency files and to challenge, correct, or amend the material. The major provisions of the act:

• Permit an individual to have access to personal information in federal agency files and to correct or amend that information.
• Prevent an agency maintaining a file on an individual from making it available to another agency without the individual's consent.
• Require federal agencies to keep records that are necessary, lawful, accurate, and current, and to disclose the existence of all databanks and files containing information on individuals.
• Bar the transfer of personal information to other federal agencies for non-routine use without the individual's prior consent or written request.
• Require agencies to keep accurate accountings of transfers of records and make them available to the individual.
• Prohibit agencies from keeping records on an individual's exercise of First Amendment rights unless the records are authorized by statute, approved by the individual, or within the scope of an official law enforcement activity.
• Permit an individual to seek injunctive relief to correct or amend a record maintained by an agency and permit the individual to recover actual damages when an agency acts in a negligent manner that is "willful or intentional."
• Exempt from disclosure records maintained by the Central Intelligence Agency; records maintained by law enforcement agencies; Secret Service records; statistical information; names of persons providing material used for determining the qualification of an individual for federal government service; federal testing material; and National Archives historical records.
• Provide that an officer or employee of an agency who violates provisions of the act be fined no more than $5,000.
• Prohibit an agency from selling or renting an individual's name or address for mailing list use.
• Require agencies to submit to Congress and to the Office of Management and Budget any plan to establish or alter records. Virtually all agencies of the executive branch have issued regulations to implement the Privacy Act.

To locate a specific agency's regulations, consult the general index of the Code of Federal Regulations under "Privacy Act" or search in www.USA.gov, "Privacy Act."

USA PATRIOT Act

Following the terrorist attacks of September 11, 2001, Congress passed the USA PATRIOT Act (Uniting and Strengthening America by Providing Appropriate Tools Required to Intercept and Obstruct Terrorism; PL 107-56). Included in the USA PATRIOT Act are provisions that:

• Amend the federal criminal code to authorize the interception of wire, oral, and electronic communications to produce evidence of chemical weapons, terrorism, and computer fraud and abuse.
• Amend the Foreign Intelligence Surveillance Act of 1978 (FISA) to require an application for an electronic surveillance order or search warrant certifying that a significant purpose (formerly, the sole or main purpose) of the surveillance is to obtain foreign intelligence information. The administration of President George W. Bush aggressively defended its use of wiretaps approved by the Foreign Intelligence Surveillance Court, which handles intelligence requests involving suspected spies, terrorists, and foreign agents. Established under FISA, this court operates secretly within the Justice Department.

USA PATRIOT Improvement and Reauthorization Act of 2005 and USA PATRIOT Act Additional Reauthorizing Amendments Act of 2006

Some provisions of the USA PATRIOT Act were set to expire at the end of 2005. After a lengthy battle Congress voted to reauthorize the act with some of the more controversial provisions intact, including the FISA amendments and the electronic wiretap provisions. Civil libertarians were concerned with issues regarding four provisions: sections 206 (roving wiretaps), 213 (delayed notice warrants), 215 (business records), and 505 (national security letters). The Senate addressed some of these concerns in a separate bill, S 2271, USA PATRIOT Act Additional Reauthorizing Amendments Act of 2006.

On March 9, 2006, the president signed into law the USA PATRIOT Improvement and Reauthorization Act of 2005 as well as the USA PATRIOT Act Additional Reauthorizing Amendments Act of 2006.

The reauthorized USA PATRIOT Act allows for greater congressional oversight and judicial review of section 215 orders, section 206 roving wiretaps, and national security letters. In addition, the act included requirements for high-level approval for section 215

FISA orders for library, bookstore, firearm sale, medical, tax return, and educational records. The act also provided for greater judicial review for delayed notice ("sneak and peek") search warrants. Fourteen of sixteen USA PATRIOT Act provisions were made permanent, and a new sunset date of December 31, 2009, was enacted for sections 206 and 215.

Homeland Security Act of 2002

The Homeland Security Act of 2002 was also passed in the aftermath of the September 11, 2001, terrorist attacks. It contains provisions that:

- Establish the Homeland Security Department.
- Exempt from criminal penalties any disclosure made by an electronic communication service to a federal, state, or local government. In making the disclosure, the service must believe that an emergency involving risk of death or serious physical injury requires disclosure without delay. Any government agency receiving such disclosure must report it to the attorney general.

Direct the secretary of homeland security to appoint a senior department official to take primary responsibility for information privacy policy.

Protect America Act and Subsequent Follow-up Legislation

On August 5, 2007, President George W. Bush signed the Protect America Act, which amended the Foreign Intelligence Surveillance Act of 1978 (FISA), declaring that nothing under its definition of "electronic surveillance" shall be construed to encompass surveillance directed at a person reasonably believed to be located outside the United States. Prior to this act, no court permission was obtained for surveillance of parties located outside the United States, though a warrant was required for electronic surveillance of targets within the United States. The Protect America Act allowed the Attorney General or the Director of National Intelligence to direct a third party (i.e., telecommunications provider) to assist with intelligence gathering about individuals located outside the United States and shields such parties from liability without a warrant from the FISA Court. The act did provide FISA Court oversight via requiring the Attorney General to submit to the FISA Court the procedures by which the government determines that such acquisitions do not constitute electronic surveillance. The Attorney General was required to report to the congressional intelligence and judiciary committees semiannually concerning acquisitions made during the previous six-month period.

The Protect America Act was designed as a temporary act to allow intelligence policy officials six months to establish a permanent law. The act expired 180 days later in January; it was briefly reauthorized and expired in February 2008. The Senate passed the FISA Amendments Act of 2007 (S. 2248) in February, which would make many of the provisions of the Protect America Act permanent. However, House leadership objected to many of the provisions. Instead, the House supported its version, the Respected Electronic Surveillance That is Overseen, Reviewed and Effective (RESTORE) Act (H. 3773). This act authorizes the Attorney General and the Director of National Intelligence to conduct electronic surveillance of persons outside the United States in order to acquire foreign intelligence, but places limitations, including: the methods must be conducted in a manner consistent with the fourth amendment to the U.S. Constitution and it prohibits targeting of persons reasonably believed to be in the United States (with exceptions). As amended, the bill allowed for limited retroactive immunity for telecommunications service providers. It provides for greater court oversight for targeting procedures, minimization procedures, and guidelines for obtaining warrants. The act is set to expire on December 31, 2009, when certain provisions of the PATRIOT Act expire. As of April 2009, the House and Senate were working out differences in language.

Name Index

Page numbers for members' committee assignments are inclusive of the entire committee listing.

Organization Index

Subject Index

Entries in **BOLD CAPITALS** are chapters; entries in **lowercase bold** indicate major subsections.